D1309152

After years of research and going through hundreds of reference books over time, I have run across a book that is a fixture on my bookshelf at work as well as my home office (having purchased two copies).

To anyone who is searching through the mounds of material out there, I offer three words: GET THIS BOOK.

It is a pleasure to read from an author that deals in real-world experience. Mark's book is well written. It is so much of a relief compared to the usual "dry" material offered by others.

Mark is now one of those authors I search out whenever I'm looking for clear and correct information, as well as real solutions.

> *Robert M. De Witte*
> *Unisys*
> *Analyst of Database/Languages/Emergency Services*

I'm currently an MCSE/MCT and am using the Microsoft Self Study guides to prepare to pass the Win2K exams. But when I want to get a clear, precise explanation of a topic, and go even deeper than just what is needed to know to answer a test question, I crack open Mr. Minasi's book.

Not only is this book well written, but Mark also has an excellent newsletter and answers his readers' e-mail questions faster than anyone I have ever dealt with. Kudos to Mr. Minasi on a job well done.

> *Kerry Keller, MCSE, MCT*
> *Courtesy of Amazon.com*

As an owner of a computer consulting firm and a past professor of computer sciences at the college level, my experience has taught me that Mark Minasi is one of the premier experts on Microsoft operating systems and problems. My first experience with one of his books was after actually trying to do roaming user profiles in Microsoft Windows NT and finding that **out of the five books I consulted only Mark Minasi's was accurate and complete.**

This book should be on the bookshelf of any administrator who is working in a Windows 2000 Server environment or anyone who wants to understand the system.

> *Harold McFarland*
> *Courtesy of Amazon.com*

As a Windows 2000 trainer since the early beta days, I can honestly say that this is by far the best book on the market for general Windows 2000 Server information. **Minasi has always been considered one of the best Windows technical writers, and this book is no exception.** Well written, highly informative, and even entertaining, this book will teach you things that Microsoft never will.

> *Robert Bush, MCT*
> *Courtesy of Amazon.com*

If you only have one Win2000 book on your shelf, make sure this is it! This book has been an invaluable to me during a large Win2000 migration at a Fortune 50 company. Mark's writing style is unique, making it easy to retain and understand important concepts. He leaves no technical stones unturned and even has a companion Web site and newsletter to update the book and correct/clarify any technical issues.

Bernhard Klinder
Editor, LabMice.net
Courtesy of Amazon.com

Mark, this book is awesome! I went through Microsoft training on NT 5/Windows 2000 for more than one year, and I can honestly say I have learned more from this book than that training. Well done and thanks!

Mike Steinberg
Windows NT/2000 Support Engineer,
Microsoft Corp.

As usual, Mark's information is detailed and honest. He tells it how it is. He tells us things that Microsoft will not admit and sometimes does not even want us to know. *Mastering Windows 2000 Server* is one of many reference books written by Mark Minasi that are in constant use by myself and others around me. Great job to all that put the book together!

Donald Dessert
Network Systems Engineer, Ciber Inc.

There's a reason why your books have sold so many copies. Your book has saved my ass more than once. It's simply the best as far as information and *readability*. You have a gift for *great* writing. Keep up the good work.

Alan Lloyd
NT Administrator, J.D. Edwards

I've been attending course 1579 this week and have been able to furnish answers from the book numerous times. I've made a believer out of the other class members. Most will be placing orders this week. I'm glad it arrived last week!

Warren Bierley
Technology Consultant,
Compaq Computer Corporation

The name resolution flow charts are a wonderful summation of an entirely too complex subject. Thank you.

Benj Todd
Lead Systems Engineer,
Regence BlueCross/BlueShield of Oregon

I've just started reading the book, but, as usual, I am enjoying it very much already. (I insist that Mark sit down and write a novel someday. **He actually knows how to *write*, instead of just jamming technical data down our digestive system.**)

Craig Dayton
EDS

Got it yesterday and haven't put it down since. This book rocks! Looking forward to your newsletter. Again, great book!

Alan D. Crowetz, MBA
President/CEO, InfoStream, Inc.

There were two Windows 2000 books available at the store, Microsoft's and yours. In the interest of reality, I bought yours. That was yesterday and I'm only on page 31, but I'm not asleep, which is way better than any Microsoft manual I've read—much better writing style.

Bruce A. MacNeill
Systems Analyst, Unisys

As an aspiring MCSE with one test to go, I would like to thank you for all the information you have given me with a significantly reduced learning curve. Your writing is detailed but not dry. I love the *Mastering* series (NT 4 and Win2K) …keep up the excellent work. **I only hope that I can help my students the way you have helped me.**

Bruce Stovall, MCP
Computer Technician/MS Instructor

I just wanted to let you know that you are a superb writer. I was weaned on *Mastering NT 4 Server*, and I just purchased *Mastering Windows 2000 Server*. You really present the info in a great way to understand and I know that **I don't have to worry about a Windows 2000 deployment because all I need to know is sitting on my desk right now.** Thanks for the great work; I appreciate every millisecond of it.

Ryan A. Klym
Information Technology Manager,
The Schumacher Group

I just wanted to thank you for *Mastering Windows 2000 Server*. It is truly a great book. I didn't need a "dummies" book; rather, I needed a book that considered both the small home test network I'm currently setting up as well as the largest WAN. An MSCE friend of mine recommended the book, as I have been assigned to the company's Windows 2000 team. He was absolutely right that this is the book for me. I'm approaching the project as a developer, and I'm amazed at how much I've been able to accomplish on the SysAdmins side of things because of the book. **I've actually started having critical input in the domain structure and AD design meetings.** Only one problem, I guess: I've not had a good night's sleep since buying the book.

William Hicks
Senior Application Developer,
Tricon Restaurants International

As an administrator getting ready to migrate from Banyan to Win2K (and as someone who has also worked in an NT shop), I have found your book to be excellent. I've attempted to read a few other Win2K or AD books and have either been bored (no pictures, no discussions) or overwhelmed. Thanks for putting out such a great reference book. **I find your AD discussion worth the money alone!**

Mark Homewood, MCP
Information Systems Support Specialist

Despite Mark's comment about not being an exam prep guide, **it does help for preparing for the exams, as well as using the product.**

Carey Chin
Computer Specialist, National Institute of Health

I just got the book today, but I've already found solutions to several questions I had about our server! Looking forward to reading the rest.

Rod Peterson
IT Manager, Sterilis, Inc.

I once thought that the O'Reilly book, *DNS and Bind*, was the single best learning source on the complicated subject of DNS. Minasi has proven me so wrong with the third edition of *Mastering Win2K Server*. **This guy has turned one of the most complex subjects that there is into "child's play" for me.** ... *One of the things that I appreciate most about your work, is that you are "example" and "for-instance" freaks...* Mark, you and your team are definitely the ranking members of the tech writing world.

Tom Oatman

Mastering
Windows 2000 Server, Fourth Edition

Mastering™
Windows® 2000 Server,
Fourth Edition

Mark Minasi

Christa Anderson

Brain M. Smith

Doug Toombs

SYBEX®   San Francisco   London

Associate Publisher: Neil Edde

Acquisitions and Developmental Editor: Chris Denny

Editors: Brianne Agatep, Donna Crossman, Jim Compton, Pete Gaughan

Freelance Editor: Kim Wimpsett

Production Editor: Kylie Johnston

Technical Editor: James Kelly

Graphic Illustrator: Tony Jonick

Electronic Publishing Specialist: Maureen Forys, Happenstance Type-O-Rama

Proofreaders: Laurie O'Connell, Yariv Rabinovitch, Nancy Riddiough

Indexer: Ted Laux

CD Coordinator: Dan Mummert

CD Technician: Kevin Ly

Book Designer: Maureen Forys, Happenstance Type-O-Rama

Cover Designer: Design Site

Cover Illustrator: Tania Kac, Design Site

This book is dedicated to the teachers out there, the hardworking and often underpaid people who guide their students to write their first essays, hang their first doors, take their first double integrals, or set up their first domains.

My life would be smaller were it not for the dozens of people who have willingly and graciously shared with me the formal and informal lessons of my life. I cannot pay them back, so with this and my other books I hope to "pay them forward," to share with others whatever small lessons I'm able to offer.

To all my teachers, thank you.

Acknowledgments

THE INITIAL TWO EDITIONS of this book were among the greatest challenges in my experience of book writing. Windows 2000 is so completely new, different, and larger than earlier versions of NT that I simply could not have turned out a volume this comprehensive by myself in less than three years—and I somehow got the feeling that all of you needed it before then! What that means is that, while no book is the work of just one person, this book relied more than most on the close working of the team of writers and editors, all of whom deserve more thanks than I can offer.

My first- and second-edition coauthors—Christa Anderson, Brian M. Smith, Doug Toombs, Lisa Justice, John Jensen, Darren Mar-Elia, and Tyler Regas—all did a yeoman's service, working with an operating system that was both unfinished (still in beta form) and complex, as Windows 2000 is without doubt the largest, most complex piece of shrink-wrap software produced to this day. I appreciate all of their efforts, and I hope you enjoy their work.

In the third edition, I got the time to step back, take a breath, and refine and expand upon the work of the first two editions. But I couldn't have done all that—and we'd never have put out a third edition—without the kind support of you readers, so thank you. Some of you went further and offered helpful errata, enabling me to make the third edition a cleaner edition. I've probably lost a name or two—sorry!—but some of the folks who were thoughtful enough to send in errors and suggested fixes to the book included Brian Nottle, Bruce Mackenzie-Low, Tom Verrijk, Joe Richards, Joel J. Garrett, Erik Rozman, Joshua Heslinga, George Perkucin, Trevor Coltham, Dave Poppel, Tom de Leon, Jim Konkler, Wendy Brookshire, Jon Forrest, Stephen Pruitt, Jim Fleshman, Mariano Velasquez, Geoff Haim, Diane Sherriff, Vincent Alberico, Brian Goldberg, Pete Solomon, Joel Bonvicini, John Shank, Mike Rizzo, Bob Smith-Vaughan, Jeffrey G. Truedson, Bruno Sandre, Blue Michael Plante, Brett Sherpan, Michael Horowitz, Edward Eldred, Ryan A. Klym, Dave Barcelou, Christopher Ard, Jon Sabberton, Mike Truitt, Isaac Breitman, Pete Schmidt, Mike Lorenson, Alain Letourneau, Holger Luebson, Bob Curtis, Ian Moran, James Tinney, Gino Tucci, Tony Ott, Howard Roberts, Chris Moller, and Steve Marfisi, in no particular order. Thanks very much, all!

The fourth edition let me greatly expand upon what the other three editions covered; far fewer errata gave me time to add completely new sections. I haven't room to list all of the folks who helped in some way with this, but thanks so much to you all.

I'm probably not the first person to compare managing book projects to juggling cats, but I cannot sufficiently thank those who mastered this book's flying felines. Chris Denny and Neil Edde got the ball rolling, and Brianne Agatep, Donna Crossman, and Kim Wimpsett edited the chapters, with help from Pete Gaughan and Jim Compton. Many thanks also to technical editor Jim Kelly for his painstaking checking and verifying.

There is, of course, the whole production crew to thank as well. Without them, all we'd have is a collection of electronic files. Kylie Johnston steered the project smoothly through the production channels, as she did with previous editions; Maureen Forys, creative wizard that she is, transformed the manuscripts into the handsome book before you; and the proofreaders— Laurie O'Connell, Yariv Rabinovitch, and Nancy Riddiough—scrutinized the many pages to ensure that no stone was left unturned.

My assistant, Jennifer Williams, proofread things, arranged pictures, and generally performed mountains of the necessary scut work that goes with publishing. It's tough work picking meticulously through someone else's text, and she did a great job.

Finally, we could not have done this without the assistance of Microsoft, who not only created the product but also allowed us to see it before it was finished.

Contents at a Glance

Introduction . . . . *xxxiii*

Chapter 1 • Windows 2000 Server Overview 1

Chapter 2 • History: The Story So Far 23

Chapter 3 • The Windows 2000 Registry 45

Chapter 4 • Setting Up and Rolling Out Windows 2000 61

Chapter 5 • The Windows 2000 Server UI and MMC 151

Chapter 6 • Understanding and Using TCP/IP in Windows 2000 Server 193

Chapter 7 • Building a Windows 2000 TCP/IP Infrastructure:
                    DHCP, WINS, and DNS 299

Chapter 8 • Understanding and Using Active Directory 445

Chapter 9 • Managing and Creating User Accounts 617

Chapter 10 • Managing Windows 2000 Storage 741

Chapter 11 • Creating and Managing Shared Folders 805

Chapter 12 • Software Installation 867

Chapter 13 • Configuring and Troubleshooting Network Print Services 903

Chapter 14 • Connecting Clients to Windows 2000 Server 963

Chapter 15 • Supporting Clients with Windows Terminal Services 979

Chapter 16 • Connecting Macintoshes to Windows 2000 1065

Chapter 17 • Web, Mail, FTP, and Telnet Services in Windows 2000 Server . . . 1093

Chapter 18 • How Running a Big Windows 2000 Network Is Different 1219

Chapter 19 • Integrating NetWare with Windows 2000 Server 1233

Chapter 20 • Tuning and Monitoring Your Windows 2000 Network 1259

Chapter 21 • Preparing for and Recovering from Server Failures. 1313

Chapter 22 • Installing and Managing Remote Access Service in
Windows 2000 Server 1403

Chapter 23 • Installing Hardware in Windows 2000 1473

Appendix • Performance Objects in Windows 2000. 1499

Index *1507*

Contents

Introduction. xxxiii

Chapter 1 • Windows 2000 Server Overview 1

Microsoft's Overall Goals for Windows 2000. 2
    Make NT an Enterprise OS 2
    Modernize NT. 4
    Make NT Easier to Support 4
Specific New Capabilities and Features 5
Making Windows 2000/NT More "Enterprising". 5
    Active Directory 5
    Network Infrastructure Improvements 5
    New Security Infrastructure. 8
    Distributed File System. 8
    Junction Points and Mounted Drives 10
    Remote Storage 11
Modernizing NT 11
    Win2K Can Plug and Play 12
    NT Gets a User Inter-Facelift 12
Lowering TCO and Warming Administrators' Hearts 13
    Remote Installation Services 13
    Windows Terminal Server Becomes Standard 14
    Group Policy Objects Replace System Policies 14
    Installer Service and Application Deployment. 15
    Better Remote Control and Command Lines 16
    Better Admin Tools: A More Powerful Command Line 17
    Unix's SU Comes to Windows 2000 17
    Disk Quotas. 18
    Backup Continues to Improve 18
    Client-Side Caching/Offline Files 19
    Internet Connection Sharing and Network Address Translation. 19
Bad News. 20
    DHCP Won't Be Fault-Tolerant. 20
    No Fax Server Software. 20
    Requires Powerful Hardware, but No Longer Supports the Alpha 21
    Hardware/DirectX Support Is Still Spotty. 21
    AD Is Inferior to Existing Directory Services. 21
    There Are Still Far Too Many Reboots 22
Summing Up 22

Chapter 2 • History: The Story So Far 23

What's the Point of Networks and Networking? 23
    Client and Server Software 25
    Everything Must Be Physically Connected 27

All Devices Must Speak the Same Network Language or "Protocol" 28
Keeping the Bad Guys Away: Security 29
Names: Finding Servers. 33
Summary: The Necessary Evils 39
So Why Use NT/2000?. 40
It's the Market Leader. 40
Its Familiar GUI Makes It Easier to Get Started 40
Many Tools Come "in the Box". 41
A Brief History of NT 42

Chapter 3 • The Windows 2000 Registry **45**
What Is the Registry?. 46
Registry Terminology 47
Subtrees 48
Registry Keys 49
Key-Naming Conventions 49
Value Entries, Names, Values, and Data Types 49
Working with the Registry: An Example 51
How Do You Find Registry Keys? 53
Even More Cautions about Editing the Registry. 53
Where the Registry Lives: Hives 55
A Look at the Hive Files. 55
Fault Tolerance in the Registry 56
Remote Registry Modification. 57
Backing Up and Restoring a Registry. 58
REGEDIT Versus REGEDT32 59

Chapter 4 • Setting Up and Rolling Out Windows 2000 . . . . **61**
Planning and Preparation 62
System Hardware Requirements. 62
Preparing the Hardware. 64
Preparing the BIOS. 65
Partitioning 65
Filesystems 66
Server Name. 67
Network Connection and Options. 67
Setting Up and Installing 72
Preinstallation: Phase 1 72
Text-Based Setup: Phase 2 74
Graphical-Based Setup: Phase 3 77
Postinstallation Procedures 82
Troubleshooting an Installation 83
The Recovery Console 84
Performing Unattended Installs: An Overview 86
Scripting 87
Delivery: CD-ROM or RIS. 87
Sysprep 88
Command-Line Automation: Controlling WINNT[32] 88

Scripts, Part I: Basic Answer Files with Setup Manager 91
Improving Setup Manager's Script 97
Trying Out the Completed Script 98
Improving the Script More 99
Scripts, Part II: Distribution Shares and OEM 102
Installing Windows 2000 with Remote Installation Services 109
RIS Overview 110
RIS Limitations 111
Steps to Making RIS Work 112
Getting Ready for RIS 113
Authorizing RIS in Active Directory 115
Installing RIS 116
Running RISETUP 117
Enabling RIS for Clients 120
Installing Windows 2000 Professional on a Workstation from the RIS Server 120
Creating a 2000 Professional System Image with RIPrep 125
Reconfiguring the Prototype 128
Delivering a RIPrep Image to a Target PC 128
Enabling Users to Start RIS Transfers 128
Creating the Installers Group 129
Restricting RIS Image Choices 131
Advanced RIS 131
Ghost's Little Helper: Sysprep 146
Using Sysprep: Overview 147
Get a New Sysprep 148
Set Up the Computer 148
Create a New Administrative User 148
Log In as the New User 149
Copy Sysprep to C:\Sysprep 150

Chapter 5 • The Windows 2000 Server UI and MMC **151**
Where Are They Now? 151
Where'd They Put the Network Control Panel? 152
What Happened to User Manager and User Manager for Domains? 158
No More Server Manager? 160
Domain Management Functions 161
Where Is the Disk Administrator? 162
What Happened to the Device Management Tools in the Control Panel? 163
Where Is the Services Control Panel? 164
What Is This Network and Dial-Up Connections Tool? 166
Where Did They Put NT Diagnostics? 167
Fixing Windows 2000's GUI 167
A Microsoft Management Console Primer 168
What Is This MMC Thing? 169
Why Is MMC Good and Not Evil? 169
MMC Terms to Know 169
The Computer Management Console 171
Other MMC Tools 173

Creating Microsoft Management Consoles 175
  Building a Simple Microsoft Saved Console 175
  Designing Tools with Taskpad Views 179
  Packaging Up the Tool for Users 190
  Distributing the Tool 192
  Editing a Custom Console Tool 192

Chapter 6 • Understanding and Using TCP/IP in Windows 2000 Server 193
A Brief History of TCP/IP 194
  Origins of TCP/IP: From the ARPAnet to the Internet 194
  Goals of TCP/IP's Design 197
The Internet Protocol (IP) 198
  A Simple Internet 198
  Subnets and Routers: "Should I Shout, or Should I Route?" 199
  IP Addresses and Ethernet Addresses 199
  IP Routers 201
  Routing in More Detail 202
Class A, B, and C Networks, CIDR Blocks, Routable and
Nonroutable Addresses, and Subnetting 203
  A, B, and C Class Networks 204
  Routable and Nonroutable Addresses 205
  You Can't Use All of the Numbers 207
  Subnet Masks 208
  Subnetting a Class C Network 210
  Classless Inter-Domain Routing (CIDR) 211
  What IP Doesn't Do: Error Checking 214
TCP (Transmission Control Protocol) 215
  Sequencing 215
  Flow Control 216
  Error Detection/Correction 216
Sockets, Ports, and the Winsock Interface 216
  How Ports and Sockets Work 217
  PAT and NAT: Routing the Nonroutable 218
  Winsock Sockets 221
Telling Software to Use TCP/IP Over Other Protocols: Network Binding 221
Internet Host Names 223
  Simple Naming Systems (HOSTS) 223
  Domain Name System (DNS) 224
  E-Mail Names: A Note 225
Getting onto an Intranet 227
  Dumb Terminal Connection 227
  SLIP/PPP Serial Connection 228
  LAN Connection 228
  Terminal Connections versus Other Connections 228
  So Where Do I Get My IP Addresses? 230
The Basics of Setting Up TCP/IP on Windows 2000 with Static IP Addresses 230
  Installing TCP/IP Software on a Windows 2000 Machine 231
  Configuring TCP/IP with a Static IP Address 233

Testing Your IP Configuration. 234
Configuration II: Setting Domain Names. 236
Handling Old Names: Configuring Your Workstation for WINS. 242
Adding IP Addresses to a Single NIC 244
Setting Up Routing on Windows 2000, NT, and 9x Machines 245
An Example Multirouter Internet 246
Adding Entries to Routing Tables: Route Add 246
Understanding the Default Routes. 247
Adding the Default Gateway 250
All Routers Must Know All Subnets 252
Using RIP to Simplify Workstation Management. 253
An Alternative Dynamic Routing Protocol: OSPF 253
Using an NT Machine as a LAN/LAN Router. 253
More Complex Static Routing. 258
Using a Windows 2000 Server as an Internet Gateway/Router 259
The Overview. 260
Collect the Pieces and Get Started. 262
Test the ISP Connection 262
Configure RRAS on the Gateway 263
Lower-Cost LAN-to-WAN Routing with Internet Connection Sharing 269
Step One: Connect the Internal Network—and Meet APIPA 270
Step Two: Get Connected to Your ISP 270
Step Three: Turn ICS On 274
Beyond ICS: Setting Up Network Address Translation (NAT) on Windows 2000 . . . 275
Understanding IPSec. 284

Chapter 7 • Building a Windows 2000 TCP/IP Infrastructure:
DHCP, WINS, and DNS. 299
DHCP: Automatic TCP/IP Configuration. 299
Simplifying TCP/IP Administration: BootP. 300
DHCP: BootP Plus. 300
Say No to Static IP: Use DHCP Everywhere!. 301
Installing and Configuring DHCP Servers 301
Creating a Range of Addresses: DHCP "Scopes". 304
Monitoring DHCP. 319
DHCP on the Client Side. 320
DHCP in Detail. 320
Getting an IP Address from DHCP: The Nuts and Bolts 321
Designing Multi-DHCP Networks 329
Name Resolution in Perspective: Introduction to WINS
(Even for Windows 2000) and DNS. 329
Two Different Lineages, Two Different Names 330
Application Program Interface = Modularity 330
NetBIOS and Winsock 331
Name Resolution Defined. 332
Handling Legacy and NetBIOS Names: The Windows Internet Name Service 332
NetBIOS atop TCP/IP (NBT). 332
B Nodes, P Nodes, and M Nodes 333

Microsoft Follows the RFCs, Almost. 333
M Node versus H Node 334
Understanding the NBT Names on Your System 334
Name Resolution Before WINS: LMHOSTS. 337
How WINS Works 339
Installing WINS 341
Configuring a WINS Server. 342
Designing a Multi-WINS Network 344
Avoiding WINS Problems 349
WINS Proxy Agents 351
Name Resolution in More Detail 352
Review: Winsock versus NBT 352
DNS/Winsock Name Resolution 352
Controlling WINS versus DNS Order in Winsock 355
NetBIOS Name Resolution Sequence 355
DNS: Name Central in Windows 2000 358
Why DNS Matters to 2000 358
Anatomy of a DNS Name 359
DNS Names Are Segmented 359
The Computer Name Is the Leftmost Part. 359
The DNS Namespace: The Key to DNS 360
Introducing the Hierarchy: Back to Left-to-Right 360
Why Build the DNS Hierarchy This Way? 361
The Root, Top-Level, Second-Level, and Child Domains. 362
DNS Definition: "Authoritative" 366
Zones versus Domains (and More on Delegation) 367
Forward and Reverse Lookup Zones 369
Basic DNS Record Types. 369
A Records (Hosts) 370
Cheap "Clusters": Building Fault Tolerance with Multiple A Records
and Round-Robin DNS 371
Simple Load Balancing: Subnet Mask Ordering 372
SOA Records (Start of Authority). 372
Name Server/NS Records (DNS Servers) 372
CNAME Records (Aliases) 373
MX Records (Mail Exchange) 373
Pointer (PTR) Records (Reverse Host Records). 374
SRV Records 374
Fault Tolerance: Primary and Secondary DNS Servers. 375
Secondary DNS Servers Hold Read-Only Zone Copies 376
How Primary and Secondary DNS Servers Synchronize 376
Transferring Zone Data. 377
Building a Simple DNS Zone 377
Introducing bigfirm.biz 377
Some Important Notes about This Example. 378
Creating the Primary DNS Server 379
Installing the DNS Service 380
Creating the bigfirm.biz Zone 381
Creating the Reverse Lookup Zone 383

Cleaning Up after the Wizard 386
Creating Host Records 389
Identifying the Second Name Server 390
Creating the MX Record. 390
Giving the Web Server a Second Name 391
Creating a PTR Record for BIGDOG 393
Creating a Secondary DNS Server for bigfirm.biz. 393
Testing the Configuration 396
Creating Subdomains in DNS. 397
Tell bigfirm.biz to Delegate ecoast.bigfirm.biz 398
Creating the Lower-Level Domain, ecoast.bigfirm.biz 400
Peeking at the Zone Files 400
SOA Record in Zone File Format 401
A Records in Zone File Format. 402
NS Records in Zone File Format and "Glue" Records 402
CNAME Records in Zone File Format 404
MX Records in Zone File Format 404
Directly Manipulating Zones Files: An Example 404
Dynamic DNS (DDNS). 405
Seeing DDNS Work 405
What Triggers DDNS Registrations? 406
DDNS Registrations in More Detail 406
WINS Registration versus DDNS Registration 412
DDNS Security Is Weak, If You Care 413
Active Directory–Integrated Zones. 415
DNS Resolution in Detail. 418
Step 1: Check HOSTS and the Client Cache 418
Step 2: The Preferred DNS Server Looks in Its Cache 420
Step 3: The Preferred DNS Server Looks in Its Zones 421
Step 4: The Preferred DNS Server Finds and Queries My DNS Server 423
Designing Your DNS Architecture 426
Many Resolvers versus One Cache 426
DNS Forwarders: The Best of Both Worlds 427
Uprooting a DNS Server: When Forwarders Are Grayed Out 429
Separate Internal and External DNS 430
Securing Internal DNS Servers: Slaves 434
DNS Troubleshooting: Understanding the DNS Boot, Cache, and Zone Files 435
DNS Boot Order 436
The BOOT File 437
The CACHE.DNS File. 440
Application: Building a Private Root 441
Application: Disaster Recovery Summary 443
Application: Grafting an Active Directory Domain into an Enterprise with
Old DNS Servers. 444

Chapter 8 • Understanding and Using Active Directory . . . . • 445

What We'll Accomplish in This Chapter 445
A Word on This Chapter's Structure 446

Active Directory for NT Newcomers. 446
    Security: Keeping Track of Who's Allowed to Use the Network and Who Isn't 447
    Searching: Finding Things on the Network. 449
    Creating New Types of "Subadministrators" 450
    Delegation: Subdividing Control over a Domain. 452
    Satisfying Political Needs 453
    Connectivity and Replication Issues 453
    Scalability: Building Big Networks 454
    Simplifying Computer Names or "Unifying the Namespace" 455
    Satisfying the Lust for Power and Control 456
Active Directory: The Basics for NT Veterans 457
    How Active Directory Affects Existing One-Domain Enterprises. 457
    How Active Directory Affects Multidomain Enterprises 458
Understanding and Using Active Directory's Features 463
    Domains 464
    User (and Now Machine) Groups 465
    Organizational Units (OUs) 473
    Sites. 477
    Building Multidomain Structures I: Trees 477
    Building Multidomain Structures II: Forests 478
    The Case for an Empty Root 485
    Logons under Active Directory 486
Building an Active Directory: Some Hands-On Experience 487
    Building the First Domain. 487
    Creating a Second Domain 498
    Other Active Directory Objects: Contacts, Shared Folders, and Printers 515
AD-Related DNS Design and Troubleshooting. 517
    Choosing Your Top-Level Domain 518
    Building an AD-Friendly DNS Infrastructure 518
    Using DNS to Troubleshoot DCPROMO and Logon Problems 523
Operations Masters/FSMOs. 525
    Multimaster versus Single-Master Replication. 525
    But Not Everything Is Multimaster 526
    Domain Naming: A FSMO Example 526
    Why Administrators Must Know about FSMOs. 527
    FSMO Roles 528
    Transferring FSMO Roles the Hard Way 536
Forestwide Time Synchronization 538
Local AD Replication. 540
    AD Local Replication Starts as a Loop 540
Sites Revisited 556
    How Sites Work 557
    Defining a Site 558
    Defining a Subnet and Placing It in a Site 558
    Placing a Server in a Site. 558
Inter-Site Replication 560
An Application of Active Directory: Group Policy Overview 562
    Differences in System Policy and Group Policy Implementation 563

Group Policies Apply to Sites, Domains, and OUs—Not Groups (Mostly) 563
Policy Filtering and Group Policies 564
Group Policies Only Apply to Windows 2000 Machines. 564
Group Policies Undo Themselves When Removed 564
You Needn't Log In to Get a Group Policy 565
What You Can Do with Group Policies 565
Watching the Network: Auditing with the Active Directory 566
What You Can Audit 566
How to Audit. 568
The Bottom Line: Logs Are Expensive...Maybe Too Expensive 571
Migration Strategies 572
In-Place Upgrade 572
Clean and Pristine Migration. 574
A Free Migration Tool: NETDOM 577
Another Free Migration Tool: ADMT 578
Active Directory Oddities 582
If Two Admins Both Modify a Group, One's Changes Get Lost 582
Make Changes on DCs Near the Target Client 582
In Single-Domain Enterprises, Make All Domain Controllers Global Catalog Servers . . . 583
Choose Your Domain Names Well. 583
Planning Your Active Directory Structure. 584
Examine Your WAN Topology. 584
Lay Out Your Sites 584
Figure Out Which Existing Domains to Merge and Merge Them 584
What Needs an OU and What Needs a Domain? 584
Choose an OU Structure for Delegation, Then for Group Policies. 585
Use Just One Domain if Possible 585
Develop Names for Your Domains/Trees. 585
Get the DNS Infrastructure Ready. 585
Use the Power of Inheritance 586
Overall AD Design Advice 586
Understanding and Using Certificates 586
Public Key Pieces I: Public Keys, Private Keys, and Authentication. 589
Public Key Pieces II: Encrypted Communications (SSL) 591
Public Key Pieces III: Certificates and Certificate Authorities 593
Trusting Certificate Authorities 599
Running Your Own Certificate Authority with Windows 2000 602
Using PKI in Windows 2000 610
Revoking Certificates 614

Chapter 9 • Managing and Creating User Accounts **617**
Creating Local and Domain User Accounts 617
Use Computer Management for Local Accounts. 617
Use Active Directory Users and Computers for Domain Accounts. 620
Understanding Groups 636
Creating Groups 636
Group Types: Security Groups versus Distribution Groups 639
Group Scope: Locals, Domail Locals, Globals, and Universals. 641

Working with Security Groups 643
How Do Organizational Units Fit In? 652
Zen and the Art of Login Scripts 652
Understanding User Permissions and Rights 658
Object Permissions, ACLs, and ACEs 658
User Rights 660
Local and Domain-Based Group Policies 663
Group Policy Benefits 664
Group Policies Compared to System Policies 665
Local Group Policies: Security Templates 666
Working with Templates 668
Group Policy Concepts 672
Local Policies and Group Policy Objects 674
Creating Group Policies 676
Group Policy Troubleshooting: GP Application Order 681
Delegating Group Policy Administration 687
User and Computer Configuration Settings 689
Managing Group Policies 702
Troubleshooting Group Policies 707
Working with Roaming User Profiles 709
Anatomy of a User Profile 711
Configuring Your Own User Profile 713
Birth of a Local Profile 715
Roaming Profile Basics 716
Preconfiguring User Profiles 719
Mandatory Profiles 729
Setting Up a Group Template Profile 731
How Does an NT 4 Client Choose between Local, Roaming, and
Mandatory Profiles? 732
Which Type of Profile Is Right for My Network? 736
Comparing Windows NT 3.51, NT 4, and 95/98 Profiles 739

Chapter 10 • Managing Windows 2000 Storage **741**
Using the Disk Management Tool 741
Disk Management Terminology 742
Installing a New Physical Disk 752
Using Basic Disk Features 752
Using Dynamic Disks 760
Creating a Volume Set 763
Creating a Stripe Set 764
Establishing a Mirror Set 765
Establishing RAID 5 Volumes 768
Advanced Disk Management Topics 772
Hardware or Software RAID? 780
Performing Disk Maintenance 781
Background: Disk Geometry and File Formats 781
Formatting Disks 781

Defragmenting Disks 787
Using CHKDSK. 790
Using Encrypted NTFS 794
How Win2K Encryption Works. 794
Encrypting Files 795
Decrypting Files 800
Enough of That! Managing Disk Quotas. 800
Background: How Quota Management Works. 800
Setting Up User Quotas 801
Managing Quota Entries 803
Summary 804

Chapter 11 • Creating and Managing Shared Folders 805
Basics of File Sharing 805
Creating Shared Folders 806
Creating Shares from Explorer. 807
Remotely Creating Shares with the Computer Management Console . . . 809
Publishing Shares in the Active Directory. 810
Managing Permissions. 811
Share Permissions 811
File and Directory Permissions 814
Auditing File and Directory Access 831
Enabling Auditing. 831
Hidden Shares 833
Common Shares 835
C$, D$, and So On 835
ADMIN$. 835
PRINT$ 836
IPC$ 836
REPL$ 836
NETLOGON 836
Connecting to Shares via the Command Line 836
Introducing net use. 837
Using a Different Account with net use 837
"A Set of Credentials Conflicts" 837
net use-ing over a WAN 838
The Distributed File System 838
Dfs Terminology. 840
Stand-Alone versus Fault-Tolerant Dfs 841
Creating a Dfs Root 842
Adding Links to a Dfs Root 845
Configuring Dfs Replicas 847
Dfs Replication 848
Managing Dfs. 848
Web Sharing. 852
Using Offline Files/Client-Side Cacheing 854
Introducing Offline Files. 854
How Offline Files Works 854

Enabling Offline Files on Your Desktop: The Basics 855
Getting and Keeping Things in the Offline Files Folder 857
Offline Files in Action: Before the Trip 859
Working and Making Changes on the Road 860
Back in the Office: Syncing Up 861
Applying Offline Files to the Office: When Servers Fail 862
Controlling Synchronization for Non-Mobile Users 863
Cleaning Out Offline Files 865

Chapter 12 • Software Installation **867**
Publishing a Package to Users 868
Step One: Copy adminpak.msi to a Network Share 868
Step Two: Create a GPO 869
Step Three: Filter the GPO 869
Step Four: Add the Package to the GPO 870
Filtering Group Policy 872
Using Organizational Units 873
Assigning a Package to Users or Computers 874
Step One: Running the Administrative Setup 874
Step Two: Create a Group Policy Object 875
Step Three: Add the Package to the GPO 876
Step Four: Customize the Package Properties 877
Removing a Package 878
Redeploying a Package 879
Creating Your Own MSI 879
Step One: Create a Clean Computer 880
Step Two: Take the Before Snapshot 880
Step Three: Install the Application and Reboot 881
Step Four: Test the Application 882
Step Five: Take the After Snapshot and Compare 882
Step Six: Make Any Customizations 883
Step Seven: Test the Application Installed by the New MSI 885
Distributing the Easy Way: Using ZAP Files 886
Step One: Create a ZAP File 886
Step Two: Share the ZAP File and Installation Files 887
Step Three: Add a Package to a GPO 887
Checking Out Those Off-the-Shelf Applications 888
Customizing Packages 888
Creating an MST 889
Using an MST 896
Upgrading Applications 898
Getting NT Apps to Work 900
Loosen Up the Registry Permissions 900
Identify Failed System32 Overwrites 901
Use DLL Redirection to Let Apps Use Their Own DLLs 901

Chapter 13 • Configuring and Troubleshooting Network Print Services **903**
Print Services Terminology 904

The Win2K Printing Model 904
   The Graphics Device Interface. 905
   The Printer Driver 905
   The Print Spooler. 905
   The Printing Process. 908
Setting Up a Printer Connection 909
   Installing a Printer on a Print Server 909
   Preparing for Web Printing 913
   Getting the Printer to the Clients 918
   Using Client-Side Printers in a Terminal Server Environment 926
   Automatically Installing Printers 929
Securing Printers 933
   Tuning Printer Permissions 933
   Group Policy Settings for Printers 940
Configuring Printer Settings 946
   Creating Multiple-Personality Printers 948
   Defining Port Settings. 948
   Using Separator Pages. 951
   Setting Printer Priorities 953
Adjusting Print Server Settings 953
   Choosing Form Settings 954
   Configuring Server Port Settings 955
   Adding or Updating the Printer Driver on a Windows 2000 Print Server 956
   Keeping Track of Your Printing. 958
Managing Print Jobs. 959
Troubleshooting Printer Problems 961
   Basic Troubleshooting: Identifying the Situation 961
   Using Online Resources 962

Chapter 14 • Connecting Clients to Windows 2000 Server 963
Connecting Windows 95 and Windows 98 Workstations. 963
   Configuring the Workstation 964
   Attaching to the Network 965
   Accessing Network Resources 967
   Accessing the Active Directory. 968
Connecting Windows NT Workstations. 968
   Configuring the Workstation 968
   Accessing Network Resources 972
Connecting Windows for Workgroups Workstations 973
   Attaching to the Network 976
Connecting DOS Workstations 977

Chapter 15 • Supporting Clients with Windows Terminal Services 979
Why Care about Terminal Services?. 979
   Centralized Deployment of Applications 980
   Supporting PC-Unfriendly Environments. 981
   Less Processing Power Required on the Client 982

Simplifying the User Interface 983
Providing Help Desk Support 984
The Terminal Server Processing Model 984
Anatomy of a Thin Client Session 985
Server and Client Requirements 991
Server Hardware 991
Client Hardware 994
Installing (or Removing) Support for Terminal Services 996
Adding Core Terminal Server Support 996
Changing or Removing Terminal Services 998
Adding TSAC Support 999
Creating a New Terminal Server Client 999
PC-Based RDP Clients 999
Setting Up and Connecting a Windows-Based Terminal 1003
Setting Up a Handheld PC 1005
Creating, Deleting, and Modifying Connections 1005
Connections with the RDP5 Client 1006
Connections with the Remote Desktop 1010
Client Catch-22s 1013
Troubleshooting Connection Problems 1015
Editing Client Account Settings 1016
Remote Control 1017
Session Time-Outs 1018
Setting Client Path Information 1020
Configuring Terminal Services for All Connections 1024
Terminal Services Licensing 1029
The Win2K Terminal Services Licensing Model 1030
Understanding Session Licensing 1031
The Terminal Services Licensing Tool 1033
Application Licensing 1037
Configuring Applications for a Multiuser Environment 1037
Choosing Applications 1037
Making Your Applications Play Well with Others 1039
Managing Terminal Sessions 1050
Introducing Command-Line Tools 1050
Using the Terminal Services Manager 1051
Do I Need MetaFrame? 1061
Using Remote Administration Mode 1062
How Much Will Remote Administration Mode Affect Server Performance? 1062
How Do I Connect to the Terminal Server? 1062
How Many People Can Log in to the Server? 1063
Can I Run Any Management Tool from a Terminal Session? 1063

Chapter 16 • Connecting Macintoshes to Windows 2000 1065

Getting Started 1066
10Base-T, 100Base-T, or 1000Base-T? 1066
Knowing the Macintosh 1066
File and Print Server Considerations 1070

Installing the Servers for Macintosh. 1071
    Creating Macintosh Shares 1073
    Sharing Printers 1076
Accessing Server Resources 1082
    Accessing Shared Folders. 1083
    Accessing Shared Printers 1085
Implementing Security 1086
Setting Advanced Options. 1088
Supporting Applications across Platforms 1090
Network Alternatives 1090
    AppleShare IP 6 1091
    So, What Are You Saying? 1092

Chapter 17 • Web, Mail, FTP, and Telnet Services in Windows 2000 Server. 1093
A Closer Look: What IIS Can (and Can't) Do 1094
    World Wide Web (HTTP) Server 1094
    File Transfer (FTP) Server. 1094
    Network News (NNTP) Server. 1095
    Simple Mail Transfer (SMTP) Server. 1095
Installing Internet Information Services 1096
    Default Configuration 1096
Global IIS Configuration. 1097
Setting Up a Web Site and Configuring Web Services 1100
    Creating a New Web Site 1101
    Modifying Web Site Properties 1107
    Virtual Directories 1123
Setting Up an FTP Site and Configuring FTP Services 1127
    Creating a New FTP Site 1127
    Modifying FTP Site Properties 1129
    Virtual FTP Directories 1136
    Using FTP for File Transfer 1138
Setting Up an NNTP News Server and Configuring NNTP Services 1143
    Creating a New NNTP Server 1144
    Modifying NNTP Virtual Server Properties. 1146
    Defining NNTP Server Expiration Policies 1155
    Virtual NNTP Server Directories 1157
Setting Up an SMTP Server and Configuring SMTP Services 1158
    Internet E-mail Protocols 1158
    Creating a New SMTP Server 1159
    Modifying SMTP Virtual Server Properties 1161
    Maintaining Your SMTP Server. 1171
A Free E-mail Server for Windows 2000 1174
    Setting Up Your Mail Server: IMS Limitations. 1175
    How the IMS Software Works. 1175
    Downloading the EMWACS Software 1176
    Unzipping the EMWACS Software 1176
    Installing the Services 1176
    Adding Registry Entries 1177

Setting Users to Log In As Batch Jobs 1177
Configuring the Services 1178
Setting Up Your E-mail Client. 1180
MailSite: "EMWACS Pro" 1180
E-mail Security Concerns 1181
Using Telnet for Remote Login 1182
Early Telnet Uses 1182
Modern Uses for Telnet 1182
Setting Up the Telnet Server 1182
Communicating Securely with SSL 1184
Requesting a Certificate. 1185
Securing a Site or Directory 1188
Configuring and Troubleshooting Indexing Service and Building Web-Based Query Pages . . 1189
What Indexing Service Does 1189
The Annoying Thing about Indexing Service: Little Documentation 1189
How You'll Use It (Why You Care). 1190
Using the Catalog: Querying Indexing Service from Manage Computer 1195
Using the Catalog: Querying Indexing Service from the Web. 1197
Troubleshooting Failed Queries 1203
Windows 2000 Internet Security: Some Thoughts 1203
If You're Not Using IIS, Turn It Off 1205
Get and Apply the Latest Service Packs and Hotfixes 1205
Simplifying Hotfix Application 1206
Use IIS and NTFS Permissions. 1207
Disable Indexing. 1208
Disable All Nonessential Ports 1208
Move wwwroot. 1208
Get Rid of the IIS Admin, Documentation, Web-based Printing, Extra
    Directories, and Samples. 1209
Disable Unnecessary Services on Your Servers. 1209
Consider Disabling Microsoft File and Print Sharing 1210
Eliminate Nonessential ISAPI 1210
Detecting Outside Attacks. 1211
Deterring Attacks 1211
Don't Forget Hazards from Within 1217

Chapter 18 • How Running a Big Windows 2000 Network Is Different 1219

Active Directory Design Issues 1219
Enterprise Forests. 1219
Modifying the Schema, Merging Forests: Limited Flexibility 1220
Sites. 1221
Organizational Units. 1222
GPOs. 1222
Replication Issues. 1224
SYSVOL 1224
Dfs 1225
How GPO Replication Is Different and Special 1226

Deploying Infrastructure Services. 1226
  DNS 1227
  Global Catalog Servers 1228
  Operations Masters. 1230
Domain Migration Strategies and Downlevel Coexistence 1231
  Migration Options 1231
  Downlevel Coexistence 1231

Chapter 19 • Integrating NetWare with Windows 2000 Server. 1233
Integration versus Migration 1233
  Integration 1233
  Migration. 1234
Getting Started. 1234
  Adding Protocol Support 1235
  Adding Client Support 1237
  Verifying Client Connectivity. 1238
Integrating NetWare and Windows 2000 Server. 1239
  Configuring Gateway Services for NetWare 1239
  File and Print Services for NetWare. 1243
Migrating from NetWare and NDS to Windows 2000 and Active Directory. 1244
  DSMT Overview and Conventions 1245
  Installing and Configuring the DSMT. 1246
  Importing Bindery/NDS Data 1250
  Manipulating NDS Data in the DSMT. 1252
  Writing Objects to Active Directory 1254
  Migrating File Resources. 1255

Chapter 20 • Tuning and Monitoring Your Windows 2000 Network. 1259
Roundup of Tuning Support Tools and What to Do with Them. 1260
  System Monitor 1260
  Performance Logs and Alerts. 1260
  Event Viewer. 1261
Observing Performance Patterns with the System Monitor 1262
  Creating a Chart. 1263
  Remote Performance Monitoring. 1273
  Saving Chart Data. 1274
Logging Performance Data 1276
  Understanding Log Types 1276
  Creating Logs. 1276
  Viewing Log Data. 1283
Whattheckhappened? Troubleshooting with the Event Viewer. 1284
  Understanding Log Types 1285
  Viewing Remote Event Log Data. 1286
  Reading Log Entries 1287
  Managing and Archiving Log Contents 1288
Quick Looks: Using the Task Manager. 1291
Basic Tuning Stuff. 1295
  Optimizing Server Processing Power 1295

Editing Virtual Memory Settings 1296
Tuning the System Cache 1297
Server Tuning 1299
Using the Most Current Drivers 1300
You Knew It Was Coming: Hardware and Other Performance Recommendations . . . 1303
Configuring Network Browsing 1305
Solving the Directory Service Problem 1305
How Browsing Works 1308
Choosing a Master Browser 1308
Stupid Browser Tricks 1311

Chapter 21 • Preparing for and Recovering from Server Failures **1313**
Preventing Stupid Accidents 1314
Power-Protect Servers 1314
Keep the Servers Pure 1315
Limit Access to Servers 1316
Use Passwords Effectively 1316
Backup Programs and Approaches 1318
Basic Backup Procedures 1319
Advanced Backup Options 1322
Scheduling Automated Backups 1331
Backing Up to Tape 1335
Automating Tape Backups 1345
Viewing Backup Logs 1351
Restoring Data 1352
Backing Up and Restoring the Active Directory 1356
Troubleshooting Hardware with the System Information Tool 1360
System Summary. 1361
Hardware Resources 1362
Components 1363
Software Environment 1364
Internet Explorer 1365
Saving System Configuration Information 1367
Understanding the Boot Process 1369
Prequel: The Hardware Must Work 1369
Step One: Load NTLDR 1370
Step Two: Run NTDETECT 1370
Step Three: Load NTOSKRNL 1370
Fixing Minor Problems with the Advanced Options Menu 1372
Using Safe Mode Options. 1373
The Last Known Good Configuration 1374
Enable VGA Mode 1377
Enable Boot Logging. 1377
Debugging Mode 1378
Preparing for Recovery 1378
Installing the Recovery Console 1378
Creating the Emergency Repair Disk 1379
Creating a Boot Floppy. 1381

Repairing—or Recovering—a Damaged Installation 1382
    Understanding Repair Options 1383
    Using the Recovery Console 1383
    Using the Emergency Repair Disk 1391
Troubleshooting Login Failures: "No Domain Controller Found" 1393
    Check the Basics 1395
    If You're Dialing In 1395
    If You're Local 1395
    Tell the Workstation to Be More Patient 1396
Troubleshooting Startup Mysteries: How Do I Get Rid of That Program? 1396
Planning for Disaster Recovery 1397
    Creating a Disaster Recovery Plan 1397
    Implementing Disaster Recovery 1397
    Make a Recovery "Coloring Book" 1398
    Making Sure the Plan Works 1399

**Chapter 22 • Installing and Managing Remote Access Service in
Windows 2000 Server 1403**
Common Applications for Remote Access Service 1404
    Connecting to the Internet 1404
    Accepting Incoming Calls from Remote Clients 1405
    Connecting to a Private Network 1405
    Acting as an Internet Gateway 1405
    Accepting VPN Connections from Remote Clients 1405
    Dialing Up a Remote Network and Routing Traffic 1406
Bandwidth Planning and Considerations 1406
    Remote Node 1406
    Remote Control 1410
RAS Hardware Requirements 1410
    Case in Point: Choosing the Right Modems 1411
    Analog Modems 1412
    ISDN 1413
    Direct Options (Null Modem, Parallel, and Infrared) 1414
    X.25 1415
    Frame Relay 1415
RAS Installation and Setup 1415
    Installing Devices for Remote Access 1415
Connecting to the Internet 1417
    Optional Internet Connection Settings 1421
Accepting Incoming Calls from Remote Users 1425
    Remote Access Server Installation and Setup 1426
    Granting Dial-In Permissions to User(s) 1429
    Changing RAS Server Configurations after Installation 1430
    Client Configurations 1436
    Managing Connected Users 1440
Connecting to a Private Network 1441
Acting as an Internet Gateway 1444
    Configuring Windows 2000 Server to Act as an Internet Gateway 1445

Accepting VPN Connections from Remote Clients. 1450
    VPN Overview. 1451
    A Brief History of VPN: PPTP, L2F, and L2TP. 1452
    Implementing VPN via PPTP and L2TP. 1452
    VPN Performance Considerations 1460
Dialing Up a Remote Network and Routing Traffic 1460
    Sample Network. 1461
    Setting Up the First Server 1461
The Most Common (and Poorly Documented) RAS Problems 1469
    "I've connected to a RAS server from my home PC, but I can't browse
      anything on the network!". 1469
    "How can I keep RAS connections alive when a user logs off of their
      workstation?". 1470
    "No matter what I try, I can't seem to get a modem connection from a
      workstation to my RAS server.". 1470
    "Can I make a RAS client automatically dial in to a RAS server at a s
      pecified time?" 1471
    "My dial-up users aren't getting the WINS and DNS addresses that are
      defined on our network.". 1472
    "I don't want my dial-up users to get the WINS and DNS addresses that
      are defined on our network.". 1472

Chapter 23 • Installing Hardware in Windows 2000 . . . . **1473**

Hardware Resources: The Basics. 1474
    I/O Addresses 1474
    DMA Channels 1477
    Interrupt Request Levels (IRQs) 1478
    ROM Addresses 1481
Practical Hardware Tutorial 1481
    Adding New Hardware to a System 1481
    Removing Hardware 1485
Windows 2000 Hardware Management 1485
    Device Manager 1486
    Driver Signing 1492
    Add/Remove Hardware Wizard 1493
    Found New Hardware Wizard 1494
    Hardware Profiles 1495
    Troubleshooter 1496

Appendix • Performance Objects in Windows 2000 . . . . **1499**

Index *1507*

Introduction

"OH, NO," I HEAR YOU CRY, "a whole new version of NT! And just when I'd figured out NT 4." Hey, relax, you're gonna love Windows 2000. You can do all kinds of things that you couldn't do before. Remote control and administration's easier. Rolling out applications to users' machines from a central location is simpler; heck, rolling out entire PC configurations, operating system and all, is easier. You can build far larger networks than with NT 4. You can automate more processes.

It won't *all* be good news, admittedly. Yes, it's also a *new* operating system, so we've spent a lot of the past two years discovering bugs as we figured out new features (and, sadly, applying hotfixes to patch frightening new security holes). And Windows 2000's hardware requirements are sufficiently onerous that you'll probably *have* to go get new hardware before you dare set up your new Windows 2000–based domains. But, as a wise old head once commented to me, "Hey, if this stuff ever gets easy, lad, we'll all have to go find jobs."

Why a Fourth Edition?

The fourth edition of *Mastering Windows 2000 Server* is the latest and most complete of my series of guides to using Windows 2000 to get your job done. I've aimed in this book to show you how Windows 2000 Server works, what it can—and *can't*—do, and to show you the shortest path to getting any particular job done. My coauthors and I have tried to make this a guide that you can use on a day-to-day basis to simplify the task of managing networks. And, furthermore, I intend to continue helping you out through a free online newsletter that I hope you'll sign up for... but I'll tell you about that at the end of this introduction (which is a sneaky way to try to entice you to stay with the intro to the end).

But why a fourth? Two reasons: first, in the year since the third edition, I had the opportunity to learn about and work with more aspects of Windows 2000, and I wanted to make sure that information was in the book. That's pretty much the reason that you've seen a version of this book or its NT 4 predecessor annually: it gives me a chance to add the new technologies that I've learned about, to report on new things that Microsoft has added, and to fix errors in previous editions. So, in other words, I could have guessed years ago that this edition, or something like it, would appear. But I didn't expect the second reason: security.

A New Security Focus

As every system administrator who lived through Code Red, SirCam, Code Blue, Nimda, and the zombie attacks of 2001 knows, 2001 was a *rough* year for computer security (to say nothing of the *other* security-related events of 2001). The year 2001 saw the discovery of some very serious security holes in Windows 2000's Internet Information Services, Indexing Service, and Media Player, and, worse, later saw a bunch of new worms, viruses, and Trojan horses exploiting those holes. Network administrators have always, of course, had a responsibility to secure their networks, but I think 2001 changed the *reason* why they've got to do that.

Prior to 2001, my main concern in securing my network was in ensuring that the bad guys didn't attack me. In theory, then, if I didn't care about my data and left my network wide-open, then the only person that I was affecting was me. But the new worms changed that reality. One unprotected Internet Information server can be infected, and that IIS server can then spend all of its free time trying to find and infect other servers. So when I put an insecure IIS box on the network, then I'm not just potentially hurting myself—no, I've actually joined the Other Side and provided a tool that the weasels can use to magnify their mischief and destruction. I guess the first great truth of computing in the 21st century seems to be that security isn't optional... not for anybody. So I think you'll notice a bit of a trend in the "all-new" stuff in this edition; you might think of the fourth as *Mastering Windows 2000 Server: The Security Edition.*

A Useful Administrator's Handbook, Not an Exam-Cram

But before going on to enumerate the fourth edition's benefits, having said what the book is, let me say one thing that it's not, or at least not intended to be: an MCSE study guide. Over the years, I have heard from literally thousands of people who've told me that they have used some of my books to successfully study for Microsoft certification exams, and I'm always happy to hear that. I'm also happy to hear that people are making use of this book to study for their Windows 2000 certifications. And, in fact, I sat down one day in 2001 and took all four of the core Windows 2000 certification exams cold, just to see how I'd do. I honestly knew only two things about the exams: (1) There are four core tests, and (2) everyone says that something called "network infrastructure" is hard. My reasoning for taking these exams was this: Many people choose to use the book as a guide to preparing for the exam, and pretty much everything I know is in the book. So, I thought, if I could take the tests cold and pass them, then I guess the book *could* help others study for the exams. Well, I passed 'em all, so if you know this book back to front, then you've probably got a chance at doing well on the four core tests and the Active Directory design test. (And no matter how you study, best of luck!) But, again, I want to stress that the goal of this book is to help you get your job done rather than to help you pass a test.

If you own a copy of the second or third edition and you're wondering if it's a good idea to "upgrade," then allow me, if you will, to tell you why I believe that you'll find a copy of the fourth a good investment. In short, this edition contains 20 completely new sections ranging in size from 2 to 30 pages, a new focus on security, a wealth of new Active Directory (AD) and DNS design and troubleshooting advice, dozens of significantly rewritten and expanded sections, and some looks ahead to .NET Server (the next version of NT), where appropriate.

All-New Sections

As I said before, my original goal in the fourth was to get a chance to add coverage of a bunch of built-in Windows 2000 technologies that are useful but that I simply didn't have the time to include before. The rash of security problems that beset Windows NT and 2000 in 2001 spurred me to tighten up my own network, and I've included what I've found works and doesn't work security-wise in this edition. I think you'll find these completely new sections useful. (And, if you don't own any previous editions, please note that I'm jumping straight into techie jargon in the following points so as to provide a short overview for veteran readers. I will explain all of this terminology in the book.) The new sections include:

DNS-Related AD Troubleshooting   Probably the source of the greatest number of AD questions. Helpful if you're having trouble logging onto a new AD or adding a new domain controller to an AD. Simple diagnostic steps to prove whether the problem is or isn't DNS-related and, if it is, then how to fix it in Chapter 8.

Using Security Templates and SECEDIT   I've been kicking myself since the third edition came out for not covering this completely essential tool. How'd you like to control user rights, local group membership, NTFS permissions, Registry security, auditing, and account policies remotely on any system on your network? Simple ASCII templates let you control it all. Learn about it in Chapter 9.

Auditing Security Events, File and Directory Access   If you're like most of us, then you know that Windows 2000, like NT, provides a wealth of potential reporting on who did what and when and where he did it. But how to use it? Chapters 8 and 11 include all you need to know about using auditing to track what's happening in your network.

IPSec Explained and Demonstrated   IP Security—IPSec to its friends—is a useful way to secure traffic between any two (or more) systems, even over the Internet. What's even better, though, is that this works for virtually every Internet-enabled application. Windows 2000 includes it free and it's well worth your time to get to know it. The write-up is about 20 pages at the end of Chapter 6.

Certificates, Public Key Infrastructure, and Certificate Authorities   PKI is a huge—vast—topic but an important one. Certificates provide a way to authenticate users outside of your network and potentially not even running a Windows operating system. Just as the publicly-defined TCP/IP protocol freed us from the proprietary protocols like NetBEUI and IPX/SPX, PKI is moving us away from proprietary authentication systems. Notice I said "moving"—2000's support of certificates is important but incomplete. Even if you do not intend to use PKI now, read this anyway. Sometime in the next five years you'll have to understand and wrestle with this. There are over 30 pages on the topic at the end of Chapter 8.

Securing IIS Servers and Reading IIS Logs   We can lock our file and print servers behind firewalls, but we have no choice about where our Web servers go—they've got to be out on the public Internet. Chapter 17 offers 16 pages of advice on protecting your Web server. You'll also find a new section in that chapter showing you how to keep track of who's been knocking at your door by reading your IIS logs.

Configuring and Using Indexing Service   If you are building or maintaining an IIS-based Web site, then you'll usually want to offer your visitors a flexible search engine. Windows 2000's Indexing Service is a surprisingly useful tool that is, unfortunately, nearly completely undocumented—and that includes some truly frightening default settings, security-wise. Chapter 17 includes a new section on setting up and securing Indexing Service, as well as some ready-to-use Active Server Page scripts to provide you a basic search engine.

Troubleshooting Group Policies   If you have an Active Directory, then you'll soon discover the power of group policies. But sometimes they don't seem to work exactly as advertised, and then it's up to you to figure out what's wrong. Chapter 9 always included a section on GPs, but for this edition I've doubled its size and added new sections, including the troubleshooting section.

Removable Storage Manager and Automated Backups with NTBackup   I try whenever possible to use the tools that are in the box, mainly because I'm cheap, and so I use NTBackup. But making NTBackup work so that it automatically does scheduled backups turned out to be a major challenge, because while 2000's NTBackup backs up to tapes, as it always did, it now works through a complex intermediary named Removable Storage Manager, or RSM, in order to write to tapes. Chapter 21 explains RSM in detail and presents some fairly intricate—and useful, I hope—batch files that you can, with a little modification, plug right into your system and get your backups working automatically.

Troubleshooting Network Address Translation and Internet Connection Sharing   I can tell from the amount of letters that I get about ICS and NAT that a lot of you want to use your Windows 2000 computers as a way to share a single routable Internet address with a number of machines. So I created a new section in Chapter 6 offering advice on how to methodically examine and fix a nonfunctioning ICS or NAT connection.

Making Older Apps Work under Windows 2000   Two new sections talk about a couple of tricks that you can do to manage that small number of NT 4 apps that simply don't want to run under 2000. The sections cover a couple of undocumented tricks—shutting off Windows File Protection temporarily and using something called "DLL redirection" to accommodate applications that absolutely must have their own versions of system DLLs—you can solve some of the more annoying compatibility problems.

DHCP User and Vendor Classes, Command-Line Tools   At first glance, DHCP didn't change all that much under Windows 2000 . . . but there were actually a few quite interesting improvements. One was a whole new set of command-line tools that basically let you do all of your DHCP administration from the command line (and therefore scripts). The other was the notion of vendor and user "classes," which let you create a set of machines in your network that get a different set of DHCP settings than others, even if the others are on the same subnet. Chapter 7 includes this information.

Major Rewrites and Changes

Many chapters include significant rewrites. There truly isn't space to list them all, but here are the bigger ones.

Chapter 4, on Setup, includes a new section that I think you'll really like. It shows you how to build setup scripts and remote installation servers that do unattended, automated rollouts of Windows 2000 Server and Professional . . . but these servers arrive with the latest service packs and hotfixes from the first boot. **Chapter 6, on TCP/IP basics,** not only includes the pieces that I've already described, but a couple of reader requests as well: a table of common port numbers and a description of how to use network binding order to improve system performance.

I have felt very strongly for a while now that there isn't a really good reference for running DNS on Windows 2000, and so I've worked hard to make this book that reference. To that end, the **DNS coverage in Chapter 7** now includes details on primary/secondary replication, securing zone transfers between servers, and subnet mask ordering (with thanks to Robert Eggleston for pointing it out). I've also added coverage about what to do when you find yourself in a mixed DNS environment—a legacy non-2000 DNS network that you must blend somehow with a 2000-based DNS system. Even if you don't use 2000-based DNS servers, the built-in dynamic DNS clients on your Windows 2000 systems will give your legacy DNS servers fits when they constantly try to register with those systems. You'll see in that chapter how to shut the 2000 boxes up and give those old BIND systems a rest!

Two years of post-beta experience has also taught me that the sort of DNS design called "split-brain" DNS or, as I like to think of it, "keeping two sets of books" isn't an advanced or optional architecture—no, I think today's security environment requires it. So I've got a lot more discussion of split-brain architecture. You'll even build a split-brain DNS system if you follow my step-by-step example of creating a DNS domain called "bigfirm.biz." The example previously employed only routable addresses, which isn't a reality for most folks; it's now built around a more commonly-used IP address range, and will "plug and play" better into test networks and home-based networks where you're likely to have only one routable address and the rest all non-routable. Even better, I have redesigned the example (it used to be "bowsers.com") to integrate perfectly with the sample build-your-own Active Directory in Chapter 8; that should make the examples work on a much wider variety of systems.

Speaking of **Chapter 8, on Active Directory**, it too has gotten some major revisions (it is probably the most extensively revised chapter in this edition) as I try to cover more and more AD planning, installation, management and troubleshooting concepts. You'll see even more DNS in this chapter, as it is AD's most necessary evil. Chapter 8 sees more practical DNS help in the form of nuts-and-bolts troubleshooting techniques as well as planning issues—should Acme choose acme.com, acme.local or acme.pri for their AD domain name? The section on migration is considerably larger, with an expanded discussion of the pros and cons of the two main migration approaches.

The AD chapter also includes more AD nut-and-bolts, with an explanation of the "other" AD objects—shared folders, printers, and contacts—as well as domain local groups. I honestly didn't find them all that useful in my AD work, but found that Microsoft asked about them quite a bit in the MCSE exams, so I figured that it couldn't hurt to pump up the DLG coverage. I still don't think they're useful, but read up on 'em and you'll get three or four more questions right on the AD test.

Time and Knowledge Base articles have given us some cool new fixes for seemingly impossible problems. Fixes for some annoying domain controller and global catalog discovery problems are now available with Service Pack 2 and a few Registry zaps. They're in Chapter 8 as well. I realized that I'd covered how to delegate control of an organizational unit, but I'd neglected to explain how to undo that—how to "undelegate"—but the chapter covers that now. I found that my original explanation of AD replication internals was a bit off-kilter, so I deleted most of it and rewrote it, and also added some info on using a tool called REPADMIN to track replication. Working with some very large firms on designing their Active Directories has taught me that the peculiar nature of the schema under Active Directory—one size fits all—can pose some problems, and I tell you about them in the chapter. And you've already read about the new sections on audits and certificates.

Chapter 9, on user accounts, also got a serious reworking. We'd covered profiles for NT 4 workstations, thinking that profiles were passé. Turns out that they're not, so I updated the section to cover profiles on 2000 and XP systems. You already know about the rewrite of the group policies section and the new sections on SECEDIT, but there are, again, more nuts and bolts on a smaller scale. How to set complex password policies, how to change passwords from the command line, how to read (and write) the LDAP-ese that some tools require, and a rewrite of how user permissions and rights work are all in Chapter 9.

Chapter 10, on storage and drives, revisits and amplifies upon the problems of making mirrored disks work properly, including creating and using a Windows 2000 boot disk to let you boot from a mirrored disk. **Chapter 11** needed, I felt, a better and fuller explanation of 2000's newer way of representing ACLs, so there's a new section on understanding allow versus deny permissions, as well as an in-depth explanation of the lowest-level permissions—what I call the 13 "atomic permissions." And you've already read about the new section on auditing file and directory access. I hope that after reading this chapter you'll never get confused about NTFS permissions again.

Chapter 17, the chapter on IIS/FTP/e-mail/telnet, has a number of new sections, as you've read, including securing your Web server, reading the logs, and adding Indexing Service. This chapter also has a section showing you how to build an Active Server Page that sends e-mails automatically. I use it to inform me of system events. The book's coverage of EMWACS IMS, the free e-mail server for Windows 2000, is updated with new URLs—as the tool is free, it kind of has to live wherever it's welcome. Many of you have expressed frustration with setting up multiple Web sites on a single server, so I've added a step-by-step example of doing that. That leads to some more in-depth discussion of SSL on Web sites. Finally, **Chapter 21, the disaster recovery chapter**, includes the new section on RSM that you've already read about. On top of all of these changes are many small improvements, error fixes, and tweaks.

All in all, I'm quite proud of this new edition. I hope that you choose to pick it up and, more important, I hope that you're pleased with it. And if you're *still* on the fence about whether this edition is worth your time and money, here's the kicker: by popular demand, the CD version of the book is back. A fully searchable version of the book is on a CD-ROM bound into this volume.

What Was New in the Third Edition

At just about the same time that Windows 2000 shipped, so also did the second edition of this book. At the time, I thought the fact that Win2K had finally shipped would mean that I could slow down a bit and take things a bit easier.

Boy, was *I* wrong.

Many organizations and individuals who'd decided to ignore Win2K until it shipped (or, as many wryly remarked, "*if* it ships") created a large demand for consulting and seminars when 2000 finally *did* ship.

The consulting gave me an opportunity to work with 2000 in real-life situations that you just plain couldn't duplicate during the beta process, and that experience made me reevaluate some of 2000's strengths and weaknesses, as well allowed me to see some better ways to use 2000. All of the companies and government agencies that I visited had differing needs, but one thing that they all wanted to know more about was, "How do we roll out Windows 2000 Server and Professional most easily?" As a result, Chapter 4, the Setup chapter, is much larger and now covers scripting, Remote Installation Services (including a bunch of undocumented RIS goodies), and Sysprep.

That was the benefit that I got from the *consulting*; in addition, the *seminars* gave me the opportunity to see that while the book was good, it needed reorganization and expansion.

I found that, in particular, the whole issue of when to introduce Active Directory bedeviled me. I put it in Chapter 2 of the earlier editions because it seemed to me that AD was so central to Windows 2000 that I *had* to introduce it early on. But understanding Active Directory requires understanding Domain Name System (DNS), and DNS was covered much later in the book. DNS was covered later in the book because when I first started writing about NT back in 1993, TCP/IP was an "advanced topic," and so made sense in the back of the book. It finally dawned on me that if you're doing Windows 2000, you're pretty much *compelled* to use TCP/IP—which meant that I needed to explain TCP/IP, 2000's routing functions, DHCP, WINS, and DNS very early in the book. (And if you don't know what those things are, don't worry—I'll explain them all in detail.) In fact, the quality of 2000's DHCP, WINS, and DNS services is so improved over that of their counterparts in NT 4 that they'd justify moving to 2000 even *without* Active Directory! Furthermore, you shouldn't even *think* of implementing an AD without a good solid DNS infrastructure.

But how many of us NT 4 expert types *really* had to know that much about DNS? Well, the fact is that NT 4 never really relied on DNS all that much, and so most of us never had to progress beyond the basics. But 2000 relies on DNS heavily, and so I added a mini–DNS book inside this book. If you don't know what a forwarder or a slave is, if you're fuzzy on how *primary* DNS server is different from *authoritative* DNS server, or if you haven't a clue how to set up a DNS server so that your internal network sees a completely different set of names than the external Internet sees—or why you'd want to—then don't skip Chapter 7! And once you're comfortable with building a big-time DNS system, then you'll appreciate the expanded coverage of Active Directory, which has moved from Chapter 2 to Chapter 8. The AD chapter is about twice the size of the AD chapter in the previous editions, and includes new discussions of sites, replication, operations masters, and migration approaches and tools, as well as expanded discussion of the old material.

In addition to the changes prompted by consulting and teaching, the third included enhancements brought about by your letters. For example, many of you wrote to tell me that you needed some more background material. Not everyone's been with us since the NT days, you said, so how about explaining a bit more about what a domain is in the first place? To all of those who wrote asking for that intro, Chapter 2 now offers it. And in response to many requests, I've shown how to set up network address translation routers in Chapter 6.

But I wasn't the only contributor to the third edition. Brian M. Smith returned to completely rework his chapter on file sharing. He rewrote the section on file and directory permissions to better explain how 2000's allow/deny system works, and to explain in greater detail how the Distributed File System (Dfs) works. (To show you how determined he was, Brian was working on edits up to the day before he got married—congratulations Brian, and thanks for the hard work!) Christa Anderson revisited her chapter on storage with greater coverage of dynamic disks, expanded her Terminal Services chapter to include updated information as well as Microsoft's not-to-be-missed free Terminal Server Advanced Client, added coverage of authoritative restores and showed how to beef up the Recovery Console in the disaster recovery chapter, and explained how to set up Internet printing in the printing chapter. Doug Toombs enlarged his already-huge chapter on Remote Access Services and added some terrific real-world tips on securing Internet Information Services.

What's in This Book

To misquote Douglas Adams in *The Hitchhiker's Guide to the Galaxy,* "Windows 2000 is big *really* big." So here's a guide to what's in this book so you'll know what to expect.

Chapter 1 is a brief introduction to the goods and bads about Windows 2000. When I say "brief," I mean it, even though the chapter is about 30 pages long. One could probably spend three times that just getting started explaining everything that Windows 2000 does. And in Chapter 2, I bring any Microsoft networking newbies up to speed with an explanation of Microsoft's basic networking terminology and concepts, as well as a little history. If you're an old NT veteran, then feel free to skip that chapter. Chapter 3 introduces a necessary evil of NT/2000 networking: the Registry. If you've worked with a Microsoft product with a Registry before, then there's very little new there; if you don't know what a Registry is, then you'll find the chapter essential.

After three chapters, you'll probably be getting impatient to install 2000 and do something with it, so that's Chapter 4. In this large chapter, you'll first learn how to do a basic install of 2000. Then you'll see how to write scripts to do unattended installs of 2000, how to extend the power of scripting with a tool called Remote Installation Services, and how to use a free tool called Sysprep to make it possible to use disk-copy tools like Drive Image Pro and Ghost to quickly distribute prebuilt system images to new computers.

Once you've got Windows 2000 set up, you'll need to get around in it, and you're going to soon find that you *can't find a bloody thing*—or rather it'll seem that way sometimes. Where is the blasted Network Control Panel? How do I stop a service? Why doesn't the Control Panel *do* anything anymore? As the user interface has changed somewhat, you may find yourself saying quite often something like, "Where are they now?" To answer that question, I asked Lisa Justice to write Chapter 5. Lisa and I worked together years ago, and she developed the excellent coverage on user profiles in *Mastering Windows NT Server*. Lisa takes it a step further, however, and shows you how to use the Microsoft Management Console to build your *own* network management tools.

After that, the next two chapters take up the issues surrounding TCP/IP in a network environment. Where TCP/IP was once a mildly exotic networking alternative, Windows 2000 essentially forces you to adopt TCP/IP as your primary networking protocol—so you'd better be ready to implement and support it. In Chapter 6, I explain how TCP works specifically in Windows 2000 and how Windows 2000 handles the essential infrastructure issues of IP routing. Then, in Chapter 7, I show you how to design and implement an IP infrastructure with the Dynamic Host Configuration Protocol (DHCP), the Windows Internet Name Service (WINS)—despite what you may have heard, it's *not* dead, sadly, so be sure to read the section on WINS—and the Domain Name System (DNS). DNS gets its own very large section where we take you from basic concepts to step-by-steps on how to build and implement a world-class DNS infrastructure.

By then, you're ready for Active Directory, Windows 2000's crown jewel. Chapter 8 starts off with a discussion of what motivated Microsoft to throw away its old user account system and replace it with AD. You'll get some hands-on experience in setting up a small AD, and then you'll learn about creating and managing an AD of any size, including migration approaches and advice.

Lisa returns in Chapter 9 to explain the ins and outs of creating and managing user accounts. That's a *big* topic, including not only the Windows 2000 successor to profiles, but also group policies, the Windows 2000 successor to NT 4's system policies.

Windows 2000 handles storage differently than NT did, as you'll learn in Chapter 10. In that chapter, Christa Anderson shows you how to connect, partition, and format drives, as well as covering Windows 2000's RAID functions. Christa was a coauthor for the first two editions of *Mastering Windows NT Server* and is now a major contributor for *Windows 2000 Magazine*, as well as the author of an upcoming Sybex title on Windows Terminal Server. That's followed by Brian M. Smith's chapter covering shared folders, including how to secure those shares with both share and NTFS permissions—they're quite a bit different from NT 4's permissions—and coverage of Windows 2000's new Distributed File System and the File Replication Service. Brian is a consultant who's been working in many NT shops since NT 3.5 and has done just about every kind of job imaginable in an NT/2000 shop, so he brings a wealth of hands-on expertise to his chapters. Chapter 11 ends with a piece by me about offline folders, a modification of the network redirector that offers greater network response, laptop synchronization support, and network fault tolerance.

John Jensen joins us in Chapter 12 to describe an all-new feature of Windows 2000: central distribution of applications. John is a long-time NT C programming Giant Brain type of a guy, and being an applications programmer gave him a few advantages in analyzing and describing the built-in software distribution tool that Windows 2000 offers. Christa returns in Chapter 13 to describe how to network printers under Windows 2000. Brian then explains, in Chapter 14, how to connect client PCs to a Windows 2000 network, whether those PCs are running DOS, Windows, or whatever.

Christa then warms to a favorite topic of hers in Chapter 15, where she covers the built-in Terminal Services feature of Windows 2000. And if you have no idea what Terminal Services does, check out that chapter: Terminal Services makes your Windows 2000 system a multiuser computer, in many ways combining the best of the PC and the mainframe! Then in Chapter 16, Tyler Regas shows you how to connect your Macintosh to a Windows 2000 network.

Once your organization is connected to the Internet, you'll probably want to get a Web server up and running. Windows 2000 offers that and more, and Doug Toombs shows you how to set up the Internet Information Services version 5, including not only the Web piece but also the FTP server piece, the NNTP news server piece, and the SMTP mail server, all in Chapter 17. Doug is another *Windows 2000 Magazine* contributor and a consultant (`www.netarchitect.com`) who has put together many an NT network for clients. In the end of the chapter, I show you how to set up the telnet server built into every NT server, explain how to set up a free Internet mail server, and discuss Internet security a bit.

I needed someone to write Chapter 18 who actually works with large Win2K networks. The first person who came to mind was Darren Mar-Elia, a network manager with Charles Schwab. Schwab is one of the early implementers of Windows 2000, and so Darren was able to offer with authority some sage advice for those designing a large Windows 2000 enterprise.

And speaking of enterprises, most large ones have at least a little bit of software somewhere written by Novell, hence Chapter 19 discusses NetWare coexistence. For that chapter, I tapped Doug. Then, in Chapter 20, Christa offers some advice and instruction on tuning and monitoring a Windows 2000–based network, and then in Chapter 21, she looks at disaster recovery—never a happy topic, but a necessary one. Doug then returns for a lengthy and quite complete look at dial-up, ISDN, and frame relay support in Remote Access Service (RAS) in Chapter 22.

Brian finishes the book off with a chapter on handling hardware: Windows 2000's new Plug-and-Play hardware support is something of a mixed blessing, but Brian shows you how to make almost any new hardware work under Win2K. ("Almost" because, as was the case with NT, we Windows 2000 users are the poor stepchildren when it comes to driver availability. Even lawn mowers seem to come with Windows 98 drivers these days, but 2000/NT–compatible hardware is a little more scarce, although it's getting better with time!)

Conventions Used in This Book

As you know, when discussing any network technology, things can get quite complex quite quickly, so I've followed some conventions to make them clearer and easier to understand.

Windows 2000 versus NT

Throughout this book, you'll see me refer to *Windows 2000*, *NT 4*, and just plain *NT*. I don't want to confuse, so let me clarify what I mean when I use those terms.

When I say "Windows 2000" or "NT 4," then of course I mean those particular products. But when I say "NT," I'm referring to the various versions of the NT operating system that have come out, including both NT 4 and Windows 2000. Despite the name change from NT-version-some-thing to Windows-model-year, under the hood, NT 4 and Windows 2000 are quite similar. The underlying kernel, the piece of the operating system that manages memory, handles multitasking, and loads and unloads drivers, is largely unchanged from NT 4, with the very important exception of the new Plug-and-Play capabilities. So it seems appropriate to me to refer to either an NT 3.*x*–based, NT 4–based, or Windows 2000–based network as an "NT network."

Windows

Microsoft is working so hard to "brand" the name Windows that now they've attached the name to three totally different operating systems. The first of the "original" Windows—versions 1.0, 2.0, 2.1, 3.0, 3.1, 3.11, Windows for Workgroups 3.1 and 3.11, Windows 95 and 98—is an ever-evolving oper-ating system built to extend the life of Microsoft's cash cow, MS-DOS. The second was NT, a project intended originally to extend an older operating system named OS/2. And the third is Windows CE, an OS designed for smaller diskless computers, including the of-dubious-value "AutoPC," a computer designed for your car's dashboard. (Oh, great, now I get to worry that the bozo in front of me in traffic will be distracted playing Quake; good call, Bill.) Therefore, it's getting a bit ambiguous when someone says "Windows"—so what I mean when I use the term all by itself, without a qualifier like "2000," "NT," "CE," or the like, is "Windows Classic"—Windows 3.*x* or its cousin, Windows 95/98. I can't wait until Microsoft sends Pella and Andersen cease and desist letters enjoining them from using the word "Windows" in their corporate name and product-line descriptions.

Directories

By default, Windows 2000 installs into a directory named \winnt on some drive. (See, it really *is* still NT.) You can decide at installation time to put the operating system somewhere else, but almost no one does. As a result, I have a bit of a problem: I often need to refer to the directory that Win-dows 2000 is installed into, and I need a phrase less cumbersome than "whatever directory you installed Windows 2000 into" or the brief and technically accurate but nonintuitive %systemroot%. So you'll see references to the \winnt directory, which you should read as "whatever directory you've installed Windows 2000 into."

Similarly, \winnt contains a directory I'll refer to now and then called system32; I'll refer to that as \winnt\system32.

Register to Stay Up-to-Date!

With the first version of this book, I tried out a way to keep you folks informed about book errata, changes to Windows 2000, or just plain new stuff that I've learned. No matter how old 2000 gets, we'll *never* know everything about it—there will always be new things to learn. And certainly I'll include the things that I learn into new editions of the book—but why wait for the next edition? I'd rather get you at least *some* of that new information immediately!

So I'm extending the following offer to my readers. Visit my Web site at www.minasi.com and register to receive my free Windows 2000/NT newsletter. Every month that I can, I'll send you a short update on tips and things that I've learned, as well as any significant errata that appear in the book (which I'm praying don't appear). It won't be spam—as the saying goes, "Spammers must die!"—just a short heads-up on whatever I've come across that's new (to me) and interesting about Windows 2000. Past newsletters have also included lengthy articles on DNS troubleshooting, Indexing Service, and IPSec, so I think you'll find it a worthwhile newsletter for the price.

Well, okay, about the spam part: there will be *one* bit of naked marketing—when the next edition of the book comes out, I'll announce it in the newsletter.

For Help and Suggestions: Check the Newsletter and *www.minasi.com/gethelp*

As always, if I can help, I'm available on e-mail. Got a question the book didn't answer? Visit my FAQ page at www.minasi.com/gethelp and, if that doesn't help, there are instructions on how to e-mail me. I can't promise that I'll have the answer, but I'll sure try! I'm often traveling, sometimes for weeks at a time, and I don't pick up e-mail when I'm on the road, so if I take a week or few to respond, don't worry, I'll get back to you as soon as I can. It's easiest to help with questions which are specific but brief—please understand that I sometimes open my e-mail to find more than a hundred questions waiting for me!

In addition to offering help, I'd appreciate *your* help and feedback. Sybex and I have been able to get a new edition of this book out roughly annually since NT Server first appeared in 1993. I don't know everything about NT or Windows 2000—I'm not certain *anyone* does—and through the years, reader suggestions and "book bug reports" have been a tremendous source of assistance in making the NT books better and better. ("Gasp! An *error*? In *my* book? No, say it isn't so!") Got a tip, something you want to share with the world? Pass it along to me, and I'll include it in the next edition and acknowledge your contribution.

And by the way, to all of you reading this book: thank you so much, and I hope you enjoy our coverage of Microsoft's flagship networking platform!

Chapter 1

Windows 2000 Server Overview

AFTER YEARS OF TALK about "Cairo" (the original Microsoft code name for what became Windows 2000) and even more years of work, Microsoft finally shipped Windows 2000. After training us to expect roughly annual releases of new versions of NT—NT 3.1 shipped in 1993, 3.5 in 1994, 3.51 in 1995, and 4 in 1996—NT 5 finally arrived, but it was considerably later than a year after the release of NT 4. Furthermore, NT 5 arrived with a new name: Windows 2000. But the name's not all that's new.

So what took so long? Was it worth the wait? For many, the answer will be "yes." Much of NT's foundation—the internal kernel structure, how drivers are designed, how Windows 2000 multitasks—hasn't changed all that terribly much from NT 4, but network professionals really don't see that part of NT. Instead, we network types notice that the *above-ground* structures, the tools built atop the foundation, are so different as to render Windows 2000 Server almost unrecognizable as a descendant of NT 3.*x* and 4.*x*. For comparison's sake, and to extend the structural metaphor, think of using Windows NT 3.1 Advanced Server as renting a room in someone's basement, using NT 4 as renting a two-bedroom apartment, and using Windows 2000 Server as living in Bill Gates's mansion on Lake Washington: more rooms than anyone can count, all filled with new and wonderful electronic gadgets.

In the mansion, many of the things that you know from the basement room are unchanged—the electricity comes out of sockets in the wall, the pipes are copper or PVC, bathrooms have sinks and commodes in them—but there's so much more of it all, as well as so many new things, both useful ("Hey, cool, a garden, and automatic sprinklers for it!") and of debatable value ("What does this bidet thing do, anyway?"). That's not to say that NT's underpinnings will never change, not at all—the next (and still-unnamed) version of NT will go a step further, digging up NT's 32-bit foundation and replacing it with a 64-bit one.

The main point, however, is this: If you're an NT network administrator, be prepared for culture shock. In some of their parts, the difference between NT 4 and Windows 2000 is at least 10 times as great as the difference between NT 3.1 and NT 4. And if you've never worked with NT in any flavor, be prepared to find Windows 2000 both delightful and frustrating—as is the case with most Microsoft software.

It would be somewhat shortsighted of me to simply say, "Here are the new features you'll find in Windows 2000," and then to just dump the features—it sort of misses the forest for the trees. So let me start off by briefly discussing the big picture and what Microsoft's trying to accomplish; then I'll move along to those new features and, finally, take a look at a few of Windows 2000's shortcomings.

Microsoft's Overall Goals for Windows 2000

The changes in Windows 2000 from NT 4 are quite significant, but they were long in coming. What was the wait all about?

Make NT an Enterprise OS

Microsoft wants your company to shut off its mainframes and do your firm's work on big servers running NT. That's why there is a version of Windows 2000 Server called Datacenter Server. Microsoft is also hoping that "enterprise" customers will exploit new Windows 2000 Server facilities such as Active Directory and Microsoft Application Server (nee MTS) and COM+ to write gobs of new and hardware-hungry distributed applications. Before they can accomplish that, however, they need to clear three hurdles: reliability, availability, and scalability.

NT MUST BE MORE RELIABLE

Since their appearance in the late '70s, microcomputer-based network operating systems have been seen as fundamentally different from "big-system" OSes like IBM's MVS and OS/400, Compaq's OpenVMS, and the myriad flavors of Unix. PC-based network operating systems weren't exactly seen as toys, but neither were they seen as something that one would base one's business on, if that business was truly critical. For example, it's hard to imagine the New York Stock Exchange announcing that they'd decided to get rid of their current trading system and to replace it with a NetWare 4.1 or NT 4–based client-server system. PC-based stuff just wasn't (and largely still isn't) seen as sufficiently reliable yet to take on the big guys.

Nor is that an unfair assessment. Most of us would be a bit uncomfortable about discovering in mid-flight that the state-of-the-art airliner taking us across the Pacific was run by NT, or that the Social Security Administration had decided to dump their old mainframe-based software in favor of a Lotus Notes–based system running atop NT. Years ago, many firms discovered that NT servers crashed far less often if rebooted weekly; it's hard to imagine running a heart-and-lung machine on something like that.

But Microsoft wants to shed that image. They want very much to build an OS that is sufficiently industrial-strength in reliability so that one day it wouldn't be silly to suggest that AT&T's long distance network could run atop some future version of NT, Windows 2000-something. With Windows 2000, Microsoft believes that they've taken some steps in that direction.

NT MUST BE MORE AVAILABLE

A server being rebooted to change some parameters is just as down as one that is being rebooted after a Blue Screen Of Death, the symptom of a system crash that is all too familiar to NT 4 veterans. Many Windows 2000 parameters can be changed without a reboot, where a change to the corresponding parameter in Windows NT 4 would require one. Unfortunately, as we will see, some of the most common parameter changes still require a reboot.

NT Must Be Able to "Scale" to Use Big Computers

Reliability's not the only big-network issue that Microsoft faces. The other is the limit on the raw power that NT can use—to use a word that the PC industry created a few years ago, NT must be more *scalable*.

Being an "enterprise" operating system requires two different kinds of scalability, which are somewhat at odds with each other: performance scalability and administrative scalability. The first asks, "If I need to do more work with NT, can I just run it on a bigger computer?" The second asks, "If I need to support more users/computers/gigabytes of hard disk/etc., can I do it without hiring more administrators?"

Performance Scalability

CPUs are simply not getting all that much faster in terms of the things they can do. To create faster or higher-capacity computers, then, computer manufacturers have been putting more and more CPUs into a box. And while NT has in theory been designed to use up to 32 processors since its first incarnation, in reality, very few people have been able to get any use out of more than 4 processors. With Windows 2000, Microsoft claims to have improved the scalability of NT—although I've not yet heard anyone say with a straight face that Windows 2000 will "run like a top" on a 32-processor system.

Besides the ability to use a larger number of CPUs, there were internal restrictions within Windows NT—such as the number of users that a SAM database would allow—that simply had to go. With Active Directory, many restrictions, including this one, have been removed.

The three versions of Server support different numbers of CPUs. Windows 2000 Server supports 4 processors. Windows 2000 Advanced Server supports 8 processors, and Windows 2000 Datacenter Server supports 32 processors.

NOTE   *Oh, and if you're looking in your Webster's for a definition of* scalability, *don't bother; it's not a real word. Microsoft made it up a few years ago. Basically,* scalable *roughly means, "As the job's demands grow, you can meet them by throwing in more hardware—processors and memory—and the system will meet the needs." It has become an issue because, while NT has theoretically supported 32 processors since its inception, much of the basic NT operating system itself can't use many processors—for example, adding a ninth processor to an eight-processor domain controller won't produce any faster logins. That's also true of NT programs; depending on whom you ask, SQL Server maxes out at four or eight processors. Beyond that, adding more processors does nothing more than run up the electric bill.*

Administrative Scalability/Manageability

Large enterprises do not like to add headcount in their core business areas, much less just to administer Windows NT. Windows 2000 Server contains a number of facilities such as Intellimirror, designed to allow customers to support more users running with more complex desktop environments with fewer support personnel. Microsoft typically refers to this area as "manageability," though I think "administrative scalability" better captures the flavor of the topic.

In this area, one of the most important additions to Windows 2000 is its support for both issuing and honoring digital certificates in place of userids and passwords for identification and authentication. The overall system needed to manage the life cycles of digital certificates and verify their authenticity and current validity is called Public Key Infrastructure (PKI). PKI-based security is both more secure and vastly more administratively scalable than userid+password-based security, but it is also much, much more technically complex.

Modernize NT

Three years can be an awfully long time in the computer business. The years of Windows 2000's development (1996 to 1999) saw the emergence of Universal Serial Bus, IEEE 1394, Fiber Channel, and 3-D video cards, just to name a few areas of technological growth, as well as the introduction of hundreds of new network cards, video boards, sound cards, SCSI host adapters, and so on. A new crop of network-aware PCs has appeared, PCs that understand networking right in their BIOSes and that are designed to be taken straight out of the box without anything on their hard drives, plugged into the network, and started up from the network rather than from any on-disk software. And on a more mundane note, nearly every PC sold in the past six years supports a hardware system called Plug and Play (PnP).

NT supports none of these things right out of the box. Some of these devices can be made to work, but some can't. Hardware support has always been something of an afterthought in NT, and it's amazing that Microsoft shipped NT 4 without any Plug-and-Play support, save an undocumented driver that could *sometimes* make a PnP ISA board work but that more commonly simply rendered a system unusable. NT 4's offhand support of PC Card laptops and its near-complete lack of support for Cardbus slots forced many an NT-centric shop to put NT Server on their servers, NT Workstation on their corporate desktops, and Windows 95 on their laptops.

One of Windows 2000's goals, then—and an essential one—is to support the new types of hardware and greatly improve the way that it works on laptops.

Make NT Easier to Support

The 1990s saw the rise of the graphical user interface (GUI), which brought a basically uniform "look and feel" to PC applications and made learning a PC application and PCs in general so much easier for users. We've seen programming tools go from some very simple development environments that crashed more often than they worked to today's very stable 32-bit suite of programming tools, making it possible for developers to create large and powerful 32-bit applications. Users and developers are better off—sounds good, doesn't it?

Well, it is, for them. But many of us fall into a third category: support staff. And while some things have gotten better—the graphical nature of many of NT's administrative tools helped get many new admins started on a networking career—the actual job of support hasn't gotten any easier. Consider this: Would you rather rebuild a `CONFIG.SYS` file to stitch back together a damaged DOS machine from memory, or would you prefer to pick through a broken Registry trying to figure out what's ailing it?

Microsoft's competition knew that support was the Achilles' heel of both Windows and NT, and so in the mid '90s, Sun and others began extolling the importance of considering the total cost of ownership (TCO) of any desktop system. It wasn't hard to make the argument that the biggest cost of putting Windows on a desktop isn't the hardware or the software—it's the staff hours required to get it up and keep it running.

With Windows 2000, Microsoft starts to reduce desktop TCO. A group of Windows 2000 improvements called Change and Configuration Management tools makes life easier for support folks and network administrators in general.

Specific New Capabilities and Features

So much for the good intentions. What about the new goodies?

Microsoft lists pages and pages of enhancements to Windows 2000—the PR people have, after all, had more than three years to cook up those lists. I'm sure they're all of value to someone, but here are the things that I find most valuable in Windows 2000, arranged according to my three earlier categories—making NT more enterprise-ready, modernizing NT, and improving its administrative tools/lowering TCO.

Making Windows 2000/NT More "Enterprising"

Several functions help push NT's latest incarnation to a place in the big leagues. In particular, the most significant "big network" changes to NT include:

- ◆ Active Directory
- ◆ Improved TCP/IP-based networking infrastructure
- ◆ More scalable security infrastructure options
- ◆ More powerful file sharing with the Distributed File System and the File Replication Service
- ◆ Freedom from drive letters with junction points and mountable drives
- ◆ More flexible online storage via the Removable Storage Manager

Active Directory

The crown jewel of Windows 2000, Active Directory is also the single most pervasive piece of the OS. Many of the things you'll read about in this book, many of the compelling features of Windows 2000, simply cannot function without Active Directory. Group policies, domain trees and forests, centralized deployment of applications, and the best features of the Distributed File System (to name a few) will not operate until you've got a system acting as an Active Directory server.

NOTE *The whys and wherefores of Active Directory are complex enough that they'll get a chapter all their own. In Chapter 8, you'll read about what Active Directory is trying to accomplish, how it does so, and how you can best design the Active Directory for your enterprise. But the short version is this: Active Directory is an open-ended database that stores information about who and what is on your network, and what they're allowed to do. (But that's only the barest possible explanation, as you'll see in Chapter 8.)*

Network Infrastructure Improvements

Anyone building an NT-based network around the TCP/IP protocol needed three important infrastructure tools:

- ◆ The Windows Internet Name Service (WINS), which helped Windows 2000– and NT-based servers and workstations locate domain controllers (which handled logins and authentication in general) as well as file and print servers.

♦ The Dynamic Host Configuration Protocol (DHCP), which simplified and centralized the once-onerous task of configuring TCP/IP on workstations.

♦ The Domain Name System (DNS), which did the same kind of job as WINS—keep track of names and addresses—but instead of helping workstations locate domain controllers and file/print servers, DNS helps programs like Web browsers and e-mail clients to find Web and mail servers. Some firms have avoided moving their networks to TCP/IP, staying instead with IPX (a protocol that owes its popularity to Novell's networking products) or NetBEUI (the main protocol for Microsoft networking prior to 1995). But with Windows 2000, pretty much everyone should be using TCP/IP, making DHCP, WINS, and DNS essential parts of any Windows 2000–based network.

WINS

Why did NT have two services—WINS and DNS—that kept track of names? Because of a questionable choice that Microsoft made back in 1994. Of the two, WINS was the most troublesome and, for some networks, unfortunately the most vital. Thus, it was to many people quite excellent news when Microsoft announced that Windows 2000 would be the end of WINS.

Reports of its death, however, turned out to be greatly exaggerated. The actual story is that, if you have a network that is 100 percent Windows 2000, both on the workstation and server, then yes, you can stop using WINS. But most of us won't have that for years, so Windows 2000 still has a WINS service. Thankfully, it's greatly improved; one expert commented to me that it's ironic that Microsoft finally "fixed" WINS, just as they were about to kill it. Chapter 7 shows you how to set it up and make it work.

DNS

DNS was something of a sidelight under NT 4, as NT didn't really need it—DNS's main value was to assist Internet-oriented programs like Web browsers, FTP clients, and POP3/SMTP mail clients in finding their corresponding servers. Under Windows 2000, however, DNS takes center stage. Without it, Active Directory won't work. And that bears underscoring:

WARNING   *Don't even think about planning and implementing an Active Directory until you have a DNS infrastructure planned and implemented. Or you'll be very sorry!*

NT 4's DNS server was a pleasure to work with, although that's just my opinion; I've spoken with people who tell me that it couldn't handle high volume loads. *I* didn't have any bad experiences with it, so I can't comment. NT 4's DNS wrapped a well-designed GUI around a standard DNS implementation, making basic DNS tasks simpler than they would be for a Unix DNS implementation at the time. Windows 2000 takes that a step further with improved wizards. First-time DNS administrators will find that Windows 2000's DNS server almost does all the hand-holding you could need.

Additionally, Windows 2000's DNS supports dynamic updates, a process wherein adding information about new machines to a DNS database can be automated. Based on the Internet standard document RFC 2136 (the Internet's standards are described in documents called Request for Comments, or RFCs), it combines the best of NT 4's WINS and DNS servers. The DNS server also supports another Internet standard, RFC 2782, which greatly expands the kind of information that

DNS servers can hold onto. For example, a pre-2782 DNS server could tell you which machines acted as mail servers for a given Internet domain, but not which machines were Web or FTP servers. 2782-compliant DNS servers can do that, and more: Active Directory now uses RFC 2782 to allow DNS to help workstations find domain controllers and other Active Directory–specific server types.

NOTE *Chapter 7 covers how Active Directory uses RFC 2782 in more detail.*

DHCP

DHCP frees network administrators from having to walk around and visit every single desktop in order to configure the TCP/IP protocol. The basic idea is that a workstation broadcasts over the network, seeking an IP address (every computer on an intranet must have a unique IP address); a DHCP server hears the plea and assigns that computer its own unique IP address.

The End of Rogue DHCP Servers

Generally, this is great, but now and then some dodo would decide to "practice" with DHCP by setting up a DHCP server on some PC. The budding new administrator's new DHCP server would then start handing out completely bogus addresses to unsuspecting workstations. Those workstations would then have IP addresses, but they'd be worthless ones, and as a result those workstations would be unable to function on the company's network.

With Windows 2000, however, not just anyone can create a DHCP server. Now, DHCP servers must be authorized in the Active Directory before they're allowed to start handing out addresses. This is a great advance, the end of what we used to call "rogue" DHCP servers.

DHCP Works with DNS to Register Clients

You read before that the new DNS supports dynamic updates, a process standardized in RFC 2136 whereby the DNS server will automatically receive address information about machines on the network from those machines. This is an improvement over NT 4's DNS server because that DNS server couldn't get DNS information about machines automatically—you, the administrator, had to type the names and IP addresses of new machines into the DNS Manager administration tool.

Windows 2000's DNS server collects its information about machines on the network with the help of those machines. When a machine starts up, one of the things it's doing while booting up— one of the reasons that booting modern PCs takes so long—is contacting the DNS server to tell the DNS server that the machine exists. In effect, each workstation and server on the network must know to *register* itself with the DNS server.

Unfortunately, as RFC 2136 is a fairly recent development in the DNS world, most existing operating systems—DOS, Windows for Workgroups, Windows 9*x*, NT 3.*x*, and 4.*x*—do not know to register themselves with a DNS server. That's where Windows 2000's DHCP server helps out. You can optionally tell the DHCP server to handle the DNS registrations for non-2136-aware workstations. This is a very useful new feature because, without it, dynamic updates wouldn't be worth much except for the rare firm that runs solely Windows 2000 on its desktops, laptops, and servers.

NOTE *You can read more about DHCP in Chapter 7.*

QUALITY OF SERVICE

The Internet's underlying protocol, TCP/IP, has something of an egalitarian nature; when the Net's busy, it's first come, first served. But TCP/IP has always had a built-in capability that would theoretically allow an Internet operator to give greater priority to one user over another, to dial in a better response time for some than for others. That's called quality of service, or QoS. It was always there but not really implemented, as it sort of ran against the way the Net was run.

The growth of corporate intranets, however, changes that story. Network operators in corporate networks aren't serving a mass public; rather, they're serving a diverse and hierarchical organization whose leaders may well want to be able to say, "We direct that this individual get more bandwidth and faster access to network resources than this other individual." That's possible if you're using expensive Cisco routers—but now you can do it if you use Windows 2000 machines as your IP routers as well.

New Security Infrastructure

As one security expert once said to me, "We knew that NT had 'made it' when hackers started targeting it." Hardly a month goes by without word of a new security hole in NT 4 and the hot fixes that are intended to plug that hole. Patch a plaster wall with Spackle enough, and eventually you have to wonder if you've got a plaster wall or a Spackle wall—so Microsoft must have decided early on that one of the things that Windows 2000 couldn't live without was a new security system.

So they built *two.*

Originally, Windows 2000 was supposed to replace NT 4's authentication system, known as NTLM (for NT LAN Manager), with a system popular in the Unix world called Kerberos. Kerberos is well understood and works well in large-scale systems, assisting Microsoft in their "scalability" (there's that nonword again) goal.

Partway through the Windows 2000 development process, Microsoft decided to supplement Kerberos with a *third* security system, a public key system based on the X.509 standard. They did that mainly because a public key system is considered far more scalable than either an NTLM or Kerberos system. Several companies offer hardware readers that allow users to log in by inserting credit card–sized devices called *smart cards* into the readers.

Kerberos and public key provide as a side effect a feature that NT administrators have asked after for a long time—transitive trust relationships.

Distributed File System

NT's first and probably still most prevalent job is as a file server. And as time has gone on and versions have appeared, it's gotten better at it. Some benchmarks have rated it as fast or faster than NetWare, the guys to beat. And where NT 4's file server software was largely unable to deliver throughput faster than 90Mbps, Windows 2000 can transfer data almost 10 times faster.

DISCONNECTING PHYSICAL LOCATIONS FROM NAMES

But NT's file server system is hampered by the way it addresses shares on servers. A share named DATA on a server named WALLY would be accessed as \\WALLY\DATA.

NOTE   *If you haven't worked with any Microsoft networking products before, then the two preceding backslashes before* WALLY *are just Microsoft's way of saying, "I'm about to name a server." I guess this is so there's no confusion—two backslashes always mean "a server name's next" in Microsoft networking-ese. The item after the server name is the name of the shared data, as servers can have more than one data share. In the* \\WALLY\DATA *case, I'm being uncreative and calling* WALLY's *data share* DATA.

Although that makes sense, it's limiting. Suppose the WALLY server goes up in a puff of smoke? We install a new server, perhaps named SALLY rather than WALLY, restore the data from WALLY, and re-create the DATA share. But now it's \\SALLY\DATA rather than \\WALLY\DATA, and configurations that are hardwired to look for and expect \\WALLY\DATA will fail. In other words, if a share's physical location changes, so must its "logical" location—its name. It'd be nice to be able to give a share a name that it could keep no matter what server it happened to be on.

Windows 2000 takes NT beyond that with the Distributed File System. In combination with Active Directory, Dfs—note the lowercase in the acronym; apparently someone already owned *DFS* when Microsoft started working on the Distributed File System—allows you to give all of your shares names like \\domainname\sharename rather than \\servername\sharename. You needn't know the name of the file server that the share is on.

FAULT TOLERANCE

You probably know that Windows 2000 offers you many ways to add reliability to your network through RAID storage and two-system computer clusters. RAID boxes aren't cheap, and clusters require a lot of hardware (two identical machines, external SCSI storage, extra network cards, and either the Advanced or Datacenter edition of Windows 2000 Server). But there are some very inexpensive fault-tolerance options for Windows 2000 networks as well; Dfs provides one.

If you have a file share that you want to be available despite network misfortune and failure, then one way to accomplish that is with a *fault-tolerant Dfs share.* To create one, just create two or more file shares that contain the same information, then tell Dfs to treat them like one share. So, for example, in a domain named ROCKS, you might have a share named STUFF on a server named S1 and a share named STUFF on a server named S2. To the outside world, however, only one share would be visible as \\ROCKS\STUFF. Then, when someone tries to access \\ROCKS\STUFF, Dfs will basically flip a coin and either send her to \\S1\STUFF or \\S2\STUFF. It's not full-blown fault tolerance—if S1 goes down, nothing automatically transfers people from \\S1\STUFF to \\S2\STUFF—but it's a low-cost way to increase the chance that a given share will be available, even under network "fire."

FILE REPLICATION SERVICE

Fault-tolerant Dfs requires that you maintain several network shares all containing the same information. That can be a lot of work, but then fault-tolerant Dfs sounds like it could be worth it.

For example, as you'll read later, Windows 2000 makes deploying applications from a central location or a few central locations possible. So instead of having to visit hundreds of desktops to install Office 2000, you can put Office 2000's distribution files on a server and set up everyone's system to install Office 2000 from that server. Hmmm, hundreds of people all trying to download an application package from one file share, all at the same time, won't be very satisfactory.

It'd be better to have exactly the same application package copied to perhaps 10 other shares. You *could*, of course, create the 10 shares and copy the package to each one—but you needn't. Windows 2000 includes the File Replication Service, or FRS. FRS is a vastly improved version of an old NT feature called Directory Replication. Anyone who's ever tried to use NT 4's Directory Replication knows that it needed work—FRS is the happy result.

Junction Points and Mounted Drives

All of this helpful misdirection in file shares—the ability to disconnect file share names from their physical locations—is pretty useful. In fact, it'd be nice to be able to start doing some of that physical/logical misdirection on *local* drives—and you can.

NT's always been hampered by the fact that it can only support 26 storage volumes, A: through Z:. Tying storage volumes to letters in the alphabet was a great idea when CP/M (an early pre-PC microcomputer operating system) started doing it back in 1978, but nowadays it seems more a bug than a feature.

With NT 4, you created partitions on drives and then assigned drive letters to those partitions. With Windows 2000, in contrast, you can tie any number of drive partitions to a single drive letter. The trick is this: You first create a folder (a subdirectory) in any existing NTFS drive. (NTFS is a filesystem format that—not surprisingly—only NT supports, rather than the FAT filesystem that DOS uses or the FAT32 filesystem that Windows 95/98 uses.) You can then associate—*mount* is the modern term—any drive partition with that folder.

Thus, for example, suppose you have a drive D:, which is NTFS. (If you want to follow along with this example—although you needn't in order to understand it—you'll need a drive D: formatted as NTFS and an H: drive formatted in any way, it doesn't matter.) You've got a bunch of partitions on your system and you're up to drive P:. You'd like to free up drive letter H: so you can use it to map to a home directory. Well, under NT 4, you *could* just highlight the partition currently assigned to H: and change its drive letter to Q: or some other still-unused letter.

Under Windows 2000, however, you can both free up the H: drive letter *and* keep access to the partition, *without* having to use another drive letter. First, create an empty directory on D:. (It needn't be D:; any NTFS drive will do.) Just for the sake of example, call it `D:\OLDH`—again, any directory name will do. Then you'd go into the Disk Manager, Windows 2000's version of the Disk Administrator. You do that by right-clicking My Computer, choosing Manage, opening up Storage in the left pane, and then opening up Disk Management inside *that*. Find the H: partition, right-click it, and choose Change Drive Letter and Path.

Where NT 4 only allowed you to associate *one* drive letter with a partition, Windows 2000 lets you associate a partition with as many drive letters as you like. Now, that won't help us much because we're trying to get *rid* of a drive letter—but the very same dialog box that allows you to add a new drive letter also lets you associate a partition with "an empty folder that supports drive paths"—in other words, with `D:\OLDH`. Once you've added `D:\OLDH` as an acceptable "name" for the partition, you can type either **DIR H:** or **DIR D:\OLDH** and you'll see the same files, because both names refer to the same directory.

But the plan was to free up H:, and we haven't done that yet. Returning to the Disk Manager, again right-click the H: partition and choose Change Drive Letter and Path. This time, you'll see that H: has two acceptable names, `H:` and `D:\OLDH`. Highlight H: and choose Delete. Once you reboot (yes, you've got to reboot for this change to take effect; some things never change), H: will be free and you'll only be able to access the partition's data through D:\OLDH. And if you didn't want to do all of that with a GUI tool, there's a command-line tool named MOUNTVOL that allows you to mount and unmount drives.

NOTE   *You can read more about mounting drives in Chapter 10, "Managing Windows 2000 Storage."*

Remote Storage

As you've already read, the Distributed File System and the File Replication Service appeared in Windows 2000. As you'll read later, Windows 2000 includes disk quotas (finally) and there's a better backup. Clearly, storage was an issue for the Windows 2000 design team. But perhaps the most unusual new storage-related capability is Remote Storage, a program whose goal is to allow you to mix tape-drive space and hard-disk space as if they were one thing.

The idea with Remote Storage is this. Suppose you have a 24-GB hard disk on your server; perhaps it's a nice amount of storage but not quite enough for your users' needs. Suppose also that you've got a tape backup device, a carousel device that can automatically mount any one of 16 tapes into the tape drive without the need for human intervention. Perhaps it's a DLT loader and each tape can store 20 gigabytes of data; that works out to about 320GB of tape storage and, again, 24GB of hard-disk storage. Here's what Remote Storage lets you do:

It lets you lie about the amount of hard-disk space you have.

You essentially advertise that you've got a volume containing 320 plus 24, or 344, gigabytes of online storage space. As people save data to that volume, Remote Storage first saves the data to the hard disk. But eventually, of course, all of that user data fills up the hard disk; at that point, Remote Storage shows off its value. Remote Storage searches the hard disk and finds which files have lain untouched for the longest time. A file could have, for example, been saved eight months ago by some user but not read or modified since. Remote Storage takes these infrequently accessed files and moves them from the hard disk onto the tape drives, freeing up hard-disk space.

Ah, but what happens if someone decides to go looking for that file that was untouched for eight months? Remote Storage has been claiming that the file is ready and available at any time. If some user tries to access the file, Remote Storage finds the file on tape and puts it back on the hard disk, where the user can get to it. Yes, it's slow, but the fact is that many files are created and never reexamined, which means there's a good chance that putting the file on tape and off the hard disk will never inconvenience anyone.

I worked with mainframe systems that did things like this years ago, and it was quite convenient—files untouched for six months or so would be said to be "migrated" to tape. I could "unmigrate" the tapes, and of course that would take a while, but it wasn't that much of a nuisance and it helped keep the mainframe's disks free.

NOTE   *You can read more about Remote Storage in Chapter 10.*

Modernizing NT

NT is an operating system first introduced in the '90s, so it couldn't have needed all *that* much modernizing. But it was getting awfully embarrassing not to be able to plug and play, so Microsoft fixed that. And while they were at it, what's a new release of Windows or NT without a bit of fiddling with the user interface?

Win2K Can Plug and Play

In what may be the feature awaited for the second-longest time (disk quotas are no doubt the longest-awaited feature), Windows 2000 finally offers a version of NT that knows how to do Plug and Play.

That's good news, but, as when PnP first appeared in Windows 95 and ever since, sometimes the playing doesn't happen right after the plugging. Sometimes it works that way, but inserting a new board into a system often still requires a knowledge of interrupt request levels (IRQs) and other hardware characteristics, as well as a bit of CMOS spelunking. Still, it's nice to be able to finally shut up those Windows 95 people smirking about how easy it is to add new cards to their systems.

NOTE   *You can read more about this in a special CD-only chapter devoted solely to adding new hardware to a Windows 2000 system, Chapter 23.*

NT Gets a User Inter-Facelift

Windows 95 introduced a brand-new, more Macintosh-like user interface to the Windows world. NT 4 followed that but didn't exactly copy the Windows 95 UI, instead improving upon it. Internet Explorer 4 brought Active Desktop, which brought a more Web-like feel to the Windows/NT Desktop, although at an often unacceptable cost in performance. Perhaps Active Desktop's best innovation was the Quick Launch bar, a portion of the Taskbar that can hold any number of tiny icons representing oft-used programs: One click and the program starts. Windows 98's user interface built further upon that, and Windows 2000's Desktop offers even more new features, many of which are quite useful.

For example, as time goes on, your Start/Programs menu will probably actually get *smaller*. Windows 2000 tracks how often you use programs, and if you don't use a program for a while, the program disappears off the Start/Programs menu. It doesn't disappear forever, however—instead, Windows 2000 displays a set of chevrons at the end of the menu. To see the programs (and even groups) that have disappeared because of disuse, just click the chevrons and the entire program menu returns. The Control Panel also uses this frequency-of-use information; as you no doubt know from experience with Windows 9x and/or NT 4, the Control Panel's Add/Remove Programs allows you to uninstall programs. That's still true with Windows 2000, but in addition to telling you what programs you can uninstall, Windows 2000 tells you how often you *use* that program. Pretty neat—if you need some more disk space and you're trying to choose which program to remove in order to *get* that space, the Control Panel even gives you useful hints about which programs you won't miss!

The "user inter-facelift" isn't an unalloyed blessing, however. When I first installed beta 2 of Windows 2000, it took me about 10 minutes to find the Network Control Panel. After many years, I was used to just opening up the Control Panel, then opening the Network applet—but here, no go. Instead, I right-click My Network Places (the name for Network Neighborhood's replacement), choose Properties, then find Local Area Connection in the resulting screen, then right-click *that*, and choose Properties again. Intuitive, no? Well, okay, intuitive NO. In any case, enough things have moved around that it seemed a good idea to include a short chapter on where everything's moved to, so if you can't find the Network Control Panel, or can't figure out where to turn off a service, or are baffled about where to go to partition a hard disk, turn to Chapter 5.

Lowering TCO and Warming Administrators' Hearts

Okay, I hear you thinking, "So now Windows 2000 lets us build bigger NT networks than before—heck, maybe there's a couple of bucks in overtime to be made from larger networks—and now there's Plug and Play, great, so long as there are drivers, and by the way, many NT 4 drivers will not work under Windows 2000, so there had *better* be drivers—and now the new user interface has hidden or rearranged all of the tools that I know and lo... well, like."

So you're probably thinking, "Tell me again why I'm going to like this."

You're going to like Windows 2000 because it's got a bunch of new tools. Several tools, like the Remote Installation Services (RIS), Terminal Services, the Group Policy Editor, and the Microsoft Installer Service, will make rollouts easier; they'll simplify getting an operating system on a new computer and then simplify getting applications onto that computer. Some tools, like (again) Terminal Services, Windows 2000's new built-in telnet server, and Windows Management Instrumentation, will make remote control easier. As you'll see, it's far easier to administer Windows 2000 servers from a distance than it ever was to administer NT 4 servers remotely. And some tools, such as disk quotas, client-side caching, RUNAS, a more powerful command line, and the Internet Connection Sharing feature, are either very effective administrative tools or just plain cool.

Remote Installation Services

Those choosing to put NT not only on their servers but on their workstations as well have never had an easy time of it. Rolling out DOS or Windows 9*x* to hundreds of similarly equipped machines is relatively simple: Set up the operating system on one "model" computer, get it configured the way your firm needs it, and then essentially "clone" that entire configuration byte-by-byte from the model computer's hard disk to the hard disks of all of the similarly equipped computers. From there, all that needs doing is usually a bit of fiddling on each of the new workstations to customize and make each machine unique in some way. Products like Ghost and Drive Image Pro are excellent tools for getting that job done, in effect "photocopying" a master disk image from the central model computer to other computers.

Unfortunately, NT has never lent itself to that. Its secure nature has always required that an administrator run NT's Setup program separately on every would-be NT system, making big NT Workstation rollouts a painful process. The Ghost and Drive Image Pro folks have built some tools to try to allow administrators to use those mass-copying programs to get NT onto a computer's hard disk, but those solutions have never been sanctioned by Microsoft, putting anyone who uses them in a kind of support "Twilight Zone."

Windows 2000 solves that problem with two new tools. First, you can now Ghost with impunity using something called Sysprep, a tool that "cleanses" a 2000 installation so that you can use tools like Ghost to exactly copy an image to as many systems as you like. Second, 2000 provides a great new tool called the Remote Installation Services. As with Ghost-like programs, RIS directs you to first create a workstation the way that you want it configured, then a wizard (RIPrep) copies that workstation's disk image to a server—it can be any Windows 2000 server. (By default, RIS won't help you install Windows 2000 Server, just Windows 2000 Professional. But if you know a few tricks—and you'll learn them in Chapter 4—then you can convince RIS to roll out Server images as well.) Just take a new computer out of the box, then attach it to the network, and boot it with a floppy whose image ships with Windows 2000. It asks you to identify the user who will work at that computer, and from that point on, it's a hands-off installation. RIS copies the disk image down to the new computer, runs a hardware detection to ensure that the system gets the correct drivers, the new computer reboots, and Windows 2000 Professional is up and running on the new system. (For some reason, Microsoft chose to name Windows 2000 Workstation "Windows 2000 Professional.")

NOTE   *You can read more about RIS in Chapter 4.*

Windows Terminal Server Becomes Standard

Centralized systems like mainframes were great for support people because all of the user data and configuration information resided on a small number of central locations. Solving a user's problem was then easier, as most support calls could be handled from one location. Centralized systems also meant easy backup.

On the other hand, centralized systems like mainframes weren't very good at highly interactive "personal productivity" applications, such as word processors or spreadsheets, or more modern applications like Web browsers. The decentralized nature of desktop PCs solved that problem. Unfortunately, having computers scattered geographically around an enterprise made for a tougher support job.

How, then, to have a system that allows users to run highly interactive PC-type applications and at the same time keep all of the computing and storage in a centrally located, cheaper-to-support place?

Windows Terminal Services, that's how. WTS turns an NT machine into a kind of a mainframe. You attach dumb terminals—or PCs running programs that make them look like dumb terminals— to the terminal server over a network or dial-up connection, and for all intents and purposes it looks as if the user's just running a standard Windows 2000 Professional Desktop. But all the user's machine is doing is providing keystrokes and mouse clicks and receiving graphic images of the desktop. Everything else—all the data and all of the computation—is going on in the centrally located Windows 2000 servers.

Now, Windows Terminal Services first shipped late in NT 4's life, but it was a separate product. Windows 2000 lets you convert *any* Windows 2000 server into a terminal server with just a few mouse clicks by activating Windows Terminal Services. Additionally, users on a Windows 2000 terminal server have more options than did users on an NT 4 Windows terminal server. And best of all, you can even make a Windows 2000 Professional Desktop remote-controllable with NetMeeting 3.0—so there's no need to buy pcAnywhere for all of the desktops!

NOTE   *You can read more about Terminal Services in Chapter 15.*

Group Policy Objects Replace System Policies

One way to reduce TCO in a firm with dozens, hundreds, or thousands of Windows or NT desktops is to standardize those desktops and to control in some way what gets done on those desktops.

Windows NT 4 had a feature called *system policies* that let an administrator lock down a desktop to a certain extent. If applied in full, system policies would allow an administrator to create a user workstation that could run just a few applications—say, Word, Outlook, and Internet Explorer— and nothing else.

But system policies were difficult to work with, and some of them just plain never worked. Furthermore, it was impossible to apply system policies to a group of *machines*—only groups of users. So Microsoft went back to the drawing board and redesigned the idea from the ground up. The result is Group Policy Objects. The associated Active Directory tool, the Group Policy snap-in, creates and assigns "group" policies. The word *group* is in the name to underscore something missing from NT 4's system policies. It was simple to apply some kind of control to one user, but it was more difficult to apply policies to groups of users, which is really the only reasonable way to create and manage a control structure—it's far easier to manage a large enterprise wholesale, with groups, than to manage in a retail fashion, user by user.

NOTE *The odd part about group policies is that they don't* apply *to groups. Instead, they apply to subunits of Windows 2000 domains called* organizational units, *which you'll read about in the Active Directory chapter. You can certainly control whether a policy affects a particular individual or machine based on what group or groups they belong to, but you can't apply a policy to a group—instead, you apply policies to organizational units. (That's only basically true, as you can also apply policies to particular domains or geographical areas called* sites, *but you'll read more about that in Chapter 8.)*

NT 4–style system policies furthermore required building some files with the desired policy information, placing those files on a domain controller, and having to ensure that those policy files replicated properly among the other domain controllers. Group policies live in the Active Directory, meaning that they get replicated automatically without any necessary fussing from the administrator.

But that's not all you'll like about group policies. The list of available system policies was relatively short, and the vast majority of those policies were of no value. In contrast, there's a rich variety of group policies in the Group Policy snap-in, and many of them will solve some common administrative nightmares.

NOTE *You'll read more about group policies throughout the book, but much of the coverage appears in Chapters 9 (user accounts) and 12 (deploying applications).*

Installer Service and Application Deployment

While I commented earlier that support people had gotten the short end of previous NT upgrades, that's not the case in Windows 2000. As part of their Zero Administration Windows initiative, Microsoft has built a tool into the Group Policy snap-in that allows an administrator to sit in a central location and place applications on a user's desktop without having to visit that desktop.

Previously, firms wanting to do this needed to buy and deploy the Microsoft's Systems Management Server (SMS) tool to accomplish deployment at a distance; with Windows 2000, it's built right in. But that's only the first part of the story.

We usually install programs by running the Setup program that they come with. But we never know beforehand just what the Setup program's going to do; what messes it may make on the computer. Windows 2000 has an answer for that, as well: the Installer service.

The idea with the Installer service is that you no longer run Setup programs to install applications. Instead, you feed to the Installer a file called a *Microsoft Installer* file; they're recognizable because they have the extension .msi. But an MSI file isn't a program. Instead, it's a set of commands telling the Installer how to install an application—what Registry entries to create, where to copy files, what icons to place on the program menu, and so on. And you can examine an MSI file before installing it to find out what it's going to tell the Installer to do—which means you can head off trouble at the pass.

NOTE *You'll read more about the Installer in Chapter 12.*

Better Remote Control and Command Lines

One of my pet peeves with NT has always been that there are very few good remote administration tools. For example, if you want to create a file share on a remote machine, you can do it, but it's cumbersome and involves a different tool—you create a local file share from the Explorer, but you must use NT 4's Server Manager to create remote shares. Even then, Server Manager won't let you control share permissions on remote shares; for that, you've got to look to the Resource Kit and its `Rmtshare.exe` program. And that's just one example: In general, it seems as if NT 4's administrative tools are originally built to only control the local machine; any remote administration abilities either don't exist or have a distinctly "tacked on afterward" feel. Beyond that, one of 2000's greatest strengths is that most of its tools work exactly the same whether they're controlling the local computer (i.e., the one you're sitting at) or you're controlling a remote computer. Where NT 4 made you learn two UIs—the one for the local tool and, when you were lucky enough to even *have* a remote tool, the UI for that one—2000 both offers more remote tools, and unifies them with the local tools. It can do that largely due to something called Windows Management Instrumentation, as you'll see in the next section.

WINDOWS MANAGEMENT INSTRUMENTATION

While Windows 2000 doesn't completely solve that problem, you'll find that most administrative tools work as well on remote computers as they do on the local machine. Virtually all hardware functions are now built around something called the Windows Management Instrumentation (WMI), an eminently "remoteable" software interface. As a result, Device Manager lets you view and modify hardware settings not only for the computer you're sitting at, but any machine on the network that you can see (and on which you have administrative rights); the same is true for storage management. Where Disk Administrator let you format and partition disks, it only operated on locally attached disks—its successor, Disk Manager, lets you do any of those things locally or over the network. (Finally, we network administrators will have the respect we deserve! Just think: "Call *me* a geek, will ya? I'll just attach to your computer across the network and reformat your drive." Just joking, just joking— we network types would *never* use our powers for Evil.)

WINDOWS 2000 INCLUDES A TELNET SERVER

Furthermore, every Windows 2000 Server and Windows 2000 Professional ships with a telnet server. If you choose to run the telnet server on a server, you can then connect to that server with any telnet client.

Odd as it may sound, you may sometimes find yourself telnetting to your own local machine. Why? Because when you log in with a telnet session, you identify yourself with a name and password. That means that, if you're currently logged in to a machine as a user and you need to run some administrative-level command, you need to make the machine suddenly recognize you as an administrator. Telnetting is one way—but there's another as well, a new command called RUNAS that you'll meet in a bit.

Better Admin Tools: A More Powerful Command Line

That kind of leads me into my discussion of tools that aren't so much classifiable as rollout tools or as remote control tools; rather, they just fall into a category of "neat new administrative tools." Telnet offers me a segue.

Once connected, the telnet session then gives you a command-line prompt. From there, you can run any *command-line* application remotely. "But," you may be wondering, "what good is the command line? Can I create user accounts, reset passwords, and the like from the command line?" Well, according to Microsoft, one of the "must-do" items on its Windows 2000 things-to-do list was to ensure that you could do all of your administration from the command line, that in theory you would never have to use a GUI tool. I've not found that I can do *everything* from the command line, but there's a whole lot more that you can do from a command line, as you'll see throughout this book.

Unix's SU Comes to Windows 2000

I often find myself, as mentioned before, needing to change status in the machine's eyes. For example, suppose I'm at a user's workstation trying to figure out a computer problem that's plaguing her. I realize that something's set incorrectly on her workstation and I know how to fix it, but she's currently logged in, and she only has user-level privilege, so I can't execute whatever administrative command I had in mind. What to do?

As mentioned earlier, I *could* telnet to the system as an administrator, as there's a telnet server built into every 2000 Professional box, but that'd only help me if I were running a text-based program. What about if I needed a GUI-based tool? I could ask her to log off, and then I could log in with my administrative account. But I might not want to do that—sometimes I've got a roaming profile set up and I don't want to wait for the profile to download *and* I don't want to have to worry about deleting that profile off the user's machine. The answer? RUNAS.

The scenario described above, where someone's logged in to the system as a user and needs to briefly take on administrative powers, and perhaps doesn't want to have to wait for a logoff/logon sequence, is an old one in the Unix world. That's why most Unix implementations have a so-called Super User (SU) command. It lets you run *just one program* with a different set of credentials (and, of course, that one program *could* be CMD.EXE, the command prompt—so any program that I launched from that command window would also have elevated credentials). In the Windows 2000 world, the command's name is RUNAS—in other words, "*run* this particular application *as* if someone else— presumably an administrator—were running it."

You must run RUNAS either from the command line or from Start/Run. RUNAS's syntax looks like this:

```
runas /user:username command
```

Username is the administrative username, and *command* is whatever command you want to run as an administrator. If the administrator's account is not in the same domain as the Windows 2000 Professional machine, then you may have to include the name of the administrator's domain as well. For example, if I wanted to modify a user account, I would do it with the Directory Services Administrator (which you'll meet in Chapter 8), a file named dsa.msc. If my administrative account were named Bigmark from a domain named LANGUYS, I could start up the DSA like so:

```
runas /user:languys\bigmark dsa.msc
```

Under Windows 2000, you have *two* ways of identifying an account—through the old NT 4–flavor "domain\username" approach, as I used earlier, or through a newer user-specific logon name called the *user principal name*. A UPN looks a lot like an e-mail address; for example, Bigmark's UPN might be bigmark@languys.com. I could use that formulation as well in my RUNAS command:

```
runas /user:bigmark@languys.com dsa.msc
```

You'll learn about UPNs in Chapters 8 and 9. Oh, and by the way, in case you were wondering, when you do a RUNAS, the system prompts you to enter a password; merely knowing an administrative account name isn't sufficient to become an administrator.

What's that you say, you don't want to have to type that RUNAS stuff? No problem. If you right-click the Start Programs icon for a program, choose Properties, and click the Shortcut tab, you get the option to run the program under a different username.

Disk Quotas

Let's get a drum roll on this one. After years of waiting, it's now possible to control how much space a given user takes up on a given volume. You can only set quotas on NTFS volumes.

The disk quota system is fairly simple: You can only set quotas on entire volumes, not directories, so you could, for example, say that Joe couldn't use more than 400MB of space on E, but you *couldn't* say that he couldn't use more than 200MB in E:\DATA1 and 200MB in E:\DATA2—you can't get directory-specific.

Oddly enough, you also cannot set quotas on particular user groups. Instead, you determine a good generic quota value and set that on the volume; that's the disk space limitation for each user. So, for example, suppose you set the quota to 20MB. That means that each user's personal quota is set to 20MB. You can then override that for any particular user. Sound cumbersome? It is; if you have 1000 users from 10 different groups that access a particular volume and you want to set each user's quota based on their group membership, there's not much to do save to hand-set each user's quota amount, one at a time. But it's free, and at least it's of more value than Proquota, the profile size quota manager available under NT 4.

Backup Continues to Improve

Few things grow as rapidly as the apparent need for storage space. In the late '70s, network file servers were often built around a single shared 10 MB hard disk; nowadays, it's not unusual for a desktop *workstation* to have one thousand times that much disk space.

Hard drives have gotten larger, faster, cheaper, and more reliable. But one thing that hasn't changed is the need for backup. NT's always come with a backup program, but it's always been a bit limited. It could only back up to a tape drive, so you couldn't use the NT Backup program to back up to a Jaz drive or network drive; it didn't support robotic tape changers, carousels that could automatically change the tape in a tape drive; and it was very cumbersome to use for a full server recovery.

With Windows 2000, those three objections go away. If you want to save to tape, then of course you can do that, but now you can also save to anything with a drive letter—Jaz, SuperDisk, some Web-based backup system, or the like. If you use tapes but your server's disks are larger than the capacity of a single tape, you need no longer baby-sit the server waiting for the chance to swap tapes: Windows 2000 supports many tape loaders. And if you find yourself with a dead server that you need to revive quickly, you can take a new computer and the most recent backup tapes from the dead server and quickly get the contents of those tapes onto the new computer. The new computer acts in the role of the server, making disaster recovery simpler and quicker than it was under NT 4.

Client-Side Caching/Offline Files

This next aspect of Windows 2000 is not really a server function, it's a workstation (Windows 2000 Professional) function, but it'll gladden the hearts of users and administrators alike. Called either *client-side caching* or *Offline Files* by Microsoft, this function makes the network more reliable and faster and simplifies laptop/server file synchronization for mobile users.

Offline Files acts by automatically caching often-accessed network files and storing the cached copies in a folder on a local hard drive. Your desktop computer then uses those cached copies to speed up network access (or rather, they speed *apparent* network access), as subsequent accesses of a file can be handled out of the local hard disk's cached copy rather than having to go over the network. Offline Files can also use the cached copies of the files to act as a stand-in for the network when that network has failed or isn't present—such as when you're on the road.

You'll like Offline Files for several reasons. As these oft-used cached files will reside on the local hard disk, you'll immediately see what seems to be an increase in network response speed; opening a file that appears to be on the network but is really in a local disk directory will yield apparently stunning improvements in response time, as little or no actual network activity is actually required. It also produces the side effect of reducing network traffic, as cached files needn't be retransmitted over the LAN. Having frequently used files on a local cache directory also solves the problem of "What do I do when the network's down and I need a file from a server?" If you try to access a file on a server that's not responding (or if you're not physically connected to the network), Offline Files shifts to *offline* mode. When in offline mode, Offline Files looks on your local Offline Files network cache, and if Offline Files finds a copy of that file in the cache, it delivers the file to the user just as if the server were up, running, and attached to the user's workstation.

Anyone who's ever had to get ready for a business trip knows two of the worst things about traveling with a laptop: the agony of getting on the plane only to realize that you've forgotten one or two essential files, and the irritation of having to make sure that whatever files you changed while traveling get copied back to the network servers when you return. Offline Files greatly reduces the chance of the first problem because, again, often-used files tend to automatically end up in the local network cache directory. It greatly reduces the work of the second task by automating the laptop-to-server file synchronization process.

NOTE *You can read more about Offline Files in Chapter 11, "Creating and Managing Shared Folders."*

Internet Connection Sharing and Network Address Translation

A very large percentage of us have some kind of connection to the Internet, whether it be a simple dial-up connection, cable modem, or DSL. A substantial portion of us have more than one PC in our house, which leads to one of the most common pieces of e-mail that I get: "How do I share my Internet connection with all of the computers in the house?" Once, the answer to that question was a fairly lengthy discussion of routers and proxy servers.

Now, however, the answer's easy: Just use Internet Connection Sharing (ICS). Anyone who's ever used Windows 9x or NT 4 to dial in to an ISP will be able to use ICS without any trouble—using it involves little more than just checking a box.

Here's how it works. You run ICS on the computer that's dialed in (or cable modemed or DSLed) to the Internet. That computer can be running either Windows 2000 Professional or Windows 2000 Server. (It can even be running the updated version of Windows 98, Win 98 Second Edition.) You check a box labeled Shared Access in your connection's properties; this activates ICS. At this point, the ICS machine acts as a DHCP server (which provides the other computers at home with their IP addresses) and as a router (which ensures that their packets get from the home LAN to the Internet and back).

NOTE   *ICS is a very neat feature and will no doubt be pretty popular; you can read more about it in Chapter 6.*

But ICS is actually a pretty simple routing protocol and doesn't offer much flexibility—all of your local computers can initiate conversations out to the public Internet, but no computer on the public Internet can initiate a conversation to one of your internal computers. That might not be what you'd like, as you might want to make one of your internal computers into a DNS, mail, or Web server visible to the public Internet. To pull *that* trick off, you'll need a more powerful kind of routing called network address translation (NAT). Windows 2000 can do that too, as you'll read in Chapter 6.

Bad News

It's not all wine and roses with Windows 2000, however. While it's a great improvement over NT 4, it still lacks in a number of ways.

DHCP Won't Be Fault-Tolerant

The Dynamic Host Configuration Protocol (DHCP) is an essential bit of network infrastructure, and when it goes down, the network is at least partially crippled. Adding some kind of fault tolerance to DHCP made good sense, and Microsoft told us it would offer it. Unfortunately, however, to implement fault tolerance on DHCP, you must invest tens of thousands of dollars in hardware and software for a server cluster—a great answer for a large corporation, but impractical for the rest of us.

No Fax Server Software

NT's all-in-one small business version, BackOffice Small Business Edition, shipped with a nice, basic fax server—nothing so fancy that it would put the third-party fax server folks out of business, just a basic system that is to fax servers what WordPad is to word processors.

For some reason, Microsoft did not ship a fax server with Windows 2000, however. There *is* fax support, but only on a workstation-by-workstation basis. Thus, you could walk over to a server equipped with a fax modem and fax something from there, but you couldn't fax from your desktop using the server. This seems odd given that Microsoft clearly has NT-ready fax code, but perhaps the fear of Justice has stayed their hand on this matter.

Requires Powerful Hardware, but No Longer Supports the Alpha

Every new version of NT (or Windows, for that matter) renders entire product lines of formerly useful computers useless. For example, NT 3.1, 3.5, and 3.51 ran relatively well on 486 computers, but running NT 4 on a 486 was a quixotic venture. In the same way, Windows 2000 puts the final nail in the Pentium and the MMX coffins. Yes, you *can* run Windows 2000 on a Pentium—some of this book was written on a 266MHz MMX laptop, and some of my braver (or patient) coauthors did their testing on 133MHz and 166MHz machines—but at a noticeable loss in speed. Anyone wanting to get anything done on Windows 2000 needs at least a 350MHz Pentium II and 128MB of RAM. Domain controllers will run best with two physical hard disks. Much of the same advice goes for anyone wanting to run the Workstation version of Windows 2000, Professional; at the moment all I'm doing on my Professional workstation is editing this chapter with Word 97, and I'm using 96MB of RAM—so 96MB to 128MB minimum is definitely indicated!

Worse yet, I'd normally recommend to you that, if you need serious megahertz, you should look into buying one of Compaq's Alphas—but Windows 2000 does not support the Alpha anymore, sadly. It's a real shame, as the Alpha used to be *the* way to get some serious silicon juice. But rumor has it that the next version of NT might restore Alpha support—we can only hope.

Hardware/DirectX Support Is Still Spotty

One of the great frustrations about NT, whether in its 3.*x* and 4.*x* versions or in its current Windows 2000 incarnation, is its relatively thin hardware support, particularly when compared to its Windows 9*x* little brother. Windows 2000 improves upon this as it supports a wider range of hardware and because Plug and Play now makes it easier to install that hardware—but there are still many boards that plain won't work.

Furthermore, Windows 2000 claims to support the DirectX interface, the interface that most modern games are written to, but in actual fact, DirectX's performance makes the few games that I've tried on Windows 2000 unplayable. "What's that?" you say, "Games are irrelevant on servers"? Well, yes, that's probably true—but if *one* much-touted but easily tested subsystem of Windows 2000 (DirectX) doesn't work, isn't it reasonable to be concerned about the other subsystems, the ones that aren't so easy to test?

NOTE *I wrote the previous paragraph in the first edition; here's an update worth noting. After I installed Service Pack 1 on my 2000 systems, the DirectX game that was giving me trouble (Master of Orion II) stopped failing. It was worth waiting for that 89-MB service pack to download, I guess!*

AD Is Inferior to Existing Directory Services

Directory services have been around for ages. I recall working with a competing network operating system named Banyan VINES almost 10 years ago, when Banyan introduced a directory service called StreetTalk. StreetTalk was more flexible in 1992 than Active Directory is now. For example, it's inconceivable that you cannot take two existing domains and join them into an Active Directory forest (you can read more about forests in Chapter 8)—such "pruning and grafting" has been possible in Novell Directory Services (NDS) for years. Nor are Active Directory's weaknesses the fault of NT somehow; Banyan has been selling an implementation of its StreetTalk directory service for NT for at least three years, and Novell's got a version of NDS for NT as well.

Granted, Active Directory's relative weakness probably stems from the fact that it's a "version 1.0" product. But will it improve? As with all companies, Microsoft isn't primarily motivated to create good products; instead, they're motivated to sell a lot of whatever they make—and making good stuff is usually one good way to sell a lot of stuff. But that's not the only way. Sometimes the battle for market share is won by effective advertising rather than quality. And if Microsoft wins the directory services war with marketing, then there won't *be* any incentive to improve the product.

There Are Still Far Too Many Reboots

Back in 1992, I interviewed one of the higher-ups in the NT project, a fellow named Bob Muglia. Bob is a heckuva nice guy and he provided me with a lot of useful information. But I remember one comment that he made to me, a promise that we're still waiting to see fulfilled.

"NT's going to be stable," he told me. "Once you get it set up with your drivers and applications, you should never have to reboot it. If you do, then we've failed."

I've run into Bob since then on several occasions, and I've never had the heart to needle him about his quote. But what he told me in 1992 made eminent sense: At minimum, an enterprise-quality operating system *doesn't need to be rebooted all the time*. And in fact, Microsoft has gone to some pains to advertise that you needn't reboot Windows 2000 as often as you did NT 4. The number of necessary reboots *has* been reduced, but it's still too much.

Summing Up

Having observed the positive and negative aspects, how does Windows 2000 come out in the balance? It depends on your expectations. If you wanted a vastly improved version of NT 4 with a raft of cool new doodads like Internet Connection Sharing, then you'll like Windows 2000 quite a bit. On the other hand, if you were hoping for a rock-solid, enterprise-capable network operating system that could potentially replace your existing MVS, VMS, or Unix systems, then Windows 2000 may disappoint you—while it's good, I wouldn't feel really confident about the Dow Jones running solely on Windows 2000, nor would I be very happy about finding out that the airliner I was sitting in depended on Windows 2000. But it's definitely a positive step, a step in the direction of more power and better reliability.

As you can see, there's a lot of fun new stuff to play with and learn about in Windows 2000. But Windows 2000 is sort of the "second book" in a series—NT 3.1, 3.5, 3.51, and 4 were basically chapters in the first book. Some of you have been following along with the NT story and so you're ready for the new 2000 stuff; but for those of you just joining us, we've got the next chapter, which brings up to speed those who are new to NT networking. So if you're already NT-savvy, then skip ahead to Chapter 3. If you're new to the Microsoft networking game, or just want a short refresher, then turn the page and let's review The Story So Far.

Chapter 2

History: The Story So Far

IN A LOT OF ways, Microsoft Windows 2000 should be named "NT 2.0." Anyone coming into the Microsoft networking story without any pre–Windows 2000 experience with NT probably feels just as lost as someone who gets dragged into a movie theater to see *The Empire Strikes Back* while knowing nothing of the original *Star Wars*. They end up asking things like, "Who *is* the tall guy with the black shiny mask and the bad attitude; and speaking of attitude, what is *with* that woman whose hairdo looks like she strapped a couple of Danishes on her head?"

In this chapter, I'll give you a bit of history on 2000 and then take a very high-altitude look at why we're using Microsoft NT networking in the first place. This is *not* intended to prepare you for a test on networking essentials, nor is it a complete book on NT 3.*x* and 4 networking. What I'm trying to accomplish in this chapter is to answer the questions:

◆ Why should I care about all of this 2000 networking stuff, anyway?

◆ Why does 2000 approach networking the way that it does? Here, I'm referring to the fact that much of why 2000 works the way that it does is simply *because NT always did it that way*—so knowing more about NT's history makes 2000 make more sense.

What's the Point of Networks and Networking?

In a way, this chapter is penance for my youthful misdeeds.

When I was in the seventh grade, I had a math teacher named Mr. Schtazle. Seventh-grade math was a kind of potpourri of mathematical topics—I recall one chapter that took pains to drill into our heads the difference between precision and accuracy—and I'd plague the poor man at the beginning of every chapter by asking him, "how will we use this," sort of a slightly-more-polite version of "why do we care?" Well, nowadays I find that when I'm teaching a room full of people about Windows 2000, *I've* got to be careful to answer that question—"why do you care?"—even if it isn't asked. Because if I don't answer that, then many people in the room will leave the class with a pretty good notion of *how* to accomplish a bunch of tasks but not a really good feel for *why* they'd do the tasks in the first place. And you know what? Answering the "why do I care?" question can be pretty rough some times.

So, Mr. Schtazle, if you're out there…my apologies.

Let's consider the two questions that I asked a paragraph or two back: Why network in the first place, and if we agree that networking is a good thing, why do we do it this way? The answer to the first question will turn out to be pretty straightforward: Networking solves a set of problems for us. The answer to the second question is a bit longer.

First and foremost, you're doing this to try to solve some problem that networking can help you with. Your company might want, for example, a great Web site, or to be able to send and receive e-mail, or a simple file and print server for a small office. These are the goals; a network is the means or tool to reach them. The ultimate goal of any networking project is to provide some kind of service. Everything else is just a necessary evil—but there's a *lot* to those necessary evils!

Second, each service you want to provide will need appropriate software. We build networks to provide various sorts of network-based services; for example, suppose you wanted to set up a Web site on the Internet. Services like Web sites need two main pieces: a server piece and a client piece. To put up that great Web site, you'll create the site itself with HTML and drop that HTML onto a Web server. One way to get a Web server is by taking one of your computers and putting a piece of software on it that makes that computer function as a Web server. (And in order to enjoy that Web server's content, the people on the other end of the networking picture, your users/clients/ customers/visitors, will need a piece of client software called a *Web browser.*)

Third, you need to ensure that there's a way for your information to get from your server to your clients—a physical system that the service can travel over. If the clients and servers are in the same building, then you only need a local area network (LAN)—and setting that up only requires pulling wires through the building. If, however, you want to offer your service to the world, as in the case of a Web server, then you'll need some kind of WAN (wide area network) connection to the Internet. In other cases, you'll need a WAN connection, but not to the Internet: many organizations with more than one location connect those locations via private communications links with names like "leased line," "T1," or "frame relay."

Fourth, to provide a service over a network, your server and your clients must agree on how to transmit information over that network. That agreement is called a *network protocol*, and the one that you'll most probably use in the Windows 2000 world is called the Transmission Control Protocol/ Internet Protocol (TCP/IP). You may have heard of it before, as it's the network protocol that the Internet uses—but you needn't be on the Internet to use it.

Fifth, once you've got the channels open, and before information starts flowing in both directions, you'll almost certainly need to worry about security. While you use the tool that is networking, you want to be sure it doesn't increase your risk, and in fact you can shape the tool so it reduces hazards.

Sixth and finally, once you've set up that terrific network service, then you need a way for people to *find* that great service. You do that with a "naming" system. Windows 2000 has two of them— one that appeared years ago before the first version of NT, and a newer (to NT, anyway) method that the Internet's been using for years.

Let's examine these pieces in order, take a closer look at why they work the way that they do, and get some insight into how Windows 2000 in particular handles them.

Client and Server Software

The reason that we network computers in the first place is so that computers acting as "clients" can benefit from the services of computers acting as "servers." For example, suppose you want to visit my Web site, www.minasi.com. Two of the ingredients that we'll need to make that possible are software:

- ◆ You'll need a computer running a program that knows how to request Web information and then how to receive it—in other words, a *client application.*

- ◆ I'll need a computer running a program that knows how to listen for requests for Web information and then how to deliver that information—in other words, a *server application.*

As sometimes seems *too* often in the computer business, you've got choices about both the client and the server.

THE CLIENT PIECE: A WEB BROWSER

I've said that first, you'll need a computer, of course, running a Web browser program like Netscape Navigator or Internet Explorer. But let's rephrase that in basic network client-server terms.

There is technically no such thing as "the World Wide Web." Instead, there is an agreement about how to transfer text, pictures, and the like, and that agreement is called the HyperText Transfer Protocol—which is normally shortened to HTTP. The phrase World Wide Web just refers collectively to all of the HTTP servers on the Internet. When you think you're just surfing a Web page, what really happens is this:

1. Your client computer asks the Web server (oops, I meant "the HTTP server") something like, "Do you have any documents?"

2. The Web server responds by saying, "Here's my default document," a simple text file that is the so-called "home page" for that Web server. The Web server sends that file to your client using the HTTP protocol.

3. Once your client receives the text file, it notices that the page is full of references to *other* files. For example, if the home page that you requested has pictures on it, your Web browser (HTTP client) didn't originally know to ask for them, so the Web server (HTTP server) didn't send them. Your client notices the lack of the images and requests that the server send them, which it does—again using the HTTP protocol.

Here, "HTTP client" just means a program that knows how to speak a language that transfers a particular kind of data—Web data. Your computer is deaf to the Web unless it knows how to request and receive data via HTTP.

Notice what "client" means here. It doesn't refer to you, or even to your computer. Instead, it just means a program that your computer runs.

THE SERVER PIECE: A WEB SERVER

Next, let's consider what's sitting on my side of the conversation.

I'll need a computer running a special piece of software that is designed to listen for your computer (or anyone else's for that matter) requesting to see my Web pages via the HTTP protocol, and that can respond to those requests by transferring those pages to the requesting client software. We *might* call such a piece of software an "HTTP server" program, although almost no one calls it by that name. We'd more *commonly* call it "Web server" software. There is a variety of Web server software that I might run on my Windows 2000 computer, but I'm most likely to run the one that comes free with Windows 2000, a program called Internet Information Services (IIS) 5.0. Alternatively, I might find, download (probably using HTTP!), and install a popular piece of free Web server software called Apache.

Once again, notice carefully what "server" means here. It does not really refer to the particular computer hardware that I've got stashed in my network room connected to the Internet. Instead, "server" means "the program running on Mark's computer that listens for HTTP requests and knows how to fulfill them."

Now that we've gone through all of that, let's consider again the question that I asked at the beginning of the chapter—why are you bothering with a network? The answer is probably "because you want to offer a Web site, either internally or on the public Internet, and you that think that IIS is the best (highest-performance, cheapest, or some combination of the two) Web server software around"—which means that you must use 2000, as it's the only operating system that supports IIS.

OTHER TYPES OF SERVERS

I'll tend to use the Web client-server example for this discussion. But I don't want to lose sight of the fact that there are quite a few client-server systems, besides Web servers, that are in common use and that you may want to use 2000 to create. Returning to the theme of this chapter, then—"why do I care or why do I need this stuff?"—networks offer several valuable services, and you may want to set up a computer to act as a server and offer some of those services. Here are a few besides the Web server example.

File Servers

File servers act as central places to store data files. Why put them on a server rather than just keep them on your local computer? Well, in some cases someone else created the file, and placing a file on a central server is a simple way to make the files available to others. The other good thing about storing files in a central location is that they're more easily backed up that way. 2000 comes with file server software built in.

Print Servers

Print servers let you share printers. Not everyone wants to put a printer on their desk, and besides, if you share the printers, you can afford more expensive (and presumably better) models. 2000 comes with print server software built in.

E-Mail Servers

Mail servers are essential if you're going to do e-mail. Some computer (or computers) must act as the "post office," collecting e-mail from the local users and sending it to other mail servers across the Internet, and acting as a receiving point for other mail servers to send mail destined for your organization. You *can* outsource this function by letting your ISP act as your mail server, but running your own mail server gives you more flexibility. (However, it *does* require a persistent connection to the Internet.) 2000 does *not* ship with a complete mail server—Microsoft wants to sell you Exchange for that. But 2000 *does* come with a partial mail server. Part of IIS can send mail, but it cannot receive and distribute mail. What's it good for, then? Many Web sites need the ability to mail out confirmations or other data, so giving your Web server the ability to act as a low-octane, outgoing-only mail server turns out to be useful.

Group Scheduling Servers

The centralized nature of servers means that they're a great place to keep track of scarce resources like meeting rooms or your time. 2000 does not come with a scheduling server, as Microsoft wants to sell you Exchange to do that sort of thing. But there are alternatives to Exchange; there are some terrific (and free) Web-based scheduling tools that work great on 2000—for one example, take a look at `http://mkruse.netexpress.net/scripts/calendar/`.

E-Commerce Online Stores

If you've got something great to sell, then the Web's one place to do it. There are thousands of online stores on the Web, and a good number of them run on 2000. While 2000 includes a Web server, it doesn't include the other software that you'd need to create a complete online store. But there are a lot of consulting and programming firms that would be happy to help you create an online store atop 2000!

Everything Must Be Physically Connected

If I want to offer a server service and ensure that you can enjoy that service, then we'll both need to be physically attached to the same network—the same series of cables, satellite links, or whatever— or your computer's requests will never get to my computer in the first place. That probably means that we're both on that huge network-of-networks called the Internet, but we could just be working for the same company in a single wired building, or a multilocation firm connected by a private intranet.

Now, notice that if I'm going to run a Web server, then I'll need to be connected to our common network (Internet or otherwise) persistently: I couldn't just decide to run a Web server out of my house and just dial in to the Internet now and then. Of course, if I'm only serving some private network that we share, then an Internet connection is unnecessary, as we already have connection to a common network.

People who worry about the physical connection part of networking concern themselves with getting cables run through walls, calling the phone company to arrange for persistently connected data links of various kinds, links with names like DSL, cable modem, frame relay, leased lines, T1 or T3 lines, and then with a family of hardware that helps get the bits going off in the right direction— devices with names like switches, hubs, and routers.

Does 2000 help us with this part of the job? In some parts, it can. Switches and hubs are very basic, simple devices, and 2000 has nothing to do with them—although clearly 2000 depends on their presence in order to network! Routers are, however, more complex devices. You probably know that the market leader in the router world is a firm named Cisco Systems, but you may not know that a router is really just a small, single-purpose computer. If you wanted to, you could use a computer running Windows 2000 to replace a Cisco router. Additionally, if you wanted to allow people outside your network to dial in to your network, you could use a Windows 2000 server to make that possible.

All Devices Must Speak the Same Network Language or "Protocol"

But simply being connected to the same wire isn't enough—we need a common communications language. If I were to pick up a phone and dial some number in Beijing, I'd have a physical connection with whatever poor soul picked the phone on the other end—but that would be the extent of our interaction. In the same way, computer networks need to agree on things like "what's the biggest block of data that I can ever send you?" and "how shall I acknowledge that I actually *got* that block of data" or "should I bother acknowledging receipt of data at all?" and hundreds of other questions.

The answers to all of those questions are contained in the "network language" or, in network techie terms, the *network transport protocol*. It probably won't surprise you that more than one network transport protocol exists, and over the years NT has generally supported three of them:

◆ NetBEUI (Network Basic Input/Output System Extended User Interface), an old Microsoft/IBM/Sytek protocol designed to support small networks

◆ IPX/SPX (Internet Packet Exchange/Sequenced Packet Exchange), the protocol that Novell NetWare predominantly used for years

◆ TCP/IP (Transmission Control Protocol/Internet Protocol), the protocol of the Internet and intranets

Although you have three choices, it's a good bet that your Windows 2000 network uses TCP/IP. Why TCP/IP? Well, there have been some really great protocols over the years, but as the Internet uses TCP/IP and as the Internet is so popular, TCP/IP has sort of "trumped" any of the other protocols. In fact, it's impossible to do a fair number of things that 2000 is capable of *without* TCP/IP, so I'm going to assume for our discussion and indeed for most of this book that your network will use TCP/IP.

Oh, and one more thing—once you've decided that TCP/IP is your network protocol of choice, then you'll need to install several *more* servers to support TCP/IP's infrastructure. And here again, when I say "more servers," I'm not suggesting that you have to buy more PCs, although you might—what I mean is that you'll have to install software on some computer or group of computers to perform three basic pieces of "plumbing" or "infrastructure" jobs:

◆ A Domain Naming System (DNS) server keeps track of the names of the computers in your network (an important task, believe it or not).

◆ A Dynamic Host Configuration Protocol (DHCP) server configures the specifics of TCP/IP on each computer in your network, both great and small.

◆ A Windows Internet Name Server (WINS) does something like what DNS does—keeps track of names—but isn't really necessary on a "pure" Windows 2000 network—its main job is to support older Microsoft operating systems like Windows 95, 98, ME, and NT 3.*x* and 4.

You'll learn more about the specifics of DNS, DHCP, and WINS in Chapter 7. I should point out that if you're a one-person shop, then you might not need all of that, as your ISP might be handling it for you—but I'm assuming throughout this book that you are probably a network administrator/manager for a network of at *least* a few computers, and possibly for a tremendous number of computers.

Keeping the Bad Guys Away: Security

Once you've gotten the first four things done, then your job's finished, in a sense—people can now read and write files on that file server, view pages on that Web server, print to that shared printer, set up meetings with you over your scheduling server, and so on. I mean, hey, networking's all about sharing, so just open the doors and let 'em in!

As you've probably realized, there's a missing piece here: security. Security boils down to two things:

- First, you want to be able to identify who's entering your network.

- Second, once you know who's just arrived, you need a way of keeping track of what that person is and isn't allowed to do.

AUTHENTICATION

The first part of security is called *authentication,* and we usually accomplish it through usernames and passwords, although as time goes on we'll eventually use the more "science fiction" means of authentication: One day, the computer may recognize you by your fingerprint, face, voice, retina blood vessel pattern, or some other item that's distinctly "you."

For now, however, it's user accounts and passwords that identify users. I realize that nearly everyone who's reading this book has undergone an authentication at some point—you've all logged in to a network some time. It all sounds simple, doesn't it? And yet user accounts and passwords present special problems.

Storing Account/Password Information

First, we'll need some kind of program that lets administrators create user accounts and store them in a file. That's no big deal—it's a very simple database, and there are tons of database programs out there—but don't forget that we need to *encrypt* that information. Otherwise, there's the possibility that someone could come along and steal the file, take it home and perhaps crack it for your user's passwords.

Just such a thing happened to NT 4. NT stored user information in a file named SAM. If you leave me in the same room as your server, then I can copy that SAM onto a floppy and take it off-site to analyze it. Wasn't it encrypted? Well, yes, but sometimes encryption isn't enough—a group of hackers figured out how to crack SAM's encryption. With just a bit of work, anyone could extract passwords from an NT SAM. (Which is a good reason to keep your servers behind lock and key, so that it's harder for someone to steal your account files.) Windows 2000 uses a more sophisticated encryption scheme on its user account/password file (which is named NTDS.DIT, not SAM), and hopefully it won't be cracked any time soon.

The tool that lets administrators create, modify or delete user accounts is called Active Directory Users and Computers. "Active Directory" refers to 2000's system for storing user names and passwords. It's called a "directory" because "directory" is the current network lingo for "database of user accounts." Personally, I think it's kind of confusing—in my mind, "directory" conjures up visions of drive letters, like "C:\DOS"—but it's the current argot, so it's worth knowing. And, in case you're wondering, the "Active" part is just Microsoft marketing; don't look for any deep meaning there.

Doing Logons without Compromising Security

Next, we'll need a way to check a user account and password. Let's suppose I'm sitting at my Windows 2000 workstation and I want to get to some files on a file server named files-r-us.acme.com. Before files-r-us will give me access, I've got to submit myself for authentication, or as we more commonly say, I need to "log in." One of the many programs that comes with Windows 2000 is called `winlogon.exe`, and it's the program that pops up when you first turn your workstation on, asking you to punch in your username, password, and domain. (I'll explain what a "domain" is in a minute.)

So let's imagine that I'm trying to access some data on files-r-us. Files-r-us responds by asking my workstation, "What's his name and password?" *Now* I've got a problem.

You see, what I'd *like* to do is to just say over the network line, "This is Mark and his password is 'swordfish.'" Then files-r-us can just look in its directory file of usernames and passwords and see if it has a user named Mark with a password of *swordfish*. If so, then it lets me in. If not, it doesn't. Simple, eh?

Well, there's one flaw here—the part where my workstation passes "swordfish" over the network. A class of programs called "sniffers" can record and display any data that passes over a network wire. So passing passwords around on an unencrypted Ethernet cable isn't a great idea. That means we've got another challenge: how to prove to a server across the network from you that you've got Mark's password without actually showing that password to the server.

Over time, networks have come up with different answers, but Windows 2000 uses an old authentication method called Kerberos, first invented at MIT in the mid '80s. It replaces an older method employed by NT 3.*x* and 4 called NTLM, which was short for NT LAN Manager, a reference to one of NT's predecessors. What follows is an extremely simplified version of how Kerberos works. (It's actually a wildly inaccurate description, but it'll help the more complete explanation that you'll see in the next section.)

Let's return to files-r-us. I try to access its data, so files-r-us needs to first log me in. It does that by saying, "I'll tell you how to access my data," and sends me some instructions on how to get to its data. But the data is *encrypted*—with my password! In other words, *anyone* could claim to be me, and files-r-us would happily send this vital instructions-for-connection. But only I could decrypt those instructions, so only I could benefit from them. So files-r-us ensured that only someone with my password could gain access, without sending my password over the wire.

Sharing User Account Information: "Domains"

But my simple example about trying to access one file server is, well, a bit *too* simple. Most companies will end up with more than one server, and in fact it's not unusual to end up with dozens or hundreds of servers. And that leads to the following problem. Recall that I said a page or so back that if we're going to employ user accounts, then we'll need a file to store them in. But what if we have more than one server? What if in addition to the server named files-r-us.acme.com, I've also got a mail server named postoffice.acme.com and a Web server named www.acme.com? I might want to log in to any one of those three, so they *all* have to be able to accomplish logons. But now let's examine what that actually means in terms of keeping track of user accounts. Should each server contain a complete copy of `NTDS.DIT`, the file containing the names and passwords for users?

That might work, but it'd be a pain, for several reasons. First, `NTDS.DIT` can get pretty big, and we'd end up burning up a lot of disk space copying it to every server in our enterprise. Second, if servers are connected by low-speed WAN links, the process of copying the changes to `NTDS.DIT` to all of the servers on our network (a process called "directory replication") would take up a lot of time and network bandwidth. Third, do we *really* want to have to create a network "storm" of file copying amongst the servers every time someone just changes their password? And finally, what about the issue of securing the `NTDS.DIT` file in the first place? If we copy `NTDS.DIT` to every single server in the enterprise, there are bound to be a few that are out in the open, not physically secured. It'd be easy for an intruder to copy the `NTDS.DIT` from a poorly secured computer and spirit it off-site in the hopes that someone will come up with an `NTDS.DIT` cracker.

The "better idea" that we've used in networks for years is to put the user directory—the `NTDS.DIT`—not on every single server, but instead on a relatively small subset of the servers. Those `NTDS.DIT`-holding servers then serve in the role of *logon server*, doing the job of authenticating for the other servers. In Microsoft parlance, a logon server is more commonly called a *domain controller*. So, to return to the example of accessing data on files-r-us, let's imagine that files-r-us is *not* a domain controller and doesn't contain a copy of `NTDS.DIT`, and that another computer, vault.acme.com, *is* a domain controller and contains a copy of `NTDS.DIT`. In this newer arrangement, I don't directly log into files-r-us, but instead enlist the aid of vault.acme.com in order to authenticate with files-r-us.

In a purely Windows 2000 network, vault.acme.com would help me log in to files-r-us with Kerberos. In order to understand how Kerberos works, you first need to understand that under Kerberos, not only do the users have passwords, the server programs do also. Thus, the file server program running on files-r-us has its own password. So both the user and the server each have passwords—remember that.

When I tell my workstation to try to get some data from files-r-us, my workstation sees that it'll need to get me logged in to files-r-us. It does that by asking the domain controller, vault, to give me something called a "ticket" to the file server service on files-r-us. The domain controller responds by handing my workstation an encrypted piece of data, which is the Kerberos ticket.

The ticket can be decrypted with my password, making its contents a mystery to anyone but me (or my workstation, which obviously knows my password). My workstation decrypts the ticket, which contains two things. First, it contains a message saying "your special one-time-only password for accessing the file server at files-r-us is 'opensesame.'" Second, it contains *another* encrypted message—but this one's not encrypted with my password, so I can't decrypt it! But my workstation knows to send it to the file server, which decrypts it successfully, as the file server has its own passwords. Once the file server receives and decrypts the part of the Kerberos ticket that I sent it, the file server sees that that ticket piece says something like "the special one-time-only password for communicating with Mark is 'opensesame.' And by the way, you should have gotten this message from Mark sometime between 10:45 A.M. AND 11:15 A.M., from his IP address, which should be 117.39.82.3."

Once the file server gets its half of the Kerberos ticket, it knows a few things:

◆ The user claiming to be Mark who wants access to the file server is indeed Mark.

◆ Any messages from that now-authenticated person named Mark should have originated from IP address 117.39.82.3.

◆ If Mark and the file server really want to maintain a secure connection, they could even encrypt their communications using this shared—but secret—password, opensesame.

SECURITY ROLES AND DEFINITIONS: DOMAINS, DOMAIN CONTROLLERS, AND MEMBER SERVERS

Armed with this information, I can define a few Microsoft networking terms.

Domain

You just saw an example where one machine (vault) let me log in to another machine (files-r-us). I haven't mention this yet, but before I could get *anywhere* I needed to log in to the computer at my desk, my workstation—and when I first tried to log in to my workstation, it was once again vault.acme.com that authenticated me. Clearly, then, my workstation and files-r-us "trust" vault.acme.com in some fashion.

The collection of machines that share the same list of user accounts, the same `NTDS.DIT`, is a *domain*. Or, to put it a bit more specifically: several computers hold a copy of `NTDS.DIT` and are willing to act as "logon servers" (domain controllers) with that `NTDS.DIT`. The collection of machines that are willing to accept logons from those domain controllers (in Microsoft terms, who "trust" those domain controllers) and the domain controllers themselves are collectively called a domain. So my workstation, vault, and files-r-us are all part of the same domain.

Domain Controller

A server, such as vault.acme.com, that contains a copy of the user account/password data, and that therefore can let users log in to servers, is a *domain controller*. Domain controllers exist to centralize the user account/password information so that we needn't put the `NTDS.DIT` on every server.

Member Server

A machine that is running Windows 2000 Server or NT Server but *not* acting as a domain controller will not contain a copy of `NTDS.DIT` and therefore can't authenticate domain members. Such a machine is called a *member server*.

DEFINING USER PERMISSIONS

Once a server has determined that I am indeed me, does that mean that I'll get access to the server's information? Not necessarily. Authentication just identifies me. The next step in security is access control, also known as (depending on what network operating system you are using) *rights*, *permissions*, or *privileges*.

Windows 2000 has a very flexible system of file and directory permissions, as did earlier versions of NT. As you'll see later in this book, you can exert very fine-grained control, such as specifying that Mary can read or write to a given file, that Bill can only read it, and that June cannot access the file at all.

ACCESS TO EARLIER SECURITY SYSTEMS

The last challenge that Windows 2000's security designers faced was the so-called "legacy" support—ensuring that Windows 2000 could interact with the security systems built into Windows for Workgroups, Windows 9x, NT 3.x and 4. I've described in very broad strokes how Kerberos works, but Windows and NT didn't use anything like that and in fact *couldn't* do Kerberos logons. Microsoft knew that you wouldn't be very happy if they required you to throw away all of your old Windows and NT systems before you could implement Windows 2000, so 2000 knows a variety of logon methods—NTLM 1.2 for Windows and NTLM 2.0 for NT, in addition to Kerberos.

It's hard to overstate the importance of security. For example, in the past, one of Novell's *main* advantages over NT was in the way that it stored user accounts and handled logins—Novell's security was faster and more flexible. Sure, one could argue that Novell moved data around file servers more quickly, but not so much more quickly that anyone would really modify a buying decision. Basically, people were buying Novell for Novell's security system, something called NetWare Directory Services (NDS)—NDS was essentially a "big time" user database, something with a more "enterprise" feel to it than NT's older SAM-based system. In sum, security is *important*.

Names: Finding Servers

When PC-based networking first appeared, we didn't do much Web work—the earliest common LAN functions were file and print services. So from the very beginning (all of 15 years ago) of PC-based networking, we've done file and print services; they're the most basic network services. But now suppose that you've got a network with more than one server on it, and you want to find out which server has a printer available for sharing, or you can't remember which server holds that share called `hrdocuments`; how do you search for network functions?

That's one of the oldest problems in networking, and not just in Microsoft networking. Microsoft's most current answer to the "how can I find resource X on the network?" is to store that information in the Active Directory database. But they're not there by any means yet and, even if you have an all–Windows 2000 network (which is unlikely), you'll find that by default the Active Directory isn't all that much help in finding file and printer shares. I'm sure that's going to change as new versions of NT appear, but for now, we 2000 users are pretty much stuck with an old technology known colloquially as the Network Neighborhood—now renamed for Windows 2000 as My Network Places. Here's where it came from and how it works.

How would we set up a system that provided a centralized directory of services on a network, a kind of "yellow pages" that let a user quickly find a file share or shared printer? Microsoft networking uses a kind of name server system called the *computer browser* or *browse services*—it has nothing at all to do with the Web, it's had that name since before the Web existed—where you, the network administrator, don't have to do *anything*; the name servers set themselves up automatically. Sounds good? Well, it *is* for small networks, but it gets troublesome for larger ones—which is why 2000 is trying to phase it out.

The servers in a Microsoft network that contain information about network services are called *browse masters* or *master browsers*. What's different about the concept of Microsoft browse servers is that no one computer is fixed as the browse master. Instead, when your computer logs in to your network, it finds a browse master by broadcasting a request for one, saying, "Are there any browse masters out there?" The first browse master to hear the workstation (there can be multiple browse masters, as you'll see) responds to the workstation by saying, "Just direct all your name service requests to me."

When a server starts up, it does the same thing. It broadcasts, "Are there any browse masters out there?" and when it finds one, it says to it, "I am a server with the following shares. Please add me to your list of servers." The list of servers that a browse master maintains is called the *browse list*, not surprisingly.

TIP   *This is the really irritating thing about the browse list: it's broadcast-based. That means that if your network isn't 100 percent broadcast-friendly, then you'll sometimes end up with an incomplete list of servers on your network. So if you have a network built in more than one segment (and who doesn't?), or you use some kinds of Ethernet switches rather than hubs, then you may experience missing servers in the browse list. That's part of why Microsoft is trying to phase out the browse list. But for now, understand that the browse list is a largely lame and unreliable technology. You'll see later on, in Chapter 7, that you can install a service called the Windows Internet Name Service (WINS) to reduce the chance that the Browser breaks, but trust me—you'll eventually come to a point where you've done everything that you can do, but the Browser still doesn't work. When that happens, don't feel bad—we've all been there. I'll suggest some ways to make it work better and reduce your dependence on the Browser a bit later in this section.*

By now, you may be wondering, "How come I've never seen one of these browse lists?" You have. If you ever work with earlier versions of NT or with Windows for Workgroups, then you would see Figure 2.1 when you opened the File Manager and clicked Disk/Connect Network Drive.

FIGURE 2.1

Sample browse list from Windows for Workgroups or Windows NT version 3.*x*

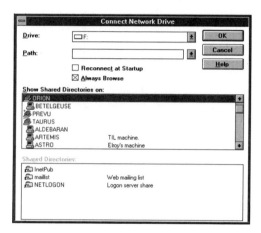

From Windows 95 or Windows NT 4, you can see a browse list by opening the Network Neighborhood folder, as in Figure 2.2.

FIGURE 2.2

Sample browse list from Windows NT 4 or Windows 95/98

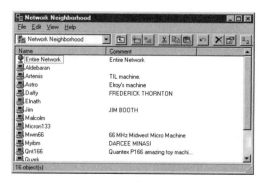

From DOS or indeed any command line, you can see a browse list by typing **net view** or **net view** *machinename*. You see a screen like the one in Figure 2.3.

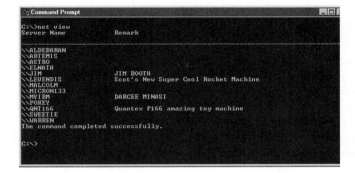

NOTE   *What's with that* \\ *thing? Microsoft's network software has, since 1985, used a way of writing the names of servers and of* shares *on servers called a Universal Naming Convention or UNC. It looks like* *servername**share-name. So, for example, if I had a server named "bigserver" that contained a file share called "mydata," I'd refer to that share as* *bigserver**mydata—that would be the UNC for that share. You'll learn more about this in Chapter 11, on file shares, but I wanted to explain the mystifying* \\ *briefly here. And by the way, you pronounce "**" as "whack-whack" in the Microsoft world. Now, to my way of thinking, that'd mean that a regular forward slash—* / *—would be pronounced "backwhack" in Microsoftese, but I've never gotten confirmation on that.*

Each figure shows you the list of servers available: Aldebaran, Artemis, and Astro. Other servers—Daffy and MWM66—appear only in some of the browse lists because a few minutes passed between taking the screen shots, and a few "test" servers went up or down in those few minutes. In all three cases, the workstations that these screens were taken from got their browse lists from a local browse master.

You can drill down further into these browse lists, as well. In Windows 95/98, Windows NT 4, or 2000 (in 2000, open My Network Places), you can double-click any one of those servers and see the list of shares that the servers offer; that, too, is information from the browse list. In Windows for Workgroups or Windows NT 3.*x*, you'd just click a server once, and the list of its shares would appear in the bottom pane of the dialog box. From DOS, you'd get the list of servers by typing **net view**, as you've already seen, and then you get the list of shares for any given server by typing **net view** *servername*, where *servername* is the name of the server whose shares you want to see.

WHEN BROWSE LISTS GET TOO LARGE: WORKGROUPS TO THE RESCUE

As I've described them so far, browse lists seem pretty convenient. But in the little test network that I used for the previous screen shots, you saw only a few servers. Hell, *everything* works fine on *small* networks.

Now let's talk about *your* network. Sit down at a corporate network of any size and you see dozens, hundreds, or *thousands* of servers. Scrolling down through a 500-server browse list would be a bit time-consuming—to say nothing of how much work the browse master would have to do to keep it up-to-date! The problem to solve is, then, managing the size of the browse list. There are two ways to do that:

◆ Reduce the number of servers in your enterprise.

◆ Divide the enterprise-wide browse list into several smaller browse lists called *workgroups*.

Disable Peer-to-Peer Sharing on Workstations

The first answer is actually a bit off the main topic, but let me digress for a moment and talk about it before returning to the main item: workgroups. When I say, "Reduce the number of servers," I'm talking about an unfortunate side-effect of running Windows for Workgroups, Windows 95, Windows NT, and 2000 workstations—they all have the capability to become peer-to-peer servers. The browse masters don't distinguish between industrial-strength servers running NT Server and low-octane peer-to-peer servers, so you could end up with a browse list that's *supposed* to only list your servers, but *actually* lists all of your servers and workstations. In general, I think peer-to-peer networking is a bad idea. If a piece of data is important enough to be used by two employees, then it's a company asset that should be backed up regularly and so should go on a managed file server, not a desktop machine that's probably backed up once a decade. My recommendation is this: Disable the peer-to-peer sharing option on your Windows for Workgroups, Windows 95, Windows NT, and 2000 workstations. How you do this depends on the operating system of the workstations in question. In NT 3.*x* and 4, open the Control Panel and then the Services applet; locate the service called Server and stop it, as well as disabling it for future reboots. In Windows 9*x*, go to Control Panel/ Network/File and Print Sharing and make sure both options, to share files and printers, are unchecked. In Windows for Workgroups, make sure the sharing control in Network Setup is set *not* to enable file or printer sharing.

Not only will your network have less traffic—workstations will no longer have delusions of serverdom, so they won't be chattering at the browse master all of the time—but not loading the server part of the workstation's operating system saves RAM on the workstation.

Divide the Browse List into Workgroups

The other approach to keeping a browse list to a manageable size is to subdivide it in some way. That's a reasonable thing to suggest if you realize that, no matter how large an organization *seems* to be, it's usually composed of lots of smaller groups, such as Manufacturing, Sales, Marketing, Accounting, Finance, Personnel, Senior Management, and so on. Each of those groups can be called *workgroups*, and you can pretty much chop up your enterprise into workgroups in any way you like (but a rule of thumb says that a workgroup should be a group of people for whom 95 percent of the data generated by that group stays within that group).

From a more network-technical point of view, the minimum definition of a workgroup is just *a group of workstations that share a browse list*. (That's my definition, not Microsoft's.) The idea is that when someone in Accounting opens up her browse list, you want her to see just the Accounting servers, not the Manufacturing servers, as she has no use for the Manufacturing servers. (Besides, there's a good chance that she doesn't have permission to access the Manufacturing servers anyway—but I'll get to workgroups and security in a little bit.) How do you join a workgroup? See the sidebar "How Do I Join a Workgroup?"

HOW DO I JOIN A WORKGROUP?

Generally, all you need to do is to tell the networking software on your workstations and servers that they're members of a given workgroup. There isn't any "security" in being part of a workgroup—you pretty much just declare yourself a member and you are a member. (As a matter of fact, if you misspell the name of the workgroup, you end up accidentally founding a whole new workgroup all by yourself, which I'm sure was not your intention!)

Specifically, you designate which workgroup you're a member of in one of the following ways:

From a DOS or Windows for Workgroups workstation

In the [network] section of the SYSTEM.INI file you'll find a WORKGROUP= parameter. (You'll have a SYSTEM.INI even if you're just running DOS, because the network client software creates one.) You can also set the workgroup from the MS-DOS Network Client Setup program, or in the Windows for Workgroups' Network applet of the Control Panel.

From Windows 95/98   Open the Control Panel and double-click the Network icon. In the property sheet that you see, click the Identification tab. You see the place to fill in the workgroup name.

On Windows NT 3.x   Open the Control Panel and double-click the Network applet. You'll see a button labeled Domain or Workgroup. (NT has a kind of confusing way of blurring workgroups and domains, which I'll make clearer later in this chapter.) Click that button, and you can change the workgroup you're a member of. Again, NT complicates choosing a workgroup somewhat, so read the rest of this chapter if you want to change an NT workgroup.

On Windows NT 4   Open the Control Panel and double-click the Network applet. Like Windows 95, Windows NT 4 has a property sheet with an Identification tab. Click Change to change the workgroup. Again, with NT you may see no references to workgroups at all; instead you see references to domains. Read on to understand the differences.

On Windows 2000   If you're a member of a domain, then *do not* join a workgroup—I'll explain that in a minute. Otherwise, right-click My Computer and choose Properties. Click the Network Identification tab and then the button labeled Properties. Fill in a new workgroup in the field named Workgroup; then close the dialog box and reboot.

NOTE   *Workgroup names are like Windows 9x and NT 3.x/4.x machine names, and can be up to 15 characters long.*

So, to review what we've seen so far:

◆   Network browse lists allow a user at a workstation to see all of the servers on the network, and from there to see all of the shares on a given server.

◆   Browse lists can get fairly long, so you can partition your entire network into *workgroups*, which are just groups of people that share a browse list.

◆   When you request a browse list, you don't get the entire list of servers in your enterprise network, you only get the list of servers within your workgroup.

◆ Each workgroup has one or more servers that act as gatherers of browse information. They're called browse masters or master browsers, and they're picked automatically.

◆ Machines that are only workstations and don't act as servers even in a peer-to-peer capacity do not appear on browse lists.

As the question of what machines go on a browse list and what machines don't is important to the length of a browse list, let me list the kinds of machines that can act as servers in a Microsoft enterprise network:

◆ Windows 3.*x* (with the Workgroup Add-On for MS-DOS clients)

◆ DOS (with Workgroup Add-On for MS-DOS clients)

◆ Windows for Workgroups

◆ Windows 95

◆ NT Workstation

◆ NT Server

◆ Windows 2000 Professional

◆ Windows 2000 Server, Advanced Server, or Datacenter Server

HOW DO I VIEW A BROWSE LIST?

Microsoft has built different browse programs into its various network client software.

From a DOS or NT/2000 Command Line   Type **net view**. That shows you the list of servers. You can view the shares on a given server by typing **net view *servername***. To see the browse list for a workgroup other than your own, type **net view /workgroup:*workgroupname*.**

From NT or 2000, don't use **/workgroup:** in the command; instead, use **/domain:.**

From Windows for Workgroups or Windows NT 3.*x*   Open the File Manager, click Drive, and then click Connect Network Drive. You'll see a window with two panes. The browse list for your workgroup and a list of the other workgroups on the network appears as the list of possible servers in the top pane and, when you click a server, that server's shares appear in the bottom pane. To see the browse list for a workgroup other than your own, double-click the name of the workgroup in the top pane.

From Windows 95/98 or Windows NT 4   Open the Network Neighborhood folder. You'll see the servers in your workgroup represented as PC icons in a folder. Double-click one of the servers, and a folder will open up showing you the shares. To see the browse list for a workgroup other than your own, double-click the Entire Network icon and you'll see a list of workgroups. On Windows NT 4, click Entire Network and then Microsoft Network, and then you'll get a list of the other workgroups.

From Windows 2000   If your system is in a workgroup, then open My Network Places and then the icon labeled Computers Near Me. If your system is part of a domain, then that icon isn't available. Instead, open My Network Places and then the icon labeled Entire Network, then the icon named Microsoft Windows Network. You'll see one or more icons representing the workgroups on your network—open the one representing your workgroup and you'll see your workgroup's browse list.

As it's an unusual product, let me just explain that the Workgroup Add-On for MS-DOS is a separate Microsoft product that lets you use a DOS machine as a peer-to-peer server. (Also, it's pretty old, so I have no idea where you'd get a copy these days.) Again, I recommend that you disable file and print sharing on all of these machines except, of course, for the machines dedicated to the task of being servers, all of which are probably running NT Server.

And once you're in a workgroup, you'll no doubt want to see your browse list; "How Do I View a Browse List?" tells you the specifics.

Now, if you *tried* that on a working network, then you might have gotten one of NT and family's less helpful responses, like "System error 1230 has occurred." That gives me the chance to offer another important bit of advice for anyone using a modern Microsoft operating system—how to convert a numeric error code into a bit of explanatory English text.

How to Convert a Numeric Error Code to English Text

Just type **net helpmsg** *number*, where *number* is the error code. For example, you'll probably stumble across error 5 now and then: "access is denied." It means that you didn't have the right to do something that you tried to do. Another common one is error 53, "the network path was not found." It means that you tried to access some server that the system can't find or, as is usually the case for me, you misspelled the server's name.

Before leaving the topic of the Browser, let me offer one more piece of advice: try to avoid it, as it's unreliable. If your users need access to particular file shares, then you can deliver access to those shares in a few ways. First, you can "map" file shares, which means that you can create imaginary drive letters on your user's workstations. In other words, if the user often uses \\server1\compdata, then you could set up her workstation so that she'd see a new drive "V:" which isn't a local hard disk—it *looks* like a local hard disk—but is instead a network drive. Or you could simply create a shortcut to the UNC on her desktop. You'll learn how to do both of those things in Chapter 11.

Summary: The Necessary Evils

I hope in this section that I've provided a bit of an answer to the question, "Why do we have to worry about all of this stuff just to get a mail server up and running?"

◆ First, you need a piece of server software that can accomplish whatever it is that you're trying to do—Web server, mail server, or whatever.

◆ Next, you need to be compatible with and connected to a physical network that connects to your clients—either the public Internet or a private network of some kind.

◆ Then your server must move its data around in the same way that your clients' machines do, using the same network language or protocol, probably TCP/IP. TCP/IP itself will require some server functions as well, to maintain it.

◆ It wouldn't be necessary in a perfect world, but in our imperfect world your network needs to protect its data with a security system, and in today's world that unfortunately means an *elaborate* security system.

◆   Finally, you'll need some way of finding what you put in that network, once you've got it working. Active Directory will become that way in the future, but for now it's a kludgy thing called the Computer Browser that you see in My Network Places.

So presumably you now see why your network needs so many moving parts. Why buy them from Microsoft?

So Why Use NT/2000?

I hope that by now I've convinced you that networking seems like a good thing. But you could build your network atop any number of operating systems, including Unix, Linux, Novell NetWare, IBM's OS/400 or MVS, or Compaq's VMS, just to name a few. Why NT or its most recent incarnation, Windows 2000 Server?

Well, understand when I answer that question that (1) I'm not from Microsoft, (2) I'm not here to sell NT/2000 to you, I'm just here to tell you how to make it work, and (3) the reality of the matter is that every one of the OSes that I just named are good products that have not only their adherents and detractors, but that also have many solid positive features—after decades of business computer use, the market has filtered out both the truly terrible products, and some perfectly good but inadequately marketed products, leaving only products that are at least competent (and always well-marketed). So if you want to read that 2000 is not only your best choice, but also that you're a total fool to try to use anything else, then I'm afraid you've come to the wrong place. Yes, I like NT, including its latest incarnation (2000), but it's not the only answer.

But it *is* a very good answer. Here's why.

It's the Market Leader

Most stats that I see say that the NT/2000 family of operating systems has the largest market share—38 percent of servers according to the last set of numbers that I saw. Being part of the biggest market share means that it's easier to find consultants, support, and third-party tools. Oh, and it *also* means that there's plenty of demand for your services once you become an expert!

Its Familiar GUI Makes It Easier to Get Started

The fact that Windows 2000 Server uses a GUI that is basically the same as Wintendo—oops, I meant Windows 95, 98, and Me—means that hundreds of millions of people already know how to navigate the 2000 desktop. Yes, some things have been moved around, but in general once you know Windows, you know how to get around on 2000.

In contrast, I have recently done a lot of work with Linux and, while it's a quite powerful operating system, the user interface is *not* for novices; even its multitude of GUIs are still clumsy, although that'll probably change with time. (That's not to say that you shouldn't use Linux—just that I think the Microsoft OSes have an easier-to-use GUI.) With 2000, you can often figure out how to solve a problem by noodling around in the GUI—it lends itself more to exploration than would an operating system that relies mainly upon command-line commands to control it.

Many Tools Come "in the Box"

When NT 3.1 first came out, it was pretty amazing that it came with a dial-in module and a host of other goodies that you had to buy separately in order to run its competition at the time, Novell Net-Ware. NT had a free TCP/IP stack when many other OSes were charging big bucks for it, a free Web server, and so on. Since then, other server operating systems have continued to include more and more things with the basic operating system—for example, the variety of tools that come with Linux is nothing short of stunning—but Microsoft has kept the heat on the competition by including a variety of new tools with every release. At this point, the basic version of 2000 Server includes (in addition to its basic functionality of a file and print server) a Web server, an FTP server, a sophisticated Internet router, automated workstation rollout tools (Remote Installation Services), centralized software distribution tools (Group Policies), a two-level disk storage system (Remote Storage Manager), encryption (Encrypted File System), and lots of other tools.

Not all of the tools are stellar; for example, the disk quota system, which allows you to keep any given user from stealing all of the disk space on the shared file servers, is pretty lame. But because 2000 provides at least a basic quota functionality, the many shops that are trying to minimize the number of vendors they deal with can get an awful lot of their networking needs met in just one package: 2000 Server.

When you view Microsoft products, bear in mind that you usually won't encounter really cutting-edge tools; in my judgment, that's not Microsoft's market niche. Instead, they seem to focus on incrementally improving existing products, as well as adding new tools by imitating competitors. Not being the first on the block can sometimes be a pretty good thing, as you get to watch the competition's mistakes. Very little in Win2K is truly never-seen-before-in-the-world new. Instead, it's a distillation of a lot of other people's good ideas. Yes, some may see that as *stealing* other people's good ideas, and there's some merit to that view. And Microsoft has what some might call an unfair advantage in that they've got enough money to keep trying and trying and trying; for example, their first two networking products, MS-NET and LAN Manager, were pretty weak compared to the competition's, but they had the money and tenacity to keep slugging away it, finally releasing the far-better NT product. Another example of this strategy occurred in 2001, with Microsoft's release of the Pocket PC 2002 operating system. They're trying to crush the PalmOS guys in the palmtop market, and they've made two weak attempts with Windows CE 1.0 and 2.0, but they're learning. I don't know if Pocket PC will beat PalmOS—as a long-time Palm user, I tend to think not—but they'll *definitely* steal more of PalmOS's market share with Pocket PC than they ever did with Windows CE.

And while Microsoft's detractors like to paint Microsoft as nothing but a bunch of rip-off artists, it's actually hard to find who *originated* these ideas. Some say that Microsoft stole Novell and Apple's best ideas; well, Novell certainly didn't invent networking, and their IPX/SPX protocol is blatant "theft" of a Xerox protocol. Apple didn't invent the GUI that Microsoft supposedly stole—Xerox did. (Hmmm, maybe there's a pattern here.) In any case, it *is* something of a comfort for people to be able to buy a single product that is a decent fit for just about all of their networking needs, instead of looking for the "best of breed" in each area. Why? Anyone who's ever tried to trouble-shoot a multivendor network problem knows why: Both vendors just point the finger at the other vendor and say "that's him—he's the guy causing your problem." (They're hoping you'll get tired and go away. Most of us do, sadly.)

In contrast, the same people are developing all of 2000's pieces; so you have to believe that at some point *someone* would have noticed if they didn't fit together. Or that if someone didn't notice it *before* they shipped, they'll get around to fixing it afterward.

In sum, why use 2000? It's fairly reliable, it does most of what you want a network operating system to do, it's reasonably priced, and enough other people use it that you're probably not going to go terribly wrong.

A Brief History of NT

Let's finish this chapter with a look at how NT has grown and changed since its early days.

Even in the early 1980s, Bill Gates knew that networking was a key to owning the computer business. So, on April 15, 1985, Microsoft released its first networking product, a tool called MS-NET, and its companion operating system, DOS 3.10. Most people knew about the new DOS and were puzzled at its apparent lack of new features. What it contained, however, were architectural changes to DOS that made it a bit friendlier to the idea of networks.

Now, Microsoft wasn't big enough at that time to create much hoopla about a new network operating system, so they let others sell it—no matter how high or low you looked, you couldn't buy a product called "MS-NET." Instead, it sold mainly as an IBM product under the name of the IBM PC Network Support Program; IBM viewed it as little more than some software to go along with their PC Network LAN boards and, later, their Token Ring cards. The server software was DOS-based, offered minimal security, and, to be honest, performed terribly. (Believe me, I *know*; I used to install them for people.) But the software had two main effects on the market.

First, the fact that IBM sold a LAN product legitimized the whole industry. IBM made it possible for others to make a living selling network products. And that led to the second effect: the growth of Novell. Once IBM legitimized the idea of a LAN, most companies responded by going out and getting the LAN operating system that offered the best bang for the buck. That was an easy decision: NetWare. In the early days of networking, Novell established itself as the performance leader. You could effectively serve about twice as many workstations with Novell NetWare as you could with any of the MS-NET products. So Novell prospered.

As time went on, however, Microsoft got better at building network products. 3Com, wanting to offer a product that was compatible with the IBM PC Network software, licensed MS-NET and resold it as their "3+" software. 3Com knew quite a bit about networking, however, and recognized the limitations of MS-NET. So 3Com reworked MS-NET to improve its performance, a fact that didn't escape Microsoft's attention.

From 1985 to 1988, Microsoft worked on their second generation of networking software. The software was based on their OS/2 version 1 operating system. (Remember, Microsoft was the main driving force behind OS/2 from 1985 through early 1990. Steve Ballmer, Microsoft's number two guy, promised publicly in 1988 that Microsoft would "go the distance with OS/2." Hey, the world changes and you've got to change with it, right?) Seeing the good work that 3Com did with MS-NET, Microsoft worked as a partner with 3Com to build the next generation of LAN software. Called Microsoft LAN Manager, this network server software was built atop the more powerful OS/2 operating system. As with the earlier MS-NET, Microsoft's intention was never to directly market LAN Manager. Instead, they envisioned IBM, 3Com, Compaq, and others selling it.

IBM did indeed sell LAN Manager (they still do in the guise of OS/2 LAN Server). 3Com sold LAN Manager for years as 3+Open but found little profit in it and got out of the software business. In late 1990, Compaq announced that they would not sell LAN Manager because it was too complex a product for their dealers to explain, sell, and support. Microsoft decided then that if LAN Manager was to be sold, they'd have to do the selling, so on the very same day as the Compaq withdrawal, they announced that they would begin selling LAN Manager directly.

NOTE *Interesting side note: Ten years after Compaq decided that their sales force couldn't sell network software, they reversed direction and said that they'd sell a special version of Windows 2000 called Datacenter Server. It's special because you cannot buy it from Microsoft—you* must *buy it pre-installed on specially certified vendor hardware. In other words, the hardware vendors (Compaq's not the only one selling Datacenter) now believe that they can sell complex network operating systems. I wish them the best of luck, but stay tuned to see the outcome of this particular marketing maneuver!*

LAN Manager in its first incarnation still wasn't half the product that Novell NetWare was, but it was getting there. LAN Manager 2 greatly closed the gap, and in fact, on some benchmarks LAN Manager outpaced Novell NetWare. Additionally, LAN Manager included administrative and security features that brought it even closer to Novell NetWare in the minds of many network managers. Slowly, LAN Manager gained about a 20 percent share of the network market.

When Microsoft designed LAN Manager, however, they designed it for the 286 chip (more accurately, I should say again that LAN Manager was built atop OS/2 1.*x*, and OS/2 1.*x* was built for the 286 chip). LAN Manager's 286 foundation hampered its performance and sales. In contrast, Novell designed their premier products (NetWare 3 and 4) to use the full capabilities of the 386 and later processors. Microsoft's breakup with IBM delayed the release of a 386-based product and, in a sense, Microsoft never released the 386-based product.

Instead of continuing to climb the ladder of Intel processor capabilities, Microsoft decided to build a processor-independent operating system that would sit in roughly the same market position as Unix. It could then be implemented for the 386 and later chips, and it also could run well on other processors, such as the PowerPC, Alpha, and MIPS chips. Microsoft called this new operating system NT, for new technology. Not only would NT serve as a workstation operating system, it would also arrive in a network server version to be called LAN Manager NT. No products ever shipped with that name, but the wallpaper that NT Server displays when no one is logged in is called `LANMANNT.BMP` to this day.

In August 1993, Microsoft released LAN Manager NT with the name NT Advanced Server. In a shameless marketing move, they labeled it version 3.1 in order to match the version numbers of the Windows desktop products. This first version of NT Advanced Server performed quite well. However, it was memory-hungry, lacked Novell connectivity, and had only the most basic TCP/IP connectivity.

September 1994 brought a new version and a new name: Microsoft Windows NT Server version 3.5. Version 3.5 was mainly a "polish" of 3.1; it was less memory-hungry, it included Novell and TCP/IP connectivity right in the box, and it included Windows for Workgroups versions of the administrative tools so network administrators could work from a Workgroup machine rather than an NT machine. Where many vendors would spend 13 months adding silly bells and whistles, NT 3.5 showed that the Microsoft folks had spent most of their time fine-tuning the operating system, trimming its memory requirements, and speeding it up.

In October 1995 came NT version 3.51, which mainly brought support for PCMCIA cards (a real boon for us traveling instructor types), file compression, and a raft of bug fixes.

NT version 4, 1996's edition of NT, got a newer Windows 95–like face and a bunch of new features, but no really radical networking changes. Under the hood, NT 4 wasn't much different from NT 3.51.

From mid 1996 to early 2000, no new versions of NT appeared, an "upgrade drought" such as we'd not seen in quite some time from Microsoft. Then, in February of 2000, Windows 2000 shipped. And as to *its* new features—well, you're holding a book on the topic in your hands! But that's not the last part of the story. In 2001, Microsoft released Windows XP, which fixes some of 2000's troubles and adds some new features. *That* in turn will pave the way for yet another version of NT, code-named Blackcomb, but let's wait for another edition or two of this book to cover *that* product.

Well, I hope this chapter wasn't boring for those already expert in NT—I *did* warn you!—and helped bring the newbies up to speed. No matter what version of NT you're running, however, you'll soon find that you'll want to (or *have* to) tweak some setting in 2000 (or NT 4 or NT 3.*x*) to make it work just the way that you want. That's why I've got to next show you where 2000 *stores* those settings. The settings storage place is called the Registry—and you'll learn how it works in the next chapter.

Chapter 3

The Windows 2000 Registry

ANY EXPLANATION OF HOW to solve problems and get things done in Windows 2000 will soon turn to a bit of software fiddling called "modifying the Registry" or "hacking the Registry." This chapter explains exactly what the Registry is, why you care about it, and how to work with it. If you've already worked with Windows 95, 98, Me, or a previous version of NT, then this will be old stuff. But the newcomers should read carefully!

Anyone who works with Windows 2000, whether as a user or as an administrator, makes a fair number of adjustments to it—from the small ones, such as changing a background color, to larger ones, like changing a network IP address. Similarly, when you use an application, you inevitably end up configuring it as well, directing it where to save files, how the application should start up, whether to automatically run macros, and the like. And, of course, when you reboot Windows 2000 or whenever you start up an application, you expect your configurations to still be in effect—the things that you tell an operating system or application to do should survive a reboot. But where are these customizations stored?

Over the years, different operating systems have answered that question in different ways. Windows 2 and 2.1 actually stored a lot of their configuration information inside their own program files, which unbelievably meant that every time you made a change like installing a new video card, the Windows Setup program would build an entirely new copy of Windows with that driver's information embedded in the Windows program itself! Not every configuration change in Windows 2.x required a rebuild of the operating system, thankfully, as Windows 2.x and then 3.x used ASCII text files with names like WIN.INI, SYSTEM.INI, CONTROL.INI, and so on to store configuration information. INI files weren't a bad thing overall—their ASCII nature made changing them simple, a task for Notepad or an easy-to-write BASIC program—but the growing complexity of Windows in both its 9x and Windows NT incarnations created a need to be able to store more complex configuration information.

Microsoft's answer to that increased need arrived with the first version of NT, Windows NT 3.1, in the summer of 1993. The answer was a group of files with the collective name of the *Registry*. (Microsoft always capitalizes it—the Registry—so I will, too, but it always seems a bit overdone, don't you think?) The Registry is terrific in that it's one big database that contains all of the

Windows 2000 configuration information. Everything's there, from color settings to users' passwords. (In case you're wondering, you can't directly access the part with the passwords.) Even better, the Registry uses a fault-tolerant approach to writing data to ensure that the Registry remains intact even if there's a power failure in the middle of a Registry update.

So you've just *got* to like Windows 2000's Registry. Except, of course, for the *annoying* parts about the Registry, including its cryptic organization and excessively complex structure. But read on and see what you think.

What Is the Registry?

The Registry is a hierarchical database of settings that describe your user account, the hardware of the server machine, and your applications. Any time you make some change with the Control Panel or some other MMC snap-in, the effect of that change is usually stored in the Registry. (I say "usually" because some information is stored in the Active Directory, which is separate from the Registry.)

If you can make changes to your system and they're then stored in the Registry, you might ask, "Who cares? What's the value of the Registry?" Well, consider how much time you spend configuring a new workstation or server. If that machine died for some reason, you'd want to set up another machine to replace the now-dead one—do you really want to spend all that time reconfiguring the replacement machine to look like the original? No, of course not. You would much prefer to be able to just put Windows 2000 on the new machine and then restore all of the preferences and settings in one fell swoop, and you can do that, *if* you've got a backup of the old machine's Registry. Then all you need do is to put Windows 2000 on the replacement machine and then restore the old machine's Registry to the new machine. That, then, is the Registry's first value: when backed up, it preserves much of a machine's "state."

NOTE   *Of course, another way to preserve the state of a Windows 2000 Professional machine is to store its image on a Remote Installation Services (RIS) server, as described in Chapter 4. Unfortunately, however, you can't use RIS to store the state of a member server or domain controller.*

Preserving user settings is nice, but it's not the Registry's sole value. In addition to storing the settings that *you've* made in the Registry, Windows 2000 saves many settings that you never see, such as dynamic settings that Windows 2000 makes to itself every time it boots—for example, whenever Windows 2000 boots, it creates a census of the hardware attached to it and stores that census in the Registry. The Registry also contains internal adjustments that Windows 2000's designers preset with the intention that you would never touch them—and *that's* where the fun begins, at least for us noodlers.

Ninety-nine point nine percent of Windows 2000's settings are of no interest whatsoever. But a few are quite powerful and largely undocumented or documented solely by obscure Knowledge Base articles. The occult nature of these Registry settings has predictably become the source of countless "tips and tricks" about how to tune up NT's and Windows 2000's performance or how to solve some knotty problem. Perhaps the most remarkable of these appeared a few years ago when NT internals expert Mark Rossinovich discovered that the only real difference between NT Workstation 3.51 and NT Server 3.51 was *a few Registry settings!* Twiddling the Registry, then, is often of value to Windows 2000 troubleshooters.

The tough part about working with the Registry for NT/Windows 2000 is in grasping the programs and terminology used in editing the Registry. You're just supposed to *understand* sentences like these:

> *When you receive upon logon the message 'A domain controller for your domain could not be contacted ' then you may need to increase Netlogon's timeout value.*

> *To increase the amount of time Netlogon waits before timing out during an interactive logon using a Domain User account, the following registry setting can be used... In the subkey* `HKEY_LOCAL_MACHINE\SYSTEM\ CurrentControlSet\Services\Netlogon\Parameters`, *create a new value* `ExpectedDialup- Delay` *of type* `REG_DWORD` *and fill in a value between 0 and 600, representing the new Netlogon delay.*

Sentences like these are a major reason for this chapter. You will come across phrases like that in Microsoft literature, magazine articles, and even parts of this book. Much of that information contains useful advice that will make you a better network administrator if you understand how to carry it out—in fact, these snippets are incredibly useful if you've got a busy network and people are having trouble logging in. My goal for this chapter, then, is to give you a feel for the Registry, how to edit it, and when to leave it alone.

Registry Terminology

What did that stuff with all the backslashes mean? To get an insight, let's look at the Registry. You can see it by running the program `REGEDT32.EXE` (it's in the `\Winnt\SYSTEM32` directory); just click Start/Run and fill in **REGEDT32.EXE**. There is another Registry Editor as well named `REGEDIT.EXE`—there are two because NT originally had REGEDT32, and then Windows 95 shipped with a different editor for *its* Registry named REGEDIT. We still have both editors because REGEDT32 has a few features that REGEDIT doesn't, and vice versa. (Oddly enough, this state of affairs has existed since mid 1996; you'd think that by the time Windows 2000 shipped, Microsoft would have just merged all of the best of both editors into a single one, but they haven't.)

Run REGEDT32 and click the `HKEY_LOCAL_MACHINE` window. You'll see a screen like the one in Figure 3.1.

FIGURE 3.1

Registry Editor screen

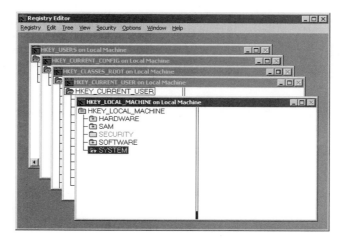

The terms to know in order to understand the Registry are *subtree, key, value, data type,* and *hive.*

WARNING *It's easy to accidentally blast important data with the Registry Editor, so it might be a good idea at this point to put the Editor in* read-only *mode by clicking Options, then Read Only Mode. You can always reverse the read-only state whenever necessary in the same way. It is truly simple to render a server completely unusable with a few unthinking Registry edits, so be careful, please. Unfortunately, only REGEDT32 has a read-only mode—REGEDIT doesn't.*

Subtrees

Windows 2000's Registry is spread out physically as it is saved in several separate files (called *hives*), as you'll learn later, and the Registry is also spread out *logically* into separate parts called *subtrees.*

The main reason for this is that the Registry stores all information about a computer and its users by dividing them up into five subtrees, as shown in Table 3.1.

TABLE 3.1: THE FIVE SUBTREES OF THE REGISTRY

SUBTREE	DESCRIPTION
HKEY_LOCAL_MACHINE	Contains information about the hardware currently installed in the machine and the settings for systems running on the machine. You do most of your work in this and the next subtree.
HKEY_CURRENT_USER	Contains the user profile for the person currently logged on to the Windows 2000 Server machine. Contains user preferences and settings for desktop applications running on this machine.
HKEY_USERS	Contains a pointer to the HKEY_CURRENT_USER subtree and also to a profile called the DEFAULT profile. The DEFAULT profile describes how the machine behaves when no one's logged on. For example, if instead of a blue background you wanted a machine to display a green background when no one was logged on, or if you wanted to display a particular wallpaper when no one was logged on (which I've found quite useful for keeping clear in my mind which machine was which when using a keyboard switch or just a table full of identical-looking machines), then you'd modify that DEFAULT profile.
HKEY_CLASSES_ROOT	Holds the file associations, information that tells the system, "Whenever the user double-clicks a file with the extension .BMP in Windows Explorer, start up PBRUSH.EXE to view the file." It also contains the OLE registration database, the old REG.DAT from Windows 3.*x.* This is actually a redundant subtree, as all its information is found in the HKEY_LOCAL_MACHINE subtree. It also gets placed in the HKEY_CURRENT_USER\SOFTWARE\CLASSES key.
HKEY_CURRENT_CONFIG	Contains configuration information for the particular hardware configuration you booted up with.

In general, you'll do most of your work in the first two subtrees. Some Registry entries are specific to a machine (HKEY_LOCAL_MACHINE, HKEY_CLASSES_ROOT, HKEY_CURRENT_ CONFIG), and some are specific to a user (HKEY_USERS, HKEY_CURRENT_USER, as well as other Registry files that are in the

\Documents And Settings\USER ID directories, which you'll meet later—but for now, just understand that the \Documents And Settings folder is where Windows 2000 machines store user preference information). That's important, and it's a great strength of the Registry's structure. The entries relevant to a particular machine should, of course, physically reside on that machine. But what about the settings relevant to a user: the background colors you like, the programs you want to see in your Start menu, the sounds you want on the system? These shouldn't be tied to any one computer; they should be able to move around the network with that user. Indeed, they can. Windows 2000 supports the idea that "roving users" can have their personal settings follow them around the network via *roaming profiles*, which you will learn more about in Chapter 9.

Registry Keys

In Figure 3.1, you saw the Registry Editor display five cascaded windows, one for each subtree. HKEY_LOCAL_MACHINE was on top; you can see the other four subtrees' windows, too. HKEY_CURRENT_USER's window has a right and left pane. The pane on the left looks kind of like a screen from the Explorer or the old Windows 3.1 File Manager.

In the File Manager, those folders represented subdirectories. Here, however, they separate information into sections, kind of in the same way old Windows INI files had sections whose names were surrounded by square brackets, names like [386enh], [network], [boot], and the like. Referring back to the HKEY_LOCAL_MACHINE picture shown in Figure 3.1, let's compare this to an old Windows 3.*x*–style INI file. If this were an INI file, the name of its sections would be [hardware], [sam], [security], [software], and [system]. These folders or sections are actually called *keys* in the Registry.

But here's where the analogy to INI files fails: You can have keys within keys, called *subkeys* (and sub-subkeys, and sub-sub-subkeys, and so on). Let's open the SYSTEM key. It contains subkeys named ControlSet001, ControlSet002, CurrentControlSet, Select, and Setup, and CurrentControlSet is further subkeyed into Control and Services.

NOTE *If you use REGEDIT, it will show you where you are in the Registry at the bottom of the window. That's one of the things it does that REGEDT32 doesn't. REGEDIT also lets you copy that entire Registry key path to the clipboard so that you can easily paste it into a document—a very nice feature.*

Notice, by the way, the key called CurrentControlSet. It's very important. Almost every time you modify your system's configuration, you do it with a subkey within the CurrentControlSet subkey.

Key-Naming Conventions

The tree of keys gets pretty big as you drill down through the many layers. CurrentControlSet, for example, has dozens of subkeys, each of which can have subkeys. Identifying a given subkey is important, so Microsoft has adopted a naming convention that looks just like the one used for directory trees. CurrentControlSet's fully specified name would be, then, HKEY_LOCAL_MACHINE\SYSTEM\CurrentControlSet. In this book, however, I'll just call it CurrentControlSet to keep key names from getting too long to fit on a single line.

Value Entries, Names, Values, and Data Types

If I drill down through CurrentControlSet, I find subkey Services, and within Services, there are many subkeys. In Figure 3.2, you can see some of the subkeys of CurrentControlSet\Services.

FIGURE 3.2

The subkeys of `Current-ControlSet\ Services`

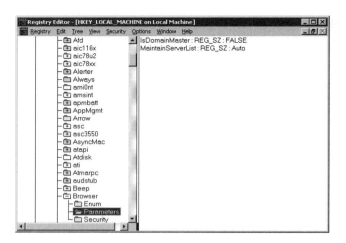

One of those keys, `Browser`, contains subkeys named `Enum`, `Parameters`, and `Security`. Once we get to `Parameters`, however, you can see that it's the end of the line—no subkeys from there. Just to quickly review Registry navigation, the key that we're looking at now is in `HKEY_LOCAL_MACHINE\ SYSTEM\CurrentControlSet\Services\ Browser\Parameters`.

In the right pane, you see two lines:

```
IsDomainMaster : REG_SZ : False
MaintainServerList : REG_SZ : Auto
```

This is how the Registry says what would be, in the old INI-type files, something like this:

```
IsDomainMaster=False
MaintainServerList=Auto
```

Each line like `IsDomainMaster:REG_SZ:False` is called a *value entry*. The three parts are called *name*, *data type*, and *value*, respectively. In this example, `IsDomainMaster` is the *name*, `REG_SZ` is the *data type*, and `False` is the *value*.

Microsoft notes that each value entry cannot exceed about 1MB in size. It's hard to imagine one that size, but it's worth mentioning.

What is that `REG_SZ` stuff? It's an identifier to the Registry of what *kind* of data to expect: numbers, messages, yes/no values, and the like. Microsoft defines five data types in the Registry Editor (although others could be defined later), shown in Table 3.2.

TABLE 3.2: DATA TYPES AS DEFINED BY THE REGISTRY EDITOR

DATA TYPE	DESCRIPTION
REG_BINARY	Raw binary data. Data of this type usually doesn't make sense when you look at it with the Registry Editor. Binary data shows up in hardware setup information. If there is an alternative way to enter this data other than via the Registry Editor—and I'll discuss that in a page or two—then do it that way. Editing binary data can get you in trouble if you don't know what you're doing. The data is usually represented in hex for simplicity's sake.

Continued on next page

TABLE 3.2: DATA TYPES AS DEFINED BY THE REGISTRY EDITOR *(continued)*

DATA TYPE	DESCRIPTION
REG_DWORD	Another binary data type, but it is 4 bytes long.
REG_EXPAND_SZ	A character string of variable size, it's often information understandable by humans, like path statements or messages. It is "expandable" in that it may contain information that will change at runtime, like %username%—a system batch variable that will be of different sizes for different people's names.
REG_MULTI_SZ	Another string type, but it allows you to enter a number of parameters in this one value entry. The parameters are separated by binary zeroes (nulls).
REG_SZ	A simple string.

Those who first met a Registry with Windows 95 will notice a few differences here. Windows 95 has six subtrees, but only three data types—*string*, which encompasses REG_SZ, REG_MULTI_SZ, and REG_EXPAND_SZ; *dword*, which is the same as REG_DWORD; and *binary*, which is identical to REG_BINARY.

And if you're wondering how on earth you'll figure out what data type to assign to a new Registry value, don't worry about it; if you read somewhere to use a particular new value entry, you'll be told what data type to use. Failing that, I usually just guess REG_SZ if it's textual in nature, REG_DWORD if it's numeric.

Working with the Registry: An Example

Now, I know you want to get in there and try it out despite the warnings, so here's an innocuous example. Remember, it's only innocuous if you *follow* the example to the letter; otherwise, it will soon be time to get out your installation disks.

That's not just boilerplate. Don't get mad at *me* if you blow up your server because you didn't pay attention. Actually, you *may* be able to avoid a reinstallation if the thing that you modified was in the CurrentControlSet key; Windows 2000 knows that you often mess around in there, and so it keeps a spare. In that case, you can reboot the server and, when the boot menu prompts "Please select the operating system to start:," press F8 for the Windows 2000 Advanced Options menu. One of the options you'll get will be Last Known Good Configuration. That *doesn't* restore the entire Registry; it just restores the control set. Fortunately, the current control set is a *lot* of the Registry. It doesn't include user-specific settings, however, like "What color should the screen be?" Thus, if you were to set all of your screen colors to black, rendering the screen black on black (and therefore less than readable), rebooting and choosing Last Known Good Configuration wouldn't help you.

In any case, let's try something out, something relatively harmless. Let's change the name of the company that you gave Windows 2000 when you installed it. Recently my firm changed names from TechTeach International to MR&D. Suppose I'd already installed a bunch of Windows 2000 machines and filled in TechTeach International when prompted for an organization. Suppose also that I want to change that so the Help/About dialog boxes say that I'm Mark Minasi of MR&D, but I don't feel like reinstalling. Fortunately, the Registry Editor lets me change company names without reinstalling:

1. Open the Registry Editor. From the Start menu, choose Run.

2. In the command line, type **REGEDT32** and press Enter.

3. Click Window and choose HKEY_Local_Machine. Maximize that window and you'll see a screen somewhat like the one in Figure 3.3.

FIGURE 3.3

The Registry Editor HKEY_LOCAL_MACHINE on Local Machine dialog box

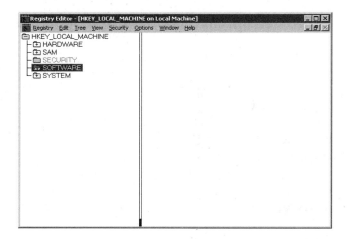

4. We're going to modify the value entry in HKEY_LOCAL_MACHINE\Software\Microsoft\ Windows NT\CurrentVersion. Double-click the Software key, then double-click the Microsoft key, then double-click the Windows NT key, and, finally, double-click the CurrentVersion key. You'll see a screen like the one in Figure 3.4. In the left pane, you'll still see the Registry structure. On the right, you'll see the value entry RegisteredOrganization.

FIGURE 3.4

CurrentVersion RegisteredOrganization

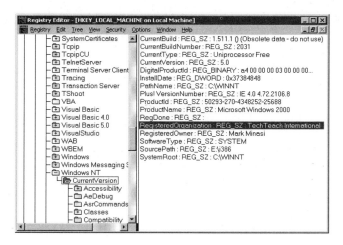

5. Double-click `RegisteredOrganization`, and a String Editor screen appears.

6. Highlight the old value and replace it with **MR&D**. Click OK, and close up the Registry Editor.

Now click Help/About for any program—even the Registry Editor will do—and you'll see that your organization is now MR&D.

WARNING *Click all you like; you will not find a Save button or an Undo button. When you edit the Registry, it's immediate and it's forever. So, once again, be* careful *when you mess with the Registry.*

How Do You Find Registry Keys?

How did I know to go to `HKEY_LOCAL_MACHINE\Software\Microsoft\Windows NT\CurrentVersion` in order to change my organization name? I found it by poking around the Registry.

If you have the Windows 2000 Resource Kit from Microsoft—and if you don't, then *get it!*— you'll find 150 pages detailing each and every key. (That, by the way, is why there isn't a complete key guide in this book. First of all, there wasn't anything that I could add to what's in the Resource Kit; second, Microsoft has already published the Kit; and third, 150 pages directly lifted from someone else's publication is a pretty serious copyright violation. I don't think it's possible to paraphrase 150 pages of reference material.) Additionally, the Registry keys are documented in an online help file. Unfortunately, some keys aren't documented anywhere except in bits and pieces on Microsoft Tech-Net or the like, and I'll mention *those* in this book.

In my opinion, the Registry Editor has a glaring weakness: no effective search routine. Suppose you knew that there was something called `RegisteredOrganization` but you had no idea where it lives in the Registry? You'd be out of luck. REGEDT32 includes a View/Find Key, but it only searches the names of *keys*, not value entries. In contrast, the newer `REGEDIT.EXE` *can* search keys, values, and names. I could then search for "RegisteredOrganization." I'll contrast REGEDT32 and REGEDIT later on in this chapter.

Even More Cautions about Editing the Registry

If you're just learning about the Registry, you're probably eager to wade right in and modify a value entry. Before you do, however, let me just talk a bit about using caution when you manipulate the Registry. (I know I've mentioned it before, but it's important, so I'm mentioning it again.)

The vast majority of Registry items correspond to some setting in the Control Panel, Active Directory Users and Computers, or some other MMC snap-in. For example, you just saw where we could change the `RegisteredOrganization` directly via the Registry Editor. I only picked that example, however, because it was fairly illustrative and simple to understand. In general, *don't use the Registry Editor to modify a value that can be modified in some other way.*

For example, suppose I choose to set a background color on my screen to medium gray. That color is represented as a triplet of numbers: 128 128 128. How did I know what those color values meant? Because they're the same as Windows 3.*x* color values. Color values in Windows are expressed as number triplets. Each number is an integer from 0 to 255. If I input a value greater than 255, the Registry Editor would neither know nor care that I was punching in an illegal color value. Now, in the case of colors, that probably wouldn't crash the system. In the case of other items, however, the system could easily be rendered unusable. For example, I'm running Windows 2000 Server on a system with just a single Pentium II processor, so the Registry reflects that, noting in one of the HARDWARE keys that Windows 2000 is running a "uniprocessor" mode. Altering that to a multiprocessor mode wouldn't be a very good idea.

Why, then, am I bothering to tell you about the Registry Editor? Three reasons.

First, there are settings—important ones—that can only be altered via the Registry Editor, so there's no getting around the fact that a Windows 2000 expert has to be proficient in the Editor.

Second, you can use the Registry Editor to change system value entries on remote computers. To use a very simple example: I'm at location A and I want to change the background color on the server at location B, and to do that I have to physically travel to location B in order to run the Control Panel on the Windows 2000 machine at that location. Instead of doing that, however, I can just start up the Registry Editor, choose Registry/Select Computer, and edit the Registry of the remote computer. (This assumes that you are running Windows 2000 Server and you have the security access to change the Registry of the remote computer—that is, you're a member of the Administrators group on that computer.)

Third, a program comes with the Resource Kit called REGINI.EXE that allows you to write scripts to modify Registries. Such a tool is quite powerful; in theory, you could write a REGINI script to completely reconfigure a Windows 2000 setup. Again, however, before you start messing with that program, please be sure that you have become proficient with the Registry. I've explained the various kinds of mischief that you can cause working by hand with the Registry Editor. Imagine what kinds of automated disasters you could start at 450MHz with a bad REGINI script!

By the way, there's another way to automate Registry changes, through REGEDIT. You can create an ASCII text file with the desired Registry changes, then use an undocumented /s (for "silent") switch to introduce the changes.

The file has a particular format. The first line must be Windows Registry Editor Version 5.00, followed by a blank line. Then you enter a line with the full name of the Registry key that contains the value that you want to modify, surrounded by square brackets. Then type a line for each value that you want to modify, with the name of the value, an equal sign, and the desired value. Strings should be surrounded by quotes, and numbers—as in the DWORD type—should be prefixed by DWORD:; for example, consider the following file:

```
Windows Registry Editor Version 5.00

[HKEY_LOCAL_MACHINE\SOFTWARE\Microsoft\Windows NT\CurrentVersion]
"RegisteredOrganization"="MR&D"
"NumberOfLicenses"=dword:00000003\
```

The first line identifies the file as a set of Registry changes. That first line is probably to keep someone from accidentally feeding some random file to REGEDIT, causing untold havoc from just an ill-thought-out mouse click. Then there's a blank line and then the description in square brackets. The line afterward sets the RegisteredOrganization, as described earlier, and the final entry is just an imaginary setting that I created just to show how to do a number. If I put those five lines—it's *five*, remember the blank line—into a file and called it `mystuff.reg`, I could make REGEDIT modify the Registry with it like so:

```
Regedit /s mystuff.reg
```

And by the way, here's a useful tip: if you use REGEDIT's "export" function (Registry/Export Registry File), the resulting exported file is ASCII and in the proper format for using `/s` to apply the values to another computer.

Where the Registry Lives: Hives

The Registry is mostly contained in a set of files called the *hives*. ("Mostly" because some of it is built automatically every time you boot up your system. For example, Windows 2000 doesn't know what devices are on a SCSI chain until you boot.) Hives are binary files, so there's no way to look at them without a special editor of some kind, like the Registry Editor. Hives are, however, an easy way to load or back up a sizable part of the Registry.

Most, although not all, of the Registry is stored in hive files. They're not hidden, system, or read-only, but are always open, so you're kind of limited in what you can do with them.

A Look at the Hive Files

The machine-specific hive files are in the `\WINNT\SYSTEM32\CONFIG` directory. The user-specific hive files are in the `\WINNT\DOCUMENTS` and `SETTINGS\USER ID` directories. You can see the hive files that correspond to parts of the subtree listed in Table 3.3.

TABLE 3.3: HIVE FILES

SUBTREE/KEY	FILENAME
HKEY_LOCAL_MACHINE\SAM	SAM (primary) and SAM.LOG (backup)
HKEY_LOCAL_MACHINE\SECURITY	SECURITY (primary) and SECURITY.LOG (backup)
HKEY_LOCAL_MACHINE\SOFTWARE	SOFTWARE (primary) and SOFTWARE.LOG (backup)
HKEY_LOCAL_MACHINE\SYSTEM	SYSTEM (primary) and SYSTEM.ALT (backup)
HKEY_USERS\DEFAULT	DEFAULT (primary) and DEFAULT.LOG (backup)
HKEY_USERS\Security ID	NTUSER.DAT
HKEY_CURRENT_USER	NTUSER.DAT
HKEY_CLASSES_ROOT	(Created from current control set at boot time)

Table 3.3 needs a few notes to clarify it. First, about the HKEY_CLASSES_ROOT subtree: It is copied from HKEY_KEY_LOCAL_MACHINE\SOFTWARE\Classes at boot time. The file exists for use by 16-bit Windows applications. While you're logged on to Windows 2000, however, the two keys are linked; if you make a change to one, the change is reflected in the other.

The user profiles now live in \Documents and Settings*username*, where each user gets a directory named *username*. For example, I've got a user account named mark, so there's a directory named \Documents and Settings\mark on my computer. If I look in it, I find the files ntuser.dat and ntuser.dat.log.

To summarize, then, the core of the Registry is the four *S*s and DEFAULT:

◆ SAM

◆ SECURITY

◆ SYSTEM

◆ SOFTWARE

SAM contains the user database; SECURITY complements SAM by containing information such as whether a server is a member server or a domain controller, what the name of its domain is, and the like. SYSTEM contains configuration information like what drivers and system programs the computer uses, which should be loaded on bootup, and how their parameters are set. SOFTWARE tends to contain more overall configuration information about the larger software modules in the system, configuration information that does *not* vary from user to user. And then every user has an NTUSER.DAT with their specific application preferences in it.

One question remains about the hive files, however. Why do all the files have a paired file with the extension .LOG? Read on.

Fault Tolerance in the Registry

Notice that every hive file has another file with the same name but the extension .LOG. That's really useful because Windows 2000 Server, and Windows 2000 workstations for that matter, uses it to protect the Registry during updates.

Whenever a hive file is to be changed, the change is first written into its LOG file. The LOG file isn't actually a backup file; it's more a journal of changes to the primary file. Once the description of the change to the hive file is complete, the journal file is written to disk. When I say "written to disk," I *mean* written to disk. Often, a disk write ends up hanging around in the disk cache for a while, but this write is "flushed" to disk. Then the system makes the changes to the hive file based on the information in the journal file. If the system crashes during the hive write operation, there is enough information in the journal file to "roll back" the hive to its previous position.

The exception to this procedure comes with the SYSTEM hive. The SYSTEM hive is really important because it contains the CurrentControlSet. For that reason, the backup file for SYSTEM, SYSTEM.ALT, is a complete backup of SYSTEM. If one file is damaged, the system can use the other to boot.

Notice that HKEY_LOCAL_MACHINE\HARDWARE does not have a hive. That's because the key is rebuilt each time you boot so Windows 2000 can adapt itself to changes in computer hardware. The Plug and Play Manager, which runs at boot time, gathers the information that Windows 2000 needs to create HKEY_LOCAL_MACHINE\HARDWARE.

Confused about where all the keys come from? You'll find a recap in Table 3.4. It's similar to Table 3.3, but it's more specific about how the keys are built at boot time.

TABLE 3.4: CONSTRUCTION OF KEYS AT BOOT TIME

KEY	HOW IT'S CONSTRUCTED AT BOOT TIME
HKEY_LOCAL_MACHINE:	
HARDWARE	Plug and Play Manager
SAM	SAM hive file
SECURITY	SECURITY hive file
SOFTWARE	SOFTWARE hive file
SYSTEM	SYSTEM hive file
HKEY_CLASSES_ROOT	SYSTEM hive file, Classes subkey
HKEY_USERS_DEFAULT	DEFAULT hive file
HKEY_USERS\Sxxx	Particular user's NTUSER.DAT file
HKEY_CURRENT_USER	Particular user's NTUSER.DAT file

Remote Registry Modification

You can modify another computer's Registry, perhaps to repair it or to do some simple kind of remote maintenance, by loading that computer's hive. You do that with the Registry Editor by using the Load Hive or Unload Hive command.

You can load or unload the hives only for HKEY_USERS and HKEY_LOCAL_MACHINE. The Load Hive option appears only if you've selected one of those two subtrees. Unload Hive is available only if you've selected a subkey of one of those two subtrees.

Why, specifically, would you load a hive or a remote Registry?

First of all, you might load a hive in order to get to a user's profile. Suppose a user has set up all of the colors as black on black and made understanding the screen impossible. You could load the hive that corresponds to that user, modify it, and then unload it.

Second, you can use the remote feature to view basically *anything* on a remote system. Suppose you want to do something as simple as changing screen colors. You'd do that on a local system by running the Control Panel, but the Control Panel won't work for remote systems. Answer: Load the Registry remotely.

You could load and save hive files to a floppy disk, walk the floppy over to a malfunctioning machine, and load the hive onto the machine's hard disk, potentially repairing a system problem. This wasn't possible if you used NTFS on the boot disk of an NT 4 system unless you had multiple copies of NT 4— there wasn't an easy way to get to a system with an NTFS boot drive. Under Windows 2000, however, you can go to the advanced boot options and boot to a command prompt even if the system's damaged.

There is yet another way to control Registries remotely, through something called system policies, which are covered in Chapter 9.

Backing Up and Restoring a Registry

By now, it should be pretty clear that the Registry is an important piece of information and that it should be protected. It protects itself pretty well with its LOG files, but how can you back it up?

Unfortunately, the fact that Registry hive files are always open makes it tough to back up the Registry since most backup utilities are stymied by open files. The NTBackup program that comes with Windows 2000 works well, and, while it's a bit primitive, it *can* back up the Registry hive files. So if you use NTBackup—and it's pretty good, when you consider its price—then you should tell it to back up your Registry every night.

NT 4 had a terrific tool named RDISK that would back up your entire Registry with just a few keystrokes, but that's nowhere to be found in Windows 2000. The replacement for RDISK can be found in the Backup program, which offers to create an Emergency Repair Disk, just as RDISK did, through these steps:

1. Launch Backup (Start/Programs/Accessories/System Tools/Backup).

2. Click the Backup tab.

3. Make sure all directories and files are unchecked.

4. Look under My Computer's list of drives; the last option will be System State; check that.

5. Next to the list box labeled Backup Media or File Name, fill in a filename or click Browse and choose a filename; this is where the Registry backup will go.

6. Click the Start Backup button.

7. In the next dialog box, click the Advanced button.

8. Uncheck Automatically Backup System Protected Files with the System State.

9. Click OK to dismiss the dialog box.

10. Click Start Backup. Backup will then save the Registry. You can restore the Registry with Backup as well.

What if you want to back up only a portion of the Registry? The Windows 2000 Resource Kit includes a program called `REG.EXE` that lets you back up the Registry from the command line and while the system is running—but only *one subtree at a time*. It looks like `REG SAVE HKLM\` `subtreename destination`, where *destination* is the place that you want the backup to go, and the subtree names are, of course, `SECURITY`, `SAM`, `SYSTEM`, and `SOFTWARE` in the case of `HKEY_LOCAL_MACHINE`. Note also the abbreviation: REG accepts `HKLM` in place of `HKEY_LOCAL_MACHINE`, `HKCU` in place of `HKEY_CURRENT_ USER`, `HKCR` in place of `HKEY_CLASSES_ROOT`, and `HKCC` in place of `HKEY_ CURRENT_ CONFIGURATION`.

A complete Registry backup to a directory named `C:\RB` would, then, require several lines:

```
Reg save HKCR c:\rb\hkcr
Reg save HKCC\Software c:\rb\hkccsoft
Reg save hkcc\system c:\rb\hkccsys
```

And so on. You'd restore the Registry with REG as well.

REGEDIT Versus REGEDT32

Since Windows NT 4 arrived, we've had a choice of Registry editors. NT 3.*x* always shipped with REGEDT32, but Windows 95 included REGEDIT and Microsoft decided to offer it for NT 4 (and Windows 2000, of course) as well. Are there good reasons to use one or the other?

REGEDT32 has a couple of features that REGEDIT lacks. For one thing, you can set the size of the display font that REGEDT32 uses. That may not sound exciting, but I get a lot of use out of it when teaching classes. It seems like more and more Microsoft administration tools use *really* tiny fonts, making online demonstrations difficult in a room holding more than about 20 people. REGEDT32's greater strength, however, is its ability to set security on Registry keys. As with everything else in Windows 2000, each key in the Registry has a *security descriptor* or *access control list (ACL)*, a description of who is and who isn't allowed to modify that key. Sometimes Microsoft will discover a "hole" in Windows 2000 security caused by some incorrect security setting, and you must use REGEDT32 to seal that security hole—REGEDIT can't do the trick here.

For most other work, I use REGEDIT. First of all, I like the fact that the status bar at the bottom of its window always tells me the complete path to my current position in the Registry. The ability to search for any string is convenient as well. For example, one time I'd gotten my system so confused that it kept asking for a particular program every time I booted up. Clearly the command to start this program was somewhere in the Registry—but where? A quick search solved the problem, showing me where in the Registry the problem lay, making it easy for me to undo the problem. Perhaps the best capability, however, is in REGEDIT's built-in Registry modification language. As mentioned earlier in this chapter, it's a convenient way to record favorite software settings in an ASCII file and then play them back onto a new system whenever you want.

No one *wants* to play around in the Registry, but in real life, most network administrators will find a bit of Registry spelunking to be the only answer to many problems. Knowing how the Registry is organized and what tools are available to modify it will prove valuable to all Windows 2000 fixers.

Chapter 4

Setting Up and Rolling Out Windows 2000

EVERY NEW VERSION OF Windows or its big brother, NT, is a mixed blessing. We usually get more capabilities, but also more complexity. Now, you'd think that a more complex operating system would be more complex to set up, but here's a case where Microsoft has done a pretty decent job, as their setup routines get better and better with each OS version.

If you've ever set up an NT 3.x or NT 4 system, then you're probably used to struggling with Setup to get it to accept third-party hardware drivers, but Windows 2000's Plug and Play largely solves that problem. Older NT required us to decide whether a computer would be a domain controller at setup time, but in the Windows 2000 world, all servers are born equal—you don't have to decide which will be domain controllers until after the servers are deployed.

Even better, Windows 2000 comes with a variety of tools to assist you in rolling out servers unattended. You can script an install, as before, but scripts are easier. If you choose to use a disk-cloning routine like Ghost or Drive Image, Windows 2000 now has a tool named Sysprep that solves the problem that made many people chary of using cloners, something called the "duplicate SID problem." And 2000 includes my personal favorite rollout routine, the Remote Installation Services. As third-edition coauthor Brian Smith has observed, "Anyone with a half-decent collection of hardware components and the 'click Next to continue' capabilities of a 7 iron can probably install Windows 2000 Server and get it to boot up on the first try, almost every time."

The hard part comes when you want not only a stable, reliable installation, but also a *repeatable process*. This repeatable process will allow one-stop shopping for all of your installation needs and give you that clean and efficient install every time. However, to produce those perfect results time and time again, the planning and preparation phase of the install becomes even more important. Failure to properly plan out an install will most certainly result in a reinstall.

Throughout this chapter, I'll cover key fundamental planning steps, help you prepare your system for Windows 2000, run through an install, and, finally, troubleshoot the mess we got ourselves into.

Planning and Preparation

First of all, what is all this hubbub about planning? Well, anyone who has done a significant number of NT installs has had to format and start over at least once. Usually this is due to a lack of planning. In my case, it is usually that I partitioned wrong, built a member server when it should have been a domain controller, or some other simple lack of foresight. (For those who haven't worked with NT, this was a major pain: as I suggested earlier, there was quite literally no way to convert a member server to a domain controller or vice versa without completely wiping out the server and rebuilding it. People would often write me to ask what program they should use to convert a member server to a domain controller and the best answer I could offer was "fdisk, then Setup.") In contrast, with Windows 2000 you first create a member server and, once you are up and running with a stable server, you can promote it to a domain controller.

Next comes Plug and Play. Yes, NT 4 gave you some quasi plug-and-play functionality, but it was spotty at best and only applied to *ISA* Plug and Play, which is fairly unusual, rather than the more common PCI-based PnP boards. Windows 2000 takes another step in that direction. Plug and Play is *supposed* to make your life easier in the hardware preparation department. Sometimes, however, even the most modern Plug-and-Play–based system will trip over its drivers, and hybrid PnP/legacy systems can be a bit of trouble to install. For good or ill, however, you probably won't run into too many systems with a combination of Plug-and-Play and non-PnP boards, as you'll find that Windows 2000's demands on hardware are so great that you'll probably only be installing Windows 2000 on relatively new hardware—which is likely to be entirely Plug and Play. Windows 2000 also has a Remote Installation Services option, which can serve as a central, Ghost-like source for distributing Windows 2000 across your network.

These enhancements, improvements, and new features increase the possibility of a smooth installation process but still define why it's best to plan ahead of time. Planning doesn't just save you from making mistakes. It can make your installation do a lot more than just installing Windows 2000. With proper planning, you can use Windows 2000's features and enhancements to save time for each install and build an entire installation process for use throughout your enterprise.

System Hardware Requirements

Once again, Microsoft has upped the ante on system requirements. Let's see what you'll need, minimum, to build a system with decent performance.

CPU NEEDS

No longer can we get by with a 486 Intel processor. A Pentium is in order, running at 166MHz or higher, although the truth of the matter is that you really should have at least a Pentium II–class processor: a Celeron, a Xeon, or a Pentium II or III. The so-called "front-side bus" on the processor should be a minimum of 100MHz, which means that your system should be a 350MHz or faster system. The one exception: the 366MHz processor is *not* a 100MHz front-side bus, it's only a 66MHz and so should be avoided.

RAM REQUIREMENTS

However, while processing dictates how fast your computer will do the job, *memory* decides *whether* your computer can do the job. Where NT 4 let you get by with 16MB of RAM, Windows 2000

Server will not let you install with anything less than 64MB on an Intel box. When deciding how much memory you will need, try to consider what your server will be doing. Simple file and print sharing is not as resource intensive on a server as running applications like Exchange, SQL Server, Web services, and so on. Any time you put the server side of a client/server application on your system, it means that your server is performing processing that would have otherwise been done by the workstation. This directly influences your memory and processor requirements. For example, a system that is merely serving a few print queues and shared directories can get by with the bare minimums. On the other hand, tack on Web hosting, mail servicing, and user logon validation for several thousand users, and you may need memory well up into the triple digits, and a processor that could fry eggs. I'd put a *minimum* of 128MB of RAM on a Windows 2000 member server (96MB for a Windows 2000 Professional workstation) or 256MB for a domain controller.

More memory means more places for the memory hardware to fail, however, and that's why you need ECC (error-correcting code) memory. You may recall something called *parity*, a set of circuits attached to memory systems of PCs in the '80s whose job was to monitor the memory and detect data loss in a PC's RAM. Such data loss could be caused by a bad memory chip (which you can ward off by testing your RAM with a good RAM tester program like CheckIt or QAPlus before deploying the server), but random events also cause data loss; static electricity, power surges, and (believe it or not) infrequent extremely low-level radioactivity from the memory chips *themselves* can damage memory data. (Don't worry, you won't get cancer or mutations from your memory chips. Many, many everyday things in our world are mildly radioactive: the bricks cladding your house and, indeed, most kinds of ceramic produce an extremely small amount of radioactivity. Memory chips produce a radioactive particle once in a great while, and when they do, that particle may happen to cross paths with a location in memory—and when *that* happens, the memory bit may be flipped from a 0 to a 1 or vice versa!)

In any case, parity was kind of frustrating in that it could detect that *something* was wrong, but it didn't know *what* was wrong. PCs with parity memory were usually designed to simply shut down the PC when a memory error was detected using the parity method (which the error message would usually incorrectly call "a parity error" rather than a "memory error"—after all, if parity detected the memory error, then parity was working fine!), and shutting down an entire system just because parity discovered one damaged bit is a trifle extreme.

In contrast, most modern Pentium II–based systems (which, again, include the Xeon, Celeron, and of course the Pentium III) can go a step further and implement ECC. ECC is cool because it not only *detects* memory errors, it *corrects* them automatically. So when that stray alpha particle or (more likely) power glitch scrambles a bit, ECC finds that problem and fixes it without ever bothering you.

Now you may be wondering, "How much would such a wonderful feature cost?" Well, back in the old days, I worked on minicomputer systems with ECC that cost thousands of dollars. But most Pentium II–based systems can do it for about $20 per 128MB of RAM. Here's the trick: most PC memories these days are implemented as synchronous dynamic random access memory, or SDRAM, packages. SDRAMs come in a 64-bit version or a 72-bit version. When I last priced 256MB SDRAMs, the difference between a 64-bit and 72-bit SDRAM was $50 on a $420 SDRAM, a fairly cheap "insurance policy" in my opinion.

TIP   *Recently I've noticed that people selling RAM don't label it as "64-bit" or "72-bit"; rather, they've taken to calling all memory modules "64-bit" and then adding the phrase "w/ECC" or the like. If you're in doubt about what you're buying, insist that a phrase like "with enabled ECC memory" or something similar be in the invoice.*

You may have to go into your system's setup BIOS in order to turn on the ECC feature. Not all systems activate ECC by default.

STORAGE REQUIREMENTS

Hard-disk space requirements for Windows 2000 Server have been upped to 850MB plus an additional 100MB for each 64MB of system RAM. Of course, this will vary depending on your optionally installed components and future intentions for the server. I would recommend 1.2GB as the bare minimum and up to 2GB for servers that have numerous server components installed.

A *bootable CD-ROM drive*, although not required, is always highly recommended. A time always comes when your server crashes and you need a reinstall fast. Rather than scrambling for boot disks to get you connected to your installation source on the network, you simply pop the CD in and off you go.

A network-bootable system—one that supports the Preboot Execution Environment (PXE) standard, version 0.99C or later—would be a real plus. This lets you set up a computer to boot from the network. You'll like having this feature because it makes installing 2000 from a central RIS server *much* easier.

All of your hardware requirements can be further summed up by referencing the *Hardware Compatibility List (HCL)*. Every piece of hardware in your system should be on the list. Anything not on the list could generate problems from application failures to system crashes and probably won't even install at all. Why? Most likely, if your hardware is not on the list, you will have a hard time locating a driver. Should you happen to have an OEM driver that came with the hardware, you are risking system instability because Microsoft hasn't tested or guaranteed it to work. Why do you care? Because if you get on the phone to Microsoft and give them the requisite $200 in order to get them to help you with a problem, and *then* you tell them that you've got hardware that's not on the HCL, the Microsoft support person gets to say, "Golly, I'm sorry, your stuff isn't on the HCL, that's the problem," and hang up. Result: a free two hundred bucks for Bill and no solution for you. If you trust the manufacturer of the hardware who provided the driver to have fully tested it with all aspects of Windows 2000, fine. Be cautious, though. The best recommendation is that if you are buying new hardware, consult the list first. You can find the HCL on your Windows 2000 CD (`\Support\ HCL.txt`) or on the Web at `www.microsoft.com/hcl/default.asp`.

Preparing the Hardware

Once you have your hardware, it is highly advisable that you get it working and compatible first. Throughout the process, Setup will examine, activate, reexamine, configure, poke, and prod at every piece of hardware in your system that it can find. This is where the Plug-and-Play intricacies come in. If everything in your system is true Plug and Play, this process should go off without a hitch. Mix in a few older devices that don't fit this bill and you could get some serious problems, including complete setup failure.

In this section, we'll do whatever we can to avoid these problems before we even launch Setup. To resolve these same issues after the installation is complete, see Chapter 23, which is available on the CD that came with this book.

Preparing the BIOS

Most machines have highly configurable BIOSes, which can really play an important role in how Windows 2000 operates. For the pre-Setup phase, you can look for obvious settings that may interfere with your installation. Your boot device order may need customizing to allow you to boot to the CD. This, I find, is one of the most convenient ways to do an install. But then again, if you weren't expecting the CD to be bootable, you could inadvertently keep rebooting into the initial install phase from the CD over and over again, thinking you were getting the hard drive. Nothing major, but it has happened to the best of us.

The most important parts of the BIOS you'll prepare are Plug-and-Play configuration and interrupt reservations. Because most systems capable of running Windows 2000 are fairly modern by default, this step gets a little bit easier. The problem comes when you try to add older, non-Plug-and-Play components into your Plug-and-Play system. For example, you may have a non-Plug-and-Play device that is an old ISA network adapter, hard-coded for interrupt 10. When your Plug-and-Play devices come online, you may have one that prefers to initialize on interrupt 10, not knowing that your ISA card will soon request the same. As soon as the driver initializes the ISA card, there's conflict.

The best thing to do is to configure interrupt 10 under your Plug-and-Play BIOS settings to be reserved for a non-Plug-and-Play card. This tells any Plug-and-Play device to leave that interrupt alone. But now we have the problem of determining *what* those interrupts are *before* we start the install. Your non-Plug-and-Play device may have a configuration disk that programs it for specific settings. There may be jumpers on the hardware. Most troublesome, there may be no obvious clue as to what it is set for. In this case, a DOS-level hardware analyzer may be required to identify those resources being used.

TIP *Actually, let me rephrase that last topic sentence. The best thing to do is to* only buy Plug-and-Play–compatible hardware for your server. *Period.*

Once you have identified and recorded all required hardware information, return to your BIOS configuration. You may have a Plug-and-Play configuration screen that lets you define whether certain interrupts are available for general use—including being allocated by Plug-and-Play boards—or whether they should be reserved for ISA boards. Since non-Plug-and-Play boards are generally not BIOS-aware, they will continue to use the interrupt that has been reserved, but note that when your Plug-and-Play boards initialize, they will be denied the resource usage as defined by the BIOS.

In most cases, the procedure of reserving resources through the BIOS will allow all hardware to work in harmony. If not, you may find it necessary to remove all nonessential, non-Plug-and-Play devices from your system before you begin. Then, once you have a successful install, add your hardware.

NOTE *See Chapter 23 on the CD for more details.*

Partitioning

In my opinion, planning the partitioning scheme seems to be one of the most overlooked portions of the installation process. Although Windows 2000 gives you some more advanced features for managing your partitions after the install, what you decide on prior to the install will most likely stick with you throughout the life of your server.

Knowing what type of server you are building plays a tremendously big part in the planning process. Let's go back to our simple member server that serves out several shared directories and a few print queues. You may find it more convenient in the long run to keep your data on one partition and the system on another. Keeping that in mind, you may want to size your system partition based on your minimum requirements (400MB) plus some breathing room (let's say a few hundred MB) plus some extra room to grow as your business needs grow. Planning this extra room is a delicate balance between how much you anticipate adding to the server side for running applications and how much additional data space your users may require. With storage space as cheap as it is today, I wouldn't create a system partition on any less than 2 gigabytes.

If you are intending to use the Remote Installation Services, then be sure to set aside a *big* partition solely for its use. RIS cannot store system images on either the boot partition (the partition that the system boots from, usually C:) *or* the system partition (the one containing \winnt).

With the introduction of dynamic volume attachments, you will find your partitions more easily expandable in the future. This will help eliminate the problem of having too small a system partition. Simply mount a new partition to any directory on your NTFS 5 partition, and you're back in business.

Filesystems

Choosing filesystems for your partitions is usually a bit more straightforward. You have your standard choices of FAT, FAT32, and NTFS. NTFS offers obvious advantages over FAT and FAT32, which will play an extremely large part in your filesystem decisions.

In the NT 3 and 4 days, we faced something of a dilemma: use FAT or NTFS for the boot drive? The main arguments against NTFS C: drives were (1) it made dual-booting Windows 9*x* difficult (which is pretty irrelevant for a server), and (2) fixing a damaged C: drive was easier with the DOS-based disk tools, which required FAT. Thankfully, that's no longer an issue—Windows 2000 now includes a Recovery Console, a DOS-like command-line interface that you can get up and running even if your system is otherwise dead. So, in sum, I recommend a minimum 2GB NTFS C: partition.

WARNING   You used to have a safe feeling when you made your system partition NTFS—that no one could simply sit down at the console, pop in a DOS boot disk, reboot your server, and have full access to your data. NTFS was not readable from a DOS boot disk, and the NTFS filesystem itself was just too big to fit on a single disk. Well, those safe feelings can now be tucked into the same category as the feelings you get when sitting in your car at a stoplight in downtown Washington, D.C., with your wallet lying casually on the passenger seat and your windows rolled down. Anyone can download the necessary drivers to boot up a simple DOS disk with NTFS access, and Linux has always been able to read NTFS drives (but not write them). My point here: NTFS is more secure than FAT, but NTFS only provides the same level of protection as locking your car door and rolling up the windows. If someone wants your data and has access to your server, they can get it. Physically securing the server is the only way to truly protect your data.

When choosing NTFS for Windows 2000, there are still considerations to be made. Windows 2000 has new features added to NTFS that are not available in NT 4, pre–Service Pack 4. Those features unique to NTFS 5 are:

◆ Encryption

◆ Dynamic volume extensions

- Disk quota capabilities

- Distributed link tracking

- Volume mount points

- Indexing

NOTE   *For all the details on filesystem considerations, refer to Chapter 10, which covers Windows 2000 storage issues.*

Knowing what type of filesystems you will want for your finished product is essential prior to installation, but just in case there is any question, go with the lowest common denominator, which is FAT. You can always convert up to NTFS later, but you can't convert NTFS back to FAT.

Server Name

This seems like a no-brainer, but it's a good idea to plan your naming convention. There are two ways that most people make living with server names difficult. The first is underestimating the importance of server names. The second is overdoing it when it comes to a standard convention.

By underestimating naming conventions, you end up with server names like GEORGE, ELROY, JUDY, and ASTRO on your network. This is fine for a small office LAN that will never grow too far beyond your ability to remember these names. When you start getting more than those few servers, it gets difficult to remember who is what.

Sometimes people overdo standard conventions by defining so many formats, items, and indexes into the name that it becomes just as confusing. Some of the things people put in a name is the server's geographic location, building location, room number, role, and an index. For example, a server in Annapolis residing in the Commerce Center building that is an Exchange server might be named ANNCCBEXC01. This information is fine, but keep it to useful information that resembles the important features in your network. Does your network and its users really care what building the server is in? What about the city? What if you add another Exchange server in the courthouse? That would be named ANNCRTEXC01. Perhaps a better method here would be to put the EXC first. Simplicity is key. You may want to define your network into systems and that's it. If you had two Exchange systems, one for the Commerce Department and one for the Treasury Department, you may want COMMAIL01 and TREMAIL01. This may allow a better grouping of servers.

The bottom line here is to really think about it. Get the customers and the people who will manage the network involved. Get a consensus on what is important and what is not important. Although you can easily change the name of the server later, you can't easily change the hundreds or thousands of users' workstations that connect to them.

WARNING   *And never name the machine and the user the same! Several errors crop up when you're logged in to a machine named X using a user account that's also named X.*

Network Connection and Options

Not knowing your network configuration ahead of time isn't usually going to be a showstopper. Knowing it can save you time though.

PROTOCOLS

You will most likely be using the TCP/IP protocol. If you're not in charge of your network configuration, then double-check this beforehand—for legacy reasons, there's at least a chance that your network still runs the NetBEUI or IPX protocols. (Locate those reasons and stomp 'em flat!) Find out this protocol info ahead of time—those network gurus are never around when you need them in mid-install. By default, Windows 2000 installs only TCP/IP, which has some configuration concerns that will make a tremendous difference in your ability to connect to the network later. If you use TCP/IP, do you have a DHCP server on the network? (And if you haven't got a clue about what those things are, then either read Chapters 6 and 7 or get some help from your local TCP/IP techie.) If you don't have a DHCP server, you will need static information. The most critical elements are your IP address, subnet mask, and some sort of name resolution, whether WINS, DNS, or a HOSTS or LMHOSTS file. Without those components, you will not get anywhere with TCP/IP. If the servers you need to contact are on another subnet, you will need to define your default gateway.

NOTE   *See Chapter 6 for more details on what your IP address, subnet mask, and name resolution settings are and how they work.*

If you are using NetBEUI on your network, you don't have the same concerns with configuring the protocol. NetBEUI is a simple, straightforward protocol designed for small LANs and has extremely low configuration requirements. It does, however, have another concern. NetBEUI does not route. This means that your routers between subnets of your network will not pass the NetBEUI protocol. You are as good as stranded. If you use bridging between subnets, you're back in business. Find out how your network is configured before you try to rely on NetBEUI. If you can, however, avoid NetBEUI—locate and eradicate it from your network.

TIP   *Resistance is futile. Just use TCP/IP.*

DOMAIN MEMBERSHIP

Almost every server will be a member of a domain rather than a workgroup. Windows 2000 makes this decision easier. In NT 3.*x* and 4.*x*, you had the choice of making your server a member of a workgroup, a member of a domain, a primary domain controller, or a backup domain controller. This was a critical decision during the install. You could switch a server from a workgroup to domain and back very easily, but you could not change roles between a member server and domain controller. You also could not change the domain you controlled. Once you had a domain controller in one domain, you couldn't then make it a controller of another domain. You don't need to make that decision to install Windows 2000. You'll only have the choice of joining a workgroup or domain.

If you're joining a domain, you will need to have a computer account created in the domain. A computer account is almost identical to a user account, and like a user account, it resides in the accounts database held with the domain controllers. If the server is a member of a domain, it can assign rights and permissions to users belonging to its member domain or any of its trusted domains. This is important to your users. They should log in once to the network and never have to be asked for a password again. If the server resides in a workgroup, then the ability to give rights to domain users is out of the question, causing multiple login points.

Whether you're a member of a workgroup or a domain, you can promote the server to a domain controller later by running the Active Directory Installation. This feature sounds like a nice, simple advantage, but it has a bigger impact than is obvious. In an NT 4 environment, you have to define a standard installation for member servers and one for domain controllers. Let's say you want to automate the installs for NT servers across the network. Defining which domain you want a server to control can get tricky. Do you build a different installation setup for each domain? Do you force someone to sit at the console during the installation to answer this question? With Windows 2000, you can build one installation for all servers by putting them in a workgroup and change the membership later.

UPGRADING DOMAIN CONTROLLERS

Speaking of domain membership, here's an important note about domain *controllers*. If you are thinking of upgrading an NT 4 box that is acting as a domain controller, then I urge you to think once and twice before upgrading! You can cavalierly upgrade just about any other computer, but the domain controllers need some planning, or you'll be very, very sorry!

You see, upgrading an NT 4 domain controller has an important side effect: it upgrades your NT 4 domain to a Windows 2000 Active Directory—the Windows 2000 name for a domain. Windows 2000 doesn't allow you to upgrade any of your backup domain controllers until you've upgraded the *primary* domain controller. So you might want to think twice before simply upgrading your existing DCs. Personally, I prefer a domain upgrade technique called "clean and pristine," and I'll discuss it in Chapter 8, the Active Directory chapter. You might want to read up to that chapter before doing any NT-to-2000 surgery on your domain controllers. Basically, however, I advocate building a brand-new, empty Windows 2000 Active Directory domain, then moving the user accounts over to that domain, leaving your old NT 4 domains in place "just in case" as you migrate.

NETWORKING COMPONENTS

These are the additional services to be installed, like Internet Information Services and DNS Server. This is where I like to say things like "Ooh… Quality of Service Admission Control Protocol… sounds neat, gimme that." That's exactly what we shouldn't say. Don't overdo it here. Every option selected installs another service or utility that will consume more resources on your server.

Also be aware of the effect certain services may have on the rest of your network. Some services will require clients to be connected explicitly to a given server. On the other hand, some, like DHCP Server, act on a broadcast level and can affect clients just by being present. In addition, most services, just by being present, have an adverse effect on available system resources. Hard-disk space is consumed for additional files, memory is taken up by loading more programs, and processor cycles are consumed by running excessive services that really don't have anything to do with what your server is intended to do. Unless you will specifically be using the service on this particular server, don't install these additional components.

SERVER LICENSING

Licensing options remain the same in Windows 2000. You are given per-seat or per-server licensing modes:

◆ Per-seat licensing requires that every client on the network that accesses your server has its own license. This is the easiest method of adding up your licensing, because you only account for how many clients you have; you don't need to worry about either concurrent connections from those clients into a single server or to how many servers each client holds a connection.

◆   Per-server licensing differs in that each client-to-server connection requires a license. If a client connects to 25 different servers, that client will take up 1 license on each server, totaling 25 licenses. You may know this as a "concurrent use license." It's simpler because it's easy to track—once that 26th person tries to attach, he's just denied the connection—but it's usually more expensive because you then have to buy a bunch of licenses for *each* server.

Which way to go? Well, the short answer is: Per-seat is almost always the right technique. But if you want more details...

Per-seat is usually the cheapest licensing method if you have more than one server. Under per-seat licensing, you buy a client access license, or CAL, for every *computer* that will attach to your enterprise's servers. Again, that's *computer*, not person. So if Joe Manager reads his Exchange mail from the computer on his desktop sometimes, reads it on the road with his laptop sometimes, and once in a while comes in through the firewall from home, then you need to buy *three licenses for Joe Manager*. Surprised? Most people are. On the one hand, it means that if three people share a computer, then those folks only need one CAL. On the other hand, nowadays everyone has one *or more* computers, so CALs start to add up. By the way, CALs list for around $40, although you can buy them in bulk more cheaply and large organizations usually have some kind of an unlimited-client deal. But you don't want to run afoul of the software watchdogs, so if you go with per-seat licensing, then be darn sure that you've got every computer covered! (And, sadly, that may mean that you have to disallow employees from checking their e-mail or using other corporate resources from their home, unless they're using a company-issued laptop.)

Per-server licensing is simpler. You tell a server that you've purchased some number of CALs. The server's Licensing Service (a built-in part of Windows 2000) then keeps track of how many people are connected to the server at any moment. If you have X licenses and the $X+1$st person tries to attach to the server, that person is denied access.

This sounds simple, but the problem is that you've got to buy a CAL for each connection for each server. For example, suppose you have 4 servers, 25 employees, and 40 workstation PCs—there are more PCs than employees because of laptops and "general access" PCs. Suppose your goal is that all 25 employees can access any and all servers at any time.

Under per-server licensing, you'd have to buy 25 CALs for *each* server, or 100 CALs total.

Under per-seat licensing, you'd license each of the machines—all 40 of them—with a CAL. That one CAL would enable someone sitting at a machine to access any and all of the servers, no matter how many domains your system contains. Thus, in this case, 40 CALs would do the trick. In general, you'll find that per-seat is the cheaper way to go, but again, be careful about remembering to license all of the laptops and (possibly) home PCs.

Most likely, especially in larger environments, the licensing has already been worked out ahead of time. Prior to starting your first install, make sure that your licensing is best suited not just for your network, but also for the way your clients use the network.

INSTALLATION TYPE

Finally, you need to decide whether you will be upgrading an existing operating system or performing a clean install. In most cases, this decision is a no-brainer; however, with each type also comes some unique advantages and disadvantages, which will affect your decision.

For the decision phase, let's start with a machine that is currently an NT 4 server that you want to upgrade to Windows 2000. Before you jump straight into an upgrade, you should think about how a Windows 2000 clean install will compare. Maybe your partitioning scheme currently has your system partition maxed out. Perhaps your NT 4 installation has left you with some residual problem that has just never gone away. Even if you're reinstalling the same operating system, there are performance benefits to running a clean install every so often anyway. The Registry has a unique ability to grow, and grow, and grow, without ever cleaning itself up.

There are reasons for and against upgrading versus a simple wipe-and-replace. In wipe-and-replace's favor, consider: If you have ever installed a disk defragmenting utility, you also know how fragmented a well-used system can become. When it comes to fragmentation, one of the heaviest-hit files happens to be the system pagefile, which takes enough of a toll on system resources as it is. All of this clutter and excessive work being placed on your system just so it can manage itself consumes excessive amounts of otherwise free cycles left to serve your users. Backing up your data and system information, and even wiping your partitions, could yield a cleaner, more efficient, and even more stable server following the install.

In contrast, doing a wipe-and-replace sometimes impels people to go overboard. When doing a clean install, many people want to revisit server options, service configurations, and even naming conventions. Although this is the best time for the system administrator to reinvent the wheel, it puts an unnecessary burden on your users. The more integrated your systems become, the more effect one slight configuration change will have on another. You must take careful note of all services, configurations, shares, and other settings that are defined within your system. A full system backup and a rollback plan are invaluable. If you are rebuilding an NT 4 primary domain controller, you will want to promote a backup to primary before you do anything. This will ensure that all of your account and security information is secured on another system. Finally, be ready to test every function of the server from the client's point of view when you are done. This will give you the necessary lead time to resolve any problems before your users discover them.

If you've decided on a clean install, there isn't much more you need to do. If you're running an upgrade, there are still a few considerations. The last thing you want to do is upgrade a cluttered system and carry over any issues that belong to the clutter. Many people sit in front of the server so much that they install their mail client, office suite, and other programs and utilities that are not related to what the server is supposed to be doing. These should all be uninstalled before running an upgrade. Look at your services on the server. Any third-party services, such as antivirus, Web publishing, disk defragmenting, or other types of software, should also be removed prior to beginning an upgrade. By doing so, there is much less to get in the way of your install.

Which way is the best? That depends on your needs and those of your users, but let me finish this section with a bit of advice that you'll probably find unpleasant. When you look at the time involved in rebuilding user accounts, shares, services, permissions, and who-knows-what else, you'd think that upgrades are the way to go. But in my experience upgrading from NT 3.1 to 3.5 (I lost my printer shares), 3.5 to 3.51 (some domain controllers simply refused to work), and 3.51 to 4 (several miscellaneous problems), I must admit that I'd be *very* wary of simply upgrading a machine, particularly a domain controller, to Windows 2000. If there's any way at all to do a clean install of Windows 2000 on your former NT 4 servers, I strongly recommend it. I should stress that this isn't a fear based on any actual NT 4–to–Windows 2000 problems that I've experienced, just general experience with upgrades.

Setting Up and Installing

Now that we have analyzed the life out of planning for an install, we should be ready to go. The actual installation is broken into three stages. The first is the preinstallation setup wizard. You'll only see this if you're installing Windows 2000 from inside NT 4—that is, if you've popped the 2000 install CD into a system running NT 4. This process defines those options that configure *how* to do the install. The second stage is the text-based setup, which simply defines where to install. Finally, the graphical-based setup stage, also called a setup wizard, customizes everything from installed protocols and services to computer name and domain membership to the system time and date. After this final stage is complete, your server should be ready for final cleanup.

Preinstallation: Phase 1

The first thing you need to do is, of course, connect to your install source. Preferably, you would connect directly to your CD or a network copy of the CD. However, certain circumstances may make this impossible, such as, for example, a system with no operating system, no CD drive, and no DOS-based network drivers to connect you to your install source. In these cases, you'll need the dreaded boot disks. Once you have connected to your source, you need to be in the directory that corresponds to your processor—I386 for Intels. With boot disks, you simply boot the system to the first disk.

WINDOWS 2000 SETUP BOOT DISKS

Boot disks are no longer created using the WINNT command-line parameters. Disk images are stored on your Windows 2000 CD's bootdisk directory with a simple batch file and utility that allows you to create them. Another change is that boot disks no longer come in sets of three; instead, they come in sets of four. (As we all know, bigger software is always better, right?) Here's how you create the disks:

1. Prepare four blank 1.44MB floppy disks.

2. Change to your CD's bootdisk directory.

3. Execute **makeboot.exe:**.

4. Follow all prompts to create the four disks.

From MS-DOS, Windows 3.1, or Windows for Workgroups 3.11, you will need to start your setup in the DOS-based mode found with winnt.exe.

From a Windows 9*x* system, or earlier versions of NT, you'll launch the installation from the winnt32.exe. This GUI version of the setup executable gives you that user-friendly, yes-or-no click method of initiating the install. For this example, I'm using the drive letter F: as the CD source on an Intel-based system. To follow along, select Start/Run and enter the following:

```
F:\I386\winnt32.exe
```

If you have a system that can be upgraded to Windows 2000 Server, you will immediately reach the prompt to decide whether to run a clean install or an upgrade. If you do not have an upgrade-capable machine, you will be informed that an upgrade is not available, and the upgrade option will be grayed out.

NOTE   *Only Windows NT servers can be upgraded to Windows 2000 Server. Windows 9x and Windows NT work-stations can be upgraded to Windows 2000 Professional.*

Following the licensing agreement, you may continue to the Special Options screen. The special options let you define language options, advanced options, and accessibility options:

◆ Language options give the choice of installing multiple languages by holding the Ctrl key down while selecting or deselecting languages with the left mouse button. You can also select your default language, which Setup uses to define all default date, time, currency, number, character set, and keyboard layouts.

◆ Advanced options customize the way the installation actually happens (see Figure 4.1):

FIGURE 4.1

Advanced Setup options

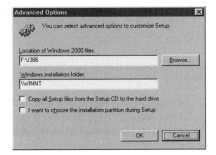

◆ Location of Windows 2000 Files refers to the place from which you will be installing Windows 2000. I'm installing from an Intel system from F:\I386. This entry is filled in based on where you launch the install. However, if you would like to redirect Setup to another location, enter that location here.

◆ Windows Installation Folder indicates the directory under which Windows 2000 will be installed. This defaults to \winnt, but it can be changed to another directory if desired. If dual-booting with other installations of NT or Windows 2000, you may need to specify a unique directory name. Do not include the drive letter designation.

◆ Copy All Setup Files creates a complete setup source on one of your local hard drives under the directory \win_nt.~ls. Under this directory, you will find the I386 source we are so familiar with.

NOTE   *Most systems won't need the Copy All Setup Files option selected. Windows 2000 will do a pretty good job of loading the right drivers to reconnect you to your source after the reboot. However, if you fail to find your source for the text-based setup, this option will get you back on track.*

◆ I Want to Choose the Installation Partition During Setup allows you to define which partition you will be installing Windows 2000 in. If selected, you will get a prompt following the reboot to choose your partition.

◆ Accessibility options available for Setup include the Narrator and Magnifier. By selecting these options now, the tools will be available during the next installation phase.

At this point, the installation files will be copied to your hard disk, the system will be prepared for the text-based portion of Setup, and you will be prompted for a reboot.

ANATOMY OF A MACHINE READY FOR SETUP PHASE 2

Ever wonder what makes a system continue along its setup path after a reboot? Or have you ever started into the second phase of the setup, had all sorts of problems, and wanted to start from scratch? It will help to know exactly what causes the second phase to start upon reboot so you can easily remove it later. These components are going to be present on your system after completion of the preinstallation phase of the setup:

◆ On the boot partition, a directory named win_nt.~bt has been created.

◆ All critical Windows 2000 boot files, including enough drivers to access the network or CD source, have been copied to the win_nt.~bt directory.

◆ In the win_nt.~bt directory, a file named winnt.sif contains the information you provided from the first phase of the setup.

◆ The Windows 2000 boot files have been copied to the boot partition (unless you've overridden them with a winnt or winnt32 option) if not already present. The system is now Windows 2000 bootable. (Note that when I say "boot" I mean it in the standard this-is-the-drive-that-the-computer-boots-from meaning, rather than Microsoft's "official" definition—for some reason, they define the partition that contains the bulk of the operating system files as the "boot" partition, and the partition that you boot from as the "system" partition. Don't ask me why...)

◆ The boot.ini is configured to default to the win_nt.~bt\bootsect.dat after 5 seconds.

Text-Based Setup: Phase 2

The text-based portion of Windows 2000 Setup is very similar to previous versions of Windows NT, only less cluttered. We get our welcome screen, make a few selections on where we want to do our install, and then we sit back and watch the Setup program copy a whole bunch of files. It's a really simple click-Next-to-continue process, but there are some gotchas hiding in the deeps.

NOTE *This is the* first *phase you'll see if you're installing by booting from the CD-ROM.*

As soon as your machine boots into the text-based portion of Setup, you may notice a prompt at the bottom of the screen that tells you to press F6 if you need to install additional SCSI or RAID drivers. If you don't want these additional drivers, just wait a few seconds and it will go away. In the real world, you don't use that F6 selection a whole lot anyway, so it is more convenient to just wait a few seconds rather than to keep having to say, "No, I don't want additional drivers." It's kind of like the press-F1-tab-F10 or some other machine-specific command to enter the BIOS setup. How would you like to have to press Escape to bypass the BIOS setup utility every single time you reboot your machine? To make a long story short, this F6 prompt comes up quickly. If your system has a SCSI or RAID controller that you know isn't going to initialize without an OEM-provided driver, you'll need to pay attention and hit F6.

The install starts off with a Welcome to Setup screen. You have the choice to set up Windows 2000, repair an existing Windows 2000 installation, or quit. The Press F3 to Quit option will live with you throughout this phase of the setup. If at any time during this phase you decide that you want to abort your setup attempt, this will be your escape route. Upon this exit, your system will be rebooted, but be aware that your `boot.ini` file has not been changed. Subsequent reboots will still by default cause your machine to restart the setup after 5 seconds at the boot menu. To get rid of this permanently, edit your `boot.ini` to reflect the default equal to your other operating system boot path of choice. My machine looked like the following:

```
[Boot Loader]
Timeout=5
Default=C:\$win_nt$.~bt\bootsect.dat
[Operating Systems]
multi(0)disk(0)rdisk(0)partition(2)\winnt="Microsoft Windows 2000
Server"/fastdetect
C:\="Microsoft Windows 98"
C:\$win_nt$.~bt\bootsect.dat="Microsoft Windows 2000 Server Setup"
```

To restore my machine to its original boot preferences, I changed the Default line back to my Windows 2000 Server boot selection and deleted the entire Windows 2000 Server Setup option. Consequently, my `boot.ini` looked like this:

```
[Boot Loader]
Timeout=5
Default=multi(0)disk(0)rdisk(0)partition(2)\winnt
[Operating Systems]
multi(0)disk(0)rdisk(0)partition(2)\winnt="Microsoft Windows 2000
Server"/fastdetect
C:\="Microsoft Windows 98"
```

To continue along with the setup, press Enter, and you'll arrive at the Disk Partitioning and Installation Location Selection screen. Be careful here. There are two things to do. The most obvious is the selection of the partition in which you want Windows 2000 installed. Highlight the partition where you would like Windows 2000 installed, and press Enter.

Let's take this a step further. Beneath this screen is a very handy disk-partitioning utility. From here, you can completely redo your partitioning scheme. You can delete existing partitions, create new partitions out of unpartitioned space, and format partitions in either the NTFS or FAT format file systems.

NOTE *You can find more information on disk partitioning in Chapter 10.*

Before we begin partitioning our drives, let's go back to the planning session we had earlier. Let's say our ideal goal is to have a 1GB Windows 98 C: partition (on which we will leave our current operating system), a 2GB system partition on drive D:, and a 4GB data partition on drive E:. Just to give us all the necessary scenarios to describe how the setup phase partitions drives, we'll assume we have a current partition scheme of a 1GB C: with Windows 98, a 1GB D:, a 2GB E:, and a 3GB F: partition. To go from a 1-1-2-3 gigabyte partition scheme to a 1-2-4 gigabyte partition scheme, we are forced to delete almost all partitions, since we cannot reorder partitions. In other words, we cannot massage our existing second partition of 1GB into a 2GB partition without giving it more room first.

Let's start by deleting the 1GB D: partition. Use the arrows to highlight the D: partition, and press D to delete. A confirmation screen will appear asking you to now either press L to continue the partition deletion or Escape to abort.

WARNING   *Always take this opportunity to second-guess yourself. Once you press L to confirm the deletion of the partition, your partition and everything that was on it is gone. Ask yourself what data was on the D: drive. Make sure you can afford to lose it all. Do you have a backup of the data? If it contains a previous NT or Windows 2000 installation, do you have a backup of the security and accounts databases? If rebuilding a domain controller, have you promoted someone else to PDC? Do you have a recent Emergency Repair Disk available? If you are 100-percent confident that you don't need anything on the partition, press L.*

When you come back to the main Disk Partitioning screen, you'll see that the second partition of 1GB is now marked as unpartitioned space. Of course, it does no good to repartition this space now because the most you'll get is 1GB again. That would defeat the purpose of the exercise. You need 2GB. So move on down the list to what was the 2GB E: partition and delete it in the same fashion. When you return to the main screen again, after confirming the deletion of the 2GB partition, you'll find that the adjacent, unpartitioned spaces have turned into a single block of unpartitioned space equaling 3GB. Just to keep it simple, we now have our 1GB C:, a 3GB unpartitioned space from our combined, deleted 1GB and 2GB partitions, and a remaining 3GB partition.

At this point, we'll go ahead and create our new 2GB D: partition. Highlight the 3GB free space and press C for create. You'll move into a new screen where you're shown the total available space within which you can create a partition and are asked how large a partition you want to make. By default, the maximum available space is filled in: 3GB. We want to drop that down to 2GB. Press Enter and presto! We have a 2GB new (unformatted) partition, followed by our remaining 1GB that we left out and the 3GB data partition.

After we delete our 3GB partition, it will melt into the adjacent 1GB partition, forming a 4GB unpartitioned space. We can create the new 4GB space and we're set with partitioning anyway.

Now we still have to format our partition before we can use it. To format a partition, highlight the space listed as New (Unformatted) and press Enter to select the partition as your Windows 2000 installation directory. Really, you're not selecting a partition to format; you're just selecting a partition in which to install Windows 2000. If Setup finds that your chosen installation partition is not formatted, you'll get an additional screen to do just that. You are shown options to format FAT or NTFS. Once again, go back to our planning phase of the setup. We should already know what format we want. Once the format is complete, we continue onward with the installation.

TIP   *If you want to simply partition and format drives without continuing to do an installation, you can always choose to go backward after the format and select another partition to format or install to, or you can simply exit the installation program.*

Setup will now examine your disks. This examination is not an intensive look into the reliability of your disk. It merely runs a CHKDSK-like utility to verify a clean file and directory structure. After the examination, Setup will copy all Windows 2000 files to your chosen install location. Finally, the system will ready itself for the graphical setup phase and reboot.

CHANGES IN THE WINDOWS 2000 TEXT-BASED SETUP

You may notice some things missing from this phase of the Windows 2000 setup compared to the setup for previous versions of Windows NT. You no longer get the options to define the following:

◆ Basic PC type

◆ Video system

◆ Keyboard

◆ Country layout for keyboard (defined in phase 1)

◆ Mouse

Perhaps these deletions from the text-based setup can be attributed to the better hardware detection found with Plug and Play. With these changes, or reductions, to the text-based setup, you will find this stage much quicker and easier than it was in NT.

Graphical-Based Setup: Phase 3

As soon as you boot into the graphical-based setup phase of the install, Windows 2000 will run a Plug-and-Play detection phase to configure all your hardware. (This will take a while—it's often the most lengthy part of Setup—so now's a good time to go grab a Pepsi, check the voicemail, or run 5 miles.) Surprisingly enough, Windows 2000 did a better job on my particular system than Windows 98 ever did. How could that be? It's simple, really. The Plug-and-Play detection phase tries to attach the correct driver to each device in your system, so a driver must be present for each device. If no driver is available, you'll get an "unknown device" message, or a generic device driver will be installed.

Since Windows 2000 has a more recent compilation of drivers, you can expect that some newer hardware will show up for Windows 2000 that otherwise wouldn't in Windows 98. More than anything, this should stress the importance of the Hardware Compatibility List (HCL). Once again, it doesn't hurt to double-check the HCL. Look at www.microsoft.com/hcl/default.asp for any recent updates or additions to the list. Some devices that were once thought unsupported may be found. If your device isn't on the HCL, it won't have a driver immediately available. You will be able to install a device driver later, however, if one becomes available.

TIP   If you have a device that isn't supported on the HCL or doesn't have a prepackaged device driver on the CD, you can use the /copysource or /copydir switch to copy an additional directory to be used during the setup. This can be used to make your device drivers available for detection. Look for more details in "Performing Unattended Installs" later in this chapter.

Once the Plug-and-Play detection phase is finished, the first dialog we come to is the Regional Configuration screen. This stop defines settings such as number, currency, time, date, and keyboard locale formats.

Next is the Name and Organization dialog. The name and organization listed here show who the product is registered to; it isn't used for anything related to the computer name or other means of defining the server on the network.

The next dialog configures your licensing options, which are the same as previous versions of NT. There is per-seat licensing and per-server licensing. Enter this information in accordance with how you purchased Windows 2000.

Next comes the computer name and administrator password definition. The computer name has already been thought out. The administrator password, especially for a clean install, is extremely important. For a clean install, this is going to be your only way to log in. Don't forget this. And please don't leave it blank unless this is just a machine you're playing around with. The default Administrator account is both powerful and dangerous because, by default, it can't be locked out. That means that someone can potentially crack your system by running a program that tries to log in with the default Administrator account by trying every word in the dictionary or every combination of numbers, letters, and characters. Make their work harder by putting a long and complex—numbers, letters, and characters—password on your default Administrator account. Then be sure to write that Administrator password on a sticky note and put it on the side of your monitor so you won't forget it. (Just kidding.)

The Components Selection dialog defines the additional server components that are bundled with Windows 2000, including:

- Certificate Services

- Internet Information Services

- Management and Monitoring Tools

- Connection Manager Component

- Directory Services Tools

- Network Monitor Tools

- SNMP

- Message Queuing Services

- MS Indexing Services

- MS Script Debugger

- Networking Services

- COM Internet Services Proxy

- Domain Name System

- Dynamic Host Configuration Protocol

- ◆ Internet Authentication Services

- ◆ QOS Admission Control Service

- ◆ Simple TCP/IP Services

- ◆ Site Server LDAP Services

- ◆ Windows Internet Name Service

- ◆ Other Network File and Print Services

- ◆ File Services for Macintosh

- ◆ Print Services for Macintosh

- ◆ Print Services for Unix

- ◆ Remote Installation Services

- ◆ Remote Storage

- ◆ Terminal Services

- ◆ Terminal Server Licensing

Individually select each component that will be used on your server, and click Details to view sub-components (see Figure 4.2). A white box with a check mark means the entire component, including all subcomponents, will be installed. A white box with no check mark means that none of the components or subcomponents will be installed. A gray check box with a check mark means that only some of the subcomponents of the main component will be installed.

FIGURE 4.2

Windows
Components

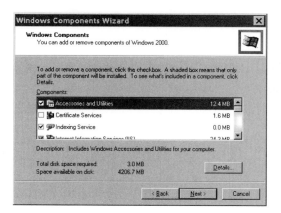

If a modem was detected, a modem configuration screen will be next. This is where you define your calling options—in particular, your area code and what number to dial to get an outside line. These options are included in the setup so that you (hopefully) won't have to configure each dial-up session in the future to dial a 1 for long distance, a 9 for an outside line, and so on. This little part was not included in the setup phase of previous versions of Windows NT.

The standard date, time, and time zone configuration gives you a last chance to set your system clock. Setting the correct time zone is important, especially in networks that span multiple time zones. Many utilities automatically take into account the time zone and adjust the displayed time accordingly. A server configured with the wrong time zone, even if the time is correct, would display the wrong time.

WARNING *Windows 2000's Active Directory needs fairly good—although not exact—time synchronization, so Microsoft included a pretty neat time service with Windows 2000. Basically, every time a server boots up (and regularly thereafter), that server looks to another server to get the right time. Called the Windows Time Service, you can read more about it in the Active Directory chapter. But the important thing is this: it's no big deal if your time is a bit off—it's the time zone that's important, so make sure that's set for each server.*

The network settings give you two choices: typical and custom. The typical settings assume that you will want the Client for Microsoft Networks, TCP/IP using DHCP addressing, and File and Print Sharing.

By choosing custom settings, you can add, remove, or customize protocols, clients, and services. If you want to assign static IP information, highlight TCP/IP and click Configure. By clicking the Add button, you will be given a choice of Client, Protocol, or Service. This is also reminiscent of a Windows 9*x* machine. You can add more clients, like Client for Novell Networks, more protocols, like NetBEUI, or more services.

NOTE *The terminology for network settings has changed in Windows 2000. For NT-based systems, there is the Server service, which is responsible for passing information out to the network, and the Workstation service, which is responsible for accessing other servers and your local system. Windows 2000 has adopted the Windows 9x terminology. Instead of having a Workstation service per se, you have a Client service. It means the same thing, but it more explicitly defines the Workstation service as a client, which corresponds to Client for Microsoft and Client for Novell. The Server service is now broken into two standard services: File Sharing for Microsoft Networks and Print Sharing for Microsoft Networks.*

At the WORKGROUP/DOMAIN selection page, you can join either a workgroup or domain by selecting the appropriate radio button and typing the workgroup or domain name in the corresponding box. If you join a domain, you must have an account created for your machine name. You can do this two ways.

The first way is to select the Create Computer Account button. After clicking OK to join the domain, you will be asked to enter an administrative account name and password. This account must be one with either Administrator or Account Operator rights. If you're using an account from the domain you are joining, enter the account name and password. If you're using an account from a trusted domain of the one you are joining, type the full domain and account name in the *DOMAIN\USERNAME* format. This will inform the validating domain controller of the location of your account. The account creation will be initiated from the server you are installing.

The second method is to not select Create Computer Account but have one created ahead of time. You may want to employ this method if the person running the install doesn't have the appropriate rights and doesn't want to hunt down an administrator when this step comes up. In this scenario, go to Server Manager for the NT 4 domain on which you want to add the server and select Computer/ Add to Domain, or go to Active Directory Users and Computers and select New/Computer. Select NT Workstation or Server and type the name of the computer. During the installation of the server, leave the Create Computer Account option unselected, enter the correct domain name, and you should be set.

Because of security concerns, though, the computer account you create will change its password immediately upon a successful joining of the domain. This means that if, for some reason, you redo a clean install of a machine that already has a computer account, you can't have your new install assume that account. You must either delete and re-create the account with the same name or build the new server with a different name.

COMPUTER ACCOUNTS

Computer accounts are just like user accounts, and you can see them in the Active Directory Users and Computers tool (which we'll discuss in Chapter 8) or in Server Manager on NT 3.*x* and 4. If you have enabled auditing of successful account management on the domain, you will see an Account Manager security event #624 logged in the PDC of an NT 4 domain or a similar event on any DC of an AD domain. A 624 event is a "create user account" event. Let's say we create a computer account for a new server named CADDY in the LAB domain. Under the details of the security event, the account name that was created will show as CADDY$. This CADDY$ account will be used for all communication between the server and the domain, such as validating user passwords. Once the new server and the PDC "shake hands," the server will initiate a password change for the CADDY$ account. Every 7 days thereafter, the server will again initiate a password change. The same procedure of account and password maintenance is used between domains for trust relationships.

So why is changing a password such a big deal? Well, the server is going to assign permissions to its resources based on domain user accounts. The server isn't going to blindly trust that anyone who claims to be from the LAB domain is a valid user; it wants to make certain that they are in fact a LAB user from the real LAB domain. By having this unique account with a highly secured password, the server can do just that. If the server asks the LAB domain to validate a user but the LAB domain doesn't recognize the correct CADDY$ account and password, authentication fails. This makes it nearly impossible to transport a server out of its domain and gain access to its data.

We're just about done with the install. The Setup Wizard finishes copying the files, configures the system, and performs a final cleanup. The `boot.ini` will now be changed to reflect the new Windows 2000 install as the default boot option. There is, however, one more step that can optionally be done here. If you need to run another program, perhaps a setup program for some utility or application, then you can tell Setup to run it automatically, using the `winnt32.exe` command-line parameter /cmd:*command*. (Of course, using this command-line parameter means that you needed to add that /cmd option when you *started* running Setup, so if you've been doing Setup while following along, this advice is a bit late.) This could be used to run a batch file or utility to perform such tasks as transferring user data, installing programs, or other means of further automating your installs. (This is covered in more detail later in this chapter in the section on unattended installs.) The system will now reboot into a full-fledged Windows 2000 operating system.

TIP   But if it doesn't, *then try running winnt32 with its* debug *switches, winnt32 /debug2 or /debug3, which offer more information. Debug3 gives more information than debug2 and, in case you're wondering, debug1 is just the default.*

Postinstallation Procedures

After the installation is complete, there are still a few more steps to perform to finalize the server and prep it for production:

- On the first reboot, the Server Configuration Wizard will pop up automatically. It will identify the last few steps that must be completed to configure your server based on the additional network components you installed. It will also ask you some questions about your existing network to help you determine whether you want to install an Active Directory.

NOTE *See Chapter 8 for more information about Active Directory and when and how to launch the Active Directory Installation Wizard.*

- Check your device manager for undetected or nonfunctioning hardware components. If you removed any hardware prior to the install due to conflicts, add them back in now. Before we are truly done with the install, every piece of hardware should work properly.

NOTE *See Chapter 23 on the CD to learn how to manage hardware from within Windows 2000.*

- You'll want to finalize your disk partitions. In many clean install scenarios, you may have unpartitioned space left on your hard drive. Refer to Chapter 10 and take care of these partitions now.

- For most new installations using TCP/IP, a DHCP address will be in effect. This may not be a standard practice for production servers. If necessary, acquire and configure the appropriate static TCP/IP information.

- In many larger network environments, certain services, utilities, tools, or other programs are loaded on all servers. For example, some sites may utilize enterprise management tools that require the usage of an agent that runs on the server to collect and pass information up to a management console. Most likely, some sort of backup software will need to be installed also. Find out what additional software is needed and install it now.

TIP *You always want to completely configure a server and install all of its additional components before it goes into production. By production, we mean the point at which the first user connects to the server. Since many additional services, configurations, and software components will require a reboot, you'll want this out of the way up front to avoid further disruptions of your users' work.*

- Run through the Control Panel applets to set all server configurations the way they should be for the long haul. Especially noteworthy are the System Control Panel settings for the pagefile and maximum Registry size.

NOTE *Check Chapter 20 for information about Control Panel applets.*

- At this point, you may get the urge to walk away. Well, hold on just a minute. Too many times, people make some last-minute changes, like the Control Panel settings, and leave it at that.

Even though you were never told to reboot the system—your changes were instantly accepted—there may be some unexpected side effects the next time you reboot. Just in case, give it another reboot now, before your users begin counting on the server being available.

◆ If the system is a dual-boot machine, which is usually not the case on a server, boot into all operating systems to make sure the system integrity is intact and all data is available from all required operating systems.

◆ Once the system itself is complete, create an emergency repair disk. And as an extra safeguard, you may also want to run a full backup.

◆ Finally, a step we rarely perform is documenting the server. Ask yourself if anyone else could take care of the server should you decide to take a week off for a golf vacation. If there are any special things you have to do, like restart a service every day, it should be documented. This is a step you *must* take before you can consider your operating system "installed." See Chapter 21, which covers preparing for and recovering from server failures, for more details.

At this point, you should have a production-ready server and a method for creating this same server time and time again. It seems like a lot of extra work is required in addition to actually installing Windows 2000 Server, but it is well worth the trouble.

Troubleshooting an Installation

Windows 2000 produces a relatively smooth installation. Plug and Play helps in many ways by eliminating the need to know and preconfigure all of your hardware prior to launching an install. There will be a few instances where you will have problems, though.

We discussed failed hardware components earlier. If your system locks up during the hardware detection and configuration phase, you have something that does not play nicely in the sandbox. Sometimes it will be obvious which component is the culprit. Sometimes it won't be so easy. Start with the obvious methods of troubleshooting—the /debug setup parameter discussed in the "Command-Line Automation" section later in this chapter. This will definitely help identify where the install goes wrong. The next step is to either resolve or work around the problem.

If you have hardware conflicts causing problems with your install, you have a couple of options. First, you could configure the hardware and BIOS, as was discussed earlier in "Preparing the Hardware," to get along with the other hardware. Maybe the troublesome hardware is a sound card that refuses to accept the detection phase. Rather than spend x amount of time trying to get it to work, pull it out of the system. Get your Windows 2000 system running first. Then add the component later.

Let's say you completely blow an install at some point. You want to start over from scratch, but you don't want to format your partition and lose potential data. There are three things on your hard drive related to the install that you will want to clean up before starting over:

◆ The win_nt.~ls directory if you copied all files to the system

◆ The win_nt.~bt directory

◆ A line in your boot.ini pointing to win_nt.~bt\bootsect.dat

Removing these entries will make your system completely forget that an install was ever happening, allowing you to start over at square one. Be careful when modifying the `boot.ini`. If you're reverting to an old operating system, make sure your `boot.ini` default is put back to the way it was. Leaving an entry pointing simply to C:\ will let your DOS or Windows 9x operating system's files boot the system. Here's a sample `boot.ini` file for a dual-boot Windows 2000 and Windows 98 machine:

```
[boot loader]
timeout=30
default=C:\
[operating systems]
multi(0)disk(0)rdisk(0)partition(2)\winnt="Microsoft Windows 2000 Server"
C:\="Microsoft Windows 98"
```

The [boot loader] section defines how your boot menu will act. This example shows a time-out of 30 seconds, at which point the default operating system on C:\ will be booted. Once the boot process continues to the C:\, it will require the standard boot files of that operating system. In Windows 98's case, that is the `MSDOS.sys` and `IO.sys`. The [operating systems] section defines the selection menu and where the operating system corresponding to each choice resides. Here, Windows 98 resides in C:\, and Windows 2000 resides on `multi(0)disk(0)rdisk(0)partition(2)\winnt`. This translates into the \winnt directory of the disk and partition defined by the address of `multi(0)disk(0)rdisk(0)partition(2)`.

NOTE *See Chapter 10, "Managing Windows 2000 Storage," for complete details on how logical drives are defined in Windows 2000.*

NOTE *If you want to get rid of the Windows 2000 boot menu altogether and return to your single bootup in Windows 9x, you must delete the* `boot.ini`*,* NTDetect *and* NTLDR *from your boot partition. After they are gone, you will need to re-SYS your boot partition to make it fully DOS- or Windows 9x–bootable again. The best way to make sure this will work is to first boot into your DOS or Windows 9x operating system, format a bootable floppy, and copy* sys.com *to the floppy. Delete the Windows 2000 boot files listed above, reboot your system to the floppy, and run a* SYS C: *command.*

The Recovery Console

Windows 2000 has a nifty new Recovery Console that can go miles farther than the old methods of fixing broken installations. Take this scenario—one that I've dealt with numerous times. An important system file gets corrupted, umm deleted. You know how it goes, "Let's see, `NTFS.SYS`, I never use `NTFS.SYS`, let's just delete it to make more space." The next time you reboot, the system won't come up. Go figure. Now you need to copy a new `NTFS.SYS` to your hard disk. You make a bootable floppy, put `NTFS.SYS` on it, reboot to the floppy, and find out that your system partition is NTFS. We all know that you can't boot to a DOS floppy and access an NTFS partition. Enter the Recovery Console.

What is the Recovery Console? It is a scaled-down cross between a DOS command-line environment, certain Windows 2000 setup functions, and partition-correcting utilities, all with the capability to access NTFS partitions.

The first thing you need to do is get into the Recovery Console. There are two ways to do this. First, you can launch the WINNT32 Setup program with the /cmdcons parameter. A brief setup routine and file-copying session will take place to create your console. Once completed, your `boot.ini` will reflect a new operating system selection, Microsoft Windows 2000 Command Console. Simply boot your machine and then select that menu item. Of course, this method would only work if one had the foresight to install the console before the system broke down. If you haven't created it ahead of time, don't worry, you can get there from the normal setup routine.

Launch Setup like you normally would—from the CD, the boot floppies, whatever you prefer. At the Welcome to Setup screen, select the repair option. From there, you will get the option to repair your installation using either the emergency repair process or the Recovery Console, and off you go.

Once you enter the console, you get a selection of all Windows 2000 installations on the system. Enter the number of the installation you want to work on and press Enter.

NOTE *When entering the console from Setup, you go straight into the console. When entering the console from your boot menu, you'll need to press F6 at the "Press F6 " prompt to install SCSI drivers. This will let you access your SCSI hard drives or CD-ROMs that require a driver.*

The next step is validation. One of the major differences between the FAT and NTFS filesystems is security. Even though you can see the NTFS partitions now, you still need to have access to the filesystem. The console will ask you to enter the Administrator password. After you enter the password, you are dropped at a command prompt in the systemroot directory of the installation you chose. Simple!

Well now what? You're at this command prompt. What do you do with a command-prompt-only version of Windows 2000? Start off with a HELP command, which shows you a list of all available commands. You can do things like copy files, change directories, format drives, and other typical DOS-like file operations. To resolve the current problem, you would just copy your NTFS.SYS from your floppy to your Windows 2000 installation folder and you should be back in business. In addition, there are some other commands that can help you get back into Windows 2000:

DISKPART   This command will launch a disk partitioning utility almost identical to the utility we used during the text-based phase of setup.

FIXBOOT   This command will make a new boot sector on your drive of choice and make that partition your new boot partition. If you happened to destroy your boot sector information and can't boot at all, this may be your best bet.

FIXMBR   This command will repair the master boot record on the selected drive.

DISABLE   If you are having problems with a device that is not letting Windows 2000 boot completely—let's say you accidentally changed a device's startup parameter or installed a new service that keeps killing your system—the DISABLE command will let you prevent that service or device from starting.

ENABLE   This is just the opposite of DISABLE. Let's say you disabled an important boot device; reenabling it may be the easiest solution.

LISTSVC   Both the DISABLE and ENABLE commands require that you tell it *which* service or device to alter. This command will give you a list of all devices and services.

SYSTEMROOT   This command gives you a quick return path back to your `systemroot` directory without having to fight those long, pesky CD commands. It also helps you when you forget which drive and directory your chosen Windows 2000 installation resides in.

LOGON   The logon command takes you back to your first prompt of the Recovery Console so you can choose another installation to repair.

HELP   In case you can't remember the command, this is a nice little reminder.

Now that you know what the Recovery Console does, let's run through a couple of examples. We'll take the first example from our scenario earlier, a known missing or corrupt `NTFS.SYS`. Once we've logged in to the Recovery Console for our Windows 2000 installation and copied a fresh `NTFS.SYS` to our A: drive, we need to copy it to our `systemroot` directory. We should already be in the `systemroot` directory, but just to be sure, we type **systemroot**. Now, we type **copy A:\NTFS.SYS**. Easy huh?

Here's another problem. We have recently installed a new service named BillyBobY2KChecker. It is set to start automatically during boot up, but as soon as it does, blue screen! Into our Recovery Console we go. At the prompt, type **listsvc**. We should see, among our many devices and services, BillyBobY2KChecker service set to automatic. Now, we type disable **BillyBobY2KChecker**. Next time we reboot into Windows 2000, we should get in just fine and should probably uninstall the problem software.

The Recovery Console is a handy utility that can get you out of a lot of trouble. Once you have installed Windows 2000, it might not be a bad idea to run the `winnt32.exe` with the `/cmdcons` parameter. This won't actually launch setup, just configure the console. You will always have the console available in your boot menu, although it won't be set as default.

Performing Unattended Installs: An Overview

Got 50 servers to install? Getting a little tired of shoving CD-ROMs into drives and baby-sitting the setup process, answering the same dumb questions over and over again? Then you need to learn about unattended installs!

An unattended install is simply a method of providing the answers for the setup questions before they are asked in order to automate the installation process. There is no other difference in the install itself. But why do we need to automate? Usually, automation is most beneficial in large networks where Windows 2000 machines will frequently be built. By automating these installs, numerous hours can be spared that would otherwise be spent sitting at the console. Another benefit of unattended installs is that they can be run by non–Win2K experts and produce the same wonderful results every time. This could help in those environments where the only on-site server operator is not an experienced administrator. Rather than spend hours walking them through an install to your specifications, you can merely give them a single command line and be done with it.

Win2K provides three different tools to make it possible for you to do unattended installations, and I'll explain them to you in the remainder of this chapter. Before getting into the details of these tools, however, I want to provide some perspective on how you'd use these tools. We'll cover three major areas:

- ◆ Scripting installations
- ◆ Using Remote Installation Services
- ◆ Using Sysprep

Scripting

In its simplest form, a script is just a file that preanswers all of those questions that Setup asks—what shall we call the computer, what is your name, what's the product ID value, that sort of thing. So what's to learn? Well, first of all, you have to learn the language of scripts; like most computer things, scripts have a specific syntax that you must follow or they won't work. It's not a *hard* syntax—I don't want to scare you away—but there's a syntax nonetheless. Microsoft has made your script-writing job pretty easy, in that they've included with 2000 a program that asks you some questions and then spits out a script. It's only a basic one, and you'll have to add a few lines to make it useful, but it's a good start.

Once you've done a little scripting, however, you'll soon want more flexibility and power out of the scripting language—and you can get it. There's a whole next level of scripting power via what are called the OEMPreinstall options, and you'll learn them next.

Delivery: CD-ROM or RIS

All a great script does is to save you having to answer questions while running Setup—but first you've got to get Setup running in the first place. The next set of tools simplifies the process of delivering all of the setup files to the new PC to begin with.

The simplest way to start up a setup is to shove a CD into the computer's CD-ROM drive and then boot from the CD. But how to supply the script? With a trick, as you'll see—put the script on a floppy disk and call the script `winnt.sif`. But who wants to walk around with a CD-ROM, and, besides, what if you want to deploy more than just the operating system? Well, under NT 4, you'd have to create a network share that contained all of the NT installation files, then you'd have to figure out how to get a computer with nothing on its hard disk connected to the network in the first place.

Windows 2000 again simplifies matters with a tool called Remote Installation Services (RIS). With RIS, you can store prebuilt Windows 2000 installation files and scripts on a server—a RIS server. Then RIS eliminates the need to wonder how you're going to get your new computer attached to the network in the first place by supporting a network boot standard that many new computers support called PXE, the Preboot Execution Environment. And if you don't have a PXE-compliant computer, that's not a problem; RIS can generate a generic floppy disk that will allow most desktops and some laptops (laptops are the weak point here, as you'll see) to connect to a RIS server, with no built-in PXE support needed.

By the way, if you know a bit about Windows 2000 already, then you might be thinking, "Wait a minute, Mark—RIS only distributes 2000 *Professional*. You can't use it to deliver *Server*." But you *can*. There's an undocumented technique to let RIS deliver Server, and you'll read about it a bit later in this chapter.

Sysprep

For some folks, the two things that I've just described—scripting and delivering setups—is the slow way to do things. Many firms prefer to first create a computer that looks just exactly as they'd like all of their computers to look. Then they create hundreds of exact duplicates of that prototype computer, "cloning" the prototype's hard disk, and in the process quickly roll out hundreds of ready-to-work desktop or server computers.

The only problem with this method is that until the advent of 2000, Microsoft hadn't supported people who do that, as cloning results in computers that lack unique SIDs, security identifiers. But Microsoft now has a tool that makes a prototype computer "clonable," called Sysprep.

Now we're almost ready to get into the details of scripting—but before we do, let's take a quick look at the program that starts off a Windows 2000 setup in the first place or, rather, the *two* programs that start a Windows 2000 setup: `winnt.exe` and `winnt32.exe`.

Command-Line Automation: Controlling WINNT[32]

When you simply boot a system from the CD-ROM, then you're not aware of the name of the program that starts off the setup process. But you can also initiate a Windows 2000 setup from the command line with one of two commands: `winnt32.exe` if you're starting the setup from a computer that's already running Windows NT or 2000, or `winnt.exe` for a system running DOS or Windows 3.*x* or 9*x*. The command-line parameters of these programs tell the Setup program where your source installation files are, where you want to install Windows 2000 Server, where your answer file is located, and other information needed to prepare for the setup. A command-line parameter can also be used to copy an additional folder to your setup source so that those files will be available during the installation. This is handy when you have OEM drivers for the hardware you want to install during the setup rather than waiting until afterward.

Before you start using command-line parameters, it is important to *really* understand them. They can have a very profound impact on the installation process, so let's go over the `winnt32` options:

/checkupgradeonly   Whenever Windows 2000 Setup begins, it checks to see if an upgrade is possible. Setup will not attempt to actually run the install.

/cmd:*command*   This option will launch the given command line before the setup process has completed, which will allow you to perform some additional customization or launch other programs.

/cmdcons   If you have a failed installation on your system, this option will add a Recovery Console item to your `boot.ini` operating system selection menu.

/copydir:*folder*   When you're doing automated installs for a large number of machines, this may be one of the most useful options in your arsenal. How many times have you been stopped in the middle of an installation because your network card drivers are, well, on the network? You resort to copying files to a floppy, spend 10 minutes trying to find one, format it, copy files, and hike them back to your server. What a bother. The /copydir option can really help you out here. It will copy the specified folder to your installation directory during setup—while you're still connected to your network.

/copysource:*folder* Similar to the /copydir option, the /copysource option copies a specified folder to your installation directory. The major difference between the two is that the /copysource directory is deleted after setup is complete.

/debug[*level*][:*filename*] You can tell Setup to log debugging information to a given file based on the following criteria. Level 0 logs severe errors only, 1 adds regular errors, 2 includes warnings, 3 adds all informational messages, and 4 incorporates detailed information about the setup for complete debugging purposes.

/m:*folder* This option can be dangerous. When the setup process begins to copy files, the /m option tells it to look in the specified folder first. If that folder contains files to be used in setup, those files be will used. If the files are not present, they will be retrieved from the regular installation source. This can be helpful if a hotfix or alternative version of a file that you choose to use for every install (rather than the default version on the CD) is available. Instead of running your install and then running an update or replacing files, you can use /m and perform these tasks in one swift step.

/makelocalsource Have you ever had problems reconnecting to your installation source after you've rebooted and started the setup? This could be due to things like Setup not recognizing your CD-ROM or network card. This option tells Setup to copy the entire source to your hard drive so that you can guarantee it will be available later.

/noreboot There may be times when you want to launch the first stage of Setup, get your machine ready for the installation, but not reboot quite yet. This option will bypass the screen at the end of the first setup wizard and return you to your existing operating system without a reboot. When you do reboot, though, Setup will continue.

/s:*sourcepath* This seems like a redundant switch. You've already found your source path if you've gotten as far as launching the setup. Setup even knows where it's coming from. This parameter does help identify where your source is—the I386 directory—but it also does something better. You can specify multiple source paths and have Setup copy files from each simultaneously. This can really save you time if you have a slow CD and a slow network. Be careful, though; the first source path identified must be available or Setup will fail.

/syspart:*drive* Another very powerful option here when you're considering mass deployments is the /syspart parameter. This will start your setup to the specified drive and mark that drive as active. Once Setup is complete, you can physically take that hard drive out of the system, place it in a new system, and boot right into Setup. You must use the /tempdrive parameter with /syspart.

/tempdrive:*drive* Setup will use the specified tempdrive to place temporary setup files. If you have space concerns with drives or merely a preference on where you want temporary files to go, use this parameter.

/unattend The /unattend option will do an automated, no-input-required upgrade of your previous operating system. All configurations and settings of the old operating system will be used for the upgrade.

/unattend[*num*]:*answer_file* This launches one of the most powerful features of unattended installations: the answer file. The answer file is a text file containing any or all answers to be used throughout the entire setup process. We'll talk about building the answer file in the next section. If your current operating system is Windows 2000, you can also specify a time delay for the reboot, determined by [*num*].

/udf:*id*[,*udf_file*] One of the problems with automated installations is that you can't fully automate an install unless you provide a name for the server, and all servers—all machines for that matter—on your network *must* have a unique name. This requires that you either enter the name during the setup or use an answer file on all machines, giving them the same name. Neither of those are viable options. The /udf parameter allows you to specify unique information about each installation based on the file specified in the UDF file—uniqueness database file. Here's how it works. In the UDF file, there is a listing of names and a section matching each name with computer-specific information. Usually the computer-specific information will be just the computer name, but anything you put in this file will override the same entry in the answer file. Take a look at a sample UDF file named `unattend.udf`:

```
;SetupMgrTag
[UniqueIds]
    BS01=UserData
    BS02=UserData
    BS03=UserData
    BS04=UserData
    BS05=UserData
[BS01:UserData]
    ComputerName=BS01
[BS02:UserData]
    ComputerName=BS02
[BS03:UserData]
    ComputerName=BS03
[BS04:UserData]
    ComputerName=BS04
[BS05:UserData]
    ComputerName=BS05
```

I have five specified, unique computers defined—BS01 through BS05. If I'm sitting down to install a Windows 2000 machine for BS03, I would send the /udf:BS03,unattend.udf parameter. The Setup program will look in the UDF file and have any entries under the BS03 section override those in the standard answer file. So if the ComputerName entry in the answer file is BSxx, Setup will substitute BS03 in its place for my installation.

Those are all of the possible command-line parameters that you can feed the WINNT32 program. To better see how they work, let's try a few samples of running WINNT32 from the CD located in F:.

We are installing to a server that is very specific about using OEM drivers for the network card. If we start the setup and reboot, the default drivers with Windows 2000 won't get us back online. We'll use the /copysource option to copy down our drivers from the network folder of Z:\NIC\OEM. Just to be on the safe side, we also want to use a /makelocalsource option so we have all files available for use. We'll launch the following command:

```
F:\I386\winnt32 /copysource:z:\nic\oem /makelocalsource
```

During the first phase of Setup, the entire z:\nic\oem directory will be copied to the hard drive to be used during the installation. Once completed, the directory will be removed to free up our space again. We will also get a complete copy of the I386 directory copied to our local installation source. Between the two, we should have no problems with the installation not being able to find files.

Now, we want to launch a setup using an answer file named C:\w2k\setup\unattend.txt and a uniqueness database file named C:\w2k\setup\unattend.udf. To keep parity with the earlier scenario, we'll install this machine with the BS03 ID. In this case, we run this command:

```
F:\I386\winnt32 /unattend:c:\w2k\setup\unattend.txt
/udf:BS03,c:\w2k\setup\unattend.udf
```

WINNT supports a subset of those options—/s, /t, /u, and /udf—as well as these:

/e: Specifies a command to execute after Setup finishes

/a Enables accessibility options

/r: Tells Setup to copy a folder to the target machine, leaving it in place after Setup finishes

/rx: Like /r:, but deletes the folder after Setup finishes

Scripts, Part I: Basic Answer Files with Setup Manager

The easiest way to get started with scripts is to let a Windows 2000 program called Setup Manager build one for you.

INSTALLING SETUP MANAGER

Setup Manager isn't installed by default—here's how to get it.

1. Insert the Windows 2000 Server CD into your computer's CD drive.

2. Open the folder named Support and, inside that, another folder named Tools.

3. In Support\Tools, you'll see a file named deploy.cab. Double-click it to open it.

4. Select all of the files in deploy.cab, right-click, and choose Copy.

5. Create a directory named DepTools on your computer's hard disk. Right-click the DepTools folder and choose Paste.

6. Open the DepTools folder and double-click the Setupmgr.exe icon.

RUNNING SETUP MANAGER

That starts up Setup Manager, which is a wizard and therefore starts off with a "welcome" screen. Click Next to get past it and you'll see a screen like Figure 4.3.

FIGURE 4.3

New file or modify an old one?

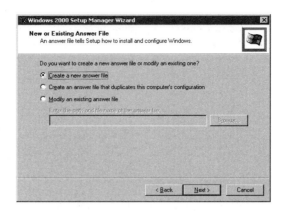

As you can see, Setup Manager will either create a new script file or edit an existing one.

WARNING *In general, I recommend that you never use Setup Manager to edit an existing script, because when starting up Setup Manager to change just one thing in a script, I find that it sometimes gets a bit rambunctious and decides whatthehey, while I'm here why don't I fix all of these other bad ideas that I see in this script?*

Tell it that you're creating a new script and choose Next. You'll see a screen like Figure 4.4.

FIGURE 4.4

What kind of script?

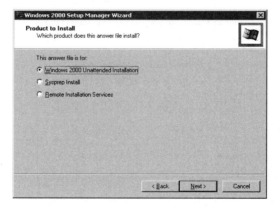

Setup Manager can build scripts that you can use either for a simple unattended install, for RIS, or for Sysprep. We're doing just a simple install, so choose that and click Next. You'll then see a screen like Figure 4.5.

Setup Manager will create scripts to install either Professional or Server; choose Server and click Next to see Figure 4.6.

FIGURE 4.5

Professional or
Server?

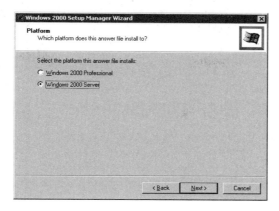

FIGURE 4.6

Just how hands-off?

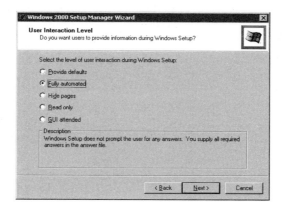

This screen advises Setup Manager how thorough it should be in creating the script. In theory, choosing Fully Automated will cause Setup Manager to fill in enough information that you can just start an install using winnt or winnt32, walk away for 45 minutes, return, and be done. In actual fact, you'll have to include a few other things, as you'll see. Choose Fully Automated and click Next to see a screen like Figure 4.7.

From this point on, the Setup Wizard mainly asks the same kinds of questions that Setup has already asked, so I'll go through them quickly. First, there's the end-user license agreement (EULA). As with every other piece of software nowadays—both Microsoft and non-Microsoft—2000 comes with a sign-it-or-else "contract" called a software license. The point of the software license is to give the software vendor more ability to restrict what you do with the software than they'd normally get from copyright laws. By agreeing to it here, you avoid having the Setup program stop and ask you to agree to the EULA in mid-install. Check the box and click Next to fill in your name and organization, and then Next to fill in the client licensing option, per-seat or per-server. Click Next to see Figure 4.8.

FIGURE 4.7

Agreeing to the
EULA

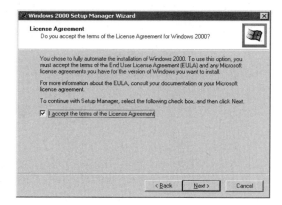

FIGURE 4.8

Machine names and
automatic UDFs

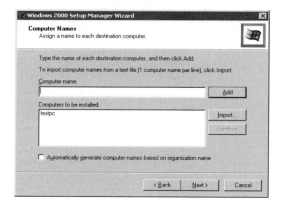

Here, I've entered a machine name of testpc and clicked Add. Computer names aren't very interesting, but what *is* interesting is that you can use the Setup Manager to create a UDF, like the one you saw earlier in this chapter.

The following two wizard panels are self-explanatory. The first lets you specify a password for the local default Administrator account, and the one following lets you specify your system's video resolution. Then you choose whether to use the default network settings or to customize them in some fashion, as you see in Figure 4.9.

You'll usually choose Typical Settings, but let me take a moment and point out one of Setup Manager's strengths. If you decide to take 2000's default networking settings, then you'll get a pretty basic setup script—you'll use DHCP to get your IP address (and if you don't know what DHCP is, don't worry, I'll be explaining it in the next few chapters—for now, just understand that it makes the process of setting up the TCP/IP software on a computer far easier). But what about if you *didn't* want to use DHCP for configuration—what if you wanted to script an install with a specific set of TCP/IP configuration parameters, like a specific IP address? Here's where Setup Manager shines. Perhaps it's the fact that I seem to be afflicted with AFS (After-Forty Syndrome), but I can never remember the combination of script commands needed to specify an IP address. So I cheat by just running Setup Manager and telling it to set up a simple script for a system with a prespecified IP address. I can then look at the resulting script and cut and paste to create my desired script. That's not to say that Setup Manager knows how to create *every* possible kind of script, but it's pretty smart, making it a kind of automated "cheat sheet."

FIGURE 4.9

Typical or custom network settings?

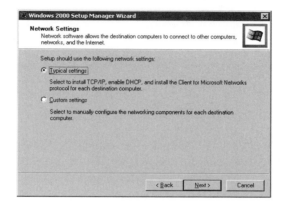

Anyway, after deciding to do typical network settings and clicking Next, you'll get a panel that lets you specify whether you're going to join a domain or a workgroup; the panel after that sets the time zone—and let's stop here again for a moment to point out a real improvement in 2000 scripting over NT scripting. 2000 supports a few dozen time zones (yes, there are more than 24 time zones, for political reasons), but you specify a time zone with just a number. For example, the U.S. Eastern time zone, which I live in, is number 35, and the command to tell 2000 install to put its machine in the Eastern time zone looks like

```
TimeZone = 35
```

Not impressive, eh? Well, consider: under NT 4, you had to type in a descriptive label, like

```
TimeZone = "Eastern Time Zone (GMT -5)"
```

Or something like that—but in any case, if I'd misspelled Eastern or inserted an extra blank, then the script was No Good and the setup routine would stop dead. Now, the worst thing that happens is that my user's computer thinks it's in Karachi. (Which, given the kind of interesting food they serve in Karachi, might not be so bad, after all.)

Next, you'll be asked whether or not you want to edit the "additional settings"; skip that for now, but play around with them another time. The "additional settings" let you set up a modem, regional settings, and languages—three items that were a real pain to script under 4. But my favorite in the "additionals" is the browser settings. It really irritates me that every time I set up a new computer and start Internet Explorer for the first time, it jumps out to MSN; I've always wanted to say to NT and now 2000's Setup programs, "Look, I swear, I will *never ever use MSN in my entire life*—so stop making me either wait for MSN to load or have to click the Stop button!" When I start up a browser, I want it to start *immediately*, so my home page is "about:blank." I can make that happen in a script with the following commands:

```
[Branding]
BrandIEUsingUnattended = Yes
[URL]
Home_Page = about:blank
```

Anyway, you'll next get the option whether to Create a Distribution Folder or to just simply write out the script; choose No to write out the script and Setup Manager will write the script for you.

EXAMINING SETUP MANAGER'S SCRIPT

The script that Setup Manager created for me looks like this:

```
;SetupMgrTag
[Data]
    AutoPartition=1
    MsDosInitiated="0"
    UnattendedInstall="Yes"

[Unattended]
    UnattendMode=FullUnattended
    OemSkipEula=Yes
    OemPreinstall=No

[GuiUnattended]
    AdminPassword=*
    OEMSkipRegional=1
    TimeZone=35
    OemSkipWelcome=1

[UserData]
    FullName="Mark Minasi"
    OrgName=MR&D
    ComputerName=testpc

[LicenseFilePrintData]
    AutoMode=PerSeat

[Identification]
    JoinDomain=testdomain.com
    DomainAdmin=machineguy
    DomainAdminPassword=swordfish

[Networking]
    InstallDefaultComponents=Yes
```

This is a pretty basic script, but let's go through it, then add a few commands that I think are essential. For starters, an answer file is like a typical INI file, around since the early days of Windows; it's a simple ASCII file that you could, if you wanted to, create with Notepad. There are sections of the file that are broken up into groups; they're identified by their headers and surrounded by square brackets, like [*HEADER1*]. Within each section are different settings and the corresponding values to be used during the setup, formatted as *ITEM=VALUE*.

The first section is called [Data] and it's pretty much "boilerplate," simply you-gotta-have-them instructions. MSDOSInitiated should equal 0 if you're doing an install from the CD-ROM, or 1 if you're doing a RIS install. AutoPartition must be equal to 1, or Setup will stop and ask you which partition to install 2000 into. UnattendedInstall should be, um, obvious.

The [Unattended] section tells Setup what level of user interaction to expect, and you see Full-Unattended, which is the script-syntax equivalent of the Fully Automated option we chose from Setup Manager. OEMSkipEula just says "don't make him accept the license agreement." OEM-Preinstall is a *very* powerful command that we'll meet later. Turning on the OEMPreinstall features will, as you'll see, unlock a whole bunch of extra automated setup capabilities—but now, let's stick with the basics.

[GUIUnattended] controls the second, graphical part of Setup, answering many of the questions that section asks. Without OEMSkipWelcome=1, Setup would stop at the beginning of Setup and ask if you want to continue. (Now, what part of FullUnattended did you not understand, Windows 2000?) Note AdminPassword=*; that doesn't say to set the password equal to an asterisk; rather, it says to make it blank.

[UserData] lets you brand the PC with your name and organization, and the name of a PC. [LicenseFilePrintData] just specifies how you're going to license the clients. [Networking] is simple in this example; it just says to take the defaults.

Look at the [Identification] section, and let's consider what that does. You want to join this computer to a domain, and of course you'll need at least *some* level of administrative control to do that. That's what that administrative name and password are for—to give Setup the authorization to create a computer account. But obviously you might not be too happy about the idea of putting the account name and password of a domain administrator into an unencrypted ASCII file. Fortunately, you can create a lower-power administrator that can only create and destroy *machine* accounts—it can't mess with user accounts or anything else on the domain—and you'll learn how to do that at the end of the chapter.

Improving Setup Manager's Script

We didn't ask Setup Manager to do anything fancy, which is why we got a pretty short script—I just wanted to create a basic script. But you really can't use that script yet to try out unattended installations; we'll need to add a couple of lines.

PRODUCTID

As with NT, Windows 2000 needs you to punch in a machine-specific product ID. On Win2K, it's a 25-character sequence of letters and numbers. (If you work for a large company then you'll probably have a version of the installation CD called the Select CD—they don't require you to punch in a product ID.)

You specify a product ID with the ProductID command, which goes in the [UserData] section, like so:

```
[UserData]
    FullName="Mark Minasi"
    OrgName=MR&D
    ComputerName=testpc
    ProductID="11111-22222-33333-44444-55555"
```

(And no, that code won't work, it's just an example.) Some people worry about the licensing issues involved if you use the same product ID for every one of your servers. Well, the 2000 *software* certainly doesn't mind: You can have every server running the same product ID and they'll work fine. And if the software police come knock down your door and want you to prove that you actually *do* have sufficient licenses to run 10 servers, then *they* don't care about your product IDs either: they want to see the receipts showing that you paid for 10 Server licenses. So it's perfectly fine to use the same ID on every system.

REPARTITION

The one other essential command is Repartition=Yes, which goes in [Unattended]. This command tells Windows 2000 Setup to delete all partitions on the first physical drive and create one big NTFS drive. If you *don't* use the Repartition command, then you have to either prebuild the partitions on the computer somehow (there are third-party tools that can do that) or accept that Setup will stop partway through the text portion and prompt you to ask which partition to place 2000 on.

Trying Out the Completed Script

Once finished, the script will look something like this:

```
;SetupMgrTag
[Data]
    AutoPartition=1
    MsDosInitiated="0"
    UnattendedInstall="Yes"

[Unattended]
    UnattendMode=FullUnattended
    OemSkipEula=Yes
    OemPreinstall=No
    TargetPath=\winnt
    Repartition=Yes

[GuiUnattended]
    AdminPassword=*
    OEMSkipRegional=1
    TimeZone=35
    OemSkipWelcome=1
```

```
[UserData]
    FullName="(Fill in your name)"
    ComputerName=mypc
    ProductID="11111-22222-33333-44444-55555"

[LicenseFilePrintData]
    AutoMode=PerSeat

[Identification]
    JoinDomain=(yourdomain)
    domainadmin=(admin account)
    domainadminpassword=(password)

[Networking]
    InstallDefaultComponents=Yes
```

Of course, you'll have to fill in the items relevant to your system—the ones that I put in parentheses—and you'll need a valid product ID. And if you don't *have* a domain to join, then you can make a much simpler [Identification] section like this to join a workgroup:

```
[Identification]
    JoinWorkgroup=(your workgroup name--anything will do)
```

Want to try it out? To do so, you'll need just a few ingredients:

◆ First, of course, you'll need a computer. Note that as I've included the Repartition=Yes command, this will blow away any partitions on its first physical hard disk.

◆ Next, you'll need to copy your script file to a floppy. The floppy needn't be bootable. Rename the script file name to `winnt.sif`. That's a "magic" name—if you name it something else, then this won't work. Put the floppy in the A: drive.

◆ After that, insert the Windows 2000 installation CD in the CD-ROM drive.

◆ Finally, in your computer's BIOS you need to rearrange the boot order.

Ideally, you'd like a system that lets you tell it to first boot from the CD-ROM and then, if that wasn't bootable, to try the C: drive, and only if *those* two weren't available, to boot from A:. Now, with the CD-ROM in its drive and the floppy in the A: drive, boot the system. It'll ask you to press a key to boot from the CD-ROM and, if you don't, then it boots from the hard disk.

Then you just walk away.

What's going on? A trick built into Windows 2000. If it boots from its setup CD, it then looks on the A: drive for a file named `winnt.sif`. If it finds one then it presumes that the `winnt.sif` file is the script that it should use to do an unattended install. Pretty neat, eh? Hey, stay tuned, it gets even better.

Improving the Script More

Once you've got a basic script like that working, you can take it considerably further, as the script language is pretty extensive. Look back in the directory where you copied the files from `deploy.cab` and you'll see a large WordPad document named `unattend.doc`—a roughly 180-page document—that documents all of the scripting parameters. Here are a few suggestions.

MOVE DOCUMENTS AND SETTINGS

Windows 2000 stores the user profiles by default in a directory `C:\Documents and Settings`; if you want to move that, then add the line ProfilesDir=*path* to put the profiles somewhere else.

AUTOMATICALLY CHOOSE A COMPUTER NAME

If you've supplied an organization name, then you can just set the ComputerName equal to an asterisk, and Setup will then create a unique name for the computer, building on the organization name. Put that command in [UserData].

USE COMPONENTS TO SKIP GAMES AND LOAD TERMINAL SERVICES

Want to skip Solitaire, Minesweeper, and Pinball? Add this section:

```
[Components]
Solitaire=Off
Minesweeper=Off
Pinball=Off
```

Alternatively, you can use Components to activate the built-in Terminal Services module of Windows 2000 Server, the piece that lets you do remote administration using simple "Windows terminals," as you'll learn in Chapter 15. Just add some commands in [Components] and some in another section, like so:

```
[TerminalService]
ApplicationServer=0
PermissionsSetting=1
[Components]
LicenseServer=off
TsEnable=off
TsClients=on
```

I strongly recommend turning Terminal Services on for all of your servers, and I'm told by Microsoft folks that it's best to turn Terminal Services on *before* you start loading server applications like SQL, Exchange, and the like, so adding Terminal Services in the script is a great convenience.

PRECONFIGURE INTERNET EXPLORER

As I mentioned a few pages back, you can configure Internet Explorer in the script as well. For example, here's a piece from a script that I use:

```
[FavoritesEx]
    Title1="Mark Minasi Home Page.url"
    URL1="http://www.minasi.com"
[Branding]
    BrandIEUsingUnattended=Yes
[URL]
    Home_Page=about:blank
```

The first section preloads my home page into my Favorites. The second just warns Setup that we'll be configuring IE via a script, and the third section defines my home page as about:blank.

Now, for those of you who are IEAK (Internet Explorer Administration Kit) wizards, then your hard work isn't wasted—there's a script setting that tells Setup to find the file containing your IEAK settings and then to apply them. (Run Setup Manager and you'll see the option.)

POSTINSTALL POLISHING: ADDING SUPPORT AND BRANDING INFO

Now that you've got your system set up, let's add a bit of branding and support info. (Truthfully, the branding info is a bit silly—though fun—but the support info isn't silly, it's useful.)

Try this: log in to your Windows 2000 system as Administrator (that's probably the only account you've got built yet anyway), and find the icon on the Desktop labeled My Computer in the upper-left corner. Right-click it and choose Properties. You'll see a multi-tabbed properties page like the one you've seen elsewhere in Windows. You can add a picture (or any bitmap) to it in the empty space on the left side, like so:

◆ Take any bitmap that's roughly 175×175 pixels.

◆ Name it `oemlogo.bmp`.

◆ Place it in `\winnt\system32`.

Next, let's add some support information. You can "brand" a computer to describe its model, and also add an arbitrary set of lines of text for support information by including a file in `\winnt\system32` named `oeminfo.ini`. This is an ASCII text file with two sections, [General] and [Support Information]. It looks like this:

```
[General]
Manufacturer=<descriptive vendor name>
Model=<particular model>
[Support Information]
Line1=<first line of text>
Line2=<second line of text>
Line3=<and so on >
```

For example, you might have an `oeminfo.ini` file that looks like the following:

```
[General]
Manufacturer=Clonetronics
Model=DeskWidget 820 (60 GB disk, 733 Processor)
[Support Information]
Line1=For Tech Support call:
Line2=(555) 555-1212
Line3=After hours, call Bill
Line4=(If you can find him)
```

After inserting a simple bitmap and the above `oeminfo.ini` file, I got a My Computer Properties page that looks like Figure 4.10.

If you were to click the button labeled Support Information, then you'd see the four lines of support info.

FIGURE 4.10

My Computer
Properties

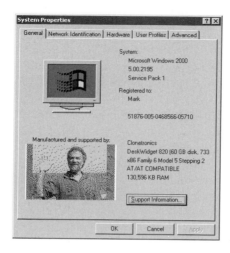

Scripts, Part II: Distribution Shares and *OEM*

You've seen that one way to start an unattended install is to shove a floppy and a CD into a system, boot, and walk away. But that's really only of value if you just want to install the operating system with the basics. Next, let's see how to load a whole *bunch* of new software, and also do some other great stuff, including installing applications on top of the OS.

STARTING A SETUP WITH WINNT/WINNT32

Like previous versions of NT, Windows 2000 ships on a CD and includes a large directory called I386. Inside I386 are a pair of programs that you've already met, winnt.exe and winnt32.exe. As you've already read, one way to start Windows 2000's Setup program is to just type **winnt** or **winnt32** with a sequence of options. You *could*, then, install Win2K on a system this way (I don't recommend it, although there's a good reason why I'm explaining it):

1. Clean up about 2GB of space on a drive on a computer's hard disk.

2. Copy the I386 directory on the CD and its subdirectories to the drive with 2GB or more space.

3. Change directories over to the copied I386 directory that is now on the computer's local hard disk.

4. Open a command line and type either **winnt** or **winnt32** with whatever options are appropriate at the time, depending on what kind of install you want to do. (And, again, use **winnt** if you're currently running DOS or Windows 9*x*, winnt32 to start a 2000 Setup from inside NT or 2000.)

WINNT[32] AND DISTRIBUTION SHARES

Now, why did I explain this to you if I recommend that you not use it? Because many people *do* use a variation on this theme. Over the years, many of us have done WINNT/WINNT32 installs not by copying I386 to the target machine, but instead by putting I386 on a shared folder (called a "distribution share" or "distribution folder") on a file server. *Then* you walk over to the machine that you want to put 2000 on, connect to the file share, and type **winnt** or **winnt32**. Summarized, then, the idea with a distribution share is that you first copy the I386 files over to some share on the network; then to put Windows 2000 on a new machine, you just walk over to the machine, log in to the network, connect to the distribution share, run the WINNT program in the share, and Setup starts. You can, of course, script an installation this way as well, and so the whole process can become basically unattended.

The Chicken and the Egg

The only problem with this whole approach has always been that part about taking a brand-new machine and logging in to the network with it—namely, how the blazes do you *do* it? Computers with empty hard disks don't know jack about networks (at least, not usually—stay tuned for the RIS section to see the alternative), so simply stuffing an Ethernet card into a new PC and hooking it up to the company network accomplishes nothing besides making another LED on the Ethernet switches light up. You need a network stack—protocols, a network file client, all that kind of stuff. It's always sort of been true that "you need to be on the network to be able to connect to the software that you'll need to install in order to get onto the network." Kind of a chicken-and-egg thing.

Microsoft used to offer a two-floppy set of code called the MS-DOS Client for Microsoft Networks that helped a bit. You'd first stick DOS on the new machine, then load the MS-DOS Client for Microsoft Networks, then reboot the system. That would let you log in to a domain and from there attach to a distribution share—but it was an awful lot of installing just to start off the NT or 2000 Setup programs. Worse yet, the Client didn't include drivers for any NICs built after the Punic Wars, so you always had to hunt around for a set of DOS-compatible drivers for the modern network card in your computer.

With a bit of luck and determination, I was sometimes able to fit the whole mess onto a floppy, and that wasn't so bad—just boot the new computer from the A: drive and I'd be connected to the network. Of course, I had to reengineer the floppy for every different model of NIC, which partially explains why I (a) only bought 3Com Ethernet cards for years and (b) resisted going to 100-megabit Ethernet a year or two longer than I should have—I was reluctant to have to create a new network boot floppy.

Where does that leave you nowadays? Well, to my knowledge, Microsoft doesn't distribute the Client any more. You can solve the "how do I get to the distribution share in the first place" problem in one of three ways:

♦ Find an old copy of the MS-DOS Client for Microsoft Networks and cook up network boot floppies. (And please don't e-mail me, I can't distribute them—they're copyrighted.)

♦ Given that many new systems ship with Wintendo (Win 9*x*) on them anyway, you already have a network-aware operating system sitting on your new computer's hard disk. Use that to connect to the distribution share.

♦ A lot of new computers have the ability to do a PXE or "network boot." Windows 2000's Remote Installation Services (RIS) is built to support PXE boots, and so can let a computer with even an empty hard disk get to a RIS server and then to install 2000 from a server. Unfortunately, RIS only supports Windows 2000 *Professional*, not Server. Fortunately, there's an undocumented way to get around that and thus deploy Server via RIS but we'll get there in a bit.

EXTENDING *I386*: PREINSTALLING SERVICE PACKS

Let's presume, then, that you've figured a way to get your workstations attached to a network distribution share. Now we can start reaping the benefits of doing installs from a share on a hard disk rather than a CD-ROM: we can *add* to the data on the CD.

The first terrific thing that we can do is to preinstall service packs. As I write this, Service Pack 1 has been out for a while. You can download it as an 89MB file named sp1network.exe. SP1 lets you attach it to an I386, "assimilating" itself so that when you do an installation from that I386, you instantly have a copy of Windows 2000 with Service Pack 1 installed, rather than having to first install 2000 and *then* apply the service pack. Here's how.

1. Create a directory on a server's hard disk and copy the I386 folder to it. Let's say for example's sake that you put it in C:\I386.

2. Put the sp1network.exe file on that computer's disk (it doesn't matter where), open a command line, and type **sp1network -x** to extract all of the Service Pack 1 files. It'll ask you where to put them, so specify a directory wherever it makes sense for you.

3. Once sp1network has extracted itself, look in the directory that sp1network created. In it is a directory named I386\update. In there you'll find a program named update.exe.

4. Run update.exe with the –s option and point it at the drive containing I386, *not* the I386 directory itself. For example, if you put I386 on C:, then type **update –sc:** to put the service pack files into C:\I386.

Microsoft says that the –s stands for "slipstream," but I tend to think that it stands for "aSsimilate," as that's what the service pack does—assimilates itself into the I386. Notice that, because the service pack will only take the name of the directory *above* I386 as an input, you really *must* store the data from the CD's I386 folder in a folder also named I386. This isn't a great hardship—most distribution shares I've ever seen are named I386—but now there's a reason that you really *have* to call the directory I386.

TIP   *Now that you've seen how to automatically install a service pack, you're probably wondering how to automatically add the latest hotfixes. I'll show you how to do that in the upcoming section "Tell Setup to Run Commands with* cmdlines.txt."

OEM: MORE *I386* POWER

Look back at my example script and you'll see, in the [Unattended] section, a command OEM-Preinstall=No. Let's change that No to Yes and unlock a bunch of convenient unattended setup features:

◆   You can tell Setup to create directories and files on the newly installed machine.

◆   You can tell Setup to run any number of commands at the end of setup—for example, commands to tell Setup to install other applications.

◆   You can supply Setup with newer device drivers than the ones that ship with Windows 2000, or device drivers for hardware that didn't even exist when 2000 shipped.

♦ You can specify that you want to install a particular Hardware Abstraction Layer (HAL). You wouldn't do this very often (so I'm not going to cover the topic any further), but once in a while you'll try to build a setup script for a system that needs a custom HAL, and this is the only way to tell Setup to use it while unattended.

Here's how to use the power of OEM. Inside an I386 directory, create a directory named OEM. For example, suppose you'd copied the I386 directory to the E: drive and then perhaps slipstreamed Service Pack 1 onto it. Before starting to do installs from that E:\I386 directory, create a directory named E:\I386\OEM. We'll do our work in that directory.

Setup Bitmaps and Logos

While the Setup program runs on a user's machine, you might want to include instructions or information on the screen. You can do that with the [OEM_Ads] section. Create a section in your script with a logo= and a background= command, like so:

```
[OEM_Ads]
logo=ourlogo.bmp
background=backgrnd.bmp
```

Place the files ourlogo.bmp and backgrnd.bmp in the \I386\OEM directory. They must be simple Windows-type bitmap files—you can't use GIF or JPEG files. The background file will display as the background, centered on the Setup screen. Don't use a bitmap larger than 640 × 480, as that's the resolution that Setup runs in.

And by the way, here's an important tip: Try out the bitmap and logo before using it for a user's system install. Setup puts a couple of big dialog boxes up that obscure most of the background, so if you actually want to pass along some information, then you'll have to be careful about where you place the info on the bitmap or logo; otherwise, the information won't be readable.

Create Directories and Copy Files

If you create a directory inside OEM with a one-letter name, like I386\$OEM$\E or I386\$OEM$\D, then Setup will copy any file (or directory) in that directory to the drive letter of the same name on the newly-installed computer. For example, suppose I want my computers to all have a directory on C: called Data, which will contain a file named basic.txt. Let's assume that I've got the I386 distribution share on a server, on its D: drive, so I've got the setup files in D:\I386. To ensure that every new system created from this share has a directory named C:\Data and containing the basic.txt file, all I need do is this:

♦ Create a directory named D:\I386\OEM\C.

♦ Create a directory inside *that* directory named Data –D:\I386\OEM\C\Data.

♦ Place the basic.txt file inside the D:\I386\OEM\C\Data directory.

OEM also has a few "magic" directory names that you can exploit to place files into the system folders. First, there's the $$ directory. Anything in I386\$OEM$\$$ goes to winnt. What's the value of that? Well, when you're writing an installation script, you might not know beforehand which drive winnt will go on. Rather than having to create a directory named I386\$OEM$\C\winnt and then accidentally try to use that to put files in winnt on a system that puts its operating system on the D: drive, putting files in I386\$OEM$\$$ will ensure that those files will end up in winnt on the drive that contains the operating system.

So, for example, if you liked the idea of including support information on your system, then recall that you store the support and branding information in a file named oeminfo.ini, which must sit in \winnt\system32. You could create an oeminfo.ini file and then place it in a distribution share at I386\$OEM$\$$\system32, and the file would then automatically get copied to the system32 directory of any newly-installed systems. You'd be ensuring that every new system gets the support information without requiring any extra work on your part.

Including Updated Drivers

Windows 2000 includes a pretty large collection of drivers in its initial offering. But the 2000 code "went gold" back in December of 1999, and as time goes on, it'll be more and more likely that either you have a piece of hardware that didn't exist at the time of 2000's birth (and therefore 2000 lacks a driver for it), or the hardware's manufacturer has created a newer and better driver. You can automate the process of telling 2000 to use a new or updated driver, using the OEMPnPDrivers command.

Create the directories for new or updated drivers in OEM, then specify them in OEMPnP-DriversPath. For example, suppose I've got some new video and audio drivers, and I place the new video drivers into a directory named I386\$OEM$\$1\newvid. Then I put the new audio drivers in I386\$OEM$\$1\newaud. I can then tell Setup to look for them by adding this line to the [Unattended] section of my setup script:

```
OEMPnPDriversPath="newvid; newaud"
```

Notice that we describe directories by their path below OEM. Don't include "I386\OEM" in the path.

WARNING *Note that you should keep the list of directories to 40 or fewer characters. This is a limitation of OEM-PnPDriversPath. But don't make them single-character directory names, or Setup will try to create files on drive C:, D:, E:, etc., on the target machine!*

Tell Setup to Run Commands with cmdlines.txt

Once your system is set up, you might want to install some applications beyond the basic operating system, or you might want to delete some little-used files that Setup leaves behind, or you might want to accomplish any number of other small tasks. You can do that with a file named cmdlines.txt, which must be located in the OEM directory.

cmdlines.txt is just a list of command-line commands that you want Setup to execute. That may sound to you as if I'm suggesting that cmdlines.txt is an old DOS-style batch file, but it isn't. For some reason, it needs a specific format. The first line must be [Commands] on a line all by itself. Then, you list the commands that you want Setup to run—but you must surround the commands with double quotes. For example, consider this example cmdlines.txt file:

```
[Commands]
"msiexec /i \\server\share\somefile.msi"
"regedit /s myhacks.reg"
```

As you see, the first line is just [Commands]. Then, the second line is the first command that you want Setup to run. If you've never heard of MSIEXEC, then let me introduce you—it's a command that you'll use a lot when building `cmdlines.txt` files. You see, under Windows 2000, you install an application using a new service called the Windows Installer service. Instead of installing programs with a traditional `setup.exe` program, you install programs by handing a "package" to the Installer. This package is the collection of files that you need to run the program, as well as a set of instructions about how to install the program—"this file goes here, this icon goes on the Start menu, create these Registry entries"—and the Installer looks at the instruction file (which, by convention, has the extension `.msi`) and carries out its instructions. (You'll learn more about this in the chapter on software deployment; I'm just giving you the barest of sketches about how it works here.)

Normally you deploy an MSI-type package using Active Directory, as you'll learn a bit later in this book. But if you want to install an application from the command line, then you'll use a new Windows 2000 program called `msiexec.exe`. The /i option says to install the program from its MSI, silently. Again, you'll learn more about where you get MSI files from a bit later in the book—I just thought that an `msiexec /i` example would be useful.

TIP *In order to make this work,* `msiexec.exe` *must be in the* `$OEM$` *directory; copy it from a functioning Windows 2000 installation.*

The second command may be familiar to NT 4 experts. Sometimes the easiest way to set up NT or 2000 to work *exactly* the way you want is to apply a bunch of Registry hacks. The REGEDIT command offers a pretty neat command-line way to modify the Registry.

For example, I find the AutoRun feature of CD-ROMs *really* annoying. I don't want 2000 offering to install every time I pop the 2000 CD into a drive just to get a file or two. Now, I *could* shut off AutoRun by opening up a Registry Editor, navigating down to `HKEY_LOCAL_MACHINE\SYSTEM\ CurrentControlSet\Services\Cdrom`, and then editing the entry labeled AutoRun, setting its value to 0. But I don't want to hand-edit the Registry—and that's where REGEDIT comes to the rescue. Just create a four-line ASCII file (call it `CDFix.reg`) with these contents:

```
REGEDIT4

[HKEY_LOCAL_MACHINE\SYSTEM\CurrentControlSet\Services\Cdrom]
"AutoRun"=dword:00000000
```

Note the blank line between "REGEDIT4" and "[HKEY "; you need that. Now open up a command line and tell REGEDIT to apply this change by typing **regedit /s cdfix.reg**; the /s means "be Silent, Regedit!" and so you won't get a message. But reboot your NT machine and you'll find that AutoRun is now disabled. Notice how what I could call the REGEDIT "command language" works: the first line is REGEDIT4, then a blank line, then you indicate what key you want to work with, in brackets, and then the value entry. And that line starting with [HKEY_LOCAL_MACHINE is just one line when typed, no matter how long. You can put a whole bunch of changes into a single file, or create different `.reg` files and apply them sequentially.

As with `msiexec.exe`, be sure to put `regedit.exe` in the `$OEM$` folder, or this won't work. And you may be wondering, how did I figure out how to create a file in "REGEDIT format?" Simple. I just highlighted a key that I wanted to apply and then exported it. The exported file turned out to be a simple ASCII format—and an import showed that REGEDIT imports files in the same format as it exports.

Using CMDLINES.TXT *to Install the Latest Hotfixes*

Here's an even more valuable use for `cmdlines.txt`: preinstalling hotfixes. Hotfixes are files that fix some critical problem in Windows 2000, things that will eventually make their way into the next service pack but that Microsoft felt were important enough that they couldn't wait for the next service pack. You can find them by going to `www.microsoft.com/security` and then clicking the Security Bulletins link. Now, that works as of the time that I am writing this, but Microsoft is fond of rearranging their Web site, so if that doesn't work, then just do a search for "security bulletins" on their site and you'll find them. For step 1, download them and collect them into the `$OEM$` directory. They'll have names like `q123456_w2k_sp3_x86_en.exe`, which tells you

◆ that you can find out about what this fixes in Knowledge Base article Q123456,

◆ that you apply this to Windows 2000 (w2k),

◆ that it is intended for inclusion in Service Pack 3,

◆ that it's meant for the Pentium (x86) version of Windows 2000, rather than some other architecture like an Itanium, and

◆ that it works on the version of the operating system that is localized for English.

If you've ever applied a hotfix, then you know that you just run it as a program, which is nice and simple. But what's *not* so simple is that every time you install a hotfix, the stupid hotfix insists that you reboot the computer. Let's see, 16 hotfixes in the post-SP2 world… figure a minute a reboot… I've only got 1000 computers to do this on. Naaah. But there's good news. Fortunately, most hotfixes written since mid-2000 have two options, –m and –z, that tell the hotfixes to install quietly and not to force a reboot. But apply a bunch of hotfixes, and you'll see that they can conflict with one another unless you install them in just the right order. That's where Microsoft's `qchain.exe` comes in. You can probably find it by searching the Knowledge Base for article Q296861, which will provide a link to download it. Use `qchain` after you've installed a whole bunch of hotfixes with the –m and –z options but before rebooting, and `qchain` will rearrange all of the hotfixes so that they do not conflict with one another.

Make sure that all of the hotfixes and `qchain.exe` are in the `$OEM$` directory. Then modify `cmdlines.txt` to invoke each of the hotfixes with the –m –z options, and finally run `qchain.exe`. A simplified `cmdlines.txt` with four imaginary hotfixes—I'll spare you the 16-liner that I actually use—might look like this:

```
[Commands]
"msiexec /i \\server\share\somefile.msi"
"regedit /s myhacks.reg"
"q302755_w2k_sp3_x86_en.exe -m -z"
"q303984_w2k_sp3_x86_en.exe -m -z"
"q301625_w2k_sp3_x86_en.exe -m -z"
"qchain c:\logfile.txt"
```

Notice, as we've said before, that you must surround the commands in quotes.

Pretty nifty, eh? I used to roll out test machines without hotfixes mostly because I felt that it took too much time, but too many of those machines fell prey to the Worm of the Week. Now I'm (relatively) secure from the first power-up.

I hope I've convinced you that OEM holds some pretty powerful capabilities. If you use it and the OEMPreinstall=Yes command, then you can extend the power of an unattended installation pretty far.

GUIRunOnce

I haven't included this section in my example scripts yet, but I should mention that you can include a section, [GUIRunOnce], in a setup script. It tells 2000 to finish installing and then to reboot. Once 2000 reboots, it then lets you log in. Once you've logged in, Setup runs the commands in GUIRunOnce—typically these are setup commands for applications. They run under whatever user account you logged in as, so if you're installing something that requires Administrator-level privileges, then be sure to log in with a powerful-enough account.

Items in the [GUIRunOnce] section must be surrounded by quotes. One example that I've seen of GUIRunOnce's power is the automatic starting and running of DCPROMO, the program that creates domain controllers. You'll learn more about DCPROMO in Chapter 8.

So you can see that you can do pretty neat things with scripts and the OEMPreinstall features. But let me not oversell this; let's remember that there's still that chicken-and-egg problem of "how do I get on the network to get to the network share in the first place?" We'll solve that problem next, with Remote Installation Services, or RIS.

Installing Windows 2000 with Remote Installation Services

Well, by now, you've probably tried shoving the CD-ROM into some computer's drive and installed Windows 2000. You may well have had some luck at it and found that after a bit of twiddling, you could make it work quite well. "Cool," you might have thought, "Installing Windows 2000 will be a snap."

But then, you probably realized that you'd have to do it for *several hundred machines*. Let's see now, doing the exact same set of twiddling several hundred times would take... well, more patience and time than many of us have. It would be nice to be able to spend a fair amount of time on just one computer, getting it just right, and then to "photocopy" that configuration onto dozens or hundreds of other computers.

And for years, many of us did just that. Back when I worked in training labs teaching Windows 3 running atop DOS 5, it was a simple matter to just boot up a workstation with a floppy containing the Novell client software, format the workstation's C: drive, and then XCOPY an entire drive image from a Novell shared volume onto the workstation. The whole process was completely automated once I got it started, and took no more than about 20 minutes.

Later on, with the advent of bigger operating systems like Windows 95, drive copier programs like Ghost and Drive Image Pro came out. These drive copiers didn't care what files were on a computer; they'd just copy a physical hard disk or partitions from that hard disk to a network folder for you. Then you could set up a new computer to look just like the prototypic computer by booting the new computer from a floppy and then pulling down the Ghost or Ghost-like (would that be "Ghostly"?) image.

That worked fine for Windows, but not for NT, as NT is secure, and so each computer with NT installed on it has long and machine-specific strings of numbers embedded in it, numbers called security IDs, or SIDs. Cloning one machine's NT image onto thousands of machines would lead to thousands of machines with identical SIDs. While that might not *sound* terrible, it could have some very bizarre side effects.

For example, suppose you start up a new PC with a cloned copy of NT Workstation or Windows 2000 Professional on it, logging in the first time as the default administrator. The first order of business is then to create a local user account for yourself. But inside NT, that account would get an SID. As this is the first account created besides the built-in Administrator and Guest accounts, that account's SID will be the first available in the range of SIDs on this machine.

Now imagine that Janice down the hall, who has a machine containing the exact same cloned image on her system, also logs in to her new machine as its default administrator and creates herself an account. It'll have a different name than your account—but that won't matter. NT doesn't really care what your name is; it cares what your SID is. And what value SID does Janice have? Well, as it's the first created account, you guessed it—her account now has the same SID as yours.

What does that mean? Well, suppose you made your local account an Administrator account. That means that when she's logged in to her own machine with her own account, she can use Windows 2000's remote control tools to do administrator-like things to your system over the network. That's not a good thing, unless you and Janice are really good buddies.

As a result, disk-cloning vendors have come up with "SID scrambler" programs. You copy the cloned image onto a new machine and then run the SID scrambler. It creates a unique set of SIDs on the newly cloned machine and all should be well. Microsoft, however, says that the SID scramblers from the two big players, Symantec's Ghost and PowerQuest's Drive Image Pro, won't do the whole job. I honestly don't know if this true or if it's just Microsoft... well, being Microsoft. In any case, now Microsoft has a method for rolling out a single workstation image to dozens, hundreds, or thousands of machines while simultaneously ensuring that each machine has a unique SID. It's a tool called the Remote Installation Services (RIS). In this section, you'll learn how to set it up and how to get those images out to all of those PCs hungering for an operating system.

RIS solves the other big rollout problem, as well: the "how do I get a computer with nothing on its hard disk connected to the network so that I can do a network-based install?" problem. You'll see how to do that in this section, but before I go further, let me offer this warning:

WARNING *I've included RIS in this chapter because it's a rollout and deployment tool, but RIS won't work unless you have an Active Directory infrastructure in place, as well as have some knowledge of another infrastructure tool called the Dynamic Host Configuration Protocol (DHCP), and are also comfortable with file and directory permissions on NT/2000 disk drives. If any of that sounds a bit scary, then just skip this RIS section and go on to the Sysprep section. Then, once you've gotten through the TCP/IP and Active Directory chapters, come revisit this section.*

RIS Overview

RIS lets you designate a server or a set of servers as *RIS servers*. A RIS server contains the files necessary to install Windows 2000 onto a computer from across the network. RIS can deliver an operating system to a waiting PC in one of three formats:

Simple I386-based Installation   In this simplest form, RIS is just a place to store the Windows 2000 installation files. How is it different from just putting I386 onto a directory on any old file server and then sharing that directory? Not very much except in one important way: it solves the "how do I get to the network in the first place?" problem. You can go to the PC that you intend to put Windows 2000 on and boot it with just one floppy, and you'll be off and running, no messing around with the DOS Client for Networks or the like. Of course, once this installation starts up, you must sit at the computer and answer all of Setup's questions, baby-sitting the computer while Setup runs.

Scripted *I386* Install This installation is like the preceding situation, with the added benefit of unattended installation. You just go out to the target PC, boot the floppy, and away it goes. These first two options are called *CD image format* images.

Complete System Image with Minimal Setup Interaction This option is really the more interesting, although you can only do it when deploying Windows 2000 *Professional*—you can't do this with Server. In this situation, you build an entire prototypical machine, complete with applications, then use RIS to create an image of that machine on a RIS server. You then boot the target PC with a RIS-built floppy again, and RIS transfers the entire disk image, complete with operating system and applications, to the target PC. It's not entirely hands-off, however, as it needs a bit of machine-specific customization: you need to punch in a unique machine name, for example. This kind of image is called a *RIPrep image format* image.

RIS Limitations

Before getting too excited about RIS—it's nice, but the Ghost guys needn't worry about being put out of business—let's look at what it *can't* do.

RIS CLIENTS MUST HAVE PARTICULAR PCI NETWORK CARDS; MOST LAPTOPS WON'T WORK

I'll cover this later, but you can only get a RIS system image onto a computer that knows how to ask for one, and the only way that a system knows how to ask is if the system supports something called the Preboot Execution Environment (PXE) protocol, version 0.99C or later. If you've seen computers that can be "network managed," then there's a good chance that the computer has PXE support in its BIOS. In addition to PXE support, you'll need a NIC that works with PXE. No ISA NIC that I know of supports PXE, and I've only heard rumor of PCMCIA/PC Card/CardBus laptop NICs that support PXE. Most PXE-compatible NICs are PCI cards. Laptops aren't completely shut out, as some laptops now ship with an integrated NIC built to the "mini PCI" specification—I've seen some IBM ThinkPads that fit in this category. Such a laptop might be RIS-compatible. (And believe me, RIS's convenience is sufficiently great that PXE/mini-PCI compliance will be a "must-have" characteristic of all of my future laptops!)

What if your computer doesn't support PXE? RIS comes with a program called `RBFG.exe`, the RIS Boot Floppy Generator. It's a program that lets your computer support PXE, so long as your computer has one of the particular 25 NICs that `RBFG.exe` supports. It's annoying that RIS doesn't really support pre–year 2000 laptops and most pre-1998 desktops, but truthfully that's Windows 2000's story from start to finish—it can solve many of your existing problems, so long as you don't mind replacing most of your hardware and software.

RIS CAN ONLY IMAGE THE C: DRIVE

When you build a prototype computer whose image you will then propagate all over the enterprise, you'd better build a computer with just one hard-disk partition C:. RIS will merely copy the C: drive and whatever's on it.

RIS HAS A FAIRLY SPARSE ADMINISTRATIVE UI

While RIS doesn't require a *lot* of administration, there are few tasks that you'll do frequently, and RIS doesn't provide a very good way to do them. For example, if you had a RIS server that contained many system images, but you didn't want every user to see every possible image (which is very likely—odds are that you'd have one image for the accounting folks, another for the programmers, and so on), then the only way to restrict the choice of images that a user sees is through NTFS permissions rather than via some simple administrative interface.

Steps to Making RIS Work

The first time you set up a RIS server, it can seem a bit complicated if you're not ready for it, as RIS is a bit different from other Windows 2000 services. What I'm referring to is that to install most Windows 2000 network services, like IIS or WINS, you just install them on a server, reboot the server, and you're done. Setting up RIS on a server, however, requires fiddling a bit with Active Directory.

TIP *Before you can use RIS, you must have a Windows 2000–based domain running with an Active Directory domain controller. You also need a functioning DNS server integrated with the Windows 2000 domain—that is, a DNS server that supports RFC 2782 SRV records and RFC 2136 dynamic updates, as described in Chapter 8.*

WARNING *In order to explain how to set up RIS, I'll need to assume that you already know what a DHCP server is. If, however, you have not worked with previous versions of NT and so probably don't know DHCP, then don't worry about it—just skip this section until you've learned about TCP/IP, DHCP, and Active Directory in the next few chapters, then return to this section. (And in that case, please accept my apologies for making you jump around the book.)*

To get a RIS server working, follow these steps:

1. Set up a Windows 2000 server and make it a member of a Windows 2000 domain. The server must have a fairly large NTFS drive available, and that drive can't be the boot drive or the drive containing the operating system.

2. Authorize the soon-to-be-RIS server in the Active Directory as a Dynamic Host Configuration Protocol (DHCP) server, even though it's *not* a DHCP server.

3. Add the Remote Installation Services service to the server and reboot it.

4. Run RISetup, the Remote Installation Setup Wizard, to prepare the large drive for receiving RIS images and to put an initial image on the drive—it's just a simple copy of I386.

5. At that point, the RIS server is ready. You can add new images to it with a wizard called RIPrep.

We'll examine each of these steps in the following pages.

Getting Ready for RIS

RIS's job is to let you take a PC with an empty hard disk, attach the PC to your enterprise network, put a RIS-created floppy disk into the PC's A: drive, and boot the PC. The small program on the floppy disk is just smart enough to get an IP address for the PC, then locate an Active Directory domain controller, and ask the Active Directory domain controller where to find a RIS server. Once the PC finds the RIS server, it can then start the process of pulling down a particular system image so that the PC becomes useful.

NECESSARY INFRASTRUCTURE

But Windows 2000 needs some infrastructure to make all of this work right. The PC gets an IP address from a DHCP server, so you'll need at least one DHCP server running in your enterprise to make RIS work. (In case you've never worked with an IP-based NT network before, DHCP's job is to automatically assign unique network addresses to each server and workstation on the network. TCP/IP *requires* that every machine have a unique IP address, or the network software just doesn't work.) Once it has an IP address, the PC finds an Active Directory server by looking it up in DNS—so you'll need a DNS server. And the PC can't query an Active Directory domain controller for the location of a RIS server unless you've got an Active Directory domain controller—so you'll need an Active Directory–based domain (as opposed to a bunch of Windows 2000 servers in a domain built out of NT 4 domain controllers). Of course, if you're running an Active Directory–based domain, then you've *got* to have DNS running, so the simplified list of things you'll need before RIS will work is an Active Directory–based domain and at least one DHCP server.

A DRIVE FOR SIS

Furthermore, the RIS server needs a partition to store the RIS images. For some reason, RIS will not store images on the boot partition—which is usually drive C:—or the system partition, which is the drive that contains \winnt and the other NT system files. I found this kind of frustrating the first time I went to set up RIS, as the server that I intended to put RIS on had only two drive letters and Windows 2000 installed on the D: drive. C: was the boot, D: the system, and so RIS wouldn't install. I reinstalled Windows 2000 on the C: drive, freeing up D:, and RIS worked fine. You can have other things on RIS's drive, like files of other types; you just can't have the system files on the drive. Remember that while RIS will make an image of whatever filesystem is on the original workstation, it must be placed onto an NTFS partition on the server.

While it's not entirely clear to me why RIS is allergic to system files, there's a very good reason why it wants a drive pretty much to itself. Imagine a RIS server that contained 20 system images—how much space would that need? Well, Windows 2000 Professional itself takes up about 450MB on a hard disk, so let's be generous and say that the applications added to the image only total 50MB, leading to a 500MB image; it's just easier to calculate this way. Ten half-gigabyte images totals 5 gigabytes. But now let's look more closely at those 10 images. The vast majority of the files in the images are identical: For example, each image contains a file named `Drivers.cab` that's nearly 50MB in size, and the file is exactly the same for each of the 10 images. That's a terrible waste of space—500MB to store 10 identical copies of a 50MB file!

RIS solves that problem with a service called the Single Instance Store, or SIS. SIS is a service called the SIS Space Groveler (is that a great service name, or what?) that runs in the background and searches a particular drive letter—for some reason, it's only built to attach itself to a single drive letter rather than system-wide—looking for duplicate files. It then frees up space by deleting the duplicate files, putting in their place a directory entry that makes it appear as if the duplicate is still in place. In actuality, however, the duplicate is no more than a sort of pointer to the complete copy of the file. Clearly a trick like this will require a bit of magic, and that magic comes from a combination of SIS and Windows 2000's version of NTFS—that dedicated-to-RIS drive must be an NTFS volume.

EXTENDING SIS: SIDE NOTES

It's a shame that SIS only loads as part of RIS; I could easily imagine many cases wherein recovering space from duplicate files could be beneficial, such as in the case of a server containing hundreds of users' home directories—there's likely to be *plenty* of duplication there.

Actually, if you're feeling a bit brave, then you actually *can* get SIS to run on other drives, according to Knowledge Base article Q226545. It says that SIS identifies which drives to do its magic on by looking for three things:

◆ First, the drive must be an NTFS drive.

◆ Second, the drive must contain a hidden folder in its root named SIS Common Store.

◆ Finally, that SIS Common Store folder must contain a file named MaxIndex.

I honestly have not tried this myself, but I pass along the information in case it's of help. So, for example, to apply SIS to any given file server, just install the RIS service on that system (even if you do not intend to make the server a RIS server), place a hidden folder named SIS Common Store in the root of whatever drive you want SIS to work on, and don't forget MaxIndex.

While I'm on the subject of advanced SIS maintenance, here's another tidbit from the Knowledge Base, article Q272149. You can, if you want to, tell SIS to ignore a particular directory in this way:

1. Start up a Registry-editing tool.

2. Navigate to the key named HKEY_LOCAL_MACHINE\SOFTWARE\Microsoft\Windows NT\ CurrentVersion\Groveler\ExcludedPaths.

3. Create a new value entry with any name that you like, of type REG_SZ.

4. In the data for that value entry, include the name of the directory without the drive letter.

For example, suppose I wanted SIS to ignore a directory named mystuff on a SIS volume. I'd just go to the key named above and create a new value entry. I could call that value entry NoMyStuff. I'd make it of type REG_SZ, and in the entry I would place the string "\mystuff." Then I'd either have to reboot to see the changes take effect, or I'd have to stop and start the SIS Space Groveler service.

WARNING   *Be aware, however, that I'm told that unless you back up this drive with a backup program that is Windows 2000–aware, then SIS drives aren't backed up properly. Sometimes the backup program thinks that it's backing up a file, but it actually just backs up SIS's pointer to a drive. Restoring that pointer without the file is usually not helpful.*

Authorizing RIS in Active Directory

Microsoft figured—probably rightly—that you wouldn't want just *anybody* putting a RIS server on the network. So before you can get the RIS service working on a server, that server must be authorized in the Active Directory. For some reason, however, you don't authorize it as a RIS server; you authorize it as a DHCP server.

To do that, find a DHCP server and log in to it with an account with administrative powers. Click Start/Programs/Administrative Tools/DHCP. Click Action on the menu bar, and you'll see the option Manage Authorized Servers, which is shown in Figure 4.11.

FIGURE 4.11

DHCP Action menu

Choose Manage Authorized Servers and you'll see the list of currently authorized DHCP servers like the one in Figure 4.12.

FIGURE 4.12

List of current authorized servers

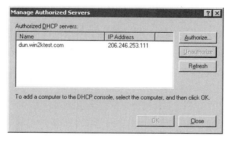

Click Authorize and you'll get a dialog box like the one in Figure 4.13, letting you punch in the IP address of the server that you're going to make into a RIS server.

FIGURE 4.13

Entering IP address of new RIS server

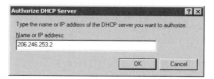

Click OK, and it'll confirm your choice, as Figure 4.14 shows.

FIGURE 4.14

Confirming the new server

NOTE *If you* don't *know the IP address of the soon-to-be RIS server, go over to that server and log in to it. Then open a command prompt (Start/Programs/Command Prompt), type* **ipconfig***, and press Enter. It will report the IP address; if you have several IP addresses, take the one in the section labeled Ethernet Adapter Local Area Connection rather than PPP Adapter.*

Now that Active Directory is ready for RIS, let's get RIS ready.

Installing RIS

Next, you'll put the RIS service on the server:

1. Log in to the server that you want to add RIS to, using an Administrator account, and open the Control Panel (Start/Settings/Control Panel).

2. Start the Add/Remove Programs applet.

3. Choose the Add/Remove Windows Components icon.

4. A wizard screen labeled Welcome to the Windows Components Wizard will appear; click Next and it will show you the optional server components, as you see in Figure 4.15.

FIGURE 4.15

Windows Components screen

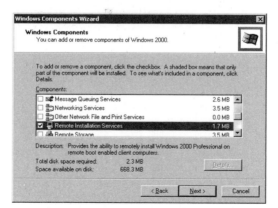

5. Scroll down and check the box labeled Remote Installation Services. Then click Next and Finish.

6. You'll be prompted to reboot, so reboot the server.

Running RISETUP

When installing most Windows 2000 services, you just choose the option in Windows Components, wait for the Control Panel to pull the new service off I386, reboot the computer, and it's up and running. RIS is a bit more work than that, however, as RIS must claim its drive and set up SIS. For good measure, RIS also creates a first image. That first image is the simplest one possible—it's just a copy of the I386 directory from the Windows 2000 Professional CD-ROM.

Log in to the would-be RIS server with an administrative account and run RISETUP (either from a command prompt or click Start/Run, fill in **risetup**, and press Enter) and the Remote Installation Services Setup Wizard starts. The initial screen is shown in Figure 4.16.

FIGURE 4.16

RISetup initial screen

Click Next and the wizard will quickly scan your drives looking for a likely place to keep RIS's files. In my case, it found drive F:. It wants to create a directory named RemoteInstall, as you can see in Figure 4.17.

FIGURE 4.17

Suggested location for RIS images

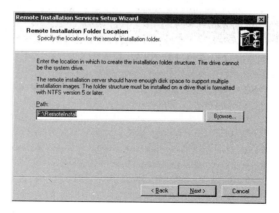

After you click Next, RISetup will ask you if you want the server to respond to requests from PCs for operating systems, as shown in Figure 4.18. Inasmuch as you don't have any useful images on the RIS server at the moment, tell the server not to respond to those requests.

FIGURE 4.18

Telling RIS to ignore requests until we're done configuring it

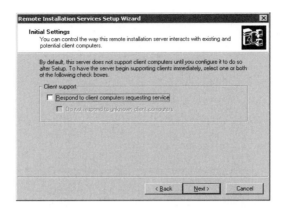

Click Next and, as you can see in Figure 4.19, RIS will ask where to find a Windows 2000 Professional CD-ROM.

FIGURE 4.19

Looking for a fresh copy of Windows 2000 Professional

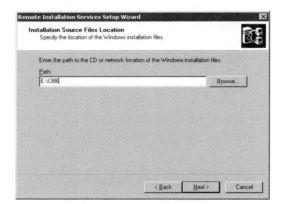

Now's a good time to pop the Windows 2000 Professional disc into your CD-ROM drive—more than likely you've *currently* got the Windows 2000 *Server* disc in there from when you installed RIS. RISetup usually isn't bright enough to know that the files are in I386, so it'll typically just suggest the drive letter of your CD-ROM. For example, if your CD-ROM drive is G:, it'll suggest that the Windows 2000 Professional files are at G: rather than G:\I386, so you'll probably have to help it out and tell it where to find the files. Alternatively, if you have Windows 2000 Professional's I386 directory on one of your hard disks, you can point RISetup there. Click Next and you'll get the screen you see in Figure 4.20.

Recall that a RIS server can have many images on it. Each image gets a folder within the Remote-Install folder. This first, simple I386 image needs a name too, and RISetup suggests just win2000.pro, which is probably fine for our needs. Click Next to continue and you'll see a screen in which you can describe the image, as shown in Figure 4.21.

FIGURE 4.20

Folder name for the simple I386 option

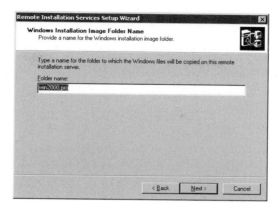

FIGURE 4.21

Describing the simple image

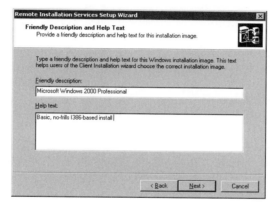

When someone plugs a new machine into the network and boots from the RIS-prepared boot floppy, he may be offered several choices of OS images to download. (After all, one of the things that RIS is supposed to offer is the ability to keep a bunch of images around for different uses.) This screen lets you add some descriptive text. Click Next and you'll get a summary "this-is-your-last-chance" screen like the one in Figure 4.22.

FIGURE 4.22

Checking on the settings

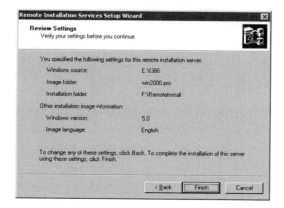

Click Finish and go away for a while. A screen like Figure 4.23 will appear.

FIGURE 4.23

Progress indication
screen

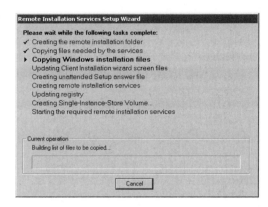

As you see from the screen, RISetup has a lot to do. It copies the I386 files over to its local folder, starts SIS, and does other housekeeping. Expect it to take 10 minutes or so at least.

Enabling RIS for Clients

Amazingly, after RISetup does its work, the RIS server does not reboot! But it's time to put the RIS server to work, or at least to respond to requests for I386 installs. Make sure you are logged in as a domain administrator at the RIS server, then click Start/Run, fill in DSA.MSC, and press Enter. If the RIS server happens to be a domain controller, then it's even easier—just click Start/Programs/ Administrative Tools/Active Directory Users and Computers. (Notice that you've got to start the DSA from Start/Run because for some reason Setup *installs* the Active Directory tools on all servers, but only puts entries for those tools on the Start/Programs menus of domain controllers.)

In the left pane of the window, you'll see an icon depicting several computers, intended to represent your domain. Open it (double-click or click the plus sign) and it'll open to some folders, including one named Computers. It's likely that your RIS server is there. Right-click the RIS computer's icon and choose Properties. You'll then see a properties page.

My RIS server is named D (it came after A, B, and C... and yes, some days I'm just not as creative as I would like to be), and there are several property tabs, one labeled Remote Install. Click that and you'll see a page like the one in Figure 4.24.

There's not much in the way of an administrative and management interface for RIS, just this page and a few tabs on the Advanced screen, which you'll see a bit later.

On this screen, there's not all that much to do except to turn it on. Check Respond to Client Computers Requesting Service, and it's ready to go!

Installing Windows 2000 Professional on a Workstation from the RIS Server

It's working; let's give it a try. The RIS server is up on the network and the Active Directory knows about it. Suppose I have a computer that I want to put Windows 2000 Professional on (call it the target computer); these are the steps.

FIGURE 4.24

FIGURE 4.24

Remote Install tab
of the properties
page for RIS server

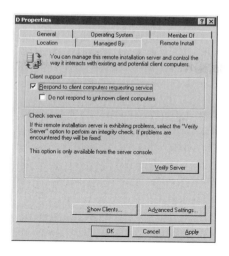

NOTE   *I know, you're wondering, "What's this stuff about 2000* Professional*? Let's do* Server*!" I'm getting there, but I'm going to do Professional first—and I promise, the reason for that will be clear once I get to the section on deploying Server with RIS.*

The target computer gets the attention of the RIS server through something called the Preboot Execution Environment protocol, abbreviated PXE and pronounced "pixie." Some computer vendors sell PCs with PXE in the BIOS. To connect a PXE-equipped PC to a RIS server, you don't even need a floppy disk; you just plug it into the network, turn it on, and you'll eventually get a prompt like "boot from the network y/n?" If you let it boot from the network, it'll first seek out a DHCP server, then find an Active Directory server with DNS, and kick off RIS—all the code for doing that is in the PC's BIOS ROM.

NOTE   *You may have to adjust your system's CMOS settings in order to tell it to try to boot from PXE rather than the hard disk, floppy, or CD-ROM. Exactly how you do that depends on your system. On my IBM T21 ThinkPad, I press F12 when I turn on the computer to tell it to choose to boot from the "Intel Boot Agent." I've seen Dells where you tell it to boot "from MBA." Basically, though, here's the approach: start up your system's BIOS setup routine. You'll usually—sorry for the weasel words, but this does vary from system to system, and not every system even allows you to do a PXE boot—see an option to arrange the boot order. On my T21, I get the five options for devices to boot from: the floppy, the hard disk, the CD-ROM, the Intel Boot Agent, and "Network Boot," which I haven't found a use for yet. I can then rearrange the boot order, so as to tell my system, "First try to boot from the Intel Boot Agent, and if that's not available then try the CD-ROM, and if that doesn't work then boot from the hard disk, and if that doesn't work, then boot from the floppy, and never try to boot from 'Network Boot.'"*

But your system needn't support PXE to do RIS, however. Microsoft includes a utility with RIS that will generate bootable floppy disks that replace the PXE BIOS for the PXE-deaf among us. It's called `RBFG.exe`, and you'll find it on any RIS server in the `\RemoteInstall\Admin\I386` directory. Run it and you'll see a screen like Figure 4.25.

FIGURE 4.25

Remote Boot Disk
Generator dialog box

Running it is pretty simple—just put a floppy into A: and click the Create Disk button. A great improvement over its older cousin, the Network Client Administrator, the Remote Boot Disk Generator doesn't require that you provide it with blank floppies. That's the good news.

The *bad* news is that this will only work if your computer has PCI expansion slots and one of the 25 supported PCI network cards. Fifteen years' experience with network software has made me conservative enough that almost all of my NICs are made by 3Com—not because I think 3Com makes a better card, but because I don't want to have to search after drivers—and so RBFG supports all of my machines. But that might not be the case for all of your systems.

Actually, let me take that back. Not *all* of my systems will work with an RBFG floppy—my laptops won't. Laptops don't have PCI slots in them (unless they're in some kind of docking station), so if your laptop connects to a network with a PC Card or CardBus slot (as 99.9 percent of them do), then you won't be able to use RIS to get Professional on your system, sadly. Thankfully, a growing number of brand-new (late model year 2000) laptops have integrated NICs that use a variation on PCI called the "mini-PCI" specification. (That's why I bought the T21.) Some of those also have PXE in their BIOSes and so will work with RIS.

But what about the fact that new network cards appear all of the time? It's not unreasonable at all to suggest that a year after Windows 2000's release you might find yourself trying to install Professional on a system with a brand-spanking-new network card that RBFG simply doesn't know how to handle. How do you introduce RBFG to a new set of drivers?

Unfortunately, you can't. Microsoft has said that they'll update RBFG.exe regularly and perhaps distribute it over the Web, and it could be that they will—but we'll see. (As I write this, 2000's been out for almost a year and we haven't seen an update.) But let me stress that you may never need a PXE boot disk if you're buying new computers. Any computer with a PXE BIOS and an integrated NIC can use RIS without any floppies at all—these computers have been *designed* to support RIS, so to speak, and so won't need a floppy. As time goes on, it's reasonable to hope that more and more computers will be "net-bootable."

I have also found that several vendors now offer PCI-based Ethernet NICs with PXE ROMs right on the NICs. I have personally installed an Intel PRO/100+ Management Adapter into an old (circa 1998) APM system and successfully enabled it thereby to PXE boot. I've also used the 3Com model 9C905C-TX-M, a modified version of their standard 100BaseT NIC that contains what 3Com calls the Integrated Managed PC Boot Agent, a fancy name for a ROM. Both cards were reasonably priced and were real godsends for me, as they extended the life of a bunch of 400MHz systems. (I say "extended" because I'm never buying a system again that doesn't do PXE boots—RIS is just too convenient!)

In any case, if you generate a PXE boot disk, stick it into the target machine and boot the machine. You'll see a screen with something like the following text:

```
Windows 2000 Remote Installation Boot Floppy
  Copyright 1999 Lanworks Technologies Co. a subsidary of 3Com Corporation
All rights reserved.
3Com 3C90XB / 3C90XC EtherLink PC
Node: 00105AE2859F
DHCP...
TFTP................
Press F12 for network service boot
```

Press F12, and a text screen appears that says:

```
Welcome to the Client Installation wizard. This wizard helps you quickly and easily
set up a new operating system on your computer. You can also use this wizard to
keep your computer up-to-date and to troubleshoot computer hardware problems.
In the wizard, you are asked to use a valid user name, password, and domain name to
log in to the network. If you do not have this information, contact your network
administrator before continuing.
Press Enter to continue
```

You are looking here at some client software downloaded from the RIS server called the Client Install Wizard. Look back to the first screen and notice the TFTP with all the periods after it—that was the Trivial File Transfer Protocol transferring a very simple text-based operating system to your computer.

TIP *But what if you don't get a response from PXE? If your system just searches and searches for DHCP but gets no response, then check your network switches. I once worked at a site where we couldn't get a PXE boot to work to save our lives. Then someone noticed that the Ethernet switches had a feature called "minimal spanning tree" enabled. Apparently it filtered or slowed down the DHCPDISCOVER broadcasts that the workstation did to find a DHCP server, and so the workstation never got an IP address from DHCP. So check your network infrastructure before you assume that a RIS client has bad hardware. And if it still doesn't work, then think about putting a network packet analyzer on the network segment so that you can watch the DHCP/TFTP process. Also check the NIC. I had one RIS server that worked perfectly for 90 percent of my workstations, but 10 percent just plain couldn't see it. The problem? It had a 10-megabit NIC and they had a 100-megabit NIC. Why that should trouble some 100Mb NICs and not others is a mystery to me, but you might want to be careful about matching 100Mb client NICs with 100Mb NICs on RIS servers.*

What's kind of interesting about this initial RIS setup screen is that the introductory screen, and all of the other text screens that you'll see from the Client Install Wizard, are built on a slightly modified version of HTML. You can see the "source code" for that first screen by looking on the RIS server in \RemoteInstall\OSChooser\English directory and examining the file named welcome.osc. It looks like the following:

```
<OSCML>
<META KEY=ENTER HREF="LOGIN">
```

```
<META KEY=F3 ACTION="REBOOT">
<META KEY=ESC HREF="LOGIN">
<META KEY=F1 HREF="LOGIN">
<TITLE>  Client Installation Wizard
    Welcome</TITLE>
<FOOTER>  [ENTER] continue </FOOTER>
<BODY left=5 right=75>
<BR>
<BR>
<BR>
Welcome to the Client Installation wizard. This wizard helps you quickly and easily
set up a new operating system on your computer. You can also use this wizard to
keep your computer up-to-date and to troubleshoot computer hardware problems.
<BR>
<BR>
In the wizard, you are asked to use a valid user name, password, and domain name to
log in to the network. If you do not have this information, contact your network
administrator before continuing.
</BODY>
</OSCML>
```

If you've got any familiarity with HTML, then understanding this is simple—things surrounded by angle brackets <> are *tags*, commands to the computer. They're often in pairs like right and left parentheses—<oscml> starts the "program," </oscml> ends it. That forward slash (/) indicates that it's the end of a command—for example, <TITLE> Client Installation Wizard</TITLE> indicates that there's a command, <TITLE> (which, as you can guess, puts a title in the screen), then there's the text that's supposed to go into the title, and then </TITLE>, which says, "That's the end of the title text." Again, they're like left and right parentheses. The <META KEY> commands tell the wizard what to do when you press particular keys. <META KEY=ENTER HREF="LOGIN"> means, "When the user presses the Enter key, run the program login.osc." <META KEY=F3 ACTION="REBOOT"> means that if the user presses the F3 key, then just reboot the system.

My intent here isn't to document the entire programming language—Microsoft hasn't completely documented it yet, to my knowledge—but to point out that you could *easily* change the generic welcome text to something customized to your particular company.

Anyway, once you press Enter, you're prompted for a username, password, and domain. The account that you log in with must have the ability to create new computer accounts. You'll next be advised that the process will delete any data on the existing hard disk:

```
The following settings will be applied to this computer installation.
Verify these settings before continuing.
Computer account: ADMINMARK1
Global Unique ID: 00000000000000000000000105AE2859F
Server supporting this computer: D
To begin Setup, press Enter. If you are using the Remote Installation Services boot
floppy, remove the floppy diskette from the drive and press Enter to continue.
```

Here, the RIS client software has chosen a name for the computer, ADMINMARK1, that it constructed by taking my login name—ADMINMARK was the account I used at the time—and adding a number to it. The Global Unique ID, or GUID (pronounced "gwid"), is just an ID number that RIS assigned to that computer. PXE-capable machines all have a GUID built right into them, but machines using RIS boot floppies get a GUID constructed for them consisting of 20 hex zeros followed by their NIC's MAC address. Finally, the Client Install Wizard tells you the name of the RIS server that it's getting its image from. Once you press Enter to confirm, pop the floppy out of the A: drive and walk away for a half hour or so. When you return, Windows 2000 Professional will be installed completely hands-off on the machine.

RIS sets the system up like so:

◆ The new machine joins the RIS server's domain.

◆ RIS repartitions the machine's hard disk into just one large partition and formats that partition as NTFS, no matter how the drive was previously partitioned.

◆ The new Windows 2000 Professional system has all of the settings you'd find in a typical install.

Want to change any of that? Then you'll need to create some system images.

Creating a 2000 Professional System Image with RIPrep

Even doing a no-frills installation on a new system with RIS is pretty nice. But it would be nicer to provide not only a vanilla operating system but perhaps a few settings and certainly an application or two—now, *that* would make the Ghost guys sweat! (But not sweat all *that* much, as you'll see. Ghost is still better than RIS. But Ghost costs money, and RIS comes free with Windows 2000.) You can do such a thing, creating what's called a *RIPrep image format* image. Here's how you do it:

1. Set up a prototypical Windows 2000 Professional system as you'd like it. (You can't do this with Server, to my knowledge.) Make sure that all of the code and data are on drive C:—no other drives will be copied by RIS.

2. Run the Remote Installation Preparation Wizard (RIPrep), which strips the SIDs off the prototypical machine.

3. Once the image is on the RIS server, it's available to new systems for installation.

For my example, I've installed Office 2000 onto a Windows 2000 Professional workstation. To create the RIPrep image, I log in to that prototypical machine with a domain administrator account. I then open up My Network Places and navigate over to my RIS server, the machine named D. RIS creates a share called REMINST on every RIS server. I open REMINST, then I open up the folder inside labeled Admin, and then I open the folder inside that labeled I386. Inside is a file named riprep.exe. I double-click it and see the opening screen, as shown in Figure 4.26. Click Next to see the screen shown in Figure 4.27.

You can send the resulting image to any RIS server; I'll choose the one I've been working with, the server named D, and click Next, which leads to the screen in Figure 4.28.

FIGURE 4.26

Opening screen of RIPrep

FIGURE 4.27

Choosing the destination RIS server

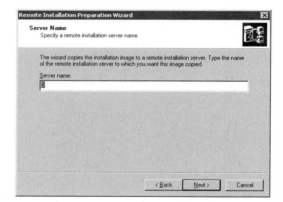

FIGURE 4.28

Naming the new folder

As with the CD image that RISetup insisted upon, this new image will need a folder name. Once I name the folder and click Next, a screen in which I add a description appears, as shown in Figure 4.29.

Finally, in the next two screens (Figures 4.30 and 4.31), I confirm that I want RIPrep to actually do the work.

FIGURE 4.29

Describing the new folder

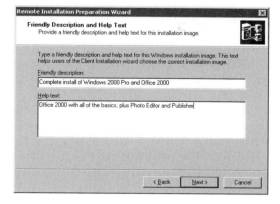

FIGURE 4.30

Confirming my choices

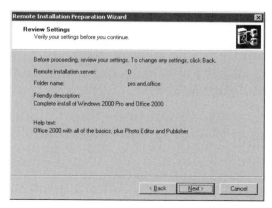

FIGURE 4.31

RIPrep finishes with informational messages

Reconfiguring the Prototype

After transferring the system image to the RIS server, you're directed to reboot the prototype. You'll then see something odd—it looks as if the prototype is running Windows 2000 Setup all over again! In order to make the prototype's image usable to RIS, RIPrep scrubs all of the user-specific settings and SIDs off the machine. Once you reboot, your system runs a kind of "mini-setup" to restore that information. Once the system reboots, you'll be prompted to do the following:

◆ Agree to the license agreement.

◆ Choose a keyboard and localization.

◆ Fill in a username and organization.

◆ Specify a computer name and password for the default Administrator account.

◆ Pick a time zone.

◆ Decide whether to do typical or custom network settings.

◆ Join either a workgroup or domain.

The mini-setup doesn't take nearly as long as Setup did, however, as it's not necessary to run Plug and Play.

Delivering a RIPrep Image to a Target PC

Now how do you deliver that operating-system-with-applications image to a target PC? In exactly the same way that you got the first one onto a target PC. Either press F12 when the PXE ROM tells you to or boot from an RBFG-generated floppy.

NOTE   *You do not need to build a separate RBFG-generated floppy for each system. You can build just one and carry it with you, using it to start as many different RIS image transfers as you'd like. Or, as you've already read, your newer systems may already have PXE boot abilities in their BIOS, and you therefore don't need a floppy to get a RIS install started.*

Now that you've got more than one image on your server, the Client Installation Wizard will offer you one more screen. After you log in, it'll list the available images and their descriptions, allowing you to choose one. Then, as before, it'll remind you that it's about to destroy any data on the hard disk and, from there, all you need do is to pop that RBFG floppy out of the floppy drive, walk away, and come back in a half hour—the entire install is hands-off.

WARNING   *Once again, don't take the "this will zap the hard disk" warning lightly. If (for example) your RIPrep image is based on a system with a 1500MB C: drive formatted as FAT32, then RIS will repartition and reformat the C: drive of the target PC to 1500MB and FAT32 no matter how the drive was partitioned on the target PC before. RIS will leave any remaining space unpartitioned.*

Enabling Users to Start RIS Transfers

The idea, then, with RIS is this: Joe comes into your office and tells you that his computer's hosed and would you reinstall his operating systems and applications when you get a chance? You reply that you've got an even better idea and hand him an RBFG floppy. You tell him to boot it, press F12 when prompted, then log in to the Client Installation Wizard and choose the Standard Productivity Desktop option, an image that you've built with all of the company's standard desktop software— Office, Palm's HotSync software, and Lotus Organizer.

Now, if Joe goes back and tries this, he'll see an error message like this:

```
The user Joe currently logged in to this computer does not have the permissions
needed to create a computer account or modify the computer account NEWPC (NEWPC$)
within the domain apex.com.
This error may also indicate that the server D supporting this client cannot
contact the directory service to perform the operation.
Restart this computer and try again. If the problem persists, contact your network
administrator for assistance.
```

What's going on here is that, in the process of installing the RIS image on Joe's machine, RIS must also create a *machine account*—remember, in Windows 2000 domains, machines have accounts just as people do—and not just any old user can create machine accounts. By the way, he also has to be able to delete machine accounts, as there's probably already a machine account floating around that has the same name as the one he's about to create, as well as a few other machine permissions.

You *could* make him a member of the Account Operators group for just a day so that he could do the install, but that's an awful lot of power to give a user just so he can kick off a RIS image transfer. So instead, let's create an altogether new group called Installers, which will have the power to create and delete machine accounts but nothing else. Now, creating the Installers group will be a bit of a lengthy procedure, but you'll only have to do it once. Once you have the Installers group defined, you can then just simply add any user to that group before giving him an RBFG floppy to reinstall his system. (And for safety's sake, you can remove him the next day, after he's got his system back up and running.)

NOTE *This is a neat example of something that you're going to learn in an upcoming chapter about 2000. The Active Directory part of 2000 lets you create groups of administrators with sets of powers that you can control very finely. It's part of a process called* delegation, *and we'll take it up in detail in the Active Directory chapter.*

Creating the Installers Group

You'll find creating the Installers group easiest while sitting at a domain controller:

1. Log in using an account with domain administrator rights and then start the Directory Service Administrator DSA.MSC by clicking Start/Programs/Administrative Tools/Active Directory Users and Computers. In the left pane, you'll see an icon representing your domain with a plus sign next to it; click the plus sign to expand the domain.

2. Next, create the Installers group. Right-click the Users folder and choose New/Group.

3. That raises a dialog box called Create New Object–(Group). In the field Name of New Group, fill in **Installers**. This will create a global group named Installers, which is what we want, so click OK and the dialog will close.

4. Back in the DSA's menu, click View/Advanced Features. That will show the Security tab on the properties page, which will be essential to give Installers the permissions that it needs.

5. Next, we're going to give some domain-wide permissions to the Installers group, so right-click the domain's icon and choose Properties. You'll get a dialog box named *Domain Name* Properties.

6. Click the Security tab in the properties page. Installers doesn't currently have any permissions, so we'll need to add a record for them. Click the Add button and you'll now see a dialog named Select Users, Computers or Groups.

7. Click the Installers group, click Add, and then click OK to dismiss the dialog box.

8. Back in the *Domain Name* properties page, find Installers in the Name list box and click it, then click the Advanced button.

9. You'll see a dialog box labeled Access Control Settings for *Domain Name*. Again, locate Installers—this part of the operating system isn't intended for regular old users, so the UI's a bit convoluted here—to indicate the Installers record that you created. It'll currently have some very basic permission like Read or the like. Click the View/Edit button.

10. Now you'll see a dialog named Permission Entry for *Domain Name*. Scroll down in the list box labeled Permissions to find the Create Computer Objects permission. You'll see two columns of check boxes, one labeled Allow and the other Deny. Check the Allow box and do the same for the next permission, Delete Computer Objects. In the list box labeled Apply To, choose This Object and All Child Objects. What you're doing here is giving Installers the right to create and destroy new objects in the directory, but *only* computer objects—machine accounts. Click OK to clear the Permission Entry for *Domain Name* dialog box.

11. That permission made the folders accept the new machine objects. But once created, Installers have no control over the machine accounts themselves, so we'll add another permission record to give Installers complete control over machine accounts. From the Access Control Settings for *Domain Name* dialog box, click Add, choose Installers, and click OK. The Permission Entry for *Domain Name* dialog box then appears.

12. Click the Apply Onto drop-down list box and choose Computer Objects. Check the Allow box next to the Full Control permission. Click OK and Windows 2000 will return you to the Access Control Settings for *Domain Name* dialog box.

13. Scroll down in the Permission Entries list box and you'll see that there is now a new entry for Installers, a "create/delete" permission—that's what you just created—as well as a "full control" record for "machine objects."

14. Click OK to dismiss the Access Control Settings For dialog box.

15. Click OK to dismiss the *Domain Name* properties page.

Now that that's done, you can put Joe into the Installers group:

1. Open the Users folder and locate the Installers group.

2. Right-click Installers and choose Properties.

3. Click the Members tab.

4. Click the Add button.

5. Find Joe's account, click Joe, click OK, and then click OK again.

Finally done. Yes, that was a bit of work, and you'd kind of wonder why Microsoft didn't just build the group for us. I sure don't know.

Restricting RIS Image Choices

Once you turn Joe loose with that floppy, you just might not want him accidentally loading the wrong image. He might just decide that he'd *love* to download the Programmer's Workstation image, complete with the C++ and Java compilers, interactive debuggers, and the like—none of which he has any use for. You can, as it turns out, keep him from seeing all of the images on the RIS server. But you'd never guess how you do it.

The RIS server has a set of directories that exist in \RemoteInstall\Setup\English \Images. If you've got a simple I386 installation called win2000.pro, then its image is in \RemoteInstall\Setup\ English\Images\Win2000.Pro. Each RIS image, then, has a directory inside \RemoteInstall\ Setup\English\Images; remember that.

Each image contains a folder named I386, which contains yet *another* folder named Templates. *That* folder contains a file named with the extension .sif. It's an answer file that RIS uses to be able to do the installation without any user intervention. So, for example, if you have an image called Programmers, there's an SIF file in \RemoteInstall\Setup\English\Images\I386\Templates.

The way that you keep Joe out of the Programmers image is to set the NTFS permissions on the SIF file so that he's denied Read access. Once RIS sees that he's not supposed to see the file, the Programmers image won't even be offered to him.

Advanced RIS

Those are the basics about Remote Installation Services. But before you go running off to take advantage of them, you should know about some fine points, including why you haven't seen Windows 2000 Server RIS yet.

ADVANCED RIS I: ROLLING OUT SERVER

Thus far, my examples have referred mainly to Windows 2000 Professional rather than Windows 2000 Server. There's a reason for that:

You see, RIS was never built to let you roll out Server—only Professional.

There's a way around it, as I'm about to show you, but the work-around won't let you build and store prebuilt Server images in the same way that you can get a copy of Professional "just so" and then put that complete workstation image in cold storage on a RIS server. Still, being able to do scripted Server installs from RIS will turn out to be useful.

Okay, ready? Here's the trick. You'll start from a Server I386 directory on a hard disk—a hard disk because you'll need to modify one file in that directory. The file's name is txtsetup.sif, and you need to change the line ProductType=1 to ProductType=0. Then you'll tell RIS to offer that

I386 as one of its optional images. Now, normally RIS looks over the I386 to double-check that it's a Professional I386, not a Server I386, but that change we'll make will fool it. After RIS accepts and copies the I386, you'll go back and change `txtsetup.sif` back so that ProductType=1—or you'll get some very confused copies of Server! Finally, we'll add scripts and end up with a pretty extensive RIS-based tool for rolling out Server. Here's the step-by-step.

1. Copy the I386 directory from a Server installation CD to one of your RIS server's hard disks. I'll use D: for my example, so in my case I'd end up with the I386 files in D:\I386.

2. As long as we're doing this, let's apply Service Pack 1. Assuming that you've got the whole 89MB `sp1network.exe` file around, expand it by typing **sp1network -x** and, when it asks where to install itself, just tell it D:\sp1.

3. Once Service Pack 1 has expanded itself into D:\sp1, you then cd to D:\sp1\ I386\update and type **update −s:d:** to tell Service Pack 1 to slipstream itself into the D:\I386 files.

4. Now let's make that change that RIS needs in order to swallow our Server image. Use Notepad to edit D:\I386\txtsetup.sif. Find the line ProductType=1 and change the 1 to 0, then save `txtsetup.sif` and exit Notepad.

5. Now RIS will accept this I386. Let's tell it to create a new image using that I386. Start up Active Directory Users and Computers (it's either on your Start menu as Start/Programs/Administrative Tools/Active Directory Users and Computers, or click Start, then Run, type **DSA.MSC**, and press Enter).

6. Open the folder labeled `Computers` and find the RIS server. Right-click its icon and choose Properties, then click the tab labeled Remote Install.

7. At the bottom of that tab, you'll see a button labeled Advanced Settings; click it. You'll see another properties page with three tabs labeled New Clients, Images, and Tools. Click the Images tab and you'll see something like Figure 4.32.

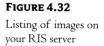

FIGURE 4.32

Listing of images on your RIS server

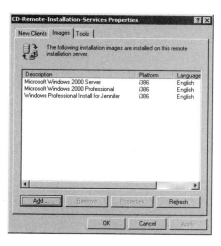

8. You'll see a listing of the images that your RIS server has, as in Figure 4.32. If you've just installed it, then you'll probably only have one image, with a name like Microsoft Windows 2000 Professional. Click the Add button at the bottom of the page and you'll see a screen like Figure 4.33.

FIGURE 4.33

Adding a new image

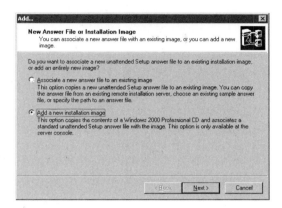

9. Notice that RIS lets you create an "image" simply by writing a script and associating that with an existing I386 directory, or it'll let you introduce a whole new I386 directory, as I've checked. Choose Add a New Installation Image and click Next.

10. That starts off a wizard that basically just asks you where to find the image (D:\I386, in this example) and what to call it, as you see in Figure 4.34.

FIGURE 4.34

What to call the new folder

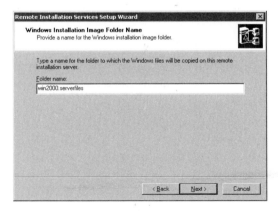

11. Here, I've called it win2000.serverfiles. That means that the I386 files will go on your RIS server's SIS drive into a folder named \RemoteInstall\ Setup\English\Images\win2000 .serverfiles. Click Next and RIS will want a "friendly name" for this image, as you saw when you created other RIS images. Click Next from that and you'll see a question about the "client installation screens," as you see in Figure 4.35.

FIGURE 4.35

What to do with the client installation screens

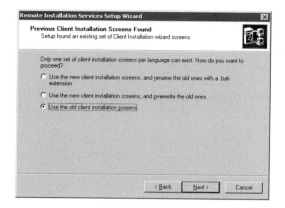

12. The client installation screens are the HTML-like files that control what the user sees when first connecting to the RIS server. I'd just leave them as is, as you see on the screen. Click Next a couple more times and RIS will copy the I386 into the `\RemoteInstall\Setup\English\Images\win2000.serverfiles` directory (or whatever you named it) and add that image to its list of images.

13. Finally, once RIS has finished copying the files, change the ProductType value back. Look in `\RemoteInstall\Setup\English\Images\`*whateveryoucalled-yourfolder*`\I386` and you'll find `txtsetup.sif`. Just locate the ProductType=0 line and change the 0 to 1, then save the file.

Congratulations—you've just smuggled a Server I386 onto your RIS server.

ADVANCED RIS II: USING OEM

Once you start getting a bit fancy with your RIS-based installs, you'll soon pine for the power of the OEM folder. So you might tunnel down into your `\RemoteInstall\ Setup\English\Images\`*whateveryoucalledit*`\I386` folder and place a OEM folder inside that I386 folder, hoping to see some of OEM's power transferred to RIS.

But it won't work.

The problem? For some bizarre reason, RIS installs need the OEM folder *at the same directory level* as I386, not inside it. So, for example, if I created an image folder just called `serverinst`, then I'd place the OEM folder at `\RemoteInstall\Setup\English\Images\serverinst\$OEM$`, not `\RemoteInstall\Setup\English\Images\serverinst\I386\$OEM$`.

ADVANCED RIS III: BUILDING RIS SCRIPTS

If you've used the above trick to put a Windows 2000 Server image on a RIS server, and then PXE-boot a computer to that RIS server and tell RIS to load that Server image, then RIS will wipe the first physical hard disk on that computer, make that first drive one big NTFS volume, and do a mainly unattended installation of Windows 2000 server—"mainly" because it'll prompt you for a product ID.

Unattended is good; *mainly* unattended isn't. So let's see how to script a RIS install. As with the winnt.sif-style scripts, you can use the Setup Manager to create RIS scripts. But I find that the Setup Manager isn't much help here. I pretty much use Setup Manager to create a basic script, then I hand-adjust it, as you saw earlier in this chapter.

But there's no need to have Setup Manager create a basic script for RIS—you see, every RIS install gets its own basic script, called ristndrd.sif. Look in the I386 directory of any RIS image directory and you'll see a directory named Templates. Inside *that* is a file named ristndrd.sif. Mine looks like the following.

```
[data]
floppyless = "1"
msdosinitiated = "1"
OriSrc = "\\%SERVERNAME%\RemInst\%INSTALLPATH%\%MACHINETYPE%"
OriTyp = "4"
LocalSourceOnCD = 1

[SetupData]
OsLoadOptions = "/noguiboot /fastdetect"
SetupSourceDevice = "\Device\LanmanRedirector\%SERVERNAME%\RemInst\%INSTALLPATH%"

[Unattended]
OemPreinstall = no
NoWaitAfterTextMode = 0
FileSystem = LeaveAlone
ExtendOEMPartition = 0
ConfirmHardware = no
NtUpgrade = no
Win31Upgrade = no
TargetPath = \winnt
OverwriteOemFilesOnUpgrade = no
OemSkipEula = yes
InstallFilesPath = "\\%SERVERNAME%\RemInst\%INSTALLPATH%\%MACHINETYPE%"

[UserData]
FullName = "%USERFIRSTNAME% %USERLASTNAME%"
OrgName = "%ORGNAME%"
ComputerName = %MACHINENAME%

[GuiUnattended]
OemSkipWelcome = 1
OemSkipRegional = 1
TimeZone = %TIMEZONE%
AdminPassword = "*"

[LicenseFilePrintData]
AutoMode = PerSeat

[Display]
```

```
ConfigureAtLogon = 0
BitsPerPel = 8
XResolution = 640
YResolution = 480
VRefresh = 60
AutoConfirm = 1

[Networking]
ProcessPageSections=Yes

[Identification]
JoinDomain = %MACHINEDOMAIN%
CreateComputerAccountInDomain = No
DoOldStyleDomainJoin = Yes

[NetProtocols]
MS_TCPIP=params.MS_TCPIP

[params.MS_TCPIP]
; transport: TC (TCP/IP Protocol)
InfID=MS_TCPIP
DHCP=Yes

[NetClients]
MS_MSClient=params.MS_MSClient

[params.MS_MSClient]
InfID=MS_MSClient

[NetServices]
MS_Server=params.MS_Server

[params.MS_Server]
; service: SRV (Server)
InfID=MS_Server
BroadcastsToLanman2Clients = No

[ServicesSection]

[RemoteInstall]
Repartition = Yes
UseWholeDisk = Yes

[OSChooser]
Description ="Microsoft Windows 2000 Server"
Help ="Installs Windows 2000 Server"
LaunchFile = "%INSTALLPATH%\%MACHINETYPE%\templates\startrom.com"
ImageType =Flat
Version="5.0"
```

This won't need all that much in the way of changes because, after all, it's already able to direct an almost-unattended installation. But here are a few changes that I made to make my Server-installing RIS image more useful for me.

First, I added a ProductID= line to the [UserData] section. That kept it from stopping to prompt me for a product ID.

Next, I changed OEMPreinstall=No to OEMPreinstall=Yes, so I could then set up a OEM directory (at the same directory level as I386, recall, not *inside* I386) and get the benefits of OEM— cmdlines.txt, preloaded files and directories, extra driver directories, and so on. That also let me include an [OEM_Ads] section to specify background and logo bitmaps for the install—not necessary items, but I like them and clients like when I set them up, as it makes an install look like a "company brand" install rather than a Microsoft commercial.

Then I changed the [Identification] section. RIS normally uses some command that refers to an "oldstyledomainjoin" that seems to work fine if you let RIS pick the machine name, but if you want to pick your own, then it seems not to work unless you do it by specifying a user account and password that can create and destroy machine accounts. Again, it needn't be an actual domain administrator—just someone from the Installers group will do fine.

Then I changed the [Display] section so that the systems come up on 1024×768 resolution rather than the unwieldy 640×480. I used [Components], as before, to remove the games and to enable Terminal Services, and [FavoritesEx] to preconfigure defaults for Internet Explorer. I ended up with a script that looks like this; I have highlighted the lines that I added or modified:

```
[data]
floppyless = "1"
msdosinitiated = "1"
OriSrc = "\\%SERVERNAME%\RemInst\%INSTALLPATH%\%MACHINETYPE%"
OriTyp = "4"
LocalSourceOnCD = 1

[SetupData]
OsLoadOptions = "/noguiboot /fastdetect"
SetupSourceDevice =    "\Device\LanmanRedirector\%SERVERNAME%\RemInst\%INSTALLPATH%"

[Unattended]
Repartition = Yes
UseWholeDisk = Yes
OemPreinstall = yes
NoWaitAfterTextMode = 1
ExtendOEMPartition = 0
ConfirmHardware = no
NtUpgrade = no
Win31Upgrade = no
TargetPath = \winnt
OverwriteOemFilesOnUpgrade = no
OemSkipEula = yes
InstallFilesPath = "\\%SERVERNAME%\RemInst\%INSTALLPATH%\%MACHINETYPE%"
```

```
[OEM_Ads]
background=backg.bmp
logo=logo.bmp

[UserData]
FullName = "%USERFIRSTNAME% %USERLASTNAME%"
OrgName = "%ORGNAME%"
ComputerName = %MACHINENAME%
ProductID="11111-22222-33333-44444-55555"

[GuiUnattended]
OemSkipWelcome = 1
OemSkipRegional = 1
TimeZone = %TIMEZONE%
AdminPassword = "*"

[LicenseFilePrintData]
AutoMode = PerSeat

[Display]
ConfigureAtLogon = 0
BitsPerPel = 16
XResolution = 1024
YResolution = 768
VRefresh = 72
AutoConfirm = 1

[Networking]
ProcessPageSections=Yes

[Identification]
JoinDomain=%MACHINEDOMAIN%
DomainAdmin=machineguy
DomainAdminPassword=swordfish

[NetProtocols]
MS_TCPIP=params.MS_TCPIP

[params.MS_TCPIP]
; transport: TC (TCP/IP Protocol)
InfID=MS_TCPIP
DHCP=Yes

[NetClients]
MS_MSClient=params.MS_MSClient

[params.MS_MSClient]
```

```
InfID=MS_MSClient

[NetServices]
MS_Server=params.MS_Server

[params.MS_Server]
; service: SRV (Server)
InfID=MS_Server
BroadcastsToLanman2Clients = No

[ServicesSection]

[Components]
Solitaire=Off
Minesweeper=Off
Pinball=Off
LicenseServer=Off
TSEnable=On
TSClients=On

[TerminalService]
ApplicationServer=0
PermissionsSetting=1

[FavoritesEx]
Title1="Mark Minasi Home Page.url"
URL1="http://www.minasi.com"
[Branding]
BrandIEUsingUnattended=Yes
[URL]
Home_Page=about:blank

[RemoteInstall]
Repartition = Yes
UseWholeDisk = Yes

[OSChooser]
Description ="Microsoft Windows 2000 Server"
Help ="Installs 2000 Server with Service Pack 1 and Terminal Server"
LaunchFile = "%INSTALLPATH%\%MACHINETYPE%\templates\startrom.com"
ImageType =Flat
Version="5.0"
```

Now, how did I make that change take effect? Simple—I made the changes to the `ristndrd.sif` file and just resaved `ristndrd.sif` to its original location. Alternatively, I could have written another script and then gone to the Advanced button of the RIS page on Active Directory Users and Computers, as you saw me do a few pages back. If I wanted to, I could have any number of scripts all doing unattended installs from the same Server I386 directory.

ADVANCED RIS IV: MODIFYING THE CLIENT WIZARD

If you implemented something like the above script, then you might have noticed a sort of annoying thing about RIS: machine names. By default—and it takes a bit of doing to defeat the default, so to speak—RIS names the first machine that you install *yourusername*1, the second *yourusername*2, and so on. For example, I just started a RIS install of a server and, when the Client Installation Wizard asked me to log in, I logged in as ADMINMARK so RIS named the server ADMINMARK1. I'd much prefer it if the Client Installation Wizard would just *ask* me what to call the server. Look back to the line in the `ristndrd.sif` script that names the server:

```
ComputerName = %MACHINENAME%
```

So, clearly some kind of environment variable is set by RIS, and the value in the environment variable is then used to name the machine. As a matter of fact, a close look at `ristndrd.sif` shows *several* of these environment variables—%MACHINEDOMAIN%, %TIMEZONE%, %ORGNAME% and the like—that RIS somehow constructs and then passes to the Setup routine on a computer that RIS installs.

Is there a way for us to *directly* control those variables, and therefore to have greater control over how RIS installs the server? Yes. As a matter of fact, you can even create new environment variables—but to see how that works, let's go back and reexamine all of those `.osc` files. On your RIS server, there's a directory named `\RemoteInstall\ Oschooser\English`. In that directory, you'll find (on my system, anyway) 42 text files with the extension `.osc`. I don't pretend to understand entirely how they work, but here's what I've pieced together, with some trial and error, the help of my third-edition coauthor Doug Toombs, and a few Knowledge Base articles.

When you first connect to a RIS server, you get a screen driven by the file `welcome.osc`. Let's revisit that file:

```
<OSCML>
<META KEY=ENTER HREF="LOGIN">
<META KEY=F3 ACTION="REBOOT">
<META KEY=ESC HREF="LOGIN">
<META KEY=F1 HREF="LOGIN">
<TITLE>Client Installation Wizard
    Welcome</TITLE>
<FOOTER>[ENTER] continue </FOOTER>
<BODY left=5 right=75>
<BR>
<BR>
<BR>
Welcome to the Client Installation wizard. This wizard helps you quickly and easily
set up a new operating system on your computer. You can also use this wizard to
keep your computer up-to-date and to troubleshoot computer hardware problems.
<BR>
<BR>
In the wizard, you are asked to use a valid user name, password, and domain name to
log in to the network. If you do not have this information, contact your network
administrator before continuing.
</BODY>
</OSCML>
```

First, notice the <META> commands. They define what happens when you press one key or another. I've seen two variations on the <META> command—the HREF and the ACTION variations. For example,

```
<META KEY=ENTER HREF="LOGIN">
```

This tells the Client Installation Wizard that if the user presses the Enter key, then the Wizard should next find and load the file login.osc. Like an HTML "<A>" tag, it provides a link to another OSC file. But now consider this <META> command:

```
<META KEY=F3 ACTION="REBOOT">
```

This time, pressing F3 doesn't take you to a file reboot.osc. Instead, "REBOOT" means just what it sounds like—it tells the wizard to reboot the computer. Other ACTION= values that I've seen include

LOGIN   Take the information on the screen (this shows up in the wizard panel that asks you to log in) and try to log in to an Active Directory domain.

ENUM IMAGES   This seems to tell RIS to take all of the operating system images available on this server and only show users the options that they have access to—remember that you can keep users from seeing images by adjusting the file and directory permissions on that image.

Clearly, then, the job of welcome.osc is to get you to press Enter so that you'll next go to login.osc. That looks like this:

```
<OSCML>
<TITLE>Client Installation Wizard
   Logon</TITLE>
<FOOTER>[ENTER] continue    [ESC] clear    [F1] help    [F3] restart
computer</FOOTER>
<META KEY=F3 ACTION="REBOOT">
<META KEY=F1 HREF="LOGINHLP">
<META KEY=ESC HREF="LOGIN">
<META ACTION="LOGIN">
<BODY left=5 right=75>
<BR>
<BR>
Type a valid user name, password, and domain name. You may use the Internet-style
logon format (for example: Username@Company.com).
<BR>
<BR>
<BR>
<FORM ACTION="CHOICE">
  User name: <INPUT NAME="USERNAME" MAXLENGTH=255>
   Password: <INPUT NAME="*PASSWORD" TYPE=PASSWORD MAXLENGTH=20>
<BR>
Domain name: <INPUT NAME="USERDOMAIN" MAXLENGTH=255>
</FORM>
<BR>
```

```
<BR>
<BR>
Press the TAB key to move between the User name, Password, and Domain name fields.
</BODY>
</OSCML>
```

Looking at the <META>s up top show that they either reboot you, get help, or—<META ACTION="LOGIN">—commence the Active Directory logon. But where do we go next? To see that, look at the <FORM ACTION="CHOICE"> command. Look at that and the next four lines. This defines a simple "form" on the screen. The form gathers three pieces of information—your username, your password, and the name of the domain that your account is a member of. Here, then, is what this <FORM> command is doing: first, it collects values for USERNAME, PASS-WORD, and USERDOMAIN. Then, once you press Enter to indicate that you're done entering those values, the form moves you along to "CHOICE." But what is CHOICE? Well, apparently the "ACTION=" parameter means something a little different in a <FORM> than it does in a <META>, as it just takes you to the screen defined by choice.osc.

But here's where things get a bit weird. Here's what's in choice.osc:

```
<OSCML>
<META KEY=F3 ACTION="REBOOT">
<META KEY=F1 HREF="CHOICHLP">
<META SERVER ACTION="DNRESET">
<META SERVER ACTION="FILTER CHOICE">
<TITLE>Client Installation Wizard
    Main Menu</TITLE>
<FOOTER>[ENTER] continue    [F1] help    [F3] restart computer</FOOTER>
<BODY left=5 right=75>
<BR>
<BR>
Use the arrow keys to select one of the following options:<BR>
<P left=8>
<FORM>
<SELECT SIZE=10>
<OPTION VALUE="OSAUTO" TIP="This is the easiest way to install an operating system
on your computer. Most installation options are already configured by your network
administrator.">
Automatic Setup
<OPTION VALUE="CUSTOM" TIP="With this option, you can define a unique name for this
computer and specify where the computer account will be created within the
directory service. Select this option if you are setting up this computer for
someone else within your company.">
Custom Setup
<OPTION VALUE="RESTART" TIP="A previous remote installation attempt has been
detected on this computer. Select this option to restart a previously started
installation.">
Restart a Previous Setup Attempt
<OPTION VALUE="TOOLS" TIP="This option gives you access to tools for keeping your
computer up-to-date and for troubleshooting problems.">
```

```
Maintenance and Troubleshooting
</SELECT>
</FORM>
</P>
<BR>
<BOLD>Description:</BOLD>  
<TIPAREA>
</BODY>
</OSCML>
```

Here's the weird part: *I've never seen this screen appear, no matter how I set up RIS.* But I *did* notice that a screen flashes by very quickly with the words Main Menu in its upper-right corner (one of the benefits of working with slow machines is, I suppose, that you can see a little more of what they're up to—with an 800MHz box, I might not have seen the Main Menu) before moving to a screen that is clearly created by a different file, `oschoice.osc`.

I theorized that the two <META SERVER> commands were the things causing me to skip ahead to `oschoice.osc`, so I tried removing them and my Client Installation Wizard did indeed stop at a screen labeled Main Menu. Even better, one of the options in the Main Menu was to specify my machine's name! Why, then, did Microsoft write `choice.osc` so that it always zips past any user input? I haven't a clue. But if you remove the two lines, as I did, and choose the Main Menu option Automatic Setup, then the script seems to say that next the wizard panel `osauto.osc` should load. It's just one line:

```
<META SERVER ACTION="CHECKGUID OSCHOICE DUPAUTO">
```

Which *seems* to tell the system to run the `oschoice.osc` panel, so let's look at that next:

```
<OSCML>
<META KEY=F3 ACTION="REBOOT">
<META KEY=ESC HREF="CHOICE">
<META SERVER ACTION="ENUM IMAGES">
<TITLE>Client Installation Wizard
    OS Choices</TITLE>
<FOOTER>[ENTER] continue     [ESC] go back     [F3] restart computer</FOOTER>
<BODY left=5 right=75>
<BR>
<BR>
Use the arrow keys to select one of the following operating systems:
<P left=8>
<FORM ACTION="WARNING">
<SELECT NAME="SIF" SIZE=12>
%OPTIONS%
</SELECT>
</FORM>
</P>
<BOLD>Description:</BOLD>  
<TIPAREA>
</BODY>
</OSCML>
```

This seems to figure out which images you're eligible to install. It appears the server passes the list of images to a form (<FORM ACTION="WARNING">) through a variable called %OPTIONS%. Whichever you choose goes into an environmental variable called SIF and it appears to next take you to warning.osc—which basically just puts up a "warning, you're about to blow away anything on the hard disk, are you sure?" kind of message; when you press Enter, it takes you to install.osc, which looks like this:

```
<OSCML>
<META KEY=ESC ACTION="REBOOT">
<META KEY=ENTER ACTION="REBOOT">
<TITLE>Client Installation Wizard
    Installation Information</TITLE>
<FOOTER>[ENTER] continue</FOOTER>
<BODY left=5 right=75>
<BR>
<BR>
The following settings will be applied to this computer installation. Verify these
settings before continuing.
<BR>
<BR>
Computer account:                 %MACHINENAME%
<BR>
<BR>
Global Unique ID:                 %GUID%
<BR>
<BR>
Server supporting this computer:  %SERVERNAME%
<BR>
<BR>
<BR>
To begin Setup, press ENTER. If you are using the Remote Installation Services boot
floppy, remove the floppy diskette from the drive and press ENTER to continue.
</BODY>
</OSCML>
```

This panel also basically just displays some information. But notice something odd about the <META> commands—they say that no matter whether you press ESC or Enter, you'll reboot. But you'd *think* that "reboot" would, well, reboot the computer—which would sort of abort the whole RIS process. But no—on this particular panel, "reboot" means "full speed ahead!" for the RIS install. So, we've seen that a standard RIS install progresses from welcome.osc to login.osc to choice.osc (in "stealth" mode) to osauto.osc (also "stealthed") to oschoice.osc to warning.osc and then finally to install.osc. Here's where I'm going to make use of this to control the machine name: I'll add an extra panel between oschoice.osc and warning.osc and include a form that gives the user the ability to enter a machine name.

Looking back at oschoice.osc, you recall that we *got* from oschoice.osc to warning.osc by way of the form in oschoice.osc: the <FORM ACTION="WARNING"> command. *That's* where I'll break the chain from `oschoice.osc` to `warning.osc`, by modifying that one item in `oschoice.osc` from "<FORM ACTION="WARNING">" to <FORM ACTION="PICKNAME">. Using the other .`osc` files as a model, I then come up with this file, which I name `pickname.osc`:

```
<OSCML>
<META KEY=ESC ACTION="REBOOT">
<META KEY=F3 HREF="OSCHOICE">
<TITLE>Client Installation Wizard
    Choosing Names</TITLE>
<FOOTER>[ENTER] continue     [ESC] Reboot F3 Pick Install</FOOTER>
<BODY>
<FORM ACTION="WARNING">
Machine Name: <input NAME="MACHINENAME" VALUE=%MACHINENAME% maxlength=20><br>
%OPTIONS%
</SELECT>
</FORM>
</BODY>
</OSCML>
```

This file starts off by defining ESC as "reboot" and F3 as "return to `oschoice.osc`." Then it defines title and footer text for the screen. Then it defines a form that will progress to the `warning` .`osc` panel, once you press Enter for this form. Inside the form is just one field—an input field that lets you type a machine name of up to 30 characters. The NAME="MACHINENAME" means that whatever you type will go into the environmental variable named MACHINENAME. The VALUE=%MACHINENAME% tells the Client Installation Wizard to offer as default text the name that RIS *wants* to use, like ADMINMARK1.

Still not sure this would be useful? Then consider this: Suppose you had to roll out hundreds of servers, each with static IP addresses—as a large international Web-hosting ISP had to recently. They built themselves some RIS Client Installation Wizard panels that let them type in IP addresses and subnet masks, then passed that information to the `ristndrd.sif` file. Now, in my example, I used the built-in environment variable named MACHINENAME, but there's nothing keeping you from making up your own environment variable. For example, what if I'd added these two <input> commands to my `pickname.osc` file:

```
IP address:<input name="IPADR"><br>
Subnet mask:<input name="SUBMSK">
```

Then, inside `ristndrd.sif`, I just adjust the script so that it doesn't get IP addresses from DHCP, but instead assigns static IP addresses. Part of the revised `ristndrd.sif`, then, would include these lines:

```
IPAddress=%IPADR%
SubnetMast=%SUBMSK%
```

You can create as many new environmental variables you like—IP address is just one example. RIS offers a lot of flexibility—so much so that it's changed my PC hardware buying habits. From now on, it's all PXE machines for me.

ADVANCED RIS V: NEW NIC DRIVERS

Now, all of this will work fine, *unless* your computer requires a NIC driver that's not on the Windows 2000 distribution CD—say, if you had a relatively new computer whose NIC made its market debut after February 2000. Supposing that this new computer can PXE boot, then it'll boot to the RIS server all right and Setup will start. But just a few minutes into the text mode Setup, you may see this message:

```
The network server does not support booting Windows 2000. Setup cannot continue.
Press any key to exit.
```

You see, once Setup kicks in, it does a quick check to see if it can fire up your network card; for some reason, it won't use the TFTP transfer ability built into PXE to copy the Setup files. As the NIC is newer than the drivers that Setup knows about, Setup can't initialize the card, and stops.

But wait—what about that OEMPnPDrivers command? If you put the drivers for the new NIC into OEM and pointed to them with OEMPnPDrivers, then Setup ought to be able to use those drivers, right? Well, not exactly. Windows 2000 likes its drivers digitally signed, and many sets of drivers don't come with digital signatures. You can work around that by adding this line to the `ristndrd.sif` script:

```
DriverSigningPolicy = Ignore
```

Put that in the [Unattended] section. Then put the NIC drivers on the RIS server in OEM as before, but Microsoft recommends a more specific procedure. Create a directory \$OEM$\$1\ Drivers\NIC and put the NIC drivers there. Create an OEMPnpDrivers command that looks like OemPnpDriversPath=\Drivers\Nic in the `ristndrd.sif` file, and then you ought to be able to get RIS started on a system with a new NIC. (And yes, I *did* recommend that you keep the names of driver directories short due to the 40-character limit on the OemPnpDriversPath command, but I wanted this text to be clear, so I used a longer name. You'd do fine with a directory named \$OEM$\$1\DR\NIC instead of \$OEM$\$1\Drivers\NIC.)

Apparently a driver has to be in the I386 directory for the text mode portion of Setup to see it, so Microsoft says in Knowledge Base article Q246184 that you've got to put the INF and SYS files from the network driver into the I386 directory on the RIS server. You may have to do a bit of experimenting to find out exactly which SYS and INF files you actually need in the I386 directory, because you don't want to *have* to put `oeminfo.inf` in I386—after all, it seems like every board comes with an `oeminfo.inf`.

Microsoft *also* advised in the Q article that you restart the BINL service in the Services applet of Manage Computer. (Right-click My Computer, choose Manage Computer, open Services and Applications, and then click Services. In the right pane you'll see a service named Boot Information Negotiation Layer. Right-click it and choose Restart.) Using this process, I have successfully set up RIS for several computers with very recent—post-2000—NICs.

Ghost's Little Helper: Sysprep

RIS and scripting are cool, but the fastest way to blast an image onto a new system continues to be Ghost or something like it. The idea is to first create a server or workstation just the way you like it, as you would before RIPrep-ing a system. Then use a disk-copying tool like Symantec's Ghost or

PowerQuest's Drive Image Pro to essentially "photocopy" the drive—these tools don't look at files, they just copy an entire partition from one drive right atop another. (Or, for about $1000, you can forgo buying Ghost or Drive Image and buy a drive-to-drive copier. These are pretty neat—you plug the source hard disk into one side, pop some empty drives into the "receiver" receptacles, push the Start button, and walk away. I'm told that some of these can copy a gigabyte a minute!)

This drive-copying method works great for Windows 9*x*, but it's a terrible idea for NT and 2000, as each NT or 2000 system has a unique set of numbers embedded into it called its security identifiers or SIDs. Copying a drive copies the SIDs, making the network unable to tell the difference between the two drives. Unfortunately, the consequences of having systems with identical SIDs wasn't severe enough to warn people off from cloning drives, so many firms do drive cloning. In response to the need to handle the duplicate SID problem, the Ghost and Drive Image folks have written "SID scramblers," which create a unique set of SIDs on every computer. And while that ought to solve the duplicate SID problem, Microsoft won't support a computer that's been cloned, even with an SID scrambler.

I once asked a Microsoft techie why they wouldn't support a cloned system, even if it had its SIDs scrambled. Does it actually cause a repeatable problem, I asked, or was Microsoft refusing to support cloned systems just to play it safe? The Microsoft support person said, "Well, we can't prove any problems with cloning—but we've seen cloned systems that had problems that went away when we wiped their hard disks and did a fresh install." I looked at him with one eyebrow raised and said, "You do realize that wiping and reinstalling is a technique that we use all of the time, on systems both cloned and noncloned, don't you?" He had nothing to say.

Using Sysprep: Overview

In any case, Microsoft knows that many people use cloning products and that they'd do well to help their customers use those cloning products. So Windows 2000 comes with a "SID scrubber" called System Preparation Tool (`Sysprep.exe`). Sysprep's simple to use—here are the basic steps.

1. Put Sysprep on a directory named `C:\Sysprep`. You can then script it, and if you do, put the script in `C:\Sysprep`, calling the script `sysprep.inf`.

2. While you were acting as the administrator and setting the system up, you probably created some default software settings that would be convenient for others to have. Copy the local Administrator's profile to the Default Users profile so that anyone who gets a clone of this system gets those software settings.

3. Run Sysprep. It strips the SIDs off your computer and shuts down your machine.

4. *Do not reboot your computer under 2000.* Instead, boot from a floppy (probably to DOS) and run your disk-cloning program—Ghost, Drive Image Pro, or whatever. You do not want to let the computer boot up because when it does, it will realize that it is SID-less and will generate a new set of SIDs—which is what you ran Sysprep to get rid of in the first place.

Let's look at this in more detail. And I *will* go into a bit more detail than usual here; I know that many of you are already quite facile with NT and perhaps with 2000, but for those who are just starting out in 2000, then *everything* seems confusing, so I'll take you through these steps, one at a time.

Get a New Sysprep

Before you even get started with Sysprep, get on Microsoft's Web site and get the latest one. The one I've seen, version 1.1a, greatly enhances what Sysprep can do. But I should mention one thing that Sysprep *can't* do:

WARNING *You cannot Sysprep a domain controller.*

You can find the latest Sysprep at:

`www.microsoft.com/windows2000/downloads/deployment/sysprep/default.asp`

Set Up the Computer

Start off by creating a computer—whether a server or a workstation—and get it just the way that you want it. Don't bother joining a domain—that complicates this process a trifle, so instead of joining a domain, join a workgroup of whatever name you like—again, it's just temporary and doesn't matter.

Add whatever applications you'll need, configuring the software settings as you think they should be. For example, I hate all that Web content in the Explorer folders and turn it off immediately. But it'd be nice to *always* have it turned off, and I can do that. The idea is this: while I've been logged in as an administrator, I've been making changes to 2000 and 2000 remembers those changes—but only while I'm logged in as administrator! If I create a second user account and log in as that person, then I won't keep any of my settings, and have to reteach 2000 how I like it to work.

Create a New Administrative User

Once you've got the computer the way you want it, you'll want to copy the administrator's profile to `Default User`, so we need another user account to do that, because an administrator can copy any profile in the system *except* his/her own. You need a second admin account in order to be able to copy the first admin account. Here's how to create an admin account.

1. Click Start, then Run, and fill in **compmgmt.msc**, then press Enter to start the Computer Management snap-in.

2. In the left pane, you'll see an icon labeled Local Users and Groups with a plus sign next to it. Click the plus sign to expand it to two folders named, not surprisingly, Users and Groups. Right-click the Users folder and choose New User.

3. That'll give you a dialog box that will let you create a user account that is only recognized by this computer. Let's call it ADMIN2. Fill in the rest of the dialog box and the password, however you like. Click Create, then Close.

4. Click the `Users` folder to show the users in the right pane. Right-click ADMIN2 and choose Properties.

5. In the resulting Properties page, click the tab labeled Member Of (which shows the groups that ADMIN2 is a member of) and then the Add button.

6. That will display the list of local groups on this computer. Choose Administrators, then Add, then OK, then OK again.

7. Close the Computer Management snap-in.

Log In as the New User

Now log out of the default Administrator account and log back in as ADMIN2.

Locate the folder named Documents and Settings—it's probably on the same drive as the operating system—and open it. You'll see a folder or two in there—these folders store the user profiles (i.e., the settings and preferences) for the people who've used this computer. You'll probably see one for the Administrator. You want to copy this to a profile called Default User—but there are two things standing in your way. First, Default User's profile folder is hidden by default, so unless you've told 2000 to show you hidden folders, then you won't see the folder. Second, you can't copy one profile to another just by copying the folder contents—you have to use a Control Panel tool.

First, let's see that Default User folder. If you haven't done it yet, open the Documents and Settings folder. Click Tools, then Folder Options, and then, on the resulting properties page, click View. Click the radio button labeled Show Hidden Files and Folders, then OK, and Default User should pop into view. Next, let's copy the Administrator profile to the Default User profile.

Open the Control Panel (Start/Settings/Control Panel) and then the System applet. The System applet will show five tabs: General, Network Identification, Hardware, User Profiles, and Advanced. Click User Profiles and you'll see a list of profiles stored on this computer. Locate the one named *machinename*\Administrator of Type "Local," and click the Copy To button; you'll see something like Figure 4.36.

FIGURE 4.36

Copying the Administrator's profile

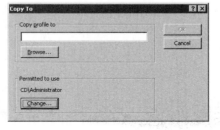

First, click the button labeled Change in the group labeled Permitted to Use. Right now, only the Administrator account can use this profile—let's change that so that anyone can use it. You'll get a list of possible groups and users, one of which is called, appropriately, Everyone. Choose Everyone and click OK.

Next, copy the profile to \Documents and Settings\Default User. Either type in the whole path name (including whichever drive letter you have Documents and Settings on), or use the Browse button and navigate to the folder. Once you've got \Documents and Settings\Default User in your sights, click OK and the deed is done!

Copy Sysprep to *C:\Sysprep*

Now your system's ready for Sysprepping. Once you've downloaded the new Sysprep, unzip it and put all of its files into `C:\Sysprep`. Now just open a command line and type

```
cd \sysprep
sysprep -pnp
```

Sysprep will then strip the SIDs off of your system and shut the computer down. Now copy its hard disk in whatever way you prefer—with a hardware copier or by booting from a floppy or CD-ROM and running Ghost, Drive Image Pro, or something like that.

Now, whenever you copy that disk image to a new hard disk and boot a computer from that hard disk, then the copy of Windows 2000 will recognize that it lacks SIDs, and so it'll generate some. In the process, it has to rejoin the domain, ask for a product ID, and so on. Don't want to have to baby-sit the 2000 systems every time they're first Ghosted? No problem. You can make a Sysprep setup script, which is actually just a minor variation on the scripts we've been doing all chapter. Even better, Setup Manager will make a basic Sysprep script for you, and then you can tweak it for your particular needs. Here's the only thing you've got to do in order to make the Sysprep script work. First, you must name the script `sysprep.inf`. Second, you must include the `sysprep.inf` file in the `C:\Sysprep` directory before Sysprepping your model machine. As before, you've got to add the ProductID entry if your copy of Windows 2000 requires product IDs, and you can use "computername=*" as you've already seen to have the computer create its own unique, random name.

That's all there is to it—and it's well worth looking into Sysprep, as many people are finding that the absolutely fastest way to get a 2000 image on a system is to take a Sysprepped and Ghosted image that's been burned onto a CD, boot the new computer from that CD, and then Ghost the image to the computer's hard disk.

If you've made it with me this far, then you've probably seen that Windows 2000 offers us a considerably improved set of rollout tools than the ones we had with NT 4. Start playing around with scripting, RIS, OEM, and Sysprep, and you may find that deployment's not so bad after all!

Chapter 5

The Windows 2000 Server UI and MMC

WHEN I FIRST INSTALLED Windows 2000, it looked to me a lot like Windows NT 4. So they added a couple of snazzy new icons on the Desktop—big deal. "This'll be a snap," I thought. "What's all the fuss?" But then I opened the Control Panel. Don't bother looking for the Network applet, because it's not there. And it's not the only thing missing. The Services Control Panel? Gone. The Administrative Tools group is still there, but most of our old friends, like Server Manager and User Manager for Domains, have been eaten by this ever-present thing called the Microsoft Management Console (MMC).

Where is everything? What's an old administrator to do? If you've already been fooling around with the Windows 2000 betas, then you know the answers to these questions and you can safely skip this chapter. If you are completely new to Windows 2000, this chapter will help you find those tools in their new homes. Plus, we'll take a peek into the MMC framework and get you started customizing MMC tools to fit your administrative needs.

Where Are They Now?

When NT 4 was released, NT 3.51 administrators were comforted by the fact that most of the administrative tools were the same. We didn't have to relearn those everyday tasks. To add network services and protocols, you went to the Network Control Panel; for user and group configuration, you went to User Manager and User Manager for Domains. To administer servers and shares and services remotely, we had Server Manager. So it is very disconcerting to see, upon loading Windows 2000 Server, that the three most commonly used tools seem to have disappeared. Microsoft has decided the Control Panel will now be for user options and simple configuration changes, so several items have been moved out of the Control Panel and integrated into new administrative tools.

In this section, we'll take a look at some of the most glaring interface changes that an NT 4 administrator must face, and I'll show you the new procedures for those common tasks. I won't bore you with too many details; rather, I just want to get you pointed in the right direction. Specifically, I'll answer these questions:

◆ Where'd they put the Network Control Panel?

◆ What happened to the User Manager and User Manager for Domains?

◆ No more Server Manager?

◆ Where is the Disk Administrator?

◆ What happened to the device management tools in the Control Panel (SCSI, Tape Device, etc.)? Where do I install a new device now?

◆ Where is the Services Control Panel?

◆ What is this Network and Dial-Up Connections tool?

◆ Did they do away with NT Diagnostics?

This quick reference should help you weather the interface changes gracefully and have you navigating Win2K like a pro in no time at all.

Where'd They Put the Network Control Panel?

Under NT 4, to configure almost any network-related information, you only had to open the Network applet in the Control Panel. There you could change the machine name and workgroup name, join a domain, and add/remove adapters, protocols, and network services like DHCP, WINS, or DNS. Win2K takes a different approach. These functions have been dispersed into several different tools.

CHANGING A MACHINE NAME OR WORKGROUP/DOMAIN

To change a machine's name or a workgroup name or to join a domain, open System Properties by choosing Start/Settings/Control Panel/System (or just right-click My Computer on the Desktop and choose Properties). Select the Network Identification tab, shown in Figure 5.1. The rules that apply for joining a workgroup or domain in NT 4 also apply to Windows 2000; you must be logged on as a local administrator, and if you wish to join the computer to a domain, you must also have a valid username and password to create the machine account. Also, please note that if the machine is a domain controller, you will not be able to change the identification information here.

Click the Properties button to bring up the Identification Changes dialog box, shown in Figure 5.2. From here, you can change the machine name and workgroup or domain affiliation. Click the More button if you wish to change the DNS suffix (domain name) or the NetBIOS name for the computer as well.

FIGURE 5.1

The Network Identification tab in the System Control Panel

FIGURE 5.2

The Identification Changes dialog box

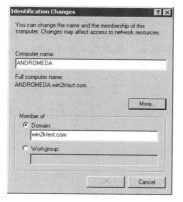

ADJUSTING NETWORK PROTOCOLS

Under Windows 2000, you use Network and Dial-Up Connections to install protocols. Click the Start button and choose Settings, then Network and Dial-Up Connections (or right-click My Network Places on the Desktop and select Properties). As shown in Figure 5.3, each connection will display an icon. For instance, if the server has a modem and two network cards, you'll see an icon for each network adapter (they are labeled Local Area Connection by default, but you can rename them), one for each dial-up networking connection, plus the Make New Connection icon. The dial-up networking connections don't represent different modems, but rather what we used to call Address Book entries in NT 4. You can see the type of connection and status on the left in the window when you highlight the icon. It's a good idea to rename the Local Area Connection icons to something meaningful, especially if the machine has multiple networking devices.

FIGURE 5.3

The Network and Dial-Up Connections window

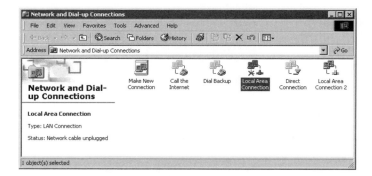

To add a protocol, select the Local Area Connection icon for the device that will use the protocol, then right-click it and choose Properties. Figure 5.4 shows the property page. Now, this is beginning to look familiar. Click the Configure button to display the device information, or click Install to add a client, protocol, or service to this device.

FIGURE 5.4

The Local Area Connection Properties page

Figure 5.5 shows the dialog box where you select a network component to install. Choose to add a protocol, and you'll be shown a list (Figure 5.6). If you add a protocol, it becomes available to every connection. Likewise, if you remove a protocol, as opposed to just unchecking the box (shown back in Figure 5.4) that indicates the device driver is to use that protocol, it is removed for all connections. Also, you can't add or remove all of the same network components here as you could in NT 4's Network Control Panel, but you can add and remove the Microsoft and NetWare redirector and server components.

FIGURE 5.5

The Select Network
Component Type
dialog box

FIGURE 5.6

The Select Network
Protocol dialog box

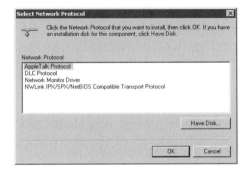

ADJUSTING AND ADDING/SUBTRACTING NETWORK SERVICES

To load, unload, or configure Microsoft File and Print Services or the Gateway (and Client) Services for NetWare, use the property page for the correct connection in the Network and Dial-Up Connections window, as described in the preceding section. By the way, the Workstation service is now called the Client for Microsoft Networks, and the Server service is called File and Printer Sharing for Microsoft Networks. Presumably this provides consistency with Windows 95 and Windows 98. However, they are still called the Server and Workstation services if you want to stop, pause, or restart them.

Services like DNS, WINS, and DHCP are added using Add/Remove Programs. Open Control Panel/Add Remove Programs/Add or Remove Windows Components. This kicks off the Windows Components Wizard. After the initial screen, select Networking Services and choose Details. Figure 5.7 shows some of the networking services components that can now be loaded.

If you still happen to be using the Web Content view instead of the classic view for your folders, there is also a helpful link (called Add Network Components) in Network and Dial-Up Connections, visible on the left side of the window. This link opens the Windows Optional Networking Components Wizard. Although Web Content for folders is generally annoying, and I'll show you how to turn it off later in the chapter, this link is worth mentioning because it saves you a few mouse clicks (or touch-pad taps, as the case may be). As you see in Figure 5.8, this wizard offers a subset of the components from the Windows Components Wizard, namely management tools like SNMP and Network Monitor, Other Network File and Print Services (Print Services for Unix, Services for Macintosh), plus the full list of networking services shown in Figure 5.7.

FIGURE 5.7

The Networking
Services dialog box
in the Windows
Components Wizard

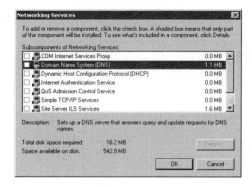

FIGURE 5.8

Optional networking
components

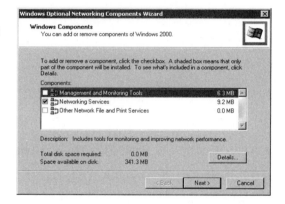

CONFIGURING AND INSTALLING/REMOVING NETWORK ADAPTERS

How do you add a network adapter under Win2K? Hopefully, you won't have to. Plug and Play takes away most of your hardware woes. But once in a while you might need to add an adapter manually. For instance, at one point I wanted to load the Microsoft loopback adapter on my laptop to run some tests. In case you don't already know, the loopback adapter is a software-based *virtual adapter* that allows you to load network protocols and services without having an actual network card installed. The problem is, it's not Plug and Play–compliant, as you would deduce—how do you auto-detect a virtual adapter? The trick to remember here is that an adapter (even the Microsoft loopback adapter) is considered hardware. So you'll need to invoke the Add/Remove Hardware Wizard.

To add an adapter, follow these steps:

1. Choose Start/Settings/Control Panel and then Add/Remove Hardware. You can also open the System applet, go to the Hardware tab, and click the Hardware Wizard button (see Figure 5.9).

FIGURE 5.9

Access the Hardware Wizard by clicking its button in the System Properties page

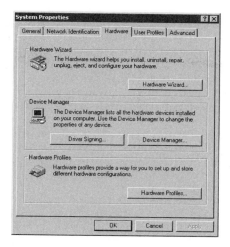

2. From the Welcome screen, choose Next, then select Add/Troubleshoot a Device in the next window, as shown in Figure 5.10. The annoying thing is that the wizard now searches for new Plug-and-Play hardware. It would be nice to have an option to skip the detection attempt.

FIGURE 5.10

Choosing a hardware task

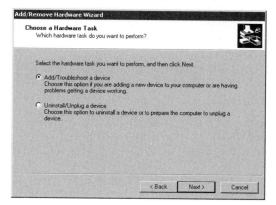

3. Next, the wizard presents a list of devices installed on your system. Select Add a New Device and click Next (see Figure 5.11).

4. The wizard now asks you whether to search for new hardware (again!) or choose it from a list. Actually, if you choose to search for new hardware, Win2K searches for hardware that is not Plug and Play–compatible. If you choose to select your device from a list, the wizard will display a list of device types, as shown in Figure 5.12. Scroll through the list and choose the device type you wish to install, such as a network adapter, and click Next.

FIGURE 5.11

Adding a new device

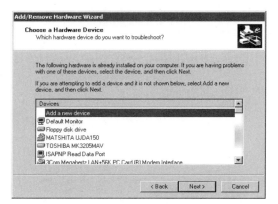

FIGURE 5.12

Choosing the type of
hardware you want
to install

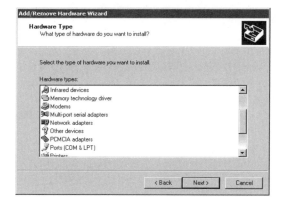

5. Next, select your adapter from a list of known devices (see Figure 5.13), or choose Have Disk
if it's not on the list and you have the driver from the manufacturer. Then click Next.

If you've selected from a list of known devices, just confirm the choices you've made and finish the wizard. If you've chosen Have Disk, point the wizard to the driver files (on a disk,
floppy, or other location). From that point, the installation procedure depends on the device.
Depending on the device, you may or may not be prompted for device settings.

What Happened to User Manager and User Manager for Domains?

We'll discuss user and group management more thoroughly in Chapter 9, but for now, just remember
that where NT 4 created both local user accounts and domain accounts with slightly different versions of the User Manager, Windows 2000 stores local user and domain accounts in very different
places and with somewhat different tools. *Local* user accounts (on stand-alone and non–domain controller systems) are created in Local Users and Groups using the Computer Management tool, and
domain accounts, or any accounts on a domain controller for that matter, are created with Active
Directory Users and Computers (by the way, what an awkward name for an admin tool).

FIGURE 5.13

FIGURE 5.13

Selecting the adapter
to install

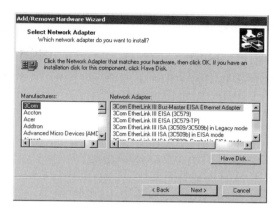

These Win2K tools can be used to add and modify user accounts; assign home directories, login scripts, and profiles; create and manage groups; and reset a user's password. However, you may recall that the NT 4 User Manager tools are also used to set account password and lockout policies, assign user rights, and even create trust relationships. Except for trust relationships, these functions are now administered using Group Policy or the Local Security Policy tool.

CONTROLLING ACCOUNT PASSWORD AND LOCKOUT POLICIES

To set account password and lockout policies for the local machine, use the Local Security Policy tool. However, if your system is part of an Active Directory domain, you'll set the domain-wide password and lockout policy using the Domain Security Policy tool. Details about setting local and group policies are included in Chapter 9, but here's a quick rundown, from the domain perspective. Log on to a domain controller as a domain administrator and follow these steps:

1. Start the program named Domain Security Policy in the Administrative Tools group.

2. In the left pane, open `Account Policies` (shown in Figure 5.14). From this point on, setting account and lockout policies for the domain is very similar to using the Local Security Policy tool to set policy for a stand-alone server. Expand `Password Policy` or `Account Lockout Policy` and double-click the policy items that appear in the right pane. You'll see check boxes to turn on the policy (such as Define This Policy Setting) and, depending on the policy, parameters to set, like Minimum Password Age or Account Lockout Duration.

FIGURE 5.14

Setting the machine's
password policy

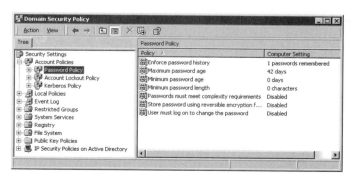

3. Once you've defined your setting, click OK and you'll see the changed setting displayed in the right pane of the window. Simply close the tool and the change is saved. There is no menu item to apply or save changes.

Audit policy, user rights, and some other miscellaneous security options that were previously only available by editing the Registry (or using some Resource Kit tool) are found in the Local Policies component under Security Options.

BUILDING TRUST RELATIONSHIPS

In Windows 2000, you shouldn't have to create trust relationships at all; trust is implicitly built when new domains are created in an existing forest. See Chapter 8 for an explanation of Active Directory domains, forests, and trees. Only when you wish to set up access to resources in other preexisting forests or Windows NT 4 domains will you need to create trust relationships. This is done by going to Administrative Tools/Active Directory Domains and Trusts. Right-click the icon representing your domain. Choose Properties and you'll see a property sheet with a tab labeled Trusts. From that point, it's just like establishing a trust relationship in NT 4. You can add a trusted domain or add domains that trust your domain.

No More Server Manager?

There is no more Server Manager tool in Windows 2000. Okay, it's still there, like the File Manager from NT 3.51 persisted in NT 4. It's not included in the Administrative Tools group anymore, but you can open it by clicking Start/Run, then filling in **srvmgr.exe**. And Server Manager is still useful for administering NT machines in a domain. But the problem with the Server Manager tool lies in the fact that it attempts to cover two different areas of remote administration: those functions that are machine-specific, such as shares and services, and those functions that relate to domain administration, such as promoting backup domain controllers. Win2K attempts to clear up the confusion by separating types of functions into separate components (although not necessarily into separate tools).

TIP   You'll find that Windows 2000 comes with several tools that Microsoft didn't put in Start/Programs. Many of those tools have been implemented as MMC snap-ins (see "A Microsoft Management Console Primer" later in this chapter for more information on MMC), and a great way to locate them is to search for ***.msc** *files with Start/Search/For Files or Folders.*

The functions of Server Manager that are machine related (such as shares and services) have moved to the Computer Management tool. Those related to domain management have moved to Active Directory Users and Computers and, to a lesser extent, Active Directory Sites and Services.

SHARES, SERVICES, AND ALERTS

To create and manage file shares on your local machine or on a remote machine, open Computer Management in the Administrative Tools group. If you want to create a share remotely, highlight Computer Management, choose Connect to Another Computer from the Action menu, then select the remote machine from the list. Expand System Tools to Shared Folders, and then open Shares, as shown in Figure 5.15.

FIGURE 5.15

Viewing shared folders

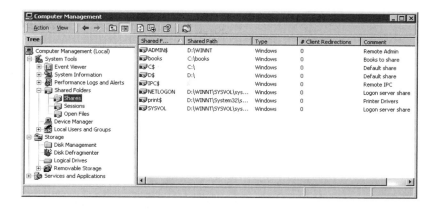

From the Action menu, or by right-clicking in the details pane (on the right), you have the option to create a new file share. This kicks off the Create Shared Folder Wizard. This new wizard allows you to select the directory to share by browsing; you can even create a new folder, which is a big improvement over the remote sharing in Server Manager, where you had to magically remember the full path of the directory you wanted to share. Once you've supplied the necessary info, like the local path, share name, and description, click Next and choose one of the basic share permissions or set custom permissions. Click Finish to create the share. Now, right-click the new share and choose Properties to change the description or share permissions and to set NTFS security on the directory. The Shared Folders tool also allows you to view user sessions and open files as Server Manager did, with the option to disconnect the session or the file if necessary.

To configure alerts for particular events on specific servers, there is now a special tool in Computer Management/System Tools called Performance Logs and Alerts. Now you can configure alerts without opening the Performance Monitor. The application doesn't have to be running in the foreground anymore to do performance logging or generate alerts. Plus, now you can configure Win2K to respond to alert events by creating log events, by sending a network message, or by running a command file. These are Big Improvements.

NOTE   *See Chapter 20 for specifics on configuring performance alerts.*

Domain Management Functions

To create a new machine account in a domain, open Active Directory Users and Computers, then select the domain and container where you want to add the machine account. There is already a Computers container for computer accounts, but you don't really have to use it. Select the Computers container (for example), and choose New/Computer from the Action menu. Supply the computer name in the dialog box that appears. If you are creating an account for an NT machine, be sure and check the box to allow pre–Windows 2000 computers to use the account. Now click OK to create the new machine account. See Chapter 8 for a complete overview of Active Directory.

PROMOTE/DEMOTE A DOMAIN CONTROLLER

Windows 2000 doesn't require a primary domain controller (PDC) as NT 4 did. In Win2K, these are called *replica domain controllers*, and all domain controllers are more or less equal, although there is a PDC emulator to accommodate certain requirements of legacy clients. So we really don't promote and demote domain controllers in the NT 4 sense of the words. However, a stand-alone machine or a member server may become a domain controller (without reinstalling!), and a domain controller can become a stand-alone machine or a member server (also without reinstalling). You will still have to reboot the machine after running DCPROMO to complete the transformation, though.

To create a new domain controller account, go to Active Directory Sites and Services in the Administrative Tools group. Open the Sites folder and choose the site where you want to create the new domain controller. Right-click Servers and choose New/Server. When prompted, supply the name of the new domain controller.

It's also possible to create the domain controller account during the process of converting a non–domain controller into a domain controller, if you have the appropriate local and domain administrative rights. Run DCPROMO.EXE from the Start/Run menu on the machine to be promoted, and a wizard kicks in that lets you join the machine to a domain, create a new domain, or become a domain controller in an existing domain.

CONTROL SERVICES ON A REMOTE MACHINE

To view and configure services on a remote machine as you did in Server Manager, go to the Computer Management tool. From the Action menu, choose Connect to Another Computer and select the remote machine from a list, or just type in the machine name. Once you are connected to the remote machine, expand Services and Applications to reveal the Services node. Highlight Services and you'll see, in the right pane, a list of services on the remote machine. You can now stop, start, and even restart services using your ever-useful right-click function, or you can use the Action menu. You can even use those cute tape recorder–like icons on the toolbar. The Properties option leads you to the equivalent of the old (NT 4) Configure button with more information and configuration options, such as a Recovery tab and a Dependencies tab.

NOTE *The Services tool in the Administrative Tools group also replaces the Services Control Panel; see "Where Is the Services Control Panel?" later in this chapter for more details.*

Where Is the Disk Administrator?

The Disk Administrator is now called Disk Management, and it can be found in the Storage component of Computer Management (see Figure 5.16).

Disk Management deserves a separate discussion (see Chapter 10), but let's just say that all the old functions are still there, more or less intact, plus the tool is now "remoteable." In other words, you can create and remove partitions on remote Win2K machines, with the proper administrative credentials, of course. But if you're in a rush and need to partition and/or format a drive, then open Computer Management (Start/Programs/Administrative Tools), then open the folder labeled Storage, and then open the folder inside *that* labeled Disk Management. From there, partitioning, volume naming, and formatting are all GUI-driven.

FIGURE 5.16

The Disk Management tool

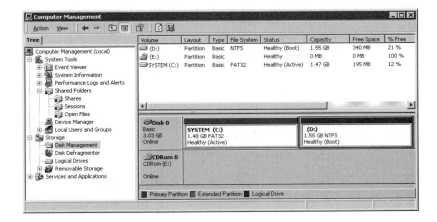

What Happened to the Device Management Tools in the Control Panel?

Some of the applets in the Control Panel—like Mouse, Display, and Sounds and Multimedia—still exist, but Win2K now takes the attitude that the Control Panel is for user-level options and not for advanced configuration. So you can still adjust your display and mouse settings, but the SCSI and Tape Device applets have gone away (see Figure 5.17 for a typical view of the new Control Panel applets). The Devices applet is also no more, replaced by the long-awaited and much more useful Win2K version of Device Manager (accessible through the Hardware tab of the System Control Panel or the System Tools component of the Computer Management tool). Actually, the Win2K Device Manager is much more useful than its Windows 9*x* predecessors because it is remoteable. That's right, now you can view devices and update drivers on your servers from the comfort and luxury of your own cubicle, assuming that you have administrative privileges on the remote machine.

FIGURE 5.17

A typical view of the Control Panel

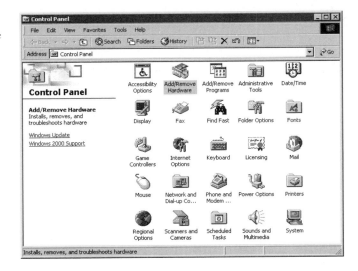

To view existing devices and drivers on a local or remote machine, go to the Computer Management tool in the Administrative Tools group. For a remote machine, highlight the root of the console (Computer Management) and choose Connect to Another Computer from the Action menu. Then go to the System Tools component and open Device Manager. From here, right-click the machine name at the top (or any device type on the list) to scan for hardware changes. For anything that is not detected, however, go to Add/Remove Hardware in the Control Panel on the local machine. This wizard allows you to manually add and configure a device.

If you haven't noticed already, it will be a relief to learn that the System Control Panel persists, although with a noticeable face-lift; virtual memory settings and environmental variables, as well as startup and recovery options, are configured using the Advanced tab (see Figure 5.18).

FIGURE 5.18

The System Control
Panel's Advanced tab

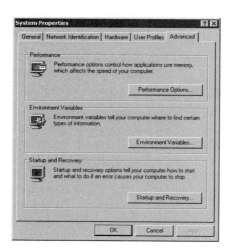

Where Is the Services Control Panel?

The functions of the Services Control Panel are now managed and configured using the Services tool. This is accessible as a stand-alone administrative tool but also takes the form of a snap-in or an extension, where it can be used remotely in the Computer Management tool. Choose Start/Programs/ Administrative Tools/Computer Management, or right-click My Computer and choose Manage. Expand Services and Applications, then Services, as shown in Figure 5.19. Here you see a list of services on the computer. Right-click them to stop, start, pause, or resume. Also, when you do, notice that there is a Restart option; with one button, you can stop and then start a service.

Win2K has improved on the old Services Control Panel significantly; you can now see a brief description of the service (so you don't accidentally disable something important) and its current status, start-up value, and security context all in one view. At least, you could if the descriptions weren't as long as postdoctoral theses.

To configure a Win2K service, highlight a service and double-click it, or right-click and choose Properties, and you'll see the new, improved configuration options for Win2K services. Figure 5.20 shows the General tab, which allows you to change the description and even the display name of the service. You can change the description of a service to something meaningful, such as "Do not stop this service under any circumstances." You can also change the status or the start-up value here. To change the security context (to have the service log on as a particular user) or to change the password of the user account the service uses, select the Log On tab.

FIGURE 5.19

Services in Computer Management

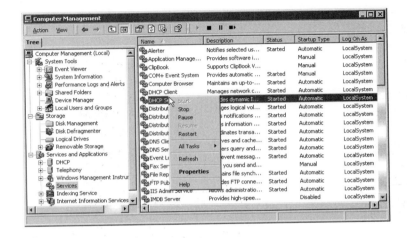

FIGURE 5.20

The property page of a service

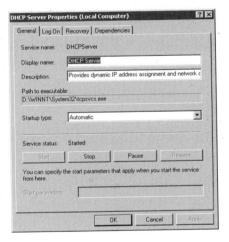

The Recovery tab, shown in Figure 5.21, displays a new set of options, including what to do if the service fails. In addition to choosing the response (from Take No Action all the way to Reboot the Computer) that will occur on the first, second, and subsequent attempts, you can provide the details. There is also a Dependencies tab to tell you what services depend on this one and what services this one depends on, which is good to know *before* you stop the service. In NT 4 you had no way of knowing about dependencies (other than from experience or a separate Resource Kit application) until you tried to stop the service.

NOTE   *It's a small thing, but when you right-click a service, you'll notice that in addition to Stop, Start, Pause, and Continue, there's a new option, Restart. This is deceptively cool—you see, choosing Restart causes Windows 2000 to stop a service and then start it again in just one click, a great time-saver compared to NT 4, where you had to first stop the service, then wait for the service to stop, and then start it again.*

FIGURE 5.21

Options in the
Server Properties
Recovery tab

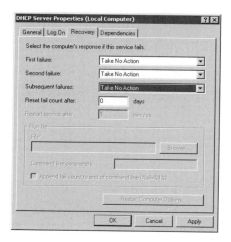

What Is This Network and Dial-Up Connections Tool?

The Network and Dial-Up Connections tool brings together the functions of Dial-Up Networking and NT 4's Network Control Panel. The idea here is that a connection is a connection, whether it's a serial cable to another computer on your desk, a dial-up connection to the Internet, or a network connection using an Ethernet card that provides access to the corporate network in your office.

Each connection represented in this tool contains the necessary device and protocol-specific information for its purposes. In other words, each connection's properties and configuration information is specific to the connection type and instance. For example, a Dial-Up Connection is much like an Address Book entry in NT 4 Dial-Up Networking; it knows which device (modem), phone number, and authentication protocol to use, and there are network protocols and services specified for it. A Local Area Connection entry is really not so different, containing information about the device to use (the network card type and hardware address), as well as network protocols and services to be used.

Figure 5.4 (a few pages back) shows the properties of a sample local area connection. Microsoft has just simplified the Network Control Panel options here by removing the Network Identification and Services configuration options. Different types of connections are all grouped together in this tool. So you may see several different dial-up connection entries (the dial-up icon includes a telephone), just as you saw multiple Address Book entries in Dial-Up Networking under NT 4, but you'll also see different Local Area Connection icons if you have multiple network cards (the connection in the network icon appears to be a BNC T-connector). If your server contains another type of networking device, such as an X.25 card or ISDN device, it will have an icon as well.

Where Did They Put NT Diagnostics?

WINMSD is gone. Well, the tool as we knew it is gone, replaced by a tool called System Information, which can be found in the Computer Management console under System Tools. Like many other tools we knew under NT 4, WINMSD has been replaced by a snap-in to the MMC. However, if you enter **WINMSD** in the Start/Run dialog box, the System Information tool opens by itself in a console, as shown in Figure 5.22. So if you really want to, you can put a shortcut to WINMSD in your `Administrative Tools` folder and feel right at home. The System Information tool is a huge improvement over `WINMSD.EXE` and an invaluable resource for system information.

FIGURE 5.22

The System Information tool

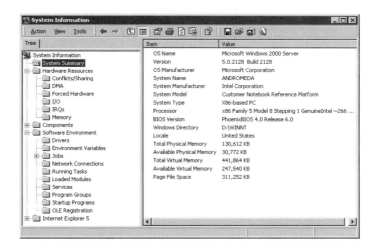

Fixing Windows 2000's GUI

If you're an administrator, then you may find Windows 2000's slightly new Desktop a bit annoying. Personally, I find the Web content that appears on the left-hand side of every window to be just a waste of space. Additionally, whenever I want to go do some maintenance in the `Program Files` or `System` directories, I've got to click past patronizing user-proofing screens that essentially say, "Hey, look, buddy, you're probably too stupid to mess with these files, are you *sure* you want to see this directory?" I need to see the hidden and system files, and in general, Details view is best for maintenance operations. Additionally, I've never found the address bar or standard buttons of much value in administrative tasks; they just rob me of screen space.

The first thing that I must do, then, when faced with a new system is to get it into "administrator-friendly" mode. To save you time, here are the steps:

1. Open My Computer.

2. From its menu bar, choose Tools/Folder Options.

3. In the General tab, under Web View choose Use Windows Classic Folders.

4. Click the View tab.

5. Check the box labeled Display the Full Path in the Title Bar.

6. Click the radio button labeled Show Hidden Files and Folders.

7. Uncheck the box labeled Hide File Extensions for Known File Types.

8. Uncheck the box labeled Hide Protected Operating System Files (Recommended) and click Yes when it asks you to confirm your choice.

9. Click OK.

10. Back in the main My Computer folder, click View/Details.

11. Right-click any blank space to the right of the menu bar and uncheck Standard Buttons.

12. Right-click any blank space to the right of the menu bar and uncheck Address Bar.

13. Hold down the Shift key and then click the close icon on the My Computer window—the icon in the upper right-hand corner that looks like an X. Hold down the Shift key so that the user interface will remember these settings.

Now that you've "saved" these settings with Shift+close, you'll reopen My Computer and apply those settings to all folders:

1. Click Tools/Folder Options.

2. Click the View tab.

3. Click the button toward the top of the page labeled Like Current Folder.

4. Click Yes to confirm the message.

5. Click OK to close Folder Options.

6. Close My Computer.

From now on, you'll be ready to get work done instead of appreciating the lovely "Web content"!

A Microsoft Management Console Primer

Let's face it, NT 4 admins. Our old familiar administrative tools—like the User Manager and User Manager for Domains, Server Manager, Event Viewer, and even Disk Administrator—have been assimilated into these things called Microsoft Management Console (MMC) tools.

I've discussed the shocking absence of Network Control Panel and how to deal with it. I've explained how to add a protocol or service. If only that were enough. To master Win2K's graphical changes, you must fully understand the Microsoft Management Console. In this section, I'll explain how MMC is not evil just because it has assimilated our friends, discuss key MMC terms you should know, briefly look at the Computer Management console, and, finally, introduce you to creating your own MMC-based administrative tools.

What Is This MMC Thing?

In NT 4, administrators had to master multiple administration tools. A whole set of built-in tools, plus independent third-party tools, made administration sort of a mess. Although many admin tools functioned remotely, you had to install some of them separately (unless your desktop happened to be an NT server), and with third-party tools, you often had to jump through hoops to get them to work remotely, if at all. Even worse, with menus, buttons, toolbars, wizards, tabs, HTML, Java (you get the picture), just learning how to navigate new software was a chore. Also, there was no simplified version of User Manager for Domains that could be given to account operators and no way to hide menu items in administrative tools for those without full administrator rights.

So we complained. "As administrators, we need to be able to administer our networks from the comfort and luxury of our cubicles. And we don't want to waste time exploring all the windows, wizards, and tabs in every new tool. And we need more flexible tools," we said. Behold, Microsoft has heard our cries, and their response was the Microsoft Management Console.

MMC is a framework for management applications, offering a unified interface for Microsoft and third-party management tools. MMC doesn't replace management applications; it integrates them into one single interface. There are no inherent management functions in MMC at all. It uses component tools called snap-ins, which do all the work. MMC provides a user interface; it doesn't change how the snap-ins function.

Why Is MMC Good and Not Evil?

MMC offers the following benefits:

◆ You only have to learn one interface to drive a whole mess of tools.

◆ Third-party (ISV) tools will probably use MMC snap-ins. At best, Microsoft is encouraging software vendors to do so.

◆ You can build your own consoles, which is practical and fun. Admins can even create shortcuts on the console to non-MMC tools like executables, URLs, wizards, and scripts.

◆ By customizing MMC consoles, admins can delegate tasks to underlings without giving them access to all functions and without confusing them with a big scary tool.

◆ Help in MMC is context sensitive; it displays help subjects for only the appropriate components. Okay, that's not really new, but it's still cool (the Action menu is also context sensitive, but nobody uses menus anymore; everybody just right-clicks instead).

MMC Terms to Know

This section defines important terms you'll need to know when working with MMC.

A *console*, in MMC-speak, is one or more administrative tools in an MMC framework. The prebuilt admin tools, like Active Directory Users and Computers, are console files. You can also make your own consoles without any programming tools—you needn't be a C or Visual Basic programmer, as I'll discuss a bit later. The saved console file is a *Microsoft saved console (MSC)* file and it carries the .MSC extension.

NOTE   *It's important to distinguish between Microsoft Management Console and console tools. MMC provides a framework to create customized console-based tools.* MMC.EXE *is a program that presents administrators (and others creating console tools) with a blank console to work with. It might help to think of a new instance of* MMC.EXE *as providing the raw material for a tool. In that case, Microsoft Management Console provides the rules and guidelines for building the tool, and the new console you create is the finished product.*

Snap-ins are what we call administrative tools that can be added to the console. For example, the DHCP admin tool is a snap-in, and so is the Disk Defragmenter. Snap-ins can be made by Microsoft or by other software vendors. (You *do* need programming skills to make these, in other words.) A snap-in can contain components called nodes, or containers, or even leaves, in some cases. Although you can load multiple snap-ins in a single console, most of the prebuilt administrative tools contain only a single snap-in (including the Computer Management tool).

An *extension* is basically a snap-in that can't live by itself on the console but depends on a stand-alone snap-in. It adds some functionality to a snap-in. Some snap-ins work both ways. For example, the Event Viewer is a stand-alone snap-in, but it's implemented as an extension to the Computer Management snap-in. The key point is that extensions are optional. You can choose not to load them. For example, Local Users and Groups is an extension to the Computer Management snap-in. If you remove the extension from the COMPMGMT.MSC file used by your support folk, or simply don't include it in a custom console that uses the snap-in, those who use the tool won't have the option to create or manage users and groups with the tool. They won't even see it. (Please note that this will not prevent them from creating users and groups by other means, if they have the correct administrative privileges.)

Admins can create new MSC files by customizing an existing MSC file or by creating one from a blank console. The MMC.EXE plus the defined snap-ins create the tool interface. Also, it's possible to open multiple tools simultaneously, but each console runs one instance of MMC. Open an MSC file and look in Task Manager while it's running—you only see the MMC.EXE process running, not the MSC file, just as you see WINWORD.EXE running in Task Manager, but not the Word document's name.

By default, prebuilt console tools open in *User mode*. Changes cannot be made to the console design. You can't add or remove snap-ins, for example. To create or customize a console, use *Author mode*. When a user is running a tool and not configuring it, it should be running in one of the *User modes*. The tool will actually look different in User mode than it does in Author mode.

Figure 5.23 shows a sample console tool, with the parts of the interface labeled. This console is running in Author mode to show all the parts of the MMC interface. This is a custom console, but to open any existing tool in Author mode, invoke it from the Start/Run dialog box with the **/a** switch.

In Figure 5.23, the Main MMC window is present because the tool is open in Author mode. In User mode, the Main MMC window, with menus and buttons, is hidden and you only see the Console window. The Console menu in the Main window is basically a File menu, but it's also used to add and remove snap-ins and set console options. The Console window Action menu is context sensitive and will reflect the options of the selected snap-in tool or component. The hierarchical list of items shown by default in the left pane is called the *console tree* (hence the "tree" label on the tab), and at the top is the *console root*. The Favorites tab displays any created links to places in the console tool. The right pane is called the *details pane*. Snap-ins appear as nodes on the console tree. The contents of the details pane change depending on the item selected on the console tree.

FIGURE 5.23

Anatomy of a console tool

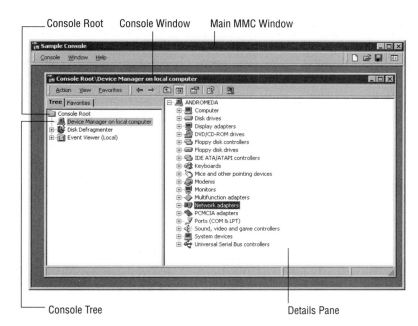

Console Root   Console Window   Main MMC Window

Console Tree   Details Pane

The Computer Management Console

The Computer Management console is *the* main tool for administering a single server, local or remote. If you only have one server on your network and you only want to use one admin tool, Computer Management fits the bill. To open the Computer Management console, select the tool from the `Administrative Tools` folder or right-click My Computer and choose Manage. You can also right-click the machine's icon in Active Directory Users and Computers and choose Manage.

There are three nodes in the Computer Management console tree: System Tools, Storage, and Services and Applications (see Figure 5.24). Notice that the focus is on the local machine by default; to connect to other computers on the network, highlight the Computer Management icon at the root of the tree and choose Connect to Another Computer from the Action menu.

Expand the nodes in the Computer Management console tree to reveal the configuration tools and objects, as shown in Figure 5.25. Most of the core functions are under System Tools. Some functions even work remotely on NT 4 machines (you can view a remote machine's Event Logs, for example), but new features require the remote machine to be a Win2K box.

FIGURE 5.24

The Computer Management console tree

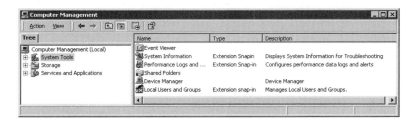

FIGURE 5.25

The expanded Computer Management console tree

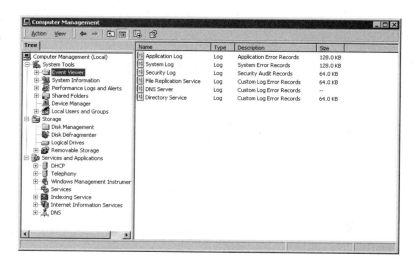

In the System Tools node, you can complete the following tasks:

◆ View events and manage the Event Logs. Basically, the Event Viewer tool turned into an MMC snap-in. Notice that some services, such as DNS and Directory Service (Active Directory software) now have their own logs.

◆ View system information. The export option in these consoles is great for generating reports and documenting your server configuration. System Information provides details about hardware resources, system components configuration information, and software components (see Figure 5.26).

◆ Set up performance logs and alerts without opening Performance Monitor (see Chapter 20 for specifics on configuring performance alerts).

◆ Manage shared folders. View, create, and manage shares; view sessions and open files; and disconnect sessions. This replaces those functions in the Control Panel's Server applet for local management and the remote shares management feature in Server Manager.

◆ Manage devices. The long-awaited Device Manager is fully remoteable and a great place to track down information about your hardware, update drivers, and troubleshoot resource conflicts.

◆ Create and manage local users and groups (Chapter 9 is all about creating and managing users and groups).

The Storage node (shown back in Figure 5.25) includes options for managing removable storage (a new feature), along with the new Disk Defragmenter tool and the Disk Management tool, which is the equivalent of the Disk Administrator in NT 4. There is also a component to view logical drives, including network drive mappings, and their properties. This is useful if you want to quickly view free space or set NTFS security at the root of a partition, for example. Too bad you can't browse directories like you can in Explorer. Oh well, I guess we don't need *another* desktop shell program, do we?

FIGURE 5.26

Viewing system information

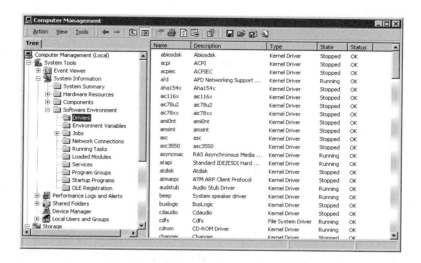

The Services and Applications node (also shown in Figure 5.25) includes telephony settings, services configuration, Windows Management Instrumentation (WMI), indexing, and IIS management stuff, the last of which is also available in the Administrative Tools group by itself (the tool is called Internet Services Manager, while the extension in Computer Management is called Internet Information Services). The Services tool replaces the Services Control Panel and the remote service management feature of Server Manager. Expect the components available in the Services and Applications node to change depending on what services are installed. For instance, if the server is a DHCP server or is running DNS, these management components will appear under Services and Applications—otherwise, you won't see them.

Other MMC Tools

If you're like me, you don't want to click here and click there and basically get carpal tunnel syndrome just to open something from the Administrative Tools group. If you prefer to use Start/Run to invoke your tools, it's nice to know their filenames. Table 5.1 outlines some of the core MMC-based tools files to save your hand and your sanity. Keep in mind that some tools, like DNS and DHCP, might not be present on the system if the corresponding service is not installed. Also, you need to include the program extension in the Start/Run box. Just entering **DSA**, for example, doesn't work. You'll need to enter **DSA.MSC**.

TABLE 5.1: Main MMC-Based Files

MSC FILE	COMMON NAME
MSINFO32.MSC*	System Information
COMPMGMT.MSC	Computer Management
DCPOL.MSC	Domain Controller Security Policy

Continued on next page

TABLE 5.1: MAIN MMC-BASED FILES *(continued)*

MSC FILE	COMMON NAME
DEVMGMT.MSC	Device Manager
DFRG.MSC	Disk Defragmenter
DFSGUI.MSC	Distributed File System
DISKMGMT.MSC	Disk Management
DOMPOL.MCS	Domain Security Policy
DOMAIN.MSC	Active Directory Domains and Trusts
DSA.MSC	Active Directory Users and Computers
DSSITE.MSC	Active Directory Sites and Services
EVENTVWR.MSC	Event Viewer
FAXSERV.MSC	Fax Service Management
FSMGMT.MSC	Shared Folders
GPEDIT.MSC	Group Policy
LUSRMGR.MSC	Local User Manager
NTMSMGR.MSC	Removable Storage Manager
PERFMON.MSC	Performance Monitor
RRASMGMT.MSC	Routing and Remote Access
SECPOL.MCS	Local Security Policy
SERVICES.MSC	Services Configuration
TAPIMGMT.MSC	Telephony
COMEXP.MSC*	Component Services
DHCPMGMT.MSC	DHCP
DNSMGMT.MSC	DNS
IIS.MSC*	Internet Information Services

Another caveat: most of these tools are found in the \winnt\system32 directory and are therefore in the default search path. A couple, however, are found in other directories that are not included in the default search path. The tool to manage Internet Information Services (IIS.MSC) is a good example; it's found in \winnt\system32\inetsrv. These errant tools are marked with an asterisk (*) in Table 5.1. The quickest way to find them is to use the Search option on the Start button. Once you locate them, there are a bunch of options. You can copy the tool to \winnt\system32 or just put a shortcut right on the desktop if you don't mind the clutter. The other alternative is to change the search path to include these directories. It's a bit more of a pain; you'll need to open the System applet in Control Panel, then go to the Advanced tab and choose the Environmental Variables button. Edit the system variable called Path. Oh, yes, and then reboot. Is it worth it? Many don't think so. One strategy I like to use combines these approaches. I copy all the tools I want to a separate directory, then add *that* directory to my search path. That way I don't have to edit the path variable multiple times. I just edit it once to add my tools directory, then copy tools into the directory to make them quickly accessible from the Run routine. You may think this is a lot of trouble to use a couple of tools, but just wait until you install a bunch of third-party tools on your server. They all use their own installation directories. Although Microsoft is reportedly requiring new third-party admin tools to go in the \winnt\system32 directory, they've caved in on requirements before, so it's best to be prepared.

Creating Microsoft Management Consoles

If the existing MMC tools don't fit your needs exactly, you can create a customized tool with your most frequently used components. Creating your own admin tool is easy using the MMC framework and snap-ins provided by Microsoft and third-party software vendors. Yes, keep in mind that your next version of a backup program or virus scanner or who knows what could be managed by a vendor-supplied MMC snap-in.

Although it's actually quite simple to create a customized MMC tool, there are so many options for customizing that I can't tell the full story here. Nevertheless, no discussion of the new Win2K interface would be complete without an example or two of authoring administration tools.

Building a Simple Microsoft Saved Console

To configure your own custom admin tool, open a blank MMC in Author mode by opening Start/Run and typing **mmc.exe**. This will open up an untitled console (Console1) and display a generic console root, shown in Figure 5.27. You can now open existing MSC files (just as you open DOC files in Word or XLS files in Excel) by choosing Open from the Console menu. These files will automatically open in Author mode if you open them in a blank console. If you wish to open and fiddle with existing MSC files, most (but not all) of them are in the \winnt\system32 directory. Just be sure to leave the original MSC files intact; you might need them again. In the example that follows, you'll be creating a tool from scratch, starting with a blank console and loading snap-ins.

FIGURE 5.27

A generic console root

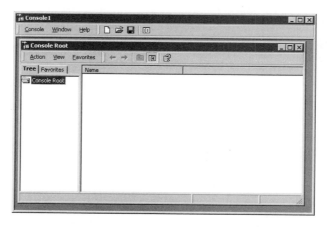

Suppose you need a tool for hardware management and troubleshooting. To create it, follow these steps:

1. Start by renaming the console root Hardware Tools; right-click the console root and choose Rename (you can actually do this step later if you prefer).

2. Now you're ready to add snap-ins. Choose Add/Remove Snap-in from the Console menu in the Main window. As you can see in Figure 5.28, you must choose where to add the snap-in. Right now, it's only possible to add snap-ins to the console root (now called `Hardware Tools`), but you can also group related tools by first adding folders to the console root.

FIGURE 5.28

Choosing where to add snap-ins

3. To add folders to the console root, choose the Add button to open the Add Standalone Snap-In dialog box (see Figure 5.29). You'll now see both dialog boxes, sort of cascaded. Items chosen from the list in the Add Standalone Snap-In dialog box will appear in the list of snap-ins in the parent dialog box. Scroll through the list until you see a folder called `Folder`. Choose Add, and the folder appears in your list of snap-ins in the Add/Remove Snap-In dialog box. Choose Add again and you'll see two. Close the Add Standalone Snap-In dialog box to return to Add/Remove Snap-In, then click OK to close it.

4. Back at the console in progress, right-click the folders to rename them. Figure 5.30 shows a Hardware Tools console with three folders, renamed to `Disk Tools`, `Other Tools`, and `Web Sites`.

5. The `Web Sites` folder will contain snap-ins that are actually hyperlinks to hardware vendor and support sites. To add links to the `Web Sites` container, open the Add/Remove Snap-In dialog again (choose Add/Remove Snap-In from the Console menu), select the `Web Sites` folder as the container, choose Add, then scroll through the list until you find Link to Web Address. Click the Add button, and from this point, it's just like creating a new Internet

shortcut; fill in the URL and give the shortcut a friendly name. Choose OK to close the Add/Remove Snap-In page and return to the console. When you select the link in the console tree, the Web page will appear in the details pane. You can actually surf the Web from the console, although you'll technically need links to get off that particular site.

FIGURE 5.29

The Add Standalone Snap-In dialog box

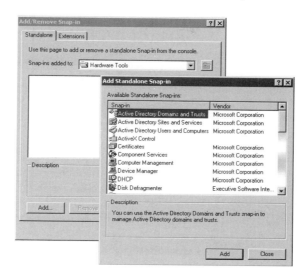

FIGURE 5.30

Customizing the console

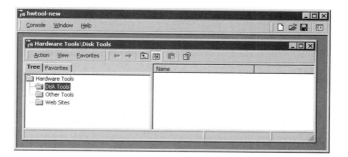

To add tools to the other folders, go through the same process and choose the appropriate tools from the list of snap-ins available. Presumably, third-party software vendors will provide tools as snap-ins, so this list will expand and vary with the configuration and software installed. Some tools will prompt you to select a computer to manage. Others, such as the Event Viewer snap-in, also present the option to choose the machine when you start the tool from the command line, as shown · in Figure 5.31. To change the focus of the tool when you kick it off, enter **tool.msc /computer=** *computername* in the Start/Run box or at a command prompt.

FIGURE 5.31

Selecting a computer
for the snap-in to
manage

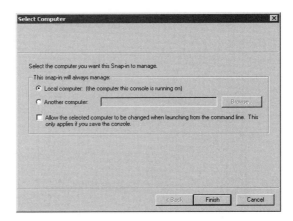

While adding the stand-alone snap-ins, be sure to check out the available extensions for them. It's interesting to note that the Computer Management snap-in components are all implemented as extensions (see Figure 5.32), although most also exist as independent snap-ins. You can load the Computer Management snap-in and deselect the extensions that aren't needed for your custom tool. All available extensions are added by default.

FIGURE 5.32

Select or deselect
extensions

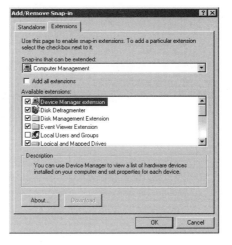

In Figure 5.33, you can see what your final tool could look like: a customized Hardware Tools console. This one consists of a Disk Tools folder (with Defragmenter and Disk Management), a folder called Other Tools that includes the Device Manager and System Information, and a Web Sites folder that can be filled with helpful hardware support–related links.

To save the custom console, open Save from the Console menu, name the file and specify a path to save it in, then click Save. Now the MSC file is ready to use.

FIGURE 5.33

A custom Hardware
Tools console

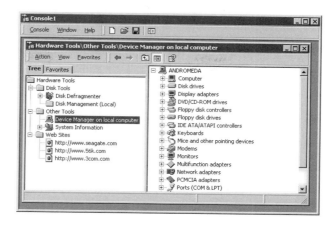

Designing Tools with Taskpad Views

It's possible to design simple views of an MMC tool for newbie administrators, foregoing their need to learn the different tools and navigate the console tree nodes. You might also wish to present a limited set of tasks and hide others that are normally available in a regular MMC tool view. Taskpad views fill this need and allow you to create a tool that looks like the one shown in Figure 5.34. This tool presents a limited set of tasks instead of the entire console tree structure. Now novice administrators can perform delegated tasks without drilling down through the tree, expanding and collapsing, hoping to find the right tool, then looking for the choice on the Action menu. Instead, they can just click the icon and go right to the task.

FIGURE 5.34

A simple
taskpad tool

Taskpad views are HTML-based pages that can include links to console menu commands, wizards, scripts, other executables, even URLs. At least one snap-in is required to create a taskpad view, although you can create links to tasks that are unrelated to the snap-in, such as scripts. To include menu command and property page tasks, however, the corresponding snap-in must be loaded beforehand.

Before designing a console with taskpad views, or any type of console for that matter, put your thinking cap on and visualize the tool you need. What tasks will the tool include? Which snap-ins will be required? You'll need to be somewhat familiar with the available snap-ins and their functions. Will your tool include only one taskpad view with a bunch of tasks in a single window? Or do you need a tool with several tabs, each containing a set of related tasks? Figure 5.34 shows a tool with only one taskpad view; tasks are all together in one window, and the console tree is hidden from the user. Figure 5.35 illustrates a multiple taskpad tool, perhaps for a more experienced support person who needs to perform several different types of tasks and doesn't want to load a different tool for each one.

FIGURE 5.35

A multiple taskpad tool

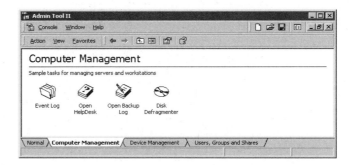

There are a couple of possible strategies for creating taskpad views. One is to just assemble a specific set of tasks into one or more taskpad views. For example, when the tool is opened, you might see a single taskpad view called Routine Admin Tasks with links labeled Create New User or Create New Share. If you to click the link called Create New User, the dialog box or wizard to create new users appears. In a tool like this, you might want to hide the console tree to prevent users from navigating around and present only the taskpad view.

Another technique is to create taskpad views for particular items in the tree, for example a taskpad for Users and Groups, another for Shared Folders, and a third for the Event Viewer. Again, you might choose to hide the actual console tree and normal views for this tool. In that case, you should create a main taskpad with links to the other taskpads located at different branches of the tree. So imagine a taskpad view called Main Taskpad, which contains links called Open Services and Manage IIS. Click the former and another taskpad appears, with a list of services and links to stop, start, or restart a service. Use the Forward and Back buttons on the toolbar (as we do in Explorer) to return to the Main Taskpad view.

Alternately, you might choose to present these taskpad views in addition to the normal views without hiding the console tree. In this case, the taskpad will enhance the functionality of the console tool by presenting a set of simple task options (for people who don't like playing Marco Polo in admin tools) without imposing any limitations on what the user can see or access.

Whichever approach you choose, keep in mind that taskpad views are meant to simplify and facilitate the use of a console. They can even limit, to some extent, the administrative options that are presented. However, you should not consider them a foolproof way to limit admin types from performing certain tasks. Even if they can't get around the limitations of the custom console, which is by no means certain, they may have access to other tools that are not restricted. The best way to limit another admin's power is to use all of the other built-in security options that are available in appropriate combinations:

security group memberships, rights, group policies, and delegation of control are some of the more reliable tools for this purpose. Don't rely on a customized, locked-down console tool instead.

In this section, I'll show you how to create a Main Taskpad view for the Computer Management snap-in and how to create tasks. Then I'll demonstrate how to set up taskpad views for particular items in the console tree, with links from the Main Taskpad. Finally, I'll reveal how to customize the interface to hide the console tree and present a simplified interface to the user.

CREATING TASKPAD VIEWS

Once you've decided which tasks your user or admin person will perform with this tool and identified the necessary snap-ins, you are ready to create the console. In this example, you'll create a view and a select set of tasks from the Computer Management snap-in to keep things simple. This tool will be for gathering information; we'll use the Event Logs, System Information, and Device Manager functions. Open a blank console as described earlier (Start/Run and enter **mmc.exe**) and load the required snap-ins. You can also use an existing custom console that contains the necessary snap-ins as long as you open it in Author mode.

To follow along with this example, load the Computer Management snap-in in your blank MMC console; it encompasses all the tasks for this tool. It's also possible to add the three snap-ins separately (Event Logs, System Information, and Device Manager), but the Computer Management snap-in has a special capability that will facilitate remote information gathering, as you'll see in a moment.

To create a taskpad view at the top of the Computer Management node, follow these steps:

1. Select the Computer Management node in the console tree, right-click it (or pull down the Action menu), and choose New Taskpad View.

2. A New Taskpad View Creation Wizard appears. Click Next to continue.

3. Next, select the style of the taskpad view (shown in Figure 5.36). Choose whether to display the actual items that would normally appear in the details pane (such as a list of users or a list of services), and if so, whether you want a vertical list (to accommodate lots of columns) or a horizontal list (for longer lists). In this case, we're just going to create a view of links and don't want to see the details pane information, so choose No List. If you were to choose a list type, however, you would use the List Size option box to determine how much of the window pane can be taken up by the list. I'll demonstrate a taskpad view with a list in a moment. Now, select the style you want for your task descriptions. If you needed a longer explanation to appear alongside the link, you would choose Text. However, we want a description that just pops up when you hover over the link, thus leaving more room for task links, so choose InfoTip. All of the tasks created later will use this style. Choose Next to continue.

4. In the next screen (Figure 5.37), you must decide whether to apply the view to the selected tree item only or to any other tree item of the same type. If you choose the latter, you have the option to change the default details pane display for those items to the taskpad view (although the normal view will still exist). However, let's choose to apply the view only to the selected tree item. This taskpad view will only display when the Computer Management root node is selected. Choose Next.

FIGURE 5.36

Configuring the style of the taskpad

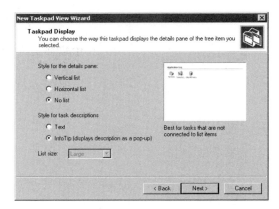

FIGURE 5.37

Selecting a taskpad target

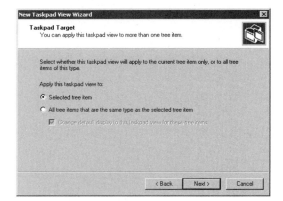

5. Now, supply a name for your taskpad (mine is called Main Taskpad) and a description if you wish. The description you supply will appear under the title in the details pane. That's it! In the final screen of the wizard, you have the option to kick off the New Task Wizard and start creating tasks (uncheck the box beside Start New Task Wizard to avoid creating a new task for now). Click Finish to close the wizard and create the new taskpad view.

Figure 5.38 shows the new taskpad before any tasks are created. Notice the squared-off tabs that allow you to move between the taskpad view and the normal view of the details pane. In a moment, I'll show you how to hide the console tree on the left and remove the normal view tab to achieve the look and feel of the console shown in Figure 5.34.

If you want to create another taskpad view, like the one in Figure 5.35, just choose New Taskpad View again from the Action menu. Or choose Delete Taskpad View to delete a selected one. If you want to make changes to a taskpad, select Edit Taskpad View from the Action menu (you may have to click the taskpad's tab first—blast those pesky context-sensitive menu commands!). In the taskpad view property page, shown in Figure 5.39, you can go back and change the style of the view and add, remove, or modify tasks.

FIGURE 5.38

A console with a taskpad view

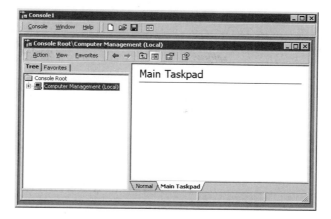

FIGURE 5.39

The taskpad property page

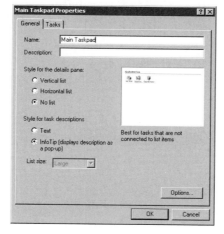

CREATING A TASK

To create tasks for the new taskpad, select the Start New Task Wizard check box in the last screen of the Taskpad View Creation Wizard, or choose Edit Taskpad View from the Action menu. Move to the Tasks tab and click New to start the same wizard. The following steps illustrate how to create a task that uses the Connect to Another Computer command (in the Computer Management Snap-in):

1. In the New Task Wizard, click Next to begin creating a new task. The wizard asks whether the task will be a menu command (from the context or Action menu in the console), a shell command, or a navigation command, which points to a link in the Favorites tab (see Figure 5.40). Although shortcut menu commands are limited to the functions of a loaded snap-in, a shell command could be an executable (like a wizard), a shell script or other type of script, even a URL. In any of these cases, the shell command task actually kicks off the command called, so

in that sense, it's just a taskpad's version of a shortcut to something outside of the tool itself. For example, you can create a shell command task and point it to the Calculator (CALC.EXE) if you want (that way, it's handy for those binary-to-decimal conversions). Click the radio button beside the desired type of task. We'll create a menu command in this example, but if you choose to create a shell command at another time, you'll need to specify the path to the command and any command-line parameters (also called *arguments*), the "start in" directory, and whether the command should run in a normal window, minimized, or maximized. Figure 5.41 shows the dialog box where you create a shell command task.

FIGURE 5.40

Creating a new task

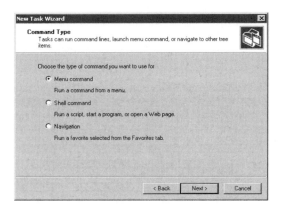

FIGURE 5.41

Creating a shell command task

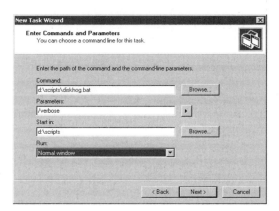

NOTE   *In contrast to shell command tasks, which refer to commands outside the tool, navigation command tasks are shortcuts to places within the console. For instance, if you want a shortcut to the Disk Defragmenter, find it in the tool, then add it to the tool's favorites (just choose Add to Favorites from the Favorites menu). Then, when you create your task, just choose the shortcut to Disk Defragmenter from the list of existing favorites. Once the shortcut is created, clicking the task icon whisks you down to the Disk Defragmenter tool.*

2. After choosing to create a menu command, select a source for the command in the next screen (see Figure 5.42) and choose a command from those available on the right. You can choose whether the source of the command will be an item in the details pane or a specific item in the console tree. In this case, we are creating the latter, a tree item task. Now you'll see the Computer Management node in the left pane and Connect to Another Computer is among the available commands on the right. Highlight Connect to Another Computer and click Next.

FIGURE 5.42

Selecting a menu command

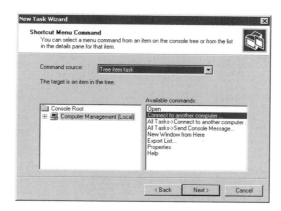

3. Give the task a name and a description. The description you supply will either appear alongside the task icon or will pop up when you hover over it, depending on the style choice you made for the taskpad. Click Next.

4. In the next screen (shown in Figure 5.43), choose a task symbol. Unfortunately, the selection of symbols is pretty limited. However, some tasks have recommended symbols; the wizard may highlight one for you but will of course leave the final choice up to you. Click Next.

FIGURE 5.43

Choosing an icon for Figure 5.44: the task

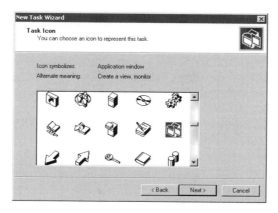

5. The wizard confirms your task creation (see Figure 5.44), displaying a list of created tasks and giving you the option to run the wizard again to create another task. Click Finish, then click OK to close the taskpad property page. The new task will appear in the taskpad as a link. Just click the link once to run it.

FIGURE 5.44

Completing the New Task Wizard

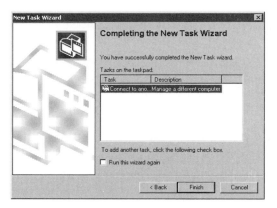

6. Just for practice, run the New Task Wizard again, creating a new menu command based on another tree item. Scroll through the Computer Management tree and locate Shares under Shared Folders. The task you're looking for is New File Share. Create a task to create a new share on the computer. Now your taskpad should look like the one shown in Figure 5.45. Using the tasks you've created, you can now connect to remote machines and create shares on them.

FIGURE 5.45

A taskpad with tasks

Steps 1 through 5 illustrate how to create a task to connect to another computer, which is important if the tool is to function remotely. This is why the Computer Management snap-in was used instead of the individual component snap-ins. When adding individual component snap-ins like the Event Viewer, you must choose to have it always manage the local machine or a particular remote machine.

TIP   When you load a snap-in, there is an option to specify the machine to be managed when the tool is started from the command line, but this requires that you close and reopen the tool to administer a different machine; that's just too much trouble. With the Connect to Another Computer task that's built in to the Computer Management snap-in, you can easily change the focus for any task created without closing and reopening the console.

SOME NOTES ABOUT TASKPADS AND TASKS

When you were creating the taskpad in our example, you had the choice in step 4 to apply the view to the selected tree item only or to any other tree item of the same type. When a taskpad view is applied to the selected tree item, it will only be visible when you navigate to the node in the console tree or use a link such as a Favorite to get there. When a taskpad view applies to other tree items and is set to display by default instead of the normal details pane view, the taskpad would theoretically contain mostly generic menu commands, like Open or Properties, so that as you navigate to a certain part of the tree, you see a consistent taskpad view and set of link commands in the details pane on the right. Unfortunately, Microsoft is still working out the kinks in this area, because taskpad views created in this way don't seem to display except at the node where they are created, and the documentation is pretty silent about it.

When you're choosing a menu command source, if your command source is the list in the details pane, your choices are limited to menu commands available at that level. However, you can still create tree item tasks that point to any item on the tree. Menu item command tasks are not limited by the item to which the taskpad is linked. So why would you want to create tasks that are limited to the commands in the details pane at all? Well, this capability is useful if you need to apply the same tasks to different items in the list. You see, with tasks that use the command list in the details pane, you first choose the item from a horizontal list in the taskpad, for example; then you choose the task link. The command applies to the selected item. As an example, let's create a taskpad view for the Services node and create tasks to stop, start, and resume the selected service in the taskpad:

1. First, create the new taskpad for services configuration. Go to the Services node in the console tree (it's under Computer Management/Services and Applications/Services) and choose New Taskpad View from the Action menu. The wizard will open. Click Next to continue.

2. Select display options for the taskpad. For Services, there will be a long list, so a vertical list is appropriate, although selecting a horizontal list will allocate more room to display the columns. I also recommend leaving the task description style on InfoTip, as this will allow more room for task links. Click Next.

3. Choose to apply the taskpad view to the selected tree item. These commands will be specific to the Services node. Choose Next.

4. Give the taskpad a name (I just called mine Services) and a description, which will appear under the name in the details pane. Click Finish to create the taskpad and start the New Task Wizard (if you left the box checked, it's selected by default).

5. To create a task, click Next in the New Task Wizard. Choose to create a menu command and click Next.

6. This time, in the Shortcut Menu Command page, you'll choose your command from the list in the details pane for Services. As you can see in Figure 5.46, these are also the commands that are available in the context menu when you select a service and right-click it. Select Restart (it doesn't really matter which service is selected on the source side at this point) and click Next.

FIGURE 5.46

Creating a service configuration task

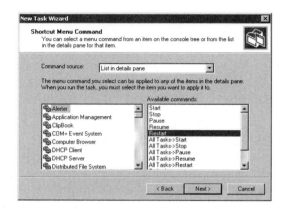

7. Supply a name for the task and a short description. I changed the description for the Restart task because the default description, which appears when you hover your cursor over the symbol in the taskpad, was incorrectly service- and machine-specific (another small kink). Click Next.

8. Choose an icon from the list, click Next, click Finish in the confirmation page, and you're done.

9. Repeat steps 5 through 8 as necessary to create tasks for Start, Stop, Pause, Resume, and Properties.

Now the Services taskpad should appear with the list of services displayed in a list. The tasks you've created appear alongside (or under) the details pane. To restart a given service, select it from the list and click Restart. Figure 5.47 shows the final Services taskpad with several service-related tasks, although you might not want to include the Properties task if you don't want the user of the tool to change the configuration of the services.

CUSTOMIZING THE CONSOLE INTERFACE

You can give the customized tool a simplified look and feel by hiding the console tree and those navigation tabs that allow users to move between the normal view and the taskpad views.

Ya know, that reminds me, if we hide the console tree and the navigation tabs, lock the tool down, and prevent the user of the tool from navigating the console tree, they have no way of getting to the Services taskpad we created in our earlier example. They'll be stuck at the Main Taskpad. So before we customize the console interface, we need a task in the Main Taskpad that acts as a link to the Services taskpad. There are two ways to accomplish this, and both seem to work equally well.

FIGURE 5.47

The Services taskpad

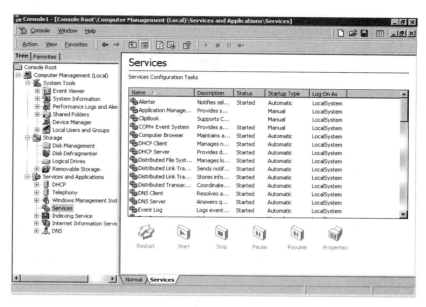

The first way to create a link to another taskpad is to navigate to the node while the console tree is visible in Author mode and add that location to the list of Favorites. Then, create a navigation task in the Main Taskpad and select the Services Favorite as the destination. The Favorites link must exist, however, before you can create a navigation task for it.

If you don't want to use the Favorites method, create a menu item task in the Main Taskpad and select as the source a tree item task. Navigate down the tree to Services and select the command Open (shown in Figure 5.48). This will create a task to open the Services node where the taskpad will display by default.

FIGURE 5.48

Creating a task to
open a console
taskpad view

Now, to customize the console interface, choose Customize from the View menu in the Console window. A set of view options is shown in Figure 5.49. Items are shown when the boxes are checked and hidden when they are cleared. While clearing the Console Tree check box does hide the Tree tab in the console pane on the left, it doesn't hide the pane itself; you'll still see the Favorites tab. If that's not agreeable to you, use the Show/Hide Console Tree button on the toolbar. It actually hides the entire tree side of the Console window.

FIGURE 5.49

Customizing the view of a console

Hide the Action and View menus by clearing the Standard Menus check box. Removing the Action menu prevents the user from selecting an item from a horizontal or vertical list in a taskpad and pulling down the Action menu to see a complete set of task options, but they can still use the context menu by right-clicking if you don't disable it (see the next section for instructions on disabling the context menu). If you clear the check box labeled Standard Toolbar, the toolbar with the forward and back buttons (as well as the Up One Level and Show/Hide Console buttons) disappears. You need those buttons if the tool has to navigate the tree. Consider our earlier example of the Main Taskpad with a link to the Services taskpad. If the Standard toolbar is removed, you cannot return to the Main Taskpad from the Services taskpad without a link in the Services taskpad. If the console tool is only running wizards or scripts, however, removing the navigation buttons won't be a problem. To really simplify the window, clear both the Status Bar and the Description Bar check boxes (the status bar is displayed by default, but the description bar is not). Clear the Taskpad Navigation Tabs check box to remove the Normal tab from the bottom of the details pane, and users will only be able to view the taskpads you've created.

Each snap-in can have its own menu items and toolbar buttons. To hide these for all snap-ins in the tool, clear the two check boxes in the Snap-In section of the dialog box. You can't pick and choose which toolbars and buttons to hide; you either hide them for all snap-ins or reveal them for all snap-ins.

Packaging Up the Tool for Users

When the tool is ready to be published, choose Options from the Console menu of the Main window and change the tool's name (from Console1 to something descriptive), as shown in Figure 5.50. The new name will now appear in the title bar. You might also want to assign a different icon than the generic MMC icon. Finally, assign a default mode to the MSC file. Choose Author mode, and it will always open with the main MMC window and main menu/toolbar, allowing changes to be made to the tool. Otherwise, only the Console window is available. If you aren't sure what I mean by the terms *Main MMC window* and *Console window*, glance back at Figure 5.23, "Anatomy of a console tool." Use one of the three User modes to prevent changes, such as adding and removing snap-ins. The three different User modes represent varying degrees of restrictions, including whether the user can open multiple windows. Limited Access Single Window is the most restrictive.

FIGURE 5.50

The Console
Options dialog box

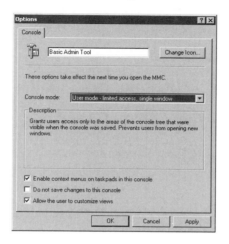

Notice the three configuration check boxes at the bottom of Figure 5.50. To disable all context menus on all taskpads in the console, uncheck the box that says Enable Context Menus on Taskpads in This Console. If you created that Services taskpad and left out a Properties task, for example, the user could still right-click a service in the list and choose Properties, unless the context menus are disabled (see the preceding section for instructions on removing the Action menu, which also shows a full set of possible tasks when an item is selected). Check Do Not Save Changes to This Console to prevent users from saving any changes to the console. Users can customize views by default. To prevent this, uncheck the box that says Allow the User to Customize Views. Choose OK, then save the console as an MSC file if you haven't already.

Figure 5.51 shows our basic admin tool running in User mode with limited access and a single window. The console tree and taskpad navigation tabs, as well as the Action and View menus, are hidden. This tool does reveal the Standard toolbar, however, since it's necessary to be able to go forward and back in the tool. Too bad you can't hide some buttons and not others. The buttons to show the console tree and to go up a level are also available.

FIGURE 5.51

The final product

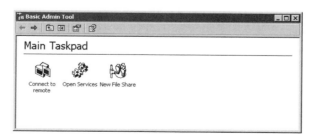

Distributing the Tool

When the tool is finished, just distribute it as you would a normal file; e-mail it to someone, put it on the network file server in a shared folder, or use Active Directory services to publish it. Appropriate administrative permissions for the tasks and access to the snap-ins, either on the local machine or on the network, are required to use the tool.

Unfortunately, these custom tools will only run on other Win2K machines, unless Microsoft has plans to distribute a compatible version of MMC for Windows 9x and NT 4 clients.

Editing a Custom Console Tool

Making changes to the console is easy, even when the tool opens in User mode by default. The tool can be opened in Author mode using one of several methods. If you open it using Start/Run and enter the filename with the **/a** switch, the MSC file will open in Author mode. Right-clicking the file's icon and choosing Author is another method. Also, you can open a blank console using Start/Run and entering **mmc.exe** and then choose open from the Console menu to pull up any MSC file in Author mode. But how can you keep others from making changes to the tool using these tricks? Chapter 9 explains how to restrict access to Author mode, and even particular snap-ins, using group policies.

In this chapter, you learned how to gracefully weather the user interface changes that come with administering Windows 2000 Server. You should now feel confident configuring network software without the Network Control Panel, among other things. We also explored the Microsoft Management Console and learned a few of its inner secrets. Now you are ready to unleash the real power of MMC, by using its authoring features to create consoles that fit the needs of your MIS/IT department.

Chapter 6

Understanding and Using TCP/IP in Windows 2000 Server

WHEN NT FIRST APPEARED, TCP/IP was the mildly scary, obscure, complex protocol used by just a few—those "oddballs" in research, education, and government who were attached to that large but still-private club called "the Internet." Most of us chose either NetBEUI in small networks for its simplicity or IPX for its partial interoperability with Novell NetWare.

Since the early '90s, however, IPX has been dethroned as the corporate protocol of choice and TCP/IP has replaced it. Furthermore, most of the basic pieces of Windows 2000 that separate it from earlier implementations of NT—a directory structure integrated with the Domain Name System, a workstation installation tool (Remote Installation Services), and other components first introduced in Windows 2000—simply must have TCP/IP to run. In a very large sense, TCP/IP is *the* mandatory protocol for Windows 2000.

TCP/IP is a big subject, so the book takes three chapters to cover it. In this, the first of those, I'll explain what TCP/IP is and how its networks—both the worldwide Internet and your firm's intranet—work. In this first chapter, you'll see how to build a basic intranet and you'll understand some of the vexing-but-necessary parts of putting one together—in particular, you'll learn about IP addresses, subnet masks, and IP routing. I'd like to be able to tell you, "You needn't worry about any of that—just run the Intranet Creation Wizard" or some other mythical tool, but sadly such tools are just that—mythical. However, things like subnet masks sound scarier than they actually are, which is why I'm going to take you through the ugly details.

In the next chapter, we'll look at three very basic and essential TCP-related technologies that allow you to create an infrastructure for your network—the Dynamic Host Configuration Protocol (DHCP), the Domain Name System (DNS), and the Windows Internet Name Service (WINS).

Then, in Chapter 17, you'll see how to set up the server service that is perhaps the most popular type of server on TCP/IP-based networks—a Web server, with the built-in Internet Information Server (IIS) shipped with Windows 2000.

A Brief History of TCP/IP

Let's start off by asking, "What *is* TCP/IP?" TCP/IP is a collection of software created over the years, much of it with the help of large infusions of government research money. Originally, TCP/IP was intended for the Department of Defense (DoD). You see, DoD tends to buy a *lot* of equipment, and much of that equipment is incompatible with other equipment. For example, back in the late '70s when the work that led to TCP/IP was first begun, it was nearly impossible to get an IBM mainframe to talk to a Burroughs mainframe. That was because the two computers were designed with entirely different *protocols*—something like Figure 6.1.

FIGURE 6.1

Compatible hardware, incompatible protocols

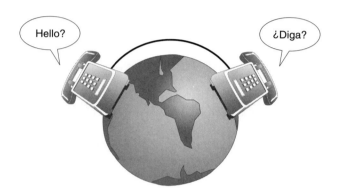

To get some idea of what the DoD was facing, imagine picking up the phone in the U.S. and calling someone in Spain. You have a perfectly good hardware connection, as the Spanish phone system is compatible with the American phone system. But despite the *hardware* compatibility, you face a *software* incompatibility. The person on the other end of the phone is expecting a different protocol, a different language. It's not that one language is better or worse than the other, but the English speaker cannot understand the Spanish speaker and vice versa. Rather than force the Spanish speaker to learn English or the English speaker to learn Spanish, we can teach them both a universal language such as Esperanto, the universal language designed in 1888. If Esperanto were used in my telephone example, neither speaker would use it at home, but they would use it to communicate with each other.

That was how TCP/IP began—as a simple *alternative* communications language. As time went on, however, TCP/IP evolved into a mature, well-understood, robust set of protocols, and many sites adopted it as their *main* communication language.

Origins of TCP/IP: From the ARPAnet to the Internet

The original DoD network wouldn't just hook up military sites, although that was an important goal of the first defense Internetwork. Much of the basic research in the U.S. was funded by an arm of the Defense Department called the Advanced Research Projects Agency, or ARPA. ARPA gave, and still gives, a lot of money to university researchers to study all kinds of things. ARPA thought it would be useful for these researchers to be able to communicate with one another, as well as with the Pentagon. Figures 6.2 and 6.3 demonstrate networking both before and after ARPAnet implementation.

FIGURE 6.2

Researchers before
ARPAnet

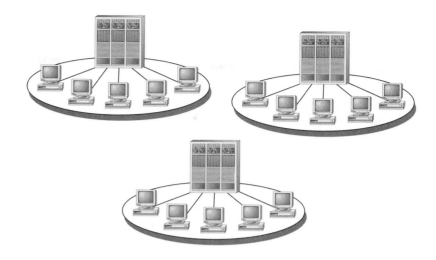

FIGURE 6.3

Researchers after
ARPAnet

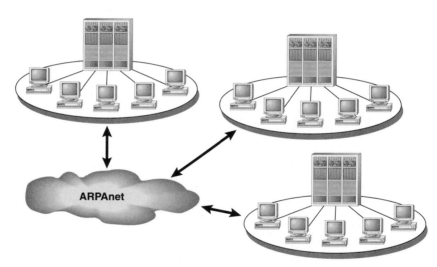

The new network, dubbed ARPAnet, was designed and put in place by a private contractor called Bolt, Baranek, and Newman. For the first time, it linked university professors both to each other and to their military and civilian project leaders around the country. Because ARPAnet was a network that linked separate private university networks and the separate military networks, it was a "network of networks."

ARPAnet ran atop a protocol called the Network Control Protocol (NCP). NCP was later refined into two components, the Internet Protocol (IP) and the Transmission Control Protocol (TCP). The change from NCP to TCP/IP is the technical difference between ARPAnet and the Internet. On 1 January 1983, ARPAnet packet-switching devices stopped accepting NCP packets and only passed TCP/IP packets, so in a sense, 1 January 1983 is the "official" birthday of the Internet.

ARPAnet became the Internet after a few evolutions. (Well, that's a "few evolutions" unless you happen to believe that Al Gore invented it in his spare time while a senator.) Probably the first major development step occurred in 1974, when Vinton Cerf and Robert Kahn proposed the protocols that would become TCP and IP. (I say *probably* because the Internet didn't grow through a centralized effort, but rather through the largely disconnected efforts of several researchers, university professors, and graduate students, most of whom are still alive—and almost *all* of whom have a different perspective on what the "defining" aspects of Internet development were.) Over its more than 20-year history, the Internet and its predecessors have gone through several stages of growth and adjustment. Ten years ago, the Internet could only claim a few thousand users. Nowadays, hundreds of millions of people are on the Internet. The Internet appears to double in size about every year. It can't do that indefinitely, but it's certainly a time of change for this huge network of networks.

Internet growth is fueled not by an esoteric interest in seeing how large a network the world can build, but rather by just a few applications that require the Internet to run. Perhaps most important is Internet e-mail, followed closely by the World Wide Web, and then the File Transfer Protocol (FTP) but more on those later in Chapter 17.

Originally, the Internet protocols were intended to support connections between mainframe-based networks, which were basically the only ones that existed through most of the 1970s. But the 1980s saw the growth of Unix workstations, microcomputers, and minicomputers. The Berkeley version of Unix was built largely with government money, and the government said, "Put the TCP/IP protocol in that thing." There was some resistance at first, but adding IP as a built-in part of Berkeley Unix has helped both Unix and the Internet grow. The IP protocol was used on many of the Unix-based Ethernet networks that appeared in the '80s and still exist to this day. As a matter of fact, you probably have to learn at least a smidgen of Unix-like commands to get around the Internet—but don't let that put you off. In this chapter, I'll teach you all the Unix you need and show you how much of the old Unix stuff can be fulfilled by Windows 2000. You will find, however, that most ISPs are still driven by Unix.

In the mid-1980s, the National Science Foundation created five supercomputing centers and put them on the Internet. This served two purposes: It made supercomputers available to NSF grantees around the country, and it provided a major "backbone" for the Internet. The National Science Foundation portion of the network, called NSFnet, was for a long time the largest part of the Internet. It is now being superseded by the National Research and Education Network (NREN). For many years, commercial users were pretty much kept off the Internet, as most of the funding was governmental; you had to be invited to join the Net. But those restrictions have been relaxed and now the majority of Internet traffic is routed over commercial lines rather than government-run lines. In fact, commercial and private users dominate the Internet these days, so much so that the government and educational institutions are now working on a faster "Internet 2."

It's customary to refer to the Internet as the information superhighway. I can understand why people say that; after all, it's a long-haul trucking service for data. But I think of it more as "Information Main Street." The Internet is growing because businesses are using it to get things done and to sell their wares. Much of this book was shipped back and forth on the Internet as it was being written. Heck, that sounds more like Main Street than a highway.

Nowadays, nearly every firm has at least some presence on the Internet; not having a Web page is almost like not having a phone. Remember when fax machines became popular in the early '80s? Overnight, people stopped saying, "Do you have a fax?" and just started saying, "What's your fax number?" It's getting so that if you don't have an Internet address, you're just not a person. For example, my Internet mail address is `help@minasi.com`.

Goals of TCP/IP's Design

But let's delve into some of the techie aspects of the Internet's main protocols. When DoD started building this set of network protocols, they had a few design goals. Understanding those design goals helps in understanding why it's worth making the effort to use TCP/IP in the first place. Its intended characteristics include:

- Good failure recovery
- Ability to plug in new networks without disrupting services
- Ability to handle high error rates
- Independence from a particular vendor or type of network
- Very little data overhead

I'm sure no one had any idea how central those design goals would be to the amazing success of TCP/IP both in private intranets and in *the* Internet. Let's take a look at those design goals in more detail.

GOOD FAILURE RECOVERY

Remember, this was to be a *defense* network, so it had to work even if portions of the network hardware suddenly and without warning went offline. That's kind of a nice way of saying the network had to work even if big pieces got nuked.

CAN PLUG IN NEW SUBNETWORKS "ON-THE-FLY"

This second goal is related to the first one. It says that it should be possible to bring entire new networks into an intranet—and here, again, *intranet* can mean your company's private intranet or *the* Internet—without interrupting existing network service.

CAN HANDLE HIGH ERROR RATES

The next goal was that an intranet should be able to tolerate high or unpredictable error rates and yet still provide a 100-percent reliable end-to-end service. If you're transferring data from Washington, D.C., to Portland, Oregon, and the links that you're currently using through Oklahoma get destroyed by a tornado, then any data lost in the storm will be resent and rerouted via some other lines.

HOST INDEPENDENCE

As I mentioned before, the new network architecture should work with any kind of network and not be dedicated or tied to any one vendor.

This is essential in the twenty-first century. The days of "We're just an IBM shop" or "We only buy Novell stuff" are gone for many and going fast for others. (Let's hope that it doesn't give way to "We only buy Microsoft software.") Companies must be able to live in a multivendor world.

VERY LITTLE DATA OVERHEAD

The last goal was for the network protocols to have as little overhead as possible. To understand this, let's compare TCP/IP to other protocols. While no one knows what protocol will end up being *the* world protocol 20 years from now—if any protocol *ever* gets that much acceptance—one of TCP/IP's rivals is a set of protocols built by the International Organization for Standardization (ISO). ISO has some standards that are very similar to the kinds of things that TCP/IP does, standards named X.25 and TP4. But every protocol packages its data with an extra set of bytes, kind of like an envelope. The vast majority of data packets using the IP protocol (and I promise, I *will* explain soon how it is that TCP and IP are actually two very different protocols) have a simple, fixed-size 20-byte header. The maximum size that the header can be is 60 bytes if all possible options are enabled. The fixed 20 bytes always appear as the first 20 bytes of the packet. In contrast, X.25 uses dozens of possible headers, with no appreciable fixed portion to it. But why should *you* be concerned about overhead bytes? Really for one reason only: performance. Simpler protocols mean faster transmission and packet switching. We'll take up packet switching a little later.

But enough about the Internet for now. Let's stop and define something that I've been talking about—namely, just what *are* TCP and IP?

Originally, TCP/IP was just a set of protocols that could hook up dissimilar computers and transfer information between them. But it grew into a large number of protocols that have become collectively known as the *TCP/IP suite*.

The Internet Protocol (IP)

The most basic part of the Internet is the Internet Protocol, or IP. If you want to send data over an intranet, then that data must be packaged in an IP packet. That packet is then *routed* from one part of the intranet to another.

A Simple Internet

IP is supposed to allow messages to travel from one part of a network to another. How does it do this?

An intranet is made of at least two *subnets*. The notion of a subnet is built upon the fact that most popular LAN architectures (Ethernet, Token Ring, and ARCNet) are based on something very much like a radio broadcast. Everyone on the same Ethernet segment hears all of the traffic on their segment, just as each device on a given ring in a Token Ring network must examine every message that goes through the network. The trick that makes an Ethernet or a Token Ring work is that, while each station *hears* everything, each station knows how to ignore all messages except the ones intended for it.

You may have never realized it, but that means that in a single Ethernet segment or a single Token Ring ring, there is *no routing*. If you've ever sat through one of those seemingly unending explanations of the ISO seven-layer network model, then you know that in network discussions, much is made of the *network layer*, which in ISO terms is merely the routing layer. And yet a simple Ethernet or Token Ring never has to route. There are no routing decisions to make; everything is heard by everybody. (Your network adapter filters out any traffic not destined for you, in case you're wondering.)

But now suppose you have *two* separate Ethernets connected to each other, as you see in Figure 6.4.

FIGURE 6.4

Multisegment
intranet

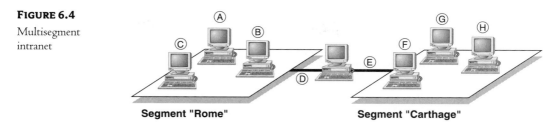

In Figure 6.4, you see two Ethernet segments, named Rome and Carthage. (I was getting tired of the "shipping" and "finance" examples that everyone uses.) There are three computers that reside solely in Rome that I've labeled A, B, and C. Three more computers reside in Carthage, labeled F, G, and H.

Subnets and Routers: "Should I Shout, or Should I Route?"

Much of intranet architecture is built around the observation that PCs A, B, and C can communicate directly with each other, and PCs F, G, and H can communicate directly with each other, but A, B, and C *cannot* communicate with F, G, and H without some help from the machine containing Ethernet cards D and E. That D/E machine will function as a *router*, a machine that allows communication between different network segments. A, B, C, and D could be described as being in each other's "broadcast range," as could E, F, G, and H. What I've just called a broadcast range is called more correctly in intranet terminology a *subnet*, which is a collection of machines that can communicate with each other without the need for routing.

For example, F and H can communicate directly without having to ask the router (E, in their case) to forward the message, and so they're on the same subnet. A and C can communicate directly without having to ask the router (D, in their case) to forward the message, and so they're on the same subnet. But if B wanted to talk to G, it would have to first send the message to D, asking, "D, please get this to G," so they're not on the same subnet.

Now, this whole trick of somehow knowing that F and H are on the same subnet and so do not need to enlist the aid of a router—F can just "shout" the message and H will hear it—or knowing that A and F are on different subnets—so A would need the help of D to get to F and F would require E's assistance to get to A—is IP's main job. Essentially, IP's job is to figure out "should I shout, or should I route?" and then, if routing's the way to go, IP has to figure out which router to use, assuming there's a choice of routers.

IP Addresses and Ethernet Addresses

Before continuing, let's briefly discuss the labels A, B, C, and so on and how those labels actually are manifested in an intranet. Each computer on this net is attached to the net via an Ethernet board, and each Ethernet board on an intranet has two addresses: an *IP address* and an *Ethernet address*. (There are, of course, other ways to get onto an intranet than via Ethernet, but let's stay with the Ethernet example as it's the most common one on TCP/IP intranets.)

ETHERNET ADDRESSES

Each Ethernet board's Ethernet address is a unique 48-bit identification code. If it sounds unlikely that every Ethernet board in the world has its own unique address, then consider that 48 bits offers 280,000,000,000,000 possibilities. Ethernet itself only uses about one quarter of those possibilities (2 bits are set aside for administrative functions), but that's still a lot of possible addresses. In any case, the important thing to get here is that a board's Ethernet address is predetermined and hard-coded into the board. Ethernet addresses, which are also called Media Access Control (MAC) addresses (it's got nothing to do with Macintoshes), are expressed in 12 hex digits. (*MAC address* is synonymous with *Token Ring address* or *Ethernet address*.) For example, the Ethernet card on the computer I'm working at now has MAC (Ethernet) address 0020AFF8E771, or as it's sometimes written, 00-20-AF-F8-E7-71. The addresses are centrally administered, and Ethernet chip vendors must purchase blocks of addresses. In the example of my workstation, you know that it's got a 3Com Ethernet card because the Ethernet (MAC) address is 00-20-AF; that prefix is owned by 3Com.

NOTE *You can see an NT machine's MAC address in several ways. You can type* **net config workstation** *or* **net config server** *(it's the string of hex in parentheses). Or you can run the System Information snap-in (*\Program Files\ Common Files\Microsoft Shared\MSInfo \Msinfo32.msc*), then open up the* System Information *folder, then the* Components *folder inside that, then the* Network *folder inside that, and finally the* Adapter *folder inside the* Network *folder. One of the reported pieces of information will be the MAC Address.*

IP ADDRESSES AND QUAD FORMAT

In contrast to the 48 bits in a MAC address, an IP address is a 32-bit value. IP addresses are numbers set at a workstation (or server) by a network administrator—they're not a hard-coded hardware kind of address like the Ethernet address. That means that there are four billion distinct Internet addresses.

It's nice that there's room for lots of machines, but having to remember—or having to tell someone else—a 32-bit address is no fun. Imagine having to say to a network support person, "Just set up the machines on the subnet to use a default router address of 10101110100-101010010101100010111." Hmmm, doesn't sound like much fun—we need a more human-friendly way to express 32-bit numbers. That's where *dotted quad* notation comes from.

For simplicity's sake, IP addresses are usually represented as *w.x.y.z*, where *w*, *x*, *y*, and *z* are all decimal values from 0 to 255. For example, the IP address of the machine that I'm currently writing this at is 199.34.57.53. Each of the four numbers is called a *quad*; as they're connected by dots, it's called *dotted quad* notation.

Each of the numbers in the dotted quad corresponds to 8 bits of an Internet address. (*IP address* and *Internet address* are synonymous.) As the value for 8 bits can range from 0 to 255, each value in a dotted quad can be from 0 to 255. For example, to convert an IP address of 11001010000011110101010000000001 into dotted quad format, it would first be broken up into 8-bit groups:

11001010 00001111 10101010 00000001

And each of those 8-bit numbers would be converted to its decimal equivalent. (If you're not comfortable with binary-to-decimal conversion, don't worry about it: Just load the Win2K Calculator, click View, then Scientific, and then press the F8 key to put the Calculator in binary mode. Enter the binary number, press F6, and the number will be converted to decimal for you.) Our number converts as follows:

11001010	00001111	10101010	00000001
202	15	170	1

which results in a dotted quad address of 202.15.170.1.

So, to recap: Each of these computers has at least one Ethernet card in it, and that Ethernet card has a predefined address. The network administrator of this network has gone around and installed IP software on these PCs and, in the process, has assigned IP addresses to each of them. (Note, by the way, that the phrase "has assigned IP addresses to each of them" may not be true if you are using the Dynamic Host Configuration Protocol, or DHCP, which I'll describe in detail in the next chapter. For most of this chapter, however, I'm going to assume that you're not using DHCP and that someone must hand-assign an IP address to each Ethernet card.)

Let me redraw our intranet, adding totally arbitrary IP addresses and Ethernet addresses, as shown in Figure 6.5.

FIGURE 6.5

Two-subnet intranet with Ethernet and IP addresses

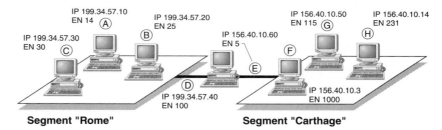

IP Routers

Now let's return to the computer in the middle. It is part of *both* segments. How do I get one computer to be part of two networks? By putting two Ethernet cards in the computer in the middle. (A computer with more than one network card in it is called a *multihomed* computer.) One of the Ethernet cards is on the Rome subnet, and the other is on the Carthage subnet. (By the way, each computer on an intranet is called a *host* in TCP-ese.)

Now, each Ethernet card must get a separate IP address, so as a result, the computer in the middle has *two* IP addresses, D and E. If a message is transmitted in Rome, adapter D hears it and E doesn't. Then, if a message is transmitted in Carthage, adapter E hears it but D doesn't.

How would we build an intranet from these two subnets? How could station A, for example, send a message to station G? Obviously, the only way that message will get from A to G is if the message is received on the Ethernet adapter with address D and then re-sent out over the Ethernet adapter with address E. Once E resends the message, G will hear it, as it is on the same network as E.

In order for this to work, the machine containing boards D and E must be smart enough to perform this function whereby it resends data between D and E when necessary. Such a machine is, by definition, an *IP router*. It is possible with Windows 2000 to use a Win2K computer—any Win2K computer, not just a Windows 2000 Server computer—to act as an IP router, as you'll learn later.

Under IP, the sending station (A, in this case) examines the address of the destination (G, in this case) and realizes that it does not know how to get to G. (I'll explain exactly *how* it comes to that realization in a minute.) Now, if A has to send something to an address that it doesn't understand, then it uses a kind of "catchall" address called the *default router* or, for historical reasons, the *default gateway* address. A's network administrator has already configured A's default router as D, so A sends the message to D. Once D gets the message, it then sees that the message is not destined for itself, but rather for G, and so it resends the message from board E.

Routing in More Detail

Now let's look a little closer at how that message gets from A to G. Each computer, as you've already seen, has one *or more* IP addresses. It's important to understand that there is no relation whatsoever between an Ethernet card's address and the IP address associated with it: The Ethernet MAC address is hardwired into the card by the card's manufacturer, and the IP addresses are assigned by a network administrator.

But now examine the IP addresses and you'll see a pattern to them. Rome's addresses all look like 199.34.57.*z*, where *z* is some number, and Carthage's addresses all look like 156.40.10.*z*, where, again, *z* can be any number. The Ethernet addresses follow no rhyme or reason and are grouped by the board's manufacturer. That similarity of IP addresses within Rome and Carthage will be important in understanding routing.

Now, let's reexamine how the message gets from A to G:

1. The IP software in A first says, "How do I get this message to G—can I just broadcast it, or must it be routed?" The way that it makes that decision is by finding out whether or not G is on the same *subnet* as A is. A subnet is simply a broadcast area. Host A then, is asking, "Is G part of Rome, like me?"

2. Station A determines that it is on a different subnet from station G by examining their addresses. A knows that it has address 199.34.57.10 and that it must send its message to 156.40.10.50. A has a simple rule for this: If the destination address looks like 199.34.57.*z*, where, again, *z* can be any value, then the destination is in the same subnet and so requires no routing. On the other hand, 156.40.10.50 is clearly *not* in the same subnet.

   If, alternatively, G *had* been on the same subnet, then A would have "shouted" the IP packet straight to G, referring specifically to its IP and Ethernet address.

3. So station A can't directly send its IP packets to G. A then looks for another way. When A's network administrator set up A's IP software, she told A the IP address of A's *default router*. The default router is basically the address that says, "If you don't know where to send something, send it to me and I'll try to get it there." A's default router is D. So now A has a sort of subgoal of getting a message to nearby D, with IP address 199.34.57.40. We're almost ready to hand this over to the Ethernet card—*except* that Ethernet cards don't understand IP addresses; they understand MAC addresses.

   TCP/IP's got an answer for this: Address Resolution Protocol (ARP). A just sends a broadcast to the local segment, saying, "If there's a machine out there that goes by the IP address 199.34.57.40, please send me back your MAC address." D hears the request and responds that its MAC address is 100.

A then sends an Ethernet frame from itself to D. The Ethernet frame contains this information:

- ◆ Source Ethernet address: 14
- ◆ Destination Ethernet address: 100
- ◆ Source IP address: 199.34.57.10
- ◆ Destination IP address: 156.40.10.50

4. Ethernet card D receives the frame and hands it to the IP software running in its PC. The PC sees that the IP destination address is not *its* IP address, so the PC knows that it must route this IP packet. Examining the subnet, the PC sees that the destination lies on the subnet that Ethernet adapter E is on, so it ARPs to get G's MAC address; G responds, "My MAC address is 115," and then E sends out a frame, with this information:

- ◆ Source Ethernet address: 5
- ◆ Destination Ethernet address: 115
- ◆ Source IP address: 199.34.57.10 (note this is A's address, not E's)
- ◆ Destination IP address: 156.40.10.50

5. G then gets the packet. By looking at the Ethernet and IP addresses, G can see that it got this frame from E, but the original message really came from another machine, the 199.34.57.10 machine.

That's a simple example of how IP routes, but its algorithms are powerful enough to serve as the backbone for a network as large as the Internet.

TIP   There are different kinds of routing algorithms in TCP/IP. Windows 2000 supports the Routing Information Protocol (RIP) version 2, Open Shortest Path First (OSPF), and IGMP version 2. For other routing approaches, or for very high-capacity routing needs, you need either third-party software or a dedicated hardware router to build large, complex intranets with Windows 2000. But Windows 2000 can handle a considerably larger set of routing tasks than did its predecessors.

Class A, B, and C Networks, CIDR Blocks, Routable and Nonroutable Addresses, and Subnetting

Before leaving IP routing, let's take a more specific look at networks, subnets, and IP addresses.

The whole idea behind the 32-bit IP addresses is to make it relatively simple to segment the task of managing the Internet or, for that matter, *any* intranet.

To become part of the Internet, you'll need a block of IP addresses and a name (like acme.com) or a set of names. Find a local Internet service provider (ISP) for the block of addresses. ISPs may also handle registering names for you, but it's just as easy to register a name yourself with Network Solutions or another name registrar; surf over to www.internic.net to find out how.

But how do the *ISPs* get their IP addresses? Originally, an organization named the Internet Assigned Numbers Authority (IANA) handed out addresses. In 1993, however, an Internet document RFC 1466 (the rules describing how things work in the Internet are called Requests for Comment, or RFCs) explained that it made more sense to distribute the job as the Internet became bigger. The IANA, which is now in the process of becoming the Internet Corporation for Assigned Names and Numbers (ICANN), divides its number-assigning authority among three Regional Internet Registries (RIRs, inevitably): RIPE (R seaux IP Europ ens, or European IP Networks) handles Europe, the Middle East, Africa, and the better part of Asia; APNIC (Asia Pacific Network Information Center) handles the rest of Asia and the South Pacific; and ARIN (American Registry for Internet Numbers) handles the Americas. Rather than say "The IANA/ICANN, RIPE, ARIN, APNIC, or one of their suborganizations," however, I'll just say "IANA" when referring to the IP-allocating groups.

A, B, and C Class Networks

The IANA or an ISP assigns a company a block of IP addresses according to the company's size. That block of addresses is called a *network*. (As you'll soon see, a subnet is just a subdivision of that set of assigned addresses, hence "sub" net.) Big companies get class A networks (there are none left; they've all been given out), medium-sized companies get class B networks (we're out of those, too), and others get class C networks (they're still available). Although there are three network classes, there are five kinds of IP addresses, as you'll see in Figure 6.6.

FIGURE 6.6

Internet network classes and reserved addresses

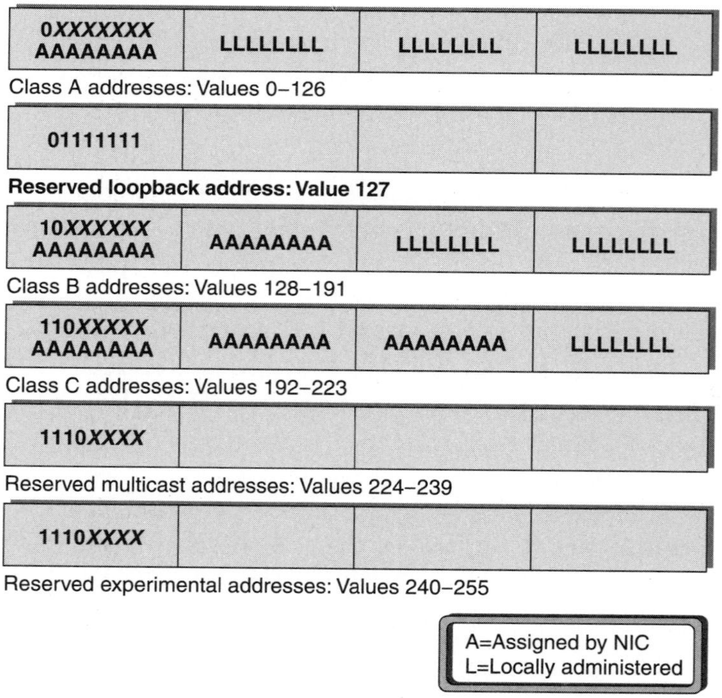

Because it seemed, in the early days of the Internet, that four billion addresses left plenty of space for growth, the original designers were a bit sloppy. They defined three classes of networks of the Internet: Large networks, medium-sized networks, and small networks. The creators of the Internet used 8-bit sections of the 32-bit addresses to delineate the difference between different classes of networks:

Class A Networks   A large network would have its first 8 bits set by the NIC, and the network's internal administrators could set the remaining 24 bits. The leftmost 8 bits could have values from 0 to 126, allowing for 127 class A networks. Companies like IBM get these, and there are only 127 of these addresses. As only 8 bits have been taken, 24 remain; that means that class A networks can contain up to 2 to the 24th power, or about 16 million, hosts. Examples of class A nets include General Electric (3.*x.y.z*), BBN (4), IBM (9), Xerox (13), Hewlett-Packard (15), DEC (16), Apple (17), MIT (18), Ford (19), Eli Lilly (40), DuPont (52), Merck (54), Boeing (55), the U.S. Postal Service (56), various defense groups—remember who built this—and some unexpected ones: Networld+Interop, which has the 45.*x.y.z* network set aside for its use (not bad, an A network for two week-long conferences a year!), the U.K. Department of Social Security (51), and Norsk Informasjonsteknologi (32).

Class B Networks   Medium-sized networks have the leftmost 16 bits preassigned to them, leaving 16 bits for local use. Class B addresses always have the values 128 through 191 in their first quad, then a value from 0 to 255 in their second quad. There are then 16,384 possible class B networks. Each of them can have up to 65,536 hosts. Microsoft and Exxon are examples of companies with class B networks. (So Apple and IBM have class A networks and Microsoft only has a class B. What do you want to bet that this kind of thing keeps Bill up late nights?)

Class C Networks   Small networks have the leftmost 24 bits preassigned to them, leaving only 8 bits for local administration (which is bad, as it means that class C networks can't have more than 254 hosts), but as the NIC has 24 bits to work with, it can easily give out class C network addresses (which is good). Class C addresses start off with a value from 192 to 223. As the second and third quads can be any value from 0 to 255, that means that there can potentially be 2,097,152 class C networks. (That's what my network, minasi.com, is.) The last C network, when it's assigned, will be 223.255.255.*z*; remember that the owner of that network will be able to control only *z*.

Reserved Addresses   Some addresses are reserved for multicast purposes and for experimental purposes, so they can't be assigned for networks. In particular, address 224.0.0.0 is set aside for *multicasts*, network transmissions to groups of computers.

Routable and Nonroutable Addresses

Once upon a time, getting hold of a bunch of IP addresses was easy. But nowadays, they're scarcer and scarcer. Four billion possible addresses sounds like a lot, but the A/B/C class approach tends to waste addresses on large companies and those who just got in line at the right time: With all due respect to the organizations involved, it's hard to believe that certain universities, Apple, and the Network+Interop conference really need 48 million unique IP addresses. Don't misunderstand me, I'm not suggesting that we change their address allocation—first come, first served in the IP land rush is a reasonable first approach to allocation. But big and small firms alike need IP addresses, and they're not as plentiful as they once were.

We've heard for years that the Giant Brains of the IP world are working on promoting a replacement for IP called IPV6, a 128-bit–based addressing scheme that would allow more IP addresses than there are electrons in the universe, but then I've been hearing about the "imminent" nature of IPV6 since about 1993. Until it's more widely accepted, we need some way to stretch our IP addresses. And there *is* a way that's been widely adopted.

In RFC 1918, the Internet folks defined three nonroutable ranges of IP addresses. They are:

♦ 10.0.0.0–10.255.255.255

♦ 172.16.0.0–172.31.255.255

♦ 192.168.0.0–192.168.255.255

The original idea with the ranges of nonroutable addresses was to set aside some addresses that people could use to build "test" intranets without having to go to the IANA for a range of numbers—anyone can build an IP-based network using these addresses. Furthermore, even if networks based on the above addresses *were* attached to the Internet, then they couldn't cause any mischief, because Internet routers are programmed to *ignore* them! As messages sent from these ranges won't be routed on the public Internet, they are logically called the *nonroutable* ranges.

This means that literally millions of networks in the (for example) 192.168.1.0–192.168.1.255 range could exist, all at the same time, because they cannot communicate with the public Internet, and therefore can't cause any trouble. And that offers a kind of side benefit to companies choosing to use the nonroutable addresses: security. Clearly if my system has address 10.10.10.10, then I'm protected from outside hackers, because if they can't connect to me, then they can't cause trouble, right?

Because of this, most companies use at least two sets of IP addresses: Addresses used in their company's *internal* Internet (or "intranet," as we say nowadays) and a range of "official" Internet addresses obtained from an ISP or directly from a part of the IANA.

Now, from what I've said so far, it sounds like the folks whose machines have nonroutable addresses are sort of left out in the cold; they can route *inside* their company's network, but they're shut out of access to the public, *routable* Internet. But not any more. In fact, a little technological trick has made it possible for companies to offer public Internet access to their nonroutable addresses. You see, there is a class of routers called network address translation (NAT) routers that can perform a small bit of magic and let you use private, non-IANA–assigned IP addresses on your company's intranet and still be able to communicate with the Internet.

So, for example, suppose your firm had obtained a class C address range from the IANA or an ISP: 256 addresses. Although you have thousands of computers, the fact that there are only 256 addresses is no problem as the NAT router can handle communications with the Internet. NAT is kind of interesting in that it lets machines with nonroutable addresses *initiate* conversations with machines on the routable public Internet, but doesn't allow machines out on the Internet to initiate conversations in the other direction. For example, if I were sitting at a machine with IP address 192.168.1.17 behind a NAT router and tried to surf www.microsoft.com, then I'd get in, no problem. But if someone in the public Internet tried to connect to my system at 192.168.1.17, they'd be rebuffed, as *their* local router would know better than to pass a request to a nonroutable address.

We'll see a bit more about NAT (and an important partner, PAT (*port* address translation) later in the chapter. And in case you wondered, NAT and PAT have a *down*side: under the wrong circumstances, NAT and PAT *can* let the bad guys in.

You Can't Use *All* of the Numbers

There are some special rules to IP addresses, however. There's a whole bunch of numbers that you can never give to any machine. They're the default route address, the loopback address, the network number, the broadcast address, and the default router address.

THE DEFAULT ROUTE ADDRESS

As you'll see later, the address 0.0.0.0 is another way of saying "the entire Internet." But as 0.*x.y.z* is in the class A range of addresses, all of 0.*x.y.z* must be set aside—all 16 million addresses.

THE LOOPBACK ADDRESS

The address 127.0.0.1 is reserved as a loopback. If you send a message to 127.0.0.1, then it should be returned to you unless there's something wrong on the IP software itself; messages to the loopback don't go out on the network, but instead stay within a particular machine's IP software. And so no network has an address 127.xxxxxxxx .xxxxxxxx.xxxxxxxx, an unfortunate waste of 16 million addresses.

THE NETWORK NUMBER

Sometimes you need to refer to an entire subnet with a single number. Thus far, I've said things like "My C network is 199.34.57.*z*, and I can make *z* range from 0 to 255." I was being a bit lazy; I didn't want to write "199.34.57.0 through 199.34.57.255," so I said "199.34.57.*z*."

It's not proper IP-ese to refer to a range of network addresses that way. And it's necessary to have an official way to refer to a range of addresses.

For example, to tell a router, "To get this message to the subnet that ranges from 100.100.100.0 through 100.100.100.255, first route to the router at 99.98.97.103," you've got to have some way to designate the range of addresses 100.100.100.0–100.100.100.255. We could have just used two addresses with a dash between them, but that's a bit cumbersome. Instead, the address that ends in all binary 0s is reserved as the *network number*, the TCP/IP name for the range of addresses in a subnet. In my 100.100.100.*z* example, the shorthand way to refer to 100.100.100.0 through 100.100.100.255 is "100.100.100.0."

Notice that this means you would never use the address 100.100.100.0—you never give that IP address to a machine under TCP/IP.

For example, to tell that router, "To get this message to the subnet that ranges from 100.100.100.0 through 100.100.100.255, first route to the router at 99.98.97.103," you would type something like **route add 100.100.100.0 99.98.97.103**. (Actually, you'd type a bit more information, and I'll get to that in the upcoming section on using your NT machine as a router, but this example gives you the idea.)

IP BROADCAST ADDRESS

There's another reserved address, as well—the TCP/IP broadcast address. It looks like the address of one machine, but it isn't; it's the address you'd use to broadcast to each machine on a subnet. That address is all binary 1s.

For example, on a simple class C subnet, the broadcast address would be *w.x.y*.255. When would you need to know this? Some IP software needs this when you configure it; most routers require the broadcast address (as well as the network number). So if I just use my class C network 199.34.57.0 (see how convenient that .0 thing is?) as a single subnet, then the broadcast address for my network would be 199.34.57.255.

DEFAULT ROUTER ADDRESS

Every subnet has at least one router; after all, if it didn't have a router, then the subnet couldn't talk to any other networks, and it wouldn't be an intranet.

By convention, the first address after the network number is the default gateway (router) address. For example, on a simple class C network, the address of the router should be *w.x.y.*1. This is not, by the way, a hard-and-fast rule like the network number and the IP broadcast address—it is, instead, a convention.

Suppose you have just been made the proud owner of a class C net, 222.210.34.0. You can put 253 computers on your network, as you must not use 222.210.34.0, which describes the entire network; 222.210.34.255, which will be your broadcast address; and 222.210.34.1, which will be used either by you or your Internet Service Provider for a router address between your network and the rest of the Internet.

Now, once you get a range of addresses from the IANA or an ISP, then you are said to have an *IP domain.* (*Domain* in Internet lingo has nothing to do with domain in the Win2K security sense.) For example, my IP domain (which is named minasi.com, but we'll cover names in a minute) uses addresses in the 206.246.253.*z* network, and I can have as many Win2K domains in there as I like. However, from the point of view of the outside Internet, all of my Win2K domains are just one Internet domain: minasi.com.

Subnet Masks

If you had a trivially small intranet, one with just one subnet, then all the devices in your network can simply transmit directly to each other and no routing is required. On the other hand, you may have a domain so large that using broadcasting to communicate within it would be unworkable, requiring you to subnet your domain further. Consider IBM's situation, with a class A network that can theoretically support 16 million hosts. Managing *that* network cries out for routers. For this reason, it may be necessary for your IP software on your PC to route data over a router even if it's staying within your company. Let's ask again, and in more detail this time, "How does a machine know whether to route or not?"

That's where subnets are important. Subnets make it possible, as you've seen, for a host (a PC) to determine whether it can just lob a message straight over to another host or if it must go through routers. You can tell a host's IP software how to distinguish whether or not another host is in the same subnet through the *subnet mask.*

Recall that all of the IP addresses in Rome looked like 199.34.57.*z*, where *z* was a number between 1 and 255. You could then say that all comembers of the Rome subnet are defined as the hosts whose first three quads match. Now, on some subnets, it might be possible that the only requirement for membership in the same subnet would be that the first *two* quads be the same—a company that decided for some reason to make its entire class B network a single subnet would be one example of that. (Yes, they *do* exist: I've seen firms that make a single subnet out of a Class B network, with the help of some bizarre smart bridges. And no, I don't recommend it.)

When a computer is trying to figure out whether the IP address that it owns is on the same subnet as the place that it's trying to communicate with, then a subnet mask answers the question, "Which bits must match for us to be on the same subnet?"

IP does that with a *mask*, a combination of 1s and 0s like so:

11111111 11111111 11111111 00000000

Here's how a host would use this mask. The host with IP address 199.34.57.10 (station A in Figure 6.5) wants to know if it is on the same subnet as the host with IP address 199.34.57.20 (station B in Figure 6.5). 199.34.57.10, expressed in binary, is 11000111 00100010 00111001 00001010. The IP address for B is, in binary, 11000111 00100010 00111001 00010100. The IP software in A then compares its own IP address to B's IP address. Look at them right next to each other:

11000111 00100010 00111001 00001010 *A's address*
11000111 00100010 00111001 00010100 B's address

The leftmost 27 bits match, as does the rightmost bit. Does that mean they're in the same subnet? Again, for the two addresses to be in the same subnet, certain bits must match—the ones with 1s in the subnet mask. Let's stack up the subnet mask, A's address, and B's address to make this clearer:

11111111 11111111 11111111 00000000 *the subnet mask*
11000111 00100010 00111001 00001010 A's address
11000111 00100010 00111001 00010100 B's address

Look down from each of the 1s on the subnet mask, and you see that A and B match at each of those positions. Under the 0s in the subnet mask, A and B match up sometimes but not all the time. In fact, it doesn't matter whether or not A and B match in the positions under the 0s in the subnet mask—the fact that there are 0s there means that whether they match is irrelevant.

Another way to think of the subnet mask is this. The IANA and friends give you a range of addresses, and you allocate them as you see fit. Of the 32 bits in your IP addresses, some are under your control and some are under the IANA & Co's control. In general, however, the bits that the IANA controls are to the left, and the ones that *you* control are to the right. For example, the IANA controls the leftmost 8 bits for a class A network, the 16 leftmost bits for a class B network, and the leftmost 24 bits for a class C network.

How do you know what value to use for a subnet mask? Well, if you have a class C number and all of your workstations are on a single subnet, then you have a case like the one we just saw: A subnet mask of 11111111 11111111 11111111 00000000, which, in dotted-quad terminology, is 255.255.255.0. Remember that, by definition, the fact that I have a C network means that the IANA has "nailed down" the leftmost or top three quads (24 bits), leaving me only the rightmost quad (8 bits). Since all of my addresses must match in the leftmost 24 bits and I can do anything I like with the bottom 8 bits, my subnet mask must be 11111111 1111111 11111111 00000000, or 255.255.255.0. Again, with subnet masks, the 1s are always on the left and the 0s on the right— you'll never see a subnet mask like "11111111 11110000 00001111 11111000" or "00000000 11111111 11111111 11111111."

Getting back to my C network, however, that 11111111 11111111 11111111 00000000 mask assumes that I'll use my entire C network as one big subnet. Instead, I might decide to break one class C network into two subnets. I could decide that all the numbers from 1 to 127—00000001 to 01111111—are subnet 1 and the numbers from 128 to 255—10000000 to 11111111—are subnet 2. In that case, the values inside my subnets will only vary in the last 7 bits rather than (as in the previous example) varying in the last 8 bits. The subnet mask would be, then, 11111111 11111111 11111111 10000000, or 255.255.255.128.

The first subnet is a range of addresses from *w.x.y.*0 through *w.x.y.*127, where *w.x.y* are the quads that the NIC assigned me. The second subnet is the range from *w.x.y.*128 through *w.x.y.*255.

Now let's find the network number, default router address, and broadcast address. The network number is the first number in each range, so the first subnet's network number is *w.x.y.*0 and the second's is *w.x.y.*128. The default router address is just the second address in the range, which is *w.x.y.*1 and *w.x.y.*129 for the two subnets. The broadcast address is then the *last* address in both cases, *w.x.y.*127 and *w.x.y.*255 respectively.

Subnetting a Class C Network

If you're going to break down your subnets smaller than class C, then having to figure out the subnet mask, network number, broadcast address, and router address can get kind of confusing. Table 6.1 summarizes how you can break a class C network down into one, two, four, or eight smaller subnets with the attendant subnet masks, network numbers, broadcast addresses, and router addresses. I've assumed that you are starting from a class C address, so you'll only be working with the fourth quad. The first three quads I have simply designated *w.x.y.*

TABLE 6.1: BREAKING A C CLASS NETWORK INTO SUBNETS

NUMBER OF DESIRED SUBNETS	SUBNET MASK	NETWORK NUMBER	ROUTER ADDRESS	BROADCAST ADDRESS	REMAINING NUMBER OF IP ADDRESSES
1	255.255.255.0	*w.x.y.*0	*w.x.y.*1	*w.x.y.*255	253
2	255.255.255.128	*w.x.y.*0	*w.x.y.*1	*w.x.y.*127	125
	255.255.255.	*w.x.y.*128	*w.x.y.*129	*w.x.y.*255	125
4	255.255.255.192	*w.x.y.*0	*w.x.y.*1	*w.x.y.*63	61
	255.255.255.	*w.x.y.*64	*w.x.y.*65	*w.x.y.*127	61
	255.255.255.	*w.x.y.*128	*w.x.y.*129	*w.x.y.*191	61
	255.255.255.	*w.x.y.*192	*w.x.y.*193	*w.x.y.*255	61
8	255.255.255.224	*w.x.y.*0	*w.x.y.*1	*w.x.y.*31	29
	255.255.255.	*w.x.y.*32	*w.x.y.*33	*w.x.y.*63	29
	255.255.255.	*w.x.y.*64	*w.x.y.*65	*w.x.y.*95	29
	255.255.255.	*w.x.y.*96	*w.x.y.*97	*w.x.y.*127	29
	255.255.255.	*w.x.y.*128	*w.x.y.*129	*w.x.y.*159	29
	255.255.255.	*w.x.y.*160	*w.x.y.*161	*w.x.y.*191	29
	255.255.255.	*w.x.y.*192	*w.x.y.*193	*w.x.y.*223	29
	255.255.255.	*w.x.y.*224	*w.x.y.*225	*w.x.y.*255	29

For example, suppose you want to chop up a class C network, 200.211.192.*z*, into two subnets. As you see in the table, you'd use a subnet mask of 255.255.255.128 for each subnet. The first subnet would have network number 200.211.192.0, router address 200.211.192.1, and broadcast address 200.211.192.127. You could assign IP addresses 200.211.192.2 through 200.211.192.126, 125 different IP addresses. (Notice that heavily subnetting a network results in the loss of a greater and greater percentage of addresses to the network number, broadcast address, and router address.) The second subnet would have network number 200.211.192.128, router address 200.211.192.129, and broadcast address 200.211.192.255.

In case you're wondering, it is entirely possible to subnet further, into 16 subnets of 13 hosts apiece (remember that you always lose three numbers for the network number, router address, and broadcast address) or 32 subnets of 5 hosts apiece, but at that point, you're losing an awful lot of addresses to IP overhead.

I should note that in some cases, subnetting won't work the way I've said it does. Suppose I chop up my C network using the 255.255.255.192 subnet mask. I've said that this gives me four subnets: 199.34.57.0, 199.34.57.64, 199.34.57.128, and 199.34.57.192. You can set up the network like that, and in every case I've ever encountered, things will work fine. But there may be cases where you'll run into trouble, so it's fair to warn you that RFC 950, the RFC that defines how to subnet an IP network, says this:

> *In certain contexts, it is useful to have fixed addresses with functional significance rather than as identifiers of specific hosts. When such usage is called for, the address zero is to be interpreted as meaning "this," as in "this network." The address of all ones are to be interpreted as meaning "all," as in "all hosts." For example, the address 128.9.255.255 could be interpreted as meaning "all hosts on the network 128.9." Or the address 0.0.0.37 could be interpreted as meaning "host 37 on this network." It is useful to preserve and extend the interpretation of these special addresses in subnetted networks. This means the values of all zeros and all ones in the subnet field should not be assigned to actual (physical) subnets. In the example above, the 6-bit wide subnet field may have any value except 0 and 63.*

What this means in English is this: RFC 950 says to use neither the first subnet nor the last subnet. Thus, if you're going to be completely RFC-compliant (which is never a bad idea), you would *not* be able to use subnets 199.34.57.0 and 199.34.57.192. And my earlier example of dividing 199.34.57.0 into two subnets by using subnet mask 255.255.255.128 would not work at all.

Should you care? If you're using modern routers or NT machines for routers, you won't run into trouble using all possible subnets. But if you've got some routers that are sticklers for the rules, you might cause trouble by using those other subnets. It's kind of a shame, as the 255.255.255.192 subnet for a C network yields four 62-address subnets, and staying strictly RFC-compliant means you only get *two* 62-address subnets.

Oh, and one more reason to understand RFC 950's restrictions: If you take any exams, such as the Microsoft or Cisco certification exams about TCP/IP, the RFC 950 answer will be right—the practical answer will be "wrong," even if it *would* work in the real world.

Classless Inter-Domain Routing (CIDR)

Now that we've gotten past some of the fine points of subnet masks, let me elaborate on what you see if you ever go to the IANA or an ISP looking for a domain of your own.

The shortage of IP addresses has led the IANA to curtail giving out class A, B, or C addresses. Many small companies need an Internet domain, but giving them a C network is overkill, as a C network contains 256 addresses and many small firms only have a dozen or so computers that they want on the Internet. Large companies may also want a similarly small presence on the Internet: For reasons of security, they may not want to put all of the PCs (or other computers) on the Internet but rather on an internal network not attached to the Internet. These companies *do* need a presence on the Internet, however—for their e-mail servers, FTP servers, Web servers, and the like—so they need a dozen or so addresses. But, again, giving them an entire 256-address C network is awfully wasteful. However, until 1994, it was the smallest block that an ISP could hand out.

Similarly, some companies need a few hundred addresses—more than 256, but not very many more. Such a firm is too big for a C network but a bit small for the 65,536 addresses of a B network. More flexibility here would be useful.

For that reason, the IANA now gives out addresses without the old A, B, or C class restrictions. This newer method that the IANA uses is called Classless Inter-Domain Routing, or CIDR, pronounced "cider." CIDR networks are described as "slash *x*" networks, where the *x* is a number representing the number of bits in the IP address range that IANA controls.

If you had a class A network, then the IANA controlled the top 8 bits and you controlled the bottom 24. If you decided somehow to take your class A network and make it one big subnet, then what would be your subnet mask? Since all of your A network would be one subnet, you'd only have to look at the top quad to see if the source and destination addresses were on the same subnet. For example, if you had network 4.0.0.0, then addresses 4.55.22.81 and 4.99.63.88 would be on the same subnet. (Please note that I can't actually imagine anyone doing this with a class A net; I'm just trying to make CIDR clearer.) Your subnet mask would be, then, 11111111 00000000 00000000 00000000, or 255.0.0.0. Reading from the left, you have eight 1s in the subnet mask before the 0s start. In CIDR terminology, you wouldn't have a class A network; rather, you would have a *slash 8* network. It would be written "4.0.0.0/8" instead of "4.0.0.0 subnet mask 255.0.0.0."

With a class B, the IANA controlled the top 16 bits, and you controlled the bottom 16. If you decided to take that class B network and make it a one-subnet network, then your subnet mask would be 11111111 11111111 00000000 00000000, or 255.255.0.0. Reading from the left, the subnet mask would have 16 1s. In CIDR terms, a B network is a *slash 16* network. So if your firm had a B network like 164.109.0.0 subnet mask 255.255.0.0, in slash format that would be 164.109.0.0/16.

With a C class, the IANA controlled the top 24 bits, and you controlled the bottom 8. By now, you've seen that the subnet mask for a C network if you treated it as one subnet is 11111111 11111111 11111111 00000000. Reading from the left, the subnet mask would have 24 1s. In CIDR terms, a C network is a *slash 24* network. Thus, one of my C networks (206.246.253.0, mask 255.255.255.0) can be written "206.246.253/24." Grasping this /24 nomenclature is important because you'll see it on some routers. My Ascend router never asks for subnet masks—just slashes.

Where the new flexibility of CIDR comes in is that the IANA can in theory now not only define the A-, B-, and C-type networks, it can offer networks with subnet masks in between the A, B, and C networks. For example, suppose I wanted a network for 50 PCs. Before, IANA would have to give me a C network, with 256 addresses. But now they can offer me a network with subnet mask 11111111 11111111 11111111 11000000 (255.255.255.192), giving me only 6 bits to play with. Two to the sixth power is 64, so I'd have 64 addresses to do with as I liked. This would be a *slash 26* (/26) network.

In summary, Table 6.2 shows how large each possible network type would be.

TABLE 6.2: CIDR NETWORK TYPES

IANA NETWORK TYPE	"SUBNET MASK" FOR ENTIRE NETWORK	APPROXIMATE NUMBER OF IP ADDRESSES
slash 0	0.0.0.0	4 billion
slash 1	128.0.0.0	2 billion
slash 2	192.0.0.0	1 billion
slash 3	224.0.0.0	500 million
slash 4	240.0.0.0	250 million
slash 5	248.0.0.0	128 million
slash 6	252.0.0.0	64 million
slash 7	254.0.0.0	32 million
slash 8	255.0.0.0	16 million
slash 9	255.128.0.0	8 million
slash 10	255.192.0.0	4 million
slash 11	255.224.0.0	2 million
slash 12	255.240.0.0	1 million
slash 13	255.248.0.0	524,288
slash 14	255.252.0.0	262,144
slash 15	255.254.0.0	131,072
slash 16	255.255.0.0	65,536
slash 17	255.255.128.0	32,768
slash 18	255.255.192.0	16,384
slash 19	255.255.224.0	8192
slash 20	255.255.240.0	4096
slash 21	255.255.248.0	2048
slash 22	255.255.252.0	1024
slash 23	255.255.254.0	512
slash 24	255.255.255.0	256
slash 25	255.255.255.128	128

Continued on next page

TABLE 6.2: CIDR NETWORK TYPES *(continued)*

IANA NETWORK TYPE	"SUBNET MASK" FOR ENTIRE NETWORK	APPROXIMATE NUMBER OF IP ADDRESSES
slash 26	255.255.255.192	64
slash 27	255.255.255.224	32
slash 28	255.255.255.240	16
slash 29	255.255.255.248	8
slash 30	255.255.255.252	4
slash 31	255.255.255.254	2
slash 32	255.255.255.255	1

I hope it's obvious that I included all of those networks just for the sake of completeness, as some of them simply aren't available, like the slash 0, and some just don't make sense, like the slash 31—it only gives you two addresses, which would be immediately required for network number and broadcast address, leaving none behind for you to actually use. The smallest network that the American subgroup of the IANA, ARIN, will allocate to a network is a slash 20, a 4,094-address network.

CIDR is a fact of life if you're trying to get a network nowadays. With the information in this section, you'll more easily be able to understand what an ISP is talking about when it says it can get you a slash 26 network.

What IP *Doesn't* Do: Error Checking

Whether you're on *an* intranet or *the* Internet, it looks like your data gets bounced around quite a bit. How can you prevent it from becoming damaged? Let's look briefly at that, and that'll segue to a short talk on TCP.

An IP packet contains a bit of data called a *checksum header*, which checks whether the header information was damaged on the way from sender to receiver.

Many data communications protocols use checksums that operate like this: I send you some data. You use the checksum to make sure the data wasn't damaged in transit, perhaps by line noise. Once you're satisfied that the data was not damaged, you send me a message that says, "OK—I got it." If the checksum indicates that it did *not* get to you undamaged, then you send me a message that says, "That data was damaged—please resend it," and I resend it. Such messages are called ACKs and NAKs—positive or negative acknowledgments of data. Protocols that use this check-and-acknowledge approach are said to provide *reliable* service.

But IP does not provide reliable service. If an IP receiver gets a damaged packet, it just discards the packet and says nothing to the receiver. Surprised? I won't keep you in suspense: It's TCP that provides the reliability. The IP header checksum is used to see if a header is valid; if it isn't, then the datagram is discarded.

This underscores IP's job. IP is not built to provide end-to-end guaranteed transmission of data. IP exists mainly for one reason: routing. We'll revisit routing a bit later, when I describe the specifics of how to accomplish IP routing on a Win2K machine.

But whose job *is* end-to-end integrity, if not IP's? The answer: its buddy's, TCP.

TCP (Transmission Control Protocol)

I said earlier that IP handled routing and really didn't concern itself that much with whether the message got to its final destination or not. If there are seven IP hops from one point to the next, then each hop is an independent action—there's no coordination, no notion of whether a particular hop is hop number three out of seven. Each IP hop is totally unaware of the others. How, then, could we use IP to provide reliable service?

IP packets are like messages in a bottle. Drop the bottle in the ocean, and you have no guarantee that the message got to whomever you want to receive it. But suppose you hired a "message-in-the-bottle end-to-end manager." Such a person (let's call her Gloria) would take your message, put it in a bottle, and toss it in the ocean. That person would also have a partner on the other side of the ocean (let's call him Gaston), and when Gaston received a message in a bottle from Gloria, Gaston would then pen a short message saying "Gloria, I got your message," put *that* message in a bottle, and drop that bottle into the ocean.

If Gloria didn't get an acknowledgment from Gaston within, say, three months, then she'd drop *another* bottle into the ocean with the original message in it. In data communications terms, we'd say that Gloria "timed out" on the transmission path and was *resending*.

Yeah, I know, this is a somewhat goofy analogy, but understand the main point: We hired Gloria and Gaston to ensure that our inherently unreliable message-in-a-bottle network became reliable. Gloria will keep sending and resending until she gets a response from Gaston. Notice that she doesn't create a whole new transmission medium, like radio or telephone; she merely adds a layer of her own watchfulness to the existing transmission protocol.

Now think of IP as the message in the bottle. TCP, the Transmission Control Protocol, is just the Gloria/Gaston team. TCP provides reliable end-to-end service.

By the way, TCP provides some other services, most noticeably something called *sockets*, which I will discuss in a moment. As TCP has value besides its reliability feature, TCP also has a "cousin" protocol that acts very much like it but does *not* guarantee end-to-end integrity. That protocol is called UDP (User Datagram Protocol).

That's basically the idea behind TCP. Its main job is the orderly transmission of data from one intranet host to another. Its main features include:

- Handshake
- Packet sequencing
- Flow control
- Error handling

Whereas IP has no manners—it just shoves data at a computer whether that computer is ready for it or not—TCP makes sure that each side is properly introduced before attempting to transfer. TCP sets up the connection.

Sequencing

As IP does not use a virtual circuit, different data packets may end up arriving at different times and, in fact, in a different order. Imagine a simple intranet transferring four segments of data across a network with multiple possible pathways. The first segment takes the high road, so to speak, and is delayed. The second, third, and fourth do not and so get to the destination more quickly. TCP's job on the receiving side is to then reassemble things in order.

Flow Control

Along with sequencing is flow control. What if 50 segments of data had been sent and they all arrived out of order? The receiver would have to hold them all in memory before sorting them out and writing them to disk. Part of what TCP worries about is *pacing* the data—not sending it to the receiver until the receiver is ready for it.

Error Detection/Correction

And finally, TCP handles error detection and correction, as I've already said. Beyond that, TCP is very efficient in the way that it does error handling. Some protocols acknowledge each and every block, generating a large overhead of blocks. TCP, in contrast, does not do that. It tells the other side, "I am capable of accepting and buffering some number of blocks. Don't expect an acknowledgment until I've gotten that number of blocks. And if a block is received incorrectly, I will not acknowledge it, so if I don't acknowledge as quickly as you expect me to, then just go ahead and resend the block."

Sockets, Ports, and the Winsock Interface

Just about anything that you want to do with the Internet or your company's intranet involves two programs talking to each other. When you browse someone's Web site, you have a program (your Web browser, a *client* program) communicating with their Web server (obviously, a *server* program). Using the File Transfer Protocol (FTP), which I'll discuss later in this chapter, requires that one machine be running a program called an *FTP server* and that another computer be running an *FTP client*. Internet mail requires that a mail client program talk to a mail server program—and those are just a few examples.

Connecting a program in one machine to another program in another machine is kind of like placing a telephone call. The sender must know the phone number of the receiver, and the receiver must be around his or her phone, waiting to pick it up. In the TCP world, a phone number is called a *socket*. A socket is composed of three parts: the IP address of the receiver, which we've already discussed, the receiving program's *port number*, which we *haven't* yet discussed, and whether it's a TCP port or a UDP port—each protocol has its own set.

Suppose the PC on your desk running Windows 2000 wants to get a file from the FTP site, which is really the PC on *my* desk running Windows 2000. Obviously, for this to happen, we have to know each other's IP addresses. But that's not all; after all, in my PC I have a whole bunch of programs running (my network connection, my word processor, my operating system, my personal organizer, the FTP server, and so on). So if TCP says, "Hey, Mark's machine, I want to talk to you," then my machine would reply, "Which *one* of us—the word processor, the e-mail program, or what?" So the TCP/IP world assigns a 16-bit number to each program that wants to send or receive TCP information, a number called the *port* of that program.

The most popular Internet applications have had particular port numbers assigned to them, and those port numbers are known as *well-known ports*. You can see some well-known ports in Table 6.3.

TABLE 6.3: INTERNET PROTOCOLS AND PORT NUMBERS

INTERNET PROTOCOL	PORT NUMBER
FTP	TCP 20/21
Telnet	TCP 23
Simple Mail Transport Protocol	TCP 25
DNS	UDP and TCP 53
Trivial FTP (TFTP)	UDP 69
Hypertext Transfer Protocol (Web)	TCP 80
Kerberos logons	UDP and TCP 88
Post Office Protocol v3 (POP3)	TCP 110
Network News Transfer Protocol (NNTP)	TCP 119
Simple Network Time Protocol (SNTP)	UDP 123
NetBIOS	UDP and TCP 137, UDP 138, TCP 139
IMAP4	TCP 143
SNMP	UDP 161/162
LDAP	TCP 389
Secure HTTP (SSL)	TCP and UDP 443
SMB over sockets (CIFS)	TCP/UDP 445
ISAKMP (key exchange for IPSec)	UPD 500
SQL Server	UDP/TCP 1433

Specific programs may use their own particular ports, as in the case of Active Directory's global catalog server, which uses port 3268. Someone in the Navy has put up a nice page collecting many more ports at `www.nswc.navy.mil/ISSEC/Docs/Ref/Networking/new_ports.html`.

How Ports and Sockets Work

So, for instance, suppose I've pointed my HTTP client (which you know as a Web browser, like Internet Explorer) to an HTTP server (which you know as a Web server like a copy of Internet Information Server). Let's also assume that I'm going to visit www.acme.com, that acme.com's Web server is at 123.124.55.67, and that my computer has IP address 200.200.200.10.

My Web browser tries to contact the machine at 123.124.55.67. But just knowing a machine's IP address isn't sufficient; we need also to know the port address of the program that we want to talk to because, for example, this computer might also be a mail server, and I want to surf its Web pages, not send or receive e-mail. My Web browser knows that by convention the Web server lives at port 80. So my Web browser essentially "places a call"—that is, sets up a TCP/IP session—with port 80 at address 123.124.55.67, sometimes written 123.124.55.67:80, with a colon between the IP address and the port number. That combination of an IP address and a port is called a *socket address*.

In order for the Web server computer to chat with my computer, the Web server computer must be *ready* to chat—there's got to be someone at the Web browser "listening" when I "call." That's a lot of what a Web browser program does—it just sits and waits, "listening" on port 80. When the Web browser first starts up, it says, "If anyone calls on port 80, wake me up—I'm willing to take calls on that port." That's called a *passive open* on TCP.

So my Web browser talks to the Web server at the Web server's port 80. But how does the Web server talk back—what port does it use on *my* computer, what port on my computer is now listening for the server's response? Well, port 80 might seem the logical answer, at first—but it can't be. Here's why: suppose I'm sitting at a computer that's *running* a Web server and I fire up Internet Explorer to surf a different Web site. Could that Web site talk back to my computer at port 80? No, because port 80 on my computer is *already* busy, as *my* Web server would be running there.

Instead, the Web server negotiates with my Web browser to pick a port that my system's not using. So the conversation might look like

1. (From my computer to the Web server): "Hi there, anyone home at port 80 on 123.124.55.67?"

2. (From the Web server to my computer): "Sure; how should we talk?"

3. (From my computer to the Web server): "Ummm, how about port 40000?"

4. (From the Web server to my computer): "Great, then, let's set up a connection to 40000."

So my questions to the Web server go to 123.124.55.67:80, and the answers come back on 200.200.200.10:40000. (And yes, I've left a few steps out, like "how did the Web server ask which port to use in the first place," but I'm trying not to turn this into a whole *book* on TCP/IP!) Here's the point that I want to make: Communications to a server employ a well-known port, like 80 on HTTP. In contrast, however, communications back to a client don't use any particular predefined port—the server and client just agree on one "on-the-fly."

NOTE   *And in case you're wondering, servers can carry on more than one conversation over a given port. If 500 people are all surfing a Web server, then the Web server can keep those conversations separate.*

PAT and NAT: Routing the Nonroutable

Now that you know about ports, I can tell you how a bit of magic that you'll see a little later works. Windows 2000 includes a couple of tools called Internet Connection Sharing (ICS) and port address translation (PAT) that let you share a single routable IP address with any number of computers, even though those computers all bear *non*routable addresses. Let's look at how the simpler one, ICS, works.

INTERNET CONNECTION SHARING OVERVIEW

Suppose you have a bunch of computers in your home, all connected via an Ethernet network. Suppose also that you've got a high-speed Internet connection like a DSL or a cable modem connection.

Those kinds of connections usually come with one—and one only—routable IP address, which you give to one of your computers.

But what about the other ones? How can you get all of your Windows 9x, NT 4, and Windows 2000 boxes in the house *all* on the Internet at the same time? After all, only one computer can use a given IP address, so trying to put that one routable IP address on every computer in the house not only won't help, it'll hurt—the Internet connection will work fine as long as only one computer's using the DSL or cable modem vendor-supplied address, but put it on a second system and *neither* system will be able to get to the Internet. Instead, here's how to put everyone in the house on the Internet.

First, connect all of the computers to your home Ethernet. Do not give those computers an IP address; instead, tell their TCP/IP software to obtain IP addresses "automatically" (and I promise, we'll do that soon; I'm just explaining the outline of the method right now). Next, give the routable IP address (let's make it 200.200.200.10 for the sake of example) to a Windows 2000 computer. Finally, turn on a Windows 2000 feature called Internet Connection Sharing—there are specifics on this at the end of this chapter. Then reboot all of the computers except for the one with the routable IP address. Result: once rebooted, all of those computers will be able to access Internet resources.

How ICS Shares a Routable Address with Nonroutable Machines

What happened? Well, first of all, the routing computer—the one running ICS—distributes unique IP addresses to all of your other computers. But *what* IP addresses? Well, it's not kosher to start making up routable IP addresses and handing them out unless you actually *own* those addresses, so the routing computer hands out "safe" IP addresses from one of the nonroutable ranges specified in RFC 1918, the range from 192.168.0.2 through 192.168.0.254, and gives itself an extra IP address, 192.168.0.1. So far, so good—the computers in your home network can all "see" each other, even the routing computer.

Here's where the magic happens. Suppose one of your nonroutable computers (let's give it address 192.168.0.10) wants to surf my Web site at 206.246.253.200. That nonroutable computer says to the routing computer, the only one with a routable, acceptable-on-the-Internet address, "Please connect me to the Web server at 206.246.253.200." Now, clearly, the 192.168.0.10 system can't directly talk to my Web server, as 192.168.0.10 is a nonroutable address and no router will pass any 192.168.*y.z* traffic over the Internet. But the routable computer can employ its 200.200.200.10 address to establish that connection to the Web server at 206.246.253.200. The routable computer at 200.200.200.10 acts as a kind of "relay" to forward the nonroutable computer's request to my Web server, passing messages back and forth. My Web server hasn't a clue that the *real* client is sitting on a nonroutable address; as far as my Web server's concerned, it's talking to 200.200.200.10.

But the 200.200.200.10 computer running ICS can go further than that, as it can simultaneously relay requests for every single computer in your nonroutable network. So could you have 15 machines in your nonroutable network all talking to my Web site at the same time? Sure. But my Web site would think that the machine at 200.200.200.10 was holding 15 simultaneous conversations with it—peculiar, perhaps, but not unallowable. But what if each of the 15 people sitting at the 15 computers were surfing *different* pages on my Web site—how would the routing computer on your network keep it all straight? With ports. It could be that the session between the first nonroutable computer and my Web site took place on 200.200.200.10:40000, the second on 200.200.200.40001, and so on. The routing computer is then using the incoming port number to figure out which of its local, nonroutable computers made a particular request, so that it can *translate* that incoming port into a nonroutable address, so to speak. That's why the process is called *port address translation* or PAT. ICS is a piece of PAT routing software built into Windows 2000.

PAT IS ALMOST A FIREWALL, BUT ONLY *ALMOST*

PAT is, then, a pretty neat bit of routing magic. Say your ISP only gives you one routable IP address—here's a way to stretch it across dozens of machines. Even better, PAT offers a simple, basic kind of anti-hacker security. Consider that your nonroutable computers can access e-mail, Web, and other services on the public Internet, but still remain basically invisible in the sense that your internal computers can *initiate* a conversation with a server on the Internet, but no computer on the public Internet can initiate a conversation with one of your nonroutable computers. It's harder, then, for jerks—oops, I mean hackers—to attack your internal machines.

Harder, yes, but not impossible, I should point out. Once one of your internal, nonroutable systems establishes contact with a computer on the public Internet through your PAT routing computer, then there's obviously a channel now open from that computer on the public Internet and your nonroutable computer. While I'm not a security expert by any means, I'm told by people that I trust that this "open port," as they call it, can be a method for "e-bottom feeders" to potentially attack your system. And no matter what sort of security you use, remember that once you've downloaded a program to one of your internal computers and run that program, then the program can have malicious intent. Remember also that many kinds of files can contain programs nowadays: Web pages can contain VBScript macros, Word files can contain programs, and you might end up downloading and installing a kind of program called an ActiveX object simply by viewing a Web page. (That's why I keep my security settings fairly paranoid in Word, Outlook, and Internet Explorer, and I recommend that you do also—look in Tools/Macro/Security in Word and Outlook, or Tools/Internet Options/Security in Internet Explorer.)

And by the way, I've cast my PAT example as a home-based one, but don't think that only homes and small businesses can use it. Most large organizations only assign their routable addresses to a small number of systems, and put nonroutable addresses on the vast majority of their machines. Then they use PAT or PAT-like routers to let their employees access the Internet.

NAT VERSUS PAT

PAT's a nice piece of routing software built into 2000, but not the only one. ICS is nice, but it's pretty inflexible. It's supplemented by a more powerful bit of routing software called network address translation (NAT). In fact, it's far more likely that you've heard of NAT before than PAT, because many PAT routers are mistakenly called NAT routers. (And understand that while a purist might quibble about whether a router is a PAT or NAT router, the fact is that the definitions have blurred so much in popular usage that in actual fact you'll probably *only* hear the phrase "NAT" rather than "PAT." In fact, as you'll see later in this chapter, 2000 contains software that will do both NAT and PAT, but calls the capability "NAT routing." So after this section, I'll surrender and just refer to NAT rather than PAT.)

A simple NAT router lets you connect a particular routable IP address with a particular nonroutable IP address. Thus, for example, if you had a Web server on a machine with the nonroutable address 10.10.10.50, then the outside world couldn't see or access that Web server. But suppose you had a few dozen routable addresses, including (for example) 100.50.40.10? You could put those addresses on a NAT router and tell the NAT router for example, "connect the routable 100.50.40.10 address with the nonroutable 10.10.10.50 address." When someone on the public Internet tried to surf the Web site at 100.50.40.7, then, the NAT router would transparently redirect all of that traffic to the system at the nonroutable address 10.10.10.50.

There's yet another permutation of port address translation that we'll see, built into Windows 2000's NAT routing software. In NAT, as you saw, the router completely assigned an entire routable IP address to a machine with a nonroutable IP address. But Windows 2000 also lets you assign a particular port on one system to a particular port on another system. So, for example, I could tell a Windows 2000 system acting as a router, "Whenever traffic comes in for 100.50.40.7 on port 80, send it to the nonroutable 10.10.10.50 system, on port 5000." (I'm not saying you would *want* to do it, I'm just explaining that it's possible.) So, in that case, you would set up the Web server on the 10.10.10.50 system and reconfigure the Web server so that it didn't use the standard port 80, but rather port 5000—and yes, IIS lets you do that, as you'll see in Chapter 17.

Winsock Sockets

Before moving on to the issue of Internet names (rather than all this IP address stuff that we've been working with), let me define a term that you'll hear in the 2000 TCP/IP networking business: *winsock* or "windows sockets." The value of sockets is that they provide a uniform way to write programs that exploit the underlying Internet communications structure. If, for example, I want to write a networked version of the game Battleship, then I might want to be able to quickly turn out versions for Windows, OS/2, the Mac, and Unix machines. But maybe I don't know much about communications, and don't *want* to know much. (I'm probably supposed to note here that Battleship is a registered trademark of Milton Bradley or someone like that; consider it done.) I could just sit down with my C compiler and bang out a Battleship that runs on Unix machines. Just a few code changes, and *presto!* I have my PC version.

But the PC market requires some customization, and so a particular version of the sockets interface, called Winsock, was born. It's essentially the sockets interface but modified a bit to work better in a PC environment.

The benefit of Winsock is that all vendors of TCP/IP software support an identical Winsock programming interface (well, identical in theory, anyway) and so TCP/IP-based programs should run as well atop FTP software's TCP/IP stack as they would atop the TCP/IP stack that ships with NT and 2000, as well as Windows for Workgroups, Windows 9*x*, and Windows Me. That's why you can plop your Netscape Web browser on just about any PC with TCP/IP and it should work without any trouble.

Telling Software to Use TCP/IP Over Other Protocols: Network Binding

This discussion has covered a particular set of network protocols—TCP/IP—so far, and TCP/IP is a pretty flexible protocol. You can use it for just about anything that you'd need a network protocol for, and in fact many networks use only TCP/IP. But your network might include other protocols running alongside TCP/IP on your Ethernet cables; in particular, it's not unusual to see Microsoft networks running IPX/SPX or NetBEUI in addition to TCP/IP. You might be running IPX/SPX because you've also got some Novell servers around, or you might be running NetBEUI because you still have some older Microsoft operating systems, either on clients or workstations. If either of those things are true, then you might have to run NetBEUI and/or IPX/SPX on your Windows 200x systems as well. And that leads me to discuss network binding.

Suppose I have a workstation running TCP/IP, IPX/SPX, and NetBEUI protocols, trying to talk to a file server that runs only TCP/IP. The workstation and server employ several pieces of software to set up the workstation-to-file-server file sharing connection:

◆ There's a piece of software on the workstation that knows how to ask the file server for data; technically, we could call it the *file-server-client software*, the client part of the file sharing client-server software. Microsoft calls it the Client for Microsoft Networks.

◆ The client software gets to the network by choosing a protocol to use to communicate over the wire to the server. If the workstation runs TCP/IP, IPX/SPX, and NetBEUI, then the Client for Microsoft Networks doesn't know which to choose, so it uses them all, duplicating its request to the file server over all three.

◆ The protocols run over the network cables to the server. As we've seen, the server doesn't respond to all of them, as it's not running software to make it aware of IPX/SPX or Net-BEUI. But it *does* understand TCP/IP.

◆ The server-side piece of the file sharing software connects to the one protocol running on the server, TCP/IP.

What's wrong with this? Nothing really, except that it's a bit inefficient. The workstation essentially makes the "server, please talk to me" request over one protocol, then another, and then, if there's no response, finally the third protocol. So the order in which a piece of software tries different protocols can speed up or slow down a computer's performance. You could probably pretty easily imagine some not-so-great scenarios here; for instance, suppose this three-protocol-using workstation lived in an environment with 20 file servers, and 19 of the 20 file servers used TCP/IP exclusively. Suppose also that this workstation always first tried IPX/SPX, then NetBEUI, and then TCP/IP whenever it wanted to contact a file server. Clearly that'd run terribly.

The word for the order in which a given piece of network client or server software—like the Client for Microsoft Networks—taps a protocol is called the *network binding order*. You can control that from a Windows 200x system like this.

1. Right-click My Network Places.

2. Choose Properties.

3. You'll see a Network and Dial-Up Connections dialog box that contains icons that represent your different ways of connecting to a network, whether a network adapter or a dial-up connection.

4. Do *not* right-click Local Area Connection—surprised you, eh? Instead, look at the Network and Dial-Up Connections icon, and notice that it's got an unusual item on its window menu—Advanced. Click Advanced and then Advanced Settings; *that* will raise another window, labeled Advanced Settings, with Adapters and Settings and Provider Order tabs. Click Adapters and Settings.

5. The resulting property page has an upper and lower part. The upper lets you choose which adapter you want to arrange bindings for; click it and you will see the applications that communicate through that adapter.

In the lower part of the dialog box, you'll see the various network applications running on your computer. For example, most systems run Client for Microsoft Networks (the file sharing client software) and File and Printer Sharing for Microsoft Networks (the server piece of the file sharing software). Under each application, you'll see the protocols that use it. Up- and down-arrow buttons then let you choose the order of the protocols to try—the *binding order* for that application. In my example where you've got a client computer in a network that incorporates 20 file servers, 19 of which use only TCP/IP, then, it'd make sense to adjust the bindings for the Client for Microsoft Networks to use TCP/IP before IPX/SPX or NetBEUI.

Internet Host Names

Thus far, I've referred to a lot of numbers; hooking up to my Web server, then, seems to require that you point your Web browser to IP address 206.246.253.200, TCP port number 80, which is written "206.246.253.200:80" in socket terminology.

Of course, you don't actually do that. When you send e-mail to your friends, you don't send it to 199.45.23.17; you send it to something like robbie@somefirm.com. What's IP got to do with it?

IP addresses are useful because they're precise and because they're easy to subnet. But they're tough to remember, and people generally prefer more English-sounding names. So TCP/IP allows us to group one or more TCP/IP networks into groups called *domains*, groups that will share a common name like microsoft.com, senate.gov, army.mil, or mit.edu.

NOTE *Internet naming, and in particular the Domain Name System (DNS), is a big topic—in fact, it'll take up the majority of the next chapter; this section is just a brief summary. Stay tuned to Chapter 7 for the truly ugly (but necessary) details.*

Machines within a domain will have names that include the domain name; for example, within my mmco.com domain I have machines named micron133.mmco.com, narn.mmco.com, minbar.mmco.com, zhahadum.mmco.com, and serverted.mmco.com. Those specific machine names are called *host names*.

How does TCP/IP connect the English names—the *host* names—to the IP addresses? And how can I sit at my PC in mmco.com and get the information I need to be able to find another host called archie.au when archie's all the way on the other side of the world in Australia?

Simple—with HOSTS, DNS, and (in the next chapter and if you have pre–Windows 2000 machines on your network) WINS. The process of converting a name to its corresponding IP address is called *name resolution*. Again, how does it work? Read on.

Simple Naming Systems (HOSTS)

When you set up your subnet, you don't want to explicitly use IP addresses every time you want to run some TCP/IP utility and hook up with another computer in your subnet. So, instead, you create a file called HOSTS that looks like this:

```
199.34.57.50  keydata.mmco.com
199.34.57.129 serverted.mmco.com
```

This is just a simple ASCII text file. Each host goes on one line, and the line starts off with the host's IP address. Enter at least one space and the host's English name. Do this for each host. You can even give multiple names in the HOSTS file:

```
199.34.57.50   keydata.mmco.com markspc
199.34.57.129  serverted.mmco.com serverpc bigsv
```

You can even add comments, with the octothorp (#):

```
199.34.57.50   keydata.mmco.com markspc #The Big Dog's machine
199.34.57.129  serverted.mmco.com serverpc bigsv
```

Ah, but now comes the really rotten part.

You have to put one of these HOSTS files on *every single workstation*. That means that every single time you change anyone's HOSTS file, you have to go around and change *everybody's* HOSTS file. Every workstation must contain a copy of this file, which is basically a telephone directory of every machine in your subnet. It's a pain, yes, but it's simple. If you're thinking, "Why can't I just put a central HOSTS file on a server and do all my administration with *that* file?"—what you're really asking for is a *name server*, and I'll show you two of them, the Domain Name System (DNS) and the Windows Internet Name Service (WINS), in this chapter.

You must place the HOSTS file in \WINNT\SYSTEM32\DRIVERS\ETC on an NT or Windows 2000 system, in the Windows directory on a Windows for Workgroups or Windows 95/98 machine, and wherever the network software is installed on other kinds of machines (DOS or OS/2).

HOSTS is reread every time your system does a name resolution; you needn't reboot to see a change in HOSTS take effect.

Domain Name System (DNS)

HOSTS is a pain, but it's a necessary pain if you want to communicate within your subnet. How does IP find a name outside of your subnet or outside of your domain?

Suppose someone at exxon.com wanted to send a file to a machine at minasi.com. Surely the exxon.com HOSTS files don't contain the IP address of my company, and vice versa?

Well, back when the Internet was small, HOSTS was sufficient—the exxon.com and minasi.com machines *would* have found each other in HOSTS back in 1980. The few dozen people on the early Internet just all used the same small HOSTS file. With the Internet's machine population in the hundreds of millions, however, that's just not practical; we needed something better.

The Internet community came up with an answer in 1984: Distribute the responsibility for names. That's done by the Domain Name System (DNS). There is a central naming clearinghouse for *the* Internet, the Internet Corporation for Assigned Names and Numbers (ICANN), which you met earlier in this chapter. (Obviously, if you're only running a private intranet, then *you* perform the function of name manager.) ICANN is the overall boss of DNS naming, but it delegates particular domains to particular *name registrars*, as for example when it delegates keeping track of all of the .com domains to VeriSign's Network Solutions subsidiary.

Instead of trying to keep track of the name and IP address of every single machine in the Internet, ICANN and its delegated registrars require that every Internet domain have at least two machines (although some now only require one) running that contain a database of that domain's machines. These machines are called *DNS servers*.

ICANN then needs only to know the IP address of the domain's DNS servers, and when a request for a name resolution comes to ICANN's servers, ICANN's servers just refer the questioner to the domain in question's local DNS machines. (We'll see how this works in greater detail in the next chapter.)

Thus, if you wanted to visit my Web site at www.minasi.com, you'd start up your Web browser and point it at `www.minasi.com`. Before your browser could show you anything, however, it would need to *find* the machine named www.minasi.com. So it would fire off a DNS query, "What's the IP address of www.minasi.com?" to its local DNS server. The local DNS server probably wouldn't know, and so it would ask ICANN's DNS servers. ICANN's servers would know that the IP address for minasi.com's DNS server is 206.246.253.111 and would tell your local DNS server that it could find www.minasi.com's IP address by asking the question of the 206.246.253.111 machine. So your local DNS server would then re-ask the question, this time of my local DNS server, and would then get the answer "206.246.253.200." And most DNS servers remember past queries for a few hours or perhaps a day, so if you revisited my Web site the same day, when your Web browser asked your local DNS server for the IP address of www.minasi.com, your local DNS server would respond, "206.246.253.200," without hesitation.

You've no doubt noticed that many Internet domains end with `.com`, but there are other endings as well. Back in the pre-ICANN days, the InterNIC (ICANN's predecessor) started off with six initial naming domains: EDU was for educational institutions, NET was for network providers, COM for commercial users, MIL was for military users (remember who built this?), ORG was for organizations, and GOV was for civilian government. For example, there is a domain on the Internet called white-house.gov; you can send Internet e-mail to the President that way, at `president@whitehouse.gov`. There are more root domains these days, such as `.int`, `.museum`, `.name`, and a long list of two-letter codes for countries such as `.fi` for sites in Finland, `.uk` for sites in the United Kingdom, and so on.

What kind of computer do you need to run a DNS server? Just about any kind—there's DNS server software for IBM mainframes, DEC Vaxes, Unix and Linux, and of course, Windows 2000—in fact, a DNS server module not only ships with Windows 2000, you can't even run an Active Directory without a DNS server. You'll see how to set up a DNS server in the next chapter.

E-Mail Names: A Note

If you've previously messed around with e-mail under TCP/IP, then you may be wondering something about these addresses. After all, you don't send mail to minasi.com, you'd send it to a name like `help@minasi.com`. `help@minasi.com` is an e-mail address. The way it works is this: A group of users in a TCP/IP domain decide to implement mail.

In order to receive mail, a machine must be up and running, ready to accept mail from the outside world (that is, some other subnet or domain). Now, mail can arrive at any time of day, so this machine must be up and running all of the time. That seems to indicate that it would be a dumb idea to get mail delivered straight to your desktop. So, instead, TCP mail dedicates a machine to the mail router task of receiving mail from the outside world, holding that mail until you want to read it, taking mail that you want to send somewhere else, and routing that mail to some other mail router. The name of the most common TCP/IP mail router program is *sendmail*. The name of the protocol used most commonly for routing e-mail on the Internet, by the way, is the Simple Mail Transfer Protocol (SMTP).

Once e-mail is sitting on your local mail server, you then retrieve it via another mail protocol, the Post Office Protocol (POP3).

Unfortunately, Microsoft did not include an SMTP router or POP3 program in either the workstation or the server version of NT, so either you have to connect up to an existing mail router in order to get Internet mail or you have to buy a third-party mail product to work under NT or Windows 2000.

You can see how mail works in Figure 6.7.

FIGURE 6.7

The interrelation of host names, e-mail names, and the Internet

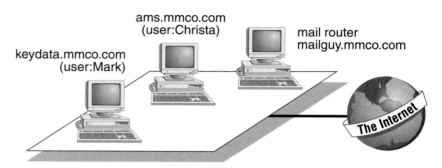

In this small domain, we've got two users: Mark and Christa. Mark works on keydata.mmco.com, and Christa works on ams.mmco.com. Now, suppose Christa wants to send some mail to her friend Corky, executive director for Surfers of America; Corky's address is `corky@surferdudes.org`. She fires up a program on her workstation, which is called a *mail client*. The mail client allows her to create and send new messages as well as receive incoming messages. She sends the message and closes her mail client. Notice that her mail client software doesn't do routing—it just lets her create, send, and receive messages.

The mail client has been configured to send messages to an SMTP server, which is running in this subnet on mailguy.mmco.com. mailguy is kind of the post office (in Internet lingo, a *mail router*) for this group of users. The SMTP server on mailguy.mmco.com stores the message, and it then sends the message off to the machine with the DNS name surferdudes.org, trusting IP to route the message correctly to surferdudes. Hmmm...there's no one machine named surferdudes.org; where should the mail go? As you'll learn in the next chapter, a DNS administrator can advertise that e-mail should go to a particular machine. Thus, surferdudes.org might have a machine named po.surferdudes.org; when mailguy.mmco.com tries to send the mail to corky, mailguy first asks DNS, "What machine is supposed to get mail for surferdudes?" and DNS replies, "po.surferdudes.org."

Additionally, the SMTP server knows the names Christa and Mark. It is the workstation that is the interface to the outside world vis-a-vis mail. Note, by the way, that *DNS* has no idea who Mark or Christa is; DNS is concerned with *host* names, not *e-mail* names. It's DNS that worries about how to find mailguy.mmco.com.

A bit later, Corky gets the message and sends a reply to Christa. The reply does *not* go to Christa's machine ams.mmco.com; instead, it goes to mailguy.mmco.com because Corky sent mail to `christa @mmco.com`. The mail system sends the messages to mmco.com, but what machine has the address mmco.com? Simple: DNS directs it to send mail for mmco.com to mailguy.mmco.com.

Eventually, Christa starts up the mail client program once again. The mail program uses POP3 to send a query to the local mail router mailguy.mmco.com, saying, "Any new mail for Christa?" There *is* mail, and Christa reads it.

Getting onto an Intranet

So far, I've talked quite a bit about how an intranet works and what kinds of things there are that you can do with an intranet. But I haven't told you enough yet to actually get *on* an intranet, whether it's your company's private intranet or *the* Internet.

- ◆ You can connect to a multiuser system and appear to the Internet as a dumb terminal. This doesn't happen much any more, so it's unlikely that you'll do this.

- ◆ You can connect to an Internet provider via a serial port and either a protocol called the Serial Line Interface Protocol (SLIP) or one called the Point-to-Point Protocol (PPP) and appear to the Internet as a host. This is what you're doing when you dial up with a modem to an Internet service provider (ISP) such as AOL.

- ◆ You can be part of a local area network that is an Internet subnet and then load TCP/IP software on your system and appear to the Internet as a host. This is probably how most people get on the Internet—either when the computer on your desk connects to the Internet via your company's network, or if you connect at home via a cable modem or DSL.

Each of these options has pros and cons, as you'll see. The general rule is that in order to access an intranet, all you basically have to do is to connect up to a computer that is already on an intranet.

The essence of an intranet is in *packet switching*, a kind of network game of hot potato whereby computers act communally to transfer each other's data around. Packet switching is what makes it possible to add subnetworks on-the-fly.

Dumb Terminal Connection

This was once a common way to attach to the Internet. You'd dial up to a multiuser system of some kind—usually a Unix box of some stripe—and do simple terminal emulation. You'd then have a character-based session with typed commands only—no mouse, no graphics. Very macho, but not as much fun as surfing with a graphical Web browser. On the other hand, the distant multiuser machine did all the heavy lifting, computing-wise.

Unfortunately, this terminal access approach was kind of limited. Suppose, for example, that I live in Virginia (which is true) and I connect to the Internet via a host in Maine (which is not true). From the Internet's point of view, I'm not in an office in Virginia; instead, I'm wherever the host that I'm connected to is. I work in Virginia, but if I were dialing a host in Maine, then from the Internet's point of view I'd be in Maine. Any requests that I make for file transfers, for example, wouldn't go to Virginia—they'd go to my host in Maine.

Now, that can be a bit of a hassle. Say I'm at my Virginia location logged on to the Internet via the Maine host. I get onto Microsoft's FTP site—I'll cover FTP in Chapter 17, but basically FTP is just a means to provide a library of files to the outside world—and I grab a few files, perhaps an updated video driver. The FTP program says, "I got the file," but the file is now on the host in

Maine. That means that I'm only half done, as I now have to run some other kind of file transfer program to move the file from the host in Maine to my computer in Virginia.

SLIP/PPP Serial Connection

If you've got one of those $10/month or $20/month Internet accounts, then you fit in this category.

A somewhat better way to connect to a TCP/IP-based network—that is, an intranet or the Internet—is by a direct serial connection to an existing intranet host. If you use PCs, then you may know of a program called LapLink that allows two PCs to share each other's hard disks via their RS232 serial ports; SLIP and PPP are similar ideas. An intranet may have a similar type of connection called a SLIP or PPP connection. The connection needn't be a serial port, but it often is. SLIP is the Serial Line Interface Protocol, an older protocol that I sometimes think of as the *simple* line interface protocol. There's really nothing to SLIP—no error checking, no security, no flow control. It's the simplest protocol imaginable: Just send the data, then send a special byte that means, "This is the end of the data." PPP, in contrast, was designed to retain the low overhead of SLIP and yet include some extra information required so that more intelligent parts of an intranet—items like routers—could use it effectively. The Point-to-Point Protocol works by establishing an explicit link between one side and another, then uses a simple error-checking system called a *checksum* to monitor noise on the line.

Which protocol should you use? The basic rule that I use is that SLIP doesn't provide error checking but uses less overhead, and PPP provides error checking and uses more overhead. Therefore, when I'm using error-correcting modems, I use SLIP. On noisy lines and without error-correcting modems, I use PPP.

You may use PPP even if you *don't* have an account with an ISP. Windows 2000 supports PPP via Routing and Remote Access Service (RRAS), so if you dial into your company's servers, you do that with PPP. Windows 2000 only supports SLIP on the client side: You can dial into a SLIP server with Dial-Up Networking, but RRAS won't let you set up a Windows 2000 system as a SLIP server.

LAN Connection

The most common way to connect to an intranet is simply by being a LAN workstation on a local area network that is an intranet subnetwork. Again, this needn't be *the* Internet—almost any LAN can use the TCP/IP protocol suite.

This is the connection that most Windows 2000 servers will use to provide TCP/IP services. Microsoft's main reason for implementing TCP/IP on NT is to provide an alternative to NetBEUI, as NetBEUI is quick and applicable to small networks but inappropriate for large corporate networks. In contrast, TCP/IP has always been good for intranetworking, but one suffered tremendously in speed. That's not true anymore, however; for example, a quick test of TCP/IP versus NetBEUI on one of my workstations showed network read rates of 1250K/sec for NetBEUI and 833K/sec for TCP/IP, and write rates of 312K/sec for NetBEUI and 250K/sec for TCP/IP. Again, TCP's slower, but not by a lot. And NetBEUI doesn't go over routers.

Terminal Connections versus Other Connections

Before moving on to the next topic, I'd like to return to the difference between a terminal connection and a SLIP, PPP, or LAN connection. In Figure 6.8, you see three PCs on an Ethernet attached to two minicomputers, which in turn serve four dumb terminals.

FIGURE 6.8

When Internet con-
nections involve IP
numbers and when
they don't

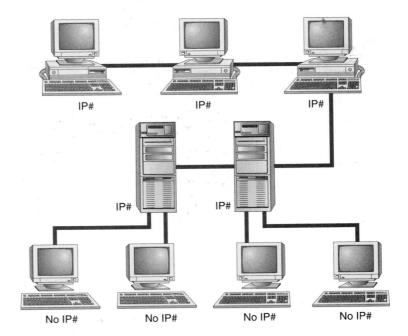

The minicomputer-to-minicomputer link might be SLIP or PPP, or then again they might be LANed together. Notice that only the *computers* in this scenario have Internet Protocol (IP) addresses. Whenever you send mail to one of the people on the PCs at the top of the picture, it goes to that person's PC. If you were to scrutinize the IP addresses—and most of the time, you will not—you'd see that everyone had the same IP address. In contrast, the people at the *bottom* of the picture get their mail sent to one of the minicomputers, and so in this example, each pair of terminals shares an IP address. If Shelly and George in your office access your company's intranet through terminals connected to the same computer, then a close look at mail from them would show that they have the same IP address. But, if you think about it, you already knew that; if you send mail to `george@mailbox.acme.com` and to `shelly@mailbox.acme.com`, then the machine name to which the mail goes is the same; it's just the usernames that vary.

So, in summary: If you want to get onto *the* Internet from a remote location, then your best bet is to sign up with a service that will bill you monthly for connect charges, like Delphi. To attach to a private intranet, you need to dial up to a multiuser computer on that intranet, or you need a SLIP or PPP connection, or you have to be on a workstation on a LAN that's part of that intranet. You then need to talk to your local network guru about getting the software installed on your system that will allow your computer to speak TCP/IP so that it can be part of your intranet.

NOTE *There is one case where Figure 6.8 isn't complete. If one of the terminals pictured is not simply a dumb ASCII terminal attached to a minicomputer but is instead a Windows Terminal—still a dumb terminal, but one built to work specifically with Windows 2000 Terminal Services, Windows Terminal Server 4, or Citrix Metaframe—then that terminal will have its own IP address.*

So Where Do I Get My IP Addresses?

You can't get anywhere in the next section without some IP addresses. How does what you've read so far in this chapter relate to where you should go to get IP addresses?

◆ If you're part of a large corporation, there is almost certainly a group who manages (or doles out, in other words) the IP addresses; if so, go to them for the IP addresses you'll need.

◆ If you're just playing around with this, then you can use any addresses you like, provided you're not connected to the Internet. But it's a good idea to use one of the RFC 1918 ranges in any case—it's a good habit.

◆ If you're with a small firm and it's your job to get the firm on the Internet, then you have two tasks. First, you've got to figure out how you'll be connected. Do you need constant, 24/7 connection to the Internet? You will if you intend to run your own Web or mail servers on your site, and in that case, you'll probably need to get a frame relay connection to your ISP. On the other hand, does your firm just need periodic access to the Internet? Then you may be perfectly happy with the cheaper alternative of some kind of shared dial-on-demand system, either using analog modems or ISDN. Second, how many IP addresses do you need? If you put in a NAT router, by purchasing one from Cisco or some other router vendor, or if you use a Windows 2000 machine as a NAT router (you'll read later how to do that), then you'll only need one dedicated IP address from your ISP. On the other hand, if you want all of your firm's computers to have their own routable IP addresses, then you should expect to have to pay your ISP a bit more for them than you would for just one IP address—but having all routable IP addresses keeps things simpler, in my experience.

◆ If you're a home user with an existing Internet connection, such as a dial-up modem, an ISDN dial connection, cable modem, or DSL, and you want to share that connection with other machines on a home network, then just use Internet Connection Sharing, which you'll read about later in this chapter.

The Basics of Setting Up TCP/IP on Windows 2000 with Static IP Addresses

Enough talking about TCP/IP internetworking; let's do it, and do it with Windows 2000.

Traditionally, one of the burdens of IP administrators has been that they must assign separate IP numbers to each machine, a bit of a bookkeeping hassle. You can adopt this "static" IP address approach, and in fact you will *have* to assign static IP addresses to at least a few of your systems. In actual fact, however, you'll find that assigning a static IP address to every single IP-using computer in your enterprise soon palls, and you'll assign IP addresses to most systems automatically with the Dynamic Host Configuration Protocol, covered in the next chapter.

No network can completely avoid static IP addresses, however, so we'll start out with this older method of putting an IP address on a Windows 2000 computer. In the next chapter, we'll take up dynamic IP addressing with DHCP.

Here's the most basic set of TCP/IP configuration tasks, and the first ones we'll tackle:

1. Load the TCP/IP protocol on the Windows 2000 system.

2. Set the IP address and subnet, default gateway, and DNS server.

3. Prepare the HOSTS file, if you're going to use one.

4. Test the connection with Ping.

Let's take a look at those steps, one by one.

Installing TCP/IP Software on a Windows 2000 Machine

Before you can configure TCP/IP on a Windows 2000 system, you've got to have TCP/IP loaded. Now, the chances are very good that you already have TCP/IP loaded because it is the default protocol—if you installed Windows 2000 and chose Typical Settings in the Network Setup part, then you've already got TCP/IP on your system, so skip ahead to the next section, "Configuring TCP/IP with a Static IP Address."

If not, however, it's simple to install it. Open the Control Panel (Start/Settings/Control Panel) and then open the Network and Dial-Up Connections applet that you'll find in Control Panel. You'll see something like Figure 6.9.

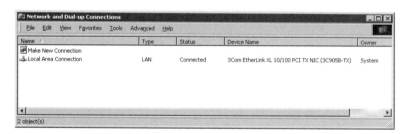

This window describes each NIC in your system and also lists every item in your Dial-Up Networking directory—so if you've got your system set up to be able to dial an ISP or perhaps a distant Windows 2000 network, then you'll see a line for each of those DUN directory entries—as well as an icon that can start a wizard to add new DUN directory entries. This computer hasn't got a modem and therefore has never dialed up anywhere, so there are just the two entries. If this machine had two NICs, then you'd see two Local Area Connection entries.

I want to install TCP/IP on the NIC, so right-click that and choose Properties, and you'll see a dialog box like Figure 6.10.

I set up this example machine with just the NetBEUI protocol, as you see in the dialog box. To add TCP/IP, click the Install button and you'll get a choice of things to install, as you see in Figure 6.11.

Click Protocol and Add and you get a list of protocols that you can add. Select Internet Protocol (TCP/IP), as you see in Figure 6.12.

FIGURE 6.10

Properties for the
NIC

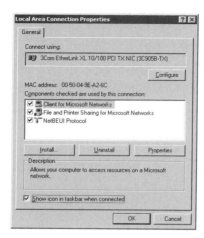

FIGURE 6.11

Choosing to install
an adapter, protocol,
or service

FIGURE 6.12

Choosing to add
TCP/IP

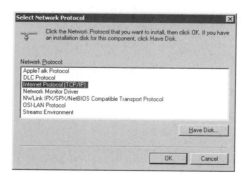

Click OK, and the machine will run the disks for a while as it installs TCP/IP with the default settings, which will automatically configure TCP/IP on this system with DHCP. We're going to change that in the next section, but you've now got TCP/IP on your system.

Configuring TCP/IP with a Static IP Address

Now let's apply an IP address to the TCP/IP software on this system. If you're not already there, get to the Local Area Network Connection properties page—right-click My Network Places, choose Properties, then right-click Local Area Connection in the dialog box that follows, and choose Properties on the resulting context menu. (You can also get to it from the Control Panel, as described in the preceding section.) It'll look something like Figure 6.13.

FIGURE 6.13

LAN Connection properties page

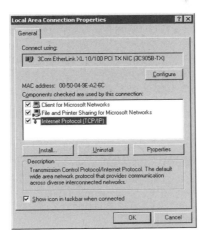

Click Internet Protocol (TCP/IP) and then the Properties button. You'll see a dialog box that looks like Figure 6.14, or anyway it will once we're through with it.

FIGURE 6.14

IP Properties page after modification

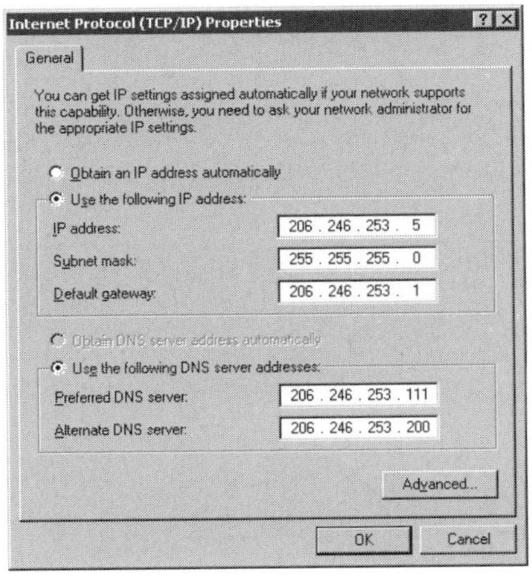

When you first see this dialog box, the Obtain an IP Address Automatically and Obtain DNS Server Address Automatically radio buttons will be selected. You should click the Use the Following IP Address and Use the Following DNS Server Addresses radio buttons. As mentioned earlier, you'll need to know four things to configure this screen: your IP address, the subnet mask, the IP address of your default gateway, and the IP addresses of one or more DNS server. In the case of the computer I'm configuring here, the IP address is 206.246.253.5, the subnet mask is 255.255.255.0, the default gateway is 206.246.253.1, and I've got two DNS servers, at 206.246.253.111 and 206.246.253.200. You might not use any DNS servers (although I can't imagine why); in that case, be sure to set up a HOSTS file and remember that it goes in the machine's \winnt\system32\drivers\etc directory.

WARNING   *Do not—and I repeat, do not—simply type in numbers to make your dialog box match mine. I can pretty much guarantee that if you type in IP addresses from my network at your location, it's not going to work. Again, you must get IP addresses from either your local network folks, an arm of the IANA, or an ISP.*

Click OK to clear the IP and LAN properties pages, and you'll have your IP address configured. But does it work? Read on.

Testing Your IP Configuration

There are two basic tools you'll use to verify that TCP/IP's working on your system: IPConfig and Ping.

IPCONFIG

First, check your IP configuration by opening a command prompt and typing **ipconfig /all**; you'll then see a screen like Figure 6.15.

FIGURE 6.15

Output of
`ipconfig /all`

`ipconfig /all` should be your first step when checking a TCP/IP installation or when trouble-shooting one. This particular IPConfig output starts out with some general information about this machine and then displays specific information about the Ethernet adapter. It's laid out like this because, in some cases, you may have two or more NICs in a system, and each NIC will have an IP address. Additionally, you may have a modem on your system and may be connected to the Internet via a dial-up connection. In that case, you'd again have more than one IP address—your Ethernet card would have an IP address (the one you just assigned it if you were following along with the previous text), and your modem would have an IP address that your ISP gave it when you dialed up.

Anyway, looking at the IPConfig output, CA is the machine's name—I was just using short names the day that I was setting this machine up.

WARNING   *In general, you should avoid underscores in your computer names. Microsoft's old-style NetBIOS-based networking doesn't mind it, but the Internet document on legal Internet names, RFC 1123, doesn't permit underscores. According to RFC 1123 in its "assumptions" section, each piece of an Internet name can be no more than 24 characters long—that is, each piece between the periods—and the only legal characters are a–z, 0–9, and the hyphen/minus sign. In fact, the earliest 32-bit Microsoft TCP/IP software, the code that shipped with Windows for Workgroups 3.11, would simply refuse to work on a machine with an underscore in its name. That's not true anymore, and in fact, the Active Directory uses a fair number of underscored names, but that's acceptable, as AD communications will mainly just go on amongst computers running Microsoft software. But avoid underscores in workstation names as it may potentially cause trouble when trying to use resources on the Internet, which may be running on computers that aren't running Microsoft software.*

Node Type answers the question, "How does the system convert an old-style NetBIOS name like \\SNOOPY into an IP address?" That's a long and complicated story, and we'll take it up in the next chapter. IP Routing Enabled asks whether this computer is acting as an IP router. As you saw in the example in the beginning of the chapter with machines A through H, you've got to have two IP connections to do that, so this clearly isn't a potential router—but I'll show you before the end of the chapter how to make a Windows 2000 machine into an IP router. I'll explain WINS Proxy Enabled in the next chapter.

Looking at the specific information under Ethernet Adapter Local Area Connection, the first entry is Connection-Specific DNS Suffix. This refers not to a Windows 2000 domain but to an Internet domain name, such as minasi.com, microsoft.com, or whitehouse.gov. Back in the NT 4 and earlier days, NT's TCP/IP software would only let you put a machine in just one Internet domain. That wasn't a big deal for most of us, but some people wanted their systems to be able to seem to be members of several domains, to have a sort of multiple citizenship in two or more domains. Such a machine might have a NIC in it that was connected to acme.com's network, and it might have another NIC in it connected to apex.com's network. If the machine's name were tadpole, then it might want to be able to be recognized both as tadpole.acme.com and tadpole.apex.com.

Now, when configuring tadpole under NT 4, you would have had to choose whether tadpole was in acme.com or apex.com—you couldn't choose both as you had to choose domain membership for the whole machine. Under Windows 2000, however, you can say that one NIC is a member of acme.com, and that the other is a member of apex.com. In my particular case, I really have no need to do that, which is why Connection-Specific DNS Suffix is empty. In fact, I haven't set the Internet domain name for the adapter *or* the entire machine as I'm going to get to that a bit later in this chapter.

Next are the IP addresses of the two DNS servers, an English-like description of the NIC, and the NIC's MAC address. DHCP Enabled indicates whether I punched in the IP address directly or let DHCP set the IP address for me. As I set the IP address myself, the value is No. If it were Yes, then—as you'll see in the next chapter—IPConfig would furnish more DHCP-specific information. Finally, IPConfig reports the IP address, subnet mask, and default gateway.

PING

So all of the settings are correct—but can you reach out to the outside world? TCP/IP has a very handy little tool for finding out whether your TCP/IP software is up and running and whether you have a connection to another point: Ping.

Ping is a program that lets you send a short message to another TCP/IP node, asking, "Are you there?" If it is there, then it says "yes" to the ping, and Ping relays this information back to you. You can see an example of Ping in Figure 6.16; the first line of the screen shows you the syntax, `ping ipaddress`.

FIGURE 6.16

A sample Ping output

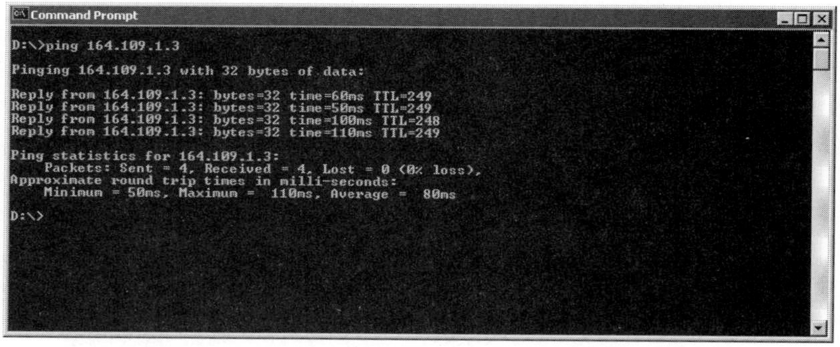

In the figure, I pinged the IP address of a server I know of on the Internet. The ping was successful, which is all that matters, and it's a very telling test as the address that I pinged is across the Internet from my system—the fact that I got a response from 164.109.1.3 means that not only is my TCP/IP software working across my segment and across my enterprise, but across the Internet as well.

But when *you're* testing your Internet software, don't use that IP address as there's no sense in flooding the Digital Express guys, the folks who own that machine. Instead, go ahead and ping my router—206.246.253.1. (I used to use www.microsoft.com as my Ping example, but now they've got their system rigged so that it won't respond to pings. I guess they couldn't figure out a way to charge for them.)

Use the approach outlined in the sidebar "How Do I Make Sure That TCP/IP Is Set Up Properly?" to get the most out of Ping.

Configuration II: Setting Domain Names

Thus far, my computer's name is just plain CA, which is a mite shorter than most Internet names; one might expect a name more like a.minasi.com or the like, a name that looks like *specific machine name.organization name.root*, where *root* is a suffix like *com*, *gov*, or some country identifier.

I intend for my computer CA to be part of an Internet domain named win2ktest.com, so its complete Internet name, or FQDN (fully qualified domain name), will be ca.win2ktest.com. What that really means, in essence, is that if someone pings ca.win2ktest.com, I want the machine to respond. If I decide to run Web server software on it later, then I want people to be able to see whatever content is on it by pointing their Web browsers to http://ca.win2ktest.com rather than having to use http://206.246.253.5. (I know this probably seems obvious to many of you, but stay with me, there's a point coming.)

HOW DO I MAKE SURE THAT TCP/IP IS SET UP PROPERLY?

With these Ping tests, you're demonstrating two things: First, that your IP software can get a packet from your computer to the outside world (in other words, that your IP connectivity is functioning), and second, that your connection to a DNS server for name resolution is working.

First, test IP connectivity by pinging specific IP addresses.

In most cases, your connection will work the first time. Start out with an overall "does it work?" test by pinging some distant location on the Internet. As mentioned in the text, you're welcome to ping my router, 206.246.253.1. If that responds correctly, then you've demonstrated that your IP software can get out to the Internet and back.

If it doesn't work, then try pinging something not so far—your default gateway. (Actually, the next thing to do is to look around back and make sure the network cable is still in place. There's nothing more embarrassing than calling in outside network support only to find that your LAN cable fell out of the back of your computer.) If you can successfully ping the default gateway but not my router, then either your firm's external Internet routers have failed or perhaps your default gateway is configured incorrectly. Another tool you might try is tracert, a souped-up Ping that shows you each of the hops that the IP packet had to use to get from your machine to the destination. It's a command-line command: Just type **tracert** followed by an IP address or DNS name. You can see a sample output in the following figure.

If you can't get to the default gateway, then try pinging another computer on your subnet. If you can get to another machine on your subnet but not the gateway, then perhaps you've got the wrong IP address for the gateway or perhaps the gateway is malfunctioning.

If you can't get to another system on your subnet—and I'm assuming that you've already walked over and checked that the other machine is up and running—then it may be that the IP software on your computer isn't running. Verify that by typing **ping 127.0.0.1**.

127.0.0.1 is the "loopback" address. IP software is designed to *always* report success on a ping to 127.0.0.1, if the IP software is functioning. Recheck that you've installed the TCP/IP software and rebooted after installing.

Once you're certain that IP works, try out DNS. Try pinging a distant location, but this time, don't do it by IP address, do it by name—try pinging www.whitehouse.gov, www.internic.net, or www.minasi.com. If the ping works, great; if not, check that you've got the right address punched in for your DNS server and then check the DNS server.

I would have guessed that unless I found some way to tell CA that its full name was actually ca.win2ktest.com, it wouldn't know to respond when someone pinged it by its full name. But, as it turns out, that's wrong.

If you're sitting at your computer and you type **ping ca.win2ktest.com**, then your computer asks your local DNS server what ca.win2ktest.com's IP address is. *Then* your computer just pings that IP address, and ca.win2ktest.com never even knows *what* name your computer originally called it by. If one of the people running IBM's DNS servers were to decide on a whim to insert an entry into IBM's DNS database that said "iguana.ibm.com has IP address 206.246.253.5," then anyone anywhere pinging iguana.ibm.com would end up pinging my computer.

The point is, then, that in order to have my computer named CA recognized as ca.win2ktest.com, I've got to be concerned more with informing win2ktest.com's DNS server of CA's IP address than I should be concerned about telling CA that it's in win2ktest.com. So how do I ensure that win2ktest.com's DNS server finds out about CA? As it turns out, there are three ways to do this. (And even though handling DNS servers is a topic I won't get into until next chapter, it's worth covering this here.)

ADD A STATIC DNS ENTRY

The first way to make the DNS server for the Internet domain win2ktest.com know that there's a machine named ca.win2ktest.com whose IP address is 206.246.253.5 is for an administrator to simply sit down at the DNS server and *tell* it. Depending on what kind of machine the DNS server is running on, the admin will either edit a file or run some kind of management tool. (Again, you'll see how to do that with Windows 2000's DNS server in the next chapter.)

JOIN THE WINDOWS 2000 DOMAIN OF THE SAME NAME

The second way to tell the DNS server for the Internet domain win2ktest.com to include ca.win2ktest.com in its list of known hosts is for CA to join the win2ktest.com *Windows 2000* domain. This is a positive side effect of Windows 2000's unifying of Windows 2000 domain names and Internet (DNS) domain names. If the server named CA joins a *Windows 2000* domain named win2ktest.com, then by default the DNS server for the *Internet* domain named win2ktest.com adds a record in that Internet domain for ca.win2ktest.com. Doing that is fairly easy as long as you have a domain administrator account on win2ktest.com.

While logged onto CA with an account with local administrative powers, right-click the My Computer icon and choose Properties. You'll see a properties page with several tabs, one of which is labeled Network Identification. Click that tab and you'll see a screen something like Figure 6.17.

As you can see, this machine is not currently a member of a domain. (It doesn't matter that the workgroup is called win2ktest; workgroups are unrelated to domains insofar as we're concerned here.) Note that the full computer name is simply CA, not CA with anything after it. I'll join CA to the win2ktest.com domain, and we'll see that change. I click Properties and see something like Figure 6.18.

Note that I've already filled it in, changing the Workgroup radio button to the Domain radio button and filling in the domain name win2ktest.com. When I click OK, though, the dialog box stops and asks me to demonstrate that I'm an administrator with the ability to create new domain accounts in the win2ktest.com domain, as you see in Figure 6.19.

FIGURE 6.17

Network Identification tab

FIGURE 6.18

The change-domain dialog box

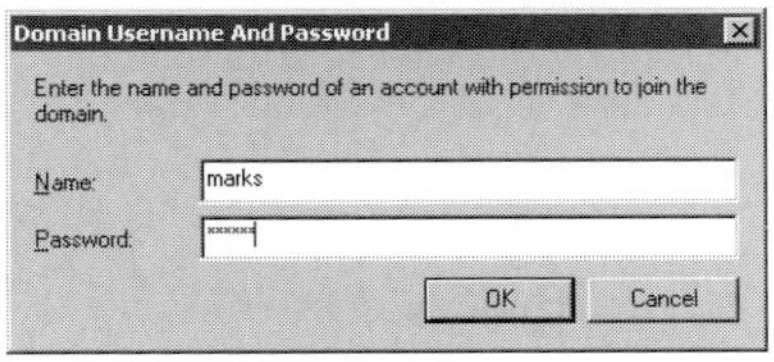

FIGURE 6.19

Checking domain administration credentials

I fill in an administrator name and password and click OK. The system runs the hard disk for a while and finally I get the message "Welcome to the win2ktest.com domain." And—no surprise—I've got to reboot to make it take effect. (Interestingly, the screen in Figure 6.17, when it returns, reflects the name change I've just done, with a yellow "caution" triangle indicating that the changes don't take effect until after I reboot.)

After the reboot, two things happen: First, another look at the Network Identification tab shows that the machine's full computer name is now ca.win2ktest.com. Second, a peek in the DNS database for win2ktest.com shows that there's now an entry for ca.win2ktest.com with IP address 206.246.253.5. But how does the DNS server know? Because all Windows 2000 domains are partially built around a DNS server, and in particular a DNS server that accepts RFC 2136–compliant dynamic updates. When CA booted up, it saw that it was a member of win2ktest.com, so it located the win2ktest.com DNS server and added its name to the win2ktest.com names database.

DIRECTLY ENTER THE DOMAIN NAME INTO NETWORK IDENTIFICATION

But wait—this may not always make sense. Phillip Morris owns Kraft Foods and Miller Brewing Company. From an internal corporate point of view, it may be (I don't know, as I've never worked for any of the three entities) that everyone working for any of the three thinks of themselves as "Phillip Morris employees," and Phillip Morris could be headquartered in one large complex in Richmond, Virginia. So from an internal management and IT point of view, they're one organization.

But to the outside world, the three entities seem to behave like separate firms, particularly on the Internet: A visit to www.kraft.com or www.millerbrewing.com gives no clue that Phillip Morris owns them. It just might be, then, that Phillip Morris doesn't want to be forced to make its DNS names jive with its Windows 2000 domain names. And they aren't, with Windows 2000. You just have to do a little fiddling in the Network Identification tab.

Now that CA is a member of the win2ktest.com Windows 2000 domain, let's say for the sake of example that we wanted it to be part of the minasi.com Internet (DNS) domain.

I start renaming CA DNS-wise by returning to Network Identification: Right-click My Computer, choose Properties, and click the Network Identification tab. As before, click Properties. This time, however, click the More button and you'll see a dialog box like Figure 6.20.

FIGURE 6.20

NetBIOS computer and domain names dialog box

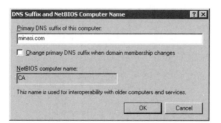

Notice the check box that says Change Primary DNS Suffix When Domain Membership Changes—*that's* the only thing connecting Internet domain names with Windows 2000 domain names! To let this computer be part of the minasi.com Internet domain but still be part of the Windows 2000 win2ktest.com domain, I just uncheck the box, and in Primary DNS Suffix of This Computer, I just fill in minasi.com. Of course, after such a momentous change, a reboot is required!

Before leaving this topic, I should point out that there is one more side effect to associating a machine with a domain: the domain search order. Bring up TCP/IP properties—again, right-click the Local Area Network Connection icon and choose Properties, then click Internet Protocol

(TCP/IP) and then click the Properties button—and then click the Advanced button, and you'll get a properties page with four tabs, one labeled DNS. Click the DNS tab and you'll see a screen like Figure 6.21.

FIGURE 6.21

DNS advanced properties page

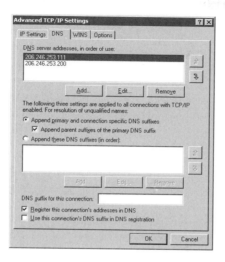

The top field in the screen, DNS Server Addresses in Order of Use, is a bit mislabeled; it really means "these are the DNS servers that IP will use to resolve DNS names." The section in the middle of the dialog box is the part that I'm mainly interested in here, the part that starts at the radio button labeled Append Primary and Connection Specific DNS Suffixes through the radio button labeled Append These DNS Suffixes (in Order).

To understand domain search order, consider the following question. Suppose you're part of the research division of American Rocketry, Ltd., working in its Tidewater regional offices in southeast Virginia. American Rocketry might have divided up their DNS domain, americanrocket.com, into three divisions: research, management, and manufacturing, each with its own child domains: research.americanrocket.com, mgmt.americanrocket.com, and manufacturing.americanrocket.com. Furthermore, the folks running the research.americanrocket.com DNS server might have decided to divide up the DNS management job further with two child domains as there are two research facilities—one in the Tidewater area and one at the Bonneville Salt Flats in Utah—so they've created child domains tidewater.research.americanrocket.com and bonneville.research.americanrocket.com. If you work in Tidewater as a researcher and your computer's name is surveyor, then the complete DNS name of your computer is surveyor.tidewater.research.americanrocket.com. If there's a Web server down the hall that holds all of the content that you use in your intranet named memoryalpha, then to get to it you've got to start up your Web browser and point it at `http://memoryalpha.tidewater.research.americanrocket.com`—which could get a bit tedious.

The value of domain search order is this: Your system will be configured with a computer name of surveyor and a domain name of tidewater.research.americanrocket.com. Now that Windows 2000 knows your domain name, you can refer to another system in tidewater.research.americanrocket.com by its computer name rather than having to type in the FQDN; you could point the Web browser to `http://memoryalpha` and the browser would find the Web server without any trouble. Just type in a computer name without any periods in it, and your system will know to add your domain name to the end before querying DNS.

By default, Windows 2000 does just that—it adds your domain name to the end before querying DNS, and that's how NT 4 operated as well. But as Windows 2000 offers you the ability to put different NICs in different Internet domains, you may have a system with multiple-domain citizenship; that's what Append Primary and Connection Specific DNS Suffixes refers to.

But what if you're working for a firm like my mythical Pepsi example, where a workstation might be in tacobell.com, pizzahut.com, pepsi.com, or kfc.com? Then you might want to have your system try a whole *bunch* of DNS queries before giving up. That's why you have the option later in the dialog box to enter domain names to search.

Before leaving this dialog box, note Register This Connection's Addresses in DNS. Remember that the DNS servers associated with an Active Directory enterprise can accept dynamic, RFC 2136 DNS updates so that a workstation or server can insert itself into the DNS name database rather than requiring an administrator to sit down and enter that machine's IP address and name by hand. Windows 2000 machines automatically seek out their local DNS server and try to add themselves to that DNS server's list of names and IP addresses. If, for some reason, you do *not* want your workstation to do that, then you can just uncheck the box.

Handling Old Names: Configuring Your Workstation for WINS

While in that advanced properties page for TCP/IP, click the WINS tab and you'll see something like Figure 6.22.

Now, if you're *really* lucky, then you'll never have to look at this screen. But I doubt that you're that lucky.

FIGURE 6.22

WINS client configuration tab

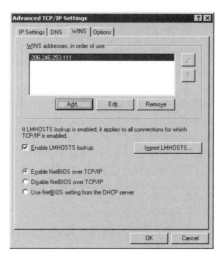

I'll cover WINS in detail in the next chapter, but for now all you need to understand is that you have one or two Windows 2000 (or possibly NT) servers acting as name resolvers or WINS servers. This dialog box lets you fill in the names of a primary and secondary WINS server.

In brief, here's what WINS is all about. As you've read, most of the Internet in general as well as Windows 2000 uses something called DNS to convert network names to network addresses (or, in network lingo, to "resolve network names"), but now I'm saying that we'll *also* use something else, called WINS, to do what sounds like the same thing. What's going on? In truth, you shouldn't really have to set up WINS at all; NT and Microsoft enterprise networking in general should use DNS for all of its name resolution, but it didn't in Windows for Workgroups, Windows 9*x*, NT 3.*x*, and NT 4. It wasn't until Windows 2000 shipped that Microsoft networking started relying on Winsock and DNS.

The reason is that Microsoft wanted NT's networking modules to work like the already-existing LAN Manager system, and LAN Manager used a naming system based on its NetBIOS application program interface. A computer's NetBIOS name is the computer name that you gave it when you installed it. When you type **net view \\ajax**, something must resolve \\ajax into an IP address—a NetBIOS-to-IP resolution. WINS does that. In contrast, the rest of the Internet would see a machine called ajax as having a longer name, like ajax.acme.com. If there were a Web server on ajax, then someone outside the company would have to point her Web browser to `http://ajax.acme.com`, and some piece of software would have to resolve ajax.acme.com into an IP address. That piece of software is the socket or Winsock interface, and in either case, it will rely upon not WINS but DNS to resolve the name. In a few words, then, programs written to employ NetBIOS will use WINS for name resolution, and programs written to employ Winsock use DNS for name resolution.

I can probably guess what you're thinking now, and, yes, DNS and WINS should be integrated, and they eventually were, but not until Windows 2000 arrived. Why would you continue to have WINS servers if you've got Windows 2000? Because it's pretty likely that you've still got some Windows for Workgroups, Windows 95 or 98, and/or NT 4 servers and workstations still floating around. All of the time that they were working on Windows 2000, Microsoft kept promising us that WINS would no longer be necessary once Windows 2000 came out, but there was some fine print, namely "so long as you throw away all of your old machines or put Windows 2000 Professional or Server on them." Most of us can't afford to do that, so we'll be living with WINS servers for the time being—which means that your Windows 2000 systems must know where those WINS servers are; hence this dialog box.

In Figure 6.22, I told this computer that there's a WINS server at 206.246.253.111 by clicking Add, filling in the IP address, and clicking OK. You could only tell pre–Windows 2000 systems about two WINS servers, but for some reason Windows 2000 allows you to list as many WINS servers as you like in this dialog box.

Even at its best, WINS couldn't do the whole name resolution job. Some tough name resolution problems could only be solved with a HOSTS-like file called LMHOSTS. The Enable LMHOSTS Lookup check box lets you use an LMHOSTS file if you've got one installed on your system. I'll explain LMHOSTS in detail in the next chapter.

The Enable NetBIOS over TCP/IP versus Disable NetBIOS over TCP/IP radio buttons embody a deceptively momentous choice, so it's odd that the choice is tucked away in this obscure properties page. Another way of phrasing the WINS-versus-DNS dichotomy is to say that all of the Microsoft operating systems prior to Windows 2000 built all of their networking tools atop a programming interface called NetBIOS, and Windows 2000 breaks with that tradition by instead using another programming interface called Winsock. An all–Windows 2000 network would be perfectly happy running only network programs—Web servers, e-mail, file servers—that used Winsock. But if those servers want to communicate with older Windows and NT systems, then they must use older networking programs that are compatible with these old systems, and those older networking programs are built atop NetBIOS.

That means that if your Windows 2000 system is acting as a file or print server for any older machines, it needs to keep NetBIOS around. If it's running any applications built for pre–Windows 2000 versions of NT, it'll probably need NetBIOS. Put simply, you can't shut off NetBIOS until you're free of both old client machines and old network applications. But one day you'll be able to axe NetBIOS, and when you can, you should, as it'll reduce network chatter and free up server memory and CPU power.

Adding IP Addresses to a Single NIC

If you're still in the Advanced TCP/IP Settings page, click the IP Settings tab, and you'll see something like Figure 6.23.

FIGURE 6.23

IP Settings advanced properties tab

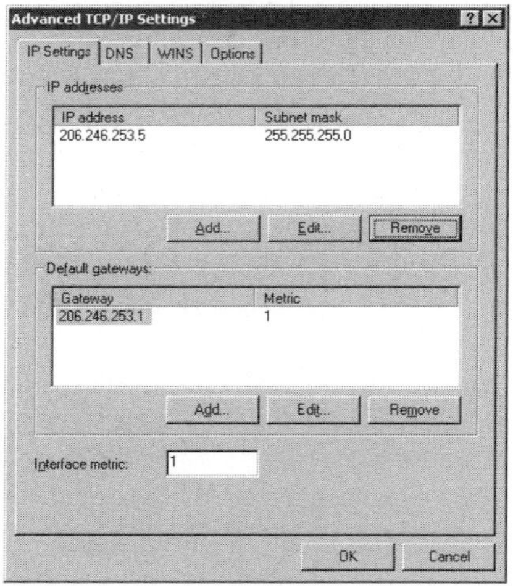

This NIC already has the 206.246.253.5 IP address that I gave it earlier. But notice the Add button. This lets you attach different IP addresses to the NIC to assign more than one IP address to a single NIC.

Why would you want to do that? Normally, you wouldn't. But there *is* one case where it would be very useful: when you're hosting multiple Web sites on a single Web server.

For example, suppose I've got two Internet domains, minasi.com and win2kexperts.com. I intend to put up a Web site for minasi.com (`www.minasi.com`) and another for win2kexperts.com (`www.win2kexperts.com`). But I want them to be very different Web sites; perhaps the minasi.com site is a personal site and the win2kexperts site is a business site. Even though `www.minasi.com` and `www.win2kexperts.com` are both hosted on a machine at 206.246.253.100, I don't ever want anyone visiting the business site to see pictures of my last vacation, and I don't think my friends care much about my professional résumé.

I separate the two by creating two *virtual sites*. There are two basic ways to give a single Web server "multiple personalities." You'll read more about how to do that with Internet Information Server in Chapter 17, and in that chapter you'll learn *one* way to create multiple virtual sites. That method doesn't work with old browsers—Netscape 1.*x*, Internet Explorer 1.*x* and 2.*x*, Spyglass—but only with *really* old browsers, so what you'll read in Chapter 17 may well be all you need. But if you ever need the slightly more expensive (and when I say *expensive* here, I mean that you'll have to use an IP address for each virtual site) method that works with *any* browser, then here's briefly how to do it—and it's a great example of why you'd put multiple IP addresses on a single NIC:

1. I assign an extra IP address to the Web server so that it now has two addresses—let's say they're 206.246.253.100 and 206.246.253.101.

2. I then set up DNS so that `www.minasi.com` points to the first address, 206.246.253.100, and `www.win2kexperts.com` points to the second address, 206.246.253.101.

3. I've already got the minasi.com Web site running, so I'll need a place to put the win2kexperts.com content. I just create a folder on the Web server called `w2kx` and put the HTML, images, and so on for win2kexperts.com there.

4. I next tell the Web server to create a "new site." It then basically needs to know two things: where to find the content (`C:\w2kx`) and which IP address to associate with the site. I've got to tell it to "start" the site, and I'm in business.

The important thing here is to understand that every one of these sites, each of these "personalities" of your Web server, burns up an IP address, and as you see, you use the IP Settings property tab to add those extra IP addresses to your Web server's NIC.

Whew! Getting IP running on that system was a bit of work. Good thing we can do most of our machines automatically with DHCP—but even that requires configuring, which is why we went through all of this detail. Now that I've got IP on a system, I can return to some of the more techie infrastructure issues—like IP routing.

Setting Up Routing on Windows 2000, NT, and 9*x* Machines

Up to now, I've assumed that all of your TCP/IP-using machines had a single default gateway that acted as "router to the world" for your machines. That's not always true, as real-life intranets often have multiple routers that lead a machine to different networks. I've also assumed that your Windows 2000 network is connected to the Internet, or to your enterprise intranet, via some third-party (Compatible Systems, Bay Networks, Cisco Systems, or whomever) router. That's also not always true, as NT machines can act as IP routers.

Routing problems aren't just *server* problems; they're often workstation problems, as well. So, in this section, I'll take on two topics:

♦ How to set up routing tables on your workstations and servers

♦ How to use your Windows 2000 servers as IP routers

An Example Multirouter Internet

Suppose you had a workstation on a network with two gateways, as shown in Figure 6.24.

FIGURE 6.24

A workstation on a
network with two
gateways

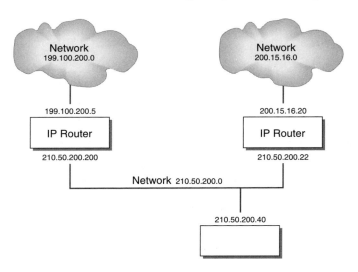

As is the case for most of these diagrams, a multinetwork picture can be cryptic, so here's an explanation of what you are looking at.

First, there are three separate Ethernet segments, three separate subnets. They are all class C networks, just to keep things clean. Two of the networks are only represented by clouds; thus, the cloud on the left containing 199.100.200.0 is just shorthand for an Ethernet with up to 254 computers hanging off it, with addresses ranging from 199.100.200.1 through 199.100.200.254. Notice that I said 254, not 253, because *there is no default gateway for these subnets*. As there are only three subnets, this is an intranet, not part of the Internet. One side effect of not being on the Net is that you can use the .1 address for regular old machines. I left the Internet out of this first example because I found that it confused me when I was first trying to get this routing stuff down. I'll add it later, I promise.

There is also another cloud, to the right, representing a network whose addresses range from 200.15.16.1 through 200.15.16.254—network number 200.15.16.0.

In between is a third subnet with address 210.50.200.0. You see a rectangle representing a PC in the middle that has only one Ethernet card in it, and its IP address is 210.50.200.40. The rectangles on the right and left sides of the picture are routers, computers with two Ethernet cards in them and thus two IP addresses apiece. Each has an address on the 210.50.200.0 network, and each has an address either on the 200.15.16.0 network or on the 199.100.200.0 network.

Adding Entries to Routing Tables: Route Add

Having said that, let's now figure out how to tell the machine at 210.50.200.40 how to route anywhere on this network. These are some of the facts it needs to know:

◆   To get a message to the 199.100.200.0 network, send it to the machine at 210.50.200.200.

♦ To get a message to the 200.15.16.0 network, send it to the machine at 210.50.200.22.

♦ To get a message to the 210.50.200.0 network, just use your own Ethernet card; send it out on the segment, and it'll be heard.

You tell a workstation how to send packets with the `route add` command. Simplified, it looks like this:

```
route add destination mask netmask gatewayaddress
```

Here, *destination* is the address or set of addresses that you want to be able to get to. *Netmask* defines how *many* addresses are there—is it a C network with 250+ addresses, something subnetted smaller, or perhaps a "supernet" of several C networks? *Gatewayaddress* is just the IP address of the machine that will route your packets to their destination.

The `route add` command for the 199.100.200.0 network would look like this:

```
route add 199.100.200.0 mask 255.255.255.0 210.50.200.200
```

This means, "Send a message anywhere on the 199.100.200.0 network, send it to the machine at 210.50.200.200, and it'll take care of it."

TIP   If you just type the `route add` *statement as you see it in the previous text, then your system will forget the routing command when next you boot. You can tell it to remember that route next time with the* `-p` *("permanent") switch, as in* `route -p add 199.100.200.0 mask 255.255.255.0 210.50.200.200`. *This only works on NT and 2000; you can't make routes permanent under Windows 9x.*

Just a reminder on subnetting, for clarity's sake: Suppose the network on the upper left wasn't a full C network, but rather a subnetted part of it. Suppose it was just the range of addresses from 199.100.200.64 through 199.100.200.127. The network number would be, as always, the first address (199.100.200.64), and the subnet mask would be 255.255.255.192. The `route add` command would then look like this:

```
route add 199.100.200.64 mask 255.255.255.192 210.50.200.200
```

Anyway, back to the example in the picture. Add a command for the right-side network; it looks like this:

```
route add 200.15.16.0 mask 255.255.255.0 210.50.200.22
```

That much will get a Windows 2000, NT, XP, 9x, Me, or even DOS-based TCP/IP system up and running.

Understanding the Default Routes

Even if you don't ever type a `route add` command at a Windows workstation, you'll find that there are routing statements that are automatically generated. Let's look at them. First, we'd need an explicit routing command to tell the 210.50.200.40 machine to get to its own subnet:

```
route add 210.50.200.0 mask 255.255.255.0 210.50.200.40
```

Or, in other words, "To get to your local subnet, route to yourself."

Then, recall that the entire 127.*x.y.z* range of network addresses is the loopback. Implement that like so:

```
route add 127.0.0.0 mask 255.0.0.0 127.0.0.1
```

This says, "Take any address from 127.0.0.0 through 127.255.255.255 and route it to 127.0.0.1." The IP software has already had 127.0.0.1 defined for it, so it knows what to do with that. Notice the mask, 255.0.0.0, is a simple class A network mask.

Some Internet software uses intranet multicast groups, so the multicast address must be defined. It is 224.0.0.0. It looks like the loopback route command:

```
route add 224.0.0.0 mask 255.0.0.0 210.50.200.40
```

The system knows to multicast by *shouting*, which means communicating over its local subnet.

VIEWING THE ROUTING TABLE

Let's find out exactly what routing information this computer has. How? Well, on Windows 2000, Windows NT, Workgroups, and 95/98 workstations, there are two commands that will show you what the workstation knows about how to route IP packets. Type either **netstat -rn** or **route print** at a command line—the output is identical, so use either command—and you see something like Figure 6.25.

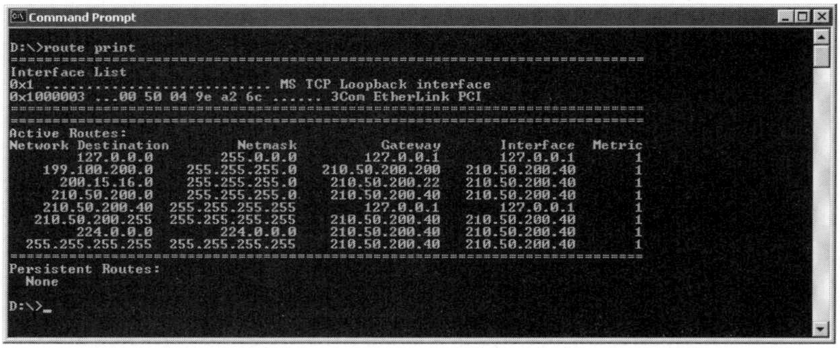

FIGURE 6.24

Sample **route print** output

Notice that the output of `route print` is similar to the way you format data in `route add`. Each line shows a network address, which is the desired destination; the netmask, which indicates how many addresses exist at the desired destination; and the gateway, which is the IP address that the workstation should send its packets to in order to reach the destination. But note two more columns: Interface and Metric.

THE INTERFACE COLUMN

Interface asks itself, "Which of my local IP addresses—the ones physically located inside me, like my loopback and all the IP addresses attached to all of my network cards—should I use to get to that gateway?" On this computer, it's a moot point because it only has one network card in it.

What might this look like on a multihomed machine, like the router on the left side? It has two IP addresses, 199.100.200.5 and 210.50.200.200. A fragment of its route print output might then look like this:

```
Network Destination  Netmask         Gateway         Interface    Metric
199.100.200.0   255.255.255.0  199.100.200.5  199.100.200.5        1
210.50.200.0    255.255.255.0 210.50.200.200 210.50.200.200        1
```

There are two networks that the router machine can get to (obviously, or it wouldn't be much use as a router), and each one has a gateway address, which happens to be the local IP address that the router maintains on each network. But now notice the Interface column: Rather than staying at the same IP address all the way through, this tells the computer, "I've already told you which gateway to direct this traffic to; now I'll tell you which of your local IP addresses to employ in order to get to that gateway in the first place."

THE METRIC COLUMN

The Metric column (what, no English option?) tells IP how many routers it will have to pass through in order to get to its destination. A metric value of 1 means "your destination is on the same subnet." A metric value of 2 would mean "you have to go through one router to get to your destination," and so on. Since the .40 workstation must go through a router to get to either the 199.100.200.0 or the 200.15.16.0 network, both of those networks get a metric of 2.

TIP   *Just think of it this way: Metric = the number of routers you must travel through plus 1.*

Ah, but how did the computer know that it would take a router jump to get to those networks? Well, you see, *I* told it.

I have to confess here that I left off a parameter on the route add command, simply to make the explanation palatable. As I knew that the metric was 2 for both routes, I just added the parameter metric 2 to the end of both route add statements. The revised, complete commands look like this:

```
route add 200.15.16.0 mask 255.255.255.0 210.50.200.22 metric 2
route add 199.100.200.0 mask 255.255.255.0 210.50.200.200 metric 2
```

You'll learn a bit later that a protocol called RIP will make this process automatic, but for now I want to stick to this manually constructed set of routing tables. (Using hand-constructed routing tables is called *static routing*; the automatic methods like RIP are called *dynamic routing*, and I'll get to them later.)

ROUTE PRINT OUTPUT EXPLAINED

Now that you can decipher each column in the route print output, I'll finish up explaining the output.

The first line is the loopback information, as you've seen before. It's automatically generated on every NT/Workgroups/9x machine running the Microsoft TCP/IP stack. The second and third lines are the manually entered routes that tell your machine how to address the 200.15.16.0 and 199.100.200.0 networks. The fourth line is another automatically generated line, and it explains how to address the 210.50.200.0 subnet, which is the local one. The fifth line refers to 210.50.200.40

itself. The mask, 255.255.255.255, means that these aren't routing instructions to get to an entire network, but rather routing instructions to get to a particular computer. It basically says, "If you need to get data to 210.50.200.40, send it to the loopback address." The result: If you ping 210.50.200.40, then no actual communication happens over the network. The sixth line defines how to do a local subnet broadcast. Again, it doesn't point to an entire network, but rather to the particular subnet broadcast address. The seventh line serves Internet multicasting, as you saw before. And the final address is for something called the *limited broadcast address*, a kind of generic subnet broadcast address.

Adding the Default Gateway

Suppose you wanted to set up my 210.50.200.40 machine. How would you do it? More specifically, you'd ask me, "Which is the default gateway?"

Well, in the TCP/IP configuration screen that you've seen before, you'd obviously be able to supply the information that the IP address should be 210.50.200.40 and the subnet mask should be 255.255.255.0. But what should you use to fill in the Default Gateway field? I mean, there are *two* gateways, 210.50.100.22 and 210.50.100.200. Which should you use?

The answer? Neither. A *default gateway* is just another entry in the routing table, but it's not specific like the ones you've met so far; it's a catchall entry. This network doesn't get to the Internet, and it can only see two other subnets, each with their own routers (gateways), so I left the Default Gateway field blank. And there's an advantage to that.

"DESTINATION HOST UNREACHABLE"

If I were to try to ping some address not on the three subnets, such as 25.44.92.4, then I wouldn't get the message that the ping had timed out, or experienced an error, or anything of the sort; rather, I'd get a "destination host unreachable" message. That's important: "Destination host unreachable" doesn't necessarily mean that you can't get to the destination host, but it *does* mean that your workstation doesn't know *how* to get to that host—it lacks any routing information about how to get there at all. Do a `route print` and you'll probably be able to see what's keeping you from getting to your destination.

BUILDING A DEFAULT GATEWAY BY HAND

When *would* a default gateway make sense in our network? Well, let's add an Internet connection to the network, as shown in Figure 6.26.

Now we need another `route add` command—but what should it look like? I mean, what's the generic IP address of the whole Internet?

Believe it or not, there *is* such an address: 0.0.0.0. Think of it as "the network number to end all network numbers." Remember, any given network's number is just the first address of the network. And what's the first address of the Internet? 0.0.0.0. And the network mask? Well, since it doesn't matter *what* address bits match which other address bits—after all, no matter what your address is, you're still on the particular "subnet" that is the entire Internet—the subnet mask is also 0.0.0.0. So the command looks like this:

```
route add 0.0.0.0 mask 0.0.0.0 210.50.200.1
```

FIGURE 6.26

Network with an
Internet connection

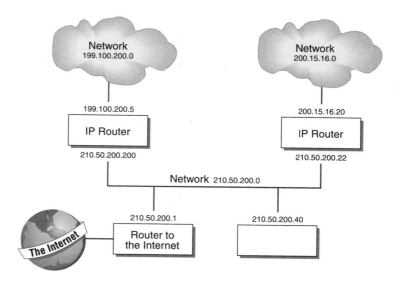

HANDLING CONFLICTS IN ROUTING INFORMATION

However, it appears that there are some conflicts here. Look at some of the instructions that you've given the IP software about how to route:

♦ There's a rule about handling the specific address 210.50.200.40: Just keep the message local at 127.0.0.1, no routing.

♦ There's a rule about how to handle the range from 210.50.200.0 through 210.50.200.255: Shout it out on the subnet, no routing.

♦ There's a rule about how to handle the range from 199.100.200.0 through 199.100.200.255: Send it to 210.50.200.200.

♦ There's a rule about how to handle the range from 200.15.16.0 through 200.15.16.255: Send it to 210.50.200.22.

♦ There's a rule about how to handle *all* Internet addresses: Send the messages to 210.50.200.1.

Here's what I mean about a conflict: Suppose you want to send an IP packet to 200.15.16.33. You have one rule that says, "Send it to 210.50.200.22" and another that says, "Send it to 210.50.200.1." Which rule does the software on your workstation (or server) follow?

Answer: When in doubt, first look for the route with the smallest metric. If there is more than one candidate, then take the *most specific* one—in other words, choose the one with the most specific subnet mask.

In this case, there are two entries in the routing table that point to the destination, 200.15.16.33. I haven't shown you their metrics, but both of them require hopping over one router, so each route has metric 2. As their metrics are tied, you look next to the subnet mask. As the 210.50.200.1 route has a very generic subnet mask (0.0.0.0), your machine would ignore it in comparison to the more specific 210.50.200.22's subnet mask of 255.255.255.0.

Suppose workstation 210.50.200.40 wanted to get a message to another machine on the subnet; let's say that its address is 210.50.200.162. Again, there's a routing conflict, as one route entry just says to send it to 210.50.200.40—in other words, don't route, shout! There's another routing entry—the 0.0.0.0 one again—that says it can also get the IP packet to 210.50.200.162, as it claims it can get any packet *anywhere*. Which to choose? Well, if constructed correctly, an excerpt of the routing table will look something like this:

Destination	Netmask	Gateway	Interface	Metric
0.0.0.0	0.0.0.0	210.50.200.1	210.50.200.40	2
210.50.200.0	255.255.255.0	210.50.200.40	210.50.200.40	1

The first entry is the default gateway. It's got metric 2 because you've got to hop over at least one router to get to the Internet. (In actual fact, it's probably not a bad idea to set this value a bit higher, just to be sure internal IP packets *never* try to get sent over the Internet.) The second entry basically says, "To send data to your local subnet, just say it out loud on your Ethernet card"—again, don't route, shout. As the Internet metric is higher, your machine will know not to try to send a local message by sending it to the default gateway.

One more thing: You wouldn't, of course, want to have to type in those **route add** commands every time you start up your computer. So you'd use a variation on the **route add** command. Just type **route -p add**. When you add the **-p**, that entry becomes permanent in your system's routing table.

All Routers Must Know All Subnets

I've talked about how I'd set up my sample network from the point of view of a workstation. It would work, but you can see that it's a real pain to punch in all of those **route add** statements for each workstation. The answer is to make the routers smarter; *then* you can just pick one router to be the default gateway for the .40 workstation, and the workstation needn't worry about anything. So let's take a minute and see how each of the three routers in this system would be set up.

The first router is the one on the left, which routes between 199.100.200.0 and 210.50.200.0. It must know three things:

◆ It can get to 199.100.200.0 through its 199.100.200.5 interface.

◆ It can get to 210.50.200.0 through its 210.50.200.200 interface.

◆ It can get to the Internet through 210.50.200.1, which it gets to through its 210.50.200.200 interface.

In fact, you would not have to type in routing commands telling it how to get to 199.100.200.0 or 210.50.200.0; assuming it's an NT machine, the NT routing software figures that out automatically. But you can tell it to get to the Internet by setting a default gateway:

```
route add 0.0.0.0 mask 0.0.0.0 210.50.200.1 metric 2
```

The routing software is then smart enough to realize that it should get to 210.50.200.1 via its 210.50.200.200 interface.

The second router, the one on the right, routes between 200.15.16.0 and 210.50.200.0. It can get to both of those networks directly, and, as with the first router, we don't have to tell it about them. But to get to the Internet, it must route packets to 210.50.200.1, and so, like the first router, it should have a default gateway of 210.50.200.1.

Now let's tackle the third router, the machine at 210.50.200.1, which is the Internet gateway. It must know that it should use the Internet as its default gateway. For example, on my Compatible Systems routers, there is a magical address WAN that just means the modem connection to the Internet. I essentially tell it, "Route add 0.0.0.0 mask 0.0.0.0 WAN," and packets travel to and from the Internet over the modem. The router must then be told of each of the three subnets, like so:

```
route add 210.50.200.0 mask 255.255.255.0 210.50.200.1 metric 1
route add 199.100.200.0 mask 255.255.255.0 210.50.200.200 metric 2
route add 200.15.16.0 mask 255.255.255.0 210.50.200.22 metric 2
```

Using RIP to Simplify Workstation Management

Thus far, I've shown you how to tell your workstations how to exploit routers on the network. In most cases, you won't need to build such large, complex routing tables by hand, and in almost no case will you *want* to build those tables.

Ideally, you shouldn't have to type in static tables; instead, your workstations could just suck up routing information automatically from the nearby routers, using some kind of browser-type protocol. You *can* do such a thing with the Routing Information Protocol (RIP).

RIP is an incredibly simple protocol. Routers running RIP broadcast their routing tables about twice a minute. Any workstation running RIP software hears the routing tables and incorporates them into its *own* routing tables. Result: You put a new router on the system, and you needn't punch in any static routes.

RIP version 2 ships as part of Windows 2000. The Microsoft implementation supports both IP and IPX. Routes detected by RIP show up in `route print` statements just as if they were static routes.

An Alternative Dynamic Routing Protocol: OSPF

Although RIP has been around for some time, it's an awfully chatty protocol. Twice a minute, each RIP router broadcasts its entire routing table for all to hear. A more intelligent and bandwidth-parsimonious but more complex to set up dynamic routing protocol is available in the form of the Open Shortest Path First (OSPF) protocol. You have to feed the routers a bit more information about the layout of your sites, but once you do, OSPF quickly generates the shortest routes for your packets.

Using an NT Machine as a LAN/LAN Router

In the process of expanding your company's intranet, you need routers. For a network of any size, the best bet is probably to buy dedicated routers, boxes from companies such as Cisco Systems, Bay Networks, or Compatible Systems.

Dedicated routers are fast and come with some impressive management tools: neat GUI programs that let you control and monitor your network from your workstation. But routers have one disadvantage: They're expensive. I haven't seen an Ethernet-to-Ethernet IP router available for less than $3,000. Again, don't misunderstand me: These routers are probably worth what they cost in terms of the ease that they bring to network management and the speed with which they route data. But you might have more than one subnet on a given site, and you might *not* have the three grand, so you're looking for an alternative.

How about a software alternative? Any Windows NT 4 workstation or server can act as a simple IP router—all you need is a multihomed PC (one with two or more network cards installed in it) and Windows NT 4. Just open the Control Panel, open the Network applet, then the Protocols tab, and the TCP/IP protocol. Click the Routing tab, and you see an option called Enable IP Routing. That's how you turn on NT's routing capability.

Making a Windows 2000 system a router is a bit more complex. Let's see how to set up this router. Let's return to that cross-Mediterranean rivalry and set up a LAN-to-LAN router for Carthage and Rome. Imagine you have an intranet that looks like Figure 6.27.

FIGURE 6.27

A sample intranet

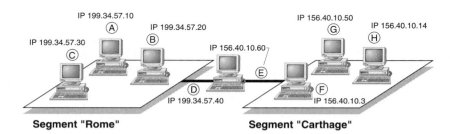

We're going to use the machine that's on both Rome and Carthage as the router. (Actually, there's no choice here, as it's the *only* machine in both TCP/IP subnets, and any router between two subnets must be a member of both subnets.) First I'll look at how to set up the machine with adapters D and E as a router, and then I'll take a slightly more complex example:

1. The machine between Rome and Carthage—let's call it MEDITERRANEAN—needs two Ethernet cards. Install two network cards (let's use Ethernet for this example) in a Windows 2000 system machine. Microsoft *intended* for you to only be able to use Windows 2000 Server, but you can use Professional as well with a Registry hack, so long as you're only doing static routing—I haven't been able to figure out how to make Professional do RIP or OSPF routing.

2. Configure the Ethernet card on the Rome subnet with IP address 199.34.57.40 and the Ethernet card on the Carthage subnet with IP address 156.40.10.60. Here's how: Once you've got a second NIC installed in the MEDITERRANEAN system, open up Network and Dial-Up Connections and it'll look like Figure 6.28.

FIGURE 6.28

Network and Dial-Up Connections with two NICs

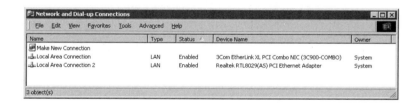

3. Right-click either of the two connection objects and choose Properties, and you'll then see the screen that lets you modify the TCP/IP properties for that NIC, including its static IP address. Once I've set the IP addresses properly, an **ipconfig /all** looks like Figure 6.29.

FIGURE 6.29

ipconfig /all before enabling routing

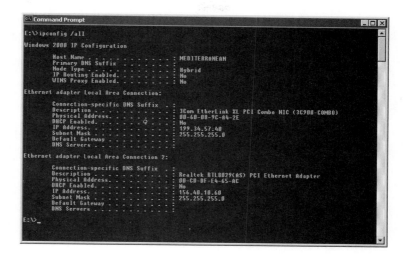

Note that this IPConfig output is larger than the previous ones, mainly because it's got to report on two NICs. There's no DNS server specified and no domain name specified because (1) it simplified the IPConfig output and (2) routers usually needn't have DNS names for their interfaces. Note also that IP Routing Enabled is No. That's important—just because a Windows 2000 system has NICs attached to different subnets doesn't automatically mean that the system will act as a router.

4. Next, turn on routing. You can turn on simple static routing for either a Windows 2000 Server or Professional machine by looking in the key HKEY_LOCAL_MACHINE\System\CurrentControlSet\Services\Tcpip\Parameters for the value named IPEnableRouter, which will be set to 0. Change the value to 1, reboot the system, and it'll do static routing between the subnets that it's directly connected to.

I suggested the Registry hack because it's the only way that I've found to make a Professional machine an IP router—which is odd, because under NT 4 Workstation there was a check box in the Control Panel to enable IP routing. Maybe it was an oversight, or perhaps Microsoft wants to sell you a copy of Server if you want to do IP routing?

In any case, if the routing machine is running Windows 2000 *Server*, then no Registry fooling-around is needed. Instead, click Start/Programs/Administrative Tools/Routing and Remote Access, which will show you an MMC console like Figure 6.30.

Click the plus sign next to MEDITERRANEAN. You'll see a red arrow pointing down, indicating that routing hasn't been turned on yet. To turn routing on, right-click MEDITERRANEAN in the left pane and choose Configure and Enable Routing and Remote Access. That, not surprisingly, starts off a wizard, the Routing and Remote Access Server Setup Wizard. Click Next and you'll then see a screen like Figure 6.31.

FIGURE 6.30

Opening RRAS administrator screen

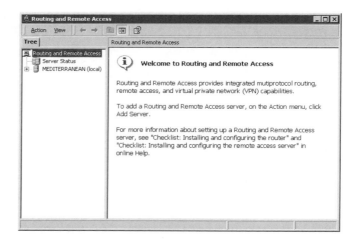

FIGURE 6.31

Initial RRAS setup wizard screen

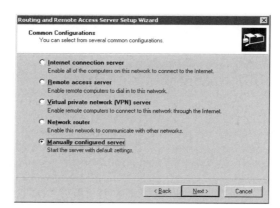

Setting up a router can be a bit challenging, so Microsoft decided fairly late in the Windows 2000 development process to try to build four "precooked" router setups and then offer them in combination with a fifth option that allowed you to build the router as you like. Take that fifth option, Manually Configured Server, and click Next and then Finish to complete the wizard. Windows 2000 will beep and ask you if you want to start the Routing and Remote Access Service; click Yes. You'll then see a screen like Figure 6.32.

FIGURE 6.32

RRAS management console with routing enabled

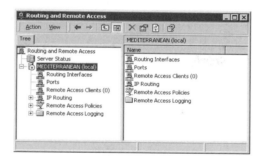

With Windows 2000, Microsoft combined what were two separate functions under earlier versions of NT: IP routing and remote access. (Actually, they combined them with an optional add-in called Routing and Remote Access, or by its beta name, Steelhead, but not many people used it. I was amused when at a briefing a Microsoft developer surprised the audience by referring to Steelhead as "merely a technology demonstration," presumably rather than something they were serious about. It was, after all, a bit late to have told us that!)

As we chose manual setup, Windows 2000 turned on some things that we don't want—in particular, Windows 2000 turned on dial-up connections, which don't make sense on this server, as it lacks a modem. We can fix that by right-clicking MEDITERRANEAN and choosing Properties, which shows a dialog box like the one in Figure 6.33.

FIGURE 6.33

Reconfiguring the router

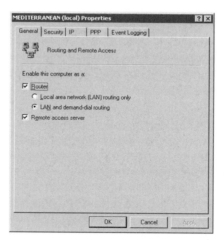

You can see that this router is set up as a remote access server; uncheck Remote Access Server and then click the radio button labeled Local Area Network (LAN) Routing Only, then click OK to make those changes take effect. You'll be asked if it's all right to restart the router software; click OK to let it.

There's nothing more to do. As MEDITERRANEAN's routing is turned on and because it's directly connected to both the 199 and 156 networks, it will automatically route packets between the networks. Of course, the machines on both networks must know to use one of MEDITER-RANEAN's NICs, either via a `route add` statement or by referring to MEDITERRANEAN's local NIC as their default gateway. By the way, if you set up a machine like this one, to do NIC-to-NIC routing but not any remote access, and then change your mind, just go back to the RRAS snap-in and right-click the server and choose Disable Routing and Remote Access. Once RRAS is disabled on a server, you can just right-click the server and once again choose Configure and Enable Routing and Remote Access; the wizard will again run, and you can change any of your RRAS configuration choices then.

One more point before moving on. You've already learned how to use `route add` from the command line to add a static route. RRAS lets you do that from the GUI as well. In the left panel, you see an object labeled IP Routing. Open it and you'll see two other objects, one labeled General and the other labeled Static Routes. Right-click Static Routes and choose New Static Route, and you'll see a dialog box like Figure 6.34.

FIGURE 6.34

Dialog box for adding a new static route

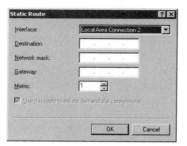

Okay, so it's not a very useful dialog box—I could probably type the `route add` command more quickly than I could open this dialog box and punch in its values—but at least it's not another three-screen wizard that only asks one question, right?

More Complex Static Routing

By now, you've set up an IP router to move traffic from one subnet to another. It will *not*, however, route traffic among three or more subnets. Why not? Well, the default router software isn't very smart. Look at Figure 6.35, and you'll see what I mean.

Here, you see an intranet with just three subnets: 200.200.1.0, 200.200.2.0, and 200.200.3.0. For ease of discussion, let's call network 200.200.1.0 "network 1," 200.200.2.0 "network 2," and 200.200.3.0 "network 3." The network 1 to network 2 router, machine A, has addresses 200.200.1.1 and 200.200.2.40, and the network 2 to network 3 router, machine B, has addresses 200.200.3.75 and 200.200.2.50.

Once you turn on IP routing in machine A, it's smart enough to be able to route packets from network 1 to network 2 and packets from network 2 to network 1. But if it receives a packet from network 1 intended for network 3, it has no idea what to do about it.

Machine B has the same problem, basically. It knows how to go from network 2 to network 3 and from network 3 to network 2, but it has no idea how to find network 1.

FIGURE 6.35

An intranet with three subnets

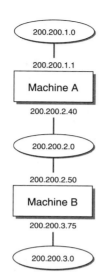

How do you solve this problem? Either with static routes or with RIP. The best answer is probably to put the RIP router on both machine A and machine B, and they will end up discovering each other's routes through the RIP broadcasts. But how would you tell machine A how to find network 3 and how would you tell machine B to find network 1? With static `route add` commands.

On machine A, tell it about network 3 like so:

```
route add 200.200.3.0 mask 255.255.255.0 200.200.2.50
```

(Or, if you're feeling GUI, use RRAS.) You're saying to this machine, "In order to find network 200.200.3.0, use the IP address 200.200.2.50; it's attached to a machine that can get the packets to that network." For the sake of completeness, you might add the "metric 2" parameter to the end.

On machine B, tell it about network 1 in a similar way:

```
route add 200.200.1.0 mask 255.255.255.0 200.200.2.40
```

Remember that in both cases the "mask" information says, "I'm giving you information about a subnet, but the mask says how useful the information is." And if you want the router to *remember* these routes through reboots, don't forget the -p option to make the route permanent.

Using a Windows 2000 Server as an Internet Gateway/Router

Consider this. Your company has purchased a full-time PPP account from some Internet provider. You have your LAN running TCP/IP with IANA-approved IP numbers. All you need is a machine that will route your local traffic over the Internet when you want to FTP, use e-mail, or do whatever.

From a hardware point of view, it's pretty easy: You just need a PC containing both an Ethernet card and a serial port, with a dial-up PPP connection. That machine is essentially doing the job of TCP/IP routing. How do you do that in Windows 2000?

The Overview

There are several "what ifs" that you have to consider if you want to use your NT machine as a LAN-to-WAN Internet gateway.

CONSIDER A DEDICATED ROUTER AS AN ALTERNATIVE

The first piece of advice is: Don't, if you can avoid it. In my company, I use the Compatible Systems mr900i, a terrific box that I picked up for $850. It's easy to manage, comes with a nice Windows-based router management program, does RIP, is much cheaper than buying a Pentium and a copy of NT, and is as fast as the wind. I'd recommend it as the way to go if you want to hook up your net to the Net. On other networks, I've used the Lucent Pipeline router, another quite good product in the $550 to $2000 range, which includes an optional security package to turn the router into a firewall-like device. In another network, I've used the Cisco 1602, at a cost of about $1500, if I recall right. I liked the Compatible box best of the three, as it had both the best tech support and, again, a Windows-based router management program—the others could only be controlled by a cryptic command-line interface or a complex text-based menu structure.

Whatever you choose (if you choose not to go the way of a Windows 2000–based router), there are many good options that are far more stable software-wise than something as complex as an off-the-shelf PC acting as a server. And that's not a slam at Windows 2000, just a recognition that anything with a greater number of "moving parts," so to speak, is more likely to break—there's no floppy drive, hard disk, video card, or dozens of drivers written by dozens of different companies running in a dedicated router, unlike a Windows 2000 box.

WAN CONNECTION OPTIONS

But there are times that I don't have access to a dedicated router, and perhaps I'd like to use my Windows 2000 machine as my Internet router. So let's see how to accomplish that. Take a look at Figure 6.36.

FIGURE 6.36

LAN/WAN router overview diagram

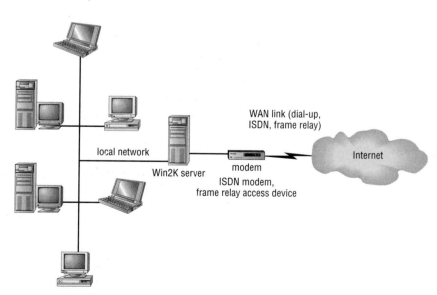

To the left in Figure 6.36, you see your company's local area network connected to the Windows 2000 machine that will act as the gateway server. There's nothing special there, it's just a regular network. I'll assume for the purposes of this explanation that you've obtained IANA-approved IP addresses for each of the machines in your network.

To the right is the connection between your gateway and the Internet. It could be several different possible types of connections, but the most likely are modem, ISDN, or frame relay.

WARNING *In general, cable modem and DSL would* not *be possible connections for a configuration such as I've described here, where you obtain IP addresses from an ISP and put them on your local machines and then use a gateway to connect to the Internet. Although there's no technical reason why that's so, I don't know of any cable modem or DSL provider who offers more than one IP address to a customer; every one that I've asked just looks at me helplessly. Restricting cable modem and DSL customers to just one IP address is unfortunate, as cable or DSL would make for a low-cost, high-speed way to connect a lot of PCs to the Internet. But, then, perhaps that's the point: If you've got a lot of machines to connect, then I guess the provider wants to charge more. However, there is a way for one computer to share a cable modem or DSL (or any other type) connection with all of the PCs on its local network, a tool called Internet Connection Sharing. The difference is that you must use network address translation (NAT) routing, where all of your local machines get nonroutable IP addresses. You'll read about Internet Connection Sharing a little later in this chapter.*

Modem and ISDN connections are dial-up connections, not continuous connections. If you intend to host any Internet servers on your local network, such as if you want to run your own DNS, Web, FTP, or e-mail servers, then your network needs a *persistent* connection; it must be connected to the Internet 24 hours a day, 365.24219878 days a year (to be *nearly* exact, that is).

Dial-up is a pain for building consistent connections because it's hard to keep up and connected. Years ago, when I had my company connected to the Internet on a shoestring budget, I connected our network to our ISP with a 14.4Kbps modem. I used a "flat-rate" phone account, one that cost $25 a month with no charges for local calls. The call to the ISP was local, so I figured I'd just dial up and not hang up. Essentially, I figured, $25 a month bought me a moderately noisy 14.4K dedicated line to the Internet—good deal, right?

It was a constant pain, and let me try to convince you not to try it for your routed Internet connection. First of all, the phone company computers go around and periodically disconnect any dial-up connection that's been up and running too long. Second, most ISPs think *fault-tolerant* refers to their belief that customers will tolerate the ISP's faulty infrastructure, so many ISPs end up rebooting their systems periodically, which kicks anyone off the modems and drops the dial-up connection.

Back in 1992, when I had the 14.4 connection running, I had to establish the dial-up connection myself, and when the connection would drop periodically, I'd have to reestablish it with a few commands at the router. You'll see that RRAS has a feature called *on-demand dialing*, which is supposed to sense whenever anyone on the local network needs to get to the Internet, and when the Windows 2000 router senses that need, it dials up the Internet. It *sounds* as if this might be the way to ensure that a dial-up connection dials up and stays up: Why not just run a simple batch file that does a ping to somewhere out on the Internet and use the Scheduler service to automatically run the batch file every 20 minutes or so? Seems like a great idea, but in my experience the demand dialer has trouble figuring out whether the modem is currently connected. I've had RRAS tell me that a demand-dial connection was up and running when I could clearly see that the "carrier detect" light on the modem was off.

ISDN offers some of the same problems with the extra fact that you usually get charged by the minute for ISDN connections, which can run up the meter fairly quickly.

The answer for many may be a dedicated connection called a *frame relay* connection. You're charged a flat monthly rate for it, depending on things like how far away you are from the ISP and how fast the connection is. In my experience, a fairly low-speed, 56Kbps frame relay runs around $150–$200 per month. That's just the telco charges for the frame, however; the ISP will levy additional charges to rent you the IP addresses, route your packets, and whatever other services they offer. Instead of a modem to connect your server to the frame relay, you get a frame relay access device, or FRAD, which is either an external box that looks something like a modem and connects to your server with a serial port or a board that plugs into a slot inside the server. In any case, a frame relay connection ends up looking to Windows 2000 like a Dial-Up Networking connection, and whoever sells you the FRAD will include a "modem driver" for the FRAD so that Windows 2000 will understand how to use the FRAD. (Be *very sure* that a Windows 2000 driver exists before buying a FRAD. Make sure they know how to make it work with Windows 2000.)

Collect the Pieces and Get Started

Before beginning, make sure you have the following information close to hand:

◆ Addressing information from the ISP: your range of IP addresses, subnet mask, and router IPs.

◆ DNS server addresses from your ISP.

◆ If you are dialing into the ISP, correct phone numbers.

◆ Account name and password for the ISP.

◆ Verify that your system will be able to log in "hands off" with either a protocol called CHAP (Challenge Handshake Authentication Protocol) or PAP (Password Authentication Protocol). Although it's unlikely, there are some ISPs that actually still require you to pop up a dumb terminal screen and punch in an account name and password. RRAS can't handle that kind of login as far as I can see (even with a prebuilt script), so double-check that you can PAP or CHAP in.

Once you've collected that information, get started by doing the following:

◆ Get network cards in all of the local machines and in the server.

◆ Install the TCP/IP protocol on them and assign the ISP-assigned IP addresses to the local machines (DHCP's the easiest way).

◆ Attach the WAN connection device—modem, ISDN, FRAD, or whatever—on the gateway.

Test the ISP Connection

In a minute, we'll show RRAS how to connect your LAN to the Internet via a WAN. But before doing that, we'll figure out how to connect to the ISP in the first place.

No two connections work the same way. Some ISPs automatically assign IP addresses as you connect, and some require you to preconfigure your system with a particular IP address. If you're dialing up with a modem, you may have a choice of phone numbers and a bit of experimentation may reveal that one of them gets a high-speed connection more consistently. ISDN is always a challenge to get working, and frame relay can be pretty easy once you've done it a few times. Essentially what I'm suggesting is that you do a "dry run" of hooking up to the outside world. Plan to do it on a Tuesday morning, when your ISP's help desk is fully staffed and has recovered from answering all of the questions from the wave of frustrated people who couldn't connect all weekend (when there's no one or only a small staff at the help disk) and so angrily called on Monday.

Of course, you'll be using your system as a Dial-Up Networking client computer. If you need help on setting up a dial-out to the Internet, read Chapter 22, which discusses both DUN and its server-side partner, Remote Access Service (RAS).

Configure RRAS on the Gateway

Next, start up RRAS on the gateway—Start/Programs/Administrative Tools/Routing and Remote Access. As before, right-click the icon representing the gateway and choose Configure and Enable Routing and Remote Access. That'll start a wizard you see in Figure 6.37.

FIGURE 6.37

Starting the RRAS wizard

Click Next, and you'll see several options for routing, as you see in Figure 6.38.

FIGURE 6.38

Routing options

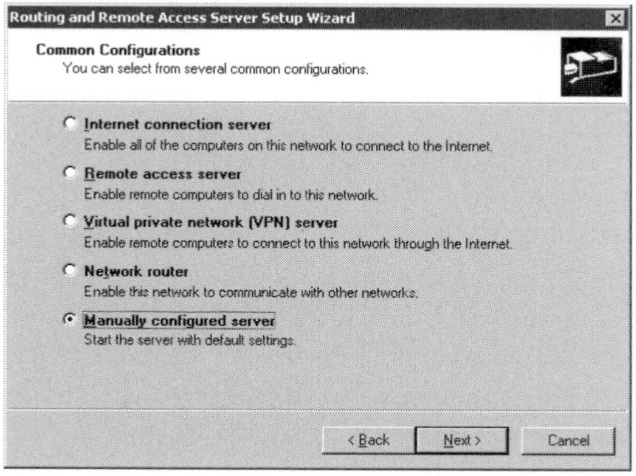

Again, take the Manually Configured Server option and click Next; you'll then see something like Figure 6.39.

FIGURE 6.39

Completing the RRSA wizard

Click Finish and you'll be asked if it's all right to start the service. Click Yes and the service will start. You'll then see a RRAS screen that looks like Figure 6.40.

FIGURE 6.40

RRAS management console

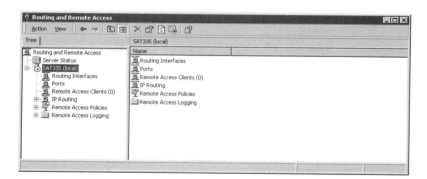

Now, by default this machine will accept dial-ins, so unless you *want* dial-ins, let's disable them for security reasons. Right-click the server name and choose Properties, and you'll see a screen like Figure 6.41.

Uncheck Remote Access Server, then click OK. You'll be asked if it's all right to restart the routing service; click Yes to indicate that it's fine. You'll be back at the RRAS screen. Click the Routing Interfaces object in the left pane and you'll see something like Figure 6.42.

I should note that at this point the folks who are doing a full-time connection, like frame relay, are done. You may have to do something to tell RRAS that you have "dialed" that connection—sorry I'm being vague, but this varies from vendor to vendor and that's why you want to be very sure that they've got good Windows 2000 support before buying their FRAD—but other than that, you've now got a connection out to the Internet, a connection to your local network, and routing is enabled.

FIGURE 6.41

RRAS properties

FIGURE 6.42

RRAS screen with server opened

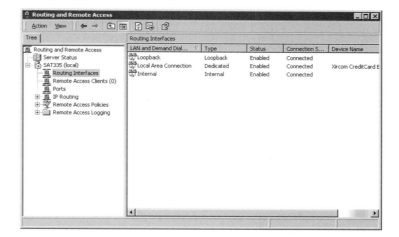

For those with modems and ISDN, however, we're not done, so we'll move on to Figure 6.42.

Now right-click the Routing Interfaces object and choose New/Demand-Dial Interface, which kicks off yet another wizard, the Demand Dial Interface Wizard. I'll spare you the first screen, but if you click Next from the opening screen, you'll see a screen like Figure 6.43.

Give the connection a name and click Next, and the wizard will show you something like Figure 6.44.

As RRAS handles virtual private network (VPN, covered in detail in Chapter 22) connections as well as more common dial-up type connections, the wizard next asks you which type of connection you're creating. Choose the modem/ISDN option and click Next, and you'll see the next panel, as in Figure 6.45.

FIGURE 6.43

Naming the direct-dial interface

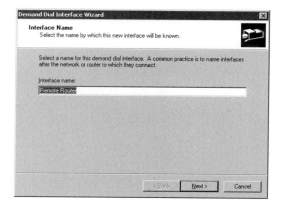

FIGURE 6.44

VPN or direct-dial?

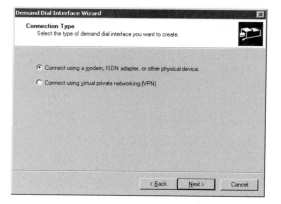

FIGURE 6.45

Which device to use?

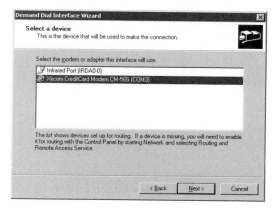

You'll only see this screen if you have multiple potential devices for WAN connection. Now, in my world, infrared isn't much of a WAN link, but I guess it's just a matter of taste. Click the modem, ISDN box, or whatever you're going to use to dial out, and click Next, and you'll see something like Figure 6.46.

FIGURE 6.46

What number to dial?

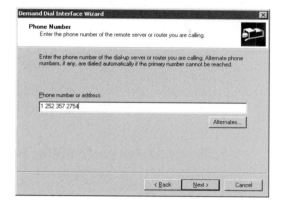

Enter the number that the modem should dial and click Next to see Figure 6.47.

FIGURE 6.47

Configuring the routing connection

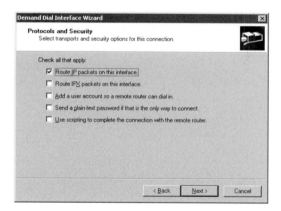

I've clicked only Route IP Packets on This Interface, and then clicked Next to see Figure 6.48.

Here, Domain is only relevant if you're dialing into a Windows 2000 or NT 4 RAS/RRAS server. For dial-up to a standard ISP, just leave Domain blank. Fill in the user account name and password, then click Next (one *would* think that they could have consolidated a few of these wizard screens, hmmm?), click Finish and then click the Routing Interfaces object, and you'll see a screen like Figure 6.49.

Notice that Remote Router is one of the listed interfaces. Right-click it and choose Properties, and you'll see a properties page for the interface. Click Options and you'll see something like Figure 6.50.

FIGURE 6.48

User ID for dial-in

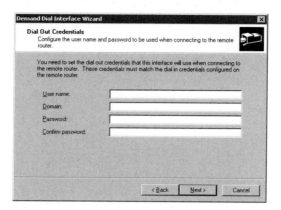

FIGURE 6.49

Routing Interfaces
listed

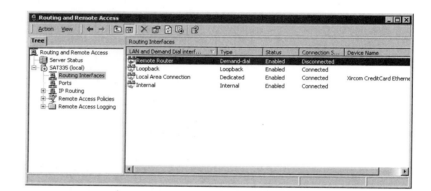

FIGURE 6.50

Making the interface
persistent

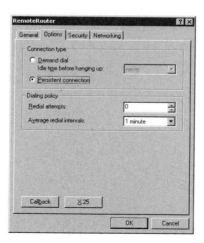

By default, the modem only dials up when the gateway senses that one of the local systems needs to access the Internet. I suspect that you'll find that a somewhat unsatisfactory option because of the relatively large amount of time that the gateway will require to dial up and establish the Internet connection. For example, suppose I sit at one of the local machines and type **ping www.whitehouse.gov**; it will probably take so long for the gateway to complete the Internet dial-in that the ping will have long ago timed out. A better answer, I believe, is to just click the Persistent radio button. That way, RRAS tries to establish the dial-up connection and keep it up.

Lower-Cost LAN-to-WAN Routing with Internet Connection Sharing

The preceding section explained how to connect a set of machines on a LAN connection using the traditional method—get a connection device of some kind, get a bunch of IP addresses from an ISP, and so on. But that can be an expensive proposition. Newer routing technologies make it possible for you to connect as many computers as you like to the Internet through a gateway machine. What's new about that? Well, as with the example we just saw, all of those computers are connected to the gateway with a local area network, and the gateway is connected to the Internet somehow. What's *different* is this:

- The only machine on the network with a "regulation," IANA- or ISP-issued IP address is the gateway.

- The other machines have nonroutable addresses.

- All of the "heavy lifting," routing-wise, is being done by the gateway computer. In fact, the ISP has no idea whatsoever that all of those other computers are accessing the Internet via the gateway.

This functionality, generically called network address translation (NAT) routing, was until recently fairly expensive to implement, requiring special routers. But Windows 2000 comes with the software to turn a Windows 2000 server into a NAT router. Even more amazing, Microsoft included this capability in Windows 2000 *Professional* as well—and even in the revised version of Windows 98, the "second edition"! Called Internet Connection Sharing, this will work on any kind of Internet connection, whether it's a modem, ISDN, cable modem, DSL, or whatever.

NOTE *Just to be on the safe side, check your "use agreement" with your ISP. Some ISPs specifically forbid any kind of sharing.*

In the remaining part of this chapter, I'll walk you through setting up ICS with a Windows 2000 machine. Basically, there are just a four steps:

1. Attach all of your internal computers together in a network.

2. Connect one of the computers (the one running ICS) to the Internet either via a modem or another Ethernet card. (Yes, that's *another* Ethernet card—you can't put the Internet connection on the same segment as the connection to the internal, nonroutable machines.)

3. You'll now have two connections on the ICS computer—one to the local Ethernet connecting the internal nonroutable machines, and one to the Internet. On the Internet connection, turn on ICS.

4. Tell all of the internal, nonroutable computers to automatically get their IP addresses (which they'll end up getting from the ICS machine), then reboot them.

Once you do all that, the internal systems will have nonroutable IP addresses in the range 192.168.0.2–192.168.0.254—but they'll be able to access the Internet.

Step One: Connect the Internal Network—and Meet APIPA

This is easy. Just put an Ethernet card in every computer in your home, small business, or whatever set of machines you need ICS for. (I'm kind of hoping you've already done this, or it's reasonable to wonder why you're reading this book!) When configuring the TCP/IP settings as you saw back in Figure 6.14, don't bother punching in any values; instead, just click the radio button labeled Obtain an IP Address Automatically.

Now boot the systems and do an **ipconfig /all**. You'll find that they all have IP addresses in the range between 169.254.0.1 through 169.254.255.254. Where did *those* addresses come from? They're a new feature of Windows 2000 called Automatic Private IP Addressing (APIPA).

The idea in most IP-based networks, as you'll see in the next chapter, is to set up a kind of server called a Dynamic Host Configuration Protocol (DHCP) server somewhere on the network. That DHCP server then automatically supplies IP addresses to all systems on the network, freeing you from having to walk around to every system and punch in a different IP address. But what happens if you have a system that (1) expects to find a DHCP server and therefore doesn't *have* a static IP address, but that (2) finds itself on a network without a DHCP server? Well, under NT 4, that system would basically just disable its TCP/IP software. Under 2000, however, it randomly assigns itself an address in the range of 169.254.0.1 through 169.254.255.254, checking to make sure that no one else has this address. Granted, it's not a terribly useful way to get IP addresses on important Web servers, but for a small network that's not intending to talk to any other network, it's not a bad answer. But it's only a temporary answer, as we'll see, because ICS actually includes a basic, no-configuration-necessary DHCP server inside it, and so when we get ICS running, then its DHCP server will hand out more useful addresses to the machines on your internal network.

Step Two: Get Connected to Your ISP

The next step is just to get connected to your ISP.

GET CONNECTED TO YOUR ISP (DIAL UP)

NOTE   If you connect via DSL or cable modem, then skip this section and go to the next, "Get Connected to Your ISP (Cable Modem/DSL) and Internal Network."

Right-click My Network Places and choose Properties, and you'll see a screen like Figure 6.51.

Double-click the Make New Connection icon, and you'll get the inevitable welcome screen from a wizard that will help set up the connection to the ISP. Click Next to get past it, and you'll see Figure 6.52.

FIGURE 6.51

Creating a new connection

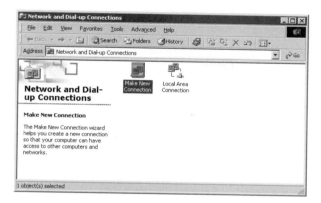

FIGURE 6.52

How to connect?

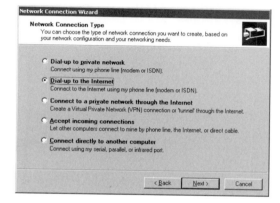

Tell the wizard that this is just a modem dial-up to the Internet by clicking the radio button labeled Dial-Up to the Internet and click Next. For some reason, this kicks off the Internet Connection Wizard (the wizardry is getting a trifle thick for my taste) and you'll see Figure 6.53.

FIGURE 6.53

Introducing the Internet Connection Wizard

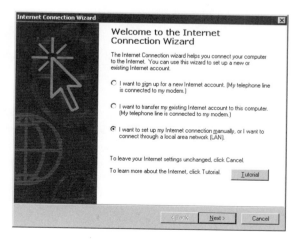

Pick the last option, and click Next. You'll see something like Figure 6.54.

FIGURE 6.54

Dial or direct connect?

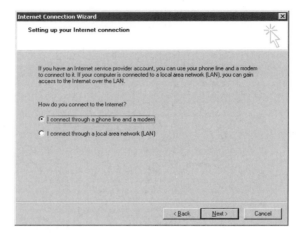

As you're dialing in, select the phone line option. (Again, though, didn't you already answer that question back in Figure 6.52? Maybe Microsoft needs to run the "hearing test wizard.") Click Next and you'll fill in the phone line, as you see in Figure 6.55.

FIGURE 6.55

Phone number to call

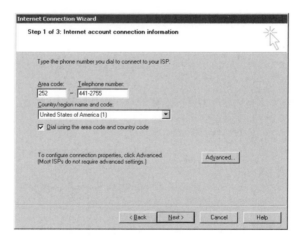

Although that's a fairly self-explanatory item, I included Figure 6.55 to point out that there's an Advanced button on the screen. I had to use it to set up my ISP's connection and you may also, so let's take a look at what it does. Click Advanced and you'll see a properties page with two tabs, one labeled Connection (which you'll probably never have to worry about) and another labeled Addresses (which you may have to worry about). You see the Addresses tab in Figure 6.56.

FIGURE 6.56

Setting the DNS
server addresses

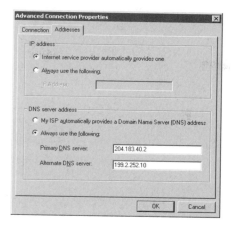

Although it's possible for an ISP to automatically configure your system when you dial in, giving your system an IP address and telling it where to find the DNS servers, not all do. In my experience, most of them can do the IP address, as nearly everyone dials in with PPP nowadays—I say *nowadays* because as recently as 1995 many ISPs still only supported the simpler SLIP protocol—and PPP does the IP address assignment to the client (that is, your dialing-in PC) with no trouble. But many ISPs still require you to punch in the addresses of their DNS servers—here's where you do it. There's room to fill in up to two DNS servers; then click OK to return to the screen where you fill in the phone number, and click Next. In the next screen, you can enter your user account name and password; click Next, and you can give the dial-up entry a descriptive name—I used Coastal Net ISP—then click Next.

After that, the wizard wants to set up an e-mail account, asking, "Do you want to set up an Internet mail account now?" Click the No radio button and then Next. You can at this point click Finish and the system will dial up to the Internet, but don't do that yet—uncheck the box labeled To Connect to the Internet Immediately, Select This box and Then Click Finish, and *then* click Finish. Network and Dial-Up Connections will look something like Figure 6.57.

Now skip the next section, and jump to "Step Three: Turn ICS On."

FIGURE 6.57

Dial-up object
created

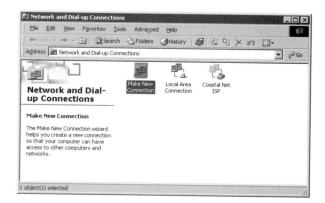

GET CONNECTED TO YOUR ISP (CABLE MODEM/DSL) AND INTERNAL NETWORK

If you connect to the Internet via DSL or cable modem, then you won't be creating one of those Dial-Up Networking objects. (Or, to use Microsoft's phrase, you won't create any *connectoids*—where they get these words is beyond me.) Instead, you connect to your cable modem or DSL through Ethernet—usually, the DSL or cable modem provider sells you an Ethernet card, which attaches to an interface box of some kind. The chances are that all you've got to do is to just pop the Ethernet card into your computer, hook a cable from the Ethernet card to the DSL/cable modem interface, and boot your computer. You might have to load a NIC driver for the Ethernet card, or perhaps Windows 2000 already has the driver. Then, when you're configuring the IP stack on the Ethernet card, just take the option labeled Obtain an IP Address Automatically. This says to let the DSL/cable modem system give you an address automatically via a system called DHCP, which we'll talk about in the next chapter.

Get that hooked up before going any further. Make sure that the Windows 2000 machine attached to the DSL/cable modem connection can surf the Net without any trouble. (And I apologize for being vague about how to get your 2000 box on DSL/cable modem, but I've never lived anywhere that either service was available, so I'm just going from having looked at friends' systems.)

You might, therefore, be tempted to put a hub on that cable modem or DSL connection and then just hang your other internal PCs off that hub. *Don't.* At least, not if you want ICS to work. Make sure that the computer running ICS, the one acting as the Internet sharing computer, has two Ethernet cards in it—one connected to the DSL or cable modem connection, and the other connected to the internal network of nonroutable systems.

Step Three: Turn ICS On

If you haven't already done it, go to Properties for My Network Places (right-click My Network Places and choose Properties), and you'll see a dialog box like the one that you saw back in Figure 6.9, Network and Dial-Up Connections. You'll see at least one Ethernet connection, probably labeled Local Area Connection or Local Area Connection 2, which represents the NIC attached to the internal network. Then you'll see an object representing the connection to the Internet—it'll either be a Dial-Up Networking connectoid if you dial up to the Internet, or another Local Area Connection object if you're using DSL or cable modem to connect to the Internet. (Come to think of it, you'd also see a second Local Area Network object if you were just connecting a separate small network to your Internet-attached corporate network.)

Locate the object that connects to the Internet—either the connectoid or the Local Area Network connection—and right-click it. Choose Properties, and you'll see a properties page with several tabs, one of which is labeled Sharing; click that tab, and you'll see a screen like Figure 6.58.

Check Enable Internet Connection Sharing for This Connection, and the On-Demand Dialing section will change from grayed to enabled. If the connection is not a full-time connection, then check Enable On-Demand Dialing. That will tell your gateway to dial out whenever anyone on the network needs to get on the Net. Again, call setup time may mean a long wait at first, so tell people to do something like a ping to some outside IP address and wait a minute or so to give the connection enough time to get set up, and *then* to start up the Web browser, e-mail program, or whatever.

FIGURE 6.58

Shared access dialog box

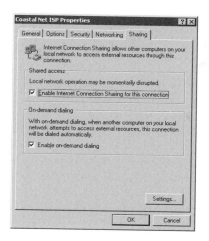

When you click OK to clear the properties page, you'll get a confirmation message saying something like this:

> When Shared Access is enabled, your LAN adapter will be set to use IP address 192.168.0.1. Your computer may lose connectivity with other computers on your network. If these other computers have static IP addresses, you should set them to obtain their IP addresses automatically. Are you sure you want to enable Shared Access?

The "192.168.0.1" address is part of the nonroutable IP addresses. Your computer then becomes a DHCP server, believe it or not, and if you set the computers on the local network to get their addresses from DHCP and reboot them, they'll all be able to communicate with each other *and* with the gateway, and the gateway will get their packets to and from the Internet without trouble. Try it—you'll see that those 169.*x.y.z* addresses have now become 192.*x.y.z* addresses, *and* that all of the internal systems can ping the public Internet, surf Web sites, and the like.

Beyond ICS: Setting Up Network Address Translation (NAT) on Windows 2000

ICS is great, but what if you want more? On the one hand, ICS lets you easily connect a bunch of internal machines to the Internet via one routable address—it's quite literally a matter of a click or two and you're done. But you can't change the range of addresses that ICS's mini-DHCP server gives out. Nor can you facilitate *incoming* traffic—ICS is basically a simple port address translation router. Any system inside your network can initiate an outbound conversation, but outside systems on the public Internet can't initiate an incoming conversation. Furthermore, ICS really only makes sense if you only have one routable IP address. That won't always be true—and so you'll sometimes want to configure network address translation rather than ICS.

For simplicity's sake, let me assume that your Internet connection is via a NIC of some kind—DSL, cable modem, or perhaps you've built an isolated network within your Internet-connected business—rather than a dial-up connection. For example, consider a training lab: Most medium- to large-sized companies have a room or two filled with a bunch of networked computers used for teaching classes. Those computers typically get nonroutable addresses but sometimes need outside Internet access, and so corporate IT departments usually need to set aside a routable address or two for the training lab and then need to somehow share those routable addresses with the training lab's nonroutable addresses. Most places use a Cisco router to accomplish that sharing, but there's no reason why a Windows 2000 server that's already in the training lab can't do that job and save the training department the cost of the Cisco router.

And, before we go any further, let me clarify that the machine sitting between the private non-routable network and the public Internet is a Windows 2000 Server machine. It *can't* be a 2000 Professional machine, as Pro only offers ICS—no NAT. For the sake of this explanation, let's call that in-between box W2KBOX. As you've already read, looking in Properties for My Network Places will show two Local Area Network connection objects. To enable ICS, right-click the one that's attached to the Internet and choose Properties. In the properties page that results, click the Sharing tab, check the box labeled Enable Internet Connection Sharing for This Connection, click OK, and then click Yes to the resulting dialog box. No news here—you just read how to do that. After a brief delay, ICS will start working. The NIC attached to the private network now has the static IP address 192.168.0.1. Your Internet-attached computer now runs a simple kind of DHCP server that hands out IP addresses in the private network range of 192.168.0.0 through 192.168.0.255. Set the computers on the internal network to look to DHCP for their IP addresses and reboot them, and they will get addresses on the 192.168.0.0 network and will look to the 192.168.0.1 system as their default gateway. Try a ping from any system on the internal network and you'll see that network now has Internet connectivity.

ICS LIMITATIONS

But ICS is limited in several ways. First of all, you cannot configure anything about the DHCP server built into ICS. Second, while any system on the internal network can access systems on the Internet, it's not possible for systems on the Internet to access the systems on the private network— if I were to ping your system at (for example) 192.168.0.100 from a computer on the Internet, I would not get a response from your system. That could be good from a security point of view, and so many people might not see this as a disadvantage at all.

But suppose you had a Web server on an internal machine hosting a terrific site that you wanted to offer to the public Internet. And suppose a *different* machine, also on the internal network, ran a mail server that, of course, won't be much good unless it can both send mail and receive mail. You could, of course, also just install the mail server and Web server software on W2KBOX, but you might not want one box acting as router, mail, and Web server—to make that work you'll have to abandon ICS and instead use NAT and its support of "inbound" connections. But NAT's a bit more complex to set up, so let's start out by duplicating ICS's functions, then we'll add inbound connections.

RRAS/NAT SETUP TO DUPLICATE ICS

Start off by disabling Internet Connection Sharing on W2KBOX; let me start this explanation by first using NAT to simply reproduce what ICS does. *Then* we can add on it. Assign the address 192.168.0.1 to the NIC attached to the internal network. (You needn't use *that* IP address in general—I'm just duplicating ICS's functionality as closely as I can.) Next, 2000 requires that we enable our old friend Routing and Remote Access. I've walked you through RRAS a few times now, so I'll be brief:

1. Click Start/Programs/Administrative Tools/Routing and Remote Access.

2. You will see an icon representing your Windows 2000 server system in the left panel of the MMC screen. Right-click it and choose Configure Routing and Remote Access, which starts the RRAS setup wizard.

3. Click Next to get to the first screen, choose Manually Configured Server, then Next and Finish, then confirm that you do indeed want to start the service.

4. By default, RRAS enables a bunch of things that you probably don't need, including RAS. Let's shut that stuff off: Back in the RRAS snap-in, right-click the icon representing your server and choose Properties. Beneath the Router check box, choose the radio button labeled Local Area Network Routing Only and uncheck the Remote Access Server check box, then click OK and confirm that you want to restart RRAS. To see a RRAS snap-in screen, look back to Figure 6.32.

5. Next, tell RRAS that you'd like to create a NAT router. In the left pane of the snap-in, open the server object and you'll see an object labeled IP Routing; open it, then right-click General, and choose New Routing Protocol. You'll get several options, as in Figure 6.59.

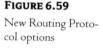

FIGURE 6.59

New Routing Protocol options

6. In the New Routing Protocol dialog box, choose Network Address Translation (NAT) and click OK. Back in the snap-in you'll see that the left pane now contains, under IP Routing, an object labeled Network Address Translation. Right-click that object and choose Properties, and you'll see a dialog box as in Figure 6.60.

7. This dialog box lets you tell NAT to act as a DHCP server as ICS did. In the properties page, choose the Address Assignment tab. And although it's not a full-blown DHCP server—you'll get to see one of *those* soon, and trust me, they can get a bit complex—you'll see that this dialog box lets you define the range of addresses that your NAT router will give out to the machines on the private network. Check the box labeled Automatically Assign IP Addresses by Using

DHCP, and choose the range of addresses that you want to hand out. For example, to continue to hand out addresses in the 192.168.0.*z* range, just fill in 192.168.0.0 for the IP Address, and 255.255.255.0 for the Mask value. Then click Exclude and exclude 192.168.0.1, as it's already taken—remember, you gave it to *this* machine's Ethernet card!

FIGURE 6.60

NAT properties

8. Before leaving this dialog box, click the tab labeled Name Resolution. Then check the box labeled Clients Using DNS (Domain Naming System). This lets your NAT router act as a kind of a DNS "proxy." The machines on the private network look to the NAT router to resolve DNS addresses; the NAT router then goes to its local DNS server to resolve those addresses, and passes the IP addresses to the machines in the internal network. Click OK— but don't try to route from the internal network yet, you're not quite done.

Although it *ought* to be obvious to NAT at this point that its job is to route between the network with the nonroutable addresses and the network with the routable addresses, it isn't, so you've got one more task: Tell NAT about the two NICs, and tell NAT which is the internal network and which is the Internet-connected one:

1. Right-click Network Address Translation and choose New Interface to get a dialog box like Figure 6.61.

2. With ICS, you associated Internet Connection Sharing with the NIC with the routable address; here, you tell NAT which NIC *doesn't* have routable interfaces as well. Click the one connected to the Internet, and you'll get a dialog box like Figure 6.62.

3. Click the radio button labeled Public Interface Connected to the Internet, which is NAT-ese for "this is the NIC with the routable addresses." Also check Translate TCP/UDP Headers (Recommended), as it's the only way that NAT can do the magic of making one TCP/IP address serve many systems simultaneously, and then click OK to clear that dialog box. You've told it where to find the Internet—now tell it which segment to share that Internet connection with. Right-click Network Address Translation again and choose New Interface again.

Choose the NIC connected to the nonroutable network and this time, choose the radio button labeled Private Interface Connected to Private Network; click OK.

FIGURE 6.61

Choosing the NIC to run NAT on

FIGURE 6.62

Choosing the Internet-connected NIC

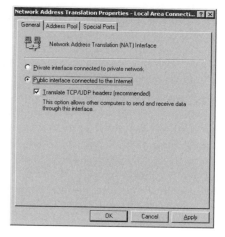

Reboot the systems on the internal network and they should yet again see the router as a DHCP server handing out IP addresses in the 192.168.0.0 subnet.

BEYOND ICS I: PORT MAPPING

Now we've duplicated ICS's functionality in NAT. Let's take it further.

Discussions of sharing a single routable address, or a small number of routable addresses, with a larger number of machines on a *nonroutable* network usually have DSL or cable modem connections in mind. But that's not the only potential "target market," so to speak, for NAT. As you've read elsewhere in this chapter, sharing a routable address via ICS only allows the internal (nonroutable) computers to initiate conversations to the outside Internet, not the reverse. For example, an internal computer could surf an external Web site; but if you were to set up one of the internal 192.168.0.0

computers as a Web server, then it would be impossible for a computer on the routable public Internet to surf that Web server. Is there a way around this? Well, if your internal-network-to-Internet connection is just a machine running ICS, then you're stuck—but with NAT, you can easily arrange matters so that external computers can connect to resources on your internal network.

How you'd let the Internet access an internal Web server (or mail server, FTP server, or whatever else; I'll stick to Web servers here for simplicity, but making any type of server available works the same) depends crucially on one question: How many routable IP addresses do you have available? Let's first consider the case wherein you only have one routable IP address available. In case it's not obvious, you have no choice about what to do with that address: You've got to assign it to the computer acting as the router (which, for simplicity, I'll just call the router).

One way to offer a public Web server in this one-address case would be, of course, to set up IIS on the router. But you might not want to do that, either because NT (and therefore 2000) has never been all that good at doing a lot of different things on one machine, or perhaps because you need a system with more horsepower to run a complex site.

Just to make this explanation concrete, let's arbitrarily assign a few IP addresses. Let's say that the router has a routable IP address of 206.246.253.9, and that its internal nonroutable address is 192.168.0.1. Let's suppose the computer on the internal network that's running the Web server is on the internal nonroutable address 192.168.0.10. That Web server needs a routable address to be visible to the public Internet, but you've already used your only routable address on the router—what to do?

NAT allows you to redirect a particular port from the router to a particular port on a particular computer on the internal network. Web connections usually come into a Web server on port 80, so you just tell the router to refer any incoming communications on the router's port 80 to port 80 on 192.168.0.10. 2000's NAT software calls such a port-to-port connection a *special port*. Here are the specifics on how I would create a special port on my simple example network. First, I go to the routable machine at 206.246.253.9 and open Routing and Remote Access (Start/Programs/Administrative Tools); I then see an MMC console with my router machine shown as an icon, with a plus sign next to it. I then click the plus sign to open the router's options—if it's already open, that's probably because the RRAS MMC snap-in seems to recall some of what you did the last time that you ran it.

In the right pane, I see objects representing routing options. I open the one labeled IP Routing, and inside that, I see Network Address Translation (NAT). I left-click that and my router's public (206.246.253.9) and private (192.168.0.1) interfaces will appear in the right pane. Then I right-click the public interface and choose Properties, and click a tab labeled Special Ports. There aren't any special ports on the router yet, so I'd then have to click Add to create one. *That* leads to the dialog box I've been waiting for, one labeled Add Special Port; you can see it in Figure 6.63.

It asks you to specify an incoming port, private address, and outgoing port. Fill those fields in with **80**, **192.168.0.10**, and **80**, respectively, and click OK.

To review what I'm trying to accomplish here: A request comes in to the Web server at 206.246.253.9 or, in other words, a request comes in to 206.246.253.9:80, as 80 is the HTTP port. What I want NAT to do is move the request over to the machine addressed as 192.168.0.10, and address it to port 80 on that machine. When might I have set the incoming and outgoing ports to different values? In my experience, you *wouldn't* do it all that often, but if for some reason you wanted to set up the Web server at 192.168.0.10 on port 10000, then you'd fill in **10000** on Outgoing Port so that traffic from the Internet—which expects to do Web business on port 80—would get to the Web server.

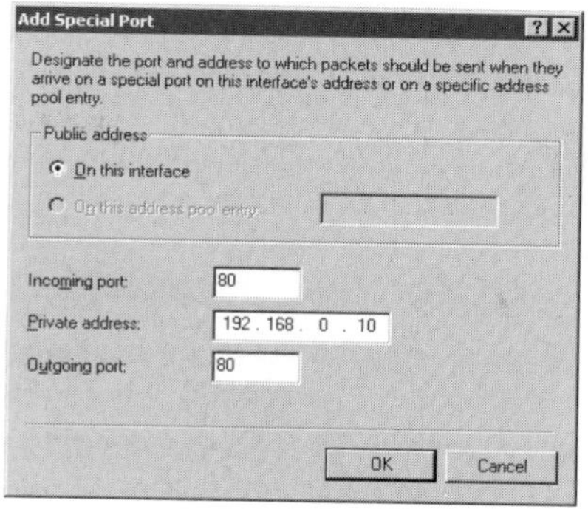

FIGURE 6.63

Connecting an incoming port on the router to a port on an internal machine

BEYOND ICS II: TRUE NAT

But perhaps you've spent a few more bucks and gotten more than one IP address from your ISP, or you're working in a corporate environment and you've wheedled a few more addresses out of IT; in that case, you've got a few more options. With a few more IPs in hand, you may be able to go a step further in connecting your internal systems to the public Internet. Presuming that your ISP sells you a block of routable IP addresses rather than just one IP address, you'll need a router on your site to handle routing those addresses. Let me underscore that so far we've only used 2000's routing function to serve systems on the nonroutable 192 network, as previously the ISP only gave us one IP address. In fact, this hasn't (from a purist's point of view) been NAT, but *PAT*—port address translation.

With NAT, you can "glue" one address to another. For example, if my ISP gave me a range of addresses from 206.246.253.180 through 206.246.253.183, I *could* give one of those addresses to a particular nonroutable machine. So, for example, I could take the 206.246.253.181 address and glue it to the machine with IP address 192.168.0.10 on the nonroutable internal network. The net effect would be exactly the same thing as if I put the 192.168.0.10 system on the routable public Internet, giving it address 206.246.253.181.

Doing that sort of thing requires three main steps:

1. First, the outside Internet has to recognize your NAT router as "the place to go" when routing traffic in the range that the ISP gave you.

2. Then, your NAT router has to be ready to *accept* those addresses—someone's got to inform it of its new duties.

3. Finally, you've got to tell the router to "glue" the particular routable address to the particular nonroutable address.

If you've been following this chapter up to now, then Step One is easy. Either you connect your 2000-running NAT server to whatever links you to your ISP—frame relay, DSL, or whatever—or you connect your 2000 NAT box to your company's internal Internet-attached network, then you make sure that the people running the ISP or your company's network have configured their routers to direct traffic for your little range of routable addresses to that 2000 box. In other words, the first step is Someone Else's Problem.

In Step Two, you've got to tell the router to *expect* that traffic. Once you've got your router connected to both sides, it's time to set up the static routes and, if you've read the preceding part of this chapter, then that shouldn't be difficult. Normally, giving a router a bunch of addresses lets the router act as a static router, acting as a go-between for two or more subnets, all of which contain routable addresses. And while it might be nice to have enough routable addresses to give one to each system in our internal network, we often don't. So when we get those few new routable addresses, we won't hand out a routable address to each system in the internal network. Instead, we'll continue to set up the router to do port address translation in most cases, meaning that most traffic from the internal network to the external network will be simple port address translation, as ICS performs—no change there. What'll be different is this: We'll set up the NAT router to essentially "glue" a routable address to one of the computers on the internal, nonroutable network—that's Step Three.

I'll explain this using a specific example, to keep it easier to follow. Assume that the Windows 2000 system acting as the router is connected to the public Internet via an Ethernet connection with IP address 206.246.253.9. Let's also presume that our local ISP, IT department, or whomever has given me a small range of addresses, from 206.246.253.180 through 206.246.253.183. In IP network terms, this means that I've got network number 206.246.253.180 with subnet mask 255.255.255.252. Of course, as I can't use the first or last address in a subnet, that leaves me with only two routable addresses: 206.246.253.181 and 206.246.253.182. I'll need the first one for the router itself, so all I've got left to assign to an internal system is the second address, 206.246.253.182.

On the internal network, suppose I have a mail server at 192.168.0.10 that I'd like the outside world to see. My goal, then, is to associate the routable address 206.246.253.182 to the non-routable address 192.168.0.10, so that (for example) someone on the public Internet could ping 206.246.253.182 and unknowingly receive answers to that ping not from the router, but from the internal machine at 192.168.0.10.

There are three steps to this process: First, tell routers in the public Internet to route traffic intended for the two 206 addresses to the machine acting as the router. But, again, you won't do this step; your ISP or IT department will. They'll have to set up their routers to point to your 2000 system as the "official router" of 206.246.253.181 and .182.

Second, you must prepare the router to accept incoming traffic in that address block. You do that by right-clicking the object in the Routing and Remote Administration snap-in that represents the NIC that's attached to the public Internet. Then choose Properties and you'll see a properties sheet with three tabs on it labeled General, Address Pool, and Special Ports. Click Address Pool and you'll see a screen like Figure 6.64.

Tell it about the range of addresses by clicking Add, then fill in the resulting dialog box. Click OK when you fill in the dialog box; now the system's ready to act as the router for that range of addresses.

Finally, glue 206.246.253.182 to 192.168.0.10. In the same Address Pool tab on the properties page of the publicly attached NIC, you'll see a button labeled Reservations—you can see it in Figure 6.64. Click it and then Add and you'll see a dialog box looking like Figure 6.65.

Fill in the field asking Reserve This Public IP Address with the routable value (the 206 number, in my example); fill in For This Computer on the Private Network with the nonroutable IP address of the computer that you want externally visible (the 192 address, in my example); and finally check the box labeled Allow Incoming Sessions to This Address. Click OK to close the dialog box and you're done. In this example, someone pinging 206.246.253.182 would "touch" the machine at 192.168.0.10.

FIGURE 6.64

Informing the router what addresses it's responsible for

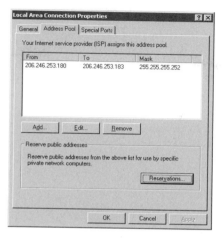

FIGURE 6.65

Mapping a routable address to a non-routable address

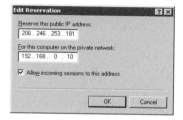

TROUBLESHOOTING ICS AND NAT

If this doesn't work, then be methodical. There are three components to any intranet-to-Internet routing system—the Internet, the gateway (the box running ICS, NAT, or whatever—the thing acting as a router), and the intranet (the machines inside your network that want to get to the Internet).

First, check that the gateway PC can communicate with the Internet. First check with a ping to an IP address, *not* a DNS address—check IP connectivity without confusing things vis-à-vis name resolution; for example, ping 206.246.253.1. *Then* do a ping to some location by its DNS address; for example, ping www.minasi.com. If these don't work, then either your connection to the outside world (cable, DSL, or whatever) has failed, or you've got something strange going on in your routing table that makes it try to route to the Internet via the internal network. If IP pings work but DNS pings don't, then check DNS.

Next, check that the gateway can communicate with the intranet. Ping systems inside your network, again by IP address and then DNS. Same approach here—check routing if it's an IP problem, DNS/WINS if it's a name problem.

Then check that the intranet systems can ping the gateway. As before, ping the IP address (the intranet side, 192.168.0.1, or whatever you set it to), then the name.

Finally, check that the intranet systems can ping the outside world through the gateway, by IP and by name. Using this simple methodology breaks down the problem into something tractable.

Understanding IPSec

Basic garden-variety IP lacks security, and that's fine in most cases—if you're just visiting my Web page, then you really don't care much if anyone were to snoop on you, unless of course your boss had issued an edict against visiting my site. And it's possible but very unlikely that someone on the Internet, sitting on a computer between you and me, would take the time to somehow intercept the data that my Web site were sending your browser, modifying it before sending it to you so as to produce a falsified page.

But many communications *do* need security. If you were to visit my Web site to buy something online, then you'd want *that* communication secured. SSL solves that problem, but it's pretty much restricted to a Web-only protocol. If a company had two offices across the country from one another but used the Internet to connect a server in one site to a server in the other site, then the company would probably want to ensure that any communications between those two servers both couldn't be snooped upon and couldn't be modified along the way by evildoers. SSL wouldn't really be the answer for that.

Instead, another set of protocols called IP Security (IPSec) seek to provide a generic answer for securing IP-based networks. IPSec operates at the same layer as IP, rather than SSL, which, again, is an application-layer protocol. IPSec is also a necessary part of using the Virtual Private Network (VPN) protocol L2TP—you can't run L2TP without IPSec.

IPSec lets you choose how secure a communication between two computers will be. Basically, it offers four levels of security:

◆ Block transmissions

◆ Encrypt transmissions

◆ Sign transmissions

◆ Permit transmissions to travel unchanged, without signing or encrypting them

Let's examine those in a bit more detail.

BLOCK TRANSMISSION

This does just what it sounds like: It blocks transmissions. When you tell IPSec to "block" traffic from machine X to machine Y, then the IPSec code on machine Y just simply discards any traffic coming in from machine X.

Although this might seem at first blush to be kind of useless, if you think about it then you'll see that it isn't at all. In some senses, blocking traffic is the most extreme option for security, right? For example, my firm might have a competitor whose systems run on subnet 200.200.100.0, and I don't want them to be able to send me mail, visit my Web site, or communicate with my network in any way. (These could clearly be mortal-enemy types of competitors.) I could set up IPSec on my systems to block that subnet, just discarding any packets that arrive.

ENCRYPT TRANSMISSION

Here, I *want* to allow traffic to pass from machine X to machine Y, but I'm worried that someone will eavesdrop on the network connection between X and Y. So I tell IPSec to use a protocol called the Encapsulating Security Payload—and I'll bet you didn't need to be precognitive to guess that its acronym is ESP—to encrypt the traffic before putting it on the network. Snoopers will only see an unreadable, random-looking stream of bytes.

Notice how convenient it is that IPSec works way down at the network protocol layer—it can encrypt *anything*. Do you like the convenience of Telnet but hate that it sends its information in clear-text? Just tell IPSec that whenever machine X and machine Y are using Telnet to communicate that IPSec should use ESP to encrypt the communication. No modification required at all to the Telnet server or client.

When would encryption be useful? Perhaps you have a few machines inside your intranet that handle very sensitive information—payroll info or perhaps customer credit cards. The data might be kept on a machine named SQL1, and it might be entered and edited only from workstations WS1, WS2, and WS3. You might fear that an insider might set up a sniffer on the network to trap this traffic as it goes by, collecting privileged information. You can keep people from accessing SQL1's database in the first place with permissions, as you already know. But you can keep people from listening on the wire by creating IPSec policies on SQL1 that force it to encrypt any communications to and from WS1, WS2, or WS3, and you can create similar policies on those workstations.

Or, in another instance, suppose you had a server in Chicago and offices all around the country, containing workstations that need to access data on that server. Suppose also that the only way that the offices connect to Chicago is over the public Internet, and you're (rightly) concerned that running company data over the public Internet might not be the best idea, security-wise. You could create an IPSec policy on the Chicago server so that it will only accept encrypted traffic—it never accepts cleartext communications. You would then create IPSec policies on the workstations so that they only communicate with the Chicago server via ESP.

NOTE *And in case you're thinking, "What if that company had firewalls at every location—would IPSec work through a firewall?" The answer is yes. You must open UDP port 500 and permit protocols number 50 and 51.*

SIGN TRANSMISSION

In certain kinds of network attacks, the bad guys fool your computer into thinking that transmissions from them are transmissions from someone that you trust. Or other attacks involve grabbing transmission packets somewhere between you and the trusted person, modifying the packets and sending them along to you—a so-called "man-in-the-middle" attack. IPSec lets you guard against this with a protocol called Authentication Header (AH). AH is a method for digitally *signing* communications. If your computer and mine are performing signed communications, then we're *not* encrypting our data—anyone listening on the wire could overhear our communications. Instead, digital signing adds a bit of data to the end of our network packets that we can use to verify that the data wasn't changed in transit.

PERMIT TRANSMISSION

Permit is IPSec's phrase for "no security at all." It just tells IPSec to let the traffic pass without any changes to it and no checks on its integrity. This is basically what happens in a TCP/IP-based network that doesn't include any IPSec. Why, then, have a "permit" action at all? So that you can create rules that restrict some things but not others, such as a rule (which you'll see us build later) that says, "Block all incoming traffic *except* for traffic on ports 80 and 443—permit that traffic."

IPSEC FILTERS

Now that you know what IPSec can do, let's examine an important flexibility about IPSec—its filters. In my examples so far, I've said that you can direct IPSec to encrypt traffic between two particular systems. In another example, I said that you could tell IPSec not only to encrypt transmissions between two particular systems, but that you could further refine IPSec's mission by saying that it should encrypt transmissions between those two systems *only when running Telnet.* In the section on blocking traffic altogether, I suggested that you might want to tell your Web server to block any traffic at all from subnet 200.200.100.0.

More specifically, you can use filters to restrict IPSec to securing communications:

◆ By the source computer's IP address, IP subnet, or DNS name

◆ By the destination computer's IP address, IP subnet, or DNS name

◆ By the port and port type (TCP, UDP, ICMP, and so on)

All of this makes for a very nice amount of flexibility in IPSec-ing.

IPSEC RULES = IPSEC ACTIONS + IPSEC FILTERS

Blocking, encrypting, signing, or permitting traffic is said to be an IPSec *action.* You've just met IPSec filters. But to use IPSec, you combine a filter and an action to produce a *rule.* For example, suppose you want to tell the IPSec system on a given computer, "Encrypt all Telnet traffic from the computer at 10.10.11.3." *That's* a rule. It has a filter part and an action part:

◆ The *filter* part says, "Only activate this rule if there is traffic that is (1) from IP address 10.10.11.3, and (2) uses TCP port 23." (In case you didn't know, Telnet uses port 23.)

◆ The *action* part says, "Encrypt the traffic."

We'll build some IPSec rules, filters, and actions in a bit, once I've gotten a few more concepts out of the way.

SIGNING AND ENCRYPTING NEED ONE MORE PIECE: AUTHENTICATION

To make either digital signatures or encryption work, you need a set of agreed-upon *keys*—passwords, basically. So whenever you create an IPSec rule, then you'll have to tell IPSec how to authenticate.

Microsoft's IPSec supports three methods of authenticating: Kerberos, certificates, or an agreed-upon key. The Kerberos option only works between computers that are either in an Active Directory domain, or in AD domains that trust one another. Simply having two computers that have Kerberos clients won't be sufficient and, insofar as I can see, even two Windows systems that are members of the same Unix-based Kerberos version 5 realm (the Kerberos version of what we call a domain in the Microsoft world) can't use IPSec to communicate while authenticating with Kerberos. Perhaps Microsoft should have called this options "Active Directory" rather than "Kerberos."

The *certificates* option allows you to use Public Key Infrastructure (PKI) certificates to identify a machine. The *preshared key* option lets you use a regular cleartext string as the key. Not very secure, but as Microsoft is always very careful to say, "Hey, it was in the RFC, so we had to include it." *I* love the preshared key option, myself, as it's great for experimentation. No need to set up a certificate or an AD domain—just tell both machines to use a preshared key and they type in some text, like "this is a secret" on both machines. I wouldn't use it in a production environment, but for teaching and testing purposes, it's great.

WARNING   *Microsoft's IPSec implementation of authentication has a sort of annoying habit: It demands an authentication method whether IPSec needs it or not. You see, simply permitting traffic through without changing it, or blocking it altogether, does not require any agreed-upon keys, so in theory any rule that only includes permitting and blocking should not require choosing an authentication method—it'd be like the Department of Motor Vehicles asking you whether you put regular or high-test gas in your electric car when you registered it. But, again, Microsoft's IPSec asks you for an authentication method anyway, even though it'll never use it. So if you're building an IPSec rule that only permits and/or blocks, then go ahead and choose any authentication method; it doesn't matter.*

HOW IPSEC WORKS IN WINDOWS

That was the theory. Let's see how to actually do IPSec in Win2K and later OSes. There isn't really an "IPSec manager" program built into Windows; instead, Microsoft set things up so that you do IPSec entirely through policies, whether local policies or domain-based policies.

NOTE   *I know we haven't covered domain-based group policies yet, but don't worry—I'll show you how to do this with a local policy. Then, as you'll learn later when we cover domain-based group policies, the only real difference between local policies and domain policies is that you can centrally create a domain policy on an Active Directory domain controller and it then gets distributed to machines around the network. That's convenient because it means that you needn't travel around to each machine on your network to configure IPSec—or any of the hundreds of other things that domain policies can do.*

To make IPSec do our bidding, we'll first open the Local Security Policy snap-in: Click Start/Programs/Administrative Tools/Local Security Policy, or Start/Run and type **secpol.msc** and press Enter. It's a standard MMC snap-in, and in the left "command" pane, you'll see icons for Account Policies, Local Policies, Public Key Policies, and one called IP Security Policies on Local Machine—click on that. You'll see a screen like Figure 6.66.

FIGURE 6.66

Initial IPSec policies

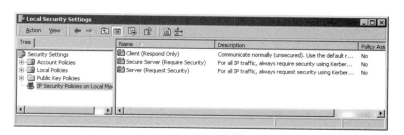

In the right pane, you see three policies—Client (Respond Only), Secure Server (Require Security), and Server (Request Security). Those are three prebuilt policies that Microsoft ships with the OS. In the extreme right column, you see No next to each one; that means none of them are activated or *assigned* in Windows lingo. You can activate any policy by right-clicking it and choosing Assign. But you can only have one policy assigned at a time, that's important—if you want to add some functionality to a current IPSec policy, then you can't just create a new policy and assign it, as that will *unassign* whatever policy is currently in force.

So, for example, suppose I were configuring IPSec on a server and I wanted to instruct that server to always encrypt communications when talking to server SV1 and to always digitally sign communications when talking to server SV2. I could create a policy that forces my system to encrypt when talking to SV1 and a second policy that forces my system to sign when talking to SV2. But if I did, then I'd see that I can only have one policy in force at a time. The *correct* way to see to handling SV1 and SV2 correctly would be to create *one* policy that contained *two* rules—one for SV1 and one for SV2. And note that you do not have to have *any* IPSec policies assigned at a given time—in fact, in Figure 6.66, no policies were assigned.

Let's review what we've seen so far about IPSec:

◆ You control and enable IPSec on Microsoft operating systems through policies. You can only have one IPSec policy active on any given machine.

◆ Policies contain rules, which tell IPSec what to do, and authentication methods, which tell IPSec how the receiver (or receivers) and the transmitter (or transmitters) will exchange a password. They will then use that password in order to sign or encrypt the traffic. Even though permit and block rules don't use authentication, Windows requires that you specify an authentication method.

◆ IPSec lets you authenticate via the Active Directory, PKI certificates, or a preshared key.

◆ Rules contain a filter or filters that tell the rule when to kick in, and rules contain actions that tell the rule what to do.

◆ There are four possible actions: block, encrypt, sign, or permit.

If that sounds like perhaps more work than you bargained for just to get a bit of secure traffic, then wait, don't run away—Microsoft has prebuilt three nice, generic policies that might just fill the bill for you. So you might not have to write any policies at all—just find the one that works for your needs and turn it on.

Default IPSec Policies

The three policies that come with IPSec are called Client (Respond Only), Server (Request Security), and "Secure Server (Require Security).

The Client (Respond Only) policy tells a computer not to use IPSec unless requested. So, for example, suppose you set this policy on your workstation and try to access a Web site on a system that doesn't support IPSec. In that case, the server (the Web server) won't try to initiate IPSec with your computer, so your computer won't insist on IPSec-ing the transaction, so all is well. But if your computer tries to connect to a server that *does* do IPSec, then the server will say to your workstation, "let's do IPSec," and your workstation will be able to oblige.

The Server (Request Security) policy should cause your computer to attempt to initiate IPSec whenever possible. But if the client computer either can't or won't use IPSec, then your computer should talk to it anyway.

As you'd expect, the Secure Server (Require Security) policy is designed to disallow any communications that don't use IPSec.

Creating a Custom IPSec Policy

Let's walk through a simple example of setting up an IPSec policy that will ensure an encrypted connection between two machines. Suppose you work at home and have a persistent connection to the Internet—DSL, cable modem, or the like—with a static IP address of 199.10.10.3. Your job involves updating a database on a machine across the Internet from you, a machine at 206.20.20.10. You want that connection to be encrypted and, just for simplicity's sake, we'll use a preshared key. In this simple example, I'll assume that the only system that 199.10.10.3 wants to IPSec with is the 206.20.20.10 machine, and vice versa.

We'll need two policies—one for the 199.10.10.3 machine and one for the 206.20.20.10 machine. Each has two rules in addition to the default rule. The first rule for 199.10.10.3 will consist of this:

- ◆ Filter: Trigger the rule whenever there is traffic to 206.20.20.10, over any port.

- ◆ Action: Encrypt the data.

- ◆ Authentication: Preshared key, key "secret."

The second rule is the reverse—trigger the rule whenever there is traffic *from* 206.20.20.10; the rest of the rule is the same as the first.

The easiest way to create a rule is to first define filters and actions, and *then* create the rule out of the new filter and action.

Defining a Filter   In Local Security Policy, right-click the object labeled IP Security Policies on Local Machine and choose Manage IP Lists and Filter Actions. You'll see a dialog box like the one in Figure 6.67.

FIGURE 6.67

Dialog box to manage filters and actions

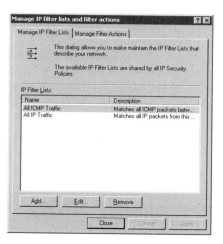

Notice that there are already two filters—All ICMP Traffic and All IP Traffic. They are there because Microsoft needed them to define the three prebuilt policies. I'll create the "traffic to 206.20.20.10" rule by clicking Add to open the dialog box in Figure 6.68.

FIGURE 6.68

Creating a new
filter, part 1

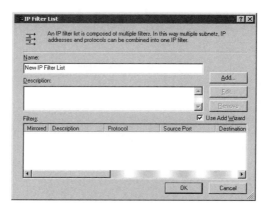

This dialog box doesn't actually let you create a new filter; it's sort of a staging area for new filters. (Don't ask me why they built it this way.) Give the filter a name, such as "Comms with 206.20.20.10." Then, to define the filter, uncheck Use Add Wizard and click Add to raise the dialog box you see in Figure 6.69.

FIGURE 6.69

Filter Properties
dialog box

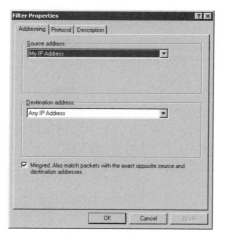

For Source Address, leave it as is. For Destination Address, click the drop-down dialog box and you'll see five options: My IP Address, Any IP Address, A Specific DNS Name, A Specific IP Address, and A Specific IP Subnet. Choose A Specific IP Address, and punch in **206.20.20.10**. If you like, click the Description tab and describe the filter. If we were going to specify only traffic on a particular port, then we'd click the Protocol tab—it lets you specify the protocol type (UDP, TCP, ICMP, and others) and a port number.

One more thing before you click OK—the Mirrored check box. Leave it checked. *Mirror* means to use the rule in both directions—don't just activate it from "my address" to 206.20.20.10; also activate it from 206.20.20.10 to "my address." This saves us the trouble of creating that second rule—quite convenient. Now you're ready to click OK until you're back to the Manage IP Filter Lists and Filter Actions dialog box.

Defining an Action Next, click the tab labeled Manage Filter Actions. You'll see something like Figure 6.70.

FIGURE 6.70

Default filter actions

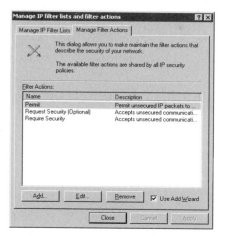

As before, skip the wizard—it's of no help. Uncheck Use Add Wizard, and click Add to show a dialog box like Figure 6.71.

FIGURE 6.71

Defining the action

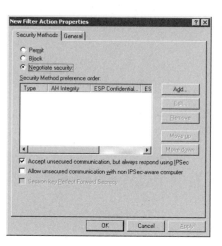

Thus far, I've said that IPSec offers four possible actions, but you see only three here—Permit, Block, and Negotiate Security. That's because Negotiate Security includes signing and encryption. You can see the check box that tells your system to accept nonsecured information, but leave it unchecked: We want to be sure that this communication is either secured, or we don't want to do it at all. To specify the encryption, ensure that the radio button Negotiate Security is chosen, and then click Add to see a dialog box like the one in Figure 6.72.

Click High (ESP) and OK to choose encryption. As you can see, you could choose signing-only by clicking Medium (AH). Click OK to clear the dialog box and return to New Filter Action Properties. Click the General tab and give the filter a name, such as "Require encryption." Click OK to return to the Manage IP Filter Lists and Filter Actions dialog box, and then click Close to close that dialog box.

Building an IPSec Rule   Now let's assemble the filter and action into a rule. In Local Security Policy, again right-click the object labeled IP Security Policies on Local Machine and choose Create IP Security Policy. That will start a wizard; click Next and it will prompt you for a name and description of the rule. Name it **Secure comms to 206.20.20.10** and click Next.

Next, the IPSec Policy Wizard will ask if you want to include the "default response rule." Uncheck the check box—skip the default response rule—and click Next, then Finish. You'll see a dialog box like Figure 6.73.

FIGURE 6.72

Choosing signing or encryption

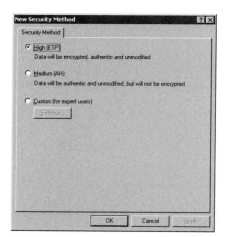

FIGURE 6.73

Showing rules in the policy

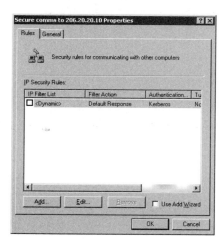

Make sure that the Use Add Wizard check box is unchecked, and click Add to show a dialog box like you see in Figure 6.74.

FIGURE 6.74

Defining a rule

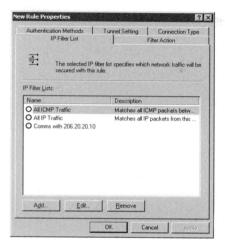

You've done most of the hard work; now just stitch a filter to an action, choose an authentication method, name the rule, and you'll be done. Choose the filter by clicking its radio button—Comms with 206.20.20.10 in my example—and click the Filter Action tab to reveal the possible actions. Click the radio button next to your desired action—I called mine "require encryption"—and click the tab labeled Authentication Methods. You'll see a dialog box like the one in Figure 6.75.

FIGURE 6.75

Authentication methods

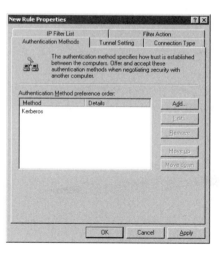

Click Add to choose the authentication method, and you'll see the dialog box in Figure 6.76.

FIGURE 6.76

Choosing an authentication method

Here you can see the three options for authentication—Kerberos, certificate, or a preshared key. If both machines were in the same Active Directory domain, then the easiest thing to do would be the default—Kerberos, which I've suggested should be labeled "Active Directory" instead. But for simplicity's sake, I'll use a preshared key. So I click the Use This String... option and type in a phrase. I used the extremely-hard-to-guess phrase, "this is a secret." Then I click OK twice and then Close, and I'll be back in Local Security Settings. In the right pane, I see the possible IPSec policies, and the one that I just created will be there. I right-click that policy and choose Assign.

Now I'm done on the 199.10.10.3 side. Next, I'd go to the 206.20.20.10 machine and create an identical policy, *except* that I'd replace the references to 206.20.20.10 with 199.10.10.3. But how could you check that you've actually got encryption working between the two systems? With a program called Ipsecmon—just click Start/Run and type **ipsecmon** and click OK. Ipsecmon isn't very pretty, but it *will* identify systems that you are communicating with via IPSec and what level of security you are using.

USING IPSEC TO PROTECT SYSTEMS THROUGH PACKET FILTERING

Here's another neat thing that you can do with IPSec—filter packets. It's not a common use of IPSec, but it works pretty well.

One way to at least partially secure a system is to shut down unused ports, to tell your system, "Don't accept any traffic except on the following ports." For example, suppose you've got a Windows 2000 system that is solely a Web server; that's all that it does. You *could* decide to tell that system, "only accept incoming traffic on TCP ports 80 and 443," as TCP port 80 is the port that, by default, Web browsers will use to access a Web site. Point your browser to www.acme.com and your browser will ask the machine at www.acme.com, "Please accept this request at your port 80." Your Web server uses port 443 for *secured* communications—SSL. In this section, I want to show you how to use IPSec to disable every port on your system except 80 and 443. But before I do, two notes on this process.

First, you probably know that you can do this far more simply via the built-in filtering ability of TCP/IP. If not, take a look at the Advanced properties of your IP stack—right-click My Network Places, choose Properties, and you'll see an icon for your network adapter. Right-click *that*, and choose Properties, and you'll see a properties sheet that includes objects for, among other things, an object called Internet Protocol (TCP/IP). Left-click that object, then click the Properties button, and you'll get a properties page on your TCP/IP stack. In that page, click Advanced and then Options. The "Options" page will probably offer two items—IP Security and TCP/IP Filtering. Click on TCP/IP Filtering and then the Properties button.

You'll see a dialog box that allows you to tell your system, "Only accept the following ports." So, with a few clicks, you could tell your system to only accept traffic on TCP ports 80 and 443— believe me, far fewer clicks than will be required with IPSec. So why do it this way? For three reasons: First because it's a nice, easy example of working with IPSec. And second, and more importantly, you wouldn't want to have to walk around to every system and do all of that clicking; you issue IPSec commands to your system via group policies, either local policies or domain-based policies. It's *very* convenient to be able to describe a port filter once in the form of an IPSec policy, then use group policies to apply that filter to dozens of machines with just a few clicks in the Active Directory. And, finally, although the built-in TCP/IP filtering is nice, it only lets you shut down every port *except* a small list of ports. What if you wanted to do the reverse—allow every port *except* a few? You can't do that from TCP/IP filtering. You *can* easily do it from IPSec. When might this be useful? Consider that you'd also like to secure machines that *don't* run a Web server. As you know, Microsoft seems obsessed with installing IIS on just about every machine, so you may have a lot of Web servers running that you never knew about. But so many viruses attack Web servers, so you *really* want to protect these "accidental" Web servers. One way might be to create a policy that is the reverse of what I'm doing here—create an IPSec policy that passes everything *except* ports 80 and 443. Then apply that policy to every machine *except* the Web servers.

My second caveat is to note that simply filtering ports 80 and 443 on a Web server is a very simple approach to security, and probably *too* simple. The built-in SMTP server that runs on every IIS box by default wouldn't work, as SMTP needs port 25. And, worse, any remote access tool, such as Telnet or Terminal Services, wouldn't work either, as they employ ports other than 80 and 443. You would then have to do all of you Web server administration by sitting down at the Web server and logging in locally. If you were *really* going to secure your system, you'd want to do a bit more research to discover which ports your particular installation uses.

The Rules

As before, we'll first create the filter and the action, and then assemble it into a rule. (I'll spare you the dialog box screen shots; the process is the same as in the earlier example. I'll just focus on what you'll need to know to make this work.) This time, we'll need more than one rule—four, actually. If they don't make sense upon an initial reading, don't worry—I'm about to explain them. In IPSec-ese, then, you'd state the objective "block all traffic except the traffic coming in on TCP ports 80 and 443" with four rules:

- If network traffic of any kind or any port *enters* this computer from any other computer, block it.

- If network traffic of any kind or any port *originates* at this computer and is addressed to go to go to any computer on the Internet, let it pass.

- If TCP traffic on port 80 enters this computer from any other computer, let it pass.

- If TCP traffic on port 443 enters this computer from any other computer, let it pass.

Upon first reading those four bullet points, you're likely to say, "Wait…the first rule says to block *all* traffic of any kind, and the third one says to allow TCP port 80 traffic. Doesn't that conflict?" It looks that way, but it's the only way that we can give IPSec an even mildly complicated filtering rule. When IPSec comes across a conflict in rules, it takes the more specific of the conflicting rules. Let's stress that.

NOTE *The rule about conflicting IPSec rules is this: The specific rule beats the more generic rule.*

So, for example, suppose traffic comes in on TCP port 80. Rule One says, "It's incoming data; ignore it." Rule Three says, "It's incoming data *on port 80*; keep it." Rule Three is more specific, so it wins.
Let's see how to build the policy's four rules.

Building Rule One

Rule One says, "Block all incoming traffic." Let's break that down into its filter and its action. As you've seen, you create a filter by specifying this:

 ◆ Source address: the address that the potentially filtered data comes from

 ◆ Destination address: the address that the potentially filtered data is going to

 ◆ Port and protocol: the protocol and port that the data travels to or from

 ◆ Mirroring: Whether or not to automatically mirror the filter

A filter that wants to describe "all incoming traffic" would have these values:

 ◆ Source address: any IP address

 ◆ Destination address: my IP address

 ◆ Port and protocol: any

 ◆ Mirroring: no

Notice that you do *not* want mirroring. That's because I want to block all incoming traffic and permit all outgoing traffic. If I wanted to do that same thing to both incoming and outgoing traffic, then I'd mirror the rule. As all four rules are *asymmetric*, we won't mirror any of them.
Rule One's action is to block traffic, so create a block action. Stitch the "all incoming traffic" filter with the "block" action, and you've got Rule One.
But what about authentication? Recall that blocking and permitting don't modify the data, they just pass it through or discard it, so they don't need any password. But IPSec wants to see authentication, so pick any type that you like—it won't matter. (Although if you pick Kerberos on a system that is not a member of an Active Directory domain, then the GUI will offer a dire-sounding dialog box that basically says, "Are you sure?" Just tell it that yes, you're sure.)

Building Rule Two

The second rule permits all outgoing traffic. The filter is very much like the last one, although source and destination are reversed:

 ◆ Source: my IP address

- Destination: any IP address

- Ports and protocols: any

- Mirroring: no

For an action, choose the already-built Permit one. Assemble the rule and, again, choose any authentication method that you like.

Building Rules Three and Four

Next, we'll build the rules that pass traffic on ports 80 and 443. The filter is a trifle more complicated; here's the criteria for the port 80 one:

- Source address: any IP address

- Destination address: my IP address

- Ports and protocol: port 80 on TCP

- Mirrored: no

When building the filter, first set the source and destination addresses, and then uncheck the Mirror check box. Then click the Protocol tab to see something like Figure 6.77.

FIGURE 6.77

Configuring a protocol filter

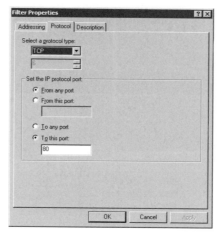

In the Protocol tab, first choose TCP under Select a Protocol Type, and then click the radio button To This Port and fill in **80**.

For the action, choose the Permit action. Again, do anything that you like for Authentication, as it does not matter. Do the same thing for Rule Four, except specify port **443** instead of port 80.

Once you've got your policy assembled, assign it and then try it out. You won't be able to ping your Web server, nor will you be able to access its SMTP server, nor an FTP server if you have one running on that system. But you *will* be able to access its Web pages, both secured and unsecured.

ONE A FEW FINAL THOUGHTS ABOUT IPSEC

I haven't covered all of IPSec here, as IPSec could probably fill a book—I've just tried to hit the high points. But I don't want to leave without mentioning a few things.

First, IPSec will *not* work in conjunction with Network Address Translation. If your workstation sat behind a NAT router, at, say, 192.168.23.3, and you wanted to create a secure IPSec connection with a server on the public Internet, then you would not be able to use IPSec.

Second, I've been talking about IPSec as a one-to-one way for systems to communicate. But IPSec also has a feature called *tunneling* whereby most of your systems needn't be IPSec aware at all. Instead, they'd funnel all of their communications through a single IPSec-aware computer that is prepared to "relay" their communications to another IPSec-aware computer on a remote site. Thus, if you had 100 machines at one location and 100 machines at another location, and you wanted machines at each location to be able to talk to all of the machines on the other location, but you wanted security while the data traveled from one location to another, then you could just designate one machine at each location as a sort of "firewall" box. Those boxes would tunnel IP traffic from one site to another.

Third, IPSec is a standard, not just a Microsoft functionality. So in theory you should be able to use Microsoft's IPSec to communicate with other vendor's tools. But test that before you start to rely upon it—I've heard that many non-Microsoft implementations can run into trouble trying to talk with IPSec-enabled Windows boxes.

Fourth, IPSec first appeared with Windows 2000. Earlier versions of the operating system—and lamer ones, like Windows Me—cannot do IPSec communications.

Well, by now, you're on an intranet in the traditional way. Microsoft adds two possible options to this setup: the Dynamic Host Configuration Protocol (DHCP) and the Windows Internet Name Service (WINS). We'll meet these two, as well as the essential third (Domain Name System, DNS) and a few other services, in the next chapter.

Chapter 7

Building a Windows 2000 TCP/IP Infrastructure: DHCP, WINS, and DNS

WHETHER YOU'RE HOOKING UP a two-computer intranet in your house to share an Internet connection or weaving a world-spanning Internet, you've got to solve two basic problems. First, every system on the network needs a unique IP address and requires configuration—it needs to know the address of its default router, what its domain name is, where the nearest DNS server is, and the like. And second, it needs help finding its way around the network: How do I send mail to Jane over at Acme Industries? How do I connect to the server that will let me buy books or shoes online? Or, more mundanely, how do I find a server that will log me in?

TCP/IP-based Windows 2000 systems use three technologies to accomplish IP configuration and name management: the Dynamic Host Configuration Protocol (DHCP), the Domain Name System (DNS), and the Windows Internet Name Service (WINS). Of the three, WINS is something of a relic, a technology that in *theory* you can forgo altogether, but in practice you can only do it if your network is both purely Windows 2000–based (all machines run Windows 2000) and if your network-aware applications are built for Windows 2000 rather than NT 4 or earlier operating systems. Furthermore, this chapter is *essential* because if you don't do a great job designing your DNS architecture, then Active Directory will run terribly; in many ways, DNS is the foundation of Active Directory.

DHCP: Automatic TCP/IP Configuration

In Chapter 6, you learned how to set up IP on a Windows 2000 system. Ah, but now ask yourself, "Do I really want to walk around to 3000 workstations and do this by hand?" Auuugghhhh! Oops, sorry, what I really meant was, "Of course not." Who wants to have to remember which IP address you gave to *that* machine so you don't put the address on *this* machine? Or how'd you like to get a phone call every time some visiting dignitary needs an IP address for his laptop? No thanks. DHCP will greatly simplify the task, so let's see how to set it up.

WARNING   By the way, this discussion assumes you've already read Chapter 6; don't think that if you decided from the start to go with DHCP then you could jump in here without reading the preceding chapter.

Simplifying TCP/IP Administration: BootP

"I have a little list/it never can be missed." Well, OK, that's not exactly what Pooh-Bah sings in *Mikado*, but it fits here. You see, back when I first put TCP/IP on my company's computers, in 1993, I had to keep this list of PCs and IP addresses in a notebook. It was basically a kind of master directory of which IP addresses had been used so far.

Obviously, I had to consult it whenever I put TCP/IP on each new computer. Obvious, sure, but what's unfortunate is that I never seemed to have the notebook with me when I needed it. So I started keeping this list of computers and IP addresses on one of my servers, in a kind of common HOSTS file. It served two purposes: First, it told me what IP addresses were already used, and second, it gave me a HOSTS file to copy to the local computer's hard disk.

But, I recall thinking, this is silly. Keeping track of IP addresses and the machines using them is a rote, mechanical job—you know, the kind of job computers are good at.

Unknown to me, the Internet world apparently had a similar feeling and so invented a TCP/IP protocol called BootP, which became DHCP, as you will see. With BootP, a network administrator would first collect a list of MAC addresses for each LAN card. I've already mentioned the 48-bit identifiers on each network card, which are good examples of MAC addresses.

Next, the administrator would assign an IP address to each MAC address. A server on the company's intranet would then hold this table of MAC address/IP address pairs. Then, when a BootP-enabled workstation would start up for the day, it would broadcast a request for an IP address. The BootP server would recognize the MAC address from the broadcaster and would supply the IP address to the workstation.

This was a great improvement over the static IP addressing system that I've described so far. Administrators didn't have to physically travel to each workstation to give it its own IP address; they needed only to modify a file on the BootP server when a new machine arrived or if it was necessary to change IP addresses for a particular set of machines.

Another great benefit of BootP is that it provides protection from the "helpful user." Suppose you have user Tom, who sits next to user Dick. Dick's machine isn't accessing the network correctly, so helpful user Tom says, "Well, *I'm* getting on the Net fine, so let's just copy all of this confusing network stuff from my machine to yours." The result was that both machines ended up with identical configurations—including identical IP addresses, so now neither Tom *nor* Dick can access the network without errors! In contrast, if Tom's machine is only set up to go get its IP address from its local BootP server, then setting up Dick's machine identically will cause no harm, as it will just tell Dick's machine to get *its* address from the BootP server. Dick will get a different address (provided that the network administrator has typed in an IP address for Dick's MAC address), and all will be well.

DHCP: BootP Plus

BootP's ability to hand out IP addresses from a central location is terrific, but it's not dynamic. The network administrator must know beforehand all the MAC addresses of the Ethernet cards on the network. This isn't *impossible* information to obtain, but it's a bit of a pain (usually typing **ipconfig /all** from a command line yields the data). Furthermore, there's no provision for handing out temporary IP addresses, such as an IP address for a laptop used by a visiting executive. (I suppose you could keep a store of PCMCIA Ethernet cards whose MAC addresses had been preinstalled into the BootP database, but even so, it's getting to be some real work.)

DHCP improves upon BootP in that you just give it a range of IP addresses that it's allowed to hand out, and it just gives them out first come, first served to whatever computers request them. If, on the other hand, you want DHCP to maintain full BootP-like behavior, then you can; it's possible with DHCP to preassign IP addresses to particular MAC addresses (it's called *DHCP reservation*), as with BootP.

With DHCP, you only have to hardwire the IP addresses of a few machines, such as your BootP/DHCP server and your default gateway.

WARNING *Both DHCP and BootP use UDP ports 67 and 68, so you won't be able to install both a BootP server and a DHCP server on the same computer. Now, Microsoft does not supply a BootP server; this note would mostly be relevant only if you tried to install a third-party BootP server. But Windows 2000/NT also allows you to make a computer a BootP forwarding agent. If you enable that software on a DHCP server, the server stops giving out IP addresses.*

Let's see how to get a DHCP server up on your network so the IP addresses will start getting handed out, and then we'll take a look at how DHCP works.

Say No to Static IP: Use DHCP Everywhere!

In a minute, I'll get into the nitty-gritty of setting up DHCP servers and handing out IP addresses. But before I do, let's address a big, overall network configuration question: Which machines should have static IP addresses, and which machines should get their addresses from DHCP servers?

In general, the answer is that the only machines that should have static IP addresses should be your WINS servers, DNS servers, and DHCP servers. In actual fact, you'll probably put the WINS, DNS, and DHCP server functions on the same machines.

"But wait!" I hear you cry, "Are you suggesting that I let my domain controllers, mail servers, Web servers, and the like all have floating, random IP addresses assigned by DHCP willy-nilly?" No, not at all. Recall that you can assign a particular IP address to a particular MAC address using a DHCP reservation. My suggestion, then, is that you sit down and figure out which machines need fixed IP addresses, get the MAC addresses of the NICs in those machines, and then create reservations in DHCP for those machines. (You'll see how a bit later.)

Installing and Configuring DHCP Servers

DHCP servers are the machines that provide IP addresses to machines that request access to the LAN. DHCP only works if the TCP/IP software on the workstations is *built* to work with DHCP—if the TCP/IP software includes a *DHCP client*. Microsoft offers TCP/IP software with DHCP clients for Windows for Workgroups and DOS. NT 3.5, 3.51, and 4 workstations as well as Windows 95 and 98 workstations are already DHCP-aware. Of course, Windows 2000 Professional machines also include DHCP clients.

INSTALLING THE DHCP SERVICE

To get ready for DHCP configuration:

- ◆ Have an IP address ready for your DHCP server—this is one computer on your network that *must* have a hardwired ("static") IP address.

- ◆ Know which IP addresses are free to assign. You use these available IP addresses to create a pool of IP addresses.

You install the software to make your server a DHCP server in the same way that you install most other network services, from the Add/Remove Windows Components applet of the Control Panel. Step-by-step, it looks like this:

1. Open the Control Panel (Start/Settings/Control Panel).

2. Open Add/Remove Programs.

3. Click Add/Remove Windows Components and wait a bit while the Windows Components Wizard starts up. (Why we needed a wizard when a dialog box would do, particularly when a dialog box would appear 15 seconds more quickly than the wizard, is a mystery. But, then, I guess all of the wizards I've ever read about were mysterious to me.)

4. Click Next to bring up the list of Windows components.

5. Click Networking Services and then the Details button.

6. Click the check box next to Dynamic Host Configuration Protocol (DHCP).

7. Click OK to return to Windows Components.

8. Click Next to install the service. The system will say that it is "Configuring Components" for a while, probably a few minutes. A couple of rounds of FreeCell, and the Completing the Windows Components Wizard screen appears.

9. Click Finish to end the wizard.

10. Click Close to close Add/Remove Windows Components.

And best of all, you needn't reboot afterward. You control DHCP with the DHCP snap-in, which you'll find in Administrative Tools: Start/Programs/Administrative Tools/DHCP. Start it up, and the opening screen looks like most MMC snap-ins, with the left and right panes. This particular one lists your server, with a plus sign next to it. Click the plus sign and you'll see a screen like Figure 7.1.

Notice that this snap-in lists the server in the left pane. That's because you can control as many DHCP servers as you like from this program. All you need do to add a DHCP server to the list of servers that you control is to just select Action/Add Server.

FIGURE 7.1

DHCP manager
opening screen

AUTHORIZING DHCP SERVERS (FOR ACTIVE DIRECTORY USERS)

Now, before we go any further, I have to add a note here about DHCP and Active Directory because if you're running AD, then you won't be able to make your DHCP server work without a little adjustment—hence the note *now* rather than in the next chapter. If you're not running AD, then feel free to skip this section, but just remember that you saw this—or it'll come bite you *later*, when you've gotten your AD up and running.

Look at the small icon that sort of looks like a tower computer in Figure 7.1. There's a small circular blob next to it. It's sort of small, so you may not be able to see it in the screen shot, but to the left of "dun.win2ktest.com [206.246.253.111]" is a small arrow that points downward—in color, it's red. That arrow represents a nice touch on Microsoft's part.

You see, under NT 4, 3.51, and 3.5, anyone with an NT Server installation CD could set up NT Server on a computer and make herself an administrator of that server. With administrative powers, she could then set up a DHCP server. Now, the job of a DHCP server, recall, is to hand out IP addresses to computers who want to be part of the network. The problem arises when the administrator of this new server decides just for fun to offer a bunch of meaningless IP addresses, a range of addresses that your firm doesn't actually own. The result? Well, the next time a machine in the company needs an IP address, it asks any server within earshot for an IP address. The server with the meaningless addresses responds, as do the valid servers—but the server with the bogus addresses is likely to respond more quickly than the valid servers (it doesn't have anything else to do) and so many client PCs will end up with IP addresses from the server with the bogus addresses. Those addresses won't route and so those people won't be able to get anything done on the network.

Why would someone set up a server with bogus addresses? Usually it's not for a malicious reason. Rather, it's more common that someone's just trying to learn DHCP and sets up a server to play around with, not realizing "test" DHCP servers are indistinguishable from "real" DHCP servers to the client machines. Such a DHCP server is called a *rogue* DHCP server.

Windows 2000 solved the problem of rogue DHCP servers by disabling new DHCP servers until a domain administrator "authorizes" them in the Active Directory. With Windows 2000, anyone can set up a DHCP server, but the server won't start handing out addresses until authorized. This isn't foolproof, as only machines that are members of Active Directory–based domains seek to be authorized. Someone who wanted to maliciously set up a rogue DHCP server could simply install a copy of Windows 2000 Server and not join it to the domain, *then* set up a DHCP server—but, again, that's not the most common problem.

You authorize a server with the DHCP snap-in, and, again, you've got to be logged in as a domain administrator to do this. From the DHCP snap-in, click the server and then select Action/Authorize, and you'll see a dialog box like the one in Figure 7.2.

You can see that there are no servers authorized yet, so let's authorize this one. Click Authorize and you'll see the dialog box in Figure 7.3.

FIGURE 7.2

List of authorized
DHCP servers

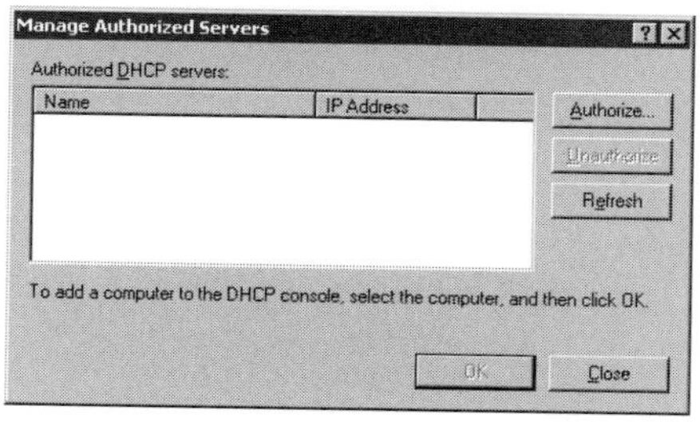

FIGURE 7.3

Authorizing a new
DHCP server

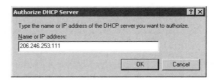

I've filled in the IP address of this server. Click OK, and you'll be asked to confirm that you do indeed want to add this server. Click the Yes button, and you'll return to the list of authorized servers. Click Close to close that dialog box and you'll see the DHCP snap-in looking as in Figure 7.1, save that the red down-pointing arrow is now a green up-pointing arrow.

NOTE   *You should be able to click the server and then press F5 to refresh the display to see the green arrow. In my experience, however, you usually have to close the DHCP manager and then reopen it to see the green arrow appear. (Once I not only had to close and reopen it, I also had to press F5. Clearly the DHCP manager isn't one of those chatty kinds of entities that constantly yammer on about their current condition—no, this app is downright reticent about its mood.)*

Now you can offer IP addresses with this server.

If you *don't* have an Active Directory running, then you needn't authorize the server, as clearly there wouldn't be anything to authorize it *with*. But here's an interesting side effect of how Windows 2000 authorizes DHCP servers. (Again, I know that some of you don't even *have* an Active Directory yet, but pay attention to this, or it'll bite you when you first set up your AD.)

If you are running a DHCP server on a network without an Active Directory, and all of a sudden bring up an AD, then the DHCP server will sense that, *even if it's not part of the AD domain*. It will then shut itself down. This *always* trips me up when I'm doing a class and I'm demonstrating Active Directory—first I get the DHCP and DNS servers up and running, then I create the AD, but then forget to authorize the already-running DHCP server that conveniently sniffs out the Active Directory and consequently disables itself. Anyway, just thought I'd mention it—now let's get back to the whys and wherefores of DHCP setup.

Creating a Range of Addresses: DHCP "Scopes"

That DHCP snap-in isn't really much to look at, is it? Well, it won't be, as there are no scopes set up yet. Scopes? What's a scope?

CREATING THE SCOPE

For DHCP to give out IP addresses, it must know the range of IP addresses that it can give out. Microsoft calls a range of IP addresses, and the descriptive information associated with them, a *scope*. To create a scope, right-click the server's icon and choose New Scope, which starts the New Scope Wizard. Click Next from its opening screen and you'll see a screen like the one in Figure 7.4.

In this screen, you simply identify the scope, giving it a name and a comment. In my experience, I've never really figured out why there's a name *and* a comment, as the name has no real use; it could well *be* a comment, in effect. Fill in appropriate values for your network, and click Next to see a screen like Figure 7.5.

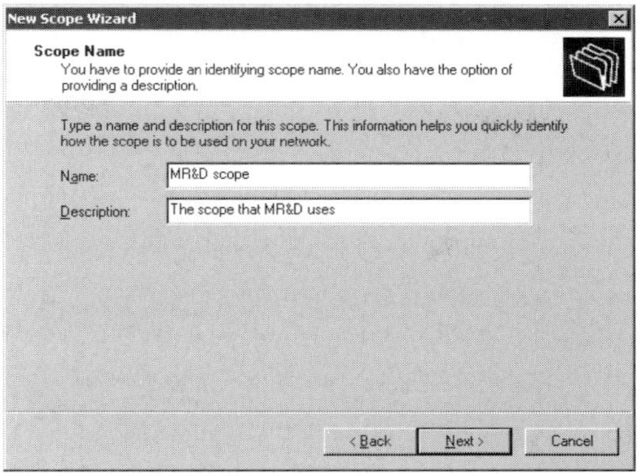

FIGURE 7.4

Naming the scope

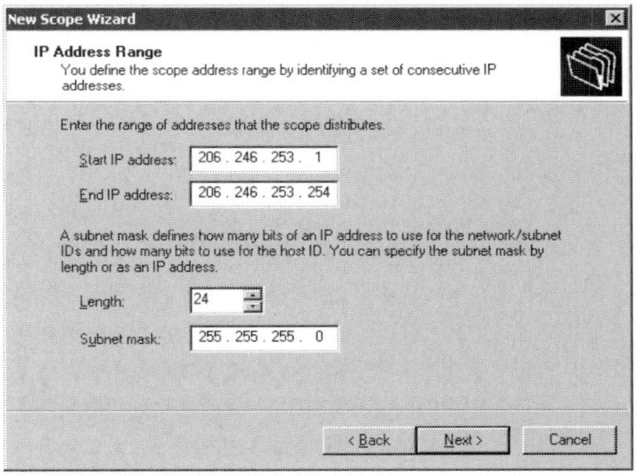

FIGURE 7.5

Defining the IP address range

SPECIFYING IP ADDRESS RANGE

A scope is simply a range of IP addresses—a pool from which they can be drawn. In the example in Figure 7.5, I've created a scope that ranges from 206.246.253.1 through 206.246.253.254—in other words, I'm going to use DHCP to manage the entirety of my class C network.

NOTE   I don't want to get too sidetracked on the issue of scopes just now (we'll cover multiscope considerations later), but let me mention why you'd have more than one scope on a DHCP server. You can assign a scope to each subnet serviced by your DHCP servers—and, yes, it is possible for one DHCP server to handle multiple subnets. In contrast, however, a DHCP server won't let you create more than one scope in the same subnet. I will, however, show you how to get more than one server to act as a DHCP server (for the sake of fault tolerance) in a minute.

I put DHCP in charge of giving out *all* of my Internet addresses, but clearly that makes no sense, as I must have at least *one* static IP address around—the one on my DHCP server. So I need to tell the DHCP server not to give *that* one away, but how to do it? Click Next twice—the wizard seems to need two clicks on the Next button here—to see the next screen, where I'll tell the server what addresses to avoid, as in Figure 7.6.

FIGURE 7.6

Excluding address ranges

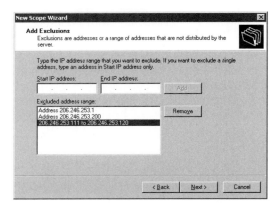

As you see, I've excluded several addresses: The .1 address is a dedicated LAN/WAN router, the .200 machine has a static address, and while working on this book I temporarily set aside the .111 through .120 addresses for static IP. Notice that you can specify one address by itself; you don't *have* to specify starting and ending addresses in a one-address range.

SPECIFYING MORE RANGES: SUPERSCOPES

As you read in Chapter 6, in general there's a one-to-one relationship between physical network segments and subnets. IP was designed to let systems that could directly "shout" at each other do that, communicating directly rather than burdening routers.

Sometimes, however, you'll see two separate subnets on a single segment. That's often because a single network can't accommodate all of the segment's machines. For example, if you started your enterprise with 180 hosts and acquired a slash 24 network, you'd have enough addresses for 254 devices, presuming that you didn't subnet. But what about when your firm grows to need 300 machines? You might go out to your ISP and get another slash 24, another 254 addresses.

Now you've got two networks. You *could* break your network up into two segments and apply one set of network addresses to each segment. But you might not want to: Suppose your one segment can support all of your machines and you can't see the point in messing around with more routers— what then?

You create a *superscope*. The idea with a superscope is that it contains more than one range of IP addresses—more than one scope—but applies them to a single segment. You can do it simply—just define two separate scopes on a DHCP server, then right-click the server, choose New Superscope, and you'll have the superscope. You can then add scopes to the superscope as you like; don't forget that you might have to change the subnet mask to reflect the larger range of addresses.

But what about the mechanics of a superscope? When you put a new machine on this subnet and it broadcasts to find a DHCP server and get an IP address, will it get an IP address from the first scope or the second? The answer is that it doesn't matter. If you're just shoehorning two IP subnets onto the same physical segment simply because you're out of IP addresses on an existing subnet, then it doesn't matter whether a workstation gets an IP address from the first range of IP addresses or the second range of IP addresses, as all of the enterprise's routers know how to find either range.

Once in a while, however, you have two ranges of IP addresses on the same physical network for a reason—perhaps one range is composed of IANA- or ISP-assigned IP addresses and the other is composed of nonroutable addresses. You probably have good reasons, then, to put some computers on the routable addresses and some on the nonroutable addresses. But how to get DHCP to help there? After all, both the routable and nonroutable ranges are in the same shouting radius, so to speak. When a workstation asks DHCP for an address, how would DHCP know whether to give that workstation a routable or nonroutable address?

The answer is that DHCP can't—there's no magic here. There would have to be some kind of setting on the client that the client could use to give DHCP a clue about what network it wanted to be a member of, the routable or nonroutable. What you must do in a situation like that is decide which machines go in the routable network and which go in the nonroutable network and then enter their MAC addresses by hand into DHCP with *reservations* (which we'll cover later), much as network administrators must when using BootP instead of DHCP.

SETTING LEASE DURATION

Returning to the wizard, click Next and you see a screen like Figure 7.7.

FIGURE 7.7

Set lease duration.

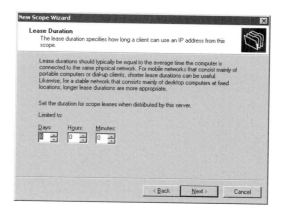

As you'll read in a few pages, when I explain the internals of DHCP, the DHCP server doesn't give the client PC an IP address to use forever. The client PC only gets the IP address for a specific period of time called a *lease*, and by the time the lease period's up, the client must either lease it or another address from a DHCP server, or the client must stop using IP altogether, immediately. But how long should that lease be? Although that was something of an issue when DHCP first appeared in NT 3.5, it doesn't matter all that much what you set it for now, so long as you set it for longer than a few days; the default of eight days is probably good. We'll talk more about lease durations when we discuss DHCP internals later. Click Next to move to Figure 7.8.

FIGURE 7.8

Configure DHCP options.

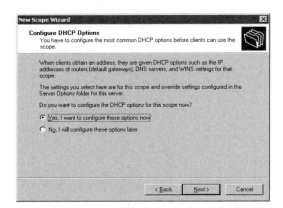

SETTING CLIENT OPTIONS

Remember all of those options in the Advanced tab for TCP/IP Properties when you configured static IP addresses in the preceding chapter? Well, you needn't travel around to the workstations and set them, as DHCP lets you configure those things right from the server. DHCP can provide default values for a whole host of TCP/IP parameters, including these basic items:

◆ Default gateway

◆ Domain name

◆ DNS server

◆ WINS server

Notice I said *default*. You can override any of these options at the workstation. For example, if you said that by default everyone's DNS server was 10.0.100.1 but wanted one particular PC to instead use the DNS server at 10.200.200.10, then you could just walk over to the PC and use the Advanced button in the TCP/IP properties page (see Chapter 6 if you don't recall how to find that) to enter a DNS name. Even though the DHCP server would offer a DNS server address of 10.0.100.1 to the PC, the PC's DHCP client software would see that the PC had been configured to use 10.200.200.10 instead and would use that address rather than 10.0.100.1. Any other DHCP-supplied options, however, wouldn't be ignored. The general rule is, then, that anything configured on the client overrides anything that DHCP suggests.

Click Next to see the first client option, shown in Figure 7.9.

You may recall that in the last chapter I said that when configuring TCP/IP on a Windows 2000 machine, the "big four" characteristics, so to speak, are IP address, subnet mask, IP address of the default gateway, and address or addresses of local DNS server(s). By its nature, any DHCP lease gives the first two; this is the third.

Although you *can* enter any number of gateways, there's no point in entering more than one, as I've never found a situation wherein Microsoft's IP could use a second, third, or fourth possible gateway upon discovering that the first gateway is down. I've only specified one gateway, as you see in Figure 7.9. Click Next to see the next option screen, as in Figure 7.10.

FIGURE 7.9

Set default gateway.

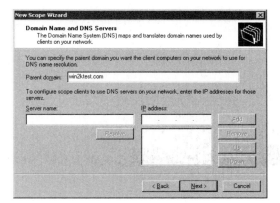

In this wizard screen, you tell the DHCP server that whenever it leases a client PC an IP address from this scope, it should also set that client PC's DNS domain name to some value—win2ktest.com, in this case—and to tell the client PC that it can find DNS servers at some address. I've chosen *not* to specify DNS servers, however, because *all* of the scopes in my enterprise share two DNS servers, and I don't want to have to reenter these DNS servers for every scope. As you'll see in a few pages, I can instead just tell this server, "Give this particular DNS server to *all* scopes." Click Next to see the next screen, as in Figure 7.11.

Most of us will still have the necessary evil of WINS servers; here's where you tell the client where to find your enterprise's WINS servers.

FIGURE 7.11

Set WINS server(s).

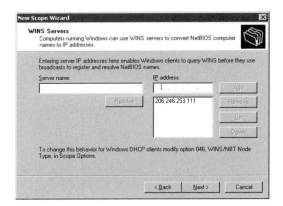

ACTIVATING THE SCOPE

Click Next and you can get the scope started, as you see in Figure 7.12.

FIGURE 7.12

Activate the scope.

    That's all for the basic scope options, so the wizard's done. On the way out, it asks if you're ready for this server to start handing out leases on IP addresses. Click Yes and Next, and the wizard will finish, starting the scope in the process. The DHCP snap-in then looks like Figure 7.13.

    Taking a minute and looking at the hierarchy in Figure 7.13 underscores a few things about how DHCP works. The snap-in enables you to control any number of DHCP servers from a central location, although you see only one in this example screen, the machine at 206.246.253.111. Each server can have several subnets that it serves, with one range of IP addresses for each subnet. The ranges are called scopes, and again this example machine only shows one scope, but could host many—I've seen one large corporate DHCP server that hosts 1200 scopes! Within the scope there are several pieces of information: the range of addresses (Address Pool), the list of addresses that this server has given out (Address Leases), addresses that we've preassigned to particular systems (Reservations, which we'll cover a bit later), and particular TCP/IP settings that the DHCP server should give to any clients (Scope Options). Notice that the options include something we didn't set—WINS/NBT Node Type. That's DHCP-ese for the fact that the client PC will be set up to use a WINS server—in other words—that the client will be set up as something called a *hybrid node*, which I'll cover later in this chapter in the WINS section.

FIGURE 7.13

DHCP snap-in with activated scope

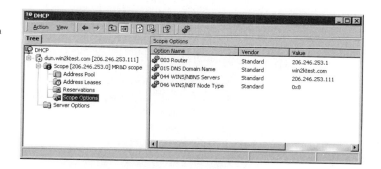

SETTING OPTIONS FOR ALL SCOPES

Notice the folder lower in the interface labeled `Server Options`. The server options are useful when you're putting more than one scope on a server. It could be that if you have three different subnets and a couple hundred machines, you've only got two DNS servers, and those machines serve your entire enterprise. When configuring those scopes, it would be a pain to have to retype in those DNS servers—the same two DNS servers—for all three scopes. `Server Options` solves that problem by allowing you to set options for *all* of a given server's scopes in one operation. Just right-click the `Server Options` folder and choose Configure Options to see a dialog box like the one in Figure 7.14.

FIGURE 7.14

Server Options dialog box

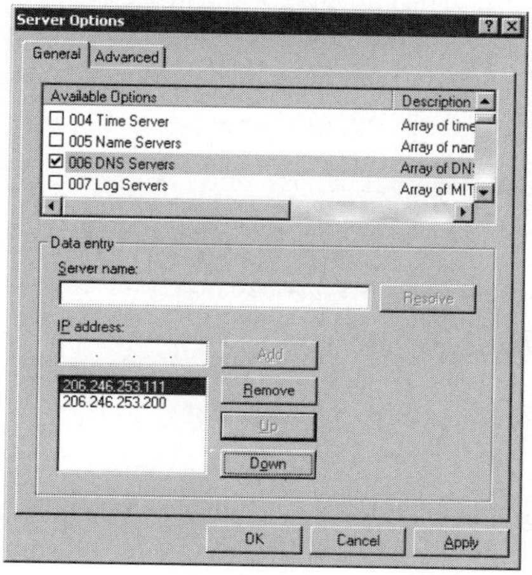

Here I've clicked DNS, and you can see that it allows me to enter DNS server addresses, as the wizard did. A bit of scrolling down shows that there are a *lot* of potential DHCP options. But, despite the fact that there seem to be bushels of sadly unused parameters mutely begging to be used, *don't.* Even though they exist, the Microsoft DHCP *client*—the part of Windows, DOS, Windows 95/98, NT, and Windows 2000 that knows how to get IP addresses from a DHCP server—does not know how to use any options save the ones I just mentioned. Microsoft included the other things just to remain compatible with BootP.

FORCING A PARTICULAR IP ADDRESS ON A CLIENT: DHCP RESERVATIONS

Sometimes, BootP doesn't seem like a bad idea. There are times that you'd like to be able to say, *this* computer gets *that* IP address. Fortunately, it's easy to accomplish that with DHCP reservations.

Look at the DHCP snap-in and you'll see a folder labeled `Reservations`. Right-click that folder and choose New Reservation. You'll see a dialog box like the one in Figure 7.15.

Here, you see that I'm assigning the .115 address to a machine with a particular MAC address.

FIGURE 7.15

Reserving an IP address

So far, it sounds like DHCP pretty much hasn't changed since NT 4, and in large measure that's true. But it has added superscopes and support for dynamic DNS even on systems that don't understand dynamic DNS. And there's one more neat difference. Once you've created a reservation, open the `Reservations` folder and you'll see an object representing that reservation. Right-click it and you'll see Configure Options; click that and you'll see that you can set things like DNS server, domain name, WINS server, and the like for one specific reservation! Now, that's a pretty neat new feature.

ADVANCED OPTIONS: USING AND UNDERSTANDING USER AND VENDOR CLASSES

As you've seen, you can assign different DHCP options either to all scopes (the `Server Options` folder) or to a particular scope. You've even seen that you can assign DHCP options to a particular machine's reservation! But there's another way to assign options, through *user classes* and *vendor classes*. Here's how you use them:

◆ You can make a machine a member of a user class by just telling the computer that it's a member of that class. You could have classes such as laptop or test-computers.

◆ Machines are also potentially members of vendor classes, but you can't control that—it's hardwired into their operating systems. For example, all Windows 2000 machines are automatically members of a vendor class called Microsoft and one called Microsoft Windows 2000; Windows 98 and Me computers are automatically members of vendor classes Microsoft and Microsoft Windows 98. Vendor classes determine what options are available for you to give to your DHCP client.

◆ You can use DHCP to apply a particular option to a particular system. The vendor class determines which options are available to the system—"default" includes the basic by-the-RFC stuff you've always seen, Microsoft vendor options would offer nonstandard new options that would only be relevant to a system running a Microsoft operating system—and the user class determines whether to apply that option. Thus, you could use user and vendor options to say, "If this system is a member of the IBM-laptops class (a user class), then set the Router option (which is in the DHCP Standard Options vendor)."

You can see the user and vendor class controls like so:

1. Open the DHCP snap-in (Start/Programs/Administrative Tools/DHCP).

2. Open either a scope's options or the server options by right-clicking the `Scope Options` or `Server Options` folders and choosing Configure Options.

3. Click the Advanced tab. You'll see something like Figure 7.16.

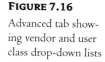

FIGURE 7.16

Advanced tab showing vendor and user class drop-down lists

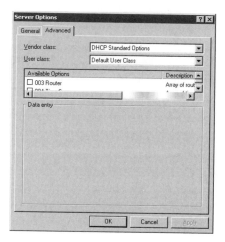

Prebuilt Vendor Classes

Click the Vendor Class drop-down list and you'll see four options: DHCP Standard Options, Microsoft Options, Microsoft Windows 2000 Options, and Microsoft Windows 98 Options. While DHCP Standard Options is enabled, notice that you get all of the usual options—router, domain name, time server, name server, and so on. But click Microsoft Options, and you'll see a few non-RFC options that Microsoft added:

◆ The Microsoft Disable NetBIOS Option tells the computer to shut down the NetBIOS-over-TCP (NetBT) interface. If you don't know what NetBT is, then don't worry—I'll cover it right after I finish DHCP. But briefly, it's a piece of software that pretty much all NT-aware software built before Windows 2000 depends upon. If you've got an NT 4 workstation logging onto a Windows 2000–based domain, then you need NetBT. Most modern networks still have enough pre-2000 stuff around that they still need NetBT, but in time—2004 or 2005, I'd guess—most of us will be able to shut NetBT off. The result, once you can do it, is a noticeably faster network. To enable this—that is, to shut off NetBT—check the box next to Microsoft Disable NetBIOS Option, which will enable the Data Entry/Long field; enter **0x2**.

◆ Check the Microsoft Release DHCP Lease on Shutdown Option and fill the Data Entry/Long field with **0x1** to enable. This tells a Windows 2000 system to release its DHCP lease upon shutdown, as the name indicates. Why is this useful? Consider this scenario: An employee works at her laptop in the office during the day, with her laptop connected to the company network via an Ethernet connection. The user shuts down the machine and takes it home. At home, she wants to check her mail, so connects her laptop to a phone line to dial in. She turns on the computer, which sees that it has an Ethernet card that has a DHCP lease. It tries to re-contact the DHCP server but fails, but that's no problem—it's got time on the lease and merrily sets up a TCP/IP stack atop an Ethernet card that's not attached to anything. The user dials up and now the computer has *two* IP stacks—one that actually goes somewhere, via the modem, and one that doesn't do anything. Some services bind to the useless Ethernet card and the user either experiences failures or slow service. One answer: Tell the user to disable the Ethernet card. Another answer: Tell the user to type **IPCONFIG /RELEASE** before shutting down the laptop at work. But the easier answer is to enable this feature—shutdowns lead to DHCP lease releases. (This would also bedevil users with Ethernet connections at home, so it's a good practice in that case also.)

◆ The third option lets you modify the default metric of DHCP-supplied gateways. I'm honestly not sure where this would be useful.

Click Microsoft Windows 2000 Options, and you'll get the same three options. Click Microsoft Windows 98 Options, and you won't see any options—apparently Microsoft has hard-coded the vendor class into 98 but didn't do much with it. Again, you cannot create new vendor classes of your own.

Prebuilt User Classes

Next, click the User Class drop-down list, and you'll see three prebuilt user classes: Default User Class, Default BOOTP Class, and Default Routing and Remote Access Class. Here's where you'll see each of the classes:

Default BOOTP Class   All of your Windows 2000 systems will be members of this class.

Default User Class   The class that a system reports if it lacks class (finds belching in public funny, blue screens just for the heck of it, that kind of thing) or, more likely, has a DHCP client that simply doesn't understand what a user class is in the first place—DHCP user classes weren't even a fully accepted RFC standard when Microsoft released Windows 2000. An NT 4.0 system, then, would end up with Default User Class.

Default Routing and Remote Access Class   If you're connected via RRAS, then you're in this class. This is potentially a pretty useful class; for example, the DHCP Help for Windows 2000 shows you how to set the lease times for dial-in users—members of the Default Routing and Remote Access Class—to smaller values than for other users; that way, folks who typically only visit a site for a day end up with a day-long rather than a week-long lease.

You can see which user classes a system belongs to (there is no way to view the vendor classes for a system) by typing **ipconfig showclassid ***; a sample run might look like the following:

```
C:\>ipconfig /showclassid *

Windows 2000 IP Configuration

DHCP Class ID for Adapter "LAN":
        DHCP ClassID Name . . . . . . . . : Default BOOTP Class
        DHCP ClassID Description  . . . . : User class for BOOTP Clients
        DHCP ClassID Name . . . . . . . . : Laptop
        DHCP ClassID Description  . . . . : Identifies laptops
```

Here, this computer is a member of two user classes—Default BOOTP Class (it's a Windows 2000 computer) and a class called "Laptop" (which I created).

User-Defined User Classes

How did I define my own user class? In two steps. First, I told the DHCP server about the new user class and, second, I told some of my workstations that they were members of the class.

You create a new user class in the DHCP snap-in. Right-click the server's icon and choose Define User Classes, and you'll get a dialog box like the one in Figure 7.17.

FIGURE 7.17

DHCP user classes

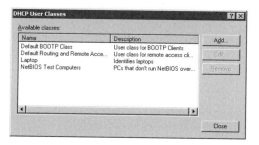

This dialog box doesn't show the Default User Class; however, your DHCP server—*every* 2000-based DHCP server, in fact—has it. Mine shows four rather than the two you'll have because I created the other two. Let's create a new user class and use it. Suppose I want all of the people in building 12 to have the domain suffix "b12.bigfirm.biz." To create the new user class, I click on Add and fill in the dialog box, as you see in Figure 7.18.

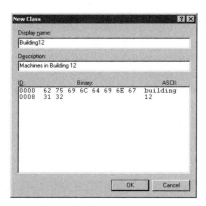

FIGURE 7.18

New user class for building 12

The only non-straightforward part of filling out the dialog box was the ID part; it's not obvious, but you've got to click the mouse in the empty area below the word *ASCII* to be able to type in the class identifier. You can't have blanks in the identifier. Click OK and Close to return to the DHCP snap-in. Now right-click Server Options again and choose Configure Options, click Advanced, and notice that under User Class, there is now a class called "building12." (Case matters—as you'll see in a minute, this won't work unless you add the client machines to a class spelled "building12" exactly—case and all.) Choose building12 under User Class. Now we want to assign a particular DNS suffix to the Building12ers, and that's in the default options, so for Vendor Class just choose DHCP Standard Options. Look for the line 015 DNS Domain Name, choose it, and in the Date Entry/String Value field, enter **b12.bigfirm.biz.** and click OK. You're ready on the server side. Don't worry about the hex on the left side; it's just an alternative way of entering the data.

Next, find a machine and make it a member of the building12 user class. Open a command line and type this:

```
ipconfig /setclassid "Local Area Connection" building12
```

Then type **ipconfig /renew** and you should get an output something like this:

```
Windows 2000 IP Configuration

Ethernet adapter LAN:

        Connection-specific DNS Suffix  . : b12.bigfirm.biz.
        IP Address. . . . . . . . . . . . : 206.246.253.135
        Subnet Mask . . . . . . . . . . . : 255.255.255.0
        Default Gateway . . . . . . . . . : 206.246.253.1
        DHCP Class ID . . . . . . . . . . : building12
```

Two notes on this:

◆ First, notice in the `ipconfig /setclassid` line where I have `"Local Area Connection"` in quotes. That is the *name* of your network adapter. Didn't know that it *had* a name? Recall that we saw that in Chapter 6. To see it, right-click My Network Places and choose Properties. The page that results will have an icon for a LAN connection and the name next to it. The default name is *Local Area Connection*, but you can rename it. If you have more than one NIC, then you'll have a different name.

◆ If this doesn't work the first time that you do it, don't be surprised—this always behaves a bit flaky the first time you use it—I have no idea why. Try an `ipconfig /release` after you do the `/setclassid` command before the `ipconfig /renew`.

The DHCP user class will survive reboots; to clear the user class info, type this:

```
ipconfig /setclassid "Local Area Connection"
```

And if your NIC has a different name than "Local Area Connection," then substitute that, of course.

If you script your installs, then you can also set an adapter's class ID by adding this parameter to its `[MS_TCPIP parameters]` section:

```
DHCPClassId = name
```

ADVANCED SERVER CONFIGURATION

Before leaving configuration, let's take a look at some overall server configuration items—in particular, logging and DNS client registration. In the DHCP snap-in, right-click the server and choose Properties. You'll see a page with three tabs. The first is named General, as you see in Figure 7.19.

FIGURE 7.19

General server configuration page

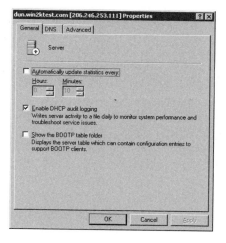

The main thing to notice here is the logging option. It's a default option, so don't worry about having to check it. But where is the log kept? Well, for one thing, there are seven logs, one for each day of the week—that makes finding a record for an action on a particular day easier. The logs are in simple ASCII format, so you can examine them with Notepad, although it would be nicer if the DHCP snap-in would go get them *for* you. They're in \winnt\system32\dhcp in files whose names include the day of the week. Part of one log looks like the following:

```
63,07/03/99,00:44:30,Restarting rogue detection,,,
51,07/03/99,00:45:30,Authorization succeeded,,win2ktest.com,
```

```
11,07/03/99,00:47:09,Renew,206.246.253.135,
PC400.win2ktest.com,00105A27D97A
10,07/03/99,00:48:00,Assign,206.246.253.2,
PC400.win2ktest.com,5241532000105A27D97A000000000000
10,07/03/99,00:48:00,Assign,206.246.253.3,
PC400.win2ktest.com,5241532000105A27D97A000001000000
63,07/03/99,01:51:51,Restarting rogue detection,,,
51,07/03/99,01:52:52,Authorization succeeded,,win2ktest.com,
```

Rogue detection is a process whereby the DHCP server seeks to find unauthorized DHCP servers. To entrap these dastards, the DHCP server craftily pretends it is just a PC looking for an IP address. It gets offers from other DHCP servers, and the DHCP server then checks their IP addresses against the list of authorized DHCP servers in the Active Directory. If it finds a scoundrel, then it reports that in the Event Viewer.

On the third line, you see that the machine at 206.246.253.135 has "renewed" its IP address—that is to say, it has said to the DHCP server, "You once gave me this IP address and the lease is running out. May I extend the lease?" The two "assign" statements give the .2 and .3 addresses to PC400 to then hand out—you see, PC400 is a RAS server and needs IP addresses to give away to dial-in clients. RAS has given those two addresses for PC400 to use.

The Advanced properties page has another interesting tab, the DNS tab. Click it, and you'll see a screen like the one in Figure 7.20.

FIGURE 7.20

Configuring the dynamic DNS client from DHCP

Although DNS is a topic for later in this chapter, let me jump ahead a bit and explain briefly how it works. DNS is a database of machines and names: My local DNS server is the machine that knows there's a machine named dun.win2ktest.com with an IP address of 206.246.253.111. But how does it *know* that? With DNS under NT 4, I'd have to start a program called the DNS Manager and hand-enter the information. But under Windows 2000, dun.win2ktest.com is smart enough to talk to its local DNS server and say, "Listen, I don't know if you knew this, but I'm a machine on the network, my name's dun.win2ktest.com, and my IP address is 206.246.253.111." Additionally, the DNS server—which is running Windows 2000—is smart enough to *hear* this information; older DNS servers wouldn't be expecting machines to register themselves with their local DNS server, and the local DNS server wouldn't have a clue about what to do with the information anyway. But post-1998 DNS servers have a feature called *dynamic* DNS, which enables them to accept this name/address (*name registration*) information from other machines rather than having to have a human type the information in.

There are two important points to notice in the preceding paragraph. First, the DNS server's got to be smart enough to listen to and act upon the name registrations when they come from the clients. Second, the clients have to be smart enough to *issue* name registration information! If my workstation's running NT 4 rather than Windows 2000, then it hasn't been programmed to offer name/address information to its DNS server because the whole dynamic DNS technology didn't even exist in 1996 when Microsoft wrote NT 4! From the point of view of the state-of-the-art DNS server running on the Windows 2000 server, then, the old Windows 9*x*, Windows for Workgroups, and NT clients are just plain dumb. Or, more exactly, from the point of view of the DNS server, those clients *don't even exist*. There's no way that the DNS server could figure out they are there.

That's what the dialog box in Figure 7.16 accomplishes. The Windows 2000 DHCP server will notice when it's handing out an IP address to a machine that doesn't know about dynamic DNS; although the DHCP server cannot modify the code running on the older client, it can fill in for the older client's lack of knowledge, and register the client's name/address with DNS for it. Notice the option labeled Enable Updates for DNS Clients That Do Not Support Dynamic Update; that's the feature I've been discussing here. Make sure that box is checked.

COMMAND-LINE CONFIGURATION AND BACKUP: NETSH

Windows 2000 and later versions of Windows Server are more and more controllable from the command line. DHCP is particularly so, which makes for easier disaster recovery.

There are a bunch of commands for controlling DHCP, but they all start out with `netsh dhcp`. But you only need to know one:

```
netsh dhcp dump
```

It dumps out all of the `netsh` commands that you'd need to rebuild the DHCP server. So you could capture that output to a file named `dhcpbackup.txt` like so:

```
netsh dhcp dump>dhcpbackup.txt
```

And then you can rebuild the DHCP server with this command:

```
netsh dhcp exec dhcpbackup.txt
```

Monitoring DHCP

Once you've got a DHCP server set up and running, you may want to find out how many leases remain, who's got those leases, and the like. Open the `Address Leases` folder and you'll see something like Figure 7.21.

This folder displays all of the leases that DHCP has currently outstanding, which machine (by name) has them, as well as the machine's MAC address.

FIGURE 7.21

Assigned leases

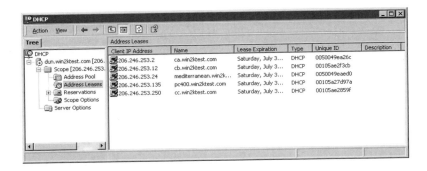

But how many addresses are left? Right-click any scope and choose Display Statistics, and you'll see a message box like Figure 7.22.

FIGURE 7.22

Lease statistics

With just a few clicks, you can bring up this message box and find out whether your network's hunger for IP addresses is being met.

DHCP on the Client Side

Now that you've set up DHCP on a server, how do you tell clients to use that DHCP? Simple. Any Microsoft operating system from Windows for Workgroups to Windows 9x to NT 3.x to NT 4.x to Windows 2000 all have DHCP configuration as an installation option, although some of those clients refer to it as "automatic" configuration rather than DHCP configuration. (By the way, the Microsoft Client software for DOS and Windows supports DHCP as well.)

Once a system has gotten an IP address, you can find out what that address is by going to that system, opening a command line, and typing **ipconfig /all**. On a Windows 95 workstation, click Start/ Run, and then type **winipcfg** and press Enter. Windows 98 supports both IPConfig *and* WINIPCFG. Windows NT only supports IPConfig. IPConfig's useful for other DHCP client–fiddling, as well. You can force a DHCP client to abandon its DHCP-supplied IP address and look for a different one by typing first **ipconfig /release** and then **ipconfig /renew**.

DHCP in Detail

That's setting up DHCP. But how does it work, and unfortunately, how does it sometimes *not* work? DHCP supplies IP addresses based on the idea of *client leases.* When a machine (a DHCP client) needs an IP address, it asks a DHCP server for that address. (*How* it does that is important, and I'll get to it in a minute.) A DHCP server then gives an IP address to the client, *but only for a temporary period of time*—hence the term *IP lease*. You might have noticed you can set the term of an IP lease from DHCP; just right-click any scope and choose Properties, and it's one of the settings in the resultant window.

The client then knows how long it's got the lease. Even if you reboot or reset your computer, it'll remember what lease is active for it and how much longer it's got to go on the lease.

TIP   *On a Windows 3.x machine, lease information is kept in* DHCP.BIN *in the* Windows *directory. On a Windows 95 machine, it's in* HKEY_LOCAL_MACHINE\System\CurrentControlSet\Services\VxD\DHCP\Dhcp-infoxx, *where xx is two digits. And if you want to enable or disable the error messages from the DHCP client on a Windows 95 machine, it's the value PopupFlag in the key* HKEY_LOCAL_MACHINE\System\CurrentControlSet\Services\VxD\DHCP; *use "00 00 00 00" for false, or "01 00 00 00" for true. Alternatively, opening a command line and typing* **ipconfig /release** *will erase this information. To find the place in the Registry holding DHCP lease information on an NT machine, run REGEDIT and search for DHCPIPAddress in* HKEY_LOCAL_MACHINE\System\CurrentControlSet. *The key or keys that turn up are the location of the DHCP lease info. On a Windows 2000 system, it's probably* hkey_local_machine\system\currentcontrolset\services\TCPIP\parameters\ Interfaces; *within there you'll find GUIDs (Global Unique IDs, the things that look like* {CE52A8C0-B126-11D2-A5D2-BFFEA72FC}) *for each adapter and potential RAS connection. There's a DHCPIPAddress value in each adapter that gets its addresses from DHCP.*

So, if your PC had a four-day lease on some address and you rebooted two days into its lease, then the PC wouldn't just blindly ask for an IP address; instead, it would go back to the DHCP server that it got its IP address from and request the particular IP address that it had before. If the DHCP server were still up, then it would acknowledge the request, letting the workstation use the IP address. If, on the other hand, the DHCP server has had its lease information wiped out through some disaster, then it will either give the IP address to the machine (if no one else is using the address), or it will send a *negative acknowledgment* (NACK) to the machine, and the DHCP server will make a note of that NACK in the Event Log. Your workstation should then be smart enough to start searching around for a new DHCP server. In my experience, sometimes it isn't.

Like BootP, DHCP remembers which IP addresses go with what machine by matching up an IP address with a MAC (Media Access Control, that is, Ethernet) address.

Normally a DHCP server can send new lease information to a client only at lease renewal intervals. But DHCP clients also "check in" at reboot, so rebooting a workstation will allow DHCP to reset any lease changes such as subnet masks and DNS services.

Getting an IP Address from DHCP: The Nuts and Bolts

A DHCP client gets an IP address from a DHCP server in four steps:

1. A *DHCPDISCOVER* broadcasts a request to all DHCP servers in earshot, requesting an IP address.

2. The servers respond with *DHCPOFFER* of IP addresses and lease times.

3. The client chooses the offer that sounds most appealing and broadcasts back a *DHCP-REQUEST* to confirm the IP address.

4. The server handing out the IP address finishes the procedure by returning with a *DHCPACK*, an acknowledgment of the request.

INITIAL DHCP REQUEST: DHCPDISCOVER

First, a DHCP client sends out a message called a DHCPDISCOVER saying, in effect, "Are there any DHCP servers out there? If so, I want an IP address." Figure 7.23 shows this message.

FIGURE 7.23

DHCP step 1:
DHCPDISCOVER

**DHCP
client**

**DHCP
server**

Enet addr: 00CC00000000
IP addr: 0.0.0.0

Enet addr: 00BB00000000
IP addr: 210.22.31.100

"Is there a DHCP server around?"

IP address used: 255.255.255.255 (broadcast)
Ethernet address used: FFFFFFFFFFFF (broadcast)
Transaction ID: 14321

You might ask, "How can a machine communicate if it doesn't have an address?" Through a different protocol than TCP—UDP, or the *User Datagram Protocol*. It's not a NetBIOS or NetBEUI creature; it's all TCP/IP-suite stuff.

Now, to follow all of these DHCP messages, there are a couple of things to watch. First of all, I'm showing you both the Ethernet addresses (Token Ring addresses for those of you using Token Ring) and the IP addresses because you see that they tell somewhat different stories. Also, there is a *transaction ID* attached to each DHCP packet that's quite useful. The transaction ID makes it possible for a client to know when it receives a response from a server exactly *what* the response is responding to.

In this case, notice that the IP address the message is sent to is 255.255.255.255. That's the generic address for "anybody on this subnet." Now, 210.22.31.255 would also work, assuming that this is a class C network that hasn't been subnetted, but 255.255.255.255 pretty much always means "anyone who can hear me." If you set up your routers to forward broadcasts, then 255.255.255.255 will be propagated all over the network; 210.22.31.255 would not. Notice also the destination Ethernet address, FFFFFFFFFFFF. That's the Ethernet way of saying, "Everybody—a broadcast."

DHCP OFFERS ADDRESSES FROM NEAR AND FAR

Any DHCP servers within earshot—that is, any that receive the UDP datagram—respond to the client with an offer, a proposed IP address, like the one shown in Figure 7.24. Again, this is an offer, not the final IP address.

This offering part of the DHCP process is essential because, as I just hinted, it's possible for more than one DHCP server to hear the original client request. If every DHCP server just thrust an

IP address at the hapless client, then it would end up with multiple IP addresses, addresses wasted in the sense that the DHCP servers would consider them all taken, and so they couldn't give those addresses out to other machines.

FIGURE 7.24

DHCP step 2: DHCPOFFER

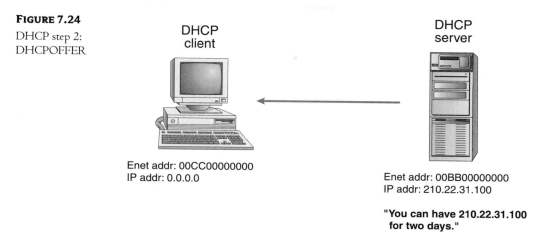

DHCP client

Enet addr: 00CC00000000
IP addr: 0.0.0.0

DHCP server

Enet addr: 00BB00000000
IP addr: 210.22.31.100

"You can have 210.22.31.100 for two days."

IP address used: 255.255.255.255 (broadcast)
Ethernet address used: 00CC00000000 (directed)
Transaction ID: 14321

SIDE NOTE: LEAPFROGGING ROUTERS

Before going further, let's consider a side issue that may be nagging at the back of your mind. As a DHCP client uses *broadcasts* to find a DHCP server, where do routers fit into this? The original UDP message, "Are there any DHCP servers out there?" is a broadcast, recall. Most routers, as you know, do not forward broadcasts—which reduces network traffic congestion and is a positive side effect of routers. But if DHCP requests don't go over routers, then that would imply that you have to have a DHCP server on every subnet—a rather expensive proposition.

The BootP standard got around this by defining an RFC 1542, a specification whereby routers following RFC 1542 would recognize BootP broadcasts and would forward them to other subnets. The feature must be implemented in your routers' software, and it's commonly known as *BootP forwarding*. Even if you live in a one-subnet world, by the way, that's worth remembering, as it's invariably a question on the Microsoft certification exams: "What do you need for client A to communicate with DHCP server B on a different subnet?" Answer: The router between A and B must either "be RFC 1542–compliant" or "support BootP forwarding."

Okay, so where do you *get* an RFC 1542–compliant router? Well, most of the IP router manufacturers, such as Compatible Systems, Cisco, and Bay Networks, support 1542. New routers probably already support it; older routers may require a software upgrade. Another approach is to use a Windows 2000 or NT system as a router, as Windows 2000 and NT routing software includes 1542 compliance. But what if you've got dumb routers, or router administrators that refuse to turn on BootP forwarding? Then you can designate an NT or Windows 2000 machine as a *DHCP relay agent*.

A DHCP relay agent is just a computer that spends a bit of its CPU power listening for DHCP client broadcasts. The DHCP relay agent knows there's no DHCP server on the subnet (because you told it), but the relay agent knows where there *is* a DHCP server on another subnet (because you told it). The DHCP relay agent then takes the DHCP client broadcast and converts it into a directed, point-to-point communication straight to the DHCP server. Directed IP communications can cross routers, of course, and so the message gets to the DHCP server.

What do you need to make a DHCP relay agent? Well, with NT 4, you could use any NT machine—workstation or server. For some annoying reason, Windows 2000 only includes software to make a DHCP relay agent with Server.

To make an NT machine into a DHCP relay agent, just open the Control Panel, then the Network applet. Click the Protocols tab and double-click the TCP/IP protocol. In the resulting dialog box, you'll see a tab labeled DHCP Relay. Click it, and you'll see a dialog box like the one shown in Figure 7.25.

FIGURE 7.25

Configuring an NT 4 computer to be a DHCP relay agent

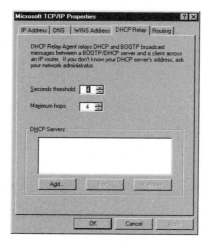

To make this work, just click the Add button and fill in the IP address of a DHCP server or servers. The dialog box is simple, but there are two things that confuse people about making a computer into a DHCP relay agent, so let me note them in the following tip and warning.

TIP   *The NT DHCP relay agent runs on a computer on the subnet, not a computer acting as a router on a subnet. However, the Windows 2000 DHCP relay agent can run on a router PC or a nonrouter. You should only have one DHCP relay agent on each subnet.*

WARNING   *Under no circumstances should you make a DHCP server into a DHCP relay agent. The net effect will be for the DHCP server to essentially "forget" that it's a DHCP server and instead just forward every request that it hears to some other DHCP server. This prompts me to wonder why the silly DHCP relay agent function isn't grayed out altogether on a DHCP server—certainly the Obtain an IP Address from a DHCP Server option is.*

To make a Windows 2000 system—remember, server only—into a DHCP relay agent, you've got to use Routing and Remote Access Service. Basically any RRAS configuration will do; you needn't enable WAN routing or dial-in. Look back to Chapter 6 to see how to configure an RRAS system—again, click Start/Programs/Administrative Tools/Routing and Remote Access, then right-click the server's name and choose Configure and Enable Routing and Remote Access to start the wizard, then choose Manually Configured Server, and finish the wizard. You'll see a screen like the one in Figure 7.26.

FIGURE 7.26

RRAS main screen

Open the IP Routing object (click the plus sign) and one of the objects you'll see will be DHCP Relay Agent. Choose it and the RRAS management console will look something like Figure 7.27.

FIGURE 7.27

RRAS console with DHCP Relay Agent highlighted

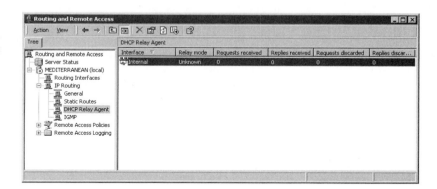

Double-click the Internal object and you'll get a dialog box that lets you configure hop counts, in the unlikely event that you'll need to do that.

You've got to configure the agent, so right-click it and choose Properties and you'll see a dialog box like the one in Figure 7.28.

You configure the agent by telling it where to find DHCP servers. Enter the IP address of the DHCP server and click Add to add a server to the list. Finally, you've got to enable the agent to listen on the local network for DHCP requests to forward. Right-click DHCP relay agent and choose New Interface. Choose Local Area Connection and the agent will then be active on the network.

FIGURE 7.28

Relay agent configuration screen

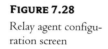

Discussion of relay agents and 1542-compliant routers leads me to yet another question. What if a DHCP server from another subnet gave an IP address to our client? Wouldn't that put the client in the wrong subnet? If a DHCP server serves a bunch of different subnets, how does it know which subnet an incoming request came from? DHCP solves that problem with BootP forwarding.

Assuming that your routers implement BootP forwarding, then a client's original DHCP request gets out to all of them. But how do we keep a DHCP server in an imaginary subnet 200.1.2.z from giving an address in 200.1.2.z to a PC sitting in another imaginary subnet, 200.1.1.z? Simple. When the router forwards the BootP request, it attaches a little note to it that says, "This came from 200.1.1.z." The DHCP server then sees that information, and so it only responds if it has a scope within 200.1.1.z.

Anyway, notice that although to the higher-layer protocol (UDP) this is a broadcast, the lower-layer Ethernet protocol behaves as though it is not, and the Ethernet address embedded in the message is the address of the client, not the FFFFFFFFFFFF broadcast address. Notice also that the transaction ID on the response matches the transaction ID on the original request. End of side trip, let's return to watching that client get its address from DHCP .

PICKING FROM THE OFFERS

The DHCP client then looks through the offers it has and picks the one that's "best" for it, or so the Microsoft documentation says. In my experience—and I've done a bunch of experiments—"best" means "first." It seems that the first server that responds is the one whose offer it accepts. Then it sends another UDP datagram, another broadcast, shown in Figure 7.29.

It's a broadcast because this message serves two purposes. First, the broadcast *will* get back to the original offering server if the first broadcast got to that server, which it obviously did. Second, this broadcast is a way of saying to any *other* DHCP servers who made offers, "Sorry, folks, but I'm taking this other offer."

Notice that both the Ethernet and the IP addresses are broadcasts, and there is a new transaction ID.

FIGURE 7.29

DHCP step 3:
DHCPREQUEST

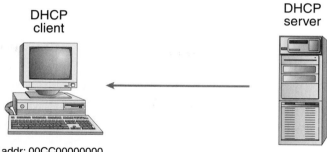

Enet addr: 00CC00000000
IP addr: 0.0.0.0

Enet addr: 00BB00000000
IP addr: 210.22.31.100

"Sure; also take this subnet
mask, DNS server address,
WINS server, node type,
and domain name."

IP address used: 255.255.255.255 (broadcast)
Ethernet address used: 00CC00000000 (directed)
Transaction ID: 18923

THE LEASE IS SIGNED

Finally, the DHCP server responds with the shiny brand-new IP address, which will look something like Figure 7.30.

It also tells the client its new subnet mask, lease period, and whatever else you specified (gateway, WINS server, DNS server, and the like). Again, notice it's a UDP broadcast, but the Ethernet address is directed, and the transaction ID matches the previous request's ID.

FIGURE 7.30

DHCP step 4:
DHCPACK

Enet addr: 00CC00000000
IP addr: 0.0.0.0

Enet addr: 00BB00000000
IP addr: 210.22.31.100

"Can I have the 210.22.31.100 IP address,
and thanks for the other offers, but no thanks."

IP address used: 255.255.255.255 (broadcast)
Ethernet address used: FFFFFFFFFFFF (broadcast)
Transaction ID: 18923

You can find out what your IP configuration looks like after DHCP by typing **ipconfig /all**. It may run off the screen, so you may need to add **|more** to the line. This works on DOS, Windows for Workgroups, and NT machines. You can see a sample run of **ipconfig /all** in Figure 7.31. Windows 95 machines have a graphical version of IPConfig called WINIPCFG.

FIGURE 7.31

Run of IPConfig

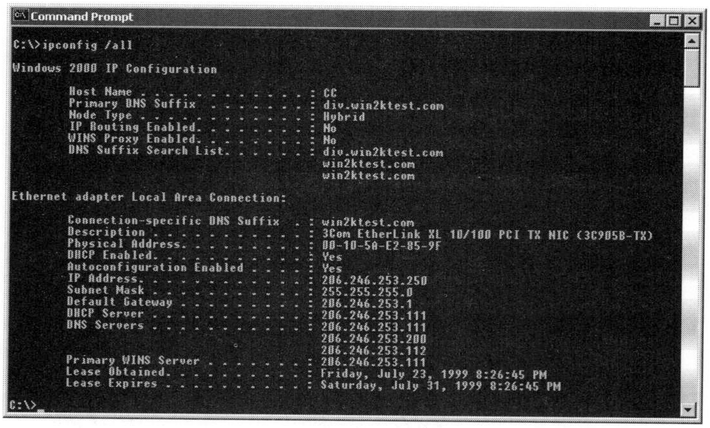

LOST OUR LEASE! MUST SELL!

What happens when the lease runs out? Well, when that happens, you're supposed to stop using the IP address. But that's not likely to happen.

When the lease is half over, the DHCP client begins renegotiating the IP lease by sending a DHCP request to the server that originally gave it its IP address. The IP and Ethernet addresses are both specific to the server.

The DHCP server then responds with a DHCPACK. The benefit of this is that the DHCPACK contains all of the information that the original DHCPACK had—domain name, DNS server, and so on. That means you can change the DNS server, WINS server, subnet mask, and the like, and the new information will be updated at the clients periodically, but no more than 50 percent of the lease time.

Now, if the DHCPACK doesn't appear, then the DHCP client keeps resending the DHCP request out every two minutes until the IP lease is 87.5 percent expired. (Don't you wonder where they get these numbers from?) At that point, the client just goes back to the drawing board, broadcasting DHCPDISCOVER messages until someone responds. If the lease expires without a new one, the client will stop using the IP address, effectively disabling the TCP/IP protocol on that workstation.

But if you've messed with the DHCP servers, then the renewal process seems to get bogged down a bit. It's a good idea in that case to force a workstation to restart the whole DHCP process by typing **ipconfig /renew** or, better, **ipconfig /release** followed by **ipconfig /renew**; that will often clear up a DHCP problem.

Even with an infinite lease, however, a DHCP client checks back with its server whenever it boots. Therefore, you can often change from infinite to fixed leases by just changing the lease value at the server. Then stop and restart the DHCP service.

Designing Multi-DHCP Networks

Clearly the function of the DHCP server is one that shouldn't rest solely on the shoulders of one server (well, okay, servers don't have shoulders, but you know what I mean). So, how can you put two or more DHCP servers online to accomplish some fault tolerance?

Microsoft seems, however, a bit confused about how to go about providing multiple DHCP servers for a given subnet and has offered different advice at different times.

In one document, *Windows NT 3.5 Family Upgrade Course,* it said several things. First, "There is *no* mechanism in DHCP that allows two or more DHCP servers to coordinate the assignment of IP addresses from overlapping IP address pools."

No argument there. If you had two different DHCP servers on the same subnet, and they both thought that they could give out addresses 202.11.39.10 through 202.11.39.40, then there would be nothing keeping the first server from giving address 202.11.39.29 to one machine while simultaneously the other server was giving out that same 202.11.39.29 address to another machine. (It's almost as if helpful Tom has returned!)

Then, it goes on (pages 147 and 148) to demonstrate two different machines running DHCP server and each machine having a different scope. Both scopes are, however, taken from a single subnet.

In contrast, the NT Resource Kit (version 3.5, but 3.51 has no updates on the matter) takes issue with the idea of more than one scope referring to a subnet like so: "Each subnet can have only one scope with a single continuous range of IP addresses."

What this boils down to is this: I don't know what the official Microsoft approach to DHCP fault tolerance *is.* I *do,* however, know what works and what has worked for me. Like many people, I came up with an approach such as the one in the NT training guide. I just run DHCP on multiple machines and create multiple scopes that refer to the same subnet. I make absolutely sure that the ranges of addresses in the scopes do not overlap at all, and everything seems to work fine.

Name Resolution in Perspective: Introduction to WINS (Even for Windows 2000) and DNS

Consider the two following commands, both issued to the same server:

```
ping server01.bigfirm.com
```

and

```
net use * \\server01\mainshr
```

In the `ping` command, the server is referred to as server01.bigfirm.com. In the `net use` command, that same server is called server01. The difference is important for these reasons:

♦ Ping relies upon a traditionally Internet-oriented programming interface called *Winsock,* and any program running Ping generally needs access to something called a *DNS server* in order to execute the `ping` command.

◆ net use relies upon a traditionally Microsoft networking–oriented programming interface called *NetBIOS,* and any program running net use generally needs access to something called a *WINS server* to execute the net use command.

Let's do a bit of background work in order to understand Winsock, DNS, NetBIOS, and WINS.

Two Different Lineages, Two Different Names

The ping command is clearly a TCP/IP/Internet kind of command. You can't run it unless you're running TCP/IP, and as a matter of fact, it's a valid command on a Unix, VMS, Macintosh, or MVS machine so long as that machine is running a TCP/IP protocol stack.

In contrast, net use is a Microsoft networking command. You can do a net use on an NT network no matter what protocol you're running, but the command usually wouldn't be valid on a Unix, VMS, Macintosh, or whatever kind of machine; in general, Microsoft networking is pretty much built to work on PCs. (Yes, I know, NT is in theory architecture-independent, so you could find an Alpha machine using net use commands, but on the whole, NT is an Intel *x*86 operating system at this writing—and I haven't seen announcements of an NT/390 for the IBM mainframe world, NT VAX for the Digital world, or NT SPARC for the Sun world.)

Application Program Interface = Modularity

The difference is in the network application programming interface (API) that the application is built atop. API? What's that?

Well, years ago, most PC software had no understanding of networks at all. But that's not true anymore; there are many "network-aware" programs around. For example, the software that lets a Windows 2000 system be a file server is network aware; what good would a file server be without a network? Other network-aware server software includes Web servers such as Internet Information Server or e-mail servers such as Exchange.

Desktop machines—*clients*—use network-aware software as well. The program that lets you browse file servers with My Network Places on Windows 2000 systems, browse Network Neighborhood on Windows 9*x* and NT 4 systems, or do command-line commands such as net view (which lets you view the servers in a workgroup or the shares on a server) or net use is generically called a "client for Microsoft networking" and is network aware. So also is a Web browser (the client software for a Web server) or an e-mail client.

But the programmers who build network-aware applications such as file server clients or Web browsers aren't generally the programmers who write the rest of the networking software—the NIC drivers, the protocols, and so on. Different pieces of network software are usually designed to fit together in a modular fashion. But the only way that the folks who write the Web browsers can remain compatible with the folks who write the TCP/IP code is if the application developers and the protocol developers agree on an interface, a kind of "software connector" between the two pieces of software. More and more, designers build software to be modular specifically so that the Web browser people don't have to coordinate closely with the TCP/IP protocol–writing people.

The interface between a protocol and the applications that rely on it is called the *application programming interface* (API). Think of an API as being something like the controls you use when driving a car. Your car's steering wheel, accelerator, and other controls form the interface that you see, and you learn to use them to operate the car. You might have no idea while you're driving what's under your car's hood—you just push down the accelerator and the car goes faster. If someone snuck into my garage tonight and replaced the internal combustion engine in my Honda with a magic engine that didn't use gas, I would have no idea, nor would I care until I eventually noticed that the gas gauge seemed to be broken. As a driver, I really don't have to know anything at all about engines—all I've got to know is that the pedal on the right makes the car go faster. So long as the magic engine makes the car go vroom-vroom when I push down the right pedal, I'm happy.

The "automobile API" consists of a few "primitive" commands: Brake the car, accelerate the car, shift the car's transmission, and so on. There is no command "back the car out of the driveway," and yet I can still back a car out of a driveway by just assembling several of the primitive commands into the actual action of backing a car out of a driveway. The best part about this generic automobile API is that once you learn how to drive one car, you can instantly use another. In other words, you are an "application designed for the car driver controls API."

In contrast, consider how private pilots learn to fly. They have two pedals on the floor of their plane, but the left pedal turns them left and the right pedal turns them right. Someone trained as a private pilot would be an "application designed for the private plane API." Taking someone who can fly a plane and plunking him down in a car without any other training wouldn't work too well. In the same way, if an application is built for *one* network API, then it won't work on another. But if you built a car whose controls acted like an airplane's, airplane pilots could drive the car without any trouble.

NetBIOS and Winsock

I'm stretching a point a bit here, but I could say that cars and planes are just different ways of solving the same problem: transportation. In the same way, various network vendors over the years have tackled the same problem and come up with different solutions. In particular, Microsoft has, since 1985, built its network applications atop a network API of its own creation called the Network Basic Input-Output System (NetBIOS). The Internet world, on the other hand, has used a different network API called *sockets*. In the PC world, we've got a special version of sockets called *Winsock*.

Recall that the value of an API is that it separates your network applications from your network vendor—you needn't buy your network operating system from the same people you bought your network fax software from. For example, if you buy a network fax application designed for a network API named NetBIOS, you should be able to run that network fax application on any network at all, so long as the network supports the NetBIOS API. Similarly, at one time there were several vendors selling a version of TCP/IP for Windows for Workgroups back in 1992–1994. If the Winsock implementations on each of those TCP/IP versions were built right, then you should have been able to run the exact same copy of Eudora Light (a free Internet e-mail program) or Netscape Navigator on any of them.

Can your network live with just Winsock or NetBIOS programming interfaces? Probably not. You want to run the NetBIOS-based programs because anything written for Microsoft networks prior to Windows 2000 was written to run on NetBIOS. And you want to run Winsock-based programs because so many Internet-type applications exist—the Web and e-mail stand out, but there are many more—and they're built to work with Winsock.

NOTE   *In fact, one of the major changes in NT wrought by Windows 2000 was that all of Windows 2000's networking will work fine on Winsock and doesn't need NetBIOS at all. But any Windows 9x, Workgroups, or NT system needing to access data on Windows 2000 servers will do so via NetBIOS. Similarly, any pre–Windows 2000 applications running on a Windows 2000 system can only run atop NetBIOS, even if all of the systems in the network are Windows 2000 systems. The result is that virtually all Windows 2000 systems need a complete NetBIOS infrastructure.*

Name Resolution Defined

Something that both NetBIOS and Winsock have in common is that they both want to support easy-to-work-with machine names. Yes, every machine on the Internet and on most Windows 2000 networks (I say *most* because probably a few people are left not using IP) has a unique IP address, but no one wants to use that to identify servers: Opening My Network Places should show servers with names such as \\PERSONNEL rather than 220.10.99.32, and Amazon wants to be able to tell you to shop for books at www.amazon.com rather than 208.216.182.15. So we need some kind of data-base server around that can translate www.amazon.com to 208.216.182.15 and \\PERSONNEL to 220.10.99.32. This problem of converting a name into an IP address is called *name resolution*. For NetBIOS and Winsock, it's the same problem but with two different solutions. NetBIOS looks for its name resolution from a Windows Internet Name Service (WINS) server; Winsock looks for its name resolution from a Domain Name System (DNS) server.

NetBIOS versus Winsock still not clear? Then consider one more analogy. Think of the APIs as communications devices. Telephones and the mail service are communications devices, also, so I'll use them in an analogy. Ping's job is to communicate with some other PC, and **net use** also wants to communicate with some PC. But Ping uses Winsock (the telephone) and **net use** uses NetBIOS (the mail). If you use the telephone to call a friend, then that friend's "name" as far as the phone is concerned may be something like (707) 555-2121. As far as the mail is concerned, however, the friend's "name" might be Paul Jones, 124 Main Street, Anytown, VA, 32102. Both are perfectly valid "names" for your friend Paul, but they're different because different communications systems need different name types. In the same way, server01.bigfirm.com and \\server01 are both perfectly valid, but different, names for the same server.

Handling Legacy and NetBIOS Names: The Windows Internet Name Service

Anyway, for those of you NT 4 vets hoping that WINS would bite the dust in Windows 2000, sorry, looks like we've still got to support it. So let's see how to support this "legacy name resolving system." (*Legacy* is computer industry-ese for "crappy old stuff that we hate and that's why we upgraded in the first place, but we can't seem to get rid of all of it and so now we have to support both the new incomprehensible stuff *and* the crappy old stuff." But *legacy* sure makes it sound better, at least to me.)

NetBIOS atop TCP/IP (NBT)

The NetBIOS API is implemented on the NetBEUI, IPX/SPX, and TCP/IP protocols that Microsoft distributes. That makes Microsoft's TCP/IP a bit different from the TCP/IP you find on Unix (for example), because the Unix TCP/IP almost certainly won't have a NetBIOS API on it; it'll probably only have the TCP/IP sockets API on it. (Recall that as with all PC implementations of TCP/IP, Microsoft's TCP/IP form of sockets is called the Winsock API.)

NetBIOS on the Microsoft implementation of TCP/IP is essential, again to make older operating systems and applications happy. And NetBIOS over TCP (which is usually abbreviated NBT or NetBT) needs a name resolver.

Now, basic old NetBIOS converted names to network addresses by just broadcasting—"Hey, I'm looking for \\AJAX; if you're out there, \\AJAX, tell me your IP address!"—but clearly that's not going to be the answer in a routed environment; all of those "name resolution shouts" will stop dead at the routers. If \\AJAX is across a router from us, our software will never find \\AJAX.

NetBIOS name resolution over TCP/IP is, then, not a simple nut to crack. Many people realized this, and so there are two Internet RFCs (Requests for Comment) on this topic, RFC 1001 and 1002, published in 1986.

B Nodes, P Nodes, and M Nodes

The RFCs attacked the problem by offering options.

♦ The first option was sort of simplistic: Just do broadcasts. A computer that used broadcasts to resolve NetBIOS names to IP addresses is referred to in the RFCs as a *B node*. To find out who server01 is, then, a PC running B node software would just shout out, "Hey! Anybody here named server01?"

Simple, yes, but fatally flawed: Remember what happens to broadcasts when they hit routers? As routers don't rebroadcast the messages to other subnets, this kind of name resolution would only be satisfactory on single-subnet networks.

♦ The second option was to create a name server of some kind and to use that. Then, when a computer needed to resolve a name of another computer, all it needed to do was send a point-to-point message to the computer running the name server software. As point-to-point messages *do* get retransmitted over routers, this second approach would work fine even on networks with routers. A computer using a name server to resolve NetBIOS names into IP addresses is said to be a *P node*.

Again, a good idea, but it runs afoul of all of the problems that DNS had. *What* name server should be used? Will it be dynamic? The name server for NetBIOS name resolution is, by the way, referred to as a NetBIOS name server, or NBNS.

♦ The most complex approach to NetBIOS name resolution over TCP/IP as described in the RFCs is the *M node*, or *mixed* node. It uses a combination of broadcasts and point-to-point communications to an NBNS.

Microsoft Follows the RFCs, Almost

When Microsoft started out with TCP/IP, it implemented a kind of M node software. It was "point-to-point" in that you could look up addresses in the HOSTS file, or a file called LMHOSTS, and if you had a DNS server, then you could always reference that; other than those options, Microsoft TCP/IP was mainly B node-ish, which limited you to single-subnet networks. (Or required that you repeat broadcasts over the network, clogging up your network.) Clearly, some kind of NBNS was needed, and the simpler it was to work with, the better. As the RFCs were silent on the particulars of an NBNS, vendors had license to go out and invent something proprietary and so they did—several of them, in fact, with the result that you'd expect: None of them talk to each other.

That's where WINS comes in.

WINS is simply Microsoft's proprietary NBNS service. What makes it stand out from the rest of the pack is Microsoft's importance in the industry. They have the clout to create a proprietary system and make it accepted widely enough so that it becomes a de facto standard.

Microsoft's NetBIOS-over-TCP client software not only implements B, P, and M nodes, it also includes a fourth, non-RFC node type. Microsoft calls it an H, or Hybrid, node.

But wait a minute; isn't *M node* a hybrid? Yes. Both M nodes and H nodes (and note well that at this writing, M nodes are RFCed and H nodes aren't) use both B node and P node, but the implementation is different:

◆ In M node, do a name resolution by first broadcasting (B node) and then, if that fails, communicate directly with the NBNS (P node).

◆ In H node, try the NBNS first. If it can't help you, then try a broadcast.

M Node versus H Node

"Hmmm," you may be saying, "Why would anyone want to first broadcast, *then* look up the answer in the name server? Why clutter up the network cable with useless broadcasts when we could instead go right to the source and reduce network chatter?"

The answer is that it's a matter of economics. Recall that the RFCs on NetBIOS over TCP were written back in the mid '80s, when a typical PC had perhaps an 8MHz clock rate and a 5MHz internal bus. An Ethernet full of XTs would have had a lot of trouble loading the network enough for anyone to even notice. The bottleneck in networks in those days was the CPU or disk speed of the network server. But if the network includes routers—and if it doesn't, then broadcasting is all you need—then consider what the routers are connected to: wide area network links, probably expensive 9600, 14,400, or 19,200bps leased lines. In a network like this, the LAN was a seemingly infinite resource, and wasting it with tons of broadcasts was of no consequence. In contrast, creating more traffic over the WAN by having every machine ask for NetBIOS names (presuming the NetBIOS Name Server was across the WAN link) could greatly reduce the effectiveness of that expensive WAN. Besides, the reasoning went, the vast majority of the time a PC only wanted to talk to another PC on the same LAN, so broadcasts would suffice for name resolution most of the time. The result? M nodes.

The economic picture in 1994, when Microsoft was inventing WINS, was another story entirely: LANs were clogged and WAN links were far cheaper—so H nodes made more sense.

You can force any DHCP client to be a B, P, M, or H node. One of the options that you can configure via DHCP is the WINS/NBNS Node Type. You give it a numeric value to set the client's NetBIOS name resolution technique. A value of 1 creates a B node, 2 is used for a P node, 4 for an M node, and 8 for an H node, the recommended node type.

Understanding the NBT Names on Your System

A major part of the NetBIOS architecture is its lavish use of names. A workstation attaches up to 16 names to itself. Names in NetBIOS are either group names, which can be shared—workgroups and domains are two examples—or normal names, which can't be shared, like a machine name. As you'll soon see that WINS keeps track of all of these names, you may be curious about what all of them *are*—so let's take a minute and look more closely into your system's NetBIOS names.

You can see the names attached to your workstation by opening a command line from a Windows for Workgroups, Windows 95, NT, or Windows 2000 machine and typing **nbtstat -n**. You get an output like this:

```
Node IpAddress: [199.34.57.53] Scope Id: []
      NetBIOS Local Name Table
   Name       Type     Status
---------------------------------------------------------------------------
MICRON133  <00> UNIQUE   Registered
ORION      <00> GROUP    Registered
MICRON133  <03> UNIQUE   Registered
MICRON133  <20> UNIQUE   Registered
ORION      <1E> GROUP    Registered
MARK       <03> UNIQUE   Registered
```

In this example, the ORION group names are my workgroup and domain. MICRON133 is my machine's name, and MARK is my name—notice that NetBIOS registers not only the machine name, but the person's name as well. You can see the list of registered names on any computer in your network by typing **nbtstat -A <ip address>**, where the -A *must* be a capital letter.

But why is there more than one MICRON133? Because each different part of the Microsoft network client software requires names of its own, so they take your machine name and append a pair of hex digits to it. That's what the <00>, <20>, and the like are—suffixes controlled by particular programs. For example, if some other user on the network wanted to connect to a share named STUFF on this computer, she could type **net use * \\micron133\stuff**, and the redirector software on her computer would then do a NetBIOS name resolution on the name MICRON133<00>, as the <00> suffix is used by the redirector. Table 7.1 summarizes suffixes and the programs that use them.

TABLE 7.1: EXAMPLES OF MACHINE NAMES

UNIQUE NAMES	WHERE USED
computername>[00h]	Workstation service. This is the "basic" name that every player in a Microsoft network would have, no matter how little power it has in the network.
computername>[03h]	Messenger service.
computername>[06h]	RAS Server service.
computername>[1Fh]	NetDDE service; will only appear if NetDDE is active or if you're running a NetDDE application. (You can see this by starting up Network Hearts, for example.)
computername>[20h]	Server service; name will only appear on machines with file/printer sharing enabled.

Continued on next page

TABLE 7.1: EXAMPLES OF MACHINE NAMES *(continued)*

UNIQUE NAMES	WHERE USED
<computername>[21h]	RAS Client service.
<computername>[BEh]	Network Monitor agent.
<computername>[BFh]	Network Monitor utility.
<username>[03h]	Messenger service; any computer running the Messenger service (which is just about any MS networking client) would have this so that NET SEND commands to a user could be received.
<domain name>[1Bh]	Primary domain controller.
<domain name>[1Dh]	Master browser.
<domain name>[00h] or *<workgroup name>*[00]	Domain name; indicates that the computer is a member of the domain and/or workgroup. If a client is a member of a workgroup whose name is different from a domain, then no domain name will be registered on the client.
<domain name>[1Ch]	PDCs and BDCs would share this; if a machine has this name registered, then it is a domain controller.
<domain name>[1Eh] or *<workgroup name>*[1Eh]	Used in browser elections, indicates that this computer would agree to be a browser. Will only show up on servers. (Potential browser.)
MSBrowse	Domain master browser.

No matter what kind of computer you have on a Microsoft enterprise network, it will have at least one name registered—the *<computer name>*[00] name. Most computers also register *<workgroup>*[00], which proclaims them as a member of a workgroup. Those are the only two names you would see if you had a DOS workstation running the old LAN Manager network client without the Messenger service or a Windows for Workgroups 3.1 (not 3.11) workstation that had file and printer sharing disabled.

Most modern client software would also have the Messenger service enabled and so would have the *<computer name>*[03] and *<username>*[03] names registered, as well.

Adding file and/or printer sharing capabilities to a computer would add the *<computer name>*[20] name. Servers all agree to be candidates for browse master by default, so unless you configure a machine to *not* be a candidate for browse mastering, then the *<workgroup name>*[1E] name will appear on any machine offering file or printer sharing. If the machine happens to be the browse master, it'll have *<workgroup name>*[1D] as well. Workstations use the [1D] name to initially get a list of browse servers when they first start up: They broadcast a message looking to see if the [1D] machine exists, and if it does, then the [1D] machine presents the workstation with a list of potential browsers.

Browse masters get the network name [01][02]__MSBROWSE__[02][01] as well—it's a group name, and only the *master* browsers are members. Master browsers use that name to discover that each other exists.

Name Resolution Before WINS: LMHOSTS

Clients written prior to WINS, or clients without a specified WINS server, try to resolve a NetBIOS name to an IP address with several methods. The tools they'll use, if they exist, are:

- A HOSTS file, if present

- Broadcasts

- An LMHOSTS file, if present

- A DNS server, if present

You met HOSTS before—it's just a simple ASCII file. Each line contains an IP address, at least one space, and a name. LMHOSTS works in a similar way to HOSTS. And yes, you'd do well to understand LMHOSTS, as it solves many name resolution problems with pre–Windows 2000 servers and perhaps even Windows 2000 servers in an enterprise with both Windows 2000– and NT 4–based domains.

TIP *Let me stress that: Don't skip this section. It's not a history lesson; it can sometimes be the only way to fix a Win2K problem, believe it or not.*

INTRODUCING LMHOSTS

Recall that HOSTS is an ASCII file that lists IP addresses and Internet names, such as the following:

```
100.100.210.13 ducky.mallard.com
211.39.82.15 jabberwock.carroll.com
```

Microsoft reasoned that if a simple ASCII file could supplement or replace DNS to resolve Winsock names, why not create an ASCII file to hold NetBIOS names? The result is the LMHOSTS file. LMHOSTS consists of pairs of IP addresses and names, like HOSTS, but the names are 15-character *NetBIOS* names, not Internet-type names:

```
100.100.210.13 ducky
211.39.82.15 jabberwock
```

I assumed in the previous example that the NetBIOS name is identical to the leftmost part of the Internet name, although that's not necessary, as you may recall from the earlier discussion in this chapter about setting up TCP/IP on a system.

REPRESENTING HEX SUFFIXES IN LMHOSTS

But how to handle the nonprinting characters in a NetBIOS name, the <1B> used by the primary domain controller, the <1C> used by all domain controllers? Recall that the hex suffixes are always the 16th character in a NetBIOS name, so write out a suffixed NetBIOS name like so:

- Enclose the name in quotes.

- Add enough spaces to the end of the name so that you've got 15 characters in the name.

- After the spaces, add \0x followed by the hex code.

For example, suppose I had a domain named CLOUDS and a domain controller named \\CUMULONIMBUS at address 210.10.20.3. I'm creating an LMHOSTS file that I can put on systems around the network so that they can find \\CUMULONIMBUS and recognize it as the primary domain controller for CLOUDS. The LMHOSTS file would look like this:

```
210.10.20.3 cumulonimbus
210.10.20.3 "clouds          \0x1B"
```

This indicates that the machine at IP address 210.10.20.3 has two names (or at *least* two names). As CLOUDS is a six-letter word, I added nine spaces to the end of it.

A SPECIAL SUFFIX FOR DOMAIN CONTROLLERS: #DOM

In most cases, the only hex suffix you'll care about is <1C>, the suffix indicating a domain controller. You can create an entry for it as previously, with a \0x1C suffix, or you can use a special metacommand that Microsoft included in LMHOSTS: #DOM.

To indicate that a given entry is a domain controller, enter a normal LMHOSTS entry for it, but add to the end of the line #DOM: and the name of the domain controller. In the CUMULONIMBUS example, you could register CUMULONIMBUS's name and the fact that it was a domain controller for CLOUDS like so:

```
210.10.20.3 cumulonimbus #DOM:clouds
```

But \x01C and #DOM behave a bit differently, in my experience. If you enter a \x01C entry in an LMHOSTS, then NT will use it and only it, ignoring WINS or any other information—so if you're going to use an \0x1C entry, make sure it's right! Furthermore, if you try to tell NT about more than one domain controller in a given domain using the \0x1C suffix, it will only pay attention to the *last* one mentioned in the LMHOSTS file.

"LISTEN TO ME!": THE #PRE COMMAND

This is a bit out of order, as I haven't taken up WINS in detail yet, but as long as I'm discussing LMHOSTS, it kind of fits. As you'll learn later, a normal H node type of client will first send a name resolution question to a WINS server before consulting its local LMHOSTS file, if one exists. Only if the WINS server returns a failure, saying, "I'm sorry, I can't resolve that name," does the client look in its LMHOSTS file. But sometimes you want to tell a PC, "I have a particular entry here in LMHOSTS that is more important than anything that WINS tells you. If you need to look up this particular NetBIOS name, use the LMHOSTS entry rather than looking at WINS." For those entries, you can use the #PRE metacommand. In the case of CUMULONIMBUS, the line above would look like:

```
cumulonimbus  #DOM:clouds #PRE
```

#PRE's job is this: If WINS and LMHOSTS offer conflicting answers to the question, "What's the IP address of CUMULONIMBUS," then in general the client listens to WINS rather than LMHOSTS—in other words, by default WINS, uh, wins. But #PRE gives an LMHOSTS entry precedence over anything that WINS has to say.

CENTRALIZED LMHOSTS: #INCLUDE, #ALTERNATE

LMHOSTS is powerful, but could include a fair amount of running around, because for a user's PC to benefit from LMHOSTS, *the LMHOSTS file must be on the user's PC*. Yuck. That means you'd have to go out Amongst The Users, a happy time for some but a—ummm—mixed blessing for others. Every time you changed LMHOSTS, you'd have to walk around replacing the old LMHOSTS file with a new one on every single machine—ugh, double yuck. Is there a better way?

Sure. You can put a small LMHOSTS file on a user's machine with just one simple command: "Go to this server to read the 'main' LMHOSTS file." Even better, you can specify as many backups for this server as you like. You do it with the #INCLUDE and #ALTERNATE metacommands. Here's a sample LMHOSTS:

```
#BEGIN_ALTERNATE
#INCLUDE \\shadows\stuff\lmhosts
#INCLUDE \\vorlons\stuff\lmhosts
#INCLUDE \\centauri\stuff2\lmhosts
#END_ALTERNATE
```

You can use #INCLUDE without the #ALTERNATEs, but it seems to me that if you're going to go to all the trouble of having a central LMHOSTS, you might as well add some fault tolerance, right? And I would hope that it would go without saying that \\SHADOWS, \\VORLONS, and \\CENTAURI would either have to be on the same subnet as the client PC, or you should add a few lines above the #BEGIN ALTERNATE to tell the PC where to find those three servers.

#INCLUDE also takes local filenames:

```
#INCLUDE D:\MORENAME
```

LMHOSTS is a pretty powerful tool, and it still makes sense in today's NetBIOS-using networks because, as you'll see, WINS is not without its flaws.

How WINS Works

You've seen that the world before WINS was a rather grim place, where everyone shouts and many questions (well, resolution requests) go unanswered. Now let's look at what happens with WINS.

WINS Needs NT or Windows 2000 Server

To make WINS work, you must set up an NT Server or Windows 2000 Server machine (it won't run on anything else, including NT Workstation) to act as the WINS server. The WINS server then acts as the NBNS server, keeping track of who's on the network and handing out name resolution information as needed.

WINS Holds Name Registrations

Basically, when a WINS client (the shorthand term for "any PC running some kind of Microsoft enterprise TCP/IP network client software designed to use WINS for NBT name resolution") first boots up, it goes to the WINS server and introduces itself, or in WINS-speak, it does a name registration. (In fact, as you recall, most machines have several NetBIOS names, so clients register each of those names with WINS.) The client knows the IP address of the WINS server either because you hard-coded it right into the TCP/IP settings for the workstation or because the workstation got a WINS address from DHCP when it obtained an IP lease.

You may recall that the client actually gets *two* IP addresses, one for a "primary" and one for a "secondary" WINS server. The client tries to get the attention of the primary and register itself on that machine. But if the machine designated as a primary WINS server doesn't respond within a certain amount of time, the client next tries to register with the secondary WINS server. If the secondary will talk to the client and the primary won't, the client registers with the secondary. You can tell that this has happened by doing an **ipconfig /all** at the client. Among other things, this reports the address of the primary WINS server. If that address is the *secondary's* address, then you know that the primary was too busy to talk—and that turns out to be an important diagnostic clue, as you'll see later when I discuss how to design multiserver WINS systems.

In the process of registering its name with a WINS server, the workstation gets the benefit of ensuring that it has a unique name. If the WINS server sees that there's another computer out there with the same name, it will tell the workstation, "You can't use that name." The name registration request and the acknowledgment are both directed IP messages, so they'll cross routers. And when a workstation shuts down, it sends a "name release" request to the WINS server telling it that the workstation will no longer need the NetBIOS name, enabling the WINS server to register it for some other machine.

WINS CLIENT FAILURE MODES

But what if something goes wrong? What if you try to register a name that some other workstation already has, or what if a workstation finds that the WINS server is unavailable?

Duplicate names are simple—instead of sending a "success" response to the workstation, the WINS server sends a "fail" message in response to the workstation's name request. In response, the workstation does not consider the name registered and doesn't include it in its NetBIOS name table; an **nbstat -n** will not show the name.

But if a workstation can't find the WINS server when it boots up, then the workstation simply stops acting as a hybrid NBT node and reverts to its old ways as a Microsoft modified B node, meaning that it depends largely on broadcasts but will also consult LMHOSTS (and perhaps HOSTS, if configured to do so) if they're present.

IT'S MY NAME, BUT FOR HOW LONG?

Like DHCP, WINS only registers names for a fixed period of time called the *renewal interval*. By default, it's 6 days (144 hours), and there will probably never be a reason for you to change that. Forty minutes seems to be the shortest time that WINS will accept.

In much the same way that DHCP clients attempt to renew their leases early, WINS clients send "name *refresh* requests" to the WINS server before their names expire—*long* before. According to Microsoft documentation, a WINS client attempts a name refresh very early after it gets its names registered—after one-eighth of the renewal interval. (My tests show that it's actually *three*-eighths, but that's not terribly important.) The WINS server will usually reset the length of time left before the name must be renewed again (this time is sometimes called the *time to live*, or TTL). Once the client has renewed its name *once*, however, it doesn't renew it again and again every one-eighth of its TTL; instead, it only renews its names every one-half of the TTL. (My tests agree with that.)

Installing WINS

Installing WINS is much like installing all the other software that we've installed elsewhere in this chapter and in the book.

When you're planning how many WINS servers you need and where to put them, bear in mind that you need not put a WINS server on each subnet (which is one of the great features of WINS). It *is* a good idea to have a second machine running as a secondary WINS server, however, just for fault tolerance's sake. Remember that if a workstation comes up and can't find a WINS server, it reverts to broadcasting, which will limit its name resolution capabilities to just its local subnet and will cause it to do a lot of shouting, which adds traffic to the subnet. Why would a WINS client not find a WINS server if there's a working WINS server?

Well, normally the client would find the server just fine, but in some small percentage of the cases, the WINS server might be too busy to respond to the client in a timely fashion, causing the client to just give up on the server. That will probably only happen very rarely, unless you're overloading the WINS server. Unfortunately, a very common way to overload a WINS server is to put the WINS server function on the same machine that's also acting as a domain controller. Think about it: When is a WINS server busiest? First thing in the morning, when everyone's booting up and registering names. When's a domain controller busiest? First thing in the morning, when everyone's logging in. That leads to a warning.

WARNING   *If possible, don't put the WINS server function on a domain controller.*

That's where a secondary is useful. If you have a backup domain controller, then put a WINS server on that machine as well. The WINS software actually does not use a lot of CPU time, so it probably won't affect your server's performance unless you have thousands of users all hammering on one WINS server. If *that's* the case, I'd dedicate a computer solely to WINS-ing.

To get a WINS server set up, follow these directions:

1. Open the Control Panel (Start/Settings/Control Panel).

2. Open Add/Remove Programs.

3. Click Add/Remove Windows Components and wait a bit while the irritating Windows Components Wizard starts up.

4. Click Next to bring up the list of Windows components.

5. Click Networking Services and then the Details button.

6. Click the check box next to Windows Internet Name Service.

7. Click OK to return to Windows Components.

8. Click Next to install the service. The system will say that it is "Configuring Components" for a while, probably a few minutes. A bit later, the screen labeled Completing the Windows Components Wizard appears.

9. Click Finish to end the wizard.

10. Click Close to close Add/Remove Windows Components.

No reboots needed anymore—thanks, Microsoft—and you'll see in Start/Programs/Administrative Tools that you've got a new snap-in to control WINS. Start it up, click the plus sign next to the server, and it will look like Figure 7.32.

FIGURE 7.32

The initial WINS manager screen

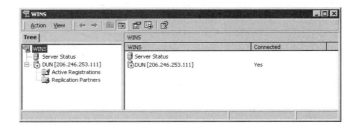

No need to authorize WINS servers, in case you're wondering. The first thing you should do on your WINS server is inform it of the machines on your subnet that are not WINS clients but use NetBIOS on TCP/IP. There won't be many of them, but they may exist; for example, you may have some old pre-1995 Microsoft Windows machines around. Machines with hard-coded IP addresses don't need to be entered, so long as they use WINS: If they know the address of a primary or secondary WINS server, they will register their names with that server. If you *do* have an old system requiring a static mapping, right-click Active Registrations and choose New Static Mapping. You then see a dialog box like the one shown in Figure 7.33.

FIGURE 7.33

The Static Mapping table

Alternatively, if you have an existing LMHOSTS file, you can click Action at the top menu, then Import Hosts, and the program will take that information to build a static-mapping database.

Configuring a WINS Server

Right-click the server in the left pane of the WINS snap-in, and choose Properties. You'll see a properties page like the one in Figure 7.34.

FIGURE 7.34

Server configuration
properties page

WINS will regularly back up its database—a good disaster recovery step—if you fill in a directory name in Default Backup Path. You can even use a UNC, such as \\ajax\central\wins or the like. A check box allows you to tell WINS to also do a backup specifically when the server is shut down.

Click the Database Verification tab, and you'll see a page like Figure 7.35.

FIGURE 7.35

Configuring WINS
verification

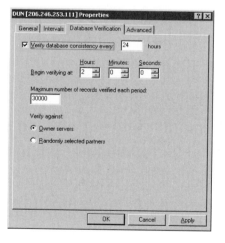

This is a real improvement in WINS over NT 4's WINS service. WINS has always had trouble as a distributed database: Name records get transmitted around the network and databases get corrupted. The corruption spreads and before you know it, you're erasing your WINS databases and starting all over. The option at the top of the screen tells your WINS server to periodically check its records against those of any other server in your enterprise. It's a good idea. If you enable it, I'd let it check every 24 hours, as is the default, and to check against the *owner* rather than a random server. *Owner* in WINS terminology means "the WINS server that generated the original name record." Thus, it could be in a multi-WINS server world that I registered my PC's name with WINS Server 1, which then told WINS Server 2 about me. (This happens automatically, recall—you needn't do anything to get your system registered with WINS except to specify a WINS server in your TCP/IP settings.) WINS Server 2 might run into some kind of trouble and corrupt the record about my machine. But checking with WINS Server 1 would point out the problem, and WINS Server 2 would be set straight.

Click the Advanced tab and you'll see a page like the one in Figure 7.36.

FIGURE 7.36

Advanced WINS server configuration

The first interesting thing here is logging. You can leave logging enabled, but think twice about logging detailed events. Basically, if you enable this, then WINS adds a lot of chatter to the Event Viewer, and WINS gets *really* slow. It's not a bad idea if you're trying to get some insight into what WINS does on a small network, but I've had it freeze a WINS server right up on me.

Enable Burst Handling is a work-around to handle an old WINS problem. WINS is busiest first thing in the morning, when everyone's logging on and trying to register their system names. Before registering a name, however, WINS must check its database to ensure that there's no duplication, that no one's trying to register a computer name that already exists. But that takes time, so WINS cheats.

The chances are good that early morning (the busy time) registrations are simply reregistrations, so WINS goes into burst mode, meaning it pretty much agrees to every registration request. It then says, "Come back and reregister in a few minutes," which gives it a chance to *really* check a registration when things are slower. It only shifts into burst mode when it has a lot of outstanding registration requests in its queue. How many? That's what the radio buttons are for—to set how soon WINS goes into burst mode. The default is probably fine, but if you're getting a lot of refused registrations—where WINS simply doesn't respond—then set the threshold to Low.

Designing a Multi-WINS Network

Thus far, I've discussed a situation where you have one WINS server and a bunch of clients. I've *also* mentioned the notion of a secondary WINS server, suggesting that at least one additional WINS server would be in order. How should you set up this second WINS server? And how about the third, fourth, and so on? And while we're at it, how many WINS servers should you have?

FROM MANY SERVERS, ONE DATABASE

The theory with multiple WINS servers is that you might have one in Europe, one in Africa, and one in North America. Europeans do their registrations with the European server, Africans with the African server, and Americans with the North American server. Then, on a regular basis, the three WINS servers get together and create a master worldwide list of WINS records, a kind of sort/merge amalgamating three different databases. But how to do it? We certainly don't want to have to transmit—*replicate* is the WINS term—the entire African name serving database over WAN links to Europe and America, particularly because the database probably hasn't changed all that much since yesterday.

As a result, WINS time-stamps and sequence-numbers name records so that it can take up less WAN bandwidth. That's great in theory, but in practice it means that WINS servers that are being asked to *do* all that sorting and merging will be pretty occupied CPU-wise, which will of course mean that they're falling down on the job as name resolvers. It also means that it might be a good idea to designate a relatively small number of servers—say, perhaps *one*—to essentially do nothing but the sort/merges.

MINIMIZING THE NUMBER OF WINS SERVERS

People assume that as with domain controllers, it's a great idea to have a local WINS server, and lots of them. But it's not, and in fact you should strive to keep the WINS servers to an absolute minimum.

A local WINS server would be great because it could quickly perform NetBIOS name resolutions for nearby machines. And in fact it would be great if you could install a WINS server in every location that only did name resolutions—but remember that every WINS server does *two* things: name resolutions and name registrations. This, in my opinion, is the crux of why multiple WINS networks can be a pain. If you could simply say, "Go to local machine X for name resolutions, but for those infrequent occasions when you need to do a name *registration*, go across the WAN to the central WINS server named Y," then WINS would be more trouble free. Sure, a morning logon would get a bit slower, as the registration would happen over the WAN, but you'd not get the corrupted WINS databases that are sadly so common in big WINS installations.

Why this happens is easy to understand. Merging two WINS databases and "boiling them down" to one database is simple. Merging three is harder, and merging 100 could be, well, a lot of work, perhaps more than WINS's database engine is capable of. That's why for years, Microsoft has maintained that no enterprise on the entire planet needs more than 14 WINS servers. More than that, and database corruption becomes far more likely.

People want a local WINS server for name resolution, but actually they're not getting much for it. If your WINS server were across the WAN from you, how much time would a name resolution take? Well, an entire name resolution request and response is only 214 bytes. Let's see, at 56Kbps that would be, hmmm, three-hundredths of a second. Here's a case where the wide area network will *not* be the bottleneck! WINS may have its drawbacks, but one thing that it was designed to do, and designed well, is to respond to name resolution requests quickly. Even a 66MHz 486 running NT 4's WINS server can handle 750 resolution requests per minute—so when it comes to WINS servers, remember: Less is more.

ADDING THE SECOND WINS SERVER

Of course, having said that, a *second* WINS server isn't a bad idea.

When setting up a Microsoft TCP/IP client, you're prompted for both a primary and a secondary WINS server address. When your PC boots up, the PC goes to the primary WINS server and tries to register the PC's NetBIOS name with that WINS server. If it's successful, it never even tries to contact the secondary WINS server unless a subsequent name resolution attempt fails.

What that implies is important: Suppose you've been a good network administrator and created a backup WINS server, and then you've pointed all of your workstation's Secondary WINS Server fields to that backup. The primary goes down. Where are you?

Nowhere very interesting, actually. You see, that secondary WINS server doesn't know much, as no one has ever registered with it. If a WINS client successfully registers with its primary server, it does not try to register with the secondary server.

If the primary goes down and everyone starts asking the secondary to resolve names, the secondary will end up just saying, "Sorry, I can't answer that question." So you've got to convince the primary to replicate to the secondary. Fortunately, there's an easy way: *push/pull partners*.

KEEPING THE SECOND SERVER UP-TO-DATE

In general, you've got to configure two WINS servers to be push/pull partners, but it's possible to have them discover each other with a setting in the WINS snap-in. Right-click the `Replication Partners` folder, choose Properties and click the Advanced tab, and you'll see a screen like Figure 7.37.

FIGURE 7.37

Choosing automatic discovery of replication partners

Here, I've checked the box Enable Automatic Partner Configuration, which will cause the WINS server to periodically broadcast (well, actually it will *multicast*) to find other WINS servers and from there to automatically replicate. This will, however, usually only work for WINS servers on the same subnet, as most routers don't pass IP multicasts. On a big network, this is a bad idea, but for a small network it'll save the administrator a bit of time and trouble.

Alternatively, you've got to introduce the replication partners. WINS database replications transfer data from a push partner to a pull partner. Those terms *push* and *pull* aren't *bad* terms description-wise, but they need a bit of illumination. Suppose for the purposes of the example that you have two machines named Primary and Secondary. Suppose also that Primary is the machine that gets the latest information, as it is the *primary* WINS server, and that all we really want to do with Secondary (the name of the machine that is the secondary WINS server) is have it act as a kind of backup to Primary's information. Thus, Secondary never really has any information to offer Primary. In that case, we'd have to set up Primary to *push* its database changes to Secondary.

You can tell a WINS server to create a push, pull, or push/pull relationship with another WINS server by right-clicking the folder labeled `Replication Partners` and choosing New Replication Partner. You're prompted for the IP address of the WINS server with which you want to establish a replication relationship.

In a push/pull relationship, data gets from Primary to Secondary in one of two ways. First, Secondary (the pull partner) can request that Primary (the push partner) update Secondary, telling Secondary only what has changed in the database. Alternatively, Primary can say to Secondary, "There's been a fair amount of changes since the last time I updated you. *You really should request an update.*" I italicized the last sentence to emphasize that it's really the pull partner that does most of the work in initiating the database replication updates. All the push partner really "pushes" is a suggestion that the pull partner get to work and start requesting updates.

Having said that, could I just tell Secondary to be a pull partner with Primary, without telling Primary to be a push partner for Secondary? Wouldn't it be sufficient to just tell Secondary, "Initiate a replication conversation with Primary every eight hours"? It would seem so, as there wouldn't any longer be a need for Primary to do any pushing—but there's a catch. If Secondary starts pulling from Primary, Primary will refuse to respond to Secondary's pull request unless Primary has been configured as a push partner with Secondary, because WINS servers are configured by default to refuse replication requests from all machines but partners, remember?

TIP *WINS services are totally independent of Windows 2000 domain security, as is DHCP. A WINS server can serve workstations throughout your network. In fact, if your network is connected to the Internet and doesn't have a firewall, you could actually publish your WINS server address, and other networks across the Internet could share browsing capabilities! (Whether you'd want to do that is another issue.)*

CONTROLLING REPLICATION

So now we see that the right thing to do is to make Secondary a pull partner with Primary and make Primary a push partner with Secondary. What triggers the replication? What kicks off the process of WINS database replication? To see, right-click any server listed in the `Replication Partners` folder, choose Properties, and click the Advanced tab. You'll see a screen like the one in Figure 7.38.

Well, recall that either the push partner or the pull partner can start the conversation. In the case of the former, you configure a push partner to tap its partner on the shoulder and suggest a replication session based on the number of database changes. You can tell Primary, "Notify Secondary whenever 50 changes have occurred to the WINS database on Primary," or whatever number you like, so long as you like numbers above 19; 20 is the minimum number of changes that NT will allow you to use to trigger replication. (You can alternatively trigger replication from the WINS snap-in.) The default, zero, essentially turns off push triggers.

A pull partner, in contrast, can't possibly know how many changes have occurred and so needs another way to know when to request updates. So pull partners request updates based on time—you configure a pull partner to contact its partner every so many minutes, hours, or days.

FIGURE 7.38

Configuring WINS replication

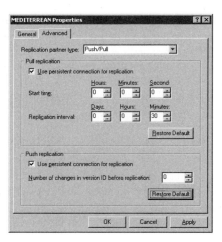

TIP   *The bottom line, however, is that most of us will just set up our WINS replication relationships to the defaults, particularly if we set up our WINS enterprise as a hub-and-spoke design, as you're about to read. You might want to set your partners to replicate less often in a large enterprise.*

REPLICATION DESIGN

Now that Microsoft has had four years' experience supporting big clients using WINS, some Microsofties have recommended to me a push/pull partner architecture something like a hub-and-spoke design. You see it pictured in Figure 7.39.

FIGURE 7.39

Suggested primary/ secondary WINS server configuration

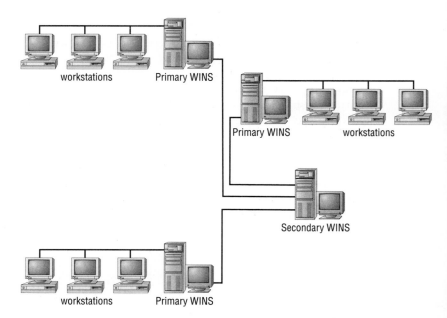

The goal of this design is to keep WINS servers responsive while still handling replication. In the picture, you see three different networks, each served by a WINS server labeled Primary WINS. In each network, each workstation points to the local WINS server as its primary server and the central machine labeled Secondary WINS as its secondary. In other words, then, every machine in the enterprise designates that one central machine as their secondary WINS server and a closer machine as their primary WINS server.

The main job of the central WINS server is to gather the three primary servers' databases, aggregate them into one enterprisewide WINS database, and replicate that database out to the local primaries. Each primary WINS server, then, designates the central WINS server as its sole push/pull partner.

Many firms implement a mesh-type structure, where every WINS server designates every other WINS server as a push/pull partner. The result is a nightmare of corrupted WINS databases and lost records. To add another WINS server, just make sure that it has some kind of connectivity to the central WINS server and make it a push/pull partner of that machine. If you end up with too many WINS servers for one central machine, just put hubs and spokes on the ends of the hubs and spokes, building a hierarchy.

WARNING *No matter what kind of WINS replication architecture you create, ensure that there are no loops in your replication. For example, if WINS server A replicated to B, which replicated to C, which replicated to A, then records can be replicated and re-replicated, causing WINS problems.*

Avoiding WINS Problems

Sources inside Microsoft tell me that WINS generates more support calls than any other of NT's "core" network technologies. That won't be surprising to anyone who's ever tried to track down a WINS problem. Here are a few tips to save you some time and help you avoid having to pay Microsoft more money to keep the product that you bought from them working.

WINS SERVERS SHOULD POINT TO THEMSELVES AS A PRIMARY WINS SERVER ONLY

When you're configuring the TCP/IP stack on a WINS server, do not fill in a value for a secondary WINS server, and in the Primary field, fill in the server's own value. This avoids a situation wherein the WINS server is busy but needs to reregister its own address. As it is busy, however, it cannot—believe it or not—respond quickly enough to *itself*. As a result, the WINS client software on the WINS server seeks out another WINS server, and so WINS server A's name registrations end up on WINS server B. The result is WINS instability, as the WINS server software is built assuming that each WINS server's name is registered on its own database.

BE CAREFUL REPLICATING TO "TEST" WINS SERVERS

Don't set up a "test" WINS server, register a few names on it, have a "production" WINS server pull the names from the test server, and then shut off the test WINS server for good. WINS will refuse to delete names that it got from another server, no matter how old and expired they are, until it can do a final double-check with the WINS server that it got the names from originally; if you shut off the test and never turn it back on, those records will never go away without a bit of operator intervention!

To remove all of the records created by a defunct WINS server, go to one of its replication partners and start WINS Manager. Right-click the `Active Registrations` folder, then choose All Tasks/Delete Owner. That allows WINS to finally purge the old owner's records.

DON'T MAKE A MULTIHOMED PC A WINS SERVER

A PC with more than one NIC can hear communications from several subnets. That's gotten WINS in trouble when a WINS server is multihomed, as WINS sometimes gets confused about where a name registration came in from. Several service packs have claimed to fix it, but each service pack brings more trouble reports. My suggestion: Don't make a multihomed machine a WINS server.

By the way, the same advice goes for PDCs. Multihomed PCs shouldn't be PDCs. The reason is that the PDC ends up being the master browser in a domain, and again, having workgroup announcements coming in from several different network segments causes problems for the browser software.

DON'T MAKE A DC A WINS SERVER

As explained earlier, both the domain controller and WINS functions are at their busiest at the same time. Mixing DC and WINS responsibilities on a single machine will make a mediocre DC and a mediocre WINS server. (Of course, on a small network this isn't the case; if you have 25 users, feel free to make one machine your domain controller, WINS, DHCP, DNS, and file server—but be sure you know how to do disaster recovery on it!)

DELETING AND PURGING WINS RECORDS

You'll eventually look at your WINS name database and realize that there are a bunch of old, useless records that you'd like to get rid of. Some of those records may be, as mentioned earlier, garbage left over from an old, now-defunct WINS server. Those are easy to get rid of—just choose the Delete Owner function, as described earlier.

For other records, though, the approach is a bit different.

Consider how a record gets created and propagated around an enterprise. A machine named TRAY (what server doesn't have a tray?) registers itself with WINS Server 1. That generates a record in WINS Server 1's database. WINS Server 1 is said to be the "owner" of that record.

Now suppose WINS Server 1 replicates TRAY's name record (or more likely, records) to WINS Server 2. WINS Server 2 now contains copies of those records, but it also knows that WINS Server 1, not itself, originated—"owns"—those records. Working at WINS Server 2, an administrator deletes the TRAY record. (In `Active Registrations`, right-click a record and choose Delete.) But the record still exists on WINS Server 1, and in time WINS Server 1 will rereplicate that record to WINS Server 2, so TRAY's record will reappear.

The alternative to deleting is *tombstoning*. When you tombstone a record, you don't remove it from the database; rather, it marks it as being in a *tombstone state*.

The purpose of the tombstone is this: WINS Server 2 has already written TRAY off, but it knows that the rest of the enterprise doesn't know that TRAY is history. So the next time WINS Server 1 replicates a TRAY record to WINS Server 2, WINS Server 2 may be tempted to insert a new record in its database for a machine named TRAY—but then it sees the tombstone record with TRAY's name and so can say, "Ah, I should just ignore that record; I have more up-to-date information than WINS Server 1 does." When WINS Server 2 next replicates to WINS Server 1, it'll tell WINS Server 1 that TRAY is tombstoned, and so WINS Server 1 will tombstone TRAY in its database as well. Eventually TRAY will be marked as tombstoned in the entire WINS enterprise.

By the way, tombstoned entries don't get purged from a WINS database until WINS runs a *scavenging operation*. That happens every three days by default, or you can initiate a scavenging operation from the WINS Manager by right-clicking a server, then choosing Scavenge Database.

TIP *If for some reason you stop the WINS service more often than every three days, your WINS database will never be scavenged. If that's the case, manually initiate scavenging from the WINS Manager.*

A badly designed WINS replication structure may need a bit of tombstoning help, and here Windows 2000's graphical WINS Manager is of assistance. When you click Delete Mapping, you get an option—delete or tombstone? You'd use tombstone *always* if you want to delete a record on server X but you're working from server Y. You'd typically delete rather than tombstone if you're sitting right at the server that owns the record that you're about to delete. And if you found that you'd been trying to get rid of a record but it keeps coming back, you'd tombstone it.

WINS Proxy Agents

Using an NBNS (NetBIOS naming server) such as WINS can greatly cut down on the broadcasts on your network, reducing traffic and improving throughput. But, as you've seen, this requires that the clients understand WINS; the older network client software just shouts away as a B node.

WINS can help those older non-WINS-aware clients with a *WINS proxy agent*. A WINS proxy agent is a regular old network workstation that listens for older B node systems helplessly broadcasting, trying to reach NetBIOS names that (unknown to the B node computers) are on another subnet.

To see how this would work, let's take a look at a simple two-subnet intranet, as shown in Figure 7.40.

Here, you see two class C subnets, 1.1.1.0 and 1.1.2.0. There's a router between them. On 1.1.1.0, there are two workstations. One is a WINS-aware client named HELPFUL, which is also running a WINS proxy agent. The other is an old B node client named HOPELESS, which is not WINS-aware. On 1.1.2.0, there are a couple of servers, a machine acting as a WINS server and a regular old file server.

FIGURE 7.40

An example of a two-subnet intranet

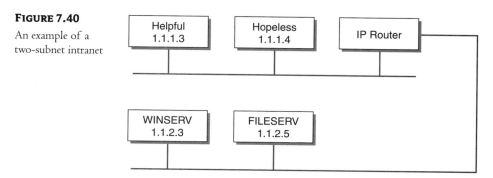

When HOPELESS first comes up, it'll do a broadcast of its names to ensure that no one else has them. The machine that it really should be talking to, of course, is WINSERV, but WINSERV can't hear it. HELPFUL, however, hears the B node broadcasts coming from HOPELESS and sends a directed message to WINSERV, telling it that there's a workstation named HOPELESS trying to register some names.

WINSERV looks up those names to ensure that they don't already exist. If they *do* exist, then WINSERV sends a message back to HELPFUL, saying, "Don't let that guy register those names!"

HELPFUL then sends a message to HOPELESS, saying, "I'm sorry, but *I* already use the name HOPELESS." That keeps HOPELESS from registering a name that exists on another subnet.

Assuming that HOPELESS names do *not* currently exist in the WINSERV database, however, WINSERV does *not* register the names; putting a WINS proxy agent on 1.1.1.0 doesn't mean that the non-WINS clients will have their names registered with WINS. That means that it's okay to have the same NetBIOS name on two different computers, so long as they are both B node clients and are on different subnets.

Suppose then that HOPELESS does a `net use d: \\fileserv\files`—in that case, the name \\fileserv must be resolved. Assuming that HOPELESS does not have a HOSTS or LMHOSTS file, HOPELESS will start broadcasting, saying, "Is there anyone here named FILESERV? And if so, what's your IP address?" HELPFUL will intercede by sending a directed IP message to WINSERV, saying, "Is there a name registered as FILESERV, and what is its IP address?"

WINSERV will respond with the IP address of FILESERV, and HELPFUL will then send a directed message back to HOPELESS, saying, "Sure, I'm FILESERV, and you can find me at 1.1.2.5." Now HOPELESS can complete its request.

TIP   Make sure there is only one WINS proxy agent per subnet! Otherwise, two PCs will respond to HOPELESS, causing—how do the manuals put it? Ah yes—"unpredictable results."

Name Resolution in More Detail

Now that you know how to configure DNS and WINS, you may be faced with a troubleshooting problem in reference to name resolution. Perhaps you try to FTP to a site inside your organization, but you can't hook up. Even though you know that `ftp.goodstuff.acme.com` is at one IP address, your FTP client keeps trying to attach somewhere else. You've checked your DNS server, of course, and its information is right. Where else to look?

Review: Winsock versus NBT

Remember first that there are two kinds of name resolution in Microsoft TCP/IP networking, Winsock name resolution and NetBIOS name resolution. A `net view \\`*somename* needs NetBIOS-over-TCP name resolution, or NBT name resolution. In contrast, because FTP is, like Ping, an Internet application, it uses Winsock name resolution. So, to troubleshoot a name resolution problem, you have to follow what your client software does, step by step.

DNS/Winsock Name Resolution

I type **ping lemon**, and get the response "unknown host lemon." But I suspect there's a LEMON out there, and I'm not talking about a computer from a certain Texas computer company. How did Windows 2000 decide that it couldn't find LEMON? It certainly takes long enough to decide that it can't find lemon, after all—usually on the order of 20 to 30 seconds on a 400MHz system. *Something must be going on.*

When faced with a question such as this, I turned to the Microsoft documentation for help, but there wasn't much detail. So I ran a network monitor and issued `ping` commands to computers that didn't exist, to see the sequence of actions that the network client software tried in order to resolve a name. The HOSTS and LMHOSTS files do not, of course, show up in a network trace, so I inserted information into those files that didn't exist on the DNS or WINS servers and then tried pinging again, to demonstrate where the HOSTS and LMHOSTS files sit in the name resolution hierarchy. (And if you think about it, LMHOSTS and WINS should have nothing at all to do with a Winsock resolution. Perhaps in a non-Microsoft world, but not in Windows 2000.) Pinging for a nonexistent "apple," I found that the name resolution order proceeds as shown in Figure 7.41.

FIGURE 7.41

The name resolution order

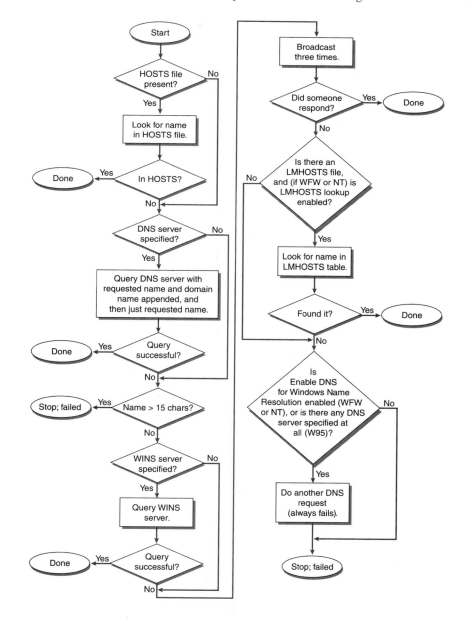

Step by step, it looks like this:

◆ First, consult the HOSTS file, if it exists. If you find the name you're looking for, stop.

◆ Next, if there's a specified DNS server or servers, then query them. First, query apple. NT machines then query apple.mmco.com, tacking on the domain name; Windows 95 workstations don't do the second query.

This happens whether or not the box Enable DNS for Windows Name Resolution (found in the Advanced Microsoft TCP/IP Configuration dialog boxes of NT 3.51 and Windows for Workgroups—there's no corresponding option in Windows 2000) is checked. If DNS has the name, then stop.

◆ After that, the client looks to see whether the name has 16 or more characters, or whether it has a period in its name. If it does, then the process stops, a failed name resolution attempt.

◆ Next, if there's a specified WINS server or servers, then query the WINS server(s). The name WINS looks for is apple <00>, the name that *would* be registered by the Workstation service, if the apple machine existed.

◆ If that fails, then do three broadcasts looking for a machine with NetBIOS name apple <00>, requesting that it identify itself and send back its IP address. Again, this would succeed with a workstation running some NetBIOS-over-TCP/IP client, even a relatively old one, as it would have registered the apple <00> name already, if only on its own name table. Unfortunately, this only works if the machine is on the same subnet.

◆ If the name still hasn't been resolved, read the LMHOSTS file. (Under NT 3.51 and Windows for Workgroups, do not do this if the Enable LMHOSTS Lookup box is unchecked; skip this step.) As with the earlier steps, stop if you find a match; if not, keep going.

◆ If you're running an NT or Windows for Workgroups machine with the box Enable DNS for Windows Name Resolution checked (the option seems not to exist in Windows 2000), then you've instructed your system to do a DNS lookup every time a WINS lookup fails. If that box is checked, then a second and last DNS lookup will happen. If, on the other hand, you *don't* have the Enable DNS box checked, then there's nothing left to do.

Look at that sequence: HOSTS, DNS, WINS, broadcast, LMHOSTS, and DNS again. This surprised me for a couple of reasons. First, it seems that every unsuccessful name resolution results in broadcasts, the *bête noire* of those of us trying to keep the network traffic to a minimum. My guess is that the broadcasts aren't part of an according-to-Hoyle IP stack, but Microsoft just threw them in for good measure and the WINS query as well. Then, if you've checked Enable DNS for Windows Name Resolution, the client software performs a DNS lookup as a matter of course after any failed WINS lookup; unfortunately, that leads to a redundant DNS lookup here. In short, if your Windows 95 workstation knows of a DNS server, it will use that DNS server when doing both DNS and NetBIOS name resolutions.

The broadcasts are a pain, but they *would* be of benefit when you tried to execute a TCP/IP command on a computer in your network but wanted to use the shorter NetBIOS name rather than the longer DNS name, such as apple instead of apple.mmco.com.

Getting back to an earlier question, what happened on that workstation that could not access the FTP site? There was an old HOSTS file sitting in the Windows directory that pointed to a different

IP address, an older IP address for the FTP server. HOSTS is read before anything else, so the accurate information on the DNS or WINS servers never got a chance to be read. So be very careful about putting things in HOSTS if they could soon become out-of-date!

There is an explicit Enable DNS for Windows Name Resolution check box in Windows for Workgroups and NT 3.51 clients, but how do you control whether DNS gets into the act on a Windows 95 client? You can't, at least not entirely; where Workgroups and NT 3.51 separate the options about whether to specify a DNS server and whether or not to use that DNS server as a helper when resolving NetBIOS names (that's what Enable DNS for Windows Name Resolution means), Windows 95 seems not to do that.

Controlling WINS versus DNS Order in Winsock

Now, what I just showed you is the order of events by default in NT, Windows 9*x*, or Windows 2000 clients. But if you feel like messing around with the way that Winsock resolves names, you can. As usual, let me take this moment to remind you that it's not a great idea to mess with the Registry unless you know what you're doing.

Look in the Registry under `HKEY_LOCAL_MACHINE\System\CurrentControlSet\Services\Tcpip\ServiceProvider` and you see `HostsPriority`, `DnsPriority`, and `NetbtPriority` value entries. They are followed by hexadecimal values. The lower the value, the earlier that HOSTS, DNS (and LMHOSTS), and WINS (and broadcasts) get done. For example, by default DNS's priority is 7D0 and WINS's is 7D1, so DNS goes before WINS. But change DNS's priority to 7D2, and WINS does its lookup and broadcast *before* the client interrogates the DNS server.

Again, I'm not sure *why* you'd want to do this, but I include it for the sake of completeness and for the enjoyment of those who delight in undocumented features.

NetBIOS Name Resolution Sequence

Readers send me many questions about NT and 2000, but unfortunately I usually can't help much, usually because the problem boils down to either some hardware or software that I'm not familiar with, so all I can do is to make a few suggestions to help them try to smoke the problem out on their own. Of all of the troubleshooting suggestions that I make, however, here's the most common one.

Many problems sound like "I can't get X machine to connect to and communicate with Y machine," as in "I have a file server named ABEL that workstation BAKER can't access." Most people don't realize the very important fact there are *two* problems to troubleshoot here:

◆ First, you must have IP connectivity.

◆ Second, you must have proper name resolution—and "proper" means DNS/HOSTS if the application is Winsock-based, or WINS/LMHOSTS if the application is NetBIOS-based.

I know I've touched on this elsewhere, but I really want to hit home with this point. First, make sure that the two systems can ping each other. Do a ping from each side to the other. Without the ability to transfer IP packets back and forth, your network can go no further—"don't mean a thing if you ain't got that ping," y'know.

Once you're sure that you have IP connectivity, check that your systems can resolve each other's names. Here's where I find that readers sometimes go wrong. Someone will tell me that workstation

\\ABEL can't contact server \\BAKER, "even though I pinged BAKER from ABEL." In other words, the reader typed **ping baker** or something similar while sitting at ABEL. But Ping doesn't use NetBIOS to resolve the name "baker," of course—it uses DNS. That's no help, although it *does* demonstrate that there's IP connectivity. We need to test that ABEL can resolve the name \\BAKER via *NetBIOS*, not DNS. I'm not sure why, but Microsoft doesn't include a NetBIOS-based Ping in NT and 2000, and I wish it did. It'd make life a lot easier. About the closest thing that you can get to a NetBIOS-based ping is probably a `net view` command, as in `net view \\baker`. That command will list the shares on the BAKER server, but it's not a great test, as other irrelevant factors can cause it to fail.

To really chase down a NetBIOS name resolution problem, you've got to understand what's going on under the hood, exactly how the "WINS client"—the word for the piece of software that runs on your workstation and resolves NetBIOS names—operates.

I'll assume for this discussion that you haven't modified the way that the WINS client resolves NetBIOS names—that is, that you haven't told the client to disable the LMHOSTS file—and that you are using WINS. (Come to think of it, that's an important troubleshooting step: Make sure that all of the communicating parties are either connected to the same WINS server, or to WINS servers that replicate to each other.)

Summarized, the name resolution sequence appears in Figure 7.42.

The NBT name resolver uses the following steps; if any succeed, then it stops looking:

◆ The resolver caches the result of NetBIOS-name-to-IP-address resolutions that have succeeded in the past 30 seconds, and looks first in that cache. You can see the current state of your NetBIOS name cache by typing **nbtstat -c**. You can clear the cache by typing **nbtstat -R**.

◆ If the client is a Windows 98, Me, NT 4, or Windows 2000 system, then the first thing to check is whether the name to the right of the \\ is either an IP address or a recognizable DNS name—that is, that it has a period in its name. If the name is just an IP address, as in a command like `net use * \\199.33.29.15\Stuff`, then forget the name resolution and just go to that IP address. If it's a DNS name, like `net use * \\myserver.region8.acme.com\files`, then resolve the name using the *DNS* client, not the WINS client (and you'll read about how DNS resolves names in the remainder of the chapter).

◆ If the name wasn't IP or DNS—or the client was too old to be able to respond to that—then the next part is the WINS client, if the client software is WINS aware. If WINS is disabled under Windows 95, or if there is no WINS server specified in Workgroups or NT 3.51, then the client skips this step.

◆ If WINS isn't being used, then the client does three broadcasts. For example, `net view \\apple` causes three broadcasts looking for a workstation with the name apple registered rather than apple.mmco.com or the like.

◆ Next, if LMHOSTS is enabled—and it appears that LMHOSTS is *always* enabled on Windows 95/98/Me/2000 clients but must be enabled with the Enable LMHOSTS check box for NT 3.51 and Workgroups—then the client looks up the name in LMHOSTS. Surprised? When doing NBT name resolutions, LMHOSTS gets consulted *before* HOSTS, a reversal over Winsock name resolutions. Recall that LMHOSTS only contains 15-character NetBIOS names, not longer DNS-like names.

♦ If you've checked Enable DNS for Windows Name Resolution in Workgroups or NT 3.51, or if you have specified a DNS server in Windows 95/98/Me/2000, then the workstation's client software will look at HOSTS, and if HOSTS can't help, it will interrogate the DNS server (or servers, as you can specify up to four DNS servers).

FIGURE 7.42

Name resolution sequence under NetBIOS

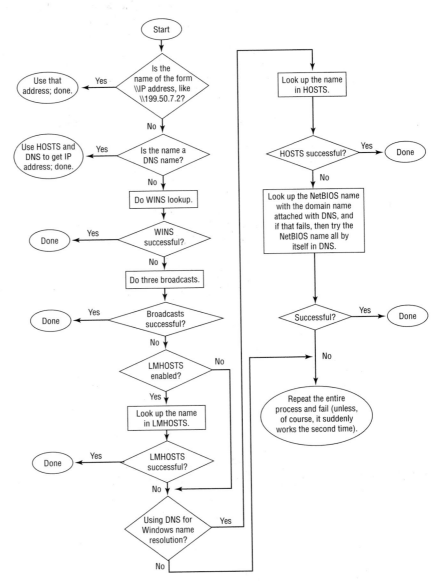

The NT/Workgroups clients and the 95/98 clients use DNS differently. The NT/Workgroups clients do a DNS query for the name with the domain name appended to it and then a DNS query of just the name. For example, if your domain is acme.com and you're doing a `net view \\myserver`, then an NT workstation will ask DNS first to resolve the name myserver.acme.com—it automatically adds the domain name for the first resolution. Then, if the DNS server can't resolve the name with the domain name attached, the client will request that the DNS server just resolve myserver.

In contrast, the Windows 95/98 client software only asks the DNS server to resolve the name with the domain name appended; in my example, a Windows 95/98 workstation would ask DNS to resolve myserver.acme.com but would not ask about myserver.

Then there's a final step in NetBIOS name resolution—it's an odd one. If the client software is the NT client (not the Workgroups or Win95/98 clients), and if it has been unsuccessful so far, then it goes back and does it all over again, I suppose in the hope that it'll work the second time.

DNS: Name Central in Windows 2000

Windows 2000 turned names in Microsoft networking on its head. From 1985's MS-Net through the versions of LAN Manager through Windows for Workgroups, Windows 9x, and NT 3.x and 4.x, NetBIOS reigned supreme and anyone running a TCP/IP-based network needed WINS or, before WINS's appearance, LMHOSTS files to support NetBIOS names, as you've just read. DNS, where it existed, was something of an afterthought.

With Windows 2000, all of that changes. The heart of naming in Windows 2000 is DNS. As you've already read, in a network of *only* Windows 2000 systems and applications, WINS would be completely unnecessary. Whether you've got old systems in your Windows 2000–based network or not, however, DNS is all-important: The Active Directory simply cannot run without it.

DNS is, for those just joining us, a name resolution system invented in 1984 for the Internet. It enables you to point your Web browser to a "friendly name" such as www.continental.com when you want to look up Continental Airlines' flight schedule rather than having to know that Continental's Web server is at IP address 208.229 .128.54. It makes e-mail work smoother through its MX records (which you'll read about later) and has proven itself to be an easily expanded way of maintaining names in the largest network in the world. DNS's ability to grow—its *scalability*—is a real plus for the Active Directory, as Microsoft hopes that the AD will be the basis of some very large networks.

Why DNS Matters to 2000

Why is DNS a big deal all of sudden? After all, in truth NT 4 experts could get away with knowing basically nothing *about* DNS, and in fact you could probably even have passed the NT 4 TCP/IP elective exam without answering any of the DNS questions. So why's it so important now?

You should care about DNS for several reasons, but here's the main one: DNS is now the central name repository for Active Directory, replacing WINS's role in NT 4. Yes, WINS will be around for a good time longer—so long as you have pre-2000 operating systems and application software running anywhere on your network—but WINS is in its twilight years. (Or so we hope, anyway; I rather doubt that many would attend a "WINS wake," unless they were serving drinks and *hors d'ouevres*). That's because although basic NT 4 services accessed the network via NetBIOS, which relies upon

WINS for name resolution, Windows 2000 instead accesses the network via Winsock, which uses DNS for its name resolution.

To see how the importance of names has shifted from WINS to DNS, consider this example: Both NT and 2000 use a set of machines called *domain controllers* to act as the keepers of the enterprise's user accounts. When one domain controller learns something new about a user, such as a new password, that machine must pass that information on to the other domain controllers. But how does it *find* those domain controllers? Well, an NT 4 DC would find another DC via WINS. But a Windows 2000 DC would find another DC via DNS. Similarly, before your workstation can log you in first thing in the morning, that workstation must find a DC—which it needs in order to log you in—with DNS. So where DNS access was a kind of "nice to have" feature of NT 4, in Windows 2000 DNS is really a "need to have" feature—no DNS, no logon.

DNS, then, is now a basic service, no less important than electricity, at least as far as your network is concerned.

Anatomy of a DNS Name

DNS has rules for naming computers, rules that are in some senses actually more restrictive than the ones that we lived with under NetBIOS.

DNS Names Are Segmented

DNS names are arranged in pieces separated by periods so that, for example, a PC name such as mypc.test.minasi.com has four pieces to it. Each piece can't exceed 63 characters in length, and the entire name can't exceed 255 characters total. The only acceptable characters in a DNS name (according to RFC 1123—as you'll see, 2000 bends this rule) are A–Z, a–z, 0–9, and a "-"—that is, a hyphen or a dash, no underscores allowed under RFC 1123.

That's worth keeping an eye on if you're upgrading systems from pre–Windows 2000 operating systems. NetBIOS lets you use considerably more characters than DNS does.

The Computer Name Is the Leftmost Part

When picking apart a DNS name, the leftmost piece is the computer name, and the remaining pieces to the right are the computer's "DNS domain" or "DNS suffix." (Some sources call it a *DNS domain*, others a *DNS suffix*. I think the Microsoft literature favors *DNS suffix* because it's easy to get confused between *DNS* domains and *Active Directory* domains.) So, for example, in the machine mypc.test .minasi.com, visualize two pieces:

mypc + test.minasi.com, or

machine name + DNS domain name/suffix

Now that I've pointed out that the leftmost part is the machine name, let me answer a question that might be in the minds of those who've used NT. I said a couple of paragraphs back that each piece of a DNS name can be up to 63 characters long. Is that *really* true when it comes to the leftmost piece—can I *really* assign a machine name that is that long?

Well, it depends. Windows 2000's NetBIOS software is only really aware of the leftmost part of the name, so from NetBIOS's point of view mypc.test.minasi.com would simply be named \\mypc.

But NetBIOS doesn't like computer names longer than 15 characters, so any Windows 2000 system with a machine name longer than 15 characters but shorter than 64 characters (and remember we're talking about just the leftmost piece here—mypc, not mypc.test.minasi.com) would be able to communicate from a Windows 2000 PC to a Windows 2000 PC, but pre-2000 systems would not be able to see a computer with a 16+ character name, so Windows 2000 keeps a *truncated* NetBIOS name in that case. That might not be a problem—but if two systems with long computer names both truncated to the same name, as would be the case with a system named marksfavoritepc0001 and marksfavoritepc0002—then the NetBIOS software on one of those systems would simply shut itself down, as duplicate names are a no-no for NetBIOS, and thus pre-2000 systems would not be able to access that second system.

The DNS Namespace: The Key to DNS

The huge size of networks that DNS can handle naming for is downright amazing. Given the name of any computer on the Internet, it can give you the IP address of that computer, and usually in just a few seconds. How many computers *are* there on the Internet—how big is the database that DNS is searching for you when it resolves a name? Honestly, I don't know the exact number of machines on the Internet, but I'm sure that "hundreds of millions or more" is a reasonable guess. The database of machine names for the entire Internet is a *big* database, and it changes all the time—but it works. From any computer on the Internet, you can find the address of any other computer on the Internet, using the worldwide DNS hierarchy or "namespace." Furthermore, you can get that information relatively quickly, usually in a few seconds.

How does a DNS hierarchy or namespace work? You need to know this for a couple of reasons. First, even if you create a DNS hierarchy that *isn't* connected to the public DNS hierarchy, you still need to create a hierarchy, and the tiniest DNS namespace works exactly the same as the public DNS namespace, it's just smaller. Second, if you *do* decide to build your DNS so that it's a part of the public DNS hierarchy, then you'll need to know how that hierarchy works. (And, I suppose, the third reason would be that it's just interesting to understand how this essential part of the Internet works.)

You'll see people use the term *namespace* and *hierarchy* when referring to DNS. I'll tend to use *hierarchy* here, but if you read something that refers to a *DNS namespace*, then just substitute *DNS hierarchy* and you'll be correct.

Introducing the Hierarchy: Back to Left-to-Right

As I suggested in the first paragraph of the last section, you read DNS names left to right, whether they're names in the worldwide DNS hierarchy or in your own private four-computer private DNS hierarchy. But what are you reading? Let me explain this in some detail, and use it as my vehicle to introduce how the DNS hierarchy works.

To rephrase a question I posed a couple of paragraphs ago, "How on Earth could a database as large, widespread, and everchanging as the DNS machine-name-to-IP-address database be managed and maintained and yet still offer reasonable query times?" Well, as you'll see later in this chapter, the *only* reason that it's possible is because no one person or organization must keep track of those names. Instead, the responsibility for keeping track of the name-to-IP-address relationship is maintained locally—if you point your browser to www.minasi.com and your local DNS server then tries to figure out the IP address of www.minasi.com, then your local DNS server is soon going to be talking to *my* local DNS server to resolve that name. That means that it's *my* job to make sure that you can find the www machine in the minasi.com domain because minasi.com is my domain. If by contrast you go looking for www.acme.com and *Acme* drops the ball on keeping track of *their* domain, then it only affects the people trying to get to the Acme systems—you wouldn't be hampered at all in trying to find a computer in the minasi.com domain.

Let's look again at the PC whose full name is mypc.test.minasi.com to start examining how the hierarchy works. What do the placements of the periods in the name—the parts of the name—tell us?

First, we know that its machine name is mypc. Second, we know that its domain is test.minasi.com.

But what *is* test.minasi.com? Well, reading left to right, you see that *test* is a subdomain or child domain (RFCs use both terms, so I don't think one is the "official" name) of another domain named minasi.com. That means that whoever created the test.minasi.com domain needed the permission of whoever's in charge of the minasi.com domain in order to create the test.minasi.com domain.

Next let's move to the right, and consider *minasi.com*. What is this domain? It is a child domain of a domain named, simply, com. (Yes, there is such a domain.) To create the minasi.com domain, someone (well, *me*, actually) needed to contact the people in charge of the com domain and get permission to create a subdomain of com named "minasi" or, in other words, "minasi.com." That's what you do when you visit www.networksolutions.com to try to register a new "dot-com" domain.

But where did the com domain come from; is it a child of some other domain? Well, if it weren't for a very common bit of sloppiness, then it'd be more obvious. You see, mypc.test.minasi.com isn't, strictly speaking, a complete DNS name—instead, mypc.test.minasi.com. *is*. What's the difference? Look again—the correct one ends with a period. The com. domain is actually a child domain of a domain named just "." that is, by the way, pronounced "dot" and is called the *root* of the DNS hierarchy. And as long as I'm introducing terminology, the phrase *complete DNS name* isn't really correct—the Internet-speak phrase is *fully qualified domain name* (FQDN).

Notice why I've been calling the way that DNS stores names a "hierarchy"—DNS distributes responsibility. To create the com domain only required the permission—granted *once*—of whomever owned the root (.) domain. (Originally it was the U.S. government, but that responsibility has moved to a nonprofit group called the Internet Corporation for Assigned Names and Numbers, or ICANN). I got to register minasi.com because I provided some information and a credit card number to the people who run the com domain, Network Solutions. (They're a division of a for-profit firm named VeriSign.) Now, if someone were to come to me and ask to create a domain named thisistheplace.minasi.com, then she wouldn't have to talk to ICANN or VeriSign—she'd only have to talk to me.

Let me underscore that. To create minasi.com, I only needed the permission of the people who run the .com domain. I didn't have to get permission from other .com companies, such as microsoft.com, ibm.com, or saralee.com—I just needed the OK from the .com parent domain, which is controlled by Network Solutions. In the same way, if I wanted to create a subdomain of minasi.com, such as hq.minasi.com, then I not only needn't tell microsoft.com, ibm.com, or saralee.com, I also needn't tell Network Solutions.

Why Build the DNS Hierarchy This Way?

Let's back up for a bit and see what led to DNS looking as it does today. In the TCP/IP world, anything with an IP address is called a *host*. Back in the early '80s, when the Internet (which wasn't yet *called* the Internet—it was the ARPAnet then) consisted only of a few hundred computers, a server on MIT's campus held a file that listed the names and IP addresses of those few computers. That file was named HOSTS because it listed all of the hosts on the Internet. When someone at some distant site added a computer to their local network and attached that computer to the ARPAnet, then he or she would just contact someone at MIT, who'd update the HOSTS file, and once a day everyone would attach to that MIT server and download the latest HOSTS file.

As you know, the HOSTS file still exists, although in a much less important role. But why not keep running things the old way, with one big central HOSTS file? Well, let's see: Assume 200 million computers on the Internet, and about 40 characters per HOSTS line; that'd be about 8 gigabytes. So every day you'd have to connect to some location and download 8 gigs— yuck. Even worse, every single time you put a computer on your network, adding pc0012 to acme.com, you'd have to tell someone at the one worldwide central repository of the HOSTS file, and hope that they'd update the file in a timely fashion. And when you added a new system to your network, or perhaps assigned a name to a different IP address—such as when you move www.acme.com from one machine to another, changing an IP address in the process—then you'd better hope that everyone out there in Internetland who you'd *like* to be able to find your Web server is working from the latest HOSTS file—ugh, double and triple yuck.

The Root, Top-Level, Second-Level, and Child Domains

Having explained how the hierarchy *doesn't* work, let's look at how it *does* work. Take a look at Figure 7.43.

FIGURE 7.43

The public DNS hierarchy

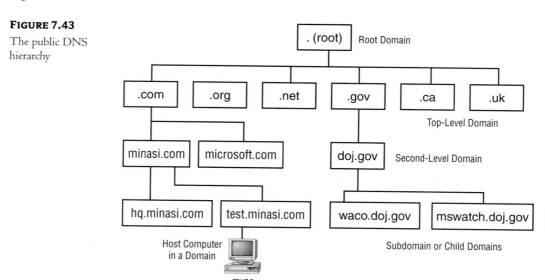

TOP-LEVEL DOMAINS

Below the root are hundreds—yes, hundreds—of *top-level* domains. Most of the ones we tend to think of around the world are .com, .net, and .org, as they've become sort of the worldwide "catch-all" domains. Then, each country has its own top-level domain—the United States has .us, Canada .ca, the United Kingdom .uk, and so on. Some countries have decided to offer their top-level domain for registrations, as in the case of the Cocos Keeling Island, the owners of the .cc top-level domain that many are using as an alternative to .com, .org, or .net. The island has a total population of 604 and in 1995—the last year I could find data for—their main export was copra. Who knows, perhaps nowadays they're all sharing the wealth from being the "kings of dot-cc." In another example, the somewhat-larger (population 10,000) island nation of Tuvalu ended up with the top-level domain with the salable name of .tv. Top-level domains .gov, .mil, and .edu tend to point to U.S. government, military, and educational institutions—remember who invented the Internet—although I guess in theory, groups of those types in other countries might register names under those top-level domains as well.

In November 2000, ICANN announced it'd soon approve several new top-level domains. I don't exactly get why they did some of them, but they are presented in Table 7.2.

TABLE 7.2: NEW TOP-LEVEL INTERNET DOMAINS

DOMAIN	PURPOSE	CONTROLLING ORGANIZATION
.aero	Aerospace-oriented firms, including airlines	Societe Internationale de Telecommunications Aeronautiques (Belgium)
.biz	Basically an "expansion area" for .com	JVTeam, LLC
.coop	Business cooperatives	National Cooperative Business Association
.info	Information sources	Afilias, LLC
.museum	Museums, clearly	Museum Domain Management Association
.name	People's names (see text)	Global Name Registry (the U.K.)
.pro	Various professional groups—doctors, lawyers, accountants, that sort of thing	RegistryPro (Ireland)

The top-level domains .biz and .info are both wide-open domains that anyone can register names in. If you're Acme Termite Inspection service and acmetermite.com, acmetermite.net, and acmetermite .org are taken, then you might still be able to get acmetermite.biz or acmetermite.info. The domain .pro is *not* wide open; there are people running various subdomains there. For example, you couldn't (as far as I can see) just register engineer.pro; rather; someone would administer engineer.pro and you'd get a name below that, like janesconstruction.engineer.pro. (As I write this, there's already a cpa.pro, medical.pro, and legal.pro.) The idea behind the .name domain is that someone would create an overall registry of people whose last name was Minasi and therefore control the minasi.name domain. I'd then get a subdomain under that called mark.minasi.name.

Different organizations control different top-level domains. For example, clearly Ottawa designates who hands out registrations under .ca, and the .tv sellers couldn't be doing those sales without the permission of the Tuvalans. The top-level domains that are biggest by far, however, are of course .com, .net, and .org, all administered by a company called Network Solutions, based in northern Virginia—but you may hear this company referred to by several names. Before the late '90s, a consortium of U.S. government agencies called the InterNIC controlled the entire DNS naming hierarchy, and they contracted with Network Solutions, a private firm, to handle the nuts and bolts of keeping the .com, .org, and .net top-level domains working. As a result, people have a tendency to use the terms *Network Solutions* and *the InterNIC* interchangeably, although they're not the same thing, and the InterNIC has become pretty irrelevant now that the U.S. has ceded control of the public DNS hierarchy to ICANN. Network Solutions is also not the same as ICANN—ICANN worries about *all* of the top-level domains. You might even see people refer to Network Solutions as VeriSign, the e-commerce security folks; that's because VeriSign bought Network Solutions in 1999.

ROLL-YOUR-OWN TOP-LEVEL DOMAINS: FOR INTERNAL USE ONLY!

Before I move to second-level domains, I wanted to toss in something that we'll be covering in detail later. Although the public Internet only uses a handful of top-level domains (TLDs in geek-speak), that doesn't mean you can't create others of your own sometimes. As you'll see, I strongly recommend that the DNS servers that support your Active Directory *not* be visible on the public Internet, if you can avoid it. You can, as you'll learn, create a DNS server that is perfectly capable of resolving names on the public Internet, but that also hosts a domain that is "invisible" to the public Internet. (You'd do this for security's sake.) You can accomplish this in several ways, but one simple way is just to use a domain name with a nonstandard TLD. For example, suppose your company's publicly visible Internet domain name were acme.com; you might choose to create an Active Directory domain name of acme.local. Never heard of a domain called something-dot-local? No wonder—there's no such TLD on the Internet. But you can do anything you like on your *intra*net, creating domains with any TLD that you like. So I guess I *could* have an e-mail name of mark@minasi—but only people inside my company could use it! Again, we'll cover more on this later, but I wanted to plant that idea in your head now so I can expand on it later.

SECOND-LEVEL DOMAINS: SEARCHING THE HIERARCHY

Sadly, ICANN's not about to give me my own .minasi top-level domain, so I guess I won't be able to change my e-mail address to mark@minasi any time soon. So the second-level domains are the more interesting ones for most of us.

As you just read, you can create a second-level domain with the permission of the owner of the parent domain. To create your second-level domain, the parent domain only has to do one thing: "delegate" name responsibility for your second-level domain to some machine. That's an important concept, and I'll get to it in a minute. But first, let's see how DNS uses its hierarchical nature with an example.

Suppose you point your browser to www.minasi.com. Your browser needs to know the IP address of the www.minasi.com machine, so it asks your local DNS server to resolve www.minasi.com into an IP address. (This is a simplified example—we'll consider a more complete one later.) Where should your local DNS server go to ask the IP address of the www machine in the domain minasi.com? Simple—it should go to the DNS server for minasi.com. That's a perfectly correct answer but not a very helpful one. How is your DNS server supposed to find the DNS server for minasi.com? Well, in general, you can find the address of a domain's DNS server by asking the domain's *parent's* DNS server—in other words, the DNS servers in the com domain can tell you the addresses of the DNS servers in the minasi.com domain.

But we're still not done, because *now* the question is, "What is the IP address of the DNS server (or servers) for the com domain?" Well, as you just learned, you get a domain's DNS server addresses from the DNS servers in that domain's parent's DNS server, so you'd get com's DNS server address from the DNS servers for com's parent, "."—the root.

Hmmm...if you've been patient enough to keep following this so far, then you've probably realized that we've run into a bit of a brick wall. You find the DNS servers for minasi.com by asking the DNS servers for com, and you find the DNS servers for com by asking the root, but who do you ask to find out the DNS servers for the root, as the root has no parent? (Hey, that'd be a great computer trivia question: Which is the only "orphan" DNS domain?)

The answer is, "you cheat." Every piece of DNS server software that I've ever seen comes with a kind of a cheat sheet called the *root hints file*, which contains the name and IP addresses of the 13 root DNS servers. On a Windows 2000 DNS server, you'll find a file named `cache.dns`—an ASCII file that you can examine with Notepad—in `\winnt\system32\dns` on any server that you've installed the DNS server service on. Anyway, once your DNS server has located a root DNS server's address in its root hints file, it asks that root DNS server for the addresses of the DNS servers for the com domain, then asks one of the com DNS servers for the address of the minasi.com DNS server, *then* asks the minasi.com DNS server for the address of the machine named www in the minasi.com domain and finally resolves the name for you. To summarize what happened when your local DNS server tried to resolve www.minasi.com:

1. First, your DNS server decided to find the minasi.com DNS server.

2. To find the minasi.com DNS server, your DNS server decided to look for the addresses of the com domain's DNS servers, as com is minasi.com's parent domain.

3. To find the com domain's DNS server, your DNS server decided to look for the root DNS servers.

4. It knew the IP addresses of the root DNS servers through its local root hints file.

5. Using the IP address of a root DNS server, it asked that root DNS server for the address of a DNS server for the com domain.

6. The root DNS server told your DNS server the addresses of the com domain's DNS servers.

7. Your DNS server then took one of those addresses and asked that com DNS server for the addresses of the minasi.com DNS servers.

8. That DNS server for the com domain told your DNS server the addresses of minasi.com's two DNS servers.

9. Your DNS server then asked one of minasi.com's DNS servers to resolve the name www.minasi.com.

10. The minasi.com DNS server resolved the address, returning the IP address of www.minasi.com.

THIRD LEVEL, CHILD, OR SUBDOMAINS: MORE ON DELEGATION

Now suppose I choose to divide my domain into subdomains or child domains. Suppose I create a subdomain named hq.minasi.com. What's involved? Delegation.

You saw from the previous example about resolving www.minasi.com that a DNS server resolves a name by working its way up the DNS hierarchy until it gets to the root, then works its way back down until it finally finds the DNS server that can answer its question. But, in some senses, *shouldn't* the root servers be able to resolve www.minasi.com? After all, www.minasi.com *is* in their domain, sort of. Or I could argue that the DNS servers for the com domain should be able to resolve www.minasi .com, as that address is inside the com domain, *sort* of "once removed," so to speak.

The answer is no, the root and com domains should *not* be able to resolve www in the minasi.com domain because they have *delegated* name resolution responsibility for minasi.com to a set of DNS servers, the minasi.com DNS servers. More specifically, the root domain contains records called NS (name server) records that delegate the responsibility for the com domain to the com DNS servers, and the com domain's DNS servers contain NS records that delegate name server responsibility for the minasi.com domain to the minasi.com servers. In fact, the people who maintain the database for the com zone *could* keep the name resolution record for www.minasi.com in the com database, but that would defeat the whole purpose of the hierarchy, and it would be a pain for me—if I ever moved the Web function from one of my computers to another, I'd have to bother the Network Solutions people and ask them to change the name resolution record for www.minasi.com.

So why would I create a subdomain of minasi.com? Perhaps I've got the same kind of problem that Network Solutions does—that is to say, perhaps I want to enable a group to use DNS names within my domain, but I don't want to have to do the maintenance on the DNS records. Suppose, for example, that I buy a company in Singapore, 12 time zones away from me. Now suppose they put a new machine online and need a name resolution record for that machine installed in the minasi.com DNS database. They can't call me when they need that, as it's not only a long way away, but also because I'm usually asleep while they're working. That gets kind of annoying and after a while they say, "Can't you just give us control of the name resolution for our own machines?" Well, I'm not particularly keen about giving them control of the whole minasi.com domain, but I'd like to grant their request for local control of their machine names. So I create a subdomain and call it test.minasi.com. Making their subdomain a reality requires two things:

- First, they'll need to make one of their computers into a DNS server for the test.minasi.com subdomain. That machine will, of course, need to be on the Internet persistently.

- Second, I'll need to tell the rest of the world to look at their server when resolving names in the test.minasi.com domain. I do that by delegating name server responsibility, by placing an NS record in my minasi.com DNS database that says, "There's a subdomain named test in the minasi.com domain, and if you want to look up any names in that, then don't ask me, ask this other DNS server, the one in Singapore."

You'll learn more about NS records a bit later, when I get more specific about building DNS zones, but in a nutshell that's all there is to delegation—it's a one-line command in a parent DNS server's database that says, "Hey, don't ask *me*—go talk to this other DNS server."

DNS Definition: "Authoritative"

Before moving on to my next DNS topic, let me define a term: *authoritative*. I've been telling you that to look up names in minasi.com you need to find minasi.com's DNS servers, and that you find minasi.com's DNS servers by asking the DNS servers in minasi.com's parent domain, com. The names of the minasi.com DNS servers that the com servers report to you are called the authoritative servers for minasi.com.

In other words, I could, in theory, have 50 DNS servers set up for minasi.com running on my network. (Don't ask me why I'd do that; I can't think of a reason offhand.) But if the com domain's DNS servers only know about three of those minasi.com DNS servers, then when people ask the com domain's servers for the names of the minasi.com servers, then the com domain servers will only contain three NS records for minasi.com, so they will only report the three minasi.com DNS servers that they know about. In the same way, if my imaginary Singapore office ran 47 DNS servers but I had only entered one NS record in the minasi.com DNS database for test.minasi.com, then only the one DNS server named in that NS record would be authoritative for test.minasi.com.

Zones versus Domains (and More on Delegation)

I've been talking about how DNS servers maintain a database for a "DNS domain," but strictly speaking, DNS servers don't hold name information for domains, they hold them for *zones*. What, then, is a zone? It's a DNS-specific term that basically means "the range of Internet addresses that this DNS server will be concerned about." To see how this works, consider Acme Industries (acme.com), a firm familiar to any Warner Bros. cartoon fan. And, in the process, we'll also consider another example of delegation.

When Acme got its Internet connection, it set up a primary DNS server at its corporate headquarters in Chicago and gave DNS names to their machines. There are machines with names such as jills-pc.acme.com, bigserver.acme.com, www.acme.com, and so on.

As time went on, however, Acme began to feel the bite of competition from its hated and longtime rival, Apex Limited (apex.com). So it moved its "gadgets" group—the guys who brought us Acme Instant Hole, Acme Rocket Sled, or Acme Spring-Powered Shoes—to Mexico in the hopes of lower prices. Meanwhile, Acme bought a munitions firm in Belgium and decided to close its other big domestic division, the "explosives" group, and sell the Belgian explosives instead.

At this point, Acme has three loci of operation: the suits in Chicago, the gadgeteers in Mexico, and the demolitions folks in Belgium. The question for Acme's network engineers is, "How do we arrange our DNS?" They decide to create two child domains, explosives.acme.com and gadgets.acme.com. Although some machines will stay in the top acme.com domain—the Web server, www.acme.com, is an obvious choice—many machines will be either *machinename*.explosives.acme.com or *machinename*.gadgets.acme.com. Why split up the domain into child domains? Any of several reasons, but one obvious one might be just simplicity—you can look at a machine's name and immediately figure out to which department it belongs.

NOTE *Please note that I'm talking about DNS domains, not Windows 2000 domains. Windows 2000 allows Acme to divide up its DNS names into subdomains as much as it likes, while still being able to keep all of its machines and users in as many or as few domains as it likes.*

Acme has two basic options for setting up its DNS, shown in Figures 7.44 and 7.45.

In Figure 7.44, Acme keeps things as they've been: There is one server that is the primary authority for all of Acme's machines. It's a perfectly fine answer, but not everyone may like it, as you'll probably guess if you recall my earlier example of my mythical Singapore office.

FIGURE 7.44

Acme with one
DNS zone

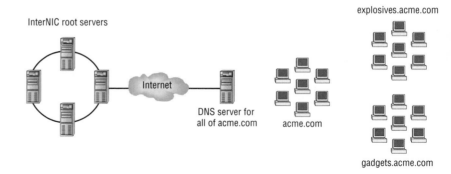

FIGURE 7.45

Acme with three
DNS zones

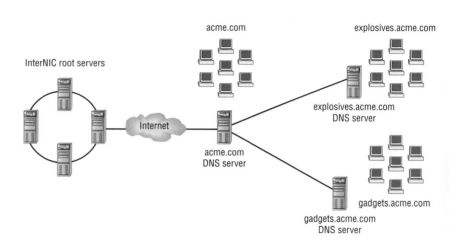

This is not, understand, a *wrong* answer; it's just one of several possible answers, and some may not like it. The folks in Belgium must rely on some network operators in Chicago to keep their machines properly listed in the DNS database, and it may be that every time Belgium needs some new machines and IP addresses stuffed into the database, it's morning in Belgium and the middle of the night in Chicago, so the Belgians get to wait. And, as they're the explosives guys, that might weigh heavily on the minds of the suits in Chicago when the Belgians ask for their own DNS server. Mexico could experience the same kinds of long-distance administration problems as the ones that Belgium faces. That could lead to the setup shown in Figure 7.45.

In Figure 7.45, Explosives has its own DNS server, and Gadgets has one of its own as well. The acme.com DNS server in Chicago has a pretty sparse database—basically, it just names a few machines in Chicago and then contains a few records that say, "While I *am* the acme.com DNS server, don't ask me about anything with a name like something-dot-explosives.acme.com or something-dot-gadgets.com; rather, go ask these other machines." Recall that in DNS terms, we'd say that the acme.com server has *delegated* name resolution for gadgets.acme.com to some DNS server in Mexico and delegated name resolution for explosives.acme.com to some other DNS server in Belgium.

Now, acme.com is still just one domain, but its DNS responsibilities—techies would say "DNS namespace duties"—have been spread out. What, then, to call these subsets of domains for which Acme's new DNS servers are authoritative? The term is *DNS zone* or *zone*. In Figure 7.44, Acme implemented its DNS as one zone. In Figure 7.45, Acme has three zones: its top-level acme.com zone, the explosives.acme.com zone, and the gadgets.acme.com zone.

How is this relevant to Windows 2000? Well, if your Windows 2000 network uses domains—and it will—then each domain requires a DNS zone of its own. So, for example, from the point of view of DNS, Acme could implement acme.com, explosives.acme.com, and gadgets.acme.com as either one big zone, two zones, or three zones. Acme won't retain that flexibility if it creates Windows 2000 *domains* named acme.com, explosives.acme.com, and gadgets.acme.com; Windows 2000 would, in that case, require three separate zones.

Forward and Reverse Lookup Zones

Thus far, I've described DNS's main task as converting host names such as kiwi.fruit.com to IP addresses such as 205.22.42.19. But DNS can do the reverse as well; you can ask a DNS server, "What host name is associated with IP address 205.22.42.19?"

The process of converting a host name to an IP address is called a *forward name resolution*. The process of converting an IP address to a corresponding host name is called *reverse name resolution*.

DNS maintains information about a given domain such as fruit.com in files called *zone files*. Fruit.com, then, has a zone file that DNS can use to look up kiwi.fruit.com's IP address. But where does DNS go to look up the host name associated with IP address 205.22.42.19?

Well, recall that the Internet authorities hand out blocks of addresses. There's a DNS zone called a *reverse lookup zone* for each Internet network. So, assuming that fruit.com's working with a class C network 205.22.42.0, it's someone's job to keep a reverse lookup zone for 205.22.42.0.

The *name* of the reverse lookup zone is odd, though. To construct it, take the dotted quads that the Internet authorities gave you—drop the ones that you control—and reverse them, then add .in-addr.arpa to the end of the name. Thus, whoever is responsible for 205.22.42.0 would create a reverse lookup zone 42.22.205.in-addr.arpa. A few other examples:

- 164.109.0.0/16, a class B network, would drop the two zeroed quads and reverse the remaining two to yield a reverse zone name of 109.164.in-addr.arpa. Notice there were only two dotted numbers, as it's a B network and the owner controls the bottom two quads.

- 4.0.0.0/8, a class A network, would have reverse zone 4.in-addr.arpa. In the case of an A network, only the top quad is set, so there's only one number in the reverse zone.

- 200.120.50.0/24, a class C network, would drop the zeroed quad and reverse the numbers to get a reverse zone name of 50.120.200.in-addr.arpa.

Basic DNS Record Types

I've been referring vaguely to "DNS databases." Now let's consider in more detail exactly what these databases look like and what's in them. DNS databases contain several kinds of database records—there's more there than just names and IP addresses. Take a look at Figure 7.46, and you'll see a listing of some DNS records at the minasi.com domain. Don't worry that you haven't seen the DNS snap-in before; I'm just providing this figure to show a few examples as I introduce each record type.

FIGURE 7.46

Sample DNS
records for a domain

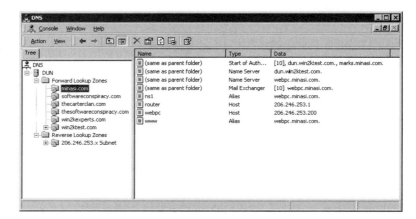

A Records (Hosts)

The simple record that says that webpc.minasi.com is at IP address 206.246.253.200, the record that relates names to IP addresses, is called an *A* record or *host record*. (It's called an A record because DNS's internal database, a set of ASCII files called *zone files*, uses an *A* to indicate that a record is a host record. You'll learn about zone files later.) As you saw in Figure 7.46, A or host records are usually the most numerous—there's one for a machine named webpc at 206.246.253.200 and one for a machine named router. The router entry, by the way, does indeed point to the network's router. Giving the router a name isn't necessary; it just makes pinging it easier.

NOTE   *I know I'm calling them* A records *even though the graphical UI doesn't call them that. But I'm doing it because, again, zone files use the* A *designation—webpc's record in a zone file might look like* **webpc A 206.246.253.200**—*and I believe that you'll agree by the end of the chapter that you can get a lot done with zone files, from both an administration and troubleshooting standpoint. So throughout this section, I'll be presenting the records both as Windows 2000 refers to them and as zone files refer to them.*

And because I've introduced information from an actual Internet domain, let me add the following important warning.

WARNING   *This is very important. Please note that minasi.com and win2ktest.com are domains that I host. I use sample screen shots from them, but* please do not use the domain name win2ktest.com or minasi.com in your network. *If you're live on the Internet, that will make your system attempt to log in to my domain controllers and register records in my win2ktest.com or minasi.com zones (and that's just not polite, if you know what I mean!). That goes for other names that you'll see in this chapter as well, such as the acme.com or bigfirm.biz domains that I use as examples. Other people own these domains and would view attempts to log in to their domains or add records to their DNS servers as hostile acts, and take action accordingly. (After all, what would* you *do if you found some stranger taking up residence in your front room?) I strongly suggest when you're playing around with DNS zones that you ensure that you're not connected to the Internet, that you register a DNS domain name with the proper DNS name authorities such as www.networksolutions.com, or that you set up "split-brain DNS," which I'll describe later. That will ensure that you're a "good Internet citizen." Thanks!*

Cheap "Clusters": Building Fault Tolerance with Multiple A Records and Round-Robin DNS

This isn't a record type, but as long as I'm talking about A records, let me explain a great (and free!) way to handle a lot of Web traffic.

Suppose I've got a Web server at IP address 206.246.253.100. I've named it www.minasi.com because, well, that's what people expect the Web server at minasi.com to be named. But now let's suppose that several thousand people all decide at the same time to hit my Web site to find out how to hire me to speak at their next engagement. (Hey, it could happen.) At that point, my poor Web server's over-loaded, lots of people get some kind of "server is too busy to respond to you" message, and I lose lots of potential business. That would be bad. Really bad.

Alternatively, I could set up three more machines with IIS on them, at IP addresses 206.246.253.101 through 206.246.253.103. Then—and here's the clever part—I just enter host name records, A records, for each of them and name *all* of them www.minasi.com. My DNS snap-in might then look like Figure 7.47.

FIGURE 7.47

Preparing for round-robin DNS on www.minasi.com

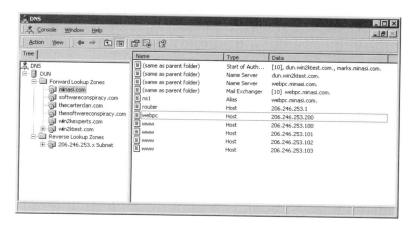

Now that I've got all four machines each named www.minasi.com, suppose someone points her browser to www.minasi.com. My DNS server is then asked by *her* DNS server to resolve the name www.minasi.com. So my DNS server looks at the four addresses that have www.minasi.com and responds with the four IP addresses, saying, "You can find www.minasi.com at 206.246.253.100, .101, .102, and .103." Then, seconds later, someone else's DNS server asks my DNS server what IP address goes with www.minasi.com. My DNS server then responds with the same information, but in a different order, offering first 206.246.253.101, then .102, .103, and finally .100. The DNS client will usually take the first address offered first, so the first visitor will tend to go to .100, and the second to .101. The third person to ask about www.minasi .com gets the four addresses in the order of .102/.103/.100/.101, the fourth as .103/.100/.101/.102, and then for the fifth, DNS cycles back to .100/.101/.102/.103.

This process, called *round-robin DNS*, spreads out the load on a machine. If I had these four Web servers set up, they each would get roughly one-fourth of the incoming Web requests. In that way, I could build a "scalable" Web site. Now, understand that this *isn't* a replacement for Windows 2000

Advanced Server and multisystem clusters. DNS has no idea what's going on with the various Web servers, and if one of them goes down, DNS knows nothing of the problem and just keeps giving out the bad server's IP address to every fourth inquirer. But it's a free way of doing load balancing and worth a try before spending tens of thousands of dollars on cluster systems.

NOTE   *Note that although I used an example of four consecutive IP addresses, you need not use consecutive addresses for your round-robin groups.*

Simple Load Balancing: Subnet Mask Ordering

If you've set up round-robin DNS, where you have several systems that have the same name but different IP addresses, then Windows 2000 DNS servers can not only do round robin for you, they can also load balance.

Suppose I have 10 machines all named server1.minasi.com and 10 subnets on my network. Then suppose I have one of these machines on each subnet. Think about what happens when a computer on a particular subnet asks DNS to resolve server1.minasi.com. Simple round robin would just offer the 10 IP addresses in some random order. But clearly it'd make life easier on the routers if I could somehow tell DNS, "Listen—when someone asks for the IP address of server1.minasi.com, *and* if one of the server1.minasi.com systems is on the same subnet as that someone, then always offer the IP address of the *local* server1.minasi.com first." Windows 2000's DNS server will do that—it's called *subnet mask ordering*. It is enabled by default. (You can turn it off in the Advanced tab of the DNS server's Properties page, which you'll meet a little later.)

SOA Records (Start of Authority)

Every domain has a *start of authority* record, abbreviated in zone files as an *SOA* record. It's the record that names the primary DNS server for the domain, provides an e-mail address for an administrator for the domain, and specifies how long it's okay to cache its data. (I'll explain what a "primary" and a "secondary" DNS server are a bit later, but here's the short version: The primary DNS server for a zone contains the only read/write copy of the zone. Secondary servers—there can be as many as you like—contain read-only copies of the zone, so they can help.) It also alerts the outside world when any of the domain's records have changed through a serial number. In Figure 7.46, the [10] in the SOA record is the domain's serial number and indicates that since the domain was set up, there have been 10 changes—new records, deleted records, modified records. Secondary DNS servers can use this to see whether data on the primary server has changed, requiring them to go get updates from the primary DNS server.

Name Server/NS Records (DNS Servers)

Name server records (called *NS* records in a zone file) define the name servers in the domain. The two NS records name the two DNS servers currently supporting the domain.

NOTE   *By the way, a single machine running DNS server software can act as a DNS server for as many zones as you like, within the limits of CPU power and memory space. You need not dedicate one server to one zone. Actually, you saw that in Figure 7.46; notice that this DNS server acts as a name server for several domains.*

Notice that both records look like "(same as parent folder) Name Server *servername.*" There's a couple of interesting points to be made here. First, notice that the servers' IP addresses aren't listed anywhere here. That's because they are both servers on another domain—to find their IP addresses, you'd search DNS for their A records in win2ktest.com.

Second, notice the "(same as parent folder)"; what that means is that these are name servers for this domain. But you can also use the NS records to delegate authority to a subdomain, a zone. An NS record for an imaginary zone westcoast.minasi.com might look like (in zone file terms):

```
westcoast    NS  surfers.earthlink.net.
```

That record would say, "To resolve names for *somename.*westcoast.minasi.com, go to surfers .earthlink.net." Knowing how to create NS records that point to DNS servers for subdomain zones will come in handy later when we're seeing how to cope with non–Windows 2000 DNS servers.

CNAME Records (Aliases)

Many times, you'll need a host to respond to more than one name. For example, webpc.minasi.com does several different things, including serving as the Web server. I'd like the 206.246.253.200 machine to respond to webpc.minasi.com as well as to ns1.minasi.com and www.minasi.com. I do that with a *CNAME* record (the GUI tool calls them *Aliases*). A CNAME record says something like, "If you need a machine to respond to www in this domain, then point to the machine at webpc.minasi.com." Notice how a CNAME record looks:

```
www Alias webpc.minasi.com.
```

Notice that the left portion only says *www*, not *www.minasi.com.* If you create a CNAME within a given domain, the CNAME must be for a name that ends with the domain's name, hence www rather than www.minasi.com. In contrast, the machine that it's being equated to, webpc.minasi.com, need not be in the domain, and so its full name is entered in the DNS record, *including* the trailing period—leave off the period and it'll just add the zone's name and so it'll think that you mean to equate www.minasi.com to webpc.minasi.com.minasi.com!

CNAME, by the way, stands for *canonical name.* I don't know why they didn't use Alias from the very beginning—it's got the same number of letters—but for whatever reason, we call these CNAME records in the DNS business.

MX Records (Mail Exchange)

If I send mail to `bill@acme.com`, then I've told my e-mail program that I want the mail to go to someone named Bill and that Bill has an account on some server in the acme.com domain. What I *haven't* told my e-mail program is where exactly to send the e-mail for Bill, what his mail server's name is. If it's not immediately obvious why this is important, consider: If you know that my domain is named minasi.com, how do you know where to find my Web or FTP server? There's an *informal* convention in the world that I'd call my Web server www.minasi.com and my FTP server ftp.minasi.com, but nothing *requiring* that. You can't simply tell your Web server, "Go check out the minasi.com Web site." But you *can* tell an e-mail program, "Send this mail to minasi.com." That's because DNS includes something called a *mail exchange* or *MX* record, which answers the question, "Which machine is the mail server for minasi.com?" This particular one says that mail for `someone@minasi.com` should go to the machine named webpc.minasi.com.

Notice that the MX record has a "preference" number in brackets, [10]. That lets you specify more than one MX record for a given domain. If I wanted to be sure that some server could pick up mail even if webpc.minasi.com was down, I could set up e-mail software on an "emergency backup" machine. But I wouldn't want anyone delivering mail there while webpc.minasi.com was functioning, so I'd use the preference number to control that. With the preference number, you indicate to DNS which mail server you prefer—lower numbers are preferred over higher numbers. I could, then, create the emergency mail server and give it a preference number higher than 10. It would then be ignored for mail unless webpc.minasi.com was down. If you specify two MX records of the same priority, then DNS will end up load-balancing the two mail servers.

Pointer (PTR) Records (Reverse Host Records)

Those are the common record types you'll find in a forward lookup zone. Look in a reverse lookup zone, however, and you'll find one more type—a pointer record. Look at Figure 7.48 for an example.

FIGURE 7.48

Example reverse lookup zone

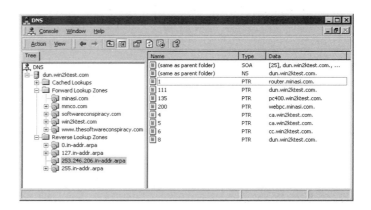

A *pointer record* works just like a host record—an A record—except that where you use an A record to look up the IP address associated with a given host name, a pointer record lets you look up a host name associated with a particular IP address. As you'll see later, you probably won't have to worry too much about these, as Windows 2000's DNS snap-in will, upon request, create pointer records automatically whenever it creates a host record.

SRV Records

The record types you've read about so far have been around for quite some time. But SRV records are new—they first appeared in RFC 2052 (a 1995 document) and were later revised in RFC 2782. They are, however, essential to the Active Directory. You simply cannot run an Active Directory without DNS servers that understand SRV records.

SRV records are fairly long; here's an example:

```
_kerberos._tcp.marksite._sites.dc._msdcs 600 SRV 0 100 88 dc1.win2kbugs.com.
```

SRV records let DNS become a sort of "directory of services" for a domain. For example, if I tell you that my domain's name is minasi.com, how would you know the name of the Web server for that domain? By convention, you'd guess—it's just a guess—that the name of the Web server for minasi.com is www.minasi.com. But what if I wanted to call my Web server something other than "www" and still have you able to find it? I can't, as our common convention for naming Web servers is inflexible. Similarly, how would you find my FTP server, if I had one? You'd guess that its name would be ftp.minasi.com. Fine so long as I only have one FTP server and want to call that computer ftp.minasi.com, but troublesome otherwise.

If it's still not clear why this might be a problem, consider this real-world example: Suppose I go to Acme's headquarters to apply for a job. How would I find the HR office in the Acme building, presuming that's where I go to apply for a job? Well, if we assigned rooms in corporate buildings the way that we assign names for Web and FTP servers, then we'd have some kind of convention such as, "The HR office is room 120." Sound like it might cramp your style? It probably would, which is why we have a building directory on the first floor of most buildings.

Put simply, an SRV record lets you say, "If you're looking for this kind of server, it's over there." The previous example lets you find a type of server called a *Kerberos* server. Kerberos is an authentication protocol, and it normally operates on port 88. Why do you care? Well, inasmuch as the Active Directory authenticates using Kerberos, *this* is how workstations use DNS to find domain controllers. Ignoring some of the details, the above SRV record says, "To find a Kerberos server that communicates on TCP port 88 and which is located on the site named marksite, just go to the machine named dc1.win2kbugs.com."

Additionally, you can have more than one record of this type—and so you can have more than one domain controller for a given domain in a given site.

Fault Tolerance: Primary and Secondary DNS Servers

Next, let's consider how to make this DNS database highly available and fault-tolerant.

If a ton of people all decide at the same time to come surf www.minasi.com, then that means that a ton of *DNS servers* will all be trying at the same time to resolve the address www.minasi.com. But what if I only have one DNS server? That's asking for trouble. It'd be nice if I had more than one DNS server containing a copy of the minasi.com zone file; then those servers could share some of the burden of name resolution. (Of course, those extra DNS servers had better be listed in the DNS servers for the com domain—if a DNS server isn't recognized as authoritative by being listed in its parent's DNS servers, then no one will ever know to even *try* to query the DNS server.)

But that might be a bit chaotic. Suppose I've got five DNS servers that all hold a copy of the minasi.com zone file. When I want to make a change to the zone file, perhaps to add or delete an A record, how do I do that? Must I make the identical change to each of the five copies of the zone file by hand? That doesn't sound like much fun.

Fortunately, I needn't do that. DNS has a built-in system for managing updates to a zone's file. Here's how it works. Each domain has one and only one "primary" DNS server. That's the one that you make changes and updates to the zone file on. And when you set up a DNS server for a particular domain, you must tell the DNS server whether it is the primary DNS server for that domain. As I suggested a few pages back, you designate which DNS server is authoritative for a given zone by naming that DNS server in the SOA record for the zone. You can have only one primary DNS server for a given zone.

Secondary DNS Servers Hold Read-Only Zone Copies

You can have as many *secondary* DNS servers for a zone as you like, however. When you set up a zone on a DNS server, you tell the DNS server whether it should act as the primary DNS server or secondary DNS server for the zone. If it's to be a secondary DNS server, then you must tell the DNS server who is the primary DNS server for that zone, so that the secondary knows where to go to get the "official" copy of the zone files.

NOTE *Note that any DNS server can act as the primary server for more than one zone. In fact, a DNS server can simultaneously act as the primary server for several zones while at the same time also acting as a secondary server for several zones. DNS servers can hold any number of zones.*

How Primary and Secondary DNS Servers Synchronize

As the zone files change, we need some kind of mechanism to update the zone files on the secondaries on a regular basis or, to use Windows 2000 lingo, to "replicate" the zone files. Here are the mechanics of how DNS servers stay in sync.

Recall that you make any changes to a zone on the primary DNS server for that zone; if you were to make a change to a zone on a secondary server for that zone, then the change would be lost. So how do those changes on the primary get synchronized to the secondaries?

When the primary learns something new, it does *not* contact the secondaries; rather, it's the job of the secondaries to ask the primary periodically if there are any changes. They do that every few minutes, and "few minutes" is defined by an item in the Start of Authority record. SOA records contain two bits of information essential to a secondary DNS server: the serial number and the refresh interval.

The refresh interval is a period of time specified in seconds; 900 seconds—15 minutes—is Windows 2000's DNS default. That tells the secondary DNS server for a zone to ask the primary every 15 minutes, "May I see your SOA record?" The secondary asks about the primary's SOA record because it will then use the *serial number* on the primary to determine whether something has changed. What's the serial number? Well, every time you update a zone file on the primary, then the DNS server increments the serial number; if it was 44 before you added a new host, then the serial number goes to 45 after you add that host.

So for example, let's say that the secondary has updated its zone from the primary at 10:00 A.M., learning among other things that the latest serial number for the zone is 237. At 10:01, you add a new host A record at the primary. The primary stores that new A record and increments the serial number to 238. The secondary, of course, knows nothing of this.

But 15 minutes after the last synchronization, the secondary asks the primary for the SOA record. When the primary responds, the secondary notices that the serial number is now larger than it was the last time that it asked, so something must have changed. The secondary requests an update on the zone records, and now it's in sync. Fifteen minutes later, it requests the SOA record again and, if the serial number hasn't changed, does not request an update. The secondary thus polls the primary every 15 minutes, whether things have changed or not.

You can, by the way, change this behavior and tell the primary to tap the secondaries on the shoulder when new information comes in. It's called *notifying*, and you'll see a bit later how to tell the primary DNS server to tell any or all of the secondaries to come get the latest zone data.

Transferring Zone Data

Until recently, DNS servers replicated data to their secondaries in a fairly primitive way.

The secondary servers in a domain periodically contact the primary DNS server and copy its database to theirs. The *whole* database. So if a zone file contained 4000 lines of information and only one line changed, the secondary servers got the whole file when they requested an update. RFC 1995 changed that, allowing for "incremental zone transfers." Put simply, RFC 1995–compliant DNS servers would know how to transfer just the few records that have changed, rather than re-sending the whole zone file. Windows 2000's DNS server is RFC 1995–compliant, and you can configure it to only do incremental zone transfers. (I'll cover the DNS management tool later, but for the curious, you open the DNS MMC snap-in—Start/Programs/Administrative Tools/DNS—and right-click the icon representing the server, click Properties, then click the Advanced tab on the resulting properties page. Uncheck the box labeled BIND Secondaries and click OK or Apply, and the server will do incremental zone transfers to all other DNS servers.)

Secondary DNS servers are just machines that hold a backup copy of the primary DNS server's database. They can also satisfy DNS name resolution queries when asked. They cannot accept changes to the zone files. When the primary DNS server will be down for some time, you can promote any secondary to be the primary DNS server for a domain. In general, however, that's something that an administrator's got to initiate—secondary DNS servers will not promote themselves.

Microsoft's DNS server can do all of the things that I've described so far; it follows the RFCs, the rules of the road for the Internet. But it can do more as well, offering a non-RFC mode that lets you create a zone that is neither a standard primary nor secondary zone, but instead an "Active Directory–integrated zone." These zones offer a few features, but the one that's relevant here is that all DNS servers in an AD-integrated zone are equal when it comes to replication and updates—you can make a change to an AD-integrated zone no matter on which DNS server you're working. The DNS servers then keep track of these changes without the need for a single primary DNS server through a process called *multimaster replication*. Does that mean that you should use AD-integrated zones? As time goes on, I find that I like them for AD-related DNS work more and more. I particularly like that they let you secure a dynamic zone—something that we'll take up a bit later. And the multimaster feature is nice. But I'd prefer not to put my DNS servers on domain controllers, so there are pros and cons. We'll return to AD-integrated zones later.

Building a Simple DNS Zone

I've got plenty of other things to explain about DNS, but by now you're probably feeling a bit itchy to try all of this out. So let's build a DNS zone for an imaginary bigfirm.biz zone. This zone will contain several computers, but if you want to follow along then you only really need one computer, to act as the DNS server.

Introducing bigfirm.biz

Suppose for the sake of argument that I'd like to set up a domain named bigfirm.biz, pictured in Figure 7.49. It has its network set up as a nonroutable class C network at 192.168.0.1.

FIGURE 7.49

bigfirm.biz servers

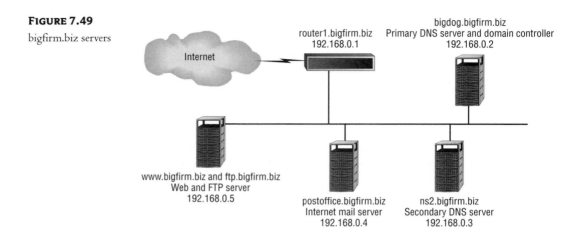

There are just a few machines important enough that they must have entries in DNS:

- As I've mentioned before, it's convenient to name the router at 192.168.0.1.

- The mail server for bigfirm.biz is a machine named postoffice.bigfirm.biz, at 192.168.0.4.

- The Web server for bigfirm.biz is a machine named www.bigfirm.biz, at 192.168.0.5.

- That same 192.168.0.5 machine is also the FTP server, and we want it to respond to the name ftp.bigfirm.biz.

- There is a machine that will act both as a domain controller (once we set up AD in the next chapter) and as the primary DNS server; it's named bigdog.bigfirm.biz, at 192.168.0.2192.168.0.2. If you intend to actually sit down at a machine and follow this example along, then this is the only actual computer you've got to set up. Understand that its domain controller role will be irrelevant right now, as we don't have a domain set up—just a simple workgroup.

- There's another DNS server that also acts as a file server at ns2.bigfirm.biz with address 192.168.0.3.

Some Important Notes about This Example

In the next chapter, I'll take up the Active Directory. AD doesn't work well if DNS isn't set up right, and I get an awful lot of mail from people who try to set up a simple Active Directory with just a machine or two and fail. The reason is almost always the same thing: They didn't set up their DNS infrastructure correctly before trying to set up their domain controllers. So to make things easier for the experimenters, I've integrated *this* example—a simple DNS setup—into next chapter's simple AD setup. So if you're planning to play with next chapter's simple AD example, then don't forget to follow along here for DNS.

Also note that I've assigned addresses in the 192.168.0.0 range, which is a range of nonroutable addresses. (Recall that you learned about nonroutable addresses and Network/Port Address Translation in the previous chapter.) This implies a few things:

♦ If you set up this example with a few machines of your own, then these machines will be unable to access the public Internet, *unless* your router is a NAT/PAT router. Just set up the machine or machines with one of the IP addresses in the example, and set the subnet mask to 255.255.255.0 and the default gateway to 192.168.0.1.

♦ You may recall from the previous chapter that Windows 2000 and later operating systems can act as NAT routers and that there's a kind of simplified NAT router called ICS that you can set up with just a click or two. ICS is set up to use addresses 192.168.0.1–192.168.0.254, which is one reason why I designed this example with those addresses. Where I've got a hardware router pictured in Figure 7.49, you could be running a Windows 2000 or later system acting as the ICS router. In that case, you needn't set its IP address to 192.168.0.1 because, as you learned in the last chapter, enabling ICS automatically sets the IP address on the Ethernet card on the intranet side of the router to 192.168.0.1. Or, alternatively, your NAT/PAT router might simply be an existing corporate router or a DSL/cable modem dedicated router.

♦ Recall that systems with nonroutable addresses accessing the Internet via a NAT/PAT router such as ICS have the ability to *initiate* communications to the public Internet and systems on the public Internet can respond to queries from the systems with the nonroutable addresses, but systems on the public Internet cannot *initiate* conversations with nonroutable addresses. That means that these servers can only serve computers in their 192.168.0.x network. Systems on the public Internet could not access the Web or DNS servers, for example, unless you configured the NAT/PAT router to map ports on the publicly visible router to particular ports on servers in the 192.168.0.x network, or if you had extra routable IP addresses that you could then use the NAT/PAT router to assign to particular systems in the 192.168.0.x network. You saw in the previous chapter how to do that.

Creating the Primary DNS Server

To see all of this at work, I'll need a computer acting as the bigdog.bigfirm.biz machine, where I'll set up the DNS server service. Name servers must be running a DNS server service of some kind, and although they needn't use Microsoft's DNS server program, it's free (and probably the one that you bought the book to learn how to use), so I'll use that one. In case you want to follow along and build a small DNS zone of your own—you needn't in order to understand this—then build a Windows 2000 server (it must be Server; Professional can't run the Microsoft DNS Server service) like so:

♦ Give it the machine name BIGDOG.

♦ You needn't join it to any domain, as you probably don't have one running yet. I joined mine to a workgroup called "bigfirm," but that's not necessary.

More specifically: Install Windows 2000 Server on a machine. Give it the machine name BIGDOG and a static IP address of 192.168.0.2, a subnet mask of 255.255.255.0, and a default gateway value of 192.168.0.1. (Or, if it's doing double-duty as the ICS or NAT/PAT machine, then set its IP address on the Ethernet card on the internal network to 192.168.0.1, subnet mask 255.255.255.0, and no default gateway—refer to previous chapter for more details on ICS and NAT if you're going to do this.) Then change its DNS name to bigdog.bigfirm.biz in the Network Identification tab. More specifically, if you're following along, then these are the steps:

1. Right-click My Computer and choose Properties.

2. Click the Network Identification tab.

3. Click the Properties button.

4. In the Identification Changes dialog box, click the More button to raise the DNS Suffix and NetBIOS Computer Name dialog box.

5. In the field labeled Primary DNS Suffix for This Computer, fill in bigfirm.biz and click OK.

6. Click OK three more times, then Yes to close all of the dialog boxes and reboot the server.

Once the system has rebooted, try an `ipconfig /all` command. You should see that the Host Name is bigdog and the Primary DNS Suffix is bigfirm.biz.

Installing the DNS Service

Once BIGDOG has rebooted and thinks its DNS suffix is bigfirm.biz, let's get the DNS Server service running on it.

The steps to installing DNS are exactly the same as for installing any of the other network services—DHCP or WINS—but here's what you do:

1. Open the Control Panel (Start/Settings/Control Panel).

2. Open Add/Remove Programs.

3. Click Add/Remove Windows Components and wait a bit while the irritating Windows Components Wizard starts up.

4. Click Networking Services and then the Details button.

5. Click the check box next to Domain Name System (DNS).

6. Click OK to return to Windows Components.

7. Click Next to install the service. If you get a page asking about Terminal Services Setup, just click Next. The system will say that it is "Configuring Components" for a while, probably a few minutes, and may need the original Server installation CD. A bit later, the Completing the Windows Components Wizard screen appears.

8. Click Finish to end the wizard.

9. Click Close to close Add/Remove Windows Components and then close Control Panel, if you prefer.

10. Return to your IP properties and set the Preferred DNS Server on BIGDOG to point to itself—192.168.0.2.

TIP *That's a general rule—you should usually set up DNS servers to point to themselves for name resolution; specify the server's IP address in the Preferred DNS Server field. If you configure the server via a DHCP reservation, then you can specify the server's preferred DNS server address in the reservation as well.*

You needn't reboot. Click Start/Programs/Administrative Tools/DNS and you'll see the DNS snap-in. You'll see an icon representing your server in the left pane; click the plus sign next to it and you'll see a screen like Figure 7.50.

FIGURE 7.50

Initial DNS snap-in screen

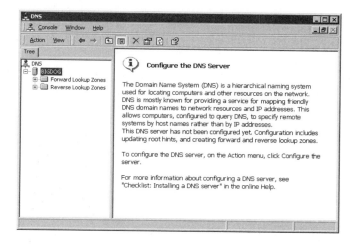

Creating the bigfirm.biz Zone

Notice that under your server's icon are two folders, Forward Lookup Zones and Reverse Lookup Zones. I'll create the bigfirm.biz zone—a forward lookup zone—by clicking the plus sign next to Forward Lookup Zones, then right-clicking the Forward Lookup Zones container and choosing New Zone, which invokes a wizard, as you see in Figure 7.51.

FIGURE 7.51

New Zone Wizard opening screen

It'd be really nice if Windows 2000 came with an expert mode setting that would let us bypass these wizards, but there isn't one. Perhaps in Windows 2002 Server. In any case, click Next to see Figure 7.52.

FIGURE 7.52

Choosing a zone type

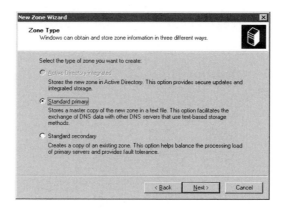

Here, you tell the wizard whether to create a primary or secondary zone. Choose Standard Primary. The first option, Active Directory–Integrated, is grayed out because this is a stand-alone server. If, however, I were to build a Windows 2000 domain named bigfirm.biz, then I would have the option to convert this zone to an AD-integrated zone (but we'll look at AD-integrated zones in more detail later). Click Next, and you'll see Figure 7.53.

FIGURE 7.53

Name the zone.

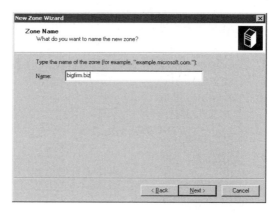

Here, I tell it the name, bigfirm.biz, and click Next to see Figure 7.54.

In this figure, you see a really nice feature of this server software. It suggests a name for the zone file that it's about to create, which is not a big deal. What's really nice, however, is that you can choose any filename—and, more important, you can point the server at an already-existing zone file by clicking Use This Existing File. *That* means that disaster recovery on DNS servers is a snap: Just install the

DNS service on a new system, set its IP address to equal the IP address of the DNS server that it's replacing, copy the zone files from the old server (or its backups) to the new server, and then just re-create the zones with a few clicks of the wizard. You then point the wizard at the already-existing files—meaning that you needn't re-create any DNS records—and in a few minutes you've completely rebuilt your DNS server.

FIGURE 7.54

Name the zone file.

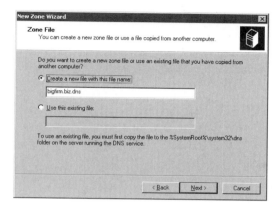

Click Next, and you'll get a confirmation screen like the one in Figure 7.55. Click Finish, and you've got your zone.

FIGURE 7.55

Wizard confirma-
tion screen

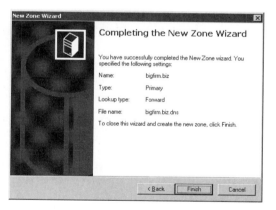

Creating the Reverse Lookup Zone

Next, let's get the reverse lookup zone created so that when I create host records in the forward zone, there's a reverse zone in which to create pointer records.

Before I do that, however, I should point out that you may not ever have to *create* a reverse lookup zone. Some ISPs insist on managing the reverse zones, so the ISP that bigfirm.biz got its C network from might say, "You've got DNS responsibility for bigfirm.biz, and you've got the addresses in such-and-such range of IP addresses, but we'll keep track of its reverse lookup zone for those IP addresses." So, for example, I work with a C network of 206.246.253.0, and so its reverse lookup zone would be 253.246.206.in-addr.arpa. By default, my ISP creates and maintains that reverse lookup zone—not because they're control freaks or anything like that, but just because many people probably don't feel like running their reverse lookup zones.

Try to get them to allow you to run the reverse lookup zone, if you can, because I've found that Windows 2000 works much better when you control them both, or at least when you're careful to have records in the reverse zone *at least* for your DNS servers. As you'll learn a bit later, there's a useful tool you can use for diagnosing DNS troubles called NSLOOKUP. My ISP was good enough to let me manage my reverse lookup, but there's no guarantee that yours will. However, inasmuch as we're building our own nonroutable network, then no one will complain if we run our own reverse lookup zone!

More specifically, here's why you'll care if you don't have a reverse lookup zone that corresponds to your forward zone or zones. In the example that I'm working through now, the DNS server for bigfirm.biz is bigdog.bigfirm.biz at 192.168.0.2192.168.0.2. But remember that your TCP/IP configuration doesn't ask you to tell it the *name* of your DNS server—it wants the *IP address* of your DNS server, and that seems to lead to the potential trouble.

What I've seen is that if I start NSLOOKUP, then it knows only the IP address of the DNS server that it's supposed to be using. NSLOOKUP's first act is to contact the *reverse lookup zone* for the DNS server's IP address in order to obtain the DNS server's DNS name. NSLOOKUP wants to interrogate your DNS hierarchy to say to it, "I have your IP address, but what's your host name?" So somewhere, *some* reverse lookup zone had better know about the DNS server!

For example, if I started NSLOOKUP on a system that looked to 192.168.0.2 as its DNS server, then NSLOOKUP would ask bigdog.bigfirm.biz the host name of the machine with IP address 192.168.0.2. If whoever's running the 0.168.192.in-addr.arpa zone hasn't added a pointer record for 192.168.0.2, or if you're running a completely private DNS system that is unconnected to the Internet's DNS hierarchy and no one has created the reverse lookup zone, then NSLOOKUP for some reason acts like it can't find a DNS server.

WARNING   *I should point out that just because NSLOOKUP can't do the reverse resolution, NSLOOKUP will still work—it'll just produce an annoying set of error messages every time you use it.*

In any case, to create the reverse lookup zone, click the plus sign next to the Reverse Lookup Zones folder, and then right-click the that Reverse Lookup Zones folder and choose New Zone, which will kick off the same wizard that you just saw. The first two panels are identical—choose to create a primary zone again—and you'll see the third panel, which looks different, and looks like Figure 7.56.

Here, the wizard makes life easy for you—you just type in the network number of your block of IP addresses and it flips the numbers around, and when you click Next, the wizard adds the .in-addr.arpa suffix, as you see in Figure 7.57.

Again, you can either create a new zone here, or revivify a dead zone by pointing the wizard at an old zone file. Click Next and Finish, and you've got two zones, as you see in Figure 7.58.

FIGURE 7.56

Defining the reverse lookup zone

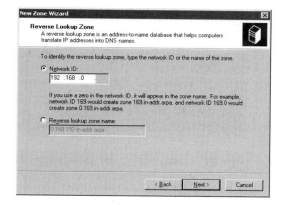

FIGURE 7.57

Choosing a zone filename

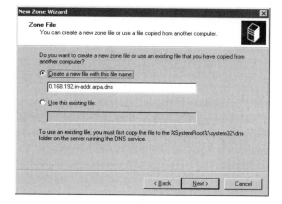

FIGURE 7.58

DNS snap-in with forward and reverse zones

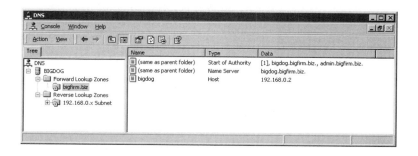

Note that there isn't always a one-to-one relationship between forward and reverse lookup zones. For example, on my network, which is just one class C network, I host the windowsnetworking.info, learnwindows.biz, mmco.com, minasi.com, win2ktest.com, win2kbugs.com, win2kexperts.com, softwareconspiracy.com, and thesoftwareconspiracy.com domains. All machines in those nine domains have IP addresses somewhere in my 206.246.253.0/24 network range. Thus, I've got nine forward lookup zones but only one reverse lookup zone.

Cleaning Up after the Wizard

The wizard makes a few assumptions about your zones that you might not agree with, so it's worthwhile to take a closer look at its work. I right-click the bigfirm.biz container and choose Properties, which brings up a five-page property sheet. The first tab is labeled General, as you see in Figure 7.59.

FIGURE 7.59

General property tab with dynamic updates options exposed

This tab points to the zone file, which is how you'd tell DNS to go work with a backup file if the original zone file were somehow corrupted. Notice that there's a button to pause this zone, meaning to tell the DNS server to stop responding to resolution requests for this zone, and a button that'll let you change the server's status from primary for the zone to being one of potentially many secondaries for the zone. This is an important button because *this* is the way that you promote a secondary DNS server to become the primary for the zone.

The setting you'll probably want to fool with, however, is the one labeled Allow Dynamic Updates. As you'll learn a bit later in this chapter, Internet standard RFC 2136 defines a neat tool called *dynamic DNS* (DDNS). As you'll see, DDNS is not only useful in a Windows 2000–based network, it's *essential* if your Win2K-based network will use Active Directory domains—which it probably will. By default, the wizard disables that feature for security reasons, which will cause you *big* problems if you want this DNS server to serve a Windows 2000 domain. DNS servers for Windows 2000 domains *must* be able to accept dynamic updates, or you simply can't set up a Win2K domain. Presuming that bigfirm.biz will one day become an Active Directory domain, let's enable DDNS by clicking the Allow Dynamic Updates drop-down and changing the setting from No to Yes.

TIP *If you click the drop-down list, then you'll only see the Yes and No options. But later on we'll see that if you make a zone an Active Directory–integrated zone, then you'll get a third option, Only Secure Updates. That's a great option if you're using AD-integrated zones, as it keeps outsiders from registering on your zone. If you ever create an AD-integrated zone in some real-world setting, be sure to choose Only Secure Updates.*

Next stop is the Start of Authority (SOA) tab. It looks like Figure 7.60.

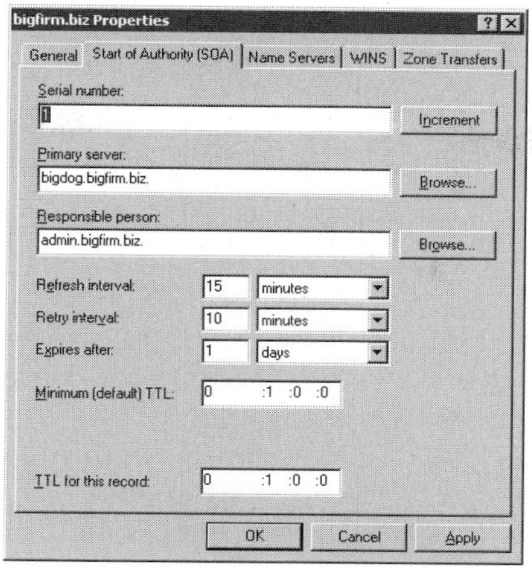

FIGURE 7.60

Start of Authority
properties page

What Microsoft's done here is just to GUI-ify the fields that you find in a standard SOA record. And although putting graphical interfaces on many tools often seems hardly worth the effort, it's much appreciated here. Let's take a look at each of these fields.

First is Serial Number, which indicates how many changes have been made to the zone since it was created. Here you see a serial number of 1 because I haven't done anything to it yet. In general, leave this alone and let the server increment it automatically as needed.

Primary Server identifies the DNS server authoritative for this domain. As you know, I'm using bigdog.bigfirm.biz, which is of course a member of this DNS domain. But don't expect that to always be the case—it's common for small domains to pay their ISP to maintain the DNS servers for those domains. In that case, the primary DNS for bigfirm.biz might be in another domain altogether.

Responsible Person names the e-mail address of someone to whom to send problems and questions. It's an e-mail address, but it's formatted strangely—admin.bigfirm.biz is the way that an SOA record stores the address `administrator@bigfirm.biz`. In any case, it's wrong, as I'm the person setting this up, so I'd replace administrator.bigfirm.biz with help.minasi.com because my e-mail address is `help@minasi.com`.

The next three numbers instruct secondary servers how to get information from the primary server. Refresh Interval tells all secondary servers to query this primary server at least once every 15 minutes. That's the Windows 2000 default, but truthfully seems a bit short—I'd set it to an hour minimum. (Or you could set up your zone so that the secondary doesn't come bug the primary to see if there are changes; instead, as explained elsewhere in this chapter, you can tell the primary to *notify* the secondary whenever there's a change.) If the secondaries try to connect with the primary and can't, however, the Retry Interval option instructs the secondaries to try to communicate with the primary every 10 minutes. Expires After tells the secondaries that if they are unable to communicate with the primary DNS server for an entire day, they should assume the information that they have is too far out-of-date and discard it. In other words, when a secondary cannot access the primary for more than one day, then the secondary basically just stops answering name resolution queries.

The final two entries direct other DNS servers how long to cache name resolution data. TTL stands for *time to live* and is expressed as days:hours:minutes:seconds.

Minimum (Default) TTL advises other DNS servers how long to cache information received from this server. It's 60 minutes by default, so any DNS server that does a name resolution on bigfirm.biz and then needs the same name resolved 59 minutes later need not requery one of the bigfirm.biz DNS servers. Sixty minutes is the Microsoft default, and personally I think it's a bit short—I'd set it somewhere between four hours and a day. The field is called Minimum TTL because every single record in a DNS zone file can have its own separate TTL. The vast majority of the time, however, you won't assign a specific TTL to a specific DNS record, so this "Minimum" TTL is probably more properly called a "Default" TTL.

The final field, TTL for This Record, allows you to set a different TTL just for this SOA record. As you just read, you can, if you want, set specific TTLs for each and every record in any given DNS zone.

The next tab is the Name Servers properties page, as you see in Figure 7.61.

FIGURE 7.61

Name Servers properties page

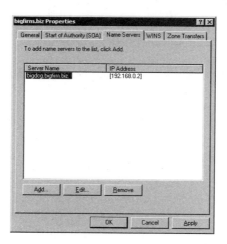

This is where you specify the names of other name servers. We'll use this later to add ns2.bigfirm.biz to our list of name servers. The next page is the WINS page, and although it was an interesting feature under NT 4, I can't recommend it now, so click the Zone Transfers tab to look at that page, as you see in Figure 7.62.

For a secondary DNS server to operate, it has to copy the information in the primary DNS server's zone files to its own zone files—to ensure that its database of names and IP addresses is up-to-date. Copying zone information from one server to another is called *zone transfers*, as you've already read. Why control this? Security. You might not want just *anyone* being able to just make themselves into secondary DNS servers on one of your zones.

By default, this DNS server will transfer the contents of its zone files to any server that asks. But knowing the names of your system's machines can help bad guys compromise security on your network, so Windows 2000 gives you the option to disallow transfers altogether, to name a set of acceptable DNS servers to limit transfers to, or to just transfer to the other name servers listed on the Name Servers page—a quite logical option. If you've got a group of people in your organization who set network security policy, then check with them before leaving zone transfers open to just anyone.

FIGURE 7.62

Zone Transfers prop-
erties page

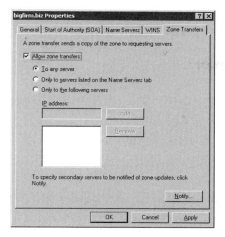

I'm done working with bigfirm.biz's configuration, so I click OK to close the properties page. Then I need to do the same thing to 0.168.192.in-addr.arpa's zone—fix the responsible party and allow dynamic updates, at the very least, and possibly modify the time intervals in the SOA record.

Creating Host Records

DNS's main job is simple name resolution—ask it the IP address of a machine named postoffice .bigfirm.biz, and it tells you that the IP address is 192.168.0.4. DNS knows that information via host or A records.

Right-click the `bigfirm.biz` folder and choose New Host and you'll see a dialog box like Figure 7.63.

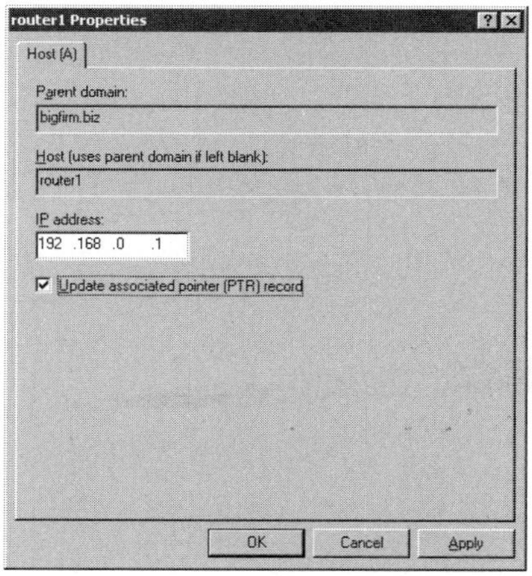

FIGURE 7.63

New host dialog box

In that figure, I've filled in the information about bigfirm.biz's LAN/WAN router, at 192.168.0.1. I've also checked Update Associated Pointer (PTR) Record, which will create a pointer record in the reverse lookup zone. I click OK. Then I create the other hosts:

Router1	192.168.0.1
ns2	192.168.0.3
postoffice	192.168.0.4
www	192.168.0.5

Once done, my DNS snap-in looks like Figure 7.64.

FIGURE 7.64

Host names all entered

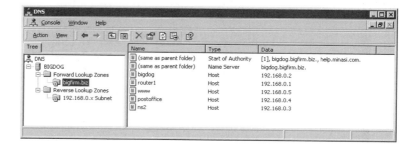

If you thought it was a pain to punch in a handful of A records, then you might be wondering how you're going to create a DNS zone in the real world, where you might have dozens or hundreds of servers and hundreds or thousands of workstations. *That's* where the relatively new notion of dynamic DNS is useful. As you'll learn later, you can, with DDNS, tell the workstations and servers to create their *own* A records in the DNS server—but we'll get to that in a bit.

Identifying the Second Name Server

Next, I'll tell the network that there's another DNS server around. I can't click New Name Server or anything like that. Again, I've got to right-click the `bigfirm.biz` container and choose Properties, then click the Name Servers page. It has an Add button on it, and when I choose it and fill in ns2's information, it looks like Figure 7.65.

Here, I've filled in its name and IP address, although just the IP address is sufficient.

Creating the MX Record

We run our SMTP/POP3 server on postoffice.bigfirm.biz at 192.168.0.4, but there's no way for people either on our intranet or out on the public Internet to know that—mail to someone@bigfirm.biz will never get to us. (Again, as this is a nonroutable address, the outside world couldn't even *communicate* with this server, unless the NAT router provides postoffice with an externally visible address. But this is useful even for internal-only mail.) I'll fix that by adding an MX record for postoffice. Right-click the bigfirm.biz container and choose New Mail Exchanger and a dialog box like Figure 7.66 appears.

FIGURE 7.65

Defining ns2 as a DNS server for the domain

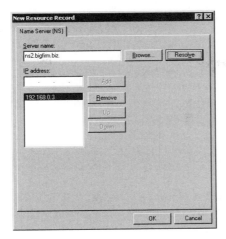

FIGURE 7.66

Making postoffice the designated mail server

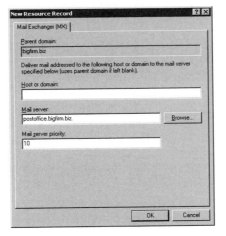

Notice that this dialog box wants to see postoffice's full DNS name, postoffice.bizfirm.biz. That's because a machine on an entirely different domain might be the desired mail server. By default, the DNS server suggests a mail preference value of 10, and because there's only one mail server on this domain, it doesn't matter what value we set here—there's no other server to "prefer."

Giving the Web Server a Second Name

The last initial configuration job to get out of the way is the FTP server. We've got a machine that acts both as a Web server and as an FTP server. Its current name is www.bigfirm.biz, so people will clearly have no problem finding our Web server. But people assume that an FTP server will have the name ftp, so it'd be nice if the machine also answered to ftp.bigfirm.biz. We add this second name with the CNAME or Alias function; right-click bigfirm.biz and choose New Alias and you'll see a dialog box like the one in Figure 7.67.

FIGURE 7.67

Assigning an alias to the Web server

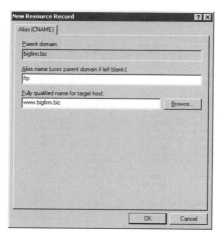

As the alias is to be an alias relevant to this domain, you don't fill in the domain name—**ftp** is sufficient. (In fact, you *can't* enter **ftp.bigfirm.biz** in that field and have it work properly.) The alias could, however, refer to a machine outside of the domain—perhaps www.smallfirm.com holds the FTP libraries for both bigfirm.biz *and* smallfirm.com—and so you fill in the second field with a complete DNS name.

At this point, bigfirm.biz looks like Figure 7.68 in the snap-in.

The reverse lookup zone doesn't know about ns2, so it's worthwhile opening its properties page and adding ns2 to its list of name servers. And of course, my work's not done yet—postoffice had better be ready to accept mail, the Web and FTP server programs on www need to be running, and the secondary zones on ns2 need setting up—but the basics are out of the way.

FIGURE 7.68

bigfirm.biz's state after configuration

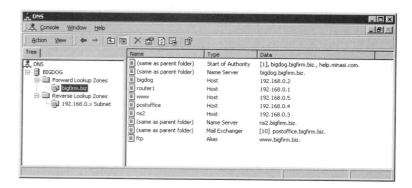

Creating a PTR Record for BIGDOG

As we've been creating A records for all of the systems in bigfirm.biz, then the DNS snap-in has been conveniently creating reverse lookup—PTR—records for each system. But we never created an A record for BIGDOG—the DNS snap-in did that automatically.

Unfortunately, it doesn't create a PTR record automatically. So we'll need to create one. Right-click the reverse lookup zone, the folder labeled 192.168.0.x Subnet, and choose New Pointer. It'll ask for the last quad of the IP address and a fully qualified name for BIGDOG; fill in **2** and **bigdog .bigfirm.biz.** as you see in Figure 7.69 and click OK.

FIGURE 7.69

Creating a PTR record for BIGDOG

Creating a Secondary DNS Server for bigfirm.biz

We've got one DNS server set up; now let's set up a secondary for a bit of backup, safety, and fault tolerance. Recall that we've planned for a secondary DNS server named ns2.bigfirm.biz at 192.168.0.3.

SETTING UP THE SECONDARY ZONE

Install Windows 2000 Server on that system, give it the IP address 192.168.0.3, set its name to ns2 and its DNS suffix to bigfirm.biz as I did with BIGDOG (which, you'll recall, requires a reboot). Set the IP stack to point to itself—192.168.0.3 for preferred DNS server, and start up the DNS snap-in.

Notice that so far I've not done anything to make this server a "secondary" DNS server, and in fact there *is* no such thing as a secondary DNS server—there are only secondary zones hosted on a particular DNS server. Recall that a DNS server can host many zones. When you set up any given zone on a DNS server, you identify whether that DNS server's role will be primary or secondary *for that zone.* In fact, it's quite common to see DNS servers that are primary for some zones but at the same time serving as secondary, "backup" servers in other zones.

To make ns2.bigfirm.biz a secondary DNS server for bigfirm.biz, I start the process of creating a new zone as before—in the snap-in, I right-click the `Forward Lookup Zones` container and choose New Zone and the wizard appears. Clicking past the first screen, I see the screen that asks what type of zone this will be, as you see in Figure 7.70.

FIGURE 7.70

Opting for a secondary zone

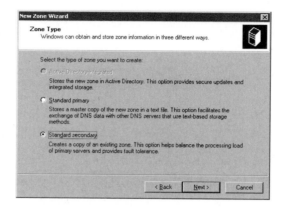

By clicking the Standard Secondary radio button, I warn the wizard to ask me different things. When I click Next, it asks me, as it has before when creating primary zones, for the name of the zone and what to call the zone files. But the next screen asks something new, as you see in Figure 7.71.

FIGURE 7.71

Identifying the primary DNS server

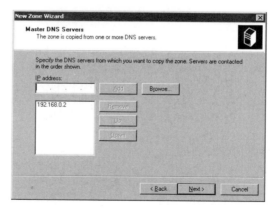

As this is to be a secondary server, serving mainly to back up information from another server, the secondary server must know where to find the original information. I enter the IP address of bigdog .bigfirm.biz and click Add and Next, then Finish, and the secondary is created. In a moment or two, you'll see a zone in `Forward Lookup Zones` named bigfirm.biz; open it, and you'll see all of the big-firm.biz records.

SECURING ZONES

Creating secondary DNS servers presents some potential security questions. When you set up a secondary DNS server, you'll see that all you really have to do is to say, "I want to be a secondary DNS server for domain xyz.com, and you'll find the primary DNS server for xyz.com at 10.10.10.17." Your new secondary server then contacts that primary server and asks it for a copy of the entire xyz.com zone.

But does the primary obey the request? In some cases, the primary's administrators might not think so. One could argue that DNS zones contain information that would make life easier for a hacker—and, to an extent, that's right. So one way for a hacker to immediately retrieve all of the available information about a given zone would be to just set up a secondary DNS server for that zone.

If you don't feel you have anything particularly worth stealing in your zone file, then don't worry about this. But if it's a concern, then consider securing zone transfers. You can do that from the *primary* DNS server for bigfirm.biz; right-click the zone, choose Properties, and then click the Zone Transfers tab. You'll see a dialog box like the one in Figure 7.72.

FIGURE 7.72

Zone Transfers tab in bigfirm.biz

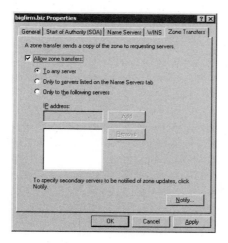

By default, a Windows 2000 system acting as a primary DNS server for a zone will allow any DNS server to request that it transfer a copy of the entire zone. But, as you see in the dialog box, you can choose to restrict transfers only to name servers named in the NS records—the Name Servers tab—or to a specific list whose IP addresses you specify. Or, for truly higher security, you could disallow zone transfers altogether; but then you couldn't have secondary DNS servers.

You can also change the way that DNS servers replicate by clicking the Notify button. As you read earlier, by default it is the secondary servers that poll the primary for changes. But if you click the Notify button, then you'll get a dialog box that lets you instruct the primary to inform any or all of the secondaries when there's been a change in the zone files and that they therefore should come get the changes.

Testing the Configuration

Well, by now, your DNS server should be up. But how to check it? With a diagnostic tool called NSLOOKUP. It's a command-line utility, one of those old cryptic Unix utilities. If DNS is a server, think of NSLOOKUP as a simple diagnostic client. It'll talk to any DNS server and let you make simple queries, queries that mimic an outside computer trying to resolve a name. When you type **nslookup**, it responds with a > prompt. I'll work at BIGDOG for this example. These are the commands I'll use:

◆ First, I type **nslookup** to start the program. The system will respond with the IP address of the DNS server that it's currently using to resolve names. Notice it's 192.168.0.2, BIGDOG. Make sure you've got the reverse lookup zone enabled as well, or this won't work.

◆ Then **ls -d bigfirm.biz** says, "List everything you know about bigfirm.biz." That will show me what BIGDOG knows.

◆ Now that I've seen that BIGDOG answers queries about the domain correctly, let's try out the backup, ns2.bigfirm.biz. The command **server 192.168.0.3** or **server ns2.bigfirm.biz** tells NSLOOKUP to direct its name queries to that server from this point on.

◆ Let's try a different type of query. **set type=any** and **bigfirm.biz** displays a summary of information about bigfirm.biz.

◆ **exit** exits NSLOOKUP.

You can see the session in Figure 7.73.

FIGURE 773

Running NSLOOKUP to test the DNS server

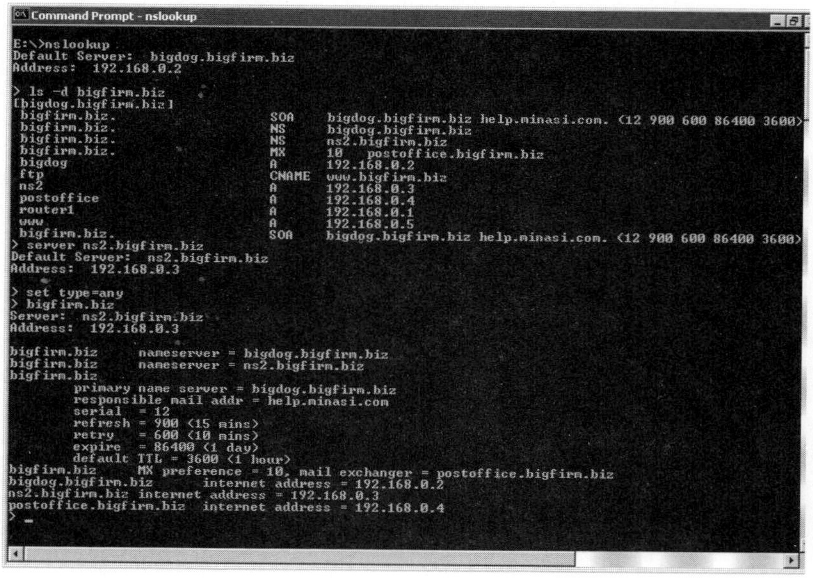

Creating Subdomains in DNS

Now bigfirm.biz is running well. But suppose we wanted to delegate control of some of Bigfirm to another group within the organization, as you see in Figure 7.74.

FIGURE 7.74

Expanded
bigfirm.biz DNS
structure

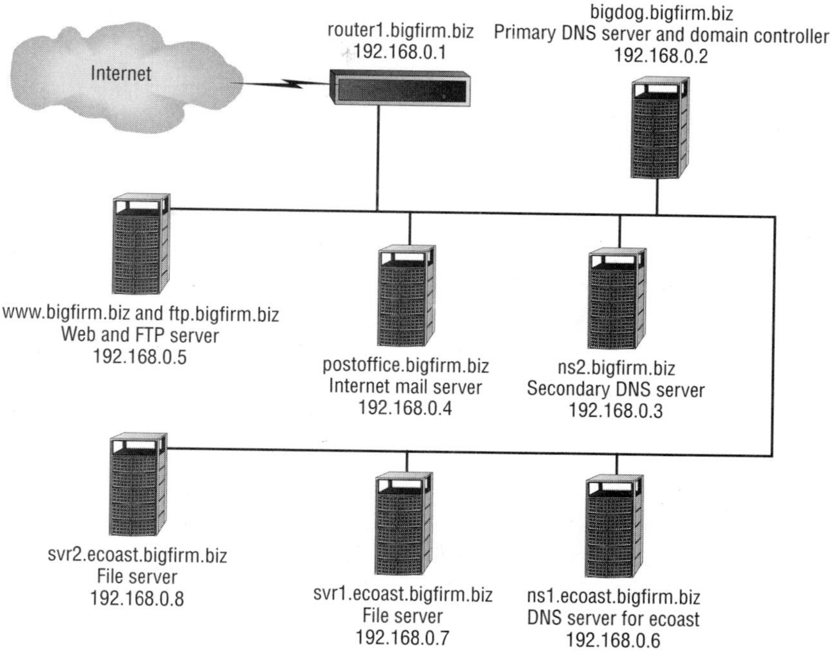

In that figure, I've added three systems: ns1.ecoast.bigfirm.biz (192.168.0.6); svr1.ecoast.bigfirm .biz (192.168.0.7), a file server of some kind, and svr2.ecoast.bigfirm.biz (192.168.0.8). Notice that all of the names have gotten longer—they're all *something*.ecoast.bigfirm.biz—and that means that we'll need another DNS server. For whatever reason, the bigfirm.biz IT management decided to let the ecoast.bigfirm.biz folks administer their own DNS, and so wants to give them a new subdomain, ecoast.bigfirm.biz. There are three parts to setting up a new subdomain that someone else's DNS server keeps track of:

- ◆ Tell the upper-level domain that there will be a lower-level domain under another system's control.

- ◆ Tell the upper-level domain's DNS server where to find a DNS server for the new lower-level domain.

- ◆ Set up the new lower-level domain's DNS server.

In DNS-ese, we'd call this *delegating control of a zone*. (And if you find yourself nodding off, then let me plead with you to pay attention here—many of you will use this to make the Active Directory fit into an existing Microsoft-hostile DNS infrastructure!) Briefly, do it this way:

1. Right-click the upper-level domain (bigfirm.biz) in the DNS snap-in and choose New Delegation.

2. That starts a wizard that basically wants to know just three things: what the subdomain will be called, and what are the name and IP address of its first authoritative DNS server. Tell it that the new delegated domain is named "ecoast" (it adds the bigfirm.biz all by itself), that the name server for ecoast.bigfirm.biz is called ns1.ecoast.bigfirm.biz, and that its IP address is 192.168.0.6.

3. Go to the new DNS server for the new ecoast.bigfirm.biz subdomain (that server is ns1.ecoast.bigfirm.biz, recall) and set up the new ecoast.bigfirm.biz subdomain in the exact same way that you've already created other DNS domains.

Here's a look at a step-by-step example of how to do it in bigfirm.biz.

Tell bigfirm.biz to Delegate ecoast.bigfirm.biz

There are actually a few steps under the hood to telling bigfirm.biz that it needn't worry about name resolution for anything whose name ends with ecoast.bigfirm.biz, and in the days before the DNS snap-in you'd have to do those steps one at a time. The DNS Delegation Wizard, however, handles them all for you. I right-click the `bigfirm.biz` folder and choose New Delegation, which starts up a wizard. Click Next past its title screen and you'll see a screen like Figure 7.75.

Here, I fill in the name of the subdomain "ecoast," not the whole ecoast.bigfirm.biz domain. Again, it's just the new part of the domain name, ecoast rather than ecoast.bigfirm.biz. I then click Next and see something like Figure 7.76.

This panel wants to know the name and IP address of the DNS server (or servers) for the new subdomain. I can enter a name/IP address pair by clicking Add, which shows the dialog box in Figure 7.77.

FIGURE 7.75

Naming the subdomain to delegate to

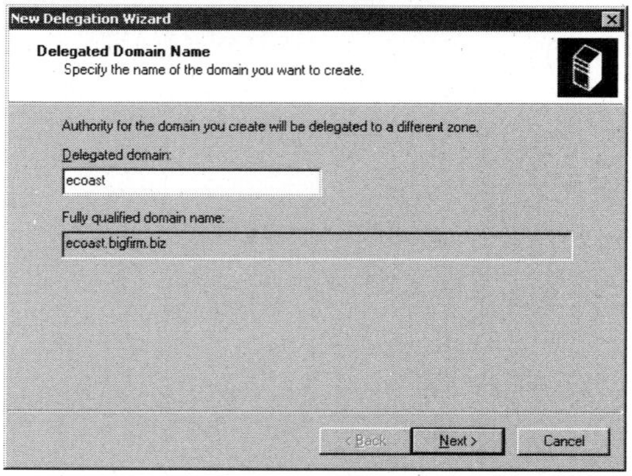

Here, you've got to fill in *both* IP address and name to satisfy this dialog box. I then click OK and Next, and the final screen is a confirmation. Click Finish, and the delegation is done. The snap-in now looks like Figure 7.78.

FIGURE 7.76

What DNS server to delegate to

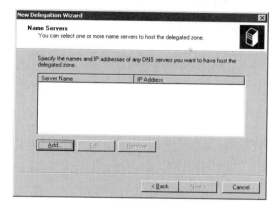

FIGURE 7.77

Specifying the DNS server

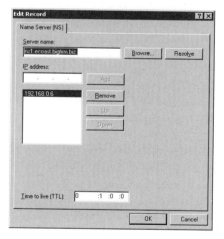

FIGURE 7.78

DNS snap-in with delegated domain

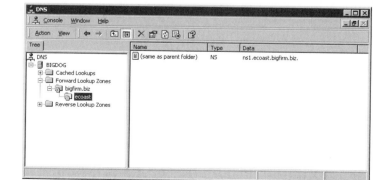

It doesn't look very different on a black and white page, but that **ecoast** folder has gone from a light yellow color to gray, indicating it's a delegated domain. You may not see the color change on your system immediately—you may have to click **bigfirm.biz** and/or **ecoast** and press F5 to see it. At this point, the work's done on this server; time to go work at ns1.ecoast.bigfirm.biz.

Creating the Lower-Level Domain, ecoast.bigfirm.biz

Working from ns1.ecoast.bigfirm.biz, run its DNS snap-in, right-click its **Forward Lookup Zones** folder and choose New Zone. From this point on, it ought to look familiar. You create a subdomain with exactly the same wizard you used to create the domain.

In fact, if you think about it, it makes perfect sense. If you get a domain name from Network Solutions with a name such as bigfirm.biz, then Network Solutions has already gone to *its* domain named simply com and delegated control of a subdomain of com—that is, bigfirm.biz. We don't think about that much because it's not anything we worry about normally. But the second part of the process, creating the zone, we *do* think about, as that's usually our job as network engineer types.

Peeking at the Zone Files

Before I leave our simple zone, let's take a look beyond the GUI and see how the DNS data is stored for a delegation. So long as you do not choose to create an Active Directory–integrated zone, then Windows 2000's DNS server stores your DNS records in the same format as a Unix DNS server would—in a simple ASCII file called a *zone file*. The 2000 DNS server stores these zone files in the \winnt\system32\dns folder; look there, and you'll see a file named bigfirm.biz.dns.

Why would you bother doing this? Troubleshooting or recovery. Sometimes it's just easier to stop the DNS service and then directly examine the zone files. (You must stop the DNS service, because if you modify a zone file without first stopping the DNS service, then your changes will be lost.) We'll see a bit more about recovery a bit later in the chapter.

Returning to the bigfirm.biz.dns file, after a bit of editing to rearrange the records (which doesn't affect DNS's behavior at all) and remove some comments, mine looks like this:

```
@ IN  SOA bigdog.bigfirm.biz.  help.minasi.com. (
   12            ; serial number
   900           ; refresh
   600           ; retry
   86400         ; expire
   3600       ) ; minimum TTL


@ NS bigdog.bigfirm.biz.
@ NS ns2.bigfirm.biz.

bigdog      A      192.168.0.2
ns2         A      192.168.0.3
postoffice  A       192.168.0.4
router1     A      192.168.0.1
www         A      192.168.0.5
ns1.ecoast  A      192.168.0.6
```

```
ecoast      NS      ns1.ecoast.bigfirm.biz.
ftp         CNAME   www.bigfirm.biz.
@           MX 10   postoffice.bigfirm.biz.
```

This zone file contains SOA, NS, A, CNAME, and MX records. Let's see what they say. As you've seen so far:

- The A records relate host names to IP addresses.

- The NS records identify name servers for particular zones.

- The MX records identify mail servers for particular machines or zones.

- The SOA record describes the characteristics of the zone and who to contact if there's a problem with the zone.

- The CNAME record lets you add an extra recognized name to an IP address.

Most records have three pieces of information on them: the object being described, the record type, and the descriptive information. For example, consider a record like this:

```
postoffice  A      192.168.0.4
```

This would mean, "The host named postoffice in this domain has IP address 192.168.0.4." Notice that the leftmost part of the text says postoffice rather than postoffice.bigfirm.biz. Within zone files, descriptive labels in general are assumed to be only host names, and zone names are appended automatically. If you *don't* want that to happen, put a period at the end of the name, as in:

```
postoffice. A      192.168.0.4
```

Notice the period after "postoffice." That would assign the IP address to a host whose fully qualified domain name was simply postoffice, with no .com or the like after it.

I've mentioned TTL, or time to live, information. None of the previous records have TTL information, but if you wanted to put a TTL on a record, then just put the number of seconds that it's good for. So, for example, to tell the world that postoffice.bigfirm.biz has the IP address 192.168.0.4, but to check back with us on that information every day, we might have this A record:

```
postoffice  86400  A  192.168.0.4
```

SOA Record in Zone File Format

The first record is the SOA record:

```
@ IN  SOA bigdog.bigfirm.biz.  help.minasi.com. (
```

It's basically saying, "This the start of authority record for bigfirm.biz."

Waitaminute—I don't see "bigfirm.biz" anywhere in that line. Where'd I get that this is the SOA for bigfirm.biz? The answer is the @ sign. It's got a magic meaning inside zone files completely *different* from the magic meaning that it has in e-mail addresses. Instead of separating an e-mail name from a user's domain, the @ here is shorthand for "this zone." So, because this is the bigfirm.biz zone, @ is just a shorthand way of saying bigfirm.biz. If you wanted to, you could write the SOA record as this:

```
bigfirm.biz. IN SOA bigdog.bigfirm.biz. ...
```

This is why you can't type the e-mail address of the responsible person for the zone with an @. If you did, DNS would just expand the @ to `bigfirm.biz`, leading to a pretty funny-looking e-mail address.

The `IN` is a holdover from the early days of DNS—it stands for *Internet* and refers to the fact that at one point it appeared that there would be other namespaces that DNS would worry about. Strictly speaking, every one of these records needs the `IN` part—I've worked with older DNS servers that wouldn't function without it—but it appears that the Windows 2000 DNS server doesn't need it. You might have to edit zone records to insert an `IN` before the record type—for example, all of the As might have to become `IN As`—if you wanted to put a Windows 2000 DNS zone file on an older DNS server.

Following the `@ IN SOA` is `bigdog.bigfirm.biz.`—that's the DNS name of the primary DNS server for this zone.

NOTE   *Notice—that's the* primary *DNS server, which is not necessarily the* authoritative *DNS server. How can you tell by looking at this zone file which server is authoritative? You can't. You find out which DNS server is authoritative, recall, by looking in the zone files of the* parent *domain to find out how the parent delegates name resolution responsibility for the child.*

Following that is the e-mail address of the technical contact for the domain, the e-mail address of the person to mail to if there's a problem with the domain. Then there are the five numbers that the SOA record uses to describe the domain data, as explained earlier.

A Records in Zone File Format

As with most zones, the bulk of the records are A records:

```
bigdog        A     192.168.0.2
ns2           A     192.168.0.3
postoffice    A     192.168.0.4
router1       A     192.168.0.1
www           A     192.168.0.5
ns1.ecoast    A     192.168.0.6
```

There are just two points to make about these records. First, notice that all of the names do not end in periods, so they're relative to the zone name. In other words, "www" is short for "www.bigfirm.biz." Second, notice that you *can* have periods in the middle of a name. Even though ns1.ecoast.bigfirm.biz is not, strictly speaking, in the bigfirm.biz zone—it should be in the separate ecoast.bigfirm.biz zone—you can still include its A record by labeling that record `ns1.ecoast` and, as DNS just tacks on the domain name by default, it ends up being clear (to the DNS server, anyway) that this is an A record for ns1.ecoast.bigfirm.biz. (Remember that record—I'll have more to say about it in a minute.)

NS Records in Zone File Format and "Glue" Records

Next are two NS records, as follows:

```
@ NS bigdog.bigfirm.biz.
@ NS ns2.bigfirm.biz.
```

These records say that the name servers for this zone, bigfirm.biz, are bigdog.bigfirm.biz and ns2.bigfirm.biz. Again, this works because @ gets automatically translated by the DNS server to "this zone" or, in this case, `bigfirm.biz`. They could have just as well been written like so:

```
bigfirm.biz  NS  bigdog.bigfirm.biz.
bigfirm.biz  NS  ns2.bigfirm.biz.
```

There's another NS record further down:

```
hounds        NS  ns1.ecoast.bigfirm.biz.
```

Now, *this* one has a different job than identifying the DNS servers for bigfirm.biz. Can you figure out what it does? It's an NS record, so its job is to identify a DNS server for a zone. But it doesn't refer to @ or `bigfirm.biz.`, it refers to `ecoast`, and notice that there's no period at the end of it. That means that we're supposed to add the zone name, `bigfirm.biz`, to get its full name. Expanded, then, the DNS server reads this record like so:

```
ecoast.bigfirm.biz  NS  ns1.ecoast.bigfirm.biz.
```

This is the delegation record for the ecoast subdomain. *This* is the record that essentially "creates" the ecoast.bigfirm.biz zone. If you were to look in the (huge) zone file that serves the com domain, then you'd see a similar record for your "dot-com" domain (assuming you have one). This is half of what the wizard that performed the domain delegation did. The *other* half of what the New Delegation Wizard did was to add an A record for ns1.ecoast.bigfirm.biz that could be written in one of two ways:

```
ns1.ecoast.bigfirm.biz.   A  192.168.0.6
```

or

```
ns1.ecoast    A   192.168.0.6
```

Notice that the first example includes a fully qualified name, as it ends with a period. That A record (however you enter it) for NS1 is called a "glue" record. Let's see why.

Suppose you want to resolve a name in the subdomain ecoast.bigfirm.biz. How does your DNS server do it? Well, it wants to find the DNS server for ecoast.bigfirm.biz so that it can query that DNS server about whatever name it's trying to resolve. As we've seen, you find the DNS server for ecoast.bigfirm.biz in the DNS server for bigfirm.biz. Specifically, your DNS server asks the bigfirm.biz DNS server for any NS records that are relevant to ecoast.bigfirm.biz. And, as you can see, the DNS server would return the answer, "You can find a DNS server for ecoast.bigfirm.biz at the machine named ns1.ecoast.bigfirm.biz."

If that were *all* that the bigfirm.biz DNS server said, then it wouldn't be very useful. So to look up a name on ecoast.bigfirm.biz, I ask a machine named ns1.ecoast.bigfirm.biz? Okay, then I guess I need to find the IP address of that machine named ns1.ecoast.bigfirm.biz; I wonder who I'd ask about that? Well, let's see, ns1.ecoast.bigfirm.biz is part of the ecoast.bigfirm.biz domain, so the DNS server I'll query to find the IP address of ns1.ecoast.bigfirm.biz would be…umm…ns1.ecoast.bigfirm.biz. So, in other words, the only way to get the phone number for Mel's Grocery is to call Information, but before I can call Information I must know the phone number for Information, and the place to call to find all numbers (including Information) is Information.

To avoid this chicken-and-egg situation, DNS zones often contain A records for hosts that aren't part of that zone. In some senses, you might say that they're out of place—but without them, we'd never be able to find the IP address of ns1.hounds .bigfirm.biz. So adding this seemingly out-of-place A record solves the problem. Such an A record is called a *glue record*.

CNAME Records in Zone File Format

Next, you see a CNAME record:

```
ftp          CNAME  www.bigfirm.biz.
```

This CNAME equates ftp.bigfirm.biz to a machine named www.bigfirm.biz. The result is that anyone seeking to resolve ftp.bigfirm.biz gets returned the IP address of www.bigfirm.biz.

MX Records in Zone File Format

The last record is an MX record, like so:

```
@            MX 10  postoffice.bigfirm.biz.
```

Notice how it's laid out; again, starting with an @ to indicate it refers to the entire domain, then the record type MX, then the preference value, and finally the name of the mail server. I could have more than one, but this zone only has one.

Directly Manipulating Zones Files: An Example

I'll return to looking at the ASCII files that drive a standard DNS server (and a Windows 2000 DNS server, provided that you don't make your zones AD-integrated) a bit later, but before leaving the topic for now, let me offer some step-by-step advice on working directly in a zone file.

Suppose you wanted to add a host name entry—an A record—for a machine named test.bigfirm.biz, at address 192.168.0.10. You could do it via the GUI, but here's how to add the entry to the zone files directly. Basically, you stop the DNS service, modify the zone file, then start it up again. In steps:

1. In the DNS snap-in, right-click the icon representing the DNS server and choose All Tasks/Stop. This stops the DNS service on that server.

2. Look in \winnt\system32\dns to find the zone file named bigfirm.biz.dns. Edit it with Notepad.

3. Add test A 192.168.0.10 to the end of bigfirm.biz.dns, and as you type it, you need only remember to start the line with test, then leave at least one space, then the capital A, then at least one space, then the IP address.

4. Increase the numeric value in the Serial Number entry of the SOA record by one so that the other servers (well, there aren't any here, but there would be in a real-world scenario) know there's new data in the zone.

5. Save the file.

6. Return to the DNS snap-in, right-click the server, and choose All Tasks/Start.

Once the DNS server has started again, take a look in the bigfirm.biz zone. You'll see that test's entry is visible. Once again, why would you modify the ASCII file instead of just clicking? Well, you might not—but you *might* decide to make large-scale changes to the zone via some program or macro that you wrote, a program that reads and massages the ASCII zone file. You'd follow basically the same approach in that case—stop the DNS service, run the program that modifies the zone file, then start the DNS service.

Dynamic DNS (DDNS)

Well, I've been dropping hints about it for the past 40 pages or so—so let's talk about *dynamic DNS*, or DDNS to the acronym-oriented.

For years, WINS has been a pain in the rear for many reasons. But it was better than DNS in one important way: Its database was automatic and dynamic. What I mean is that you almost never had to tell a WINS server about a machine out on the network. Instead, the machines would tell WINS about themselves automatically; whenever they booted up or renewed their DHCP leases, they'd go back and reregister themselves with WINS. The result? WINS automatically kept a database of machines on the network.

Now DNS, in contrast, wasn't automatic. You had to punch in A records for every one of your machines by hand, either by editing a zone file or by clicking in a GUI. It would have been pretty nice if DNS servers could collect information about the names and addresses of the machines on the network in a similar way to WINS.

Well, now DNS can, with DDNS. RFC 2136 describes a process whereby DNS clients—the workstations and servers that rely upon DNS for name resolution—can register themselves with DNS automatically, telling DNS to create an A (or any other type) record for them, without requiring any work on an administrator's part.

Seeing DDNS Work

Want to see it in action? You can, if you've been following along and built the bigdog.bigfirm.biz machine. Just put Windows 2000—Professional or any flavor of Server—on a computer. Call that computer MYPC. Give it a static IP address of 192.168.0.20, subnet mask 255.255.255.0, don't fill in the default gateway, and set the DNS server to 192.168.0.2—that is, BIGDOG. Finally, set the DNS suffix to bigfirm.biz and reboot the computer.

Once MYPC has rebooted, go over to BIGDOG, start the DNS snap-in, and open the bigfirm.biz forward lookup zone. You will see an A record for MYPC with an IP address of 192.168.0.20—an A record created automatically.

Next, stop the DNS service so that the zone data gets flushed out to the zone files, and take a look at \winnt\system32\dns\bigfirm.biz.dns. You'll see an A record for MYPC that looks like this:

```
mypc 1200 A 192.168.0.20
```

Notice the 1200—remember what that is? It's a time to live value for the A record. 1200 seconds is 20 minutes. So when MYPC registered with the DNS server, it basically said, "I'm mypc.bigfirm.biz and I'm at 192.168.0.20, but if anyone asks about me, tell them that I might be a different address in 20 minutes—so don't cache the data for any longer than that."

NOTE *You can change that value if you care to by creating a REG_DWORD value entry called DefaultRegistration-TTL in* HKEY_LOCAL_MACHINE\SYSTEM\CurrentControlSet\Services\Tcpip\Parameters. *Fill the value entry with the length in seconds that you'd like the TTL set to. I can't think of a reason why you'd mess with it, but I include this for the curious. Please note that this is* not *how often your system reregisters with DDNS—there really isn't a Registry entry to affect that, as you'll see later in this chapter.*

Now look at the reverse lookup zone for 0.168.192.in-addr.arpa. You'll see a PTR record for 192.168.0.20—the computer registered both its forward and reverse entries! Now, that might *not* be true if you didn't make the 0.168.192.in-addr.arpa or the bigfirm.biz zone willing to accept dynamic entries—remember that zones aren't dynamic by default. You can easily check that both zones accept dynamic updates. In the DNS snap-in, right-click the folder representing zone, then choose Properties and click the General tab. Then choose Yes under Allow Dynamic Updates.

What Triggers DDNS Registrations?

If you'd forgotten to make the zones dynamic until after MYPC booted, how can you force MYPC to re-try registering? Well, clearly you could turn MYPC on and off, but who wants to do that? Instead, open a command line at MYPC and type this:

```
ipconfig /registerdns
```

Then check the zones—you should now see the updates.

How do the registrations work? Well, remember that DDNS registrations are *initiated by the client*. The DNS server does not ask the client to register; instead, the client requests the registration of the server. Five events cause a client to register or, more likely, to *re*register:

◆ The computer has been rebooted and the TCP/IP software has just started.

◆ You've changed the IP address on a system with a static IP address.

◆ Your computer gets its IP address from DHCP and the computer has just renewed its DHCP lease.

◆ You type **ipconfig /registerdns**.

◆ 24 hours has passed since the last time the system registered with DDNS.

You can change that 24-hour period to another one with a Registry change to HKEY_LOCAL_MACHINE\SYSTEM\CurrentControlSet\Services\Tcpip\Parameters; add a new value entry Default-RegistrationRefreshInterval of type REG_DWORD. You can then specify how often to reregister in seconds. The default is 86,400, the number of seconds in a day.

DDNS Registrations in More Detail

My simple example with one workstation—MYPC—and just one DNS server—BIGDOG—obscured some of the complexity of a DDNS registration. Here is more specifically how a registration happens.

ON A SYSTEM WITH A STATIC IP ADDRESS

1. First, the client computer asks its local DNS server to retrieve the SOA record for the client computer's DNS suffix. So, for example, because MYPC sees that its DNS suffix is bigfirm.biz, it asks its local DNS server (which happens to be BIGDOG) to go find the SOA record for bigfirm.biz.

2. The local DNS server queries its DNS hierarchy for the answer to the client's question. In the case of BIGDOG, it already *knew* the answer, as BIGDOG contained the zone files. But if MYPC had been hooked up to a different DNS server, that DNS server could still have queried other DNS servers to get the SOA record for bigfirm.biz, and returned that information to MYPC.

3. Inside the SOA is, you may recall, the name of the DNS server that is primary for the big-firm.biz zone. That's why MYPC wanted the SOA record: It has to register (or reregister) with the DNS server that acts as the primary DNS server for the bigfirm.biz zone because recall that only the primary DNS server can change a zone. Even if a secondary DNS server for bigfirm.biz chose to accept MYPC's registration, it wouldn't be any good because that secondary DNS server wouldn't replicate MYPC's A record to other DNS servers, and they wouldn't listen if it tried anyway. The registration must be done at the primary (unless you build an Active Directory–integrated zone).

4. Now that MYPC knows the name of the primary DNS server for bigfirm.biz, it contacts that DNS server and sends its registration requests: "Please create an A record for mypc.bigfirm.biz at 192.168.0.20."

5. But it's not done yet—now it needs to register a PTR record with the reverse zone. So it asks for the SOA record for the reverse zone and then uses that SOA record to identify the primary server for the reverse zone. Once it knows the primary server for the reverse zone, it asks the reverse zone's primary server to register it.

ON A SYSTEM THAT USES DHCP

That's how MYPC worked, as it has a static IP address. But if MYPC had gotten its IP address from DHCP, then things would work just a bit differently.

When a system gets its address from DHCP, then the system only registers its *forward* record—the A record—rather than the PTR record. The DHCP server handles registering the reverse zone's PTR record. Furthermore, you may, if you like, tell the DHCP server to handle *all* registrations, both forward and reverse. Look back to Figure 7.20 in the section on DHCP and you see the DNS tab on a DHCP scope's properties. It's not the default, but you can choose a radio button labeled Always Update DNS and, if you do, then the clients don't do registrations, the DHCP server does.

Remember that I said that DDNS registrations are initiated by the client. But what about if the client *isn't* running Windows 2000? A Windows 98, Windows Me, or NT 4 system wouldn't know how to register itself in DNS, nor would it know that it even had to. Recall that also back near Figure 7.20, I explained—and it seems a good time to say again—that the Windows 2000 DHCP server is also smart enough to detect systems that don't know to register themselves with DNS. In that case, the DHCP server will register both the forward and reverse entries for those systems. (Unless you tell it not to; that's an option.)

MUST MY SYSTEM REREGISTER?

Anyone with a good knowledge of how WINS works will probably assume, as I did, that you *must* reregister with DDNS on a regular basis, or the DDNS server will simply "forget" your system's dynamically registered records.

By Default, 2000 Does Not Clean Out Old Records

Actually, though, that's not true. At least, not by default.

In fact, if you leave the Windows 2000 defaults in place, then your workstation really need only register once. Once it has told the DNS server to create an A record and a PTR record (and whatever other records it may need created), then those records stay in the zone file indefinitely.

Scavenging: Cleaning Out the Old

That may sound a tad inelegant. I mean, dynamic DNS is supposed to be *dynamic*, right? So if one day I shut down the machine named pc152.bigfirm.biz and never start it up again, then I really shouldn't have to go root around in the bigfirm.biz zone file and delete its records. Can't the system do this kind of housekeeping itself?

Yes, it can. The process is called *scavenging*. Scavenging is a process whereby a DNS server periodically (you can configure how often, as you'll see) checks its dynamically created records to see how long it's been since they were registered (or reregistered). Then, if the scavenger finds records that haven't been registered or reregistered in a long time (and you can configure how long "a long time" is), then it deletes them from the zone file.

Controlling Scavenging: Just Three Numbers

To see how to set up scavenging, right-click the DNS server's icon in the DNS snap-in and choose Set Aging/Scavenging for All Zones and you'll get a dialog box like Figure 7.79.

FIGURE 7.79

Setting scavenging parameters

Check the box labeled Scavenge Stale Resource Records to enable scavenging. But what about those two time values, the No-Refresh Interval and the Refresh Interval? Well, there are three numbers relevant to how scavenging works; here, you see two of them—and I'll explain them in a minute.

To see the third, right-click the server again, choose Properties, and click the Advanced tab. You'll see something like Figure 7.80. Check Enable Automatic Scavenging of Stale Records to kick off the scavenger on a regular basis. (I've set it to one hour, but you'll probably choose a much longer value, perhaps running the scavenger weekly.)

FIGURE 7.80

How often to scavenge?

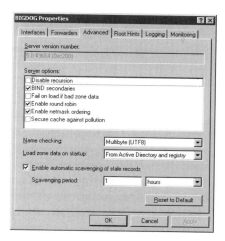

The No-Refresh Interval   Look back to Figure 7.79 and you'll see the first value, something called the No-Refresh Interval. It creates a period of time wherein your computer *cannot* reregister itself in DNS. So, for example, if the no-refresh interval were one day and your computer had reregistered at 9:00 A.M. on Tuesday morning, then any attempts to reregister itself before 9:00 A.M. Wednesday morning would simply be ignored by the DDNS server.

Why'd Microsoft bother with something like this? Mostly because you have the option, as I've mentioned (and will discuss later in some detail) to store your zones not in a traditional zone file, but instead in the Active Directory, a so-called "Active Directory–integrated zone." Any time that your system reregisters, that creates a change in the AD, and any change in the AD must be replicated to every other AD controller in the enterprise. Replication traffic can clog your WAN links and slow down the DCs, so I guess the idea with the no-refresh interval is to reduce the burden imposed on the AD by overzealously reregistering systems.

If you're experimenting and want to force an immediate reregistration within the no-refresh interval, just open the zone in the DNS snap-in and use the GUI to delete the A record for the system that you want to register. Then go to the system that you want to reregister and type **ipconfig /registerdns** at a command line.

The Refresh and Scavenging Intervals   Figure 7.79 also includes a field called the Refresh Interval. But that's not a very descriptive name. The better name would be "The Remainder of the Immunity from Scavenging Period." It's an interval that says to the scavenging routine, "If this record's age is less than the sum of its no-refresh and refresh intervals, then don't even *think* of scavenging it."

For example, suppose I've got a no-refresh interval of one day and a refresh interval of two days. And let's suppose that the scavenging routine runs every day. (You set the scavenging interval as you see in the dialog box in Figure 7.80.) Your system registers at 9:00 A.M. Tuesday morning. As you read before, that means that the DDNS server would be deaf to any attempts by your system to reregister. Let's say that the scavenging routine runs every evening. It sees that the no-refresh plus the refresh intervals equals three days. The scavenger then sees that your workstation's A record is less than a day old. That age is less than three days, so the scavenger leaves the record alone.

Let's suppose that you're on vacation for the week. So 9:00 A.M. Wednesday morning is when your DDNS server would accept a reregistration for your system, but your system's not on, so it doesn't try to reregister. Wednesday evening, the scavenger sees that your workstation's A record is about a day and a half old—still too young to scavenge. The same thing happens Thursday night, when the scavenger sees a two-and-a-half-day-old record. But on Friday night, your workstation's A record is three-and-a-half days old, so the scavenger munches it.

Choosing a Good No-Refresh and Refresh Interval   There really isn't any relationship between the scavenging interval and the no-refresh/refresh intervals. But you should take a minute to ensure that you don't set the no-refresh/refresh intervals too small. The sum of those two should be larger than the frequency of reregistration.

Here's an exaggerated (and impossible) example of what I mean. Suppose your system reregisters with DDNS only once every 30 days. But then suppose you set a no-refresh interval of six days and a refresh interval of seven days, and a scavenging interval of one day. Let's follow the process through from Jan. 1:

1. On Jan. 1, your system registers with DDNS.

2. The DDNS server will not accept another registration from your system until Jan. 7, but that's no problem—your system doesn't intend to reregister until Jan. 31.

3. Every day until Jan. 14, the scavenger runs and sees that your system's A record is less than 13 days (6 plus 7) old, and so leaves it alone.

4. Around Jan. 14, however, the scavenger runs, finds the record older than 13 days, and deletes it.

Remember that this is a client-driven registration system, so there's no method for the DDNS server to give the client a heads-up that it's time to reregister.

So, clearly you should set the sum of your no-refresh and refresh intervals so that they always exceed the maximum possible interval between subsequent reregistrations. But what's the maximum possible interval between reregistrations? Recall the things that trigger a reregistration: They happen every 24 hours (if the system stays up), upon a DHCP lease renewal, or when you turn your computer on. So the longest you'd probably ever go between reregistrations would be as long as you ever have your computer off—seven days, perhaps, unless you're in the habit of taking two-week vacations.

Setting Scavenging: A Note
If you decide to turn on scavenging, you'll run into an oddity. For some reason, you must turn on scavenging at the server level (as you saw in Figure 7.79) and *then* you've got to turn it on for each zone that you want to scavenge. You do that by right-clicking the zone and then choosing Properties. Click the General tab and you'll see an Aging button; click it and you'll get a dialog box that looks like Figure 7.81.

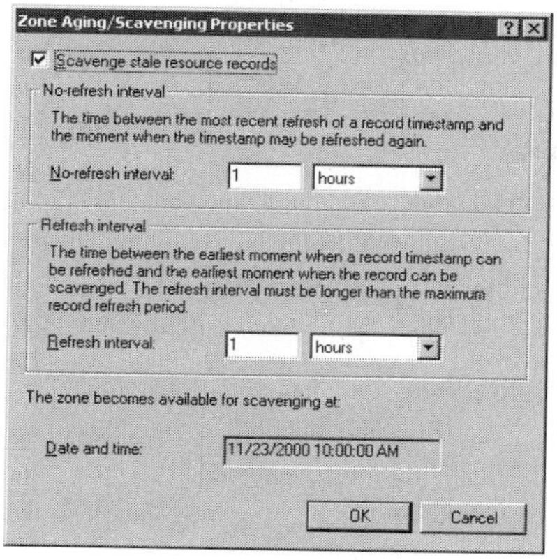

FIGURE 7.81

Scavenging settings for a zone

Don't set your intervals to one hour, as you see in that dialog box—I was just experimenting. The defaults of seven days apiece are probably just fine. Notice the information field at the bottom of the dialog box—that says when scavenging could next occur. If you look in the zone file at a dynamic record after you've turned on scavenging, you might see an entry like this:

```
ca   [AGE:3505395]  96  A  192.168.0.21
```

You should recognize the `ca 96 A 192.168.0.21` part—that's just an A record for a host named ca.bigfirm.biz at address 192.168.0.21 with a TTL of 96 seconds. The `[AGE:3505395]` is the "birthday" of this record, the hour in which it was created. As near as I can tell, this is a value measured in hours since January 1, 1600, or thereabouts, and don't bother with decimals—it seems that scavenging works in units of hours or larger.

WARNING   *Note something about that `[AGE:]` entry—it's not a standard part of a DNS record. Therefore, if you turn on scavenging, then you'll still have zone files, but they won't be portable to non-Win2K-based DNS servers anymore, at least not without some work—you'd have to edit the zone files to remove the `[AGE:]` items before trying to transplant a 2000 zone file onto another kind of DNS server.*

In sum, then, to enable scavenging you must remember to:

♦ Set the no-refresh and refresh intervals for the server as a whole, as in Figure 7.79.

♦ Turn on scavenging, as in Figure 7.80.

♦ Set the no-refresh and refresh intervals for each zone.

Viewing When a Record Will "Go Stale"

If you want, you can find out when a particular record will go stale, although not directly. Start up the DNS snap-in and choose View/Advanced. Then right-click any record and choose Properties; you'll then see something like Figure 7.82.

FIGURE 7.82

Viewing a record's properties with View/Advanced enabled

Here, I took the ns2 system and deleted its record in the zone on bigdog, after turning on scavenging on bigfirm.biz. Then I went over to the ns2 system and typed **ipconfig /registerdns** to make ns2 reregister itself dynamically with BIGDOG. The date that you see of 12/7/2001 at 7:00 A.M. isn't telling me that this record goes stale at that time; instead, it's telling me that this record *was created*—registered—at that date. To find out when it'll go stale, I'd have to first add the no-refresh plus the refresh intervals. Suppose the no-refresh interval is two days, the refresh interval is three days. That'd tell me that the earliest time that this record can go stale is five days later at 7:00 A.M. on Dec. 12, 2001. But, of course, that's not the *only* information that I need. Recall that stale records only get deleted when the scavenging routine runs, so I'd need to know when the scavenging routine runs to determine exactly when this record will disappear.

Viewing Scavenging Logs

Windows 2000 Server reports what happened in every scavenging cycle in the Event Viewer in the System log. Just look for a DNS event with event ID 2501.

WINS Registration versus DDNS Registration

Now that you've seen how DDNS registration works, you might have committed a bit of mental shorthand (I know *I* did when I first learned this) along the lines of "DDNS for Winsock is equivalent to WINS for NetBIOS—and so many of the same issues apply." That's *partially* right; but there's one significant difference between WINS and dynamic DNS, and that difference will affect how you decide how many DNS servers you need, and where to place them.

As you've seen, every TCP/IP-enabled computer gets a "primary WINS server" and a "preferred DNS server." At first blush, it looks like a system's primary WINS server and its preferred DNS server do basically the same thing, and in some senses they do: Your preferred DNS server is the DNS server that resolves DNS names for you, and your primary WINS server is the WINS server that resolves NetBIOS names for you. But here's the difference: Your system needs to register both with the WINS and DNS databases. Your system registers its NetBIOS name with its primary

WINS server, but it *doesn't* register its DNS name with its *preferred* DNS server; instead, it registers its DNS name with the *primary* DNS server for its zone.

As you've previously read, every WINS server has two very different tasks. First, it resolves NetBIOS names from its database. Second, it collects names to populate that database. Clearly a WINS server that serves one-fifth of the organization would only receive registrations from one-fifth of the organization, and therefore would be ignorant of the other four-fifths—and so any time that one of the WINS clients asked that WINS server to resolve a machine name in the organization, there'd be an 80-percent chance that the WINS server wouldn't know the name. That's silly, so, as you've read, any enterprise that uses more than one WINS server must set that WINS server up to share its database with the other WINS servers to accept databases from other WINS servers and to merge those other databases with its own so that it (and every other WINS server) has a consistent, enterprisewide database of machine names, hence the Microsoft "14 WINS servers worldwide" rule of thumb. That's a shame from the name resolution side—it'd be really great to be able to somehow scatter dozens of WINS servers all over the place to resolve names. But that'd be a nightmare if all of those dozens or hundreds of WINS servers each contained a little database that needed to be merged with all of the other databases—that's just asking for database corruption. Wouldn't it be cool if you could just create a kind of "low-octane WINS server" incapable of accepting registrations, a kind of "resolving-only" WINS server? You'd get it a copy of the WINS database somehow and it could focus only on resolving names; and with tons of them around, then each one could serve just a small number of clients, with the result that all of those clients received very snappy response on their name resolution requests.

Well, sadly, you can't do that with WINS, which brings me to the major point about how WINS and DDNS are different.

Should you limit yourself to 14 servers total with DNS? Absolutely not. In WINS, the machine that you register with *must* be the one that you use to resolve names. With DNS, the machine that resolves names is your preferred DNS server. You register with a different computer—the primary DNS server for your zone. The result is terrific—you can place any number of DNS servers in your organization whose only job is to resolve names and therefore help your network respond to clients more swiftly.

DDNS Security Is Weak, If You Care

One thing that troubles some people about vanilla, by-the-RFC DDNS servers is that they will accept a registration from anyone. So, for example, if bigfirm.biz's DNS server were "live" on the Internet, then anyone anywhere could just set their Windows 2000 computer's domain suffix to bigfirm.biz and type **ipconfig /registerdns**. This would work even if that machine's local DNS server didn't do DDNS. Remember, all that your preferred DNS server must do is be able to retrieve the SOA record for bigfirm.biz—and any DNS server can do that.

Should the bigfirm.biz people care that people are registering on their domain? So what if the machine at 62.11.99.3 registers itself as poindexter.bigfirm.biz? A Microsoft person told me that it might matter. For example, he explained, consider the 128-bit downloadable versions of Internet Explorer. In the past, you weren't supposed to be able to download them if you weren't in the United States or Canada. Microsoft's Web site determined whether you're in the United States or Canada by looking at your domain. If bigfirm.biz's record in the Network Solutions database showed a U.S.

address, then the download was okayed, so someone from outside the United States or Canada could sneak in that way.

Presumably, a hacker could first register with bigfirm.biz, then try to hack some system. If the system administrator of the attacked system noticed that he was being hacked by someone at bigfirm.biz, that might make for a bit of a hassle for the bigfirm.biz administrator. Particularly if the hacker was trying to crack an NSA or CIA site.

Not every brand of DDNS server software is wide open. I once set up a Linux box running BIND, the standard free-of-charge Unix DNS server software that the vast majority of DNS servers run around the world. I created a few dynamic DNS zones on it and told my Windows 2000 boxes to create an Active Directory—but to use the Linux box as their DNS server, not a 2000 box. It worked great. While I was setting the zones up on the BIND server, however, I noticed that BIND has a nice, effective, basic kind of security for zones. You can tell it, "This zone takes dynamic updates, but only from the following subnets." You could then punch in your firm's subnets. A bit of a pain to first set up, but useful. In contrast, Microsoft's DDNS is wide open, unless you enable Active Directory–integrated zones.

MAKING WINDOWS 2000/XP COMPUTERS *NOT* DO DYNAMIC REGISTRATION

Windows 2000 and later Microsoft operating systems automatically attempt to register their host names and IP addresses with the primary DNS server of the DNS domain that they belong to, as you've seen. But that can cause some problems in places that haven't adopted the Active Directory or that use static DNS servers for some reason.

I had a client that used Unix-based BIND servers and that hadn't made their DNS zone dynamic. (There wasn't any reason, as they weren't using the AD yet.) The PC guys rolled out a few hundred Windows 2000 Professional systems.

The BIND guys—a different group—noticed.

All of a sudden, the DNS server logs were chock-full of warnings and errors about all of these computers trying to register with their static DNS zones. That worried the BIND guys, so they tracked it down to all of these new PCs. What to do? Well, the BIND folks could have just ignored the messages. But that *does* seem a bit inelegant. So rather than lowering the river, why not just raise the bridge? In other words, how to get the 2000 boxes to stop bugging the DNS servers?

You can tell a Windows 2000/XP/.NET computer to forgo registering altogether either from the GUI or with a Registry hack. The Registry hack is in `HKEY_LOCAL_MACHINE\SYSTEM\Current-ControlSet\Services\Tcpip\Parameters`. Add a new value entry, DisableDynamicUpdate—it's a REG_DWORD entry—and set it to 1 and reboot the computer. That'll keep the computer from attempting a dynamic update, whenever the computer has a static address or got it from DHCP.

You can tell the computer not to try to update DNS in the GUI, as well; it's in the Advanced TCP/IP Settings property page, on the DNS tab. Uncheck the Register This Connection's Addresses in DNS box.

But what if you want to distribute this setting to bazillions of machines? The best solution is probably a custom policy; either a system policy would work (if you've got Windows 2000/XP workstations on an NT 4 domain) or a group policy (if you're running the AD). Custom policies are a big topic, though, so I won't go through the step by steps here—see Chapter 9 on how to create a custom system policy. Microsoft has a Knowledge Base article that explains how to build a group policy to tell a workstation to stop trying to register with their DNS servers at Q294832.

Active Directory–Integrated Zones

You've read that DNS zones come in two flavors: primary and secondary. But Windows 2000's DNS offers you a third type of zone called an *Active Directory–integrated* zone. As I see it, AD-integrated zones offer two main benefits: multimaster zone replication and a DDNS registration process that is both load-balanced and secured. But they've got a drawback as well: They stray from the RFCs for DNS a bit—but *just* a bit—and you've got to make your domain controllers into DNS servers. Let's see how to make a zone an AD-integrated zone, then look into the pluses and minuses in some detail.

CREATING AN AD-INTEGRATED ZONE

Go to any primary zone on a Windows 2000 DNS server and right-click it, then choose Properties. The resulting properties page looks like the one back on Figure 7.59. To convert between a primary and an AD-integrated zone, click the Change button and you'll see a dialog box like the one in Figure 7.83.

FIGURE 7.83

Changing the zone type

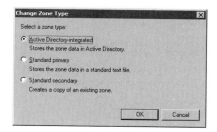

If you've been following along in the bigfirm.biz example, then your Active Directory–integrated zone option will be grayed out. That's because you can only host an AD-integrated zone on an Active Directory domain controller, and the DNS server that we created for bigfirm.biz—BIGDOG—isn't a DC. (Recall that in fact we haven't created any domains at all yet.)

This dialog box shows that if you want to experiment with an AD-integrated zone versus a standard primary zone, then you can, with no fear of being stuck with an AD-integrated zone that you can't convert back to a primary. Just a mouse click or two converts a zone from primary to AD-integrated or vice versa.

Once you make a zone an AD-integrated zone, then a visit back to the General tab of the Properties page for that zone (right-click the zone in the DNS snap-in and choose Properties) will show that under Allow Dynamic Updates there is now, in addition to the two old Yes and No options, a new option, Only Secure Updates.

MULTIMASTER ZONE REPLICATION

You've already read that under standard DDNS, only one computer can accept registrations in a given zone—the computer that happens to be the primary DNS server for that zone. That means that a worldwide company might think twice about using DDNS (and therefore the Active Directory), because no matter where a 2000-based workstation or server was situated, it would have to find and communicate with that *one* computer in the world every time that it wanted to reregister. And recall that Windows 2000–based computers want to reregister whenever they renew their DHCP lease, reboot, every 24 hours, or when you type **ipconfig /registerdns**. So if your worldwide enterprise has an office in Khartoum with 200 machines and a primary DNS server in New York, then every single time the computers in Khartoum want to reregister, they've got to do it live-on-the-WAN to New York. That might be impractical.

With an AD-integrated zone, you can have as many "primary" DDNS servers as you like. Any one of these DDNS servers can accept DDNS registrations. They then replicate this information among themselves. So you could have a domain controller in Khartoum that not only handles logons for the users, but also handles machine registrations. Then, instead of requiring every system to talk to New York one at a time, the Khartoum DC just chatters with the closest DC now and then, perhaps a machine in Cairo, and tells the Cairo DC about the new DDNS registrations. Cairo's DC might forward that to the Paris DC, which sends it to the New York DC, and so eventually every DNS server knows about the Khartoum DDNS registrations.

Is it a lot of work to tell Khartoum how to find Cairo and then telling Cairo how to find Paris and so on? Not really, but here's the important point: As you'll see in the next chapter, you'd have to set this up to have a worldwide Windows 2000 domain anyway. The DCs would share this information as part of their normal DC-to-DC chatter. So once you've set up the DCs to be able to send normal domain information back and forth, then you don't have to do anything at all to enable them to send DDNS registration information back and forth.

Once you've converted a zone to an Active Directory–integrated zone, you can install the DNS server service on any other DC for that domain. You enable that DNS server to assist in name resolution and registration for the domain by just creating a new forward zone, as you've seen, just as if you were creating a secondary zone for an existing domain—but instead of choosing Secondary Zone, you choose Active Directory–Integrated Zone. From that point on, everything's automatic. Windows 2000 will then automatically tell some machines to register with one DDNS server, others with a different DDNS server, and so on.

SECURE DDNS REGISTRATION

I've got several domains running in my network, but I have one main Windows 2000 Active Directory domain in my network, named win2ktest.com. It needs, as you've read, a dynamic DNS zone to support the Active Directory, and besides I liked the whole idea of DDNS, so I set up win2ktest.com as a DDNS zone early on, back in the Windows 2000 Beta 3 days. I made it a standard primary zone rather than an AD-integrated zone.

Then the first edition of this book came out.

Because I sometimes take screen shots from an actual running network—mine—my examples tend to show dialog boxes from the DDNS server that hosts win2ktest.com. Unfortunately, some readers don't understand that win2ktest.com is only an example domain name, rather than the one that they should use, so they just create domains named win2ktest.com on their test networks. Unfortunately, if those readers are sitting at machines with routable IP addresses attached to the public Internet, then their Windows 2000 machines will attempt to find the primary DDNS server for win2ktest .com and then to register themselves with that machine's zone files.

In other words, with *my* machine.

I didn't imagine that this would be a big problem when the book's first edition came out. But I happened to look in the win2ktest.com zone files about four weeks after the book came out and found that *1000* machines had registered with win2ktest.com from around the world—yikes! Clearly I needed to do *something* to keep the *rest* of the world from registering with my domain, but what? The simplest answer was to convert my zone from a simple primary zone to an AD-integrated zone and then to enable Only Secure Updates on that zone. (That's two steps—just converting the zone to an AD-integrated zone doesn't set dynamic updates to Only Secure Updates. You have to go to Properties for that zone and drop down the Allow Dynamic Updates list box to select Only Secure Updates.)

The value of doing that was this: Machines can only register DNS records with an AD-integrated zone on a DDNS server by first *logging in to the AD domain*. So any random Windows 2000 machine on the other side of the world that happens to have a DNS suffix of win2ktest.com can't register itself with my DDNS server unless it has a machine account on the win2ktest.com domain.

And for those new to NT networking, there is indeed such a thing as a machine account, nonintuitive as it might seem! When you first attach a machine to an NT or a AD domain, you must have at least some administrative powers, as you're asking the domain to create an account much like a user logon account. Unlikely as it seems, every time that you turn your Windows 2000– or NT-based computer on, it goes out to the Windows NT or Windows 2000 domain and *logs in*. That's how AD-integrated zones keep my zone from growing beyond the size of my computer's hard disk!

As time has gone on, it has become clear that converting the zone to an AD-integrated one was a good idea. Just a few minutes ago, I briefly converted the win2ktest.com zone back to a standard primary zone to get a screen shot *just for 30 seconds* and, when I changed it back, I noticed that *two* machines had registered on the temporarily opened win2ktest.com zone! So if you see a message like this in your Event Viewer, then you'll know that your system tried to register with my DDNS server and was rebuffed:

```
The system failed to register network adapter with settings:

    Adapter Name: {994A8620-8987-4D4A-ABA9-507122C08F28}
    Host Name: dodo
    Adapter-specific Domain Suffix: win2ktest.com
    DNS server list:
      206.246.253.111
    Sent update to server: 206.246.253.111
    IP Address(es):
      210.20.10.4

The reason it could not register was because the DNS server refused the dynamic
update request. This could happen for the following reasons: (a) current DNS update
policies do not allow this computer to update the DNS domain name configured for
this adapter, or (b) the authoritative DNS server for this DNS domain name does not
support the DNS dynamic update protocol.

To register a DNS host (A) resource record using the specific DNS domain name for
this adapter, contact your DNS server or network systems administrator.
```

POTENTIAL AD-INTEGRATED PROBLEMS

So is Active Directory integration the answer for you? Probably. The whole idea of basing my DNS infrastructure on a nonstandard Microsoft implementation troubled me at first, but the more I think about it, the less troublesome it seems. Let's consider the issues.

First of all, does using AD-integrated zones force you to use only Microsoft DNS servers? Not at all. You can use other DNS servers as secondary servers on an AD-integrated zone. Those secondary servers receive zone transfers from the AD-integrated servers, as before. Yes, it *is* true that the AD-integrated servers must all be Microsoft Windows 2000 DDNS servers, but what's the harm in that? If we were to stay with a standard BIND-type DNS implementation, then we'd be restricted to just one primary DNS server: In effect, all AD integration does is to expand the number of possible "primary" DNS servers. I have tested a Linux box running BIND as a secondary DNS server on an Active Directory–integrated zone and experienced no trouble whatsoever.

Second, once you "go Microsoft," is there no going back? Not at all. A few mouse clicks converts an AD-integrated zone back to a standard primary zone. Once you converted a zone back to standard primary and shut down the DDNS server, then you'd have a standard ASCII zone file that you could place on a non-Microsoft DNS server, instantly "migrating" your DNS hosting from a Windows 2000 box to some other DNS system.

No, if I have a complaint with AD-integrated zones, it's this one: The only machines that can be AD-integrated servers are Windows 2000 domain controllers. That worries me because I've always thought it a bad idea to put the name registration services on the same computer that does the logons. Remember that whenever you reboot your computer, it tries to reregister with DDNS. When do most people boot their computers? First thing in the morning. But what else do people do first thing in the morning? Log in to the domain. Early in the day, then, is when the domain controllers are busiest, logging people in. It seems to me that the busiest time of the day for a DDNS server is *also* first thing in the morning. Why take two functions that are both busiest at the same time and put them on the same machine? It seems somewhat unwise. But consider the alternative: If you use only a single primary DDNS server, then you've set up your enterprise so that if that one machine goes down, DDNS registrations don't happen. (But, on the other hand, don't forget that if you haven't turned on scavenging, then it's not going to be a big deal.)

What's the right answer, then? I can't say that I have the 100-percent best answer, but on balance I'd say that using AD-integrated zones makes the most sense in a predominantly Windows 2000–based shop.

DNS Resolution in Detail

Now that we've seen how to set up a 2000-based DDNS server, let's look at how DNS works from the *client's* point of view. And in the process, I'll get a chance to discuss several important concepts I haven't covered yet.

Let's say you're sitting at a Windows 2000 machine attached to the Internet. You start up Internet Explorer or Netscape and point it to my Web site, www.minasi.com. Your browser hasn't a clue that www.minasi.com is the DNS name of the machine with IP address 206.246.253.111, so it needs something to do that name resolution for you—a local DNS server. I'll assume you're sitting at work while doing this, and that your firm has at least one local DNS server, which needn't be a Windows 2000 DNS server. Here are the specific steps that your workstation and the local DNS server perform to turn www.minasi.com into 206.246.253.111.

Step 1: Check HOSTS and the Client Cache

On a Windows 9x or NT 3.x or 4 computer, the first thing that your workstation would do to resolve www.minasi.com would be to ask the local DNS server, "What's the IP address for www.minasi.com?" But Windows 2000's DNS client—that is, the built-in software that knows how to ask DNS servers to resolve names—has an extra new feature: It caches the results of name resolution requests.

As has been the case with Microsoft DNS clients from the beginning, your workstation will first look in \winnt\system32\drivers\etc for an ASCII file named hosts. If the DNS name that it's looking for is there, then your workstation will use that IP address and not look any further.

VIEWING THE DNS CLIENT CACHE

You won't use a HOSTS file very often, though. Instead, your system will probably resolve many names out of its own DNS cache; here's how that works: Suppose you pointed your browser to www.minasi.com first thing in the morning; that causes your workstation to go ask the local DNS server to search the public DNS namespace for the IP address of www.minasi.com. But then suppose you returned to www.minasi.com later that day; in *that* case, your workstation wouldn't *have* to ask a DNS server for the IP address of www.minasi.com because the Windows 2000 DNS client software remembers the answers to old name resolution requests. Want to see what DNS names your workstation currently knows? Open up a command line and type this:

```
ipconfig /displaydns
```

You'll see a list of names and addresses, as well as the TTL in seconds. Like a DNS server, the Windows 2000 DNS client will only cache information for as long as the TTL specifies. Thus, if your system asks my DNS server to resolve www.minasi.com, then my system says, "Its IP address is 206.246.253.111 and its TTL is one hour," so for the next hour your system wouldn't bother to try to re-resolve www.minasi.com, choosing instead to assume that the address hadn't changed.

Adding caching on the DNS client was a good move on Microsoft's part precisely because, recall, 2000 uses DNS the way NT used WINS, as the basic workhorse naming system. There are probably servers in your network that your workstation communicates with all the time; relieving the local DNS servers of having to resolve and re-resolve the names lightens the burden on those servers and reduces network chatter.

REMEMBERING RESOLUTION FAILURES: "NEGATIVE" CACHING

Once in a while, however, you'll want the DNS client to *forget* what it's learned. For example, suppose you'd built the simple bigfirm.biz DNS system, but misspelled BIGDOG as the machine, accidentally miskeying it as BGIDOG or something like that. You then sit down at some other machine and type **ping bigdog.bigfirm.biz**, and your system tells you that there's no machine by that name. You realize the error and go over to BGIDOG, renaming it to BIGDOG and rebooting it. You go over to your workstation and try another **ping bigdog.bigfirm.biz**, but it *still* tells you that there's no such system. Huh? You *fixed* the silly thing—*now* what's wrong? What's wrong is called *negative caching*. The DNS client not only caches the *successes*, it also caches the *failures*, remembering any failed name resolution attempts for five minutes. So if you wait a few minutes more, then **ping bigdog.bigfirm.biz** will work. But who wants to wait? You can alternatively tell your system to forget all of its cached entries with this command:

```
ipconfig /flushdns
```

So remember: When you're doing network troubleshooting, flush your DNS cache regularly so you don't get errors arising out of previously failed DNS resolutions that *shouldn't* fail anymore but that do anyway for some mysterious reason. Negative caching is the reason, so flush that cache after re-trying any failed command! And if you decide that five minutes is too long or too short a period to remember failed name resolutions, you can change that. Just look in the Registry in `HKEY_LOCAL_MACHINE\SYSTEM\ CurrentControlSet\Services\Dnscache\Parameters` to find the value entry named NegativeCacheTime. It's a value in seconds.

But if you've never tried to resolve www.minasi.com before from this workstation, then clearly the IP address for my Web site won't be in your cache. So in that case it would be time to check with the local DNS server.

Step 2: The Preferred DNS Server Looks in Its Cache

If the local DNS cache didn't have the answer, then your workstation must ask for the help of a DNS server. When configured, every computer running TCP/IP gets the IP address for a *preferred DNS server*. That's the server that the workstation should first go to when it needs a name resolved. You can include a second choice DNS server, which the TCP/IP software will query to resolve a name *only* if the preferred DNS server doesn't respond at all. (You can also offer a third, fourth, fifth, sixth, seventh, and eighth choice server.)

DNS QUERIES GO TO PORT 53

The client—your workstation—queries the DNS server on port 53. (In the network traces that I've done, the queries seem to all run on *UDP* port 53, but there might be a TCP-based implementation.) The workstation also supplies a port number for the DNS server to respond on; as is usually the case with TCP or UDP communications, the port for server-to-client responses isn't a "well-known" port; it's basically just a random value—in effect, the client says, "Well, I've *got* to address DNS queries on port 53. What port should the DNS server use to talk back to me? How about 1066? Yeah, that sounds good, 1066—Battle of Hastings and all that. Hey, listen, DNS server, can you resolve www.minasi.com for me, and send me back the answer on port 1066 here at my IP address, 210.10.20.11? Thanks."

DNS SERVERS ALSO HAVE CACHE

Like the Windows 2000 DNS client, the Windows 2000 DNS server caches entries for places that it's already visited. In fact, that's been true for as long as I can remember for DNS servers of all kinds, Microsoft and otherwise. So if someone has asked your DNS server to look up www.minasi.com in the past 24 hours—the TTL that I set on my www.minasi.com record—then that DNS server need not query any other servers to resolve www.minasi.com. Instead, it just looks into its cache and finds the answer.

You can see what your Windows 2000 DNS server has in its cache by enabling the Advanced View (in the DNS snap-in, click View and look at Advanced; if it's not checked, then click Advanced) and you'll see a folder in the snap-in labeled `Cached Lookups`. Open it and you'll see all of the places that DNS has cached. You can clear the cache, should you want to—perhaps for troubleshooting purposes—by right-clicking the `Cached Lookups` folder and choosing Clear Cache. Typing **ipconfig /flushdns** while sitting at the DNS server will not clear the cache; instead, it would only clear the *DNS client cache* on that particular computer.

Step 3: The Preferred DNS Server Looks in Its Zones

But what if the DNS server *hasn't* been asked to resolve www.minasi.com recently? Is it time to go out to other DNS servers on the Internet? Maybe, but maybe not. It depends on whether this DNS server contains any zones.

LOCAL ZONES TAKE PRIORITY

If you were sitting on a workstation computer in my local network, then it's likely that the preferred DNS server for that computer would be the same DNS server that acts as the primary DNS server for minasi.com. In that case, the workstation's primary DNS server would be the perfect machine to ask the question, "What's the IP address for www.minasi.com?"

When queried, DNS servers look in their local zones—whether primary or secondary—before querying other servers on the Internet (or, if your DNS hierarchy isn't connected to the public DNS system, other servers in your private DNS hierarchy).

DNS DECEPTION: "SPLIT-BRAIN" DNS

You're going to learn a bit later in this chapter that sometimes you quite deliberately want to present one set of DNS names to your private internal intranet and quite a different set of names to the external Internet—I think of it as "keeping two sets of books" DNS-wise. (Some people call it "split-brain DNS.") But I want to offer a simple example to underscore how a DNS server resolves, and that locally held zones take priority over anything on the Internet.

An Example: Faking dell.com

Suppose you wanted to visit Dell and buy a computer from them over the Web. You'd start out by pointing your browser to `www.dell.com`, and your preferred DNS server would search the Internet's other DNS servers to get the IP address of Dell's Web site. So far, so good—nothing that I said in the preceding sentence should run counter to your real-life experience.

But now suppose you were to do this: Go over to your local DNS server and create a new forward lookup zone called "dell.com." Make it a primary DNS zone. Then insert an A record for "www" in the dell.com zone, pointing it to some Web server on your network. Flush your local DNS cache and point Internet Explorer to `www.dell.com`. You'll see that you get a Web page—but not Dell's.

WARNING *If you tried this, then do yourself a favor and delete that zone now. I guarantee that if you don't, then you'll forget it's there and your users will soon be banging on your door wondering why they can't get to Dell's Web site.*

Let's review what you did. By putting a new primary zone called dell.com on one of your local DNS servers, you caused anyone who uses that particular DNS server as their preferred DNS server to be unable to get to the real Dell. You didn't crash Dell's worldwide empire—*everyone else on the Internet can still find Dell without a problem.* Sure, you've got a bogus dell.com zone, but it doesn't affect anyone else, because there would be no reason for anyone to visit your DNS server to resolve www.dell.com.

The only people who *would* use that DNS server to resolve www.dell.com would be those people who happen to use that DNS server as their preferred DNS server.

Another Example: Introducing Internal versus External acme.coms

Let me jump off of the Dell example to discuss split-brain DNS. I'm going to cover it later, but I want to introduce the idea here.

This notion that local zones always win can be used to let you run a dynamic DNS service in a company that perhaps doesn't want to put a DDNS server on the public Internet. For example, imagine that Bigfirm already *has* an externally hosted zone called bigfirm.biz, and you want to create an Active Directory internally called bigfirm.biz. The external bigfirm.biz zone is probably run by some ISP on a static DNS server—*they're* not about to make their zone dynamic just to make you happy. Sure, you *could* take charge of—that is, become authoritative for—your zone, but it's not necessary.

Suppose you set up a DNS server—a dynamic one—of your own, with a bigfirm.biz zone on your intranet. As long as all of your workstations used that DNS server as their preferred DNS server, then any time that a workstation or server asks that DNS server to resolve a bigfirm.biz name, then the DNS server will notice that it *holds* a zone file for bigfirm.biz. It with then say to itself, "Heck, I don't have to go out on the Internet to resolve this name—I'm 'the guy' for this zone! *I* have the answers!" Systems could then register names for bigfirm.biz with this DNS server and your AD would work like a charm. *That's* the basics of how I recommend that you set up your DNS server. But we'll cover this in more detail later in this chapter; for now, let's get back to seeing how resolution occurs.

DEFINITION: A "CACHING-ONLY" DNS SERVER

Before leaving this section, it's worth briefly defining a term: *caching-only* DNS server. I've just explained that a DNS server that contained a zone for some domain would look in that zone first, rather than searching the Internet. But I haven't explicitly pointed out yet that you might well be running DNS servers *that contain no zones at all*—in fact, the majority of DNS servers are "zoneless." What's the point of a zoneless DNS server? Simple: It focuses solely on searching other DNS servers to resolve name resolution questions. The fact that the server caches the answers to DNS queries that it has received previously leads to the name of this kind of DNS server—a "caching-only" server.

If it's not clear why a caching-only DNS server can be useful, consider Figure 7.84.

FIGURE 7.84

Simple SOHO
Internet connection

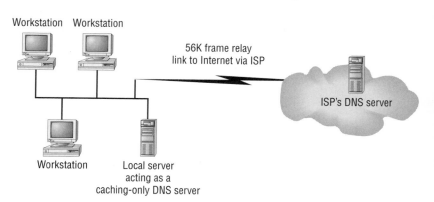

In Figure 7.84, you see a typical small office/home office (SOHO) connection between a small LAN and the Internet. The SOHO setup has a persistent 56K frame relay connection between it and the Internet. Does 56K sound unreasonably slow? It's not—first of all, if you want more than one IP address, then your ISP typically doesn't connect to you via cable modem or DSL, and, second, the vast majority of the world doesn't have the option for DSL or cable modem.

So here's the question: What DNS server should we use as the preferred DNS server for the workstations in the small office? The ISP runs a DNS server and is perfectly happy for us to point all of our workstations to that DNS server as their preferred DNS server. The ISP then worries about keeping the thing up and running, and we needn't buy a DNS server.

Alternatively, however, we could set up a DNS server locally. It wouldn't have to be a dedicated machine, and as you've seen we could just add the DNS server function to an existing Windows 2000 (or Linux or Novell or you-name-it) server. That server would know how to search the other DNS servers on the Internet, and we'd configure all of the workstations to use that local DNS server as their preferred DNS server. Which is the better answer?

I think most network architects would go with the latter approach—set up a local DNS server. To see why, ask this: What's the bottleneck in this network? It's a common one for many networks, namely, the connection to the Internet. The fact that a DNS server caches the responses to name queries keeps us from burning up that WAN link. For example, suppose four people in the company decide to visit Microsoft's Web site. In the case where we use the ISP's DNS server, that's four DNS queries that go over the WAN link. But with a local DNS server, then the local DNS server queries other DNS servers on the Internet once to find the IP address of Microsoft's Web site. The local DNS server can resolve the subsequent three queries from its own cache, meaning that those three queries stay on the fast local network. So caching-only servers are a pretty good idea.

Step 4: The Preferred DNS Server Finds and Queries My DNS Server

Well, presuming that the local DNS server can't resolve the query from its local cache or zone files, what next? As you read earlier in this chapter, your local DNS server will next try to locate a DNS server that is authoritative for minasi.com and then go query *that* server. But how to find that authoritative server? Recall from the discussion earlier in this chapter that

- ◆ your local DNS server wants to find the zone for the com domain because that will contain the record pointing to the DNS server for minasi.com,

- ◆ but before your DNS server can query the com server, it needs to know the DNS server for com,

- ◆ and the way it gets *that* is by querying the root servers,

- ◆ and the way it knows how to find the root servers is that your DNS server comes pre-packaged knowing the names and addresses of the 13 root servers.

Once your DNS server obtains the IP address of the minasi.com domain's DNS servers, then your DNS server will go ask one of the minasi.com DNS servers to resolve www.minasi.com, and report the value back to your computer.

At least, that's what I told you a few sections back—that's basically right, but it left out some detail. Now let's fill in more of the details.

TALKING TO THE ROOT

Let's back up a minute and consider what the client asked of the server. The DNS client software running on your workstation said to your local DNS server, "Please resolve the name 'www.minasi.com.'" But it said more than that: More completely, it said, "Please search for the answer, even if you have to talk to a bunch of DNS servers." And your local DNS server will do that, doggedly following the trail of other DNS servers until it gets the answer or discovers that no answer is possible.

In contrast, let's consider what happens when your local DNS server queries a root server. I've been saying up to now that your local DNS server asks the root for the address of the com DNS server so that it can ask the com server the address of the minasi.com DNS server, but that's not exactly true. Actually, your DNS server asks the root server, "What's the IP address of www.minasi.com?"

Now, the root server *could* choose to go root around (no pun intended) and get that answer for my DNS server. But it doesn't want to do any more work than is necessary—hey, it's pretty busy, just 13 root servers for the entire DNS hierarchy of Planet Earth means 13 pretty overworked computers—so instead of answering the question, the root server says in effect, "I could find that answer for you, but I'm not going to. But here's what I'll do instead—I'll give you the name and address of the *next* DNS server that you should ask the question of." Your DNS server then re-asks the question, "What's the IP address for www.minasi.com?" of the DNS server that the root server referred it to. That subsequent server might be designed to go get the complete answer for your DNS server, or it might just be set up to work like the root servers, saying, "I won't give you the answer, but here's the next guy to try." For example, here's what the conversation might look like when your DNS server tries to find www.minasi.com:

1. Your DNS server asks a root server, "What's the IP address of www.minasi.com?"

2. The root server probably answers, "Don't ask me, ask one of these servers," and lists the names and addresses of the DNS servers for the com domain.

3. Your DNS server picks one of those names and says to the DNS server for the com domain, "What's the IP address of www.minasi.com?"

4. The com DNS server answers, "Don't ask me, ask either the DNS server at 206.246.253.111 or the one at 206.246.253.112." (Those are the IP addresses of my two DNS servers and, yes, one of them is the same computer as the Web server.)

5. Your DNS server asks my DNS server, "What's the IP address for www.minasi.com?"

6. My DNS server responds, "www.minasi.com is at 206.246.253.111."

DEFINITION: RECURSIVE VERSUS ITERATIVE QUERIES

So we've seen that your DNS server will go to great lengths to answer a query. Mine works that way, too, and so will most DNS servers with which you'll ever work. But those root servers, and the DNS servers for the com domain and other top-level domains, don't do that. That's because DNS recognizes two kinds of queries: recursive and iterative.

A *recursive* query is the kind that you make against your local DNS server. You tell it to keep asking the questions until it gets an answer.

An *iterative* query is what the root servers do. When asked to resolve a name, they'll only resolve the name if they have the information right there in their zone files. If not, they just pass along the name of the next DNS server—or servers, usually—in the chain.

Down at the programming level, it's possible for a DNS server to specify when querying whether it wants a recursive or iterative answer. But that won't matter if the server has been configured to only answer recursively.

CONTROLLING RECURSIVE AND ITERATIVE BEHAVIOR

By default, the Windows 2000 DNS server answers queries recursively, searching as long as is necessary. But you can modify that behavior. In the DNS snap-in, right-click the icon representing the DNS server, click Properties and then the Advanced tab, and you'll see a screen like Figure 7.85.

FIGURE 7.85

Advanced DNS properties

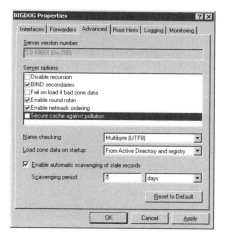

By checking the box labeled Disable Recursion, you cause the DNS server to respond in an iterative ("Go ask this guy for your answer") rather than a recursive ("I looked all over and here's your answer") manner.

Summarizing, then, the major steps that happen when your Windows 2000 workstation needs a DNS name resolved:

1. First, look in the local file named `hosts`.

2. If that doesn't help, look in the DNS client's local cache.

3. If the local cache can't help, then contact the workstation's preferred DNS server, asking it to resolve the name.

4. The preferred DNS server looks in its cache and then its zones to answer the query.

5. If it can't, then the local DNS server looks for the DNS server that *can* answer the query, the DNS server (or, usually, servers) that are authoritative for the domain in question. It does that by asking the root servers, which direct it to the next level of DNS servers, finally getting the IP addresses of the authoritative DNS servers.

6. The local DNS server then directly queries the authoritative DNS server, getting the IP address of the target system.

7. Finally the local DNS server returns the answer to the workstation.

Designing Your DNS Architecture

By now, you've got many pieces of DNS knowledge. Let's stitch it all up together to see how to design a system of DNS servers that will serve your organization's needs.

A DNS architecture typically needs to solve several problems.

◆ First, you'll probably want to install several caching-only DNS servers into your network, to provide fast name resolution.

◆ But you'll want to exploit the power of caching. As each DNS must build its own cache, caching argues *against* many servers and in favor of just one big server. What's the right balance? You can strike that balance with a concept called *forwarding*.

◆ Most firms will want to present one set of DNS names internally and a different one externally so that the outside world only sees a small subset of that firm's computers. You will, then, need to know how to maintain a separate namespace internally and externally.

◆ Finally, intranet DNS servers can present a potential security threat. Through a concept known as *slaving*, you can protect those DNS servers from outside attack.

Many Resolvers versus One Cache

As time goes on, the percentage of computers in your network that are Windows 2000 (or later, once Whistler ships) will grow. As the Windows 9x and NT 4 computers fade away, WINS will become less important and DNS will become more so. Every time that a system needs to find a file server, or every time a system needs to find a domain controller to perform an authentication—virtually every time one system needs to communicate with another—it'll need a DNS name resolution.

Now, thankfully Microsoft put a DNS cache on every workstation, so we might hope that most of those name resolutions will be resolved by the workstation itself, out of its DNS cache. Despite that, though, there will be an awful lot of name resolutions in your network that can't be handled by the 2000 DNS client's cache, and so network designers will constantly face this inescapable truth: Networks that resolve names slowly will be perceived as slow networks.

Fast name resolution isn't the only thing that you'll need for a fast network, but you can't have a fast network without it. So how do we plan to provide fast name resolution?

On the face of it, the answer would seem to be DNS servers, and lots of them. If you have lots of DNS servers sprinkled around your network and a low DNS client-to-server ratio, then client machines will see fast response, won't they? Well, yes, except for one consideration: caching on the DNS servers.

THE "MANY SERVERS" SCENARIO

Imagine that we're designing the DNS architecture for Megabucks Corporation, a firm with 2000 employees on a single large campus. Megabucks is attached to the Internet via a few T1 lines that are always busy transmitting and receiving e-mail, Web traffic, and streaming multimedia. Every unnecessary access to the Internet creates congestion on those lines.

We figure that one DNS server for every 100 employees seems like a good ratio (I just made that up, please don't take it as an actual rule of thumb—I don't think it'd be possible to come up with a rule of thumb for DNS servers that would be simple and useful, sadly), so we set up 20 DNS servers that we'll call ns01.megabucks.com through ns20.megabucks.com. Then let's watch them work.

First thing in the morning, people show up and start working. One employee, Mary, sits at a workstation whose preferred DNS server is NS01. She points her browser to www.cnn.com to get the headlines, and so her workstation asks NS01 to resolve www.cnn.com. NS01 hasn't been asked for www.cnn.com yet today, so it's got to go out on the Internet to get the answer. When other people whose workstations subsequently go to www.cnn.com, NS01 has the name already resolved and so can respond to their name resolution requests instantly.

But now Bill sits at his workstation, starting off his day with the headlines at www.cnn.com. *His* workstation, however, uses ns02.megabucks.com as its DNS server. NS02 hasn't been asked for www.cnn.com's IP address yet, so it has to go out to the Internet to answer that query. Similarly, NS03, NS04, and so on—each of the 20 DNS servers—each have to separately learn the IP address of www.cnn.com. (That's presuming that they have to learn it at all—for example, NS17 might only serve a bunch of people who might only use their computers to do work rather than the high-tech equivalent of reading the paper in the office.) In other words, if our servers could somehow get together on what they know in their caches, then we could reduce by up to 20-fold the amount of WAN bandwidth that the DNS servers suck up.

THE "ONE BIG SERVER" SCENARIO

Or we could take a different tack. Instead of installing DNS on a bunch of machines, some of which might also be serving in other roles, we go spend some of the company's money for a monster eight-CPU system with several gigabytes of RAM. Then we point *every* workstation in the plant to this system. The benefit? One server means one cache. After Mary causes the server to resolve www.cnn.com, then Bill's subsequent resolution request can be answered instantaneously.

If *this* scenario makes you a bit queasy, then it should. Although one big cache would be nice, putting all of my eggs in one basket has always made me wish for a titanium basket. Is there a way to both unify the cache and get the benefits of scattering DNS servers all over the place?

DNS Forwarders: The Best of Both Worlds

We *can* centralize the cache and yet keep our 20 DNS servers. The trick is called *forwarding*. Figure 7.86 shows how it works.

You've read how a DNS server would normally resolve a name—look in its cache, its zones, and then start looking out on the Internet for the authoritative DNS server. With forwarding, we add an intermediate step. At Megabucks, we'd set up a 21st machine as a DNS server and then tell the 20 other DNS servers to use that 21st machine as a *forwarder*. Then they'd resolve a name in this way:

1. As before, look in the local cache and zones.

2. If the local cache and zones don't have the answer, then don't go out on the Internet. Instead, query the forwarder.

FIGURE 7.86

A DNS forwarder

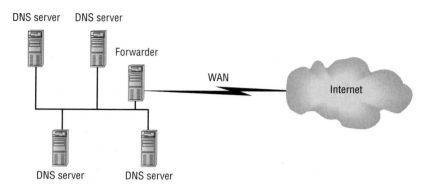

3. If the forwarder has the answer in its local cache or zones, then it can answer the question. If not, then the forwarder searches the DNS servers on the Internet, as you've already learned.

4. Once the forwarder has the answer, it sends that back to the querying DNS server.

5. *But* if the forwarder doesn't respond in a reasonable amount of time, then the querying DNS server just gives up on the forwarder and searches the DNS servers on the Internet itself.

Now, at first blush, it might look like we've just made things slower by adding a new step in the resolution process—querying and then waiting for the forwarder. But consider how the forwarder communicates with the local DNS servers—through the company LAN. That LAN's likely to be 100 megabits per second or faster—almost certainly in any case faster than the WAN link to the Internet. The value of the forwarder at Megabucks is this: Mary and Bill still have separate DNS servers, but their DNS servers don't ever have to communicate on the Internet. Because Mary first looked up www.cnn.com, that caused her DNS server (NS01) to try to resolve the name. It asked the forwarder, who also didn't know the IP address for www.cnn.com. So the forwarder went out over the WAN link to the Internet to find out www.cnn.com's IP address, and told Mary's DNS server. Minutes later, when Bill's DNS server (NS02) needed to resolve www.cnn.com, it asked the forwarder to go look it up—and the forwarder responded instantly over the company's LAN because the forwarder already had the answer in its cache. The result? Now www.cnn.com is in the caches of NS01, NS02, and the forwarder—but we only went out on the Internet once.

Telling a Windows 2000 DNS server to use a forwarder is simple. Just open the DNS snap-in and right-click the icon representing the DNS server, choose Properties, then click the Forwarders tab on the properties page. You'll see a screen like Figure 7.87.

In that figure, you see that I've checked the Enable Forwarders box, which is unchecked by default. You can also see that you can specify several forwarders by IP address. Finally, you can see that you can set the length of time that your DNS servers should wait for the forwarders to respond before giving up on them and doing the Internet-based search themselves.

Does the forwarder need to be a particularly powerful machine? Not really; answering a query out of the cache isn't that stressful for a system. But you'd do well to give the forwarder a *lot* of RAM. The more RAM, the more items it can cache without having to page them out to disk.

FIGURE 7.87

Configuring a DNS forwarder

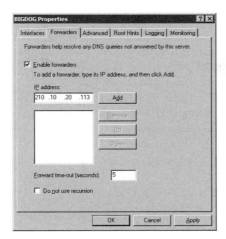

Uprooting a DNS Server: When Forwarders Are Grayed Out

Time for a short digression. If you've just set up your DNS server and are following along with the book, then you might have seen something disconcerting—the Enable Forwarders check box is grayed out. Click on the Root Hints tab, and you see the same thing. What happened? You've got a "false root."

What's happening here is that your DNS server thinks that it is *the* only DNS server in the world, that it is the root of the public DNS hierarchy. How'd it happen? Certain circumstances—I've never nailed them down—cause the DNS server upon first startup, the first time you start the DNS snap-in, to ask you if it's true that this is the only DNS server around. As there are plenty of things to worry about when setting up a network, it's only normal to click OK—actually I think it's Next, as it's presented by a wizard—and forget it.

Until you try to change a forwarder or a root hint. *Or*—and here's the part that will drive you crazy—you try to resolve a name out on the public Internet.

Installing a private root on a DNS server tells it that there *isn't* any other DNS server around to which to refer questions. So if your DNS server doesn't have a zone that it can look something up in, then it just assumes that no one knows the answer.

Anyway, that's what went wrong. How to undo it? Here are three ways to reintroduce your DNS server to the rest of the world. All three share the same basic approach; they delete the root domain from your DNS server. I'm explaining all three approaches so that I can also offer some insight into how to do a bit of under-the-hood work on DNS.

First, there's the command-line approach. This needs a command called DNSCMD.EXE, which doesn't automatically install with Windows 2000 Server, but *is* included in the Server Tools add-on, which you can find on the 2000 Server CD in the \SUPPORT\TOOLS folder. Once DNSCMD is installed, you can de-root your DNS server with one command:

```
dnscmd /ZoneDelete .
```

Note the spacing—first `dnscmd`, then a space, then the option `/ZoneDelete`, then another space, then ".", the name of the zone to delete. I notice that there's an option `/dsdel` that you must run to delete the zone if it's Active Directory–integrated, but I'm not quite sure how you'd end up with an AD-integrated root domain, at least not without a lot of work! Uppercase and lowercase seem not to matter. Once you execute the command, I would recommend restarting the DNS service. Then open up the DNS snap-in, and try to examine the Forwarders or Root Hints tabs on the server's Properties page—you'll see that they're no longer grayed out.

You can also de-root a DNS server from the DNS snap-in. Open up the `Forward Lookup Zones`, and you'll see a folder whose name is simply "."; as you now know, that's the root domain. Right-click that folder and choose Properties. In the Properties page, check that the zone type is Primary rather than Active Directory–integrated; if it *is* AD-integrated, just click the Change button next to the type and convert it to a standard primary zone. Close the Properties page.

In the `Forward Lookup Zones` folder, right-click the root zone and click Delete. Close the DNS snap-in, restart the DNS Server service, and re-open the DNS snap-in. You'll see that Forwarders and Root Hints are no longer grayed out.

Finally, for those who enjoy a bit of Registry tweaking, here's a third uprooting procedure. As far as I know, this only works on a standard primary zone. First, stop the DNS Server service, either from the GUI or from the command line with this:

```
net stop "DNS Server"
```

Then edit the Registry to altogether remove the key at `HKEY_LOCAL_MACHINE\SYSTEM\CurrentControlSet\Services\DNS\Zones\.` and, again, notice that final period—that was part of the key, not the end of the sentence. Restart the DNS service, and you're back in the public DNS hierarchy.

Of course, now and then you might actually *want* a DNS server with a private root; I'll tell you how to set one up a bit later in this chapter.

Separate Internal and External DNS

Well, we figured out how Megabucks Corporation should place the DNS servers that will resolve names for their internal folks. But now they've got another problem: How should they set up the DNS servers that will hold the megabucks.com zone files? For most firms, it's not as easy as just running the Create New Zone Wizard. Let's look at the kinds of decisions that Megabucks has to make when configuring their IP subnets and DNS names, given that they are both running their own intranet and are connected to the Internet.

ONE SCENARIO: COMPLETELY OPEN ON THE INTERNET

We know that Megabucks has about 2000 employees, so let's suppose it has about 2500 computers and therefore needs about 2500 IP addresses. That'd be about 10 class C–sized subnets. In the simplest network layout we could imagine, Megabucks goes out and gets 10 class C networks from an ISP. Every one of those 2540 IP addresses are fully routable on the public Internet. They put one IP address on each one of their computers, and so each computer can ping anywhere on the Internet. (And anyone on the Internet can ping any one of those computers.) They then register the domain megabucks.com with Network Solutions. When Network Solutions asks for the IP addresses of two DNS servers that will act as the authoritative servers for the megabucks.com domain, the Megabucks folks just give them the addresses of two Windows 2000 servers, and then run the DNS service on those machines—let's call those two machines primary.megabucks.com and secondary.megabucks.com.

Then they create a primary megabucks.com forward lookup zone on one of the two Windows 2000 DNS servers (primary.megabucks.com, as you've no doubt guessed), and a secondary megabucks.com forward lookup zone on the other Windows 2000 DNS server, secondary.megabucks.com. They enable dynamic DNS updates on the megabucks.com zone, and so the megabucks.com zone is soon filled with about 2500 A records naming every system on the Megabucks network.

Notice that for an internal Megabucks system to resolve the name of another internal Megabucks system, then that system (or its DNS server) ends up asking either primary.megabucks.com or secondary.megabucks.com. Notice also that whenever someone in the public Internet tries to resolve a megabucks.com name, such as when she tries to visit www.megabucks.com or sends mail to somebody@megabucks.com, her DNS server also gets its name resolution query answered by the same two servers, primary.megabucks.com and secondary.megabucks.com, using the very same megabucks.com zone.

What's wrong with this? Well, technically there's nothing illegal about it, but this scenario would trouble most security experts. Using the same DNS server for your internal network as you use to allow external people to resolve names in your domain exposes your entire domain to the Internet. What concerns the security folks—and please understand that I do not by any means consider myself a security expert—is that there's a general principle of security that goes something such as, "The less that you tell the weasels, the harder it is for the weasels to attack you."

For example, suppose a potential slimeball looked at all of those A records. That's a complete listing of the names and IP addresses of all of the workstations on your network. Everybody knows that many users are pretty lax about things like passwords and security on their own workstations, so they'd be a good starting point—probably an easier cracking job than the servers. If you're running Active Directory, then you get even more information from DNS than usual; for example, DNS will tell you the names of the system's domain controllers. That's not a bug—DNS under Windows 2000 is *supposed* to do that, remember? The bottom line is that most firms would prefer for the DNS server that the public Internet sees to only know a few records—the obligatory SOA record and NS records, as well as an MX record or two so that the company can receive Internet e-mail, as well as A or CNAME records for its Web and perhaps FTP servers.

A BETTER SCENARIO: SPLIT-BRAIN DNS

Now let's see if we can do a better job for Megabucks.

TIP   *This is the recommended scenario for many folks, so be sure to give this a good, close look!*

It likes those 2500+ routable IP addresses, so it decides to stay with them. But it'd like the public to see just a small subset of the megabucks.com DNS information, while allowing its internal users to see everything—and that not only means everything in the internal megabucks.com network, but the rest of the Internet as well. Take a look at Figure 7.88 to see how Megabucks can change its network to make things work a bit more to its liking.

To keep the diagram simple, I reduced the number of internal name-resolving DNS servers from twenty to just two—instead of NS01 through NS20, we've only got NS01 and NS02. There are several concepts in that diagram, but the single most important is that now we have *two* primary DNS servers for megabucks.com and two sets of secondary DNS servers for megabucks.com.

FIGURE 7.88

Using *two* sets of primary/secondary DNS servers for megabucks.com zone

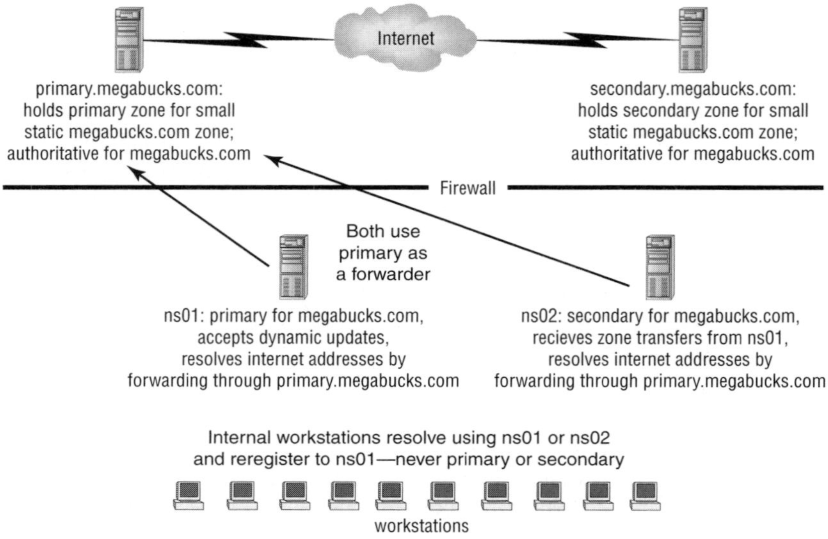

primary.megabucks.com:
holds primary zone for small
static megabucks.com zone;
authoritative for megabucks.com

Internet

secondary.megabucks.com:
holds secondary zone for small
static megabucks.com zone;
authoritative for megabucks.com

Firewall

Both use
primary as
a forwarder

ns01: primary for megabucks.com,
accepts dynamic updates,
resolves internet addresses by
forwarding through primary.megabucks.com

ns02: secondary for megabucks.com,
recieves zone transfers from ns01,
resolves internet addresses by
forwarding through primary.megabucks.com

Internal workstations resolve using ns01 or ns02
and reregister to ns01—never primary or secondary

workstations

The servers primary.megabucks.com and secondary.megabucks.com are still primary and secondary servers for the megabucks.com domain, and they are still the two authoritative DNS servers for the domain, as far as Network Solutions is concerned. But now those zones are static, not dynamic, and they contain just a handful of records, as I suggested at the end of the last section. There's an SOA record, two NS records (one for primary and one for secondary), MX records to point to the publicly available mail servers, and A or CNAME records to point to the Web servers, FTP servers, and any other servers that Megabucks wants the outside world to see. These two DNS servers are *not*, however, the primary and secondary DNS servers as far as the internal Megabucks systems are concerned.

TIP *Let me underscore this. I'm asked often, "We have a registered Internet domain, and we're going to do Active Directory. Right now our ISP hosts our zone—do we have to take that back? Must we become authoritative for our zone?" The answer is, "Absolutely not." Go ahead and leave the public zone on an ISP, where it's (hopefully) safe, sound, and secure. (And someone else's problem.) It'll handle the external requests, and as you'll see, you'll run some servers of your own for the internal ones.*

Instead, the DNS servers that previously only did name resolution, the ones that were caching-only servers, now contain a zone: the megabucks.com zone. We told ns01.megabucks.com that it was the primary DNS server for megabucks.com, as well as authorizing dynamic updates for the zone. We told NS01 that the megabucks.com zone had a secondary DNS server as well, ns02.megabucks.com. We did *not* tell it that primary.megabucks.com and secondary.megabucks.com (the external DNS servers) held megabucks.com zones; as far as NS01's concerned, it and NS02 are the only DNS servers for megabucks.com. ns02.megabucks.com has been set up as a secondary server on megabucks.com and told to pull its zone file from NS01.

Additionally, the workstations inside megabucks.com only know about NS01 and NS02 vis-a-vis DNS servers. Some machines are configured with NS01 as their preferred DNS server, and some are configured instead with NS02 as their preferred DNS server. No workstations are configured with primary.megabucks.com or secondary.megabucks.com as their preferred DNS server. Whether they query NS01 or NS02 for an SOA record for megabucks.com, they'll be told the same thing—that NS01.megabucks.com is the primary DNS server for megabucks.com and therefore is the place to go to reregister with dynamic DNS. (This works just as well if NS01 and NS02 are Active Directory domain controllers and their megabucks.com domain is set up as an Active Directory–integrated domain, in case you're wondering.)

Let's follow a few name resolutions through to see how this meets Megabucks' needs.

First, what happens if someone in the public Internet tries to resolve www.megabucks.com? That person's local DNS server will ask the root servers where it can find the DNS servers for megabucks.com, and the root servers will reply, "Either primary .megabucks.com or secondary.megabucks.com can answer your name queries about megabucks.com." The person's local DNS server will then ask primary or secondary and will get back the address of the Web server that Megabucks wants the outside world to see.

Well, how about if that person on the outside Internet tries to resolve ns01.megabucks.com? Again, their local DNS server will be directed to primary or secondary. The megabucks.com zone sitting on primary and secondary doesn't include a record for NS01, and there's no way for that person out on the public Internet to know that there are other DNS servers on megabucks.com that could answer the question. As a result, the attempted name resolution for NS01 will fail. That includes any attempts to find domain controllers for the megabucks.com Active Directory, whenever it gets the domain running. So, summarized, outsiders can't see into the megabucks.com intranet's naming service.

Let's look at it from the reverse point of view. What would a person on an internal system be able to do?

Well, first, suppose someone inside Megabucks tried to resolve www.microsoft.com, and presume that information wasn't in their system's local DNS cache. In that case, their workstation would contact one of the internal DNS servers (NS01 or NS02). If the internal DNS server had been asked the question recently, then it'd have the answer in cache. If not, the internal DNS server would forward the request out to secondary.megabucks.com, which would be able to get the answer and reply back to the internal DNS server.

NOTE *Note that secondary could forward to any external DNS server. In fact, if primary and secondary were indeed on the ISP's DNS servers, then it wouldn't make all that much sense to forward to it, as the ISP's DNS servers are busy and across a WAN link from the internal DNS servers. Megabucks might alternatively just put a simple DNS server outside of its firewall (but still on the Megabucks premises) that contained no zones at all. As it's outside the firewall, it should spend some time hardening it against attack, of course. And for security's sake, don't forward the internal servers to the outside, slave them—you'll learn how in a page or two.*

Next, consider the case where someone inside Megabucks tries to resolve the name of another machine inside Megabucks. No problem there—NS01 contains a megabucks.com zone that knows the names of every internal machine, as they all register with NS01, and NS02 has a copy of that zone, as it's a secondary.

Basically, then, split-brain DNS on megabucks.com lets us create a kind of "two-way mirror": People outside the domain can't see in, but people inside the domain can see out.

There *is* one case where things get a little tricky. What about if someone at one of the internal megabucks.com systems tries to resolve www.megabucks.com or one of the other publicly visible Megabucks systems? From what we've seen so far, that resolution attempt would fail. The internal system would address its query to NS01 or NS02, and both DNS servers contain a zone for megabucks.com. But would there be a www record in that zone? Not by default, as the Web server wouldn't register itself with the dynamic DNS servers—it's supposed to be visible on the public Internet, so its preferred DNS server would likely be either primary.megabucks.com or secondary.megabucks.com.

That leads to the unusual side-effect that the only people on the planet who can't get to www.megabucks.com are the people who work for Megabucks. Which might not be so bad, if Megabucks were planning to announce the layoffs on the Web.... Seriously, though, the fix here is easy: Just add a static entry into NS01's megabucks.com zone for www, as well as records for the mail, FTP, and any other servers.

YET ANOTHER: DIFFERENT NAMES

I just explained how to create one set of DNS names internally and another externally, but that's not the way that everyone handles their inside/outside name dichotomy. Some firms just register two different DNS domains and use one on their internal network and the other on their external network. For example, before Compaq bought them, Digital Equipment Corporation used to use digital.com for their externally visible network and dec.com for their internal network.

Other firms register both the .net and .com versions of its company name, so Megabucks might use the megabucks.com DNS domain for their externally visible systems and megabucks.net for their internal systems.

Still others create child domains. Megabucks might decide to create a child domain named internal.megabucks.com. All of the internal systems would have names like *machinename*.internal.megabucks.com, and we'd place an internal.megabucks.com zone on all of the DNS servers on the internal network. The DNS servers for the parent level, megabucks.com, would all live out on the external network, but there would be no delegation records on that external DNS server to indicate that there is a child domain of megabucks.com called internal.megabucks.com.

Whatever names you decide to use internally, make sure they're registered with the worldwide DNS hierarchy. Otherwise, someone *else* could unwittingly register a domain with that name, and as a result your internal users couldn't resolve any names in that domain. If that's not clear, think back to my example about what would happen if you created a dell.com zone on your internal network: Whenever one of your users tried to surf to www.dell.com, they'd be directed to one of your Web servers, not the actual Dell ones.

Securing Internal DNS Servers: Slaves

Before we leave DNS, let's consider one more issue: networks employing nonroutable addresses on their internal networks. As you learned in the previous chapter, it often makes a lot of sense to set up your internal systems with nonroutable IP addresses. Despite their "nonroutable" name, systems with nonroutable addresses can still access the public Internet through network address translation and/or port address translation. As you recall from the previous chapter, one of the nice things about a

NAT/PAT-driven Internet connection is that your internal systems can *initiate* a conversation with a system on the public Internet, but no system on the public Internet can initiate a conversation with one of your internal systems, providing a bit of Internet security.

Now let's take that last bit of information and apply it to the internal DNS servers on our internal network. Recall that in the scenarios that I've laid out so far, an internal DNS server contains the zone for the internal network and therefore can immediately resolve any internal name. When it wants to resolve an external name—the DNS name of a system on the Internet—then it uses another DNS server that is still on the company network but visible to the external Internet (and probably on the other side of a firewall), using that externally visible DNS server in the role of a "forwarder." If security is our concern, then forwarders make even more sense than they did before. Suppose we have 20 internal DNS servers and two external forwarders. As all external DNS name resolutions are accomplished by the two external forwarders, then those two are the only two DNS servers that we've got to worry about securing—the 20 internal DNS servers present no issue at all, as they're behind the firewall, right?

Almost, but not quite. Remember how a DNS server uses a forwarder? It passes queries along to the forwarder and waits for the forwarder to search the Internet's DNS servers to resolve those queries. But remember that it only waits *so* long; if the forwarder doesn't respond in a particular period of time (a configurable period, but it's five seconds by default on Windows 2000 DNS servers), then the internal DNS server just takes the bull by the horns and searches the Internet itself.

That's the troublesome part. If a server from behind a firewall initiates a conversation with a DNS server on the public Internet, then that server is essentially asking a question and waiting for an answer. To allow the server on the public Internet to answer the query of the system behind the firewall, address translating routers must temporarily leave a link in place, an open port on the firewall leading back to the internal DNS server. Why's that bad? I don't actually see it as a terribly heinous thing, but the security experts that I know worry about it. Suppose, they say, someone had cooked up a bogus DNS server on the public Internet that grabbed those incoming ports leading back behind the firewall and tried somehow to use that to compromise the internal DNS server. I'm not sure *how* you'd do that, but then I'm neither a computer criminal nor a security expert, so I'll take their word for it when they say that "bad things could happen."

The fix is simple. Just modify your internal DNS servers' behavior when they send queries to the forwarder. Tell your internal DNS servers, "If the external forwarder doesn't respond to your query, too bad—just consider the attempt failed." This is called *slaving* the internal DNS server to the forwarder. To see how to do that, look back at the tab on a DNS server's properties page that controls forwarding (look back to Figure 7.87). Just check the box labeled Do Not Use Recursion, and you've slaved the server. Slaving a DNS server to another DNS server is, then, nothing more than a restricted form of forwarding a DNS server to another DNS server.

DNS Troubleshooting: Understanding the DNS Boot, Cache, and Zone Files

Thus far, we've worked with the Windows 2000 DNS server via its GUI interface and wizards. They're fine for many tasks, but in my experience they're a bit "fragile"—the DNS tree is built from a chain of data, and if any of those links aren't in place, then the GUI may refuse to run at all.

Starting up the DNS snap-in and having it refuse to work is pretty scary—"Do I have to reinstall *all* of Windows 2000 to fix this?" most of us would wonder—but there's a way to work with and fix many DNS problems by just modifying a few ASCII files. (Unless your zones are Active Directory–integrated. If they are, of course, then you can always temporarily convert them back to standard primary or secondary zones; then you'll get ASCII files to work with.) You'll find that one of the best DNS troubleshooting tools is Notepad, believe it or not.

There's another reason for understanding these DNS ASCII files. Other DNS server implementations, such as NT 4's DNS server and most Unix implementations of DNS servers, are driven by almost the same ASCII files and file formats as Microsoft's Windows 2000 DNS server. Learning how to do a bit of under-the-hood work with Windows 2000's DNS server, then, equips you to work with other DNS server implementations as well.

DNS Boot Order

First let's take a look at what files DNS reads to get started and in what order it reads them. There are just a few files that control a DNS server's behavior: one named **boot**, another named **cache.dns**, and one zone file for each of the zones for which the DNS server is responsible:

◆ **boot** has two main jobs. First, it tells a DNS server whether the server is a root name server. Second, it tells the DNS server what domains it acts as the primary DNS server for and which domains it acts as the secondary DNS server for. Non-Microsoft DNS server implementations have always kept this "boot" information in a file called **boot**, but for some reason Windows 2000 DNS servers store the information in either the Active Directory, the server's Registry, or a normal BOOT file. By default Windows 2000 DNS servers store the BOOT information in the Active Directory, but for purposes of failure recovery and troubleshooting, I prefer to use the traditional method of saving the information in a separate file named **boot**. I'll show you how to change your DNS servers so that they use a BOOT file instead of Active Directory or the Registry as well, a little later.

◆ **cache.dns** is a file listing the names and IP addresses of your DNS hierarchy's top-level root name server or servers. For people attached to the Internet, **cache.dns** contains the addresses of the 13 ICANN root servers. For someone in a private DNS system, **cache.dns** would contain the addresses of the private DNS's name servers. Microsoft's Windows 2000 DNS server software uses a file named **cache.dns** to store its root server information (rather than Active Directory or the Registry), so in this way the DNS server software that Microsoft ships with Windows 2000 Server behaves precisely like other DNS servers.

NOTE   *Not every machine has a* **cache.dns**: *A DNS hierarchy's root name servers do not have* **cache.dns** *files.*

◆ A DNS server will have a zone file for each zone for which it is a primary or secondary server. A zone file contains all of the zone's data—who its name servers are, its SOA record, its host name records, MX records, CNAME records, and the like. As with **cache.dns**, Microsoft's Windows 2000 DNS server software behaves like other DNS servers and maintains zone information in simple ASCII files, formatted in the same way as other DNS servers. You've already seen how zone files are arranged.

The BOOT File

BOOT files connect a DNS server to the hierarchy of DNS servers and tell the DNS server which zones it is authoritative for. By default, however, the DNS server software that comes with Windows 2000 doesn't use BOOT files—so let's change that.

The first way to change how a Windows 2000 DNS server stores BOOT information is through the GUI:

1. Open the DNS snap-in.

2. Locate the icon depicting your DNS server.

3. Right-click the server's icon and choose Properties. A properties page will appear with tabs labeled Interfaces, Forwarders, Advanced, Root Hints, Logging, Security, and Monitoring. Click Advanced.

4. You'll see a single-selection drop-down list box labeled Load Zone Data on Startup; choose Boot from File.

5. Click OK.

6. Close the DNS snap-in.

If that sounds like too much clicking, then open up your Registry Editor of choice, navigate to `HKEY_LOCAL_MACHINE\System\CurrentControlSet\Services\DNS\Parameters`. Look for the key `BootMethod`; if it's not there, then create it—it's of type REG_DWORD. Set its value to 1. (If the value is 2, the BOOT information is stored in the Registry and if the value is 3, it's stored in Active Directory.)

Windows 2000's DNS server stores all of its configuration files—`boot`, `cache.dns`, and any zone files—in `\winnt\system32\dns`.

There are only three kinds of records you'll see in a BOOT file: *Primary* tells a DNS server that it's a primary DNS server for a zone, *secondary* tells the DNS server that it's a secondary DNS server for a zone, and *cache* tells the DNS server where to find the list of root servers.

PRIMARY RECORD

BOOT files often contain a line like the following:

```
primary    minasi.com    minasi.com.dns
```

This record tells this DNS server that it is the primary DNS server for the minasi.com zone, that it is authoritative for the zone. It also identifies the file that contains minasi.com's zone information—`minasi.com.dns`. You don't *have* to name a zone's file with a name of zone name +.dns, but it's customary.

In the primary record, the word *primary* is followed by at least one space, then the name of the zone, then at least one space, and finally the zone filename.

When a DNS server is the primary root server, it has this line in its BOOT file:

```
primary    .    root.dns
```

As you recall, the name of the root of the DNS namespace is . (a period); the zone file's name is often `root.dns`, but it could be anything. All you're doing in this line is telling the DNS server where to find the file that contains the root zone information.

SECONDARY RECORD

You might see this line in a BOOT file:

```
secondary win2ktest.com 210.10.30.11 win2ktest.com.dns
```

This tells this server that it is a secondary DNS server for the win2ktest.com zone. The format of the record is similar to the primary record, save for an extra bit of information—the IP address of the *primary* DNS server for that zone.

A secondary root server would have a line in its BOOT file that looked like this:

```
secondary  .  124.99.21.3  rootfile.dns
```

That line would tell the server that it was a secondary DNS root server, that the primary root server was at IP address 124.99.21.3, and that the server could find the root zone file information in a file called `rootfile.dns`.

CACHE RECORD

Primary and secondary records tell a DNS server, "You are authoritative in some manner for some given zone." Cache records say, "In case you need to find a name server for a particular zone quickly and don't feel like searching around, here's the name of a file that contains a list of name servers for that zone." Such a list is sometimes called a *hints* file.

I suppose you *could* put all kinds of hints files on your DNS—perhaps you access Microsoft's Web site so much that you can't *stand* the idea of having to wait while your DNS servers work their way around the Net to get the address of Microsoft's DNS servers—but I've never seen it. So far as I've ever seen, the only destination worth storing hints about was the root of the DNS hierarchy, the root of the namespace. You point your DNS server at any hints files with the cache record. It looks like this:

```
cache  zone-name  name-of-file-containing-list-of-DNS-servers-for-that-zone
```

As I said, the place you're most likely to store hints about is the root domain, the one named ., and by convention the name of the file that you store the root hints in is called `cache.dns`. The most common cache record that you'll see in BOOT files is, then:

```
cache  .  cache.dns
```

But if you *did* want to keep that file that listed all of Microsoft's DNS servers, then you might call that file `microsoft.cache`, and you'd tell your DNS server about it by adding this line to the BOOT file:

```
cache  microsoft.com  microsoft.cache
```

BOOT EXAMPLES: DNS DISASTER RECOVERY (1)

Okay, ready for the secret of disaster recovery under DNS? It's so easy you won't believe it. Let's assume you have the `cache.dns` and zone files for a dead DNS server, but the server stored its BOOT information in the Active Directory, as is the default—so you've got cache and zones, but no BOOT file to start the process off! How do you take those files and get DNS back up and running in no time?

Well, step one is to install the DNS service on a new server. Step two is to get it to boot from the BOOT files rather than from something in the Registry or Active Directory. Step three is to stop the DNS service so you can restore the `cache.dns` and zone files. Step four is to rebuild a BOOT file— so let's use a few examples to review what a BOOT file would look like.

In one simple example, suppose we're rebuilding a DNS server that was the primary DNS server for apex.com. The zone file for apex.com is the default, `apex.com.dns`. The server wasn't a root server. The BOOT file then looks like this:

```
primary      apex.com     apex.com.dns
cache        .            cache.dns
```

Now let's try one where the server was primary for apex.com (zone filename `apex.com.dns`), acme.com (zone filename `acme.com.dns`), and secondary for reliable.com (zone filename `reliable.com.dns`). The primary DNS server for reliable.com has IP address 201.10.22.9. This server's not a root server. The BOOT file then looks like this:

```
primary      apex.com     apex.com.dns
primary      acme.com     acme.com.dns
secondary    reliable.com 201.10.22.9  reliable.com.dns
cache        .            cache.dns
```

For the final example, suppose we have a server just like the last one, but it's the root server. The root domain needs a zone file and we've decided to follow tradition and call it root.dns. The BOOT file would then look like this:

```
primary      apex.com     apex.com.dns
primary      acme.com     acme.com.dns
secondary    reliable.com 201.10.22.9  reliable.com.dns
primary      .            root.dns
```

Notice that the cache record goes, replaced by a primary record for the root.

DNS Disaster Recovery (2)

This is a might off-topic, but inasmuch as I brought up disaster recovery in the previous section, I wanted to take a moment and talk about the more straightforward way to do disaster recovery on a DNS server.

Recall that primary zones store simple ASCII text files called *zone files*. They're all you need to rebuild a DNS server. They live in `\winnt\system32\dns` and all have names such as *domainname*.dns; for example, the zone file for bigfirm.biz would be bigfirm.biz.dns. All you need do to easily recover a DNS server is to back up its zone files regularly.

Then just set up the DNS service on another system. Stop the service. Restore the backedup zone files to `\winnt\system32\dns` on the new system. Start the service. Run the wizard to create a new zone, but when it asks you what to call the new zone file, recall that it gives you the choice to create a new zone file or use an existing one. Tell it to use an existing one and give it the name of the restored zone file, and you're back in business.

If the zone is an Active Directory–integrated zone, then the data is in the AD database itself; any other domain controller can access the zone data.

The *CACHE.DNS* File

If you're connected to the Internet and your DNS servers are part of the worldwide DNS namespace, then you'll probably never have to look at this file. But if you're working with a private root, then you *will* have to modify the file—so let's take a look at one. With the comments (the lines starting with semicolons) removed, the one on my DNS servers looks like this:

```
@                          NS  a.root-servers.net.
a.root-servers.net.        A   198.41.0.4
@                          NS  b.root-servers.net.
b.root-servers.net.        A   128.9.0.107
@                          NS  c.root-servers.net.
c.root-servers.net.        A   192.33.4.12
@                          NS  d.root-servers.net.
d.root-servers.net.        A   128.8.10.90
@                          NS  e.root-servers.net.
e.root-servers.net.        A   192.203.230.10
@                          NS  f.root-servers.net.
f.root-servers.net.        A   192.5.5.241
@                          NS  g.root-servers.net.
g.root-servers.net.        A   192.112.36.4
@                          NS  h.root-servers.net.
h.root-servers.net.        A   128.63.2.53
@                          NS  i.root-servers.net.
i.root-servers.net.        A   192.36.148.17
@                          NS  j.root-servers.net.
j.root-servers.net.        A   198.41.0.10
@                          NS  k.root-servers.net.
k.root-servers.net.        A   193.0.14.129
@                          NS  l.root-servers.net.
l.root-servers.net.        A   198.32.64.12
@                          NS  m.root-servers.net.
m.root-servers.net.        A   202.12.27.33
```

As you can see, it is 13 pairs of records. Each pair starts off with an @ sign, then NS, then a DNS name. The following line starts off with the DNS name, then a capital A, then an IP address. There is at least one space between each of the line's parts. The people at Microsoft formatted the file so that the As and NSs line up nicely, but that's not necessary.

The records with NS in them are *name server* records. Their job is to identify a name server—a DNS server—for any given zone. You read them right-to-left: "a.root-servers.net is a name server for the zone named @." Sounds good, but what domain is @? @ is just a shorthand way of saying, "Look, you already know what zone we're talking about, so don't make me write it out all over again, Okay?" As we're talking about the root—recall, the cache record in boot identified this as a file of hints about the root—the @ signs are just a short way of writing .; and yes, I know—typing . is as easy, if not easier, than typing @ —but it's one of those matters of convention that everyone seems to follow. Blame it on the Unix guys. As you'll see later when we examine zone files where the zone names are longer than one character, however, that @ can be quite useful. In any case, we read that first NS record as saying, "a.root-servers.net is a name server for the root domain."

The A records are called *host* records because they identify host names. An A record's job is simple: It links a DNS name and an IP address. Read these left to right; the first one would be read, "The machine named a.root-servers.net is at IP address 198.41.0.4."

Now the reason for the pairs of records is a bit clearer: The NS record says, "You can find a root name server at a.root-servers.net," but to find the server we ultimately need the IP address more than we need the name, and so the A record answers the question, "Okay, so now I know that a.root-servers.net is the machine I want, what's its IP address?" And there are 13 pairs of records because the ICANN runs 13 root servers.

In contrast, what would this look like if you were running a private namespace, a private DNS hierarchy? For example, suppose you had only two root DNS servers, one named root1.acme.com at 100.100.20.17 and another called root2.acme.com at 100.100.20.18. For the purposes of hints, we don't care which is primary and which is secondary. Your `cache.dns` file would then look like this:

```
@                     ns    root1.acme.com
root1.acme.com.       a     100.100.20.17
@                     ns    root2.acme.com
root2.acme.com.       a     100.100.20.18
```

Like the other DNS files, cache/"hints" files go in `\winnt\system32\dns` and, as they are ASCII, can be easily edited with Notepad.

Application: Building a Private Root

Okay, now you're a zone file maven. Let's put that knowledge to work. First project: Create a private root. But first, let's review what that means.

You've read that DNS servers are smart enough to work their way up to the top of the DNS server hierarchy, and that at the top of that hierarchy is a bunch of servers run by ICANN. That's usually true, but not always. Your DNS servers might *not* be attached to any machine in the outside world. You might have your own little private intranet not attached to the Internet for reasons of security or cost. In that case, however, you must still have a DNS server hierarchy. The difference is that *you* build all of it. In that case, your DNS hierarchy is said to have a *private root*.

Recall that you learned earlier in this chapter that the public DNS hierarchy has a topmost level domain called *root* but spelled "."—a period. Below that are the top-level domains such as com, net, edu, biz, and the like. But every hierarchy, big or small, needs a root.

If you want your own DNS hierarchy instead of using the public DNS system, you can easily accomplish that with Windows 2000's DNS server. All there is to building a private root is really to just create a zone for . and populate it with the proper information; in this section, we'll see how.

Oh, and I forgot the other reason for building a private root: It makes for a great joke at the company. You set up the private root DNS server, choose some victim, and point his machine at your DNS server, where you've got bogus domains built for cnn.com, microsoft.com, and so on. (Just kidding—it would be a fair bit of work just for a few sadistic yuks.)

Suppose you've got two DNS servers (we could do more, but it would get monotonous), one named ns1.apex.com at 10.10.10.10 and the other named ns2.apex.com at 10.10.10.20. We'll configure it so that ns1.apex.com will be the DNS name hierarchy root, the top of the namespace. Then we'll configure ns2.apex.com in the same way that we'll configure *all* DNS servers that aren't root servers. Just to keep this clear, we're not going to set up any zones yet, not even apex.com—just the root structure.

SETTING UP THE ROOT SERVER (METHOD 1)

First, be sure that the machine at ns1.apex.com thinks its name is ns1.apex.com. As there isn't a DNS server around to tell it that, you'll have to enter it in the Network Identification page: Right-click My Computer, choose Properties, then click the Network Identification page. Click the Advanced button, then the More button. Uncheck Change DNS Domain Name When Domain Membership Changes, and in the field labeled DNS Domain Name of This Computer, enter **apex.com** and click OK until you're back at the Desktop. You'll have to reboot. This renaming step isn't absolutely necessary, but the DNS server's GUI interface will make a bit more sense this way.

Also, as this is a DNS server, make sure it looks to itself for DNS services; in the IP Properties screen, the address in Preferred DNS Server should be its own IP address.

Next, make the DNS server boot from the BOOT file, either from the snap-in or with a Registry Editor. Then stop the DNS server service on ns1.apex.com so that you can monkey with the DNS files.

The root server's BOOT file will have one line:

```
primary   .    root.dns
```

By now, you know that this just says that this server is the primary DNS server for a zone that happens to be called .; furthermore, the zone's zone file is named `root.dns`. Looking in `root.dns`, we see a pretty straightforward zone file:

```
@  IN SOA ns1.apex.com. joe.apex.com (1 900 600 86400 3600)
@  NS  ns1.apex.com.
ns1.apex.com.  A    10.10.10.10
```

The first line is the SOA record, as always. I copied the numbers from Windows 2000's defaults. The second says, "A machine named ns1.apex.com is the name server for this zone (which is the root)." The third supplies an IP address for ns1.apex.com. And remember that both **boot** and **root.dns** go in `\winnt\system32\dns`.

Notice that I had to spell out ns1.apex.com; that's because the zone we're working from here is the root zone, not the apex.com zone.

Start up the DNS server service again and your root's up and running.

SETTING UP THE ROOT SERVER (METHOD 2)

In case you don't want to mess with BOOT files, here's how to install a private root from the GUI:

1. In `\winnt\system32\dns`, delete the `CACHE.DNS` file. (There should be a backup in `\winnt\system32\dns\samples`, but you might check before deleting `CACHE.DNS` anyway.)

2. Open the DNS snap-in.

3. Create a new forward zone called just . with the wizard.

4. Restart the DNS service.

5. Close the DNS snap-in.

6. Open the DNS snap-in.

Right-click the icon for the server. You will see that the Enable Forwarders box is grayed out, as are the Root Hints.

WAIT, NSLOOKUP IS COMPLAINING!

At this point, you may be tempted to try to run NSLOOKUP to see if you can resolve names. You'll get an error message along the lines of "can't find server" or the like. You didn't do anything wrong, don't worry.

Remember, the first thing that NSLOOKUP does is a reverse lookup on the DNS server's IP address. Recall that IP Properties stores the IP address of a DNS server, not its name. So if NSLOOKUP can't get its reverse lookup request fulfilled, it can't report the name of the server.

The answer is simple. Just be sure to set up a reverse lookup zone if you control your in-addr.arpa zone, or ask your ISP to enter the records for your DNS servers if they control the reverse lookup zone. Once you set up the reverse lookup zone, put in PTR records for all of your DNS servers. Then NSLOOKUP will be happy. And to put NSLOOKUP though its paces, **set type=any**, then press Enter, and then **apex.com** and Enter, and you should see the SOA information as well as the name server information.

SETTING UP THE OTHER DNS SERVERS

Next, let's see how to set up the other DNS servers. As before, first change their `BootMethod` value to tell the DNS server to use the BOOT file, and then stop the service while you modify the files. Ensure that the DNS server points to itself in the Preferred DNS Server field of IP Properties.

The BOOT file will just contain a cache record to help NS2 find the DNS root server. The BOOT file is one line:

```
cache  .  cache.dns
```

But don't use the `cache.dns` file that automatically ships with Windows 2000; that points to ICANN root servers to which you can't get. Instead, it'll point to your one root server, and its contents then look like:

```
@              ns   ns1.apex.com
ns1.apex.com.  a    10.10.10.10
```

Start the DNS service and your DNS enterprise—both servers—now recognizes NS1 as the root. For the third and later servers, just repeat the steps you just did for this second DNS server.

Application: Disaster Recovery Summary

As you've seen, you can rebuild a DNS server easily with these ingredients:

◆ The **boot** file

◆ The `cache.dns` file

◆ The zone files

In a pinch, it's not hard to build `boot`, `cache.dns`, or zone files from scratch. Given the files, get DNS running on a new computer, stop the DNS service, put the files in place, and start the service again. You need not even reboot.

Application: Grafting an Active Directory Domain into an Enterprise with Old DNS Servers

Suppose you bring Windows 2000 into your firm, acme.com. At a meeting of the IT planning staff, you sell the CIO on the whole idea of the Active Directory as a directory service. Everyone loves the idea (or at least no one has attacked you with a sharp object) until you enthusiastically say something like, "And Microsoft was even smart enough to use DNS as its naming infrastructure!"

All of a sudden, the Unix guys, who have been scowling in the corner, say in unison, "Whaaaaaat????" They're not dumb. They know what this means. You see, if your firm is like many, your internal DNS servers are probably running on Unix boxes rather than something else. The program that the Unix box is running, BIND, is well understood and fairly stable. The Unix folks know that if the Active Directory uses DNS as its naming system, then that almost certainly means that Windows 2000 comes with a DNS server—and while they were able for years to safely shoot down any ideas about using NT 4's DNS server, Windows 2000's DNS server is pretty well integrated with the Active Directory. No, you don't *have* to use Windows 2000's DNS server to make the Active Directory work, but the Unix guys see the writing on the wall. No way they're polluting their BIND system with some less-reliable DNS server from Redmond, they say. The Active Directory? "I say it's spinach," they say, "and I say I don't like it."

You've got several answers to this objection. First of all, you may be able to make them happy and keep using BIND. Any DNS server that supports RFC 2136 dynamic updates and RFC 2052 SRV records and that allows you to put underscores—which are not exactly kosher, RFC-wise—into host names will support Active Directory. You needn't use Microsoft's DNS server. As you've read, the latest version of BIND meets those criteria, and in fact I've set up the Active Directories using only BIND-based DNS servers.

But perhaps your enterprise is on an earlier version of BIND or some other DNS server and doesn't want to upgrade. What to do? Simple: Get them to delegate a subdomain to your DNS servers. That way, if acme.com doesn't want to have all of its DNS servers assimilated into the Microsoft DNS Collective, then they needn't be. The Unix servers can continue to handle the acme.com top-level domain. You just ask for a subdomain such as win2k.acme.com (some people are proposing ds.*domainname*, as in ds.acme.com—the *ds* stands for *directory service*) or some such, and you then put all of the Windows 2000 machines in the subdomain. The DNS server that keeps track of them can then be a Windows 2000 server without affecting the rest of acme.com.

Why is this an application of understanding zone files? Because someone may decide to make it *your* job to add the records to the BIND servers that delegate the win2k.acme.com zone to your Windows 2000 server. And this way, you'll be able to just sit right down and make the necessary modifications. Although, now that I mention it, there's this Vi editor thing you should know about.

I know that this was a big chapter, but believe me, it was the shortest that I could make it without skipping important details. WINS, DHCP, and DNS are as essential to a functioning network as electricity. I promise you that if you take the time to design and implement a good WINS/DHCP/DNS infrastructure, you'll avoid many troubleshooting sessions.

But what did we set all of that infrastructure up for? One reason was to enable us to build a sturdy Active Directory. In the next chapter, you'll learn how AD works and how to *make* it work.

Chapter 8

Understanding and Using Active Directory

THE FIRST THING THAT you probably ever heard about Microsoft's latest network operating system, Windows 2000, was that it can support larger networks than its predecessor, Windows NT Server 4, with something called the Active Directory. To read the marketing literature, you'd think that Microsoft believes that the Active Directory is the single most important piece of Windows 2000.

Well, actually, it probably thinks that because the AD probably *is* the single most important piece of Windows 2000. Unfortunately, it's also one of the most complex parts of Windows 2000 and one of the most pervasive—virtually every major feature of Windows 2000 requires the Active Directory, with the possible exception of Plug and Play.

What We'll Accomplish in This Chapter

Veterans of NT 4 networks get a tired, resigned look on their faces when I talk to groups about AD. The new Active Directory name and the new user interface for AD's management tools make most NT 4 experts feel that all of their hard-won expertise is now useless, that "everything they know is wrong." There are a bunch of new terms relevant to AD—*trees, forests, organizational units,* and so on.

If you're one of the despairing, then cheer up, I've got good news! AD is really nothing more than NT 4 domain structures with a bunch of cool improvements. The problem is, of course, that Microsoft not only came up with a bunch of new features and gave them new names, it gave most of the old concepts new names as well. But if you're pretty up-to-speed on NT 4 networks, then you actually won't find AD terribly daunting, once someone gives you the NT-4-to-Windows-2000 decoder ring. Think of this chapter as that ring.

In this chapter, I'll explain what Microsoft's motivation was in designing this major change to its domain structure model. What kinds of problems was it trying to solve? What could justify Windows 2000 Server's increased complexity? And once we understand those problems, the next questions are how do we solve those problems with this Active Directory thing, and how well does AD solve them?

A Word on This Chapter's Structure

Before diving into the chapter, let me explain what you'll find here. This chapter first motivates the whole idea of the Active Directory, then discusses exactly what problems AD was supposed to solve. Then I'll give you the quick-and-dirty overview of what AD offers, trying to summarize as briefly as possible what forests, trees, organizational units, and other new AD concepts mean and why you should care. Then I'll walk you through some of the practical procedures, some step-by-step examples to help you understand the techniques that you'll need in order to actually build an Active Directory—which brings me to the chapter's main problem. *Then* we'll build upon that to see how to create a well-running AD.

There *is* one odd thing about this chapter's structure: It's got two introductory sections. I did that because it seems likely that this book's audience is composed of two groups. Members of the first group are old hands at NT 4 administration; they know how to run an NT 4 network and want to build on that knowledge to make the transition to Windows 2000. (Notice I didn't say that they would transition to Windows 2000; *transition* is a verb to only marketing people and consultants.) The second group is altogether new to Microsoft networking and perhaps new to networking in general.

I decided to serve both groups by writing *two* different overviews—one for each group. I'll start off in this chapter with an explanation of the kinds of things that modern networks require and examine both how NT 4 met those requirements and how Windows 2000 meets those requirements. Although it may be of interest to NT 4 veterans, it's not primarily intended to serve their needs—it's for the newbies. Following that, I have a shorter rundown for the vets that basically answers the question, "What does Windows 2000 do for me that NT 4 didn't?" Then I'll get into the specifics of building an Active Directory.

However you read the rest of the book, though, remember: I strongly recommend that you do some real AD planning before you install your first system. Whether you're an old-timer to NT or a newcomer, you will find that you can't just start installing Windows 2000 on some systems, build a few domains, and *then* plan your Active Directory. You really must understand enough of AD to sit down and make a plan before you shove the first CD into the first drive. As the business management books say, "Failure to plan is a plan to fail," or something like that. (I never *was* any good at that management stuff.) And don't even think about setting up an AD until you have a solid DNS structure in place.

First, then, let's introduce the Active Directory to the NT newbies; again, the NT 4 experts out there may choose to skip it and move straight on to "Active Directory: The Basics for NT Veterans."

Active Directory for NT Newcomers

Not that long ago, networks were small (remember when the only "networks" you cared about were CBS, NBC, and ABC?) and so were their problems. But nowadays it's not unusual to see worldwide networks connecting hundreds of thousands of PCs and users. Managing that kind of complexity brings up big problems—oops, we're supposed to call them *challenges*, I always forget. One of the answers to the obvious question, "Why bother with Windows 2000, anyway?" is that it was designed with some of those challenges in mind. That's important because NT 4 *didn't* address many of those problems.

Security: Keeping Track of Who's Allowed to Use the Network and Who Isn't

A network's first job is to provide service—central places to store simple things like files or more complex things like databases, shared printing, or fax services. To make it possible for people to communicate in ways like e-mail, videoconferencing, or whatever technology comes up in the future. And, more recently, to make it easier for people to buy things.

Fast on the heels of that first job, however, is the second job of every network: security. Once, most computer networks were unsecured or lightly secured, but human nature has forced a change and there's no going back. Just as businesses have locks on their doors, file cabinets, and cash registers to protect their physical assets, so also do most modern firms protect their information assets. And no matter what vendor's network software you're using, computer security typically boils down to two parts: authentication and authorization. To see why, consider the following example.

Acme Industries sells pest control devices. They have a sales manager named Wilma Wolf; Wilma wants to see how the sales of a new product, Instant Hole, is doing. Acme has it set up so that Wilma can review sales information through her Web browser—she just surfs over to a particular location on one of the company's internal Web servers and the report appears on her screen.

Of course, Acme management wouldn't be happy about just *anybody* getting to these sales report pages, so the pages are secured. Between the time that Wilma asked for the pages and the time that she got them, two things happened:

Authentication   The Web server containing the sales reports asked her workstation, "Who's asking for this data?" The workstation replied, "Wilma." The server then said, "Prove it." So the workstation popped up a dialog box on Wilma's screen asking for her username and password. She types in her name and password, and assuming that she types them correctly, the server then checks that name and password against a list of known users and passwords and finds that she is indeed Wilma.

Authorization   The mere fact that she has proven that she's Wilma may not be sufficient reason for the Web server to give her access to the sales pages. The Web server then looks at another list sometimes known as the *access control list*, a list of people and access levels—"Joe can look at this page but can't change it," "Sue can look at this page and can change it," "Larry can't look at this page at all." Presuming Wilma's on the "can look" list, the server sends the requested pages to her browser.

Now, the foregoing example may not seem to contain any deep insights—after all, everyone's logged into a system, tried to access something, and either been successful or rejected—but understanding how Windows 2000 Server and in particular the Active Directory is new requires examining these everyday things a bit. Here's a closer look at some of the administrative mechanics of logins.

MAINTAIN A "DIRECTORY" OF USERS AND OTHER NETWORK OBJECTS

Every secure system has a file or files that make up a database of known user accounts. NT 4 only used a single file named SAM, short for the less-than-illuminating Security Accounts Manager. It contained a user's username (the logon name), the user's full name, password, allowed logon hours, account expiration date, description, primary group name, and profile information. Of course, the file was encrypted; copy a SAM from an existing NT 4 system and pull it up in Notepad, and you'll see only garbage.

But Windows 2000's Active Directory, which is SAM's successor—I suppose we could call AD the "Son of SAM"—stores most of its user information in a file called NTDS.DIT. But NTDS.DIT is different from SAM in a few ways. First, NTDS.DIT is a modified Access database, and Windows 2000 Server actually contains a variant of Access's database engine in its machinery. (Microsoft used to call the Access database engine JET, which stood for Joint Engine Technology—no, the meaning isn't obvious to me either, I think they just liked the acronym—but now it's called ESE, pronounced "easy," which stands for the equally useful name Extensible Storage Engine. But I'm kidding a bit when I say that it's an Access database. Microsoft needed Exchange to have a pretty good database engine while shuffling around both information about Exchange user accounts as well as the mail itself. That's probably why they renamed it.) Second, as you'll see demonstrated over and over again, NTDS.DIT stores a much wider variety of information about users than SAM ever did.

The information in NTDS.DIT and the program that manages NTDS.DIT are together called *the directory service*. (As a matter of fact, most folks will never say "NTDS.DIT"; they'll say "directory service.") Which leads to a question: What exactly is a "directory"?

It would seem (to me, anyway) that what we've got here is a database of users and user information. So why not call it a *database*? No compelling reasons; mostly convention, but there *is* one interesting insight. According to some, databases of users tend to get *read* far more often than they get *written*. That allows a certain amount of database engine "tweaking" for higher performance. This subset of the class of databases gets a name—*directories*. I guess it makes sense, as we're used to using lists of people called *office directories* or *phone directories*. I just wish the folks in power had come up with some other name; ask most PC users what a directory is, and they start thinking of hard disk structures. "C:\WINDOWS--isn't that a directory?"

CENTRALIZING THE DIRECTORY AND DIRECTORIES: A "LOGON SERVER"

"Please, can't we set things up so I only need to remember *one* password?"

Consider for a moment when Windows 2000 Server will use that user information located in the Active Directory. When you try to access a file share or print share, the Active Directory will validate you. But there's more at work here. When fully implemented, the Active Directory can save you a fair amount of administrative work in other network functions as well.

For example, suppose your network requires SQL database services. You'll then run a database product such as SQL Server or Oracle on the network. But adding another server-based program to your network can introduce more administrative headaches because, like the file and print servers, a database server needs authentication and authorization support. That's because you usually don't want to just plunk some valuable database on the network and then let the world in general at it—you want to control who gets access.

So the database program needs a method for authentication and authorization. And *here's* where it gets ugly: In the past, many database programs have required their administrators to keep and maintain a list of users and passwords. The database programs required you to duplicate all that work of typing in names and passwords—to redo the work you'd already done to get your Novell, Linux, NT, or whatever type LAN up and running. Yuk. But it gets worse. Consider what you'd have to do if you ran both NT as a network operating system *and* Novell NetWare as a network operating system: Yup, you're typing in names and passwords yet again. Now add Lotus Notes for your e-mail and groupware stuff, another list of users, and hey, how about a mainframe or an AS/400? More accounts.

Let's see—with a network incorporating NT, Oracle, NetWare, and Notes, each user owns *four* different user accounts. Which means each user has *four* different passwords to remember. And, every few months, four different passwords to remember to change.

This seems dumb; why can't we just type those names and passwords once into our Windows 2000 Server and then tell Oracle, NetWare, and Notes to just ask the local Windows 2000 Server machine to check that I am indeed who I say I am rather than making Oracle, NetWare, and Notes duplicate all of that security stuff? Put another way, we have a centralized computer that acts as a database server, another that acts as a centralized e-mail server, another as a print server—why not have a centralized "logon" server, a centralized "authentication" server? Then our users would only have to remember (and change) one password and account name rather than four.

Centralized logons would be a great benefit, but there's a problem with it: How would Notes actually *ask* the Win2K server to authenticate? What programming commands would an Oracle database server use to ask a Microsoft "logon server" (the actual term is *domain controller*, as you'll learn later) whether a particular user should be able to access a particular piece of data?

Well, if that domain controller were running NT 4, the programming interface wouldn't have been a particularly well-documented one. And third parties such as Oracle, Lotus, and Novell would have been reluctant to write programs depending on that barely documented security interface because they'd be justifiably concerned that when the *next* version of NT appeared (Windows 2000 Server), then Microsoft would have changed the programming interface, leaving Lotus, Novell, and Oracle scrambling to learn and implement this new interface. And some of the more cynical among us would even suggest that Lotus and Oracle might fear that Microsoft's Exchange and SQL Server would be able to come out in Windows 2000 Server–friendly versions nearly immediately after Windows 2000 Server's release.

Instead, Microsoft opted to put an industry-standard interface on its Active Directory, an interface called the Lightweight Directory Access Protocol (LDAP). Now, LDAP may initially sound like just another geeky acronym, but it's more than that—what Microsoft has done by putting an LDAP interface on the Active Directory is to open a doorway for outside developers. And here's how important it is: Yes, LDAP will make Oracle's or Lotus's job easier should they decide to integrate their products' security with NT's built-in security. But LDAP also means that it's (theoretically, at least) possible to build tools that create Active Directory structures—domains, trees, forests, organizational units, user accounts, all of the components. It means that if Windows 2000 Server gets popular, but Microsoft's Active Directory control programs turn out to be hard to work with, then some clever third party can just swoop in and offer a complete replacement, built atop LDAP commands.

This, after you spend a bit of time with the Microsoft Management Console, may not seem like a bad idea—but I'll leave you to make your own judgment about that once you meet the MMC.

Searching: Finding Things on the Network

Thus far, I've been talking about the directory service as if it only contains user accounts. But that's not true—the DS not only includes directory entries for people, it also contains directory entries describing servers and workstations. And that turns out to be essential, for a few reasons.

FINDING SERVERS: "CLIENT-SERVER RENDEZVOUS"

Client-server computing is how work gets done nowadays. You check your e-mail with Outlook (the client), which gets that mail from the Exchange machine down the hall (the server). You're at your PC (the client) accessing files on a file server (the server). You buy a shirt at L.L. Bean's Web server (the server) from your PC using Internet Explorer (the client).

In those three cases, the copy of Outlook on your desktop had to somehow know where to find your local Exchange server, you couldn't get files from your file server until you knew which file server to look in, and you couldn't order that shirt until you'd found the address of the L.L. Bean Web server, www.11bean.com.

In every case, client-server doesn't work unless you can help the client find the server, hence the phrase *client-server rendezvous*. In the Outlook case, your mail client knows where your mail server is probably because someone (perhaps you) in your networking group set it up, feeding the name of the Exchange server into some setup screen in Outlook. You may have found the correct file server for the desired files by poking around in Network Neighborhood in Windows 95/98, or in the My Network Places if your workstation is running Windows 2000 Professional, or perhaps someone told you where to find the files. You might have guessed L.L. Bean's address, saw it on a magazine ad, or used a search engine like Yahoo! or AltaVista.

Those are three examples of client-server rendezvous; many more happen in the process of daily network use. When your workstation seeks to log you in, the workstation must find a domain controller, or to put it differently, your "logon client" seeks a "logon server." Want to print something in color and wonder which networked color printers are nearby? More client-server rendezvous.

In every case, the Active Directory can simplify the process. Your workstation will be able to ask the Active Directory for the names of nearby domain controllers. You can search the Active Directory for keywords relevant to particular file shares and printers. And Exchange 2000 stores its user information in the Active Directory.

NAME RESOLUTION AND DNS

But merely getting the name of a particular mail, Web, print, or file server (or domain controller) isn't the whole story. From the network software's point of view, www.11bean.com isn't much help. To get you connected to the Bean Web server, the network software needs to know the *IP address* of that server, a four-number combination looking something such as 208.7.129.82. That's the second part of client-server rendezvous.

In the case of a public Website such as Bean's, your computer can look up a Web server by querying a huge network of publicly available Internet servers called the Domain Name System, or DNS. The public DNS contains the names of many machines you'll need to access, but chances are good that your company's internal network doesn't advertise many of its machines' names on the Internet; rather, your internal network probably runs a set of private DNS servers.

After its inception in 1984, DNS didn't change much. But 1996 and 1998 brought two big changes referred to as RFC 2782 and RFC 2136 (you read about them in Chapter 7), transforming DNS into a naming system that's good not only for the worldwide Internet but also for internal intranets. Many of the pieces of DNS software out in the corporate world don't yet support 2782 and 2136, so it's a great convenience that Windows 2000 Server's DNS server supports those features.

Creating New Types of "Subadministrators"

The next network challenge becomes apparent after a network has grown a bit. When a network is small or new, a small group of people do everything, from running the cables and installing the LAN adapter boards to creating the user accounts and running the backups. As time goes on and the network gets larger—and more important to the organization—then two things happen. First, the organization hires more people—*has* to hire more people because there are more servers to tend and user accounts to look after—to handle all the different parts of keeping a network running. And second, networks get political: All of a sudden, some of the higher-ups get clued to the fact that *what those network geeks do affects our ability to retain our power in this organization.*

Both of those things mean that your firm will soon start hiring more network helpers. In some organizations, these newly created positions get to do much of the scut work of network administration, stuff that is (a) pretty simple to train people to do and (b) of no interest to the old-timer network types. Examples of the I-don't-want-it-you-can-have-it jobs in a network include:

Resetting Passwords   For security's sake, we usually require users to change their passwords every couple months or so. We also inveigh against the evils of writing those passwords down, so it's pretty common for users to forget what their most recently set passwords are. Resetting passwords to some innocuous value is something that really needs to be done quickly—the natives get restless when you take a week to let them back on the network—and it's a relatively simple task, so it's perfect for the newly hired, minimum-wage network assistant.

Tending the Backups   For tediousness, nothing matches the sheer irritation of backups. Most of us are forced to use tape drives for backups and, well, some days it seems like tape drives were invented by someone who was abused by network administrators as a small child. They're balky, prone to taking vacations at random times, and you never can predict exactly how much data you can get on 'em—eight gigs one day, three the next, and as a result, *someone* has to be around ready to feed in another blank tape. And somebody's got to label them and keep track of them; ask most network admin types what job they'd most like to give someone else to worry about, and backups are likely to be at the top of their wish list.

Hiring a few low-wage backup watchers and password fixers also gives a firm a sort of a "farm team," a place to try out folks to see if they're capable enough to learn to eventually become network analysts with more responsibilities (and, they hope, more salary).

But regular old users can't do things like resetting passwords and running backups—you need at least some administrative powers to do those things. Recall that we'd like to hire this "network scut-work" person or persons at a pretty low hourly rate, and that's troublesome from a security point of view. If he can leave this job and go off to one with the same pay level but whose main challenge is in remembering to say, "Would you like fries with that?," then it might not be the brightest idea to give him full administrative control over the network. Is there a way to create a sort of "partial administrator"?

NT 4 gave us *some* of that, as there was a prebuilt group called Backup Operators, but there wasn't a Reset Password Operators group, and besides, all NT 4 offered was a small set of prebuilt groups of types of administrators—the groups were called Server Operators, Account Operators, and Backup Operators—with different levels—there wasn't a way to create a new type of group with a tailor-made set of powers. Windows 2000 Server changes that, offering a sometimes bewildering array of security options.

Delegation: Subdividing Control over a Domain

In the last section, I offered two examples of things that might motivate changing how the network works—a growing set of network duties that require some division of labor (which I covered in that section) and growing attention from upper management as it becomes increasingly aware of the importance of the network in the organization. That second force in network evolution is perhaps better known as *politics*. Despite the fact that it's something of a bad word, we can't ignore politics—so how does Windows 2000 Server address an organization's political needs?

To see how, consider the following scenario: Some fictitious part of the U.S. Navy is spread across naval facilities across the world, but perhaps (to keep the example simple) its biggest offices are in Washington, D.C., San Diego, Calif., and Norfolk, Virginia. There are servers in D.C., San Diego, and Norfolk, all tended by different groups. For all of the usual reasons, the officers in charge of the Norfolk facility don't want administrators from D.C. or San Diego messing with the Norfolk servers; the D.C. folks and the San Diego folks have similar feelings, with the result that the Navy technology brass wants to be able to say, "Here's a group of servers we'll call Norfolk and a group of users we'll call Norfolk Admins. We want to be able to say that only the users in Norfolk Admins can control the servers in Norfolk." They want to do similar things for San Diego and D.C. How to do this?

Well, under NT 4, they could do it only by creating three separate security entities called *domains*. Creating three different domains would solve the problem because separate domains are like separate *universes*—they're not aware of each other at all. With a D.C. domain, a Norfolk domain, and a San Diego domain, they could separate their admins into three groups who couldn't meddle with one another. It's a perfectly acceptable answer and indeed many organizations around the world use NT 4 in that manner—but it's a solution with a few problems.

For one thing, enterprises usually want *some* level of communication between domains, and to accomplish that, the enterprises must put in place connections between domains called *trust relationships*. Without a trust relationship, it's flatly impossible for a user in one domain to access something—a printer, a file share, a mail server or the like—in another domain. The simple process of having a user in one domain access a resource in another requires a logon; the domain that contains the resource (printer, file share, mail, and so on) must recognize and log in the user. But there's no way for the resource-owning domain to even *try* to log in a user from the user's domain unless the two domains have been "introduced"—that is, unless administrators from each of the two domains have agreed to allow their domains to trust one another.

Unfortunately, trust relationships are a quirky and unreliable necessity of any multidomain enterprise using NT 4. With Windows 2000 Server, in contrast, the Navy need only create *one* domain and then divide it up using a new-to-NT notion called *organizational units*, usually abbreviated *OUs*.

More specifically, the Navy would solve their problem in this way:

◆ They'd create one domain named (for example) NAVY.

◆ Inside NAVY, they'd create an organizational unit named Norfolk, another called DC, and a third named San Diego. They would set up their servers and then place each server into the proper OU.

◆ Also inside NAVY, they'd create a user group named Norfolk Admins, and two others named San Diego Admins and DC Admins. They'd create accounts for their users and place any administrators into their proper group, depending on whether they were based in D.C., San Diego, or Norfolk.

At this point, understand that the San Diego Admins (kinda sounds like a baseball team, doesn't it?) don't yet have any power: There's no magic in Windows 2000 Server that says, "Well, there's an OU named San Diego and a group named San Diego Admins, I guess that must mean I should let these Admin guys have total control over the servers in the San Diego OU." You have to create that link by *delegating control* of the San Diego OU to the user group San Diego Admins. (There's a wizard that assists in doing this, as you'll see when we walk through a delegation example later in this chapter.) We'll see that OUs are a useful tool for building large and useful domains.

Satisfying Political Needs

"That's *my* data, so I want it on *my* servers!" As information has become the most important asset of many firms—for example, I once heard someone comment that the majority of Microsoft's assets resided in the crania of their employees—some firms have been reluctant to yield control of that information to a central IT group. Nor is that an irrational perspective: if you were in charge of maintaining a five-million-person mailing list, and if that list generated one half of your firm's sales leads, then you might well want to see that data housed on a machine or machines run by people who report directly to you.

Of course, on the other side of the story there is the IT director who wants Total Control of all servers in the building, and her reasoning is just as valid. You see, if a badly run server goes down and that failure affects the rest of the network, it's *her* head on the chopping block.

So on the one hand, the department head or VP wants to control the iron and silicon that happens to be where his data lives, and on the other hand, the IT director who's concerned with making sure that all data is safe and that everything on the network plays well with others wants to control said data and network pieces. Who wins? It depends—and that's the "politics" part.

What does Windows 2000 do to ameliorate the political problems? Well, not as much as would be nice—there is no "make the vice presidents get along well" wizard—but Windows 2000's variety of options for domain design gives the network designers the flexibility to build whatever kind of network structure they want. Got a relatively small organization that would fit nicely into a single domain, but one VP with server ownership lust? No problem, give her an OU of her own within the domain. Got a firm with two moderately large offices separated by a few hundred miles? Under NT 4, two domains and a trust relationship would be the answer, and you could choose to do that under Windows 2000, but that's not the only answer. As Windows 2000 is extremely parsimonious with WAN bandwidth in comparison with NT 4, you might find that a single domain makes sense as it's easier to administer than two domains, but not impossible from a network bandwidth point of view. And bandwidth utilization is our next topic.

Connectivity and Replication Issues

More and more companies don't just live in one place. They've purchased another firm across the country, and what once were two separate *local* area networks are now one firm with a wide area network need. If that WAN link is fast, then there's no network design headache at all: Hook the two offices up with a T1 link and you can essentially treat them as one office.

That's beneficial because each site will usually contain a domain controller—one of those servers that host the Active Directory database and which act as machines to accomplish logins. But those domain controllers must communicate with each other whenever something changes, as when a user's password changes or when an administrator creates a new user account. This is called *Active Directory replication*. The same thing happened with NT 4, as NT 4 also allowed you to put multiple domain controllers in an enterprise.

In NT 4, suppose we've got two offices connected by a slow WAN link. Suppose further that we've got a domain controller in each of these offices. They need to replicate their SAM database between domain controllers (recall that NT 4 used a user database named SAM; Windows 2000's database is called the Active Directory). NT 4's domain controller updates happened every five minutes. That means that a domain controller might try to replicate changes to another domain controller every five minutes, even if they're only connected with a very slow link. All that chatter could well choke a WAN link and keep other, more important traffic from getting through.

Windows 2000 improves upon that by allowing you to tell Windows 2000 domain controllers about how well they're connected. The idea is that you describe your enterprise in terms of *sites*, which are basically just groups of servers with fast connections—groups of servers living on the same local area network, basically. You can then define how fast (or probably, slow) the connections *between* those sites are, and Windows 2000 will then be a bit smarter about using those connections.

In particular, Windows 2000 Active Directory servers compress data before sending it over slow WAN links. Taking the time to compress data requires a certain amount of CPU power, but it's well worth it, as AD is capable of a 10:1 compression ratio!

Not only do we often face slow links, we often must live with *unreliable* links, ones that are up and down or perhaps only up for a short period of time every day. Windows 2000 lets you define not only a WAN link's speed but also the times that it is up.

NT 4's directory replications require a real-time connection called a *remote procedure call* (RPC). RPCs are like telephone calls—the domain controller programs on each side must be up and running and actively communicating simultaneously. Inasmuch as domain controllers can be more or less busy as the day wears on, requiring this kind of shared concentration to get a simple directory replication accomplished is a bit demanding. It might be nicer if replications could work less like a telephone call and more like a mailing—and to a certain extent, Windows 2000 allows this, or rather points to a day in the future when it'll be possible.

It's possible for one domain controller to simply *mail* part of its replication data to another domain controller. Then, even if the receiving domain controller is not currently online, the mail message is still waiting for it, ready to be read when the receiving domain controller is again awake. Sounds good, but unfortunately, not *all* of the directory replication can happen over mail. Microsoft says that'll change in a future release, but not in Windows 2000.

Site control will make life considerably easier for those managing multilocation networks.

Scalability: Building Big Networks

Large enterprise networks found NT 4 lacking in the number of users that its SAM database could accommodate. Although you could theoretically create millions of user accounts on an NT domain, it's not practical to create more than about 5000 to perhaps 10,000 user accounts in a domain. (If you took the MCSE exam for NT Server and are looking at that number oddly, it's because they made you memorize 40,000 as the answer to the question, "How many user accounts can you put on an NT domain?" In my experience, that's just not realistic, hence my 5000–10,000 number. (And in fact a handful of big companies *have* successfully maintained SAMs with 40,000 users, but they all told me that it's no simple feat.)

Five thousand user accounts are more than most companies would ever need. But some large firms need to incorporate more user accounts into their enterprise, forcing them to divide their company's network up into multiple domains—and multiple domains were to be avoided at all costs under NT 4 because of the extra trouble in maintaining them.

The Active Directory can accommodate many more user accounts than NT's SAM. Microsoft claims it has stress-tested Windows 2000 domains with 1.5 million users in them, and, in one impressive example, Compaq built an AD with 100 million users in it. Although it'll be a while before we get enough real-world experience to know exactly how many users we can reasonably expect to add to Windows 2000 networks, it's clear that Windows 2000 systems will support far larger lists of users than did NT 4.

Furthermore, the Active Directory enables you to build larger networks by making the process of building and maintaining multidomain networks easier. Where once an administrator of a multidomain network had to build and maintain a complex system of interdomain security relationships—the *trust relationships* I've already referred to—now Windows 2000 will let you build a system of domains called a *forest*. A forest's main strength is that once a group of domains has been built into a forest, the trusts are automatically created and maintained. There are additionally smaller multidomain structures called *trees* that also feature automatic trusts; you'll read more about trees and forests later.

Simplifying Computer Names or "Unifying the Namespace"

We discussed this in the previous chapter, but it's worthwhile revisiting the topic of names, particularly if you're new to 2000.

Devices on a network mainly identify themselves by some long and unique identification number. On an intranet or the Internet, it's a unique 32-bit address called an *IP address*. Networks also commonly exploit a 48-bit address burned into each network interface card called a *MAC address*. Any Ethernet, Token Ring, ATM, or other network interface has one of these addresses, and conventions that network manufacturers have agreed upon ensure that no matter from whom you buy a NIC, it will have a 48-bit address that no other NIC has. Some parts of NT identify PCs by their IP address (or addresses—a machine with multiple NICs will have an IP address and MAC address for each NIC), others by the PC's MAC address or addresses.

But people don't relate well to long strings of numbers—telling you that you can send me mail to `mark@1100111011110110111110111001000` is technically accurate (presuming that you can find a mail client that will accept network addresses in binary) but not very helpful. It's far more preferable to be able to instead tell your mail program to send mail to `help@minasi.com`, which you can do. Somehow, however, your mail client must be able to look up minasi.com and from there find out where to send mail for minasi.com. In the same way, pointing your web browser to `www.microsoft.com` forces the browser to convert `www.microsoft.com` into the particular IP address or addresses that constitute Microsoft's website. This process of converting from human-friendly names such as minasi.com to computer-friendly addresses such as 1100111011110110111110111001000 is called *name resolution*. It's something every network must do.

So why is name resolution a problem with NT? Because most of the networking world uses *one* approach to name resolution, and up through version 4, NT used a different one.

Most every firm is either on the Internet or has an internal intranet, or both. Intranets and the Internet use a form of name resolution called the Domain Name System, or DNS. DNS names are the familiar Internet names such as www.microsoft.com. In contrast, Microsoft networking has for years used a different and incompatible naming system called NetBIOS names, which are simpler—no more than 15 characters long, no periods.

PCs resolve DNS names by consulting a group of servers around the world called, not surprisingly, *DNS servers.* Your company or Internet Service Provider operates one or more DNS servers and your Internet software uses these nearby DNS servers to resolve (for example) www.minasi.com to the Internet address 206.246.253.200.

NT-based networks using Internet software don't use DNS for much of their work. Instead, Microsoft invented its own name servers somewhat like DNS but using NetBIOS names; they called these name servers Windows Internet Name Service, or WINS, servers.

That leads to this problem: Nearly every firm is on the Internet—*has* to be on the Internet—and so every firm must give DNS names to their computers. But if they're also using NT, then they need to give their systems NetBIOS names. That in and of itself is not a great burden; what *is* a burden is that these names are important to the programs that use them, and programs can typically need one of the two names and can't use the other of the two.

Let's take an example. Suppose someone wants to log in to an NT 4 domain at Acme Technologies. To accomplish that, her workstation must find a domain controller for that domain. Her workstation does that by searching for a machine with a particular NetBIOS name. Let's say that Acme does indeed have a domain controller around named LOGMEIN (its NetBIOS name) that *also* acts as a Web server with the DNS name reptiles.pictures.animalworld.com, as it hosts pages of pictures of local reptiles. Let's also suppose that for some reason Acme has no WINS servers but has a great network of DNS servers.

DNS names are of no value to the workstation looking for a logon. You could have the finest set of DNS servers in the world, but it would make no difference—without a functioning WINS server, that workstation would probably be unable to locate a domain controller to log you in. On the other hand, if someone sitting at that same workstation sought to view the reptile pictures on http://reptiles.pictures.animalworld.com, she'd just fire up Internet Explorer and point it at that URL. Internet Explorer is, of course, uninterested in NetBIOS names, relying mainly on DNS names. The workstation would quickly locate the Web server and browse its pages, even as that same workstation was unable to detect that the very same server could perform logins.

Windows 2000 solves this problem by largely doing away with WINS, using DNS for all of its name resolution needs. Unfortunately, however, Windows 2000 uses DNS for all of *its* name resolution needs—older Windows 9x and Windows NT 4 systems still rely on WINS. So while WINS's role is diminished, it'll still be around until you've pulled the plug on the last Windows 9x and NT machines.

Satisfying the Lust for Power and Control

Well, okay, maybe it's not *lust,* but it's certainly *need.* Put simply, there just plain aren't enough support people around and no shortage of users to support. In 1987, many firms retained one support person for every 100 users; in many companies nowadays, that ratio is more like one support person for every 2,000 users.

That means that where once it was once possible for a support person to physically visit every user's PC to perform support tasks, it's just not reasonable to expect any more. Support people need tools that allow them to get their support work done from a central location as much as is possible.

And, although not every user is all that happy about it, one way to simplify a support person's job is to standardize each PC's desktop. In some cases, support staffs need software tools to allow them to *enforce* that standard desktop. (As you can imagine, it's a political issue for many firms.)

In NT 4, Microsoft started helping support staffs centralize their desktop control with something called *system policies*. But system policies were lacking in a few ways. The Active Directory improves upon system policies with a kind of "system policies version 2" called *group policies*.

Better security, more flexible administration options, wiser use of bandwidth, and providing god-like control to administrators: That's basically what the Active Directory is trying to accomplish. But how does it accomplish that? To find out, turn to the section named "Understanding and Using Active Directory's Features." Unless, of course, you want to just keep reading—in the next section, I explain what AD means to those who are already accustomed to NT 4.

Active Directory: The Basics for NT Veterans

What does the Active Directory mean for those of us who've been working with NT domains, trust relationships, and the like since 1993? Are things all that different?

How Active Directory Affects Existing One-Domain Enterprises

Well, let's first get the easy part of the answer out of the way: If your firm currently runs a single-domain NT enterprise, or even just a bunch of NT servers in a workgroup without a domain, then no, the Active Directory won't change your life all that much. You'll probably choose to remain as one domain. You'll still create user accounts, albeit with a different tool than User Manager for Domains. There are still user groups, file permissions, and the like. You may have to learn a thing or two about DNS if you've never done anything with it, but even then a small network can get away with a fair amount of DNS ignorance with impunity. You *will* have to learn a lot of new management tools—as I just suggested, the User Manager for Domains is dead and is largely replaced by the Active Directory Users and Computers—and you'll likely have to buy new servers, as Windows 2000 requires some horsepower (350MHz Pentium II and 256MB RAM *minimum* for a domain controller), but that's about it.

That's not to say, by the way, that you should not upgrade to Windows 2000; it just means that the Active Directory won't turn out to offer the biggest benefits of Windows 2000 to your enterprise. Windows 2000 *does* offer some really cool other things, however. In particular, you'll probably like Plug and Play and the Change and Configuration Management (formerly known as Zero Administration Windows) tools. CCM will simplify the task of getting Windows 2000 Professional (the name for Windows 2000's version of NT Workstation) onto a computer, it'll make protecting users' data an easier task, and it'll enable you to distribute applications onto users' desktops from a central point with just a few mouse-clicks.

That's the good news. The bad news for smaller enterprises (and, well, for larger ones as well) is that although getting Plug and Play is great, the reality is that Windows 2000 runs horribly slowly on all but the most recent computer hardware, implying that you'll probably need to not only upgrade your operating system but your network's hardware as well to make Windows 2000 useful. And although CCM puts some wonderful centrally controlled user support tools in your hands, CCM's benefits only extend to users running Windows 2000 Professional on their desktop PC, again implying that you're going to be buying some hardware if you really want to enjoy Windows 2000's benefits.

How Active Directory Affects Multidomain Enterprises

For many NT 4 users, even the vaguest outlines of AD's capabilities sound like manna from heaven. Bigger domains and more flexible domain structures—it all sounds great.

But how much new stuff will you have to learn? Is it true that "everything that you know is wrong"? Well, some things are very different, yes. But they're rooted in what you already know.

WINDOWS 2000 STILL HAS DOMAINS

First of all, Windows 2000 still has domains, and in many ways they still look like NT 4 domains. Where NT 4 stored information about user and machine accounts in a file named SAM, Windows 2000 stores that—and much else—in a file called NTDS.DIT. Under NT 4, a user in a multidomain environment had to identify both herself and the name of the domain whose SAM contained her user account. That's still true under Windows 2000, but it gets a bit easier, as Windows 2000 has a database called the *global catalog* that knows every user and what domain she's from. The GC knows every user by a *user principal name*, or UPN. A UPN looks like an e-mail address—joeblow@acme.com. A user can then either decide to log in as "Joe from domain sales.acme.com," in which case his workstation will contact a domain controller from domain sales.acme.com, or he could log in as joe@acme.com, which would prompt his workstation to ask the GC what domain joe@acme.com belongs to. The GC would respond that he's from sales.acme.com, and the workstation would then contact a domain controller from sales.acme.com to get the information that it needs to log Joe in.

Notice another thing about domains: Where NT 4 had domains with 15-character names, Windows 2000 uses DNS-style naming for domains—but more about that in a minute.

WINDOWS 2000 DOMAINS CAN BE BIGGER

You can fit about 5000 user accounts comfortably in an NT 4 domain, forcing large enterprises to create multiple domains in order to accommodate all of their user accounts; such a domain design was called a *multimaster* model. In contrast, a Windows 2000 domain can fit 1.5 million users (or more, depending on whom you talk to) into its Active Directory database—which ought to be sufficient user accounts for even the largest companies. Windows 2000 will allow many large companies that were forced to use multiple domains because of the sheer size of their workforce to consolidate all of their user account domains into a single domain. Such domains can be large enough that many large enterprises can probably get away with one domain—for example, at this writing, a very large oil company is trying to implement their entire worldwide enterprise as a single Windows 2000 domain.

MANY MORE ENTERPRISES CAN BE A SINGLE DOMAIN

Not only can domains be bigger, they can be wider—or at least more widely dispersed geographically.

Under NT 4, some relatively small companies decided to implement multidomain enterprises because of geography. Say a company's got an office uptown and another downtown, with 1000 or so employees in each location and about 3000 employees in total. Should they be one domain or many? Three hundred user accounts fit comfortably in one domain, but then there would probably have to be a domain controller in each location. Say for example that the PDC is in the uptown office and a BDC is in the downtown office. As there's a DC in each office, everyone can be logged in by a local DC. Those two DCs must, however, be connected with some kind of full-time connection (let's suppose it's a 56K frame relay link) so that the PDC can inform the BDC of any changes to user accounts, passwords, and the like.

Password-changing day comes along and all 3000 employees dutifully change their passwords. The folks in the downtown office will find changing passwords quite slow, unfortunately, because although a BDC can log a downtowner in, it can't help with password changes; logins require only reading the SAM, and a BDC can do that just fine. But changing a password requires modifying the domain's SAM, and only the PDC can do that. Password-changing traffic, then, must go over the frame relay link. (The downtowners have no idea that this is why password changing is so slow, by the way.) To add insult to injury, the frame relay link will be excessively slow on password-changing day, as the PDC will be using much of the frame relay's bandwidth to *tell* the BDC about these new passwords. This becomes so frustrating that the firm eventually decides to create two different domains, one for the uptown office and one for the downtown office.

Windows 2000 lets them get back together for two reasons. First, all DCs can accept changes, so a downtowner can conduct the entire password-changing ritual while talking to the local DC. But when the downtown DC updates the uptown DC about the new passwords, won't that choke the frame relay? No, not at all. Where NT 4 used the same chatty, bandwidth-wasting protocol to update BDCs whether they were connected with a fast or slow link, Windows 2000 detects DCs with slow connections and compresses its data before sending, and compresses it well—tests show about a 10:1 compression ratio. This firm can become one domain again.

In general, intersite replication is far more efficient than it was under NT 4. That means that where previously under NT 4 you might have wisely chosen to implement a network in two separate cities as two domains so as to reduce replication traffic over a slow WAN link, under Windows 2000 you might just as wisely choose to build a single domain spread over a wide geographic area.

DOMAINS CAN BE DIVIDED INTO SUBDOMAINS

But perhaps there's another concern—politics. The woman running the downtown office insists that the people who run the servers uptown not have admin control of "her" servers downtown. Now, in the NT 4 days, she could segregate her servers security-wise by just keeping them in a different domain. But there wasn't a simple way to "protect" a set of servers in domain X from some subset of domain X's domain administrators.

With Windows 2000, however, there is. The domain's architects can just create a subdomain called an *organizational unit* (call it Downtown Servers) and put the downtown servers in that OU. Next, they create a group called Downtown Admins or something like that and put the downtown administrators' user accounts into the Downtown Admins group. Finally, they tell Windows 2000 to allow only the Downtown Admins group to administer the Downtown Servers OU. This process of assigning control of an OU's contents to a group is called *delegating,* and Windows 2000 even has a wizard to assist in the process.

IT'S EASIER TO BUILD AND MAINTAIN MULTIPLE-DOMAIN NETWORKS

If it sounds like I'm a proponent of single-domain networks, I am. The more "moving parts" (read: trust relationships) in your network, the more things there are to break. So Windows 2000's ability to support bigger and more diverse single-domain networks is pretty cool.

If, however, after examining Windows 2000's capabilities you still choose to remain with a multi-domain model, you'll find multidomain Windows 2000 networks a bit easier to manage than multidomain NT 4 networks.

If you choose to have more than one domain, Windows 2000 makes it easier to automatically build trust relationships among them by letting you create a *forest* of domains. Forests of domains can be subdivided into *trees*; the main reason you'd do that is, as you'll see, to make it easier to integrate your domain naming scheme with your DNS naming scheme.

Multiple Domains with NT 4

For example, consider the following NT 4 domain structure, pictured in Figure 8.1.

FIGURE 8.1

NT 4 domain
structure

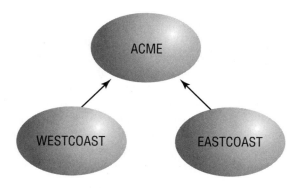

Here, Acme has decided to create three domains—ACME, which probably contains all of the *user* accounts in the entire enterprise; EASTCOAST, which probably contains all of the workstation and server accounts in their East Coast office; and WESTCOAST, which probably contains all of the workstation and server accounts in their West Coast office. They wanted the two "resource domains," EASTCOAST and WESTCOAST, to trust the master domain, ACME, hence the arrows from EASTCOAST to ACME—"eastcoast trusts acme"—and from WESTCOAST to ACME ("westcoast trusts acme"). For whatever reason, Acme's divided itself geographically, whether for political or bandwidth reasons.

To set this up, the Acme NT 4 administrators had to do these steps:

1. Create the ACME domain and populate it with user accounts.

2. Create the EASTCOAST domain and populate it with server and workstation accounts.

3. Create the WESTCOAST domain and populate it with server and workstation accounts.

4. Build a trust relationship between EASTCOAST and ACME so that EASTCOAST trusts ACME. (In case you've forgotten what trust relationships are, they are a necessary first step when you intend to do some kind of sharing across domain lines. They're sort of like the initial treaties that former enemy countries sign so as to enable trade relations and begin selling things to one another.)

5. Build a trust relationship between WESTCOAST and ACME so that WESTCOAST trusts ACME.

6. Go to every machine in WESTCOAST, log in as a local administrator, and add ACME's Domain Users group to that machine's local Users group. Also, add ACME's Domain Admins group to that machine's local Administrators group.

7. Go to every machine in EASTCOAST, log in as a local administrator, and add ACME's Domain Users group to that machine's local Users group. Also, add ACME's Domain Admins group to that machine's local Administrators group.

Sound like fun? It's not. And the fun's not over. The Acme admins really should do a few other things as well. For one, they should sprinkle backup domain controllers from the ACME domain in both the East Coast and West Coast offices so that people at both offices can easily log in. Furthermore, those administrators should expect to have to monitor the two trust relationships, as they're prone to "breaking."

And remember—that example was almost the simplest multidomain example imaginable. Real-world enterprises often incorporate *hundreds* of domains.

Multiple Domains with Windows 2000

Now let's see what's involved with doing this under Windows 2000. Assuming that Acme would stay with three domains (a questionable assumption, recall, but let's use it to illustrate how much easier multidomain enterprises are under Windows 2000), their domain structure would probably look like Figure 8.2.

FIGURE 8.2

Corresponding Windows 2000 domain structure

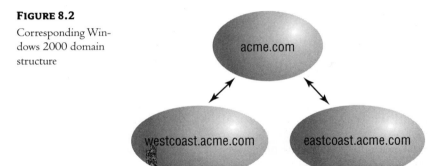

Looks similar at first glance, but a closer look shows differences. First of all, notice the names for the domains. NT 4 domain names had to be 15 characters or fewer in length, and periods in the names were a bad idea. Windows 2000 domain names are hierarchical and can be basically as long as you like. Notice also the .com suffix: Windows 2000 uses a DNS-type naming system, and for good reason—Windows 2000 *uses* DNS to keep track of domain structure. By default, one of the domain controllers in acme.com is a DNS server.

NOTE *Does this mean that you must use Microsoft's DNS as your DNS server? No, it doesn't require that. You can run a Unix-based DNS server (or some other DNS server, for that matter), but that DNS server software will have to be pretty modern as it's got to implement some DNS features that only entered the DNS standards in the spring of 1997. Refer back to the previous chapter if you need to know more about DNS.*

Notice also that the lines between the domains are *two-way* arrows. That symbolizes the fact that the trusts are all two-way, unlike NT 4's one-way trusts. Furthermore, those trusts are *transitive*, which means that trust "flows through" domains. As eastcoast.acme.com trusts acme.com, and acme.com trusts westcoast.acme.com, then eastcoast.acme.com trusts westcoast.acme.com. This could never have happened under NT 4—to make East trust West, we'd have needed to build a separate trust relationship between them.

You can extend the hierarchical naming structure as far as you like. For example, if you wanted to subdivide eastcoast.acme.com into engineering, administrative, and research divisions, you could create three more domains named engineering.eastcoast.acme.com, administrative.eastcoast.acme.com, and research.eastcoast.acme.com. The hierarchical naming structure of DNS has always been DNS's strength, and Windows 2000 exploits that.

Enough of the high-level stuff—how does this make life easier for administrators? Here are the steps that admins would take in order to create the three-domain system in Figure 8.2:

1. Create the acme.com domain by running a program called DCPROMO. DCPROMO is a wizard that asks questions of the admin and from there decides how to build the domain. The admin must tell DCPROMO that acme.com is a new domain, that the domain is the first domain in a new tree, and that the new tree is the first tree in a forest.

2. Once DCPROMO finishes its work—about 20 minutes of database creation—the admin creates the user accounts. If he has an ASCII file listing the desired names, passwords, and the like, then Windows 2000 comes with a built-in VBScript program to do that automatically.

3. Next, locate a different Windows 2000 Server machine and create the eastcoast.acme.com domain, again with DCPROMO. This time, the admin tells DCPROMO that eastcoast .acme.com is a *child domain* of acme.com. Join any machines/servers to eastcoast.acme.com.

4. Do the same thing for westcoast.acme.com.

At this point, the admin is *done*. Windows 2000 automatically creates trust relationships between acme.com and eastcoast.acme.com as well as between acme.com and westcoast.acme.com. It also does all of the work necessary so that users in acme.com are recognized as users in the two child domains. Furthermore, there's an already-created group called Enterprise Administrators whose members can seize control of any domain in the forest, potentially allowing them to actually *be* "Enterprise" administrators. Much easier than NT 4.

ACTIVE DIRECTORY ENABLES MANY OF WINDOWS 2000'S NEW FEATURES

In addition to making domain building simpler and more flexible, the Active Directory makes a bunch of Windows 2000's new features possible.

Basically, AD is a database, as you've already read. But in addition to being a database of users and machines, it's also the place that Windows 2000 stores much of its administrative information. In the following sections, I'll give you some examples.

AD Stores Zero Administration Info

Ever had to rebuild a user's workstation from scratch? How long did it take—would you measure it in minutes, hours, days, or weeks? There are commercial tools such as Symantec's Ghost that can assist in that task, but Windows 2000 has a Ghost-like tool built right in called the Remote Installation Services, as you read in Chapter 4. RIS lets you take a new computer right out the box, plug it into the network, and boot a floppy. The floppy gets the computer onto the network and locates an Active Directory server. From there, AD takes over and directs the process of getting a working disk image onto the workstation in 30 to 45 minutes, unattended. The information about where to keep those disk images and who gets which ones is stored in AD.

Anyone who's ever struggled with system policies under NT 4 knows that they're no picnic: You've got to generate a `NTCONFIG.POL` file, put it on a domain controller, and set up replication for `NTCONFIG.POL` among domain controllers. With Windows 2000, however, all of the system policy stuff—which is now called *group policies*—is stored and automatically replicated by AD.

Ever tried to "push" out an application with SMS or a similar tool? Again, no fun. But one of AD's functions is to store and decide who gets what applications.

AD Supports Directory-Enabled Networking

Windows 2000 allows you to control bandwidth within your intranet using QoS (Quality of Service) control in TCP/IP. You can, then, say that a particular person should get more bandwidth on Tuesday afternoons when she needs it for videoconferencing. And where is that information stored? In the Active Directory.

AD Will Eventually Replace the Browser

Over the years, Microsoft has gamely tried to support a simple way of browsing the servers on your local network. First called the Browser, then Network Neighborhood, the whole idea was that you could just open up a window and see what was available on your company's network. You'd first see the servers, and then you could drill down into a particular server to see its file and print shares.

The problem with the Browser has always been that Microsoft's networking model grew out of a peer-to-peer paradigm rather than a client-server model. Rather than letting a central server maintain a list of available servers, Microsoft's Browser depended on servers finding each other and electing one of their numbers to act temporarily as the keeper of the server list. It was a good try, but it never really worked that well and over the years, the cry, "Why can't I see [my computer, some server, anything at all] in Network Neighborhood?" has wasted person-millennia of support time.

The Browser still exists in Windows 2000, but it's slowly being supplemented by a central list of servers and shared resources maintained on the Active Directory. That list includes the names of servers, the shares available on the system, and the printers available on the system. As more and more Windows 2000–aware applications appear, we'll see AD act more and more as the place to go to find network services.

Understanding and Using Active Directory's Features

With the overview out of the way, let's next dig into some details. And AD has a *lot* of details!

NT 4 domain designers had just a few tools: domains, user accounts, machine accounts, groups, and trust relationships. Windows 2000 designers, in contrast, have all of those things and also the extra tools of organizational units, trees, forests, and sites.

In this section, I'll give you an overview of Windows 2000's main enterprise-building tools:

◆   Domains

- ◆ User and machine groups
- ◆ Organization units
- ◆ Sites
- ◆ Trees of domains
- ◆ Forests of trees of domains
- ◆ Group policies

Domains

The typical way to explain an NT domain is to say that it is "the unit of NT security." That's true, but it's not very illuminating, so let's see what it means.

As you've read earlier in this chapter, every network with any kind of security at all needs to keep a list of information about users—the names, passwords, and other information about people authorized to use the system. In a one-server system, that list sits somewhere on the one server. But when you add a second server, the question arises: How do we tell the *second* server about the users that the *first* server knows about? There are two basic approaches: either duplicate the user list onto the second server, or enable the second server to somehow use the first server's list.

The first option initially sounds like the simpler of the two. Suppose you've got 200 users—you set up the first server, type in 200 names, and the first server now knows about the 200 users. Go to the second server, and either retype the 200 names (ugh, yuck) or just copy the file containing the list of the 200 users to the second server (better, but still not perfect). There are two problems with this. First, not every network operating system lets you copy the file that contains the list of users—in particular, NT 4 did not. You typed names into a file named SAM on one server and you could not just copy that SAM to another server. Assuming you can get past the first problem, a second problem soon appears: password-changing day. Users may not realize that their user accounts appear on two different servers, and so they may not know that when they want to change their passwords they must do it in *two* places. And of course things get more complex when you add the third, fourth, and five-hundredth server.

Windows 2000 still uses a SAM. SAM is the name of the file that Windows 2000 machines—servers and workstations—use to store *locally built* and maintained accounts. If you wanted to, you could implement dozens of Windows 2000 servers, *not* create a domain, and only use their local SAMs. I have no idea why you'd want to do that—you'd have to retype usernames and worry about how you'd keep user passwords in sync across all of the servers—but you could choose to do that if you liked.

The better answer for any type of network is not to attempt to maintain dozens or hundreds or thousands of separate parallel user account lists, but rather to build just one list and share it some-how. NT 4 solved the problem with a networked SAM, a single machine with a central SAM.

Windows 2000 still does something very like that, although technically the networked file isn't a SAM, it's called `NTDS.DIT` or, more commonly, the Active Directory.

A relatively small number of machines hold a copy of the `NTDS.DIT` database file. Other machines needing authentication refer to the `NTDS.DIT` holders. Through a process called *multimaster replication*, the `NTDS.DIT` holders ensure that they all have a consistent set of data in their `NTDS.DIT`.

But "machine that holds a centralized `NTDS.DIT`" is a bit cumbersome, so let's define a few terms to make this all easier to refer to. Any one of the machines holding a copy of `NTDS.DIT` is called a *domain controller*, *Active Directory server*, or, sometimes, *logon server*. The group of machines that refer to a set of domain controllers for authentication is collectively called a *domain*. So presume that you join Acme, which for the moment we'll say is a one-domain company. Someone "builds your user account," which means they add a record to the user database describing you and giving you a password. When you try to log in to your workstation, the workstation wants to know who you are so that it can figure out whether to let you log in; you respond by telling it your name, password, and the fact that you're from domain acme.com. The workstation then locates an Active Directory server for acme.com and verifies your identity.

As with NT 4, Windows 2000 locates user accounts in a particular domain; *locate* here means "place a record in the Active Directory database." You wouldn't say that a particular user lives in a particular forest or tree—you'd refer to a given user account as being in a domain. NT machines and Windows 2000 machines also have accounts (called *machine accounts,* not surprisingly) that live in a particular domain. In the last paragraph I said that the group of machines that refer to a set of domain controllers for authentication is called a *domain*—the machines in that group all have machine accounts in that domain. As you read earlier, Microsoft says that you can put up to 1.5 million user accounts on a domain.

NOTE   *That's not a hard limit, however. As I mentioned earlier, a Compaq techie put 100 million records in an Active Directory and not only did it work, it worked* fast! *AD could respond to queries on that directory in a second or two.*

Let's stop and summarize how NT 4 and Windows 2000 store user information:

◆   Both NT 4 and Windows 2000 will let you create local user accounts, accounts only recognized on the one system upon which they reside. The file that these accounts are stored in is called SAM in both cases.

◆   NT 4 offered a centralized SAM that would sit on a machine called a domain controller.

◆   In contrast, when Windows 2000 centralizes a list of users, it doesn't use SAM, it uses a differently structured database file called `NTDS.DIT`. Just as with NT 4, any Windows 2000 server with a copy of the central user list on it is called a domain controller.

That's basically how domains are structured; now let's look at a great time-saver for managing access to things in a domain: groups.

User (and Now Machine) Groups

Much of a network engineer's job involves using the built-in security features of a network OS to enforce company policy. For example, there might be files on the network that only the managers of the Manufacturing division should see. If people were all trustworthy, then you could just mark a file "Manufacturing managers only, please" and leave it at that. But sadly, they aren't, so Windows 2000, like virtually all network OSes around today, includes the notion of file *permissions*, meaning that you can attach a list to any file or group of files, a list that describes who may access those files and what level of access they should enjoy. So you can protect that Manufacturing-only file by applying permissions to it that restrict its access to Manufacturing managers only.

But how to apply those permissions to just the Manufacturing managers? Well, of course you *could* figure out which of the user accounts belong to those managers, then you could grant access to each of those accounts one at a time. That'd be a lot of work, however, and furthermore, it would *remain* a lot of work, as you'd have to shuffle permissions around every time someone joined or left the ranks of the Manufacturing managers.

A far better answer, and one that Windows 2000 enables, is to create a special kind of account, which is neither a user account nor a machine account, called a *group*. You'd create a group named Manufacturing Managers—any name will do, actually. Then you can choose particular user accounts to add to that group. Finally, you'd modify the file permissions by granting access rights not to a particular user account or accounts, but instead to the group. Anyone in the group would essentially inherit file access by virtue of being a member of the group.

In other words, if Jane, Sue, and Tom are all promoted to Manufacturing manager and you were then directed to give them access to the 10 shares that Manufacturing managers have exclusive access to, then without groups, you'd have to visit each one of those shares, adding the three names to each one. In contrast, with groups, then you would have already visited those shares a long time ago and just told the shares that anyone in the group Manufacturing managers had access to those shares. Having done that in the past, *now* all you have to do is to just add Jane, Sue, and Tom to the Manufacturing managers group, and they instantly get access to the 10 shares.

BOTH USERS AND MACHINES CAN EXIST IN GROUPS

NT 4 didn't let you put machine accounts into a group, and that was unfortunate, as it would have often been convenient to create groups of machines upon which to apply system policies. Windows 2000 fixes this, and you can now have groups that contain machines, users, or a combination of those two. You cannot, however, apply policies to groups, oddly enough—you apply them to organizational units, covered a bit later, and yes, you can put machines into OUs.

GROUPS CAN EXIST INSIDE GROUPS INSIDE GROUPS INSIDE GROUPS

Sometimes it's convenient to put a group inside a group. For example, every server has a group built into it called Administrators. Anyone in the group is, as you'd guess, treated by that server as an administrator, someone with the power to perform any task on that server. But what if I had a group in the enterprise that I wanted to be able to act as administrators on *every* machine? Well, I *could* walk over to every single machine in the company and add each of those enterprise-wide administrators' names to the local Administrators group of each machine. Yuk. No fun.

It's a bit easier to create a group on some computer somewhere called BigDogs or something like that and make all of the enterprisewide administrators' user accounts a member of BigDogs. Then I can visit each machine in the company and just add the BigDogs group to each of those machines' Administrators group. Sure, it's still a lot of work, but this way I only have to add *one* thing—the BigDogs group—to each Administrators group, instead of having to add a whole bunch of user accounts to each Administrators group. And if someone gets fired or hired, I need only delete/add a user account to BigDogs, and it'll automatically be recognized as a former or present BigDog.

So putting groups inside groups was something of a convenience for administrators. But Microsoft didn't want to have to worry about what might happen if you put group A inside group B, then put group B inside group C, and then accidentally put group C inside group A; that could be confusing for NT to decode. As a result, Microsoft simplified the groups-inside-groups abilities of NT. In general, it figured that there would be groups like Administrators, which really only describes a specific machine; being a member of Administrators for machine X doesn't mean that you have any power at all on machine Y—you'd have to be a member of machine Y's Administrators group for that. As these groups were really only relevant to their local machines, they were called *local* groups.

In contrast, groups such as BigDogs get created on some machine, but they're not really connected to that machine closely. BigDogs was interesting because it could be placed into the local Administrators group of some other machine. Such groups could, one supposes, be called traveling or export groups, but Microsoft called them *global* groups.

To ensure that you couldn't put a group inside a group, which was inside another group, and so on—the more exact way to say that would be "to ensure that you couldn't *nest* groups in more than one level"—Microsoft designed NT to allow you to put global groups into local groups. As a global could not go into a global, and as a local couldn't go into anything, you could not nest groups beyond one group inside another group. The net effect was one level of nesting—a global goes into a local and that's that.

Windows 2000 extends the notion of groups by increasing the number of group types from two to four and allowing more nesting levels. The old local group has been replaced by two types of local groups: *machine local* groups and *domain local* groups. Global groups work largely as they did before, although they're a bit more flexible. And an entirely new type of group, a *universal* group, lets you do just about anything that you want with it, albeit at a price in performance and compatibility with NT 4. Let's take a look, then, at Windows 2000's four kinds of groups:

◆ Machine local groups

◆ Domain local groups

◆ Domain global groups

◆ Universal groups

Machine Local Groups

Machine local groups do pretty much what they did before. Every machine has a prebuilt group called Administrators, one named Users, another named Backup Operators that defines a person powerful enough to run the backups but not powerful enough to get into the kind of mischief that a full-fledged administrator could. If you're a member of the Users group, you can log in to that machine and perform basic functions. If you're a member of the Administrators group, you can do anything. There are other groups as well; you can see a machine's machine local groups by right-clicking My Computer, then choosing Manage. An MMC window will appear. In its left panel, open System Tools. Within that, open Local Users and Groups. Within *that*, open Groups. You'll see something like Figure 8.3.

FIGURE 8.3

Machine local groups for Windows 2000 machine

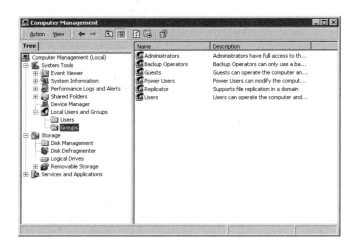

Machine local groups can include global groups, as always. They can also contain:

◆ Universal, global, or domain local groups from their home domain

◆ Universal or global groups from any trusted Windows 2000 domain

◆ Global groups from any trusted NT 4 domain

Domain Local Groups

NT 4 keeps its list of user accounts and groups in a file called SAM, as you've read before. Windows 2000 machines still have SAMs, but only workstations (Windows 2000 Professional) and member servers actually *use* their SAMs.

NOTE   *They won't use them much, however. In an NT 4–based network with an NT 4 domain, it never made much sense to create a bunch of user accounts on the local SAM as user accounts built on the domain SAM were more flexible. That's still true for Windows 2000 networks: You'll almost always want to use accounts built in a domain's Active Directory rather than on a local SAM.*

Domain controllers, in contrast, don't use SAMs; they keep all of their account information in `NTDS.DIT`—the Active Directory, recall. But DCs can find use for local groups as well—an Administrators group, Backup Operators group, and so on—and so the Active Directory has local groups as well. As they're not implemented in SAMs, however, I guess Microsoft felt that it needed a new name, leading to *domain local groups*.

You don't use the My Computer/Manage sequence to see domain local groups. Instead, you run the MMC snap-in called Active Directory Users and Computers. You'll either find it on the Administrative Tools program menu, or just click Start/Run and fill in **dsa.msc** and press Enter.

TIP   *The* dsa *in* `dsa.msc` *stands for Directory Services Administrator, its name in Windows 2000 prior to beta 3. You'll still hear people refer to the program as the DSA, probably because saying* Active Directory Users and Computers *takes way too long to say, and ADUC just really doesn't cut it as an acronym.*

You'll see your domain name with a plus sign next to it; open it and you'll see several folders. Open the Users folder and it'll look something like Figure 8.4.

FIGURE 8.4

Groups in an Active Directory folder

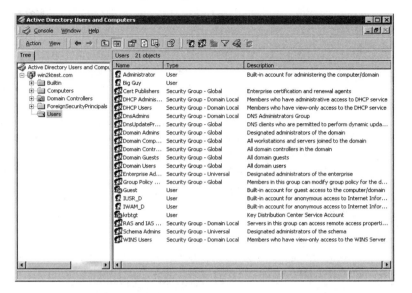

You see all three kinds of groups here—domain locals, globals, and universals. You'd use a domain local group as you'd use a machine local group; they're just on domain controllers, and you *can't* create machine locals on a DC…it's just not possible. But that's not all that they can do. You can put domain local groups into the local group of any machine on the domain. (I'll cover domain local groups in some more detail in the next chapter.) You can put the following things in domain local groups, in addition of course to user accounts:

◆ Universal, global, and other domain local groups, provided they are from the same domain

◆ Universal or global groups from any domain in the same forest

Global Groups

I didn't mention it earlier, but NT 4 experts already knew that global groups were a bit more "special" than NT 4 local groups because you could create a global group only on a domain controller. That's still true in Windows 2000; global groups can be created only on a DC. You use global groups as before—a place to collect a bunch of user accounts that you will then place inside some local group. Besides user accounts, the only thing you can put in a global group is another global group from the same domain.

Universal Groups

If the artificial division between groups that mainly receive other groups and user accounts (local groups) and groups that mainly exist to be placed in other groups (global groups) seems a bit contrived, well, perhaps it is. Why not just have a type of group that can contain other groups (as with a local group) and that can also "travel" to other groups (as with a global)? Windows 2000 has just such a group, called a *universal* group. A universal group can contain *any* global or universal group from *any* domain in the forest.

NOTE *Despite the "universal" name, a universal group cannot contain anything from a domain outside of the forest. Forests don't share any security information unless you explicitly create a trust relationship between their domains. And there's no way to make two forests trust each other—you can only make two domains trust each other. So I suppose there is a way to make two forests trust each other: Just go to each domain in each forest and make that domain trust every domain in every other forest, one domain at a time. No, on second thought, I don't think so.*

Figure 8.5 summarizes the "what kind of group goes into what other kind of group?" relationships.

FIGURE 8.5

Group nesting relationships

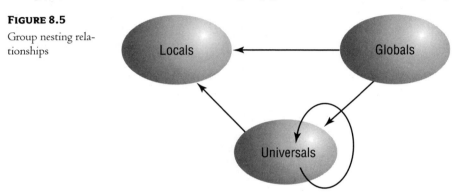

The next logical question, then, is "Okay, why don't we use universal groups whenever we need groups?" Two reasons: First, you can't create a universal group until all of your domain controllers are Windows 2000 machines (NT 4 machines can be backup domain controllers in a Win2K domain), and second, universal groups have a significant effect on the size—and therefore the responsiveness—of something called the *global catalog*.

NOTE *One reader objected to that last paragraph in a previous edition, saying that an NT 4 machine couldn't be a backup domain controller (BDC) in an Active Directory for the simple reason that there is no such thing as a BDC under the Active Directory. The issue apparently troubled him mightily as he went on to question my competence and parentage. So in case you too are troubled, here's why the paragraph's right. First of all, the NT 4 domain controllers in an Active Directory domain don't even know that they're in an AD and, in fact, haven't a clue about what an Active Directory is. They think they're BDCs in a Windows NT 4 domain, and one—that's right, just one—AD domain controller is, to the NT 4 BDCs, the primary domain controller. They will accept account updates from no other computer. Second of all, although Microsoft likes to say that all DCs are equal under Windows 2000, it's plainly not true. Some domain controllers assume a particular role called Flexible Single Master of Operations (FSMO)—something you'll read about elsewhere in this chapter—and one of those roles is called the Primary Domain Controller FSMO. If you shut the PDC FSMO down without first anointing another DC as the PDC FSMO, then some pretty bad things will happen to your network. Yes, Microsoft has largely decentralized the role of domain controller with Active Directory when compared to NT 4's domain controllers, but not completely decentralized those roles. It seems reasonable, then, to refer to the system running the PDC FSMO role as "the PDC" and the other domain controllers as "backup domain controllers," even if it isn't regulation Microsoft terminology. (And third, as to that parentage thing, my folks had been married a good five years before I was born, I have records to prove it.)*

Mixed versus Native Mode and Universal Groups

For compatibility's sake, Windows 2000 domains can include NT 4 domain controllers as backup domain controllers. But because NT 4 domain controllers don't have the same abilities as Win2K machines, a Windows 2000 domain that includes NT 4 domain controllers must forgo some of its capabilities. One of those capabilities is the notion of heavily nested groups. As universal groups are the most "nestable" of Windows 2000 group types, a Windows 2000 domain can't support universal groups until all of its domain controllers are Windows 2000 machines; the last NT 4 domain controller must be shut off.

When first installed, Windows 2000 domains assume that there's at least one NT 4 domain controller around. For safety's sake, then, all new Windows 2000 domains start up in Mixed mode and will not create universal groups.

Once all of your domain controllers are Windows 2000 machines, you can shift your domain to Native mode, which will allow universal groups. You can view your domain's mode by clicking Start/Programs/Administrative Tools/Active Directory Domains and Trusts, or Start/Run and typing **domain.msc**. You'll see a list of domains in your forest; right-click the new domain and choose Properties and you'll see something like the Figure 8.6.

FIGURE 8.6

Currently in Mixed mode, can shift to Native mode

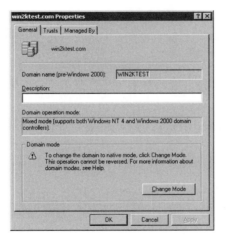

If you click the button to change your domain to Native mode, it'll ask you if you're sure. Once you do and then close `domain.msc`, you'll be alerted that this change doesn't happen immediately.

Once all of the DCs in the domain have gotten the message that they should switch over, and after you reboot all of those DCs, your domain will be in Native mode.

TIP   *If you're sure that you're never going to incorporate any NT 4 domain controllers, install the first Windows 2000 domain controller in your new Windows 2000 domain and shift it over to Native mode immediately. That way, you don't have to run around rebooting domain controllers, and any DCs installed after you've shifted to Native mode will automatically be in Native mode.*

The Global Catalog and Universal Groups

One reason that you sometimes wouldn't use universal groups is because of their effect on something called the *global catalog*. But what's a global catalog?

As I've hinted so far and as you'll read a bit later, Windows 2000 helps you build big multidomain networks by allowing you to create a multidomain structure called a *tree* or a larger structure called a *forest*. Without stealing the later tree-and-forest section's thunder, let me motivate the global catalog discussion by saying that one of the benefits of having a tree/forest of domains is that anyone from any domain can log in to any workstation from any other domain in the tree/forest. This is great in theory but in practice constitutes a major performance hassle. Suppose we had a forest with 50 domains: Every time you wanted to log in to a workstation, that workstation would have no idea which of the 50 domains to query to authenticate your logon. So it would have to search one domain after the other ("Hey, do you know a guy named Ralph023?"), and the result could be *extremely* slow logons.

The global catalog (GC) solves that problem. It's an abbreviated version of *every domain in the forest*. Clearly this could get to be pretty big, but the GC remains manageable in size because it only contains a small subset of information from the Active Directory: What users each domain includes and what domain they're from is one of those pieces of information. (There's another value here as well, but I'll cover it later when I discuss forests and trees.)

Another piece of information stored in the GC is the name of each global group in each domain in the forest. That wouldn't constitute too much space and wouldn't make the GC grow too much. But universal groups are a completely different story: The GC not only knows all of their names, it also knows what users are members of each universal group! As a result, heavy use of universal groups could considerably slow down network logons—so it's a good idea to use universals sparingly.

In case you're wondering, there is not, as far as I know, any tool that lets you directly browse or examine the global catalog—although some search operations use it.

GROUP SIZE IS LIMITED TO 5000 MEMBERS

Groups can also contain groups, as you'll see later in this chapter, and that turns out to be useful. For some reason, groups cannot contain more than 5000 members, meaning that if you need a group with more than 5000 members, you'll have to create several groups, each with under 5000 members, and then place *those* groups into a single "super" group, then apply whatever permissions you want to that "super" group. Yes, it's a pain, but it's probably one of those things they've left undone so we'll have a reason to buy Whistler (the code name for the next version of Windows 2000).

Thus far, we've seen domains, which are a way of defining a collection of users and machines that share the same security rules, and groups, which make managing access to servers easier. Next, let's see how to subdivide a domain, with organizational units.

NOTE   *If the max size on a group is 5000, then what happens with Domain Users? Every user is a member of that group, and if you build an AD larger than 5000 users, then Domain Users doesn't crash. What's going on? The answer is that Domain Users isn't really a group—it just looks like one. It can be any size you like.*

This limitation is fixed in the 2002 edition of NT, Windows .NET Server. You can have millions of users in a group in .NET Server.

NOTE *There are a few more details about groups, but I'll leave for them now and cover them in more detail in Chapter 9.*

Organizational Units (OUs)

Sometimes a domain is too large an area to cede control of. For example, suppose you've got to hire some people to act as backup operators, and suppose that your domain is spread out geographically. You might not want someone who can get to your system from a St. Louis machine to be able to waltz into the San Francisco office and log in to one of those machines. You'd like such people to have backup operator power, but not over the entire network—just over a subset of the network.

Or perhaps you need a staff of people who can reset passwords, or manage printers, or adjust permissions on a set of servers. But you don't want those folks to have those powers over the entire domain. That could be true for either geographic reasons (St. Louis and San Francisco) or organizational reasons (for example, the Marketing department might want their own password-changer person).

The answer in each case is to subdivide the domain into organizational units, or OUs.

ORGANIZATIONAL UNITS ARE FOLDERS

OUs look like folders when viewed with Windows 2000's administrative tools. When you create a user account in a Windows 2000 domain, you can choose to either create the account right in the domain or create it inside one of the folder-like things that you'll see in that domain. When you first create a Windows 2000 domain, you'll automatically get a folder named Users and another named Computers. Although it may *seem* that user accounts should go into the Users folder and machine accounts should go in the Computers folder, that's not the case at all. (That'd be too obvious.) Instead, the only real reason for the Users and Computers folders, which are somewhat like OUs but lack some important powers of OUs (for example, you can't assign group policies to Users or Computers), is so that Windows 2000 has a place to put any user accounts and machine accounts from an upgraded NT 4 domain. The folders are also useful because, if you use some third-party tool to create user accounts and the tool was built for NT 4, then Windows 2000 will sense that and put any user accounts the tool creates into the Users folder.

WHAT YOU CAN DO WITH OUS

OUs have two main uses. You can:

♦ Give control of a set of user and/or machine accounts to a set of users, allowing you to, for example, define a set of people who can reset passwords in a particular department, without having to make them administrators of greater power than might be desirable, and furthermore restricting the range of people whose passwords they can change to a small set of users.

♦ Control and lock down user desktops through the use of group policy objects, control tools like NT 4's system policies; despite their name, however, group policies aren't applied to user groups—they apply to organizational units, domains, or sites.

Using OUs to Create Subadministrators

Or suppose the Graphics department has a bunch of expensive printers shared on the network. They don't want the regular IS people controlling the printers for some reason; they want their local techies to serve as the printer admins. In that case, you could create an OU called Graphics Printers or the like and put the fancy printers into that OU. Then you can give control of that OU and, in the process, of the printers in the OU to a particular user account or perhaps a group containing the names of the admins that Graphics likes.

NOTE *The process of giving a user or group of users control of an OU is called* delegating control *of that OU. Right-click the OU and you can run the Delegation Wizard to make that adjustment.*

If the International Trade and Arbitrage department's VP insists on a separate set of administrators for her servers, OUs can meet her needs. Again, just create a separate OU for her servers, a group for her admins, and delegate control of the OU to the group.

You'll see plenty more on the topic of delegation later in this chapter.

Using OUs to Apply Policies

NT 4 introduced the idea of a *system policy*. Policies let you control user desktops through those users' Registries. You'd place in a centrally accessible location a file called `NTConfig.pol` that contained instructions about what you wanted changed on the user's Registries. NT 4 workstations would then automatically read that file and make changes to their Registries according to the file's orders. In this way, you could control desktops from a central location.

But what if you wanted to control just a subset of a domain, a collection of machines or users? You couldn't apply a system policy to a collection of machines. You could apply a system policy to a group of users, or at least in theory you could. In practice, groups and policies didn't work so well.

Windows 2000 has a much farther-reaching kind of policy called a *group policy*. You can apply group policies to subsets of a domain. The subset? Not a group, as the name suggests, but an OU.

There is one exception to this: policies about passwords and accounts in general. You can control things such as whether you need complex passwords, how often to change passwords, how long passwords should be, or account lockout policies with group policies, but only on policies applied on the domain level. The AD happily lets you create password-related group policies on organizational units and doesn't even complain about them; it just ignores them.

MULTIPLE DOMAINS VERSUS OUs: WHEN EACH MAKES SENSE

Notice in each case cited here that you could *also* accomplish those same ends with multiple domains. International Trade could be its own domain with its own administrators and trust relationships to the rest of the firm. Ditto Graphics. In the first case, all of the administrators could be lumped into a domain off by themselves, and indeed that's been done many times with NT 4—and could still be done for Windows 2000.

When, then, should you use one domain divided into OUs, and when should you have different domains? Well, in general, my rule of thumb would be, "Don't use multiple domains unless you must." So the real question, then, is, "When do multiple domains make sense?" In a few cases:

Replication Problems Due to Poor Bandwidth Probably the best reason. All domain controllers in a domain really need to be online to each other all of the time. If one office is in Timbuktu and the other is in McMurdo Base and they don't really share much save for very limited WAN support, make them separate domains. Think of it this way: Suppose you had one office in Chicago and another in Sydney (Australia) with an expensive, low-bandwidth link between the two. Suppose also that you had 20,000 people in the Chicago office and 150 in the Sydney office. Every time the Chicago people changed their passwords, you'd have to replicate all of that traffic over the expensive-and-slow WAN link to the domain controllers in Sydney. Not a great use of WAN links. It'd be better to just build two domains.

Different Account Policies   As with NT 4, you could set account policies—things such as how often users must change their passwords, whether to lock out users who've entered too many incorrect passwords, and how many is "too many"—but you could only set them on a domain-wide basis.

Early in the beta process, Windows 2000 let you set password lengths, frequencies, and the like on an OU-by-OU basis rather than domain by domain. But, as you read a page or two back, the final released copy of Windows 2000 did not allow that. If you want to give a set of people a different set of account policies than the account policies that you give to another set of people, then you'll have to put those sets of people into different domains.

You Don't Trust the Branch Office   Suppose you're a one-domain company with a large corporate headquarters and a bunch of small branch offices. You've got a branch office somewhere with 15 employees. So you put a server—just one—in that building. It serves as the local domain controller, Exchange server, file server, and print server. (And when you're not around, they use it as the receptionist's workstation.)

This server is left out in the open. Yes, there's a lock on the main front door of the office suite, but it's only locked at night. As the server isn't physically secured, someone could steal it or, with just a screwdriver and a few minutes, could steal its hard disk. That hard disk holds a copy of the Active Directory for the entire company, as you work for a one-domain firm.

If this happened under NT 4, you might end up compromising the passwords of all of your users companywide, as there are programs around that can read a SAM and crack its passwords, producing clear text. But no one will ever write an AD password "cracker," right? Unfortunately, they already have. I'm told the latest version of l0phtcrack (**www.atstake.com**) will extract Active Directory passwords, although the Web site says nothing about that (and I didn't feel like spending $250 to download it and find out). But whether an AD password cracker is currently available is irrelevant to what I'm saying...there will eventually be one, rest assured. So physical security is a top priority—these cracker programs in general will only work if you're physically sitting at the DC.

As a result, you can see that by putting one or more of your domain controllers in a location that's not physically secure, you potentially threaten every password in your enterprise. In that case, you might consider separate domains. That way, if the bad guys compromise a single domain's passwords then at least they haven't compromised *all* of the enterprise's passwords.

Politics   Same as it ever was.

We Just Found It This Way, Honest!   Your firm buys another firm, and you have to blend the two organizations. There are third-party tools around that will help assimilate the new domain into your existing domain, but that'll be a big undertaking and maybe you don't have the time to do that just at the moment. In that case, you're living in a multidomain world for a while. Multi-*forest*, most likely. If you can, however, I recommend you consider merging the two domains with a tool like Active Directory Migration Tool, which we'll cover later in this chapter.

I know I've said it already, but let me weigh in again with my opinion about multiple domains, or rather, why I'd avoid them. First of all, NT 4 multiple domain enterprises were a major pain, as trusts tended to break. Supposedly this won't happen under Windows 2000 and thus far I haven't seen it, but in general, the fewer "moving parts" in my enterprise, the better. Additionally, NT has had its growing pains over the years about security. What if the next "NT security hole" appears in Windows 2000 trusts?

And then there's the issue of bugs in general: I'd prefer to work with the parts of Windows 2000 that have been tested most thoroughly. For example, my personal experience with multiple-processor machines running NT is that they're more fragile and a bit more crash prone. I can't prove it, but my guess is that, if Microsoft has 200 people on campus testing Windows 2000, the majority of them have a single-processor machine on their desks. Isn't it logical to assume then that NT has been better tested on single-processor machines than multiprocessor machines? For the same reason, ask yourself: Of all of the people beta-testing Windows 2000 (or Windows 2000 Service Pack 1 or Windows 2000 Service Pack 2 or whatever), do you think most of them tested it in a single-domain or multidomain environment? My guess is the former—which would imply that it's the better way to go for reliability. Understand, however, that these are just guesses on my part.

OUs versus Groups

So far, I've described two kinds of things that hold other things—that is, I've described something called a *group*, which can contain users and/or machines, and I've described something *else* called an organizational unit, which *also* can contain users and/or machines.

So what's the difference? Well, in an oversimplified sense, you put the things that you want to control into an OU. Then you grant that control to a group. If you wanted to, for example, create a sub-group of an enterprise like a department and then designate a group of people who could act as administrators to that department, then the department would be an OU and the desired administrators would be a group. You'd then delegate authority for the OU to the group. But here's some more detail.

A user account can only be in one OU, but it can be a *member* of as many groups as you like. A user account or machine account exists in only one domain in a general sense, but the account may also live in an OU *inside* that domain, much as you or I can live inside some city in a state, but we each live in only one city. In contrast, no matter which city you live in, you can be a member of as many associations—groups—that you like.

You can use groups to assign permissions—you can, for example, deny access to a file to anyone in a given group. Windows 2000 won't let you do any permission work with OUs; you can't deny access to a printer or a file share to an entire OU.

OUs let you define *logical* divisions in a domain. But knowing about the *physical* subdivisions is important as well: I might not want to transfer that half-gigabyte file to server DISTRIBUTE01 if I knew that it's only connected to the rest of the domain with a 56K link. That's where sites come in handy.

Sites

As you read earlier in this chapter, one of NT 4's weaknesses was the fact that domain controllers replicate data among themselves in a very "chatty," bandwidth-intensive way. That's not a problem for domain controllers on the same LAN, as there's typically bandwidth to burn on a LAN, but WAN links are nothing to toss away lightly.

Windows 2000 improves upon that with the notion of *sites*. In addition to knowing about machines and users in an enterprise, the AD also keeps track of the geographic aspects of an enterprise. Each LAN-connected area is called a *site*. Windows 2000 uses the insights that you give it about your physical layout to figure out where the WAN links—the slower and more expensive part of your network—are. It then does two very helpful things: First, it compresses the replication traffic (again, by a factor of as much as *10*, quite impressive!), and second, it uses route costing information that you supply to figure out how best to route the replication traffic at lowest cost.

The Active Directory also uses sites in a feature called Distributed File System or Dfs. With Dfs, you could create a file share that contains some important information and then create a "replica" version of that file share on each of your sites. A tool called the File Replication Service would ensure that all of those file shares contained the identical information. If you've got four sites, for example, then you'd have four replicas. But the four of them all look like just one share to users. When a user attaches to a Dfs share with replicas on multiple sites, then, Dfs uses the AD's site information to ensure the user gets connected with the *local* replica, if possible.

By the way, if you've got experience with Exchange, then all of this will sound somewhat familiar, and it should—Exchange first pioneered the idea of sites several years ago. In fact, I once heard a Microsoft speaker say, "You may have participated in the five-year beta process for Active Directory; you may have known it as Exchange 4.0, 5.0, and 5.5." (He was, in case you're wondering, clearly speaking with his tongue in his cheek.)

At this point, you've met domains, groups, organizational units, and sites. Next, let's meet two ways of organizing *collections* of domains: trees and forests.

Building Multidomain Structures I: Trees

Real-world experience with NT from version 3.1 through 4 showed that people needing multiple-domain enterprises tended to build *hierarchies* of domains, what computer people call *tree structures* despite the fact that computer trees tend to have their roots up top in the air and their "leaves" at bottom. Microsoft designed Windows 2000 to use DNS as a naming system, and DNS is hierarchical in nature anyway, so Windows 2000 exploits this happy coincidence and encourages you to build multidomain enterprises as hierarchies.

NOTE *As you read in the DNS chapter, hierarchies of names are sometimes alternatively called* namespaces. *Thus, if Acme is divided into acme.com, westcoast.acme.com, and eastcoast.acme.com, then you might hear the Acme managers refer to the Acme namespace or perhaps the Acme's Active Directory namespace. All* namespace *means here is "the system that we use to choose names that make some kind of sense."*

The first Windows 2000 domain that you create is called the *root* of the tree. Suppose, following the earlier example, that the root's name is acme.com. Domains below it are referred to as *child domains*, as you've read. You can decide to divide your organization geographically—for example, eastcoast.acme.com and westcoast.acme.com—or organizationally, as perhaps manufacturing.acme.com, finance.acme.com, and sales.acme.com. In case it's not clear, here's the rule for naming child domains: A child domain must have a name like *name.parentdomainname*. So, for example, a child domain of acme.com must have a name like *name*.acme.com—so eastcoast.acme.com or westcoast.acme.com would be fine, and apex.com would *not* be fine, as it doesn't include "acme.com" in it.

You can then create another level if you choose—perhaps sales.ecoast.acme.com, manufacturing .ecoast.acme.com, finance.ecoast.acme.com, and sales.wcoast.acme.com, manufacturing.wcoast.acme .com, and finance.wcoast.acme.com (six domains!)—and another and another, to create as complex a system as you want. Windows 2000 helps you by automatically creating trust relationships between each domain and its child domains. For example, merely creating wcoast.acme.com automatically creates a two-way trust relationship between wcoast.acme.com and acme.com. This two-way trust means that acme.com administrators may choose to extend file and print permissions to finance.acme.com users and vice versa.

And as I mentioned earlier, Windows 2000 trust relationships are *transitive*. Creating finance.wcoast.acme.com creates a two-way trust relationship between finance.wcoast.acme.com and wcoast.acme.com, but it doesn't stop there: Because wcoast.acme.com and acme.com *also* have a two-way trust, finance.wcoast.acme.com ends up with an automatic trust relationship with acme.com. (If that doesn't sound interesting, then you didn't work with NT 4 and earlier versions, which required you to hand-build every single trust relationship.) Thus, because ecoast.acme.com trusts acme.com and acme.com trusts wcoast.acme.com, then ecoast.acme.com trusts wcoast.acme.com.

Building Multidomain Structures II: Forests

Domain trees, then, offer the benefits of automatic trust relationships, a very good thing. But there's just one minor problem with that—all of the domain names must fit into a nice hierarchy. The child domains must contain the names of the parent domains.

FOREST BASICS

Suppose in contrast that your enterprise divides into acme.com and apex.com, two former rivals that have merged. Suppose further you've decided to go with a multiple-domain enterprise and want to keep some of your firm as acme.com and some as apex.com.

It looks like two things are true, then: First, you're probably going to have two domains, and second, those two domains won't fit into a tree.

You can choose to build these two Windows 2000 domains into a unified structure, but it can't be a tree because of their dissimilar names. Instead, you can choose to create a *forest*. A forest is just a group of trees, as you see in Figure 8.7.

Here, you see a forest built from the acme.com and apex.com trees.

Other than different naming hierarchies, the trees in the forest act like one tree in terms of their trust relationships—Windows 2000 builds transitive trusts automatically. So, for example, as eastcoast.acme.com trusts acme.com, acme.com trusts apex.com, and eastcoast.acme.com trusts apex.com—all automatically.

YOU MUST BUILD TREES AND FORESTS TOGETHER

This sounds great, and of course it's a terrific improvement over NT 4. But hidden in this potentially rich notion of many domains joined into a tree and many trees joined into a forest is a dirty little secret.

FIGURE 8.7

Example Active
Directory forest

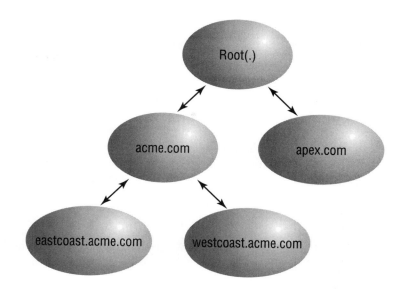

WARNING *You cannot join already-existing domains into a tree. Nor can you join already-existing trees into a forest. The only way to add a domain to a tree, or a tree to a forest, is to build it from scratch onto an existing tree or forest.*

You Can't Glue Domains Together

So suppose I were to create an AD domain named acme.com on one network. Then, on a completely separate network totally unconnected to acme.com's network, I create an AD domain named eastcoast.acme.com. I cannot then attach the two networks and effect a tearful reunion of parent and child domain. Nor could I build apex.com and acme.com AD trees in isolation and then connect them, after the fact, to create a forest.

Attaching existing domains to existing trees or forests is called *pruning and grafting* and it can't be done, at least not with the tools supplied by Windows 2000. Thus, for example, if Exxon buys Mobil, and Exxon already has a domain named exxon.com and Mobil's got a domain named mobil.com, it's not possible to join them together in a tree with the supplied Windows 2000 tools.

"...But Only the AD Wizard Can Make a Tree"

(My apologies to Joyce Kilmer.) Let's review what I'm saying here. If I've created an AD domain named acme.com and want to create a child domain in its tree named eastcoast.acme.com, then I sit down at the machine that I want to be the first DC in eastcoast.acme.com and create the eastcoast.acme.com domain, explaining to the Active Directory Installation Wizard (which you'll meet a bit later) that I want it to be part of an existing tree, acme.com. Before the wizard will go any further, it demands the name and password of an administrator for the acme.com domain. Windows 2000 will refuse to create a child domain unless it can contact the parent domain right at that moment and get permission. In the same way, if you want to create a second tree in a forest, then the wizard will require that you tell it the name and password of an administrator for the first tree. (What about the third tree or fourth tree—what account do *they* need to provide? From the second to the millionth tree in a forest, you've got to provide an admin account from the *first* tree in the forest. As you're about to read in the next section, that first tree is "magic.")

TIP *You're probably wondering exactly* what *administrative account you need to create new domains in a forest. The answer is, any account that is a member of a group called Enterprise Admins. You will only find that group in the very first domain that you create in a forest. And just to make things a bit confusing, you can create* some *domains without having to be a member of Enterprise Admins—simply being a member of the group called Domain Admins in that very first domain works as well, so long as you are either creating another tree in the forest, or if you are creating a child domain of that first domain in the forest. Yes, I know, this sounds odd, but it's what I've found works.*

Combining Domains, Trees, and Forests: The Future and .NET Server

So suppose you *do* have separate domains, trees, or forests that you want to attach to existing domains, trees, or forests—what do you do? Well, the *best* answer would be if you could link those objects with one of those nifty new Windows 2000 two-way transitive trust relationships. In some senses, that's all there *is* to a tree or forest; it's just a bunch of domains strung together with two-way transitive trusts. So if you could build two-way transitive trusts between domains, trees, or forests, then you could essentially build whatever kind of AD structure that you liked.

But you can't do that under Windows 2000's version of AD. Under NT 3.*x* and 4, you could create a trust relationship between any arbitrary two domains, but that trust relationship was only a one-way trust, and it wasn't transitive. Windows 2000 lets you create trusts between any arbitrary two domains as well—but those are only old NT 4–style trusts, one-way and non-transitive. In what is probably the most important Active Directory–related feature in Windows .NET Server, you can create transitive trust relationships from forest to forest. Create just one trust from Apex's forest to Acme's forest, and every domain in the Acme forest trusts every domain in Bigfirm's forest, and vice versa.

There are a few gotchas on this nifty forest-to-forest trust, though. First of all, it will only work if every single domain controller in both forests is running Windows .NET Server. And, second, transitive trusts may not do everything you want, inasmuch as two forests that trust each other do not have a single unified global catalog. (Perhaps that'll appear in Longhorn, the code name for the *next* version of NT, slated for a 2003 release.)

Using Migration Tools to Combine Domains, Trees, and Forests

The other answer is to go spend some money to buy a so-called "migration" tool, such as the ones offered by Fastlane, NetIQ, Aelita, and Entevo, or Microsoft's Active Directory Migration Tool, which is free but a bit limited (we'll cover it later). These tools copy user and machine accounts and permission information between one domain and another. You would, then, "merge" two domains by creating an empty domain in the same tree/forest as one of the domains, then copying the objects from the other domain.

For example, suppose I had two distinct domains, acme.com and apex.com, and wanted to merge them into a forest. Using a migration tool, I'd work something like this:

1. Create a new empty domain named apex2.com (or something like that—you'll run into trouble if you try to work with two domains both named apex.com) in acme.com's forest, using the Active Directory Installation Wizard.

2. Build an old-style NT 4 trust relationship between the apex.com domain and the apex2.com domain.

3. Build an old-style NT 4 trust relationship in the other direction, between the apex2.com domain and the apex.com domain.

4. Use the migration tool to copy the user and machine accounts from apex.com to apex2.com.

5. Now tell the users in apex.com to no longer log in to apex.com, but instead to log in to their accounts on apex2.com.

The process isn't trouble-free, but it works.

TRUSTS IN MORE DETAIL

Just in case you ever *do* need to create a trust between Windows 2000 and NT or 2000 domains, here's some more information on them. Old NT 4–style trusts are one-way only, even if they're between two Windows 2000 domains. In this section, when I say "trust," I mean "NT 4–style trust."

NT 4 Trusts Include the Trusting and the Trusted

Any trust between two domains has a trusting and a trusted domain. The trusting domain is willing to accept login information and authentications from the trusted domain. For example, suppose I have two domains—an NT 4 domain named FACTORY and a Windows 2000 domain named acme.com. Suppose also that FACTORY is a domain that contains very few user accounts; instead, it contains the machine accounts for several hundred servers. People with user accounts in acme.com need to get access to data in FACTORY's servers.

This is an example of a fairly common NT 3.*x* and 4 domain model called a *master/resource model*. The idea was to build at least two domains, a "master" domain and then one or more "resource" domains. You'd put all of the company's user accounts into the master domain (acme.com, in this case) and then put the servers into a resource domain or, in most cases, you'd have several resource domains, and each server would have an account in the resource domain that made the most sense. (Don't worry too much about the details on this, as it's really not an issue anymore. If you really want to read about it in great detail, I'd suggest reading Chapter 12 in my book *Mastering Windows NT Server 4*. But you don't need to do that to follow this discussion.)

So in the master/resource scenario, you'd have servers in the resource domain and users in the master domain. The users would want to access data on the servers, so the servers needed to be able to recognize and accept login data not from their own (resource domain) domain controllers, but rather from the DCs in the user's (master) domain. So we need FACTORY's servers to accept logins from acme.com's domain controllers.

Or, in other words, we need the FACTORY domain to *trust* the acme.com domain.

If you've not messed around with trust relationships in the past, then go back and read that again so you're clear on it. The primary goal was to allow acme.com people access to FACTORY's data. But FACTORY's servers will not, of course, let any users get to that data unless they can authenticate those users. But FACTORY can't authenticate the users, only their home domain's DCs can. Therefore, FACTORY must begin accepting authentication from acme.com. That's the definition of "to trust" here: to accept authentications. So acme.com folks get to use FACTORY's data because acme.com is *trusted*, and FACTORY lets them because it is *trusting*.

There are a couple of ways to create a trust relationship—the GUI way and the command-line way. The command-line way is preferable because it creates a more flexible trust and is actually *essential* if you intend to use a migration tool to copy user accounts from an existing NT 4 domain to a Windows 2000 domain and want to employ something called *SID histories*—and yes, I'll explain all of that later. But I want to show you both ways of creating trusts because most people will consider the GUI approach easier and, if you don't care about being able to create SID histories—again, a topic for a bit later—then you needn't work with the command line.

Creating a Trust with the GUI

To create a trust relationship between two domains requires a bit of work both on the part of the trusted domain and the trusting domain—administrators for both domains must participate. The tool for creating trusts in NT 4 is the User Manager for Domains, located on NT 4 servers at Start/Programs/Administrative Tools/User Manager for Domains. You bring up the dialog box that lets you work with trust relationships (Figure 8.8) by clicking Policies, then Trust Relationships.

FIGURE 8.8

Trust Relationships dialog box in NT 4 User Manager

You can then designate domains that you trust, as well as domains that you permit to trust you. (Odd as that sounds, it's true. I can see why the *trusting* domain would need the permission of its administrator to start trusting—accepting logons from other domains is a big deal—but I've never quite figured out why it makes sense to have to get an admin's approval to *be* trusted.)

The tool for creating trusts in Windows 2000 is Active Directory Domains and Trusts, also in Start/Programs/Administrative Tools. In the left pane, you'll see a listing of the domains in your forest. To change a domain's trust relationships, right-click the icon representing the domain, and click Properties. You'll see a properties page that includes a tab labeled Trusts, as in Figure 8.9.

The screen shot in Figure 8.9 is from a simple forest that I created whose root domain was named win2ktest.com. It was a two-tree forest, and this is the list of trusts for win2kexperts.com, the second tree. It has a child domain named va.win2kexperts.com. I did not have to create these trusts—creating the forest created them.

It's pretty simple to see how to create a trust between two domains—just fill in the proper domain names into the "trusted" or "trusting" sections of the interface. But here's a trick to make the process faster:

When setting up a trust, first go to the *trusting* domain and tell it to trust the trusted domain. Then go to the trusted domain and tell it that it's okay for the trusting domain to trust it. For example, recall that we wanted the NT 4 domain FACTORY to trust the Windows 2000 domain acme.com. That's easiest with these steps:

1. As FACTORY will be the trusting domain, go first to that domain. Start up User Manager for Domains and click Policies, then Trust Relationships.

2. In the section of the dialog box labeled Trusted Domains, click Add and fill in **acme**. You wouldn't use "acme.com" because NT 4 will only recognize older NetBIOS names. Click OK and confirm any messages.

3. Then move to a server on the acme.com domain and start up Active Directory Domains and Trusts. Find acme.com in the left pane, then right-click it and choose Properties, and then click the Trusts tab.

4. In the area labeled Domains That Trust This Domain, click Add and fill in **factory** and then press Enter. Do not allow it to verify the trust unless you are simultaneously logged in as an administrator for both domains. Close AD Domains and Trusts.

The trust should work now. To create a trust between two AD domains, it's the same process, except of course that both domains use AD Domains and Trusts rather than the User Manager.

FIGURE 8.9

Trusts tab on a domain's properties page

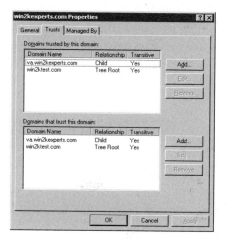

When the Trust Doesn't Work

Sometimes I can't make this work. No matter what I do, User Manager for Domains (often) or AD Domains and Trusts (less frequently) complains that it cannot contact a domain controller for the other domain.

That could be because of something very simple. If one system can't ping the other system, then you can't establish a trust. Trust also could fail if one system cannot resolve the other system's name—the NetBIOS names, if it's an NT-4-to-2000 trust, or DNS names, if it's a 2000-to-2000 trust. So check basic connectivity, WINS, and DNS if you can't get one domain to acknowledge another's existence.

But once in a while, there's simply nothing that you can do to make an NT 4 system see a 2000 domain controller. So in that case, you need to employ the "emergency measures"—a file called LMHOSTS. As you read in the previous chapter, LMHOSTS is an ASCII file that you place in \winnt\system32\drivers\etc. You can use it to help one domain find another domain's primary domain controller—which NT needs to find if it's to create a trust. In each domain controller, create an LMHOSTS entry that points to the other domain controller by entering a line like this in LMHOSTS:

```
IPaddress-of-other-DC   "name-of-other-domain <spaces to fill to 15 chars> \0x1B"
```

That should be typed as just one line, even if it broke on the printed page. The idea here is that we're creating an LMHOSTS entry that points to a DC whose ID is "1B" hex, which designates the primary domain controller. For example, if the domain controller for acme.com that is acting as something called the *PDC emulator* or PDC FSMO (we'll get to FSMOs very soon, I promise) had the IP address 25.7.4.11, then I'd enter this line into the LMHOSTS on the primary DC on FACTORY:

```
25.7.4.11   "ACME            \0x1B"
```

Notice that the name in the entry is the domain's name, not the PDCs. As ACME is four characters long, I added 11 spaces after its name, before the \0x1B. And you must use the double quotes. That entry goes into the LMHOSTS file on the PDC for FACTORY so that it can find the PDC for acme.com. In all likelihood, that'll work; but if the acme.com system still claims to be unable to find the PDC for FACTORY, then find out the IP address for FACTORY's PDC—let's say that it's 25.10.10.19—and put *this* entry in the LMHOSTS file on acme.com's PDC FSMO:

```
25.10.10.19 "FACTORY         \0x1B"
```

This time, I padded the name with eight spaces, not eleven, as FACTORY is seven characters long.

Creating a Trust from the Command Line

You can create a two-way trust relationship between an NT 4 domain (call it NT4DOM) and a Windows 2000 Active Directory domain (call it win2kdom.com) with the following command:

```
netdom trust nt4dom /D:win2kdom.com /UserO:ntadmin
➥/PasswordO:ntpassword /UserD:win2kadmin
➥/PasswordD:win2kpassword /Add /Twoway
```

ntadmin and *ntpassword* refer to the name and password for an account with Domain Admin privileges in the NT domain, and *win2kadmin* and *win2kpassword* refer to the name and password for an account with Domain Admin privileges for the Windows 2000 AD domain. And although that command broke into multiple lines on the printed page, be sure to type it as all one line.

WARNING   *If you will be using SID histories (described later), then it is very important that you create this NT-domain-to-2000-domain trust using the netdom.exe program that comes in the 2000 Resource Kit or the Resource Kit subset that ships on the 2000 Server CD. If you instead create the trust by running the User Manager for Domains on the NT side and Active Directory Domains and Trusts on the 2000 side, then you will have what Microsoft calls a downlevel trust, which would be the same kind of trust that you'd have gotten if you stuck with the GUI. In fact, I recommend that you create all trusts with netdom.exe.*

You can find `netdom.exe` on the Windows 2000 Server CD, in the `\Support\Tools` folder. Look in the file named `support.cab`–NETDOM is in there.

The Case for an Empty Root

Look back to Figure 8.7. In that figure, I drew an extra root domain in addition to apex.com, acme.com, and acme.com's two child domains. I did that to make the diagram "look" right—we're used to seeing hierarchies end up at a single point.

In a tree, it's simple to see which domain is the root or top-level domain—it's simple to see that apex.com is the top of the apex.com tree and that acme.com is the top of the acme.com tree. But when we build two trees (apex.com and acme.com) into one forest, then which domain is the "top" or "root" domain? Or isn't there a root; perhaps all trees are equal?

In an Active Directory forest built of several trees, there *is* a single forest domain root. It's just not obvious which one it is.

NOTE   *The root domain of a Windows 2000 AD forest is the first domain that you installed in the forest.*

So suppose you came across an AD forest that contained just three domains—acme.com, apex.com, and consolidated.com. Which domain is the forest root? The answer isn't obvious because the three domains seem to sit at the same level. I don't know of a quick way to find out which domain is the forest root, but here's a slightly slower one. Remember that only the forest root domain contains a group named Enterprise Admins; that's how we'll find the root.

Start Active Directory Users and Computers (Start/Programs/Administrative Tools/Active Directory Users and Computers). In the left pane of the MMC snap-in, you'll see an icon representing a domain; it looks like three tower PCs clustered together. Right-click that icon and choose Find. In the resulting dialog box, there's a drop-down list box labeled In, which lets you tell the program which domain to search in; click it and you'll see that you have the ability to search any one of your forest's domains. Choose one of your top-level domains. Then notice the field labeled Name; enter **enterprise*** and press Enter. If the search found a group called Enterprise Admins, then you've found the root. If not, drop down the In list box and try another domain until you locate the one with Enterprise Admins.

Suppose acme.com turned out to be the root domain in my acme/apex/consolidated example. There are probably three domains because there are or were at some time three different business entities that for some reason are one firm now. Who *cares* if the Acme guys happen to be the forest root?

Well, the Apex and Consolidated guys, that's who—whether they know it or not. You see, members of the Enterprise Admins group, which happens to live in the Acme domain, have powers in *every domain in the forest*. They're not members of the Domain Admins group in those domains, but they might as well be, as Enterprise Admins have Domain Admin–like powers everywhere.

That means that although in *theory* Acme, Apex, and Consolidated have separate domains, with those nice, convenient security boundaries, in *practice* the Apex and Consolidated folks have to just kind of hope that the Acme guys don't get the lust for power one day and decide to do something scary in the Apex or Consolidated domains. So you can see why Apex and Consolidated might be a bit nervous.

The answer? Don't create three domains, create four. The first domain—the root domain—should be some domain that you're never going to use, e-gobbledygook.com or something like that. Create one administrative account in that domain, including it in the Enterprise Admins. Let the CIO create it and then have her write down that account name and password, and then stuff the paper on which she's written them into her safe. At the same time, create the other three domains—you'll need the CIO for a while, she'll have to type in the username and password for that Enterprise Admin account in order to create those three domains. Then you can put away the Enterprise Admin account and you'll only need it now and then.

This idea of creating a first domain and then populating it with only an account or two, then doing nothing else with it, is called an *empty root* AD design.

Some firms create an empty root domain even if it's just a one-domain enterprise in case it acquires other companies at some time in the future. It's not a bad bit of bet-hedging, and I'd recommend it to some. Of course, the downside of it is that you've got to have a DC or, better yet, two DCs, sitting around running, doing nothing to support the root domain. But, again, it may not be a bad investment——an empty root is one case where I'd break my single-domain-preferred preference.

Logons under Active Directory

All of the machinery that the Active Directory includes enables Windows 2000 to be a bit smarter about logons than NT 4 was. Here's a brief look at how AD uses sites and DNS to log in machines and users.

When you start up your Windows 2000 desktop machine, it must log in to your Windows 2000 domain—machines log in as well as people (or at least machines running Windows 2000 or NT must log in—Windows 9x systems don't).

The hard part about logons is in finding a domain controller—that is to say, a computer that offers Kerberos logon services (on port 88) and LDAP query services (on port 389). Once your system has found a DC, then transacting all of the Kerberos back-and-forth stuff about checking your password and user ID (or your machine's password and user ID) is very simple. The problem is finding a machine to *present* these credentials to.

In its most basic form, a machine finds a domain controller by asking DNS, "I'm a member of the win2ktest.com domain. Do you know of any machines in that domain that are registered as servers using port 88 and 389?" "Ports 88 and 389" is Internet-ese for "Kerberos and LDAP server," and machines communicate with domain controllers using LDAP. Therefore, asking for a Kerberos/ LDAP server is the same as asking for a domain controller.

But actually DNS servers under Windows 2000 are even smarter than that, as they not only have a list of Kerberos/LDAP servers for a given domain, they also have a list of sites for that domain *and* a list of Kerberos/LDAP servers broken down by site. Thus, a machine can say to DNS, "Give me the name of a domain controller in the downtown site and the win2ktest.com domain." Now, not every site may *have* a domain controller. In that case, DNS just hands the system the address of any old domain controller.

Once the client machine has a DC's address, it opens communications with the DC. Part of the DC's job, however, is to make sure that the client is talking with a nearby DC if at all possible. That's necessary because a laptop may have been installed at the Nome site but has been carried to the Miami site. The laptop queries DNS for a Nome DC, and DNS gives the laptop the address of a

Nome DC. When the laptop starts logging in via the Nome DC, however, the Nome DC notices that the laptop has an IP address (which the laptop got from a local DHCP server in Miami) that indicates that it's in Miami. The Nome DC then looks that address up in the Active Directory and deduces that the laptop is currently in Miami. The DC then queries DNS for the name of a DC in Miami, or at least close to Miami, and then tells the laptop to instead log in with that closer machine rather than communicating all of the way up to Nome.

Summarized, then, Windows 2000 systems find domain controllers by first using their knowledge of their site locations and domain names to query DNS for the names of nearby domain controllers. The machines then contact the nearby domain controllers and ask them to log them in. The DC that agrees to log them in first checks that it is the closest DC available, and if it is *not*, then it redirects the machine to a closer DC.

You can find out which server logged you in by opening a command prompt and typing **set**. One of the pieces of information that you'll get is a line starting with LOGONSERVER=; to the right of the equals sign is the name of the DC that logged you in.

Building an Active Directory: Some Hands-On Experience

Let's take a break from the heavy concepts for a while and do a little hands-on work. Let's build a small tree of domains to get a feel for what the Active Directory process looks like. In this tree, I'll create two domains: one called bigfirm.biz and another, a child domain called div.bigfirm.biz. As I'll want an account that can act as an administrator across the whole tree, I'll also create a user named bigguy with those powers.

If you want to do something like this, you'll need two machines because, under Windows 2000, a single machine can only be a domain controller for one domain; two domains, therefore, would require two machines—more, in fact, if you wanted to start adding replica DCs or member servers.

Building the First Domain

One of the really nice things about Windows 2000 is that Microsoft separated the process of installing Windows 2000 from the process of creating a domain controller. You can do a fairly vanilla installation of Windows 2000 Server (or have an equipment supplier preinstall Windows 2000 Server, as companies such as Dell, Compaq, HP, or IBM do) without having to worry about two of NT 4's biggest pains— that you needed to designate a machine as a domain controller during Setup, and that you couldn't install a backup domain controller unless your computer was connected live on the LAN to the domain's PDC. So you can start this process from pretty much any machine running Windows 2000 Server. But before you do, consider four caveats: memory, DNS, NTFS, and disks. Let's take a minute and consider those.

HARDWARE: MEMORY, DISKS, AND NTFS

The memory part is easy. As far as I can see, any Windows 2000 domain controller uses *at least* 136MB of memory. You don't *need* to have 136MB of actual RAM in a machine before using it as a Windows 2000 domain controller, but if you *don't* have at least that much, be prepared for nearly constant disk activity as Windows 2000 pages pieces of itself on and off disk. It's a matter of taste, but I found all of that disk chattering extremely annoying and so I originally upgraded my machines to 256MB of RAM—thank heavens memory's finally dropped in price—and I'm now in the process of upgrading them to 512 MB. You'll hear a lot of people talking about how you need giga-hertz-plus systems to run XP or 2000, but in my experience it's RAM that's important. (And don't forget to use ECC RAM!)

Next, you'll get better performance out of your Active Directory servers if you can put two sepa-rate physical SCSI hard disks in your system—and yes, they *must* be SCSI for best performance, because you'll get that good performance if both hard disks can run simultaneously, and Win-dows 2000 only supports simultaneous access on SCSI drives, not EIDE.

The third consideration is relatively easy. Active Directory servers *need* an NTFS partition, so before trying to make a server a domain controller, be sure that it's got at least one NTFS partition.

DNS: AD'S FOUNDATION

The final, and most important, caveat is about DNS. The Active Directory stores its list of domain controllers and global catalog servers in DNS, as you've already read, and it uses dynamic DNS to do it. Recall that a computer registers itself with the dynamic DNS zone by first requesting the SOA record for that zone and then reading the SOA record to determine the name of the primary DNS server for that zone. Then the computer contacts the primary DNS server and registers itself. That means that for you to even *think* about setting up a domain called bigfirm.biz your would-be new domain controller must do the following:

◆ Ask its preferred DNS server to get the SOA record for bigfirm.biz. Thus, before you try to convert a Windows 2000 system to an Active Directory domain controller, then you should really reexamine the DNS server or servers that this system will use to make DNS requests. You're almost certainly doing split-brain DNS of some kind, so double-check that when your soon-to-be domain controller asks DNS for the name of the primary DNS server for bigfirm.biz that it gets the right answer.

◆ Your soon-to-be DC will then try to send dynamic updates to the DNS server pointed to by that SOA record. That DNS server had better be willing to accept those updates, or you are not going to be able to make this computer a domain controller.

As I've said, my example will create an AD domain called bigfirm.biz. That's a domain that I've registered, and I run a zone by that name *that is not dynamic*. I registered the domain and set up a simple nondynamic zone on it for some specific reasons. First, I didn't want to use a domain example that someone was using, as I was concerned that they might not like having lots of people trying to register with their no-doubt-nondynamic DNS server. Second, I wanted to *ensure* that the primary DNS server associated with bigfirm.biz wasn't dynamic so as to be 100-percent sure that you'd have to master split-brain DNS before you could get the AD to work.

If you followed my instructions in the previous chapter, then you have a system running with IP address 192.168.0.2 (or perhaps .1) called BIGDOG running a DNS server that contains a local zone for bigfirm.biz. That machine points to itself for a preferred DNS server, and so when it asks, "Who's the primary DNS server for bigfirm.biz?" then the answer will be, "You are." If you've fol-lowed previous chapter's instructions, then you also have that zone set up to be dynamic, and so we'll be able to make this an Active Directory domain controller.

As a matter of fact, inasmuch as you've set up split-brain DNS, you *could* call your AD anything. You could create a microsoft.com AD. But if you *did*, then recall that your DNS server would never be able to find the *real* microsoft.com!

Before going any further, you might want to just take a moment to find out which DNS server your computer will try to send the updates to. Do it with NSLOOKUP, which you start from a command line:

```
E:\>nslookup
Default Server:  bigdog.bigfirm.biz
Address:  192.168.0.2

> set type=soa
> bigfirm.biz
Server:  bigdog.bigfirm.biz
Address:  192.168.0.2

bigfirm.biz
        primary name server = bigdog.bigfirm.biz
        responsible mail addr = admin.bigfirm.pri
        serial  = 48
        refresh = 900 (15 mins)
        retry   = 600 (10 mins)
        expire  = 86400 (1 day)
        default TTL = 3600 (1 hour)
bigdog.bigfirm.biz      internet address = 192.168.0.2
>exit
```

As you saw in the previous chapter, NSLOOKUP starts out by telling you which server it's getting its answers from and, as I want BIGDOG to point to the DNS service on itself, then the results are encouraging initially. Then I type **set type=soa** because I want to retrieve the SOA record. Then I enter **bigfirm.biz** and NSLOOKUP retrieves and displays the info in the SOA record, which includes the *primary name server*. That is the machine at 192.168.0.2, so I'm in business.

Of course, you may have modified your AD setup and, if so, then use NSLOOKUP to ensure that your computer returns the results that you wanted. For example, if you've decided to call your AD mydomain.com, then you'd be asking NSLOOKUP for SOA information on mydomain.com. Also, recall that I'm setting things up so that the primary DNS server and the DC for bigfirm.biz are the same systems; there's no particular reason why you'd have to do that, unless you wanted to create an Active Directory–integrated zone (remember that AD-integrated zones are great, but they only allow you to put DNS on domain controllers). If you've got enough machines, then go ahead and set up this DC on a machine at 192.168.0.10 or something. Just make sure that the system's preferred DNS server points at whatever machine is the primary for bigfirm.biz or at a DNS server that acts as a secondary for bigfirm.biz. For example, if you've got three machines and wanted to build an example that mimicked big networks more closely, then you might do this:

◆ On a computer running Windows 2000 Server at IP address 192.168.0.2, set up DNS and create the primary zone for bigfirm.biz, as we've already done. Call the system BIGDOG.

◆ On a computer running Windows 2000 Server at IP address 192.168.0.6, set up DNS and make it a secondary DNS server for bigfirm.biz. It's kind of like what we did in the previous chapter with the machine named ns1.ecoast.bigfirm.biz, but without the delegated subzone. Call the system ns2.bigfirm.biz.

◆ On yet another computer running Windows 2000 Server, give it IP address 192.168.0.20 (these are all arbitrary addresses that I'm using, of course). Don't put DNS on it. But set its "preferred DNS server" to the address of either DNS server.

You needn't build your example with this much complexity, of course; I just didn't want you to get the idea that in the real world there's only one DNS server in an enterprise, or that every DC must be built on the same machine as the primary DNS server for a zone.

Of course, none of this is a problem if all you're going to do is just read the text and follow along with the screen shots.

RUNNING DCPROMO

To convert a Windows 2000 server to a domain controller—it must be a server, you can't make a Professional machine a DC—click Start/Run and then type in **dcpromo**. That starts the Active Directory Installation Wizard, as you see in Figure 8.10.

FIGURE 8.10

Starting
DCPROMO

You use this not only to convert member servers into domain controllers, but the reverse as well, to "demote" a domain controller to a member server. The wizard asks a series of questions and then, based on the answers to those questions, sets up a new tree, forest, or domain or creates a replica domain controller in an existing domain. Click Next and you'll see a screen like Figure 8.11.

The way that you create a new domain is simple: Set up a machine as the first domain controller for that domain. Building a domain's first domain controller and creating a new domain are exactly the same thing. But you wouldn't have just one domain controller for most domains. For one thing, each site within a multisite domain will usually have at least one DC, to enable logons. Another reason you'd have multiple DCs on a single domain—whether single- or multiple-site—is to handle many logon requests. As you know, login requests don't space themselves out nicely throughout the day. Instead, most login requests happen all around the same time, first thing in the morning. The more DCs, the more logons your domain can handle. The second, third, fourth, and further domain controllers in a domain were called *backup* domain controllers under NT prior to Windows 2000, but Windows 2000 doesn't give them any special name because they're all supposed to be equal. As you'll see in the later discussion on FSMOs, however, that's not true.

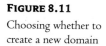

FIGURE 8.11

Choosing whether to create a new domain

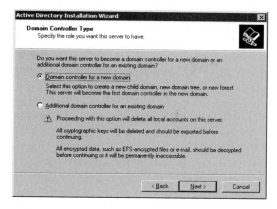

TIP   *So would it be a good idea to make all of your Windows 2000 servers into domain controllers, to speed logons? No. Making a server a DC takes up memory and CPU power. Additionally, too many DCs means extra LAN chatter as they keep each other updated on changes to the Active Directory. The warning at the bottom of the screen is trying to say that non-DCs have a SAM with local accounts, and DCs instead have an* `NTDS.DIT`*.* `DCPROMO` *deletes a computer's SAM contents when the computer becomes a DC. There's a kind of optimal number of DCs that you should have in a network and that number varies from network to network. Personally I monitor the* `lsass.exe` *process to get a feel for when to add a DC.*

The first question that DCPROMO asks, then, is whether to create a whole new domain or just another DC in an existing domain. We're creating a new domain, so I select that and click Next. That leads to the screen in Figure 8.12.

FIGURE 8.12

Choosing to create an altogether new tree or a child domain in an existing tree

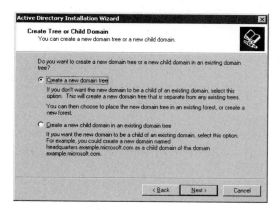

This is the first domain in a new tree, so I choose that and click Next. The screen then looks like Figure 8.13.

FIGURE 8.13

Choose a new forest or an existing forest.

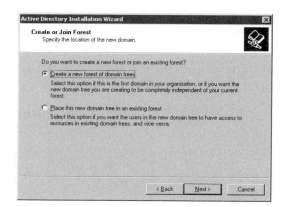

Recall that Windows 2000 lets you build domains into trees and trees into forests, so logically the Active Directory Installation Wizard must know where to put this new tree—in an altogether new forest or in an existing forest? Again, this is a new forest, and I select that and choose Next, leading to a screen like Figure 8.14.

FIGURE 8.14

Full name of the new domain

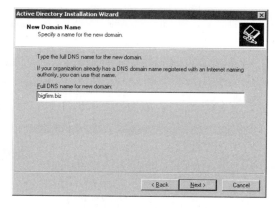

Sometimes these wizards are a bit chatty; here's an example. Just type in the name of the new domain, which in this case is bigfirm.biz. Clicking Next leads to the screen in Figure 8.15.

Unless your network is 100-percent Windows 2000, both servers and workstations, then your network contains machines running network software written in the NT 3.*x* and 4.*x* days, when domain names could be no more than 15 characters long and could not have a hierarchy of any kind. Those older systems—and you know, I tend to want to call them *legacy* systems, as that's been the *chic* term for old software for about 10 years now, but it seems that the current Microsoft term is *down-level* systems—wouldn't understand a domain named bigfirm.biz, and so they need a more familiar name. For that reason, Windows 2000 domains have two names—their DNS-like name (for example, bigfirm.biz) and an old-style domain name (which can be anything that you want, but bigfirm seems like a good choice; but whatever you do, *do not* include periods in downlevel domain names—it'll give you headaches later). As network names under NT 3.*x* and 4.*x* were chosen to accommodate an old network programming interface called NetBIOS, this old-style domain name is also called a *NetBIOS name*. The wizard will by default offer the text to the left of the leftmost period, so it here offers the NetBIOS name BIGFIRM, which is fine. I click Next and the screen in Figure 8.16 appears.

FIGURE 8.15

Legacy domain name

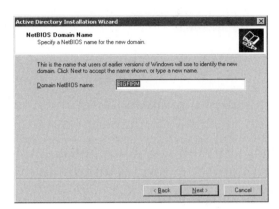

FIGURE 8.16

Placing system files

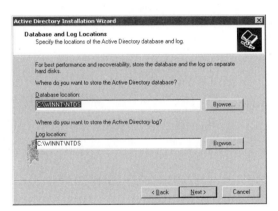

Windows 2000 stores the Active Directory database in two parts, as is often the case for databases—the database itself and a transaction log. Two things to bear in mind here are that the actual Active Directory database file should be on an NTFS volume for better performance and that it's a good idea to put the transaction log in a different physical hard disk than the Active Directory database. (You see them on the same drive in the screen shot because the machine I was doing this on had only one physical hard disk.) Putting the transaction log in a different physical drive means that the system can update both the AD database and the log simultaneously, and believe me, in a production environment, you'll see a significant difference in performance by using a two-drive system rather than a one-drive system. But, as I mentioned earlier, that'll only work if the two drives are *SCSI* drives—the 2000 driver for EIDE isn't smart enough to run two EIDE drives simultaneously. But we're not finished with drives yet; click Next and you'll see why, in Figure 8.17.

FIGURE 8.17

Placing the
SYSVOL volume

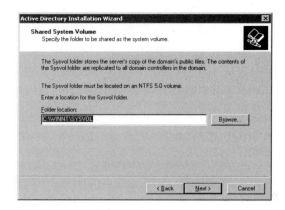

Remember the caution earlier on that you need at least one NTFS drive on an Active Directory server? This is where you'll use it. Anyone who's ever set up an NT 4 domain controller will soon realize how cool this is. You see, NT 4 stored a lot of important user configuration and control information in a directory named NETLOGON on the primary domain controller—system policy files, default profiles, and login scripts. But *backup* domain controllers needed the NETLOGON information as well, so network administrators had to somehow ensure that all of the files from the PDC's NETLOGON would somehow get copied to the BDC's NETLOGONs. With Windows 2000, however, that's not a problem: All of that data goes into a directory called the Sysvol directory, which is *automatically* replicated to other domain controllers. It's an excellent labor saver and a hidden "plus" for Windows 2000! I click Next, and it's time to start worrying about DNS.

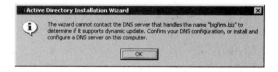

Here, DCPROMO has tried to find and contact the DNS server for bigfirm.biz. (See, I *told* you that DNS was important!) Some trouble occurred along the way, leading to this warning message. This message means one of two things:

♦ **DCPROMO didn't get a response from any of the DNS servers for bigfirm.biz.** In the particular case of bigfirm.biz, I registered it with Network Solutions, as I mentioned earlier. (Reread Chapter 7 if you're still fuzzy on how DNS hierarchies work.) To register a domain with Network Solutions, you must tell them the IP addresses of two machines that will serve as DNS servers for the domain. I told them that the primary DNS server would be on this *particular* machine, and as I'm still in the process of setting it up, there's not a DNS server running—hence this error message.

♦ **DCPROMO *got* a response from the DNS servers for bigfirm.biz but found that they didn't accept dynamic updates.** Suppose I'd already set up a machine as the DNS server, but the machine was an NT 4 server. The DNS service that shipped with NT 4 didn't include support for RFC 2136, probably because NT 4 shipped before RFC 2136 was released. RFC 2136 supports the idea of dynamic updates, which are very important to the way that Windows 2000 maintains information about domains and other Windows 2000 services. I tend to get this error a lot because when I set up my DNS zones beforehand, I sometimes forget to make the zones accept dynamic updates.

If you get this error message then it means you don't have DNS set up right. I strongly recommend you cancel DCPROMO and fix DNS before going any further. If you don't, however, and if you click OK, then the screen shown in Figure 8.18 appears.

FIGURE 8.18

Permission to set up a DNS server

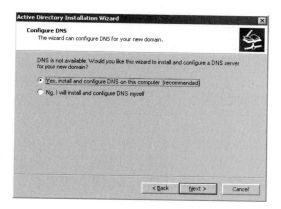

If Windows 2000 stumbles in its attempt to find a DNS server for your new domain, it'll offer to automatically set up DNS for the domain. (If, on the other hand, it *finds* the DNS server but the DNS server can't take dynamic updates, *then* you'll get a different error message to the effect that DCPROMO can't go on.) I recommend against this, but if you do it then be aware that you now have a primary DNS server for bigfirm.biz—make sure that other DNS servers pull the bigfirm.biz zones from it and that all other systems in your network look to either this machine or one of the secondary DNS servers as their preferred and alternate DNS servers.

TIP *If you're still having trouble with DNS, then take a look at the upcoming section "AD-Related DNS Design and Troubleshooting."*

Click Next and one more warning appears, as you see in Figure 8.19.

This message only appeared starting in later betas of Windows 2000. Apparently, as the message indicates, in order to allow NT 4 RAS servers to authenticate dial-in users, Windows 2000 has to loosen up its security structure a bit—not a very appetizing prospect given the raft of security problems that have plagued its NT 4 predecessor. Make this judgment call yourself, but it looks like it might be a good idea to think about upgrading your NT 4 RAS servers if possible. Click Next, and you'll get a screen like Figure 8.20.

One of Windows 2000's at-boot-time options is to rebuild a damaged Active Directory database to restore it to an earlier version that is internally consistent, but which has probably lost a lot of information. You don't want just anyone doing that—a malicious individual telling Windows 2000 to rebuild its database is basically telling it to *destroy* its database—so Windows 2000 asks for a password that it'll use to challenge anyone trying to rebuild the AD database. Fill that in and click Next, and you'll see the screen in Figure 8.21.

FIGURE 8.19

Choose whether NT 4 RAS servers will be in the network.

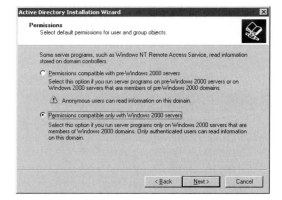

FIGURE 8.20

Directory Services repair password

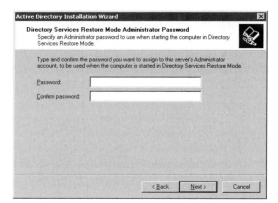

FIGURE 8.21

Confirming your choices

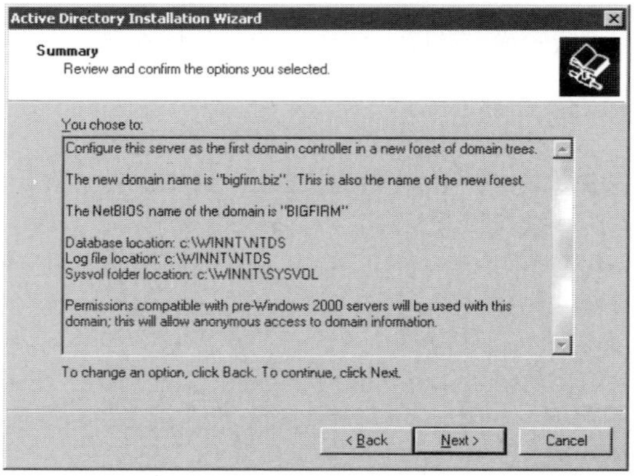

Read this last screen carefully, and if you did anything you didn't like, back up and make the changes before clicking Finish! The reason is simple: Once the Active Directory setup process starts, you'll see a screen like Figure 8.22.

FIGURE 8.22

Starting up the AD creation process

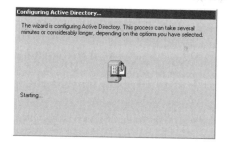

You'll be seeing *that* screen for a goodly time, at least 20–30 minutes in my experience. You can speed that up a bit with two SCSI hard disks, as mentioned before, but it takes a while. The reason to be double-sure before clicking Finish is that, if you realize after the AD creation process is underway that you want to go back and redo something, then you have to *first* sit through the entire AD creation process, *then* you get to reboot the server—never a quick process with Windows 2000—and *then* you get to run the Active Directory Installation Wizard again to break down the domain, *then* you get to reboot again, and finally you run the Active Directory Installation Wizard a *third* time, getting all the settings right this time, and of course, once that's done, it's another 20–30 minutes waiting and a reboot. Total elapsed time between "Oops, I clicked Finish and didn't mean it" and "Ah, now it's finally fixed" can be on the order of an hour and a half—plenty of time to kick yourself. Anyway, once the directory's ready, the wizard ends with a screen like the one in Figure 8.23.

FIGURE 8.23

Final DCPROMO report

Once it's done, you'll have to reboot this new domain controller.

SHIFTING MY DOMAIN TO NATIVE MODE

Windows 2000 domains have two possible modes, Mixed and Native. When first created, domains are in Mixed mode, which means they can accept NT 4 domain controllers as one of their own. That's theoretically terrific, but in actuality you'll find that much of Windows 2000 doesn't work until you move your domain from Mixed mode to Native mode. You'll do that with just a few steps.

Once the new domain controller has rebooted, you log in as Administrator with whatever password you assigned to that account. Click Start/Programs/Administrative Tools and choose Active Directory Domains and Trusts. You'll see an icon labeled with the name of your new domain; right-click it and choose Properties and you'll see a button labeled Change Mode, just like the screen that you saw back in Figure 8.6. Click the button and accept the confirmation. Surprisingly, no reboots necessary.

Creating a Second Domain

Now let's create a child domain for bigfirm.biz, div.bigfirm.biz. But, as before, we'll need to do a little prep work.

CREATING A FORESTWIDE ADMINISTRATOR

Before creating div.bigfirm.biz, I'll need to create an administrative account that will be recognized as an administrator throughout this domain forest that I'm creating. Creating user accounts is covered later in Chapter 9, but here's a quick cheat sheet on creating a forestwide admin.

Once that first domain controller for bigfirm.biz is up and running, I log in as its local administrator as that's the only extant account at the moment. Because bigfirm.biz was the first domain created in the tree, it's a little bit special and, you may recall, is called the *forest root*—special because any other trees or domains that you create after this first domain sit below that first domain.

Running Active Directory Users and Computers

Anyway, once logged into the bigfirm.biz domain controller, I click Start/Programs/Administrative Tools. The first time you do this, you'll notice that you've got three new tools: Active Directory Sites and Services, Active Directory Domains and Trusts, and Active Directory Users and Computers. As you can guess, you create user accounts with Active Directory Users and Computers, the DSA. This application is also the tool you use to modify user accounts. When started, its first screen looks like Figure 8.24.

FIGURE 8.24

Opening DSA screen

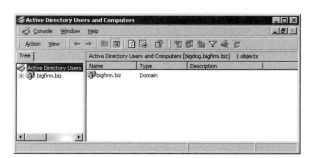

This is showing you the current domain, bigfirm.biz. Click the plus sign to open that branch and you see a screen like Figure 8.25.

FIGURE 8.25

Default domain contents

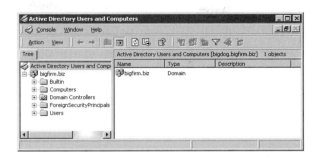

Now you see five things that look like folders—`Builtin`, `Computers`, `Domain Controllers`, `ForeignSecurityPrincipals`, and `Users`. Although it'll be no surprise when I tell you that the folder labeled `Users` contains user accounts, I want to stress that it's not necessary to use that folder—the folder is just created to provide a default place to keep user accounts. If for some reason you wanted to create all new user accounts in the folder labeled `Computers`, nothing would stop you and you could make everything work just fine. If you knew at this point that your domain would be subdivided into an OU called Hatfields and another called Mccoys, then you could create those OUs right now and create each new user account in either the Hatfields OU or the Mccoys OU.

Creating a New User Account

I'm going to be unoriginal here, however, and just create a user account in the `Users` folder. To do that, I just right-click the `Users` folder. The context menu will offer a submenu labeled New, and one of the options will be User; I choose that and get a screen like Figure 8.26.

FIGURE 8.26

Creating the new user account

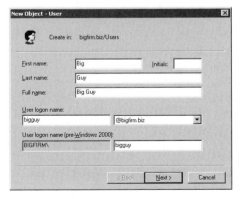

Much of this is self-explanatory, but let's go through this screen. First you fill in a first and last name as well as a full name. These three characteristics are largely just labels of very little use save for displays and searching. The fifth field, User Logon Name, is the "magic" name, the one that this user will use to log in. Note that you can add an @ suffix to the name and a domain name, giving you a logon name that looks like an e-mail name. Now, there's some complexity in that name that's not immediately apparent, so let me digress a bit about logon names.

User Principal Names (UPNs) or Logon Names

If you worked with NT 4, then you'll recall that it was possible to have an enterprise built of many different domains that trusted each other, where *trusted* in this context means "allowed each other to share security information and logins." Thus, if I had a user account named Mark that was built in a domain named ORION but wanted to log in to a machine that was a member of a different domain named AQUILA, then the AQUILA machine would in general refuse to log me in unless the AQUILA domain *trusted* the ORION domain. I'd then log in to the machine from AQUILA by telling it three things: my username, password, and domain. If I'd merely tried to log in as Mark from AQUILA, the login would have been refused, as no AQUILA domain controller would have a Mark account—only the ORION ones would. By saying that I was "Mark from ORION," I told the AQUILA machine how to find a domain controller that could vouch for me—I was telling it, "Go find one of the ORION domain controllers, they can verify that I'm me."

In a multidomain Windows 2000 world, you can still do that. If I already had div.bigfirm.biz built and I wanted to log in to a div.bigfirm.biz machine with a Mark account from bigfirm.biz rather than div.bigfirm.biz—two different domains, recall—then I could sit down at a div.bigfirm.biz machine and, as before, say "I'm Mark from bigfirm.biz," by typing **mark** into the username field, selecting Bigfirm in the Domain drop-down list, and filling in my password. The div.bigfirm.biz machine would then know to go find a bigfirm.biz domain controller to verify my login. But Windows 2000 offers *another* way to identify myself at login as well—I can use a user principal name (UPN), a term for a name looking like name@domainname. (Personally, I'd just call it a universal login name or the like, but who knows, maybe Microsoft liked UPN as an acronym better than ULN.) Sit down at a Windows 2000 Pro or XP Pro desktop and type a name followed by an **@**, and you'll see the Domain field gray out.

Getting back to this account that we're creating, you see that by default Windows 2000 suggests that BigGuy's UPN should be bigguy@bigfirm.biz. Presuming that I agree and create his account with that UPN, he can then sit down at any machine in the forest and log in with just bigguy@bigfirm.biz, and a password, without having to fill in a domain name.

UPN Suffixes and the Global Catalog

At this point, you may be thinking, "Big deal—how does that save any typing?" Whether you type in that you're someone@somedomain and a password, or whether you alternatively type in that you're "someone" from "somedomain" with a given password, what's the difference? What's the big deal?

Well, now, *that's* the interesting part.

You see, you can basically specify any domain name that you like after the name. If I wanted to, I could give BigGuy's UPN the suffix @microsoft.com, even though I clearly don't own the microsoft.com domain name. The latter part of a user's UPN need not have *anything to do with the user's domain*. You could have domains acme.com, apex.com, and greatstuff.com, with user accounts scattered throughout the three domains, but could then give everyone UPNs like somename@acme.com. You can see the specifics on how to add more possible UPN suffixes to your AD in the "How Do I Add a UPN Suffix?" sidebar.

How Do I Add a UPN Suffix?

In the example about UPN suffixes and the global catalog, I suggested that I could give myself a UPN of mark@microsoft.com. But a bit of clicking around the DSA doesn't yield any obvious ways to give myself the microsoft.com suffix. How do I get the DSA to let me use another suffix? Follow these steps:

1. Click Start/Programs/Administrative Tools/Active Directory Domains and Trusts.

2. In the left pane, there's a list of the domains in your enterprise. Above that list is a line Active Directory Domains and Trusts; right-click that and choose Properties. You'll see a dialog box like the one shown here.

3. Fill in the suffix that you'd like, such as microsoft.com or whatever. Click Add.

4. Click OK.

5. Close Active Directory Domains and Trusts.

So What's the Point of Using E-Mail–Like Logon Names?

This raises two questions. First, why would you do this, and second, how does it work? The answer to the first question is that obviously Microsoft intended the name to be your e-mail name, such as joe.blow@acme.com.

At this point, I must confess that I figured Microsoft did this merely to give me yet another reason to buy Exchange. But I wronged them. Here, instead, was Microsoft's reasoning.

In large corporations, you might have hundreds of domains, and those domains don't have nice names such as THIRDFLOOR or MARKETING; instead, they're the CORP0123X domain. So when teaching a user how to log on, techies had to tell the user, "You are johnax12 from domain CORP0123X with password YiKeSiWiLlNeVeRrEmEmBeRtHiS72." Folks had trouble remembering all of that. So Microsoft wanted to simplify it. It wanted to give every user a unique name. So Microsoft asked: Do users currently have a name that is relatively unique? And the answer was yes, their e-mail name. So if johax12 has the email name johnax@acme.com, or perhaps j9391@aol.com, then we can let him use that as his logon name. And note that I offered an AOL e-mail name. There's no reason why you can't give a user an e-mail name from another domain because it's *not really an e-mail name*. The system never *uses* it as an e-mail name.

Basically, Microsoft let us have users log onto forests using names that *look* like e-mail names for one and only one reason: It makes user training easier.

That leads to the second question: How do we make this work? Sure, it's lovely that I can log on to my very complex corporate network as mark@microsoft.com, but how does my workstation find out that my *real* logon name is mmina in a domain named acme.com? By adding a new step to logons. I log in as mark@microsoft.com, and then my workstation has to say to itself, "Well, mark...*if* that's your real name! Let's find out who you *really* are" and then proceeds to "crack" my logon name. But how does it do that? With the help of an Active Directory service mentioned a few times before in this chapter called the *global catalog* (GC). The GC service runs on one or more domain controllers, and among other things, it keeps an index relating people's UPNs—their logon names—to the names of their actual domains. Thus, if I created an account for myself with UPN mark@microsoft.com and tried to log in to a bigfirm.biz machine, that machine would quickly pop over to a local GC server (which, by the way, the machine finds by looking it up in DNS—that's one of the many examples of Active Directory services that systems use DNS to find) and ask the GC server, "Where does mark@microsoft.com *really* live?" The GC server would reply, "In bigfirm.biz," and so my workstation would then contact a domain controller in bigfirm.biz (finding a DC for bigfirm.biz in DNS) and log me in. So the GC is a pretty positive thing, as it speeds up logons. But it *does* have one disadvantage: It can keep you from being able to log in.

WARNING   *If your workstation cannot find a global catalog server in a multidomain Active Directory forest, then you cannot log in. So it's a good idea to have more than one around. (As far as my experiments show, you don't need a GC to log in to a single-domain forest.)*

TIP   *You can, however, tell your workstations to accept logons even when they can't find a GC with a Registry entry, according to Microsoft Knowledge Base article Q241789. Just create an entry in* HKEY_LOCAL_MACHINE\System\ CurrentControlSet\Control\Lsa *called IgnoreGCFailures of type REG_DWORD and set it to 1. It's not a really good idea, however, as it means that your workstation will skip a security step while logging you on—it bypasses checking your universal group membership. That's important because you may be a member of a universal group that has been denied access to the workstation, and normally that'd be a reason to deny you the logon. But I mention it for those cases when a successful logon that ignores a universal group denial is more important than denying a logon because a workstation can't find a global catalog.*

I guess it's worth digressing for a moment, then, and explaining how to create more global catalog servers. Only domain controllers can be global catalog servers. You can make any DC a GC by opening a tool called Active Directory Sites and Services (it's in Administrative Tools). In the left pane, you'll see an icon—or icons—representing different geographic sites on your network. (If you've only created a basic AD and haven't done any work on sites yet, then AD will have automatically created one site called Default-first-site.) Open the sites and you'll find folders labeled Servers. Open them and you'll see icons representing every domain controller. Open any domain controller's icon and you'll see a folder named NTDS Settings, as you see in Figure 8.27.

FIGURE 8.27

Active Directory
Sites and Services

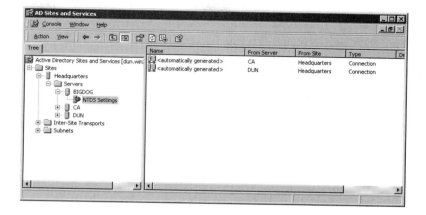

NOTE *By the way, note the reference in this and some other future screen shots to a win2ktest.com domain; that's a different domain from bigfirm.biz, of course—I needed a test domain with four DCs and gave it that name. This would all work the same on bigfirm if you were to build a bunch of DCs for it as well.*

Right-click that folder and choose Properties, and you'll see a properties page like the one in Figure 8.28.

To make a DC act as a GC, just check the box labeled Global Catalog, click OK, and then close AD Sites and Services. As a rule of thumb, you'd like to see two GCs on every site. And if you're a one-domain enterprise, then you should, at least according to a Microsoft AD expert, make every *one* of your DCs into global catalog servers.

FIGURE 8.28

NTDS folder
settings

Finishing Up the User Account

Anyway, back to creating bigguy, notice that Windows 2000 simultaneously creates a downlevel username. This is the name that bigguy would be recognized as if he tried to log in to an NT 4 or earlier server. Simply sticking with bigguy for a downlevel name seems fine, so I click Next and the screen changes to Figure 8.29.

FIGURE 8.29

Setting a password

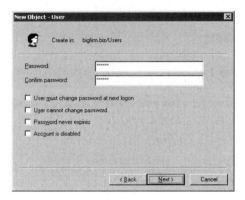

A straightforward screen; click Next and I'm asked to confirm the account information and click Finish. Opening the Users folder, I can see that bigguy is now created, as you see in Figure 8.30.

FIGURE 8.30

Contents of the Users folder after creating bigguy

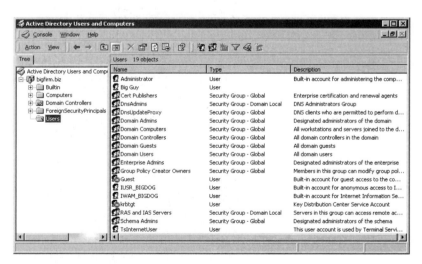

Notice the groups that Windows 2000 automatically creates when you build a domain controller. The one we're interested in is the group named Enterprise Admins; as you read earlier, anyone in that group is recognized as an administrator all around the forest. Adding bigguy to that group is simple.

First, I open the Enterprise Admins group by either double-clicking it or by right-clicking it and choosing Properties, and I see something like Figure 8.31.

Clicking the properties page Members tab shows the list of members of Enterprise Admins, as you see in Figure 8.32.

FIGURE 8.31

Enterprise Admins folder properties

FIGURE 8.32

Members of Enterprise Admins

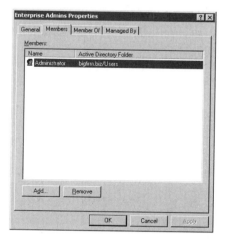

Notice that the local administrator account for the bigfirm.biz domain controller is an Enterprise Admin. Windows 2000 causes that to happen automatically. Recall that bigfirm.biz is the root domain, and there's got to be at least one forestwide administrator. By clicking the Add button, I get a dialog box like Figure 8.33.

I just highlight the bigguy account, click Add and OK, and bigguy's a forestwide administrator.

FIGURE 8.33

Adding bigguy to Enterprise Admins

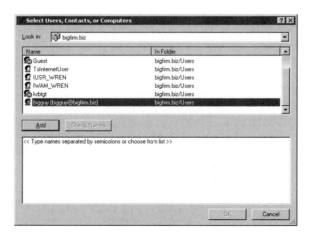

TIP   By the way, even now bigguy isn't a complete Superman in this domain. There is a group that the Enterprise Administrators aren't a part of—the Schema Administrators. This group can, as its name suggests, make changes to the forest's schema, which includes changing what the global catalog stores. By default, the only member of the Schema Administrators group is the default Administrator account on the PDC of the domain that is the forest root (or, for the purists, "the default administrator on the machine that happens to serve in the role as PDC FSMO for the domain that is the forest root"). Also, machines in the domain would not allow bigguy to sit down and administer them—they would not recognize him as an administrator. To fix that, put bigguy in another group, Domain Admins. So to make bigguy truly a Big Guy, add him to Schema Administrators and Domain Admins. Or put Enterprise Administrators inside Schema Administrators.

BUILDING SUBDOMAIN CONTROL WITH AN ORGANIZATIONAL UNIT

You've read earlier that one of Windows 2000's strengths is that it can let you grant partial or complete administrative powers to a group of users, meaning that it would be possible for a one-domain network to subdivide itself into Uptown and Downtown, Marketing and Engineering and Management, or whatever. Let's look at a simple example of how to do that.

Let's suppose that there are five people in Marketing: Adam, Betty, Chip, Debbie, and Elaine. They want to designate one of their own, Elaine, to be able to reset passwords. They need this because "I forgot my password, can you reset it for me?" is probably the number one thing that Marketing calls the central IS support folks for. The central IS folks are happy to have someone local to Marketing take the problem off their hands, freeing them up to fight other fires.

Here's the process:

1. Create an organizational unit called Marketing. (You can call it anything that you like, of course, but Marketing is easier to remember later.)

2. Move Adam's, Betty's, Chip's, Debbie's, and Elaine's already-existing user accounts into the Marketing OU.

3. Create a group called MktPswAdm, which will be the people who can reset passwords for people in the Marketing OU. (Again, you can actually give it any name that you like.)

4. Make Elaine a member of the MktPswAdm group.

5. Delegate password reset control for the Marketing OU to the MktPswAdm group.

If you want to follow this along as an exercise, get ready by creating accounts for Adam, Betty, Chip, Debbie, and Elaine as you did for BigGuy, except don't make them administrators.

Creating a New Organizational Unit

Creating a new OU is simple. Just open up the DSA (recall, the Directory Service Administrator, also labeled Active Directory Users and Computers), right-click the domain's icon in the left pane, and choose New/Organizational Unit. A dialog box will prompt you for a name of the new organizational unit. Fill in **Marketing** and click OK and you're done.

Moving User Accounts into an OU

Next, to move Adam, Betty, Chip, Debbie, and Elaine to the Marketing OU, open the DSA, open your domain (mine's bigfirm.biz, yours might have another name), and then open the Users folder. (If you created the five accounts somewhere other than Users, then look there.)

Choose all five user accounts by clicking Adam, then holding down the Control key and left-clicking the other four accounts. Then right-click one of the five accounts and you'll get a context menu that includes a Move option; select Move and you'll get a dialog box asking you where to move the "object." It'll originally show you your domain name with a plus sign next to it; just click the plus sign and the domain will open to show the OUs in your domain. Choose Marketing and click OK, and all five accounts will move to the Marketing OU. In the DSA, you can open the Marketing OU and you will see that all five accounts are now in that OU.

Creating a MktPswAdm Group

Next, to create a group for the folks who can reset Marketing passwords. Again, work in the DSA. Click Action/New/Group. (You can also right-click the Marketing OU and choose New/Group.) You'll see a dialog box like Figure 8.34.

FIGURE 8.34

Creating a new group

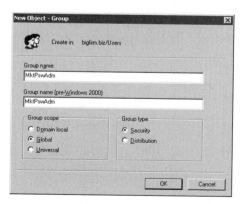

You see that the dialog box gives you the option to create any one of the three types of groups in an Active Directory. A global group will serve our purposes well, although in this particular case—the case of a group in a given domain getting control of an OU in that same domain—then either a domain local, global, or universal group would suffice. I've called the group MktPswAdm. Click OK and it's done.

Next, put Elaine in the MktPswAdm group. Right-click the icon for MtkPswAdm and choose Properties, as you did earlier when creating bigguy. Click the Members tab, then the Add button, then Elaine's account, then Add, then OK, and you'll see that Elaine is now a member of Mkt-PswAdm. Click OK to clear the dialog box.

Delegating the Marketing OU's Password Reset Control to MktPswAdm

Now let's put them together. In the DSA again, locate the Marketing OU and right-click it. Choose Delegation and the first screen of the Delegation of Control Wizard will appear, as you see in Figure 8.35.

FIGURE 8.35

Opening screen of the Delegation of Control Wizard

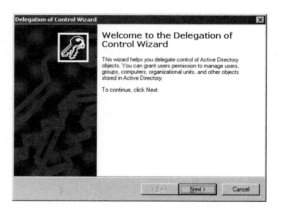

The wizard is a simplified way to delegate, and it'll work fine for our first example. Click Next and you'll see Figure 8.36.

FIGURE 8.36

Before selecting a group

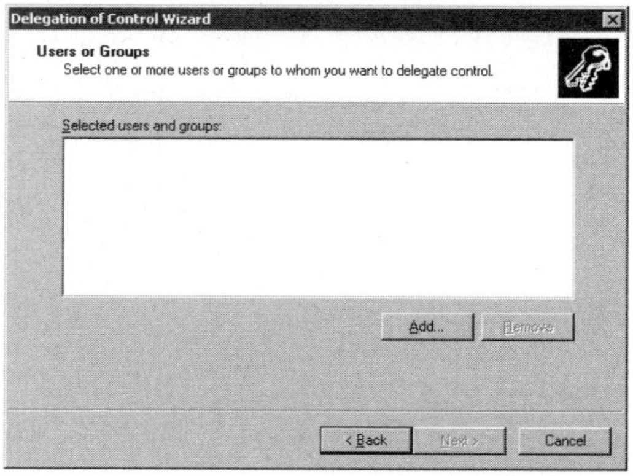

Next, you've got to tell it that you're about to delegate some power to a particular group, so you've got to identify the group. Click Add and choose the MktPswAdm group. Note that when the DSA shows you user accounts in the Add function, it ignores OUs and just lists all accounts and groups in the domain. This is quite handy as it makes finding a particular account much simpler. After choosing MktPswAdm and clicking OK to dismiss the Add dialog box, the screen looks like Figure 8.37.

FIGURE 8.37

MtkPswAdm selected

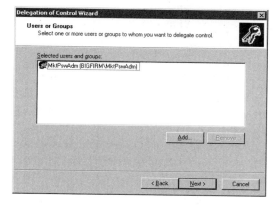

Now click Next, and you'll get a menu of possible things to delegate, as you see in Figure 8.38.

FIGURE 8.38

Options for delegation

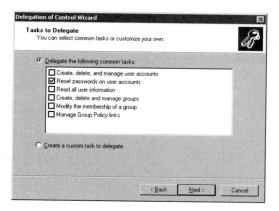

Once we do a bit of exploring here, you'll see that there are many, many functions that can be delegated. Rather than force you to wade through a long list of things that you'll never care about, however, Microsoft picked the top six things that you'd be most likely to want to delegate, one of which is the ability to reset passwords. I've checked that in the figure; press Next and the final screen in the wizard appears, as you see in Figure 8.39.

FIGURE 8.39

Confirming your choices

Click Finish, and it's done.

Remember, delegation lets you designate a set of users who have some kind of control over a set of users and/or computers. You accomplish that by putting the controlling users into a group, the things that you want them to control into an OU, and then delegate control of the OU to the group.

TIP *Or, to put it in a bit more eccentric fashion, think of it this way: The victims go into an OU, the oppressors into a group.*

ADVANCED DELEGATION

Although that's a nice—and useful—example, it only hints at the power of delegation. You actually needn't use the wizard to delegate, it just makes things simpler for a range of common applications. Here's how to more directly manipulate delegation.

First, open up the DSA and click View/Advanced Features. New things will pop up on the screen, as in Figure 8.40.

FIGURE 8.40

DSA with View Advanced Features enabled

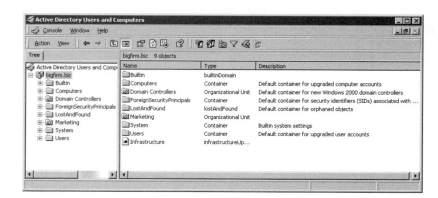

Right-click `Marketing` and choose Properties. You'll get a properties sheet with a tab labeled Security. Click it, and you'll see something like Figure 8.41.

Here, I've scrolled down a bit to see what the dialog box tells us about the MktPswAdm group. It appears that the group can't do anything—until you click the Advanced button, which results in a screen like Figure 8.42.

FIGURE 8.41

Security tab on Marketing OU

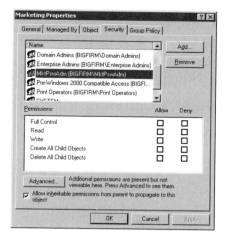

FIGURE 8.42

Advanced security settings for Marketing OU

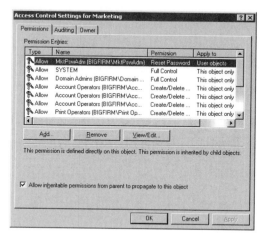

Again scrolling down to highlight MktPswAdm, there's not much said here—Reset Password control of user objects. Reset Password is one specific set of administrative powers, but there are many other specific sets of admin power that you can build to suit your need. To dive further into the delegation structure of an organizational unit and see those specific abilities, click View/Edit, and you'll see something like Figure 8.43.

FIGURE 8.43

Specific MktP-swAdm abilities

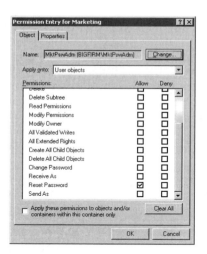

As you can see from the figure, there are a *lot* of powers that you can grant to a particular group in controlling a particular OU!

Where might you make use of this? Well, you gave MktPswAdm the ability to change passwords, but you didn't take it away from the groups who originally had it—the domain admins, enterprise admins, and the like can still reset passwords. That's not a bad idea, but if you really ever *do* come across a "feuding departments" scenario, wherein Marketing wants to be sure that they're the *only* people who can administer accounts, then you'd first delegate the Marketing OU to some group, and then you'd go in with the Security tab and rip out all of the other administrators.

TIP   *And to see a step-by-step example of a more advanced delegation, look back to the end of Chapter 4, where we created a new kind of group called Installers.*

HOW DO I FIND OUT WHAT DELEGATIONS HAVE HAPPENED, OR UNDELEGATE?

Time for some bad news.

Suppose you're not the administrator who set up the Active Directory. Suppose, instead, you're the *second* administrator, the person hired to clean up a mess that some guy—who's now gone—made. You know these kind of administrators, the "mad scientist" variety: the guys who just click on things in the administrative tools until they solve the problem...they think. And *document*? Heck, real administrators don't document. After all, this network was hard to design, it should be hard to understand!

So you're wondering what this guy did. How did he change the company's AD from the default AD that you get when you run DCPROMO? That's a hard question to answer. First, of course, the OUs that he created are obvious—just look in Active Directory Users and Computers and you'll see the new folders. But what delegations did he do?

Sad to say, there is no program you can run that will compare the standard AD structure and delegations to the current AD structure and delegations and spit out a "this is what changed" report. About the best you can do is to right-click all of the containers—the domain itself, Users, Computers, and any OUs—and choose Properties and look in the Security tab. (Don't forget to do View/ Advanced before doing that, or the Security tab won't appear.) So let me offer a really heartfelt piece of advice: Always document delegations. *Always.* Try to control who can do delegations and make clear that delegations are only authorized sparingly.

While I'm here, I should also mention that although the Delegation Wizard is a nice little tool, it's only a *delegation* wizard, not an *un*delegation wizard. If you want to remove MktPswAdm's ability to change Marketing passwords, you've got to go into the Security tab, find the references to Mkt-PswAdm, and rip them out.

CREATING A SECOND DOMAIN

But suppose we're not happy with just one domain; that OU stuff just wasn't enough for the boss. Resigned to politics, I'm ready now to create the second domain, div.bigfirm.biz. Recall that one machine can only be a domain controller in one domain, so I need a second machine to act as DC for div.bigfirm.biz before I can create that domain. As before, I need a machine running some variation of Windows 2000 Server and I start DCPROMO on it.

DCPROMO starts out as before. I tell it that I'm creating a new domain but not a new tree: The new domain will be a child domain to the existing bigfirm.biz domain. But I can't create a child domain under bigfirm.biz without bigfirm.biz's permission—which is where bigguy will become useful. Once I tell DCPROMO that I'm creating a child domain, I get a screen like Figure 8.44.

FIGURE 8.44

Establishing credentials for creating a child domain

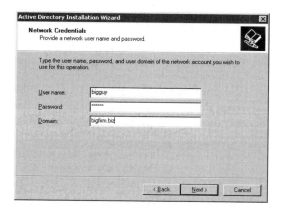

Here, I've filled in bigguy's login information. DCPROMO pauses a bit to authenticate the bigguy account. Once I've filled that in, I click Next and the screen in Figure 8.45 appears.

DCPROMO now needs to know which domain to add a child to and what to call the child. I fill in that the parent's name is bigfirm.biz, or I could have just pressed the Browse button and chosen from the domains in the forest. The child domain will be named div.bigfirm.biz, but DCPROMO just wants you to type in **div** for the child name, and it then assembles it and the parent domain into the complete name div.bigfirm.biz for the child domain.

I then progress through DCPROMO much as with the first domain, so I'll spare you the screens—but notice Figure 8.46.

FIGURE 8.45

Naming the child
domain

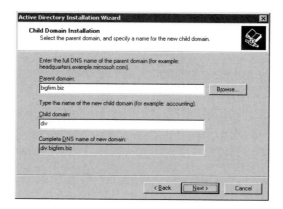

The bigfirm.biz domain got the downlevel name (or NT 4 or NetBIOS name, take your pick, they all mean the same thing) of bigfirm. But how to name the child domains with the more complex names—just take out the periods and take the leftmost 15 characters? Do some kind of truncated name with tildes on the end, in the same way that long filenames get converted to 8.3 names? Well, you can actually give your domains any downlevel name that you like, but the default ones are just the leftmost portion of the domain name, as you see in the figure. As *div* is the leftmost portion of the domain name, the domain gets the downlevel name div by default.

From this point on, I just answer DCPROMO's questions as I did for the first domain, so I'll spare you those screens. Another 20 to 30 minutes of Active Directory setup and the second domain is done.

FIGURE 8.46

Downlevel name for
child domain

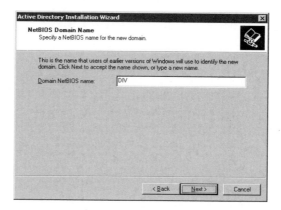

Before leaving here, let me make a few points about using DCPROMO to build domains. First, as you've already read, get DNS ready before starting. Second, DCPROMO's kind of rigid about the order in which you create domains. The first domain that you create in a forest is the forest root domain, and there's no changing that. Third, you've got to add domains by creating them; you can't create a domain green.com and another yellow.com separately and then decide later to merge them into a forest. Instead, you must first create green.com as the first domain in a forest and then create yellow.com as the first domain in a new tree but in an existing forest.

Other Active Directory Objects: Contacts, Shared Folders, and Printers

You might have noticed when you right-clicked the domain in the Active Directory and chose New, there were three other things that you can create:

◆ Contact

◆ Shared Folder

◆ Printer

None of them are quite what they appear to be, so let's take a minute and see what they're good for.

CONTACTS

Well, in the case of Contacts, that last sentence might have been "...see what they're *not* good for." A contact is something that acts very much like a user account...but isn't a user account. It doesn't have a password and cannot log on to the network.

So what good is it?

Open up a real-live user account, and you'll see that it's got bunches of tabs. There are places for information such as street address, e-mail address, manager's name, phone numbers, home page, and other items. You can, therefore, use your Active Directory as a kind of low-octane Human Resources database. This won't be news to Exchange users, as Exchange has kept a database like this for years. So, for example, if you created a bunch of users and took the time to type in all of their managers' names in the Manager fields, then you could do queries such as, "Show me all of the users whose manager is Evelyn Wilson."

If that sounds interesting, then you might want to be able to include information on people who *aren't* users on your network—friends, family, business associates, and so on. Contacts let you do that. Once you create a contact, you'll see that it has fields for that same kind of information as user accounts do: phones, addresses, managers, and the like. From a Windows 2000 system, then, you could click Start/Search/For People and, in the Look In drop-down box, specify the Active Directory. The Search for People dialog box then lets you search by names, e-mail addresses, and the like. Once you find a person, you right-click his record and choose Send Mail and it starts up your mail client, with the e-mail address all filled in. AD, then, becomes a kind of simple contacts database.

The whole notion of first looking up a name in AD and then right-clicking to send that person mail is a bit cumbersome. I think, however, that this wasn't Microsoft's main idea; I believe, instead, that you can make this more useful if you're running Exchange 2000. I don't use Exchange 2000, however, so I can't say. Additionally, as you *can* query the Active Directory with LDAP, you could in theory build or use any of a number of tools to query your AD-based contacts database. I say *in theory* because also in theory you should be able to look up names in Outlook 2000 from an LDAP-compatible server. As I said, I don't use Exchange. But I *do* use Outlook as a mail client, so I've tried telling it to look up people's names in the AD. So I should be able to type into the To field a name in the database, such as Mike Smith and then Outlook should automatically fill in Mike's e-mail address. I've not been able to make that work and the folks that I've asked at Microsoft about it just kind of look bewildered and say, "Well, I guess it *should* work, but we all use Exchange, so I've never tried it...."

The bottom line is that contacts are apparently of quite limited value unless you're running Exchange 2000.

SHARED FOLDERS

You'd think that creating something called a *shared folder* in the Active Directory would, well, *share* a folder. But that's not what happens. Instead, creating a shared folder in the Active Directory just puts a notice in the AD saying, "Someone shared a folder at the following location, and it's got the following stuff in it." This is known as *publishing* a share in the AD.

For example, suppose we create a directory on C:\ on BIGDOG called JUNK and share it as JUNK. (Just create the directory JUNK in C:\, then right-click its folder and choose Sharing.... Click the radio button Share This Folder, and then OK.) Then copy a few files to the folder, so that there's something in there.

Now go to Active Directory Users and Computers and right-click some folder—the domain icon, the Users folder, or whatever—and choose New, then Shared Folder. You'll see a dialog box like the one in Figure 8.47.

FIGURE 8.47

Creating a shared folder in AD

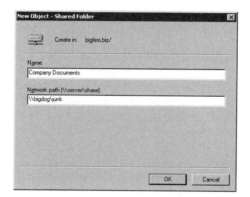

Create a name for it—I've used "Company Documents—and fill in the address of the share as *servername**sharename* and click OK. You'll then see an icon that looks like a hard disk on a network cable in Active Directory Users and Computers. Double-click it and you'll see something like Figure 8.48.

FIGURE 8.48

Modifying the shared folder object's properties

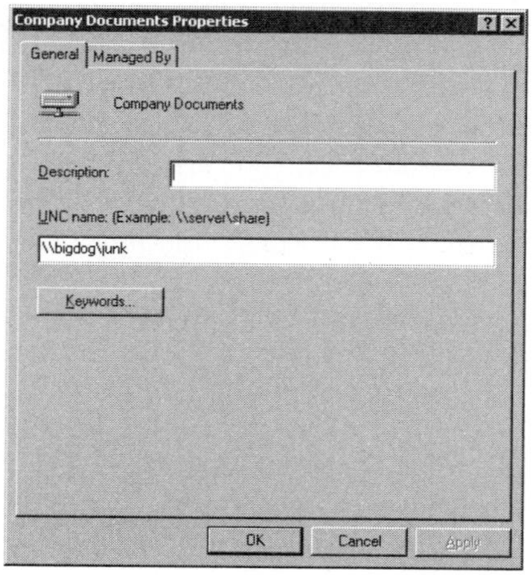

Take a look here and you can see where this would be useful. You can fill in the Description field, or, even better, you can click Keywords and fill in words that describe the share.

Now how's that useful? Just as with the contacts, you can search for shared folders. Open up Active Directory Users and Computers, right-click the domain and choose Find, and you'll see that one of the things that you can search for are shared folders—just type in keywords and you'll get the folders that match those keywords. Click on the folders and they'll take you straight to the shared data.

This has several advantages over the standard Network Neighborhood operation that you're probably familiar with:

Keywords   First, obviously, you can search for the content that you're seeking, rather than wandering around Network Neighborhood hoping that someone has named a share in a meaningful way.

No Broadcasts   All of that data in Network Neighborhood/My Network Places gets there because every single server and, usually, every single workstation broadcasts its presence every 12 minutes. You'd be amazed how much network bandwidth is wasted with those broadcasts. Once you shut them off by disabling NetBIOS over TCP/IP—which you can't do in a practical sense now, but will make sense for many networks by 2005 or so—then you'll get a bunch of bandwidth back, up to 15 percent on some networks.

You Disconnect the Users from the UNCs   To find this company data in a standard non-AD system, I've got to just somehow know that the data is sitting on BIGDOG in a share called Junk. In such a network, you refer to the share by its UNC (Universal Naming Convention), \\bigdog\junk. But what if I moved the data to \\server1\data? Then I'd have to tell everyone to stop looking on BIGDOG and instead look on SERVER1. *But* if everyone is instead searching the Active Directory, or if they know that the folder published in the AD as Company Data is the place to go, then they are completely unaware of the data's UNC. When I move the data from \\bigdog\junk to \\server1\data, then, all I need do is to modify the published item in the Active Directory.

All in all, this notion of publishing shares is a big step forward. It *does* require teaching users to find and exploit shared folders a bit differently, though.

You may have one question: Why do you have to go through the extra step of publishing a share? When you shared \\bigdog\junk in the first place, why wasn't there a little check box on the Sharing dialog box saying something such as, "Publish to the Active Directory?" I have no idea. And do you want to hear something totally bizarre? In the Windows 2000 beta, *the check box was there.*

Even stranger: printers. A *printer* isn't really a printer, it is, like a shared folder, just a published entry in the AD to the effect that there's a printer shared somewhere, complete with descriptive information on it. But here's the odd part: When you share a printer, *it publishes itself.* You need do nothing. Strange, no?

AD-Related DNS Design and Troubleshooting

We covered DNS in the previous chapter, but mostly from the point of view of DNS in a generic setting—the things that you need to make DNS work with or without the Active Directory.

Choosing Your Top-Level Domain

DNS is connected to names and so part of your AD planning involves coming up with an AD name, and of course the first part's easy—if you're Acme or Bigfirm, then that'll be your AD name. But is it bigfirm.biz? Or something like bigfirm.local? What's .local all about?

Well, if you're going to run your own DNS system and don't care if it's visible to the outside Internet, then you needn't use a standard .com, .org, .biz, (and so on) top-level domain. Many folks use .local, as in bigfirm.local. Or there's an Internet standard working its way through the committees that suggests using .pri—for *private*. So if you want to be "with it" name-wise, then go with *something*.pri.

Does it matter what TLD you use? Possibly, but not likely. Here's the scenario that we're concerned about: You call your AD bigfirm.local. Then, a few years down the road, ICANN approves a new TLD, .local. Someone else registers the now-publicly-available bigfirm.local domain and sets up a Web server, mail server, and so on. Someone inside your network tries to access their stuff but can't get to those servers, as the local domain has that name.

In my opinion we won't see a .local TLD anytime soon, so I'm not sure that it matters whether you use .local, .pri, or, as some are doing, .ds for *directory service*.

Building an AD-Friendly DNS Infrastructure

In my example Active Directory, I made life a bit easier for you by starting out with a guaranteed AD-compatible DNS infrastructure, one built atop a dynamic DNS zone running on a Windows 2K or later server. But you may not have the luxury of a network whose DNS options are wide open, and you don't *need* that luxury—AD works well with non-Microsoft DNS servers, and I've built a couple of forests without any Microsoft-based DNS servers at all. In this section, you'll first understand what AD needs of DNS and then you'll see the various ways to make different DNS configurations work with AD.

WHAT AD NEEDS FROM A DNS SERVER

The Active Directory absolutely needs two things of its DNS server:

- Support of underscores in DNS names. Yes, I know I told you not to use underscores in your machine names, but no one told Microsoft apparently—some important subdomains of your AD need underscores in their names. Every DNS server that I know of will tolerate underscores, but not all do by default, so you might have to turn this feature on with yours. Microsoft's DNS servers from NT 4 onward tolerate underscores by default. (I'm not even sure that it's *possible* to make a Microsoft DNS server reject names with underscores.)

- Support of SRV records. Recall that SRV records are a generic way to store information about a server's abilities in DNS. Simplified, SRV records store two pieces of information about a server's abilities—the protocol that it supports and the port that it runs that protocol on. For example, you could in theory use SRV records to ask a domain, "What is your Web server's address?" by making an SRV record request for a server running the HTTP protocol (the Web protocol, as you may know) on port 80 (the most common Web server port). Similarly, Windows 2000, XP, and .NET systems locate Active Directory domain controllers via SRV records, asking the domain's DNS servers, "Do you have any SRV records for a server running the Kerberos protocol on port 88?" They also locate global catalog servers—which, recall, are essential for logons—by requesting SRV records for servers running the LDAP protocol on port 3268. Without those records, machines cannot find a domain controller…and not much happens in AD if you can't find a DC.

Furthermore, AD is light-years easier to run if it supports:

◆ Dynamic DNS. You've already seen that 2K, XP, and .NET Server systems register their host records via dynamic DNS. But AD domain controllers rely upon dynamic DNS for more than that—DCs create subdomains and register SRV records via dynamic DNS. Now, DDNS isn't 100-percent essential, as you could simply punch in all of the SRV records by hand—sounds like fun, doesn't it? —but I strongly recommend that you make your DNS zone dynamic.

YOU DO *NOT* NEED TO USE A MICROSOFT DNS SERVER

I said this before, but I want to stress it. Most people use a Unix or Unix-derivative machine running a program called BIND to act as their DNS server. Windows 2000 can work perfectly well in an environment where a Unix-based BIND server acts as its DNS server, so long as it's a version of BIND that supports SRV records (RFC 2782) and dynamic updates (RFC 2136) and permits machine names with underscores. (I know—I've done it. I successfully created a three-domain AD forest using a single DNS server running BIND on Linux. Worked like a charm.) Or you might be using Lucent's QIP DNS/DHCP replacement, a good alternative to either BIND or Win2K's DNS.

In that case, you need not configure a Windows 2000 system as a DNS server.

WHAT TO DO IF YOUR CURRENT DNS SERVER ISN'T AD FRIENDLY

But, as the song goes, we can't always get what we want. What do you do if you don't have a DNS infrastructure doesn't want to do things Microsoft's way? You do have a few alternatives.

Generally the issue is that DNS admins are concerned about enabling dynamic DNS. They think—rightly—that it creates one more potential security problem. But all's not lost in that case. Let's examine the possibilities.

If Your DNS Supports SRV and Underscores but Not Dynamic DNS

If you can't convince your DNS folks to adopt any of the of the suggestions that follow this one, then let me get the "worst case DNS scenario" out of the way. In this scenario, we'll leave dynamic DNS shut off.

I hope that none of you ever have to *do* this, but it's a chance to highlight an interesting feature of AD that you may find useful for troubleshooting. It's a last-ditch way to stitch together a DNS zone that will make an AD happy.

Let's say that we're working with a modern DNS server that supports SRV records and underscores, but no dynamic updates. How to make it AD friendly? With the help of a file named `netlogon.dns`.

Back when Microsoft was first putting AD together, they talked to a lot of their big customers about what AD would require and some of those customers balked. They had a big BIND infrastructure that, well, *worked*—Unix-based systems often have the interesting characteristic of being complex to get working, but once they're working, you can pretty much leave them alone and they require almost no care and feeding—and so they didn't want to change those servers one whit.

"Not changing them one whit" included dynamic DNS—it has to be admitted that dynamic DNS offers some potential security issues, and so flipping the switch to turn their BIND servers into *dynamic* BIND servers met some opposition. SRV records were no problem; underscores were no problem. But DDNS was a sticking point.

So Microsoft engineered the AD to offer a compromise.

Every DDNS-aware computer writes its own A (host name) records into DDNS by itself. But the AD *really* relies upon all of those SRV records, and *they* are written to the zone files by the Netlogon service. Whenever you reboot a domain controller, or restart its Netlogon service, or if some time has gone by without an update, then the Netlogon service contacts the primary DNS server and registers its SRV records.

But it also does something else: It writes those records to an ASCII text file called `NETLOGON.DNS`, stored in `\WINNT\SYSTEM32\CONFIG`. Try it—go to any AD domain controller and use Notepad to look at `\WINNT\SYSTEM32\CONFIG\NETLOGON.DNS`. It's a bunch of SRV records.

Those companies that are *completely* anti-dynamic DNS, then, *could* set up their DNS to support AD like so without dynamic DNS. Here's how our fictitious bigfirm.biz domain might do it, using an NT 4.0 DNS server – you'd do the same thing with a non-dynamic BIND server:

1. First, set up a bigfirm.biz zone as a primary zone on a DNS server. Call the zone file bigfirm.biz.dns.

2. Enter A records for each domain controller.

3. Go to each AD domain controller and restart its Netlogon service.

4. Copy the \WINNT\SYSTEM32\CONFIG\NETLOGON.DNS file from that DC to a floppy or a file on the network.

5. Once you've got all of the NETLOGON.DNS files, merge them all into one big ASCII file on the primary DNS server for bigfirm.biz.

6. At the bigfirm.biz DNS server, stop the DNS service.

7. In \WINNT\SYSTEM32\DNS, open the file bigfirm.biz.dns with Notepad.

8. Add in the extra lines with the SRV records that you collected when you merged all of the NETLOGON.DNS entries into a single file into bigfirm.biz.dns.

9. Save the bigfirm.biz.dns file.

10. Restart the DNS service (or, if it's a Unix box, the daemon).

That DNS server—and any of its secondaries—can now support an Active Directory. So why wouldn't everyone do this? Well, first of all, it's a lot of work collecting all of those `NETLOGON.DNS` files. And, second, it's not very, well, *dynamic*. If you ever take one of these DCs offline, you'd have to delete its zone records. And every time you put a new one on your network, you'd have to collect and merge *its* SRV records. Not much fun…but definitely possible. If all else fails DNS-wise, you can always do this dynamic-DNS-by-hand approach to DNS.

Using NT 4 DNS Servers in an AD

Can you use NT 4.0 DNS servers for an AD? Sure, with some work. My first guess was that NT 4's DNS didn't do SRV records, as their RFC appeared not terribly long before NT 4's release. And in general I was right. But if you install Service Pack 6a on an NT 4 system a funny thing happens…the DNS server now supports SRV records! So, if you wanted, you could do the hand-built zone file routine that I outlined previously.

Sounds like too much work? It probably is. But there's a completely useful potential function for an NT 4 DNS server in an AD.

Use it as a *secondary* DNS server. Recall that a simple standard DNS setup for a given zone has just one primary DNS server and any number of secondary DNS servers. And recall that the only DNS server that accepts changes to a zone is the primary. The secondaries just accept their zone copies from the primary using a standard zone transfer—in other words, secondary DNS servers really don't ever need to support dynamic DNS.

You could, then, have a single Windows 2000-based DNS server as the primary server in a zone. That would accept all of the dynamic updates from the various servers and workstations and boil them down to a standard DNS zone file. Then it would copy that zone file to the secondaries, which could be running NT 4 with Service Pack 6a. Then, whenever a workstation needed to look up an SRV record so that it could find a global catalog server or a DC, the NT 4 systems could easily answer the request.

Upgrade to DDNS/SRV Compliance or Replace It

If you have DNS servers that don't support underscores and SRV records, then you must change your DNS infrastructure to make the AD work. Either upgrade your existing non-Microsoft DNS servers to newer versions of their software that support DNS or replace them with Windows 2000 or later servers. Heck, those Unix guys are *always* eager to replace their well-known BIND systems on the Sun boxes with Microsoft stuff—they're all closet Microsoft junkies, really! (Joking, joking….)

Create and Delegate Your Domain to an AD Child Domain

If bigfirm.biz had an existing set of DNS servers that do not and never will support SRV, DDNS, and the like, then one answer is to create a child portion of your current DNS names and delegate the control of those names to a Windows 2000 system. For example, if you've already got several hundred Unix, Windows, and NT machines in an Internet domain named bigfirm.biz and the DNS server for bigfirm.biz is an ancient BIND implementation, then you can always tell the old BIND server that there's a new subdomain (a *zone* in DNS-ese) called win2k.bigfirm.biz (which would contain machines with names such as bluebell.win2k.bigfirm.biz, rover.win2k.bigfirm.biz, or metrion.bigfirm .biz) that will have its own name server. Of course, that name server will be one of your new Windows 2000 servers. The Active Directory doesn't insist upon having RFC 2782, 2136, and underscore support for *all* of the company's machines—just the AD DCs.

Delegate the AD-Specific Subdomains

The previous solution is a good one, but it troubles many people, as they want their systems to have names such as *something*.bigfirm.biz instead of *something*.win2k.bigfirm.biz. So they'd like the AD situated at the firm's "top level," so to speak, but they don't want the top-level DNS to be AD friendly. There *is* a work-around in this case. But it's a bit trickier.

Create an Active Directory and look in the DNS zone and you'll see that the AD has created a bunch of folders in your DNS zone, as you see in Figure 8.49.

FIGURE 8.49

DNS subfolder structure in an AD domain

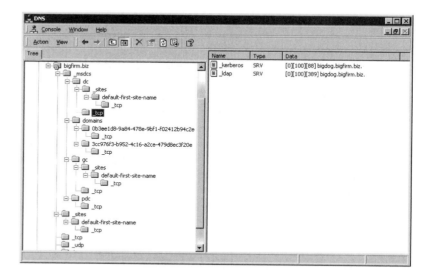

Notice that bigfirm.biz has four folders:

◆ _msdcs

◆ _sites

◆ _tcp

◆ _udp

Thus, just as there's a DNS domain named bigfirm.biz, there are also now subdomains named _msdcs.bigfirm.biz, _sites.bigfirm.biz, _tcp.bigfirm.biz, and _udp.bigfirm.biz; DCPROMO created them. (I'm sure you've noted the underscores in the subdomain names—what *were* those Microsoft folks thinking, anyway?) Those are subdomains just like one named win2k.bigfirm.biz would be. DCPROMO created them as simple folders in the same zone file as bigfirm.biz, but there's no reason why you couldn't have created them as four separate domains, four separate zone files potentially on four different servers.

Recall that the really important DNS records aren't so much the A (host) records for the DCs, it's the SRV records. So if you leave the top bigfirm.biz zone static and just punch in the host records by hand and then create the subdomains by hand *on a DNS server that supports DDNS*, then everyone's happy—the DCs can write their SRV records and the workstations.

So if bigfirm.biz's zone were hosted on a static DNS server, then all you'd have to do would be to first set up a DNS server that supports dynamic DNS (and SRVs and underscores, of course). Then, on the new DNS server, set up the four subdomains. Then go to the static DNS server with the bigfirm.biz zone and delegate the four zones to the new DNS server—just as I showed you how to create the ecoast.bigfirm.biz zone in the previous chapter. Set the four new zones to dynamic. Finally, hand-enter A records for the domain controllers in the static bigfirm.biz zone— and you're done.

Create a Parallel "Split-Brain" Windows-Based DNS for Your Microsoft Systems

You saw in the previous chapter how to do this. If you want to run an AD named bigfirm.biz, then one way to do it is to set up a Windows 2000 server as a dynamic DNS server. Then create a bigfirm .biz zone and make it dynamic. Do *not* register this server as an authoritative server with Network Solutions or whoever the parent domain is—you do *not* want visitors from the public Internet. Then set up the Microsoft boxes so that they all look to this one DNS server as their DNS server. As that server has a zone named bigfirm.biz, then any queries about bigfirm.biz will end up being answered out of that zone. The DNS server will also accept dynamic DNS registrations. You can take it a step further and set up more DNS servers so as to spread out the name resolution load in your intranet, and use DHCP to tell different Microsoft systems to use different DNS servers. But make sure that these DNS servers are secondary DNS servers for the internal bigfirm.biz zone. Forward the DNS servers to a server outside your firewall—actually, *slave* the internal DNS servers for security's sake.

And don't forget to copy any externally visible records for bigfirm.biz, such as www.bigfirm.biz to the internal bigfirm.biz's zone. Again, I've discussed this in greater detail in the previous chapter, so look that over before adopting this approach.

Using DNS to Troubleshoot DCPROMO and Logon Problems

After all that hard work you still might run into a DNS-related AD problem. It might show up in one of three cases:

◆ You're trying to add a second (or third or fourth or *whatever*th) domain controller to an existing domain, or

◆ You're trying to create a new domain in an existing forest, or

◆ You're trying to log on to a domain and you get an error message along the lines of "no domain controller found."

Furthermore, you wouldn't *see* an error message necessarily, but if a member server couldn't find a DC to log it on for more than a week then that member server would probably not find itself a member of the domain any more, as workstations and member servers are expected to change their passwords once a week.

Now, if the problem crops up when you're running DCPROMO on the *first* domain controller on the first domain in the forest, then I've already covered what to do about it—check the SOA record and ensure that your would-be domain controller is contacting the correct DC. But if you see any of these other symptoms, then the probable cause is this: The machine contacted DNS to look up the SRV records for a domain controller and was unsuccessful. But you have a terrific troubleshooting tool at your fingertips—NSLOOKUP.

AD stores the SRV records for domain controllers and global catalog servers under the following names:

◆   Global catalog servers are stored on a site-by-site basis under the name _ldap in domains named _tcp.*sitename*._sites.gc._msdcs.*domainname*, and all of the domain's global catalog servers are stored under the name _ldap in the domain named _tcp.*sitename*.gc._msdcs.*domainname*. In both cases, the SRV records for GCs will use port 3268.

◆   Domain controllers' SRV records are stored also on a site-by-site basis under the name _kerberos in domains named _tcp.*sitename*._sites.dc._msdcs.*domainname*. An all-in-one collection of all domain controllers in all sites is stored under the names _kerberos in a domain named _tcp.dc._msdcs.*domainname*.

So, for example, suppose my workstation lives in a site named default-first-site-name in a domain named bigfirm.biz. To find a domain controller, it would ask DNS if there was an SRV record named _kerberos._tcp.default-first-site-name._sites.dc._msdcs.bigfirm.biz. An NSLOOKUP run would look like this:

```
C:\>nslookup
Default Server:  bigdog.bigfirm.biz
Address:  192.168.0.2

> set type=srv
> _kerberos._tcp.hq._sites.dc._msdcs.bigfirm.biz
Server:  bigdog.bigfirm.biz
Address:  192.168.0.2

_kerberos._tcp.hq._sites.dc._msdcs.bigfirm.biz  SRV service location:
          priority      = 0
          weight        = 100
          port          = 88
          svr hostname  = bigdog.bigfirm.biz
bigdog.bigfirm.biz        internet address = 192.168.0.2
>
```

In this way, you can, from the command line, do exactly what your computer does when looking for a DC on your site. (Remember to substitute the name of your site for hq and the name of your Active Directory domain for bigfirm.biz.) If your system can't find a DC in its site, or if no DCs in the site respond, then it simply asks for the complete list of all DCs in all sites. This is clearly a short list in my simple one-DC network, but the SRV lookup is, again, for _tcp.dc._msdcs.*domainname* or, in my case, bigfirm.biz:

```
> _kerberos._tcp.dc._msdcs.bigfirm.biz
Server:  bigdog.bigfirm.biz
Address:  192.168.0.2

_kerberos._tcp.dc._msdcs.bigfirm.biz     SRV service location:
          priority      = 0
          weight        = 100
```

```
        port            = 88
        svr hostname    = bigdog.bigfirm.biz
bigdog.bigfirm.biz      internet address = 192.168.0.2
>
```

You can do the same searches for global catalogs by just replacing the ".dc." with ".gc." and "_kerberos" with "_ldap"—you can see an example here, where I search for all global catalog servers across all sites:

```
> _ldap._tcp.gc._msdcs.bigfirm.biz
Server:  bigdog.bigfirm.biz
Address:  192.168.0.2


_ldap._tcp.gc._msdcs.bigfirm.biz        SRV service location:
        priority        = 0
        weight          = 100
        port            = 3268
        svr hostname    = bigdog.bigfirm.biz
bigdog.bigfirm.biz      internet address = 192.168.0.2
>
```

Notice the port, 3268; you will see other records returned in some cases that have the _ldap name but that only run on port 389—those are not global catalog servers.

I cannot stress how powerful these NSLOOKUPs are. They are the *key* to troubleshooting logon failures—and, as logon failures make creating new DCs or simply logging on fail, they're pretty useful.

Operations Masters/FSMOs

Let's return now to some concepts, starting with the notion of *operations masters*. But first, a bit of review on a basic concept: *multimaster replication*.

Multimaster versus Single-Master Replication

One of the things that differentiates Windows 2000 DCs from earlier versions of NT's DCs is multimaster replication. Under NT 4 and earlier products, you had one DC called the primary domain controller, which held a copy of the SAM, the file that contained the user accounts. That SAM on the PDC was the only one that you could modify. All other DCs in an NT 4-and-earlier domain were *backup* DCs. They could authenticate people, but not accept changes to their accounts. If, for example, you work out of your firm's Tulsa, Oklahoma, office, which has a BDC, then that local BDC can log you in sometime in the morning without having to communicate with the PDC, which I'll place for the sake of argument in Columbus, Ohio. But if a local Tulsa administrator wants to change your password, then she starts up the NT tool named the User Manager for Domains. It's not obvious, but at that point User Manager for Domains locates and connects with the DC in Columbus over a WAN link. At that point, the administrator can do things like create new accounts or perhaps reset your password, and the DC in Columbus would eventually replicate that new information to the BDC in Tulsa (and other BDCs as well, of course). But if the WAN link is down, then User Manager for Domains will refuse to let her do any account maintenance. Because only one DC holds the "master" or writeable copy of the SAM, this approach to maintaining a database of users is called a *single-master* replication system.

Windows 2000 improves upon that with multimaster replication. Under multimaster, *any* DC can accept changes to the user account, so in the Tulsa example, a local Tulsa admin could start up an administration tool such as User Manager's successor, Active Directory Users and Computers, and make a change to a user's account, even if the link between Tulsa and Columbus was down. As any DC can accept changes, any DC is then a "master," hence the phrase *multimaster*.

WARNING *You only get multimaster replication once your AD domain is in Native mode. Mixed-mode domains use a single-master replication scheme.*

But Not Everything Is Multimaster

In general, the Active Directory tries to carry this notion of decentralized control throughout its structure. In general, all DCs are equal, but, to paraphrase George Orwell, some DCs are more equal than others. Those DCs are the ones that serve in any of five roles called either *operations master* or Flexible Single Master of Operator roles. By the way, no one says *flexible single master of operator*; it gets acronym-ized to FSMO and is pronounced "fizz-moe." Strictly speaking, FSMO was the phrase that Microsoft used through most of Windows 2000's development process, but renamed FSMOs to *operations masters* late in the beta process. As a result, you'll hear some people say *operations master*, but the FSMO name has stuck with many, probably because it's quicker to say "fizz-moe." So, for example, the phrases *domain naming operations master* and *domain naming FSMO* refer to the exact same thing.

Certain jobs in the AD just need to be centralized, and so we end up with FSMOs. For example, take the job of creating new domains. Suppose I've got a domain acme.com and someone decides to set up a new domain controller and thereby create a child domain, hq.acme.com. Creating a domain causes AD to build a lot of data structures—a domain for hq.acme.com, more work for the global catalog, changes to the overall forest AD database, and so on. Now imagine that two people both try to create a new domain named hq.acme.com at roughly the same time. That could be a nightmare—the parent domain would be receiving conflicting requests to modify the AD database, there might be potential security issues, and it might keep the whole forest from functioning.

Domain Naming: A FSMO Example

What's that you say? The chances of trying to create two identical domains "at roughly the same time" is unlikely? Not necessarily. If you have two offices in your enterprise, and you only connect the two offices to synchronize their domain controllers once every few days—and you can do that; AD only *requires* that you sync DCs every 60 days at the maximum—then you could easily have two different people try to create a domain with the same name, in each office, within a span of a few days. We don't want that happening, so AD chooses one DC to act as a sort of central clearinghouse for new domain creation and whenever you run DCPROMO to create a DC in a previously nonexistent domain (and therefore to create a new domain), DCPROMO stops and locates the one DC in the entire forest that is the "keeper of the domain names." That DC is said to be the *domain naming FSMO* or *domain naming operations master*. If DCPROMO on the new would-be DC cannot establish contact with the domain naming FSMO, then it flatly refuses to go any further.

Let me repeat that: If you have a worldwide enterprise with hundreds of offices all around the world, and you're sitting in the Lisbon office trying to create a new domain in your company's AD forest, then the computer that you're using to create that new domain will need to be live-on-the-wire to the one computer in your entire worldwide network that approves new domain names—the domain naming operations master or FSMO.

Why Administrators Must Know about FSMOs

Lest you get the idea that I'm saying that this is a terrible failing on AD's part, understand that I'm *not* saying that. You don't create domains all that often, one hopes, so this isn't much of a hardship, in my opinion. In general, you won't think about the DCs that act as FSMOs in your forest much at all. But you *do* need to do a little planning about which DCs will be FSMOs, and you need to know how to assign a particular FSMO role to a particular DC.

Which reminds me you *do* have to manage the FSMO roles by hand. The AD automatically picks a particular DC to act in each FSMO role—the first DC that you install—but it's not bright enough to move those roles around. So, for example, consider this scenario. Your company decides to play around with AD and sets up its first DC on a "junk" machine in a test lab—say, the old 133MHz system with 64MB of RAM. They see that AD works pretty well, and so start buying some "big guns" to be the production DCs—Pentium 4s, Itaniums, or whatever. They roll out these big DCs and things seem to work pretty well.

Until one Monday, folks come to work and the AD apparently still thinks it's the weekend because AD's not working. Administrators find that they can't create new user accounts or join machines to a domain. Someone has tried to install Exchange 2000, but it complains about not having the authorization to change something called the *schema*. The Cleveland office was scheduled to create a new child domain, but that's refused, too. The remaining NT 4 domain controllers—perhaps the firm has decided to run in Mixed mode for a while—complain that they can't find the PDC, and account changes like password resets are clearly not getting to those NT 4 backup domain controllers.

What happened? Well, someone was playing around in the lab that weekend and needed an extra machine with which to do some experimenting. The 133MHz system was just sitting there, still running Windows 2000 and acting as an AD domain controller. But it wasn't really relevant anymore, the weekend noodler reasoned, as the firm now has several dozen big DCs running. So our experimenter wipes the hard disk on the 133MHz system and puts Linux on it.

You see, by default, AD assigns the FSMO roles to the first DC that you install. Which means that 133MHz system has been quietly serving in a very important role. But now it can't. And AD isn't smart enough to figure that out and then to nominate a new computer in that role. You might say that our "sparkling" forest has lost its "fizz moe." It's now your job to transfer the FSMO roles to other DCs.

That's why you care about FSMOs.

NOTE *Actually, there is one case where AD automatically moves the FSMO role: when you use DCPROMO to convert a domain controller that holds one or more FSMO roles into a member server. DCPROMO finds another appropriate domain controller and moves the FSMO roles to that DC. In that case, decommissioning the Pentium 133 would have resulted in no problems. So perhaps the best advice here is, "When you want to get rid of a domain controller, always use DCPROMO to decommission it before FDISKing it."*

FSMO Roles

There are five FSMO roles in AD:

- ◆ Schema
- ◆ Domain naming
- ◆ RID
- ◆ PDC
- ◆ Infrastructure

There is only one schema FSMO in the entire forest, and similarly only one domain naming FSMO. Each domain in the forest, however, has its own RID, PDC, and infrastructure FSMO.

SCHEMA

Schema is the word for the structure of the AD database—the fields. It's the list of things in the database, like username, password, and so on. In some senses, it's the directory to your Active Directory.

Examining the Schema with the Schema Snap-In

You can look at the schema with the Active Directory Schema snap-in. It's not sitting in Administrative Tools, however; follow these steps to run it.

1. Click Start/Run and enter **mmc /a**, then press Enter to start the Microsoft Management Console in Author mode.

2. Click Console, then Add/Remove Snap-in.

3. In the resulting dialog box, click the button labeled Add, which will raise yet another dialog box, Add Standalone Snap-in.

4. In the Add Standalone Snap-in dialog box, locate and click the object labeled Active Directory Schema, then click the Add and Close buttons. If Active Directory Schema isn't in the list, then run the file named `adminpak.msi` in the `\winnt\system32` directory of any Windows 2000 server, then try again.

5. Back in the Add/Remove Snap-in, dialog box, click OK to close.

You'll then see a screen like Figure 8.50.

Here, I've highlighted the part of the schema that tells us that there's an attribute called user-PrincipalName, which, you know by now, is the login name. Double-click it and you'll see a dialog box describing its properties, but they'll probably be grayed out, even if you're an Enterprise Admin. Recall that even Enterprise Admins can't modify the schema—you must be a member of the Schema Admins group to do that. But if you're a Schema Admin, then you'll see the properties page with everything enabled, as in Figure 8.51.

Notice the check box labeled Replicate This Attribute to the Global Catalog. You can, using the Schema Manager, control what does and doesn't replicate in the GC.

FIGURE 8.50

Schema Manager
snap-in

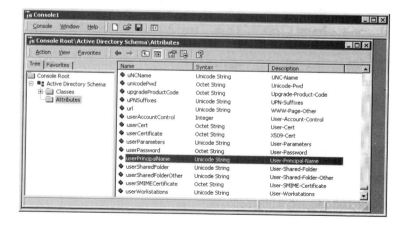

FIGURE 8.51

Properties page for
user principal name

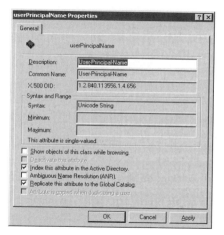

The Schema and Your AD

But will you change the schema very much? Probably not. But there are few things that you should bear in mind.

First, remember that there is only one schema for the entire forest; it's not meaningful to talk of changing the schema for a particular domain, as any changes to the schema are changes to the schema of an entire forest. So a bit of innocent schema-dabbling will affect every domain controller in every domain in the forest, as all of those DCs will have to be notified of the changes and thus will have to make room for the new schema items in their copy of the schema, which burns up some CPU and disk time.

Second, when will you change the schema? Usually the only thing that you'll do that will cause the schema to change will be adding new server-based applications such as Exchange 2000, server-based apps that were designed with the Active Directory in mind.

Keeping Schema Changes Orderly

Inasmuch as schema changes affect the whole forest, it's reasonable to say that the schema *does* change—we want it to change in an orderly fashion—it'd be really bad if two people both modified the schema at the same time.

For that reason, and because there's only one schema for the entire forest, there's only one computer that can approve schema changes in the entire forest. That computer is said to have the *schema FSMO* role. By default, the AD places the schema FSMO role on the first domain controller that you install in the first domain of the forest. So the first DC that you set up should be a well-protected one!

You can see which computer is the schema FSMO computer, or move that role to another computer, like so:

1. Right-click the object labeled Active Directory Schema and choose Change Domain Controller.

2. In the resulting dialog box, click Specify Name and type in the name of the domain controller to which you want to transfer the schema FSMO role. If you're not going to transfer the FSMO role, then any DC will do.

3. The snap-in will think for a minute and refresh its screen. Then right-click the Active Directory Schema object and choose Operations Master to see a dialog box like Figure 8.52. Note that win2ktest.com has returned!

FIGURE 8.52

Changing the schema FSMO

4. Click the Change button and the system will ask you if you really want to make the change; confirm that you do.

5. Oddly enough, the dialog box for changing the FSMO remains up on the screen, but doesn't offer an OK button (it's disabled)—it only offers a Cancel button, which you'd *think* would un-do moving the FSMO. But it doesn't; the FSMO's already moved. Click Cancel to clear the dialog box, and you've successfully moved the schema operations master.

You must be a Schema Admin to move the schema FSMO role.

Planning for Schema Changes…and Conflicts

Before leaving the subject of the schema, let me offer a thought about how it will affect your organization. As I write this in early 2002, there are truthfully very few AD-aware applications. But now let's consider what happens in the near future, when there are many of them.

Let's imagine that we work at a big university with a lot of independent departments. The university's forest has many domains—Chemistry, English, Microbiology, Astronomy, Music, Geology, and others—that all live in a single forest and therefore have only one schema. Now imagine that Astronomy just got a cool new application that will aid its professors in researching something, and so they put it on the AD. It adds a few dozen things to the schema, including a Magnitude field, which stores a star's brightness. Then suppose Geology buys some neat new application that will help them in seismology research, which also adds a few things to the schema—such as a Magnitude field, where they'd store information on earthquake power. What happens when Geology tries to install an application that wants to create a schema field whose name already exists? Well, to make a long story short, it depends…and not all possible outcomes are good.

My point is this: Geology should have *known* when it first installed its app that the app would conflict with an existing one. But how could they have known? Well—and here's the part you won't like—every forest should consider keeping a testing lab up and running all the time, with a DC or two that run a working but independent version of your forest. Prior to rolling out any server-based apps, you should test them out on the test lab to see if they create schema changes that will make AD bellyache.

What's that you say? That Astronomy and Geology are used to running things independently, not having to ask each other's permission to run applications? Yes, I can believe that—research and educational institutions have that tradition. But once you make the decision to stitch your organization together into a single forest, then your organizational components must communicate a bit more to keep things working. And *somebody's* going to have to keep that test lab up and running all the time. Which means staffing it and finding space, machines, and software for it. Golly, that argument about how Windows lowers total cost of ownership (TCO) doesn't seem quite as compelling now.…

In case it's not clear, I think this is a bit of a weakness in the Active Directory. Basically, in this case, the AD is just another piece of software that says, "If you want to use me, you'll have to modify the way that you do business," and that seems awfully backwards to me—sort of like a mouse manufacturer saying, "Gosh, we're sorry that our revolutionary mouse design doesn't fit your hand…have you perhaps considered surgery?"

Global Catalog Changes and the Schema in Windows 2000

While I'm here discussing the schema, there's one more side effect of schema changes that you ought to know: what happens when you change the global catalog's structure.

Recall that every schema item has a check box telling AD whether to include it in the global catalog. Check the box, and you tell the GCs, "Listen, there's about 1000 items in the AD, but I only need you to extract a few dozen of them for the GC. I just added a new item." That leads to a nonintuitive result. (At least, nonintuitive from my point of view.)

Suppose the GC used to keep track of, say, 25 items in the Active Directory. You check a box and so now the GC must build a slightly larger GC. How does it do it? Now, *I* would guess that it would just say to itself, "Well, I've got 25 of the 26 already…so I'll just contact my DC partners in the other domains and go get that 26th item."

But it doesn't.

Instead, it says, "Hmm...things have changed. The only way to be absolutely sure that I'm not missing something important is to just *dump the whole global catalog and start over.*" Yikes! This means that any change to the list of items in the GC kicks off a message to every global catalog server in the forest to just flush its copy of the GC and to start contacting other DCs to rebuild the GC from scratch. In other words, get ready for some network activity and a set of global catalog servers that will be fairly unresponsive for a while.

What can you do about this? Two things: Install the server-based apps early on, where there is only a small number of global catalog servers, or wait a bit and make sure that all of your domain controllers are running a version of NT that is later than Windows 2000.

In the first approach, you start out creating your Active Directory by creating your first DC, and you immediately install the server-based applications to that DC. Then, any future DCs will have your augmented schema and global catalog structure from the very beginning, and you'll never see the global catalog servers decide to quit working and have a party in mid-day just because someone installed an application on a server. Some apps make that easier to do; for example, Exchange 2000's Setup program has an option that allows you to only modify the schema. It doesn't install any files— it just makes room for Exchange's schema needs, should you ever decide to install an Exchange server later. If you're even thinking about running Exchange, I suppose it's not a bad idea to pump up the schema in anticipation of a possible Exchange future. (Although I should point out that installing Exchange on a virgin AD roughly triples the number of fields in the schema.)

The second approach just says something like, "Don't do the Active Directory until you get your hands on .NET Server or a later edition of Windows 200x Server." .NET Server helps out by changing the global catalog's behavior. Under a forest populated by post-Windows 2000 global catalog servers, changes to the GC only cause the global catalog servers to contact other DCs for just the changes—adding a 26th item to the GC would only cause GC servers to go get the 26th item and add it to the GC, rather than dumping the whole thing and starting over.

DOMAIN NAMING FSMO

You've already met this one—I used this FSMO as my example earlier of why you'd need an operations master in the first place. There is only one of these for the entire forest. As with the schema operations master, the AD places the domain naming operations master role on the first domain controller that you install on the first domain that you install.

You change the domain naming operations master role with the Active Directory Domains and Trusts tool, which we've already met. Just open AD Domains and Trusts and right-click the object in that MMC snap-in labeled Active Directory Domains and Trusts, then choose Connect to Domain Controller, and you'll see a dialog box like Figure 8.53.

In this dialog box, you'll point AD Domains and Trusts to the DC that you want to serve as domain naming FSMO. Fill in its domain name in the field labeled Domain, then fill in the text field labeled Change To with the name of the desired DC, then click OK. Then once again right-click the object labeled Active Directory Domains and Trusts and this time choose Operations Master. In the resulting dialog box, click the Change button and confirm that you do indeed want to transfer the operations master role. Click Close to clear the Change Operations Master dialog box, and you've moved the domain naming FSMO role.

FIGURE 8.53

Changing the domain naming operations master

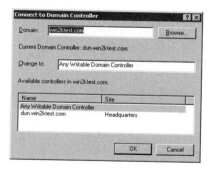

WARNING *The domain naming FSMO role should only be placed on a DC that is also a global catalog server. Apparently the AD developers got a little lazy and decided that, inasmuch as the global catalog knows about things from all over the forest, the domain naming FSMO could exploit the GC's knowledge.*

You must be an Enterprise Admin to change the domain naming FSMO.

RID POOL FSMO

One of the things that any Native-mode AD domain controller can do is to create new accounts (user and machine) without having to go find some "central" or "primary" DC. In the NT/2000 world, everything has a unique identifier called its *security ID* or SID. SIDs look like this:

S-1-5-21-*D1-D2-D3-RID*

The 1-5-21 applies to all SIDs. What I've called *D1, D2,* and *D3* are actually three randomly generated 32-bit numbers. When AD first creates a domain, it generates these three unique 32-bit numbers, and they remain constant for any SID generated in that domain. And it's not just a matter of a separate D1/D2/D3 for a domain—the local SAM on a workstation or member server also has its own set of three unique 32-bit numbers.

NOTE *I know, you're wondering, "How does AD ensure that your computer's D1/D2/D3 is different from one built randomly in, say Pocatello?" My answer is: I don't know. I'd guess that they partially build the D1/D2/D3 from something unique, like the MAC address on the domain controller. But that's just a guess.*

So, for example, if I created a domain named acme.com and it happened to come up with D1=55, D2=1044, and D3=7, then every SID in acme.com would look like S-1-5-21-55-1044-7-*something*, where *something* is a 32-bit number. In other words, all SIDs in a domain are identical, save for the last 32 bits. That last 32 bits is the only *relative* difference between SIDs and is therefore called the *relative ID* or RID. Some RIDs are fixed; for example, the SID for the default Administrator account on a computer.

Anyway, if a DC needs to generate a new SID, then it *knows* what the first part of the SID will be. It just needs a unique RID. So there's one DC in every domain that hands out pools of 500 RIDs at a clip. Each DC can, then, create up to 500 accounts before it has to go back to this one central DC, which then doles out 500 more RIDs. (Actually, DCs don't wait until they're "on empty;" they refill their pool sooner than that.) The computer that hands out the 500-RID bunches is called the RID operations master or the RID FSMO. By default, it is the first DC installed *in a domain*. Note that there is a RID FSMO for each domain, not just one per forest.

You move the RID FSMO function from one DC to another with Active Directory Users and Computers. Open up ADUC, right-click the object representing the domain, and choose Connect to Domain Controller, then choose a DC as you did for the domain naming FSMO. Then return to the icon representing the domain, right-click it again and choose Operations Masters to see a dialog box like the one in Figure 8.54.

Notice that there are three tabs on that dialog—RID, PDC, and Infrastructure. Those three FSMO roles are domain specific, not forest specific, and you use this dialog box to transfer any of those roles to another DC. By default, AD assigns those roles to the first DC created in a domain.

As you saw in transferring the domain name FSMO role, just click Change and confirm the change, and ADUC will transfer the FSMO role to the DC that you've indicated.

You must be a Domain Admin for a given domain to transfer the RID FSMO role for that domain.

FIGURE 8.54

Transferring RID, PDC, or infrastructure operations masters

INFRASTRUCTURE AND PDC FSMOS

In a multidomain network, it is, according to the Microsoft folks, difficult to quickly reflect changes to group and user accounts across domains. So you might rename a user, or put a user in a group in the domain that you administer, but that change might not show up in other domains for a while. Something called the *infrastructure operations master* speeds this process up. You change its role in the same way that you'd change the RID FSMO. There is one infrastructure FSMO per domain.

WARNING   *There's one oddity about the infrastructure operations master role: Don't make a DC that is a global catalog server into an infrastructure FSMO, unless every DC in your domain happens to be a global catalog server.*

You must be a Domain Admin for a given domain in order to transfer the infrastructure FSMO role for that domain.

Finally, there's the PDC emulator FSMO. It's a very important one.

In many cases, computers running a pre–Windows 2000 operating system need to find the PDC of the domain that they're a member of. Some of those cases will be obvious: For example, clearly an NT 4 BDC will look for its PDC when the BDC needs to update the information in its SAM. But there are many other cases where only the PDC will do; here are a few significant ones:

◆ The Network Neighborhood/My Network Places is populated by a computer acting as the "master browser" that collects the names of local computers. By default, the PDC acts in that role.

◆ When Windows 95 systems log in, they look for a file of system policies called `config.pol`— but they'll only look to the PDC for that file; BDCs are no good, as far as they're concerned.

◆ If an NT 4 domain is trying to establish a trust relationship with an AD domain, then the NT 4 domain will need to contact the PDC for that AD domain. That's because NT 4 doesn't understand multimaster replication and therefore thinks that it *must* do its negotiation with the one writeable version of the domain—the PDC.

Arbitrarily dubbing one of an AD domain's DCs as the "primary" DC, then, makes sense. And while an AD domain is in Mixed mode, the PDC emulator FSMO is more than just an emulator; it's the only DC that can accept account changes.

But does that mean that a PDC emulator becomes irrelevant once you're in Native mode and have no pre-2000 boxes around? Not at all. The PDC emulator still serves in two extremely important functions. Although we haven't covered replication yet, you probably know that replicating AD changes can take time—sometimes a significant amount of time. So suppose the following happens: I'm working in St. Louis and need my password changed. So I call the company help desk, which is, unknown to me, in Ottawa. The help-desk person changes my password, and it seems that all will be well.

But consider: What DC did the help-desk person change my password on? Well, she probably did it on a DC that was physically close to her, a DC in Ottawa. So an Ottawa DC knows my new password. But how long will it be before my local St. Louis DCs know my new password? Well, it could be hours. So does that mean that I'll have to just twiddle my thumbs for a few hours waiting for my new password to find its way to Missouri? Well, if we were talking about any other attribute besides a password, then the answer would be yes—but passwords are special.

When an admin changes a password on some DC somewhere, that DC immediately contacts the system acting as the PDC emulator FSMO for that domain. So the PDC FSMO almost always knows the most up-to-date passwords. When I try to log in to the domain, it is a local DC that tries to log me in. As I tell that DC my new password, the local DC is inclined at first to decline my logon, as the password that I offer doesn't match what the DC has. But before declining my logon, the DC connects to the PDC emulator FSMO for its domain and double-checks—and if the password that I gave my local DC matches the new one that the PDC has, then I'm logged in. This "high-priority replication" also occurs for one other user attribute—account unlocks. Thus, when a user forgets his password and then re-tries to log on with the wrong password over and over, then not only does he need a new password, he's probably also locked himself out of his account. So when the administrator resets the user's password, then the admin probably also has to unlock the account. Immediately replicating the new password without replicating the account unlock wouldn't be very helpful.

That's one important job for the PDC FSMO—what's the other one? We'll cover that in an upcoming section, "Forestwide Time Synchronization."

You can change the PDC FSMO from Active Directory Users and Computers, as you did with the infrastructure or RID FSMOs. You must be a Domain Admin for a given domain in order to transfer the PDC FSMO role for that domain.

Transferring FSMO Roles the Hard Way

Transferring FSMO roles is very simple via the GUI, as I've shown you. But there's a catch: You can only use the GUI to transfer a FSMO role *if the present FSMO is up and running*. If you FDISK-ed the computer that was acting as your PDC FSMO, then there's no one around to "approve" transferring the PDC FSMO role to another computer. In that case, you don't just *transfer* the operations master role—you "seize the master."

If your PDC FSMO or infrastructure FSMO will be temporarily offline, then it's perfectly safe to transfer those FSMO/operations master roles to another computer, and you can actually do it through the GUI. It'll tell you that the operations master is offline and that you can't transfer the role, but ignore it and click Change anyway. You'll get the usual confirmation request and then *another* dialog box, like this:

After a bit more thought, you'll get a *final* confirmation dialog box:

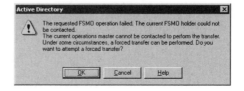

But to transfer the RID, domain naming, or schema FSMO, you'll need to use a command-line tool, NTDSUTIL. You start it from the command line by typing **ntdsutil**. Then do this:

1. Type **roles**; NTDSUTIL will respond by changing the prompt to `fsmo maintenance:`.

2. Type **connections** to point to the computer that you are going to transfer the FSMO role to. NTDSUTIL will respond by changing the prompt to `server connections:`.

3. Type **connect to** *servername*, where *servername* is the server that you want to transfer the FSMO role to.

4. Type **quit** to return to FSMO maintenance.

5. Type **transfer** *fsmotype* **master**. You'll get a request for confirmation if NTDSUTIL finds that it cannot contact the current FSMO to get its approval. Confirm that you want to force a transfer.

6. If that works—if there are no error messages—then you're done. But if the transfer fails, then type **seize** fsmotype **master**. A bit more drastic, but it always works.

7. Type **quit** twice and you should be done.

For example, here is a session where I seized the RID master role from a computer called ca.win2kexperts.com to a computer named bigdog.win2kexperts.com (what I typed is in bold, the computer's responses are in roman):

```
C:\WINNT\system32>ntdsutil
ntdsutil:roles
fsmo maintenance:connections
server connections: connect to server bigdog.win2kexperts.com
Binding to bigdog.win2kexperts.com...
Connected to bigdog.win2kexperts.com using credentials of locally logged on user
server connections:quit
fsmo maintenance:transfer rid master
ldap_modify_sW error 0x34(52 (Unavailable).
Ldap extended error message is 000020AF: SvcErr: DSID-032104F7, problem 5002
(UNAVAILABLE), data 1722
Win32 error returned is 0x20af(The requested FSMO operation failed. The current
FSMO holder could not be contacted.))
Depending on the error code this may indicate a connection, ldap, or role transfer
error.
Server "bigdog.win2kexperts.com" knows about 5 roles
Schema - CN=NTDS
Settings,CN=BIGDOG,CN=Servers,CN=Headquarters,CN=Sites,CN=Configuration,
DC=win2ktest,DC=com
Domain - CN=NTDS
Settings,CN=BIGDOG,CN=Servers,CN=Headquarters,CN=Sites,CN=Configuration,
DC=win2ktest,DC=com
PDC - CN=NTDS
Settings,CN=BIGDOG,CN=Servers,CN=Headquarters,CN=Sites,CN=Configuration,
DC=win2ktest,DC=com
RID - CN=NTDS
Settings,CN=CA,CN=Servers,CN=Headquarters,CN=Sites,CN=Configuration,DC=win2ktest,
DC=com
Infrastructure - CN=NTDS
Settings,CN=CA,CN=Servers,CN=Headquarters,CN=Sites,CN=Configuration,DC=win2ktest,
DC=com
```

Hmmm—transfer didn't work. Let's seize:

```
Attempting safe transfer of RID FSMO before seizure.
ldap_modify_sW error 0x34(52 (Unavailable).
Ldap extended error message is 000020AF: SvcErr: DSID-032104F7, problem 5002
(UNAVAILABLE), data 1722
Win32 error returned is 0x20af(The requested FSMO operation failed. The current
FSMO holder could not be contacted.))
```

```
Depending on the error code this may indicate a connection, ldap, or role transfer
error.
Transfer of RID FSMO failed, proceeding with seizure...
Synchronizing server bigdog.win2kexperts.com with its neighbours
This operation may take a few minutes....Failed.
fsmo maintenance:quit
ntdsutil:quit
```

To transfer or seize the RID FSMO, type **transfer rid master**, or **seize rid master** as you see above. For domain naming operations master, use **domain naming master**; for the schema operations master, use **schema master**.

WARNING *If you seize a RID, domain naming, or schema master, make sure that the old master never comes online again. The AD havoc will result! If need be, boot it from a DOS/Win 9x floppy and FDISK it.*

Forestwide Time Synchronization

As you'll read in the upcoming sections on replication, the AD needs all of its domain controllers to pretty much agree about the current time and date. They don't have to be *exactly* the same, but they need to be close. Under NT 4 and earlier, establishing time synchronization across a domain was difficult to accomplish. But Windows 2000 includes a service called the Windows Time Service that keeps all of your Windows 2000 workstations and servers in good time sync.

Win2K does that in the following way. The PDC emulator FSMO of the forest root—the first created domain's first domain controller, recall—is the Master Time Server Dude. All other servers automatically create a hierarchy, sort of like a "telephone tree," to distribute time synchronization information. Everyone below that top dog automatically gets time synced from someone above it in the hierarchy. But who syncs that top dog, the forest root domain's PDC FSMO?

First of all, odd as this sounds, you *needn't* sync the FSMO. All that matters in W2K is that all of the servers think it's the same time. Sure, it'd be nice if it was the *actual* time, but that's not necessary. If your whole enterprise was five minutes early, that would constitute no problem for AD, as long as *all* of the servers are five minutes early.

But as long as we've got this hierarchy, let's do it right. You could use an atomic clock, one of those roughly $100 things that read the official time off some AM signals out of Colorado or other places. Or you could save a buck or two and just let the Internet set your time.

The suite of Internet standards includes a way of sharing time information called the Simple Network Time Protocol (SNTP). Many, many machines on the Internet serve as SNTP servers and will provide up-to-date time information to any machine running an SNTP client. Fortunately, Windows 2000 includes an SNTP client. You can tell a Windows 2000 machine to synchronize its clock from a given Internet time server with this command:

```
net time /setsntp:DNSNAME
```

For example, if a machine named clock.atomictime.org were an SNTP server, you could tell your system to use it to synchronize with this command:

```
net time /setsntp:clock.atomictime.org
```

You can specify multiple time servers by separating them with spaces and surrounding them with double quotes, like so:

```
net time /setsntp:"clock1.acme.com clock2.acme.com clock3.acme.com"
```

If you forget what server you told the clock to sync with, you can find out by typing this:

```
net time /querysntp
```

By default, the forest root's PDC FSMO will try to synchronize with its time source once every 45 minutes until it successfully connects with the time source. Then it does it again in 45 minutes, and again 45 minutes later. It keeps resynchronizing every 45 minutes until it has successfully synchronized three times in a row. Then it reduces its frequency to once every eight hours. You can change this with a Registry entry, although I'm not sure why you'd need to. (All Time Service parameters are in `HKLM\ System\CurrentControlSet\Services\W32Time\Parameters`.)

But where to find an SNTP server? Oddly enough, there are many around. Most ISPs' big DNS servers seem to act as SNTP servers. You can find out if a particular machine is an SNTP server with a neat little free tool called `ntpquery.exe` from `http://www.bytefusion.com/ntpquery.html`. You just point it at a DNS name or IP address and if that machine is a time server, you get a screen full of incomprehensible long numbers.

There doesn't seem to be a way to enable success/failure logging to the Event Log. But there is a diagnostic program that you can use to figure out if you're connected to a useful time server. Shipped on all Windows 2000 Professional and Server machines, the program is called `w32tm`. Although it's not as pretty as `ntpquery.exe`, it's free and integrates with the time service.

W32TM will not work if the time service is working, so you have to take the time service offline before running W32TM. You can do that from Manage Computer as always, or you can do it from the command line like so:

```
net stop w32time
```

That stops the service; **net start w32time** starts it again. If you run W32TM without options, it sits there and seems to do nothing, as it is now acting as a time server. You can force it to cough up help about its legal options by starting it with a nonsense option, like **w32tm -iwishihadBill'smoney** or whatever you like. In any case, what you want to do is to check that your Windows 2000 server can get to your chosen time server, and that time server is responding to it. You have already set the time server's name with the `/setsntp:` option. Test it with this command:

```
w32tm -v -once
```

That tells W32TM to synchronize just once and to do it verbosely. You'll get a fair amount of output, but inside it there should be a line that looks like this:

```
W32Time:     Recv'ed from server 48 Bytes...
```

That indicates that your system can find the time server and that the time server acknowledged the synchronization request. Don't forget to restart the time service once you've finished testing it.

This service requires that port 123 be open to the outside world, so set your firewalls appropriately.

TIP *You can even use this if you don't have an Active Directory running. If, for example, your home machine were a Windows 2000 Professional or XP machine, then you could use* `net time /setsntp` *to give your workstation the name of a time server, and the workstation would periodically resynchronize with that server. But only do this if you're connected to the Internet via cable modem or DSL...it might be quite unsettling to have your workstation dial up Earthlink at 3:30 in the morning just to get the time!*

Local AD Replication

You've already read that AD uses a multimaster replication scheme, which means that any change to AD object—a new machine account, a modification to a machine account, a new user account, and so on—can happen on any domain controller. As replication takes time, that means that at any given second it could be possible that every single DC in a domain might have a slightly different copy of the AD database for that domain. But if left alone for long enough (that is, if no one changed anything about the AD), then every copy of the AD database sitting on all of the DCs would eventually be identical.

WARNING *Note that this is only true if your Active Directory is in Native mode. Mixed-mode ADs will employ single-master replication.*

How does this work—how can we have many different sources of changes to a database and not end up with a hopelessly garbled database? Let's start off by understanding local AD replication, the way that AD replicates at a single site. (Recall that a site is a collection of networks connected at high speed—say, for example, a bunch of Ethernets. Any device in a site should be able to communicate with any other device in a site at millions of bits per second.) We'll add WAN considerations later.

AD Local Replication Starts as a Loop

If you set up a site containing more than one domain controller, then those domain controllers will discover each other (not a terribly hard thing to do, as they're all publicized via DNS and the AD) and then they'll automatically work out a replication sequence. So as to avoid chaos, every DC doesn't replicate to every other DC. Simplified, AD replication in a site with four DCs named DC1, DC2, DC3, and DC4 works like this: DC1 replicates it info to DC2, which takes DC1's news, adds it to DC2's news, and passes all of that news to DC3. DC3 then takes the things that it learned from DC2 (which included DC1's changes), adds them to its (DC3's) changes and then sends all of *that* to DC4. DC4 then takes everything that it's learned from DC3, as well as any changes that DC4 knows of, and sends them to DC1, closing the loop.

I said that was the simplified version. Now let's fill in a few details and complicate things a bit.

WELL, ACTUALLY, IT'S *TWO* LOOPS

First of all, there isn't just one loop, there are two—you might say that AD replicates in both a clockwise and counterclockwise direction, as you see in Figure 8.55.

FIGURE 8.55

AD replication loops
on a small site

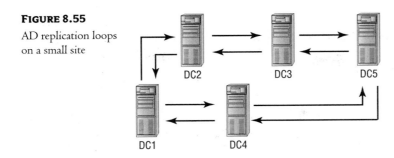

In that picture, notice that every domain controller replicates with two other DCs. DC1 replicates any changes that it receives to both DC4 and DC2. And notice that this points out one way in which my simple text example above was inaccurate: If replication actually worked as I suggested, then when DC1 received a bit of news, it would pass that news to DC2, who'd pass it on to DC3, who'd pass it on to DC5, who'd pass it on to DC4, who'd end up telling it again to DC1. But that *won't* happen. Suppose we modify the user account for a user named Tom to reflect the fact that he has a new manager. Instead, DC1 will tell its news ("Tom has a new manager!") to both DC2 and DC4. DC4 will soon tell DC5 about Tom's new manager, and at about the same time, DC2 will tell DC3 about Tom's new boss. A short while later, DC3 will try to tell DC5 Tom's news—but DC5 will tell DC3, "Thanks, but I already knew that." Result? The news has made its way around the AD fairly quickly.

And by the way, I've been writing things like "DC1 tells its news to DC2," and that's a little incomplete. More specifically, AD replication is always "pull" replication. More correctly, I should say, "DC1 notifies DC2 that it's got some news and eventually DC2 asks DC1 to communicate any changes that DC1 has seen" but that's a bit cumbersome to write. (The techie phrase that the AD uses is "pull replication with notification"—DC1 notifies, DC2 pulls.)

LOCAL REPLICATION HAPPENS EVERY FIVE MINUTES

Domain controllers within a site replicate to their two replication partners—what you might call their "clockwise" and "counterclockwise" partners—every five minutes. As far as I know, that's a hard-wired value; you can't change it. If there's nothing to say, then a DC says nothing at those five-minute intervals. But if a DC doesn't hear from either of its replication partners for an hour, it nudges that partner anyway, saying, "Are you *sure* you don't have anything new to tell me—that is, are you still alive?"

THE KCC MAKES THE LOOPS

Who forms this loop? Who decides which DC will be the two replication partners for a given DC? A program that runs on every DC called the Knowledge Consistency Checker (KCC). It pops up every 15 minutes, looks around, and asks, "Have we lost any DCs or gotten any new ones since the last time I looked?" If the DC population has changed since the last time, then the KCC—or rather KCCs, as there's one running on every DC—adjusts the loops.

TIP　*You can't see the KCC in Task Manager because it's part of* LSASS.EXE. *But watching* LSASS.EXE *can be a great way to figure out whether you need another DC. Using Performance Monitor, log the Process object and look at* LSASS.EXE's *percentage of CPU use over time. If it grows considerably—or if you find that when* LSASS.EXE *is busy then the total CPU utilization is usually 100 percent—then you know that it's time for an extra domain controller.*

How can you find out the names of the replication partners for a given DC? With Active Directory Sites and Services. Open it (it's in Administrative Tools) and you'll see icons that look a bit like a tall building with windows in it. You may have more than one of those icons, as you get one for each site. Open one of the site icons and you'll see a folder named Servers and, inside that, icons representing each DC. Open any server icon and you'll see a folder named NTDS Settings; open *that* and you'll see something like Figure 8.56.

FIGURE 8.56

Viewing DUN's
replication partners

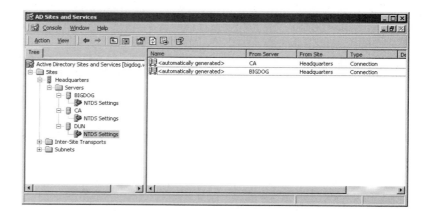

In that simple domain, there are three DCs, named BIGDOG, CA, and DUN. You can see that DUN replicates with both CA and BIGDOG—two separate rings. Notice that you are seeing the *pull* partners here. DUN pulls data from CA and from BIGDOG.

If you *really* want to, you can lay out the entire replication scheme. Just right-click in the right pane and choose New/Connection, and you can specify which DCs replicate to what DCs. I recommend against it, *but* you might do it when in a troubleshooting situation.

You can force the KCC to run by installing a program called repadmin.exe and then typing **repadmin /kcc.** REPADMIN is one of the Resource Kit tools that you get free with Windows 2000 Server—look in the \Support\Tools folder and install the tools by double-clicking the file named W2KRSKT.MSI.

BUT SOMETIMES IT'S NOT A LOOP, IT'S A MESH

This sounds pretty good, until you start thinking about what might happen in a company with *lots* of domain controllers? Suppose you had 200 DCs. That'd mean that if one DC started replicating some change to the Active Directory, the change could take up to 100 replications to get to all other DCs. Let's see: 100 replications, each of which happens at roughly five-minute intervals—500 minutes—that's *more than eight hours.* That's not an acceptable interval for replication within a site!

Well, no, it isn't, and Microsoft didn't think so, either. So the KCC looks around and asks, "Are any DCs more than three hops apart?" If so, the KCC just adds more links, converting the loop into a mesh. You can see an `NTDS Settings` folder that demonstrates that in Figure 8.57.

FIGURE 8.57

Example of mesh replication

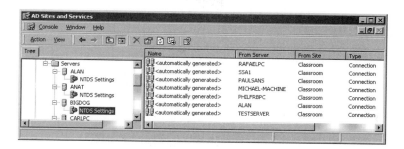

I've been calling the process of moving an AD change though a set of domain controllers a "loop," but as you see, it might not *be* a loop; it might be a mesh. That's why Microsoft has a different term to describe the path that an AD change might take through a set of DCs: the *replication topology*.

THERE IS MORE THAN ONE REPLICATION TOPOLOGY

Even a simple network, however, is a bit more complex than I've described. I've described a single loop—oops, I mean replication topology—but every forest will have more than that. Every forest has at least three replication topologies.

To see why, recall that a forest is a collection of domains. Each domain has its own "private" information that it (mostly) only replicates among the DCs for that domain. (For example, the information in your user account, such as your name and password, stays in your domain's replication topology. If we were to create a new user account in one domain, then the other domains would know nothing of that, so it wouldn't generate replication in the *other* domains, save for a bit of activity on the global catalog servers.) That domain-specific data is one replication topology: the pathway for updates from one DC to another within a domain. But recall that there is some data that is specific to the *forest*, not the domain; that data needs to be seen by *every* DC, no matter what domain that DC is a member of. The forestwide data is called the *schema and configuration naming contexts*, and it replicates among all DCs in the enterprise, not just the DCs in one domain, so the KCC creates a replication topology for that data that is distinct from the replication topology that any single domain uses.

NOTE *Just a word on that phrase* naming context. *It's an LDAP term that Microsoft adopted, unfortunately in my opinion. It just means "a database that must be replicated amongst a bunch of computers." So when you read a high-falutin'-sounding phrase such as, "The KCC creates a replication topology for the acme.com domain naming context," you can translate it to this: "The KCC figures out which DCs replicate to which DCs so that they can replicate acme.com's domain info, such as usernames, attributes, passwords and the like."*

There is also, recall, a database that consists of a subset of data from all of the domains: the global catalog. The KCC creates a replication topology that global catalog servers use to replicate the GC as well.

This all means that you could have *quite a few* replication topologies running. For example, a four-domain forest would have one replication topology for each domain, then one for the forestwide data, and then finally one for the global catalog—six, in all. You can see a simpler example—replication in a two-forest domain—in Figure 8.58.

FIGURE 8.58

Two domains, three
replication topologies

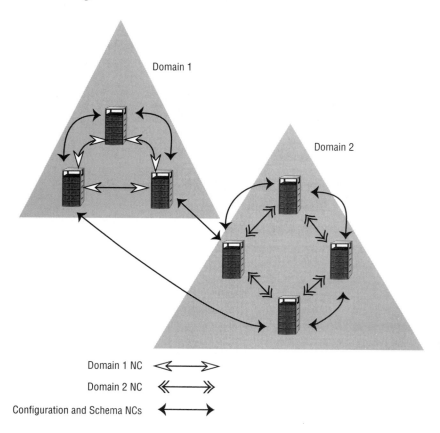

In this example, you see the two triangles labeled Domain1 and Domain2—recall that Active Directory diagrams always use triangles to represent AD domains. Domain1 has three DCs that have formed a two-way loop to replicate their domain information amongst themselves, and Domain2 has four DCs that have created a similar loop. There is also a third loop that incorporates all of the DCs, which replicates the schema and configuration naming contexts. (For simplicity's sake, I left out one replication path, the global catalogs.)

BUT WHAT ABOUT "REPLICATION CRASHES"?

Recall that back in my picture with the five DCs, named DC1 through DC5, I said that if we changed Tom's manager then the information would replicate its way both clockwise and counter-clockwise until it hit DC3 and DC5 at about the same time. Then either DC3 would try to replicate to DC5 or DC5 would try to replicate to DC3, and at that point the would-be receiver of the news would say, "Thanks, but I already know that."

But what if *this* had happened. An administrator connected to DC1 changes Tom's manager to one value. At about the same time, an administrator connected to DC5 changes Tom's manager also but to a different name.

Who wins?

To see, let's look a bit under the hood at replication. Back when we created Tom's user record, someone probably filled the Manager field with the name of Tom's manager—as in the words of Paul Simon's old *Graceland* album, let's call him Al. AD stored something like this:

Object	Tom's user account
Attribute	Manager
Value	Al Jones
Version number	1
Modified	1 December 2000 1:01 PM

A couple of months later, the admin attached to DC1 updates Tom's user record to reflect the fact that his new manager is named Beth Meadows. DC1 then stores (and replicates) this database information:

Object	Tom's user account
Attribute	Manager
Value	Beth Meadows
Version number	2
Modified	5 February 2001 4:22 PM

Notice that in addition to the new Value, there's a new timestamp and a new "version number." Version numbers are simple: a DC is just supposed to increment them when it changes an attribute. As the previous value had version number 1, the change gets version number 2. If we change it again, it'd be version number 3, and so on.

Now, over at DC5, another administrator thinks that he's supposed to update Tom's record with Beth's name, but he figures that Beth must *really* be Elizabeth, so he enters that, resulting in DC5 storing and replicating this data:

Object	Tom's user account
Attribute	Manager
Value	Elizabeth Meadows
Version number	2
Modified	5 February 2001 4:25 PM

Notice that the version number here is 2, not 3. That's because from the point of view of the domain controller DC5, this *is* the second version. It doesn't yet know that DC1 has changed the record.

DC1 then tells DC2 about Beth, and DC5 tells DC3 about Elizabeth. Soon thereafter, either DC2 tries to replicate to DC3 or vice versa—it's just a matter of chance. It's then clear that there's a conflict: two different items are trying to update the same attribute of the same record. Time for conflict resolution. How does AD do that? Fairly simply:

If one candidate has a later version number, then it wins. If they have the same version number, then the later one wins.

See why time synchronization is so important? In both cases, the version number is 2, so that's irrelevant. But Elizabeth appeared three minutes after Beth, so she wins.

It's just a might sleazy, but I should mention that there is, therefore, a way that the admin at DC1 could have improved the chances that his changes would be more collision-proof. If he'd changed the manager to Beth, then beth, then back to Beth," then his replicated record would have had a version number of 4, because by AD's lights, the attribute had changed three times in just a few moments. The Beth record would have had a higher version number than the Elizabeth record, and it would have won, even if it were an older record.

AD REPLICATION NUTS AND BOLTS

I hope you will never have to worry about how the AD gets its data from one DC to another. But just in case you need to troubleshoot replication, here's how it works under the hood.

A note on this explanation, though: Recall that Active Directory is a database. It stores a lot of information about the objects in its database, and recall that some examples of those objects are user and machine accounts, but there are many other kinds of things stored in AD. For the purposes of explaining AD replication, however, I'm going to simplify just a bit and use only user account creations and modifications in my examples.

AD in a One-Domain Controller World

Let's consider what happens when you connect to a DC and create a user account. Again for purposes of readability, I'll simplify the structure of a user account record and say that user accounts only keep track of these things:

- The user's name

- The user's UPN (logon name)

- The user's password

- The name of the user's manager

Suppose I create a user named Dawn, with a UPN of dawn@dell.com. (You've already seen that we can assign any UPN suffix that we like, and I was getting tired of acme.com. I'm sure the Dell folks won't mind.) Let's say that her password is "swordfish" and her manager's name is Wally. Let's say that I'm creating Dawn's account on a domain controller called DC1.

Now, you'd think that all that AD would store was something like "created a user account; name= Dawn, UPN=dawn@dell.com, password=swordfish, manager=Wally, time and date of creation= 10:00 AM 28 February 2001." But it's a bit more complex than that. I only mentioned this in passing, but AD does not replicate entire *records*; instead, it replicates *single attributes*. So if I change Dawn's manager to Jane in a few months, then AD won't replicate "name=Dawn, UPN=dawn@dell.com, password= swordfish, manager=Jane;" instead, it'll only say something like "for Dawn's record, manager now equals Jane." That's important because it implies that we must keep track of updates to each attribute, not each record.

Introducing Update Sequence Numbers (USNs)

The AD keeps a running total of changes that it has seen in its history called an *update sequence number* or USN. Every DC has its own set of USNs, as you'll see, but for now let's just stick with the one DC that I'm creating Dawn on. It might have seen 5000 changes since I first created its Active Directory, so it would associate Dawn's name with USN=5001. You may recall also that AD keeps version numbers on each attribute, so it'd store a version=1 for that attribute. Creating Dawn's user record, then, would cause the DC to do the following things:

◆ "Got a new object in the database. It's a user account that I'll give a SID of 1-5-21-43-534-83-1188."

◆ "Got a new user name for 1-5-21-43-534-83-1188, Dawn. It's the 5001st thing that I (the DC) have learned, so I'll associate her name with USN=5001. Version number is 1."

◆ "Got a UPN for 1-5-21-43-534-83-1188, value=dawn@dell.com. It's the 5002nd thing I have learned, so I'll give it USN=5002. Version number is 1."

◆ "Got a password for 1-5-21-43-534-83-1188, value=swordfish. It's the 5003rd thing I have learned, so I'll give it USN=5003. Version number is 1."

◆ "Got a manager for 1-5-21-43-534-83-1188, value=Wally, USN=5004, version number is 1."

So now we've created a user account for Dawn. She logs in the first time, and her workstation asks her to change her password, so she changes it to "secret." AD stores that new password like so:

◆ First, it computes a USN for the new password. We've probably created other user accounts and done maintenance on other accounts between the time that we first created Dawn's account and now, so it's likely that the latest USN is higher than 5004. Let's just say that this DC's USNs are up to 5716.

◆ Next look at the previous version number for the password attribute for Dawn. It was version=1, so the new password will have version=2.

◆ AD then stores something like "got a password for 1-5-21-43-534-83-1188, value=secret, USN=5716, version number is 2."

The following table summarizes what DC1 knows about Dawn.

Attribute	Value	USN	Version
Name	Dawn	5001	1
UPN	dawn@dell.com	5002	1
Password	secret	5716	2
Manager	Wally	5004	1

But if an AD increments its USN number every single time there's a change, won't it run out of USNs? Then what happens? Well, the USN is a 64-bit number, so you could have 18,446,744,073,709,551,616—that's more than 18 quintillion—changes before it becomes a problem. Remember that I said earlier that someone at Compaq had created an AD with 100 million members? Well, if you created an AD that large, then you could apply on average more than 18 billion changes apiece to each of those accounts before you maxed the USNs out. Or, in other words, if you made 1000 changes a second, then it would take about 18 quadrillion seconds to cause the USNs to roll over. Eighteen quadrillion seconds is (if I've done the calculation right) more than 500 million years.

And you just *know* that Microsoft will come out with a radically different update to the Active Directory by then...so we'll have to reset our USNs at that time anyway, and the count will start all over again!

Adding a Second Domain Controller

Well, thus far, we haven't done anything with replication, inasmuch as there's only been one DC. Let's add one named (you guessed it) DC2. It's got a brand-new, basically empty AD database file. It connects to DC1 and gets the current state of the domain's AD. Let's suppose that the very first account that it gets from DC1 is Dawn's account. Dawn's name, UPN, password, and manager will then get USNs 0–3, as you see in the following table:

Attribute	Value	USN	Version
Name	Dawn	0	1
UPN	dawn@dell.com	1	1
Password	secret	2	2
Manager	Wally	3	1

Notice something *very* important here. USNs from one domain controller do not have to match USNs from another domain controller. If we had a third domain controller that also held a copy of Dawn's user account information, then that DC's Dawn records would almost certainly have a different set of USNs.

Limiting Replication: Using USNs and Introducing "High-Water Marks"

What, then, does a USN do? Basically this: It helps replication partners know how much replication they have to do. DC1 replicated everything that it knew to DC2, item by item, and there were plenty more records than just Dawn's to pass along. As DC1 told things to DC2, it also told DC2 the USNs—that's DC1's USNs—for each piece of data. Let's suppose that the highest USN in DC1's AD database at the time was 6729. In general, DC2 doesn't care all that much about DC1's USNs. But as DC1 finished replicating to DC2, then DC2 made a note to itself, saying "The last time that I replicated from DC1, DC1's highest USN was 6729." That is DC2's *high-water mark* value for DC1.

Five minutes later, DC2 wants to replicate again from DC1. But how much of DC1's database does DC2 need in order to be up to date? We certainly don't want to replicate all of DC1's AD database to DC2 every five minutes! To avoid that, DC2 starts out the replication process by asking

DC1, "What's your currently highest USN?" The replication conversation could, then, go something like this:

DC2:   What's your currently highest USN?

DC1:   It's 6729.

DC2:   Hmmm, let's see—my high-water mark value for you is also 6729. As that was the last USN that you replicated to me, I already *have* that change, so I guess I'm up to date. Thanks, I guess we're done!

Alternatively, if DC1 had said, "My currently highest USN is 6800," then DC2 would know that it had missed 71 changes to AD and so could ask DC1 to send along the changes associated with DC1's USNs 6730 through 6800. That would lead to these events:

- DC2 would record DC1's changes in its copy of the Active Directory.

- Those changes would have USNs *on DC2*, and so DC2's highest USN is now higher.

- DC2 would now know that its high-water mark value for DC1 is no longer 6729, but instead now 6800.

A Problem: Infinite Loops

Reviewing, then:

- Each DC maintains a separate copy of the Active Directory on its domain.

- That AD contains USNs for each item in the AD.

- USNs in one domain controller's copy of a given AD record will generally not match the USNs in another DC's copy of the AD for the same record—if Mary Smith's password has USN 10030 on one DC, that same password for Mary will be stored on a different DC, but with a different USN.

- Each DC remembers the highest USN that it has heard from each of its partners. Those highest-USNs-so-far are called the *high-water mark* values for each replication partner.

- DCs use the high-water marks to be able to tell their replication partners, "Only tell me what's new since the last time we spoke."

So far, so good. But so far, there's no way to avoid an infinite loop. To see that, let's suppose that we start off with our two domain controllers, DC1 and DC2. Let's say that DC1's highest USN is 5000, and DC2's highest USN is 1000. The system is quiescent, so DC1's high-water mark for DC2 is 1000, and DC2's high-water mark for DC1 is 5000.

Now suppose an administrator makes a change on DC1—we change the value for Beth's Manager field. DC1 gives that AD change—that "update" in AD-ese—a USN of 5001.

DC2 says to DC1, "What's your highest USN?" DC1 responds, "5001."

DC2 now knows that it's hopelessly behind and so seeks to get back "in sync" with its buddy DC1. So it says, "Send me all of your updates with USNs higher than 5000." DC1 responds with the new information. DC2 records this new manager for Beth dutifully, and that change gets USN 1001 on DC2. DC2 also records that DC1's high-water mark is now 5001.

Eventually DC1 says to DC2, "What's new?" Or, in AD-ese, "Do you have any updates after that last one that I got from one, any greater than 1000?"

DC2 says, "Sure, I've got a 1001." (Which is true.) So DC1 realizes that now *it* is hopelessly behind the times (which is not true) and asks DC2 for this new information. DC2 responds by telling DC1 about Beth's "new" manager. DC1 records this information, bumping its highest USN up to 5002 and recording that DC2's latest high-water mark value is 1001.

But now what happens the next time that DC2 says to DC1, "What's your highest USN?" Well, of course DC1 replies, "5002," and the whole mess starts all over again. Although this would make for very busy-looking domain controllers, it wouldn't be of much use...so Microsoft included a "propagation dampening" feature to stop the loops. It's got two parts: the originating USN and the up-to-date vector.

Originating USNs: Credit Where Credit Is Due

I've told you so far that whenever a DC stores an update (update=change, recall) to the Active Directory, then it identifies the update by a USN, and that USN is local to that DC—all other DCs in the domain will eventually know the information included in that update, but those DCs will all end up assigning a different USN to the information.

But what I *didn't* tell you was that DCs also store some more information: the name of the *originating DC* and the USN on that DC. So the table that I showed you a few pages back of how part of DC2's AD might look after replicating from DC1 might be more completely represented like so:

Attribute	Value	USN	Version	Originating DC	Originating USN
Name	Dawn	0	1	DC1	5001
UPN	dawn@dell.com	1	1	DC1	5002
Password	secret	2	2	DC1	5716
Manager	Wally	3	1	DC1	5004

As before, this table shows four attributes and values for a user named Dawn. Each attribute has a USN that is a *local* USN, the USN that DC2 created when copying the records from DC1, and a version number. But now we've got originating DC, which identifies the DC that *first* made the change, and that DC's USN. Thus, even if we had 100 DCs here, they'd all have their own different USNs on their local copies of Dawn's information—but every one of them would remember that the first DC with this information was DC1 and would remember DC1's corresponding USNs.

Up-to-Date Vectors: Breaking the Loop

What good are those originating USNs? They're the key to stopping the infinite loops. You've already heard that each DC remembers the highest USN that it's ever heard from each of its partners. Those numbers are, again, called the *high-water mark* table for that DC. Now let me add a bit more information that's kept by each DC: the highest *originating USN* that it's ever heard, *from all DCs*—not just the replication partners. This table of highest originating USNs is called the *up-to-date vector*.

Thus far, I've told you this (incomplete) story about how DCs update each other: One DC remembers the high-water mark that it's seen so far from its partner, and so it asks the partner, "What records do you have in your AD with a higher USN than this high-water mark that I have for you?" In actuality, the more complete request goes, "What records do you have in your AD with a higher USN than this high-water mark that I have for you, *but that do not include any originating USNs less than or equal to my table of up-to-date vectors?*"

A Replication Example Using High-Water Marks and Up-to-Date Vectors

Let's revisit my earlier DC1/DC2 replication example. Suppose our story starts as follows:

DC	Highest USN	High-Water Mark for Partner	UTD Vectors	
			DC1	DC2
DC1	5000	1000	4817	388
DC2	1000	5000	4817	388

I'm making this example easier by starting from a quiescent, "everybody knows exactly the same things" state. Things work as well otherwise, but this is clearer. DC1 knows DC2's highest USN accurately, DC2 knows DC1's accurately, and they each have the same UTD vector. (Note that every DC's table includes its *own* highest originating USN as well!)

Now, suppose an administrator is connected to DC1 and makes a change—again, Beth's manager works fine. In storing this new item, DC1 gives it USN 5001, identifies the originating DC as DC1, and the originating DC's USN as 5001. DC1 also updates its UTD vector to reflect that the latest originating USN that it knows of from DC1—itself—is 5001.

Now DC2 asks DC1, "What items do you have in your AD that have a USN greater than 5000 (DC2's current high-water mark for DC1) *and* whose originating USNs are greater than the ones that I have in this up-to-date vector: DC1=4817, DC2=388?"

DC1 now examines everything with a USN higher than 5000. It finds one record, the one that describes Beth's new manager. DC1 examines its originating DC/USN and finds that it originated on DC1 with a USN of 5001. DC1 then looks at the up-to-date vector that DC2 sent it and sees that as far as DC2's concerned, any item that originated at DC1 after USN 4817 is news...so DC1 sends the info about Beth's manager along to DC2.

DC2 then stores this information as local USN 1001, originating DC=DC1 and originating DC's USN=5001. It also notes that the highest originating USN from DC1 is 5001, and a high-water mark for DC1 of 5001. The current state of replication then looks like this:

DC	Highest USN	High-Water Mark for Partner	UTD Vectors	
			DC1	DC2
DC1	5001	1000	5001	388
DC2	1001	5001	5001	388

Next, DC1 seeks to replicate with DC2. DC1 last knows of USN 1000, so it asks DC2 for any updates after 1000, provided that their originating USNs exceed the ones in DC1's up-to-date vector; DC1 includes the contents of its current up-to-date vector.

DC2 notes that it has a USN 1001 and considers sending it to DC1. But then it makes a second check of originating DC and USN and notes that the record came from DC1. So it then asks, "What is the latest originating USN from DC1 that DC1 knows about?" and the answer is 5001. DC2 then says to itself, "Well, this record was new to me…but clearly DC1 already knows about it, as it knows all of the DC1-originated records up to the one with a DC1 USN of 5001."

DC2 then replies "No, I don't have anything that you don't know. But my highest USN is now 1001." DC1 makes a note of that, and the replication is done—we're back to quiescence.

Adding More Domain Controllers

Let me wrap up this discussion of replication nuts and bolts with a somewhat more complex example. To demonstrate how all of that works, I set up four computers as DCs on a domain that I created called win2ktest.com, machines named BIGDOG, CA, CLONE300, and DUN. DUN holds all of the FSMO roles, but other than that is indistinguishable from the others. After giving them 15 minutes to run the KCC and settle down into a replication structure, I opened four copies of AD Sites and Services to show the NTDS Settings folders for all four, as you see in Figure 8.59.

FIGURE 8.59

Replication partner settings for BIGDOG, CA, CLONE300, and DUN

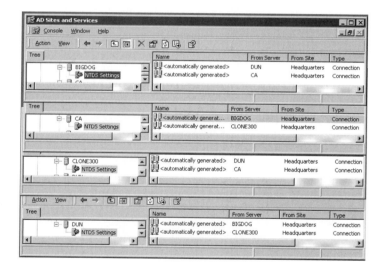

By the way, you can use the NTDS Settings folder to force replication. Just right-click any replication partner and you'll see an option to Replicate Now; that will force the DC to replicate with that replication partner immediately.

Sketched out, the win2ktest.com replication structure looks like Figure 8.60.

Recall that each domain controller has an up-to-date value for every other DC—not just its replication partners. You can see the entire up-to-date vector for any domain controller with a command-line tool called REPADMIN. REPADMIN is part of the mini-Resource Kit that comes with Windows 2000 Server that I mentioned earlier. Recall that you can install it by looking in the \Support\ Tools folder of the Server CD for a file called W2KRSKT.MSI; double-click it and answer the prompts and you'll get several useful and interesting tools.

FIGURE 8.60

win2ktest.com's
replication topology

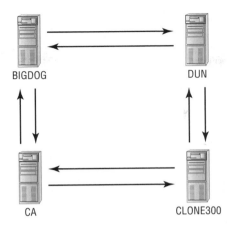

BIGDOG   DUN

CA   CLONE300

REPADMIN runs from the command line, and it's as cryptic as most command-line Resource Kit tools. To see the up-to-date vector for a domain controller, make sure that you're sitting at the domain controller and open up a command prompt, then type this:

    repadmin *naming-context* /showvector

where *naming-context* is just the name of your domain, but written strangely. Take each part of the AD DNS-like domain name and write it as **DC=***firstpart***,DC=***secondpart***,DC=***thirdpart* and so on for as many parts as the domain name includes. For example:

win2ktest.com becomes DC=win2ktest,DC=com

hq.acme.com becomes DC=hq,DC=acme,DC=com

Why REPADMIN wants it this way has to do with the internal representation and storage of the Active Directory. AD is built to use a database-access language called the Lightweight Directory Access Protocol (LDAP), and that's how LDAP refers to domain names. There's far more to know about LDAP, but I've been trying my hardest to spare you its cryptic nature, so you won't hear any more LDAP stuff than is absolutely necessary. You can see a sample run of repadmin /showvector in Figure 8.61. Or, to see the up-to-date vector of a DC that you're *not* logged into, just add its name DC=hq,DC=acme,DC=comto see the vector on bigdog.win2ktest.com, type **repadmin dc=win2ktest,dc=com /showvector bigdog.win2ktest.com.**

FIGURE 8.61

Displaying the up-
to-date vectors for
all of the DCs

I ran that on CA, and you can see that CA's up-to-date vector even includes an entry for itself. Notice that CA has not four entries but five, even though there are only four domain controllers. The fifth entry doesn't have a name, but instead a long string of letters and numbers. That string of letters and numbers is called a *globally unique ID*, or GUID. What you're seeing is this: I *used* to have a fifth domain controller on this network, but I decommissioned it. The GUID is the only information left about that old DC —the AD recognizes that it no longer exists, but the process of demoting a DC does not direct the other DCs to scrub its up-to-date value from their up-to-date vectors. (Old DCs never really die apparently; they just fade away.)

Now, let's suppose that I change the AD, again by modifying Beth's manager while attached to DUN. Clearly DUN is going to replicate that account to its partners, BIGDOG and CLONE300; that part's easy to understand. But it's just as clear that BIGDOG will want to replicate the new account to CA—*and* that CLONE300 will want to replicate the account to CA. Clearly we don't want CA getting any more replication traffic than is necessary, so how does AD keep CA from getting the same report twice?

Step One: Create the New User on DUN

First, let's change Beth's manager at DUN and review what happens to CA. When things start out, CA has the following up-to-date vector:

CA	4747
BIGDOG	6454
DUN	39469
CLONE300	4968

Let's assume that the AD is quiescent when I change Beth's manager, so those are also the current high-water values for those domain controllers. I make the change to Beth's account on DUN and, as you saw earlier, DUN's highest USN increments. Let's say that the update on DUN has a USN of 39473. I'll simplify this example and focus mainly on the up-to-date vector, as I hope that the highest-USN and high-water mark's use is clear by now. (Also, explaining a complete four-DC replication with all the bells and whistles takes pages and pages and pages.) DUN bumps up its up-to-date vector for itself to 39473.

Step Two: DUN Replicates the New User to BIGDOG

After a little while, DUN says to its two replication partners BIGDOG and CLONE300, "I've got a new USN; you might want to come replicate with me." Let's say that BIGDOG responds a bit more quickly than CLONE300, saying, "Send me all the new entries whose originating USNs exceed 4747 if it came from CA, 6454 if it came from BIGDOG, 39469 if from DUN or 4968 if from CLONE300." DUN sees that the record's originating DC is DUN but that the originating USN is 39473—which is larger than 39469. So it sends along Beth's new manager. BIGDOG increments its USNs and stores away the information about Beth's new manager, including the fact that the information originated at DUN with USN of 39473. BIGDOG also changes the value in its up-to-date vector entry for DUN up to 39473.

Step Three: BIGDOG Replicates to CA and DUN

Armed with this new information, BIGDOG taps both CA an DUN on the shoulder and says, "Hey, check out my new USN." Perhaps DUN responds first, saying "Tell me any new stuff as long as it originated with CA after 4797, BIGDOG after 6454, DUN after 39473, or CLONE300 after 4968." BIGDOG says, "Hmmm, I guess this info about Beth's manager isn't all *that* new...it's from DUN and has a USN of 39473. Never mind, DUN."

CA responds similarly but not identically: "Tell me any new stuff as long as it originated with CA after 4797, BIGDOG after 6454, DUN after 39469, or CLONE300 after 4968." Notice that CA's got an older up-to-date vector entry for DUN. BIGDOG sees that the info on Beth's manager is originally from DUN but has a USN larger than 39469 and replicates the information to CA. CA stores it, noting again that the information originated with DUN—not BIGDOG, even though he's the one that passed the info along—and that DUN's USN for the information was 39473. CA updates its value in the up-to-date vector table for DUN to 39473.

Step Four: DUN Updates CLONE300

While BIGDOG is updating CA, the chances are good that CLONE300 finally responded to DUN, saying, "What's new since the last time we talked, DUN? But only tell me things if they originated with CA after 4797, BIGDOG after 6454, DUN after 39469, or CLONE300 after 4968." (As you can see, CLONE300 has the same up-to-date vector that CA had a moment ago.) DUN sees that the only new record that it has originated at DUN but has a USN of 39473, and so replicates it to CLONE300. CLONE300 stores that information, including the fact that the information originated with DUN and updates its up-to-date vector table entry for DUN to 39473.

Note that as of now, all four DCs have the latest information. Additionally, all four DCs have an up-to-date vector table entry for DUN of 39473. Thus, when any DCs consider sending the information on Beth's new manager to any other DC, then they stop, as they see the other DC's up-to-date vector and realize that the other DC already knows!

Peeking at AD Replication

How can you monitor AD replication? You've already seen how to use REPADMIN to find up-to-date vectors. It'll do other stuff, too.

Finding Replication Partners Repadmin will also tell you what systems are replication partners with a given DC Just type **repadmin /showreps** *DCname* here DCname is just the DNS name of a domain controller. Here's an excerpt of the output:

```
DSA Options : IS_GC
objectGuid  : c735fab4-d564-4a2a-9dc0-225a232d71cf
…  INBOUND NEIGHBORS …
DC=win2ktest,DC=com
    Headquarters\BIGDOG via RPC
        objectGuid: cf78b375-063a-4c5b-899f-8caff22c7f36
        Last attempt @ 2001-03-17 19:57.52 was successful.
```

Here's what this is telling you: First, notice the `DSA Options: IS_GC`; that tells you that this server is a global catalog server. Second, you see that this replicates with BIGDOG, which is in the site named Headquarters. (We'll cover sites in a moment.) Finally, you see when it last replicated.

Seeing High-Water Marks You can see a DC's high-water marks with the /showreps option. It looks like this:

```
Repadmin /showreps namingcontext dcname /verbose
```

So, for example, to see the high-watermark table for DUN as seen from BIGDOG's perspective, type this:

```
Repadmin /showreps dc=win2ktest,dc=com bigdog.win2ktest.com /verbose
Excerpted, the output might look like
==== INBOUND NEIGHBORS =====…
    Headquarters\DUN via RPC…
        USNs: 59228/OU, 59228/PU
```

You'll see a line for each replication partner. The high-watermark value is the number followed by the /OU—59228, in the case of that example. That's the highest USN from DUN that BIGDOG has seen.

Forcing Replication It would be convenient sometimes to tell AD to get off its butt and replicate *now*, and it'd be really great if there one command to do that. There isn't, unfortunately. But you *can* tell a given DC to replicate with all of its partners with repadmin via the repadmin /syncall *destinationDCname namingcontext* /force command. So, for example, to tell BIGDOG to replicate with all of its replication partners in win2ktest.com, I'd type this:

```
repadmin /syncall bigdog.win2ktest.com dc=win2ktest,dc=com /force
```

Logging Replication Info to the Event Log Those are the basics of how the AD shuffles information around its various sites and domain controllers without duplicating efforts. Would you like to watch the replication process for yourself? Then look in HKEY_LOCAL_MACHINE\SYSTEM\CurrentControlSet\ Services\NTDS\Diagnostics. There are about a dozen value entries in there, and they can all accept numeric values between 0 and 5. 0 means "don't tell me anything"; 5 means "fill up the Event Log with lots of replication details!" And I *do* mean fill it up. It's interesting stuff, but there's a *lot* there.

Sites Revisited

Once you've built your TCP/IP infrastructure, you've got to tell the Active Directory about it. There are several reasons for that, but the most important is that the Active Directory is smarter than the old SAM-based NT 4 domain system in the way that it uses bandwidth. When replicating from domain controller to domain controller, it needs to know whether it's communicating via a high-speed link, and thus can be voluble without worrying about choking the link, or if perhaps it's talking to its domain controller sibling over a 56K link and then will take the time to compress the data a bit, becoming a trifle more terse and bandwidth friendly.

But the domain controller can't know the answer to that question unless you help it. A DC knows that it can communicate at high speed with another DC if they're both in the same *site*. But how does it know that?

How Sites Work

The answer is this: They look to find themselves in the Servers container of one of the Sites containers of the Active Directory. There is a separate container for each *site*, where a site is defined as "a collection of subnets that communicate with each other at very high data rates." You define sites and then place domain controllers in sites.

Workstations and servers, however, don't get that help. They've got to choose domain controllers to log them and their users in, and clearly they want to be logged in by a nearby domain controller. They determine who's nearby by examining what subnet *they're* in, then the subnet that each domain controller's in to figure out which DC is nearest. They need to know which subnets are close to one another—in other words, which subnets are in the same sites.

"But," you might wonder, "how did the Active Directory figure out what sites it had, what subnets it had, and which subnets go into what sites?" *That's* the part that requires a little administrative elbow grease, so let's see how to apply that elbow grease. Our tool of choice will be a snap-in called Active Directory Sites and Services, located in Administrative Tools. Open it and you'll see a screen like Figure 8.62.

FIGURE 8.62

Initial Active Directory Sites and Services screen

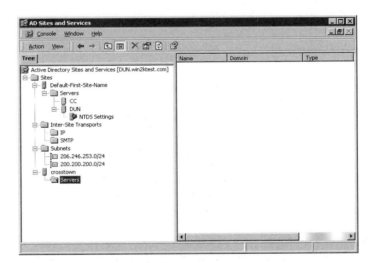

Notice that there's only one site, one called Default-First-Site-Name. When you create an Active Directory forest, the AD just creates a site by that name and assumes that everything's in it. Open up Default-First-Site-Name, and you'll see that your domain controllers are in there. The idea with setting up AD's site topology is that you must:

◆ Define each site.

◆ Define each subnet.

◆ Assign each subnet to a site.

From there, the domain controllers figure out by themselves to which site they belong.

Defining a Site

Suppose I set up another site, across town from my first site. The Active Directory needs to know about that site. Right-click the Sites folder and choose New Site, and you see a screen like Figure 8.63.

FIGURE 8.63

Creating a new site

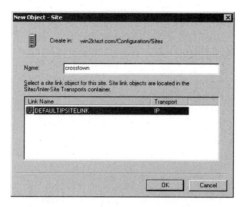

I just fill in a name for the new site (crosstown) and click OK. When I do, I get a message box like Figure 8.64.

FIGURE 8.64

Checklist for hooking up the new site

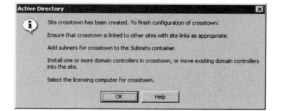

Defining a Subnet and Placing It in a Site

Next, we'll describe the subnets in our enterprise. Suppose the original site is at 206.246.253.0 and the crosstown site is at 200.200.200.0. I need to tell Site Manager about these subnets. You see me creating a new subnet in Figure 8.65.

Notice that AD then asks me to associate the subnet with a particular site. I'll define another subnet for the crosstown site, 200.200.200.0, as well, and now Active Directory Sites and Services will look like Figure 8.66.

Placing a Server in a Site

Figure 8.66 shows that I opened up the first site to display a container inside it called Servers, and then inside that I've got a server named CC. If CC were actually in Crosstown, then I could tell AD that by moving the server to Crosstown; I just right-click CC and choose Move and I'll see a dialog box like Figure 8.67.

FIGURE 8.65

Creating a
new subnet

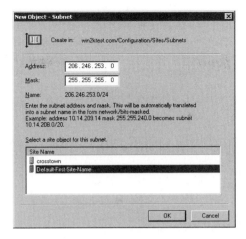

FIGURE 8.66

Sites and Services
after defining sites
and subnet

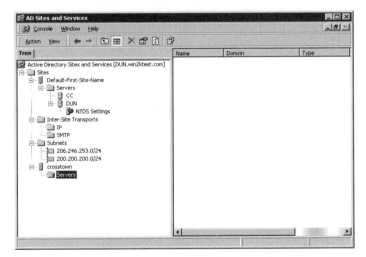

FIGURE 8.67

Moving a server

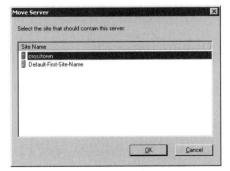

It's a little bit of work, but arranging your servers in Sites and Services Manager pays off if your enterprise spans WAN links.

Inter-Site Replication

Now that you've seen how to create subnets and a site, let's see how to get them to communicate with one another.

You already know that within a site, AD replicates by building a replication topology that is either a two-way loop (in a site with seven or fewer DCs) or a mesh. But a loop or mesh topology across WAN links would be inefficient, so AD instead creates a minimal spanning tree, meaning that it creates a set of site-to-site replication paths that minimizes the load on your WAN bandwidth. Take a look at the AD Sites and Services snap-in shown in Figure 8.68.

FIGURE 8.68

AD Sites and Services for a two-subnet, two-site enterprise

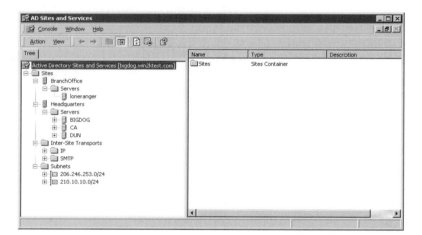

This is obviously a very simple "enterprise." But it'll serve fine to let me explain what you've got to worry about in a multisite world. You see, once you set up your sites, then they figure out how to replicate all by themselves, *within the site*. But across sites, they need a little help. You need to define how bits get from (in the example pictured) Headquarters to BranchOffice.

Huh? The AD needs you to tell it how to get from point A to point B? Hasn't it ever heard of IP? I mean, Ping can figure out how to get from Headquarters to BranchOffice—why can't the AD?

The AD can easily figure out how to get from one place to another, but it doesn't know three things:

◆ If you have more than one connection from point A to point B, as you might in an intranet or the Internet, is there a connection that you'd prefer that the AD uses over another one?

◆ Is the connection available all the time, or only part of the time?

◆ Would you like to use real-time RPC connections to replicate, or e-mail-based SMTP connections?

You tell AD about connections between sites by creating *site links*. Right-click either the IP or SMTP folders, choose New/Site Link, and you'll see a dialog box like the one in Figure 8.69.

In this dialog box, I tell AD which sites this link will join, name the link, and click OK. An icon will then appear in Active Directory Sites and Services in the IP folder (or the SMTP folder if you created it in there, but the chances are that you'll almost always create site links with IP, as you'll see). Double-click the site link object and you'll see a dialog box (Figure 8.70) that looks just a little different from the one that let you create the site link.

FIGURE 8.69

Creating a new site link

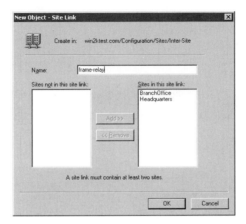

FIGURE 8.70

Site link properties

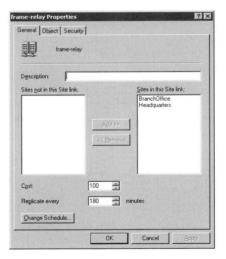

This dialog box is *very* important for three reasons. First of all, notice the spinner box labeled Cost; you'll use that to nudge the AD to use a link more or less. The AD will choose lower-cost links over higher-cost links. Second, you can control how often the AD tries to replicate over this link. Notice that site-to-site linking is quite different from intrasite links; replicating across a WAN link every five minutes might not be a low-cost approach for a wide-area based directory service, unless you put up all of those WAN links solely for AD's convenience! The minimum interval that you can specify for a replication across a WAN link is 15 minutes—the maximum intrasite time for replication. Click the Change Schedule button, and you'll see a dialog box like Figure 8.71.

FIGURE 8.71

Setting the replication schedule

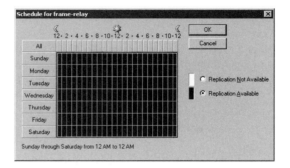

It could be that the Headquarters-to-BranchOffice link is a dial-up link that's only up from 2 P.M. to 3 P.M. on Tuesdays. In that case, you can tell AD not to bother trying to replicate before then.

WARNING *AD sites must replicate at least once every 60 days or less. AD throws away objects that have been "inactive" for 60 days, so if one site and another didn't talk for a few months, then they'd start deleting objects from their copies of the AD that they weren't using but that other DCs in other sites were still using.*

Finally, you create a site link either in the IP or SMTP folder to indicate how to replicate. SMTP *sounds* like a great answer: It doesn't need to be running all of the time, the link needn't be up that often—heck—we might even be able to send replication updates via Hotmail!

Unfortunately, it's not that useful. First of all, you can only replicate the forestwide schema and configuration naming contexts, so you could not, for example, update one domain controller in domain X from another domain controller in domain X that was on a different site using only SMTP. They must replicate with RPC, a real-time connection. And, second, you can't use just any old mail server. You need a public key certificate on that server to ensure secure mail before security-conscious AD will let you use it to replicate. (Oddly enough, you *could* do domain replication in the betas that appeared mid-way through Windows 2000's gestation.)

Once you tell AD all of these things about sites, a souped-up version of the Knowledge Consistency Checker called the Inter-Site Topology Generator or ISTG—there's one ISTG DC at each site, and they choose themselves, so there's no FSMO seizing to worry about here, it's automatic—talks to the other ISTGs and figures out which links to use so as minimize cost.

An Application of Active Directory: Group Policy Overview

I've talked so far in mildly vague terms about how you can accomplish different kinds of control in an Active Directory. The specific tool for exerting much of that control is group policies, the successor to NT 4's system policies. Here's an overview of what they do and how they work.

Differences in System Policy and Group Policy Implementation

With NT 4's system policies, you could control a wide variety of things—you could give a user a particular Start/Programs menu, give him a particular look to a desktop, restrict the user from running many programs, and the like. All of these restrictions would be collected into a single file called `NTCONFIG.POL`, which you'd then place on each of the domain controller's NETLOGON shares. You can't have more than one NT 4 policy file.

In contrast, with Windows 2000 there is no tangible and separate file for policies. Instead, Windows 2000 stores the policy information in the Active Directory. You put this information into the AD in the form of *group policy objects*, or GPOs. You can put as many or as few particular policies into a given GPO as you like. For example, suppose you wanted to accomplish three things with policies:

- ◆ You want everyone to be able to change the system time on their workstations. (By default, normal users can't modify the time on their Windows 2000 workstations.)

- ◆ You want everyone's `My Documents` folder to be stored on the network rather than (as is default) on the local hard disk, so that everyone's documents can be centrally backed up.

- ◆ You want to deploy Word 2000 to everyone from a central server.

I've simplified this by saying that I want these things to happen to *everyone*; you'll see later how to restrict these policies to a smaller set of users. In any case, the point I was trying to make about GPOs is this: You could create a single GPO and include all three of these policies in it, then apply that one GPO to everyone. Or you could create three separate GPOs, put only one policy in each, and then apply each of the three policies to everyone, or any in-between option—one GPO with two of the policies and another with the remaining policy, with both GPOs applied to everyone, would once more produce the same effect.

Well then, it's reasonable to ask, why *would* you create multiple GPOs or separate GPOs? The fewer the GPOs, the faster the logins. Every time a user tries to log in, the Active Directory must scan all of its GPOs to see which of those GPOs applies to that user. On the other hand, you might create different GPOs if you wanted to apply different policies to different people—if you wanted the folks in one OU to be able to change their workstation times but wanted a different OU's `My Documents` folder on the network, then you'd create one GPO that allowed users to change their workstation time and apply that GPO to the first OU, and you'd create a different GPO moving `My Documents` to the network, and then you'd apply that to the second OU.

Group Policies Apply to Sites, Domains, and OUs—Not Groups (Mostly)

Why did I use OUs in my previous example rather than groups? Because oddly enough, "group" policy objects don't apply to groups—they can apply either to sites (which would let you exert control over all machines in a particular site), domains, or OUs. You can't directly say, "Everyone in the ACCOUNTANTS group gets QuickBooks Pro 2002 deployed to their desktop." Now, if ACCOUNTANTS were an OU rather than a group, then you *could* deploy QuickBooks Pro 2002 to all of the accountants. (As I write this, there isn't a QuickBooks Pro 2002, but I'm guessing that there will be.)

Is it *completely* impossible to apply a policy to a group, then? Well, not exactly.

Policy Filtering and Group Policies

What I said in the preceding section wasn't completely true—you *could* deploy an application to a group. But how you do it is a bit sneaky.

As you've read, Windows 2000 lets you apply policies to sites, domains, and/or organizational units. Microsoft even has an acronym for those three—SDOU. But you can use someone's group membership to influence whether or not he gets the effect of a particular policy.

I've already said that GPOs are not files, but they share one thing with files: they have permissions associated with them. And you can apply permissions to groups. One of the permissions associated with GPOs is Apply Group Policy; if this permission isn't granted, then the policy doesn't apply.

To apply a policy to just the ACCOUNTANTS group, then, we'd apply a policy to the entire domain, but then we'd set permissions for the Domain Users group so that Apply Group Policy was not allowed, and then we'd add a separate permission for just the Accountants group, allowing them to apply the group policy.

Policy filtering is a bit troublesome for two reasons. First, it can greatly complicate trying to figure out what someone else did when setting up policies: If you were to walk into an already-configured enterprise without any documentation and try to figure out what policies are supposed to do for that enterprise, you'd have your work cut out for you. As a matter of fact, there's an acronym relevant to that: RSOP, which stands for Resultant Set of Policy. To see what it means, consider the following question. I've got a new user, Bob, in a given organizational unit, which is in a particular domain, and Bob's machine is in a particular site. That means that the site may have policies that apply to Bob, the domain may have policies that apply to Bob, and the OU may have policies that apply to Bob. And don't forget that OUs can live inside OUs, so there might be an entire hierarchy of OUs that Bob lives in—each of *those* OUs could have policies attached to them. And on top of it all, policy filtering may affect whether or not all of those policies apply to Bob. The question is, which policies apply to Bob? It's not an easy question—you have to thread through which policies apply, the order in which they apply—a later policy generally overrides an earlier policy, although it can be configured differently—and then policy filtering must be taken into account. Determining the set of policies that actually affect Bob—his RSOP—is a difficult computational task, and you'll see a class of applications called *RSOP modelers* whose job is to do that very thing.

The second concern about policy filtering is that it slows down the process of applying GPOs to a user when logging in, which slows down the login process.

Group Policies Only Apply to Windows 2000 Machines

Although group policies are great, they're similar to so many of Windows 2000's best-sounding features—they only work on Windows 2000 machines. If your users are still running Windows 95 or 98, you can only use system policies to control their desktops; if they're running NT 4, you'll have to use NT system policies to control their desktops.

Group Policies Undo Themselves When Removed

One of the troublesome things about NT 4's system policies is that once a system policy is applied to a user account or a machine, the policy remains in place even if it is removed from the domain controllers. So, for example, if for some reason you'd created a system policy to set everyone's background color to green, then the Registry of every computer that logs in from that point on will be changed to set the background to green. If enough users screamed about this and you removed the policy, their screens would remain green. They could certainly *change* the color themselves, but it'd be nice if the policy had undone itself on the way out. With Windows 2000, that happens: Remove a policy and its effects are reversed. This can be quite powerful: For example, if you've used a group policy to deploy an application and then remove the policy, the application uninstalls itself!

You Needn't Log In to Get a Group Policy

NT 4 only applied system policies at start-up (for machine policies) and logon (for user policies). In contrast, Windows 2000 applies group policies every 90 minutes or so for workstations and member servers and every five minutes for domain controllers.

What You Can Do with Group Policies

You can do basically anything with group policies that you could do with system policies, and lots more. Here are a few examples:

Deploy Software   You can gather all of the files necessary to install a piece of software into a *package*, put that package on a server somewhere, and then use group policies to point a user's desktop at that package. The user sees that the application is available, and again, you accomplish all that from a central location rather than having to visit every desktop. The first time the user tries to start the application, it installs without any intervention from the user.

Set User Rights   You may know from NT 3.*x* and 4.*x* that NT had the notion of "rights," the ability to do a particular function. One such example is the one I've already used about a standard user not being able to change his workstation's time and date. Under NT 4, you had to visit a machine to modify user rights; now it's controllable via a GPO, meaning again that you needn't wear out any shoe leather to change a distant machine's rights.

Restrict the Applications That Users Can Run   You can control a user's desktop to the point where that user could only run a few applications—perhaps Outlook, Word, and Internet Explorer, for example.

Control Settings on Windows 2000 Systems   The easiest way to control disk space quotas is with group policies. Many Windows 2000 systems are most easily controlled with policies; with some systems, policies are the *only* method to enable and control those systems.

Set Logon, Logoff, Startup, and Shutdown Scripts   Where NT 4 only supported logon scripts, Windows 2000 allows any or all of these four events to trigger a script, and you use GPOs to control which scripts run.

Simplify and Restrict Programs   You can use GPOs to remove many of the features from Internet Explorer, Windows Explorer, and other programs using GPOs.

General Desktop Restriction   You can remove most or all of the items on a user's Start button, keep her from adding printers, or disallow her from logging out or modifying her desktop configuration at all. With all of the policies turned on, you can really lock down a user's desktop. (Too much locking down may lead to unlocking the automatic rifles, however, so be careful.)

There's lots more to work with in policies, but that was a basic introduction to get you started. (You can read more in the next chapter, and you'll see references to group policies throughout the rest of the book.) Let's return now to the larger issues of AD—namely, how best to get it on your system.

Watching the Network: Auditing with the Active Directory

You *know* they're out there, don't you?

You know—the bad guys. The ones who are trying to Take Down Your Network.

Okay, that's a big exaggeration. There really aren't all that many people attacking networks, and, truthfully, most networks face more threats from *inside* people than outsiders. So my pathetic scare tactic in the first three sentences wasn't all that effective. Hmmm, let's see if I *can* find a scenario sufficiently frightening to the average administrator to get your attention. Ah, got it! How about this one: Something goes wrong, or it seems that something went wrong, and so the boss asks: "What kind of network activity have we had recently? Are there any clues to who's logged on recently, or tried to?"

And you have look at her and say, "Ummm, I really don't know."

Now, *that's* scary. So let's see how to answer that question with verve and aplomb, or at least some of how to answer that question with verve and aplomb—through audits.

What You Can Audit

AD will optionally track a number of activities and save what it finds about those activities in Event Log entries, in the Security log. (And let me warn you, some of those entries are somewhat less than totally useful—but this is still worth doing.) Windows 2000 supports several kinds of audits:

- Audit account logon events
- Audit logon events
- Audit account management
- Audit directory service access
- Audit policy change
- Audit system events
- Audit process tracking
- Audit object access
- Audit privilege

LOGON EVENTS

Audit logon Events and Audit Account Logon Events are two slightly different items that are both quite valuable in tracking who did what where to whom. As you know, domain-based networks rely on a small number of computers to validate—logon—users. So a user Ray might try to access a member server \\SV1, and \\SV1 might try to authenticate that user at a domain controller \\DC2. Here's what these two settings would track:

◆ Audit Account Logon Events would tell \\DC2 to log the fact that it was asked to validate Ray and did. That would appear in \\DC2's log.

◆ Audit Logon Events would tell \\SV1 to log the fact that it needed to check to see that Ray was a recognized user prior to letting him access something on that machine. The log entry would appear on \\SV1's log.

Did you notice the point about where the entries live? That's important: *There is no central domain repository of logs.* Part of your job as an administrator is to collect and manage the logs of all of your systems. Fortunately, the only logs you typically need are the ones for the domain controllers and members servers...although workstation logs can be sometimes useful as well.

OBJECT ACCESS

Audit Object Access is possibly the most important, or at least shares the most important spot in my opinion with the logon events audits. Why? Because you can ask your systems to keep track of who reads, writes, deletes, or creates any file or any group of files on themselves. Wondering if the user deleted his e-mail PST file or it disappeared all by itself? With object access auditing, you'd be able to look at the user's workstation's logs and tell exactly when the file met its maker.

Tracking files and directories on a given machine—or tracking any other object, for that matter, as printers count as objects as well— requires *two* steps: First, enable object access auditing on the computer that stores the object and, second, tell the computer to audit that particular object. You see, by default simply turning object access on at a particular computer won't result in a single entry in the Security event log. You've got to then say, "watch this directory" or "watch this file" or even "watch this file, but only when Joe is working with it." You'll see more about how to do that in Chapter 11.

ACCOUNT MANAGEMENT

As its name implies, this is also a good item to audit. Any changes to user or group accounts get logged here. Create a user, create a group, modify a group's membership, change a password, and you're logged.

POLICY CHANGE

Think of this as an audit of the auditors: Turn off logging to do something sneaky, and you will have left behind an entry that tells when you turned logging off. It also logs changes in user rights— why exactly did that administrator let that user log on locally to the domain controller between 9:50 and 10:10, anyway—and changes in trust policies.

PRIVILEGE USE

This is a potentially useful tool but, boy, does it generate output. Every single time that you exercise a right—not a permission—then it's logged here. You'd be surprised how often you exercise rights— logging on, shutting down a system, changing the system time, taking ownership, and so on—so be prepared for larger logs if you turn this on. It'd be great if you could just turn on one or two particular privileges, but I've not found a way to do that.

SYSTEM EVENTS

System Events doesn't generate all that many entries and is probably worth running. It logs whenever you restart the computer or shut down the computer and also logs whenever you do something that "affects the system security or security log," in the documentation's words. My experience is that it tracks the security log—when you cleared it, resized it, and so on.

DIRECTORY SERVICE ACCESS

This is a kind of catch-all that logs any activity that trips a permission on the Active Directory. Think of the Active Directory as a container and users, machines, policies, organization units, and the like as just objects in that container, such as files in a directory. Just as NTFS permissions on a directory tell you when someone's been creating or deleting files, this setting tells you who's been doing things that modify the AD. I have not found much use for this. It *seems* as if anything that causes an Account Management logging entry also causes a Directory Service Access entry.

PROCESS TRACKING

It's a programmer thing…we admins wouldn't understand. This tracks activity between a program and the operating system—creating handles, starting execution, calling other programs, and the like. You probably won't find this useful.

How to Audit

You audit network activity by enabling one or more kinds of auditing on the computer in question. Let me stress that: If you've got 1000 machines in your network, then you may need all 1000 machines to have auditing turned on, depending on what you want to audit. For example, tracking file and directory changes requires having object auditing enabled, so if you wanted to track files on every workstation, then you'd need auditing enabled on every workstation.

You turn auditing on for a particular machine via a policy, either a local policy or a domain-based group policy. We'll discuss local versus domain policies in the next chapter, but here's the short version of the differences: You've already read about the kinds of things that you can do with domain-based group policies, and you can probably see that domain-based group policies are pretty powerful. Ideally in a network with an Active Directory domain then you'd use the power of domain-based group policies to centralize the process of enabling auditing, and I'll show you how in a minute.

You don't always *have* an Active Directory domain, however, and in case you've not yet built yours but want to start auditing immediately, then here's how to enable auditing: with a tool called the Local Security Policy snap-in. Start it up clicking Start/Programs/Administrative Tools, then Local Security Policy. (You may recognize it from our work with IPSec in Chapter 6.) You'll see an icon in the left pane called Security Settings and, underneath it, folders labeled Account Policies, Local Policies, Public Key Policies, and IP Security Policies. Open up the Local Policies folder, and you'll see three folders inside: Audit Policy, User Rights Assignment, and Security Options. (Aren't they *all* security options? And aren't the Account Policies referred to in the top-level folder by that name referring to the *local* system? The names for this tool perplex me.) Open up `Audit Policy` and you'll see something like Figure 8.72 in the right window.

FIGURE 8.72

Auditing Options

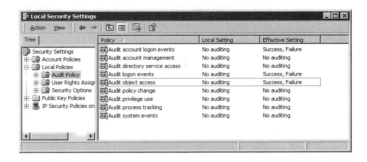

You may recall that domain-based group policies override any local group policies, and the computer in this screen shot lives in a domain. That's what the Effective Policies column shows.

But you probably don't want to have to go visit every single computer to turn this stuff on. That's where a group policy can make life easier. To enable auditing using domain-based group policies, then create a group policy object and look in the Computer Configure/Windows Settings/Local Policies/Audit Policy. Apply that object to the particular machines for which you want to enable auditing. So, for example, if it's something generic that you want to apply to every machine, then create the group policy object on the domain. But if it only applies to the domain controllers, then apply the policy to their OU. Or, if there's a different group, then use policy filtering—it's covered in the next chapter. (And to see what you actually *see* when you look at a log in the Event Viewer, look to Chapter 20.)

MANAGING LOGS

What, then, should you audit? I can't tell you what's right for you—there's no good answer because you must trade off log management versus coverage level. Look at this way: If you turn on all logging on every single machine, then in theory you'd have a wealth of knowledge...but you'd need terabytes of storage space to store it all, and in practical terms you'd never get a chance to review it.

At minimum, I'd log logon failures. Logging all logons is potentially interesting, but so many successful logons occur in a day that you end up filling the log with the information. Policy change and system events aren't too numerous—they won't cost much in terms of numbers of events. Privilege use can be valuable but creates more log clutter.

You should also consider how to manage log size with the log settings. Open up any event log in Manage Computer, right-click the log's icon, and choose Properties, and you'll see a dialog box like the one in Figure 8.73.

Notice how the system manages the amount of space that a log takes: You set an amount of disk space for the system to set aside for that log file. The log can't exceed that space. This is actually a security measure; otherwise, an attacker could bring your system down by doing things that the system would log, such as a failed logon attempt. Merely by deliberately trying and failing to log on, the attacker could make the log grow if it weren't set to a maximum size to actually fill your hard disk—crashing your system.

FIGURE 8.73

Configuring the
Security log

So fixed log sizes protecting you from fill-the-hard-disk attacks are the *good* news; the bad news is that a fixed-size log can be filled up. So you're faced with some more tough choices: What to do to keep that from happening? The system will, at your request, do one of three things when the log fills:

♦ Just overwrite the oldest events. Not a terrible low-maintenance answer, particularly if you provide enough space for the logs. (I recommend that you set the size of each log to 10MB— it's fairly hard to fill up that much space for logging.) But it leaves you open to an attacker doing something bad and then deliberately causing some series of innocuous events to happen over and over again so as to fill up the log with those innocuous events. So let's say that I'm a bad-guy administrator who's just created an administrative account that I will then use for fell purposes. I don't want you to know that I created the account, so I write a little batch file that does something like open a file over and over and over again…"Oops, I guess there was a bug in my batch file," I'll just say. As I know that you're auditing object access to the opened file, then every time that the batch file opens the file, an event gets added to the log. If I let the batch file run long enough, then soon there will be nothing in the log but reports that a batch file opened a file over and over again.

♦ Overwrite events after X days. The default behavior; the system erases events after seven days. For complete coverage, you'd have to back up the logs, although with hope you'd know about intrusions within seven days. Old logs are mainly useful for assessment of how long the bad guy's been around.

♦ Clear logs manually. This never erases anything. It's the most secure approach, but again requires you to "touch" every system periodically to back up, archive, and clear the logs. There's also the issue of, "What happens if the log fills?" In that case…

By the way, what happens if the log *does* fill up, as in the case that you've told it to keep all events for X days or you've told it to never delete events? That's up to you. In that case the system would by default just stop logging new events but keep running. There is a policy that you can set with group policies, however, that causes the server to stop altogether. I don't generally recommend this setting, as it could be clearly used to crash a server—fill the log and the system freezes. And, again, I'd set the logs to 10MB in size. You have to work *really* hard to fill up 10MB in an evening, so it'd be tough for an attacker to use a full log to cover his tracks.

That leads me to another point: What we've talked about so far is not, by far, the hardest part of auditing. The hardest part is managing the darn logs. Ten thousand machines means 10,000 logs. They get larger every day, they fill up, and they've got to be regularly stored somewhere and cleared to make space for more logs. I have not come across an automated way to do that, so we're talking about creating a nontrivial amount of administrative work. Given the size of modern hard disks you certainly could let the event log grow to gigabytes in size, so you wouldn't have to back it up and clear it very often, but then what happens when the bad guy clears the log? All you've got—as you've not backed it up often—is a record of the seemingly suspicious activity that someone cleared the log. Sure, you can look 'em in the eye and ask why they did it, but they can always say it was a mistake.

Logs are only useful if they're respected. Harsh as it sounds, to make them useful you must protect them. There should be a specific procedure for clearing logs, perhaps something that requires two administrators' sign-off. Anyone clearing a log otherwise should face disciplinary review and if security is important enough then you might make clearing a log without authorization an "instant termination" offense. Sound harsh? I don't know—what would you do to a bookkeeper who'd deliberately thrown out a few week's receipt and disbursement records?

The Bottom Line: Logs Are Expensive...Maybe *Too* Expensive

Let me leave the issue of auditing and logs with a splash of cold water:

It may well make good sense for you not to bother with auditing and managing event logs.

In the perfect world, you turn logging on for every server and workstation. You also collect the logs on all of those machines to some central place regularly—certainly every day or two—and archive them. You additionally peruse those logs before archiving them, looking for traces of wrongdoing or just incipient system failures.

You've got time for that, right?

Unfortunately, most admins don't. There are third party tools—Mission Critical's got one called Operations Manager that it sold to Microsoft, who's now renamed it Microsoft Operations Manager—but they are expensive, costing you per-user (all users, not just administrators) fees that mount quickly. So here's my final advice on logs: Do the math. Figure out how much in terms of personnel time, equipment, media, and the like that a decent auditing process will cost. And try to assess your downside—what *would* it cost you not to be able to answer the kinds of questions that logs can answer? Present these numbers to the boss and if she still wants you to audit, then tell her how many more people and servers you're going to need.

I live about three quarters of a mile from the Atlantic Ocean in a hurricane-prone area. In the perfect world, I'd have a cool 100-foot-high seawall buried in the ground with a set of huge motors that would spring that seawall up into a deployed position at a few minutes' notice. Gargantuan pumps would stand ready to pump floodwaters away from my house. Massive generators would, at my command, spring to life and power the whole process while driving motors that shutter my house's windows. But in the real world that stuff costs money, and so I've just got insurance, some good waterproof containers for my important documents, and I back up my servers daily. I had to accept a practical level of disaster preparedness...and so does your firm. But *make* the boss examine this trade-off, and do it now—she won't want to hear about this on the morning that you discover that you've been hacked, while you're trying to explain why the logs have been cleared. In practice, you'll come up with some compromise between fully backed up and monitored logs and no logging at all—but get everyone's agreement on it.

Migration Strategies

I strongly suggest that you put together a test network with a few computers, install Windows 2000 on them, and set up an Active Directory so that you can play around with the AD's basic tools before you try to implement it on your actual enterprise network. But eventually the day will come that you'll have no choice but to do the *real* install, the there's-no-turning-back install. One day, you're going to have to migrate your current NT 4 domain—or domains—to the Active Directory. (Unless you're starting from scratch, in which case your job is far easier.) Here's some advice on how to approach the migration.

There are two basic philosophies about NT-to-AD migration: "in-place" upgrades versus "clean and pristine" migration.

In-Place Upgrade

In the in-place upgrade approach, you let Windows 2000's Setup program convert your domain's current SAM file to an Active Directory.

GETTING READY FOR THE UPGRADE

Before you do this, make absolutely sure you've got your DNS infrastructure in place. And just to be certain that you've got something of a fallback position, go to one of your NT 4 backup domain controllers and synchronize it, and then take if offline. Then, if worst comes to worst, you can always just shut down the new AD domain controller, turn the BDC back on, promote it to PDC, and then walk around to the other BDCs and force them to synchronize with the newly anointed PDC. (But let's hope it doesn't come to that.)

HOW TO DO AN IN-PLACE UPGRADE

You must do this at the primary domain controller; if you try to upgrade a backup domain controller then Windows 2000's Setup program will simply stop and refuse to go any further.

But before you do it, you need to make a change to your PDC's Registry. (And the Registry of *any* NT 4 domain controller that you intend to upgrade in place to Windows 2000.) Navigate to `HKEY_Local_Machine\System\CurrentControlSet\Services\Netlogon\Parameters` and add a new value entry called NT4Emulator of type REG_DWORD. Set its value to 1. (I'll talk about what it does later.)

TIP   I've gotten a fair amount of mail asking me something like, "I want to do an in-place upgrade, but I want my new Pentium 4 system to be the PDC. How do I do this?" Simple. First, install NT 4 on the Pentium 4, and tell it that you want the new computer to be a backup domain controller on the existing NT domain. Then, once it's installed, use the NT 4 Server Manager to promote that new BDC to the PDC. Then put the Windows 2000 Server CD into the new PDC's CD-ROM drive and do an in-place upgrade.

When you do an in-place upgrade on an NT 4 domain controller, then the normal Windows 2000 Setup runs as usual. But the first time that you boot the machine after Setup, it immediately starts up DCPROMO and goes directly to the screen asking whether you want to create a new tree or a child domain in an existing tree. DCPROMO runs as you've seen it run before, with one important difference: You don't get to choose the NetBIOS name for the domain. The new Windows 2000 AD domain will have the old NetBIOS name of the old NT 4 domain, whether you like it or not. You can, however, give the new AD domain any *AD* name that you like. So, for example, if you're upgrading the PDC on an NT 4 domain named AUTOSERVICE, then your new Windows 2000 AD domain—which you can make part of an existing tree or forest, or create your own new forest—could be named acme.com. But its NetBIOS name would continue to be AUTOSERVICE, so that the old NT and Windows systems would still be able to find it, as they know it by the AUTOSERVICE name.

NOTE   *Let me stress that, as I get a lot of letters on it—the "downlevel" NetBIOS name needn't be connected at all to the Active Directory domain name. If your domain was called ABC under NT 4 and you upgrade it, then its NetBIOS name is still ABC. You can give it any AD domain name that you like—mycoolnewdomain.org, for example. Then the DC responds to old-style NT 4 (or any NetBIOS) request to the domain ABC, and any AD requests for mycoolnewdomain.org.*

OLD DCs STILL WORK

At this point, you've now got an Active Directory with only one of your DCs actually running Windows 2000, and the others are still running NT 4. As I've said before, this is why there's a Mixed mode—the lone AD DC knows that it *could* do a lot of cool things, but that then its domain data would be incomprehensible to the NT 4.0 BDCs. So it denies itself a few features—multimaster replication and universal groups are the most important ones—and continues to work fine with the NT 4 BDCs.

As soon as you can, you'll want to get those BDCs upgraded. Once the last one's done, then you can shift over to Native mode and get all of the features for which you paid. That's worth stressing.

NOTE   *Native mode only requires that your DCs all be Windows 2000. Contrary to what I've heard a lot of people say, you can be purely Native mode while still having as many NT 4 member servers and workstations in your domain as you like.*

AVOIDING TROUBLE WITH THE WINDOWS 2000 MACHINES

There is one quirk about in-place upgrades that you should be aware of.

Suppose, as is that case for many people, that you've introduced a bunch of Windows 2000 member servers and workstations into your NT 4 domain, and then you upgrade a single DC to AD. You'll see a curious effect. Once you have a single 2000-based domain controller in a Mixed mode environment, all of the 2000 Professional machines will only go to *that* machine to log in. When those 2000 Pro machines saw only NT 4 domain controllers, then they'd log in to any one of them. But if there is at least one 2000 DC in the domain, then the 2000 Pro boxes will only log in with that one (and any other 2000 DCs in the domain).

So if you have an NT 4 domain with a lot of 2000 Professional systems in it, then you'll probably want to upgrade those BDCs quickly. Or you can make the Registry change that I suggested at the beginning the section. That keeps the 2000 boxes from becoming fixated on one DC. But you *must* make that Registry change before upgrading. If you make the Registry fix *after* you upgrade, then any 2000 boxes who have logged onto the domain since the upgrade will remain fixed on that one DC. The only fix is to run around to all of those 2000 boxes and unjoin them from the domain, then rejoin them.

IN-PLACE UPGRADES: PRO

To summarize, then, the things in favor of in-place upgrades are the following:

◆ They don't require new machines.

◆ Your users keep their old SIDs and the domain keeps its old trust relationships, so any servers in other domains—resource domains containing perhaps file and print servers or e-mail servers, for example—will still recognize those users without trouble.

◆ The users keep their old passwords.

◆ It's simple, just a quick upgrade.

IN-PLACE UPGRADES: CON

Although in-place upgrades have a lot going for them, I recommend that many people *not* do them; here's why:

◆ You cannot make your former NT 4 PDC into a domain controller on an existing Windows 2000 domain; upgrading a PDC will always result in the creation of a new AD domain.

◆ You cannot set the new domain's NetBIOS name, as it's automatically set equal to the old NT 4 domain's name.

◆ You cannot merge your old NT 4 domain into an existing Windows 2000 domain.

◆ You upgrade *all* of the accounts, and it's a one-way trip—there's no AD rollback wizard. (Although you can, as I've suggested, keep an NT 4.0 BDC "on ice" as an emergency measure.) I prefer more gradual approaches.

◆ Any leftover junk in your old NT 4 domain SAM remains in your new Active Directory database.

Clean and Pristine Migration

The other approach is called *clean and pristine* (C&P). In this approach, you leave your existing NT 4 domains alone and create a new, empty AD domain. Then you use a program called a *migration tool* to copy user and machine accounts from the NT 4 domain (or domains) into the new AD domain.

C&P IS GRADUAL

In most cases, I prefer the C&P approach. For one thing, it's gradual. With an in-place upgrade, you walk your domain through a one-way door. If you find later that 2000 just isn't the thing for you, then too bad; you're stuck. But if you have a new domain and you copy some subset of your users over to that domain, then you just tell those users to log in to this new domain. If they start using the new domain and you find after a week or two that the AD's just not the tool for you, then you can always just tell the users to go back to their old NT 4 account.

Another thing that troubles me about an in-place upgrade is that I suspect that 2000's Setup program is more reliable when setting up a new empty domain than it will be in trying to create an AD domain out of an NT 4 domain; writing Setup programs that can upgrade existing systems has always seemed to me like trying to replace the carpet in a room without lifting any of the furniture. I'm impressed that anyone would try it, but it seems a task that's likely to fail. Furthermore, I have to wonder how well tested the upgrade option is; sure, large numbers of people tried out 2000 during its beta phase, but how many actually tried the beta to upgrade existing useful domains? Not many, I'd guess. But understand that I can't point to any one known bug in Setup's upgrade routine; it's just paranoia based on 27 years of working with computer software.

Handling Permissions with the New Domain

Now, it might look like this will cause you a bunch of extra work. Suppose Joe in the old NT 4 domain has permissions to access some server in some other NT 4 domain. Can he still? After all, the permissions allow Joe-at-the-old-domain to access the server; Joe-at-the-new-domain is a completely different user account. How can you get that server to let Joe's *new* account access that server? There are two approaches: re-ACLing and SID histories.

Re-ACL the Server

One approach is the obvious (and somewhat laborious) way: Just walk over to all of those old servers and just add Joe's new account to the permissions lists on those servers. This is called *re-ACLing* because the other name for a list of permissions on a network service is the access control list. It can be a real pain, but some migration tools will do that for you automatically.

Use SID Histories

You know that every user has a SID; that's been true since NT 3.1. But the Active Directory lets users have more than one SID. As migration tools create the new AD user accounts, those accounts of course get new SIDs. But the migration tools can tack the user's old SIDs onto the new user account as well, exploiting a feature called *SID history*.

What SID Histories Do Then, when a user tries to access some resource that he had access to under his old account, his workstation tries to log him in to that resource, using his new Active Directory account. Unless you've re-ACLed the resource, the logon is refused, as the server that holds the resource doesn't recognize the new account. But if the user has a SID history, then the workstation tries again to log him in, but this time uses the old NT 4 SID. This time the logon succeeds, and he's in.

What You Need to Create SID Histories Several notes about SID histories are important:

◆ You need a migration tool that knows how to create SID histories. Microsoft's free Active Directory Migration Tool, which I'll cover a bit later in this chapter, can do that.

◆ Migration tools create SID histories as they copy user accounts from older NT or 2000-based domains to your new native mode domain. Before a migration tool can work, you must create a trust relationship between the old and new domains. But no matter which migration tool you've got, your migration tool cannot create SID histories unless you have created that trust relationship with NETDOM. I covered this earlier in the section "Creating a Trust from the Command Line."

◆ You can only create SID histories in a native mode AD domain. So when you create that new clean-and-pristine AD domain, then make sure that it's already shifted into native mode before creating the trust relationship and running the migration tool.

How SID Histories Work   SID histories do their magic in a kind of clever fashion. To allow you to keep an old SID from a different domain, SID histories are just old user SIDs that masquerade as global group SIDs. For years it's been true that when you get authenticated on a domain, then the DC tells your server or workstation, "This is Mark, his SID is such-and-such, and here are the SIDs of the global groups that he belongs to." With SID histories, a DC just stretches the truth a bit and when it lists your global group SIDs, it includes the SID of your old domain account.

Getting Rid of old SID Histories   You can keep SID histories for quite a while—systems running Service Pack 2 can store up to 120 old SIDs. But SID histories are really just temporary measures, as you really only need your old SIDs as long as your old domains are around. That probably won't be for long. Once you've moved all of your servers and workstations out of the old domain, then the old SID is of no value. So it'd be convenient to be able to trim those old SID histories off of your user accounts. You can do that with a short VBScript that Microsoft describes in their Knowledge Base article Q295758.

DISADVANTAGES OF CLEAN AND PRISTINE

Although I've said that C&P has the advantage of reversibility, thus helping you to manage your risk, it's not without costs.

◆ First of all, you need more machines than you would if you were just upgrading. You'll need machines to act as domain controllers in the new domain.

◆ Most migration tools cannot copy passwords. The users will then have to create new passwords the first time that they log in to the new AD domain. This isn't terrible, but it's annoying to some.

◆ You've got to buy a migration tool. There *is* a free one that you can get from Microsoft called the Active Directory Migration Tool, but it's really intended for small-scale migrations of a few hundred users at best. These tools aren't cheap, costing somewhere in the neighborhood of $10 per user. That's *per user*, not per administrator, so those pictures of Alexander Hamilton start adding up.

◆ You cannot create a Windows 2000 domain with the same NetBIOS name as the old NT 4 domain, because that would require you being able to create two domains with the same Net-BIOS name (since you don't decommission the old NT 4 domains when you do a clean and pristine migration).

◆ It's more work. You've got to worry about when to move any given set of users, you may have to re-ACL, and so on.

CLEAN AND PRISTINE ADVANTAGES

To summarize its advantages:

- ◆ C&P lets you do gradual upgrades.

- ◆ C&P *copies* user accounts, not *moves* them. The old accounts are still there if something goes wrong.

- ◆ C&P lets you create your DCs from clean installs, avoiding the extra complexity and potential bugs of an in-place upgrade.

- ◆ C&P lets you consolidate domains, collapsing a morass of many domains into just one, or just a few.

A Free Migration Tool: NETDOM

Suppose you decide to migrate an NT 4 resource domain, merging it into a new AD domain. First, recall from NT 4 that a resource domain, in theory, has very few user accounts, just a lot of machine accounts. The strategy then will be to first convert both the master domains and the resource domains to Windows 2000. Next, you'd create OUs for each of the old resource domains. Then you've got to move the machine accounts from the old NT 4 domain to the new AD domain. What's that, you say, you don't want to pay for a migration tool to do all that machine account moving? Well, pop your Server CD into your CD-ROM drive and take a look in `support.cab`, a file that you'll find in the `\Support\Tools` folder. Among other things, you'll see a program called `netdom.exe`.

To use NETDOM, you'll need a user account in the old resource domain that has administrative powers; a user account in the master domain, again with administrative powers; the name of the master domain—the one that you want to move the machine's account to—as well as the name of the organizational unit in the master domain that you want the machine's account in. The NETDOM command then looks like this:

```
netdom move machine_name /d:destination_domain_name
➥/uo:current_domain_admin_account_name
➥/po:password_for_current_domain
➥/ud:new_domain_admin_account_name
➥/pd:password_for_new_domain /ou:OU_name /reboot
```

Thus, for example, suppose you were moving a machine named lemon.fruit.com from a domain named fruit.com to a domain named citrusfruits.com. Suppose also that you have an administrative account in the old domain, fruits.com, named fruitboss with password rind, and an administrative account in citrusfruits.com named VitaminC with password ascorbic. Let's say also that lemon is going into an OU called yellowfruits in the citrusfruits.com account. You could sit down to any command prompt and type the following command, which would move lemon.fruit.com to the citrusfruits.com domain in the yellowfruits OU:

```
netdom move lemon.fruit.com /d:citrusfruits.com
➥/uo:fruit\fruitboss /po:rind /ud:citrusfruits\vitaminc
➥/pd:ascorbic /ou:yellowfruits /reboot
```

The `/reboot` option remotely reboots lemon, as that's necessary for the changes to take effect.

Another Free Migration Tool: ADMT

About a month after releasing Windows 2000, Microsoft posted a free migration tool on its Web site. Named the Active Directory Migration Tool (ADMT), the tool is (or was when I wrote this—just search the Microsoft site if this URL doesn't work any more) at `http://www.microsoft.com/ Windows2000/library/planning/activedirectory/admt.asp`.

The NetIQ folks built this under contract to Microsoft. ADMT does a lot of things, but mainly it moves large numbers of user accounts, groups, and similar information *en masse* from an existing NT 4 or Windows 2000 domain into an existing Native-mode Windows 2000 domain.

USING ADMT: AN EXAMPLE

Here's how it works. Suppose you had an NT 4 domain named OLDDOM with several thousand users in it (to say nothing of machine accounts) and a domain named OLDDOM2 with several thousand *more* user accounts in it. Some higher-up comes along and tells you to combine them into one larger domain named NEWDOM. How do you do it?

Well, first you'd have to somehow re-create all of the OLDDOM and OLDDOM2 user accounts in NEWDOM. Now and then, you'd find that OLDDOM contained a user account whose name also appeared in OLDDOM2, resulting in a "collision." If both domains contain a jsmith, then somebody's going to have to become jsmith01 or something like that.

How to create those user accounts? You could, of course, just type them in one at a time. Or you could use a command-line tool like the ADDUSER tool in the Resource Kit, as many have. But what about the name collisions? ADDUSER's not too good at that. And let's take it a step further: suppose that NEWDOM is a Windows 2000 domain, meaning that it can contain organizational units. It might be nice to be able to plunk all of the Persons Formerly Known as OLDDOM Members (in the NT world, all users are Princes—sorry, couldn't resist) in one OU and the OLDDOM2 folks in a different OU. ADDUSER won't help there either—but ADMT will.

In a case like this, you could first use ADMT to copy the user accounts from OLDDOM (which ADMT calls a "source" domain) to NEWDOM (which ADMT calls a "target" domain.) Then you'd fire up ADMT again to copy user accounts from the OLDDOM2 source domain to the NEWDOM target domain.

To transfer the OLDDOM accounts, first install ADMT on a Win2K system, server or Professional, in the target domain. One restriction you *must* pay attention to, however, is this: the target domain, NEWDOM—which, as it's a Win2K domain, would more likely be called allfolks.com or something like that—*must* be a native mode Win2K domain; mixed-mode domains need not apply.

ADMT starts out in a standard MMC window, but all of its tasks are built to work as wizards, so they're pretty self-explanatory. Choosing the User Migration Wizard tells ADMT to copy user accounts over to the target domain. Try it and you'll notice a few things.

First, ADMT has a "test" mode. In test mode, ADMT will run through the User Migration Wizard, doing everything but actually writing out the user accounts. Second, while ADMT calls itself a migration tool, it's more of a "gradual account movement" tool. What I mean is this: ADMT didn't *move* the user accounts from OLDDOM to NEWDOM—it *copied* them. The difference is significant. Now every user has both an "old" OLDDOM account and a "new" NEWDOM account—meaning that if you move your users over to NEWDOM and you realize a couple of weeks into the process that something's gone terribly awry, you can always just tell them to log in with their old accounts! Third, ADMT can't copy *passwords* when it copies user accounts, not surprisingly, so it must instead assign simple initial passwords to the newly created user accounts in the target domain, and the users must then log in with those passwords the first time and change them immediately. ADMT lets you choose to either set the password initially equal to the username, or ADMT will alternatively create a complex password for the new user account. It then stores the new passwords in a text file, so that you can read the file and tell the users their new passwords. Fourth, ADMT will create SID histories.

CREATING NT-TO-2000 TRUSTS

ADMT requires that you create a trust from NEWDOM to OLDDOM, create one from OLD-DOM to NEWDOM, and then that you include your NEWDOM administrative account in the local Administrators group of the OLDDOM domain controllers. (And by the way, the local Administrators group still exists on Win2K domain controllers, but it's tucked away in the `Builtin` folder, rather than the `Users` folder.) I found that many functions would not work on member servers in the source domain unless I took the extra step of placing the target domain's Domain Admins group into the member server's local Administrators group.

WARNING   *Recall that you must use the NETDOM program on the Windows 2000 Server CD or the 2000 Resource Kit. If not, then you'll get a "downlevel trust," and ADMT cannot create SID histories if you only have a downlevel trust.*

INSTALLING ADMT

After downloading ADMT, you'll have a file called `admt.exe`. Run it and it'll install Active Directory Migration Tool. I find that it runs a bit more trouble-free if you run it on a domain controller. ADMT's setup program puts an icon to the program in the Start/Programs/Administrative Tools group.

READ THE HELP FILE

Once you've installed ADMT, start it up and you'll notice that it has a pretty extensive Help file. I strongly recommend that you read it; all I'm doing here is giving you a general overview of how to use ADMT, and the Help file has more detail to it.

SET UP YOUR ADMIN ACCOUNTS

You'll need to be an administrator on both domains in order to accomplish the migration. In my experience, this works:

◆ Create an account with domain administrative power in the target domain—that is, the new Windows 2000 AD domain.

◆ As there is a two-way trust relationship between the old NT 4 domain and the 2000 domain, you should be able to log in to one of the NT 4 systems, run User Manager for Domains, and add the Windows 2000 domain admin account to the Administrators group on the NT 4 domain controllers.

◆ Install ADMT on a domain controller for the target domain, the Windows 2000 Native-mode domain.

◆ Log in at that domain controller using the domain admin account that you created a few steps back.

Now you're ready to run the wizards.

MIGRATE THE GROUPS AND USERS

Right-click the Active Directory Migration Tool icon and you'll see that you can run several wizards. First run the Group Migration Wizard, where you can either test the migration or just do it. (Do the global groups first.) Running a test first is a good idea, of course. The next panel lets you choose the global groups to migrate from the NT 4 domain to the Windows 2000 domain. After that, the wizard prompts you to choose where to put the global groups— which OU, that is. Then you set options for the migration, as you see in Figure 8.74.

FIGURE 8.74

Setting options for group migration

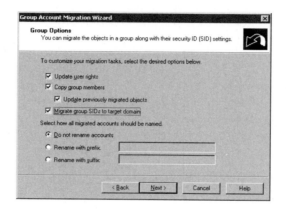

Update User Rights just duplicates whatever rights a global group has on the NT 4 domain on the Windows 2000 domain; for example, if Domain Users has the right to change the workstation time on the NT 4 domain controllers, then that group will have the same right on the Windows 2000 DCs. Copy Group Members tells ADMT to copy both groups and user accounts. I've found that this option works fairly well and saves me the trouble of having to go back and copy user accounts. Migrate Group SIDs to Target Domain to Target Domain tells ADMT to create SID histories, both for the groups and user accounts. You can then tell ADMT how to name conflicting accounts, so that, for example, if you tried to migrate a user account named Jack into a domain that already *had* an account named Jack, then ADMT could automatically add a prefix or suffix to the name. You might tell ADMT to add the suffix *NT*, resulting in Jack's new user account name on the 2000 domain being jackNT.

Click Next a couple of times and you'll see another options screen (Figure 8.75).

Two things are relevant here. First, as I mentioned before, ADMT cannot transfer passwords, so it has to create them. It can either just cook up some complex passwords and store them in a file for your convenience, or simply set the password equal to the username. Second, ADMT will convert roaming profiles, meaning that you won't lose your profile simply because you've moved domains— an old irritant.

A few panels more and the wizard converts the user accounts, and you've migrated your NT 4 users!

FIGURE 8.75

User migration
settings

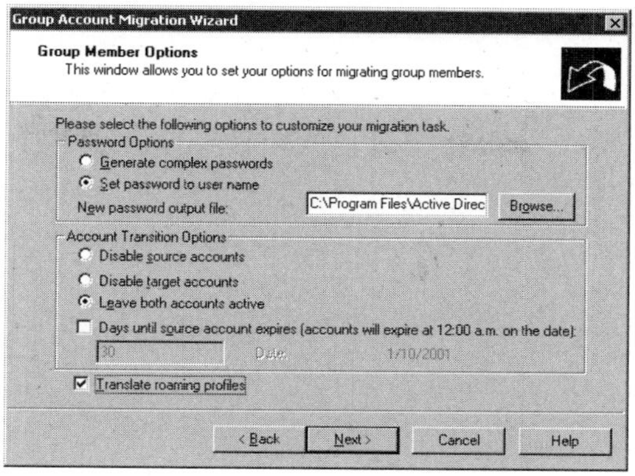

RE-ACLING WITH ADMT

Suppose now that you've moved the user accounts from OLDDOM to NEWDOM. As I've suggested, you'd like to make this a nice, gradual move that'll be easy to back out of. Now that the users have new accounts, you'll have to tell the file and print servers that they use about these new accounts—re-ACLing them. You could use SID histories to handle the permission issue, but ADMT will re-ACL for you. You might, for example, have a large share on a server in OLDDOM that the people with user accounts in OLDDOM can get to, but you also want their new NEWDOM accounts to be able to access those old shares on OLDDOM as well. (Eventually you'll move that server out of the OLDDOM domain and into the NEWDOM domain, so this is just an interim step.) In other words, if Paul has a OLDDOM account that gives him read/write access to some share on a member server in OLDDOM, and now Paul has an NEWDOM account, then we want ADMT to go tell that member server in OLDDOM to add Paul's NEWDOM account to its share, giving Paul's NEWDOM account read and write access as well. ADMT will do that, with the Security Translation Wizard, a tool that will not only add the new target domain accounts to share permission lists, it can also re-create user rights, NTFS permissions, user profiles, and local group memberships for the new NEWDOM account to give that new account all of the abilities of the old one.

But consider how difficult a job it is to find all of the share permissions, NTFS permissions, user rights, and the like that refer to Paul's old OLDDOM account so as to duplicate those for the new NEWDOM account. That could be a pretty slow process over the network, so ADMT remotely installs programs called "agents" to the servers that you direct it to translate security settings for. *That*, however, can cause a bit of trouble, in my experience: as I mentioned earlier, I found that source domain's member servers often would reject ADMT's attempt to remotely install its agent unless I'd placed the target domain's Domain Admins group into the source domain's local Administrators group—then it all installed fine. You re-ACL with ADMT via the Computer Migration Wizard.

There is a lot more that ADMT can do; all I've done here is to get you started. Again, I strongly recommend that you study the Help files before doing anything drastic with ADMT. But I think you'll like what the tool can do for you.

Active Directory Oddities

We're almost done with the Active Directory but, before I forget, I want to alert you to a few "gotchas" in AD. I'll list them briefly.

If Two Admins Both Modify a Group, One's Changes Get Lost

One of AD's strengths in comparison to NT is its replication model. Instead of a single read-write domain controller backed up by a bunch of read-only domain controllers, every DC is read-write and a complex multimaster replication structure makes sure that each DC knows about the changes that each other DC receives. Replications over slow WAN links compress data 10 to 1 before transmitting, and administrators can schedule when those replications happen. When you changed a single attribute about a user account under NT 4, NT replicated the user's entire record; AD only replicates the changed attribute.

So where's the problem? AD stores a group's membership as one attribute. Group membership as an attribute in combination with multimaster replication creates another potential problem: membership change collisions. The demise of the single-master model makes the following scenario possible: Suppose there's a DC in St. Louis and another in Ottawa, both part of the same domain. A group called FaxServerOperators contains, not surprisingly, the names of the users allowed to administer some mythical fax server software. Now suppose that Julie, a domain administrator in Ottawa, adds herself to the FaxServerOperators group, and at roughly the same time Steve, an admin in St. Louis, adds himself to that group.

They've each changed the members attribute that is part of the record that describes the FaxServerOperators object. Ottawa starts replicating Julie's change locally and across the WAN, St. Louis starts replicating Steve's change, and eventually they collide. Who wins? There's a long algorithm that AD uses to figure that out, but basically it's whoever's change happened last.

What to do about this? Well, it might be that you don't modify group memberships all that often, and so there's nothing to worry about. But if you want to ensure that changes to group memberships don't collide, then you could return to the days of NT 4, so to speak, by choosing one of your domain's domain controllers as a kind of "administrative clearinghouse," telling all of your administrators around the globe that before they change a group's membership, they should first focus Active Directory Users and Computers on that "clearinghouse" domain controller. You can do that, by the way, by right-clicking the icon representing your domain. Then choose Connect to Domain Controller and fill in the name of the DC that you want to work with.

Or you could always use the sneaky "version number" trick that I showed you a few pages back (heh, heh).

Make Changes on DCs Near the Target Client

The group collision discussion leads to some general advice for administrators in geographically scattered domains: Don't assume that AD's replication structure will respond quickly enough to serve your clients' needs. Let's return to St. Louis and Ottawa, but this time let's make Steve in St. Louis a regular user without any administrative powers, and Julie an admin in a centralized, company-wide help desk. Steve needs something changed in his AD account, perhaps because he's in a different department or his phone extension has changed. He contacts Julie and asks her to update his AD record, and she does.

But how long will it be before Steve sees the changes?

Both St. Louis and Ottawa contain DCs. When Steve queries AD about his account, he's most probably talking to a DC in St. Louis. When Julie makes an AD change, however, she's likely to be communicating with a DC in Ottawa. If she and Steve worked on the same site, then all of the domain controllers on the site would know of the change that Julie made within a fairly short time—DCs replicate any changes to the other DCs in their site in 15 minutes. But what about replication across WAN links—how fast is that and how quickly would Steve's local DCs know about Julie's changes? That's up to whoever designed your AD replication structure. Frequent updates across WAN links mean that news of account changes travels quickly, but it also sucks up WAN bandwidth, so if Julie and Steve's company is parsimonious in its use of WAN bandwidth for replication then it might be a while before Steve's local DCs see Julie's changes. But Julie can change that by focusing Active Directory Users and Computers on a DC near to Steve. By initiating the AD change in St. Louis rather than Ottawa, Julie ensures that Steve's local DCs will see the account changes more quickly. The cost is that Julie must do account changes through a DC that's communicating with her at WAN speeds rather than LAN speeds—but what price customer service?

You're probably thinking, "What about changes to passwords? Will they suffer from slow replication?" What if Steve asks Julie to give him a new password, as he's forgotten his old one, and so she does—but while she's connected to an Ottawa DC, not a St. Louis DC. Will Steve have to wait for however long it takes for Ottawa to replicate the new password to St. Louis? No: Windows 2000 treats passwords a bit differently. Suppose Steve tries to log in immediately in St. Louis, before any of the St. Louis DCs know of his new password. His attempted logon fails, but before the St. Louis DC reports that failure, the St Louis DC communicates with the single DC in the domain, which acts as something called the PDC Flexible Single Master of Operations, even if that PDC FSMO is across a WAN link. That machine always has the most up-to-date password, and can authenticate Steve for St. Louis.

In Single-Domain Enterprises, Make All Domain Controllers Global Catalog Servers

You've learned that the global catalog is essential for facilitating logins in multidomain forests. But what about single-domain forests? In a single-domain forest, it's just as clear that there's no question about what domain can log you in, so the GC seems sort of irrelevant, doesn't it? Well, yes and no, according to a few Microsoft experts. According to these Redmond techies, it's true that single-domain forests shouldn't need a bunch of GC servers, but apparently some server applications—they didn't say which—seek out a GC server regardless of the number of domains in a forest, so it'd be useful to have as many GC servers around as is possible, to keep that sort of application happy.

Making a domain controller a global catalog server is expensive in terms of server performance in a multidomain forest, but not in a single-domain world: the process of distilling a single domain down into a global catalog is trivial. So if you've got a single-domain forest, then you might consider making all of your domain controllers into global catalog servers.

Choose Your Domain Names Well

Some things never change. Once you've created a domain, you can't change its name. Of course, there are work-arounds to that: You could always create a new domain with the newly desired name, then use some directory migration tool to copy user and machine accounts over to that new domain, but that's a nontrivial process, no matter how easy our friends at NetIQ, Fastlane, Entevo, and Aelita are trying to make it.

Additionally, you can't rename a domain controller, at least not without a bit of work. As long as a PC is a DC then you can't rename it. But remember that in Windows 2000 you can shift a computer's role from domain controller to member server and back without reinstalling—so you could run DCPROMO and convert the DC to a member server, rename it, and then convert it back to a DC. But that's quite a bit of work to rename a DC.

Planning Your Active Directory Structure

The idea of this chapter has been to give you an overall idea of how AD's pieces work. I strongly suggest that you peruse the rest of this book before starting in on building your AD structure, as the AD *permeates* Windows 2000. But here are few hints on how to get started on designing your AD structure.

Examine Your WAN Topology

Domain controllers in a domain must replicate among themselves in order to keep domain information consistent across the domain. DCs need not be connected exactly 24/7—you *could* just dial connections between branch offices and the home office every day or so and then try to force replication to occur, although it's not simple and may lead to problems down the road—but on the whole you'll find that domains work best if they have constant end-to-end connection. If you have an area that's poorly or sporadically served by your WAN connections, perhaps it's best to make it a separate domain.

Lay Out Your Sites

Once you know where the WAN connections are, list the sites that you'll have, name them, and figure out which machines go in what sites. Also document the nature of their connections—speed and cost—to assist Windows 2000 in using the intersite bandwidth wisely.

Figure Out Which Existing Domains to Merge and Merge Them

You'll probably want to reduce the number of domains in your enterprise. One way to do that would be to merge old resource domains into an old master domain. The idea here would be that you first upgrade the master domain to Windows 2000, then merge the old NT 4 resource domains into that master domain as organizational units, using NETDOM, ADMT, or whatever other migration tools you might buy.

What Needs an OU and What Needs a Domain?

As you read earlier, you can divide up enterprises either by breaking them up into multiple domains or by creating a single domain and using organizational units to parcel out administrative control, or you can do any combination of those.

This is partially a political question, but you can get a head start by looking at the perceived needs of the organization. Is administration centralized or decentralized? Do the company's divisions work together closely, or is there not very much collaboration? And be sure to get corporate sign-off on these matters from the executive suite or be prepared to deal with the bruised egos later.

From a technical point of view, there are really only a few reasons to use more than one domain, as you've read. The biggest reason is replication traffic. If you have two large domains connected only by a slow WAN link, then you may find that it makes sense to keep them as separate domains. But think carefully about it—Windows 2000 is very efficient at using WAN links for domain replication traffic. There's also the "we don't trust the branch office" reason, as well as the far less likely reason that you need to grant different account policies to some group.

Choose an OU Structure for Delegation, Then for Group Policies

I haven't discussed group policies all that much in this chapter—they'll get more coverage later in Chapters 9 and 12 and other places—but one thing worth noting about group policies is that they're a tool for controlling users and computers.

As you read earlier, group policies don't really apply to groups; they apply to OUs. That would seem to mean that you should organize groups of people that you want to control into OUs so that it's easy to create and apply group policies to them.

On the other hand, recall that the great strength of organizational units under Windows 2000 is that you can create groups of users, which you can give varying degrees of control (*delegate*) over those OUs. In the end, you'll find that delegation can affect system performance more than group policies, so when you're chopping up your domains into OUs, choose OUs that make sense from a delegation point of view. Does Manufacturing want their own local administrators? Put the Manufacturing users into an OU. Does Publicity want to control their own printers? Then put their printers into an OU. In any case, you probably won't find much conflict between an OU structure that's group policy–centric over an OU structure that's delegation-centric: after all, any group that wants to share an administrator probably also wants that administrator to have control over it through group policies.

Use Just One Domain if Possible

Sorry for the repetition, but let me say one more time: minimize the number of domains. In fact, minimize them to just *one* domain, if possible. Windows 2000 domains can be truly huge, able to contain millions of objects, large enough for almost any enterprise. And Windows 2000's site-awareness allows it to make good use of your low-speed, expensive wide area network bandwidth.

Develop Names for Your Domains/Trees

Windows 2000 allows a wider variety of domain names than NT 4 allowed, but sometimes you can have too much of a good thing, too *many* options. If you're going multidomain, how will the domains fit together? Do you divide geographically, by division, by function? Where are the lines of control in the organization now?

Get the DNS Infrastructure Ready

I hope I've beaten this one to death enough so far, so I'll keep this short. Remember:

- Create a DNS zone whose name matches your AD domain's and don't be afraid to use an imaginary top-level domain.

- Make sure it's dynamic or do the jiggery-pokery with delegating the three zones.

◆ You needn't use a Microsoft DNS server, but it's not a bad idea, particularly with AD-integrated zones.

◆ Split-brain DNS is a good idea to protect your zones from external prying eyes.

◆ If you're having trouble creating extra domain controllers, joining machines to the domain or just plain logging in, use the NSLOOKUP tool to check the SRV records for global catalog and domain controllers.

Use the Power of Inheritance

The notion of things existing inside things runs throughout Windows 2000: organizational units can exist inside other OUs, and of course all OUs ultimately exist inside domains, domains exist inside trees, and trees exist inside forests.

When you set a permission or some other security policy on an object (*object* here meaning an OU, domain, forest, or tree), then anything created thereafter inside that object takes on that security policy. This is called *inheritance*. So, for example, if you wanted every user account in a forest to have to change its password every 10 days, it's far easier to set that rule up at the top of the forest before creating other domains, trees, OUs, and the like, because in general, from that point on, any new trees, domains, or OUs created in the forest will have the 10-day-password-change rule. (I said "in general" because it's possible to block inheritance; it's possible for an administrator to configure an object to ignore effects from higher-level objects.)

Overall AD Design Advice

There's lots to consider in building your AD and only you know what your organization needs and wants—I can't pass along a standard one-size-fits-all design for an AD. But overall, remember these things:

◆ Use sites to control bandwidth and replication.

◆ Use organizational units to create islands of users and/or computers, which you can then delegate administrative control over.

◆ Use domains to solve replication problems and possible political problems.

◆ Use forests to create completely separate network systems. If, for example, your enterprise had a subsidiary that wasn't completely trusted (in the human sense, not the NT sense) and you were worried that the automatic trust relationships (in the NT sense) created by common membership in a forest might lead to unwanted security links, then make them separate forests. The value of separate forests is that there is no security relationship at all between two forests unless you explicitly create the relationship using NT trust relationships.

Understanding and Using Certificates

Before leaving the Active Directory, let's cover a tool that enhances some of the AD's abilities. You've probably heard the terms *digital certificate* or, more likely, simply *certificate* and perhaps *public key* or *public key infrastructure*, or its inevitable TLA, "PKI." You've probably also heard that Microsoft has included

PKI infrastructure components into its NT-based OSes since Windows 2000. So what can it do for you, and how can you make Windows 2000 do it?

PKI is a topic so large that I'd need a fair-sized book to do it real justice, so this section is just an overview of PKI under 2000. The two most significant points that you should get out of it, however, are the following:

- PKI is a standards-based and OS-independent way to authenticate you—to prove who you are.

- Although it's got a lot of promise, PKI's not heavily used in Windows 2000 yet save in a few applications.

So to answer the "what does this do for you" question broadly: A certificate is a kind of ID card, a passport that proves with a high degree of reliability that you are indeed you. But they're only good for identifying people—they work for servers as well or, for that matter, just about anything that needs to prove its identity.

But there's more to it than just that. Certificates aren't a Microsoft invention; they're based on standards and vendors other than Microsoft support them, and in fact some of Microsoft's competitors have been heavy users of PKI for years before Microsoft noticed the field. Of course, that may not be a bad thing; after all, that means that Microsoft's PKI tools are based on the latest versions of well-understood technologies. One standard that you'll hear of a lot is X.509, a certificate format that Microsoft adopted for their certificate services.

That was the good news. The bad news is that PKI on Windows 2000 is still something of a work in progress. If you were to, for example, "get religion" about PKI and decide that you'd like to rip out the standard underlying Microsoft security systems and replace them with just PKI, then you can't. You can't, for example, tell domain controllers to stop authenticating each other with Kerberos and start using PKI. You *could* set your users up to log on using certificates, but it'd be a bit expensive (see the following comments about smart cards). Here's what you can do with PKI under Windows 2000:

- **Create and use certificates to allow two systems from different domains use IPSec.** As you read in Chapter 6, IPSec is a very nice way to authenticate and/or encrypt IP communications between two (or, actually, more than two) systems across the Internet. But those systems need to be able to authenticate and Microsoft (and the RFCs) only offer three options: Both sides share a simple phrase as the password (yuck), both sides authenticate via Kerberos (not bad, but only works if their systems are in the same forest), or via certificates. Certificates are really the only way that two systems that are not members of the same forest can accomplish IPSec.

- **Securing Web access.** One of the many ways that you can control who accesses your Web sites is via certificates.

- **Create and use certificates to secure e-mail inside an organization.** You can create user-specific e-mail certificates that users can use either to authenticate or encrypt their e-mail communications. The only problem is that all parties involved must accept as valid certificates that *your* server creates. Clearly that's a doable thing if we're talking about one company or a couple of companies in partnership, it but wouldn't work so well to secure mail to the great wide world. For that, you need to go to a generally trusted certificate source such as Thawte, which we'll cover later.

◆ **Smart card logons.** Certificates are a neat tool…but can we use them for logons? After all, that's the authentication that I'm most interested in most mornings. Sure, you can use them…but there is the small problem of entering the certificate to begin with. In a normal logon with a normal user account and password, you type in your logon name, such as jane@acme.com, and a password. But typing in a certificate would be pretty difficult, as they can be thousands of bytes long. So you *can* log onto a Windows 2000 system with a certificate, but only if you've got that certificate stored on a credit-card-sized device called a *smart card*. You also need a smart card *reader* on your system to do this. I found that add-on USB smart card readers cost about $70 apiece—not a deal-breaker, but probably a bit much to spend for a technology that's just getting started in the Microsoft world. In any case, smart cards relate to certificates in this way: If you want to do smart cards, then you *must* use certificates.

◆ **EFS recovery agents.** The Encrypted File System lets you set up people who can decrypt your files in the event that you don't remember your password. You designate new *recovery agents*—the emergency decrypter guys—with certificates.

◆ **Signing programs.** As you probably know, Windows 2000 and later operating systems support the idea of "signing" a given program, software installation package or driver, ensuring either the software's provenance or that it's been tested by Microsoft's hardware lab. That signing is done with certificates.

All of this is a good thing, but as I say it's just an interim step. In the future, it'll be possible (as a matter of fact, this is possible now, but it's unusual) to carry around one smart card that holds your personal certificate. Now suppose you have an account that you use on a Novell network, one on a Windows 2000 Active Directory forest, a One-Click account at Amazon.com, and so on. Here's how public key will make your life easier: You give a copy of your certificate to the Novell network's administrator, the AD forest's admin, Amazon, and the other folks who have an account of yours. They then make an association between the your certificate and the local account that they keep for you, a process called "mapping the certificate to the account." From that point on, your smart card gets you access to all of those accounts. Just one password to worry about, and finally that Holy Grail of account management—single logons. Log on once at your PC and you're connected everywhere.

Of course, that's not the only way that PKI could work. You could keep a certificate encrypted on your workstation and then use a standard login to decrypt it; it would then get you logged onto your Novell, Amazon, and other accounts. Or why not just put the certificate on a floppy? That'd work too…but in every case security is the issue, and as floppies are easy to copy and hard to secure I suppose that's why you don't see this answer. It's a shame, though, because although smart cards are a neat idea, it's going to be years (if ever) before smart card readers are standard on PCs. (And then we get to fight over which vendor's smart card technology we adopt, and, well, you've seen that movie before.) So personally I wish that we could use floppies as a sort of interim smart card, but I don't imagine it's going to happen soon.

Let's look a bit at how PKI works under the hood, then look at some of the specifics of PKI in Windows 2000.

Public Key Pieces I: Public Keys, Private Keys, and Authentication

Certificates and PKI terminology includes a lot of references to *public* and *private* keys. Let's see what they are and how they let people identify themselves to others. For example, suppose I want to negotiate a contract with you electronically, over e-mail. It's easy enough to send proposed documents back and forth, but the last part—the legally binding signature indicating agreement—that's been tough to do over e-mail. But what if I could send you an e-mail saying "I agree" that you could be 100-percent sure came from me? That'd do the trick.

All I'm looking to do here is prove that I sent it. There's nothing secret in the e-mail, so I have no need to encrypt it; I just want to *authenticate* it, or, in public key terminology, to "sign" it.

KEY FACTS ABOUT KEYS

To do this, I ask my computer to generate two numbers called a *private* key and a *public* key. They're called *keys* because I can use them to lock (that is, encrypt) some bunch of data, or to unlock (that is, decrypt) that data. (I know I just said that I don't want to encrypt the e-mail, but we *will* need to encrypt a bit of data, as you'll see.) PKI can be easy to understand, but you'll find it puzzling unless you're clear on a couple of things:

- ◆ Again, there are two different "keys" generated.

- ◆ They are quite long numbers, hundreds of digits long. That's so that it'd be nearly impossible for someone to just try every combination with a computer program—some keys are so long that the fastest computer in the world would take trillions of years to try every combination! (And by then, I probably wouldn't worry about the attacker cracking my data.)

- ◆ PKI uses the keys for encryption and decryption of data.

- ◆ We arbitrarily choose one of the two keys to be the private key and keep it hidden—no one should ever see this. The other key is the public key, and we can hand out it to anyone. For a long time, cryptographic algorithms used "symmetric" encryption, meaning that you used the same key to *encrypt* as to *decrypt*. But in 1970 or 1976—depending on who's story you believe—mathematicians came up with an interesting new kind of cryptographic method that uses *one* key to encrypt and a *different* key to decrypt. This is called *asymmetric* encryption. PKI uses asymmetric encryptions.

NOTE   I say "depending on whose story you believe" because for a long time the researchers credited with first describing and making practical an asymmetric encryption technique were two American mathematicians named Whitfield Diffie and Martin Hellman, who first presented their technique in 1976. In 1997, however, a British cryptologist named James Ellis claimed he'd created the idea for British intelligence back in 1970.

- ◆ If you encrypt something with the public key, only the private key can decrypt it. If you encrypt something with the private key, only the public key can decrypt it. Things encrypted with the public key *cannot* be decrypted with the public key, and things encrypted with the private key cannot be decrypted with the private key.

PREPARING AND SIGNING A MESSAGE

So let's see how I can use public and private keys to send some secured e-mail.

First, I run a program to generate a public/private key pair. I hide the private key somewhere safe on my hard disk. I make my public key easily available to anyone who wants it—hand it out on floppies, put it on my Web site, whatever. (We're going to refine this process soon, I promise, but for now let's just hand out public keys this way.)

Next, I prepare my message for you, something like "I agree to the following contract," followed by the text of the contract. That's our message body. I give it to my e-mail client and tell the client to "sign" the message.

The e-mail client then runs the message text through a program called a *hash function* that boils down the message to just a few bytes, a *digest*. Hash functions are also called *one-way functions* because you stuff in some data (your message, in this case) and get out a digest, *but you can't necessarily reverse the process*. That's not necessary. For example, suppose I wanted to hash the message "Meet me at the bridge." I want to boil that down to just a single number. I could do that by noticing that text files are all ASCII and that ASCII codes are numeric—"m" is 109, "e" is 101, a space is 32, and so on. My message then becomes this:

```
m e e t <space> m e <space> a t <space> t h e <space> b r i d g e
109+101+101+116+32+109+101+32+97+116+32+116+104+101+32+98+114+105+100+103+101 = 1,920.
```

Thus, I've boiled down the message into a single number, a digest. We're going to use that in a minute to prove that the message did indeed come from me. But before I do, let's notice why this is a one-way function. There would be no way to deduce from 1920 that the original message was "meet-me-at-the-bridge" short of generating all possible messages, computing their digests and then looking at the messages whose digests were 1920—and there'd be a lot of them—and guessing which one was my original message. (And, by the way, I just showed you the simplest hash function possible—crypto systems actually use more complex ones.)

So let me stress—digests aren't for *transmitting* data; they're for *authenticating* a data stream's author, or at least that's what we're about to try to do.

Now we've got a message body and a digest created from that message body—now it's time to do some encrypting. Using my private key, my e-mail program encrypts the digest. It then sends you an e-mail containing two things: the message text and the encrypted digest of the message text.

RECEIVING AND VERIFYING THE MESSAGE

Now let's see what you do on your end. Your e-mail client receives the message and notices that it is signed. Time to check the signature! So the e-mail program takes the message and, using the same hashing function as my e-mail client, computes a digest for the message.

Now, if the digest that I sent you (based on the message text that I sent) is the same as the one that you compute (based on the message that you received), then we can be pretty sure that you received the message accurately. But how do you know that the message came from *me*? That's where the encrypted digest comes in. You compute that the digest of the received message equals 1920. You want to check that against the digest that I sent you—but it's encrypted. Remember that I encrypted it using my private key. The only key that can decrypt it, then, is my public key—which you've already gotten. So your e-mail program decrypts the digest and sees that the decrypted value is 1920.

You could only have gotten a decrypted value of 1920 from my public key if the original value that encrypted the digest was my private key. You got a matching value—1920—so the message digest must have been sent by me. If anyone had tampered with the message en route, then you'd have a message that would lead to a different message digest value.

In this way, we can use public keys to verify that a message did indeed come from a particular sender.

WHY THIS IS IMPORTANT: NO "SHARED SECRETS"

Notice something about that communication—I sent something to you that I was able to guarantee came from me using encryption; I was able to perform the equivalent of physically signing a contract, but at a distance. We didn't *need* public and private keys to do that, however. Alternatively, I could have just called you up at the beginning of our negotiation process and said, "Let's do this over e-mail, but to make sure that we authenticate each communication, we'll send along encrypted digests of the mails." So far, this is no different from what we did. But if we didn't have public key technology, then you'd say to me, "Okay, how do I decrypt these digests?" I'd then have to say, "Hmmm...for this negotiation, I'll encrypt the digests with the password u8Kj$3NsF. Use that password to decrypt the digest." In other words, we'd do the same thing as we did before, but instead of using an asymmetric encryption method, we'd use a symmetric encryption method. That involves no great brain power, as people have been doing symmetric encryption for centuries. This password, which is known to us both, is called a *shared secret*, and all symmetric encryption methods require shared secrets.

But do you see the weaknesses in this method?

I'd have to get on the phone with you and read you a password—quite a pain. You might mistranscribe it, as uppercase and lowercase matter. You'll probably write it down somewhere, certainly as you're taking the message from me. And what if it's just plain difficult to find a time when we both can get on the phone, such as if you're on the other side of the Earth? (That may be the reason we're creating a business agreement electronically to begin with.) Or I guess I could just send it to you in an e-mail, but then I'm sending a password over the Internet—the not-so-secure Internet—and then I'd have to worry that someone intercepted that password.

Additionally, I'd have to come up with a different password every time I negotiated something via e-mail, as I wouldn't want to use the same password with more than one person—if word got out that I always used rutabaga as my password, then anyone could digitally impersonate me.

That's the neat part about public/private key pairs. I didn't have to tell you anything except my public key, and I don't care *who* has that.

Public Key Pieces II: Encrypted Communications (SSL)

You've seen that one of the keys—no pun intended—to PKI is encryption. We just used it to verify a message's sender, but we didn't really encrypt much of anything—just a few bytes of a message digest. But sometimes we want to carry on an entire conversation in secret, to encrypt the entire transmission.

For example, let's consider an encrypted transmission method that you've probably used quite a bit over time—a Secure Sockets Layer, or SSL, communication. You do one every time you buy something on the Internet and that little lock icon appears in your Internet Explorer status bar. That communication depends upon public and private keys, as you'll see.

Suppose you're going to buy something from Bigfirm on its Web site. You click the Buy Now link next to some piece of merchandise, and your Web browser sees that the destination of that link wants security—the URL of the page is `https://something` rather than `http://something`. (The extra *s* means *secure*.)

Your browser and Bigfirm's Web server will communicate via symmetric encryption. They'll agree on some key and then they'll use that key to encrypt transmitted data and also use that same key to decrypt received data. (Why not asymmetric encryption, you ask? Well, for one thing, it takes a *lot* more CPU time than symmetric encryption.)

So your Web browser and Bigfirm's Web server say, "Okay, just for today we'll agree that we'll use the key KD39z82fRnx+H to encrypt and decrypt. If we ever talk again, we'll pick another random key for *that* session—but use this one for this particular session."

Simple, eh? Sure, except for one problem: *How do they agree on the key?* The whole idea is that you don't want someone to be able to just listen in on the communication and decrypt the traffic as it goes by, particularly if that traffic includes the information "Joe Smith lives at this address and his credit card number is such-and-such." So we encrypt the communication, and so no one can listen in. Sounds good, except for one little thing.

How does Bigfirm's Web server tell your Web browser, "Let's use the key KD39z82fRnx+H?" Clearly it shouldn't communicate that information in cleartext (that is, unencrypted text), or the bad guys will just make use of the very same key to listen in on (and perhaps even modify) the conversation. So symmetric encryption will help us…if only we can get the whole thing started with a secure exchange of keys.

That's where *asymmetric* encryption comes in. Let's see how.

To begin with, Bigfirm's Web server has a public and a private key. Your Web browser, on the other hand, does not. (Why not? Well, do you remember telling it to create one? No? Then it hasn't got one. And even if it did, it wouldn't use it in this context, trust me.) So how could we use encryption to exchange keys? Well, the Bigfirm Web server *could* generate a session key—that's the phrase for these use-'em-one-and-throw-them-away keys, like that KD39z82fRnx+H key I've been talking about—and encrypt it before sending it to your Web browser.

But consider this: If Bigfirm encrypts the key with its private key, then the public key will decrypt it…but *everyone* has Bigfirm's public key. Well, then, what if Bigfirm encrypts the key with its public key? Well, then, you'll need Bigfirm's private key to decrypt it, and the bad guys don't have Bigfirm's private key, so they won't be able to steal the session key.

Unfortunately, *you* won't be able to use it either, as you also lack the private key. What to do?

Let's look at the other way around: What if *your Web browser* were to suggest the session key? Here's how it works:

◆ Your Web browser knows Bigfirm's public key and uses it to encrypt the session key.

◆ Your Web browser then sends the encrypted session key to Bigfirm's Web server, which uses its private key to decrypt.

◆ *Now* you've got an agreement on a key that you can use for encrypting traffic between your Web browse and Bigfirm's Web server!

You will hear the phrase *key exchange* a lot in PKI. It usually means the same thing: We intend to establish some communication that we want to encrypt using a symmetric encryption algorithm. But to agree on a key in the first place, one side encrypts a suggested session key with the *other* side's public key. The other side can then decrypt it, and no one can snatch the session key as it goes by on the wire but the intended recipient.

Public Key Pieces III: Certificates and Certificate Authorities

Thus far, we've seen that we can "sign" or "authenticate" a communication, leaving the communication in cleartext but allowing the receiver to verify that I'm the message's sender and that the message wasn't modified along the way. We've also seen that we can use public and private keys to exchange session keys that we can then use to encrypt an entire transmission, both authenticating it and ensuring that no one snoops on it.

But there's something I've kind of swept under the rug so far—how those public keys get disseminated. How would your Web browser get a copy of Bigfirm's public key? How would your e-mail client get my public key to use in verifying my message in the first place? I kind of waved my hands and said that I could give you my public key on a floppy or put it on my Web site, and that's only partly true. Yes, I could put my public key on a floppy, but then how would I get it to you? If you lived down the street, then I could hand it to you. If you lived far away, I could FedEx it to you, but that would get kind of expensive, and takes time. Sure, I could put my public key on my Web site, but then we're faced with a chicken-and-egg question: How do you know that you're actually looking at my Web site when you grab that public key and not a clever copy that some bad guy creates while somehow diverting your DNS lookups of www.minasi.com? You can't, so we need another method of handing out public keys. That method is called *certificates*.

WHAT'S IN A CERTIFICATE

A digital certificate isn't a physical certificate with an attractive border and your name in big fancy letters; instead, it's just a bunch of bytes that contain, at minimum:

- The name of the thing that the certificate describes—it might be a person (the e-mail example), a server (the SSL example), or anything else. Certificate documents call this the *entity,* as it's a nice generic name for "person, server, or whatever."

- The public key of the entity. (Notice how quickly we slip into that cert-speak—entity.)

- When this expires. Certificates have an expiration date. For example, the SSL certificate on my Web server expires every two years.

- What kind of certificate this is. There are certs for securing e-mail, certs for identifying servers for IPSec, certs for securing Web servers via SSL, and so on.

- Who issued the certificate: I'll explain this in a minute.

- Other identifying information, which varies with the type of the certificate.

GETTING A CERTIFICATE

That's what's *in* a certificate—but what *is* a certificate? Put simply, it is a public key and some identifying information about you, as you saw in the previous bullets, all collected and then digitally signed by someone else. The idea is that when I need to give you my public key then, as I said before, I can't just hand it to you unadorned, as you have no real way to know that it came from me. So instead I hand it to you...but the bytes that I hand you have been digitally signed by some third party that both you and I trust.

If that's not clear, let's see what happens a bit more specifically. First of all, I need a certificate before I can give one to you. Here are the steps to getting one.

First, I generate a public/private key pair. But why would anyone believe that it was actually me that generated the pair or, actually, the public key, as I'll never show you the private key? That's where the next step comes in.

Next, I contact a company that issues certificates, a *certificate authority*, or CA. Examples of such companies would be VeriSign, Thawte, or Baltimore. I give them my public key and ask them to create a certificate. Only *they* can create a certificate signed by them, as only they have their private key, and they generally charge for the service. (Or, in some cases, I might instead create my *own* CA and start minting my own certificates. I'll show you how to do that later.)

After that, the CA wants to make sure that I'm actually me, so they usually want to see something that validates my claim. For example, if I want a certificate for www.minasi.com, then I've got to prove that I actually own minasi.com and am doing business under that name. Verifying *some* certificate types is easy; to validate an e-mail certificate, you've just got to send the certificate to that e-mail address.

Once the CA is satisfied that I'm me, they build the certificate, including my name, public key, expiration date, and who they—the issuing CA—are. Then they run it through their hashing function and the digest for the certificate pops out. They then pull out their private key and encrypt the digest. Put it all together and it's a certificate. They e-mail it to me and I install it on the appropriate software—it might be Outlook if it's a "Hey, I'm really Mark Minasi" certificate for e-mail, or IIS if it were a Web server certificate.

USING A CERTIFICATE

Once I've installed the certificate on my system, here's how it gets used. Suppose again that I send you a piece of e-mail that I want to digitally sign. I'll take you through the steps on it, but first let's cover certificate types.

Types of Certificates

I'm about to explain how I could use a certificate to prove that a piece of e-mail that I send you actually came from me. But I want to note that while I've been just saying "certificate" as if they were all the same, they are *not*, not by any means. Certificates associate some identity and usually some attribute to a computer, user, or service. For example:

E-mail I've already mentioned e-mail signing certificates and encrypting certs without actually saying that they are two different kinds of certs. You can get a certificate that does both, but you sometimes won't. Inside that certificate would be a bit of information that says "This certificate can be used for e-mail signing," or "This certificate can be used for e-mail encryption," or both. *Why* would you have two different certificates for signing and encryption? Because you use them in different ways. You need the encryption key to decrypt encrypted mail that people send you. You need the signing key to prove that you are you over e-mail. You'd have two keys because you want to back up the encryption key, *and you never want to back up the signing key*. If you lost the encryption key, then you would not be able to read any old or new encrypted mail, so you'd want to restore that key. But if you lost your *signing* key, then there's no problem—you just get another one. But you would never want to back up your signing key because if someone got a hold of the backup and installed it on her system then she could impersonate you! Email certificates are typically associated with a user.

Web Browser   Suppose you want to access a restricted Web site. How do you prove who you are? One way is to create a Web browser certificate and associate it with your user account. This is different from an e-mail certificate because it is typically associated with a particular user account *on the Web server*.

Server   If I wanted to use IPSec to secure communications between two computers and wanted to use certificates, then each of those computers would have to have server certificates—a certificate associated with a computer rather than a person.

CAs   CAs have certificates that identify them as certificate-issuing authorities.

EFS Recovery Agents   You can designate extra people who can recover encrypted files, *EFS recovery agents*, only by issuing certificates identifying those people.

Software   Microsoft signs drivers with certificates that are not user or computer-oriented, but instead certify that someone has tested a piece of software.

Using a Certificate to Sign an E-Mail

First, I create the message. As before, Outlook runs the message through a hashing function and gets a digest. It then uses *my* private key to encrypt the digest. Outlook then assembles the e-mail message by combining the message and the encrypted digest as before, but then adds *a copy of my certificate*, sending them all as one digitally signed e-mail message.

After a bit, your computer receives it. It sees that there's a certificate attached to the message and looks in the certificate for the issuing CA. (Let's just say that it was Thawte. They'll give you an e-mail certificate just for the asking at /www.thawte.com/getinfo/products/personal/join.html.)

Next task: to validate this certificate. Remember that your system isn't validating my message; that'll come in time. Instead, this is your e-mail client—let's say you run Outlook also—saying, "I'm going to use Mark's public key to validate his message, but I only know that it's his public key because Thawte says that it is. But how do I *know* that Thawte actually generated this certificate? Ah, the certificate contains an encrypted digest *of the certificate*. I can check that..." and so it hashes the certificate to get a digest *of the certificate*, not the message. It then wants to compare to the digest attached to the certificate to the one that it just computed. But how does your computer decrypt this digest so that it can compare it to the one that it just computed? Well, Thawte created the e-mail certificate with its private key, so your computer needs Thawte's public key. But where does your computer get Thawte's public key?

You may be surprised to learn that it's already on your hard disk. So let's make a slight digression and talk about certificate stores and how to see the ones on your system.

Certificate Stores: User, Computer, and Service

Your computer has a place in its Registry called its *certificate store*. And not only does your *computer* have a certificate store, your user account also have one. It's also in the Registry. Services running on a system even have certificates. (I'm not going to cover certificates for services much here, so I won't mention this again, but whenever I refer to computer and user certificate storage, remember that there's a certificate storage for each service as well.)

That's an extremely important point, so let me say it again: There is more than one certificate store on a computer. Sometimes you'll want a certificate in your user store rather than your computer store or vice versa. For example, you will find that your copy of Windows in just about any version comes with copies of certificates containing the public keys of Thawte, VeriSign, Baltimore, and dozens of other CAs. Those sit in the computer's certificate store, not yours.

To underscore how that might affect you, consider what might happen if a brand-new certificate authority appeared, Joe's Discount Certificates. Where VeriSign wants hundreds of dollars to issue a certificate to your Web server so that you can do SSL transactions, Joe will issue one for five bucks. So a favorite vendor of yours, Acme Closeout Center (ac-close.com), buys and installs some Joe's Discount SSL certificates, saving themselves a few bucks.

You notice this the next time that you try to visit ac-close.com. Your computer wants to set up a secure SSL session with ac-close.com and when it examines ac-close.com's certificate, then your computer wants to validate that certificate. It sees that Joes' Discount Certificates signed the certificate, and so it wants to validate Joe's Discount Certificates...but your computer can't, as it doesn't already have a copy of Joe's public key in a certificate. So IE pops up a scary-looking message informing you that it can't validate the SSL transaction.

The Acme guys know this and have placed a note on their Web page explaining that you need to first download and install Joe's certificate containing his public key. So you download the certificate. But here's the question: Do you download it to your machine's certificate store or your user account's certificate store? It depends. If your user account roams then you might want to have Joe's public key in your user store, as it'd roam with you. No matter what computer you were sitting at, the copy of IE on that computer could set up secure SSL sessions with Acme Closeouts, as it'd find a certificate for Joe's, the issuing CA for Acme's SSL certificate. On the other hand, if you wanted anyone who sat at a particular computer to be able to connect to Acme without any complaints, then put the certificate into the machine's certificate store.

NOTE   *I should mention here that if you're using the Active Directory then a lot of this stuff becomes automatic. I'm showing you the simpler non-AD setup so that you can understand what's going on under the hood.*

WARNING   *If you're using Netscape Navigator, then things work a bit differently—for some reason, the PC version of Netscape doesn't use the certificate store built into the operating system. So assume that when I'm referring to some behavior in a Web browser I'm referring to Internet Explorer.*

Installing the MMC Certificates Snap-In

But how do you acquire, view, and remove certificates? You manage certificates with an MMC snap-in. We're going to create a custom MMC that will let us manage certificates for both our accounts *and* our computer's account:

1. Start up a blank MMC: Click Start, then Run, then fill in **mmc**, and press Enter.

2. In the MMC, choose Console, then Add/Remove Snap-in, then Add and choose Certificates, and click "Add" again.

3. As you can manage certificates for your user account, your computer's account or a service's account, the MMC needs to know which you intend, and offers you all three choices. Tell it that you will manage certificates for Computer Account rather than My User Account or Service Account, then click Next and Finish.

4. Now we'll add a *second* Certificates snap-in, but this second one will manage your user account's certificate store. In Add Standalone Snap-In, Certificates will already be highlighted. Click Add again to add it to your MMC the second time. This time, when asks whether you'll manage a computer, user or service account, just click Finish.

5. Now click Close to clear the Add Standalone Snap-In dialog box and OK.

6. We're going to save this snap-in, so let's do a bit more cleanup. Click Console, then Options.

7. Where you see Console Mode, choose User Mode—Limited Access, Single Window.

8. Next to the icon at the top of the dialog box, click the Change Icon button so we can find a better icon than that lame old hammer.

9. In the Change Icon dialog box, click the Browse button. It'll take you to `winnt\system32`. Navigate to `C:\WINNT\system32\certmgr.dll` and double-click it to display its icons.

10. Pick an icon and click OK.

11. Click OK to clear the Options dialog box.

12. Let's put this MMC tool on the Start Programs menu. Click Console/Save As and in the File Name field, fill in a name, such as **Certificate Manager** and then the Save button.

13. Close the MMC. Your Administrative Tools menu should now include Certificate Manager. Click Start/Programs/Administrative Tools/Certificate Manager.msc," and if you expand all of its folder then you'll see something like Figure 8.76.

FIGURE 8.76

Certificate Manager for user and computer certificate stores

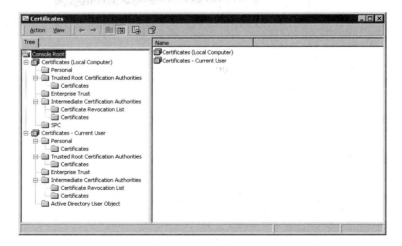

TIP *You may well have other folders in your Certificate Manager, particularly if you're on a system that's a member of an AD. Don't worry about it, all of what I'm describing will still work.*

Look in the folders named `Trusted Root Certification Authorities\Certificates` under both the computer and the user store, and you'll see the certificates that I mentioned—VeriSign, Baltimore, Thawte, and dozens of others.

But even though it *looks* as if all of those CAs have certificates in your user store, they don't really. Instead, when you log onto a system, you temporarily "inherit" all of the certificates that the machine's store holds. You can see this with a little more clicking.

Click on Certificates (Local Computer) and then choose View/Options. You'll see a Physical Certificate Stores check box; check it and click OK. Then click Certificates - Current User and, again, choose View/Options and check Physical Certificate Stores. When you open the folders under Trusted Root Certification Authorities, then your MMC will look something like Figure 8.77.

FIGURE 8.77

Certificate Manager with physical stores revealed

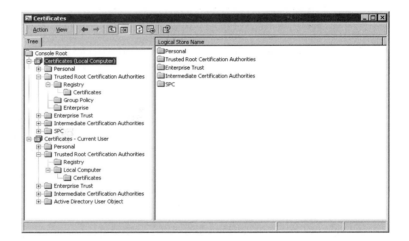

Notice that under the computer's folder, there are three folders—`Registry`, `Group Policy`, and `Enterprise`. This reflects the three places that together make up the machine's certificate store. Click Registry/Certificates and you'll see all of the CAs that you saw before. But now look under the Current User's icon for Trusted Root Certification Authorities—there is a Registry folder again (which you'll probably find is empty), and a folder called `Local Computer` with a folder inside it called `Certificates`.

That `Local Computer` folder is nothing more than a kind of "shortcut" to the *machine's* certificate store! Click there and you'll see all of the same CAs that you just saw.

And in case you're wondering, the "SPC" folder holds certificates of software publishers that you have agreed to trust—or at least Help says that it's supposed to be. Mine's empty even though I've trusted Microsoft and Macromedia software signing certs in the past.

Outlook Verifies the E-Mail Key

Now that I'm done with the side-trip about certificate stores, let's finish up the signed e-mail example. Recall that your computer had just gotten the e-mail and needed to verify the certificate. Your system has a copy of Thawte's public key and uses it to decrypt the digest on the certificate. It checks out—the digest created by Outlook from the certificate's contents matches the decrypted digest attached to the certificate—and so Outlook knows that it can trust the information on the certificate.

Now that Outlook knows that it can trust the information on the certificate, it reads *my* public key from the cert. It can then use that public key to verify the message that I sent, by again computing a digest, this time on the entire message, and then decrypting the enclosed digest and comparing them.

Trusting Certificate Authorities

Thus far, we've seen that:

- ◆ Public/private key pairs provide a way to authenticate or sign communications and to encrypt communications without having to use shared secrets.

- ◆ I need your public key for us to communicate, and you enclose it in a certificate when providing it to me.

- ◆ I want to know that this is indeed *your* public key and so you ask a certificate authority to digitally sign the certificate.

- ◆ To validate that CA's digital signature I need the CA's public key, also provided in the form of a certificate.

- ◆ This could lead to the question "who validates the CA's certificate" *ad infinitum*, so Microsoft makes life easier on us by pre-storing the certificates of major CAs on my computer in a certificate store.

- ◆ Computers and user accounts (and services as well) each have their own certificate stores.

The fact that Microsoft preloads Thawte's certificate on my computer relieves me of having to worry about how to get an honest-to-God copy of that certificate. But what if I want to use a CA other than the ones preinstalled? And that's not an unlikely circumstance, as two very common events would require me to answer that question:

- ◆ My company will probably set up its own CA for issuing certs that it will use internally.

- ◆ My firm might also have business partners, and we might have agreed to trust each other's certificates. Thus, if Bigfirm and Acme agree to give each other some amount of access to each other's servers, then they need to authenticate each other. Certificates can be quite a useful way to do this. If Bigfirm agrees to accept Acme's certificates, then Bigfirm will need to install a certificate containing Acme's CA's public key on its systems, and Acme will need to do the same things for Bigfirm's CA's public key.

TRUST AND SELF-SIGNED CERTIFICATES

Consider that *trust* word I've been using. What does it mean in a certificate sense? Consider a real-world thing that is sort of like a certificate: my driver's license. Suppose I want to get on an airplane. The gate attendant needs to see my ID or I don't get on the plane; let's see why.

The airline's desire is to verify that the ticket issued to Mark Minasi is indeed in the hands of Mark Minasi. It tries to do that by reasoning in this way: First, match the written name on the ticket to the written name on the driver's license. Then, verify that the name Mark Minasi goes with the person holding the driver's license by looking at the picture on the driver's license and then comparing it to the face of the person holding the license. (Gate attendants almost never actually do this part, so the system is pretty much invalid—but let's stay in the realm of the theoretical here.) Finally, we know that the license, which associates the name Mark Minasi with the face in the picture, is trustworthy because it was issued by the state of Virginia.

That's the key to understanding trust here—they don't really trust the driver's license, they trust that the state of Virginia has done some work to validate my identity. If a driver's license is a certificate, then, Virginia is the certificate authority.

But why should they trust Virginia? I mean, they don't have an army, issue currency, or have treaties with foreign countries; they don't have a seat on the UN, so why trust them? The answer is, "Because we just do." Even if I'm in a state other than Virginia, the driver's license is still accepted—Florida residents, for example, trust Virginia. As a matter of custom and convenience, at some point you choose to trust some authority for identification.

But that doesn't always work. Most places outside of the United States don't accept driver's licenses issued by U.S. states as proof of identification. Instead, they want a passport. But let's imagine that some country, say, Turkey didn't require a passport, and instead accepted U.S. driver's licenses as proof of ID. Why would Turkey "recognize" Virginia? It probably wouldn't. Instead, Turkey might reason in this way: "We have treaties with the US; we believe that they are a viable and relatively reliable political entity. Now we look at this certificate—driver's license—for this guy Mark Minasi. We don't know him, but he's got this ID issued by some 'state' called Virginia. We don't know *them*, either, but they're vouched for by the U.S. government—and *them*, we know! So we accept that this guy is indeed Mark Minasi."

This is an example of a "hierarchy of trust." Let's apply it to the email example. To review:

- You wanted to validate my certificate, which was signed by Thawte.

- So you needed Thawte's public key to check my digest.

- You found that in Thawte's certificate, which was sitting in your certificate store.

But now let's take it a step further: How do you validate Thawte's certificate, the one that Microsoft put in your certificate store when you installed Windows on your system? Well, if you take a look at Thawte's certificate, then you will see that it, too, is digitally signed and therefore can be validated.

But who signed it?

Thawte, that's who. The certificate containing Thawte's public key is signed, all right—using Thawte's public key. It's a "self-signing" certificate.

Well, what the heck good is *that*? Well, it's a *little* useful. After all, it's at least *internally* consistent; if the certificate's digest didn't match an actually computed digest, that'd be bad. But in the end analysis, you are simply trusting—in the colloquial sense of the word—that Thawte is a well enough run company that they won't give out bogus certificates (it'd be bad if Thawte gave some hackers a certificate for a Web server that said "Yes, this is the dell.com Web server") and that Microsoft didn't put the wrong certificate for Thawte into your copy of Windows.

In the PKI sense, "trusting" a CA means that you have installed their certificate in your certificate store.

TRUST MODELS

So you've seen that PKI can't work without trust and that a given machine trusts certificates issued by a given CA by placing that CA's root CA certificate in the machine's certificate store. You might call this the *Web trust* model—just as Microsoft has placed 106 root CA certificates in your Windows 2000 certificate store (107 for XP or .NET Server), you can add root CA certs for other CAs as well.

But there's one more piece to trusting that's worth mentioning here—delegation of trust. It's possible for your organization to have a *hierarchy* of CAs. Instead of just one machine issuing all of the firm's certificates, a number do. Why divide up the job? Three basic reasons—to spread out the work, to let subdivisions of the organization control their own machines acting as CAs and to *truly* secure the root CA machine.

The first reason should be obvious. I haven't mentioned this yet, but if you integrate your PKI with the Active Directory then every user and machine account *automatically* requests a certificate. With a large organization of tens of thousands of people, it'd be just impossible to get fast enough turnaround from one machine. So perhaps the Chicago office gets its own CA, Minneapolis gets one, and so on. But instead of having to run around and tell every machine to trust certs from Chicago, Minneapolis, and the other cities, you just tell them all to trust your root CA. What happens, then, when a machine gets a certificate created by a subdivision's CA? Well, recall the sequence of trust— you used my e-mail cert's signature to trust it because it was signed by some CA and you trusted that CA because it had a certificate which was signed ...by the CA itself. With a lower-level or "subordinate" CA, you just add a layer: A machine in Minneapolis has a cert signed by the Minneapolis CA, which has a cert signed by the root CA, which has a cert signed by itself. No more administration, but a good way to balance out the load. Nice—very scalable.

The second reason may happen if your firm's divisions tend to run their own IT infrastructure. Maybe Engineering wants their own CA. Or perhaps you view different kinds of certs as more or less important—maybe you want to secure the system that hands out SSL certificates more than the one that hands out e-mail certificates. In any case, it's the same approach. The subordinate CA has a certificate signed by the root CA.

The final reason is kind of interesting. I did some work for a large public certificate authority and at one point, they said "Would you like to go see the Root CA?" (I could just hear the capital letters in their voices.) Sure, I said. They took me through this vault into a room with layers and layers of security, which led to a room that contained...a computer. Just a computer, no network connections. Just a stand-alone machine. The idea is this: Companies such as VeriSign, Thawte, Baltimore, and the like don't have just one CA, they have many machines. But it's a hierarchy and *something's* got to be at the top. So they build a bunch of subordinate machines that generate certificates. Once that's done, there's really not much for the root CA to do but to generate certificates for the subordinate CAs. Once that's done, it probably makes good sense to keep the top dog off the network, as the hierarchy of trust ends with it. If someone were to hack that system and steal its private key, then they could issue bogus certificates in the CA's name...and they'd be instantly out of business. This way, the worst thing that happens is that a subordinate CA gets hacked. Then *it* could be impersonated, but not the entire CA.

Running Your Own Certificate Authority with Windows 2000

Let's sit down and try it. We'll build a simple CA with Windows 2000 and create a few certificates.

CREATING A CERTIFICATE AUTHORITY

All you need to make a Windows 2000 Server a CA is to install Certificate Services…and convince some systems to trust your certificates! I'll establish a CA called Avian Secure CA on a system called SPARROW , a system without an Active Directory.

To install the Services, open Control Panel, choose Add/Remove Programs, and then choose Windows Components. Click Certificate Services and Details and you'll see a dialog box like Figure 8.78.

FIGURE 8.78

Details view of Certificate Services

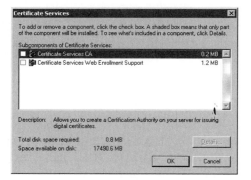

Check both boxes if they're not already checked. Click OK and the Control Panel will check that you really mean it, warning you that "After installing Certificate Services, the computer cannot be renamed and the computer cannot join or be removed from the domain. Do you want to continue?" Choose Yes and OK so that Control Panel reconfigures your server. You'll get a few screens that ask about how to configure this certificate server; the first looks like Figure 8.79.

FIGURE 8.79

Which kind of certificate server?

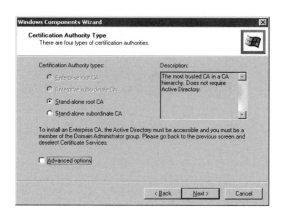

I've chosen Stand-Alone Root CA for my example here. If this system were an AD domain controller, then you'd have the Enterprise options that are grayed out here. Click Next, and you'll see a screen like Figure 8.80.

FIGURE 8.80

Describing the CA

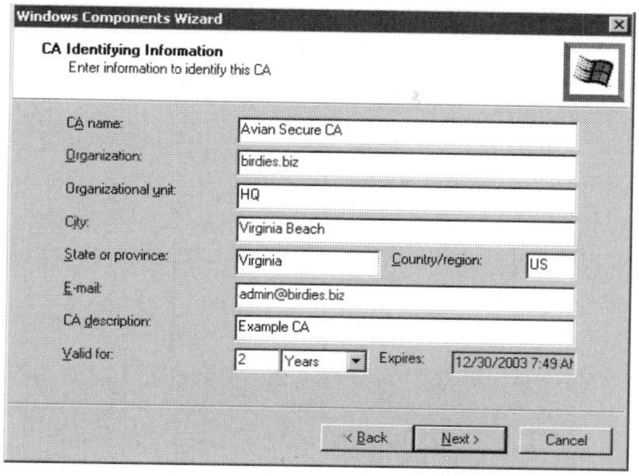

This is mostly just descriptive stuff (although if this were a real CA then there's no "just" about it—you need to provide this information so that people can see who you are. Fill it in and click Next, and you'll see something like Figure 8.81.

FIGURE 8.81

Where to store
the certificate
information

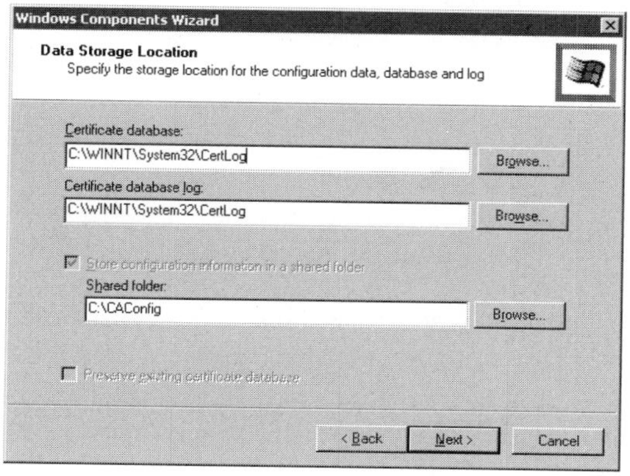

When installing Certificate Services on a test system, I found an unusual behavior. The first time that I installed the services, the system created a directory called `C:\CACONFIG` and shared it as \\servername\CertConfig. I removed Certificate Services, unshared CACONFIG and deleted the folder. Then I reinstalled Certificate Services. It tried to use CACONFIG, but only as \\servername\CertConfig. So if you're reinstalling Certificate Services, then be sure to create a folder for it beforehand and share it. Click Next and Finish and the software's installed.

CREATING AND INSTALLING CERTIFICATES

Now that the Avian's CA is up and running, let's issue a certificate. Let's suppose that I've got a system named WREN that wants a server certificate, so it asks SPARROW for one.

There are three steps to getting a certificate: You first request that the CA issue you one, then the CA decides to actually give you the certificate, and then you download and install it.

Requesting the Certificate

I request the certificate from a Windows 2000 CA by pointing my Web browser to the enrollment pages, prebuilt forms that I can get to by typing in the CA's DNS address and adding the phrase /certsrv to make a URL. As WREN is requesting a certificate from SPARROW , another computer on its same intranet, I just log onto WREN as an administrator, start up IE and type **http://sparrow/certsrv** to see a screen like Figure 8.82.

FIGURE 8.82

Opening certificates
Web page

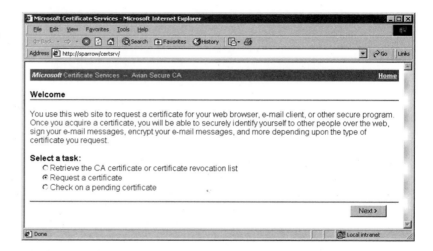

You see that there are three options here, but the one that will get us a cert is clearly Request a Certificate, so I'd click that if it's not already clicked and then the Next button to see a screen like Figure 8.83.

I guess the most commonly requested certificates are e-mail certs and Web browser certs, hence their presence here. But we're just looking for a basic server certificate, so I'll need to click Advanced Request and click Next *twice*. That shows Figure 8.84.

I had to fill in two items, the name of the server and a contact e-mail. Then I chose the type of certificate that I was looking for under Intended Purpose:— Server Authentication Certificate. But there's more to see here also, so I scroll down in the browser to see something like Figure 8.85.

Notice a few things in this option screen. First, recall that I talked earlier about the fact that you might sometimes want a separate key for signing and encryption; we see that here in the Key Usage options—Exchange means "use for encryption." You can set the key length—longer keys are more secure but require more CPU power to encrypt and decrypt. I tend to use the default. The only thing that I changed here was checking Use Local Machine Store. I do this because it's me running IE, and so by default any actions that I do—including creating certificates—will by default be associated with me rather than the computer. But this is a *server* authentication cert, and so it goes in the *machine's* store of certificates, not mine. This check box ensures that the key goes to the right place.

FIGURE 8.83

What kind of certificate?

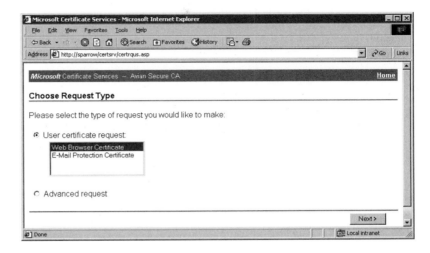

FIGURE 8.84

More details on certificate type

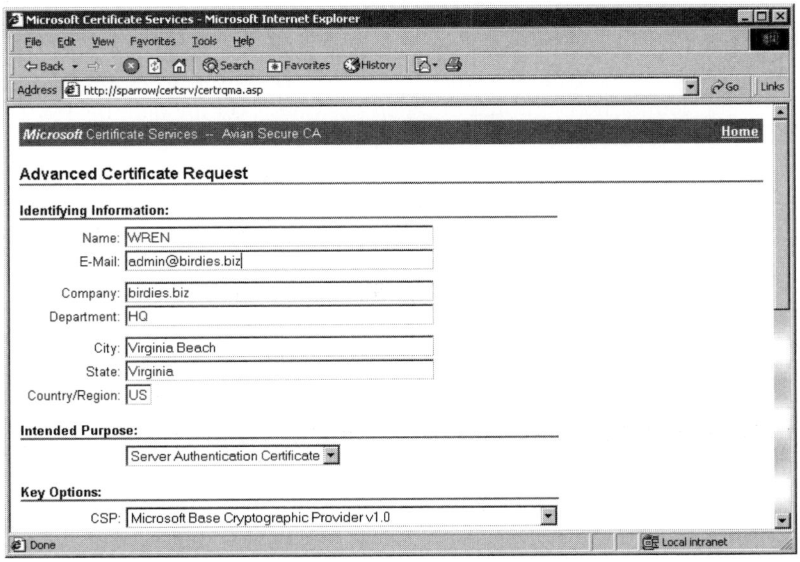

FIGURE 8.85

Putting the certificate in the machine store

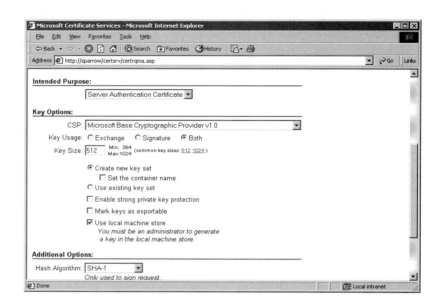

I click Submit to start the process. Wren creates a private and public key pair, encrypts the private key and stores it and the public key somewhere in the Registry, and sends the public key to the CA so that the CA can bind it into the certificate. I then get a message that the request was submitted, and to return later to retrieve the certificate.

The CA Issues the Certificate

Now the certificate request sits at the CA, waiting to be approved by an administrator. (That "administrator" would be me in this case.) So I log onto the CA computer, SPARROW, to approve the certificate.

There's a tool on SPARROW that arrived with the Certificate Services—an MMC called Certificate Authority. I start it and click the Pending Requests folder to see Figure 8.86.

FIGURE 8.86

Certificate Authority snap-in

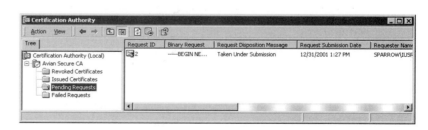

You see the certificate request in the figure; I need only right-click it and choose Issue (my only other option is Deny) and the certificate is issued.

NOTE *You can, if you want, tell your CA to automatically generate any CA requested. Just open up the Certificate Authority snap-in and right-click the icon for the server. Choose Properties (no surprise there, eh?) and the Policy Module tab. In that tab, click the Configure button and choose the Default Action tab in the resulting policy page. On that tab you'll see two radio buttons telling the CA what to do when it receives a certificate request—Always Issue the Certificate and Set the Certificate Request Status to Pending. Administrator Must Explicitly Issue the Certificate. The latter choice is enabled by default on a stand-alone CA, but you could change it, although I can't see why you'd do that—handing out certificates to any old random person doesn't sound very "secure."*

Retrieving the Certificate

Moving back to Wren, I return to `http://sparrow/certsrv` and this time I choose the radio button for the task Check on a Pending Certificate and click Next to show me a page like Figure 8.87.

FIGURE 8.87

Choose a pending certificate request

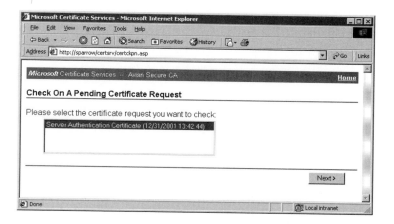

There's only one pending request so I just click Next and get the news that it's been issued, as you see in Figure 8.88.

I click the Install This Certificate link and get a final Web page telling me that it installed without a hitch.

WARNING *Remember, I'm assuming that you're using Internet Explorer. You've got to do more work to make this work with Netscape.*

Remember that I checked that box telling the system to create the key pair in the local machine store? I can check that now by opening up the Certificate Manager snap-in. The new cert is *either* in the `Personal` folder on the Local Computer store or the user store, as you see in Figure 8.89.

Notice that the certificate turns out to be in the Local Computer store, as I wanted. But if I were to do everything else the same then the certificate would end up in the user store. That's not to say that I couldn't *move* it from the user's `Personal` folder to the computer's `Personal` folder by just cutting and pasting in the Certificate Manager snap-in—but specifying where to put it from the beginning saves a bit of work.

FIGURE 8.88

The certificate is ready for installation

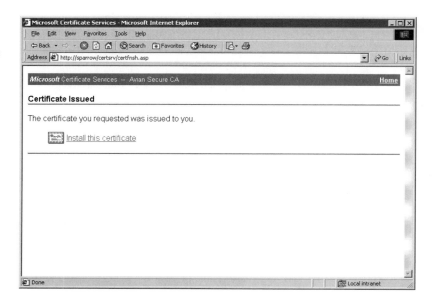

FIGURE 8.89

The new certificate is installed.

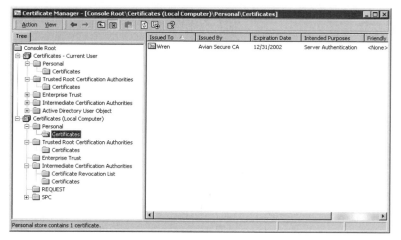

NOTE *In an Active Directory–integrated CA, your machine would automatically* request the certificate, the CA would *automatically issue the cert, and the machine would automatically install it.*

TRUSTING THE NEW CERTIFICATE AUTHORITY

So Wren now has a certificate created by a certificate authority called Avian CA—but isn't something missing here? *Wren doesn't trust Avian CA!* We never introduced them! So what happens when a system holds a certificate created by a CA that it doesn't trust? Well, you can see that by double-clicking on the certificate and then the Certification Path tab, as in Figure 8.90.

FIGURE 8.90

Certification path
for new certificate

Hmmm...now, is *that* odd—it seems that Wren likes this certificate and the whole idea of the Avian CA altogether. What's going on here? A look in the Trusted folder shows that *there's an Avian certificate in there.* Windows 2000 got a little sneaky and stayed one jump ahead of us—when it installed the new certificate for Wren, it also installed the root CA certificate for the CA that created the certificate. Well, that saves us some work.

But sometimes you'll want a system to trust a CA even if that system *doesn't* hold any certificates issued by that CA. In that case, you need to download and install the root CA certificate for that CA.

There's an easy way to do it, via the /certsrv URL that you've already met. You might have noticed that one of the options on the first page was to Retrieve the CA Certificate or Certificate Revocation List. Click that and you'd see a screen like Figure 8.91.

Click Install This CA Certification Path, and you'll get the CA's root certificate. But, as we've seen before, IE puts the certificate not in the Local Computer's store, but instead, maddeningly, in the user's certificate store. That's no problem, it's just a few more clicks to move it to the Local Computer certificate store—in your Certificate Manager, just locate the Trusted Root Certification Authorities\Certificates folder under Certificates - Current User. Find the certificate that IE just installed and right-click it, then choose Cut. Now locate and right-click the Trusted Root Certification Authorities\Certificates folder under Certificates (Local Computer) and choose Paste, and then confirm the action when the operating system asks if you're sure. (There may be an easier way, but I've not found it yet.)

Windows 2000–based CAs also maintain a URL for direct download of their root CA: http://*servername*/certenroll/*servername*_*CAname*.crt, where *servername* is the DNS name of the server and *CAname* is the certificate authority's name. So, for example, if the certificate server's DNS name were swallow.bigfirm.biz and the CA's name were Avian, then the URL would be http://swallow.bigfirm.biz/certenroll/swallow.bigfirm.biz_Avian.crt. You can represent blanks in a URL with %20—for example, as our CA's full name is Avian secure CA on a server simply named swallow, its URL would be http://swallow/certenroll/swallow_avian%20secure%20ca.crt.

FIGURE 8.91

Fetching the root CA's certificate

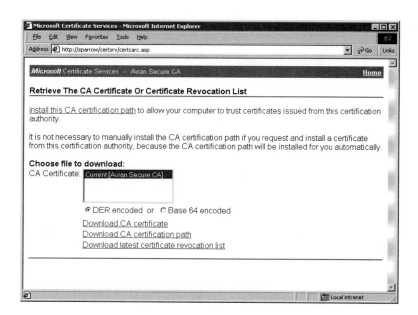

Using PKI in Windows 2000

Now that you've seen how to get a simple certificate, let's look at the specifics of getting some of Windows 2000's PKI-aware components to work.

IPSEC

You read in Chapter 6 that IPSec is a pretty powerful and flexible way to sign and/or encrypt communications between two machines or amongst a greater number of machines. But IPSec needs authentication and only supports three kinds—Kerberos (which is simple but only works between machines from the same domain), a shared secret (which is all too easily compromised, as all sides must agree upon the secret), and certificates. If you want to use IPSec to secure communications between two systems in different domains, or for that matter any set of systems that might be in any number of domains or workgroups, then certificates are the way to go.

Using certificates for IPSec is simple, once you know what *kind* of certificate to use. First of all, you're looking for a certificate that goes on the Local Computer certificate store, so use the Advanced Request and check the Use Local Machine Store. Under Intended Purpose, choose either Client Authentication Certificate or IPSec Certificate. (For some reason, a *server* authentication certificate won't let two servers communicate via IPSec. Go figure.) Make sure that all systems that want to use IPSec to talk to each other have a certificate from the same CA.

Finally, when you select the authentication method for your IPSec rule, then choose Use a Certificate from This Certificate Authority and click Browse; you'll see a list of the CAs that the system recognizes. Choose the one CA that all of your IPSec-ing systems, and IPSec will work like a charm.

But before you try this the first time, do yourself a favor: Get the IPSec working, and *then* add the certs. If you're unfamiliar with both IPSec and certificates then you're bound to miss a step somewhere and not know where to go. Start out with a simple shared secret for authentication—it's just a configuration step. Once IPSec's working, get the certificates from the CA onto the machines and check their Local Computer stores to ensure that the certs are there and are the right type. *Then* change the IPSec rule to use certificates.

E-MAIL

As I've already said, a Windows 2000 PKI can generate certificates for signing and/or encrypting e-mail. It's even fairly simple to create the certs because, as you may recall, e-mail certs are one of the two "one-click" certificates in the Web-based request page. But there are few specific wrinkles about e-mail certificates that you should know.

First, recall that when you request a certificate you must fill in a small form. Two of those items are Name, which you can use to name the certificate, and e-mail address, which was pretty irrelevant in the server certificates that we've talked about so far. (In fact, I've often left the field blank, and it works fine.) But for e-mail, that's not the case: Whatever e-mail account you fill in there is the only e-mail account that can use this certificate. If you regularly use several e-mail addresses, then you'll need at least one certificate for each one.

Second, when you *do* request the certificate, either through the simplified or Advanced Request interface, the type of certificate that you want is called an E-Mail Protection Certificate. You *can* use the simplified interface, but you might choose to use the Advanced Request interface for two reasons.

◆ First, you can mark the private key as exportable in Advanced; you can't do that in Basic. Why would you want to? Because you can export the keys to a floppy and lock them away somewhere. Then, if your system crashes, you can reinstall (*import* is certificate-ese) the keys to the new system.

◆ Advanced lets you create separate certificates for signing and encryption. (Recall that for some reason Advanced calls encryption certificates *Exchange* certificates.) *That's* important because you *would* export and store your *encryption* keys, you'd never export and store your signing keys. If you lose a signing key, just revoke its certificate (more on that later) and request a new one.

Third, both the sender and receiver of a piece of e-mail may both need certificates. If all I want to do is send you a piece of signed e-mail, then all I need is an e-mail certificate issued by an authority that you recognize. You need not have any certs. But if I want to send you *encrypted* e-mail, well, that's a bit tougher.

Recall how SSL encryption worked: The server has a certificate and the client (your Web browser) usually doesn't. So they need to agree on a password for symmetrical encryption in their session. But how to agree on that key without sending it in plaintext? Simple—the client offers a password (*session key* is the better phrase, actually) to the server by encrypting it *with the server's public key*. No one can decrypt this but the server, so the secret's safe.

Now suppose I want to encrypt some e-mail to you. As with SSL, I'll use *your* public key to encrypt the mail that I want to send to you. But e-mail's not a real-time communication process, so you might not even be online when I try to mail you. Therefore, I would have no way to *get* your public key unless you send it to me beforehand! To send you encrypted mail, then, I'd *first* have to ask you to send me a piece of mail with your public key on it. *Then* I could use that from this point on to encrypt mail to you.

Finally, you must tell your e-mail client software to use your certificates and when to use them. As there are a ton of popular e-mail clients, I can't explain how to do it on all of them—but most clients have an Options/Security or the like. You can usually tell your system whether to sign and/or encrypt everything (which seems a might extreme to me), or just pick which items to sign or encrypt.

Remember also that the e-mail certs that you issue with your CA won't be much good on the public Internet. But Thawte is generous enough to hand out Internet-friendly e-mail certs for free, so if you'd like to start signing your e-mails then visit `www.thawte.com/getinfo/products/personal/join.html`.

WEB BROWSER

Browser certificates are popular in so-called "extranet" situations, where you want to secure a Web site—that is, you don't want just anyone to be able to access it—but you want some people outside your firm to be able to get to the pages. So how do you limit access to a Web page or pages?

One simple way is to secure the pages with NTFS permissions. You can say that only Joe, Jane, and Sue can read `blahblah.htm` on your Web site; so if anyone tries to access `http://yourwebservername/blahblah.htm`, then a logon dialog box will pop up in Internet Explorer asking for a name, password, and domain. NTFS permissions on Web pages are simple to set up and secure for logons—that dialog box does a challenge-response authentication, so no passwords are flying around in cleartext.

But that means that you've got to create user accounts for Joe, Jane, and Sue and, worse, that means that you've got to maintain them. Even worse yet, it's really only going to work if Joe, Jane, and Sue sitting on-site at that other company are using Windows and Internet Explorer! A better answer is a client authentication system that works across platforms and X.509 certificates are a good one. An in-depth discussion of this would require more details about IIS than I've got space for here, but here's the overview.

Setting Up Certificate-Based Access Control

Basically you can limit who gets access to a Web site server in a few steps.

WARNING   *Notice that this will only apply at the Web site level—you cannot use certificates to control access to particular Web pages.*

1. First create and install a Server Authentication Certificate from your internal CA. Don't forget to tell the enrollment page to place the certificate in the local computer's certificate store. Now the certificate is on the server and IIS sees it, but IIS doesn't know which, if any, Web sites to associate the certificate to.

2. Then attach it to this particular Web site in IIS. In the Internet Services Manager, right-click the icon for the Web site that you want to secure, choose Properties and click the Directory Security tab. Then click the Server Certificate button to start a wizard. Click Next and choose Assign an Existing Certificate and Next again, and then choose the certificate that you just installed, then Finish.

3. Next, require people to use certificate-secured communications; in the same Secured Communications area as the Server Certificate button that you just pushed. Click Edit and, in the

resulting dialog box, check the Require Secure Channel (SSL) box and Require Client Certificates. Click OK twice to clear the dialog boxes.

4. That Web site can only be accessed with URLs starting with `https://` rather than `http://`, so set up all of your hyperlinks accordingly on pages that refer to your newly secured site.

5. Clients will also need certificates. Just run the Web enrollment page as you've seen before, and this time choose a Web Browser Certificate.

Now when a client tries to connect to the Web site they will be refused unless they've got a certificate from a CA trusted by the IIS machine.

Tightening Up Certificate and IIS Security: The Certificate Trust List

Notice that—all you need is a certificate from *any* trusted CA. Unfortunately, that's probably not what you wanted.

To see what I mean, suppose ABC company wants to set up a Web site that a few of XYZ company's employees can access. So ABC does what I just described—set up the Web site, create a CA, put a server authentication certificate on the Web server, tell IIS to use that certificate for directory security, require secure channel, and hand out Web browser certificates to the small number of XYZ employees who they want mucking around on their Web site. This will work fine, and those XYZ employees will be able to access the ABC Web site.

Unfortunately, so will other people.

All IIS requires in this case is a Web browser certificate from *any* CA that the IIS server's operating system trusts. Therefore, any Joe Blow coming to ABC's restricted Web site will get access even *without* a Web browser certificate from ABC's CA; a Web browser certificate from Thawte, VeriSign, Baltimore, or any of the dozens of other in-the-box, "pre-trusted" CAs will do.

Fortunately, IIS has a mechanism to restrict the CAs that it should accept certificates from to authenticate to a particular Web site. It's called a *certificate trust list*. When you create and activate one, you modify IIS's behavior in this way: Where it previously would take certs from any trusted CA, now it only takes certs from the specific CAs that you list. To create one:

1. Open up Internet Services Manager (Start/Programs/Administrative Tools/Internet Services Manager).

2. Right-click on the site that you've secured with certificates, and choose Properties.

3. Click the Directory Security tab.

4. In the Secure Communications section, click Edit.

5. In the resulting dialog box, check Enable Certificate Trust List.

6. You'll need to create a CTL now. Click the New button to start a wizard. Click Next to get to the first page.

7. In the Certificates in the CTL page, click Add from Store and choose the CAs whose certificates you want IIS to accept for access to your Web site. Once you've done that, choose Next.

8. In the following panel, fill in the fields to describe the CTL. Click Next and Finish.

Other Certificate Uses In IIS

You can take this further if you like, with *one-to-one* or *one-to-many*" mapping. The idea here is that you could create a set of local or domain user accounts and associate particular certificates with particular user accounts. So if the Web browser certificate Lara Wilson is associated with—*is mapped to*—a Windows 2000 user account lwilson then you can use IIS's normal security features to control Lara's access. But Lara can get to the Web site using, again, non-Windows desktops. In a *many-to-one* situation, you do something similar but instead of mapping certs to users one by one, you write some rules that the system uses to do that mapping on the fly.

If you use auditing, then you should be aware of a somewhat annoying side effect of certificates: Anyone accessing a secure Web site with certificates always generates a "logon failure" item in the Security event log. It's kind of annoying, as it gives the false impression that you're under a major hack attack.

You'll read more about IIS in Chapter 17.

EFS CERTIFICATES

You'll read more about the Encrypting File System in Chapter 10, but the basics are that it lets you encrypt and thereby protect files. But if you forget your password to your user account, then you can't decrypt your files. That's why EFS requires that you create at least one account that has the ability to decrypt files, an *EFS recovery agent*. As you'd probably guess by now, there's nothing to it. Just create an EFS Recovery Agent certificate—you'll have to use Advanced request—and install it on the target machine, using the Local Security Policy snap-in under the Public Key Policies/EFS Recovery Agent folder—just right-click it, choose Add, and a wizard lets you assign the new Recovery Agent. The only catch is, as usual, that the system must accept certificates from the CA.

Revoking Certificates

This whole PKI/certificate thing is pretty neat, but there are a few wrinkles to be aware of. For one, what happens when you've got to get rid of a certificate? For example, suppose my laptop has a certificate on it and someone steals it. I sure don't want them sending e-mail with my digital signature on it! There is an answer—certificate revocation. In this section, we'll see how that works.

Revoking a certificate is straightforward. Just start up the Certificate Authority snap-in and look in the Issued Certificates folder. Find the certificate that you want to revoke and right-click it and choose Revoke Certificate. It'll offer you the chance to record one of seven reasons (including Unspecified), and the certificate then goes into the Revoked Certificates folder.

So the certificate is now officially *persona non grata* around the network? Well, not exactly, not just yet. Remember that one of the great strengths of certificates is the fact that they rely on a hierarchy of trust—that is, if your system holds a cert that's signed by a server whose cert your system also holds, then the system won't stop every time that it examines the cert to locate and contact the root CA or even the issuing CA. So it takes a little time for a client (or a server) to realize that a certificate is no longer any good.

In the PKI world there is an important acronym, CRL. It stands for Certificate Revocation List. CAs issue CRLs on a regular basis, weekly by default, but you can make it more or less often. (In Certificate Authority, right-click the Revoked Certificates folder and choose Properties and you'll see a Publication Interval, which you can change.) Or you can force a CA to generate—*publish* is PKI-ese—a new CRL—by right-clicking the Revoked Certificates folder and choosing Publish.

Different client systems check CRLs at different intervals and upon different events. But most will automatically get a new CRL when the old one expires, so you might want to set the expiration time to be more frequent than the weekly default value. Of course, that means more network traffic.

If you need to find out the age of the CRLs on an IIS server, look in `\Documents and Settings\ Default User\Local Settings\Temporary Internet Files\` for files with the `.crl` extension. (They are probably in folders *inside* that folder.) Double-click on the CRL files, and you'll see when they were published and when the next update will be.

Need to have an IIS server immediately recognize a revoked certificate? Then do this: First, force the CA that issued the certificate to publish a new CRL. Second, go to the IIS server and find and delete the CRL file for the CA that issued the certificate. Finally, restart IIS—not just the one site, but the entire IIS service. (Again, just the service—you needn't reboot the entire server.) Clients trying to access the Web site will see an "HTTP 403.13 - Forbidden: Client certificate revoked" message.

By now, we've covered a lot of theory and a smaller amount of concepts. Let's move to more nuts and bolts, starting with a discussion of user accounts—in the next chapter.

Chapter 9

Managing and Creating User Accounts

BY NOW YOU'VE LEARNED the basics of Active Directory, how to install and configure major components of Windows 2000 Server, the ins and outs of the new user interface and MMC, as well as the care and feeding of the Registry. Now let's tackle something at the heart of an administrator's job: creating and managing users and groups. In this chapter, you'll first learn how to create user accounts, both in a workgroup and domain-based environment. You'll then see how to use groups—there are four types—to simplify your administration tasks. After that, you'll understand how to use policies to simplify user management, extend user rights, and lock down Desktops. Then you'll learn how to use and manage profiles.

Creating Local and Domain User Accounts

While most of you will be using Active Directory, some of you might still be using NT 4 domain controllers, and so, of course, you'd create any of those user accounts the old way, with User Manager for Domains. But if you need to create a *local* account on a Windows 2000 system, then you can still do that. There isn't a local User Manager any more, though; instead, it's Computer Management. In the next two sections, I'll show you how to create user accounts both locally and on an Active Directory domain.

Use Computer Management for Local Accounts

The bulk of the chapter assumes an Active Directory context. By this point, you have already read about domains, forests, and trees and know the benefits of using Active Directory on your network. In many cases, particularly if you have NT 4 workstations or Win2K systems as clients, it's desirable to create a domain (even if you only have one server) in order to take advantage of all the additional features of Active Directory. However, it's possible that a small organization might want to keep life very simple or even (brace yourself here) that the company's primary network OS is not Win2K/NT. For example, in a network that is Unix- or NetWare-based, there may be a need to set up a special-purpose NT server without all that AD stuff. In that case, if your Win2K machine is not a domain controller (DC) and you aren't using Active Directory, create your user accounts using the Computer Management tool (COMPMGMT.MSC). Users and groups created with COMPMGMT.MSC are local accounts, which is to say they exist and are valid on that local machine only. However, COMPMGMT.MSC is a remote enabled tool, so you can use it to create and manage local users and groups on remote member servers in a domain or on remote stand-alone servers. Just choose Connect to Another Computer from the Action menu to do this.

TIP   The Action menu is the menu that you see (instead of the File menu) at the top left in the Microsoft Management Console tools. See Chapter 5 for an overview of MMC and console anatomy.

TIP   If the machine you are working on is a domain controller, you have to use Active Directory Users and Computer (DSA.MSC) to create accounts. On a domain controller, the Local Users and Groups node is disabled in COMPMGMT.MSC, and there is an X in a red circle over the function to indicate that it's deactivated.

Creating user accounts on a non–Active Directory server in Win2K is pretty much the same as creating local accounts on a non-DC in NT 4, except that you use the Computer Management tool instead of User Manager. In COMPMGMT.MSC, open System Tools and then Local Users and Groups, as shown in Figure 9.1. Notice the users and groups that are created by default when you install Win2K. On a stand-alone server, with no particular network services such as IIS, Terminal Services, DHCP, or DNS installed, the only built-in accounts are Administrator and Guest. The Guest account is disabled by default as a security precaution. This account, on a stand-alone server or in an AD context, is used primarily to blow a huge hole in the security of a system by allowing unauthenticated access. That's right, unauthenticated access. No password is required for the Guest account. You can use it without any knowledge of a username or password, which is why it's disabled by default. It's a good thing that Guest is a very poor account as far as powers and abilities are concerned. The Administrator account, of course, has powers and abilities well beyond those of mortal users. It cannot be deleted or disabled, even if you set stringent account-lockout policies (which lock the account after a certain number of bad logon attempts). The Administrator account is not ordinarily subject to this policy and therefore cannot be locked out, even after a million bad logon attempts, which could be more than enough to crack a weak password.

TIP   You could deny the Administrator account access to the computer from over the network. Then the would-be hacker would have to physically sit at your computer to try those million passwords. You'll see how to do that later, when we talk about user rights and policies.

FIGURE 9.1

Computer Management/ Local Users and Groups

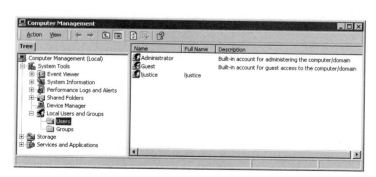

NOTE *One common security practice is to rename both the Guest and Administrator accounts. This hinders a would-be intruder from taking advantage of the well-known usernames when attempting to log in.*

The standard local groups that are built into a stand-alone server are Administrators, Backup Operators, Guests, Power Users, Replicator, and Users. Additional built-in groups are created on a domain controller system, as you'll see in a moment. These built-in groups have a predefined set of rights and permissions. To empower users with those rights and permissions, just make those users members of the appropriate group. For a rundown of the built-in groups and their rights, see Table 9.2 later in this chapter.

To create a new user account on a non-DC Win2K system, open the Users folder under Local Users and Groups. Then choose New User from the Action menu, or right-click Users in Local Users and Groups and choose New User. Fill in the fields for User Name, Password, and Confirm Password (the others are optional) as shown in Figure 9.2, and choose Create. To change account properties, or to assign group memberships, a logon script, and a home folder, or to grant dial-in permission to the user, right-click the user account and choose Properties. To set a user's password, highlight the account and right-click, then choose Set Password. All of these options and more will be discussed a bit later when we're creating AD accounts.

FIGURE 9.2

Creating a local user

NOTE *The local accounts you create on a stand-alone server, member server, or workstation are stored in the SAM (Security Accounts Manager) database, just as they are in NT 4. The SAM is still located in* `\winnt\system32\config`.

That's it! If you want to set account policies such as lockout restrictions or auditing, use the Local Security Policy tool (`SECPOL.MSC`) or the Group Policy snap-in (`GPEDIT .MSC`). The process is very similar to configuring Group Policy with the Active Directory tools except that, since the machine is not a domain controller, changes will apply to the local policy for the machine. (I'll show you how to use the Group Policy snap-in to set account lockout and password policy for the domain later in the chapter.) The policies created will be local policies, which will live in the local machine's Registry database. Not surprisingly, the scope of policy settings is more limited for local polices than for group policies in an Active Directory environment. I'll also discuss group policies and how they differ from local policies later in this chapter.

Use Active Directory Users and Computers for Domain Accounts

In Win2K, Active Directory Users and Computers (DSA.MSC) is the primary administrative tool for managing user accounts, security groups, organizational units, and policies in a single domain or in multiple domains. As a Microsoft Management Console (MMC) application, the tool can be run on any Win2K machine, although it's only installed on Win2K servers (and it only appears in the Start menu programs on domain controllers) by default. To run DSA.MSC on a Win2K non-DC system, you can publish the application using Active Directory, and it can then be installed on Win2K Server or Professional desktops using Add/Remove Programs. There is a prepackaged set of admin tools called the Admin Pack (found in \winnt\system32\ADMINPAK.MSI) that can be published using Group Policy, which installs the three Active Directory tools on a machine. See Chapter 12 for more information on publishing software in the Active Directory. DSA.MSC is also useful for managing computer accounts, organizational units, resources like printers and shared folders, and even DCs. However, the focus in this chapter is on creating and managing users and groups, including management of users' environments and group policies.

TIP   Computer accounts in Windows 2000 are more like user accounts in that they can be included in groups and organizational units.

WHERE DO USER AND GROUP ACCOUNTS LIVE?

As in NT 4, local user accounts on a stand-alone server, member server, or Win2K Professional workstation are stored in a Security Accounts Manager (SAM) database, usually located in C:\winnt\system32\config, but it depends on where you created your WINNT (system root) directory.

For Active Directory, the file is called NTDS.DIT, and it's found in %systemroot%\NTDS by default, but you can specify a path in the DCPROMO routine. As you learned in Chapter 8, the NTDS.DIT database stores a lot more information than the SAM does. It also stores information about servers and workstations, resources, published applications, and security policies. NTDS.DIT and the software that runs it are generally referred to together as the *directory service* or the Active Directory. This data structure is replicated throughout the domain to all domain controllers in a given domain for fault tolerance and load balancing. It's actually a database that uses an engine similar to the one used by Access, but one that programs control via the Lightweight Directory Access Protocol (LDAP) specified in RFC 1777. Unfortunately, you can't open it in Access or otherwise view or edit it directly. It can, however, be queried and modified using the Active Directory Service Interfaces (ADSI) or, for the braver, LDAP verbs. As I'll discuss later, the Resource Kit for Win2K includes several VBScript files created for just that purpose.

SECURITY IDENTIFIERS

User accounts, when first created, are automatically assigned a *security identifier (SID)*. A SID is a unique number that identifies an account. SIDs have been used since NT began; the system doesn't really know you by your name, but rather by your SID. User IDs are just there for the human interface. SIDs are never reused; when an account is deleted, its SID is deleted with it. SIDs look like this:

S-1-5-21-D1-D2-D3-RID

S-1-5 is just a standard prefix (actually, the 1 is a version number, which hasn't changed since NT 3.1, and the 5 means that the SID was assigned by NT); 21 is also an NT prefix; and D1, D2, and D3 are just 32-bit numbers that are specific to a domain. Once you create a domain, D1 through D3 are set, and all SIDs in that domain henceforth have the same three values. The *RID* stands for relative identifier. The RID is the unique part of any given SID. Each new account always has a unique RID number, even if the username and other information is the same as an old account. This way, the new account will not have any of the rights and permissions of the old account and security is preserved.

QUICK TOUR OF USER- AND GROUP-RELATED FUNCTIONS IN *DSA.MSC*

Active Directory Users and Computers provides the network administrator with the means to perform the following tasks:

- Create, modify, and delete user accounts

- Assign logon scripts to user accounts

- Manage groups and group memberships

- Create and manage group policies

Open DSA.MSC by running it from the Start menu, or choose Start/Programs/Administrative Tools/Active Directory Users and Computers. DSA.MSC seeks out any nearby domain controller if you're in native mode; if you're in mixed mode, then of course it must contact the PDC operations master, as mixed mode means that you've still got a single-master model. In DSA.MSC, you will see the name of the contacted DC at the top of the console tree and your domain name right under the console root, as shown in Figure 9.3.

In the left pane, you see listed a set of containers and organizational units that were created automatically with the domain: Builtin, Computers, Domain Controllers, ForeignSecurityPrincipals, and Users (Tech Services and Marketing are organizational units created by an administrator). As with all the console applications, click an object in the console tree (on the left) to see its contents and information in the details pane (on the right). Notice also that the description bar for the details pane tells you how many objects there are in the container. The description bar, like the status bar and the toolbars, can be hidden if you want a more simplified view. Just choose Customize View from the Action menu and uncheck the Description Bar check box.

FIGURE 9.3

AD Users and Computers console

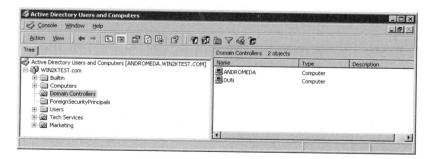

The Users and Computers containers are the default places to put user, group, and computer accounts when a machine is upgraded from NT 4. They gotta go somewhere. But you don't have to put new ones there, and you can move them to OUs as needed. As you'll quickly discover, you can put a user account in any OU, even directly in the "domain" container. When I first created a few user and group and machine accounts, I just created them in the domain root, then moved them to OUs as they were set up.

Builtin is the container for those special built-in local groups—such as Administrators, Account Operators, Guests, and Users—that exist on every Win2K Server machine, including domain controllers. More on this in a bit.

Domain Controllers is the default OU for new Windows 2000 domain controllers. This is where the accounts are located when you first create a DC. Like the accounts in the Computers container, DC accounts can be moved to other OUs.

ForeignSecurityPrincipals is a default container for objects from external, trusted domains. In this chapter, we'll be working only with users and groups from this domain.

To create something new, select the container object where you want to locate it, then select New from the Action menu or right-click to select New from the Properties context menu. As shown in Figure 9.4, you can choose to create a shared folder, a user account, a printer, an OU, a group account, a contact, or a computer account. Any of these choices kicks off a corresponding wizard to create the object. In each case, to fill in all the details, go back and edit the properties of the object after creating it (right-click the object and choose Properties).

FIGURE 9.4

Creating a new object

Because they aren't really OUs, but instead mere "containers," you can't create an OU inside the Users or Computers containers, and you can only create users, computers, and groups inside the Builtin container.

Right-clicking an object brings up its context menu. The choices displayed change with the object you right-click. Right-click a user account and you have the option to disable it or reset the password, for example; right-clicking a computer account reveals options like Move and Manage (Manage opens up COMPMGMT.MSC connected to the selected computer).

This chapter is really not about managing machine accounts or printers or shared folders, so we'll leave those discussions for another chapter. However, contacts and OUs do relate to user and group management, so we'll take a look at those new items in a moment.

PREBUILT ACCOUNTS: ADMINISTRATOR AND GUEST

If you have just created a new domain, you'll notice that two accounts called Administrator and Guest are built already. The Administrator account is, as you've guessed, an account with complete power over a machine or a domain, depending on the context. You can't delete the Administrator account but you can rename it.

You assigned the password for the Administrator account when you installed Win2K and then again when you ran DCPROMO.EXE to create a new domain. The first was a local Administrator account and password, but once you created a domain, the new Administrator account and password for the domain replaced it. Don't lose that password, as there's no way to get it back! (Well, you can always rebuild from scratch, but that's no fun.)

The other account is the Guest account. *Guest* means "anyone that Win2K doesn't recognize." By default, this account is disabled, and it should *stay* that way. If you've ever worked with a different network, like a Unix or NetWare network, you're probably familiar with the idea of a guest account—*but Win2K works differently, so pay attention!* You can get access to most other operating systems by logging in with the username Guest and a blank password. That Guest account is usually pretty restricted in the things it can do. That's true with Win2K as well, although the Everyone group also includes guests.

Here's the part that *isn't* like other operating systems. Suppose someone tries to access a shared printer or folder on a Win2K server or domain that has the Guest account enabled. She logs on to her local machine as melanie_wilson with the password happy. Even without an account on the server or domain, Melanie can still work on her local machine. Windows 95/98 machines don't care who you are, having no local accounts at all. On an NT 4 or Win2K workstation, she would have to log in to an account on the local machine. However, none of these operating systems require you to log in to a server or domain in order to get access to the local workstation. Suppose that this domain or server doesn't even *have* a melanie_wilson account. Now she's working at a computer and tries to access a domain resource. Guess what? She gets in.

WARNING   *Even though an explicit domain login requires that you use a username of Guest, you needn't explicitly log in to a domain to use guest privileges. If your network is attached to my network and your Guest account is enabled, I can browse through your network and attach to any resources that the Guest account can access. I needn't log in as Guest; the mere fact that there is an enabled Guest account pretty much says to Win2K, "Leave the back door open, okay?" So be careful when enabling the Guest account.*

CREATING A NEW USER ACCOUNT

Before I discuss the ins and outs of account properties, UPN names, profile information, and all the other user settings, let's just go through the steps to create a new user account with the wizard. Then I'll go back and discuss all the settings for the newly created account.

To create a user account, in DSA.MSC select the Users container (or any other container/OU where you want the account to be located), then select New/User from the Action menu (shown in Figure 9.4 a few pages back). A wizard appears with a dialog box shown in Figure 9.5. Fill in the First Name, Initials, Last Name, and Full Name fields as shown in the figure (Initials and Last Name are optional fields). Next, fill in the user logon name (jblomberg) and choose the Universal Principal Name (UPN) suffix to be appended to the username at logon time; recall that we discussed UPNs in Chapter 8. For logging in to an NT 4 or Windows 95/98 machine, there is also a downlevel logon name, which uses the old-style *DOMAINNAME\username* syntax from previous versions of NT.

FIGURE 9.5

Creating a new user

Usernames in Win2K must follow these rules:

◆ The name must be unique to the machine for local accounts (or unique to the domain in the case of domain accounts). However, a domain user account name may be the same as a local account name on a non-DC that is a member of the domain, a fact that causes much confusion because they are completely separate entities.

◆ The username cannot be the same as a group name on the local machine for a local account (or the same as a group name on the domain in the case of domain accounts).

◆ The username may be up to 20 characters, upper- or lowercase or a combination.

◆ To avoid confusion with special syntax characters, usernames may not include any of the following:

   " / \ [ ] : ; | = , + * ? < >

◆ The name may include spaces and periods, but may not consist entirely of spaces or periods. Avoid spaces, however, since these names would have to be enclosed in quotes for any scripting or command-line situations.

Before going on, I want to point out that there are *three* significant user names in Figure 9.5. First, the Full Name is Joao Blomberg. That was nothing but decoration in NT 4, but it's significant in Active Directory, as it is part of your LDAP name. Joao's LDAP name would look like this:

```
cn="Joao Blomberg",cn="Users",dc="win2ktest",dc="com"
```

(You might care what Joao's LDAP name is if you were ever to use a tool that "spoke" in LDAP or if you were to do some scripting in a LDAP-aware language.) In LDAP-ese, cn is container, and yes, user accounts are containers. So there's a container named Joao Blomberg inside a container named Users (the Users folder), and that folder is in a domain named win2ktest.com. You describe domain names in LDAP in terms of their components, the pieces separated by a period—in the case of win2ktest.com, it'd be win2ktest and com. You separate those with dc, which means domain component. If Joao's account were not in the Users folder, but instead were in an OU called, say, UptownUsers, then you'd replace the cn (container) with ou:

```
cn="Joao Blomberg",ou="UptownUsers",dc="win2ktest",dc="com"
```

The second name, jblomberg@win2ktest.com, is the Active Directory logon name or UPN (user principal name). You read in Chapter 8 that while this *looks* like an e-mail address, it's not—it's just a convenient, easy-to-remember name to give a user instead of making the user remember a domain name and username.

The third name, win2ktest\jblomberg, is the older-style NT 4–type logon name. You could use this name when logging on from a Windows 9*x* workstation or an NT 4 workstation. Or you might find yourself using it on older programs that run fine on Windows 2000/XP/.NET systems, but that don't understand UPNs. I find, for example, that some Resource Kit tools require you to identify yourself, but don't understand a logon name like mark01@win2kexperts.com; they need to see something like win2kexperts\mark01.

Once you've filled in all the username information, choose Next. In the following screen, shown in Figure 9.6, set a password for the user account and confirm it. Set the password and account options summarized in Table 9.1, then choose Next. None of the account options are selected by default, so it's a good idea to go ahead and select User Must Change Password at Next Logon.

FIGURE 9.6

Setting password and account options

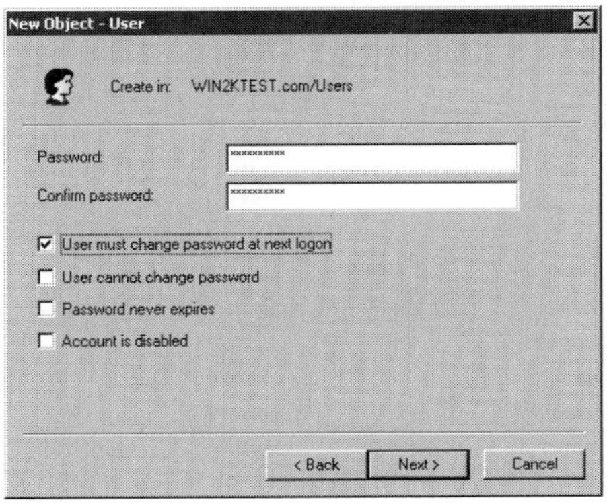

TABLE 9.1: PASSWORD AND ACCOUNT OPTIONS FOR CREATING A NEW USER ACCOUNT

OPTION	DESCRIPTION
User Must Change Password at Next Logon	Forces a user to change their password the next time they log in; afterward the box will be unchecked.
User Cannot Change Password	If checked, prevents the user from changing the account's password. This is useful for shared accounts and accounts that run services like Exchange.
Password Never Expires	If checked, the user account ignores the password expiration policy, and the password for the account never expires. This is useful for accounts that run services and accounts for which you want a permanent password (such as the Guest account).
Account Is Disabled	If checked, the account is disabled and no one can log in to it until it is enabled (it is not, however, removed from the database). This is useful for accounts that are used as templates and for new user accounts that you create well in advance, such as new hires that will not begin work for several weeks.

The final screen of this Create New Object Wizard, shown in Figure 9.7, simply confirms all the information you've supplied, including the container/OU where the account will live, the full name, the logon name, and the password or account options selected. Choose Finish and your user account is created.

FIGURE 9.7

Confirming new user information

USER ACCOUNT PROPERTIES

Now let's go back and look at the properties of the account we just created. Right-click the user account object and you'll see several options in the context menu, shown in Figure 9.8. From here you can quickly copy the account, manage the user's group memberships, disable or enable the account, reset the user's password, move the account to a different container or OU, open the user's home page, or send him mail (these last two require that the home page URL and e-mail address be specified in the account information). You can also choose to delete or rename the user account from this menu.

FIGURE 9.8

User's context menu

WARNING   *Each user and group account is assigned a unique identifier, called a SID, when it is created. Deleting a user or group account deletes the unique identifier. Even if you re-create an account with the same name, the new account will not have the rights or permissions of the old account.*

Choose Properties from the context menu to bring up the full user account information. In the General tab, shown in Figure 9.9, you can add a description of the user account, put in the name of the office where the user works, and add telephone numbers, an e-mail address, even Web page addresses. The Address tab in Figure 9.10 shows fields for a user's mailing address. The Telephones tab (Figure 9.11) offers a place for home, pager, mobile phone, fax, and IP phone numbers, as well as a place to enter comments.

FIGURE 9.9

User Properties General tab

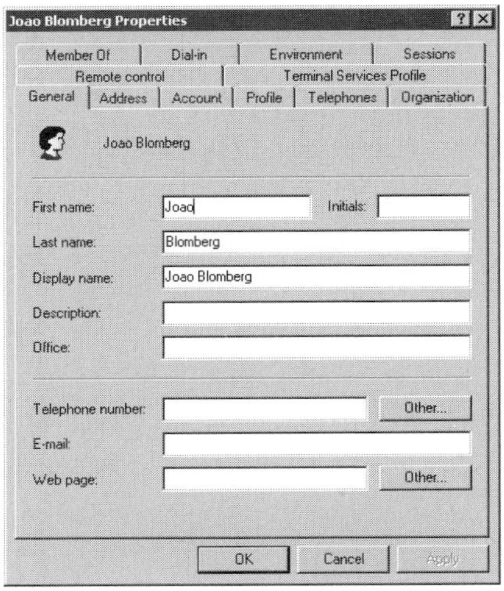

FIGURE 9.10

User Properties
Address tab

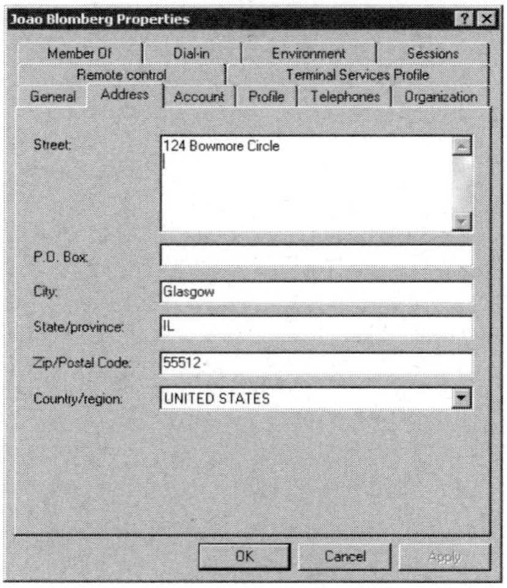

FIGURE 9.11

User Properties
Telephones tab

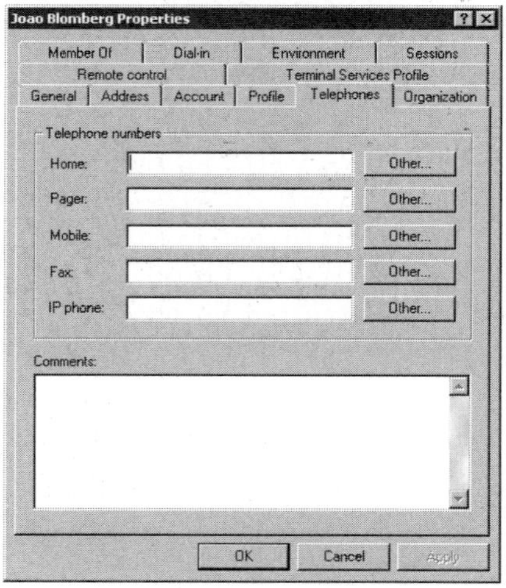

In Figure 9.12 you see the Organization tab, where you can enter information about someone's actual job title and her position in the pecking order of the organization.

So four of the tabs in the user account properties are about contact information, not what we old-time NT admins would call account properties. You know, you could enter almost all of this stuff in the Exchange mailbox properties. So I know you are wondering, as I did, "What's the deal, are they integrated now? Will Exchange actually use Active Directory to create mailboxes?" It depends. With Exchange 5.5, yes, you need some method of creating Exchange accounts for users. But with Exchange 2000, Exchange *has* no separate method for creating user accounts; it just uses the information that AD has about the user.

FIGURE 9.12

User Properties
Organization tab

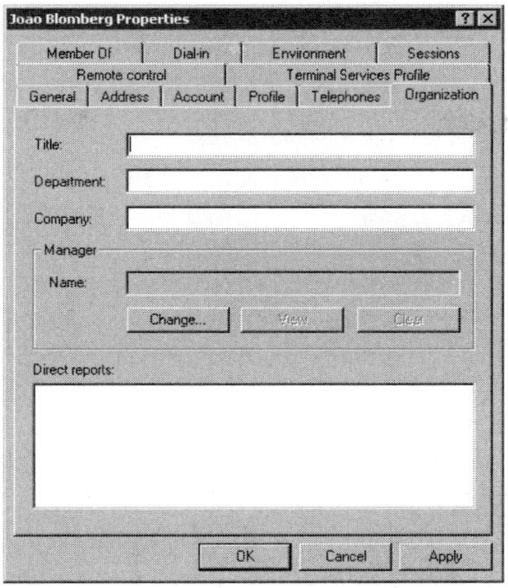

We'll leave the Dial-In tab to Chapter 22, which covers Remote Access Service. The next few sections deal with managing account settings, profile information, and group memberships.

NOTE *If Terminal Services is installed on your Win2K box, several additional User Properties tabs must be configured. See Chapter 15 for more information.*

Account Settings

If you need to modify the user's logon name or UPN suffix, go to the Account tab (Figure 9.13). This is also the place to specify permissible logon hours, account options, and all that stuff. By default, users are allowed to log in any day of the week at any time of the day (24/7), but you can choose the Logon Hours button to designate particular permitted hours and days (see Figure 9.14).

FIGURE 9.13

User account properties

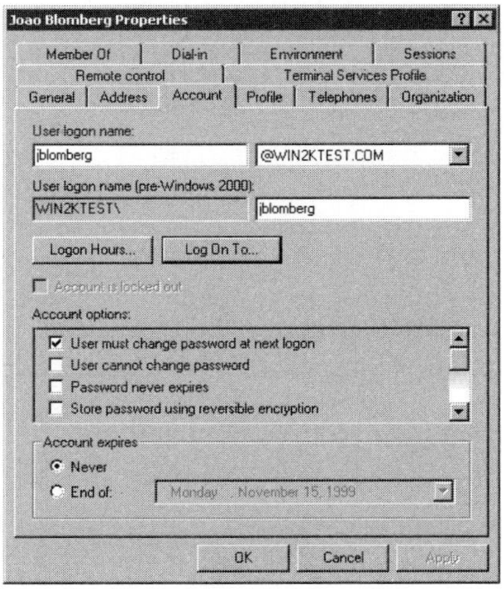

FIGURE 9.14

Setting logon hours

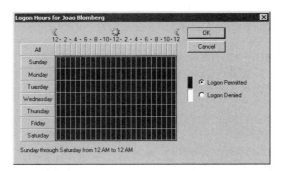

NOTE *By default, a user will not be logged off automatically when logon hours expire, but there is a setting to accomplish this. The setting is called Automatically Log Off Users When Logon Hours Expire, and it's found in the Group Policy snap-in, under* `Computer Configuration\Windows Settings\Security Settings\Local Policies\Security Options`. *This parameter can also be set using the Domain Security Policy tool or the Local Security Policy tool (depending on the context). In either case, look for the setting under* `Local Policies\ Security Options`. *(We'll look at Local Security Policy and group policies a bit later in this chapter.)*

By default, users can log in to the domain from any workstation, but logon workstations may still be specified by NetBIOS names (see Figure 9.15). However, you must still be using NetBIOS on your network in order for this to be enforced.

FIGURE 9.15

Permitted logon workstations

Looking back at the Account tab (Figure 9.13), you see the Account Is Locked Out check box. If the account is locked as a result of bad logon attempts (configurable using one of the various Policy tools, as I'll explain later), the box will show up as checked and available. If you wish to manually unlock the account, just uncheck the box. At the bottom of the Account tab you see the account expiration setting. By default, an account never expires, but if you enable the option, the default interval is six weeks. Notice also that more account options are available than in NT 4 (scroll down in the Account Options box to see all the options). Several of these, like User Must Change Password at Next Logon, are familiar to NT 4 administrators and fairly self-explanatory to others.

Several options are new and more obscure. The Store Password Using Reversible Encryption option is used for Windows 95/98 clients. Some Web authentication schemes also require this. That's not really new; it was just not an exposed option in NT 4. The smart card option is new and to be used if you opt for a public key infrastructure such as X.509. Select the Do Not Require Kerberos Preauthentication option if the account will use an implementation of the Kerberos protocol other than the one supplied with Win2K. Not all versions of the Kerberos protocol use this feature, but Windows 2000 does. Select the Use DES Encryption Types for This Account option if you need the Data Encryption Standard (DES). DES supports multiple levels of encryption, including MPPE Standard (40-bit), MPPE Standard (56-bit), MPPE Strong (128-bit), IPSec DES (40-bit), IPSec 56-bit DES, and IPSec Triple DES (3DES).

Notice that the user's password cannot be reset from the Account tab. To reset the user's password, close the account properties sheet and right-click the username in the details pane of DSA.MSC. Choose the option to reset the password, and you will be able to type in and confirm a new password, as shown in Figure 9.16. There is also a convenient check box to force the user to change their password at the next logon.

FIGURE 9.16

Resetting a user's password

Profile Information

The Profile tab, shown in Figure 9.17, is the place to specify a user's profile path, a logon script, and a home folder. Mostly, these options are for *downlevel clients* (a condescending new term for any pre-Win2K clients), because the same settings and many more can be specified with Group Policy settings. However, Group Policy only works on Win2K systems, and it may be a while before companies begin to standardize on Win2K Professional desktops. Until then, you'll want to use the options in the Profile tab. I'll discuss user profiles and logon scripts in more detail in the sections to come, but the following paragraphs give you the basics about these features.

A user's Desktop settings, from Start menu content right down to a color scheme and mouse orientation, can be stored in a network location so that the user can log in from any system on the network and see the same Desktop. You can specify a shared network location for that purpose. This is also useful if you want to force a user (or group of users) to keep the same settings all the time. Such an arrangement is called a *roaming profile* if it's not forced on a user and if they can make changes. If the user is compelled to load that profile and can't log in without it, it's called a *mandatory profile* (or a *shared mandatory profile*, if more than one user is shackled to it). Win2K group policies allow you to configure folder redirection and other Desktop settings, eliminating much of the need for NT 4–style roaming and mandatory profiles, so this feature is most useful for NT 4 clients. For many more details, refer to "Working with Roaming User Profiles."

FIGURE 9.17

User profile properties

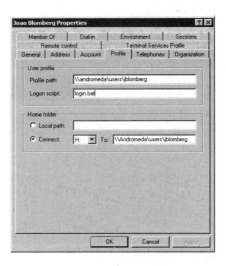

A *logon* or *login script* is one that runs at logon time to configure a user's environment and assign network resources, such as mapped drives and printers. Though the art of the logon script is well known in other network operating systems, including NetWare, logon scripts in Microsoft networks have not always been emphasized. Many Microsoft networks were small in the beginning, and users could "browse" for network resources. Login scripts are, however, filling a more important role for Windows environments; today's networks are larger, and administration of resources and users is becoming increasingly more complex. See "Zen and the Art of Login Scripts" later in this chapter for details, but for now, you should know that Win2K has a default path where the logon script will be stored (in the SYSVOL, which is by default in the \WINNT directory, but it's configurable). That's why you only need to specify the script's name in the dialog box. However, it is possible that the logon script could be stored in a subdirectory of SYSVOL, for example in SYSVOL\Sales\saleslogin.bat. In that case, you would need to specify the relative path from the SYSVOL root, such as Sales\saleslogin.bat.

A *home folder*, also known as a *home directory*, is a folder assigned to the user for their private use. Although applications may have their own default folder for saving and opening files, the home folder will be the default working folder for a user at the command prompt. You can specify a local path for a user's home folder, but it's only useful if the user will be logging in locally to the machine. For users logging in from the network, you need to choose the Connect option and specify a network path following the UNC convention *machinename**servername**directoryname*. You can also use a variable as a folder name, *%username%*, to indicate that the home folder name is the same as the user ID.

When you specify a home folder path for the user, if the network share already exists and you have permission to write to it, Win2K will create the user's home folder automatically. This saves admins a lot of time. If you need a step-by-step procedure to create and assign home folders, see Chapter 11, which covers creating and managing shared folders.

In any discussion about home folders, questions about how to limit disk space consumption are bound to arise. NT 4 had no built-in mechanism to set or enforce disk quotas at all. One strategy was to set up a separate partition for user directories, confining the problem to that partition (kind of like growing horseradish). The hapless admin sometimes ran routine "diskhog" scripts and asked, begged, or publicly humiliated users into cleaning up their home folders. Others threatened to start deleting files at random if users didn't comply. But the best option was to purchase a third-party disk quota tool. Now Win2K comes with a simple quota management system. You simply enable it for a volume and then set thresholds for warnings and so forth. Read about it in Chapter 10.

Group Memberships

To specify group memberships for a user account, open the Member Of tab in the account properties sheet. As you see in Figure 9.18, by default a new user is a member of the group Domain Users. The Active Directory Folder column on the right indicates the container or OU path for the group. To add a user to another group, choose Add and select from a list of available groups (Figure 9.19). Highlight the group name, and double-click it or click the Add button to add it to the bottom pane. If scrolling through the list is too tedious for you, just type in the group names, separated by semicolons. Then use the Check Names button to confirm that the names you typed are valid group names. Choose OK and you're back at the Member Of tab with the new groups showing in the window. Choose OK again and you're done. To remove users from groups, use the Remove button in the Member Of tab. See the section "Working with Security Groups" for the skinny on group memberships.

FIGURE 9.18

Setting group memberships

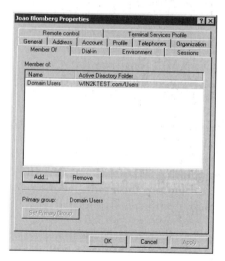

MANAGING ACCOUNTS

In the preceding sections, I discussed how to make changes to a single user account. Now let's talk about how to make changes to several (or many) accounts at once. While we're on the subject, I'll cover a couple of other multiple-account issues, including how to create a bunch of users at a time.

FIGURE 9.19

Selecting users and groups

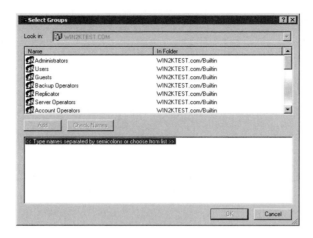

In DSA.MSC you can select multiple accounts in the details pane by holding down the Shift key while you work the down arrow key or you can hit the Ctrl key as you click each of the accounts and then right-click to see the context menu while those accounts are selected. As you see in Figure 9.20, you can choose to move them all to another container or OU, add them to a group (to remove members of a group, you'll need to go to the properties sheet of the group itself), disable accounts, or enable accounts. You can also send them all mail, assuming you have specified e-mail addresses for the accounts.

TIP   Remember, changes to a user's account, such as group memberships, will not take effect until the next time the user logs in.

FIGURE 9.20

Selecting multiple users in DSA.MSC

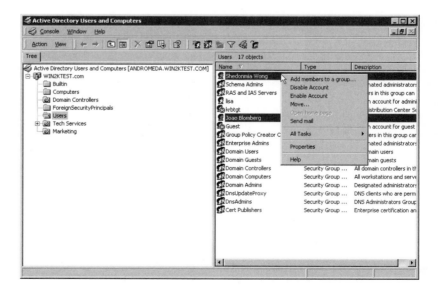

To create users with like settings, you can create an account template and copy it. Properties that are copied include account settings (such as Password Never Expires), group memberships, account expiration date (if supplied), and the UPN suffix. The profile information (home directory, user profile path, and logon script) is also copied, and if you used the %username% variable to set up the template user's home folder, it will be created automatically for new users when the account is copied.

Okay, those are nice options, but where is the Select Members by Group option from our old friend the User Manager for Domains (USRMGR.EXE)? With that tool you were able to select all the members of a given group at once instead of scrolling through a list and selecting the users one by one. Come to think of it, you were able to manage a wider set of account properties with USRMGR.EXE, including logon hours and home directories, and even make all users change their passwords at next logon. There doesn't seem to be a way to do these things with DSA.MSC. I actually did stumble across a Properties on Multiple Objects dialog box (by selecting several accounts and pressing Alt+Enter), but it didn't work. It only set the properties of the first account selected.

So how do you make changes to several users at once, and how can you create, say, 50 or 500 users at a time?

The answer to these questions seems more complicated than it has to be, unless Microsoft is hiding something from us. The Active Directory can be queried and modified using the Active Directory Service Interfaces (ADSI). So if you master ADSI and learn about Active Directory class objects and attributes and so forth, and if you know some VBScript or JScript, some Java or VB or C, or even some C++, you could create your 50 users at a time, presumably. Even better, some bright, shining third-party vendor will figure it out for us and slap a user-friendly interface on it. We only have to wait for it to appear.

NOTE *The Resource Kit includes several VB scripts that run in conjunction with the Windows Scripting Host. These scripts, with names like* CREATEUSERS.VBS *and* USERGROUP.VBS, *allow you to use the command line or an input file to create, modify, and delete user and group accounts. Once you get the hang of the naming conventions for AD objects, these scripts are extremely useful.*

RESETTING PASSWORDS

The most commonly changed part of a user's account is the password. You can reset a password from the GUI by right-clicking the user's account in Active Directory Users and Computers, but how about changing it from the command line?

Well, if it's a local user account, then simply type **net user *username newpassword***, so, for example, to change the local admin's password to bigsecret, you'd type the following:

```
net user administrator bigsecret
```

But that only works for local accounts. To change a password on a domain account, add the /domain option. So to change the default administrator password on the domain to reallybigsecret, type this:

```
net user administrator reallybigsecret /domain
```

And there's also a great 2000 Resource Kit tool, cusrmgr, that will set a password to a *random* value. Why would you want that? Personally, I don't want people using the default Administrator account, but it's so hard to break them of the habit. So I randomize the password, make people use their own Domain Admin account, turn on auditing and threaten Severe Punishment to anyone caught setting the Administrator password back to something else—unless there's a good reason. Cusrmgr randomizes passwords using the -u option to select the user account and the -p (lowercase!) option to randomize, like so:

```
cusrmgr -u Administrator -p
```

Understanding Groups

Assigning users to groups makes it easier to grant them rights to perform tasks as well as permissions to access resources such as printers and network folders. Assisting you in this endeavor are several built-in groups with built-in rights that you should be familiar with. You'll also want to create your own user groups and assign them certain rights and permissions. The members of the groups you create can, in turn, be granted the ability to administer other groups and objects, even whole organizational units. To top it all off, groups in Win2K can now contain computers and contacts as well as users and other groups. They can also be used as e-mail distribution lists. So it's important to understand the different types of groups that exist in Win2K and how to work with them to delegate control, grant access to necessary resources, and configure rights. That is the subject of the next few sections.

Creating Groups

To create a new group in Active Directory Users and Computers, navigate to the container where you want the group to live. Groups can be created at the root of the domain, in a built-in container such as Users, or in an OU. While you have the container highlighted, choose New and then Group from the Action menu (Figure 9.21). Supply the name of the group (Engineering) and the downlevel name if it will be different; then choose the group scope and group type, shown in Figure 9.22. By default, the group scope is Global and the type is Security. For an explanation of group types and group scope, see the upcoming sections. Choose OK to create the group in the selected container.

Now let's fill in the rest of the group information and add users to the new group. Find and double-click the group you just created to open the Group properties sheet. In the General tab shown in Figure 9.23, fill in a description if you wish and an e-mail address if a distribution list exists for the group.

FIGURE 9.21

Creating a new group

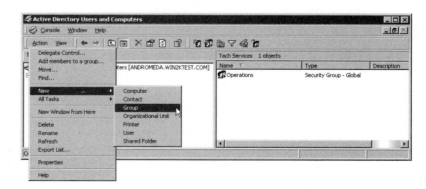

FIGURE 9.22

Information for a new group

FIGURE 9.23

A group's properties on the General tab

To populate the group, go to the Members tab and choose Add. As you see in Figure 9.24, Win2K allows users, other groups, and even computers to belong to groups (although there are rules for group nesting, as you'll read in the next few sections). Group members can also come from different OUs. Highlight the users or groups and choose Add, or type in the names separated by semicolons; then choose Check Names to verify the typed-in names (it's not necessary to check the names if you selected them from the list). Choose OK to finalize your additions and return to the properties pages. To view or modify the local and universal groups to which Engineering, for example, belongs, open the Member Of tab (Figure 9.25). The Managed By tab is for optional contact information and does not necessarily reflect any direct delegation of control.

Another way to add members to a group is to right-click the user account and choose Add Members to a Group. If you want to add several selected users to the same group at once, hold down the Ctrl key as you select the users, then right-click and choose Add Members to a Group. There's also a button on the toolbar to add one or more selected objects to a group. As I mentioned earlier, unfortunately no option is available to select all of the members of a group, which would allow other account properties to be managed as well.

FIGURE 9.24

Adding users to a group

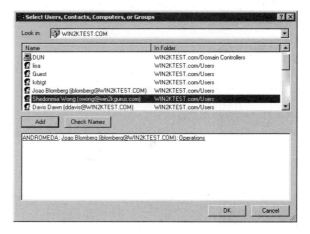

FIGURE 9.25

Nested groups

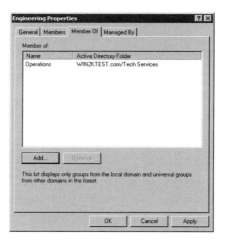

One final how-to note: It will probably be necessary to move a group from one container to another at some point, since having groups in OUs facilitates delegation. To do this, right-click the group icon in the details pane of the console and choose Move. Navigate to the container that will be the new home for the group (Figure 9.26), select it, and choose OK. But you can only move users and groups from one OU to another *inside the same domain*; there's no easy way to move them between domains in a forest.

FIGURE 9.26

Moving a group to
another container

Group Types: Security Groups versus Distribution Groups

When creating group accounts in Win2K, you have the option to classify a group as a *security group* or as a *distribution group*. Security groups are not really new; they are equivalent to user groups as we knew them in all versions of Windows NT. Their new name serves only to distinguish them from distribution groups, which are sort of "nonsecurity groups" and *are* new to Win2K.

SECURITY GROUPS OVERVIEW

Security groups are groups used to assign rights and permissions. Like user accounts, security groups are assigned SIDs. When you view or edit an object's Access Control List (ACL), for example, the group names that appear on the list are security groups (sometimes they show up as SIDs if the friendly names are slow to resolve). These user and group SID entries on the ACL are matched up with a user's credentials to permit or deny access to the object.

There are three major types of security groups: local, global, and universal—although you might prefer to think of them as four different groups: local, domain local, global, and universal.

Local groups are the kind of groups you find on a stand-alone server, a server that is a member of a domain, or a Win2K Professional workstation. Local groups are local to the machine. That is, they exist and are valid only on that workstation or that non-DC server.

Domain local group is the special name for a local group that happens to be on a domain controller. Domain controllers have a common active directory that is replicated between them, so a domain local group on one DC will also exist on its sibling DC. As you'll see when we get into the details, domain local groups are different from other local groups.

Global, universal, and, of course, domain locals live on the DCs in the Active Directory. Global groups are still pretty much like they were in NT 4; they are used to grant access rights and permissions across machine (and domain) boundaries.

Universal groups are new to Win2K and can also serve the function of global groups, granting rights and object permissions throughout domains and between domains. Universals are more useful than globals or locals because they are infinitely more flexible with regard to nesting, but you can really use them only when your domain has gone "native," which requires that all NT 4 domain controllers be upgraded to Win2K.

DISTRIBUTION GROUPS AND CONTACTS

In NT 4, every group was a security group and could be used for controlling access to resources and granting rights. A distribution group is simply a nonsecurity group. Distribution groups don't have SIDs and don't appear on ACLs. So what are they for? If you've worked with Exchange or a similar product, you are familiar with distribution *lists*. These are groups of recipient addresses. It's easier to send mail to ACME Managers, for example, than to individually select each manager's name from a list.

Assuming that you have entered mail addresses for your users, your security groups in the Active Directory are also unofficial distribution lists. Just right-click a group name in DSA.MSC and you'll see the option to send mail to the group members, just as you see the option to send mail to a user account when you right-click it. This kicks off your default mail-handling program, and the system will try to send mail using the e-mail address supplied in the account information. So, if you have a set of people working in the finance department and you place all those people in a security group called Finance, you can not only assign permissions for resources to the Finance group, but you can also send mail to the members of the Finance security group, assuming you have filled in the e-mail information for each member.

In other words, distribution groups are basically only useful if you've adopted Exchange 2000. I can't resist saying it: "Resistance is futile. You will purchase our technology..."

It's part of Exchange 2K's raison d'être: it merges the list of e-mail users (the "directory") that Exchange 5.5 and earlier versions had to maintain separately from the list of domain users kept on domain controllers. E2K basically doesn't *have* a directory any more. Instead, it just exploits AD's directory "parasitically."

Distribution lists are not always the same as security groups, though. For instance, say your company is a communications provider and has a distribution list called Outage Alert. This distribution list is used to notify certain people in the case of a major outage that will affect service to your customers. The members of this list might include people from operations, customer relations, even the chief executive officer. Plus, the distribution list could include external e-mail addresses of key business partners (also known as *contacts*). These people will not have a security group in common, and it's silly to have to create a separate security group just because you need a distribution list. Since Microsoft is so determined to integrate Active Directory and Exchange, you can classify a group in the Active Directory as a distribution group, a group with no security privileges. No security identifiers are created for a distribution group, so the membership is not included in a user's credentials at logon time. You can't grant printer permissions to a distribution list because it doesn't appear in the ACL. This group is strictly for e-mail. Presumably, this will allow us to manage a good part of Exchange mailboxes and distribution lists without using a separate Exchange administration tool.

NOTE *You can change a security group to a distribution group and back again, but not if you're still running in Mixed mode. As with everything else that's truly useful in Win2K, this action requires that you be running in Native mode.*

Similarly, contacts are objects that store information about people, including e-mail, telephone, and related information. Contacts can be members of security or distribution groups, but they are not accounts, so contacts have no security identifier (SID) and cannot be assigned user rights or permissions.

Group Scope: Locals, Domail Locals, Globals, and Universals

Where are they recognized and what can they contain? These are the main issues surrounding local, domain local, global, and universal groups. Since they are used to grant rights and permissions, we need to know where that group membership means something, where it is accepted (kind of like American Express). Since we want to nest groups to simplify the granting of rights and permissions, we need to know the rules and recommendations for nesting as well.

LOCAL OR MACHINE LOCAL GROUPS

The basic local group, also called a "machine" local group, is the only type of group that exists on stand-alone servers and Win2K Professional systems. A stand-alone server or Professional workstation, neither of which is a member of a domain, is like an island nation with no knowledge of the outside world. It only recognizes its own local groups and users. Local groups are the only ones that can be granted permission to access resources, and membership is limited to local users. When the machine joins the domain, however, that island nation becomes a member of a greater governing body, like a federation of island nations. It can have local user accounts, as we saw earlier in this chapter, but it can also accept user accounts built on a domain controller—the domain controller's Active Directory is a centralized database of user accounts, saving you the trouble of re-creating them on every single machine.

A machine uses its local groups to simplify administration. For example, suppose I've got a server with a printer on it and I want to control who can use the printer. I create a local group called PrinterOK and give the PrinterOK group permission to print to the printer. But there's no one in PrinterOK initially, so I'd better populate the group. Perhaps I want to let people from the domain print on the printer. I *could* insert user accounts from the domain into PrinterOK one by one, but that's too much work, so it's more convenient to just grab a group that already *contains* those domain users and stuff the domain-based group into the local group. Just a few clicks and I'm done.

But I got a bit sneaky when I just said "domain-based group"—I left out a bit of important information. You can't insert local groups in local groups. You'd *think* that you ought to be able to just drop Group A into Group B indiscriminately, but you can't, mainly due to the fact that NT 4 and earlier versions didn't let you. (And in case you're wondering, there was never a good reason for NT's inability, at least in my opinion.) That's why local groups are called *local* groups, to differentiate them from the other kinds of groups. The other kinds of groups—there are three types—can only be built on domain controllers. A local group can contain any of the three domain-based groups—they're called global, domain local, and universal—in itself.

GLOBAL GROUPS

The first domain-based group type is the *global group*. (It resembles NT 4 global groups, if you're familiar with them.) They can only contain user accounts from the domain, as with NT 4 global groups. But Active Directory gives them a bit more power—global groups can exist inside other global groups, so long as the global groups are in the same domain.

You can put a global group inside a local group of any domain that trusts the global group's domain. So you could stuff a global group into a local group for a member server in the same domain as the global group or into a local group for any other domain in the forest. Think of global groups as "traveling groups." They're a convenient collecting point for domain user accounts.

DOMAIN LOCAL GROUPS

The second kind of domain-based group, one that didn't exist until Windows 2000, is called a domain local group. I'll warn you right up front that I'm still not quite sure why they exist or what good they do. Put in just a few words, they're basically low-functionality versions of global groups.

You just read that global groups are groups built on a domain controller, can contain user accounts from the local domain and can be placed in any local group in any machine in any domain that trusts the global group's domain. So if you have a global group built in domain A and domain B trusts domain A, then you can put that global group in any local group on any machine in domains A or B. A domain local group acts just like a global group, *except* you can only put a domain local group into the local groups of machines in the same domain as the domain local group. In the this example, then, a domain local group created in domain A could only be placed in a local group on a machine on domain A. Even if domain B trusts domain A, you still can't put any of domain A's domain local groups into domain B's local groups.

You can also put a domain local group into any other domain local group in the same domain. But the big question is what good are they? To tell you the truth, I'm just not sure. I can think of one benefit only: domain locals do not increase the GC's workload; globals do. The global catalog includes, among other things, names of all global groups in all domains in the forest. In contrast, the global catalog does not contain any information about the domain local groups. So I guess a domain local group has a smaller impact on a global catalog. But, in any case, it's not much of a difference.

One reason you *do* want to know about domain local groups is if you intend to take the Microsoft certification exams. Now, *they* like domain local groups. You'll get a question or two that will try to trip you up by offering you a solution that involves putting a domain local group into a local group of a different domain. You always know *that* answer's wrong.

UNIVERSAL GROUPS

The third, and coolest, type of domain-based group is a universal group. Summarized, a universal group can do *anything*, just about. You can only create them on a domain controller, as with domain local and global groups. But you can do the following:

♦ Put a global group from any domain in the forest into a universal group

♦ Put a universal group into a local group (that's a machine local—universals will have no truck with domain locals, as far as I can see)

♦ Put a universal group inside a universal group (this is the cool part)

Finally, the group that we've always wanted. Just like the Russian *matryoshka* dolls (those dolls that open to contain a doll, which can be opened to contain a doll and so on), you can have universal groups in universal groups inside universal groups. . . .

So the logical question is why don't we just use universal groups for everything and not even worry about domain local or global groups anymore? There are two reasons. First, universal groups can only be used in Native mode. Native mode is only possible after you have upgraded all NT 4 domain controllers; the NT 4 DCs can't handle this universal group thing. Second, if you use only universal groups, your global catalog will become bloated and replication issues could occur. You see, universal group names and membership are both replicated to the other global catalog servers (typically, one for each site); global group names, in contrast, appear in the global catalog, but their members don't. With multiple domains, the global catalog contains replicated information for every domain in the forest, and the size (and replication time) will increase exponentially if universal groups contain a large number of objects. Answering the question of whether Joe is a member of the universal group Guys can be difficult, if Guys contains the groups CoolGuys and LessCoolGuys, particularly if CoolGuys contains a bunch of groups, and so on. Global catalog servers take the time to pre-expand global groups, a process that takes time and RAM. A close examination of universal groups, then, leads me to echo Microsoft's general advice about them: they're pretty neat, but use them sparingly.

OTHER FACTS ABOUT GROUPS

You should know two other things about groups.

First, you can put machine accounts in groups. You couldn't do that in NT 4; you could only put user accounts in groups prior to Windows 2000. Why would you *want* to create groups of machines? Well, when you start messing around with group policies, then you'll want to create policies that apply only to *some* people or machines. Groups with machines in them are an essential part of accomplishing that.

Second, there's a limitation in Windows 2000's Active Directory that limits a group's size to about 5000 members. That's fixed in Windows .NET Server, but you should keep it in mind if you're using Windows 2000. So if you want to have a group with 15,000 members, you have to break it up into, say, three smaller groups and then put those smaller groups into a group together.

If you're unsure about which kind of groups go into which kinds of groups, then I've summarized it in the following Figure 9.27

FIGURE 9.27

Group relationships

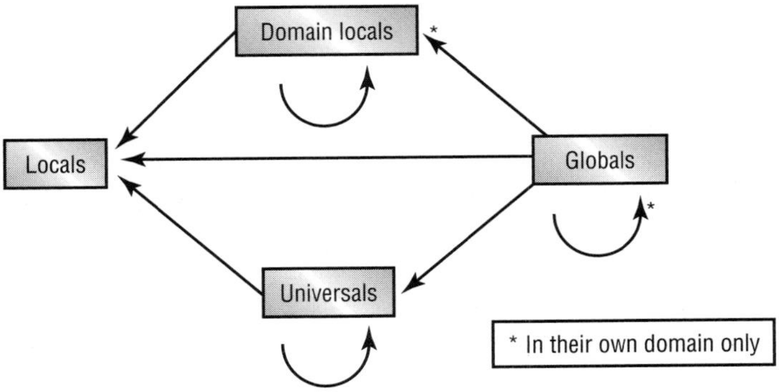

Working with Security Groups

All right, enough talk about global, local, domain local, and universal groups. You need some examples of how this works. However, let me first emphasize how important it is to think about your group structures ahead of time. Once you've "prenested" your larger membership groups (including the local and universal groups) and granted access to the local groups when you set up your resources, you'll only have to fiddle with global and universal group memberships from then on. This will save time and simplify the task of granting object permissions.

Some good, basic nesting examples can be drawn from the nesting patterns that are set up automatically within a domain. One is the nesting of administrator groups. The Administrator account on a Win2K machine draws its powers from membership in the local Administrators group. Take Administrator out of the Administrators group, and the account has no special powers or abilities (but I don't recommend it). The Active Directory automatically creates the Domain Admins global group, although it doesn't assign broad admin rights to the group as you might think. When a Win2K machine joins a domain (or becomes a DC), the global group Domain Admins and the universal group Enterprise Admins are automatically placed in the membership of the local Administrators group. Figure 9.28 shows the membership of the domain local group Administrators for the win2ktest.com domain.

FIGURE 9.28

Members of the Administrators domain local group

The net effect of this nesting is that a member of the Domain Admins or Enterprise Admins group is a local administrator on every member machine in the domain. You can override this default behavior by removing Domain Admins or Enterprise Admins from a machine's local Administrators group, but again, I don't recommend this unless you have a special reason to do so. You can replace the Domain Admins or Enterprise Admins group membership in the local Administrators groups with more specific Admin-type global groups, such as F&A Admins or CS Admins. However, having no global or universal groups at all in the local Administrators group limits control to local Administrator accounts and unnecessarily complicates remote administration tasks.

Another example of group nesting is the membership of the local Users group. On a domain member or domain controller, Users automatically includes Domain Users. When you create a new user account in a domain, the new user is automatically assigned to the Domain Users group. It's sort of an All Users in the Domain group. The net effect is that a user account in a domain is automatically granted local user privileges on every domain member machine by default. The user account goes into the global group Domain Users, and the global group Domain Users goes into the local group Users, which is granted local rights and permissions on a system.

You should also know, just for the record, about a couple of other nestings: Domain Guests is automatically a member of the local group Guests on all domain member machines, and Enterprise Admins (a universal group) is a member of the local Administrators group.

Now let's look at the fictional case of the aforementioned Green Onion Resources (GOR), a national IT consulting and integration firm. Green Onion uses Win2K's Active Directory with both Win2K and NT 4 domain controllers. The company has grouped its IT resources into domains by regional offices—for example, GOR South domain, GOR West domain, and GOR East domain. Finance and Accounting (F&A) people are similarly grouped into global groups by region, as are other functional units of GOR. So there are global groups called F&A South, F&A West, and F&A East. Keeping the Finance people in different global groups within different domains allows finer control of region-specific resources and administration. Some central resources, however, must be accessible to all F&A people at GOR. Those resources are located in the Central Finance share on the Win2K server called GOR_ALPHA1. Now, administrators (or their delegates) have set up a local group called F&A Central on GOR_ALPHA1 and have put each global group (F&A South, F&A West, and F&A East) into the local group called F&A Central. The local group F&A Central has access to the shared resource Central Finance. The following diagram illustrates the GOR strategy for F&A Central access:

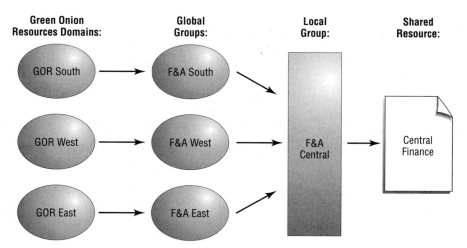

This will work and is definitely the way to go in Mixed mode. When someone leaves or is hired for one of the F&A departments, admins have only to add or remove the user account from the global group to grant or deny access. This will also grant access to the region-specific resources already accessible by the global groups. But when Green Onion Resources upgrades all existing NT 4 domain controllers, they go into Native mode and the fun begins. Now they can keep the granularity of having global groups by functional unit and region, and can also group these F&A regional groups into a new universal group called GOR F&A. The GOR enterprise admins put the three groups, F&A South, F&A West, and F&A East, into the universal group GOR F&A. They can now use the universal group to directly permit access to F&A organization-wide resources, such as the Central Finance folder, instead of using the three global groups—although it's still considered good form to put the universal group into a local group and grant access to the local group. The following diagram illustrates the adjustment once GOR switches to Native mode.

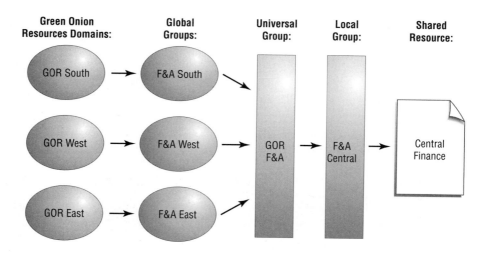

Why should we keep nesting global and universal groups into local groups even after switching to Native mode? Certainly, you can instead just put a bunch of accounts into the GOR F&A universal group. If you have a single domain for your organization and never plan to add more, this strategy is perfectly acceptable. With multiple domains, however, remember that the global catalog must replicate the names and members of all universal groups throughout the forest. Having all 600 or so bean-counter accounts from the various domains in one universal group therefore becomes a replication (read "performance") issue.

You can also grant access to the shared resource directly to the universal group and bypass the local group nesting altogether. Current thinking holds that it's easier to just set up access on the resource once, then modify it by manipulating the membership of the group that has access. This was especially true under NT 4, when managing permissions on remote shares was a bit cumbersome, but Active Directory management is likely to change all that. Granting access directly to the universal group seems to be in keeping with that principle, though, if you plan to keep universal group membership down and limit it to other groups. The drawback is that domains and their global groups might come and go—especially in Win2K, since an entire domain can be wiped out without reinstalling the operating system. If ACL entries refer to global or universal groups that are no longer recognized as the result of a defunct domain or a broken trust relationship, ACL will report an entry as "Account Unknown" and the Forces of Darkness will increase and multiply and chaos will reign...Well, maybe not. But it's messy. If you *always* grant access to a local group, the machine will *always* recognize it. Then you can simply grant or deny access to a resource by manipulating the membership of that local group.

BUILT-IN DOMAIN LOCAL GROUPS

You might have noticed in our earlier tour of DSA.MSC that all the built-in user accounts, like Guest and Administrator, are placed by default in the Users container. Users also contains predefined global groups. But some groups are listed under the Builtin container. As you see in Figure 9.29, the groups in the Builtin container are labeled Builtin Local, and the ones in the Users container

(Figure 9.30) are Domain Local, Global, or Universal. What's the difference? Well, for one thing, recall from Chapter 2 and our earlier discussion here that local groups are specific to the machine, whereas global groups can be accepted throughout the domain or in a trusted domain. Built-in local groups have predetermined rights and permissions for the purposes of administration. Membership in these (or any) groups grants the user all the powers and abilities granted to the group. This is a way to quickly assign well-defined administrative roles rather than having to create them from scratch. For example, Server Operators have an inherent set of rights for creating file shares and managing services. Backup Operators have the right to back up files and directories, even if they don't have permission to read or modify them.

FIGURE 9.29

DSA.MSC Builtin container

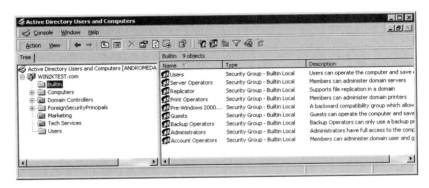

FIGURE 9.30

DSA.MSC Users container

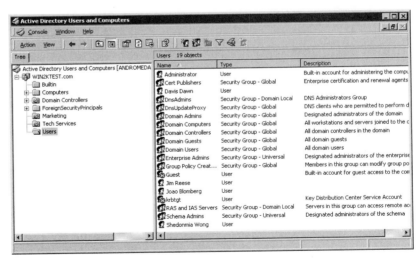

Table 9.2 lists the built-in domain local groups and their special abilities. Built-in local groups are common to all Win2K systems of the same ilk (server/DC/workstation) and provide convenient container groups for granting local administrative authority. Note that you can't delete these groups. You can, however, create other users and groups in the container, although they won't have any special rights unless you assign them.

TIP   In general, rights grant the ability to do something, often something admin related or otherwise restricted. Permissions, on the other hand, give us the ability to access resources such as files and printers as well as Active Directory objects such as group policies.

TABLE 9.2: BUILT-IN GROUPS AND THEIR RIGHTS

USER RIGHTS	MEMBERS CAN ALSO
Group: Administrators	
Log on locally	Create and manage user accounts
Access this computer from the network	Create and manage global groups
Take ownership of files	Assign user rights
Group: Administrators	
Manage auditing and security log	Manage auditing and security policy
Change the system time	Lock the server console
Shut down the system	Unlock the console
Force shutdown from a remote system	Format the server's hard disk
Back up files and directories	Create common program groups
Restore files and directories	Keep a local profile
Add and remove device drivers	Share and stop sharing directories
Increase the priority of a process	Share and stop sharing printers
Group: Server Operators	
Log on locally	Lock the server
Change the system time	Override server's lock
Shut down the system	Format the server's hard disk
Force shutdown from a remote system	Create common groups
Back up files and directories	Keep a local profile
Restore files and directories	Share and stop sharing directories
	Share and stop sharing printers
Group: Account Operators	
Log on locally	Create and manage user accounts, global groups, and local groups[1]
Shut down the system	Keep a local profile

Continued on next page

TABLE 9.2: BUILT-IN GROUPS AND THEIR RIGHTS *(continued)*

USER RIGHTS	MEMBERS CAN ALSO
Group: Print Operators	
Log on locally	Keep a local profile
Shut down the system	Share and stop sharing printers
Group: Backup Operators	
Log on locally	Keep a local profile
Shut down the system	
Group: Backup Operators	
Back up files and directories	
Restore files and directories	
Group: Everyone	
Access this computer from the network	Lock the server[2]
Group: Users	
(None)	Create and manage local groups[3]
Group: Guests	
(None)	(None)
Group: Replicator	
(None)	(None)

1. *They cannot, however, modify Administrator accounts, the Domain Admins global group, or the local group's Administrators, Server Operators, Account Operators, Print Operators, and Backup Operators.*

2. *In order to actually do this, the member of the group must have the right to log in locally at the server.*

3. *In order to actually do this, the user must either have the right to log in locally at the server or have access to the DSA.MSC tool.*

Administrators Administrators have almost every built-in right, so members are basically all-powerful with regard to administration of the system.

Backup Operators Members of Backup Operators have the right to back up and restore files, whether or not they have permission to access those files otherwise.

Server Operators The Server Operators local group has all the rights needed to manage the domain's servers. Members can create, manage, and delete printer shares at servers; create, manage, and delete network shares at servers; back up and restore files on servers; format a server's fixed disk; lock and unlock servers; unlock files; and change the system time. In addition, Server Operators can log in to the network from the domain's servers as well as shut down the servers.

Account Operators   Members of the Account Operators local group are allowed to create user accounts and groups for the domain and to modify or delete most of the domain's user accounts and groups. Members of Account Operators cannot modify or delete the following groups: Administrators, Domain Admins, Account Operators, Backup Operators, Print Operators, and Server Operators. Likewise, members of this group cannot modify or delete user accounts of Administrators. Nor can they administer the security policies; but they can add computers to a domain, log in at servers, and shut down servers.

Print Operators   Members of this group can create, manage, and delete printer shares for a Win2K server. Additionally, they can log in at and shut down servers.

Power Users   This group exists on non-DCs and Win2K Professional systems. Members can create user accounts and local groups and can manage the membership of Users, Power Users, and Guests, as well as administer other users and groups that they have created.

Users   Users can run applications (but not install them). They also can shut down and lock the workstation. If a user has the right to log in locally to a workstation, they also have the right to create local groups and manage those groups they have created.

Guests   Guests can log in and run applications. They can also shut down the system, but otherwise their abilities are even more limited than Users. For instance, Guests cannot keep a local profile.

Replicator   This group is strictly for directory replication. A user account is used to run the Replicator service, and that user should be the only member of the group.

In the Users container, other predefined domain local groups and global groups may be created as part of the configuration of a certain service. These groups might serve to allow users access to certain services (DHCP Users and WINS Users, for instance) or to provide a group container for administrators of the service, as in the case of DHCP Administrators and DNS Admins. These and other predefined global groups may also have special rights and/or permissions for particular actions, but not the broad rights and permissions of Administrators, Server Operators, or another built-in local group.

NOTE   *Some predefined groups, including Domain Computers and Domain Controllers, are designated for machine accounts, although you can add a user account to Domain Computers if it gives you a thrill.*

Win2K has several built-in global groups, among them Domain Admins, Domain Users, and Domain Guests. These will only appear on domain controllers. In fact, it's impossible to create global groups anywhere *other* than on domain controllers. Although you might use an administration tool while sitting at a non-DC to create the global groups, the groups will exist only on domain controllers. Table 9.3 describes the most important built-in global groups.

TABLE 9.3: BUILT-IN GLOBAL GROUPS

GROUP	WHAT IT DOES
Domain Admins	By placing a user account into this global group, you provide administrative-level abilities to that user. Members of Domain Admins can administer the home domain, the workstations of the domain, and any other trusted domains that have added this domain's Domain Admins global group to their own Administrators local group. By default, the built-in Domain Admins global group is a member of both the domain's Administrators local group and the Administrators local groups for every NT or Win2K workstation in the domain. The built-in Administrator user account for the domain is automatically a member of the Domain Admins global group.
Domain Users	Members of the Domain Users global group have normal user access to, and abilities for, both the domain itself and any NT/Win2K workstation in the domain. This group contains all domain user accounts and is by default a member of every local Users group on every NT/Win2K workstation in the domain.
Domain Guests	This group allows guest accounts to access resources across domain boundaries if they've been permitted to do so by the domain administrators.

SPECIAL BUILT-IN GROUPS

In addition to the built-in local and global groups, several special groups that are not listed in DSA.MSC (or Computer Management Users and Groups for that matter) will appear on Access Control Lists for resources and objects, including the following:

INTERACTIVE   Anyone using the computer locally.

NETWORK   All users connected over the network to a computer.

NOTE   Incidentally, the INTERACTIVE and NETWORK groups together form the Everyone local group.

SYSTEM   The operating system.

CREATOR OWNER   The creator and/or owner of subdirectories, files, and print jobs.

AUTHENTICATED USERS   Any user who has been authenticated to the system. Used as a more-secure alternative to Everyone.

ANONYMOUS LOGON   A user who has logged in anonymously, such as an anonymous FTP user.

BATCH   An account that has logged in as a batch job.

SERVICE   An account that has logged in as a service.

DIALUP   Users who are accessing the system via Dial-Up Networking.

How Do Organizational Units Fit In?

Organizational units (OUs) are logical containers in a domain. They can contain users, groups, computers, and other OUs, but only from their home domain. You can't put global groups or computers from another domain into your domain's OU, for example.

The usefulness of OUs is strictly for administration. Administrators can create and apply group policies to an OU and can delegate control of OUs, as well. The idea is to have a subdivision of a domain but still share common security information and resources. Grouping users, groups, and resources into organizational units allows you to apply policies in a more granular fashion and also to decide specifically who manages what and to what extent. So when you're advised about how to group your OUs, keep in mind that the tool must fit your hand; your organization may be unique, so your approach to OUs may be as well.

Rather than creating OUs for locations (that's what sites are for), departments, and so on, think about how your organization will be administered. Design your OUs with delegation in mind. Keep it simple for your own sake. Thousands of nested OUs just make more work for you. Also, OUs are unrelated to the process of locating resources on your network, so you needn't group them with a browse list in mind, either.

What's the difference between an OU and a container? An OU is a container, but not just a container like the Users container in DSA.MSC. You can delegate control of a container (you can delegate control of anything), but you can't apply Group Policy to one.

How are OUs different from groups? A user can be a member of many groups but can only be in one OU at a time. Like groups, OUs can contain other OUs. Group names appear on ACLs, so you can grant or deny access to groups. OUs do not appear on ACLs, so you can't give everyone in the Finance OU access to a printer, for example. On the other hand, you can't assign a designated set of Desktop applications to everyone in a security group, but you can publish or assign the company accounting package to the entire Accounting OU.

Zen and the Art of Login Scripts

Login scripts are an ancient revered method for configuring a user's working environment and assigning network resources. Before we had Network Neighborhood, in a time before Microsoft networks came into prominence, network clients were relatively unenlightened about the network around them. Login scripts were written in the common language of the client and ran from the server on the client at the time of logon. These scripts would create local drive mappings to the servers, redirect local ports to assign printers, synchronize the system clock with a central designated time server, and perform other honorable related tasks. One could say, Grasshopper, that logon scripts reached their peak in the Age of NetWare, when the color red blanketed the networking world. In the Age of NT 4, networking clients become more aware of the network around them. In small isolated networks, the Art was all but abandoned, but logon scripts still flourished in large complex environments, prized for their eternal usefulness. During this time, the Art became more sophisticated. While logon scripts are now used to perform increasingly complex tasks, the essential Art, the True Art of Login Scripts, has remained unchanged.

Today Win2K offers us the ability to use not only logon scripts but also logoff scripts, startup scripts, and shutdown scripts. We're no longer confined to a limited set of shell commands, either. Organizations now use a myriad of scripting and even programming languages to accomplish eye-popping configuration feats compared with those of 10 years ago. There is no way to do justice to everything that's out there in the few pages allotted here, but I will discuss your choices of scripting language, take a look at an example logon script, and tell you how to assign a logon script in Win2K.

SCRIPTING LANGUAGES

A wide variety of scripting environments and languages are available today, including DOS/NT/Win2K shell commands, Windows Scripting Host (WSH), KiXtart, XLNT, Perl, VBScript, JScript, even Python. You can use literally any language that is useful to you and is understood by your client machine. Login scripts are only limited by a couple of things: developers and clients. A script developer (that includes you) must know how to use the chosen tool. It's no good to try writing a logon script in C if you can't even figure out how to make it say "Good morning." The vast majority of us aren't programmers, so we must use simpler tools, such as shell scripts or special logon script languages like KiXtart or XLNT. The client, as well, must understand the language of the script, so if you want to use Perl, for example, you need a Perl interpreter installed on each client system.

Win2K/NT/Windows 9x shell commands are an obvious choice for logon scripts. No special client software is required. If you have pre-NT clients, your command set is rather limited, but the NT 4 command-line language is actually fairly robust in comparison to the earlier set of commands. Plus, all of the NT 4 scripts I've tried on Win2K systems still work, so there is a great deal of backward compatibility built into the Win2K shell language. In my humble opinion, however, NT/Win2K shell scripting is still less flexible or intuitive than any of the various Unix shell languages. Remember that Windows software (even Win2K and NT) was not designed primarily for command-line geeks, but for people with mice (the electronic kind). However, Microsoft is showing some improvements in the command-line arena, so let's encourage them.

KiXtart 95 was designed by Ruud van Velsen at Microsoft Benelux. It is a freeware logon script processor that also serves as an enhanced batch language. KiXtart is extremely flexible and easy to use. A version was released in the NT 4 Resource Kit, but you will want to download the latest version from kixtart.to/script/. There is also an online manual at this site. Again, I am assuming that most of your clients will not be Win2K Professional systems yet, although the KiXtart scripts I use run perfectly well on Win2K machines.

Perl (Practical Extraction and Reporting Language) was initially developed for system administrators as a tool to run reports. It has become much, much more. Platform independent like Java, but without the memory overhead of the Java virtual machine, Perl has proven its usefulness to Unix administrators and developers and has become one of the more popular scripting languages in the Windows world as well. You will have to install a Perl interpreter and modules on your clients, although this process is relatively painless. Alternately, there is a utility called Perl2Exe that converts Perl scripts to executables. If you don't mind the overhead of running a program that's around 700K (script, interpreter, and any modules) across the network whenever users log in, download it from www.demobuilder.com. The latest version of Perl for Windows 95/98/NT, ActivePerl, is available from www.activestate.com/ActivePerl/. ActivePerl includes Perlscript, an ActiveX scripting engine like VBScript or JScript. There is also a wealth of information on Perl in bookstores and at www.perl.com.

The Windows Scripting Host (WSH) is an environment for running Visual Basic Scripting Edition (VBScript) and JavaScript natively on Windows 95/98, NT, or Win2K. The Scripting Host (and a Script Debugger) are included with Win2K, and WSH is an installation option for Windows 98, but if you need WSH for 95 or NT you'll need to download it from `msdn.microsoft.com/scripting/` `windowshost`. The site is also a good source of information and offers a link to `wsh.glazier.co.nz/`, a site that focuses on using WSH for logon scripts. You'll find examples of WSH logon scripts there.

There are numerous other scripting environments, including C shell, PythonWin, XLNT, and the MKS Toolkit by Mortice Kern Systems, Inc. (MKS is a toolkit for you Unix-heads; it includes Korn shell, Vi editor, AWK, and more). All these offerings are available for evaluation or as freeware from `www.microsoft.com/NTServer/nts/exec/vendors/freeshare/develope.asp`. (Yes, Microsoft does have a third-party software download area. Really!)

ASSIGNING THE LOGIN SCRIPT

Specify a logon script in the user account profile information in `DSA.MSC`, or assign scripts using Group Policy. Either way, the scripts and any other necessary files must be in the `SYSVOL` share, found in `\winnt\SYSVOL\sysvol`. Pre-Win2K clients look for a share called `NETLOGON` to get to the script. Win2K machines create a `NETLOGON` share in `\winnt\SYSVOL\sysvol\domainname\scripts` for backward compatibility. If you have Win2K Professional machines as clients, Group Policy can be used to assign a logon script. Scripts assigned to Win2K machines using Group Policy run asynchronously in hidden windows, so the user shell may actually start before logon script processing is complete. Scripts assigned in account properties run synchronously in visible windows by default. In that case, the user shell does not start until the script is done.

EXAMPLE LOGIN SCRIPTS

The following sample scripts serve to illustrate the types of things you can do in a logon script. This project is an abbreviated version of an actual logon script; as they used to say on that old TV show, "The names have been changed to protect the innocent." In this configuration, `login.bat`, the designated logon script, calls the main script (`login.scr`), which uses KiXtart 95 scripting language to map drives according to group memberships. At the end of `login.scr`, a script called `setmail.bat` is called to check for a user's Exchange mail profile and to create one if it doesn't already exist. The `setmail` script is not included here, but I show the `call` command in the main routine as an example of using logon scripts to ease configuration tasks other than the mapping of network drives.

The KiXtart script (`login.scr`) uses semicolons for comments, which I have supplied to explain what the script commands are doing. `Login.bat` uses native shell scripting, so comment lines are preceded by the command `REM`. Since this is a sample logon script and not a textbook example of shell scripting or KiXtart scripting, I've included numerous comments instead of a line-by-line explanation, and instead of the usual commented-out statements in the script, to let you know what's going on.

All of the executables used in the scripts are kept in `NETLOGON` for simplicity's sake (we have NT 4 workstations and a few straggling Windows 95 clients).

Example 9.1: Login.bat *(Designated Login Script)*

First, turn off the command echo:

```
@echo off
```

Since NT and 95/98 call logon scripts differently, let's check the `%OS%` variable to see if it's set to Windows_NT and, if it isn't, skip to the subroutine for Windows 95/98 clients:

```
@if not "%OS%"=="Windows_NT" GOTO 95OS
```

NT machines can run the script with a UNC path. The `kix32` executable takes as its argument the name of the script:

```
:NTOS
\\SERVER1\NETLOGON\kix32.exe \\SERVER1\netlogon\LOGIN.scr
GOTO EOF
```

Windows 95/98 machines temporarily map the Z: drive to NETLOGON during the logon sequence. They cannot run the script using a UNC path. The path statement is not for KIX32.EXE, but rather for other executables called later:

```
:95OS
path=z:\
z:\kix32.exe z:\Login.scr
GOTO EOF
:EOF
EXIT
```

Example 9.2: Login.scr *(KiXtart Login Script Called by* Login.bat*)*

```
:STAGE1
```

Statements preceded by a question mark (?) cause the text that follows on the same line to be displayed on the console screen, much as ECHO does in the native shell language:

```
? "NXT login script now processing..."
? "Querying your System Information..."
```

We need to check again for 95/98 versus NT machines, because variables are set differently for each. @INWIN is a KiXtart variable used for this purpose. Again, the script processing skips to the appropriate subroutine, SETVARNT or SETVAR95, depending on the OS. Win2K boxes will process like NT machines and Windows 98 systems will process like Windows 95 machines:

```
IF @INWIN = 1
    GOTO SETVARNT
ELSE
    GOTO SETVAR95
ENDIF
```

These commands set variables on 95/98 clients using SHELL and WINSET.EXE. SHELL is a KiXtart routine to call a native shell command, and WINSET.EXE is actually an executable from the Windows 95 CD that sets environmental variables. @USERID and the other words preceded by @ are variables that KiXtart understands. Thus, we are using KiXtart variable values to set actual system environmental variables:

```
:SETVAR95
SHELL "winset.exe USERNAME=@USERID"
SHELL "winset.exe ADDRESS=@ADDRESS"
SHELL "winset.exe COMPUTER=@WKSTA"
SHELL "winset.exe DOMAIN=@DOMAIN"
SHELL "winset.exe COMMENT=@COMMENT"
SHELL "winset.exe FULLNAME=@FULLNAME"
SHELL "winset.exe HOMEDIR=@HOMEDIR"
```

```
SHELL "winset.exe HOMESHR=@HOMESHR"
SHELL "winset.exe LSERVER=@LSERVER"
SHELL "winset.exe PRIV=@PRIV"
GOTO STAGE2
```

On NT and Win2K boxes, the following commands set variables without "shelling out" to the native command environment. The SET command sets user variables, and SETM defines system variables:

```
:SETVARNT
;set variables on NT clients using set command
SET USERNAME="@USERID"
SETM ADDRESS="@ADDRESS"
SETM COMPUTER="@WKSTA"
SETM DOMAIN="@DOMAIN"
SET COMMENT="@COMMENT"
SET FULLNAME="@FULLNAME"
SET HOMEDIR="@HOMEDIR"
SET HOMESHR="@HOMESHR"
SET LSERVER="@LSERVER"
SET PRIV="@PRIV"
```

KiXtart includes a special executable to query for group memberships. I put it in the NETLOGON share for convenience.

```
:STAGE2
? "Querying your group memberships..."
;SHELL "\\server1\netlogon\kixgrp.exe /s"
```

Time synchronization is an important function in many logon scripts. The SERVER1 listed here is a designated time server that synchronizes regularly with a reliable external time source:

```
? "Synchronizing your system's clock"
;synchronize with time server
SETTIME \\server1
```

Next, we check to see if the time synchronization was successful. If it wasn't, a message box pops up to get the user's attention.

```
IF @error = 0
   ? "System clock synchronized"
ELSE
   MESSAGEBOX ("Cannot synchronize the system clock.
   Please inform your administrator.","XYZ Login Script", 0)
ENDIF
?
```

The following commands will use group membership to map network drives. Just in case, we'll first delete any preexisting drive mappings. Again, if there are errors while deleting previous drive mappings, a message box will get the user's attention.

```
? "Now mapping network drives..."
```

```
?
;delete any previous drive mappings and check for errors
USE "*" /DELETE
IF @error = 0
    ?"Previous mappings deleted..."
ELSE
    MESSAGEBOX ("Cannot delete previous drive mappings.
    Please inform your administrator.",
    "XYZ Login Script", 0)
ENDIF
;MAP Drives by Group Membership
;Map Domain F & A to M: drive
IF INGROUP ("Domain F & A") = 1
    use M: "\\server1\F&A Control"
    ? "F & A Drive Mapped"
ENDIF
;Map Domain Sales to S: drive
IF INGROUP ("Domain Sales") = 1
    use S: \\server1\Sales
    ? "Sales Drive Mapped"
ENDIF
;Map Domain Tech Services to T: drive
IF INGROUP ("Domain Tech Services") = 1
    use T: \\server1\TechSvcs
    ? "Tech Services Drive Mapped"
ENDIF
;Map common drives for Domain Users
IF INGROUP ("Domain Users") = 1
    use G: \\server1\apps
    use P: \\server1\public
    use N: \\server1\infosys
    use H: @HOMESHR
    ? "Global Drives and Home Directories Mapped"
ENDIF
```

Finally, the script will call the setmail.bat script for NT boxes only. (It only runs this for NT boxes because some of the executables used in the script don't work reliably on the few remaining 95 machines on our network.) SETMAIL.BAT checks the system for the existence of an Exchange mail profile for the user and, if one does not exist, automatically creates one.

```
IF @INWIN = 1
    ? "Checking for your Mail Profile..."
    shell setmail.bat
ENDIF
? "Login Script Complete"
EXIT
```

Understanding User Permissions and Rights

Much of what we've got to do as administrators is to both provide our users with access to *some* network resources and keep the users *from* other network resources. Ever since NT 3.1, Microsoft operating systems have let you control access with two tools: permissions and rights.

Object Permissions, ACLs, and ACEs

You've seen some references to permissions so far, and you'll see a lot more of them in the next chapter, which is on file and directory shares. Basically, a *permission* is just a setting that controls your level of access to some object on the network. For example, I could create a file called MYSECRETS.TXT and set its file permissions so that only I can read, write, and delete it and so that some other user—perhaps a father-confessor figure?—can read it, but nobody else can access it at all. Permissions let me do that; they control access to an object.

We mainly think of permissions in terms of files and directories, but there are many more things in the NT family of Microsoft operating systems that have permissions. A few include the ability to control things like the following:

◆ Registry keys, which determine who can read or modify a given key or value entry

◆ Contents of domains and organization units, which determines who can add things (for example, users or machine accounts) to a domain or an OU

◆ System services, so you can control who can start or stop a given service

◆ Directories and files, both of which have permissions

As you'll learn throughout the rest of the book, many things have permissions. You can usually find an object's permissions by right-clicking on the object and choosing Properties. In the resulting property page, there is usually a tab labeled Security. That's not always true, and in some cases, the UI doesn't reveal the underlying security items. In other cases, you may have to take some extra steps to see the permissions. For example, you will not see the Security tab on a domain or organizational unit in Active Directory until you choose View/Advanced in Active Directory Users and Computers, as you may recall in the "Advanced Delegation" section in Chapter 8.

Here's a simple example of permissions. I've right-clicked a file named TESTIT.TXT on my hard disk, chosen Properties and then the Security tab. It shows me Figure 9.31.

You see from it that an account named mark@minasi.com has full control, and the Everyone group can only read this file. You also see that this object has five possible permissions: Full Control, Modify, Read and Execute, Read, and Write. Collectively, this set of permissions is called an access control list or ACL (pronounced *ackel*). Each entry in the ACL—the mark@minasi.com and Everyone entries, I mean—are called access control entries (ACEs). But there's a lot more detail possible; click the Advanced button to see more, and you'd see a dialog box like the one in Figure 9.32.

You can get this dialog box from *any* Security dialog box, as far as I can see, by clicking the Advancedbutton. It makes more or less sense, depending on the object type. In the case of this file, you can see that it really doesn't show us much that we didn't already know. But the other two tabs are useful; Auditing lets you tell the system whether or not to audit access to this file and what level of detail to log, and Owner lets you find out who owns the file and lets you change the owner. (In

Microsoft terms, an object's "owner" is a person who has an unstoppable right to change permissions on that object. We'll discuss that in greater detail in the next chapter.)

FIGURE 9.31

Security tab for a file

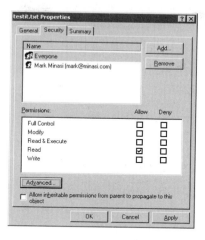

FIGURE 9.32

Access Control Settings dialog box

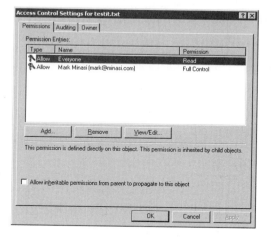

To find out the most nitty-gritty details that you can about the ACE for Everyone, click it and then View/Edit. That shows you a dialog box like the one in Figure 9.33.

Again, you'd see a dialog box *like* this for any object that has ACLs, but the exact contents of the dialog box would vary from object to object. In this particular case, you see 13 very specific permissions, the lowest-level permissions possible on a file. The five permissions that you saw in the first dialog box (Full Control, Modify, Read and Execute, Read, and Write) aren't really permissions at all—they're *groups* of these 13 lowest-level permissions.

FIGURE 9.33

Lowest-level permissions for a file

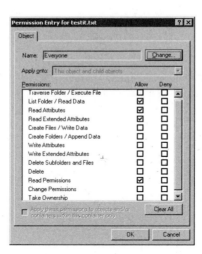

User Rights

In contrast to permissions, there are rights. Permissions give you different access to different objects; rights give you the ability to do particular things. And yes, the line between permissions and rights *is* fuzzy in Windows 2000 and later operating systems. For example, is the ability to create user objects a permission or a right? Well, under the hood, a user is just an object in a particular "container" called the domain. So creating a user in a domain is very similar to creating a file in a directory, and it is permissions that control that. But what about the ability to physically sit down at a server and log on? That's not a permission; that's a right.

In general, rights tend to apply to a particular system (for example, the right to log on to the system, the right to change its time, and the right to shut it down). So I guess, in a sense, Microsoft could simply have considered any given system to be a "container" and then made those powers (local logon, time change, shutdown) into ACLs on the system. But they didn't, and so we have rights.

Additionally, some rights are basically system-specific powers that override ACLs. For example, one right is the right to back up files. Clearly, you'd think that you can't back up files if you can't read them, but anyone with the back-up right *can* back up any file on a system, including the ones that he or she is denied access to—rights trump permissions. But don't worry about your privacy, because the Backup Operators group's rights are only valid in conjunction with a backup routine. Backup Operators can't just open files on the server and read the contents, for example.

Win2K's built-in groups have certain rights already assigned to them. You can also create new groups and assign a custom set of user rights to those groups. As I've said before, security management is much easier when all user rights are assigned through groups instead of to individual users.

To view or modify the local rights assignment for a user or group, open the Local Security Policy tool from the Administrative Tools group on a non-DC or use the Domain Controller Security Policy tool for a DC. Open `Local Policies\User Rights Assignment`. A listing of rights and the users or groups to which those rights have been granted will be displayed in the details pane on the right, as shown in Figure 9.34.

FIGURE 9.34

Local user rights policy

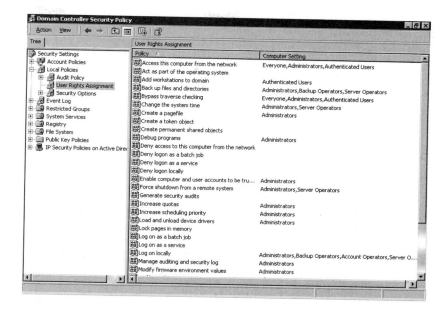

To add or remove a right to or from a user or group, double-click the right as displayed in the details pane or right-click the selected right and choose Security. In Figure 9.35 you see the Security information for the right to change the system time. To remove this right from a group, highlight the name of the group and choose Remove. To add a group or user to the list, choose Add and in the Select Users or Groups dialog box, type in a name or choose Browse to select a name. Table 9.4 lists user rights with descriptions.

FIGURE 9.35

Local security policy setting for a user right

Table 9.4: Local User Rights

User Right	Description
Access this computer from the network	Connect over the network to a computer.
Act as part of the operating system	Act as a trusted part of the operating system; some subsystems have this privilege granted to them.
Add workstations to domain	Make machines domain members.
Back up files and directories	Back up files and directories. As mentioned earlier, this right supersedes file and directory permissions.
Bypass traverse checking	Traverse a directory tree even if the user has no other rights to access that directory. For example, if I have no access to C:\Files but *do* have access to C:\Files\Department\Sales, then I can't access C:\Files\Department\Sales *unless* can bypass traverse checking.
Change the system time	Set the time for the internal clock of a computer.
Create a pagefile	Create a pagefile.
Create a token object	Create access tokens. Only the Local Security Authority should have this privilege.
Create permanent shared objects	Create special permanent objects.
Debug programs	Debug applications.
Deny access to this computer from the network	Opposite of the "Access this computer from the network" right; specifically revokes the right to users/groups that would normally have it.
Deny logon as a batch job	Revokes the right to log in as a batch job.
Deny logon as a service	Revokes the right to log in as a service.
Deny logon locally	Revokes the right to log in locally.
Enable computer and user accounts to be trusted for delegation	Designate accounts that can be delegated.
Force shutdown from a remote system	Allows a computer to be shut down from a remote system.
Generate security audits	Generate audit log entries.
Increase quotas	Increase object quotas (each object has a quota assigned to it).
Increase scheduling priority	Boost the scheduling priority of a process.
Load and unload device drivers	Add or remove drivers from the system.
Lock pages in memory	Lock pages in memory to prevent them from being paged out into backing store (such as PAGEFILE.SYS).

Continued on next page

TABLE 9.4: LOCAL USER RIGHTS *(continued)*

USER RIGHT	DESCRIPTION
Log on as a batch job	Log on to the system as a batch queue facility.
Log on as a service	Perform security services (the user that performs replication logs in as a service).
Log on locally	Log on locally at the server computer itself.
Manage auditing and security log	Specify what types of events and resource access are to be audited. Also allows viewing and clearing the security log.
Modify firmware environment values	Modify system environment variables (not user environment variables).
Profile single process	Use Win2K profiling capabilities to observe a process.
Profile system performance	Use Win2K profiling capabilities to observe the system.
Remove computer from docking station	Remove a laptop computer from its docking station.
Replace a process level token	Modify a process's access token.
Restore files and directories	Restore files and directories. This right supersedes file and directory permissions.
Shut down the system	Shut down Windows 2000.
Synchronize directory service data	Update Active Directory information.
Take ownership of files or other objects	Take ownership of files, directories, and other objects that are owned by other users.

Many rights, such as the right to debug programs and the one to profile a single process, are useful only to programmers writing applications to run on Win2K and are seldom granted to a group or user. When would you mess with these? Some third-party applications require you to extend some set of rights to a user before you can run the application.

You can set user rights on a machine-by-machine basis with Local Security Policy or, as you'll learn soon, SECEDIT.EXE; you can set rights wholesale over a number of machines with Group Policies.

Local and Domain-Based Group Policies

An administrator's work is never done. Users are constantly fiddling with their settings. It's hard to maintain "standard builds," and rolling out new applications is a big headache in large networks or small. It's a pain to package up applications, remote management systems like SMS are unnecessarily complex, and Admin privileges are needed to install many applications on NT or Win2K machines. What a marketing opportunity!

When it comes to configuration management, there are a lot of buzzwords flying around these days: system policies, Group Policy, Change and Configuration Management (CCM), Intellimirror.

What do these words mean to an everyday admin who just wants to maintain some continuity in Desktop configurations?

CCM and Intellimirror are marketing monikers for a group of Win2K Desktop management features, including roaming profiles and folder redirection, offline folders, software distribution, and Desktop configuration control (I mean management). Despite the fancy terms, many of these features (including folder redirection, software distribution, and remote Desktop configuration) are easily implemented with group policies.

Group Policy Benefits

The term for the most broad-reaching control and support technology, however, is *group policies*. It's a confusing term because it doesn't really refer to groups. There are two kinds of group policies, the kind *with* a domain to back them up and the kind *without* a domain. (In case you're wondering, *domain* here means Active Directory domain.) Without a domain you use a tool called Local Security Policies and a command-line tool called SECEDIT, *with* a domain you use domain-based group policies (where the Active Directory does much of your work).

But what exactly can you *do* with group policies? Here's a brief list:

◆ Publish or assign software packages to users or machines.

◆ Assign start-up, shutdown, logon, and logoff scripts.

◆ Define password, lockout, and audit policy for the domain.

◆ Standardize a whole bunch of other security settings for remote machines—settings previously configurable only by editing the Registry or using a third-party security configuration tool. Some features, like the ability to enforce group memberships and services configuration, are completely new.

◆ Define and enforce settings for Internet Explorer.

◆ Define and enforce restrictions on users' Desktops.

◆ Redirect certain folders in users' profiles (such as `Start Menu` and `Desktop`) to be stored in a central location.

◆ Configure and standardize settings for features like offline folders, disk quotas, and even Group Policy itself.

Many of these features are discussed in sections of their own throughout this book. Software distribution is covered in Chapter 12, "Software Installation." Chapter 11, "Creating and Managing Shared Folders," touches on offline folders. User profiles are discussed later in this chapter. Folder redirection is really a lightweight approach to user profiles ("Profiles Lite"), allowing you to use a subset of the full, roaming profile features, so we'll talk about that, too, later in this chapter. The key point here is that Group Policy provides a single point of administration, allowing administrators to easily install software and apply standardized settings to multiple users and computers throughout an organization.

Group Policies Compared to System Policies

Before Win2K, a much smaller subset of these things, mostly just Desktop restriction and a few security settings, were accomplished using system policies. Group policies have improved on system policies in a couple of major ways.

THE ACTIVE DIRECTORY HANDLES REPLICATION

With NT system policies, you had to see to it that a file named `NTCONFIG.POL` was properly replicated to every domain controller's NETLOGON share. You did that by setting up the NT directory replication service, which was a nice try but tended to be a bit flaky. In contrast, domain-based group policies live partially in the Active Directory and partly in Sysvol, the Window 2000-and-later replacement for NETLOGON. Both Active Directory and Sysvol replicate themselves automatically, with no work required on your part.

DOMAIN-BASED GROUP POLICIES UNDO THEMSELVES WHEN REMOVED

NT 4–type system policies write permanent changes to the Registry when they are applied. This phenomenon is commonly called *tattooing*. Remove the policy and the settings remain. You actually have to "reverse the policy" (by applying a policy with opposite settings) or change the settings manually. Group policies, on the other hand, write their information only to certain parts of the Registry and so are able to clean up after themselves when the policy is removed.

For example, suppose you'd created an NT 4–type system policy that set everyone's background color to some nauseating hue and also set up a policy that kept them from changing the color back. Those changes got written into the system's Registries. So if you deleted the policy, then they'd still have those items in their Registries, and therefore the ugly background as well. You'd actually have to write a *second* policy to undo the Registry effects. With domain-based group policies, that's not necessary. Just removing the policy will undo its effects.

YOU NEEDN'T LOG ON TO GET DOMAIN-BASED GROUP POLICIES

System policies are applied only once: at logon for user settings and at start-up for computer settings. Group policies are applied this way, too, but they are reapplied at specific intervals. Furthermore, Windows NT always had the peculiar characteristic of taking its policies from the user's domain. Why's that a problem? Well, suppose your workstation was a member of a domain called MACHINES and your user account was a member of a domain called USERS. Presumably, you'd want the machine policies that affect your machine to come from the machine's domain, MACHINES. But under NT 4, that never happened. Instead, when the user logged on, the machine would go grab a `NTCONFIG.POL` file from the user's domain, USERS. It would then hand any machine policies to itself and any user policies to the user. Under Windows 2000 and later with Active Directory, machines get their policies from their domain when they power up (recall that machines log on also) and users get policies from *their* domain when they log on.

Additionally, workstations check with Active Directory every 60 to 120 minutes to see if there are new policies and, if there are, then the workstations apply them—both user and machine policies. Further, group policies do a lot more than just modify Registry settings.

GROUP POLICIES ONLY WORK ON WINDOWS 2000 AND LATER MACHINES

The bad news about group policies, both locally and domain-based, is that they only work on Win2K Server or Professional machines, and they require Active Directory, although it is possible to apply a more limited set of "local policies" without AD.

You can only use group policies to control Windows 2000 Server and Windows 2000 Professional machines. If your users run Windows 95/98 or Windows NT Workstation 4 on their Desktops, you'll have to use the same old tools as before—Windows 9x profiles and system policies and Windows NT 4 profiles and group policies. Yes, you read that right—you may have to worry about one set of policies for the Windows machines, another for the NT 4 machines, and a set of group policies for the Win2K machines. Similarly, you might have a set of profiles for Windows 9x users, another for the NT 4 users, and a third set for the Win2K users. If it's any consolation, you can store *all* of these things on a Win2K server—you don't have to keep an old NT 4 server around to hold the NT profiles.

In the sections that follow, you will learn how group policies work and how to create and modify them. You will become familiar with the different nodes and settings in the Group Policy snap-in and look at a few examples of deploying group policies in your organization. Finally, we'll discuss some of the dos and don'ts of group policy.

Local Group Policies: Security Templates

You'll see in a minute that having a domain around to hang domain-based group policies on is a pretty attractive thing. But if your domain is still an NT 4–based domain, (or perhaps if you have Windows 2000 and XP systems around in a network based on Unix, Novell, or some other network OS), then you will still want to be able to accomplish what policies can do, and you can, in the main, albeit with a bit more work. That's where local group policies come in.

You've already met the Local Security Policy snap-in; it's the simple, GUI way to control a particular right on a particular machine. But domain-based group policies let you do considerably more than the Local Security Policy snap-in does, so we need something a trifle more powerful, and Windows 2000 and its descendants have that: a very useful tool called security templates. Let me suggest that if you've been overlooking them, then you've *got* to start using them. In this section, you'll see why.

Worms, viruses, disgruntled employees, and our ever-growing reliance on computers all add up to one thing: a need for security. Clearly there are more and more reasons to secure our computers and, for most of us, there are more and more computers around to secure! But who wants to make security a full-time job? Not me. That's why you should know about a set of tools that can simplify your job of locking down 2000 (and later) boxes.

Let's say that you've decided that you want to ensure that the Power Users groups on your workstations should be empty—you don't want anyone in those groups. You also are awfully tired of stomping out Code Red on all of those computers that installed IIS by default, so you're going around and disabling Web Publishing Service on all servers that don't need it.

But, man, that's a lot of work. So you adopt Plan B: The Security Requirements Document. In this document, you outline exactly what must be done for any workstations or servers approved here at Acme Corporation. You distribute the document. And no one has time to read it. Nor is there any easy way to check up on systems to see if they meet the requirements. Or so it seems.

Wouldn't it be great to just push a button and make those changes on every system? You can, with a few tools: `secedit.exe`, an MMC snap-in named Security Configuration and Analysis, and Security Templates.

WHAT TEMPLATES CAN DO

Basically, a security template is an ASCII file that you feed into a program named `SECEDIT.EXE`. That template is a set of instructions—basically a script—that tells secedit to make various kinds of changes in your system.

Templates don't let you modify anything that you couldn't modify otherwise; they just provide a nice, scripted, reproducible way to make modifications and then easily audit systems to ensure that they meet the template's requirements. You could make any of these changes by hand with the GUI, but it'd be time-consuming. With templates, you can change the following:

NTFS permissions If you want the directory `C:\STUFF` to have NTFS permissions of System/ Full Control, Administrators/Full Control, and to deny access to everyone else, then a template can make that happen. And as you can apply templates not only to one machine but to many (provided you're using group policies), you could enforce that set of NTFS permissions on the whole domain.

Local group membership Perhaps you have a policy that workstations are set up so that the only accounts in the local Administrators group should be the local Administrator account and the Domain Admins group from the domain. But now and then, some support person "temporarily" elevates a user account to the Administrators group, with the innocent intention of undoing the action "as soon as the need is over." And, as that support person is as busy as all support folks are, that undoing never gets done. By applying a security template that says that "only Administrator and Domain Admins can be in the local Administrators," reapplying the template kicks everybody out who's not supposed to be there.

WARNING *Templates just automate the process of setting some security information, just as if you'd sat down and done it from the GUI. There's no magic "guardian angel" that constantly monitors a system to ensure that your desired template settings are always enforced. The only way to ensure that your settings remain in force is either to reapply the template on some regular basis or create a group policy to apply the template, as group policies reapply themselves to a system roughly every 90 minutes.*

Access to turn on and off IIS, and control who can turn them on and off Want to shut off IIS on all machines but a few? That can be a pain, as Windows 2000 installs IIS on every server by default. With a security template, you can turn off or even disable services. Templates also let you control who has the permissions to *change* that—you can restrict who can turn a service on or off, or you can grant that power to some user that you want to be able to do that, but that you don't want to make into an administrator.

Registry key permissions The Registry contains a lot of information that users can read, but can't change. For example, you may have noticed that there are a number of Desktop applications that worked fine under NT 4 and that allowed someone with just user privileges to run them, but those same applications won't let a user run them under Windows 2000 Professional—only an administrator can run them. What's the difference? There are a few keys in the Registry that users could both read and write under NT 4, but that they can only read under Windows 2000. Thus, if you have one of those applications—AutoCAD is one example—and you want users to be able to run those apps on their Windows 2000 Desktops, then you can either just make all of your users local administrators (which may not sound like a great idea) or just loosen up the permissions on the Registry keys to dial them back to their NT 4 settings. You could do that painstakingly from REGEDT32.EXE, but it's so much easier to just apply a template to accomplish the same thing.

Local security policy settings   Every machine has dozens of local security settings, things like "should I show the name of the last person who logged in?," "how often should passwords on locally stored accounts be changed?," and "who should be allowed to change the time on this system," to name a few. Under NT 4, you set these things through the local version of User Manager, lusrmgr.exe. In Windows 2000, as you've seen, you use the Local Security Policy snap-in, or secpol.msc. It helps you build templates.

Working with Templates

It's easiest to show you how to work with templates with an example, so let's build a template to do three things:

◆ We'll ensure that no one is in the local Power Users group.

◆ We'll set NTFS permissions so that a directory C:\SECRET will only be accessible to the local Administrators group.

◆ Finally, we'll shut down Internet Information Service, that pesky Web server that seems to install itself on every operating system that Microsoft makes.

First, we'll need some tools. As with most W2K tools, they fit into the MMC. We'll give it two snap-ins: Security Templates and Security Configuration And Analysis. Set it up like so:

1. Click Start, then Run, and type **mmc /a** in the Open field, then press Enter to bring up the empty MMC.

2. In the empty MMC, click Console, then Add/Remove Snap-in. You'll see the Add/Remove Snap-In dialog box.

3. In the Add/Remove Snap-In dialog box, click the Add button. That raises the Add dialog box.

4. In the Add dialog box, click Security Configuration and Analysis and then the Add button. Then click the Security Templates object and Add.

5. Click Close and then OK.

You'll see a screen like Figure 9.36.

FIGURE 9.36

MMC with Security
Templates and Secu-
rity Configuration
and Analysis snap-ins

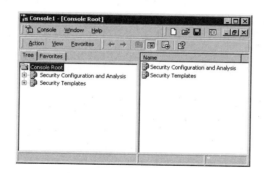

Click any of the folders under Security Templates, and you'll see, in the right pane, folders corresponding to everything that you can control with security templates—Account Policies (password, lockout, and Kerberos policies), Local Policies (audit settings, user rights, and security settings), event log settings, Restricted Groups (control of what goes into and stays out of various local groups), System Services (turns services on and off and controls who has the rights to change any of that), Registry security (permissions to change or view any given Registry key and sets which keys will have changes audited), and File System (control NTFS permissions on folders and files). That looks like Figure 9.37.

FIGURE 9.37

Folders showing
what a template can
control

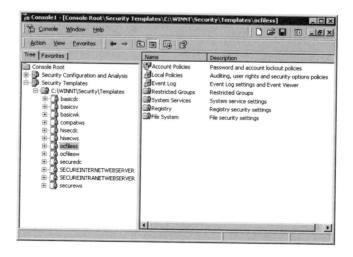

Notice that there are a number of pre-built templates. My system includes a bunch that you probably don't have, but you do have at least nine of them. BASICDC, BASICWS, and BASICSV restore a domain controller, workstation, or member server to their out-of-the-box security settings—very useful when you've been experimenting and want to undo the day's exploration! COMPATDC, COMPATWS, and COMPATSV set a domain controller, workstation or server to NT 4–level security settings. Yes, NT 4 was less secure than Windows 2000 out of the box. Finally HISECDC, HISECWS, and HISECSV set security settings higher than you'd find in the standard configuration.

But we're interested in building a new template from scratch. You do that by right-clicking the template path—it's `E:\WINNT\Security\Templates` on my system, but it'd be different on yours—and choosing New Template, and then picking a name. It'll appear as a folder in the left pane, next to the pre-built templates. I've named mine Simple. First, let's clean out the Power Users group:

1. Open Simple.

2. Inside Simple, you'll see a folder named Restricted Groups. Click it so that it appears in the left pane.

3. Right-click Restricted Groups and choose Add Group. Note that if you are working on a domain controller, then you won't, of course, have a Power Users group.

By default, including a group in a security template tells the template to remove everyone from the group, so we're done. If you wanted to use the security template to put someone in the group, then just right-click the group and choose Security, which lets you specify users—or, if appropriate, groups—to a group.

Next, let's set up the security template so that any system with a folder named `C:\SECRET` will only be accessible to the local administrators.

1. Back in the left pane, right-click File System and choose Add File.

2. In the dialog box that appears, you can either browse to a particular directory or simply type the directory name in. Yes, the menu item was Add File, but you can choose directories as well. Type `C:\SECRET`.

3. You'll then see the standard Windows 2000 NTFS permissions dialog. Delete the Everyone/Full Control information and add Administrators/Full Control.

4. The program will ask if you want these permissions to apply only to this folder or to all child folders. Set it as you like.

5. Click OK.

Finally, let's shut down IIS.

1. Click System Services.

2. In the right pane, right-click World Wide Web Publishing Services and choose Security.

3. Check the Define This Policy Setting in This Template check box, and click the Disabled radio button.

4. Click OK.

Now save the template—right-click Simple or whatever you called the template and choose Save. You now have a file named `simple.inf` in your `\WINNT\Security\Templates` folder.

CREATE A SECURITY DATABASE

Now, you'd think that all you need do to apply this template would be to just, well, apply it. But you can't. Instead, you have to essentially compile it from its simple ASCII form to a binary form called a "database." You do that from the other snap-in, Security Configuration and Analysis.

1. Right-click Security Configuration and Analysis and choose Open Database to open the Open Database dialog box, which asks what database you want to load.

2. Within the Open Database dialog box, you want to create a new database, but there's no option for that; instead, just type the name of the new database. In my example, I type **Simple** and press Enter. Typing in a name of a new database causes the snap-in to realize that you want to *create* a new database, so it then asks which template to build it out of. (Yup, it's non-intuitive.) By default, a dialog shows you the files with `.INF` extension in the `WINNT\Security\Templates` folder.

3. If you're following my example, choose `simple.inf`. Before you click, though, notice the Clear This Database before Importing check box. That's useful. Otherwise, when you're experimenting with a template, the snap-in makes your changes cumulative (which might well be your intention, but it's not usually mine) rather than wiping the slate clean and starting from scratch.

4. Choose the template and click Open. Nothing obvious has happened, but the snap-in has now "compiled" (which is my word, not Microsoft's, but it seems a good shorthand for the process of converting your ASCII template into a binary security database) the template into a security template named `security.sdb` in `My Documents\Security\Database`.

Next, right-click Security Configuration and Analysis and you'll see two options: Analyze Computer Now and Configure Computer Now. Analyze doesn't change the computer. Instead, it compares the computer's state to the one that you want to create with the template. It then shows you—and saves a log file that explains—how your system varies from what the template instructs.

But who wants to just find out how a system varies from our (administrative) desires? It'd be far more interesting to just tell the system, "Do this." And you can. Instead of choosing Analyze Computer Now, pick Configure Computer Now, and it'll modify the permissions to fall into line with the template.

That's all very nice, you may be thinking, but how do I apply it to dozens of computers? Do I have to visit each one? No; you can use a command-line tool for that. A command-line program called `SECEDIT.EXE` will both convert templates into databases and apply databases. Probably the most useful is this one, which reads a template, applies it, and creates a database in the process:

```
secedit/configure/cfg templatefilename/db databasefilename/overwrite/loglogfilename
```

You could, then, include the `secedit` command in a logon batch file, and reapply it with every logon. Or you could enable the telnet server on the Windows 2000 machines and just apply the template whenever you like.

And by the way, there's another way to create a template, although you can't build a complete template—Restricted Groups and other functions of this snap-in aren't included here—by opening Local Security Policies and right-clicking Security Settings. Then choose Reload and Export Policy to create a template.

USING DOMAIN-BASED GROUP POLICIES TO APPLY TEMPLATES

`Secedit` is nice, but involves a lot of messy editing of logon batch files. Also, it only gets applied at logon time. How do you enforce security settings more often? With group policies.

Domain-based group policies have a few benefits. First of all, it's easy to control whom they apply to, much easier than having to figure out which batch files go where. Second, they reapply themselves not only at logon time, but also throughout the day—the workstation seeks them out every 60 to 120 minutes. So, if domain-based group policies sound neat, then read on—we're just about to get started with them!

Group Policy Concepts

Let's start with some important concepts, terms, and rules you need to know to master Group Policy. In the process of explaining the functionality of Group Policy, I will mention several settings without actually showing you how to turn them on in the Group Policy snap-in. Just focus on the concepts for now. Later on in this section, we'll take a full tour of the Group Policy console, and I'll point out the all settings (such as No Override and Block Inheritance) that are discussed in this section.

Administrators configure and deploy Group Policy by building *group policy objects (GPOs)*. GPOs are containers for groups of settings (*policies*) that can be applied to users and machines throughout a network. Policy objects are created using the Group Policy snap-in, usually invoked with the Group Policy tab in `DSA.MSC` or `DSSITE.MSC`. The same GPO could specify a set of applications to be installed on all users' Desktops, implement a fascist policy of disk quotas and restrictions on the Explorer shell, and define domainwide password and account lockout policies. It is possible to create one all-encompassing GPO or several different GPOs, one for each type of function.

There are two major nodes in the Group Policy snap-in, User Configuration and Computer Configuration. User configuration policies apply to user-specific settings such as application configuration or folder redirection. The computer configuration policies manage machine-specific settings such as disk quotas, auditing, and Event Log management. However, there is a good bit of overlap between the two. It's not unusual to find the same policy available in both the User Configuration and Computer Configuration nodes. Be prepared for a certain amount of head scratching as you search for the policy you want to activate, and decide whether to employ the user-based policy or the computer policy. Keep in mind that you may create a policy that uses both types of settings or you may create separate User and Computer Configuration policy objects.

Contrary to their name, group policies aren't group oriented at all. Maybe they are called group policies because a bunch of different configuration management tools are *grouped* together in one snap-in (maybe "assorted policies" just didn't have the same ring to it). Regardless, you cannot apply them directly to groups or users, but only to sites, domains, and OUs (Microsoft abbreviates these collectively with the term *SDOU*). This act of assigning GPOs to a site, domain, or OU is called *linking*. GPOs can also be linked to local policy on a particular Win2K machine, as you'll see in a moment. The GPO-to-SDOU relationship can be many-to-one (many policies applied to one OU, for example) or one-to-many (one policy linked to several different OUs). Once linked to an SDOU, user policies are applied at logon time, and computer policies are applied at system start-up. Both policies also periodically refreshed, with a few important exceptions.

NOTE *Group policies aren't just Registry changes. Several policies are applied with Client Side Extension (CSE) DLLs. Examples are disk quota policy, folder redirection, and software installation. In fact, there is a CSE DLL that processes the Registry changes,* USERENV.DLL.

NOTE *When I said GPOs were stored in the AD, that wasn't exactly accurate. Group policy objects are stored in two parts, a Group Policy Container (GPC), and a policy folder structure in the* SYSVOL. *The container part is stored in the Active Directory and contains property information, version info, status, and a list of components. The folder structure path is* WINNT\SYSVOL\sysvol\Domainname\Policies\GUID\ *where* GUID *is a Global Unique Identifier for the GPO. This folder contains administrative templates (ADM files), security settings, info on available applications, and script filenames with command lines.*

NOTE *Group policy objects are rooted in the Active Directory of a domain. You can't copy them to other domains, but you can link them across domain boundaries (although it's not recommended).*

POLICIES ARE "ALL OR NOTHING"

Each GPO contains many possible settings for many functions; usually you'll configure only a few of them. The others will be left "inactive," sort of like putting REM in front of a command in a script or using a semicolon at the beginning of a line in an INF file. Win2K still has to read the whole policy, but it only acts on the options you've enabled. However, once you've configured a set of policies and told AD that "this GPO is linked to the win2ktest.com domain," for example, the individual settings or types of settings cannot be selectively applied. All User Configuration settings will be applied to all users on Win2K systems in the linked domain. All Computer Configuration settings will be applied to all Win2K machines in the domain. Remember that neither will be applied to NT 4 or 95/98 clients.

Now, let's say you've created a GPO that deploys a set of standard Desktop applications like Word, Excel, and Outlook, and you threw in a bunch of shell restrictions to prevent users from changing their configurations. If you don't want your IT support group users to be subject to those ridiculously stringent shell restrictions (although those users may need them most of all!), you can do a couple of things. You can create a separate GPO for those policies and link it to a lower-level container, such as an OU that contains all the regular users. But that OU will be the only one that gets the Office applications. You can alternately set permissions on the GPO that prevent the policy from being applied to the IT support group (this is called filtering). However, if you use filtering to solve this problem, none of the settings in the GPO will apply to the IT support group at all.

Group policy application is all or nothing, so sometimes you really need separate policies for separate functions. The best way to approach this might be to create a GPO for standard software deployment, and a GPO for shell restrictions. Both could be applied at the domain level, but shell restrictions can be filtered for the IT support group. The point is, it's not possible to create one monolithic policy and then specify who gets what settings, and you wouldn't want to do that anyway. At least, you wouldn't want to troubleshoot it.

POLICIES ARE INHERITED AND CUMULATIVE

Group Policy settings are cumulative and inherited from parent Active Directory containers. For example, win2ktest.com domain has several different GPOs. There is a domain-level policy that sets password restrictions, account lockout, and standard security settings. Each OU also has a policy to deploy and maintain standard Desktop applications as well as folder redirection settings and Desktop restrictions. Users and computers who are in both the domain and the OU receive settings both from the domain-level policy and from the OU-level policy. So some blanket policies can be applied to the entire domain, while others can be hashed out according to OUs.

REFRESH INTERVALS FOR GROUP POLICY

Policies are reapplied every 90 minutes, with a 30-minute "randomization" to keep the domain controller from getting hit by dozens or even hundreds of computers at once. Policies on DCs are refreshed every 5 minutes. There is, however, a policy to configure all of this, as you'll see in the section coming up, "Group Policy Policies." (So, if I set a policy for the refresh interval on Blanket Vanilla Policy Policy, would that be referred to as a Blanket Vanilla Policy Policy policy?) Exceptions to the refresh interval include folder redirection and software installation. These are only applied at logon or system start-up time; otherwise, you might end up uninstalling an application while someone is trying to use it. Or a user might be working in a folder that is being redirected to a new network location. That would be bad.

Local Policies and Group Policy Objects

When you use Active Directory Users and Computers or Active Directory Sites and Services to create and link group policies, you are working with group policy *objects* to specify a collection of settings to be applied at user logon or machine boot time. The information in the GPO says things like "change this, change that, install this, disable that." But administrators also need to be able to view the actual settings for these policies sometimes.

In NT 4, it was possible to use the System Policy Editor to view and edit those Registry entries for the local machine (rather than creating or editing a policy, you chose to open the Registry). As such, the System Policy Editor served as a more user-friendly Registry editing tool than either REGEDIT.EXE or REGEDT32.EXE. Similarly, the Group Policy snap-in provides the ability to view local policy settings on a machine.

When you open the Group Policy tool provided with Win2K (GPEDIT.MSC), it automatically focuses on the local machine, as shown in Figure 9.38. Administrators can use the tool as they would use the Local Security Policy tool to configure account settings (such as minimum password length and number of bad logon attempts before locking the account) and to set up auditing. With the exceptions of software installation and folder redirection, all of the settings from Group Policy are also available for local policy configuration.

FIGURE 9.38

Group Policy snap-in

NOTE *The local Group Policy folder structure is equivalent to that of other GPOs and is found in* \winnt\system32\ GroupPolicy.

To focus on another computer's local policy, you must have Administrator rights on that machine. You can select a computer while adding the Group Policy snap-in to a custom management console, as shown in Figure 9.39. If you know the name of the computer, just fill it in or choose the Browse button. The snap-in can focus on a local machine or on a group policy object; the Browse button allows you to locate and find group policy objects linked to sites, domains, OUs, or computers (Figure 9.40). Additionally, if you select the Allow the Focus to Be Changed option when opening the snap-in from the command line, it's possible to select the policy object as an argument when you start the console. GPEDIT.MSC, the Group Policy console that ships with Win2K, has this option turned on.

FIGURE 9.39

Adding the Group Policy snap-in

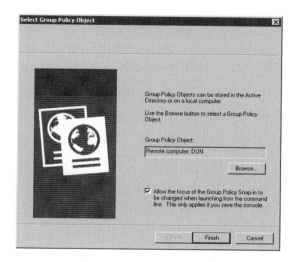

FIGURE 9.40

Selecting a group policy object (GPO)

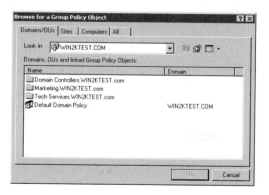

The syntax to open GPEDIT.MSC and look at the local policy on a remote machine is as follows:

GPEDIT.MSC /gpcomputer: *machinename*

So you could type, for example:

GPEDIT.MSC /gpcomputer: dun
Or you could type:

GPEDIT.MSC /gpcomputer: dun.win2ktest.com

Be sure to include a space between **/gpcomputer:** and the machine name, though.

There is one important limitation when using GPEDIT.MSC to modify policy on a remote machine. The security settings extension to the Group Policy snap-in will not work when the tool is focused on a remote machine. That's worth saying again. You cannot open GPEDIT.MSC with the switch **/gpcomputer:** *computername* and modify the security settings on a remote machine. Apparently, Microsoft considers it a security vulnerability to allow it. Another example of software telling us what's best for us?

NOTE   *If you are using group policies, local policy is always processed before site, domain, or OU group policies.*

Creating Group Policies

Now that you understand the major concepts involved in group policies and know the difference between local policies and group policy objects, let's go through the steps of creating and editing a group policy object. In this section, I'll show you all the settings we discussed in the preceding "theory" section.

To open the Group Policy snap-in in DSA.MSC, right-click your domain name at the root of the console and choose Properties from the context menu. Move to the Group Policy tab, shown in Figure 9.41, to see what GPOs have been linked at the domain level. If you haven't already created other policies, you'll see only the default domain policy listed. Notice the Block Policy Inheritance check box at the bottom left of the Group Policy tab. It prevents any group policy settings at a higher level from trickling down to this one. Remember the order in which policies are applied: first is the site level, then the domain level, then policies for OUs.

NOTE   *To view the GPOs that are linked to a container (site, domain, or OU), right-click the object in the console (DSA.MSC for domains and Ous and DSSITE.MSC for sites) and choose Properties from the context menu. Then navigate to the Group Policy tab. From that point, the interface to configure policies is the same regardless of the container it's linked with.*

To turn on No Override, highlight the policy and choose Options, then select the No Override check box (see Figure 9.42). When this setting is on, other policies applied down the line are prevented from defeating the settings of this policy, even with Block Inheritance enabled. Note that Block Policy Inheritance is turned on at the link level (site, domain, or OU), whereas No Override is enabled per policy. Check the Disabled box to turn off the policy so that it won't be processed or applied at this level. Disabling the policy doesn't disable the object itself. For example, the same policy, disabled at the domain level, could theoretically be applied at the site or OU level. If either option (No Override or Disabled) is turned on, there will be a check in the corresponding column of the Group Policy tab. You can activate both options using the context menu for the policy. Just right-click a selected policy to view the context menu.

FIGURE 9.41

A domain's Group Policy properties

FIGURE 9.42

Group Policy options

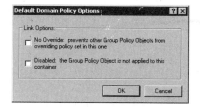

Back in the win2ktest.com properties sheet, choose New to create a new GPO. Win2K will create a policy called New Group Policy Object and then allow you to rename it. If you miss that opportunity and end up with a policy called New Group Policy Object, just highlight the policy, right-click, and choose Rename from the context menu.

Choose Properties to view and modify your new group policy object's properties. The General tab shown in Figure 9.43 shows creation and revision information as well as options to disable the User or Computer Configuration portion of the policy. Depending on how you subdivide your domain into OUs, you may choose to create some policies with only computer settings and others with only user-specific settings. In that case, if the unused portion of the GPO is disabled altogether, policy application and updates are faster. If, however, your cold medicine has caused a momentary lapse of reason and there are important settings in the node you disable, those settings will be removed from the client machine. So Win2K will ask you to confirm that move, just to be sure.

FIGURE 9.43

Group Policy General properties

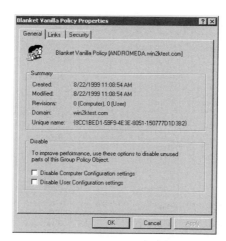

The Links tab gives you the opportunity to search for sites, domains, or OUs that use this GPO, if there are any. Because searching for other links takes a few moments and some resources, no linked containers will be displayed until you perform the search. Click the Find Now button to start the search.

The Security tab in the properties sheet reveals the GPO's default permissions (see Figure 9.44). Highlight a name at the top to view the permissions in the lower section. Notice that Domain Admins and Enterprise Admins have Read and Write permissions as well as Delete and Create All Child Objects, whereas the Authenticated Users group only has Read and Apply Group Policy. Read and Write are required to change a policy; Read and Apply are required to be a recipient of the policy.

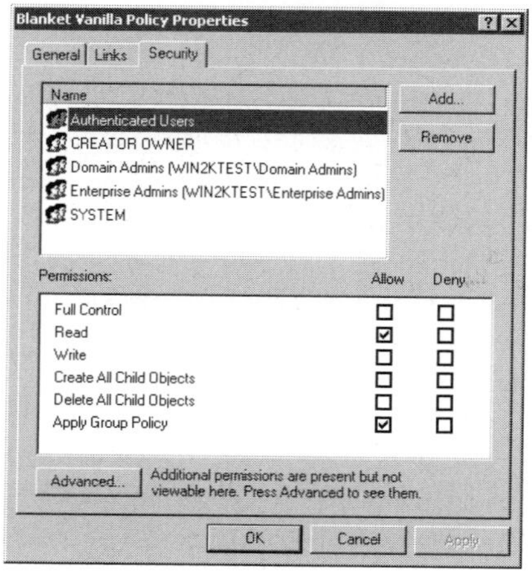

FIGURE 9.44

Group Policy permissions list

NOTE *Don't think that Domain Admins and Enterprise Admins are not subject to a group policy's settings just because they are not granted Apply Group Policy permission by default. Users will have all the permissions of all their groups; therefore, as members of Authenticated Users, the members of Domain Admins and Enterprise Admins will also be granted Apply Group Policy permissions.*

Back in the Group Policy tab of our win2ktest.com domain properties page, if you highlight the new GPO that you have just created and choose the Up or Down button, you can move the policy up or down in the window. This is an important tidbit to know: When multiple GPOs are linked to one container, as is the case in Figure 9.45, they will be applied from the bottom up, so the one at the top is applied last. Therefore, GPOs higher in the list have a higher priority. If there are conflicting settings, the higher policy wins.

FIGURE 9.45

Increasing the priority of group policy objects

To delete a GPO, or to just remove it from the list, highlight the policy and choose Delete. Win2K will present you with the option to delete it altogether (Figure 9.46) or to remove it from the list while preserving the policy to be linked to another container at another time.

FIGURE 9.46

Removing a group policy object

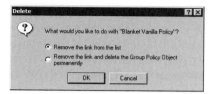

Choose the Add button on the Group Policy tab to link an existing group policy object to the desired container. As you see in Figure 9.47, you can look for GPOs that are linked to other domains/OUs or to other sites, or you can just ask for a list of all GPOs. It took me a minute to grasp this simple operation: Click the container name (the OU for Marketing.win2ktest.com, for example) to view the policies linked to it. Then highlight the policy and choose OK to add it to the list back on the Group Policy tab.

FIGURE 9.47

Adding a group policy link

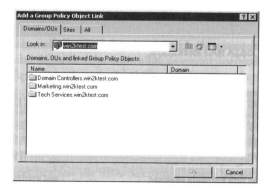

Now let's view and modify our new policy. Back in the Group Policy tab, highlight the policy and choose Edit. This will open the Group Policy snap-in in a separate window, and you'll see the policy object name at the root of the namespace, in this case Blanket Vanilla Policy [DUN.win2ktest.com] Policy. This indicates to us what policy is being viewed and edited. Figure 9.48 shows the policy expanded in the console tree to show the major nodes of the group policy object.

FIGURE 9.48

Group Policy namespace

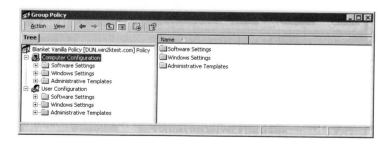

There are two major types of settings, as I mentioned earlier. Computer Configuration settings are applied to machines at start-up and at designated refresh intervals. User Configuration settings are applied to the users' working environments at logon and at designated refresh intervals.

We'll explore the various policies according to subject matter later, but prepare yourself for the fact that policies are not all configured in a uniform way as far as the interface is concerned. You'll need a few examples to see what I mean:

◆ To specify software packages under `Software Settings\Software Installation`, open the folder and choose New/Package from the Action menu. An Open dialog box asks for the location of the package. Once it's been located and selected, you configure the package properties.

◆ To set the interval that users can wait before changing passwords, go to `Computer Configura-tion\Windows Settings\Security Settings\Account Policies\Password Policy`. Double-click Maximum Password Age in the details pane on the right, enable the setting by clicking the box that says Define This Policy Setting, and supply a time interval value.

◆ To set a policy that restricts group memberships, go to `Restricted Groups` under `Security Settings` in `Computer Configuration\Windows Settings` and choose Add Group from the Action menu. A dialog box asks you to enter a group or browse for it. Once the group is added to the list in the details pane on the right, double-click the group name to open a dialog box and supply the names of the users that must be or are allowed to be in the group. You can also define group memberships for the group itself.

◆ To set up folder redirection, go to `User Configuration\Windows Settings\ Folder Redi-rection` and choose a folder (for example, `Start Menu`). The details pane on the right will be blank. Right-click white space in the details pane (or pull down the Action menu) and choose Properties. The properties page appears and you can now specify a location for the Start menu and configure redirection settings.

The point of this wild ride through the Group Policy snap-in interface is not to disorient you, but rather to illustrate the fact that the Group Policy snap-in contains several nodes to accomplish various tasks, and procedures to specify settings will vary with the node and the task. There is no one way to configure a setting, although many do follow the pattern of the second example. So, when in doubt, right-click or look at the Action menu. It's a strategy to live by.

Once you've configured your Group Policy settings, simply close the Group Policy window. There is no Save or Save Changes option. Changes are written to the GPO when you choose OK or Apply on a particular setting, although the user or computer will not actually see the change until the policy is refreshed.

Group Policy Troubleshooting: GP Application Order

Now that you've got a GPO or two running, you'll soon find the troublesome part of group policies: figuring out what they're doing. Imagine, for example, that a user calls up and says, "Why is my background purple?" You then realize that there are a *lot* of places that your system gets policies from, and they might disagree on things like, for example, background color. So which one *won*?

POLICIES EXECUTE FROM THE BOTTOM UP, IN THE GUI

Let's start out by just considering a simple situation: just policies on a domain. Suppose I look at my domain in Active Directory Users and Computers. I right-click the domain, then choose Properties and click the Group Policies tab to see something like Figure 9.49.

In this (admittedly fanciful) situation, the domain has five group policies, four of which attempt to set a workstation's background color to gray, green, red, or blue. (The other is the Default Domain Policy, which has nothing to say on the issue.) Who wins? Gray, red, green, or blue? The answer lies in two basic conflict resolution rules for group policies:

Rule 1   Listen to the last policy that you heard from.

Rule 2   Execute policies from the bottom up, as they appear in the GUI.

FIGURE 9.49

Multiple policies in a domain

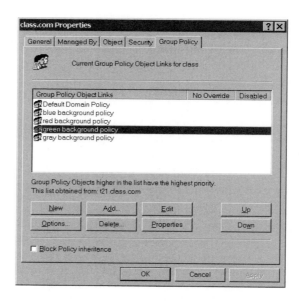

Reading from the bottom of the dialog box up, you see that the system will first see the policy that sets the background gray, then the one that sets it green, then the one that sets it red, and finally the one that sets it blue. As blue is the last one heard from, it wins, and the effects of the previous three are obviated.

But what if you *want* the red background policy to win? Notice the Up and Down buttons in the figure? You can shuffle them around to your heart's content.

GROUP POLICY APPLICATION ORDER

But that example only considered domain policies. But you can apply policies to different levels:

◆ Sites can have policies, and no matter what domain's machines and users are in that site, those policies apply. (That's why you've got to be an Enterprise Administrator to create site policies.)

◆ OUs can have policies. And OUs can contain OUs, and OUs can contain OUs that contain OUs, and so on.

◆ There are also *local* policies, don't forget.

So, again, who wins? Policies are applied in the following order: local policy, sites, domains, organizational units, then OUs inside of OUs. If the domain policy says, "You must be logged in before you can shut down the machine," and the OU policy says, "Allow shutdown before logon," the OU policy takes precedence because it is applied last. If one policy says, "Lock it down," and the next one says, "Not configured," the setting remains locked down. If one policy says, "Not configured," and the next one says, "Lock it down," then it's locked down in this case, as well. If one policy says, "Leave it on," and the next one says, "Turn it off," it's turned off. If one policy says, "Turn it off," and another, closer one says, "Turn it on," then a third one says, "Turn it off," guess what? It ends up turned off. However, for the preservation of your sanity, it is desirable to avoid these little disagreements between policies.

ACL-ING POLICIES: FILTERING GROUP POLICY

But we're not *nearly* finished here. It *could* be that while it looks as if many policies apply to your system, in fact, only a small number do. The reason: group policies have ACLs.

Right-click the container linked to any given GPO (in our example, the domain) and choose Properties. Select the Group Policy tab and highlight the policy you wish to filter. Choose the Properties button and go to the Security tab (shown again in Figure 9.50). Now you see the access control list (ACL) for the policy object.

FIGURE 9.50

Group Policy Security settings

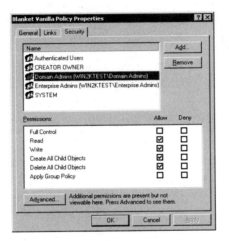

As I pointed out before, Domain Admins and Enterprise Admins have Read and Modify permissions, and Authenticated Users have Read and Apply Group Policy. It may happen that you create a policy to restrict Desktops and you don't wish to apply it to a certain group of people. The group Authenticated Users includes everyone but guests, so by default, the policy will apply to everyone but guests; that means even Domain Admins and Enterprise Admins will receive the policy settings. To prevent Domain Admins and Enterprise Admins from receiving this policy, you must check the box in the Deny column next to Apply Group Policy (Figure 9.51). A member of both groups will only need the Deny setting for one of the two groups, but you'll need to check the Deny box for both groups if the members of Domain Admins and Enterprise Admins are not the same people. To "excuse" others from receiving the policy, put them all in a security group and add that group to the list. It is not enough to "not check" the granted box for Read and Apply Group Policy; the users in your special security group are also members of Authenticated Users, so you actually need to choose the Deny option for them as well. Deny takes precedence over Allow.

FIGURE 9.51

Denying the Apply Group Policy permission

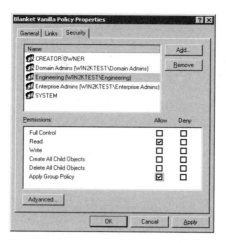

If you wish to filter policy for a certain Win2K machine (or group of machines), follow the same strategy. Add the computer accounts to a security group, add that group to the ACL for the policy object, then deny the group Read and Apply Group Policy permissions.

There is an alternative to adding a security group to the ACL and denying them Read and Apply permissions. You could also remove Authenticated Users from the ACL altogether, preventing anyone from receiving the group policy. Then you would simply add entries to the ACL for any security groups you *do* want to receive the policy. Be sure, though, to allow them *both* Read and Apply Group Policy. Figure 9.52 shows the permissions list for Blanket Vanilla Policy in which Authenticated Users has been removed and the Engineering group has been added. This is a useful strategy if you don't want the policy to apply to all users and computers in the linked container by default.

FIGURE 9.52

Group Policy ACL without Authenticated Users

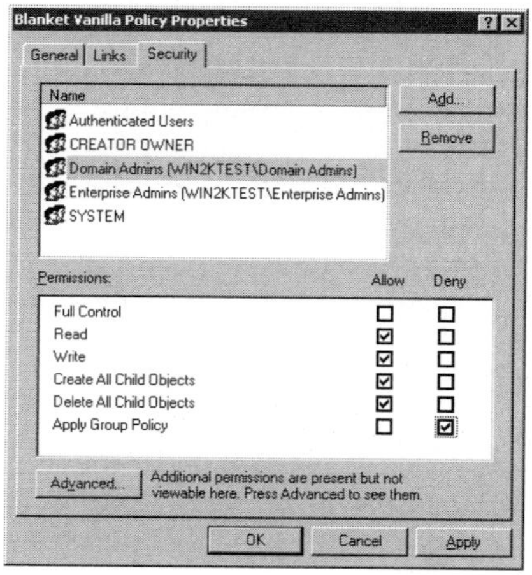

By the way, there is nothing to prevent you from adding individual users to the permissions list for a group policy object. Let me stress, then, that policy filtering is incredibly powerful—you might say that it's the tool that lets you oppress individuals or groups. In the real world, however, adding ACLs to a policy can be a nightmare for the poor fool trying to figure out two years later why a policy is attached to a domain but *isn't bloody applying to most of the people in the domain!*

No Override and Block Inheritance

Just as filtering can be used to counter the blanket application of policies, Block Inheritance is a special setting on a policy to prevent higher-level policies from trickling down. When Block Inheritance is turned on, the settings of higher policies will not be applied to lower containers at all. For example, if you create a GPO for a specific OU, say Accounting, and set up all the necessary settings for the Accounting OU, and then you want to prevent the win2ktest domain GPOs from affecting the Accounting OU, you'd turn on Block Inheritance. The only policies applied will be the Accounting OU policies.

There is also a counter to the Block Inheritance counter. (Isn't this becoming like a *Batman* episode? "Robin, they've blocked our transmission. It's time for the block-anti-block Bat-transmitter!") When No Override is turned on for a policy, settings in subsequent policies are prevented from reversing the ones in the No Override–enabled policy. For example, if domain admins have a set of highly disputed settings turned on at the domain level and those renegade Accounting admins set up their own OU with its own policies and turn on Block Inheritance, the Accounting OU effectively escapes the disputed settings but only until the domain admins get wise and turn on No Override. Then the domain admins win, and the Accounting OU people have to live with the same restrictions as everyone else. No Override beats Block Inheritance (just like paper covers rock).

Like all secret weapons, No Override and Block Inheritance are best used sparingly. Otherwise, in a troubleshooting situation it becomes rather complicated to determine what policies are applied where. This could be detrimental to the mental health of a network administrator.

Whew! To summarize the factors that can decide which group policy object wins:

◆ Examine policies in this order: local policies, then site policies, then domain policies, OU policies, and any OUs inside the OUs, and so on.

◆ Within any unit—site, domain, or OU—examine the policies as they appear in the GUI, from the bottom up.

◆ If policies conflict, only pay attention to the last one that you examined, *unless* you already saw a policy that said No Override—that means that no matter what policies come afterward, you should ignore them if they conflict with the No Override policy.

◆ Before you actually apply a policy, check its ACLs—if you don't have the Read and Apply Group Policy ACLs, then the policy doesn't apply.

Group Policy Example: Forcing Complex Passwords

Before leaving this, let's look at a conflict resolution example that will also offer an example of a useful policy. You may recall that an early NT 4.0 service pack (either 2 or 3, I forget) included a file called `passfilt.dll` which, if installed on your domain controllers, would force users to select "strong" passwords, where Microsoft's definition of "strong" ("complex" seems more appropriate to me) is that a password must fit the following criteria:

◆ Be at least six characters long

◆ Contain three of the four types of characters: uppercase letters, lowercase letters, numbers, or "special" (punctuation, etc.) characters

◆ Not contain your username

Under NT 4, you just installed `passfilt.dll` on all of your DCs. To make your Windows 2000 Active Directory domain require complex passwords, however, you use a different process.

First of all, you needn't install `passfilt.dll` and, in fact, you won't find it anywhere on the 2000 CD; its functionality is built into Windows 2000. You need only turn that functionality on, with a group policy. The short version of how to do that is to enable the Passwords Must Meet Complexity Requirements of Installed Password Filter policy. Here are some more step-by-step details:

1. Open up Active Directory Users and Computers.

2. In the left pane (the "command pane") you'll see a three-computer icon representing your directory. Right-click it and choose Properties, then click the Group Policies tab in the resulting property page.

3. This policy is a machine policy, not a user policy. (This surprised me, as it seemed as if it should be a user policy—after all, we're controlling how users set policies, no? But I guess this is a policy that affects any action on this particular machine—i.e., the domain controller.) Therefore, open up the Computer Configuration computer icon.

4. Within that, open Windows Settings and then Security Settings. There may be a bit of a pause here, but don't worry, just give it a few seconds. Then open Account Policies and finally the Password Policy folder.

5. Inside the Password Policy folder, you'll see a Passwords Must Meet Complexity Requirements of Installed Password Filter policy. Double-click it.

6. Check the Define This Policy Setting check box.

7. Click the Enable radio button.

8. Close the GP Editor.

But you're not done yet—don't expect this to take effect immediately. Domain controllers reapply policies every five minutes, but they can only apply a policy that they know about, so you've also got to wait for the policy information to replicate to other domain controllers. (Obviously, if you have only one DC, then replication isn't a problem.)

Now, I *did* all that, and then created a user account and tried to give it a short one-character password, expecting to get an error message. But I didn't; 2000 accepted the short password despite the new policy. I even opened a command line and typed **secedit /refreshpolicy machine_policy**, hoping that would push the system into seeing the policy. But it still didn't work.

Here's what I forgot. Domains automatically get a policy called Default Domain Policy. When I created my new policy, Complex Password Policy, then the Group Policies user interface placed it below the Default Domain Policy, as the UI does by default—reading top to bottom, you can see the order in which policies were created and/or linked to the domain. I hadn't realized it before, but the Default Domain Policy object *disables* strong passwords!

So there's a conflict in policies here. My Complex Password Policy said to use complex passwords, and the Default Domain Policy said not to. Who wins? Well, by default, a system pays attention to the *last* command that it heard, and the system executes policies from the one at the bottom of the list in the user interface to the top. (It's true, believe it or not.) So the system first got the command to force strong passwords, and then as it worked its way up the UI it came across the Default Domain Policy, which said to *not* force strong passwords. So no strong passwords.

The answer? I could have simply set my Complex Password Policy object to No Override. Instead, I just moved it above Default Domain Policy in the UI. Result: strong passwords.

And one more note, embarrassing as it may be: I thought originally to just try this strong password policy out on an organizational unit, but the policy didn't work. Then I remembered—duh—that account policies don't apply to OUs; you've got to make account policies on domains or they'll be ignored.

Delegating Group Policy Administration

The ability to delegate creation and configuration of group policies to Administrative personnel (or to others, for that matter) is extremely useful, especially in a large organization. In this section I'll explain how to allow persons who are not members of Domain Admins or Enterprise Admins to create and manage policies for designated sites, domains, or organizational units.

Group policy objects, by default, can be created by a member of the Administrators group for the domain or by members of the global group called Group Policy Creator Owners. However, while members of Administrators have full control of all GPOs, members of Group Policy Creator Owners can only modify policies they themselves have created, unless they have been specifically granted permission to modify a policy. So, if you put a designated group policy administrator into the security group Group Policy Creator Owners (that's almost as awkward as Active Directory Users and Computers), that person can create new policy objects and modify them.

It's one thing to create a group policy; linking that GPO to a site, domain, or OU is another matter. Administrators have this power by default, but a special permission called Manage Policy Links must be granted on the ACL of the site, domain, or OU before anyone else can create policy links to it. Also, there doesn't seem to be a way to create a group policy without linking it to something, at least initially. So if you want to use the Group Policy Creator Owners security group, you need to go ahead and set permissions on a container object to allow them to manage policy links. You'll need to use the Delegation of Control Wizard to accomplish this.

To allow members of Group Policy Creator Owners to create links to a particular OU, for example, right-click the OU in DSA.MSC. Choose the option Delegate Control from the context menu. Choose Next in the initial screen to go to the part where you add the users and groups to whom you will delegate control. Choose Add and select Group Policy Creator Owners from the list. Choose Add again, then OK to return to the Users or Groups window, as shown in Figure 9.53. The GP Creator Owners will appear in the Selected Users and Groups box. Choose Next; then select Manage Group

Policy Links from the predefined common tasks to delegate (see Figure 9.54). Choose Next and confirm your choices in the last screen by clicking the Finish button.

FIGURE 9.53

Delegation of Control Wizard's Users or Groups window

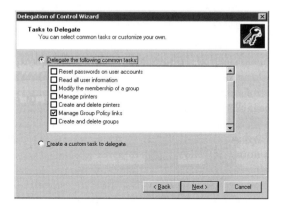

FIGURE 9.54

Delegating management of Group Policy links

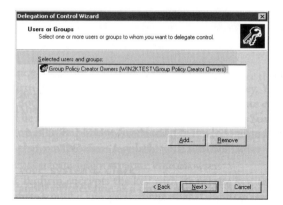

Members of Group Policy Creator Owners can now create new GPOs linked to that OU. They can also modify policies that they have created, but if there are other policies on the OU, members of Group Policy Creator Owners can't edit them by default. You'll have to grant the group Read and Write permission on the policy object's ACL.

Designating a regular user or junior admin as a member of Group Policy Creator Owners and giving them the ability to manage group policy links, even if it's just at the OU level, is a real exercise in faith and quite taxing for us control freaks (I mean letting-go-challenged people). If you want finer control when delegating group policy administration tasks, set up a custom MMC console. You may even elect to limit administration to a certain GPO by loading the Group Policy snap-in focused on that GPO. Enable only the extensions you want your delegate to use. It's further possible to configure a policy to permit the use of certain Group Policy snap-in extensions and prevent the use of others, just in case the delegate stumbles on to Author mode by accident. See the section "Group Policy Policies" later in this chapter for specifics.

TIP   *See Chapter 5 for a discussion on customizing Microsoft Management Consoles.*

That was a lot of information, so let's review the primary requirements for creating and editing GPOs:

◆   To create a GPO, you must be a member of either the Administrators group (and this includes nested groups, so membership in Domain Admins is acceptable, for example) or of Group Policy Creator Owners. If you insist on the McGyver approach, however, you at least need access to a domain controller, Read/Write permissions on SYSVOL, and Modify permission on the directory container. When creating an "OU God," then, make sure the would-be OU God is a member of the domain's GP Creator Owner group.

◆   To edit a policy, a user must (a) have full Administrator privileges, or (b) be creator owner of the GPO, or (c) have Read and Write on the ACL of the GPO.

User and Computer Configuration Settings

Now that you've learned all about creating and linking and delegating administration of Group Policy, we'll explore some of the policy settings themselves in the next few sections. Since you can use various types of policies to configure a range of settings, we won't try to cover every single setting in the pages allotted to this chapter (otherwise it could be a book all by itself!). Rather, think of this section as an overview of what group policies can accomplish to make your life easier as an administrator. To follow along, open the Group Policy snap-in for a GPO by navigating to the Group Policy tab in the container's properties pages, highlight an existing policy, and click the Edit button.

As you see in Figure 9.55, there are two main nodes to the Group Policy snap-in: User Configuration and Computer Configuration. Both nodes have the following subnodes: Software Settings, Windows Settings, and Administrative Templates. The difference between the two is this: Policies set for User Configuration will apply to the user's settings, and those set for Computer Configuration will apply to the machine configuration. For example, if Registry settings are involved, as is the case with Administrative Templates, the changes will be written to HKEY_CURRENT_USER (HKCU) for User Configuration stuff and to HKEY_LOCAL_MACHINE (HKLM) for Computer Configuration settings. Otherwise, the differences aren't so obvious and there is some overlap in the settings, just as HKCU contains some of the same entries as HKLM. You may wish to create separate policies for machines and users, to keep things straight, but be on the lookout for any conflicts. If a value set in the computer settings is also specified in the user policy settings, the User Configuration settings will take precedence by default.

FIGURE 9.55

Group Policy nodes and subnodes

For both User Configuration and Computer Configuration, the `Software Settings\ Software Installation` subgroup can be used to publish, assign, update, and even remove applications from a user's Desktop. See Chapter 12, "Software Installation," for the full story on using group policies to set up application packages.

SPECIFY SCRIPTS WITH GROUP POLICY

You can specify logon and logoff scripts, as well as scripts to run at system start-up and shutdown, using `Windows Settings` in either the User Configuration node or the Computer Configuration node. Expand `Windows Settings` to reveal `Scripts`, then select the script type (Start-up, Shutdown, Logon, or Logoff) in the details pane on the right; Figure 9.56 shows the scripts available in User Configuration. From here, double-click the script type (such as Logon) or highlight it and choose Properties from the Action menu. Add scripts to the list using the Add button (see Figure 9.57). Supply a script name and parameters when prompted. To edit the script name and parameters (not the script itself), choose Edit. If more than one script is specified, use the Up and Down buttons to indicate the order in which the scripts should run.

FIGURE 9.56

Group Policy start-up scripts

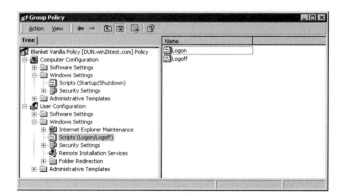

FIGURE 9.57

Adding a script to Group Policy

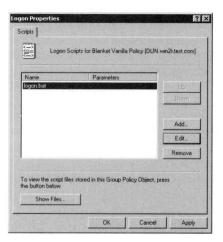

The scripts you create and assign should be copied to the following path in the SYSVOL directory: \winnt\SYSVOL\SysVol*domainname*\Policies\{GUID}\Machine\ Scripts\Startup or Shutdown (or User\Scripts\Logon or Logoff, depending on whether you are assigning scripts to the Computer Configuration or to the User Configuration node). The Global Unique Identifier (GUID) for the group policy object is a long string that looks like {FA08AF41-38AB-11D3-BD1FC9B6902FA00B}. If you wish to see the scripts stored in the GPO and possibly open them for editing, use the Show Files button at the bottom of the properties page. This will open the folder in Explorer.

As you may know, you may also specify a logon script in the properties page of the user account in DSA.MSC. Microsoft calls these *legacy logon scripts* and encourages us to assign scripts with Group Policy for Win2K clients. Of course, Windows 95/98/NT clients don't use group policies, so you'll still assign their logon scripts in the account properties. Other than that, the only real advantage to using the Group Policy scripts is that they run asynchronously in a hidden window. So if several scripts are assigned, or if the scripts are complex, the user doesn't have to wait for them to end. Legacy logon scripts run in a window on the Desktop. On the other hand, you might not want the scripts to run hidden (some scripts stop and supply information or wait for user input). In that case, there are several policy settings available to help you define the behavior of Group Policy scripts. These settings are located in the Administrative Templates node under System\Logon/Logoff for User Configuration and under System\Logon for Computer Configuration. There you'll find settings to specify whether to run a script synchronously or asynchronously and whether it should be visible or invisible. Legacy logon scripts can be run hidden, like Group Policy scripts, by using the setting shown in Figure 9.58. The Computer Configuration settings also include a maximum wait time for Group Policy scripts, which is 600 seconds by default. This changes the time-out period, which is the maximum allotted time allowed for the script to complete.

FIGURE 9.58

Policy to run legacy scripts hidden

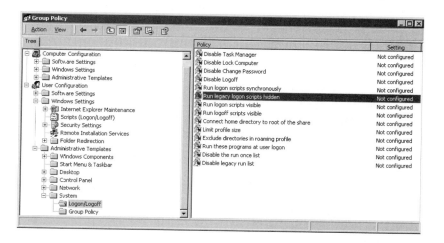

FOLDER REDIRECTION

One of the more useful things you can do with User Configuration settings in Group Policy is to arrange for a user's Application Data, Desktop, Start Menu, or My Documents folder to follow her around from computer to computer. These folders are important elements in a user's working environment. Application Data stores application-specific user information (Internet Explorer uses it, for example), and Desktop may contain important folders and shortcuts that need to be just one click away for the user. Start Menu contains program groups and shortcuts to programs; My Documents is the default place to save and retrieve files, sort of like a local home directory. With user profiles in NT 4 and now Win2K, you can preconfigure these folders' contents and assign network locations. With the System Policy Editor for 95/98 or NT, it was also possible to specify a location for these folders. But, unlike the Default User profiles behavior, redirected folders live in one designated place all the time. They are not copied to each machine the user logs in to, causing "profile build-up." Instead of using the folder in the user's local profile, she will be *redirected* to the location specified in the group policy. Group policy folder redirection replaces and enhances those functions offered previously in system policies, with additional options to manage the redirected folder behavior.

There are several good reasons to use folder redirection. For one thing, it's convenient for users who log in to different machines. Also, if you specify a network location for some or all of these folders, they can be backed up regularly and protected by the IT department. If roaming profiles are still in use, setting up folder redirection speeds up synchronization of the server profile with the local profile at logon and logoff, since the redirected folders need not be updated. Redirecting the Desktop and Start Menu folders to a centralized, shared location facilitates standardization of users' working environments and helps with remote support issues, because help desk personnel will know that all machines are configured in the same way. Best of all, you can mix and match. It's possible to specify a shared location for the Desktop and Start Menu folders while allowing each user to have his own My Documents and Application Data folders. Let's take a look.

To set a network location for the Start Menu folder in Group Policy, go to User Configuration\ Windows Settings\Folder Redirection\Start Menu, right-click the highlighted Start Menu folder, and choose Properties from the context menu. The properties page reveals that no policy is specified by default for Start Menu redirection. Choose Basic from the drop-down list to specify a single location for the Start Menu folder, to be shared by all the users; or choose Advanced to set locations based on security group membership. If you want a single location for a shared Start Menu folder, just fill in the target location with a network path or browse for it. To designate different locations, first choose a security group and then specify a network path. Figure 9.59 demonstrates redirecting the Start Menu folder for all members of Win2KTEST\Engineering to the Central share on the server Andromeda. In our example, all of Engineering will use the same Start Menu folder, but in any case, it's possible to set up individually redirected folders by appending %username% to the path. This creates a subfolder named after the user. Next, click the Settings tab to configure the redirection settings.

For the sake of completeness, the redirection settings for My Documents are shown in Figure 9.60. The redirection settings for all the other folders are the same except that My Documents has the My Pictures subfolder, so there are a couple of extra items to configure.

The options you see in Figure 9.60 show default selections for the My Documents folder. The user will have exclusive access to the folder, so uncheck this box if everyone is sharing the folder.

The contents of the corresponding folder will be copied to the new location by default. Even after the policy is removed, the folder will remain redirected unless you say to "un-redirect" it. One notable exception is the Start Menu folder. We can pretty much assume that a redirected Start Menu folder is a shared Start Menu folder (otherwise, why bother?), and making it private or copying over it would generally be a bad thing. Therefore, both the option to grant exclusive rights and the option to move the contents of a user's Start Menu folder to the new location are grayed out in the Settings tab.

FIGURE 9.59

Policy to redirect the user's Start Menu folder

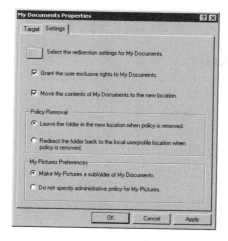

FIGURE 9.60

Policy to redirect the My Documents folder

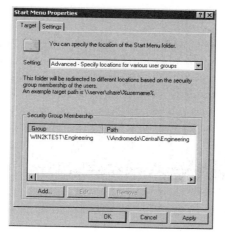

SECURITY SETTINGS

Security Settings, along with Administrative Templates, make up a large part of Group Policy. The default security settings for Win2K security are purposely open, to keep down administrative headaches and to ensure that users and applications work as intended. As security increases, users and applications have more restrictions and support time goes up. In other words, security is inversely proportionate to convenience. As you start locking down systems, something is bound to stop working. Hey, regular users can't even install applications on a Win2K system by default. When you start enforcing passwords that are 8 characters or more, contain both letters and numbers, can't use any part of a user's name, and cannot be reused until 15 other passwords have been used, things get complicated for the everyday Joe. As important as security is, Microsoft judged (wisely, I believe) that functionality had to come first. For organizations that want to increase security, there are tools and guidelines. But there is one problem with this approach. A big problem.

If you've ever "hardened" an NT server according to established military or other high-security guidelines, you know that you have to set particular permissions on particular folders, that you must change the default permissions on certain Registry keys, and change or create other Registry entries as well. All in all, it takes a few hours of work on a single server, even for an efficient admin. What if you have 50 servers and 500 Professional workstations? Some things can be scripted, but others can't. Try as they might, there is no Microsoft or third-party tool that does everything automatically for all machines.

Here's where Group Policy comes to the rescue. Assuming you are going to standardize throughout the organization somewhat, you only have to change those sticky Registry permissions and settings once, using Group Policy. You only have to set the NTFS permissions once. They can even be set up in one policy and copied to another. Whether you need a lot of security or just a little more than the default, chances are you'll want to make at least some standardized changes, and the `Security Settings` node will certainly make your life easier. The bulk of Security Settings are found under `Computer Configuration\Windows Settings\Security Settings`, although public-key policies are also found in the `User Configuration` node in the same path. The following summarizes the major categories of settings under Security Settings:

Account Policies   Specify password restrictions, lockout policies, and Kerberos policy.

Local Policies   Configure auditing and assign user rights and miscellaneous security settings.

Event Log   Centralize configuration options for the Event Log.

Restricted Groups   Enforce and control group memberships for certain groups, such as the Administrators group.

System Services   Standardize services configurations and protect against changes.

Registry   Create security templates for Registry key permissions, to control who can change what keys and to control Read access to parts of the Registry.

File System   Create security templates for permissions on files and folders to ensure that files and directories have and keep the permissions you want them to have.

Public Key Policies   Manage settings for organizations using a public key infrastructure.

IMPORTING SECURITY TEMPLATES

A full discussion of all these security settings is certainly beyond the scope of this chapter, but you should be aware that security settings templates are available and installed with Win2K Server to ease the burden of wading through and researching all the settings. It's also safer to configure settings offline and then apply them, than it is to play with a live working group policy.

As you read in the earlier section on *local* group policies, the security settings templates take the form of INF files and are found in `\WINNT\Security\templates`. There are several to choose from, from basic workstations or servers to secure, highly secure, and dedicated DC configurations. When applied directly or via Group Policy, the templates incrementally modify the default settings. You can view and modify the templates using the Security Templates snap-in, shown in Figure 9.61. As you see in the figure, these settings are the same as those found in Group Policy Security Settings, with the exception of Public Key Policies and IP Security Policies, which cannot be configured with templates. The values for the settings in each template are preconfigured to meet the necessary level of security. These templates, or new ones you create, can then be applied directly to a Win2K machine's local policy by using a command-line program called SECEDIT.EXE or they can be imported into Group Policy.

FIGURE 9.61

Security Templates snap-in

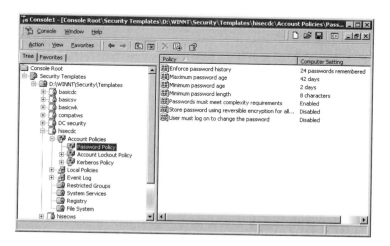

Every fresh installation of Win2K gets a standard set of local computer policies with default security settings. For this reason it's a good idea to export your existing settings to a file by using the Group Policy snap-in focused on the local machine (GPEDIT.MSC will open that way by default) before making any drastic changes. Security settings for upgraded systems do not have their local policy changed in case the configuration has been customized. For upgraded Win2K servers, Microsoft suggests we first apply the Basic configuration template and then apply an appropriate security settings template with all the settings specified explicitly.

Remember that I promised you when I discussed templates how to apply them with domain-based group policies? This is how: To import a security template into Group Policy, go to Computer Configuration\Windows Settings\Security Settings and right-click Security Settings. Choose Import Policy from the context menu, then select your policy from the list of templates. Group Policy automatically looks for the template in \WINNT\Security\templates, but you can tell it to look someplace else if necessary. The INF file will be imported to modify the settings in the selected group policy object.

In the spirit of this template idea, the various subcomponents of Security Settings (like Account Policies or Local Policies) also support a copy-and-paste function, which appears in the context and Action menus when the subcomponent is selected. An admin person can actually copy that part of the template information to the Clipboard and apply it to another policy.

ADMINISTRATIVE TEMPLATES

`Administrative Templates` is the part of Group Policy that is most like System Policies in NT. The settings available here are based on template files (ADM files, like those used in NT and Windows 95/98 System Policies). These settings specify Registry entry changes to adjust various aspects of a user's environment or a machine configuration, including those famous options to restrict a user's Desktop to the point where they can only run a limited set of programs and nothing else.

The user changes specified in `Administrative Templates` are written to `HKEY_CURRENT_USER\Software\Policies`, and computer changes are written to `HKEY_LOCAL_MACHINE\Software\Policies`. The two ADM files used by Win2K are `system.adm` and `inetres.adm`, found in `\WINNT\inf`. Capabilities of `Administrative Templates` can also be extended with custom ADM files.

NOTE *When you load an Administrative Template, the ADM files are copied to* `\SYSVOL\Domainname\ Policies\GUID\Adm`.

What's the difference between User Configuration and Computer Configuration with regard to Administrative Templates? Good question. Depending on the nature of the configuration settings, some live in the user part of the Registry (HKCU), while others live in the machine part (HKLM). Other settings exist in both places, which makes things really confusing. Settings for Task Scheduler, for example, are exactly the same in both places. So, other than asking yourself, "Which node has the setting I want?" the difference is whether the policy should apply to the machine, regardless of who logs in, or whether the policy should apply to the users and follow them from machine to machine.

What can you do with Administrative Templates settings? Among the primary functions is "Keep users from changing *X*" or "Disable or hide option *Y*." But mostly it's just a large collection of configuration options loosely organized together to ease our administrative burden and help us achieve the power and control of our networks and users that we crave and feel we truly deserve. An attempt to catalog each subnode and all of its policy settings would be a boring and futile exercise in the Microsoft style of documentation and is best left to those who write the Resource Kits. Besides, many of these policies should not be discussed in a vacuum and are best approached in the context of the particular application or service they configure.

Nonetheless, this section would be lacking if it did not include at least a few pointers on individual policies. So the following sections offer a few highly opinionated comments on some of the settings you'll find in Administrative Templates. For more suggestions on how to lock down a user's Desktop, see the system policies section later in this chapter. You'll find the same options (and more) in Group Policy as in the System Policy Editor.

WINDOWS COMPONENTS

For every setting in Internet Explorer, there seems to be policy to disable it. Considering that a good deal of time at work is spent surfing the Web, it's a particularly cruel and clever thing to impose such control over IE settings. Unfortunately, many companies use Netscape Navigator instead of Internet Explorer.

Though you might want to implement those cool Windows Explorer restrictions to the Map Network Drive and Disconnect Network Drive options, or remove particular drives in My Computer, this will only work with inexperienced users. Anyone who can access a command line can circumvent these restrictions, so be sure and check out the method to restrict the programs that can run from Windows Explorer. A more useful setting is the one to "not track shell shortcuts during roaming." This tells Explorer to resolve shortcuts in roaming profiles to local paths rather than tracking the source and attempting to open a program or file on a remote computer (this caused me much gnashing of teeth and pulling of hair before I figured out how to stop it).

The same principle applies to the Start menu and Taskbar and Desktop options. Experienced users will not be prevented from running unblessed programs just because Run is removed from the Start menu. But the Explorer settings may be useful to guard against inexperienced users' tendency to fiddle with things randomly. Plus, there is something to be said for a simplified and consistent Start menu and Desktop throughout an organization. I personally appreciate the options to hide "Computers Near Me" or "Entire Network" in My Network Places; with these hidden, users are not tempted to poke around on different servers to see what they can access.

CONTROL PANEL SETTINGS

The `Control Panel` node includes several options to disable or remove all or part of the Add/Remove Programs applet. Disabling Add/Remove Programs will not prevent users from running setup routines in other ways, however.

The Display policies prevent users from changing Display settings such as screen resolution, screen savers, and background wallpaper—in other words, customizing the display. Although it is desirable to prevent a user from changing the display to settings incompatible with hardware, it's not really necessary because Win2K does include safeguards against that eventuality. Unless the machine is in a library or school or someplace where a standardized Desktop appearance is necessary, I see no point in preventing access to these settings. Unless you work someplace where everyone has to wear a blue or black suit every day, and the Desktops are subject to the same dress code, there are better ways to reassure ourselves of our superiority as network administrators.

The policies that prevent users from adding or deleting printers are useful if your users are in the habit of doing that and then calling you to ask, "Why can't I print?" Also, it is helpful to specify an Active Directory path for printers to assist with searches.

SYSTEM SETTINGS

Under `System`, use the Century Interpretation for Year 2000 entry to set programs to interpret two-digit date references consistently and correctly. This parameter, when enabled, defaults to 2029, so a reference to 01/06/29 is interpreted as 2029, while 01/16/30 is interpreted as 1930.

Disabling Registry editing tools prevents users from running `REGEDT32.EXE` and `REGEDIT.EXE`, which is not a bad idea, although regular users only have Read access to the vast majority of the Registry anyway.

The famous setting Run Only Allowed Windows Applications is found in the `System` node under User Configuration (not Computer Configuration). If you enable the policy, you must add a list of allowed applications or users will be unable to run anything at all. Figure 9.62 shows the policy enabled with a sample list of allowed applications. Use of this policy is often combined with the policy to hide My Network Places and Internet Explorer from the Desktop, remove Run from the Start menu, and apply other restrictions found in the `Windows Explorer` policies node.

FIGURE 9.62

Policy to run only
allowed applications

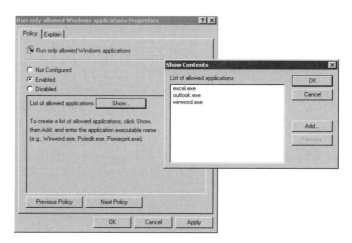

USING GROUP POLICY TO SET PASSWORD AND ACCOUNT LOCKOUT POLICY

In NT 4, any account policies set in User Manager for Domains applied to domain account and password functions; the audited events, such as restarts, failed logon attempts, and security policy changes, were those occurring on domain controllers. Group policies in Win2K are much more powerful. If you choose to create a policy at the domain level, the settings will apply to all domain member machines—servers, workstations, and domain controllers included. It is possible, however, for OU policies to override local policy settings such as auditing and user rights.

One big note about password, account lockout, and Kerberos group policies: They are applied at the domain level only. Domain controllers will receive their settings from domain-level account policies and will ignore the settings in policies linked to OUs. In fact, you'll see an error in the Event Log if an OU-level policy contains these settings. So unfortunately, you still can't make administrator types change their passwords more often than everyone else does (not without a big stick, anyway). Differing Local Policy settings can be applied to OUs, however, so audit policy can be stricter on "high security" OUs and more lax on others.

Password Policy includes the following options:

Enforce Password History Enable this option and supply several new passwords that must be unique before a given password can be used again.

Maximum Password Age This option sets the amount of time for which a password can be used before the system requires the user to pick a new one.

Minimum Password Age The value set here is the amount of time for which a password must be used before the user is allowed to change it again.

Minimum Password Length This option defines the smallest number of characters that a user's password can contain. Eight characters is a good length for passwords.

Passwords Must Meet the Complexity Requirements of Installed Password Filter Password filters define requirements such as the number of characters allowed, whether letters and numbers must be used, whether any part of the username is permitted, and so forth.

Store Passwords Using Reversible Encryption   Windows 95/98 clients and Macintosh clients need to authenticate with a lower-level encryption.

User Must Log On to Change Password   This option prevents unauthenticated users from changing an account password through brute force attacks. It also prevents a user from changing a password after it's expired.

Account Lockout Policy, once enabled, prevents anyone from logging in to the account after a certain number of failed attempts:

Account Lockout Threshold   This value defines how many times the user can unsuccessfully attempt to log in before the account will be locked out.

Reset Account Lockout Counter After   This setting defines the time interval after which the count of bad logon attempts will start over. For example, suppose you have a reset count of two minutes and three logon attempts. If you mistype twice, you can wait two minutes after the second attempt and you'll have three tries again.

Account Lockout Duration   This setting determines the interval for which the account will be locked out. After this time period expires, the user account will no longer be locked out and the user can try to log in again.

USING GROUP POLICY TO MANAGE MMC

Delegation is a great feature of Win2K, and the Microsoft Management Console is a big part of that. Many Win2K administrators will want to create consoles to accomplish particular tasks and distribute them to the responsible parties. Group Policy offers options to control MMC so that others can't make changes to existing MMC tools or access snap-ins and extensions that are off-limits, not the least of which are the Group Policy snap-ins and extensions.

You see, in NT 4, users could either run the Server Manager tool or they couldn't. If they could run the tool, they might only be able to create machine accounts (if they were members of Account Operators) but not to promote domain controllers. That didn't keep users from seeing the option in the menu or from attempting operations that were not permitted in their security context. With Win2K, not only can you design a tool that includes just the snap-ins and extensions that you want your admin types to use, but you can also explicitly forbid any changing of the tool (by preventing Author mode). What's more, you can completely forbid access to a particular snap-in, regardless of the tool employed by the user. Please note that this does not actually set a user's security level (that's what security groups and rights are for), but it can effectively limit access to certain administrative tools. Cool, eh?

The Microsoft Management Console policies are found under `Administrative Templates` in the User Configuration node (see Figure 9.63). The main policies shown in this figure are to restrict Author mode (which prevents the user from creating console files and from adding or removing snap-ins) and to restrict users to an explicit list of permitted snap-ins. These two policies are not exactly mutually exclusive, as you might think; nor does enabling the first policy eliminate the need for the second.

FIGURE 9.63

MMC group policies

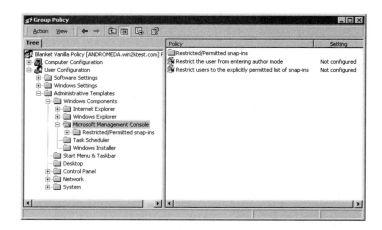

A user who is not permitted to enter Author mode is unable to do any of the following:

◆ Run `MMC.EXE` from the Start menu or a command prompt; it opens, by definition, in Author mode with a blank console window.

◆ Open any console with the `/a` (Author mode) switch.

◆ Open any console that is configured to always open in Author mode.

All of the prebuilt administrative consoles that are included in `Administrative Tools` are User mode tools, so they can be used when the restriction is activated. However, if you create a console and distribute it but forget to set it to open in User mode, the user will not be able to access the tool with this policy in effect.

If the policy to restrict users to only the expressly permitted list of snap-ins is enabled, users will not be able to add or remove restricted snap-ins or extensions to console files when in Author mode (they will not even appear in the list of available snap-ins). More importantly, if a console file already contains a restricted snap-in or extension, when the tool is run by a user who is subject to this policy, the restricted snap-in or extension will not appear in the console. For example, if you don't have access to the Group Policy tab for Active Directory tools (set this policy in the Group Policy node under `Restricted/Permitted Snap-Ins`), you won't even see the tab in Active Directory Users and Computers (or AD Sites and Services) when you open the properties of the site, domain, or OU.

If you do choose to restrict users to only the expressly permitted list of snap-ins, be sure to filter the policy for exempt admin types. Also, you need to go to the `Restricted/Permitted Snap-Ins` folder and enable those snap-ins that you want to be available. Otherwise, *no snap-ins will be available* to nonexempt users regardless of their power and status on the network. This could be very bad, so think carefully before you disable access to the Group Policy snap-in, or you might not be able to reverse the damage.

Even if you don't enable the policy to restrict snap-in and extension use, you can still deny access to certain snap-ins. You see, if the policy Restrict Users to the Explicitly Permitted List of Snap-Ins is configured, enabling a certain snap-in means that it *can* be used. But if you leave this policy turned off, enabling a certain snap-in means that it *cannot* be used.

Figure 9.64 shows the snap-ins that can be permitted or restricted. There is a separate list of extension snap-ins that can be restricted/permitted (Figure 9.65). Extensions are implemented as dependent modules of snap-ins, but sometimes they do the same things as full-blown snap-ins. For example, the Event Viewer is a snap-in and can exist by itself in a console, as it does in the Event Viewer administrative tool, but it is also implemented as an extension in the Computer Management tool. So you'll need to know whether the thing you want to restrict is a full snap-in or an extension. See Chapter 5 for additional information on MMC consoles and snap-ins.

FIGURE 9.64

Permitted or restricted MMC snap-ins

FIGURE 9.65

Permitted or restricted MMC extensions

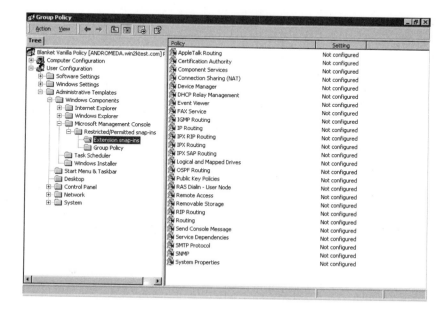

There is a separate folder for the Group Policy snap-in and related extensions (Figure 9.66). These allow you to restrict or permit access to the individual parts of Group Policy so that delegated admin types can assign software to be installed, for example, without having access to the Security Settings node. *Be careful when restricting access to the GP snap-ins.* This policy should be filtered for trusted, responsible (and polite) administrators.

FIGURE 9.66

Setting up Group Policy snap-in restrictions

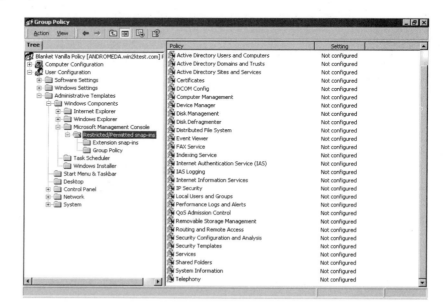

A final note about MMC policies: If the user doesn't have all the necessary components installed on her machine, the MSC file won't work properly and may not even run. There is a very useful policy called Download Missing COM Components, which directs the system to search for those missing components in the Active Directory and download them if they are found. For some reason, this policy is found in `User Configuration\Administrative Templates\System` and in the corresponding path of `Computer Configuration`.

Managing Group Policies

In the preceding section, we touched on using Group Policy settings to restrict access to certain MMC snap-ins and extensions, including the Group Policy snap-ins. Let's finish up our discussion of group policies with an exploration of the other Group Policy configuration options that are actually included as group policies (Group Policy policies). Then I'll close with a few select observations and suggestions for configuring and managing group policies in your organization.

GROUP POLICY POLICIES

Policies to control Group Policy are found in `Administrative Templates` of both the `User Configuration` and `Computer Configuration` nodes (`Administrative Templates\System\Group`

Policy). Figures 9.67 and 9.68 show the User Configuration and Computer Configuration options for Group Policy. The following paragraphs summarize the most important configuration options.

FIGURE 9.67

User Configuration settings for Group Policy

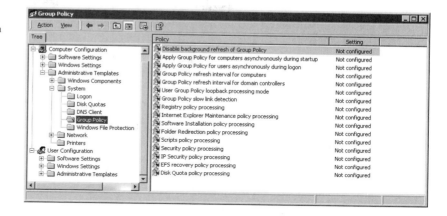

FIGURE 9.68

Computer Configuration settings for Group Policy

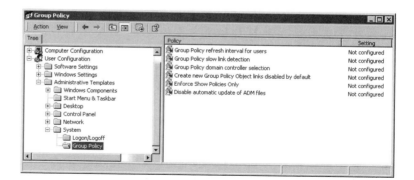

Group Policy Refresh Intervals for Users/Computers/Domain Controllers   These separate policies determine how often GPOs are refreshed in the background while users and computers are working. These parameters permit changes to the default background refresh intervals and tweaking of the offset time.

Disable Background Refresh   If you enable this setting, policies will only be refreshed at system start-up and user logon. This might be useful for performance reasons, since having 1500 computers refreshing policies every 90 minutes could cause congestion on an Ethernet.

Apply Group Policy for Users/Computers Synchronously During Start-up   Enable this setting to prevent users from logging in until all group policies have been applied. Otherwise, policies apply in the background and a user will be able to log in while policy settings are still changing.

Policy Processing Options   These policies, with names such as Registry Policy Processing and Folder Redirection Policy Processing, are available to customize the behavior of the different GPO components. Each policy (see Figure 9.69 for an example) presents at least two of the following three options:

Allow Processing Across a Slow Network Connection   For slow connections, some policies can be turned off to enhance performance (you can define what a "slow link" is by using the Group Policy Slow Link Detection setting). Security settings and Registry policy processing will always apply, however, and cannot be turned off.

Do Not Apply During Periodic Background Processing   Specify which components will be refreshed periodically. Software installation and folder redirection policies will never be refreshed while a user is logged in, so the option is not available for them.

Process Even If the Group Policy Objects Have Not Changed   To conserve network and system resources, GPOs are, by default, not refreshed if there have been no changes. To increase security, however, and guard against a user's changing a policy setting, enable the policy to ensure that all settings are reapplied at each refresh interval. Please note that enabling this policy may cause noticeable performance degradation.

FIGURE 9.69

Scripts policy processing options

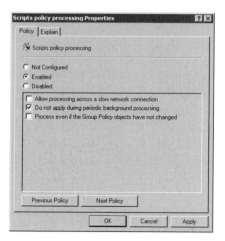

When You Want *User* **Settings on a Particular** *Machine*: **Loopback Processing Mode**   By default, user policies are processed after Computer Configuration policies, and user policies will take precedence if there are conflicts. Also by default, users receive their policy regardless of the machine they use to log in. Sometimes this is not appropriate and policies need to be applied according to the computer's policy objects instead ("loopback processing"). For example, if I log in to a server to do administration, it's not appropriate for my office productivity applications to start installing themselves. Another example of when you would want computer policies to override user policies is if you want to apply more stringent policies for machines that are exposed to the anonymous public (machines in libraries, university computer labs, or kiosks in shopping malls and tourist attractions, for instance). Two modes are used to control this behavior (see Figure 9.70): Merge mode and Replace mode.

Merge Mode   Process user policies first, then computer policies. Computer policies will therefore override conflicting user policies.

Replace Mode   Disregard user policies and processes only computer policies.

FIGURE 9.70

User Group Policy loopback processing mode policy

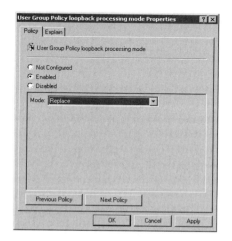

GROUP POLICY OVER SLOW LINKS

Group Policy still works over slow links such as dial-up connections. Even better, it's applied whether users log in using Dial-Up Networking or whether they log in with cached credentials and then initiate a connection. However, application of Group Policy over slow links can pose performance issues, so Win2K includes policy settings to define a slow link and to define how policies are applied over a detected slow link.

The default definition of a slow link, as far as group policies are concerned, is anything under 500 kilobits per second. The system performs a test using the Ping utility to determine the speed of the connection. If the Ping response time is under 2000 milliseconds, the connection is fast. You can change the definition of a slow link, however. This policy setting, called Group Policy Slow Link Detection, is available in both the User Configuration and Computer Configuration, under `Administrative Templates\System\Group Policy` (see Figure 9.71 for the properties page of the policy). To change the default parameter, enter a number in Kbps or enter 0 to disable slow-link detection altogether. If you disable slow-link detection, all policies will be applied regardless of the connection speed.

As I mentioned in the preceding section, policy processing settings for individual policy components (these have names such as Folder Redirection Policy Processing and are found in the same path

as the Slow Link Detection setting, under `Computer Configuration\Administrative Templates\`
`System\Group Policy`) allow you to specify whether a portion of the policy object will be processed
over a slow-link connection. Again, this is not an option for Registry-based policies or for security
settings; these will always be processed, even over slow links. The other modules will not be applied
over slow links by default.

FIGURE 9.71

Group Policy's slow-
link detection prop-
erties

To have logon scripts run over slow links, for example, open the policy called Scripts Policy Processing. Enable the policy, as in Figure 9.72, and check the box beside Allow Processing Across a
Slow Network Connection. Choose OK and the policy is set. Repeat as necessary for the other policy processing entries.

FIGURE 9.72

Policy processing
options

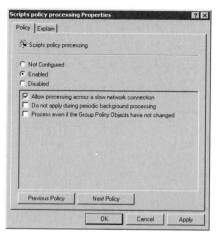

Troubleshooting Group Policies

In case it's not clear by now, group policies are powerful…and also complex. And they can be kind of opaque—sometimes you create a bunch of policies on a domain controller that you intend to control some Desktop, then restart the Desktop, log in, and wait to see the effects of the new policies…but nothing happens.

There aren't a lot of *great* group policy troubleshooting tools—at least, none that are inexpensive or included in the box—but here are a few.

GPRESULT

GPRESULT.EXE is a Resource Kit tool that will display a wealth of information about group policies. To use it, you must be physically sitting at the user's machine while the user is logged in—that's the downside of GPRESULT. But it *does* provide some nice info:

◆ User rights information

◆ The DC that the workstation got the policies from

◆ When the policies applied

◆ Which policies applied

You can get more detailed information with options:

◆ /v says to give more verbose information: gpresult /v.

◆ /s says to give even *more* information; it is the "super-verbose" option. You'd use it as in gpresult /s.

◆ If you know that you're zeroing in on just a machine policy, then add /m; if you're only interested in user policies, add /u. So, for example, to get the maximum information about the user policies applied to this system, add gpresult /s /u.

GPOTOOL

Sounds like the Resource Kit's only Irish program, doesn't it? GPOTOOL.EXE checks all of your group policies to ensure that they are "whole." Group Policies exist in two parts: First, there is a text file in Sysvol for each policy which is called the Group Policy Template (GPT), and, second, each policy shows up as a record in the Active Directory called the Group Policy Container (GPC). If one replicates and the other one does not, then the policy won't work.

GPOTOOL checks each policy and ensures that it has replicated both in the GPC and GPT. But GPOTOOL has one annoying feature, in fact, a feature shared by many GP tools: it doesn't refer to policies by their English name or "friendly name," as Microsoft calls it. Instead, it reports on policies by their globally unique ID (GUID), a scary-looking hexadecimal string. You can look up a GUID's friendly name with some techniques outlined in a Knowledge Base article (Q216359) or with this script:

```
set RootDSE = GetObject("LDAP://RootDSE")
Domain = RootDSE.get("DefaultNamingContext")
wscript.echo "The domain name is: " & domain & vbCrLf
```

```
Set GPCContainer = GetObject("LDAP://cn=Policies,cn=System," & domain)
For Each object in GPCContainer
    wscript.echo "Friendly name: " & object.displayname
    wscript.echo "Container GUID: " & object.guid
    wscript.echo vbCrLf
Next
```

(That's from the book *Windows 2000: Group Policy, Profiles, and IntelliMirror*, ISBN 0-7821-2881-5, by Jeremy Moskowitz, from Sybex. If you want more details on handling group policies, it's *the* resource.) You make the script work by opening Notepad and typing those lines into Notepad. Save the file as c:\seepols.vbs, ensuring that Notepad doesn't tack on an extra .txt. Then open a command prompt and type **cscript c:\seepols.vbs** and you'll get a list of all policies and their GUIDs and friendly names.

REGISTRY KEYS TO REVEAL POLICIES

The Registry can help unlock policies. It actually keeps a record of what policies applied to your computer and your account in HKEY_LOCAL_MACHINE\Software\Microsoft\Windows\CurrentVersion\Group Policy\History for the machine settings and HKEY_CURRENT_USER\Software\Microsoft\Windows\CurrentVersion\Group Policy\History for user settings. You can also enlist the Registry's aid in logging GP information with a couple of keys.

In HKEY_LOCAL_MACHINE\Software\Microsoft\Windows NT\CurrentVersion, create a completely new key—not a value entry, a key—named Diagnostics. In that new key, create a value entry RunDiagnosticLoggingGroupPolicy of type REG_DWORD and set it to 1. Reboot the computer. You'll get a tremendous amount of information about what group policies applied to this computer. (Turn it off when you no longer need it, or you'll gain new skills, like learning how to make the Event Log larger and how to clear it. Those policies can be a bit voluble!)

USERENV.DLL is a DLL that drives much of group policies as well as handles your roaming profiles. It reveals some of what it's doing with a Registry change: Go to HKEY_LOCAL_MACHINE\SOFTWARE\Microsoft\Windows NT\CurrentVersion\Winlogon and create a new entry UserenvDebugLevel and set it to 1. You'll get an ASCII log file in WINNT\Debug\UserMode\userenv.log. It's a log file, so it doesn't reset itself with every reboot; if you're about to do some troubleshooting, then go delete or rename any existing userenv.logs, or you'll make the job of picking through its cryptic output even harder.

A FEW FINAL THOUGHTS ON GROUP POLICY

In the last few sections, I have discussed the concepts of group policies, including local policies. We have created a sample group policy and seen how to turn on the various settings, like No Override and Block Policy Inheritance. We have looked at filtering policies for security groups and delegating policy administration to others. We have explored many of the actual policy settings, including administrative templates for Desktop control, security settings, folder redirection, MMC management, even Group Policy policies. But before you close this chapter and begin to configure group policies on your network, there are two more significant issues that you want to be very aware of. One is that group policies affect network and system performance. The other is that group policies are difficult to troubleshoot if something goes wrong.

The performance issue is pretty simple: the more policies to apply, the longer the logon time. Each time a user logs in (or a computer is restarted), each of the GPOs associated with the user's or computer's containers (SDOUs) is read and applied. This can slow down logons considerably, and users may start calling the help desk to ask, "What's wrong with the network?" Therefore, you should keep the number of policies to a minimum. Another thing that can bog down a machine or a network is the background refresh rate. Refresh your policies too often and you'll see a hit because the machine is always busy asking for policy changes. Think about disabling the background refreshes altogether unless you're worried about users changing their settings to escape policies. With the background refresh disabled, user and computer policies are only reapplied at logon and start-up, respectively. The worst thing you could do for performance is have a bunch of different policies in effect and tell Group Policy to reapply at each refresh interval even if there are no changes. Another way to streamline GPO processing is to avoid assigning GPOs from different domains. Just because you can do it doesn't mean it's a good idea.

The problem with troubleshooting policies stems from an inability to view the cumulative policy settings that are actually in effect for a user or machine. This capability to display actual policy settings, referred to as the Resultant Set of Policy (RSOP), is necessary for managing and troubleshooting policies. Without it, you have to look at the properties of each site/domain/OU to see which policies and containers are linked. Then you must view the ACLs to see if there's any filtering, and check out the disabled, Block Policy Inheritance, and No Override options. Finally, you need to view the settings of the policies in question before you can get to the bottom of things. You'll need to take notes.

So until Microsoft comes out with an RSOP tool, promised soon after the release of Win2K, here are a few suggestions to help minimize troubleshooting time:

◆ Keep your policy strategy simple. Group users and computers together in OUs if possible, and apply policy at the highest level possible. Avoid having multiple GPOs with conflicting policies that apply to the same recipients. Minimize the use of No Override and Block Policy Inheritance.

◆ Document your group policies heavily, individual settings as well as framework. You may want to visually depict your policy structure and put it on the wall, like your network topology diagrams. That way, when a problem arises, you can consult the documentation to see what's going on before you go fishing.

◆ Finally, test those group policies before deployment! This is absolutely essential to save your help desk and ensure that applications and system services continue to run properly.

Working with Roaming User Profiles

As you use Windows—any version of Windows—and applications, you end up customizing your Desktop and the applications on your Desktop to your particular preferences. Things like your choice of Desktop fonts and color, how an application should start up (e.g., minimized or windowed), and how you want the application to work are all part of something called your *user profile*. You've got one, whether you want it or not, stored on your computer's local hard disk.

But as you move from computer to computer in an organization, it'd be nice to have those settings follow you around. Or, even if you don't use more than one workstation, it'd be nice to be able to wipe that workstation's hard disk clean, reinstall the OS and applications from scratch, and not lose your Desktop and applications settings. You can accomplish that with a variation on a user profile: a *roaming* profile. Not every version of Windows supports roaming user profiles, but NT 3.*x* and later do. (Although, truthfully, they weren't of much value until NT 4.) In this section, we'll see how they work and what you can do with them.

NOTE   *Let me stress that NT 4, Windows 2000, XP, and .NET Server all handle profiles almost identically. Even though this discussion uses Windows 2000 examples, everything will work the same way if you're supporting NT 4 or XP workstations. The main difference is the name of the profile directory, as you'll learn in a page or two, for some incomprehensible reason, Microsoft moved profiles from* \WINNT\PROFILES *to* Documents and Settings. *Just make that substitution in your head and you'll be able apply all of this to NT workstations. XP workstations also work the same, but they continue to use* Documents and Settings.

I said that these settings may be configured by a user who wishes to personalize her Desktop, but they can also be set by a system administrator responsible for configuring Desktops, or by a combination of the two. In other words, a user may create shortcuts and select a screen saver, while an administrator may configure special program groups for the user's Desktop. However, the two are not mutually exclusive. By default, every user on an NT 4 machine (except members of the Guests group) keeps a local profile directory that NT names after the user ID. Guests are not allowed to keep local profiles.

User profiles can be implemented in several different ways, according to the needs of your organization. In situations where a network-based solution is not feasible or not desirable, there are still several options to keep in mind:

Local Profiles   Users keep only local profiles and create and configure these profiles themselves. User settings don't follow a user around in this case, and a wiped-and-rebuilt workstation won't keep its settings.

Preconfigure the Default User Profile   Users keep only local profiles, but an administrator preconfigures a "magic," locally stored user profile called the "default" user profile. Anyone who logs onto this system gets that default user profile as a jumping-off point for their personal user profile.

Preconfigured Local Profiles   Users keep only local profiles, but an administrator preconfigures all or part of the local user profiles. (This can be labor intensive.)

Enabling roaming user profiles, which are of course networked, can exploit the centralizing power of networks and opens up four more possibilities:

Roaming Profiles   Add a user profile path to the user's account information to automatically create and maintain a copy of the user profile in a network location (the user can configure her own profile).

Preconfigured Roaming Profiles   Add a user profile path to the user's account information and copy a preconfigured profile to the network location specified (the user can make changes to her profile, but the administrator creates the initial state of her profile).

Network Default User Profiles   Create a default user profile and copy it to the `NETLOGON` share of the authenticating domain controller(s). This will hand out default profiles to all new users (users can make changes to their profiles). This option can be used in conjunction with roaming or local profiles.

Mandatory Profiles   Add a user profile path to the user account, copy a preconfigured profile to that path, and use special filename and directory name extensions to specify that this is a mandatory profile. The user must use the profile and cannot make any changes. A mandatory profile can be shared by a group of users.

Anatomy of a User Profile

A local user profile is created automatically by the system the first time a user logs in to an NT machine. This profile directory is located in `%SYSTEMROOT%\PROFILES` on an NT 4 machine or a Windows 2000 machine that was upgraded in-place from NT 4. On a cleanly installed Windows 2000, XP, or .NET Server system, the profiles are stored in a directory called `Documents and Settings` on the same drive as the operating system. (You can change that location if you like, but you've got to do it at setup time by scripting the install.) Figure 9.73 shows the contents of the `Documents and Settings` directory on a Windows 2000 system.

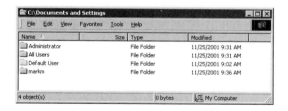

The `Documents and Settings` directory contains a profile for every user who logs in to the NT machine (in this case, user markm and the user Administrator), as well as a directory called `All Users` and one called `Default User`. The `All Users` directory stores common program groups (programs available to all users on a specific machine) and shortcuts that will appear on every user's Desktop on that machine. For example, Administrative Tools is stored in the `All Users` folder, so the programs listed in this group will be made available to anyone logging in to the machine. The `Default User` folder, which is hidden by default, exists because the operating system uses it as a template for creating individual profiles for new users. Figure 9.74 shows the contents of an individual user profile directory, `C:\Documents and Settings\joel`.

Each user's profile contains several folders with links to various Desktop items plus the `NTUSER.DAT` file, which contains configuration settings from the Registry. `NTUSER.DAT.LOG` is a transaction log file that exists to protect `NTUSER.DAT` while changes are being flushed to disk. (You won't find an `NTUSER.DAT.LOG` for the `Default User` profile directory because it is a template. The other folders store information on the contents of the user's Desktop and Start Menu items, including shortcuts and program groups. Remember that a user's profile also includes the common program groups and shortcuts indicated in the `All Users` folder. Table 9.5 describes the various folders in a user profile.

FIGURE 9.74

An individual profile directory

TABLE 9.5: FOLDERS IN AN NT 4 USER PROFILE

FOLDER	EXPLANATION
Application Data*	A place for applications to store user-specific information.
Desktop	Any file, folder, or shortcut in this folder will appear directly on the user's Desktop.
Cookies	Internet Explorer cookies
Favorites	Shortcuts to favorite Web sites and bookmarks can be stored here.
Local Settings*	A part of a profile that does *not* roam, even if you make the profile roam. A place for things like temporary files, which can be large and disk-hungry but don't have a reason to network.
NetHood*	Shortcuts placed here will appear in Network Neighborhood.
Personal or My Documents	You'll see Personal on NT 4 systems, My Documents on later systems. It's the place that Microsoft recommends that applications save user data, so that your documents are all in one place. You can change the location of My Documents through policies, so don't be alarmed if you have a profile that doesn't have a My Documents.
PrintHood*	Shortcuts placed here will appear in the Printers folder.
Recent*	NT automatically puts shortcuts to recently used files here. Linked to Documents in the Start menu.
SendTo*	Place shortcuts to apps, printers, and folders here to quickly copy an item to a predefined place, to open a file within a specific application (such as Notepad), or even to print a file.
Start Menu	Contains personal program groups and shortcuts to program items.
Templates*	Contains shortcuts to templates created by applications such as PowerPoint and Word.

These folders are hidden by default. NT and 2000 hide different combinations of the folders.

In addition to the folders, a user profile includes numerous user-definable settings for Windows NT Explorer (View All Files, Display Full Path in the Title Bar, and Show Large Icons); the Taskbar (Auto Hide, Show Small Icons in Start Menu, and Show Clock); Control Panel (command prompt, mouse, and display preferences); and Accessories (Calculator, Clock, and Notepad). Network Printer, Drive Connections, and Windows NT Help bookmarks are also saved in the user profile. Virtually any application written for Windows NT can remember user-specific settings. These settings, not directly linked to Desktop items, are contained in the `NTUSER.DAT` file.

`NTUSER.DAT` is the Registry part of a user profile. It corresponds to the `HKEY_ CURRENT_USER` subtree in the Registry Editor (`REGEDT32.EXE`).

Configuring Your Own User Profile

Before you configure user profiles on your network, you will need to master techniques for configuring your own profile. You can then use these skills to configure profiles for other users.

The `NTUSER.DAT` file for the user currently logged in may be edited using a Registry editing tool such as `REGEDT32.EXE` or `REGEDIT.EXE`, although these tools are not particularly intuitive (an understatement if I have ever heard one). The System Policy Editor (`POLEDIT.EXE`), a tool that originated in NT 4 for creating system policies (which are covered in an appendix on the CD, in case you've got NT 4 Desktops to worry about), is more user-friendly and can be used to directly edit several selected settings in the local Registry. (It comes with NT Server and all flavors of Windows 2000, but for some reason it's not installed with XP by default. It's not necessary, though, just convenient.)

The System Policy Editor is a "selective" Registry editor and is easier to use, as it does not require any knowledge of Registry syntax or structure. While this application offers several options that are not available in the graphical interface, very little would be of interest to normal users setting up their own profiles, even assuming that they have access to the application (it's not included with NT Workstation). Even though the System Policy Editor can be used to edit the machine's local Registry, as shown in Figure 9.75, most of the Local User options focus on restricting a user's Desktop. Joe User probably would not do that to himself. However, this little piece of information will come in handy when *you* want to restrict other users' Desktops.

FIGURE 9.75

Using the System Policy Editor to change the local Registry

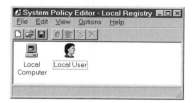

Actually, the best way to configure the `NTUSER.DAT` part of your profile is simply to configure your Desktop. By using the applets in the graphical interface to change your color scheme, map network drives, and connect to printers, you are making changes to `NTUSER.DAT`. Use a Registry editor only when you want to make a change that is not offered in the Control Panel. For example, under NT 3.51, the only way to change the icon title font, size, and style was in the Registry, under `HKEY_ CURRENT_USER\CONTROL PANEL\DESKTOP`. In NT 4, 2000, and XP, however, these and other formerly unavailable options can be adjusted using the Appearance tab in Control Panel/Display.

WARNING   As I've warned you before, you're just asking for trouble if you start playing with your machine's Registry for no good reason. Don't edit the Registry if you can make the changes using the Control Panel.

To configure the Taskbar, program items, and shortcuts in your profile folder, right-click the Taskbar and choose Properties. The General tab of the Taskbar and Start Menu Properties dialog box (Figure 9.76) allows you to adjust a couple of things in the Taskbar.

FIGURE 9.76

Specifying Taskbar options in the Taskbar and Start Menu Properties dialog box

Notice that if you are running NT 4, then you won't see the Use Personalized Menus option, but don't worry about it—you won't need it here. Toggle the check boxes to see how your display will change. The Advanced tab (Figure 9.77) allows you to add and remove shortcuts and folders from the Start menu. (Again, an NT 4 version of this will look a trifle different.) The Add and Remove buttons are the easiest way to go, but the Advanced button gives you more flexibility.

FIGURE 9.77

Customizing the Start menu in the Taskbar and Start Menu Properties dialog box

The Advanced button takes you directly to your Start Menu folder in Explorer (Figure 9.78). Add a folder to create a program group and add a program. Folders and shortcuts may be added in

NT Explorer or by double-clicking My Computer on your Desktop. Either way, changes to the folders in your profile directory show up right away on your Desktop.

FIGURE 9.78

The `Start Menu` folder in Explorer

TIP *You can create shortcuts and drag them right onto your Start menu button to create a shortcut at the top of the Start menu. The shortcuts to* `PSP.EXE` *shown in Figure 9.78 were created in this way. You can also create a folder in this location with shortcuts to several program items. Microsoft calls these* custom program groups.

TIP *Add a few shortcuts to the* `SendTo` *folder in your profile. If* `SendTo` *contains shortcuts to your home directory, to word processing or spreadsheet applications, and to printers, you'll be able to right-click a file to copy it to your home directory, open it in Word, or even print it!*

Birth of a Local Profile

The next step in mastering user profiles is to understand how 2000 (or NT or XP) creates a user profile and how a user obtains one. In short, when a user (we'll call him Corwin) logs in for the first time, there is no profile for him yet. So the system creates a new profile folder for him. The Default User profile information is copied to that new directory. This information, along with the shortcuts and program items found in the `All Users` folder, is then loaded to create Corwin's Desktop. The new profile now exists in a folder named after the user in the same path as the `Default User` profile directory, `\Documents and Settings\Corwin`. (Again, if this were an NT 4 workstation, the local profile would instead be located in `%SYSTEMROOT%\PROFILES` After 2000 creates the local profile, any user-specific changes made by Corwin, to elements such as Desktop color schemes, shortcuts, persistent network connections, or personal program groups, will be saved to Corwin's profile. (For information about ownership and permissions, see Chapter 11.)

NOTE *Only users who are members of the local Administrators group may make changes to the* `All Users` *folder.*

By the way, if that profile is created on an NTFS partition, Corwin will be the *owner* of the profile because he created it. Permissions will be set to allow him to modify his own profile. SYSTEM and Administrators will also have full access to the profile. The system sets the permissions like so:

◆ SYSTEM gets Full Control.

◆ The local Administrators group gets Full Control.

◆ The user's account gets Full Control.

◆ Other users will be denied access to Corwin's profile folder.

So, to summarize: If you log onto a workstation either with a local or domain account you and don't have a roaming profile, then the workstation needs to find one for you *somewhere*. First, the workstation looks in its profile directory and, if it finds one for your account, then it uses that one. If there *isn't* one for your account, then the workstation needs to create one and uses the "template" profile stored in Default User.

That's how *local* profiles work. Now let's see how things change when we network the profiles, as "roaming" profiles.

Roaming Profile Basics

A network administrator might choose to specify a path on the network to store a user profile. A profile is a *roaming profile* (rather than a local profile) when the user account information indicates a profile path, even if that path is local. In the simplest of scenarios, the administrator has simply created a share on the server, set appropriate permissions on the share (and directories), and indicated in `Computer Management/System Tools/Local Users and Groups` or `Active Directory Users and Computers` that a copy of the user's profile should be stored there.

Thus far, we haven't given Corwin a roaming profile; so far, he's just created a local profile on the Windows 2000 workstation that he uses all the time and that workstation keeps the one and only copy of that profile locally, on `C:\Documents and Settings\Corwin`. (Notice that this would apply whether Corwin has a local account or a domain account; merely having a domain account doesn't confer a roaming profile. But let's say for the sake of the example that Corwin's account is on an Active Directory domain.)

Suppose now that Corwin is downstairs in Eric's office and wants to get to the domain. Eric logs off, and Corwin logs on. Corwin doesn't yet have a roaming profile, and so Eric's computer doesn't have a clue about how Corwin likes his system set up, so it creates a new profile for Corwin from its—Eric's workstation's—Default Users profile. That means more work for Corwin. We'd like his Desktop settings to follow him around. So we'll give him a roaming profile. Here's howto specify a roaming profile path for a user in two easy steps:

1. Create a shared directory. I like to create a share and name it `profiles` or `PROFILES$` (to hide it from the browse list). Set share-level permissions to Change or Full Control to allow all users storing profiles to alter their profiles. You do not have to create profile directories for the users. The workstation operating system will create the profile directory for the user and set appropriate permissions.

2. Open Active Directory Users and Computers, navigate to the user account in question, open its properties page, go to the Profile tab, and fill in the path for the user profile directory as shown in Figure 9.79. The figure shows the user's roaming profile located in \\`Bigserve\Pro-files\Corwin`. `Profiles` is the name of the share, not the directory name, so if you created a hidden share for the profiles, as mentioned in step 1, you'll need to use `PROFILES$` instead. Use %USERNAME% in place of the username if you are specifying roaming profiles for more than one user account. You may also specify the user profile path as the user's home directory, as also shown in Figure 9.79.

FIGURE 9.79

The Profile Path and Home Directory ("Home Folder") fields on the Profile tab of the user account's properties page

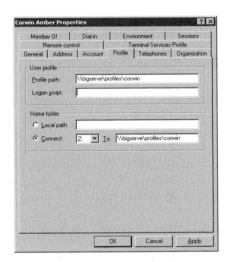

So Corwin has logged onto his local system in the past, and his local system has a profile for him. Now that we've specified a profile path, the Active Directory has set aside a place for a roaming profile. But how does AD fill that place, how does it create the user's profile? As it turns out, that can be a bit complex. Let's first consider the case where Corwin has been granted a roaming profile, but already has one on his workstation.

CREATING A ROAMING PROFILE WHEN A LOCAL ONE EXISTS

The next time Corwin logs in, the workstation will see that there is a network path specified for the profile. Recall that Corwin already has a local profile in his workstation. This appears to pose a problem, however—there is no profile on the server yet, but one does exist on the local machine. So, the workstation simply loads the local profile and creates a directory on the server to store the roaming profile. When Corwin logs out, the workstation operating system (NT, 2000, or XP) will copy the local profile directory to the network path. In other words, the OS used the preexisting local profile to create the roaming profile directory on the server. From now on, whenever Corwin logs in, the workstation operating system will check to make sure that the profiles still match (using a time stamp) and will load the most recent version. The workstation operating system will save any changes

Corwin makes to both profiles: the local copy and, when Corwin logs out, Corwin's profile directory on the server.

Okay, why all this rigmarole about saving the user profile to the local path and to the server? The server is the first option, but by default, the workstation operating system will always keep a local profile folder to ensure that the user can access his profile if the network profile is unavailable. This is also useful with slow network connections.

If the profile directory on the server is unavailable for some reason when Corwin logs in (perhaps because the server is down), the workstation operating system will simply let Corwin know this and load the local copy. In that case, the workstation operating system will not attempt to copy changes to the server when Corwin logs out. The next time he logs in, the workstation will display another dialog box saying, "Your local profile is more recent than your server profile." Corwin can then choose which profile to load. (In case you are wondering, this scenario for Win2K and XP Desktops can be managed with group policies.)

CREATING A ROAMING PROFILE WHEN THERE IS NO LOCAL PROFILE

Next, let's consider what happens if a user logs onto a workstation and a domain for the first time. What if newcomer Bleys also has a roaming profile path specified in the Active Directory and he logs in to his workstation for the first time? Like Corwin, Bleys doesn't have a profile directory on the server at all. Unlike Corwin, he has no local profile on the workstation. In this case, the workstation operating system will use the information in `Default User` on the local machine to create a local profile and will also create a profile directory in the network path. Just as with Corwin, when Bleys logs out, the workstation will copy his local profile, including any changes, into the newly created directory.

Table 9.6 illustrates the order for loading a user profile, given the two scenarios we've discussed.

TABLE 9.6: LOADING A USER PROFILE WHEN THE ROAMING PROFILE IS NOT YET CREATED

SITUATION	WHAT THE WORKSTATION OS DOES
A local profile exists.	The workstation OS loads the local profile and creates a roaming profile directory on the server. Changes to the local profile are updated automatically. When the user logs out, the contents of the local profile directory are copied to the server profile directory.
No local profile exists.	The workstation OS uses a Default User profile to create a local profile. The local profile is updated dynamically. A roaming profile directory is created on the server. When the user logs out, the OS copies the contents of the local profile directory to the server.

NOTE *Although it is possible to specify a roaming profile for a local account on an NT workstation in* DSA.MSC, *it's not really useful unless you are preconfiguring mandatory profiles for the local machine. And it's not really a roaming profile at all in this case, because it cannot be loaded when the user logs in elsewhere. Also, do not expect consistent roaming profile behavior if the user is logging in locally and has a roaming profile path specified on the local machine.*

WARNING   *Note that if you log onto more than one kind of Desktop—that is, if you sometimes log on to workstations running NT 4, sometimes ones running XP, and sometimes ones running 2000, and if you log on with a roaming profile, then you'll see some odd behavior. For example, if you have a profile first created on a 2000 workstation and you log onto an NT 4 workstation, then the icons look odd and you'll get a few error messages. It's not the end of the world, but it can be unsettling to the non-technical user. Or it can just be annoying; for example, when I first set up an XP system on my Active Directory domain, I logged on as my normal domain account, which dragged my profile over to the XP system. XP then set my colors to all of the goofy bright XP colors, giving my Desktop a kind of Playskool look.*

Preconfiguring User Profiles

This idea that people start out from some Default User profile is all well and good, but we'd probably like to gussy that thing up a bit, perhaps customize it to look like a corporate standard or perhaps to simplify the Desktop a bit for our less-techie users or the like. So one way to make things easier for users would be to preconfigure the Default User profile. (It'd be even better to preconfigure one profile that would affect the whole domain, but we'll get there in a minute. For now, let's just see how to make the Default User profile do our bidding on a given workstation.)

To preconfigure the Default User profile, just create a bogus user account and set it up just as you want Default User to be. Then copy that bogus user's account to the Default User account. (First, log off the bogus user account and log back on as a local administrator.)

Now you can copy the contents of the newly created profile over the existing contents of the Default User profile on the local machine, using Control Panel. On a 2000 or XP system, remember that you must first unhide the Default User folder or just set the Explorer settings to show hidden files and folders.

You can also copy that profile folder to a server location, to implement a preconfigured roaming profile. You can even change the name and assign appropriate permissions during the process if you use the System applet to perform the copy rather than Explorer or another file management utility. Although a copy from Explorer would work in some scenarios, you would still have to set the directory permissions separately. Also, in certain other procedures regarding user profiles, the operating system needs to know that we are dealing with *profiles* here, not just files and directories. Get into the habit of using the System applet when dealing with user profiles.

Figure 9.80 shows the User Profiles tab in the System applet. Select the profile you have configured (Corwin, in my case) and choose Copy To. Specify the path for the copy as shown in Figure 9.81, and remember to change the Permitted to Use information or only the bogus user (Corwin) will be able to load the profile.

This procedure can be used for several functions, depending on the path you specify. On the local level, you can copy the customized profile to `C:\Documents and Settings\DEFAULT USER` to preconfigure profiles for all new users on the NT workstation who do not already have a roaming profile stored on a server. It's also possible to copy the customized profile to other workstations if you have administrative rights on them. Take advantage of the fact that the system root directory on all of the workstations is shared as `ADMIN$`. Use the path `\\MACHINENAME\ADMIN$\Documents and Settings\DEFAULT USER` to preconfigure the Default User profile on other workstations.

You can easily overwrite existing user profiles by typing in **Documents and Settings***username,* or the appropriate UNC path; but again, don't forget to set permissions. You also need permission to overwrite the user's existing profile.

FIGURE 9.80

The User Profiles tab in the System applet

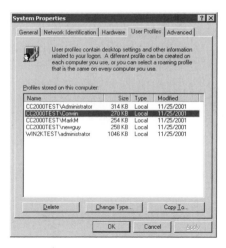

FIGURE 9.81

Copy the profile over Default User

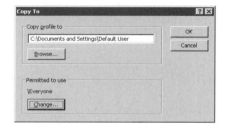

HOW DO I CREATE AND COPY A PRECONFIGURED USER PROFILE?

1. On a Windows 2000 Professional workstation, create a new user account using Manage Computer\System Tools\Local Users and Groups, as you learned earlier in this chapter. For this example, I'll call the new user account Corwin. Corwin doesn't need any particular user rights or group memberships. Either unhide the Default User folder in Documents and Settings or tell Explorer to show hidden files.

2. Log off and log back in to the workstation as Corwin. 2000 will create a user profile for Corwin using the default.

3. Customize Corwin's Desktop. Create any Desktop shortcuts and put those shortcuts into the Start menu. Set up persistent network connections. Using Explorer or by right-clicking the Taskbar and choosing Properties, you can add new program groups or shortcuts to the Start Menu folders. By default, any user can change his profile.

4. When the profile is exactly the way you want it, log out. The system will now save the changes in the user's profile directory (\Documents and Settings\Corwin). Actually, they are flushed to disk as you make changes to the profile.

Continued on next page

HOW DO I CREATE AND COPY A PRECONFIGURED USER PROFILE? *(continued)*

5. Log back on to the workstation as a local administrator. Right-click My Computer and choose Properties to get the System applet (also accessed through Control Panel/System). Choose the User Profiles tab. You should see at least a user profile for your administrator account and for Corwin. If no one else has ever logged in to the workstation, that's all you will see.

6. Use the mouse to highlight the template profile, then choose Copy To. Browse to the location of the directory or type in the path. This may be a local path or a network path. NT will create the profile directory where you specify as long as you have permissions to write to that path. Be sure to give the Everyone group (or the appropriate users or groups) permission to use the profile; Corwin is the only user that has access right now. Choose OK to start the copy process. Figures 9.80 and 9.81 show the dialog boxes you will be using in this step.

7. Log off. You're done!

PRECREATING ROAMING PROFILES

Set up preconfigured roaming profiles by copying the profile to the same UNC path you specified in the user account properties. In other words, if Corwin has never logged onto any system, then you could precreate a profile for him and copy the profile to the path `\\MACHINENAME\PROFILES\Corwin` and also use that path as the user profile path for Corwin's domain account.

Preconfigured local profiles may be set up this way, but you must specify a path in the user's local account information. Do not try to put the directory into the Documents and Settings directory: NT, 2000, or XP have no way of linking that profile with the new user, so the machine will just create a new directory (for example, `Corwin001`).

PRECREATING A *DEFAULT* ROAMING PROFILE

If you want to pre-create roaming profiles for a lot of users, then you don't want to have to put a precreated profile into each user's directory. And you needn't. You can copy the profile to the NET-LOGON share on a domain controller to set up a domainwide Default User profile. You see, if a user is logging in to a domain, the machine first looks for a Default User directory in the NETLOGON share (recall that Win2K provides a NETLOGON share in `\WINNT\SYSVOL\sysvol\`*domainname*`\SCRIPTS` to support Windows 95/98 and NT clients) of the authenticating domain controller. Only if no Default User directory is found in the NETLOGON directory does the machine use the local Default User information. If a DEFAULT USER directory exists in this network path (where logon scripts and system policies are also stored), all new domain users with NT workstations will use this directory as the domainwide Default User template, instead of using the local Default User directory. Specify the path as `\\MACHINENAME\SYSVOL\`*domainname*`\SCRIPTS\DEFAULT USER`. Alternatively, you can save the profile directly to the NETLOGON share (`\\MACHINENAME\NETLOGON\DEFAULT USER`) if you are in the Administrator group (by default, the Everyone group has Read permission only to the share, while the Administrator group has Full Control permission). Be sure to name the directory Default User and grant permission to Everyone (or another appropriate group) to use the profile.

In any of the scenarios described above, users can still modify their own profiles once they are created. A variation of this procedure is used to set up mandatory profiles; it will be discussed later.

EDITING THE *NTUSER.DAT* HIVE FILE IN NT 4

You can change many user profile settings by editing the contents of the folders or by configuring the Desktop. However, if you want to place restrictions on the preconfigured Default User or roaming profile to protect the system from inexperienced users, you will need to edit the hive file (NTUSER.DAT) of the template profile. To do this, you will need a Registry-editing tool.

WARNING   *As always, do not edit the Registry unless you really know what you're doing. Editing the Registry can have disastrous consequences: you could ruin your system configuration and have to reinstall your whole operating system. Be careful!*

NOTE   *Unfortunately, you cannot log in as a user named Default User and make changes directly to the Default User profile. If you try it, the operating system will get really confused. If you create a user DEFAULT USER and set the profile path in User Manager as %SYSTEMROOT%\PROFILES\DEFAULT USER, of course the OS will use the* Default User *directory to create the profile. The OS will also create a* DEFAULT USER.000 *profile directory for the user, and any changes you make to the profile while logged in as DEFAULT USER will not be saved to the* Default User *directory. In fact, they won't be saved to* DEFAULT USER.000, *either. You might even find that changes the user makes do not even apply on the Desktop!*

USING *REGEDT32.EXE*

To edit user profiles using REGEDT32.EXE, open HKEY_USERS, as shown in Figure 9.82. Typically HKEY_USERS only contains two keys: .DEFAULT and the SID of the user currently logged in. The key .DEFAULT is not the Default User hive file, as you might think. That is located in \Documents and Settings\PROFILES\DEFAULT USER\NTUSER.DAT. The hive file represented in Figure 9.82 is loaded from C:\WINNT\SYSTEM32\CONFIG\.DEFAULT and is known as the *system default profile*. Microsoft describes it as the profile in effect when nobody is logged in. This seems to be a dangling chromosome from NT 3.51 profiles, when each profile was its own hive file.

The system default and Default User profiles are independent of each other. That is, changing the color scheme in the Registry for the .DEFAULT hive will not affect the Default User profile hive in Documents and Settings. Otherwise, when I set the system default (.DEFAULT) profile to use some neat (I mean practical and informative) bitmap wallpaper, any user who logged in without an already established profile would also get stuck with my wallpaper.

FIGURE 9.82

HKEY_USERS subkey

NOTE *Have you ever wanted to change that default Windows bitmap you see on the screen when nobody is logged in? Well, that bitmap is the wallpaper for the SYSTEM profile (also known as the system default profile). Since SYSTEM is a user (or at least an entity) under NT, it makes sense that SYSTEM should have a profile, right? The SYSTEM default profile is the profile in effect when no one is logged in (you see the Ctrl+Alt+Del login dialog box). Simply use a Registry editor such as* REGEDT32.EXE *or* REGEDIT *to specify different wallpaper. The entry is found in* HKEY_USERS\.DEFAULT\CONTROL PANEL\DESKTOP. *Edit the value entry for Wallpaper, specifying the full path of the bitmap that tickles your fancy as the value of the string. You will be editing the hive file* %SYSTEMROOT%\SYSTEM32\CONFIG\DEFAULT. *Screensavers in effect when no one is logged in can be specified in the same way. By the way, this works for Win2K systems as well.*

You can use REGEDT32 to edit a user profile other than the system default and the profile that is actively loaded. Be sure to use REGEDT32—REGEDIT can't do this job! It's been around since NT 3.1, pretty much unchanged. (In fact, this upcoming example is from NT 4. It works the same in 2000 or XP.) And one more point: You don't *have* to do the following Registry hacks to control how a profile gets loaded. System and group policies can handle all of that stuff; look back to the group policies section for more info or read the section on NT 4's system policies on the CD if you're using NT 4 Desktops.

Load the hive file using the Load Hive option from the Registry menu (Figure 9.83). This may be the NTUSER.DAT file from the Default User profile directory or any NTUSER.DAT file; you can browse for it (Figure 9.84). NT will prompt you for a temporary key name (Figure 9.85) and will then load the hive into the Registry Editor, as shown in Figure 9.86. Make changes to the Registry settings of the Default User profile. To finish up, select the loaded hive and choose Unload Hive from the Registry menu to save changes and clear the hive from the Registry Editor.

FIGURE 9.83

Loading the hive in REGEDIT.EXE

FIGURE 9.84

Browsing to find the hive file

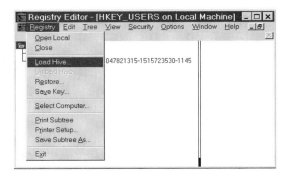

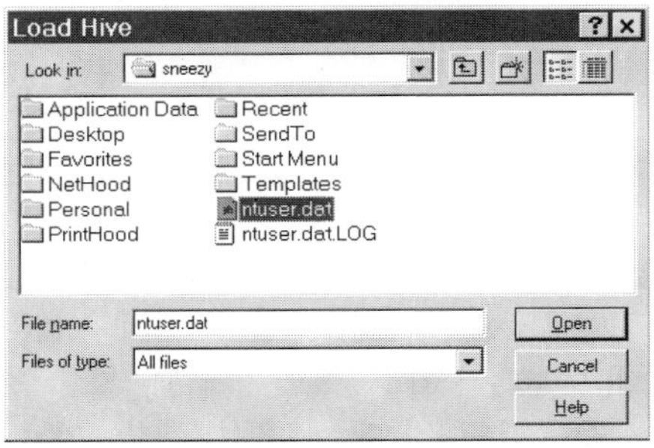

FIGURE 9.85

Assigning a tempo-
rary key name

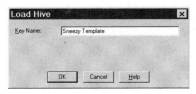

FIGURE 9.86

The hive is loaded.

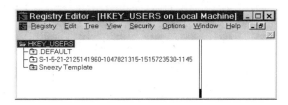

So which changes do you make once the hive is loaded? Ah, that is the real question. You might configure all profiles to wait for logon scripts to execute before starting the user's shell. That way, any drive mappings or environmental variables specified in the logon script will take precedence over those in the user's profile. This entry is called `RunLogonScriptSync` (run logon scripts synchronously) and is found in `HKEY_USERS\KEYNAME\SOFTWARE\MICROSOFT\WINDOWS NT\CURRENTVERSION\WINLOGON` (Figure 9.87). Although I could suggest a couple of other Registry entries to modify, the fact is that `REGEDT32.EXE` and `REGEDIT.EXE` are not all that user-friendly. Without spending copious amounts of our time reading Registry documentation (which is not always helpful) and experimenting, we do not know what is possible. We need a GUI Registry Editor. At this point, the System Policy Editor steps back onto the scene.

FIGURE 9.87

The `RunLogon-`
`ScriptSync` entry

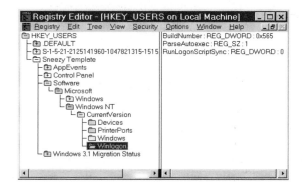

NT 4 SYSTEM POLICY EDITOR TO THE RESCUE

Instead of trying to hack everything out in `REGEDT32.EXE`, you can use the System Policy Editor to place restrictions directly on the profile. Run the System Policy Editor (`POLEDIT.EXE`) while logged in as the template user SNEEZY. In this scenario, you will be using the Policy Editor as a user-friendly Registry Editor, instead of as a tool to impose system policies on your network.

Choose File/Open Registry/Local User, as shown in Figures 9.88 and 9.89. Now you can actually read about your options in English (Figure 9.90). Apply your restrictions. You'll notice that you can take away the Run, Find, and Settings in the Start menu, as well as many other potentially dangerous built-in options on the Desktop. You'd better be careful, though: Changes will apply immediately to the open profile you are configuring, so you might want to make that the last thing you do when configuring the profile. Also, don't touch Local Computer or you will be making changes to your other local hive files (like the System hive). These restrictions are written to the Registry.

FIGURE 9.88

Open local Registry

FIGURE 9.89

Local User/Local Registry

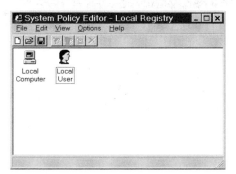

You can now go back and view the edits by looking under HKEY_CURRENT_USER\SOFTWARE\MICROSOFT\WINDOWS\CURRENTVERSION\POLICIES\EXPLORER (Figure 9.91). When you finish, close POLEDIT.EXE, log out, log back in as an administrator, and follow the steps outlined earlier to copy the profile, restrictions and all, to the Default User or Roaming Profile path.

FIGURE 9.90

Local User proper-
ties in
`POLEDIT.EXE`

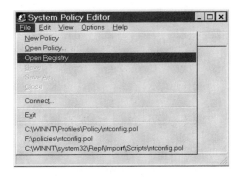

FIGURE 9.91

REGEDIT32 poli-
cies subkey

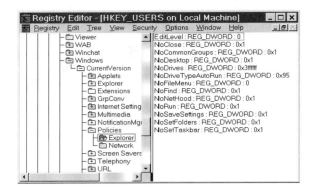

If you are configuring a domainwide default profile, log in to the domain as a new user; you will get the preconfigured default profile and any restrictions you built in. This will be a good opportunity to inspect your work and look for any loopholes or problems. And remember to create your own profile or an administrator profile before doing this stuff, or it will apply to you as well!

THE BAD NEWS ABOUT NT 4 PRECONFIGURED DEFAULT PROFILES

The problem with a "powerless, preconfigured" Default User profile becomes apparent when a new administrator or some such person logs in for the first time. Your new administrator's profile will be created from this template, and she will be the irritated but unintentional recipient of a highly restricted Desktop (oops). In this case, you would need to keep a stash of unrestricted profiles in reserve somewhere (preconfigure them or make a copy of an untouched Default User profile). Users who should not get these powerless, preconfigured profiles must have unrestricted profiles specifically assigned to them. Furthermore, these profiles will have to exist in the network path specified in User Manager or User Manager for Domains before the user ever logs in. If she has already logged in and received the altered Default User profile, you have to delete her profile from the local machine and from the server to remedy the situation. In other words, the user will need to start over with a new profile and will lose any changes made to customize her Desktop. (That's why people tend not to use profiles to restrict user behavior—they use policies instead.)

Problems with Preconfigured and Roaming Profiles

As you create profiles for users or simply allow user's to have roaming profiles, keep in mind that a user profile includes settings on screen placement, window sizes, and color schemes. The display adapters and monitors on the workstations should be taken into consideration. If Corwin has a 21-inch monitor with the latest and greatest AGP card and sets up his Desktop accordingly, he may get an unpleasant surprise when he logs in to Eric's machine equipped with lesser video capabilities. When preconfiguring a profile for a user, sit at a computer that has the same video capabilities as the user's primary workstation. If you are configuring a Default User profile or one that will be used by multiple users, those workstations must have the same video capabilities. Alternately, you can use the lowest common denominators to ensure that the settings will work on all platforms.

A Special Note about Shortcuts and Link Tracking   Video problems are not all of it. If you are installing applications on the Desktop, always use default installation directories so that short-cuts created will resolve more smoothly. Also, keep in mind that NT shortcuts will first attempt to resolve using the *link tracking method*, which is the *absolute* path for the shortcut. Failing that, the shortcut will try to resolve with the *search method*, which means it will search the local drive. In other words, if you created a shortcut to Notepad on \\WOMBAT, saved the profile as a roaming profile, then sat down and logged in at \\POLECAT, the shortcut would first try to resolve to \\WOMBAT\WINNT\SYSTEM32\NOTEPAD.EXE. If the user cannot connect to \\WOMBAT, the system will supposedly search for the program in %Systemroot%\SYSTEM32\NOTEPAD.EXE. But if \\WOMBAT exists, the user is prompted for a username and password to access \\WOMBAT\C$, the hidden drive share that's reserved for remote administration. This leaves users scratching their heads, saying, "What did I do?"—or worse, calling the help desk to ask, "What did you do?" To prevent this problem, when creating shortcuts, use expandable variables (such as %WINDIR%, %SYSTEM-ROOT%) whenever possible. Luckily, shortcuts work just fine when they point to a shared directory on the server, as long as they are created properly and permissions are appropriate.

Another consideration to keep in mind is that when users on your network regularly move from one NT machine to another, every machine they use will store a copy of their local profile. These will eventually add up and consume a chunk of disk space. An administrator can delete local profiles periodically, using the Delete option in the User Profiles tab of the System applet. You may also use System Policy Editor to compel the NT workstations to delete cached copies of roaming profiles when the user logs out, as shown in Figure 9.92. This is a machine-specific setting, that is implemented in the Registry in HKEY_LOCAL_MACHINE\SOFTWARE\MICROSOFT\WINDOWS NT\CURRENTVERSION\ WINLOGON. The name of the value entry should be DeleteRoamingCache, with a datatype REG_DWORD and a value of 1; it should read

```
DeleteRoamingCache:REG _DWORD:1
```

Active Directory's group policies have a policy like this also; in the GP editor, look in Computer Configuration\Administrative Templates\System\Logon, and there's a policy named Delete Cached Copies of Roaming Profiles.

Finally, accessing roaming profiles across a WAN link is not recommended. Whenever possible, load profiles from a server locally. Besides eating up network bandwidth (when the profile is sucked off the server at logon and copied back to the server at logoff), time-out intervals for slow connections will cause numerous problems in synchronizing the local and server copies of the profiles.

FIGURE 9.92

Delete roaming cache

"CACHED" PROFILES: A TIP

Talking of mandatory profiles reminded me of a peculiar behavior of NT, one that may bedevil you if you're extremely security conscious.

Suppose I've given you an NT 4 workstation (again, 2000 or XP will work the same way) named \\PC027, but I've not created a local account for you. Instead, I've given you a domain account on the SONGBIRDS domain and told you to log in from that. Thus, every morning you sit down at your workstation and tell your machine that you want to log in from a SONGBIRDS account, not a PC027 account. That is, you want your workstation's Local Security Authority *not* to look in your workstation's SAM but rather to use NETLOGON to communicate with one of the DCs in SONGBIRDS, and then to ask one of those controllers to look up your user account in the domain SAM.

Sounds good—but what about those times when you get that dratted "No domain controller found" error message? If your workstation's NETLOGON can't find a DC, it seems that there's no way for your local LSA to establish your credentials. That seems to mean also that if there's no DC around, you can't get on your workstation, doesn't it? Or does it?

The first time this happened to me, I was somewhat taken aback to see that my NT workstation logged me in *anyway*, using "cached credentials." The idea is that, if you got in all right *yesterday*, we'll give you the benefit of the doubt *today*, even if the local LSA *can't* find a DC. Cool, eh? Well, yes, it might be cool for many—but the more security-conscious among us might be quite unhappy about the idea that if a network administrator modifies or deletes your account on Tuesday, by Wednesday your workstation might not know about it.

Fortunately, there's a Registry setting that you can use to make a workstation require a domain logon. Just go to HKEY_LOCAL_MACHINE\Software\Microsoft\Windows NT\CurrentVersion\Winlogon and create a value entry called CachedLogonsCount, of type REG_DWORD, and set its value to 0. Make this change on every NT workstation on which you want to require strict logons. And if making all of those Registry changes sounds like a lot of work, stay tuned—a little later I'll show you how to use a tool called *system policies*, a neat way to let you remotely (and automatically) control Registries.

NOTE   DELPROF.EXE, *a command-line utility included in the NT Workstation and NT Server Resource Kits, allows administrators to delete user profiles on a local or remote computer running any version of Windows NT through 4, but not Windows 95/98. Of particular interest is the utility's ability to delete profiles that have been inactive for x number of days.*

Mandatory Profiles

So far in this discussion, all types of user profiles allowed users to make changes to customize their own profile (assuming you did not set up System Policy Editor to discard changed settings at logoff). Another option for controlling user profiles is to assign a *mandatory profile* to the user or to a group of users.

NOTE   *I don't really recommend using mandatory profiles. Their goal is to lock down a user's Desktop and, as I've indicated before, the better tool for that is policies, not profiles. But I include information about them for the sake of completeness.*

A mandatory profile is a read-only profile that the user must use. Mandatory profiles are a tad more work because the profile must exist ahead of time and must exist in the path you point to or the user cannot log in. Remember, with roaming profiles, we could just let NT copy the profile to the network path unless we wanted Corwin to use a profile we created for him.

The mandatory profile is a type of roaming profile, in that you must specify a profile path in the user's account information. To create a mandatory profile directory, name it with the extension .MAN (for example, \\ALDEBARAN\PROFILES\Corwin.MAN). This tells the operating system that the profile is mandatory and that the user will not be able to log in if the profile is unavailable. In that case, the user will see a dialog box that says "Unable to log you in because your mandatory profile is not available. Please contact your administrator."

Also, rename the NTUSER.DAT file to NTUSER.MAN so that the user cannot save changes to the profile. Once the local profile is created on the workstation, the locally created copy of the profile will also be read-only. This does not set permissions on the profile *per se*, so it works on both FAT and NTFS. Nor does changing the name to NTUSER.MAN set the read-only attribute on the file. It's just a special extension for the profile that tells NT not to save changes at logoff (changes will apply while the user is logged in but will be lost when the user logs out). This feature is useful if you want to assign one profile to a group of users and you do not want these users to be able to save changes. In other words, everybody shares a copy of the same profile, and it is protected against users' "personal touches."

NOTE   *Strangely enough, if the* .MAN *directory does exist in the specified path, but permissions on the directory do not grant at least read access to the user, that user will be able to log in using a default profile. The user encounters the following message (this was actually a problem in the* USERENV.DLL *and is corrected in Service Pack 3): "You do not have permission to access your central profile located at* \\SERVERNAME\SHARENAME\USERNAME.MAN. *The operating system is attempting to log you on with your local profile."*

The following are your options for setting up mandatory profiles:

Use a Read-Only Profile   Simply rename the file NTUSER.DAT to *NTUSER.MAN* before you assign the profile to the user or users. Keep in mind that when a user first logs in, NT does not know that this user's profile is a mandatory profile (because the directory name is *USERNAME*, not

USERNAME.MAN). If the profile is unavailable, the system will load a local or default profile. However, once the system loads the mandatory profile from the profile path, the System applet on the workstation shows the profile as mandatory. The user or users will not be able to save changes to the Desktop. At this point, if the network profile becomes unavailable, the system will load the local profile, but because NT now considers it a mandatory profile, changes will not be saved.

Incidentally, renaming the NTUSER.DAT file to NTUSER.MAN can be done as an afterthought, as well. In other words, if a user formally has a local and configurable profile, you can go to the C:\WINNT\PROFILES\USERNAME directory and rename the hive file. It will be read-only from that point on.

Force the User to Load a Particular Profile   If you specify the directory path on the server as DIRECTORYNAME.MAN but you do not rename the hive file to NTUSER.MAN, the operating system will not see it as a mandatory profile. If the hive file is not named NTUSER.MAN, the workstation will classify it merely as a roaming profile. At logon, however, the user will not be able to log in if the profile directory does not exist in the specified path. Users can make changes to their Desktops, however, since it's not a real mandatory profile to NT.

Create a Read-Only Profile That Must Be Used   Specify the directory name as DIRECTORY-NAME.MAN and rename the NTUSER.DAT file to *NTUSER.MAN*. This is ideal if you want to force users to load a profile off the network and you want to prevent them from making any changes.

How Do I Configure a Mandatory Profile?

Mandatory profiles are created in much the same way preconfigured profiles are created. Mandatory profiles can be assigned to individual users or to groups. Here is how to create a shared mandatory profile and assign it to everyone in a particular group (Research Users):

1. Create a user, log in as that user, and set up the Desktop.

2. Apply any restrictions you want at the time, using the System Policy Editor as described earlier. Log off.

3. Log back on to the machine as an administrator.

4. Use the System applet (under Control Panel/System/User Profiles) to select the profile and copy it to a shared directory on the network, naming it *SOMETHING*.MAN. Remember to set permissions to allow your user (or a group) at least Read and Execute access to the profile and its contents. As you can see in the following Copy To dialog box, I named the directory researchusers.man and assigned permissions to the group Research Users.

5. Use Explorer or your favorite file management tool to rename the copied NTUSER.DAT file to NTUSER.MAN.

6. In the properties sheet for the user account, fill in the profile directory path, pointing to your mandatory profile directory.

7. You are now ready to have users log in and receive their mandatory profiles.

Continued on next page

HOW DO I CONFIGURE A MANDATORY PROFILE? *(continued)*

You can see what profiles are saved on a local NT machine, and what type they are, in the System applet—the same place you go to copy profiles. The following properties sheet shows all three types on a machine:

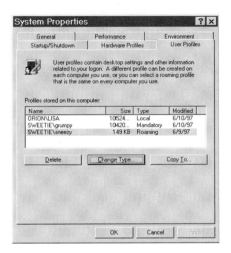

Setting Up a Group Template Profile

As you can see, it's relatively easy to assign "shared" profiles to users and groups. However, any time two or more users are pulling their profiles from the same profile directory, they should be pulling a mandatory profile. Otherwise, changes made by each user to the group profile directory on the server will be saved. Happy and Eric will have to deal with Corwin's Eggplant color scheme or Ninja Turtles icons.

How much more trouble is it to preconfigure and assign profiles based on, say, group membership, which will then be under the control of the individual user? This would not be a mandatory profile but just a point of departure for the user. Actually, it's a lot more trouble. Sure, you can make profile templates for groups, but how do you assign them and still let users customize the Desktop according to their own preferences or needs? Let's see how to do this.

ASSIGNING USER-CONFIGURABLE PROFILES TO GROUPS

If you use the standard preconfigured user profile procedure, follow these steps.

First, make group template profiles by creating three security groups (CLEAVERS, ADAMS, and CLAMPETTS). Then create three bogus group member accounts, naming them, for instance, CLAMPETTS TEMPLATE, ADAMS TEMPLATE, and CLEAVERS TEMPLATE (you were getting pretty tired of Corwin and Eric, weren't you?). Log on and off as each bogus user, and then configure the group profiles.

Before you add Ward or June user to the CLEAVERS group, open the System applet and copy the CLEAVERS group template profile to a shared profile directory, renaming it after the new user you are about to create. Then create the user, specifying his profile path as *MACHINENAME*\ *PROFILESHARENAME**USERNAME*, where *PROFILESHARENAME* is the directory where you copied the profile.

This process is not complicated overall, but you do have to remember to copy a new profile to the shared directory and assign the profile to that specific user each time you create a new account.

How Does an NT 4 Client Choose between Local, Roaming, and Mandatory Profiles?

In all of this discussion about locally cached profiles, roaming profiles stored on a server, and mandatory profiles, it's important to understand the order in which NT, 2000, or XP look for a profile and how the system chooses among the three. Plus, there are a couple of considerations that I haven't yet explained. To make this simple, let's view the scenarios from two perspectives: that of a user who has never before logged in to that workstation (Morticia), and that of a user who has logged in to the machine already (Gomez).

Morticia logs in to her newly assigned Windows 2000 workstation. Assume that there is no profile path specified for Morticia in her account information. She only has a local profile. The workstation must create a profile for her from a `Default User` directory. If Morticia is logging in to a Win2K domain, the operating system will first look in the `NETLOGON` share for a Default User profile (it has to look there anyway for the logon script; why not just kill two birds with one stone?). There's no `Default User` directory in the `NETLOGON` share? Oh well, the system will just have to use the Default User info from the local machine.

If there *is* a profile path specified for her account, however, the system looks in that path for the profile directory. If the profile exists, the Desktop loads it and uses it to make a local copy. This may be a roaming or a mandatory profile. If no profile exists in the path and the path was indicated as mandatory—\\SERVERNAME\SHARENAME*USERNAME*.MAN, for example—the user will not be allowed to log in at all! If there is no profile in the specified path and a roaming profile is specified (\\SERVERNAME\SHARENAME*USERNAME*), the workstation will make one. Again, for a Win2K domain logon, the system first checks in `NETLOGON`. If no `Default User` directory is found there, the system creates Morticia's profile from the local `Default User` directory.

So far, so good. Now let's tackle Gomez, who has been using his workstation for a few weeks already. If no profile is specified in his account information, nothing changes for Gomez. He continues to use his locally stored profile.

On the other hand, if by chance you decide to implement roaming profiles one evening or weekend and Gomez comes in the next morning and logs in, his workstation has to check a few things. First, if a profile path exists in the account info, his workstation must first check to see if Gomez has changed his roaming profile type back to local. Aha! You see, Gomez might have grown tired of waiting for his roaming profile to load off the server and decided to tell his workstation not to bother, to just use the local copy all the time. He can do this by opening the System applet and the User Profiles tab, selecting his own profile, and choosing Change Type. Gomez then sees the dialog box shown in Figure 9.93. Gomez could not do this if the profile was mandatory, and of course, you cannot change a local profile to a roaming profile unless you are changing it *back* to a roaming profile.

FIGURE 9.93

Changing a user profile from roaming to local

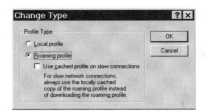

Any user may change an unrestricted roaming profile back to local and may also choose the option to automatically "Use cached profile on slow connections." If Gomez checks that box, he's saying to his operating system, "If there is a slow network connection, just go ahead and load my local copy and don't bother me." What qualifies as a slow connection? That depends on an interval set in the Registry, called `SlowLinkTimeout`. The default interval is two seconds. Generally, if the two-second interval is exceeded, Gomez will see a dialog box stating that a slow network connection has been detected and asking whether to load the local or the roaming profile. By default, Gomez has 30 seconds to choose (that value is determined by a Registry entry called `ProfileDlgTimeout`), after which time the system will load the local profile. But if Gomez enables the option to "use cached profile on slow connections," the workstation will automatically load the local profile without asking Gomez. Hmmm.

The Registry entries affecting detection of slow network connections are found in `HKEY_LOCAL_MACHINE\SOFTWARE\MICROSOFT\WINDOWS NT\CURRENTVERSION\WINLOGON`. All of the following values can be set using the System Policy Editor:

SlowLinkDetectEnabled   Has a data type of `REG_DWORD` and possible values of 0 (disabled) or 1 (enabled). Slow-link detection is enabled by default, and the system is told to be aware of slow network connections.

SlowLinkTimeOut   Has a datatype of `REG_DWORD` and a default value of 2000 (2 seconds expressed in milliseconds). Possible values are 0–120,000 (up to 2 minutes). When this threshold is exceeded and `SlowLinkDetectEnabled` is set to 1, users can log in by using a local profile instead of the roaming profile.

ProfileDlgTimeOut   Has a datatype of `REG_DWORD` and a default value of 30 (expressed in seconds). This value determines how many seconds a user has to choose between a local or server-based profile when the value of `SlowLinkTimeOut` is exceeded.

Assuming that there is no slow network connection and assuming Gomez has not changed his roaming profile back to a local profile (he hasn't had a chance yet, right?), the system will check to see whether (1) the profile is mandatory or (2) the profile on the server is more current.

If either (1) or (2) is true, the system will load the server copy. If neither is true, then Gomez gets a pesky dialog box. You see, if (2) is not true, then the profile on the server is not more current than the local copy. This implies that there was a problem in synchronizing the profiles the last time Gomez logged out. So the operating system will announce that the local profile is more recent than the network profile and will ask if Gomez wants to load the local instead.

Whew! That was a bit complex, so maybe the following flow charts will help. Figures 9.94 and 9.95 describe Morticia (new user to the workstation, with local profile and roaming profile), and Figure 9.96 follows Gomez (an existing user with locally stored profile). Finally, I've thrown in Figure 9.97 to show how a user's profile is saved at logoff.

FIGURE 9.94

How a new user gets a local profile

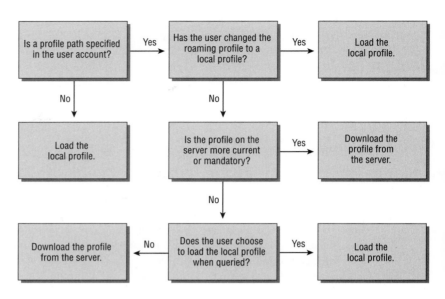

FIGURE 9.95

How a new user gets a roaming profile

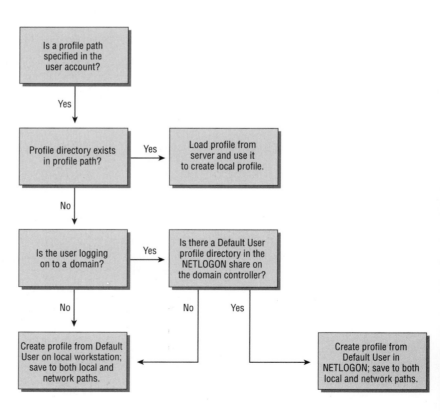

FIGURE 9.96

How a user with a local profile gets a roaming profile

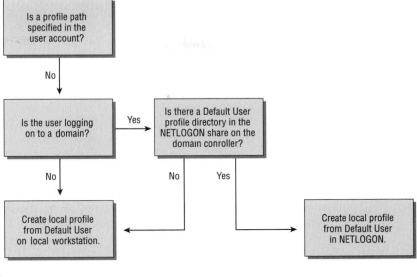

FIGURE 9.97

How user profiles are saved at logoff

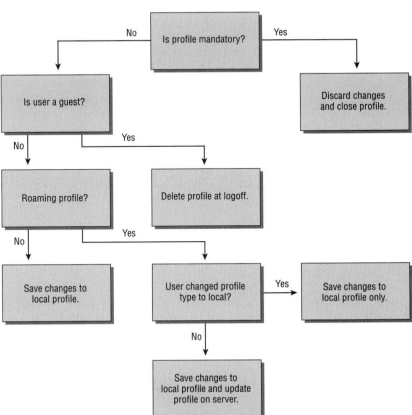

Which Type of Profile Is Right for My Network?

Now that you are a Microsoft user profile guru, you'll need to decide what kind of profiles to implement on your network. Even if you do nothing, you are still making a choice to let users just keep local profiles. To help you decide, the following paragraphs summarize the pros and cons of the different types of profiles:

Local Profiles Only   Local profiles may be the best choice in a mixed client environment or where users don't need to roam. Windows 95/98 profiles are not interchangeable with NT/2000/XP Workstation profiles, though the Desktop is similar, so users moving from one client OS to another need *either* local profiles only *or* two roaming profiles. (Do you feel a migraine coming on?) This option has the lowest administrative overhead and offers the fewest options for preconfiguring profiles and controlling Desktops. However, you can still use System Policy Editor to configure Desktops and impose restrictive policies without implementing roaming profiles.

Roaming Profiles   A roaming profile has two major benefits: mobility and fault tolerance. Not only can users move from Desktop to Desktop and have their preferred settings follow them, they also have a "backup" of their profile stored on the server. If you have to reinstall the workstation, the user doesn't necessarily have to reconfigure the Desktop. Plus, you can let NT create the profile for you as long as there are no special settings to hand out to users.

This is also the option to use if you want profiles to be centrally located and controlled. The downside is that roaming profiles may follow you to another machine but may not work flawlessly once they are downloaded. Shortcuts to applications that exist only on the user's "home workstation" and different video adapters and monitors are only two of the possible problems users may encounter. Also, roaming profiles shooting across your Ethernet every time a user logs in or out will generate more traffic and slow down user logons. If it's a consideration at 10Mbps, think of the problems if you have an ISDN connection at 64Kbps.

Finally, remember that NT, 2000, or XP will store a local copy of the profile for every user that logs in to a given machine. If users roam and roam and roam, they leave copies behind, taking up hard drive space as well as presenting a security issue (my Desktop may have a few items on it I don't want to leave behind). To address this problem, set up the machines to delete cached copies of roaming profiles.

Mandatory Profiles   Mandatory profiles, because they are also roaming profiles, have the benefit of being mobile and fault tolerant. They can also be centrally located and controlled, like roaming profiles. Plus, mandatory profiles are the only way you can force a user to load a particular profile. Because it is read-only, users can share a profile; you keep fewer profiles stored on the server instead of one for every single user. While mandatory profiles offer more control than roaming profiles, they also require more setup on your part. You must manually create a mandatory profile and place it in a network path; the operating system can't create a mandatory profile for you. Finally, if a user attempts to log in and the mandatory profile is unavailable, NT will not allow the user to log in. This prevents a malicious user from logging in with the Default User profile and running amok, but it can also be a drawback if you are preventing a legitimate user from logging in, thus causing loss of productivity in the organization.

Network Default User Profile   One of the best things about a domainwide Default User profile is that it can be implemented in conjunction with roaming profiles. This offers a great way to preconfigure all new user profiles, and although it does not help you hand out special program groups to, say, the accounting department, it can be used as a point of departure. You can use the System Policy Editor to hand out custom Start menu items to group members. However, if you place heinous restrictions on the Default User profile in the NETLOGON share, you'll have to create a special roaming profile and assign it to folks who shouldn't get the restrictions (such as new MIS employees).

IMPLEMENTING USER PROFILES: AN EXAMPLE

Let's see what we've learned by looking at a sample situation and determining the best way to use profiles.

Suppose you manage several computer labs at a university, and each lab has 35–100 NT 4, 2000, or XP workstations. Up to 10,000 students at the university, who all have accounts on the university-wide system, visit various labs using various machines. A few students cause problems in the network. Some of these students are malicious, while some are just inexperienced. If you stand by and do nothing, users will leave profiles behind when they log out. You'll have to periodically delete profiles. If you allow users to have access to all possible tools on the Desktop, administrative overhead increases as you troubleshoot problems and reinstall the OS on the workstations.

Solution #1: Preconfigure a Domainwide Default User Profile

With this solution, you may have to create more than one domainwide Default User profile if user accounts are in multiple domains. Restrict profiles as necessary, assign roaming profiles, and delete cached copies of roaming profiles using System Policy Editor or the Resource Kit utility, DELPROF.EXE.

This is a good solution, but it poses one big problem. Even if users have restrictions placed on the profile, with roaming profiles for every user, the network servers will hold thousands of copies of the very same profile. Not only that, but savvy users may be able to change their own Registry settings and break free of restrictions.

Actually, there is a very simple solution to the profile detritus problem. Rather than going to the trouble of setting up a policy to delete cached copies of roaming profiles, editing the Registry of every machine, or running DELPROF.EXE at regular intervals, you can make every user a guest at the local machines in the lab. Although this approach has several other implications that might make it unfeasible for your situation, it would take care of profile buildup. Members of the Guests group are not allowed to keep local profiles unless they are also members of the Users group.

Solution #2: Create a Shared Mandatory Profile

A better solution is to create a restricted profile directory, name it USERS.MAN, rename the hive file to NTUSER.MAN, and assign this as a shared mandatory profile to all users. You'll also need to delete cached copies of roaming profiles. This way, even if a user manages to edit the Registry settings to remove the restrictions, changes will be discarded at logoff. You also save space on the network servers.

WARNING   *There is one possible problem with this solution, if you're still using NT 4: If many students try to download the mandatory profile at exactly the same time, they may experience sharing violations (NT 4 Service Pack 2 fixed this problem).*

DISTRIBUTING USER PROFILES

You may also want to keep several copies of the mandatory profile (for example, one in each lab) for load balancing. There is a way to distribute user profiles across domain controllers using the undocumented environment variable %LOGONSERVER%: You create a share of the same name on each DC, put the mandatory profiles into each of the shared directories, then indicate the profile path in account properties as something like \\%LOGONSERVER%\PROFILES\USERS.MAN. To prevent major profile synchronization problems, don't use this variable with regular roaming profiles; use it only with mandatory profiles.

What if you don't want to store profiles on the DCs, or what if not every lab has one? If the students logged in at the same lab every time, there wouldn't be any problem. You could just point to the local server for that lab in the user account's information. Unfortunately, you can't count on such regularity.

You can tell the workstation where to look for the profile by creating a new environmental variable on each of the workstations. The new environmental variable will be %SERVERNAME% and will point to the local lab server keeping the mandatory profile.

HOW DO I MAKE USERS LOAD PROFILES FROM LOCAL SERVERS?

Use the System applet's Environment tab to set a system variable pointing to the local server, as shown in the following System properties sheet. Fill in the information as shown. In this case, the local lab server will be LAB01FSUNC. (Do not include % signs or \\ as part of the variable.) Choose the Set button and click OK. The new variable will be set, but you will need to restart the computer before these settings take effect (since the operating system reads the system variables at start-up).

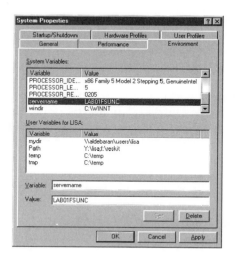

Once you have defined the %SERVERNAME% variable on each of the workstations (REGINI.EXE, a Resource Kit utility, can be pretty handy for that type of thing), created a share of the same name on each server, and copied the mandatory profiles to those shared directories, you can then indicate the profile path in the user's account properties as \\%SERVERNAME%\PROFILES\USERS.MAN.

Comparing Windows NT 3.51, NT 4, and 95/98 Profiles

As described in the preceding sections, there's a lot that can be done with NT 4 user profiles in an NT/Win2K Server environment. However, in case you are not yet managing a network of just NT 4 clients, let's round out our discussion with a quick rundown of the differences between NT 3.51, NT 4, and Windows 95/98 user profiles. The important thing to keep in mind is that Windows 95/98, NT 3.51, and NT 4 profiles are not cross-platform profiles. In other words, a user who requires a roaming profile and customarily sits at several types of clients would need a Windows 95/98 profile *and* an NT profile for each version.

NT 3.51 PROFILES

In NT 3.51, each user profile is a single hive file (found in `%SYSTEMROOT%\SYSTEM32\ CONFIG`), and profiles are stored with the rest of the Registry hive files (see Figure 9.98). Instead of a bunch of folders and a hive file, everything is included in the one file, for example, LISA000.

FIGURE 9.98

NT 3.51 user profile

NT 3.51 supports per-user profiles (equivalent to roaming profiles) and mandatory profiles. The profile path for an NT 3.51 personal profile would be specified as `\\SERVERNAME\SHARENAME\ USERNAME.USR` in the User Manager for Domains, and for a mandatory profile, `\\SERVERNAME\ SHARENAME\FILENAME.MAN`.

Because there was no System Policy Editor under NT 3.51, options for restricting profiles were limited. NT 3.51 did provide a tool called User Profile Editor (`UPEDIT.EXE`), shown in Figure 9.99, which allowed you to log in as your bogus user, configure the Desktop, and save a configured profile with a skimpy set of restrictions to the current user or system default. This was also the tool used to save the profile to a specified path when implementing per-user or mandatory profiles.

NT 4 profiles use the Windows 95/98 profile structure, so NT 3.51 profiles will be converted to NT 4 profiles when upgrading from 3.51 to NT 4. NT 3.51 per-user profiles were simply files, whereas NT 4 profiles are entire directories, so NT 3.51 profiles formerly named `USERNAME.USR`, for example, will be converted to a directory called *USERNAME.PDS*. Likewise, mandatory profiles named `USER.MAN` will be converted to a directory called `USER.PDM`. If a user is in a mixed environment, she will have a separate profile for each version, and they will not be synchronized (changes made to one won't show up in the other) if changes are made after the initial migration.

FIGURE 9.99

User Profile Editor

WINDOWS 95/98 PROFILES

In Windows 95/98, individual profiles are not created by default but must be enabled in Control Panel/Passwords. If roaming profiles are enabled on the Windows 95/98 machine, they will be stored automatically in the user's home directory and will then operate in the same way as the NT Workstation profiles. You need not specify a profile path for the user in Active Directory Users and Computers.

Individual mandatory profiles can be used in Windows 95/98, but shared mandatory profiles cannot. For this reason, the administrator must create a profile for each user and copy it to that user's home directory.

The structure of a Windows 95/98 user profile contains differences from an NT user profile. Instead of an `NTUSER.DAT` file, Windows 95/98 has a `USER.DAT` file. Instead of `NTUSER.DAT.LOG` (the log file that stores changes to the `NTUSER.DAT` file), Windows 95/98 uses a file called `USER.DA0`. These two files are not exact equivalents. Windows 95/98 uses `USER.DA0` as a "backup," writing a copy of `USER.DAT` to `USER.DA0` every time the user logs out. NT 4 uses `NTUSER.DAT.LOG` as a transaction log file to protect the hive file while it is being updated. To create a read-only mandatory profile, rename the 95/98 `USER.DAT` file to `USER.MAN`. NT 4 and Windows 95/98 use basically the same folder structure, except that the `Application Data` folder does not exist in Windows 95/98.

Additional differences in Windows 95/98 profiles include the following:

◆ Not all Desktop items will roam; only LNK (shortcuts) and PIF (program information) files will.

◆ Common program groups aren't supported in Windows 95/98.

◆ Windows 95/98 can't use a centrally stored Default User profile.

NOTE *If you're still supporting NT 4 and Windows 9x clients, then don't skip the chapter on the CD about system policies for NT and 9x clients!*

Chapter 10

Managing Windows 2000 Storage

WHETHER YOUR WIN2K SERVER is a print server, an e-mail server, a Web server, or whatever kind of server you can think of, it's still in many ways a file server. No matter what kind of resources a server is providing to the network, the server has to store a lot of files to support those resources.

A lot of files means a lot of storage, and a lot of storage means maintaining it. In this chapter, I'll talk about the tools Win2K includes to help you maintain your disks and other storage media. At one time, this mostly meant the Disk Administrator. We're going to start with the Tool Formerly Known As The Disk Administrator (now called the Disk Management tool), but there's a lot more to it than that: encryption, new disk formats, and disk quotas.

Using the Disk Management Tool

Server disks must be faster, more reliable, and larger than their workstation-based cousins. How do you achieve those goals of speed, reliability, and size? Well, there's always the simple answer: Spend more money for a drive with more of those three characteristics. But there is another solution: a group of drives can band together and, acting in concert, provide speed, capacity, and fault tolerance. This solution is called *Redundant Array of Independent Disks (RAID)*. Until relatively recently, putting RAID on your server required buying an expensive hardware-based RAID system. However, this changed with Windows NT and continued with Windows 2000. With the Disk Management tool in Windows 2000, you can take a bunch of hard disks and "roll your own" RAID system. This doesn't make hardware-based RAID obsolete by any means, since hardware RAID is more flexible than software and, as we'll discuss later, a heck of a lot easier on your computer—one particular kind of software RAID can be ruinous to computer performance. Software RAID just offers a less-expensive option for those who want this kind of data protection but can't afford hardware RAID solutions. This section explains the Windows 2000 disk management paradigm, describes your organization and protection options, and shows you how you can use the Disk Management tool to best arrange your data for your particular situation.

The Disk Management tool is not just a warmed-over version of the Disk Administrator from NT 4. Whereas the Disk Administrator required you to reboot after any change to the partition system, or possibly if you breathed too hard on the hard disk, here you can create and delete volumes without rebooting. You can mount partitions to paths on other NTFS volumes instead of just assigning drive letters to new volumes. You can format volumes while creating them rather than having to format them from the command prompt or from Explorer as was necessary in the past. All in all, it's a good tool and a *great* improvement over previous iterations of the Disk Administrator.

With the Disk Management tool, you can do the following:

◆ Create and delete partitions on a hard disk and make logical drives.

◆ Get status information concerning these items:

  ◆ Disk partition sizes

  ◆ Free space left on a disk for making partitions

  ◆ Volume labels, their drive-letter assignment, filesystem type, and size

◆ Alter drive letter and file mounting assignments.

◆ Enlarge disk volumes.

◆ Create, delete, and repair mirror sets.

◆ Format any volume.

◆ Create and delete stripe sets and regenerate missing or failed members of stripe sets with parity.

Don't recognize some of these terms? Hang on, they're defined in the next section.

Disk Management Terminology

Before we get into the discussion of how you can use the Disk Management tool to arrange and protect your data, you need to know some of the terms that we'll be tossing around. These terms will be explained further in due course, but this section introduces them.

SLED

An acronym for *single large expensive drive*, SLED is a way of arranging your data on one very large, very (hopefully) reliable drive. SLED has historically been a popular method of arranging data for two reasons:

◆ It's simple. You only have to buy one disk and store your data on it.

◆ Dedicated RAID hardware has been expensive in the past. Even though it's not as expensive as it used to be, it still reflects an added cost.

Trouble is, if that one very large and very reliable drive fails, then your data goes with it. That's where RAID comes in.

RAID

"Apply a shot of RAID, and all those nasty data problems will be gone!" No, it's not really a household product. RAID (Redundant Array of Independent Disks) is a method of protecting your data by combining the space on hard disks to improve disk fault tolerance and/or data throughput. Most of the discussion of RAID in this chapter will focus on its fault-tolerance attributes. There are many kinds of RAID implementation, each of which works in a different way and has different applications. Win2K Server supports levels 0, 1, and 5, also known as striping without parity, disk mirroring, and striping with parity, respectively. We'll talk about exactly what these *mean* later in this chapter.

NOTE   *RAID isn't always redundant. RAID level 0 (disk striping without parity) isn't fault tolerant because it contains no redundant data to help you re-create lost data.*

Basic Disks versus Dynamic Disks

Win2K supports two kinds of disk storage: dynamic and basic. The main difference between them is the difference between broad support and disk flexibility. Any OS can detect a basic disk, even if it can't read the logical volumes on that disk. Only Windows 2000 can detect dynamic disks, but you must use dynamic disks to use multidisk volumes.

Basic Disks

Basic storage is the kind of storage that has been around since the DOS days, allowing for primary and extended disk partitions and logical drives. If you're upgrading NT 4 to Win2K, then the basic disks may still include the mirror sets, volume sets, and stripe sets that you created under the previous version of the operating system.

Basic disks have their limits. For compatibility reasons, they conform to the four-partition limit imposed by the structure of the disk partition table (a 64-byte file in the first sector of any disk; the partition table lists the physical locations of any logical partitions on the disk but can only describe four partitions because each description takes up 16 bytes). Basic disks also don't support new fault-tolerant volumes. If you want to use Win2K's RAID, you'll need to upgrade the basic disks to dynamic disks.

Dynamic Disks

Dynamic disks are new in Windows 2000 and are not supported by any earlier Windows operating system. If you want to use any kind of fault-tolerant or multidisk volumes, then you'll need to use dynamic disks.

Dynamic disks work together in Win2K in logical units called *disk groups*. When you make a disk dynamic, you're writing a 1MB database of information at the end of that disk volume. This database contains all the partition information for all the dynamic disks in the server and identifies the disk type as system ID 42, which tells Win2K, "look at the on-disk database to find out what volumes are present." The contents of the databases for each disk are identical. (The changes are time-stamped, so that if a disk happens to be missing for a while, the newer changes will be copied to the disk when it returns.) If you import a "foreign" disk (a disk belonging to another dynamic disk array on another computer) to the mix, then the database entries in the new array are copied to that new disk, and any entries on the foreign disk are copied to the database of the disk array you're importing the disk into. In other words, importing the foreign disk merges the two databases. If importing just overwrote the imported disk's database, then it'd lose any existing volumes.

When you upgrade a basic disk that already has partitions on it (as the system disk will) to dynamic, you've got a partition table to deal with. The contents of that table are copied to the database. The rest of the disk is then identified in the table as "42" and reserved for new volumes that will be recorded *only* in the database, not in the partition table.

When you boot a computer with dynamic disks in it, the BIOS reads the partition table and reports the boot partition to work from. Finding the operating system, it goes through the boot process described in Chapter 21, "Preparing for and Recovering from Server Failures." The drivers for supporting dynamic volumes—DMLoad, DMAdmin, and (if the volume is a boot volume) DMBoot—are loaded early in the process of loading all Win2K drivers.

You need to use dynamic disks to use multidisk volumes with Windows 2000. Does that mean that you should *always* upgrade disks to dynamic? The answer is no—not even to Microsoft. In multidisk systems, dynamic disks can be very useful, but think about upgrading a disk before doing it. Dynamic disks are visible only to Windows 2000 and later versions of Windows. They're incomprehensible—in fact, invisible—to any locally installed operating system other than Win2K. Additionally, although you can revert a dynamic disk to a basic disk, you can only do this so long as the dynamic disk doesn't have any volumes on it. In other words, if you upgrade a basic disk that already has data on it to a dynamic disk, you'll have to delete the volumes in which that data is stored (and thus delete the data) before you can revert the disk to basic.

In short, to create new fault-tolerant volumes or multidisk volumes, you'll need to upgrade your disks to dynamic. If you need local compatibility with other operating systems, then stick with basic disks. If you've only got one disk in the server and don't plan to add more, you might as well leave it basic and save yourself the 1MB of space that the dynamic metadata would use, because dynamic disks have no benefits in single-disk computers.

NOTE *Dynamic disks are not supported on laptops. See the later section "Not All Disks Are Upgradable" for the details.*

FREE SPACE VERSUS UNALLOCATED SPACE

The definition of *free space* seems obvious. "Free space on a disk is just space that's free, right?" It's not. Free space does not refer to unused areas within established drives. Rather, *free space* is an extended partition that doesn't yet have any logical drives in it, or the space within that partition not yet divided into a logical drive. (Hang on—I'll get to what extended partitions and logical drives are in a minute.)

This definition of free space is different from the one used in NT 4 and previous versions, where free space was space on a disk that was not part of a volume. Disk space formerly called free space is now called *unallocated space*. It's not committed to be part of any volume or partition. Both basic and dynamic disks may have unallocated space.

PHYSICAL DISKS VERSUS LOGICAL PARTITIONS

To understand disk management, you must understand the difference between physical disks and logical drives or partitions. A *physical disk* is that contraption of plastic and metal that you inserted in your server's case or have stacked up next to it. The Disk Management tool identifies physical drives by numbers (Disk 0, 1, 2; CD 0, 1, 2) that you cannot change.

NOTE   *If you have multiple disks in your computer, they're numbered by their status on the drive controller. For example, in a SCSI chain, the disk with SCSI ID 0 will be Disk 0, the drive with the next SCSI ID will be Disk 1, and so on. The SCSI ID and the disk number are not directly related and will not necessarily match—the only correspondence lies in the disk's priority in the system.*

You cannot change the size of a physical disk. The size given to it when it was low-level formatted (something you almost certainly don't have to worry about if you're installing Win2K on the disk; you can't low-level format an EIDE drive and don't need to low-level format a SCSI drive—it's done before you buy it) is the size the drive will remain.

In contrast to a physical disk, a *partition* or *volume* or *logical drive* is a way of organizing space on that physical disk that the Disk Management tool assigns a drive letter to or mounts to a path on an NTFS volume. You can change drive-letter assignments and adjust the sizes of logical partitions, as they have no physical presence. A logical partition can be part or all of a physical disk or even (in the case of volume sets, mirror sets, and stripe sets) extend across more than one physical disk.

In short, a physical disk is a solid piece of hardware with a fixed size. A partition/logical drive/ volume is a way of organizing the space on that piece of hardware, but it has no physical existence. Basic disks have partitions and logical drives, and dynamic disks have volumes, but if I say "partition" or "volume" or "logical drive," I'm speaking generally of the same thing: a way of organizing physical disk space.

Wondering what it means to mount a drive to a path? Read on.

MOUNTED DRIVES

The Disk Administrator you used with previous versions of NT identified each logical disk volume by a drive letter. This method is simple and has the advantage of making a really short way of leaping to that partition: you type the letter representing it. The disadvantage, of course, is that so long as Win2K insists on using the Roman alphabet, you're limited to a total of 26 letters for all local drives and mapped network connections. It also means that it is not possible to add more space to an existing logical drive. To get around these limitations, Win2K supports mounting volumes to empty folders on NTFS volumes. Mounted volumes work *only* with NTFS, because they depend on some attributes not found in FAT or FAT32. However, they work with both basic and dynamic disks.

The basic idea of mounting a partition to a folder is that you're redirecting to the partition all read and write requests sent to that folder. Mount a new partition to `X:\Mount Volume Here` and every file I/O request you send to `X:\Mount Volume Here` will be rerouted to the new partition, even if the original drive X: is on a different physical disk entirely. You can mount a volume to as many paths as you like. The only restrictions are that the folders must be empty at the time of mounting and not mapped to any other volumes, and they must be on NTFS volumes on the local computer. NTFS 5 is the only file format that Win2K supports that can use the reparse points that redirect path information.

The mounted volumes show up as subfolders in the path you mounted them from, but as you can see in Figure 10.1, the mounted volumes show up as drives instead of folders.

FIGURE 10.1

Mounted volumes
within a folder

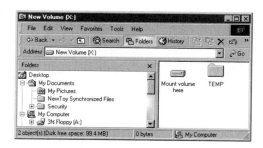

Why bother with mounting volumes to NTFS paths? Three reasons. First, it means that you're in no danger of running out of drive letters for local and network partitions. Mounted drives render the 26-letter limitation irrelevant.

Second, you can use this technique to effectively enlarge a volume on a basic disk, which you cannot do otherwise. For example, say that drive X: is running short of room. It's on a basic volume, so you can't make drive X: any bigger. Instead, you add a new disk and create a 2GB volume on that disk, then map the new 2GB volume to an empty folder on drive X:. Drive X: is now effectively 2GB larger.

Third, you can use this technique to create a fault-tolerant area on a non-fault-tolerant volume. That 2GB volume you created can be a stripe set with parity or a mirror set, even if the disk containing drive X: is a basic disk and therefore does not support fault-tolerant volumes. For example, you could create a new folder on drive X: called Home Directories, then map a RAID volume to that folder. Whenever someone saves a file to any subfolder of X:\Home Directories, it's going to the RAID volume even if the rest of drive X: is *not* fault tolerant.

Volume mappings are transparent to the user base, incidentally. Just as a user doesn't have to care whether drive X: is on the computer he's working on or on a file server, the same user doesn't have to care whether the folder he's saving to is located on the same physical disk as the rest of drive X: or on another disk altogether. You can also mount a drive to multiple paths or both mount it and assign it a drive letter.

Experiment with mounting drives to NTFS paths. They're a really cool addition to Win2K's storage management capabilities.

DIVIDING BASIC DISKS

Although mounted drives are not specific to basic or dynamic disks, the ways that you can arrange the space on physical disks are. Basic disks support three kinds of organizational divisions: primary partitions, extended partitions, and logical drives.

Primary Partition and Extended Partition

I mentioned earlier the difference between physical disks and logical drives, partitions, or volumes. Although the latter three are all organizational divisions of physical disk space, they're not all the same thing. A *partition* is a portion of a hard disk set up to act like a separate physical hard disk, rather like splitting a single physical hard disk into several logical drives. There are two kinds of partitions: primary and extended.

A *primary partition* is a portion of a physical hard disk that the operating system (such as Win2K) marks as bootable. Under DOS, you can only have one primary partition. Under Win2K, NT, or Windows 9x, you can have multiple partitions on a drive; one partition at a time is marked "active," meaning you can boot from it. You can't break primary partitions into subpartitions, and you can create only up to four partitions per disk because that's all there's room for in the partition table. You might partition your hard disk so one primary partition is running Win2K and another is running Linux.

Four logical divisions on the disk aren't enough? You can create an *extended partition* from unallocated space on a physical disk. Once you do, you'll see a new area of free space on the drive, with a dark green border. The dark green border identifies the extended partition's area. You can only have one extended partition on a physical disk, but you can supplement it with up to three primary partitions.

You can't put any data into an extended partition or assign it a drive letter—it's just free space. To make it able to hold data, you'll need to create one or more logical drives in that extended partition.

Logical Drive

A *logical drive* is a logical division of an extended partition that behaves like an entity unto itself. You can divide an extended partition into as many logical drives as you like, so long as you make each partition the minimum size required (this minimum size will be shown in the wizard helping you to create the partition).

Logical drives are indicated in the Disk Manager display with a royal-blue stripe. Because they're part of an extended partition, they'll have a green border that encompasses all drives in the partition and any free space left in it after you create the drives.

DIVIDING DYNAMIC DISKS

I hate to keep hammering this home, but it's important and, I've found, not intuitive: You'll use dynamic disks any time that you want to use any kind of multidisk logical divisions of disk space. Forget RAID, forget fault tolerance... the key point to dynamic disks is their support for storage areas that may extend over more than one disk. Of those areas, dynamic disks support volumes, mirror sets, stripe sets with parity, and RAID 5 volumes.

Volume

A *volume* is a logical division of the unallocated space on a dynamic disk. It works like a logical drive or primary partition except for one major difference: Whereas logical drives and primary partitions must be confined to a single disk and can't be made larger, volumes using NTFS may either exist on a single disk or encompass space on more than one, and you can add more unallocated space to them. This makes volumes much more flexible—and potentially more space efficient—than partitions or drives. As you can see in Figure 10.2, it's much easier to figure out how to fit 30MB of data into a 35MB volume set than it is to fit it into one 20MB logical drive and one 15MB logical drive. Especially if that 30MB is a single database.

Win2K supports two kinds of volume sets: simple volumes, which start out only taking up space on one disk, and spanned volumes, which start out taking up space on multiple disks. You can extend either kind of volume; if you extend a simple volume onto another disk, then it becomes a spanned volume. You cannot make the volume set smaller unless you delete it and create a new one.

FIGURE 10.2

How a volume
set works

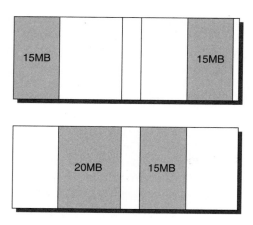

In this figure, 65MB of free space is available, but no more than 20MB of this space is contiguous. To get the most efficient use of this space, you could combine it in a volume set so all of the data is considered in one large chunk. Once this free space has been made into a volume set, you could store a 65MB chunk of data in it, even though the largest contiguous space is only 20MB in size.

NOTE *You can only extend NTFS-formatted volumes created on a dynamic disk. Volumes made from converted logical drives or partitions may not be extended.*

Volume sets do not protect your data; they only let you use available drive space more efficiently. If something happens to one of the hard disks used in a volume set, that volume set is dead, even if the other hard disks are fine. Because the more hard disks you have, the more likely it is that one will fail at any given time, be sure to back up volume sets regularly.

Mirror Set

Mirror sets are the simplest form of Win2K data redundancy, writing two copies of all data onto volumes on two separate disks so that if one disk fails, the data is still available. If anything happens to the disk storing your original data, you still have an identical copy on the other half of the mirror set.

Collectively, the two volumes are called a *mirror set*, or RAID 1. They have a couple of advantages:

♦ You can mirror an existing simple volume set, making it fault tolerant.

♦ You only need two physical disks to create a mirror set, instead of the minimum of three that RAID 5 volumes require.

Disk mirroring is simpler to use in Win2K than it was in NT 4. You can create mirrored volumes without rebooting and don't have to regenerate data to recover it if one of the disks supporting the mirror crashes. The data will remain available—it just won't be fault tolerant until you mirror it again.

If you've ever heard or read anything about disk mirroring, you've probably also heard the term *disk duplexing*. As shown in Figure 10.3, disk duplexing is much the same as disk mirroring, except that duplexing generally refers to mirroring information on two separate disks—each with its own disk controller—so that the data is not vulnerable to controller failures. When Win2K Server talks about disk mirroring, it is referring to both duplexing and mirroring.

Mirror sets secure data well, but they're not very space efficient because every piece of data that you record has an identical twin on the other half of the mirror set. You need exactly twice as much storage space as you have data.

FIGURE 10.3

Disk mirroring versus disk duplexing

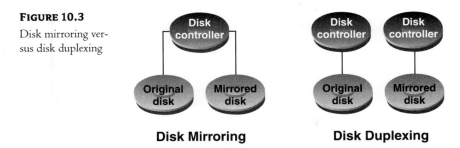

Stripe Set

Volume sets are useful because they allow you to combine many differently sized areas of unused disk space into a single volume. However, they don't offer any performance benefits. To use space on multiple disks and decrease read and write times, consider using disk striping without parity, also known as RAID level 0.

When you create a stripe set from free space on your disks, each member of the stripe set is divided into stripes of equal size. Then, when you write data to the stripe set, the data is distributed over the stripes. A file could have its beginning recorded onto stripe 1 of member 1, more data recorded onto stripe 2 of member 2, and the rest on stripe 3 of member 3, for example. If you're saving data to a stripe set, a file is never stored on only one member disk, even if there is room on that disk for the entire file. Conceptually, striping looks something like Figure 10.4.

If you take free space on your disks and combine it into one stripe set with its own drive letter, the disk access time for that drive will be improved since the system can read and write to more than one disk at a time. To do striping without parity information included, you need at least two, but not more than 32, disks.

Disk striping has a speed advantage over volume sets, but consider this:

◆ You cannot extend a stripe set as you can a volume or extend it over more disks once it's created. The size that you make the stripe set is the size it will stay.

◆ You cannot mirror a stripe set with software, although you *can* mirror a simple volume. There is simply no way to make a stripe set fault tolerant other than backing it up.

If you're looking for performance, use nonparity stripe sets. If you're looking for flexibility, expandability, or fault tolerance, use simple or spanned volume sets.

FIGURE 10.4

Stripe set without parity

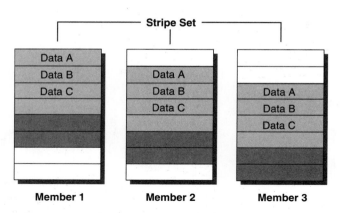

Different data files are represented here with different shades of gray. As you can see, an entire data file is never all put onto one member of the striped set. This improves read time since, if Data A is called for, the disk controllers on all three members of the set can read the data. With a SLED data arrangement, only one of the members could read the data.

RAID 5 Volume

For data protection, or to decrease your disks' read time, you can select areas of unallocated space on your disks and combine them into a *RAID 5 volume*, also known as a *stripe set with parity*. RAID 5 volumes are the most cost-effective form of RAID that Win2K supports because they require less space for redundant data than mirroring does. The catch is that they're also very processor intensive.

How Disk Striping with Parity Works   Every time you write data to a RAID 5 volume, the data is written across all the striped disks in the array, just as it is with regular disk striping (RAID level 0). Parity information for your data is also written to disk, always on a separate disk from the one where the data it corresponds to is written. That is, there isn't a separate "parity" disk, although RAID 4 (not supported in Windows 2000) organizes data that way. Rather, each disk supporting the RAID 5 volume may contain a piece of original data or the parity information needed to reconstruct that original data, but not both the original and its parity information. That way, if anything happens to one of the disks in the array, the data on that disk can be reconstructed from the parity information on the other disks. This is shown in Figure 10.5.

If you think about it, writing parity information every time you save a document could turn into a big waste of space and time. Take, for example, the document I'm creating for this book. If I've protected my data with level 5 RAID and parity information is stored to disk every time this file is saved, does that mean that there is parity information for every incarnation of this document from the time I began writing? If so, how can all the parity information and data fit on the disks?

The answer is, of course, that it doesn't, and this is what produces the performance degradation that's unavoidable in striped disk writes. Every time a document is saved to disk, its parity information must be updated to reflect its current status. Otherwise, you would have to keep backup parity information for every version of the document that you ever saved.

FIGURE 10.5

Disk striping with
parity information

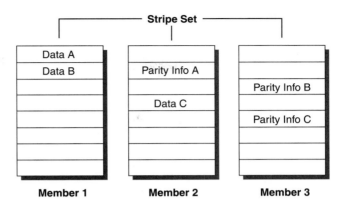

As you can see, no single member of the stripe set keeps all the original data or all the
parity information. Instead, the data and parity information are distributed throughout the
stripe set so, if one member disk fails, the information can be reconstructed from the
other members of the stripe set.

Updating the Parity Information   There are two ways to update the parity information. First, since
the parity information is the XOR (exclusive OR) of the data, the system could recalculate the XOR
each time data is written to disk. What is an *XOR?* On a *very* simplistic level, the XOR, or *exclusive OR
arithmetic,* is a function that takes two 1-bit inputs and produces a single-bit output. The result is 1 if
the two inputs are different or 0 if the two inputs are the same. More specifically:

$$0 \text{ XOR } 0 = 0 \quad 1 \text{ XOR } 0 = 1 \quad 0 \text{ XOR } 1 = 1 \quad 1 \text{ XOR } 1 = 0$$

When you're XORing two numbers with more than one bit, you match the bits up and XOR
each pair individually. For example, 1101010 XOR 0101000 equals 1000010. The result you get
from this function is the parity information, from which the original data can be recalculated.

Recalculating all the data stored in the volume each time you wrote to disk would take quite a
while. A more efficient way of recalculating the parity information, and the one that Win2K Server
uses, is to read the old data to be overwritten and XOR it with the new data to determine the differences. This process produces a *bit mask* that has a 1 in the position of every bit that has been
changed. This bit mask can then be XORed with the old parity information to see where *its* differences lie, and from this the new parity information can be calculated. This seems convoluted, but
this second process only requires two reads and two XOR computations rather than one of each for
every drive in the array.

RAID 5 volumes are great in theory, but in Windows 2000's implementation they don't work so
well. First, needing to generate parity information for every write to disk slows down the write
process. Second, and really more important, RAID 5 represents a serious drain on processor time. In
high-end hardware RAID, the hardware RAID configuration has its own processor that handles all
the calculations necessary. Software RAID, such as what we're discussing in this chapter, relies on the
server's processor to do all that calculating. You almost certainly won't use software RAID 5 much on
a production server, because of the performance toll it extracts. Certainly, never use it on a terminal
server.

Installing a New Physical Disk

When you first add a new hard disk to your computer, Win2K will not recognize the new disk even if it shows up at boot time (SCSI or IDE). You must add support for the new drive, either manually or by following the Write Signature and Upgrade Disk Wizard. The wizard will start up automatically when you open the `Disk Management` folder in the Computer Management tool and have new physical disks attached.

There are two steps to setting up a new hard disk: writing a disk signature and choosing whether the disk should be basic or dynamic. Win2K writes disk signatures automatically when it detects the disks or as part of the Write Signature and Upgrade Disk Wizard.

To add a new disk, follow the wizard. It's not really much of a wizard anymore (in early betas of Win2K, it was longer, asking you to specify disks that you wanted to sign instead of just writing the signature automatically). All you're doing is picking disks to upgrade to dynamic, something you should think through before doing because, as you'll see, you can't always undo it very easily. Win2K will write a signature to the disks automatically when it detects a new disk and upgrade any that you choose.

Using Basic Disk Features

Basic disks, recall, are the default in Win2K. A basic disk is a normal disk, available from any operating system and using primary and extended partitions to divide up physical disk space into logical units. You'll need to stick with basic disks if you want to make disks available to operating systems other than Win2K. This will keep you from using RAID, but then again, even before Win2K introduced dynamic disks you couldn't access mirrored or other RAID volumes from any operating system other than NT anyway. On basic disks, you can create primary partitions, extended partitions, and logical drives.

USING PRIMARY PARTITIONS TO STORE OPERATING SYSTEMS

Although you'll set up the initial disk partitioning when you install Win2K Server, you can use the Disk Management tool (in the Computer Management section of the MMC; Computer Management is in the Administrative Tools program group) to edit the logical divisions of your disk after you've installed Win2K.

Forgetting dynamic disks, you normally boot a computer from a primary partition. When you install Win2K, the Setup program will automatically create a primary partition to put Win2K on. Once Windows 2000 is installed, you can create more bootable partitions, or just another partition to store data that's separate from your system partition. Right-click any area of unallocated space on the hard disk and choose Create Partition to start the Create Partition Wizard. Click through the welcome screen, then choose the type of partition you want to create (see Figure 10.6).

In the next screen of the wizard, specify the size of the primary partition. It can be anywhere from the minimum specified in the wizard to the full size of the unallocated space. Make sure that you make the partition as big as it will ever need to be, because you can't extend primary partitions. Even if you make the disk a dynamic disk, you won't be able to extend the partition space—only volumes created on dynamic disks from the beginning may be extended.

FIGURE 10.6

You can create primary partitions from unallocated space.

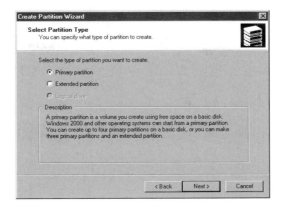

In the next wizard screen (see Figure 10.7), you have three options: choose a drive letter for the new primary partition, mount it to an empty folder on an NTFS volume, or do neither.

FIGURE 10.7

Pick an identifier for the partition.

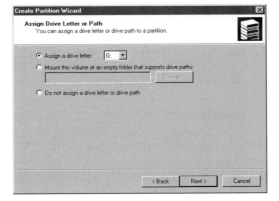

NOTE   *At some point, you'll have to assign the partition a drive letter or path if you want to use it. You can't save data to an area of the disk that isn't named or format it with Explorer—there's no way to get its attention, so to speak.*

Next, you'll be prompted to choose a format for the disk (see Figure 10.8). Win2K supports NTFS (the default file format), FAT, and FAT32. You'll only have the option to compress the volume if you format with NTFS. Quick formats, which just wipe the disk without checking it for errors, are available with any format type.

You don't actually have to format the partition now—you can format a volume at any time by right-clicking it and choosing Format from the shortcut menu—but you'll have to format it before you use it.

FIGURE 10.8

Choose a disk format.

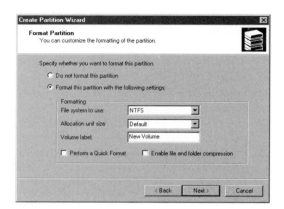

When you've finished, you'll see a finish screen like the one in Figure 10.9. Review your choices to make sure the new partition is set up the way you want it, and click Finish.

FIGURE 10.9

Review your choices before finishing the logical drive.

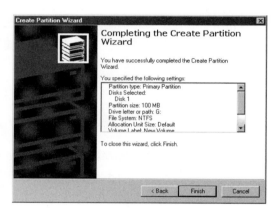

USING LOGICAL DRIVES TO ORGANIZE INFORMATION

Even if you rely on the SLED model for your data storage, you may want to divide that single large physical drive into smaller logical ones. You could, for example, keep all the accounting information on logical drive C:, the engineering information on logical drive D:, the personnel information on logical drive E:, and so on. As discussed earlier, you can also mount logical drives to NTFS volumes on other local disks to effectively enlarge the other volumes. Although you can also do all this with primary partitions, logical drives have an advantage: no four-division limit per physical disk.

To create a logical drive, you must first take unallocated space and convert it to an extended partition. Creating an extended partition is much like creating a primary partition, except for the different partition type that you'll choose in the first page of the wizard and the fact that you won't be asked to format or label the new partition. The new extended partition will be labeled Free Space.

I'll talk about the benefits and drawbacks of the filesystems Win2K supports shortly, but when experimenting with creating partitions, you might wonder why some filesystems are available for some partitions but not for others.

The filesystems available will depend on the size of the partition you're formatting and the tool you're using to do it. If you format with the Disk Management tool as described here, you can format a partition smaller than 4GB (4096MB) with any filesystem that Win2K supports: FAT, FAT32, or NTFS. For volumes larger than 4GB, the Disk Management tool will only offer the formats of FAT32 or NTFS. For partitions larger than 2GB but smaller than 4GB, FAT will be an option, but when you choose that filesystem you'll see a message warning you that the partition you're formatting will not be compatible with previous versions of Windows, since the filesystem will use clusters bigger than 32KB. If the partition is larger than 4GB, then only NTFS and FAT32 will appear in the Disk Management tool's list of acceptable file formats.

If you're formatting partitions with Explorer, then all three filesystems will appear in the list of available file formats regardless of the size of the partition. If I'm formatting a partition 4GB or larger, then FAT will still appear in the list of available file formats; when I click the OK button to begin the format, Win2K will chug away as though formatting the volume. However, when it apparently finishes I'll see an error message saying that the format couldn't be completed. The partition you tried to format will be unformatted, in its original condition, and any data on the volume before the intended format will still be there.

Once you've created the extended partition, you're ready to create a logical drive so that you can store data. To do so, right-click free space in the extended partition and choose Create Logical Drive from the shortcut menu. This will start the Create Partition Wizard that you've seen before. Click through the first screen, and you'll see the one shown in Figure 10.10.

FIGURE 10.10

Choose to create a logical drive.

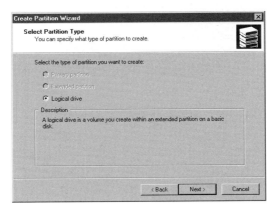

Notice that you only have one option here; you can't create partitions within an extended partition. Click Next to open the next page of the wizard and choose the size of the drive you want to create (see Figure 10.11).

FIGURE 10.11

Specify the size of the new logical drive.

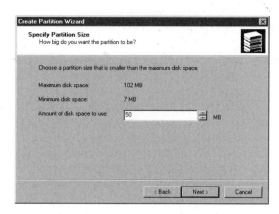

In the next screen of the wizard, you can once again choose to either mount the drive or assign it a drive letter. Format the drive with the filesystem you want, and you'll arrive at the finish screen showing you the options you picked. Click Finish, and the logical drive will appear in the extended partition.

DELETING A BASIC DISK PARTITION OR DRIVE

To delete any basic disk volume, right-click it and choose the Delete Partition or Delete Logical Drive option (whichever applies). A dialog box will pop up and warn you that any information in the volume that you're deleting will be lost and ask if you're sure you want to continue. (Surprisingly, the default option is Yes, which strikes me as a bit dangerous.) Click Yes to delete the volume.

The deleted basic disk volume will revert to whatever it was before you created the volume. Primary partitions and extended partitions revert to unallocated space on the drive; logical drives revert to free space.

CONVERTING A BASIC DISK TO A DYNAMIC DISK

Even after you partition it, you can convert a basic disk to a dynamic disk so that any new volumes you create can span multiple physical disks. Before you start converting, however, there's a few things you should consider.

You Can't Easily Undo This

If you don't read another word in this section before skipping to the instructions, read this. If you upgrade a disk to dynamic, then you cannot make that disk a basic disk again without deleting every volume on it. There is no way to preserve a dynamic disk's organizational structure when making it a basic disk.

Not All Disks Are Upgradable

These instructions will not work on every disk. If you don't see an option to upgrade a basic disk, there may be a reason:

◆   Only fixed-disk drives may be dynamic disks. Removable disk drives such as Jaz drives and CD-Rs can only be basic disks. The reasoning is simple: A dynamic disk volume may extend over more than one physical disk. A removable disk might not always be present.

- If the disk has a sector size larger than 512 bytes, then you won't be able to upgrade it. Notice that that's the *sector* size, not the *cluster* size. I'll get into the difference more in the later section on formatting, but for the moment just understand that (a) this is a problem you're unlikely to encounter, and (b) you can't change the sector size of your disks with a Win2K format. Cluster size, yes; sector size, no.

- You can't make disks on a laptop computer dynamic—Win2K doesn't support this. The logic is that laptops normally only have a single physical disk. First, this means that they can't reap any of the benefits of dynamic disks, since those benefits are all tied into RAID. Second, if a laptop has a second hard disk that's available when the laptop is in a docking station, then the database containing information about the dynamic disks in the computer would easily become out of date if the two dynamic disks only sometimes worked together.

- For those using Windows 2000 Advanced Server or Windows 2000 Datacenter Server, you can't make the shared storage system in a cluster dynamic.

What's Happening to My System and Boot Partitions?

Before upgrading, consider what effect the change will have on existing system data—both for Win2K and for any other operating systems on the computer:

- You will *not* be able to install Win2K onto a volume on a dynamic disk unless the volume was upgraded from a basic disk. That is, the volume must have existed on the physical disk before you upgraded it to dynamic. Although Windows Setup can "see" a native dynamic volume— i.e., it will appear in the list of available partitions for installation—if you select it, Setup will not be able to recognize the partition and will ask you to pick another one.

- You can (usually) upgrade the disk with the system partition on it, but the upgrade will not take effect until you restart the computer. (Actually, this is true for any disk that has files open during the upgrade, not just the system partition.) This is one of the few times that you'll need to restart the computer for a change in the Disk Management tool to take effect.

- You can't upgrade a basic disk with a system partition if that disk has NT 4 RAID volumes on it.

- You will not be able to access the dynamic disks from any locally installed operating system other than Win2K. That is, you'll be able to get to them from across the network, but in a dual-boot computer, the other operating systems will not be able to see the dynamic disks. That, by the way, includes *booting* from those dynamic disks, so don't convert the disk with other operating systems on it.

Keep in Mind What You Have

You may not *want* to upgrade a basic disk to dynamic. Seriously. You'll need to do it to get the full benefits of Win2K's multidisk volumes and software RAID support, but upgrading can be hard to reverse and a pain to resolve if you can't. Keep the following in mind:

- If you upgraded NT 4 to Win2K, the basic disk may have RAID volumes (stripe sets or mirroring) on it. To continue using these multiple-disk volumes as fault-tolerant volumes, you must upgrade each disk in the RAID volume to dynamic.

◆ You cannot extend the volumes on the converted disk if the volumes were originally created on a basic disk. Only volumes originally created on a dynamic disk may be extended to other disks or made larger with unallocated space on the same disk.

◆ Although you always have the option of converting dynamic disks back to basic disks, you must delete any volumes on the disk first.

Upgrading the Basic Disk

Now that you're thoroughly intimidated, let's go through the process of doing the conversion:

1. In the Disk Management tool, right-click the gray area on the left side of the physical disk you want to convert (see Figure 10.12).

FIGURE 10.12

You must start from the physical disk, not from one of the logical volumes on the disk.

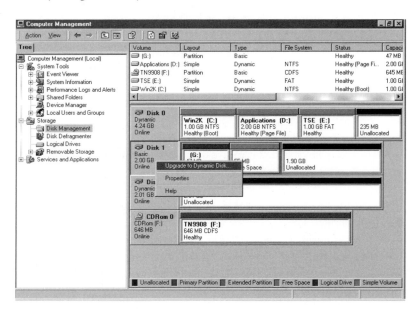

2. From the shortcut menu that appears, choose Upgrade to Dynamic Disk to open the dialog box in Figure 10.13. All basic disks on the computer that are available to be converted (recall, this includes only fixed-disk drives) will be listed and identified by number.

FIGURE 10.13

Choose the basic disk(s) you want to convert.

3. Click OK, and the Disk Management tool will then display a list of the disks it's going to convert. This dialog box is much like the preceding one except for a Details button. Click this button, and you'll see a list of the logical drives on the physical disks (see Figure 10.14).

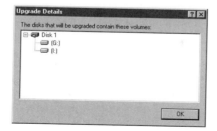

4. Exit the Details box and return to the Disks to Upgrade box by clicking OK. If you're still sure you want to upgrade, click the Upgrade button. You'll see a message like the one in Figure 10.15, warning you that previous versions of Windows will no longer be able to boot from this disk. Click Yes, and you'll get *another* message warning you that all mounted file paths will be dismounted. (If you regret upgrading a disk to dynamic, it's not going to be Microsoft's fault.) Click OK to get through this message box.

Once you've clicked OK, the hard disk will grind away for a couple of minutes. When the operation is completed, any partitions or logical drives that had previously been on the disk will now be simple volumes. If the disk had open files—as with the system disk—then you'll need to reboot.

Why Didn't the Upgrade Work?

That's how it's supposed to work. If you're attempting to upgrade disks that should work (see "Not All Disks Are Upgradable") and the upgrade doesn't take, then something may be wrong with the disks or with a volume on the disk.

When Disk Management attempts to convert a basic disk to dynamic, it first does a system check to make sure that the conversion will take. The disks must be working (you can't write a 1MB database of disk information to a disk that's having I/O errors), and the volumes on the disks have to be working and visible to the Win2K Volume Manager. For instance, if you create a partition with a tool other than the Disk Manager, then until you restart the system the Volume Manager may not be able to "see" it. If the Volume Manager is unaware of that volume, it will stop the disk conversion process. If multidisk volumes are on the basic disks (as you might have if you were upgrading from

NT 4—otherwise, this won't be an issue), then it makes sure that all the parts of those volumes are there.

Using Dynamic Disks

You'll need to use dynamic disks if you want to use Win2K's software RAID protection. Read on for more information about how to create and delete RAID volumes and use them to improve fault tolerance and/or disk performance.

CREATING A DYNAMIC DISK VOLUME

Creating a dynamic disk volume is much like creating a volume on a basic disk, but you'll have some more options depending on the number of dynamic disks you have available and the kind of volume you're creating. The basic process goes like this:

1. In the Disk Management tool, right-click unallocated space on any dynamic disk to open the shortcut menu. Choose Create Volume.

2. You'll open the Create Volume Wizard. Click past the opening screen to the one shown in Figure 10.16. Pick a type of volume to create.

FIGURE 10.16

Choose a type of dynamic volume to create.

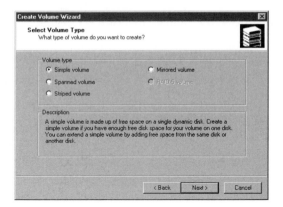

NOTE *Not all volume types will always be available. If you have available only a single dynamic disk with unallocated space, you'll only be able to create a simple volume. Two dynamic disks with unallocated space available will permit you to create a stripe set, spanned volume, or mirror set. To create a stripe set with parity, at least three dynamic disks with unallocated space must be present.*

3. In the next screen, choose the disk or disks that you want the volume to be on. The currently selected disk will be in the list on the right side (see Figure 10.17) and the available disks will be on the left side. Select a disk and click the Add or Remove buttons to pick the disks you want the volume set to be on.

FIGURE 10.17

Choose the disks that should support the volume.

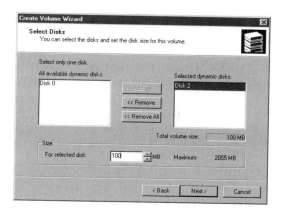

4. In the same screen of the wizard, pick the size you want the volume to be. By default, the new volume will be as large as possible, based on the amount of unallocated space available on the disks you've chosen. You can make it smaller than this size, down to 1MB, but you obviously can't make the volume bigger.

5. In the next screen of the wizard (see Figure 10.18), choose a drive letter or map the new volume to a path on an NTFS volume. Although you don't have to do either at this time, you will need to call the new volume *something* before you can use it.

FIGURE 10.18

Choose a drive letter or mount the volume to a drive path.

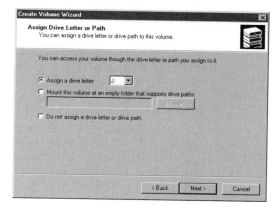

6. Click to open the next screen of the wizard and choose a disk format for the new volume: NTFS, FAT32, or FAT. Again, as you can see in Figure 10.19, you don't have to format the volume while creating it, but you will need to format it before you can use it.

NOTE *You can always perform a quick format on a volume (just wiping the volume and not checking for bad clusters), but file and folder compression—and other features such as disk quotas and file encryption—are only available for NTFS volumes.*

FIGURE 10.19

Format the new volume.

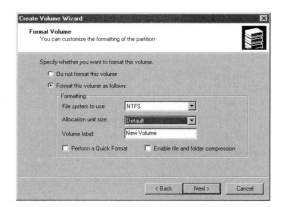

The final screen of the wizard displays the choices you've made so that you can go back and change them if need be. Otherwise, click Finish, and the new volume will be accessible as soon as it's formatted—no rebooting required.

DELETING A DYNAMIC DISK VOLUME

Deleting a dynamic disk volume is straightforward: right-click the volume to delete and pick Delete Volume from the shortcut menu. You'll see a message like the one in Figure 10.20, warning you that you're about to delete any data on that volume. Click Yes to continue deleting the volume, and it's instantly gone—no rebooting or further warnings required.

FIGURE 10.20

Deleting a volume permanently deletes the data stored on that volume.

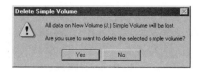

CONVERTING A DYNAMIC DISK TO A BASIC DISK

If you mistakenly upgrade a basic disk to dynamic, all is not lost. You can reverse the process. The only catch is that you can't revert volumes on a dynamic disk to basic disk volumes, because they don't exist in the disk's partition table—just in the dynamic disk database. If you have volumes on the disk, then the Revert to Basic Disk option in the disk's shortcut menu will be grayed out. You'll need to delete all volumes before this option becomes available.

Assuming that the disk is empty, however, the process is simple for a data disk. Right-click the gray area of the physical disk (all the way to the left in the Disk Management tool's display) and choose Revert to Basic Disk. That's it. No reboot required.

Creating a Volume Set

I explained how to build any dynamic disk volume in the earlier section, "Creating a Dynamic Disk Volume." The only volume-set-specific parts to remember are these:

◆ Simple volume sets will only use space on one dynamic physical disk.

◆ Spanned volume sets may use space on from 2 to 32 dynamic physical disks.

Other than that, the process of creating a simple or spanned volume is now blessedly simple: pick the disks to place the volume on, pick a size for the volume, assign the volume a drive letter or mount it to a path, format it, and you're done.

ENLARGING A VOLUME SET

If it turns out that your NTFS-formatted volume set is smaller than you need it to be, it's not necessary to delete it and re-create it from scratch. Instead, you can *extend* it by adding areas of free space to its volume.

NOTE   *You cannot make a volume set smaller. To do that, you must delete the volume set and create it again.*

To extend an existing simple or spanned volume set, follow these steps:

1. Right-click the simple or spanned volume set you want to expand and choose Extend Volume from the shortcut menu. You'll start up the Extend Volume Wizard.

2. Click through the initial page of the wizard to display the screen shown in Figure 10.21. From here, choose the disk or disks onto which you want to extend the volume set. Only dynamic disks with unallocated space will be available.

FIGURE 10.21

Pick the disks to add to the volume set and specify how much space you want to add.

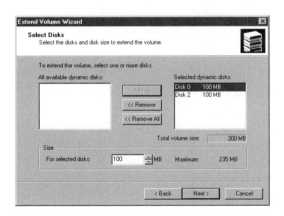

3. In this same screen, choose the amount of unallocated disk space you want to add from the new disk. The Disk Management tool will display both the amount of space that you're adding and the total size of the newly extended volume.

4. The final screen of the wizard will show the choices you've made. Review them and click either Back to make changes or Finish to extend the volume set.

The volume set is now the larger size that you specified, and all the area in it will have the same drive letter. The unallocated space that you added is automatically formatted to the same filesystem as the rest of the volume set—NTFS.

There are a few catches to extending volume sets:

◆ You can only extend NTFS volumes, so you'll need to reformat or convert FAT or FAT32 volumes to NTFS before you can extend them.

◆ Although converting a basic disk to dynamic makes any partitions on the disk become simple volumes, you cannot extend *those* simple volumes. Only volumes originally created on a dynamic disk are extensible. (Any volumes you create on that disk after it's converted to dynamic are extensible, however.)

◆ Again, you cannot use this procedure to make a volume set smaller. To do that, you need to delete the volume set and create a new one.

◆ You cannot combine two volume sets, nor can you add a logical drive to a volume set.

Creating a Stripe Set

Creating a stripe set without parity is just like creating any other dynamic disk volume: make sure that you've got at least two dynamic disks with unallocated space available, right-click an area of unallocated space, and choose Create Volume to start the wizard. In the first screen that includes any data, make sure that you've selected the Striped Volume type as shown in Figure 10.22.

FIGURE 10.22

Choose striped volumes to reduce disk access times.

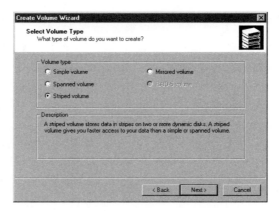

From here, the volume creation process is the same for all dynamic volumes, as described in the earlier section, "Creating a Dynamic Disk Volume." Just keep in mind the following:

◆ Stripe sets must include at least 2 and no more than 32 physical disks.

- ◆ Each stripe will be the same size. That is, if the largest area of unallocated space on Disk 0 is 50MB, then the largest stripe set you can create on three disks is 150MB, even if Disk 1 and Disk 2 each have, say, 200MB of unallocated space.

- ◆ Stripe sets do not include any parity information, so the volume size the wizard lists is an actual reflection of the amount of data you can store on the striped volume.

If anything happens to any member disk of your nonparity stripe set, all the data in the set is lost. It doesn't hurt the other disks in the stripe set, but it means that the data in the stripe set itself is unavailable.

DELETING A STRIPE SET

If you make a stripe set too small or too big, there's no way to resize it. You'll need to delete the stripe set and start over. Just right-click it and choose Delete Volume from the shortcut menu. As always, you'll be prompted to confirm that you want to delete the volume, and when you do, the stripe set—and all the data stored on it—will disappear.

Establishing a Mirror Set

To create a mirror set, you can either start from unallocated space on a dynamic disk or mirror an existing simple volume.

NOTE *You cannot mirror a volume on a basic disk. The only mirrors that Win2K supports on basic disks are those left over from upgrading NT to Win2K.*

To create a mirror set from unallocated space, right-click an area and choose Create Volume from the shortcut menu. Go through the wizard as described in the earlier section, "Creating a Dynamic Disk Volume," noting the following:

- ◆ You'll need two dynamic disks with unallocated space on them.

- ◆ Both halves of the mirror set will be the same size. You cannot mirror a large volume with a smaller one.

- ◆ A mirror set can use any disk format: NTFS, FAT32, or FAT.

To mirror an existing simple volume, right-click the volume and choose Add Mirror from the shortcut menu. You'll open a dialog box like the one in Figure 10.23, asking you to select the disk that you want to create the mirror on. Click the disk so that it's highlighted—this won't work otherwise.

NOTE *Only dynamic disks with areas of unallocated space big enough to mirror the selected volume will be listed. If no area of unallocated space is big enough, then you won't have the option of mirroring the volume.*

Click the Add Mirror button, and the Disk Management tool will create in the unallocated space a partition that's the same size as the simple volume being mirrored. The partition will be formatted to match the filesystem on the original volume, and the redundant data will be regenerated. (Depending on the size of the volume you're mirroring, this may take a while. It's not a fast process on large volumes.)

FIGURE 10.23

Choose a dynamic disk to hold the mirrored data.

The new partition will have the same drive letter or mounted path as the one you mirrored and will be available immediately—no reboot required.

GETTING RID OF AND RECOVERING DATA FROM A MIRROR SET

If you don't want to maintain redundant information anymore, then the mirror set is history. *How* you get rid of it depends heavily on what you're trying to do:

- If you don't want any of the information in the mirror set anymore, then *delete* the mirror set.

- If you only want to keep half the data in the mirror set (either the original volume or the redundant half), then *remove* the mirror set.

- If you want to keep all the data—original and redundant—but don't want to mirror it anymore, then *break* the mirror set.

You don't have to delete, remove, *or* break a mirror set to keep using its data if half of it fails—it just won't be fault tolerant until you replace the failed disk and establish a mirror again.

Deleting a Mirror Set

To destroy all data in a mirror set, right-click the mirrored volume and choose Delete Volume from the shortcut menu. The Disk Management tool will ask you if you're sure; click Yes to continue deleting the mirror.

This will delete both halves of the mirror set—and destroy the partition—so only do this if you don't need the data or you've backed up. (Strictly speaking, you shouldn't mess around with your data unless you've backed up anyway, but this time you'll *definitely* delete it.)

Removing a Mirror Set

If one of the disks dies, the data on the still-functioning disk will still be accessible, but it won't be protected anymore (see Figure 10.24).

To protect it again, you'll need to remirror the volume. However, you can't *re*mirror a mirrored volume, and even if half of it's dead, the mirror itself is still valid. To start protecting the data again, you'll need to get rid of the original mirror.

FIGURE 10.24

If one of the disks supporting a mirrored volume dies, then the mirror set is displayed as failed.

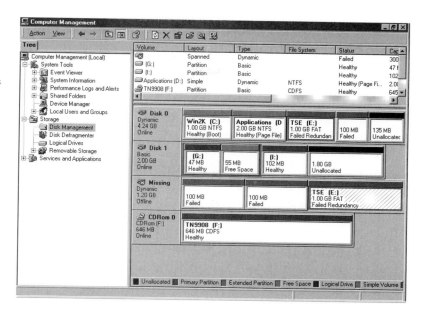

To delete one half of the redundant data and stop mirroring, remove the mirror set. Right-click the mirror set and choose Remove Mirror from the shortcut menu. You'll see a dialog box like the one in Figure 10.25.

FIGURE 10.25

Pick a half of the mirror set to remove.

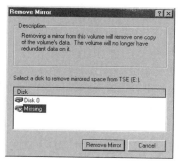

Be sure to pick the half that you *don't* want to keep. When you click Remove Mirror, the Disk Management tool will ask if you're sure. Click Yes to continue. The partition you selected will be deleted. The mirrored partition that you *didn't* select will become a simple volume. Its data will not be affected.

Breaking a Mirror Set

If both halves of the disk are still working, but you don't want to mirror the data anymore, then you can break the mirror set and thus make the two volumes act again like simple volumes. Both volumes will begin their new lives with all the data they had as their half of the mirror set; breaking the set does not affect the data.

To break the mirror set, right-click a mirror set that's still functioning (if the mirrored volume has failed, then you'll have to remove the mirror, not break it) and choose Break Mirror from the short-cut menu. You'll see a message asking if you're sure and warning you that your data will no longer be fault tolerant. Click Yes to continue.

NOTE *If an application is referencing data stored in the mirror set—even if its contents are just displayed in Explorer—you'll see an error message telling you that the volume is in use. Stop using the mirror set before breaking it if you want to copy the data currently being viewed to both halves of the mirrored volume.*

The two halves of the mirrored volume will now become simple volumes. One half will retain the drive letter that had belonged to the mirrored volume, and the other will have the next available drive letter.

MIRRORING CONSIDERATIONS

As you're deciding whether or not to protect your data by mirroring it, keep these things in mind:

◆ Mirroring to drives run from the same drive controller does not protect your data from drive controller failure. If any kind of controller failure occurs, you won't be able to get to the backup copy of your data unless you are mirroring to a disk run from a separate controller.

◆ For higher disk-read performance and greater fault tolerance, use a separate disk controller for each half of a mirror set.

◆ Disk mirroring effectively cuts your available disk space in half. Don't forget that as you figure out how much drive space you've got on the server.

◆ Disk mirroring has a low initial cost, since you must purchase only one extra drive to achieve fault tolerance, but a higher long-term cost due to the amount of room your redundant information takes up.

◆ Disk mirroring will slow down writes, as the data must be written in two places every time, but will speed up reads, as the I/O controller has two places to read information from. It gets the best performance of the two fault-tolerant RAID levels.

◆ You cannot extend a mirrored volume. The size it is when mirrored is the size it will stay.

Establishing RAID 5 Volumes

To create a RAID 5 volume on a computer, follow these steps:

1. Right-click any area of unallocated space on any dynamic physical disk. From the shortcut menu that appears, choose Create Volume.

2. Click through the opening screen of the wizard. On the first real screen, select RAID 5 Volume, as shown in Figure 10.26.

FIGURE 10.26

Choose RAID 5 to establish a stripe set with parity.

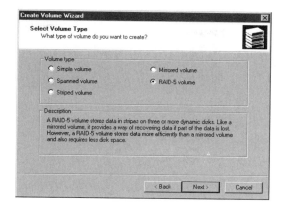

3. In the next screen (see Figure 10.27), choose at least three disks that you want to be involved in the stripe set. The disk you started with (the one with the area of unallocated space) will be in the right column of disks to use; the other dynamic disks with unallocated space will be on the left side. In the figure, I've selected three disks to use. To add a disk to the stripe set, select it in the list of all available dynamic disks and click the Add button. To remove a disk from the stripe set, select it in the list of selected dynamic disks and click the Remove button.

FIGURE 10.27

Select the disks to be in the stripe set and the size of the set.

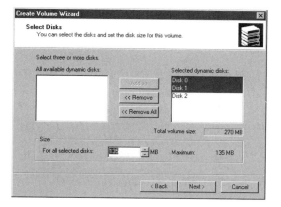

4. In this same dialog box, pick the size of the stripe set. In the Size box, the Disk Management tool will display the maximum size of the stripes based on the unallocated space on the chosen drives. You can go smaller than this amount, but not bigger. The value in Total Volume Size will reflect the total amount of room available for *data*, not the total space in the stripe set. Since $1/n$ of the space in a RAID 5 volume (where n is the number of disks in the set) is used for parity information, the more disks you have, the larger percentage of room for data you'll get.

NOTE *The amount of unallocated space on each physical disk will determine the size of the stripe set. Each section of the stripe set must be the same size, so if one disk has only 50MB unallocated space on it, then the entire stripe set can be no more than 150MB, even if the other disks have 500MB of unallocated space each. That said, not all the unallocated space must be contiguous. If a disk has one chunk of unallocated space that's 50MB and another that's 100MB, then the disk can contribute to the RAID 5 150MB volume.*

   5. Choose to assign a drive letter or mount the volume to an NTFS path (see Figure 10.28).

FIGURE 10.28

Assign the volume a
drive letter or path.

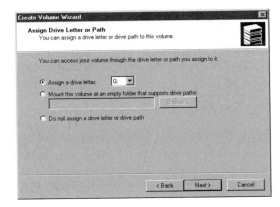

   6. Choose whether or not to format the new volume right away and the disk format you want to use (see Figure 10.29).

FIGURE 10.29

Pick a format for the
volume.

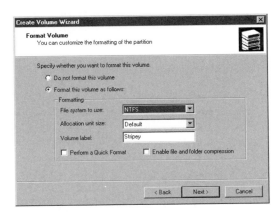

   7. Review your choices, backing up to change any of them or clicking Finish to create the RAID 5 volume.

   Win2K will grind away for a few minutes, setting up the new stripe set. When it's done, the RAID 5 volume will be immediately ready to use.

RETRIEVING DATA FROM A FAILED STRIPE SET

If an unrecoverable error to part of a stripe set with parity occurs, you'll still be able to read and write to the volume, but the volume will be marked Failed in the Disk Management tool (see Figure 10.30). This is a warning: lose one more disk, and the data will be inaccessible and unrecoverable.

FIGURE 10.30

You can still read and write to failed RAID 5 volumes, but they're no longer fault tolerant.

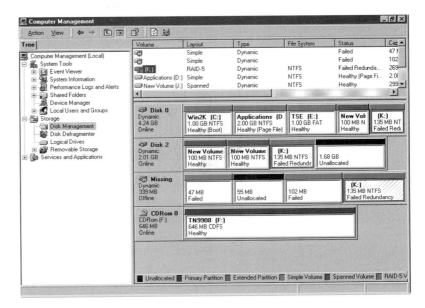

To make the volume fault tolerant again, replace the failed disk, rescan the disks, and reactivate the disk. If this doesn't make the volume healthy again, then right-click the stripe set and choose Reactivate Volume. The computer will chug away for a couple of minutes, rebuilding the missing data with the parity information on the remaining disks, and the stripe set will be back in one piece. You don't have to reboot.

DELETING A STRIPE SET

Deleting a stripe set is quite simple. Right-click the volume and choose Delete Volume from the shortcut menu. You'll see the usual warning message telling you that you're about to delete the volume and lose data; click through it, and the stripe set will again be unallocated space. Don't forget that deleting a stripe set destroys the data in it—even the parity information.

THINGS TO REMEMBER ABOUT DISK STRIPING WITH PARITY

Keep these things in mind when it comes to disk striping with parity:

◆ Striping with parity has a greater initial hardware cost than disk mirroring does (it requires a minimum of three disks rather than two). Nevertheless, it allows you to get more use out of your disk space.

◆ You cannot make a stripe set bigger (even if more unallocated space becomes available) or extend it to another physical disk.

◆ Although you can access the information in a stripe set even after one of the members has failed, you should regenerate the set as quickly as possible. Win2K Server striping cannot cope with more than one error in the set, so you're sunk if anything happens to the unregenerated stripe set.

◆ Striping with parity places greater demands on your system than disk mirroring, so add more memory and processor power to the server if you plan to use disk striping. I strongly recommend that you never use RAID 5 volumes on a terminal server.

◆ If you have fewer than three dynamic disks on your server with unallocated space, you cannot make stripe sets with parity.

Advanced Disk Management Topics

The earlier sections in this chapter covered the basics, introducing the grammar of disk management in Windows 2000 Server and showing you how to set up the various kinds of logical divisions of physical disks. So long as all you're ever planning on doing is setting up volumes once, you're fine.

Things rarely remain that simple, however. What if you want to install a second copy of Windows 2000 on the same computer—what kind of volume can it reside on? Dynamic disks on the same computer, as you've learned, share information. If you move a physical disk from one computer to another, then what happens to that shared information? For that matter, how do you recover from a boot disk failure if you mirrored it? That's what we're going to talk about here.

FORMATTING AND LABELING A LOGICAL DRIVE OR PARTITION

Let's start with a simple one. Formatting the volume while it's being created is an option (a nice change from NT 4) but not required. If you don't format a volume while creating it, you'll need to do so before you can use the disk. You may also want to reformat an already-formatted volume to quickly delete all data.

To format a volume from the Disk Manager, right-click it and choose Format from the shortcut menu. You'll open the dialog box shown in Figure 10.31.

Type in any name you like, then choose the disk format you want to use: NTFS, FAT32, or FAT. Click OK, and Win2K will format the selected volume. Of course, any data already on the disk will be irrevocably deleted in the course of the format, so if you're reformatting, be sure that you've already saved any data on the volume that you want to keep.

FIGURE 10.31

Format and label the new partition or drive.

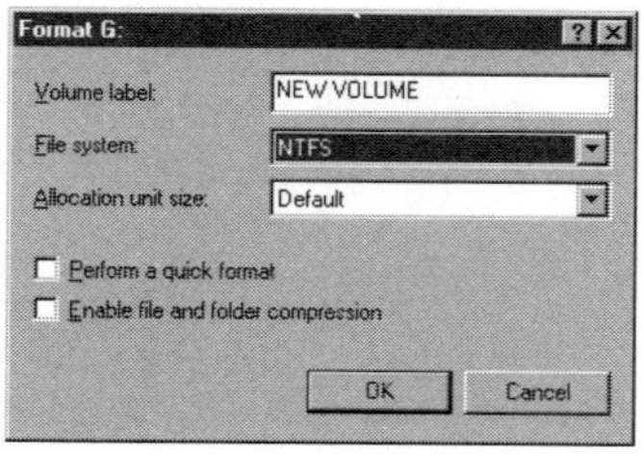

NOTE   *If you open Windows Explorer and try to access the new drive letter before you format it, you'll get a message telling you that the disk is not formatted and asking if you want to format it now. Say OK, and the Format dialog box will open. Oddly enough, if you start the format in this manner, the default file format is FAT, not NTFS.*

WINDOWS 2000 SETUP AND DYNAMIC DISKS

Say that you've installed Windows 2000 Server on a computer, fudged around with the Disk Management tool a bit, and now want to create a parallel installation of the OS. If you have dynamic and basic disks and a variety of the divisions of those disks available, where can you install Windows 2000?

If you're attempting to install to a basic disk, it's easy. You can install Windows 2000 on a primary partition or on a logical drive within an extended partition. (It's okay to install on an extended partition. Win2K will make it a boot partition.) Or, if the basic disk has enough unallocated space, you can use Setup to create a new partition. If you've ever installed Win2K, you know all about installing to basic disks.

Dynamic disks make life more complicated. Setup (and the Recovery Console described in Chapter 21) only recognizes dynamic disk partitions that are *hard-linked*, or created when you upgrade a basic disk to dynamic and the basic disk had preexisting primary partitions or logical drives configured. Each of the preexisting partitions retains a legacy-style partition table entry (type 42 for primary and type 05 for extended), even after upgrading the disk to dynamic. These special hard-linked entries allow Setup to recognize them as valid partitions for installation. In other words, you cannot install Windows 2000 to a volume that you created after upgrading the disk to dynamic. The disk may appear in the list of available options in Setup when you're picking the partition to install to; Setup will display a drive letter for the dynamic volume, so if your dynamic disk had only one volume, you might be fooled into thinking everything is okay. However, if you select the native dynamic volume, Setup will tell you that it can't recognize it and ask you to pick another option. This means that you cannot install Windows 2000 onto a RAID 5 volume, spanned volume, stripe set without parity, or a simple volume created on a dynamic disk, since by definition all those volume types are created from unallocated space on a dynamic disk. You can install Windows 2000 onto a dynamic disk if you pick a partition that existed before you upgraded the disk and is now a simple volume or even half of a mirror set. The partition had to exist while the disk was a basic disk, so that Setup can find the disk location in the disk boot record.

Good so far? Here's where things get strange. Microsoft will tell you that creating partitions on a dynamic disk using Setup will screw up the disk by confusing it as to its basic/dynamic identity. More exactly, re-creating a volume during Windows 2000 Setup changes the partition table information from type 0x42 (which means, "Go read the dynamic disk database to get partition information") to a normal partition table entry: 0x06 for FAT, 0x0B for FAT32, or 0x07 for NTFS. This, supposedly, will render the disk unreadable and cause the Logical Disk Manager Service to display that disk as Dynamic Unreadable in Disk Management.

My experience is a little different. If you have a dynamic disk, and you get ready to install Windows 2000, then you actually can't create a new partition on it—not at first. Say that you're creating a parallel installation of Win2K and attempt to install it onto a dynamic disk. Any unallocated space on the dynamic disk appears as unformatted or damaged space to Setup, not unpartitioned space. If you delete an existing dynamic partition and attempt to create a new partition, the partition won't format and, when you reboot to your original installation, it will be a basic disk. If you delete the "damaged" partition—not touching the volume already on the disk—so you can create a new partition in the available space, you'll delete all partitions on the disk but will be able to create new partitions on the disk. (The installation won't work properly, but you will be able to create the partitions and the files copied during the initial portion of Setup will be there.) In other words, creating new volumes on a dynamic disk during Setup won't render the disk unreadable, but will destroy any data currently on the disk and convert it to basic without warning.

WARNING   *Don't create partitions on dynamic disks during Setup.*

In short, keep the following in mind when choosing a location for a secondary Windows 2000 installation:

◆   Any partitioned or unpartitioned space on a basic disk: good.

◆   Any hard-linked volume on a dynamic disk: good.

◆   Any soft-linked volume on a dynamic disk: impossible.

◆   Creating new partitions on a dynamic disk: very bad.

Frankly, if you want to make the system partition fault tolerant, then the easiest way is to install Win2K onto a basic disk and then upgrade that disk to dynamic. The primary partition that you installed Win2K into will become a simple volume, and you can mirror that volume onto another dynamic disk. Which leads us nicely to our next topic: making the system disk dynamic.

UPGRADING A SYSTEM DISK TO DYNAMIC

When you upgrade disks in Windows 2000 from basic to dynamic, all partition information is moved into a private database at the end of the disk. Only one partition table entry of type 0x42 is entered in the master boot record (MBR) at sector 0.

The process of becoming dynamic is different for disks containing the system or boot partition. The process with system/boot disks is called *rooting*. When Win2K roots a disk, the system partition remains intact, but the Filesystem ID fields are changed to 0x42 to show that they are dynamic volumes recorded in the database at the end of the volume. The system partition remains intact so that the BIOS knows how to communicate with the disk and can boot Win2K. This is done so that the BIOS can load the kernel and other files necessary to start the Disk Management driver files to read the dynamic volumes. If there is any unallocated space on the volume, an entry is added similar to those of other dynamic volumes (not rooted) that encompasses the rest of the space.

If you want to revert the system disk, you're a bit stuck. As noted earlier, the option to revert volumes from dynamic to basic only exists if the disk is empty and unpartitioned. You can't delete the system partition when you're using it. Backing up the system configuration, reformatting the disk, and reinstalling is really your only option.

MOVING A DYNAMIC DISK

You might want to move a dynamic disk to a new computer, say, if you're moving half a mirror set to re-create duplicate data on a different computer. Recall that Win2K organizes dynamic disks into disk groups. When you move a dynamic disk from one computer to another, you're moving it to a new group, because even if those disk groups have the same name (as they will, since Win2K only supports one disk group per computer and they're numbered starting with 0), they're not the same group. Therefore, to make this work, you'll need to introduce the disk you're moving to its new disk group—*without* deleting the volume information on the disk you're moving.

NOTE *In case it's not obvious, when you move the last dynamic disk from a computer, the disk group no longer exists, since dynamic disk information is stored only on dynamic disks.*

Prep Work

Before you start swapping disks around, take a look at what you've got. First, if any multidisk volumes don't show up as Healthy in Disk Manager, then fix them before moving the disk. Second, if you're planning to move more than one dynamic disk from the same disk group and containing parts of the same multidisk volume, it is a *very* good idea to move all those disks at once. Spanned volumes won't work unless all their disks are present—you will lose their data if you only move one of the disks supporting a stripe set or spanned volume—and fault-tolerant volumes may get out of sync. For instance, say that you have a mirror set on server ALPHA. If you *break* that mirror set and move half of it to server BETA, then you don't have a problem. But if you keep the mirror set intact, move half of it to server BETA, and keep using the disks on both systems (you can keep writing to a failed mirror set in Win2K, it'll just show up as Failed Redundancy in the Disk Manager), then try to move the other half from ALPHA to BETA, the data on the two mirror halves will be inconsistent. In such a case, Win2K will re-create the mirror set with the data from the physical disk moved first to BETA.

In this discussion, I'm going to call the computer you removed the disk from the *source* computer and the computer you moved it into the *destination* computer. When you remove a dynamic disk from a computer, information about it and its volumes is retained by the remaining online dynamic disks. The removed disk is displayed in the Disk Management tool on the source computer as a Dynamic/ Offline disk with the name Missing. You can remove this Missing disk entry by removing all volumes or mirrors on that disk, and then use the Remove Disk menu item associated with that disk.

Introducing the New Disk

After you physically connect the disks to the destination computer, open the Action menu and choose Rescan Disks. The new disk will show up as Dynamic/Foreign. By default, Dynamic/Foreign disks should be brought online automatically, but if it's not, then right-click the disk and choose Online.

To use Foreign/Dynamic disks, you'll need to *import* them. Right-click one of the moved disks and choose the Import Foreign Disks option. The importing procedure works slightly differently depending on whether there's already a disk group on the new computer. If there are no preexisting online dynamic disks, then the disk group is brought online directly as it is, except that you'll lose any nonredundant information partially contained on disks you didn't move (e.g., if you moved only one disk supporting a stripe set). The disk group remains the same as it was; the database doesn't change. If a disk group was already present on the destination computer, then Win2K's Volume Manager will merge the old disk group information with the new disk group information, so that all the dynamic disks can work together. The new disks will become members of the local disk group.

Can I Use the Data on the Moved Disks?

So what happens to the volumes on the dynamic disks you moved? Depends on whether you moved enough data for the volume to work. Either the data or the redundancy data to re-create the data must be on the destination computer.

Simple volumes, which are contained on a single disk, should be fine if they were fine before you moved the disk.

If you moved only part of a multidisk but non-fault-tolerant volume, such as a volume set or stripe set, that volume is disabled on both the source and destination computers until and unless you move the disks containing the rest of it. So long as you don't delete the volume on either the source or destination computer, you should be able to move the rest of the volume to the destination computer and re-enable it, but you will need to move all the disks supporting that multidisk volume. If you delete and overwrite part of the volume, you can't rebuild the volume.

If you move a disk containing part of a RAID 5 volume, then the data may be available even if you didn't move the entire volume to the destination computer; this depends on whether you moved enough parity data to regenerate what's missing. If the parity information is valid, one disk of the RAID 5 volume can be missing and the volume should still work, just as it would if one of the disks in the volume failed.

If you move a mirror set that's up to date, then you can use the data on the new computer or even (if you broke the mirror set on the source computer) re-create the mirror set on a dynamic disk on the destination computer. If you move the two halves of the mirror set at different times, then reaffixing the mirror set on the source computer will cause the first mirror half to overwrite any data on the second mirror half. Even if you made changes to the second mirror half, those changes will be lost, not merged when the two halves come together again.

WARNING *All these comments apply to data disks. If you move the system disk to a new computer, the computer will not boot unless the right Plug-and-Play ID information for the mass storage controller is already in the Registry. Otherwise, Win2K will not be able to load the right drivers. The simplest way to avoid this situation is to only move system disks to computers that are identical to the source computer.*

CHANGING A SYSTEM DRIVE LETTER

Under a couple of circumstances, you might need to change the system drive letter. If you mirrored the boot disk and the main disk fails, then when you break the mirror, the second—working—partition will automatically be assigned the next available drive letter. Which means that if Win2K still thinks that, say, C: is the boot drive, you're going to have a hard time booting if the only working system drive is now called J:. Or, as one reader wrote:

> *I made the mistake of leaving an alternate drive in my laptop when I installed [DOS followed by] W2K on the primary drive. Now the boot disk (which ought—in the natural order of things—to be "D", as I have the DOS partition) is H:. And of course, the W2K tools won't let me reassign the drive letter at all. (In NT, you could reassign the drive letter—but you had to reboot when you left Disk Manager.) Know of any way that I can get that H: to D:?*

Trouble is, if you right-click the system volume in Disk Management and choose Change Drive Letter and Path from the shortcut menu, then although you'll be able to open the dialog box you'd normally use for this purpose, when you click the Edit button to do the actual editing you'll see an error message telling you that you can't modify the drive letter of your system or boot volume. What to do?

To change or swap drive letters on volumes that cannot otherwise be changed using the Disk Management snap-in, you'll need to edit the Registry. For example, say that you want to swap H: and D:. Open REGEDIT and go to the `HKLM\SYSTEM\MountedDevices` key. Within that key are values for each of the lettered drives on your computer. In the list, find `\DosDevices\D:`. Right-click it and choose Rename to edit it to `\DosDevices\Y:` (or some drive letter not currently being used).

TIP   To make this change, you'll need Full Control over the `HKLM\SYSTEM\MountedDevices` *key. Security settings are available in the Security menu of REGEDT32, but to rename this key as described here, you'll need to use REGEDIT.*

Next, right-click `\DosDevices\H:` and change it to `\DosDevices\D:`. Finally, right-click `\Dos-Devices\Y:` and rename it to `\DosDevices\H:`. (If you're only changing one drive letter, then you don't need to do the swapping—just change the drive letter to the unused letter.) You'll then need to restart the computer.

RECOVERING A FAILED DATA DISK

Recovering from simple disk failure isn't too bad, if the disk that died is not the disk with the operating system files on it. If you accidentally switch off an externally mounted drive, or if the drive comes loose in the box, any volume sets or nonparity stripe sets that depended on that disk will be temporarily dead—reasonable, because for all practical purposes, one of its disks has failed. The missing disk either will not show up in the Disk Manager at all (if you rebooted with the disk off) or will show up with a Missing note on it (see Figure 10.32).

FIGURE 10.32

A dead drive in the Disk Management tool

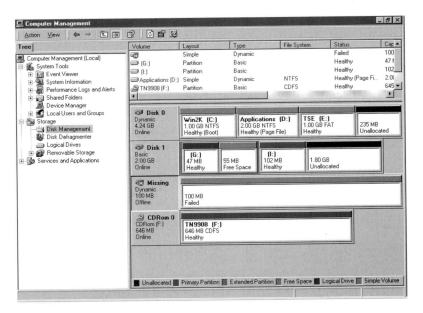

If it's a simple matter of a loose cable or an accidentally flipped power switch, just reconnect the cable or switch the drive back on. After you've done so, right-click the Disk Management tool's icon in the left pane with the rest of the Computer Management tools and choose Rescan Disks. You'll see an informational dialog box telling you that the Disk Management tool is rescanning. When it's done, right-click the failed volume and choose Reactivate. Win2K will caution you to run CHKDSK on the volume. Click OK, and your disk will appear as it was before and the volume set will again have a drive letter and be operational.

Or, if you're just recovering from a single failed data disk in a fault-tolerant disk volume (mirror set or RAID 5 volume), you can use the procedures I described earlier to regenerate the missing data and make the volume fault tolerant again. Even before you do so, the data will still be available.

CREATING AND USING A FAULT-TOLERANT DYNAMIC DISK FOR SYSTEM RECOVERY

A lot of people ask whether they can use a dynamic disk for their boot disk and thus make it fault tolerant. The answer is yes… to a point. Since you can't install Windows 2000 onto a native dynamic disk partition (Setup and the Recovery Console rely on the partition table, not the disk group's database, to find disk partitions) you can only use mirroring to protect a system disk. A RAID 5 volume is, by definition, a native dynamic disk volume, but a mirror may be built from a partition on a basic disk later upgraded to dynamic.

NOTE *Just a reminder: you will need at least two physical hard disks in the server to mirror its system partition.*

To mirror the system files, install them onto a basic disk as you would normally; we'll call this Disk 0. Having made sure that there is an area of unallocated space of equal size to the system partition, on another disk—Disk 1—upgrade Disk 0 to dynamic. Upgrade Disk 1 to dynamic as well. Now, right-click the system partition on Disk 0 and choose Add Mirror. As described earlier in this chapter, select the dynamic disk with the empty space that you want to copy the original system data to, and create the mirror. The data on the newly mirrored system partition will be copied—*regenerated*, in Disk Management tool lingo—to the blank half of the mirror set, as shown in Figure 10.33.

FIGURE 10.33

Building a mirrored boot partition

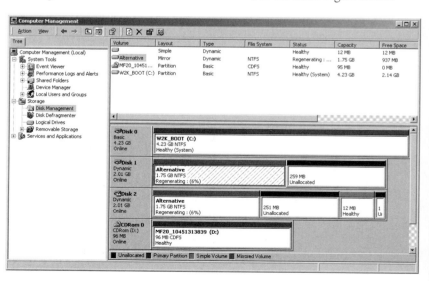

EDITING BOOT.INI TO BOOT TO THE MIRRORED PARTITION

If you've never looked at a BOOT.INI file before, its syntax can be a bit intimidating. Break it down a bit, however, and it's not so bad. This file is the workings for the boot menu, and has two pieces: [boot loader] and [operating systems]. [boot loader] tells the computer which path is the default and how long the computer should wait before choosing the default option. It looks like this example pointing to the \WINNT folder on the first partition of the first disk in the computer:

```
[boot loader]
timeout=30
default=multi(0)disk(0)rdisk(0)partition(1)\WINNT
```

[operating systems] lists all the available operating systems on the computer, their disk and partition location, the name of the system directory, and the name by which each operating system is identified on the boot menu. For example, it could look like this:

```
[operating systems]
multi(0)disk(0)rdisk(0)partition(1)\WINNT="Microsoft Windows 2000 Professional"
/fastdetect
multi(0)disk(0)rdisk(0)partition(1)\WIN2KSRV="Microsoft Windows 2000 Server"
/fastdetect
C:\CMDCONS\BOOTSECT.DAT="Microsoft Windows 2000 Recovery Console" /cmdcons
```

Take a look at the format of the entries in [operating systems]. The multi section tells Windows 2000 to rely on the computer's BIOS to load system files, and may be found on either SCSI or IDE computers. The disk part should always be 0 if you're using the computer's BIOS to boot. The rdisk part identifies the physical disk to boot from, starting with 0 for the first disk and moving up; it has nothing to do with SCSI IDs, just the location of that disk in the chain. Finally, the partition part identifies the partition you want to boot from, starting with 1 instead of 0. Know where your mirrored OS is so you can point to it, and you should be able to recover from a dead system partition.

The system disk is now fault tolerant. Good thing, because the next time you boot the computer, you see a message like this:

```
Windows 2000 could not start because of a computer disk hardware configuration problem.
Could not read from the selected boot disk. Check boot path and disk hardware.
Please check the Windows 2000(TM) documentation about hardware disk configuration and
your hardware reference manuals for additional information.
```

This message does not inspire happy thoughts. What we've got here is a failed primary partition. In a perfect world, if the original half of a mirrored system partition failed, Windows 2000 would boot anyway, saying, "Hey—the partition I normally boot from isn't working. I guess I'll boot from this mirrored system partition that was so cleverly built for me and then tell the sysadmin that the primary boot partition failed so they can fix the mirror." Sadly, Win2K is not that smart. Instead, you'll need to get a bootable Windows 2000 floppy, edit BOOT.INI to boot from the mirrored partition, and then boot to the mirror so you can fix the problem. Specifically:

1. Create a Windows 2000 boot disk by formatting the disk from a Win2K computer and copying BOOT.INI, NTDETECT.COM, and NTLDR to the floppy disk.

TIP   *It's important to format the floppy from a Windows 2000 computer. Doing so will make the disk's boot record point to* NTLDR. *When* NTLDR *runs, it loads the available operating system selections from the* BOOT.INI *file. In other words, if you use a preformatted disk instead of explicitly formatting the floppy from a Win2K computer, the boot floppy may not work.*

2. Edit BOOT.INI to point to the installation on the good half of the mirror set. If you're not sure how to do this, then see the sidebar "Editing BOOT.INI to Boot to the Mirrored Partition."

3. Boot from the Windows 2000 boot disk to get into Win2K. From there, break the mirror set and replace the broken disk with a good one, then reestablish the mirror to make the boot drive fault tolerant again.

4. If the drive letter changed when you broke the mirror, then change the system drive letter (using the procedure described earlier in this chapter) to the original drive letter. Otherwise, you won't be able to boot.

Hardware or Software RAID?

Purely software RAID is simple to set up, and if you own an operating system that supports it, you can experiment with RAID with no additional costs other than those for the drives needed to support your chosen RAID model. However, for serious applications it's wanting. Here's why.

Accessibility   Windows 2000 RAID volumes are invisible to any operating system other than itself. Even NT can't read Windows 2000 RAID volumes, since Windows 2000 requires the use of dynamic disks supported only by that operating system.

Recovery time   You've got a mission-critical system up and running, and one of the four drives in a stripe set with parity goes to The Land Where Hard Drives Are Eternally Blessed. Your next move is to bring the server down, replace the bad drive with a new good one, and then reintegrate that new one into the stripe set in order to keep the data fault tolerant. You must do this as quickly as possible, because the data is no longer fault tolerant and the more disks you're depending on, the greater the likelihood that one of them will fail. To do this, however, you must bring down this mission-critical server while you take out the old drive, install a new drive, and put the stripe set back together. We're not talking about a two-minute fix here. In contrast, you could buy a *hardware* RAID system: a box containing several drives that act as one and that look to the Win2K system like just one drive. An external RAID box costs a bit more, but a hardware-based RAID system can rebuild itself faster than can Win2K software. And best of all, most hardware-based RAID systems allow you to "hot-swap" the bad drive—that is, to replace the bad drive without bringing down the server.

Management   Software RAID volumes are individual disk partitions grouped to create a single RAID partition, which can complicate management—with software RAID and three disks, it's easy to set up three parallel RAID 5 partitions, each requiring its own parity calculations that stress the server. Hardware RAID generally treats disks as single-partition entities.

Most people who use Windows 2000's built-in RAID use its mirroring capability, since the processing required to support RAID 5 seriously degrades server performance. However, if you're serious about data protection for Windows 2000, you'll probably look at hardware RAID, preferably one of the more advanced sorts offering its own processor and the ability to hot-swap failed disks.

Performing Disk Maintenance

The job doesn't end with setting up disk volumes on the physical disks. To keep those volumes working well, you'll need to perform some routine maintenance on them.

Background: Disk Geometry and File Formats

Before getting into disk formats, disk defragmenting, and CHKDSK, let's take a quick look at the relationship between Win2K and hard disks and how this relationship makes all these tasks necessary.

A hard drive is actually not one but several disks called *platters*. Each platter is divided two ways: pie-shaped wedges and concentric circles. The pieces defined by the intersection of these divisions are called *sectors* and are the physical units of storage on a hard disk. Each sector on a disk is normally 512 bytes in size.

Win2K doesn't know a sector from a hole in the ground. To let its file storage component store and retrieve data on the disk, Win2K must impose some kind of logical structure over the physical structure of the disk. That logical structure is called a *disk format*, and it groups sectors together in logical units called *clusters*. The number of sectors in a cluster varies, depending on the size of the disk partition (all other things being equal, larger disks typically have more sectors per cluster) and the disk format you're talking about. All clusters have at least one sector in any filesystem that Win2K supports.

A cluster is the smallest organizational unit that the filesystem can recognize, which means that you can only store one file per cluster. If a file is too big to fit into a single cluster, then it will be spread over multiple clusters, as close together as possible. If a file is smaller than the cluster size, it will still fit into a single cluster and any unused space in that cluster goes to waste. Larger clusters reduce the likelihood that files will get fragmented, but smaller clusters generally use file space more efficiently.

Sound irrelevant? Trust me: you'll need this background on clusters and sectors when it comes to performing basic disk maintenance.

Formatting Disks

Win2K is the first generation of NT sensible enough to let you format volumes while creating them with the Disk Management tool. However, you can still format volumes from Explorer or from the command prompt, as you needed to do in NT 4.

DISK FORMATS SUPPORTED IN WIN2K

Win2K supports three disk formats: the old FAT format that includes long-filename support, the FAT32 file format introduced with Windows 95 OSR 2, and an updated version of the NTFS format that's been around since NT 3.1.

FAT and FAT32

FAT is the granddaddy of Microsoft filesystems, the one that all Microsoft operating systems support. It uses a simple catalog called the *file allocation table* to note which cluster or clusters a file is stored in. If a file's stored in more than one cluster, then the cluster includes a pointer to the next cluster used for that file until the final cluster includes an End of File marker.

FAT and FAT32 have a great deal in common: a simple set of attributes that note creation and access dates and the settings of the hidden, archive, system, and read-only bits. The main difference between FAT and FAT32 lies in their relative cluster sizes. FAT is actually FAT16, which means that it uses a 16-bit addressing scheme that allows it to address up to 2^{16} (that is, 65,536) clusters. To address very large volumes that include a lot of sectors, therefore, FAT must organize those sectors into very large clusters and can't format a volume larger than 4GB.

FAT32, in contrast, has 32-bit addresses, which means that it can name up to 2^{32} (that is, 4,294,967,296) clusters. Because of this, FAT32 can use much smaller clusters even on large volumes; on volumes up to 8GB, it uses 4KB clusters. Other than this difference, however, it's the same as FAT.

The main reasons FAT and FAT32 are included with Win2K is for backward compatibility with other operating systems. Most often, the advanced features of NTFS will make it your first choice for a server filesystem.

NTFS

NTFS is the filing system especially designed for use with Win2K and NT Server:

♦ NTFS is designed for system security (that is, setting file permissions); FAT and FAT32 are not. (You can, however, restrict access to *shared* directories even when using FAT.) To learn how file permissions work, see Chapter 11, "Creating and Managing Shared Folders."

NOTE   *NTFS originally had a couple of bugs in Windows 2000. One allowed Windows Installer to write files to folders write-protected with NTFS, and another prevented interactive users from accessing removable media formatted with NTFS. Both bugs are fixed in SP2.*

♦ Only NTFS volumes support Win2K file encryption, disk quotas, volume mounting, and data compression. Only volumes formatted with NTFS may be extended.

♦ NTFS keeps a log of activities in order to be able to restore the disk after a power failure or other interruption. It won't replace *data* on the NTFS drives, but if it's interrupted in the middle of a write procedure, it will restore the volume structure. This prevents the disk's volume from becoming corrupted.

Win2K uses a later version of NTFS than NT 4 does. Not only that, if you install Win2K onto a machine with NT 4 already installed, Win2K will automatically upgrade the NTFS volumes to NTFS 5, rendering those volumes unreadable by NT 4. The good news is that NT 4 can read and write to the latter version of NTFS if you install Service Pack 4 or later. To set up a dual-boot system, install NT 4, install SP4 or later, then install Win2K. That way, when NTFS volumes exist, you'll never have a time when you can't read the NTFS volumes from NT 4.

One of the other things that NTFS can do is find its own shortcuts when you move the file that the shortcut points to—even if the shortcut is on a different computer from the one where the file is located.

For example, say that there's a file called `myfile.txt` on \\serpent\workingfiles, a shared directory. You refer to `myfile.txt` often, so you create a shortcut to that file (using its UNC \\serpent\workingfiles\ `myfile .txt`) on the desktop of your workstation so you don't have to drill down to find the file. Even if the file gets moved on SERPENT, the shortcut on your computer will still work because the properties of the shortcut will note the new location.

NAMING CONVENTIONS FOR LONG FILENAMES

All disk formats in Win2K support long filenames. Even FAT uses the extensions that make this possible. Filenames in Win2K can be up to 256 characters long with the extension, including spaces and separating periods. You can use any upper- or lowercase character in a long or short filename except the following, which have special significance to Win2K:

? " / \ < > * | :

Even though NTFS supports long filenames, it maintains its compatibility with DOS by automatically generating a conventional FAT filename for every file. The process doesn't work in reverse, however, so don't save a file with a long filename when working with an application that doesn't support long filenames, or else you'll only have the abbreviated name to work with. If you do, the application that doesn't like long names will save the file to the short name and erase all memory of the long filename. The data won't be erased, however; only the descriptive filename is affected.

When converting a long filename to the short format, Win2K does the following:

◆ Removes spaces.

◆ Removes periods, all except the last one that is followed by a character—this period is assumed to herald the beginning of the file extension.

◆ Removes any characters not allowed in DOS names and converts them to underscores.

◆ Converts the name to six characters, with a tilde (~) and a number attached to the end.

◆ Truncates the extension to three characters.

Given how long filenames convert to 8.3 conventions, you may want to keep that in mind when using long filenames so that your filenames make sense in both versions. For example, you could name a file `PRSNLLET-Personal letters file.DOC`, so that the shortened name would be `PRSNLL~1.DOC`.

You can't format a floppy to NTFS format. There's a good reason for this: the NTFS file structure is complex so that finding data on large disks is fast and easy, but it takes up more room than a floppy disk can supply. Floppy disks don't need NTFS.

However, you can create files with long names on a floppy, since the Win2K version of FAT supports 256-character filenames. Win2K keeps two names for floppy files, the long name that you originally assigned and a truncated 8.3 name. DOS sees the shorter 8.3 name, however, making it possible for you to work with files that have long names under Win2K but short names under DOS.

Which Filesystem?

Which filesystem should you use? Table 10.1 gives you an at-a-glance comparison of NTFS and the FAT filesystems.

TABLE 10.1: COMPARING NTFS AND FAT IN WIN2K

FEATURE	NTFS	FAT32	FAT
Filename length	256 characters	256 characters	256 characters under Windows 9x, NT, Win2K; 8.3 under DOS
File attributes	Extended	Limited	Limited
Associated operating system	Win2K and Windows NT	Win2K, Win98, Win95 OSR2	DOS
Organization	Tree structure	Centrally located menu	Centrally located menu
Software RAID support?	Yes	Yes	Yes
Accessible when you boot the computer from a DOS floppy?	No	No	Yes
Maximum volume size supported	1024GB	32GB (and will not format volumes smaller than 512MB)	4GB
Cluster size on a 1GB volume	2KB	4KB	32KB
Supports extensible volumes?	Yes	No	No

NTFS supports file compression, file encryption, transaction logging that can keep your disks from becoming corrupted due to aborted writes, and granular local security. It's more efficient in the way it uses disk space, particularly on the large disks so common these days. You need to use it to support drive mounting and extended volumes, discussed earlier in this chapter. It builds strong bodies 12 ways. (Okay, maybe that was Wonder Bread.) When *shouldn't* you use NTFS?

The only times NTFS won't work for you is when you need to support other operating systems *on the same computer as Win2K.* (When it comes to network access, the filesystem does not matter—a Windows 98 computer can read an NTFS volume across the network.) FAT is widely supported by other operating systems, so you should use it on any volume that you'll need to have accessible to other OSes on the same computer. (You'll also need to put those volumes on a basic disk, recall.) The exception to this is Windows 95 OSR 2 or Windows 98. FAT32 is more space efficient than FAT, so you should use FAT32 on any volumes that need to be locally accessible to both Win2K and Windows 9x. FAT32 volumes are *not* readable by NT 4 without the FAT32 support available for purchase from www.sysinternals.com, so if you need to keep data for NT 4, Windows 9x, and Win2K and don't have this tool, you should use FAT.

SHOULD I USE FAT ON THE SYSTEM PARTITION?

Mastering Windows NT Server 4 recommended that you format the system partition with FAT. If you did this, then you could copy the installation files from the CD to the system partition. That way, if you needed to reinstall, you could reinstall from the hard disk after booting from a floppy instead of using the slower CD.

The only trouble with keeping all system files and said installation files on a FAT-formatted partition is that doing so is enormously wasteful of disk space. Like many of the rest of us, Win2K/NT has gotten fatter as it's gotten older. The \I386 folder on the Win2K CD is 327MB. The NTFS-formatted Win2K system directory on one Win2K server—*not* including the \I386 folder—is about 850MB. (For comparison, the FAT-formatted system partition on an installation of Windows NT 4, Terminal Server Edition I have is 427MB, not including any installation files.) To be pretty sure I wouldn't run out of room, I'd need a system partition at least 2GB in size. You can format a 2GB partition with FAT—barely. That's the largest amount of disk space that FAT can "see" under Win2K. But doing so is horribly wasteful. As discussed earlier in this chapter, the FAT filesystem is wasteful of space on large partitions because it organizes the disk into very large clusters. 2GB might not be enough to store all the system files.

Thankfully for the bloat problem, a new tool in Win2K called the Recovery Console makes formatting the system drive with FAT no longer necessary. I'll go into the Recovery Console in detail in Chapter 21, but the short version is that it's an NTFS-compatible command-line recovery tool that you can use to get at your system directory and make repairs. You can install support for the Recovery Console while you still have a working OS, and can also get to this tool from the Win2K Setup program. So as long as you have the original CD or the Setup boot floppies, you can get to the Recovery Console and fix things, which means that it's fine to use NTFS on the system partition.

FAT system partition or no, it's still a good idea to copy the installation files to the hard disk. That way, you've always got an easily accessible copy of them when you need them to install a new driver or service.

USING THE FORMATTING TOOLS

Formatting a volume outside of the Disk Management tool is simple. If you access an unformatted volume (one you created but didn't format) from Explorer, you'll see a message telling you that the disk (volume, really, but it says "disk") isn't formatted and asking if you want to format the volume now. Click Yes to format the disk, and you'll open the Format dialog box in Figure 10.34.

FIGURE 10.34

Choose a filesystem for the new volume.

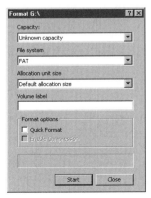

In the Format dialog box, choose the filesystem that you want to use on the partition: FAT (the default, for some reason), FAT32, or NTFS. If you format with NTFS, you can even change the cluster size—but don't do that. The default works fine for most uses. For best security, make all of your partitions NTFS, which is locally accessible to Win2K (or to NT with Service Pack 4 or later installed) and to any operating system across the network. The Recovery Console (discussed in Chapter 21) makes it no longer necessary to format the system partition with FAT for recovery purposes.

Formatting with Win2K is a little different from formatting in NT. First, fault-tolerant volumes can use any format that Win2K supports, not just NTFS. Second, you can use the Quick Format option to format the volume on any new volume, even fault-tolerant volumes, which you could not do with NT 4.

Click the Start button to begin the format. A dialog box will appear and ask you to confirm the format; click OK and the format operation will begin. A dialog box will show you the process of the format. Be warned: although the dialog box has a Cancel button, canceling the format won't necessarily restore the partition to its original condition.

If you're addicted to the command prompt, you can still use it to format disks. To do so, open the Command Prompt located in the `Accessories` folder and type the following:

```
format driveletter: /fs:filesystem
```

driveletter is, of course, the drive letter of the logical drive, and *filesystem* is FAT, FAT32, or NTFS. For example, to format a newly created drive E: as NTFS, you would type **format e: /fs:ntfs**. You must specify a file format—there's no default.

CONVERTING FAT OR FAT32 TO NTFS

If you have FAT or FAT32 volumes on your disk that you'd like to be NTFS, you don't have to back up their data, reformat the disks, and then start over. Instead, you can use the CONVERT command-prompt utility. Its format is simple:

```
convert driveletter: /fs:ntfs
```

So, for example, to convert drive P: to NTFS, you'd type **convert p: /fs:ntfs**. You'd see output like the following:

```
The type of the file system is FAT32.
Determining disk space required for filesystem conversion
Total disk space:            51200 KB.
Free space on volume:        50395 KB.
Space required for conversion:  2303 KB.
Converting file system
Conversion complete
```

Notice that you must have a certain amount of free space (in this case, *free space* means unused space in the partition) on the volume to convert it. That's a place to store data while the clusters are being reorganized. If you don't have enough free space, then you can't convert the volume. Thus, it's a good idea to convert volumes before they get too full.

You cannot convert to any filesystem other than NTFS, and you cannot reverse the process. You also can't convert the current drive, which means that you cannot convert the system drive to NTFS without rebooting. The conversion will happen during the reboot process.

NOTE *A bug in Windows 2000 may have prevented you from converting FAT32 volumes larger than 20GB to NTFS, due to a problem with logical-block addressing on some IDE drives. This bug was fixed in SP2.*

Defragmenting Disks

One of the simpler ways you can improve disk performance is to regularly defragment disks that need it, thus putting all the parts of each file into the same place on the disk for easier retrieval.

Defragmenting? Recall that each cluster can hold only one file at most, even if the data file is 1KB and the cluster is 8KB. If a file is too big to fit into a single cluster, then the remaining file data will go in the next available cluster, and the next, and the next, until the file is completely stored. Each cluster that the file's stored in contains a pointer to the next cluster where that file's data is contained, until you get to the last cluster containing data for that file and the pointer says "that's all, folks." When you open a file stored on disk, the filesystem driver looks in the file catalog at the top of the disk and finds the clusters that the file is stored in. It then pulls the data from those clusters and reads it into memory.

How Disks Get Fragmented and Why You Care

When a disk is new, the available clusters are all next to each other, so it doesn't matter much if a file is distributed among several clusters. As you use a disk, however, this is likely to change. Create and delete files, and clusters get freed up unevenly. And the filesystem driver doesn't look for a run of clusters big enough to store all a file's data in one place; it just stores data in the first clusters available. If clusters 1–3, 10, and 15–100 are available, file A needing five clusters will go into clusters 1–3, 10, 15, and 16, not into clusters 15–20. When a file is spread among several noncontiguous clusters, it's said to be *fragmented*.

NOTE *Because large FAT volumes use much bigger clusters than large NTFS volumes, files on NTFS volumes are more likely to be fragmented. This isn't an argument in favor of using FAT—those larger clusters also imply more wasted disk space, and you don't get the other benefits of NTFS—but an observation about how clusters work. You can increase the cluster size on NTFS volumes if you'd like to reduce file fragmentation.*

Data is stored in the cluster it's originally put in—if a more convenient cluster becomes available, then the data isn't moved. Even if clusters 4–9 become free when a file is deleted, file A will keep using the same clusters it started with.

This isn't terrible. You'll still get all the data from the file, even if the file is fragmented. However, it will take a little longer to open fragmented files, and in case of serious disk errors, it's harder to recover badly fragmented files than ones stored in contiguous clusters. A *very* fragmented system disk can actually cause Win2K to crash if it takes too long to find a file that it needs. Therefore, it's a good idea to keep your disks defragmented.

Using the Defragmenting Tool

Win2K comes with a defragmenting tool. To defragment a volume or see whether it needs to be defragmented, right-click the volume in Explorer and open the volume's property sheet. Turn to the Tools tab that's shown in Figure 10.35.

FIGURE 10.35

The Tools tab contains all disk maintenance tools.

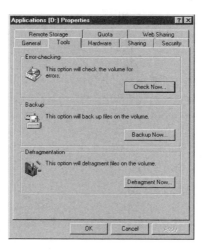

Click the Defragment Now button to open the screen shown in Figure 10.36. Notice that only local volumes are listed. You can't defragment volumes across the network.

FIGURE 10.36

The Disk Defragmenter shows all logical volumes on the computer.

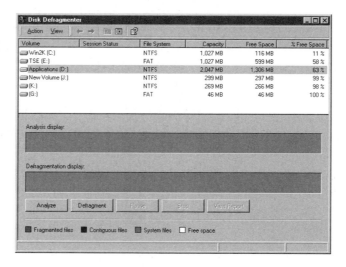

First, see whether the disk needs to be defragmented at all. Highlight the volume in the list and click the Analyze button. The defragmenter will chug away for a minute (it's pretty fast—a 2GB volume took only a few seconds to analyze) and then display its recommendation (see Figure 10.37).

FIGURE 10.37

Analyze disks before defragmenting them.

If you want to see more information about how fragmented your disk is, click the View Report button to open the dialog box shown in Figure 10.38.

FIGURE 10.38

View the report to see how badly the disk is fragmented.

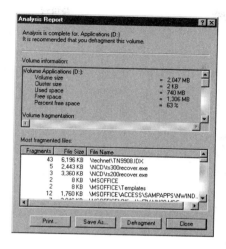

What are you looking at here? The top part of this dialog box displays six types of information:

◆ Basic volume statistics

◆ Volume fragmentation

◆ File fragmentation

◆ Pagefile fragmentation

◆ Folder fragmentation

◆ Directory table fragmentation

Most of the information about the volume should be pretty simple to figure out: the volume size is the size of the partition, the cluster size is the size of each logical storage unit on the drive (in this case, 2KB, or 4 sectors), and the rest of the section describes how much space on the disk is currently used, how much is free, and what the percentage of free space is.

The Volume Fragmentation section below the Volume Information section is a little more relevant to the question of how much file reads are delayed, describing the status of the files themselves. The total fragmentation describes how fragmented the entire disk is; the file fragmentation how fragmented the used parts of the disk are (that is, the proportion of files that are fragmented), and the free space fragmentation describes how fragmented the unused space on the disk is. Free space fragmentation matters when it comes to creating new files—the more fragmented the unused space, the more likely it is that new files will be fragmented too.

File Fragmentation gives you file-level fragmentation information. This area lists the total number of files on disk, the average size of a file, the total fragments, and the average number of fragments per file. Ideally, the value for fragments per file should be as close to 1.00 as possible, as that number indicates that all files are contiguous. In this example, the ratio is 2.09, which indicates that files are, on average, fragmented into three clusters (three, because that .09 that won't fit into the second cluster). The Most Fragmented Files window at the bottom of this dialog box gives you more specifics about which files are most fragmented, but you don't need to worry about this unless you're interested in comparing the "before" and "after" results.

TIP *If you are interested in comparing the "before" and "after" readings, click the Save As button to save the entire fragmentation report as a text file.*

The rest of the information shows fragmentation for specific parts of the disk volume structure so you can see just how fragmented the pagefile and directory structure are.

That's the current status of your volume. To fix it, close any files (including application files) using the fragmented volume, then click the Defragment button. The tool will start reorganizing the files on the disk to put them into contiguous clusters. Defragmenting the disk will *not* free up space on the disk, but it will group all free space together to allow it to be used more efficiently.

NOTE *You can defragment a volume with open files, but it will take much less time if you close all files first. This makes it difficult to defragment the system volume.*

By the way—defragment your disks before they get too full. The Disk Defragmenter requires 15 percent of free volume space to store data that it's rearranging. If the volume is too full, you'll need to remove files or (if possible) extend the volume before you can defragment it.

Using CHKDSK

File data is stored in clusters. If a file is stored in more than one cluster, then each cluster the file's stored in contains a pointer to the next cluster holding file data. If those pointers are lost, you can't pull up the entire file from disk.

NTFS's transaction logging prevents this from happening. Each NTFS volume maintains a *transaction log* of all proposed changes to the volume structure, checking off—*committing*—each change as it's completed and only then. When you restart the system, NTFS inspects the transaction log and rolls the state of the disk back to the last committed change. Basically, it's similar to the Last Known Good option that you can choose on startup to restore your server to its status at the last successful boot, except that transaction logging and rollback is automatic. Notice that transaction logging works only for *system* data, not for user data. If the disk failed in the middle of a write action, then the data that was supposed to be written to disk is lost. However, the volume structure of the disk will be all right. Any data already written to disk will be recoverable.

FAT and FAT32 do not have transaction logging. If the disk fails—perhaps due to a kicked power cord—before a write action is completed and you restart the disk, there's no record of the last valid disk structure. You may need to run CHKDSK to check the pointers used in the file allocation table. This isn't to say that there's never any need to run CHKDSK on an NTFS volume—NTFS protects the integrity of filesystem data, or *metadata*, not user data. You can use the command-line version of the tool to edit the size of the transaction log or to check the disk for bad sectors (sectors to which the filesystem shouldn't write because they're damaged and might not read properly). Read on to learn more about what CHKDSK is doing and how to use the graphical and command-line versions.

WHAT IS CHKDSK DOING?

Let's take a look at how CHKDSK works on an NTFS volume. When you run CHKDSK, you're telling the tool to make three passes over the specified drive to examine the structure of the metadata on the disk—again, that's the data describing how user data is organized on the disk. Metadata tells the filesystem what files are stored in which clusters, how many clusters are free and where they are, and what clusters contain bad sectors. In addition, it provides pointers to files.

During CHKDSK's first pass over the selected drive, it scans each file's record in the master file table (MFT). It examines each file's record for consistency and lists all the file records in use and which clusters those file records are stored in. It then compares this record with the drive bitmap stored in the MFT. Any discrepancies between the two are noted in CHKDSK's output.

During the second pass, CHKDSK checks the drive's directory structure. It makes sure that each index record in the MFT corresponds to an actual directory on the drive and that each file's record in the MFT corresponds to a file stored somewhere in the volume. CHKDSK also makes sure that all time and date stamps for all files and directories are up to date. Finally, it makes sure that no files with an MFT entry but no existence in any directory are present on the volume. If the MFT entry is complete, the file can usually be restored to the directory where it should be kept.

The third pass of CHKDSK is for checking the integrity of the security descriptors for each file and directory object on the NTFS volume. During this pass, CHKDSK makes sure that all security settings are consistent. It does not check the security settings to make sure that they're appropriate to a particular folder or even to make sure that the group or user account named exists. Rather, the security pass of CHKDSK simply makes sure that, assuming all security information is correct, the security settings for the files and directory objects in the volume will work.

The final and optional pass of CHKDSK (done only if you use the /R switch) tests the sectors in the volume reserved for user data (the metadata sectors are always checked) to see whether all of them can be read from and written to correctly. If CHKDSK finds a bad sector, then it marks the placement of this sector in the volume report. If the sector was part of a cluster that was being used, CHKDSK will regenerate and move the data to a new cluster that contains only good sectors if the volume is fault tolerant, or fill the bad sector with a string that means "no data should be stored here." As you can see, the data in the bad sector won't be recovered unless there's some redundant data to copy it from, but at least the filesystem won't store more data in the cluster containing the bad sector.

How long does this process take? Depends on the size of the volume, the depth of the check, and what else the computer is doing during the check. CHKDSK is extremely CPU and disk intensive, and if it must contend with other processes for CPU time, then the check will necessarily take longer. The best rule of thumb is that, if you can avoid it, you shouldn't run the disk checker on a computer that is actively trying to do something else. In any case, you can't run CHKDSK on a volume that currently has files open. If you attempt to do so, CHKDSK will tell you that it can't get exclusive control of the volume and ask if you want to schedule the check for the next time the computer restarts.

There are two forms of CHKDSK in Win2K: the graphical tool and the command-line utility. The graphical tool is simpler, but the command-line utility has many more options and is more flexible.

NOTE *The version of CHKDSK that came with NT 4 is not compatible with Win2K because Win2K's NTFS file structure is different. To check NTFS volumes under Win2K, you'll need to use the version of CHKDSK that comes with the OS.*

RUNNING CHKDSK FROM EXPLORER

The simplest way to run CHKDSK is from Explorer, as this tool doesn't demand that you know the command syntax and just uses the default options. To use the tool, select a drive in Explorer and open its property sheet. Turn to the Tools tab, then click the Check Now button to open the dialog box in Figure 10.39.

FIGURE 10.39

The graphical disk checker

There are two options available from the graphical version of CHKDSK. If you tell CHKDSK to attempt to fix filesystem errors, then it will try to resolve any orphaned files—files that have entries in the filesystem catalog but don't appear in a directory on the volume. If you check the box that tells CHKDSK to scan for and attempt recovery of bad sectors, you're telling it to make the optional fourth pass of checking each sector on the disk instead of just the ones containing metadata. As you'll recall from the description of just what CHKDSK is doing, data in bad sectors will not always be recoverable—only if the volume is fault tolerant and CHKDSK can get the data's redundancy information elsewhere is the data recoverable.

To begin checking the selected volume, click the Start button. The computer will begin grinding away using the options you supplied. (If you don't check either box, CHKDSK runs in read-only mode. Since the graphical tool doesn't display a report, read-only mode doesn't help you much.) The dialog box will display each phase of the disk check and display a status bar showing how far along each pass is until it's completed.

When the disk check is done, a message will appear telling you that the disk has been checked. No report of bad sectors or other information will appear. You can check another disk by exiting the current drive's property sheet and selecting another drive from Explorer.

RUNNING CHKDSK FROM THE COMMAND PROMPT

You have little control over how CHKDSK works when you run it from Explorer. If you'd like more control, you'll need to use the command prompt. The command-line options can be a little tricky to use, but they're faster and more flexible than the GUI once you get accustomed to them.

Without any arguments, CHKDSK runs in read-only mode on the current drive. You'll see command-line output showing the progress of each pass over the volume, and then you'll get a report like the following, showing you how the total disk space is used:

```
2096450 KB total disk space.
1011256 KB in 9214 files.
   2248 KB in 539 indexes.
      0 KB in bad sectors.
  31116 KB in use by the system.
```

```
   4096 KB occupied by the log file.
1051830 KB available on disk.

   2048 bytes in each allocation unit.
1048225 total allocation units on disk.
 525915 allocation units available on disk.
```

You should recognize the terminology used from the previous discussions of how NTFS organizes files on disk. The indexes are in fact directories on the disk. The log file is the transaction log used to record changes to the volume metadata so that any incomplete changes can be rolled back. The allocation units are clusters.

So—you've got a disk report, but that report doesn't allow you to do anything. To control the process, you'll need to plug in one or more of the switches explained in Table 10.2.

TABLE 10.2: COMMAND-LINE SWITCHES FOR CHKDSK

SWITCH	WHAT IT DOES
/f	Tells CHKDSK to attempt to fix filesystem errors, such as orphaned files. The help file for this switch says that it fixes errors on the disk, but that's not really accurate. It fixes inconsistencies in the filesystem catalog.
/v	Has different results depending on whether you use the switch on FAT volumes or on NTFS. On FAT volumes, this switch lists the full path of every file on the volume. On NTFS volumes, it runs CHKDSK in verbose mode, reporting any cleanup messages relevant to fixing filesystem errors or missing security descriptors.
/r	Checks every sector on the disk to make sure it can be written to and read from. Any bad sectors are marked as bad.
/x	Forces the volume to dismount first if dismounting is necessary to run CHKDSK (that is, if there are open handles to the chosen volume). Choosing this option will dismount all volumes.
/i	Tells CHKDSK not to check the indices on NTFS volumes. In other words, CHKDSK will skip the second pass of the disk checking operation. Although selecting this option can save you quite a bit of time on volumes with a lot of directories, it's not a good idea to use this switch unless you must since any inconsistencies in the directory structure will go unnoticed.
/c	Tells CHKDSK not to check for cycles on the NTFS volume. Cycles are a rare kind of disk error wherein a subdirectory becomes a subdirectory of itself, creating an infinite loop. You can probably turn this switch on safely since cycles are rare, but it won't save you much time.
/l[:size]	On NTFS volumes, specifies a new size for the transaction log. The default size is 4096KB, and for most purposes that's just fine.
volume	Specifies the mount point, volume name, or (if followed by a colon) the drive letter of the logical volume to be checked.
filename	On FAT volumes, tells CHKDSK to evaluate the specified filename to report on how fragmented it is. This option does not work on NTFS volumes.

The order of the switches is as follows:

```
chkdsk [volume[[path]filename]]] [/f] [/v] [/r] [/x] [/i][/c] [/l[:size]]
```

Using Encrypted NTFS

One of the new features of Win2K is its support for native public key encryption, allowing you to secure your documents and folders so that only you—or the people you give the key to—can view the documents. It's a handy way of keeping even shared documents private or of protecting files on a machine that can be easily stolen, such as a laptop.

Encryption doesn't conceal the fact that the documents exist. Rather, when you attempt to open an encrypted file, Win2K checks to see whether you have a key to that file. If you don't, then you're forbidden access to the file. This denial is not application dependent—for example, a Word document won't be accessible in Word *or* WordPad. The user without the public key can't open the file object at all.

TIP   The process of checking for an encryption key is pretty compute intensive, so it's probably best not to encrypt files stored on a terminal server or other CPU-bound server.

Since encryption is an attribute, like compression or the archive bit, it's only supported on NTFS 5 volumes.

How Win2K Encryption Works

When you encrypt data, you're generating a request for a new security certificate identifying you to Win2K as who you say you are. A *cryptographic service provider (CSP)* generates two 56-bit keys: a public key, used for encrypting data for you, and a private key, used for decrypting that data. The two keys are unrelated—knowing a public key does not give you the ability to guess the private key.

The CSP passes the public key to the certificate authority, which uses it to create a public key for you. The certificate and public key are stored in the `Personal/Certificates` folder located in the Certificates add-in to the MMC (see Figure 10.40).

FIGURE 10.40

Personal encryption certificate

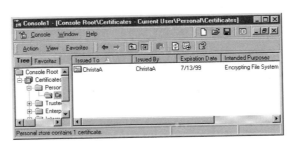

NOTE   Don't worry about the certificate expiration date of 7/13/99, which would seem to imply that I can no longer use this certificate to prove my identity and decrypt files. Microsoft only used two-digit numbers in the MMC to show when certificates would expire. If you open the certificate and look at the Details tab, you'll see that the certificate expires on July 13, 2099.

Win2K users can encrypt data across the network, but the data is only encrypted when written to a disk, not while traveling across the network—you'll need network encryption for that. Also, the certificate will always be originally on the Win2K machine where the data is stored. The private key is stored in the Registry of the computer where the data is stored.

Only Win2K users and clients will be able to encrypt and decrypt data. Even though NT and Windows 9*x* users can read and open files on NTFS 5 volumes—and even though encryption standards apply to them, too—the NT and Windows 9*x* users don't have the tools they'd need to encrypt the data unless they're running a Win2K session.

This information isn't required when it comes to encrypting or decrypting your own data, but it could come in useful when it comes to recovering someone else's encrypted data or protecting laptop encryptions. We'll do the simple part first, then return to the question of why you need to protect certificates and how you can do it.

Encrypting Files

To encrypt a file or folder from Explorer, right-click the file or folder (you cannot encrypt entire volumes) and open its property sheet. On the General tab, there's an Advanced button.

TIP   *If there isn't an Advanced button, make sure that you're looking at an NTFS volume, not a FAT or FAT32 one.*

Click that button to open the Advanced Attributes dialog box shown in Figure 10.41.

FIGURE 10.41

Encryption is an advanced NTFS attribute.

You can either compress or encrypt file data, not both. Check the option you want and click OK. If the folder containing the file is not encrypted, you'll be warned of this and prompted to encrypt both the folder and the file. Normally, it's a good idea to let Win2K encrypt the folder as well. If you leave the folder unencrypted, changes to the file that make it appear to be a new file will leave the file unencrypted. All new files created within a folder inherit the folder's encryption attributes.

TIP   *If using encryption, encrypt the* My Documents *folder for all users (*%userprofile%\My Documents*) to ensure that the personal folder, where most Office documents are stored, will be encrypted by default.*

The encryption attribute is now set. If anyone but you, even someone with administrator privileges, attempts to open the file or run the encrypted executable, they'll be denied access. There are no obvious visual cues (such as blue text) telling you that certain files or folders are encrypted, but if you look in the left pane of the Win2K Explorer window when an encrypted file is displayed, you'll see the listing.

COPYING AND MOVING ENCRYPTED FILES

New files in a directory inherit the encryption attributes of that directory: if the directory is encrypted, the file will be encrypted as well. If the directory is not encrypted, the file won't be encrypted. What about files *copied* to a directory? This is where it can get a little tricky:

◆ If you copy or move an unencrypted file to an encrypted NTFS directory, that file will become encrypted.

◆ If you copy or move an encrypted file to an unencrypted NTFS directory, the file will remain encrypted.

◆ If you copy or move an encrypted file to a FAT or FAT32 directory, that file will no longer be encrypted (since encryption is an NTFS attribute).

You can also encrypt files from the command prompt with the CIPHER command. To encrypt a single folder in the current directory, type **cipher /e** *foldername*, where *foldername* is the name of the folder you want to encrypt. To decrypt the same folder, replace the /e switch with /d, like this: **cipher /d** *foldername*. The command will report back to you whether the operation succeeded or not. You can't encrypt or decrypt a folder's contents if it's in use (or even displayed in an Explorer window), so be sure that no one's looking at files that you're attempting to manipulate.

NOTE   Again, you can't encrypt compressed data or vice versa. If you attempt to encrypt a compressed file or folder with CIPHER, you'll get an Access Denied error. Uncompress the file or folder and try again to encrypt it, and the operation should work.

Normally, CIPHER will only encrypt the files in the immediate folder you specify, not the subfolders. It will also only encrypt parent folders if told to, leaving the files' parent directories unencrypted. To keep from accidentally decrypting a file (by apparently making it new in a decrypted folder), encrypt the folder as well by typing **cipher /e /s:**foldername **/a**. This will encrypt all files within the specified folder and all subfolders to that folder.

ENFORCING ENCRYPTION

Encrypted files don't have any obvious differences alerting people to their off-limits status, and the contents of an encrypted folder are displayed like any other shared or locally available data. The only way you can tell that you've attempted to open an encrypted file is that you won't be able to do so.

Sadly, the error messages you get when attempting to access files that someone else has encrypted represent a help-desk call waiting to happen. Whether accessing the encrypted file locally or from the network, from Win2K or from an earlier operating system, you'll see an error message like the one in Figure 10.42.

FIGURE 10.42

Windows 9*x* and NT 4 users may not be sure why they can't open an encrypted file.

What about administrators? If someone with administrator privileges opens the file's property sheet and edits the encryption attribute, they'll be unable to apply the change—they'll be denied access. What happens if an administrator takes ownership of the file? File ownership doesn't actually matter to encryption. Even if you (as the administrator) take ownership of an encrypted file, you won't be able to read it.

Sometimes, you may want to know just who encrypted a file. The Explorer UI will tell you that a file *is* encrypted, but not *who* encrypted it. It'd be sort of annoying to find that someone had encrypted a bunch of files in some public network share, leading to a rash of calls from users who are suddenly unable to access those files. And yes, that can actually happen—if you create a file and are that file's owner, but you allow me read and write permissions on the file, then I can encrypt it, and then you can't see its contents anymore because you're not the one who encrypted it.

As an administrator, you can fix things by decrypting the files—but wouldn't you like to know the identity of the moron who caused the trouble? You can, with a command-line Resource Kit utility named EFSINFO.

For example, run EFSINFO with the /u option (to show user information) and /r (to show recovery agent information), like this:

```
efsinfo /U /r /:c:\working somefile.doc
```

and it'll tell you who encrypted `somefile.doc` and who can decrypt it, like this:

```
c:\working

.: Encrypted
  Users who can decrypt:
    LABRYNTH\ChristaA (CN=ChristaA,L=EFS,OU=EFS File Encryption Certificate)
  Recovery Agents:
    GEEKTOY\Administrator (OU=EFS File Encryption Certificate, L=EFS,
      CN=Administrator)

somefile.doc: Encrypted
  Users who can decrypt:
    LABRYNTH\ChristaA (CN=ChristaA,L=EFS,OU=EFS File Encryption Certificate)
  Recovery Agents:
    GEEKTOY\Administrator (OU=EFS File Encryption Certificate, L=EFS,
      CN=Administrator)
```

PROTECTING ENCRYPTION KEYS

Microsoft positioned Win2K's encryption services especially for laptop users who wanted to keep their data secure even if their laptop was stolen. However, there's one major hole in this security plan. If someone *does* steal a laptop and can log in with administrator rights, they can edit the certificate settings in a way that allows them to decrypt the data.

NOTE *Of course, if you don't password-protect your laptop, then decrypting your files is as easy as logging in as you.*

To avoid this problem, Microsoft recommends exporting each user's certificate and saving it to disk, then deleting the certificate on the computer. To do so, follow these steps:

1. In the MMC, add the Certificates snap-in.

2. In the `Personal` folder, open the `Certificates` folder. The per-user certificates on the computer will be displayed in the right pane.

3. Right-click the certificate that you want to export as a file and choose Export from the All Tasks menu. This will start the Export Certificate Wizard, which asks whether you'd like to export the private key along with the certificate. You'll need the private key to decrypt data.

4. In the next screen, choose the export options, including the file type, the strength of encryption you want to use, and what you want to do with the local key if the export works. (Personally, I'd delete it manually once I was sure that the export had worked rather than letting Win2K delete it for me.)

5. If you chose to export the private key, you'll need to supply a password to import the key again. Choose this password carefully, as it's protecting your encryption.

6. Choose a filename for the key by either typing a path or browsing for it. You can save the file on any volume, not just NTFS.

7. The final screen of the wizard will display your choices. Review them carefully, then click Finish to export the keys. If the export operation worked, Win2K will pop up a quick message box to tell you so.

Save the certificate on a floppy disk or, better yet, a safe network location where it can get backed up, then delete it from the computer. You'll be able to open encrypted files, but the certificate will no longer be on the machine.

To import the certificate to another computer or replace it on the same one, open the same `Personal` folder, right-click the `Certificates` folder, and choose Import from the All Tasks menu. This will start the Import Certificate Wizard:

1. Browse for the file you saved.

2. If the certificate you're importing includes the private key, you'll need to supply the password assigned when the key was exported. Type it in and choose the degree of control you want over the private key.

3. Specify where the new key should go. For user keys, the `Personal` folder should be fine.

4. Review the importing options, then click Finish to import the key. Win2K will tell you if the importing action succeeded.

NOTE *For more about certificates, see Chapter 8.*

RECOVERING ENCRYPTED FILES

If I encrypt a file, how do I recover the file? EFS won't let you encrypt files unless you have at least one account set up as what Windows 2000 calls an EFS Recovery Agent. By default, workstations and member servers' recovery agents are just the default Administrator account—not members of the Administrators group, but the Administrator *account*. The default recovery agent for a domain is the default administrator for the computer that was the first domain controller installed for that domain.

To recover a file for someone, you must move that file to a computer with a recovery agent, then log in as the recovery agent and decrypt the file, either through the GUI by removing its encryption attribute in the Advanced section of the file or folder properties, or with the `cipher` command that we discussed earlier:

```
cipher /u/a filename
```

In other words, EFS doesn't see any difference between you, the person who originally encrypted a file, and the recovery agent; if you had an encrypted Word file and the recovery agent tried to open it, she'd see your file. If you've denied the recovery agent access to your Word file, then she won't be able to open it. Of course, if the recovery agent doesn't have access to your file, then she also can't decrypt it for you—but that's easily remedied by an administrator who can take ownership of the file and then grant read and write access for the file to the recovery agent. Again, if you haven't changed the defaults, then the recovery agent is the default Administrator. That account can do just about anything anyway, so getting control of a file is no trouble.

Let's look a bit further into the recovery agent account. First, do you really want to have to use the default Administrator account for anything? Probably not—that's a lot of power to give to the person in charge of making sure users can read their files—so how do you change which account can handle emergency decryptions? It's harder than you might expect. EFS encrypts and decrypts your files using a simple symmetrical algorithm; the same "password" (not a user password that you can change, but a "password" that you give to EFS to permit it to encrypt and decrypt) encrypts and decrypts your files. But it *stores* that password using an asymmetric, public key–type encryption method. When you encrypt a file, EFS encrypts the password using your public key and stores the now-encrypted password in NTFS. When EFS needs to decrypt a file, it asks NTFS for that encrypted password. NTFS passes the request to an independent module of the EFS driver that handles all reads, writes, and opens on encrypted files and directories, as well as operations to encrypt, decrypt, and recover file data when it is written to or read from disk, and which passes the information back to NTFS. NTFS then gives the password to the EFS driver, which uses your private key to decrypt the password. Now that it has the password, it can decrypt the file. (You've probably guessed by now that encrypting files slows things down a trifle.) How does EFS, then, allow more than one person to decrypt a file? By again exploiting NTFS: Not only can it store the file's password encrypted with your public key, EFS will also include that same password encrypted with the public key or keys of as many recovery agents as you like.

Where things get sticky is in the process of introducing EFS to a prospective recovery agent's public key/private key pair: you need a hierarchy of certificate authorities recognized by your computer. Without a certificate hierarchy, there are no certificates, and without certificates, you can't introduce EFS to new recovery agents. (With an exception—stay tuned.) So you'll need at least a certificate server or two running before you can monkey with the list of recovery agents. In an Active Directory environment, that's not too hard to accomplish, although it does require some work: AD doesn't install a certificate hierarchy by default. And in a stand-alone server environment, you could, if you wanted, install a certificate server to act as a one-server hierarchy and issue certificates with that.

NOTE *On a stand-alone 2000 Professional system, you'd have to first create a certificate authority on a system run-ning Server, then get the Professional system to accept the certificates from the server, and then create the certificates and export them to the Professional system. That's an awful lot of work. Practically speaking, then, stand-alone Professional sys-tems may have no option but to leave their default Administrator as the sole recovery agent. For laptop users, that means two things: Really, truly, don't use the Administrator account for day-to-day logins, and there's yet another reason to password-protect that account.*

But wait—at least one account has a certificate without having to go through all of the certificate-authority stuff. Where did the first recovery agent, the default Administrator, get its certificate? Appar-ently EFS generates a self-signing certificate for the default Admin. I've not been able to find a way to get it to build certificates like that for other accounts; it'd be a nice, low-overhead way to add some flexibility to EFS administration.

Decrypting Files

Decrypting encrypted files is a simple matter if you're the person who encrypted the file in the first place. When you open it, the file is automatically decrypted—the action is completely transparent to the user.

That decryption is temporary, however—as soon as you close the file, it's encrypted again. If you want other people to be able to use the file, then you'll need to decrypt it. To decrypt a file or folder from Explorer, open its property sheet and click the Advanced button on the General tab. Uncheck the box next to Encrypt Contents to Secure Data. The file is now open to anyone who has access to it.

Enough of That! Managing Disk Quotas

Many administrators found NT 4 incomplete in one way or another, and one of the perennial com-plaints was its lack of quota management tools. Without quota management, it's hard to control the amount of disk space people on the network use; even in these days of cheap and plentiful storage, there comes a limit to the amount of time and money you want to put into storing every single JPEG John Doe receives.

Several NT-compatible quota management applications exist, but adding quota management to NT has historically not been cheap. To help those who need a basic form of quota management, Win2K now includes simple quota management tools. Win2K's tools don't include all the function-ality some third-party products do—one big shortcoming is that you must assign disk quotas on a per-user basis—but they're a start and have the usual advantage: you've already paid for them.

Background: How Quota Management Works

The process of quota management is straightforward: The quota manager keeps an eye on writes to the disk of protected lettered volumes based on criteria set by the network administrator. If the pro-tected volume reaches or exceeds a certain level, then a message is sent to the person writing to the volume warning them that the volume is near quota, or the quota manager prevents the user from writing to the volume altogether, or both. The mechanics of how all this works varies from product to product, but the basic effect is the same: users can't write to volumes that are at or exceed their preset quota.

Win2K's quota management is based on user identity and the folder the user is storing information in, so you can control not only how much space a person uses but *where* they're using it.

Setting Up User Quotas

By default, Win2K quotas are turned off. To start working with quota management, open Explorer and right-click the volume you want to protect. This can be any NTFS 5 volume with a drive letter, whether local or a drive letter mapped from another server. Turn to the Quota tab shown in Figure 10.43.

FIGURE 10.43

Disk quotas are disabled by default.

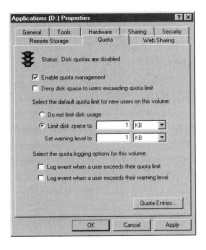

NOTE   *You cannot set quotas on a folder within a volume; you can only set them on the entire volume.*

The first order of business is to enable quotas. To turn on disk quotas and make the management options available, check that box. You can set up all the options before clicking OK or Apply to enable quotas. Choose Apply to keep the property sheet open.

Next, choose whether to enforce quotas by denying disk space to anyone violating a quota. If you don't check this box (it's not checked by default), then people violating their disk space quotas will still be able to write to the volume.

WARNING   *Never enforce a quota on a system partition and deny disk space to those exceeding it. When booting, Win2K writes data to the disk. If you enforce quotas, then the system may not be able to boot. Actually, there's really no reason to put quotas on the system partition if it's separate from the data partition.*

Third, set a default quota limit. Notice that the default value is 1KB, which means that unless you're in a particularly draconian mood, you're going to want to change the default to something a bit more reasonable. You might, for example, limit each user's quota on the volume containing home directories to 10MB.

Finally, set the logging options, sending events to the System log in the Event Viewer tool when users exceed their quotas or reach the warning level. Users will be identified by name in the System event log, so you know who is running out of assigned disk space.

You've now done the basic job of setting up quota management on the volume. Next, you'll need to create quotas for each person who'll be using that volume. To do so, click the Quota Entries button to open the screen in Figure 10.44.

FIGURE 10.44

Add quota entries to the list.

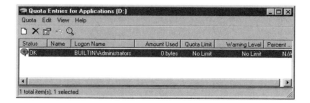

When you start, the only entry will be the default one for the local server's administrator. To add a new entry, choose New Quota Entry from the Quota menu. You'll see the dialog box in Figure 10.45.

FIGURE 10.45

All user accounts on the domain or the local server will be listed.

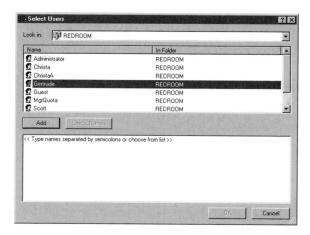

You can choose accounts from either the local user account database or the one for the domain. When you've selected the names for which you want to create entries, click the Add button to display the names in the lower half of the window. Once the names are displayed, you can click OK to move to the next stage of creating the entry.

TIP   Because quotas are enforced on a per-user basis, you can't create quota entries on a per-group basis. However, you can create quota entries for multiple users by Ctrl+clicking the names. All users will start with the same settings.

In the window shown in Figure 10.46, choose whether to enforce quotas for the new entries, and (if so) how much disk space in the volume they get. The amounts shown in this window will be the default you set on the Quota tab.

In this same box, specify the level at which the users will be warned that they're about to run out of disk space. The warning level, obviously, should be less than the quota limit. Win2K will fuss at you if the warning level is more than the quota and make you edit the value so that the warning level is less than or equal to the quota.

FIGURE 10.46

Specify the amount of disk space allocated to the new quota entry.

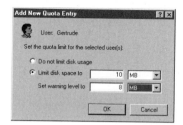

Click OK, and you'll return to the list of quota entries. The new entries will be listed and take effect immediately. If a user attempts to write to the volume and is over quota, she will get a write error. The exact nature of the error message will depend on what application users are using when they attempt to write to the volume, but the basic idea will be the same: they're denied access to the volume because it's now write-protected. To write to the volume, they'll need to delete some of their files to get below quota or have someone else take ownership of their files.

NOTE *Some quota management software allows users a "grace write" when they're over quota, permitting them to save the file they're working on before locking them out. Win2K's quota management does not.*

If you want to use the same quota limits on more than one NTFS 5 volume, you can export the quotas and import them on the new volume. To export a quota, select it in the list in the Quota Entries management tool and choose Export from the Quota menu. The extension for the export files is not displayed. Choose a name for the file and save it. To import the quota settings, open the Quota Entries management tool for that volume and choose Import. Browse for the file, and you can import the quotas.

Quotas may not work as expected on volumes that you originally formatted with FAT or FAT32 and then converted to NTFS. Any files that users created on the FAT volumes will appear to the quota manager to belong to the Administrator, not to the person who created them, since the FAT filesystems don't distinguish file ownership like NTFS volumes do. Therefore, the files that people created on the FAT volume before it was converted to NTFS won't be charged to their quotas, but to the Administrator.

Managing Quota Entries

Some time after you implement quotas in your network, people will start running up against them. If you open the `Quota Entries` folder, you'll see three possible statuses for quotas. Quotas may be within acceptable limits, at warning levels, or over quota (if you haven't prevented users from writing to volumes for which they're over quota).

Win2K doesn't include any messaging tied up to quota limits, so you'll need to keep an eye on this yourself. You can sort the entries in the list by clicking the columns, so if you need to find all the people (for example) who have crossed the warning threshold for quotas, you'd click the Status column. Sadly, there's no mechanism from here to send people messages; you'll need to rely on e-mail or some other messaging technique.

Summary

Win2K's storage management includes many features new to the operating system—features for which many network administrators have clamored for years. In this chapter, you've seen how the new Disk Management tool works to protect data and system disks, learned about the options available when it comes to choosing a disk format, and learned how to use some of the new advanced features of NTFS: disk quotas, encryption, and file compression. Using these tools, you should be better able than ever to protect and manage your data files.

Chapter 11

Creating and Managing Shared Folders

MICROSOFT THREW ALL SORTS of new services, features, and functions into Windows 2000 Server, but at the heart of it all is still the requirement to be a good file server. Windows 2000 took the solid file sharing capabilities of Windows NT, extended them with the Distributed File System (Dfs), and made permissions and shares easier to manage—not to mention that this is all on top of a more stable and powerful operating system. In this chapter, we will talk about what file sharing really is, how those permissions work, and how to set it all up. Next, we'll dig into the Dfs. We'll find out what it is, how it works, and how to make it work for you. Finally, we'll take all of the basic file sharing capabilities and push them right out to our users' web browsers, making files available for offline use.

Basics of File Sharing

The core component of any server is its ability to share files. In fact, the Server service in all of the Windows NT and now Windows 2000 lines handles the server's ability to share file and print resources. But what exactly does that mean, and why is it so important? By default, just because you have a server running doesn't mean it has anything available for your users. Before they can actually get to resources on the server, you must share out your resources. Let's say you have a folder on your local I: drive named APPS with three applications in subfolders, as shown in Figure 11.1.

When you share this folder out to the network under the name of APPS, you allow your clients to *map* a new drive letter on their machines to your I:\APPS folder. By mapping a drive, you are kind of placing a virtual pointer directly to where you connected. If you map your client's M: drive to the APPS share of the server, their M:\ will look identical to the server's I:\APPS. (Don't worry, I'll slow down and explain how to create this share later, and I'll explain how to connect to it in Chapter 14.) See how a client connection of M:\ being mapped to the server's APPS share— Figure 11.2—looks identical to the real I:\APPS from Figure 11.1?

FIGURE 11.1

Subfolders in
I:\APPS

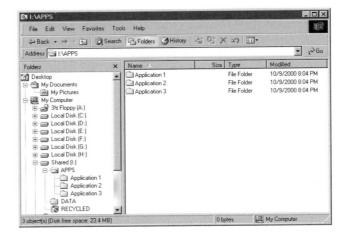

FIGURE 11.2

M:\ mapped to
I:\APPS

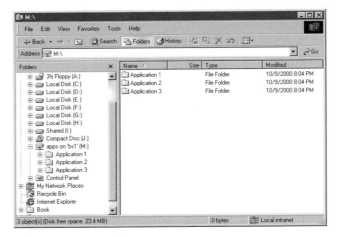

That's really all there is to it. Sharing resources means that you will allow your users to access those resources from the network. No real processing goes into it as far as the server is concerned; it just hands out files and folders as they are.

Creating Shared Folders

Before you can create a shared folder, you must have appropriate rights to do so. This requires that you are either an administrator or a server operator. You can create shares in several ways: You can use the Explorer interface when sitting at the server, use the Computer Management console from the server, or do it remotely.

Creating Shares from Explorer

If you're sitting at the server, the Explorer interface provides a simple and direct means for creating and managing all properties of a share. Let's go back to the I:\APPS folder that you want to make available to the network under the name of APPS.

NOTE   Don't forget that not all clients can handle names longer than eight characters. This applies to shares as well. If you have old DOS LAN Manager clients, they wouldn't be able to interpret share names longer than eight characters such as if we named the share Applications instead of APPS. For this chapter, I am assuming a Windows 98 user base, so long filenames and share names won't be a problem.

In Explorer, right-click the APPS folder and select the Sharing menu option. This will bring up the properties dialog box for the folder APPS, already set to the Sharing properties page. To share the folder, click the Share This Folder radio button, as shown in Figure 11.3.

FIGURE 11.3

Properties for the APPS share

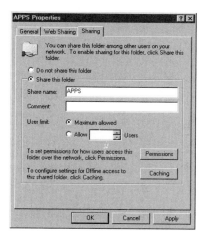

NOTE   Incidentally, if you want to stop sharing this folder later through the Explorer interface, go back into the properties as we just did and select the button to not share this folder.

The Share Name option is the most critical entry. The share name is how your users will reference this share. For our purposes, we are sharing this folder as APPS. The Comment field is used to provide more descriptive information about this share. Technically, the comment has no real bearing on the server or client; it just makes browsing a little less cryptic—I'll comment my share as "Network Applications Share." This information will be visible to the users when they browse My Network Places for available shares, as shown in the Explorer window in Figure 11.4.

The next step is securing your share. Using the Permissions button, you can define your share permissions. I'll discuss this in more detail later in this chapter.

FIGURE 11.4

Browsing network shares

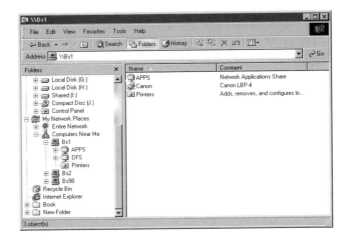

Another new feature you can enable on the Sharing page lies behind the Cacheing button. Cacheing allows offline file and folder access for your users. Once again, this will be covered a bit later, in the "Using Offline Files/Client-Side Cacheing" section.

Once you select OK, your share is enabled and ready for immediate use by your users.

SETTING USER LIMITS

You can also configure how many users can connect to a share simultaneously (in the User Limit area of the Sharing properties page). Let's say the applications under your share are each licensed for 100 concurrent users. Even though you may have 200 users on your network, you can configure your server share to maintain a limit of only 100 users at a time. As users connect to the share, they build up to the user limit. As users log off, or disconnect from the share, the number drops. This type of licensing enforcement can be handy in reducing your licensing costs.

Be careful on your licensing. Not all applications have a concurrent license mode, as compared to a client license mode. (Unfortunately, as Microsoft has abandoned concurrent licensing, more and more other firms have stopped offering this useful licensing option.) In such cases, the manufacturer doesn't care how many users are accessing the application at any given time, they just care about how many people have installed the application altogether. This user-limit option will not protect you in these cases.

Another thing to keep in mind is that this user-connection concurrency limit is based on the entire share. It cannot be defined further to each folder within a share. If Application 1 under the has a concurrency limit of 100, and Application 2 and Application 3 are unlimited, you don't want to inadvertently limit those other applications.

Finally, you need to consider how your users connect to the share to use these applications before you limit them based on concurrency. If your users all connect to the share upon logging in, but don't disconnect until logging off, your concurrency limit may be used up based on who shows up for work first. If connections are made only when actually using the application, the user limit will work quite nicely. Otherwise, you will have 100 people using up your concurrency limit, although maybe only a small percentage of them are actually using the application.

Remotely Creating Shares with the Computer Management Console

Within your Administrative Tools program group, you have the Computer Management console. With this tool you can, among other things, create and manage shares locally or remotely. In contrast, within the Explorer interface, if you right-click a folder that is not local to your machine, you won't see the Sharing menu option. If you are going to be creating a share using the Computer Management console from your local machine, you're set. If you want to manage a share on a remote server, you have to first connect to that server. Right-click the Computer Management (Local) icon, and select Connect to Another Computer. From there, you can type in the name of the server you want to manage or browse the network for the computer you want.

To begin with the share management, you need to drop down to `Computer Management\System Tools\Shared Folders\Shares`, as shown in Figure 11.5. (You might notice that I've already deleted my `APPS` share so we can start fresh here.)

FIGURE 11.5

Computer Management, Shares

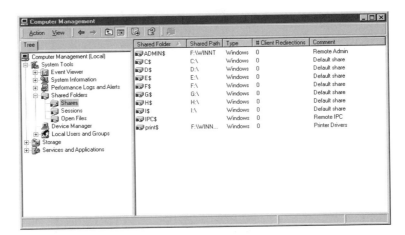

You can now either hit the Action button or right-click in the Shares window, then select New File Share. A new wizard-like dialog box, shown in Figure 11.6, greets us with spaces to enter all essential components of a share. First, select the folder you want to share out. You can browse through the given drives and folders, or you can create a new folder on-the-fly by simply typing out the full drive and folder name in the Folder to Share box. Again, we want to share the `I:\APPS` folder. Enter the name you want this share to be given, along with a brief description, and select Next.

From here, we jump straight to defining our share permissions. In this next dialog box, you are given four options for defining permissions: All Users Have Full Control allows everyone to exploit the maximum amount of access as allowed by the file and directory access permissions. Administrators Have Full Control; Other Users Have Read-Only Access ensures that your users cannot modify or delete anything within the share but still gives your administrators the appropriate rights to manage the data.

Administrators Have Full Control; Other Users Have No Access seems like an odd choice. Why would you share something out to the network and not allow anyone except administrators in? Of course, you could want a share used by administrators only to access certain network management resources, but more importantly, this option is a good way to keep security under control. When creating a share, you don't have to start with a wide-open door. Why not start off with a closed door and open it up per your specifications later? Well, the logic behind this argument seems moot when looking at the next option—Customize Share and Folder Permissions—but it really isn't. The customize option lets you define permissions based on specific users or groups you desire. However, if you don't know which users and groups belong just yet, don't sweat it. Select the second Administrators Have Full Control option, as shown in Figure 11.7; other users will have no access for now, and you can open the door when you finish collecting the information you need.

FIGURE 11.6

Giving a folder location in the Create Shared Folder dialog box

FIGURE 11.7

Controlling computer access in the Create Shared Folder dialog box

Publishing Shares in the Active Directory

One of the great things about the Active Directory is that it can unify all resources in an enterprise into a single directory, whether it's printers, groups, users, organizational units, or just about anything you can dream up—or more appropriately, serve up. This counts for shares too. The benefit is that you won't need to first browse to the exact server that the share resides on, you'll just simply browse into your Active Directory from the Windows Explorer and find your resources organized by your organizational unit structure—which should make more sense to your users than a bunch of server names.

To publish a share, you need to be in your Active Directory Users and Computers management console. Right-click the organizational unit of choice and select New/Shared Folder. From there, you'll be asked to provide a name for this publication of the share and, of course, the share name. That's all there is to it—your share is now published in the Active Directory. However, it is published under the name you provided, and not as its original share name. So if I want to publish the share \\BS1\APPS as `Network Applications`, that is all the users will see.

Managing Permissions

Now that you've shared out your resources to the world, it's time to protect them *from* the world. There are numerous ways to secure your server and its resources, but the two most efficient are *share permissions* and *file and directory permissions*. These permissions let you control who accesses your data and what they can do with it.

Share Permissions

Share permissions are possibly the easiest forms of access control you will deal with in Windows 2000. Consider share permissions such as an access pass to a secure building. When you walk up to the front door, you get a pass that tells you your access level for everything else on the inside. If your pass says "Level One access," then everything else in the building will give you Level One access—at the most. Once inside, try to get into a room with Level Two access requirements, and it won't work. By defining share permissions, we can safely control the access level for each person at the front door.

An important thing to understand is that this front door—or share-level permission—isn't the entire picture. The share-level permission only represents the *maximum* level of access you will get on the inside. If you get read permissions at the share, the best you can do once inside the share is read. Likewise, change permissions will grant change at best. If you want full control to *anything* inside the share, you need full control *at* the share.

Finally, understand that when I say the share permission is the *maximum* level of access you will get inside the share, it is entirely possible to restrict access more once inside. You could get full control at the share, but an object inside can still say that you can read, but not change.

NOTE *There are cases every once in a while where you will choose one of the FAT file systems for your logical drives. FAT has no file and directory permission capabilities, leaving your data very insecure. However, you can alleviate some of these pains through share permissions. Even on FAT partitions, you can share out folders and assign whatever level of share permissions you like. In this scenario, the share permissions are it—they won't be overridden by file or directory permissions because there aren't any. If you get change to the share, you get change to everything within the share. Unfortunately, this still doesn't prevent an intruder from accessing data directly at the console. Physical security of the server is your only surefire protection.*

DEFINING SHARE PERMISSIONS

To define share permissions, we will work through the Computer Management console. Select the share you want to secure by right-clicking the share name and selecting Properties. You can get to the same place from Explorer by right-clicking the locally shared folder, selecting Sharing, and then clicking the Share Permissions tab, shown in Figure 11.8.

FIGURE 11.8

The Share Permissions tab

NOTE   The properties dialog box you see now is different from what you may be used to. You will notice that there is the familiar Security tab and a new Share Permissions tab. The Security tab takes you straight to the folder permissions.

You are shown a Name box that lists users and groups assigned to the share; when a user or group is selected, the permissions for that user or group to access the share are revealed. You can assign different levels of permission for different users and groups. At the share level, we have the following types of permission:

Permission	Level of Access
Full Control	The assigned group can perform any and all functions on all files and folders through the share.
Change	The assigned group can read and execute, as well as change and delete, files and folders through the share.
Read	The assigned group can read and execute files and folders, but has no ability to modify or delete anything through the share.

Our example in Figure 11.8 shows full-control access for Everyone. If we want to restrict share permissions to give Everyone read-only rights and administrators full control, we will need to reduce Everyone's rights to read-only and add a new set of rights for administrators. While sitting on the Everyone selection, clear the check boxes for Change and Full Control. Now you need to add full control for administrators. Select the Add button, then find the Administrators group and click Add. You will come back to the Share Permissions tab with the Administrators group added to the display. Select the Full Control check box, and as you can see in Figure 11.9, everything else is checked automatically.

FIGURE 11.9

Share permissions, full control for administrators

Again, keep in mind that share-level permissions are just your first filter. Whatever level of permissions you get at the share level will be the highest level of permissions you can get for files and directories. If you get read-only rights to the share, but full-control rights to the file, the share will not let you do anything other than read.

UNDERSTANDING ALLOW AND DENY

NT 4 veterans may be a bit put off by these permissions—they're not the way things looked under NT! Well, believe it or not, NT supported this notion of "allow" and "deny"; it just never showed it to us in the user interface, so we never used it.

Share permissions are just about the simplest set of permissions that we'll deal with, so they're a great place to explain this "allow" and "deny" notion. Here's how they work:

◆ An administrator of a share, file, user account, or whatever can change permissions on that object. (That's almost a complete definition of an administrator actually.) There are several kinds of permissions—Full Control, Change, or Read in the case of shares. Anyone can be allowed or denied by the administrator, or the administrator can choose to clear *both* Allow and Deny, leaving a user with neither allow nor deny on that permission.

◆ If the user has no permissions, no allow or deny, then the user does not have access to the object.

◆ If the permission is checked Allow, then the user can exercise the permission, and if Deny is checked, then the user can't. I know that's obvious, but let's see how it affects more complex situations.

Objects may have more than one permission on them. Figure 11.8 shows just one permission—Everyone/Full Control—but you'll see Security dialog boxes with many entries giving different permissions to different individuals or groups. (Recall that these entries are called Access Control Entries or ACEs, and the entire list is called an Access Control List or ACL, pronounced "ackel.") There may be conflicts in that case. For example, suppose I want to access some share, and there's an

ACE for the group Domain Users that has neither the Allow nor Deny box checked. (I'm a member of that group.) Suppose there's also an ACE naming a group called Managers (which I'm a member of) where the Allow box is checked. Finally, suppose there's an ACE that names me specifically and checks the Deny box. What wins?

The operating system looks at all of the ACEs relevant to me and computes this way: First, it ignores any "no checked" entries. No allow or deny from Domain Users. Next, it looks for any Allow checks. If I have none, then I don't get in. But I *do* have an Allow check, as I'm in Managers. So far, I've got one Allow check and no Deny checks. Finally, it looks for any Deny checks. If it finds even one of them, then I'm denied. And there is one, in the third ACE. Rephrased, then: I get a permission if I have at least one Allow checked and no Deny checks. I am denied a permission if I have no Allow checks at all, or if I have at least one Deny check.

For example, then, to deny just one person access to something, then just add an ACE with their name on it and check Deny. To allow only one person access to something, then remove all ACEs from the object and add that one person with an Allow check. Do *not* add that one person with an Allow check and then add Everyone with a Deny check—that one person is a member of Everyone, and so would have a Deny check...and would be denied access.

Here is where it gets dangerous. What if we have a share to which we allow read permissions for the Domain Users group, then we explicitly deny read permissions for another group called Employees? I log in as a user who just so happens to be both a Domain User and Employees member. Now what? When I connect to that share, every group that I belong to, as well as my username, is checked against the permissions list for that share. If any one of those groups or my username comes up in the Deny column, I'm denied—end of story. Likewise, if through one group I'm allowed full control, but another group I belong to has Deny change, I can read but not change. So be careful when using Deny permissions on a share. In practical uses, you might find it extremely helpful to Deny specific individuals. You might want to create a group for Offenders that you want to specifically block. Denying general groups, though, could get you into more of an administrative nightmare than you bargained for.

File and Directory Permissions

The old days of Microsoft networking utilized share-level permissions only. Once connected to a share with a given set of permissions, you had those permissions for everything under the share. If you had 1000 users who all wanted private access to their data, you would have to create 1000 shares with specific permissions on each share. Then, with the introduction of Windows NT to the Microsoft networking platform, you could create one share for all users, and customize access via file and directory permissions—permissions that could be assigned directly to the files and folders. With this new feature came an unending ability to customize the security of your data.

You may hear a lot about how NTFS, in conjunction with file and directory permissions, can help you protect the server itself from an intruder. Theoretically, this is true. Assuming that you do not know an administrator username and password, if you sit down at the server, you cannot gain access to the server's data. The idea is that NTFS will not let you boot to anything less than the NT operating system and view files. This feature lets us relax a bit about the physical security of the server. We know that no one can log into the server, and that our partitions are NTFS. Pop a DOS boot disk in, reboot the server, and you can't see a thing on the hard drive.

Well, it was only a matter of time. Someone *did* come up with a utility that allows us to gain access to NTFS partitions via a simple boot disk. (Actually, it was Microsoft—the Recovery Console that you get when you boot from the Windows 2000 Server or Professional CD lets you do it. But seriously, there was a package before RC that did it—Sysinternals's ERD Commander, which you can find out about at `www.sysinternals.com`.) So to be secure, go back to square one: Lock your server up so no one can sit at its keyboard.

PERMISSION TYPES

Before we assign permissions to our files and folders, we need to have a good understanding of what those permissions mean and how they work. Now, there are two different levels of permissions.

To see the higher level, go to any NTFS folder, right-click it and choose Properties, and then the Security tab. You'll see a permissions dialog box like the one in Figure 11.10.

FIGURE 11.10

Top-level NTFS permissions dialog box

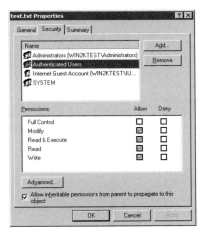

Compare Figure 11.10 to Figure 11.9, a standard share-level permissions dialog box. Notice that share-level permissions only offered three permission types—Full Control, Change, and Read. Very simple, and note that there was no Advanced button in the dialog box, unlike Figure 11.10. You've already seen in Chapters 8 and 9 that most permissions dialog boxes have an Advanced button that lets you drill down to a lower, more-specific level of permissions. The permissions you see in Figure 11.10 are actually built up out of the lower-level permissions. For example, the high-level permission List Folder Contents comprises five lower-level permissions—Traverse Folder, List Folder, Read Attributes, Read Extended Attributes, and Read Permissions. I think of them as "molecular" and "atomic" permissions. There are 13 atomic permissions for NTFS. You'll see that other object types have more or less atomic permissions; for example, any Active Directory object (a user account, a machine account, an organizational a group policy object, and so on) has 38 atomic permissions. (Which leads to some odd things: What would a child object be for a group policy? The answer is of course that there *is* no such thing. But other sorts of Active Directory objects, such as organizational units, *can* have child objects [you can create users and other OUs inside OUs].) All AD object types share the same set of atomic permissions, even the ones that are irrelevant—go ahead and grant someone the ability to create child objects for a group policy object; it'll be about as useful as granting someone at a brick factory the ability to set the sex of the bricks.

Look at Table 11.1 to see how groups of atomic permissions in the left column make up molecular permissions.

TABLE 11.1: ATOMIC AND MOLECULAR PERMISSIONS

ATOMIC	WRITE	READ	LIST FOLDER CONTENTS	READ AND EXECUTE	MODIFY	FULL EXECUTE
Traverse Folder/Execute File			x	x	x	x
List Folder/Read Data		x	x	x	x	x
Read Attributes		x	x	x	x	x
Read Extended Attributes		x	x	x	x	x
Create Files/Write Data	x				x	x
Create Folders/Append Data	x				x	x
Write Attributes	x				x	x
Write Extended Attributes	x				x	x
Delete Subfolders and Files						x
Delete					x	x
Read Permissions	x	x	x	x	x	x
Change Permissions						
Take Ownership						x

SOME PERMISSIONS DO DOUBLE DUTY: FILES VERSUS DIRECTORIES/FOLDERS

Notice in that table that some permissions have two names, such as Traverse Folder/Execute File or Create Folders/Append Data. What in the *blazes* does that mean? It's just one more little hurdle to get past when understanding permissions.

You see, NTFS permissions apply both to directories (or *folders*—the terms are interchangeable) and files. And Microsoft only allocated so much space on a file or folder for describing permissions—13 bits, to be exact. They use that same 13 bits whether describing a person's access level to a file or a folder.

But the kinds of things that you can do with files and folders are not exactly the same. Sure, they're similar—you change permissions on a file or folder, you read attributes of a file or folder—but some things are a bit different and in a few cases you end up with a file operation that has no corresponding action on folders and vice versa. For example, there's the "execute file" permission.

You use this when you've got a file that is actually an executable file, such as `winword.exe`. If I deny you the Execute File permission, then you can't run Word, plain and simple. It's a useful permission, so it's good that Microsoft included it.

But there is *nothing* even remotely similar to it for folders. You don't execute folders.

So Microsoft looked around for a permission that was useful and that applied to folders, but that lacked a file analog. That permission is Traverse Folder. The idea is this: Suppose there's a folder you'd like to get to that is several levels deep, say a folder named `C:\toplevel\level2\level3\level4`. You have been denied access to `C:\toplevel`, `C:\toplevel\level2`, and `C:\toplevel\level2\level3`... but have Full Control of `C:\toplevel\level2\level3\level4`. So you have godlike powers inside level4...if you can just *get* there.

The Traverse Folder permission lets you bypass all of the locks on the upper levels and essentially "beam yourself" right into level4. Like Execute File, it's a useful permission, but it has nothing to do with files. What's happening is this: When NTFS is examining a permission, then it pulls up the 13 bits. When looking at the first one, then it asks itself the question, "Is this a file or a folder?" If it's a file, then it interprets that first bit as Execute File permission. If a folder, then it's Traverse Folder permission. You'll see this in a somewhat less extreme manner on some of the other permissions as well.

Let's look at the other atomic permissions in some detail.

ATOMIC PERMISSIONS

We'll start at the atomic level. These permissions are the building blocks of the permissions that we normally speak of, like Read, Modify, and Full Control. You will probably never see these permissions, much less refer to them on their own.

Traverse Folder/Execute File   We just covered these in the previous section.

List Folder/Read Data   List Folder permissions allow you to view file and folder names within a folder. Read Data permissions allow you to view the contents of a file. This atomic right is the core component of Read.

Think of the separation between these two atomic permissions. Is there really much of a difference? Yes, but probably not for long. Remember the days when we called everything files and directories? Now the file and *folder* terminology has become mainstream. Just when we start really getting used to it, another term is coming into play: *objects*. Everything on your machine is an object—both files and folders. This atomic permission could almost be rephrased to *read object*. Regardless of whether this permission applies to a file or folder, this right lets you examine the contents of an object.

Read Attributes   Basic attributes are file properties such as Read-Only, Hidden, System, and Archive. This atomic-level permission allows you to see these attributes.

Read Extended Attributes   Certain programs include other attributes for their file types. For example, if you have Microsoft Word installed on your system, and you view the file attributes of a DOC file, all sorts of attributes will show up, such as Author, Subject, Title, and so on. These are called *extended attributes*, and they vary from program to program. This atomic permission lets you view these attributes.

Create Files/Write Data The Create Files atomic permission allows you to put new files within a folder. Write Data allows you to overwrite existing data within a file. This atomic permission will not allow you to add data to an existing file.

Create Folders/Append Data Create Folders allows you to create folders within folders. Append Data allows you to add data to the end of an existing file, but not change data within the file.

Write Attributes This permission allows you to change the basic attributes of a file.

Write Extended Attributes This permission allows you to change the extended attributes of a file.

Delete Subfolders and Files This atomic permission is strange. Listen to this: With this permission, you can delete subfolders and files, even if *you don't have Delete permissions on that subfolder or file*. Now how could this possibly be? If you were to read ahead to the next atomic permission—Delete—you would see that that permission lets you delete a file or folder. What's the difference? Think of it this way: If we are sitting at a file or folder, Delete lets us delete it. But let's say I'm sitting at a folder and want to delete its *contents*. This atomic permission gives me that right. There is a very vague difference between the two. One lets us delete a specific object, the other lets us delete the *contents* of an object. If we are given the right to delete the contents of a folder, we don't want to lose that right just because one object within that folder does not want to give us permissions. Hey, it's my folder, I can do with it what I want.

Delete Plain and simple this time, Delete lets you delete an object. Or is it plain and simple? If you have only the atomic permission to delete a folder but not its big-brother atomic permission to delete subfolders and files, and one file within that folder has no access, can you delete the folder? No. You can't delete the folder until it is empty, which means that you need to delete that file. You can't delete that file without having either Delete rights to that file, or Delete Subfolders and Files rights to the file's parent folder.

Read Permissions The Read Permissions atomic permission lets you view all NTFS permissions associated with a file or folder, but you can't change anything.

Change Permissions This atomic permission lets you change the permissions assigned to a file or folder.

Take Ownership We'll talk about what ownership is and what it does in more detail later, but this atomic permission allows you take ownership of a file. Once you are the owner, you have an inherent right to change permissions. By default, administrators can always take ownership of a file or folder.

MOLECULAR PERMISSIONS

A full understanding of what atomic permissions do and of Table 11.1, which shows the atomic makeup of molecular permissions, provides exceptional insight into what these molecular permissions are and how they work. This section will try and put the atomic makeup of permissions in better perspective, but flip back and forth to the table while you read about these permissions. This information will form a solid foundation to help you manage permissions later.

Read Read permissions are your most basic rights. They allow you to view the contents, permissions, and attributes associated with an object. If that object is a file, you can view the file, which happens to include the ability to launch the file, should it be an executable program file. If the object in question is a folder, Read permissions let you view the contents of the folder.

Now here is a tricky part of folder read. Let's say that you have a folder to which you have been assigned Read permissions. That folder contains a subfolder, to which you have been denied all access, including read access. Logic would say that you could not even see that subfolder at all. Well, the subfolder, before you even get into its own attributes, is *part of* the original folder. Because you can read the contents of the first folder, you can see that the subfolder exists. If you try to change to that subfolder, then—and only then—will you get an Access Denied.

Write   Write permissions, as simple as they sound, have a catch. For starters, Write permissions on a folder let you create a new file or subfolder within that folder. What about Write permissions on a file? Does this mean you can change a file? Think about what happens when you *change* a file. To change a file, you must usually be able to open the file, or read the file. To change a file, Read permissions must accompany your Write permissions. There is a loophole though: If you can simply append data to a file, without needing to open the file, Write permissions will work.

Read and Execute   Read and Execute permissions are identical to Read, but give you the added atomic privilege of traversing a folder.

Modify   Simply put, Modify permissions are the combination of Read and Execute and Write, but give you the added luxury of Delete. Even when you could change a file, you never really could delete the file. You'll notice that, when you select permissions for files and folders, if you select Modify, then Read, Read and Execute, and Write are automatically checked for you.

Full Control   Full Control is a combination of all previously mentioned permissions, with the abilities to change permissions and take ownership of objects thrown in. Full Control also allows you to delete subfolders and files, even when the subfolders and files don't specifically allow you to delete them.

List Folder Contents   List Folder Contents permissions apply similar permissions as Read and Execute, but they only apply to folders. List Folder Contents allows you to view the contents of folders. More important, List Folder Contents is only *inherited* by folders, and is only shown when looking into the security properties of a folder. It will allow you to see that files exist in a folder—similar to Read—but will not apply Read permissions to those files. In comparison, if you applied Read and Execute permissions to a folder, you would be given the same capabilities to view folders and their contents, but would also propagate Read and Execute rights to files within those folders.

INHERITED PERMISSIONS

Another new tool in the Windows 2000 file server toolbox is the *inherited permissions* feature. In Windows NT, if you wanted to set permissions for all files and directories for an entire directory tree, you had to check a box to apply permissions down from the root. When that happened, the server literally went through every single file and set the permissions as defined—what a tedious process. Now, there is inheritance. If a file or folder is set to inherit permissions, it really has no permissions of its own; it just uses its parent folder's permissions. If the parent is also inheriting permissions, you simply keep moving up the chain of directories until you get one that actually has some cold, hard permissions assigned. That being said, the root directory cannot inherit permissions.

For example, I have a folder named APPS, with three subfolders and files. All of the subfolders and files allow inheritable permissions. If I set my permissions on APPS to allow read and execute permissions for Users, all subfolders and files automatically mirror those new permissions. What if I want to customize the permissions on Application 1 so that users can also write? I right-click Application 1, select Properties, and then click the Securities tab. From there, I can see the Allow Inheritable Permissions from Parent to Propagate to This Object option (there's a mouthful for you). This says that the object we are looking at—Application 1—has permissions inherited from its parent—APPS. To get rid of those inherited permissions, I clear the check box and am immediately presented with the dialog box shown in Figure 11.11.

FIGURE 11.11

You're warned when you remove inheritance.

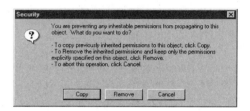

What is happening now is that this object is no longer going to be using inherited permissions; it will be using its own permissions. The problem is, it really doesn't have permissions of its own yet. This dialog box is asking us how to start. Do we want to use the original parent permissions as a guide or baseline, or do we want to start from scratch with no permissions for anyone? If we already had highly customized permissions, we'd probably want to choose to copy those permissions and tweak them down a little further. In our case, we'll choose to copy the original permissions, and then we can just add the required write permissions on top of those.

We've covered removing the inherited permissions, but what about down the road, when we want to reset everything back to the standard top-level permissions at APPS? Just as easy. Under our APPS properties, Security tab, we click the Advanced button and see another check box, Reset Permissions on All Child Objects and Enable Propagation of Inheritable Permissions. This will effectively remove any custom, explicitly defined permissions of those objects and simply revert to inherited permissions. Be careful when resetting propagation. If you had any customized permissions on any child objects, they are gone forever after this change is applied.

ASSIGNING FILE AND DIRECTORY PERMISSIONS

Once you understand what different permissions mean, assigning them to files and folders is a piece of cake. We'll start off in Explorer. Find the file or folder you want to assign rights to, right-click it, select Properties, and then select the Security tab. Take a look at Figure 11.12.

The top window shows the different groups or users to whom permissions are assigned, and the bottom window shows the permissions assigned to the selected user or group. I'm starting off in my APPS folder. Ideally, because this is for applications, I want all users to have Read and Execute permissions and not have the ability to change, add, or delete anything. I want to get rid of that Everyone entry because it opens a door to my data that is extremely dangerous. I also want to keep administrators in full control, so they can still maintain the data. So I'll start off by adding Administrators and giving them full control. Click the Add button, and a list of users and groups is displayed like the one shown in Figure 11.13.

FIGURE 11.12

The Security properties tab

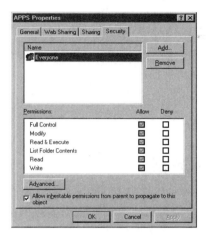

FIGURE 11.13

Selecting users and groups

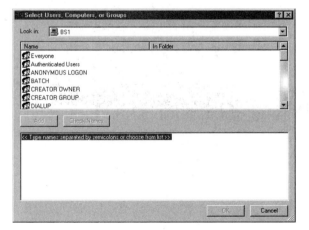

We'll try and do both groups at the same time. Select the Administrators group and click Add. Likewise, select the Users group and click Add. (If you don't want to spend the time searching for the group or user, you can type it in the Name box, click Add, and then click Check Names. That would cross-check your manually typed entry with the actual list of names to find a match.) Once we have added Administrators and Users, our dialog box should look like the one shown in Figure 11.14.

FIGURE 11.14

Adding the Administrators and Users groups

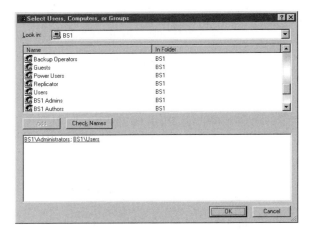

Click OK, and we see the two newly added groups, along with our Everyone group in the upper box—as shown in Figure 11.15.

FIGURE 11.15

The new groups in the Security tab

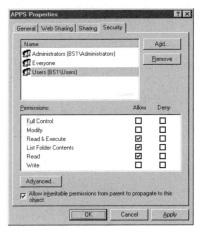

Just to finish cleaning things up, go ahead and select the Everyone group and click Remove. Hmm. When I tried to do that, I got the error message shown in Figure 11.16.

FIGURE 11.16

Error removing the Everyone group

What happened is that the inheritance check box in the lower portion of the Security tab says to use the parent folder's permissions. In this case, the parent's permissions give Everyone full control. Obviously, we want to get rid of that inheritance. Uncheck the inheritance option and let's choose Remove. This will take the Everyone permissions received from the parent and throw them away. Fine. Notice how it didn't remove the entries we just created? This saves us from having to go back and do the whole thing over again.

We are now down to just our Administrators and Users groups. All we have to do is assign the correct permissions. For administrators, we wanted full control. Highlight the Administrators group, and check the Full Control box in the Allow column. The Security tab should now look like Figure 11.17. Then repeat this process for Users: Highlight Users and check Read & Execute.

FIGURE 11.17

New permissions

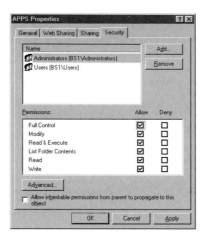

NOTE *You need to be careful when selecting some permission levels. Selecting Read & Execute includes all of the rights of Read, so Read is automatically checked. If, on the other hand, you want to clear Read & Execute, unchecking the Read & Execute box won't automatically uncheck Read.*

You could click OK here and let the permissions take hold, but let's look into the advanced properties first by clicking the Advanced button. Some of the information shown here is the same as what we saw in the Security properties page, just reworded a bit (see Figure 11.18).

The Permission Entries box shows your selected groups and users, with a description of their rights that you have assigned. Nothing different there. The Allow Inheritable Permissions from Parent to Propagate to This Object check box is the same. But here we get a new check box: Reset Permissions on All Child Objects and Enable Propagation of Inheritable Permissions. Again, there's a mouthful. In part, this is the same as the Windows NT version of applying permissions to all files and subfolders, but Windows 2000 doesn't do it quite the same way. The second part of that statement—*enable propagation of inheritable permissions*—says that it will give all subfolders these permissions by turning on each one's Allow Inheritable Permissions from Parent to Propagate to This Object check box.

FIGURE 11.18

Advanced access
control properties

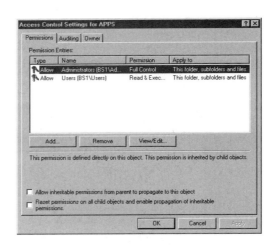

The next feature of the Access Control Settings dialog box is the ability to tailor your extended permissions. Select Users, then click the View/Edit button. You'll get the options shown in Figure 11.19.

FIGURE 11.19

Advanced
permissions

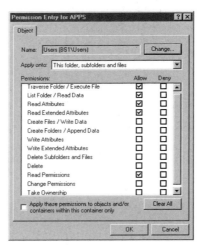

These permissions break down Read and Execute into smaller parts. If you want your users to have all the benefits of Read and Execute, but don't want to allow them to view permissions, you could simply clear the Read Permissions box. From there, you also have more specific means of propagating these custom permissions. The Apply Onto drop-down list lets you assign advanced permissions to any combination of the current folder, the current folder's subfolders, and the files. To use the Apply Onto selection, though, you must check Apply These Permissions to Objects and/or Containers within This Container Only."

CONFLICTING PERMISSIONS

You can assign permissions to files, and you can assign permissions to directories. Just as share permissions can conflict with file and directory permissions, file permissions can conflict with directory permissions. In share-level conflicts, the share wins; in file and directory permission conflicts—the file wins. If you assign read-only rights to a directory, but you assign change rights to a file within that directory, you will still be able to change the file.

Of course, there *must* be an exception to every rule, and here it is: deletions. Let's say a directory says that you do have rights to delete files, but the file itself says that you *cannot* delete it. In this case, the directory wins, and you will be able to delete the file. How can this be? Imagine the file with read-only permissions. You open the file and try to save it—the *file itself* is being changed. But if you delete a file, are you *really* changing the file? Not really. All you are changing is the directory structure. You are removing the entry within the directory for that specific file, but aren't doing anything to the file itself. Similarly, you can still rename a file, even though you have no permissions on the file.

MULTIPLE PERMISSIONS

Now for another problem. We have given our Administrators group full control over a file, and everyone else has read permissions only. Here is where permissions once again come into conflict. Everyone is everyone. Even Administrators are part of Everyone. Hmmm. How does this work? Well, in the case of multiple permissions, the *least restrictive* permissions will prevail. Let's say we have an administrator named Bob. Bob is part of the Everyone group, which has read-only rights. Bob is also part of the Administrators group, which has full control. In this case, Bob will get full control because it is least restrictive.

DENY PERMISSIONS

We talked about Deny permissions on shares earlier. The same thing applies in file and directory permissions, but in a way that's just a tad bit more complex because of the increased number of security options. Think of a corporate bonus-award spreadsheet file that you are trying to protect. You want everyone to see the file, but you only want the managers to be able to actually change the file. It makes sense: Grant Employees read-only rights and Managers full control. Let's imagine that somewhere along the line, some low-level supervisor falls into both groups. They need to be part of Managers for some things, but are more like Employees in others. If you leave the permissions as we just described, this supervisor is going to get the best of both worlds with this spreadsheet—full control. For this reason, you decide that you explicitly don't want anyone in Employees to have full control. Now what?

Easy enough: We simply deny those excess permissions. What you need to do is find out which permissions you specifically do *not* want Employees to have, and instead of checking those permissions in the Allow column, check them in the Deny column. Figure 11.20 shows how you would make sure that Employees have read-only rights.

Notice how we've only denied Write permissions? Wouldn't we want to deny Full Control and Modify permissions as well? Not really. Whenever you select Full Control, everything else is automatically selected because Full Control *includes* all permissions. What this means is that if you select to deny Full Control, you also deny Write, Read, Read and Execute, and Modify. If you deny Modify, you deny Read and Execute, Read, and Write. If you deny Read and Execute, you also deny plain old Read. It all cascades down the line. Just take note when clicking various check boxes, as one check on one side could really mean several on both sides being changed.

FIGURE 11.20

Deny permissions

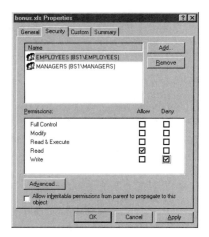

Back to our example—we want to allow Read and deny Write. We don't care so much about Read and Execute for this type of file, and in either column, Modify or Full Control overrides the other column's Read or Write. When you click OK to have these new permissions take effect, you'll get a warning that tells you that Deny permissions override Allow permissions. Now, in the case of the multiple-permissions scenario, the Deny takes precedence, and even if our supervisor in question has both Managers and Employees memberships, he'll get cut off with the Deny.

OWNERSHIP

Through the course of assigning and revoking permissions, you are bound to run into the problem where no one, including the administrators, can access a file. And you can't change the file's permissions because you need certain permissions in order to assign permissions. This could be a really sticky situation. Fortunately, ownership can help you out.

There is an attribute of every object called an *owner*. The owner is completely separate from permissions. There will always be *some* owner for *every* object. Yeah, that's great, but how does that help me? Well, the owner of an object has a special privilege—the ability to assign permissions. So if I'm the owner of a file, but don't have access to the file, I can take advantage of my ownership to reassign permissions to myself. Neat-o.

Well, how do I get to be the owner anyway? For starters, whoever creates an object is the default owner. Should that person be a regular user, that's the owner. If there is no apparent creator of the object, which is the case for many system files and folders, ownership is set to the domain's Administrators group.

Here is another problem: The file you are trying to get to but have no permissions for was created by a user and therefore is owned by that user. So you don't have permissions, and you're not the owner, which means that you can't reassign the permissions. Aha. There is a right that is assigned to

Administrators that allows them to take ownership of objects. With this right, you can go into that restricted object, seize ownership, and then use that new ownership to reassign permissions.

Let's walk through this whole scenario: I have a share called USERS. Under USERS is a folder named `Brian`, to which I have installed Full Control permissions for Brian only. While logged in as Administrator, I try to access the `Brian` folder and receive an Access Denied message. The time has come for me to check out what Brian has been up to. I right-click the `Brian` folder and select Properties, then select the Security tab. I receive the dialog box shown in Figure 11.21.

FIGURE 11.21

Permissions for the `Brian` folder

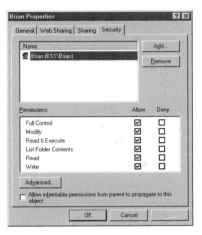

We can see that Brian has full control, but no one else is in the access list at all. But wait a minute, if I'm not in the access list, how am I even seeing these permissions? I select the Advanced button, and then select the Owner tab. A dialog box like Figure 11.22 appears, showing my ownership.

FIGURE 11.22

Advanced security properties, showing current owner

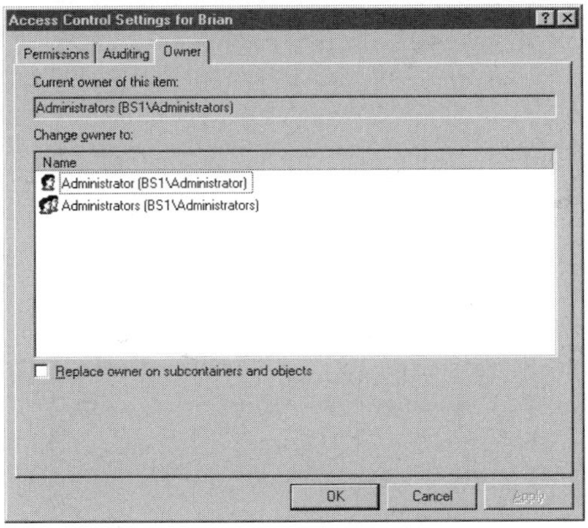

That's right, I was the one who originally created the folder `Brian`, so I'm the owner. As the owner, I can reassign permissions. That does it, I'm adding Administrators to the access list with full control. I cancel out of the advanced properties dialog box and return to the permissions screen. I select Add, find the Administrators group, and then grant them full control. My permissions now look like Figure 11.23.

FIGURE 11.23

New permissions

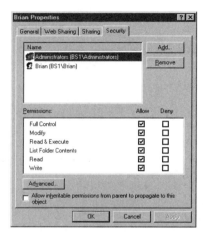

Now, back to Explorer, I click the `Brian` folder and I'm in, only to find a folder that Brian created, named `Secret`. I click that folder—Access Denied. Easy enough, I'll just go in and do the same thing. I right-click `Secret`, select Properties, and then select Security. This time, I get a different message, as shown in Figure 11.24.

FIGURE 11.24

I have no permissions for this folder.

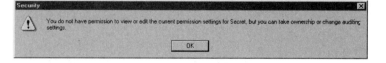

I don't have permissions, but I can take ownership. Why is it different this time? Well, last time I had created the folder named `Brian`, so I was the owner; therefore I could still view and change permissions. This time Brian created the folder, which means that Brian is the owner, so I—Administrator—have no inherent rights to even see the permissions. This becomes obvious when I see the Security properties tab, shown in Figure 11.25.

I am looking at the Security properties tab, but I can't see who has what permissions. I also can't add or change permissions. In fact, everything in this dialog box is grayed out, except for the Advanced button. Well, let's hit it. Under the advanced properties, I see a similar sight—the advanced Permissions tab options are grayed out entirely. So I select the Owner tab (see Figure 11.26).

FIGURE 11.25

Permissions when
not the owner

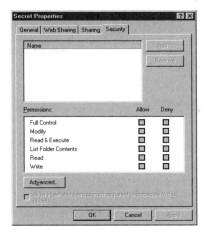

FIGURE 11.26

Unknown owner

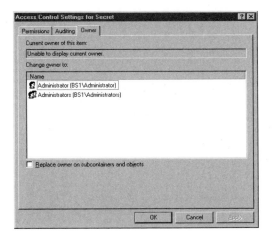

I can't tell who the owner is, but it is safe to say that it isn't me. From here, I want to take ownership. Under the Change Owner To box, you will see the different users or groups that you belong to
who have rights to take ownership. As you can see, I can select either Administrator or Administrators.
Do I want to use the individual Administrator account or the Administrators group? In this case, I
won't want every administrator on the network to be able to view Brian's secret folder, so I'll just select
Administrator. If I simply select Administrator and hit OK, I'll be given rights to the folder, but will
probably run into the same roadblock with subfolders and files. To get it all over with in one shot, I
select Replace Owner on Subcontainer and Objects. A translation of this into old Windows NT
terms would be Replace Owner on Subdirectories and Files. I hit OK and return to the permissions
dialog box. I'm still grayed out, so I'll hit OK again to close out and implement the changes.

Now I'm the owner. I try to change into the `Secret` folder again—Access Denied! Being the owner, I don't yet have rights to the objects, but I now have rights to change permissions. I right-click the `Secret` folder, select Properties, and then select Security. Aha! (See Figure 11.27.)

FIGURE 11.27

Permissions are now visible.

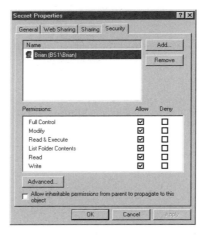

As shown in Figure 11.27, I can now see that Brian has full control. What I need to do next is add the Administrator account with full control. I select Add, and enter the Administrator account. Again, before I close out, I want to make sure that I get this for all subcontainers and objects, so I select Advanced, then check Reset Permissions on All Child Objects and Enable Propagation of Inheritable Permissions, as shown in Figure 11.28.

FIGURE 11.28

Enabling propagation

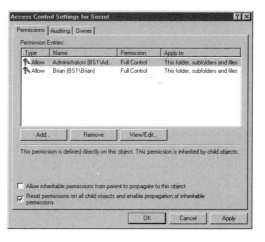

This will pass my new permissions down throughout the entire `Secret` directory structure. When I return to the Explorer window now, I finally have full control.

Auditing File and Directory Access

Security's no good unless you use it. Who deleted that file out of the common share? Who modified that file? You can use NTFS's permissions to track that stuff to the event log.

There are two steps to logging file and directory access: First, you've got to tell your computer to enable auditing, and, second, you've got to tell your system which files and directories to audit.

Enabling Auditing

I don't know why you can't simply say to an NT/2000/XP/.NET system, "Log any accesses to this to file," but you can't, at least not without first enabling the whole idea of auditing. I'm guessing it's a performance issue—auditing must be driven by some kind of "watchdog" routine that peeks at file accesses and logs those accesses it's been told to log. But I guess the watchdog must suck up some CPU time, hence disabling auditing by default.

You turn on auditing as you read in Chapter 8, but here's a review. You enable auditing either on a system-by-system basis with the Local Security Policy snap-in, or you can flip it on for groups of machines via group policies. To turn it on a particular system, click Start/Programs/Administrative Tools, then Local Security Policy. Then open up Local Policies and then Audit Policy. You'll see something like Figure 11.29.

FIGURE 11.29

Auditing options

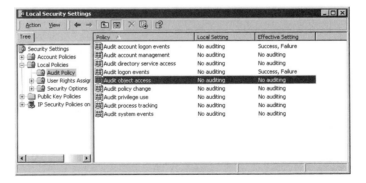

To track file and directory access, double-click on the Audit Object Access item, and you'll see a dialog box like Figure 11.30.

FIGURE 11.30

Enabling object auditing

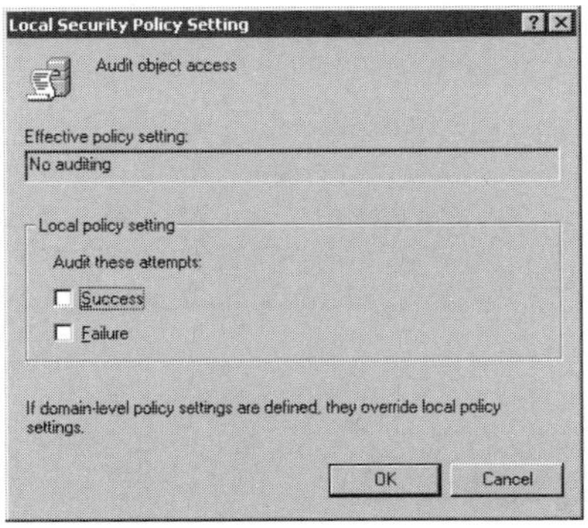

Notice that, as you learned in Chapters 8 and 9, any domain-based group policies will override local group policies—but of course if you don't have an Active Directory, then there won't *be* any domain-based group policies. You saw the effect of group policies back in Figure 11.29 in the Effective Setting.

To enable auditing using domain-based group policies, then create a group policy object and look in the Computer Configure/Windows Settings/Local Policies/Audit Policy. Apply that object to the particular machines for which you want to enable auditing.

All you've done at this point is make auditing *possible*. Now tell the system which files you want to audit. Do that by getting to the Security tab of any file or folder (right-click the file or folder and choose Properties, then the Security tab) and then the Advanced button to raise the Access Control Settings for *objectname* property page. That will have three tabs: Permissions, Owner (both of which we've already looked at), and Auditing. Click Auditing and you'll see something like Figure 11.31.

FIGURE 11.31

Auditing property page

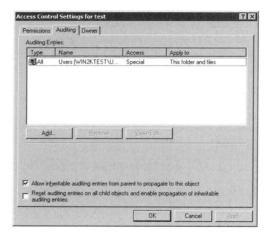

In this one, I've already entered an audit instruction—you probably won't see any on your page. Note the two dialog boxes that control whether to propagate these changes to folder contents and whether to reset any *existing* audit settings once this setting is enabled.

Click Add and you'll be prompted for the users to audit—you've seen this dialog box before, so I'll spare you the figure—and you can say that you only want to watch a particular user (we've always had our eye on that Leslie character, haven't we?) or a group, including the all-encompassing Everyone, Authenticated Users, Users, and the like. You *then* see the atomic permissions dialog box, which, again, you've also seen before. But where the previous atomic screen shot gave you an Allow or Deny check box, this one gives you a Successful and Failed check box.

Thus, you could decide that you only want to know when someone transfers ownership of a file and don't care if someone tries and fails to modify ownership. The atomic permission is Take Ownership. You'd check the Successful check box because you only care if someone actually *changed* ownership—if he failed in his attempt, then you don't care. (Understand that I'm not *recommending* you only audit ownership changes; this is just an example.)

Once you've set auditing for a directory (or a file), you can see who's been working with it by looking in the security log. For example, an event type 560—a file write—shows the following information:

```
Object Open:
    Object Server: Security
    Object Type:    File
    Object Name:    D:\test\test.txt
    New Handle ID: 208
    Operation ID:  {0,5892625}
    Process ID: 1208
    Primary User Name:   jane
    Primary Domain:   BIGFIRM
    Primary Logon ID: (0x0,0xE90B)
    Client User Name: -
    Client Domain: -
    Client Logon ID:  -
    Accesses    READ_CONTROL
        SYNCHRONIZE
        ReadData (or ListDirectory)
        WriteData (or AddFile)
        AppendData (or AddSubdirectory or CreatePipeInstance)
        ReadEA
        WriteEA
        ReadAttributes
        WriteAttributes
```

You see from this that we're opening a file named D:\test\test.txt and the person doing it is named "jane" in a domain called BIGFIRM. You can then see the various atomic permissions that Jane exercises (whether she knows it or not) when she closes a file in Notepad that's changed.

Everything that you read in Chapter 8 about auditing applies here: Be sure to do something about managing the logs. They can get large quickly. And remember that logging is of no value if you don't check them now and then!

Hidden Shares

As we've seen before, once we share a folder out to the network, it becomes visible to the user community. But what if we don't necessarily want everyone to see the share? For example, I have created an installation source share on my server so that whenever I go to a user's workstation, I can install whatever applications I need to without having to bring CDs. It's really just a convenience for me, but at the same time, I don't want the users clicking away through the shares, installing every program they can get their hands on. Sure, I could limit the share to allow permissions only to me, but that is kind of a pain, too. I don't want to log off the user and log in as myself every time I do an install, especially if user profiles are being used. This is where creating hidden shares can help. I want the share to be there and available, but just not as easily visible. Although not a completely secure solution, it is a deterrent to the overly browse-active.

To create a hidden share, proceed as normal in sharing a folder, except place a dollar sign at the end of the name. That's it. Now, whenever the server registers its information to the browse list with its available resources, it simply will not register that hidden share.

The share that I am creating will be called INSTALL$, which will be shared from `D:\Install`. I create the share as normal, making sure to call it INSTALL$ instead of INSTALL (see Figure 11.32).

FIGURE 11.32

Creating a hidden share

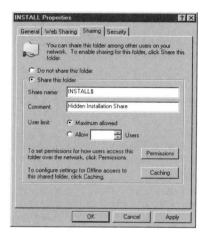

Now, from my client workstations, I will not see the INSTALL$ share listed in the browse list, but can still map a drive to the INSTALL$ drive connection if I manually type the share name, as I've done in Figure 11.33.

FIGURE 11.33

Mapping to a hidden share

Although the hidden share will not show from your Explorer browse list, the share is visible through the Computer Management console. This helps keep you from forgetting which hidden shares you have created.

Common Shares

In Windows 2000, you may find that several common shares have already been created for you. Most of these shares, you will find, are hidden shares (see Figure 11.34).

FIGURE 11.34

Common hidden shares

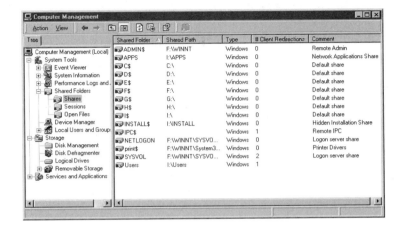

C$, D$, and So On

All drives, including CD-ROM drives, are given a hidden share to the root of the drive. This share is what is called an *administrative share*. You cannot change the permissions or properties of these shares; however, you can stop sharing them altogether. These shares come in handy for server administrators who do a lot of remote management of the server. Mapping a drive to the C$ share will be the equivalent of being at `C:\` on the server.

NOTE   *Only administrators or backup operators can map to administrative shares.*

ADMIN$

ADMIN$, like its C$, D$, and other drive share counterparts, is an administrative share. This share maps directly to your system root, or where your Windows 2000 operating system resides. I installed my Windows 2000 operating system to `D:\Winnt`, so that's where my ADMIN$ maps to.

Why is this necessary? Let's say I manage 50 servers, and I want to copy an updated INI file to all servers to have them configured differently. (Of course, I have already tested the configuration change thoroughly. The last thing you want to do remotely is change the configuration of an operating system without knowing exactly what is going to happen when you reboot or otherwise initiate the change.)

The problem is that about half of my servers are new Windows 2000 servers with the system installed into `C:\Winnt`. The other half are a mixed bag of old upgraded servers and random installs performed by different admins, so my system root can be anything from `D:\Winnt` to `C:\Windows2k` to who knows what. Thus the ADMIN$ share. I have one common connection point that I can connect to across the board, with no guesswork required.

PRINT$

Whenever you create a shared printer, the system places the drivers in this share. See the chapter on printing services (Chapter 13) for more information.

IPC$

The IPC$ share is probably one of the most widely used shares in interserver communications. We know how you can map a drive letter to a share on a server, and use that drive to access files and folders. What about other resources? How do you read the event logs of another computer? You don't actually map a drive, you use *named pipes*. A named pipe is a piece of memory that handles a communication channel between two processes, whether local or remote.

REPL$

Whenever the replication service is used, a REPL$ share is created on the export server. The export server sends a replication pulse to import servers. The individual import servers connect back to the export server to get a replicated set of the data. This REPL$ share is where your import computers will connect. This share is a critical element of replication, so it's best to leave it alone.

NETLOGON

The NETLOGON share is used in conjunction with processing logon requests from users. Once users successfully log in, they are given profile and script information that they are required to run. This script is usually going to be a batch file. For example, I have a common batch file that I want all of my users to run every time they log in. This allows me to have all clients run a standard set of commands, like copying updated network information, mapping standard network drives, and so on. These batch files, scripts, and profiles go in the NETLOGON share.

Connecting to Shares via the Command Line

Now that you have these shares, how do people use them? Assuming that I've got a share called APPS on a server called BS1, how would someone attached to the network get to that share? There are several ways to use the GUI to get to shares:

- Right-click My Network Places and choose Map Network Drive, then follow the wizard that starts.

- Browse the network from My Network Places.

- Look for a share in the Active Directory.

All of those techniques are convenient, but they require a fair amount of network "superstructure"—they only work well if the network's working well. But sometimes you need to attach to a share when things aren't working so well—in fact, sometimes you need to attach to a share specifically *because* things aren't working so well, and the share contains some tools to help you get it working right. That's where the command line comes in handy.

Introducing *net use*

The command I'm talking about is net use. In its basic form, it looks like this:

```
net use driveletter \\servername\sharename
```

For example, to attach to the share APPS on the server named BS1, and then to be able to refer to that share as drive V: on my system, I'd open a command prompt and type this:

```
net use v: \\bs1\apps
```

If I didn't want to worry about figuring out which drive letters are free, I'd just use an asterisk instead of a drive letter, as in the following:

```
net use * \\bs1\apps
```

net use will then just choose the first available letter.

Using a Different Account with *net use*

Sometimes you're logged in to one account and need to connect to a share, but you only have permissions to access that share from another account. In such a case, you can tell net use to try to connect you with the share while using that different account with the /user: option. With this option, net use looks like this:

```
net use driveletter \\servername\sharename password
➥/user:domainname\username
```

So, for example, if I were logged onto a domain named CANISMAJOR (note we're talking older NetBIOS-type domain names here; net use seems not to understand the newer DNS-type names) under an account named Joe, and I wanted to access a share named DATA on a server named RUCHBAH on a domain named CASSIOPEIA, then I might have a problem, particularly if the CASSIOPEIA domain doesn't have a trust relationship with CANISMAJOR. But perhaps I have an account named Mark on the CASSIOPEIA domain, with password "halibut." I could then type this:

```
net use * \\ruchbah\data halibut /user:Cassiopeia\mark
```

You needn't type the password, in case you're concerned that someone might be watching. Leave it off, and net use will prompt you.

"A Set of Credentials Conflicts"

Sometimes when you're trying to attach to a share, you'll get an error message that says something like, "A set of credentials conflicts with an existing set of credentials on that share." What's happening there is this: You've already tried to access this share and failed for some reason—perhaps you mistyped a password. The server that the share is on has, then, constructed some security information about you that says that you're a deadbeat, and it doesn't want to hear anything else about you. So you need to get the server to forget about you so that you can start all over. You can do that with the /d option. Suppose you've already tried to access the \\BS1\APPS share and apparently failed. It might be that you *are* actually connected to the share, but with no permissions. (I know it doesn't make sense, but it happens.) You can find out what shares you're connected to by typing just **net use** all by itself. Chances are, you'll see that \\BS1\APPS is on the list. You have to disconnect from that BS1 server so that you can start over. To do that, type this:

```
net use \\bs1\apps /d
```

But then do another **net use** to make sure that you've got all of those connections cleaned up; you may find that you have *multiple* attachments to a particular server. *Then* your **net use** will work. Or... in a few cases, you may have to disconnect *all* of your file shares:

```
net use * /d
```

net use-ing over a WAN

Now we are into one of our most difficult networking areas: connecting to our resources across long distances and great unknowns. If you've ever had to rely on remote computing, you know well not to rely on it. We have a new little function set in our **net use** arsenal that takes a lot of the "unknown" out of the picture. Instead of relying on getting to the appropriate name resolution server, getting through to that server, and getting accurate reliable resolution over an inaccurate and unreliable network link, we can now just map a drive straight to our server via its IP address. Granted, you now need to know that IP address, but it is a good failsafe. In my case, I work from several different locations connected with frame relay WAN links. My Network Places isn't always so good about being able to convert server names into IP addresses, so **net use** **bs1** usually tells me that my machine couldn't *find* \\BS1. Even if it *does* work, name resolution—converting a name such as BS1 to a network address—takes time.

If you know the IP address of the server that you're trying to contact, then you can use the IP address in lieu of the server's name. I know that BS1's IP address is 134.81.12.4, so I can simply type this:

```
net use \\134.81.12.4\apps
```

And, as you're probably connecting from a different network, you might have to add the /user: information. And it's never a bad idea to add /persistent:no so that your system doesn't spend five minutes trying to reconnect to it the next time that you start up. So, for example, if BS1 is a member of a domain named bigfirm.biz and I have an account on bigfirm.biz named "boss," I could ensure that BS1 will know who I am and log me on like so:

```
net use \\134.81.12.4\apps /user:bigfirm\boss /persistent:no
```

Know the **net use** command; you'll find it useful.

The Distributed File System

One of the new and exciting features in Windows 2000 is the Distributed File System (Dfs). With Dfs, you can create a single share that encompasses every file share–based resource on your network. Think of it like a file share home or "links" page. Under this one share, you have links that point to all of your other shares across numerous servers. Now, using this Dfs share, your users only need to remember one place to connect.

Let's say you had the following set of shared resources across the network, with users mapping to those shares as shown:

UNC Path	Users' Mapping	Resource Description
\\BS1\APPS	G:	All generic applications
\\BS2\APPS	G:	The same applications as \\BS1\APPS

UNC Path	Users' Mapping	Resource Description
\\BS99\SALES	S:	The corporate sales data
\\BS20\USERS	H:	All user directories
\\BS20\FINANCE	Q:	The corporate financing data
\\BS21\APP2	P:	Miscellaneous applications

This could become a real pain for users, who have to remember where to go to connect to their various resources. There are five different servers housing resources. This also means that if a client needed to access APPS, SALES, USERS, and FINANCE all at the same time, they would be required to make four different connections. Well, four doesn't sound too bad, but I have been in large networks where there were literally no more available drive letters left on clients to map another share; every single letter from A: to Z: was mapped to something. You also have to remember which clients connect to \\BS1\APPS and which connect to \\BS2\APPS. Again, not a big deal in this particular example, but if you had 50 servers containing the same set of APPS, this could become a nightmare to keep track of.

NOTE   *As you can probably see, Dfs is going to be most beneficial in large enterprises, and probably not worth the effort in small office networks.*

Now, let's put this same scenario into a Dfs instead. We would have one Dfs Root—we'll call it CORP—with all of our corporate shares listed within. I'll show you how to do all of this later, but our end result will look like Figure 11.35.

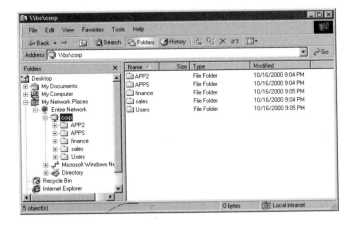

FIGURE 11.35

Dfs root view

All resources, no matter where they reside, show up under the domain's CORP Dfs root volume. The links to the other shares show up to the users as subdirectories under CORP. Users don't know, see, or ever care what server each of those subdirectories point to, nor will they ever even need to know that there *are* other servers involved at all. To them, it is one big share with everything they need.

Understand, though, that Dfs isn't *really* a new kind of file server. In a sense, it's not a file server at all—it is, instead, a way of putting a kind of "table of contents" on a bunch of existing file shares. Dfs does *not* create file shares; you must create all of the file shares on the various servers first, *then* use Dfs to impose some order. To underscore that point, here's another fact about Dfs: the file shares needn't be NT or 2000 file shares. If you had Unix NFS, Banyan VINES, and Novell NetWare client software on your computer, then you could actually create a Dfs "share" that only points to NFS, VINES, and NetWare volumes!

But does that mean that this new Dfs root—this "table of contents"—constitutes a new single point of failure? If that one server that houses the root—the place where all of our users go to find their resources—goes dead in the water, so do our users, right? Not necessarily. Combined with the Active Directory, Dfs roots can be fault tolerant. Instead of the actual, physical root being housed on one server, it can be stored in the Active Directory, which is maintained across all domain controllers. Now, if one of those servers housing the root—in the Active Directory—goes down, our users pick it up automatically from another domain controller without even a hiccup.

Again, let's stress the function of Dfs. "Fault-tolerant Dfs" doesn't mean that we're backing up the data in the file shares. It only means that the "table of contents" that is a Dfs root gets backed up, so that if the computer hosting the Dfs root goes down—and sorry to be stressing this point, but again there's a good chance that the machine hosting the Dfs root *does not contain one single byte of shared files*, just the pointers to the servers that contain those files—then there's another computer standing by to assume the role of "table of contents server" or, in 2000-ese, Dfs root.

But *can* we somehow protect those file shares and their data with some kind of fault tolerance? Yes, with *link fault tolerance*. We saw earlier that we had two different servers with an APPS share. Assuming that those servers contain identical sets of APPS data, there is no need for them both to be listed in our Dfs. We can have one APPS link listed, with users being referred to either one of the replica sets. It's a great way of streamlining your network, but has its shortcomings. If we set up our Dfs-based APPS link to point to both \\BS1\APPS and \\BS2\APPS, the users will be randomly diverted to one or the other link. We don't have much in the way of customizing how one replica is chosen over another. We'll need to keep this in mind when configuring replica links across a WAN. The last thing you want to do is redirect your users across a slow line if you don't have to.

But how do we ensure that \\BS1\APPS and \\BS2\APPS contain the same data? With the File Replication Service. Just like the old Directory Replicator service of Windows NT 4 days, we have replication capabilities within our Dfs. Using the File Replication Service, Dfs can keep all copies of replica links in sync with each other. With our two APPS shares, we make a change on the master copy, and Dfs takes care of getting those changes out to the replica copies. Again, this has shortcomings—this time, in principle, not in the technical details. If you have dynamic data within a link at all—and by dynamic I mean anything that changes as the users access it, such as Word documents, spreadsheets, databases, or anything else that requires users to change data on the server—you can't replicate it. Why? If a user is working on the master link, their changes will trickle down to all users. If they are on a link that is a replica, their changes will get overwritten next time the replication occurs. Use caution when using link replicas and replication.

Dfs Terminology

Before we go much farther, we need to understand the terminology. Just like with the Active Directory, a whole new set of concepts and terms comes into play.

You start with a *root*. This translates roughly into the share that will be visible to the network. In our example, CORP was our root. You can have many roots in your site, but each server can house only one root. A root is shared out to the network, and actually operates like any other share. You can have additional files and folders within the shared folder.

Under a root, you have a *Dfs link*. The link is another share on the network that is placed under the root. I guess the term *link* is part of our never-ending terminology shift. In this case, it seems to be shifting to more of an Internet nomenclature. The link within the Dfs hierarchy is like a hyperlink on a web page that automatically directs you to a new location. You don't need to know where. Once you find your home page (the Dfs root), you can place hyperlinks to any other website you want (your Dfs links). These newly placed links will now work like any other folder underneath the root.

A *replica* can refer to a root or a link. If you have two identical shares on the network, usually on separate servers, you can group them together within the same link, as *Dfs replica members*. You can also replicate an entire root as a *root replica member*. Once replicas are configured, the File Replication Service manages keeping the contents of roots in sync.

Stand-Alone versus Fault-Tolerant Dfs

Before we begin making a Dfs, we need to decide which kind of Dfs we want. This will be primarily decided based on whether we have an Active Directory. The big difference is going to be on the root. In an Active Directory–based Dfs, or fault-tolerant Dfs, the root itself can have replicas. In other words, that one single point of failure—the root—has been spread out into the Active Directory. Using root replicas, if you have 27 servers housing the Active Directory, you have 27 places where the Dfs information lives. Well, not all Dfs information, just enough information to point clients to one of the Dfs root replicas. With that, as long as the Active Directory is alive and available, the Dfs is too. Also, when integrated into the Active Directory, link replicas can be configured to use automatic replication. With automatic replication, the File Replication Service takes over the synchronization of the contents of replicated folders to ensure that all replicas contain the same information. It might be safe to say that if you have an Active Directory–based domain, you should choose the fault-tolerant Dfs.

But here's the really cool part of an Active Directory–based Dfs. If I host my Dfs in the Active Directory of the bs.local domain, not only do my users not need to know which server a particular share is on, but now they don't even need to know which server the Dfs itself is on. Instead of having to map a drive to \\servername\dfsname, my users could map a drive to \\bs.local\dfsname. Now, using the same logic a client uses to find an available domain controller for the Active Directory, it can search for a host of the Dfs. If one fails, the client just calls on another.

A domain-based Dfs automatically publishes its topology in the Active Directory. What this means is that the actual Dfs hierarchy—the root(s), links, replica members—is published into the Active Directory so that all domain controllers will know where the Dfs lives, what it looks like, and how to get to it. It *doesn't* mean that every domain controller is a Dfs root replica server, and it *doesn't* mean that the Dfs publishes its root share so that all users can peek into the Directory and find it. Of course, you can go into Windows Explorer and type **\\bs.local\dfsname**, but you can't go into Windows Explorer, browse through the Entire Network directory, and find that root share. If you want your users to be able to browse to the root, you need to publish the share in the Active Directory Users and Computers management console. You saw how to publish a share earlier in this chapter.

If you've gotten this far, you probably don't have an Active Directory to publish to. What about the non-AD-based networks? A lot of companies are in positions where they can begin the migration to Windows 2000 (and many are doing so) even if only to put up a few member servers here and there. The Dfs provides an enhancement to the basic file server that lets an enterprise step out of its physically bound shackles into a more user-friendly and manageable state. A stand-alone Dfs is a solid step forward into the world of Windows 2000, without requiring a major Active Directory initiative. With a stand-alone Dfs, you don't get the nice fault tolerance of the root itself, you don't get the automatic replication, and you don't get the Dfs published in the Active Directory. But you still get all the other goodies, like combining all of your network shares into a single namespace and finally killing the dependency on physical server names and locations when it comes to getting your users to their resources. In just a little bit, we'll talk about how these new benefits brought to you by the Dfs can be put to use in a practical environment—with or without an Active Directory—but first, let's jump into learning how to actually build these things.

Creating a Dfs Root

To get to the Dfs manager, select Start/Programs/Administrative Tools/Distributed File System. Now, the first thing you need to do is create the root. Right-click the Distributed File System in the left pane, and select New Dfs Root Volume. Of course, a wizard greets you. Select Next at the welcome screen, and you are then asked which kind of root you want to create (see Figure 11.36).

FIGURE 11.36

Select the Dfs root type.

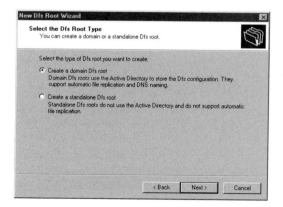

Your choices for the root type are domain Dfs root and stand-alone Dfs root. A domain root will publish itself in the Active Directory, while a stand-alone root will not. This fundamental difference is the source of all other differences. Most important, a domain root must be hosted on a domain controller, so that there is an Active Directory to post to. One of the most important benefits of being published in the Active Directory is that domain roots can have replica roots. Again, a root replica lets us have any domain controller host the root, which greatly improves fault tolerance. Because the roots require the Active Directory to be replicas at this level, stand-alone roots cannot be or have replicas. Because my server, BS1, is already a domain controller, I'll choose a domain root.

The next step is choosing a domain that will host the Dfs, as shown in Figure 11.37. If you were to select a stand-alone Dfs, you would not get this option.

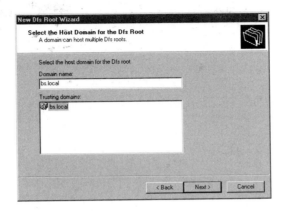

The purpose behind selecting a domain to host the root is to publish the Dfs into the Active Directory. This clues us into yet another *big* advantage of using fault-tolerant roots. Jump forward in your mind, if you will, to what this may look like to the clients later on. If you publish this root called CORP into the Active Directory on the domain bs.local, you will later see this shared out to the world under the name of `bs.local\corp`, as well as `bs1.bs.local\corp`. If you were using a stand-alone root, you would only be able to see this as `bs1.bs.local\corp`. How does this help? This is one less thing you have to configure at the workstation level. Simply point all of your clients to bs.local, and they never need to worry about which server houses which resources.

After you select which domain will host the root, you select the server that will host the root, as shown in Figure 11.38. This is where the actual resource will reside.

Now you define the actual share for the root. Remember, this can be a regular share. You can select an existing share on your host server to be the root of your Dfs, or you can create a new one on-the-fly (see Figure 11.39).

FIGURE 11.38

Select a server to host Dfs.

FIGURE 11.39

Select a share for the Dfs root.

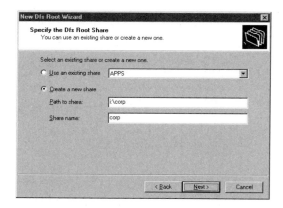

I've decided to make a new share called CORP. This is going to be my CORP-orate resource Dfs root. I don't already have one, so I've chosen to create a new share. If the path for the share does not exist, it will be created automatically, so don't worry about Alt+Tabbing back and forth just to get your folder set up ahead of time. Finally, you select a name for the Dfs root (see Figure 11.40).

FIGURE 11.40

Provide a Dfs root name.

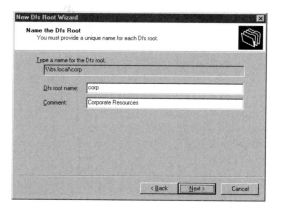

The name for each root must be unique for the domain. Unlike shares, whose names could be the same as long as they were on different servers, there can only be one CORP Dfs root per domain. This is a side effect of having the Dfs root accessible from the domain instead of the server. I would say a very acceptable side effect. Also, notice in Figure 11.36 how the path appears as \\bs.local\ corp, not \\bs1.bs.local\ corp or even \\bs1\corp.

Finally, you are shown a confirmation dialog box with all of your selections, and the root is created. When we return to the Dfs manager console, we see the new root listed as \\bs.local\corp, as shown in Figure 11.41.

FIGURE 11.41

The new root

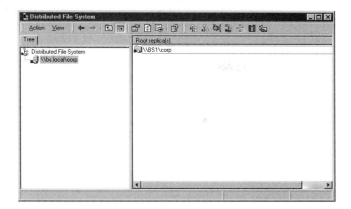

Adding Links to a Dfs Root

Once we have our root, we need to add our Dfs links. Let's start with APPS. First, you want to select your new root in the left pane of the console. You will notice that in the left pane, our root is \\bs.local\corp, indicative of its membership with the domain, whereas the right pane shows that the share, or the physical location of the resource, is \\bs1\corp. Right-click the root—that would be \\bs.local\root—and select New Dfs Link. This is where you add another network resource to your Dfs. We're going to start with the \\BS1\APPS share (see Figure 11.42).

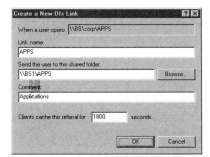

FIGURE 11.42

Add the Dfs link.

Pay attention to the terminology in this dialog box: When a User Opens \\BS\CORP\—Link Name blank—Send the User to This Shared Folder—blank. To fill in the blanks in our example, we want to say, "When a user opens \\BS\CORP\APPS, send the user to this shared folder: \\BS1\APPS." The first blank—Link Name—doesn't have to exist already. Simply type it in. The second blank— "Send the user to this shared folder"—is the name of an existing share on the network. You can enter the UNC for the share, or browse your network for the share that you want to point users to. Sorry, but you can't create a share on-the-fly here; it must already exist.

The Clients Cache This Referral for [blank] Seconds value tells the client how long to wait before they check back with the hosting server to update share information. When a client connects to \\BS\CORP\APPS, they are told by the hosting server, which happens to be \\BS1, to connect to

\\BS1\APPS, *but* check back with me in 1800 seconds. At that time, the client will call back the Dfs host to see if everything is okay. If you take a link offline—applicable when you have replica links, or if you simply redirect a link to a different share, the client will be told this information at that time, and will be directed back to the appropriate share accordingly. Think about this value carefully. The shorter the interval, the higher the network traffic. The longer the interval, the longer it takes a client to check back for an update. Let's say you have defined an interval of 3600 seconds, or one hour. A client connects to \\BS\CORP\APPS at 10:00 exactly, and is redirected to \\BS2\APPS. They won't check back until 11:00. At 10:10, you find out that you need to take the server down. You want to take BS2 offline, and redirect all clients to a replica member of APPS on BS1. (We'll cover replicas in a minute.) So you configure your replica set to have BS2 offline. If you take BS2 down now, your client who connected at 10:00 could lose data. The best thing to do is wait until all clients have reported back so they can see that BS2 is offline, and redirect to BS1. This means that you may have to wait the longest possible interval before shutting down your server—an hour. If your interval was 10 minutes, then you could be fairly comfortable that within 10 minutes, BS2 would be free from any client connections to APPS.

Going back to the network resources given earlier, we will repeat the above process to create all child nodes—except for \\BS2\APPS—using the information below:

When a User References	Send the User To
\\BS\CORP\APPS	\\BS1\APPS
	\\BS2\APPS
\\BS\CORP\SALES	\\BS99\SALES
\\BS\CORP\USERS	\\BS20\USERS
\\BS\CORP\FINANCE	\\BS20\FINANCE
\\BS\CORP\APP2	\\BS21\APP2

When we're done, the Dfs console will look like Figure 11.43.

FIGURE 11.43

The new child nodes in the Dfs console

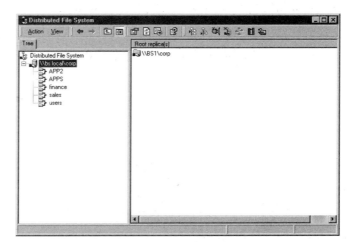

Configuring Dfs Replicas

Now we want to make a replica link of APPS. Remember how we had \\BS1\APPS and \\BS2\APPS? We want to combine those into one logical resource: \\BS\CORP\APPS. Right-click the APPS link, and select New Replica. What you get is a condensed version of the dialog box that created the Dfs link in the first place (see Figure 11.44).

FIGURE 11.44

Add a new Dfs replica member.

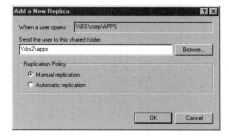

Enter the path for the next share that is to be available as part of this resource, and check whether you want automatic or manual replication configured. (We'll go over replication in a minute.)

Select OK, and you will see in your console that your child node now shows two shares in the right pane—one for \\BS1\APPS, and one for \\BS2\APPS (see Figure 11.45).

FIGURE 11.45

Replica members

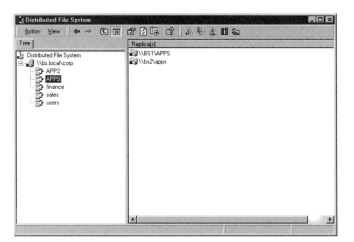

From now on, when our clients connect to \\BS\CORP\APPS, they will be directed to either \\BS1\APPS or \\BS2\APPS.

To remove a replica member, right-click the member and select Remove Replica. If I want to take \\BS2\APPS out of the replica set, leaving only \\BS1\APPS, I could remove it from the Dfs just like that. When removing a replica member, however, nothing on the replica member's server is altered in any way. \\BS2\APPS will still be shared, and all data will still be available within that share. The only thing that is affected is the Dfs topology.

Dfs Replication

Replication itself is simple. In a stand-alone Dfs, the replication is manual, and one link replica is the master. In other words, changes from that particular master server propagate to all other replica servers. If the physical share you want to keep synchronized resides on an NTFS volume on a Windows 2000 Server, replication is automatic and uses multi-master replication. With multi-master replication, you can modify files on any one of the link replicas, and the changes will be automatically copied to the other members. Really, with automatic replication, there is no such thing as a master after the initial replication. The first replication will need a master to ensure that all shares have the same starting point. It is advised, though, that you do not mix automatic and manual replication within a single replica set.

To enable replication, right-click the child node with multiple members, and select Replication Policy. The dialog box shown in Figure 11.46 will be presented.

FIGURE 11.46

The Replication Policy dialog box

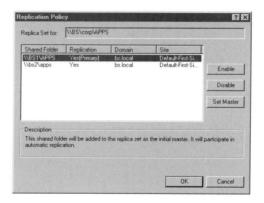

Each member within the replication set is shown, along with its replication properties. In Figure 11.46, \\BS1\APPS is configured to replicate and is set as the primary system for replication—in other terminology, the export server. All other members of the replication set will have their data synchronized by the primary system. Members can be replica child nodes, but cannot actually be replication partners. To change the replication configuration of each member, highlight the member in the Replication Policy dialog box, and select either Enable or Disable. Similarly, if you want to change which server is to act as the primary, or export, server for replicated data, highlight the member, and select Set Master.

Managing Dfs

After you have configured your Dfs, there are a few certain steps you must go through to properly manage the roots, links, and clients connected to it.

TAKING REPLICA MEMBERS OFFLINE/ONLINE

When you have multiple members belonging to a replica set, you may find occasions to take one offline. This could be because you need to perform maintenance on a server. You don't want to just take a server down and have users lose their connections. You also don't want to go through the process of dropping a member from the replica set and adding it again later once your maintenance is done. Instead, right-click the member share and select Take Replica Member Offline/Online. This will toggle a member's status. When offline, a small yellow warning icon will appear over the member, as shown in Figure 11.47.

FIGURE 11.47

An offline member

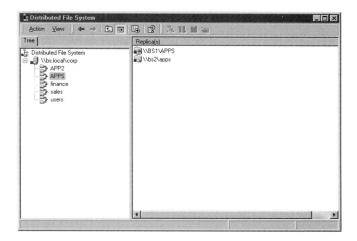

CHECKING NODE STATUS

Periodically, you should verify the status of each link within the Dfs topology. To check the status of a link, right-click the share in question and select Check Status. A green check mark indicates that the node is working properly. A red icon with an X through it indicates a problem (see Figure 11.48).

FIGURE 11.48

A failed node

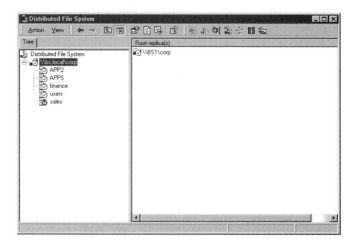

A failed node indicates that there is a problem accessing the shared folder to which the child node refers. Try checking out the share directly to make sure it is still available to the network. More severely, the entire server that hosts the child node could be down.

DELETING CHILD NODES

In Figure 11.48 above, the SALES node has failed. (It really failed because I stopped sharing SALES on the server where the resource actually resided.) Now I want to completely remove SALES from my Dfs. Right-click the child node in the left pane and select Remove Dfs Link. This will remove the SALES folder from the CORP hierarchy, but will not touch the actual SALES share or any of its data on the remote server. Users will still be able to connect to \\BS99\SALES directly. If I wanted to finish this job, I could stop sharing and delete SALES from BS99.

CONNECTING AND DISCONNECTING FROM ROOTS

Within the Dfs management console, you can connect to any Dfs root on your network to manage. Right-click the Distributed File System line in the top of the left pane, and select Display an Existing Dfs Root. From there, you can browse your network for roots or type in the location of the root. For my CORP root hosted on BS1, I could type in **bs****corp**. To remove a Dfs root from the console, right-click the root and select Remove Display of Dfs Root.

THE PHYSICAL ROOT

One of the problems with understanding this whole concept of a logical root with no physical bounds is trying to figure out what—physically—this Dfs is. For starters, let's go back to the Dfs we've been creating throughout this chapter. Originally, I put my root on BS1 in the folder I:\corp. From there, I've created links of APPS, USERS, FINANCE, and APP2. If we look at I:\corp, we see a folder structure like that of Figure 11.49.

Notice anything? Those folders were all created automatically under I:\corp as I created the links. If I try to look into one of those folders under I:\corp, I get an Access Denied because the system has those areas protected in order to handle the Dfs referrals—the process of passing users to a respective link member, rather than the physical subdirectory.

FIGURE 11.49

The physical root

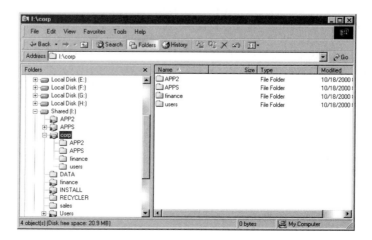

Speaking of referrals, when a client goes to hit the APPS folder within the Dfs CORP, what exactly happens? Using the Network Monitor, you can trace out the referral process. There are two important transactions between the client and the server. The client initially tries to access APPS just as it would any other directory within a share, except the server returns a message that tells the client to get a referral link. Why can't the server just direct the client there in the first place? Well, if you had the root server act as a middleman to the entire process—every share, folder, and file access—your bandwidth would go through the root to and from that server. You have to force the client to make the connection to the actual link member. By getting this "error" message, the client has to go to Plan B, which in this case is find out who—if not the root—has the data in question. Now the client sends a Get Dfs Referral message to the root server, requesting a filename of \bs.local\corp\APPS. The root server responds to the referral with the actual share name that the client needs to contact. In this case, the server has chosen BS2, so it responds with \bs2\APPS. It also includes a Dfs TimeTo-Live value equal to the parameter configured for the client cacheing interval.

PRACTICAL USES

Before you start setting up your root, throwing in some links, and reorganizing the way your users access their resources, let's take a quick look at some good ways that Dfs can actually add value to your network. Remember, it's not about playing with cool new features; it's about making life easier.

Consolidated Enterprise Resources

The example Dfs we've worked through in this chapter would be a good way to consolidate enterprise resources. You can take all of your shared resources across the network and put them under one logical share. Then, instead of having to know which logical drive a resource resides on, you only need to know the subdirectory. The neat thing is that actually configuring the Dfs has absolutely no impact on the configuration of your network. You can build and experiment with Dfs configurations all day long in a production environment without anyone even knowing that it exists. All of the old shares on your network remain in place, data is untouched, and users don't see anything different. Once you're ready with your new Dfs, the hard part comes in—changing your users' drive mappings from one drive per \\server\share to one drive for all shares. Don't underestimate this task. It's more than just mapping a new drive letter to the Dfs root. All applications need to know that they will no longer be on drive X:, but drive Y:.

Life-Cycle Management

The good news is that with Dfs, this is the last time you'll ever deal with changing drive mappings. If you need to move data from one server to another for purposes of life-cycling a new server in and an old one out, you don't need to play the game of backing up data, wiping the server, rebuilding it new with the same name, and restoring data to make it look like it is the same physical machine. With Dfs, you can set up a brand new server and configure it as an offline link replica for the share you want "moved." After you verify that all data has been ported over successfully, bring it online and take the old one off. The users don't know that they are hitting a new server. The Dfs handles it all in stride.

Web Sharing

Web sharing is another new feature of Windows 2000. It allows you to share folders directly for use via HTTP requests coming from web browsers.

NOTE *You must be running Internet Information Services for this option to be available. If your server doesn't support web access at the server level, it won't matter whether your shares are "web-enabled." Your users won't be able to get to those shares through their web browsers anyway.*

Configuring web sharing is extremely simple. Within your Windows Explorer, right-click the folder you want to share out to the Web and select Sharing. At the top of the folder properties dialog box that appears, you'll notice a Web Sharing tab (see Figure 11.50). Selecting that tab allows you to configure how this folder will be shared out to the Web. I'm going to enable web sharing for my Marketing folder.

FIGURE 11.50

Web Sharing folder properties

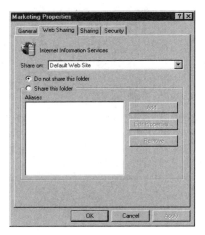

At the top of the Web Sharing tab is a Share On drop-down list. In that list are the different websites that have been created via the Internet Services Manager. Select the website that you want to add this folder into. Most of the time, the default website will be just fine, and this is where I am choosing to place my Marketing folder.

The next step is to select the radio button for Share This Folder. Once selected, a dialog box will pop up to configure the web alias for this folder, as shown in Figure 11.51.

The alias is what web clients will refer to in order to access this resource. Choose which permissions you would like web clients to have for the data in this share. You can select any combination of Read, Write, Script Source Access (which allows clients to execute scripts through this share), and Directory Browsing (which allows clients to see folder lists without being required to enter a valid filename to view). Choose the application permissions level from None, Scripts, and Execute. Once completed, you will be returned to your Web Sharing tab and will have the new alias shown as a configured alias (see Figure 11.52).

FIGURE 11.51

The Edit Alias dialog box

FIGURE 11.52

The configured web alias

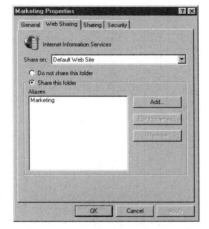

You can add more aliases for this folder by selecting the Add button, or remove unwanted aliases by selecting the alias and clicking the Remove button. You can also revisit alias properties by selecting the alias and clicking Edit Properties.

Once you click OK, the alias will be registered to your selected server's website and ready for browsing. Go to your web browser and enter the URL for this alias. On my machine, that would be `http://BS1.bs.local/marketing/`. Because I enabled directory browsing for my alias, I can see the files and folders within that folder, and I see the web page shown in Figure 11.53.

WARNING   *I tried to combine a few of these features into one step by enabling my CORP share—which is my Dfs root—as a web folder. When I look at* `\\BS\CORP` *within the regular Explorer, I can see the full Dfs. But if I try to look at my own* `I:\CORP` *folder, I can see all the directories corresponding to my child nodes, but since they are not real resources on my machine—rather redirections to other shares somewhere else—the server gives me an Access Denied message. When I enable web sharing for the CORP share on my server, and try to access* `http://BS1.bs.local/corp`—*access is denied again. When navigating through the web browser function, the client never gets a chance to ask for a link referral.*

FIGURE 11.53

Browsing the web folder

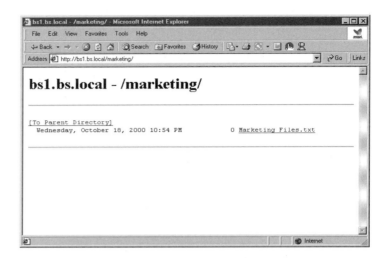

Using Offline Files/Client-Side Cacheing

As you've seen, Windows 2000's file server functionality has grown to include Dfs as well as web folders, while retaining the old NT file server capabilities. But it doesn't stop there: Not only does Windows 2000 improve the *server* side of file servers, it also jazzes up the *client* side.

Introducing Offline Files

Although many of Windows 2000 Server's new capabilities will largely appeal to network administrators, Win2K's Offline Files, or Client-Side Cacheing (Microsoft uses both names interchangeably), feature will appeal to almost anyone who uses a network. Offline Files provides three main advantages: It makes the network appear faster to its users, smoothes out network "hiccups," and makes the now-difficult task of keeping laptop files and server files in sync simple and transparent.

How Offline Files Works

Offline Files acts by automatically cacheing often-accessed network files, storing the cached copies in a folder on a local hard drive, a folder not surprisingly called `Offline Files`. Offline Files then uses those cached copies to speed up network access (or apparent network access), as subsequent accessing of a file can be handled out of the local hard disk's cached copy rather than over the network. Offline Files can also use the cached copies of the files to act as a stand-in for the network when the network has failed or isn't present—such as when you're on the road.

Offline Files is a write-through cacheing mechanism; when you write a file out, it always goes to the network, and it is also cached to your local hard disk. And when you want to access a file that Offline Files has cached, then as you've already read, Offline Files would *prefer* to give you the cached (and faster) copy, but first Offline Files checks that the file hasn't changed at the server by examining the file date, time, and size both on the server and in the cache; if they're the same, then Offline Files can give you the file out of the cache without any worries; otherwise, Offline Files fetches the network copy, so you've got the most up-to-date copy.

As a network file could easily be modified by someone else when you're not using it, there's a pretty good chance that the network copy of a file would often be different from the cached copy. But if *that*'s the case, then what good is Offline Files? After all, if the file changes on the network a lot, then you'll just end up having to retrieve it from the network instead of enjoying the speed of getting it from cache. Offline Files increases the chances that it has the most up-to-date copies of your cached files by doing background synchronizations in several user-definable ways. This synchronization is largely invisible to the user, who simply utilizes My Network Places or a UNC to access network files, as has been the case with earlier versions of NT and NT client software.

NOTE *Offline Files only works on Windows 2000 machines; you can't get this benefit if you've got Windows 9x or NT 3.x or 4.x on your Desktop. If you are using a Win2K Desktop, however, Offline Files will be useful even if you're accessing a server running pre–Windows 2000 software, such as NT 3.x or 4.x.*

You'll like Offline Files for several reasons. As these oft-used cached files will reside on the local hard disk in the `Offline Files` folder, you'll immediately see what seems to be an increase in network response speed: Opening a file that appears to be on the network but that is really in a local disk folder will yield apparently stunning improvements in response time, as little or no actual network activity is required. It also produces the side effect of reducing network traffic, as cached files needn't be retransmitted over the LAN. Having frequently used files in a local cache folder also solves the problem of "What do I do when the network's down, and I need a file from a server?" If you try to access a file on a server that's not responding (or if you're not physically connected to the network), Offline Files shifts to "offline" mode. When in offline mode, Offline Files looks in your local Offline Files network cache and, if it finds a copy of that file in the cache, it delivers the file to you just as if the server were up, running, and attached to the user's workstation. And anyone who's ever had to get ready for a business trip knows two of the worst things about traveling with a laptop: the agony of getting on the plane, only to realize that you've forgotten one or two essential files, and the irritation of having to remember when you return to make sure that whatever files you changed while traveling get copied back to the network servers. Offline Files greatly reduces the chance of the first of those problems because, again, often-used files tend to automatically end up in the local network cache folder. It greatly reduces the work of the second task by automating the laptop-to-server file synchronization process.

Enabling Offline Files on Your Desktop: The Basics

When you first install Windows 2000, Offline Files does not work by default. You must turn it on in one of two ways: either by telling Offline Files to keep track of a particular file, or by going to Folder Options—it's available in the Control Panel, or in the Tools menu of any folder window. Then just check the box labeled Enable Offline Files.

Once activated, Offline Files will often *automatically* cache a file just as a side effect of you using the file. (I'll get to why it *often* rather than *always* does this in a bit.) You can, however, tell Offline Files to *ensure* that a particular file or an entire folder on the network is always in the `Offline Files` folder (recall, the name for the Offline Files cache) in just two steps: First, find the desired file (or folder) in My Network Places. Second, right-click the file. My Network Places will then display the file's context menu with the usual items—Open, Rename, Delete, and the like—but some files' context menus will include the option Make Available Offline, as you can see in Figure 11.54.

FIGURE 11.54

"Pinning" a file so that it is always in the `Offline Files` folder

Forcing Offline Files to keep a copy of a particular file in the `Offline Files` folder (that is, forcing Offline Files to keep a copy of a file on the PC's local hard disk) is called *pinning* that file or folder. The first time that you pin a file, Offline Files will start up a configuration wizard, called the Offline Files Wizard, that asks a few questions, then sets up Offline Files to run based on your answers. And although it *sounds* like a great idea, be careful about making entire folders available offline, as that has the effect of copying the entire folder and all of its contents to your local hard disk. That can take some time when it's first set up, and of course it can be a bit chagrining when it fills up your hard disk. (Subsequent synchronizations may be quite quick, as you'll read later.)

If you choose Tools/Folder Options, you'll see the property page shown in Figure 11.55.

FIGURE 11.55

Options for Offline Files

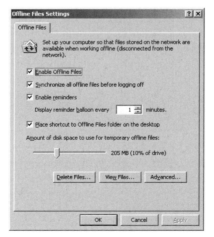

In the Offline Files Settings page, the first check box tells a Windows 2000 machine to enable its Offline Files capability. The second tells Offline Files to compare every file in the `Offline Files` folder with the file's "actual" values out on the network servers, forcing Offline Files to synchronize its local file copies with the file originals every time you log off. (That's only one of *several* options you have for controlling offline file synchronization, and you'll read more about those options later.) The next check box controls how Offline Files tells the user that one or more servers are not currently available, leading Offline Files to place that server or servers into offline mode. If you'd like, you can tell Offline Files to remind you every so often that one or more servers are in offline mode, with a ToolTip-like balloon such as you see in Figure 11.56.

FIGURE 11.56

Offline Files reminding you that you're offline

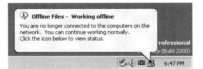

If you know that one of your servers is about to go offline, or if you're a mobile user about to go on a trip, then you will often need to know whether a particular file is already in your PC's cache, its `Offline Files` folder. You can see which files are in the local `Offline Files` folder, as well as their status, in a few ways: In the Offline Files Settings page, click the View Files button. Alternatively, in a check box on the same page, you can direct Windows 2000 to place a shortcut to your `Offline Files` folder right on your Desktop.

While the whole idea of network file cacheing is attractive, there's a built-in limitation to how many files can be cached on a user's local hard drive. There are often tens of gigabytes worth of files out on the network, and under a gigabyte of free space available on most workstations. It is entirely possible that you could, in a short period of time, examine more files on the network than would fit on your hard disk. Clearly, if left to itself, Offline Files could use up all of your free disk space, but you can control how much free space Offline Files is allowed to fill up in the Offline Files Settings page. However, you can only control how much space Offline Files allocates to the automatically cached files, and when that space is exhausted—by default, it's 10 percent of your disk's space—then Offline Files just drops the file that hasn't been used in the longest time to make room for more automatically cached files. In contrast, you can pin as many files as you like, forcing Offline Files to cache *them*—but you of course could run out of disk space doing that. If that happens, Offline Files just pops up a dialog box directing you to either unpin some files or to free up some disk space.

Getting and Keeping Things in the Offline Files Folder

Once you've turned Windows 2000's Offline Files feature on, how do you use it? In a given day, you may access many files on a network—which ones get copied into the `Offline Files` folder?

It's easier to conceptualize how Offline Files caches files if you understand that files get into the `Offline Files` folder in one of two ways: either you *direct* Offline Files to cache a file by pinning it (recall that you do that by choosing Make Available Offline from a file's context menu) or Offline Files decides by itself to cache some files without you having to ask it to. Offline Files calls these automatically cached files *temporary offline files*.

SITUATIONS IN WHICH FILES WON'T CACHE

You can't always cache network files, however. Sometimes you'll look at a network file's context menu and the Make Available Offline option doesn't appear; when that happens, Offline Files won't cache the file either by pinning or by making it a temporary offline file. One of three things causes this cacheing prohibition: First, if the file is on a non-SMB server, such as a NetWare server, then you don't get the option to cache the file. Offline Files can only cache files on SMB servers, which means that it can cache files from NT 3.x and 4.0 servers and workstations as well as Windows 9x machines running File and Printer Sharing services. (Of course, it can also cache files from Windows 2000 servers and workstations.) Second, if you have disabled Offline Files by unchecking Enable Offline Files in Folder Options, the option won't appear. Third, you will not get the option to pin a file if the shared folder that the file resides in has been declared non-cacheable by a network administrator. A network admin may declare a share non-cacheable in the share's property page at that share's server. They just right-click the shared folder and choose Sharing, then click the Cacheing button. A dialog box like the one shown in Figure 11.57 will appear.

If the network administrator unchecks the Allow Cacheing of Files in This Shared Folder option, then no one will be able to cache files in that folder.

FIGURE 11.57

Adjusting cache settings for a shared folder

MANUAL AND AUTOMATIC CACHEING

Assuming you're working at your workstation and trying to access a network file that *can* be cached, pinning that file will prompt Offline Files to immediately copy the network copy of the file to your local Offline Files folder; a dialog box appears showing you the progress of that copy.

Other files get cached in the Offline Files folder if the files are in a network share on a Windows 2000 machine and if that share has been designated for *automatic* cacheing. Using the Cacheing Settings dialog box, an administrator can designate a share as Manual Cacheing for Documents—the default setting—or as either Automatic Cacheing for Documents or Automatic Cacheing for Programs. Either of the latter two server-cacheing settings will cause automatic cacheing. When you open any file from a share configured for automatic cacheing, then that share's server tells your workstation, "While you're at it, cache this file." Your workstation then makes a local copy in the Offline Files folder, noting that the copy is a temporary offline file. The only difference between cacheing for documents or for programs is that Offline Files will run an EXE in a cached-for-programs folder without checking to see whether it's up to date—without synchronizing that file first. It's a bit quicker that way, though of course it could cause trouble if you modified that EXE frequently.

How Offline Files Manages Cache Space

Offline Files allocates space for pinned files a bit differently than it does for temporary offline files. Recall that the Offline Files Settings page includes a slider that you can use to control how much of your hard disk space to allow Offline Files to use. A second look shows that this amount only applies to the *temporary* offline files. The space taken by the files that you *pin* into the cache does not count against the space allocated in the Offline Files Settings page. As I said earlier, if the Offline Files folder is full and Offline Files automatically caches a new temporary offline file, it must drop one or more older files from the Offline Files folder to keep the size of the temporary offline files below the maximum allowed amount given in Offline Files Settings.

And don't bother looking on your hard disk for the Offline Files folder—it's actually a series of folders inside \Winnt\Csc hidden not with the Hidden attribute, but the System attribute. You can find it, but first you've got to go to the Winnt folder, then choose Tools/Folder Options, then go to the View tab and uncheck Hide Protected Operating System Files (Recommended) and confirm the choice. You'll then be able to browse through \Winnt\Csc. What you *won't* find there are useful file-names—all cached files are tagged with long numerical names rather than their actual names.

Offline Files in Action: Before the Trip

Now that you've got Offline Files set up, let's put it to work. It's useful to both mobile and fixed-location users, but its benefits are most dramatic for those mobile users, so here's a step-by-step look at how someone might use Offline Files to make life on the road easier.

Putting the Files in the Cache

A user named Jim is about to go on a trip. He connects his laptop into his company's corporate network and opens a share named Shareac on a server named Coral. Jim's network administrator has set up the Shareac share as an Automatic Cacheing for Documents share. Shareac contains two files that Jim needs, file1.txt and file2.txt. Jim right-clicks those files and chooses Make Available Offline. Over the course of the day, he also accesses file3.txt and file4.txt, although he does not pin them.

Ensuring They're in the Cache

Before shutting down the laptop prior to getting on the road, Jim wants to double-check that copies of file1.txt and file2.txt are on his laptop's hard disk. He opens his Offline Files folder and sees a screen something like the one in Figure 11.58.

FIGURE 11.58

Jim's Offline Files folder contents after accessing the Coral server

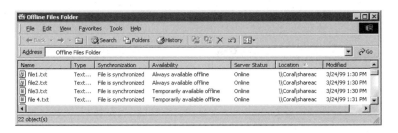

Note that under the Availability column, `file1.txt` and `file2.txt` are designated as Always Available Offline, meaning that they've been pinned; note also the little (blue) modification to the files' icons, indicating that they are pinned. Note also that `file3.txt` and `file4.txt` are in the `Offline Files` folder, even though Jim didn't pin them—Offline Files automatically cached them. You can tell this because under the Availability column head, these files are noted as being Temporarily Available Offline. They could end up pushed out of the Offline Files cache without warning, were Jim to reattach to his corporate network and start accessing other cacheable files.

Note also that the server status of Online means that Jim's still attached to the corporate network and that Coral is online. Actually, his laptop will consider Coral online until the laptop notices that Coral is not responding to attempted communication. Jim can view his `Offline Files` folder either via a shortcut on the Desktop (assuming he has configured his system to show one), or he can navigate to the Offline Files Settings page and click the View Files button.

GETTING THE MOST RECENT VERSION OF THE FILE

If Jim has even more files to synchronize, perhaps entire folders, then he can employ Mobile Sync, available by choosing Start/Programs/Accessories/Synchronize. When started, its screen looks like Figure 11.59.

FIGURE 11.59

Choosing shares to synchronize with Offline Files

Mobile Sync lists all of the folders that contain pinned files that Offline Files knows of. Jim can then check the folders he's interested in synchronizing and click the Synchronize button. Clicking Properties just displays the contents of the `Offline Files` folder, and the Setup button allows Jim to configure synchronization when he's *not* traveling (see the later section "Controlling Synchronization for Non-Mobile Users").

Working and Making Changes on the Road

On the plane to a client site, Jim starts up his laptop and opens My Network Places. His Desktop looks the same as it did back at the office, except now his system tray contains a small icon depicting a PC. Moving a mouse over the PC icon gets the message "Offline Files—the network is not available."

Right-clicking that icon offers a context menu that includes Status, which will simply report again that the network is not available; Synchronize, which obviously won't accomplish much until he's reconnected to the network; View Files, which opens up the `Offline Files` folder; and Settings, which brings up the Offline Files Settings page.

ACCESSING "NETWORK" FILES ON THE ROAD

Despite the fact that Jim is not attached to any network, My Network Places shows a "networked folder" icon for Shareac on Coral. If he opens up that folder, he'll see `file1.txt`, `file2.txt`, `file3.txt`, and `file4.txt`, just as if he were connected to the corporate network. He could open a command window and type **net view \\coral** to get a list of shares available on Coral, including Shareac. He could alternatively find `file1.txt` in the `Offline Files` folder.

Jim sees a problem with `file1.txt` and edits the file and saves it, and Offline Files allows Windows 2000 Professional to make it seem as if he's attached live on the corporate network. He also makes a few changes to `file2.txt`. After a meeting, he creates a completely new file, `file5.txt`, and saves it in the Shareac volume, again as if he were connected to the company network.

WARNING: SOMETIMES OFFLINE FILES DON'T WORK

Oh, by the way, this all sounds good, but sometimes it has gone haywire on me. In the typical traveling scenario, I've got a laptop and a file server, and I pin some files or perhaps a complete share or folder on the file server. Whenever you pin an entire folder, you have to wait a minute or two while Offline Files goes out and copies all of the files from the pinned folder to your local hard drive. In the case where my laptop is a member of a different domain than the file server, I've seen Offline Files *look* like everything syncs up fine when I pin the folder. But when I disconnect from the network and try to *access* the files, I've gotten error messages like "The network name is not available." I've also had situations where I originally logged in under a particular username and then had to enter a different username to access some share. When I then pinned that share, again Offline Files looked as if it were copying every single file. When on the road, however, Offline Files refused to let me view or work with the file, claiming that it didn't exist at all. My advice follows in the warning.

WARNING   *If you are going to depend on Offline Files, make sure that your laptop, file server, and user account are all in the same domain. If that's not the case, be absolutely sure while you're still in the office to disconnect the network cable after synchronizing your pinned files and double-check that you can access those files. Offline Files is great, but don't trust it until you can be really sure of it!*

Back in the Office: Syncing Up

After Jim returns from his trip, he plugs his laptop into his company's network and powers up the computer. He has updated `file1.txt` and `file2.txt` and created a completely new file, `file5.txt`, and he wants all three of these new or modified files written to the network servers.

As his laptop's operating system loads, it senses that it's back on the corporate network and tries to update the three files on Coral's share. `file1.txt` and the new `file5.txt` are no problem—the version of `file1.txt` is the same as it was before Jim left, so Offline Files overwrites the server copy with Jim's updated copy. `file5.txt` didn't exist before, so there's no conflict and Offline Files writes it to the server share. But unknown to Jim, someone *else* modified `file2.txt` while he was on the road. This presents a conflict to Offline Files, a conflict that it can't resolve by itself, so it prompts Jim for guidance (see Figure 11.60).

FIGURE 11.60

Resolving a file version conflict

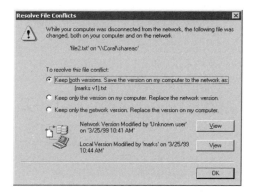

Jim uses the View buttons to examine both versions and decides that his update has more recent information, so he clicks the Keep Only the Version on My Computer button and then clicks OK. At this point, the files on his laptop and the ones on the network servers are synchronized.

Applying Offline Files to the Office: When Servers Fail

But suppose you're not a traveling user. What does Offline Files offer you? Greater network reliability and speed. By cacheing commonly used documents, Offline Files offers you a safety net in the event that the network fails.

BULLETPROOFING WORD WITH OFFLINE FILES

Suppose you're working on a Word document. You keep the DOC file on a server rather than your local hard disk so that you can work on it from any workstation and because it'll be automatically backed up every night. But Word's frequent background saves and AutoRecover writes mean that your workstation must often communicate with the server where the document resides. A network failure or even a short hiccup in network or server response can cause problems that can lead to Word losing your document. With Offline Files, Word has a much softer landing. Once the server becomes unresponsive, Offline Files automatically shifts all of that server's folders to offline mode. Your first clue that there's a network problem, other than the initial delay from an unresponsive network, is that the Offline Files PC icon has appeared in your system tray, and a balloon message tells you that the server you were working with is now offline. You can continue to work with and save the file, but of course it'll really save to the `Offline Files` folder, at least until you reconnect to the server and synchronize. Additionally, you'll see this kind of network fault-tolerant behavior on *any* cached file, whether a pinned file or a temporary offline file. As you saw before, Offline Files will cache any file that you access on an automatically cached share, or any file that you pin in a manually cached share. This suggests that you should consider either pinning all of the Word files that you use from a server or set the server shares' cacheing settings to Automatic Cacheing for Documents.

RESUMING NORMAL OPERATION

When the server is available again, Offline Files will sense that and modify its icon to the one shown in Figure 11.61. Click the Offline Files icon, and you'll see a dialog box (Figure 11.62) offering to reestablish connection to the server.

FIGURE 11.61

Ready for reconnection

FIGURE 11.62

Reestablishing network connection with Offline Files

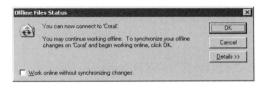

Click OK and you'll get a warning to close whatever files you are working on, as Windows 2000 will have to close any open files before it can synchronize them.

Controlling Synchronization for Non-Mobile Users

In addition to its fault-tolerant-like benefits, Offline Files's other great strength for non-mobile users is that it can improve a user's network experience by reducing the time between when a user requests a file on the network and when the user gets that file. There's no magic in that quick response, of course: Offline Files gets those files to the user so quickly because the files are already sitting on the user's hard disk in the `Offline Files` folder. But that's really only half the story. Sure, it's nice to get your files quickly—but are they the *right* files? The answer is yes, but there's a lot of underlying machinery ensuring that.

Before offering the locally cached file copy as correct, Offline Files does a quick synchronization with the original network file. That synchronization need not be an entire copy; instead, it is a simple consistency check. For example, try pinning a 100+MB file to your `Offline Files` folder. The initial synchronization will be a simple file copy, and it'll take a good long time. But then right-click the large file and do a synchronization, and you'll see that synchronization finish in seconds. This is true even for large files; for example, in one test, a 4MB JPEG file on a network server was pinned to a workstation's `Offline Files` folder, then the JPEG file was modified by another workstation, reducing its size by 30 percent. Synchronizing the first workstation to the JPEG file's new size took less than 5 seconds.

So you might find when accessing a file via the `Offline Files` folder that there is a short delay while your workstation synchronizes with the offline file's original copy. That might be acceptable, but Offline Files improves further upon that performance by periodically resynchronizing its offline files *before* you need them.

In addition to the synchronizations that occur when you reconnect after being offline, when actually accessing the file, or after choosing Synchronize on a pinned file's context menu, you can also configure your Windows 2000 workstation to synchronize at logon, at logoff, when the workstation is idle, or at particular times of day. You configure these synchronizations either by starting Mobile Sync via Start/Programs/Accessories/Synchronize and then clicking the Setup button, or by opening a folder and choosing Tools/Synchronize and then clicking the Setup button on the resulting page. You get a properties page like the one shown in Figure 11.63.

FIGURE 11.63

Initial synchronization configuration screen

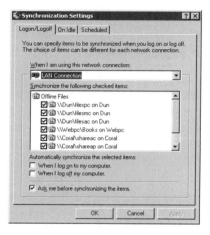

There are three tabs on this properties page: Logon/Logoff, On Idle, and Scheduled. The first two have a single-selection drop-down list box, When I Am Using This Network Connection, that allows you to specify whether you want this synchronization done over a LAN or WAN connection.

In the first tab, you can instruct Offline Files to synchronize at logon or logoff or both. And if you think that synchronizing might be a lengthy process and would like to be able to skip it, you can select the Ask Me Before Synchronizing the Items option, and Offline Files will display the Mobile Sync screen, letting you choose which—if any—folders to synchronize.

The second tab allows Offline Files to essentially synchronize in the background, waiting until your computer sits idle (see Figure 11.64).

FIGURE 11.64

Controlling foreground/background synchronization

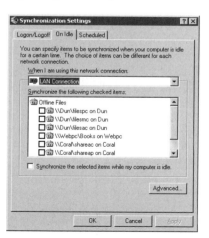

As with the Logon/Logoff tab, you can specify which folders to synchronize. The Advanced button lets you control how long your workstation should be idle before synchronizing, and how often to synchronize if the computer is idle for long periods of time.

The final tab, Scheduled, lets you set up synchronizations for particular times of day. You can tell it to synchronize every *n* days, every day, or every weekday.

Cleaning Out Offline Files

Sometimes Offline Files won't go away, however. Say you once connected to a server named MANGO and pinned a couple of files. You'll never see MANGO again and the files aren't important any longer, but the system keeps wanting to synchronize with MANGO and you get an error message every time you log in or log off. What to do?

Simple. Go to the `Offline Files` folder and unpin all of the files (or perhaps folders) in MANGO. Alternatively, you should be able to do that in My Network Places. Unpin everything related to MANGO, reboot, and you *should* hear no more about MANGO. Sometimes, however, it just stays around forever. In that case, zap *all* of the cached files. (Be sure to synchronize the folders that are still relevant first!)

You might want to flush out all offline files for several reasons. You might be about to give a laptop or desktop to someone and don't want them poking around inside your `Offline Files` folder or `\Winnt\Csc`. Or maybe you've just gone a bit pin-crazy and have so much stuff cached that you don't have any hard disk space left. In that case, unpin what you can first. But finish the job by choosing Start/Programs/Accessories/System Tools/Disk Cleanup. You'll notice that one of the things that Disk Cleanup will do is to wipe out your offline files.

WARNING   *Again, make sure there's nothing cached that you want to synchronize with the file server before doing this; if you've made changes and haven't synchronized, cleaning out the* `Offline Files` *folder will lose your changes!*

You'll probably first notice Offline Files when you see how much easier it makes keeping laptop files and network files in lockstep. But you may soon notice that your in-house network is a bit snappier, and that the occasional network failure doesn't keep you from getting work done. And if *that* isn't a killer app, what is?

Chapter 12

Software Installation

ONE OF THE MOST common problems a network administrator faces almost daily is software installation and distribution. Isn't it heartwarming when your boss comes into your office and tells you, "We just bought a site license to XYZ Application. Can you install it on all 400 of our computers by the end of next week? Thanks!" Doesn't her confidence in you just make you proud?

Trust me—if it does, then it's likely that you haven't done this before.

At the firm where I work, we've tried everything from Microsoft's SMS to third-party solutions to home-grown solutions to alleviate this problem. Some work okay—most don't. Well, I suspect that a network administrator must have snuck onto the Windows 2000 development team because Software Installation (SI) is one of the most significant time-saving (and therefore money-saving) features in Windows 2000.

What Microsoft has done is integrate software installation into the operating system—and with that, allow it to be centrally controlled, distributed, and managed. You can automatically install an application company-wide or restrict it to a specific list of locations or a group of individuals. When you are done with it, or when you discover the licensing doesn't allow you to roll it out to the entire company, then you can forcibly remove it from all computers in one fell swoop. All of this is integrated into the operating system and Active Directory.

To help implement SI, Microsoft made some changes to the Winlogon service, OLE automation (COM), and the shell. Aside from that, these are the components of SI:

- Software Installation in Group Policy

- The Windows Installer Service

- The Add/Remove Programs applet in the Control Panel

You use Software Installation within group policy objects (GPOs) to control and manage the applications you are distributing, called *packages*. Everything else is used to install or remove the packages based on what you set up in Group Policy. There are two ways you can distribute a package to a user or to computers: *publishing* or *assigning*. When you publish a package, you're making it available to users or computers, and it gets installed at their option. To install it, the user simply goes to the Add/Remove Programs icon in the Control Panel. You cannot publish a package to computers. When you assign a package to users or computers (you *can* assign packages to computers), you are basically stating that they must have this package and that it will be installed for the users the next time they log in (sort of, but more on that later) and for the computers the next time they boot up.

These GPOs are stored in the Group Policy Container, which is a Directory service object—yet another benefit of Active Directory. The Group Policy Container also stores the class store. The class store is where all programs and APIs are stored for the publication and assignment of packages.

NOTE *"But where do you get packages from?" I hear you cry. Microsoft is pushing software vendors hard to offer their new software releases in MSI (Microsoft Installer) format. If you see a file on a vendor's distribution CD with the extension* `.MSI`, *then that vendor has created a ready-for-Windows-2000 package. Alternatively, as you'll read later in this chapter, you can build your own packages with third-party products, including one that comes free with Windows 2000—VERITAS's WinInstall. (Find it on the Windows 2000 installation CD under* `\valueadd\3rdparty\mgmt\winstle`*.)*

Publishing a Package to Users

Let's start off with an example that fixes a headache that's plagued Windows NT administrators for years: Windows 2000 and NT 4 only install domain administration tools on the servers. Most administrators are not always sitting at a server when they need these tools. So, as they gained experience, they would copy the tools with any extra DLLs to a network share and create shortcuts that ran the tools from the network share. This worked fine under NT 4. However, under Windows 2000, the administration tools are all COM objects, and as COM objects, they must be registered before they can be used. On Windows 2000 domain controllers, Microsoft includes `adminpak.msi`, which allows you to publish the administrator tools any way you want.

NOTE *As suggested earlier, MSI is a new file type that is the data file for the Windows Installer—the service that performs all of the work for SI. MSI stands for Microsoft Software Installer. A package can be just the MSI or it can include other files as well.*

Here are the steps to publish the package:

1. Copy `adminpak.msi` to a network share.

2. Create a GPO called AdminPak (you can call it anything you like).

3. Filter the GPO so that only enterprise admins and domain admins can install the package.

4. Add the package to the GPO.

Step One: Copy *adminpak.msi* to a Network Share

This first step is easy. I created another subdirectory called `C:\Packages` and shared it as `Packages`. Within `C:\Packages`, I created yet another subdirectory and called it `AdminTools`. Then I copied `adminpak.msi` from `C:\winnt\system32` to my new `AdminTools` subdirectory. Figure 12.1 shows what I did.

FIGURE 12.1

Copying `admin-pak.msi` to a network share

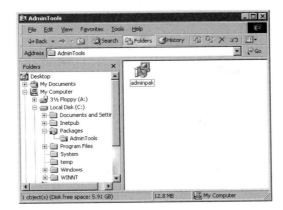

Step Two: Create a GPO

Next, start up the DSA (also known as Active Directory Users and Groups), and then right-click the domain name and choose Properties. Click the Group Policy tab, then the New button, type **Admin-Pak**, and hit Enter (see Figure 12.2).

FIGURE 12.2

Naming the GPO that deploys AdminPak

Step Three: Filter the GPO

The default behavior for Windows 2000 is to apply GPOs to all users in an organization, but with filtering, you have complete control. It's a good habit to get into because you can choose the users and computers to which a GPO applies. I'll cover filtering later in this chapter.

To apply a filter, click the Properties button, then the Security tab. Make sure the Apply Group Policy permission is unchecked for all groups but Domain Admins and Enterprise Admins. Then click OK. When you first create a GPO, it does not apply to administrators. For this example, we want it to apply as Figure 12.3 shows.

FIGURE 12.3

This GPO applies to Domain Admins.

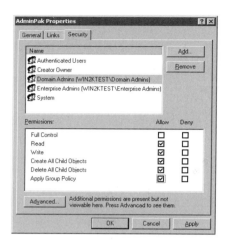

Step Four: Add the Package to the GPO

Next, click the Edit button. This will launch the Group Policy snap-in with your new group policy open and ready to be edited. At this point, you must make a decision. When you add a package to a group policy, you can assign or publish the package to users, or you can assign it to computers. Packages are added to the GPO under `Software Settings\Software Installation` in either `Computer Configuration` or `User Configuration`, as Figure 12.4 shows.

FIGURE 12.4

Add packages to a GPO in `Software Installation`.

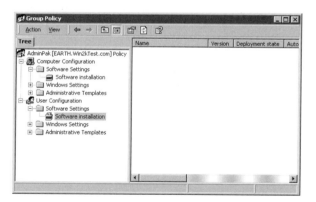

We'll add the `adminpak.msi` to `User Configuration\Software Settings\Software Installation`. To do that, right-click `User Configuration\Software Settings\Software Installation` and choose New/Package. Now find the `adminpak.msi` on your network. Mine is located on `\\EARTH\Packages\AdminTools\adminpak.msi`, so I'll just type it in. Then click OK.

NOTE *Be sure to use the full UNC path name. If you don't, the Windows Installer will not be able to find and install the package and all installations will fail. Luckily, the Group Policy snap-in warns you if you don't use a network path.*

At this point, we are prompted for the package deployment method, as shown in Figure 12.5. Choose Published and click OK. The next time you create your own package, don't worry too much about getting the deployment method right. It can be changed later by right-clicking the package and selecting Assign.

FIGURE 12.5

Specifying that
the package will be
published

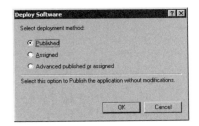

We now have the `adminpak.msi` ready for installation by any domain or enterprise administrator. To test the package, go to a Windows 2000 Professional workstation that is a part of your domain and log in as a domain or enterprise administrator. Go to the Control Panel and click Add/Remove Programs and then Add New Programs. You should see a screen like the one in Figure 12.6.

FIGURE 12.6

From Add/Remove
Programs, you can
install published
packages.

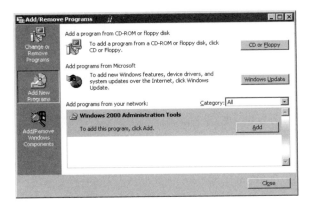

As you can see, all you need to do to add Windows 2000 Administration Tools is click the Add button. After you've installed the package, it then shows up under Add New Programs as Installed and Change or Remove Programs.

NOTE *You can repair any published application by clicking Add/Remove Programs in the Control Panel, then clicking Change or Remove Programs, and then clicking the Support Information link. A dialog will be displayed with some basic support contact information and a Repair button to reinstall the package.*

Filtering Group Policy

In the first example, we touched on what filtering group policies does for us in Software Installation. Simply put, thanks to filtering, we can place a GPO anywhere in our domain organization and use security to control who will get the software packages the GPO contains. No matter what the reason, be it licensing, security, or politics, you can control who gets a package. You can decide that one user gets the package or a thousand users get it, one computer or a thousand computers—it doesn't matter where in the organizational structure the user or computer falls.

Filtering is completely controlled by using the Security tab on the GPO's properties dialog box, which you see in Figure 12.7. Any user, computer, or security group (or any security group the user or computer is a member of) in the Name list will get the package if the Allow check box for the Apply Group Policy permission is checked, unless, of course, the Deny check box next to Apply Group Policy is checked for the user, computer, or security group (or any security group the user or computer is a member of). Authenticated Users refers to any validated domain user on the network.

FIGURE 12.7

Set up filtering from the Security tab on the GPO's properties dialog.

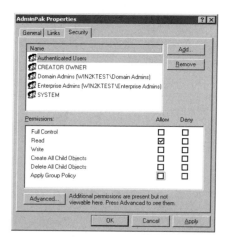

Don't expect the Security tab for the GPO to grant rights to users so they can use the features or information of an application. It won't. You can set the AdminPak GPO to apply to any domain user and any domain user would be able to install it—and that's it.

So, what happens if a GPO that had applied to a user or computer no longer applies? Let's say we have a user called LittleMutt who was in the Domain Admins group. When we set up our AdminPak GPO, it applied to all members of the Domain Admins group, including LittleMutt, and LittleMutt installed the package. Well, later we discover that LittleMutt is too young and inexperienced for the far-reaching power granted by being a member of the Domain Admins group, so we remove him from the group. Now the AdminPak GPO no longer applies to him, so what happens to the package he already installed? Does it get removed? The default behavior is that it doesn't—unless you have checked Uninstall This Application When It Falls Out of the Scope of Management.

You can check this option by right-clicking the package once you are editing your GPO. Click on the Deployment tab and you'll see a dialog like the one shown in Figure 12.8.

FIGURE 12.8

The Deployment options tell Windows 2000 what to do when a GPO no longer applies to users or computers.

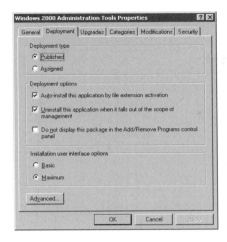

Using Organizational Units

You can also use organizational units (OUs) to control package distribution within Active Directory. Your OUs will sometimes follow your company's organizational structure, which makes the use of OUs very natural for package distribution for two reasons. The first reason is that you can use OUs for beta-testing both the application and the rollout of the application. The second is, of course, politics.

Whenever you roll out a new application, you probably assign a group of users and computers to be your beta testers. The users and computers in this group will usually change based on the application, but it is useful to have, let's say, a Beta Testers OU. You can add any users or computers you like to that OU and then create the GPO that will control the new application's package. You would create the GPO with the correct security and security group membership in place and test the rollout and the application. You could then add the GPO to other Beta Testers OUs within other sites of your company to test the remote install of the new package. When you are ready to roll the package out to the rest of the company, simply add the GPO to any other OU or to the domain and remove it from the Beta Testers OUs. This leaves the GPO and package completely unchanged and eliminates the need for any last-minute changes. Last-minute changes are frequent causes of problems with package distributions or implementations.

In addition, if you are rolling out a new version of an application currently in use, you can isolate the new version to the members of your Beta Testers OU while all other users continue to use the prior version. This is a powerful technique to aid you during upgrades.

With politics, the reasons are different but the methods and results are the same. The GPO that controls your package is added to the OUs that want the package. You can still have one security group to help manage which users or computers get the package within the OUs that are supposed to get it.

As with GPO filtering, when a user or computer no longer belongs to an OU, then any package that was installed because of membership in the OU will be uninstalled if you've checked the check box Uninstall This Application When This GPO No Longer Applies to Users or Computers on the package's properties dialog.

Assigning a Package to Users or Computers

Assigning a package to a user or a computer is the coolest thing about this Software Installation stuff. As with publishing an application, the current user doesn't need administrator privileges on the computer and the package will still get installed. However, if the package is assigned to a user, it gets installed when the user logs in. If the package is assigned to a computer, it gets installed when the computer boots up and no one needs to be logged in. If the user tries to delete the application, the package will be reinstalled or repaired. When you assign a package to a GPO, the package is *advertised* to every user and computer that GPO applies to.

The interesting thing about assigning a package is that it gets only partially installed at login or boot. An install program for an application typically does only a few relatively simple things: copy files to the computer, associate file types to the application, register any COM objects, and set up Start menu shortcuts. Well, at login or boot time, the Winlogon process only performs *part* of the installation of your package; it takes care of the shortcuts, file associations, and COM registration. To the user, this makes it appear that the software is installed. Consider Microsoft Excel, for instance. Excel is on the menu, and if any file with the .XLS extension is opened, Excel will launch. In addition, the icon for all XLS files is changed to the Excel icon. The user can't see that COM objects are registered, but we know that they are there. We can see them by running REGEDIT and looking in the HKEY_CLASSES_ROOT for the Excel.Application key, followed by several others. The installation is finished when the user clicks the application shortcut in the Start menu or opens any file associated with the application.

There are a couple of cool things about this. First, only those applications used by the user, or even the parts used by the user, will get completely installed. This saves time and disk space. Second, when the user logs into another computer, assigned packages follow her and appear to be already installed. Perhaps the user is on another computer temporarily because she has gotten a new computer. If all of her applications have been assigned, they will get installed as she uses them.

To demonstrate how a package is assigned, we'll use Microsoft Office 2000 Premium. Distributing a package by assignment is very much like publishing one. Here are steps to assign the package:

1. Run the administrative setup.

2. Create a group policy object called Office 2000 (you can call it anything you like).

3. Add the package to the GPO.

4. Customize the package properties.

Step One: Running the Administrative Setup

Start by installing a network-accessible copy of Office 2000 on some file server. You can run the administrative setup by clicking Start/Run, typing **d:\setup /a d:\data1.msi**, and clicking OK. You are then asked for your CD key and the location to which you want to install Office 2000. After a couple of minutes, the install is done and we're ready to begin.

NOTE *Be sure to enter your CD key. If you don't, your users may be prompted for one when the product is installed when they click the Start menu, unless you've got the Microsoft Select CDs—they don't require keys.*

The first thing I'm going to do is set up a Beta Testers group within my Corporate HQ OU and move the LittleMutt user to that group, as shown in Figure 12.9. Your OUs may be different, but I ended up with what is in Figure 12.9. Remember that we removed LittleMutt from any administrators groups, so he is a regular user without any administrator privileges on the domain and he doesn't need them on our test workstation either.

FIGURE 12.9

This is the Beta Testers OU.

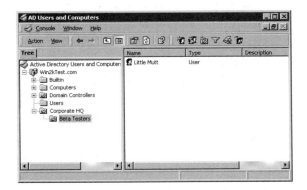

Step Two: Create a Group Policy Object

Next, start up the DSA, right-click the Beta Testers OU, and choose Properties. Click the Group Policy tab, then the New button, type **Office 2000**, and hit Enter (see Figure 12.10).

FIGURE 12.10

Creating an Office 2000 GPO

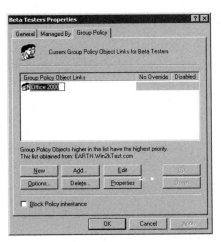

Now press the Properties button and click the Security tab. By default, the GPO is created so that it applies to Authenticated Users (as you can see in Figure 12.11), which means to any user or computer that is in our OU. This is perfect for our example, so we'll leave it as it stands. Click OK to close the dialog.

FIGURE 12.11

This GPO applies to all authenticated users.

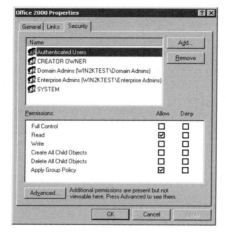

In the real world, it's at this point that you'd probably want to set up your own filtering because you wouldn't want all users (that's what the Authenticated Users group means) to get Office 2000. You can do this by clicking the Add button and selecting the security group you want the GPO to apply to.

Step Three: Add the Package to the GPO

The next step is to click the Edit button. This will launch the Group Policy snap-in with the Office 2000 GPO open. We want to add the package to `User Configuration\Software Settings\ Software Installation`, as Figure 12.12 shows. Right-click Software Installation (or right-click in the empty right window pane) and choose New/Package. My Office 2000 is located on `\\EARTH\ Packages\O2KPremium\data1.msi`, so I'll just type it in. Then click OK. Be sure to use a network path or the package installation won't work.

FIGURE 12.12

The Software installation for the Office 2000 GPO

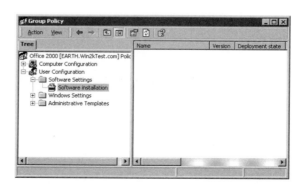

At this point, we're prompted for the package deployment method, shown in Figure 12.13. Choose Assigned and click OK.

FIGURE 12.13

Deploying Office 2000 via assignment

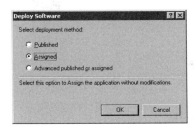

Step Four: Customize the Package Properties

Next, double-click the package; this will bring up the properties dialog. The first thing we want to do is make sure the Uninstall This Application When It Falls Out of the Scope of Management option is checked. Also, set Installation User Interface Options to Basic to minimize the dialogs that the users will see. Figure 12.14 shows the Deployment tab for the package as I've set it up.

FIGURE 12.14

Select Uninstall This Application When It Falls Out of the Scope of Management.

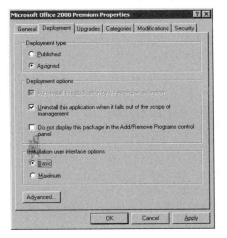

Now click OK and we are ready to test our deployment. To test the deployment, we need to log on as user in our Beta Tester OU. That is good ol' LittleMutt, so go to a Windows 2000 workstation that is part of your domain and log on as LittleMutt. Now, in addition to the standard messages in the logon dialog, toward the end you will see "Applying software installation settings." It is at this point that the Winlogon process is performing the first half of the installation. It's doing things like associating file types, registering COM objects, and setting up Start menu shortcuts.

These associations, registered COM objects, and shortcuts are exactly what you and I are used to. They are advertised components and features of an application. By "advertised," I mean that they are available and ready to be used but not completely installed and copied to the local hard drive. Remember when I said that some changes were made to the Winlogon server, OLE Automation, and the shell? Well, we know how Winlogon changed; now comes an explanation of how OLE Automation and the shell changed. The first time an advertised COM object is used, the modified shell will install the feature via the Windows Installer Server, and the same thing happens the first time an advertised shortcut is used.

Since you are now logged on as LittleMutt, you should see the Office 2000 shortcuts on the Start menu. Click the Excel shortcut and you'll see a Windows Installer dialog like the one shown in Figure 12.15. This is the rest of the installation taking place, where the application is actually being copied to the computer.

FIGURE 12.15

Windows Installer is beginning the Excel install.

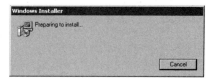

Removing a Package

The process for removing packages is very easy and very powerful. It is the same regardless of whether the package is published or assigned. Bring up the Group Policy snap-in to edit the GPO that contains the package you wish to remove. Next, right-click the package and choose All Tasks/Remove. You will then see a dialog like the one shown in Figure 12.16. Now we have two choices.

FIGURE 12.16

Deciding how Windows 2000 is to handle the already installed copies of the package

If we select the first option, we can immediately remove our package from the users or computers to which it is published or assigned. What *immediately* really means is that the package will be removed the next time the user logs in (if the package is published or assigned to the user) or the next time the computer boots (if the package is assigned to the computer). While this may not be immediate in the literal sense, it will uninstall your package from wherever SI previously installed it, so make sure this is what you want to do before you click OK. The next time the user logs on, he will get the message "Windows Installer removing managed software *name of package*," where *name of package* is the name of the package you just removed.

If, on the other hand, we select the second option, any existing installations of our package will remain where they are and no new installs will take place. One word of caution: Once you select the second option and remove the package, the existing installations of your application are orphaned and you no longer control them. In other words, if you decide later that they should be removed, your only choice is to go to every workstation that has the application and manually remove it yourself.

Redeploying a Package

With software distribution, it is often useful to have the ability to force the package to be reinstalled everywhere. Maybe you've added modifications to a package. For this and other reasons, Microsoft included a feature that gives you that ability. Within the Group Policy snap-in, right-click the package you wish to redeploy, then choose All/Tasks/Redeploy Application and you'll get the dialog like the one shown in Figure 12.17.

FIGURE 12.17

The redeploy warning

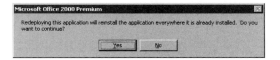

Be sure this is what you really want to do since your package will get reinstalled for all users and computers—even if it means 10 thousand users or computers.

Creating Your Own MSI

In the not-so-distant future, applications will come with an MSI that we can deploy via Software Installation. But what do we do for now? Well, Microsoft's answer is to include the VERITAS Software Console and WinINSTALL Discover. The VERITAS Software Console allows you to view and edit an MSI and WinINSTALL Discover helps you to create one. Now don't confuse WinINSTALL Discover with the WinInstall service. They are very different—just named alike. WinInstall installs packages via an MSI. WinINSTALL Discover allows you to create an MSI from an application that was installed using an old-style install or setup program.

The big picture on how you create your own MSI is this: You take a *Before snapshot* of a computer, install the new application, then take an *After snapshot* of the computer; then the two snapshots are compared and the differences are output to the MSI. The steps are as follows:

1. Create a clean computer.
2. Take the Before snapshot.
3. Install the application and reboot.
4. Test the application.
5. Take the After snapshot and compare.
6. Make any customizations.
7. Test the application installed by the new MSI.

Step One: Create a Clean Computer

A clean computer is one that has only the operating system and its operating system service packs installed. If you install any other software on the computer prior to creating the Before snapshot, you run the risk of making the new application dependent upon the other software being installed first. The reason for this is simple. WinINSTALL Discover only notices the differences between the Before and After snapshots. It won't care that the new application didn't install a DLL or make a needed Registry entry because the DLL or Registry entry was already there.

Here's an example that will help me explain my point. Windows 2000, with the latest and greatest service packs installed, has version 1.0 of the `ABC.DLL`. You then install some other software that, unknown to you, upgrades the `ABC.DLL` to version 1.1. Then you take the Before snapshot. Now your new application also needs version 1.1 of the `ABC.DLL`. However, when you run the setup for your new application, it probably will not copy the `ABC.DLL` again because it sees that it is already there. Even if it did, WinINSTALL Discover will see no difference between the Before and After version of the `ABC.DLL`. The bottom line is that your new application will not work when installed with the MSI unless the other software is installed first. The same thing goes for Registry entries. The goal of this whole procedure is to find out everything your new application needs and include it in the MSI.

By the way, having a clean computer also means you shouldn't install VERITAS Software Console and WinINSTALL Discover. You wouldn't want your new application to require VERITAS Software Console or WinINSTALL Discover for it to work, would you?

Step Two: Take the Before Snapshot

Go to your clean computer and log on as a user with administrator privileges on that computer. This is, of course, so that you can install the new application. Now run WinINSTALL Discover. It's best to run it from the Start/Run menu and to run it from the network without mapping a drive to a network share. My command was `\\Earth\C$\Program Files\VERITAS Software\Wininstall\ DiscoZ.exe`, but of course, yours will be different.

The first dialog that comes up gives you a brief explanation of what WinINSTALL Discover is about to do. Click the Next button and the next dialog asks for your new application name, the location and name of the MSI, and whether the application is a 16- or 32-bit application. For this example, I installed the Windows 2000 Resource Kit, so I answered the questions as Figure 12.18 shows.

FIGURE 12.18

Defining your new application

Next you're asked for a drive to store temporary work files. This can be a local drive or a network drive, but it's best if you use a local drive. Don't worry, the temporary work files won't show up in your MSI.

The next dialog asks which drives to scan. These are the drives WinINSTALL Discover will use to take the Before snapshot. It is important to be careful to select any drive that might change as a result of installing your new application. You wouldn't, though, want to select network drives, CD-ROM drive, and so on. Figure 12.19 shows what I selected.

FIGURE 12.19

Telling Win-INSTALL Discover which drives to watch for changes (which drives to scan)

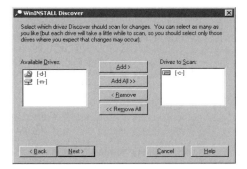

After you click Next, you are asked what files to exclude from the scan, as shown in Figure 12.20. I kept the defaults, but you can, of course, change them to exclude any other files you need excluded. This is where the temporary work files that are a part of WinINSTALL Discover's Before snapshot process are excluded from the scan.

FIGURE 12.20

You can select files to exclude from scanning.

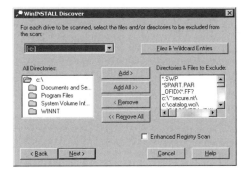

After you click Next, the process begins. It will take a few minutes as each drive you selected, and the Registry, is scanned.

Step Three: Install the Application and Reboot

This part sounds pretty simple, and it is. You simply need to install your new application exactly as you want the MSI to install it. You should reboot the computer, since many application setup programs install the last couple of files they need during the next reboot. This is often because the setup program needs to replace a file that is currently in use. So to be safe, we reboot.

Step Four: Test the Application

Now you need to configure and test the application to ensure that it is working as you want and expect it to. The only thing you need to keep in mind is that any change you make will probably end up in the MSI.

Step Five: Take the After Snapshot and Compare

Again, you need to log on as a user with administrator privileges on what was the clean computer. Then run WinINSTALL Discover again to take the After snapshot. It's a good idea to run it from the Start/Run menu and to run it from the network without mapping a drive to a network share. My command was \\Earth\C$\Program Files\VERITAS Software\Wininstall\DiscoZ.exe, although, again, yours will be different.

The first dialog you'll see will look like Figure 12.21. Now WinINSTALL Discover knows that it has taken the Before snapshot on this computer already, so it asks whether you want to take the After snapshot or abandon the Before snapshot so you can start the process over.

FIGURE 12.21

Beginning the After snapshot

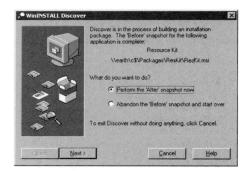

When you're creating your own MSI, it is quite likely that you will need to do the entire "Before snapshot—Install the application—After snapshot" process a couple of times. Keep in mind that if you do, your computer is no longer clean and you should get it back to a clean state before starting over. Yes, that may mean reinstalling Windows 2000.

Luckily for us, WinINSTALL Discover remembers all of the long path names we typed in so we don't have to type them in again. Make sure Perform the 'After' Snapshot Now is selected, as it is in Figure 12.21, and click Next.

Now as soon as you click Next, WinINSTALL Discover is off and running, taking the After snapshot. This will take about as long as taking the Before snapshot. As it takes the After snapshot, it compares that to the Before snapshot and writes any differences it finds to your new MSI. When it's done, you may see a dialog like Figure 12.22.

This dialog means that WinINSTALL Discover was successful but here are the peculiarities it found. You'll typically get warnings at this point, and you should look through them to see if any throw red flags for you. Other than that, it means you need to test the application when it is installed by your new MSI.

FIGURE 12.22

The new MSI has been generated.

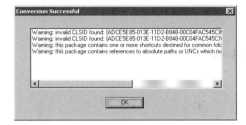

Step Six: Make Any Customizations

What you want to do now is take a look at the MSI you just made and possibly modify it. You can do so by using the VERITAS Software Console. From the Start menu on the server that has your new MSI, choose Program Files/VERITAS Software/VERITAS Software Console. Then choose File/Open and select your new MSI. Once you've opened your MSI, you should see a window that looks somewhat like Figure 12.23.

FIGURE 12.23

The opening window with the MSI opened

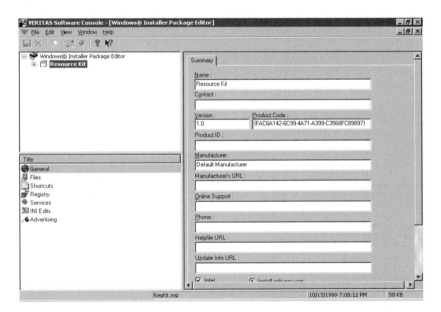

The General information contains the basics, but the really useful information is under the other titles. If you click Files in the lower-left section of the window, you should see something like Figure 12.24. These are all of the files in your MSI. This is how you can find out what files are being installed by the package—whether it's your new MSI or an MSI provided by an off-the-shelf commercial application.

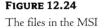

FIGURE 12.24

The files in the MSI

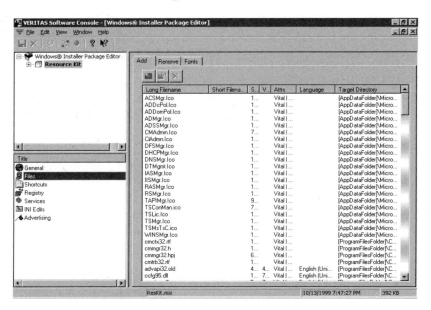

Why is this useful? What would we want to change here? If an application requires these files, we probably shouldn't remove any, right? Well, each application we install on a workstation (or server, for that matter) has its own set of required files. And of those files, at least some are shared by other applications. It is the shared files, typically DLLs, that cause us trouble.

For instance, say we have an application called Abc that requires a DLL called `shared.dll` version 2. Also, let's say we have another application, Def, which also requires `shared.dll`, but this time it needs version 1. Because we install application Abc and then Def, we end up with version 1 of `shared.dll` and application Abc ends up not working. By using VERITAS Software Console to edit your MSIs, you can do something about the problem.

Scroll down the file list, find a file called `comdlg32.ocx`, and double-click it (Figure 12.25). You know the shared file problem? Well `comdlg32.ocx` is one of the most widely shared ActiveX controls around. It seems that every application nowadays installs its own version of it.

At the bottom of the dialog is a drop-down list called Component. This is the part of the application that needs this DLL—write the number down or print the screen and then click OK to close the properties dialog. Now in the tree in the upper-left portion of the console window, double-click Resource Kit. The tree will open up and display another line labeled Resource Kit; double-click that one as well.

NOTE *An MSI is the install database of an application. So the first level in the tree is the name of the application. Within the application there are features, the second level of the tree. Within features are components, the last level of the tree.*

Now scroll down and click the component you took note of earlier. Click the General title and you will see, as shown in Figure 12.26, where all of the files for this component will be installed.

FIGURE 12.25

The install file properties of `comdlg32.ocx`

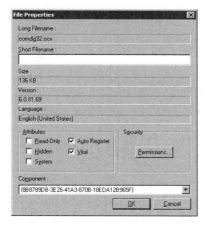

FIGURE 12.26

The install location of `comdlg32.ocx`

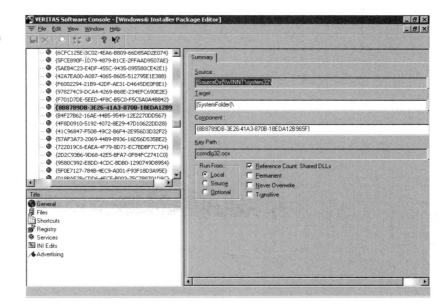

This is the install location of `comdlg32.ocx`. You can change it here if you like. If you click the File title, you can also delete the file from the MSI, skipping its installation altogether.

Step Seven: Test the Application Installed by the New MSI

Now this is the moment of truth. You need to use the new MSI to install the new application on several different computers and to test all of its features. This is how you determine if this entire process worked. You need to test all of the new application's features to see if any part of the installation was missed.

You can install and test the application on a clean computer, but you need to install and test it on one that is not clean as well. This is so you can find out whether the new application will conflict with other applications, and it is by far the most important and time-consuming part of the process.

Distributing the Easy Way: Using ZAP Files

What if you can't or don't want to create your own MSI? Maybe you don't have the time, or maybe the installation is complex or unique enough that you don't want to risk breaking it. Well, instead of creating MSIs, you can use ZAP files.

ZAP files give us a way to publish an application's installation program through the Windows 2000 SI feature. That saves a lot of time up front. Since we are publishing the package, we can still control which users are allowed to install it. Notice that I didn't mention computers. Remember, we cannot publish packages to computers; we must *assign* packages to computers. ZAP files can only be published to users.

When you use a ZAP file to publish a package to users, the user can use Add/Remove Programs in the Control Panel to install the application. Once it's installed, you can use Add/Remove Programs to reinstall or remove the application as if it were an MSI installation. What you don't get is the ability to have applications repaired automatically, nor do you get the ability to upgrade the application automatically through SI.

ZAP files do borrow a function from the process for assigning a package. In the ZAP file, you can associate a file extension with the package installation so that, when a user double-clicks a file with that extension, the package installation is launched. Now this is not what we think of as normal file association, because the file type is not really associated with the installation program. Windows 2000 simply knows that if the file is not associated with any program, it shouldn't run the installation program.

These are the steps to publish an application via a ZAP file:

1. Create a ZAP file.

2. Share the ZAP file and installation files.

3. Add a package to a GPO.

Step One: Create a ZAP File

A ZAP file is nothing more than a text file with a `.ZAP` extension. The example I am using here is listed below, and as you can see, it has the format of an INI file:

```
[application]
FriendlyName = "WinZip Version 7.0"
SetupCommand = \\Earth\Packages\WinZip\WinZip70.EXE
DisplayVersion = 7.0
[ext]
ZIP =
```

The first line in the `application` section is FriendlyName and is simply the name that you and I will see for a package description in the GPO editor and that the users will see when they install the package. The next line is SetupCommand. This is the actual installation program that will be run when the user selects the application in Add/Remove Programs or double-clicks a file with the right extension (`.ZIP` in this example). DisplayVersion is exactly what it sounds like and is displayed with the package in the GPO editor.

The next section is `ext` and it needs to contain any file extension you want associated with the installation. In our example here, `ZIP =` is all we need to tell Windows 2000 to run what we've defined for the SetupCommand if no program is associated with the file extension.

Step Two: Share the ZAP File and Installation Files

We've been doing this all along with SI. I created a directory called `WinZip` in the `Packages` share on `Earth`, so the full path of my installation program is `\\Earth\Packages\WinZip\WinZip70.exe`. My ZAP file was placed right next to it, and its full path is `\\Earth\Packages\WinZip\WinZip.zap`.

Step Three: Add a Package to a GPO

You can either create a new GPO or add a new package to an existing GPO. To create a new GPO, first start the DSA, right-click the OU you want to contain the GPO (I used Beta Testers again), then choose Properties. Click the Group Policy tab, then the New button, and give your GPO a name. Once you have the GPO created, just click it and hit the Edit button to start the GPO editor.

Now we must add the package to User Configuration/Software Settings/Software Installation. Right-click Software Installation (or right-click in the empty right window pane) and choose New/ Package. My ZAP file's full path is `\\Earth\Packages\WinZip\WinZip.zap`. As Figure 12.27 shows, be sure to change the file type to ZAP files. Then click Open.

FIGURE 12.27

Selecting a ZAP file for the package

At this point, we are prompted for the package deployment method shown in Figure 12.28. Notice that we cannot choose Assigned. Choose Published and click OK.

FIGURE 12.28

Publishing a ZAP file

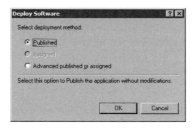

Once that is done, so are we—other than testing of course. The users that the GPO applies to can install the package at any time. The next time those users log in, they will be able to double-click a ZIP file and install WinZip.

Checking Out Those Off-the-Shelf Applications

You can use the VERITAS Software Console for more than just editing your own MSI. You can use it to edit the MSI that comes with any off-the-shelf application. "Why in the world would I want to do that?" you ask. Thanks for the lead-in; I'm glad you asked. The answer is pretty simple: you want to find out what the installation is doing and where it's doing it.

Installation programs copy DLLs to all parts of your hard disk, make Registry entries, and register COM objects. Nothing stops them from overwriting another application's DLLs, Registry entries, or COM objects. Nothing but you, that is. With the VERITAS Software Console, you can now take a look at any install (provided it's an MSI) and see what it is doing. If you browse an application's MSI and find that it is overwriting a DLL that is critical to another application or to the operating system, you have the chance to do something about it early on. At the very least you now know what applications to test. If you want to take a more proactive course of action, you can change the location to which the DLL is copied to a place where only the new application can get to it. Another option is to remove the file completely from the MSI. The same choices are available to you if you find Registry entries being made that overwrite another application's.

If you do decide to edit the MSI, you should keep in mind that doing so is a tricky business. For instance, some software publishers will support you grudgingly, if at all, if you have modified their MSI. On the technical side, your required thoroughness increases dramatically. Also, be warned that today's applications use COM quite a bit. What this means to us is that if we change the location to which a DLL is copied and that DLL is a COM object, then one of two events could occur. The first is that the COM object won't work and the new application fails and maybe other applications will fail as well. The second is that the new application works fine, but other applications may or may not fail because they are still using the new COM object. Keep in mind that COM objects are not retrieved by their full path on the hard disk. They are retrieved by the location specified in the Registry. Simply put, applications will be able to find a COM object (and its DLL) no matter where you put it on the hard disk as long as the COM object is properly registered.

Customizing Packages

So far, I've only talked about how you can deploy an application using an MSI. Unless you edit it using VERITAS Software Console, you are deploying the application unmodified. We have another option available to us called *modifications*.

Modifications are files similar to MSIs in that they describe how an application is to be installed. While MSIs define the official way an application is to be installed (according to the software publisher), modifications describe how it will be installed differently from what is in the MSI—kind of like saying, "Yes, but this is how I really want to do it this time." Modifications have an `.MST` extension (because they were originally called *transforms*). Modifications provide a safe way to customize the installation of an application.

NOTE *MST is a new file type for the modification files. These files give you a way to customize the application installation without actually editing the MSIs.*

You can make an MST by using a tool provided by the software publisher. For instance, to create one for Microsoft Office 2000, you need the Custom Installation Wizard found in the Office 2000 Resource Kit (which you can download from Microsoft). Once you have an MST, using it is quite easy—but you only have one chance to use it.

NOTE *MSIs can only be applied when first adding a package to a GPO. You must choose Advanced Published or Assigned in the Deploy Software dialog.*

Creating an MST

The first thing you need to do is to download and install the Custom Installation Wizard if you don't already have it. To download the wizard, go to `www.microsoft.com/office/ork/2000/appndx/toolbox.htm` and download the `ORKTools.exe`. Once you've extracted and installed the Office Resource Kit Tools, you can start the Custom Installation Wizard by selecting Start/Programs/Microsoft Office Tools/Microsoft Office 200 Resource Kit Tools/Custom Installation Tools.

The first dialog of the wizard is the welcome screen giving a short description of the wizard's features. Click Next and you'll come to the dialog shown in Figure 12.29. Here we'll use the same MSI we've been using for Office 2000, `\\EARTH\Packages\O2KPremium\data1.msi`. In the dialog, the wizard is assuring us that nothing will happen to our MSI. Keep in mind that the purpose of the MST is to customize the MSI without changing it.

FIGURE 12.29

Opening the MSI that you'll be customizing

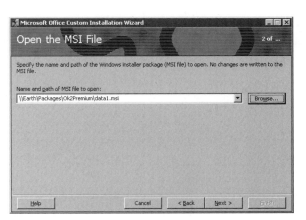

Click Next and you'll see the dialog in Figure 12.30. Here we either create a new MST or open an old one. For this example, we want to create a new one, so make sure Do Not Open an Existing MST File is selected, then click Next.

FIGURE 12.30

Opening an existing
or new MST

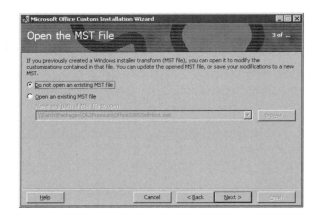

At the dialog in Figure 12.31, we are only asked for the new MST's path and filename. There's really not much to this step since we don't have to worry about where the MST is actually stored at this point. In order to use the MST with an MSI in a package, the MST must be located in the same directory (which also must be network accessible). Click Next.

FIGURE 12.31

Naming the
new MST

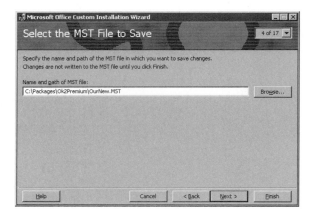

The dialog in Figure 12.32 begins our customizations. First, you can change where Office 2000 will be installed. Second, you can change your company name. While you may not want to change the location of Office 2000, you probably will want to fill in your company name. Once you've done that, click Next.

The Remove Previous Versions dialog in Figure 12.33 is where you decide whether you want earlier versions removed during the Office 2000 installation or you want to leave it up to the user. The Default Setup Behavior option leaves it up to the user—but only to a point. If any earlier versions of Office are found, the user is asked if she wants *all* previous versions removed. She won't be able to leave the old version of Excel and remove the old version of Word. She can only leave them both or remove them both. The second option is where you decide now to remove old versions. If you select this option, the user will not have a choice and the old versions will simply be removed.

FIGURE 12.32

The Office install path

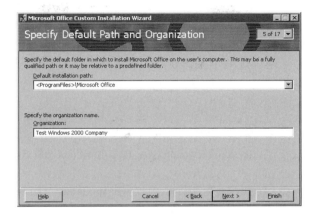

FIGURE 12.33

Removing previous versions

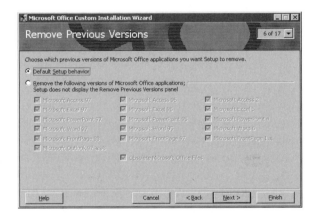

Figure 12.34 shows you how you can select which features of Office to install and, if installed, the location from which they will be run. Your choices are Run from My Computer, Run from Network, and Installed on First Use. If you select the first choice, the program files will be installed locally. For the second, the program files will be used from the network. And for the third, files will be installed locally the first time the user tries to use the program.

That said, keep in mind that the MSI and the MST you are building can be run interactively. When you run them interactively, all of the options in the preceding paragraph are available. If you distribute everything in a package, then the standard behavior of SI will take precedence and program files will be installed the first time they are used. By the way, some of the little disk pull-downs are gray because they have more installable features beneath them. The white ones are the end of the line. Click Next to move on to the next screen.

FIGURE 12.34

Setting feature installation options

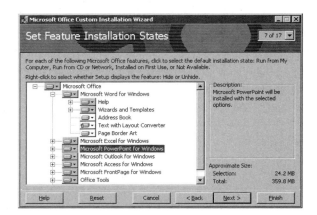

Now for you Office gurus out there, there is the dialog shown in Figure 12.35. It allows you to get really fancy with your installs of Office. It does this by utilizing yet another part of the Office Resource Kit, the Office Profile Wizard (also downloadable from Microsoft's site). With the Profile Wizard, you can customize the behavior and look and feel of Word and Excel at install time—things like toolbars, dictionaries, templates, and the default save format. The standard options are good enough for our example, so click Next.

The Add Files to the Installation dialog in Figure 12.36 means exactly what is says. You can use it to install your own dictionaries, templates, and the like, or even your own programs, with the Office install. This makes for a much cleaner install of the "company standard." No longer do you have to install Office and then figure out how you get the company standard dictionary installed as well. Click Next.

FIGURE 12.35

You can customize the application settings using an OPS file from the Profile Wizard.

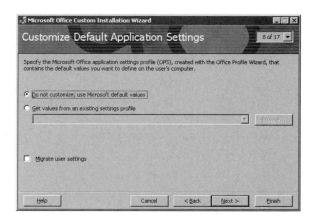

The Add Registry Entries dialog in Figure 12.37 does for the Registry what the preceding dialog does for files. You can make your own Registry entries a part of the Office install. Click Next.

The dialog in Figure 12.38 allows you to control where Office shows up on the Start menu. You can also add new items to the menu for your own programs that you added to the install. Click Next.

FIGURE 12.36

Adding your own files to the installation

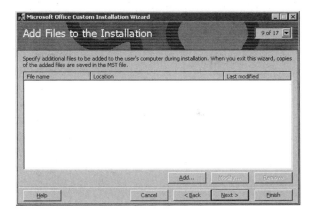

FIGURE 12.37

Adding your own Registry modifications to the installation

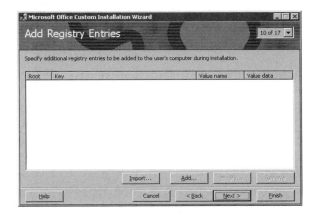

FIGURE 12.38

Changing where Office shows up on the Start menu

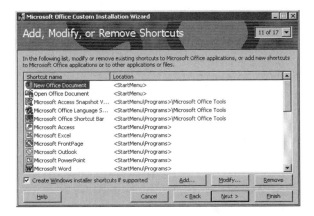

The Identify Additional Servers dialog in Figure 12.39 lets you set up multiple sources for the installation files. These are the servers and shares from which the Windows Installer will pull files when it needs to. They are used when you first install Office from the network onto a computer and when you've selected Installed on First Run. Click Next.

FIGURE 12.39

Adding additional installation sources

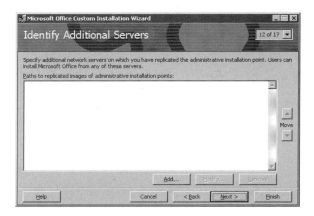

In Figure 12.40, we see yet another way you can add your own stuff to the installation. Here you can specify additional programs to be run after the Office install is complete. Any programs you add are run one after the other, in the sequence you specify. When one ends, the next will be launched. If one hangs, then the trailing programs won't be run. Click Next.

FIGURE 12.40

Adding your own programs to the installation

In the dialog in Figure 12.41, you can customize the default Outlook profile. Keep in mind that Outlook stores the user's profile in the system part of the Registry. If the user does not have the required rights to make changes to that part of the Registry, she will not be able to change her Outlook profile. Click Next.

FIGURE 12.41

Customizing
Outlook

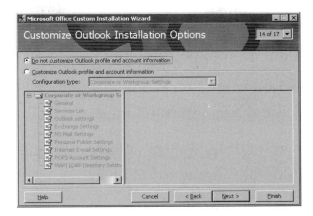

The dialog in Figure 12.42 lets you define how you want to install Internet Explorer 5, which is required for some features of Office. If you're installing Office on a Windows 2000 computer, it should already have Internet Explorer 5 installed. Click Next.

FIGURE 12.42

Setting up the installation of Internet Explorer 5

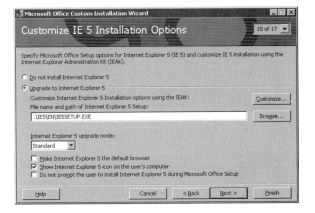

Many of the choices you made throughout this process are stored as properties of the setup. These are shown in the dialog in Figure 12.43, where you also can change anything you like. You can't remove any of the standard properties, but you can add, change, or remove your own. Click Next and you are asked to save your changes. Click Finish to do so.

The dialog in Figure 12.44 wraps up the MST creation. You are also given a command line you can use to test the Office install with your new MST.

FIGURE 12.43

Changing the installation properties

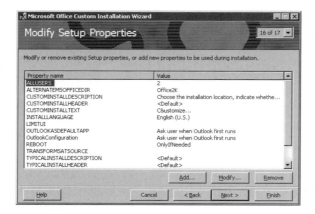

FIGURE 12.44

Completed creation of the MST

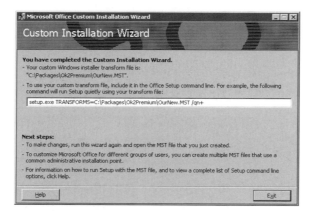

Using an MST

To create a package with an MSI and an MST, you start off the way you would normally begin to add a package—by editing your GPO in the Group Policy snap-in, right-clicking User Configuration/Software Settings/Software Installation, and choosing New/Package. Then select your MSI (a ZAP file cannot be used). Once the MSI is selected, you will see the Deploy Software dialog, shown in Figure 12.45.

FIGURE 12.45

Select the Advanced Published or Assigned option.

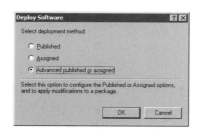

In the Deploy Software dialog, select Advanced Published or Assigned and then click OK. If you choose either Published or Assigned, you won't be able to add modifications to your package. Your only option will be to delete the package (not the MSI) and start over.

Now click the Deployment tab shown in Figure 12.46. Here you can select your deployment method, either Published or Assigned. You may also want to check Uninstall This Application When This GPO No Longer Applies to Users or Computers. To minimize interaction with the user, select Basic under Installation User Interface Options.

FIGURE 12.46

You define how to deploy your application in the Deployment tab.

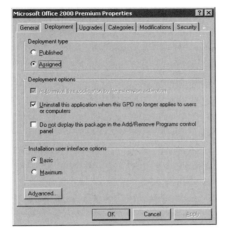

Next, click the Modifications tab and click the Add button. Select your MST and click OK.

NOTE   *Be sure your MST is in the same directory as your MSI. If not, your package will not work properly.*

Once you've selected your MST, you should see something like Figure 12.47. At this point, you can add other MSTs if you like and control the order in which they are applied.

Now click OK and you can begin testing your package.

FIGURE 12.47

All modifications for the Office 2000 package

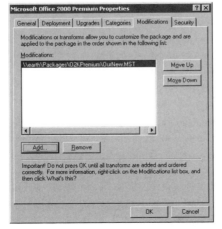

Upgrading Applications

So you've been on Windows 2000 for some time now, and you've deployed all of your applications via packages with MSIs. Then you get a new version of an application—now what? Well, the answer is, of course, to upgrade the application with another MSI.

Upgrading an application is very easy and not much different from distributing any other application. Very simply, you start with any package that is based on an MSI. Now this is the package that *is* the upgrade. For my example, I'm using Office 2000. So to begin, start with the GPO in the Group Policy snap-in, right-click the package, and select Properties. Then click the Upgrades tab and you'll see something like Figure 12.48.

FIGURE 12.48

Starting with an empty Upgrades tab

Now click the Add button to see a dialog like Figure 12.49. You can upgrade an application in your current GPO, or you can select another GPO and any package within it. There is one exception: you cannot upgrade a package that is based on a ZAP file. To continue our example, select A Specific GPO, then click Browse.

FIGURE 12.49

The Add Upgrade Package dialog

NOTE   *You cannot upgrade a package that is based on a ZAP file. Packages must be installed via an MSI for them to be upgradable.*

At the Browse for a Group Policy Object dialog shown in Figure 12.50, click the All tab. You can browse any way you like, but I find using the All tab easier. However, if I had thousands of GPOs, I'm sure I'd think differently.

FIGURE 12.50

Browsing for all GPOs in the domain

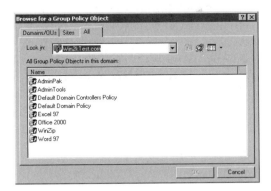

The package I want to upgrade with Office 2000 is Word 97, so select it and click the OK button. Now we're back at the Add Upgrade Package dialog, only this time, we see all the packages in the GPO, as in Figure 12.51. In this example, there is only Microsoft Word 97, so select it. Now there is a decision to make: what should be done with the old application? The first choice is to uninstall it before installing the new application; the second choice is to leave the old application alone and install the new application on top of it. Select Uninstall the Existing Package, Then Install the Upgrade Package; then click OK.

FIGURE 12.51

Selecting Microsoft Word 97

Now the GPO properties dialog shows that Office 2000 is replacing Microsoft Word 97, as shown in Figure 12.52. Click the Required Upgrade for Existing Packages option. Once we click

OK, any user who is managed by the Word 97 GPO will have Word 97 uninstalled the next time they log in. The icon for Word will remain on the Start menu until selected. Then, Office 2000 will be installed.

FIGURE 12.52

Office 2000 is replacing Microsoft Word 97.

I hope you can see how extremely useful Software Installation can be. This is not just a cool new feature that we would like to use and that would give us more capabilities. It actually saves us time, and headaches, day to day. It gets most of its power from its tight integration with Windows 2000's Active Directory and the heavy reliance on security and group policy objects. Unfortunately, because of that integration, to get the most from Software Installation, Windows 2000 must be installed on your users' computers, not just your servers.

Also, this is the first implementation of this feature integrated into the operation system. As more and more software publishers begin using MSIs and MSTs to install their products, our jobs will become well, maybe not easier, but at least more consistent. In future versions of Windows 2000, Microsoft will likely improve the process even more, giving us even more useful features—features we haven't even thought of yet.

Getting NT Apps to Work

Now and then, you'll run across an app that worked fine under NT but won't under 2000. But 2000 is a sort of minor upgrade kernel-wise, so what would cause this? If it works under NT, then it ought to work under 2000, no? There are few things that you can try to make a balky NT app work.

Loosen Up the Registry Permissions

As you read in Chapter 9, Window 2000 tightened up on the access control entries on Registry keys in HKEY_LOCAL_MACHINE\SOFTWARE. Try the prebuilt templates COMPATWS.INF, COMPATSV.INF, and COMPATDC.INF to loosen up the permissions back to the NT 4 level and see if that makes the applications run.

Identify Failed System32 Overwrites

Sometimes the problem arises because applications write files into \winnt\system32 that overwrite existing system files. Under NT 4, an application developer could write a modified version of some system DLL, EXE, OCX, or SYS file and tell the application's Setup program to delete the version of the file that shipped with the operating system, replacing it with the developer's version. Sometimes it wasn't a bad idea, but all too often it resulted in an unstable system.

Under Windows 2000, that Setup program would be foiled. The operating system includes a feature called Windows File Protection (WFP) that detects whenever a file with the extension .OCX, .SYS, .EXE, or .DLL in the System32 directory is deleted. (Or, more specifically, it detects if the deletion of one of those files *if it shipped with the operating system;* other OCX, DLL, EXE, or SYS files aren't protected even if they *do* live in System32.) WFP then grabs a copy of the erased file out of a hidden cache directory, \winnt\system32\dllcache, and restores it to its original version. (Service packs update the cache, in case you're wondering.)

WFP works silently; the only way that you'll find out that it did anything is to look in the System Event Log. You'll see an event ID 64002, with a message something like this:

```
File replacement was attempted on the protected system file
c:\winnt\system32\sol.exe. This file was restored to the original version to
maintain system stability. The file version of the system file is 5.0.2138.1.
```

If you load a program that worked under NT and doesn't under 2000, then take a peek in the Event Viewer to see if the app's Setup program woke up WFP. If it did, then note the names of the files.

Next, go get the app's version of the files. No, we're not going to let it overwrite DLLs in System32, but there is a way to provide for peaceful coexistence, wherein an application can have its own modified copy of a system DLL without having to affect the way that the rest of the OS works.

First, turn off Windows File Protection. In HKEY_LOCAL_MACHINE\SOFTWARE\Microsoft\ Windows NT\CurrentVersion\Winlogon, create or modify an entry called SFCDisable—it's a REG_DWORD—and give it the hex value FFFFFF9D. Reboot the system and WFP is asleep. Now reinstall the app and grab the files that it overwrites from System32. Restore the SFCDisable value to 0 and reboot.

Use DLL Redirection to Let Apps Use Their Own DLLs

So now here's the situation: You've discovered that the operating system relies upon a DLL called window.dll (there isn't any real DLL by that name, it's just an example), but the application that you're trying to install ships with a window.dll of its own. The application is used to overwriting the operating system's DLL with its own, but it can't. How do we set things up so that the application can use its own window.dll without disturbing the rest of the OS? With "DLL redirection;" keep reading to see how it works.

Suppose you have an application called somecadapp.exe. It's in a directory C:\SOMECAD. You put its special version of window.dll into C:\SOMECAD. Now, if you run somecadapp.exe, it will look for window.dll, but by default, the operating system responds to requests for DLLs by first looking in SYSTEM32. As the OS *has* a copy of window.dll in that directory, it never gets around to looking in C:\SOMECAD, and so somecadapp.exe continues to be non-functional....

Unless you know a trick.

The trick is called *DLL redirection.* You can instruct Windows 2000 to look for DLLs first in the same directory as the application, *rather* than first looking in SYSTEM32. To do that, just create a file with the same name as the application, but with the extra extension .local. Thus, in my example, you'd create a file called somecadapp.exe.local and put it in the same directory as somecadapp.exe. *Now* the OS will find somecadapp's "personal" windows.dll.

In this chapter, you've seen how to roll out apps using Windows 2000's new tools. Get to know them and you can save yourself a lot of visits to user desktops!

Chapter 13

Configuring and Troubleshooting Network Print Services

"PAPERLESS OFFICE," MY SORE head. Even after years of interoffice e-mail and online documents, in many offices it's not official until you hold the printed evidence in your hand. Printing isn't sexy, but it's an inescapable—and vital—part of life in the networked office.

It's simply not practical—or necessary—to provide everyone in the office with a personal printer. Instead, you connect a printer to a print server and share the printer from there so that dozens or hundreds of people can use one printer. Of course, once dozens or hundreds of people depend on a single piece of equipment, that piece of equipment becomes pretty crucial. It needs to be up and running, dependable, and accessible to those who need it but off-limits to those who don't.

Hence this chapter. In the following pages, I'll talk about how to use Windows 2000 Server to complete the following tasks:

- Create a new local printer or connect to one already set up on the network or Internet.

- Secure the printer so that only those people who should be using it have access to it.

- Configure printer settings to help people find and troubleshoot print jobs.

- Speed up printing by making multiple printers look like one.

- Connect to a printer from a variety of different platforms.

- Troubleshoot the printing problems that will inevitably occur.

In the course of this chapter, I'll use the Microsoft terminology for referring to printers and printing functions. If you're not familiar with this vocabulary, read on before jumping in.

Print Services Terminology

Contrary to what you might have believed, a *printer* is, in fact, not that putty-colored box that you put paper into and printed documents come out of. In the Microsoft world, a printer is a logical device that's an intermediary between user applications and the *print device* (the thing that actually does the printing). All configuration settings apply to printers, not to print devices. The ratio of printers to print devices is not necessarily 1:1. You can have one printer and one print device, two printers for a single print device, or one printer and several print devices. I'll talk about *why* you might want to do any of these in the course of this chapter.

When you send documents to a printer, they become part of the printer's *queue*, the group of documents waiting to be printed. Although in other operating systems, such as OS/2, the queue was important as a primary interface between the application and printing devices, in Windows 2000 (and all forms of Windows NT), the printer plays this role.

Most often, the printer is accessible to the network via its connection to a *print server*, the computer on which printer drivers are stored. Most of this chapter will operate under the assumption that your network's printers are connected to a print server running Windows 2000. A *network-interface printer* is a printer directly connected to the network via a built-in network card.

NOTE   *Even if the rest of your network is running Win2K, your print server doesn't have to be—and vice versa. A print server can run Windows for Workgroups, Windows 9x, any version of NT Workstation or Server, LAN Manager, or (if you installed MS-Net) Windows 3.x or DOS. The options available to you will depend on the operating system; if your print server runs an operating system other than Win2K, then some of the information in this chapter may not apply to you.*

GETTING ACQUAINTED WITH THE WINDOWS 2000 PRINTING INTERFACE

As with much of Win2K, the first step in learning how to administer printers is to find out where all the printer management tools *are*. I won't get into the details of how to use these tools just yet, but when you're looking for the right tool for the job, this sidebar should help you find it.

To set up the printer for using forms, to configure printer ports, to add or update printer drivers, or to set spooling or error management options, you'll need to configure the printer server, not the printer or print device. Printer server properties are available from the Properties option in the File menu of the Printers window. The Printers window is accessible from the Control Panel, or from the Settings section of the Start menu.

Individual printer properties, such as the printer's description, sharing options, port used, spooling options, and device settings, are set from printer-specific properties pages. You can get to them either by right-clicking a printer's icon in the Printers menu or by choosing Properties from the File menu of a particular printer's queue window. Editing one printer's properties pages has no effect on any other printer.

The Win2K Printing Model

The process of printing is a bit more complex than it (hopefully) looks from the outside. The Windows 2000 model uses several components to render application data for graphical output, get the data to a printer, and then help the printer manage multiple print jobs. Some of the following information on *how* Win2K printing works is background, but it's also helpful when it comes to troubleshooting, so wade through it if you can.

The main chunks of Win2K printing are the Graphics Device Interface (GDI), the printer driver, and the print spooler.

The Graphics Device Interface

The Graphics Device Interface (GDI) is the portion of Win2K that begins the process of producing visual output, whether that output is to the screen or to the printer. Without the GDI, WYSIWYG output would be impossible. To produce screen output, the GDI calls the video driver; to produce printed output, the GDI calls the printer driver, providing information about the print device needed and the type of data used.

The Printer Driver

Printer drivers are the software that enable the operating system to communicate with a printer. They're incompatible across operating systems, so although any Win32 operating system can print to a Win2K Server print server without first installing a local printer driver—they'll just download it from the print server—you'll have to make sure the drivers are available for the clients that will be using the printer. That means that even though you've attached the printer to a Win2K computer, you'll need to install the Windows 98 printer drivers if any network client computers are running Windows 98.

Win2K printer drivers are composed of three subdrivers that work together as a unit:

◆ Printer graphics driver

◆ Printer interface driver

◆ Characterization data file

The printer graphics driver renders the GDI commands into Device Driver Interface (DDI) commands that can be sent to the printer.

You need some means of interacting with and configuring the printer, and the role of the printer interface driver is to provide that means. The printer interface driver is your intermediary to the characterization data file, providing the information you see in a printer's properties pages.

The characterization data file provides information about the make and model of a specific type of print device, including what it can do: print on both sides of a piece of paper, print at various resolutions, and accept certain paper sizes.

The Print Spooler

The print spooler (SPOOLSS.DLL, in %*systemroot*%\system32) is a collection of dynamic link libraries (DLLs) and device drivers that receive, process, schedule, and distribute print jobs. It's implemented with the spooler service, which is required for printing, and is composed of the following components:

◆ Print router

◆ Local print provider

◆ Remote print provider

◆ Print processors

◆ Print monitor

THE PRINT ROUTER

When a Win2K client computer connects to a Win2K print server, communication takes place in the form of remote procedure calls from the client's print router (`WINSPOOL.DRV`) to the server's print router (`SPOOLSS.DLL`). At this point, the server's print router passes the print request to the appropriate print provider: the local print provider if it's a local job, and either the Windows or NetWare print provider if sent over the network.

THE PRINT PROVIDER

To find the right print provider, the print router polls the Windows print provider. This provider then finds the connection that recognizes the printer name and sends a remote procedure call to the print router on the print server. That local print provider then writes the contents of the print job to a spool file (which will have the extension `.spl`) and tracks administration information for that print job.

TIP   By default, all spool files are stored in the `%systemroot%\system32\spool\printers` directory. If you like (perhaps if you've installed a faster hard drive that you'd prefer to spool from), you can change that location by adjusting the value of the print server settings on the Advanced tab. To get there, open the Printers Control Panel and choose Server Properties from the File menu. Move to the Advanced tab, and you'll see the spooler settings, including the location of the spool file.

Win2K normally deletes spool files after the print job they apply to is completed because they only exist to keep the print job from getting lost in case of a power failure to the print server. If you want to keep track of such data as the amount of disk space required by spool files and what printer traffic is like, you can enable spooler event logging.

THE PRINT PROCESSOR

A print processor works with the printer driver to "de-spool" spool files during playback, making any necessary changes to the spool file based on its data type.

Er—*data type?*

The data type for a print job tells the print spooler whether and how to modify the print job to print properly. This is necessary because methods of print job creation aren't standardized; for example, a Win2K client won't create a job the same way a Linux client does. Therefore, a variety of print server services exist to receive print jobs and prepare them for printing. Some of these print services assign no data type (in which case Win2K uses the default data type in the Print Processor dialog box), and some assign a data type.

The spool file can accept data from the print provider in one of two forms: Enhanced Metafile (EMF) or RAW. EMF spool files are device-independent files used to reduce the amount of time spent processing a print job; all GDI calls needed to produce the print job are included in the file. Once the EMF file is rendered, you can continue using the application from which you were printing. All the rest of the print processing will take place in the background. Unlike EMF spool files, which still require some rendering once it's determined which printer they'll be spooled to, RAW spool files are fully rendered when created. Modern NT-based operating systems such as Win2K and NT 4 use RAW spool files for local print jobs, for Encapsulated PostScript print jobs, or when otherwise specified by the user. Windows 9x uses EMF files for local printing but sends RAW data to a networked print server. Windows NT 4 uses EMF files for both local and networked printing, and NT 3.x uses RAW whether printing locally or to a network printer.

NOTE *All else being equal, EMF spool files are normally smaller than RAW spool files because they're generic instructions for rendering, not complete renderings.*

WinPrint, the Win2K/NT print processor, understands four versions of EMF data files (1.003–1.008), three kinds of RAW data files, and TEXT files, which have the characteristics shown in Table 13.1.

TABLE 13.1: WHICH DATA TYPE DO I NEED?

DATA TYPE	DESCRIPTION	SUPPORTED BY
EMF	Tells WinPrint that the job was created in Windows and is already partially rendered. WinPrint works with the GDI and printer driver to complete the rendering, then returns the job to the local print provider.	NT and Win2K print clients
RAW	Tells WinPrint not to modify the print job at all, but to return it to the local print provider.	All printer clients
RAW [FF Auto]	Tells WinPrint to check for a form-feed command at the end of the print job. If one isn't there, WinPrint adds it and then returns the job to the local print provider.	All printer clients
RAW [FF Appended]	WinPrint adds a form-feed command to the print job and then returns the job to the local print provider.	All printer clients
TEXT	Tells WinPrint that the print job is ASCII text to be printed as hard copy and as is. WinPrint uses the GDI and the printer driver to produce this output, then sends the new job to the local print provider.	All printer clients

The default data type is RAW, supported by all Windows clients. To select a different data type, open a printer's properties pages and turn to the Advanced tab. Click the Print Processor button to display a list of possible print processor types. Select a different data type from the list and click OK. The new data type will be used for all print jobs that don't specify that another data type should be used.

That said, don't change the data type unless you're *sure* it's a good idea. If a print client can use EMF files, it will do so even if the default data type is RAW, so you're not losing anything by making RAW the default. In contrast, if you make EMF the default data type, then Windows 9x clients won't be able to print. No error messages will appear on the client that initiated the print job, and no errors will show up on the print server, but the print jobs they send along will disappear into the ether.

THE PRINT MONITOR

The print monitor is the final link in the chain getting the print job from the client application to the print device. It's actually two monitors: a language monitor and a port monitor.

The *language monitor*, created when you install a printer driver if a language monitor is associated with the driver, comes into play only if the print device is bidirectional. A bidirectional print device can send meaningful messages about print job status to the computer. In this case, the language monitor sets up the communication with the printer and then passes control to the port monitor. The language monitor supplied with Win2K uses the Printer Job Language. If a manufacturer created a printer that spoke a different language, it would need to create another language monitor, as the computer and print device must speak the same language for the communication to work.

The *port monitor's* job is to transmit the print job either to the print device or to another server. It controls the flow of information to the I/O port to which the print device is connected (a serial, parallel, network, or SCSI port). The local port monitor supplied with Win2K controls parallel and serial ports; if you want to connect a print device to a SCSI port or network port, you must use a port monitor supplied by the vendor. Regardless of type, however, port monitors interface with ports, not printers, and are in fact unaware of the type of print device to which they're connected. The print job was already configured by the print processor.

By default, only the locally required print monitor is installed. To use another monitor, you'll have to create a new port in the printer configuration settings.

The Printing Process

Those are the parts of the printing process. Here's how they fit together when printing from a Win2K client:

1. The user chooses to print from an application, causing the application to call the GDI. The GDI, in its turn, calls the printer driver associated with the target print device. Using the document information from the application and the printer information from the printer driver, the GDI renders the print job.

2. The print job is next passed to the spooler. The client side of the spooler makes a remote procedure call to the server side, which then calls the print router component of the server.

3. The print router passes the job to the local print provider, which spools the job to disk.

4. The local print provider polls the print processors, passing the print job to the one that recognizes the selected printer. Based on the data type (EMF or RAW) used in the spool file, any necessary changes are made to the spool file in order to make it printable on the selected print device.

5. If desired, the separator page processor adds a separator page to the print job.

6. The print job is de-spooled to the print monitor. If the printer device is bidirectional, then the language monitor sets up communications. If not, or once the language monitor is done, the job is passed to the port monitor, which handles the task of getting the print job to the port the print device is connected to.

7. The print job arrives at the print device and prints.

That's how Win2K sees printing. Good stuff to know when it comes time to troubleshoot printing problems. For the rest of the chapter, however, we'll concentrate on how *you* see printing.

Setting Up a Printer Connection

The day hasn't yet come when you can always plug a printer into a Windows 2000 server and expect the server to find it without your help. Until it does, if you want to use a printer from Win2K, you'll need to either create the printer locally or connect to a printer on the network. You will need to set up support for a printer to use it from a computer if any of the following conditions apply:

◆ You're installing support for a printer connected directly to one of the parallel or USB ports of the local machine.

◆ You're installing support for a network-interface printer.

◆ You're defining a printer that sends information to a file (as opposed to a print device).

◆ You're making a second printer for a print device.

I'll describe first how to set up a new printer and then how to connect to a printer already installed on the network.

Installing a Printer on a Print Server

If you're coming to Win2K from NT 3.5*x*, then you're used to setting up a new printer from the Print Manager. The Print Manager, however, went out with NT 4—all functions of the Print Manager are now part of the Printers window, available either from its shortcut in the Control Panel or from the Settings folder off the Start menu. There's an Add Printer Wizard in the Printers folder that you must run to set up a printer on the local computer.

Unlike NT 4, the Win2K Add Printer Wizard prompts you for all options before installing the printer drivers. To create a new printer connected to the local machine, follow these steps:

1. Open the Printers menu and click the Add Printer icon you'll see there. Click Next in the opening screen of the Add Printer Wizard (the opening window isn't important; it tells you only that you're using the Add Printer Wizard in case you hadn't figured that out) to get to the screen shown in Figure 13.1. For this example, choose the default option, Local Printer, and click Next.

FIGURE 13.1

Specify first whether the printer is connected to the local computer or on the network.

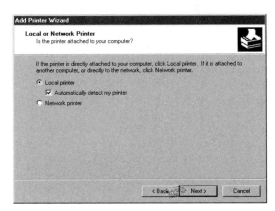

2. If you're using a Plug-and-Play printer, you can tell Win2K to detect it by clicking the check box visible in Figure 13.1. If not, or if you're creating a printer to send output to a file, you will have to tell the Add Printer Wizard which port the printer is connected to. Indicate the port the printer is connected to (see Figure 13.2). Most times, the one you want should be fairly obvious—just make sure you've selected the port the printer is plugged into. If you don't see the port you need listed, perhaps if you're setting up support for a network interface printer, then click the Create a New Port radio button and choose Standard TCP/IP Port from the drop-down list. To create a printer that stores print information in a file, choose the FILE option near the bottom of the list. Click Next.

FIGURE 13.2

Choose the printer's port from the list.

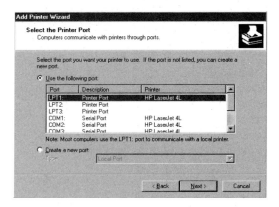

NOTE *Any TS ports (e.g., TS0001) near the bottom of the list represent printers connected to a terminal server client. Don't connect a printer to them unless you're manually redirecting a printer to a terminal client session.*

3. Next, you'll choose the driver needed for your particular printer. From the list presented, choose the printer's manufacturer from the left and the printer model from the right. By default, Win2K will use its own printer driver. If you've got a newer one from the manufacturer or from the manufacturer's Web site, click the Have Disk button and provide the path to the driver. If the Win2K server is connected to the Internet, you can alternatively click the Windows Update button to automatically download a newer driver from the Microsoft Web site, if one is available. Click Next.

TIP *If the driver you need is already installed on the system—perhaps for a different printer that you already created—Win2K will ask if you want to use the existing driver or replace it with the new one. Generally speaking, newer is better.*

4. After you've chosen a driver to use, the Add Printer Wizard asks you to name the printer using, by default, the printer's model name (see Figure 13.3). The name cannot contain a comma, backward slash, or exclamation point, but it has few other restrictions. The name you choose can be quite long—up to 220 characters—but I don't recommend making the name any longer than is strictly necessary to be descriptive. Click Next to move on.

FIGURE 13.3

Choose a local name for the printer.

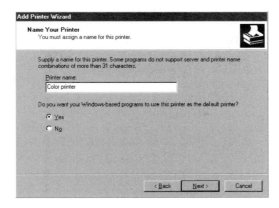

TIP *Keep printer names short. First, if you're ever connecting to or managing the printer from the command line, do you really want to have to type "This is the printer by the coffee machine; it's got a single paper tray and faces west" when prompted for the name of the printer? Even identifying the printer in the Printers dialog box is harder if all the printers have overly long names because the names get cut off in the display. Second, some applications can't work with a name longer than 31 characters. If you can't fully identify a printer without creating a long name, you can always add a location and printer description, as I'll describe in a moment.*

5. Next, if you're sharing the printer, choose a share name for it. If the name you've given the printer has more than one word or a forward slash, the wizard will delete the spaces and combine the words until it has a single word up to eight characters long (see Figure 13.4). The reason for this is backward compatibility: DOS clients won't be able to connect to printers with names more than eight characters long or with spaces.

FIGURE 13.4

By default, the Add Printer Wizard will make a DOS-compatible name for the printer.

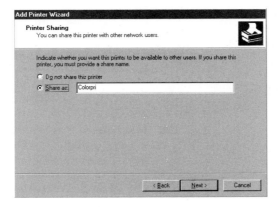

If you don't have DOS clients to worry about, you can make a new name for the printer. Once again, the name may be up to 220 characters long and include spaces, but it can't contain commas, backward slashes, or exclamation points.

6. In the next stage of the installation, you'll have a chance to describe the printer and location (see Figure 13.5). The usefulness of these descriptions varies. All clients (DOS, NT, Windows 9x) will display the information you enter into the Comment text box, but they won't be able to display what you enter into the Location box. Win2K clients will be able to display both. Therefore, unless your network is composed entirely of Win2K servers and clients, all important information should go into the Comment box. Click Next to move to the next screen.

FIGURE 13.5

Only Win2K clients will be able to see all the descriptive information you enter here.

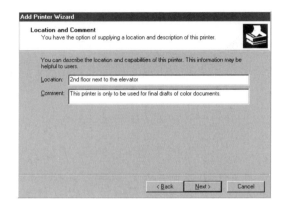

7. The next screen asks whether you'll want to print a test page when you're done. Choose the Yes or No radio button and click Next. Can't hurt—it's a good way of seeing whether you set up the printer properly *before* you try to use it.

8. The final screen in the information-gathering part of the Add Printer Wizard (see Figure 13.6) shows the options that you entered at each stage so you can go back and change options if necessary. Review your choices and click the Finish button if you want to keep the settings.

FIGURE 13.6

Review your choices before committing yourself with the Finish button.

9. The Add Printer Wizard will prompt you for the location of the setup files. Put the Win2K installation CD in the CD-ROM drive, or provide the path to the installation files if you copied them to disk. Win2K will copy the drivers needed and, if you told it to do so, print the test page.

At this point, you have one printer for one print device. If you'd like to create a second printer—perhaps to configure a different set of permissions for it—you can do so in the same way you created the first printer. Follow the procedure I just described, making sure you do two things:

◆ Give the new printer a different local name and share name.

◆ Choose the exact same settings (port, printer manufacturer and model, and so on) you chose for the first printer.

Sending documents to the new printer will cause them to print on the same print device. The only difference will lie in the configuration options you set for the new printer.

Preparing for Web Printing

One of Win2K's new features is its support for Web-based printing, allowing users to print or manage documents from their Web browsers. It takes a little more prep work than sharing a printer with the local network, but it can be handy.

What Can (and Can't) Web Printing Accomplish?

Handy how? Your first thought might be that Web printing will be a good way to add remote printer access so that people who don't work in your office could send print jobs to your printers. For example, I recently had to FedEx 50 pages of a presentation to an office, which meant that I had to print out the presentation, put the thing in an envelope, fill out the slip, and call FedEx to pick up the package. If the recipient had set up their printer for Internet printing, then I could have just sent the print job to their printer directly and skipped the FedExing part, right?

Well, maybe not right. First, the flow of information is no different from that of an ordinary print job, except that you've added a Web server into the mix. Print jobs are *big*, bigger than the files they're printing, because spooling a print job requires extra information. If you try to send a big print job across a slow link, it may take a while to get there.

What about printing shorter documents? It would be possible to use Internet printing just as you would a fax. Win2K doesn't support network faxing, and so long as you only used the printer like you would a fax—you don't often fax 50-page PowerPoint presentations, do you?—then you'd be okay. But doing that requires setting up a printer explicitly for this purpose, and it does open up a security hole because you're allowing people to log in to the domain. If I were doing this, I'd set up a network printer (remember, printers are logical representations of the boxes that do the printing, not the boxes themselves) just for anonymous users to connect to, and explicitly deny those anonymous users from doing anything else on the network. I'd also set up the Internet print server outside the network's DMZ, so that access to the printer server didn't give people access to other network computers.

Frankly, the best use I've seen for Web printing is that it really streamlines the printer setup process for the client. As you'll see in the "Internet Printing" section (on setting up client access to the printer via the Web), this process is much simpler than using the Add Printer Wizard: You tell the user to run

Internet Explorer 4 or later, connect to the print server by typing **http://*printservername*/printers** in the Address section of the browser, then click the printer they see there—since you will have used security permissions to make sure that they can only see the printer they're supposed to connect to. The user clicks the link for that server, then clicks the Connect link to automagically download the driver to their computer. That's it—the printer is installed and available to any application.

SETTING UP A WEB PRINT SERVER

The protocol used in Web printing depends on whether the printer is available on the LAN or on a WAN. Web printing uses the Internet Printing Protocol (IPP), encapsulated within the HyperText Transfer Protocol (HTTP) used for browsing the Web. Printers on the local LAN will use the faster remote procedure calls (RPCs) to send jobs to the printer, just as they do for traditional print jobs. Because an Internet print server must be able to accept incoming HTTP traffic to communicate with print clients not on the LAN, the print server must also be a Web server. For a Win2K Server print server, this means that you'll need to install the Internet Information Services (IIS) on the print server and run the service. (Win2K Professional print servers will use the Personal Web Server.) If you previously chose not to install IIS—it's installed by default on Win2K servers—install it from the Add/Remove Windows Components tool in the Add/Remove Programs applet in the Control Panel.

SECURING A WEB PRINT SERVER

Once you've got IIS installed, the print server can accept clients connecting to it from IE, but you should do some security tweaking before opening the printer to the world—as it stands, the printer is open to everyone who connects to it, and you do *not* want just anyone connecting to network computers—or even just anyone printing large print jobs. Open the Internet Services Manager in the Administrative Tools program group. All the Web servers in the domain will be listed below the `Internet Information Services` folder. Find the Web print server in this list. Within its `Default Web Site` folder, look for the `Printers` folder. At this point, your management console should look something like the one in Figure 13.7.

FIGURE 13.7

Find the `Printers` folder for your Web printer.

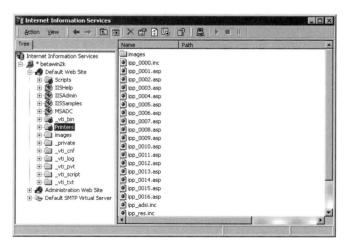

Now, right-click the `Printers` folder and choose Properties from the context menu that appears. You'll see a tabbed properties page like the one in Figure 13.8.

FIGURE 13.8

The properties page for the `Printers` folder

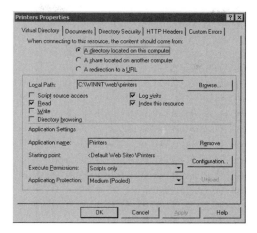

On the Virtual Directory tab shown here, make sure the entry points to the right information for printing. Secure access to the printer from the Directory Security tab (see Figure 13.9).

FIGURE 13.9

Printer security settings

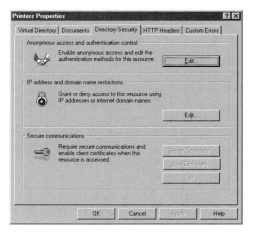

User authentication is set from the Authentication Methods dialog box (see Figure 13.10), accessible from the Directory Security tab when you click the Edit button for Anonymous Access and Authentication Control. Web folders may be set up for anonymous access, using the terminal server account, with the privileges assigned to that account. Edit this account to use any domain account by clicking the Edit button and browsing for a new account to use (see Figure 13.11).

FIGURE 13.10

Choose an authentication method for Web print management.

FIGURE 13.11

You can choose a different account for people accessing the `Printers` folder.

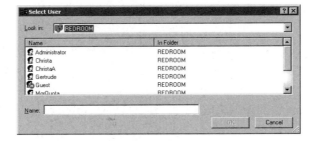

Alternatively, you can require that anyone connecting to the printer via the Web get authenticated on the network first. Set up the `Printers` virtual folder for basic authentication if you want people to be able to manage printers from any browser. Win2K will fuss at you for choosing this option because it sends passwords in clear (unencrypted) text, but if you choose Kerberos (Integrated Windows authentication) or challenge/response (Digest authentication) for greater security, you'll limit yourself to managing printers from Internet Explorer 4 or later. By default, authentication will be based on the domain that the Web printer is part of; to choose a different domain, click the Edit button and browse for the domain you want to use. If the box in the Browse dialog box is blank, the local domain will be used for authentication.

Another method you can use to restrict access to a Web printer is to permit only members of a particular domain or only those with a specific IP address. To do so, go back to the Directory Security tab and click the Edit button for IP Address and Domain Name Restrictions. You'll see a dialog box like the one in Figure 13.12.

When you first open this dialog box, no one will be specifically denied or granted access. (Note that you can use this dialog box to either explicitly permit or deny access.) To add an entry to the list, first click the appropriate radio button to indicate whether you're adding a "denied" entry (the Denied Access radio button) or a "permitted" entry (the Granted Access radio button). When you've made your choice, click the Add button to open the dialog box in Figure 13.13. You must *deny* someone print access to keep them off the printer. Even if you delete the Everyone group and remove the explicitly given permission, people will still be able to print unless denied print access.

FIGURE 13.12

A list of permitted or forbidden domains and networks

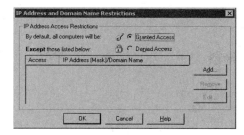

FIGURE 13.13

Choose the domain name, IP address, or network to which you want to permit or deny access to the Web printer.

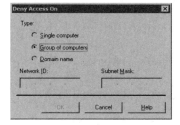

TIP   *Be sure to pick the right radio button (Granted Access or Denied Access) before you define the IP address to which you're permitting or denying access. Otherwise, you'll have to re-create the entry.*

To permit or deny a single IP address, use the Single Computer option. Of course, if that single computer is getting its IP address from a Dynamic Host Configuration Protocol (DHCP) server, this option won't always apply to the same computer. A more effective method of restricting printer access is to define access for a group of computers, using the network IP address and the subnet mask (when you click each option, the boxes to fill in change accordingly). You *can* also permit or deny access to the computer based on domain membership, but this is an expensive operation. If you identify a domain by name, the name must be resolved on both ends of the connection before the Web server can identify the domain, and this will slow down print jobs considerably.

Once you've identified the computer(s) for which you want to permit or deny access to the Web printers folder, they'll appear in the list in the IP Address and Domain Name Restrictions dialog box, as shown in Figure 13.14. Permitted addresses will have a key icon; denied addresses will have a lock icon. The print server is then ready to accept print requests from clients.

FIGURE 13.14

List of networks permitted access to the **Printers** folder on the Web server

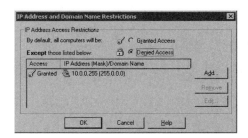

WARNING *Make sure you apply SP2 to any Web print server—or any Web server, for that matter. The ISAPI extension used to allow print jobs to travel over HTTP has a bug that could allow an intruder to get complete control of the server.*

Getting the Printer to the Clients

The method you use to connect a client workstation to a networked printer depends on the operating system the client is using. DOS clients must connect from the command line and need locally installed drivers, 16-bit Windows clients can connect from the graphical interface and need their own drivers, and 32-bit Windows clients connect from Network Neighborhood or My Network Places and don't even need locally installed printer drivers.

NOTE *As you may recall, 16-bit Windows is not an operating system, it's a graphical operating environment for DOS. All DOS workstations must have locally installed printer drivers. You may need to install the driver more than once or install it to application directories to make sure the applications see the printer. You'll also need to manually update drivers should new versions become available (unlikely as that is).*

CONNECTING FROM DOS

To set up LPT1 from DOS, type **net use lpt1: ***server******printername* at the command prompt, where *server* is the name of the Win2K print server and *printername* is the name of the printer. If you want to reconnect to this printer every time you log in to the network, add the **/persistent:yes** switch to the end of the command. Just typing **/persistent** won't do anything, but if you leave off the switch altogether, the connection will default to the persistency settings previously defined.

TIP *Not sure of the name of the print server or the printer? Type **net view** at the command prompt to see a list of all servers. Type **net view ***servername* *to see a list of all resources shared from that server.*

For example, suppose you're setting up network printer support for a DOS workstation that does not have a locally connected printer. Some older DOS applications don't give you a chance to select an output port—it's their way or the highway. Therefore, you'd like to automatically redirect *any* output sent to LPT1 to be intercepted by the network-accessible printer HP5 attached to the Win2K server BIGSERVER. You want to remake this connection every time you log in to the network so that you don't have to worry about printer support.

The command to fulfill this set of conditions would look like this:

```
net use lpt1: \\bigserver\hp5 /persistent:yes
```

CONNECTING FROM WINDOWS 3.X OR WINDOWS FOR WORKGROUPS

To connect to a shared printer from network-enabled Windows or from Windows for Workgroups, select the Printers icon in the Control Panel. You should see a dialog box that shows the printer connections you already have, like the one in Figure 13.15.

What you do from here depends on whether you're just reconnecting to a previously established network connection, creating a new network connection to a printer you can support, or starting at the beginning by installing local support for the printer.

FIGURE 13.15

A list of installed
printers for Windows
for Workgroups

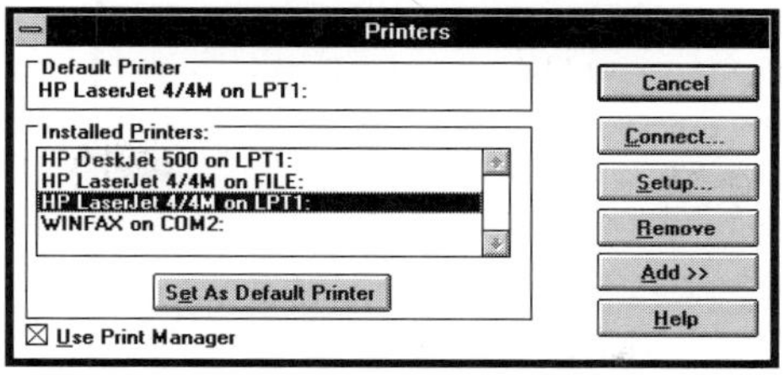

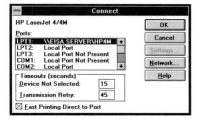

Connecting to an Available Printer

To connect to any of these previously connected printers, you'd just click the Connect button to
open the dialog box shown in Figure 13.16. Click OK, and you're done.

FIGURE 13.16

Connecting a Win-
dows for Work-
groups client to a
previously installed
network printer

Creating a New Network Connection

If you're connecting to a new printer, then instead of clicking Connect, choose the Network button to
open the dialog box shown in Figure 13.17. Find the print server and printer you want and click OK.

FIGURE 13.17

Creating a new con-
nection to a net-
worked printer

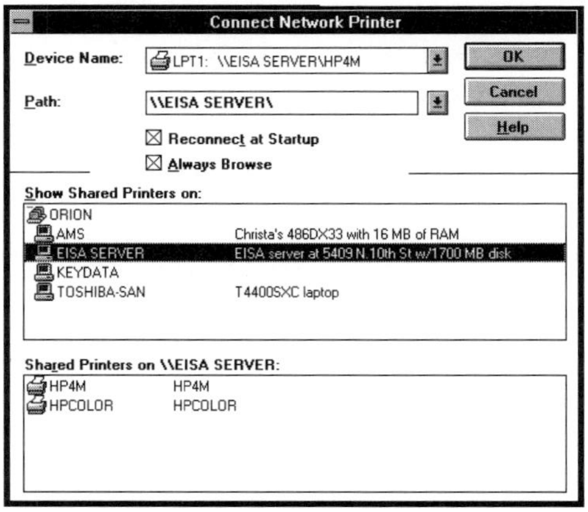

Installing a Printer Driver for Win16 Operating Systems

If you haven't already installed support for the printer, you've got a couple steps ahead of you. Rather than clicking the Connect or Network button, click Add to see a list of installed printers and available printer types (see Figure 13.18).

FIGURE 13.18

A list of available printer types

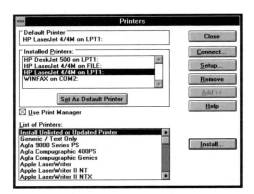

Find the printer you want from the list and click the Install button. The system will prompt you for the location of the printer drivers. Browse for the drivers or insert the requested disk. Once you've installed the correct driver, you can create the network connection to the printer and connect to it.

CONNECTING FROM WINDOWS 95 OR NT CLIENTS

The first time I connected to an NT printer from an NT Workstation back in 1993 (NTW pre-dated Windows 95, you may recall), I thought that I must have missed a step—it was too easy. You don't have to install local driver support at all; just connect to the printer. 32-bit Windows clients don't use locally stored drivers but instead reference the ones you've installed on the server to support them. This not only saves you a step in the process of installing printer support, it makes it much easier to update printer drivers. When there's a new driver out, you don't have to run around to each client with a floppy disk or set up some kind of remote installation script—you just install it to the server, and when the clients connect, they'll use it automatically.

To install a printer from Windows 9*x* or Windows NT, open the `Printers` folder, accessible as a shortcut from the Control Panel, and start the Add Printer Wizard. Click the Next button to open the dialog box shown in Figure 13.19.

Be sure to say that the printer will be managed by a printer server, not locally. Click Next and choose the printer you want from the list, as shown in Figure 13.20. Click Finish and the printer is locally available.

TIP   *If you want to connect to multiple printers, you must do so one printer at a time.*

You can also connect to network-accessible printers from the NT and Windows 9*x* Network Neighborhood. Open Network Neighborhood and double-click the appropriate print server. As shown in Figure 13.21, Network Neighborhood will then display all resources shared from that server, including printers.

FIGURE 13.19

Specify that the printer is connected remotely, not locally.

FIGURE 13.20

Choose a printer from the list of servers and printers.

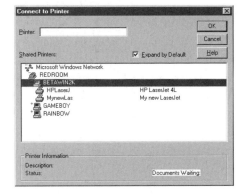

FIGURE 13.21

Installing printer support from Network Neighborhood

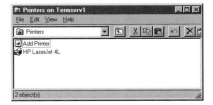

From here, you can right-click the appropriate printer and either capture the printer port (redirecting all output sent to, say, LPT1 to the network printer) or install support for the printer to make it accessible with UNC nomenclature.

CONNECTING FROM WINDOWS 2000

The Add Printer Wizard in Win2K looks a little different from the one in Windows NT or Windows 9*x*, but the basic effect is much the same:

1. Start the Add Printer Wizard and click through the obligatory Welcome to the Add Printer Wizard opening screen. When asked whether you want to create a local or network connection to a printer, choose the network option, as shown in Figure 13.22.

FIGURE 13.22

When connecting to a network printer, be sure to specify the network connection.

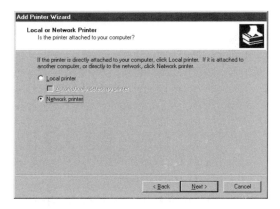

2. Next, indicate the printer's location. What happens here depends on whether your network is using NT 4 domains or the Win2K Active Directory.

   If you're connecting from a Win2K computer that's part of an NT 4 domain, then, as you can see in Figure 13.23, Win2K supports connecting to printers either in terms of the printer's name or by an intranet/Internet address, like this:

   `http://`*printservername*`/printers/`*printername*`/.printer`

   where *printservername* and *printername* are what they sound like: the print server and its share name. If you aren't sure of the printer's name, you can leave that space blank and browse for the print server. The browse function doesn't work for printers with their own name or URL; you must enter a valid name for the printer if you choose that option.

FIGURE 13.23

Type the name of the printer's server or its URL.

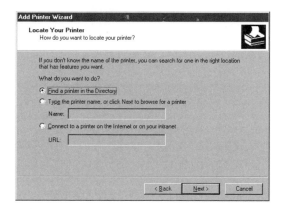

TIP *Frankly, if you're connecting with a URL, it's a lot easier to do it from a browser so you can click links to printers rather than having to know their share names. One mistyped letter in that URL and you get an error message telling you that the printer setup utility could not connect to the printer. If you're using a browser, all you need to know is the name of the print server.*

3. If you choose to browse for a printer, you'll see a browse list like the one in Figure 13.24, showing the printers on the network and the servers they're connected to. As you can see, any location information or comments attached to a printer will show up when you select a printer, so you can easily find the one you want.

FIGURE 13.24

Scan the list of available printers and choose the one you want to connect to.

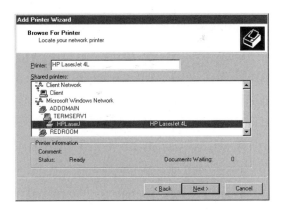

If you're connecting from a Win2K computer using the Win2K directory structure, you have another option: searching the Active Directory for the printer you want. Check the box that says Find a Printer in the Directory and click Next, and instead of browsing as described previously, you'll open a dialog box from which you can browse for printers by a collection of different criteria and in different parts of the Active Directory (users, computers, domain controllers, and so forth). You can also search for printers based on their name or on other criteria, such as what features they support.

TIP   *The simplest method of finding a printer in the Active Directory is to leave all boxes blank and click the Find Now button. If you mistype any search criteria, your search will come up empty.*

Three tabs in the dialog box for finding printers in the Active Directory include all the search options. From the Printers tab, you can search for printers by name, location, or model number of the printer. From the Features tab, you can look for printers that have certain capabilities, such as double-sided printing, color printing, and stapling. On this same tab, you can specify minimum requirements in pages per minute printed and in the paper sizes the printer supports. The Advanced tab contains the same settings on the Printers and Features tab, only in more detail, allowing you to find printers even if you're not sure of their names and letting you choose from a more defined feature set. Choose the options you want to search for and an area of searching in the In box, and click the Find button.

4. Once you've chosen the printer, the wizard will ask if you want to set up the printer as the preassigned printer for all applications (Figure 13.25). If you've already got a preassigned printer, the default option is No; if this is the first printer connection you're setting up, the printer is set up as the default without any prompting from you.

FIGURE 13.25

Specify whether the new printer should be the one all applications choose to print to.

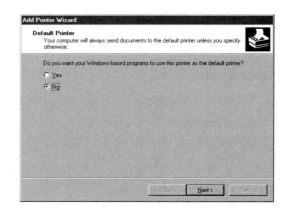

NOTE *The default printer will have a check mark on its icon in the* `Printers` *folder.*

5. Finally, the Add Printer Wizard will show you the options you've chosen so far, letting you click either Finish to install support or Back to change an option. If you've already got the drivers installed, that's it—you can use the new printer immediately. Otherwise, you'll have to copy the new drivers from the CD or your installation directory.

The printer should appear in the Printers dialog box. Its icon will look like that of a locally connected printer, with the addition of a network connection attached to it.

INTERNET PRINTING

If your network clients are running Internet Explorer 4 or later and you're having users connect to their own printers, forget the Add Printer wizards: There's now a better way. If your print server is running IIS, people can connect to any shared printers from a browser and it's *really easy.*

NOTE *Although the documentation implies that this procedure might work with Netscape, I haven't been able to make it work. I'd stick with Internet Explorer.*

You have a couple of options when it comes to connecting to a printer via a Web browser. If you know the print server's name but not the name of the printer you want to connect to, then in the Address box in IE type **http://***servername***/printers** to open a browser page like the one in Figure 13.26. In this example, the name of the print server is CLONE300 (original, yes). You do need to know the print server's name. There's no "browse the network for printers" option built into this.

NOTE *If you're one of the people who avoids the pesky* `http://` *prefix by typing* www *instead (I do it because that means I don't have to squint at the screen to see that I typed both the colon and the two forward slashes) you should know that the* www *prefix won't work here. If connecting locally, you can just skip the* `http://` *prefix altogether, though, like this:* **//***printservername***/printers**.

To connect to a particular printer, click its link in the list to open the screen in Figure 13.27. You're not connected yet, you just have the option.

FIGURE 13.26

List of all available printers on a print server

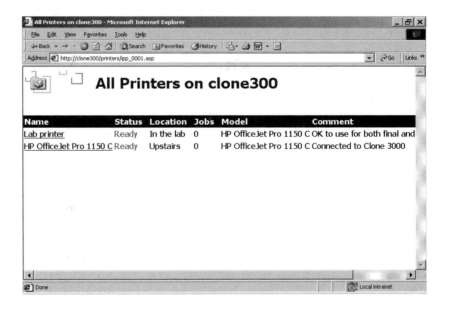

FIGURE 13.27

You must explicitly connect to a printer to use it.

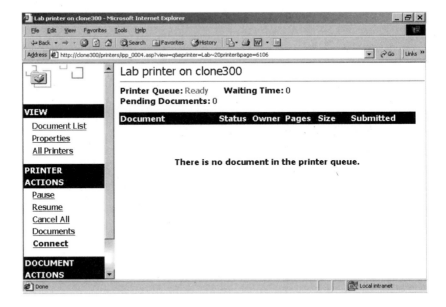

To connect to the printer, click Connect in the list of printer actions. A small status bar will display the progression as the print server sends you the drivers you need, and you'll be connected just as you would had you connected from the Add Printer Wizard. The only difference is that because the installation process is so simplified—you connect to a printer and you click Connect—you never get the option of setting the new printer as the default. If you want to make the new printer the default over an existing printer, you'll need to open the Printers folder, right-click the printer in question, and choose Make Default from the context menu.

TIP   If you know the name of the printer, you can link to it directly like this: `http://servername/printername`. *If you have permission to access the printer, then that puts you directly into the printer's information screen, from which you can connect to the printer.*

As I said earlier, Internet printing represents an excellent way of simplifying client-side printer setup. If you have a corporate home page, you could put a link on the home page, something along the lines of "click HERE to connect to a printer." The user clicks THERE, they go to the page where the printers are listed (and, by tweaking security settings, you can make sure that they only see the printer they're supposed to connect to), they click the printer, and then click to connect. This works for any client that can run IE4. If you're connecting across the Internet, a dialog box appears asking for the domain name, username, and password; if you're connecting locally, this dialog box does not appear.

Using Client-Side Printers in a Terminal Server Environment

When the Terminal Services Edition of Windows NT was first released, the display protocol—the protocol downloading application output to the client machines and uploading keystrokes and mouse clicks to the server—had some holes in it. Remote and local sessions didn't share a Clipboard, so you couldn't cut and paste between applications running on the client and those running on the server. Remote control of sessions wasn't supported. Session clients couldn't use their locally connected printers without sharing them from the network and then connecting to them from the terminal server session.

Win2K filled some of these holes, including the problem of getting local access to client-side ports. Using the new desktop client, clients can access their local printer from a terminal server session without sharing the printer with the network. The only catch is that it's not quite as simple as that for all clients.

NOTE   Win2K supports redirected client-side printers connected to COM and LPT ports, not those connected to USB ports.

Win32 (Windows 9x, NT, and Win2K) desktop client print requests sent to local printers will be automatically redirected to the local printer so long as you've previously installed the driver needed for the printer on the terminal server. You'll have to manually configure Windows terminals and Win16 clients to use locally attached printers.

AUTOMATICALLY REDIRECTING PRINTERS

Other than making sure the driver is installed on the terminal server, you don't have to do anything to set up an automatically redirected printer. When a person with a client-side printer logs onto a terminal server and initiates a session, a fake print job owned by the Administrator is sent to the printer. This isn't a real print job, just a notice to the printer that it's being redirected for use with the terminal server session—you'll probably never notice it if you don't deliberately look at the status box for the printer during the second or two required for the redirection to take place. Behind the scenes, what's happening is that the Win2K terminal server checks the name of the printer driver on the client and looks for the same printer driver on the terminal server's `NTPRINT.INF` file. If Win2K doesn't find that driver name, then the Event Viewer will log error messages and the redirection won't work.

CORRECTING DRIVER NAME MISMATCHES

Not finding the driver name isn't an entirely out-of-the-way problem. For example, Hewlett-Packard supplies Windows 98 and NT 4 drivers for the DeskJet 722C printer. This driver is called HP DeskJet 720C Series v10.3. The Windows 2000 version of the same driver is called HP DeskJet 722C. Driver name mismatch=no working printer. Before SP2 came out, Microsoft's recommended fix for this problem was editing `NTPRINT.INF`, which worked but broke the digital signature on the file, making the system display a pop-up warning every time you installed a new printer. After you apply SP2 to the Windows 2000 terminal server, however, you can edit the Registry to point to a secondary INF file with the printer information, in case Windows 2000 can't find the driver it's looking for in `NTPRINT.INF`. End result: automatic print mapping even for mismatched printer names and an unsullied `NTPRINT.INF`.

To make this work, first apply SP2 to the terminal server. When you've done so, open the Registry and go to `HKLM\SYSTEM\CurrentControlSet\Control\Terminal Server\Wds\rdpwd`. Add two new values. `PrinterMappingINFName`, data type REG_SZ, should contain the name and complete path of the INF file to which you want to send lookups for drivers not found in `NTPRINT.INF`. `PrinterMappingINFSection`, data type REG_SZ, should have a value of the name of the section of the INF file you created where the printer driver mappings are described.

After adding these new Registry values, create an INF file to include the user-defined mappings from the client-side to server-side drivers. These names must match exactly, with identical spacing; the names are also case sensitive. For example:

```
[Version]
Signature="$CHICAGO$"
[Printers]
"HP DeskJet 720C Series v10.3"  =  "HP DeskJet 722C"
```

Save this file with the name you specified in `PrinterMappingINFName` when editing the Registry, and be sure to name the section mapping old and new printer names with the name of the section you specified in `PrinterMappingINFSection`.

Assuming the redirection does work, if you look in the `Printers` folder for the terminal server session, you'll see the redirected printer there, identified by its name, the name of the computer it's connected to, and the number of the terminal server session. For example, the printer HPLaser that's connected to the computer MONSTER, using Session ID4, will be identified in the `Printers` folder as `HPLaser\MONSTER\Session 4`. No one else on the network will see this printer unless you've shared it with the network.

For automatic printer mapping to work, all of the following must be true:

◆ The name of the printer driver on the client and the server must be identical. It's not enough that they be the drivers for the same printer—the names have to match.

◆ The printer must be connected to an LPT port on a client. Win2K Terminal Services does not support redirection of USB printers.

◆ The client session must have printer redirection enabled.

If the printer *doesn't* automatically redirect, check the System event log in the terminal server to find out why.

TIP   *You can automatically redirect a network printer to a terminal session by creating a persistent mapping for that printer on that client. For example, if you always want a user to connect to the same network printer, then you can employ the* net use *command to connect it, like this:* `net use lpt3 \\`*`servername`*`\`*`printername`* `/persistent:yes`. *In this example,* servername *is the name of the print server and* printername *the name of the shared printer you're connecting to. You could, of course, substitute* `lpt1` *or* `lpt2` *in this example, if no local devices are using those ports.*

MANUALLY REDIRECTING PRINTERS

Win16 clients and those using Windows-based terminals (WBTs) will need to manually redirect printers. This may not always be possible with a WBT because the RDP client for older WBTs may not have been updated to version 5 (version 4 does not support redirection of client-side printers). However, new WBTs generally have the RDP5 client, and you should be able to get an updated client for older terminals that don't already include it.

NOTE   *You cannot manually redirect a printer connected to a USB port.*

To manually redirect a printer for a terminal services client, follow these steps:

1. Get the name or IP address of the client device. (If your Window's terminals don't use names—not all do—you'll need to use the terminal's IP address.) Start a terminal session from that client machine.

2. Start the process of manually adding a locally connected printer to the terminal server.

3. In the part of the wizard where you're choosing the port the printer is connected to, scroll down in the list until you see the name or IP address of the client computer with the printer attached, like this:

   Ts002 CLIENTPC LPT1

4. Choose that port to attach the printer to, and install the printer normally.

When a client disconnects or logs off a session, the printer queue is deleted and any incomplete or waiting print jobs are deleted. Once you have manually redirected a printer for a terminal session, that redirection will take place automatically thereafter, and the print queue will be automatically created from the information stored on the client.

PREVENTING PRINTERS FROM BEING REDIRECTED

But what if you don't want clients to use their local printers during terminal server sessions? You may not, especially if the client is connecting to a printer across a dial-up connection. Sending a print job from terminal server to client-side printer may be acceptable at LAN speeds but unwise over a 56Kbps modem connection since sending the print job back to the client for printing can make the connection slow to a crawl. Or you may want people to use a networked printer for their terminal server sessions for auditing purposes. Whatever the reason, you want to disable printer redirection.

To prevent printer redirection on a per-user basis, open the user account's Properties pages and turn to the Environment tab. On that tab is a section called Client Devices, underneath which are three check boxes that control whether that person has access to client-side drives and client-side printers and whether that client should automatically print to the client-side default printer. By default, all three boxes are checked, enabling all client-side printers and drives. To keep the client's printer from being redirected to the terminal session, uncheck the box that says Connect Client Printers at Logon. To permit the user to redirect client-side printers but to keep the default printer from changing to the client-side default, uncheck the box that says Default to Main Client Printer.

If you don't want *anyone* connecting to the terminal server via a given display protocol to use their local printers, you can do this as well. Open the Terminal Services Configuration tool that's in the Administrative tools section of the terminal server. Click the `Connections` folder in the left pane so that the installed display protocols (only RDP, unless you have MetaFrame installed) appear in the right. Open the properties pages for RDP and turn to the Client Settings tab.

There are two sections on this tab. The Connection section on the top is a duplicate of the Client Devices section of the per-user Environment properties discussed above. By default, the per-user settings control, but if you want to apply the settings discussed previously not just to individual users but to everyone using the display protocol, you can deselect the option that says Use Connection Settings from User Settings and edit the entries accordingly. The section at the bottom of the Client Devices tab controls which client-side resources are disabled. Disable client-side printing as follows:

- ◆ To prevent users from redirecting any client-side printers, deselect Windows printer mapping.

- ◆ To prevent terminal users from redirecting client-side printers attached to parallel ports, disable LPT port mapping.

- ◆ To prevent terminal users from redirecting client-side printers attached to serial ports, disable COM port mapping.

Automatically Installing Printers

You've seen now how to get printers to people by walking through the installation wizards. However, this method requires you either to permit users to create their own printers—which is prone to error—or to install them yourself on each computer. In the interests of saving a little time, let's take a look at some methods of simplified printer deployment.

INTERNET PRINTING

As I mentioned earlier, the best use of Internet printing is not, in fact, allowing people to send print jobs over the Internet—it's a security hole and will require an awful lot of bandwidth. Instead, consider using Internet printing to automatically set up printers. When a person connects to the printer via the Web page (which you have locked down as described earlier so that only their approved printers show) the driver is automatically downloaded to the client computer if it's not already there.

PROGRAMMATICALLY INSTALLING PRINTERS

If you don't mind doing a little scripting, then you can also automatically install printers on the basis of user or computer identity when the user logs on—and then unmap the printer connection when a particular user logs off. As is true of scripting in general, this takes some work up front. However, for any task you'll be repeating on a regular basis, scripting it will save you an awful lot of time and trouble. This will only fully work on NT-based operating systems such as NT, Windows 2000, and Windows XP, but if you preinstall drivers onto Windows 9*x* computers it will work there as well.

NOTE *A Resource Kit tool called PrintAdmin enables you to programmatically install and manage printers on the local computer or remote computers running NT or Windows 2000. To use it, you'll need to know how to use VBScript, and, to be perfectly frank, I think the method I'm describing here is easier and completely adequate if installing is your main goal.*

I don't have space for a complete treatise on scripting Windows 2000 here, but the basic idea is this: Win32 operating systems support a scripting environment called Windows Scripting Host (WSH) that enables you to run VBScript and JScript scripts to perform tasks that you'd normally have to perform by hand. In scripting, real objects such as printers are represented by scripting objects, which you manipulate by addressing the *properties* (characteristics) of those objects and exploiting their *methods* (things they can do). Objects are nouns, properties are adjectives, and methods are verbs. WSH is supported on all Win32 operating systems. WSH abstracts the interface to a number of Win32 objects. One of these is `WshNetwork`, a collection of network resources—shared drives and printers. It can also "see" the name of the computer the script is running on and the name of the person currently logged on; the computer name (`.ComputerName`), username (`.UserName`), and computer domain (`.UserDomain`) are all properties of the `WshNetwork` object.

TIP *For those who've never touched scripting before, create scripts in a text editor such as Notepad and save them with a* `.vbs` *extension. Windows 2000 cannot interpret VBScript—this isn't a command-line language like the* **net** *commands.*

For our purposes, we care about only `WshNetwork`'s printing-related methods. To map a printer explicitly to a port as you would with **net use**, use the `.AddPrinterConnection` method. To create a Windows printer connection (and automatically install the driver on NT-based operating systems such as NT, Windows 2000, and Windows XP) use the `.AddWindowsPrinterConnection` method—this is the method I'll use here. To set the default printer for a computer, use the `.SetDefaultPrinter` method.

Creating a Generic Printer Connection

Good so far? Let's take a look at the simplest way of accomplishing this with VBScript:

```
Option Explicit
Dim oNetwork, sPrintPath
Set oNetwork = CreateObject("WScript.Network")
sPrintPath = "\\sandworm\printer"
oNetwork.AddWindowsPrinterConnection sPrintPath
oNetwork.SetDefaultPrinter sPrintPath
Set oNetwork = vbEmpty
Set sPrintPath = vbEmpty
```

In this example, I've defined the variables the script will use (so that if I mistype a variable name then I'll get an error message instead of a new variable), created a connection to the WshNetwork object (which we must do to call on its properties and methods), assigned the UNC path to the shared printer path to the *sPrintPath* variable to make the path information easier to deal with, and then called on the appropriate methods to create the printer and make it the default, supplying the variable representing the printer path as an argument. Finally, I've been a good little coder and set the variables I used equal to vbEmpty now that I'm done with them so that the memory required to support those variables may be released. So long as I assign a valid path in line 4, then this script will work on any NT-based computer. To make this script work for yourself, just replace the highlighted path in line 4 with a valid shared printer UNC path.

Incidentally, there's nothing stopping you from using this script to install support for more than one printer but making one of those printers the default. You'll need one variable for each separate UNC path to the printers for which you want to install support.

Creating a Computer- or User-Specific Printer Connection

Thing is, you probably don't want to install the same printer on every computer in the network. Rather, you'd prefer to establish a connection based on user identity or computer name—particularly the latter because it's often more important that the printer you use be close to where you're sitting than assigned to you personally. That script could look something like this:

```
Option Explicit
Dim oNetwork, sPrintPath
Set oNetwork = CreateObject("WScript.Network")
Select Case oNetwork.ComputerName
  Case "Gamma"
      sPrintPath = "\\sandworm\printer1"
  Case "Geektoy"
      sPrintPath = "\\sandworm\printer2"
   Case Else
      sPrintPath = "\\sandworm\printer3"
End Select
oNetwork.AddWindowsPrinterConnection sPrintPath
oNetwork.SetDefaultPrinter sPrintPath
Set oNetwork = vbEmpty
Set sPrintPath = vbEmpty
```

As you can see, this script starts out just like the other one: I've defined the variables I'm using and established a connection to the WshNetwork object. By including the Select Case statement, however, I've allowed the script to read the local computer name and make a decision about what printer to install based on that information. I've included two valid options, but just so I don't have to create options for *every* computer on the network I've also included a Case Else option that says in effect, "If you can't do anything else, do this." The value of the computer name determines the value for *sPrintPath*, which then gets plugged into the .AddWindowsPrinterConnection and .SetDefault-Printer methods as in the previous example. Again, replace my computer names and printer paths with yours.

I could have done exactly the same thing using the name of the user logged in as the argument for Select Case. Taking only the Select Case snippet, that could have looked like this:

```
Select Case oNetwork.UserName
  Case "Christa"
      sPrintPath = "\\sandworm\printer1"
  Case "Mark"
      sPrintPath = "\\sandworm\printer2"
   Case Else
      sPrintPath = "\\sandworm\printer3"
End Select
```

The rest of the script looks just like the previous example. User-specific mappings are not persistent, incidentally. If Christa logs on and gets her printer mapped, then logs off, when Mark logs on and gets his printers mapped he will not see both Christa's printers and his printers—just his. If you want to disable a computer-specific mapping or a mapping not replaced by another mapping, however, you'll need to manually remove the printer or use the .RemovePrinterConnection method to WshNetwork, supplying the printer path as an argument as you did to add the printer. For example, you could create a script to include in the logoff script for Windows 2000 computers.

Creating a Location-Specific Printer Connection

The previous example allows us to create a default printer based on which computer the script runs on. As you can see, though, you'll need to either create options for each computer on the network, or make up more than one version of the script to distribute according to computer location. In a large network, either option could get cumbersome. There is a third way: you could ask the user to tell you where they are in broad terms (e.g., "library" or "second floor") and then install the appropriate printer based on that information. For example:

```
Option Explicit
Dim oNetwork, sPrintPath, sLocate
Set oNetwork = CreateObject("WScript.Network")
sLocate =_
   InputBox("Where are you? Type 'Lab', 'Library', or 'Reception'.")
Select Case sLocate
  Case "Lab"
      sPrintPath = "\\sandworm\printer1"
  Case "Library"
      sPrintPath = "\\sandworm\printer2"
  Case "Reception"
      sPrintPath = "\\sandworm\printer3"
  Case Else
      Wscript.Echo "That is not a valid choice." :Wscript.Quit
End Select
oNetwork.AddWindowsPrinterConnection sPrintPath
oNetwork.SetDefaultPrinter sPrintPath
Set oNetwork = vbEmpty
Set sPrintPath = vbEmpty
```

What I've done here is create an input box prompting the person running the script to tell me where they are. Based on that input, the script will assign a printer to their computer. If they type an invalid choice, then the script nags at them and ends—that's what the `Wscript.Quit` method does. Alternatively, you could assign a generic printer if the person running the script didn't choose one of the three valid options. This script does require user input, but so long as you trust your user base to know what part of the building they're in, it should work.

TIP *Use the location-specific printer installation script as a template for creating default printers based on user location. If you use group policies to disable the Add Printers applet in the Control Panel and hide shared printers by ending their names in a dollar sign ($), then people will be able to connect to only the printers programmatically assigned to their username, computer name, or location—and you can set the default. This will keep the people in Lab A from mistakenly sending their print jobs to Lab Z, three buildings away.*

`WshNetwork` methods are not the only ways to manage printers through VBScript, but without getting into Windows Management Instrumentation (WMI) and the Active Directory Services Interface (ADSI), they are the simplest. For much more information about scripting Windows 2000 administration, check out *Windows 2000 Automated Deployment and Remote Management* (Sybex, 2001), a guide to using VBScript for Windows 2000 management for anyone who's used to working from the GUI.

Securing Printers

Just because you've networked a printer doesn't mean you want everyone with a domain account to be able to use it. Maybe you'd like to reserve the color printer for people who need to use the more expensive ink, or you want to keep people from printing their résumés after hours. Perhaps it's something as simple as wanting to make sure people connect to the right printer so you're not plagued with people complaining that their job didn't print when they've actually sent five copies to the wrong printer. In this section, let's talk about what you can do to make printers available only to the people you say at the times you say.

TIP *Printer security doesn't always give you the degree of granularity you need to give everyone the permissions they need and no more. Consider setting up multiple printers for each print device, setting different permissions for each, and only giving people access to the printer tuned for their needs.*

Tuning Printer Permissions

You can make printers available all the time to everybody, or you can pick and choose the times and circumstances under which the printer will be available. Here's how.

SETTING AVAILABLE HOURS

By default, a printer will always accept print jobs. You can determine the hours during which a printer will send jobs to the print device. If a print job is sent to a printer after hours, the job will be queued but not printed until the printer is again available.

To edit a printer's hours of availability, turn to the Advanced tab of its properties pages (see Figure 13.28) and set new times. All that this does is tell Windows 2000 to hold print jobs in the spooler until the printer is again available, so the new settings won't affect any jobs that have already been sent to the printer.

FIGURE 13.28

Define times for the printer to be available.

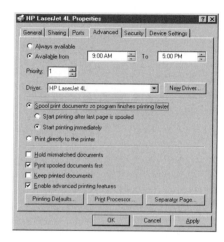

If you want a print device to be always available to some users and only available during certain hours to others, you'll need to create multiple printers for the single print device. Once you've done so, you can configure the printing hours separately for each printer, with the results as shown in Figure 13.29.

FIGURE 13.29

Restricting printer hours for a specific group of users

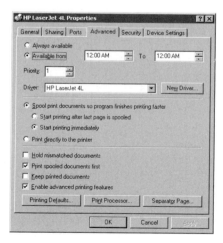

SETTING PRINTER PERMISSIONS

Those familiar with the NT/Win2K argot will remember that you secure a Win2K network by defining user rights for what people can *do* on the network and setting permissions for the resources that people can *use*. Printer security is controlled with permissions on a per-group or per-user basis.

To set or edit the permissions assigned to a printer, log in with an account that has Administrator permissions, open the printer's properties pages, and turn to the Security tab. You'll see a dialog box like the one in Figure 13.30.

FIGURE 13.30

Default printer permissions

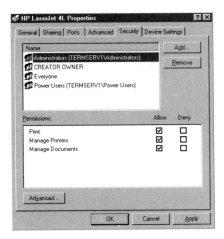

TIP *If you turn to a printer's Security tab and see a list of Security IDs (SIDs) instead of user or group names, and the cursor changes to an hourglass when over the dialog box, don't panic. The print server is retrieving the names from the domain controller and will show the user and group names after a few seconds. If this doesn't happen—if the SIDs never resolve to user and group names—then there's something wrong with either the domain controller or the connection between the two servers.*

From here, you can edit the basic permission sets of the groups for whom some kind of printer access has been defined, denying or granting explicit access in three areas: printing (the ability to send print jobs to the printer), managing print jobs (the ability to control whether a print job is printed or the order in which it's printed relative to other jobs), or managing the printer.

NOTE *Table 13.2 includes a complete list of all permissions and how they apply to printers.*

Not sure how to interpret the check boxes? If a permission is checked, then it's explicitly enabled or disabled, depending on which box is checked. If a permission is clear on both sides, then it's implicitly enabled. Shaded permission boxes imply that a permission is granted or denied through inheritance. You can explicitly enable or disable the permission by checking the appropriate box.

Fine-Tuning Printer Access

The Security page only shows the default groups and the basic permissions they've been assigned. For more control over the permission process, click the Advanced button to open the dialog box seen in Figure 13.31.

FIGURE 13.31

Setting advanced
printer permissions

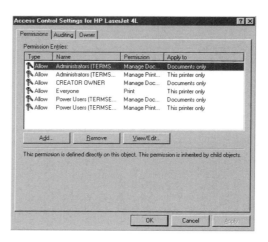

From here, you can see the state of the defined permissions. A key icon symbolizes a granted permission; a padlock symbolizes a denied one. (When you first open this dialog box, you should only see keys—no permissions are explicitly denied by default.) The comment below the list of users and groups notes whether the highlighted permission applies to the basic membership of that group only or to subgroups within that group.

You can adjust these permissions either by adding new users or groups to the list (getting them from the domain controller) or by editing the permissions of the groups already there.

To define permissions for a new user or group, click the Add button. The print server will retrieve a list of users and groups from the domain (or server; you can pick either from the list) displayed in the Look In box. Choose a user or group from the list and click it. You'll open a dialog box like the one in Figure 13.32. The permissions listed here have the characteristics outlined in Table 13.2.

FIGURE 13.32

Defining the permis-
sions of a new user

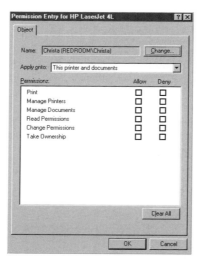

TIP   If the user or group you want isn't displayed in the list, type it into the Name box. If you've already created an account for this user or group, you'll be able to edit its permissions.

TABLE 13.2: PRINTER PERMISSIONS AND THEIR IMPLICATIONS

ACCESS TYPE	EFFECT	TIED TO
Print	User can send jobs to the printer.	Read permissions
Manage Printers	User can change printer properties and permissions.	Print, read permissions, change permissions, and take ownership of the printer
Manage Documents	User can control document-specific settings and pause, resume, restart, and delete spooled print jobs.	Read permissions, change permissions, and take ownership of the printer
Read Permissions	User can see the permissions all users and groups have for that printer.	NA
Change Permissions	User can change the permissions all users and groups have for that printer.	Read permissions (although this won't be checked)
Take Ownership	User can take ownership of the printer.	Any permissions assigned to Creator/Owner of the printer

You can customize user permissions by explicitly permitting some actions and denying others. For example, permission to manage printers normally implies permission to change permissions for that printer. However, you can get around this by allowing printer management while denying the ability to change permissions. This doesn't always work—you can't permit people to print yet deny them the ability to read permissions—but it's worth experimenting to see whether you can get the degree of granularity you want in access permissions.

NOTE   Printer permissions can apply to the printer only, to documents only, or to both the printer and the documents printed on it.

Changing permissions for an existing user or group works in much the same way: Select a name, click the View/Edit button, and you'll see the same set of options to explicitly grant or deny permissions.

Auditing Printer Access

Curious to know who's doing what to the printers under your care? Turn to the Auditing tab (accessible from the Advanced button of the Security section of a printer's properties) to set up auditing to list events in the event log.

SETTING UP PRINTER AUDITING

Win2K does not audit by default. For auditing to work properly, you'll have to first turn on auditing. This is a bit more of a pain than it was in NT 4, but once you get comfortable with the Microsoft Management Console, it'll get easier.

The Group Policy snap-in is an extension of the Computer Management snap-in, and you'll need to make sure you've got it in your management tools.

To enable auditing, run the Microsoft Management Console and add the Group Policy add-in under Computer Management. Under `Computer Configuration\Windows Settings\Security Settings\Local Policies`, you'll find the `Audit Policy` folder. Enable the logging types you're interested in.

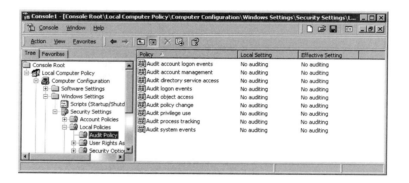

By default, Win2K doesn't log printer use or security events, so the list on the Auditing tab of a printer's properties pages will be empty when you originally turn to it. To add events to audit, click the Add button to move to the dialog box. If you need to choose a different domain, click the down arrow for the Look In box as shown in Figure 13.33.

FIGURE 13.33

Choose a group or user to audit.

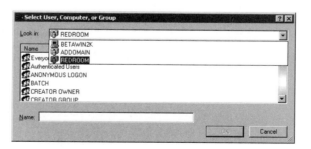

As when setting printer permissions, you'll first choose a group or user to audit from the list, then you'll choose events to audit. After you've chosen a group or user to audit and clicked OK, you'll move to a dialog box like the one in Figure 13.34.

FIGURE 13.34

Choose the events
to audit.

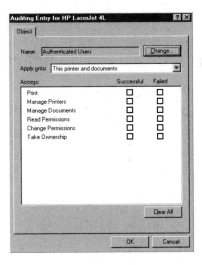

The dependencies shown here work the same way as the ones described in Table 13.2. The main difference is that here you're monitoring the attempts to *do* these things, not granting or denying permission to do them. Also, the Successful and Failed columns aren't mutually exclusive like the Allow and Deny ones are—you can monitor both failed and successful attempts to take ownership of a printer, for example. When you've finished tweaking the auditing options, click OK to return to the main Auditing tab, which will now look something like the one shown in Figure 13.35. Entries for these audits will now appear in the Security portion of the event log.

FIGURE 13.35

A list of users and
events to audit

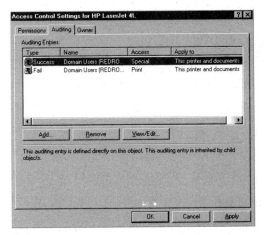

Assigning an Owner to a Printer

Administrators can give the printer to a new owner from the Owner tab of the Access Control Settings dialog box accessible from the advanced security options. The options are the person who made the printer in the first place and an administrator of the domain, as you can see from Figure 13.36.

FIGURE 13.36

A list of possible owners for the printer

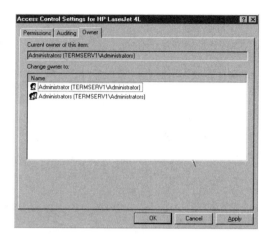

HIDING SHARED PRINTERS

The best way to secure any network resource is to conceal the fact that the resource even exists. Printers are no exception to this rule. To keep a shared printer (or any other shared resource, for that matter) out of the browse list, put a dollar sign at the end of its name, like this: PRINTER$. The printer name will not show up in the browse list, but a user who knows that the printer exists and which server it's connected to will be able to connect to it with **net use**, like this:

```
net use \\servername\printername
```

Anyone using the scripts we discussed earlier will also be able to connect to the printers.

Group Policy Settings for Printers

Win2K has some group policies that you can edit to configure how much control users have over adding and removing printers and over how those printers appear in the Active Directory.

PRINTER-SPECIFIC GROUP POLICY SETTINGS

The Group Policy settings in the Microsoft Management Console include some policies you can tweak to configure how the printer appears in the Active Directory or in the domain (see Figure 13.37). To get to these settings, open the Group Policy snap-in and move to the Administrative Templates section of the Computer Configuration settings. As you can see from Table 13.3, some of these settings apply only to Win2K clients, but others apply to any client.

FIGURE 13.37

Group policies
controlling printer
publishing

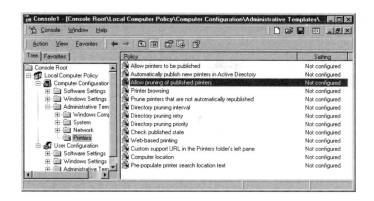

TABLE 13.3: PRINTER PUBLICATION POLICIES

POLICY	DEFAULT VALUE (WHEN NON-CONFIGURED)	DESCRIPTION
Allow Printers to be Published	On (permits publishing)	Toggles to allow printers to be published. If a printer isn't published, clients can't find it in the Active Directory. When configured, overrides Automatically Publish New Printers in Active Directory policy.
Allow Pruning of Published Printers	On (will prune)	Controls whether the pruning service may remove printers that it can't find when browsing for them. If you enable this option, you can tune it with the pruning interval, retry, and priority policies.
Downlevel Printer Pruning	Never	Controls the circumstances under which a printer connected to a downlevel print server (that is, one running an operating system other than Win2K) will be removed from the browse list. Choosing to prune only if the server is found means the printer will only be removed from the browse list if it's confirmed that the printer is gone. Choosing to prune whenever the printer is not found means the printer can be removed even if it's not confirmed that the printer is gone because the browse service can't find the print server. By default, missing printers will not be pruned. Printers connected to Win2K print servers are not affected by this setting because they're automatically published by default.

Continued on next page

TABLE 13.3: PRINTER PUBLICATION POLICIES *(continued)*

POLICY	DEFAULT VALUE (WHEN NON-CONFIGURED)	DESCRIPTION
Automatically Publish New Printers in the Active Directory	On (will publish)	Controls whether printers are published automatically or whether you have to publish them. If Allow Printers to Be Published policy is set, this policy is ignored.
Directory Pruning Interval	8 hours	Determines the interval at which printers that haven't announced themselves recently are removed from the directory of published printers. The pruner reads this value every hour, so changes will not take effect immediately.
Directory Pruning Retry	2 tries	Determines how many times the pruning thread will attempt to contact a print server before giving up and deleting that printer's entry from the Active Directory.
Directory Pruning Priority	Normal	Tunes the priority of the pruning thread, responsible for deleting outdated printer entries in the Active Directory. The higher the priority of the pruner thread (or any thread), the more often it will get CPU cycles and thus the more often the Active Directory will be updated—but the fewer CPU cycles the other threads will get. You can set this value to Lowest, Below Normal, Normal, Above Normal, or Highest.
Check Published State	Never	Verifies that published printers are indeed in the Active Directory. You can set this value to Never (the default) or at varying intervals ranging from 30 minutes to 1 day.
Printer Browsing	Off in domains using the Active Directory; on in NT 4 domains dependent on browsing to publish resources	Controls whether the print subsystem can add printers to the browse list. In a Win2K domain that uses the Active Directory, the print subsystem does not announce printers to the master browsers in the domain. If you disable printer browsing, you prevent the print subsystem from announcing the printers even in an NT 4 domain.

Continued on next page

TABLE 13.3: PRINTER PUBLICATION POLICIES *(continued)*

POLICY	DEFAULT VALUE (WHEN NON-CONFIGURED)	DESCRIPTION
Prune Printers That Are Not Automatically Republished		Controls the circumstances under which a printer connected to a computer running an operating system other than Win2K or a printer published outside its own domain may be pruned. Choosing Never means that the printer will never be pruned. Choosing Only When the Print Server Is Found means that the printer will be pruned if the print server is found but the printer isn't available. Choosing Only When the Printer Isn't Found prunes printers that are not automatically republished. This setting applies only to printers published from Active Directory Users and Computers, not from the Printers section of the Control Panel.
Web-Based Printing	Off	When disabled, won't accept print requests sent via HTTP, or publish printers to the Web.
Custom Support URL in the Printer Window's Left Pane	Off	Ordinarily, the left window of the `Printers` folder displays the Microsoft URL and (if available) the URL for the printer's maker. If you enable this policy and type in a URL, you can point people to a different location—perhaps a customized troubleshooting guide on the company Web site.
Computer Location	Used to help people figure out not only where a printer is, but where the printer server it's connected to is	Identifies the location of the printer server.
Pre-populate Printer Search Location Text	On	Enables location tracking (based on the subnet of the printer server and the client) and a browse feature.

When you first install Win2K, none of these settings will be configured. To enable or disable a policy, right-click that policy and choose Properties from the pop-up list that appears. You'll see a dialog box that looks like the one in Figure 13.38.

Click the check box to check or clear the box. If you need more information about what a policy actually does if enabled, turn to the Explain tab. Once you've chosen to actively clear or check a box, the policy's entry will change from Not Configured to Enabled or Disabled.

FIGURE 13.38

Configuring print
server policies

TIP *You can run through the list of policies with the Previous Policy and Next Policy buttons without exiting and reentering the policy Properties box. The only catch is that if you click Cancel, you'll cancel every policy change you made while the window was open.*

USER-SPECIFIC PRINTER SETTINGS

To edit user settings for adding and removing printers, click Start/Programs/Administrative Tools/ Active Directory Users and Computers. Click the Active Directory container of the domain you want to manage (an organizational unit or a domain). Right-click that container, and then click Properties. On the Group Policy tab, click New to create a new group policy, then Edit to open the Group Policy Editor. The settings you're looking for are in User Configuration/Administrative Templates/Control Panel/Printers and are described in Table 13.4.

WARNING *These settings generally apply to the Add Printer Wizard. If someone uses the Add Hardware tool to add a printer, for example, then they can circumvent Disable Addition of Printers.*

TABLE 13.4: GROUP POLICIES FOR USER CONTROL OVER PRINTERS

POLICY	DESCRIPTION
Disable Deletion of Printers	Prevents users from deleting local and network printers. If a user tries to delete a printer, such as by using the Delete command in the Printers tool in the Control Panel, Windows displays a message explaining that the action is prevented by a policy. This policy does not prevent users from running programs to delete a printer.

Continued on next page

TABLE 13.4: GROUP POLICIES FOR USER CONTROL OVER PRINTERS *(continued)*

POLICY	DESCRIPTION
Disable Addition of Printers	Removes the Add Printer Wizard from the Start menu and from the Printers folder in Control Panel.
	Also, users cannot add printers by dragging a printer icon to the `Printers` folder. If they try to use this method, a message appears explaining that the action is disabled by a policy.
	This policy does not prevent users from using the Add/Remove Hardware wizard to add a printer. Nor does it prevent users from running programs to add printers. This policy does not delete printers that users have already added. However, if users have not added a printer when this policy is applied, they cannot print.
Browse the Network to Find Printers	Permits users to browse the network for shared printers in the Add Printer Wizard.
	If you enable this policy, when users click Add a Network Printer but do not enter the name of a particular printer, the Add Printer Wizard displays a list of all shared printers on the network and prompts users to choose a printer. If you disable this policy, users cannot browse the network; they must enter a printer name.
	This policy affects the Add Printer Wizard only. It does not prevent users from using other tools to browse for shared printers or to connect to network printers.
Default Active Directory Path When Searching for Printers	Specifies the Active Directory location in which searches for printers begin.
	The Add Printer Wizard gives users the option of searching Active Directory for a shared printer. If you enable this policy, these searches begin at the location you specify in the Default Active Directory Path box. Otherwise, searches begin at the root of Active Directory.
	This policy only provides a starting point for Active Directory searches for printers. It does not restrict user searches through Active Directory.
Browse a Common Web Site to Find Printers	Adds the path to an Internet or intranet Web page to the Add Printer Wizard. You can use this policy to direct users to a Web page from which they can install printers, making it easy for users to find the printers you want them to add.
	If you enable this policy and enter an Internet or intranet address in the text box, Windows adds a Browse button to the Locate Your Printer page in the Add Printer Wizard. The Browse button appears beside the Connect to a Printer on the Internet or Your Company's Intranet option. When users click Browse, Windows opens an Internet browser and navigates to the specified address to display the available printers.

Configuring Printer Settings

Sharing a printer with the network and securing it isn't generally the end of the story. You haven't yet added support for separator pages used to help dozens of printer users avoid picking up each other's documents, and you haven't configured messaging so the right people get printer messages. And what about setting up printer priorities so that Windows 2000 will print user documents on the right printer, without user intervention?

NOTE   *The options described in this section apply to both network and locally connected printers.*

To configure a printer's settings, right-click its icon in the printer's properties pages and choose Properties from the pop-up menu that appears (see Figure 13.39).

FIGURE 13.39

Use this dialog box to fine-tune a printer's settings.

Most of the basic configuration options, such as name changes and sharing, are pretty self-explanatory once you look at the screen. I'll go over the more complex options, but if you're trying to figure out where an option is configured, refer to Table 13.5 for a quick guide to what's where.

TABLE 13.5: PRINTER OPTIONS AND LOCATIONS

OPTION TO CHANGE	LOCATION	REASON TO EDIT
Add more client drivers	Additional Drivers dialog box, available from the Sharing tab	Load drivers for printer clients so they can be automatically downloaded to the client (available for 32-bit Windows only).
Add more ports	Ports tab	Restore ports that you've deleted or add support for direct network connections to the printer.

Continued on next page

TABLE 13.5: PRINTER OPTIONS AND LOCATIONS *(continued)*

OPTION TO CHANGE	LOCATION	REASON TO EDIT
Change port time-outs	Ports tab when you click the Configure Port button	Increase port time-out settings to make ports wait longer to receive printer data. Helps if the print job isn't getting to the printer quickly enough.
Edit printer settings	Device Settings tab	Edit the printer settings, including the amount of memory installed, fonts installed on the printer, page protection, and the like.
Edit user or group permissions to the printer	Security tab	Edit the list of users or groups with access to the printer or change the permissions they have.
Set the hours printer will accept print jobs	Advanced tab	Edit to shut off a printer after certain hours, perhaps when the workday is over.
Identify local printer name	General tab	Use for local printer identification.
Identify network printer name	Sharing tab	Use for printer identification on the network.
Set the page order	Layout tab of Printing Preferences dialog box, available from the Printing Preferences button on the General tab or the Printing Defaults button on the Advanced tab	Toggle between printing pages in normal or reverse order.
Set paper orientation	Layout tab of Printing Preferences dialog box, available from the Printing Preferences button on the General tab or the Printing Defaults button on the Advanced tab	Toggle between portrait and landscape orientation of printer output.
Identify the paper source	Paper/Quality tab of Printing Preferences dialog box, available from the Printing Preferences button on the General tab or the Printing Defaults button on the Advanced tab	Choose a different paper tray to print from, perhaps for higher-quality paper or printing from transparencies.
Set the print processor	Advanced tab	Toggle between default print formats (EMF, TEXT, or RAW).
Set the printer spooling	Advanced tab	Toggle between using printer spooling and sending documents directly to the printer.
Edit separator pages	Advanced tab	Specify a new separator page for print jobs.

Creating Multiple-Personality Printers

Sometimes, it's not easy to choose a single set of options for a particular print device. Disparate groups of people are using the printer, and the same permission sets don't really work for all groups. In a situation like this, one easy way to manage access to a print device is to create multiple printers for a single print device. Multiple printers means support for multiple device settings, including:

◆ Printer names and comments

◆ Hours the printer is available

◆ Kind of access to the printer users and groups have

◆ Default paper tray used

And there are others. Any options that you configure from a printer's properties pages, you can fine-tune by creating a second printer for a single print device. Once you've edited the new printer's settings, you can assign printer access to the appropriate people. There's no upper limit on the number of printers you can make for a single print device, although the more printers you make, the more complicated your printer management will be. You can't manage all the printers for a single print device from a single console even though it's only one print device and it's connected to the print server.

The process of adding a second (or third, or fourth, and so on) printer is nearly identical to that of adding the first one. Start the Add Printer Wizard from the `Printers` folder and follow the instructions as prompted. Just make sure that you choose a new name for the printer and choose the same printer driver the original printer uses.

At this point, you can configure each printer as you see fit, as described in the following sections.

WARNING *Not all options set in a printer's properties pages are printer specific. Port time-outs, for example, apply to any parallel port on the print server. One printer's time-outs will apply to* all *printers.*

Defining Port Settings

Port settings control how the print server sends print jobs to its ports. You can't do too much to configure ports other than define which port a printer sends print jobs to and, in the case of parallel ports, how long the printer is willing to wait for an expected print job before reporting an error condition. Unless I say otherwise, you'll be controlling most port settings from the Ports tab (see Figure 13.40).

ASSIGNING A PRINTER TO A NEW PORT

If you move a print device from one port to another, you'll need to edit the device's port settings. Open the printer properties pages, turn to the Ports tab, and check the box next to the correct port. Notice that you can select multiple ports only if printer pooling is enabled.

Not sure what all those ports are? TS ports are printer ports of terminal server sessions. LPT ports are parallel (8-bit) ports. COM ports are serial (1-bit) ports. Finally, any port prefaced with a server name indicates a network connection. The terminal server session ports show the ports attached to currently connected terminal server clients and can be used to manually redirect ports, as described in "Manually Redirecting Printers."

FIGURE 13.40

The Ports tab for a printer

CREATING A PRINTER POOL

As I mentioned in the beginning of this chapter, the ratio of printers to print devices isn't always 1:1. You've already seen how you can create multiple printers for a single print device. I'm talking here about how to make a single printer support multiple print devices.

Why would you want to do this? It's mostly a matter of efficiency. Even with the fast printers (I'm talking about the actual piece of hardware now), busy offices may have more print jobs coming through than one printer can handle. To keep things running smoother and reduce delays, you can distribute print jobs among multiple printers, as shown in Figure 13.41. Print clients will all send their print jobs to the same printer, but the jobs will go to the printer that's least busy at any given time. This is called *printer pooling*.

FIGURE 13.41

Use printer pooling to reduce printing delays.

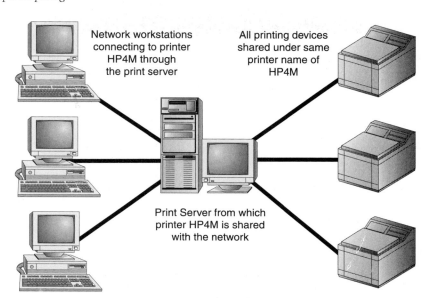

Network workstations connecting to printer HP4M through the print server

All printing devices shared under same printer name of HP4M

Print Server from which printer HP4M is shared with the network

To set up a printer pool, turn to the Ports tab for the printer. Make sure the box enabling printer pooling is checked, then select all the ports to which printers in the printer pool are attached. These ports can be local ports, ports connected to terminal server clients, or network ports.

There are a couple catches to printer pooling. First, the printers in the pool must be identical to each other—same make, model, and amount of installed memory. Second, I highly recommend putting the pooled printers in the same physical location. It's not going to endear you to your user base if they have to wander from place to place looking for their print jobs.

TIP   Consider using separator pages with usernames in printer pools since users will not necessarily know which printer their job went to.

SENDING DOCUMENTS DIRECTLY TO THE PRINTER

As I explained in the description of the Win2K printing model at the beginning of this chapter, Win2K normally creates a spool file that's sent to the printer for printing rather than sending documents directly to the printer port. Spooling documents means the application you're printing from is only tied up for the time it takes to create the spool file, not to print the entire document. This is called *printing in the background*.

If you can't use print spooling for some reason—perhaps if the print server's hard disk is so full that it can't create the spool file—then you can send documents directly to the printer port, without creating a spool file or using print server resources. Turn to the Advanced tab of the printer's properties pages and select Print Directly to the Printer, as shown in Figure 13.42.

FIGURE 13.42

Disabling print spooling

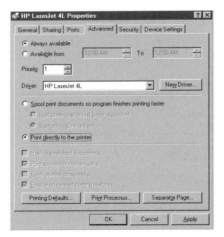

This is not something you'll often want to do. Spool files allow you to print large and complex documents without running out of printer memory. They also allow users to regain control of their applications quicker. Only disable print spooling if you can't print otherwise.

Using Separator Pages

When a lot of people are using the same printer, keeping print jobs organized can get complicated. To help you minimize the number of people who wander off with each other's print jobs, Win2K supports separator pages. These extra pages are printed at the beginning of documents to identify the person doing the printing, the time, the job number, or whatever other information is defined in the page. (I'll explain how you can tell what information a page will print, and how you can create your own custom separator pages, in a minute.)

TIP   Like other printer options, separator pages are assigned to printers, not to print devices, so you can use a different separator page for each printer.

CHOOSING A SEPARATOR PAGE

By default, printers don't use separator pages. To use one of the default separator pages provided with Win2K, move to the Advanced tab of a printer's properties pages and click the Separator Page button. You'll see a dialog box like the one in Figure 13.43.

FIGURE 13.43

Choose a separator page.

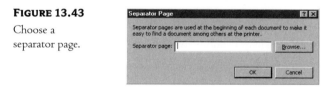

Type the name of the separator page or click the Browse button to open the %*systemroot*%\ `system32` folder (where the pages are stored) and find the one you want. Table 13.6 describes the four separator pages that come with Win2K.

TABLE 13.6: DEFAULT SEPARATOR PAGES

PAGE NAME	DESCRIPTION	COMPATIBILITY
SYSPRINT.SEP	Prints a blank page before print jobs	PostScript
PCL.SEP	Switches a dual-language printer to PCL mode	PCL
PSCRIPT.SEP	Switches a dual-language printer to PostScript mode	PostScript
SYSPRTJ.SEP	Prints a blank page before print jobs sent to a PostScript printer	PostScript

There's one catch to choosing a separator page: The page must be available locally. Although you can choose an SEP file stored in a network-accessible folder, a separator page that's in a networked location will not print. The system won't fuss at you either when you choose the SEP file or when you send a print job to a printer, but print jobs will have no separator page.

CREATING A NEW SEPARATOR PAGE

Given that the separator pages that come with Win2K are mostly necessary in specific instances, you'll probably want to create your own separator pages if you use them at all. Separator page files are just text files, so you can create the file in Notepad.

On the first line of the new file, type a single character—any character will do—and press Enter. This character will now be the escape character that alerts Win2K that you're performing a function, not entering text, so make it one that you won't need for anything else. Dollar signs ($) and pound signs (#) are both good escape characters, but the only rule is that you can't use the character as text.

Once you've picked an escape code, customize the separator page with any of the variables shown in Table 13.7. Be sure to include the escape character before each function, as I've shown in this table with a dollar sign.

TABLE 13.7: SEPARATOR PAGE FUNCTIONS

VARIABLE	FUNCTION
BS	Prints text in block characters created with pound signs (#) until you insert a $U. Be warned—printing text like this takes up a lot of room. You probably don't want to use this option.
$D	Prints the date the job was printed, using the format defined on the Date tab of the Regional Options applet in the Control Panel.
$E	Equivalent to the Page Break function in Word; all further functions will be executed on a new page. If you get an extra blank separator page when you print, remove this function from the SEP file.
$F*pathname\filename*	Prints the contents of the specified file to the separator page, starting on a blank line. As separator pages are strictly text-only, only the text will be printed—no formatting.
$H*nn*	Sets a printer-specific control sequence, where *nn* is a hex ASCII code that goes directly to the printer. Look in your printer manual for any codes that you might set this way and for instructions on how and when to use them.
$I	Prints the job number. Each print job has a job number associated with it.
$L*xxx*	Prints all the characters following (represented here with *xxx*) until it comes to another escape code. Use this function to print any customized text you like.
$N	Prints the login name of the person who submitted the print job.
$*n*	Skips *n* lines (where *n* is a number from 0 to 9). Skipping 0 lines just moves printing to the next line, so you could use that function to define where line breaks should occur.
$T	Prints the time the job was printed, using the format defined on the Time tab of the Regional Options applet in the Control Panel.
$U	Turns off block character printing.
$W*nn*	Sets the line width, where *nn* is a number of characters. Any characters in excess of this line width are truncated. The default (which you don't have to define) is 80 characters.

For example, the following SEP file

```
$
$N
$O
$D
$L This is a separator page. Only use these pages to organize
$L print jobs because they're otherwise a waste of paper.
$l
$T
```

produces this output:

Christa

1/31/02 This is a separator page. Only use these pages to organize print jobs because they're otherwise a waste of paper.

3:49:11 PM

Notice that there are only line breaks if you specifically include them. Without the $n codes, all output will be on a single line.

When you're done, save the separator page file with an .sep extension to the %systemroot%\ system32 folder if you want to store it with other separator pages. Otherwise, you can store the page anywhere locally available to the print server. To use the new page, just load it as you would one of the defaults.

Setting Printer Priorities

You can set printer priorities to give one person's print jobs higher priority than those of others. This can be handy if you're sharing a printer from your Windows 2000 workstation and want to make sure your print jobs have first crack at the printer, or if the print jobs that one group of people create are more important than those most other people are creating. Regardless of priority, all print jobs are scheduled, but the jobs sent to the higher-priority printer will be spooled first to the print device.

Set printer priorities from the Advanced tab of the printer's properties pages (see Figure 13.44). The default value is 1; higher numbers (up to 99) have higher priority.

You can only set one priority on a single printer—you can't set one priority for one group, a second for a particular user, and a third for yet another group. Instead, you'll need to create one printer for each set of priorities you want to assign.

Adjusting Print Server Settings

To edit server-wide printer settings, open the Printers folder, make sure that no installed printers are highlighted, and choose File/Server Properties. You'll see a dialog box like the one in Figure 13.45.

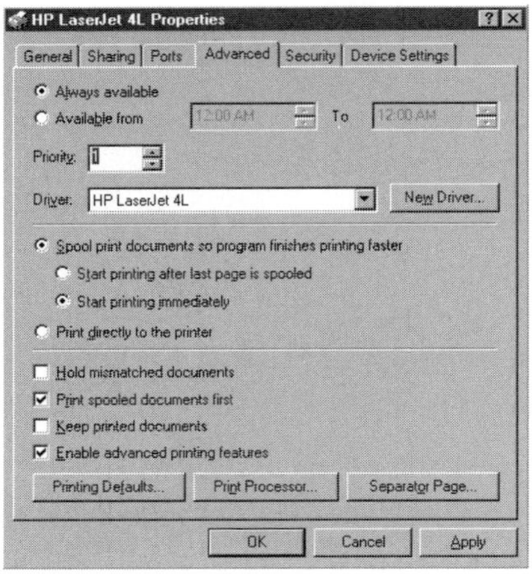

FIGURE 13.44

Raise printer priorities if you want jobs sent to a certain printer to be processed first.

FIGURE 13.45

Edit server properties to change settings that apply to all printers.

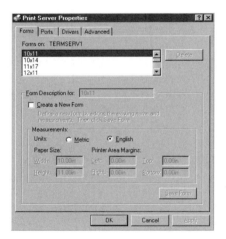

TIP *To make sure you're editing serverwide settings, highlight the Add Printer icon in the* Printers *folder before choosing Server Properties from the File menu.*

Choosing Form Settings

Windows 2000 spaces its print jobs based on forms, which define a template for where text should appear. Win2K comes with a long list of predefined forms (see Figure 13.46) you can choose from, but it also allows you to define your own form settings for customized needs such as printing to company letterhead.

FIGURE 13.46

Serverwide form
settings

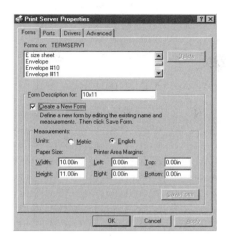

Win2K is set up to print on blank 8.5×11 paper (the standard size). To choose a new form, find it in the list. To create a new form, edit the settings in the dialog box, choose a new name for the form, and then click the Save Form button.

NOTE   You must choose a new name for the form. You can't overwrite or delete the forms provided with Win2K.

Configuring Server Port Settings

Although you can configure the following settings from any printer's properties pages, I think it's less confusing to edit them in the server properties. That way, you're reminded that the settings you make here apply not just to a single server but to all affected servers.

ADDING AND DELETING PORTS

Most people won't need to add or delete ports, but here's how you do it if you need to:

1. Open the print server's properties pages and turn to the Ports tab. You'll see a list of the currently installed ports.

2. Click the Add Port button to open the Printer Ports dialog box.

3. Click the New Port button and provide a name for the port in the text box that appears, then click OK.

4. Back in the Printer Ports box, click Close to return to the Ports tab.

The new port should appear in the list of installed ports.

NOTE   Add COM ports if you have a multiport serial adapter and will support more than four serial printing connections. Add network ports if you're supporting a printer connected directly to the network.

This will add a new port listing to HKLM\Software\Microsoft\Windows NT\ CurrentVersion\ Ports—no reboot required.

To delete a port, just select it in the list and click the Delete Port button. You'll be prompted to confirm that you really want to delete the port. When you do so, the port listing will immediately disappear from the Registry.

OOPS! I DELETED A PORT I WAS USING!

It is easy to replace accidentally deleted parallel ports. Click the Add Port button and choose to add a local port. Give the port the appropriate name (such as LPT1) and you're done.

It is *not* so easy to replace an accidentally deleted serial port. In that case, you'll need to add the port, then edit the Registry to define it as a serial port. Add the port as described earlier, then open REGEDT32 and move to HKLM\Software\Microsoft\Windows NT\Current Version\Ports. Find the value for the port you deleted, then double-click it to edit its value to 9600,n,8,1. Unless you deleted every COM port, you'll have other COM port values there for reference.

Parallel, file, terminal client, and network connections have no values in the Registry—just entries.

EDITING PORT TIME-OUTS

A print device connected to a parallel port (identified as LPT*x*) will wait a certain interval from the time it expects to receive a print job to the time it gets it. If the print device doesn't get the job within that time, it will notify the person sending the print job that there's an error. Technically speaking, it's not the printer that's complaining, but the parallel port.

You can adjust the interval of time that a parallel port will wait before complaining that it hasn't yet received an expected print job. Turn to any printer's Ports tab, select a port, and click the Configure Port button. You'll see a dialog box like the one in Figure 13.47.

FIGURE 13.47

Edit the value to increase or decrease the transmission time-out.

The normal time-out period is 90 seconds. Raise or lower this value by typing in a new number. The lower the value, the more sensitive the port will be to delays. Higher values may make the printer more forgiving of transmission delays, but if you do have a real problem printing, it will take longer for you to discover this.

Adding or Updating the Printer Driver on a Windows 2000 Print Server

One of the cool things about using Win32 clients for network printing is that you don't have to install local driver support anymore. This really speeds up the client installation process and makes it easier to update drivers since you no longer have to run from workstation to workstation with the new disk.

For this to work, however, you *do* need to install support for those clients on the server end so that the client can access them as necessary. Drivers are added on a serverwide basis—if you have more than one printer of the same type connected to your print server, you'll update all drivers at once, not just the ones that printer is using.

To add a driver:

1. Turn to the Drivers tab of the printer server's properties pages. You should see a list of installed drivers that looks like the one in Figure 13.48.

FIGURE 13.48

Drivers previously installed on the server

2. Click the Add button on this screen to start the Add Printer Driver Wizard. Click through the opening screen to the point where you can choose the manufacturer and printer model for which you're adding support.

TIP   The list of available printer drivers includes only those that come on the Win2K installation CD. If you've got an updated driver, click the Have Disk button and provide the path to the driver file.

3. From the list that appears (see Figure 13.49), choose all the Win32 clients that will be connecting to this printer from the network. Win2K supports drivers for the following operating systems and platforms:

   ◆ Alpha (NT versions 3.1–4)

   ◆ Intel (Win2K, NT versions 3.1–4, Windows 9*x*)

   ◆ PowerPC (NT versions 3.51 and 4)

   ◆ MIPS (NT versions 3.1–4)

NOTE   Remember, the fact that DOS and Windows 3.x drivers aren't listed doesn't mean that you can't print from those clients. It just means that those drivers are not included with Win2K, and the clients will need to have them locally available.

FIGURE 13.49

Choose the clients that you'll need to support.

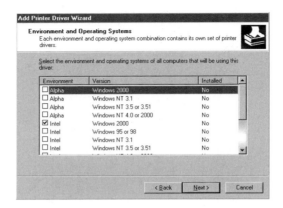

4. When you click Next, you'll see the wizard's final screen, telling you what driver support you have added.

Updating a driver is simpler:

1. From the Drivers tab of the server's properties pages, highlight the driver you want to update and click the Update button. Win2K will ask you whether you're sure you want to update the driver.

2. You'll be prompted for the location of the driver files—either the installation CD or a floppy or network connection.

That's it—the driver's updated.

TIP *Not sure where to get driver updates? Forget any floppy disks that came with your hardware—those drivers are apt to be very out of date. Instead, go to the printer manufacturer's Web site and look for a Downloads section. The most recent drivers should be available there.*

Keeping Track of Your Printing

Win2K offers some messaging and logging capabilities that you can use to monitor the printing process or refer to for troubleshooting when something's not going right. To configure these capabilities, turn to the Advanced tab of the server's properties pages (see Figure 13.50).

Most of these options are fairly self-explanatory. The spooler error, warning, and information events go into the logs visible from the Event Viewer. They don't record every print job sent to the printer (thank goodness, or you'd end up with a huge event log), only spool events.

Messaging is configured from the same tab. By default, the person originating a print job gets a message when the print job is completed or if there's a problem with it. You can disable messaging here, send the error message to the *computer* originating the job, or set up the print server to beep when there's a printing error. Most of the time, the default options will work fine.

FIGURE 13.50

Set logging and messaging options for your print server.

Managing Print Jobs

Managing print jobs is pretty straightforward whether you're doing it from the `Printers` folder or from the Web.

MANAGING PRINTERS AND DOCUMENTS FROM THE *PRINTERS* FOLDER

If you double-click a printer's entry in the `Printers` folder, you'll see all print jobs currently waiting to be printed and the following information (see Figure 13.51):

- The filename of the document being printed
- The job's status (printing, spooling, or paused)
- Who sent the job to the printer
- How many pages are in the job and how many remain to be printed
- The file size of the print job
- The time and date the user submitted the job

FIGURE 13.51

A job waiting to be spooled to a printer

When you select a job in the list, you can use the tools in the Document menu to pause a job, resume a paused job, restart a print job from the beginning, or delete a print job. The only catch is that you have to do all this while the job is still spooling to the print device. You can't control the parts of the job that have already spooled to the physical printer's memory from this console.

If you pause a print job, you can edit its priority or printing times in the middle of printing. From the Document menu, choose Properties to open the dialog box in Figure 13.52.

FIGURE 13.52

Properties of a print job

From here, you can view many properties inherited from the printer and passed to the job, and you can raise or lower the job's priority. The higher a job's priority, the higher its place in line, so you can use this feature to manipulate the order in which jobs print even if one job got to the printer before another did. This can be very useful on those occasions when the person printing the 200-page manual sends their job to the printer before the person creating a cover sheet for the FedEx package that has to be ready by 3:30.

MANAGING PRINTERS AND DOCUMENTS FROM A BROWSER

You can't completely manage a printer from a browser—you can't adjust printer settings, paper sizes, and the like—but you can do Basic Printer and Document Management Stuff.

You can pause, resume, or cancel all print jobs for a particular printer. From the printer's page, click the link naming what you want to do to the printer.

You can pause, resume, or cancel individual print jobs from the Web browser. When print jobs are active, they're displayed on the printer's Documents page, visible when you click the Documents link under Printer Actions. Each print job has a radio button next to it; to select a print job, click it so that it's highlighted. When you've selected the print job, you can pause, resume, or delete it using the links provided there.

Troubleshooting Printer Problems

Printing under Windows 2000 is usually pretty trouble-free, but every once in a while you may run into problems. The remainder of this chapter describes some of the more common printing problems and tells you how to solve them.

Basic Troubleshooting: Identifying the Situation

First, try to figure out *where* the problem lies. Is it the printer? The application? The network? If you can tell where the problem lies, you'll simplify the troubleshooting process.

TIP   The printing problem that frustrates me most is paper jams. Getting that last shred of jammed paper out of the printer can drive you to madness. To minimize paper jams, store paper somewhere with low humidity (curled paper jams easier), don't overfill the paper tray, and keep paper neat before it goes in the tray.

Printer troubles can happen due to any combination of three different causes:

◆ Hardware errors

◆ Software errors

◆ User errors

TIP   One basic part of printer troubleshooting is to make sure the person is connected to the right printer and knows which print device is associated with that printer. Some troubleshooting jobs end with the task of finding the printer with five unclaimed print jobs on top of it.

No One Can Print

If no one can print, check the print device and network connection. Check the easy stuff first: Is the printer on and online? Does the cartridge have ink? Is the printer server up and running? Did the printer *ever* work, or is this its maiden voyage? If it never worked, make sure you've got the right driver installed, or try downloading a newer one from the manufacturer's Web site.

From the console, check the port settings. Is the printer sending data to the port the print device is connected to?

Also, see if you can print from the print server. There could be a network problem preventing people from reaching the print server.

Make sure there's enough space on the print server's hard disk to store spool files. If the print server can't create spool files, it can't print from a spool.

Make sure the printer is set up to use the proper print processor.

Some People Can't Print

What do those people have in common? Are they all in a single subnet? In the same user group? Using the same application? Printing to the same printer? Find the element they have in common, and that's probably the element that's causing the printing problem. For example, if everyone who's printing from NT clients can print and everyone printing from Windows 9*x* clients can't, then check the data type (on the Advanced tag of a printer's properties—click the Print Processor button to see what the currently selected default data type is). Unless the data type is RAW, then print jobs that people create from Windows 9*x* clients will disappear—you won't see any error messages, they just won't print.

ONE PERSON CAN'T PRINT

If only one person can't print, try to narrow down the source of the problem. Can the person print from another application? Can the person print from another computer? If this person can't print at all, see if someone else can print from their computer. If so, check the permissions attached to the person who can't print. They may be denied access to the printer altogether.

TIP   If only one person is having printing problems, try rebooting the computer and retrying the print job. Some applications (such as Netscape Navigator 4.51) have a problem if they crash in the middle of creating a print file—they won't accept another one because they think the previous job is still being created. Sometimes, this problem will prevent any application from printing from that computer. In such a case, the only thing to do is reboot and try again. Logging out and in again won't do it.

Using Online Resources

If you get completely stuck, try the links included in the left pane of the `Printers` folder. (Note that these links will be visible only if you've got Web content enabled. If you disabled Web content to clean up the desktop, you can reenable it for this folder only by opening Tools/Folder Options and, on the General tab of the Folder Options dialog box, choosing Enable Web Content on My Desktop.)

The More Info link leads to a printer page on the Microsoft Web site at `www.microsoft.com`, the manufacturer's link leads to their printing page (if they have one), and the Microsoft Support link leads to the printing home page in the Microsoft support area of its Web site. (I'd provide the link, but given how often Microsoft rearranges its Web site, by the time you read this it wouldn't be accurate.) If your print server has an Internet connection, you can connect directly from the `Printers` folder, but if not, you can still plug the URLs into a browser to see if the online resources can help you with your question.

TIP   Considering how often Microsoft reorganizes its Web site, you might be better off using the URL policy I described earlier to link to a custom home page with a troubleshooting guide and perhaps the latest drivers. Nothing is more frustrating than being desperate enough to try the Web tool but then discovering the link is dead.

Unglamorous as printing is, it's an essential service for just about any organization. In the previous pages I've talked about how to set up printers for local use or for your network, how to get those printers to the people who need them, how to automatically deploy printers through Internet Printing and simple administrative scripts, and how to keep those printers from those who haven't any reason to be using them. After reading this chapter, you should feel ready to do your part to help keep those recycling bins full.

Chapter 14

Connecting Clients to Windows 2000 Server

YOU'VE BUILT YOUR SERVER, created your users, and shared your resources. Now you need to get your clients to that server. In this chapter, I'll show you how to set up various workstations with networking components, how to log in to the network, how to connect to shared resources, and, when applicable, how to find and connect to the Windows 2000 Active Directory.

Throughout this chapter, I'm going to use the various operating systems to connect to the same server, on the same domain, and with the same user account.

- ◆ My username is bsmith.

- ◆ My resource server name is BS01.

- ◆ My computer name is BS99.

- ◆ My domain is BS.

- ◆ My full domain name is BS.COM.

Connecting Windows 95 and Windows 98 Workstations

Connecting a Windows 95 or Windows 98 workstation to the network *can* be an easy thing to accomplish. We have Plug and Play on our side, which (usually) takes the guesswork out of installing the network card, and networking is an inherent capability of our workstation. In other words, the installation and configuration of all networking components does not require us to do much more work or know much more than would be required to simply install the client itself. In contrast, the older Windows 3.*x* clients had a whole slew of manual configurations and additional files to modify: protocol.ini, autoexec.bat, config.sys, system.ini, etc. Those older Windows platforms just weren't network-ready. Theoretically, installing your networking components in Windows 95/98 *and* making them talk to the server are as easy as point, click, and go—as long as you know where to point and click. The coverage in this section applies to both Windows 95 and Windows 98, as their networking components work nearly identically.

Configuring the Workstation

To start off, I'll assume that your workstation is fully up and running with Windows 95/98 and has no networking components installed. We start in the Network Control Panel (select Start/Settings/Control Panel, then open up the Network applet). You should see an empty network configuration dialog box like the one shown in Figure 14.1.

FIGURE 14.1

The Configuration tab of the Network Control Panel for Windows 98

You need to have at least one type of networking *client*, at least one *protocol*, and at least one network *adapter*. Additionally, you can add a *service*, such as file and print sharing. Since you presumably have none of these, you'll click the Add button. You are now asked which type of networking component you wish to add (see Figure 14.2).

FIGURE 14.2

The Select Network Component Type dialog box

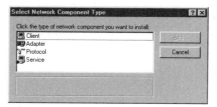

We'll start off by adding an adapter. From the list of component types, select Adapter and then click Add once again to open up the dialog box shown in Figure 14.3.

In the Select Network Adapters dialog box, you'll see a list of adapter manufacturers on the left and corresponding adapters on the right. Choose your adapter and click OK. After a quick file copy or two, you'll find yourself back at the Network Control Panel applet. Here's the neat thing: an adapter is useless without both a client to bind to and a protocol to talk with. Windows knows this and installs a set of defaults to make your life easier. In Windows 95, you usually get the Client for Microsoft Networks as your client, and IPX/SPX and NetBEUI as your default protocols. In Windows 98, as you can see in Figure 14.4, you get the Client for Microsoft Networks, but the only protocol listed is TCP/IP.

FIGURE 14.3

The Select Network Adapters dialog box

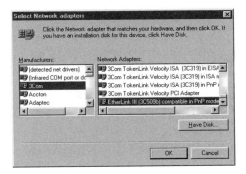

FIGURE 14.4

A full complement of networking components is installed by default.

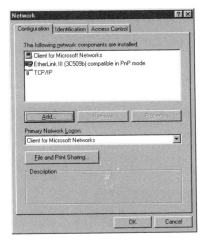

For convenience' sake, TCP/IP is configured to use DHCP automatically. If you need to change this to reflect the configuration of your particular environment, you can choose the protocol in the Network Control Panel, then select Properties. Likewise, you can configure your network adapter particulars to suit your needs.

Attaching to the Network

As shown in Figure 14.4, in addition to the Configuration tab, you'll find two additional tabs in the Network Control Panel. Pay particular attention to the Identification tab, which is shown in Figure 14.5.

As you can see, the computer name for me is BS99. The computer name must be unique, just like in Windows NT and Windows 2000 machines. The workgroup is BS.

NOTE *BS? My domain is BS. Why is my workgroup BS? The workgroup is where your computer belongs. When you open up your Network Neighborhood, this is where you start. By putting your machine into the same workgroup as your domain, your domain resources will be more readily available to your workstation with less browsing required. Also, if your Windows 95/98 workstation is running a service, such as file and print sharing, it registers itself into the browse list of this workgroup.*

FIGURE 14.5

The Network Control Panel's Identification tab

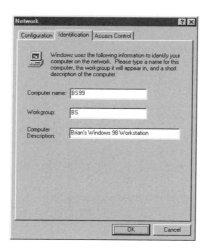

Now we'll talk about our domain. Unlike a Windows NT or Windows 2000 machine, and more like a Windows for Workgroups machine, a Windows 95/98 machine does not have to *belong* to a specific domain in order to log in to the domain. This lets us be in one workgroup, but still log in to any domain. Back in the Configuration tab of the Network Control Panel, you can specify the properties of your Client for Microsoft Networks by either double-clicking the client, or selecting it once and clicking Properties. You'll see the dialog box shown in Figure 14.6.

FIGURE 14.6

Client for Microsoft Networks Properties

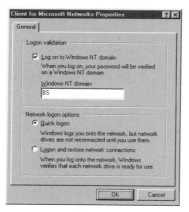

By placing a check in the Log On to Windows NT Domain box, you're telling your workstation that you are going to want to be validated with an official domain user account before you get into the operating system. In the Windows NT Domain box, enter the domain where your user account resides.

NOTE *Here, you are only specifying that Windows 95/98 requires you to log in to a domain. Again, Windows 95/98—unlike its Windows NT and Windows 2000 counterparts—is not secure and will not require you to log in to access the workstation. When prompted to log in, you can simply click Cancel, and you're in—to the workstation, but not the domain.*

From this point on, you'll get a handy logon-request dialog box every time you boot up your workstation. Changing passwords is a snap, too. If your password expires, you'll get a handy little message, along with a separate dialog box in which to change it.

Accessing Network Resources

Now that we're in, we need to find and connect to the resources that drew us to the network in the first place. We're going to find our resources by double-clicking the Network Neighborhood icon on the Desktop (my Network Neighborhood is shown in Figure 14.7).

FIGURE 14.7

Network Neighborhood

What you are looking at in your Network Neighborhood is your browse list for your workgroup—or domain, if the name is the same. In my domain, BS, BS01 is the only server registering into the browse list. Double-clicking the server reveals a list of shared resources on that server, shown in Figure 14.8.

FIGURE 14.8

BS01 shared resources

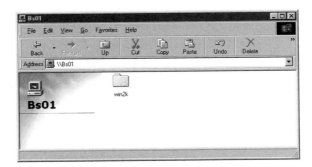

In Figure 14.8, you can see that my only share is Win2K. (If you've shared any printers, printer shares will also be visible here.) You can browse deeper into the files and folders of a shared folder, or map a drive directly to the share by right-clicking the share and choosing Map Network Drive. To attach to a printer, you can choose Start/Settings/Printers; from there, choose Add Printer, and select your resource as we did earlier.

Accessing the Active Directory

There's another neat feature for Windows 95 and 98 clients. On the Windows 2000 CD, under the Clients directory, is a Win9x directory. In that directory, you will find a single executable, which installs the Directory Service Client for Windows. This Directory Service Client allows your Windows 9x client to see the new Active Directory in Windows 2000. The installation is a simple click-next-to-continue and reboot process. No configuration issues, no selections to make.

Now that we have this Active Directory client installed, exactly what is it that we have? There is no utility that brings up the Active Directory, and there is no new program installed. Most importantly, what we do have are new options and capabilities under the Find menu within the Windows Explorer. A previously unavailable choice in the Find menu is Printers. Another new option is integrated with a new version of the Windows Address Book; it lets you find People published in the Active Directory. (The Windows Address Book is updated during the Active Directory client installations.) Obviously, this little client installation doesn't give you a direct tap into the heart of the Active Directory, but it does give you the essential functionality required to make your Active Directory published resources available to your Windows 9x clients.

Connecting Windows NT Workstations

Windows NT workstations, even more so than Windows 95/98 clients, come networking-ready. All of the essential components of networking are inherent to and already included in the basic installation of Windows NT. If you've installed Windows NT, chances are you've already installed all the networking components required to get you going. Just to be on the safe side, we'll walk through the key requirements. This section, like the previous one, will assume that you have a fully functioning operating system; it covers the configuration of networking components and, finally, shows you how to connect to Windows 2000 resources.

Configuring the Workstation

Windows NT will have almost all of your networking components installed by default—the Workstation service, the Server service, and a dial-up adapter or network adapter if you have either a modem or network card present in your machine. However, you will probably want to revisit all of these options just to make sure you are set up for your particular network. To do this, you need to open the Network Control Panel. Obviously, the foundation of networking lies with a network adapter. So select the Adapters tab. To install your network card, click Add; you will be shown a list of supported network cards, as shown in Figure 14.9.

FIGURE 14.9

Selecting a network adapter

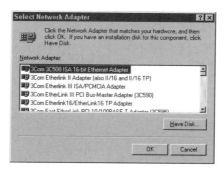

Scroll down to find your network adapter, or select Have Disk to locate a driver or an unlisted—but supported—network adapter. The next step is selecting protocols. This selection is entirely dependent upon your specific network. To install additional protocols, select the Protocols tab, then select Add. You will be shown a list of supported protocols to select from. To configure an installed protocol, if required (as is the case with TCP/IP), highlight the protocol and select Properties. The TCP/IP properties page is shown in Figure 14.10.

FIGURE 14.10

TCP/IP properties

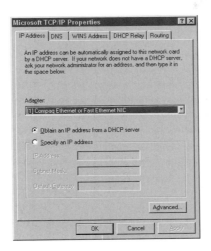

In the real world, you will have a static IP address for 99 percent of your servers 99 percent of the time. For workstations, however, the reduced administration requirements of DHCP will almost always prevail. With that said, we will continue using DHCP with our clients. If you select the Obtain an IP Address from a DHCP Server radio button, TCP/IP will be assigned a DHCP address. By selecting this option, the DHCP server can supply any or all values to your TCP/IP configuration, and not just the actual IP address. Your local network configuration will have everything to do with how these settings are assigned. Keep in mind, though, that any entries within the TCP/IP properties pages—such as DNS servers, WINS servers, default gateways, or domain names—will override any setting that the DHCP server gives you.

Another section of note in the NT Network Control Panel is the Services tab. Services here are referred to differently than we have become used to in Windows 9x and Windows 2000. In Windows NT, terms like *Client for Microsoft Networks* and *File and Print Sharing* are replaced by the terms *Workstation* and *Server*. Take a look at Figure 14.11.

The Workstation service is our basic network client. This is the one that gives us the ability to use the network. The Server service allows us to share our resources. These basic components require little to no configuration for the workstation to operate effectively as a network client.

In the Network Control Panel's Identification tab, you will see your computer name and domain or workgroup membership configuration. Unlike a Windows 9x or 3.x client, a Windows NT machine—whether it is a Windows NT workstation or Windows NT server—must have a computer account created in the domain it wishes to belong to. Because the computer account is nearly identical to a user account, you must have Account Operator or Administrator privileges to join a domain. On the other hand, to join a workgroup, you do not need to hold any special domain privileges. Of course, to change these settings in either case, you will need Administrator rights on the local workstation or server.

FIGURE 14.11

Network services

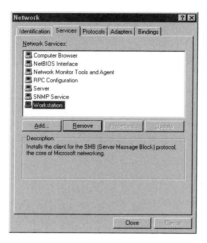

Well, it sounds like a real pain—joining a domain—so why bother? If a Windows NT workstation or server is only in a workgroup, domain users cannot be assigned permissions to any resource on the workstation or server, nor can they log in with that account. This creates a nightmare situation when you want to log in to a machine and still be able to access resources on a domain. To make a long story short, you will want to join the domain.

To join a domain, select the Change button from the Identification tab. You will be shown your current domain and workgroup membership, along with your current computer name. You can change either your computer name or your workgroup/domain membership option. As soon as you begin changing one, the other becomes grayed out, so if you want to change both, you'll have to come back after changing the first. My computer name, BS99, is fine, but I want to join the BS domain (see Figure 14.12).

LOGGING IN TO WINDOWS NT MACHINES AFTER JOINING A DOMAIN

When a Windows NT workstation or Windows NT server joins a domain, users from that domain can—if assigned the appropriate permissions—log in directly to that machine. They will not have to have separate accounts on the local machine and domain to access resources in both places.

It doesn't end there, though. Users from any domain that is trusted by the domain in which the machine belongs can be assigned permissions to and, if allowed, log in directly to the local machine.

Um, let's clarify that a bit. My machine, BS99, belongs to the BS domain. The BS domain trusts the MANAGEMENT domain. I can add users and global groups from both the BS and MANAGEMENT domains into my BS99 local groups and assign permissions for my resources to those users—including the right to log in to BS99. If there is another domain out there, SALES, that is not trusted by BS, users cannot log in to BS99 with their SALES accounts.

FIGURE 14.12

Changing domain

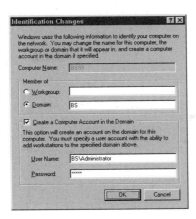

In the Identification Changes dialog box, select the Domain radio button to type your domain choice in the corresponding text box. Before clicking OK, you need to have a computer account for your machine. If one has already been created, either from Server Manager for Domains or within the Active Directory Users and Computers management console, you should be set to go. If not, check the Create a Computer Account in the Domain check box. Once checked, you can fill in a username and password to be used to actually create the computer account. This username and password, as I mentioned earlier, must have either Account Operator or Administrator rights on the domain you are joining. I always like to be on the safe side and enter the full domain qualified name. Instead of simply typing **Administrator**, I type **BS\Administrator**—this ensures that I use Administrator from the BS domain.

After you've completed the domain membership change, you will be prompted to reboot the server for the changes to take effect. After you reboot, your logon dialog box will allow you to enter the username and password for the domain that you just joined.

WHY REBOOT?

If all you did was change your domain and workgroup membership, you don't really have to reboot to let the changes take effect. What the reboot does is allow all services to register with the new domain membership. Without the reboot, you will still be part of the domain and will still be able to use the new domain membership.

This is helpful to know if your workstation or server ever loses its "trust relationship" with its domain. This happens when the NT machine account password gets out of sync between the machine and the domain. To correct this, you need to remove the machine from the domain—join a workgroup—delete the machine account from the domain, and, finally, rejoin the domain, creating a new computer account as you go. You could be forced to reboot twice, or simply ignore the reboot suggestion and do it all in one shot. If the machine in question is a workstation, you shouldn't run into problems, but on production servers, I would recommend rebooting every chance you get.

After you have configured all of your adapters, services, and protocols, you will probably find a request to reboot upon closing the Network Control Panel. Do so, and you should be ready to connect to your Windows 2000 server.

Accessing Network Resources

In Windows NT, when you come to the Logon Information screen, you will notice that you can't manually enter a domain name in the Domain selection box. Instead, you are given a predefined list of domains from which to choose. This list goes back to our conversation about Windows NT machines joining a domain. We can log in with accounts from our own local machine (like my BS99, which will not have domain access) accounts from our own domain that we are a member of, and accounts from any domain that our domain trusts.

TIP   Why the option of logging in with accounts from a trusted domain? Let's say I am in a network that has a Windows NT master domain model. To make it simple, I have the ACCOUNTS domain, where all accounts reside, and the RESOURCE domain, where all resources reside. When I add a Windows NT workstation to the network, where should I add it? Many people think that it belongs in ACCOUNTS, so that I can log in with my user account from that domain. But that's not really the best place. I put the workstation in the RESOURCE domain instead. When I log in to my machine, my domain choices will be my own machine (of course), the RESOURCE domain, which has no accounts, and finally, the ACCOUNTS domain. Placing NT workstations and member servers in the RESOURCE domain instead of the ACCOUNTS domain will keep your network more organized.

To connect to a network resource with a Windows NT client, you can simply right-click Network Neighborhood and choose Map Network Drive. A dialog box will appear, similar to the one shown in Figure 14.13.

FIGURE 14.13

Mapping a drive

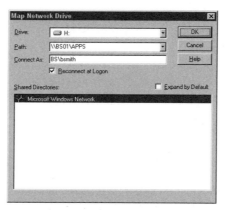

This dialog box works just like it does with any other client, except we have that additional feature of *Connect As*. The Connect As option allows you to connect to a network share with a different set of credentials or another user account. Simply type the username in the Connect As box, or as I have shown, type in the full *domain\username* to let the target machine know exactly which domain the username belongs to. One thing to keep in mind when using this option is that Windows NT can only map to a given server with one set of credentials. If I have already connected to a server, I can't specify a different username for a new connection, even if connecting to a different share.

There are times, though, that you may get the error message that your credentials conflict, indicating that you are already connected to a server under a different username but don't have any drive connections to that server. What you need to do is go to a DOS prompt and type a **net use** statement. Chances are, you will see a connection to that machine's IPC$ share without a drive letter specified. This happens when you do things like open Server Manager for Domains or Event Viewer to a machine. You don't realize that you have connected to that server already, but you have. First, make sure all programs using that connection are closed, then drop the connection by typing **net use** *server**share* **/d**. For example, if I had opened Event Viewer to BS01 and saw a net use connection to \\BS01\IPC$, I would type **net use** \\**bs01****ipc$** **/d**.

If you don't specify a user to connect as, Windows NT will use the credentials of the logged-in user to establish the network connection. Click OK and you'll either be connected or, if you used a different set of user credentials, be prompted for a password. That's all there is to it.

Connecting Windows for Workgroups Workstations

Before creating a Windows for Workgroups to Windows 2000 Server relationship, you need to be aware of basic limitation. The Active Directory—and all the benefits that come with it—is not available. You are pretty much limited to basic network share access. I know that in today's world, you probably won't find many occasions to connect Windows for Workgroups computers to the network, but when that occasion does arise, it might not hurt to be prepared. It's probably safe to say that we have all gotten too used to the Windows 9*x*, Windows NT, and Windows 2000 Desktop interface to be efficient when sitting in front of an old Windows for Workgroups machine. Everything is in a different place. That Program Manager just sits on top of our desktop. There's no Start menu! How embarrassing would it be to sit down at a workstation—you being the senior server administrator—and not have the slightest clue how to connect to your servers? Well, relax. In this section, we'll walk through configuring the basic networking components of Windows for Workgroups, and we'll touch back on how to connect to network shares.

It is very common—even on a machine with a network adapter present—to have a Windows for Workgroups machine that is completely ignorant of your network. In the Program Manager window, you'll find a Network program group, which contains a Network Setup icon. Launching that icon will present a dialog box like the one shown in Figure 14.14.

FIGURE 14.14

The Network Setup dialog box

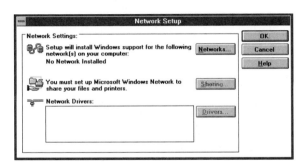

The dialog box in Figure 14.14 shows no configured networking support. To add this support, select the Networks button to install what we would call in Windows 9*x* or 2000 terminology your Client for Microsoft Networks (see Figure 14.15). In the Networks dialog box, select the Install Microsoft Windows Network button.

FIGURE 14.15

Selecting networks

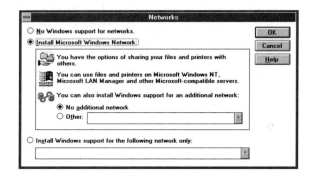

The next step is installing our adapter. Go back to the Network Setup dialog box and select the Drivers button; the resulting dialog box will contain both network adapters and protocols. Click the Add Protocol button, and you will see a list of all supported network adapters (see Figure 14.16). You can find your adapter in the list, or, if you're brave, you can click the Detect button to have the Setup program attempt to detect it for you.

FIGURE 14.16

Selecting an adapter

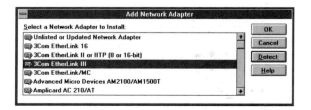

I say you have to be "brave" to use the Detect button because the Windows for Workgroups programming predates Plug and Play by quite some time. The risk of system lockup during this detection phase is substantial. Nevertheless, on my old 486 with a 3Com EtherLink III ISA network adapter, the Setup program was able to detect my adapter.

After selecting your adapter, you'll be returned back to the Network Drivers dialog box. You will see, as shown in Figure 14.17, that a set of default protocols has been automatically installed as well.

If the default protocols, NetBEUI and IPX/SPX, don't meet your needs, you can remove whichever protocol your don't want by highlighting it and clicking Remove. You can then add new protocols by clicking the Add Protocol button. In the event that multiple protocols are used, you can easily select a primary protocol by highlighting the protocol of choice and clicking the Set as Default Protocol button. Likewise, if a protocol such as TCP/IP needs configuring, you can highlight the protocol and click the Setup button.

FIGURE 14.17

Installed networking components

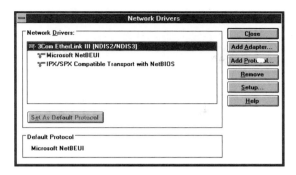

Once you have added and configured all required protocols—and have done your suggested reboot—you should be almost set to go networking. To finish things off, you need to configure your workgroup and logon settings. Now that you've set up a network, there is a new applet in your Control Panel, the Network applet. Launching that will present a screen like the one shown in Figure 14.18.

FIGURE 14.18

The Network applet in Windows for Workgroups

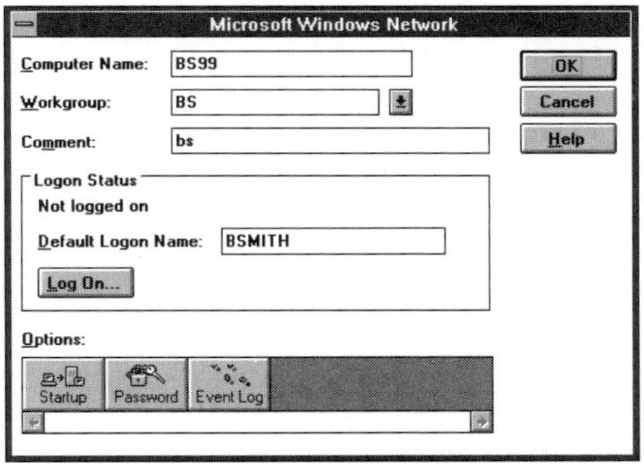

In this screen, you can configure your computer name and workgroup. These settings determine how your system will register itself on the network and how it will receive browse lists. Finally, you need to configure who you log in to the network as—and where you log in. Clicking the Startup button will present you with the screen shown in Figure 14.19.

FIGURE 14.19

Startup options

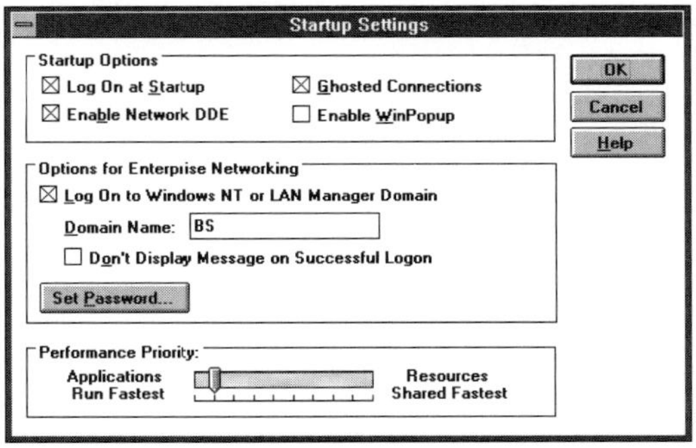

Some key parameters in this window are Log On at Startup, which tells Windows for Workgroups to present you with a logon dialog box before the Program Manager loads your desktop, and Log On to Windows NT or LAN Manager Domain. The latter option allows you to specify which domain you want to be authenticated in.

NOTE *Windows for Workgroups will require the NetBIOS name of the domain—BS, in my case—and will not be able to use the fully qualified BS.COM.*

Attaching to the Network

Now that your Windows for Workgroups client is configured, you need to log in to the domain and connect to your resources. Logging in with Windows for Workgroups is a little different and a bit more simplistic than it is with its bigger brothers Windows 9*x*, NT, and 2000. The desktop—Program Manager in this case—is not tied in to any user-specific information like the Windows Explorer is. Every user who logs in to a Windows for Workgroups machine—and those who do not log in at all—receives the same program groups, desktop, and program settings. User profiles simply do not exist. What does this mean to Windows for Workgroups? You can log in and out from within the Program Manager or the Network program group, or (if you checked the Log On at Startup option) you can restart Windows to get the same old familiar logon box with fields for username, password, and domain.

After you log in, you can go to the File Manager and find a new set of commands in your menu bar: Connect To and Disconnect Network Drive. Selecting these will bring up a dialog box like the one shown in Figure 14.20. In it, you can browse the network for available shares, or type in a share name. Once connected, the drive will show up in your File Manager window, and you can go to work.

NOTE *Sorry, but you can't view or access Active Directory information with a Windows for Workgroups client.*

One of the limitations of Windows for Workgroups clients is that they can't run commands via full UNC names. If I have a share on my server named \\BS01\Install that contains a batch file named `setup.bat`, I can't simply run a new command line of \\BS01\Install\`setup.bat`. Instead, I have to map a drive—I'll call it Z:—to \\BS01\, install, then launch Z:\`setup.bat`.

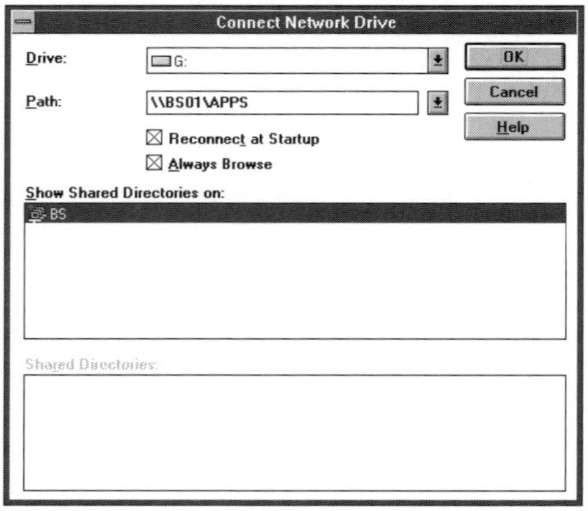

FIGURE 14.20

The Connect Network Drive dialog box

Connecting DOS Workstations

Now we enter into the realm of the forgotten GUI-less operating system: DOS. You may recall that in the days of Windows NT 3.*x* and 4.0, we had two convenient, or at least semi-convenient, tools at our disposal. The first was the MSCLIENT, a built-in DOS client. The second was the Network Client Administrator utility, which allowed us to make DOS-based, network-bootable floppy diskettes that helped us connect to our installation source. Needless to say, both of those little tools are gone with Windows 2000. Why? Well, there are a couple of reasons. Probably in the forefront of Microsoft's mind is the simple little fact that DOS is no longer a "supported" operating system. By not "supported," I mean that if you decide to burn up a handful of extra money to call up the Microsoft support folks and tell them that you are having problems connecting your DOS workstations to a Windows 2000 server, then you will find that the satisfaction of burning extra money is all you get. Another reason for the lack of DOS tools on the Windows 2000 Server CD is that there are new and improved installation methods. You used to not be able to pop in a CD, reboot your machine, and have the CD fire up an install. Instead, you had to boot to a DOS diskette with CD or network drivers and then connect to your install source. You also now have more capable installation methods: You don't need to wipe a machine clean before trying to do an install. You can instead put faith in an upgrade—that is, when you are upgrading from one *supported* operating system to Windows 2000 Server. In short, the inclusion of DOS tools on the CD is merely for the purposes of launching an install. That's it. They aren't there so you can run around the office and set up all the workstations as DOS-only machines. With that being said, you still have options in this department of install. You can boot to the CD, you can create setup boot floppies, you can launch the install from an existing operating system, etc.

NOTE *See Chapter 4 for more details on connecting to and launching the Setup program.*

Now comes our other problem: connecting to our installation source covers only half of our need to have DOS on hand, and doesn't do anything for the real issue we face. The real issue is connecting clients to Windows 2000 servers. Again, Windows 2000 Server doesn't come with a handy utility to create your DOS installation or even your DOS network driver installation, so if you absolutely *must* have a prepackaged DOS installation, you are going to need to get your hands on an NT 4.0 Server CD. To summarize a DOS installation ready for networking, you have at least three components:

- A `config.sys` that loads a driver for your network card

- An `autoexec.bat` or `config.sys` that loads a program to handle networking functions

- A command-line utility that executes network commands, like `net.exe`

What we are going to focus on is the third component, the `net.exe` program.

NOTE *Actually, I have found that a lot of people don't realize that NET is a self-standing utility. They type* **net use** *and* **net view** *and all sorts of* net *commands all day, but fail to see how it really works.* net *simply calls up your network program, while the next parameter, like* use, *is the function you want to perform. Next, depending upon the function called, are parameters to tell the function where or on what to perform that function. Understand that* net *is a simple command-line utility, and everything else is a little less confusing.*

In DOS, we will focus on three major functions of the `net` command. First and foremost is `logon`. This actually logs you in to your domain. For me, to log in with my user credentials as identified in the beginning of this chapter, I type **net logon bsmith /domain:bs**. What I am doing is logging in as BSMITH, in the domain BS. Be careful, though: the domain entry is the downlevel domain name, not the new, fully qualified domain name of BS.COM—DOS doesn't recognize those types of domain names.

The next function is `view`. The `net view` statement is more important for DOS clients than for any other. This is because DOS has no browser to show you a nice, neat list of resources across your network. Instead, you have to manually find them with `net view` commands. You have two ways to focus your `view`. First is at the domain. For me, typing **net view /domain:bs** will provide a list of servers that are registered on the BS domain. From that list, you can focus your `view` at each individual server for a list of shared resources. If I want to see all shares on my server—BS01—I would type **net view \\bs01**.

Now we've found our target share, which is APPS under BS01, and we need to connect to it. You can't really make much use of programs and printers via a `net` interface, so you need an actual drive letter or printer port connection. Enter `use`. If I want to map the G: drive to the above listed server and share, I type **net use g: \\bs01\apps**. This must be in the UNC format of *servername**share*. Similarly, if I want to map my LPT1 printer port to a printer shared from BS01 as CANON, I would type **net use lpt1: \\bs01\canon**.

There are also some other `net` functions worth mentioning. `net logoff` logs you off the domain you logged into. `net time \\bs01` synchronizes my computer clock with that on the server BS01. `net password /domain:bs bsmith old new` changes my BSMITH account password on the BS domain from old to new.

That's really all there is to it. Sure, you may only deal with DOS workstations about once for every thousand workstations you visit, but there is still some good foundation knowledge hiding inside that little black box known as the DOS prompt. I hate to say it, but all those fancy little buttons and browse lists just combine the different functions of the native `net.exe` command into a simple user-friendly environment. Make certain that you know how to connect to your network with a DOS workstation—it will always be your lowest common denominator and can come in handy when you're stuck. Besides, would you rather have a command prompt or a wizard?

Chapter 15

Supporting Clients with Windows Terminal Services

MULTIUSER WINDOWS, SERVER-BASED COMPUTING, thin client computing—whatever you call it, it's part of Windows 2000's server line. Multiuser Windows has been around for quite a while. Citrix created MultiWin, the set of extensions to Windows NT that enables it to run multiple user sessions from the same machine. The first MultiWin product was multiuser NT 3.51, Citrix's WinFrame. Starting in July 1998, Microsoft began shipping its Terminal Server Edition of NT 4 (TSE).

So, the support for Terminal Services in Win2K Server isn't new. What *is* new about multiuser support in Win2K is that this is the first time that support for server-based computing has been an intrinsic part of the Windows Server operating system. Terminal Services is now something you can turn on or off as needed, making it just one more handy tool in the operating system like Remote Installation Services or Internet Information Services.

Installing Terminal Services on a Windows 2000 server is easy. Creating a working terminal server capable of supporting multiple users, all running different applications and wanting to use their client-side resources, may not be. You'll need to do a fair amount of tweaking once you get past the basic step of running Notepad from the terminal server. If you're serious about administering a terminal server, I *highly* recommend you make the Terminal Services section of the Microsoft Knowledge Base your favorite pleasure reading because this is relatively new territory to Microsoft and it's still working the bugs out. This chapter will do all the basic legwork for you, however.

Why Care about Terminal Services?

Terminal Services gives you secure remote access to a computer and requires little enough bandwidth that you can use it over low-speed connections. So?

The first reason to care about Terminal Services applies to anyone using Windows 2000 Server, not just people wanting to support an application server. Terminal Services has two modes: Remote Administration (the default) and Application Server (which I'll concentrate on in this chapter). Remote Administration enables you to manage Windows 2000 Server computers from across a network, without limiting your access to tools within the Microsoft Management

Console (MMC) or even requiring you to use Windows 2000 as the operating system. If you don't use Terminal Services for anything else, use it for managing servers without having to physically move from console to console. Turn to the section "Using Remote Administration Mode" to read more about the requirements for remote management access.

NOTE   *With the newest generation of Windows, Microsoft seems to have really caught onto the potential of Terminal Services. In the preliminary versions of .NET Server, Terminal Services is enabled for Remote Administration mode by default. Even Windows XP has a limited Terminal Services capability called Remote Desktop. Only one person can use a Windows XP computer at a time, but that person can be either working at the computer's console or connecting across the Terminal Services connection.*

In this chapter, however, I'll focus on how you can use Application Server mode—the "terminal server" part of Terminal Services—to support clients. If any of the following are important to you, then seriously consider how you could use Application Server mode:

◆ Simplifying application deployment and management

◆ Reducing the impact of hardware failures or misconfigured computers that keep people from working

◆ Getting out of the hardware rat race that constantly requires more updates to support the latest and greatest software

◆ Using computers in environments that are not compatible with desktop computers

◆ Simplified help desk and training support

Centralized Deployment of Applications

One great benefit to Terminal Services is how it simplifies application deployment to the clients. Windows 2000 Server has some application deployment tools in the form of group policy objects (GPOs), and Chapter 9 discusses those tools in detail. If you use GPOs to deploy applications to the Desktop you can create packages that enable you to run applications on the client computer while making those applications "maintainable" from a central point. GPOs have their failings, however. First, you can't use GPOs with just any Win32 operating system; instead you must use Windows 2000 Professional or Windows XP clients. Second, setting up GPOs effectively is not necessarily a simple matter. Third, you can't always use GPOs to deploy applications across a low-bandwidth network connection well—the application packages may not be small. Finally, all these factors make GPOs a questionable method of application deployment for any applications that need to be updated frequently (as some database clients do). The more often you need to deploy an application across the network, the greater the chance something weird will happen along the way. (The technical term for the time between unexpected and inexplicable failures is *Mean Time Between Weirdness*—MTBW—and the concept is probably familiar to you.)

Using Terminal Services to deploy applications has its own difficulties—namely, getting all the applications and all the users to play nicely in the same space—but it avoids the problems and limitations associated with GPOs. For example, when you update an application installed on a terminal server, it's instantly updated for everyone using that server. Any operating system that has a Remote

Desktop Protocol (RDP) client (and, these days, that can include Macintosh and Linux clients as well as Win32) can use the terminal server, so you're not limited to deploying applications to the higher-end clients. A Terminal Services connection requires little bandwidth, so you can use it on busy or slow network connections. And, because you're not actually sending applications or data across the network or installing applications on the clients, the MTBW rating for clients using Terminal Services is low—so long as nothing changes and it's working right in the first place.

Running applications on a terminal server is not a trouble-free process; getting things set up properly and keeping people from fiddling with the terminal server can be tricky. Some applications won't work at all in a multiuser environment. And in case you thought installing applications on a terminal server meant you could support many users with a single license, think again—you'll still need to pay for application licensing for each user or computer connecting to the applications published on the terminal server. However, this basic fact remains true: Set a compatible application up once on the terminal server, and its updates are available to everyone who has access to the terminal server, without the need for any changes to the client.

Supporting PC-Unfriendly Environments

The dream of "a PC on every desktop" will remain a dream, if for no other reason than in some environments the conditions are bad for the PC or the PC is bad for the conditions. In other words, you can't run a PC everywhere.

First, there are environments that are bad for PCs. PCs do not like dust, excessive heat, or vibration, and *you* will not like maintaining the PCs if you try to use them in an environment that has any of these characteristics. PCs are also a commodity item; if you leave them unattended and unguarded where just anyone can get to them, they will disappear. For these reasons, Windows terminals are becoming a popular choice in environments that are PC-unfriendly but still need access to Windows applications. Warehouses and unattended trucker kiosks (where the truckers can log in to display and print their shipping orders from a terminal) are two good examples of how to use Windows terminals in PC-unfriendly environments. I've also seen terminals in health club cafés and coffeehouses set up so that only the monitor is visible, thus reducing the chances of someone dropping a strawberry-banana low-fat smoothie with a shot of wheatgrass juice down the vents. For that matter, if someone does drop said smoothie down the terminal's vents, then, because the applications are installed on and running from the terminal server, replacing the device to provide an identical environment is as simple as unplugging the sticky terminal and plugging in a new one. If you drop the smoothie down a computer's vents, then restoring an identical working environment is significantly more complicated.

What about PCs being bad for the conditions? Clean rooms where chips and boards are made are good candidates for Windows terminals. You can't have dust in a clean room, and the fans in a PC kick up dust. Additionally, becoming sanitized to enter a clean room is neither simple nor inexpensive; you don't want to put devices that need care and feeding from the IT staff in there. Another factor applies to many situations, not just clean rooms: Anyplace where space is at a premium is a good candidate for Windows terminals.

This section isn't to sell you on the idea of Windows terminals but to point out that sometimes they're useful—and you can't use them without a terminal server.

POWER STRUGGLES

Another aspect of the environment-unfriendly PC applies to the power a desktop PC uses. Inspired by the California energy crises of 2000 and 2001, my cohort Steve Greenberg and I did a couple of lab and real-world studies to see how desktop-centric computing and server-based computing compared in terms of power usage. What we found was sobering: A server-based computing network required less power to provide application support than did a desktop-centric environment, even when the client computers for accessing the terminal server were desktop computers instead of terminals. In fact, the Windows terminals used so little power that the use of terminals increased the difference dramatically.

If you're interested in the results of our research, you can download the main study at www.thin-client.net (look in the "What's New" section for the link), but here are the highlights: The desktop PCs we tested had a constant power draw of about 85 watts when running applications locally (excluding a 15" CRT monitor, which drew an additional 85 watts). Running applications from a terminal server, the desktop PC power usage dropped to 69 watts—not a big difference on a small scale, but this difference increases as the network grows. The terminals we tested drew less than 10 watts, or 24 watts with a built-in LCD display. If you're assuming (as many did) that the power use of the terminal server was great enough to offset the gains realized by using server-based computing, think again. Although a terminal server used an average of 141 watts in our testing (the power draw fluctuated depending on how many people were using it), a terminal server can support many clients, so its greater power draw is offset by the number of people it's supporting.

The power savings realized become more dramatic as the network gets larger—and as power gets more expensive. If you'd like to figure out how much you're spending on power, then calculate the result of $n*p*h*52$ to get the number of kilowatts (kW) your client computers use each year, where n is the number of desktop devices, p is the power (in kW) used by each device, h is the number of hours each week that the devices are turned on, and 52 is the number of weeks in a year. For example, say your network has 5,000 client computers, each powered on 50 hours a week. If the 5,000 clients are PCs with CRT displays running applications locally (.17kW), then they'll use 5000*1.7kW*50*52, or 2,210,000 kW each year. If the 5,000 clients are thin clients with integrated LCD panels (.024kW), they'll use 5000*.024kW*50*52, or 31,200kW each year. Say those 5000 thin clients need 200 servers (.141kW) to support them, and those servers are on 24/7. In that case, the calculation is 200*.141kW*168*52, or 246,355.2, giving you a total of 277,555.2kW.

Based on these calculations, at 0.20 per kW, serving applications with the PC network costs $442,000 to run each year. Serving applications via a thin client network—with servers on all the time—costs $55,511.04. And we haven't even begun to talk about other aspects of Total Cost of Ownership or the investment required to keep IT hardware up and running. Nor have we talked about how reducing power usage reduces power costs because dissipating two units of heat (generated by power-sucking devices—put your hand on a CRT lately?) requires one unit of energy.

Saving on power costs is not the only reason to use Windows terminals, but, if you're tossing around the idea of replacing PCs with terminals, it's a compelling argument in favor of it.

Less Processing Power Required on the Client

First, about those ever-more-powerful computers: Does it take a 2GHz Pentium II with 256MB of RAM installed to check e-mail, do accounting, and poke around on the Web a bit? Of course it doesn't, but, as of late 2001, that's not an unusual hardware profile for a desktop computer. Not that these computers are too expensive in absolute terms; I'm wryly amused that every time I buy a new computer, I pay less for a system more powerful than the last one I bought. But although they're not too expensive in absolute terms, the new computers aren't always worth it because what you're doing doesn't demand all that much from your hardware. Ironically, unless your job is something demanding such as computer-assisted design, you're often more likely to need a powerful computer at home than at work because game hardware requirements are so high. It takes more computing power to play a few swift rounds of Diablo II than it does to write this chapter. (Fighting demons is hard work!)

The trouble is, sometimes you do need those more powerful computers if you're planning to keep up with existing software technology. True—you don't need the world's fastest computer to do word processing. You may, however, need a computer faster than the one you have if you're going to keep up with the latest and greatest word processing package that everyone's using. If you want to be able to read all those charts and graphs, you can't always do it when the word processor you're using is six years old, even if it still suits your in-house needs. Trouble is, if your computer is also six years old, you may not be able to run the newest word processor. This is annoying. Keeping up with those new hardware requirements can get expensive and time consuming. But making new software work on old hardware can be just as much of a headache when you discover that although that old Pentium is still as fast as you need, it won't run Win2K Professional.

If you're using Terminal Services to support applications, the client only displays applications running on the terminal server, rather than running them locally—you don't have to concern yourself with whether the applications will run on the client computer, just the server. If the application will run on the terminal server, then it will display on the client. As I'll discuss in this chapter, you may need to tweak an application to make it run *well* on the terminal server and some applications won't run well at all, but you can use Terminal Services to get an application to a computer that would not normally support it.

Simplifying the User Interface

Another potential benefit to Terminal Services is it can simplify the user interface (UI). I'm not sure why Microsoft keeps talking about how using a computer is getting easier and easier. Speaking as the favorite source of free tech support for my parents (and some of my friends and *their* parents), I, for one, am not buying this idea. Experienced users may find it easier to customize their interface, but those who are less experienced find all sorts of pitfalls when it comes to using their computers: so many options that they get confused and too many ways to break something. Colorful icons with rounded corners do not a simple UI make.

Terminal Services does not automatically make the UI simpler. In fact, to use Terminal Services effectively, you'll need to make sure you've locked down the user environment pretty securely because many people will be using the same computer and one deleted file can screw up a lot of people. But, as I'll explain later in this chapter, it's possible to run either a complete desktop from a terminal server or a single application. If the people you're supporting only need a single application, then you can save yourself and them a lot of grief by providing a connection that runs it and nothing else. This is particularly true with Windows-based terminals, which are little more than a monitor, a box, a keyboard, and mouse.

Providing Help Desk Support

Finally, Terminal Services can make application support easier, not just in terms of installing new applications and applying fixes but in helping people learn to use those applications. Windows 2000 Terminal Services supports a feature called Remote Control that you can use to connect to another person's terminal session. (This isn't the security hole it may seem—you must have permission to do this, and by default the person to whom you're connecting has to permit the connection before you can see their screen.) When you have remote control of another user's session, you can either watch what they're doing and coach them (perhaps over the telephone) or actually interact with the session so that you can demonstrate something. This beats standing over someone's shoulder saying, "Click the File button at the top left. No, *File*. The FILE button..." or trying to figure out what they're doing when your only information comes from their description of the screen. I'll talk more about how to use Remote Control later in this chapter.

The Terminal Server Processing Model

Regardless of whether you're using TSE, Windows 2000 Terminal Services, or MetaFrame, in a broad sense they all work pretty much the same way. *Thin client networking* or *server-based computing* (same thing, different emphasis) refers to any computing environment in which most application processing takes place on a server enabled for multiuser access, instead of a client. The terms refer to a network by definition, so it leaves out stand-alone small computing devices such as personal digital assistants (PDAs) or handheld PCs, although you can add thin client support to some of these devices. What makes thin client networking and computing "thin" is neither the size of the operating system nor the complexity of the apps run on the client, but how processing is distributed. In a thin client network, all processing takes place on the server, instructions for creating video output travel from server to client, and all video output is rendered on the client.

You may have heard thin client networking described as *a return to the mainframe paradigm.* (I have heard this less politely phrased as "You just reinvented the mainframe, stupid!" Sheesh.) This comparison is partly apt and partly misleading. It's true that applications are stored and run on a central server, with only output shown at the client. However, the applications being run in the thin client environment are different from those run in a mainframe environment; mainframes didn't support word processing or slideshow packages, and the video demands on the graphical Windows client are necessarily greater than they were with a text-based green-screen terminal. Yet the degree of control that thin client networking offers is mainframe-like, and I've heard one person happily describe thin client networking and the command it gave him over his user base as "a return to the good old mainframe days."

Why the move from centralized computing to personal computers and back again? Business applications drove the development of PCs—the new applications simply couldn't work in a mainframe environment. Not all mainframes were scrapped, by any means, but the newer application designs were too hardware-intensive to work well in a shared computing environment. But those applications came back to a centralized model when it became clear that the mainframe model had some things to offer that a PC-based LAN did not:

- Grouping of computing resources to make sure none are wasted

- Centralized distribution and maintenance of applications

- Clients that don't have to be running the latest and greatest operating system with the latest and greatest hardware to support it

- Client machines that don't require power protection because they're not running any applications locally

All in all, reinventing the mainframe has its advantages.

Anatomy of a Thin Client Session

A thin client networking session has three parts:

- The *terminal server*, running a multiuser operating system

- The *display protocol*, which is a data link layer protocol that creates a virtual channel between server and client through which user input and graphical output can flow

- The *client*, which can be running any kind of operating system that supports the terminal client

THE TERMINAL SERVER

In Win2K Server, Terminal Services is one of the optional components you can choose to install during Setup, similar to Transaction Services or Internet Information Services. If you've enabled Terminal Services, then when Win2K boots up and loads the core operating system, the terminal service begins listening at TCP port 3389 for incoming client connection requests.

TIP Because Terminal Services is essential to the operation of a terminal server, you can't shut this service down. If you try it from the command line with the `net stop termserv` *command, you'll get an error. Click the service in the Services section of the Computer Management tool, and you'll see that the options to pause or stop the service are grayed out in the context menu. If you want to keep people from logging onto the terminal server for a while (perhaps while you're doing maintenance on it), then open the Terminal Services Configuration tool and disable RDP. This will end any current connections and prevent anyone else from logging on until you enable the display protocol again.*

Understanding Sessions

When a client requests a connection to the server and the server accepts the request, the client's unique view of the terminal server is called its *session*. In order to start these sessions as quickly as possible, the terminal server creates two dormant sessions. When clients connect to the dormant sessions, Terminal Services will create more dormant sessions so that it's always got two ready to go. In addition to the remote sessions, a special client session for the console (that is, the interface available from the terminal server itself) is created.

NOTE Some have asked if there's any way to make Windows 2000 Professional multiuser. Nope—no Microsoft desktop operating system supports full-fledged Terminal Services, and there is no way to add it. Even Windows XP, which has the Remote Desktop feature that allows someone to connect to the computer via the RDP display protocol, can only support one connection at a time—console or terminal session. The Terminal Services I discuss in this chapter is solely a Server-class feature.

All sessions have unique Session IDs that Windows 2000 uses to distinguish the processes (roughly equivalent to executable files) running within different terminal sessions on the same computer. The console session is assigned Session ID 0. When a client connects to the terminal server, the Virtual Memory Manager in Win2K generates a new Session ID for the session and passes it to the Session Manager once the SessionSpace for that session has been created.

Every session, whether displaying an entire Desktop or a single application, runs the processes shown in Table 15.1.

NOTE *In NT and Win2K, an executable file is internally known as an* image. *This is because, technically speaking, an application isn't the piece getting CPU cycles but instead is a collection of commands called* threads *that get CPU time to do whatever they need to do. The threads have an executing environment called the* process *that tells them where to store and retrieve their data. You don't really have to worry about these details except to understand what these processes and images the administration tool refers to are. Technically speaking, a process is an environment for the parts of an application that run, not an executable component itself. The EXE is the executable image of this process—the part that includes the code that needs processor cycles. For the sake of consistency with the interface, I'll refer to programs running on the terminal server as* processes.

TABLE 15.1: PROCESSES COMMON TO TERMINAL SERVICES SESSIONS

COMPONENT	FUNCTION
Win32 Subsystem	Win32 subsystem required for running Win32 applications (including the Win2K GUI).
User Authentication Module	Logon process responsible for capturing username and password information and passing it to the security subsystem for authentication.
Executable Environment for Applications	All Win32 user applications and virtual DOS machines run in the context of the user shell.

The other processes in the session will depend on the applications the user is running. The crucial points to be learned from this are that every session has its own copy of the Win32 subsystem (so it has a unique Desktop and unique instances of the processes that support the Desktop) and its own copy of the WinLogon application that authenticates user identity. In practical terms, what this means is that every separate session a single person runs on the terminal server is using memory to support these basic files. I said earlier that you could set up terminal sessions that display only single applications—no Desktop. The flip side of this convenience is that supplying a full suite of applications connected separately requires a lot more memory on the terminal server than supplying all those applications from a single Desktop in a terminal session. That is, if you create one session to use Microsoft Word, one session to use Outlook, one session to use AutoCAD, and one session to use Solitaire, this will place a heavier strain on the server than running all those applications from a single Desktop session.

NOTE *Win2K Terminal Services are more parsimonious with memory allocation than TSE was. The amount of memory reserved for the SessionSpace has been reduced from 80MB to 60MB, and the per-session mapped views have been reduced from 48MB in TSE to 20MB in Win2K. This is a Good Thing—greater efficiency in memory allocation means support for more users, all else being equal.*

The terminal session keeps per-session processes from corrupting each other or viewing each other's data. However, although the sessions are allowed to ignore each other, they still have to coexist. All sessions use the same resources—processor time, memory, operating system functions—so the operating system must divide the use of these resources among all of the sessions while keeping them separate. To do so, Windows 2000 identifies the processes initiated in each session not only by their Process ID but by their Session ID as well. Each session has a high-priority thread reserved for keyboard and mouse input and display output, but ordinary applications run at the priority they'd have in a single-user environment. Because all session threads have the same priority, the scheduler processes user input in round-robin format, with each session's input thread having a certain amount of time to process data before control of the processor passes to another user thread. The more active sessions, the greater the competition for processor time.

The number of sessions a terminal server can support depends on how many sessions the hardware (generally memory but also processor time, network bandwidth, and disk access) can support and how many licenses are available. When a client logs out of his session, the virtual channels to that client machine close and the resources allocated to that session are released.

Memory Sharing on a Terminal Server

Win2K does not necessarily have to run a separate copy of each application used in each session. When you start an application, you're loading certain data into memory. For example, say that running WordMangler loads files A–E into memory. If you start a second instance of WordMangler, is it really necessary to load a second instance of all those files into memory? You could do this, but as more and more sessions started up on the terminal server the duplicated DLLs and EXEs would cause the server to quickly run out of memory. But if you let all instances of WordMangler use the same copies of A–E, then if one instance needs to change a file that's in use, all other instances will be affected. To get around the wasted-space/data-corruption dilemma, Win2K uses *copy-on-write* data sharing. "Helper files" are available on a read-only basis to as many applications that need them and are able to reference them. Let an application *write* to that data, however, and the memory manager will copy the edited data to a new location for that application's exclusive use. Copy-on-write works on any NT-based operating system, not just a terminal server, but because terminal servers are likely to be running multiple copies of the same application simultaneously, they greatly benefit from this memory-sharing technique.

The catch to copy-on-write is that only 32-bit applications really benefit from it. The reason for this has to do with how 16-bit applications run in a 32-bit operating system. Namely, they don't: To run a 16-bit application, NT-based operating systems have to create a 32-bit operating environment called a *NT virtual DOS machine* (NTVDM) that contains the 16-bit application. The NTVDMs can do copy-on-write data sharing, but the 16-bit applications they're hosting cannot. Therefore, all else being equal, Win16 and DOS applications will use more memory than Win32 applications.

THE REMOTE DESKTOP PROTOCOL

You can run all the sessions you like on the terminal server, but that won't do you any good unless you can view the session output from a remote computer and upload your input to the terminal server for processing. The mechanism that allows you to do both is the *display protocol.*

How RDP Works

A display protocol downloads instructions for rendering graphical images from the terminal server to the client and uploads keyboard and mouse input from the client to the server. Win2K natively supports the Remote Desktop Protocol (RDP) version 5, and with Citrix's MetaFrame add-on to Terminal Services, it supports the Independent Computing Architecture (ICA) protocol. RDP is based on the T.120 protocol originally developed for Net Meeting, and as such has some theoretical capabilities that aren't realized in the release product. The way it's implemented now, the RDP client that comes with Win2K Server provides a point-to-point connection dependent on TCP/IP that displays the Windows 2000 Server Desktop or a single application on the Desktop of a client running RDP.

NOTE *Yes, you can run multiple sessions from a single client and even multiple sessions for a single user (although for reasons of profile maintenance and memory usage, this may not be the best plan—I'll get into this later). However, each session is still a point-to-point connection rather than a one-to-many connection such as that possible with Citrix MetaFrame's Seamless Windows connection.*

The processing demands placed on the client are reduced by two factors. First, the display protocol only supports up to 256 colors, so the demands on the video card won't be all that great. As you can see from the "Will the Real RDP Please Stand Up?" sidebar, this will change with .NET Server, but you will be able to reduce this color depth for less capable clients and low-bandwidth connections. Second, RDP has a feature called *client-side caching* that allows the client to "remember" images that have already been downloaded during the session. With caching, only the changed parts of the screen are downloaded to the client during each refresh. For example, if the Microsoft Word icon has already been downloaded to the client, there's no need for it to be downloaded again as the image of the Desktop is updated. The hard disk's cache stores data for a limited amount of time and then eventually discards data using the Least Recently Used (LRU) algorithm. When the cache gets full, it discards the data that has been unused the longest in favor of new data.

NOTE *In Win2K, the image on the screen is updated about 20 times per second when the session is active. If the person logged in to the session stops sending mouse clicks and keystrokes to the server, then the terminal server notes the inactivity and reduces the refresh rate to 10 times per second until client activity picks up again.*

Note that in addition to each client session, there's also a session for the server's use. All locally run services and executables run within the context of this server session.

Understanding RDP Channels

The way that the Desktop or single application in a terminal session look and interact with the client's computer depends on the *channels* used in the display protocol. Channels work like roads between two locations in that they must be open on *both sides* to work. For example, Route 29 in Virginia presents a straight shot between two cities: Charlottesville and Gainesville. If either Gainesville or Charlottesville shut down their end of the road—in other words, if the road became unavailable on either side—then traffic could no longer travel along that road. It doesn't matter that Gainesville's end is open if Charlottesville is closed. Channels work the same way: They're like roads between the terminal server and the client. If the road is not available on one side, it does not matter if it's available on the other.

The capabilities of any one version of RDP are entirely dependent on what channels that version exploits. RDP has room for lots of channels for doing different things, and each version of RDP enables more of them. Because it uses more of its channels, RDP in Win2K has features that were not supported in TSE's implementation of RDP. The Clipboard now works between local and remote applications, so you can copy text from the copy of Microsoft Word running on the terminal server to your local instance of Notepad. RDP5 supports client-printer mapping, which allows client-side printers to become available from a terminal session without the client having to share them with the network and connect to them from the terminal session. (This mapping is automatic for Win32 clients; you can set it up manually for Win16 clients.) To speed screen redraws over slow links, RDP5 improves *bitmap caching*, which stores frequently used bitmaps in a cache on the client so that the client can draw from its local cache instead of getting the updates from the server. (This is helpful over dial-up connections and other slow links, but it's limited to PC clients because the cache resides on a hard disk.) Finally, as I mentioned earlier, RDP5 supports *remote control* (what Citrix and the Win2K command line calls *session shadowing*), which enables you to take control of someone else's terminal session and either see what they're doing or manipulate the Desktop for them, all from another terminal session. All these capabilities—shared Clipboard, remote control, printer mapping, and so forth—are enabled through the use of channels. To get the full feature set, you must have RDP5 support on both client and server ends. Therefore, if you install the RDP5 client on a computer but connect to a TSE terminal server, only those channels that RDP4 uses will be available to the connection. Figure 15.1 shows how the use of channels enables Microsoft to add more features to the existing display protocol but also limits the connection's capabilities to the least common denominator.

NOTE *Although you can update the RDP client component by downloading the latest client from the Microsoft Web site or getting it from the Setup CD for Windows XP, you cannot update the RDP server component that goes on the terminal server. There is no way to make a TSE terminal server's RDP component as capable as a Windows 2000 terminal server, or a Windows 2000 terminal server as capable as a .NET Server terminal server (see the "Will the Real RDP Please Stand Up?" sidebar).*

FIGURE 15.1

RDP is a collection of channels conveying data between the terminal server and terminal client.

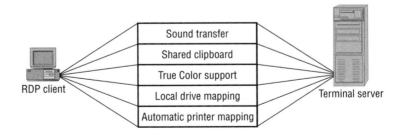

Notice something about channels: The more capable the RDP version—that is, the more channels it uses—the more bandwidth is required to support those channels. Just because each version of RDP is written more efficiently than its predecessors, this doesn't mean TSE connections are more responsive than sessions using Windows XP's Remote Desktop. In fact, quite the opposite is true—the most recent version of RDP is pretty snappy. However, the more channels your RDP connection is using, the more bandwidth they'll need. Therefore, you will not always want to enable all these channels. I'll show you how to selectively enable and disable them in the course of this chapter.

WILL THE REAL RDP PLEASE STAND UP?

Windows 2000 Terminal Services comes with an RDP client. You can download something called the Terminal Services Advanced Client (TSAC) from Microsoft's Web site. Also available for download is something called the Remote Desktop. Which version is which, and which one do you want?

Microsoft released its first version of multiuser Windows in July 1998 with its Windows NT, Terminal Server Edition (TSE). TSE had basic functionality but frankly wasn't all that when it came to supporting users. If you wanted support for client-side mapped printers or hard drives, applications published as part of a Web page, remote control of user sessions, or a Clipboard shared between remote and local applications so you could cut and paste text between the two, you needed an add-on product—almost inevitably Citrix MetaFrame.

With Windows 2000, RDP became a lot more capable. When supporting Windows 2000 Terminal Services, you should worry about three potential RDP clients. First, there's the one that comes with Windows 2000 Terminal Services and, if you choose to install the client software with the service, is stored on the terminal server in \system32\clients\tsclient\win32\disks\disk1. (That's the path for the Win32 RDP client. If you happen to have Windows for Workgroups around, then install the Win16 client located in the folder of the same name.) Run Setup.exe on client computers to install this RDP client.

TSAC, which you may have heard about, came out after Windows 2000 did. Capability-wise, it's identical to the RDP client that installs with Windows 2000 Terminal Services, but its packaging is a little different. The TSAC Web Package is an ActiveX control you can use to initiate and run terminal sessions from within Internet Explorer (IE), and it includes a downloadable ActiveX control and sample Web pages you can use as a starting point for running Windows-based programs inside IE. Available from the same Web page as the TSAC are the Terminal Services Connections MMC snap-in, which you can use to run terminal sessions from within the MMC (and thus more easily manage servers running Terminal Services in Remote Administration mode), and the Terminal Services Full Client Windows Installer (MSI) package, which you can use to distribute the RDP client via Intellimirror or Systems Management Server. You can download the TSAC, MMC snap-in, and the MSI packaging of the RDP client from www.microsoft.com/windows2000/downloads/recommended/tsac/default.asp.

Windows XP and .NET Server (the latter is not yet out as of this writing) both have a new version of RDP that is more capable than RDP5 in Windows 2000. The new display protocol supports automatic mapping of client drives to terminal sessions, making it easy to copy and paste files between the client computer and the terminal session. It also supports sound, which at first glance doesn't sound very useful but can be your friend when it comes to training videos with voice-overs and the like. Finally, the new version of RDP supports a maximum color depth of 24-bit True Color, instead of the 256-color maximum that restricted previous versions of RDP and kept some people with color-dependent applications from using Terminal Services. (You can reduce the color depth to fewer colors with the new version of RDP; 24-bit color is just the top end.) Windows XP comes with the RDP client (and, as I said, a limited server capability) built in. You can also download the new client from Microsoft's Web site at www.microsoft.com/windowsxp/pro/downloads/rdclientdl.asp. However, there is one catch to the next generation of RDP. Because the full capabilities of the RDP client depend on the channels between client and server, you currently can only get these full capabilities when connecting to a Windows XP Remote Desktop. Terminal Services clients will have to wait until .NET Server, and its server-side support of the next generation of RDP, becomes available. That said, all versions of RDP are backward compatible, so you never have to worry about having a client or server RDP component that's too advanced to work with humbler versions.

THE CLIENT

So you've got a terminal server running sessions and a display protocol to pass information to and from the sessions. All you're missing now is someone to use the sessions.

A client session is *connected* when a client computer chooses a terminal server from the RDP interface and gets far enough to see the login screen. The session becomes *active* when the user successfully logs onto the domain or onto the terminal server's local account. During this session, client input in the form of mouse clicks and keystrokes is uploaded to the server via a virtual channel. The commands to render bitmaps showing the interface are downloaded to the client via another virtual channel. If client-printer mapping is enabled for the connection, the communication between terminal server application and client-printer takes places along yet another channel. A buffer supports the shared Clipboard data for local and remote sessions, too.

NOTE *Session 0—the console session—does not use the same keyboard and video drivers that client sessions use. Whereas Session 0 uses the Win2K video and keyboard drivers, the client sessions use drivers based in the RDP.*

Once the graphics-rendering instructions download to the client, the client-side CPU and RAM create the images for display. During the course of the session, the user can work on the terminal server as though he or she were physically at the terminal server, using the client machine's keyboard and mouse. As the client runs applications, loads data into memory, and accesses shared resources on the network as though logged on directly (clients are not restricted to accessing the terminal server), the client uses the hardware on the server. The only restrictions on the client are those defined by security settings.

Server and Client Requirements

The computing model for thin client networking means that the horsepower is typically concentrated on the server end, not the client end. Because the server will be supporting a couple of dozen people—maybe more—this is not the time to skimp on power.

Server Hardware

The notion of using a bigger server so that you can skimp on client-side hardware isn't new. That's all a file server is: a computer running a big, fast hard disk so that you don't have to buy big, fast hard disks for everyone in the office. Terminal servers are designed on a similar principle: If most of the processing takes place in a single location, you can concentrate the hardware resources needed to support that processing in a single location and worry less about power on the client end.

CORE HARDWARE RECOMMENDATIONS

For the purposes of running an efficient terminal server, the bare minimum required to run Win2K won't cut it. It was technically possible to run a TSE session from a terminal server with a Pentium 133 and 32MB of RAM—I've done it. It worked fine...so long as only one person wanted to use the terminal server. Although there are no hard and fast specifications for a terminal server, some general guidelines for server sizing follow.

TIP *If you're upgrading a TSE terminal server to Windows 2000 Terminal Services, be sure to allow for the greater demands of the core operating system. Windows 2000 Terminal Services allocates less memory to individual sessions than TSE did, which helps, but Windows 2000 Server is resource-hungry in itself, let alone when a couple of dozen people are using the server at the same time.*

Processor Faster is better…to a point. More important than a fast processor is one with enough cache so that it doesn't have to reach out to the (slower) system memory for code and data. Faced with a choice between more cache and more speed, go with more cache. It's a.good idea to at least *plan* for a multiprocessor computer. Although only multithreaded applications will actually use more than one processor, if there are two processors, then threads needing execution can line up at both. At this point, however, I'd stick with two processors. Processor time is not the only bottleneck in a terminal server and using more servers instead of fewer removes some of the other bottlenecks.

Memory Terminal servers tend to be memory bound, not processor bound. Get high-speed, error-correcting memory, get plenty of it, and be prepared to add more as you add more users or applications to the terminal server. The amount of memory you'll need depends on the applications that people use, the number of concurrent sessions, and the memory demands of the files opened in those sessions—CAD programs will stress the system more than, say, Notepad. Most terminal servers I've seen use from 512MB to 1GB of RAM. Service Pack 2 addresses a number of memory leaks that, although not specific to terminal services, will impact a server that needs all the memory it can get.

Disk Use SCSI disks on a terminal server if at all possible. A SCSI disk controller can multi-task among all the devices in the SCSI chain, unlike an EIDE disk controller that can only work with one device at a time. This is an important capability in any server, and especially so in a terminal server.

Network Even if it were easy to get ISA network cards these days, you'd want to use PCI and its higher data-transfer speeds instead. On a busy terminal server, consider load-balancing network cards, which can assign multiple NICs to the same IP address and thus split the load of network traffic. Another alternative is a multi-homed server with one NIC dedicated to terminal session traffic. So far as network *speed* goes, sending application output and client-side input back and forth requires little bandwidth, but client-print jobs sent to mapped printers can take quite a bit. Mapped drives (for those using Windows XP connections or .NET Server) will also increase the load by making it possible to copy files back and forth across the RDP connection. Be sure to only support client-mapped printers and other bandwidth-intensive features over networks that can handle it, or (particularly important for those using Windows 2000 terminal servers) get helper software to reduce the size of print jobs.

NOTE *Print helper software will also generally remove the need for supporting individual client printers on a terminal server by providing a universal printer driver. However, universal print support is only half the battle—look for compression and reduced bandwidth requirements, as well.*

Video The client display depends on client capabilities, not server capabilities, so client computers will display 256 colors even if the server has a lower color depth.

USING THE SYSTEM MONITOR

The Windows 2000 System Monitor discussed in Chapter 20 can help you get an idea of how test terminal sessions are stressing the server. Server load will scale linearly with the number of people using the server, so as long as you pick a representative group of around five people, you should be able to extrapolate your needs for larger groups. The key objects and counters for measuring general server stress introduced in that chapter will help you size terminal servers, too. But, when you enable Terminal Services on a Windows 2000 Server computer, you'll add a couple of additional System Monitor objects that are worth examining.

First, the Terminal Services object has counters representing the number of active sessions (sessions where the user has connected to the terminal server and successfully logged on), inactive sessions (where the user is still logged onto the terminal server but has stopped using the session), and the total combined. Mostly, this object is useful for keeping track of how many sessions a terminal server has to support. Chapter 20 discusses performance logging and alerts; if you find that a terminal server functions best below a certain number of connections, you could set up an alert log with that threshold and then, if the server breaches that tolerance, use the `change logon /disable` command to disable the server for new connections and send you a message to alert you.

Although you can get some session-level information from the Terminal Services Manager, a performance object called Terminal Services Session provides quite a bit more. Use the Terminal Services Manager to find the session you want to monitor (because they're identified to System Monitor by their session numbers, not user login name) and then add counters to monitor that session. Each session object has processor and memory counters that should look familiar to anyone who's used System Monitor, but it's also got session-specific counters such as the ones in Table 15.2. I haven't included all the counters here, just the ones to show you the kind of information that will be useful when you're calculating the load on the server and looking at the kind of performance the sessions are getting.

NOTE *If you click the Explain button in System Monitor when adding counters, you'll see a description of these counters, but the explanations for counters similar to those found in other performance monitoring objects may have been copied straight from there. Don't worry about this—just substitute session for process.*

TABLE 15.2: KEY TERMINAL SERVICES SESSION SYSTEM MONITOR COUNTERS

COUNTER	DESCRIPTION	SEE ALSO
% Processor Time	Percentage of time that all of the threads in the session used the processor to execute instructions. On multi-processor machines the maximum value of the counter is 100 percent times the number of processors.	
Total Bytes	Total number of bytes sent to and from this session, including all protocol overhead.	Input Bytes, Output Bytes
Total Compressed Bytes	Total number of bytes after compression. Total Compressed Bytes compared with Total Bytes is the compression ratio.	Total Compression Ratio

Continued on next page

TABLE 15.2: KEY TERMINAL SERVICES SESSION SYSTEM MONITOR COUNTERS *(continued)*

COUNTER	DESCRIPTION	SEE ALSO
Total Protocol Cache Hit Ratio	Total hits in all protocol caches holding Windows objects likely to be reused. Hits in the cache represent objects that did not need to be re-sent, so a higher hit ratio implies more cache reuse and possibly a more responsive session.	Protocol Save Screen Bitmap Cache Hit Ratio, Protocol Glyph Cache Hit Ratio, Protocol Brush Cache Hit Ratio
Working Set	Current number of bytes in the Working Set of this session.	Virtual Bytes, Page Faults/Sec

WARNING   When experimenting with terminal sessions to find out how many users you'll be able to support for each session, do not set up a license server; let the terminal server issue its temporary 90-day licenses for this purpose. Although this sounds counterintuitive, using the temporary licenses prevents you from unwittingly assigning per-seat licenses to test equipment. See the "Terminal Services Licensing" section for an explanation of how licensing and license allocation works.

Client Hardware

When connecting to a Win2K terminal server via a native RDP client, you'll use a PC with a Win32 operating system loaded, a Windows terminal, or a handheld PC using Windows CE.

NOTE   In this context, a native RDP client means one available from Microsoft and thus implies Win32 or (rarely) Win16. Although Microsoft does not support other platforms, Hoblink sells a cross-platform (Windows, Mac, Linux, DOS) Java client at `www.hob.de/www_us/produkte/connect/jwt.htm`, *and there is a free Linux RDP client available at* `www.rdesktop.org`.

WINDOWS TERMINALS

In its narrowest definition, a Windows terminal is a network-dependent device running Windows CE that supports one or more display protocols such as RDP or ICA, the display protocol used to connect to MetaFrame servers. Many Windows terminals also support some form of terminal emulation.

NOTE   In this section, a Windows terminal is any terminal device designed to connect to a Windows terminal server; it can run any operating system that's got an RDP client. A Windows-based terminal (WBT) is such a device that's running a Windows operating system locally—CE or (more rarely) Embedded NT—and follows the Microsoft system design requirements for WBTs.

The main thing defining a Windows terminal is its thin hardware profile: Because the main job of most Windows terminals is to run a display protocol, they don't need much memory or processing power, and they don't use any storage. A Windows terminal includes a processor, some amount of memory, network and video support, and input devices: a keyboard (or equivalent) and mouse (or equivalent). The terminals don't generally have hard disks, CD-ROMs, or DVD players. The operating system (these days, Windows CE, one version or another of NT Embedded, or Linux) is stored in local memory. Beyond those similarities, Windows terminals range physically from a "toaster" form factor to a pad to a small box that can attach to the back of a monitor—or even be part of the monitor itself.

Although most Windows terminals are entirely dependent on their terminal server, a small set of them can run applications locally. The devices still don't have hard disks; the applications are stored in ROM like the operating system. The types of applications available depend on the terminal's operating system since locally stored applications must run locally instead of just being displayed. Generally speaking, however, it's more common for Windows terminals to depend on a terminal server for applications.

TIP *That's a quick and dirty definition of Windows terminals. If you're interested in more details and some product reviews, then read "Evaluating Windows Terminals" in the April 2000 issue of* Windows 2000 Magazine.

Windows terminals are most popular in environments where people are using a single application, where supporting PCs would be logistically difficult, or anywhere else that PCs aren't a good fit. However, PCs still outnumber Windows terminals as thin clients, if for no other reasons than that companies already have PCs and taking away a powerful PC to replace it with a less-powerful PC can be a difficult political decision—even for people who don't need a whole PC.

PC CLIENTS

At this point, people are using more than twice as many PCs as Windows terminals for terminal server client machines. This isn't surprising. First, unless they're starting afresh, people already have the PCs. Even though WBTs are a little less expensive than low-end PCs—not much, though—they're still an added cost. Second, not all applications work well in a terminal server environment. It's often best to run some applications from the terminal server and some locally. Unless you're buying new hardware and don't anticipate any need to run applications locally, you're likely to have to work with PCs for at least some of your terminal clients.

To work with Win2K's Terminal Services, the PCs must be running a Win32 operating system, have support for the RDP display protocol installed, and have a live network connection using TCP/IP and a valid IP address.

HANDHELD PCs

I'm surprised that handheld PCs (H/PCs) aren't more popular than they are, given how handy they are and how much time I spend explaining to curious people what mine is. They're a terrific substitute for a laptop—inexpensive, lightweight, and thrifty with their power so that you can actually use them during the entire flight instead of having to give up two hours after takeoff. (You can also use one on a plane without worrying that the person in front of you will suddenly recline their seat and crack your laptop's display.) Usually, they run WinCE and, thus, only WinCE-compatible applications such as Pocket Office. But by downloading and installing the Terminal Services client for handheld PCs and getting network support if it isn't already built in, you can use wired, wireless LAN, or dial-up connections to connect to a terminal server.

NOTE *Because Microsoft rearranges its Web site regularly, there's no use providing a link to the RDP client—it'll be outdated twice by the time you read this. Look in the Downloads section of the WinCE area on* www.microsoft.com; *you should be able to find it there.*

What a handheld PC looks like depends on who makes it. Some (mine among them) look like a laptop's baby brother. Others fold into a little portfolio shape or are a flat tablet. Some devices known as handheld PCs are small pocket-sized deals that are, in my personal opinion, too small to really work on. Some—the ones I prefer—have keyboards; others have only pointers. What all this comes down to is that a handheld PC isn't really in a position to replace a desktop PC. Instead, it's usually used in cooperation with a desktop machine with which it's partnered.

Installing (or Removing) Support for Terminal Services

Terminal Services is one more service you can run under Win2K. As such, you can turn this capability on and off by installing or uninstalling the service. Installing Terminal Services enables the multiuser capabilities of Win2K and adds some administration tools to the Administrative Tools group, and uninstalling the services makes Win2K single-user again and removes the tools. You must reboot after installing or removing support for Terminal Services.

As discussed earlier, with the advent of the TSAC allowing users to connect to the terminal server from a Web browser, installing support for Terminal Services became a two-part job. First, you need to make sure that Terminal Services is installed on the Win2K server. Then you need to add support for the TSAC to that server (along with support for Internet Information Service, if it's not installed already—by default, the IIS is installed on all Windows 2000 servers unless you explicitly choose to not install it).

Adding Core Terminal Server Support

To add Terminal Services to a Win2K server:

1. Open the Add/Remove Programs applet in the Control Panel.

2. Choose Add/Remove Windows Components.

3. From the list available, check the box next to Terminal Services (see Figure 15.2). You do not need to install Terminal Services Licensing on all terminal servers to run terminal sessions, although you'll need to install the licensing tool on *some* Win2K servers in the network to keep track of terminal license use.

FIGURE 15.2

Check the Terminal Services box to enable Win2K's multiuser capabilities.

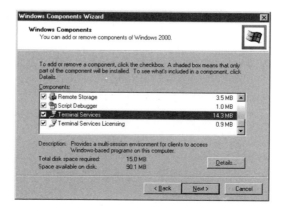

4. If you click the Details button to display the screen shown in Figure 15.3, you'll see that you can install the client creation files and/or the files needed to supply Terminal Services. Check the options you need (both are selected by default) and click OK.

FIGURE 15.3

You can install either the client files or the Terminal Services capabilities, or both.

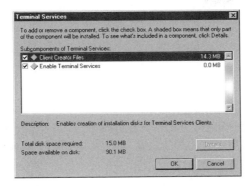

5. Click Next to move to the Terminal Services Setup screen. As you can see in Figure 15.4, you have two choices for setting up Terminal Services. Remote Administration mode allows you to make up to two connections to the Win2K server for administrative purposes only; you can't use these connections to serve applications, and the server will be set up to give equal time to all processes instead of favoring those in the foreground. This is the default option. Application server mode is the mode of Terminal Services I'll talk about in the course of this chapter, and the one you'll need to choose to permit users to run applications from the terminal server. Choose the option you want and click Next.

TIP   You might install Terminal Services in Remote Administration mode on a server you want people to use as a work area in one instance: small-time development. That is, you could create a Windows 2000 server to act as a development platform for up to two people at a time, so long as you do not mind those people having Administrator-level access to the computer.

FIGURE 15.4

Win2K allows you to install Terminal Services either for administrative purposes or for supporting client application needs.

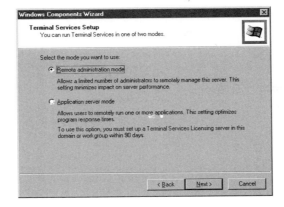

TIP   *Choose wisely. The modes do not run in parallel (which, sadly, means that to manage a terminal server from a session, you have to use up a TSCAL) and to change modes you have to reinstall the service.*

6. Choose the security context you want to use for Terminal Services (see Figure 15.5). This is one of the less intuitive parts of installing Terminal Services. Basically, this screen is asking is whether you want to allow applications full access to system files (in case they need to change them while running) or read-only access. If you're not sure, then pick Permissions Compatible with Windows 2000 Users, which allows only read-only access to system files. If the applications won't run, you can always change the security settings from the Terminal Services Configuration tool.

FIGURE 15.5

Choose how securely to grant permissions.

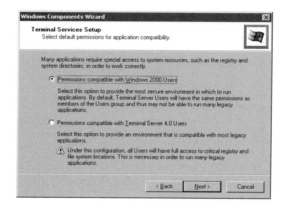

7. Win2K will copy the files from the installation CD (or, if you didn't insert it, will prompt you for the path to the files). When it's done, you'll be prompted to restart the computer to make the changes take effect.

Changing or Removing Terminal Services

When you restart the server, the Terminal Services tools will be added to the Administrative Tools folder. These tools will be available whether you installed Terminal Services in Remote Administration mode or in Application Server mode.

To change the mode of a terminal server between Application Server and Remote Administration, reinstall the service and pick the appropriate setting. To remove Terminal Services from a Win2K server, follow these steps:

1. Open the Add/Remove Programs applet in the Control Panel.

2. Choose Add/Remove Windows Components.

3. From the list available, check the Terminal Services box.

4. Click Next, and wait for Win2K to check for the existence of all the files it needs to run the services that you still have loaded (it will do this even if you loaded those services earlier).

Restart the machine when prompted. The Terminal Services tools will be removed from the Administrative Tools program group.

Adding TSAC Support

Once you have the core Terminal Services installed, you're ready to install the TSAC. Go to the TSAC page on the Microsoft Web site (currently at `www.microsoft.com/windows2000/downloads/recommended/TSAC/default.asp`), make sure that Web Package is listed in the drop-down list on that page, and then choose Next.

The following page lists the server requirements for TSAC, lets you choose a language version, and explains how to install and uninstall the package. Choose a language version and click Next.

The next page holds the end-user licensing agreement (EULA) for the TSAC. To start the download, click the I Accept – Download Now button. You'll see the Save As dialog box pointing to a location where you can save `TSWEBSETUP.EXE` onto your computer or network. Browse to the location you want—it doesn't matter where, so long as it's on a network location that terminal servers can access—and click Save. The file isn't very big (about 314KB), so it shouldn't take long to download.

NOTE `TSWEBSETUP.EXE` *is also on the CD for Windows 2000 SP1, in the* `\Valueadd\TSAC` *directory, but it's not automatically installed when you install the service pack.*

The installation is simple. Run `TSWEBSETUP.EXE` on the terminal server, either locally or from a network connection. Agree to the EULA, then when prompted either browse to the location in which you want to put the sample Web pages or agree to the default of `C:\inetpub\wwwroot\tsweb`. Click OK. Setup will copy files to the selected folder, then offer to show you the release notes. You can use the sample pages that come with the TSAC server-side support—there's one for connecting to a single server and one for connecting to multiple servers—or snip the client code from the source into your own Web pages. Just make sure you share the directory holding the Web pages containing the client connection content, and the server's ready to accept user input.

Creating a New Terminal Server Client

The procedure for connecting a client to the terminal server varies slightly depending on whether you're talking about PC clients, handheld PCs, or WBTs.

PC-Based RDP Clients

To connect a PC-based client to Terminal Services, you have to run a short installation program on the PC to install client support for RDP. This process is quite simple and (wonder of wonders in the Windows world) does not require that you reboot the computer afterward to use the client. The only catch is that you have to *get* those installation files to the client.

How you go about this depends on the operating system your clients are using and how many clients you have to get the RDP client to (and, by extension, the effort that you're willing to put into creating a deployment plan). You can create installation disks with the Terminal Services Client Creator, share the client files on the network and run the Setup program from the client, or deploy an MSI package with Group Policies.

CREATING SETUP DISKS

From the terminal server, run the Terminal Services Client Creator found in the Administrative Tools program group on the terminal server. You'll see a dialog box such as the one shown here.

Notice that each client type requires a different number of disks: the Win16 client requires four, and the Win32 client requires two. Notice also that only Intel clients are supported for Win2K terminal services; although beta versions of Win2K included support for Alpha Win32 clients, this support is no longer included, even for NT4 clients running on Alphas. The client creator doesn't format the disks by default, but I choose to format mine on general principles (after making sure that nothing important is on the disks, of course). I'm unlikely to remember that anything else important is on a disk labeled "RDP Client for Windows NT (Intel)."

You can't create a disk to any location other than a floppy drive. To make the client setup network accessible, your best bet is to share the directories where the client files are stored.

I've included these instructions mostly for the sake of completeness, but as you've probably noticed, this is a pretty clumsy and slow method of distributing client files. You must have a working network to use Terminal Services in the first place, so let's use that working network and forget the steps to the Floppy Stroll.

DISTRIBUTING VIA NETWORK SHARE

To install the files, follow these steps:

1. From the terminal server, share the folder %*systemroot*%\system32\clients\tsclient\net. There are two folders within the net folder: Win16 (for Windows for Workgroups clients) and Win32 (for x86-based Windows 9x and NT clients).

TIP *If you're having your users install their own client files, it's important to make sure they install the right files for their operating system. To avoid user misunderstandings about which installation files to use, you could share each client installation set individually. If you really want to eliminate the possibility that someone will install the wrong files, set user- or group-specific permissions on the shares so that only those who need access to each client type have access. This level of control is probably overkill for most people, but it's worth noting.*

2. From each client Desktop, locate and connect to the share, tunneling to the Disk 1 folder within the appropriate directory and running Setup.exe from there.

INSTALLING AND CONFIGURING THE RDP 5 CLIENT

However you choose to get the Setup program to the PC clients, the process of installing it is the same—and much like installing any Microsoft application. Supply your name and the name of your company, agree to the EULA requirements, and choose a destination directory for the files if you don't like the default location of a new folder in the `Program Files` directory.

Start the copying process, and that's the end of it. A few seconds later, you'll see a message box stating that the client was successfully installed. Click OK, and you're ready to use the client. It will be in the Terminal Services Client program group on the client.

TIP *You can set up the Terminal Services client to run from the terminal server's console, and it's a good idea to do so. You can't remotely control user sessions from the console, but only from within another session. If you're working on the console, you can shadow a session only by starting a terminal server session—even one on the same terminal server. For more on how to remotely control user sessions, turn to the later section "Taking Control of User Sessions."*

INSTALLING AND CONFIGURING REMOTE DESKTOP

Although Windows XP comes with RDP preinstalled in the form of the Remote Desktop, you can use Remote Desktop on any Win32 operating system: Windows 9x, Windows Me, Windows NT, or Windows 2000. Download `msrdpcli.exe`, currently available from `www.microsoft.com/windowsxp/pro/downloads/rdclientdl.asp` and run the executable to install Remote Desktop. Again, the Remote Desktop will only have the capabilities of Windows 2000 RDP if you're connecting to a Windows 2000 terminal server, but it's got a nice UI and having it already distributed will make it easier when you get around to installing .NET Server—your clients will already have the updated RDP client.

WARNING *Just so you know, if you install Remote Desktop on a computer that's already got the RDP5 client installed, the RDP5 client will disappear. Also, be sure to reboot the Windows 2000 terminal server after upgrading any clients to Remote Desktop. I've seen some strange errors—mostly cookies that no longer worked—after installing Remote Desktop, but they went away after a reboot.*

Installing Remote Desktop is as simple as installing any other RDP client. Once you run the EXE and start the installation wizard, follow these steps:

1. Agree to the terms of the EULA.

2. Enter your name and company if Setup does not populate these fields for you and indicate whether you want the Remote Desktop available to anyone who uses the computer or just you.

3. Click Install to let the Setup wizard copy the files, and the Remote Desktop icon will be added to Programs/Accessories/Communications.

You don't need to reboot when you're finished.

DEPLOYING THE CLIENT AUTOMATICALLY

That's how you can do it manually, but, frankly, the easiest way to install the Terminal Services client is to automate the process. You can do this with just Win2K in any of a few ways: use the TSAC to distribute client connection files through Web pages, distribute the Terminal Services client files using Group Policy (this requires using the Active Directory and clients that can connect to the Active Directory), or run a simple logon script that you can use whether or not you've set up group policies.

Using the TSAC with Internet Explorer

For clients to connect to a terminal server from Internet Explorer, they need to navigate to the location where the page including the connection ActiveX control is located, even if it's just like this: *servername**sharename**page.htm*, where this is the UNC name of the Web page in the shared directory. Say, for example, that you're just using the Default.HTM page that comes with TSAC, and this page is located on gammawin2K in the shared tsweb folder—the UNC would look like this: \\gammawin2K\tsweb\Default.HTM.

Say you're the user connecting to this page. When you connect, you'll see a screen prompting you to supply the name of the server you want to connect to and the resolution. There's also a slot to provide security credentials: username and logon domain. When you click the Connect button, if the TSAC ActiveX control isn't already installed on your computer, you'll see a dialog box asking if you want to install and run the Terminal Services ActiveX Control. Click OK to install it.

Using Group Policies

I don't want to rehash Chapter 9's discussion of GPOs, but another way to distribute the RDP client is to create an installer package for the Terminal Services client and distribute it to specified people or computers. This is a good technique if you have a lot of Windows 2000 Professional desktops to get the client to but don't want to use the Web interface to RDP. Essentially, what you'll do is download the MSI package from the TSAC downloads page, create a group policy to deploy the package to certain users or computers, and refresh the domain policy. See Chapter 9 for specifics of how to create and deploy GPOs.

Using the Command Prompt

If you're only distributing the client to a few people, aren't using Windows 2000 Professional clients, and/or don't have the Active Directory set up, you can just create an unattended installation for the RDP client.

To install the files from the command prompt, make sure you're in the path for the right version of the Setup files on the terminal server and type **setup /q1** to install the RDP client. This method ensures that when the installation is done, the user has to click OK on the Installation Was Completed Successfully box. To install without any user interaction, go to the command prompt and type **setup /qt**.

So, for example, you could create a short script to automate this process:

```
net use j: \\sandworm\net /persistent:no
j:\win32
setup /qt
c:
net use j: /delete
```

In this example, sandworm is the terminal server where the client installation files are located, and \net is the share name for %*systemroot*%\system32\clients\tsclient\net. As you can see if you've ever used the command line, this script connects you to the share, changes to the Win32 directory in that share (since \NET contains files for both Win16 and Win32 clients), runs a silent unattended install, changes back to a local drive, and then disconnects from the remote drive.

To uninstall the RDP client from the command line, type **setup /u /qnt**.

Setting Up and Connecting a Windows-Based Terminal

Setting up a WBT for the first time is pretty simple. It's largely a matter of plugging everything in (power supply, monitor, network connection, mouse, and keyboard) and supplying the information the WBT needs to interact with the terminal server. For this example, I'll set up a Windows CE–based Windows terminal on a LAN. Although some Windows have different options from others, the basic setup information required is the same on all CE-based Windows terminals.

NOTE *Setting up Linux-based Windows terminals gets a bit more complicated. Sadly, there is no standardized way of doing this, so you'll need to peruse your Linux terminal's documentation for instructions. You'll be providing much the same information to the Linux-based terminal that you're providing to the Windows-based terminal.*

SETTING UP THE TERMINAL

Once everything is plugged in and you've powered on the unit, choose to begin creating a new connection. The Setup Wizard walks you through the following steps:

1. First off you're faced with the EULA, which states that use of the unit with Terminal Services is predicated upon your having a valid Terminal Services user license and that you must follow the licensing for any applications run from the terminal server. You must click Accept to continue with the wizard.

2. Indicate whether the WBT is connecting to the terminal server via a LAN (the default) or a dial-up connection.

3. Choose the display protocol that should be used to make connections. You have the option of the Microsoft Terminal Server Client (the default, which I'll use here) or the Citrix ICA client, which you'd choose if connecting to a terminal server running WinFrame or MetaFrame. Most modern Windows terminals also offer some kind of terminal emulation support, but you will not use this to connect to a Windows terminal server.

4. The Setup wizard will attempt to locate a DHCP server on your network. If it can't find one, the wizard will tell you so. You'll have the option of telling the wizard to use the IP information supplied by DHCP or supplying a static IP address.

TIP *If you have a DHCP server and the wizard doesn't detect it, make sure the DHCP service on the server is up and running properly and that the server is connected to the network. If they are, then restart the wizard to see whether it finds the DHCP server. Don't just tell the wizard to use DHCP information if it's not able to find it, or you may run into problems in getting an IP address assigned to the terminal. No IP address, no connection to the terminal server.*

5. If you choose to supply a static IP address, you'll be prompted for it, the subnet mask, and (if applicable) the default gateway. The IP address, recall, is the identifier for the network node, and the subnet mask identifies the network segment that the node is on. The default gateway is only necessary if the network is subnetted and the terminal will need to connect to another subnet.

6. Next, you'll be prompted to supply the servers used for name resolution: WINS, DNS, or both. You'll need to know the IP addresses of the servers, as there is no browse function. If

you're using one of the name resolution services, be sure to check the box that enables that service. Otherwise, the connection won't work, and you'll have to edit it to use the IP address instead of the NetBIOS name. To establish support for WINS, you'll need to reenter the unit's network setup.

7. Choose a video resolution. One possible option is Best Available Using DDC. DDC, which stands for Display Data Channel, is a VESA standard for communication between a monitor and a video card. If it supports DDC, a monitor can inform the video card about its capabilities, including maximum color depth and resolution.

When you click the Finish button in the final screen, you'll be prompted to restart the terminal to make the settings take effect. After restarting the system, you'll begin the second half of the terminal setup: the connection.

TIP   To manually restart a WBT, turn the unit off and back on again. If you're one of those people (like myself) who normally leave a PC on, don't worry. Turning off a WBT is equivalent in seriousness to turning off a printer. Doing so will disconnect any current sessions you have open, but it's not like rebooting a computer.

CREATING A NEW CONNECTION

To create a new connection, follow these steps:

1. Choose a name for the new connection and the name of the terminal server to which you're connecting. If you're using a dial-up connection instead of a LAN, be sure to check the Low-Speed Connection box so that RDP will compress the data a little further.

2. To configure the terminal for automatic logon to the terminal server session, fill in the name, password, and domain of the person using the terminal. If you leave this section blank, you'll have to explicitly log in each time you connect to the terminal server. For tighter security, leave it blank; if it doesn't matter whether someone can log in to the terminal server, you can set it up for automatic login.

3. Choose whether you want the terminal server session to display a Desktop or run a single application. Once again, there's no browse function, so you need to know the name and path (from the server's perspective) of any application you choose. If you don't provide correct path information, the connection will fail.

At this point, the connection is set up and you're ready to go. The Connection Manager displays a list of the available connections. To use one, select it and click the Connect button. You'll see a logon screen (assuming you didn't set up the connection for an automatic login). Type your name and password, and you're in.

TIP   If you have a Windows terminal set up to work with Windows Terminal Server and are wondering how you're going to update it to work with the server you updated to Win2K, relax. When you make a preset connection, the terminal will connect to the Win2K terminal session without a hitch, with no help from you. The only catch is that the terminal manufacturer will need to supply the flash update that you can use to upgrade the terminal from RDP 4 (used by NT Terminal Server Edition) to RDP 5 (used by Win2K and required for the advanced features of Terminal Services in Win2K). Win2K won't automatically update the client on the terminal.

Setting Up a Handheld PC

To use a handheld PC (H/PC) to connect to a terminal server, you must install the RDP client on the H/PC and then create a session on the client.

First, you must get the RDP client. Go to the Microsoft Web site and navigate to the Downloads section of the WinCE section. You'll have to go through some screens where you agree that you understand that having the RDP client installed does not imply that you're licensed to access a terminal server. (There's also a link to a place where you can buy more licenses if needed.) Download the 1MB-client setup program (`hpcrdp.exe`) to the desktop partner of the H/PC.

NOTE   *As of this writing, the Windows CE RDP client is located at* `www.microsoft.com/mobile/downloads/ts.asp`, *but it may have moved by the time you read this. It's also on your Win2K Server CD in the* `\valueadd\msft\mgmt\mstsc_hpc` *directory.*

To install the RDP client on the H/PC, follow these steps.

1. Turn on the H/PC and connect it to the desktop partner. Make sure that they're connected.

2. Run `hpcrdp.exe` to start the installation wizard.

3. Click Yes to agree to the EULA.

4. Choose an installation folder for the client on the desktop partner. The default location is a subfolder of the `Windows CE Services` folder, which you'll have installed in the course of partnering the desktop machine and the H/PC.

5. The installation program will start copying the files to the H/PC. This may take a few minutes if you're using the sync cable instead of a network connection—a sync cable is a serial connection.

6. Once the files have been copied, click Finish on the desktop side to end the Setup program.

To set up a connection, go to the H/PC and look in Start/Programs/Terminal Server Client. There are two options here: the Client Connection Wizard and the Terminal Server Client.

To use the default connection settings, click the Terminal Server Client and type in the name or IP address of the terminal server to which you want to connect. Click the Connect button, and the client will search for that terminal server. You'll need to log in as if you were logging into the server or domain.

For a little more control over the connection settings, run the Client Connection Wizard. You don't have as many options as you do when running the similar wizard for the PC client, but you can specify a connection name, provide your username and password for automatic logon, and choose whether to run an application or display the entire Desktop. Click the Finish button, and the wizard will put a shortcut to that connection on your H/PC's Desktop.

Creating, Deleting, and Modifying Connections

Now that the client is installed, you're ready to connect to the terminal server. Let's take a look at how to do this from a PC.

Connections with the RDP5 Client

The simplest way to connect to a terminal server is to run the Terminal Services Client found in the Terminal Services Client program group. When you do, you'll see a dialog box like the one in Figure 15.6, showing all available terminal servers on the network.

FIGURE 15.6

Use the Terminal Services Client to connect to a terminal server using default settings.

To connect to a server, select its icon in the list and choose the resolution you want the client session to use. If the server you want isn't listed, try typing its IP address in the Server box at the top of the dialog box.

NOTE *A lower resolution doesn't give you a lower-resolution full-screen client session; it gives you a smaller window. For example, if your client computer's local resolution is 1024×768 and you choose a terminal server session resolution of 800×600, the session window will be smaller than your Desktop but will have the same resolution as the Desktop, instead of looking as it would if you changed your display settings to make the display 800×600.*

Once you click the Connect button, the client will find the selected terminal server and begin a session. If you included logon information in the settings, they'll be logged in; if not, they'll see the usual Win2K logon screen. Clients should supply their domain username and password, and they'll be logged in.

TIP *If the client gets an error message saying that the terminal server is busy and try again later, check the client TCP/IP settings and make sure that it has a valid IP address and subnet. If it doesn't, the client will get the "too busy" message.*

The Terminal Services Client is easy to use, but the default options aren't always what are needed. To set up client custom settings, skip the Terminal Services Client and choose the Client Connection Manager from the same program group. From here, you can create new connections with personalized settings, save those connection settings for future reference, edit the settings later, and delete session settings if you no longer want to use them.

CREATING A NEW CONNECTION

To create a customized connection, choose New Connection from the File menu and complete the following steps:

1. Choose a name for the new connection and a server to which to connect. If your network includes a WINS or DNS server, you can use the name of the server. If not, then supply the terminal server's IP address. (The RDP client, recall, requires TCP/IP.) If you don't know what terminal servers are available, click the Browse button to display a list of available terminal servers in the domain, as shown here.

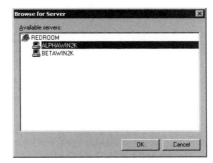

2. If you want to automatically log in to the server when starting the connection, check the box and fill in the appropriate account name, password, and domain or workgroup.

3. Choose the session display settings, including the session display resolution and whether the session should run in a window or take up the entire screen. You can only choose a resolution less than or equal to the client window size. That is, if your client computer's display is set for 1024×768, the session resolution can be no greater than 1024×768.

TIP   For a completely seamless feel to your Terminal Services session, run the Desktop in full-screen mode so that only the remote session is displayed. You can switch back and forth between the session Desktop and the local Desktop by pressing Ctrl+Alt+Break.

4. Indicate whether you'd like to use data compression and bitmap caching to improve performance. Data compression is most important over a slow network (such as a dial-up connection). Using bitmap caching will store a copy of bitmapped images locally so that RDP will only have to update them if there are changes.

5. Specify whether you want the session to display an application or the entire Desktop. If you choose the Desktop, you'll be able to run any application accessible to your user account. Running a single application means that only that application will be displayed, and that if you exit the application, the session will end. You must know the name and path of the application to connect to—there's no browse function.

NOTE *Although it might seem logical to name the application location by its Unicode name, this isn't how it works. Instead, you must enter the path as it appears from the terminal server's perspective—for example,* C:\msoffice\office\ winword.exe. *This may seem odd, but it's because you're connecting to the application locally, not via the network.*

6. Specify how the session will be displayed. You can add the connection to the Terminal Services Client program group (or to another program group that you specify if, for example, you'd like users to be unaware that they're running the application from the terminal server) so that you can use it without running the Client Connection Manager. You can also edit the connection's icon, perhaps to that of the application that the session will open.

TIP *Use the Search tool in 32-bit Windows to find icons, which have an* .ico *extension.*

When you've entered all this information, you'll see a Finish screen. The client connection settings will be ready to use immediately. You can make as many connection settings as you need to different terminal servers or different applications or at different resolutions. Just keep in mind that each separate session running on the terminal server, whether it's an application or a full Desktop, uses resources on the terminal server and gets a time slice of the CPU cycles.

REUSING CONNECTIONS ON OTHER COMPUTERS

You can also transfer connection settings to another client computer without typing them in again. First, save the connection to a file. Highlight it in the Client Connection Manager and choose Export from the File menu. Choose a name for the file and click Save. If password information was part of the connection settings, you'll be asked whether you want to save the password along with the rest of the configuration information for that connection. If you do, then click Yes—just don't forget that doing so means that anyone logging in to the terminal server with that connection will use the identity of the person for whom the connection was originally created. The exported connection will be saved with a .cns extension and will be quite small—around a kilobyte.

To start using that connection, open the Client Connection Manager at the client computer that you want to have access to the terminal server. Choose Import from the File menu, move to the location of the saved connection, and select it.

NOTE *Be careful if you're trying to reuse connection files originally created with TSE. When you import a TSE client connection file using the* conman /import:file.cns *command (where the connection is named* file.cns*), the connection may appear in the Terminal Server Client menu instead of the Terminal Services Client menu. Use the graphical tools to import TSE connections.*

Incidentally, if you copy and paste a connection's icon to the Windows 2000 Desktop (for easier access), you may see an access violation. If you do, be sure to apply SP2 to the client computer.

EDITING AND DELETING CONNECTION INFORMATION

Not all session settings are engraved in stone after you've created the connection. To edit a connection, highlight it in the Client Connection Manager and choose File/Properties (see Figures 15.7, 15.8, and 15.9).

Finally, to delete a session from the Connection Manager, just highlight it and press the Delete key.

FIGURE 15.7

The General tab is for editing the name of the server, its description, and any automatic logon information.

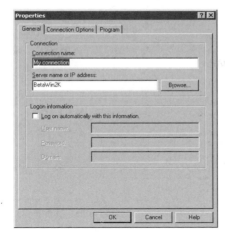

FIGURE 15.8

The Connection Options tab covers session display settings, including the size of the window and the speed of the connection between server and client.

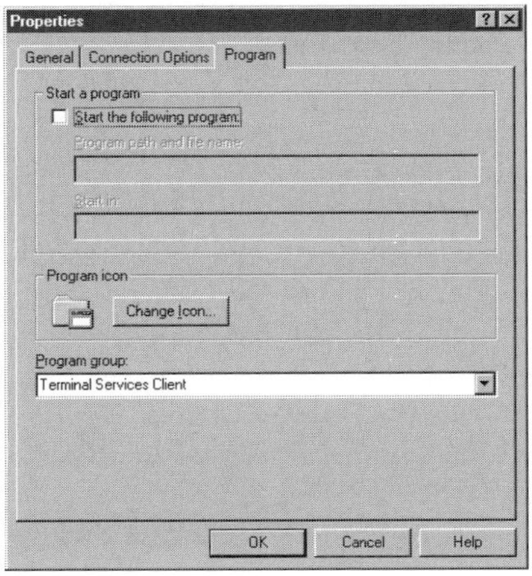

FIGURE 15.9

In the Program tab, choose a new application to run in the terminal server session, or change the icon or program group associated with the session settings.

Connections with the Remote Desktop

If you install the Remote Desktop RDP client, the setup and adjustment procedures will look a little different from those in the Windows 2000 RDP client.

To use the Remote Desktop client, open it (Programs/Accessories/Communications/Remote Desktop). When you first run the tool, no servers will be selected, but you can either type a server's name or browse for them by clicking the down-arrow button in the Computer box and choosing Browse for More to open the dialog box shown in Figure 15.10.

FIGURE 15.10

Browsing for terminal servers from the Remote Desktop

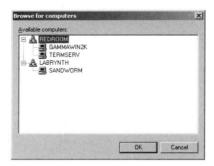

When you've found the terminal server to connect to, double-click on it or click it select OK to return to the main login window, which should now have a server selected, as shown in Figure 15.11. To connect to this server with the default settings, just click the Connect button. This will connect you to the selected terminal server and prompt you to log in. When you have successfully logged in, by default the session will run in full-screen mode with a sizing bar at the top so that you can easily minimize or resize the window to show the local Desktop.

FIGURE 15.11

To use the selected terminal server with the default settings, click the Connect button.

Notice that I didn't touch the Options button in Figure 15.11. If you're using the default settings, you'll never need to touch it. Let's take a look at what those settings involve.

When you first click the Options button, you'll see the General tab, as shown in Figure 15.12. From here, you can choose user credentials to log in with, save or open shared connection settings, and, if you like, pick another server to log into. The only part that might cause confusion (and with reason) is the box prompting you for your user password. Even if you supply this information, you'll still be prompted for your password when you connect to the terminal server.

The Display tab controls all session settings relating to display. The default settings shown in Figure 15.13 may not apply to the terminal session—you need the newest RDP server component to get 24-bit color, and Windows 2000 Server does not have it, but the full-screen mode will. The connection bar at the top of the terminal session window is useful for full-screen sessions, as it offers an easy way to minimize the session and reach the local Desktop. The resolution for the setting will depend on the local client settings—the settings for Remote Desktop size apply only to the window's size.

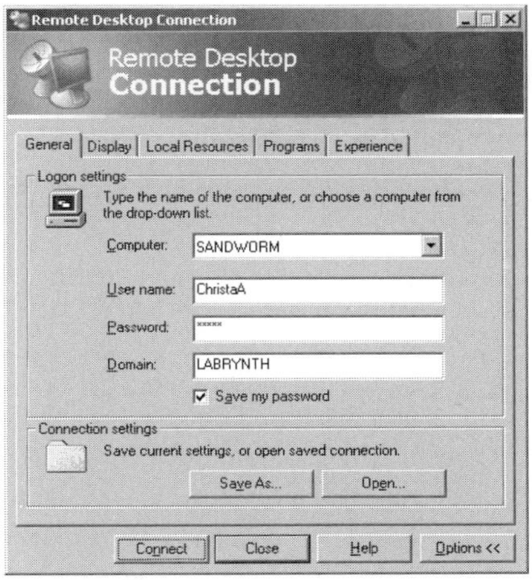

FIGURE 15.12

Use the General tab to supply user credentials and save connection settings to a file.

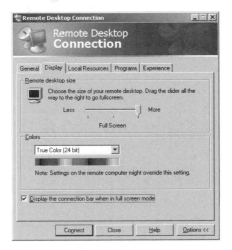

FIGURE 15.13

The Remote Desktop display settings are intended to mimic a user's local Desktop.

The Local Resources tab shown in Figure 15.14 is a little more in-depth, but (again) unless you're connecting to a Windows XP Desktop or a beta of .NET Server, you don't need to worry about most of the options. The Sound settings at the top offer you three options—Bring to This Computer, Do Not Play, and Leave at Remote Computer—but these settings don't apply to sessions hosted by Windows 2000 terminal servers. The key combinations settings do apply and specify whether standard Windows key combinations should apply to the remote session only in full-screen mode, all the time, or always apply to the local session. The default option of full-screen mode is probably the one that people will find easiest to use because it will send the keystrokes to whichever view of the Desktop is most prominent. Finally, the Local Devices settings may or may not apply. Printer mappings (enabled by default) will work with Windows 2000 terminal sessions, as will serial mappings, but local drive mappings are only available with the newest version of the RDP server.

FIGURE 15.14

Not all Local Resources settings will be available to sessions hosted by a Windows 2000 terminal server.

The Programs tab displayed in Figure 15.15 is pretty self-explanatory if you've used Terminal Services before. If you choose a program to run here, then that program will be the only one available—if the user closes it, then they'll end their session. The starting folder settings supply a working directory for the program if you don't want to use the default (often My Documents), but this is an optional setting.

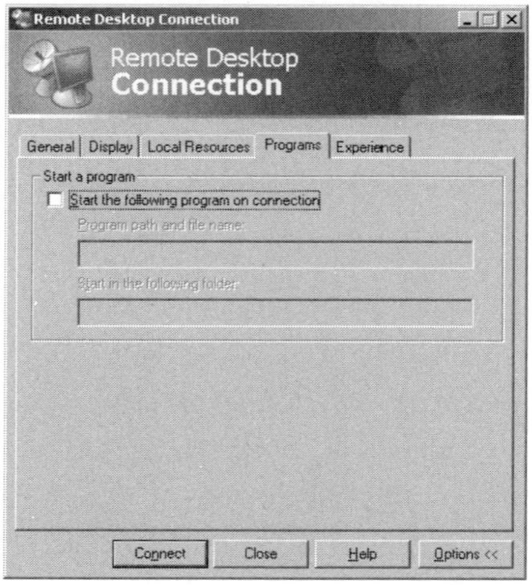

FIGURE 15.15

Choose a single program for terminal sessions.

Finally, the Experience tab determines some features to enable based on Microsoft's guesses about what will work best on the selected connection speed (see Figure 15.16). Although you can manually check or uncheck boxes to enable and disable features, for each network speed offered Remote Desktop will have some default settings.

TIP   Although you can't control printer mapping from here, when creating a connection to work over a slow network, seriously consider disabling printer mapping.

FIGURE 15.16

Enable or disable
session features
depending on the
network speed the
connection will be
using.

Client Catch-22s

By and large, using a connection to the terminal server is largely idiot-proof once you've got everything set up. However, there are a couple of things your users should be aware of before they use one of their terminal server connections. Some apply to all PC users (but not to Windows terminals), and one applies only to Win16 clients.

NORMAL KEYBOARD SHORTCUTS DON'T WORK

You're accustomed to using keyboard shortcuts to navigate between applications on your Desktop, and you can see how to enable Desktop shortcuts for use with Remote Desktop. You may wonder how to make the shortcuts work in your terminal server session running on your PC and using the RDP5 display protocol. The simple answer is that you can't—those shortcuts are picked up by the local buffer for use on the local console. Instead, you'll need to substitute keyboard shortcuts as shown in Table 15.3.

The copy, cut, and paste commands will work as usual in both local and remote sessions. The commands will apply to whichever session is in the foreground. If you copy in one session and then move the other session to the foreground to paste, the text will be pasted in the second session.

TABLE 15.3: KEYBOARD SHORTCUTS IN TERMINAL SERVICES CLIENT SESSIONS

FUNCTION	LOCALLY USED COMBINATION	SESSION-SPECIFIC COMBINATION
Brings up application selector and moves selection to the right	Alt+Tab	Alt+PgUp
Brings up application selector and moves selection to the left	Alt+Shift+Tab	Alt+PgDn
Swaps between running applications	Alt+Esc	Alt+Insert
Opens the Start menu	Ctrl+Esc	Alt+Home
Right-clicks the active application's icon button in the upper left of the application window	Alt+spacebar	Alt+Del
Brings up the Windows NT Security window	Ctrl+Alt+Del	Ctrl+Alt+Esc

YOU NEED TO LOG OFF TO END A SESSION

Just closing the terminal server window doesn't terminate the session; it disconnects it so it's in a sort of trance state on the server, maintaining the user's session until the user decides to come back to it. If you want to *terminate* a session, then log out as you would if logging out of the domain.

WARNING   *Do train users to terminate sessions correctly, not just disconnect them. Every user connected to the terminal server has their own HKCU section in the server's Registry, left open until the session is terminated. If you're having trouble with painful, swollen Registries, then disconnected-and-never-terminated sessions could be one reason. You can also configure Windows 2000 Terminal Services to automatically terminate disconnected sessions after a predetermined period of inactivity.*

PROBLEMS WITH PASSWORD-PROTECTED SCREENSAVERS

Frankly, you shouldn't be using screensavers with terminal sessions anyway because generating the output takes a tool on the CPU for no good reason. But if you do, and if a user minimizes the session, then when they try to log back in to the password-protected screensaver, they'll get a blank screen in the session window. There's nothing to be done about this; the user will need to terminate the session and then restart it. All in all, it's just one more reason not to use screensavers with terminal sessions. If a user needs to secure a session without terminating it, then tell them to disconnect. They'll need to log on again to reconnect to the session.

CONNECTING WITH THE WIN16 CLIENT

Windows for Workgroups clients must save their domain password in their password list when logging on (there's a check box in the logon screen that allows them to do this). Otherwise, they'll get an unhelpful error message: "Error code: 0x906 SL_ERR_SECCTXTINITFAILED (0x906) SL: InitSecurityContext call failed." All this means is that the domain controller can't find the password. This does not apply if your network is organized as a workgroup, only if it's using domain security.

Troubleshooting Connection Problems

When you set up a connection properly, it should work—but *should* is a nice word that doesn't always apply to reality. Table 15.4 lists a few error messages that users might encounter when trying to access a terminal server, either in Application Server mode or in Remote Administration mode.

TABLE 15.4: CONNECTION ERROR MESSAGES

ERROR MESSAGE	PROBABLE MEANING
The local policy of this system does not allow you to log in interactively.	The user attempting to log in does not have the "logon locally" permission available under `Security Settings\Local Policies\User Rights Assignment\Log On Locally`. Modify the appropriate GPO to grant the user or group this permission.
You do not have access to this session.	The user attempting to log in does not have sufficient permissions on the RDP-TCP connection. Modify the RDP-TCP permissions by using Terminal Services Configuration to grant the user or group the logon permission.
Your interactive logon privilege has been disabled. Please contact your system administrator.	The user attempting to log in does not have the Allow Logon to Terminal Server check box selected on the Terminal Services Profile tab of their account. Use Active Directory Users and Computers to modify this setting.
The terminal server has exceeded the maximum number of allowed connections. The system cannot log you on (1B8E). Please try again or consult your system administrator.	The user is attempting to log in to a terminal server in Remote Administration mode, but the server has reached its connection limit. Terminal servers in Remote Administration mode allow a maximum of two concurrent sessions, active or disconnected.
Terminal server sessions disabled. Remote logins are currently disabled.	The user is attempting to log in to a terminal server where an administrator has disabled additional logons by issuing the `CHANGE LOGON /DISABLE` command. To enable logon, issue the `CHANGE LOGON /ENABLE` command.
Because of a network error, the session will be disconnected. Please try to reconnect.	The user is attempting to log in to a terminal server where an administrator has specified a maximum connection limit, and the limit has been reached. To change this value, open the Terminal Services Configuration MMC snap-in, click Connections, double-click a connection—i.e., RDP-TCP—then select the Network Adapter tab. At the bottom of this tab are two options, Unlimited connections and Maximum connections.

Continued on next page

TABLE 15.4: CONNECTION ERROR MESSAGES *(continued)*

ERROR MESSAGE	PROBABLE MEANING
The client could not connect to the terminal server. The server may be too busy. Please try connecting later.	The user is attempting to log in to a terminal server where an administrator has disabled one or more connections. To check this, open the Terminal Services Configuration MMC snap-in, click Connections, right-click a connection—i.e., RDP-TCP—and select All Tasks. If Enable Connection is an option, the connection is currently disabled. There will also be a red *X* over the icon for the specified connection when disabled. This is also known as the World's Most Unhelpful Error Message because it may appear for any number of problems that don't have anything to do with the server being busy. For example, if your client can't find the subnet where your terminal server is, you'll see this error message.
ICA clients unexpectedly disconnect.	This is a MetaFrame problem, not a RDP one, but because both Microsoft and Citrix have addressed it, it's worth including. Install SP2 for Windows 2000 Server and get the hotfix from Citrix.

Editing Client Account Settings

Everything's ready to go on the client side, but you may still have some work to do to get the server side configured. The following are optional—but useful—settings that allow you to define how long a session may last, whether someone can take remote control of a user's terminal session, how the RDP protocol is configured, and client path and profile information. The location of these settings depends on whether you've set up the member accounts on the terminal server itself (as a member server) or are editing the main user database on a Win2K domain controller. If the former, the settings will be in the Local Users and Groups section of the Computer Management tool in the Administrative Tools folder. If the latter, the settings will be in the Active Directory Users and Computers tool in the Administrative Tools folder.

In this example, I'll use the Active Directory Users and Groups tool, shown in Figure 15.17. The settings for user accounts in the Local Users and Groups option are the same as the ones in the user accounts stored in the Active Directory, the only difference being that the Active Directory account properties have tabs related to user contact information.

Open the Users folder, find the user you want, then right-click it and choose the Properties item. This properties page controls all user settings, so I'll concentrate on the settings that apply to Terminal Services.

NOTE *Unfortunately, you have to configure all user settings—for Terminal Services and in general—individually, rather than configuring settings for groups or organizational units. This is definitely suboptimal, but that's the way it is.*

FIGURE 15.17

Edit account properties from the Users folder in Active Directory Users and Computers.

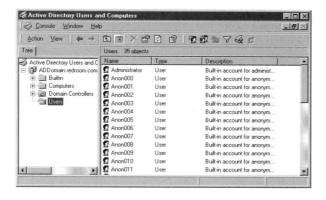

Remote Control

The ability to take remote control of a user's session comes in handy when troubleshooting time comes. Rather than trying to blindly talk someone through a series of commands ("Okay, find the Programs folder. Got it? Now look for the icon that says 'Microsoft Word'"), you can take over the session, manipulating it from your session while displaying it also for the user. The person whose session you're controlling will be able to see exactly how to complete the task and will have it done for them.

The settings for the kind of remote control that you can take are defined on the Remote Control tab of each user's properties pages, shown in Figure 15.18.

FIGURE 15.18

Setting remote control options for taking over user sessions

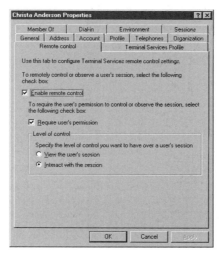

First, you must specify whether remote control is even permitted for the session (by default, you can take control of any session, no matter what rights the owner of the session has). Specify also whether the user whose session is being shadowed must permit the action before the remote control can begin. If you choose this option, the person who originated the session will see a message box telling them that such and such person of such and such domain is attempting to control their session, offering the chance to accept or refuse the control.

NOTE *If a user refuses the remote control connection, you can't control or view the session even from an account with Administrator privileges.*

The final option on this tab determines what kind of control you can have over this user's session. For troubleshooting purposes, you'll find it most useful to be able to interact with the session, so you can actually show the user how to do something (or just do it for them). Choosing this option means that both the original user and the person with remote control over the session can send mouse clicks and keystrokes to the terminal server for interpretation. Graphical output is displayed on both the original session and the remote control view of the session.

If you're choosing the option to view the user's session, the person remotely controlling the session isn't really controlling it, but is only able to watch and see what the original user is doing. The person who set up remote control can't use the mouse or keyboard with the remotely controlled session. This could potentially be a troubleshooting tool if you're trying to find out exactly what someone's doing wrong and help them correct it, while making sure that you can't interfere. Most often, however, I find the option to take control of the session more useful than the ability to watch.

Session Time-Outs

The status of a client session isn't a binary proposition. Rather than on/off, the state of a client session may be active, disconnected, or reset. An *active* session is what it sounds like: a session that's actively in use. In a *disconnected* session, the client has shut off the client interface to the session, but the session—and all its applications—is still running on the server. When a client *resets* a session with the Logoff command, the session ends and all applications in the session are shut down.

Although the distinction may not sound significant at first, it's important. When clients disconnect from their sessions, all their data is still loaded into memory and their applications are running, exactly as they left them. This means that a client can disconnect while going to lunch, and thus secure the session without having to start over. The only catch to a disconnected session is that it still uses up processor cycles and some memory because the session thread still gets its crack at the processor and because all the user data is still active. However, as the data stops being accessed, Win2K will swap it out to the paging file on the hard disk and replace it in physical memory with more recent data; when the client reconnects to the session and tries to use the data, the data will be paged back in. The still-running client session also won't impact available network bandwidth much because the terminal server will detect that the session is idle and stop sending video updates to the client machine.

If a user attempts to reconnect to the terminal server with more than one disconnected session running, a dialog box will display the disconnected sessions, their resolution, and the time that they've been disconnected. The user can then pick the session to reconnect. If the user doesn't pick a session in a minute or so, the highlighted session will be reestablished. The other session will remain on the terminal server, still in its inactive state.

Win2K gives you the option of controlling how long a session may stay active, how long it may stay disconnected without being terminated, how long active but idle sessions may stay active before they're disconnected—and even whether a particular user may connect to the server at all. These settings are controlled from the Sessions tab, as shown in Figure 15.19.

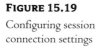

FIGURE 15.19

Configuring session connection settings

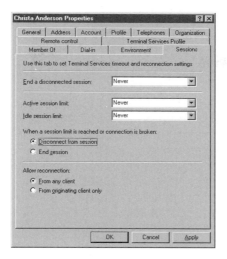

You can control how long the setting may remain active before being disconnected or terminated. If you want to prevent people from forgetting to log out from their terminal session at the end of the day or at lunch, use this setting.

As I already discussed, a disconnected session is still using up terminal server resources—in the page file if nowhere else. This is by design, so that users can reconnect to a session and have all their applications and data still loaded, but if a session is permanently abandoned, there's no point in leaving it up. Choose a time-out period that reflects the amount of time you're willing to give a user to get back and use their connection before their applications are all closed.

You can determine also how long a session can be idle before being disconnected or terminated. This isn't quite the same setting as the first one, which limits connection time whether or not the session is still getting input. Rather, this setting limits the amount of time that a session can be idle before being shut down. This setting is a little more useful in most cases, given that the session must be unused for a certain period before it is shut down.

The default for all three settings is Never, meaning there's no restriction on how long a session may be running, disconnected, or idle. The maximum time-out period is two days.

TIP If you want to gather some statistics about how long people are staying logged in, or how long disconnected sessions are remaining idle on the server, you can get this information from the Terminal Services Manager. System Monitor can tell you how many active or inactive sessions are currently running on a given terminal server.

The settings on the bottom of the tab determine how disconnected and reestablished connections should be handled. You may have noticed that two of the time-out options gave you the choice of disconnecting or terminating the session at the end of the time-out session, but no option for specifying which it should be—disconnection or resetting the connection. The answer depends on whether you pick Disconnect (the default) or End (which resets the connection) for broken or timed-out connections. The other option controls how users may reconnect to disconnected sessions. ROP sessions can reconnect to their client session from any client machine. Only ICA sessions can be forced to reestablish the connection from the same machine from which they started. If a user has more than one disconnected session running on the same terminal server, when they reconnect they'll have a choice of which session they want to use. The session(s) not chosen will continue to run on the terminal server.

Setting Client Path Information

Win2K spreads per-user files all over the place. Unless you specify otherwise, user home directories are in subfolders of the terminal server's Profiles folder and are identified by username. Their temporary directories are subfolders of the terminal server's temporary directory and identified by Session ID. To keep all per-user information in a single place, you may want to specify a new home directory. This will give you a fighting chance of applying per-user system quotas and keeping all files in one place for easier recovery—not to mention keeping the home directories off the terminal server, which could ultimately take up a lot of room.

PROFILE PATHS AND HOME DIRECTORIES

Roaming profiles are stored on a profile server instead of a local machine, so the user can log in with the same settings wherever she connects to the network. The other option is locally stored profiles, stored on the computer where they're displayed. When a profile is applied, it makes per-user changes to the Registry of the computer the person is logged in to that apply only to that user. So far, this is just like NT profiles have been for years.

With Terminal Services, it still works more or less the same way. The profiles may still be stored either locally or on a profile server—but in this case *locally* means on the terminal server. As you probably know, you can't *not* use a profile with Win2K—if you don't specify one, then you'll get the Default User profile.

You have a couple of options when it comes to profiles and Terminal Services. If you only provide a path for the user profile, then that path applies to both "normal" user settings and settings for terminal sessions that the user starts up. Filling in only the information the Profile tab in a user's profile will have this effect—the person will have the same profile path and home directory for terminal sessions as they do normally.

This may sound like a good plan, but in most cases it's not. First off, what works well when logging in from a Win2K Pro computer may not work well when logging onto a terminal session. For one example, the screensaver you might use on Win2K Pro without a second thought is a resource-draining vanity in a terminal session. For another, the colors that look great in a 16-million color environment look odd when the maximum color depth is 256 colors. Both color scheme and preferred screensaver are part of the profile. For another, using the same profile for both ordinary sessions and terminal sessions leaves you exposed to lost profile changes. Consider how profiles work. When you open a profile and make changes to it, those changes are stored locally and don't get written back to the profile server until you log out. So what happens if you have two copies open, make a change in one and then log out, then make a change in the other copy and then log out? Right—you lose all the changes made to the first one because the copy you saved last to the profile server overwrote the copy you saved first. This can happen any time you open a profile more than once—it's not just a problem with Terminal Services—but you're not likely to log in two or more times when you're logging in to the domain from a fat client. Log in to both the fat client (since you needed to log in to the domain to get to a computer from which you could run the terminal session) and to the terminal server, and you immediately have two copies open. For these reasons, it's probably best to use different profiles for terminal sessions and fat client sessions.

How about roaming profiles for terminal sessions, if those profiles are different from the ordinary user profiles? This is still not a good idea because of the possibility that you'll have multiple copies of your profile open at once. Particularly if your terminal session is set up to only serve applications and you use more than one application, you're likely to open multiple copies of your profile at the same time.

So does this mean that local profiles are the way to go? Nope—not if you have many users to support and those users won't always log in to the same server. When you use local profiles, they're stored on the terminal server. If you have 60 users, each with his or her own profile, and you can't predict which of four servers those 60 users will connect to, then that means that you've got to store those 60 profiles on each server. That's a lot of room to munch up on the terminal server's system drive. It can also lead to inconsistency in the user environment if a user changes his profile on one server and not on another. It's especially important to not keep user profiles locally if you're using load balancing of any kind because doing so would mean that people would never know which profile they'd get.

For this reason, the best plan might be to use mandatory profiles, which are just ordinary profiles with a .man extension. Users can edit mandatory profiles to the degree their system policies allow them to, but those changes don't get saved to the server. Limiting to the user experience, perhaps, but if you use mandatory profiles with terminal sessions, then you avoid the problems of lost profile edits from multiple copies of the profile being opened. To specify a profile location, set the path location for the Terminal Services profile from each user's properties pages, as shown in Figure 15.20.

The Allow Logon to Terminal Server check box controls whether the person is permitted to log in to the terminal server at all. By default, anyone with an account on the domain or server may do so.

FIGURE 15.20

Specify the path to the user profile and home directory in the Terminal Services Profile tab.

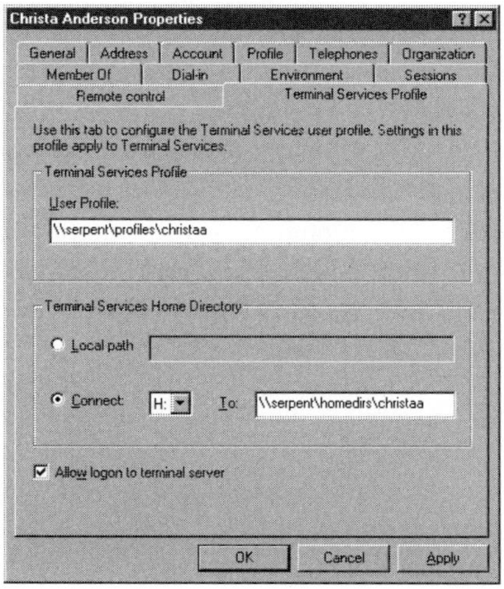

COMMAND-LINE UPDATES TO PROFILE INFORMATION

To change or set user profile information for one user account is no big deal: Open Active Directory Users and Computers, open the user account's Properties sheet, turn to the Terminal Services Profile tab, and make the change. Multiply this procedure by 50, 500, or 5000 users, however, and it gets less easy. ADSI doesn't expose the Terminal Services profile path for user accounts, so you can't use VBScript to programmatically change user account profile information. However, all is not lost: You can make these edits with the `tsprof` command-line tool.

`Tsprof` supports three actions: You can update account profile information, you can copy it to another user account, or you can query a user account to make sure your changes took or see what the current profile settings are. The basic syntax for these commands looks like this:

```
TSPROF /UPDATE  [/DOMAIN:domainname|/LOCAL]  /PROFILE:<path> username
TSPROF /COPY    [/DOMAIN:domainname|/LOCAL]  [/PROFILE:<path>] sourceuser  destinationuser
TSPROF /Q       [/DOMAIN:domainname|/LOCAL]  username
```

Make sure you don't include extra spaces in the command, or you could accidentally query the domain name as though it were a username.

For example, say that my Terminal Services users don't have session-explicit user accounts; they're using the same accounts they typically use to log on to the domain. The profile settings that work well for a full-color session on a single-user computer might not translate well to a terminal session, so I want to edit that account information to C:\profiles. I can do so from the command line, like this:

```
tsprof /update /domain:redroom /profile:c:\profiles\profile.man christa
```

In this example, the user account is in the REDROOM domain, the profile path is C:\profiles, and the user account I'm editing is named Christa. This command will spit back the following information:

```
Terminal Services Profile Path for redroom\christa is { c:\profiles\profile.man }
```

If the curly brackets don't contain any information, I haven't set a Terminal Services profile for that user account. The /update argument doesn't tell you what the profile path information was *before* you changed it, so if you want to ensure that it needs to be updated, query the account. To perform the query, use the /q argument, like this:

```
tsprof /q /domain:labrynth christa
```

If you used `tsprof` with TSE, notice that the command now is /q, not /query. The command changed in Windows 2000.

Finally, you can copy profile-path information from one account to another. The /copy command works similar to /update, except you must provide the source and destination account names, in this case, Christa and Vera, respectively:

```
Tsprof /copy /domain:redroom christa vera
```

The system will now copy Christa's profile account information to Vera's user account; if I query Vera's account, the profile information will be there.

Be careful when you use these tools. `Tsprof` can't tell whether a profile path is valid any more than the graphical user account management tools can; `tsprof` will enter whatever information you give it. If the account name is invalid, `tsprof` will generate an error when it attempts to update the information—`Failed Setting User Configuration, Error = 1332 (0x534)`—but won't show any problems when you perform a query.

DEFINING THE SESSION ENVIRONMENT

The Environment tab in the properties pages sets the Terminal Services environment for the user, replacing any related settings (such as an application to run at logon) that might already appear in a user's client logon settings. If you want to automatically run an application at logon, type its path in the Program File Name box (sadly, there's no browse function). The working directory goes in the Start In box. Notice that supplying the name of an application does not limit the terminal server session to only running that application and then ending when the application is terminated. All this does is run the application when the session starts—the main Desktop still remains available. If you want to provide a terminal session running only a single application, and then closing when that application closes, then you'll need to set that up when configuring the client connections, as described earlier in this chapter.

The settings in the Client Devices section at the bottom of this tab don't all apply to Win2K clients. The first one, Connect Client Drives at Logon, applies only to sessions where remapping client drives for use in terminal server sessions is enabled (and it may confuse users as to whether they're saving files to their local drives or to the terminal server, so I wouldn't use it if I were you). The printing options, however, do apply to RDP clients. Checking Connect Client Printers at Logon specifies that any printers mapped from the terminal server session should be reconnected. Default to Main Client Printer specifies that the client should use its own default printer, not the one defined for the terminal server.

SETTING THE LOCATION OF TEMPORARY DIRECTORIES

Rather than using the default location for user temporary files, you can specify a new one in the user's home directory. Unlike the other settings we've discussed, this one is not set from the user properties pages. Instead, you'll use the `flattemp` command and edit user system settings.

First, log in as the user for whom you're making the change and open the System applet in the Control Panel. Turn to the Advanced tab, and click the Environment Variables button to open the dialog box shown in Figure 15.21.

TIP   Rather than logging in as the person whose environment you're editing, you can remotely control a terminal server session that that person is running. This allows you to edit their settings as though you were that person.

FIGURE 15.21

Editing the location of temporary files

Double-click the values of TEMP and TMP and type the new location in the dialog box that appears. When you've done this for every user, you're ready for the next step. From the command line, run `flattemp /enable`. This will tell Win2K to point all users either to a single temporary directory or to one specified for them in the System applet. To reverse this, run `flattemp /disable` to point all users back to the default location for their temporary files.

*WARNING**   If user home directories are located on a network share instead of on the terminal server, then you'll be vulnerable to application errors if an application attempts to write to the temporary directory when there's a network error. This won't hurt the disk volume, but the application will respond as it would if the disk had died, and you may lose data. You can avoid this problem by keeping terminal server home directories on the terminal server, but you'll end up with a lot of data clogging up the server. Sadly, you can't use Offline Files with a terminal session—as you no doubt have noticed if your office keeps a community laptop for people to take on the road, Offline Files is a machine-specific setting.*

Configuring Terminal Services for All Connections

You can configure general settings for all Terminal Services connections from the Terminal Services Configuration tool in the Administrative Tools folder (see Figure 15.22). If you're running Terminal Services alone, you'll have only the RDP connection in this folder; if you have other multiuser Windows components added (like MetaFrame's ICA protocol or direct video support), they'll be in the folder as well.

FIGURE 15.22

Configure display protocol settings from this tool.

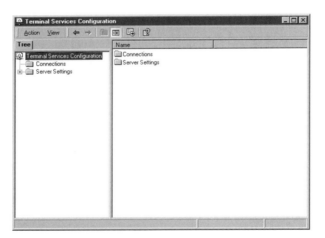

What can you do here? The `Server Settings` folder contains settings that apply to all connections made to the server. The `Connections` folder shows all installed display protocols (if you're running Win2K only, then RDP will be the only object in this folder).

*NOTE**   Win2K only supports one RDP connection per network adapter. If your terminal server has more than one NIC installed and you're using RDP with both of them, you can configure the RDP protocol for each adapter separately.*

THE *SERVER SETTINGS* FOLDER

The `Server Settings` folder (see Figure 15.23) contains options that control the creation and deletion of per-session temporary files and the types of access permitted to the terminal server. The options here are identical whether the server is set up to be an ordinary server with remote administration capabilities or an application server.

FIGURE 15.23

Server Settings
folder for a terminal
server in Remote
Administration mode

As discussed earlier in the section "Installing (or Removing) Support for Terminal Services," the terminal server mode indicates what kind of access is permitted to the terminal server. The server may be set up as an application server or as an ordinary server that can be remotely administered. Application servers permit as many users as you have licenses for to run terminal sessions on the server. Remote Administration mode is for administrative work only.

Deleting the temporary folders on exit means that when a user logs out of a terminal server session, the temporary folder they used—and all the TMP files in it—is deleted. This setting, set to Yes by default, keeps the terminal server from getting cluttered with TMP files, but ensures that those files are only deleted when they're no longer needed. Using temporary folders per session means that a separate TMP folder will be created for each session started, with those new folders (identified by Session ID) being placed by default in subfolders to the main Win2K `Temporary Files` directory.

The Internet Connector licensing option affects *all* terminal server sessions, not just those that come through the Internet, so only enable this option for terminal servers accepting only Internet connections. Frankly, I haven't yet heard of anyone with an application for these licenses and no one at Microsoft has been able to give me a possible application for them. The only scenario I can envision that they'd work in is if you were an ISV offering your software via the Web for people to sample on an anonymous basis. Even application service providers (ASPs) have a different licensing scheme.

The second-to-last option lets you turn off the Active Desktop on the terminal server sessions. Unless you really need it for some reason, I'd turn it off and save the resources. Finally, you can choose the type of permissions you want to apply to this terminal server: TSE 4 file access is compatible with all applications (but may leave some system folders vulnerable to changes from user applications) or Win2K file access that may not work with all applications (because it denies permissions to some system folders) but does not allow users—or applications—to tamper with those files.

THE *CONNECTIONS* FOLDER

Use the `Connections` folder to configure protocol-wide settings. First, you can disable RDP so that no one can connect to the server, something you might want to do if you know you're going to be taking the server down for maintenance and don't want to have to bother with kicking people off. Since you can't turn off the terminal server service, this is the easiest way to keep people off the server while still keeping it running. To do so, just right-click the protocol and choose Disable Connection from the All Tasks part of the pop-up menu. The command to reenable the connection is in the same All Tasks section.

For more detailed control of RDP, choose the Properties option from the pop-up menu. Most settings in the RDP-Tcp dialog box work the same way as their counterparts in the per-user connection settings, which normally take precedence. For a more uniform set of protocol configurations, you may edit the settings here and check the boxes that tell the protocol properties not to inherit their settings according to the user. The two settings that aren't configurable on a per-user basis control security are found on the General and Permissions tabs.

THE GENERAL TAB

The General tab shown in Figure 15.24 controls the degree of encryption used with RDP.

FIGURE 15.24

Configuring RDP
access security

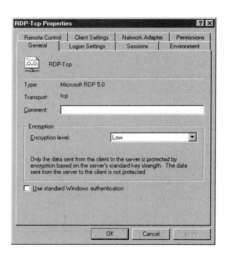

By default, the protocol is set for Medium encryption, meaning that all communications between client and server are encrypted with the standard 40-bit algorithm (56-bit if the client is running Win2K Professional). Low encryption only protects communications from the client to the server—not the other way around—and High encryption protects communications in both directions with 128-bit encryption. The level of encryption depends on the server—the RDP client will negotiate the security level that the server's using.

TIP The greater the level of encryption, the worse the session performance will be, due to the encryption/decryption overhead at both ends of the connection. Only use Medium or High encryption over slow networks if you're concerned about the signal being intercepted.

You don't have to worry about the Use Standard Windows Authentication check box unless you've installed a third-party authentication package on the server. In that case, checking this box tells Win2K to use its native authentication scheme to validate terminal session user logons, rather than using the third-party package. If you have a third-party Gina.dll file installed, however, you'll want to be sure you've applied SP2 to the Windows 2000 terminal server; otherwise the server will use the third-party authentication package for console logons regardless of your settings.

PERMISSIONS

Those familiar with the NT/Win2K argot will remember that you secure a Win2K network by defining user rights for what people can *do* on the network and setting permissions for the resources that people can *use.* Terminal Services security is controlled with permissions, on a per-group or per-user basis.

To set or edit the permissions assigned to terminal server sessions, turn to the Permissions tab. You'll see a dialog box like the one in Figure 15.25. From here, you can edit the basic permission sets of the groups for whom some kind of access to terminal server functions has been defined.

FIGURE 15.25

Default terminal server permissions

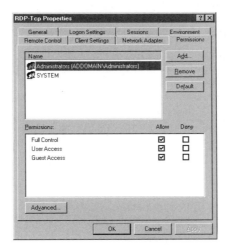

TIP   *If you turn to the Permissions tab and see a list of security IDs instead of user or group names, and the cursor changes to an hourglass when over the dialog box, don't panic. The terminal server is retrieving the names from the domain controller and will show the user and group names after a few seconds. If this doesn't happen—if the SIDs never resolve to user and group names—then there's something wrong with either the domain controller or the connection between the two servers.*

Not sure how to interpret the check boxes? If a permission is checked, then it's explicitly enabled or disabled, depending on which box is checked. If a permission is clear on both sides, then it's implicitly enabled. You can explicitly enable or disable the permission by checking the appropriate box.

Fine-Tuning Access to Terminal Server Functions

The first page shows only the default groups and the basic permissions they've been assigned. For more control over the permission process, click the Advanced button to open the dialog box shown in Figure 15.26.

FIGURE 15.26

Setting advanced permissions

From here, you can see the state of the defined permissions. A key icon symbolizes a granted permission; a padlock symbolizes a denied one. (When you first open this dialog box, you should only see keys—no permissions are explicitly denied by default.) The comment below the list of users and groups notes whether the highlighted permission applies to the basic membership of that group only or to subgroups within that group.

You can adjust these permissions either by adding new users or groups to the list (getting them from the domain controller) or by editing the permissions of the groups already there. To define permissions for a new user or group, click the Add button. The terminal server will retrieve a list of users and groups from the domain displayed in the Look In box. Choose a user or group from the list and click it. You'll open a dialog box like the one in Figure 15.27.

FIGURE 15.27

Defining the permissions for a new user

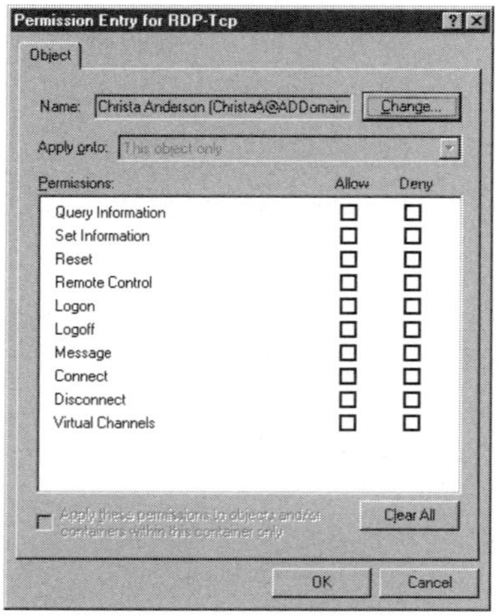

TIP If the user or group you want isn't displayed in the list, type it into the box. If you've already created an account for this user or group, you'll be able to edit its permissions.

By default, new users and groups have limited permissions. If you add a new user—even a domain administrator—using the Add button on the Permissions tab, then the new user will only have Logon permission (Guest access) if you don't specify otherwise. You will need to specify the access you'd like to grant or deny to the groups and users you're adding to the list.

The permissions listed here have the characteristics outlined in Table 15.5 I'll talk more about how to use these functions in the later section "Managing Terminal Sessions."

TABLE 15.5: TERMINAL SERVICES PERMISSIONS

ACCESS TYPE	EFFECT
Query Information	Allows users to gather information about people using the terminal server, processes running on the server, sessions, and so forth
Set Information	Allows users to set the level of control other users have over the session
Reset	Allows users to reset other connections, ending them and logging the other user off the computer
Remote Control	Allows users to take control of or view other user sessions
Logon	Allows users to connect to the terminal server
Logoff	Allows users to disconnect from the terminal server
Message	Allows users to send messages to other terminal server clients
Connect	Allows users to connect to other terminal servers
Disconnect	Allows users to disconnect from other terminal servers
Virtual Channels	Enables virtual channels for that group

Changing permissions for an existing user or group works in much the same way: Select a name, click the View/Edit button, and you'll see the same set of options to explicitly grant or deny permissions.

TIP If you want to cancel all permission changes for a user or group and start over, click the Cancel button. If you want to remove every granted or denied permission associated with a user or group, click Clear All.

Terminal Services Licensing

Licensing single-user computers is complicated enough. Bring terminal servers into the equation, and the complication increases. Do you have to pay for only the operating system? Only the client sessions active at any given time? Only some client sessions? What about applications—an application is only loaded on one machine, so you should only have to pay for one license, right? And who's in charge of keeping track of all these licenses, anyway?

Licensing is never fun and it's not glamorous, but it's part of the cost of doing business. Read on to make some sense of the Terminal Services licensing model.

The Win2K Terminal Services Licensing Model

First, let's take a look at how the licensing model works in Win2K. In TSE, licensing was handled by a license manager service that came with TSE. You told the license manager how many Terminal Services licenses you had, and it kept track of how they were used. This is no longer true in Win2K. Instead, you have a license server, which may not be the terminal server. A new player is also involved. No longer can you just tell the license server how many TS licenses you have—now you have to get official licenses from Microsoft.

As shown in Figure 15.28, several players cooperate to make Terminal Services licensing work in Win2K:

◆ The terminal servers

◆ The license servers

◆ The Microsoft clearinghouse that enables the license servers and the access licenses

FIGURE 15.28

The Win2K Terminal Services licensing model

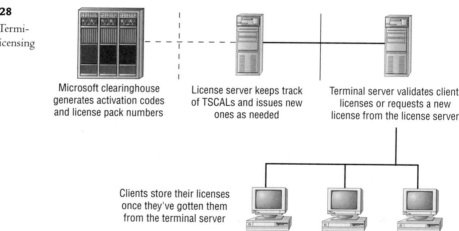

Microsoft clearinghouse generates activation codes and license pack numbers

License server keeps track of TSCALs and issues new ones as needed

Terminal server validates client licenses or requests a new license from the license server

Clients store their licenses once they've gotten them from the terminal server

The first time a client connects to a terminal server, one of two things happens. The terminal server will take the license the client proffers—I'll get to the question of just how a client would *have* such a license in a minute—or, if the client doesn't have a license, the terminal server will find the license server by discovery (broadcasts in workgroups and NT 4 domains or by polling the domain controllers in Win2K domains) and request a license from the license server. If the license server has a license to issue, it will give it to the terminal server, who will issue it to the client *computer* that's attempting to make the terminal connection. The client can then present its license to the terminal server and log in. If the license server does not have an available license—even a temporary license— then the client cannot log in. If the terminal server can't connect to the license server for some reason, then the terminal server will accept preexisting licenses, but clients without valid temporary or permanent licenses will not be able to log in to the terminal server.

Notice something critical here. In the scenario as I've described it, the client computer gets its license when it *connects* to the terminal server, not when the user initiating the session logs in. In the later section "Reclaiming TSCALs," I'll describe a post-SP2 hotfix that will allocate licenses only when the user has successfully logged in.

When a client disconnects from the terminal server, it retains its license—the license does not go back to a pool. Therefore, if I log in to the terminal server once from my office desk and once from my home office, I'll use up two separate licenses. You cannot give these licenses back to the license server; they're marked in the license server's database as given to a particular machine, identified by GUID.

Understanding Session Licensing

When Microsoft first released Windows NT, Terminal Server Edition, it made a terrible marketing decision. Any client connecting to the terminal had to have a valid NT Workstation license. At $400 a pop, NTW licenses aren't cheap, so a lot of people looked at TSE and said, "Nice, but not worth the money." In an effort to win those people back, in February 1999 Microsoft revamped their licensing structure, giving NT Workstation clients a built-in license to access the terminal server but requiring you to purchase terminal server licenses (which cost approximately $150 per seat instead of $400) for computers running any other operating system. However, access to the server running Terminal Services is licensed on a per-seat basis, not per user—computers are licensed, not people.

In Win2K, the licensing structure includes four license types:

♦   Terminal Server Client Access Licenses

♦   Terminal Services Internet Connector Licenses

♦   Built-in licenses

♦   Temporary licenses

NOTE   *Not all Terminal Services functions use licenses. When you're running Win2K's Terminal Services capabilities in Remote Administration mode (an option when you're installing Terminal Services), you don't need TSCALs because Remote Administration mode comes with two administrator's licenses.*

TERMINAL SERVER CLIENT ACCESS LICENSES

Terminal Server Client Access Licenses (TSCALs) are for named user accounts in the domain and issued on a per-seat basis. Anyone in a company who's using the terminal server must have a TSCAL, regardless of whether they're connecting to the terminal server via Microsoft's RDP display protocol or Citrix's ICA display protocol (which they would if you'd installed MetaFrame for Windows 2000). To access a Win2K server at all, of course, a client also needs a 2000 Client Access License (2000 CAL). TSCALs are sold for the retail trade in 5-packs and 20-packs; a 5-pack costs $749 retail and an upgrade from a TSE 5-pack costs $349. (For those not mathematically minded, that comes to just under $150/head retail, which is about what TSE TSCALs cost.)

License Packaging

The way you buy TSCALs determines how you pay for them and how much flexibility you have in the purchase. Most people who buy small volumes of Microsoft products will buy their TSCALs as part of a 5-CAL or 20-CAL Microsoft License Pak (MLP). Physically, an MLP is a thin cardboard envelope that contains the EULA denoting the number of CALs purchased. The MLP for TSCALs in Win2K also includes a license code, a 25-character alphanumeric code that indicates what the license is for and how many TSCALs it purchases (so that you can't fudge the entries and say that you bought 20 TSCALs when you really only bought 5). You can only install an MLP once. Small to medium customers will get their licenses through a program called Microsoft Open License, which allows you to purchase a user-specified quantity of licenses, after which Microsoft issues you an Open License Authorization and license numbers for the licenses, which you can install as many times as you need to. Select and Enterprise Agreements for large customers work like open licenses, except that the customer provides their Enrollment Agreement number instead of the Open License numbers.

Reclaiming TSCALs

Once allocated to a computer, a TSCAL belongs to that computer and is identified as such in the license server's database. You cannot release TSCALs from a computer, so the visiting consultant who logs in to the terminal server once leaves with a TSCAL. Not only that, but if you wipe a computer's hard disk and reinstall, then there's no record of that TSCAL on the computer and it will have to request a second one. If you need to reclaim TSCALs, then you'll have to telephone the Microsoft clearinghouse and ask them to give you more licenses to make up for the ones you lost.

That is, that's the case unless you install a post-SP2 hotfix on your terminal servers and license servers. Currently available for download from www.microsoft.com/windows2000/downloads/critical/q287687/default.asp, this hotfix resolves two problems with Windows terminal server licensing. First, after you install the hotfix, clients will only take a license after they have successfully logged onto the terminal server, not after they have created a connection and can see the domain logon screen. Second, it will allow unused licenses to slowly make their way back to the pool of available licenses. Notice that these changes apply only to licenses issued *after* you apply the hotfix.

The hotfix doesn't allow you to personally put TSCALs back in the license pool, but it allows unused ones to revert there—slowly. Rather than permanently assigning TSCALs to clients, after you apply the hotfix to all terminal servers and license servers, the license server will give first-time requesters a TSCAL with a time-out period (a randomly assigned interval between 52 and 89 days). When the user logs onto the terminal server, the terminal server tells the license server that the license has been validated (used by someone with permission to log onto the terminal server). The TSCAL is then assigned to that machine. Every time someone connects to the terminal server from that machine, the terminal server will check the expiration date on the TSCAL. When the expiration date is less than 7 days, the terminal server renews the TSCAL assignment to that machine for another 52 to 89 days. Should the client machine not log into the terminal server before its TSCAL expires, its TSCAL will return to the pool of available licenses. Although this fix doesn't make Windows terminal services licensing perfect, the ability to reclaim licenses (and only give licenses to machines used by people authorized to use a terminal server) is better than being on first-name terms with the people working at the Microsoft licensing clearinghouse.

INTERNET CONNECTOR LICENSES

The Windows 2000 Terminal Services Internet Connector License (TSICL) allows a maximum of 200 concurrent users to connect anonymously to a terminal server via the Internet. That's right— you can't use a TSICL to dial into the network from home but will instead need a TSCAL for your home computer. The TSICLs are solely for the purpose of demonstrating Web-enabled applications to Internet users. Not only that, but according to Microsoft, you can't install the TSICL pack on a Win2K terminal server that's for employees. The server will only allow client access to terminal services through the Internet—anyone who logs onto that server will use one of the TSICLs and will connect as an anonymous user. A 200-pack ICL for Win2K costs $9999, and these ICL packs are only available to Microsoft Select volume customers.

Frankly, the TSICLs aren't good for much because you can't legally use them to give employees home access to terminal services. Although it might sound as though the TSICLs are useful for application service providers (ASPs, which are companies that lease applications to people via a dial-up connection), they're really not—ASPs have a different licensing model. As noted earlier, the only use I can see for these licenses is for people offering samples of their software via a Web site.

UNLIMITED AND TEMPORARY LICENSES

The two remaining license types are simpler. Win2K Professional computers can draw from the license server's pool of unlimited licenses. Finally, the license server issues temporary licenses when a terminal server requests a license and the license server has none to give (perhaps because you haven't installed a license pack yet). The license server then tracks the issuance and expiration of the temporary licenses.

Byzantine enough for you? Table 15.6 is a cheat sheet.

TABLE 15.6: TERMINAL SERVICES PERMANENT CLIENT ACCESS LICENSE TYPES

SITUATION	TERMINAL SERVICES LICENSE TYPE REQUIRED	COST
Users connecting from Win2K Professional desktops	Unlimited pool	N/A
Users connecting from any desktop not using Win2K Professional	Terminal Server Client Access License (TSCAL)	A 5-pack of TSCALs costs $749 retail, and an upgrade from a TSE 5-pack costs $349.
Anonymous users connecting to the terminal server via the Internet	Terminal Services Internet Connector License (TSICL)	200 simultaneous anonymous connections cost $9999.

The Terminal Services Licensing Tool

To help you keep track of the licenses used, Win2K includes the Terminal Services Licensing tool, found in the Administrative Tools program group of any Win2K Server with the Terminal Services Licensing service running on it.

TIP Terminal Services Licensing is one of the services you can install during Setup, like support for Terminal Services itself. To add it after installing Win2K Server, open the Add/Remove Programs applet in the Control Panel and click the Add Windows Components icon. Follow the Windows Components Wizard and just pick the component from the list of available options. In a purely Win2K domain, with no NT domain controllers, this license server must be on a domain controller. In a Mixed domain, the license server may be on a workstation.

When you first start the licensing tool, it will browse for license servers on the network and then report back with the ones it found, as shown in Figure 15.29.

FIGURE 15.29

Use the Terminal Services Licensing tool to manage license usage.

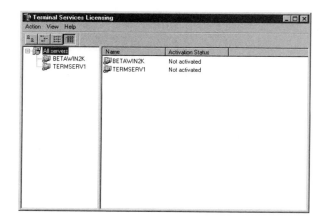

Win2K Terminal Services took a cue from Citrix and set up the same kind of licensing-enabling procedure. You can't just plug in the terminal server, tell the license server how many licenses you've bought, and let people log in. Although the temporary licenses will function for a limited time (90 days), to fully enable the terminal server licenses, you'll need to activate the server and download the license key.

Until Win2K, only Citrix products (MetaFrame and WinFrame) required activation. Activation is essentially a way of making sure you've really paid for the licenses you're using. (According to Citrix, it also helps technical support keep track of you for better customer support, but I have a sneaking suspicion that the "let's make sure people are paying for what they use" issue is a little more important—not that it wouldn't be important to me, of course.) When you activate a license, you're providing your product number to Microsoft. Microsoft then runs an encryption algorithm on it and sends you back the results as your activation code. You then give Microsoft back the activation code, they run another encrypting algorithm on it, and they send you a license code that corresponds to that activation code. This is an extra step, and that's annoying, but the procedure itself really isn't too arduous.

When you first open the Terminal Services Licensing tool, it looks like Figure 15.29. As you can see, the licensing server is present but not yet activated, so it can only issue temporary licenses that expire after 90 days. To make the license server ready to monitor license usage and to issue TSCALs, you'll need to activate the server and install the license pack assigned to that server. To do so, follow these steps:

1. Right-click the server and choose Activate Server from the context menu. Click through the opening screen.

2. Choose a method of contacting Microsoft to get a license. You have four options for contacting Microsoft to give them your product number. The Internet, the default option, gives you a direct connection to Microsoft but requires that the license server have an Internet connection. Other options include the Web (whether from the license server or another computer with an Internet connection), the telephone, or fax. For this example, I'll choose the Web (see Figure 15.30) and click Next.

FIGURE 15.30

Choose a way of contacting the Microsoft clearinghouse to get an activation code and valid license packs.

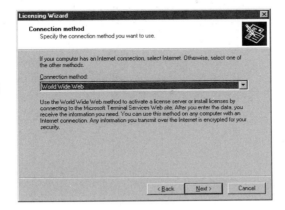

NOTE *If you choose to contact the licensing people via telephone or fax, the next screen of the wizard will display a list of countries to choose from so that you've got a shot at making a toll-free call. If you're licensing TSCALs for the MSDN version of Win2K, you'll need to call the clearinghouse.*

3. Now I need to take the product ID displayed in the screen (see Figure 15.31) and go to `https://activate.microsoft.com`. On this Web page, you'll have a choice of activating a license server or installing license packs. Choose to activate the server and choose Next.

FIGURE 15.31

Take the product ID here and send it to Microsoft to generate an activation code.

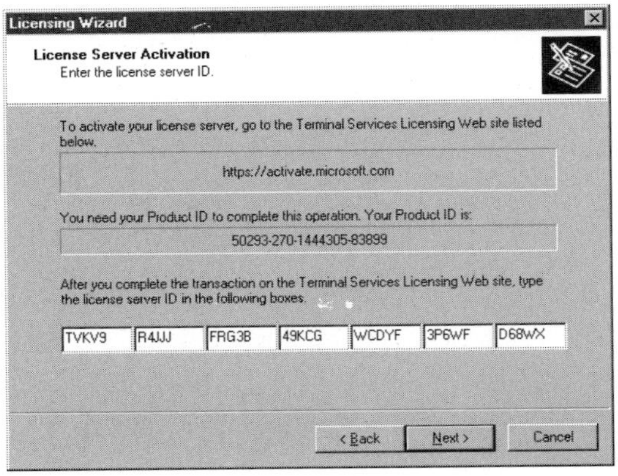

TIP   *When you try to activate a Terminal Services license server, you may see an error message telling you the licensing wizard cannot connect to the selected license server and prompting you to make sure the licensing service is installed and running. Additionally, the selected license server's activation status is unknown. This can happen if you're logged in with a roaming profile and the terminal server is set up to delete the roaming profile cache. It's also possible for this to happen if you're using a mandatory profile. The problem is that activating the server requires editing the profile, and in either case, you can't. SP2 addresses the problem if you're using roaming profiles with profile deletion enabled, but you can't activate a server when using a mandatory profile.*

4. On the next screen of the wizard, fill in the required product ID number, personal information, and purchase method (Select or Enterprise, Microsoft Open License, or Other to install via a retail licensing code). Click Next, review the information on the screen, and then click Next again to submit it. The Web site will spit out your activation code. Give it to the wizard to activate the server, which will then appear in the licensing tool with a status of Activated (green, and with a little picture of a certificate instead of the red X that unactivated servers get).

WARNING   *Be sure you have entered the product ID correctly, or the activation code won't work on your server. The Microsoft licensing clearinghouse generates that activation code by performing an algorithm on your product ID.*

5. Back on the Web site, you can quit now and enter the activation code you just got into the activation wizard, or, while still in the wizard, you can get client licenses based on the code displayed. You'll need client licenses, so you might as well continue. Click Yes to move to the next screen of the licensing tool, where you'll need to fill in the codes of all the license packs you have (the MLP number, or your Open License or Enrollment Agreement number, depending on what kind of customer you are). Again, confirm the information that you've entered and click Next to submit it.

6. The Web site will spit out a valid license pack number that will work with the server you activated, and which you can plug into the license server. Notice that it will only work with this server, and, if the license pack number is for a retail purchase, you can only install it once. To install the license pack number, return to the Terminal Services Licensing tool, right-click the activated server, and choose Install Licenses from the context menu. When prompted, fill in the license pack number as shown in Figure 15.32.

FIGURE 15.32

Installing the client access licenses

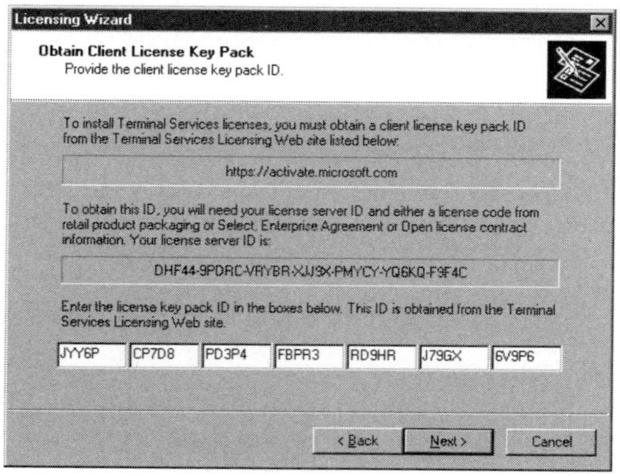

Once you install the license pack, the license server is ready to go.

TIP *If the license server won't accept a license pack and you're sure you typed it correctly, the database might be damaged. If it is, you can rebuild by uninstalling the licensing service, reinstalling it, and then reactivating the server.*

All that said, here's a warning: You have 90 days to activate a TSCAL license server. Use those 90 days to make sure you're running the licensing service on the computer that you want to take the job. The client licenses you create will only work on the server you've activated, and the activation code is based on the product ID.

Application Licensing

Application licensing in a terminal server environment is simpler than you might think: Whatever licensing that is applied to a product in a single-user environment applies to the terminal server environment. For example, Microsoft Office 2000 is licensed on a per-seat basis. If you install Microsoft Office onto the terminal server, then every computer that will ever run a Microsoft Office application will need to have an Office license, even if the application only runs once a year. However, because Office is licensed on a per-seat basis, if you already have a licensed copy of Office installed on a PC client running terminal services, that client may use Office in the terminal session (perhaps when dialing into the terminal server from home) without purchasing an additional Office license because that computer is already licensed to run the application suite. Be sure to get familiar with the licensing a given application requires so you can see how it will work in the multiuser environment.

Configuring Applications for a Multiuser Environment

Not all applications work well in a thin client environment. Some use up too many processor cycles or too much memory; some can't tell the difference between a user and a computer; some store information in locations inappropriate to a multiuser operating system. Sometimes you're stuck with these problems, and if you really need to run those applications, you'll need to do it from the client Desktop. However, some problems are fixable, if you take a little time.

Choosing Applications

First, which applications should you be trying to run at all? An application suitable for a terminal server environment fits the following profile:

- Undemanding of processor cycles and memory
- Modular in video output for better caching
- Stores user data in per-user spaces, not in per-machine spaces
- Identifies users by username, not computer name
- Stores global data in global locations, not local ones

> *WARNING*   *Poorly designed applications that can function in a single-user environment will bring a terminal server to a screeching halt. For example, the effect of memory leaks in an application is exponentially increased because multiple instances of the application—all leaking—may be running. (I keep mentioning SP2, but one of the things that SP2 does is fix some memory leaks in parts of the operating system—not a bad idea on a terminal server.)*

In addition to these traits, consider the operating system for which the application was originally designed. Although some Win16 and DOS applications can work in a multiuser environment, Terminal Services works best for Win32 applications. The reason for this has to do with how Win2K runs Win32 and Win16 applications. As a Win32 operating system, Windows 2000 can't run Win16 applications on its own. Instead, it creates a Virtual DOS Machine (VDM), which is a 32-bit application, and runs the Win16 application within the context of that VDM. Whereas Win32 applications running normally on Win2K can share files and structures among themselves, so long as they're not changing those files or structures, applications running within VDMs can't "see" each other to share files. The practical upshot of this, combined with the fact that translating 16-bit calls to the operating system into 32-bit calls takes some overhead, means that Win16 applications perform less well in this environment than Win32 applications. They'll work—a good thing because you may not have a choice about running them if that's what you're using—but they'll use more memory than Win32 apps.

DOS applications present another kind of problem. Actually, they present two other kinds of problems. First, DOS applications were written for a single-user, single-tasking environment. To be as responsive as possible, DOS applications constantly poll the keyboard buffer, looking for input that's meant for them. This means that a DOS application in the foreground, even when not doing anything, is using up an astounding amount of CPU time. This is acceptable in a single-user environment, but won't work when that CPU time has to be shared with a dozen people.

TAMING DOS APPLICATIONS

Windows NT, Terminal Server Edition (TSE), includes a utility called DOSKBD that modifies a program's keyboard polling to improve system performance when you run DOS-based programs. Essentially, DOSKBD puts a program to sleep when it polls the keyboard buffer too often and negatively affects server performance. Win2K doesn't include a copy of DOSKBD, and the TSE version doesn't work with Win2K Server Terminal Services.

I'm told that the Win2K Resource Kit will eventually include a Win2K-compatible version of DOSKBD, but it doesn't now. Until it does, according to Microsoft, people who need to use DOSKBD can't upgrade to Win2K Terminal Services—they're stuck with TSE. (And this means that new users of Terminal Services are out of luck, as Microsoft stopped making TSE in August 2000, and the only copies for sale are those made before that time.) However, there's another option. Go to www.mindspring.com/~dgthomas/tame.htm and check out Tame, a tool for tuning DOS applications in a Win2K environment. Until the resource kit utility is ready, that's the advice you'll get from Microsoft Support if you ask about tuning DOS applications.

Also, DOS applications with a graphical UI don't use Windows graphics rendering instructions, but bitmaps. Bitmaps take much longer to download to the client than GDI rendering instructions, so session responsiveness will suffer. Bitmap-displaying applications are jerky at best in a terminal server environment and more often are completely unusable, particularly on slower connections.

Another problem with DOS applications in a multiuser environment is that you can't run them in full-screen mode. Because full-screen mode requires loading a different font set from the Windows one used for DOS applications running in a window (and thus increased memory overhead), Microsoft decided not to permit this.

You *can* run DOS and Win16 applications in a terminal server environment. They just won't cooperate with other applications as well as Win32 applications will. DOS applications in particular probably won't look as good as they would running locally.

However, you can often tweak an application to make it work better in a multiuser environment than it would if left to its own fell devices. Installing applications in a multiuser environment takes a little more care than does installing them for a single-user environment, but that's part of the price of thin client networking.

Making Your Applications Play Well with Others

Even if an application doesn't need any massaging to make it work right when shared among multiple people, you can't install it in the same way you would if installing it for a single person's use.

To work properly in a multiuser environment, applications should edit the HKCU branch of the Registry to add user-specific information, rather than HKLM. Otherwise, those settings apply to the machine, not to the user. This means that not only are per-user settings available to everyone using that particular machine, but the settings will only be available at that machine—if the user logs in to another machine, the settings won't be available. If you've only got one terminal server in your network, it won't matter for this reason if application settings are machine specific, but a single terminal server will generally only serve a couple of dozen people, tops, and maybe fewer than that if client demands are high. Even if you do only have one terminal server, you've still got the problem of trying to keep user-specific information limited to the people who set it up. For example, say that Web browser bookmarks are stored in a machine-specific area. In a terminal server environment, that means everyone will have the same bookmarks—and will overwrite each other's settings at will.

Point being: User-specific settings should go into HKCU, not HKLM. However, you can't *install* applications into HKCU. HKCU applies only to the current user, not all users, and the identity of the current user will change depending on who's logged in—the contents of HKCU are different for each terminal server session. To get around this dilemma you need some user-specific settings, but you need to keep them someplace all users can get to, at least at first. Win2K manages this by providing a global installation mode that exploits the machine-wide settings of HKLM.

INSTALLING APPLICATIONS FOR MULTIPLE USERS

Each Terminal Services session has two operating modes: Execute and Install. The names are descriptive of what the modes are for: Execute mode is for running applications or installing for single users, and Install mode is for installing applications to be available to multiple users. The mechanics of installing an application depend on which mode you're in when running the application's Setup program.

If you install an application while in Execute mode, it installs and edits the Registry as it would if you installed it for use on a single-user computer. When a session is in Install mode, all Registry entries created during that session are shadowed under HKLM\Software\Microsoft\Windows NT\CurrentVersion\Terminal Server\Install. Any edits that an application makes to HKCU or HKLM are copied to HKLM\Software\ Microsoft\Windows NT\CurrentVersion\Terminal Server\Install\ Machine. You don't have to know all this to install applications. What you *do* have to know is that when the session is in Execute mode, if an application attempts to read an HKCU Registry entry that doesn't exist, Terminal Services will look in HKLM\Software\Microsoft\Windows NT\CurrentVersion\ Terminal Server\Install for the missing key. If the key is there, Terminal Services will copy it and its subkeys to the appropriate location under HKCU, and copy any INI files or user-specific DLLs to the user's home directory. For users without home directories, the files go to their personal folder within %*systemroot*%\Profiles. In short, Win2K makes the basic settings for each application machine specific, then copies these base settings into the user Registry entries so that the user can customize the application. Notice that this doesn't mean the application keeps returning to its pristine state every time the user runs it—the keys are only copied from their Install mode location to their user location if the keys don't already exist under HKCU. Some applications (such as Microsoft's TechNet) allow you to bypass Add/Remove Programs because the Setup program isn't named Setup.exe.

NOTE *Unfortunately, there's no way to spoof a user's identity to install an application for an individual while logged in with another account (if you logged in as Administrator and wanted to install an application for a particular user, for example). Nor can you specify a subset of users who should have access to a particular application. If you only want some people to use an application stored on a terminal server, the easiest way to manage that is to limit the people allowed to use that server.*

So how do you put the server into Install mode? On a Windows 2000 terminal server, it's easy: If you attempt to install an application from its Setup program without using the Add/Remove Programs applet, the installation will fail, and Win2K will nag you to run the Add/Remove Programs applet to put Win2K into Install mode. You cannot install an application for a single user if you've set up the server to be an application server.

When the application's Setup program finishes running, you'll go back to the wizard, which will prompt you to click the Next button. Finally, you'll see a dire-looking dialog box (see Figure 15.33) telling you to click the Finish or Cancel buttons when the installation process is complete, but warning you in capital letters not to do so *until* the installation is complete. Clicking Finish or Cancel returns the session to Execute mode.

FIGURE 15.33

Don't click the Finish button until the application is completely installed, or the settings won't all get copied.

Install mode's usefulness isn't limited to the installation process. Using application compatibility scripts or hand tuning, you can use Install mode to configure an application with general settings to apply to all users. Outside of Add/Remove Programs, you can put a session into Install mode with the change user command-line utility. change user has three options:

◆ /execute, the default, in which applications install in single-user mode

◆ /install, used to put the session into Install mode so that applications will be available to all users

◆ /query, which reports the mode that the session is in, like this:
   Application EXECUTE mode is enabled.

So, before running a setup program, open a command prompt and type **change user /install**. This will cause Win2K to shadow new Registry entries, as I described earlier, so that they'll be copied to each user's personal Registry settings as the user runs the application for the first time. Just bear in mind that *any* changes you make to an application while in Install mode will be copied to that Registry key and therefore apply to all users using the application for the first time.

NOTE   *If you notice that users are sporadically losing settings, or that settings from one user may appear in another user's profile, install SP2. This fix addresses a problem in Windows 2000 wherein running entries in a user profile's* RunOnce *key could switch the server to Install mode. If other software makes Registry changes during this time, the changes may be recorded and distributed to all other users on the server.*

USING APPLICATION COMPATIBILITY SCRIPTS

Given that just about all of the applications the terminal server users will be running were originally designed for a single-user environment, many applications require a little manipulation to get them optimized for a multiuser system. Win2K Server includes application compatibility scripts for some commonly used applications. You can find the scripts for the applications in Table 15.7 in *%system-root%*\Application Compatibility Scripts\Install.

TABLE 15.7: COMPATIBILITY SCRIPTS INCLUDED WITH WIN2K

APPLICATION	SCRIPT
Corel Office 7	Coffice7.cmd
Corel Office 8	Not supported
Eudora Pro 4.0	Eudora4.cmd
Lotus Notes 4.*x*	Lnote4u.cmd
Lotus Smart Suite 9	Ssuite9.cmd
Lotus Smart Suite 97	Ssuite97.cmd
Microsoft Access 2.0	Office43.cmd

Continued on next page

TABLE 15.7: COMPATIBILITY SCRIPTS INCLUDED WITH WIN2K *(continued)*

APPLICATION	SCRIPT
Microsoft Access 7.0	Office95.cmd
Microsoft Access 97	Office97.cmd
Microsoft Excel 5.0	Office43.cmd
Microsoft Excel 7.0	Office95.cmd
Microsoft Excel 97	Office97.cmd
Microsoft Excel 97 (stand-alone installation)	Msexcl97.cmd
Microsoft Exchange 5.0 and higher	Winmsg.cmd
Microsoft ODBC	ODBC.cmd
Microsoft Office 4.3	Office43.cmd
Microsoft Office 95	Office95.cmd
Microsoft Office 97	Office97.cmd
Microsoft Office 2000	Requires Transform file
Microsoft Outlook 97	Outlk98.cmd
Microsoft Outlook 98	Outlk98.cmd
Microsoft Outlook Express	Outlk98.cmd
Microsoft PowerPoint 4.0	Office43.cmd
Microsoft PowerPoint 7.0	Office95.cmd
Microsoft PowerPoint 97	Office97.cmd
Microsoft Project 95	Msproj95.cmd
Microsoft Project 98	Msproj98.cmd
Microsoft Schedule+ 7.0	Office95.cmd
Microsoft SNA Client 4.0	Sna40cli.cmd
Microsoft SNA Server 3.0	Mssna30.cmd
Microsoft SNA Server 4.0	Sna40srv.cmd
Microsoft Visual Studio 6.0	MSVS6.cmd
Microsoft Word 6.0	Office43.cmd
Microsoft Word 7.0	Office95.cmd
Microsoft Word 97	Office97.cmd

Continued on next page

TABLE 15.7: COMPATIBILITY SCRIPTS INCLUDED WITH WIN2K *(continued)*

APPLICATION	SCRIPT
Microsoft Word 97 (stand-alone installation)	Msword97.cmd
Netscape Communicator 4.0x	Netcom40.cmd
Netscape Communicator 4.5x	Netcom40.cmd
Netscape Communicator 4.6x	Netcom40.cmd
Netscape Navigator 3.x	Netnav30.cmd
Peachtree Complete Accounting 6.0	PchTree6.cmd
PowerBuilder 6.0	PwrBldr6.cmd
Visio 5.0	Visio5.cmd

These scripts are designed to customize the application's setup to be appropriate for terminal server users, first setting up the command environment, then making sure that the session is in Install mode, checking the Registry for evidence of the application to be configured, and finally editing the Registry as needed. The contents of the scripts vary based on the application, but generally speaking, they do things like turn off CPU-intensive features (such as the FindFast utility that comes with Microsoft Office), add multiuser support to the application, or set user-specific application directories for applications that need them.

To use the scripts, just run them right after you install the application they customize, before anyone has had a chance to use the application. For example, when you run the script for Office 97, Notepad will open and display the `RootDrv2.cmd` file, prompting you to pick a drive letter for the customized installation to use. Provide a drive letter, save the file, and close Notepad, and the script will run. Log out and log back in, and the new settings will be applied.

TIP *To make sure that no one tries to use the application before you've run the compatibility script, disable the RDP connection while finalizing the application setup.*

The release notes on the Windows 2000 CD detail the customization requirements for each application and inform you of any limitations that exist on these applications in a multiuser environment. Rather than reproduce the entirety of this very complete documentation, a simple example will show you why this kind of customization is necessary and how the script works.

You've probably encountered the Dr. Watson program a time or two in the past. If an application crashes, Dr. Watson runs and saves the debugging information to a file that you can send to the application manufacturer. The default location for this file is the system root directory, which normal users do not have permission to access and to which you don't *want* to *give* those users access. If an application crashes, Dr. Watson will not be able to write the debug files to its usual location and will prompt the user for a new file location.

If you want to keep things simple—and don't want to have to wonder where the debugging files are being written—then run the Dr. Watson application compatibility script. This will edit the application's settings to save the debugging files to the user's home directory, as specified in `RootDrv2.cmd`.

You're not limited to using the default settings included in these scripts. To edit one of them, right-click the script's icon and choose Edit from the context menu to open the file in Notepad. Before changing anything, I recommend that you inspect the readme file on the Win2K installation disk, so you know what you're doing.

What if your application doesn't have a script made for it? The `Templates` folder in the `Install` directory includes KEY files (you can open these in Notepad as well) that show you where each Registry entry for application settings is located and what the values should be. Based on this information and using an existing CMD file for a template, you can use the Windows scripting language to create a new script. Alternatively, you can manually edit the user settings from the application interface while the session is in Install mode, as described in the later section "Hand-Tuning Applications."

INSTALLING MULTIUSER-ENABLED APPLICATIONS

As Terminal Services becomes more widespread, it's probable that more applications will come with multiuser installation packages. Microsoft Office 2000 is one that presently does. If you try to run the normal installation program on a terminal server, you'll see a nag screen telling you that you can't do that and prompting you to use the installation files provided with the Office 2000 Resource Kit:

1. First, get the terminal server transform file, `TermSrvr.mst`, and place it in an accessible location for the installation. You can obtain the transform file from the `\ORK\PFiles\ORKTools\Toolbox\Tools\TermSrvr` folder of the Office 2000 Resource Kit CD, or in `\Program Files\ORKtools\Toolbox\Terminal Server Tools` if you installed the Resource Kit.

2. Install Office Disc 1 on the Terminal Server computer.

3. In the Control Panel, double-click Add/Remove Programs, click Add New Programs, and then click CD or Floppy. Click Next, then click Browse, and then move to the root folder of the installation CD and select **Setup.exe**. Click Open to add **Setup.exe** to the Run Installation Program box.

4. Don't run it yet. On the command line, append the following command after **Setup.exe**, separated by a space: **TRANSFORMS=*path*\TermSrvr.mst**, where *path* is the location where you copied `TermSrvr.mst`.

5. From here, all goes as expected. In successive windows of the installation wizard, provide your customer information and accept the EULA, then choose Install Now. When you see a message telling you that the installation completed successfully, click OK, click Next, and then click Finish.

HAND-TUNING APPLICATIONS

If you don't need to edit many per-application settings, it might be simpler to make the changes from the user interface while in Install mode, rather than trying to create a new compatibility script. You can also manually edit applications that *have* compatibility scripts but don't include some settings that you need to configure, like turning off the animated Help feature in Microsoft Office.

Turn Off Processor- and Bandwidth-Stressing Features

Terminal servers are designed to squeeze every last bit of juice out of system resources so that nothing is wasted. Therefore, they're often stressed—they're *supposed* to be stressed. Given that, don't waste processor cycles on producing effects that don't necessarily add any real content to the end product, and don't waste network bandwidth on sending those useless effects to the client. In Microsoft Office, for example, turn off sparkle text and the Office Assistant. In other applications, look for pretty effects that don't do anything constructive and see whether you can disable them.

Provide Path Information

Many applications have settings for file locations—places to save files to, places to open files from, template locations, and so forth. However, those locations will often be different for different users. To make sure that file locations for each user are correct, enter a drive letter—and then map that drive letter to different locations for each user. For example, the Save As location for all Word users could be H:, but H: would direct each user to their private home directory.

USING THE REGISTRY TO TUNE APPLICATIONS

Of course, if an application doesn't have a setting in its interface, you can't use Install mode to tune that setting. However, all is not necessarily lost. You can edit some application settings directly within the Registry, in `HKLM\Software\Microsoft\Windows NT\CurrentVersion\Terminal Server\Compatibility\Applications`. (Obligatory warning follows.)

WARNING *Be careful when editing the Registry. Neither REGEDIT nor REGEDT32 has an Undo feature, and neither will tell you if you edit a value to a meaningless entry. Back up the Registry before you edit it, and remember that a mistyped entry in the wrong place can wipe out needed information or render Win2K unbootable.*

More specifically, keep the following in mind:

- When editing value data, notice whether the values are shown in hex, decimal, or binary. When you're editing string values, you can choose to display them in any of those formats. Just be sure that you're entering the data in the chosen format. 15 decimal is F hex, but 15 hex is 21 decimal. You can guess how mixing up hex and decimal could get very ugly very quickly.

- If you're replacing a key (and, if you try out these hacks, you will be), be sure that the key that's selected is the one you want to replace. Restoring a key deletes all the present information in the key and replaces it with what's in the restored key. For example, say that you want to replace the contents of the `MSOFFICE` key that's a subkey of `Applications`. If you have `Applications` selected when you restore the saved REG file, you will wipe out every subkey of `Applications` and replace it with the information that should have gone into `MSOFFICE`.

- Never run a REG file unless you know exactly what it contains and what it will do. Executing a REG file imports the contents of that file into the Registry—permanently. There is no Undo feature.

Now that you're thoroughly intimidated, read on to see how to make your applications play well with others and call you by your name.

Bad! Bad Application! Go to Sleep! Reducing Demands of Windows Applications

Even if you turn off processor-hogging effects, some applications are just more cycle-hungry than others. In a terminal server environment, this is a Bad Thing. Not only do CPU-sucking applications themselves underperform in a multiuser environment because they're contending with other applications, but they hurt other applications' performance by denying them cycles. You can edit the Registry to make Win2K keep a closer eye on Windows application management, denying processor cycles to applications that use too many, known internally as Bad Applications. Doing so will give more cycles to the other applications that the processor-sucker was starving, but will also make the errant application less responsive itself.

To make the edit, open REGEDT32 and turn to the key HKLM\Software\Microsoft\ Windows NT\CurrentVersion\Terminal Server\Compatibility\Applications. As you can see in Figure 15.34, within the Applications key, you'll see a long list of keys for installed applications.

FIGURE 15.34

The contents of the Applications subkey

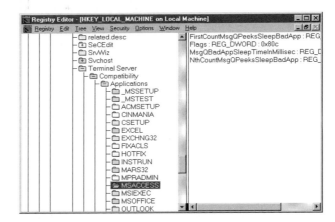

NOTE   *Use REGEDT32, not REGEDIT, for this process. You'll need tools found only in REGEDIT32.*

First, check to see whether the application you want to configure is already listed; if it is, then a key with the name of the application will be present. If the key exists, then open it. If the key doesn't exist, or doesn't include the values you need to edit, then you'll need to get the values elsewhere. Find the SETUP key, designed for Win32 applications.

NOTE   SETUP1 *is almost identical to* SETUP. *The only difference is in its Flags value, which is set for both Win16 and Win32 applications.*

Open SETUP and look at the values within it, which are described in Table 15.8.

TABLE 15.8: BAD APPLICATION REGISTRY VALUES

VALUE NAME	DESCRIPTION	DEFAULT VALUE
FirstCountMsgQPeeksSleepBadApp	Number of times that the application will query the message queue before Win2K decides the application is a Bad Application. The lower this value, the sooner Win2K will decide that the application is bad, and the more quickly the other two values will apply.	0xf (15 decimal)
MsgQBadAppSleepTimeInMillisec	The number of milliseconds that a suspended application will be denied CPU cycles. The higher this value is, the longer the application will sleep.	0
NthCountMsgQPeeksSleepBadApp	The number of times that a Bad Application can query the message queue before Win2K will put it to sleep again. The lower this number, the more often the misbehaving application will go to sleep.	0x5 (5 decimal)
Flags	Describes the type of application to which these settings apply. Your options are 0x4 for Win16 applications, 0x8 for Win32 applications, or 0xc for both types.	0x8 (Win32 only)

Assuming you're starting from scratch, you're going to save the SETUP key, import the key to a new (or existing) key for the application, and then edit these settings:

1. First, highlight SETUP, choose Save Key from the Registry menu, and as shown in Figure 15.35, save the key to the default directory with some name and a .reg extension.

2. Now, highlight the Applications key and choose Add Key from the Edit menu. In the dialog box shown in Figure 15.36, name the new key the filename of the application you're configuring, minus the extension—for example, wordstar.exe's key would be named wordstar. Leave the Class field blank, and click OK. The new key will appear below Applications.

FIGURE 15.35

Saving a Registry key

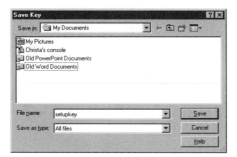

FIGURE 15.36

Creating a new
application key

3. Now, with your new key highlighted, pick Restore from the Registry menu and choose the REG file you created earlier. The Registry Editor will warn you that you're about to replace the contents of the selected key with the contents of the file you're importing. Once you're sure you're replacing the right key, click Yes.

Finally, double-click value data entries to make your edits in the dialog box shown in Figure 15.37, bearing in mind the information I gave you about what those edits will do. Make sure you've set the flags properly according to whether the application you're editing is a 16-bit or 32-bit application, and don't forget to notice whether you're making changes in hex or decimal (or binary, if you're a true glutton for punishment).

FIGURE 15.37

Edit string values
to set the Bad Appli-
cation parameters
you want.

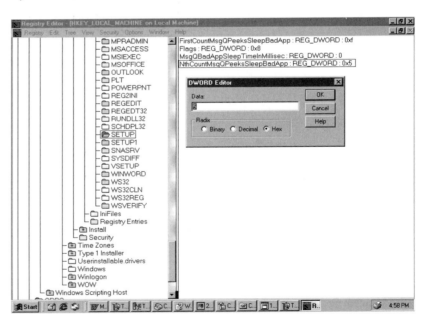

The settings will take effect when you next open the application. Because you edited a key in HKLM, the changes will apply to all instances of the application running on this terminal server.

The Hack That Was

Windows Terminal Server, and terminal sessions running on early betas of Win2K Server, had a little problem when it came to running WinChat, the graphical chat application that comes with Windows. Because WinChat referenced computers, not users, you couldn't use it from a terminal server session to talk to someone running another terminal session. Try to connect to someone, and you'd see a list of computers to choose from, as shown in Figure 15.38. Chat sessions with yourself get dull, so that made WinChat pretty well useless.

FIGURE 15.38

WinChat only provides a list of computers to connect to, not a list of users.

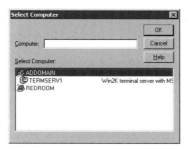

The intrepid user of Terminal Services is not foiled by such petty machinations, however. There's a cool hack you could use to make the application reference usernames instead of computer names. In `HKLM\Software\Microsoft\Windows NT\CurrentVersion\Terminal Server\Compatibility\Applications`, where you just edited the Bad Application settings, there's a value for Flags, which in the previous section was 8 or c, signifying that the settings applied to either a Win32 application or to both Win16 and Win32 applications.

TIP *To apply more than one flag to an application, add together the value of all the flags you want to use and make that the value of the Flags entry.*

You can apply several other compatibility flags to Flags with varying results. One flag tells Win2K to make the application return the version number; another tells it to make the application use the system root directory instead of the user's system directory. For our purposes, the important value is 0x10 (that is, 10 hex), which tells an application to look for users by their usernames, not their computer names. So, you could edit the value of Flags for the `WINCHAT` key to 18, telling Win2K, "Not only is this a Win32 application, but it should reference usernames, not computer names." No reboot is necessary; just restart WinChat. It wouldn't display usernames—that would have been handy, but no dice—but if you plug a username into the browse function, it would find that user and place the call.

You're probably thinking that I'm going to tell you that Microsoft fixed this problem in Win2K. In a way, you would be correct: You will no longer have problems running WinChat in a terminal server session and only being able to reference computers. This is because Microsoft has evidently decided there was no point in having a messaging application that "didn't work" from terminal server sessions available to those sessions. Now, if you attempt to run WinChat from a Windows 2000 Server terminal session, you get an error message telling you that that application can't be used from a terminal server remote session. When I asked Microsoft why they did this, the answer was that they were more interested in pushing NetMeeting than WinChat.

Well, that's *one* way to cut down on support calls, I suppose. The good news is that this hack will still work if you have any other applications that reference computer names instead of usernames—just edit that application's key as I described here. You just can't use it any longer to fix WinChat.

Managing Terminal Sessions

Thus far, you've configured client settings and set up applications. Everyone's happily typing away in their sessions. But what if they're not so happy? Win2K includes Terminal Services management capabilities that allow you to keep tabs on what's happening on the terminal server. These capabilities work both from the GUI and from the command line.

Introducing Command-Line Tools

Like the rest of Win2K, Terminal Services has some excellent GUI tools that make it easy to quickly get used to working with the service. That GUI can't do everything, however, and what it can do it can't always do *quickly.* Thus, the Win2K command-line tools that allow you to manage terminal sessions come in handy when it's time to make batch files—or just to do something quickly without taking the time to hunt down the right tool or part of the MMC. Experienced WinFrame hands may find some of these tools similar in function to command-line utilities found in WinFrame, although the tools are typically wrapped into a single tool (such as `query`) and the WinFrame tools made switches to the main Microsoft tool.

There are far too many options to go into complete detail about every one of the command-line tools listed in Table 15.9, but the following sections should help you get an idea of how you can manipulate Terminal Services from the command line and the GUI administration tool. I already discussed some of these—`flattemp` and `tsprof`, for two—earlier in this chapter.

TIP   To see a complete list of all options for a command, type its name and /? at the command line.

TABLE 15.9: SUPPORTED WIN2K TERMINAL SERVICES UTILITIES

COMMAND	FUNCTION
change logon	Temporarily disables logons to a terminal server.
change port	Changes or displays COM port mappings for MS-DOS program compatibility. For example, you could use this utility to map one port to another one so that data sent to the first would actually go to the second.
change user	Flips between Execute mode and Install mode.
cprofile	Removes unnecessary files from a user profile. You can only run this tool on profiles not currently being used.
dbgtrace	Enables or disables debug tracing.
flattemp	Enables or disables redirected temporary directories, which you can use to send TMP files to a location other than the default.

Continued on next page

TABLE 15.9: SUPPORTED WIN2K TERMINAL SERVICES UTILITIES *(continued)*

COMMAND	FUNCTION
logoff	Ends a client session specified by session name or Session ID, either on the local terminal server or on one specified.
msg	Sends a message to one or more clients.
query process	Displays information about processes.
query session	Displays information about a terminal server session.
query termserver	Lists the available application terminal servers on the network.
query user	Displays information about users logged on to the system.
register	Registers applications to execute in a system or user global context on the computer.
reset	Resets (ends) the specified terminal session.
shadow	Monitors another user's session. Cannot be executed from the console, and cannot shadow the console. Equivalent to the graphical remote control tools.
tscon	Connects to another existing terminal server session.
tsdiscon	Disconnects from a terminal server session.
tskill	Terminates a process, identified by name or by Process ID.
tsprof	Copies the user configuration and changes the profile path.
tsshutdn	Shuts down a terminal server.

Those who used TSE will notice that their tools are here, but many of the command names have changed. The utilities still provide the same functions as the commands in TSE, but you'll have to learn new names for most of them.

Using the Terminal Services Manager

To help you keep track of who's using the terminal server, what processes they're running, and the status of their connections, Win2K includes the Terminal Services Manager, found in the Administrative Tools program group and shown in Figure 15.39.

The left pane shows all domains in the network and all terminal servers within those domains. (You can use this tool to manage any terminal server that's listed; you don't need to be physically at that console.) The right pane's content depends on what's selected: If it's the domain or the entire network, then all current connections to that server (active or disconnected) and the name of the server hosting them are displayed; if it's a terminal server, then all current connections to that server are displayed; if it's a username, then all the processes running in that user's context, or information about the user session, are displayed. Notice also that the right pane is tabbed, with the contents of the tabs depending on whether you've got a domain, server, or user selected on the left. Broadly speaking, you use the administration tool to get information about:

◆ Users, including what their Session IDs are, what applications they're running, and what server they're using

◆ Sessions, including what the ID of that session is, what's running in that session, what the status of the session is, how long the client has been logged in, and information about the computer the client is logged in from (IP address, RDP version, and so forth)

◆ Processes, including the Process IDs and the executable files (*images*) with which these processes are associated

NOTE   *It's not hard to figure out what information you're looking at—a short period of poking around will teach you where everything is. More important is the question of what you can do with this tool. In the following example, I'll show you how to use the management tools to see what's running on the server, send messages to people on the server, terminate remote processes, and close user sessions. For this example, I'll refer to a bogus game called TSQUAKE, a Terminal Services—compliant version of Quake.*

FIGURE 15.39

The Terminal Services Manager tool

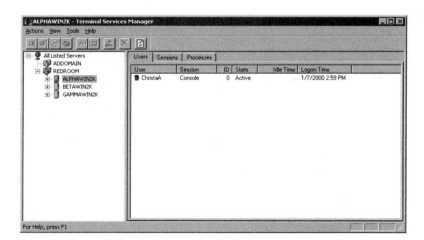

GATHERING INFORMATION

Who's playing TSQUAKE again?

To find out, you'll need to know who's logged in to the server or servers and what processes are running in their sessions. You can use both the Terminal Services Manager and the command line to get this data.

From the GUI, select the terminal server or domain for which you want information. In the right pane, three tabs will become visible: one listing users currently logged in to the terminal server, one showing the current active and disconnected sessions, and one showing the processes currently running on the terminal server.

Flip to the Processes tab associated with the domain (see Figure 15.40) to see a complete list of all processes running in the domain, the server they're running on, the session they're in, and the name of the user who owns that session. This screen will also show the Process ID (PID), which will come in handy when it comes time to terminate processes.

FIGURE 15.40

Viewing processes running on a terminal server

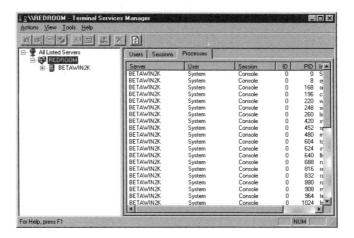

You can get more than just process information from this screen. Select a terminal server in the left pane. From the tabs that appear on the right, you can find the information described in Table 15.10.

TABLE 15.10: FINDING INFORMATION IN THE TERMINAL SERVICES MANAGER

DATA TYPE	TAB
Client computer name or IP address	Sessions
Image names for processes	Processes
Process IDs	Processes
Protocol used for each session	Sessions
Session idle time	Users
Session IDs associated with processes	Processes
Session status	Users, Sessions
User logon time	Users, Sessions
Username associated with processes	Processes
User Session IDs	Users, Sessions

Everything you need to find out—which user and which PID is associated with which session, and how busy that session is—is here. If you use the command-line `query` utility, you can get much the same information that you can from the Terminal Services Manager tool, but you have to do it a piece at a time. From the command line, there's no way to retrieve a list of all processes running in a domain or across all domains, so first you'll have to isolate the terminal server. For example, to see a complete list of all terminal servers in the current domain, type **query termserv**. Win2K will return a complete list of all terminal servers in the domain, like this:

```
Known Microsoft Terminal Servers
--------------------------------
SANDWORM*
TERMSERVA
TERMSERVB
```

Need the list from another domain? Add the domain name you're retrieving the list from to the command, like this:

query termserv /domain:_domainname_

You'll get the same output, customized for the domain you specified.

Once you've got the name of the server you need to check out, look for TSQUAKE by querying for processes, like this:

query process

Win2K will return a list of all processes running in the current session, as shown below:

```
 USERNAME        SESSIONNAME  ID    PID IMAGE
>administrator   console       0   1152 explorer.exe
>administrator   console       0   1348 osa.exe
>administrator   console       0   1360 findfast.exe
>administrator   console       0    532 infoview.exe
>administrator   console       0   2052 depends.exe
>administrator   console       0   2172 cmd.exe
>administrator   console       0    764 taskmgr.exe
>administrator   console       0   1256 tsadmin.exe
>administrator   console       0   1636 mmc.exe
>administrator   console       0   1500 winword.exe
>administrator   console       0   2092 regedit.exe
>administrator   console       0   1776 query.exe
>administrator   console       0   1652 qprocess.exe
```

To query the process list for a different user, add that person's username to the command, like this:

query process gertrude

TIP   *You can also list processes associated with a particular session name or Session ID, although for most purposes I find it easier to reference usernames.*

Okay, but what you really want is a list of everyone who's goofing off and using up CPU cycles. Although you can't get a list of all processes running in a single domain or across domains, you can retrieve a list of all users with a particular process running in their sessions, like this:

```
C:\>query process winword.exe
 USERNAME          SESSIONNAME      ID   PID IMAGE
>administrator     console           0  1500 winword.exe
 christa           rdp-tcp#1         1  1400 winword.exe
```

Use this command to track down those TSQUAKE users.

SENDING MESSAGES

Once you've got your list of people running TSQUAKE, you can let them know that they're caught. From both the GUI and the command line, you can send messages to a single person, to multiple people, and even across domains.

From the left pane of the Terminal Services Manager tool, select the terminal server the people are using. In the right, select the people to whom you want to send a message (Ctrl+click to select multiple usernames). From the Actions menu, choose Send Message to open the dialog box shown in Figure 15.41. Click OK, and the message will instantly pop up on the screen of everyone you included on the recipient list.

FIGURE 15.41

Sending a message to users

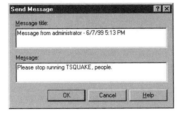

You can also send messages from the command line with the msg utility. This works much like msg did in single-user Windows, with one exception: messages sent to a username will be sent to all instances of that name, not just one. This is so that a person running multiple sessions will be sure to get their message.

msg has lots of options. Its basic syntax looks like this:

msg {*identifier*}[/SERVER:*servername*] [/TIME:*sec*] [/v] [/w] [*message*]

The *identifier* can be a username, Session ID, session name, or a filename containing an ASCII list of all users to whom the message should go. The /TIME parameter doesn't delay the message; rather, it's a time-out period that cooperates with the /w switch that waits for user response before giving control of the command prompt back to the message's sender.

NOTE   *Like the other command-line utilities,* msg *runs on the server you're connected to unless you specify otherwise.*

To send a message to a single user, run `msg` like this:

msg gertrude Gertrude, please close TSQUAKE. You're wasting processor time.

If you want some kind of record that Gertrude saw the message—or at least clicked OK—use the /v (for "verbose") switch as follows:

msg gertrude /v Gertrude, I mean it. Close the game.

You'll see output like the following:

```
Sending message to session RDP-Tcp#1, display time 60
Timeout on message to session RDP-Tcp#1 before user response
```

To send a message to everyone logged in to that terminal server, use an asterisk, like so:

msg * Hey, everyone--Gertrude's got enough free time to play TSQUAKE. Anyone got anything for her to do?

Alternatively, send a message to a preset group by typing all recipient names into a Notepad file and saving it, then referencing the file like this:

msg @users Hey, everyone--Gertrude has enough free time to play TSQUAKE. Anyone got anything for her to do?

The only catch to sending messages to multiple users is that if you add the /w option, `msg` works sequentially. That is, it will send the message to the first person in the list (going in order of Session ID) and wait for either a response or a time-out before sending the message to the second person in the list.

TERMINATING APPLICATIONS

Gertrude and the other TSQUAKE players aren't paying attention to your pleas. Time to get tough and terminate the application. Every instance of TSQUAKE that you close will exit immediately, with no warning to the user and no chance to save data.

NOTE *Before I get into this, let me distinguish between terminating and resetting. Both options close applications with no warning, but single processes are terminated and entire sessions are reset.*

To kill a single application from the GUI, select the server or domain in the left pane and turn to the Processes tab in the right. All running processes will appear here, identified by the name of the server they're running on, who's got them open, the PIDs of the processes, and other relevant information. As elsewhere, you can Ctrl+click to select multiple processes. When every process to be terminated is selected, right-click and choose End Process from the context menu (it's the only option). The selected applications will close instantly.

You can also terminate applications from the command line. Just be careful. This procedure is open to error, and you will not make people happy if you accidentally close the wrong process and lose all their data.

The command to kill terminal server applications is `tskill`, related to the `kill` command that appeared for the first time in NT 3.5's Resource Kit and which stops an application by killing its process. Like the Terminate menu command, `tskill` will stop an application as soon as it's executed, with no time allowed for saving data or other tasks. It's very intrusive, so you should only use it when there's simply no other way of getting an application to stop.

The syntax of `tskill` is as follows:

```
tskill processid | processname [/SERVER:servername] [/ID:sessionid | /a] [/v]
```

Notice that you can reference a process either by its name or its Process ID. The former is easier and necessary if you're using the `/a` switch to close all instances of an application on the terminal server. The latter is necessary if you're only trying to close specific instances of the application, perhaps leaving untouched the instance of TSQUAKE that your boss has open.

So, to kill all instances of TSQUAKE running on the currently selected server, you type:

```
tskill tsquake.exe /a
```

To kill only selected instances, get the PID by running `query process` or `query user` and plug it in, like this:

```
tskill 1875
```

Sadly, you can't list several PIDs at once to kill, so if you need to pick and choose processes without killing all instances, you'll need to terminate instances of a process one at a time.

TIP *Although you need to supply the executable extension with* `query process`, *the command won't work if you supply the extension with* `tskill`. *So, it's* **query process tsquake.exe**, *but* **tskill tsquake**.

TAKING CONTROL OF USER SESSIONS

Sometimes, the best plan isn't to just shut down applications from the terminal server. Instead, you can take control of a user session and see what they're doing (as opposed to listing processes, which just tells you what processes are active in the context of a given session). This can be especially helpful for troubleshooting purposes, such as if Gertrude says she didn't mean to run TSQUAKE but couldn't figure out how to shut it down once she had it running. Taking remote control of the session gives you the same degree of control that you'd have if logged on as that user.

You can remotely control a user's session in one of two ways: from the Terminal Services Manager or from the command line.

TIP *You can only take remote control of a terminal server session from another terminal server session, not from the console. The remote control option in the Terminal Services Manager and the* **shadow** *command-line utility won't work from the console. The session must be running at the same resolution as the session you're trying to control; you can't shadow a 1024×768 session from one running at 800×600.*

To use the GUI, start a terminal server session, logging in with an account with Administrator privileges. From within the session, start the Terminal Services Manager. Select a terminal server in the left pane and switch to the Users tab so that user sessions are showing. Find the session you want to shadow, and choose Remote Control from the Actions menu. A dialog box like the one shown in

Figure 15.42 will prompt you for the hotkey combination you want to use to end remote control of your own session (so you can get back to the original session).

FIGURE 15.42

Choose a hotkey combination to toggle back to your original session.

If the user session is configured to require user permission for control, then a dialog box will appear on the screen, letting the user know that someone has requested permission to control their session. If they permit the control, then you're in charge of their session without further ado. If they don't permit the control, then you'll see an error message telling you that you couldn't get permission to control the session.

NOTE *The degree of control you have over a user's session that you're remotely controlling depends on the settings in the user's account settings.*

The command-line utility for taking remote control of a user session is called `shadow`, after the WinFrame and MetaFrame name for remote control. Its syntax is as follows:

```
shadow {sessionname | sessionid} [/SERVER:servername] [/v]
```

To use it, start a terminal services session with administrative privileges. Open the command prompt and run **query user *username*** or **query session *username*** to find the Session ID or session name of the user whose session you want to shadow. You can't shadow based on ***username***, so you'll need this information even if you know the account name of the person whose session you're shadowing.

If shadowing a session on the same terminal server that you're logged in to, the command syntax for shadowing Session ID 1 is as follows:

shadow 1

If that session requires user permission to be remotely controlled, then you'll see the following message while your session waits for permission to take over the remote one:

```
Your session may appear frozen while the remote control approval is being
negotiated.
Please wait...
```

Once you have permission, you're in, just as you would be when using the GUI remote control option.

The only tricky part to shadowing from the command prompt is that you had best do it at least once from the GUI before trying the command-line utility. The `shadow` command does not prompt you for a hotkey combination to end remote control and return to your session. It will use the one defined for the GUI, so if you know what that hotkey combination is, you can use it. Just make sure you know how to return to your own session from the remote control.

Ending—or Preventing—User Sessions

That's it—Gertrude's kicked off the server until she can learn to stop using it incorrectly.

If you want to stop an entire terminal session, not just a single process within it, you can either disconnect or reset the connection. Disconnecting, you recall, cuts the user off from the session (although there's normally nothing to keep a user from reconnecting), but leaves all applications running and data in memory. When the user reconnects to a session they were disconnected from, then they're right back where they left off. A reset connection, in contrast, closes all applications the person had open. Disconnected sessions still use some system resources, albeit not much because their data will eventually be paged to disk and they won't have new user input to process. Reset sessions use no resources.

To disconnect or reset a session from the Terminal Services Manager tool, select it in the left pane and choose Reset or Disconnect from the Action menu. You'll see a dialog box warning you that the session will be disconnected or reset; click OK, and the selected session or sessions will be ended.

You can also end user sessions from the command line with the `tsdiscon` and `reset session` commands. The syntax for `tsdiscon` is as follows:

```
tsdiscon [sessionid | sessionname] [/SERVER:servername] [/v]
```

Once again, you can choose to identify sessions to close by session name or Session ID. To find out both, run `query session` to get output like the following:

```
SESSIONNAME  USERNAME       ID  STATE   TYPE   DEVICE
>console      Administrator  0   active  wdcon
 rdp-tcp      65537              listen  rdpwd
 rdp-tcp#2    Christa        2   active  rdpwd
                             1   idle
                             3   idle
```

Find the session name or ID you want, and plug it into the `tsdiscon` command like this: **`tsdiscon 2`**. Once you've pressed the Enter key, the user of the selected session sees a message, "Terminal Server has ended the connection," and is given a Close button to push.

TIP *I find it easiest to reference Session IDs. You always have to use a number—you can't choose to disconnect a session attached to a particular username—so you might as well choose the shortest identifier you can get away with.*

The syntax for resetting a session is similar to that used for disconnecting it:

```
reset session {sessionname | sessionid} [/SERVER:servername] [/v]
```

Once again, the user will see a dialog box telling them that Terminal Server ended the connection and prompting them to close.

What if you'd like to keep people off the terminal server altogether, perhaps while you're installing new applications on it? If no one's yet connected, you can disable the RDP protocol from the Terminal Services Configuration tool located in the Administrative Tools program group. Open the tool so that it looks like the window in Figure 15.43 and right-click the RDP protocol. From the pop-up menu that appears, choose All Tasks/Disable Connection.

WARNING *If you disable the connection from the Terminal Services Configuration tool, you'll reset any existing sessions.*

FIGURE 15.43

Resetting the RDP protocol

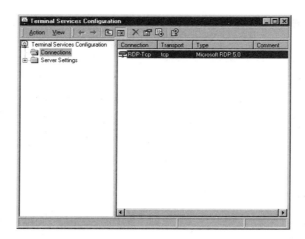

If you've reset all connections in preparation for shutting down the server, you can also shut down the server without going to the console. tsshutdn's syntax is as follows:

```
tsshutdn [wait_time] [/SERVER:servername] [/REBOOT] [/POWERDOWN]
➥[/DELAY:logoffdelay] [/v]
```

Most of these options are what they appear to be. *wait_time* specifies the amount of time (in seconds) until the server is shut down, and *servername* specifies a server if you don't want to shut down the one you're currently logged in to. /REBOOT reboots the server, and /POWERDOWN shuts it down if the server has Advanced Power Management drivers (if not, the server shuts down all server processes and displays the Click to Restart message).

So, for example, you could combine tsshutdn and msg to tell everyone that the server's going to be rebooted in five minutes. First, send the following message:

Msg * The server will go down in 5 minutes for maintenance. Please log out.

Second, run the tshutdn command with the following parameters:

tshutdn 300 /reboot

Say, however, that you don't want to shut down the server. You just want to keep any new sessions from starting. To disable the protocol for new sessions without disturbing the ones already in place, you'll need to use the change logon command utility. Its syntax is as follows:

```
change logon {/QUERY | /ENABLE | /DISABLE}
    /QUERY    Query current terminal session login mode.
    /ENABLE   Enable user login from terminal sessions.
    /DISABLE  Disable user login from terminal sessions.
```

Typing **change logon /disable** prevents any further connections from being made until you reenable the protocol. Anyone who tries to connect will see an error message telling them that remote logins are currently disabled. Disabling RDP does not, obviously, affect the console session as it's not dependent on RDP. As I mentioned earlier, you'll need to disable logins if you want to keep people off the terminal server, as the service itself does not shut off.

Do I Need MetaFrame?

That's a look at Windows 2000 Terminal Services in a nutshell. But you can't talk about Windows Terminal Services and ignore MetaFrame.

Microsoft didn't invent multiuser Windows—a company called Citrix did. Citrix still makes its multiuser Windows product, now called MetaFrame. Although MetaFrame is dependent on the presence of Windows terminal services, it adds a lot to it. With the advent of Microsoft's Remote Desktop version of the RDP client, the RDP client has just about caught up with ICA, MetaFrame's display protocol. But for some purposes you may still need MetaFrame even after .NET Server and its updated RDP server component are available.

NOTE *Incidentally, the latest version of MetaFrame is MetaFrame XP. This has no relation to Windows XP, according to Citrix—I'm told by someone who should know that Citrix came up with the "XP" moniker before Microsoft did.*

I don't have room here to discuss MetaFrame in real detail, but let's take a look at the features that might make MetaFrame XP a valuable addition to your Windows 2000 terminal servers. As you'll see, most of these features have to do with the servers, not the clients.

Multiprotocol Support Terminal Services uses RDP to pass user input and terminal output between client and server. RDP depends on TCP/IP, which means that both the client and the server must be running it. This isn't all that big a deal because the Win32 clients that Terminal Services supports all come with TCP/IP. The ubiquity of the Internet makes TCP/IP the transport protocol of choice on most networks anyway, but Terminal Services does lock you into one protocol. The ICA protocol used with Citrix's MetaFrame, in contrast, supports IPX/SPX and NetBEUI.

Application Publishing With Win2K, you can create client connections that supply only applications, but the user must know which server is running the application and make an explicit connection to it. With MetaFrame, you can create general client connections to a set of servers running a certain application, without the client having to know or care which server is providing the application. These connections may be displayed on the user Desktop (for Win32 clients) or in a folder called `Program Neighborhood`, or in a browser using MetaFrame's NFuse Web-based application publishing. NFuse is not the same as the TSAC, which is an RDP client in the form of an ActiveX control. All the TSAC does is build the RDP client into a Web page so that people can connect to the terminal server through Internet Explorer. TSAC doesn't have any application-publishing features at all.

Seamless Windows Seamless Windows—the display of applications or a Desktop that fits perfectly into the local environment—is important for a couple of reasons. From the client perspective, Seamless Windows means you can see the entire Desktop or entire published application without having to scroll or display the session in full-screen mode. From the server perspective, all sessions displayed using Seamless Windows and running on the same MetaFrame server are actually running from the same session, and thus using up less memory than connecting to each application individually.

Load Balancing Load balancing is not unique to multiuser Windows; it's the ability of multiple servers to work in tandem so that the least-busy server processes client requests. Windows 2000 Server does not support load balancing. Win2K *Advanced* Server and Datacenter Server support

Network Load Balancing for user logons, but it's restricted to load balancing according to client IP address. To get application load balancing for Win2K Server, you'll need the load-balancing version of MetaFrame XP: XPa. MetaFrame XP's load balancing allows you to allocate work among servers according to processor load, memory load, the client's IP address, the applications being run, and other rules.

All that said, Win2K Terminal Services is a perfectly serviceable tool for implementing Terminal Services in your network, particularly for smaller environments. And Win2K has one *great* advantage over third-party products: price. Although Win2K Terminal Services client access licenses (TSCALs) aren't free for most client platforms, if you install MetaFrame you'll have to purchase both the TSCALs and *additional* licenses for the MetaFrame access. And MetaFrame isn't cheap.

Using Remote Administration Mode

This chapter is generally about how to use Terminal Services to create application servers, but as I've said, Terminal Services gives you a handy way of accessing *any* Win2K server. If you've never used Terminal Services for remote management and you've just read this chapter about how to set up an application server, you may have some questions about how Remote Administration mode works and what you can do with it, so let's address those now.

How Much Will Remote Administration Mode Affect Server Performance?

You're probably aware that a terminal server requires a lot of horsepower to support all those clients and may be wondering whether Remote Administration mode is going to require you to seriously beef up your ordinary servers. Nope. Application servers require so much memory because many people are using them at once, not because the service itself is particularly power-hungry. The total memory requirements for running Terminal Services in Remote Administration mode are a little less than 2.5MB of RAM. In other words, if the server can do what it's supposed to do, unless it's very stressed, remote administration shouldn't faze it.

How Do I Connect to the Terminal Server?

If you like, you can use the Terminal Services clients described earlier in this chapter, installing them and connecting as I explained earlier. But for remote administration, there's a much cooler idea. Remember the Terminal Services Advanced Client (TSAC) I mentioned previously? In the same download area of the Microsoft Web site, there's a MMC snap-in that you can add to a Windows 2000 computer so you can manage servers from the MMC. This snap-in works on either Win2K Server or Pro computers, as it's just an interface for connecting to a server via RDP.

To get the MMC snap-in, go to www.microsoft.com/windows2000/downloads/recommended/ TSAC/default.asp, choose MMC Snap-In from the drop-down list, and click Next. The next page explains how to install the snap-in and allows you to pick the language you want to use. Click Next again, and you're at the download page. When you click the I Accept – Download Now button, you'll see a dialog box for saving Tsmmcsetup.Exe (349KB) to your network.

TIP   *Install SP1 or later before installing this tool. There's a bug in the snap-in that prevents the window from resizing if you change the size of the MMC or the child window that displays the terminal session.*

To install the MMC tool:

1. Run the EXE.

2. Agree to the EULA.

3. Accept the default location of the snap-in (`C:\Program Files\Terminal Server MMC Snap-In`) or browse for a new one. Setup will copy the files to the location you said and add a Terminal Services Connection tool to your Administrative Tools folder.

4. When you select this tool, at first it will only have an empty group for Terminal Services connections. To add a new connection, right-click and choose Add New Connection from the context menu. You'll see a dialog box prompting you to browse for servers running TCP/IP listener (running Terminal Services), or to type in a name or IP address for a terminal server, Using the boxes provided, name a server and, if you like, give the connection a name.

5. When you have picked a server, the logon information boxes allowing you to fill in your username, password, and domain for automatic login will become available. You can either fill in that information now or log in to the domain or server as you normally would when initiating a terminal connection.

TIP *If the server you're running has Terminal Services installed in Remote Administration mode, you can add it to the list of connections. If you want to shadow another remote session, you'll need to do so from a terminal session—the console doesn't support shadowing.*

6. After you have chosen a server to connect to, it will appear as a computer object below the Terminal Services connections object. To connect to a server, double-click its name. If you didn't fill in login information, you'll be prompted for it. The terminal session will be displayed within the MMC, so you can flip between as many sessions as you like.

NOTE *You can only connect to a computer for remote administration if you're a member of the Administrators group, and the server will only accept up to two connections at once. Disconnected sessions count toward the count.*

How Many People Can Log in to the Server?

When you install Terminal Services into this mode, you're permitting up to two simultaneous administrative connections to the terminal server. (Anyone whose account does not have administrative privileges on the domain will be denied access to the server, so you don't have to worry about Joe User logging into the Web server if he doesn't have an administrative account.) The licenses for these connections are built in, so you don't need additional licenses for server management—or a Terminal Services license manager—if you're only using Terminal Services for this purpose.

Can I Run Any Management Tool from a Terminal Session?

Sort of. Microsoft notes several tools that won't work in a terminal session and that you must operate from the console. Microsoft SQL Server 6.5 and 7 PerfMon counters cannot be accessed from a remote session (this is fine; you really don't want to be running System Monitor from an RDP session anyway—too many graphical updates) and must be viewed from the console. Also, Pervasive

SQL v7 has a namespace problem that prevents the tool from installing properly from a terminal session. Otherwise, though, most tools will work in a remote session.

NOTE *Although Microsoft says that the Disk Management tool won't work properly from a terminal session, and changes to volumes or disks won't show up in the terminal session until you log out and log back in, I haven't found this to be the case.*

However, you may not *want* to run all administration tools from a remote session because the display of the tool will affect how well the tool works from a terminal session. For example, don't bother trying to view performance data in System Monitor from a terminal session because the constant screen updates will be jerky and slow. Think of Remote Administration mode as a version of Telnet that has some graphical support, and you'll find it easier.

Chapter 16

Connecting Macintoshes to Windows 2000

A LARGE NETWORK IS likely to contain more than just Windows computers. If your network includes Macintosh computers, this chapter will give you the necessary information to connect them to your Windows 2000 servers for file and print services.

Though many people mistakenly think that MacOS-based computers are really only good for graphics and publishing, they remain real computers, just like Windows-based systems but with a different way of looking at things. Because of this, it is not uncommon to find Macs in many network environments, and often for graphics and publishing. Regardless of what the Macs are actually used for, however, they are often served by Windows NT–based servers running File and Print Services for Macintosh. Unfortunately, getting Macintosh support in Windows NT 4 was akin to pulling teeth. The good news is that the Windows 2000 Server Services for Macintosh (SFM) is vastly improved and better-integrated into the operating system, easing administrative woes.

That's not where it stops, though. There are two other possibilities to consider, AppleShare IP and MacOS X Server, both of which are capable of supporting Windows-based workstations for file and printer sharing. AppleShare IP 5.x and above (currently to version 6.2) has built-in support for the SMB networking protocol, the native language of Windows. MacOS X Server can have SMB support added through a utility from the Unix world called Samba.

Though it is often a good thing to have diversity in environments, as it drives innovation and lowers prices, here it helps little. We now have several potential solutions to various cross-platform problems, and the more choices we have, the more confusing it can become. And while some networks may be purely Apple-centric, which greatly eases administration, many network designers understandably recognized the power of Windows NT 4 Server for large storage server solutions. To raise the bar, Windows 2000 makes these tasks much easier, but there are still concerns for security in a mixed environment.

This chapter explains the options available in Windows 2000 for supporting Macintosh clients; it also covers other solutions from the Macintosh side of the equation.

Getting Started

Before you jump right in and install SFM, you should take a look at your existing network and its hardware and make sure everything is set up so that SFM works properly. Among the things you should consider when connecting your Macs to a Windows 2000 network is the physical hardware required.

10Base-T, 100Base-T, or 1000Base-T?

Today it is nearly a foregone conclusion that some form of Ethernet will be used in the LAN network environment. The question remains, "How fast will we go?" For you, this will be an easy decision because you can make the same choice for all of your platforms. Gone are the days of slow and incompatible LocalTalk networking. Ethernet has made major inroads into the Macintosh platform for many years now. Part of the equation depends on the type of Macintosh equipment you have (see the next section for an overview).

TIP *Your best tool in a Macintosh arsenal is GURU from NewerRAM, makers of RAM upgrades. This free utility lists every known Apple Macintosh and MacOS clone system in existence. It not only covers what NewerRAM RAM will upgrade your 7200/120, but every other technical note worth knowing about the various models. There's also an unmistakable dash of nonsense thrown in to make you laugh in between reading about maximum throughput numbers for the serial bus on the Performa 5250 and figuring out how many VRAM slots there are in a 7300/200. Pick up your copy at* www.newerram.com/products.

As for deciding which type of Ethernet to support, this depends almost entirely on two things: what you're already wired for and what your Macs support natively. As you'll see in the next section, most Power Macs come with built-in Ethernet, which can be good and bad.

Knowing the Macintosh

Understanding the systems that you work with day in and day out is crucial. If something goes down, you need to know either what to do to fix it or where to find the information that will help you. Here's some helpful information about the Macintosh that will give you an edge.

PRE–POWER MAC/68K SERIES

The venerable 68k series of Macs come in many configurations and various form factors. If your company still has these types of Macintosh in use, you may still be using LocalTalk. If you are, stop. Migrate to Ethernet. All of your legacy Mac hardware can be integrated into your Ethernet network for less than $130 per computer. Granted, the connection to the network will still only be as fast as the serial port on the Mac can handle, but 57,600 isn't too bad, considering that most operations involve small amounts of data and documents.

FIRST-GENERATION POWER MAC

The first generation of Power Macs is made up of transition systems that were meant to make the move from 68k CISC to PowerPC RISC as seamless as possible. It worked. There were very few problems associated with the complete migration to the new CPU architecture, despite the fact that all 68k operations are performed in *emulation*. The majority of these systems, based on the then-powerful PowerPC 601, came with either built-in 10Base-T Ethernet ports (RJ-45) or an AAUI-15 port, which can use an Ethernet transceiver for adaptation to Ethernet (around $30 a unit). These systems all have NuBus slots. 10/100 cards from Asante are around $300 for the few models that do not have built-in Ethernet.

SECOND- AND THIRD-GENERATION POWER MAC

Though the first-generation systems were bulletproof, the second- and third- generation computers proved that Apple could continue to develop powerful and stable machines. This was also the age of the Power Mac Performa. Almost all non-Performa systems shipped with built-in Ethernet configured in the same way as first-generation machines. This collection also spawned the best-selling Power Macs of all time, the 8500 and 9500 (the iMac has sold more than 3 million units as of this writing, making *it* the new sales leader).

TIP   *A new market for CPU replacement has emerged that allows you to upgrade even a lowly 6100/60 to a G3. How? Simple, really. The companies that sell these cards employ the little-used PDS (Processor Direct Slot) to connect a card with the necessary circuitry. Later Power Macs mount the factory CPU on a daughter card for easier upgradability. So, don't throw out those old Macs! Prices for the upgrades ranged from $199 for 240MHz and $499 for a 477MHz at the time of this writing, but be sure to check out the many Mac upgrade Web sites for the latest pricing information. They oughta know; they sell them!*

FOURTH-GENERATION AND G3 POWER MACS

Apple continued its strong lead by releasing some updates to their most popular machines. These were the 7300, 8600, and 9600. Stocked with powerful 604e CPUs, PCI slots, the ability to hold 1GB of RAM, and very easy-to-open cases, they sold well. The jig was up, though, as Apple caused sales on the latest Power Macs to go somewhat limp. Apple had already announced the successor to the 60*x* line, the G3 (known internally at Motorola as the PowerPC 740; G3 is an Apple name for the CPU). People decided that it was easier to wait a few more months and get a much more powerful computer.

The first G3 Power Macs came in a desktop case and a mini tower case that looked identical to two earlier Mac favorites, the 7300/200 and 9600/350. In fact, other than a slightly faster bus and a G3 CPU inside, they were no different, with one serious exception: they were limited to 384MB of RAM. For serious users and companies that rely on the latest, this was potentially disastrous, especially to video and sound professionals who typically have up to 1GB of RAM installed. Subsequent models, however, have proven to be better suited to their common purpose.

NOTE   *All fourth-generation Power Macs and first-generation G3 Power Macs have built-in Ethernet.*

G4 POWER MACS

In early 1999, Apple released the next-generation G4 systems. Billed as a desktop supercomputer, these systems truly have the ability to perform over 1 *billion* gigaflops per clock tick with a theoretical limit of four! A G4 500 is purported to be able to outrun—by three times, mind you—a Pentium III 600. Neato. This type of speed and raw instruction parsing power was previously only available to those who could pony up the several hundred thousand dollars it took to buy a real supercomputer. You can now buy one for $1599. Monitor sold separately.

The G4s are mostly architecturally identical to the G3s in relation to RAM (1GB max.) and drive (1TB max. in the box) space. The PCI slot arrangement has been modified a bit. There is now a real AGP 2x slot for the video card on board. The remaining slots are the same as on the previous model: one dedicated video slot and three 64-bit PCI slots for additional expansion. These new systems also have built-in 10/100 Ethernet support and an option for a 1000Base-T card to be installed.

NOTE *Apple also offers the G4 Cube, which packs an amazing amount of power and capability into its eight inches. Also available are two dual-processor G4s—one model has two 450MHz processors, and the faster model sports two 500MHz processors. For more information on Apple's G4 products, visit* `www.apple.com`.

You also may have heard that the new Power Macs do not have floppy drives. This is true. Apple decided that it would be better to leave out the cost of a floppy drive ($80 for a Mac because they have auto-eject, unlike manual Windows floppy drives that run around $20) and put that money elsewhere. There are also no traditional Macintosh expansion ports to speak of. Instead, there are USB and FireWire (also called IEEE 1394) ports, which are hot-pluggable and much, much faster.

THE IMAC

So phenomenal is the success of the iMac that it is often overlooked by systems administrators as a toy, and they'd be wrong. The first iMac came with a measly 233MHz G3, 4GB HDD, 32MB of RAM, 15-inch monitor, and 10/100 Ethernet. It also revived a slipping USB market. Today, you get a powerful 450MHz G3, 64MB of RAM, and a 20GB HDD, 15-inch monitor, and 10/100 Ethernet. They are solid performers and already have the hardware to integrate into a network.

TIP *The iMac was designed in part to act as a network computer (NC). Using a feature afforded by MacOS X Server, an iMac can be booted up over the network without requiring a local* `System` *folder. The iMac's system resides on the server and is sent to the iMac when it requests a boot session. A single MacOS X Server can use its Netboot capabilities to provide bootable systems for 50 iMacs at the same time, but more on that later.*

WARNING *The iMac does not ship with a floppy drive, nor is one available at extra cost. Though it is uncommon for anyone to actually use the little plastic guys anymore, it's a safe bet that when you drop an iMac on a user's desk, they'll immediately require one. If you need to provide workstation storage, consider a low-cost SCSI Zip drive for around $100.*

Apple has gone on to announce new iMac models, straying somewhat from the one-model ethic established at the iMac's introduction. There are now four to choose from. The basic model, which now sells for $799, was Apple's first foray into the sub-$1k market. This model comes in only one color, has a 350MHz G3 CPU, 64MB of RAM, a 7GB hard-disk drive, a CD-ROM, a 56k modem, two USB ports and a 10/100 Ethernet port.

The new iMac models—the DV (for digital video), DV+, and DV Special Edition—come in a choice of colors. The iMac DV has a 400MHz G3 CPU, 10GB hard-disk drive, a CD-ROM, two USB ports, and two 400Mbps FireWire (IEEE 1394) ports. The DV+ version has a 20GB drive and replaces the CD-ROM with a 4× DVD-ROM. The iMac DV Special Edition adds another 64MB of RAM and bumps the HDD to 30GB. The DV models are priced $999, $1299, and $1499, respectively.

One of the more attractive aspects of the new DV systems is their built-in video capabilities. Apple even goes so far as to provide the software required to perform video editing. Simply plug your digital camera into one of the supplied FireWire ports, and you're good to go (most middle- and high-end video cameras have been shipping with IEEE 1394 support for the last few years). Needless to say, this is a very inexpensive way to add video-editing capabilities to your company's toolbox.

NETWORK ADAPTERS

Ethernet provides the most cost-effective, universal, and sturdy network media format for Windows 2000 servers and yields the best transmission speeds. As you read earlier, most Power Macs come with Ethernet capabilities built in. Some, like the 7300, 8600, and 9600, offer an RJ-45 and AAUI, while most provide an AAUI-15 port, which requires a transceiver (roughly $25–$30 per unit, less in bulk). There is no loss of performance when using an AAUI interface transceiver; however, the built-in Ethernet in most of these older Power Macs is limited to 10Base-T, so an upgrade is necessary for all other speeds.

TIP *All Power Mac systems from the fourth generation to today use PCI, exactly the same as in PCs. Adapters are also available for the NuBus interface (for older Macintosh systems using the 680x0 processor and first- and second-generation Power Macs). Network adapters for Macs include Ethernet, Token Ring, Fiber Distributed Data Interface (FDDI), and fiber optic. The Ethernet adapters can be either standard 10Mbps coax or unshielded twisted pair (UTP), 100Mbps cards using Category 5 UTP cable, or the newly standardized 802.3z, also known as gigabit Ethernet. Gigabit Ethernet is now built in on G4 dual processors.*

CABLING

Though you are most likely boringly familiar with cabling, we feel it is important to mention that Macs use exactly the same cable for the job as a Windows machine would. Macs can also be added to any topology you might require or that already exists.

PHYSICAL TOPOLOGIES

As touched on earlier, Macs can participate on every physical topology that Windows 2000 can—nothing new there. It's also fair to say that Ethernet has dominated the networking world with its lower cost of implementation and its fast, reliable performance.

Today, even 100Base-T implementations of Ethernet are quite affordable and offer even better performance. Perhaps the best part of using Ethernet is that you probably already have the necessary equipment in your Windows 2000 server. If you have the proper adapter card, Macs can use coax cable to attach to older 10Base-2 or 10Base-5 networks, although this is increasingly uncommon. Twisted pair (commonly referred to as UTP; the *U* stands for unshielded) is the versatile media of choice these days. Considering how cheap a single Ethernet installation is (approximately $30–$40 per seat), it's well worth the investment to upgrade if you're still using LocalTalk, even though it is very unlikely you are. Add to this the fact that almost all Macintosh computers have a built-in Ethernet port, and making the decision is quite easy.

NOTE Since the Mac's introduction in 1984, there have been well over 60 million Macintosh computers sold. Roughly 60 percent of these computers have built-in Ethernet capabilities, including the very first Power Mac, the 6100/60, introduced in March of 1994.

Topologies available for Ethernet include the star and bus or possibly a combination of the two, depending on your needs, physical location, and reliability requirements. Bus topologies typically use either 10Base-2 or 10Base-5 coax cable to connect the nodes together, and can reach over fairly long distances (185 meters for 10Base-2 and 500 meters for 10Base-5). Star topologies allow for up to four hubs between any two nodes, for a total length of about 100 meters.

File and Print Server Considerations

Windows 2000 Server can provide file and print servers for Macintosh computers, but it does not include a client service that would allow it to connect to a Macintosh computer to retrieve files. To accomplish that task, you would need to purchase one of the NetBIOS network packages for the Macintosh computer. The most common use for the File and Print Servers for Macintosh is to provide greater storage capacities and a common drop point for both Windows and Macintosh clients.

NOTE Thursby Software makes DAVE, a NetBIOS client for the MacOS. DAVE allows the Mac to look like a Windows client to the rest of the network. A demonstration copy is available at `www.thursby.com`.

Back in the days of yore, disk partitions for the Macintosh operating system were limited to a maximum size of 2GB. But with System 7.5, the capacity rose to 16GB and then, beginning with OS 8, to 2 terabytes. With the earlier operating systems for the Macintosh, it was very important to find a server solution with greater capacity for file storage. At that time, Windows NT Server gave Macintosh users a solution for a network server with much greater storage capacities. If you are setting up the File Server for Macintosh for Macs that are not using more recent versions of the MacOS, bear in mind that they will be limited in the size of volume they can see. If you support Macs that are pre–System 7.5, they are not able to see more than 2GB in a single volume. (And if you're still supporting pre–System 7.5 Macs: ouch!) You must limit the size of the Macintosh-accessible share to 2GB for these clients, or upgrade. When you install the File Server for Macintosh, it will automatically create one shared folder to contain the Microsoft User Authentication Modules (UAMs). Unlike Windows NT 4, Windows 2000 doesn't require that you create the Macintosh-accessible volume to contain your shared files at the time of install. Instead, when you share a folder, you make the decision to provide access to Windows clients, Macintosh clients, or both. You will also be able to limit the size of the shared folder to comply with the needs of the particular Macintosh operating system version.

It's also easy to set up printing from a Macintosh to a Windows 2000 server. The Print Server for Macintosh can make any physically attached print device available on the network for Macintosh clients. It can also attach to, and even capture, AppleTalk printers on the network. When you choose to capture the AppleTalk printer, only the Windows 2000 server can send jobs to the printer.

One of the old complaints on Macintosh networks involves the use of different revisions of print drivers. Every time a Macintosh client sent a job to an AppleTalk printer, it had to load its driver on the printer first. If several Macintosh clients were doing this with different versions of the driver, it could result in a "printer war," where the printer was spending all of its time changing drivers and not actually printing. The fix was to capture the printer so it would only accept incoming jobs from the print server. Fortunately, this is no longer the case. LaserWriter 8 software is much more capable and intelligent. We'll get into the details later on.

GATHERING INFORMATION FOR THE SFM INSTALLATION

When planning for the installation of the SFM, make the effort to gather some basic information first. This will help to make the install process as painless as possible. Create a table that includes the information you'll need to configure the servers. For instance, you should document the following:

◆ The type and name of adapters in the server

◆ The IP address range that the Macs fall inside of

◆ The network number for AppleTalk, if applicable

◆ Any zone names that may have been applied inside the Mac network

◆ Whether the server will be seeding the network (*Seeding* is an AppleTalk term that describes the process of generating initial network information such as zone names and network numbers.)

Installing the Servers for Macintosh

With Windows 2000 Server, the SFM is separated into File Server for Macintosh and Print Server for Macintosh. You can opt to support both services or install only the service your clients require. When either service is installed, the AppleTalk protocol will automatically be installed, even if your Macintosh clients are using TCP/IP.

To begin the installation process in Windows 2000 Server, follow these steps:

1. Open the Control Panel and double-click Add/Remove Programs. When the dialog opens, select the Add/Remove Windows Components button.

2. Click Add/Remove Windows Components to bring up the list of available components (see Figure 16.1).

FIGURE 16.1

The Windows Components Wizard showing the Other Network File and Print Services option

3. Select Other Network File and Print Services, and click the Details button to show the sub-components.

4. Select File Services for Macintosh if you want to allow Macintosh users to access the server for files. Select Print Server for Macintosh if you wish to enable Macintosh users to print to a shared printer controlled by the Windows 2000 server. Check the boxes beside the services you want to install, and then click Next to install the components.

TIP   You will achieve better performance on your Windows 2000 server by selecting only the services you really need to install. This is true of any optional components, because every service requires system resources to run. This means that, if your Macintosh clients only need access to a laser printer controlled by the Windows 2000 server, you should only install the Print Server for Macintosh.

Once you have successfully installed the SFM, you can do some basic configuration to customize the appearance of your server on the network. One way to do this is to define a custom logon message that the Macintosh clients will see when they log in to the Windows 2000 server. To set a new message, or to edit an existing message, follow these steps:

1. Choose Start/Programs/Administrative Tools/Computer Management.

2. Expand System Tools, and then right-click `Shared Folders`.

3. Select Configure File Server for Macintosh from the context menu.

4. On the Configuration tab of the property sheet, type your message in the Logon Message text box (see Figure 16.2).

FIGURE 16.2

Type your logon message in the Configuration tab of the FSM property sheet.

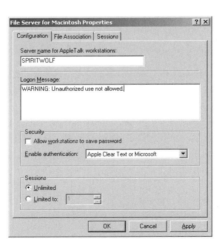

5. Click OK when you are satisfied with your changes.

The Configuration tab can also be used to define the total number of user sessions that will be allowed at one time. You can set the name of the server as it will appear to Macintosh clients, although it will default to the NetBIOS name of your server.

WARNING   *Most users—Mac, Windows, or otherwise—despise logon messages. If you must include one, make it short and sweet. If not, skip it.*

Creating Macintosh Shares

Once the File Server for Macintosh is installed, you'll be able to create shared folders that will be accessible to your Macintosh clients. Windows 2000 Server gives you the ability to create and manage shared folders with the Computer Management snap-in (`COMPMGMT.MSC`) of the Microsoft Management Console (MMC).

NOTE   *Administrators familiar with serving Macs on Windows NT 4 will find the changes made to Macintosh administration both much easier and frustratingly mislocated. All systems administration functions have been moved to the MMC, as you read in Chapter 5.*

Before you begin sharing volumes, let's go over some ground rules:

◆   You cannot share the same folder twice as two different Macintosh volumes. We've grown used to being able to do this in the Windows NT world, but it isn't allowed for Macintosh volumes.

◆   You cannot create a Macintosh volume inside of a share as another Macintosh volume. This means that if the first path listed here is shared as a Macintosh volume, you cannot have the second path as a separate Macintosh volume. The third path, however, is acceptable as long as it remains a separate path:

Good	`D:\Mac`
Bad	`D:\Mac\Programs\Graphics`
Good	`D:\MacOS\Other\Directory`

◆   Third, there are some limits on the number and naming of Macintosh volumes for the File Server for Macintosh. An underlying AppleTalk protocol buffer determines the number of volume names. The volume names can be up to 27 characters in length. If you will have multiple Macintosh volumes, you should balance the need to have clear names with the limits of the buffer space. To determine the number of volume names that can be displayed, use the following formula:

$$N \times (M + 2) \leq 4624$$

N is the number of volume names, and *M* is the average length of the names in characters (bytes). Any names that exceed this limit will not be viewable to the Macintosh clients.

NOTE   *You cannot create a Macintosh volume name with more than 27 characters using the Computer Management tool in Windows 2000 Server. If you need to create a volume with a longer name, use the* `MACFILE.EXE` *command from the command prompt.*

To create a Macintosh-accessible share, follow these steps:

1. Choose Start/Programs/Administrative Tools/Computer Management.

2. Expand the entry for System Tools, then expand Shared Folders (see Figure 16.3).

FIGURE 16.3

The Computer Management screen showing the Shared Folders group

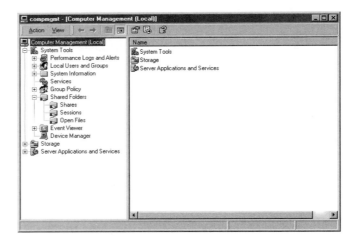

3. Right-click Shares and select New File Share. This will launch the Create Shared Folder Wizard (see Figure 16.4).

FIGURE 16.4

Creating a Mac-accessible shared folder

4. Select the folder to share by either typing the full path to the folder in the Folder to Share text box or browsing for it by clicking the Browse button to the right of the field. If the folder does not already exist, the wizard will create it for you if you type the information in the Folder Name text box.

5. In this dialog, you can set the name of the shared folder as your users will see it while browsing, and you can apply a comment to the share.

6. In the same dialog, check the box next to each operating system that will be supported for this shared folder. Options include Microsoft Windows, Novell NetWare, and Apple Macintosh clients. Click the Next button when you've checked the options you need.

7. Click Next. You may be prompted to confirm that you want to share the folder if it is located on a file system other than NTFS. If you confirm it, the permissions dialog opens (see Figure 16.5).

WARNING *You can create a Macintosh-accessible folder on either NTFS or the CD-ROM file system (CDFS). You cannot create Macintosh volumes on either FAT or FAT32. If your computer's drive is formatted with FAT or FAT32, you'll be able to install the Print Server for Macintosh, but not the File Server for Macintosh.*

FIGURE 16.5

Setting permissions for the new share

8. Select the appropriate level of permissions for your users and then click Next.

9. The Completing the Create Shared Folder Wizard dialog opens, summarizing the options you've selected. Click Finish when you're satisfied, and the wizard will create the shared folder for you. You will be asked if you would like to create more shares and given Yes and No options.

These steps will make your new share available to your Macintosh clients. In addition, you can set the permissions for the shared folder to restrict access or leave it set to its defaults to allow general access for all users.

The permissions applied to a Macintosh shared folder are different in Windows 2000 than they were in Windows NT 4. NT 4 used the standard Macintosh permissions of See Files, See Folders, and Make Changes. The File and Print Services for Macintosh in NT 4 would also apply any NTFS permissions, even though the Macintosh clients could not see them. In Windows 2000, you set permissions on the shared folder or at the NTFS level just as you would for a normal Windows share. Figure 16.6 shows the shared folder permissions for a Macintosh share.

The shared folder permissions are the same as they are in earlier versions of Windows NT, but the interface for assigning them is quite different. The available permissions are as follows:

Full Control Allows a user to do anything in the share. The user can read, write, execute, delete, change permissions, and take ownership.

Change   Allows a user to modify files and folders within the share. A user with Change permission can read, write, execute, and delete files and folders within the share.

Read   Allows the user to read and execute. The user with Read permission can view any file or folder in the share and run programs found there.

No Access   Denies any access to a user. The No Access permission always overrides all other permissions.

NOTE   *Notice that the interface (shown in Figure 16.6) no longer includes a specific option to assign No Access permission. To accomplish the equivalent of No Access, simply uncheck each permission that is listed in the dialog. By not giving any permission, you are essentially assigning No Access without the possible unexpected results, such as the administrator or even the operating system not having access.*

FIGURE 16.6

The shared folder permissions dialog for a Macintosh-accessible share

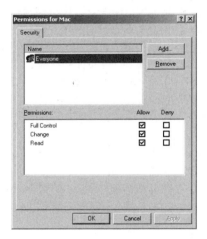

To assign permissions to a Macintosh share, use Explorer or My Computer to browse for the local path of the shared folder, and right-click the folder. Choose Sharing from the context menu and click the Permissions button. If you set the permissions through the Computer Management tool, you are actually setting NTFS permissions on the folder and files instead of setting shared folder permissions. This works as well, if not better, because you can define different permissions at any level of the hierarchy, not just at the root folder of the share.

Sharing Printers

One of the reasons most people install the services for Macintosh is to allow their Macintosh clients to access a shared printer on a Windows 2000 server. There are two basic types of printer that you can share this way: an AppleTalk print device on the network or a locally connected print device.

Macs can create print jobs in PostScript format and can have special code sent directly to the printer via a specially developed driver, but the default output format is QuickDraw, the Mac's native display engine. This allows you to provide a wide range of printer choices to both Windows-based machines and Macintosh clients.

WARNING *Another less-used technology that has moved out of favor with Apple is called QuickDraw GX. This was supposed to be Apple's next-generation graphics engine and was available as an add-on component for some time, but management problems and efforts to integrate Display PostScript, a technology familiar to Unix users, caused a premature death for the powerful technology. Apple has now wholly embraced SGI's OpenGL as its next graphics engine.*

If your Macintosh clients require printing output to be in PostScript, it is not a problem, even if the printer receiving the job is not a PostScript printer. The Print Server for Macintosh provides PostScript emulation for print jobs submitted from a Macintosh client. This means that any print job sent to a Windows 2000 server from a Macintosh will be automatically converted from Post-Script to a form suitable for the print device.

NOTE *It is important to remember that the key to good printing is a good driver. It is the driver that provides the printer with the information that correctly renders the print job. Check with the printer's vendor to see if there is a compatible MacOS driver or one optimized for network printing to an NT server providing Mac print services. They are out there.*

LASERPREP WARS?

One of the old issues with printing to a network from Macintosh clients was something Mac users called *LaserPrep wars*. A LaserPrep file is a configuration file that describes how a laser printer should handle a print job. This file comes with the PostScript driver and is specific to any version of the Chooser. What happens in a LaserPrep war is that one Macintosh client sends version 6 of the LaserPrep file and PostScript driver to the printer, then another client sends version 7 of the LaserPrep file and PostScript driver. For each version that it receives, the print device must go through a reset to change modes. The real problem with this is that things can reach a point where virtually all the print device is busy doing is switching modes.

If you maintain an older Macintosh network and have these multiple-driver-versions blues, then SFM solves the time issue by sending the LaserPrep file along with every job that is sent to the printer. This takes a little extra effort on the part of the server, but it actually results in faster performance because the print device doesn't go through the work of making the file a resident in its own memory.

Another way to smooth this process is by capturing the printer. If the Windows 2000 server captures the printer, then no one else can submit jobs to it to interfere with the settings. Using SFM can actually prevent LaserPrep wars from ever occurring.

Of course, Apple has been aware of the problem and long since fixed it. The solution is called LaserWriter 8 (LW8), and it is Apple's PostScript engine for the MacOS. A Macintosh doesn't even need to have a printer installed to use LW8. The current version is 8.6.1 and it is freely available on Apple's software updates Web site (asu.info.apple.com). If you would like to print to LaserWriter printers from your Windows NT computers, you can also download the Windows driver.

Assuming that you have installed the Print Server for Macintosh, sharing an AppleTalk print device is easy. The process is the same as redirecting a local port to a network print device. That sounds easy, doesn't it? The idea here is that you are creating a print queue for a network interface print device that communicates with the AppleTalk protocol.

To install and share an AppleTalk printer, follow these steps:

1. Open the Printers window and double-click Add Printer to start the Add Printer Wizard. (You may also go to Start/Settings/Printers and choose Add Printer if you have modified the proper settings in the Taskbar property sheet.)

2. The first choice to make is whether your printer is installed locally or on the network. Choose Local and click Next. Note that the Automatically Detect and Install My Plug-and-Play Printer option is checked by default.

3. Next, you must choose the local port to which the print device is connected (see Figure 16.7). Click the Create a New Port radio button and select AppleTalk Printing Devices from the Type drop-down list. Click Next. Windows 2000 will attempt to locate all of the AppleTalk print devices on the local network.

FIGURE 16.7

The Select the Printer Port dialog showing the AppleTalk Printing Devices setting

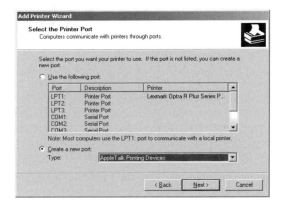

NOTE *For some interesting reason, your Macintosh clients will still be able to access file shares for Macs even if the AppleTalk service is not running. This is because Macs use TCP/IP like all other computers. Not having AppleTalk running, however, will cause you not to be able to set up an AppleTalk printer for sharing. Double-check that your AppleTalk service is in operation before beginning. The Mac clients will still be able to access TCP/IP-based printers, however.*

4. Select the AppleTalk printer that you want to install and click OK. When prompted to capture the port, select Yes.

5. The next dialog requests that you select the manufacturer and model of the print device. Choose the manufacturer from the list on the left, and then select the correct model on the right. Click Next.

6. Enter a name for the printer (see Figure 16.8). This name is only used locally on your computer; it won't display in the Active Directory or the browse list. If you already have one or more printers installed on your system, you must decide whether this printer will be used as the default printer by your Windows applications. When you have completed all settings, click Next.

FIGURE 16.8

The wizard asks you to provide a name for the new printer.

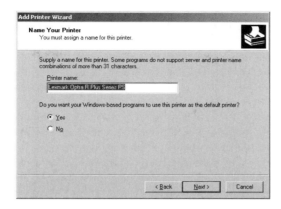

7. The next decision is whether to share the printer. Click the radio button next to Share As and then enter a name for the shared printer. This name will be displayed in the browse list and may be published to the Active Directory. Be sure to use a name that can be viewed from all network clients that will need to access this printer.

8. Click Next to open the Location and Comment dialog (see Figure 16.9). Enter a meaningful description of the location of the printer and provide a comment that gives the users any additional information they might need. Click Next.

FIGURE 16.9

The Location and Comment dialog gathers information that can be published to the Active Directory.

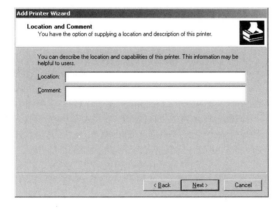

9. The Print Test Page dialog gives you the opportunity to test the printer installation by sending a test job. Click Next.

10. The final step is to confirm all selected options (see Figure 16.10). When you click Finish, the wizard will install the drivers and finalize all settings for the printer. It is a good idea to review these settings carefully before clicking Finish.

FIGURE 16.10

The final dialog of the Add Printer Wizard gives you an opportunity to verify all options before creating the printer.

NOTE   *To complete this procedure, you need to actually have an AppleTalk print device located somewhere on your local network. When a printer is shared in this way, your Macintosh clients will be sending their jobs to the printer using the AppleTalk protocol. AppleTalk over TCP/IP is nearly as fast as TCP/IP itself, so you should not be concerned about any perceptible performance degradation as a result of using this manner of printer sharing. You may, however, use an Apple-Share IP server to act as a print server for both Mac and Windows clients, as AppleShare IP allows printing over TCP/IP for both operating systems. There is another possible way to share a printer installed on a Windows 2000 server. It requires that you connect at least one of your Macs as a NetBIOS network client, attach it to the shared printer as a Windows client, and then share it again as an AppleTalk printer. Once this is done, the other Macs can print to the Net-BIOS print gateway and pass through to the Windows 2000 printer. This is more complicated, but it will work if needed. This also provides TCP/IP printing for both Mac and Windows clients, but it's more difficult to configure and maintain.*

TIP   *For more on AppleShare IP and other mixed-platform networking solutions, see "Network Alternatives" later in this chapter.*

The Print Server for Macintosh makes any printer that is installed locally on the Windows 2000 server available to your Macintosh clients. Once the printer has been installed on the server, the Print Server for Macintosh will begin advertising the printer to AppleTalk clients on the network. To install a printer to be used by your Macintosh clients, follow these steps:

1. Open the Printers window by selecting Start/Settings/Printers.

2. Double-click the Add Printer icon to start the Add Printer Wizard.

3. The first choice to make is whether your printer is installed locally or on the network. Choose Local and click Next. Note that the Automatically Detect and Install My Plug-and-Play Printer option is checked by default.

4. Next, you must choose the local port to which the print device is connected. Typically, the print device will be attached to your first parallel port, LPT1. Once you have selected the correct port, click Next.

5. In the next dialog, you will select the manufacturer and model of your print device. This will ensure that you're installing the correct driver. If you have a third-party driver to install, select Have Disk and browse for the location of the drivers.

6. Enter a name for the printer. This name is only used locally on your computer; it won't display in the Active Directory or the browse list. If you already have one or more printers installed on your system, you must decide whether this printer will be used as the default printer by your Windows applications. When you have completed all settings, click Next.

7. The next decision is whether to share the printer. Click the radio button next to Yes and then enter a name for the shared printer. This name will be displayed in the browse list and may be published to the Active Directory. Be sure to use a name that can be viewed from all network clients that will need to access this printer.

8. Click Next to open the Location and Comment dialog. Enter a meaningful description of the location of the printer and provide a comment that gives the users any additional information they might need. Click Next.

9. The Print Test Page dialog gives you the opportunity to test the printer installation by sending a test job. Click Next.

10. The final step is to confirm all selected options. When you click Finish, the wizard will install the drivers and finalize all settings for the printer. It is a good idea to review these settings carefully before clicking Finish.

After you have added a new printer to be used by the Print Server for Macintosh, it's a good idea to restart the service. This allows the print spooler to correctly recognize the new printer. In Windows 2000, this function has moved from the Control Panel's Services applet to the Computer Management console in Administrative Tools. To stop and restart the print spooler, use these steps:

1. Open Computer Management from the Administrative Tools group on the Start menu. (You can alternately right-click My Computer and select the Manage item.)

2. Open the Services and Applications item, and click Services to open the list of services available on the computer (see Figure 16.11).

3. Scroll down through the list until you find the Print Spooler service. Click this service once to highlight it and then click the Restart Service button.

4. When prompted to also stop and restart the Print Server for Macintosh, click OK. Figure 16.12 shows the prompt you will receive to restart the Print Server for Macintosh.

5. After the services have restarted successfully, close the Computer Management console application.

TIP *This technique is also used fairly often when troubleshooting the printing architecture on Windows 2000. Should documents get stuck in the print queue at any time on Windows 2000 or earlier versions of Windows NT, try restarting the print spooler to reset the spool. Many people will actually try rebooting the server or flushing the queue in this scenario, when all they really need to do is restart the spooler service.*

FIGURE 16.11

Windows 2000
Server includes the
option to stop and
restart services with
a single click.

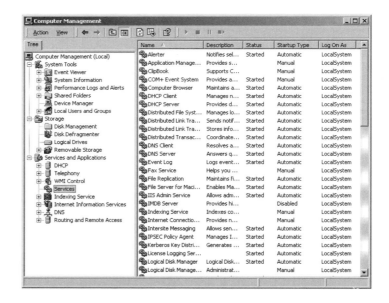

FIGURE 16.12

Restarting the print
spooler automati-
cally restarts the
Print Server for
Macintosh.

Accessing Server Resources

Once the SFM is installed on the Windows 2000 server, you will be able to begin using the resources from your Macintosh clients. This section discusses the usage from the Macintosh side of the equation.

Macintosh clients will typically use the Chooser to make network connections for printing or for files. To access the network, the Chooser requires that AppleShare be installed and running. Most Macintosh systems will attempt to make the initial connection through TCP/IP if it is installed, but they still require that the AppleTalk protocol be installed as support for the Apple-Share functionality.

There are, however, some things to be aware of. In versions of the MacOS from 8.6 onward, the Chooser is bolstered by the Network Browser, an eminently more useful network tool. Users can browse and select network resources using the Open/Save dialog box format of the Network Browser interface. The older Chooser Control Panel was somewhat cumbersome to use. This change is welcome.

NOTE   *The folks at Apple have not been resting on their laurels. They are offering a public beta of the venerable OS's next version, MacOS X. Anyone (that is, anyone with a G3 or G4 chip and at least 128MB or RAM) who wants to spend $30 for the privilege can test-drive the new system.*

The primary driving force behind all these networking capabilities is Open Transport (OT), the technology that replaced the aging and incomplete MacTCP. OT has many capabilities, one of the most powerful being the ability to change networking configurations on the fly, not requiring a restart as in Windows, NT or otherwise. A quick visit to the TCP/IP Control Panel will reveal an easy-to-use interface (to change to Advanced or Administrator views, go to Edit/User Mode and make your choice). You also have the option to restrict access to the Control Panel via a password. The Advanced and Administrator views are identical except that in the Administrator view, you can lock each individual group of items (by, of course, clicking the little lock icon to toggle it on or off as desired) to restrict option access inside the Control Panel itself.

I'll first show you how to access a Windows 2000 server for files and programs, and then, later in the section, I'll show you how to connect to a shared printer.

Accessing Shared Folders

A Windows 2000 server can make a wonderful file server for Macintosh clients. Many networks can benefit from the use of this configuration to store large multimedia files or simply to share the files for both Windows and Macintosh clients. Once you have set up the shared folders on your Windows 2000 server as discussed in the earlier sections of this chapter, you will be able to use those folders for Macintosh files and programs.

When you want to get to the shared Macintosh-accessible volume from a Macintosh client that is pre–MacOS 8.5, follow these steps:

1. From the Apple menu, select Chooser.

2. Once Chooser opens, select AppleShare (see Figure 16.13). You'll have the choice to either select the server name from the list or, if the name does not appear, click the Server IP Address button to enter the IP address of the Windows 2000 server.

FIGURE 16.13

The Chooser window showing the available connection options

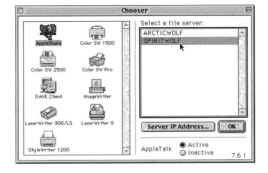

3. You'll receive a prompt to choose your authentication method (see Figure 16.14). Apple Standard UAMs will transmit the user authentication in clear text when contacting the Windows 2000 server. Microsoft Authentication will use an encrypted logon to the server. Click OK to begin logon.

FIGURE 16.14

Choose your authentication mode.

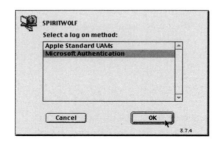

4. Enter your username and password and then click OK. If your logon is authenticated, you will receive a list of Macintosh-accessible shared folders on the Windows 2000 server, as shown in Figure 16.15.

FIGURE 16.15

The available shares on the Windows 2000 server

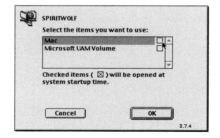

5. Click the shared folder you want to connect to. You can place a check mark beside the share name if you want the share to be connected at boot time. Click OK to continue.

TIP   *You can mount several volumes at once from a single server. Simply hold the Shift key and select each volume you would like to mount immediately. If you only select one and there are more available, you will have to go back into the Chooser or Network Browser to mount the remaining volumes.*

This will connect you to the shared folder. Any files that have been saved to the folder by Windows clients will appear as text documents with a PC label at the top of the icon. MacOS 8.*x* includes a conversion utility that will automatically change the files to a format that the Macintosh can read. The files can be worked with directly from the shared folder or copied down to the Macintosh.

WARNING *If Macintosh clients save files to the folder, the files will have the normal icons stored within their resource fork. Use caution when working with the files on the Windows 2000 server, because Windows operating systems don't use the concept of multiple forks of data within a file. NTFS provides the ability to store two data forks for a single filename, but Windows 2000 doesn't use this method of storage for itself. Fortunately, if you do move a Macintosh file in Windows 2000, a prompt will appear asking if you would like to strip the resource fork or not. Click No and be happy. There is also, oddly, an option named Forkize that allows a Windows 2000 workstation or server to add a resource fork to a file destined for use on a Mac, alleviating the need for pesky and unreliable filename extensions.*

When you want to mount the shared volumes from a Macintosh client that is running MacOS 8.5 or later, follow these steps:

1. From the Apple menu, select the Network Browser item.

2. Once Network Browser opens, select the name of the server you wish to connect to. Note that there are small, blue arrows to the immediate left of the name. Click the arrow.

TIP *For the Macintosh-uninitiated: The little blue arrows work like the plus/minus signs in a Windows tree view hierarchy. Click the arrow, and the contents of the item next to it will appear below. Additional blue arrows will appear as needed.*

3. A dialog will appear and you'll receive a prompt asking to authenticate yourself. Enter your logon information and click OK to begin logon.

4. If your logon is authenticated, a list of shared folders on the Windows 2000 server will appear in the familiar Macintosh list view.

5. Double-click the shared folder you want to connect to and its icon will appear on your desktop. If there are additional authentications required, enter the information for each one and click OK.

Accessing Shared Printers

Connecting to shared AppleTalk printers on a Windows 2000 server is much like connecting to a shared folder from the Macintosh. To connect to a shared printer with a pre–MacOS 8.5 system, follow these steps:

1. From the Apple menu, open the Chooser.

2. In the Chooser window (see Figure 16.16), select the appropriate printer type in the left pane. If you are printing to a PostScript printer other than an Apple printer, you can use the Laser-Writer 8 type to connect. Once you have selected the printer type, Chooser will display the available printers on the network.

3. Select the printer you want to connect to and click the Create button.

NOTE *The first time you install a printer using these steps, the button text in Chooser will read Create. After that first install, the text will read Setup.*

FIGURE 16.16

The Chooser showing the Setup option for a shared printer

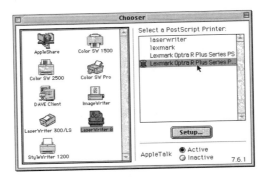

4. The Setup screen lets you choose a specific PostScript Printer Description (PPD) file, configure the settings for the printer, and retrieve printer information. When you are satisfied with the options, click the OK button.

After the last step, the printer will be created on your desktop and set as the default printer. If you have more than one printer installed, you'll need to open the print configuration panel in every open application to set the correct printer selection after installing the new printer.

When you want to access network printers from a Macintosh client that is running MacOS 8.5 or later, follow these steps:

1. From the Apple menu, select the Network Browser item.

2. Once Network Browser opens, select the name of the printer you wish to connect to.

3. Once you are connected to the printer, its icon, which you can use to drop documents onto, will appear on your desktop.

NOTE *Any Macintosh user connecting to a shared printer on a Windows 2000 server will be affected by printer permissions just as Windows clients are. The Mac user won't see any indication in his printer window as to what permissions have been assigned to him. If Macintosh users have not been given permission to use the shared printer, they will not be able to connect to it at all.*

Implementing Security

User security is an issue with Macintosh clients just like it is with any other platform. The normal user authentication provided by AppleShare networking is to require a username and password. These credentials are transmitted in clear text, making it easy for someone skilled in the ways of cracking to compromise your network's security. Microsoft has taken steps to provide encrypted user-authentication capabilities for Macintosh clients.

NOTE *The reality is that crackers, popularly and incorrectly known as hackers, are few and far between, at least any that can compromise a MacOS Web server or a well-designed Windows security model. Most self-styled "hAcKeRz" are really 15-year-olds with not much else to do and a yen for Nintendo. Don't take this to mean that you can leave your sensitive data lying about anywhere, but don't go overboard when designing your security model either.*

There are three basic modes of authentication when a user at a Macintosh computer tries to log in to a Windows 2000 server:

Guest   This option lets the users log in using the Guest account on the Windows 2000 server. This option not only has no security involved, it fails to provide any kind of audit trail to track what the users are doing on the server while connected. The Guest account is normally disabled in Windows 2000.

Authenticated User   This option requires the user to log in using a valid user account. It does provide the ability to track users through the use of auditing, but it uses the standard Apple UAM that transmits the credentials as clear text.

Microsoft Authentication   This final option requires the presence of the correct version of the Microsoft UAM for your installed version of AppleShare. Microsoft authentication will encrypt all user credentials prior to transmitting them to the server.

The heart of Windows 2000's security features for the File Server for Macintosh is the User Authentication Module (UAM). The UAM allows a Mac user to participate in standard Windows 2000 user-level security and encrypts the credentials before transmitting them to the server. The encrypted form of the credentials is stored on the Windows 2000 server. When the Macintosh user logs in to the Windows 2000 server, the credentials are encrypted and sent to the server. The Windows 2000 server then compares the credentials sent by the client to the credentials stored on the server.

WARNING   *The UAM data can also be intercepted. Windows 2000 Server comes with 40-bit encryption capabilities to satisfy United States export laws regarding, that's right, munitions. If you prove you are located in the U.S. or Canada and agree to a restrictive EULA (end-user license agreement), you may download an updater that will bring Windows 2000 to 128-bit encryption. 40-bit encryption can be beat inside of a week on a single Pentium 133, so don't feel that safe.*

The standard authentication is fine for most environments, even though it uses clear text when transmitting the password. But if your environment requires additional security, you should require your users to install the Microsoft UAM for Windows 2000.

NOTE   *If you have used the Macintosh services in Windows NT Server and then upgraded to Windows 2000 Server, you will need to install the new UAM on your Macintosh clients.*

In past versions of Windows NT Server, the installation procedure for the Microsoft UAM was to simply copy the UAM folder for the version of AppleShare that you're using to your System folder on a Macintosh computer. This wasn't too difficult, but it did require you to know exactly which version of AppleShare was supported on your computer. Choosing the wrong version meant either a hang or a fatal error any time you tried to use the authentication.

Windows 2000 Server has introduced an even easier method for installing the UAM. Macintosh users will connect to the Microsoft UAM shared folder on the Windows 2000 server and double-click the Microsoft UAM Installer. This runs a native Macintosh program to select the appropriate version of the Microsoft UAM and then automatically copy the needed files to the System folder on the client. Users will also find a document in this share that describes the need for the Microsoft UAM and how to install it.

The Microsoft UAM runs a small program on the Macintosh client when a user tries to log in. The program provides spaces for the user to enter a name and password as well as a Windows 2000 domain to log in to. Once this has been filled in, the credentials are encrypted and transmitted.

To effectively use this security for your Macintosh clients, you must configure the properties for the File Server for Macintosh to allow Microsoft encryption. You can choose between multiple security schemes to decide whether you will accept standard Apple security, Microsoft security, or both. To configure the File Server for Macintosh, follow these steps:

1. Open Computer Management from the Administrative Tools group on the Start menu.

2. Click the plus sign beside System Tools to expand it.

3. Right-click Shared Folders in either the left or the right pane of the console, and select Configure File Server for Macintosh from the context menu.

4. In the resulting dialog, select the Security drop-down list box and then choose the appropriate method of logon. Click OK to save the changes.

Enabling the Microsoft encrypted logons will let your users connect to the Windows 2000 server with encrypted credentials instead of the standard clear text. You may actually find that the standard authentication is fine for most resources and that the Microsoft encrypted logons are more trouble than they're worth. But if you require security in your network environment, this will provide an adequate level of authentication for most purposes.

Setting Advanced Options

Occasionally it may be necessary to change some of the Registry settings for the SFM instead of using the graphical management tools provided by Windows 2000 Server. Normally, you would change all of these settings by using the Computer Management tool in the Administrative Tools group. These Registry settings are found in two basic locations: the adapter key(s) and the AppleTalk parameters key.

The values in Table 16.1 are found in this location:

```
HKLM\System\CurrentControlSet\Services\AppleTalk\Parameters
```

TABLE 16.1: THE REGISTRY SETTINGS IN THE APPLETALK PARAMETERS KEY

VALUE	DESCRIPTION
DefaultPort Data type:REG_SZ	This value determines the default port to which the AppleTalk protocol will be bound. If you aren't routing AppleTalk, only the Macs located on the local network will be able to access the server. The default value set at the time the SFM is installed is the first Ethernet adapter found on the server.
DesiredZone Data type:REG_SZ	This value sets the zone in which the SFM will participate. If no data is present in this value, SFM will use the default zone for the network.
EnableRouter Data type:REG_DWORD	This value determines whether the Windows 2000 server should act as an AppleTalk router for all of its installed network interfaces. Do not enable this setting unless you have more than one network adapter in the server and wish to use it as a router.

The settings listed in Table 16.2 have to do with the network adapter and will be present in multiple keys if there are multiple adapters present. The settings are found in the following location:

```
HKLM\System\CurrentControlSet\Services\AppleTalk\Parameters\
    Adapters\<network adapter name>
```

TABLE 16.2: THE REGISTRY SETTINGS IN THE ADAPTER KEY

VALUE	DESCRIPTION
AarpRetries Data type:REG_DWORD	This hexadecimal value determines how many times the Apple Address Resolution Protocol (AARP) will attempt to resolve a network address. The default is 0xA.
DdpCheckSums Data type:REG_DWORD	This value tells Windows 2000 to use the checksums in the DDP layer of the AppleTalk protocol. The default is 0x0 (false).
DefaultZone Data type:REG_SZ	This value contains the name of the default zone. This setting is only used if the Windows 2000 server is being used to seed the network.
NetworkRangeLowerEnd Data type:REG_DWORD	This value defines the lower end of the network number range and is only used if the server is being used to seed the network. The range of acceptable values is 0x1 to 0xFEFF.
NetworkRangeUpperEnd Data type:REG_DWORD	The same as the preceding value, but this value sets the upper bound of the network numbers available on the network. Acceptable ranges include 0x1 to 0xFEFF.
PortName Data type:REG_SZ	This value assigns a name, in the form adaptername @computername, to the adapter using AppleTalk so that it may be easily identified on the network.
SeedingNetwork Data type:REG_DWORD	This values determines whether the adapter will be seeding the network. If the value is 0x1 (true), AppleTalk will read the other seed information, and, if it's correct, AppleTalk will seed the network to set the default values for the Macintosh clients.
ZoneList Data type:REG_MULTI_SZ	If the adapter will be used to seed the network, this value defines the available zone names for the network.

As always, when editing the Registry, use extreme caution. Whenever possible, adjust these settings through the graphical user interface or the command prompt.

Supporting Applications across Platforms

Many of the applications your users will be using on Macintosh computers have Windows-based counterparts. This was one of the reasons for installing the SFM that I discussed at the beginning of this chapter. Fortunately, most of these applications are well documented, and the necessary file extension information has already been entered into the SFM on Windows 2000.

Both the Windows and Macintosh platforms use some kind of file extension information to associate a document with the program that created it. If you stop and consider that these two platforms are really quite different, you'll begin to appreciate the convenience of this common approach.

With this association in place, a Macintosh user can create a Word document on his Mac and save it to the shared folder on a Windows 2000 server using the SFM. When a Windows user views the same document through a Windows share for the same server folder, she will see the icon associated with Word on her computer. She can then open the file natively in Word 97, make changes, and save them back to the network folder. When the Mac user comes along, he will find the document just as he left it, but with the changes added.

If by some chance you have an application for both platforms that is not already defined in Windows 2000 Server, you can add or modify the file extension associations. To add new file associations for the SFM, follow these steps:

1. Open Computer Management from the Administrative Tools group.

2. Expand System Tools and right-click Shared Folders.

3. Select Configure File Server for Macintosh from the context menu.

4. Click the File Association tab of the properties dialog.

5. In Files with MS-DOS Extension, enter an extension or select one by clicking the arrow. If the extension is already associated with a file type and creator, it will automatically be selected under Creator.

6. Under Creator, select a creator program and file type that you want to associate with this file extension.

7. To complete the operation, click Associate. Click OK to apply the change and close the window.

These associations affect the icons that users of each platform will see when they access the Macintosh share. When you've added a new file extension association, it will only affect files that are created after the association is made. Files that were created before the association will have the icon given to them by the creating application.

Network Alternatives

Windows 2000 is not the only player in the game. Apple's very own AppleShare IP has received many enhancements over the past two years, including the ability to serve Windows clients *natively*. That's right, AppleShare IP (ASIP) speaks SMB fluently and treats both Mac and Windows clients equally with one exception: Windows clients are limited to printing over TCP/IP only. This, however, is not often a real limitation in the modern network, as most printers are capable of being accessed over TCP/IP.

AppleShare IP 6

ASIP 6 was the first version of ASIP to offer Windows connectivity. The previous version came bundled with an AppleTalk for Windows client that allowed ASIP to see the Windows machine as a Mac on the network. This was not particularly stable or reliable. So, what does this mean to you? Easy—a Mac can be loaded with ASIP to provide your entire network with TCP/IP printer access, regardless of platform.

ASIP's more multiplatform-friendly nature makes it a great alternative to complex (and rightly so!) Windows servers. There are some caveats to this convenience. One of the reasons ASIP is so easy to administer is its simplicity. ASIP combines a file, print, mail, FTP, and Web server in one package. Apple customers demand power made simple, so ASIP was designed to fit this need. As a result, some possibly powerful security features are not present.

WARNING *Even though an ASIP server can be added to a Windows workgroup, it cannot be added to a domain. ASIP does not have the functionality it would need to participate as a domain member. It does, however, work wonderfully as a workgroup server in mixed company.*

This is not to say that an ASIP Web server is not secure. In fact, it's one of the most difficult to crack. It's quite the bear to break into a Mac Web server, as evidenced by the Crack-a-Mac challenge. The site successfully withstood constant attack by would-be crackers for three months before one particularly creative individual was able to exploit a chink in SiteEdit for Macintosh. The hacker was able to gain access to the server through another product and view all files on the drive and retrieve the passwords file. After gaining access to the SiteEdit password file, the hacker was able to use SiteEdit to modify the home page.

The fault lay in the combination of software and not in a particular security hole presented directly by a particular server product. Once this hole, which apparently was very difficult to find (the cracker maintained secrecy and did not make the hole available to the public), was patched, the Mac became secure again. The challenge has since been closed, as there is no interest in a server-cracking challenge that cannot be won.

NOTE *For some perspective, the prize that was offered was an Apple PowerBook 3400/240, much slower than the 450MHz Macs available when the site was finally taken down. The challenge was up for more than two years—a long time for a server that was constantly barraged with solicited attacks to be illegally accessed only once.*

THAT'S NOT A MAC?

For much greater security in the Mac world, one would need the services of Apple's latest arrival, MacOS X Server. Essentially OpenStep, Apple cofounder Steve Jobs's operating system based on the MACH kernel, MacOS X Server gives the familiar Mac face a real tweaking with the MacOS-compatible Unix variant. Running on the well-known Unix-like MACH 2.5 kernel, it is capable of running slightly modified Unix software, POSIX software, and the MacOS (in an emulation environment called the Yellow Box, of course), and it even includes a command line, a first for any version of the Macintosh system software.

NOTE *Familiar with the iMac? Who isn't, right? Well, MacOS X Server can use its Netboot capabilities to provide bootable systems for up to 50 iMacs from one server. Plug the iMac into the server via Ethernet, remove the HDD from the iMac, set up Netboot services on the server, and turn on the iMac. The iMac will boot directly from the server with only a cursory glance to see if there's a HDD. Each iMac has its own boot configuration and never has to store anything locally. The network computer lives!*

Despite its attractive exterior, the server is a powerful and secure engine with all the benefits of Unix and few of the interface complexities, making it quite attractive to Mac networks that were serving via Windows NT. The one major drawback? No built-in Windows serving capabilities. There is, however, a version of Samba available for MacOS X Server, and the source is available if you're familiar with modifying code for recompilation.

Its benefits? Most Windows NT/2000 administrators have at least a passing familiarity with Unix in some form or another. MacOS X Server is a powerful and inexpensive Mac-savvy server that has the ability to work hand-in with Windows on a network with a little tweaking. It also has security possibilities far above and beyond ASIP.

So, What Are You Saying?

Since you're wondering why all the Mac server talk, it's simple. Windows 2000, which has a strong foundation in Windows NT, is not the perfect solution for all problems. Any admin will agree that there are other solutions that are worth investigating. In the case of the Mac, if they do populate a portion of your network, they should be given every consideration. Most people who use Macs in an office setting would experience drastically reduced work performance if forced to supplant their old Mac for a Windows machine.

For this, it is important to remember the Mac. If they were added to the network or if they originally populated the network before your arrival, it's because someone felt it important or felt that progress could be made if some employees were offered an alternative. Give these users and the company an opportunity to use the Mac technology and leverage the available technologies that make solid use of the Mac in a network environment, even a mission-critical environment.

NOTE *There is a project at UCLA called AppleSeed that combines eight G3/400 Power Macs together via 100Base-T Ethernet and special software to create a parallel-processing supercomputer that can beat the pants off of a Cray T3E-900. Running ZDNet's PIC test-bench series, an AppleSeed four-CPU arrangement was able to finish the test in 421 nanoseconds compared to the Cray's 481. Total cost for AppleSeed? Eight Macs, 2.30GB RAM, and 48GB disk cost $22,461. Total cost for the Cray? Let's just say that eight years ago, one Cray cost $20 million. They're still not cheap.*

Just keep in mind that in the end, regardless of what we prefer or what we think will work better, it's the best solution that is most important. Windows 2000 provides all needs and more for a cross-platform network, but it can use a hand in a few departments. That's where MacOS X Server or AppleShare IP can come in. They're easy to work with and require very little maintenance. A friend of mine has a Power Mac 7100/80 that runs MacOS 8.1 and ASIP 6.1, and serves as a file server for his in-home network. The last time I asked him about it, this machine had been running, with five exceptions for restarts and one power outage, for eight months nonstop (this is a "consumer" machine!). Keep that in mind the next time someone tries to offer you the benefits of Windows over the Mac.

Chapter 17

Web, Mail, FTP, and Telnet Services in Windows 2000 Server

UNLESS YOU'VE BEEN LIVING in a cave somewhere for the past five years, you're undoubtedly aware that the Internet is becoming a major part of the way that the world works. Notice I said world, not just companies. With each passing day, the Internet is having more and more of an impact on the daily lives of countless people. The amount of information available to anyone, anywhere, at any time is simply mind-boggling, and this trend is only going to continue to grow in the future.

Not one to miss out on such a significant part of people's lives, Microsoft is doing everything that they can to be a part of this revolution. While some of their tactics might be questionable—such as tying their Internet Explorer browser directly in with their most recent operating systems—other approaches are quite beneficial. The most significant benefit is the inclusion of the latest version of Internet Information Services (IIS) with the base Windows 2000 Server operating system.

Internet Information Services is a full-featured platform capable of servicing HTTP (Web), FTP (file transfers), NNTP (news), and SMTP (e-mail) tasks for an organization. Due to its integration with the Windows 2000 operating system, it is relatively easy to set up, configure, and manage. IIS is capable of scaling to meet even the most demanding of environments—Microsoft runs their own Web site on IIS, and their site receives millions of hits per day.

Currently, Internet Information Services is enjoying second-place title as the most widely implemented Web server around, according to Web server statistics available at Netcraft (www .netcraft.com/survey/). According to the May 1999 statistics, Internet Information Services (in its various versions) accounted for 22.89 percent of 5,414,325 Web sites that were queried. So what was the first-place Web server? A package known as Apache, an open-source version of the original NCSA HTTPd Web server. In the same survey, Apache accounted for 57.22 percent of the servers sampled, and was increasing in market share.

On my most recent trip to the Netcraft Web site, I learned something very interesting: they are starting to track uptime for servers, and Windows 2000 is showing some exceptional uptime statistics! In one particular instance—Starbucks.com—it would appear that their Windows 2000–based Web site was running nonstop from April to November 2000. If the figures are correct, that's seven months without needing a reboot! Quite a change from the old days of IIS on NT.

Since Microsoft doesn't typically enjoy being second place to anyone, this could mean good things for administrators if Microsoft continues to add more features and functionality into IIS. Even if Microsoft doesn't add anything new, IIS is a robust platform that can meet the Internet needs of most organizations right out of the box. Let's start our discussion by taking a closer look at each of the services that IIS can provide.

A Closer Look: What IIS Can (and Can't) Do

Internet Information Services is really an overall umbrella for a suite of TCP/IP-based services all running on the same system. Although some of the services rely on shared components, overall they are functionally independent from one another. Just as an electrician who has different tools for different jobs, IIS has different Internet capabilities to help meet different needs. With the release of Windows 2000, Microsoft has reached version 5 for Internet Information Services. The following sections will briefly discuss some of the standard functionality included with IIS 5.

World Wide Web (HTTP) Server

If you're reading this book, and this chapter specifically, I'll assume that the World Wide Web is nothing new to you. Internet Information Services includes an HTTP server so that you can publish data that you want to the World Wide Web quickly and easily. IIS's Web service is easily configurable and reliable, and it supports security and encryption to protect sensitive data.

You can use IIS's Web service to host a Web site for your own domain or multiple domains, an intranet, and the Internet, and even allow users to pass through your IIS Web server to access HTML documents on machines within your organization. In addition, FrontPage server extensions are supported in IIS 5, allowing clients to easily publish and manage Web sites through FrontPage, Microsoft's "what you see is what you get" (WYSIWYG) Web site creation tool.

File Transfer (FTP) Server

Although the use of File Transfer Protocol is not the only way to send a file from one location to another, it is by far the most widely supported as far as the Internet is concerned. FTP was one of the original means of copying files from one location to another on the Internet, long before the days of graphical browsers, HTTP, and Web sites. Since the protocol has been around for so long, support is available on almost any platform, including midrange and mainframe systems that might not typically support HTTP.

In IIS 5, the FTP service includes support for resuming broken file transfers. This capability allows client workstations to restart an aborted file transfer at the point where it ended. This helps save on network bandwidth because clients don't have to re-request an entire file—they can simply resume where their transfer left off.

Network News (NNTP) Server

Sometimes referred to as Usenet, Network News Transport Protocol (NNTP) is something that I hope to see start taking off in the near future, simply due to the great functionality it provides. By using Internet standards (RFC 977), the NNTP service can be used as a means of maintaining a threaded conversation database on an IIS server, just like in Usenet groups on the Internet. Users with properly configured newsreader programs can navigate through and participate in these conversation databases.

Although services like Google Groups (`http://groups.google.com`) have recently made Usenet better known, it still isn't as widely used as something like HTTP. That's unfortunate, since NNTP represents such a great cross-platform protocol for managing threaded conversation databases. Hopefully, the inclusion of NNTP in with IIS 4 (and now IIS 5) will increase the use of this capability.

Simple Mail Transfer (SMTP) Server

At first glance, having a mail service included in IIS might seem as if Microsoft is cannibalizing their own e-mail platform, Exchange. Unfortunately, if you are hoping that you might use this feature as an e-mail platform for your organization, you will be a bit disappointed. Microsoft has included an SMTP service with IIS primarily for support of the other services within IIS—namely HTTP and NNTP. In other words, the SMTP server that comes with IIS is not sufficient to act as an e-mail server. If you want a Windows 2000–based mail server, you'll have to either look at a commercial product or use the free EMWACS SMTP/POP3 server discussed later in this chapter.

For example, some of the FrontPage server extensions require having a mail capability available on a Web server. If a visitor to a FrontPage Web site hosted on your IIS server fills out a form, and the results of that form are to be e-mailed to a specific e-mail address, the SMTP service is the process that will handle that. The SMTP service is missing an important component—a POP3 or IMAP service—that would be necessary for IIS to act as a full-blown mail server for an organization. POP3 or IMAP is the means by which clients retrieve their specific messages from their mailbox on a mail server.

Since SMTP is simply a transfer protocol, there is no real structure given to the storage of messages once they have been received by your system. All e-mails sent to your SMTP server will simply be dropped in a directory, in a plain-text format. Although you could manually go through each message and determine whom to send it to, I'm sure you can see that most people wouldn't want to do that. Even receiving a small amount of e-mail, daily, could make that a full-time job in itself.

However, having the SMTP service available is great if you have outgoing mail needs for your server, even beyond the support for FrontPage and NNTP. By using a properly formatted text file and copying it into the outgoing e-mail directory, you can easily have Windows 2000 send mail to any address on the Internet as long as it can connect to the target server. For example, maybe you have a nightly job that creates a summary report you would like e-mailed to customers or suppliers each day. Through some creative use of batch files and scheduling, this could easily be done with the SMTP service included in Windows 2000 Server. In fact, I use the IIS SMTP service to mail out my e-newsletter. IIS does the mailing, but I generate the mail and send it out using a free product called Asp Email from `www.persits.com`.

Installing Internet Information Services

By default, Windows 2000 Server should have installed Internet Information Services on your system automatically. However, you may want to check to make sure that all the services that you need (HTTP, NNTP, SMTP, FTP) have been installed. If for some reason they weren't, or if they have been removed since, adding them to the server again is relatively easy. The only requirement necessary to install IIS is that the TCP/IP protocol be installed on the system.

To install Internet Information Services, go into the Control Panel and launch Add/Remove Programs, then click the Add/Remove Windows Components button. This will launch the Windows Components Wizard, from which you can add or remove any parts of the Windows 2000 operating system. In the list of components, check the option for Internet Information Services (IIS), as shown in Figure 17.1.

FIGURE 17.1

Installing Internet Information Services (IIS)

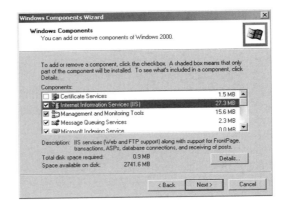

By default, selecting this option will install all of the components of IIS on your Windows 2000 Server—including support for HTTP, FTP, NNTP, and SMTP. If you would prefer to install only certain services (WWW , for example), click the Details button and uncheck the options you don't want to install. If this server will be connected to the public Internet, it might be a good security precaution to uninstall services you don't plan on using. Even though you can always disable the services once they're installed, the best security of all is to not have anything on the system that you don't need.

Click OK when you've selected the options you want to install, and Windows 2000 Server will begin installing the necessary components.

Default Configuration

If you chose to install all the IIS services (either as part of your initial setup of Windows 2000 Server or after the fact), you should end up with a default configuration similar to the following:

- Default (empty) Web site with FrontPage extensions, responding on TCP/IP port 80 on all configured IP addresses

- Administrative Web site, responding on a random TCP/IP port number on all configured IP addresses, with access restricted to the local host (127.0.0.1) IP address only

- Default FTP server, responding on TCP/IP port 21 on all configured IP addresses

- Default NNTP virtual server, responding on TCP/IP port 119 on all configured IP addresses

- Default SMTP virtual server, responding on TCP/IP port 25 on all configured IP addresses

Looking at these services through the Internet Services Manager MMC, you should see a screen similar to the one in Figure 17.2.

If you will be connecting this server to the Internet, and you know in advance that you won't be using certain services, I would recommend stopping them through the MMC interface. This will prevent anyone from using these services without your being aware of it (for example, someone using your SMTP server—if it's configured incorrectly—as a mail relay for "spam" e-mail) and protect you against any security breaches that might be found at a later date. Since some of these default sites can't be deleted, the best option is simply to disable them if you don't plan on using them. However, the documentation for IIS depends, in its default configuration, on the default Web service being available, so keep that in mind when shutting down services on your system.

FIGURE 17.2

Internet Services Manager MMC with default IIS settings

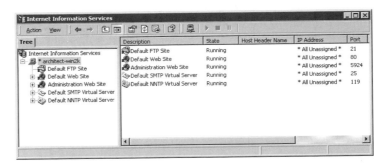

Global IIS Configuration

From the main view of the Internet Information Services MMC, you can set parameters for your system that will apply on a global (server) level by editing the server properties, or you can set parameters that will apply on an individual site level by editing the site properties as needed. Unfortunately, this can be a bit confusing because some individual site properties can override global server properties. In any case, to set global defaults and parameters for your system, right-click your IIS server in the scope pane of the IIS MMC and then select Properties to edit the properties page for your server. You should see a properties page similar to the one in Figure 17.3.

From this page, you can modify several settings for your system, including global defaults for the IIS service and default settings for the server extensions installed on the system. For example, if you know that all Web sites on your server are going to use `index.html` as their default start page instead of the Microsoft standard `default.html`, you could set that option in the master properties for the Web service. By selecting the WWW or FTP service from the Master Properties pull-down box (located under the Internet Information Services tab) and clicking the Edit button, you can define settings for sites hosted on your system. The settings you can define here are defined in the "Setting Up a Web Site and Configuring Web Services" section later in this chapter.

FIGURE 17.3

Editing global IIS server properties

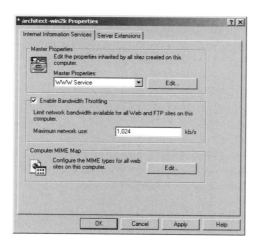

If you already have sites running and configured on your system and change the global parameters for your server, Windows 2000 will also give you the option to apply these changes to the individual Web/FTP sites on that system. For example, in Figure 17.4, I have set a limit for each Web site on my server to use no more than 5 percent of the CPU on the system. Windows 2000 is indicating that this conflicts with settings for one of the Web sites on the system.

FIGURE 17.4

Setting global properties that override individual site properties

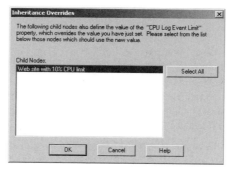

An existing Web site already has a CPU limit of 10 percent in place, so Windows 2000 is asking me if I would like to apply the new global default to the individual Web site in question. By selecting the site(s) to change and then clicking OK, Windows 2000 will apply the global defaults to the individual site(s). If you plan on hosting multiple Web sites on your server, this is a great way to make across-the-board changes to your system.

In addition to setting global defaults for Web and FTP sites, you can also use a feature called bandwidth throttling to control how much bandwidth IIS uses on your network. This option is a great feature for several reasons. First, if you have other Internet-based services on your network that require a set amount of bandwidth, setting this parameter will ensure that IIS doesn't consume all of your available bandwidth. This is good for making sure that there is enough bandwidth left on your Internet connection for e-mail, etc.

For example, let's say that you have a T1 connected to your organization's network, but you don't want the IIS process to ever consume more than one-quarter of the bandwidth on this connection. By using the figures in Table 17.1, you can see that a full T1 (1,544,000 bits per second) represents approximately 193KBps, so to limit IIS to one-quarter of your T1, you would enter a value of 48 here.

TABLE 17.1: COMMON BANDWIDTH CONVERSIONS

CONNECTION TYPE	BANDWIDTH, IN BITS/SEC	BANDWIDTH, IN KILOBYTES/SEC
56K	56,000	7
64K	64,000	8
128K	128,000	16
256K	256,000	32
512K	512,000	64
T1	1,544,000	193
10Base-T	10,000,000	1250
T3	44,736,000	5592
100Base-T	100,000,000	12,500

Bandwidth throttling is also a great feature for testing how well a Web site will perform over a slow link. Want to see how a Web site is going to look and perform for someone dialing in over a 56K connection? Try setting the bandwidth throttle down to 7 or 6KBps. It is also useful in benchmarking and scaling systems.

One important note to make about bandwidth throttling, however, is that bandwidth throttle settings on individual Web sites will override global server settings. To me, this seems a bit backward, but it is the way that Microsoft chose to implement this capability. So why not just use the individual site settings and ignore the global settings? The main reason is because there is no way to set bandwidth throttle settings for the other services in IIS.

The last option you can set for your global IIS site is the MIME (Multipurpose Internet Mail Extensions) mappings that the IIS Web service will send to client browsers when a file is requested. For most implementations of IIS, the defaults in this area should be fine. However, if you need to add, remove, or change any mappings on your system, click the Edit button and then make changes as necessary.

Under the Server Extensions tab, you can control several settings for Web sites on your system, including global security settings. The options available when setting global server extension settings are shown in Figure 17.5.

Once again, many of these same features are editable for each individual Web site, but there might be instances where you want to define a global default to be used for all sites. However, be careful when making changes to global server extension settings. Unlike other global IIS settings that will give you a warning when conflicting values are encountered, extension settings will be immediately applied to all sites on your IIS server with no regard to any existing values in place. Unless you have a specific need to define global settings, I would recommend leaving the options in this dialog box at their defaults and changing the server extension settings for each individual site as needed. Definitions for the settings available can be found later in the "Modifying Web Site Properties" section.

FIGURE 17.5

Configuring server extensions

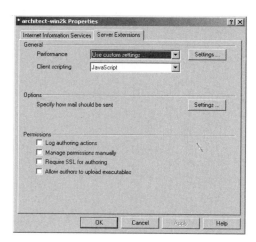

Once you have the global settings configured correctly on your server, it's time to start publishing content. In the next two sections, I will discuss setting up Web and FTP sites on your system and the configuration items associated with each. For the purposes of our discussions throughout the remainder of this chapter, I'll assume that you are configuring new sites or virtual servers in each case.

Setting Up a Web Site and Configuring Web Services

When you are ready to start building a Web site, the steps you must follow are quite easy. First, you will need to have the following information available:

◆ What IP address you want this Web server to live on (or if it should respond on all available IP addresses).

◆ What TCP/IP port number this Web server should listen to on the previously specified IP address(es). Typically, this is port 80.

◆ What TCP/IP port number this Web server should listen to for secure communications on the previously specified IP address(es). Typically, this is port 443.

◆ What *host header name* your Web site will respond to if you will be configuring multiple Web sites on a single IP address. Host header names are common Web site names, such as www.microsoft.com. (I'll explain host header records soon.)

◆ What directory on your system will house your Web site content (HTML, scripts, etc.).

Creating a New Web Site

Begin creating your Web site by selecting your IIS server in the Internet Services Manager MMC and then choosing New/Web Site from the Action pull-down menu. This will launch the Web Site Creation Wizard, which will walk you through the process to create a Web site. The first question the wizard will ask is for a descriptive name for your site. Enter an appropriate name, and then click Next to proceed to the step shown in Figure 17.6.

FIGURE 17.6

Web Site Creation
Wizard, IP Address
and Port Settings
section

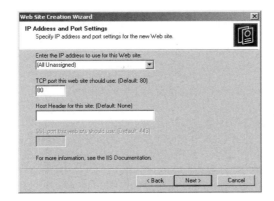

In the second step of the Web Site Creation Wizard, you will need to enter information about how your Web site can be reached. Namely, this is defined by three items: the IP address used, the port used, and any host header strings sent to your server. IIS will use any and/or all of these items to determine which Web site on your system to direct users to. If you are only hosting one Web site, the defaults should be acceptable. However, if you will be hosting multiple Web sites (for example, a private, internal Web site and a public, external Web site), the correct configuration here is important.

SERVER IP ADDRESS

The first piece of information the Web Site Creation Wizard wants to know about is which IP address to use for this Web site. This is primarily for servers with more than one network adapter or with multiple IP addresses assigned to a single network adapter. For systems with more than one network adapter, you can host a different site on each adapter by choosing the appropriate IP address in this field. If you have a network adapter with multiple IP addresses assigned to it (see Chapter 6), you can assign a different Web site to each address. Although the latter configuration is primarily seen in larger Web-hosting type arrangements, it can still be useful. If you'd prefer to have IIS simply display the same site to any IP address configured on the server, leave the default All Unassigned value in place; otherwise, select the appropriate IP address from the pull-down list.

TIP   If you are going to have an internal, private Web site published on your internal network adapter and an external, public Web site published on your external Internet network adapter, make sure that the IP address for your internal adapter is unreachable from the outside world. You can test this by trying to ping—from the public Internet—your internal IP address, or by trying to connect to it via a browser.

HTTP PORT FOR WEB SITE

The second thing the Web Site Creation Wizard needs to know is which port to use for your Web site. By default, port 80 is the standard port assigned to the HTTP protocol. If you will be hosting a public Web site, accessible to anyone, leave the selection at port 80. Browsers will try to connect to Web sites on this port when a user types in a URL. However, if you have custom needs or want to secure your Web site a bit, you can change this port to any number from 1 to 65535. To connect to your Web server with a customized port, users will need to know the port number and append it to the URL string as follows: `http://www.netarchitect.com:9000/`. This would direct a user's browser to attempt to open up an HTTP session on port 9000 instead of the default port 80. So, for example, you could access my Web site as `http://www.minasi.com/` or `http://www.minasi.com:80/` and either would work.

UNDERSTANDING AND USING HOST HEADER RECORDS

Unique IP addresses were once the way that multiple Web sites were hosted on the same physical box. However, since IP addresses are becoming more and more of a commodity, there is a means of assigning multiple Web sites to the same IP address and port number—through the use of something called host header names. A host header name is a means of including the host name a browser is requesting (e.g., `www.microsoft.com`) into the HTTP header transmitted to the HTTP server. Modern (post-1997) browsers not only say to Web sites, "Please give me your Web pages," they also say, "Please give me your Web pages—and by the way, *I* think I'm talking to `www.bigfirm.biz`." That's important because just one Web site can have several names; for example, if you type `www.minasi.com`, `www.learnwindows.biz`, `www.windowsnetworking.info`, or `www.win2ktest.com`, then you'll still end up at my Web site. It doesn't matter which URL you use to get to my site in this case. But that same Web server also runs a completely different site, `www.softwareconspiracy.com`. The IP addresses and port numbers are the same for the two Web sites, so how does IIS know which site you want? It listens to that host header record that your Web browser sent along with its HTTP request.

More specifically, when a client browser begins to open a Web site, it will (by default) look up the IP address for the host name in the URL and open a TCP connection on port number 80. Once that connection is established, it will transmit its request for a page to the server and include the host header name information in with the request. IIS will look at the host header name information, compare the name to those in its list of servers, and then respond accordingly by returning the correct pages for the corresponding site. This is a quick and easy way to host multiple sites on a single server, but clients must be using at least Microsoft Internet Explorer 3 or Netscape Navigator 2 for this to work correctly. Anyone using an older browser than that will be directed to the default Web site instead.

SSL AND SSL/HOST HEADER CONFLICTS

The last option in this phase of the wizard is to define a Secure Sockets Layer (SSL) port number to use for this Web site. SSL is the means by which Web servers and browsers can maintain secure communications between each other. You have probably used SSL if you have ever purchased anything over the Internet. Since SSL requires having an appropriate certificate installed on your IIS system (more on this later), this option will be grayed out if you don't have one installed. By default, port 443 is the correct number to use for secure communications.

Before we go on, I should warn you that SSL and host header names don't mix. If you are planning on using SSL, you can only assign one host header name to your site, since the domain name is encoded in the certificate. If you need to host multiple SSL sites on the same box, use multiple IP addresses. For example, consider my Web server. It has a certificate that identifies it as a machine named `www.minasi.com`. Recall that the very same site also has the name `www.learnwindows.biz`. You can access any page on the site using either name—for example, the page `talks.htm` about the short talks that I do can just as easily be accessed as `http://www.minasi.com/talks.htm` or as `www.learnwindows.biz/talks.htm`—either action gets you to the exact same page. But "http://" means "to make a nonsecure connection," over port 80. If you look closely at your address bar the next time that you're on a secure page, then you'll see that the URL in that bar doesn't start with "http://" but rather with "https://"—the "s" means "make this secure," which really means "connect with port 443 rather than 80." Here's where you'd see a difference between accessing a page as `https://www.minasi.com/something` versus `https://www.learnwindows.biz/something`—the first would work, the second wouldn't. For example, I have a secured page called `nwsreg-form.htm` where people can sign up for my free monthly e-mail newsletter. If you try to connect to it as `https://www.minasi.com/nwsreg-form.htm`, then you get a secured connection and you'll see the lock in the status bar of IE. But if you try to get to that very same page as `https://www.learnwindows.biz/nwsreg-form.htm`, then you'll get a warning from your browser that looks like Figure 17.7.

FIGURE 17.7

Internet Explorer warning when host header record doesn't match machine name

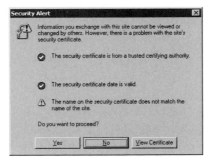

SETTING UP MULTIPLE VIRTUAL WEB SITES

With that background out of the way, let's look at how to set up more than one separate and distinct Web site on an IIS server.

In previous versions of Windows NT, hosting multiple Web sites (sometimes referred to as "virtual sites") on the same physical system was often a tricky operation, sometimes requiring modifications to the system Registry. Fortunately, this process has been made much easier in Windows 2000. For example, let's say you wanted to host two different Web sites on your server—one for `www.microsoft.com` and one for `www.sybex.com`. The steps that you would follow to make this happen are:

1. Create DNS records for each of your Web sites, each pointing to the same IP address or to unique IP addresses (for more information on creating DNS records, please see Chapter 7).

2. Choose how you want to determine which site on your server visitors are trying to reach, via one of the following options:

Host header records: The easiest of all three choices, host header records allow you to specifically enter the site name—for example, `www.microsoft.com`—in your definition of a Web site. As you've just read, modern browsers (IE 3 or Netscape 2 or later) will transmit the name of the site to the server, and the server will return the pages for the appropriate sites. Enter the appropriate host header names in the host header field shown back in Figure 17.6.

Multiple IP addresses: Whether you have multiple NIC cards installed in your server or you have programmed multiple IP addresses for a single NIC card, assigning a unique IP address to each unique Web site is one of the more common ways to host multiple Web sites on the same system. In the IP address field in Figure 17.6, enter an appropriate, unique IP address for each site that matches the DNS records you defined in step 1.

Unique port numbers: Although less common than the other two methods of hosting multiple sites, using a unique TCP port number for each site can also allow you to host multiple sites on the same system. This is more commonly seen with sites that don't need to be publicly accessible, since browsers will use port 80 by default. You can enter a custom port number in the TCP port field shown in Figure 17.6; however, client browsers will have to append the port number to their URL to be able to access the site (e.g., `http://www.microsoft.com:200` for accessing port 200).

3. Using the Web Site Creation Wizard, create two virtual Web servers on your system, one for the `www.microsoft.com` site and one for the `www.sybex.com` site. Define each site with a unique host header name, IP address, or TCP port—depending on how you want to control virtual sites on your system.

4. Place the necessary Web content for each site in the directory defined for the site.

Once you have all the information entered correctly, click Next to move on to the next step of the wizard, shown in Figure 17.8.

FIGURE 17.8

Specifying anonymous access and the path to files for a site

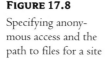

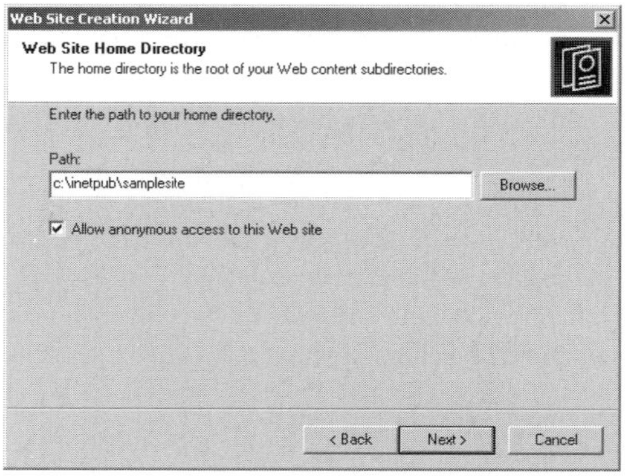

The next step of the wizard is where you will define the location for your files for this Web site, and whether to allow anonymous access to the site. The path is pretty much straightforward: enter the local path that IIS should use for files when someone connects to this site. Or, if you intend on hosting your content on another machine within your organization, you can enter a UNC path in the form of \\servername\sharename. If you choose the UNC option, the wizard will prompt you for an appropriate username and password combination to use when retrieving content from the target system.

If you will be making this a publicly accessible Web site, leave the Allow Anonymous Access to This Web Site box checked. This will allow any user to connect to the Web site without providing any form of authentication. However, if you want this to be a private, secured site, uncheck the box to remove anonymous access. Specific security settings that you can apply are discussed in the "Modifying Web Site Properties" section later in this chapter. Click Next to move on to the final step in the wizard, shown in Figure 17.9.

FIGURE 17.9

Setting Web site access permissions

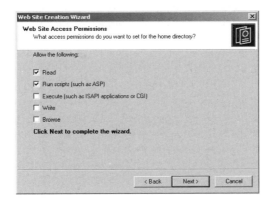

The last step in the Web Site Creation Wizard is to define access permissions to be used for this site. The permissions applied here will start at the root of the site and automatically be applied to any subdirectories below this site. Of course, you can always change the site settings later, or implement custom settings for any subdirectories below the site. Briefly, each of these access settings controls the following:

Read   Allows users to read files from your Web server. In most instances, you will want this option set for the root of a new site. The primary reason for disabling this option is for directories that contain CGI (Common Gateway Interface) or ISAPI (Internet Server Application Program Interface) applications, which will usually be set on a subdirectory level.

Run Scripts (such as ASP)   If you need to allow the execution of Active Server Pages (ASP) scripts on your site, enable this option.

Execute (such as ISAPI Applications or CGI)   If you need to allow the execution of ISAPI or CGI applications on your site, enable this option. When you enable this option, it is inclusive of the Run Scripts option as well.

Write   If client browsers either will need to upload files on your Web server or will be writing data to a file (maybe filling out a registration form, or something like that), you will need to have write permissions enabled. Personally, I prefer to only enable write permissions in subdirectories of a Web site, not the main directory itself.

Browse   If a user does not send a request for a specific file on your Web server (for example, default.html) and there is no default document defined on your system, IIS will return an HTML representation of the files and subdirectories in the root of your site. Except in special circumstances, this option should probably be left disabled.

Once you have defined the necessary security for your site, click Next to finish the wizard, and your Web site will be created. If you have HTML content to publish, you can start by putting the necessary files in the directory you defined for this site. By default, all new Web sites (unless you changed the global server properties for this option) will use default.htm or default.asp as their default home page, so make sure that the .htm or .asp file you want presented to users when they first visit your site is named appropriately. By using a client workstation with a browser, you should be able to test your site to make sure that it is operating correctly.

And don't forget the NTFS permissions! When an anonymous Web user tries to access content such as an HTML file, a JPEG, or the like, NTFS thinks that person is the user named IUSR_com-putername. If you have denied that user access, then people on the Internet won't be able to get to your Web site—IIS will pop up a box requiring them to log in.

A Multisite Example, Step-by-Step

Let's wrap up this section with an example of how you'd put a site named www.joeslabs.com and another named www.janesmarket.com on a single server—say, on a machine named spider.acme.com at 210.10.20.40:

1. Create a folder for the Joeslabs content on the spider.acme.com machine; for example's sake, let's say that you put it on E:\joeslabs. Put the files relevant to the Joeslabs site—default.htm, the JPEGs, any other HTML or script files—in E:\joeslabs.

2. Similarly, create a folder for the www.janesmarket.com content, perhaps on E:\janesmarket. Put the Janesmarket content in E:\janesmarket.

3. Ensure that DNS points to 210.10.20.40 for both www.janesmarket.com and www.joeslabs .com. In each zone, you'd probably just create a CNAME record pointing to spider.acme.com.

4. Install IIS on spider.acme.com.

5. Create the Joeslabs site: From the Internet Services Manager, right-click the icon representing spider.acme.com and choose New/Web Site, which starts up the Web Site Creation Wizard. Click Next to get past the opening screen, then type in some descriptive text for the Joeslabs Web site: **Joeslabs Web site** will do fine, although the actual text is pretty irrelevant; it's mainly to remind you as the Web administrator which of your sites does what. Then click Next to get to the IP Address and Port Settings page.

6. In the IP Address and Port Settings page (see Figure 17.6 earlier in this chapter), you'll see the three alternative methods that you can use to distinguish this site from others running on this

server: you can use a different IP address, a different port, or a different host header record. Of the three, the third option—different host header record—is by far the easiest and least costly. (Who wants to burn up an IP address for each Web site? Well, you'd have to if you were still using IIS 4!) In the field labeled Host Header for This Site (Default: None), fill in the URL that you want people to use when referring to this site—`www.joeslabs.com`.

7. Click Next and then fill in the home directory for this site, which means point the server to the folder with the content. Fill in `E:\joeslabs` and click Next.

8. Set the access permissions on this directory. In most cases, you can just take the defaults and only allow users to read files and run scripts. Click Next and then Finish, and `www.joeslabs.com` is done.

Modifying Web Site Properties

Once you are sure that your site is functioning correctly, you might find a need to fine-tune some of the parameters of the site. To change any of the settings for your site, return to the Internet Services Manager MMC and select your site in the scope pane. From the Action pull-down menu, select Properties to edit the properties pages for this site.

WEB SITE PROPERTIES

The first page in the Web site properties will look similar to the one shown in Figure 17.10. From this page, you can edit some general parameters for your Web site:

Web Site Identification Here, you can change the friendly name, IP address, TCP port number, or SSL port number assigned to your Web site. Obviously, changing any of the latter options will change the way clients access your site, so plan your changes accordingly. If you want to change the host header record for your Web site, click the Advanced button to get to the advanced identification properties for this site, and click the Add button. You should see a screen similar to the one shown in Figure 17.11.

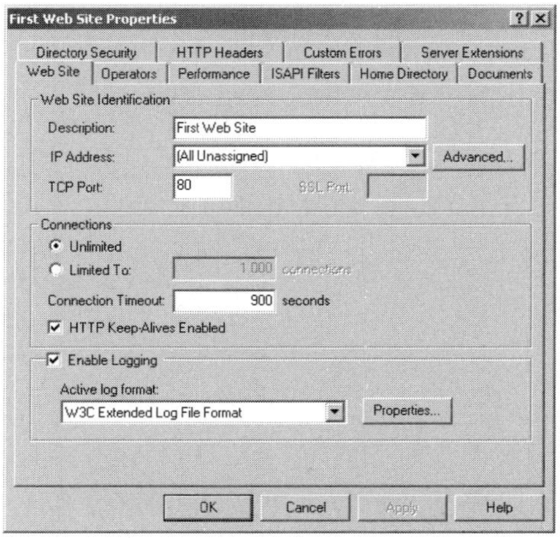

FIGURE 17.10

Web site properties for an IIS Web site

FIGURE 17.11

Advanced Web
Site Identification
properties

From this dialog box, you can change the host header name for this Web site either by adding a new identity (IP address, port, host header name) or by modifying the existing record.

Connections   Returning to the properties page shown in Figure 17.10, the next group of options you can modify is how IIS will manage incoming connections. You can limit the number of connections to your system or allow an unlimited number, enter a time-out value for IIS to close out idle connections, and enable HTTP keep-alives. Enabling HTTP keep-alives allows client browsers to maintain an open connection in between individual requests to a Web server. Since Web pages are often made up of several elements (text, graphics, etc.) that must be opened individually, this option increases performance on servers. Disabling this option could cause browsers to open a separate connection for each Web page element.

Enable Logging   You can enable or disable logging for this Web site by checking or unchecking the Enable Logging box. Since log files take up space on your system, you might consider disabling this option for an internal Web site. If you enable logging, you have format options to choose from in the Active Log Format pull-down box, including W3C Extended Log File Format, ODBC Logging, NCSA Common Log File Format, and Microsoft IIS Log File Format. Depending on which option you choose, you can edit properties for that format by clicking the Properties button. For example, choosing the ODBC Logging option and clicking Properties will take you to a dialog box where you can define the ODBC data source name, table, etc. The W3C Extended Log File Format properties will allow you to define how often new logs are created, where they are stored, and which data items to log.

OPERATORS' PROPERTIES

Moving to the next tab in the Web site properties pages will take you to the Operators page, pictured in Figure 17.12.

From this page, you can define Windows 2000 accounts that have operator privileges for this specific Web site. A user will need to be authenticated as a Win2K user, not as an anonymous user, to be able to use their operator privileges. By clicking Add, you can grant operator privileges to any users that need them. Operator privileges will grant users the rights defined below:

Web site operators can:

◆ Modify Web server access permissions and logging

◆ Modify default Web documents and Web site footers

◆ Modify page content expiration, HTTP headers, and/or content ratings

Web site operators cannot:

◆ Modify the identification (IP address, port, host header) of a Web site.

◆ Modify the anonymous user account and password.

◆ Modify bandwidth throttles.

◆ Create virtual directories or modify existing virtual directory paths.

◆ Select or deselect application isolations.

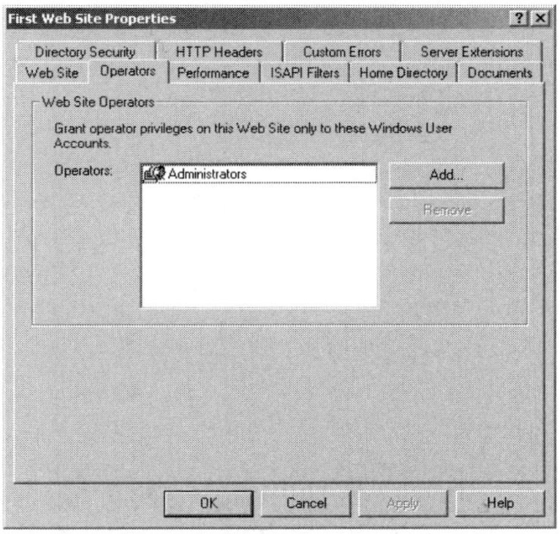

FIGURE 17.12

Operators' properties for an IIS Web site

PERFORMANCE PROPERTIES

The next options you can configure for your Web site are performance related, and can be found under the Performance properties page shown in Figure 17.13.

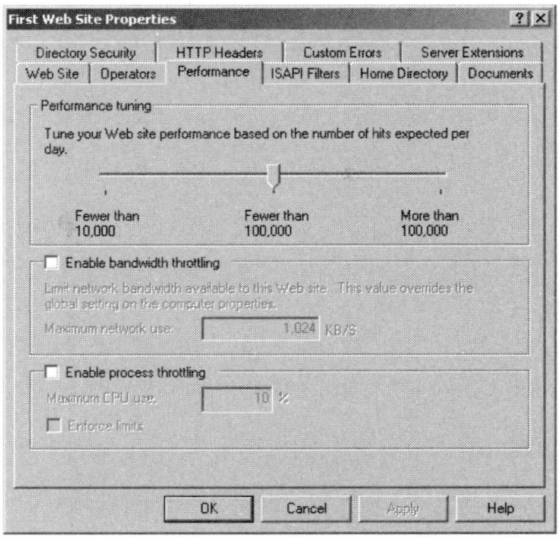

FIGURE 17.13

Performance properties for an IIS Web site

Depending on the size of your Web site and the amount of traffic you expect you will be handling, you can modify several parameters to adjust the behavior of your site:

Performance Tuning Depending on the number of hits you expect to receive in a day, you can adjust the Performance Tuning slider to one of three positions: Fewer Than 10,000, Fewer Than 100,000, or More Than 100,000. Setting this option to be slightly higher than the hits you expect to receive will yield the best performance (don't set it too high—that can actually decrease performance).

Enable Bandwidth Throttling Just as I discussed back in the global server options for IIS, you can control the amount of bandwidth that the overall server or an individual site can consume. Any settings defined here will override the global server settings. Refer back to Table 17.1 for a listing of common bandwidth sizes and their translations into kilobytes/second.

Enable Process Throttling If you will be executing applications on your server through IIS, you can limit the amount of CPU time a process can control. This can prevent an errant application from consuming all available resources on your system. Enter a percentage value for the maximum CPU use this Web site is allowed. If you would like to just receive an event log notification if this limit is exceeded, leave the Enforce Limits check box blank. Otherwise, check the box to enforce this limit, and CPU processing time will be restricted to the value you've set for this specific Web site.

ISAPI FILTERS

The next properties page—ISAPI Filters (shown in Figure 17.14)—lets you set options for which ISAPI filters are installed for a specific Web site and the order they execute in.

ISAPI filters are programs that respond to events that occur on the server during the processing of an HTTP request. The list of ISAPI filters displayed for a Web site is a combination of ISAPI filters globally defined for the server, plus ISAPI filters specifically designed for the individual Web site. If two or more filters are registered for the same event, filters with a higher priority are executed first. Filters can be added, removed, modified, or disabled from this list by using the buttons on the right side of this properties page. To change the order of execution for filters, adjust them with the up and down arrows on the left side of this page.

FIGURE 17.14

ISAPI filters properties for an IIS Web site

HOME DIRECTORY PROPERTIES

The next tab in the Web site properties pages is the Home Directory page, shown in Figure 17.15. This group of settings lets you control where IIS will look for Web content, and what security permissions to use while handling it.

FIGURE 17.15

Home directory properties for an IIS Web site

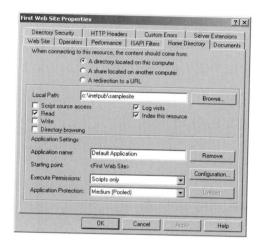

By selecting the appropriate radio button on the top of this properties page, you can control where IIS will go to look for the content for this site, or if it will send users to another Web site. Based on the selection you make, the lower portion of this properties page will change accordingly. If you select the option for a directory located on this computer, you will need to enter the local path in the lower portion of the page.

If you select the option for a share located on another computer, the Local Path field will change to a Network Directory field, where you will need to enter the correct \\servername\sharename UNC path. When you choose to use a share located on another computer for your files, you might need to enter logon credentials for the IIS service to use when it is accessing the other system. The IIS service will actually log in to the other system, retrieve the files, and present them to the user just as if the files were local. This is a great way to distribute an entire Web site throughout an organization. If individual departments are responsible for maintaining different sections of a site, you can use this feature to direct requests for their content to their servers, instead of requiring all your departments to publish their data to one system.

Lastly, if you choose to redirect users to another URL, IIS will create an HTML redirection page pointing users to the URL you specify. The Local Path field will change to a Redirect To field, where you can enter a full URL to send users to. Redirecting users to a URL can be configured through three different options: redirect users to an exact URL, redirect users to a lower subdirectory, or permanently redirect users to an exact URL. Redirecting users to an exact URL is pretty straightforward; users are sent to the exact URL you enter, just as if you typed it into their browser for them. Redirecting users to a lower subdirectory will let you create an alternate directory in your Web site structure. The last option, for permanently redirecting users to a URL, is very similar to the first option, with the exception that a permanent redirection will send a "301 Permanent Redirect" message to the browser, instead of the usual "302 Temporary Redirect." The net result of this is that some browsers will modify any bookmarks or favorites on file if they receive a permanent redirection.

If you chose either of the first two options for your content location—a directory on your IIS computer or a share on another server—several security settings will be displayed at the bottom of the properties page. These settings can be used to control what can and can't be done on your site:

Script Source Access   This option is only available when read or write access is enabled. This option allows access to source code, including scripts in ASP applications.

Read   Allows users to read files from your Web server. In most instances, you will want this option set for the root of a new site. The primary reason for disabling this option is for directories that contain CGI or ISAPI applications, which will usually be set on a subdirectory level.

Write   If client browsers will either need to upload files on your Web server or will be writing data to a file (filling out a registration form, etc.), you will need to have write permissions enabled. Personally, I prefer to enable write permissions in subdirectories of a Web site and not in the main directory itself.

Directory Browsing   If a user does not send a request for a specific file on your Web server (for example, default.html), and there is no default document defined on your system (see the next section), IIS will return an HTML representation of the files and subdirectories in the root of your site. Except in special circumstances, this option should probably be left disabled.

Log Visits   Depending on whether or not you want logging information stored about visitors to your site, check or uncheck this box. Logs will be stored in the format defined in the Web Site properties page covered earlier in this chapter.

Index This Resource   To speed searching for text data, select Index This Resource, which will cause the Microsoft Indexing Service to index all the content of this site.

Application Name   If your site is going to be the starting point for an application, this is where to enter the name of the application.

Execute Permissions   This pull-down box will let you define whether or not to allow the execution of scripts, the execution of scripts and executable files (.exe and .dll), or nothing at all.

Application Protection   To prevent errant applications from taking out other processes on your system, you can control the level of protection for each application. Low protection will allow applications to execute in the same memory space as the IIS process itself; medium protection will pool applications for this site together; and high protection will isolate each application from any others.

DOCUMENTS PROPERTIES

Continuing with our Web site configuration, the next settings tab in the Web site properties pages is the Documents tab, shown in Figure 17.16.

When users attempt to connect to your Web server without specifying a specific document to retrieve, IIS will look through the list of default documents (if enabled) to return to the user. By default, the IIS installation process will add `default.htm` and `default.asp` to this setting for the global server properties, which are then inherited by each Web site. If for some reason you would prefer to use another name—perhaps `index.html`—you can add the name to the list of default documents by clicking the Add button. IIS will look through this list, in order, and return the first matching document it finds. If you would prefer to adjust the order, use the arrows to the left of the document list to place the documents you want to look for first at the top of the list.

FIGURE 17.16

Documents properties for an IIS Web site

If you want to have every Web page within your site sent out with a common footer (for example, copyright and disclaimer information), you can have IIS do this by selecting the Enable Document Footer option. The document footer is an HTML file that IIS will merge in at the bottom of each page it displays. The footer file should not be a complete HTML file in and of itself (with `<HTML>` `</HTML>` tags, for example). Instead, it should just contain the basic HTML code you want displayed, for example:

```
<h2>This is a footer</h2>
```

This is all that would be necessary for a footer file to display the text shown as a heading type 2.

DIRECTORY SECURITY PROPERTIES

The next section of the Web site properties pages—Directory Security—allows you to control who accesses your Web site based on authentication, client IP addresses, or ACL settings on files, and gives you the ability to secure communications when clients connect to this Web site. The Directory Security properties page is shown in Figure 17.17.

The first method for securing a Web site is to define an authentication method to validate users. Since browsers—by default—will try to access a site anonymously, one option available is to remove anonymous access from your site. Click the Edit button in the Anonymous Access and Authentication Control box to edit the authentication properties of your system. The Authentication Methods dialog box is shown in Figure 17.18.

FIGURE 17.17

Directory security properties for an IIS Web site

FIGURE 17.18

The Authentication Methods dialog box

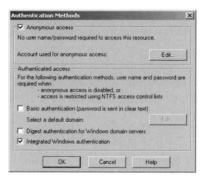

By default, Windows 2000 will allow anonymous access for Web sites and directories, unless you have overridden this option in the global server settings. There are two primary means of securing your Web site—or certain areas of your Web site. The first is to remove the check mark from the Anonymous Access box. This will effectively make your entire site a secured site and require an authentication before a user is allowed to connect at all, even to the default home page. If you choose this option, then the Authenticated Access area in the lower half of the figure becomes important in determining just how clients will authenticate themselves. If you remove anonymous access from your site, you must have some authentication option selected, or else you will effectively disable all access to your site.

The options under Authenticated Access control what level of authentication users must negotiate to get connected to your protected site. The details of each type are as follows:

Basic Authentication   This is the most basic level of authentication (and therefore the most widely supported) for validating a user accessing a Web resource. Practically all Web browsers, including Microsoft's and Netscape's, support this type of authentication. Using this authentication method, usernames and passwords are transmitted in clear text and checked against the accounts in the domain of the IIS server (if you would like to use another accounts domain for validation, click the Edit button next to Select a Default Domain). If you expect to be running a public Web site, accessed by users on various platforms and browsers, this is probably the best option for requiring authentication on your site; however, it is the least secure of all the authentication types.

Digest Authentication   A feature new to Windows 2000 Server and IIS 5, digest authentication securely transmits a hash value over the Internet instead of a password, thus keeping system passwords confidential. There are a few requirements for using this type of authentication, however. Namely, client workstations must be using Internet Explorer version 5 or later, and user passwords in the Active Directory must also be stored as clear text. This is the most secure of all the authentication types.

Windows Authentication   A new name for the Windows NT challenge/response authentication option in previous versions of IIS, Windows authentication requires users to use Internet Explorer for their Web browser. Password hashes are transmitted over the Internet, instead of the actual passwords, so this is a more secure means of authentication. User accounts are again checked against the accounts in the domain of the IIS server. Any version of Internet Explorer after version 2 can support this method of authentication. Windows authentication, like anonymous authentication, is selected by default. This is a good option for secure authentication for Internet Explorer users that haven't migrated to IE 5 or greater yet.

The second method for securing areas of your Web site is to leave anonymous authentication enabled, but to apply security settings to the specific files and directories you want to protect. This will only work on NTFS volumes (you can't define permissions on FAT volumes), and it will allow you to make some areas in your Web site open to the public while leaving other areas protected.

The method by which this works is really quite simple. When anonymous authentication is enabled, IIS will use the anonymous user account first to try to read a file and pass it back to the user requesting it. For publicly accessible Web content, without any permission settings restricting access, the IIS process should be able to access that content via the anonymous user. However, if IIS fails in accessing that file due to a security restriction, it will look to the authentication options defined previously to determine whether it should request an authentication from the user. If an authentication option is set, IIS will prompt the user for a username and password combination, and then IIS will use those credentials when accessing the file. Therefore, if you want to restrict access to specific files or directories to certain users, you must add them to the permissions applied to those files or directories, and exclude access for the anonymous user account. (For more information on placing security rights on files in NTFS, see Chapter 11.)

Another means of securing a Web site is to restrict who can access the site based on an IP address, a range of IP addresses, or a domain name. This requires knowing in advance who should be connecting to your site, and from where, but it is particularly useful when setting up Web sites designed to interface with clients or suppliers. By clicking the Edit button in the IP Address and Domain Name Restrictions area in Figure 17.17, you will see a screen similar to the one in Figure 17.19, where you can enter any restrictions you'd like.

FIGURE 17.19

The IP Address and Domain Name Restrictions dialog box

Select the appropriate radio button option to either grant access or deny access to everyone, and then enter the exception list by selecting Add. Individual IP address restrictions are useful for home or traveling users connecting to a Web site, and groups of computers can be defined by entering a network address and subnet mask. Domain name restrictions are useful as a last resort when you don't know the IP addresses of client systems that will be accessing your Web server. Since IIS only knows who is connected to it by an IP number, the server must do a reverse-DNS lookup, which means that the server will have to do quite a bit of processing just to determine if it's okay to let the user in. Unless your situation requires using domain names, it's probably worthwhile to find out the exact IP address ranges to allow into your site and configure them accordingly.

NOTE   *Many hosts out on the Internet don't actually have reverse-DNS records assigned to them, and some hosts have incorrect reverse-DNS records assigned to them. Therefore, if you were to put in a restriction based on a host/domain name, it might not work quite as well as you want it to.*

IP address restrictions can be combined along with authentication restrictions, allowing for some very secure Web site access. For example, if you have users who frequently work from home—on a computer with a fixed IP address—you could secure your site (or a portion of it) by allowing connections only from specific IP addresses, and require a secure user authentication before allowing access.

The last option for securing a Web site is to require encrypted communications between the client browser and the server, preventing anyone from intercepting data as it travels across the Internet. This is done with SSL (Secure Sockets Layer) encryption, discussed later in this chapter in the "Communicating Securely with SSL" section.

HTTP HEADER PROPERTIES

The next group of settings you can control for your IIS Web site are what headers the IIS service should include with HTTP pages it transmits. These parameters are adjusted under the HTTP Headers tab, pictured in Figure 17.20.

HTTP headers let you control several things that your Web server will transmit to Web browsers along with the HTML pages on your site. The primary things most administrators would want to control are content expiration, content ratings, and MIME file types. However, custom headers can be added as necessary for new HTML standards that haven't been implemented in IIS yet.

By checking the Enable Content Expiration box, you can effectively control how browsers will handle their cached pages when communicating with your site. If a user has visited your site before, the pages may still be in the cache of their machine; however, you may only want pages to be valid for a day or two, depending on the type of material being presented. By selecting an expiration option (to expire immediately, expire after a certain number of days, or expire on a set date) you can force browsers to request a new page from your server after the expiration interval has been reached.

FIGURE 17.20

HTTP header properties for an IIS Web site

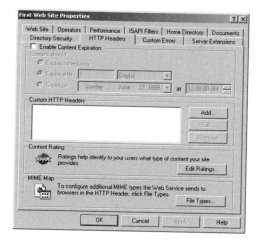

If your Web site will be hosting material that contains content some people might find objectionable, you can enable content ratings for your site or for areas of your site as needed. In the Content Rating area, click the Edit Ratings button to go to the Content Ratings properties page. From there, you can learn about the Platform for Internet Content Selection (PICS) system that was developed by the Recreational Software Advisory Council (RSAC) and is used to determine a "rating" for a Web site's content. There is also a questionnaire that you can walk through to determine an appropriate rating for your Web site. Once you have a set of ratings you want to apply to your site, click the Ratings tab in the Content Ratings properties page to begin entering those ratings (see Figure 17.21).

FIGURE 17.21

Implementing content ratings

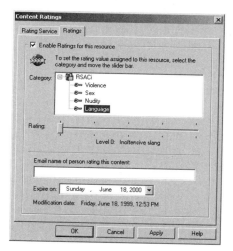

As you can see from the screen, there are four primary categories for rating a Web site—violence, sex, nudity, and language. For each of these categories, there are five levels—0 through 4—that dictate how strongly offensive the content of your site is in each category. For example, level 0 for language is defined as "inoffensive slang," while level 4 is defined as "explicit or crude language." The settings you apply here will have a direct correlation to the content settings available in Internet Explorer or Netscape Navigator, and will effectively block visitors from reaching your site if your content ratings exceed their browser settings. Set your ratings accordingly and enter an e-mail address and an expiration date for your content settings. Once the content ratings are set, IIS will transmit them out with every page on the corresponding Web site or subdirectories of the site.

If you have a need to add or remove MIME types on your IIS server, go back to the HTTP Headers tab and click the File Types button in the MIME Map area. Through the File Types dialog box that will come up, you can add additional MIME file types to your system by clicking the New Type button and entering the appropriate associated extension and content type as prompted. The content type should be in the format of *mime type/filename extension*. To remove a MIME file type, highlight the file type in the list of registered file types and then click the Remove button.

If there are custom HTTP headers you would like transmitted to browsers along with each page, you can enter them in the Custom HTTP Headers box by clicking the Add button. One thing custom headers are useful for is for HTML standards that have been developed but have not made their way into IIS yet.

CUSTOM ERRORS PROPERTIES

When building your Web server and Web sites, there may be occasions when you want to control how and what is displayed to users who receive an error. For example, you might want to have a custom HTML page displayed when a user reaches a 404 error (file not found). To customize the error messages on your site, click the Custom Errors tab on the Web site properties pages. The page for custom errors is shown in Figure 17.22.

Through this dialog box, you can choose from having a default error message, file, or URL displayed for any type of HTTP 1.1 error. The HTTP error types (along with their subtypes) are listed in the left column, the types of response are in the middle column, and the details of those responses are in the right column. In a default installation of IIS, some messages will contain default responses (just one line of text), and other errors will be defined by HTML files. Windows 2000 stores its default IIS error message files in the `%systemroot%\help\iisHelp\common` directory; you can use these as templates to define your own error messages.

To change an error message on your system, find the HTTP error number you want to change in the list (along with the subtype if necessary) and edit the properties of that error message. From the Error Mapping Properties dialog box, you can change the message type and the location of the file or URL to display (if you've chosen that type of response).

FRONTPAGE SERVER EXTENSIONS

The final tab in the Web site properties pages is for managing server extensions in a site. If you've created a new site, you probably won't see anything under this tab until you add server extensions to your site (they aren't installed by default, and don't think that you must add them—I personally find them troublesome and just write my own Active Server Page VBScripts to duplicate their function so that I can avoid having to put the FrontPage Server Extensions on my system).

FIGURE 17.22

Custom error properties for an IIS Web site

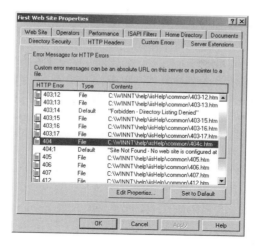

Installing FrontPage Server Extensions

To add server extensions to a site, highlight the site in the scope pane of the MMC, and select the Configure Server Extensions option from the All Tasks item in the Action pull-down menu. Or right-click your site and select the same option, as shown in Figure 17.23.

FIGURE 17.23

Adding server extensions to a site

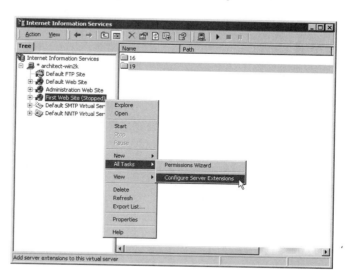

This will launch the Server Extensions Configuration Wizard, which will walk you though the necessary configurations for adding server extensions to this site. The first step of the Server Extensions Configuration Wizard is shown in Figure 17.24.

FIGURE 17.24

Defining groups in the Server Extensions Configuration Wizard

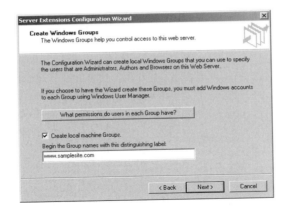

This first step in the wizard is to create special local machine groups on your system specific to the Web site you are configuring. Three groups will be created on your system, as follows:

Browsers   Users defined as browsers can browse content on this server, but can't modify any content.

Authors   Users defined as authors can both browse and modify content on this server.

Administrators   Users defined as administrators can browse and modify content on this server, in addition to being able to create new Webs, change Web settings, and control who has authoring access.

If you will be hosting multiple sites on your system, enter a distinguishing label in the Begin the Group Names with This Distinguishing Label field. For example, the Browsers group created using the example shown in Figure 17.24 will end up being named `www.samplesite.com Browsers` in the directory. Click Next to proceed to the next step of the wizard, shown in Figure 17.25.

FIGURE 17.25

Defining access control in the Server Extensions Configuration Wizard

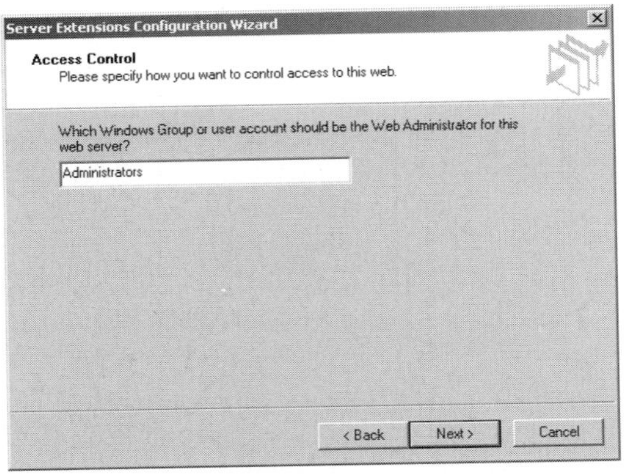

The second step of the Server Extensions Configuration Wizard allows you to define which group or user account should be the ultimate administrator for this Web server. This group has authority over the Administrators group defined in the previous step of the wizard. By default, the wizard will select the Administrators group; however, you may want to change this to another group or user on your system depending on your environment. Choose an appropriate user or group here and then click Next to move on to the last step of the wizard, shown in Figure 17.26.

FIGURE 17.26

Defining e-mail properties in the Server Extensions Configuration Wizard

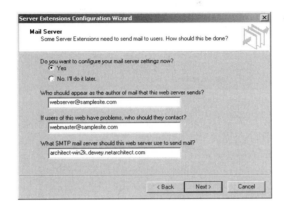

As I discussed earlier in this chapter, some FrontPage server extensions are designed to send e-mail to users. For example, a form on a Web site that collects registration information for a conference or seminar might use FrontPage extensions to have the results of the form e-mailed to a specific address. In order for those extensions to send mail, they must know how to send mail and what server to use to send it. You can configure these options during the wizard or later in the server extensions properties for this Web site. If you don't want FrontPage extensions to send e-mail out from your Web site, leaving these options unconfigured will prevent them from doing so.

If you decide to configure the mail properties, the information required is rather straightforward. In the Who Should Appear As the Author of Mail That This Web Server Sends? field, enter an e-mail address that will appear in the From: field of all outgoing messages. If you feel that you might want to collect replies from users, enter a valid e-mail address in this field, otherwise I'd recommend using an e-mail address that doesn't exist. In the If Users of This Web Have Problems, Who Should They Contact? field, enter the e-mail address of the Webmaster for this site. Lastly, you will need to enter the host name of an SMTP server that the FrontPage extensions can use in the What SMTP Mail Server Should This Web Server Use to Send Mail? field. You can either enter the name of another system here, or if you've configured the SMTP services in IIS, you can use the full name of your Web server itself (don't use the Web site name unless that is the actual name of your IIS system).

Once you have entered all of this information, click Next to finish the wizard, and the FrontPage extensions will be added to your Web. Your Web server, which might have had only a few files in it before, will now have all of the necessary subdirectories installed to support FrontPage clients.

Configuring FrontPage Server Extensions

When you have installed FrontPage extensions on a site, the Server Extensions properties page for your Web site (Figure 17.27) will finally become active and allow you to modify the properties for the site.

FIGURE 17.27

Server extensions properties for an IIS Web site

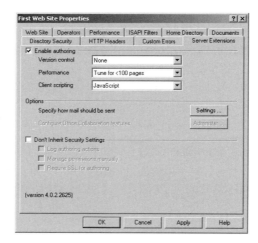

By adjusting the properties on this page, you can control the behavior of the FrontPage server extensions for this site as follows:

Enable Authoring   If you are editing the properties of a root Web, this option will be available. It will allow you to control whether users can author content on the site via FrontPage or not. The Enable Authoring option must be selected to adjust the Version Control, Performance, or Client Scripting settings.

Version Control   To keep track of who's editing Web content on your site, keep tabs on changes, and prevent one author's changes from overwriting another's, you can enable the built-in version control capabilities by selecting Use Built-In from the pull-down box.

Performance   Based on the number of pages you have on your Web site, you can adjust how the server extensions will allocate cache memory for your system. Since cached pages in memory can be returned to users quicker than pages retrieved from disk, you can increase your performance by selecting the appropriate setting here. However, since cache takes additional memory away from other system processes, don't set this value higher than necessary for the number of pages on your site—either less than 100, 100 to 1000, or greater than 1000. If you have more than 1000 pages on your site, select the Use Custom Settings performance option to fine-tune the cache parameters by hand.

Client Scripting   When the FrontPage server extensions automatically generate Web pages for users, they can handle scripts one of two ways—either creating VBScript or JScript. Choose the option that is appropriate for your environment and the users who will be connecting to your Web site.

Specify How Mail Should Be Sent   If you decide to change the mail configuration parameters that you previously specified in the Server Extensions Configuration Wizard—or if you skipped that part of the wizard—click the Settings button for this option to change these options. From there, you can change the Web server's e-mail address (the From: address your mail server will use when sending mail), the contact (usually "Webmaster") address for your site, which SMTP server to use, and the mail encoding and character set to use. The last two options are not configurable through the Server Extensions Configuration Wizard, so if you need to apply custom settings to those parameters, this is the dialog in which to do it.

Don't Inherit Security Settings   Each FrontPage root Web on your IIS server will automatically inherit the global server extension security settings of the Web server by default, as discussed earlier in this chapter. If you need to override those settings for a specific site, select this option and you will be able to manage each item individually for this site. Enabling this option will enable the Log Authoring Actions, Manage Permissions Manually, and Require SSL for Authoring items described below.

Log Authoring Actions   When an author takes action on the system (modifying content, for example), this option will log details of that transaction into the log file, `Author.log`, stored in the `_vti_log` directory of the Web site. The log will contain the name of the author performing the action, the name of the Web site the action was performed on, the remote host name, and any operation-specific data.

Manage Permissions Manually   Selecting this option will disable the normal security-changing behaviors of the FrontPage server extension administrative tools (i.e., the MMC interface). When this option is selected, any options within the FrontPage server extension properties that would normally change the security of your site (when modified) will not implement any changes.

Require SSL for Authoring   If you want to require that authors encrypt information as it is transmitted to your Web site, or if you are using basic authentication and want to make sure passwords aren't transmitted over the Internet in clear text, select this option.

Virtual Directories

As Web sites begin to grow, often there is a need to organize levels of content into subdirectories off of the main root of the site. Just like a hard drive on a computer, in time there are often too many files to manage in one directory, so subdirectories become necessary. There are two main ways to do this for a Web site. The first is to actually create a subdirectory in the site's content directory and place content into that directory. For example, let's say you have a site that is stored in `C:\Inetpub\wwwroot` and is accessed by a URL of `www.companyname.com`. If you decide you want to move all of your graphics files to a separate subdirectory, you could create a subdirectory called `C:\Inetpub\wwwroot\images` and then move all of your graphical content into that directory. To access files in that directory, client browsers would access the URL `www.companyname.com/images`.

However, what if you want to have content available as a subdirectory in your site, but you can't move the content to a normal subdirectory within your site's structure? This is where the concept of virtual roots comes into play. Virtual roots are a means of defining a subdirectory off of the root of your site (or even a lower level of your site) and then creating an alias, or a pointer to a directory somewhere else on your system or on another computer on your network. By using virtual roots, you are not forced to move all your Web content to one system and then place it in an orderly structure for visiting users. Instead, you can have content stored anywhere on your machine or on any system within your network, and users can access it through a simple directory structure.

For example, consider the diagram shown in Figure 17.28. This is representative of how I actually use virtual roots on one of my Web servers, to bring all my content into one logical structure.

As you can see from the diagram, the root of the Web site content and the two subdirectories are easily accessible from the client browser through the main URL and simple names that exist right off of the root of the URL. These three different directories are actually stored on different machines and different physical hard drives, yet to the browsing user they all seem to be in one logical structure.

I use this layout primarily for two reasons: for protected content and for data for which it is easier to create a virtual root than to move it to my IIS server. All of the publicly accessible content for my Web site is stored on a FAT volume on the same server that is running IIS. Since this content is stored in FAT (and my IIS server allows anonymous connections), anyone can get to this content without any restrictions. However, there is some content on that system that I wanted to have protected by username so that only certain users could access the content. That data has to be stored on an NTFS volume and in a protected directory (namely, the `D:\ipmonitor` directory). By creating a virtual root alias and pointing it to that directory, it appears as though it is right off of the root of my Web server, even though it is stored on a separate physical drive.

FIGURE 17.28

Sample use of virtual roots

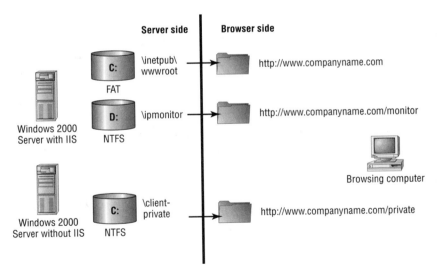

The same is true for client documents and files, which are stored on a completely separate system on my network that isn't running IIS. While I could have loaded IIS on that server and connected it to the Internet, it was easier to simply create a virtual root for that data instead. Now when clients access that directory, the data they receive actually comes from another server inside of my network.

As you can see, virtual roots can be very flexible and make structuring your Web site much easier. Like everything else in Windows 2000, Microsoft has created a wizard for defining virtual roots.

DEFINING A VIRTUAL DIRECTORY

To launch the Virtual Directory Creation Wizard, return to the Internet Information Services MMC and highlight the Web site you want to work with in the scope pane of the window. Select New/Virtual Directory from the Action pull-down menu, and the wizard will start walking you through the configuration process. The first step of the wizard is shown in Figure 17.29.

   The first thing you will need to specify for your virtual directory is the alias that refers to it. The alias is the directory name that client browsers will need to use to access the directory. For example, if a user were accessing the URL `http://www.companyname.com/documents` on your Web server, `documents` would be the alias. The alias does not need to match the name of the directory where the files are actually coming from, so you can use whatever name works best in this field. Click Next to proceed to the next step of the wizard, shown in Figure 17.30.

FIGURE 17.29

Defining an alias for a virtual directory

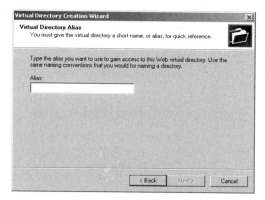

FIGURE 17.30

Defining a content directory for a virtual directory

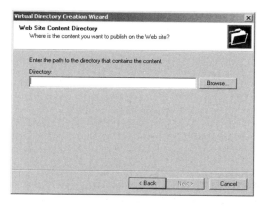

If you want to define a virtual directory that points to another directory on the same computer, enter the path name here (such as `D:\documents`). IIS will define the virtual directory as pointing to another directory on the same server. However, if you want this virtual directory to point to data located on a share on another server, enter the UNC path to that system here. When you click Next, the Virtual Directory Creation Wizard will take you to another dialog box, shown in Figure 17.31, for entering user credentials.

FIGURE 17.31

Entering a username
and password to
access shared content
via a virtual directory

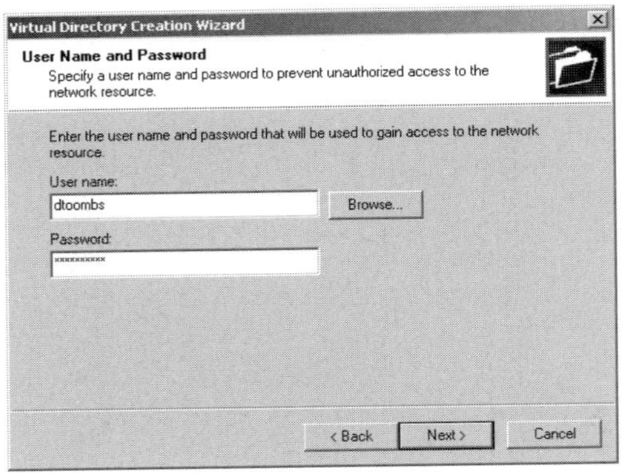

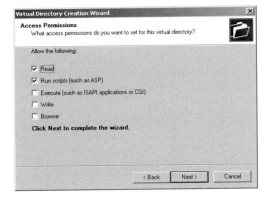

When IIS needs to contact another server for Web content, it will need to do so with a specific username and password combination. Enter an appropriate set of credentials here, one that would have appropriate access rights to the content you are trying to reach. Click Next to move to the last step of the wizard—defining access permissions—shown in Figure 17.32.

FIGURE 17.32

Defining access per-
missions for a virtual
directory

This step in the wizard is identical to the one mentioned earlier in this chapter and shown in Figure 17.9. All the definitions and permissions function the same for a virtual directory as they do for a standard directory, so return to that section for a further definition of these items.

Once you have entered all of the required information, you should have a new virtual directory item listed below your Web site. You can test this to make sure that the virtual directory responds accordingly by launching a browser and then navigating to your virtual directory. If everything has gone according to plan, IIS should return content from the appropriate location.

You can modify properties for a virtual directory in exactly the same manner that you would for a Web site—by editing the properties pages for the directory itself. You can edit the following properties pages for a virtual directory: Virtual Directory (equivalent to Home Directory for a site), Documents, Directory Security, HTTP Headers, and Custom Errors. These pages are functionally identical to the pages defined earlier in this section for modifying the properties for an entire site.

Setting Up an FTP Site and Configuring FTP Services

Although many file transfers on the Internet today take place via HTTP, FTP is still an important protocol to support if you will be running a public Web site, simply due to its broad range of client support. FTP client software has been developed for almost every computing platform imaginable— including mainframe and midrange systems. Clients who might not be able to retrieve files from your system via HTTP will most likely be able to do so via FTP.

To set up FTP services on Internet Information Services, have the following information ready in advance:

♦ What IP address you want this FTP server to listen on (or if it should respond on all available IP addresses).

♦ What TCP/IP port number this FTP server should listen to on the previously specified IP address(es). Typically, this is port 21.

♦ Whether to allow read access, write access, or both to your FTP site.

♦ What directory on your system will house your FTP files.

Creating a New FTP Site

As with most everything in Windows 2000 Server, the creation of a new FTP site begins with a wizard—in this case, the FTP Site Creation Wizard. To start the wizard, select your IIS server in the scope pane of the Internet Services Manager MMC. Select the New/FTP Site command from the Action pull-down menu, and the wizard will walk you through the necessary configuration process.

The first step in the wizard, shown in Figure 17.33, will prompt you for a friendly name to use when referencing your FTP site.

FIGURE 17.33

Entering an FTP site description in the FTP Site Creation Wizard

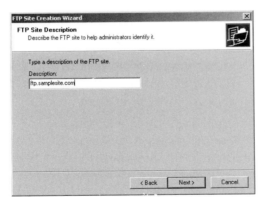

Choose a meaningful name for your site, and click Next to proceed to the next step of the wizard, shown in Figure 17.34.

FIGURE 17.34

Assigning IP addresses and ports in the FTP Site Creation Wizard

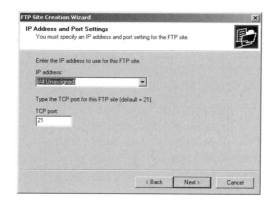

For users to be able to reach your FTP server, you need to assign an IP address and TCP port number for the service to listen to for incoming connections. By default, the wizard will want to assign your FTP server to listen to TCP port 21 on all available IP addresses on the system. If you have multiple IP addresses assigned to your server (for example, for an internal interface and an external interface), you might want to select the specific address for your system in the IP Address pull-down box. Or if you will be making your FTP site available to the Internet, but don't want to have it readily accessible on the default port of 21, you can assign it to any other port number from 1 to 65535.

TIP *Changing the port number for your FTP site is often a good idea if you will only be using it to publish or receive files for a few selected clients, suppliers, etc. One of my own clients recently had their FTP server discovered (presumably by scanning for devices responding to TCP port 21) and used by hackers as a repository for pirated software.*

If the defaults are acceptable, click Next to move on to the next step of the FTP Site Creation Wizard, shown in Figure 17.35.

FIGURE 17.35

Setting the FTP site home directory in the FTP Site Creation Wizard

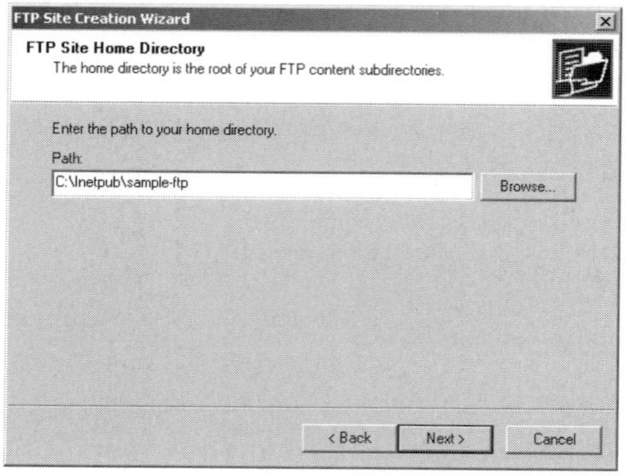

When FTP clients initially connect to your server, they will be placed in the home directory of your system and won't be able to proceed any higher on your system than the home directory. For them, the home directory that you specify will be their "root" directory. Their root directory can either be a directory on your IIS server or a share on another system on the same network. From the root directory, you can create subdirectories below your home directory in order to organize the files available for download or the files you expect to be receiving. Enter the appropriate directory name or UNC path here and click Next to proceed. If you entered a UNC path for your root directory, the next step of the wizard will prompt you for a username and password for IIS to use when accessing that share. Otherwise, if you entered a local path, the next step is the final step of the wizard, shown in Figure 17.36.

FIGURE 17.36

Setting access permissions via the FTP Site Creation Wizard

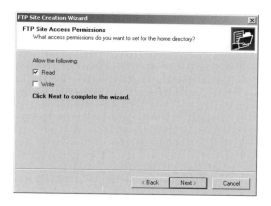

Once you have defined how your site is reachable and what directory on your system should service the site, the last thing IIS needs to know is whether or not to allow read access, write access, or both read and write access to your site. The choices here are rather self-explanatory: if you're using your FTP server simply to provide downloadable files for users or clients, then read access only would be your best choice; if you want to receive files, then select write access; if necessary, you can also select both. Click Next to finish your site, and the FTP Site Creation Wizard will build your site and start it up for you immediately.

Once your site is created, all you need to do is place the content in the home directory that you would like visitors to be able to access. This might be anywhere from a few files to a few thousand files. If you have more than a handful of files, you will probably want to organize them into some logical directory structure to make things easy to find. Whatever the case may be, make the files on your system easy to find and your users will be appreciative.

Also, it is common for FTP sites with more than just a handful of files to put index.txt and/or readme.txt files in directories throughout the site, in order to help users understand what type of content is available in each directory. After all, nobody likes trying to guess what directory names or 8.3 filenames actually mean.

Modifying FTP Site Properties

Although the FTP Site Creation Wizard does an excellent job of configuring a functional FTP site for you, there are some additional parameters that you might want to adjust for your system. For example, you might want to have a logon message displayed to users connecting to your system, or you may want to limit the number of simultaneous users on your system. In any case, to adjust the parameters for your FTP site after the wizard has created it, you will use the FTP site properties pages.

FTP SITE PROPERTIES

To reach the FTP site properties pages, highlight your new FTP site in the scope pane of the Internet Services Manager MMC and then select Properties from the Action pull-down menu. This should bring you to a dialog box similar to the one shown in Figure 17.37.

FIGURE 17.37

Editing FTP site properties

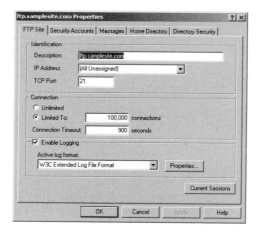

From this page of FTP site properties, you can change parameters about your site, defined as follows:

Identification   This group of controls allows you to change the "friendly name" for your site, the IP address your site listens to, and the TCP port number that it listens to. By default, the IP address for your site to listen to (unless you chose something else in the wizard) will be set to All Unassigned, causing your new site to listen for FTP users on any IP address that isn't already in use by another site on your system. To host multiple FTP sites on your system, assign each site a separate address in this field or adjust the port number.

You can change this port number as a means of securing your site (people won't know to look for an FTP server on port 28,324, for example) or so that you can host multiple FTP sites on the same IP address. You can enter a value from 1 to 65535 in the TCP Port field. However, once you change the port number, users will need to know which port number to use, since FTP client software will typically default to port 21.

Connection   Depending on the capacity and bandwidth available for your system, you may want to limit the number of simultaneous connections to your server in order to maintain adequate performance. If you are planning on running a large site and handling lots of traffic, the Unlimited option might be the best choice. If you choose to limit the connections, users who attempt to log in after the connection limit has been reached will receive a message (which you enter into the Message Properties page, described later in this section).

A "connection"—as far as IIS is concerned—is not necessarily defined as all activity from a single user. For example, a user connecting to your FTP site through a browser could launch multiple simultaneous downloads from your site. Each download session in that case would be considered a connection. Therefore, limiting your server to five connections doesn't necessarily guarantee that five users will be able to access your site at any time; one user could take up all five connection spots.

TIP *If you plan on allowing write access to your FTP site, and you know that you'll never have more than a few users connected to your FTP server at a time, you might consider limiting your system to one or two connections. If someone on the Internet were to find your server and start using it as a repository for pirated files or pornography, they'll probably start advertising its accessibility. Limiting connections is a way to at least minimize potential abuse of your system.*

To make sure that users don't stay connected to your server indefinitely, enter a time-out value in seconds in the Connection Timeout field. If for some reason an FTP session fails to close its connection appropriately, this will ensure that phantom open connections won't eventually fill up your server.

Enable Logging One of the best ways to keep track of what's happening on your system is to log the activity. Checking the Enable Logging option (enabled by default) will allow you to log activity on your site in three formats: Microsoft IIS Log Format, W3C Extended Log File Format, or via ODBC Logging. Depending on which logging option you choose, clicking the Properties button will yield a specific set of parameters you can adjust for each type of log.

Current Sessions Although this technically isn't a parameter to be adjusted, at times you may need to monitor who is connected to your FTP server and disconnect some or all of the users connected to your site. Clicking the Current Sessions button will take you to the FTP User Sessions dialog box shown in Figure 17.38.

FIGURE 17.38

Monitoring current FTP user sessions

All users connected to your FTP server will be listed in this dialog box, along with their associated IP address and the amount of time they've been connected. Users who are connected to your system anonymously—logging in via the username "anonymous" (more on this subject in the next section)—will have a question mark located in the user icon and will be listed by the e-mail address they supplied to the password prompt from the FTP server. Users who have logged in as an actual Windows 2000 user account will have a normal user icon next to the Active Directory username they're logged in as. To disconnect any users from your system, highlight their record and click the Disconnect button. To disconnect all users from your system (for example, if you're preparing to shut the system down for maintenance), click the Disconnect All button.

SECURITY ACCOUNT PROPERTIES

On an FTP server, there are generally two types of connection that users typically make: anonymous logins or user logins. Anonymous logins are overwhelmingly common on the Internet, and this is how most publicly accessible FTP servers run.

In an anonymous login, users connect to an FTP server with the username "anonymous" and an e-mail address for a password. No checking is done on this password; it is simply recorded for informational purposes. By configuring a server in this manner, any user can gain access and get files as necessary. If you plan on running a publicly accessible FTP site, it is customary to allow anonymous logins.

The opposite of an anonymous login is a user login, which requires a valid Active Directory username and password combination before logging in. User logins allow you to control user access to a greater level—you can assign security to directories on an FTP server, restricting access to certain directories based on username.

NOTE *FTP passwords are transmitted over the Internet in clear text. If you have users that will be logging into your FTP server with their Active Directory user accounts, their passwords will be in plain view of anyone who might intercept their traffic.*

Once you have decided what type of logins you want to allow, you can enforce these settings via the Security Accounts properties page, shown in Figure 17.39.

FIGURE 17.39

Editing security accounts properties

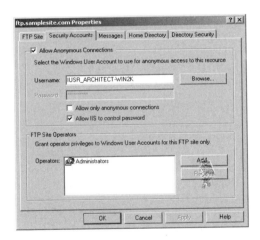

The upper half of this properties page controls what type of logins to allow on your server. If you don't want to allow any anonymous connections at all, uncheck the Allow Anonymous Connections box; this will disable the remaining options on the top half of the properties page. Otherwise, when anonymous users connect to your system, they will end up inheriting the security rights of the account defined in the Username field.

NOTE *Disabling anonymous logins will force everyone to connect to your FTP server via a username and a password. Since FTP sessions are transmitted over the Internet in clear text, this could potentially expose user passwords defined on your system to anyone who might be looking for them.*

Checking the Allow Only Anonymous Connections check box will effectively restrict any users from accessing your FTP server via a normal user login. This is particularly useful in case any user or administrative passwords within your organization are discovered—FTP cannot be used as a means to gain access via those accounts if this option is checked.

Lastly, if you choose to change the account or password for your FTP site, leaving the Allow IIS to Control Password box checked will cause IIS to change the Active Directory password of the specified user as well as store the new password to use for FTP access.

If you need to grant administrative privileges to users for managing any FTP sites on your system, add those usernames to the list of operators by clicking the Add button and then selecting users from the directory. Users who you want to make FTP site operators must also be members of the Administrators group.

TIP   *By default, most Web browsers will attempt to do an anonymous login when connecting to an FTP site. To override this behavior, you can place the username and password the browser should use in the URL string. The correct URL format for a user login via a browser is* `ftp://username:password@sitename.com`.

MESSAGE PROPERTIES

Although the FTP client interface is often cold and impersonal, you can add your own messages to your FTP server. Whether you need to inform users about new files that were recently added, tell them what site they are connected to, display a legal warning message, or just send a friendly message, you can do this through the Messages page, shown in Figure 17.40.

FIGURE 17.40

Editing message properties

The messages properties are rather self-explanatory. The Welcome message is displayed to users when they first connect to your FTP site and, if they are using a browser to access your server, on each subdirectory screen below the root. If your server has reached the maximum number of allowable connections (set in the FTP site properties discussed earlier in this section), then the Maximum Connections message will be sent to the user and their session will immediately be disconnected.

Speaking of disconnection, if a user (using something other than a browser for FTP access) disconnects properly from your FTP server, they will see the message you have defined in the Exit field. Browsers don't typically display exit messages, so if you have something important to pass along to users, it's better to put it in the welcome message than in the exit message.

HOME DIRECTORY PROPERTIES

If you read through the previous section on setting up Web sites, the properties page for Home Directory (shown in Figure 17.41) should look somewhat familiar to you. Although some of the settings and options are different for FTP sites, the general concept is the same.

FIGURE 17.41

Editing home directory properties

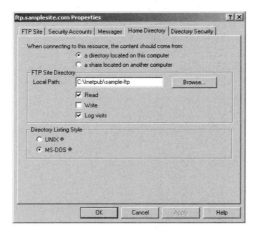

This group of settings lets you control where IIS will look for FTP files and what security permissions to use for this location:

Content Location By selecting the appropriate radio button on the top of this properties page, you can control where IIS will go to look for the content for this site, or if it will send users to another Web site. Based on the selection you make, the path information box below the radio button options will change. If you select the option for a directory located on this computer, you will need to enter the local path in the lower portion of the properties page.

If you select the option for a share located on another computer, the Local Path field will change to a Network Directory field, where you will need to enter the correct \\servername\sharename UNC path. When you choose to use a share located on another computer for your files, you might need to enter login credentials for the IIS service to use when it is accessing the other system. The IIS service will actually log in to the other system, retrieve the files, and present them to the user just as if the files were local. This allows you to build a distributed FTP site throughout your organization, even though all the files are presented to the user just as if they were all on one machine.

Security Settings Regardless of the location you choose for your content, you can control whether users are allowed read and/or write access to your files as needed. The FTP service will apply these settings for how it handles the directory overall, and these settings can be complemented by additional security permissions applied to files and directories on files stored on an NTFS partition.

Log Visits   Depending on whether or not you want logging information stored about visitors to your site, check or uncheck this box. Logs will be stored in the format defined in the FTP site properties dialog box, covered earlier in this section.

Directory Listing Style   This setting will control how IIS will return directory-listing information to users in response to the `dir` command from an FTP client—in either an MS-DOS-style listing or a Unix-style listing. This setting has no bearing on how IIS will return information in response to the `ls` command from an FTP client.

DIRECTORY SECURITY PROPERTIES

The last section of the FTP site properties pages, Directory Security (Figure 17.42), allows you to control who accesses your Web site based on client IP addresses.

FIGURE 17.42

Editing directory security properties

Through this page, you can secure your FTP site somewhat by restricting who can access the site based on an IP address or a range of IP addresses. This requires knowing in advance who should be connecting to your site and from where, but it is particularly useful when setting up FTP sites designed to interface with business partners. Select the appropriate radio button to allow access from all IP addresses by default (Granted Access) or to restrict access from all IP addresses by default (Denied Access). Create exceptions to this rule by clicking the Add button and adding an IP address or a range of IP addresses (by using a network mask). IIS will enforce these restrictions with all visitors to your site.

As with IP address restrictions for Web sites, you can set up some highly secure FTP sites by restricting access based on IP address, and then requiring authentication (i.e., denying anonymous connections) to access your site.

Virtual FTP Directories

If your FTP site begins to grow over time, you might find that you will need to add additional resources to your system as subdirectories off of the main root of the site. Just like a hard drive on a computer, in time there are often too many files to manage in one directory, so subdirectories become necessary. There are two main ways to do this for an FTP site. The first is to actually create a subdirectory in the site's content directory and place content into that directory. For example, let's say you have a site that is stored in `C:\Inetpub\ftproot` and is accessed on an FTP server at `ftp.companyname.com`. If you decide you want to move all of your executable files to a separate subdirectory, you could create a subdirectory called `C:\Inetpub\FTPRoot\bin` and then move all of your executable content into that directory. To access files in that directory, FTP clients would access the `ftp.companyname.com/bin` directory.

However, what if you want to have content available as a subdirectory in your site, but you can't move the content to a normal subdirectory within your site's structure? This is where the concept of virtual directories comes into play. Virtual directories are a means of defining a subdirectory off of the root of your site (or even a lower level of your site) and then creating an alias or a pointer to a directory somewhere else on your system or on another computer on your network. By using virtual directories, you are not forced to move all your FTP content to one system and then place it in an orderly structure for visiting users. Instead, you can have content stored anywhere on your machine or on any system within your network, and users can access it through a simple directory structure.

Virtual directories can also be used to grant different security permissions to the same set of files, based on which directory the user is in. For example, you might have an alias called "source" which points to a directory called `C:\source` on your local system. The alias is defined only with read access. You could add a second alias to your system, called "source-RW" for example, which could point to the exact same directory on your system but allow full read/write access.

DEFINING A VIRTUAL DIRECTORY

To launch the Virtual Directory Creation Wizard, return to the Internet Information Services MMC and highlight the FTP site you want to work with in the scope pane of the window. Select New/ Virtual Directory from the Action pull-down menu and the wizard will start walking you through the configuration process. The first step of the wizard is shown in Figure 17.43.

FIGURE 17.43

Defining an alias for
a virtual directory

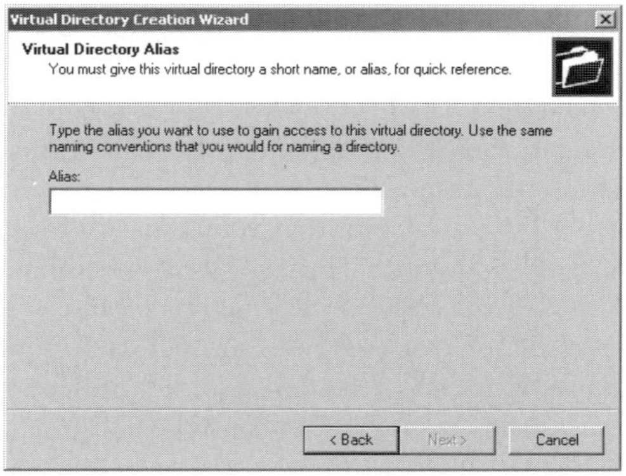

The first thing you will need to specify for your virtual directory is the alias that refers to it. The alias is the directory name that FTP clients will use to access the directory. For example, if you want to have a directory called "patches" available off the root of your site when users first connect, then "patches" would need to be the alias. The alias does not need to match the name of the directory from where the files are actually coming, so you can use whatever name works best in this field. Click Next to proceed to the next step of the wizard, shown in Figure 17.44.

FIGURE 17.44

Defining a content directory for a virtual directory

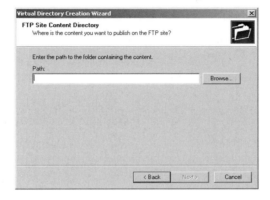

If you want to define a virtual directory that points to another directory on the same computer, enter the path name here (such as D:\patches). IIS will define the virtual directory as pointing to another directory on the same server. However, if you want this virtual directory to point to data located on a share on another server, enter the UNC path to that system here. When you click Next, the Virtual Directory Creation Wizard will take you to another dialog box for entering user credentials, shown in Figure 17.45. Otherwise, you will skip ahead to the dialog box shown in Figure 17.46.

When IIS needs to contact another server for FTP files, it will have to do so with a specific username and password combination. Enter an appropriate set of credentials here, one that would have appropriate access rights to the content you are trying to reach. Click Next to move to the last step of the wizard—defining access permissions—shown in Figure 17.46.

FIGURE 17.45

Entering a username and password to access shared content via a virtual directory

FIGURE 17.46

Defining access permissions for a virtual directory

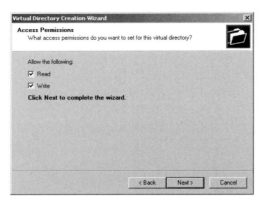

This step in the wizard is identical to the one in the FTP Site Creation Wizard mentioned earlier and shown in Figure 17.36. Decide whether you want to allow read or write access to your system, or both, and check the appropriate boxes.

Once you have entered all of the required information, you should have a new virtual directory item listed below your FTP site. You can test this to make sure that the virtual directory responds appropriately by launching an FTP client and then navigating to your virtual directory. If everything has gone according to plan, IIS should return content from the appropriate location.

You can modify properties for a virtual directory in exactly the same manner that you do for an FTP site—by editing the properties pages for the directory itself. You can edit the following properties pages for a virtual directory: Virtual Directory and Directory Security. These pages are functionally identical to the pages, defined earlier in this section, for modifying the properties for an entire FTP site.

Using FTP for File Transfer

That's FTP from the server perspective, but what about connecting to an FTP server?

If you have a PC or Macintosh on your desk, think for a moment about how you use that computer in a network situation. You may have a computer elsewhere in your building that acts as a file server, a computer that holds the files shared in your facility or your department. How do you ask that server to transfer a file from itself to your computer? You may say, "I don't do that"—but you do. Whenever you attach to a shared network resource, you are asking that system to provide your computer with shared files. Now, how you actually ask for them is very simple: You just connect to a server, which looks like an extra folder on your desktop if you're a Mac user or an extra drive letter, like X: or E:, if you are a PC user. The intranet world has a facility like that, a facility that lets you attach distant computers to your computer as if that distant computer were a local drive: It is called NFS, the Network File System. But NFS is relatively recent in the TCP/IP world. It's much more common to attach to a host, browse the files that it contains, and selectively transfer them to your local host. You guessed it: the means to do that is FTP.

There are three essentials of using an FTP client: how to start it up, how to navigate around the directories of the FTP server, and how to actually get a file from an FTP server. After that, I'll look at a special kind of FTP called anonymous FTP. So let's get started by looking at how the files on an FTP server are organized.

FTP ORGANIZATION

The first time that you get on an FTP server, you'll probably want to get right off. FTP, like much of the TCP/IP world, was built from the perspective that software must be functional and not necessarily pretty or, to use an overused phrase, user-friendly. If you're a PC user, the Unix file structure will be somewhat familiar, as the DOS file structure was stolen—uh, I mean, borrowed—from Unix. Mac users will need to find an FTP client, of which there are many.

Now, I just referred to the Unix file structure. That's because FTP servers usually use Unix. But some don't (after all, I just spent several pages talking about how to set up a Win2K FTP site), so you may come across FTP servers that don't seem to make any sense. For the purposes of this discussion, I'll assume that the FTP servers here are Unix, but again, be aware that you may run into non-Unix FTP servers. The occasional FTP server runs on a DEC VAX, and so probably runs the VMS operating system; some others may run on an IBM mainframe, and so may be running either MVS or VM. More rarely, an FTP server may run under DOS, OS/2, NT, or some other operating system. But let's get back to our look at a Unix FTP server.

FTP uses a tree-structured directory represented in the Unix fashion. The top of the directory is called `ourfiles`, and it has two directories below it—subdirectories—called `ourfiles/bin` and `ourfiles/text`, as shown in Figure 17.47. In the Unix world, `.bin` refers to executable files, files we might call program files in other operating systems, or more specifically, EXE or COM files in the PC world or load modules in the IBM mainframe world. The `text` directory contains two directories below it; one's called `contracts` and one's called `announcements`.

FIGURE 17.47

An example of how files on an FTP server are organized

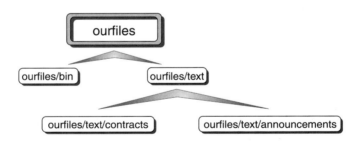

A couple of notes here. PC users may think that things look a bit familiar, but there are a couple of differences. First, notice the subdirectory named `announcements`. That name is more than eight characters long—that's quite acceptable, even though it isn't acceptable in the PC world. Unix accepts filenames of hundreds of characters. Second, notice that there are not backslashes between the different levels, but instead forward slashes; that's also a Unix feature. Now, what complicates matters for users of non-Unix systems is that FTP pretty much assumes that your system uses the Unix filesystem as well. That means that you have to be comfortable with traversing two directory structures—the one on the remote FTP server and the one on your local hard disk.

FTP CLIENT TYPES

How FTP looks to you from this point on depends on what kind of client software you use to access an FTP server. With Windows 2000, you have three choices: the standard command-line interface, Internet Explorer, or My Network Places. First, let's look at the command-line interface.

FILE NAVIGATION WITH COMMAND-LINE FTP CLIENTS

You get an FTP command line—I'll demonstrate it in a minute—that expects you to tell it where to get files from, and where to send files to, using these two commands:

◆ remote: `cd`

◆ local: `lcd`

That's because there's a tree structure on both the remote system—the one that you're getting the files from—and the local system. Let's look at a few examples to nail down exactly how all this `cd`-ing works.

Moving in FTP

When I enter an FTP site, I start out at the top of the directory structure. This top is called the root of the directory. In my example, the root is called `ourfiles`. To move down one level, to `ourfiles/text`, I could type **cd text**. That says to FTP, "Move down one level relative to the current location." Alternatively, you could skip the relative reference and say absolutely, "Go to `ourfiles/text`"—the way that you do that is by typing **cd /ourfiles/text**. The fact that the entry starts with a slash tells **cd** that your command is not a relative one, but an absolute one.

Now let's try moving back up a level. At any point, you can back up one level either by typing the command **cdup** or by typing **cd ..** . The two periods (..) mean "one level upward" to both DOS and Unix. Or you can do an absolute reference, as in cd /ourfiles.

Now suppose I'm all the way at the bottom of this structure. It's a simple three-level directory, and you often see directory structures that are a good bit more complex than this one. To move back up from `ourfiles/text/announcements` to `ourfiles/text`, you can do as before and either type **cdup** or **cd ..** . Or you could do an absolute reference, as in **cd /ourfiles/text**. To go back two levels, you can either issue two separate cdup or cd .. commands or use an absolute reference, as in cd /ourfiles. To type two cdup or cd .. commands, you type the command, then press Enter, then type the second command. Do not try to issue two commands on the same line.

AN FTP EXAMPLE OF NAVIGATION: GET A SCANDAL

There's a really neat project run by a group of volunteers called The Gutenberg Project. They take text whose copyright has expired and type it into text files. They then put these text files on both FTP and Web sites for anyone to download and read.

For example, one of my favorites of Arthur Conan Doyle's Sherlock Holmes stories is "A Scandal in Bohemia," which Gutenberg has at `ftp://sailor.gutenberg.org/pub/gutenberg/etext99/advsh10.txt`. (Their general Web home page is at `http://promo.net/pg/`.) Let's go fetch the scandal.

First, I'll FTP to `ftp.gutenberg.org`. I type **ftp ftp.gutenberg.org**, and then I get a `Name?` prompt. This site doesn't know me, so I can't log in with a local name and password. That's where the idea of anonymous FTP becomes useful. You see, you can often log in to an FTP site and download data that's been put there specifically for public use. Anonymous FTP is just the same as regular FTP except that you log in with the name "anonymous." It responds that a guest login is okay but wants my e-mail address for a password. I put in my e-mail address, and I'm in. Now, it might be that there are places on this server that I cannot get to because I signed on as anonymous, but that doesn't matter—Sherlock is in the public area. Next, I can do a dir command and see what's on this directory:

```
ftp>dir
200 PORT command successful.
150 Opening ASCII mode data connection for /bin/ls.
total 26
dr-xr-xr-x   8 0        0           512 Mar  2 13:49 .
dr-xr-xr-x   8 0        0           512 Mar  2 13:49 ..
-rw-rw-r--   1 1010     2000       1956 Feb 27  1997 README
dr-xr-xr-x   3 0        1           512 Feb 22  1997 bin
dr-xr-xr-x   2 0        2           512 Feb  3  1997 dev
dr-xr-xr-x   2 0        0           512 Feb 18  1997 etc
lrwxrwxrwx   1 0        1             4 Mar  2 13:49 ftp1 -> ftp1
drwxr-xr-x   2 1010     10000       512 Feb  5  1997 messages
drwxrwxr-x   4 0        2000        512 Nov  2  1998 pub
-rw-r--r--   1 0        1            81 Oct 30  1998 tmp.txt
dr-xr-xr-x   4 0        0           512 Feb 22  1997 usr
-rw-rw-r--   1 1010     14          913 Feb 26  1997 welcome.msg
226 Transfer complete.
ftp: 744 bytes received in 0.19Seconds 3.90Kbytes/sec.
ftp>
```

It's not a very pretty sight, but let's see what we can see. Notice the letters r, x, w, and d to the left of each entry? They represent the privilege levels of access to this file. One of the important things is whether or not the leftmost letter is d—if it is, then that's not a file, it's a directory. Notice the pub entry; that's commonly where generally available files are stored—pub is short for public.

Typing **cd pub** takes me a level down. Another dir shows a directory named gutenberg—a likely candidate—and I could keep searching around, but I found from Gutenberg's Web site that the file I'm looking for was at ftp://sailor.gutenberg.org/pub/gutenberg/etext99/advsh10.txt. I can navigate there by typing **cd gutenberg/etext99**.

Notice that there are no spaces except between the cd and the directory name, and notice also that, in general, you must be careful about capitalization—if the directory's name is Literature with a capital L, then trying to change to a directory whose name is literature with a lowercase l will probably fail. Why "probably"? It's another Unix thing; the Unix filesystem is case sensitive. In contrast, if you found yourself talking to an NT-based TCP/IP host, then case would be irrelevant. How do you know what your host runs? Well, it is sometimes announced in the sign-on message, but not always. The best bet is to always assume that case is important.

Anyway, once I get to the directory, I can do a dir command to see if advsh10.txt is there. **dir advsh10.txt** confirms that the file is there.

Before we get the file, there's one more thing that I should point out. Years ago, most files that were transferred were simple plain-text ASCII files. Nowadays, many files are not ASCII—even data files created by spreadsheets and word processors contain data other than simple text. Such files are, as you probably know, called binary files. FTP must be alerted that it will transfer binary files. You do that by typing binary at the ftp> prompt. FTP responds by saying, "Type set to I." That is FTP's inimitable way of saying that it's now ready to do a binary file transfer or, as FTP calls it, an image file transfer.

TRANSFERRING A FILE

Now let's get the file. Because it's a text file, I just type **get advsh10.txt**, press Enter, and wait. Once the transfer's done, I get some throughput statistics.

Now, when we get the file, it'll take some time to transfer. There's no nice bar graphic or anything like that to clue us about how far the transfer has proceeded. There is a command, however, that will give you some idea about how the transfer is progressing—hash. Type **hash**, and from that point on, the system will print an octothorp (#) for each 2K of file transferred. For example, say I'm on a Gutenberg system and I want to download the Bible, `bible10.zip`. (Is it sacrilegious to compress the Bible? Interesting theological question.) The file is about 1600K in size, so I'll see 800 octothorps.

Each line shows me 80 characters, so each line of # characters means 160K of file were transferred. It'll take 10 lines of # characters (10 lines!) before the file is completely transferred.

Remember that Gutenberg location. If you're ever stuck for something to read, they've literally got hundreds of books online. Even better, as they are just simple ASCII, there are programs that will transfer the files to a small computer such as a Palm handheld or a Windows CE palmtop—the easily portable, electronic book is almost here!

Downloading to the Screen

Before leaving the command-line FTP client, there's one more tip that I'd like to share with you: how to download directly to your computer screen.

Sometimes you'll come across a short file, like the READMEs that are so common around the computer world. Such a file may describe what's in an FTP directory. You'd like to examine it but the whole idea of first downloading it and then bringing up the file in Notepad seems a lot of work. In that case, download it instead to the screen.

You do that by typing **get** *filename -.*

Of course, this depends on the system that you're working with, but it may only be possible to do this "get" if your FTP session is set for ASCII transfers rather than binary transfers. You can change that by just typing **ascii** at the command line. You see the response "Type set to A."

GRAPHICAL FTP CLIENTS

In one example of how the world keeps getting better, you can often avoid command-line FTP. In many cases, all you need do is to point your browser to an FTP site by typing **ftp://***address*, like **ftp://ftp.3com.com**, in the Address field.

TIP   You need the ftp:// prefix on the address on some browsers because when you just type in an address, like ignatz.mouse.com, then the browser assumes that you want it to connect to a Web server rather than an FTP, telnet, or other server, and so it interprets the address as http://ignatz.mouse.com. What's the difference between `ftp://ignatz.mouse.com` *and* `http://ignatz.mouse.com`*? It's a matter of addresses. It's possible to have many kinds of servers running on the same system. They're distinguished by their port numbers. Just as your dentist's office might be in 210 Main Street and your dermatologist's office might also be at 210 Main Street, they probably don't share an office. The dentist's full address isn't 210 Main Street; it's more like Suite 118, 210 Main Street, and perhaps the dermatologist is at Suite 305, 210 Main Street. Different ports on a server are like different rooms in a building. Web servers are by default at port 80—but http:// is easier to remember than "connect me to port 80." FTP works on another port, actually two ports—20 and 21; telnet uses 23; and so on.*

In any case, most Web browsers can double as a graphical FTP client. You can navigate a directory structure by just clicking a directory to enter it or pressing the Backspace key to back up a level. The trouble with most Web browsers as FTP clients, however, is that they only work when you're logging in to the FTP site as anonymous; they don't give you a chance to specify a user ID and password. Thus, if the site requires an account to access it, your browser is just booted off the site.

Windows 2000 adds a new feature called FTP folders that solves that problem, however. Just open My Network Places and double-click Add Network Place. You'll be prompted to type either a UNC, like \\someserver\somevolume, or a URL, like http://www.someplace.com or ftp://ftp.someplace.com. What's particularly nice about this is that the wizard creating the new Network Place entry asks you if you need to specify a user ID and password to access the new Network Place. The FTP site then shows up in My Network Places as if it were a local set of folders, combining the simplicity of a GUI front end for FTP with the flexibility of being able to control how you log on.

That's about all that I'll say here about FTP. There is lots and lots more that FTP can do, but I've given you the basics that you can use to get started and get some work done in the TCP/IP world. If this all looks ugly, user-unfriendly, and hard to remember, then, well, it is—at least to someone used to a Macintosh or Windows. If you're not comfortable working from the command line, you may be better off with one of the graphical FTP programs available, which can make uploading and downloading files a drag-and-drop procedure more like using Windows Explorer than like using the Win2K command prompt. FTP is two things—the FTP protocol, which is the set of rules that the computers on an intranet use to communicate, and the program called FTP that you start up in order to do file transfers. The FTP protocol doesn't change and probably won't change. But the FTP program, which is usually known as the FTP client, can be as easy to use as its designer can make it. So go on out, learn to spell anonymous, and have some fun on those FTP sites!

Setting Up an NNTP News Server and Configuring NNTP Services

Newsgroups are one of the Internet's older technologies, but they're not as well known as some of the Internet's more visible counterparts—namely Web browsing and e-mail. Newsgroups are a way of collecting and threading messages posted by users together to form a sort of "conversation" database between the participants of a newsgroup.

These conversation databases can be used to discuss almost anything you can think of—questions about company benefits, organizational news releases, politics, society, technology, etc. This concept was once referred to as collaboration or groupware, in which companies within an organization could collaborate and share ideas electronically on a set of "bulletin boards" focusing on a specific topic. While some organizations have been able to implement this and make their organizations more productive, this capability still hasn't caught on as much as it should have.

The Internet is filled with literally tens of thousands of these groups, covering every imaginable topic under the sun. You name it, and there has probably been a newsgroup defined somewhere to discuss it. Thanks to IIS 5, you can easily set up and administer your own NNTP server for internal users to read, post, and reply to messages related to topics important for your organization. To get started with setting up a newsgroup server, you'll need to know the following:

◆ What IP address you want this NNTP server to listen on (or if it should respond on all available IP addresses).

◆ What TCP/IP port number this NNTP server should listen to on the previously specified IP address(es). Typically, this is port 119.

◆ Whether to allow anonymous access to your site or to require user authentication.

◆ What directories your system will use to store and manage your NNTP database files.

Creating a New NNTP Server

Even though IIS installs and configures a default newsgroup server when you set it up, you might need to have another server on your system. For example, you might need to have a public newsgroup server available to anyone on the Internet, and then a private newsgroup server available to internal staff. To start installing your server, begin by making sure that you have all of the bullet items listed above ready, and then select your IIS server in the Internet Services Manager MMC. Selecting the New/NNTP Virtual Server option from the Action pull-down menu will launch the New NNTP Virtual Server Wizard. The first step of the New NNTP Virtual Server Wizard is shown in Figure 17.48.

FIGURE 17.48

Defining a friendly name for an NNTP virtual server

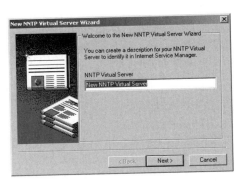

This step of the wizard wants you to specify a friendly name to use when referencing your new NNTP virtual server. This name is simply for administration purposes; your users won't see it, so choose a name that's appropriate, and then click Next to proceed to the next step of the wizard, shown in Figure 17.49.

In order to access your NNTP server, users will need to establish a TCP/IP connection to your server on a specific IP address and TCP port number. By default, NNTP servers typically communicate on port number 119. Unless you have special circumstances, you will probably want to use this as the default port number for your system.

If you are going to be running only one newsgroup server on your system, these settings might be just fine, depending on the content on your newsgroups and the configuration of your system. For example, if you were going to run an internal confidential database for the discussion of sales and marketing strategies, you probably wouldn't want to make that database available on a publicly accessible IP address. Users from the outside world could potentially connect to your system and read all of your confidential information stored in the newsgroup, so make sure you correctly determine which IP address(es) to use for your site.

FIGURE 17.49

Defining IP addresses and TCP ports for an NNTP virtual server

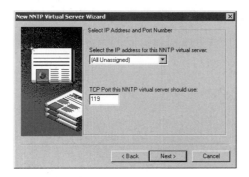

Newsgroup readers—by default—will look on port 119 for a newsgroup server, so enter 119 here in the port field. If you would prefer to change the TCP port that your server responds on (necessary if you only have one IP address and you want to run multiple newsgroup servers), you can do so here. Keep in mind that all the clients connecting to this system will probably have to manually change their configurations accordingly.

Click Next when you've completed the IP configuration, and you'll move to the next step of the wizard, shown in Figure 17.50.

FIGURE 17.50

Defining directories and anonymous access control for an NNTP virtual server

IIS requires two separate directories on your system to maintain an NNTP virtual server: one in which to store internal files for its own processing, and one to store the actual newsgroup content. In this first screen, you need to supply the directory that IIS should use for its own internal files. When you've entered this, click Next to continue to the next step, shown in Figure 17.51.

FIGURE 17.51

Defining a storage area for NNTP content files

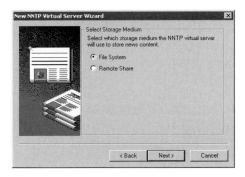

In this step of the wizard, you will be defining a "storage medium" for IIS to use when storing news content. This storage medium can be either on the IIS server itself or on another server. If you will be storing the news content directly on your IIS server, select the radio button for File System and then click Next to proceed to the next step of the New NNTP Virtual Server Wizard, shown in Figure 17.52.

FIGURE 17.52

Defining a path to store newsgroup messages

If you decide to store news content on another system, select the radio button for Remote Share. Doing so will change the next step of the wizard to prompt you for a share name and username/password combination to use to access the news content stored on another system. For the sake of brevity, I'll assume you chose the File System option and proceed directly to the next step of the wizard.

NOTE   *IIS will require approximately 548 bytes of storage in its internal working directory for each newsgroup message that will be stored on your system, in addition to the space required for the articles themselves.*

Click Finish after this step, and you will have a functional NNTP virtual server running on your IIS server.

Modifying NNTP Virtual Server Properties

Since the New NNTP Virtual Server Wizard only has a few steps to it, there are settings and parameters that you will probably need to set for your site. For example, you might want to define newsgroup names, control security, limit the size of postings, etc. To adjust the parameters for your NNTP site after the wizard has created it, you will use the NNTP virtual server properties pages.

GENERAL PROPERTIES

To reach the NNTP virtual server properties pages, highlight your new NNTP virtual server in the scope pane of the Internet Services Manager MMC and then select Properties from the Action pull-down menu. This should bring you to a dialog box similar to the one shown in Figure 17.53.

FIGURE 17.53

Configuring general settings for an NNTP virtual server

Through this page, you can change the following items to fit your needs:

Name   To modify the friendly name for your site, enter the information here. This information is only used for administrative purposes in the MMC interface; users will not end up seeing it.

IP Address   Enter the IP address for your site to use here. If you intend to have multiple IP addresses servicing the same site or you want to change the ports this site uses, click the Advanced button.

Advanced TCP Port and SSL Port   By default, NNTP sites typically use TCP port number 119 for standard connections and port 563 for secure connections. Changing these values will usually require changing the configuration of newsreader software on client computers as well.

Connection   Depending on the capacity of your server and the other jobs it's responsible for, you might want to limit the number of connections you allow into your NNTP server. By default, IIS sets this value at 1000, with a time-out value of 10 minutes (600 seconds), if you choose to enable it.

Enable Logging   If you are running an anonymous NNTP server, you might want to enable logging for your system in case you ever need to trace where a specific posting came from.

Path Header   Path headers refer to a string that is used for the "path" line in each newsgroup posting. Path lines are used to determine how a newsgroup posting will reach its destination. For more information on path lines and having newsgroup servers pass messages to each other, see RFC 1036.

NNTP SETTINGS

For settings specific to newsgroups and postings themselves, go to the Settings properties page, shown in Figure 17.54.

FIGURE 17.54

Configuring NNTP Settings for an NNTP virtual server

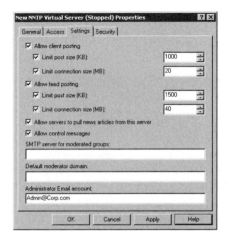

From this page, you can edit the following options:

Allow Client Posting   To disallow client posting on this system, uncheck this box. Obviously, on most systems, you will want to leave this checked.

Limit Post Size   For publicly accessible NNTP servers, you might find a need to limit the size of any one message that can be sent to your system. Otherwise, individuals might overload your system by loading huge binary files to your system, quickly filling up all the available disk space on your server. Enter a reasonable limit here, or leave the default of 1 megabyte (1000 kilobytes).

Limit Connection Size   Much like the Limit Post Size setting mentioned above, another way that individuals could potentially overload your system is by flooding it with numerous smaller messages that fit within the Limit Post Size restriction. In order to compensate for this, you can set a maximum limit, in megabytes, that an NNTP user can post during a single session to your server.

Allow Servers to Pull News Articles from This Server   If other downstream newsgroup servers will connect to your site and download a feed of messages, leave this box checked.

Allow Control Messages   Control messages are specially formatted newsgroup messages designed to control the configuration of an NNTP server; for example, to create a new newsgroup across a collection of NNTP servers, a control message can be sent out instructing all servers to create the new group. Or a control message might instruct all other participating news servers to cancel (delete) a specific message from all systems.

SMTP Server for Moderated Groups   Moderated groups (discussed a bit later in this section) are newsgroups that have their postings approved by a moderator before they are publicly posted.

This is done via e-mail, so the NNTP process needs to have an accessible SMTP server to use for sending messages. If you will be configuring the SMTP service on your IIS server (discussed later in this chapter), you can use your own system as the SMTP server.

Default Moderator Domain   When moderation e-mail messages are sent from your IIS system, they will be sent with a To: address of newsgroup_name@default_moderator_domain unless a specific moderator is specified for a group. Enter the domain portion of the address to use in this field.

SECURITY ACCOUNT PROPERTIES

In order to define operator permissions for specific user accounts on your NNTP server, click the Security tab to get to the Security properties page (shown in Figure 17.55). Here, you can define operators capable of accessing and making configuration changes to a virtual NNTP server.

FIGURE 17.55

Editing security properties

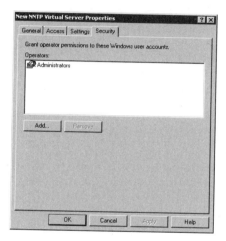

Add the Windows user accounts that should have operator privileges to this window by clicking the Add button and selecting the appropriate accounts.

ACCESS PROPERTIES

Through the Access properties page, you can make changes to how your NNTP server is to be accessed. For example, you can allow for anonymous access (this is typically enabled by default), which means that any user that can successfully connect to the IP address of your NT server can access the newsgroups contained on it. Or you can require authenticated access. You can also define SSL encryption certificates (discussed later in this chapter) to use when communicating with your server, and grant or deny connections based on IP addresses. The Access properties page is shown in Figure 17.56.

Access Control

Clicking the Authentication button in the Access Control area will take you to another dialog box, shown in Figure 17.57, for editing what type of authentication users should use when connecting to your system.

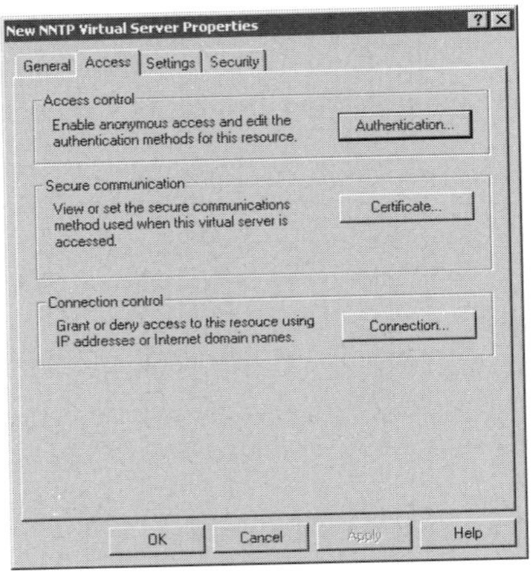

FIGURE 17.56

Editing access
properties

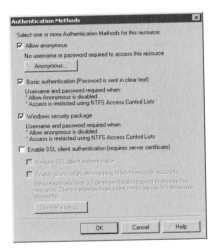

FIGURE 17.57

Editing authentica-
tion methods

By default, IIS will select all three authentication options for you—Allow Anonymous, Basic Authentication, and Windows Security Package. Anonymous access is rather straightforward; no username or password is required to connect, and all requests for content will be directed through the anonymous account defined on the Security Accounts properties page.

Basic authentication utilizes an authentication protocol built into NNTP called AUTHINFO. This protocol negotiates a username and password authentication over the Internet in clear text. This authentication method will have the widest means of support, but at the risk of transmitting passwords from your system in plain view of anyone who might be looking for them.

"Windows security package" authentication is another way of saying Windows challenge/response authentication. This typically limits client support to Windows platforms only, but it provides a secure means of authenticating users without passing clear-text passwords over the Internet.

If you would prefer to encrypt the authentication process between the client and your NNTP server, you can select the Enable SSL Client Authentication check box. This will allow your server to authenticate the client connecting to it in order to set up a secure, encrypted SSL tunnel. However, the client connecting to your server must have an SSL certificate installed for this to work. If you've enabled SSL client authentication, you can require this type of authentication for all users by checking the Require SSL Client Authentication check box. Based on the certificates that your users have installed, you can have those certificates map directly to a Windows user account by checking the Enable Client Certificate Mapping to Windows User Accounts box and then entering appropriate mappings by clicking the Client Mappings button. Doing this will basically tell IIS, "If someone hands you this certificate, assume that it is Windows user XYZ." The user does not need to actually provide a username and password; simply having the certificate is enough identification.

Connection Control

Another means of securing your NNTP server is to restrict who can access the site based on IP address, a range of IP addresses, or a domain name. This requires knowing in advance who should be connecting to your site and from where. By clicking the Edit button in the IP Address and Domain Name Restrictions area, you will see a screen similar to the one back in Figure 17.19, in which you can enter any restrictions you'd like.

Secure Communication

If you would like to protect your NNTP data as it travels from your server to the client (and vice versa), you can set up SSL communications properties through the Secure Communication area. This requires having an SSL certificate installed on your system, and is discussed in greater detail in the "Communicating Securely with SSL" section later in this chapter.

DIRECTORY PROPERTIES

Since all newsgroup content must be stored in files, you will need to define where those files are to be stored. Initially, you did that in the wizard when you provided the system with directories to use for the NNTP content. However, since the wizard assumes several "defaults" for you, you might want to edit the directory properties yourself.

To edit the directory properties, go back to the Internet Information Services MMC and expand the NNTP server item that you created. Select the item for Virtual Directories in the scope pane, and you should see the directories you originally specified in the results pane. Highlight the appropriate directory to modify, and then either select Action/Properties from the pull-down menu or right-click the directory and select Properties. An example is shown in Figure 17.58.

Once you have selected a directory to edit, you should set a properties page similar to the one shown in Figure 17.59.

You can store content in a directory on the IIS server itself or on a share on another server by clicking the Contents button in the Directory Contents portion of this properties page. If you decide to use a network share for storing your content, you will need to define an account that IIS uses to connect to the share.

FIGURE 17.58

Editing directory
properties

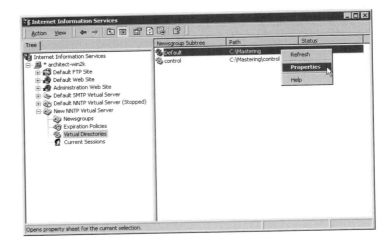

FIGURE 17.59

Directory
properties page

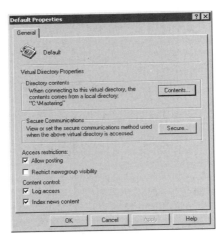

Based on the newsgroups stored in this directory, you can control some specific parameters:

Allow Posting   To disallow posting to newsgroups—that is, to the newsgroups stored in this
directory—uncheck this box.

Restrict Newsgroup Visibility   If you will be using access controls on your system to define who
can access which newsgroups, you can control what newsgroups those users will even see by selecting this option. Choosing this option can add a significant amount of processing overhead to your
system if you have a large number of groups, so you might want to leave this option disabled.

Log Access   This setting works in conjunction with the Enable Logging check box on the General properties page for the NNTP site. If you want to log access to your system, you must have
both check boxes checked. This allows you to log access to some directories as needed, without
necessarily logging all access to all directories.

Index News Content   Checking this box will instruct the Microsoft Indexing Service to index the content of this site, allowing users to search for text in postings.

Lastly, the Secure Communications section of this properties page is used to require SSL communication sessions for newsgroups stored in this directory. SSL is discussed in greater detail later in this chapter in the "Communicating Securely with SSL" section.

DEFINING GROUPS

Messages on an NNTP server are typically stored in different hierarchical groups based on their content. Levels of hierarchy are delineated by a dot between each word. For example, on the Internet, common newsgroup names such as `rec.pets.dogs` (for dog lovers) are part of the overall recreation hierarchy (`rec`), then the `pets` subhierarchy. This type of organization gives users an easy way to find the information they are looking for. Additional groups could include `rec.pets.cats` and `rec.pets.ferrets`, thus keeping the messages for each topic isolated from other messages.

Within your organization, you can also use a similar structure for newsgroups. For example, you might choose to define groups along divisional, departmental, and then topical lines. For example, a group called `accounting.payroll.withholding` could be used to handle discussion messages and questions from employees regarding their withholding from their paychecks, whereas `sales.advertising.radio` could be used to discuss the effectiveness of radio advertisements and to brainstorm for new topics.

For each level of hierarchy in the name of the newsgroup, IIS will create a separate directory in the content directory defined for your site (discussed earlier in this chapter). For example, if you create a group called `accounting.payroll.withholding`, IIS will create three subdirectories in your content directory. The first subdirectory will be called `accounting`. Within the `accounting` subdirectory, there will be another subdirectory called `payroll`, and within the `payroll` directory, there will be another subdirectory called `withholding`. If these directories are created on an NTFS volume, you can control which users can access which groups (assuming you've required authenticated access) by applying appropriate permissions to each directory. Therefore, you can restrict confidential information to only the individuals who should receive it and leave everything else open to the public.

As you can see, there are many possible uses for newsgroups. Since the default configuration of a newsgroup server doesn't typically include any groups (other than control groups, if needed), you will most likely want to add some groups to your system.

You define newsgroups from the main Internet Information Services MMC screen by expanding your NNTP server item in the scope pane, and then highlighting the Newsgroups option below it. Once you have the Newsgroups item highlighted, you can select the New/Newsgroup option either from the Action pull-down menu or by right-clicking the Newsgroups option, as shown in Figure 17.60.

Selecting New/Newsgroup launches the New Newsgroup Wizard, which will walk you through the process to define a new newsgroup. The first step of the wizard, shown in Figure 17.61, will prompt you for an appropriate name for your newsgroup. As previously discussed, enter the name for your desired newsgroup here and then click Next to proceed to the next step of the wizard, shown in Figure 17.62.

FIGURE 17.60

Setting up new newsgroups

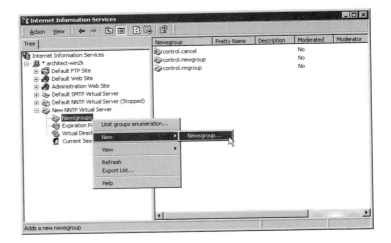

FIGURE 17.61

Defining a new newsgroup name

FIGURE 17.62

Defining a newsgroup description and pretty name

To enter descriptive information about this group above and beyond the information that the name of the group gives, use the Description field. You can also enter a "pretty name" for this newsgroup that will be returned to NNTP clients that issue a LIST PRETTYNAMES command.

Once you have entered this information, click the Finish button and your new newsgroup will be created. However, as is true with most of the wizards in Windows 2000, a few assumptions are made for this group and automatically saved as defaults. If you would like to change the properties of the group you've just created, highlight it in the results pane of the MMC and then select the Properties option either from the Action pull-down menu or by right-clicking the group. That should bring you to a group properties page similar to the one shown in Figure 17.63. In this screen, you can edit the properties you just defined for this group, plus enable some additional options, as defined next:

Read Only   If only the moderator should be allowed to post to this group, check this box. No other users will be allowed to make postings to this group.

Moderated   The default setting for new newsgroups is to leave them unmoderated—meaning that all postings are publicly available immediately; there is no "checking" process that occurs. If you prefer to have a moderator manage the messages on your system, click the Moderated option. Enter an appropriate e-mail address for the moderator in the Moderator field, or click the Set Default button if you prefer to use the moderator defined in the NNTP settings (discussed earlier in this section). Newsgroup messages will be e-mailed to the operator for approval before being published.

FIGURE 17.63

Editing group properties

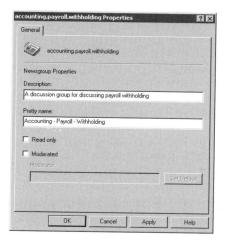

Defining NNTP Server Expiration Policies

In a perfect world, disk space would be amazingly dirt cheap, and installing terabytes worth of storage would simply be a Plug-and-Play operation. This would allow you to keep all news articles posted on your server forever and ever (amen).

Welcome to reality. If you're running an NNTP server that will be handling a fair amount of traffic, it will eventually consume all available disk space on your system, unless you expire old articles. To add an expiration policy to your system, select your NNTP server in the scope pane of the Internet Services Manager MMC and expand it. Select Expiration Policies, then select New/ Expiration Policy from the Action pull-down menu.

This will start you through a wizard in which you define which newsgroups to expire and when. The first step of the wizard will prompt you for a friendly name for your expiration policy. Enter whatever you feel is appropriate in this box and then click Next to move on to the next step of the wizard, shown in Figure 17.64.

FIGURE 17.64

Choosing all groups or selected groups

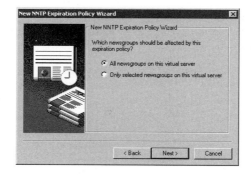

If you want to have IIS simply expire all newsgroup articles on your system after a set number of hours or days, select the radio button for All Newsgroups on This Virtual Server. Otherwise, if you want to have custom expiration policies for certain groups (for example, you might want some groups to never expire), select the button for Only Selected Newsgroups on this Virtual Server. If you choose the second option, when you click Next, you will be taken to a dialog box to enter the groups you want the policy to apply to. Enter the appropriate groups and then click Next to proceed to the last step of the wizard, shown in Figure 17.65.

This step of the wizard is quite straightforward: enter the number of hours that IIS should wait before purging a newsgroup article. The default you will find here is 168 hours, or 7 days. If you have a low-traffic site and want to keep articles around longer, then increase this value accordingly.

FIGURE 17.65

Setting an expiration interval, in hours

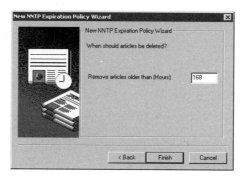

Click Finish when you are done, and you should see your new expiration policy appear in the MMC as a subitem under your NNTP server. To go back and make changes to the policy, simply edit the properties for the policy item.

Virtual NNTP Server Directories

Virtual NNTP server directories have a bit of a different function than virtual directories defined for Web and FTP sites. On Web and FTP sites, users can navigate through different directories on your system, but on a newsgroup server the only thing users can navigate to are newsgroups. So what's an NNTP virtual directory designed to do?

NNTP virtual directories are designed primarily as a means to spread newsgroup content out across systems. Content is spread across systems based on hierarchy names. For example, you might have the content for the entire `accounting.*` hierarchy stored on one server and have the content for the `sales.*` hierarchy stored on another server.

The primary benefits of doing this are increased speed and performance (you don't have one server doing all the work), and if you suddenly run out of disk space on one system, you can start spreading the content around. To create an NNTP virtual directory, begin by selecting your NNTP virtual server in the scope pane of the Internet Services Manager MMC and highlighting the Virtual Directories option below it. Select the New/Virtual Directory option from the Action pull-down menu to launch the New Virtual Directory Wizard, shown in Figure 17.66.

FIGURE 17.66

Defining a subtree for an NNTP server virtual directory

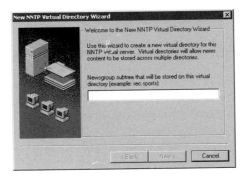

To carve off an entire section of your hierarchy structure and store it in a virtual directory, enter the left-most portion of the group name you want to store. For example, if you entered `rec.pets` in this field, you would end up storing the groups `rec.pets.dogs`, `rec.pets.cats`, and `rec.pets.ferrets` in this virtual directory, but `rec.games.chess` would still be stored in the primary directory defined for this NNTP server. Enter the appropriate hierarchy name and then click Next to proceed to the next step of the wizard.

The next step of the wizard will ask you for a "storage medium" for this content—this is exactly the same as what you saw back in Figure 17.51. The wizard will also prompt you for either a directory or a remote share and username/password combination based on your answer. The location you provide the wizard with is where all of the content for the hierarchy you specified will be stored. By clicking Finish, you will have created a virtual directory on your server for your NNTP content.

Setting Up an SMTP Server and Configuring SMTP Services

As you've seen throughout this chapter so far, there will probably come a time when your IIS server will need to send e-mail to someone. Whether it is for support of FrontPage extensions or to forward a newsgroup posting to a moderator for approval, your server will need to communicate with another host for the transfer of e-mail. The protocol you'll use to perform this communication is called the Simple Mail Transfer Protocol—SMTP for short.

Microsoft has included a basic SMTP server along with IIS 5 for exactly this reason—so that services on your server can send e-mail out to other hosts as needed. It is *not* a complete mail server, as you'll see, but it can be useful for other things.

To set up a new SMTP server on IIS, you will need to know the following information in advance:

◆ What IP address you want this SMTP server to listen to for inbound connections (or if it should respond on all available IP addresses).

◆ What TCP/IP port number this SMTP server should listen to on the previously specified IP address(es). Typically, this is port 25.

◆ A "default domain" name to use for the sending of messages.

◆ What directory on your system to use for incoming and outgoing e-mail files.

But first: what is SMTP anyway and why do we need it?

Internet E-mail Protocols

There are two main Internet e-mail protocols that most of us care about: The Simple Mail Transfer Protocol (SMTP) and the Post Office Protocol (POP3).

SMTP is the "mail" Internet e-mail protocol. SMTP grew up at a time when most users on the Internet were running Unix machines, each with its own IP address. Each Unix machine ran two mail programs. The first was a program that could package up a mail message and send it to its destination; the most common one was one named Sendmail. The second program was a so-called daemon, a program that always runs in the background, kind of like a DOS Terminate and Stay Resident (TSR) program. The daemon would constantly listen for incoming mail in the form of TCP/IP packets sent from another system running Sendmail.

The SMTP/Sendmail approach worked fine as long as every system on the Internet could run some kind of mail daemon, and so long as every system was up and running 24 hours a day, seven days a week. But primitive PC operating systems don't handle daemons well, and most people don't leave their workstations up and running all of the time, even if they are running an operating system that handles daemons well. Additionally, while many systems may run all of the time and while they may have an operating system that likes daemons just fine, they aren't connected to the Internet all of the time.

In any case, it'd be nice to enhance SMTP with some kind of mail storage system, allowing one computer to act as a kind of "post office." Suppose you have 500 people on your network with varying operating systems and uptimes. So you set up one computer that is up 24 hours a day, 7 days a week. This computer runs the mail daemon, the program that listens. You tell that computer, "Accept mail for everyone in the company, and hold onto it." That's the computer I'll call a post office. Then, when a user wants her mail, she just connects to that post office and pulls down her mail. In the Internet world, we let a client computer like the one on her desktop communicate with a post office computer with a protocol called POP3, the Post Office Protocol. Such a program is a small application referred to as a POP3 client. Actually, every POP3 client that I know of might be better referred to as a POP3 Message Receiver/SMTP Message Sender. The program only uses POP3 to get your mail; when you create a new message, it just sends it to a computer running the SMTP receiver service (the daemon), which then hands it to the SMTP delivery service (Sendmail or one of Sendmail's cousins).

In order for your office to send and receive Internet mail, you'll need a computer to act as a post office. The computer uses SMTP to talk to other post offices, and those post offices may choose to communicate with you at any hour of the day, so the computer must be attached to the Internet 24 hours a day, 7 days a week. So that your users can retrieve their mail, they'll need programs that act as POP3 clients. Finally, that post office computer will need to run a POP3 server so that it can respond to mail requests.

NOTE   *The EMWACS's Internet Mail Service (IMS) is free software that includes three services that provide most of the pieces you'll need to make a mail server. I'll talk about IMS a little later in this chapter.*

Where can you find a POP3 client? Right in Windows—the program attached to the Inbox tool (on 95) or Outlook Express (on 98, Me, 2000, or NT 4 with IE 4) can act as a POP3 client. Or, if you find the Microsoft tool not to your liking, surf on over to http://www.eudora.com/eudoralight, where you'll find Eudora Light, an excellent mail client written by the Qualcomm people. They write terrific software, and even better, they have a 32-bit version of their Eudora mail client that they give away absolutely free. You can even get the full version of the software for free if you're willing to put up the displayed ads. I'll talk about how to configure these clients a little later.

Creating a New SMTP Server

Once again, Microsoft has included a wizard to make the creation of a new SMTP server relatively straightforward.

To begin the creation of a new SMTP server, start by selecting your IIS server in the scope pane of the Internet Services Manager MMC, then select the New/SMTP Virtual Server option from the Action pull-down menu. This should bring you to the first step of the New SMTP Virtual Server Wizard, shown in Figure 17.67.

FIGURE 17.67

Defining a friendly name for an SMTP virtual server

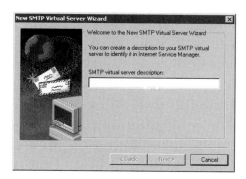

This step of the wizard wants you to specify a friendly name to use when referencing your new SMTP virtual server. This name is simply for administration purposes; your users won't see it, so choose a name that's appropriate and then click Next to proceed to the next step of the wizard, shown in Figure 17.68.

FIGURE 17.68

Defining IP addresses for an SMTP virtual server

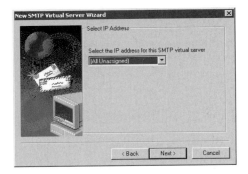

In order to access your SMTP server, other SMTP servers will need to establish a TCP/IP connection to your system on a specific IP address and TCP port number. By default, the New SMTP Virtual Server Wizard will want to have your site listen on all available IP addresses for incoming connections. If you are going to be running only one SMTP server on your system, these settings should be fine. However, if you intend on running multiple SMTP servers on your system (for example, if you plan on hosting several virtual domains on your IIS server), you might want to specify a specific IP address for this server to use.

Click Next when you've completed the IP configuration, and you'll move to the next step of the wizard, shown in Figure 17.69.

Since IIS will need a location to store incoming and outgoing e-mail messages, you must create a directory on your server to store this information. Unlike other services within IIS, in this service, you cannot define a share on another computer as the target location for your files. Instead, you must define a local path to be used for storing your SMTP content. Enter the appropriate directory to use, then click Next to proceed to the final step of the wizard, shown in Figure 17.70.

FIGURE 17.69

Defining a directory for an SMTP virtual server

FIGURE 17.70

Defining a default domain

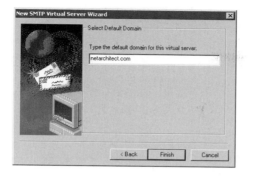

The last step of the wizard will ask you to enter the default domain that this virtual server should serve, such as netarchitect.com (you don't need to use the @ sign). Enter the appropriate domain to use, click the Finish button, and your new SMTP virtual server should be created. If you receive an error message at this point, check back in the Internet Services Manager MMC to see if the default SMTP server installed with IIS is running on the same IP address and TCP port of the system you've just defined. If it is, stop that system and then start your server again.

Modifying SMTP Virtual Server Properties

Because the New SMTP Virtual Server Wizard only asks you for a few configuration items, there are settings that you will probably want to adjust for your system. To adjust the parameters for your SMTP virtual server after the wizard has created it, you will use the SMTP virtual server properties pages.

GENERAL PROPERTIES

To reach the SMTP virtual server properties pages, highlight your new SMTP virtual server in the scope pane of the Internet Services Manager MMC and then select Properties from the Action pull-down menu. This will bring you to a dialog box similar to the one shown in Figure 17.71. From this page, you can edit options for your server, including the following:

Name To modify the friendly name for your SMTP server, enter the information here. This information is only used for administrative purposes in the MMC interface; users will not end up seeing it.

IP Address Enter the IP address for your SMTP server to use here. You can assign your server to a specific IP address or have it respond on any free IP addresses on the system by selecting the All Unassigned option. To edit the TCP port number for this SMTP server, click the Advanced button.

Connection By clicking the Connection button in this area, you can control the concurrent connection limits and time-out values for SMTP sessions going in and out of your server.

Enable Logging To keep track of what e-mails your server has sent and received, turn on logging by checking the Enable Logging box. Logging choices include W3C Extended Log Format, IIS Log File Format, NCSA Common Log File Format, and ODBC Logging.

FIGURE 17.71

Configuring general
settings for an
SMTP virtual server

SECURITY PROPERTIES

To delegate administrative controls for this server to specific users, click the Security tab to get to the
Operators properties page, shown in Figure 17.72.

FIGURE 17.72

Configuring opera-
tors for an SMTP
virtual server

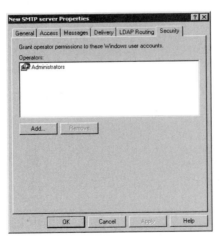

This dialog box is really quite self-explanatory. Simply click Add to add Windows server accounts
or groups to the list of administrators for this SMTP server. Users listed here will be able to change
parameters for this specific SMTP server via the Internet Services Manager MMC.

MESSAGES PROPERTIES

Because the SMTP protocol can be used to move unknown amounts of data from one system to
another, to protect yourself, you set parameters regarding the delivery of messages on your system.

Abuse via SMTP—such as someone e-mailing you a 1-gigabyte file and consuming too much disk space or the unauthorized relaying of messages—happens sometimes, so to properly protect your system you can fine-tune the message properties by selecting the Messages tab, shown in Figure 17.73.

FIGURE 17.73

Configuring message properties for an SMTP virtual server

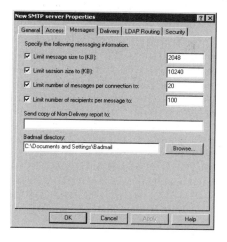

You can change a few properties here that handle how both inbound and outbound messages are controlled. They are as follows:

Limit Message Size To (Kilobytes)   To limit how large a message a mail client can send to your server, enter an appropriate value in this field. This limit will be applied after a message has been received in its entirety. The minimum for this value is 1KB.

Limit Session Size To (Kilobytes)   Instead of waiting around to receive the end of a message that has already exceeded the maximum message size, you can enter a value in this field; when a session reaches this point, IIS will close off the connection. The minimum value for this field must be equal to or greater than the previously defined maximum message size value.

Limit Number of Outbound Messages per Connection To   During a connection to an SMTP server, a client may send several messages to the system for delivery. Unfortunately, some SMTP servers are unknowingly used for the unauthorized relay of junk e-mail (often referred to as spamming), delivering hundreds of thousands of messages. By forcing a client to establish a new connection every *x* number of messages, an SMTP server becomes less desirable to a spammer for use as a relay point. I would recommend leaving the default value in this field.

Limit Number of Recipients per Message To   Although this setting would seem to limit the number of people you can send a single message to, it is really included for compliance with RFC 821, which defines SMTP. RFC 821 states that the maximum number of recipients per e-mail message is 100. But what if you have a message destined for 150 recipients? The message will be sent in one session to the first 100 recipients, and then a second session will be opened for the remaining 50 recipients.

Send Copy of Nondelivery Report To   Nondelivery of a message, for whatever reason (invalid e-mail address, etc.), will typically cause the SMTP server to generate a nondelivery report (NDR) e-mail message for the sender. If you would like to have a copy of the NDRs also e-mailed to a specific mailbox, enter the appropriate e-mail address here.

Badmail Directory   When the SMTP service sends a nondelivery report (as mentioned above), it will go through the typical delivery routine for an e-mail message. However, under certain circumstances, the nondelivery report might be undeliverable. In such cases, the SMTP service will automatically place the message in this directory and consider the message permanently undeliverable. It's a good idea to check this directory every now and then to see if anything is piling up in there.

ACCESS PROPERTIES

Although most SMTP communications across the Internet occur anonymously, you can require authenticated access to your system if you desire. If you choose to require authenticated access to your SMTP server, the Access properties page is where you will make these changes. You can also control what IP addresses and domain names can attach to your system, define secure communications, and set relay restrictions here. The Access properties page is shown in Figure 17.74.

FIGURE 17.74

Configuring access properties for an SMTP server

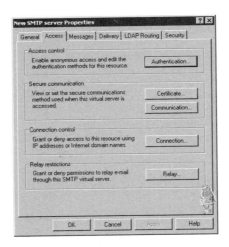

From this dialog box, you can control authentication, secure communications, address restrictions, and relay restrictions on your SMTP server by clicking the appropriate button.

Access Control

By default, SMTP connections are anonymous in nature: no authentication is required from a client accessing your SMTP server in order to send messages through it. If you want to change this behavior, click the Authentication button in this box to go to the Authentication dialog box, shown in Figure 17.75.

Anonymous Access   By default, all three authentication options are initially selected. If you don't want clients to be able to send messages anonymously through your SMTP server, uncheck this first option.

Basic Authentication   If you chose to disable anonymous access, this is the first option that you can choose for client authentication. Basic authentication works via AUTH and USER/PASS commands sent between systems in clear text. User accounts are verified against the accounts database local to the IIS machine. If a valid account is found, message processing can proceed. Otherwise, the SMTP session is never completed. Although this isn't necessarily a secure means of authentication, it will have a wider base of support than the next authentication option.

FIGURE 17.75

Configuring authentication properties for an SMTP server

Windows Security Package   Another name for the Microsoft challenge/response authentication, this option requires that both the SMTP server and SMTP client be running a Windows platform. User accounts are verified against the accounts database local to the IIS machine. If a valid account is found, message processing can proceed. Otherwise, the SMTP session is never completed.

Connection Control

If you prefer to control who accesses your SMTP server via IP addresses or domain names instead of authentications, click the Connection button in this area to edit the connection properties, shown in Figure 17.76.

FIGURE 17.76

Configuring IP address and domain name restrictions for an SMTP server

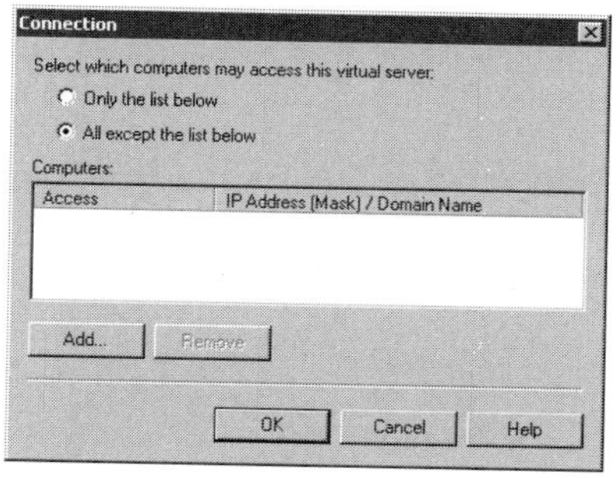

Select the radio button option to either allow only the addresses and domain names you specify or allow everyone except the addresses and domains you specify. Enter the exception list by clicking Add. From the dialog box that follows, you can either grant or deny access to a single computer (via an IP address), a group of computers (via an IP address and a subnet mask), or an entire domain (via a domain name). IP addresses are usually the best option if you know which addresses to allow or deny. Since IIS only knows who is connected to it by an IP number, the server must do a reverse-DNS lookup if you select the domain name option, which adds quite a bit of processing for the server to do just to determine if it's okay to let the user in. Unless your situation requires using domain names, it's probably worthwhile to find out the exact IP address ranges to allow into your site and configure them accordingly.

NOTE *Many hosts out on the Internet don't actually have reverse-DNS records assigned to them, and some hosts have incorrect reverse-DNS records assigned to them. Therefore, even if you were to put in a restriction based on a host/domain name, it might not work quite as well as you want it to.*

Relay Restrictions: Stopping Spammers

Because an SMTP server will typically deliver any message sent to it, abuse can become a problem if someone decides to park tens of thousands of messages on your system for delivery. Spammers will often find misconfigured third-party SMTP servers to relay their junk mail, park a few thousand messages on the system, and then move on to another server. This behavior is known as relaying a message, and it is an inherent part of the SMTP protocol—a protocol that was designed when the Internet was a more trusting, friendly place.

To defeat this behavior, many SMTP servers (including Microsoft Exchange) now include powerful relay controls that will allow you to determine whether or not the SMTP server should receive any messages for domains other than the ones that it hosts. For example, if your system lives in a domain called mycompany.com, then your SMTP server will—by default—only accept incoming messages destined to e-mail addresses ending in @mycompany.com. Any other messages will be denied, unless you specifically allow relaying by clicking the Relay button in the Relay Restrictions area and adjusting the properties page shown in Figure 17.77.

As you can see, the format of this dialog box is similar to that for allowing and denying IP address restrictions to the SMTP service as a whole. By default, all hosts are denied relay access, unless you enter specific hosts in the list box. You can either grant or deny access to a single computer (via an IP address), a group of computers (via an IP address and a subnet mask), or an entire domain (via a domain name). IP addresses are usually the best option if you know which addresses to allow or deny.

If you have enabled authentication options on your system, you can check the Allow All Computers Which Successfully Authenticate to Relay box at the bottom of this dialog box, giving anyone with an appropriate user authentication the rights to relay.

DELIVERY PROPERTIES

Click the Delivery tab (Figure 17.78) to define parameters about how messages are delivered into and out of your SMTP server.

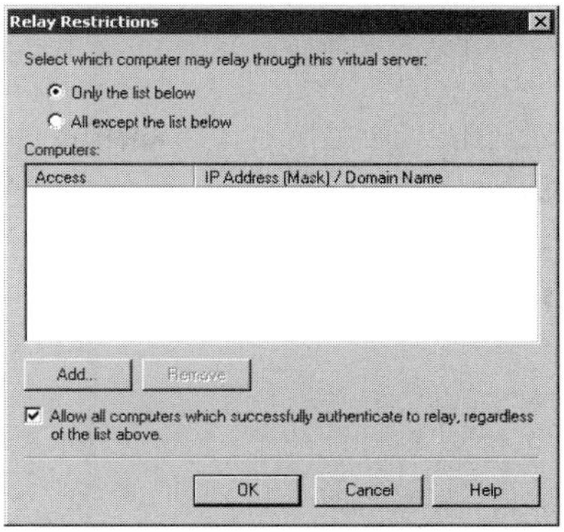

FIGURE 17.77

Configuring relay controls on an SMTP server

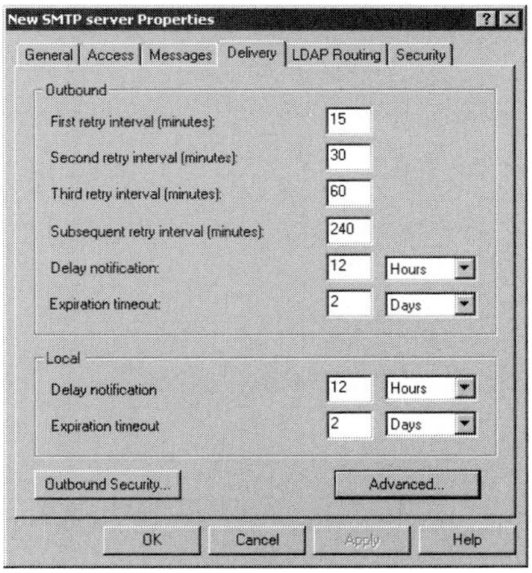

FIGURE 17.78

Configuring delivery properties on an SMTP server

This page is divided up into multiple options, both inbound and outbound, for controlling the delivery of messages.

Outbound

When an SMTP server receives a message, it will attempt to deliver it almost immediately. For various reasons, it is possible that the SMTP server will fail to deliver the message—the receiving host might be too busy, the receiving host might be down, or Internet connectivity might not be available. For whatever reason, the SMTP service will continue to try to deliver the message for the intervals specified in this section.

If the SMTP server fails at delivering the message after the first attempt, it will try again three times at the minute values specified in the First Retry Interval, Second Retry Interval, and Third Retry Interval fields. After the third retry value, if the message still hasn't been delivered, the SMTP service will attempt to deliver the message at the interval defined in the Subsequent Retry Interval field.

Eventually, if the message has failed enough times, the SMTP service will send a notification e-mail message to the user listed in the From: field of the e-mail message, letting him or her know that the message is still "in the queue" but hasn't been delivered to its destination yet. This interval is defined in the Delay Notification field. If the message eventually hits the value defined in the Expiration Timeout field, the message will be aborted and sent back to the user who sent it, along with a notification of the failure. These same values can be set for local delivery as well at the bottom of this screen.

Outbound Security

As we saw earlier in this chapter, inbound authentication controls can be set for the IIS SMTP service. If the SMTP server that your system will be communicating with requires a similar means of authorization, you will end up defining these options in the Outbound Security settings area. Click the Outbound Security button to edit the Outbound Security properties page, shown in Figure 17.79.

For more detailed information on the types of outbound authentication available, the section titled "Access Control" contains working definitions of anonymous access, basic authentication, and Windows security package. Whatever authentication your receiving systems will require, select a radio button to enable that type of security and supply the appropriate account information. For a basic authentication, click the Browse button to select a username and password to use. For Windows security package authentication, click the Modify button to define a Windows account username, domain name, and password to use.

FIGURE 17.79

Configuring outbound authentication for an SMTP server

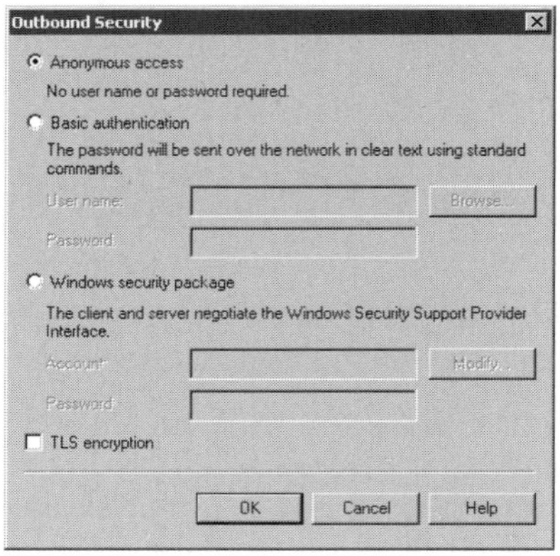

Advanced Delivery Options

The following options are advanced parameters for controlling the outbound delivery of messages. Clicking the Advanced button on the Delivery page will take you to a screen similar to the one in Figure 17.80.

FIGURE 17.80

Configuring advanced delivery properties

Maximum Hop Count   When an SMTP server receives a message, it may be sent through other servers before reaching its final destination (a mailbox). However, a pair of misconfigured SMTP servers might bounce a message back and forth between themselves indefinitely (known as ping-ponging), with the message getting larger at each step of the way and never reaching its destination. To prevent this, the SMTP service can perform a "hop count" on a message—basically, counting the number of Received headers present in a message—and reject the message if there are too many hops in the message path. By default, this is set to 15, which should be acceptable for most circumstances. If a message exceeds its maximum hop count, then the message fails and the sender gets an error message telling them that the message couldn't be delivered.

Masquerade Domain   To override the domain name in an outgoing message with a specific domain name, enter the domain name here. The domain name entered in this field—if any—will replace the existing domain name listing in the From: field of the outgoing message.

Fully Qualified Domain Name   Enter the fully qualified domain name (FQDN) of your SMTP server in this field. An FQDN typically has at least three segments to it: host.domain.tld (tld is for top-level domain).

Smart Host   If you would prefer to have another SMTP server handle all of the outgoing messages for this SMTP service, enter a domain name or host address of that host here. If you enter an IP address, Microsoft suggests entering it in brackets [ ] so that the SMTP service will immediately know that it should try to connect to the smart host via IP address and skip name resolution.

Attempt Direct Delivery Before Sending to Smart Host   If you have defined a smart host in the previous field, you can tell SMTP that it should try to deliver messages on its own first. If it cannot deliver the messages on its own, it will immediately send them on to the smart host for delivery.

Perform Reverse-DNS Lookup on Incoming Messages   When incoming messages are received by SMTP, IIS can perform a reverse-DNS lookup on the IP address noted in the header of the message and insert the fully qualified domain name of the IP address into the Received header. If the reverse-DNS lookup fails, no FQDN is put into the Received header. Reverse-DNS lookups can slow message processing, so depending on the volume of messages that you're receiving, you might want to leave this option unchecked unless necessary.

ADDING ADDITIONAL DOMAINS

By default, your SMTP server will only process messages destined for the domain you specified during the New SMTP Virtual Server Wizard. All other domain names will be considered by IIS to be "nonlocal" and therefore need to be relayed.

However, if you want to host multiple domain names on your system for e-mail or allow relaying for specific domains, you can do so by adding additional domain names through the Internet Services Manager MMC. Select your SMTP virtual server from the scope pane of the MMC and expand it. Below the SMTP server, you should see an item for Domains. Select that item, and you will see your currently defined domain in the results pane on the right side of the MMC. With the Domains option highlighted, select New/Domain from the Action pull-down menu, or simply right-click Domains and choose New/Domain, as shown in Figure 17.81.

FIGURE 17.81

Configuring additional SMTP domains

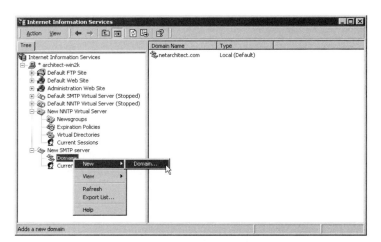

Selecting the New/Domain option brings you to a two-step wizard, the first step of which is shown in Figure 17.82.

FIGURE 17.82

Adding a domain to an SMTP server

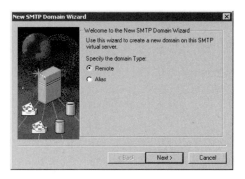

The first step of the wizard wants to know whether to add a local ("alias") or remote domain. This will define whether the SMTP service should immediately store the message in the Drop directory once it receives it (local/alias), or if it should try to pass it on to another mail system (remote). Make the appropriate selection and then click Next to proceed to the last step of the wizard, entering the actual domain name. Once you enter a new domain for your system, the SMTP server will begin receiving/accepting traffic for e-mail addresses within that domain.

Maintaining Your SMTP Server

After you've gone through all of these configuration items, you should have a fully functional SMTP server on your system servicing the domain you defined in the New SMTP Virtual Server Wizard. As with any process on your system, it will require a bit of maintaining and fine-tuning from time to time.

SMTP DIRECTORIES

If you look at the directory you defined during the setup of your site, you should see four subdirectories, titled Badmail, Drop, Pickup, and Queue.

These are the directories that the SMTP service will use when processing incoming or outgoing messages. Incoming messages to your system will end up in the Drop directory, so it is worth looking in there every once in a while to see if mail has been sent to your system. Incoming e-mail messages will be stored in .eml files and will look somewhat like this:

```
x-sender: dtoombs@usa.net
x-receiver: doug@netarchitect.com
Received: from architect1.netarchitect.com ([172.16.10.1) by ARCHITECT-
WIN2K.dewey.netarchitect.com with Microsoft SMTPSVC(5.0.1993.0993.0);
   Wed, 30 Jun 1999 23:10:42 -0400
From: dtoombs@usa.net
Bcc:
Return-Path: dtoombs@usa.net
Message-ID: <ARCHITECT-WIN2K3DEj00000001@ARCHITECT-WIN2K.dewey.netarchitect.com>
X-OriginalArrivalTime: 01 Jul 1999 03:10:44.0718 (UTC) FILETIME=[4F00A0E0:01BEC36F
Date: 30 Jun 1999 23:10:44 -0400

This is a test message - sent from dtoombs@usa.net,
to doug@netarchitect.com,
received by the Microsoft IIS 5.0 SMTP service.
```

Outgoing messages from your system will be placed in the Pickup directory, either by the Front-Page extensions or the NNTP service as needed. However, you can also use the Pickup directory for your own administrative uses by placing properly formatted messages in there for delivery. For example, if you have a service process that generates a status report every night (perhaps a backup log) and want to have it automatically e-mailed, you can simply have a process create a properly formatted text file and place it in the Pickup directory. The SMTP service will see the file there and attempt to deliver it. A properly formatted outgoing SMTP message would look similar to the following:

```
x-sender: doug@netarchitect.com
x-receiver: mark@minasi.com
```

```
From: doug@netarchitect.com
To: mark@minasi.com
Subject: Hello from Doug

Hello Mark. Hope that everything is going well with you.
```

If you intend to use the Pickup directory for your own messages, I'd recommend that you compose your text file in another directory first before placing it in the Pickup directory. If you begin to compose a message directly in the Pickup directory, the SMTP service will attempt to pick it up while you are working on it.

If the SMTP service runs into a message that it can't deliver to its intended recipient, and for which a nondelivery notification can't be returned to the sender, it will drop the message in the Badmail directory and leave it there. Every now and then it is probably worthwhile to check the Badmail directory and see if any messages have piled up.

Lastly, the Queue directory is where the SMTP service holds messages that it has pulled out of the Pickup directory. It will try sending a message immediately upon taking the message out of the Pickup directory, but if for some reason it can't deliver the message, it will hold it in the Queue directory until such time that it can be successfully delivered.

SENDING E-MAIL FROM ACTIVE SERVER PAGES

If you're building a Web site that uses IIS's built-in SMTP server, and want to mail more sophisticated things—even HTML pages—then you can do that with some built-in capabilities of IIS's Active Server pages. While this isn't a book on Web site construction, I've found this useful.

The key is an object called CDONTS, the Collaboration Data Objects for NT tool. I don't propose to explain it in detail, but I've cooked up a simple example. It sends two pieces of mail: first, a simple one-liner, and second, an HTML file.

To see this work, create the following file (see Listing 17.1). Call it mailex.asp and store it in your wwwroot directory:

LISTING 17.1: THE *MAILEX.ASP* FILE

```
<html>
<head>
<title>Mail Example</title>
</head>
<body>
<%
dim fso
htmlfile = ENTER THE NAME OF YOUR HTML FILE IN QUOTES
fromaddr = ENTER A "FROM" ADDRESS IN QUOTES
toaddr = ENTER A "TO" ADDRESS IN QUOTES
'Copy HTML file to a string variable
set fso=createobject("Scripting.FileSystemObject")
Set MyFile = fso.OpenTextFile(htmlfile,1) '1=read
HTML=""
while not myfile.atendofstream
    HTML=HTML+myfile.readline
```

```
wend
myfile.close
set fso=nothing
set myfile=nothing
'
' First mail:  create and send a simple message
'
  'Create mail object
  Set objNewMail = Server.CreateObject("CDONTS.NewMail")
  objNewMail.From = fromaddr
  objNewMail.To = toaddr
  objNewMail.Subject = "Simple mail test"
  objNewMail.Body = "Hi there; this is a test from the Web server."
  objNewMail.BodyFormat = 1  '1=text, 0=HTML
  objNewMail.MailFormat = 0
  objNewMail.Importance = 1
  objNewMail.Send
    if Err <> 0 Then  Response.write "<p>CDONTS reported an error:"  &
Err.Description & ".</p>"


'
' Second mail:  A piece of HTML mail
'
  Set objNewMail = Server.CreateObject("CDONTS.NewMail")
  objNewMail.From = fromaddr
  objNewMail.To = toaddr
  objNewMail.Subject = "Simple HTML mail test"
  objNewMail.Body = HTML
  objNewMail.BodyFormat = 0  '1=text, 0=HTML
  objNewMail.MailFormat = 0
  objNewMail.Importance = 1
  objNewMail.Send
    if Err <> 0 Then  Response.write "<p>CDONTS reported an error:"  &
Err.Description & ".</p>"
  set objNewMail=nothing
%>
</body>
</html>
```

Create a simple HTML file and put it somewhere on your Web server that the IUSR user account has read access to. For example, you might call the file `test.html` and put it in `C:\JUNK`. Then fill in values for the htmlfile, toaddr and fromaddr variables. For example, if your e-mail is `wally@acme.com`, then you might send this mail to yourself with these three lines:

```
htmlfile="c:\junk\test.html"
toaddr="wally@acme.com"
fromaddr="wally@acme.com"
```

Then run the page by opening your Web browser and calling the `mailex.asp` file. For example, if your Web server is on 192.168.0.2, then you could type into the address bar **http://192.168.0.2/ mailex.asp.** You won't see anything appear in your browser unless you've mistyped the text or IUSR is denied permission to `test.html`, but open up your mail client and you should have two pieces of mail.

A Free E-mail Server for Windows 2000

Computers all by themselves are of little value for anything more than acting as a glorified calculator or typewriter. Hooking up computers via networks has been what has really made computers useful, and of course networks are a big part of communications. But networks are of no value unless people use them—and people won't use them without a reason. This brings me to electronic mail. E-mail is often the "gateway" application for people, the application that is the first network application that they'll use; for some people, it's the only application that they'll ever use. And e-mail is probably the most important thing running on the Internet.

I just talked about setting up SMTP on your IIS server so that it could send e-mail to other hosts. However, although SMTP is the protocol used to send e-mail, setting up SMTP support does not make your IIS server an e-mail server.

Most offices have some kind of internal e-mail, such as Microsoft Exchange, Lotus cc:Mail, or the like. But connecting that e-mail to the outside world—that is, the Internet—is an expensive proposition; when we bought our cc:Mail/Internet gateway at TechTeach International, it had a list price of $4,000. That's a shame, as the protocols for Internet mail are well documented and there's lots of free code around to support them. In this section, I'll tell you about my favorite, a piece of software from the European Microsoft Windows Academic Centre (EMWACS).

EMWACS's Internet Mail Service (IMS) software can take you a good way toward the goal of setting up e-mail for both internal and external use. It consists of three services that'll run on any Windows 2000 Server machine:

◆ The SMTP receiver service, the listening "daemon" program, called `SMTPRS.EXE`. When another post office gets mail for you, it will communicate with `SMTPRS.EXE`. Similarly, if you create a new mail message and tell your mail client to mail it out, the mail client will send the message to `SMTPRS.EXE`.

◆ The SMTP delivery service, which sends messages to other post offices, called `SMTPDS.EXE`. SMTPDS only has to listen to SMTPRS. When the receiver service gets a new piece of mail, it gives it to SMTPDS, the delivery service. If the mail is destined for another post office, SMTPDS establishes a connection with that other post office and shoots the mail over there. If the mail is destined for this post office, then SMTPDS just drops the mail into the proper user's mailbox.

◆ The POP3 server. Called `POP3S.EXE`, this program responds to requests from POP3 client programs, delivering mail to those clients when requested.

One of the best parts of IMS is that it's free.

Setting Up Your Mail Server: IMS Limitations

Before you install IMS, you should be aware of some of its limitations. You must do a few things to a Windows 2000 machine before it can serve well as a post office. Because you might find some of the constraints unduly confining, let's take a look at them before you go further.

THE MAIL SERVER MUST HAVE A STATIC IP ADDRESS

Each service must be able to find the IP address of the computer that it is running on. You can check this by typing the name of each service followed by the -ipaddress parameter; for example, once you have IMS installed on a Windows 2000 machine, you can type **smtprs -ipaddress**, and you should see the IP address and DNS name of that machine.

In my experience, the IMS components can't find a machine's IP address if that machine gets its IP address from DHCP; just being in a DNS table doesn't seem to do the trick. So you've got to run IMS on a machine with a static IP address.

DNS MUST BE ABLE TO FIND THE MAIL SERVER

This ought to be kind of obvious, but I thought I'd mention it anyway. If you send mail to bob@fin.shark.com, and DNS can't find fin.shark.com, then the mail isn't going very far. The IMS services actually try to resolve the name of the computer they're sitting on when they first start. If the IMS services can't resolve the name, then they will refuse to run.

THE MAIL SERVER ONLY SERVES USERS IN ITS USERS GROUP

If the mail server receives mail for a user it doesn't recognize, it just refuses the mail. How, then, does it distinguish the users that it recognizes? They must be in the mail server's Users group. If the mail server has joined a domain, then that domain's Domain Users group will be sitting in the server's local Users group.

THE POP3S SERVER DOESN'T ACCEPT BLANK PASSWORDS

There may be a way to do this, but I haven't figured it out. If you try to get your mail, then of course you'll be asked for your username and password. If your password is empty, then POP3S will refuse your connection, and you won't be able to retrieve your mail.

THE SOFTWARE DOESN'T HAVE PERFORMANCE MONITOR COUNTERS

Unlike a lot of Windows 2000 software, the EMWACS mail software won't install System Monitor counters. Yes, yes, I know, I'm getting a bit nitpicky about a piece of free software, but it'd be nice to use the power of Perfmon with IMS.

How the IMS Software Works

You install the three services on a Windows 2000 server. Once they're up and running, anyone can send mail to *somename@servername*, where *somename* is a valid Windows 2000 user on that server and *servername* is the Internet host name of the server. So, for example, if my local server were named altair.mmco.com and my username were markm, you could send mail to markm@altair.mmco.com. Of course, you could also allow that server to accept any mail for all of mmco.com by just putting an MX record for mmco.com pointing to altair.mmco.com.

Downloading the EMWACS Software

As I write this, the EMWACS folks have progressed to version 0.8x of their mail software and stopped. The 0.8 version works fine for me, but if you want a more-developed version, then, well, you'll have to pay for it—see the section later about Rockliffe's MailSite, the program that IMS grew up to be.

IMS used to be at `http://emwac.ed.ac.uk/html/internet_toolchest/ims/ims.htm`, but that seems not to exist any more. You can now find IMS at `ftp://ftp.texasstar.net/`. Just point your Web browser to that location and you'll see the software. They also have documentation on the product in HTML format—be sure to get that, because it'll have more detailed installation instructions than you can read here.

In addition to the EMWACS server software, you can find a number of useful utilities for EMWACS at `http://www1.sica.com/IMS`.

Unzipping the EMWACS Software

As I'm using an Intel-based server for my mail system, the file I downloaded was named `IMSi386.ZIP`. Since it's a zipped file, you'll need PKUNZIP or a similar program to decompress the files.

Create a directory that you'll unzip the files into. (I called mine `C:\EMWACS`.) Copy the `IMSi386.ZIP` file there, open a command line, and type **pkunzip -d IMSi386**; that will unzip the file and create any necessary directories. Do the same with the ZIP file containing the documentation; that will create a directory called `HTML`, which will contain the documentation.

Then copy these files to the `\winnt\system32` directory:

- ◆ `SMTPRS.EXE` (the receiver daemon)
- ◆ `SMTPDS.EXE` (the Sendmail delivery agent)
- ◆ `POP3S.EXE` (the POP3 server)
- ◆ `IMS.CPL` (the Control Panel applet to control the mail server)
- ◆ `IMSCMN.DLL` (a DLL to support the programs)

You can put most of them in different directories, but I find it easiest to just stick them in the `system32` directory. The `IMS.CPL` file must go in `\winnt\system32`.

Installing the Services

Next, register the services with Windows 2000. Open up a command line, change the drive and directory to the `\winnt\system32` directory, and type the name of each service followed by **-install**:

```
smtprs -install
smtpds -install
pop3s -install
```

Each module should acknowledge that it has installed correctly. Next, tell Windows 2000 to automatically start these services whenever you start the computer. Go to the Control Panel and open the Services applet. You'll see three new services:

◆ IMS POP3 Server

◆ IMS SMTP Delivery Agent

◆ IMS SMTP Receiver

One at a time, click each service, and then click the Startup button. Choose Automatic, and the service will start when the computer does. Do this for each of the three services. Because they haven't been started yet, be sure to also click the Start button for each service.

NOTE *For the latest updates and fixes for running EMWACS under Win2K, check the URL:* http://www1.sica.com/IMS/#W2FIX. *This information moves sometimes—it's free, so it lives where some kind volunteer is willing to give it space—so if that doesn't work then try a Google search. Please understand that I can't support EMWACS IMS, so please don't send me questions on configuring it.*

Adding Registry Entries

When the EMWACS folks built IMS, NT 4 apparently included some Registry entries that Windows 2000 doesn't have. So you'll need to add a couple of Registry entries by hand to make EMWACS work:

◆ In HKLM\System\CurrentControlSet\Services\Tcpip\Parameters, create a value entry of type REG_SZ called Domain and fill it with the name of your DNS domain—for example, "acme.com."

◆ In HKLM\System\CurrentControlSet\Services\Tcpip\Parameters, create a value entry called Nameserver (also type REG_SZ) containing the IP address of your DNS server.

Setting Users to Log In As Batch Jobs

IMS requires that any user who tries to access his mailbox be able to log in to the server running IMS as a batch job. Odd as it sounds, it's necessary. Of course, Windows 2000 hasn't made it easy; here are the steps you'll need to follow:

1. While sitting at the machine running IMS, start the Group Policy snap-in: Click Start/Run, fill in **gpedit.msc**, and press Enter.

2. You'll see Local Computer Policy and Local User Policy. Open the folder labeled Local Computer Policy.

3. Within Local Computer Policy, open the folder named Windows Settings.

4. Within Windows Settings, open Security Settings.

5. Within Security Settings, open Local Policies.

6. Within Local Policies, open User Rights Assignment.

7. Inside that folder, you will see some rights. Find and double-click Log On As a Batch Job.

8. In the dialog box that appears, click Add.

9. You'll see another dialog with a list of user groups. Find the group named simply Users and double-click it to add it to the list of groups with the Log On As a Batch Job right.

10. Click OK twice to clear the two dialog boxes.

11. Close `GPEDIT.MSC`.

Adding the local Users group will work fine if the Domain Users group from your domain is a member of the local Users group—which it should be, by default.

If users aren't able to log in as batch jobs, they'll be denied login to the Windows 2000 mail server from their client software (Inbox, Eudora, or whatever). And, once again, don't forget that the mail server will refuse to receive mail from users who aren't in its local `Users` directory. So, suppose you want to set up a mail server M1 in domain RED, but you want it to accept mail for people in domain BLUE as well. First, make sure that RED trusts BLUE. Then go to Local Users and Groups on server M1 and make sure that the group M1\Users contains both RED\Domain Users and BLUE\Domain Users.

Configuring the Services

Next, you'll see an applet labeled EMWAC IMS in the Control Panel. Double-click that, and you'll see a screen like in Figure 17.83.

FIGURE 17.83

Configuring directories for IMS mail

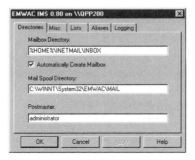

First, tell IMS where to put the mailboxes. Each user gets her own subdirectory in which IMS keeps her mail. If you check the Automatically Create Mailbox check box, then IMS will, as the label suggests, create a user's mailbox automatically. That way, IMS only creates a directory when necessary.

IMS lets you specify a couple of ways to organize user mailboxes—with the %home% and %username% variables. If you use %home% in the mailbox name, IMS will substitute the user's home directory, the one specified in the Profiles button on the User Manager. If you use %username% in the mailbox name, then IMS will substitute the user's Windows 2000 username.

For example, suppose I've got users named Sue and John as accounts on a Windows 2000 server. Their home directories are on the server at `D:\Users\username`. I could put their mailboxes in the directory `E:\MAIL` by telling IMS to set Mailbox Directory to `E:\MAIL\%username%`. As mail came in for Sue and John, IMS would end up creating directories `E:\MAIL\JOHN` and `E:\MAIL\SUE`. Mail messages would then accumulate in each directory as each user received mail. Note two things: First, `E:\MAIL` need not be shared, and second, neither John nor Sue need have File and Directory permissions on `E:\MAIL` or on either subdirectory.

Does that sound like it violates Windows 2000 security? It doesn't. You see, neither John nor Sue ever tries to access `E:\MAIL`; rather, John and Sue run programs—POP3 mail clients—that communicate in client-server fashion with the POP3S service, which in turn provides them with their mail messages. Now, it is a fact that POP3S must have access to that mailbox directory or nothing will happen.

If you set up the mailbox directories as I've just suggested, then they are very secure from user tampering. If, on the other hand, you don't care whether users can directly access their mailboxes, then use the %home% variable. For example, if you were to tell IMS to put mail in %home%\mail, John's mail would sit in `D:\USERS\JOHN\MAIL`, and Sue's would sit in `D:\USERS\SUE\MAIL`. In general, I avoid the %home% variable because, first, it confuses the mail server if a user does not have a home directory, and second, it puts the mail directories under direct user control, which isn't always the best idea.

The Mail Spool Directory is just a temporary holding directory for the mail server, and I just use the default. Postmaster is the e-mail name of the person who gets the error messages. (It's a good idea, by the way, to log in to the mail server with the postmaster's name.)

Next, click the Misc tab and you'll see the screen in Figure 17.84.

FIGURE 17.84

Misc configuration in IMS

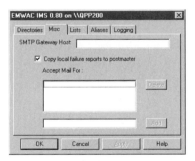

You can use this tab to tell the mail system to accept mail for other Internet domains; however, you can't use this to tell it to accept mail for other Windows 2000 domains—remember, you do that by putting global groups from other domains into the mail server's local Users group. The only thing I'd do here is to check Copy Local Failure Reports to Postmaster. That way, you can keep track of systemic problems. Finally, click the Logging tab and enable logging for each of the three services.

Once you've got IMS configured as you like it, close the Control Panel applet and start and stop each service so your configuration changes take effect. Or, if you don't want to wait around for the services to stop and start, write a batch file to do it:

```
net stop "IMS POP3 Server"
net start "IMS POP3 Server"
net stop "IMS SMTP Delivery Agent"
```

```
net start "IMS SMTP Delivery Agent"
net stop "IMS SMTP Receiver"
net start "IMS SMTP Receiver"
```

By now, you should be ready to set up your mail client.

Setting Up Your E-mail Client

A server's no good without clients. In the case of a mail server, the accompanying clients are of course called e-mail clients.

To connect to your mail server, you'll need an Internet mail client of some kind. Examples include Outlook (which can act as an Exchange client, an Internet mail client, or both), Outlook Express, Eudora (the free version or the professional version; it's a great program, and you can find it at www.eudora.com), Pegasus (free, www.pmail.com), or the mail client built into Netscape Navigator. Technically, they are all POP3/SMTP clients. Some support a third protocol, IMAP4, but that doesn't matter to us, as IMS doesn't support IMAP4, just POP3 and SMTP.

To tell your e-mail client to look to your IMS server for mail, you've got to configure it to look for your mail account. Exactly how you do that varies from client software to client software, but in every case the e-mail software will probably need to know a few things:

Do You Use POP3 or IMAP4?   POP3; again, IMS doesn't support IMAP4.

The Name of Your SMTP Server   Fill in the name of your IMS server; it acts as your SMTP server.

The Name of Your POP3 Server   Here you should also fill in the name of your IMS server as it acts in the roles of both SMTP and POP3 servers.

Your E-mail Address   Your e-mail address is *name@servername*, where *name* is your Windows 2000 user account name. For example, if your IMS server is on domain FLOWERS and you log in to the FLOWERS domain as JaneD, then your username and the name portion of your address is janed. The *servername* will either be the fully qualified domain name of the machine running IMS, such as violets.flowers.com, or just the name of the domain, if you've directed people to the server with an MX record. If an MX record for flowers.com in DNS says that mail for flowers.com should go to violets.flowers.com, then your e-mail address is janed@flowers.com. Without an MX record, e-mail addresses must specify the particular server, so in that case the address would be janed@violets.flowers.com.

Your account name and password   Fill in the Windows 2000 username and password. Even if IMS is running on a machine that's not a domain controller, you needn't include the domain prefix—in my experience, I can enter a username like **mark** rather than **orion\mark**.

From there, any other configuration options will be matters of taste—how often to check for mail and the like. Once your client's set up, send yourself a piece of mail and your mail server will be officially operational!

MailSite: "EMWACS Pro"

As you've read, I've been a fan of the free Internet Mail Service (IMS) software for NT and Windows 2000 from EMWACS for a long time. EMWACS mail doesn't do everything that I'd like; in particular, I wish that it did IMAP4, a protocol that lets you check your mail by retrieving only the headers of the mail messages rather than the entire message. That's important because I travel a lot, and it's usually just my luck to dial in to the mail server at home at 31Kbps (the actual speed of most of my "56Kbps" sessions) only to find that some idiot has put me on his "joke distribution list" and today's yuk includes a 5-megabyte bitmap. (Imagine how much laughing I do after waiting 20 minutes for this laff riot to download.) Additionally, many clients like EMWACS when I show it to them but are leery of installing software that's not supported; they're looking for something commercial, with support.

I was pleased, then, to hear that Rockliffe Systems (`www.rockliffe.com`) has taken the EMWACS IMS software, extended it tremendously, and is selling it as a product called MailSite. The core is still EMWACS, but there's a lot more, including my much-desired IMAP4. (I know, you're asking yourself, "Why doesn't he just use Exchange?" I know Exchange; I've taken and passed the Microsoft certification exam on it, have run it on client systems and even on my network for a while, but for some reason I just don't like it. All I really need is POP3/SMTP/IMAP4, and Exchange seems a bit of overkill. Basically, what I'm saying is that there's nothing wrong with Exchange—I just don't like it.)

You can go to their Web site and download MailSite and try it out for 30 days, as is the case with much software nowadays. (The program files are over 5MB in size, so pick a time of Internet quiet for the download.) The good news is that they've added a lot of nice GUI administrative support to IMS, as well as removed the need for any user-rights fiddling. The system's quite fast and of course does IMAP4 as well as all the mailing list stuff you could want. And if you're a current EMWACS IMS administrator, you won't have any trouble—it took me less than five minutes to install the software and get it running. The bad news is the price: about $700. Is it worth it? As always, it depends. If you're managing multiple mail servers, MailSite offers remote mail server administration, a big plus. The MailSite folks seemed helpful when I called their tech support line and asked a few dumb questions. And if your shop is a mixed Windows 2000/NT/Unix shop and you don't really want to be assimilated into the Exchange collective, then MailSite is something to check out. (I'm certainly enjoying it, although having to bring down the mail server every 30 days so I can go get another 30-day trial license is cumbersome... just kidding.)

E-mail Security Concerns

As the Internet grows, more and more gateways will be built to other e-mail systems. You can't get everywhere, but in time, you'll be able to reach anyone from the Internet. Now, that's a good thing, but as e-mail becomes more important, it's also essential to keep your mind on the fact that e-mail is not secure. Your mail packets get bounced all around the Internet, as you know—but think about what that means. Suppose you send a message to someone on the Internet, and my computer is part of the Internet—a piece, as it happens, that sits between you and the person to whom you're sending mail. Mail can sit in intermediate computers like mine, on the hard disk, for seconds, minutes, or hours at a time. It's a simple matter to use any number of utility programs to peek into the mail queue on the mail that's "just passing through." Never say anything on mail that you wouldn't want as public knowledge. Even if someone doesn't peek at your mail, that someone probably backs up his or her disk regularly, meaning that the message may sit on magnetic media for years in some archive. I sometimes imagine that in the middle of the 21st century, we'll see "the unpublished letters of Douglas Adams"—e-mail notes that someone stumbled across while picking through some 70-year-old backups; you know, it'll be the latter-day equivalent of going through some dead celebrity's trash. Anyway, the bottom line is this: Don't write anything that you wouldn't want your boss, your spouse, your parents, or your kids to read.

Using Telnet for Remote Login

Back in the late mid-Triassic period of computing, around 1973, you wouldn't sit at a computer; you'd sit at a terminal that was connected in some way to a computer. If a computer at the National Institutes of Health contained some database that I wanted to do analysis on, I'd put a modem on my terminal, get an account at NIH, find out the phone numbers of their dial-in modems, and then I'd dial one of those numbers. Once the modem was done squawking and I was connected at the princely speed of 300bps, I'd interact with NIH. But I'd interact solely with characters—25 lines of 80 columns of characters.

From the '60s on, the government has maintained a lot of mainframes with some very useful data on them. Before the growth of the Internet, anyone doing research could get an account and dial in to those mainframes to use the government's data—but the long-distance bills could bankrupt you.

Early Telnet Uses

But then the Internet appeared.

For early Internet—ARPAnet, actually—programmers built a set of programs, a server program and a terminal program, that would let a mainframe accept incoming connections over the Internet, much like modem dial-ins, and let someone sitting at a Unix terminal somewhere attach to that mainframe as if dialing in. The early (mid-Cretaceous, actually) programmers called the pair of programs *telnet*.

For years, telnet was a great way for groups to offer information over the Internet. Some people adapted programs used to host dial-in PC-based bulletin board systems to telnet. Others put data of general interest on telnet—for example, the University of Michigan once had census data available over telnet, and a travel agency let you book tickets on telnet. Network Solutions, the people who run DNS, had a search engine built into telnet that would let you look up a domain name to see if it was taken. Most of those are gone now, replaced with Web sites.

Modern Uses for Telnet

But telnet's still quite useful for network administrators, so it's great that Windows 2000 includes a telnet server that will support up to two simultaneous connections. Think of telnet on Windows 2000 as being sort of a low-bandwidth form of Windows Terminal Server. You can't run any graphical applications over it; you just get a C:\> style command line, but you can get an awful lot done with just that.

Before you can telnet into your machine, though, you must start up the server part of telnet. That part's easy, but you have to then configure it to accept regular telnet connections.

Setting Up the Telnet Server

Telnet is built as a service under Windows 2000. You can start it by just opening up a command line, typing **net start tlntsvr**, and pressing Enter. Alternatively, you can tell your system to always have the telnet server available by setting up the telnet service to start automatically.

Here's what you need to do to set up the telnet service to start automatically:

1. Right-click the My Computer icon, and select Manage.

2. Under Computer Management, you'll see `Services and Applications`; open it by clicking the plus sign next to it.

3. Inside `Services and Applications`, you'll see `Services`; click that and the list of services in the system will appear in the right pane of the window.

4. The service you're looking for is named just telnet; right-click it and choose Properties.

5. You'll see a single-selection drop-down list box labeled Startup; choose Automatic, then click OK to close the window. Close the Computer Management window.

While telnet is often a potential security risk because it passes passwords in clear text over the network, Microsoft has reduced that risk by modifying the way that the telnet server behaves. Instead of using clear-text passwords, it uses an NT-style authentication approach called NTLM. It requires not only a modified telnet server but a modified telnet client as well—but Windows 2000 comes with a client like that. (Other Windows operating systems will not be able to connect to the telnet server unless you edit the server's settings to allow it to accept passwords in clear text; I'll explain how to do this in just a minute.)

Assuming that you're already logged onto the domain, you can just start a session from a command line by typing **telnet** *servername*, where *servername* is the name of the server that you want to establish the telnet session on. From there, you can do anything that you can do from the command line: run batch files, run scripts, or use command-line versions of utilities.

On the other hand, you may decide that you'd like remote administrators to be able to log in with any kind of telnet client rather than just the Windows 2000 client. You can do that, but again, be warned that allowing standard telnet clients to attach requires allowing clear-text passwords—check with your security group before doing this. Here's how to tell a server's telnet server software to accept standard telnet logins:

1. First tell the telnet server to accept usernames and passwords for login security. To do that, open up a command line, type **tlntadmn**, and press Enter.

2. Choose 3 and Enter; this will let you modify a Registry setting.

3. Then choose 7 and Enter, and then y to confirm that you want to modify the NTLM option; this controls how logins occur. The default value of 2 requires a special telnet client, the one built only into Windows 2000/XP/2002. If you want non-Windows 200x systems to be able to access the Telnet server, then change this value to 1.

4. TLNTADMN will show you the current NTLM value and will confirm that you do indeed want to change it; confirm that you do by entering y and Enter.

5. Enter a new value of 1 and press Enter.

6. Again you'll be asked to confirm that you want to make this change; do so by entering y and Enter.

7. Enter 0 and Enter to exit the Registry section.

8. Enter 5 and Enter to stop the service.

9. Enter 4 and Enter to start the service.

10. Enter 0 and Enter to stop the TLNTADMN program.

11. Telnet's now ready to go. From any machine with a telnet client, you can just open a command line and type **telnet** *machine_name*, where *machine_name* is either the DNS name or IP address of your server.

Communicating Securely with SSL

We all know that the Web is a great place to find information, but I have a feeling that we've only seen the tip of the iceberg as far as the Internet is concerned. The force that is truly driving the Internet into the future is commerce. The Internet lends itself to transactional chores very well, just due to its nature and makeup. However, most commercial transactions contain some form of proprietary or confidential data, whether it's bank account numbers or corporate plans for a new product launch. All sorts of information that is confidential in nature is being transmitted across the Internet, and that trend will continue in the future.

To meet the challenge of securing confidential data, Netscape developed a protocol called Secure Sockets Layer (SSL) to be used in conjunction with HTTP as a means of providing secure communication channels between clients and servers. Through the use of certificates—encryption keys handed out by a trusted third-party organization—Web servers and Web browsers will negotiate an encrypted connection between themselves, preventing any data from being intercepted during transmission.

Some reasons to implement SSL are obvious—for example, if you intend to accept credit card numbers on your Web site from clients who are ordering products. Obviously, your clients might be concerned about their confidential information (their credit card number) crossing the Internet in the clear, so you can encrypt the ordering process to ensure that even if someone does intercept the transmission, it will be in a useless form. However, some reasons for implementing SSL are less obvious but equally as important—for example, confidential information such as brokerage statements, corporate financial statements, tax returns, medical records, etc. All are equally private as far as most individuals are concerned, and will be transmitted over the Internet more and more frequently as time goes on.

Fortunately, Microsoft has made the process of obtaining a security certificate easy in IIS 5 through the inclusion of the IIS Certificate Wizard, an administrative wizard that will create a certificate request for your system. You will, in turn, submit that request to a certificate authority—commonly referred to as a CA—which is the trusted third party. The CA will then send you a certificate that the wizard will help you install on your server. Before getting this process started, you will need to have the following ready:

◆ A functional IIS server. Although this seems obvious, there's more to it than simply having an IIS server that runs. Since certificates are highly specialized encryption keys—they even have the name of your server embedded in them—it's best to have your site working exactly how you want it first, and then add the security certificate and turn on encryption as one of the last items to do.

♦ Organizational details. Details that a CA will require from your organization include name, organizational unit, country, state, locality, and a name, e-mail address, and phone number for the contact individual requesting the certificate.

♦ Server details. Certificates are based on the server that they were requested for, and will have that server name (either an internal NetBIOS-style name or an FQDN) embedded within the key. Therefore, once you enable encryption, it's important that you don't change the name of your server—otherwise you will need to request a new certificate.

Requesting a Certificate

To begin the process of requesting a certificate, start the Internet Services Manager MMC and select your Web site in the scope pane. Then, select the Properties option from the Action pull-down menu. This will get you into the properties pages for this Web site, as discussed earlier in this chapter. Click the Directory Security tab to get to the security properties pages, shown earlier in Figure 17.17. Click the Server Certificate button to launch the IIS Certificate Wizard. The first screen of the wizard (after the welcome screen) is shown in Figure 17.85.

FIGURE 17.85

Starting the IIS Certificate Wizard

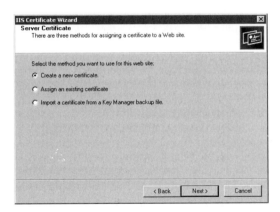

Assuming that you are requesting a new certificate for your site, select the Create a New Certificate option. Clicking Next will take you through roughly eight steps required to collect the necessary information about your organization: organization name, organizational unit, server name, contact information, etc. Enter the information requested at each step and click Next to move through the wizard. One of the final steps of the wizard will ask you where you want to store your request (assuming you selected the Prepare the Request Now, but Send It Later option in the second step of the wizard); the default is C:\certreq.txt. If this name is acceptable, click Next to proceed to the final step of the wizard.

After you have entered all of the necessary organizational and server information for your certificate request, the wizard should show you the information it has collected in a step similar to the one shown in Figure 17.86.

FIGURE 17.86

Certificate request
confirmation step

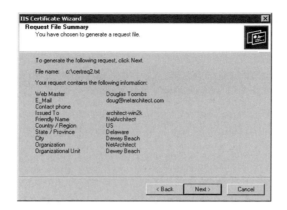

Assuming your information is correct, click Next, and the wizard will create the appropriate certificate request and place it in the file you specified. This file is simply a text file containing all of the information you entered through the wizard, encoded in a certificate request. A sample certificate request is shown here:

```
-----BEGIN NEW CERTIFICATE REQUEST-----
HIICMzOCMhACNQDwDzAYDBAGN1DECxHPRXIjSGAONWDOBXEpTjHrmtrwDAYDVQQL
EDVEZWdEeYErMEMjACUHChMMTmVOQXJjaGlOZWNOMRQwEgYDVQQHEwtEZXdleSBC
ZWFjaDERMA8GA1UECBMIRGVsYXdhcmUxCzAJBgNVBAYTAlVTMFwwDQYJKoZIhvcN
AQEBBQADSwAwSAJBANDWZ6269T1vwQ22oFxUBUf+dRVpmLFHiak9v+kyp58O/ZRz
QdTQcOlnWvxZGHWXINwDEU5cUatkOcX3ImfBxvOCAwEAAaCCATcwNQYKKwYBBAGC
NwIBDjEnMCUwDgYDVROPAQH/BAQDAgM4MBMGA1UdJQQMMAoGCCsGAQUFBwMBMIH9
BgorBgEEAYI3DQICMYHuMIHrAgEBHloATQBpAGMAcgBvAHMAbwBmAHQAIABSAFMA
QQAgAFMAQwBoAGEAbgBuAGUAbAAgAEMAcgB5AHAAdABvAGcAcgBhAHAAaABpAGMA
IABQAHIAbwB2AGkAZABlAHIDgYkAmgOYS5nRhWqlrh47DAbamYuDeux8a+ueRdAC
GKnLO6A+aORwy/qdQZfPWLollaNa/L15umsktG5agPO92QtK9WH/72gfWAjmL3og
E4UHAnrIiylWI8WdA6pvSIGB/fXDpi21GaeWUeA71su7E27apemVifiXUzVUR/kU
2NgmKrkZZZZZZZZZDANBgkqhkiG9w0BAQUFAANBAGGPAORMoqXYzK4mriO+WOhJ
yK6EjShHF2awrGrZepWliorpun5XGVWIl+UVC811bm/bxu4WacvQCXd1++IVBaB4
-----END NEW CERTIFICATE REQUEST-----
```

Once you have your request file, you need to submit that file to a CA so that they can issue a certificate to you. For my testing purposes, I chose to use VeriSign over at www.verisign.com. In any case, choose a CA that you would like to use and then submit your request file through whatever mechanism they provide.

Depending on the CA you are working with and the level of trust you want for your certificate, your request might take anywhere from a few minutes to a few days or weeks to process. Once your request has been approved, you will receive a certificate for installation on your server (a sample certificate basically looks exactly like the encryption key in the certificate request). To install the certificate, return to the Directory Security tab in the properties of your Web site (you need to install your certificate to the same site you requested it from) and click the Server Certificate button again.

This time when you launch the IIS Certificate Wizard, it will realize that you have previously requested a certificate for this Web server and it will ask you if you would like to import that certificate now, as Figure 17.87 shows.

FIGURE 17.87

Importing a certificate with the IIS Certificate Wizard

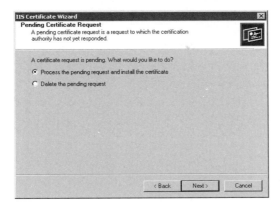

Import the certificate by entering the path to the certificate in the next step of the wizard. If everything goes as it should, you should see a summary of your certificate, similar to the one shown in Figure 17.88.

FIGURE 17.88

Summary of an imported certificate

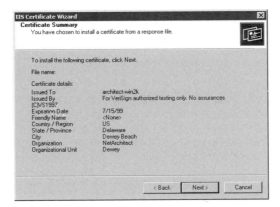

If this certificate is acceptable, click Next, and the certificate will be installed into your Web server.

NOTE *You can only install one certificate per Web site, but you can install the same certificate into multiple Web sites as long as they are referenced by the same name.*

Securing a Site or Directory

Once your certificate is installed, the Edit button should light up in the Directory Security properties page for your Web site. You can require SSL security for your entire site or in directories (real or virtual) within your site. In either case, the settings are mostly the same.

To enable encryption on a specific directory or site, go to the Directory Security properties page for that directory or site. Click the Edit button to enable security, and you will go to a Secure Communications properties page similar to the one shown in Figure 17.89.

FIGURE 17.89

Implementing secure communications

In this page, the most important setting to enable is Require Secure Channel (SSL). This will enforce secure communications for anyone trying to reach this resource (directory or site). Anyone attempting to access this resource over a standard HTTP connection will be instructed that they cannot reach the content unsecured and that they must use HTTPS to access the desired content. If you have a domestic-only build of Windows 2000 Server, you will also have the option to enable strong (128-bit) encryption, instead of relying on standard 40-bit encryption (sometimes referred to as weak).

As clients access your system, you can also accept or require client certificates as a means of authenticating who can access your system. If you want to require that only users with certificates access your system, select the Require Client Certificates radio button, and any users who do not have a client certificate installed in their system will not be able to access the secure content of your site.

Since it is possible for clients to provide certificates to your server (in addition to your server presenting a certificate to your clients), you can use this as a means of authenticating users and knowing exactly who is accessing your Web site. By checking the Enable Client Certificate Mapping check box, and then clicking the Edit button, you can "map" specific certificates to specific Windows user accounts. In effect, you are telling your IIS server, "If you receive this particular certificate, then assume that this is user John Doe accessing the Web server." If IIS knows who the exact user is, it can take advantage of permissions placed on files and directories for controlling who can access what content.

Configuring and Troubleshooting Indexing Service and Building Web-Based Query Pages

Next, let's take up an IIS-related topic: Indexing Service. Index Server has surely gotten a fair amount of press attention because it contained the security hole that the Code Red weasels used to attack Web servers around the world. But it's harder to find useful information on making Index Server *work*, and that's a shame, as Indexing Service can be a useful tool. This section describes how it works and offers some very simple Web pages that will let you exploit the service's power.

What Indexing Service Does

First of all, note that its name is Indexing *Service* rather than Index Server, as 2000 and later OSes include it "in the box." Many people (myself included) tend to erroneously call it Index Server because it was originally a separate add-on program that shipped for NT 4.0 called Index Server. Windows 2000 Server and .NET Server include it as a basic system service named Indexing Service. What it *does* is make searching today's huge hard disks a tractable affair.

Working in the background, Indexing Service examines and analyzes the files on your system, building and maintaining an index of the words that it finds there. At first blush, that'd make Indexing Service sound like something that just keeps track of every word, where "word" is just defined as a bunch of letters surrounded by spaces or punctuation. But think a bit more about it, and you'll see that Indexing Service has a harder job than that. Extracting words is simple if your document is plain ASCII text. But if it's an HTML file, how would Indexing Service know that "
," the HTML command for "break the line here," is or isn't a word? How would it understand words in a Microsoft Word document? The answer is that Indexing Service includes a bunch of *filters*, programs that understand particular file formats. Indexing Service comes with filters that let it understand ASCII files, HTML files, Microsoft Office files, and what Help calls "Internet mail and news documents." (I'm not sure what that last one means—it scans my PSTs?) Notice that there's no PDF filter; you can download it, I'm told, from Adobe's Web site at `http://www.adobe.com/support/downloads/`.

The Annoying Thing about Indexing Service: Little Documentation

The fact that Microsoft first documented it when it was Index Server means that, unfortunately, most of the Index-related documentation that you'll find on Microsoft's Web site and in books refers to the Index Server, which sort of works like Indexing Service, but not quite. To make things worse, the old Index Server documentation explained how to build HTML pages to query a cataloged directory, and for some reason Microsoft chose not to do that in the Indexing Service documentation. You're just supposed to know that things "kind of" work the same with Indexing Service as they did with Index Server, so I guess you're supposed to try the old code and hope it works. It does, sometimes; but I'll give you some basic HTML pages that you can use to create a Web page that will let you search any catalog from a Web browser. As always, once you know the magic words, then you can extract the information that you need from Microsoft's Web site.

What documentation there *is* about Indexing Service is in the Windows 2000 Server Help file. Open its Table of Contents and open the Files and Printers link. One of the sublinks that you'll see is called Indexing Service. Or just open up `\winnt\help\is.chm`.

How You'll Use It (Why You Care)

I've found Indexing Service a great tool for building a fast, flexible Web-based search engine. But you can also use it within your network or just on your computer without any Web interface at all. For example, if you had a huge directory of ASCII, Office, and HTML documents, then you could catalog that and search for particular files extremely quickly.

How It Works

You tell Indexing Service that you want to create a catalog of a particular directory by telling Indexing Service two things: what directory you want to index (catalog) and where to put that catalog—after all, the catalog files must reside somewhere. Indexing Service creates a folder named catalog.wci in the directory that you've told it to store the catalog in. That leads to the following *very* important performance concerns—ones that I learned the hard way.

◆ Do *not* put the catalog in the directory that you're cataloging. If you want to catalog C:\MYSTUFF, then nothing at all will stop you from *storing* its catalog in that same directory. But it's a bad idea, and here's why. Let's say that you put a new file into C:\MYSTUFF, and so Indexing Service notices the new file and indexes it. That indexed information goes into the CATALOG.WCI directory, which is *inside* C:\MYSTUFF. This causes Indexing Service to notice that—aha!—there is some new data in C:\MYSTUFF and... oh, no, that's just the catalog, I'll ignore it. I know this sounds insignificant, but it isn't; I created a small directory with just a couple dozen files and put the index inside the directory; Indexing Service took about 10 minutes to index it. When I put those files into a different directory and cataloged that new directory—but put the catalog in still another directory—then Indexing Service cataloged the new directory almost instantaneously.

◆ IIS *really* doesn't like catalogs anywhere in the wwwroot directory or in the directories under it. It seems to slow down both IIS *and* Indexing Service.

Managing It

Indexing Service is a service that you handle much like other services—you can start it, stop it, or restart it. A standard 2000 install sets it up as a manual rather than automatic service, so you've got to either set it up as automatic or remember to turn it on every time you reboot. (You do that in the usual way—right-click My Computer, choose Manage Computer. Under Computer Management, open the Services and Applications folder and then the object under that named Services. In Services, you'll find Indexing Service; right-click that and you'll see both Start and Properties on the resulting context menu. Start starts it right now; Properties lets you change Startup type from Manual to Automatic.) The Indexing Service snap-in looks like Figure 17.90.

Like DNS and IIS, the Indexing Service's snap-in is incorporated in Manage Computer under Services and Applications, near the Services object that you just clicked. Open it and you'll see one or more icons that look sort of like books—those are the catalogs, and we'll get to them in a minute. First, though, right-click the Indexing Service icon and choose Properties. As you see in Figure 17.91, you'll see two tabs on the page—Generation and Tracking.

FIGURE 17.90

Initial Indexing Service, showing System and Web catalogs

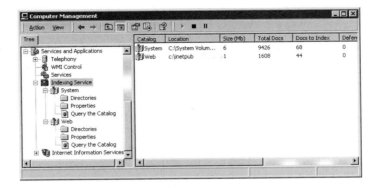

FIGURE 17.91

Indexing Service properties

Generation controls how Indexing Service creates indexes. One check box says Index Files with Unknown Extensions; it's not checked here, but if you check it, then Indexing Service just says, "Damn the torpedoes," and indexes *everything*, even if it doesn't have a filter for it. I don't use it, but I'm sure that *someone* thought it was a good idea. The other check box, Generate Abstracts, is also unchecked by default, but might be worth checking. When checked, Indexing Service tries to create an abstract of each file that it indexes. It's a nice feature but isn't always that smart; for example, it seems to create abstracts of HTML files by displaying the <h1> and <h2> elements of the document, which may not correctly characterize that document. Click the other tab, Tracking, and you'll see a page like the one in Figure 17.92.

Tracking just includes one check box, Add Network Share Alias Automatically, and it's checked by default. This ensures that if Indexing Service indexes a drive that it sees as a mapped drive letter, it remembers not only the drive letter, but the entire UNC. For example, if you've mapped \\server01\ data to X: and indexed X:, then Indexing Service would remember that those files are available at \\server01\data even *if* you don't have that UNC mapped back to X: when you try to retrieve the indexed documents.

FIGURE 17.92

Tracking tab in
Indexing Service
properties

STANDARD CATALOGS

Even if you've never used Indexing Service before, you're likely to already see two catalogs: one called System and, if you're running a Web server on the computer, another catalog called Web. As their names suggest, they index system information and whatever's on your Web server content.

Personally, the first thing I do is to delete both of them. Having my entire Web site as well as every hard disk on my server indexed gives me the heebie-jeebies. I mean, why *not* just make it easy for crackers to spy on my system once they've cracked Indexing Service? My feeling is that *I'll* decide what gets indexed on my system, thanks very much.

To delete a catalog, you must stop the Indexing Service. Then just left-click the catalog and press the Del key, or right-click the catalog—although I've seen cases where the Delete option doesn't appear on the context menu, but you can still right-click and press Del to get rid of the catalog.

CREATING A CATALOG

You create a catalog in Indexing Service by right-clicking the Indexing Service icon and choosing New and then Catalog to raise a dialog like the one in Figure 17.93.

FIGURE 17.93

Creating a new
catalog

This dialog box, labeled Add Catalog, contains just two text fields: Name and Location. In Name, just fill in the descriptive name of your catalog—no spaces allowed! This name doesn't have to relate in any way to the name of the directory that you're going to index. For example, I named the catalog for my online newsletters "Newsletters" even though they don't reside in a directory named `Newsletters`. Location is the location of the *catalog files*, not the files to be cataloged. This was what I was talking about a while back: specify a location for your catalog that is different from the actual location *to be* cataloged. For example, if I were indexing newsletters in a directory named `C:\Newsletters`, I might put the catalog's location in, say, `C:\Newsletter Index`. But no matter where you put the catalog, remember not to put it in `wwwroot` anywhere under that directory.

If Indexing Service is off when you create the catalog, you'll get a dialog to that effect: "Catalog will remain offline until Indexing Service is restarted." No surprise there.

TELL IT WHAT TO CATALOG, AND WHAT NOT TO

Now Indexing Service knows that you want to catalog *something*, but it doesn't know what. So add one or more directories to its list of things to index. Right-click the catalog's icon and choose New/Directory and you'll see a dialog box like the one in Figure 17.94.

FIGURE 17.94

Specifying the directory to catalog

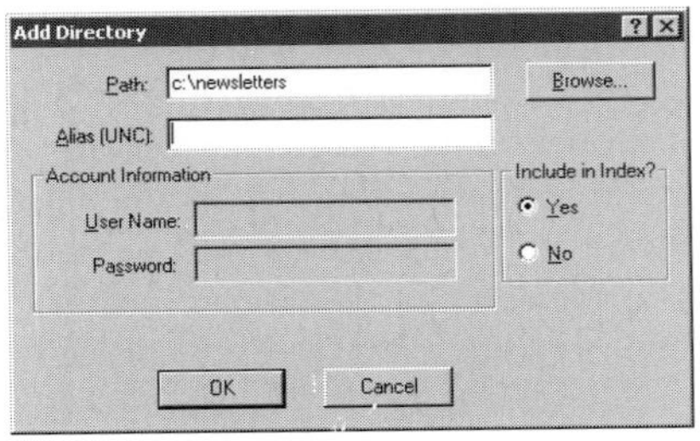

That dialog asks you to fill in the path and, if relevant, the UNC of the directory to catalog. Next to that is an odd-looking set of radio buttons asking, "Include in index?"

Is this about the dumbest question you can imagine, or what? Here you are, adding a directory to a catalog—whose sole function in life is to *index* data, and this dialog asks if you want to index the data. What were they thinking? Well, Indexing Service not only indexes the top level of the directory that you specify, but any *subdirectories* as well. So suppose I've decided to index `C:\Newsletters`, as it contains my old newsletters. But suppose that *inside* the `C:\Newsletters` directory is a `C:\Newsletters\In-Progress` directory, where I keep my newsletters that I'm still working on. Well, by default, Indexing Service would catalog *that* directory as well—so a well-placed query would let you see my newsletters before I'm even finished writing them! That's not what I want, so I might add `C:\Newsletters`, as I've described, and then add `C:\Newsletters\In-Progress`—and then tell Indexing Service *not* to include `C:\Newsletters\In-Progress` in the catalog. The net effect would be to defeat Indexing Service's natural inclination to index everything in `C:\Newsletters`, even my work-in-progress directory.

You can also block Indexing Service from cataloging a file or directory by using that file or directory's advanced properties. Right-click the file or directory, and choose Properties and then the Advanced button, and you'll see something like Figure 17.95.

Uncheck For Fast Searching..., and the folder will be essentially invisible to Indexing Service.

FIGURE 17.95

A folder's advanced
properties

CONSIDER FILE PERMISSIONS, OR YOUR CATALOG WON'T WORK

Sometimes security gets in the way of Indexing Service. So take a minute and consider the file and
directory permissions on the things that you want to index.

When I first used Indexing Service, it drove me absolutely crazy. It could index many files, but not
the ones that I wanted—not the ones on my Web server. I set up a pristine new computer, built a catalog on it with copies of the exact same data files that I wanted to index, and it worked... but not on
my Web server. Then it dawned on me: I'd monkeyed with the directory permissions on my server.

My original plan had been to adjust the permissions so that the IUSR account didn't have access
to parts of the disk that it had no need to have. But in the process of disconnecting some directory
permissions from inheriting permissions from their parent directory, I cleared all previous permissions. Including the System account.

But, as you've probably already thought, the Indexing Service runs *under* the System account. And
therein lay the problem. I'd set up the catalog right; I'd just denied Indexing Service the ability to
actually read the files that I wanted it to index. Now, in my defense, let me just squawk a bit that it'd
have been nice if Microsoft offered a verbose logging feature of Indexing Service, where I'd have gotten a clue a bit earlier... but it was still dumb on my part. So let's stop for a minute and consider
permissions.

- ◆ Indexing Service needs to be able to read whatever you want cataloged, so make sure that System can read whatever you're cataloging.

- ◆ Indexing Service needs to be able to write and modify its catalog, so be sure that System can
  write, read, and modify whatever directory you've put the catalog in.

But we're not done yet. Eventually you will want to query that catalog, using either a query tool
built into Manage Computer, which I'll show you in a minute, or perhaps through a Web interface.
Before releasing the answers to a query, Indexing Service checks that the asker has the permissions to
see the answer. So let's see what that means for my example of a Web-based search engine for my
online newsletters.

Suppose the newsletter directory gave System Full Control permissions, but denied the IUSR
account all access. What would happen? Well, Indexing Service would build the catalog for the
newsletter directory just fine. And if I logged onto the server as an administrator and queried that
catalog with some command-line tool or the built-in one that I'll show you in a minute, then perhaps

the query would work fine. But from the Web-based interface, the query failed—why? Because Indexing Service sees that the IUSR account isn't allowed to see that data.

In my experience, security is a major cause of failed queries, so keep it in mind when using Indexing Service–based tools.

Using the Catalog: Querying Indexing Service from Manage Computer

Once you've created that catalog, how do you try it out? You use a tool built into Manage Computer, under the Indexing Service icon, called Query the Catalog, as you see in Figure 17.96.

FIGURE 17.96

Sample Indexing Service query

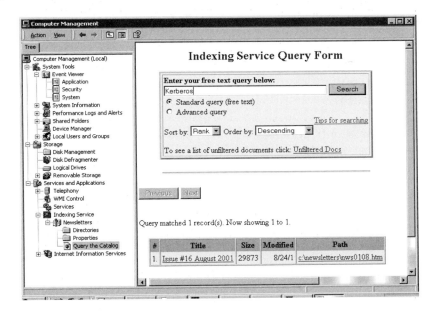

As you see in that figure, you'll see a field where you can type in your query words and a button labeled Search. The query tool will show you all of your hits and provide hyperlinks that you can click to view the files that matched your query.

This isn't really an all-purpose tool, as it's cumbersome to search a catalog unless you're physically seated at the server whose Indexing Service hosts that catalog. But it's a great debugging tool because it's a quick-and-dirty way to find out if your catalog is working. And because you're usually running it while logged in as an administrator, you typically do that test query with maximum permissions. *Then,* if you try the same query from a Web page and it fails while the Query the Catalog tool succeeds, you can be pretty sure that the problem lies with permissions rather than with something else.

Using the Catalog: The Query Language

But how do you address queries? Indexing Service has its own built-in query language that's pretty extensive but also pretty ugly. You can get the whole scoop in the Indexing Service help file, `\winnt\help\is.chm`. Open the top-level booklet icon, Indexing Service, and inside that you'll see another booklet, Advanced Topics (*using* the silly thing with queries is an *advanced topic?*). Inside there you'll find another booklet entitled Indexing Service Query Language. In this section, I'll just offer a short summary of the Indexing Service's query language and provide a few examples.

Simple Words

Of course, you can type just one word and Indexing Service will look for that. Searching for "Kerberos" will turn up any document with the word "Kerberos" in it. Indexing Service seems not to care about case—"kerberos" would turn up the same hits as "Kerberos."

Word Variations Work, Too

Indexing Service understands variations on words. For example, if you search for "patches," then you'll not only get hits that match "patches," you'll also get hits that match simply "patch" or "patching."

To do an exact search, surround the search with double quotes. Thus, if you type **patches**, then you'll get patch, patches, patching, and the like, but typing **"patches"** will only match that exact phrase.

Wildcards Are Harder

But recall that Indexing Service tries to understand text not merely as a sequence of characters, but instead as a series of *words*, so searching for "Kerb" would not yield any hits that matched "Kerberos." How, then, to do wildcards? By giving Indexing Service what Microsoft calls a phrase, wherein you surround your query with {**phrase**} and {**/phrase**}; it's sort of HTML-ish. The asterisk is the generic wildcard, as always, so to search for any line that contains "Kerb," type

```
{phrase}Kerb*{/phrase}
```

In theory, you can make Unix-style regular expressions work by surrounding them with {**regex**} and {**/regex**}, but I've not been successful making them work.

Logical Operators

Indexing Service also understands AND, OR, NOT, and parentheses. You could search for:

```
"domain controller" and (kerberos or "LAN Manager")
```

It also understands NEAR, but only in a very lame way—NEAR is defined as "within 50 words" and, no matter what the docs say, it's not possible to redefine. So this works:

```
"domain controller" near Kerberos
```

It's a pretty powerful language—it's just a little cryptic.

Filtering "Noise" Words Via noise.enu—And, Or, Numerals, Etc.

A large number of the words in English text are simple words that you probably would never search on: and, or, also, have, could, and the like. So you don't want your catalog to track every single use of *those* words. So Indexing Service includes a file called `noise.enu` in `\winnt\system32`. It's a simple ASCII file listing "noise" words—words not to index. You can change it to include (or exclude) any word, as you like. It's called `noise.enu` because it lists the *English* noise words. Look in `\winnt\`

system32 and you'll also see `noise.esn` (Spanish), `noise.deu` (German), and `noise.ita` (Italian), among others.

Using the Catalog: Querying Indexing Service from tne Web

Now that you have a working catalog and can query it from the Query the Catalog option in Manage Computer, how do you let the rest of the world (or maybe just the rest of your intranet) query the catalog? With a Web-based query client. While this isn't a programming text—nor am I an expert programmer—here's a very bare-bones, stripped-down set of Web pages that you can modify and put up to let people query some catalog.

GETTING READY

For this example, let me assume that you're going to index files in a directory called `Newsletters`, which sits in your WWWROOT directory. (Yes, you can do this for files that *aren't* in WWWROOT, but this is simplest.) You have already :

- Set up IIS on a computer (with all the current security patches, please!)

- Created a directory named `Newsletters` inside `\Inetpub\wwwroot`

- Placed a few text, HTML, or Office documents in `\Inetpub\wwwroot\Newsletters`

- Started Indexing Service on that computer

- Created a catalog called Newsletters, which indexes the `Newsletters` directory inside WWWROOT

- Tested that queries to it work with Query the Catalog

CREATING THE HTML

You'll need two files: `ask.htm`, which contains a form that lets people type in their queries, and `find.asp`, which takes the information collected in `ask.htm`, executes the query, and returns the answers. Ask.htm is pretty short, as you can see in Listing 17.2.

LISTING 17.2: THE *ASK.HTM* FILE

```
<HTML>
<HEAD>
<TITLE>Search Newsletter Archive</TITLE>
</HEAD>
<BODY>
<Form ACTION="find.asp" METHOD="POST">
Type in your query<br>
<INPUT TYPE="TEXT" NAME="SearchString" SIZE="94" MAXLENGTH="100" VALUE=" "><br>
<INPUT TYPE="SUBMIT" VALUE="Execute">
<INPUT TYPE="RESET" VALUE="Clear form">
</FORM>
</BODY>
</HTML>
```

This just prompts you to "Type in your query," then packages your query in a variable called SearchString, and then calls another HTML page called find.asp. (Both ask.htm and find.asp should be in your WWWROOT directory.)

Find.asp is a bit more complex (see Listing 17.3), as it must first perform the query and then format it nicely for the user.

LISTING 17.3: THE *FIND.ASP* FILE

```
<HTML>
<HEAD>
<TITLE>Search Results</TITLE>
</HEAD>
<BODY>
<%

'Set the search parameters

'The following line is a comment; it shows how you'd restrict the search to
'just a directory "folderinnews" inside Newsletters.
'FormScope = "/folderinnews"

'These lines set the search parameters

FormScope = "/"PageSize = 1000
MaxRecords=1000
SearchString = Request.Form("SearchString")
CatalogToSearch = "Newsletters"
SearchRankOrder="rank[d]"
OrigSearch=SearchString

'

' Create query object

set Q = Server.CreateObject("ixsso.Query")
set util = Server.CreateObject("ixsso.Util")
Q.Query = SearchString
Q.Catalog = CatalogToSearch
Q.SortBy = SearchRankOrder
Q.Columns = "DocTitle, vpath, filename, size, write, characterization, rank,
directory, path"
Q.MaxRecords = MaxRecords
'util.AddScopeToQuery Q, FormScope, "deep"

'

' Do query
```

```
set RS = Q.CreateRecordSet("nonsequential")
RS.PageSize = PageSize
response.write "<p>Your search for <b>" & OrigSearch & "</b> yielded "

If RS.RecordCount=0 then response.write "no results."
if RS.RecordCount=1 then response.write "1 result:"
If RS.RecordCount>1 then response.write RS.RecordCount & " results:"

response.write "<table
border=1><tr><td>Doctitle</td><td>Vpath</td><td>Filename</td>"
response.write "<td>Size</td><td>Write</td><td>Characterization</td><td>Rank</td>"
response.write "<td>Directory</td><td>Path</td></tr>"

'Display the results

Do While Not RS.EOF
' loop through the results.
' Build a hyperlink to the document
hlink = "<a href=""/newsletters/" & RS("filename") & """>" & RS("doctitle") &
"</a>"
' Display attributes
response.write "<tr><td>" & hlink & "</td><td>" & RS("Vpath") & "</td><td>"
response.write RS("filename") & "</td><td>" & RS("size") & "</td><td>" &
RS("write")
response.write "</td><td>" & RS("characterization") & "</td><td>" & RS("rank")
response.write "</td><td>" & RS("directory") & "</td><td>" & RS("path") &
"</td><tr>"
'Get the next result
RS.MoveNext
Loop 'end of DO WHILE loop

response.write "</table>"
set rs=nothing
set q=nothing
set util=nothing
%>

</BODY>
</HTML>
```

If you just want to try these out, then either type the lines into Notepad or copy the files from the CD to your WWWROOT directory. While still sitting at that computer, open up Internet Explorer, type **http://localhost/ask.htm**, and press Enter, and you'll see your form come up.

How the Query Code Works

To understand `find.asp`—which, again, is a very stripped-down query page—let's take it in pieces. The first part, through the <BODY> command, is just HTML. After that, we see this:

```
<%
'Set the search parameters
'The following line is a comment; it shows how you'd restrict the search to
'just a directory "folderinnews" inside Newsletters.
'FormScope = "/folderinnews"
'These lines set the search parameters
FormScope = "/"
PageSize = 1000
MaxRecords=1000
SearchString = Request.Form("SearchString")
CatalogToSearch = "Newsletters"
SearchRankOrder="rank[d]"
OrigSearch=SearchString
```

That line with just the <% tells the IIS server that a program is starting. Lines that begin with a single quote are just ignored by the server; they're comments. The next bunch of lines sets the parameters for the search. FormScope lets us tell Indexing Service that we don't want to search an entire directory, just a subdirectory. If, for example, we had a directory called \inetpub\wwwroot\newsletters\ **goodstuff** and we wanted the search to *only* look in the \goodstuff directory, then you'd change the line to

```
Formscope = "/goodstuff"
```

PageSize and MaxRecords restrict the search, limiting the number of hits that Indexing Service reports. SearchString just retrieves the search text. CatalogToSearch, of course, says to search "Newsletters." If there were other catalogs on this server, then you'd change this variable to point the search elsewhere. SearchRankOrder just says to report them from the best to the worst match. OrigSearch is just for my programming convenience.

The next set of lines forms and executes the query:

```
' Create query object

set Q = Server.CreateObject("ixsso.Query")
set util = Server.CreateObject("ixsso.Util")
Q.Query = SearchString
Q.Catalog = CatalogToSearch
Q.SortBy = SearchRankOrder
Q.Columns = "DocTitle, vpath, filename, size, write, characterization, rank,
directory, path"
Q.MaxRecords = MaxRecords
' util.AddScopeToQuery Q, FormScope, "deep"
```

```
' Do query
```

```
set RS = Q.CreateRecordSet("nonsequential")
RS.PageSize = PageSize
```

The piece towards the top is just "boilerplate," the particular magic words that you must say to ask Indexing Service a question. Note, however, types of "objects"—that's the programmer word for them—in the ServerCreateObject commands. The first in particular, ixsso.Query, is the built-in set of routines that controls queries. To find all of the developer documentation about it, search `msdn.microsoft.com` for "ixsso.query."

CONTROLLING A QUERY: WHAT TO RETRIEVE

If you did that search, you'd see that the "query" method of the "ixsso" object—I'm so glad the developers kept it simple for us—has attributes with names like Query, Catalog, SortBy, and so on. But you needn't look that stuff up unless you want to extend this example; I've already done most of the work. But you *do* have to fill those attributes with values, and that's what the Q.Query=, Q.Catalog=, and nearby lines do—they just transfer the values that we set up top into a place where Indexing Service can find it.

A couple of the lines need a bit more explaining. First, notice the Q.Columns= line; that tells Indexing Service exactly which data to retrieve.

◆ DocTitle is the title, if the file has one. HTML files have titles; ASCII files don't; Office files can have titles.

◆ Vpath is the relative path from the top of the catalog. In other words, we're looking in a directory called `\Inetpub\wwwroot\newsletters` for files, but what if the files are in a directory *inside* that directory? Vpath would show that. If it turns up a file named `\Inetpub\wwwroot\newsletters\goodfiles\hints.txt`, then the Vpath would be `goodfiles`, as it's the subdirectory inside the catalog.

◆ Filename is, logically, the filename—`hints.txt` in the previous example.

◆ Size is the size in bytes.

◆ Write is the date the file was last written to.

◆ Characterization is the "abstract" that Indexing Service can optionally create.

◆ Rank is a numeric score that Indexing Service uses to rate how well something matches a query.

◆ Directory is the complete directory path of the file `d:\inetpub\wwwroot\Newsletters\goodfiles` in the above example.

◆ Path is the combination of the filename and the directory; in the example above, it'd be `d:\inetpub\wwwroot\Newsletters\goodfiles\hints.txt`.

You can see the entire list of columns in a catalog in the Indexing Service snap-in in Manage Computer. Under the icon for the catalog itself there is a folder named Properties. Look in there and you'll the entire list of a catalog's properties or, as the query calls it, columns. (Most of them are of no value—the list above is about all you'd probably want.)

CONTROLLING A QUERY: WHERE TO LOOK

Second, note the comment that starts util.AddScope. This tells Indexing Service two things about the search: first, which directory in the catalog should it search and, second, should it search at that directory level, or search that directory and the directories *inside* of it? Recall that Indexing Service automatically *catalogs* as far down as the directory structure goes; this command doesn't affect that. Instead, it reflects the fact that Indexing Service doesn't automatically show all of its cards when you make a query—it only reveals what the query asks for.

Suppose I've got that directory structure that I mentioned before, `\Inetpub\wwwroot\Newsletters\ goodfiles\hints.txt`. Suppose also that I chose this time to index the *whole* wwwroot directory. What would that mean for the scope of the search? Without an AddScopeToQuery command, Indexing Service will only show results that it found in the top-level directory of the catalog, `\Inetpub\wwwroot`. To search the *whole* directory and the directories inside it, including `\Inetpub\wwwroot\Newsletters`, `\Inetpub\wwwroot\Newsletters\goodfiles`, and whatever else is in there, I'd use this command:

```
util.AddScopeToQuery Q, "/", "deep"
```

That says that the query defined by the object *Q* should start at the top—"/"—and should search all directories. The "deep" keyword is the part that says to search the directories inside the directories.

But what if I only wanted to search `\Inetpub\wwwroot\Newsletters`? Then I'd use a scope of /Newsletters—note that this uses the forward slash rather than backslash. The command would look like this:

```
util.AddScopeToQuery Q, "/Newsletters", "shallow"
```

Finally, what if I wanted to restrict the search to keep it out of the `\Inetpub\wwwroot` directory and start searching at `\Inetpub\wwwroot\Newsletters`, but also search directories below Newsletters? Then I'd do this:

```
util.AddScopeToQuery Q, "/Newsletters", "deep"
```

It's a *really* good idea to restrict your query scopes—you'll be surprised what Indexing Service turns up! For example, if you *did* index your entire Web site, then you'd probably be exposing things like code in progress, old code, or notes to yourself, much of which you might not want publicly visible.

To finish examining `find.asp`, the set RS= line tells IIS where to put the output of the query: into an object called a "record set" that I've unimaginatively called "RS." And finally, the rest of the program just loops through the returned values and creates a table that reports what it found. The three commands that say "set *something*=nothing" recover memory on the IIS server.

Troubleshooting Failed Queries

When you first get started with building your search pages and catalogs, you'll probably turn up a lot of failed queries. They can be frustrating; here's what to check:

◆ Permissions. SYSTEM must have read access to the data to be cataloged, full control to the directory where the catalog is stored, and, Microsoft adds (although I've not checked it), that SYSTEM must also have full control to the root of the drive where the catalog is stored. But the querying person must also have the permissions to see the documents, or Indexing Service won't even display it. So, for example, if your query fails from your Web browser, try logging onto the server as an administrator and try the query tool in Manage Computer. If *that* works and the Web browser doesn't, chances are good that IUSR doesn't have the permissions necessary to see the data. And when you're testing your Web-based app, make sure that you're not logged on as an administrator of the domain. Depending on how you have IIS set up, it may try to get you the catalog info as IUSR and, when that fails, it may automatically try again using your currently logged-on credentials as an administrator, and succeed. But non-admins won't be able to access the data.

◆ Check the query syntax. It's a bizarre language. Make sure you have a few simple queries whose syntax you *know* works.

◆ Be patient. Indexing Service is built to run in the background, which means that when you're fussing with it, then the indexing part of Indexing Service goes to sleep, waiting for the server to quiet down before it does its work. Get a cup of coffee or check your e-mail, give it a few minutes, and then try again.

◆ Dump the catalog and start over. Stop the Indexing Service, then right-click the icon for the catalog, and choose All Tasks/Empty Catalog. Then restart the Indexing Service. You start out with a fresh catalog this way, and you know that no old junk's sitting around in it.

◆ Go to the directories and files that you want to catalog, right-click them and choose Properties, then click the Advanced button. There's a check box on the resulting dialog box labeled For Fast Searching, Allow Indexing Service to Index This Folder. It's checked by default, but if someone's unchecked it, then Indexing Service will skip it altogether.

By now, you should not only have a working catalog, but also a nifty Web-based front end for it. Indexing Service is pretty cool once you get it set up, but, as always with complex tools, it's the initial setup that's the pain.

Windows 2000 Internet Security: Some Thoughts

A security engineer at a major tier-one ISP recently told me his opinion of Windows NT in regard to security. "It's an exploit in a box," he told me, very matter-of-factly, and you know what? Even though he's a "Unix guy," he's absolutely right. Windows NT is extremely permissive in its default configurations and should never be plugged directly into the Internet without being significantly patched and updated. So, you might assume that Microsoft corrected this problem in Win2K, right?

Well, sort of. In all fairness, Microsoft's current version of Windows 2000 Server is the most secure operating system that they've ever published. But does that mean that you should simply accept it with its default configuration? In the pages that follow, I'll walk through some items that you should be certain to secure on your Windows 2000 Server in order to protect it more. You'll quickly see that you shouldn't accept Windows 2000 security right out of the box.

NOTE *Although the security suggestions that follow will help secure your system, it is important to realize that there is no quick fix to Internet security. Entire volumes are published on the subject, much more than I could possibly cover in the pages of this book.*

There are, however, several types of actions you can take to detect and/or deter an outside attack. In this section, I'll talk about deterring and detecting attacks and cover security recommendations for three primary areas: accounts, file and print sharing, and network services.

Whether "security" is officially part of your job description or not, the 21st century seems to have a few new truths about it. First, we seem to be running a lot more Web servers than before: install Windows 2000, XP Professional, or .NET Server on a box with the defaults, and—congratulations—you've just installed a Web server. Even simple network-attached appliances like JetDirect modules or 3Com's Lanmodem make you control them via a Web interface, which means that—you guessed it—they've all got a Web server built into them. But what's the second truth of the 21st century? Virus- and worm-writing jerks the world over have targeted IIS. So anyone running an IIS-based Web server should understand that it is *very* likely that his or her system will be attacked by a worm; such an attack is a near certainty. But there's a third and final truth here: If you put a insecure Web server on a network, then you aren't merely a neutral party in the ongoing war between the worm-writing weasels and systems administrators; rather, you are helping the weasels.

To see what I mean by that, let's look at who would get hurt if I set up a Web server but didn't protect it from a worm. Worms like Code Red, Code Blue, Nimda, and their successors do several things. First, they usually rewrite and damage Web pages. That means that if I don't do anything to protect my Web server from infection, then I may be hurt, in that I must restore my Web pages to their predefacement state. But what if I've put a system on the Internet that runs a Web server, but only because I installed with the defaults? In that case, I shouldn't care whether a worm attacks the Web server, should I?

Of course I should, because of the *second* effect of a worm. Once planted in a Web server, worms seek out other Web servers to infect. That means that my unwitting Web server might end up as the vehicle that some weasel uses to infect an important Web server. At minimum, that's certainly not nice and I would prefer *not* to be a vector of e-infection; at worst, I might even be sued over it.

Even worse, a worm has a third effect: it chomps bandwidth. There have been days when so many copies of a given worm are busy scanning IP addresses trying to find potential victim servers that they have significantly slowed down the Internet.

The bottom line is this: If I've put an unsecured computer on the Internet, then I've put a loaded weapon into the hands of a network criminal. I've aided and abetted one of the bad guys. I worry that as more and more home users get high speed DSL and cable modem connections, and as those home users' operating systems get more and more sophisticated, that it will be possible for one cleverly written worm to simply shut the Internet down. Edmund Burke is credited with saying that all that is required for evil to triumph is for a "few good men to do nothing." Let's update that to say that all that is required for the weasels to destroy or severely damage an important artery of communication—the Internet—is for a few otherwise-good people to get lazy about securing their operating system's Web servers.

The most important point here, however, is that you can do some very simple, basic things to secure your IIS servers; let's see how.

If You're Not Using IIS, Turn It Off

Probably the most effective and simplest way to secure your Web server is to disable it if you don't want it. You can test if a computer is running a Web server in a few simple ways. First, check its services in Manage Computer: right-click My Computer, choose Manage, then locate the object labeled Services and Applications and click the plus sign next to it. That should reveal, among other things, an object named Services; click it and the right panel will show the services that your computer is running. You'll see that there isn't a service called IIS or Internet Information Service or anything like that; it's called World Wide Web Publishing Service. Right-click it, choose Properties, and you'll get a property page that lets you stop the service. But that only stops the Web server for now—reboot, and it'll probably start up all by itself. You can change that by clicking a drop-down list box labeled Startup Type, which offers you three choices: Automatic (which starts the service up at boot time), Manual (which does not start the service at boot time but lets you turn it on when you feel like it), or Disabled (which doesn't start the service and doesn't give you the option to start it). Just choose Disabled if you don't want this server to be a Web server, and then click OK.

.NET Server makes this less of a problem, as it discontinues Microsoft's practice of automatically installing a Web server on every system. Additionally, IIS 6.0 first comes up in a very "locked-down" mode, making it harder to attack an IIS 6.0 server whose administrator has chosen all of the defaults for it.

Get and Apply the Latest Service Packs and Hotfixes

Whenever a new worm appears, people castigate Microsoft for being "unprepared" for this latest attack, and administrators everywhere bemoan NT's "terrible security."

While I don't really like much of Microsoft's default security settings, I'd have to say that anyone who's ever been hit by an IIS-based worm could have avoided the infection had he just kept up-to-date with Microsoft's patches. (Up-to-date Web servers were safe from Code Red, Blue, and Nimda, for example.) The problem is that most of us are a bit sloppy about getting around to downloading and applying the latest patches, and for years that wasn't really a problem. Unfortunately, our modern-day "world of worms" has made staying on top of patches mandatory.

In Chapter 4, you learned how to preinstall—"slipstream" is Microsoft's word—service packs into an I386 so that subsequent RIS or similar installs already incorporate SP1, SP2, SP46, or whatever. You can apply service packs to already-installed systems most easily by first expanding them, as you also read in the Setup chapter, and then just using the command line. So, for example, suppose you've downloaded Service Pack 2, which comes as a file (a *big* one) named w2ksp2.exe. First, you'd expand it into a directory that I will arbitrarily call C:\WIN2KSP2 by typing

```
W2ksp2 -x
```

It'll then prompt you for the directory to expand the files into; tell it **C:\win2ksp2**. Once the files finish expanding, look in **win2ksp2** and you'll see a directory named **I386**. Inside that, you'll find a directory named **update**, and inside *that* you'll find a program named **update.exe**, which has a number of command-line switches, including "q" (just do it, don't talk to me), "u" (similar to "q"), and "n" (don't create uninstall files; I never find them useful, and they just take up disk space). From the command line, then, you could install SP2 in a hands-off manner by typing

```
\win2ksp2\i386\update\update -q -u -n
```

You can then put the expanded service pack files on a share, and use a batch file or telnet to apply service packs to machines remotely.

But service packs aren't the end of your update task. Microsoft releases patches in the form of security bulletins that you can find at http://www.microsoft.com/technet/treeview/default.asp?url=/technet/security/current.asp. This site gets rearranged on a regular basis, so if that doesn't work, just search for "security bulletin" on the microsoft.com site. The patches are EXE files with names like q335825_w2k_sp3.exe. The first part refers to the Knowledge Base article that explains what the patch does, "w2k" clearly says that it's a Windows 2000 patch, and "sp3" means that it is a *post–*Service Pack 2 fix and that this patch will eventually be part of Service Pack 3.

Simplifying Hotfix Application

If you've ever downloaded and applied a hotfix, then you're probably shaking your head and thinking, "Has this guy ever actually *done* this?" But, wait, give me a chance.

Hotfixes are a pain for two reasons. First, there are a *lot* of them. It's not unusual to see a couple or three dozen hotfixes that you need to apply *even if you have the most recent service pack*. Second, try applying one and you'll see that most of them force you to reboot after you apply them. So let's see, first I download the 18 relevant hotfixes. Then I apply the first one and wait for my system to reboot, then I do the second, and... waitaminute, you mean that I've got to do that for *all* of my computers? And then how do I check which computers have and don't have a given set of hotfixes?

Thankfully, Microsoft has offered a couple of programs to simplify the process, qchain.exe and hfnetchk.exe. You can find the link for qchain.exe at Knowledge Base article Q296861, or if that article's gone by the time that you read this, then search for "qchain.exe." You can find hfnetchk.exe at article Q303215, or, again, if that doesn't exist when you look for it, search on the program's name.

Qchain lets you apply a whole bunch of hotfixes all at once. You invoke the hotfixes—each with the options -m, -z, unattended, and don't force reboot—and then qchain rearranges them on disk and in the Registry so that they don't conflict with one another. Then you can reboot. For example, suppose you had some hotfixes with the names q335825_w2k_sp3.exe, qf843615_w2k_sp3.exe, and q745622_w2k_sp3.exe (all imaginary hotfix names, by the way). You could put them on a server named srv1 on a share called patches, and then put the hotfixes, qchain.exe, and a batch file to install the patches in that share. The batch file could look something like this:

```
set lc=\\srv1\patches\
%lc%q335825_w2k_sp3.exe -z -m
%lc%qf843615_w2k_sp3.exe -z -m
%lc%q745622_w2k_sp3.exe -z -m
%lc%qchain mylog.txt
```

Create the batch file by opening up Notepad and typing those lines into Notepad, but don't type the names of the imaginary hotfixes; instead, type one line for each of the hotfixes that you've got in that directory, prefixing them with "%lc%" and adding "-z –m" to the end. Then save them as `applypatches.bat`, again in that share. Now you can, from any machine on the network, just type

`\\svr1\patches\applypatches.bat`

And it'll apply all of the patches. You can then reboot the system, and it'll be up-to-date. But how do you check later to see what hotfixes have been applied to a given system and if it's still up-to-date? That's where `hfnetchck.exe` helps out. In its simplest form, you just run `hfnetchck.exe` on a system without any options. It then contacts the Microsoft site, downloads information about the latest hotfixes, and checks that your system has those hotfixes. It'll then report about hotfixes that Microsoft thinks that you should have but that you don't.

You can run it with the –v, verbose, switch to find out why hfnetchk thinks that you don't have a given hotfix. There are a few that apparently don't leave enough of a fingerprint behind for hfnetchk to be able to verify whether or not you actually have the hotfix installed, like one that appeared in 2001 named MS01-022. Apparently you could apply it all that you wanted, but hfnetchk couldn't find it. But running hfnetchk –v could allay your fears:

```
WARNING        MS01-022        Q296441
The XML file does not contain any file or registry details for this patch.  As a
result, this tool is unable to confirm that this patch has been applied.  Please
verify patch installation or refer to Q303215 for more information.
```

In other words, hfnetchk is saying, "Well, I can't *prove* that this is here, so I won't say that it's there... but I couldn't prove it in either case."

Use IIS and NTFS Permissions

When the bad guys get control of your IIS server, the system sees them as one of two user accounts—either the IUSR account or the System account. If they're running a script or a Web page, then they're the IUSR account. Intruders can only act as the System account in those cases where IIS has some pretty egregious bug and the intruder exploits that bug.

Let me underscore that point: visitors to your Web site are actually logged into your Web server's security system, whether a local SAM or a domain-based Active Directory. Such so-called "anonymous" Web visitors are logged in as the IUSR account. Armed with that knowledge, you can recruit NTFS to help you secure your system.

By default, Windows 2000 and earlier systems set all of their NTFS permissions to Everyone/ Full Control, and of course IUSR is a member of Everyone. I figured that IUSR didn't need access to the rest of my hard disk, however, and so I changed its permissions:

1. In wwwroot, I gave IUSR only NTFS permissions to read, execute, and list folder contents. This will work fine even if there is a script in wwwroot. You'll only need to give IUSR write permissions on any directories that Web-based scripts use to write files to.

2. In WINNT, I gave IUSR the same permissions as Authenticated Users.

3. Throughout the rest of the server's hard disk, I denied IUSR access.

TIP *Your system might need somewhat different permissions. Microsoft has a pretty nitty-gritty Knowledge Base article about required IIS 5.0 permissions at Q271071.*

Now, you might be running some set of programs or scripts that require different permissions than the ones that work for my system, so please test these things before you screw up your production Web server! Work with the content folks to find out what permissions you need for each directory but, again, in my experience IIS works very well with extremely minimal permissions for IUSR.

But IIS itself also has a set of permissions that you can use to secure your Web site. They work in tandem with NTFS permissions in the same way that file-sharing permissions work with NTFS permissions: both apply and the most restrictive ones win. IIS permissions are simpler and less flexible than NTFS permissions, as they apply to everyone accessing a site—there's no way, for example, to say that the IIS read permission (which is different from the familiar NTFS read permission) should be granted to Administrators and denied to everyone else. Instead, you just check the Read box and every visitor gets it.

Check the Execute Permissions box for every directory in your Web site as well. My site was once composed of a basic wwwroot directory that contained a bunch of directories, most of which contained only static HTML pages and images. I was surprised to find that the IIS permission on all of those directories was scripts and executables!

To view a given directory's IIS permissions, just open up the site in the IIS administration snap-in, and you'll see a folder icon for each directory. Right-click the folder and choose Properties, and you'll see the IIS permissions for that directory.

Disable Indexing

Unless you are explicitly interested in indexing a particular set of files, disable indexing both from the IIS snap-in and from NTFS.

Disable All Nonessential Ports

In Chapter 6, you learned how to use IPSec to close particular ports. Consider doing this for your Web servers. But remember, if you close all incoming ports except for 80 and 443, then you won't be able to do remote administration of your computer. You can do that from the GUI in Advanced TCP/IP, or use IPSec, as you saw in Chapter 6. Or there's a Resource Kit tool that will tell IPSec to filter all but ports 80 and 443 incoming:

```
ipsecpol -w REG -p allinone -r "Filter all but 80/443" -f [0+*] (0:80+*::TCP)
(0:443+*::TCP)
```

That should be typed as all one line.

Move *wwwroot*

By default, IIS puts its wwwroot directory on the same drive as the operating system, in the \Inetpub directory. Some particularly badly written worms can't even *find* your Web site to attack it unless the site is in Inetpub. So moving the root of your document directories will provide some small protection.

Get Rid of the IIS Admin, Documentation, Web-based Printing, Extra Directories, and Samples

IIS ships with a whole bunch of sample files and extra doodads. Many are useful, but they're also potential security holes.

For example, there is a Web-based IIS administration tool. If someone cracks that, they *own* your Web site. Get rid of it from the Control Panel in Add/Remove Programs/Windows Components. Choose Internet Information Services (IIS) and then the Details button, then uncheck Internet Services Manager (HTML). And while you're at it, if you don't use FrontPage-based Webs, then uncheck the box next to FrontPage Server Extensions. Personally, I find the FrontPage bots to be fragile, so I avoid them altogether. I would also uncheck the Documentation box. Then click Next, OK, and Finish until you're out of Add/Remove Programs. One problem that you'll notice if you do this, however, is that all of the custom error pages get deleted from \winnt\help\iishelp\common; before you zap the documentation, copy those files somewhere and then restore the directory.

You will notice that the IIS snap-in still reports a folder for IISAdmin and one for IISDocumentation; delete the folders and they're gone for good. Go ahead and also delete the FrontPage directories—the ones with VTI in their names—as well as the Printers folder to get rid of Web-based printing. In fact, before I start using a newly built IIS system, I just delete everything in wwwroot.

From the IIS snap-in, delete the folders named Printers and IISSamples. If you don't need the database connector, then get rid of the MSADC folder as well.

Disable Unnecessary Services on Your Servers

Just as Microsoft sets its servers up to be Web servers by default, it also sets them up with a bunch of other services as well. You can safely shut down unused services on Web servers or, for that matter, shut them down on *any* server—it saves CPU power and RAM, and closes any potential security holes that those services might contain. Here are some services that you might disable:

- Server service. This isn't a generic service required by all server services; instead, it's just the file and print server service. And while it's true that Web servers are a kind of file server, they do *not* need a working file server service.

- FTP service. If you need this to let Web authors upload content changes, then enable it. But be careful about running anonymous FTP sites; you'd hate to find out that you accidentally let the bad guys store their stuff on your FTP site.

- Simple Mail Transport Protocol. If your Web site doesn't do automated mail-outs, stop this service; SMTP holes have given Unix administrators fits for years.

- Indexing Service. If you aren't using it, stop it. The idea of a service running in the background to index your files so that the bad guys can find them more easily troubles me.

- IIS Admin Service, a potentially useful remote control tool, but also a potential security hole.

- Routing and Remote Access Service

◆ WebDAV. A sort of 21st-century upgrade to FTP server, it lets you do what basically looks like normal file sharing over HTTP. It's far better than FTP, but you have to wonder if it's secure. If you're not using it, get rid of it. (It's off by default.) One way to make sure that it stays off is to deny the Everyone group access to `winnt\system32\inetsrv\httpext.dll`.

But you know which service I'd *really* like to kill? The GUI. It sucks up all kinds of CPU and RAM, but what do I need it for when my Web server is just sitting in the corner waiting for requests? Maybe in Windows 2015, I guess. Here the Linux guys have the right idea.

Consider Disabling Microsoft File and Print Sharing

The same file and print sharing protocols that let you build file/print servers in your organization let you share files and printers over the Internet as well. You might want to disable that service—the Server service. Here's why.

First of all, what is it that you want to secure? I'll assume it is your data. Because you don't want an outside intruder to be able to destroy data on your servers or lock you out of your own network, let's consider this question: How could someone get access to your data?

Assume that you weren't even running a Web or FTP server; just consider what an attacker could do just to a simple file/print server that's exposed to the Internet. Attacks could come in the following forms:

◆ Someone with read access to your files could steal company information.

◆ Someone with write access to your files could modify or delete them.

◆ Someone with write access could use your file servers to store their own personal data—data they might not want to keep on their own computers, perhaps because the data is unlawful to have, like someone else's credit card numbers.

◆ Someone with write access could cripple your servers by filling up their free space with nonsense files, crashing the servers.

◆ Presumably someone could crash your mail servers by sending thousands of automatically generated pieces of mail to the servers. Enough mail messages will fill the hard disks of those servers as well.

◆ Access to your print servers could, again, let intruders fill up the print servers' hard disks with spooled files, as well as cause your printers to run out of paper.

Eliminate Nonessential ISAPI

ISAPI filters are an IIS-specific alternative to scripts and CGI programs. They were introduced back in IIS 2.0, and allow IIS to support some very fast extensions to basic Web functionality, like Active Server Pages.

You can see your system's ISAPI filters from the Home Directory tab. Click the Configuration button and then the App Mappings tab to see the file extensions associated with various ISAPI filters. Now look at the pages on your Web site—if you don't see any files with a given extension, then just delete the reference to that ISAPI filter. Code Red looked for an extension `.IDA`; had the ISAPI filter for IDA not been in place, then the virus would have gotten a Page Not Found, and wouldn't have infected that server.

Detecting Outside Attacks

Windows 2000 comes with some built-in tools to make detecting attacks easier. These do the following:

- ◆ Audit failed logons.

- ◆ Use the Performance Monitor to alert you when logon failures exceed some reasonable value.

- ◆ Periodically log network activity levels. If all of a sudden your network gets really busy at 3 A.M. for no good reason, then look closely into exactly what's going on at 3 A.M.

Deterring Attacks

The main steps to take to deter attacks include the following:

1. Don't use obvious passwords.

2. Don't enable the Guest accounts on Internet-connected machines.

3. Rename the built-in Administrator account.

4. Don't let the built-in Administrator account access the servers over the network.

5. Lock out users after a certain number of failed attempts.

6. Make passwords expire after a certain length of time.

7. Install a firewall to filter out UDP ports 136 and 137, used for Microsoft networking commands such as `net use`.

8. Put the Web, FTP, and gopher servers on a separate machine in its own domain, with no trust links to other domains.

9. Don't put any services on your DNS servers except for DNS.

It seems to me that only by directly accessing your file servers through the normal NET USE interface, via an NFS interface, or through an FTP service would someone be able to read or write data on your computers over the Internet. I'll assume that you're not going to run NFS, that you'll put the FTP server where compromising it won't matter, and that you'll focus on the file server interface.

In a nutshell, here's the scenario that you should worry about. Suppose I know that you have a server named S01 whose IP address is 253.12.12.9 and that it has a share on it named SECRET. I just create an LMHOSTS file with one line in it, like so:

```
253.12.12.9 S01
```

Now I can type **net use X: \\s01\secret**, and my Internet-connected PC sends a request to 253.12.12.9 for access to the share. Assuming the Guest account isn't enabled on S01, then S01 will first ask my PC, "Who are you?" I'll see that as a request for a username and password. When I respond with a valid username and password from the server's domain, I'm in. Actually, this is how I access my network's resources from across the Internet when I'm on a client site—two seconds' work with an LMHOSTS file, a `net use`, and I'm accessing my home directory from thousands of miles away.

To do that, I needed to know:

◆ A valid username on my network

◆ The password for that account

◆ The IP address of a server on the domain

◆ The name of a share on the domain

All right, suppose I want to hack some company with the name bigfirm.com. Where do I start? Step one is to find out what its range of IP addresses is. That's easy. Just telnet to internic.net, type **whois bigfirm.com**, and you'll get the network number and responsible person for that network. (You can alternatively run a Web-based search page with your Web browser; point it to www.internic.net.) You'll also get the IP address of their DNS name servers. The other way to find this information would be to type:

```
nslookup
set type=all
bigfirm.com
```

Bigfirm will dump the names and addresses of their DNS servers and their mail servers. Because there has to be a secondary DNS server to make the InterNIC happy, there will be at least two name servers. Now, bigfirm is probably thinking—the way most of us do—"It doesn't take much CPU power to run a DNS server. Let's put some shared directories there, too."

As Jane Slimeball Hacker, I'm thinking, "Cool—fresh meat."

You see, you've got no choice but to publish two of your IP addresses, the addresses of your DNS server and its backup. So don't put anything else on it. Once, I would suggest to firms that they just run DNS on old, slow machines. That's not an option anymore, as we now need dynamic DNS, which means you're running Windows 2000 on a system and DNS on that system. It's a shame to make a server solely a DNS server, but it might not be a bad idea from a security point of view.

Now suppose you're smart and there's nothing else on the DNS servers. So I have to fish a bit, but that's not hard, as whois told me your range of IP addresses. I'm a slimeball, but I'm a thorough slimeball (after all, I don't have a life, so I've got lots of time), and I'm willing to try all of your IP addresses to find out which ones have servers. There are even, believe it or not, freeware programs for Windows NT and Windows 2000 that will scan a range of IP addresses looking for machines attached to those addresses.

Alternatively, it's a simple matter to create an LMHOSTS file that includes a NetBIOS name for every possible IP address. For example, if I know that you have class C network 200.200.200.0, then I can create an LMHOSTS file with NetBIOS named N1, which equals 200.200.200.1; N2 equals 200.200.200.2, and so on. Then I need only do a net view \\servername for each name from N1 through N254. The IP addresses that have a computer attached to them running the server service will be the ones that challenge me for a name and password. The ones that don't won't respond at all.

What can you do? Not terribly much, except to be sure that the default Administrator accounts on those systems aren't blank—no sense in making things too easy. And it sure offers some incentive for getting rid of your old machines and applications and getting your enterprise off NetBIOS, doesn't it?

Next, I'm looking for a user account name or two. How can I get this? I don't think you can do a NET USER remotely without contacting the domain controller, which means you'll have to have a domain ID and password to get NET USER to work from the outside—whew, that's one less thing to worry about!

But there is a way to find at least some usernames. When a user logs in to a Windows 9*x*, NT, or Windows 2000 machine, the machine registers not only its own machine name on the network, but the user's name as well. It does that so alerts with that name on them can get to the proper user. For example, suppose you've asked the Performance Monitor to alert you in your username of JILL02 if a server gets low on free space. How does the network know where you are?

It's quite simple. When you log in, the Messenger Service—assuming that it's running—registers your username as one of the NetBIOS names attached to your workstation. Assuming you are logged on to a server whose IP address is 200.200.200.200, anyone doing an `nbtstat -A 200.200.200.200` would not only see the computer's name, they'd see your name as well.

So, supposing that someone named paulad was logged in at the 200.200.200.200 machine (that's physically logged in, not connected over the network), a look at the NBTSTAT output would show me that there's a user named paulad who's logged in.

So now I have a username—and probably the username of an administrative account, since paulad is logged in to a server; good news for Joe Hacker. What can you do about that? Disable the Messenger Service, and the name never gets registered. And, by the way, speaking of NBTSTAT, if you run an `nbtstat -A` and the name MSBROWSE shows up, you've found a browse master. There's a good chance that a browse master is a domain controller, right? So maybe it's a good idea to set MaintainServerList=No for the domain controllers; you make that change in `HKLM\System\CurrentControlSet\Services\Browser\Parameters`. Just let the other servers handle the browse master part; you'll remove a clue that a hacker could use. Unfortunately, however, all domain controllers have other names registered to them that pretty much identify them as domain controllers.

Now that I have a username, I need a password. Now that's a problem. Even if I could physically attach my computer to your network, I wouldn't get a password with a network sniffer—NT uses a challenge/response approach to password verification. When you try to log in to an NT domain, the domain controller sends your workstation a random number that your workstation then applies to your password using some kind of hashing function, a mathematical function that produces a number when supplied with two inputs. The result is what gets sent over the network, not the password. (As I said earlier, there is one exception to this rule; when you change your password, the new password does go over the network to the server, but that's pretty rare.)

Where do I get the password? I can do one of two things. First, taking what I know about the user, I can try to guess a password. Second, I can run a program that tries to log in repeatedly, using as passwords every word in the dictionary—this is sometimes known as a dictionary hack.

The defense against this should be obvious. First, don't use easy-to-guess passwords. Use more than one word with a character between it, like fungus#polygon. Second, don't make it easy for people to try a lot of random passwords: Lock them out after five bad tries.

That leads me to a caution about the Administrator account. If you don't have the Resource Kit, you can't lock it out. Windows 2000 Resource Kit contains a utility for locking out the Administrator account. It is called `Passprop.exe`. When enabled, the Administrator account can only be used to log in at the domain controllers, not remotely or over the network.

If you don't have the new Resource Kit, then no matter how many times you try a faulty password, the Administrator account doesn't lock. So if you don't do something about it, all the slimeballs on the Internet can spend all of their free time trying to figure out your Administrator password. What can you do about that?

There are two possibilities. First, rename the account. Don't leave it as Administrator. Second, limit its powers. You cannot delete the Administrator account, nor can you disable it. But you can remove its right to access the server over the network. By removing this right, you force someone with the Administrator password to physically sit down at the server in order to control that server. Unfortunately, that won't be easy, because the ability to log in to a server locally is granted to the Administrators group, and the Administrator account is a member of that group. You aren't allowed to remove the Administrator account from the Administrators group, so all you can do, I suppose, is to remove the entire Administrators group's right. Then just grant the individual administrative accounts the Log On over the Network right. (You'll also have to remove the Everyone group and add user accounts back in one at a time—unfortunately, the Administrator is built into the Domain Users group and can't be removed.)

Now, these measures—disabling Guest, renaming Administrator, removing Administrator's right to log in over the network, locking out repeated penetration attempts, setting Performance Monitor to alert you to excessive failed logon attempts, using well-chosen passwords—may be sufficient, and you've no doubt noticed that they're all options that don't cost a dime. But if you want greater security, then look into a firewall. The firewall doesn't have to do much, but it has one really important job: to filter out two ports on UDP.

UDP (User Datagram Protocol) is the sister protocol to TCP; just as there is a TCP/IP, there is also a UDP/IP. TCP is connection-oriented, whereas UDP is not connection-oriented; it just drops messages on the network like messages in a bottle, hoping that they'll get where they should go. Whenever you execute a Microsoft networking command, such as `net use` or `net view`, you are running an application that sends commands to a server using UDP and UDP port numbers 136 and 137. Ports are software interfaces that are used to identify particular servers; for example, when you send mail from your desktop, you usually use TCP port number 25, and when you receive mail from your desktop, you usually do it on TCP port 110. Web browsers listen on TCP port 80, in another example.

Firewalls are powerful and sometimes complex devices. Once you install them, they have a million setup options and you're likely to wonder if you've caught all the ones you need. Running NetBIOS over IP services happens on UDP ports 136 and 137; tell your firewall to filter those and it's impossible for someone to access normal file server services.

SECURING ACCOUNTS

Since an account is required to perform most actions on a Windows 2000 server, it would make sense that the accounts database should be the first line of security for any publicly connected server. Try starting with the following suggestions to harden your accounts database a bit more:

◆ Set a minimum password length of 8 characters. This one should be pretty straightforward: short passwords = easy to guess, long passwords = harder to guess. On any publicly connected system, a minimum password length of no less than 8 characters should be enforced.

◆ Set a minimum password age of 2 days. Microsoft's secure Web server recommendations call for setting a minimum password age of 2 days. This means that if someone—authorized or not—changes a password, that password cannot be changed again until 48 hours have passed. This is designed to catch situations where an attacker might know a user's password and attempt to change it temporarily for a specific purpose, with the intention of changing it back immediately afterward, going unnoticed.

◆ Set a maximum password age of 42 days. Again, common sense security practices dictate that no password should be kept forever. Therefore, setting a maximum password age of no more than 42 days is a good security precaution. Depending on your specific needs, you could set this to an even shorter interval if necessary.

◆ Keep the last 24 passwords. When used in combination with the maximum and minimum password ages, this prevents anyone from reusing any of the last 24 passwords used for an account. This is designed to defeat a common habit by some administrators of simply flipping back and forth between a few different passwords each time a change is required.

◆ Set an account lockout policy. If I could only make one recommendation for securing a publicly connected system, it would be that there must be an account lockout policy in place. In other words, if x number of invalid login attempts occur within y minutes, then the account should be locked out for a duration of z minutes/hours/days. You can use your own values for x, y, and z, but this is one of the most valuable security precautions you can take!

◆ Require complex passwords. You read how to do this in Chapter 9.

◆ Assign the Deny Access to This Computer from the Network right to the Administrator account. Windows 2000 (and Windows NT for that matter) knows whether an account is logging in from over the network or from the keyboard or mouse (or through a Terminal Services session). If you have physical access to your IIS server whenever you need it, you should strongly consider removing this right from your Administrator account. By default, most any hacker is going to know that Administrator is the default account to go after on any system, so removing this right will make it impossible to connect to the server over the network as the Administrator. This will restrict you to managing your system at the console only (or through a Terminal Server session), but it's a small price to pay for making sure that no one connects to your server over the Internet as Administrator. For more information on granting/revoking user rights, please see Chapter 9.

◆ Rename the Administrator account. As I mentioned in the last paragraph, everyone knows that the Administrator account is the default account on any Windows 2000 Server with the most privileges. Hackers want to "get Admin," so make it more difficult by renaming your Administrator account to something else—maybe something like "God," "root," "Tooth-Fairy," or something equally obscure. Some people have commented to me that this is not useful advice because it's relatively simple to actually find out the default administrator's name, and I'd have to agree that it's easy for a determined hacker to get that information. But there are many attacks that rely on very simply-built scripts or programs, and many of those programs aren't built to be very sophisticated—they assume that your home Web directory is

`Inetpub\wwwroot`, that your administrator is named Administrator, and the like. Renaming the account will slow those guys down.

◆ Create a "bait" Administrator account. If you do decide to rename your Administrator account, an additional step you can take is to create a bait Administrator account on your system. Start by renaming your Administrator account to something else. Then create a new account and call it Administrator. Give it an extremely obscure password, disable the account, and make the account a member of the Guests group only. That way, hackers can spend (and waste) their time hacking away at an Administrator account that won't yield anything if they do get the password.

◆ Disable the Guest account. By default, Windows 2000 Server will disable the default Guest account that is installed. It's worth double-checking this account to make sure that it is still disabled.

SECURING FILE AND PRINT SHARING

By default, Windows 2000 Server assumes that you'd like to enable file and print sharing on each of the interface cards installed in your server. If you have a server with multiple NICs (one for the public Internet and one for your internal network), you can disable file and print sharing on the public interface very easily.

To disable file and print sharing, start up Control Panel/Network and Dial-Up Connections and find the icon for your public interface. Right-click the public interface, then uncheck the box for File and Print Sharing for Microsoft Networks. You can test to make sure this works by mapping to a share on your server before changing this setting and then mapping to a share on your server after changing this setting.

As an additional precaution, you can instruct Windows 2000 Server not to automatically create a C$ share (and D$, E$, etc.) on your system. Again, most people who would try to compromise a server are well aware of the fact that the C$ share exists on most systems and that it's typically the root of the operating system volume. It's the "honey pot," so to speak. For a publicly connected server, no share should exist for the root of a volume!

You could delete the C$ share on your system through the MMC or the command line, but Windows 2000 Server will just re-create it the next time your system starts up. In order to tell Windows 2000 Server to never make that share, you will need to add a registry value called AutoShare-Server in the following registry value:

`HKLM\System\CurrentControlSet\Services\lanmanserver\parameters`

Define the value AutoShareServer, make it a type DWORD with a value of 0, and then reboot your server. The next time it boots, you will not have any of the default administrative shares (C$, D$, E$, etc.).

Just for kicks, if you wanted to try to "decoy" someone who might compromise your system, you could create a separate, fake C$ share on your system after you've instructed Windows 2000 Server that it shouldn't make its own. You could put in decoy `winnt` and `inetpub` directories, and if anyone hacked into your system and accessed the C$ share, they'd simply be hacking at a dummy installation of Windows 2000.

Don't Forget Hazards from Within

Finally, remember that, all too often, the bad guys aren't outside the walls; they're right inside the company with you. Here are a few thoughts to consider about internal attackers.

INTERNAL USERS CAN EASILY GET A LIST OF USER IDs

Earlier in this book, you learned how to configure a set of home directories. First, you create a share called USERS on an NTFS volume, giving the Everyone group or, better, the Domain Users group, full control permissions. Then you set the top-level directory permissions to read and execute, and assign Domain Users no file permissions at all. Users need to read and execute to navigate from the top-level directory to their individual home directories. Then you set the file and directory permissions for each directory to full control for each particular user.

The problem is that there's no way to keep a user from moving up to the top-level directory and seeing the names of all of the users' home directories. Result: Now that user has a list of all of the users' IDs, hacking is made a bit easier.

Additionally, any user on an NT Workstation or Windows 2000 Professional machine can type **net user/domain** and get a list of users in the workstation's domain. Again, these are mainly things you're concerned about for internal users, but inside hacking is probably more prevalent than outside hacking.

INTERNAL USERS CAN EASILY CRASH SHARED VOLUMES

If you haven't enabled disk quotas, any user with write access to a volume can, either accidentally or purposefully, write as much data to a shared volume as the volume can hold. The result is that now there's no space left for other users. Worse yet, if that's the volume that holds the pagefile, then the pagefile can't grow in size, which might crash Windows 2000 altogether.

It wasn't SMB file and print sharing that built the Internet or that builds e-businesses—it was and is the Web. Almost anyone working with servers will find herself the proud administrator of a Web server or two—whether she wanted to be or not. Just a bit of work can make those servers run well and run safely.

Chapter 18

How Running a Big Windows 2000 Network Is Different

THE GOAL OF THIS chapter is to take the Windows 2000 concepts you've learned about so far and expand them beyond one server or workstation to the enterprise. That is, now that you've read about the Active Directory, group policies, sites, and SYSVOL replication, how do the things you know about Windows 2000 change as you start to scale up these services? Indeed, Windows 2000 in general, and the Active Directory in particular, was designed with large enterprises in mind. Given the dizzying array of new infrastructure services, this chapter will cover some of the things you'll need to think about as you scale Windows 2000 in your own environment.

Active Directory Design Issues

As you start to think about how you will deploy Windows 2000 and the Active Directory, your first tasks will be around planning the AD namespace. That is, how many Win2K domains will you have, how many trees, and how many forests? What will be your criteria for adding new domains, trees, and forests? I can't stress enough how important it is to thoroughly plan how you intend to get from your current environment—be it NT 4, NDS, or something else entirely—to an infrastructure based on Windows 2000. This entails not only thinking about the end goal (e.g., I want to consolidate to one domain in the end), but also thinking about how you'll get there, how long it will take, and how you'll accommodate exceptions to your design.

Enterprise Forests

To start with, what are some of the issues you're likely to face as you build a large AD infrastructure? We'll start at the top—with the *forest root*. When you build that first Win2K DC into the first Win2K domain, you're asked if this is the first DC in the domain tree and the first tree in the forest. If you answer yes to both of these questions, you're innocently making some important decisions about the future of your Active Directory.

No matter how many domain trees you add into your forest, this first domain, the forest root, will play a special role in your AD infrastructure. Figure 18.1 shows an example of a forest of two domain trees. Mycompany.com was the first domain in the forest, and so it becomes the forest root. This role remains the same regardless of the fact that the subco.com domain tree is also part of the forest.

FIGURE 18.1

Viewing the forest root in a multi-domain Active Directory forest

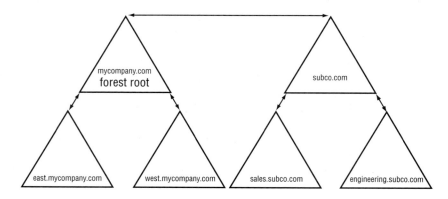

As of the current product, you can't remove or rename the forest root within the Active Directory. Because of its special role, it must remain as is for the life of your forest. Given this, consider using the forest root domain as an "infrastructure container" for your organization. That is, use this domain to house your infrastructure elements only. Build child domains underneath it to keep your business objects, like users, computer, printers, and so on. In the root domain, only keep a handful of enterprise-wide administrators who are authorized to make changes to infrastructure elements such as sites and schema and to add other domain trees.

Modifying the Schema, Merging Forests: Limited Flexibility

Another consideration as you grow your AD environment is the schema. As you know, the *schema* is the structure and relationship of your AD classes and attributes. A default schema ships with Windows 2000, but you can extend it to meet your own needs. Using the Schema AD MMC snap-in, or via the Active Directory Services Interface (ADSI)—a set of APIs for programmatically accessing the Active Directory and other directory services—you're free to add your own classes and attributes to your Active Directory. This idea works well if you have total control of your AD environment, but it presents a problem as your organization expands and contracts. This is because you can currently have only one schema per forest. What this means is that, when you define your forest, the schema in place on that first domain is replicated to all other domains in the tree and all subsequent trees that are made part of the forest.

Now let's take the scenario where either your organization buys a new company or an existing division within your organization has built its own AD infrastructure. In either case, an existing but separate forest would exist, since the acquired company would have been required to build their own forest root when they installed their first AD domain. Furthermore, each of these distinct forests may have had schema changes made to it, making it incompatible with yours. In the current release of Windows 2000, there are no tools available to merge AD forests, or schemas. What this means is that you have two choices. The first option is that you can create explicit nontransitive trust relationships between domains in one forest to allow access to domains in the other (à la NT 4 trusts). In this case, you would maintain multiple forests within your enterprise.

There are advantages and disadvantages to this, but one that should not be underestimated is the fact that there is no good solution for administration of multiple forests. In a single-forest environment, there are two universal groups that have management scope over the entire forest by default—Enterprise Admins and Schema Admins. These two groups only exist in the forest root domain. The Enterprise Admins group is automatically made a member of the local Administrators group in each subsequent child domain in the forest and in each domain tree (if your forest includes multiple domain trees). In a multiple-forest environment, there is no common administrative control. Enterprise Admins from one forest have no control over another forest unless explicitly created via trust relationships.

Another option for dealing with multiple forests is that you can decide which forest will remain, and use Microsoft-provided, or third-party, migration tools to migrate objects from one forest to the other. In the latter case, you would treat the "foreign" forests as if they were downlevel NT 4 domains to be migrated to Win2K domains. Of course, all schema changes made in the foreign forests would be lost as you migrate those objects to your enterprise forest.

Sites

Sites are boundaries of replication for the three naming contexts described in "Replication Issues" later in this chapter. Within a site, replication of these naming contexts is automatic and occurs every five minutes by default. Sites can be created to link groups of subnets that represent a set of high-bandwidth connections. Sites also cross-domain boundaries—you can have two DCs from different domains in the same site. Sites have several roles above that of just controlling replication. For example, you can create group policy objects on sites, allowing you to associate desktop management with a particular network subnet. As your Win2K network grows, maintenance of sites grows. Sites are built manually by you, the administrator. Note that sites can only be defined within the forest root domain. Even though you can load the MMC AD Sites and Services snap-in focused on a child domain controller, you won't be able to define sites there unless you're a member of the Enterprise Admins group or a member of the root domain's Domain Administrators Group. This prevents administrators in child domains from randomly defining sites that could affect your replication topology.

Associated with sites are subnet objects. You must manually define each logical IP subnet within your Active Directory infrastructure and associate those subnets with the appropriate site object. To further complicate matters, you'll need to associate sites that you define to a given site link. Site links let you group sites of equal "cost" from a network perspective. The process of both manually defining sites and site links and manually associating subnets to them can be onerous in a large AD infrastructure. To exacerbate the challenge, each site link (see Figure 18.2) and each NTDS connection object between servers in a single site give you the ability to control the replication schedule.

As you grow your AD infrastructure to hundreds of sites and dozens of site links, the task of maintaining this mass of schedules can quickly become overwhelming. Today, the only tool you have at your disposal to manage sites is the MMC snap-in for AD Sites and Services. It's clear that Microsoft will have to provide a better interface over time for managing sites in large Win2K infrastructures.

FIGURE 18.2

Viewing the replication schedule options on a site link

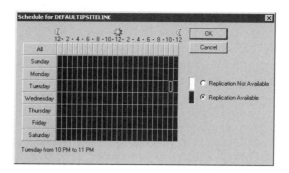

Organizational Units

The point I want to make about organizational units in a large Win2K infrastructure is this: Keep it simple! The fact that OUs exist in the AD and provide a convenient point for delegating administrative control can lead to overuse. Microsoft recommends no more than 10 levels deep of OUs, but frankly, it would be difficult to manage the complexity of such a deep hierarchy. Given the inheritance model within the AD, if you had to manage 10 levels of nested OUs—each with associated security, delegated administration, and group policy objects—you would quickly tear your hair out! The best approach as you grow your AD infrastructure is to start with as flat an OU structure as possible. This means fewer layers. You can always move objects around within a domain later as you find better groupings for users.

Think about the following trade-off: In many cases, you can either group objects by OU or by security group. For example, you could bound a set of users in the finance department either by creating a Finance OU or by creating a Finance security group within a larger OU. The path you take depends upon your goal. By bounding a group of users within an OU, you make it easier to segregate those users for purposes of delegating administration and applying group policies. However, you may find yourself creating extra work if those users get the same group policy as four or five other OUs with similar needs. In that case, you have to either create extra group policy objects or link existing GPOs from another OU to your new one.

By classifying users via security group within a larger, more generic OU structure, you may find it harder to cleanly pick those users out of the crowd when it comes to managing their special needs.

In the end, you will likely choose some combination of OUs and security groups to manage and segregate your users to provide the proper amount of administrative and configuration control.

GPOs

The group policy object is a powerful feature in Win2K, but it's also one that has the highest likelihood of causing you management nightmares as you scale up your infrastructure. This is due in part to the fact that you can define GPOs at so many different levels and in part to the fact that Microsoft provides little if any troubleshooting tools to determine what's going on during GPO processing.

To review, GPOs can be defined at the local machine, site, domain, and OU levels; they are inherited from level to level; and their effects can be filtered via security groups. Additionally, GPOs are only processed by machine or user objects. You can define multiple GPOs at each level of the hierarchy. You can have some GPOs forcibly override others, or conversely, you can prevent overriding of a GPO. Finally, each GPO contains several different *nodes* of functionality, each providing sometimes unrelated control of your users and computers. All of this makes for a potentially complex environment for controlling and managing users and computers via GPOs. So what can you do to keep a handle on GPOs as you benefit from their significant capabilities?

The answer to that is the same as the answer to managing many aspects of your AD infrastructure: Keep it simple. Just because you can define multiple GPOs at multiple levels of your AD hierarchy doesn't mean you should. As an example, each GPO contains multiple nodes of functionality—for example, Software Installation, Security, Logon/Logoff Scripts, Folder Redirection, Administrative Templates, and so on. It makes logical sense to group some of these nodes in one GPO. For example, you might define a "security" GPO that only employs the user and computer security options. In this way, you can easily delegate administration of that GPO to your security folks and be assured that they won't accidentally modify a software installation setting that unpublishes Microsoft Word for the whole enterprise.

Similarly, in addition to defining single- or limited-function GPOs, consider limiting the number of GPOs defined at the site, domain, and OU levels. Define domain-level GPOs only for policies that must have an impact on the whole domain, such as security. Leave software installation or administrative template policy to OUs. The benefits to this strategy will become apparent as you begin to think about Resultant Set of Policy (RSOP). RSOP is basically the effective policy on a given user or computer within a given container in your AD infrastructure. It means, for user x on computer y, "Tell me what my effective policy is when I log in." Microsoft will provide little or no help in this area out of the box. However, some third-party ISVs like FullArmor (`www.fullarmor.com`) provide RSOP tools to help you manage your GPO deployment. Consider obtaining these tools if you plan to deploy GPOs in any significant way in Win2K.

Another consideration is the time it takes to process GPOs at user logon or machine startup. The more GPOs a user or computer has to process, the more delay there will be in startup or logon. This is especially noticeable at user logon time, since GPOs normally process prior to the user's shell loading. You can modify this behavior via an administrative template policy, but in many cases, you won't want to. Given this behavior, it's important to do what you can to minimize the processing time of GPOs.

Microsoft has attempted to streamline the processing of GPOs in a couple of ways. First, they give you the option of disabling either the computer or user configuration settings in a particular GPO. If you've defined a GPO that only sets policy on one or the other, it's a good idea to check the box in the Group Policy property page to disable processing for that part of the GPO. This reduces the time it takes to process the GPO significantly. Additionally, GPO version will be tracked at each processing. If no changes have occurred from one logon or machine startup to the next, then the GPO will not be processed. There's an administrative template available to override this behavior, but it will add to the processing time significantly.

Modifying GPOs

One more point to consider when deploying GPOs: Because GPOs are yet another object in the Active Directory, they are subject to the same multimaster replication processes as other AD objects. Therefore, it is possible to have two people editing the same GPO at the same time. The results, of course, could be disastrous if two people make changes that cancel each other out on replication. To prevent this scenario, the Group Policy snap-in by default will always focus on the DC that currently has the PDC role within a given AD domain to edit GPOs. You can see this by selecting the View menu option while highlighting a GPO from the Group Policy MMC snap-in. You will see an option called DC Options. Figure 18.3 shows an example of the choices you have for focusing the Group Policy snap-in, with the default choice shown here.

FIGURE 18.3

Viewing the options for focusing group policy object editing

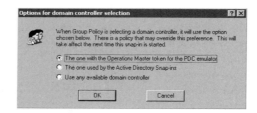

Leaving this option at the default will ensure that GPO changes are always made at the same server and reduce the chance that two people will be editing a GPO on two different DCs.

Replication Issues

Replication of various parts of the Win2K infrastructure has a big impact on reliability and availability as you scale your environment. Replication of the Active Directory, the global catalog, SYSVOL data, and Dfs can all have an impact on performance, availability, and the user experience. In this section, I'll discuss some of the main challenges you'll encounter when deploying these various services.

First, however, I want to review the concept of *naming contexts*. Win2K has three naming contexts that are replicated in a well-known way: domain, schema, and configuration. You can think of naming contexts as replication paths or loops through your Win2K environment. The domain-naming context is the replication path that only traverses domain controllers within a single domain. It is responsible for replicating changes to the Active Directory database for a given domain. The schema-naming context is responsible for replicating schema changes across the entire forest, and the configuration-naming context holds information related to replication topology and is also replicated across the entire forest.

When you define sites and site links, you're basically defining the replication topology for these three naming contexts. In addition, Win2K itself, through the Knowledge Consistency Checker (KCC) process, will define *DS connection objects* between specific DCs within your forest to fill in the details of who replicates to whom and how often. This replication topology can become very complex. Using tools such as `repadmin.exe` from the Win2K Resource Kit for diagnosing replication problems and ReplMon (also from the Resource Kit) for monitoring and manually triggering replication across DCs will go a long way toward making replication management in Win2K something less than a black art.

SYSVOL

SYSVOL, as you know, is the successor to the NETLOGON share from NT 4. In Win2K, as in NT 4, the SYSVOL share is replicated to all DCs in a domain. Under SYSVOL resides most of the data associated with GPOs, as well as any legacy NETLOGON information for your downlevel

NT 4 and Windows 9*x* devices. SYSVOL uses the new NT File Replication Service (FRS) to replicate content between all DCs in a domain. FRS replicates, by default, on the same schedule as the Active Directory, and respects site boundaries just as AD replication does.

You can change FRS's replication schedule. From the AD Users and Computers snap-in, choose the View/Advanced Features option and drill down into the System/File Replication Service feature. From there, if you highlight the Domain System Volume (SYSVOL share), right-click, choose Properties from the context menu, and then choose the Change Schedule button, you can adjust when SYSVOL replication can take place during the day. This means that, given the normal site replication schedule, you can block out hours during the day where SYSVOL replication will not happen. You should use this option sparingly, since your SYSVOL and Active Directory could easily get out of sync if you modify one and not the other. Remember that intersite replication will take longer than intrasite replication, so, for example, if you've added a new logon script to a GPO that is focused on a particular DC, then it may take a while for that script to replicate to all associated SYSVOL shares on all DCs within the domain.

Dfs

Dfs, or Distributed File System, presents a separate but important set of challenges from SYSVOL. Let's review some of the capabilities of Dfs in Win2K to see how you might get in trouble deploying it in a large infrastructure.

Dfs gives you the ability to define fault-tolerant (FT) root shares within a given domain. Note that you can only define one FT root per server. FT roots are referred to by the domain name rather than by a server name. For example, I could map a drive to the share \\us.mycompany.com\dfsroot. Underneath a particular Dfs root is any number of Dfs links. Dfs links appear as logical subdirectories to the Dfs root but physically point to any number of shares located on other servers (Win2K, NT 4, and even NetWare and Unix file systems) in your environment. Each Dfs link can have a replica associated with it as well. For example, under my fictitious dfsroot share, I might have a Dfs link called apps where I keep all of my application setup packages.

Under each Dfs link, I can add replica members. These represent shares on other servers where the same content is available. For example, my Dfs link called apps may have two replica members— shares called apps on \\servera and \\serverb. Replica members are normally used when you have some read-only content, like application binaries, that you wish to make available from more than one server. In this example, suppose servera exists in Site X and serverb exists in Site Y. Clients in Site X connecting to the Dfs share \\mycompany.com\dfsroot\apps would be redirected to \\servera\apps, and clients in Site Y would be redirected to \\serverb\apps. Thus Dfs provides some level of server affinity based on site topology.

Another feature of Dfs is to provide the file replication to all of those replica members. Dfs replication actually uses the NT File Replication Service but creates its own replication topology, which you have no control over. By default, Dfs creates a star topology between all replica members that you designate. There is also no easy way to tell when Dfs replicas have "converged" (all content changes have been replicated to all replicas). For large networks with many different replica members located across varying WAN links, you're likely to find Dfs replication inadequate. The replication available in Dfs is really meant for smaller networks where read-only content is replicated across a few servers. In fact, if you choose to use the automatic replication available in Dfs, you are limited to 256 replica members per child node. However, if, when you create Dfs links, you choose the manual replication option, you can safely support up to 1000 replica members. Note that by choosing manual replication, you are saying to Dfs that you plan to provide your own mechanisms for replicating content to each replica member—outside of the Dfs infrastructure.

You may even be tempted to use Dfs replication to replicate data that is not read-only, such as users' home folders. The current incarnation of Dfs is not really suited to this kind of approach. This is principally because you really have no control over when Dfs will "converge" replicas. As a result, if a user manages to make changes to his home folder on two different replica members before those changes have propagated, you could get into a situation where changes are getting lost. With Dfs, your best approach is to simply use the fault-tolerant feature as a way of abstracting physical location from logical share names. Let Dfs create a distributed file tree that is sensitive to site topology. If you must use Dfs replication, stick to read-only content, or purchase some other near-real-time replication software to do the actual content replication.

How GPO Replication Is Different and Special

I want to mention the special case of GPOs and how they replicate within your Win2K infrastructure. This behavior can become a major issue in larger environments with many GPOs deployed across sites with varying WAN link speeds. To review, group policy objects are actually composed of two elements. The Group Policy Container (GPC) is an object within the Active Directory that stores the reference to a particular GPO. The GPC is replicated just as other AD objects are, in a multimaster fashion, on a per-property basis. The other element of a GPO is the Group Policy Template (GPT). The GPT is really the guts of the GPO. It's the physical files that make up a GPO. Things like shutdown and startup scripts, logon and logoff scripts, administrative templates and the resulting `registry.pol` file, and security templates are kept in the GPT, which is replicated within the SYSVOL share.

Given the fact that these two elements are distinct entities with potentially different replication behavior, there exists the possibility that a GPC will replicate before its associated GPT does. What this means is that a user or computer could start processing a GPO before all of it has been replicated around the infrastructure. To prevent this from happening, it's a good idea to disable a particular GPO prior to editing it, make the changes, give them time to propagate, and then enable it again. To disable a particular GPO, load the AD Users and Computers MMC snap-in (or the AD Sites and Services snap-in if it's a site-based GPO). Focus on the container (site, domain, or OU) where the GPO resides, right-click, and choose Properties from the context menu. Select the Group Policy tab, highlight the GPO of interest, and choose the Options button. From there, you can disable or enable the GPO.

Deploying Infrastructure Services

When you're ready to start deploying a large-scale Win2K infrastructure, there are several services that you need to provide to enable proper functioning of the Active Directory and your Win2K clients. Domain Name System (DNS) and the global catalog are two such infrastructure services that are critical to the proper functioning of your Win2K environment. In this section, I'll discuss some of the challenges of deploying these services in a robust way and make some recommendations to ensure that they remain highly available.

DNS

As you know, the use of Domain Name System (DNS) is all-important in Windows 2000. It replaces WINS as the name service of choice for Win2K devices. It also serves a crucial role in the registration of special service (SRV) records related to locating Active Directory domain controllers and services such as authentication, Lightweight Directory Access Protocol (LDAP), and the global catalog. Therefore, when designing your Active Directory deployment, you'll need to put quite a bit of thought into how you'll make DNS services highly available across your network.

Remember that you can create three kinds of zones in Windows 2000. The first type, standard primary, works just like NT 4 or Unix-based DNS servers, where the zone files are kept in a text file and replication between servers is single-master based. That is, for a given zone, the server that is primary for that zone originates all changes, and those changes are replicated to standard secondary zones in a process called a *zone transfer*. This replication is one-way and can only originate from the primary. In this configuration, you could potentially have a Win2K DNS server serving as the primary for a zone that replicates to both Win2K- and Unix-based secondary DNS servers.

The second type of zone is the standard secondary, to which I've already referred. Creating this type of zone indicates that you've already defined a primary somewhere and you wish to add another replica server to it.

The third type of zone is one that is integrated into the Active Directory. An AD-integrated zone is just as it sounds. The zone file and all its records are actually stored in the Active Directory. More importantly, they are replicated from domain controller to domain controller using the same multi-master replication schedule as other directory objects. This means that the whole idea of one-way zone transfers goes away. It also means that, if you have an AD-integrated zone, you'll need to run the actual DNS service on a domain controller so it can find those zone files. There's no support for running DNS on a standard member server if you integrate your zones with the AD. So, when it comes time to add a new DNS server to your network, you simply install the DNS service on a DC, point your clients to it, and you're in business. AD-integrated zones also support the concept of incremental zone transfers. When an older-style DNS implementation needs to update secondary zones, it copies the whole of the primary zone to the secondaries regardless of whether one or one hundred records have changed since the last update. Incremental zone transfers allow a DNS implementation to update only those records that have changed since the last update. Win2K DNS supports incremental zone transfers for both AD-integrated and non-AD-integrated zones.

Earlier in this chapter, I talked about how the AD uses three naming contexts to scope replication of data. The domain-naming context replicates AD object data, and its scope is only within a single domain. If you choose to use AD-integrated zones for DNS data, then this DNS zone information is replicated using the domain-naming context. As such, AD-integrated DNS data does not replicate across domain boundaries. What this means for your DNS design is that, if you plan to have multiple domains and want to use AD-integrated zones, you'll need to either run all of your DNS servers within a single domain or have separate zones for each part of your DNS namespace—each within its own domain.

As an example, suppose you have an AD domain tree composed of mycompany.com as the root domain and usa.mycompany.com as a child domain. You may choose one of two options. In the first option, DCs in mycompany.com could host the AD-integrated zones for both mycompany.com and usa.mycompany.com. In the second option, DCs in mycompany.com could host only the zone for mycompany.com. DCs in usa.mycompany.com could then host the usa.mycompany.com zone exclusively and forward requests to servers in the root for mycompany.com. The advantage of the first scenario is that, if you place all of your DNS servers within the root domain, you can effectively isolate administration of them to DNS administrators within the root, preventing administrators in child domains from easily tampering with them.

PLACING DNS SERVERS

When it comes time to decide where to place DNS servers—be they DCs running AD-integrated zones or just member servers with standard primary or secondary zone files—you should think about this service the way you think about placing WINS servers in NT 4 today. To that end, you want your DNS servers to be highly available but not overly deployed. Remember that in Win2K, as in NT 4, client DNS resolvers cache name resolution requests to either WINS or DNS. This caching behavior reduces the frequency that a client needs to talk with a DNS server and therefore reduces concerns about name resolution traffic on the network. As such, you don't need to necessarily keep DNS servers physically close to your client segments.

This is helpful if you choose to deploy AD-integrated DNS servers in a multidomain environment where all your DNS servers reside in the root domain but your workstations reside in some child domain. For example, if you have several branch offices with workstations and servers residing in the child domain, you might consider deploying a DC from the child domain in the branch office to provide local authentication. However, if your DNS servers were located on DCs in the root domain only and your plan was to deploy a DNS server in every branch office, then you would face the requirement of deploying two DCs per branch office to achieve your result—possible, but perhaps not practical or cost effective. In that case, it probably makes more sense to keep only a few centrally located and managed DNS servers. The ultimate decision comes down to how often your clients need name resolution services, what kind of bandwidth is available between server and client, and how tolerant your client applications are of name resolution problems.

A final point to take into consideration when placing DNS servers is that clients will be unable to authenticate to your AD domain if they're unable to locate a global catalog server. This behavior can be modified to disable the requirement that a GC be available to logon. However, if you disable the GC requirement, membership in universal groups will not be available. This means that a user who is a member of universal group that has rights to a resource will not be able to get to that resource if the global catalog is unavailable. The ability to locate a GC server is in part related to how and where you place your GC servers, but it also depends on the availability of a special record within DNS. SRV resource records that point to GC servers are only stored in the DNS zone for your forest root domain under _msdcs.gc.

Global Catalog Servers

If you remember, the global catalog (GC) contains a special view of your AD infrastructure. The GC is a service that runs on select DCs within your AD forest. It contains an instance of every object within a forest—and a small subset of those objects' attributes—and is used as a quick index for searching for objects within the directory. Because the GC replicates across the entire forest rather than just within domain boundaries, it also contains any universal groups that you have defined for the forest and the members of those groups as well. This is a feature unique to universal groups and the GC. Local and domain groups are enumerated in the GC, but their membership is not stored there. It's important to keep this in mind as you build universal groups. The larger the number of universal groups you define, and the more members they contain, the larger the amount of data that will have to be replicated to all GC servers.

Remember that GC replication occurs in addition to any AD replication that goes on between DCs. This means that the amount of GC data replicating around your network becomes a function of the amount of data within the GC as well as how many servers you've designated as GC servers.

GC SERVER PLACEMENT

So, we've established that the GC plays a critical role in the proper operation of your AD infrastructure for several reasons. First, you must have a GC server available to your Win2K clients in order for them to be able to authenticate to the domain. Next, the GC holds important information about the objects in your forest and allows clients to query that information without having to go directly to the domain and server where those objects are stored. Given these roles, it's important to think about GC server placement as you roll out your infrastructure. Just as with DNS, GC servers should be highly available but not overly deployed. Too many GC servers means too much data replicating around your network. The extreme case is where every DC in your forest is also a GC server. This is generally unnecessary.

However, you might consider the method clients use to locate GC servers via DNS as a way of driving GC placement decisions on your network. That is, a client will first look for a GC server within its own site. This helps keep GC as well as authentication traffic local to the site. So, start by placing a GC server in each site—if you have a DC in a particular site, make it a GC server as well.

You can define a DC as a global catalog server from the Sites and Services MMC snap-in. Select the site where your server resides, open the Servers folder, and select the server you wish to make a GC server. Under the server, right-click the NTDS Settings container, choose Properties, and check the box to enable the GC service (see Figure 18.4).

FIGURE 18.4

Viewing the dialog within the Sites and Services snap-in for enabling the GC service

If you have more than one DC in a site and it's a large site, you might want to create a second GC server to share the load among clients within that site. Remember also that GCs span domains. You don't necessarily need a GC running on the DC in every domain. The goal is to have at least one GC in every site that has a DC.

Operations Masters

When Win2K (nee NT 5) was first announced, much ado was made about the fact that the primary domain controller (PDC) of NT 4 days went away—that changes could be made from any domain controller in your AD domain. This is only partly true in the Win2K infrastructure. The PDC role has actually been replaced and augmented in Win2K with five distinct roles, termed *operations masters* (previously called FSMO, or Floating Single Master Operation). Each operations master role must reside on a single server within a given context (your enterprise forest or per domain) and must be manually moved or changed in the event that a server holding that role becomes unavailable. The roles are as follows:

Domain Naming   The domain-naming role resides on a single server throughout the *forest* and is responsible for ensuring unique domain names. Defined in the Domains and Trusts MMC snap-in.

Schema   The schema role resides on a single server throughout the *forest*. Given the invasive nature of schema changes, it makes sense that only one server at a time be allowed to make the change, and this is the role of the schema master. Defined in the AD Schema MMC snap-in.

PDC   The primary domain controller role resides on a single server *per domain*. It is intended to provide downlevel (NT 4) backup domain controllers that reside in a Win2K domain with a PDC for backward compatibility. It's also used by the Group Policy snap-in as the default location for making changes to group policies.

RID Pool   The relative identifier (RID) pool role resides on a single server *per domain*. A RID is a sequential number assigned to any new object that is created in an AD domain. Since AD uses multimaster replication, there needs to be a way of ensuring that each DC that can create new objects does not overlap RID assignments from other DCs. The RID pool role ensures this by allocating and tracking a pool of RIDs for each DC.

Infrastructure   The infrastructure role resides on a single server *per domain* and has responsibility for maintaining interdomain consistency between AD objects—specifically for those objects that cross domain boundaries, such as sites, GC, and replication topology.

By default, each of the three domain-specific roles will reside on the first DC you build in your first domain (or child domain). In fact, all five roles will exist on the first DC you build in a new forest. For redundancy, you should plan to move at least the PDC role to a server that is separate from the other two domain roles. This ensures that failure in one will not result in failure of some critical function dependent upon these roles (e.g., the ability to create new users from NT 4). Additionally, it's probably a good idea, once you have some more DCs in your environment, to move the other roles to servers that are highly reliable and well controlled. You don't have to put each of the five roles on a separate server, but neither should you have them all on a single server. Microsoft also recommends having the PDC and infrastructure roles on separate DCs.

Domain Migration Strategies and Downlevel Coexistence

There are many issues to consider as you plan for migration of your existing NT infrastructure to Win2K. Indeed, a whole book could be written on the topic. In this section, I'll discuss some of the options you have for migration and some of the caveats as you begin to migrate to Win2K.

Migration Options

Microsoft really only provides one option out of the box for you to move your existing NT 4 domains to Win2K. That option is in-place upgrade. That is, starting with the PDC in one of your master domains, begin to upgrade DCs, servers, and workstations one by one until you're finished, then move on to the next domain. As you migrate domains into Win2K, you can use tools like Movetree and SIDWalker to consolidate domains—moving objects from many converted domains into fewer domains at your own speed. As you can imagine, this won't work for everyone. As a result, you have a couple of different options, provided by third-party vendors and Microsoft, to migrate users and computers more slowly.

The first class of tools, from vendors like BindView (`www.bindview.com`), FastLane Technologies (`www.fastlanetech.com`), and NetIQ (`www.netiq.com`), lets you take groups of users or computers defined in your NT 4 domains and re-create them in Win2K domains. The re-created accounts and groups will have, of course, lost their associated security IDs (SIDs). To get around that issue, these tools also ferret out file, printer, and other resources that were owned by the old user accounts and append an access control entry to the access control list (ACL) on each of those resources pointing to the new account. This approach not only provides a more controlled migration to Win2K, but also provides a back-out strategy, since the old accounts are usually left in place until you choose to remove them.

Another available method for migrating domains is the ability to clone a *security principal*—either a user or group. In this scenario, a user or group SID from an NT 4 account is actually placed in the SIDHistory property of the associated new Win2K group or user account, thereby providing access to resources by that Win2K user or group account without having to re-ACL those resources up front. There are tools, from Microsoft (in the Resource Kit) or the third-party vendors mentioned earlier, that use this cloning capability. (See Chapter 8 for more on the SID History options, as part of the Active Directory Migration tool.)

Downlevel Coexistence

If you have a decent-sized NT 4 infrastructure today, it's likely you'll be in a mixed NT 4/Win2K environment for some time. This is generally well supported in Win2K, but there are a couple of things to keep in mind in this kind of environment. If you remember, a Win2K domain can exist in two different modes—Mixed and Native. In Mixed mode, NT 4 backup domain controllers can still be added to your environment alongside Win2K DCs. In Mixed mode, some features within Win2K are disabled, including the use of universal security groups and group nesting.

Once you switch a domain to Native mode, these advanced features are enabled, but you can no longer add NT 4 BDCs to the domain (of course, you can still have NT 4 workstations and member servers in a Native-mode domain).

Another facet of living in a mixed environment is the challenge of management across both versions. For the most part, you can use Win2K MMC snap-ins to manage NT 4 services such as

WINS, DNS, DHCP, IIS, and others. However, the AD Users and Computers snap-in does not provide User Manager or Server Manager functionality over NT 4 domains. In that case, you'll still need to use these downlevel tools on your NT 4 or Win2K administrative workstations to manage NT 4 domains. (Again, see Chapter 8 for details on Win2K-friendly versions of these tools.)

In this chapter, we looked at some of the issues related to designing your Win2K infrastructure for a large enterprise, including the limitations of multiple forests and the schema. We examined how AD elements such as sites, OUs, and GPOs must be thought about differently as you scale them up—with a eye toward simplicity. We looked at some of the benefits and limitations of replication of objects like the SYSVOL share, Dfs, and GPOs and how to not get in trouble using these services. We looked at considerations for placing infrastructure services such as DNS, global catalog servers, and operations masters. Finally, we examined some of the options for migrating from NT 4 infrastructure to Win2K, focusing on some of the options other than in-place upgrade that you'll be able to choose from when you're ready to migrate.

Chapter 19

Integrating NetWare with Windows 2000 Server

LESS THAN A DECADE AGO, one company—Novell—owned a majority of the network operating system market. NetWare, in its various versions, reportedly enjoyed market share rates that reached into the 70 percent range. Chances were good that if you had a network in your office, Novell was the platform it was running on.

As is true with much of life, nothing lasts forever. When Microsoft came along with Windows NT, they began to—quite frankly—eat Novell's lunch in the NOS market. However, even though Microsoft was making inroads into organizations with NT, often those organizations weren't in a position to simply toss their existing Novell equipment out the window. Due to this fact, cross-platform integration became a key issue with both operating systems. As a result of this, Microsoft has included a wide variety of options for integrating Windows 2000 Server and NetWare.

Integration versus Migration

When integrating NetWare and Windows 2000 networks, a key decision will be involved very early in the design process: *migrate* or *integrate*? But no matter whether you decide to migrate to Windows 2000 and get rid of NetWare completely or integrate both networks together so that users can reach resources on both systems, Microsoft has included the tools you'll need to get the job done.

Integration

As is the case in many environments, legacy applications and systems have a tendency to just stick around. Although the year 2000 bug forced many organizations to replace outdated systems with newer ones, many legacy systems and applications still exist in the networking world, and will be sticking around for a while longer. Novell NetWare servers often fall into this category of "legacy systems."

Even if you have NetWare servers that you need to connect to that aren't necessarily considered legacy systems, Microsoft has a complete set of tools to allow for a high level of integration between Microsoft and Novell networks. These tools include the following:

IPX/SPX (NWLink) Protocol Support   Although newer releases of NetWare support the TCP/IP protocol natively, earlier versions only supported one protocol stack—IPX (Internetwork Packet Exchange) and SPX (Sequenced Packet Exchange). To successfully communicate with older NetWare servers, you will need to use this protocol (it is not installed in Windows 2000 by default).

Gateway (and Client) Service for NetWare   A wonderful little utility that allows a Windows 2000 server to attach to a NetWare server, access file and print resources on the server, and share them to its own clients as if they were hosted directly on the Windows 2000 box itself. The Gateway Service for NetWare (GSNW for short) is primarily useful for keeping only one client stack loaded on your workstations—the Microsoft networking client.

File and Print Services for NetWare networks   An optional tool (it doesn't come with Windows 2000 Server) that you can use if you would prefer to have your Windows 2000 server share its resources with NetWare clients. File and Print Services for NetWare (FPNW for short) will let your Windows 2000 Server act as if it were a NetWare server. Workstations with nothing other than a NetWare client loaded on them will be able to access resources on a Windows 2000 server running FPNW.

Migration

For some organizations, retiring NetWare systems and completely migrating to Windows 2000 is the way to go. For these instances, Microsoft has included the Directory Services Migration Tool to make that job easier.

The Directory Services Migration Tool (DSMT for short) is a great utility that will let you connect to an NDS- or a bindery-based NetWare network and import all the users, files, and security settings from the target system. The DSMT will let you do these migrations across the wire, so that you don't have to worry about accidentally destroying data on your Novell systems. You can import all of the information from the target server(s); model, rearrange, and manipulate it as necessary; and then apply the information to your Windows 2000 server.

Running the DSMT depends on having the Gateway (and Client) Service for NetWare installed on your server, and optionally the NWLink protocol for IPX support (if IPX-only servers will be migrated). Since migration will depend on these items, let's get started with installing the basic components you'll need—IPX (NWLink) and GSNW.

Getting Started

Before starting a process to migrate from or integrate with an existing NetWare network, you will need to have a few things in place no matter what you are doing. First, you will need a compatible set of protocols so that your two networks can talk to each other. Secondly, you will need the Gateway Service for NetWare components installed on any servers that need to talk to Novell systems.

Adding Protocol Support

Protocol support should be relatively straightforward, since NetWare generally only speaks two languages—IP and IPX. NetWare's native tongue is IPX, so you will find it to be the primary protocol in most NetWare 3.*x* and early 4.*x* networks. Servers running intraNetWare and later versions of NetWare could be running IPX, IP, or both protocols. In any case, load the appropriate protocols on your system so that your servers can speak with each other. Also, if you plan on running File and Print Services for NetWare, you will need to make sure that your Windows 2000 server has the same protocol loaded that your NetWare clients will be using.

If you will be installing NWLink on your Windows 2000 server in order to use IPX when communicating with NetWare systems, you may need to know the frame type used by your NetWare servers and an appropriate network address to use, if any. To add the NWLink IPX/SPX/NetBIOS protocol to your server, start by choosing Start/Settings/Control Panel and launching the Network and Dial-Up Connections icon. This will bring you to a listing of any and all network connections installed on your system—either local area or dial-up. Find the appropriate icon for the local area network connection that you will use to connect to your NetWare servers, and then edit its properties by right-clicking the icon and selecting Properties. The network properties for your LAN adapter should look similar to Figure 19.1.

FIGURE 19.1

Editing local area connection properties

As you can see from the dialog box shown in Figure 19.1, this is a local area network connection that only has TCP/IP installed on it. To add support for NWLink IPX/SPX/NetBIOS compatible transport, click the Install button and, in the dialog box that comes up, select Protocol. Clicking the Add button will take you to a listing of protocols that you can select from, shown in Figure 19.2.

FIGURE 19.2

Choosing a protocol
to add

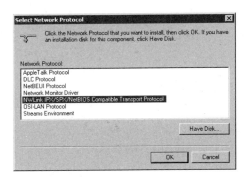

Select NWLink IPX/SPX/NetBIOS Compatible Transport Protocol from the list of supported protocols, and then click OK. Windows 2000 will add support for this protocol to the local area network adapter.

In many instances, the defaults that Windows 2000 Server will apply to the NWLink protocol will be acceptable. However, if your situation requires fine-tuning this protocol for your network environment, edit the parameters for this protocol by highlighting it on the Local Area Connection Properties page and then clicking the Properties button. This will take you to a dialog box similar to the one shown in Figure 19.3.

FIGURE 19.3

Editing NWLink
properties

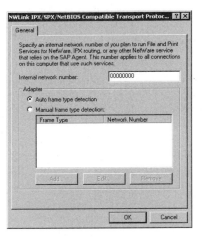

Through this dialog box, you can enter internal IPX network information and framing types to use. If you intend to have this Windows 2000 server offer services to NetWare clients (file, print, routing, etc.), enter an internal IPX network number in the field at the top of the dialog box. Make sure to use a network number that is *not* in use by any other NetWare servers on your network. Secondly, if you would like to manually configure the framing type for Windows 2000 Server to use for IPX packets, choose the Manual Frame Type Detection radio button and then click the Add button. NetWare servers running version 3.11 and earlier typically use an Ethernet 802.3 framing type, and all newer NetWare servers usually default to Ethernet 802.2 framing. Enter the appropriate framing information and IPX network numbers in the fields provided, and then click OK.

If you will be using TCP/IP to communicate with your NetWare servers, you will need to know an appropriate IP address, subnet mask, and default gateway to use for communicating with your systems. Your TCP/IP configuration on your Windows 2000 server will need to reflect those settings in order to communicate properly.

NOTE *TCP/IP should be installed on your system as an operating system default, but if it has been removed from your system for whatever reason, please see Chapter 6 for further details on installing TCP/IP.*

Adding Client Support

The next step in accessing NetWare networks is to add the necessary client support to your system. The steps for this are quite similar to adding IPX protocol support. Start from the properties page for your local area network adapter; click the Install button and select Client from the dialog box that comes up. This will bring you to a list of additional client software similar to the one shown in Figure 19.4.

FIGURE 19.4

Adding client software

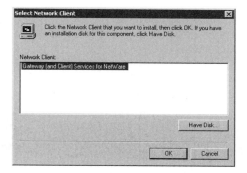

Select Gateway (and Client) Services for NetWare and then click OK to continue. Windows 2000 will require a reboot, and then the next time you log in, you will be taken to a configuration dialog box like the one shown in Figure 19.5.

FIGURE 19.5

Configuring the NetWare client

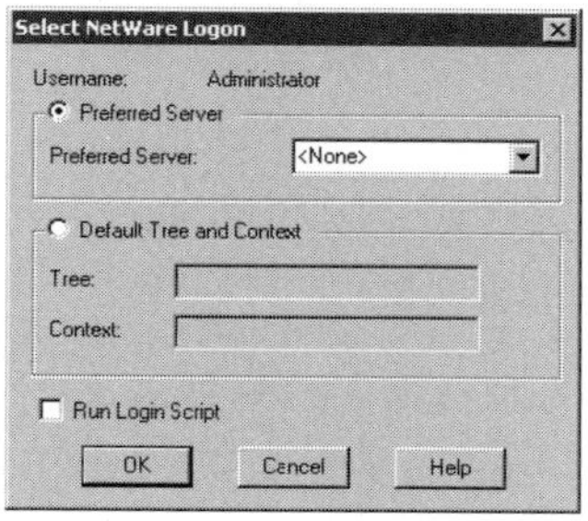

Depending on the NetWare systems you are trying to connect to, the way you configure the Select NetWare Logon dialog box will change accordingly. This dialog box will determine which server you will log into by default, or where in an NDS tree you will log in. If you plan on connecting to NetWare resources on NDS-aware servers, select the radio button for setting a Default Tree and Context and enter the appropriate tree and context information for the user account you intend to use for this system. If you will be connecting to bindery-based NetWare servers (or NDS-aware servers running bindery emulation), select the radio button for setting a Preferred Server and enter the name of the server in the data-entry field.

Lastly, if you want your Windows 2000 server to execute any NetWare login scripts during the logon process, check the Run Login Script check box. Click OK when you are finished, and the Gateway (and Client) Service for NetWare should now be installed and selected for your local area network adapter.

Verifying Client Connectivity

Once you have added the necessary client support for accessing NetWare resources, you should be able to test your configuration by opening a command prompt and typing **net view /network:nw**. If your connectivity is configured correctly, you will see a listing of NetWare servers on your network.

Try to connect to one of your NetWare servers via the Windows 2000 Explorer interface. Double-click My Network Places and then select the Entire Network option; you should have icons available to explore either the Microsoft Windows networks or NetWare networks.

Double-clicking NetWare or Compatible Networks will bring you to a window like the one shown in Figure 19.6, where you should be able to see all of your NDS trees and servers.

FIGURE 19.6

Browsing NetWare directories and servers

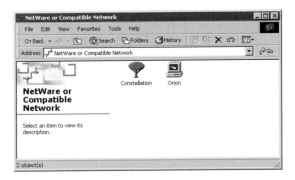

As you can see in Figure 19.6, my test network has an NDS tree called Constellation and a server called Orion. Clicking on NDS tree resources or server resources should take you further through your NetWare network. If you are having difficulty connecting to resources at this point, stop here and take the time to troubleshoot the problem before continuing, since most everything else relies on these services. Make sure that you check for proper usernames, context, passwords, etc.

Integrating NetWare and Windows 2000 Server

Now that you (presumably) have the appropriate protocol and client loaded to talk to NetWare servers, you are ready to begin integrating these two platforms together. Before beginning, however, it is important to ask yourself who will be accessing resources on which system.

Will workstations configured for Microsoft networking need to access resources on NetWare servers? If so, you have two main options for integrating these two platforms. The first option is to load a separate client stack for each platform on all of your workstations (not a desirable option in most circumstances), so that each workstation can talk directly with each server. This adds memory overhead to your client workstations, not to mention the amount of time it takes to visit every desktop to configure an additional client stack. It also potentially requires that users remember two separate logins—one for the Microsoft network, and one for the Novell network.

The second—and preferable—option for letting Microsoft networking workstations access NetWare resources is to let your Windows 2000 server act as a sort of "NetWare proxy" by configuring the gateway portion of GSNW. Your Windows 2000 server can then accept requests for NetWare-based data on behalf of the workstations, retrieve the data from the target servers, and then pass it directly back to the user. As far as the end user is concerned, they are simply accessing another shared resource on a Windows 2000 server—NetWare resources will look identical to Windows 2000 resources.

If you have NetWare clients that will need to access resources on a Windows 2000 server, your options are similar. The first option is again to load a separate client stack for each platform on all of your workstations so that each workstation can talk directly with each server. Just like before, this requires a significant amount of memory overhead on your client workstations, and usually a visit to every desktop to configure the client—not a desirable option in most circumstances.

Instead, you can have properly configured NetWare clients access resources directly on Windows 2000 servers by configuring File and Print Services for NetWare on your server. To NetWare clients on your network, your Windows 2000 server will appear to be just another NetWare server available on the network. Users will be able to connect to your server through their NetWare client stacks and access resources as necessary.

Configuring Gateway Services for NetWare

Assuming you installed the Gateway (and Client) Service for NetWare back in the "Getting Started" section, you already have part of the solution installed to provide gateway services to NetWare resources. By default, when you installed the Gateway (and Client) Service for NetWare, it walked you through the configuration for the *client* portion of the software—selecting a preferred server or tree/default context to use. The *gateway* portion of this feature is available through the Control Panel.

But before we begin configuring gateway services, you'll need to have a few things in place to make GSNW work as a gateway. They are as follows:

◆ An account defined on your NetWare server or in your NDS tree that can log in to the server(s) your Windows 2000 server will need to connect to. Appropriate permissions should be applied to this account for controlling what resources can be accessed.

◆ A group defined on your NetWare server or in your NDS tree called NTGATEWAY. The account mentioned in the previous bullet point must be made a member of this group.

◆ Resources (directories and/or print queues) on your NetWare server that have had permissions granted for the user account specified above.

Once you have these items completed, begin enabling gateway services by going to the GSNW controls page located in Start/Settings/Control Panel/GSNW. This should take you to a screen similar to the one you used when you were first installing and configuring the Gateway (and Client) Service for NetWare. Click the Gateway button on this screen to enter the Configure Gateway dialog box, shown in Figure 19.7. From this dialog box, you will end up defining two things for the Gateway Service for NetWare: the account that GSNW should use when accessing the Novell server for resources, and the file resources that it should share with the rest of the Microsoft network.

FIGURE 19.7

Configuring gateway shares in GSNW

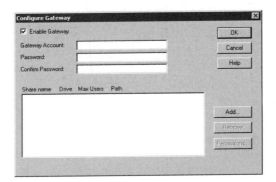

NOTE *All access to NetWare resources through GSNW will take place under the same username and context as far as NetWare is concerned. For example, you could have 30 users all accessing resources on a NetWare server, but as far as NetWare is concerned, you will only have one connection—the Windows 2000 server. This is both good and bad. The advantage is that you can squeeze your way around some Novell license restrictions if necessary. The bad news is that you can't control security permissions on an individual level; everyone accessing resources through GSNW will do so with the exact same security context, that of the gateway account.*

In the Configure Gateway dialog box, the first thing to do is check the Enable Gateway box to allow gateway services on your system. After that, you must define a NetWare (bindery or NDS) account that GSNW will use when logging into the NetWare server to access resources. This account must have adequate permissions assigned to the volumes and directories that you want to grant access to, and it must also be made a member of a NetWare group called NTGATEWAY. Personally, I always like to use an account name that makes sense to me when I see it in a Novell monitor list. I'd also recommend setting the password to never expire for this specific user; otherwise, your gateway might stop functioning on a regular basis.

DEFINING FILE SHARES

Once you have defined an appropriate gateway account for your system, you can begin to share file resources from your NetWare server through the Configure Gateway dialog box by clicking the Add button to add shares to your system. You will see a small dialog box, like the one in Figure 19.8, in which you will enter all of the necessary details for this connection.

FIGURE 19.8

Defining a new GSNW share

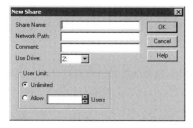

If you're familiar with sharing resources on a Windows 2000 server, this dialog box should look familiar. Enter the following information in the appropriate fields:

Share Name This is the name that Microsoft networking users will see when they list the shares available on a particular server.

Network Path This is the location of the NetWare resources that you'd like Windows 2000 Server to share. You can enter the name as a standard UNC path in the format of \\server-name\volume; for example, a UNC path of \\orion\sys would share the SYS: volume of the NetWare server ORION.

Comment If you would like to include any plain-English comments for this share (such as "These resources located on NetWare"), enter them here. Any subroutines in Windows that display share comments will display the text entered here.

Use Drive Even though you are providing a gateway service for a NetWare resource, your system will want to connect to it via a network drive letter. In a sense, you are mapping a drive, and then sharing a mapped drive (something that normally isn't allowed). Enter the drive letter that Windows 2000 Server should use for this connection.

User Limit If you would like to restrict the number of users connected to any given NetWare resource, enter a user restriction here or leave it set to Unlimited.

NOTE *In addition to defining the account for the gateway to use, the account you are* logged in with *when configuring GSNW must also have rights to the Novell server(s) you are creating gateway connections for. If this is not the case, you will see an error message indicating so when you try to create a share.*

Once you have entered the necessary information, clicking OK will create a drive mapping on your system and a share name for users to connect to. To test this, try accessing your Windows 2000 server from a properly configured workstation, and check whether you can see your NetWare share in the list of resources for the server.

DEFINING PRINT SHARES

Print shares can also be defined through GSNW , although the interface is slightly different. To share a NetWare-based printer with Microsoft networking clients, you will actually need to begin by going through the normal "add a printer" routine for Windows 2000.

Launch the Add Printer Wizard by selecting Start/Settings/Printers and then clicking the Add Printer icon. Proceed through the normal routines to add a network printer to your Windows 2000 server (for details on setting up a network printer, please see Chapter 13). At the second step of the wizard, select the radio button option to type in a printer name or browse for a printer, as shown in Figure 19.9.

FIGURE 19.9

Entering a URL for a network printer

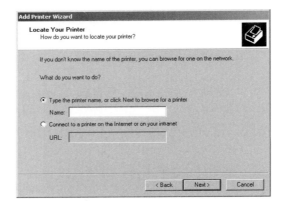

At this point, you can directly enter the URL for your NetWare print queue, or leave the field blank to browse to the print queue you want to create a gateway to. Either way, enter the appropriate NetWare print queue name in this field and then click Next to proceed to the final step of the wizard, where you can enter an appropriate print driver for Microsoft networking clients to use when accessing this resource.

NOTE   *When adding a printer to your Windows 2000 server as a gateway item, the account you are logged into Windows 2000 with when you make the connection* as well as *the gateway services account must* both *have appropriate access rights to the print queue.*

When you are finished, you should have a printer configured on your Windows 2000 server that is actually a print queue on a NetWare server. The final step necessary to make this printer available to Microsoft networking clients is to share the printer and assign it appropriate permissions. Sharing printers is covered in detail in Chapter 13, so if you are unfamiliar with this process, please check there for detailed information.

SETTING SECURITY ON PRINT AND FILE SHARES

Once you have configured the necessary items for providing gateway services for file and print shares, you may find that you want to control who can access these resources based on their Windows account.

This is controlled through setting share permissions for the resources you've created a gateway for, and works in much the same way as setting share permissions for any other resource on your system.

Share permissions are typically an "all-or-nothing" type of setting for your system. For example, with share permissions, you will either grant access to all of a printer or a set of directories, or none at all. For printers, this is a rather straightforward process and makes sense. However, for file shares you might want to control who can access certain subdirectories on the Novell volume you are sharing. Unfortunately, this can't be done when setting share permissions for a gateway resource. If a user is granted the appropriate share permissions to use the gateway resource, he or she can access all of the items available on that resource (as configured by the permissions assigned in NetWare to the gateway account used). Therefore, in setting share permissions on file resources, it really is an all-or-nothing scenario—either the user can access all of the shared resources on the NetWare server, or they can't access any.

Now, as far as read or write permissions are concerned, you can set those options via share permissions for a NetWare resource. Therefore, even though all users accessing the NetWare resources will all see the same directories and files, you can control who has read-only access and who has read-write access. Again, you can't assign these rights on a specific directory or file level, only to the entire resource you've shared. To apply share permissions to a NetWare resource, go back to the GSNW configuration page (Start/Settings/Control Panel/GSNW). Click the Gateway button, and you will see the dialog box you have previously used to define a shared NetWare resource. Highlight the share you want to modify the permissions for and then click the Permissions button to go to the Access Through Share Permissions dialog box, shown in Figure 19.10.

FIGURE 19.10

Modifying share permissions

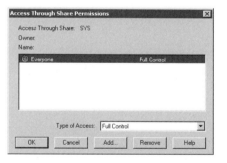

This permissions dialog box functions exactly the same as a share permissions dialog box would if you were sharing local resources from the Windows 2000 server. You can define read-only access or read-write access as necessary by modifying the permissions assigned to each user and group. For more detailed information on modifying share permissions, please see Chapter 11.

File and Print Services for NetWare

So far, in terms of integration, we've talked primarily about how to let Microsoft networking clients access resources on NetWare servers. But what if you run into a situation where the opposite is true?

What if you have some NetWare client workstations that—for one reason or another—have to stay configured as NetWare clients, but they need to access file and print resources on a Windows 2000 server?

The answer to this question is through a software package known as File and Print Services for NetWare (FPNW), a Windows 2000 Server add-on package available from Microsoft that will allow your server to *appear* as a Novell server to Novell networking clients.

By mimicking the broadcasts, protocols, and conventions that a NetWare server typically uses, your Windows 2000 server can act and behave just like a NetWare server (with the exception that you can't run NLMs on a Windows 2000 server) as far as your Desktop clients are concerned. Net-Ware clients can attach to your server, perform a standard NetWare login, and then access resources that appear to be on a standard NetWare SYS: volume. Everything appears as normal as far as the users are concerned.

Underneath it all, Windows 2000 Server is actually being quite creative by adopting several NetWare characteristics, such as listening for GetNearestServer broadcast packets, providing a SYS: volume (which is typically the `C:\SYSVOL` directory on the Windows 2000 server) to access resources, etc. If you have a need to get NetWare clients on your Windows 2000 server, but can't (or don't want to) upgrade them to a Microsoft client stack, FPNW is definitely a product worth looking into.

Migrating from NetWare and NDS to Windows 2000 and Active Directory

In the highly competitive world of computer software, making it easy for users to convert from a competitor's software package to your own is a key strategy in gaining market share. As software continues to improve, users tend to look for the latest and greatest features and capabilities, and getting those features sometimes means converting to a completely different product.

The network operating system market is no different, and I'm sure that Microsoft would like nothing better than to see Novell close up shop tomorrow (although they'd never publicly admit it). In the earlier versions of NT, Microsoft included a tool called NWConvert along with the NT operating system in an effort to make that dream a reality. NWConvert was a good tool for converting bindery-based NetWare servers to NT servers. NWConvert would copy the files, users, groups, and account restrictions over from a NetWare server, across the wire, to an NT server.

NWConvert was a useful tool, but it was limited by the fact that it could only work on bindery-based NetWare servers. NDS is being implemented more and more, which conversely has made NWConvert less and less useful. Never one to stay too far behind the times, Microsoft has rebuilt this utility (actually, Computer Associates wrote it) for Windows 2000 Server. Now, the utility is referred to as the Directory Services Migration Tool (DSMT) and is a full-blown, two-stage, project-based migration tool capable of migrating entire NDS trees or sections of trees to Active Directory–enabled Windows 2000 networks.

Although server migration is certainly no small subject, hopefully the information that follows will give you a good overview of the DSMT, what it can do, and how to use it.

NOTE *The DSMT was originally part of the Windows 2000 build; however, Microsoft decided to remove the DSMT from Windows 2000 and now offers it as part of their Microsoft Directory Synchronization Service (MSDSS). Since the capability still exists in the MSDSS add-on package as part of Services for NetWare (SFN) 5, we left the content in the book so you can understand how the technology works, and decide whether it would be useful for you when you're migrating to Windows 2000. For more information on MSDSS, visit this Microsoft Web page:* `http://www.microsoft` `.com/windows2000/techinfo/interop/mdssoverview.asp`.

DSMT Overview and Conventions

The DSMT has some unique characteristics that make it a great tool to use when migrating data and users off of NDS- or bindery-based networks. Some of the reasons why it's such a good tool include the following:

◆ It's a nondestructive, across-the-wire tool. Information is read across the network from Net-Ware servers and the NDS tree and stored on the Windows 2000 server. Nothing needs to be loaded on the NetWare server for this tool to work, and nothing is ever written back to the NetWare environment.

◆ It's a two-stage tool. Since large migrations can often be a process that must be managed carefully, you can control the pace of your migration by reading the necessary information in from the NetWare server or NDS tree. Once you have read the data, it is stored on your Windows 2000 server, where you can analyze it, manipulate it if necessary, and then write the data out to the Active Directory and your Windows 2000 server.

◆ It's a project-based tool. It isn't necessary to handle an entire NDS tree or an entire Novell server at once during a migration. You can work on migrating portions of each of these resources and work at your own pace. You can define different "projects" for different portions of your migration as necessary.

Throughout the discussion of the DSMT, there are several naming conventions that will be commonly used. They are:

Project   A DSMT container that holds one or many "views."

View   A set of object data—users, groups, organizational units, etc. Some of the view data may be imported from NetWare, some of it may have been created by hand, and some of it may have been imported from other locations. The view is the central repository for all information (with the exception of files) that you would eventually like to export to the Active Directory.

Discover   The process of importing object data (users, groups, etc.) from either a NetWare server or another location.

Configure   The process of exporting object data (users, groups, etc.) from a view to the Active Directory.

Installing and Configuring the DSMT

Depending on how you chose to configure Windows 2000 Server during installation, the DSMT may or may not be installed on your system. Let's work under the assumption that the DSMT is not installed on your computer and walk through the steps to install and configure it.

To add the DSMT to a server that doesn't have it, start by choosing Start/Settings/Control Panel and double-clicking the Add/Remove Programs icon. This will launch the Add/Remove Programs dialog box, which should have Add/Remove Windows Components listed as one of the options on the left side. Click that option and the Windows Components Wizard will launch, allowing you to add components to or remove components from your Windows 2000 server. You'll find the DSMT available as one of the options under the Networking Services component, as shown in Figure 19.11. Either install all of the networking services by checking that box, or install the DSMT individually by clicking the Details button and selecting Directory Service Migration Tool.

FIGURE 19.11

Installing the DSMT

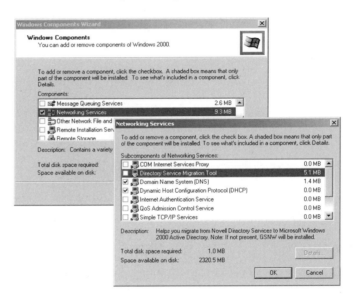

After you have successfully installed the DSMT onto your system, the program should be added to your Administrative Tools group by default. Launch the DSMT from the Start menu to begin working on your migration.

DSMT GENERAL OPTIONS

After successfully installing the DSMT, one of the first things you will probably want to do is configure the tool for your specific environment. From the scope pane of the DSMT MMC, right-click the Directory Service Migration Tool item and then select the Options command. This should take you to the first page of options you can set for the DSMT, shown in Figure 19.12.

FIGURE 19.12

Setting General
options for the
DSMT

There are very few options on the General tab. The first is to choose a location for the DSMT to store project data (users, files, etc.) that it is working on migrating. The second option is the check box at the very bottom of the dialog box, which allows you to select whether or not the DSMT should display objects from the NDS environment that don't have an exact match in the AD. Leaving this box checked will instruct the DSMT to only display NDS objects that have a corresponding counterpart in AD—anything that doesn't translate directly from NDS to AD will be ignored.

NOVELL ENVIRONMENT DISCOVER OPTIONS

When discovering items from Novell servers, there are a few options you might want to set. These parameters are defined in the Novell Environment Discover tab of the Options page, shown in Figure 19.13.

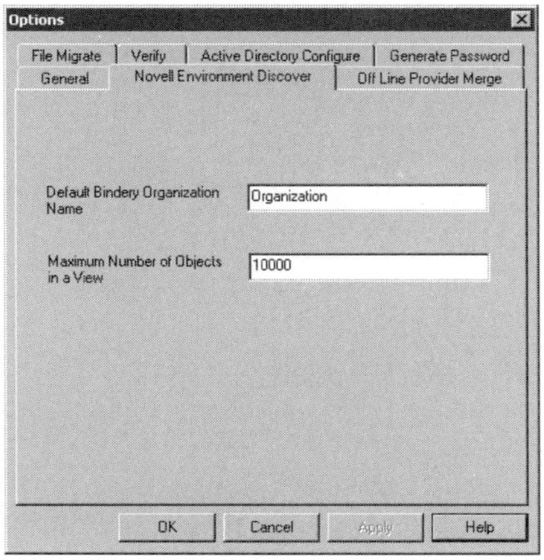

FIGURE 19.13

Setting Novell Envi-
ronment Discover
options

If you intend to import data from bindery-based systems, there will be no O= or Organization attribute (one of the highest attributes in an NDS tree) defining the overall organization. Binderies are flat by nature, simply containing user accounts and other details, so you can assign a default Organization attribute to apply when discovering data from a bindery-based Novell server by entering the name to use in the Default Bindery Organization Name field.

You can also restrict the number of objects to import during a discover operation by entering an appropriate value in the Maximum Number of Objects in a View field. This is particularly useful if you have a very large NDS structure with thousands of objects, but you don't want to import them all just yet—maybe you are testing a migration plan and want to see how it works. Entering a value here will limit the number of objects imported in a discover operation.

VERIFY OPTIONS

While discovering data from an NDS environment, the DSMT can take steps to verify the integrity of the data it is receiving. These verifications are in the form of field-length checks and counters that can be applied to the NDS structure. The Verify tab on the Options page is shown in Figure 19.14.

FIGURE 19.14

Setting Verify options

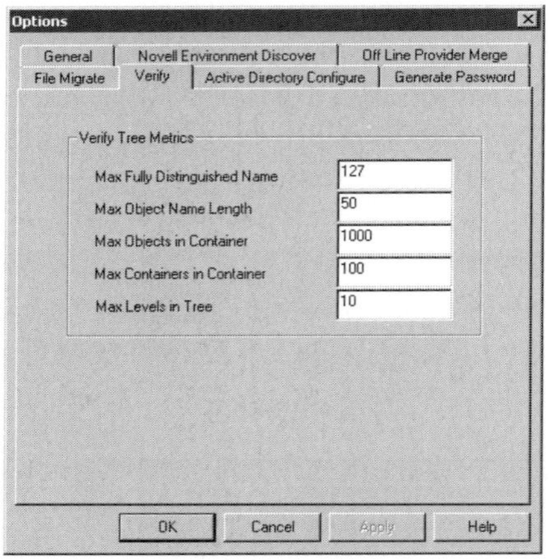

As you can see, most of these options are for setting field lengths and controlling counters during the discovery process. Here's a brief description of each of these fields:

Max Fully Distinguished Name   Controls the maximum length for the long name of an NDS object. An NDS long name includes the names of all organizational units and the organization, in addition to the object name.

Max Object Name Length   Specifies how long an individual object name (such as a username or OU) can be.

Max Objects in Container   Implements controls on how many individual objects (such as users) can be in any one container (such as an O or OU).

Max Containers in Container Implements controls on how many container objects (such as OUs) can be in any one container (such as an O or OU).

Max Levels in Tree This setting controls how many levels deep into an NDS tree that the discover process will go.

For most circumstances, the default values for these options should be acceptable.

ACTIVE DIRECTORY CONFIGURE OPTIONS

When it comes time to configure objects to Active Directory (to write the objects you've imported out to AD), the DSMT can handle multi-valued options in several ways, based on the options you choose in Figure 19.15.

FIGURE 19.15

Setting Active Directory Configure options

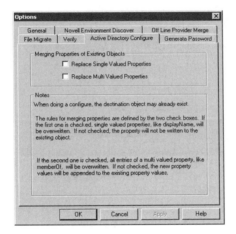

These parameters only apply in circumstances where an NDS object may already exist in your target Active Directory. For example, if you had an identical organizational unit (OU in NDS parlance) defined in a Novell environment as well as in your Active Directory environment, that would be an object that exists in both your discovered environment (NDS) and the environment you want to configure (AD). Let's look at an example.

Let's say—for whatever reason—you have a user account named Cheryl in your NDS *and* your AD structure. Now, the account for Cheryl has several "properties" associated with it. Properties are things like the user's first name, last name, what groups he/she is a member of, etc. Now, if the DSMT runs into a situation where the same object that came from the NDS environment needs to be written to the AD environment, it can do one of two things:

Replace Single-Valued Properties If this option is checked, any single-valued properties (that is, username, password, or anything else with only one value associated with it) within AD will be overwritten with the same single-valued properties from the NDS environment. For example, let's suppose that Cheryl's first name was misspelled (as Cheryll) in NDS, but was correct in AD (as Cheryl); the misspelled version of her name will overwrite the existing, correct version. Leaving this option blank will tell DSMT not to overwrite single-valued properties when configuring objects to Active Directory.

Replace Multi-Valued Properties   This option functions the same as the option for replacing single-valued properties, except it's for object properties that are multi-valued. Examples of multi-valued object properties include the listing of groups that a user account is a member of.

GENERATE PASSWORD OPTIONS

Since the DSMT can't "read" user passwords from a NetWare server or an NDS structure, you will need to choose an option for how you want to handle passwords for user objects that are migrated. The Generate Password property page, shown in Figure 19.16, will let you control what the DSMT ends up doing.

FIGURE 19.16

Setting Generate Password options

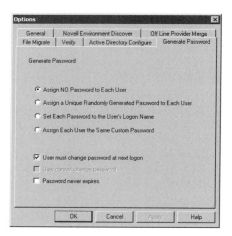

As you can see from this property page, there are four main things that the DSMT can do when it comes to the passwords for NDS users. The first option, Assign NO Password to Each User, in effect leaves the password for the newly configured AD user blank. The next option—Assign a Unique Randomly Generated Password to Each User—will create a unique 12-character password for each user. The third option, Set Each Password to the User's Logon Name, is a rather straightforward option. And finally, you can select the Assign Each User the Same Custom Password option.

Once you have selected the appropriate option for creating passwords for AD users, you can control whether or not the AD users can and should change those passwords through the three check-boxes at the bottom of the property page. These options behave exactly the same as their counterparts in defining a normal Active Directory user, so we won't discuss them in detail here.

Importing Bindery/NDS Data

Once you have configured the DSMT the way you want it, the next step for migrating data from a NetWare/NDS environment is to define a project for importing some (or all) of your NetWare/NDS data into the DSMT. The process of importing data is referred to as *discovering*, and once you have discovered data from your NetWare/NDS environment, that data is stored in the DSMT in the database location defined in the General options. Once you have a working copy of the data, you can view it, manipulate it, and generally tweak it any way you'd like before you finally end up exporting it to Active Directory.

To begin, you will need to define a new project. Start the creation of a new project by highlighting the Directory Services Migration Tool in the scope pane of the DSMT MMC and then selecting New/Project from the Action pull-down menu. The DSMT will prompt you for a project name to use and a brief description about the project. Enter an appropriate name and then click OK to continue.

Once you have a project defined, the next step is to create a "view"—basically, a set of imported data—of your NetWare resources. Start the process to create a view by highlighting your project in the scope pane of the DSMT MMC and then selecting New/View from NetWare from the Action pull-down menu. This will start the Discover Wizard that will walk you through the discovery process.

The first step of the Discover Wizard will simply ask you for a name to use for this view—personally, I like to use meaningful names for the type of data within the view. For example, if I am migrating an entire NDS organizational unit, I will name the view after the OU. Choose a meaningful name, and then click Next to move on to the next step of the wizard, shown in Figure 19.17.

FIGURE 19.17

Specifying a context to discover

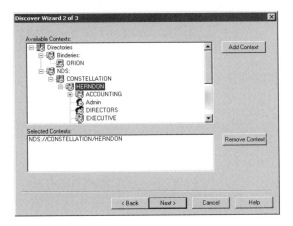

The second step of the Discover Wizard will ask you to select a bindery server or NDS context (or group of contexts) to import into the DSMT. As you can see from Figure 19.17, I have chosen to import all the data for the entire HERNDON organization within the NDS tree called CONSTELLATION. If I wanted to do a part of the tree at a time, I could have just as easily selected individual organizational units instead, such as ACCOUNTING, DIRECTORS, EXECUTIVE, etc.

In any case, navigate through your NDS structure, or your list of bindery servers, to select the context(s) or binderies that you want to discover. Click the Add Context button for each item that you want to discover, and you will then see that item listed in the Selected Contexts area of the wizard.

Click Next to proceed to the final step of the wizard (which is simply a confirmation page). When you click the Finish button in the last step of the wizard, the DSMT will start working its magic and importing all of your NDS or bindery data into this view. Once that has successfully been completed, you should see your organization, organizational units, and objects (users, groups, etc.) listed below your newly defined view in the scope pane of the DSMT MMC. As you can see from the example shown in Figure 19.18, all of the containers and objects have been successfully imported from my NDS environment to the DSMT.

FIGURE 19.18

View of the DSMT MMC after importing NDS objects

Manipulating NDS Data in the DSMT

Once you have successfully imported your bindery or NDS data from your NetWare environment, there are several things that you can do to manipulate or "tweak" the data as necessary before writing the data to your Active Directory environment.

MODIFYING OBJECTS INDIVIDUALLY

One of the first things that you can do is actually edit the properties of any of the objects the DSMT imported by double-clicking them. For example, double-clicking the user named Admin brings up the object properties in a dialog box like the one shown in Figure 19.19.

FIGURE 19.19

Modifying object (user) properties in the DSMT

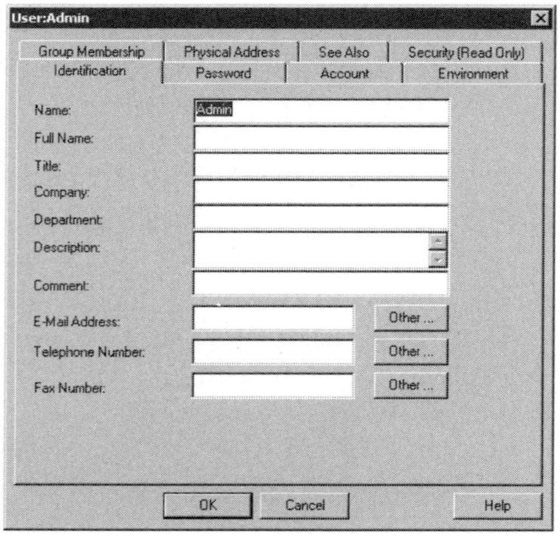

Now, we won't be going through the options listed here, because these are all fields and parameters pulled from the NDS or bindery user account imported by the DSMT. As you can see from the figure, there are multiple screens of properties for this object, all of which can be manipulated by hand while the data is still in the DSMT. The same is true for editing groups, organizational units, or any other object types the DSMT has picked up.

Also, if you would like to change the organization of individual objects—for example, move certain users and groups from one organizational unit to another—you can do this manually as well by simply dragging and dropping objects wherever you want them to be. This is a great way to correct any errors that existed in your NDS structure before writing it to the Active Directory.

CHANGING PASSWORDS (FOR USER OBJECTS)

Perhaps you forgot to configure the password options for the DSMT before running the discovery process. Or maybe you've changed your mind and want to change every user object password to blank instead of the random password option you chose earlier. If so, in the DSMT MMC, highlight either the view you want to work with or any level below the view (organization, organizational unit, etc.) and then select the All Tasks/Generate User Password option from the Action pull-down menu.

This should bring up a dialog box exactly like the one shown back in Figure 19.16, in which you can choose the password options you want to apply. Once you select an option and click Finish, the new passwords will be applied immediately. If you chose to generate user passwords on an organizational unit level, only the users listed within that specific OU will have their passwords changed. Again, remember: this information is being changed in the DSMT database only, not in your live NDS structure.

FINDING AND REPLACING TEXT IN OBJECT NAMES

Let's say that you want to globally find and replace specific text strings in object names that you've imported from NDS. For example, maybe user accounts on your system were always appended with a 01, but now you want to remove that convention. You could, of course, go through each user account by hand and change each name, but who wants to go through all that? Technology is here to make our jobs easier. So instead, in the DSMT MMC, highlight either the view you want to work with or any level below the view (organization, organizational unit, etc.) and then select the All Tasks/Find and Replace Object Names option from the Action pull-down menu. This will bring you to the dialog box shown in Figure 19.20.

FIGURE 19.20

Finding and replacing object names in the DSMT

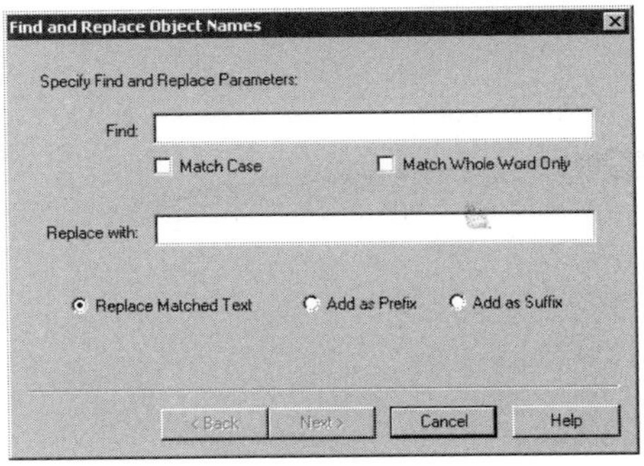

Through this dialog box, you can command the DSMT to perform a search-and-replace operation on the objects in your view (or organization, or organizational unit, depending on where you started this utility from). Enter the string that you want the DSMT to find in the Find field, the text you want it replaced with in the Replace With field, and then click Next to begin the replacement operation.

Now, just like a good word processor would do, the DSMT won't simply go through and change everything it finds that matches without checking with you first. After you define your find-and-replace strings and click Next, the DSMT will go through all the targeted objects and find the matches and ask you to select the ones you want to perform the replace operation on. Select the appropriate objects and then click Finish; your changes will be written to the DSMT copy of the data.

Writing Objects to Active Directory

Once you are certain that you have your data in the DSMT just the way you want it, one of the final steps necessary is to write the data to the Active Directory. To begin this process, in the scope pane of the DSMT MMC, highlight your organization or organizational units that you want to write to AD. From the Action pull-down menu, select the All Tasks/Configure Objects to Active Directory option, which will bring you to the wizard shown in Figure 19.21.

FIGURE 19.21

Selecting a target
AD location

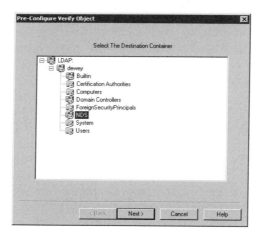

In the first screen of the wizard, you can select a target location within Active Directory to export your data to. You can export the data to any site or to any organizational unit within the site. Just to make sure that you don't overwrite any existing Active Directory objects that might have the exact same name, I would recommend creating a separate organizational unit object within your Active Directory to copy your objects into. In the example shown in Figure 19.21, I've called this organizational unit NDS, but you could call it Bindery or the specific NetWare server name if you prefer. This way, you can be sure that you are copying your objects from the DSMT to a location where they won't overwrite anything else. Once you have made the transition to AD and are certain that everything is working fine, then you can move your objects around within the Active Directory tree to their correct locations.

NOTE   *Creating a separate OU to copy your NDS records to will require you to copy each organizational unit that you've imported from NDS to AD, instead of copying the entire organization. Since it is logically impossible for an "organization" to exist below an "organizational unit"—even if it came from NDS—the DSMT will not let you do it.*

In any case, select the appropriate location to copy your objects into, then click Next. The wizard will begin copying your DSMT information into the Active Directory, checking for conflicts with any existing data. When the trial copy is completed, you will see a dialog box similar to the one shown in Figure 19.22.

FIGURE 19.22

Final verification prompt before writing DSMT data to AD

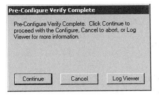

This dialog box is the last chance you'll have to change your mind before the DSMT writes its data to the Active Directory. I would recommend clicking the Log Viewer button to check to see if serious error messages have been written to the log. For example, if you try to export a username from the DSMT with the same name as a user who already exists in the Active Directory, there will be a log message indicating this error. Investigate any errors that could cause problems for your Active Directory and resolve them before writing the final data to the directory. Once you are sure that the data you will write to the Active Directory is clean, click the Continue button and the NDS and/or bindery objects will be written out to your Active Directory.

Once this task has completed, you should be able to open up the Active Directory Users and Computers MMC (from Start/Programs/Administrative Tools) and see your bindery/NDS users listed there.

Migrating File Resources

Now, migrating user accounts is a good thing, but what about the files? After all, user accounts don't do much good if there aren't any files around for the user to access, right? Well, fortunately there are two file migration options available to you through the DSMT: copying just the files from one server to another, or copying the files and their associated NetWare permissions.

Depending on which option you choose, the location where you start this operation is slightly different. The functionality is primarily the same, so we'll just discuss copying files and their associated permissions; copying just the files would simply be a subset of that operation.

To copy the files and permissions from a NetWare server to your Windows 2000 server, select your view (note, not the project or the organization, but your "view") from the scope pane of the DSMT MMC. From the Action pull-down menu, choose All Tasks/File System Migrate, which will begin the File Migrate Wizard.

The first two steps of the wizard will ask you separately if you want to migrate the security and then the files (since each can be migrated independently). Presumably, you will want to migrate both, so select Yes for each option and then click Next. This should bring you to the step of the File Migrate Wizard where you can select a source and destination for file transfer. This step of the wizard is shown in Figure 19.23.

FIGURE 19.23

Selecting a source and destination in the File Migrate Wizard

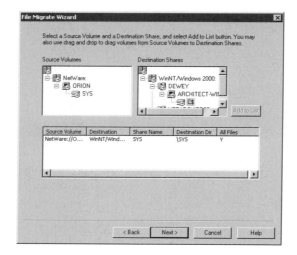

Through this interface, you can choose which NetWare volume you want to migrate files from (you must do the entire volume, as you can't select specific directories), and which Windows 2000 Server destination share you will store the files on. You do not have to store the files on the same server that you are running the DSMT on, so choose a hard drive on a server that has enough storage space available and highlight the share for that drive letter. Make sure both source and destination have been selected and then click the Add to List button to set these copy locations. Click Next to continue to the next step of the wizard.

By default, the DSMT will copy the NetWare volume to a directory on the server you've selected and give that directory the same name as the NetWare volume. The DSMT will automatically start sharing the newly created directory under the same name as well. If you wish to change the share name or target directory, the next step of the wizard will allow you to adjust the options of the file copy source and destination you've entered. If you feel like changing the target directory or share name, highlight the copy pair you wish to edit and click the Edit button. This should take you to a dialog box where you can modify the directory and share name options. Click Next to continue to the next step of the File Migrate Wizard, shown in Figure 19.24.

Assuming you are migrating files to an NTFS partition on your target server, you can control what rights are inherited by files and directories copied to your system. Since NTFS will want to automatically apply inherited rights from the parent directory (presumably the root) to all the subdirectories and files that it will create in this copy, you can view those rights through this window. If you want to change the rights that will be inherited by the files and directories that you copy over, you will need to modify the permissions assigned to your target location (again, presumably the root)—you can't change them through this interface.

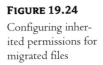

FIGURE 19.24

Configuring inherited permissions for migrated files

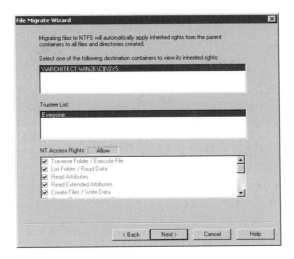

After you have verified that the rights that will be inherited look okay, click Next to finish the wizard. You will proceed through one last verification dialog box, and after that the file copy operation will begin. When the copy operation is complete, you can check the log file that has been created to verify that your data has been copied without any errors.

Chapter 20

Tuning and Monitoring Your Windows 2000 Network

IF A WINDOWS 2000 SERVER isn't performing well—if it seems unresponsive or if you're getting funny error messages—then you could install more memory or add another processor and hope for the best. Alternatively, you could try to find out what was going on and address that question specifically. Why is the server slow? Is it running short of memory? Has someone tapped into your computer and is running unauthorized processes on it? If you ask the right questions of Windows 2000's tuning and monitoring tools, then you may find out the answers. You can use these tools either from the GUI or address them through administrative scripts, since the System Monitor is a Windows Management Instrumentation (WMI) provider and, therefore, accessible to VBScript.

Whether you use the graphical tools or write scripts to reach performance or event monitoring data, the trick to using performance monitoring tools is *asking the right questions*. These tools are not omnipotent gods, but more like slightly dim-witted genies. Like such genies, performance monitoring tools are very literal-minded little cusses. They can give you the answers if you ask, but only if you ask correctly—and if you ask the wrong questions you'll drown in a sea of irrelevant data. (Somewhat less metaphorically, if you ask indiscriminate questions you'll slow down your servers and clog your network's bandwidth with unimportant queries, not to mention get a bunch of information that you can't use and that can cloud the important stuff.) Thus, in this chapter I'll talk about the genies—er, performance monitoring tools—that come with Win2K and about how you can figure out which questions to ask the oracle. Once that's done, I'll discuss the tuning you can do based on the information you gathered. To round it off, I'll describe how you can tune network browsing to make your network more responsive to the people using it.

Roundup of Tuning Support Tools and What to Do with Them

Before I get into a description of how to use these tools, here's a quick tour of the monitoring tools that come with Windows 2000:

◆ System Monitor

◆ Performance Logs and Alerts

◆ Event Viewer

NOTE *Win2K also has a Network Monitor tool that's a crippled version of the one included with Microsoft System Management Server. The one included in Win2K is pretty useless for most purposes, however, because it can only monitor data traveling between the monitored computer and the rest of the network. You can use it for monitoring network I/O to a specific computer, but not for monitoring network traffic in general.*

System Monitor

The System Monitor is Win2K's replacement for NT 4's Performance Monitor. Strictly speaking, it's not really a replacement but more of a reorganization. When you open the System Monitor, you'll see that it has two components: a Performance Monitor–like tool called the System Monitor that displays real-time performance statistics and Performance Logs and Alerts, which is the System Monitor's logging function.

TIP *To open the System Monitor quickly, type* **perfmon** *(the executable name of the Performance Monitor) into Run. Win2K will start the System Monitor with the Performance Monitor screen active. Typing* **sysmon** *into Run does nothing, by the way.*

With the System Monitor, you can do the following:

◆ Provide a simple, visual view of your servers' vital signs (one that looks great on a PowerPoint presentation of why you need more hardware) in charts, histograms, or reports

◆ Output real-time system monitoring information to a browser

◆ Keep an eye on how processes are using CPU time, I/O time, memory, and other server resources

◆ Log network data over time and export that data to a file that you can import into a spreadsheet for further analysis

◆ Open saved logs to review historical data

Performance Logs and Alerts

The other half of the Performance tools is the Performance Logs and Alerts, which takes over the logging functions of NT 4's Performance Monitor. You can do the following using the logging function:

◆ Monitor system stress and performance over a period of time, instead of watching the current output

◆ Automatically keep track of minimum, maximum, average, and current values of critical system values

◆ Send alerts to the Event log or run a program when counters exceed the tolerances you set or when important events occur

Event Viewer

The Event Viewer (located in the Administrative Tools program group) maintains several separate event logs on the server:

◆ System log

◆ Security log

◆ Application log

◆ DNS Server log

◆ File Replication Service log

◆ Directory Service log

NOTE *The Event Viewer for member servers in the domain displays only the Application log, System log, and Security log.*

The System log records the starting and stopping of services and any system-related events. This is where you'll find out that time synching isn't working, that the DHCP server has successfully cleaned up its database, or that a print job was successfully completed. If you see a message box telling you that something didn't work and to check the Event Monitor for more details, the System log is the first place to look.

The Security log records any audited events that relate to security issues, such as users accessing files or changing the Security Accounts Database. The Security log will be empty unless and until you enable security logging and specify the events that you want to monitor. I'll explain how to do that a little later in this chapter; for now, I just don't want you to wonder why it's empty.

The Application log records application-specific events that aren't far-reaching enough to make it into the System log. The name of this log can be misleading. It's not about user applications so much as about licensing, the BINL service used to back Remote Installation Services, the successful (or unsuccessful) application of security policies, performance library issues, and the like.

You'll find the System, Application, and Security logs on any Windows 2000 computer. The remaining logs only apply to computers that need them because of their role in the network. The DNS Server log (found, as you'd expect, on the DNS server) records events associated with resolving computer names to or from IP addresses. The File Replication Service log lists events relating to the File Replication Service, and the Directory Service log records events related to domain controllers keeping up with the security database.

Observing Performance Patterns with the System Monitor

If you can't measure it, you can't tune it.

As noted earlier, the System Monitor is the graphical display tool in Windows 2000's collection of monitoring tools. When you switch to this tool, you see an opening screen like the one in Figure 20.1.

FIGURE 20.1

The System Monitor tool

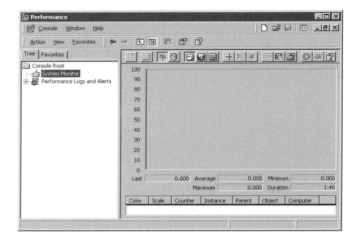

With the System Monitor, you can log minima, maxima, and averages of critical system values and get a simple, visual view of your network's "vital signs."

When you first start the System Monitor, all you see is a blank screen; you must select the objects, instances, and counters that you want to monitor. Objects, instances, and counters are defined as follows:

Object   Any Win2K system component that possesses a set of measurable properties. An object can be a physical part of the system (such as the memory or the processor), a logical component (such as a disk volume), or a software element (such as a process or a thread).

Instance   Shows how many occurrences of an object are available in the system.

Counter   Represents one measurable characteristic of an object. For example, the Processor object has several counters, including the percentage of processor time in use and the percentage of time the processor spends in Privileged and User modes.

To look at all the system areas you can monitor, click the button with the plus sign (+) on it or right-click the blank area of the System Monitor and choose Add Counters from the shortcut menu to open the Add Counters dialog box. The first item, Processor, includes information on several counters listed in the Counter box; for example, the variable that reports how many interrupts per second the system processes is called the Interrupts/sec counter. Win2K contains hundreds of counters to track system data (described in Appendix A), such as the number of network packets transmitted per second, the percentage of time a processor spends in User mode versus Kernel mode, and the number of pages swapped in and out of memory per second. However, as you can see, the System Monitor doesn't do *anything* until it is told to. So let's build a chart.

Creating a Chart

Every System Monitor chart is a custom collection of counters to monitor. To add a counter to the chart, click the button in the toolbar that has a plus sign on it. This will open the dialog box shown in Figure 20.2.

FIGURE 20.2

Add counters to the System Monitor

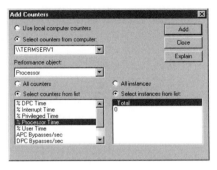

Adding counters to a chart is easy. Choose a performance object, then pick one of its performance counters. If there's more than one instance of the object (for example, if the server has more than one processor), then you'll have the choice of monitoring counters for all objects of that class or only a specific one. Click the Add button, and that counter will be added to the chart and will show up in the System Monitor, as in Figure 20.3.

FIGURE 20.3

System Monitor output

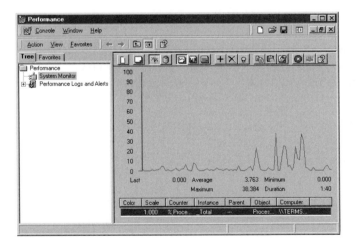

Adding counters may be easy, but choosing the counters to add and interpreting what you're seeing is not. Let's take a look at how you could pick counters to monitor.

NOTE   *The System Monitor's Add Counters dialog box has an Explain button you can click to show more information about the currently highlighted counter. However, the information that's displayed isn't always all that useful—especially for the counters new to Win2K—and not always strictly accurate. Use the information in the Explain text box as a starting point for further research if you need exact details about what a counter's monitoring, not as a final word.*

Incidentally, I've described here how to add counters to monitor on the current computer. As I'll explain a little later in this chapter, you can also—and you frequently should—monitor other computers with the System Monitor. The procedure for adding the counters is identical to adding counters to monitor locally, however.

CHOOSING OBJECTS AND COUNTERS TO MONITOR

When you first open the Add Counters dialog box, it's easy to get information overload. I haven't yet been bored enough to count all the counters for all the objects, but there must be thousands. Even if you just look at the objects, how do you tell which of the dozens available is the one you want? It's not easy, and to make the performance monitoring useful at all, you'll need to be selective. Monitoring all the counters would give you more information than you could possibly handle. You need to know what to look for.

Let me set the following scenario: You have a network up and running. But with time, the network seems to be slowing down. People are complaining. The Powers That Be start applying pressure on you to find out what's wrong and to find it out *now*. What can you do? Well, the obvious thing to do is to throw hardware at the problem, right? Go buy more memory, an extra processor if the servers support multiple processors and have slots available; get a faster network card; get a faster disk.

Doing those things *may* get you a faster server. But, hopefully, when designing the server in the first place you paid attention to server design principles and chose hardware designed for supporting many people at a time. If you didn't, then perhaps you need new hardware. But if you did, then blindly throwing new hardware at performance problems is a good way to throw money down a rat hole. If your server is spending all its time waiting for the disk drive, then getting a faster processor may indeed speed up the server—but only by a tiny percentage. If the problem is a slow disk, your money's better spent on a faster disk controller than on a faster processor. If you concentrated on the wrong problem, then you could even hurt server performance, rather than help it. The short version is this: You tune a troubled server by locating and removing its bottlenecks as much as you can. Eventually, you will bump into the limits of performance improvements, so the trick is to find the most effective performance improvements and apply them. What I want to do next is to (1) introduce you to the art of tuning, (2) point out the most likely causes of problems for file servers and application servers in particular, and (3) recommend a few counters that you can monitor to keep an eye on your network with minimum trouble.

A server's job on the network will influence the counters that are important to it: IIS Servers serving Active Server Pages (ASP) or SMTP servers providing e-mail will call on entire object classes that servers not performing those roles will never touch. If a server has no printer directly attached, then you needn't monitor the Print Queue object counters. However, there are four big sources of performance bottlenecks common to any server:

◆ Memory

◆ Disk subsystem

◆ Network card and software

◆ Processor

Resolving Memory Bottlenecks

The biggest performance drain on a Win2K system is memory. Windows applications are memory-hungry, and Win2K itself is memory-hungry—NT operating systems get more powerful and greedier with each passing generation. If you install Win2K Server with the bare minimum of memory and then actually try to use it as a server, you're not going to be happy with the result.

Background: A (Very Basic) Primer on Virtual Memory   When you're monitoring memory, you're actually monitoring both physical memory and hard disk access. The reason has to do with how Windows operating systems eke the most use possible out of physical memory—some of the apparent contents of that physical memory are actually on disk, in what's called *virtual memory*.

Virtual memory is a result of what Dorothy Parker would have said if she had been a network administrator: you can never be too rich, too thin, or have too much RAM installed. No matter how much you have, it seems, physical memory can't keep up with the data storage needs of Win2K and any applications it's running. Therefore, Windows operating systems use virtual memory, a kind of memory simulation that allows the server to support more applications and data in memory than it actually has physical memory to support. The largest Win2K servers I've seen have 1GB of RAM installed, but Windows operating systems support up to 4GB of virtual memory space—2GB to be shared among all system-level processes, and 2GB for the exclusive use of each user process running on the server. The Win2K memory manager is responsible for organizing each process's access to virtual memory so that processes don't write on each other's data in *physical* memory.

NOTE   *One of the reasons Win2K needs so much memory is because it uses a* big *chunk (like, 25 percent or so) of this memory for cacheing recently used file data. Servers that aren't file servers don't need to do this. In the "Basic Tuning Stuff" section later in this chapter I'll explain how to make Win2K stop thinking of itself as a file server and start giving you back some memory.*

Virtual memory works like this: When an application is loaded into memory, it stores its data in physical memory to store data it needs to run and present user files. As more and more applications (and the operating system) use RAM to store data, things start getting crowded. To allow applications to keep their important data in physical memory where they can get to it more or less instantly, the Win2K memory manager shuffles less important data to a file on disk called the *paging file*. The applications don't care whether data is stored in RAM or the paging file, the applications just keep referring to the data according to the virtual address where it was originally stored. Among the memory manager's many jobs is the task of keeping track of how the virtual memory storage area corresponds to the physical memory storage area, since it is almost inevitable that the physical storage area for memory will change.

What kind of data is stored in memory? Several kinds, actually:

◆ Each application (and the operating system) has a *working set* that is the sum of all the data that application is currently working with. The memory manager can trim working sets if there's a shortage of physical memory. But the smaller an application's working set, the slower the application will run, because it's going to have to keep requesting data back from the paging file, and paging data back into memory takes time.

NOTE   *If you're using Terminal Services, then there will also be a per-session working set.*

◆ *Page table entries (PTEs)* are structures the memory manager needs to map each user process's virtual address space to an area of physical memory. The memory manager needs this map to see how each process is using its view of the 2GB of user virtual memory addresses and to keep processes from overwriting each other's memory.

◆ Some operating system data must remain in memory all the time and cannot be paged to disk. The range of virtual memory addresses called the *non-paged pool* stores this data. The *paged pool* stores operating system data that can be paged to disk.

◆ The *system cache* is the data used by the entire operating system that Win2K keeps in RAM for quick access. The System Monitor Help describes the system cache as though it were synonymous with the disk cache, but it's not—the disk cache of recently used on-disk data and disk data structure is one part of the entire system cache.

The Win2K memory manager allocates memory to the system and user processes by first *reserving* it for the process that needs it (defining a range of virtual memory addresses for later use) and then *committing* it (ensuring that a place in the paging file is available to store the data the process wants to put in those virtual memory addresses). Processes can reserve all the memory they want, but when it comes time to commit that memory, some on-disk storage *must* be available to back it. Win2K has to assume that all user data will move to the paging file at some time. When a process is done with memory, it's supposed to give it back to the system to be marked as available for other processes—*free* it. Some processes do the opposite, taking more and more memory even though they're not using it or just not giving back memory that they're not using anymore until you reboot the machine. This is a result of buggy programming and is called a *memory leak*. Memory leaks are frustrating because they starve other processes without giving you any gain at all. Give them enough time, and memory leaks will shut down your server. Sadly, they're also pretty common, which is why it's pretty common practice to reboot Windows 2000 servers regularly.

The memory manager's decisions about what's important depend on the operating platform. On multi-processor x86 systems, the memory manager uses the first-in-first-out (FIFO) algorithm, which means that in a space crunch the data that's been in memory longest gets shuffled to the paging file first, regardless of how recently it's been used. On single-processor x86 systems, the memory manager uses a different priority scheme—the least recently used (LRU) algorithm, which analyzes how recently data's been used. The data that hasn't been used for a while goes to the paging file first. LRU is a bit more logical than FIFO, as it evaluates how recently you've used data instead of just assuming that anything old is less necessary. It's just a bit more complicated.

Processes can't use data that's stored on disk, so when an application calls on data that the memory manager has paged to disk, the memory manager tracks down the data's current location and executes a *page fault* to send that data to RAM where the memory controller can retrieve it for the application. End result: The application gets its data with no more than a little finger drumming at the slight delay. To the process, it looks as though the data was in memory all the time, but it really wasn't.

There is one catch to the paging file: faulting data back into physical memory takes longer than retrieving it from physical memory, because disks are slower than RAM. You measure access times (the time required to read or write data) on RAM in nanoseconds (billionths of a second) and on disk in milliseconds (thousandths of a second). So, although you can't escape paging—Windows 2000 is designed to use it, and it will, no matter how much RAM you install—you will improve server performance if you seek to minimize the amount of time your server spends paging data in and out of memory.

Important Memory Performance Counters That's not everything there is to know about virtual memory, but it's enough to make people avoid you. The important memory counters are described in Table 20.1. You can use this information to help you read other memory counters, too.

TABLE 20.1: IMPORTANT MEMORY COUNTERS

COUNTER	DESCRIPTION	WHAT THIS TELLS YOU
Memory: Available Bytes	Records the memory currently available on the server.	A low value may indicate that your server is low on memory or that one of the programs is experiencing memory leaks (especially if the number keeps decreasing). You should always have 4MB or more available. If you don't, then check for memory leaks or add more memory.
Memory: Commit Limit	Records the amount of memory that can be committed without extending the paging file. You can increase the paging file up to the limit of available space on the volume.	Extending the paging file is an expensive procedure (and requires CPU time), so it's a good idea to do this as little as possible. Make the paging file as large as you think you'll need—at least 2.5x the size of RAM you have installed.
Memory: Committed Bytes	Records the amount of memory committed to processes running on the server.	Records the amount of used RAM that requires space in the paging file in case the data must be paged to disk. Therefore, this is memory in use and unavailable to other processes, not just reserved in case a process needs it.
Memory: Pages Input/sec	Records the rate at which pages of data are written to RAM from the paging file to resolve page faults.	As this value describes hard page faults (the Page Faults counter includes soft page faults, which pull data from another area of memory and don't incur much of a hit), it's a good measure of how often you're having to pull data back from disk.
Memory: Pages Output/sec	Records the rate at which pages of data are written to the paging file to free RAM.	If the server seems to be running more slowly than it used to, monitor this counter. A high rate may indicate that the server doesn't have enough RAM to support all the data that the running applications need to keep handy.
Memory: Pages/sec	Records the current rate at which pages (4KB chunks of data on an x86 system, 8KB on an Alpha system) are read from disk back into physical memory to satisfy a page fault or are written to disk to free RAM.	A value of more than 20 pages per second implies a lot of paging and suggests that your server needs more memory.

Continued on next page

TABLE 20.1: IMPORTANT MEMORY COUNTERS *(continued)*

COUNTER	DESCRIPTION	WHAT THIS TELLS YOU
Paging File: % Usage	Records the percentage of the paging file currently in use.	If this value approaches 100%, then you need to enlarge the paging file or add more RAM. Although Win2K will make the paging file larger if need be, it's better if you do this manually so that Win2K doesn't need to use up CPU cycles to grow the paging file as needed.
Paging File: Usage Peak	Records the peak size of the paging file.	If this value is close to the maximum size of the paging file, you need to either enlarge the paging file or add more RAM. A high value implies that the paging file isn't big enough to hold all the data it must.
Physical Disk: % Disk Time	Records the percentage of time the disk spends servicing read or write requests.	Monitor this value for the physical disk that the paging file(s) are located on. If this amount seems to be increasing, check paging file usage and consider adding more memory.
Physical Disk: Avg Disk Queue Length	Records the average number of read and write requests waiting for the disk during the selected interval.	If this number is increasing at the same time the number of Memory: Page Reads/sec is increasing, that indicates that a lot of paging is going on. Monitor this value for the physical disk that the paging file(s) are located on.
Physical Disk: Avg Disk sec/Transfer	Records the length of time it takes the disk to transfer data to or from disk.	Monitor this value for the physical disk that the paging file(s) are located on to find out how responsive those disks are. This information may encourage you to move the paging file to a faster disk.
Process: Private Bytes	Records the virtual memory committed to that process.	This counter shows you how much memory a process (for all practical purposes, an application) is using. Especially if you're monitoring a terminal server, consider moving demanding applications to the client side or a different server to prevent other processes from being starved for memory.
Process: Working Set	Records the amount of RAM that the process is using to store data. The larger the working set, the more memory the process is consuming.	If a process's working set increases over time when you're not doing anything with it (like over a weekend), the process may be experiencing a memory leak.

NOTE *Notice that not all the counters you'll be monitoring for memory usage are in the Memory process object.*

Memory is complicated. Examining other potential server bottlenecks is, thankfully, a bit simpler.

Resolving Processor Bottlenecks

If you look at the counters available for the Processor object, you'll see a lot of counters for DPC and APC objects, some percentages of User and Privileged execution time, and so forth. Most of these won't help you much with server tuning. The DPC counters refer to *deferred procedure calls (DPCs)*, functions that perform a system task that is less essential than the currently executing system task, but which can grab a little processor time while the more important task is waiting for information that isn't yet ready. The APC counters refer to *asynchronous procedure calls (APCs)*, which provide a way for user programs and system code to execute code using the memory allocated to a specific application, and at a low level of priority. Basically, APCs interrupt an application that's using the CPU to make it do something else without going through the usually necessary rigamarole of shutting down the application's access to the CPU. In a broad sense, the counters for User and Privileged time refer to the percentage of time that the processor is spending executing instructions for user applications and system functions, respectively. Again, not information you can use for a lot of system tuning unless you're interested in the time that Windows 2000 spends executing system code in contrast to user code.

The information you *can* use for system tuning lies in the % Processor time and the Interrupts counters. Processor: % Processor Time tells you the percentage of time that the selected processor is doing something other than executing its "marking time" thread, the system Idle thread. Ideally, the processor is supposed to spend most of its time executing the Idle thread, because if that's the case, then the processor is available when it's needed. If Processor: % Processor Time rises above 75 percent on average, then that processor is working pretty hard and the server might benefit from a faster processor or an additional processor.

Here's one quick example of how I used % Processor Time for server tuning. When NT 3.5 came out, we were fascinated by the 3D Pipes screen saver. (We're boring. When the beta version of Windows 95 introduced Plug-and-Play support, many of the people in the company crowded around the computer running the beta, watching it discover an optical drive without rebooting.) However, using the Performance Monitor, we discovered very quickly that 3D Pipes was a serious processor hog and quit running it on any production server. According to Microsoft, changes in the NT architecture after NT 3.x (namely, moving many of the graphical components of the Win32 subsystem from user mode to the kernel so the commands to execute graphics instructions can be processed more quickly) have removed the problem under NT 4 and later. However, my experiments don't support this in Win2K. Figure 20.4 shows some output from a remote Performance Monitor session (that is, I'm monitoring the server from across the network to make sure that Performance Monitor doesn't impact the system), viewing an idle Win2K server with a 350MHz CPU. The Processor: % Processor Time counter I've selected shows the percentage of time the processor is doing something, rather than running the "idle thread" (the cybernetic equivalent of busywork) that Win2K occupies the processor with when no other threads need processor time.

NOTE *Actually, I could tell that the graphic subsystem uses the CPU time here by monitoring another counter: Processor: % Privileged Time. The graphics subsystem works in privileged mode. The high percentage of time the CPU spends in privileged mode when running the screen saver clinches the deal, given the location of the graphic subsystem.*

FIGURE 20.4

Use Performance Monitor to see how much time the processor is spending actively working.

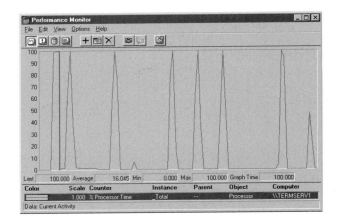

As you can see, this produces periodic spikes of nearly 100 percent utilization. As soon as I shut off the screen saver, the processor time drops to almost nothing. Now, if *that* doesn't convince you to avoid screen savers on servers, I don't know what will.

Interrupts/sec and % Interrupt time tell you how much time the processor is spending interrupting itself to handle requests from its hardware (network cards, video cards, keyboards, and so forth). If the value of Interrupts/sec exceeds 3500, then more than likely something's going wrong, either a buggy program or a board spewing out spurious interrupts. One common cause of excessive interrupts is badly designed device drivers. Are you running any beta device drivers? I've seen beta video drivers that spew out thousands of interrupts per second. You can test this by running the standard VGA driver and comparing the interrupts before and after. Another source of excessive interrupts is timer-driver programs. Some years ago, one network manager I know was seeing 4000 interrupts/second on a fairly quiet 486-based file server. After some playing around with the system, he realized that he was opening Schedule+ in his Startup group. He shut it down, and his interrupts/second dropped to a normal rate.

NOTE *I'd like to tell you that there's a System Monitor counter that lets you track interrupts/second on a program-by-program basis, but there isn't—much of this is just trial and error. Now and then I see a board that sends out a blizzard of interrupts if it's failing or, sometimes, when it's just cold. You might see this when you turn a workstation on Monday morning and it acts strangely for half an hour, then settles down.*

Resolving Disk Bottlenecks

The hard disks on your servers represent another potential sticking point for server production. For file servers, the bottleneck is obvious: the whole point of a file server is to grab data and pass it to the network for distribution. For application servers, the disk problem is more related to paging, because of the memory burden that applications incur. If you're running SQL Server or Exchange or supporting terminal server sessions, it's easy to run up against the amount of memory installed in the server—and when that happens, the server goes after your disk drive to support virtual memory.

There are a lot of counters for physical disks, but most of them don't tell you much in diagnostic terms except to help you see whether the disks are living up to their specifications. A couple that *do* are in Table 20.2.

TABLE 20.2: IMPORTANT DISK COUNTERS

COUNTER	DESCRIPTION	WHAT THIS COUNTER TELLS YOU
Physical Disk: % Disk Time	Reports the percentage of time the physical disk is busy.	If it's busy more than 90% of the time, then it's too busy—you'll improve performance if you get another disk or do less with that one.
Physical Disk: Current Disk Queue Length	Reports the current number of data transfer operations waiting for the specified physical disk (or all disks, if you choose) to handle them.	This value should be as small as possible. A high value indicates that disk waits are impacting users.

The counters in Table 20.2 can also apply to logical disks (C: drive, E: drive, and so on, as opposed to Disk 0 or Disk 1). Normally, Windows 2000 performance monitoring for logical disk objects is not enabled. To enable it, you'll need to use the `diskperf` command, which determines which disk monitoring objects are available. Diskperf has a number of arguments, but to turn on logical disk monitoring, you'll use the `diskperf -yv` switch. When you do so, you'll see a message telling you the status of disk monitoring—unless you edited the disk monitoring settings previously, both logical and physical disk performance counters will be available when you reboot—and when you reboot you'll find a new performance object in the System Monitor: Logical Disk. Logical Disk has all the same counters as Physical Disk.

All that said, you may not *need* the logical disk counters for the performance monitoring described in Table 20.2. We've already got counters telling us how many jobs are waiting in the disk queue at any given time and how often the disk is busy; monitoring logical disks instead of physical disks won't really tell us anything we didn't already know, since what we're looking at is disk stress. Logical disk counters are more useful when it comes to performance metrics such as Free Megabytes, which shows the amount of free space remaining on the selected disk. Another Logical Disk counter you might find useful for logical disks is Split IO/Sec, which keeps track of the number of split input/output actions on the disk. This counter is useful because a high number of split writes or reads (meaning that the disk controller is having to read from or write to more than one place on the disk during a single I/O action) can indicate a fragmented disk.

Resolving Network Bottlenecks

Your network's apparent speed (not what it's rated at, but how responsive it is) is a function of how much traffic there is on the network and how quickly the server can process user requests.

First, how busy is the network? You'll need to monitor the transport protocols you're running on the server. Recall that TCP/IP has several different parts—it's a suite of protocols, not a single one like NetBEUI—and the parts do different things. So, for example, a lot of IP datagrams tells you that your network card is getting a lot of regular (that is, data-related) traffic. A suddenly large number of ICMP datagrams could signify problems—or suggest that someone is pinging the heck out of your server. Look for differences in traffic levels, both on the protocol level and for the entire network card (you can monitor both). Are you getting transmission errors for inbound or outbound network traffic? How busy is the local network segment?

Second, how busy is the server? Is it seeing logon errors? How quickly are people logging in at different times of day? How many files are open on the server? If it's a terminal server session, how many users is it supporting? If it's an FTP server, then how many connections are you having to maintain? Is the server experiencing non-paged pool failures, failing to allocate memory to components that need non-paged memory because there's too little RAM installed on the system?

NOTE   *You can only get accurate network segment data if you have the Network Monitor for SMS installed. The Network Monitor that comes with Win2K only monitors data going to and from the monitored server. Therefore, you can get pretty much the same information from Network Interface that you can from Network Segment.*

Lots of questions. I'd suggest that you poke around the performance objects a bit to look for specific counters you want to monitor for your server, but Table 20.3 includes some of the more common counters you should watch.

TIP   *If your server is an Internet server of some kind (e-mail, FTP, Web, etc.), be sure to monitor the counters appropriate to its function.*

TABLE 20.3: IMPORTANT NETWORK-RELATED COUNTERS

COUNTER	DESCRIPTION	WHAT THIS COUNTER TELLS YOU
Server: Bytes Total/sec	Reports the rate at which the server is sending and receiving network data.	The total of bytes going in and out of the server per second gives you a pretty good indication of how busy the server is. If you do something to change the server load, like adding another server of that kind or added load balancing to the network, you can monitor this value to see whether the change actually did any good.
Server: Files Open	Reports the current number of files open at the moment of reporting. This is a current total, not a total of all the files that have been opened during a given time.	This counter is a good indicator of the traffic load a file server is experiencing. Sadly, there's no way to monitor file openings on a per-user or per-file basis.
Server: Pool Non-paged Failures	Reports the number of errors the server is reporting as it tries to allocate non-paged pool.	Lots of errors means that the server is running low on RAM and you'll need to add more.

Continued on next page

TABLE 20.3: IMPORTANT NETWORK-RELATED COUNTERS *(continued)*

COUNTER	DESCRIPTION	WHAT THIS COUNTER TELLS YOU
Server: Server Sessions	Reports how many people currently have connections to the server.	This counter may not tell you how busy the server is, but it can tell you how popular it is—especially if it's popular at an hour when no one should be accessing the server at all.
Network Interface: Bytes Total/sec	Reports the rate at which the network card is sending and receiving network data.	If this rate is significantly lower than what you'd expect, given the speed of your network and network card, it's time to do a little investigating to see whether something's wrong with the card.

Be sure to also monitor the protocols you've got installed for error conditions or heavy traffic at odd times.

Finally, if you're interested in using Performance Monitor like the Event Viewer, log the server object's errors. This can give you reports on failed logon attempts, file access attempts, and other attempted access that can indicate someone's trying to break into the network.

Remote Performance Monitoring

There's one big problem with running the Performance Monitor on a server: the Performance Monitor *itself* consumes resources. To keep an eye on servers on the network, consider monitoring them remotely. If you do, then you'll use a little network bandwidth but fewer resources on the monitored machine—and you'll get a more accurate reading, because you're not stressing the server by running the monitor on it.

TIP *The only time when it's to your benefit to run Performance Monitor locally is when you're monitoring counters related to network traffic. Monitoring remotely will increase network traffic and skew the results.*

Setting up remote performance monitoring is quite simple. When you're adding a counter to the monitor, you have a choice between adding the counter for the local machine or another one (see Figure 20.5). You can monitor any generation of NT computer, so if you've got a mixed environment it doesn't matter. You can also use Win2K Professional computers to do the monitoring, so you don't have to tie up a server for this task.

Make sure you've selected Select Counters from Computer, and type in the name of the computer you want to monitor with two preceding backslashes, like this: **Serpent**. (There's no Browse feature, so you have to know the name of the server you want to monitor. Annoyingly, Performance Monitor doesn't consistently "remember" the names of remote servers that it has monitored previously. Sometimes it does, and sometimes it develops amnesia.)

WARNING *Type server names carefully. If you mistype, it takes the System Monitor a while to discover that the server you've specified does not exist on the network.*

FIGURE 20.5

Adding a perform-
ance counter

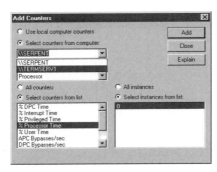

When you're done choosing the counter you want to monitor, add it as you normally would and close the dialog box. The remote computer's counter will be added to the list and identified by the computer name (see Figure 20.6).

FIGURE 20.6

Performance counters
to remote computers
will be displayed
alongside local ones.

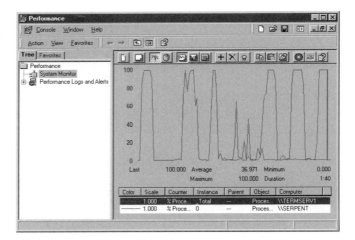

One of the cool things about doing remote performance monitoring is that it lets you compare server stress easily. If you select the same performance counter on two servers, you can compare the stress on those two servers.

WARNING *As explained in Chapter 15, Windows 2000 Server products support remote server administration using Terminal Services. Do not try to run the Performance Monitor from a Remote Administration session. The constant graphical updates made in Performance Monitor do not update smoothly on the client side. Besides, you're still running the monitor on the server and consuming resources—you're just watching from a different computer.*

Saving Chart Data

When you've identified the counters you want to monitor, you can save that information and reuse it later, either to monitor again (on the principle that what you need to monitor once, you almost certainly will need to monitor again) or to make them into an HTML file that you can display in a browser. To save chart settings, right-click somewhere in the Performance Monitor's display of current counters. From the context menu that appears, choose Save As to save the data, and you'll be prompted for the name of the HTML file. (This data will always be saved as a hypertext document.) The default folder is your personal `My Documents` folder, but you can browse for the right folder as you would with any Save As operation. Type a name for the file, and it's saved.

If you open the file, it will open in your browser as shown in Figure 20.7.

FIGURE 20.7

A saved Performance Monitor chart

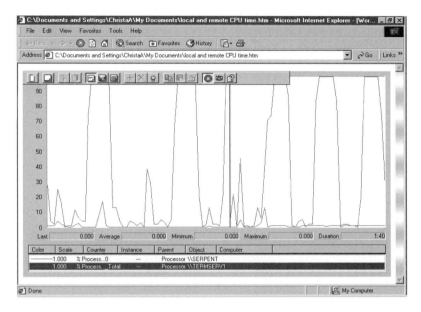

The cool part about this is that the file you're opening here will continue to display the monitored data. So long as the System Monitor is still running, you can dynamically update the output in this HTML chart. Why do it this way rather than just running the System Monitor? Mostly so you can streamline the UI. As you can see in Figure 20.7, the HTML view shows only the monitor, not the entire System Monitor tool.

To update the view steadily, click the Freeze Display button (the red button with the white X on it) in the browser to disable it. You'll see a warning that all current data will be cleared from the display; click OK. The display will clear and the browser will fill with the updated Performance Monitor data. To manually update the data (perhaps if you're making a presentation and don't want people to be distracted watching the updates to the output), then keep the Freeze Display button activated and click the Update Data button (the camera between the Freeze Display and Help buttons).

What about reusing this data in a later Performance Monitor session? I'll talk more about how to use this data in the next section.

Logging Performance Data

The NT 4 Performance Monitor included some logging support integrated with PerfMon itself. In Win2K, you've got the Performance Logs and Alerts section of the System Monitor to do that kind of work for you. Using a combination of comma-delimited and tab-delimited files and HTML documents, you can pass information between the Performance Monitor and the Logs and Alerts—or even on to another application such as Excel.

Understanding Log Types

The System Monitor supports three types of logs: counter logs, trace logs, and alert logs. *Counter logs* record data from local or remote computers about hardware usage and system service activity. *Trace logs* are event driven, recording monitored data such as disk I/O or page faults. When a traced event occurs, it's recorded in the log. *Alert logs* take trace logs one step further. They monitor counters and wait for them to exceed user-defined tolerances. When this happens, the event is logged. You can also set up an alert log to *do* something when the event happens, like send a message or run an application.

NOTE   You can either set up perpetual logging or log only for a preset period of time, so you aren't overwhelmed with data.

Creating Logs

To create a log, turn to the Performance Logs and Alerts section of the System Monitor. Open the folder for the type of log you want, so that its contents (or lack thereof) are displayed in the right details window. Right-click empty space in the Details window and choose an option for creating a new log from the shortcut menu that appears.

What happens from here depends on the type of log you're creating: a counter log, a trace log, or an alert log. Counter logs record system counters, like static versions of the performance logs we've discussed so far in this chapter. Trace logs keep track of data according to the part of the operating system that collects it. They differ from counter logs in that they provide less granularity. For example, rather than monitoring the Physical Disk object counters to get disk input and output data, you'd use a trace log. Trace logs can also draw information from non-system providers such as the Local Security Authority or the Active Directory Service to get information. Alert logs are like counter logs, but take them one step further. Counter logs just collect data. Alert logs collect performance object data for selected counters, using the same UI used for monitoring performance objects, but assess those counters against tolerances that you set when creating the log. In other words, with an alert log you don't collect *all* the data for the selected counters. Alerts are only logged when the performance data falls outside the acceptable range.

TIP   You could use counter logs to find out what's normal, then use alert logs to record aberrations from the norm. To read trace logs, you'll need to create an interpreter, so I'll stick with just describing them and focus more on how to use counter and alert logs.

Counter Logs

If you're starting from scratch, choose the New Log Settings option. Provide a unique descriptive name for the log in the box provided. Click OK, and you'll see the General tab of the log property sheet as shown in Figure 20.8.

FIGURE 20.8

When you create a new log, it will contain no counters to monitor.

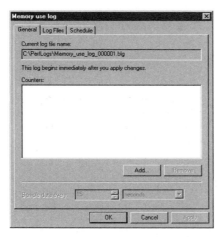

You aren't yet monitoring anything. To begin, click the Add button, and you'll open the same Select Counters dialog box you used to add counters to a Performance Monitor chart (see Figure 20.9). Make sure you've selected the computer that you want to log. As with charting, logging takes up resources, so consider running logs remotely.

FIGURE 20.9

Adding counters to log

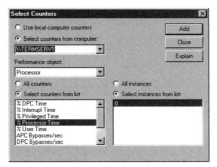

Click the Add button to add counters—you can add more than one from this window; just keep pushing the Add button—and click the Close button when you're done. The counters you selected will now be added to the Counters list on the General tab.

Back in the General tab, you can edit the sampling interval from its default of 15 seconds. The Sample Data Every box will accept an integer between 1 and 10,000, and the drop-down list of time units supports seconds, minutes, hours, or days. Pick an interval based on the duration of your expected logging time—the longer the period you're logging for, the wider you'll probably want the interval to be so you can see trends.

NOTE *You can reuse Performance Monitor counters that you've previously saved as an HTML file. If you plan to do so, start the creation process by choosing New Log Settings From in the New menu. You'll be prompted to provide the name of the saved file. After that, the process will work exactly as it does for creating a new counter log file from scratch. The General tab will display the counters used in the saved Performance Monitor file.*

Turn to the Log Files tab (see Figure 20.10) to edit file settings for the log.

FIGURE 20.10

Edit file settings to control file type, size, and name.

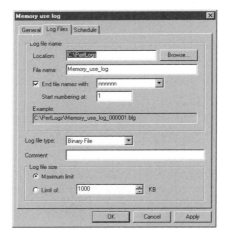

Most of these options are fairly self-explanatory, but let's take a quick tour:

◆ By default, logs are stored in a `Perflogs` folder on your Win2K server's boot partition. Unless you regularly back up this location, you might want to put the logs somewhere else for safekeeping.

◆ The name of the log is the filename. It must conform to the naming convention of the filesystem where you're storing the log.

◆ The auto filename suffix is an extension to the log filename that allows you to identify logs by their name, if you maintain more than one log with the same filename. The *nnnnnn* naming means that the files will be numbered in order (the first serial number determines the first number that will be used). Other options identify the file by the date it was created, whether by year; or month, day, and hour; or some other mechanism. Open the drop-down list to find the naming convention that works best for you.

◆ The log file comment will appear next to the list of log names in the folder, so add a comment if the log file requires further description.

◆ Unless you specify otherwise, the file is a binary file, but you can also save the data as a binary circular file, comma-delimited file (.CSV), or tab-delimited file (.TSV). CSVs and TSVs can both be opened in analysis applications such as Microsoft Excel. The only limitation to CSV and TSV logs is that they must log all at once—they can't accommodate logs that start and stop. Binary and binary circular files (both of which have .BLG extensions) are for recording data intermittently, when data collection may stop and then resume while the log is recording data. The binary files create sequential lists of all events, while the binary circular files record data continuously to the same log file so that previously written records are overwritten when new data is available.

◆ Choose whether to limit the log file size. If you're planning to log for only a certain period of time (specified on the Schedule tab), then you may not want to limit the log's size, so you don't lose any of the data you choose to save. However, if you don't plan to choose an automatic ending time, it might not be a bad idea to limit the log size so you don't get more data than you can usefully examine.

When you've edited all the file settings, turn to the Schedule tab (see Figure 20.11) to finish creating the counter log file.

FIGURE 20.11

Editing scheduling settings for the log file

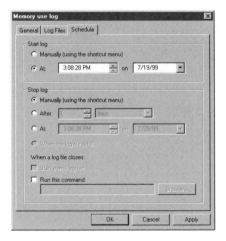

Normally, the log is set to start as soon as you finish—that is, it's set to start automatically at the time you started creating the log, which means it will begin logging as soon as you finish setting up options. You may not want to begin auditing the server as soon as you create the file if you're trying to gather information about server information under circumstances that you know will apply at a specific time. To manually start the log, choose that option here. Alternatively, you can specify a specific date and time the log should start.

Unless you specify otherwise, the log will keep collecting data until you shut it off manually. To schedule a stopping time or logging duration, click the After button and specify the time or period for which you want to log. In this same dialog box, you can also tell the System Monitor to restart the log when the preset period is ended (as you might do if you wanted to compare data from several different times of day) and name an application to run when the log is completed.

Click OK, and the new log will appear in the Details side of the Counter Logs folder. Its icon will be red until the log starts collecting data, either at the time you specified on the Schedule tab or when you right-click the log object and choose Start from the shortcut menu.

TRACE LOGS

To create a new trace log, select that object in the left pane and right-click in the right pane. As with counter logs, you can choose to either start from a saved Performance Monitor chart (New Log Settings From) or create a new log from scratch (New Log Settings). Type a unique name for the trace log when prompted, and click OK. When you do so, you'll see the General tab in Figure 20.12.

FIGURE 20.12

Choose counters for the trace log.

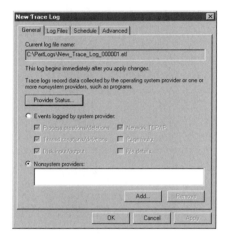

As you can see from this figure, you can collect data from two different types of providers. (A *provider* is just what it sounds like: something that *provides* information to an external application. In this case, the external application is the trace logging tool.). Services such as Kerberos can also send data to a trace log. The available non-system providers are visible when you select non-system providers to log and then click the Add button. From the list in the box that appears, you can pick available providers, such as the Active Directory service or Kerberos.

TIP   File I/O and page faults are not normally included in the trace log because of the very high values they're likely to register—a lot of I/O and page faults happen on a server operating normally. Microsoft recommends limiting the log to two hours if you want to include that data in the log.

The Log Files tab of the trace log creator works the same way the one for counter logs does, and so does the scheduler. The trace log creator includes one tab not in the counter log creator: Advanced (see Figure 20.13). Edit the settings here to make the buffers smaller or larger or to clear them periodically to make way for new data.

FIGURE 20.13

You can edit the size of the buffers reserved for a trace log.

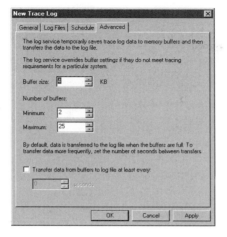

When you've edited all the trace log settings, click OK to return to the System Monitor. The log file will appear in the list. Its icon will be red until the log is running, then it'll turn green when it starts automatically or when you start it by right-clicking it and choosing Start.

ALERT LOGS

The initial stages of creating an alert log are much like those of creating a trace or counter log. Open the `Alert Logs` folder so that its contents are displayed on the right side of the System Monitor tool. Right-click anywhere in the blank area on the right of the display and choose New Alert Settings to define new counters to log or New Alert Settings From to open a saved Performance Monitor file and use its counters. Choose a name for the new alert, then click OK to open the alert log's property sheet (see Figure 20.14).

FIGURE 20.14

General tab of the alert log's property sheet

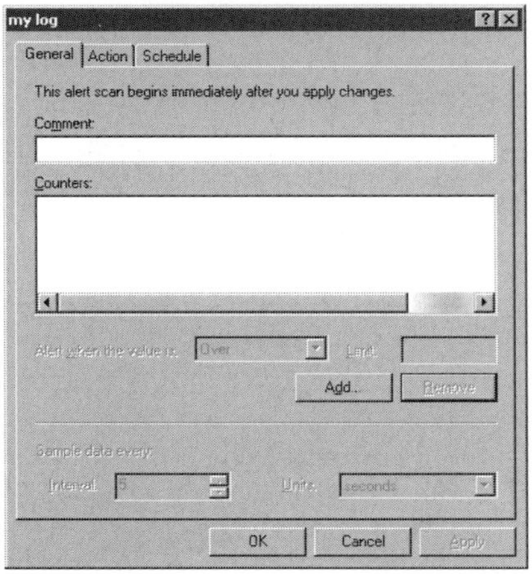

Assuming you're creating this log from new data, you'll need to add counters to the log as you did for a counter log. Click the Add button to open the dialog box in Figure 20.15, and choose the computer and performance counters you want to monitor. When you're done making selections (remember, you can add as many counters as you like by clicking the Add button), click Close to return to the General tab. The counters will show up in the list.

FIGURE 20.15

Adding counters to a log

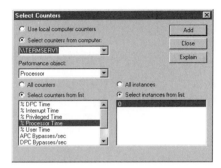

Below the list of added counters, you'll need to specify tolerances for each counter you choose. When the counter exceeds those tolerances, the alert log will add an entry to the file. For example, say that you added Physical Disk: Avg Disk Queue Length to the log. That monitors the number of read and write requests waiting for processing to the specified physical disk. If more than four requests are waiting, then that implies that the disk is too busy to handle all the demands placed on it and you need to do something about that. Therefore, you'd set the tolerances for this counter to be over four, as shown in Figure 20.16.

FIGURE 20.16

Adjust alert tolerances

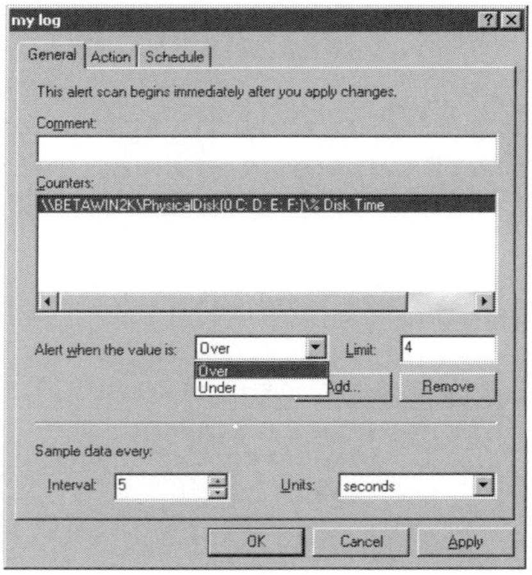

Notice that the default sampling interval for alerts (five seconds) is much shorter than the one for counters. This is because of the different nature of the log—it's assumed that you're a little more concerned about the contents of this one. Use the drop-down lists to edit the sampling intervals if you need to.

TIP *Tune alert logs carefully. The shorter interval and extra processing required to manage alerts will impact a server.*

The scheduling tab for alert logs works just like the one you used to configure counter and trace logs, but the Action tab (see Figure 20.17) is something new. From this tab, you'll need to tell the System Monitor what you want it to do when it generates an alert.

FIGURE 20.17

Edit alert settings

Normally, System Monitor just adds an entry to the Event Viewer's application Event log. If the alert isn't something that you need to know about right away, then you can leave it at that. More important alerts, however, like those generated by network errors or a severe shortage of memory, may require immediate action. From the Alert menu, you can tell System Monitor to send you (or someone else) a message when writing an entry in the alert log or even to have it run a specific application that you can use to resolve the problem. Use this tab to send arguments to the application.

Once again, when you're done editing the alert log's properties, click OK to add it to the `Alert Logs` folder. When it's running, its icon will be green.

Viewing Log Data

Setting up the log data is the easy part, once you know what you want to monitor. Reading and interpreting that data is harder. The method of viewing log output depends on the file type you've saved the log in. Sadly, you don't have a built-in reader for trace log files and you can't change their file type to open with your existing tools. Therefore, on the assumption that you're not planning on whipping up an interpreter using the Microsoft Software Development Kit, let's focus on counter and application logs.

COUNTER LOGS

Recall that when you're creating counter logs, you have a choice about how to present the data. The default option is to save the data in a binary log file (.BLG) that you can examine from System Monitor. To see this data, click the icon on the System Monitor that has the database symbol (a cylinder) on it and browse to the location where you saved the log file when setting it up. This will open the contents of the log like a static performance monitoring chart, so you can see what performance was like at a given time without having to be on the spot at that moment.

Charts are nice, but there will also be times when you want to view the information in a spreadsheet so you can manipulate the way it's presented. To do so, you'll save the log data in a tab-delimited (.TSV) or comma-delimited file (.CSV) that you can open with a spreadsheet application such as Microsoft Excel. To view the data, just open the file with Excel. If the log is still active, you'll see an error message telling you that another user or application is using the data, but you can open it as a read-only document or click the Notify option to open the file—you just can't save it to its current name while the log is still writing to the file. From there, you can use Excel's charting tools to massage the data to make a good presentation.

ALERT LOGS

Alert logs don't go into a regular file but directly to the Event Viewer's Application log (see Figure 20.18). When the counters exceed the tolerances you've set up, Win2K will add an Information record to the Application Event log.

FIGURE 20.18

Output of an alert log

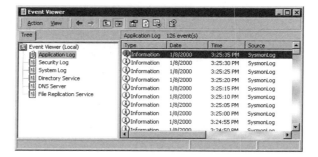

Whattheheckhappened? Troubleshooting with the Event Viewer

Win2K defines an event as any significant occurrence in the system or in an application that users should be aware of and have the chance to log. Critical events—those that can impact server availability—deserve immediate notifications, which is why you'll see "low on virtual memory" announcements on your monitor without asking for them. Less-critical but still important events are recorded in the Event Viewer, a tool in the Administrative Tools program group.

To make Win2K record, retrieve, and store logs of events, you must activate and configure event logging. You can edit just about any kind of event on a server: file and directory access, services starting (or failing to start), unexpected conditions on the server, or, as discussed earlier, alert logs based on System Monitor data.

Understanding Log Types

Win2K maintains six types of logs. Three you may recall from NT 4 and earlier: system, security, and application. System events (see Figure 20.19), the only ones logged by default, are generated by Win2K system components or related services and drivers. Security events (see Figure 20.20) record changes to any security settings or any audited access such as attempts to open files or folders. You can monitor both successful and failed security events. Application logs (see Figure 20.21) contain events generated by applications or by alert logs.

FIGURE 20.19

System log

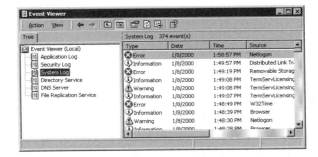

FIGURE 20.20

Security log

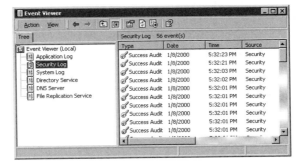

FIGURE 20.21

Application log

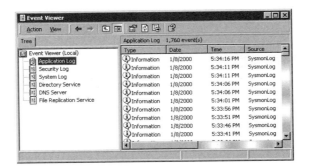

Three other logs—Directory Service, DNS Server, and File Replication Service—are new to Win2K. They're for keeping track of AD-related events. The Directory Service log entries record information regarding the NT Directory Service, problems connecting to the global catalog, and any issues regarding Active Directory in your network. The DNS Server entries record any events related to running the Directory Name Service in your Active Directory. Finally, the File Replication log entries record any notable events that took place while the domain controller attempted to update other domain controllers.

To view any log, open the Event Viewer. From the left pane showing the log types, click the type you want to view. The display in the right pane will change to show the log's contents.

Viewing Remote Event Log Data

You can connect to any NT or Win2K computer with an account in your domain (or in another, trusted domain). To do so, right-click the main `Event Viewer` folder in the left pane of the tool. From the shortcut menu that appears, choose Connect to Another Computer. You'll see a dialog box that looks like the one in Figure 20.22.

FIGURE 20.22

Choose a computer to manage.

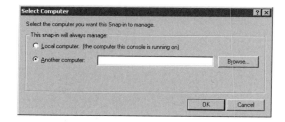

Enter the name of the computer you want to monitor (for example, **serpent**). Alternatively, you can browse for the computer you want to monitor. The other computer can be running Win2K or Windows NT or can be a LAN Manager 2.*x* server. Click Finish, click Close, and then click OK. If the new computer requires a low-speed connection, right-click the log you want to view, and then click Properties. On the Action menu, click Properties, and then click Low Speed Connection (on the General tab).

Alternatively, you can right-click the root of the Event Viewer being logged to open its shortcut menu. Click the Connect to Another Computer option and type the name of the computer you want to manage. If you're not sure of its name, click the Browse button to find the computer you want (see Figure 20.23).

FIGURE 20.23

Find a computer to manage.

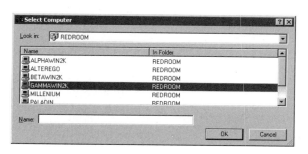

NOTE   *You can only monitor NT or Win2K computers that have a computer account in the selected domain and are currently connected to the network. All computer accounts will be listed, even if a particular computer is offline at the moment.*

When you've chosen a computer, click OK back in the Select Computer dialog box. The Event Viewer information displayed will now be the remote computer's.

Reading Log Entries

There are five categories of log entries, each identifiable by an icon:

◆ Information events describe the successful completion of a task, such as the beginning of a service. If you're using Alert logging, information events in the Application log may also indicate that an alert's been triggered, so don't assume that all information events are benign.

◆ Warning events aren't necessarily bad—they describe unexpected behavior that might point to future problems if not corrected.

◆ Error events describe fatal errors that mean a task failed. Error events may lead to data loss; they always mean that the server wasn't able to do something you asked it to do.

◆ Success events describe an audited security event that Win2K completed as requested.

TIP   *Some third-party services log successful starting as a success event instead of an information event.*

◆ Failed events describe an audited security event that Win2K could not complete as requested.

Each entry also includes the following information pertinent to the event:

◆ Date and time logged

◆ Object logging the event (such as the service that failed to start)

◆ Computer name of the server where the event was generated and, if applicable, the name of the person responsible for generating the event

◆ If applicable, the category of event, which won't tell you much—it's for the internal use of whatever server component logged the event

◆ Event number describing the event type to Win2K

Double-click any event in any log to open its property sheet (see Figure 20.24) and see more information about the event. The explanation is sometimes more than a little cryptic or is incomplete, but sometimes—and this gets easier with practice—you can glean useful information from the explanations of the events.

Troubleshooting with the Event Viewer takes a little practice. For best results, you'll need to know what your system looks like when it's running normally so you can more easily identify the events that indicate something is broken. Reading the Event Viewer on a regular basis also lets you find out about problems you may not have known you had, like misconfigured services, undetected because no one's using them much, or a drive running low on disk space. If a server seems to be acting oddly, then check the Event Viewer for warnings or informational messages that may explain what's going on. For example, reading the System log once helped me find a rogue program running on a server that I hadn't properly firewalled. A terminal server refusing connections because of a lack of licenses will also log this information in the Event log.

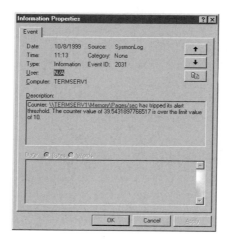

TIP *The Win2K Resource Kit includes a Windows 2000 Event Log Database that purports to list every message that could be included in any Event Viewer log. It's not especially helpful, because it doesn't include any more information than is already in the Event Viewer entries, but it's a good look at all the thousands (yes, I mean thousands) of event types you might encounter. You'll need Access installed to view this database. To run it, open the Resource Kit management console (if you've installed the Resource Kit, you can get to this from the Programs program group) and view the tools in alphabetical order.*

Managing and Archiving Log Contents

That's what you're looking at in the Event Viewer. *Managing* all that data can be a task unto itself.

DISCARDING OLD DATA

The Event Viewer logs will keep filling up according to their settings. After a while (and, if you're recording something that happens a lot, "a while" may not be long), they get full. Unless you specify otherwise, an Event log cannot get any bigger than 512KB.

To keep the data fresh, the Event Viewer normally overwrites events more than seven days old with the newer information on the principle that data more than a week old isn't helpful anymore. To edit this, open the property sheet for a log by right-clicking its icon and choosing Properties. Turn to the General tab shown in Figure 20.25.

WARNING *If you click the Clear All Events button on this tab, you'll delete all the entries in that log. Save logs before clearing them if you think you might need the data again.*

FIGURE 20.25

Edit the settings governing how data is discarded when the log is full.

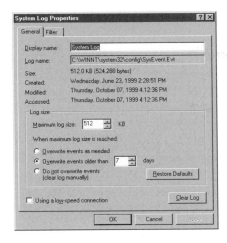

FILTERING DATA

Normally, the Event Viewer will display all records that it's collected, with the most recent entries at the top of the log. You can simplify the view of all this data by applying filters to the logged data. Filters don't affect what information is logged, only how it's displayed.

To filter a log's events, right-click the log's icon in the left pane and choose Filter from the View menu. You'll see the Filter tab shown in Figure 20.26. Choose the filtering options you want, described in Table 20.4. Only event logs with the options you specify (you can apply as many as you like) will appear in the Event log once you've applied the filter.

FIGURE 20.26

Filter data to display only pertinent information.

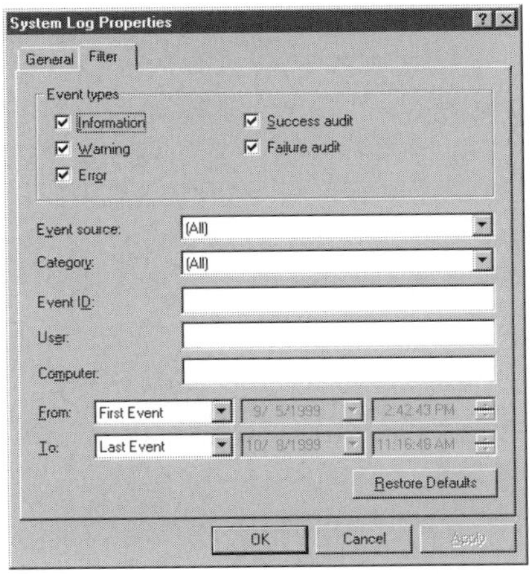

TABLE 20.4: FILTERING OPTIONS FOR EVENT LOGGING

OPTION	DESCRIPTION
Category	Includes all events within a given category. This filter is most useful for security events, as most system events do not belong to any category and the application categories are numbered, with no keys.
Computer	Includes all events on that particular computer. As the computer in question is the one you're monitoring and you can only display one computer's Event log at a time, it's not clear to me why this filter is part of the Event Viewer.
Error	Includes all error events, which are requested tasks that Win2K was unable to complete for some reason.
Event ID	Includes all events with that event ID. You can only specify one event ID at a time—you can't, for example, filter the Event log to display both event ID 7000 and event ID 4002.
Event Source	Displays events stemming from a user-specified source (a driver, system component, or service).
Failure Audit	Displays failed security events such as opening a file or changing a security setting. The events this will include depend on the security and auditing settings for the domain or computer.
Information	Displays information events. Information events typically mean that everything worked as planned, but you can use information events to reassure yourself that yes, that service started as planned, so it couldn't be a problem there.
Success Audit	Displays successful security events such as opening a file or changing a security setting. The events this will include depend on the security and auditing settings for the domain or computer.
User	Displays events that are associated with a particular user, generally the user working at the console when the event was generated. Not all events have a user associated with them—this is mostly a system log thing.
View From and To	Use these boxes to specify a range of events to display. Unless you tell it otherwise, the Event log will display all events in the log from the oldest to the newest, but you can provide starting and finishing dates and times.
Warning	Includes warning events, which tell you that something didn't go as expected (or, for alert logs, that a counter exceeded the tolerance you set up) but that the problem isn't immediately critical.

Filters work like Boolean AND statements, not OR statements. That is, if you specify event ID 7000 and check the Error box, then the log will only display entries that are errors associated with event ID 7000, not all errors and all entries with event ID 7000.

TIP *Want to view all data of a certain type but aren't sure how to filter the Event log? Click the column heading that corresponds to the type of data you want to view, and the log will sort its entries based on that type. For example, if you want to see all the entries associated with the Browser service, click the header for the Source column. All entries related to the Browser service will be grouped together.*

SAVING AND RETRIEVING LOG DATA

Like I said, logs get full. You may want the data in them for future reference, however, so you don't necessarily want to just clear all log file entries. To save a log file, right-click the log's icon in the left pane of the Event Viewer. From the shortcut menu, choose Save Log File As. A dialog box will open; type the name of the log, click Save, and you're done. You can now clear the file to begin logging afresh.

To open a saved log, right-click the Event Viewer icon in the left pane and choose Open Log File. You'll see a dialog box like the one in Figure 20.27. Browse for the .EVT file containing the saved log, choose a log type and a display name, and click OK.

FIGURE 20.27

Opening a saved
log file

When you've loaded the saved Event log, it will appear alongside the other event logs as shown in Figure 20.28.

FIGURE 20.28

Loaded event logs
don't replace existing
log files of the same
type, they supplement them.

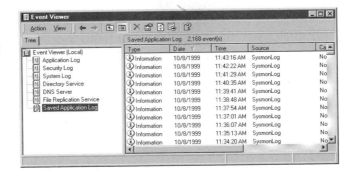

Quick Looks: Using the Task Manager

The tools we've talked about so far are good for gathering information for the long term, but setting them up and finding the relevant data takes a little time. When you want to get a quick glance at the State of the Computer, the Task Manager is the way to go. It requires almost no setup, gives you an easy way to determine which applications are hogging resources—as well as providing a shortcut to shutting down runaways—and generally offers you an instantaneous look at how the server is operating. You can't save or log data with the Task Manager, but you can see how the server is performing without having to set up performance counters. I use the Task Manager frequently on both servers and workstations.

To get to the Task Manager, press Ctrl+Alt+Del to bring up the Windows Security dialog box. Click the Task Manager button to open the box in Figure 20.29.

FIGURE 20.29

Get a visual snapshot of the server with the Task Manager's Performance tab

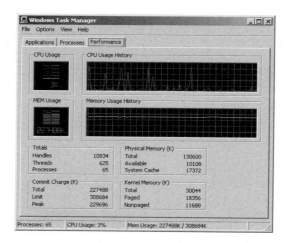

Graphically, this dialog box is pretty easy to interpret; processor-wise, it's a little stressed but not constantly, and it's using a fair amount of memory at the moment. This graphical data is collected from the time I open the Task Manager, so it will take a minute or two to get much of a snapshot of current processor and memory usage. The text on the bottom of the page takes a little more interpretation. In the Totals section in the upper left, the Processes count is a rough estimate of the number of executable files (not just user applications, but any executable file) running on the server. The Thread count represents the number of executable threads that are using those process resources and contending for processor time. The Handles count represents the number of connections that the processes have to system resources such as internal timers. Moving to the right, the Physical Memory section gives us a little more useful information: how much memory is available on the computer and how much of it is currently in use. This memory count includes only the installed RAM in the computer, not the paging file. The Kernel Memory section on the bottom right shows how much memory kernel processes (such as most of the graphical subsystem for Windows 2000) are using, and how much is paged to disk. Finally, the Commit Charge section in the bottom left shows how much memory is committed to particular processes and is not available to other processes.

The Applications tab of the Task Manager shows (some) of the executable files running on the computer, along with the data files they have open (if applicable). As you can see from Figure 20.30, you can use the buttons on this tab to navigate to running applications or end runaway applications— a runaway might show a status of Not Responding. You can also right-click on individual applications to change their window state (maximized or minimized), switch to them, close them, or find their process on the Processes tab.

NOTE *If an application crashes and is in the middle of being debugged, you can't end it until the debugger is done gathering information, and if closing the application causes the application to open a window prompting you for information (perhaps to save a file) then you'll need to either answer the prompt or choose the End Now option when prompted to override the application's prompt. Generally speaking, you're better off closing the application normally if you can.*

FIGURE 20.30

The Applications tab shows running user applications and any data files they have open

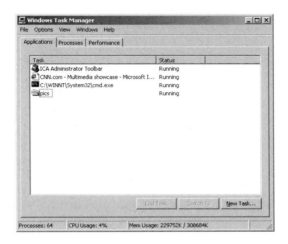

The Processes tab in the Task Manager (see Figure 20.31) takes the basic information presented with the Applications tab and significantly expands on it. The Image Name column shows the executable files associated with the applications on the Applications tab and displays all the operating system executables—that CSRSS.EXE file is the Win32 subsystem. The PID column shows the process ID for that executable, the identifier for the process created to support the needs of that executable. (I've mentioned this elsewhere, but it's worth a quick review: Executables represent sets of instructions that need to run on a computer. When you start an executable, Windows 2000 creates a process with resources—memory and the like—for that executable. That process also has at least one thread. The threads are the pieces of the process that actually run.) Windows 2000 identifies running processes both by the name of the executable file they're supporting and by their Process ID. The CPU column shows the processor that each executable is using; in a single-processor system this won't tell you anything you don't already know, but in a multi-processor system could be useful. The CPU Time column, on the other hand, shows you useful information—you can tell which executables are using the most CPU time. If all is going well, then the System Idle Process should be at the top of the list. The Mem Usage column shows the size of the working set for each executable. However, since this total includes shared pages, you can't add all these numbers up to get a complete count of the RAM installed in a particular computer.

TIP *To sort the data displayed on the Processes tab, click the appropriate column head.*

This is only a small sample of the options available to you when it comes to getting a current snapshot of the computer. When the Processes tab is in the foreground, the View menu in the Task Manager has a Select Columns option. Pick this menu item, and you'll see a dialog box like the one in Figure 20.32. The selected boxes will be listed on the Processes tab.

FIGURE 20.31

The default counters on the Processes tab represent only a small number of the counters available.

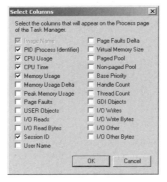

For example, notice that my Processes tab has a Session ID column, whereas yours may not. (This option will only be available if you install Terminal Services.) This column is used on servers with Terminal Services enabled, whether in Remote Administration or Application Server mode, to identify the session in which a particular executable file is running.

NOTE   *When Terminal Services is enabled in either Remote Administration or Application Server mode, the Task Manager's Processes tab displays the check box on the bottom, allowing you to show all session processes or just the ones running in the current session. (The console is Session 0.) Clear this box to get a more streamlined view of the server, or select it if you want to know what executables are running in all sessions, whether visible to you or not.*

FIGURE 20.32

Use the Processes tab to find out how much memory or processor time an executable file is using.

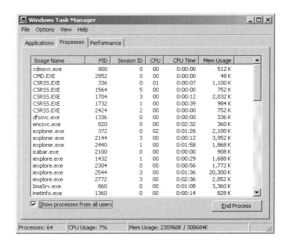

I find myself using the Processes tab most often of all the parts of the Task Manager. It's a very easy way to find out what's active on your server quickly, without mucking around with adding counters or checking the Event log. If you see what looks like an ongoing problem, then you can set up logging in the System Monitor.

Basic Tuning Stuff

So far, we've talked a lot about how to *collect* information from a server using the System Monitor, Event Viewer, and the Task Manager, but not so much about how you can exploit this information to make your servers run more efficiently. Let's open the Control Panel and see what settings we can edit now that we know a little better what state of health our servers are in.

Optimizing Server Processing Power

Windows NT Server 4 and NT Workstation had several obvious differences, but one of the major differences wasn't obvious. The core files required to run NT Server and NT Workstation were and are the same, but at boot time the OS looks in the Registry key `HKLM\System\CurrentControlSet\Control\ProductOptions`. Run REGEDT32 and look in that key on a Win2K system, and, among other information, you'll see a value for Product Type. That value was (and is—this hasn't changed) WinNT for Windows NT Workstation/Win2K Professional computers, LanmanNT for domain controllers, and ServerNT for server computers.

Why does this value matter? Based on the value of this key, NTLDR makes some decisions about how to configure the system, including runtime policy decisions such as how operating system components and user processes contend for memory and even how the processes contend for CPU time.

The most obvious result of this is that Windows 2000 Server gives a little more time to the application in the foreground than the ones in the background. But Windows 2000 Professional gives a *lot* more time to the application in the foreground, on the premise that the application you're directly interacting with is the one you want to be most responsive. If you ran, say, Microsoft Word from an Windows 2000 Server machine, it would run rather less efficiently than if you ran the application from a Windows 2000 Professional. This is because even when you were typing into Word, Windows 2000 Server would be a little distracted, checking with any other running processes to make sure they were happy and getting enough CPU time. Windows 2000 Server is meant to be a *server*, not a workstation.

NOTE *You could edit the Performance settings in the System applet of the Control Panel, but I'm talking about the way the operating systems were set to run under normal conditions.*

Ah, but what about Terminal Services? It's a server, but a server of a very special kind, since it's providing computing resources to a bunch of client machines. For that reason, Terminal Services should give more time to foreground applications than to background applications and services, as the foreground applications are the most important to the overall performance of the server.

Windows NT, Terminal Server Edition (TSE), was designed to always run foreground applications more efficiently, because if you installed TSE it was assumed you were using the server for terminal services—otherwise, you would have saved yourself some money and stuck with single-user NT. Win2K, on the other hand, comes with terminal services but doesn't have to run them—the multiuser capability is a service instead of a core part of the operating system and, as such, can be installed and uninstalled.

If Terminal Services is running and you've set up Win2K to be an application server when you installed the services, then the operating system is normally optimized for running foreground appli cations. (You've got another option of installing terminal services only for remote administration of the server, in which case the server is optimized for fulfilling server functions.)

If you're using Terminal Services for its usual function of supporting clients running applications from the terminal server, then this is fine. Under rare circumstances, however, you may want to give equal time to all running applications even when the server is supporting user applications. To do so while still running Terminal Services in Application Server mode, open the System applet in the Control Panel. Turn to the Advanced tab, and click the Performance Options button to open the dia log box you see in Figure 20.33.

FIGURE 20.33

Edit performance options.

In the Application Response section, make sure the Background option is selected. This tells Win2K to give all running applications equal access to CPU cycles. This may make your foreground applications a little more jerky, but other applications will respond to user requests more smoothly.

WARNING   *Generally speaking, you should* not *edit the Application Response options setting; this is for the exceptional case. When you install Terminal Services in Remote Administration mode, CPU time will remain in Server mode, so you won't need to edit this setting then.*

Editing Virtual Memory Settings

While we're in the Performance dialog box of the System applet, take a look at the virtual memory sections (see Figure 20.34).

The default location for the paging file is `%systemroot%\pagefile.sys`. This isn't always the best place for it, however. Generally speaking, your server will be happier if its paging file is on a separate logical disk from the operating system files. Paging files are good candidates for disk fragmentation, and a fragmented disk is not a fast disk—not good when you're trying to use an operating system from that disk.

To move the paging file from its original location, open the dialog box shown here and select the local drive where you want the paging file to go. Type in a minimum and maximum size for the pag ing file in the boxes provided. Also, select the drive where the paging file *was* and zero it out. For what should be obvious reasons, you can't put the paging file on a network-accessible drive. (In case it's not obvious, you don't want the memory manager putting important data on a disk that might not be available when the memory manager needs that data *back*.) And although removable drives (such as Jaz drives) will show up in the list of local drives that you could put a paging file on, they're displayed with a free space of 0MB, so you can't put the drives there.

FIGURE 20.34

Virtual memory settings for Win2K

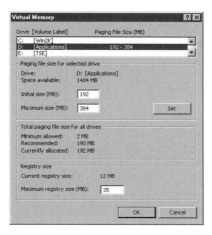

TIP   *Try to make sure that the paging file is as large as it needs to be from the beginning. Although it will get bigger as needed, the process of making the file get bigger is resource-intensive. You'll get better performance if you make the minimum size of the paging file something resembling its necessary size.*

When you finish, the size of the new paging file should be shown in the Paging File Size column next to the right drive, and that space in the original drive should be blank. Click the Set button to establish the paging file. You'll need to restart the server, but once you do, the paging file will be moved to the new location.

What if you zero out the original page file but forget to specify the location of a new one? You'll be prompted to reboot the computer as usual for changing the size of the paging file. However, when you reboot, Win2K will display a nastygram telling you that the computer either has no paging file or it's too small. It will create a temporary paging file called `temppf.sys`, storing it in the `%systemroot%\system32` folder. You must follow the instructions here (and also provided on the nastygram) for creating a new paging file on the appropriate disk. Your server will work until you do this, but it will start with no virtual memory. The new paging file will grow slowly as needed, causing you to run low on virtual memory from time to time. In other words, don't delete the paging file without creating a new one unless you want to see how the server will operate in low-memory conditions.

Tuning the System Cache

Win2K's default memory settings reflect NT's legacy as a file-sharing NOS. By default, it's set up with a large *system cache*, which is a range of virtual memory addresses reserved for holding recently used data related to file sharing, whether from hard disks, CD-ROMs, or network-accessible drives. The cache includes any data related to file reads and writes, including file contents, read and write activity to a file, or the metadata that describes a drive's structure and organization. The system cache has a range of virtual memory addresses dedicated to it, with the exact size of the range depending on the amount of physical memory installed in the server. Just as the size of the paging file increases as you install more physical memory, the system cache does, too, up to an initial limit of 512MB on an x86 system.

NOTE   You can see how much physical memory your server's system cache is using by monitoring the value of Memory: System Cache Resident Bytes. Although the System Monitor has a counter called Memory: Cache Bytes, this counter doesn't actually reflect just the System Cache working set. It reflects the entire system working set, including paged pool and any driver code and NTOSKRNL data that can be paged to disk. System Cache memory usage is also visible from the Performance tab of the Task Manager.

Up to 512MB of virtual memory addresses is a lot. If a server's supporting file sharing, then it needs this big reserved virtual memory space. However, cacheing all that data may cause a lot of disk thrashing as the data goes in and out of physical memory. If a particular server isn't doing file sharing, you can save yourself some physical memory by changing the memory usage parameters for network use. To do so, open Network and Dial-Up Connections. Right-click Local Area Connection and open its property sheet. Select File and Printer Sharing for Microsoft Networks, and open that service's property sheet as shown in Figure 20.35.

FIGURE 20.35

Server Optimization options

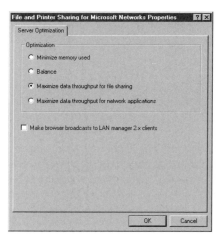

The default setting is Maximize Data Throughput for File Sharing. If you're not using the server to share files, change this setting to Maximize Data Throughput for Network Applications, or to Balance. (The Minimize Memory Used setting is only a good idea for servers serving a very few users, like fewer than 10.) This should reduce the amount of paging to disk that your server's doing.

Server Tuning

You can actually do quite a bit to make servers more responsive. Doing so requires tuning the server *and* keeping unnecessary junk off the network.

SIMPLIFY PROTOCOLS

One of the best pieces of network-tuning advice I can give you is to remove unnecessary protocols and services. Protocols and services steal memory and CPU time. Multiple protocols require multiple browse lists, which in turn steal CPU time from the machine that is the master browser, and Win2K Server machines are often elected as master browsers. One of the most common reasons a Win2K system fails to recognize a workstation, leading to a "no domain controller was available to" error message, is that the server simply has too many protocols to listen to. Try to pick *one* protocol and work with that one.

If you're using the TCP/IP stack, you find that it sometimes receives short shrift from the network because the more frenetic IPX and NetBEUI protocols grab more processor attention. (Must be an age thing—they're younger and therefore more hyper.) As a result, the TCP/IP stack may end up dropping more messages than it would if the other protocols didn't exist; one other symptom is an incomplete browse list. If you can, remove extraneous protocols. If possible, just trim down to TCP/IP. In most cases, you should be able to get away with using only TCP/IP unless you're isolating parts of the network by making them use a separate network protocol.

ONE REMEDY: SEGMENT THE NETWORK

If the network utilization is getting excessively high, you have to reduce the network traffic on that network segment. You can do that either by removing network applications—put the company Web server on a segment of its own, for instance—or by breaking up existing segments. Instead of three segments of 100 PCs, break it up into six segments of 50 PCs apiece.

But then you have to be sure to get good, fast routers to connect the network segments. Win2K servers can do the job fairly well on low-volume networks, but look to dedicated routers from companies like Compatible Systems or Cisco Systems for more heavy-traffic network segments.

RAISE SERVER PRIORITY

By default, the file server has a lower priority than the print server, potentially causing printing to slow down a dual-use server. Printing priority is set by default to 2, and file server priority is set to 1; larger numbers have higher priority. You can change the priority by modifying the Registry. Open the Registry Editor on the file server and turn to HKLM\System\CurrentControlSet\Services\lanmanserver\parameters. Add a value entry ThreadPriority of type DWORD, and set it to 2.

ENSURE THAT WIN2K CAN CONTINUE TO AUTOTUNE

Win2K's file server module includes almost two dozen tuning and control parameters. Most of them control exactly how much memory Win2K devotes to different parts of the server module. For example, what's the maximum number of sessions the server will have to keep track of at any moment in time? Win2K must know that so it can pre-allocate some RAM as working space, a place in memory to track each session. That's set by an "autotuning" parameter every time you start up a server. Similarly, what's the maximum amount of memory the server service can use at any time, both in pageable (able to be swapped out to disk) and non-pageable flavors? More autotuned parameters.

Could you choose to control these parameters yourself? If you wanted to, you certainly could, but I wouldn't recommend it. But doing some basic administrative tasks could inadvertently make it impossible for Win2K to tune its own parameters.

Elsewhere in this book, you'll see commands that start with NET CONFIG SERVER; for example, as you'll read in the upcoming section on the Browser, typing **net config server /hidden:yes** puts a server in "Romulan cloaking device" mode, wherein the server never appears in My Network Places. Alternatively, you might want to add a comment to the My Network Places display of your server by typing **net config server /srvcomment:***whatever comment you like.* In either case, using the NET CONFIG SERVER command (lower- or uppercase doesn't matter, by the way, save for whatever case you desire within the message itself) has a nasty side effect.

For some reason, when you set *one* parameter with NET CONFIG SERVER, Win2K writes out the current values of *all* the autotuning parameters. (These parameters are in HKLM\System\CurrentControlSet\Services\lanmanserver\parameters.) The nasty side effect is this: When Win2K starts up the Server service, the Server service looks in the Registry to see if these autotunable parameters are present. If they are, Windows 2000 does *not* attempt to retune them. Actually, this is true even if you never touched NET CONFIG. This matters mainly if you have changed the amount of RAM in your system. Add more RAM and reboot, and Windows 2000 will adjust all the autotunable parameters. But if they've been inadvertently cast in concrete by the simple act of hiding or naming a server, that autotuning doesn't happen.

To restore autotuning, look in HKLM\System\CurrentControlSet\Services\lanmanserver\parameters; you'll see a whole bunch of entries *if* you've done a NET CONFIG SERVER at some point. (If you've never configured the server at all, there will still be a couple for *NullSessionPipes* and *NullSessionShares*, but that's all.) Then start deleting those value entries. Don't get *too* nuts—if you've made your server a time source, don't delete TimeSource, or if you've hidden the server, don't delete Hidden, Srvcomment, ThreadPriority, or any other entry you have entered in the past for some reason.

Using the Most Current Drivers

One of the simplest things you can do to make your server happy is make sure it's always got the most recent certified drivers. (Sometimes, manufacturers release drivers on a beta basis, but I'd be cautious about using those on a production machine.) New drivers may provide better performance or add features—or fix problems caused by other drivers, like the runaway network card diagnostic service that gave me a deep and lasting appreciation for the powers of the Recovery Console (covered in Chapter 21). Buggy device drivers can also produce a blizzard of interrupts, which will slow down the CPU as it attempts to respond to all these requests for processing even if there's nothing to process.

TIP   *To detect excessive interrupts in a video board, try comparing values of Processor: % Interrupt Time or Processor: Interrupts/sec with the video in normal mode and in VGA mode. If you see many more interrupts while the video's in normal mode, try replacing the video driver.*

To update a driver in your system, open the System applet in the Control Panel and turn to the Hardware tab. Click the Device Manager button to open the Device Manager shown in Figure 20.36.

FIGURE 20.36

Check hardware settings and update drivers from the Device Manager.

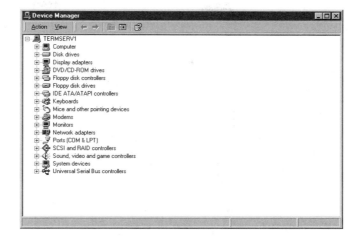

Find the category of device you want to update, then choose the particular device and double-click it to open its property sheet. (For this example, I'll update the driver on my network card.) You want the Driver tab, shown in Figure 20.37.

FIGURE 20.37

Turn to the Driver tab to view driver information and update files.

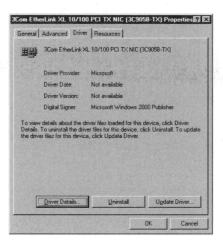

First, see what the current driver version is by clicking the Driver Details button to open the dialog box shown in Figure 20.38.

FIGURE 20.38

View driver information to check its version and creation date.

ADDING DRIVERS MANUALLY

Armed with this information, I can go to the 3Com site (www.3com.com, if you're interested) and search for new drivers. Typically, there's a Downloads section on any manufacturer's Web site. Go there and look for drivers for your class of device. You'll need to know the model number of the device, so make sure you've got that information on hand. Find the driver you want. If the version on the Web site is newer than the one installed on your server, download to a floppy disk or the network.

Armed with the location of the new driver, click the Update Driver button in the Drivers tab of the property sheet for the device. This will start the Update Device Driver Wizard. After the obligatory "Welcome to Wizard *X*" screen, you'll see the screen shown in Figure 20.39.

FIGURE 20.39

Choose whether you want Win2K to search for the driver for your device or you want to find it yourself.

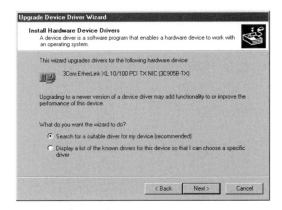

If you tell the wizard to search your drivers, select the boxes of the locations where it should look, making sure to enable the Specify Location box if you plan to update the drivers from the network.

If you tell the wizard that you want to find the driver yourself, it will search your hard disk and report back with a list of all compatible drivers located on the disk. As this list doesn't report version numbers or dates (see Figure 20.40), it's not very useful (if it only returns one driver, then it's found the one you're already using). I'd suggest letting the wizard search for appropriate drivers from CD-ROM and floppy disk.

FIGURE 20.40

The wizard will return a list of currently available drivers.

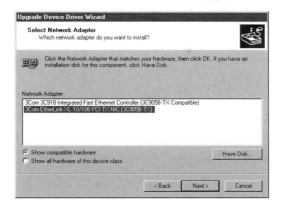

Your server will grind away for a minute as the wizard searches for INF files that match your device. When it reports back, it will tell you it found a driver already installed (if the device was already working, it did) but also give you the option of choosing another driver to use. If you enable the box asking to see the other drivers and click Next, you'll see a list showing the drivers found and reporting only which one is currently installed.

Select the driver you want to use and click Next. The wizard will install the new driver.

And hey, if that driver turns out to be a *really* bad idea, doing something distressing like causing your server to blue-screen on boot, turn to Chapter 21 to learn how to authoritatively say, "This driver never happened." (Actually, I'll tell you anyway: if you install a driver that crashes your Windows 2000 computer, you can get rid of it by booting to the Last Known Good configuration.)

You Knew It Was Coming: Hardware and Other Performance Recommendations

Finally, there's the obvious way to resolve performance problems: throw more hardware at them. By using the System Monitor, you should have a pretty good idea what hardware in your system is contributing to the bottlenecks, but here are some good starting points for choosing server hardware.

MEMORY RECOMMENDATIONS

Get more memory, if your server needs it (many, many Win2K problems can be resolved by adding more memory to a server because the OS uses so much storage). Use *fast* memory—this is the place to install that 100MHz SDRAM even if no other machines on the network get it. Make sure, too, that you're using a 100MHz (or faster) motherboard so that memory can communicate with the CPU as quickly as it's capable.

Memory problems have two main resolutions. First, you can add more memory if the memory manager is paging too much data to disk. Second, you should take care that Windows 2000 can expand the page file incrementally, so that it doesn't run out of room in the paging file. (Remember, though, that in a perfect world you'll make the paging file big enough so that it doesn't have to expand often, since expanding it takes processor time.) Don't ignore a third resolution, though: be judicious in where you run applications. If an application is using so much memory that it's straining the server, then it's probably doing something else to strain the server too: demanding lots of processor cycles, perhaps, or reading and writing from the disk a great deal. If an application is looking pushy, then think about dedicating a server to it. Some network needs can be served adequately by a server doing double duty; for example, you probably don't need to dedicate a server to supporting printing. But some tasks require their own server. If your testing or common sense indicates that you've found such an application, then indulge it.

PROCESSOR RECOMMENDATIONS

More processor power can also help. Servers will benefit from having the fastest processors (or more than one fast processor) that you can afford. Though if faced with a choice between speed and processor cache, get cache. More cache means a processor with a longer memory for what it's done recently, and this longer memory will speed up performance far more than a few more cycles per second. Too, if you have a choice between a faster processor and an additional processor, the additional processor will probably serve you better. Although many applications are not built to be multi-threaded—that is, they have only one laundry list of instructions they need to complete, and this list cannot be split over two processors—having two processors gives you two processor queues and thus shorter lines at both. A second processor won't increase performance by 100 percent for many reasons, not the least of which being that processor cycles are not the only bottleneck on a server. However, if looking at System Monitor and the Task Manager indicates that a server is processor-bound, then a second processor will probably help.

TIP   *You can pinpoint single-threaded applications by watching Process: % Processor Time and log activity on all the processors. If you have a dual-processor system and one processor is working hard (up over 50 percent utilization) while the other processor isn't doing anything at all, that pretty much proves that the application is single-threaded.*

DISK RECOMMENDATIONS

Servers should use SCSI, because SCSI devices can multitask. Even if you've got multiple EIDE drives on the server, data transfer involving one EIDE device means that data transfer with the others is on hold. Using multiple SCSI disks means that RAID works more efficiently—data transfer from a mirrored disk array is faster than to and from individual disks, because of the multiple read/write interfaces. Consider putting a page file on each physical disk in the server, so you can read and write to more than one part of the paging file at the same time.

NOTE   *For more information about disk striping and mirroring, turn to Chapter 10, "Managing Windows 2000 Storage." I'll give you one hint now, though: do not use Windows 2000's software implementation of RAID 5, disk striping with parity. If you want RAID 5 protection, then get a hardware solution with its own processor. The CPU time required to support RAID 5 will seriously task a server's processor and outweigh any read performance benefits of using RAID 5.*

NETWORKS

Even if you can find ISA network cards for your server, don't use them. PCI cards will communicate with the CPU much more efficiently than ISA and have a higher data transfer rate. If the network cards support IRQ10, use it instead of IRQ5 (which most network cards use). IRQ10 has a higher priority. And while you're thinking about networks, consider segmenting yours to isolate heavy traffic areas and keep them from impacting the rest of the network.

Configuring Network Browsing

One last bit to tuning Win2K performance is tuning browsing. Win2K is inherently the front end to the network. The faster that people can find the resources they want on the network, the happier they'll be.

I've always liked Mark's explanation of why network browsing is important in today's networks:

"Years ago, I used an IBM PC Network program. To use network resources, you had to hook up to a drive on a server by saying to the PC Network program, 'Attach me to drive E: on the machine named AVOCADO.' Nice and simple, but it begged the question: How did you know that the server was named AVOCADO and that it had shared a drive called E:? The answer is, *you had to know the name of the resource before you could connect to that resource.* There was no 'scan the network to find out what's available' feature to the network. (An IBM guy once explained to me that this was a 'security feature.' Now why didn't *I* think of that?)"

Mark wanted a "net scan" command, something that would shout to the other systems on the network, "Hey! Whaddaya got?" As it turns out, that's not very simple. The whole process of offering services on a network is part of what's known generically as *name services* or *directory services*, and they're not easy to offer. Chapter 8 covers Active Directory, which replaces the browsing that's been used in Windows operating systems up to now. However, unless you're prepared to migrate to Active Directory—and the usage stats and visual surveys I've taken at Comdex and the like suggests that you haven't yet done so—then you'll still need to think about browsing.

Solving the Directory Service Problem

How would *you* tell a workstation about every service available on the network? There's a couple ways to do this.

STATIC SERVICE LISTS

The simplest approach would be to put a file with some kind of services database on the network, kind of like one of the Yellow Pages sites on the Web. For example, you might have an ASCII file stored on each PC that says, "There is a file server on machine BIGPC with a shared disk called BIGDISK, and the computer named PSRV has a shared printer named HP4L." This approach has the advantage of being very fast and very simple to understand. If a new resource becomes available, you just add it to the service list file.

Anyone who's ever used the aforementioned Yellow Pages sites on the Web probably already knows the disadvantage of such a system: it's static. If there are any changes to the system, some poor fool (that would be *you*, the network administrator) has to go around to all the workstations and update the file. Two hundred workstations = two hundred updates. Even worse, static service lists don't take into account services that are temporarily unavailable due to a downed server or some such problem.

Although this method sounds too primitive to use, NetWare 3.x uses a variant of it. Each workstation identifies itself to the desired server via information stored in a file called NET.CFG. That's a hard-wired server name, which means that changing a server's name in this network would mean editing everyone's NET.CFG file. This is presumably the reason you don't often edit server names in NetWare 3.x world—and why Novell handles resource publishing differently in NetWare 4.x and later.

PERIODIC ADVERTISING

Another approach to resource publishing is an occasional broadcast. Every 30 to 60 seconds (depending on how the network administrator sets it up), each resource on a NetWare 3.11 network shouts to the rest of the network, "I'm here!" Novell calls this the Service Advertising Protocol (SAP) and it's a good idea, working well in many cases.

It's not the perfect answer, however. In a network with only one or two servers (a server is any computer on a network that's sharing a resource, recall) it might be okay, but imagine the traffic on a network with a fair number of servers! Periodic advertising works well on small-to-medium LANs with few servers, but on larger networks, the sheer volume of broadcasts flooding the network makes the system unworkable.

There's another reason why periodic advertising doesn't work well on an enterprise network: routers. Most networks of any size are divided into *segments*, with the segments connected with *routers* that can identify the segment traffic goes to. (For more details on how segments and routers work, turn to Chapter 6, on TCP/IP.) In general, routers move messages from one segment to another and are smart enough to avoid retransmitting messages unnecessarily. This is a Good Thing, because it means that routers cut down on network congestion.

Trouble is, routers generally do not retransmit broadcast messages, which means those SAP broadcasts don't get sent to other segments. I say "generally" because you can, in fact, configure most routers to forward broadcast traffic if you want to, but you most often *won't* want to because that defeats the congestion-reducing characteristic of browsers. In short, unless you set up your routers to forward all broadcasts, SAP announcements will remain on their local segment, effectively dividing your network into workgroups that don't talk to each other.

Larger networks, therefore, need some other method of publishing resources. One approach is through the use of name services and another (the one we'll talk about in this chapter) is the use of browse services.

NAME SERVERS

Yet another approach, and the one used by most enterprise networks, is to assign the task of keeping track of network services to a *name server*. Servers identify themselves to the name servers, which publish a list of those servers and the resources each of those servers offers. Each segment gets its own name server, but the name servers communicate to keep each other updated with currently available resources on the network. Because name servers talk to each other in one-on-one directed communication, they can communicate across routers—no broadcasts.

A name server isn't usually dedicated to that single task; often, it's another kind of server as well, such as a file server. It's a name server because a network administrator (that would be you again) set it up to become one. Setting up name servers and getting them organized is quite a bit of work, but when it works, it's a fast way of finding network resources. Sound like a good plan? Microsoft will be happy to hear that you think so—name serving is the basis of the Active Directory (just as it was the basis of the NetWare Directory Services that Novell included starting with NetWare 4). Chapter 8 talks about the Active Directory in detail, but since not everyone reading this book or using Windows 2000 is using Active Directory, we'll talk about browsing here.

BROWSE SERVICES

Browse services are actually a bit like name servers but have one major difference: rather than your having to set them up, the name servers set themselves up automatically. The Microsoft name for these automatic name servers is *browse services*. The servers that publish resources on the network are called either browse masters or master browsers—both names are correct. Master browsers are different from name servers in that no one computer is fixed as the resource publisher. When a client computer logs in to the network, it finds a master browser by broadcasting a request for a master browser and saying, "Are there any master browsers out there?" The first master browser (a network may have several master browsers, one on each segment) to hear the cry responds to the request and says, "Direct all your name service requests to me."

When a server starts up, it does the same thing, broadcasting, "Are there any master browsers out there?" When the server finds one, it tells the master browser, "I am Server AARDVARK with the following shared resources. Please add me to your list of servers." The list of servers a master browser maintains and publishes is called a *browse list*. Browse lists are the entries in Network Neighborhood on Windows 9*x* and NT 4 clients (see Figure 20.41), the contents of the `Computers Near Me` folder in Windows 2000 (see Figure 20.42), or the output you get if you type **net view** from the command prompt (see Figure 20.43).

FIGURE 20.41

Sample browse list from NT 4 or Windows 9*x* client

FIGURE 20.42

Sample browse list from Win2K client

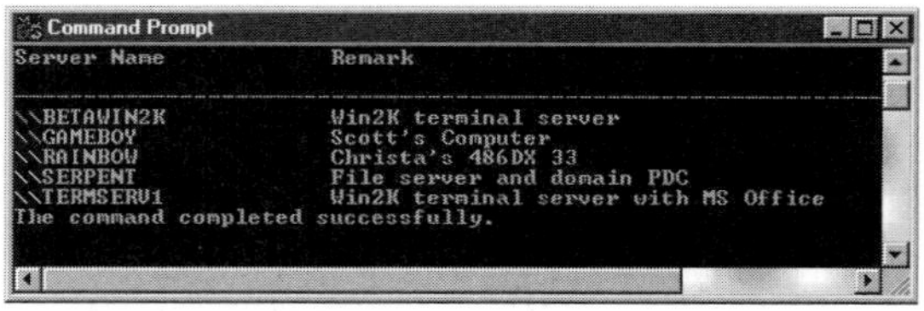

FIGURE 20.43

Sample browse list
from **net view** on
DOS or
Windows client

At the top of a Network Neighborhood or My Network Places browse list, all you see are the servers in the network—you can see what resources each server is sharing by double-clicking the server's icon. To get a complete list of shares from a server with the NET VIEW command, you'd pick a server (say, SERPENT) and type **net view \\serpent**.

Browse lists for an entire network consisting of dozens or hundreds of servers could get pretty large, so you'll subdivide your network based (usually) on your company's administrative structure. If you're not using Win2K domain security, your network will be subdivided into workgroups, which are essentially groups of computers that share a browse list. If you're using Win2K domain security, your network will be subdivided into domains. If your network has multiple domains or workgroups, you'll browse each one individually.

How Browsing Works

It can take up to 60 minutes for a browser to notice that a resource has disappeared, and in the meantime, the browser will blithely report that the resource is still available. The reason has to do with how the browser service and service advertising work.

When a server joins the network, it announces its presence then and at intervals of 1, 2, 4, 8, and 12 minutes. Thereafter, it re-announces itself every 12 minutes. A server must re-announce itself regularly to keep on the master browser's list; if a master browser does not hear from a server for three periods of 12 minutes, the master browser removes the server from its browse list.

If the network uses TCP/IP and is segmented, it's got a domain master browser responsible for updating each segment's master browser every 12 minutes. A master browser can take up to 36 minutes to realize, "Oops—that server seems to be gone from the network." If the timing is just wrong, then it might be another 12 minutes before the master browser gets around to updating its browse list with the master browser. We're up to 48 minutes. Again, if the timing's wrong, it might be as long as another 12 minutes before the domain master browser updates the browse lists on the other master browsers.

Because a server joining the network announces itself and its shared resources to the master browser when it joins, new services are advertised from the master browser almost immediately, although they may take up to 12 minutes to get to the backup browsers if the timing is off.

Choosing a Master Browser

Who are these master browsers that your servers and clients are announcing themselves to? A network set up for browsing may contain any or all of the following kinds of servers:

- Non-browser servers, which do not maintain browse lists, but announce themselves periodically to the master browser.

◆ Potential browsers, which are not master browsers but can become a browser server if necessary.

◆ Backup browsers, which maintain a browse list of servers and domains they retrieve from the master browser and share this browse list with clients.

◆ Master browsers, which receive server and domain announcements, send browse lists to backup browsers, respond to clients requesting browse server lists, promote potential browsers to backup browsers when needed, and tell the master browsers of other domains their domain name and master browser.

◆ Preferred master browsers, which are backup browsers with one extra distinction: they're given preference in browser elections. This does not mean these browsers will *always* become master browsers if there's an election, but they have more oomph in elections than those machines for which this value is FALSE.

◆ Domain master browsers, which are domains' primary domain controllers given a special bias in browser elections so they'll become master browsers. You only have to worry about domain master browsers if you're running a subnetted TCP/IP network, which, these days, means you almost certainly have to worry about domain master browsers.

◆ Each workgroup or domain elects one master browser per transport protocol used and will maintain one backup browser for each 15 computers—the master browser decides who the backup browsers are from the potential browsers available and updates them at intervals from its own list. Why one master browser for each transport protocol? If two computers aren't using the same transport protocol, they can't communicate—they can't even see each other. To make sure everyone on the network can see resources, you must maintain a separate master browser for each protocol, even though the browse lists will be merged so computers supporting multiple protocols don't have multiple browse lists.

Domain Democracy: How Elections Work

How does someone get to be a master browser? It's done with a process called an *election*. The first time a server (in the loose Microsoft sense of "a computer sharing resources with the network") joins the network, it calls out for the master browser, so that it can advertise itself, servers being the self-promoting little things that they are. If no master browser responds, the server announces, "Anarchy! We must have an election to see who will be the master browser!"

Elections are also held when any of the following events take place:

◆ A master browser is powered down gracefully.

◆ A server powers up only to discover that the existing master browser is of lower status than the server. (I'll get to the ranking system in a minute.) For example, if a Win2K Professional workstation joins the network and discovers that the master browser is, of all things, a Windows 95 machine, the Win2K workstation will experience a fit of elitism and call for elections.

◆ A computer with a YES value for the Registry entry MaintainServerList (more on this in a moment) joins the network.

If network segment has no domain controller, then an election process is started that chooses a master browser and backup browser from the computers on the segment using the following order of priority:

1. Windows 2000 Server

2. Windows 2000 Professional

3. Microsoft Windows NT 4.0 Server Enterprise Edition

4. Microsoft Windows NT 4.0 Server

5. Microsoft Windows NT 4.0 Workstation

6. Microsoft Windows 98

7. Microsoft Windows 95

8. Microsoft Windows for Workgroups 3.11

If there's a tie and one of the candidates is a primary domain controller, the domain controller will win. If neither of the candidates is a primary domain controller, then the election goes to the machine using WINS—not as a server, just a client. If both machines are using WINS, the election goes to the current master browser.

What if there's no current master browser?

◆ If there is no current master browser, the election goes to a preferred master browser.

◆ If there's still a tie (more than one preferred master browser or none), the election goes to a backup browser.

◆ If there's more than one backup browser, the current backup browser wins the election.

◆ If there's still a tie, the election goes to the computer that's been up and running longest.

◆ If there's *still* a tie, then the election goes to the computer with the name closest to the beginning of the alphabet. For example, machine AARDVARK will beat machine ZEBRA.

NOTE *A fix in Service Pack 2 eliminates a memory leak on master browsers.*

MASTER BROWSERS ON A TCP/IP NETWORK

On a TCP/IP network, the browse setup gets a little more complicated because of routers. Each segment of the network elects a master browser, as I've already described. To keep all the segments updated, one of those master browsers becomes the domain master browser (DMB). The DMB asks each segment's master browser (SMB, for lack of a better term) for an updated copy of its browse list. The DMB then replicates this updated list to the SMBs so they have a complete list of all network resources.

To give a master browser an edge in becoming the DMB, you can edit its Registry setting. In HKLM\ System\CurrentControlSet\Services\Browser\Parameters, find the value IsDomainMaster and set it to True. (The other possible value is False, which is the default.)

RIGGING ELECTIONS

It's a lot of work coming up with someone to maintain a browse list for the domain. You can simplify the election process and cut down on the number of elections by doing some backstairs finagling.

Not everyone who wants to be a master browser is a good candidate. Workstations, for one, make bad master browsers, because they're apt to get turned off, or rebooted, on a regular basis. Every time the master browser goes down, it's election time. To prevent Windows 9x computers from participating in elections, you'll need to edit a Registry value. The easiest way to do this is to open the Control Panel and run the Network applet. Turn to the Configuration tab and find the entry for File and Printer Sharing for Microsoft Networks in the list of installed network components. (If you don't find this entry, then the computer is not set up for file and print sharing and won't maintain a browse list anyway.) Click the Properties button to open the dialog box shown in Figure 20.44.

FIGURE 20.44

Edit the File and Printer Sharing properties to keep Windows 9x computers from becoming master browsers.

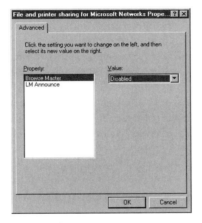

The default setting for MaintainServerList in Windows 95 and Browse Master in Windows 98 is Auto, which means "Make me a master browser if needed." If you make this value Enabled, then you're saying, "If there's a tie during an election, make me master browser" *and* "When I start up, always force an election." Instead, make the value Disabled, which makes the workstation say, "If nominated, I will not run; if elected, I will not stand" (or words to that effect). You can accomplish the same thing by editing the Windows 9x workstation's Registry so that the value of `HKLM\System\CurrentControlSet\Services\VxD\VnetSetup\MaintainServerList` is 0. A setting of 1 corresponds to an Enabled value, 2 to an auto value.

TIP *To prevent NT Workstations and Win2K Professionals from becoming master browsers, set the value of* `HKLM\System\CurrentControlSet\Services\Browser\Parameters\ MaintainServerList` *to No, instead of the default value of Yes.*

Stupid Browser Tricks

Finally, here are a couple of things you can do to optimize browsing for your network.

KEEP SHARED RESOURCES OFF THE BROWSE LIST

Just because you're sharing a resource with the list doesn't mean you necessarily want that resource to show up in everyone's browse list. To share a resource but hide it, add a dollar sign to its share name, like this: MYDRIVE$. To keep an entire *server* off the browse list, go to that server and from the command prompt type **net config server /hidden:yes.** (Yes, you're typing "server", not the name of the server you want to hide.) Go to a client on the network and refresh the browse list, and that server will be gone from the browse list.

TIP *You can still use the connection to the server and any shares it's got if you know the UNC names for those shares, like* \\serpent\freelnce.

ADJUST THE BROWSE REFRESH TIME

As I said earlier, the default refresh time for backup browsers and master browsers is 12 minutes. You can edit the refresh rate for servers in the domain, if you don't mind editing the refresh rate for *all* servers in the domain. Go to HKLM\System\CurrentControlSet\Services\lanmanserver\parameters and add a new value called Announce (if it's not already there) with a DWORD value. Unspecified, the default value is 240 seconds—four minutes. You can set this value higher or lower to decrease or increase the update interval. It's a compromise either way. If you set a shorter value, you'll increase network traffic as the browser updates its entry with the master browser. If you set a greater value, you'll cut down on network traffic but make the browse lists less up-to-date.

Chapter 21

Preparing for and Recovering from Server Failures

COINCIDENCE, GREMLINS, OR INCENTIVE from The Powers That Be to do my homework?

The day I planned to start working on this chapter, one Win2K server on my network stopped booting. I'd been out of town for a few days and so had shut all the computers on the network down (power in Virginia is notoriously chancy during the summer months). Came back, booted up the server, and it worked fine. Added support for an additional transport protocol, and rebooted as required. This time, the system couldn't find a bootable device.

Uh-oh.

Why did this happen? Dead hard disk? Something disconnected? NetBEUI ate my hard disk when I installed it? (Geez—when Microsoft makes TCP/IP the default transport protocol, they're not kidding around, are they?) The initial question, however, wasn't "What happened?" but "How badly is this going to screw me up?" Regardless of the reason *why* the machine didn't boot, the fact remains that it didn't. Had this been a production server instead of a test machine, I would have been in a world of hurt. Or could have been, if I hadn't been prepared for this kind of eventuality.

There's nothing quite like that sinking feeling when a server dies. You can't always prevent this from happening; sometimes, you're just stuck with the whims of the malignant forces in the universe. What you *can* do is either fix the problem or recover from it. That—and how to prevent problems when you can—is what I'll talk about in the course of this chapter. In this chapter, I'll cover the following:

◆ Some basics of preventing preventable disasters

◆ How to use the Windows Backup tools to create manual and automatic backups

◆ How to use the System Information tool to isolate hardware problems

◆ What's going on when your computer boots

◆ The use of the recovery tools found in Windows 2000 and how they're new or different from their counterparts in NT

◆ Disaster recovery tips

I'll explain the tools that Win2K provides to help you recover from disaster in a bit. Now, let's look at how to use common sense to avoid some disasters in the first place.

Preventing Stupid Accidents

The really clever and crafty infiltration or crashing of your network might merit a little appreciation (once you recover from it and keep it from happening again). It's the *preventable* infiltrations or server crashes that lead to gray hair. To keep your servers running and secure, you need to do the following:

◆ Physically secure your network. If the bad guys (and the careless good guys) or Mother Nature can't get to your network hardware, it's a lot harder for them to damage it.

◆ Protect your network's user and system data with a good backup strategy.

◆ Prepare for the worst with a point-by-point disaster recovery plan that anyone in your organization can follow. Don't depend on one person knowing how to return the network to working order.

◆ Understand how your server works so you can troubleshoot problems and perhaps prevent more problems in the future.

◆ Install the service packs and patches that Microsoft issues. Yes, Windows products have flaws. (Other operating systems also have flaws, but we're talking about Windows here.) Microsoft issues patches for these flaws, but if you never install these patches then they're useless.

When something goes wrong with your system, think *noninvasive*. Step 1 is *not* popping the top on the server. Three of your most valuable troubleshooting implements are the Windows 2000 installation CD, data and system state backups, and your notebook, in which you record every change you make to the network and record resolutions to problems. (The brain is Tool 3A. Sometimes it shuts off in times of stress, so you rely on the notebook.) When the time comes for troubleshooting, that notebook will be an invaluable diagnostic tool and a cheat sheet for "I know I've seen this before. How did I fix it last time?"

A basic concern in any computer security system is the need for physical security, a blanket term for the many ways in which you can protect your server and network from physical harm: stupid accidents, environmental—er—"incidents," and theft. Entire books have been devoted to the question of how to physically secure a network, so I'm not going to cover everything here. What follows is an outline of the kinds of protection you should be looking for, both physical and logical.

NOTE   *Protecting your network is a never-ending process; every safeguard has a counter. You can't protect yourself from every possible disaster, so you have to come up with a balance between how much it would cost you to recover from a disaster, how likely it is that you'll be hit by that particular disaster, and how much the protection costs. If protecting your data costs more than the data is worth, then it's time to relax a little.*

Power-Protect Servers

Always use a UPS and power conditioner to power-protect servers and network hardware such as hubs and routers. This will protect the backbone of your network from power surges and dirty power.

Power protection also will help prevent data loss and will let you shut down the servers in an orderly fashion (or shut down the servers automatically). Personally, I've had very good luck with the American Power Conversion Smart UPS series.

WARNING *Don't ground only the server room, ground the entire office. Grounding only the server room is equivalent to putting a giant "KICK ME" sign on your servers, as they'll be the easiest path to ground.*

What about client-side power protection? At one time, UPSes were so expensive that it wasn't cost-effective to protect each client station. These days, you can get a low-end UPS for less than $100, so think about the investment to give user machines power protection and a little bit of time to save documents and shut down. Power strips with surge protectors don't do the trick. Because of their high tolerance for voltage—they'll pass jolts that will damage a PC—power strips are a convenient way of plugging several devices into one outlet, but not a power-protection mechanism.

TIP *Don't plug a printer into a UPS designed for a computer only. First, it won't hurt the printer to lose power suddenly. Second, laser printers draw far more power than a PC and will drain the battery life too quickly. Do plug a monitor into the UPS. Although the monitor draws power, you'll need it to shut down the computer gracefully.*

Speaking of client power protection, one advantage to running Terminal Services instead of a traditional desktop environment is that you don't have to worry about protecting a Windows terminal—at least not for reasons of protecting data. When a Terminal Services client computer loses power, the client's session is disconnected, not terminated. That is, all client applications and data remain active and in memory on the terminal server so long as the server is running. When the session is restored, it will be exactly as it was when it was disconnected. In other words, a power outage will cause no data loss as long as the terminal server is protected. For more information about Terminal Services in Win2K, turn to Chapter 15.

For extreme quick-and-dirty power protection for network client machines, tie five knots in each computer's power cord, as close to the wall as you can. If lightning strikes the wiring, the concentration of current within the loop of the knot will kill the cord and thus break the lightning's path to the client machine. I know that this one is hard to believe, but it really works. As Mark tells it:

> During the summer of 1990, a massive electrical storm hit Washington, D.C. (where Mark lived at the time). I had tied knots in the cords of all of the computers in the house beforehand but hadn't thought to do this to the television. During the storm, one of my neighbor's houses took a direct lightning hit and a huge power surge hit my house's wiring. The cords of all the computers were warmed up a bit, but the power surge never touched the computers themselves. The television was another matter. The surge traveled straight through the cord to the TV's innards and rendered the television DOA. I couldn't have asked for a better test, although at the time I wasn't in a mood to appreciate the benefits of having had a control group.

Keep the Servers Pure

Reduce the likelihood of Bad Things happening to your servers by keeping them away from potential problems. Look for evidence of old leaks in the ceiling, and keep equipment away from them. Make sure that the server room is climate-controlled. The air conditioning used for the rest of the office might not be sufficient in an enclosed room, given all the heat that computers emit. And don't position *any* computer in direct sunlight.

Finally, avoid introducing new contaminants around the servers. Although it may be impossible to keep people from eating or drinking near their workstations, you can—and should—keep food out of the server room. If your office permits smoking, don't smoke or let other people smoke around the servers or workstations. Smoke particles inside a hard disk can chew up its surface.

Limit Access to Servers

Most people using the network don't have a valid reason to do anything to a Win2K server (except a terminal server, of course, and then they're only using it remotely). One way to keep people away from your servers is to lock said servers in a separate room. If people can't get near the servers, they can't:

◆ Reboot or shut down the server.

◆ Steal data-containing hard disks from the server.

◆ Reinstall Win2K and thus have the chance to create a new Administrator account with full access to the server.

User permissions that prevent a person from shutting down a server from the console don't prevent that same person from shutting down a server with the Big Switch. Therefore, if locking up the servers isn't an option, you can physically disable the Reset button and/or the A: drive so that people can't just shut down the server unless they have Win2K permissions to do so.

NOTE   *An OS-dependent protection utility such as* `floplock` *(in the NT 4 Resource Kit) doesn't prevent people from using the floppy drives from another operating system or from booting from a floppy—the OS isn't yet loaded when you're booting. If you want to disable the floppy drives for all operating systems, edit the BIOS to remove support for floppy drives (this setting is typically in the Standard BIOS setup) and password-protect the machine for booting. Alternatively, use a keyboard-video-mouse switch with long cables so you can keep the monitor isolated from the server to which you're providing access.*

Use Passwords Effectively

Win2K's security is built on user authentication. When you log in to a Win2K domain, your username and password are compared with the information stored in the Active Directory on the domain controller. Once you're authenticated on the network, you're assigned a security token that contains a list of your rights and permissions based on your user identity and group membership. Whenever you try to do something—read a file, install an application, whatever—the Win2K security manager compares your rights and permissions with what you want to do, and permits or denies access based on the results of that comparison.

The only thing that keeps people from impersonating each other, therefore, is the password on their accounts. Once someone has an account's password, they can use that account and all the rights and permissions associated with it. Passwords are the biggest port of entry into your Win2K network.

WHY PASSWORDS ARE VULNERABLE

Previous editions of this book included some tips on creating hard-to-crack passwords. The widespread availability of password-cracking programs such as L0phtCrack (now more innocuously known as LC3) renders most of these tips semi-obsolete for stopping anyone who *really* wants to break in and who can get physical access to the server because they give anyone with access to the network an extremely powerful tool for cracking passwords. LC3, for example, can retrieve password hashes from the Registry, from the `Repair` directory in your Win2K installation, or even from the network. Once the tool has the password file, it extracts the password hashes (encrypted passwords) and performs a series of three attacks to decrypt the hash:

Dictionary Attack   In a dictionary attack, LC3 tests all the words in a dictionary or word file (the tool itself comes with an optional word file of 250,000 words) until it finds a match.

Hybrid Attack   If the dictionary attack doesn't produce results, the next step is to see whether the user took a known word and added numbers or other characters to it, so as to foil a dictionary attack.

Brute Force Attack   The final stage is a brute force attack, in which the password hash is compared against every key combination possible. Brute force attacks take much longer (sometimes days—depends on how fast the computer doing the cracking is) than either of the other two attacks, but they can eventually crack just about any password using characters found only on a standard keyboard.

Just about any password is vulnerable to a brute force attack if given enough time. "Enough time" may mean a couple of days even on a fast computer, but if the cracker has the password hashes, then the delay won't stop the cracker unless people change their passwords during the cracking process.

NOTE   The longer and more complicated a password is, the longer it will take to crack it. Win2K is better protected in this respect than NT 4 was. Although NT 4 could technically support much longer passwords (up to 128 characters), the password-entry box in User Manager for Domains had room for only 14-character passwords. Win2K's password text box supports 128-character passwords, which will plainly take much longer to crack. Then again, can you accurately type 128 characters of mixed-case letters and numbers when you're typing blind? I can't, and I bet most of the users on your network can't either. Too, since downlevel clients such as Windows 9x and NT still don't have anywhere to type a password more than 14 characters long, you'd best take into account client OS unless you're working in a purely Win2K environment.

All that said, passwords are far from useless. You'll notice that using a tool such as LC3 requires physical access to the Win2K server or to the network. The answer? *Keep untrusted people off the network.* Protect the Administrators account, only giving Administrator rights to the most trusted people. If your network is connected to the Internet, close TCP/IP ports that you don't need, and audit failed attempts to connect to the gateway from the Internet. For the people on the inside who *do* have access to the network, institute a zero-tolerance policy for password-cracking tools for anyone without a really good reason to have them.

KEEPING OUT THE IDLE CURIOUS

Your network's security is threatened not only by the actively malicious, but also by the idle curious. Password-choosing schemes are best for keeping out those people who aren't interested enough to get serious about breaking into someone's account, but will go poking through Joe Blow's files in his private home directory if Joe makes it easy for them. To keep these people out of other people's accounts, follow the guidelines for choosing passwords below. They won't foil LC3, but they'll foil someone guessing passwords.

Impose Password Policies   Passwords must be of a minimum length, changed regularly (but not too regularly, to avoid people reusing passwords too often), and shouldn't be reused often. Set policies to require passwords to include numerals and other nonletter characters, and take advantage of the fact that Win2K passwords are CasEs3nSitiVe (hint, hint).

Don't Let People Use Easy-to-Guess Passwords   No personal names, spouse's names, dog's names, or other easy associations. Ideally, passwords should not reflect that person's job, either. A few years ago, a friend of mine doing network security for one department of the Pentagon told me that he'd had to institute this rule after discovering that the analysts in his division had all chosen passwords based on the names of battleships—words directly related to their division's mission.

Don't Write Down Passwords   The most difficult password in the world will do no good if it's on a sticky note on the base of the monitor or under the keyboard. This is the dilemma inherent to all password protection. If you make passwords easy to remember, they're often easy to guess. Make them too hard to remember or require too many of them, and users will start writing them down.

Delete or Disable Unused Accounts   An unused account is an account that isn't getting its password changed regularly and doesn't have someone using it who might notice something strange going on. If you'll need an account later, but not now, disable it so as to retain its security ID while making it impossible to use at the moment. If you'll never need an account again (perhaps for someone who has left the company), delete it.

NOTE   *If you delete an account and then re-create it, the account will have a new security ID even if it has the same username and password as the original account. You'll have to re-create all user rights and permissions from scratch.*

On a final note, those who use badges for company identification (a group that seems ever larger) can consider using biometric devices for user authentication.

Backup Programs and Approaches

Security from intrusion is important, but so is security from data loss. Backups are your first line of defense against server failures and your last recourse when all else fails. When it comes right down to it, the data on your servers is the important part. The box is replaceable, and you can reinstall the operating system if you need to. What you can't replace is the data on the drive. And if you lose that data and can't get it back, your company's life is probably over.

To help you protect your company's most important asset, Windows 2000 comes with a new version of Windows Backup, complete with more features, support for a wider array of backup destinations (unlike previous versions of Backup, which you couldn't even run if you didn't have a tape drive), and an integrated scheduler. I'll discuss this tool now, but apply SP2 if you haven't already. As you'll see in the following sections, SP2 addresses several problems with Windows 2000's NTBACKUP. I've documented some of them, but the message is basically this: Install the service pack because backups won't work consistently if you don't.

Using Windows 2000's backup program, you can back up either to files or to tapes. Backing up to a file is the simplest method, so let's start there.

Basic Backup Procedures

Experienced users of NT 4 may recall that the backup utility was in the Administrative Tools folder. In Win2K, you'll find it in the System Tools section of the Accessories folder. Open the Backup application, and you'll see the tool shown in Figure 21.1.

FIGURE 21.1

The opening screen of Windows Backup

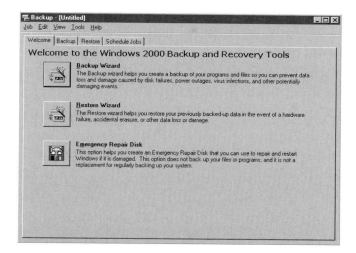

TIP *I find Remote Administration mode (discussed in Chapter 15) convenient for performing many administration tasks, but do not run backup operations from a remote computer if you want to visually monitor the process—there's too many animations and screen updates required for this to work well. You could, however, set up the backup schedule from a terminal session.*

Using this tool, you can back up data, restore data, or create an emergency repair disk. Let's start with backing up. If you click the Backup Wizard button, you'll start a wizard designed to help you create a backup set. After the opening screen, you'll see the screen shown in Figure 21.2, asking you what data you want to back up.

FIGURE 21.2

Choose a range of files to back up.

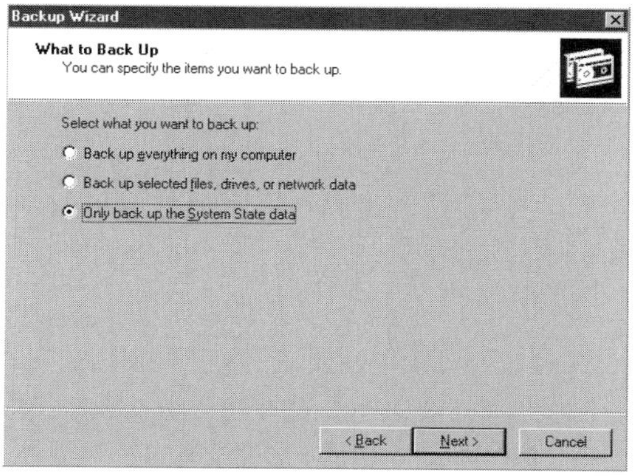

The third option allows you to only back up the System State data. The System State data, if you're wondering, is Registry information, system boot files, and the COM+ Class Registration database—system configuration information you'll need to restore your server if you have to reinstall. On Win2K Certificate Servers, this data will also include the Certificate Services database. On domain controllers, it will include a copy of the Active Directory and the SYSVOL directory, which is that server's copy of the public files shared among all domain controllers in the domain. I'll talk more about the System State data in the later section "Backing Up and Restoring the Active Directory." Backing up everything on the computer backs up all local drives (but no network drives even if they're mapped to local drive letters), and backing up selected files, drives, or network data lets you choose exactly what data you want to protect. Choose the option you want and click Next. For this example, I've chosen to back up the System State data.

You can back up either to a BKF file or, if you have a tape drive installed, to tape. Next, Backup looks for a place to put the backup catalog (see Figure 21.3). The default backup location is your floppy drive. Given that backing up the System State data alone will take upwards of 200MB on a member server, let alone a domain controller, this isn't a very practical default option, but you can browse for a new location anywhere on the local server or on a network-accessible volume. Backup does not support backing up to CD-R, CD-RW, or DVD-R devices. Once you've told Windows Backup where to put the backup file, click Next to display the final screen that displays your backup options (see Figure 21.4). If you click the Finish button, you'll start the backup.

FIGURE 21.3

Specify a backup destination.

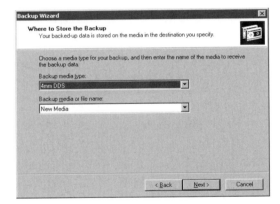

FIGURE 21.4

The final screen of the wizard displays the current backup settings.

That's a basic backup, using all the default options. If you want a little more control over how the backup is performed (that is, the options for How and When), click the Advanced button before clicking Finish to start the second part of the wizard and decide on the options listed in Table 21.1.

TABLE 21.1: ADVANCED BACKUP OPTIONS

OPTION	DEFAULT SETTING	WHAT IT MEANS
What type of backup should be performed?	Normal	You can choose from normal, copy, incremental, differential, or daily backups. These backup types are described later, under "Choosing a Backup Type."
Verify data?	No	Verifying a backup compares the data on the backup media with the source media to make sure that the data was copied correctly. Verifying a backup takes some additional time, but I'd do it anyway—it's a good way of getting a record that the data was written as expected.
Use hardware compression?	No	This option is only available if you're backing up to tape. If you choose it, then the tape will have a higher capacity than it would have had otherwise.
Append or replace existing backup sets?	Append	If the backup media already contains a backup, you have the option of either replacing that backup or adding the present backup to the catalog. The option you choose depends on which is more important to you: keeping the backup media uncluttered so you can easily find the backup set for restoration or maintaining multiple backup sets. I'd suggest replacing full backups (although you should always archive at least one full backup in case something happens to the current one) and appending incremental and differential backups.
Restrict access?	No	If you've chosen to replace any backup sets already on the media, you can choose whether to restrict access to those sets to members of the Administrators group and the person creating the backups.
What is the name of the backup and the media?	Time and date backup was created	Provide a name for the backup set. If you're using new media, or replacing the data on existing media, you can choose a new name for the tape or file.
When should the backup run?	Now	You can choose to run the backup now or pick a time at which it should run. If you're backing up a server, then you'll almost certainly want to schedule it for later, when people aren't using the data.
Back up migrated remote storage data?	No	Backs up rarely used files that have been automatically moved to remote storage.

The only Advanced backup option that might cause you any trouble is the scheduling tool, which I'll cover later in the section "Scheduling Automated Backups." When you've finished choosing options, you'll see the Finish screen again, showing the updated options.

Advanced Backup Options

I've just described the simple version of running a backup, the best version for those who want to make sure that *all* files are backed up. Those with more experience in backups will be glad to know that there are more options you can use to fine-tune your backups, including choosing files and folders to protect, choosing types of backups to perform, and scheduling automatic backups of local or network-accessible media.

CHOOSING FOLDERS TO BACK UP

Most often, you won't want to back up every file on your server. You don't have to. The Backup tool includes an Explorer-like interface from which you can pick and choose files, folders, and drives to back up.

This part works much like earlier versions of Backup. In Windows Backup, turn to the Backup tab (see Figure 21.5). You select objects for backup by checking the box next to them. You can't select every object—only those that have a clear box. Gray boxes don't represent partially selected options, as you might expect, given the meaning of gray boxes in other parts of Win2K. In Backup, the gray box means that the object cannot be selected and you must drill down into it to find the selectable objects. Notice that My Documents is in the top tier of selectable objects, which makes for a handy way to back up all your documents if you keep personal files in that folder.

Backing Up the Local Computer

Let's start with objects stored on the local server. For this example, I'll back up one folder I use for storing working data. To get to it, I double-click My Computer to expose the locally mapped drives (see Figure 21.6).

FIGURE 21.5

Windows Backup displays all drives and computers available for backup.

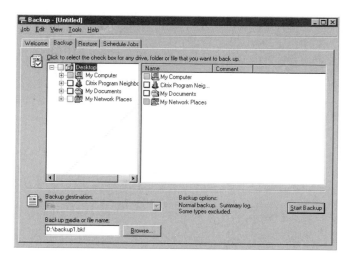

FIGURE 21.6

Contents of My
Computer

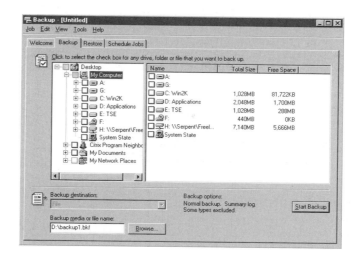

This is a list of the assigned drive letters of all partitions. The drives listed are *logical* drives, not physical drives. If you have any reason to do so, you can change their arrangement by clicking the headings of the Name, Total Size, or Free Space columns to sort the drives by one of those criteria. Notice that this list includes all drives on the server, not just fixed or local drives. Windows Backup for NT 4 didn't recognize any drives for backup but fixed media and network drives; to back up removable drives you had to go through the hassle of sharing the drive with the network from Explorer and then connecting to it from the server doing the backup. This limitation no longer exists in Win2K.

Perhaps I *think* that the Applications drive (drive D:) is the one with the data I want to protect, but I'm not sure. I can find out for sure by double-clicking the drive to see its folders. If I wanted to, I could drill down yet further within those folders to expose the subfolders, all the way down to file level. In this case, I'm going to drill down one level to see the NCD folder. I want to keep the contents of the NCD folder safe—because this is a cool add-on to Terminal Services that requires some configuring, and I want to make sure that all the files are backed up so I don't have to reconfigure them. So I check the box next to the NCD folder. If I open the NCD folder, I'll see that all the files and folders within the NCD folder are now selected.

I can deselect any object within this folder and prevent it from being backed up (see Figure 21.7). If I do so, then the check mark in the NCD folder's box will be gray, instead of the blue it is if all its contents are selected. Similarly, the box next to the logical drive that the NCD folder is stored on will have a gray check mark indicating that part of its contents are selected for backup, but not all.

You can choose as many different files and folders on as many different drives as you like to be part of a backup set. They don't have to be juxtaposed or arranged in any kind of logical form, but will retain their location on the final backup media. That is, if you choose to back up both E:NCD\ files\config and C:\My Documents\Myfile.doc, then Myfile.doc will still have its placement information so that the backup media know that the file goes in My Documents, not in the NCD folder.

TIP   *Having trouble selecting objects to back up? When the cursor changes to a check mark, you're in the box.*

FIGURE 21.7

Contents of the NCD folder to be backed up

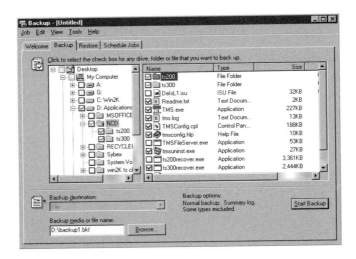

Although this drilling-down technique looks like it should work on the System State data, it doesn't. When you open My Computer to see all the local drives, you'll see another entry in the list: the System State data. If you double-click this object to view its contents, you'll see contents like those in Figure 21.8. Notice that these objects have gray boxes, so you can't select them. When using Windows Backup, you can back up all of the system data or none of it, but you can't pick and choose.

FIGURE 21.8

Contents of the System State folder

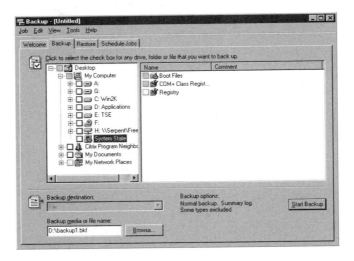

TIP   *Well, you can't pick and choose easily, but you can pick and choose. If you back up the contents of the* %systemroot%\ system32\config *folder, you'll back up the current Registry files. Then again, you can do the same thing another way, as we'll see in "Creating the Emergency Repair Disk" later in this chapter.*

Backing Up Network-Accessible Folders

You can back up the contents of any folder shared with the network from any computer on your network. Doing so is much like backing up local files and folders, except that you have to first find the computer you're looking for and then drill down as needed to the drive you want to select. There is no domainwide list of shared folders on the domain—you have to know which server contains the data you want to protect.

To get to the network server, double-click My Network Places to reach Entire Network. Entire Network will have an entry for Microsoft Windows Network. Double-click *that* and you'll get a list of all domains on the network.

Finally, within the domain you'll see a list of all computers with accounts on the domain. Select the one you want and start drilling into its shared drives to back up files as you would for a local computer. The only difference between backing up a network-accessible computer and a local one is that you can't back up the System State information for a network computer.

TIP   *If you're backing up network drives or backing up to a network location, make sure this network location is available at the time you run the backup. This is really an issue with scheduled backups, but it can be a frustrating one if it catches you unaware.*

ADVANCED BACKUP SETTINGS

Windows Backup has advanced options you can set. In either the Backup tab or the Restore tab, choose Tools/Options to go a tabbed dialog box that contains all backup and restore options.

Choosing a Backup Type

The default backup type for Windows Backup is Normal, which is a not-very-descriptive way of saying that Windows Backup performs full backups (copies all files and resets the archive bit on all copied files) unless told otherwise. If you turn to the Backup Type tab shown in Figure 21.9, you can choose one of the options described in Table 21.2.

FIGURE 21.9

Choose a new backup type if you don't want to perform full backups.

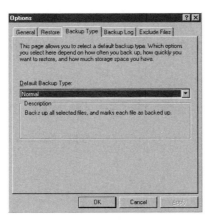

TABLE 21.2: BACKUP TYPES SUPPORTED IN WINDOWS 2000

BACKUP TYPE	DESCRIPTION
Normal	Copies all selected files and then resets the archive bit
Incremental	Copies all selected files with the archive bit set and resets the bit
Differential	Copies all selected files with the archive bit set but does not reset the bit
Daily	Copies all selected files that were edited the day the backup was performed
Copy	Copies all selected files but does not reset the archive bit

NOTE *The* archive bit *is a hidden file attribute applied to a file when it's created or edited. It's used to tell a backup or copy utility, "Hey, this file has changed." Resetting the archive bit removes the archive bit from a file; setting the bit adds it.*

You can use these backup types in combination to back up files completely and efficiently. The longest interval you'll want to have between backups is probably a day—lose more than a day's worth of work, and you're in big trouble. (Losing a day's worth of work is bad enough, which is why companies with really critical data use RAID to protect their data, as discussed in Chapter 10.) Running a normal backup every day takes up a lot of time and space, so you can run a normal backup at regular intervals, perhaps once a week, but supplement this weekly full backup with a daily differential or incremental backup. Running a daily differential backup gives you a daily copy of all the files that have changed since the last full backup; incremental backups copy all the files that have their archive bit set. Either differential or incremental backups work well as a supplement to a regular normal backup. I find differential backups easier to perform and restore because restoring a server becomes a matter of restoring the most recent normal backup and the last differential one. Restoring incremental backups is a slower process, as you must restore each incremental backup made since the last full backup individually. However, incremental backups take less time to perform than differential backups.

Daily backups aren't really a method of preserving data, but more a way of quickly finding files that you're currently using and transferring them to other media. You might find it useful to run a daily backup on a user's files to copy the ones he needs to a laptop for a business trip, if the client isn't using Win2K Pro and so doesn't have the option of using Offline Files. Copying files is only useful if you want to make a complete copy of all selected files without resetting the archive bit. A copy action like that is a way of copying files to a new location.

Choosing a Logging Type

Backup logs are a useful troubleshooting tool. If something goes wrong with the backup, then you can inspect a text-based log to see *what* went wrong. In fact, it's a good idea to at least scan the backup logs produced after each backup to make sure that the procedure went as expected.

How much information do you log? Normally, Windows Backup logs only errors and important events, but if you turn to the Backup Log tab of the Options dialog box (see Figure 21.10), you can choose not to log (bad idea, as that disables a troubleshooting tool) or to log *everything* (also a bad idea for anything other than a daily or perhaps incremental backup, as it will make your logs so big that it will be hard to find errors). Unless you need a complete record for some reason, the summary log option (the default) is probably your best bet.

FIGURE 21.10

Choose a logging option.

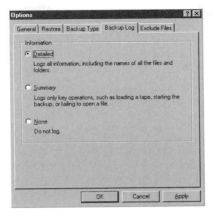

Which Files Do You Want to Back Up?

Even if you're running a full backup, you don't necessarily want to save *everything*. For example, do you really need to preserve the contents of the paging file? Probably not. For this reason, Windows Backup does not normally back up any files that don't contain real data—a user cache, a page file, temporary Internet files for the person running the backup, and the like. You can edit this list in the Exclude Files tab of the Options dialog box (see Figure 21.11).

FIGURE 21.11

Change the files to exclude, or edit the settings for excluded files.

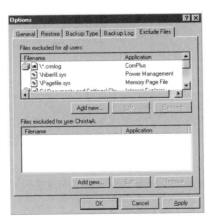

    The Add New and Remove buttons on this tab are pretty self-explanatory. Unless you have real reason to remove one of the already excluded files from the list, I suggest that you leave them alone, as the files listed are not really anything you need to back up.

To add files to exclude from the backup, click the Add New button to display the dialog box shown in Figure 21.12. The list in the upper half of the dialog box contains all the file types recognized by the server. You have to know the extension for the type of file you want to exclude from the backup, but many of the extensions are labeled so you can be sure that you've got the right one. (If an extension isn't labeled and you don't recognize it as an application file extension, files of that type are probably part of the operating system and can be reinstalled. Just be sure to check before you exclude the files from the backup.) In the Registered File Type list, click the file type that you don't want to back up, Ctrl+clicking to select more than one option at a time. When you click OK, you'll see your selection(s) added to the list of excluded file types. For example, if you don't want to back up any application files (on the principle that you can reinstall the applications if necessary), then you'd find `.exe` in the list, highlight it, and click OK.

The Custom File Mask text box is for extensions that aren't registered file types (ones you've created yourself for certain files) or for filtering files by name. The syntax for this file mask depends on whether you're filtering by filename or extension. If you want to eliminate all files *named* `abc.*` from the backup, then type **abc** in the box—no asterisks necessary. To eliminate all files with the *extension* **.abc**, then type **.abc** (note the period) in the box.

FIGURE 21.12

Choose from registered file types, or type in custom extensions.

NOTE *You must enter each custom file mask separately. If you enter two at once—say, for* `.abc` *files and* `.def` *files—then you're telling Windows Backup to skip all files with the extension* `.abc.def`. *Using semicolons or other punctuation to separate the entries doesn't work.*

By default, your file mask will apply to the entire C: drive. To edit this to apply to a different drive or only a specific folder, type in a new path or click the Browse button to open a file tree (see Figure 21.13) from which you can choose the path you want the mask to apply to.

When you click OK to exit the Add Excluded Files dialog box, the path information will be listed with the file types to be excluded on the Exclude Files tab.

The file types you've excluded will apply to all users. If you'd like to exclude file types only for the person currently logged in (there's no way to specify another user or a group), then click the Add

New button at the bottom half of the Exclude Files tab. You'll enter the same Add Excluded Files box that you saw previously, and it works the same way. The only difference is that the files you exclude will only apply to the ones you own. For example, if I chose to exclude .doc files for myself, then everyone else's .doc files would be backed up, but mine (the ones I created and own) would not.

FIGURE 21.13

Browse for the path to apply a file mask to.

TIP *The per-user masking depends on current file ownership, so if a file was created by Joe but Jane took ownership of it, the file would still be backed up if Joe added it to his personal file mask, but not if Jane did. It doesn't matter whether Joe, Jane, or Fred is running the backup: So long as Jane owns that file, then it's excluded from the backup.*

Notice that the exclude tool really only excludes files—you can't use it to include only files with certain extensions in the backup. Sadly, there doesn't seem to be any way to specify that only certain files should be backed up. Even the command-line utility NTBACKUP (which I'll discuss a little later in the "Scheduling Automated Backups" section) doesn't accept wildcards.

General Backup Options

The General tab of the Options dialog box contains the options explained in Table 21.3. These options control the settings that really don't fit anywhere else in the categories of options.

TABLE 21.3: GENERAL OPTIONS FOR BACKUP AND RESTORE OPERATIONS

OPTION	DEFAULT SETTING	WHAT IT MEANS
Compute selection information before backup and restore operations.	Enabled	This is a confusingly worded way of saying that Windows Backup will count the files and folders to be backed up or restored before actually performing the operation. I'd leave this enabled; it doesn't add much to the time required to run the operation, and this information can save you from backing up or restoring the wrong volume or backing up to media that's too small.

Continued on next page

TABLE 21.3: GENERAL OPTIONS FOR BACKUP AND RESTORE OPERATIONS *(continued)*

OPTION	DEFAULT SETTING	WHAT IT MEANS
Use the catalogs on the media to speed up building restore catalogs on disk.	Enabled	This is the fastest way for Windows Backup to create a list of all the files and folders in the backup. You should only disable this option if you're restoring data from several tapes and don't have the one with the catalog (the first tape) or if the catalog is damaged. With this option disabled, Windows Backup will scan the entire backup set and attempt to build its own catalog. Since reading tapes is a slow process, this could take a long time for a large backup set—perhaps hours.
Verify data after the backup completes.	Disabled	This compares the data on the disk with the data on the backup media after the backup has been completed and records any differences. Although verifying adds some time to a backup, I'd recommend doing it. It's a good way to be sure that files were written correctly.
Back up the contents of mounted drives.	Enabled	Normally, mounted drives (logical drives mapped to a path on another logical drive—read Chapter 10 to learn more about them) can be backed up like other media. If you check this box, the data won't be backed up—just the path information.
Show alert message when I start Backup and Removable Storage Management is not running.	Enabled	If the Removable Storage Management service isn't running, you can start it from the Services object in the System Tools folder of Local Computer Management.
Show alert message when I start Backup and there is compatible Import Media available.	Enabled	If this box is checked and you add new RSM storage media, Backup will display a message on start-up saying that it's found more media for the Import pool (to which files can be archived).
Show alert message when new media is inserted into Removable Storage.	Enabled	If this box is checked, Backup will display a dialog box when it detects new RSM media.
Always move new import media to the Backup media pool.	Disabled	If this box is checked, Backup will assume that any new media it detects should be added to the Backup media pool, and thus be available for backups.

NOTE *Removable Storage Management is used with tape drives and other archiving media. If you normally back up to a file on any kind of disk (including a removable disk like a Jaz drive) instead of tape, you don't have to worry about the Removable Storage Management settings.*

SAVING BACKUP OPTIONS

You can define settings for a backup job and save them to be used later or reused at your discretion. To do so, make sure that you've chosen the files to back up. Then, in the Windows Backup utility, choose Job/Save Selections. You'll see a Save Selections dialog box prompting you to save the backup script (normally saved in `%systemroot%\ Documents and Settings\%username%\Local Settings\ Application Data\ Microsoft\Windows NT\NT Backup\data`).

If you load a saved backup script when you have files and folders selected for backup, Backup will ask whether you want to use the currently selected folders or clear them. Clear them to load the backup script, and you'll be ready to run the backup job.

Scheduling Automated Backups

To be safe, you should back up data servers at least once a day. Trouble is, the best time to back up is late at night when everyone's off the network. With NT 4, you could use the AT command or WinAT utility to schedule backups created from the command line; with Windows 2000, you have the choice of two backup-scheduling methods, one using the GUI, and one using the AT command for running scripted backups created with an updated command-line version of `NTBackup.exe`.

There are a few ways you can schedule jobs from Windows Backup:

◆ In the Backup Wizard, one of the Advanced options asks whether you want to run the backup you've created now or schedule it for later. If you choose to schedule it for later, you'll be taken to the Schedule Job dialog box, which I'll discuss in a minute.

◆ In Windows Backup, when you create a backup job from the Backup tab and click the Start Backup button, you'll see a dialog box that prompts you for the name of the backup and allows you to start the backup now or schedule it for later (see Figure 21.14). If you click the Schedule button, you'll be taken to the Schedule Job dialog box.

FIGURE 21.14

When creating a backup job, you have the option of running it immediately or running it at a later time.

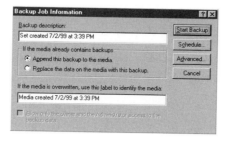

TIP   Save backup jobs before starting them. If you're scheduling a job to run later, you'll need to do this anyway, and if you think you'll ever want to run a backup job with the same parameters again, you'll save yourself some time by saving the job now.

◆ In Windows Backup, if you're creating a new backup job, you can turn to the Schedule Jobs tab, where you'll see a month calendar like the one shown in Figure 21.15. To create and schedule a backup job from the Schedule Jobs tab, click the Add Job button in the lower-right corner of the screen to start a Backup Wizard similar to the one described earlier under "Basic

Backup Procedures"—the only difference between the two wizards is that this one includes the advanced options in the main wizard, rather than through the Advanced button on the wizard's final screen. One of the options you'll be presented with is the choice of running the backup now or later, with the default time for "later" being midnight of the day you set up the backup job (see Figure 21.16). To schedule a job, select Later and click the Set Schedule button to open the scheduler.

FIGURE 21.15

The Schedule Jobs tab of Windows Backup

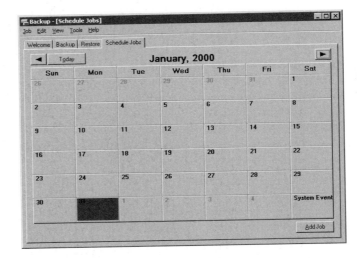

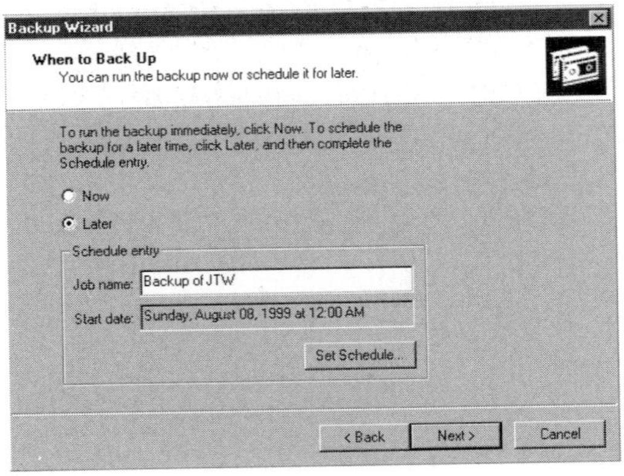

FIGURE 21.16

Default scheduling options

No matter how you get to it, the Schedule tab of the Schedule Job dialog box looks like Figure 21.17. The basic options are pretty straightforward. Choose the interval at which you want the backup job to run (once, daily, weekly, monthly, at system startup, at logon, or when the computer is idle) and the starting time and date. If you select the Show Multiple Schedules check box at the bottom of the screen, a new drop-down list will appear at the top of this dialog box, showing the varying intervals and starting times that you've chosen for this job.

TIP   If you want to run a backup job biweekly (once every two weeks), show multiple schedules and create two monthly backup jobs that start on different days.

The Advanced button takes you to the Advanced Schedule Options (see Figure 21.18), which apply only if you want to repeat the backup job, apart from any interval that you set in the main scheduling screen. Most often, you won't need to touch these options. You don't need to use them for scheduling jobs at regular intervals; this set of options would be more useful for a shorter task and one that might actually need to be run every 10 minutes or so. (Frequent backups are a Good Thing, but let's not get carried away.)

FIGURE 21.17

Choose a time and frequency for the backup job.

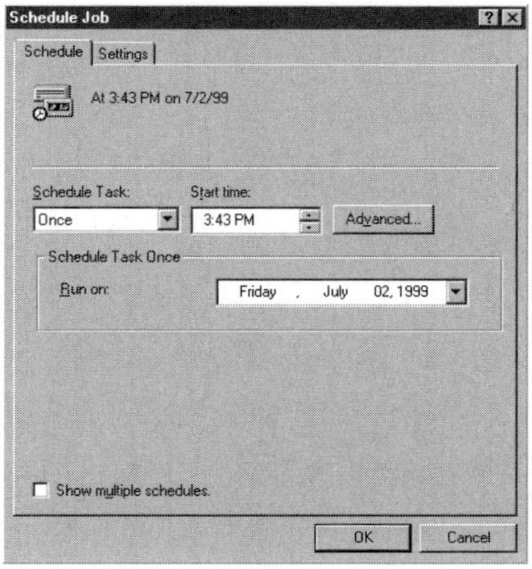

FIGURE 21.18

Advanced backup scheduling options

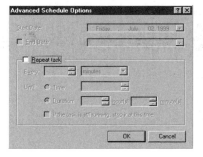

More likely, you'll use the Settings tab back in the main Schedule Job dialog box (see Figure 21.19). From here, you can specify how long the job should run (a backup job that lasts more than 72 hours seems suboptimal) and whether the job should be deleted from the list of tasks when it's done unless it's supposed to run again. The Idle Time settings could be useful, as only permitting a backup to run when the server is idle is a good way of making sure that all data files are closed (or at least unused). The only catch to this setting is that you won't be able to back up if the server is used for anything, such as being a Web server, that's likely to keep it busy at odd hours.

FIGURE 21.19

Configure job settings for the scheduled backup.

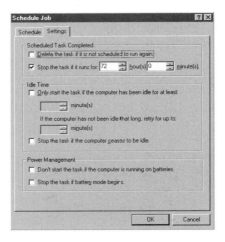

TIP *Windows Backup doesn't back up open files. If you're backing up local files only, you can make sure that all files are closed during a backup. Apply the* net stop server *and* net start server *commands; this will stop the Server service before the backup begins, but then restart it after the backup is completed.*

The final options in the Settings tab, on battery use, aren't likely to apply to a server. They help you conserve battery power by not running nonessential tasks when your power supply is limited. Accessing the hard disk takes a lot of power, so backups are an especially draining task when the power is low.

When you've finished adding jobs to the scheduler, they'll appear on the Schedule Jobs tab's calendar, as shown in Figure 21.20.

You're not stuck with the options for a scheduled job once it's created. To edit the settings for a scheduled job, just click its icon in the calendar to open the Scheduled Job Options dialog box shown in Figure 21.21.

FIGURE 21.20

Scheduled jobs appear in the calendar.

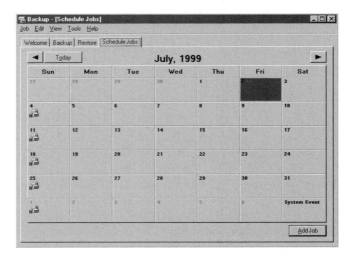

FIGURE 21.21

You can edit all job
settings even after
the job is added
to the task list.

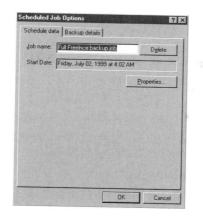

Click the Properties button to edit the timing and settings for the backup job. The Schedule and Settings tabs that appear are the same ones you saw when scheduling the job. The Task tab that also appears, however, is new. Here, you can use the command-line switches to edit the job settings, specify a new user in whose context the job should run, and create some identifying information for the job. You must know the command-line switches to NTBACKUP (discussed in the next section) to edit the settings from the Task tab.

Backing Up to Tape

Windows 2000 introduced a whole new layer of software called the Removable Storage Manager (RSM). You wouldn't think that you'd need to know anything about RSM to do backups, but RSM is the basis of Windows 2000's backup and archival capabilities. A backup program needs both drivers for the storage devices it works with and the intelligence to control those devices. NT 4's backup program directly managed the tape drives it worked with (as you may recall, NT 4's backup program only worked with a tape drive—you couldn't even *start* the program unless you had a tape drive installed). So long as you were happy with NT 4's choices, this was fine, but NT 4 was designed in a day when hard disks were a lot smaller than they are now. For example, NT 4's backup program did not support DAT *autoloaders*, systems where there's usually only one tape drive (although there can be more) with a built-in capacity to store and automatically load or unload several other tapes. If you wanted to use a DAT autoloader, you needed a third-party backup program that knew how to handle it.

NOTE *If it's not clear why you'd want an autoloader, a tape drive that can automatically insert and eject a stack of tapes, then you've never done regular backups on a hard disk (or a group of disks) whose capacity is greater than your tape drive's. For instance, 4-mm DAT drives are pretty good, fairly fast, and reliable…but only store about 8GB. To back up an entire 40GB hard disk using DAT drives, you'll need to baby-sit a backup program that prompts you every now and then to "please insert tape 4…." I'll pass.*

One way to make NT 4's backup program more flexible about its storage would be to create special tape-emulating drivers that would make *any* storage appear to be a tape drive. That is, even if the storage were, say, a CD-RW drive, then it could accept tape-related commands such as "rewind" and "retension" even though it can't use them. However, to my knowledge no such drivers exist. RSM performs a similar function by abstracting the interface not just to tape drives but to all removeable storage. Windows 2000's backup program doesn't manage its storage, RSM does.

NOTE *Even though they're not RSM aware, NT 4–era backup programs will generally run fine on Windows 2000, so long as you're not trying to back up anything that employs the new features of NTFS: encrypted files, Single Instance Store volumes, or sparse files.*

Although it's an intrinsic part of Windows 2000's backup program, RSM also supports *any* program that uses removeable storage, such as Windows 2000's archiving capabilities that back hard disk space with offline storage. In other words, RSM is not just about making backups work, but that's the part I'll focus on here.

RSM CONCEPTS: PHYSICAL LOCATIONS, LIBRARIES, DRIVES, MEDIA

To use the RSM-enabled features of backup, you'll need to know a physical location from a library from a drive from media. You can see the GUI interface for the Removable Storage Manager in Manage Computer. Right-click My Computer and choose Manage, then open up the icon labeled Storage, and you'll see something like Figure 21.22.

FIGURE 21.22

RSM before any backups

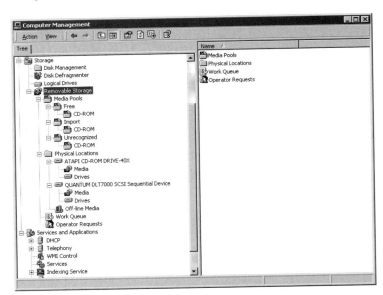

This computer has just two removable storage devices—a standard EIDE-connected CD-ROM drive and a DLT1 tape drive. There are no tapes in the DLT1 drive and NTBACKUP has never run on this system (you'll see why I mention that in a minute). Notice that under the `Removable Storage` level, there are four objects:

◆ `Media Pools`

◆ `Physical Locations`

◆ Work Queue

◆ Operator Requests

I'm going to skip the last two and just focus on the first two because they apply to backing up.

Physical Locations = Mechanical Drives

Of these two, Physical Locations is the easier to understand. In Figure 21.22, I expanded it, so you can see three objects—a drive icon representing the CD-ROM (ATAPI CD-ROM DRIVE-40X), one representing the tape drive (QUANTUM DLT7000 SCSI Sequential Device), and one labeled Off-Line Media. Physical Locations, therefore, are the drives that RSM can manage. Not the *media* in those drives, but the drives.

Library = "Autoloader" or "Stand-Alone Drive"

When I right-click either the CD-ROM or the tape and choose Properties, I get a properties page describing not the drive, but the drive's interface. I'll also see a lot of references to the device as a *library*. There is, for example, no button or check box to disable the device; instead, you'd see a Enable Library check box and un-checking it would disable the device. To RSM, a *library* is one or more drives that have an automatic changer for their tapes, cartridges, discs, or whatever. (For shorthand, I'll call them generically *tapes*.)

As you can see, Microsoft has upped the ante on its definition of the "basic removable storage doodad." Where it once was a tape, now it's a *tape library*, one or more tape drives and zero or more *changers*, the little robotic hands. My humble DLT tape drive is, then, a library consisting of *one* tape drive and *zero* changers. (Yeah, it's a lot simple. I couldn't afford that really cool HP autoloader with four drives and capacity to hold 60 tapes—$46,000 was a bit out of my budget—so I'll stick to DLT for the moment.) Microsoft even has a name for a zero-changer, one-tape-drive library: a *stand-alone library*. That's not just a CD-ROM on your system, my friend, it's an optical stand-alone library. Notice also that in addition to my DLT and CD-ROM "libraries," I have a third one called my Off-Line Media library. *Off-line media* is Microsoft's way of describing wherever you store tapes when they're not in your drives. So tapes sitting in a desk drawer or on a shelf are in a library.

This may sound odd, but it kind of makes sense once you adopt the RSM way of thinking. RSM's main job actually seems to be a kind of database that lets you keep track of your tapes. As you'll see, this database keeps track of the following information about tapes:

◆ Where they are physically located—on a shelf, in an autoloader waiting to be inserted into a drive, actually in a drive

◆ What program wrote them

◆ What sort of drive can read and write them

◆ What data is on them

RSM really only *secondarily* concerns itself with the specifics of what sort of drives you have. Calling them all libraries allows you to concern yourself with where your *data* are, not where your tapes or CDs are.

This information is not just available from the GUI; RSM has a command-line tool called RSM.EXE. To get the list of your libraries, just type **rsm view /tlibrary**. That gets this result:

```
LIBRARY

Off-line Media
ATAPI CD-ROM DRIVE-40X
QUANTUM DLT7000 SCSI Sequential Device

The command completed successfully.
```

Notice the odd spacing—there is no space between /t and library. We'll use rsm view /t again—the /t means "type of thing to view"—and its odd syntax requires no spaces between /t and the parameter describing what you want to view. As with other things in Windows 2000, though, those names are just the human-friendly names. Under the hood, Windows 2000 *really* identifies things by globally unique IDs (GUIDs), and sometimes you'll need to know what they are, as you'll see later. You can find that out by adding the /guiddisplay option, like this:

```
C:\>rsm view /tlibrary /guiddisplay

LIBRARY

Off-line Media   D49F02AE9CEA46BFB58E51AB6C7FE262
ATAPI CD-ROM DRIVE-40X   6043C178219841208E034076D0566885
QUANTUM DLT7000 SCSI Sequential Device   E30ADF03E8014BA4BB824AD69B39FBE7

The command completed successfully.

C:\>
```

Media = Tapes, Cartridges, CD-ROM Discs, Etc.

Within the CD-ROM and tape drive objects there are then, in turn, two objects, Media and Drives. *Drives* of course refers to the physical drive. But media needs some defining. To RSM, *media* means anything that you put into a drive. Tapes go in tape drives, so tapes are media. CD-ROMs go into CD-ROM drives, so they're media. But media doesn't mean a *type* of media, it means particular *instances* of media. As I suggested before, RSM's job seems to be to maintain a database that keeps track of every single tape that you ever shove into one of your tape drives.

The folder labeled Media under a drive's icon in the Physical Locations object will contain an object representing the particular tape, cartridge, or disc sitting in your drive at that moment. For example, if I insert a CD into my CD-ROM drive and click the Media folder under ATAPI CD-ROM... then I'll see something like Figure 21.23. Notice that under Loaded Media it says STREETS9. That refers to a piece of software, as this is the installation CD for a mapping program.

NOTE *In truth, RSM isn't very useful for CD-ROMs; this is just an example of how it works that you can try out on almost any system. As I've said before, NTBACKUP cannot use CD-R, CD-RW, DVD-RW, or DVD+RW drives.*

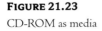

FIGURE 21.23

CD-ROM as media

I can easily use the GUI to see that my CD-ROM drive contains a CD whose label is STREETS9, but we're going to want to be able to retrieve that kind of information from the command line; for that, we'll use more of RSM.EXE. To get information on a particular tape, use the physical_media option on the rsm view command. But just typing **rsm view /tphysical_media** won't do the job— that will display *every* bit of removable media on the system at the moment. (Admittedly that's not a real problem on *this* computer, as it only contains one bit of removable media, the CD. But let's see how to do it on more real-world systems.)

To narrow the scope of rsm view /tphysical_media, add a parameter, /cg for "container GUID." As we're trying to find the GUID of the CD-ROM disc sitting in the CD-ROM drive at the moment, the container is the CD-ROM drive. As you saw a moment ago, we get that with the rsm view /tlibrary /guiddisplay command. As you can see here, to find out about the media in the drive, I'll just plug the drive's GUID into the command like this:

```
C:\>rsm view /tphysical_media /cg6043C178219841208E034076D0566885

PHYSICAL_MEDIA

STREETS9

The command completed successfully.
```

TIP   *If you're wondering how you can accurately type a GUID, don't worry. To type that command, I highlighted the GUID from the* rsm view /tlibrary /guiddisplay *output and pressed Enter, which puts the highlighted text into the Clipboard. Then I typed* **rsm view /tphysical_media /cg**, *clicked the icon in the upper-left corner of the window to drop the Control Menu for that window, then chose Edit/Paste.*

Note that as with the parameters following /t, I typed the GUID after the /cg command without any spaces after the /cg. Note also that if I needed to retrieve the GUID of the media (which we'll want to do later in with tapes), I could have added the logical_media command.

You can "drill down" even further than a given tape—physical media contain one or more partitions, and partitions contain one or more logical_media. In each case, you'd just use /guiddisplay to get the GUID of the container and then feed that with /cg as the GUID of the container to view.

MEDIA POOLS: CLASSIFYING TAPES

Thus far, I haven't shown you much of anything that has to do with tapes, so let's pop a tape into the drive and see what happens. Note that this is a *new* tape, fresh out of the box. It's never been introduced to this drive, or to NTBACKUP, before.

After inserting the tape and waiting for the tape drive to settle down, I right-click the QUANTUM DLT7000... drive and choose Refresh to force RSM to reexamine the drive's status. I then click the Media folder under the tape and see a screen like Figure 21.24.

FIGURE 21.24

Remote Storage Manager after inserting new tape

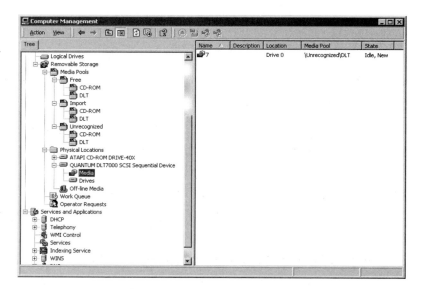

Notice that a few things happened. First, the Free, Import, and Unrecognized media pools (I'll get to what they are in a minute) now have a DLT folder underneath them, where previously they only had a CD-ROM folder there. Second, the Media folder for the tape drive now contains something called "7" that is said to be in Drive 0 in a media pool called Unrecognized\DLT; its state is reported to be Idle, New. And sure enough, clicking the DLT folder under the Unrecognized folder in the Media Pools object shows another item named 7—it's the same tape—in that folder. (If you're not crazy about naming a tape "7," then fear not. The later section "Renaming a Tape" explains how to change a tape's name.)

Basically, this is RSM-ese for "this tape is unformatted." That's not exactly right, as DLT tapes ship formatted, but RSM wants to write a bit of identifying data onto the tape. I can do that by right-clicking on the tape's icon in the right pane; I'll get a menu that offers Eject, Mount, Prepare, and Dismount. I choose Prepare and see a dialog box that says:

```
This operation will destroy the data on the media and move it to a Free media pool.
Are you sure you want to write a Free media label on the selected medium?
```

I choose Yes and get *another* confirmation message:

```
Are you sure you want to write a Free media label on 7?
```

What *are* you, hard of hearing, RSM? I click Yes again and the tape's media pool changes to Free\ DLT and its state goes to Loaded, Unprepared while the tape spins for a few minutes. It finally finishes whatever it does when "preparing" the tape, and the tape ends up in Free\DLT in a state of Idle, Available.

NOTE *There is not, as far as I can see, a command-line tool in* RSM.EXE *that will prepare never-before-used tapes. But that won't be a problem since NTBACKUP has a* /um *option that automatically erases and prepares tapes before backing up.*

Now I can explain the next RSM concept, media pools. Remember that RSM is a database of tapes. Even if you just shove a tape into a drive once, prepare it, remove it, bury it in a mine shaft, and never look at it again, RSM remembers that tape. Remember also that the RSM word for a tape is *media*. RSM wants to organize the media that it has met into categories and, by default, it categorizes media in one of three ways:

◆ *Free media* are tapes that RSM has "prepared" but that don't have any data on them. They're waiting to be used by some RSM-aware application such as NTBACKUP.

◆ *Import media* are tapes that RSM recognizes as having been prepared by RSM on this or some other machine in the past. They're RSM tapes, all right, but they're not blank (so they don't go into Free). They're also not associated with a particular RSM-aware application. As you will soon see, RSM-aware applications create their *own* media pools, and RSM will then be able to categorize some media as neither Free, Import, or Unrecognized—they'll be categorized as Backup tapes, ArcServe tapes, BackupExec tapes, or the like. So Import is a kind of catch-all category meaning, "This tape has been prepared, so it doesn't go into Unrecognized, it's not blank, so it doesn't go into Free, so some application *has* worked with it before, but I don't remember it, so it'll stay here in Import until the user decides to drop it into some application's folder."

◆ *Unrecognized media* have not been prepared to work with RSM. RSM can't do anything with them until they are.

This will make a lot more sense once we get an RSM-aware application running. When I run NTBACKUP for the first time, that causes it to introduce itself to RSM, and tells RSM to create a new fourth media pool called Backup. Now that I've run Windows 2000's backup program, any tape that NTBACKUP writes to will become essentially the "property" of NTBACKUP. As a matter of fact, if I *had* media sitting in the Import media pool that had been originally created by NTBACKUP on some other system, then the first time that I started up NTBACKUP I'd have gotten the dialog box that you see in Figure 21.25.

FIGURE 21.25

Should Backup be able to claim old backup tapes?

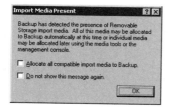

Even if you don't allow NTBACKUP to import the media now, you can do it by hand later; you can just drag any media item out of one media pool and drop it into another. (Of course, if you try to drop it into Free, then you'll get a warning that dropping it into Free will cause RSM to erase it.)

MANAGING MEDIA IN RSM

That's an overview of how RSM works—it tracks particular tapes, giving each one a GUID (which changes whenever you "prepare" a tape) and categorizing it in either an application's media pool (Backup on most systems, but if you've purchased other RSM-aware apps then you might have more than one application media pool), or one of the "holding tanks": Free, Import, or Unrecognized. Understand also that you can move media between media pools even if the actual physical tape isn't currently in the tape drive; the tape doesn't know and doesn't care which media pool it belongs to. Tapes *do*, however, carry on them the mark of their associated RSM-aware application, which is why you can take a tape created on one system, pop it into another Windows 2000 system, and it will immediately be recognized as having already been seen by RSM *and* NTBACKUP will recognize that this tape contains data written by NTBACKUP.

We're just about done with RSM, and ready to tackle NTBACKUP.

Renaming a Tape

As intuitive names for our first tape go, "7" is not ranking high. So how about we give it a more useful name? I intend to use this tape as one of two tapes that I'll store differential backups on, so I'll rename it "Diff1." To do so, I'll right-click the tape and choose Properties. The General tab has a text field that includes the name of the tape.

For some reason, renaming the tape doesn't seem to be enough to convince NTBACKUP that the tape has a new name. In my experience, you need to then put the tape in the Free media pool so that it is reinitialized.

WARNING *Moving the tape to the Free media pool deletes any data on the tape, so don't do this if there is any data on the tape that you'd miss!*

Moving a Tape to Free

Sometimes you won't be able to move a tape from the Backup media pool to the Free media pool. You must first "deallocate" it. Now, *finding* where to deallocate a tape may be a challenge.

You've already seen that by right-clicking a media object that you'll get a drop-down context menu that includes four actions—Eject, Prepare, Mount, and Unmount. Below that is a submenu, All Tasks, which on *most* MMCs would just repeat Eject, Prepare, Mount, Unmount. But *this* one includes a fifth option...Deallocate. So to free an existing tape, first right-click it and choose All Tasks/Deallocate, and then drag it to Free. (And along the way, say "yes to all of the "are you sure? messages.)

Ejecting a Tape from the Command Line

We've been going over RSM to get ready to do backups and command-line backups in particular. Over the years I've seen people write batch files for handling backups, and some folks like to end off the backup process with an `eject` command. I guess it makes for a slightly more secure backup because once the tape's ejected, then there's no hacker on earth who can convince the tape drive to reinsert the tape. (That's not true for autoloaders, of course, but it is for stand-alone drives, at least in my experience.) So how do you tell NTBACKUP to eject your tape? With RSM. The command looks like this:

```
rsm eject /pf"name of tape to eject" /astart
```

Or alternatively:

```
rsm eject /pgGUID /astart
```

In the first case, you fill in the media's name; in the second, you fill in its GUID. Note that if you let NTBACKUP prepare the tape, then it'll have a name like `Media created 1/4/2002 at 5:21 PM - 1`, and for the command to work right you'll need to type in the media name precisely.

The only real problem with this is that you probably want a fairly generic "eject" batch file, but both versions of `rsm eject` are very tape specific: You've either got to know the name of the particular tape, or you've got to know the tape's GUID. Unless you intend to use the very same tape night after night, then this won't be too useful. But consider:

◆   The GUID of the tape *drive* won't vary from day to day.

◆   If we have the tape drive's GUID, we can use `rsm view /tphysical_media` to get the GUID of the particular tape in the drive at that moment.

Here's how to put all of that together into a batch file that needs only to know the GUID of the drive in order to eject any tape in that drive. If you don't know how batch files work internally, then don't worry about following this—I'll have a ready-made batch file prepared at the end of this section that you can just type in and use (replacing my GUID with the one for your tape drive, of course).

My plan for the batch file will be that I'll use `rsm view` to retrieve the tape's GUID and put it in a variable `%tguid%`. Then I'll just issue the `rsm eject` command with the `/pg` option, specifying the GUID of the tape. We can do all that with just three lines (the second one is broken but should be all on one line):

```
set drvguid=E30ADF03E8014BA4BB824AD69B39FBE7
FOR /F "usebackq" %%i IN (`rsm view /tphysical_media /cg%drvguid% /b
➥ /guiddisplay`) DO set x=%%i
rsm eject /pg%X% /astart
```

In the first line, I'm just filling up an environment variable named *drvguid*. That long value that I'm stuffing in it, `E30ADF03E8014BA4BB824AD69B39FBE7`, is the GUID of *my* DLT drive. Yours will be different, so use `rsm view /tlibrary /guiddisplay` to get the particular GUID for your tape drive and replace my drive's GUID with yours in that line.

In the second line, I'm executing the command `rsm view /tphysical_media /cg` to get the GUID of the tape in the drive. But, as you've already seen, you must provide the GUID of a container for that to work—that's what `%drvguid%` does. You filled in your drive's GUID in the line before and that gets inserted before the command executes. The `/guiddisplay /b` says to display the GUID, and the `/b` option says to show *only* the GUID. That makes life easier, as it's only the GUID that I want. The result of that—the GUID—goes into a variable named %x. (The two percent signs are required syntax for the FOR command.)

Once I've got the GUID for the tape in X, then I can construct the last line, which executes an eject command for the tape whose GUID is in X.

Here are the steps to creating and using this batch file:

1. Get the GUID of your tape drive. From the command line, type **rsm view /tlibrary / guiddisplay**. You'll see a line for all of the removable devices on your system, including CD-ROMs. The name of the device should make clear which one is your tape drive. Grab the GUID next to that device's name—again, you can copy this value by selecting it and pressing Enter.

2. Open up Notepad and type in the batch file as you see in the previous text. In the first line, substitute your drive's GUID in place of E30ADF03E8014BA4BB824AD69B39FBE7. Note that the single quotes in the second line are *backquotes*. On many keyboards they are on the same key as the tilde (~).

3. Save the file in the WINNT directory as tapeeject.cmd.

Try it out by opening up a command line and typing **tapeeject**. The tape should eject.

TIP   *If you want to run* tapeeject *from inside a batch file, then don't just put the line* tapeeject *in the batch file; instead, use* call tapeeject, *or the batch file will end when* tapeeject *ends.*

Refreshing a Tape from the Command Line

Sometimes you'll pop a tape into a drive and try to do something with it from the GUI or the command line, and the command fails—the system acts as if there is no tape in the drive. There are two possible reasons for that. First, remember, we're working with tapes here—they're not the fastest things in the world. When you pop a tape in, the drive may take a minute or two to figure the tape out. Second, RSM for some reason doesn't always automatically figure out that you just put a tape in a drive. The *drive* knows that it's there, it's just RSM that doesn't know. So it never hurts to smack RSM upside the head before trying to do something—that's called *refreshing*.

You can refresh just about any object in the RSM by just right-clicking it and choosing Refresh. But if you're about to run a batch job to automatically back up a system, then you want a command-line method to do that. RSM lets you do that with an **rsm refresh** command. It looks like this:

```
rsm refresh /lf"drive name"
```

or

```
rsm refresh /lgdrive-GUID
```

So, for example, my drive could be refreshed either with this:

```
rsm refresh /lf"QUANTUM DLT7000 SCSI Sequential Device"
```

or

```
rsm refresh /lgE30ADF03E8014BA4BB824AD69B39FBE7
```

Notice that the drive name needs quotes and the spelling must be exact; the GUID, on the other hand, must be exact but does not need quotes.

Automating Tape Backups

You've seen that Windows 2000 conceptualizes tapes through RSM, and you've seen RSM's notions of libraries, physical media, and media pools—and that it assigns GUIDs to everything, and how much it relies upon those GUIDs. That was all necessary preparation for controlling NTBACKUP from the command line.

The basic idea with automating NTBACKUP is simple: Write a batch file that wakes up the NTBACKUP.EXE program and tells it to back up to tape. Then use the Schedule service—the AT.EXE command—to tell the operating system to run that batch file whenever you want it run—daily, every other day, or whatever.

The hardest part is usually writing the batch file. It's typically just one line, a long invocation of the NTBACKUP command. That's what we're going to focus on here. As you can see in Table 21.4, these options are enough to scare most folks off. But I'm going to simplify them as much as possible, starting from a very basic command and then adding things as we go.

TABLE 21.4: WINDOWS 2000 NTBACKUP OPTIONS

ARGUMENT	FUNCTION
backup	Tells NTBACKUP that you're running a backup operation. You must include this argument.
systemstate	Specifies that all System State data should be backed up and sets the backup type to normal or copy. As discussed earlier in this chapter, not all System State data may be backed up from a remote computer.
bks file name	This is the name of the selection information file in which the backup will be stored (if you're backing up to a file instead of a tape). More than one backup can go in the same BKS file, if you choose to append backups. You must create this file from the GUI before referencing it from the command line.
/j "job name"	Tells NTBACKUP the name of the backup job.
/p "pool name"	Tells NTBACKUP which media pool (a logical grouping of removable media, such as a tape library) to copy the backup files to. If you're using Backup, this will be the Backup media pool. You won't use this option with /g or /t, as those switches specify that a certain tape should be used; with /f, which specifies the name of a file to back up to; or with /a because you must append backup files to a specific tape, not an entire media pool.
/g "guid name"	Specifies the GUID of the tape that will be overwritten or appended with this backup job. Don't use this switch with /p, as that specifies that NTBACKUP should back up to a media pool instead of a particular tape. The GUID must be in quotes and hyphenated, so that it looks like this: "b471ff3b-101f-43bc-9d15-ffb7176cf2f3"; you must respect those demarcations must be respected—eight characters, hyphen, four, hyphen, four, hyphen, four, hyphen, 12 characters.

Continued on next page

TABLE 21.4: WINDOWS 2000 NTBACKUP OPTIONS *(continued)*

ARGUMENT	FUNCTION
/t "tape name"	Specifies the media name of the tape that will be overwritten or appended with this backup job. Don't use this switch with /p, as this specifies that NTBACKUP will use a media pool instead of a particular tape.
/n "new tape name"	Specifies the new tape name of the tape that will be overwritten or appended with this backup job. Use this switch to name a tape, but use it sparingly. Don't use this switch with /p, as this specifies that NTBACKUP will use a media pool instead of a particular tape. You also can't use this switch with /a because you can't append data onto a tape that is new or that you're renaming. Finally, it's best not to use this switch with /um since that switch is for unattended tape backups, and it may work best to let Backup name the tape on its own.
/f "file name"	Specifies the path and name of the file in which the backup will be copied. As this switch directs the backup to a file, not a tape or media pool, you can't use it with any of the switches specific to removable media: /p, /t, or /n.
/d "description"	Specifies the description of the backup set, such as "Full backup of SERPENT on 11/20/01."
/ds "server name"	Backs up the directory service on the specified Microsoft Exchange server.
/is "server name"	Backs up the information store on the specified Microsoft Exchange server.
/a	Appends the backup set to any data on the media. If backing up to a tape, you must use this switch with either /g or /t to specify the tape you want to append to. You can't use this switch with /p, as you must append to a specific tape, not an entire media pool.
/v:yes or no	Specifies whether the backup procedure should be verified or not. Verifying the data (making sure the data in the backup matches the source) takes a little time, but reassures you that the data was written correctly.
/r:yes or no	Specifies whether the tape should be available only to its owner/creator and members of the Administrators group.
/l:f or s or n	Tells NTBACKUP what kind of log file to create: full (logging every copied file), summary (logging only important events and errors), or none (in which case the backup won't be logged).
/m backuptype	Tells NTBACKUP what kind of backup to run: normal, copy, incremental, differential, or daily.
/rs:yes or no	Tells NTBACKUP whether to back up the removable storage database that records the location of archived files. If you're using removable storage, you should back up this database regularly to make sure that you can retrieve archived files.
/hc:on or off	Tells NTBACKUP whether to use hardware compression (available only if you're backing up to a tape drive, and then only if that tape drive supports it—most do). Go ahead and use hardware compression if it's available, as it will allow you to get more use out of your tapes.

Forget all the options for a minute. The basic NTBACKUP command looks like this:

```
ntbackup backup directory tapedrive
```

directory is, of course, the name of the directory (or UNC) to back up. *tapedrive* is the name of the tape drive to do the backup to. Leave that off, and the command will just not run—and it doesn't even tell you *why* unless you look for and read the log files. You specify a tape drive in one of two ways:

- /t "*name*" as in /t "Tape created on Tuesday"

- /p "*media-type*" as in /p "DLT"

- /g "*guid name*" as in /g "b471ff3b-101f-43bc-9d15-ffb7176cf2f3"

By the way, notice that RSM likes to add - 1 to tape names (apparently assuming that you have more than one tape in a set), but that name won't work with NTBACKUP. If you'd created a tape called mytape, then it'd show up in the GUI as mytape - 1—but when you use the /t option, leave the extra - 1 off. That is, use /t "mytape", not /t "mytape - 1". To identify a tape by its GUID, you must use the GUID of the logical_media *inside* the partition *inside* the physical_media that is *inside* the library.

You'll use /t and /p for different purposes. /t with /a permits you to append new backup sets to an existing tape without deleting the existing ones (which /p doesn't allow) but requires that you know the name of the tape in the drive. /p in combination with /um doesn't need the name of the tape in the drive, as it just tells NTBACKUP, "Whatever's in there, just wipe it clean and start all over!"

A BACKUP STRATEGY

For years, I've used a simple backup strategy for servers: Once a week I do a full backup, and every other day I do a differential backup. It's simple to automate with just a little manual work. I keep two tapes: the differential tape, which I leave in the drive for most of the week, and the full backup tape, which I only leave in the drive over Sunday night. (Yes, I rotate tapes, but I'm simplifying this explanation.) Here's how it works: Every Sunday morning, I remove the differential tape from my server's tape drive and put it aside. Then I insert a tape for a full system backup. On Monday morning, I remove that tape, which now has a full system backup on it, and reinsert the differential tape.

Using the Schedule service, I set up three events:

- On Sunday night/early Monday morning, I schedule NTBACKUP to back up my server's files (a "normal" backup), but first to wipe clean anything on the hard disk.

- On Monday night/Tuesday morning, I schedule NTBACKUP to do a differential backup of my server's files, but first to wipe clean anything on the hard disk. (This reinitializes the differential tape each week.)

- On the other evenings, I schedule NTBACKUP to do a differential backup of my server's files, but tell it to *append* the new backup set to the existing ones on the tape. That way, I have backup sets that represent the state of the network for every day of the week.

Furthermore, let's make this example a bit more complicated—and more useful in the real world—by specifying that the only directories that I want to back up are C:\DATA, C:\USERS, and D:\REPORTS.

THE WEEKLY BACKUP

For this backup, I want the drive wiped clean. What command does that? `ntbackup backup /p /um`. In its simplest form, that would look like this:

```
ntbackup backup directories /p "DLT" /um
```

Remember that your drive may not be a DLT; other possible values might be 4mm DDS, Travan, QIC, or others. Just look in the folder created under your Backup media pool to find out your drive's type.

But we're not out of the woods yet. How do I specify three different directories to back up?

Using a Backup Selection File

You *could* write a batch file that called `ntbackup` three times, but that's too much work. Instead, open up Notepad and type the names of the directories that you want to back up, one to a line:

```
C:\data\
c:\users\
d:\reports\
```

Then click Save As and specify that the file's name is `c:\myfiles.bks`, but don't save yet—in the Save As box, go to the Encoding box and choose Unicode.

WARNING   *This is very important. You don't have to save it in* `C:\`*, you needn't give it the extension* `.bks`*—but you've got to save it in Unicode, or NTBACKUP simply will not read it.*

Now run NTBACKUP as before, but instead of specifying a directory, specify your backup selection file's name prefixed by an @ sign. If the directory's name includes spaces, then you'll need to surround the name with quotes. The command looks like this so far:

```
ntbackup backup @c:\myfiles.bks /p "DLT" /UM
```

Choosing Logging Levels

At least until I'm sure that this thing works, I'd be happier with an extensive log. You can set logging levels with the `/l:` option: `/l:s` provides only summaries (and is the default), `/l:f` provides full logs, and `/l:n` produces no logs at all.

Hardware Compression

In theory I can get 80 gigs of stuff on this tape if I turn on hardware compression. You control that with the `/hc:` option—it's either `/hc:on` or `/hc:off`.

Verification

In general, I find that I distrust computers when it comes to my data. So I don't mind the extra time required to stop, rewind, and verify backups. You control verification with either `/v:yes` or `/v:no`. (Why `/hc` uses `on` or `off` and `/v` uses `yes` and `no` is known only to the Microsoft developers.)

Append or Replace?

In this particular case, I want to overwrite any existing backup sets, replacing any on the tape. That's the default behavior, so there's nothing to do. If I wanted the system to append its backup set to any existing sets then I'd add /a. You can't do /a if you've used /p, but you can use /a in combination with /t.

Name the Tape

By default RSM and NTBACKUP name the tape by its date and time of "creation," but you can give it any other name by adding the parameter /n followed by a name.

Back Up the Registry?

Adding the parameter `systemstate` will cause NTBACKUP to back up the System State data. The other options can go just about anywhere, but `systemstate` must go after the word `backup` and before the backup selection file's name.

Put it all together and you've got a command like this (all on one line):

```
ntbackup backup systemstate @c:\myfiles.bks /p "DLT" /UM /l:f /hc:on /v:yes
```

Create the Batch File

Finally, let's put the Schedule service to work. Put that line (with your site-specific modifications, of course) into a batch file called `c:\fullback.cmd`. Then open up a command line, type this:

```
at 2:00 /interactive /every:Monday c:\fullback.cmd
```

and press Enter. Now at 2 A.M. every Monday morning, your system will do a normal backup of the directories that you specified in `c:\myfiles.bks`.

How Do I Know It Worked?

NTBACKUP writes ASCII text files called `backup01.txt` through `backup10.txt`, maintaining logs of the last 10 times that NTBACKUP ran. (It starts reusing files once it gets to `backup1.txt`.) You cannot, unfortunately, control either the number of log files that it keeps (it's 10) or where it puts them. NTBACKUP stores the logs in `\Documents and Settings\`*username*`\Local Settings\Application Data\Microsoft\Windows NT\NTbackup\Data`...and it's that *username* thing that'll give you fits.

When you're logged in as you, Joeadmin, then the logs go to `\Documents and Settings\joeadmin\Local Settings\Application Data\Microsoft\Windows NT\NTbackup\Data`. But when the Schedule service starts the process—that is, when you're automatically scheduling a backup—it writes the logs to in `\Documents and Settings\Default User\Local Settings\Application Data\Microsoft\Windows NT\NTbackup\Data`. And don't be surprised if you have more than one of those directories—you might find that you've got a directory named `\Documents and Settings\Default User\Local Settings\Application Data\Microsoft\Windows NT\NTbackup\Data` *and* `\Documents and Settings\Default User.WINNT\Local Settings\Application Data\Microsoft\Windows NT\NTbackup\Data`. Just look in both directories and find the one with the more recent log files—those are the ones you want.

THE DIFFERENTIAL BACKUP

You set up the differential backup basically the same way, but instead of /p /um you'll use /t and a tape name—we don't want to overwrite the tapes. So you'll need to standardize on a name for a tape; I use diff1, and append a week's differentials together, so my batch file looks like this:

```
ntbackup backup systemstate @c:\myfiles.bks /t "diff1" /a /1:f /hc:on /v:yes
```

I save that as c:\diffback.cmd and tell Schedule to run it every day but Monday morning:

```
at 2:00 /interactive /every:T,W,Th,F,S,Su c:\diffback.cmd
```

And if you wanted to be really snazzy, then you could build a slightly different version that runs only on Tuesday that erases the tape first—use /p /um for that one, if you like.

MAKING RSM AND NTBACKUP SHARE INFORMATION

As I said earlier, RSM and NTBACKUP don't always see eye to eye on how to present data. RSM thinks that all tape sets have more than one tape in them, so it names tapes with a 1 at the end. NTBACKUP won't recognize the name if the 1 is there, so you have to delete the 1 before including the RSM-reported name in a batch file. Similarly, RSM reports GUIDs as unbroken strings. NTBACKUP, on the other hand, is very exacting about the way it wants to see GUIDs: It wants you to type them as eight characters, hyphen, four, hyphen, four, hyphen, four, hyphen, 12 characters. That is, the GUID RSM reports as b471ff3b101f43bc9d15ffb7176cf2f3 needs to become b471ff3b-101f-43bc-9d15-ffb7176cf2f3 for NTBACKUP to use it. Having tired of counting characters and inserting hyphens at appropriate intervals, I wrote a batch file that will grab GUID data from RSM, format it so that NTBACKUP likes it, then starts a differential backup. Just be sure to supply your own GUIDs when using this batch file!

```
@echo off
set drvguid=E30ADF03E8014BA4BB824AD69B39FBE7
FOR /F "usebackq delims==" %%i IN (`rsm view /tphysical_media /cg%drvguid%
/guiddisplay /b`) DO set tapeguid=%%i
FOR /F "usebackq delims==" %%i IN (`rsm view /tpartition /cg%tapeguid%
/guiddisplay /b`) DO set partguid=%%i
FOR /F "usebackq delims==" %%i IN (`rsm view /tlogical_media /cg%partguid%
/guiddisplay /b`) DO set logguid=%%i
set p1=%logguid:~0,8%
set p2=%logguid:~8,4%
set p3=%logguid:~12,4%
set p4=%logguid:~16,4%
set p5=%logguid:~20,12%
set bkguid=%p1%-%p2%-%p3%-%p4%-%p5%
ntbackup backup @c:\batch\files.bks /g "%bkguid%" /a /v:yes /hc:on /m
differential
```

ADVICE FOR BUILDING YOUR BATCH FILES

Now, you'll probably end up trying different things in your batch files and will have different needs than I do. So you'll have to craft your own solution, which means trial and error. There is nothing more frustrating than checking your logs in the morning only to find that for some mysterious reason *nothing seems to have happened at all.*

Here's a methodology for making command-line backups tractable.

- **Try everything out from the command line first.** Unless you're *really* good, you'll hit a few syntax snags along the way. Trying your commands out on the command line gives you immediate feedback so that you can work out the bugs quickly.

- **Build the command line gradually.** Start from the most minimal command possible, such as `ntbackup backup c:\testfiles /p "dlt" /um` or the like. Crawl before you try walking and walk before you try flying.

- **Keep track of what worked and what didn't.** You may have hardware that's cranky about some command and truthfully all tape drives are a bit flaky—something that works today may not work tomorrow unless you clean the tape or restart RSM. When you've got a command that works, make sure you've got its exact syntax saved somewhere. I use Notepad files as my logs when I'm experimenting. I use copy and paste to provide a simple log of the output from my commands.

- **Once you have the command line perfect, make a batch file.** Just copy and paste the command line into Notepad, save it with the `.cmd` extension and you're a batch file builder. Then invoke the batch file by its name—if you called the Notepad file `c:\dotape.cmd`, then open up a command line and type `c:\dotape.cmd` and make sure that it still works. If it doesn't, then check that any paths needed in the command are there.

- **Try the batch file with at.** Once you've got the batch file running so that it works as expected from the command line, test it with the Schedule service. From a command line, type **at *time* /interactive *batchfilename*** and press Enter. For *time* just punch in a time a minute or two in the future—you don't want to have to wait forever. (Remember that the Schedule service uses a 24-hour clock, so 3 P.M. should be entered as **15:00**.) If it doesn't work, then make sure that you entered the full path of the batch file.

- **Once the bugs are out, tell at to run it regularly.** Rerun the `at` command, but add the `/every:` information so that it knows which days to run the command.

Viewing Backup Logs

Unless you specify otherwise, every time you back up Backup creates a backup log. To see the contents of these logs, you can click the Report button in the dialog box that tells you that the backup is complete. Alternatively, to pick any log to view, choose Report from the Tools menu in Windows Backup. You'll see a list of backups, as shown in Figure 21.26.

FIGURE 21.26

Choose a backup log to view.

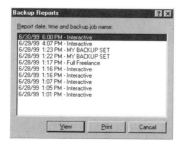

In the Backup Reports dialog box, find the report you want based on its job name or time and date stamp, and click the View button. The log will open in Notepad and provide output something such as this:

```
Backup Status
Operation: Backup
Active backup destination: File
Media name: "Media created 12/28/01 at 1:07 PM"

Backup of "H: \\Serpent\Freelnce"
Backup set #5 on media #1
Backup description: "Set created 12/28/01 at 1:23 PM"
Backup Type: Normal

Backup started on 12/28/01 at 1:23 PM.
Warning: The file \Acme\Win2K Server\2447c21.doc in use - skipped.
Backup completed on 12/28/01 at 1:29 PM.
Directories: 10
Files: 307
Skipped: 1
Bytes: 294,829,336
Time:  6 minutes and  26 seconds
```

Notice that in this log you can see what folders and directories were backed up, how long it took to run the backup, and whether any errors occurred (such as that file that didn't get backed up because it was open).

Restoring Data

Backups don't do you a lot of good unless you can put them back on the server from where they came. To restore files, open Windows Backup again. You can either run the Restore Wizard or turn to the Restore tab.

WARNING   *Windows 2000's version of NTFS uses some file attributes not found in FAT or the Windows NT version of NTFS. You may not be able to restore some data that was originally stored on an NTFS 5 volume to a downlevel volume (FAT, FAT32, or NTFS with NT 4). For example, if you back up encrypted files and then try to restore them to a FAT volume, you'll see an error message telling you that the restore destination doesn't support some system features of the original, so some files (the encrypted ones) won't be restored. What actually happens is that the file's restored, but it no longer has the encryption attribute.*

BASIC RESTORATION TECHNIQUES

To restore files from the Restore Wizard, go to the Welcome tab of Windows Backup and click the Restore Wizard icon. You'll see the usual Welcome screen. Click through it, and you'll be prompted to pick the media you want to restore from (see Figure 21.27). The options available will depend on what kind of media you've backed up to. If you've backed up to a file, you'll need to click the Import File button to import the BKF file holding your backups.

FIGURE 21.27

Available media for restoration

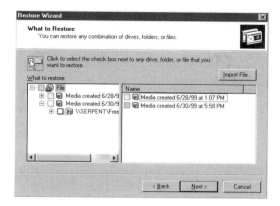

The backup sets on the media will be listed as folders, as shown in Figure 21.28. They'll be described according to volume backed up, size, type of backup, and description.

FIGURE 21.28

Each backup set on the media will appear separately.

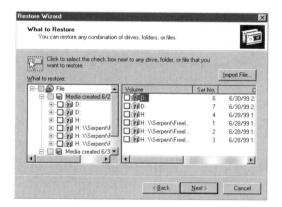

NOTE *If a backup operation was aborted for any reason—by Windows Backup or by the user—you will not be able to restore it. Such backups will still appear in the catalog but will have a question mark where their size should be. This is one more reason to ensure you can restore backups before you need them.*

Double-click a set to catalog it, and you'll be able to browse its contents. Check the boxes next to the files and folders in the backup set that you want to restore. As with selecting files for backup, a checked folder with all contents selected will have a blue check mark; if you've only selected certain files within the folder, its check mark will be gray.

NOTE *If there are any errors within the folders of a backup set, the folder will have a red exclamation point on it and the corrupted file will have another exclamation point. You will not be able to restore any damaged files.*

When you finish picking files to restore, the wizard will display a screen listing the current restore options. Click Back to edit any file or media settings, or click the Advanced button to specify a new restoration location or change the file restoration options for preexisting files and remote storage information.

WARNING *The Advanced options that you choose will apply to all future restoration operations until you change them again. For example, if you edit the options so that the files on the hard disk are always replaced with the files from the backup, that option will remain in place until you manually change it to another one.*

Where Should Files Be Restored?

Unless you tell it otherwise, Windows Backup restores files to their original location. But what if you're restoring data to a new drive with a drive letter that's different from the original? Or you want to put the contents of a daily backup on a Zip disk? From the first screen of the advanced section of the Backup Wizard, you can choose from three location options:

◆ Original location

◆ Alternate location (files and folders will be restored, folder structure intact, to the location you specify)

◆ Single folder (files will all be put within a single folder in the folder you specify, and the original folder structure will be lost)

If you tell Windows Backup to restore the files to an alternate location or to a single folder, then the wizard will display a text box where you type (or browse for) the restore path. You can only restore data to an alternate location, not system configuration information such as the Registry. Any system configuration files must go back to their original locations.

TIP *To edit this option without running the Restore Wizard, turn to the Restore tab of Windows Backup. In the lower-left corner of this tab is a drop-down list of the restoration location options. System State data must always be restored to its original location.*

What If a File with That Name Already Exists?

The second screen in the advanced section of the Backup Wizard tells Windows Backup what to do if a file with the same name as the file being restored already exists on the volume. Normally, Windows Backup will not replace the file on the existing media, on the principle that if you already have the file, you shouldn't need to replace it. However, sometimes you'll want the file from the backup, not the one on the hard disk. For example, a Word document with a macro virus may be present on the hard disk, but you don't want the infected file. To cope with some of the situations in which you might want to replace the file already on the hard disk, Windows Backup supports three replacement options:

◆ Do not replace the file on the disk (the default).

◆ Replace the file on the disk if it's older than the file on the backup.

◆ Always replace the file on the disk with the one on the backup.

Sadly, Windows Backup does not have an option to prompt you if it discovers a duplicate file on the media that you're restoring data to, or to restore the file but give it a new name on the volume if a file with the same name already exists. That would have been handy for those times when you're restoring corrupted files but don't necessarily want to replace *every* file that already exists on disk.

TIP   *To edit this option without running the Restore Wizard, choose Options from the Tools menu in Windows Backup. Turn to the Restore tab and choose the file replacement you want to use.*

What Other Data Should Be Restored?

The next screen in the advanced section of the Restore Wizard asks what nondata information you want to replace (see Figure 21.29).

FIGURE 21.29

The nondata information that you can restore depends on the file system the original data was stored in. FAT volumes only let you restore the RSM database.

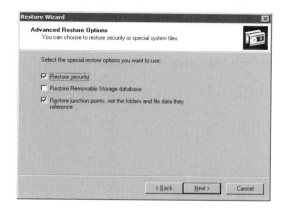

If you're restoring data backed up from a Win2K NTFS drive to a Win2K NTFS drive, you'll have the option to restore the security settings (permissions) to the files, which were backed up when you backed up the file. By default, Windows Backup will do so.

What happens if you tell Windows Backup to not restore the settings? Depends on whether the file already exists on disk:

◆ If the file exists in the location that you backed it up to, then the security settings attached to the file on disk will be applied, even if you're replacing the file.

◆ If the file does *not* exist on disk (if you're replacing a deleted file, for example) and you choose to not restore security settings, then the restored file will give the administrator of the local server and the system account full control—and wipe out any previous settings.

NOTE   *Notice that the way security settings are restored means that if you elect not to restore security settings to a file that Everyone had access to, you'll need to explicitly grant that permission again.*

Other nondata information to restore includes the RSM database and junction points. Although this option will always be available, you only need to worry about restoring the RSM Management database if you're using removable storage to archive old files. This database, stored in %systemroot%\ system32\ntmsdata, will be replaced if you choose to restore the data, so only choose this option if you're sure that the backed-up database is accurate, or you won't be able to find files.

You'll only be asked about junction points if you have mounted drives—logical drives mapped to a path on another volume—on your server. *Junction points* are physical locations on a mounted NTFS volume that point to another area of the disk or to another disk. They're used when you choose to mount a new volume to an empty folder on an NTFS volume instead of assigning that folder a drive letter. Normally, Windows Backup will restore both the junction points and the files and folders to which they point. If you check the box that tells it to restore only the points, not the data, you may lose access to the data.

When you've picked all the Advanced settings, click the Finish button on the last page of the wizard. If restoring from a backup file, Windows Backup will prompt you for the name of the file, then complete the restoration. During the process of restoring the files to disk, Windows Backup will display a Restore Progress dialog box.

VIEWING RESTORE LOGS

When a restore operation is over, the Restore Progress dialog box will remain open. Click the Report button to open the restore report in Notepad. Alternatively, you can choose Report from the Tools menu and pick the report you want from the list of available reports. The restoration report will be appended to the backup report originally created for that job, so if you don't see the information you're looking for right away, page down for it.

RESTORING CONFIGURATION SETTINGS

The process of restoring configuration data is much the same as restoring any other data—when prompted to do so, pick the System State folder from the backup set and start the restoration.

However, restoring System State data isn't as simple as restoring user data. If you restore System State data to its original location (that is, you don't specify an alternate location for it), then Windows Backup will replace the System State data currently on your computer with the System State data you're restoring. However, if you restore the System State data to an alternate location, only the Registry files, SYSVOL directory files, and system boot files are restored to the alternate location. You can't restore the Active Directory directory services database, Certificate Services database, or COM+ Class Registration database to an alternate location.

NOTE *In order to restore the System State data on a domain controller, you must first start your computer in Directory Services Restore mode, available from the Advanced Start menu when you boot Windows 2000. See the later section "Backing Up and Restoring the Active Directory" for details.*

Backing Up and Restoring the Active Directory

As I said earlier in this chapter, when you choose to back up the System State data on a computer, the contents of System State depend on the role of the computer you're backing up. If the computer is a domain controller, then System State includes the Active Directory. Backing up the Active Directory is pretty simple—you choose to back up the System State data on a domain controller. Restoring it, however, is not as simple as restoring user data. In this section, I'll talk about how to back up the Active Directory, how long you can store it, and how to restore it.

BACKING UP THE ACTIVE DIRECTORY

You can take a snapshot of the Active Directory at any time by backing up a domain controller's System State data using the procedures described earlier—either from the command line or with the graphical Backup tool. Again, on a domain controller System State data contains a copy of the Active Directory. You must perform a normal (full) backup to back up the System State data. To back up Active Directory, you must be a member of the Backup Operators group, the local Administrators group, or a group that's been given the right to back up the System State data.

WHEN GOOD BACKUPS GO BAD

Active Directory information doesn't stay good forever, and it's possible that the backups you made in the past won't work now. Read on to find out more about how older backups can go wrong.

Active Directory Backups Work Best with Service Pack 2

Remember that I prefaced the discussion of backups with a recommendation that you install Service Pack 2? Here's part of the reason why: If you restore backups made before you installed SP2, and if the transaction logs changed while you were making the backups, they may not restore properly. Since you can't fix this if it is a problem, your best bet is install the service pack and make new backups, destroying any backups made before you installed. (As you'll see next, those older backups of the Active Directory have a limited shelf life anyway.)

Service Pack 2 addresses another problem: duplicate SID events in the Event Viewer. A bug in Windows 2000 caused the creation of duplicate relative IDs (RIDs) on the domain controller. When you restore a domain controller, it should delete its current RID pool and request a new one, but because this wasn't working properly in Windows 2000, restored domain controllers were getting another RID pool without turning off their first one, leading the restored domain controller to create duplicate SIDs. End result: Install SP2 and you shouldn't see this problem.

Understanding Tombstone Lifetimes and Backup Lives

Tombstone lifetime sounds like an oxymoron. It's actually a property of the Active Directory Directory Service (NTDS) object, representing the number of days that a deleted object will exist as a "ghost" in the Active Directory before it's deleted. Tombstoned objects are still replicated but appear in the Active Directory as deleted. A housekeeping process called the *garbage collector* runs every 12 hours on each server to delete objects whose tombstone lifetimes have expired. (Personally, I would have called it the sexton to keep the metaphor going—garbage collectors don't normally have much to do with tombstones, or if they do I don't want to know about it.) Left to itself, the default tombstone lifetime is 60 days.

So what does this have to do with the useful lifetime of an Active Directory backup? Simply put, you can't restore data from a backup image older than the tombstone lifetime. If you did, the restored objects would be too old to trigger Active Directory replication and thus never be replicated to other domain controllers, and the restored domain controller would never get the replication data required to delete the objects—the records of those objects being deleted would have been removed by the garbage collector. The result would be an inconsistent Active Directory on the local server, which misses the point of a domainwide database of available resources.

If you're trying to restore a domain controller and your only backups are older than the 60-day default limit, then you have two choices. If you have at least one domain controller still up and running and its Active Directory information is good, then you have nothing to worry about—just restore the domain controller, and the remaining domain controller with good Active Directory information will replicate its data to the newly restored domain controller. If you're having to rebuild the domain from scratch, then you can pick an outdated backup, restore it to a domain controller, and replicate the other servers from the restored one.

If you *must* restore an older Active Directory backup (although I'd hate to think of what could happen to your domain that you had to lose more than 60 days of changes to get it back to working order), then you can force the change by editing the tombstone date. Because `.TombstoneLifetime` is a property of the NTDS ADSI object, you can modify it with a script or with an AD editor such as ADSIEDIT.MSC or LDP.EXE. If you do, then you can make the tombstone lifetime older than the available backup. At that point, you'll need to perform an *authoritative restore* to force the replication of this old backup to the other domain controllers since this information will be stamped as being too old for replication.

What's an authoritative restore and how would you make it happen? Read on....

PERFORMING AN AUTHORITATIVE RESTORE

During a normal file restore operation, Backup operates in nonauthoritative restore mode, restoring all files, including Active Directory objects, with their original update sequence numbers (USNs). The AD replication system uses the USNs to detect and replicate changes to the Active Directory to all of the domain controllers on the network. The Active Directory replication system updates old data with newer data from other domain controllers.

For normal operations, this is fine. It has one sticking point, though: Normally, any Active Directory data that you restore will retain its original USN used by the AD replication system to detect and spread AD changes among the domain controllers in your domain. Because of this, any data restored in nonauthoritative mode (would that be in "peon mode"?) looks like old data and won't get propagated to the other domain controllers. Not only that, but the Active Directory replication system will *replace* that restored data with the "newer" data from the other domain controllers, if any exists. If you're trying to replace bad current data with good old data, this obviously isn't what you want to happen. Authoritative restore solves this problem, forcing the domain to accept the older data and overwrite the new.

Before doing an authoritative restore, consider what effect this will have on the domain. When you restore the Active Directory database, you're restoring the following:

- User and machine accounts
- User and machine account passwords
- Trust relationships (or lack thereof) with other domains
- Objects in the Active Directory
- Etc. (See Chapter 8 for a complete description of what the Active Directory is and does in Win2K.)

However, what you're *not* doing is removing any new accounts you created since backing up the Active Directory—the AD isn't a big lump with a single USN, but a directory of objects, each with its own USN. You can pick and choose pieces of the Active Directory to restore. Also, if you perform an authoritative restore to a domain containing other domain controllers, any objects you created in the naming context (in this example, the domain naming context) after making the backup will remain in the Active Directory. Say, for example, that on Monday you create an account for ChristaA (which is then replicated to the other domain controllers in the domain), then back up. On Tuesday you create an account for Christa—also replicated to the rest of the domain. On Wednesday, you delete the ChristaA account. On Thursday, you perform an authoritative restore from the backup you made on Monday. Both the ChristaA and Christa accounts will exist in the domain, not just the ChristaA account you backed up, because the two accounts have unique USNs—they're different objects.

You can perform an authoritative restore on either all or part of the Active Directory. I'll discuss the Advanced Options boot menu later in this chapter, but because one of its menu items is crucial to restoring the Active Directory I'm going to leap ahead a bit, returning to this topic later. When you press F8 while booting a Windows 2000 Server computer, Advanced Options, as you'll see, presents you with several nonstandard ways of booting the Windows 2000 operating system. If you're booting a domain controller, then one of those nonstandard options is Directory Services Restore Mode (DSRM), used for restoring Active Directory information. When you choose this option, it will kick you back to the main boot menu, showing in text at the bottom of the screen that you're in DSRM. The system will boot in Safe Mode with Networking, run CHKDSK on all the volumes, and then present the logon screen for you to log in as the local machine's administrator.

Restoring All of the Active Directory

If you want to perform an authoritative restore of *everything* in the Active Directory, boot to DSRM. If you log in while in DSRM, you can run REGEDT32 and find a subkey called Restore in Progress within HKLM\System\CurrentControlSet\Service\NTDS. The presence of this key (created by NTBACKUP) tells the Active Directory to check all its indices the next time you boot the system normally. (You don't need to do anything with this key—it's just there.)

After you've restored the System State data but before you've restarted the server, run NTDSUTIL from the command line. At the prompt, type **authoritative restore**. Type **restore database** and press Enter, then click Yes to agree to perform an authoritative restore. You'll see output like this:

```
Opening DIT database... Done.

The current time is 11-06-01 17:51.47.
Most recent database update occurred at 11-06-01 17:03.19.
Increasing attribute version numbers by 100000.

Counting records that need updating...
Records found: 0000001484
Done.

Found 1484 records to update.
```

```
Updating records...
Records remaining: 0000000000
Done.

Successfully updated 1484 records.

Authoritative Restore completed successfully.
```

This will give all the Active Directory information on this domain the highest USNs in the Active Directory replication system, so *that* data will be replicated throughout the domain. This approach has a bit of the sledgehammer feel to it, though. For a more nuanced approach, you can pick pieces of the Active Directory to restore.

Restoring Part of the Active Directory

As I said earlier, you can use DSRM to restore individual parts of the database, not just the whole thing. For example, you could restore an accidentally deleted machine account for a domain controller. To do so, boot to DSRM and restore the System State data, then run NTDSUTIL for an authoritative restore. This time, though, instead of typing **restore database**, choose to restore part of it, like this (all on one line):

```
restore subtree "cn=domain_controller,ou=Domain
➥ Controllers,dc=domain_name,dc=xxx"
```

Here *domain_controller* is the computer name of the domain controller, *domain_name* is the domain name the domain controller resides in, and *xxx* is the top-level domain name of the domain controller, such as com, org, or net. Win2K will ask you if you're sure you want to perform an authoritative restore. When you click Yes, NTDSUTIL will open the directory information tree (DIT), note the last time it was updated and the number of entries that need updating, then read through the restore subtree command backward to find the domain, the organizational unit, and finally the computer name you want to restore. When you're done with this, type **quit** to exit authoritative restore and then **quit** again to exit NTDSUTIL, then reboot the domain controller.

TIP *If you don't know the name of the part of the Active Directory that you want to restore, use* ADSIEDIT.MSC *or* LDP *to find the name.*

Troubleshooting Hardware with the System Information Tool

If you want current nuts-and-bolts information about the hardware in your servers, you can dig out those PDF files you printed from the Web sites and read all your handwritten notes about configuration changes that you made.

For those less than thrilled about this idea, Windows 2000 has the System Information tool (see Figure 21.30), located in the System Tools section of the Computer Management (Local) MMC add-in. Using this tool, you can view the following on either the local computer or any Win2K computer:

◆ A system summary showing you the basic hardware and software configuration of the server

◆ Hardware resources used on the server

◆ Configuration information for the hardware

◆ Information about all parts of the server software environment

NOTE *The System Information tool depends on the Windows Management Instrumentation (WMI) service, which is running by default. You can see the WMI service's status among the other system services in the Services and Applications object in the Computer Management add-in.*

FIGURE 21.30

The System Information tool

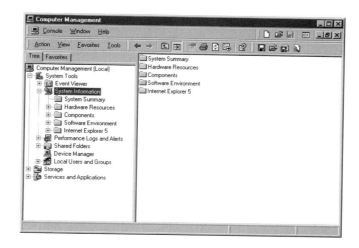

TIP *Typing* **winmsd** *or* **msinfo32** *from Run will start the System Information tool. For those who don't remember, MSD was the original Microsoft Diagnostics tool, which became WinMSD in Windows.*

The System Information tool is a neat piece of work. Unlike WinMSD, it can actually *tell* you something about your server's hardware. It's not 100-percent accurate—as I wandered through it, I found a couple of minor pieces of misinformation, such as saying that my compressed drive was not compressed and guessing at processor speed for any processor released after February 2000—but it's close. And it provides a lot more information than WinMSD ever did and in a reasonably organized manner. Read on to learn how to use this tool to inventory and monitor your Win2K server.

System Summary

The system summary information is just that—a snapshot of your system, such as the one shown in Figure 21.31. The information is roughly that which used to be on the Version tab of NT 4's Win-MSD, with the addition of BIOS version and some memory information. You can't change the data here, just see what the situation is. About the only information you need pay special attention to is the available memory. You can get memory information in *many* places around Win2K (the Task Manager is another tool that you can use for this), but here it is in black and white: how much physical and virtual memory you have available and have remaining.

FIGURE 21.31

System summary
information for a
Win2K server

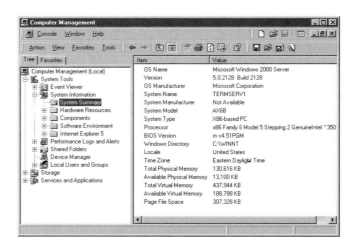

Hardware Resources

The `Hardware Resources` folder (see Figure 21.32) lists all the resources that might be used by the hardware in your services and shows what hardware actually *is* using those resources, as described in Table 21.5.

Why is this information important? Basically, everything in Table 21.5 represents either a channel for devices to pass information to the CPU for processing or a storage place for such data while it's waiting for CPU time. Each channel must have its own hotline to the CPU so that when the CPU responds to a call for processing (an *interrupt*), it knows whose data it's crunching and can pass back the results accordingly. Some devices can share some kinds of channels; IRQs, for example, can be shared by some modern hardware. But memory storage areas cannot be shared, and not all channels can be shared. If you suspect that two or more devices are using the same resources and can't share, then you can use this tool to find out.

FIGURE 21.32

The `Hardware
Resources` folder
with the contents of
one folder showing

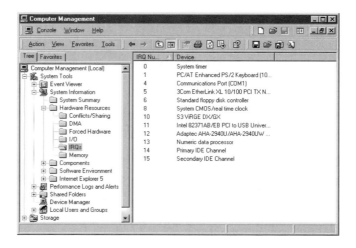

TABLE 21.5: RESOURCES USED BY SERVER HARDWARE

RESOURCE TYPE	DESCRIPTION
Conflicts/Sharing	This folder lists the components either sharing an IRQ or in conflict over one. Components sharing an IRQ should be working fine (or if they're not, the IRQ in common shouldn't be the problem). If multiple devices are in conflict over an IRQ, however, then one or all won't work.
DMA	Direct Memory Access (DMA) channels are rarely required; most often these days, they're used by audio devices. Basically, the DMA chips on the motherboard can move data from a device to RAM without the CPU having to be involved in the process. Any device that can use DMA needs its own DMA channel as its dedicated path for data moving.
Forced Hardware	Lists older devices not supporting Plug and Play that require specific IRQs.
I/O	This folder shows what devices are using what parts of virtual memory for storage. The information here is similar to what's in the Memory folder but is taken from the perspective of the memory, not the devices using it.
IRQs	Interrupt request lines, or IRQs, represent each device's hotline to the CPU. IRQs are like DMA channels in that they're specific to a given device, but are unlike them in that they don't take care of the process of shoving data to the CPU—the CPU must still be involved. Some devices can share IRQs.
Memory	This folder shows the I/O buffer areas that each device is using to store data waiting for processing. Essentially, these buffer areas are mailboxes that the CPU can use both to pick up data waiting for it and to drop off instructions for the device to which that I/O area belongs. Each device must have its own I/O area so that the CPU will drop off the appropriate instructions to each device. It's going to cause no end of confusion if the CPU asks the network card to play a sound.

Components

The Hardware Resources folder looks at the types of resources available and shows you what devices are using them. The Components folder's approach (Figure 21.33) is opposite—you look at the devices installed and see what resources they're using. But not only resources. The properties pages for the installed devices provide just about all information relevant to a piece of hardware, including resources used, driver versions, and the type of device it is.

NOTE *The Components folder is a list of all possible devices, not actual devices. For example, even if your server doesn't have a modem installed, it will still have a* Modem *folder.*

The exact data within a given object in the Components folder depends heavily on what the device it represents does. For example, the data for the display reports information such as the color density, refresh rate and resolution, video adapter's name, and other display-related information. The network's folder has three subfolders: one for the adapter, one for protocols used, and one for Winsock version information. Storage media show their size, media type, compression data, and so forth. There's even a section for problem devices, listing any devices that Win2K can tell aren't working as expected. For instance, at one time I had a SCSI removable drive attached to this server. After I removed the drive, Win2K still expected to find it, so it's now listed in the `Problem Devices` folder.

FIGURE 21.33

The contents of the `Components` folder

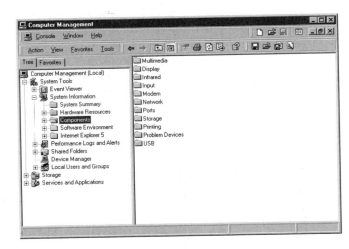

Software Environment

The information in the `Software Environment` folder (Figure 21.34) describes all of the software running on the system, who's using it, and what files and services are loaded. It includes the components listed in Table 21.6.

FIGURE 21.34

The `Software Environment` folder with one folder open

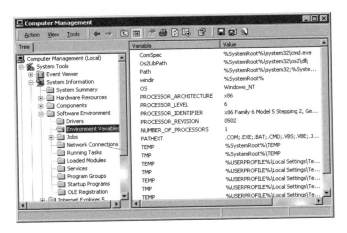

TABLE 21.6: SYSTEM PARTS DESCRIBED IN THE SOFTWARE ENVIRONMENT FOLDER

SYSTEM PART	DESCRIPTION
Drivers	This folder lists all the drivers installed on the system, and for each driver gives a brief (and more or less explanatory) description, its type (kernel driver or file system driver), its state (whether stopped or running), and its status as OK.
Environment Variables	This folder lists all the environment variables for the server, including the CPU identification, location of all temporary files, path information for system files, and OS version.
Jobs	This folder contains a folder for each kind of job that might be running on the system (for example, print jobs). The folder will list all currently running jobs of that type.
Network Connections	This folder lists all current network connections and the drive letters they're mapped to (if applicable).
Running Tasks	This sounds like it should be the job list, but it's not. Instead, it's a list of all the executable files run by the services running on the server. File path, version, file size, and file date are all listed here. If you want to know what version of a given EXE you've got, this is where to look.
Loaded Modules	This folder is like the Running Tasks folder, except that it lists all dynamic link libraries in memory. Version, size, file date, manufacturer, and path information are all displayed. If you want to know what version of a given DLL you've got, this is where to look.
Services	This folder lists all the (nonboot or system) services available on the server by name. The state of each service, its start mode (manual, automatic, or disabled), and its type are all shown.
Program Groups	This folder lists all the groups available from the Start menu. The view shows the users for whom the groups are customized (this information is stored as part of each user's profile, so you may have several different listings of the same program group, each associated with a different user). Terminal server profile associations will be displayed here.
Startup Programs	This folder lists all the programs configured to run at system start-up.
OLE Registration	This folder shows all the object linking and embedding associations used to open data files in the right kind of application.

Internet Explorer

As you can see in Figure 21.35 and Table 21.7, all the settings for IE are listed in the Internet Explorer folder, although (as with the other settings in the System Summary folder) you can't change any of them.

FIGURE 21.35

Contents of the
`Internet`
`Explorer 5`
folder

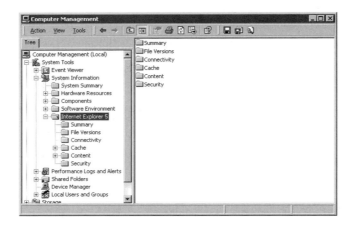

NOTE *The version information will change from version to version and if you have Internet Explorer 5.5 installed the folder is identified only as* `Internet Explorer`*. However, the information contained in these folders does not change with the installation of IE 5.5.*

TABLE 21.7: SYSTEM CONFIGURATION SETTINGS IN THE INTERNET EXPLORER 5 FOLDER

SYSTEM PART	DESCRIPTION
Summary	This folder lists basic version and path information about IE. The most useful information indicates the degree of encryption IE is set up to use, which printers are set up to work with IE, whether the Content Advisor (ratings software) is on, and whether the Internet Explorer Administration Kit is installed.
File Versions	This folder lists all the files installed that support IE, including their version number, date, size, path, and the company supplying them. If a file is expected but not present, it's still listed, but its version is recorded as "file missing."
Connectivity	This folder lists the connection settings for the browser. Most of what's here applies to proxy server settings, but also listed is whether the dialer is set up to kick in when you start IE.
Cache	This folder lists the objects in the IE cache (stored when you view online content so that when you need the images again they can be loaded from the cache).
Content	This folder lists the content controls in place on your IE setup. Again, it's indicating whether the Content Advisor is enabled. Any certificates in place (your own or someone else's) are also listed here.
Security	This folder lists the security settings you have in place for different site classes: trusted, local intranet, Internet, and restricted.

Saving System Configuration Information

All this information is great, but sometimes it won't help you get the answers you need to resolve problems with the server. That doesn't mean that it can't get someone *else* the answers they need to fix problems. The System Information tool lets you save and load configuration information. Using this capability, you can save your server's configuration to a text file or system information file. You can then e-mail that file to a tech support person with Windows 2000 installed (or not, but if not they'll have to read the text file) who can then load the file and view your computer's information as if they were connected to the server.

TIP *To save only part of the system information, select the part you want to save before starting the save procedure. For example, to save only information related to the network card's configuration, make sure that folder is selected in the left pane.*

SAVING AND OPENING SYSTEM INFORMATION FILES

To save information as a file, open the Action menu in the System Information tool and choose Save as System Information File. In the dialog box that appears, type a name for the file and click Save. The server will chug away for a minute or two as it inventories your system, and then store the file in your My Documents folder unless you specify otherwise. The file isn't too big—mine is 198KB—so you can fit it onto a floppy if necessary. The file will have an .nfo extension.

You can't open an NFO file from the System Information tool. Instead, you'll need to double-click the saved file or open an instance of the MMC. Add the System Information snap-in to the console, telling the MMC that you want information about the local computer.

Back in the console, your snap-in should now appear in the left pane. In the console tree, select System Information. From the Actions menu, choose All Tasks, and then choose Open System Information File from the menu that appears. Find the NFO file you want, and click Open. The saved file will now appear in your console window.

NOTE *You can also open the NFO file from NT's WinMSD.*

The saving-as/loading process isn't completely foolproof. Without doing an exhaustive comparison of the two files, I found discrepancies between the original system information and the contents of a system information file loaded into the MMC—for example, the server's USB information was unknown in the imported file but visible from the System Information tool. If you give a copy of this file to someone for troubleshooting help, I suggest you be prepared to answer questions based on the original information.

SAVING SYSTEM INFORMATION AS TEXT

Saving system information as a text file works much the same way as saving it as an NFO file. In the System Information tool, choose Save as Text File from the Action menu. Again, the default location is the My Documents folder. When you click the Save button, the server will inventory itself to make sure that the most current settings are saved, then put them into a TXT file that you can read with an editor such as Notepad. It's a long file; this is a partial dump of the information I collected from one server:

```
Directory           C:\WINNT
User Name           REDROOM\ChristaA
Time Zone           Eastern Standard Time
```

```
Daylight Savings Time          Eastern Daylight Time
Total Physical Memory          130612 kbytes
Available Physical Memory      14572 kbytes
Total Virtual Memory           2097024 kbytes
Available Virtual Memory       1988656 kbytes
Page File Space                311252 kbytes
Page File                      C:\pagefile.sys
```

Needless to say, I'd rather analyze the data from an organized system information file than from a 3.5MB ASCII file, but the fact that you can save the information as text means that you *can* give someone your system configuration for analysis without them having a copy of Win2K or NT handy.

NOTE *You can also print out a copy of the system configuration information, but be warned—a full copy will make several dozen pages. A sample server's file made 41 printed pages.*

SAVING INFORMATION FROM THE COMMAND LINE

You don't have to open the graphical tool if all you want to do is create a system information log. Msinfo32.exe and WinMSD.exe (same tool, different names) support the command-line switches shown in Table 21.8 to generate a local or remote system information file.

TABLE 21.8: WinMSD COMMAND-LINE OPTIONS

SWITCH	DESCRIPTION
/?	Displays Help
/msinfo_file	Opens the specified NFO or CAB file
/nfo or /s	Outputs an NFO file with the specified filename
/report	Outputs a text-format file to the specified filename
/computer	Connects to the specified computer
/categories	Displays or outputs the specified categories
/category	Sets the focus to a specific category at startup

So, for example, typing **winmsd.exe /s g:\tools\report.nfo** will generate a complete copy of the local computer's system information and store it as an NFO file in G:\tools. (Notice that I must include the file suffix even though I've specified that I want to create an NFO file—winmsd isn't smart enough to generate the suffix information on its own.) When I open this file on any computer with the MMC installed, it will show up as the local system information. If I wanted to create a text report (again, I don't recommend doing this unless you simply have no other options—it's too long), then I'd type the command like this: **winmsd.exe /report g:\tools\report.txt**.

NOTE *Generating the report takes a few minutes, even on a fast computer.*

Understanding the Boot Process

Windows 2000 includes several tools that can help you recover from problems related to the operating system, but these tools are no good if you can't get to the Advanced Options menu available at boot time for troubleshooting (discussed later) or get the Setup menu to recognize that your server does, in fact, have a hard disk. In this section, I'll describe the steps the server follows to boot, including the outward manifestations of those steps so you can figure out which step went wrong.

Prequel: The Hardware Must Work

Before you can even attack the problem of "What's wrong with Windows 2000?" you must make sure that it's not a problem of "What's wrong with the server?" You will not be able to boot the server if either of the following are true:

◆ The boot drive, the boot drive's disk controller, or the cable connecting the two is malfunctioning or incorrectly set up.

◆ The processor or the motherboard is dead.

Other hardware can give you problems, but these are the two that will really stop you in your tracks. To isolate the problem, watch and see where the problem appears:

◆ A computer that does not boot *at all*, does not make noise, does not do anything at all, is experiencing a dead (or turned off) power supply or a dead power cord.

◆ A computer that will start its fan but doesn't do anything beyond that probably has a problem with its motherboard.

◆ A computer that will count up memory but isn't displaying anything on the monitor (you can hear it, but you can't see it) and beeps at you probably has a problem with the video card.

◆ A computer that starts to load Windows 2000 (in this example) and then blue-screens before displaying the logon screen may be having memory problems.

◆ A computer that will boot and find the CD and floppy but doesn't find the hard disk controller probably has a problem with the hard disk controller.

◆ A computer that will boot and identify the hard disk controller but doesn't find a bootable hard disk probably has a hard disk problem. If you're still not positive and you have a spare system around, swap in an easy part of the computer, such as the hard disk controller, if you're not sure whether the problem lies in the disk or the controller.

TIP   Keep an eye on the fans in your servers. Those fans are vital to keeping delicate components cool. A cooked computer is a dead computer, sooner or later. A company called PC Power and Cooling (www.pcpowercooling.com) makes a temperature sensor, the 110 Alert, that fits inside a PC and squawks when the internal temperature rises above 110 degrees.

Finally—is the server plugged in? Is its UPS turned on? I know, I know—but check.

Step One: Load NTLDR

The first part of Windows 2000 that loads is NTLDR, a small program in the root directory of the boot partition of the server's hard disk. It's doing the following:

1. Shifting your processor into 386 mode

2. Starting a simple file system that allows Win2K to boot from the hard disk

3. Reading the contents of `boot.ini` to display a menu of other possible boot options

4. Accepting your choice of which OS to load

Assuming that you choose to load Windows 2000 Server, NTLDR passes control to `NTDetect.com`, a program that detects the hardware on your server.

Step Two: Run NTDETECT

`NTDetect.com` is in charge of figuring out what hardware is present on your server. It is looking for the following:

- Your PC's machine ID type

- The bus type

- The video board type

- The keyboard and mouse type

- The serial and parallel ports present on the computer

- The floppy drives present on the computer

Once NTDETECT has run without problems, it builds the `Hardware` key of the Registry, listed in `HKEY_LOCAL_MACHINE`. That part of the Registry is built each time you reboot your computer, so it will always reflect the current hardware configuration.

TIP   *If you can't get past the NTDETECT stage of system startup, there's likely some hardware conflict on your server.*

Step Three: Load NTOSKRNL

Next, the Win2K kernel (NTOSKRNL) loads with the Hardware Abstraction Layer (`HAL.DLL`), some assembly-language code that acts as an interface between the server's hardware and the operating system and allows Win2K to be hardware-independent. The kernel loads in four phases:

- The kernel load phase

- The kernel initialization phase

- The services load phase

- The Windows subsystem load phase

NOTE *NTOSKRNL and* HAL.DLL *are stored in the* system32 *directory of your Win2K installation. Both must be present on the hard disk for Win2K to load.*

KERNEL LOAD PHASE

Once HAL.DLL and NTOSKRNL are loaded into memory, Win2K loads the system settings, storing them in HKLM\System\CurrentControlSet\Services. Win2K reads the system information to determine which drivers it must load and in what order.

KERNEL INITIALIZATION PHASE

After the kernel load phase, the Win2K kernel initializes. Once Win2K has initialized the kernel's internal variables, the kernel scans the current control set for drivers with a start value of 1 and starts them. Win2K builds a new current control set, but does not yet save it. AUTOCHK.EXE, a CHKDSK-like utility, runs to make sure that the filesystem is intact. This is also the stage where the Win2K pagefile is set up.

WHICH SERVICES ARE LOADING?

Curious about which services are loading during this stage? Run the Registry Editor and turn to HKLM\System\CurrrentControlSet\Services. In this key are keys for all the services currently installed on the server. Open one of these keys and look at the start value for that service.

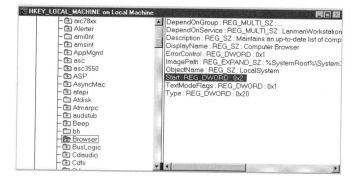

Possible values include:

0, which tells Win2K to load the service during the kernel load phase

1, which tells Win2K to load the service during the kernel initialization phase

2, which tells Win2K to start the service during the services load phase

A value of 3 indicates that the service is enabled but requires a manual start, and a value of 4 indicates that the service is disabled.

SERVICES LOAD PHASE

Next, Win2K loads the Services Manager (SMSS.EXE) and the Win32 subsystem. All services with a start value of 2 start, and Win2K writes the current control set to the System key.

WINDOWS SUBSYSTEM START PHASE

Finally, the Windows subsystem (the main part of Win2K, the one that you'll most often interact with) initializes. The Win32 subsystem starts winlogon.exe, which handles interactive user logons and logoffs. WinLogon listens for the *secure attention sequence* (Ctrl+Alt+Delete on all unmodified Win2K machines), which, in effect, tells WinLogon, "Hey! Someone's trying to log in! Listen for their username and password!" WinLogon captures the name and password and passes them to the local security authority (LSASS.EXE), which compares the username and password to the information stored in the Security Accounts Manager. If they match and the user has logon rights, another process called userinit.exe runs the shell referenced in the shell value of HKLM\Software\ Microsoft\Windows NT\CurrentVersion\WinLogon (normally explorer.exe, which loads the usual Win2K Desktop).

What *you* see of all this is the logon screen prompting you to press Ctrl+Alt+Delete to log in.

Fixing Minor Problems with the Advanced Options Menu

So that's the boot process—but what do you do if it doesn't happen quite that way?

No matter how careful you are, mistakes sometimes happen or something just goes wrong. In such a case, you'll need to fix your installation, hopefully without reinstalling the operating system. Installing Windows 2000 isn't too dreadful a prospect, but doing so takes time, especially if you must then reconfigure the server to restore all the settings you need. Sometimes you have to reinstall to make things right again, but not always. When installing isn't the only option, I prefer to spend my time doing something a little more useful.

Here's an apparently easy one: You configured the video display to a refresh rate that your monitor can't support, and you can no longer see anything. It's hard to restore the right settings when you can't see what you're doing, but the initial boot menu no longer displays a VGA setting that loads vanilla video drivers. How do you repair this kind of problem without reinstalling the operating system?

If you've made some change to your operating system that makes it unusable, all is not lost—so long as the system will boot at all and can recognize the hard disk that the operating system is installed on. The Advanced Options menu gives you several methods for fixing or debugging a broken Win2K installation. You get to this menu by pressing F8 when the boot menu appears. Do so, and you'll see a text menu like the following:

```
Windows 2000 Advanced Options Menu
Please Select an Option
Safe Mode
Safe Mode with Networking
Safe Mode with Command Prompt

Enable Boot Logging
Enable VGA Mode
```

```
Last Known Good Configuration
Directory Services Restore Mode (Windows 2000 domain controllers Only)
Debugging Mode
Boot Normally
Return to OS Choices Menu
```

NOTE *Previous versions of NT displayed the message "Press the Space Bar to display the Last Known Good Menu during the boot process." This option no longer exists. If you don't open the Last Known Good menu from the Advanced Options menu, you can't open it.*

Incidentally, the Advanced Options menu is one more reason why, if you're running a dual-boot computer supporting both Windows 2000 and NT 4, you *must* install NT 4 first. If you install NT 4 after installing Windows 2000, then you may not see the prompt to press F8 to open the Windows Advanced Options menu, the "Starting Windows" progress bar at the bottom of the screen, or the Windows 2000 startup graphic, which may be replaced by the Microsoft Windows NT 4 OSLoader screen. The problem is that NT 4 is unaware of the additional startup features of Windows 2000 and replaces the shared Windows boot files (`Ntldr` and `Ntdetect.com`). To fix this, boot from the Windows 2000 CD-ROM. At the Windows Setup screen, press R to repair the Windows installation. Then, press C to use Recovery Console. Copy the Ntldr and Ntdetect.com files from the I386 folder on the Windows 2000 CD-ROM to the root folder of the boot drive.

I discussed Directory Services Restore Mode earlier in "Backing Up and Restoring the Active Directory." Let's take a look at the other modes.

Using Safe Mode Options

The various forms of Safe Mode—with networking, without networking, with command prompt—load a minimal version of Windows 2000 with only the drivers and files needed to support that minimal version (such as NTOSKRNL). These tools can be handy when something is preventing your system from booting and you suspect an errant driver. Whichever mode you choose, during boot, Win2K will display a list of all the drivers and services as they're loading. When you log out, the machine will restart as usual.

SAFE MODE

Safe Mode starts Win2K with only the drivers and services required to boot the computer. No network drivers are loaded, and network-dependent services are changed to start option 3 (meaning that they're set for manual starting) but can't be started even from the Services section of the MMC or with `net start`. Use this version of Safe Mode to fix problems related to network services.

SAFE MODE WITH NETWORKING

Safe Mode with Networking is what it sounds like—a pared-down version of Win2K that includes network support. Use this version when you need network support and you're sure that the network drivers are not causing any problems. When you boot the computer into Directory Services Restore Mode, it's booting into Safe Mode with Networking.

SAFE MODE WITH COMMAND PROMPT

If you're expecting Safe Mode with Command Prompt to be a strictly command-line version of Win2K, you're mistaken. When you boot to this option, you'll see a list of the files that Win2K is loading, and then the graphical interface will appear, running in 640×480. However, rather than loading the Desktop, Win2K will use the command prompt for its shell.

Safe Mode with Command Prompt is a network-disabled version of Win2K that replaces the Explorer.exe shell normally used with cmd.exe. You can do anything on the local computer that you can do in the usual shell—you can even run GUI applications, if you don't mind them running with a maximum resolution of 800×600 (640×480 by default, but you can edit the Display options from the Control Panel) and 16 colors. But everything you do you must start from the command prompt or from the Task Manager (still available if you press Ctrl+Alt+Delete). Use Safe Mode with Command Prompt to run a stand-alone version of Win2K when something is wrong with Explorer that keeps Win2K from starting. You can run Explorer from this mode and gain access to the graphical Desktop, if you like, but you're not dependent on it as you are in the other versions of Safe Mode. If you don't open Explorer, you can shut down the server with the shutdown command.

TIP *To get a complete list of all the commands supported from the command prompt, type* **help | more**. *(You can just type* **help**, *but there's more commands than will fit on a single screen.) To get help with the syntax of a specific command, type* **commandname** */?*.

Please note that Safe Mode with Command Prompt is *not* the same thing as the Recovery Console. I've seen some confusion about this and want to make sure that the difference is clear. Safe Mode with Command Prompt is a minimal version of Win2K that uses cmd.exe as the default shell (operating environment) but can run any graphical tool in Win2K so long as you know the command to invoke it. The Recovery Console, which I'll discuss a little later in this chapter, is for resolving problems that can keep the computer from booting at all. It supports only a subset of commands understood in Win2K and cannot run graphical utilities under any circumstances.

The Last Known Good Configuration

One purpose of the Last Known Good Configuration option is to save you from your better ideas. For example, one time I thought I'd try installing the CD-burning software designed for a Windows 98 computer on a Windows 2000 Professional computer. While installing, I saw an error warning me that the software was not designed for Windows 2000, but I persevered. (Rules? Ha! We spit at rules.) Everything went smoothly, and I finished installing the tool. Feeling a little smug, I rebooted when prompted.

And Windows 2000 refused to start and instead displayed a blue screen. I stopped feeling smug.

Instead, I rebooted again, pressed F8 to display the Advanced Options menu, and chose to boot to the Last Known Good configuration—the configuration that had been in place the last time I'd been logged into the computer. The computer unloaded the new driver, I booted successfully, and life was good. So long as the change you made produced no system-critical errors (at the time, that is—as you can see, it's okay if the change you made prevents Windows 2000 from starting up properly), and you successfully booted and logged in to the server once before you ran into the problem, all is not lost. You can load the Last Known Good Configuration and choose from three different system start-up options:

- ◆ Using the current configuration

◆ Using the Last Known Good configuration—loaded the last time the server successfully booted and you started a session from the console

◆ Restarting the computer

UNDERSTANDING HOW LAST KNOWN GOOD WORKS

The Last Known Good Configuration option works because of the way Win2K maintains configuration information. Every time you boot the computer and log in, the configuration information for the local machine is stored in HKLM\System\CurrentControlSet. Win2K also stores a backup copy of this information and assigns it a number for organization purposes. This backup is used should the default set of configuration information—the current set—become corrupted and unusable.

NT 4 typically stored four copies of the configuration information: \ControlSet001, \ControlSet002, \CurrentControlSet, and \Clone. The CurrentControlSet wasn't really a control set but was a pointer to one of the numbered control sets, perhaps 001. ControlSet002 might have been the Last Known Good configuration, the one stored after the previous boot. The clone was a copy of the CurrentControlSet pointer.

Win2K organizes its current and backup configuration sets a little differently. As you can see from Figure 21.36, Win2K stores several copies of the configuration information, numbering them consecutively. Win2K only maintains a current control set, which is a pointer to one of the numbered sets, no clone. Another numbered set is maintained as a Last Known Good configuration, to be used if the default configuration set becomes unusable.

FIGURE 21.36

Contents of HKLM\System

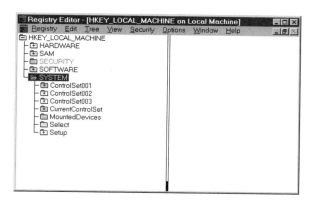

You can't tell from the numbers which configuration set your server is currently using. To find this information, look in the \Select key in HKLM\System (see Figure 21.37). There are four values here: Current, Default, Failed, and LastKnownGood. If you restart the machine and boot normally (that is, without using the Advanced Options menu), then the Default control set will be used. The value of Failed is the configuration set that had been the default when you chose to start the machine from the Last Known Good Configuration menu. Because you told Win2K to not start with that configuration set, it's now marked as Failed even if nothing is actually wrong with it.

FIGURE 21.37

The \Select key displays all current control sets.

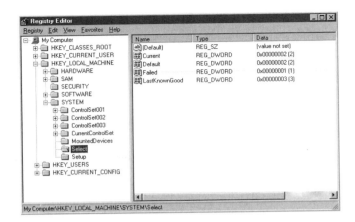

REPAIRING A SERVER WITH THE LAST KNOWN GOOD CONFIGURATION

That's just background so that you know what's happening; you don't have to tweak the Registry to make the Last Known Good option work.

If you do something that keeps the computer from starting normally, do *not* log on and try to fix it right away. Instead, restart the computer and follow these steps:

1. When the system has finished recognizing its hardware and displays the boot menu, press F8 to open the Advanced Options menu.

2. Choose Last Known Good from the boot menu and press Enter. The boot menu will now reappear with the words *Last Known Good Configuration* at the bottom of the screen. This is to remind you that, by loading that option, you're choosing to reverse all non-security-related changes made to the Registry during the last session. As I mentioned in my earlier example, this includes unloading drivers installed during the previous session.

3. If you *do* choose to use the Last Known Good configuration, Win2K will display the Last Known Good/Hardware Profiles menu. All hardware profiles created previously will be listed. If you haven't created any new hardware profiles, then your current configuration will be listed, called Profile 1.

4. Choose the profile you want, and press Enter to boot the computer.

Win2K will start with the settings with which you started your last session. After you log in, you'll see an information message telling you that Win2K couldn't start with the current configuration and is starting with a previously saved configuration.

The Last Known Good option can't always help you. It applies only so long as you have never logged in with the new configuration, but *have* logged in at least once, and can boot the computer now. That means that it won't work if any of the following apply:

♦ You have never logged in successfully (that is, if you're just installing Win2K).

◆ You edited the server's configuration, rebooted, and logged in successfully, and now want to restore your system to the way it was before the change.

◆ The change that you want to reverse is not related to control set information. You can't remove changes to user profiles or system policies with the Last Known Good menu, for example. Passwords are also unaffected by the Last Known Good option, so you can't use this option to recover from a forgotten Administrator's password.

◆ The system boots, someone logs in (even with automatic logon), and the system hangs or the problem you wanted to avoid still exists.

◆ The system won't boot at all and is unable to get to the boot menu.

Enable VGA Mode

Those familiar with NT Server will remember that in previous versions of the operating system, the boot menu had two entries for each instance of NT installed on the computer: one with whatever graphics settings you'd chosen and one designed to run in vanilla VGA mode. There was a good reason for this. In NT 3.1, there was no VGA mode, and if you set up the wrong driver and logged in (making the Last Known Good option useless), then you had to go through a complicated sequence of keystrokes to navigate blindly to the Display applet in the Control Panel and fix things. This gave you a terrific sense of accomplishment when it actually worked, but it made video problems more than a little painful to resolve.

The VGA option is no longer in the main menu, however. To get to it, you must press F8 at boot time and choose Enable VGA Mode from the Advanced Options menu. Use this option if you've installed a bad video driver and need to correct the problem. Unlike the Last Known Good menu, this option will work at any time, not just before you've successfully logged in.

Enable Boot Logging

Enabling boot logging from the Advanced Options menu starts Win2K as usual, except that it creates a file called NTBTlog.txt and stores it in the top of your system root directory. The output looks like Figure 21.38.

FIGURE 21.38

Sample output from a boot log

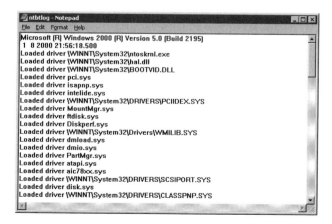

If you're running into problems, then you can check this log to see what drivers did—and did not—load. It's normal for some drivers to not load; they're available, but if you haven't got anything running that requires them, Win2K won't start them, so as to save memory. But if your network, for example, isn't working, you can scan the list of drivers to make sure that NDIS.SYS is present.

TIP   At a time when the server is working normally, enable boot logging and save the output under another name, noting the date and any new changes to the server. (You can do this pretty easily—all filesystems in Win2K support long filenames.) If something does go wrong with the machine, you can compare the healthy boot record with the sick one to find the discrepancy.

Debugging Mode

This final option in the Advanced Options menu, Debugging Mode, sends debugging information to a computer connected to a Windows 2000 computer you're booting via the serial port. The basic gist of this is that it's a way to monitor the progress of a server's boot from another server.

Preparing for Recovery

If the situation is too dire for any of the Advanced Options menu options to help you, all is not lost. Before it's time to reinstall, it's time to drag out one of Windows 2000's recovery tools: the emergency repair disk or the Recovery Console, both of which are available through the Repair option in Setup.

Installing the Recovery Console

How do you get to the recovery tools? You can install the Recovery Console from the Windows 2000 installation CD. Open the Run tool in the Start menu and type **d:\i386\winnt32 /cmdcons** where *d:* is the drive letter of your installation CD. The first time you do this, Win2K will display the message box shown in Figure 21.39.

FIGURE 21.39

Initial screen for installing the Recovery Console

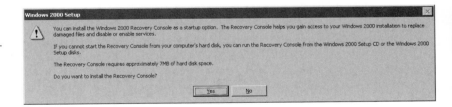

Windows 2000 Setup will copy some files from the installation CD, then prompt you to restart the computer. The Recovery Console will be in the Startup menu (the text menu you see when you start up the computer) when you reboot, listed as Microsoft Windows 2000 Command Console. To start it, just choose that option before the 30-second time-out to whatever your default startup option is.

TIP   *If you install the system partition as FAT then think, "Huh. I have this Recovery Console that I could use to repair the system partition, so I'm going to install the Recovery Console and then convert that partition to NTFS," you aren't going to like the results. The Recovery Console uses different support files for NTFS and FAT partitions, so if you install it and then convert the system partition to NTFS, the computer will hang when you choose that option from the boot menu. Convert first, then install the Recovery Console.*

Incidentally, you can install the Recovery Console onto NT computers as well. If you do so, then you can use NTFS to format the system partition without worrying that you won't be able to reach this partition if you can't boot normally.

CAN I INSTALL THE RECOVERY CONSOLE ALONGSIDE WIN2K?

Why isn't it a default option to install the Recovery Console when you install Win2K? Good question—it's so useful that you'd think it would be installed by default or that at least you'd have the option of doing so during Setup. The problem is that installing the Recovery Console deletes necessary files from the win_nt.~bt folder and thus prevents the existing Setup process from completing if the Setup process you're using writes that folder to the disk. You *can* install the Recovery Console from within another operating system if you experience a problem that prevents Setup from continuing and that the Recovery Console could fix, such as a damaged master boot record (MBR).

You can also preinstall the Recovery Console by running the winnt32 /cmdcons command from the Windows 2000 installation CD-ROM to place the files on the local hard disk. The only catch is that you must do this to a volume contained on a single physical disk, even if you later plan to mirror the system partition for system security. You can't perform a clean installation of Win2K onto a currently mirrored partition, and installing the Recovery Console has the same restriction.

INSTALLING THE RECOVERY CONSOLE POST-SP2

Installing Service Pack 1 (SP1) for Win2K should upgrade all system files, right? Not really—and among the files it doesn't upgrade are the ones related to the Recovery Console. The files in the System_drive:\Cmdcons folder are not updated. To update them, you must run the winnt32.exe /cmdcons command again from an integrated installation (also known as a *slipstreamed* installation) of Windows 2000 and SP2. Basically, a slipstreamed installation of Win2K is one to which SP2 has already been applied. If you're installing the Recovery Console from the CD as I just described, SP1 obviously isn't part of the CD. Chapter 4 explains how to create a slipstreamed \I386 directory. Once you've created the slipstreamed I386, just run the winnt32 /cmdcons as before.

Creating the Emergency Repair Disk

Every time you successfully edit your system's configuration, you should back the configuration up against the time when you unsuccessfully edit the settings. This backup disk is called the *emergency repair disk* (ERD).

TIP   *Re-create the emergency repair disk after you have successfully booted with the new configuration information. This way, you'll know that the configuration you're backing up works.*

KNOW THY ERD

It's important that you realize that the ERD you get with Windows 2000 is different from the NT 4 ERD. The Win2K ERD does not include Registry data—probably because people with complex systems could easily have a `Security` key file too big to fit on a disk. The contents of the two ERD types are shown next (the Win2K ERD is first):

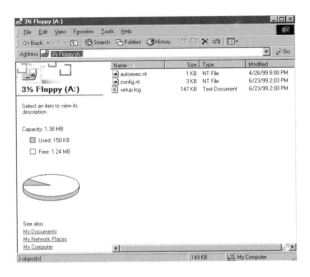

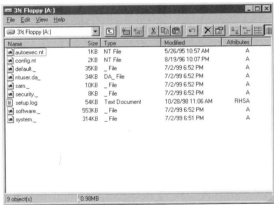

You can replace parts of the system Registry from the Recovery Console, if you update the information in the `RegBack` folder on a regular basis. (The original files are in the `\Config` folder; the backups in `\Repair\RegBack`.) Just don't expect to have that information anywhere if you don't back it up when creating the ERD.

Curious about what you *do* with the ERD? Turn to the next section.

Previous versions of NT had a utility called RDISK that you could use to create a repair disk after installation. If you're looking for RDISK in Win2K, you won't find it. Yes, Win2K still offers the same ERD functionality, but you now use a utility in the Backup program to make it, and it is *not* the same disk. Strictly speaking, the ERD is no longer a repair disk, but a boot disk to run the repair tools on the CD.

To create the ERD, follow these steps:

1. Run the Backup utility found in Accessories/System Tools. On the initial screen of the utility, you'll find buttons for three wizards: Backup Wizard, Restore Wizard, and Emergency Repair Disk. Click the Emergency Repair Disk button.

2. When prompted, put a blank, formatted disk in the A: drive and click OK. You'll have the option of copying the Registry files to the Repair directory. I strongly recommend that you do so.

NOTE *The updated files will be in* %systemroot%\Repair\RegBack.

Win2K will copy autoexec.nt, config.nt, and setup.log to the disk. The two NT files are not bootable—this isn't a boot disk. Rather, they're the files that Win2K needs to boot the files necessary for running 16-bit applications such as the Repair utility. autoexec.nt installs support for the CD-ROM (which you'll need to repair Win2K), the network redirector, and DPMI Memory. config.nt loads DOS into the upper memory block (UMB), out of conventional memory, and loads HIMEM.SYS, needed to read memory above 640KB.

Creating a Boot Floppy

The emergency repair disk is not a bootable disk. If you want to make a floppy that you can use to load Win2K when it won't load off the hard disk, you'll have to copy those files to a floppy. That floppy will not be machine-specific so long as all computers have the OS installed in the same directory, so you can keep it in your panic kit, and it's filesystem-independent.

A boot floppy is useful in any of the following situations:

- Corrupted boot sector

- Corrupted master boot record (MBR)

- Boot virus infections that keep the machine from booting

- Missing or corrupt NTLDR or NTDetect.com

- Incorrect NTBootdd.sys driver

Oddly enough, although making an NT boot floppy has been common practice for years, there's still no utility in core Win2K that you can employ to make one. (You can create Setup disks from the \bootdisk\makeboot command on the Win2K CD, but that's not the same thing. Those are Setup disks, this is a boot floppy, like a DOS boot floppy with autoexec.bat and config.sys on it.) The Windows NT floppy disk must include the files NTLDR, NTDetect.com, boot.ini, and the correct device driver for your hard drive.

CREATING A BOOT FLOPPY FROM THE CD

If you don't have another Win2K box around but do have the installation CD, then you can get the files you need. Copy Setup Disk One with the DISKCOPY command to a new floppy, then delete the files on the new disk. (If you don't have Setup Disk One, you can make it with the makeboot utility on the Win2K CD.) Don't just get a blank floppy; you need some hidden files on the disk, and this is how you're getting them. Next, copy the NTDetect.com and NTLDR files from the i386 folder on the CD-ROM to the new disk. Rename the NTLDR file to setupldr.bin.

The next step is to create the boot.ini file that Win2K uses to determine which operating system it should load and where that operating system is located. boot.ini files are just text files. For example, the following works for a single partition IDE drive with Win2K installed under \winnt; the exact value in the [operating systems] section depends upon the configuration of the Windows NT System you want to boot:

```
[boot loader]
timeout=30
Default= multi(0)disk(0)rdisk(0)partition(1)\winnt

[operating systems]
multi(0)disk(0)rdisk(0)partition(1)\winnt="Windows 2000"
```

WINNT, in this case, is the name of the system root directory.

TIP *If your computer boots from a SCSI hard drive, replace the* multi(0) *with* scsi(0)*. If you are using* scsi(x) *in the* boot.ini*, copy the correct device driver for the SCSI controller in use on the computer, and then rename it on the floppy to* NTBootdd.sys*. If you are using* multi(x) *in* boot.ini*, you do not need to do this.*

CREATING A BOOT FLOPPY FROM ANOTHER COMPUTER

If you have a working copy of Win2K around, you can copy the files you need from it. Format a floppy disk using Win2K's FORMAT command. Do a full format, not a quick format. Next, copy NTLDR and NTDetect.com from the computer to the floppy. Both NTLDR and NTDetect.com are in the root directory of the system folder.

Next, create a boot.ini file or copy one from a running Win2K computer (it's also in the root directory of the system folder) and modify it to match the computer you are trying to access.

TIP *You'll need to edit the options on the View tab of Folder options (available from the folder's Tools menu) to stop hiding protected operating system files such as* NTLDR*,* NTDetect.com*, and* boot.ini*. Just choosing to show hidden files and folders won't show this file.*

Repairing—or Recovering—a Damaged Installation

The Last Known Good menu and the Safe Mode boot options aren't always enough to get a wounded installation back on its feet again. You still have some options before reinstalling, though. As I discussed in the previous section, Windows 2000 offers two repair tools: the Recovery Console and the emergency repair disk. Both work on volumes formatted with either FAT or NTFS—one of the cool things about Win2K because this means that you can now format a system partition with NTFS but still have access to troubleshooting tools.

Understanding Repair Options

The two repair options aren't identical. The emergency repair disk is a simple procedure for those times when you don't know precisely what the problem is, but you want to fix it and get on with your life. There's little finesse involved: You start installing Win2K; when asked whether you're doing a real installation or a repair, you choose to repair; and then you plug in the ERD and let Setup repair files that are different from the ones originally installed. (There's a little more to it than that, but that's the basic story. I'll go through the procedure a bit later in "Using the Emergency Repair Disk.") So long as you haven't replaced any drivers or DLLs in your system folders with new ones, you can safely choose to restore all system files to their originals, and you'll still get your Win2K installation back as you left it—just fixed.

The Recovery Console is a little more complicated. Rather than a means of restoring damaged files, it's a command-line utility from which you can perform a variety of tasks:

◆ Copy system files from a floppy disk or CD to a hard disk (although not from a hard disk to a floppy disk).

◆ Start and stop services.

◆ Read and write data in the system directory on the local hard disk.

◆ Format disks.

◆ Repartition disks.

Use the Recovery Console when you know precisely what's wrong and what you want to accomplish. If you don't know what's wrong, this is not an easy way of finding out.

In short, if your Win2K installation is dead and you're not sure why, then use the emergency repair disk to see whether restoring the original installation files will fix the problem. If you know what the problem is—like, for example, a bad or missing SYS file or a runaway service—then you can use the Recovery Console to copy the missing file to its new location without changing any other files.

If you didn't set up the Recovery Console before Win2K became unbootable (or you want to run the ERD repair utility), then you'll need to run Setup from the installation CD. After Setup has copied all the files it needs to access the hardware it needs to run Setup, it will ask you whether you want to install Win2K, repair it, or exit Setup. Choose R to open the Windows 2000 Repair Options menu, from which you can repair an installation either with the Recovery Console (press C) or with the emergency repair disk (press R).

Using the Recovery Console

When you choose to run the Recovery Console, it will scan the disk and find any installations of Windows NT/2000 on the disk. Pick the one you want to repair. Type the number of the option you want, and supply the password for the Administrator account—*not* the account of someone in the Administrators group, the Administrator account. So long as the SAM database is present and you can be properly authenticated, you're in. (If it's not, then you need to restore the backed-up Registry files you stored in %systemroot%\repair\regback before you can use the Recovery Console.)

TIP   You can repair Windows NT Server 4 installations on dual-boot computers with the Recovery Console. Start the Repair Console as you normally would. When it returns the list of found NT installations, pick the NT 4 one.

Although it looks like an ordinary command prompt, the Recovery Console is not the command prompt that you can open from the Accessories folder. First, it supports only a few commands and only locally—this is not a network tool, and you can't run just any command-line program or utility on it. Second, those commands are specialized for this interface and only perform a limited set of functions. By default, the wildcard options in the copy command don't work in the console; by default, you can only copy files from removable media to the system partition (but not the other way around—you can't use the console to back up files to other media); and although you can move to other logical drives on the hard disk, by default you can't read files on any partition other than the system partition—or even perform a dir function on them. If you try, you'll get an Access Denied error. (As you'll see, you can change some of the security settings to make the Recovery Console more useful, but these are the defaults.) The Recovery Console is not a command-line version of Win2K, cool as that would be.

NOTE   I expected that the Recovery Console would include a command-line version of REGEDIT, like Windows 9x does. Sadly, it does not.

You can't back up files. You can't read the contents of any directory not in the system root. You can't use wildcards. You can't edit security information. What *can* you do with the Recovery Console?

Quite a lot, actually, if recovery is what interests you. As you can see in Table 21.9, the Recovery Console is a set of commands you can use to manipulate the files and structure of the system partition. As you can see, a lot of functions with duplicate commands use the same syntax; unless I specify otherwise, there's no difference between the two commands.

TABLE 21.9: SUPPORTED RECOVERY CONSOLE COMMANDS

COMMAND NAME	FUNCTION
attrib	Changes the attributes of a selected file or folder.
batch	Runs the commands specified in a text file so that you can complete many tasks in a single step.
cd or chdir	Displays the name of the current directory, or changes directories. Typing **cd..** closes the current directory and moves you up one in the tree.
chkdsk	Runs CheckDisk.
cls	Wipes the screen of any previous output.
copy or extract	Copies files from removable media to the system folders on the hard disk. Does not accept wildcards.

Continued on next page

TABLE 21.9: SUPPORTED RECOVERY CONSOLE COMMANDS *(continued)*

COMMAND NAME	FUNCTION
del or delete	Deletes one or more files (does not accept wildcards).
dir	Lists the contents of the current or selected directory.
disable	Disables the named service or driver.
diskpart	Replaces the FDISK tool with which you're probably familiar. Creates or deletes disk partitions. Only use this command on basic disks—it can damage dynamic disks.
enable	Enables the named service or driver.
extract	Extracts a compressed installation file (one with a .cab extension) to the local fixed disk. Only works if you're running the Recovery Console from the installation CD.
fixboot	Writes a new partition boot sector on the system partition.
fixmbr	Writes a new Master Boot Record (MBR) for the partition boot sector.
format	Formats the selected disk.
listsvc	Lists all the services running on the Win2K installation.
logon	If you have multiple Win2K (or NT) installations on the local hard disk, you can use this command to pick the installation you want to repair.
map	Displays the drive letter mappings currently in place. Handy for getting the information you need to use DISKPART. Only lists drives found in the partition table, not volumes listed only in the dynamic disks volume database.
md or mkdir	Creates a directory.
more, type	Displays the contents of the chosen text file.
rd or rmdir	Deletes a directory.
rename or ren	Renames a single file.
set	Allows you to display or modify four security settings governing file and folder access.
systemroot	Makes the current directory the system root of the drive you're logged in to.

WARNING   *If you thought the Registry Editor was potentially dangerous, the Recovery Console is just as bad or worse. You can really screw up your system here, to the point that the only thing to do is reinstall and reload your backups. There's no Undo feature, not all the commands ask for confirmation, and there's no Read Only setting such as the one in REGEDT32. If you're not used to working from the command line, review what you want to do and the tools you need to do it before you open the console.*

Some of the commands in Table 21.9 will look familiar to old DOS hands, but many of them work a little differently from the way they did under DOS, using a slightly different syntax or only working under specific circumstances. Let's take a look at how you can use these commands to get things back up and running.

BEFORE YOU BEGIN: FIX THE SECURITY SETTINGS

Did you notice that I said *by default* you can't copy files to external media and *by default* you can't access any partition other than the system partition? The weasel wording wasn't accidental.

Normally, from the Recovery Console you can only use the following folders:

◆ The root folder

◆ The %SystemRoot% folder and the subfolders of the Windows 2000 installation you are currently logged in to

◆ The Cmdcons folder

◆ Removable media drives such as CD-ROM drives

You also can't use wildcards with commands that would normally support them or copy data to disks.

Bah. Let's use the SET command to make the Recovery Console a bit more flexible. The SET command allows you to display or modify four environment options:

Option	Default Setting	Description
AllowWildCards	FALSE	Controls whether you can use wildcards with some commands (such as del *.tmp)
AllowAllPaths	FALSE	Controls whether you can change directories (with the cd command) to include all folders on all local drives
AllowRemovableMedia	FALSE	Controls whether you can copy files from the hard disk to a floppy disk or other recognized removable media
NoCopyPrompt	FALSE	Controls whether you can copy files without being prompted to continue when you are overwriting an existing file

Oho—so you run set AllowAllPaths = TRUE (don't forget the spaces around the equals sign) and you can navigate anywhere on the local disk, right? Almost. Before you ever start the Recovery Console, you need to edit some security settings in Win2K before the SET command will work. Depending on what kind of computer this is—a server or a domain controller—go to the Security Configuration and Analysis snap-in in the MMC, the Domain Controller Security Policy in Administrative Tools, the Domain Security Policy in Administrative Tools, or the Local Security Policy in Administrative Tools. Whichever tool you choose, look under the Local Policies, Security Options heading and locate the two security policies pertaining to Recovery Console: `Recovery Console:` `Allow Automatic Administrative Logon` and `Recovery Console: Allow floppy copy and access to all drives and all folders`.

The first policy allows you to start Recovery Console without prompting for the administrative password stored in the local computer's account database. (That's kind of handy, but it does represent a security risk.) The second policy enables the SET command while you are using Recovery Console. If you enable this policy, you can change any of the four environment variables to TRUE during a Recovery Console session.

After you enable the security policy, it must be applied (possibly across the domain) before becoming the effective policy on the local computer. This is necessary before the SET command is truly enabled and available for use during a Recovery Console session. To make it snappy, you can run `secedit /refreshpolicy machine_policy` to force a refresh of the local computer's policy after performing the policy change described previously.

After the local policy is refreshed and the enabled Recovery Console security policy is in effect, you should be able to start Recovery Console and use the SET command to enable any of the four environment options.

One last thing: You need to run SET every time you run the Recovery Console—it won't remember that you changed any settings from their defaults.

TIP *Put the SET commands you want to apply to your Recovery Console sessions in a batch file so you can run the batch file with the BATCH command when you start the Recovery Console.*

ENABLING AND DISABLING SERVICES

Why would you need to enable or disable services from the command line? Therein lies a tale.

Early in 1999, I bought a new PC. Installed Windows NT Server; ran the installation program for the 3Com network card in the server. Life was good.

Until I rebooted the computer.

You see, a diagnostic program was part of the setup for the NIC—an unavoidable part that you could not choose to not install. (Trust me: I tried, on several computers with the same set of hardware.) Whenever I started up NT, this diagnostic program would scan the system and display a message that a newer version of my NIC's driver was available—did I want to use the new driver? Click OK or Cancel, and the message box would close for a second and then reopen, with the same message. Add to this that the searching and displaying was using up 100 percent of CPU time for a 350MHz Pentium II doing *nothing else but running the diagnostic*. Running the Task Manager (when I could get a spare cycle here or there to open it) didn't help because the program wouldn't shut down even when I killed the process.

NOTE *Worried about this happening to you? Although I've run into several people who've had the same problem with one version of the driver for the 3Com 3C905X Ethernet 10BaseT card, this issue seems to be fixed in the driver published in April 1999. Other than this glitch, I've been very happy with these NICs.*

Okay, I figured—the problem is a runaway service, so if I can shut down the service I will resolve the problem. But shutting down the service is hard when you're clicking OK in a repeatedly reappearing dialog box and then frantically grabbing CPU cycles to open the Control Panel and then Services before the dialog box opens and the CPU usage starts running at 100 percent again.

In this case, I was finally able to get to the Services applet, find the service (named 3Com Diagnostics or some such, so identifying the problem child wasn't hard), and then stop and disable it. Problem solved. But it took a lot of time and mouse-clicking to get to that point. A tool that would enable me to boot to the command prompt and disable that service without having to work around the CPU-eating message box would have been nice. And that's where the services-related tools in the Recovery Console come in.

The first step to fixing a problem like this is running the `listsvc` utility. There are no arguments to this—just type **listsvc** from the command prompt, and Windows 2000 will display a list of all the services and drivers currently installed for that installation of Win2K, a short description of what they are, and their start type (boot, automatic, manual, system, or disabled). Seeing all the services will probably take a few pages of screen, but the services are listed alphabetically, so you can find the one you want fairly easily. Write down its name.

TIP   *The names of services and drivers are not case sensitive.*

Once you've found the suspected problem child, it's time for the `disable` command. The syntax is simple: `disable servicename`. Win2K will then notify you that it found the Registry entry for this service (or tell you that it can't find an entry for this service, in which case you need to check your spelling and try again). It will also display the current start type and new start type for the service. Write down the current start type for the service in case you want to start it again.

To make the change take effect, type **exit** to leave the Recovery Console and restart the computer. See whether disabling that service fixed the problem. If it did, then you're home free. (Not sure how you'd know? Depends on what the problem was. In the case of the runaway 3Com diagnostics, the fix was pretty immediate. As soon as I turned off the service, the problem disappeared.) If it didn't, then you can return to the console, enable that service, and try something else.

You don't have to disable a service to keep it from running when Win2K starts, however. Instead, you could change its start type from automatic to manual. To do so, or to reenable a service you disabled, you'll need to use the `enable` command. Like `disable`, `enable`'s syntax is simple: `enable servicename`. If run on a disabled service, using this syntax will enable the service and restore it to whatever its start type was when it was disabled.

To change a service's start type without disabling it, add the new start type to the end of the enable command, like this:

enable *servicename* start_type

where *start_type* is one of the options in Table 21.10.

TABLE 21.10: START TYPES

START TYPE	MEANING
Service_boot_start	Boot
Service_system_start	System
Service_demand_start	Manual
Service_auto_start	Automatic

So, for example, instead of disabling the 3Com diagnostic service, I could have changed its start type from automatic to manual. That way, I could have started it at any time during the Win2K session, but it wouldn't start automatically.

REPLACING DAMAGED FILES

Perhaps the problem isn't a runaway driver or service, but a corrupted part of the operating system, as in error messages that say Bad or Missing NTOSKRNL.EXE. In such a case, you may need to replace all or part of your operating system (although, if we're talking about more than a few files here or you aren't sure what's broken, you might consider hauling out the emergency repair disk). The tools most likely to apply to this scenario are the ones to create and delete directories, rename files, change attributes, and copy or extract files from other media.

Creating directories is simple. The command syntax is as follows:

```
md [drive:]path
mkdir [drive:]path
```

where *drive:* is the drive letter of the drive on which you want to create the folder, if it's not the current one, and *path* is the name of the directory you want to create. Just make sure that, if you don't spell out the location of the new directory, you're currently in the place where the new directory should be created.

The syntax for the rmdir and rd commands (for deleting directories) is the same as that for md. The only part of directory deletion that you have to watch is that you can't delete directories unless they're empty, with no subdirectories. If you try, you'll get an error message telling you that the directory is not empty, and there's no switch to make rd act like deltree (an old DOS command that would delete subdirectories).

Before you delete a directory, run the dir command to check out its contents and make sure that you really do want to remove it. Conveniently, dir displays all files, hidden or not, and shows their attributes.

Rather than deleting entire directories, however, you're more likely to need to replace individual files. That's where copy and extract come in. The copy command is what it sounds like: a method of copying a file from one location to another, with the caveat I've mentioned before that you can only copy *to* the system directory, not copy files from the system directory to removable media such as a Jaz drive. The syntax for copying files is simple:

```
copy source [destination]
```

where *source* is the name of the original file and *destination* is the directory where you're pasting the original (along with a new name, if you need it). If you don't specify a directory, the file will be copied to the directory from which you're running the command. The extract utility works the same way as copy and uses the same syntax, with one exception: You can only use extract if you started the Recovery Console from the Repair option in Setup. Neither copying utility supports wildcards (so you can't copy the entire contents of a directory very easily), but copy automatically decompresses compressed installation files for you. Both utilities will alert you if a file with the name of the one you're pasting already exists in that location.

If you're not sure that you want to replace an existing file, try renaming it and then copying the new file to the relevant location. The syntax for rename is as follows:

```
rename [drive:][path] filename1 filename2
```

`rename` works only on single files, and the renamed file must be in the same place as the original. That is, you can't use this command to move files. To do that, you'd need to use `copy`.

FIXING BOOT SECTORS AND BOOT RECORDS

Your computer uses a couple of pieces of information to navigate your hard disk. Those two pieces are the boot sector and the master boot record (MBR). Most of the time, these pieces are pretty safe, but some things (such as some viruses) can target and infect them, or they can be lost. In such a case, you'll need a way to restore them.

First, a little background. The partition boot sector contains the information that the file system uses to access the volume. The MBR (discussed next) examines the information in the boot sector to load the boot loader.

The Windows 2000 boot sector contains the following information:

◆ A jump instruction

◆ The name and version of the operating system files (such as Windows 2000)

◆ A data structure called the BIOS Parameter Block, which describes the physical characteristics of the partition

◆ A data structure called the BIOS Extended Parameter Block, which describes the location of the master file table for NTFS volumes

◆ The bootstrap code

Most of the information in the boot sector describes the physical characteristics of the disk (for example, the number of sectors per track and clusters per sector), in addition to the location of the file allocation table (for FAT volumes) or the master file table (for NTFS volumes). The layout and exact information included in the boot sector depends on the disk format used.

Given that a disk may have more than one partition, how does the hard disk know where to find the different partitions? The first sector on every hard disk (whether the hard disk has an operating system on it or not) contains that disk's MBR. The MBR contains the partition table for that disk and a small amount of code used to read the partition table and find the system partition for that hard disk. Once it finds that partition, the MBR loads a copy of that partition's boot sector into memory. If the disk is not bootable (has no system partition), the code never gets used and the boot sector is not loaded.

In short, a hard disk needs a functioning MBR to boot. The MBR is in the same place on every hard disk, so it's potentially an easy virus target.

Okay—all that said, to write a new boot sector to a drive, type **fixboot**. This will write a new boot sector to the current boot drive. To create a new MBR, type **fixmbr**.

DELETING, CREATING, AND FORMATTING PARTITIONS

The Recovery Console includes tools not only for fixing Windows 2000, but for completely wiping things out and starting over. With these tools you can repartition and reformat your hard disk. *Partitioning* is setting up logical divisions of the disk; *formatting* is placing a file system on those drives so you can store data on them.

WARNING   *You probably already know this, but just in case you've forgotten, repartitioning and formatting are* destructive. *Any data on the hard disk you've reformatted or repartitioned is history. Keep your backups.*

Before you start formatting or repartitioning, you might want to take a look at what you've already got in place. The Recovery Console's map command can help you do that. Type **map** at the command prompt, and you'll see output like the following:

```
?               0MB        Device\HardDisk0\Partition0
C:     FAT16    1028MB     Device\HardDisk0\Partition1
?               3310MB     Device\HardDisk0\Partition0
E:     NTFS     1028MB     Device\HardDisk0\Partition2
H:     NTFS     1028MB     Device\HardDisk0\Partition3
G:              1028MB     Device\HardDisk0\Partition4
?               227MB      Device\HardDisk0\Partition0
A:                         Device\Floppy0
D:                         Device\CDROM0
```

TIP   *If you're running map on a dynamic disk, only volumes created before you updated the disk (that is, volumes that were originally primary partitions or logical drives) will show up. MAP reads the partition table, and dynamic volumes created on dynamic disks are not in the partition table.*

You can see from this that logical drive G: on the hard disk hasn't been formatted because it's not showing any file system. To format it, you would use the following syntax:

format g: [/q] [/fs:*filesystem*]

Here, /q tells format to do a quick format (not checking for bad sectors), and the /fs switch is for specifying the file system to use. You don't have to specify a file system (your options are NTFS, FAT32, and FAT), but if you don't, Win2K will format it to NTFS. When you run this command, Win2K will tell you that all data on that drive will be lost and ask you to confirm that the format should proceed. Do so, and a few seconds later you will have a newly formatted drive.

TIP   *You can convert a FAT partition to NTFS, but you cannot convert an NTFS partition to FAT.*

You can format the G: drive safely, or at least without affecting any other logical drives. What you can't do, even before formatting, is repartition to make the G: drive bigger, perhaps giving it some of that space that isn't used on the disk. To do that, you need to boot the Disk Administrator and make G: part of a volume and then extend that volume—anyway, it's all in Chapter 10. If you do want to repartition the disk to reorganize its structure, run diskpart.

WARNING   *DISKPART can damage your partition table if you've upgraded the disk to a dynamic disk. Do not modify the structure of dynamic disks unless you are using the Disk Management tool.*

When you're done with the Recovery Console, type **exit** and press Enter. The computer will reboot.

Using the Emergency Repair Disk

You have two options for the emergency repair disk: Manual Repair, in which you can choose from a list of repair options (not another one!), or Fast Repair, which repairs your installation for you.

The Manual Repair option provides the following choices:

◆ Inspect startup environment

◆ Verify Windows 2000 system files

◆ Inspect boot sector

By default, all options are selected, but you can pick and choose.

INSPECT STARTUP ENVIRONMENT

This option checks the ARC path in the `boot.ini` file for a path to the Windows 2000 boot partition and `%systemroot%` folder. It does this by reading the `Setup.log` file on the emergency repair disk:

```
[Paths]
TargetDirectory = "\WINNT"
TargetDevice = "\Device\Harddisk1\Partition1"
SystemPartitionDirectory = "\"
SystemPartition = "\Device\Harddisk1\Partition1"
```

If `boot.ini` is missing, Win2K creates a new one with a valid ARC path. If `boot.ini` is present, Win2K checks the ARC path and updates it if need be.

VERIFY WINDOWS 2000 SYSTEM FILES

Selecting this option asks Win2K to refer to `Setup.log` to verify that each file in the Windows 2000 system/boot partition is good and matches the files that were originally installed. This includes the `NTLDR`, `NTDetect.com`, `ARCSetup.exe`, and `ARCLDR.exe` files used for booting various computers. The optional `NTBootdd.sys` file is never checked. Repair performs this check by comparing cyclical redundancy check (CRC) values for each file. If files are missing or corrupted, you are prompted to replace or skip the file. If you choose to replace the file, you need the Windows 2000 installation CD-ROM or an OEM driver disk that contains the correct file(s).

INSPECT BOOT SECTOR

This option repairs the active system partition boot sector and reinstalls the boot loader functionality. If the partition uses the FAT or FAT32 file system and contains a non–Windows 2000 boot sector, this repair option also creates a new `bootsect.dos` file to be used to dual-boot MS-DOS, Microsoft Windows 95, or Microsoft Windows 98 if these operating systems were previously available to be booted. If you also select the Inspect Startup Environment option and a new `bootsect.dos` file is created, Repair adds the following entry to the `boot.ini` file:

```
C:\ = "Microsoft Windows"
```

Note that the Manual Repair option does not give you a choice to repair the Windows 2000 Registry files. Believe it or not, you'll need to use the Fast Repair option for that.

FAST REPAIR OPTION

The Fast Repair option performs all the same repairs as the Manual Repair option without asking you whether you want to do them. It also attempts to load each Windows 2000 Registry file (SAM, SECURITY,

SYSTEM, and SOFTWARE). If it discovers that a file is damaged or it can't load it, then it will copy the missing or corrupted Registry file from the `%systemroot%\Repair` folder to the `%systemroot%\System32\Config` folder.

Notice that it's `%SystemRoot%\Repair`, not `%SystemRoot%\Repair\Regback`. The Registry backups you make aren't used to repair the operating system; Fast Repair reverts any damaged Registry files with those that reflect the condition of the OS when you first installed. If this occurs, you need to restore your last System State backup or manually copy a more recent version of the registry files from the `%systemroot%\Repair\Regback` folder to the `%systemroot%\System32\Config` folder. The files located in the `Regback` folder are from the last time you created an emergency repair disk and chose the option to also back up the registry files to the repair folder.

To use the ERD, start installing Win2K; when asked whether you're doing a real installation or a repair, choose to repair, make sure the ERD is in the floppy drive, and press Enter. If you don't have an ERD, you may still be able to repair the installation by pressing L to let Setup try to find the Win2K installation for you. Setup will look around to find a Win2K installation and then ask you whether the installation found at such and such a location is the one you want to repair. If it is, press Enter.

Setup will read from `Setup.log` on the ERD and then start doing the operations you selected. If it comes across any files in your existing installation that don't match the ones logged in `Setup.log`, which is a record of all files installed originally, it will tell you and then offer you a choice of skipping the file, repairing it (that is, replacing it with the one that Windows 2000 Server would install), or choosing to repair all files that differ from the original. There is no "skip all" function, so you'll have to make a decision for each file if you're pretty sure that you want to keep some of the files logged in `Setup.log`. It's inspecting the entire Win2K directory, so this may take a while.

When it's done, the computer will reboot and (hopefully) run Windows 2000.

NOTE   *If you perform a Manual fix, your security information—policies, accounts, passwords—will be as you left it. Because the Manual fix does not check Registry files, the ERD does not record or replace security information.*

Troubleshooting Login Failures: "No Domain Controller Found"

One of the most confusing and common Windows 2000 mysteries in an environment using NT domain controllers is the one that occurs when you sit down at a computer and try to log in to your domain, only to be told that no domain controller could be found to validate your login.

It can happen from any client type, whether DOS, Macintosh, Windows 9*x*, NT, or Windows 2000 Professional, and the same things tend to make it happen. But be ready for some bad news: You can't always fix it.

When you tell your workstation to try to log you in to a domain, your workstation must first find one of the machines that contains a copy of the database of domain users in passwords—in other words, a domain controller, whether primary or backup. All domain controllers announce themselves to the world by registering a NetBIOS name of *domainname*<1C>; for example, if a domain named URSAMAJOR had a domain controller named MIZAR, then MIZAR would register not only its personal NetBIOS name MIZAR<00> but also URSAMAJOR<1C>.

NOTE *<1C> is just an easily written way of saying "the hexadecimal value 1C." As all NetBIOS names are 16 characters in length and URSAMAJOR is only 9 characters long, the full NetBIOS name would look like URSAMAJOR followed by 7 blanks, 9 bytes of value hexadecimal 20—hex 20 is the ASCII code for blank—finally ending with a hex 1C. It's just easier to write URSAMAJOR<1C>, which is why I represent it that way here.*

The URSAMAJOR<1C> name is different from the MIZAR<00> name, however, as only one machine has the MIZAR<00> name, but many machines can claim the URSAMAJOR<1C> name; it's a "group" name, and each and every other domain controller in URSAMAJOR registers the name.

But how does your workstation find one of these domain controllers? Step 1 is a broadcast, a simple shout, "Is there a machine named URSAMAJOR<1C> here?" This is the first step, no matter what protocol you're using. (There is *one* way to keep this broadcast from happening—only one—and I'll cover it in a minute.) The idea is that it's always best to find a local domain controller, if one exists, and a broadcast will find that. If you're using NetBEUI, IPX, or TCP/IP in broadcast-only mode, that's as far as the workstation goes to find a domain controller. If there's not one within "earshot," so to speak, then the logon will fail.

If you're using TCP/IP with LMHOSTS, then the client will look in its LMHOSTS file for an entry with a #DOM command, like so:

```
200.116.73.18 MIZAR #DOM:URSAMAJOR #PRE
```

Sometimes that won't work, however, because of quirks in the TCP client software. An alternative form of the LMHOSTS line sometimes works better:

```
200.116.73.18 "MIZAR      \0x1C" #PRE
```

In this formulation, you directly enter the hex 1C rather than relying on the #DOM metacommand. It leads to some interesting behavior. First, entering one of these 0x1C entries *completely short-circuits the domain controller discovery process*. The machine doesn't broadcast, it doesn't talk to WINS, and it doesn't even do all that much looking around in LMHOSTS, either. In fact, if you enter several domain controller names, all using the 0x1C formulation, the NT machine will only look at the *last* one. Furthermore, if the domain controller named in LMHOSTS isn't up and available, then the NT machine simply cannot log in because, again, it doesn't even think to look in WINS or to broadcast.

Using the 0x1C formulation, then, can be quite powerful because it guarantees that a Win2K server or workstation can find a domain controller, but it has two drawbacks: It's labor intensive, as you'll have to put an LMHOSTS file on every Win2K machine; and it's not at all fault tolerant, as you end up creating a life-and-death relationship between a particular Win2K machine and its assigned domain controller.

A TCP/IP-using system that has been pointed to a WINS server will look in the WINS server's database of machine names for a machine with the URSAMAJOR<1C> name. WINS maintains a list of up to 25 domain controllers, and it sends that list to the workstation. The workstation then sends messages to all of those domain controllers, asking them if they'll log it in. The first one to respond to your workstation is the one that the workstation uses to log in.

Assuming that the workstation has located a domain controller, it then asks the domain controller to verify the requested user's credentials. The domain controller does that, and all is well. That's basically all there is to a login.

Check the Basics

So what can go wrong? There are a few basic, obvious things that can mess up a login, and, although it may seem that I'm insulting you by asking you to check them, I can only say that I've done every one of these at least once:

◆ Check that the domain name is spelled correctly. It's not possible to misspell a domain name on a Win2K or NT workstation, as you couldn't join a domain in the first place if you'd misspelled it, but it's quite easy to do so on a DOS, Windows 9x, or Mac system.

◆ Check that there's network connectivity. It may just be that the Ethernet hub had its power cord kicked out or that the network cable fell off the back of the card.

◆ Check that you typed your name and password correctly.

If You're Dialing In

Many login failures occur because you're dialing in to a Win2K network. How you attack them depends on whether you're running NT/Win2K or Windows 9x.

If you're trying to get Windows 95 or 98 to dial in to a Windows 2000 domain and for some reason can't always make it work, don't feel bad—Dial-Up Networking for Windows 9x has some problems. Fortunately, there is a solution: patch files from Microsoft. Microsoft rearranges its Web site too often for me to tell you exactly where to find it, but there is a file called `MSDUN13.exe` that completely updates the Windows 95 Dial-Up Networking code; there's a similar one for Windows 98, I'm told.

If You're Local

Local systems can also benefit from double-checking that you have a proper WINS server nearby or an LMHOSTS file. In some cases, it makes sense to have LMHOSTS even *if* you've got WINS servers—here's why.

Suppose you have a geographically scattered domain with many domain controllers, many systems whose names are registered as URSAMAJOR<1C>—WINS should know of all of them, shouldn't it? Sadly, it doesn't: WINS only remembers the last 25 domain controllers that it has heard of. If a domain controller local to you has fallen off the edge, then WINS won't tell you about it, with the result that you'll end up trying to log in over a presumably slower WAN link. Even if WINS knows of all of your domain controllers, however, how will it know which one is geographically closest to you? It doesn't.

How, then, to ensure that you find a local domain controller? Two thoughts.

First, there's always LMHOSTS. Sorry if I sound like a broken record, but it's a very useful tool.

Second, you might modify the order in which NetBIOS name resolution takes place. By default, when your system goes looking for URSAMAJOR<1C>, it first looks in its name cache in RAM. If it can't find the domain controller there, it looks to WINS. If WINS doesn't have the answer, then the PC broadcasts to find the answer, and so on.

All logins start with a single broadcast. But perhaps your local DC is busy and doesn't respond quickly enough. Can you bias things a bit more in its favor? Yes, by modifying how NetBIOS names are resolved over TCP/IP. If you tell NetBIOS to always first broadcast, *then* ask WINS, you'll be more likely to find local domain controllers if they are within shouting distance. The downside will be, of course, that every single time your workstation tries to resolve *any* name, it will broadcast first, so be aware of that. But if this sounds like a good answer to you, then change the NetBIOS node type (it's in DHCP) from hex 0x8, a *hybrid node*, to hex 0x4, a *mixed node*.

Tell the Workstation to Be More Patient

Sometimes you do everything and you still can't find a domain controller, particularly if you're logging in from an NT machine. Here's why: You may recall that NT and Win2K machines also log in to the domain, just as users do. If you try to log in the very first second that the login screen appears, your system may simply be too busy to get the login done quickly—and it times out.

The fix? Well, there are a couple of possibilities. The first one's not pretty, but it'll work: When you turn your workstation on, wait a bit and let the hard disk settle down before trying to log in.

That's about the best you can do on a Windows 9x or 3.x workstation. But if your workstations are Win2K or NT, we can do a bit better.

The problem is that the Netlogon service is the part of an NT workstation that goes out and finds a domain controller. But it's impatient and only waits about 15 seconds for a response. How to tell it to be more patient? Why, with a Registry entry, of course. Remember, you're trying to make the *client* more patient, not the server, so this Registry change goes on your workstations, although it could benefit the servers as well Recall that trust relationships can be broken if domain-controller-to-domain-controller logins across trusts don't happen quickly enough.

Anyway, the modification goes in HKLM\System\CurrentControlSet\Services\ Netlogon\ Parameters. If it's not already there, add a REG_DWORD entry named ExpectedDialupDelay. Set it to the number of seconds that you'd like your workstation to wait before deciding to give up on finding a domain controller. Minimum acceptable value is 0, maximum 600.

TIP *If you have a particularly busy network or some very overloaded domain controllers, you might consider adding this to all of your workstations via a system policy.*

Troubleshooting Startup Mysteries: How *Do* I Get Rid of That Program?

Here's a short problem and solution, but I promise you it'll be useful one day: You install some piece of software, and the install crashes, so you decide to just forget it and throw the software away. But the next time you boot the system, you see an error message because NT's trying to start the software but can't find it, or perhaps it *does* load some piece of it, leading to more error messages. What's causing the program to run?

The obvious place to look is in Start/Programs/Startup; any icons in there will run automatically when you log in. However, the contents of the Startup folder don't necessarily show everything—they show the files that have been told to put their icons in the Startup folder. Many people do not know that Win2K has a file named WIN.ini that contains a run= and a load= command, both of which can start programs. But the *really* sneaky one is a Registry key: HKLM\Software\Microsoft\ Windows\CurrentVersion\Run. In it, you'll see value entries of type REG_SZ where the value entry is some descriptive name and the data is a program's filename and any startup options. If there's a mysteriously starting program, chances are good it's in that Registry key. Delete the entry, and the program should stop starting up.

Planning for Disaster Recovery

Sometimes using the Last Known Good configuration or the Recovery Console doesn't fix your problems. Hard disk failures or natural disasters require a bit more in the way of hard-core disaster recovery.

What does *disaster recovery* mean? Essentially, it's exactly what it sounds like: a way of recovering from disaster—at best, turning a potential disaster into a minor inconvenience. Disaster can mean anything: theft, flood, an earthquake, a virus, or anything else that keeps you from being able to access your data. After all, it's not really the server that's important. Although a server may be expensive, it is replaceable. Your data, on the other hand, is either difficult or impossible to recover. Could you reproduce your client mailing list from memory? What about the corporate accounts?

Creating a Disaster Recovery Plan

The most important part of a disaster recovery plan is identifying what "disaster" means to you and your company. Obviously, permanently losing all of your company's data would be a disaster, but what else would? How about your installation becoming inaccessible for a week or longer? When planning for disaster, think about all the conditions that could render your data or your workplace unreachable and plan accordingly.

Implementing Disaster Recovery

Okay, it's 2:00 P.M. on Thursday, and you get a report that the network has died. What do you do?

WRITE THINGS DOWN

Immediately write down everything that everyone tells you: what happened, when it happened, who gave you the information, and anything else that happened at the same time that might possibly be related. Do not trust it to memory. First, you're apt to be a bit stressed at this point. Second, if it happened once, it could happen again—and if you write down the results of your interviews, you may not have to start from scratch.

CHECK THE EVENT LOGS

If you can get to them, look at the security and event logs on the server to see if you can tell what happened right before the server crashed. If you're using directory replication to maintain a physically identical file server (also known as a *hot start* server because it's ready to go whenever you need it), the log information may be on the replicated server, even if you can't get to the original.

ASCERTAIN THE CAUSE OF THE FAILURE AND FIX IT

"Easy for you to say," I hear someone muttering. It can be done, however. Once you know what events happened, it becomes easier to find out what they happened to.

Find Out If It's a Software Problem

Is it a software problem? If it is, have you changed the configuration? If you've changed something, rebooted, and been unable to boot, it's time to use the Last Known Good configuration discussed earlier. If you can boot but the operating system won't function properly, use the emergency repair disk to restore the hardware configuration.

If you have another server with a Windows 2000 Server installation identical to the server that failed, switch servers and see if the backup server works before you reinstall the operating system. If the hot start server doesn't work, you could be facing a network problem.

Find Out If It's a Hardware Problem

Is it a hardware problem? If you have a hot start server around the office, put it in place of the failed server and see if you can bring the network back up. If so, the problem lies with the dead server, and you can fix or replace it while you have the other one in place. If not, check the network's cabling.

If one drive from a stripe set or mirror set has died, the system should still be fine (if the drive that died is not the one with the system partition on it), but you should still fix the set anyway. Striping and mirroring gives you access to your data while the missing data is being regenerated, but if something else happens to the set before you regenerate the missing data, you're sunk, because the set can only deal with one error at a time.

If necessary, reload the backups.

Make a Recovery "Coloring Book"

No matter how much you know about reformatting SCSI drives or rebuilding boot sectors byte by byte, I guarantee you that the fastest way to recover from a disaster will often turn out to be a three-step process: replacing the bad hard disk and attendant hardware, installing a fresh copy of NT Server on the new hard disk, and restoring the data on the disk.

That sounds simple, but it's amazing how complex it can be in the heat of battle. Let's see, I'm reinstalling Windows 2000 Server, but what was the name of the domain? What IP address does the domain controller get? What's the WINS server address? Which services went on this server? What was the administrator's password set to?

At my shop, we decided to sit down and write a step-by-step, click-by-click instruction manual. It tells future network administrators which buttons to click and what text to type in the unlikely event that they ever need to take a new machine and rebuild our domain controller on it.

Just for an example, we have a primary domain controller on one of our domains that (as the logon traffic is relatively light) is also our DHCP, WINS, and DNS server. So, suppose the machine goes up in smoke, leaving us nothing but backup tapes—how do we rebuild that machine? We sat down and wrote out exactly what to do:

◆ Install Windows 2000 Server on a new machine.

◆ Restore the SAM and SECURITY databases.

◆ Install DHCP on the machine.

◆ Restore the old DHCP database to the machine.

◆ Install WINS on the machine.

◆ Restore the WINS database.

◆ Install the DNS server on the machine.

◆ Restore our DNS zones and records.

◆ Restore the user data.

Assume that the person who'll be doing this knows nothing more than how to click a mouse and shove CDs into drives—someone with oatmeal for brains. Sound insulting? It's not; I like to think of myself as of at least basic intelligence, but under pressure I sometimes just don't think as well as I need to—oatmeal's as good as it gets, and if I'm really pressed my brains have the power of unidentified goo. If you're good under pressure, that's great—but making the disaster recovery guide an easy read is also a big help to your coworkers.

TIP   An easier and less error-prone solution is to create unattended installations for key servers, either using answer files or Remote Installation Services. See Chapter 4 for more information about unattended installations.

Don't underestimate how long this will take: Putting the whole document together took two research assistants a couple of weeks, and it ended up being a 100+ page Word document! (Part of the reason why it was so large is that it made lavish use of screen shots wherever possible, and yours should, too. Just click the window you want to include in your document, press Alt+Prtsc, choose Edit/Paste Special in Word, choose Bitmap, and uncheck Float over Text.)

WARNING   Once you finish the document, be careful where you keep it. The document will contain the keys to your network: usernames of domain administrator accounts, the passwords of those accounts, and the like.

Making Sure the Plan Works

The first casualty of war isn't always the truth—it's often the battle plan itself.

The most crucial part of any disaster recovery plan is making sure that it works down to the last detail. Don't just check the hardware; check everything. When a server crashes, backups do no good at all if they are locked in a cabinet to which only the business manager has the keys and the business manager is on vacation in Tahiti.

In the interest of having your plan actually work, make sure you know the answers to the following questions.

WHO HAS THE KEYS?

Who has the keys to the backups and/or the file server case? The example mentioned previously of the business manager having the only set of keys is an unacceptable situation, for reasons that should be painfully obvious. At any given time, someone *must* have access to the backups.

You could set up a rotating schedule of duty, where one person who has the keys is always on call, and the keys are passed on to the next person when a shift is up. However, that solution is not foolproof. If there's an emergency, the person on call could forget to hand the keys off to the next person, or the person on call could be rendered inaccessible through a dead beeper battery or downed telephone line. Better to trust two people with the keys to the backups and server so that if the person on call can't be reached, you have a backup key person.

CALLING IN THE MARINES: DISASTER RECOVERY SERVICES

Disaster recovery isn't always fully successful. Perhaps your backups don't work or have themselves been destroyed. One more option remains before you have to tell everyone that everything they were working on for the past month is irretrievably gone: data recovery centers. Data recovery centers are staffed by people who are expert at getting data off media (most often hard disks, but not always) that can't be accessed by normal means.

Not all data recovery centers are the same. Some data recovery centers (in fact, the first data recovery centers) are staffed with people who are really, really good at getting dead hard disks back up and running. Using their skill, they can resuscitate the dead drive, copy its contents to other media, and then return the data—on the new media—to you.

Other data recovery services can retrieve data not recoverable with ordinary methods. These services operate at a binary level, reading the data from the dead media (sometimes even opening the hard disk, if the problem is serious enough) and then copying the data to your preferred media. Turnaround time is typically no more than a day or two, plus the shipping time.

The cost of data recovery depends on the following:

◆ The method of recovery used (the places that just fix hard disks tend to be cheaper but can't always recover the data)

◆ The turnaround time requested

◆ The amount of data recovered

Consider storing irreplaceable data on a different physical drive from data you can easily replace. A data recovery service can't selectively restore data. That is, if the data files and the system files are stored on a single physical disk, you can't save yourself a little money by asking the center only to recover the data files, even if the data is on two different logical partitions.

Until recently, you had to send the hard disk to the data recovery center to have its data retrieved, and this meant not having the data for at least a couple of days. Remote data recovery services can fix some software-related problems without requiring you to ship the drive anywhere or even take it out of the computer case. Using a direct dial-up connection, the data recovery center may be able to fix the problem across the telephone line.

IS SPECIAL SOFTWARE REQUIRED FOR THE BACKUPS?

Must any special software be loaded for the backups to work? I nearly gave myself heart failure when, after repartitioning a hard disk and reinstalling the operating system, I attempted to restore the backups that I'd made before wiping out all the data on the file server's hard disk. The backups wouldn't work. After much frustration, I figured out that Service Pack 2 had been installed on the server. I reinstalled the service pack from my copy on another computer, and the backups worked. I just wish I had figured that out several hours earlier.

Do the Backups Work, and Can You Restore Them?

Do the backups work, and do you know how to restore them? Verifying backups takes a little longer than just backing them up, but if you verify, you know that what's on the tape matches what's on the drive. So, as far as restoring goes, practice restoring files *before* you have a problem. Learning to do it right is a lot easier if you don't have to learn under pressure, and if you restore files periodically, you know that the files backed up okay.

Have Users Backed Up Their Own Work?

In the interest of preventing your operation from coming to a complete halt while you're fixing the downed network, it might not be a bad idea to have people store a copy of whatever they're working on, and the application needed to run it, on their workstation. People who only work on one or two things at a time could still work while you're getting the server back online.

Disasters shouldn't happen, but they sometimes do. With the proper preventive planning beforehand, they can become entertaining war stories, rather than sources of battle fatigue.

Chapter 22

Installing and Managing Remote Access Service in Windows 2000 Server

IT SEEMS LIKE IT was only a few years ago that the concept of remote computing or dial-up connectivity was relatively unknown. As far as most of the world was concerned, there was no such thing as the Internet, the idea of telecommuting hadn't been born yet, and e-mail didn't exist. Remote connectivity and dial-up modems were vague, mysterious technologies as far as the average person was concerned. Once considered the tools of businesses and technically oriented individuals to simply get "data" from one location to another, these concepts have now become part of everyday life.

Technology has changed the world in some remarkable ways, but the most amazing way is how "connected" people are these days (or, at least, can be if they *want* to). Home computers are becoming more and more common, and the average home consumer can buy a dial-up modem just as easily as a toaster or CD player. Employees are being equipped with everything from laptops to palmtops and being sent out on the road, with the expectation that they should be just as connected on the road as they are when they're in the office. For better or for worse, this onslaught of technology has brought with it a demand for "easy connectivity—anytime, anywhere."

These demands have put a heavy burden on the backs of system administrators. Not only does the typical administrator have to handle day-to-day support issues *within* the office, but with so much work happening outside the office it seems to have made an already difficult job seem impossible at times. Unfortunately, there isn't a magical solution for everyone yet (I doubt there ever will be), but Microsoft's Remote Access Service (RAS) has been designed and improved over the years to help administrators deal with some of these demands.

Originally developed in the early days of Windows NT, RAS was initially bundled as part of the base operating system. I've always felt the reason for this (at least partially) was to give NT a competitive advantage against other network operating systems out on the market—namely Novell. When remote computing was first starting to take off, Novell was the primary player in the NOS market and they had developed add-on products like NetWare Connect to support dial-up connections to NetWare networks. Products like NetWare Connect worked well and gave users the connectivity they needed, but these products had to be purchased separately and the license costs often increased in direct proportion to the number of simultaneous dial-in connections that needed to be supported.

While I can't be absolutely certain this is the reason Microsoft chose to bundle RAS in with the operating system for free, it certainly seems like a reasonable assumption. As many recent court cases have highlighted, "bundling" is a popular Microsoft tactic to gain market share. Personally, I know of at least a few organizations that started deploying NT in its early days simply because of the number of things that were included for free with the operating system—things they would have had to pay extra for with any other network operating system. Whatever the reasons were, NT began to take off, and RAS capabilities grew with each new version of the operating system.

Microsoft has improved RAS with each new version of Windows NT to the point where it has grown into a full-featured remote access platform capable of handling even the most demanding environments. By the time Windows NT 4 was released, RAS was a solid, reliable part of the NT operating system. The Internet was a few years along in its transition from the government and education environment into the commercial world, and it was becoming more common for people to try to leverage their investments in Internet connectivity to meet their remote access needs. With the release of NT 4, Microsoft included support for Point-to-Point Tunneling Protocol as a means of encapsulating RAS packets and sending them over the Internet instead of a modem. The phrase "virtual private networking" started becoming a buzzword in the vocabulary of network administrators, and Microsoft improved on the virtual private networking capabilities of NT 4 by later releasing a routing update called Routing and Remote Access Service (RRAS).

With the final advent of Windows 2000, Microsoft has put together the most comprehensive set of remote access capabilities to date, consolidating all the previous technologies and capabilities in an easy-to-use interface. But with *so* many options available, at times it can be hard to know which is your best choice. In the pages that follow, I'll discuss what some of your options are, some common scenarios you will probably run into, and the solutions for those problems.

Common Applications for Remote Access Service

For the purposes of this text, we'll assume that Remote Access Service is divided into two distinct functions: accepting inbound calls and placing outbound calls. With the advent of Windows NT 4, Microsoft now commonly refers to the latter as Dial-Up Networking (DUN for short), and receiving inbound calls has pretty much always been referred to as Remote Access Service (or RAS). Even though RAS and DUN share some of the same setup and installation routines, when you see a reference to DUN, you can assume it is for an outbound call.

With that clarification taken care of, let's take a look at some of the tasks you can accomplish with the Remote Access Service in Windows 2000 Server.

Connecting to the Internet

One of the more commonly used capabilities of Dial-Up Networking is to allow your computer to dial in to an ISP—usually via Point-to-Point Protocol (PPP)—and communicate with distant servers and hosts across the Internet. Although this might commonly be used for simple browsing and file transfers on a server, it is becoming common for e-mail and proxy servers to function entirely over dial-up connections to the Internet.

Windows 2000 Server includes several functional improvements over previous versions of Windows NT when it comes to dial-up networking. Features such as demand dialing, reestablishing failed links, and repetitively dialing nonresponsive numbers make Win2K dial-up networking a robust platform for establishing Internet connections and keeping them online.

Accepting Incoming Calls from Remote Clients

Traveling workers, telecommuters, and late-night workaholics all share one thing in common: they all eventually need access to corporate resources from remote locations. Remote Access Service can serve as a platform to get these users connected into your internal networks and servers.

Whether you need to allow access to your NT network, Novell servers, Unix hosts, or any other internal devices, RAS can act as a universal gateway for all your inbound communication needs. By accepting inbound connections from several different devices (analog, ISDN, X.25, VPN) and routing the traffic to your internal network, RAS can provide seamless networking for your users. Workstations dialed into a network over RAS will work exactly the same as they would if they were connected directly to the network (albeit a bit slower—more on that later).

Connecting to a Private Network

In addition to connecting a Windows 2000 Server to the Internet, it's often necessary to connect one network to another—perhaps to transfer data to suppliers or clients. In any case, Windows 2000 Server can be connected to another private network just as easily as to the Internet and take advantage of the same link-reliability features.

Acting as an Internet Gateway

In response to popular demand, Microsoft has added the capability for a Windows 2000 Server to share an Internet connection among clients connected to an internal network. By the addition of network address translation (NAT) capabilities in Win2K, Windows can now act as a sort of proxy for getting internal clients connected to the Internet.

NOTE   *It is worthwhile to note that this "proxy" service for getting internal clients connected to the Internet over a shared connection is completely different from the Microsoft Proxy BackOffice application, or their current version of Proxy — Internet Security and Acceleration (ISA) Server.*

Although this service will primarily be of use to small and home offices, it is a dramatic (and welcome) addition to the suite of services contained in RAS.

Accepting VPN Connections from Remote Clients

Along with the advent of the Internet in the corporate world, the concept of virtual private networking has emerged and become one of the hottest areas in networking. Virtual private networking, loosely defined, is a means of running a secure, private network over an insecure public network. Or, in plain English, you can have clients get connected (securely) to your office network by simply having an Internet connection and a valid (public) IP address and then establishing a VPN session to your RAS server. The VPN session is secure and encrypted, so your private data is protected as it passes over the public network (i.e., the Internet).

Microsoft has leveraged their investments in RAS in the development of virtual private networking in Windows 2000. By incorporating PPTP and L2TP protocols within the operating system, you can effectively set up "virtual" modems that work over IP networks, instead of analog or digital circuits. The methodology and terms used to implement these virtual modems are the same that are used for regular modems, so learning how to implement virtual private networking is made easier.

Dialing Up a Remote Network and Routing Traffic

With the addition of the Routing and Remote Access Service update to Windows NT 4, Microsoft made it easier for a Windows NT Server to act as a router, connecting to remote networks as needed and routing traffic. This type of connection between locations is commonly referred to as wide area networking or WAN connectivity.

With no more hardware than a dial-up modem at each site, internal clients and workstations can access resources on remote networks through this capability. By simply programming your internal workstations and devices to use your Windows 2000 Server as a "gateway," RAS can accept client traffic destined for a remote network, establish a connection to that network, and then pass the traffic across the connection as necessary. Since most office-to-office connectivity has traditionally been handled via costly dedicated circuits, having this ability is a tremendous benefit.

Already, this capability is helping organizations act in a completely "virtual" capacity—appearing to have a centralized network of resources that are actually individual servers spread across several sites, joined by demand-dialed dial-up connections.

Bandwidth Planning and Considerations

Before we begin discussing what types of hardware and software you need to start using RAS, it's important to make sure you have an understanding of when RAS would and wouldn't be a good solution. The two most important factors in determining this are speed and reliability.

No discussion of remote access would be complete without defining the two different types of communication that are often referred to when you hear the phrase "remote access." These are sometimes referred to as *remote-node* and *remote-control* technologies. They may sound similar, and as far as end users are concerned they're basically the same, but these two methods of remote access are in fact very different. Unfortunately, many administrators are often left with implementing vague management directives such as "make sure that our employees can work while they're on the road," which are amazing oversimplifications of remote access's complexities. It's important to understand the capabilities and limitations of each type of access so you can make the best decision for your needs.

Remote Node

RAS is a remote-node method of communication and a very flexible and versatile means of getting users or networks connected to one another. Overall, I prefer remote-node solutions over remote control for most applications, but having an understanding of how remote node works will help you recognize the best time to use it.

One of the simplest ways to visualize remote-node communication is to view the phone line connecting a client to a network as a *very* long network cable. Like any normal network cable in your office, this one is plugged into two locations. It starts at the user's workstation or laptop, goes through the phone company, and then ends at a modem in your office. Visualize that entire connection as a network cable. That modem, in turn, is connected to a RAS server (or another similar device), and the RAS server is—presumably—connected to your network. The RAS server accepts the incoming data from that dial-in user and then simply "passes" their data onto a local network segment. The same is true for outgoing data. The RAS server will see any outgoing data destined for that user on the network and transmit it over the phone line. As far as end-user functionality goes, your network should work exactly the same way in the office as it does dialing in, albeit much slower.

Since typical office network connections these days are running at speeds of upwards of 10,000,000 to 100,000,000 bits per second, throughput can be amazingly fast. So fast, that it is easy to overlook the amount of data that is actually traveling across your network. Considering the fact that the best analog modems available today are only reaching speeds of 56,000 bits per second, throughput can be a problem with remote-node solutions. Basic math indicates that there's only about 1/20th of the bandwidth available over a 56K modem in comparison to a 10-megabit Ethernet connection. That simple fact has a direct impact on the speed and performance of applications being used on the network. For example, a 2.5-megabyte Word document might open up in just a few seconds on a 10-megabit Ethernet connection in an office, but on a 56K modem connection, that document could take upwards of a few minutes to open up.

CALCULATING MODEM TRANSMISSION TIMES

Use the following formula to calculate modem transmission times:

$$\frac{\text{File size in "bytes"} \times 8}{\text{Speed of connection in "bits" (i.e., 56k = 56,000)}} = \text{Transmission time in seconds}$$

CASE IN POINT: CHOOSING THE RIGHT REMOTE ACCESS SOLUTION

If you implement a RAS solution without having some of these facts in your arsenal, you could end up with a solution that is effectively useless. Consider, for example, the case of one of my clients— let's call them the XYZ Corporation. The XYZ Corporation was in the process of moving into a new building but had to leave their accounting software and data on the file server in their old building due to several licensing and political issues. The accounting software was an old FoxPro file-based program that had served them well for many years, but it was eventually being replaced when they moved.

Their initial desire was to just have users dial in to the network in the old building and work on the accounting application as they did before. However, since the accounting application was "file-based" as opposed to being "client-server" (more on that later), the amount of data going back and forth between their workstations and servers was simply too great to make a remote-node solution work for their application. Simple analysis of their traffic indicated that their primary users of the accounting software were easily transferring 20 to 40 megabytes worth of data across their network in *as little as an hour*. If you've ever downloaded a large application from the Internet over a modem, you know how long it takes to move that much data—you probably start your download overnight and check it again the next morning.

Remembering our calculations from earlier, only about ¹⁄₂₀th of the bandwidth was available to XYZ Corporation over a dial-up remote-node connection. Quite simply, they were not going to be able to move that much data over a modem and maintain usable response times—a remote-node solution was *not* going to work for this client with this specific application.

The key factor that worked against XYZ Corporation was the fact that their critical application was file-based instead of being client-server. I can't emphasize enough how important it is to understand the mechanisms that computers typically use to move data around, so let's walk through some example applications of each of these types, see how they work, and see why some don't work well with remote-node solutions while others do.

FILE-BASED APPS VERSUS CLIENT-SERVER APPS

Consider, if you will, a simple Microsoft Access database of names and phone numbers that you have stored on your computer. For discussion purposes, we'll assume that you have not "indexed" this database (a process which makes searching databases faster) and are trying to look up the phone number for an individual with the last name of Toombs. To find this name and number, you'd launch your Microsoft Access application, open your phone number database, and then do a search on the last name. Once you submit your search, your CPU would talk to your hard drive controller, tell it to open the database on your hard drive, and retrieve the first record in the database. When the first record comes back, it turns out that it's for somebody named Anderson. The CPU realizes that Anderson doesn't equal Toombs, so it dumps the first record from its memory and then requests the second one. The second record is for Daily. Daily doesn't equal Toombs either, so once again the CPU would dump that record from memory and read the third one. And so on, and so on, until it finally got to the record for Toombs. Once it successfully finds Toombs, it displays the record on the screen.

The important factor to take note of is the repetitive process the CPU had to go through to get the data it needed. It had to keep communicating with the hard drive controller to get the next record, and then receive the response (the actual data) and check it. Given how speedy today's computers are, this all happens in the blink of an eye. But as you can see, there's a lot of communication that has to go on to make that simple operation work.

That communication, however, is all taking place between the internal components of your systems—from the CPU, across the data bus, through the hard drive controller, to the hard drive, and back again. Since these devices are directly connected to each other, they're very fast. However, suppose you move that phone number database off your hard drive and onto a file server so everyone in your office can access it. If you do the same search as before, each time Microsoft Access has to get a new record to check, the CPU will send a request to the network controller instead of the hard drive controller. The network controller will transmit the request to the server for the record and wait for the response from the file server. Once again, the CPU has to request this information over and over again from the network until it finally finds the record for Toombs. Since a hard drive on a network file-server probably isn't going to respond as fast as the hard drive in your computer, response time suffers.

To put some rough numbers to it, when the database was stored on the computer's internal hard drive, you might have had a maximum of 20 megabits' worth of bandwidth between the components inside your computer (hard drive, controller, bus, and CPU). Let's assume the last-name search took

1 second to complete. Once you move the database on your file server, your maximum bandwidth might have stepped down to only 10 megabits, assuming you're on a 10-megabit network. In theory, a search that took 1 second before could now take 2 seconds. That's still not too bad, and these are rough numbers (don't hold me to them), but they do illustrate the point we're about to make.

The 1-second query operation became a 2-second query operation when the phone number database was moved off the local hard drive and onto the network file server. Part of the reason for that is the fact that the bandwidth between our CPU and the actual data was cut in half, from 20 megabits to 10. Since the CPU had to keep requesting each record in the file, the bandwidth available between the CPU and the data source plays a key role. Now, what if someone was dialing in to the network and trying to perform the same query? If you recall the 1/20th figure discussed earlier in regards to 56K modems, you can probably see where this is heading. Cutting the bandwidth down from 10 megabits to 56 kilobytes could potentially increase our search time twentyfold. It's entirely possible that our simple query could take upwards of 40 seconds over the 56K dial-up connection.

Now, I'll be the first to admit that I'm oversimplifying things here considerably to make a point. In reality, our example query probably wouldn't take 40 seconds over a dial-up connection, but the response time would be noticeably sluggish. Even if it only took 10 to 15 seconds to retrieve the data, slowdowns like that eventually produce productivity problems. The key to all this is the fact that bandwidth is a huge factor in remote computing if you have any applications that are file-based. So what's the solution? Try to stick with applications that are client-server based.

In keeping with our name-lookup scenario above, let's assume that the data is stored in a SQL Server database instead of a standard Microsoft Access file. Using Microsoft Access (the *client* in client-server) as a "front-end" on your workstation, you can submit the same query for the last name Toombs as before. However, instead of requesting each record individually this time and checking them one by one, Access will transmit a request to the SQL Server software (the *server* in client-server) for a specific record. Access will transmit a specific request such as "get me the record(s) with a last name of Toombs." Small requests like those transmit very quickly, even over a slow connection (like a 56K modem). At that point, the responsibility of retrieving the correct data has shifted from the copy of Microsoft Access running on your CPU and is now in the hands of the SQL Server. Since the SQL Server presumably has high-speed access to the drives that store the data (most likely its own drives), it can find the answer in a few microseconds and then return an appropriate response back to Access.

The key thing to look for in determining whether an application is client-server or not is to see if there are two separate parts to the application. One part will run on your client workstations, and a second part will run on the server that stores your data (or at least on a server nearby with a high-speed connection on it). If there are two parts to your application, it is probably a client-server application and you shouldn't run into too many difficulties with remote-node users using it. However, if there aren't two parts to your application—if the only part is the client software that just uses directories and files on your file servers—you might run into performance problems using remote-node solutions.

Opening Word documents and Excel spreadsheets is—in effect—a file-based application, so it's worthwhile to look at your average document size to see how quickly it might transmit over a slow connection. Refer to the transmission times formula earlier in this section and figure out how long some sample documents would take to transmit over a modem. If most of your documents are simple and text-based, you probably won't run into too many performance issues. However, if your users typically work with large, multi-megabyte documents on your server, you might need to consider other options.

Remote Control

If remote-node communications can be viewed as using a phone line as a long network cable, then remote-control communications should be viewed as using a phone line as a long keyboard, mouse, and video cable. Remote-control solutions, by definition, allow you to remotely take control of a workstation on your network over a dial-up connection. Software on a workstation would typically have some sort of remote-control software running on it (such as pcAnywhere) and a modem attached to it. This is sometimes referred to as the host PC, since it is typically waiting to host an incoming caller. Then, presumably from another location, another workstation with compatible remote-control software would call into the host PC.

Once the two PCs have negotiated a connection, the host would begin sending its screen data to the calling computer, in effect letting the person at that calling station see everything that is on the remote screen. The calling workstation would then pass any keystrokes or mouse movements to the host PC, which would perform those actions just as if the user were sitting at the host PC doing them him- or herself. In effect, the remote-control software is tapping into the keyboard, mouse, and video input/output of the host PC and making it available to a remote PC over a phone line.

Traditionally, remote-control solutions have been a bit more expensive to develop and scale due to the increased hardware requirements on each side. Whereas one RAS server with an adequate amount of modems would theoretically be able to handle 256 simultaneous inbound modem connections, having that many simultaneous connections using certain remote-control products could require 256 computers—one to receive each of the connections. That can be rather cost prohibitive in most cases, not to mention being difficult to manage. However, it is worth mentioning because in some cases it might be the only remote access solution that would work in your environment.

It is also worth mentioning that Microsoft is including some remote-control functionality in Win2K with the bundling of Terminal Server with the base operating system (hmmm, there's that "bundling" concept again). If you are in a position where a remote-node solution won't meet your needs, you might want to take a look at it and see if Terminal Server will work for you. Terminal Server can be a worthy option since it doesn't require a separate computer to handle each inbound connection; instead, it requires one huge computer, and everybody runs a Windows session on that device (note: there are some other third party products which function in a similar manner).

NOTE   *For more detailed information on Terminal Server, see Chapter 15.*

Since you've gotten this far, I'm assuming that you feel RAS is the right solution for you and you're ready to start working with it and implementing it on your network. If that's the case, keep reading. Let's talk a bit about what type of hardware and circuits you're going to need to have in place to make this all work.

RAS Hardware Requirements

One of the first things to determine in remote networking is where you plan on connecting to and how fast you want to connect. Often, one or both of those criteria will help you determine what your available communications options are. In most instances, that will leave you with one of the following options:

Connection Type	Typical Maximum Speed	Typical Maximum Distance
Analog modem	Asymmetrical: 53Kbps down, 33.6 up	Unlimited, usually domestic
ISDN	BRI—128Kbps, PRI—1.544Mbps	Unlimited, usually domestic
X.25	2400bps—64Kbps	Global
Serial cable	Serial port max—230Kbps in most cases	"Physically near (less than 50 feet)" according to Microsoft
Infrared	Varies	Very close, line-of-sight
Parallel cable	Up to 500Kbps	Very close
Frame relay	1.544Mbps	Global

Of course, it should go without saying that any devices you are considering purchasing for use with RAS should be checked against Microsoft's Hardware Compatibility List (HCL) to make sure they are compatible with Windows 2000. By checking for HCL compatibility, you can be sure your choice of hardware has been specifically tested for compatibility with Win2K and has met the standards Microsoft has deemed necessary to be considered "compatible."

Also, if you're purchasing modems from a manufacturer that has several different models to choose from, pick your product carefully. While some modems might cost more than others due to features like voice or fax capability, if you're looking at two different models from the same manufacturer with the same capabilities, I'd suggest buying the more expensive of the two. The reason for this is quite simple: lower-cost modems are often designed by manufacturers primarily for light-duty home use applications. These are usually the modems you will see on the shelves in retail computer outlets. They are marketed to consumers and designed with tolerances and specifications targeted at the average consumer's needs. This doesn't take into consideration the more demanding needs of using modems for routing links, mail servers, etc.

Case in Point: Choosing the Right Modems

Here's a real-life case in point from one of my clients. ABC Software Company was having several problems with users calling into their RAS server. They had purchased modems built by one of the top manufacturers (if I told you the name, 90 percent of you would recognize it), but they had purchased the consumer-grade modems off their local computer store's shelf for roughly $100 each. Well, ABC Software Company seemed to always be running into odd, unpredictable problems with their remote access users. These users were unhappy and constantly calling with support issues; since their connections would randomly get dropped, they'd have trouble negotiating connections, sometimes the modems wouldn't answer at all, etc. Again, these modems on their RAS server were built by one of the top manufacturers, but they weren't the right tools for the job.

We decided to remove all the $100 modems and replace them with the $200 commercial-grade modems from the same manufacturer. The modems were the same speed and had roughly the same features, but as soon as we changed to the new modems, all the odd problems with their dial-in users disappeared. Just like that. The moral of the story: Saving money is good, but not if it ends up costing you more in the long run.

With that out of the way, let's take a closer look at your hardware and circuit options, and then we'll jump into configuring RAS on your Windows 2000 Server.

Analog Modems

Analog modems are the most commonly used connection device on RAS servers these days, so a good portion of our examples and configurations throughout this chapter will be using them.

A primer on how modems operate is in order for those of you who are unfamiliar with the technology. Modems are devices that accept binary signals (ones and zeroes) from whatever device they are connected to, convert those binary signals into audible tones, and then transmit those tones over a phone line at a prescribed speed. (This process is described as "modulation" and is the derivative of the "mo" part of the word "modem.")

On the other side of the telephone line, another modem receives these audible tones and converts them back into the binary ones and zeroes they represent. Once they have been converted back ("demodulated"), they are passed through to the device the modem is connected to as binary data. As you probably guessed, this "demodulation" process represents the "dem" in the word "modem."

Therefore, to complete a remote access or dial-up networking connection via a modem, you will need the following:

◆ Modem on the transmitting computer

◆ Modem on the receiving computer (this may be out of your control, for example, if you are dialing in to an ISP)

◆ Telephone connection between the two modems

In today's world, analog modems can transmit *and* receive data over traditional phone lines at speeds anywhere from 300 to 33,600 bits per second (sometimes referred to as the baud of the modem). As we mentioned earlier, the modems on either end of the connection convert the stream of bits to analog signals and transmit them over the phone line at a prenegotiated speed. But what about those "56K" modems?

WHEN 56K ISN'T QUITE 56K

A lot of hype and marketing has gone into the 56K modems that are currently available on the market. The modem manufacturers would love for you to believe that these modems are running at the full 56,000 bits per second, in both directions, but unfortunately that isn't quite the case. If you're planning on implementing a remote access solution for your organization, it's important to understand exactly how these modems work, what speeds you can hope to get from them, and what you can and can't expect from them.

First, you should realize that 56K modems *cannot* send and receive data at that speed in both directions. At the time of this writing, the maximum bidirectional speed anyone has been able to get out of typical analog connections is 33,600 bits per second. Much of that has to do with analog connections and the signal loss that is inherent as the analog data travels from one location to another. However, modem manufacturers are clever and have found a way to work around that limitation by removing half the analog signaling from the equation. By using a special server-side modem at one of the locations and a digital connection directly into the phone company's central office, data can be sent all the way from the server-side modem to the phone company with zero signal loss. Once the signal is within the phone company's systems, it usually travels through their system completely digital as well. The net result of this is that speeds of up to 56,000 bits per second are possible but only in one direction—the direction going from the server-side modem to the phone company. Communication in the other direction—from the location with the analog modem toward the phone company—is still limited by the inherent signal loss and peaks out at 33,600 bits per second.

Companies like Internet service providers have been the primary beneficiaries of 56K technology, and 56K modems are a great tool for getting a bit more speed when connecting to the Internet. However, it's important to realize that *you cannot purchase two identical 56K modems, plug them into regular analog lines, and expect to get a connection any higher than 33,600 bits per second between them*. Without having a server-side modem at one of your locations and a digital line from that modem to the phone company, you will be bound by the existing 33,600 limitations.

It's also worth mentioning that even when dialing in to a location with a server-side modem that supports 56K, under current FCC regulations in the United States, if you're using an analog line you will *never* get a 56,000 connection. The FCC has placed limits on the amount of voltage *any* device can transmit over a phone line, which currently restricts all modems to a maximum capability of 53,000 bits per second. However, most analyses and studies of 56K modems have revealed that reasonable speeds to expect for your connections are anywhere from 42,000 to 48,000 for data coming from the server-side modem (or "downlink speed") and, of course, 33,600 for data going to the server-side modem (or "uplink speed"). The amount of speed you get will depend on the quality of the equipment at your local phone company, the condition of the lines in your area, and your physical distance from the phone company's central office. One of my own computers was never able to get speeds higher than 42,000–44,000bps when dialing into a local ISP until I recently moved. Nothing else changed with my computer except the location it was in, but when I dialed in from my new home, I was consistently connecting at 48,000 bits per second.

ISDN

A few years ago, a 56K analog modem would be more than enough bandwidth for most remote data needs. However, as computers have grown in size and complexity, so have the files and data that computers typically need to move around. Downloading multi-megabyte items from the Internet, such as Windows 2000 Service Packs, could literally take hours over a standard dial-up connection. Fortunately, Integrated Services Digital Network (ISDN) is an option to get more bandwidth without having to get a dedicated circuit in place.

ISDN typically comes in two different flavors, ISDN Basic Rate Interface (BRI) or ISDN Primary Rate Interface (PRI). The main difference between the two is speed (and therefore, price). BRI can support data speeds of up to 128Kbps over standard copper telephone lines, and PRI supports data speeds of up to 1.544Mbps over T1 cable. Since ISDN BRI can run over the same copper wires that most people have wired in their homes, it's more commonly implemented.

ISDN BRI consists of three separate data channels on one connection. Two of the channels are 64Kbps bearer channels, commonly referred to as B channels. These two channels, when combined, make up the 128Kbps that ISDN can use to move data from one location to another. The third channel (commonly referred to as the D channel) is a special 16Kbps out-of-band channel used for signaling between your equipment and the phone company. Although all three channels add up to 144Kbps, most ISDN implementations will either use one or both B channels, so we'll refer to ISDN as being able to support 64Kbps or 128Kbps.

To use ISDN for remote access, you will need the following:

◆ An ISDN modem at each location and, optionally, an NT1 network termination device (most ISDN modems come with these built in today)

◆ A digital ISDN connection at each location

Direct Options (Null Modem, Parallel, and Infrared)

Given the affordability and broad universal support for network cards these days, using a null modem or parallel cable to connect two computers has really become more of a niche than a mainstream use of RAS. However, there may be occasions when it is the only option—maybe you have a specialty device that can't support a network card and can only communicate with the outside world via a serial or parallel port. If that's the case, a null modem cable, parallel cable, or infrared connection between your systems can be used for a connection.

Null modem cables are typically available at any computer store or through mail-order catalogs. However, according to Microsoft, standard off-the-shelf null modem cables might not be wired correctly for use with RAS. If possible, have your cabling vendor build a custom cable according to the pin configurations listed in Table 22.1. By connecting the null modem cable to the serial ports on each of your devices, you can connect your two computers together as needed. However, you will be limited to your serial port's speed and distance limitations of roughly 50 feet.

TABLE 22.1: MICROSOFT-SPECIFIED NULL MODEM CABLING REQUIREMENTS FOR RAS

9-PIN TO 9-PIN		9-PIN TO 25-PIN		25-PIN TO 25-PIN		MAC RS422/ 423 TO 25-PIN	
HOST SYSTEM	CALLING SYSTEM	25-PIN	9-PIN	HOST SYSTEM	CALLING SYSTEM	MAC	WIN2K
3	2	2	2	2	3	1	6, 8
2	3	3	3	3	2	2	20
7	8	4	8	4	5	3	3
8	7	5	7	5	4	4, 8	7
6, 1	4	6, 8	4	6, 8	20	5	2
5	5	7	5	7	7	6	—
4	6, 1	20	6, 1	20	6, 8	7	—

Source: Microsoft Corporation

Parallel connections can be made between two computers using the standard or enhanced (ECP) parallel ports of each device. By connecting devices together in this fashion, it is reasonable to expect throughput speeds of up to 500–600Kbps, but the distance between devices is again very limited. Microsoft lists a specific vendor, Parallel Technologies, in their help files included with Windows 2000 as a source for compatible parallel cables to use.

NOTE *To contact Parallel Technologies about their DirectParallel line of products, call (800) 789-4784 or visit them on the Web at* www.1pt.com.

Infrared connections are new in Windows 2000 Server and will probably serve as a useful option for small offices. Since the connection distance is limited by the strength of the infrared signal *and* a direct line-of-sight requirement, it will be an easy method of connecting (no cables!) but limited in usefulness.

X.25

X.25 is a protocol that coordinates communication between multiple machines, routing information through a packet-switched public data network. Instead of establishing direct connections from one device to another, all devices in an X.25 network simply connect to a "cloud" and pass their data to the cloud. It is up to the company that maintains and manages the cloud to ensure that the data reaches the correct destination point. X.25 is a relatively outdated technology, which is why throughput speeds top out at 56K to 64K.

So, why use X.25? Well, even though it is an extremely slow transport medium, it is also an exceptionally reliable one. There is an extensive amount of error checking and correction that occurs as a part of the X.25 protocol, which makes it a worthwhile consideration in areas with poor telecommunication services. X.25 is available globally and in some cases may be the only reasonable option for connectivity in certain countries.

Frame Relay

Frame relay is quickly becoming a preferred option to X.25 connections, as it functions on roughly the same principle—each system passing data into a data cloud—but at much higher speeds. Frame relay can support connections ranging from 56Kbps all the way up to 1.544Mbps. Since frame relay only requires a single connection from each site into the cloud, it is an excellent choice for global connectivity, since dedicated wide area network links across continents could end up being prohibitively expensive to implement.

RAS Installation and Setup

Now that we've laid the groundwork for understanding how remote access works, it's time to start working through some of the sample applications discussed earlier.

Installing Devices for Remote Access

Since a modem is one of the most widely used tools for remote access services, we'll start by quickly walking through installing your modem on a Windows 2000 Server, making sure that the correct drivers are installed, ports are selected, etc.

To begin adding modems to your system, start by clicking the Start button on the Windows Desktop. Choose the Settings/Control Panel option, and then double-click the Phone and Modem options icon. If this is your first time using this option, you will be probably be prompted for information about your area code, what type of dialing the system should use (tone or pulse), etc. After you've entered some of that preliminary information, you will be taken to the Phone & Modem Options applet. Click the Modems tab. More than likely, you won't have any modems listed. Click the Add button to launch the modem installation wizard, as seen in Figure 22.1.

FIGURE 22.1

Install New Modem wizard

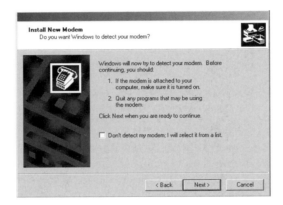

Depending on your preferences, you can either have Windows 2000 attempt to detect your modem automatically or you can select it manually from a list. If your modem is a bit older (as in, it was on the market before Win2K), you are probably safe letting Win2K attempt to find the correct driver for your modem. Leave the Don't Detect My Modem; I Will Select It from a List box unchecked, and click Next to begin the detection process.

If your modem is newer than the release of Windows 2000, or if you prefer to configure these options yourself (*I* prefer setting all these things myself), check the Don't Detect My Modem; I Will Select It from a List box, and click Next. You'll be taken to the screen shown in Figure 22.2.

FIGURE 22.2

Install New Modem selection screen

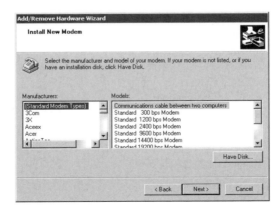

From here, you can choose from a myriad of different modem drivers. Find the driver that matches your modem, select it, and then click Next to install it. If for some reason an appropriate driver isn't listed for your modem, you can always use one of the standard modem drivers listed in the Standard Modem Types selection under Manufacturers. The standard modem drivers are reasonably good and are reliable in most circumstances. There are even standard modem drivers for 56K modems supporting the V.90, x2, and k56Flex standards. If your modem manufacturer included a driver disk along with the purchase of your modem, click the Have Disk button and insert your driver diskette in the appropriate drive. You will need to tell Windows to look in that location by giving it the appropriate path to check for the driver (usually A:\; consult your modem manufacturer's documentation for further information).

If you are installing your driver by hand, you will need to tell Windows what communications port this modem is connected to, as shown in Figure 22.3.

FIGURE 22.3

Selecting communications ports

If you have identical modems on all your communications ports, you can select the All Ports radio button. Otherwise, you should select the port your modem is currently attached to. If you have multiple modems on many ports (but not "all ports"), hold down the Ctrl key while selecting each port. When you have selected the correct ports, click Next to complete the installation. You should receive a confirmation dialog box indicating that your modem has been successfully installed.

Now that you have a modem installed, it's time to take it for a test drive. One of the easiest things to do in Windows 2000 is define a dial-up connection to the Internet, so we'll start there first.

Connecting to the Internet

It's no secret that Win2K was designed with the Internet in mind. Given that fact, Microsoft has made it easy to get your computer connected to the Internet. If you are running a Windows 2000 Server as a proxy server so your internal clients can surf the Web or if you're running it as an e-mail server, dial-up connections to the Internet are an option worth looking into. Due to some readily available "fine tuning" parameters you can set for dial-up connections, you can create a rather reliable link to the Internet with just a modem. Let's get started.

The first thing you'll need to do before connecting to the Internet is set up an account with an Internet service provider (ISP). We won't go through the specifics of how to do that here, but once you have an account you will need a minimum of three things handy to create your dial-up connection to the Internet:

◆ A local access phone number to dial (whether analog or ISDN)

◆ A username and password combination

◆ Optionally, an IP address to assign to your dial-up connection, and DNS addresses to use (most ISPs won't require you to program this information in, but in case yours does, be sure to have this handy in advance)

When you're ready to build your connection to the Internet, choose Start/Settings/Network and Dial-Up Connections. You should get a window that looks like the screen in Figure 22.4.

FIGURE 22.4

Network and Dial-Up Connections window

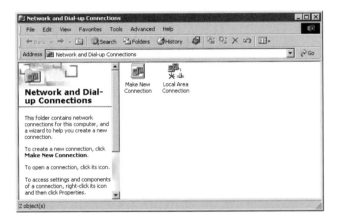

From here, double-click the Make New Connection icon to start the Network Connection Wizard, which will present you with a list of connection types you can establish. Select the Dial-Up to the Internet option and then click Next. This will launch the Internet Connection Wizard, which will walk you through the process of setting up an ISP account. The initial step of the wizard will ask you whether you want to define a new ISP account, transfer an existing ISP account, or configure your settings manually. For the purposes of being thorough, we'll walk through the manual setup option.

After selecting the I Want to Set Up My Internet Connection Manually option, you will be asked whether you want to set up your Internet connection over a modem or a LAN. If you have in-house Internet connectivity that is already running, then a LAN would be the option you would want to choose. However, since we're discussing modems, let's walk through the modem configuration.

After you select the Connect through a Phone Line and a Modem option and click Next, you will be taken through a three-step process to collect the information we discussed earlier, starting with the phone number as shown in Figure 22.5.

FIGURE 22.5

Entering account
connection
information

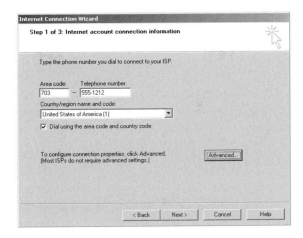

Enter the area code and phone number of your ISP's local access number in the fields provided. Select your appropriate country code, and leave the Dial Using the Area Code and Country Code field checked unless you want to override Windows 2000's ability to check the area code of the number you're dialing against its current location and adjust the dialing string accordingly.

As we mentioned before, if you need to manually assign an IP address for your server or DNS server addresses to use, this is the screen from which to do it. Click the Advanced button and you'll see a dialog box for setting the advanced connection properties of this dial-up connection. Click the Addresses tab, and you will see a screen like the one in Figure 22.6.

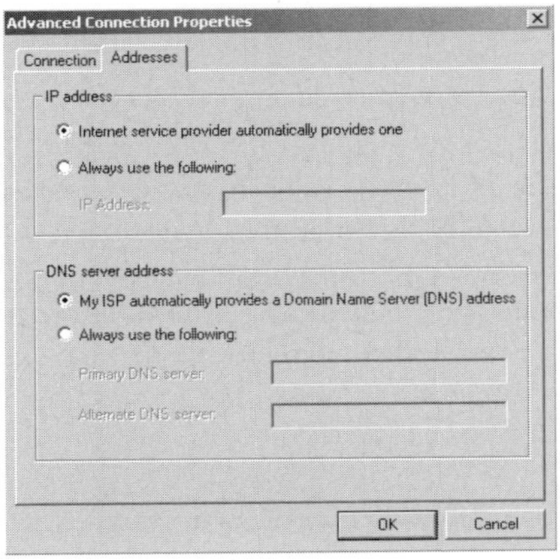

FIGURE 22.6

Advanced Connec-
tion Properties

Even though most ISPs will assign you an address automatically, if your ISP requires you to manually assign yourself an IP address, click the Always Use the Following radio button in the top of the window and enter the appropriate address in the IP Address field. Some ISPs may still require you to enter DNS server information (DNS is how Windows 2000 translates names like www.microsoft.com

into IP addresses). If so, click the Always Use the Following radio button in the bottom half of the window, and enter your primary and secondary DNS server IP addresses exactly as your ISP provided them to you. Once you're finished with any advanced settings, click the Next button to proceed to step two of the Internet Connection Wizard, as shown in Figure 22.7.

Step two of the Internet Connection Wizard is rather straightforward. Here you will enter the user credentials (username and password) your ISP has provided you for use with your account. This information will be stored along with all the other information for this dial-up networking entry so Windows 2000 doesn't have to prompt you for it every time you want to make a connection. If you don't feel comfortable having this information stored on your machine, leave the password field blank. You will receive a warning dialog box asking whether you want to proceed with a blank password. Answer Yes, we will correct this later in the text.

FIGURE 22.7

Defining user credentials in the ICW

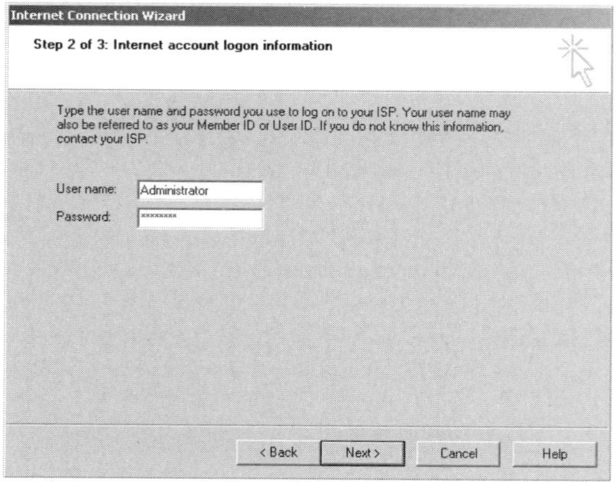

When you've entered your user credentials, click Next to complete the last step of the Internet Connection Wizard: assigning a "friendly name" to this connection. You can choose whatever you want here. Later, you will reference this connection by the name you give it. Enter a descriptive connection name, and then click Next.

If you have an Internet mail client installed on your system (namely Outlook Express), the Internet Connection Wizard will ask if you would like to configure your mail settings at this point. For the purposes of this chapter, we'll skip those settings for the time being—you can always set them later. The last thing you should see is a dialog box indicating that you have finished defining your connection.

Once you've completed defining your Internet connection, it should be shown as a grayed-out icon in the Network and Dial-Up Connections window, as shown in Figure 22.8.

At this point, you could double-click your new ISP connection and get connected to the Internet if you provided a password in step two of the Internet Connection Wizard. If that's the case, launch the icon and verify that it is working correctly. Once you're successfully connected, you should be able to connect to hosts on the Internet.

FIGURE 22.8

Network and Dial-Up Connections window with new ISP entry

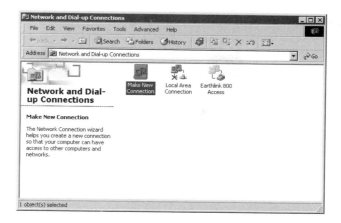

Optional Internet Connection Settings

After you've verified that your Internet connection is working properly, there are some optional settings you might find useful for controlling the behavior of this dial-up connection. Such items include:

◆ Programming a list of alternate numbers for Windows 2000 to attempt dialing

◆ Disconnecting idle connections (good for per-minute connections such as ISDN)

◆ Automatic redialing of busy or non-responsive numbers

◆ Automatic reestablishing of connections that have dropped

All these features are useful enough by themselves. However, if you're running a Windows 2000 Server that *depends* on having an Internet connection available, you'll find these extra features useful. It takes much less administration when a server can take care of establishing and reestablishing its own Internet connections without any human intervention.

To get to these options, open the Network and Dial-Up Connections window again and right-click your ISP dial-up entry. Select the Properties option, and you should get to the dialog box shown in Figure 22.9.

If your ISP has several local phone numbers available for you to use, you can program Win2K to cycle through the entire list until it gets a connection. Click the Alternates button next to the phone number, and you should see a screen like the one in Figure 22.10.

From the Alternate Phone Numbers dialog, you can enter as many numbers as you would like Windows 2000 to use to attempt to establish this connection. Click the Add button to add a new number to the list, and then use the arrow buttons on the right side of the dialog box to adjust the order of which number should be dialed first.

FIGURE 22.9

Editing general
properties of dial-up
entries

FIGURE 22.10

Entering alternate
dial-up numbers

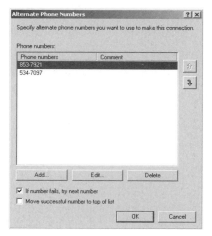

As an additional option, Windows 2000 can remember which number was successful last time you connected and try that one first if you check the Move Successful Number to Top of List option. This will make sure that if for some reason one of your ISP's local access numbers goes offline for a while, it won't stay in the top of the list and Windows 2000 won't keep trying to dial that number first.

When you're finished entering alternate numbers, click the OK button to return to the main properties dialog box for this dial-up connection. To reach the rest of the editable items for this connection, click the Options tab. This should bring you to a screen similar to Figure 22.11.

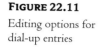

FIGURE 22.11

Editing options for
dial-up entries

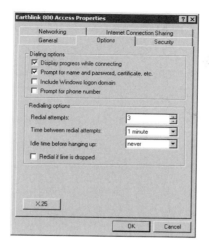

This dialog box has several options available, the most useful of which regard dialing, idle time-outs, and reestablishing broken connections. Let's go through these one by one and show how they can be used.

Prompt for Name and Password, Certificate, etc.   When you first created this dial-up networking entry using the Internet Connection Wizard, one of the steps you should have gone through (step two) was for entering a username and password to use for this connection. If you decided not to enter your password directly into the settings for this dial-up networking entry, you will want to check this option. Otherwise, Windows 2000 will simply try to use a blank password when establishing this connection. Checking this option will cause Windows to prompt you for a username and password to use instead of the existing username and password stored with this dial-up networking entry.

Redial Attempts and Time between Redial Attempts   If your local ISP has a problem with busy signals, you will appreciate these options. By choosing the number of times to attempt to redial and the time to wait between attempts, you can program Win2K to keep dialing your ISP until a number becomes available. Personally, I've found this setting to be extremely useful in times of inclement weather when everyone is stuck in their homes and clogging my ISP's lines.

Idle Time Before Hanging Up   If the same phone company that serves my area serves yours, then you are accustomed to paying for your ISDN access by the minute. These per-minute charges can add up to a rather substantial phone bill if your ISDN connection stays up all day. If your server only really needs to have a connection during business hours (for example, for proxy server clients browsing the Internet), set an appropriate idle time-out value here in minutes. Once the specified number of minutes has passed without any activity, Windows 2000 will drop the connection.

Redial If Line Is Dropped   It's simply a fact of life—dial-up connections "drop" sometimes. It just happens, but it can cause considerable headaches if people are depending on this connection being up and you happen to be away when it goes down. Checking this option causes Win2K to automatically redial and reestablish your connection if it drops. Assuming something hasn't failed on the ISP side of your connection, your link should come back up automatically within about a minute.

For this feature to work, you must have the Remote Access Auto Connection Manager service running. This service doesn't automatically start on Windows 2000 Server by default, so you will need to enable it manually. To do this, enter the Computer Management administrative tool by selecting Start/Programs/Administrative Tools/Computer Management or by right-clicking My Computer and selecting the Manage option. This will bring you into the Microsoft Management Console (MMC) for managing computers on your network. In the left pane of the MMC, you should see an option for Services under the Services and Applications group (you might need to expand Services and Applications to see it). Click the Services icon in the left pane, and you should see a listing of all the services running on your Windows 2000 Server in the result pane. The MMC screen should look like Figure 22.12.

FIGURE 22.12

Computer Management MMC for enabling RAS Auto Connection Manager

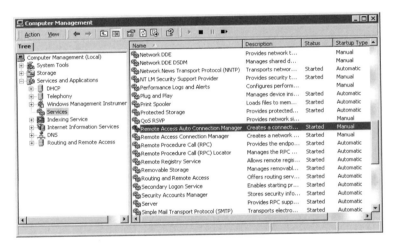

Find the Remote Access Auto Connection Manger service in the listing on the right, and double-click it to edit the properties. From here, you can start the service manually, and configure it to start up automatically every time your Windows 2000 Server boots up. The properties page for this service should look like Figure 22.13.

To start this service manually, click the Start button in the dialog box. If everything goes okay, the status of this service should change to Started. Now, to make sure that this service starts every time your Windows 2000 Server boots, select Automatic from the Startup Type pull-down box. Click OK to save your changes and then exit the Computer Management MMC.

To test the redial functionality, try establishing a connection with this ISP dial-up entry and then pull the phone plug out of your modem. Wait a few seconds so that you're sure the carrier has dropped (if you have an icon in your taskbar indicating that you're connected, it should disappear), and then plug the phone line back in. Within a minute, Windows 2000 should attempt to reestablish this connection for you without any intervention whatsoever.

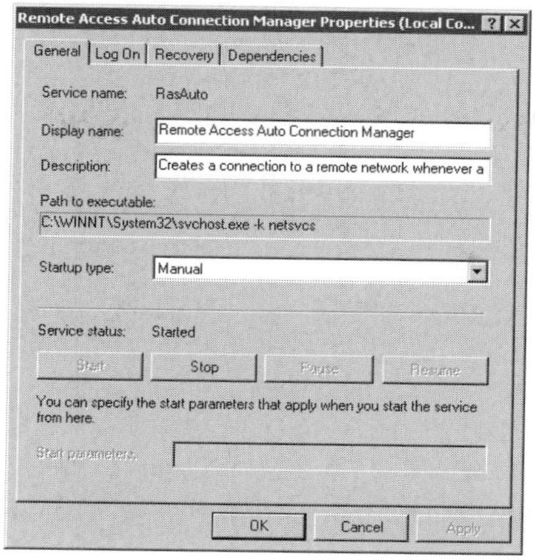

FIGURE 22.13

Service properties for RAS Auto Connection Manager

Accepting Incoming Calls from Remote Users

In today's business world, there are several buzzwords that tend to make an administrator's job a bit more challenging. Phrases like telecommuting, mobile computing, and sales force automation are all centered around one common principle—getting corporate data into the hands of people who need it, exactly when they need it, wherever they are located. In terms of systems administration, this typically means accepting inbound connections from remote clients. If you have yet to face this administrative challenge, rest assured that in the near future you most likely will. The tendency toward remote computing simply shows no signs of slowing down anytime soon.

Whatever your dial-in needs are, Windows 2000 can act as a universal gateway to get remote clients into your network. Thanks to built-in support for Point-to-Point Protocol (PPP), an RFC-defined dial-up standard, Windows 2000 can receive calls from almost any type of device. Windows PCs, Macintosh systems, Unix hosts, and even personal digital assistants (PDAs) can all establish PPP connections to remote networks. Windows 2000 can accept traffic from any of these devices and route it to the devices on your internal network, whether they're NT servers, Novell servers, Unix hosts, etc.

To start accepting incoming calls from remote clients, you will need the following:

◆ Windows 2000 Server with remote access software configured to accept incoming calls

◆ Connection device of some sort (modem, ISDN, X.25, etc.) connected to the Windows 2000 Server to accept calls from the remote clients

◆ Client computer capable of establishing a PPP session (Windows 95, 98, and NT 4; Windows 2000 Professional; Macintosh; 3Com Palm; etc.)

◆ Connection device of some sort (modem, ISDN, X.25, etc.) connected to the remote client and capable of establishing a connection to the corresponding device on the Windows 2000 Server

♦ Circuit (phone line, ISDN line, etc.) between the two devices

♦ User account on your Windows 2000 Server (or within your Active Directory) with dial-in rights granted to it

For the sake of brevity, we'll assume that you've gone through the detailed steps earlier in this chapter to add your modems (ISDN devices or whatever you might be using) to your Windows 2000 Server and they are functioning properly. With that out of the way, let's get started on accepting incoming calls from remote clients.

To be sure we're all working from the same baseline, we'll assume that you do not have the Routing and Remote Access Service installed on your computer. If you do have it installed, going through this procedure will stop your existing services and reinstall them with the answers provided to the configuration wizard.

Remote Access Server Installation and Setup

Start the installation for Routing and Remote Access Service by clicking Start/Programs/Administrative Tools/Routing and Remote Access. You will see an MMC window appear, and you should see your server listed somewhere in the left pane. Right-click your server, and select the Configure and Enable Routing and Remote Access option.

This will begin the RRAS installation process. This process is aided by a wizard that will help you configure the necessary services to allow remote clients to dial in. After a welcome dialog box (to which you will answer yes), the first dialog box you will see should look similar to the screen shown in Figure 22.14.

FIGURE 22.14

RRAS configuration wizard: role of server

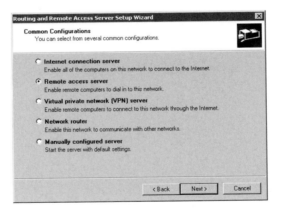

The first step of the configuration wizard is to determine what role your Windows 2000 Server will play. If you are simply looking to accept connections from dial-in clients, click the Remote Access Server radio button, and then click Next to move onto the next step of the wizard.

Figure 22.15 shows the next step of the configuration wizard, which allows you to verify that the protocols installed on your server are correct for the type of remote access you are trying to provide to your dial-in clients. The only correct answer to this dialog box is to answer Yes, All of the

Required Protocols Are on This List; answering No, I Need to Add Protocols will cause the wizard to stop at this step and abort the configuration process. Therefore, it is recommended that you select Yes and continue to the next step of the wizard, shown in Figure 22.16.

FIGURE 22.15

RRAS configuration wizard: configuring protocols

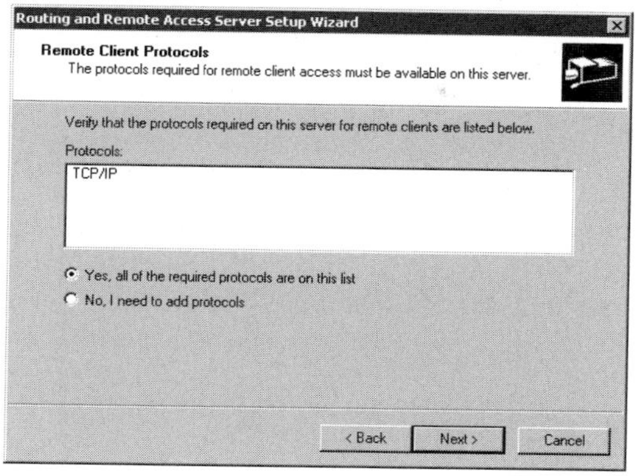

FIGURE 22.16

RRAS configuration wizard: IP address assignment

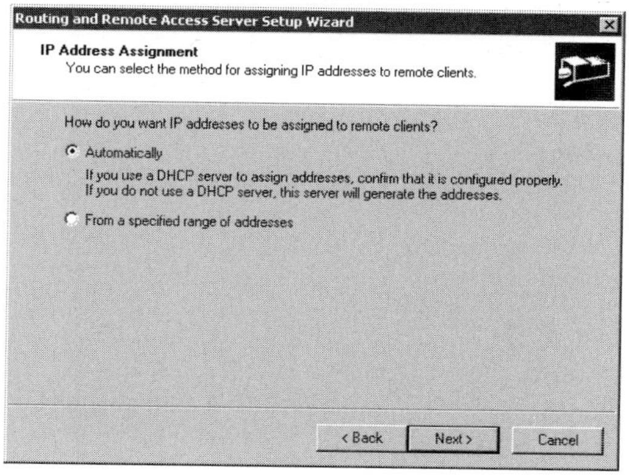

NOTE *You cannot, at this step of the wizard, specify only to use certain protocols. Although the dialog box might lead you to believe you can "select" which protocols to use, in reality the RRAS configuration wizard will automatically assume that you want to allow connections on all protocols. To remove protocols from your RRAS server, you will need to go back and manually reconfigure it after the wizard is through.*

The next step of the wizard—assuming you have TCP/IP installed on your server—will ask you how to handle assignment of IP addresses to remote dial-in clients. Since every device on the network must have its own IP address, your dial-in workstations need a way to get addresses as well. By default, RRAS will want to assign addresses to your dial-in users automatically from a DHCP server.

If you have a DHCP server running, you will probably want to accept the default Automatically option. Whether DHCP and RAS are running on the same server or on separate systems, the RAS service will attempt to obtain a DHCP-assigned address from the internal network and then pass it along to the remote client to use. The key with this option is to make sure you have a working DHCP server somewhere on your network and that it has enough IP addresses that can be used for dial-in connections.

NOTE   *For further reading on setting up a DHCP server, see Chapter 7.*

Under some special circumstances, you might want to control which IP addresses RAS hands out to dial-in clients. For example, if you have developed login scripts or other automation routines that depend on IP addresses, having a preset range might be useful. Or you might have security policies in place on your networks that only allow certain IP addresses to connect to certain devices. Either way, if you need to make sure RAS clients always fall within a certain range of IP addresses, select the From a Specified Range of Addresses option and then click Next to proceed to Address Range Assignment, shown in Figure 22.17.

FIGURE 22.17

RRAS configuration wizard: address range assignment

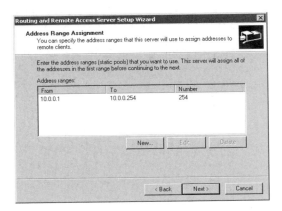

Through address range assignment, you can enter a series of IP address ranges for RRAS to use when clients dial in to your network. You can make these ranges as small or as large as you would like—just so long as you know that they are usable addresses within your network. To add a range (or ranges) to your system, click the New button and enter a start and end range of IP addresses to use. The New Address Range dialog box will automatically calculate how many addresses are in the range you provided. In the example shown in Figure 22.17, I have already entered a range of 10.0.0.1 to 10.0.0.254 for this RRAS server to use. When you have finished entering your addresses, click Next to proceed with the next step in the wizard, shown in Figure 22.18.

Although the next step of the wizard might look like it's simply asking if you have a RADIUS server available on your network, it's actually asking far more than that. This step of the wizard is asking how you would like to handle dial-in authentications. Your choices are limited to two simple options.

FIGURE 22.18

RRAS configuration
wizard: RADIUS
services

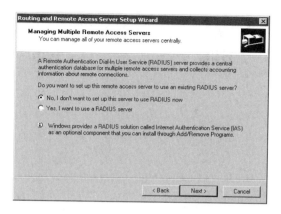

If you are currently using RADIUS services on your network (Remote Authentication Dial-In User Service) for authentication and logging of other dial-in access, you can set up your RRAS server to use the existing RADIUS server instead of using its own authentication and logging mechanisms. To specify your own RADIUS information, select the Yes, I Want to Use a RADIUS Server option, and then click Next. Since RADIUS is outside the scope of this chapter, we'll assume that you will stick to using Windows 2000's own authentication and logging mechanisms. Therefore, you can leave the default No, I Don't Want to Set Up This Server to Use RADIUS Now option, and then click Next to continue.

Since the option for RADIUS selection is the final step of the wizard, your server should be configured after you click Finish on the final panel of the wizard.

NOTE   *One of the more impressive things about Windows 2000 that was easy to overlook was the fact that the entire process for adding RAS services was completed without rebooting the server at all. I commend Microsoft on finally getting their operating system working so that it doesn't require a reboot after every minor change.*

Granting Dial-In Permissions to User(s)

Once you've successfully installed the Routing and Remote Access Service, the next thing to do is grant dial-in permissions to a user account in your Active Directory tree. (We'll assume you already have an account created for this purpose.)

NOTE   *If you need to add a new account for this exercise, see Chapter 9.*

To grant dial-in permissions to selected users, choose the Active Directory Users and Computers MMC by clicking Start/Programs/Administrative Tools/Active Directory Users and Computers. Navigate through the Active Directory tree to the user you want to grant dial-in permissions to, and right-click the corresponding record. By selecting the option to edit the properties for this user, you'll be taken to a dialog box to edit options for this user. Click the Dial-In tab, and you should be left with a screen similar to the one in Figure 22.19.

By default, the user account you've selected will probably have the Deny Access option selected at the top of the dialog box. Click Allow Access to grant dial-in permissions to this user. You also have the option to edit some user-specific settings through this dialog box.

FIGURE 22.19

Granting dial-in permissions via user properties

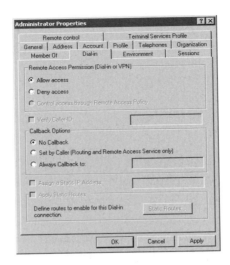

For example, if you'd like to implement an additional measure of security by making sure a certain user's remote access session always comes from a specific phone number, you have a few options available. First, if your modem and phone line supports caller ID service, you can simply select the Verify Caller-ID option box and enter the phone number this user must call in on. However, if you are using hardware that doesn't support caller ID or that service is unavailable in your area, you can achieve the same type of security by having your RAS server call the user back at a certain phone number. Selecting one of the Callback options available in the middle of the screen activates this feature.

If you have home users who dial in either via long-distance or local–long-distance, callback options might also save you some money when it comes to your remote access costs. If the telephone service you have in your office has a better per-minute rate than the rates your users typically have in their homes, you can save money on your remote access connections by having your RAS server call users back at the cheaper rates.

In addition to callback options, you can also specify a fixed IP address for this specific user to receive. This is a new feature in Windows 2000 and can be exceptionally useful when setting up internal access policies based on IP address (firewall rules, etc.).

Now, take a moment and relax. Your server is set up to receive calls. You should be able to test this by calling the number associated with your RAS server from a standard phone and getting a carrier tone. If you don't hear a carrier tone, double-check your work and make sure everything is connected properly. If for some reason you still don't get a carrier tone when you call in, try rebooting the server (oddly enough, this happened to me once, and rebooting it corrected the problem).

Changing RAS Server Configurations after Installation

Wizards are both a blessing and a curse for the Windows operating system. Although they make complex tasks easier, they also tend to assume several answers for you with no chance to change those assumptions. The RRAS configuration wizard is guilty of this practice; it will make several assumptions for you as you configure your system. You may want to check these configurations to make sure they are exactly the way you want them to be.

If you need to change any of your configuration at a later time, you can easily do so by right-clicking your server in the Routing and Remote Access MMC and then selecting Properties. Through the RRAS properties dialog boxes, you can add or remove support for certain protocols for dial-up connections, increase authentication security, and fine-tune the PPP controls for establishing connections to client systems. We'll walk through each of these areas, starting with the controls for security shown in Figure 22.20.

FIGURE 22.20

Editing security
properties for RAS
service

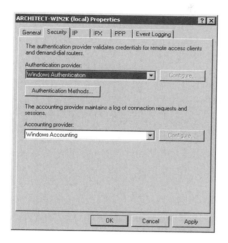

Through this screen, you can control several behaviors for the security and encryption used with your dial-up connections. Although there are pros and cons for using each (with the pros usually being increased security and the cons being limited client support), we'll discuss each option briefly so you can make your own judgements as to which is best to use.

By default, the authentication provider that should be automatically configured is Windows Authentication. If you have an external RADIUS server, you can change Windows to use the RADIUS server instead by selecting the RADIUS option from the pull-down box and then clicking the Configure button to define the RADIUS servers to use. Since RADIUS servers are out of the scope of this chapter, we'll simply stick to Windows Authentication methods.

By clicking the Authentication Methods button below the Authentication Provider pull-down box, you will be taken to a screen similar to the one shown in Figure 22.21.

FIGURE 22.21

Editing authentica-
tion types for RAS
service

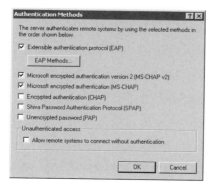

As you can see, there are several authentication options to choose from, as defined below:

Extensible Authentication Protocol (EAP)   Because security and authentication is a constantly changing field, embedding authentication schemes into an operating system is impractical at times. To solve this problem, Microsoft has included support for EAP, which is simply a means of "plugging in" new authentication schemes as needed. Currently, Windows 2000 Server only supports MD-5 Challenge and Transport Level Security (TLS, primarily used for smart-card support), but this option will allow for future authentication protocols to be plugged into the operating system easily.

Microsoft Encrypted Authentication (v1 and v2), MS-CHAP   Microsoft's derivative of CHAP, or Challenge-Handshake Authentication Protocol (see below). Using MS-CHAP allows you to encrypt an entire dial-up session, not just the original authentication, which is especially important when it comes to setting up virtual private networking sessions. MS-CHAP v2 support is included in Windows 2000 for all types of connections and in Windows NT 4 and Windows 95/98 (with the Dial-Up Networking 1.3 upgrade) for VPN connections.

Encrypted Authentication (CHAP)   Defined in RFC 1334, and later revised in RFC 1994, the Challenge-Handshake Authentication Protocol is a means of encrypting authentication sessions between a client and server. Since this protocol is defined by an RFC, it enjoys a broad base of support among many operating systems and other devices.

Shiva Encrypted Authentication (SPAP)   SPAP, short for Shiva Password Authentication Protocol, is an encrypted password authentication method used by Shiva LAN Rover clients and servers. Windows 2000 Server can act as a server when Shiva LAN Rover clients are dialing in by providing the correct authentication sequence for them.

Unencrypted (clear text) Password (PAP)   Password Authentication Protocol (PAP) is one of the last two options listed, and it is also one of the least secure. It is no more secure than a simple conversation from your server saying "What is your name and password?" to the client, the client responding with "My name is Doug and my password is 'let-me-in'." There is no encryption of authentication credentials whatsoever.

Unauthenticated Access   At first glance, this option wouldn't seem to make much sense—leaving a wide-open access point to your network with no authentication required whatsoever. However, when paired with caller ID verification, this option can make a simple and secure method for getting clients connected to your network.

If a dial-in user provides a username only, that username will be checked against the Active Directory. If there is a caller ID verification set for that user, the caller ID information will be checked and the connection will be accepted or rejected based on whether the information matches. If the user does not send a username at all, the Guest account will be used by default. Therefore, if you intend to use this option, you might want to disable the Guest account on your system (a good security practice to get in the habit of anyway).

Within the properties for the RAS service, you have the ability to fine-tune each protocol accepted by the RAS server and passed on to the internal network. By clicking the appropriate tabs (shown in Figure 22.22) for IP, IPX, NetBEUI, and AppleTalk, you can edit the following options for each protocol:

Allow *<Protocol>*-Based Remote Access and Demand Dial Connections (IP, IPX, NetBEUI, and AppleTalk)   To enable or disable support for individual protocols, check the boxes for each protocol to allow and uncheck the boxes for each protocol to reject. If you used the automatic wizard to install Remote Access Service, you might find that Windows 2000 Server enabled support for all the protocols on your system by default. However, good security practices dictate only opening up support for the protocols you need, so it's probably a good idea to remove any protocols you aren't using.

FIGURE 22.22

Editing security properties for RAS service

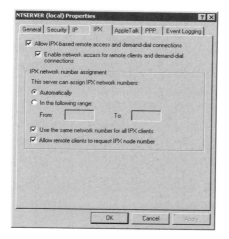

Entire Network Access for Remote Clients (IP, IPX, NetBEUI, and AppleTalk)   One way to increase the security of your dial-in system is to only allow dial-in users to access the dial-in server itself. For example, if traveling workers only need to access a set of word processing documents or spreadsheets, these could be kept on the remote access server. By unchecking the Entire Network Access for Remote Clients box, clients will only be able to access the RAS server itself.

Additionally, this is a useful option for protecting certain types of servers. For example, perhaps you only want your dial-up users to access your Windows 2000 or NT network which runs solely on TCP/IP. However, you might have Novell NetWare servers on your network running IPX that you don't want to allow access to. By removing access to the entire network for the IPX protocol, you can allow dial-in access to some systems and not others.

Dynamic Host Configuration Protocol—or—Use Static Address Pool (IP Only)   As was previously discussed in the configuration of Remote Access Service, here you can select whether your RAS server will use a DHCP server to hand out IP addresses to dial-in clients or if it will manually assign addresses from a static pool. If you choose to assign addresses from a static pool, you will need to provide the correct TCP/IP network address range and subnet mask to use.

NOTE   *For more information on calculating address ranges and subnet masks, see Chapter 6.*

IPX Network Number Assignment—Automatic or in the Following Range (IPX only)
Since IPX network numbers typically consist of two parts—a network address and a node number—you can configure what addresses RAS will assign to clients through this screen. If you have NetWare servers on your network, you may find it useful to assign a specific network number to your dial-in clients. For example, you might modify the login script on your NetWare servers to behave one way for internal clients and differently for dial-in clients, based on the IPX network number of the workstation.

Use the Same Network Number to All IPX Clients (IPX only)   If this option is checked, the RAS server will automatically assign the same network number to all IPX clients—either an automatic network number or one defined by allocating numbers. This will reduce the number of RIP announcement packets the RAS server will need to broadcast.

Allow Remote Clients to Request IPX Node Number (IPX only)   If your dial-in clients are capable of asking for a specific node number, check this option and your RAS server and dial-in client will negotiate a node address accordingly.

If you need to fine-tune the parameters for your RAS server to use when establishing PPP sessions with clients, click the PPP tab to edit the properties of these items, as shown in Figure 22.23. The default settings will be acceptable in most instances, but if needed you can enable or disable the following options.

FIGURE 22.23

Editing PPP properties for RAS service

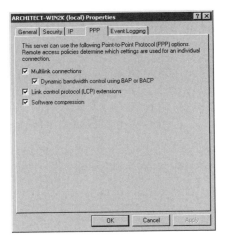

Multilink Connections   Multilink Point-to-Point Protocol (MPPP for short) was defined in RFC 1717 as a means of joining (often referred to as "bonding") two or more PPP sessions together to increase bandwidth. Effectively, you could double or triple your bandwidth between a client and a server if you had two or three modems at each location, two or three phone numbers, etc. This option must be selected if you want to be able to choose the next option.

Dynamic Bandwidth Control (BAP/BACP)   Defined in RFC 2125, Bandwidth Allocation Protocol (BAP), and Bandwidth Allocation Control Protocol (BACP) are similar in nature to Multilink protocol in that they are both used to bond connections together for increased bandwidth. However, while Multilink protocol is a "fixed" solution that will automatically join all the channels it can together, BAP/BACP will only initiate additional connections as needed due to high bandwidth utilization. This is an excellent option if you have connections that are subject to per-minute charges and don't need to have them online all the time.

LCP Extensions   Enabling Link Control Protocol (LCP) extensions is a necessary part of supporting callback security on a RAS server. If you are planning on having your system be able to call users back at a specified number, you must have this option enabled.

Software Compression   Never missing an opportunity to define a protocol for something and create another standard, Microsoft has developed the Microsoft Point-to-Point Compression (MPPC) protocol to compress data as it travels across a remote access link. MPPC is defined in RFC 2118.

In addition to configuring protocol and authentication types to use, you may also want to configure what ports on your system are used to accept incoming RRAS calls. For example, you may have some modems that are to be used strictly for dial-in and others strictly for dial-out. Unfortunately, the RRAS configuration wizard will simply assume you want to use *all* your modems for dial-in purposes.

To alter the configuration of ports on your system, return to the Routing and Remote Access MMC and expand your server in the left pane of the window. Below your server, you should see an option for Ports. Highlight that option, and then select Properties from the Action pull-down menu (or by right-clicking the item). That should take you to a window similar to the one shown in Figure 22.24.

FIGURE 22.24

Configuring RRAS ports via the Routing and Remote Access MMC

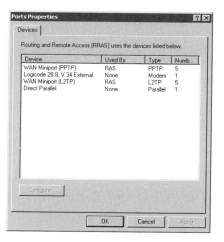

As you can see on this screen, all the interfaces that can support RRAS clients are listed for you to choose from. Highlight the interface(s) that you'd like to accept incoming calls from, and then click the Configure button. This will open the individual properties page for this device. Check the box labeled Remote Access Connections (Inbound Only) and—if you can—enter the phone number for the line connected to that device in the Phone Number of This Device field. The phone number will allow you to support BAP for devices to initiate additional connections to your server (although since this requires multiple modems and lines at each location, it might not be an option you need). Repeat this procedure for all the ports on your server.

NOTE *It is important to note that all types of ports are automatically configured for your RRAS server—including the VPN ports for PPTP and L2TP. If this server is accessible over the Internet, these ports will be "openings" that outsiders can use to try to authenticate to your network. I recommend that you change the Maximum Ports value for L2TP to zero and for PPTP to one (the minimum value allowed in RC2), unless you specifically intend to implement virtual private networking (discussed later in this chapter).*

Client Configurations

Now that you have a RAS server that's running smoothly, it's time to enable some clients and get connected into the network. While we can't cover every possible platform under the sun when it comes to remote access, we'll look at a few of the more common options, namely Windows NT 4 Workstation and Windows 9x. Windows 2000 Professional Dial-Up Networking will follow a routine very similar to the Windows 2000 Server Dial-Up Networking steps, outlined in detail in the next section.

All these client configurations assume that you have Dial-Up Networking already installed on your system and correctly configured. Assistance on installing Dial-Up Networking on other platforms is outside the scope of this book.

TIP *I frequently get calls from clients who have configured one of their users' home computers to dial in to the corporate network but are having trouble browsing the Network Neighborhood and seeing any resources. In most cases, this is due to the workgroup and domain settings on the home system not matching the settings for workstations in the office. Make sure you use the same settings in both locations.*

WINDOWS NT 4 WORKSTATION

From the Windows NT 4 Desktop, double-click My Computer and then Dial-Up Networking to bring up the main Dial-Up Networking program. If this is the first time you are using Dial-Up Networking, you might get a message about your phonebook being empty—this is okay because it is simply Windows telling you it doesn't know how to dial anyone yet. If you get that message, click OK to continue, and that should leave you at the main Dial-Up Networking screen as shown in Figure 22.25.

FIGURE 22.25

Dial-Up Networking in Windows NT 4 Workstation

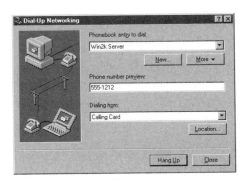

To add a new entry for your Windows 2000 Server, click the New button to start defining a new phonebook entry. The initial screen will let you enter information such as a friendly name to use for this phonebook entry, the number to dial, which modem to use, etc. Enter the appropriate information as needed and then click the Server tab to enter information about the server you are calling into. Your phonebook entry screen should look similar to Figure 22.26.

FIGURE 22.26

Selecting server options for a new phonebook entry, Windows NT 4 Workstation

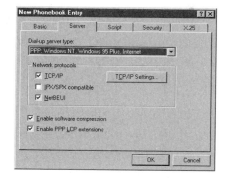

By default, Windows NT 4 Workstation will assume you are going to be dialing into a PPP-compatible server, so it will use that selection as a default for the dial-up server type pull-down box. Also, NT Workstation will assume you want to use software compression and PPP LCP extensions (as seen by the check boxes in the bottom of the window). These are also acceptable defaults for most dial-up connections and can be left checked in most cases. These settings directly correspond to the PPP settings defined on the configured RAS server.

By far, the most important settings in this dialog are the network protocol settings. In general, these settings should correspond directly to the protocols configured when installing the RAS server service, as seen back in Figure 22.15. The client workstation obviously cannot connect on certain protocols if they are not installed on your server, so make sure you are using the same protocols in each location. If you plan on using TCP/IP (which I expect most readers will), click the TCP/IP Settings button to define protocol-specific parameters if necessary. The TCP/IP Settings screen should look like the one in Figure 22.27.

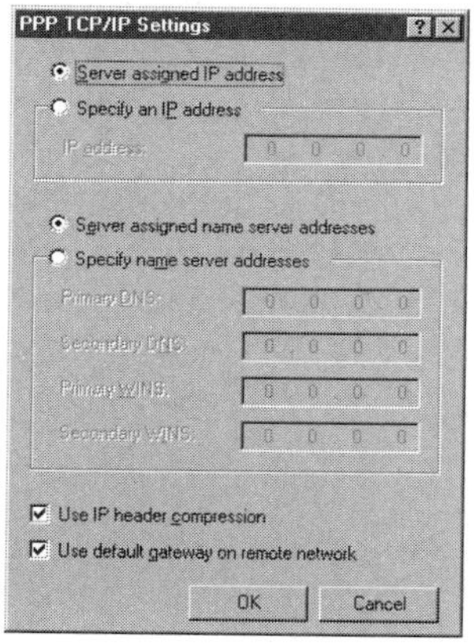

FIGURE 22.27

TCP/IP settings on Windows NT 4 Workstation Dial-Up Networking

For most installations, the default TCP/IP settings should work fine, but if your situation is a bit more specific, you can enter values for the IP address that the client should use and which DNS servers and WINS servers to use for name resolution. If you don't enter any settings for the DNS and WINS servers to use, the dial-up networking client will inherit the same values the RAS server uses itself. This is an important point, because if you are using DHCP to assign addresses, you might assume that any DHCP scope options you have added to your address space would be automatically passed along to your RAS clients. However, even if your RAS server is consulting your DHCP server for addresses to use, it will not pass DHCP scope options along to RAS clients. Settings for DNS servers and WINS servers to use will come directly from the same settings programmed into your RAS server. So, if you're using DHCP on your network, make sure you hard-code an IP address for your RAS server and program in the correct name server addresses.

Once you have set your server and protocol settings as necessary, click the Security tab to define the appropriate authentication options for your dial-in client. The security settings are shown in Figure 22.28. Just as the correct configuration for the server settings on the dial-up client depends on how your RAS server was configured, the security settings on the client will depend on how the security is configured on the RAS server as well.

FIGURE 22.28

Security settings on Windows NT 4 Workstation Dial-Up Networking

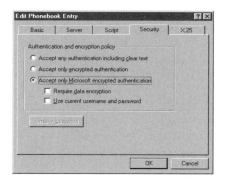

By default, Windows NT 4 Workstation selects the option to Accept Any Authentication Including Clear Text. If the RAS server is configured to only allow MS-CHAP authentication, then the Dial-Up Networking client will submit an MS-CHAP authentication and should be validated without any difficulty. If you run into problems logging in, make sure your authentication settings between your server and your client match on at least some level.

When you have completed making the necessary settings for this dial-up networking entry, click OK and then click Dial to dial in to your Windows 2000 Server. You will be prompted for a valid username, password, and domain name to log in with. Use the username(s) you granted dial-in permission to on your servers, click OK, and if everything goes according to plan your Windows NT 4 Workstation should be connected!

WINDOWS 9X

From the Windows 9x Desktop, double-click My Computer and then Dial-Up Networking to bring up the Dial-Up Networking program. If this is the first time you are using Dial-Up Networking, you might be asked to enter information about your local area code, whether to use touch tone or pulse dialing, and any prefixes you need to dial. Simply fill in the information and click OK to continue. This should bring you to the Make New Connection window shown in Figure 22.29.

FIGURE 22.29

Windows 9*x* Make New Connection

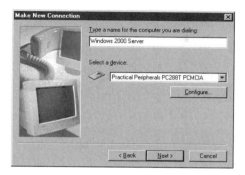

At the first step of the Make New Connection dialog box, you can enter a friendly name for this Dial-Up Networking connection and select which modem you'd like to use. Enter this information and then click Next to continue to the next step, shown in Figure 22.30.

FIGURE 22.30

Windows 9*x* Make New Connection, step two

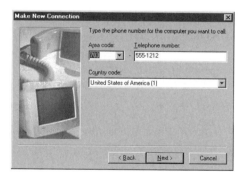

In the second (and final) step, enter the area code and phone number of your RAS server and then click Next to complete the creation of this Dial-Up Networking entry. By default, Windows 9*x* will assume several things about this Dial-Up Networking entry, including which protocols and security settings you'd like to use. For example, Windows 9*x* will select all the protocols installed on your system and try to use them over this Dial-Up Networking connection.

If you'd prefer to configure these options yourself instead of having Windows 9*x* assume what you want, go back to the main Dial-Up Networking window (the one with the Make New Connection icon) and you should see an icon for your Dial-Up Networking session. Right-click the icon, and select Properties to edit the configuration. You will see the properties pages for this Dial-Up Networking connection, as shown in Figure 22.31.

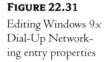

FIGURE 22.31

Editing Windows 9*x* Dial-Up Networking entry properties

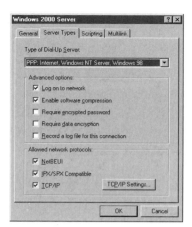

From here, you can (and should) change the security and protocol settings to match those of your RAS server. For example, if you only run TCP/IP on your corporate network, you don't necessarily need to have NetBEUI and IPX selected in your Dial-Up Networking session. Configure the settings accordingly, and then launch your session to verify that it works.

Managing Connected Users

If you need to keep tabs on users connected to your network, the Routing and Remote Access MMC can give you an overview of all remote access connections currently connected to your server. Whether connections are coming into your systems from VPN connections, serial connections, analog modems, or ISDN lines, you can get an overview of all your remote connections from one convenient console.

To manage connected users, start by launching the Routing and Remote Access MMC, by selecting Start/Programs/Administrative Tools/Routing and Remote Access. By expanding the details for your RAS server in the left pane, you should see a sub-item for Remote Access Clients listed below your system, along with a number next to it in parentheses. This number indicates the number of dial-in users currently connected to your system. This screen should look similar to the one in Figure 22.32.

From this screen, you can get an overview of how long users have been connected to your network, who is currently connected, which ports are in use, etc. By double-clicking any of the listed connections on your system, you can get advanced details about that individual connection, such as what IP/IPX addresses were assigned to the system, how much data has been transferred, etc. You can disconnect an individual connection from the same properties page by clicking the Hang Up button, or you can disconnect a user by right-clicking that user's connection in the main list of connected users. In addition to being able to disconnect a user from the main listing of connected users, you can also send a message to an individual user or to all connected users by right-clicking a connection and selecting either Send Message or Send to All, respectively.

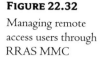

FIGURE 22.32

Managing remote access users through RRAS MMC

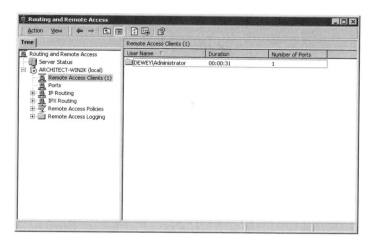

Connecting to a Private Network

Much like connecting to the Internet, at times you might need to connect your Windows 2000 Server to another private network. Maybe one of your servers needs to collect data from a client's systems or transmit product orders to a supplier. The private network might be another Win2K network, an NT network, a Novell network, or a network that contains a combination of servers and other systems. In any case, dial-up networking can get your Windows 2000 Server connected with a minimal amount of effort.

Before getting started, there are a few things you will need to have to complete making a connection to another network. Namely, you will need to have the following information available in advance:

◆ Access phone number to dial

◆ Username and password combination

◆ Protocols that will be used on the remote network

◆ Authentication the remote network will require

To get started, we'll once again be working through the Network Connection Wizard by clicking Start/Settings/Network and Dial-Up Connections and then choosing the Make New Connection icon. When the wizard starts, you should see the screen shown in Figure 22.33.

From this point, select the first option, Dial-Up to Private Network, and click Next to continue to the next step of the wizard, as seen in Figure 22.34.

Enter the phone number as prompted, and then click Next to get to the last step of the wizard, pictured in Figure 22.35.

FIGURE 22.33

Network Connection Wizard: connect to private network

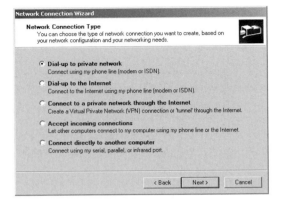

FIGURE 22.34

Network Connection Wizard: enter phone number

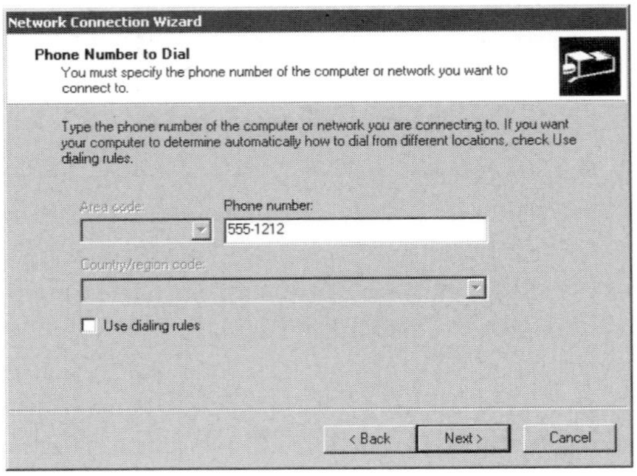

FIGURE 22.35

Network Connection Wizard: share connection

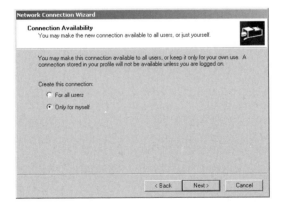

The last step of the Network Connection Wizard will ask if you would like to make this dial-up connection available to all users or to keep it just for use by the machine itself. For the purposes of simply connecting a Windows 2000 Server to another network, select the Only for Myself option here. The other option, For All Users, would end up sharing this connection for other users on the network, a topic discussed in the next section ("Acting as an Internet Gateway"). Click Next when you are finished, and you will have successfully created a Dial-Up Networking entry.

However, Win2K will have assumed several things about your dial-up networking entry that might not work for your specific situation. To double-check everything, edit the properties for this dial-up connection by right-clicking the icon for it in the Network and Dial-Up Connections window. Clicking the Networking tab on the properties page should bring you to a page similar to the one shown in Figure 22.36.

FIGURE 22.36

Dial-Up Networking entry properties

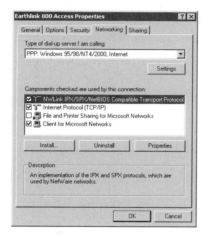

Windows 2000 will assume you want to use several defaults when you try to connect to this remote network. For example, it will assume you want to use *all* the protocols loaded on your system for this connection, it will assume it can use unsecured passwords, etc. Some of these options might not make sense in specific situations. For example, if you are connecting to an IPX-only network, it doesn't make much sense to try and negotiate a TCP/IP connection. Even though Win2K will realize that it can't establish the TCP/IP connection, why even try?

To fine-tune this connection, remove or add specific protocols as needed by checking the boxes next to the protocols listed under the Networking tab of the Dial-Up Networking entry properties pages. If you are connecting to a remote TCP/IP network and the device you are dialing in to does not provide you with an IP address or DNS server addresses automatically, you can program these in by highlighting the TCP/IP protocol and then clicking the Properties button. This will bring you to the specific TCP/IP settings to use for this connection (Figure 22.37).

On this screen you can enter the necessary information for your TCP/IP connection. If you are accessing a remote network that uses WINS servers but does not provide those addresses to you, enter them in the advanced TCP/IP settings area by clicking the Advanced button and then clicking the WINS tab.

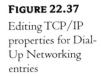

FIGURE 22.37

Editing TCP/IP properties for Dial-Up Networking entries

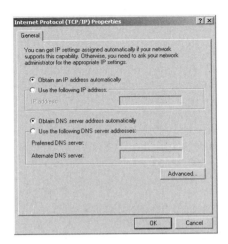

Once you have your protocols configured correctly, click OK to get back to the main properties page for this dial-up connection. If you need to edit any other properties, such as the type of security or authentication to use, click the appropriate tabs and make those settings as necessary.

If you think this looks similar to the steps to connect to the Internet described earlier in this chapter, you are correct. Basically, all the mechanisms are the same in Dial-Up Networking, but different wizards will take a different approach to the settings that are applied by default. Therefore, some of the same advanced options discussed in the "Connecting to the Internet" section (reestablishing failed links, redialing non-responsive numbers, etc.) are available for regular dial-up connections to private networks. As a matter of fact, you can even use the Dial-Up to a Private Network wizard to define a connection to the Internet. Which brings us to our next topic.

Acting as an Internet Gateway

One of the hottest little "niche" applications people always seemed to want to do with Windows NT 4 Server was to share an Internet connection with everyone else inside their organization. After all, NT servers were usually set up to share other resources (files, printers, etc.)—so it made sense that NT Server should have been able to share an Internet connection, right? Not exactly. With enough tweaking and some strict rules to follow, you *could* actually have NT Server dial an Internet connection and route traffic for internal hosts out to the Internet. However, the setup would be difficult and cumbersome, and it requires having valid (InterNIC-assigned) IP addresses available for everyone within the organization. Simply sharing a $20/month unlimited-access Internet account is not an option.

Now, Microsoft has included a variety of capabilities in Windows 2000 Server that make this task relatively easy. With the correct information about what type of connectivity you need to the outside world, Windows 2000 Server can act as an Internet gateway for your internal clients, leveraging an existing Internet connection among all the workstations in your organization.

NOTE   *The Internet gateway capabilities of Windows 2000 Server worked so well that, in the course of writing the first edition of this chapter, I was actually using my Windows 2000 Server (Beta 3) as an Internet gateway for my laptop and other test machines.*

Although Microsoft has included some great tools for sharing connections on your network, it is important to note several subtle hints Microsoft has included in their documentation for this feature of Windows 2000 Server. First and foremost, Microsoft often makes several references to small or home office networks, implying that this capability really isn't designed for use in medium-to-large environments. I would have to agree with them on this point; if you have a reasonable number of workstations on your network, you will probably be far better off going with a product such as Microsoft Proxy Server and a dedicated Internet connection.

The second point Microsoft makes repeatedly throughout their documentation is that "you should not use this feature in an existing network with other Windows 2000 Server domain controllers, DNS servers, gateways, DHCP servers, or systems configured for static IP." Since this configuration requires a very specific IP configuration to work correctly, implementing this on a network that doesn't conform to that configuration could cause lots of difficulty. I would agree with Microsoft on this point as well.

Although acting as an Internet router isn't one of the options normally available through the Make a New Connection wizard used throughout this chapter, fortunately one of the other options will configure most everything necessary. By using the steps detailed in the last section, "Connecting to a Private Network," and connecting to the Internet as the "Private" network, you can make Windows 2000 act as an Internet gateway, routing traffic from your internal clients out to the Internet and back again.

Configuring Windows 2000 Server to Act as an Internet Gateway

Start with the same steps listed in the section "Connecting to a Private Network" and go all the way up to Figure 22.34, using a local access number for your ISP as the number of the private network to dial.

This time, when the Network Connection Wizard (pictured in Figure 22.35) asks if you would like to make this connection available to all users, select For All Users instead of Only for Myself. This will enable the sharing properties for this connection. Click Next, and you should end up with a screen like the one in Figure 22.38.

FIGURE 22.38

Defining sharing options

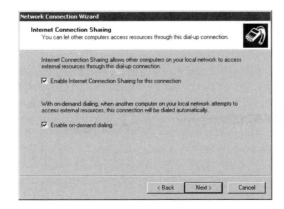

On this screen, you will have two options for how this shared connection should be handled. The first option is simply to enable sharing for this connection; leave this option checked. The second option tells Windows 2000 Server when it should establish the connection. If this box is unchecked, the only way to establish the connection to the Internet will be manually. However, users typically expect connections to be available whenever they want them, so enabling the on-demand dialing option will allow Windows 2000 Server to automatically establish this connection as needed, with no outside intervention. If you are going to be implementing a shared Internet connection, you probably want to select this option. When you check the box for on-demand dialing and click Next, you will probably receive a warning dialog box similar to the one in Figure 22.39.

FIGURE 22.39

Static IP address
change warning

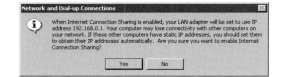

This dialog box lets you know that Windows 2000 Server will need to make several changes to its IP configuration for this functionality to work, including specifying a fixed IP address to use for the server's internal network connection. If anyone is connected to your server at this point, make sure they are disconnected before continuing, otherwise they may lose their connections to the system. Click Yes to continue, and Windows 2000 Server will make the appropriate IP changes to support sharing an Internet connection.

The last step of the wizard should ask you to assign a friendly name to this connection. Go ahead and assign a meaningful name to this connection and then click Finish. Once you have completed the wizard, you should see an icon for your shared connection in the Network and Dial-Up Connections dialog box. Launch the connection to verify that everything is working correctly. When you are prompted for your ISP username and password, enter your credentials and then check the Save Password box below the field for the domain. This will save your username and password for this connection so that when it is demand-dialed it will have what it needs. Once you have established that your ISP connection works correctly in and of itself, it's time to define a few rules as to what you want to allow across your Internet connection.

DEFINING APPLICATION AND SERVICE CONFIGURATIONS

By default, Windows 2000 Server will not automatically route any traffic from your client workstations to the Internet. You must define specific rules as to what type of traffic (i.e., what TCP/IP protocols) can go across your shared connection. To do this, begin by editing the properties for your shared Internet access connection by right-clicking the Dial-Up Networking icon in the Network and Dial-Up Connections window and then selecting Properties. Click the Sharing tab, and you should see settings for enabling shared access for this connection and on-demand dialing. At the bottom of the window is a button labeled Settings. By clicking the button, you can define settings for which applications and services can go across your shared Internet Connection. The Internet Connection Sharing Settings dialog box is pictured in Figure 22.40.

FIGURE 22.40

Configuring shared access settings

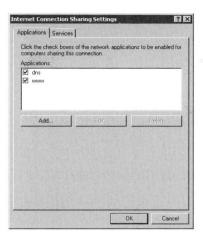

As a point of clarification, "applications" typically refer to connections that come from your internal network (for Web browsing, e-mail, etc.) and are destined out to the Internet. However, sharing an Internet connection can also allow you to accept traffic from external hosts targeted at systems within your network. For example, maybe you have a small Web server running in your organization that you would like people to be able to access. Using a shared Internet connection not only lets your users share access to the Internet, but it can be programmed to allow the Internet access to your internal shared resources as well.

This is one of the reasons why it's important to define rules as to what is allowed in and out of your shared Internet connection. Let's start by adding a few rules to allow Web browsing across the shared Internet connection. From the Settings screen, make sure you are looking at the Applications tab. More than likely you won't have any applications listed on your system (unlike the example in Figure 22.40). Click Add to add an application (in effect, a TCP/IP protocol) to your system. The dialog box to add a Shared Access Application is shown in Figure 22.41.

FIGURE 22.41

Adding a shared access application

To allow shared access for a TCP/IP application, Windows 2000 Server needs to know how that application functions. Specifically, Windows 2000 Server needs to know which ports the application uses and whether the application uses TCP or UDP connections. One of the first applications you will probably want to add will be support for DNS—the means by which clients and browsers can translate names like www.microsoft.com into IP addresses.

To add DNS support, enter a name for the application (I've used "dns" in Figure 22.41) and the port on the remote server that Win2K will be communicating with. For DNS, this port is 53, and the protocol to use for the request (with my ISP) is TCP, so I've selected the TCP radio button below the port. DNS responses from the target system will generally come back in on the same port that the client made the request from, which can be any number from 1024 to 65535. Therefore, I've put 1024-65535 in the TCP field for the incoming response to allow the DNS server to respond with the appropriate information.

As you can see, knowing how ports work is a key component of using shared Internet access. Some applications even get complicated by sending responses on UDP *and* TCP ports. For information on some commonly used Internet application ports and for the information necessary to configure your own applications as needed, see Table 22.2. Once you have configured an application for DNS, add applications as needed for the applications on your internal network.

TABLE 22.2: TCP/IP WELL-KNOWN PORTS AND SERVICES

PROTOCOL TYPE	DESTINATION PORT/PROTOCOL	RESPONSE PORT(S)/PROTOCOL(S)
FTP	21/TCP	1024-65535/TCP
Telnet	23/TCP	1024-65535/TCP
SMTP	25/TCP	1024-65535/TCP
Gopher	70/TCP	1024-65535/TCP
HTTP	80/TCP	1024-65535/TCP
POP3	110/TCP	1024-65535/TCP
NNTP	119/TCP	1024-65535/TCP

If you need to have outside clients access services on a computer on your internal network, you will need to add definitions to the services tab of the Shared Access Settings dialog box. Unless you want people from the outside world connecting to your internal systems, I would recommend leaving this blank. But if you have a Web server or FTP server that you need to have people connect to, this is the area to do it. Clicking the Services tab will take you to a screen almost identical to the one for Applications with several services listed on it. Clicking a service will allow you to define an internal host that Windows 2000 should direct that type of traffic to. Or you can click the Add button to add a service, and you will see a dialog box like the one shown in Figure 22.42.

Services work a bit differently from applications because external hosts won't connect *directly* to the IP address assigned to your internal workstation that has the destination service (especially since in most cases the internal IP addresses won't be routable addresses on the Internet). Instead, external systems will connect to your Windows 2000 Server on a specific port, and based on what port they connect to, Win2K will redirect the request to one of your internal systems. Therefore, the definitions for services vary a bit.

FIGURE 22.42

Adding a shared access service

Start defining your service by giving it a name—for example, http, ftp, etc. In the field for service port number, put the port you will expect incoming connections to come to. Again, you can use Table 22.2 to determine which ports to use. If you wanted to allow incoming HTTP traffic, for example, you would put 80 in the field for service port. Finally, in the last field for adding a service, tell Windows 2000 which of your internal computers to redirect the request to by entering either the name or IP address of the correct internal network computer. If you are using DHCP to assign addresses to your internal computers, I would recommend referencing the system by name in this dialog box.

Once you have completed this definition, hit OK and then make sure this service is checked in the Shared Access Services definition for settings. Now, if you have a connection that is demand-dialed, it's important to note that this won't typically work for incoming connections. That is, your ISP won't know that it should dial *your* server whenever someone on the Internet tries to access one of your systems. Therefore, if you are going to accept incoming service connections I'd recommend having your Internet connection online at all times.

Once you have defined the appropriate application and service settings, it's time to configure your clients to direct their Internet traffic to your Windows 2000 Server for routing.

CONFIGURING CLIENTS

Once your server is ready, you will need to tell your clients to route their Internet traffic to your Windows 2000 Server. When the Windows 2000 Server receives these packets, it will realize that they are destined for the Internet and route them as necessary (initiating your demand-dialed connection if needed). You can either program each workstation manually or let DHCP do it for you by defining the correct scope and options to use.

NOTE   *For more information on configuring DHCP scopes, see Chapter 7.*

The following information will work in your DHCP scope for getting your clients connected to the Internet (other slight variations would work as well; this is merely an example):

◆ Address range: 192.168.0.2 to 192.168.0.254

◆ Address mask: 255.255.255.0

◆ Default gateway: 192.168.0.1

◆ DNS servers to use: enter your ISP's DNS server addresses

To enter these settings manually on a Windows 2000 Professional, NT 4, or 9x client, edit the TCP/IP properties of your computer to change the IP address to something in the range listed above. The mask should be 255.255.255.0 as listed above, and the default gateway should be 192.168.0.1, the IP address your Windows 2000 Server will give itself once you enable shared access. In Windows NT 4 Workstation, this would look similar to the dialog box shown in Figure 22.43.

FIGURE 22.43

TCP/IP settings for shared access on Windows NT 4 Workstation

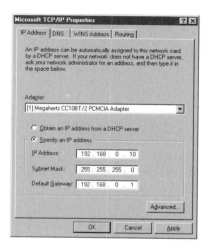

The last setting to make is the DNS server setting. Since your workstation will need to look somewhere to translate host names into IP address, you will need to put the DNS server IP addresses for your ISP into your connection settings. In NT 4 Workstation, clicking the DNS tab and adding new DNS servers to your system does this. If you don't know the IP addresses of your ISP's DNS servers, I would recommend contacting them to ask them directly or see if they list the appropriate settings somewhere on their Web site.

Once you have the correct DNS and TCP/IP settings programmed in, reboot your workstation and log back into the network. Once your computer is up and running, you should be able to allow access across your shared Internet connection for the protocols you defined on your server (DNS, Web, etc.). You should see your Windows 2000 Server automatically initiate the connection as needed whenever one of your client systems tries to access the Internet.

Accepting VPN Connections from Remote Clients

Virtual private networking is one of the hottest subjects in networking today. With the widespread presence of the Internet, it only makes sense that corporations and organizations would want to try to leverage existing investments in Internet connections for their corporate networks. But as exciting as VPN can be, it can also be a rather complex subject. Since it is basically a means of layering one logical network over another, the complexities of making a network connection are, in effect, doubled.

VPN Overview

Loosely defined, a VPN allows you to run a secure, private network over an unsecured public network. You can use virtual private networking to get clients connected to your network over the Internet and do it securely, even though the Internet is inherently an unsecured network.

One of the better analogies I've found for explaining the concepts of a virtual private network is to refer to them as "pipes." To conceptualize VPNs, think of two pipes, one large and one small. Now, imagine that the small pipe actually runs *inside* of the large one. It starts and ends at the same places the large pipe does, and it can carry materials on its own, completely independent of whatever is happening in the large pipe. As a matter of fact, the only thing the small pipe depends on the large pipe for is the determination of the start and end points. Beyond that, the small pipe can operate independently of the large pipe in terms of direction of travel, materials it carries, etc.

To add another layer to this analogy, let's assume that the large pipe is made out of a transparent material, and the small pipe is made out of metal. If anyone were to take a look at the pipe-within-a-pipe, they would easily be able to see whatever was moving through the outside (large) pipe. However, whatever was traveling through the inside pipe would remain a mystery.

If this is starting to make sense, you should be thinking to yourself that the large pipe represents the unsecured network (i.e., the Internet) and the small pipe represents the virtual private network. VPN is a way of tunneling data packets through a connection that already exists but that can't be used on its own for privacy reasons. Obviously, the Internet is a perfect example of a network that often can't be used on its own for privacy reasons.

So, what benefit does this have for the overworked network administrator? Well, for starters, it could reduce or eliminate your need to maintain a pool of modems at your site for remote dial-in users. Remote users don't need to call directly into your network to get connected; they can simply call in to a local ISP and get a valid Internet (unsecured) connection. Assuming you have a VPN/RAS server running on your network (and it's connected to the Internet), once the remote user has connected to their ISP, the client just has to establish the VPN (secured) session with the RAS server. The cost of maintaining modems and phone lines is shifted to the ISP. As long as your RAS server is connected to the Internet, you can support multiple incoming calls all over that one connection. Also, in keeping with this example, since the VPN session is being established over the Internet, there is no need for any long distance calls. If your remote user is hundreds of miles away, the cost to connect to your network is the same as if they were local, since the only call they would need to make would be to their ISP. This is a great way to support a geographically dispersed user base.

Microsoft has gone a long way toward making virtual private networking easy to implement in Windows 2000. However, if there is one piece of advice I could give everyone trying to implement virtual private networking, it is this: get a good, solid RAS server working and accepting incoming connections *first*. Use standard connections (analog modems, ISDN, etc.) on your RAS server first to make sure everything is functioning correctly. Once you are sure RAS is working correctly for standard connections, only then is it advisable to try implementing VPN connections. Since virtual private networking adds another layer of functionality "on top of" RAS, it is crucial to have a stable foundation to begin with. RAS can be peculiar in its behavior at times, so it is important to have all your configurations working correctly (DHCP address assignment, browsing, etc.). If only I had a nickel for every time I heard someone say "this VPN thing is messed up," only to find out that if they dial in to their network over a modem connection, they experience the exact same problems.

A Brief History of VPN: PPTP, L2F, and L2TP

When virtual private networking was first being developed back in the mid 1990s, two of the largest companies in the computer/networking industry tried to run with implementations of VPNs in the hopes that they would enjoy widespread implementation and therefore become an "industry standard." The two companies were Microsoft and Cisco, and each had its respective VPN technologies. Microsoft was approaching the VPN market from the operating systems point of view and had developed Point-to-Point Tunneling Protocol (PPTP) as a means to securely transmit data across unsecure networks. At the same time, Cisco was taking the lead in VPN from a strictly networking point of view with a protocol called Layer 2 Forwarding, or L2F.

Now, when either of these companies decides to develop an industry standard, they can usually get away with it if one doesn't already exist. No single standard had obtained a large enough share of the VPN market to be considered an industry standard, so the playing field was literally wide open. However, the sheer muscle and momentum that either one of these companies can put behind an initiative wasn't necessarily enough to displace the other. Each protocol had its strengths and weaknesses, and Microsoft and Cisco's offerings enjoyed moderate successes.

Now, I'm speculating a bit here, but I think that since neither industry giant was going to successfully displace the other in the VPN market, they decided it would be better to cooperate than compete. In any case, Microsoft and Cisco made the decision to collaborate on virtual private networking by merging their protocols, PPTP and L2F, into one hybrid protocol. The final product of that collaboration is Layer 2 Tunneling Protocol, or L2TP for short.

Windows 2000 Server includes L2TP support for establishing virtual private networking connections but also includes support for PPTP for backward compatibility with other operating systems. At the time this book was being written, L2TP was only supported in Windows 2000 (Server and Professional), and Microsoft had only made passing references to supporting it in Windows 98 or Me. Based on some of the white papers I've read recently, Microsoft isn't committing to L2TP support for Windows 98 or Me just yet. Therefore, the only option today for supporting legacy clients (NT 4, Windows 9x or Me) across a virtual private network is to include support for PPTP.

Okay, enough said. Let's assume you've got a good solid RAS server running and get on to the fun stuff.

Implementing VPN via PPTP and L2TP

If you went through the section "Accepting Incoming Calls from Remote Users," congratulations—you have 80 percent of what you need to support VPN connections in place already. When you install Remote Access Service, Windows 2000 Server should have added support for five PPTP connections and five L2TP connections by default. If you didn't go through the section to accept incoming calls from remote users, stop reading now and go back to complete the steps listed there. For the remainder of this section, we'll assume you have a functional RAS server in place.

We'll start by verifying that support for PPTP and L2TP is in place through the Routing and Remote Access MMC. Start the RRAS MMC by selecting Start/Programs/Administrative Tools/ Routing and Remote Access. In the left portion of the MMC window, you should see the name of your RAS server listed; expand the information for that server by double-clicking it. Right-click the listing for ports, and then select Properties to edit the ports (Figure 22.44).

FIGURE 22.44

Ports Properties

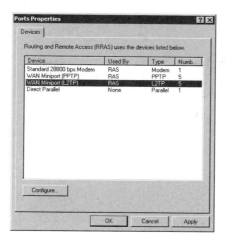

In the Ports Properties screen, you will see all the ports that Win2K has recognized and can use for Remote Access Service. Each device has a usage listed, a device name, a type, and several ports associated with it. By default, RAS should have PPTP and L2TP devices installed on your system and probably has five ports associated with each.

Depending on which type of connections you will be allowing and how many you want to allow, you can edit your protocols and circuits accordingly from here. For example, if you are only going to have Win2K clients connecting to your network over virtual circuits, you can stick with just supporting L2TP. However, if you need to support legacy clients accessing your network via virtual circuits, PPTP is your only choice. In any case, to edit the port properties for either type, double-click the item to edit or just highlight it and click the Configure button. This will take you into the port configuration screen shown in Figure 22.45 (the screen looks the same whether you are configuring PPTP, L2TP, or modem ports).

FIGURE 22.45

Configuring RAS ports (PPTP shown)

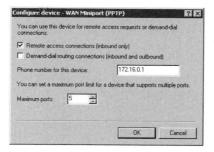

To configure your server to accept VPN connections, make sure the Remote Access Connections (Inbound Only) option is checked in the Configure Ports dialog box. For the Phone Number for This Device field, enter the public Internet IP address of your server (assuming the Internet is the public, unsecured network you will be using). This is the IP address that clients will eventually connect to across the Internet for establishing VPN circuits.

TIP   I strongly recommend that you use a fixed IP address and Internet connection for your server. Yes, you can use a dial-up connection from your RAS server to the Internet, and you can even make dynamic IP addresses work for this. But with dynamic IP addresses, your server's IP address will change every time it has to reestablish its link, quickly becoming a management nightmare.

Depending on how many simultaneous virtual private networking connections you plan on supporting, adjust the Maximum Ports value accordingly and then click OK.

TIP   I would recommend disabling any and all VPN connections that you don't plan on using. For example, if you are only going to support L2TP connections from Windows 2000 clients, disable PPTP by unchecking the Remote Access Connections (Inbound Only) option on the properties page for PPTP. This will prevent anyone from trying to establish a connection to your server via PPTP without your knowing about it.

CLIENT CONFIGURATION

To get a client workstation connected to a Windows 2000 Server running VPN protocols, you will need to have one of the following:

◆ Windows NT 4, Workstation, or Server (PPTP only)

◆ Windows 95 with the Dial-Up Networking 1.2 upgrade or better (PPTP only)

◆ Windows 98 (PPTP only now; L2TP *might* be included later)

◆ Windows 2000 Professional (PPTP or L2TP)

Since older operating systems such as Windows 95 and Windows NT 4 don't install PPTP by default, the first thing to do is add PPTP support to the client system. PPTP is a standard protocol, just like NetBEUI or NWLink, so the procedures for adding this new protocol are roughly the same.

Windows NT 4 Workstation

Assuming you already have Dial-Up Networking set up on your NT 4 Workstation, the first step to adding VPN support is to add the Point-to-Point Tunneling Protocol in the Control Panel/Network applet. Start by clicking Start/Settings/Control Panel/Network, and then click the Protocols tab. Clicking the Add button from the protocols properties page will bring you to the protocol properties dialog box, as shown in Figure 22.46.

FIGURE 22.46

Protocols properties page in NT 4 Workstation

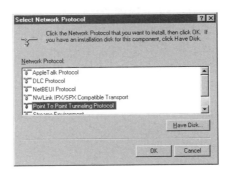

Once you have selected the Point-to-Point Tunneling Protocol and clicked OK, NT 4 Workstation will ask you how many simultaneous virtual circuits you'd like to support in the dialog box in Figure 22.47.

FIGURE 22.47

Configuring the number of virtual circuits to support

However many circuits you choose here will determine how many virtual ports Windows NT 4 will add to its configuration. Each virtual port will be called VPNx, with x referring to the specific port number. In effect, they function similarly to modems running on COM ports (COMx), so think of these VPN devices as virtual modems. If you will only be connecting to one virtual private network at a time, choose 1 and click OK.

Once you have completed selecting the number of virtual circuits to support, NT 4 Workstation will invoke RAS setup to allow you to add your new virtual modem(s) to the RAS configuration, as shown in Figure 22.48.

FIGURE 22.48

Adding VPN devices to RAS in NT 4 Workstation

Click the Add button in Remote Access Setup and you should see your VPN device in the Add RAS Device window. If you see a modem or some other device there, try pulling down the list and then selecting your VPN device. Once you have your VPN device selected, click OK and it will be added to your RAS configuration.

Once you are back to the Remote Access Setup screen, highlight your VPN device and click the Configure button. This device should be configured for Dial-Out Only, as shown in Figure 22.49.

FIGURE 22.49

Configuring VPN devices for dial-out only in NT 4 Workstation

Once everything is set correctly, click OK and RAS will start the installation routine. This will most likely require a reboot of your computer, so go ahead and restart it and get back into Windows. To use your VPN device, the last step you need to perform is creating a Dial-Up Networking entry.

Double-click My Computer and then Dial-Up Networking to begin creating a new Dial-Up Networking entry. Creating a VPN Dial-Up Networking entry is almost identical to creating a regular Dial-Up Networking entry for a phone line, except that you will use an IP address instead of a phone number to dial and the VPNx device instead of a modem. This is shown in Figure 22.50.

FIGURE 22.50

Creating a VPN Dial-Up Networking entry in Windows NT 4 Workstation

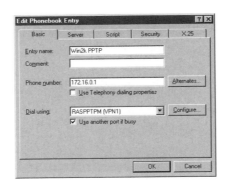

As you can see, this Dial-Up Networking entry will call a VPN server at IP address 172.16.0.1, the same IP address used in the configuration of the RAS/VPN server earlier in this chapter. As long as the VPN device is selected in the Dial Using pull-down box, everything should be set for this connection.

The first step to actually making this connection is to make sure you have an actual, valid Internet IP address before doing so. If you need to use Dial-Up Networking to connect to an ISP for this, do that first. Once you have a valid IP address available, launch your VPN Dial-Up Networking Connection to get connected to your remote system. Once you provide a set of valid user credentials, you should end up getting connected at 10,000,000 baud (10 megabits, equivalent to the speed of a 10Base-T network).

Windows 9x

Windows 9x takes a unique approach to implementing virtual private networking through the use of a Microsoft VPN adapter. Instead of adding support for PPTP or other protocols (like in other Microsoft operating systems), all you need to do is add the VPN adapter to your system to get connected.

NOTE *To add VPN support for Windows 95, you must have the Dial-Up Networking upgrade v1.2 or later installed on your system. VPN support is included in Windows 98 right out of the box.*

Start by editing the network properties of Windows 9x by selecting Start/Settings/Control Panel/Network. When the Network properties page comes up, click the Add button, and then select Adapter as the component type you'd like to install. Your screen should look like Figure 22.51.

In the list of adapters supplied, scroll down to Microsoft for the manufacturer, then select the Microsoft Virtual Private Networking Adapter listed on the right side of the screen. Click OK and Windows 9x will add the VPN adapter to its system. Of course, this will require a reboot for the changes to take effect.

FIGURE 22.51

Adding the
Microsoft VPN
Adapter to
Windows 9*x*

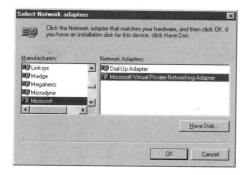

Once your system has rebooted, the next step to getting connected is creating a Dial-Up Networking entry to connect to your VPN server. From the Windows 9*x* Desktop, double-click My Computer, then Dial-Up Networking, and then Make New Connection to launch the Make New Connection wizard, shown in Figure 22.52.

FIGURE 22.52

Windows 9*x* Make
New Connection
wizard

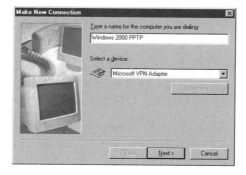

From the Select a Device pull-down box, choose the Microsoft VPN Adapter if it isn't already selected. Click Next to move to the next step of the wizard shown in Figure 22.53.

FIGURE 22.53

Entering the
IP address of a
VPN server in
Windows 9*x*

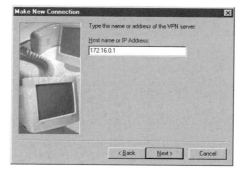

Enter the IP address or DNS name of your VPN server in the box as needed. In the example in Figure 22.53, we have used an IP address of 172.16.0.1, the same IP address used in the configuration of the RAS/VPN server earlier in this chapter. After entering the hostname or address, clicking Next will complete the wizard and place a VPN Dial-Up Networking entry on your system.

To make the VPN connection, you must make sure you have an actual, valid Internet IP address before doing so. If you need to use Dial-Up Networking to connect to an ISP for this, do that first. Once you have a valid IP address available, launch your VPN Dial-Up Networking connection to get connected to your remote system. Once you provide a set of valid user credentials, you should end up connected at 10,000,000 baud (10 megabits, equivalent to the speed of a 10Base-T network).

Windows 2000

Windows 2000 adds a few nice features to the client side of establishing VPN connections, namely the ability to automatically associate one DUN entry with another. For example, if you need to dial an ISP before you can connect with your virtual private network, Windows 2000 can join these two functions. The end result is that when you (or your users) need to connect to the virtual private network, doing so only requires launching one Dial-Up Networking session.

Like most of the remote access functionality in Win2K, to define a VPN connection, you will begin with Start/Settings/Network and Dial-Up Connections, and then the Make New Connection wizard. From the first screen of the wizard, select the option to Connect to a Private Network through the Internet, as shown in Figure 22.54.

FIGURE 22.54

Creating a VPN connection on Windows 2000

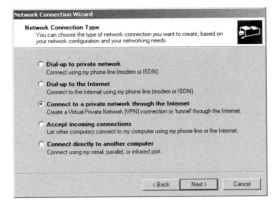

Click Next to continue, and Win2K will then ask if you need to establish a public network (Internet) connection first before establishing the VPN connection, as shown in Figure 22.55.

If the Win2K device you will be connecting already has a valid, public Internet IP address, answer Do Not Dial the Initial Connection to this question. Otherwise, if you need to obtain an IP address first from an ISP, select Automatically Dial This Initial Connection and choose the connection that will get you connected to the Internet. Doing so will cause your VPN Dial-Up Networking connection to initiate an ISP connection first. Click Next to continue on to entering the IP address or host name of the target server, as shown in Figure 22.56.

FIGURE 22.55

Creating a public connection before a VPN connection

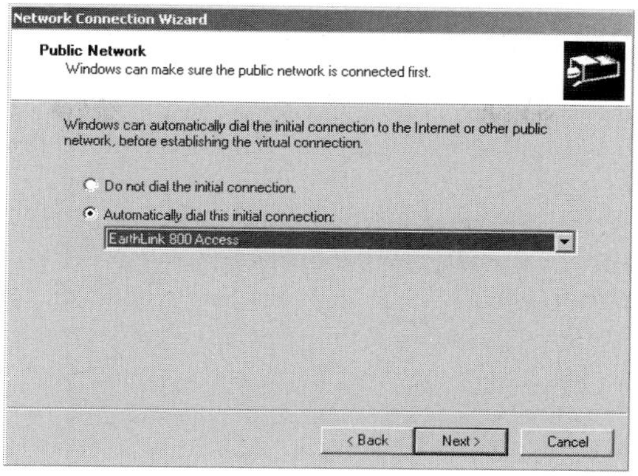

FIGURE 22.56

Entering the IP address of the VPN server

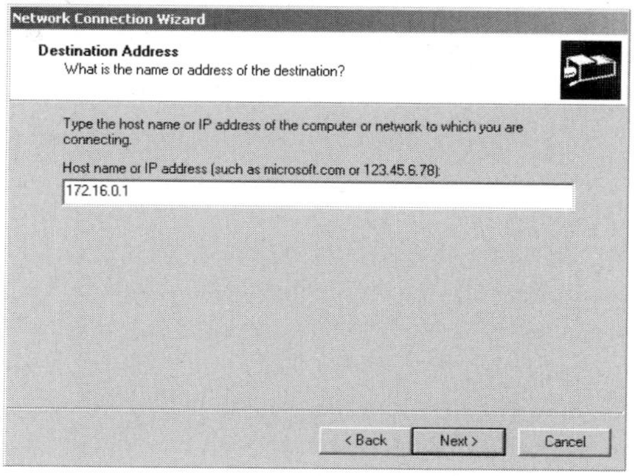

Much like many of the other client platforms we've already discussed, you will need to enter the IP address of your target system or a DNS-resolvable host name. As you can see, this Dial-Up Networking entry will call a VPN server at IP address 172.16.0.1, the same IP address used in the configuration of the RAS/VPN server earlier in this chapter. Click Next to continue, and the final step of the wizard will ask you whether you want to make this VPN connection available to all users or just yourself. For the purposes of this section, we'll assume that you just want to use the VPN connection for yourself, so click the Only for Myself radio button and click Next to finish creating the Dial-Up Networking entry.

When it comes time to actually establish this connection, if you selected the option to have Win2K dial an initial connection, you will see a dialog box like the one in Figure 22.57 asking you if the public network connection should be initiated first.

FIGURE 22.57

Windows 2000 asking if an initial public network connection should be established first

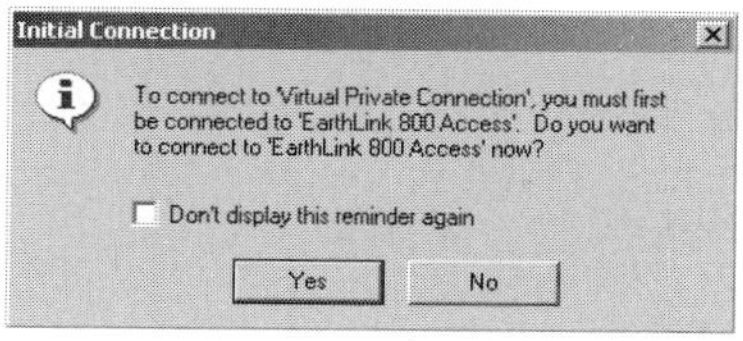

VPN Performance Considerations

Our section on virtual private networking wouldn't be complete without taking a bit of time to discuss performance issues to consider. Although virtual private networking is a neat technology, unfortunately there are some times when it just might not make sense to use it. Careful planning and consideration should help you determine if it is a solution that can add value to your organization.

In the right set of circumstances, virtual private networking can provide fast, reliable, and secure connections to remote networks across the Internet (or another unsecured network). However, in the wrong set of circumstances, a VPN can make an already slow dial-up connection seem even slower.

So what are the right circumstances? In my professional opinion, the right circumstances are when you have high-speed connectivity on your RAS server at the very least and preferably when you have high-speed connectivity on both your RAS server and your DUN client. On occasions when I have been able to implement VPN circuits at locations with a T1 or better available at both the server and client ends, performance has been wonderful and the connections reliable. However, due to the protocol overhead involved with PPTP and L2TP and the inherent latency of the Internet, if you are planning on implementing a VPN with dial-up modems on each side of your connection, I would urge you to think twice.

"But wait," you might be thinking, "I want to implement a VPN to reduce costs, not increase them." Well, I wish I could say that Microsoft's VPN implementations were going to give you the performance you might expect over modem connections, but they just won't. Simply due to the additional complexities of encrypting the data, bundling the payload data inside a TCP/IP packet, and the latency of communications across the Internet, you can expect a decrease in your performance ranging anywhere from 10 to 50 percent. Now, without getting into all the technical details, it is worthwhile to note that this isn't entirely Microsoft's fault; after all, they can't be blamed for the fact that the Internet can be inherently slow at times (or can they?). However, even with the worst-case scenario of a 50 percent reduction in performance, if there is a T1 on each side of the virtual private network, the effective speeds of the network are still roughly in the 760Kbps range. However, if you're using a 56K modem on each side of the virtual private network, which probably won't connect much faster than 48Kbps, you can easily see how a 50 percent performance penalty can make a connection go from "slow" to "unusable."

Simply put, if you are using a modem on your RAS server and a modem on your DUN client, you will get your best possible speeds by having one dial directly into the other. By doing so, there is no protocol overhead getting in the way, nor is there the need for your data to travel across dozens of routers as it works its way to its destination. By creating a direct connection, data packets go directly from the DUN client to the target network.

However, everything in life is a trade-off, and it will be up to you to decide whether this will work adequately enough for your needs. After all, what is adequate to one person might be great to another and unacceptable to yet another. In either case, expect a performance penalty when implementing virtual private networking and plan your bandwidth accordingly.

Dialing Up a Remote Network and Routing Traffic

With the release of the Routing and Remote Access Service update to Windows NT 4 Server, Microsoft was able to improve on the routing capabilities that already existed in Windows NT.

Although Windows NT 4 shipped with routing capabilities right out of the box, they were limited and cumbersome, to say the least.

Now Microsoft has included all the capabilities of the Routing and Remote Access Service update in Windows 2000 Server, making this operating system a platform capable of solving several common routing scenarios right out of the box. When you need to get data from one location to another, Windows 2000 Server might be an adequate solution for your needs.

Let's take an example of routing traffic from a central office to a remote office over an analog connection. Many organizations are often faced with a connectivity dilemma when opening remote offices, especially if there are only a small number of computers at the remote site. Installing dedicated links between locations can be cost-prohibitive depending on the number of people at the remote site, but having a group of individuals completely isolated from the organizational network usually isn't an acceptable alternative either. Windows 2000 Server is a perfect solution for this scenario, as it can establish demand-dialed links between locations whenever traffic needs to pass from one site to another. By using simple modems and ordinary phone lines, Windows 2000 can be a low-cost alternative to installing dedicated WAN links. To get started, let's walk through the details of a sample scenario.

Sample Network

Our sample network consists of the following:

- Number of sites: two (Virginia and Delaware)
- TCP/IP subnet for Virginia: 10.16.0.*x* with a subnet mask of 255.255.255.0
- TCP/IP subnet for Delaware: 172.16.0.*x* with a subnet mask of 255.255.255.0
- Windows 2000 RRAS Server in Virginia: ARCHITECT4 with an IP address of 10.16.0.4
- Windows 2000 RRAS Server in Delaware: ARCHITECT-WIN2K with an IP address of 172.16.0.1
- Phone number for analog line connected to Virginia Windows 2000 RRAS Server: (703) 555-9779
- Phone number for analog line connected to Delaware Windows 2000 RRAS Server: (302) 555-0386
- User account created in the Virginia Active Directory and granted dial-in permissions: DELAWARE-ROUTER, password: delaware
- User account created in the Delaware Active Directory and granted dial-in permissions: VIRGINIA-ROUTER, password: virginia

In effect, our network looks similar to the diagram shown in Figure 22.58.

Setting Up the First Server

To start building a demand-dialed analog connection between these two locations, you will need to have your Windows 2000 Server able to function as a router. If you've worked through any of the configurations previously discussed in this chapter, your system is probably configured to simply act as a Remote Access Server. Changing roles for the server is as simple as editing the properties for the Remote Access Service.

FIGURE 22.58

Diagram of sample network

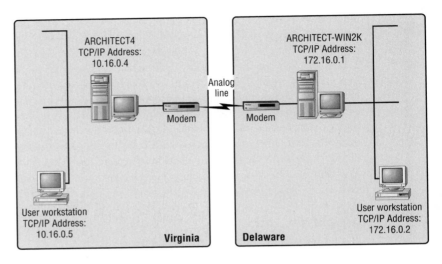

Virginia — ARCHITECT4 TCP/IP Address: 10.16.0.4, Modem, Analog line, User workstation TCP/IP Address: 10.16.0.5

Delaware — ARCHITECT-WIN2K TCP/IP Address: 172.16.0.1, Modem, User workstation TCP/IP Address: 172.16.0.2

NOTE *For the purposes of walking through the first server configuration, I will be configuring the necessary components on our Delaware router first, using the details defined above.*

To change roles for your server, open up the Routing and Remote Access MMC by selecting Start/Programs/Administrative Tools/Routing and Remote Access. Edit the properties for Remote Access Service on your server by right-clicking your server name and then selecting Properties. You should see a dialog box similar to the one pictured in Figure 22.59.

FIGURE 22.59

Editing RAS server properties to add routing capabilities

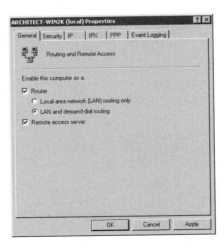

To add routing services to your system, check the box labeled Router and then select one of the two radio buttons below that option. If you will only be using LAN-based interfaces (Ethernet adapters, etc.) as your routing devices on your system, you can leave the Local Area Network (LAN) Routing Only option selected. However, if you intend to use dial-up connections (as we will in this example), demand-dialed links, or VPN connections, select the LAN and Demand-Dial Routing option. Click OK to apply the changes, and Windows 2000 Server should stop and restart the Routing and Remote Access Service to implement the changes.

When you return to the Routing and Remote Access MMC, the next step will be to enable routing support for one of the ports on your system. In the Routing and Remote Access MMC, right-click the option for Ports and select Properties to get to the ports properties pages. Once you have the ports properties pages available, double-click the device you intend to use as your demand-dialed connection (if the device you want to use isn't listed, go back to the section on adding RAS devices earlier in this chapter). The configuration page for that device should look similar to the dialog box in Figure 22.60.

FIGURE 22.60

Editing properties for the demand-dialed port

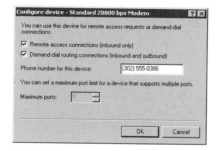

Configure this device by checking the Demand-Dial Routing Connections option and clicking OK. If you would eventually like to use Bandwidth Allocation Protocol with this configuration—to increase bandwidth by adding mode dial-up connections as needed—enter the phone number for your connection and click OK to accept the changes.

When you return to the Routing and Remote Access MMC, you might have noticed a new item for Routing Interfaces in the results pane of the window when you look at your Windows 2000 Server, as shown in Figure 22.61. This option was added when routing services were added to the server, and it is where you will begin to add your demand-dialed interface.

To start creating a demand-dialed interface, right-click the Routing Interfaces selection, and then choose the option to add a new demand-dial interface. This will launch the Demand Dial Interface Wizard, which will walk you through steps to create your demand-dialed interface. The first step of the wizard is shown in Figure 22.62.

In most cases of assigning a friendly name to a RAS or other type of connection, any name will do. However, in creating demand-dialed routing connections, the name assigned to a demand-dialed interface is important. The name assigned to a demand-dialed connection *must* match the name of the user account entered into the Active Directory at the *same* site. The same must be true on both sides of the wide area network. To quote Microsoft directly: "The username in the authentication credentials sent by the calling router must exactly match the name of a demand-dial interface on the answering router." If the username does not match a demand-dial interface name, the answering router will assume that the incoming call is a RAS *user*, not a remote router. Therefore, whatever name is entered here must also be used as a username on the same system's Active Directory. Since we're walking through setting up our Delaware remote office in our example, I've decided to call this interface VIRGINIA-ROUTER. When you have entered the appropriate name, click Next to continue to the next stage of the wizard, shown in Figure 22.63.

FIGURE 22.61

Adding a demand-dialed interface to the RRAS MMC via Routing Interfaces

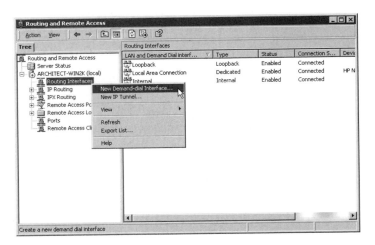

FIGURE 22.62

Defining a name for a demand-dialed interface

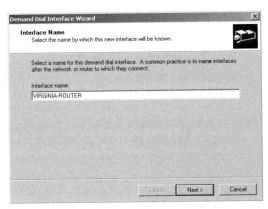

The next step of the wizard should be relatively self-explanatory. The wizard needs to know what phone number Windows 2000 Server should dial when it is attempting to establish the demand-dialed interface. Enter the number exactly as your system should dial it, including any prefixes, area codes, etc. If you have a list of alternate numbers that Windows 2000 Server can use to establish this demand-dialed connection, click the Alternates button and enter the information there. When you click Next to move to the next step in the Demand Dial Wizard, you should see a dialog box similar to the one pictured in Figure 22.64.

FIGURE 22.63

Entering the number to dial for the demand-dialed interface

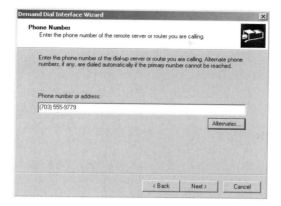

FIGURE 22.64

Selecting protocols to route, credentials to use, and connection options for a demand-dialed interface

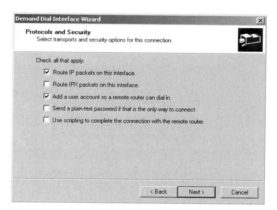

Depending on the network you are connecting to, here you can select which protocols Windows 2000 Server should route. In addition to selecting the appropriate protocols for the remote network, you can also choose to have Windows 2000 create a user account so that the remote network's router can dial into your system. Lastly, you can choose custom connection options such as sending a plain-text password if that is the only way the remote router will let you connect, or any advanced scripting options you might need. Depending on the options you select from this screen, the remainder of the Demand Dial Wizard will vary, but for the purposes of our example we'll assume you've selected IP and decided to create a user account for a remote router as seen in this figure. Click Next to continue to the next step of the wizard, shown in Figure 22.65.

FIGURE 22.65

Configuring
remote router
dial-in credentials

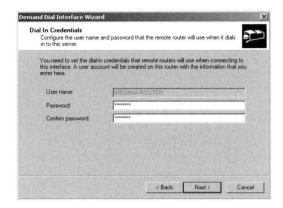

As previously stated, the friendly or descriptive name you use for a demand-dialed connection needs to be the same as the credentials for that connection, otherwise the answering router will assume the incoming caller is simply a RAS connection, not a router. Since we are defining a demand-dialed interface to call into the VIRGINIA-ROUTER device, if that device were to call the Delaware system we're configuring, it would identify itself as VIRGINIA-ROUTER. Therefore, the username field is grayed out by default, preventing you from changing it. This is an important point, because if you decide to change the user accounts used by RRAS at a later date, but don't change the interface names accordingly, you could end up with a broken routing system. Enter a password for this account to use, and make a note of it. Click Next to continue to the next screen in the wizard, as seen in Figure 22.66.

FIGURE 22.66

Configuring router
dial-out credentials

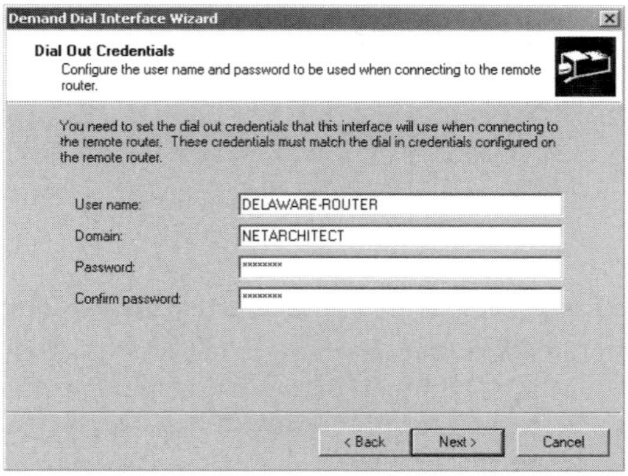

As the last step of the wizard in our sample scenario, you will need to define the user credentials your Windows 2000 Server will use when calling into a remote network. The username used here must match the name of a demand-dialed interface on the remote system exactly or else the remote system will simply assume your Windows 2000 Server is a standard RAS user. Enter the appropriate domain, username, and password combination for your configuration and then click Next to complete the wizard.

Although the wizard has completed, there is still one step remaining on your first system: defining a static route entry for the remote IP network. In effect, you will need to tell your Windows 2000 Server "whenever you need to contact these IP addresses, use this demand-dialed interface to get there." By entering a static routing entry for the remote network's IP address range and then defining the demand-dialed interface as the connection to use, Windows 2000 will know to route any packets for that network by dialing into the remote router.

To add a static route, select the IP Routing option in the left pane of the Routing and Remote Access MMC. It is an option listed under your server, so you might need to expand the view of your system. Expand the IP Routing selection by clicking the plus sign next to it, and then right-click the Static Routes option. Highlighting Static Routes and then selecting the Action pull-down menu should make a New Static Route option appear. Select this option and you should end up with a dialog box similar to the one in Figure 22.67.

FIGURE 22.67

Defining a static route to a remote network

Here you can define the necessary parameters for the remote network, starting with the interface Windows 2000 Server should use to get the packets to their destination. For the purposes of demand-dialed routing, you should make sure you have your demand-dialed interface listed in the interface section. Next, define the IP network address range by entering a destination network address and network mask in the field. Win2K will use this information to determine if packets—when it receives them—match the IP address range of the remote network. If the packets match the range defined, Win2K will route them. Lastly, you can leave the metric at 1, and make sure the Use This Route to Initiate Demand Dial Connections option is selected. Once you have all this information entered, click OK and you should see your static route appear in the results pane of the Routing and Remote Access MMC.

At this point, you have completed exactly half the work required to have your systems routing data over analog links. The other half of the job is to go through the exact same steps on the other system by configuring a demand-dial interface in the same manner just described.

Once you have both systems configured correctly, you should be able to test your connection to see if it works by doing a ping from one system to another.

NOTE *For more information about Ping, see Chapter 6.*

Start at one of your Windows 2000 Servers configured with a demand-dialed interface, go to a command prompt, and ping one of the IP addresses on the distant network. You should see your demand-dialed connection come online and start passing traffic. However, it is important to realize that for the type of communication you are attempting, your call setup times might take too long. For example, the `ping` command typically sends four ICMP echo requests, and then waits 1.5 seconds after each one for a response. All total, a test of four pings should take no longer than 6 seconds. However, if you are using analog connections, your call setup times are most likely going to be in the range of 20–30 seconds. Therefore, your connection won't come online in time to satisfy the request. For testing purposes, I would recommend using an indefinite ping by using the `-t` option on the command line, such as `ping -t 172.16.0.1`.

To solve problems like these and others, you can use some fine-tuning controls for your demand-dialed connection. For example, if you are using analog lines to connect sites and the analog lines aren't billed per-minute, it might make sense to have your demand-dialed connection online all the time. This is called making a *persistent* connection. From the Routing and Remote Access MMC, click the selection for Routing Interfaces in the left pane of the window. In the results pane, you should see your demand-dialed interface listed. Right-click the demand-dialed interface and select Properties to edit the properties page for this connection. You should see a four-tabbed dialog box similar to the one in Figure 22.68 (shown with the Options tab selected).

FIGURE 22.68

Editing router interface properties

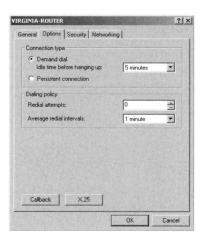

There are several settings you can control through this dialog box, but some of the most useful are listed under the Options tab shown in Figure 22.68. For example, if you are using an ISDN connection to reach your distant network and your ISDN is billed per minute, you can enter an idle time-out value in the Connection Type area of the window so your connections don't stay on any longer than necessary. Or, if the opposite is true, and you aren't billed per minute for your connections, you can select the persistent connection option to have the link stay online all the time. If for some reason the link fails, Windows 2000 Server will bring it right back online again. Set the options you would like to use, and then click OK to accept them.

When you right-click the demand-dial routing interface in the Routing and Remote Access MMC, there are also some other options you could set in addition to editing the properties of the item itself. One of the more useful items is setting the hours in which this connection can be established. If you would like to restrict the times when your demand-dialed connections can be brought online, select the Dialing Hours option when you right-click the routing interface. You should end up with an hourly grid dialog box, like the one in Figure 22.69, in which you can select the hours to allow and disallow connections.

FIGURE 22.69

Defining dialing hours for demand-dialed connections

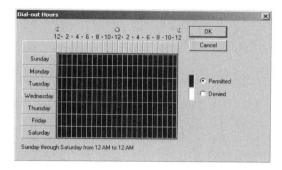

Once you have completed everything, you should have a functional wide area network running between locations and passing data as necessary. Through the use of this functionality, I have seen organizations that have set up completely "virtual" WANs consisting of multiple sites that all look as if they're operating as one large network, but in reality they are each small sites connected to a master network over analog links. Although Windows 2000 isn't designed to displace high-end routers in complex routing scenarios, it is a good solution for a lot of networking problems—some of which you may face.

The Most Common (and Poorly Documented) RAS Problems

Microsoft's RAS service is a great feature in Windows 2000—and even though they've made it simple to set up, under the hood a complex communication mechanism is working away to get packets from one system to another. Often, the Microsoft wizards will help you with setting up most of the settings necessary for RAS itself, but RAS depends on some other specific settings within Windows 2000 to function properly. In this section, we'll take a look at some common (and poorly documented) problems that users run into when they're trying to set up RAS.

"I've connected to a RAS server from my home PC, but I can't browse anything on the network!"

Okay, technically this doesn't fall under a RAS problem per se—but browsing remote networks is a problem most commonly found on RAS connections. Actually, it's the number one problem that I see posted on Usenet when people are trying to get RAS configured and running on a their network.

Let's say that you gave the phone number for the RAS server to Jane in Accounting so that she can work at home. After giving her a quick lesson on how to create a dial-up networking connection, you're hoping that Jane will be able to connect to the network from her Windows 98 PC, and then navigate through the network to get to the resources that she needs.

So Jane successfully dials in over the weekend but she can't see anything in her Network Neighborhood. If she knew how to map a drive, she'd be able to do it—but she's accustomed to double-clicking things in the NetHood to find her files. So, she can't work. On Monday, she calls for help—frustrated that she's now behind in her work.

That leaves you with the unpleasant task of remotely troubleshooting a home user's PC. Who knows, maybe her 14-year-old kid messed up the TCP/IP stack? Or maybe there's some odd problem with her modem? In any case, it might seem like it's going to be a painful issue to troubleshoot since you can't easily get your hands on the PC.

Well, here's a quick tip that could save you a lot of headaches: More often than not, when a user experiences this type of problem, it's due to a misconfigured workgroup configuration on their computer.

For example, let's say that your network domain is called COMPANY (we'll keep with down-level NetBIOS names here to make it easier). Now, most retail PCs that a user might buy for their home are configured out-of-the-box with something like Workgroup for their workgroup setting. Odds are good that the company that your user bought his or her PC from didn't give it the same workgroup setting as the name of your domain. And that's what you need for Microsoft browsing to work properly.

The solution is to configure the workgroup name on the client's workstation to be the same as the Windows NT/2000 domain or workgroup to which your users are connecting. If you've run into this problem, give it a shot and see if it works.

"How can I keep RAS connections alive when a user logs off of their workstation?"

By default, RAS connections (on Windows NT and 2000 clients) are automatically disconnected whenever a user logs out of their workstation. If you have a workstation setup at a remote site that multiple people use, you might not want this to be the case. In order to change this default behavior of Windows 2000, you'll need to modify the registry on the RAS *client*—the system that is dialing in.

Look in the following key in the registry:

```
HKEY_Local_Machine\Software\Microsoft\Windows NT\Current Version\Winlogon
```

You may see a value in that key called KeepRasConnections, but most likely you won't. It's not there by default. Add this value to your system as a type REG_SZ, and give it a value of 1 (the default behavior is indicated by a 0). This will instruct the client workstation to keep the RAS connection open, even when the user at the workstation logs out.

"No matter what I try, I can't seem to get a modem connection from a workstation to my RAS server."

If you're in this boat, you have two places to start diagnosing the problem: the server or the client. Fortunately, you might get lucky with the server diagnosis—if other users or workstations can successfully dial in to the RAS server, then it's probably not a server problem. So, the next course of action is to start troubleshooting the workstation.

The great advantage—and disadvantage—of the Windows operating system is that it hides the complexity of operating the underlying components of a system. For example, instead of knowing that to dial a modem you need to issue the command ATDT5551212 and wait for the response, you simply need to know how to enter a phone number in the appropriate dialog box within Windows.

But, what if you want to troubleshoot the dialing function? It would be helpful to see those commands as they are passed back and forth to your modem. Windows 2000 makes it an easy process to view the modem commands that RAS clients or RAS servers send.

By default, Windows 2000 will automatically log the commands that it sends to any modem. To view the log files for a particular modem, start out by selecting the Phone and Modem Options icon from the Control Panel. Click the Modems tab and then select the modem whose log file you want to view. Edit the properties for the modem, and then select the Diagnostics tab on the modem properties. You should see a View Log button on the diagnostics page—click it, and it will bring up a file named `%systemroot%\ModemLog_modemname.txt`. This file contains the history of all the commands passed back and forth between Windows 2000 and your modem.

Got a problem with a modem on a RAS server that never wants to answer calls? Try checking the log files to see if they're arguing over something. Got a RAS client that just can't seem to dial in, even though everything is configured correctly? Check the log and see if there's a problem with the initialization strings that Windows 2000 is sending.

"Can I make a RAS client automatically dial in to a RAS server at a specified time?"

Absolutely!

For example, let's say that you wanted to have an automatic routine set up for each office to call into the home server (called HOMEBASE) every night and transmit its sales figures, back up a few key data files, etc. You'll need to create the following:

♦ A dial-up networking connection with the properties for the remote server (we'll call it HOMEOFFICE in our example)

♦ A batch file to dial the dial-up networking connection and transfer the files

♦ A job in the scheduler service to trigger the batch file to run nightly

Now, the creation of the dial-up networking entry is pretty straightforward. We've covered that at length earlier in this chapter. The batch file that you create might look similar to the following (the important line to note is the RASDIAL command):

```
@ECHO OFF
CLS
ECHO Transmitting updates to HOMEBASE server
RASDIAL HOMEOFFICE
NET USE X: \\HOMEBASE\sharename
XCOPY C:\TRANSFER\*.* X: /S /E /Y
ECHO Updates to HOMEBASE server completed—hanging up
RASDIAL HOMEOFFICE /DISCONNECT
```

Now, the commands here are pretty straightforward, but the key is the RASDIAL command. This is a command-line utility that will automatically dial a dial-up networking entry. Now, for this to work you will need to have cached the username and password credentials on the dial-up networking entry that is named (HOMEOFFICE in this case). After that, the batch file runs some standard commands to connect to a share on a server, and then copy files up to the server. After the commands are completed, the RASDIAL command will hang up the connection.

Test the command out to make sure that it works properly interactively—running it from the keyboard. Once you're sure that all the timing and sequence is correct for your needs, it's time to schedule the batch file to run nightly.

By default, the scheduler service is automatically installed in Windows 2000, so setting up a job is as simple as a few point and clicks. To get to the scheduler system, start out by launching the Scheduled Tasks icon from the Programs/Accessories/System Tools menu. Click Add Scheduled Task to add a new task to your system, and then proceed through the wizard panels as prompted. Schedule the batch job to execute on a nightly basis, and then leave it alone as the system obeys and runs your batch file every night.

You could even get fancy with your batch file by trapping certain error levels—sending alert messages if there are errors, etc.

"My dial-up users aren't getting the WINS and DNS addresses that are defined on our network."

Due to the nature of the communications protocols used for dial-up connections versus local network connections, the rules are a little bit different when it comes to how clients get their WINS and DNS configurations.

For LAN connections, it's a pretty straight-forward process: the workstations will use WINS and DNS settings that are either hard-coded into the TCP/IP stack, or whatever they receive from a DHCP server's scope properties.

So, it should work the same for dial-up connections, right? The workstation should either use its own hard-coded settings or the settings defined on a DHCP server, right? *Wrong!*

Once, this little quirk had me stumped for the better part of a day at a client's site. Here's what happens—by default, Windows 2000 RAS servers will offer WINS and DNS addresses to clients based not on what the DHCP scope says, but whatever is configured for the RAS server *itself.* So, if you have your network's DHCP configuration setup perfectly, but you forgot to hard-code the correct WINS or DNS configuration in the RAS server, your RAS clients will be misconfigured when they dial in.

"I don't want my dial-up users to get the WINS and DNS addresses that are defined on our network."

Okay, so let's say that you want to override the default behavior of RAS to offer its WINS and/or DNS addresses to clients that are dialing in, without removing the WINS and DNS configuration from the RAS server itself. In that circumstance, you'll need to dive into the registry to tweak Windows 2000 a bit.

To prevent your RAS server from offering a WINS address to dial-in clients, look in the following key in the registry:

```
HKEY_Local_Machine\System\CurrentControlSet\Services\Remote Access\Parameter\IP
```

You may see a value in that key called SuppressWINSNameServers. If you do, set the value to 1. If you don't see the value in there, add it and set it to a value of 1.

To prevent your RAS server from offering a DNS address to dial-in clients, look for a value called SuppressDNSNameServers. If you see that value there, set it to a 1. If you don't see the value in there, add it and set it to a value of 1.

Chapter 23

Installing Hardware in Windows 2000

HARDWARE MANAGEMENT IN WINDOWS 2000, like many other tasks, has become much easier. With Plug-and-Play technology a working reality in Windows 2000, the Windows NT line of products takes a major stride towards seamless integration between hardware and software. Windows 2000 is, by default, a hardware hog. The operating system itself is big. It needs a lot of memory, a really fast processor, and a lot of disk space to make it all work. Put these together and you've forced yourself to get a fairly modern machine. With a fairly modern machine, you have fairly modern components. Modern components are generally going to be Plug and Play. If all components are Plug and Play, you may never find much of a need for this chapter. (Don't go away just yet, though.)

Another big step towards simplicity of hardware management in Windows 2000 comes with the variety of hardware wizards. I know what you're thinking, and I hate wizards as well. They take the skill requirements out of our profession and make it so anyone can do our job, right? Well, get over it. Sorry, I'm just kidding—kind of. Wizards do reduce the skill requirements, but they make your job easier. They make managing hardware easier. There is nothing wrong with that. Besides, wouldn't you rather spend your time doing something better?

So hardware management is easy. That's fine, but there are some serious pitfalls along the way. What if you don't have all Plug-and-Play devices? What if the wizard doesn't work? This is where the truly skilled stick out above the "click-Next-to-continue" masters. There are a lot of details to know concerning hardware components. Anything from IRQ settings to device drivers can cause device failure or system failure. In this chapter, we will discuss the common properties of hardware so that we can build a foundation for managing hardware. Next, we will go through real-world, practical hardware management issues. How do you add a device? How do you remove a device? How do you fix a device that is not working properly? Finally, we will walk through all of the hardware management components in Windows 2000 Server to apply our practical hardware foundation to the job at hand.

Hardware Resources: The Basics

There are several basic fundamentals of hardware that define how a device works with your system:

- ◆ I/O addresses
- ◆ DMA channels
- ◆ IRQ levels
- ◆ ROM addresses

The reason that you care about these hardware resources is that you can run out of them—in particular, it's fairly easy to run out of IRQs or to have *conflicts* in IRQs, I/O addresses, or the other resources. These conflicts can make new hardware fail to work, leading you to think (incorrectly) that your new hardware is no good.

Someone may have told you that you needn't worry about these conflict issues anymore because of Plug and Play. If only it were true. Plug and Play doesn't always work, and when it doesn't, it can be a very difficult beast to tame. Learn these basic concepts, and you will have some solid ground to stand on.

I/O Addresses

I/O addresses can be defined very easily. First, what is the I/O? I/O is short for input/output, of course. Every component on your computer deals with either input or output. Take, for example, a user typing an *A* on the computer. A keyboard is an input device. It takes information from some outside agent, like you, and inputs it into the computer. The CPU processes the data into something, like a digital representation of the letter A, and sends it to the appropriate output device—in this case, most likely the display adapter, which in turn sends it to the monitor.

Now there's the problem of the CPU finding the display adapter and the keyboard. The CPU needs to map an address for each piece of hardware. This address is a hexadecimal number defining each hardware location, just like a mailbox in front of your house. As each device is defined in the computer, it registers its address. From that point on, the CPU needs only to send or retrieve information from the right address.

Let's go back to our example. The CPU receives a stream of data from some I/O address number 64. This stream of data will come in the form of electrical pulses that were generated by the keyboard to specifically define an A. First, the CPU must recognize who sent this information. It came from address 64, which corresponds to the keyboard. The operating system and application have told the CPU what to do with data from the keyboard: send it to the screen. The screen can be reached via the display adapter, which resides at I/O address 3B0. The CPU generates the information for the display adapter and ships it off.

ALTERNATIVE NUMBER SYSTEMS

It's never fun, but anyone talking about hardware addresses soon runs up against having to talk in hex and perhaps binary. If you're not familiar with these alternative methods of representing numbers—or if you maybe just need a short refresher—then this sidebar is for you.

Hexadecimal numbers are used very frequently, not only in hardware applications, but in many software applications. It is very important to understand how this numbering scheme works. Before we jump into hexadecimal, let's go over the whole "numbering system" thing.

DECIMAL

Decimal numbering is what we are used to. Decimal numbering is also referred to as base 10. The *dec-* in *decimal* means 10; each place increases by a multiple of 10. From right to left, we have the 1s place, the 10s place, the 100s place, the 1000s place, etc.

Take a sample number: 175. First, figure out what each digit represents. Working down from the 100s place, we have:

$100 \times 1 = 100$

$10 \times 7 = 70$

$1 \times 5 = 5$

Now, add each digit together. $100 + 70 + 5 = 175$. Simple!

Let's go the other way. This takes some imagination. We naturally speak in base 10, but try to forget what those numbers put together mean. We do this by working down from the highest, or leftmost, digit. Start with the 1000s place just for kicks. The point here is to make sure that you start with a 0 on the left. If you start too low, then you end up with something ridiculous, like 17 10s and no 100s. So here we go:

How many 1000s are there in 175? **0**

How many 100s? **1**

Okay, we've now taken 100 out; we're left with 75.

How many 10s? **7**

We're down to $175 - 100 - 70 = 5$.

How many 1s in 5? **5**

Line those digits up in a row and you have **175**.

BINARY

Before we go into hexadecimal, let's talk binary, or base 2. Binary is equally as important as, if not more important than, hexadecimal in hardware terms. Hardware talks in electrical pulses: either on or off. On is represented by a 1, and off by a 0. Base 2 increases each digit by a power of 2, rather than by a power of 10. In this system, our digits increase from right to left with a 1s column, 2s, 4s, 8s, 16s, etc.

Continued on next page

ALTERNATIVE NUMBER SYSTEMS *(continued)*

So let's jump right into drawing out 175 in binary. First you need to get to the column that is too big for 175. Start at the smallest placeholder and work your way up until you reach a place that no longer fits: 1-2-4-8-16-32-64-128-256. Okay, obviously 256 is too big for 175.

How many 256s in 175? **0**

How many 128s in 175? **1**

$175 - 128 = 47$

How many 64s in 47? **0**

How many 32s in 47? **1**

$47 - 32 = 15$

How many 16s in 15? **0**

How many 8s in 15? **1**

$15 - 8 = 7$

How many 4s in 7? **1**

$7 - 4 = 3$

How many 2s in 3? **1**

$3 - 2 = 1$

How many 1s in 1? **1**

Put it together and you have **10101111**.

Let's work it back the other way. We'll draw out our places values from top to bottom, starting with 128, and put their corresponding binary digits next to them. We multiply them together to get the actual value for each digit.

$128 \times 1 = 128$

$64 \times 0 = 0$

$32 \times 1 = 32$

$16 \times 0 = 0$

$8 \times 1 = 8$

$4 \times 1 = 4$

$2 \times 1 = 2$

$1 \times 1 = 1$

$128 + 32 + 8 + 4 + 2 + 1 = 175$

This still sounds like a long way to put it together. Just wait, it gets necessary.

Continued on next page

HEXADECIMAL

In *hexadecimal, hex-* means 6 and *dec-* means 10. Therefore, *hexadec-* means 16. The numbers in our numeric representation increase by powers of 16. Here's where it gets interesting. With base 10, just by nature of each digit increasing by a power of 10, we had to come up with 10 different symbols to represent each value: 0, 1, 2, 3, 4, 5, 6, 7, 8, and 9. With base 2, we only need 2 symbols. Conveniently enough, we use 0 and 1.

Now we have a problem. With base 16, we need 16 different numerical symbols. Obviously we can't put a double-digit number in a single-digit place. How confusing would that be? We need more symbols beyond 9. So we improvise: 0, 1, 2, 3, 4, 5, 6, 7, 8, 9, A, B, C, D, E, and F. A = 10; B = 11; C = 12; D = 13; E = 14; and F = 15. (If it is base 16, why don't we need a symbol for 16? The 0 counts as a digit, so we only need 15 more.) Our digit places now go like this, right to left: the 1s place, the 16s place, the 256s place, the 4096s place, etc. Just keep multiplying by 16.

I'm sure you can see that 175 is going to go very quickly in hexadecimal. Again, start big. There are no 4096s in 175. There are no 256s either, so we'll start there:

How many 256s in 175? **0**

How many 16s in 175? **10**, or as we will call it, **A**

We just took 10 16s out of 175, or 160, so 175 − 160 = 15.

How many 1s in 15? **15**, or **F**

Put them together and you have **AF**.

Work it back the other way. AF translates as follows:

16 × A *or* 16 × 10 = 160

1 × F *or* 1 × 15 = 15

Add them together and you have 175.

So that's it. From now on, when you see that the I/O address for COM1 is 3F8, you will say: 3 × 256 = **768**. F × 16 = **240**. 8 × 1 = **8**. 768 + 240 + 8 = **1016**. COM1 is at address 1016. Or you can save some time by using the Windows calculator in Scientific mode. To convert 3F8 to decimal, put your calculator in Hexadecimal mode, enter **3F8**, and click the Decimal button. Voila! 1016. But what fun is that anyway?

DMA Channels

I/O channels provide a means for the CPU to talk to all hardware components. In a similar fashion, there are memory addresses, which the CPU uses to talk to different areas of memory. Memory is the lifeblood of the computer. A CPU can only process one thing at a time.

Take a simple command like 3 + 5. There are three different major components in the command. First is the 3. Next is the operator, "plus." Then comes the second argument, 5. Actually, there is a whole lot more to 3 + 5 than three simple steps. Think binary—like a computer. We want to add

011 (3) and 101 (5). First the processor receives the 011. Let's stick it in a register. (This register is an area that's *like* RAM, but isn't stored with other memory—it's actually inside the CPU, and is essential to any arithmetic or logical operation.) Now take the 101 and stick it in behind it. The addition part is where it gets tricky. How does the processor take a series of electrical pulses of 011, off-on-on, and 101, on-off-on, and somehow add them up to get 8? A portion of the processor is actually dedicated to this function. The processor will take the series of data stored in the registers and send it to the "addition" department. This is a lot of steps: Read number. Store number. Read second number. Store second number. Read operator. Determine function to run numbers through. Addition? Subtraction? Addition it is. The addition process itself takes several tiny commands to actually determine the answer. To make things worse, it hasn't even begun to determine how to make that answer show up on a screen in the form of the figure 8.

As you can see, the processor is going to get very busy when you start throwing complex commands at it. This is where DMA channels come into play. Why does the processor need to run interference on every single simple command that may be requested? Take data transfer from a file on a hard disk into memory. If every bit of that data has to go through the processor, it can get really ugly. The processor will have to read a chunk of data from the hard disk, and then write it to memory. Read a chunk; write a chunk. Read a chunk; write a chunk. With a DMA channel, you get the ability to send the data straight from the hard drive to the memory.

You're most likely to run across DMA usage in sound cards and in ECP ports, the more modern, high-speed, bidirectional version of parallel ports.

Interrupt Request Levels (IRQs)

Most hardware components in a computer work at different speeds. Compare a Pentium III processor running at 450MHz with a circa-1983 daisy wheel printer plugged into the same machine. I know, this is quite an extreme comparison, but let's go with it. The CPU wants to print, "The quick brown fox jumps over the lazy dog." Unfortunately, the CPU can't flood the printer with the whole sentence all at once, so it first says, "Print a T." Obviously, our 450MHz CPU is going to be ready to move on to the next character before the printer will. So the CPU asks the printer if it's done. No response. "Done now?" Nothing.

This can continue for an apparent eternity to our 450MHz processor. Even 1 second of wait time translates into 450 million ticks of time to the processor. Now, to the single-tasking operating system, one that can only do one job at a time, this waste of time is irrelevant. After all, it has nothing else to do but wait. But to a multitasking system like Windows 2000, this is a tremendous amount of wasted cycles that could be better spent doing other jobs. This is where interrupts come in. Instead of asking if the printer is done, the CPU tells the printer to just say when it's done, and do so on line 7. Now the CPU gets to work on other things and completely forgets about the printer. So our CPU is happily working away when line 7 lights up. It's the printer, ready for more. Take an "h."

IRQ Cascading

Now computers have a nice little system for letting every component that operates at a different speed do its own job at its own rate, but without causing the CPU to spend half its time idling. Well, not necessarily every component. Modern systems have 15 interrupt request levels. This lets 15 different components in your system interrupt the processor. Older systems had only 8 IRQs, because their interrupt-handling circuitry was built around the Intel 8259 chip, which could only handle 8 interrupts. Later (post-1984) systems needed more IRQs, so PC designers added another 8259.

But those designers didn't want to change the "newer" motherboards too radically, so they looked for a way to shoehorn those extra 8 IRQs into the PC design. But to do that, they needed to make that second 8259 a second-class citizen, putting it in line for the CPU's attention *behind* the first 8259. The *first* 8259 communicates directly with the CPU whenever it gets an interrupt—that is, whenever something activates IRQ0 through IRQ7. When one of the second 8259's IRQs—IRQ8 through IRQ15—activates, then the second 8259 doesn't tell the CPU; rather, it tells the first 8259. You can see how this works in Figure 23.1.

FIGURE 23.1

Interrupt architecture

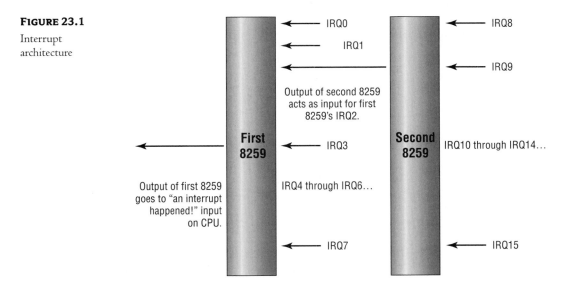

Thus, when something activates one of the IRQs between IRQ8 and IRQ15, the second 8259 responds by activating IRQ2 on the first 8259, which then responds by informing the CPU that there's been an interrupt. There are two implications of this dual-8259 architecture.

First, we *did* gain 8 more IRQs with the second 8259, but we also lost one, as IRQ2 is now dedicated to paying attention. Second, the line on the PC expansion slots that once served IRQ2 is now irrelevant, as IRQ2 is no longer available to expansion boards. IBM—the premier hardware vendor of the time—decided to just reallocate that line to IRQ9. Despite the fact that this happened 15 years ago, a lot of software and board documentation is still labeled poorly, and sometimes you'll see references to IRQ2 that *really* mean IRQ9. This whole process of having one 8259 (for IRQs 0 through 7) act as a kind of go-between for another 8259 (for IRQs 8 through 15) is called *IRQ cascading*.

TIP *Get used to hearing things like "there are 16 of something," but seeing that the highest number is 15. The zero counts too.*

IRQ PRIORITY

The 16 IRQs in the system are answered in order of priority. If, per some chance, all 16 light up at the same time, the CPU will answer IRQ0 first, then 1, then 2, and so on. Remember our cascading of IRQs 8 through 15 to IRQ2? Well, they fit in at IRQ2's priority. In other words, IRQ priority follows in order of 0, 1, 2 (8, 9, 10, 11, 12, 13, 14, 15), 3, 4, 5, 6, and finally 7. For those who really like to tweak their systems to the max, you can order your devices on IRQs based on this priority. If you have a network card and a sound card in your server, you may want to put the sound card at the lowest priority, or highest IRQ level, and the network adapter at a higher priority, or lower IRQ level. Although the sound card in a server probably won't get in the way of your network card very much, this could help the hardware in your system respond in a more appropriate manner. The common IRQs are given in Table 23.1.

TABLE 23.1: COMMON IRQS

IRQ	DEVICE	NOTES
0	Timer	You can't change this.
1	Keyboard	You can't change this.
2	IRQ9 cascade	You can't change this.
3	COM2 or COM4	Can only be one or the other COM port.
4	COM1 or COM3	Can only be one or the other COM port.
5		Usually free.
6	Floppy disk controller	
7	LPT1	
8	Clock	You can't change this.
9		Usually free, but due to its link to IRQ2, may be mislabeled as "IRQ2."
10		
11		
12	Mouse port	This is usually the built-in mouse port.
13	Coprocessor	You can't change this. The coprocessor interrupt is still used on processors with the coprocessor built into the processor chip.
14	Primary EIDE adapter	You *could* change this and the next IRQ if your system allows you to disable the EIDE adapters built onto the motherboard, but be sure that whatever host adapter you boot from uses IRQ14, or some software may give you trouble.
15	Secondary EIDE adapter	

Look through Table 23.1. At the top of the priority list is the timer. This is the system timer, which serves as the pacemaker of the entire system. Obviously, when this device says tick, the rest of the system needs to know fairly quickly. Next is the keyboard. You will pretty much want the system to respond right away to your key presses. IRQ2 comes next, which sends us to 8 through 15. Then there's the clock, which should also stay right on top of things and not lag behind when everything else gets busy. In some applications, time inconsistencies can produce very unfavorable results.

NOTE   *When looking at priority for IRQs, keep in mind that differences between priorities may mean only a few milliseconds, if that.*

Next is IRQ9, the cascading IRQ, which is sometimes available for use with an add-on card. IRQs 10 and 11 are available at the higher end of the priority list so that you can still give things like your network adapter or SCSI hard-disk controllers a good response. The farther down the priority list you go, or the higher up the IRQ-level list, the less important the device, down to the lonely old printer on LPT1.

ROM Addresses

Some hardware devices contain their own code, or ROM. This code is used for hardware to hold prepackaged routines and instruction sets. For example, a video card may have its own set of code defined to draw a circle on your monitor, which is more efficient than letting your processor stumble around trying to do something it knows little about.

The system will need a way to find, or address, that code, which is where *ROM addresses* come into play. A block of memory is set aside as the address for the device's ROM. So whenever the system needs to access the ROM, it can call up its defined memory address and cruise right along.

Watch out for ROM address conflicts. Many older devices that use ROM addresses do not allow them to be changed. Much like with some old IRQ hoarding devices, this is the case because too much software was written specifically for a certain configuration that can't be retrofitted for today's use. Most new devices, however, will let you change these addresses.

Practical Hardware Tutorial

Once you understand the nuts and bolts in hardware, it comes time to work with it. In this section, we will go over how to add new hardware, how to troubleshoot existing hardware that is malfunctioning, how to adjust hardware settings, how to remove hardware, how to configure multiple hardware profiles, and how to update device drivers.

Adding New Hardware to a System

You've bought a new hardware component. Whether a modem, a video card, a keyboard, or a monitor, you will follow the same approach to getting it integrated into your system.

Is It Supported?

Before you even begin, you want to verify that the hardware is compatible with Windows 2000 and that you have a suitable driver. Start with the Hardware Compatibility List (HCL). The HCL can be found on the Windows 2000 Server CD, under the \SUPPORT directory, as HCL.TXT. The HCL can also be found on the Web at www.microsoft.com/hwtest/hcl/.

So what is the significance of the HCL? Every item on the HCL has passed compatibility testing with Windows 2000. It is sort of like your guarantee from Microsoft that the hardware will work with the operating system. Granted, there is still a possibility that something will cause problems later down the road, but if you ever want help from Microsoft, you'll need sponsorship from the HCL. In fact, the Troubleshooter Wizard won't even continue if your hardware isn't on the list. Don't lose hope, though. The list is a living list, constantly being updated by Microsoft. Brand-new hardware may eventually show up there after the compatibility testers get their shot at it.

LOCATE A DRIVER

Beyond the mere fact of being "on the list," your hardware needs a driver. Most supported hardware will have a driver included in the Windows 2000 Server CD. If the hardware is too new to have a driver on the CD, it probably came with a driver. Look in the documentation or browse the media that came with the hardware to find the driver.

I once bought an ATI XPERT 98 Video Card. A few things on the box identified it as a potentially "compatible" card. Microsoft has a logo system that identifies hardware as being compatible with certain operating systems. At the time I bought the card, Windows 2000 wasn't mainstream, so a logo for that particular operating system wasn't stamped on the box. Instead, there were logos that said, "Designed for Microsoft Windows 95" and "Designed for Microsoft Windows 98." This told me, for one, that the recent initiatives such as Plug and Play would have been followed. (Of course, we have since started seeing logos for Microsoft Windows 2000 Server and Professional.)

The next thing to do is to look in the existing Microsoft driver files, which are included on the Windows 2000 CD. Start through the Add Hardware Wizard, and choose to add a new device. Tell the wizard that you want to select your hardware from a list, rather than try to detect one, and you will be given a list of all included drivers, broken into category. In my case, a video card falls under the Display Adapter category. By selecting the ATI Technologies manufacturer, I got a list of all ATI cards that have drivers included with Windows 2000. Well, there was no XPERT 98 listed anywhere. However, video cards are a little different in that each card is driven by a particular graphics chip, or engine as they are sometimes called. This XPERT 98 said that it was powered by the RAGE PRO PCI chip. Sure enough, under my ATI manufacturer list was the RAGE PRO PCI listing. So I took a chance that the XPERT 98 using the RAGE PRO PCI chip would work. Much to my delight, and my checkbook's, it did.

The next option for locating a driver is the Internet. Most every manufacturer has a section on their Web site from which you can download drivers for any of their supported operating systems. In my case, the Web site address for ATI Technologies was posted right there on the box. From the Web site, surf your way down through something like support or drivers. Each Web site will be different, but should be easily navigable. ("Should" is the operative word here; there is no guarantee that your manufacturer will make anything easy on you.) By following the downloading, licensing, and installation instructions from the manufacturer, you should be able to make the driver available to Windows 2000.

VERIFY HARDWARE CONFIGURATION

Windows 2000 has a neat feature within the Device Manager that lets you view your system resources and what components are plugged into them. In other words, instead of seeing a list of devices, drilling down into the properties of each, and determining what IRQs they use in order to find a free IRQ, you can simply select View Resources by Type and get a list of all occupied IRQs and their corresponding devices. This is an extremely helpful feature. From a single glance, you can see if IRQ10 is available or occupied. You can see this list of information for IRQs, DMAs, I/O addresses, or memory addresses.

Of course, if your system is entirely Plug and Play, this listing of information will not really be needed. You would merely plug your new device in and the Plug and Play Configuration Manager would take care of the rest. If this device is an older ISA card though, you may better spend your time looking into your current hardware configuration for a minute or two now, as opposed to spending an hour or two playing trial-and-error hardware configuration while watching your system lock up every time you try to boot.

The best advice here is to check all IRQs, I/O addresses, and other pertinent hardware information. Get a hard copy, and keep it handy. Every time you go to add new hardware, check your list first.

TIP   *In the Device Manager, you can generate a printed report. Once in Device Manager, select View/Print. You can print either a system summary of all components, a report on each component, or a report on just the component selected.*

INSTALL THE HARDWARE

Now for the actual hardware installation process. We will take two different approaches—one for Plug-and-Play devices, the other for non-Plug-and-Play devices.

Plug and Play

Plug-and-Play devices, by definition, will be detected by your Plug-and-Play operating system, given the appropriate resources, and be activated with no, or minimal, input required. Theoretically, it should be this simple:

◆   Shut down the server.

◆   Physically install the hardware.

◆   Boot the server.

◆   Watch Windows 2000 recognize the new hardware, and install a driver for it.

You could always be presented with the problem that a driver isn't included in the Windows 2000 device list. This will happen if the device is newer than the compilation of drivers included with the Windows 2000 source CD. In such a case, you should use the drivers that came with the device, or go to the manufacturer's Web site for the appropriate files. Given these files, though, the procedure will be a breeze.

Once again there is a catch: What if you have a non-Plug-and-Play network card in the last ISA slot that is coded to use IRQ10? Now you install a brand-new Plug-and-Play sound card in a PCI slot that for some reason prefers IRQ10 and has no clue that the ISA card will request the same. By installing this Plug-and-Play card, you have an IRQ conflict looming on the horizon. The card that used to work just fine now has to give way to the Plug-and-Play card. What to do? In Chapter 4, we talked about preparing the BIOS for Windows 2000. Your best, and by far safest, bet is to identify your non-Plug-and-Play board's resources before you even start your installation or hardware detection phase. Once identified, enter your Plug-and-Play BIOS configuration and reserve those resources for non-Plug-and-Play devices. This is how an installation of the Plug-and-Play ATI video card worked on my system:

1. I shut down the system, performing no prep work whatsoever other than preliminary research and determining that the device would be supported.

2. I popped open the case, bolted the new video card into an available PCI slot, and closed the case.

3. I plugged the monitor cable into the new video card.

4. I powered on the system and began booting into Windows 2000.

5. After logging on to the system, the dialog box shown in Figure 23.2 popped up, indicating that new hardware was detected in the form of a VGA-compatible video controller.

FIGURE 23.2

Found new VGA

6. Several seconds later, the system began searching for a driver for this new hardware (see Figure 23.3).

FIGURE 23.3

Searching for a driver

7. After searching through the devices, the system at last recognized the device as an ATI RAGE PRO PCI video card.

8. After initializing the new video card, the system detected the monitor that was attached to it and configured it into that card.

No conflicts were reported, the Plug-and-Play detection and configuration phase found a driver that was packed with Windows 2000, the driver worked, the device initialized properly, and my display worked without a problem. We'll call this the best-case scenario.

But there are a couple of different scenarios in which this process would go, well, not so smooth. First, you could have a device without a driver. In that case, you will be faced with either finding a driver or delaying the install until you can find one.

Or you could have a conflict with another card in the system, causing this new device to fail, the other device to fail, or, more commonly, both devices to fail. This will be evident by the fact that the device doesn't work or another device has stopped working, or in a last-ditch effort, errors will appear in the Device Manager window. Now, you won't always be told that there is an error in the Device Manager. This is why it becomes a good practice to go to the Device Manager after completing any device installation. Even though the installation itself went smoothly, and even if the device is working, you can't guarantee that the server is good to go for the long haul. Check it out. For a better description of what you're looking at, see the "Device Manager" section a little later.

Non-Plug-and-Play Devices

There will be occasions where ISA, EISA, and even PCI devices simply will not be detected during the Plug-and-Play detection phase. Most of the time, Windows 2000 will actually see a new device in the system. It could be reported as a totally unknown device, or it could be categorized as an unknown device of a certain type. In these situations, you have two different fundamental approaches to getting the hardware into the system.

The first method is to install the device in Windows 2000 before you actually plug the device into the system. In other words, prepare the operating system by installing the driver and telling the operating system exactly what to expect the next time it boots. Once you complete the software installation of the driver, you will be told to shut down the system and install the hardware. After it's plugged in, a reboot should bring the system up with the new device installed and working like it was there all along.

The other method is to physically install the device before telling Windows 2000 anything about it. Windows 2000 may detect and configure the device perfectly the first time around, in which case you do nothing. If the device fails detection at any level, you will have to intervene and tell Windows 2000 what the device is.

Removing Hardware

There really isn't much to removing hardware. There shouldn't be any problems with a device that isn't there, should there? Well, there is one possible error. If you remove a device without telling Windows 2000 that it is going to be removed first, it could have a problem trying to attach a driver to a device that it expects to be there. When removing devices from a Windows 2000 machine, remove the device—not the physical piece of hardware, but the listing of the device in Device Manager—from the operating system first. Once that is gone, shut down the system, physically unplug the device, and then boot the system.

Windows 2000 Hardware Management

Now that the basics about hardware are out of the way, it's time to apply them to Windows 2000 management. In this section, we will discuss the components that manage hardware, how they work, what they do, and of course, how to get to them. The different components of Windows 2000 hardware management are:

- Device Manager
- Driver signing
- Add/Remove Hardware Wizard
- Found Hardware Wizard
- Hardware profiles
- Troubleshooter

Device Manager

The Device Manager in Windows 2000 is nearly identical to the device manager found in Windows NT 4 or Windows 9x. It is a view of all hardware components in your system, how they are configured, what drivers are controlling them, and what resources they are occupying. It is also a tool for installing, removing, configuring, and troubleshooting hardware.

VIEW MODES

There are four different ways to view hardware within the Device Manager: View Devices by Type, View Devices by Connection, View Resources by Type, and View Resources by Connection. The two options View Resources by Type and View Resources by Connection are new to Windows 2000. Previous versions of Device Manager were able to tell you what IRQs, I/O addresses, and other resources certain devices were using, but if you wanted to find out which device used IRQ10, you had to go into each device until you found it. Finally, there's a better way. Instead of viewing all of the devices or device categories in your main tree view, with the details of those devices beneath them, you can select a View Resources mode that shows a listing of resources at the first level and the devices attached to those resources under each. Compare the view modes View Devices by Type (Figure 23.4) and View Resources by Type (Figure 23.5).

FIGURE 23.4

View Devices by Type

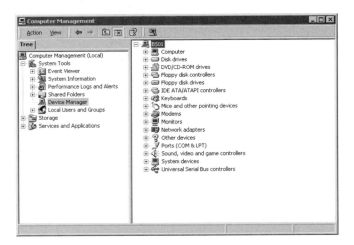

In Device Manager, you also get two different sorting methods: By Type and By Connection. The By Type mode sorts hardware based on what category of hardware the device is. All monitors go under Monitors, all modems under Modems, etc. (see Figure 23.6).

The By Connection view mode organizes your devices according to how they are physically plugged into the system. All devices on the PCI bus are shown below the PCI bus device. Since the monitor is plugged into the video adapter, you will find the listing for the monitor beneath its video adapter within the Device Manager (see Figure 23.7).

FIGURE 23.5

View Resources
by Type

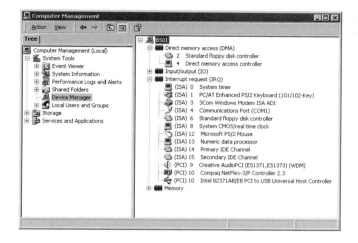

FIGURE 23.6

View Devices
by Type

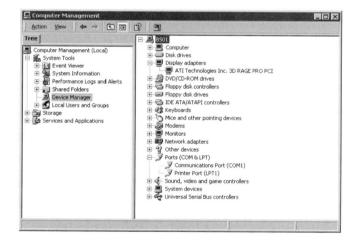

DEVICE PROPERTIES

From within each device, you can view the detailed properties of that device either by selecting the Action menu properties, right-clicking the device, and selecting Properties or by simply double-clicking the device.

General

Once within the device properties, the General tab, shown in Figure 23.8, will provide some key information.

FIGURE 23.7

View Devices by
Connection

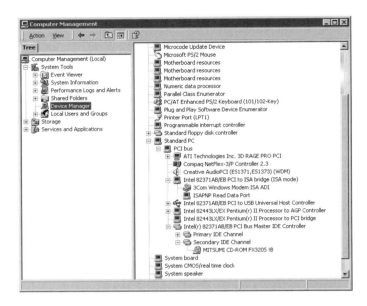

FIGURE 23.8

Device properties,
General tab

Particularly important is the Device Status window. In here, you will see whether or not the device is working and, if it isn't, a general description of why. The Troubleshooter button will launch the Troubleshooter Wizard to walk through correcting problems with a device (see the "Troubleshooter" section later in this chapter).

Also on this page is the Device Usage selection. Within this drop-down selection box, you determine when the device will be used. If your machine uses multiple hardware profiles, as is usually the case with laptop/docking station machines, you will be given the options Use This Device (Enable),

Do Not Use This Device in the Current Hardware Profile (Disable), and Do Not Use This Device in Any Hardware Profile (Disable). By not using a device in a hardware profile, you are telling Windows 2000 that in certain boot-up hardware configurations, the device either will not be installed or is expected not to be used (see the "Hardware Profiles" section, also in this chapter).

Driver

The next device properties page is the Driver tab. Important information on the driver provider, date, and version are displayed on this page (see Figure 23.9).

FIGURE 23.9

Driver details

These driver details may come in handy when working with vendors to troubleshoot faulty devices. The Driver Details button will bring up another page showing all files associated with a particular driver. If you suspect file corruption is the cause of your hardware woes, this is a simple method to find out which files you may need to replace.

Oddly, the Uninstall button is located under the Driver page; this button will completely remove the device from your system.

The Update Driver button launches the Upgrade Device Driver Wizard, which follows a series of prompts similar to those that you would go through once a new device has been detected in your system. Typically, this wizard will only be run after you have received a new device driver from the manufacturer or Microsoft that contains important upgrades to the device driver features and capabilities or bug fixes. In most cases, after launching the wizard, you will want to select Search for a Suitable Driver for My Device, as shown in Figure 23.10.

From there, you can select multiple sources in which to search for new drivers, as shown in Figure 23.11. The floppy and CD-ROM drive options will, of course, search those areas for drivers for your new device. The Specify a Location option allows you to point to a folder on your hard drive or a network drive that contains the driver files. Microsoft Windows Update will connect to Microsoft's Web site to look for the driver. To select this last option, you will need to be connected to the Internet, or have an available connection to the Internet for the wizard to use.

FIGURE 23.10

The Upgrade Device Driver Wizard

FIGURE 23.11

Locate driver files

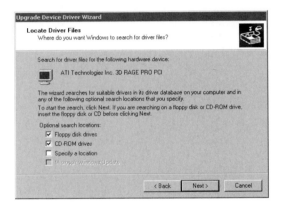

Resources

The Resources page holds the good stuff that concerns how your hardware is physically configured. All of the device's IRQ settings, ROM addresses, I/O addresses, and more are displayed in the Resources tab, as shown in Figure 23.12.

If any resources are causing conflicts, you will see a list of those conflicts and the devices that they conflict with in the Conflicting Device List area.

Some devices will also have configurable resources. By clearing the Use Automatic Settings check box, you will be allowed to change the Settings Based On options to select different prepackaged resource configurations, or, in some cases, you will be able to manually change individual resource settings by double-clicking the resource in question. If the Use Automatic Settings check box is grayed out, the device cannot be assigned new resources manually.

FIGURE 23.12

Device resources

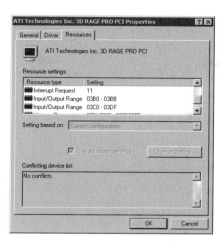

Other Tabs

Some devices will have more tabs present across the top of the device properties page. These other tabs could be labeled Properties, Settings, Advanced, or some other name. Under these pages will be hardware-specific configuration settings. For example, Figure 23.13 shows how the CD-ROM has special settings that control how the hardware works within Windows 2000.

FIGURE 23.13

CD-ROM properties

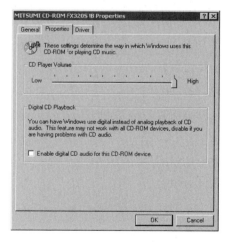

Check your devices to see which ones contain these extra pages. These settings could really come in handy to customize the performance and feel of your hardware in Windows 2000.

DEVICE MANAGER ACTIONS

Back in our Device Manager main window, there are some more actions that we can have the Device Manager carry out for us.

The Scan for Hardware Changes action works kind of like a refresh. Any changes, additions, or removals of hardware that have happened behind the Device Manager's back will be detected at this time, and the Device Manager window will be updated to reflect those changes. Any changes detected will launch the Found New Hardware Wizard, which will walk you through the installation of the Plug-and-Play device.

NOTE *The Scan for Hardware Changes action will not work with non-Plug-and-Play hardware. To install new non-Plug-and-Play devices, use the Add Hardware Wizard.*

You can also disable hardware directly from the Device Manager Action menu. Let's say you have an incompatible or faulty piece of hardware in the system that is integrated into the motherboard, and you don't want Windows 2000 to keep trying to install it every time you boot the machine. Select the device in the Device Manager window, select the Action menu, and select Disable. This action will mark the device with a red X through the device icon, and will inform Windows 2000 to leave the device alone.

Finally, you can uninstall devices by selecting the Action/Uninstall command. This will remove device drivers and information from Windows 2000, letting you physically unplug a device following a system shut down.

Driver Signing

A new option to Windows 2000, *driver signing* lets you control how Windows 2000 secures your device drivers. All drivers on the Windows 2000 CD come digitally signed. This is a verification that the driver is an authentic, Microsoft-approved driver. When updating certain software or devices in your system, the program may attempt to overwrite your existing driver, which could cause side effects that you won't be prepared for. To find the driver-signing configuration screen, you'll need to start in the System Control Panel and select the Hardware tab. From there, click the Driver Signing button. With driver signing, you get three levels of security to control how Windows 2000 notifies you about attempted changes in driver files (see Figure 23.14).

The Ignore option will not perform any signature verification and will allow any device driver file to be overwritten. The Warn option will notify you if an attempt has been made to overwrite a driver file that does not contain a signature. The Block option is the most secure option; it will not allow any driver that has not been signed to be installed.

FIGURE 23.14

Driver-signing options

NOTE   We're talking about a security feature that prevents an unwanted ability to change your device drivers. If your system partition is NTFS, then chances are, you'll need to be an administrator just to even see the folder and files where your drivers are kept. This driver-signing security is more of a feature to either keep you from accidentally overwriting drivers while performing some other installation or to keep unruly system administrators from overstepping their bounds.

Add/Remove Hardware Wizard

The Add/Remove Hardware Wizard is obviously the tool you will use whenever you add or remove hardware, but it is also used to help troubleshoot hardware or prepare the system to unplug or eject hardware like PCMCIA devices in laptops.

To launch the Add/Remove Hardware Wizard, open the System Control Panel and select the Hardware tab. Click the Hardware Wizard button, and select either to add or troubleshoot a device or to uninstall or unplug a device. By selecting the add-or-troubleshoot option, the wizard starts off with a Plug-and-Play detection phase. If new hardware is found, the Found New Hardware Wizard will appear. If no devices are found, you will be shown a list of all hardware currently installed in your system and be given an additional option labeled Add a New Device (shown in Figure 23.15).

FIGURE 23.15

The Add/Remove Hardware Wizard with the Add a New Device option

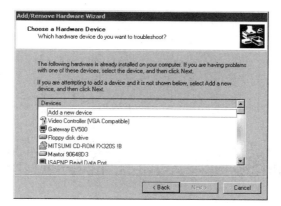

From this screen, you can either add a new device that wasn't detected through the Plug-and-Play detection or select an existing device to troubleshoot. If you select an existing device to troubleshoot, the Troubleshooter will start (see the "Troubleshooter" section later in this chapter).

If you choose to add a new device, you can either have the wizard search for new hardware or you can enter the hardware information into the system manually. This sounds redundant to have the wizard search for hardware—it just ran a Plug-and-Play detection phase two clicks ago. This detection phase, however, is a little bit different. This detection is similar to the way Windows NT 4 searches for hardware. The hardware wizard will go through all known hardware device types and try to get a response. Once the hardware responds, it should be identified and a driver should be attached. Of course, "should" is the operative word here. Some devices are more easily identified than others. If this process fails, or doesn't get it quite right, you may need to go the manual road.

To manually identify your hardware, you will first select the category of hardware that your device falls under. The next dialog box will contain a list of known manufacturers for the selected category, and, once selected, a list of supported devices for a manufacturer (see Figure 23.16).

FIGURE 23.16

Select the device driver

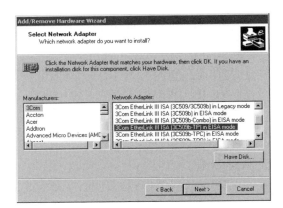

After completing the installation of the selected device drivers, your system will most likely require a reboot. Since this won't be purebred Plug-and-Play hardware that you have just manually set up, it may need the driver to initialize the device upon a reboot rather than on the fly.

Found New Hardware Wizard

The Found New Hardware Wizard shows up whenever Windows 2000 detects new Plug-and-Play hardware in your system. The first thing that happens is that the wizard tries to attach an appropriate device to the new hardware. This process is identical to the process that was used in the Upgrade Device Driver Wizard earlier. Either display a list of known devices, or search your specified locations for a suitable driver. Once the driver has been found and loaded, you are set to go.

But what if there is no device? A completely unsupported piece of hardware. I've got this system with a built-in video adapter that absolutely has no driver available for Windows 2000. Surprisingly, the Found New Hardware Wizard actually does detect a VGA-compatible display adapter, but that's about all. After searching high and low, I finally resigned to accept the choices given to me in Figure 23.17.

If no driver is available, Windows 2000 can't use the hardware. The device can either be disabled, or the installation can be skipped. If disabled, the device will be shown with a red X over its listing in the Device Manager (see Figure 23.18).

FIGURE 23.17

Failed driver files search

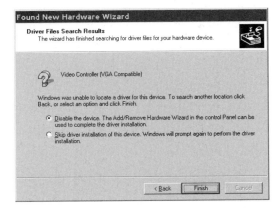

Disabled hardware

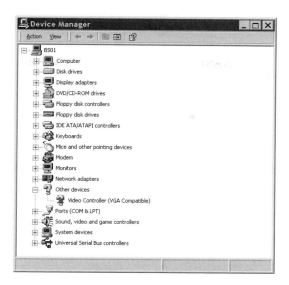

If at a later date, you obtain a driver for the device, you can launch the Add New Hardware Wizard to reinstall the device. If you elect to skip the installation, you should physically remove the hardware, or else the Found New Hardware Wizard will only go through the same process again the next time you reboot.

Hardware Profiles

Hardware profiles are used to allow your system to boot cleanly with various hardware configurations. Most commonly, this feature will be used on laptops with docking stations. In some cases, you will boot up just the laptop. In other cases, you will boot up while plugged into the docking station with additional hardware components such as a hard drive and a network card. Upon booting the system, you will get an additional menu from which you can select which hardware profile to use. By using properly defined hardware profiles, you can avoid extraneous errors and Plug-and-Play detection phases.

To configure multiple hardware profiles, you will need to start off once again in the System Control Panel and select the Hardware tab. To create multiple profiles, you'll begin by copying the first profile. Notice that you can't select to create a *new* profile. A new profile would imply a complete return to square one of the hardware detection phase. That would create a lot of unnecessary work. Instead, you just copy your current, working hardware configuration into a new profile and fine-tune it. Once you have more than one profile named in the Hardware Profile screen, you can configure your various components for usage in those profiles. To do this, go into the properties of a device from the Device Manager, then set the Device Usage to determine which profiles will use the selected component. You can either enable or disable the device for all profiles or disable the device for the current profile. It seems strange, but you cannot enable a device for just the current profile. If you want the device available for only your current profile, you will need to boot into the other profiles and select the option to disable the device in just that current profile (see Figure 23.19).

FIGURE 23.19

Hardware profiles

For each profile, you can also tell Windows 2000 if the profile is used for a portable computer or if it is docked or undocked. If Windows 2000 can determine the docking state on its own, you won't be able to change this setting.

Troubleshooter

The Windows 2000 Hardware Troubleshooter is a self-guided, point-and-click, question-and-answer help file. If you run the Troubleshooter from the Device Manger properties of a faulty device, the Troubleshooter will start off at exactly the proper place. If there's a resource conflict, it will start right at the point of how to deal with resource conflicts. If there's a driver failure, it will, of course, start right at how to deal with driver failures. The Troubleshooter can also deal with many common problems related to specific devices. It will ask questions about the nature of your problem, what does work and what doesn't work, and will eventually narrow your problem down to the source. If you are having a problem that is hardware-related, but isn't necessarily manifesting itself in the form of a warning or failure on any device, you want to start at the device that is related to the problem. From within the device properties, a Troubleshoot button will start you off with a series of very general questions to get you started (see Figure 23.20).

TIP   In some cases, you will want to start at the very top of the Troubleshooter. To get to the root level of the Troubleshooter, select Start/Help. In the left column, double-click the Troubleshooting and Other Resources book, followed by the Troubleshooting book, Troubleshooting Overview, and finally, the Troubleshooters Help option. A table on the right will show various troubleshooters, from which you can select the Hardware Troubleshooter. Another way to get into the Troubleshooter is to select a properly working device in the Device Manager, like the network adapter. Go to the Properties tab and select Troubleshooter. Some devices will start you at a device-specific troubleshooter, so you may need to try a different one.

After running through the Troubleshooter questions, you could either be presented with the solution to your problem or be given a reference to a Microsoft Knowledge Base article that provides more information on the suspected problem.

FIGURE 23.20

The Hardware
Troubleshooter
main menu

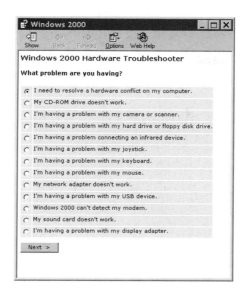

WARNING   *The Troubleshooter may ask whether your hardware is listed on the Hardware Compatibility List. If you answer No, your troubleshooting session will be terminated very abruptly. (Actually, your answer for No is given as "No, my device isn't on the HCL. I'll contact the manufacturer for further assistance.")*

Appendix

Performance Objects in Windows 2000

Win2K supports the performance objects described briefly in the following table. (I haven't included every counter in all cases, but by referring to this table you should be able to find the performance object you need to monitor the information you want.) Because the performance objects are related to the services you're running on a server and the protocols in use, your servers may include some performance counters not shown here or may not include all of the objects in this list. This is a reasonably representative sample, taken from a Win2K server running IIS and Terminal Services, having Network Monitor installed, and using TCP/IP and NetBEUI to communicate with the network. Whatever services and protocols you have installed on a server, you'll always see the objects related to disk, memory, processor, and network usage (with the exception of the Network Usage object, which will only appear if you've installed Network Monitor). I've included a little extra background for process objects relating to functions new to Win2K or that may be unfamiliar to you. For more information on unfamiliar services or features, check the index and read in more detail elsewhere in the book.

TABLE A.1: PERFORMANCE OBJECTS IN WINDOWS 2000

OBJECT	DESCRIPTION	MORE INFORMATION
ACS/RSVP Services	The ACS counters record how much network bandwidth the service is using, counting network sockets, API sockets, and the size of API notifications. The Reservation Services Virtual Protocol (RSVP) enables multimedia applications to get the amount of network space they need, based on administrator-defined policies and the amount of bandwidth available. RSVP-specific counters include timers relating to how much bandwidth an application has, the number of interfaces RSVP is aware of, and the number of message buffers it has.	Admission Control Service (ACS) allows network administrators to control the amount of network bandwidth allocated to a specific application, such as streaming video.
Active Server Pages	Monitors errors, status of client requests, the number of pending client requests, the number and duration of client sessions with the Web server, the amount of time the cache is hit (showing how efficient the Web server is in reusing data to service client requests), and the status of all ASP transactions.	Records information relating to client requests for Active Server Pages from a Web server.
Browser	Counters include the rate at which servers in the domain announce themselves to the network, the number of election packets received by the server, and the number of browse requests the server has satisfied.	Records browser activity on the network.
Cache	Records cache activity, including the number of times data can be read from the system cache without having to page it back into memory, the amount of cached information flushed (written) to disk, and the asynchronous reads that write a copy of the requested data to an applications buffer.	The disk cache is the part of RAM that's reserved for file-related data, including both recently used files and the header information that points the filesystem driver to their location on the disk.
Distributed Transaction Coordinator	The DTC counters record the status of these transactions, including the response time required, the number of committed transactions, the number of transactions aborted by the DTC or by the network administrator, and the number of transactions MTS performs per second.	The Distributed Transaction Coordinator (DTC) is the transaction-processing component of the Microsoft Transaction Server (MTS). DTC makes sure that all MTS transactions are executed only if all systems involved in the transaction carry it out.
FTP Service	Records the number of FTP clients, the number of current connections, bytes sent and received from the FTP server, files sent and received, the maximum number of connections during a session, total logon attempts (successful and unsuccessful), and other information related to providing FTP services.	The File Transfer Protocol is used for file exchange over a TCP/IP network.

Continued on next page

TABLE A.1: PERFORMANCE OBJECTS IN WINDOWS 2000 *(continued)*

OBJECT	DESCRIPTION	MORE INFORMATION
IAS Accounting Clients	Monitors information relating to accounting packets sent and received by clients, including the rate at which packets are sent and received, how many are dropped or malformed, and the total number of processed packets.	The Internet Authentication Service (IAS) provides a central point for authenticating, authorizing, accounting, and auditing dial-up or virtual private network (VPN) users connecting to RADIUS-compatible remote access servers.
IAS Accounting Server	Records information relating to IAS accounting packets sent and received by servers, including the rate at which packets are sent and received, how many are dropped or malformed, and the total number of processed packets.	
IAS Authentication Clients	Records information relating to IAS authentication packets received by clients, including the rate at which packets are sent and received, how many are dropped or malformed, and the total number of processed packets.	
IAS Authentication Server	Records information relating to IAS authentication packets received by servers, including the rate at which packets are sent and received, how many are dropped or malformed, and the total number of processed packets.	
ICMP	The ICMP counters record the number of diagnostic messages that the server has received. This object also includes ICMP packets with errors (received and refused).	The Internet Connection Management Protocol (ICMP) is part of the TCP/IP suite of networking protocols. It's used for maintaining routing tables and reporting transmission problems (the Ping command uses ICMP). Most of the time you won't need to monitor any counters associated with this object unless you're trying to detect an excessive level of Ping requests slowing down the server.
IMDB Service	The IMDB counters record the percentage of the cache currently in use, the number of tables and groups in the cache, and the current number of client connections to the cache.	The In-Memory Database (IMDB) provides database applications fast access to data. It does this by keeping the data in RAM instead of making the application wait for the file system to retrieve data from disk. This is like the file cache, but for database information only.

Continued on next page

TABLE A.1: PERFORMANCE OBJECTS IN WINDOWS 2000 *(continued)*

OBJECT	DESCRIPTION	MORE INFORMATION
Internet Information Services Global	Records activity related to serving Internet (WWW and FTP) client requests. Counters for this object record the caching and retrieval of binary large objects (BLOBs) used for handling the large strings of data associated with video and image files, and also of file handles and URLs.	This counter applies to *all* Internet-related requests, not just FTP or HTTP.
IP	The IP counters record events associated with the sending and receiving of IP datagrams, including the rate at which they're sent, received, and processed; the discard rate for outbound and inbound packets; and the discard rate. These counters also include fragmentation rates (necessary when a large packet goes onto a network that can't handle packets that big).	The Internet Protocol addresses and routes packets between hosts, using unacknowledged packets called *datagrams*. Monitoring IP traffic tells you how much data is going in and out of the network and whether it's being successfully transmitted.
Job Object	The counters associated with job objects are very similar to the ones associated with processes, monitoring total CPU time used by the job absolutely or within a specified period, the time spent in user time and kernel time, and the page fault rate for all processes in the job. The object also includes counters describing how many processes are or have been associated with a job object.	Until some new applications are written, you don't really have to worry about monitoring job objects. A job object is a nameable, securable, shareable object that controls certain attributes of the processes associated with it. Such attributes include the default working set allowed by each process within the job, its total CPU time limit, the per-process CPU time limit, the maximum number of processes associated with the job object, the priority class for the processes, and the processor affinity, if any (that's the preferred processor to use in a multiprocessor computer). The main function of a job is to allow Win2K to deal with certain processes as groups rather than separately. Most processes will not be associated with job objects, as this functionality is new to Win2K and currently few applications are written to support them.
Job Object Details	The counters work the same way as the Process Details counters except on a per-job basis.	

Continued on next page

TABLE A.1: PERFORMANCE OBJECTS IN WINDOWS 2000 *(continued)*

OBJECT	DESCRIPTION	MORE INFORMATION
Memory	These counters include values for the number of page faults, data read from and written to the paging file, the amount of memory that can be committed (promised to a process, but not yet used) without extending the paging file, the amount of system code currently in physical memory, and any other data that Win2K maintains to help you keep tabs on memory usage.	The Memory object contains many performance counters related to the way Win2K uses physical and virtual memory for user and system processes.
NBT Connection	Counts the total number of bytes sent via NBT connection to another computer or all computers, the number of bytes received, or both.	NetBIOS over TCP/IP (NBT) resolves IP addresses for NetBIOS applications. (Note that this is different from DNS or WINS name resolution; this applies to NetBIOS applications on a TCP/IP network only.)
Network Interface	This object records performance counters applying to the physical network card in the computer (or to the loopback connection, if you prefer). Records bytes and packets received and set, current bandwidth available, and the number of errors experienced.	The network interface is the physical network card.
Network Segment	Counters for this object can monitor the types of traffic on the segment (multicast or broadcast), display how much of the local network bandwidth is available, and show the total bytes and frames received on the segment each second.	Monitors traffic on the local network segment if you have SMS's Network Monitor installed.
Objects	Records the number of each type of Win2K object (processes, threads, events, mutexes, sections, semaphores) currently on the server.	Objects are Win2K's representation of system resources or computer parts. Processes represent (roughly) executable programs. Threads are the executable parts of processes. Sections are areas of memory that processes use for storing data. Semaphores are devices threads use to gain exclusive access to data they share with other threads. Mutexes make sure that only one thread is executing a given section of code. Sections may be shared among processes, so you may have fewer sections than processes.

Continued on next page

TABLE A.1: PERFORMANCE OBJECTS IN WINDOWS 2000 *(continued)*

OBJECT	DESCRIPTION	MORE INFORMATION
Paging File	Records the current or peak usage of the paging file (or of each paging file, if you have more than one).	The paging file is the area on logical hard disks where data being used is stored when RAM is too full to hold all current data.
Physical Disk	These counters can monitor the percentage of time a disk spends reading or writing data, the average size of a data transfer, the average size of the queues of data waiting to be processed, and the rate at which the disk processes read and write requests.	Records data reads and writes to each physical disk on the server. The logical disks located on each physical disk are identified, so you can tell which disk you want to monitor.
Process	These counters include data transfer required, the percentage of time a process spends executing in kernel or user mode, the amount of time the process has been running, memory use by the process, the number of threads in a given process, and the process's priority.	Monitors the resource usage by a single process running on the server or all processes. The ratio of processes to executable programs is roughly 1:1, and processes exist for all the parts of the operating system.
Processor	Monitors the percentage of time the CPU spends doing various tasks, such as handling interrupts or running user programs. Also monitors the rate at which the CPU does these tasks, measured as so many tasks per second.	The processor is the final authority in handling all processes within the computer. Monitor processor activity to make sure your CPU can keep up with the demands placed on it.
Redirector	Redirector performance counters can record the rate at which bytes/packets are sent and received on the network, the number of connections the server has to various redirector types, the number of commands currently queued for processing, and the number of network errors generated each second.	The redirector is the part of the operating system that sends client requests to the network if required and accepts incoming requests for processing.
Server	Records the status of client sessions with the server, including how many sessions there are, the rate of logons, and how many have ended due to timeouts or other errors. Server performance counters can also monitor the amount of virtual and physical memory the server is using and the rate at which the server is sending and receiving bytes.	
Server Work Queues	The server work queue describes the amount of work that's waiting for the server to get to it. Counters can record the active and available threads and the rate at which the server is transmitting bytes of data or performing read and write operations.	

Continued on next page

TABLE A.1: PERFORMANCE OBJECTS IN WINDOWS 2000 *(continued)*

OBJECT	DESCRIPTION	MORE INFORMATION
SMTP Server	Records information related to mail-handling operations, including the number of connections, the number of tries it takes to successfully send a message, the total number of bytes received over time, the number of undeliverable messages generated (according to the reasons they were undeliverable), successful and unsuccessful directory service lookups, the rate and number of DNS lookups, and the rate at which the SMTP server is sending and receiving messages and other data.	The Simple Mail Transfer Protocol (SMTP) is used for transferring mail over a TCP/IP network. Any data in this object is mail-related.
System	Records information related to the size of the Registry relative to its quota, the rate at which data is passed to the filesystem, the rate at which the filesystem handles this data, the current number of processes active on the system, the number of threads waiting for processor time, and the number of seconds since the last reboot. (That they're counting in seconds makes me wonder how optimistic Microsoft is about Win2K's stability.)	The System performance object is a server-wide look at how the components of the server are doing their jobs.
TCP	Records data relating to TCP connection status and the rate at which segments (TCP packets) are sent and received.	TCP is the protocol working with IP to make sure data gets where it's supposed to go. For speed reasons, IP doesn't make explicit connections or check to see whether data got through as planned.
Telephony	Records data relating to telephone calls serviced by the computer, including the number of existing and used lines, the rate of incoming and outgoing calls, and the number of telephone devices connected to the server.	
Terminal Services	This number will include the console and the two connections created by default for the first two users, even if no one is currently connected to them.	Records the number of active and inactive (disconnected) terminal sessions.
Terminal Services Session	Records performance data for the selected terminal session, including memory usage, cache hits, thread counts, compression data related to the display protocol, transmission errors, and the percentage of time the CPU spends processing user and kernel data for that session.	Monitor these counters to see which sessions are taking up the most resources. You might use the data you collect from these counters to identify demanding users and make them use a special terminal server so they don't affect other users.

Continued on next page

TABLE A.1: Performance Objects in Windows 2000 *(continued)*

OBJECT	DESCRIPTION	MORE INFORMATION
Thread	Records thread-related information for all threads running on the system or a selected one. Counters can display the amount of time a thread has been running, its priority, the virtual addresses it's referencing, the percentage of time it's spending executing in kernel or user mode, and its state (waiting, running, ready, terminated, etc.).	Threads are the executable parts of a process, and the parts that actually get scheduled CPU time.
UDP	These counters record the rate at which UDP datagrams are sent or received by the server.	UDP is a Transport layer connectionless protocol used for very small messages and with broadcast capabilities. You will probably never need to monitor this object; user data is sent with IP, not UDP, and Ping uses ICMP packets.

Index

Note to the Reader: Throughout this index **boldfaced** page numbers indicate primary discussions of a topic. *Italicized* page numbers indicate illustrations.

A

A (host) records
  in CACHE.DNS, 440–441
  in DNS, **370–372**, *371*
  in zone file format, **402**
/a switch
  in NTBACKUP, 1346–1347
  in tskill, 1057
  in winnt, 91
-A switch in nbtstat, 335
AarpRetries key, 1089
absolute path for shortcuts, 727
Accept Any Authentication Including Clear Text option, 1438
access control. *See* permissions; security
access control entries (ACEs), **658–659**, *659*
Access Control Lists (ACLs)
  for permissions, **658–659**, *659–660*
  for Registry keys, 59
  for security groups, 639
    ADMT tool for, **581**
    in migration, **575**
Access Control screen for Web sites, 1120, *1120*
Access Control Settings for dialog box
  for auditing, 832, *832*
  for domains, 130
  for ownership, 827–828, *827*
  for permissions, 659, *659*, 823–824, *824*
  for printers, 939, *940*
Access Denied error, 796
Access Permissions screen, 1126, *1126*, 1137–1138, *1138*
Access tab
  for NNTP servers, **1149–1151**, *1150*
  for SMTP servers, **1164–1166**, *1164*
Access this computer from the network right, 662
Access Through Share Permissions dialog box, 1243, *1243*
Accessories, profile settings for, 713
Account Is Disabled option, 626
Account Is Locked Out option, 630
Account Lockout Duration option, 699
Account Lockout Threshold option, 699
Account Operators group, 648, 650
Account Policies category, 694
Account tab, **629–631**, *629*

accounts
  auditing management of, **567**
  computer, 68–69, **81**, 129
  user. *See* users and user accounts
ACEs (access control entries), **658–659**, *659*
ACLs (Access Control Lists)
  for permissions, **658–659**, *659–660*
  for Registry keys, 59
  for security groups, 639
    ADMT tool for, **581**
    in migration, **575**
ACS (Admission Control Service), 1500
ACS/RSVP Services performance object, 1500
Act as part of the operating system right, 662
Action tab, 1283, *1283*
actions in IPSec, **286**, **291–292**, *291*
Activate Scope screen, 310, *310*
activation
  DHCP scopes, **310–311**, *310–311*
  ICS, **274–275**, *275*
  in licensing, **1034–1037**, *1035–1036*
Active Directory, 80, **445–446**, 1219
  for auditing, **566–572**, *569–570*
  backing up, 1320, **1356–1358**
  certificates for. *See* certificates
  for connectivity, **453–454**
  for contacts, **515**
  for delegation, **452–453**, **585**
  DHCP servers for, **302–304**, *303–304*
  DNS for, 358, **444**, **517–525**, *522*, **584–585**
  for domain controllers, **582–583**
  for domains, **458–459**, **464–465**
    building and maintaining, **459–462**, *460–461*
    first, **487–498**, *490–497*
    geographically dispersed, **458–459**
    names of, **583–584**
    in planning, **584–585**
    second, **498–514**, *498–499*, *503–514*
    size of, **458**
    subdomains in, **459**
  for DSMT objects, **1254–1255**, *1254–1255*
  for empty root, **485–486**
  for forests, **478–481**, *479*, *482–483*
    administrators for, **498–506**, *498–499*, *503–506*

benefits of, 455
enterprise, **1219–1220**, *1220*
global catalogs for, 472
merging, **1220–1221**
synchronization in, **538–540**
trusts in, **481–485**, *482–483*
for group policies, 463, 474, **562–566**, **584–585**,
    1222–1224, *1224*
for groups, **465–466**
    changes to, **582**
    inside groups, **466–472**, *468–471*
    size of, **472–473**
limitations of, **21–22**
logons under, **486–487**
for migration. *See* migration
for namespace unification, **455–456**
as new feature, **5**
for one-domain enterprises, **457**
and operations masters. *See* FSMOs (Flexible Single
    Master of Operators)
for OUs, **473–476**, 1222
planning, **584–586**
for political needs, **453**
for power and control, **456–457**
for printers, 923
replicating, **453–454**, 1224
    Dfs, **1225–1226**
    GPOs, **1226**
    inter-site, **560–562**, *560–562*
    local. *See* local Active Directory replication
    SYSVOL, **1224–1225**
restoring, **1356–1358**
RIS authorization in, **115–116**, *115–116*
for scalability, **454–455**
schema modification in, **1220–1221**
for searches, **449–450**
for security, **447–449**
for shared folders, **516–517**, *516*
for shares, **810–811**
for sites, 477, **556–560**, *557–559*, **584**, **1221**, *1222*
for sub-administrators, **450–451**
for trees, **477–478**
for trusts, **481–485**, *482–483*
Windows 95/98 workstations access to, **968**
Active Directory Configure tab, **1249–1450**, *1249*
Active Directory Domains and Trusts tool, 498
    for domain modes, 498
    for domain naming, 532
    for trusts, 160, 482–483
    for UPN suffixes, 501

Active Directory Installation Wizard
    for child domains, 513–514, *513–514*
    for domain controllers, **490–498**, *490–497*
    for trees, 479
Active Directory-integrated DNS servers, 1227
Active Directory-integrated zones, **415**, 1227
    creating, **415**, *415*
    multimaster zone replication in, **415–416**
    problems in, **417–418**
    secure DDNS registration in, **416–417**
Active Directory Migration Tool. *See* ADMT (Active
    Directory Migration Tool)
Active Directory Schema object, 530
Active Directory Service Interfaces (ADSI), 620, 635, 1220
Active Directory Sites and Services tool, 162, 498
    for domain controllers, 552, *552*
    for GC servers, 502, *503*
    for replication, 542, *542*, 560–561, *560*
    for sites, 557, *557*
    for subnets, 558, *559*
Active Directory Users and Computers tool, 80
    for Administrator and Guest account, **623**
    for delegation, 510–511
    for domain accounts, **620–621**
    for domain controllers, 158, 162
    for domain local groups, 468–469, *469*
    functions in, **621–623**, *621–622*
    for group policies and GPOs, 1226
    for groups
        creating, **636–638**, *636–639*
        security, **643–646**, *644–646*
    for printers, 944
    for roaming profiles, 717
    for root, 485
    for shares, 517, 811
    for Terminal Services client connections, 1016, *1017*
    for user accounts, 29, **498–499**, *498–499*, 618
        creating, **623–626**, *624–626*
        managing, **633–635**, *634*
        properties for, **626–633**, *627–633*
    for workstations, 971
Active Registrations folder, 349
Active Server Pages (ASP) for SMTP servers, **1172–1174**
Active Server Pages performance object, 1500
active sessions for Terminal Services clients, 1018
adapters
    for Macintosh computers, **1069**
    network, **156–158**, *157–158*
    for Terminal Services, 992
    for workstations, 964, *965*

Adapters and Settings tab, 222
Add, Modify, or Remove Shortcuts screen, 892, *893*
Add a Group Policy Object Link dialog box, 679–680, *680*
Add a New Device option, 157, 1493
Add a New Installation Image option, 133
Add a New Replica dialog box, 847, *847*
Add Catalog dialog box, 1192–1193, *1192*
Add Counters dialog box, 1262–1263, *1263*, 1273, *1274*
Add dialog box, 668
    for groups, 509
    for RIS images, 133, *133*
Add Directory dialog box, 1193, *1193*
Add Excluded Files dialog box, 1328–1329, *1328*
Add Exclusions screen, 306, *306*
Add Files to the Installation screen, 892, *893*
Add from Store option, 613
Add Group option, 670, 681
Add Installations and Run Programs screen, 894, *894*
Add Job option, 1331
Add Key dialog box, 1047, *1048*
Add Members to a Group option, 637
Add Mirror dialog box, 765–766, *766*
Add more client drivers option, 946
Add more ports option, 946
Add Network Adapter dialog box, 974, *974*
Add Network Components link, 155
Add Network Share Alias Automatically option, 1191
Add New Connection option, 1063
Add New Hardware Wizard, 1495
Add New option, 1327–1329
Add New Programs option, 871
Add New Quota Entry dialog box, 802–803, *803*
Add Port option, 955
Add Printer Driver Wizard, 957–958, *958*
Add Printer Wizard
    for client connections, **920–924**, *921–924*
    for Macintosh printers, **1078–1081**, *1078–1080*
    for multiple printer settings, 948
    in NetWare, 1242, *1242*
    for print server installation, **909–913**, *909–912*
Add Protocol option, 974
Add RAS Device dialog box, 1455, *1455*
Add Registry Entries screen, 892, *893*
Add/Remove Hardware Wizard, **1493–1494**, *1493–1494*
    for modems, 1416–1417, *1417*
    for network adapters, 157, *157–158*
Add/Remove Programs dialog box
    for DSMT, 1246
    for network services, 155

    for packages, 871, *871*
    for ZAP files, 886
Add/Remove Snap-in dialog box, 176–178, *176–178*, 528, 596
Add/Remove Windows Components tool
    for DHCP, 302
    for IIS, 914
    for Macintosh servers, 1071
    for Terminal Services, 996, 998
Add Special Port dialog box, 280, *281*
Add Standalone Snap-In dialog box, 176, *177*, 528, 597
Add to Domain option, 80
Add/Troubleshoot A Device option, 157
Add Upgrade Package dialog box, 898–899, *898–899*
Add workstations to domain right, 662
AddPrinterConnection method, 930
Address Assignment tab, 277, *278*
Address Leases folder, 319–320, *320*
Address Pool tab, 282, *283*
Address Range Assignment screen, 1428, *1428*
Address Resolution Protocol (ARP), 202–203
Address tab, 627, *628*
addresses
    I/O, **1474**, 1490
    IP. *See* IP addresses
    MAC, 200, 300, 455
    ROM, **1481**
Addresses tab, 272–273, *273*, 1419–1420, *1419*
ADDUSER tool, 578
AddWindowsPrinterConnection method, 930–931
ADM files (administrative templates)
    folder for, 673
    group policies for, **696**
Admin Pack tools, 620
ADMIN$ share, **835**
administrative scalability, **3–4**
administrative shares, 835
administrative templates (ADM files)
    folder for, 673
    group policies for, **696**
Administrative Templates folder, 696, 699
Administrative Templates node, 689, 691
administrative tools, **13**
Administrative Tools folder, 167
Administrator account, 618, **623**
    locking out, 1213
    renaming, 619, 1214–1215
Administrator Properties dialog box, 1429–1430, *1430*
administrators
    ADMT for, **579**
    for domains, 238–239

for encryption, 797
forest-wide, **498–506**, *498–499, 503–506*
passwords for, 78, 239
for Sysprep program, **148–149**
Administrators group, 619
nesting in, 644
rights in, 648–649
for Web sites, 1120
Administrators Have Full Control; Other Users Have
Read-Only Access option, 809–810
Administrators properties dialog box, 644, *644*
adminpak.msi file, **868**, *869*
AdminPassword setting, 97
Admission Control Service (ACS), 1500
ADMT (Active Directory Migration Tool), **578**
for ACLs, **581**
for administrator accounts, **579**
example using, **578–579**
for groups and users, **580**, *580–581*
help file for, **579**
installing, **579**
for NT-to-2000 trusts, **579**
ADSI (Active Directory Service Interfaces), 620, 635, 1220
Advanced Attributes dialog box
for encryption, 795, *795*
for Indexing Service, 1193, *1194*
Advanced Certificate Request screen, 605, *605*
Advanced Connection Properties dialog box, 272–273, *273*,
1419–1420, *1419*
Advanced Delivery dialog box, 1168–1169, *1169*
Advanced Features option, 510
Advanced Options menu, **1372–1373**
for boot logging, **1377–1378**, *1377*
for Debugging mode, **1378**
for Last Known Good Configuration, **1374–1377**,
1375–1376
for Safe Modes, **1373–1374**
for VGA mode, **1377**
Advanced Research Projects Agency (ARPA), 194–195
Advanced Restore Options screen, 1355–1356, *1355*
Advanced Schedule Options dialog box, 1333, *1333*
Advanced Settings window, 222–223
Advanced Setup options, 73, *73*
Advanced tab
for DDNS registrations, 409, *409*
for DHCP classes, 313, *313*
for DNS queries, 425, *425*
for printers
hours, 934, *934*
logging, 958, *959*

priorities, 953, *954*
searching for, 923
spooling, 906, 950, *950*
for System Control Panel, 164
for Terminal Services, 1023, 1296
for trace logs, 1280, *1281*
for user profiles, 714, *714*
for WINS
logging and burst mode, 344, *344*
replication, 346–347, *346, 348*
Advanced TCP/IP Settings dialog box, 241–245,
241–242, 244
Advanced Web Site Identification dialog box, 1107, *1108*
advertising
for network browsers, **1306**
packages, 874
.aero domain, 363
after MSI snapshots, **882**, *882–883*
AHs (Authentication Headers) in IPSec, 285
Alert Logs folder, 1281
alerts
logs for, **1281–1284**, *1281–1284*
managing, **160–161**, *161*
Alias (CNAME) tab, 392, *392*
aliases
in DNS, 392, *392*
for FTP sites, **1136–1138**, *1136–1138*
for SMTP servers, 1171
in Web sharing, 852–853
for Web sites, 1124–1125, *1125*
Aliases (CNAME) records
in DNS, **373**
in zone file format, **404**
All ICMP Traffic filter, 289
All IP Traffic filter, 289
All Newsgroups on This Virtual Server option, 1156
All tab, 899, *899*
All Unassigned option, 1101
All Users directory, 711, 715
All Users Have Full Control option, 809
Allow Access option, 1429
Allow All Computers Which Successfully Authenticate to
Relay option, 1166
Allow Anonymous option, 1150
Allow Anonymous Connections option, 1132
Allow Client Posting option, 1148
Allow Control Messages option, 1148
Allow Dynamic Updates option, 386, 406, 415
Allow IIS to Control Password option, 1133
Allow Incoming Sessions to This Address option, 282

Allow Inheritable Permissions from Parent to Propagate to This Object option, 820, 823
Allow Logon to Terminal Server option, 1021
Allow Only Anonymous Connections option, 1133
Allow permissions for shares, **813–814**
Allow Posting option, 1152
Allow Printers to be Published policy, 941
Allow Processing Across a Slow Network Connection option, 704, 706
Allow <Protocol>-Based Remote Access and Demand Dial Connections option, 1433
Allow Pruning of Published Printers policy, 941
Allow Remote Clients to Request IPX Node Number option, 1434
Allow Servers to Pull News Articles from This Server option, 1148
Allow the Focus to Be Changed option, 675
Allow the User to Customize Views option, 191
AllowAllPaths option, 1386
AllowRemovableMedia option, 1386
AllowWildCards option, 1386
Alpha processor support, 21
#ALTERNATE command, **339**
Alternate Phone Numbers dialog box, 1421, *1422*
Always Available Offline option, 860
Always move new import media to the Backup media pool option, 1330
Always Update DNS option, 407
Always Use the Following option, 1420
American Registry for Internet Numbers (ARIN), 204
analog modems for RAS, **1412–1414**
Analysis Complete dialog box, 788, *788*
Analysis Report dialog box, 789, *789*
Analyze Computer Now option, 671
AND operator in Indexing Service queries, 1196
angle brackets (<>) for tags, 124
Anonymous Access and Authentication Control settings, 1113, 1115
Anonymous Access authentication, 1164
anonymous FTP, 1132–1133, 1141
ANONYMOUS LOGON group, 651
answer files, **91–97**, *92–95*
Apache package, 1093
APCs (asynchronous procedure calls), 1269
APIPA (Automatic Private IP Addressing) feature, 270
APIs (Application Programming Interface), **330–331**
APNIC (Asia Pacific Network Information Center), 204
Append Data permission, 816, 818
Append or replace existing backup sets option, 1321
appending with backups, 1349

AppleSeed project, 1092
AppleShare, 1083, *1083*
AppleShare IP (ASIP), **1091–1093**
AppleTalk printers, 1070, **1077–1081**, *1078–1080*
AppleTalk protocol, 1073
Application Data folder
    in folder redirection, 691–692
    in NT 4 profiles, 712
Application logs, 1284–1285, *1285*
Application Name setting, 1112
application order of group policies, **681–683**, *682*
Application Programming Interface (APIs), **330–331**
Application Protection setting, 1112
applications
    cross-platform support for, **1090**
    deployment, **980–981**
    group policies for, 565
    for MSIs
        installing, **881**
        testing, **882**, **885–886**
    in Terminal Services. *See* Terminal Services
    upgrading, **898–902**, *898–900*
    in Web site security, 1112
Applications subkey, 1045–1046, *1046*, 1049
Applications tab
    for remote access, 1446–1447, *1447*
    in Task Manager, 1292–1293, *1293*
Apply Group Policy for Users/Computers Synchronously During Start-up option, 703
Apply Group Policy permission, 564, 872
APPS folder, 807
archive bits, 1326
ARIN (American Registry for Internet Numbers), 204
ARP (Address Resolution Protocol), 202–203
ARPA (Advanced Research Projects Agency), 194–195
ARPAnet, **194–197**, *195*, 362
ascii command, 1142
ASCII files
    for DNS servers, 436
    in FTP, 1142
Asia Pacific Network Information Center (APNIC), 204
ASIP (AppleShare IP), **1091–1093**
ask.html file, 1197–1198
Ask Me Before Synchronizing the Items option, 864
ASP (Active Server Pages) for SMTP servers, **1172–1174**
ASP Email product, 1095
Assign a Unique Randomly Generated Password to Each User option, 1250
Assign an Existing Certificate option, 612

Assign Drive Letter or Path screen
  for primary partitions, 753, *753*
  for RAID 5, 770, *770*
  for volumes, 761, *761*
Assign Each User the Same Custom Password option, 1250
Assign NO Password to Each User option, 1250
assigning
  login scripts, **654**
  packages, **874–878**, *875–878*
  permissions, **820–824**, *821–824*
associations for Macintosh computers, 1090
asterisks (*)
  in Indexing Service queries, 1196
  with net use, 837
asymmetric encryption, 589–592
asynchronous procedure calls (APCs), 1269
AT command, 1331
at signs (@)
  in name server records, 440–441
  in NTBackup, 1348
atomic permissions, **817–818**
attacks on Web sites
  detecting, **1211**
  deterring, **1211–1214**
Attempt Direct Delivery before Sending to Smart Host
  option, 1169
attrib command, 1384
attributes in replication, 547–548, **554–556**
Audit Policy folder, 569, *569*
auditing, **566**
  kinds of, **566–568**
  log management in, **569–572**
  printers, **937–939**, *938–939*
  shared folders, **831–833**, *831–832*
  steps in, **568–571**, *569–570*
Auditing tab, 832, *832*, 937–939, *939*
Authenticated User option, 1087
AUTHENTICATED USERS group, 651
authentication, **29–33**, 447–449
  account and password information for, **29**
  biometric devices for, 1318
  for certificates, **589–591**
  in IPSec, **286–287**
  for Macintosh computers, 1084, *1084*, 1086–1087
  for NNTP servers, 1149–1151, *1150*
  for printers, 915–916
  for RAS, **1431–1432**, *1431*, 1438
  for SMTP servers, 1164–1665, *1165*
  for telnet, 1183
  for Web sites, 1113–1115, *1114*

Authentication Access control, 1114–1115
Authentication Control settings, **1114–1115**
Authentication dialog box, 1164–1665, *1165*
Authentication Headers (AHs) in IPSec, 285
Authentication Methods, 1150, *1150*
Authentication Methods dialog box, 293, *293*
  for printers, 915, *916*
  for RAS, 1431–1432, *1431*
  for Web sites, 1113–1115, *1114*
AUTHINFO protocol, 1150
Author mode
  in MMC, 170, 175, 192
  policies for, 699–700
authoritative restores, **1358–1360**
authoritative servers in DNS, **366–367**
authorization, 447
  for database programs, 448–449
  DHCP servers, 115, *115*, **302–304**, *303–304*
Authorize DHCP Server dialog box, 115, *115*, 303–304, *304*
Authorize option, 115
Authors group, 1120
AUTOCHK.EXE utility, 1371
autoexec.bat file, 977
autoexec.nt file, 1381
autoloaders, DAT, 1335
Automatic Caching for Documents setting, 858, 862
Automatic Caching for Programs setting, 858
automatic operations
  backups, **1345–1347**
  Offline Files caching, **858**
  printer installation, **929–933**
  Terminal Services logons, 1004
Automatic Private IP Addressing (APIPA) feature, 270
Automatically Assign IP Addresses by Using DHCP option,
  277–278
Automatically Backup System Protected Files with the System
  State option, 58
Automatically Create Mailbox option, 1178
Automatically Detect and Install My Plug and Play Printer
  option, 1078, 1080
Automatically Dial This Initial Connection option, 1458
Automatically Log Off Users When Logon Hours Expire
  option, 630
Automatically Publish New Printers in the Active Directory
  policy, 942
AutoPartition setting, 97
AutoRun feature, 107
availability goals, **2**
Available Bytes counter, 1267
available hours for network printers, **933–934**, *934*

Avg Disk Queue Length counter, 1268, 1282
Avg Disk sec/Transfer counter, 1268

B

B channels, 1413
B node in NetBIOS, 333–334
Back up files and directories right, 662
Back up migrated remote storage data option, 1321
Back up the contents of mounted drives option, 1330
background
 printing in, 950
 priority for, 1295
backslashes (\) for server names, 8–9, 35
Backup application, 1318–1319, *1319*
backup argument in NTBACKUP, 1345
backup browsers, 1309
Backup dialog box, 1334, *1334*
backup domain controllers (BDCs)
 with Active Directory, 470
 communications with, 458–459, 490
Backup Job Information dialog box, 1331, *1331*
Backup Log tab, 1326–1327, *1327*
Backup Operators group, 451, 619, 647, 649
Backup Reports dialog box, 1351–1352, *1351*
Backup tab, 1322–1325, *1322–1324*
Backup Type tab, 1325–1326, *1325*
Backup Wizard, **1319–1322**, *1319–1320*, 1331–1333, *1332*
backups, **1318**
 Active Directory, **1356–1358**
 automating, **1345–1347**
 file selection for, **1322–1325**, *1322–1324*,
  1327–1329, *1327–1329*
 General tab for, **1329–1330**
 improvements for, **18–19**
 logging types for, **1326–1327**, *1327*
 Offline Files as, **862–863**, *863*
 procedures for, **1319–1322**, *1319–1320*
 in recovery plans, **1400–1401**
 for Registry, **58–59**, 1320, 1349
 restoring, **1352**
  Active Directory, **1356–1358**
  authoritative, **1358–1360**
  configuration settings, **1356**
  file selection for, **1353–1356**, *1355*
  techniques for, **1352–1356**, *1353*
  viewing logs for, **1356**
 RSM for, **1335–1336**
  libraries in, **1337–1338**
  media in, **1338–1339**, *1339*, **1342–1345**
  media pools in, **1340–1342**, *1341–1342*

physical locations in, **1336–1337**, *1336*
 saving options for, **1331**
 scheduling, **1331–1335**, *1331–1335*
 strategies for, **1347–1348**
  differential, **1350–1351**
  weekly, **1348–1349**
 sub-administrators for, **451**
 types of, **1325–1326**, *1325*
 viewing logs from, **1351–1352**, *1351*
bad sectors, 791–793
Badmail directory, 1164, 1171
Badmail Directory setting, 1164
Balance option, 1298
Ballmer, Steve, 42
Baltimore certificate authority, 594
bandwidth
 controlling, 463
 for RAS, **1406–1410**
 for replication, **474–475**
 for Terminal Services, **1045**
bandwidth throttling, **1098–1099**, 1110
Basic Authentication
 for NNTP servers, 1150
 for SMTP servers, 1165
 for Web sites, 1114–1115
basic disks
 converting dynamic to, **762**
 converting to dynamic, **756–760**, *758–759*
 deleting, **756**
 vs. dynamic disks, **743–744**
Basic Rate Interface (BRI), 1413
BASICDC template, 669
BASICSV template, 669
BASICWS template, 669
batch command, 1384
batch files
 for backups, **1349–1351**
 for IMS program, **1177–1178**
BATCH group, 651
BDCs (backup domain controllers)
 with Active Directory, 470
 communications with, 458–459, 490
"Because of a network error, the session will be
 disconnected" error message, 1015
before MSI snapshots, **880–881**, *880–881*
Best Available Using DDC option, 1004
beta testers, 873
.bin files, 1139
binary circular files, 1279
binary command, 1141
binary data type, 50

binary files
  in FTP, 1139, 1141
  for logs, 1279
binary number system, **1475–1476**
BIND system, 444, 519–520
bindery in NetWare migration, **1250–1252**, *1251–1252*
binding, network, **221–223**
biometric authentication devices, 1318
BIOS, preparing, **65**
bitmaps
  caching, 1007
  in Setup, **105**
.biz domain, 363
bks argument in NTBACKUP, 1345
.BLG files, 1279
Block option for driver signing, 1492
Block Policy Inheritance option, 676, **685**, 708–709
blocking transmissions, IPSec for, **284**, **296**
boot disks
  creating, **1381–1382**
  with NTFS, 66
BOOT files in DNS, **436–437**
  cache records in, **438**
  examples, **438–440**
  primary records in, **437–438**
  secondary records in, **438**
Boot from File option, 437
boot.ini file
  on boot disks, 1381
  boot partition path in, 1392
  defaults in, 74–75, 81, 84
  deleting, 84
  for mirrored partitions, **779–780**
[boot loader] section, 84, 779
boot process, **1369**
  Advanced Options menu in, **1372–1373**
    for boot logging, **1377–1378**, *1377*
    for Debugging mode, **1378**
    for Last Known Good Configuration, **1374–1377**, *1375–1376*
    for Safe Modes, **1373–1374**
    for VGA mode, **1377**
  in DNS, **436–437**
  hardware in, **1369**
  kernel in, **1371**
  with mirrored partitions, **779–780**
  NTDETECT in, **1370**
  NTLDR in, **1370**
  NTOSKRNL in, **1370–1371**
  Registry key construction in, 56–57

boot records, fixing, **1390**
boot sectors, fixing, **1390**, 1392
bootable CD-ROM drives, 64
bootdisk directory, 72
BootMethod key, 437
BootP protocol
  benefits of, **300**
  in DHCP, **300–301**, 323, 326
bottlenecks, System Monitor for
  CPU, **1269–1270**, *1270*
  disk, **1270–1271**
  memory, **1265–1268**
  network, **1271–1273**
brackets ([]) in scripts, 97
branding information, **101**, *102*
[Branding] section, 100
breaking mirror sets, **767–768**, 775
BRI (Basic Rate Interface), 1413
Bring to This Computer option, 1011
broadcasts
  for browse lists, 34
  in DHCP, 323, 326
  IP addresses, **207–208**
  routing tables, 253
  SAP, 1306
  with shared folders, 517
Browse a Common Web Site to Find Printers, 945
Browse for a Group Policy Object dialog box, 675, *675*, 899, *899*
Browse for computers dialog box, 1010, *1010*
Browse For Printer screen, 923, *923*
browse lists, **32–35**, *34–35*
  function of, **1306–1307**, *1307*
  viewing, **38**
  workgroups for, **35–38**
browse masters, 33, **1308–1311**, *1311*
Browse permission, 1106
browse services, 33, **1306–1307**, *1307–1308*
Browse the Network to Find Printers policy, 945
Browser, replacement for, **463**
Browser performance object, 1500
browsers
  network. *See* network browsers
  for print management, **960**
Browsers group, 1120
brute force attacks, 1317
BS separator page function, 952
built-in groups
  local, **646–651**, *647*
  special, **651**

Builtin container, 579, 621–622, 647, *647*
Builtin Local groups, 647
burst mode in WINS, 344
By Connection option, 1486, *1488*
By Type option, 1486, *1487*
Bypass traverse checking right, 662
Bytes Total/sec counter, 1272–1273

C

C$ share, **835**, 1216
C shell, 654
/c switch in CHKDSK, 793
/C switch in EFSINFO, 797
-c switch in nbtstat, 356
CA Identifying Information screen, 603, *603*
cable modems, 261, 274
cabling for Macintosh computers, **1069**
Cache Bytes counter, 1298
cache.dns file, 365, 436–437, **440–441**
Cache folder, 1366
Cache performance object, 1500
cache records in BOOT files, **438**
Cached Lookups folder, 420
CachedLogonsCount key, 728
caches
    client-side. *See* Offline Files
    for credentials, 728
    in DNS resolution, **418–421**
    in RDP, 988
    for shares, 808
    for Terminal Services, 1007
    tuning, **1297–1298**, *1298*
    for user profiles, **728–729**
    for Web sites pages, 1116–1117
caching-only DNS servers, **422–423**, *422*
Caching Settings dialog box, 858, *858*
call command, 654
Callback options, 1430
caller ID service, 1430
CALs (client access licenses)
    cost of, **70**
    for Terminal Services, **1032**
canonical names, 373
cartridges in RSM, 1338–1339
CAs (certificate authorities), 594, 1186
    creating, **602–603**, *602–603*
    for issuing certificates, **604–607**, *606*
    requesting certificates from, **604–606**, *604–606*
    retrieving certificates from, **607–608**, *607–608*
    trust in, **599–602**, **608–609**, *609–610*

cascading IRQs, **1478–1479**, *1479*
case sensitivity in FTP, 1141
catalog.wci file, 1190
catalogs in Indexing Service
    contents of, **1193**, *1193–1194*
    creating, **1192–1193**, *1192*
    querying, **1195–1202**, *1195*
    standard, **1192**
Category filtering option, 1290
CCM (Change and Configuration Management), 457, 663–664
cd command
    in FTP, 1140
    in Recovery Console, 1384
CD image format, 111
CD-Remote-Installation-Services Properties dialog box, 132–133, *132*
CD-ROM discs
    in RSM, 1338–1339, *1339*
    in unattended installations, **87**
cdup command, 1140
centralized application deployment, Terminal Services for, **980–981**
centralized logons, **448–449**
Century Interpretation for Year 2000 setting, 697
Cerf, Vinton, 196
certificate authorities, 594, 1186
    creating, **602–603**, *602–603*
    for issuing certificates, **604–607**, *606*
    requesting certificates from, **604–606**, *604–606*
    retrieving certificates from, **607–608**, *607–608*
    trust in, **599–602**, **608–609**, *609–610*
Certificate Authority snap-in, 606–607, *606*
Certificate Authority Type screen, 602, *602*
Certificate dialog box, 608–609, *609*
Certificate Manager, 597–598, *597–598*, 607, *608*
Certificate Path tab, 608–609, *609*
Certificate Revocation Lists (CRLs), 614–615
Certificate Services database
    backing up, 1320
    restoring, 1356
Certificate Services dialog box, 602, *602*
Certificate Summary screen, 1187, *1187*
certificate trust lists (CTLs), **613**
certificates, **586–588**
    contents of, **593**
    for e-mail, **611–612**
    encryption in, **591–593**
    exporting, **797–798**
    in IPSec authentication, 286–287, **610–611**
    issuing, **604–607**, *606*

keys for, **589–591**
MMC for, **596–598**, *597–598*
obtaining, **593–594**
in Outlook, **599**
PKI, 587
requesting, **604–606**, *604–606*, **1185–1187**,
1185–1187
retrieving, **607–608**, *607–608*
stores for, **595–596**
trust issues in, **599–602**, **608–609**, *609–610*
types of, **594–595**
for Web browsers, **612–614**
Certificates add-in, 794, 798
Certificates folder, 598, 794, *794*, 798
/cg switch in rsm, 1339
Change and Configuration Management (CCM), 457,
663–664
Change DNS Domain Name When Domain Membership
Changes option, 442
Change Domain Controller option, 530
Change Drive Letter and Path option, 776
Change Icon dialog box, 597
change logon command, 1050, 1060
Change Mode option, 498
Change Operations Master dialog box, 532
Change or Remove Programs option, 871
Change permission
for Macintosh computers, 1076
for shares, 812
Change Permissions permission
for printers, 937
for shares, 816, 818
change port command, 1050
Change port time-outs option, 947
Change Primary DNS Suffix When Domain Membership
Changes option, 240
Change Schema Master dialog box, 530, *530*
Change the system time right, 662
Change Type dialog box, 732–733, *733*
change user utility, 1041, 1050
Change Zone Type dialog box, 415, *415*
changers in RSM, 1337
channels in RDP, **988–989**, *989*
characterization data file, 905
charts in System Monitor
counters for, **1264–1273**, *1270*
creating, **1263–1264**, *1263*
saving, **1274–1275**, *1275*
chdir command, 1384
Check Names option, 637

Check Now option, 792
Check On A Pending Certificate Request screen, 607, *607*
Check Published State policy, 942
Check Status option, 849
Checking Disk dialog box, 792, *792*
checksum headers, 214
checksums in PPP, 228
/checkupgradeonly switch in winnt32, 88
Child Domain Installation screen, 514, *514*
child domains, 477–478
creating, 514, *514*
in DNS namespace, 361, *362*, **365–366**
CHKDSK command, **790**
from command prompt, **792–794**
from Explorer, **792**, *792*
operation of, **791**
in Recovery Console, 1384
CHOICE action, 142
choice.osc file, 142–143
Choose a Hardware Device screen, 157, *158*, 1493, *1493*
Choose a Hardware Task screen, 157, *157*
Choose Request Type screen, 605, *605*
Chooser, 1082–1083, 1085, *1086*
CIDR (Classless Inter-Domain Routing), **211–214**
cipher command, 796, 799
Cisco 1602 router, 260
Class A, B, and C IP addresses, **204–205**, *204*
Class C networks, subnetting in, **210–211**
classes for DHCP
user, **314–317**, *315–316*
vendor, **312–314**, *313*
Classless Inter-Domain Routing (CIDR), **211–214**
clean installs, 70–71
clean migration, **574–577**
cleaning out Offline Files, **865**
Clear All Events option, 1288
Clear Cache option, 420
Clear This Database before Importing option, 671
clearing logs, 570
client access licenses (CALs)
cost of, **70**
for Terminal Services, **1032**
Client Connection Manager, 1006–1008
Client Connection Wizard, 1005
"Client could not connect to the terminal server" error
message, 1016
Client Devices tab, 929
Client for Microsoft Networks service, 155, 964, 966, *966*, 974
Client Installation Wizard, 123–124, **140–145**
Client (Respond Only) policy, 288

Client Scripting setting, 1122
client-server computing, **449–450**, **1408–1410**
Client service, 80
Client Settings tab, 929
Client Side Extension (CSE) DLLs, 673
clients, 964
    caches on
        in DNS resolution, **418–421**
        in Offline Files. *See* Offline Files
    connecting. *See* connecting clients
    in DDNS registrations, 406–407
    DHCP, **320**
        leases for, **320–321**
        scope options for, **308–309**, *309–310*
    for FTP sites
        command-line, **1140–1142**
        graphical, **1142–1143**
    in IMS, **1180**
    mail, 226
    NetWare
        connectivity for, **1238**, *1238*
        support for, **1237–1238**, *1237*
    network printer connections, **918**
        from DOS, **918**
        from Internet, **924–926**, *925*
        in Terminal Server environment, **926–929**
        from Windows 3.x, **918–920**, *919–920*
        from Windows 95/NT, **920–924**, *921–924*
        from Windows 2000, **921–924**, *922–924*
    RAS, **1436–1440**, *1436–1440*
    RIS for, **120**, *121*
    software for, **25**
    Terminal Services. *See* Terminal Services
    thin, **984–985**
        client sessions in, **991**
        RDP for, **987–990**
        terminal servers for, **985–987**
    WINS, failure modes in, **340**
Clients Cache This Referral for Seconds value, 845
Clients Using DNS (Domain Naming System) option, 278
Clipboard, 989
clock IRQ, 1480
Clone key, 1375
cls command, 1384
clusters, 781, 786
cmd.exe shell, 1374
/cmd switch in winnt32, 88
cmdcons command, 1378
/cmdcons switch in winnt32, 88
cmdlines.txt file, **106–109**

CNAME (Aliases) records
    in DNS, **373**
    in zone file format, **404**
Code Red weasels, 1189
collaboration, 1143
.com domain, 225, 361–362
COM ports
    mapping, 929
    for printing, 908, 948
    for RAS, 1414
COM2 IRQ, 1480
combining domains, **479–481**
comdlg32.ocx file, 884–885, *885*
comma-delimited (.CSV) log files, 1279
command line
    for connecting to shared folders, **836–838**
    formatting from, 786
    for FTP clients, **1140–1142**
    improvements in, **16–17**
    for profile information, **1022**
    for RDP client deployment, **1002**
    for Terminal Services, **1050–1051**
    for trusts, **484–485**
    unattended installation from, **88–91**
command sources for taskpad views, 187
Command Type screen, 184, *184*
comments
    for log files, 1278
    for Netware shares, 1241
    for printers, 1079, *1079*, 1081
    for scopes, 304
    for shares, 807
Commit Charge section in Task Manager, 1292
Commit Limit counter, 1267
Committed Bytes counter, 1267
committing
    memory, 1266
    transactions, 790
Common Configurations screen, 256, *256*, 263, *263*,
    1426, *1426*
common shares, **835–836**, *835*
COMPATDC template, 669, 900
compatibility
    of filenames, 783
    of hardware, 64, 77, 1411, 1481–1482
compatibility scripts, **1041–1044**
COMPATSV template, 669, 900
COMPATWS template, 669, 900
Completing the Active Directory Installation Wizard screen,
    497, *497*

Completing the Add Printer Wizard screen, 911, *912*, 1079, *1080*

Completing the Backup Wizard screen, 1320, *1320*

Completing the Create Partition Wizard screen, 754, *754*

Completing the Create Shared Folder Wizard dialog, 1075

Completing the Delegation of Control Wizard, 509, *510*

Completing the Routing and Remote Access Server Setup Wizard screen, 264, *264*

complex passwords, group policies for, **685–687**

compmgmt.msc program. *See* Computer Management tool

Components folder, **1363–1364**, *1364*

[Components] section, 100, 137

Components Selection dialog, 78–79

compression

    for backups, 1348

    and encryption, 796

    in RRAS, 1435

    for Terminal Services, 1007

Compute selection information before backup and restore operations option, 1329

computer accounts, 68–69, **81**, 129

computer browsers, 33

Computer Configuration node, 689

    group policies for. *See* group policies and GPOs

    vs. User Configuration, 696

Computer Location policy, 943

Computer Management tool, 158

    for administrators, 148–149

    for alerts, 161

    components of, **171–173**, *171–173*

    for device management, 164

    extensions for, 178

    for groups, 467–468, *468*

    for Indexing Service, 1190, *1191*

    for Macintosh computers

        file associations, 1090

        permissions, 1076

        security, 1088

        services, 1081

        shares, 1074

    for Remote Access Auto Connection Manager service, 1424, *1424*

    for remote computer services, 162

    for shares and shared folders, 160–161, *161*, **809–810**, *809–810*

    for System Information, 167

    for user accounts, **617–619**, *618*

computer names

    Active Directory for, **455–456**

    in DNS, 359–360

    in installation, 78, 94, *94*

    in scripts, 100

    underscores in, 235

Computer Names screen, 94, *94*

Computer option for filtering, 1290

ComputerName setting, 100

computers

    assigning packages to, **874–878**, *875–878*

    Macintosh. *See* Macintosh computers

Computers container, 161, 473, 621–622

concurrent license mode, 808

config.nt file, 1381

config.sys file, 977

configuration

    Dfs replicas, **847**, *847*

    DSMT, **1246**, *1246*

        Active Directory Configure tab, **1249–1450**, *1249*

        General tab, **1246–1247**, *1247*

        Generate Password tab, **1250**, *1250*

        Novell Environment Discover tab, **1247–1248**, *1247*

        Verify tab, **1248–1249**, *1248*

    FrontPage Server extensions, **1122–1123**, *1122*

    in hardware installation, **1482–1483**

    IIS

        default, **1096–1097**, *1097*

        global, **1097–1100**, *1098, 1100*

    IMS program, **1178–1180**, *1178–1179*

    Macintosh servers, 1072

    multiuser environment applications, **1037**

    network adapters, **156–158**, *157–158*

    network browsers. *See* network browsers

    network printers, **946–947**, *946*

        multiple settings, **948**

        port settings, **948–950**, *949–950*

        priorities, **953**, *954*

        separator pages, **951–953**, *951*

    RAS

        clients, **1436–1440**, *1436–1440*

        servers, **1430–1436**, *1431, 1433–1435*

    RDP clients, **1000–1001**

    restoring, **1356**

    RRAS, **263–269**, *263–268*

    saving, **1367–1368**

    services, 164–165

    TCP/IP, testing, **234–236**, *234, 236*

    user profiles, **713–715**, *713–715*, **719–722**, *720*

    WINS servers, **342–344**, *343–344*

    workstations

        Windows 95/98, **964–965**, *964–965*

        Windows NT, **968–972**, *968–971*

configuration naming contexts, 1224
Configuration tab
    for browser elections, 1311
    for Macintosh servers, 1072, *1072*
    for workstations, 964–966, *964–965*
Configure and Enable Routing and Remote Access option,
    256, 258, **263–269**, 325, 1426
Configure Computer Now option, 671
Configure Device dialog box, 1463, *1464*
Configure device - WAN Miniport (PPTP) dialog box,
    1453, *1453*
Configure DHCP Options screen, 307, *308*
Configure DNS screen, 495, *495*
Configure File Server for Macintosh option, 1072, 1088, 1090
Configure Gateway dialog box, 1239–1240, *1240*
Configure LPT Port dialog box, 956, *956*
Configure Options option, 311–313
Configure Port option, 956
Configure Port Usage dialog box, 1455, *1455*
Configure Server Extensions option, 1119
Configuring Active Directory dialog box, 497, *497*
Confirm Password setting, 619
Conflicting Device List, 1490
conflicts, 83
    credentials, **837–838**
    IRQ, 1483
    permissions, **825**
    in ROM addresses, **1481**
    routing information, **251–252**
    in schema, **531**
    synchronization, **861–862**, *862*
Conflicts/Sharing folder, 1363
Connect access type, 1029
Connect As option, 972
Connect Client Drives at Logon option, 1023
Connect Client Printers at Logon option, 929, 1023
Connect dialog box, 919, *919*
Connect Network Drive dialog box, 34, *34*, 38, 976, *976*
Connect Network Printer dialog box, 919, *919*
Connect through a Phone Line and Modem option, 1418
Connect to Another Computer option
    for drivers, 164
    for Event Viewer logs, 1286
    for management, 171
    for services, 162
    for shares, 160, 809
    for tasks, 183, 185
Connect to Domain Controller dialog box, 532, *533*
Connect To option, 976
Connect to Printer dialog box, 920, *921*

connecting clients
    DOS workstations, **977–978**
    Windows 95/98 workstations, **963**
        Active Directory access in, **968**
        attaching to networks, **965–967**, *966*
        configuring, **964–965**, *964–965*
        network resource access in, **967**, *967*
    Windows for Workgroups workstations
        attaching to networks, **976**, *976*
        configuring, **973–976**, *973–976*
    Windows NT workstations, **968**
        configuring, **968–972**, *968–971*
        network resource access in, **972–973**, *972*
Connection Availability screen, 1441, *1442*
Connection Manager, 1004
Connection method screen, 1035, *1035*
connection names for Internet gateways, 1446
Connection Options tab, 1008, *1009*
Connection settings
    for FTP sites, **1130–1131**
    for NNTP servers, 1147
    for SMTP servers, 1161
Connection tab, 272
Connection Type screen, 265, *266*
connections
    client. *See* connecting clients
    for demand dial interface, 265, *266*
    for FTP sites, **1130–1131**
    ICS. *See* ICS (Internet Connection Sharing)
    intranet
        dumb terminal, **227–228**
        LAN, **228**
        SLIP/PPP, **228**
        terminal, **228–229**, *229*
    ISP, **262–263**, **270–274**, *271–273*
    managing, 166
    network. *See* networks and networking
    for NNTP servers, 1147, **1151**
    persistent, 261, 1468
    for print services. *See* printer connections
    for RAS
        Internet, **1417–1424**, *1418–1425*
        private network, **1441–1444**, *1442–1444*
        scheduling, **1471–1472**
        VPN. *See* VPNs (Virtual Private Networks)
    for RDP clients, **1005–1013**, *1006–1007, 1009*
    for SMTP servers, 1161, **1165–1166**, *1165*
    Terminal Services, troubleshooting, **1015–1016**
    for Web sites, 1108
    for Windows-based terminals, **1004**

Connections folder, 929, **1025–1026**
Connections settings, 1108
connectivity, Active Directory for, **453–454**
Connectivity folder, 1366
console root in MMC, 170, *171*
Console tab, 191, *191*
console tree in MMC, 170, *171*
Console Tree option, 190
Console Window in MMC, 170, *171*
consoles, 169
    creating, **175–178**, *175–179*
    in RDP, 991
    Recovery. *See* Recovery Console
consolidated enterprise resources, Dfs for, **851**
contacts
    Active Directory for, **515**
    distribution groups for, **639–640**
containers vs. OUs, 652
Content folder, 1366
Content Location settings, **1134**
Content Ratings dialog box, 1117–1118, *1117*
context menus, 622, 626
Control Panel
    for device management, 163–164, *163*
    group policies for, **697**
    profile settings for, 713
controllers
    in disk duplexing, 749
    domain. *See* domain controllers (DCs)
Conversion Successful dialog box, 882, *882*
convert utility, 786
converting
    basic disks to dynamic, **756–760**, *758–759*
    dynamic disks to basic, **762**
    FAT to NTFS, **786–787**
Cookies folder, 712
.coop domain, 363
copiers, drive-to-drive, 13, 109–110, 146–147
coprocessor IRQ, 1480
Copy All Setup Files option, 73
Copy backups, 1326
copy command, 1384, 1389
Copy Group Members option, 580
Copy Local Failure Reports to Postmaster option, 1179
copy-on-write data sharing, 987
/COPY switch in tsprof, 1022
Copy To dialog box, 149, *149*, 719, *720*, 730
Copy To option, 719, 721
/copydir switch in winnt32, 88

copying
    account templates, 635
    encrypted files, **796**
    images, **150**
    OEM for, **105–106**
    user profiles, 719–721
    zone information, 388
/copysource switch in winnt32, 89
corrupted NTFS volumes, logs for, 782
Counter Logs folder, 1280
counters in System Monitor, 1262–1263
    logs for, **1277–1280**, *1277–1279*, **1284**
    selecting, **1264–1273**, *1270*
    for Terminal Services, **993–994**
country domains, 225, 362–363
cprofile command, 1050
CPUs
    for performance, **1304**
    print, **906–907**
    requirements for, **62**
    System Monitor for, **1269–1270**, *1270*
    for Terminal Services, 992
    tuning, **1295–1296**, *1296*
    for Web sites, 1098
    for Windows terminals, 994
crashes in replication, **544–546**
Create a Computer Account in the Domain option, 971
Create a New Certificate option, 1185
Create a New Dfs Link dialog box, 845, *845*
Create a New Port option, 910, 1078
Create a pagefile right, 662
Create a token object right, 662
Create Computer Account option, 80–81
Create Files permission, 816
Create Folders permission, 816
Create Installation Disk(s) dialog box, 1000, *1000*
Create IP Security Policy option, 292
Create Logical Drive option, 755
Create New Object-(Group) dialog box, 129
Create New Object Wizard, 624–626, *624–626*
Create or Join Forest screen, 491, *491*
Create Partition Wizard
    for logical drives, **754–756**, *755–756*
    for primary partitions, **752–753**, *753–754*
Create permanent shared objects right, 662
Create Shared Folder dialog box, 809–810, *810*
Create Shared Folder Wizard, 161, **1074–1075**, *1074–1075*
Create Tree or Child Domain screen, *490*, 491
Create Volume option
    for dynamic disks, 760

for mirror sets, 765
for RAID 5 volumes, 768
for stripe sets, 764
Create Volume Wizard
for dynamic disks, **760–762**, *760–762*
for RAID 5 volumes, **768–770**, *769–770*
for stripe sets, 764–765, *764*
Create Windows Groups screen, 1119–1120, *1120*
CREATOR OWNER group, 651
credentials
cached, 728
conflicts in, **837–838**
for FTP sites, 1137
CRLs (Certificate Revocation Lists), 614–615
cross-platform application support, **1090**
CSE (Client Side Extension) DLLs, 673
CSPs (cryptographic service providers), 794
.CSV (comma-delimited) log files, 1279
CTLs (certificate trust lists), **613**
Current Disk Queue Length counter, 1271
Current Sessions settings, 1131
CurrentControlSet key, 49–51, 1375
CurrentVersion key, 52, *52*
cusrmgr tool, 635–636
Custom Errors tab, **1118**, *1119*
Custom HTTP Headers option, 1118
Custom Installation Wizard, **889–897**, *889–897*
custom program groups, 715
custom settings, 80
Custom Support URL in the Printer Window's Left Pane
policy, 943
Customize Default Application Settings screen, 892, *892*
Customize IE 5 Installation Options screen, 895, *895*
Customize Outlook Installation Options screen, 894–895, *895*
Customize Share and Folder Permissions option, 810
Customize View dialog box, 190, *190*, 621
customizing packages, **888–897**, *889–897*

D

D channel, 1414
$D separator page function, 952
D$ share, **835**
/d switch
in cipher, 796
in net use, 837–838
in NTBACKUP, 1346
daemons, 1158
Daily backups, 1326
damaged files, replacing, **1389–1390**

DAT drives, 1335
Data Encryption Standard (DES), 631
data recovery services, **1400**
[Data] section, 96–97
Data Storage Location screen, 603, *603*
data types
in Registry, **50–51**, *50*
for spool files, 906
Database and Log Locations screen, 493, *493*
Database Verification tab, 343–344, *343*
databases for security, **671**
Datacenter Server, 43
dates in separator pages, 952
dbgtrace command, 1050
DC Options option, 1223–1224
DCPROMO program
troubleshooting, **523–525**
working with, 162, **490–498**, *490–497*
DCs. *See* domain controllers (DCs)
DDC (Display Data Channel), 1004
DDI (Device Driver Interface) commands, 905
DDNS (dynamic DNS), **405**, **519–520**
operation of, **405–406**
registrations in
with DHCP, **407**
scavenging, **408–412**, *408–409, 411–412*
with static IP addresses, **407**
triggering, **406**
vs. WINS, **412–413**
security in, **413–414**, **416–417**
DdpCheckSums key, 1089
Debug programs right, 662
/debug switch in winnt32, 89
debugging in Terminal Services, 1043
Debugging mode, Advanced Options menu for, **1378**
decimal number system, **1475**
decrypting files, **800**
Default Active Directory Path When Searching for Printers
policy, 945
default.asp file, 1113
Default Backup Path setting, 343
Default BOOTP class, 314
Default Computer for user profiles, 727, *728*
Default Computer Properties dialog box, 727, *728*
Default Domain Policy, 686
Default Domain Policy Options dialog box, 676–677, *677*
default.htm file, 1113
DEFAULT key, 55
Default Moderator Domain setting, 1149
Default Printer screen, 923, *924*

Default Properties dialog box, 1151–1153, *1152*
Default Routing and Remote Access class, 315
Default Setup Behavior option, 890
Default to Main Client Printer option
    for redirection, 929
    for Terminal Services clients, 1023
Default Tree and Context option, 1238
Default User class, 314–315
Default User folder, 149, 711
Default User profile, 715, 1020
DefaultPort key, 1088
defaults
    gateways
        DHCP for, 308
        in routing, **250–252**, *251*
    IPSec policies, **288**
    printers, 923–924, 926
    quota limits, 801
    routers, 202
    routes and route addresses, **207–208**, **247–248**, *248*
    user profiles, **721–722**, **726**, 737
DefaultZone key, 1089
deferred procedure calls (DPCs), 1269
Define This Policy Setting option, 681, 686
Define This Policy Setting in This Template option, 670
Define User Class option, 315
defining
    network printer port settings, **948–950**, *949–950*
    NNTP expiration notices, **1155–1157**, *1156*
    share permissions, **811–813**, *812–813*
    sites, **558**, *558*
    subnets, **558**, *559*
    virtual directories
        for FTP sites, **1136–1138**, *1136–1138*
        for Web sites, **1125–1126**, *1125–1126*
Defragment Now button, 788
defragmenting disks, **787–790**, *788–789*
del command, 1385
Delegate Control option, 687
Delegated Domain Name screen, 398, *398*
delegation
    in Active Directory planning, **585**
    advanced, **510–512**, *510–512*
    in DNS, **365–369**, *368*, **398–400**, *398–399*
    for domains, **452–453**
    group policy administration, **687–689**, *688*
    in OUs, 459, **508–513**, *508–510*
Delegation of Control Wizard, 508–510, *508–510*,
    687–688, *688*
Delete Logical Drive option, 756

Delete Owner option, 349
Delete Partition option, 756
Delete permission, 816, 818
Delete Port option, 956
Delete Subfolders and Files permission, 816, 818
Delete Taskpad View option, 182
Delete Volume option, 762, 771
deleting. *See also* removing
    Dfs child nodes, **850**
    disks
        basic, **756**
        dynamic, **762**, *762*
    GPOs, 679
    Indexing Service catalogs, 1192
    mirror sets, **766–767**, *767*
    partitions
        in installation, 76
        Recovery Console for, **1390–1391**
    print server ports, **956**
    RDP client connections, 1008
    replica members, 847
    stripe sets, 765, **771**
    taskpad view menus, 190
    taskpad views, 182
    Terminal Services, **998–999**
    unused accounts, 1318
    user profiles, 727–729, *728*
    WINS records, **350–351**
Delivery tab, **1166–1169**, *1167*
DELPROF.EXE utility, 729
Demand-Dial Interface Wizard, 265–267, *266–268*,
    1464–1467, *1464–1466*
Demand-Dial Routing Connections option, 1463
demoting domain controllers, **162**
Denied Access option, 916–917
Deny Access option, 1429
Deny Access On dialog box, 916, *917*
Deny access to this computer from the network right, 662
Deny logon as a batch job right, 662
Deny logon as a service right, 662
Deny logon locally right, 662
Deny permissions, **813–814**, **825–826**, *826*
Department of Defense (DoD), 194
deploy.cab, 91, 99
Deploy Software dialog box
    for assigning packages, 877, *877*
    for MSTs, 896, *896*
    for publishing packages, 871, *871*, 887, *887*
deployment. *See also* packages
    centralized, **980–981**

group policies for, 565
RDP clients, **1001–1002**
Deployment tab, 872, *873*, 877, 897, *897*
DES (Data Encryption Standard), 631
description bars
    clearing, 190, 621
    contents of, 621
Description tab, 290
descriptions
    for IPSec filters, 290
    for printers, 912, *912*, 1079, *1079*, 1081
    for services, 165
    in shared folders, 517
    for taskpad views, 182
    for tasks, 185, 188
    for users, 627
    in zone files, 401
DesiredZone key, 1088
Desktop
    in redirection, 691–692
    in user profiles, 631, 712, 715
Destination Address screen, 1458, *1459*
"destination host unreachable" message, **250**
details pane, 170, *171*
Details view, 167
Device Driver Interface (DDI) commands, 905
device drivers. *See* drivers
Device Manager, **163–164**, *163–164*, 1301, *1301*
    actions by, **1491–1492**
    for disabled hardware, 1494, *1495*
    for drivers, **1489**, *1489–1490*
    for properties, **1487–1489**, *1488*
    for resources, **1490**, *1491*
    view modes in, **1486**, *1486–1487*
Device Status window, 1488
Devices applet, 163
devices in System Tools node, 172
Dfs. *See* Distributed File System (Dfs)
DHCP (Dynamic Host Configuration Protocol), **299–300**
    and Bootp, **300–301**, 323, 326
    on client side, **320**
    DDNS registrations with, **407**
    fault tolerance in, **20**
    improvements in, **7**
    installing, **301–302**, *302*
    for Internet gateways, 1449
    monitoring, **319–320**, *320*
    multi-DHCP networks, **329**
    operation of, **320–321**
        DHCPOFFER messages in, **321–323**, *322*

lease expiration in, **328–329**
lease signing in, **327–328**, *328*
proposed IP addresses in, **322–323**, *323*
reservations in, **312**, *312*
responses in, **326**, *327*
routers in, **323–326**, *324–326*
for printers, 917
for RAS clients, 1438
for RIS, 115, *115*
scopes in. *See* scope
servers for, 270
    authorizing, **302–304**, *303–304*
    configuring, **317–319**, *317–318*
    for printers, 917
    for RAS, **1427–1428**, 1433
    for Terminal Services, 1003
user classes for, **314–317**, *315–316*
uses for, **301**
vendor classes for, **312–314**, *313*
for workstations, 969
DHCP.BIN file, 321
DHCP Relay Agent Properties dialog box, 325–326, *326*
DHCP relay agents, **323–326**
DHCP Relay tab, 324, *324*
DHCP User Classes dialog box, 315, *315*
DHCPACK messages, 321, 327–328, *328*
DHCPDISCOVER messages, **321–322**, *322*, 328
DHCPIPAddress key, 321
DHCPOFFER messages, **321–323**, *323*
DHCPREQUEST messages, 321, 326, *327*
Diagnostics tab, 1471
dial-in
    login failures in, **1395**
    permissions for, **1429–1430**, *1430*
Dial In Credentials screen, 1465, *1466*
Dial-In tab, 1429–1430, *1430*
Dial Out Credentials screen, 267, *268*, *1467*
Dial-out Hours dialog box, 1469, *1469*
Dial-Up Connection, 166
dial-up for persistent connections, 261
Dial-Up Networking (DUN)
    for clients, **1436–1437**, *1436–1437*
    in RAS, 1404
    for VPNs, **1456–1459**, *1456–1459*
Dial-Up Networking dialog box, 1436–1437, *1436*
Dial-Up Networking directory, 231
Dial Using the Area Code and Country Code option, 1419
Dialing Hours option, 1469
DIALUP group, 651
dictionary attacks, 1213, 1317

differential backups, 1326, **1350–1351**
Diffie, Whitfield, 589
Digest authentication
    for printers, 916
    for Web sites, 1115
digests, 590
digital certificates. *See* certificates
dir command, 1385
direction with DLLs, **901–902**
directories, 1389
    for NNTP servers, 1145
        for groups, 1153
        properties for, **1151–1153**, *1152*
        virtual, **1157**, *1157*
    OEM for, **105–106**
    permissions for. *See* permissions
    for SMTP servers, **1171–1172**
    SSL for, **1188**, *1188*
    structure of, 791
    virtual
        for FTP sites, **1136–1138**, *1136–1138*
        for NNTP servers, **1157**, *1157*
        for Web sites, **1123–1126**, *1125–1126*
Directory Browsing option, 1112
directory-enabled networking, **463**
Directory Listing Style setting, 1135
Directory Pruning Interval policy, 942
Directory Pruning Priority policy, 942
Directory Pruning Retry policy, 942
Directory Security tab
    for certificates, 1185–1186
    for FTP sites, **1135**, *1135*
    for printers, 915–916, *915*
    for Web sites, **1113–1116**, *1114*
Directory Service Client for Windows, 968
Directory Service log, 1286
directory services, 447–448, **568**, 620
Directory Services Administrator. *See* Active Directory Users
    and Computers tool
Directory Services Migration Tool (DSMT). *See* DSMT
    (Directory Services Migration Tool)
Directory Services Restore Mode Administrator Password
    screen, 495, *496*
DIRECTORYNAME.MAN file, 730
DirectX support, **21**
Disable Addition of Printers policy, 945
Disable Background Refresh option, 703
disable command, 85, 1385, 1388
Disable Connection option, 1026
Disable Deletion of Printers policy, 944

Disable NetBIOS over TCP/IP option, 243
Disable Recursion option, 425
Disable Routing and Remote Access option, 258
/disable switch in change logon, 1060
disabled hardware, Device Manager for, 1494, *1495*
Disabled option
    for group policies, 676–677
    for printer policies, 943
disabling
    floppy drives, 1316
    peer-to-peer sharing, **36**
    RDP protocol, 1059
    services, **1387–1389**
    unused accounts, 1318
disaster recovery. *See* recovery
Disconnect access type, 1029
Disconnect option, 1059
Disconnect Network Drive option, 976
disconnected sessions, 1018–1020
disconnecting
    from Dfs root, **850**
    physical locations from names, **8–9**
    Terminal Services sessions, 1059
Discover Wizard, 1251, *1251*
discovery process in DSMT, 1245, 1251
Disk Administrator, replacement functions for, **162**, *163*
Disk Defragmenter tool, **787–790**, *788*
disk duplexing, 748–749, *749*
disk failures, recovering from, **777–780**, *777–778*
disk groups, 743
Disk Management tool, **162**, *163*, **741–742**
    for basic disks, **743–744**
        converting dynamic to, **762**
        converting to dynamic, **756–760**, *758–759*, **774**
        deleting, **756**
    for disk failures, **777–780**, *777–778*
    for disk installation, **752**
    for dynamic disks, **743–744**, **773–774**
        converting basic to, **756–760**, *758–759*, **774**
        converting to basic, **762**
        creating, **760–762**, *760–762*
        deleting, **762**, *762*
        for mirror sets, 765
        moving, **774–776**
        for system recovery, **778–780**, *778*
    for formatting and labeling drives, **772–773**, *772*
    free space vs. unallocated space in, **744**
    for logical drives, **747**, **754–756**, *755–756*
    for mirror sets, **748–749**, *749*, **765–768**, *766–767*
    mounted drives in, **745–746**, *746*

partitions in, **746–747**
   logical, **744–745**
   primary, **752–753**, *753–754*
physical disks vs. logical partitions in, **744–745**
for RAID, **743**, **750–751**, *751*, **768–772**, *769–771*,
  780
SLEDs in, **742**
for stripe sets, **749**, *750*, **764–765**, *764*
for volumes, **747–748**, *748*, **763–764**, *763*
Disk Partitioning and Installation Location Selection
  screen, **75–76**
% Disk Time counter, 1268, 1271
Disk Tools folder, 178
diskpart command, 85, 1385, 1391
diskperf command, 1271
disks and disk drives, 835
  basic
   converting dynamic to, **762**
   converting to dynamic, **756–760**, *758–759*, **774**
   deleting, **756**
   vs. dynamic disks, **743–744**
  dynamic. *See* dynamic disks
  floppy
   boot, 66, **1381–1382**
   disabling, 1316
   filenames on, 783
   in Macintoshes, 1068
  formats for, 761, *762*, **781–785**
  installing, **752**
  logical, **747**
  maintaining
   CHKDSK for, **790–794**, *792*
   defragmenting, **787–790**, *788–789*
   disk geometry and file formats in, **781**
   encryption, **794–800**
   formatting, **781–786**
  managing. *See* Disk Management tool
  monitoring, **1270–1271**
  quotas, 18, 800
   managing, **803–804**
   operation of, **800–801**
   setting up, **801–803**, *801–803*
  requirements for, 64
  for SIS, **113–114**
Display Data Channel (DDC), 1004
display fonts, 59
display protocols for thin clients, 985, **987–988**
[Display] section, 137
Display Statistics option, 320
Display tab, 1010–1011, *1011*

Display the Full Path in the Title Bar option, 168
Distributed File System (Dfs), **8–10**, **838–840**, *839*
  child node deletions in, **850**
  node status checks for, **849–850**, *849*
  replicas for, **1225–1226**
   configuring, **847**, *847*
   member management in, **848–849**, *849*
   process, **848**, *848*
  root for, **842–844**, *842–845*
   connecting and disconnecting from, **850**
   links for, **845–846**, *845–846*
   physical, **850–851**, *850*
  stand-alone vs. fault-tolerant, **841–842**
  terminology in, **840–841**
  uses of, **851**
Distributed Transaction Coordinator (DTC), 1500
Distributed Transaction Coordinator performance object, 1500
distributing
  MMC tools, **192**
  user profiles, **738**
distribution groups, **639–640**
distribution shares, **102–105**
DLLs (dynamic link libraries)
  CSE, 673
  direction with, **901–902**
  for spooler, 905
DMA channels, **1477–1478**
DMA folder, 1363
DNS (Domain Name Service), **224–225**, **358**, **455–456**,
  1227–1228
  and Active Directory, **517–525**, *522*, **584–585**
  architecture of, **426**
   DNS forwarders in, **427–430**, *428–429*, 435
   internal and external DNS in, **430–434**, *432*
   resolvers in, **426–427**
   security in, 431, **434–435**
  for dcpromo and logon problems, **523–525**
  delegation in, **365–369**, *368*, **398–400**, *398–399*
  DHCP with, 7
  disaster recovery in, **438–444**
  dynamic. *See* DDNS (dynamic DNS)
  fault tolerance in, **371–372**, *371*, **375–377**
  importance of, **358–359**
  improvements in, **6–7**
  for IMS, **1175**
  installing, **380–381**, *381*
  for Internet gateways, 1448
  load balancing in, **372**
  name resolution in. *See* DNS name resolution
  names and namespace in, **359–360**, 461

hierarchy in, **360–362**, *362*
second-level domains in, **364–365**
third-level domains in, **365–366**
top-level domains in, **362–364**, **518**
private roots in, **441–443**
with RAS, **1472**
record types in, **369–375**, *370–371*, 1103
servers. *See* DNS servers
static entries in, **238**
subdomains in, 361, **365–366**, **397–400**, *397–399*
for Terminal Services, 1003–1004
for test domains, **488–490**
troubleshooting, **435–436**
    BOOT files in, **437–440**
    cache.dns file, **440–441**
    DNS boot order, **436–437**
and WINS, 243, **355**, 380–381
zones in. *See* zone files; zones in DNS
DNS Delegation Wizard, 398
DNS Domain Name of This Computer setting, 442
DNS forwarders, **427–430**, *428–429*, 435
DNS name resolution, 278, **418**, **450**
    HOSTS and caches in, **418–421**
    preferred DNS servers in
        authoritative DNS servers found by, **423–426**, *425*
        cache searches by, **420–426**, *425*
        zones in, **421–423**
DNS namespace, **360**
    hierarchy in, **360–362**, *362*
    second-level domains in, **364–365**
    third-level domains in, **365–366**
    top-level domains in, **362–364**, **518**
DNS Server Addresses in Order of Use field, 241
DNS Server log, 1286
DNS servers, 225
    authoritative, **366–367**
    DHCP for, 308
    with ICS, 273
    for Internet gateways, 1450
    preferred
        authoritative DNS servers found by, **423–426**, *425*
        cache searches by, **420–426**, *425*
        zones in, **421–423**
    secondary, **393–395**, *394*
DNS snap-in, 381, *381*, 384, *385*
DNS Suffix and NetBIOS Computer Name dialog box, 240, *240*, 380
DNS tab, 241, *241*, 318, *318*, 407
DNSCMD.EXE command, 429–430

Do Not Apply During Periodic Background Processing option, 704
Do Not Dial the Initial Connection option, 1458
Do Not Open an Existing MST File option, 889
Do Not Play option, 1011
Do Not Require Kerberos Preauthentication option, 631
Do Not Save Changes to This Console option, 191
Do Not Use Recursion option, 435
Do Not Use This Device in Any Hardware Profile option, 1489
Do Not Use This Device in the Current Hardware Profile option, 1489
documentation
    group policies, 709
    in recovery, **1397**
    servers, 83
documents in scripts, 100
Documents tab, **1112–1113**, *1113*
DoD (Department of Defense), 194
dollar signs ($)
    for hidden shares, 834
    for separator pages, 952
    for shared printers, 940
#DOM suffix in LMHOSTS, **338**
domain accounts, 158–159
Domain Admins group, 480, 644, 650–651
domain-based Dfs, 841
Domain Computers group, 650
Domain Controller Security Policy tool, 660–661, *661*
Domain Controller Type screen, 490, *491*
domain controllers (DCs), 465, 487–488
    with Active Directory, 470
    changes to, **582–583**
    communications with, 458–459, 490
    creating accounts on, 618
    DNS for, 359
    FSMOs for, 470, **534–536**, **1230**
    as global catalog servers, 502–503, **583**
    for global groups, 469
    missing, **1393–1396**
    NTDS.DIT for, 31
    promoting and demoting, **162**
    renaming, 584
    SAM on, 525
    in security, **32**
    upgrading, **69**
    for WINS servers, **350**
Domain Controllers container, 621–622
Domain Controllers group, 650
Domain Controllers OU, 622

domain Dfs root type, 842
Domain Guests group, 650–651
domain local groups, **468–469**, *469*, 641
domain master browsers, 1309
Domain Name and DNS Servers screen, 309, *309*
Domain Name Service. *See* DNS (Domain Name Service)
/domain option with net user, 635
Domain Security Policy tool, 159–160, *159*
Domain Username And Password dialog box, 238, *239*
Domain Users group, 644, 650–651
domains. *See also* domain controllers (DCs)
    for Active Directory, **458–459**, **464–465**
        building and maintaining, **459–462**, *460–461*
        first, **487–498**, *490–497*
        geographically dispersed, **458–459**
        names of, **583–584**
        in planning, **584–585**
        second, **498–514**, *498–499, 503–514*
        size of, **458**
        subdomains in, **459**
    affiliation with, **152**, *153*
    collections of. *See* forests; trees
    combining, **479–481**
    delegation for, **452–453**
    in DNS, **367–369**, *368*
        second-level, **364–365**
        third-level, **365–366**
        top-level, **362–364**, **518**
    global catalogs for, 472
    group policies for, 563
    in installation, **68–69**
    IP, 208
    joining, **238–240**, *239*, 970–971
    migrating, **1231**
        downlevel coexistence in, 1231–1232
        options for, **1231**
    names and naming contexts, 492–493, **583–585**, 1224, 1227
        DHCP for, 308
        FSMOs for, **526–527**, **532–533**, *533*, 1230
        for TCP/IP, **236–242**, *239–241*
    native mode for, **498**
    search order for, 241–242
    in security, **30–32**
    for SMTP servers, 1161, *1161*, 1165–1166, *1165*, **1170–1171**, *1170*
    in TCP/IP, 223, **238–242**, *239–241*
    for Web sites, 1115, *1116*
    for workstations, 966, 972
Domains/OUs tab, 679–680, *680*

Domains That Trust This Domain setting, 483
Don't Detect My Modem; I Will Select from a List option, 1416
Don't Inherit Security Settings setting, 1123
DOS applications in Terminal Services, **1038–1039**
DOS workstations, connecting, **977–978**
DOSKBD utility, 1038
dotted quad notation, 200
Downlevel Printer Pruning policy, 941
downlevel systems, 492
    clients, 631
    in domain migration, 1231–1232
Download Missing COM Components policy, 702
DPCs (deferred procedure calls), 1269
Dr. Watson program, 1043
drive copier programs, 13, 109–110, 146–147
Drive Image Pro, 13, 109
drive letters, 745, 770
Driver Details option, 1489
Driver File Details dialog box, 1301, *1302*
Driver Files Search Results screen, 1494, *1494*
Driver Signing Options dialog box, 1492, *1492*
Driver tab, 1301, *1301*, **1489**, *1489–1490*
drivers, 1483–1484, *1484*
    for FRADs, 262
    in installation, **1482**
    interrupts for, 1270, 1300
    for Macintosh computers, 1070
    for modems, 1417
    for network print services, **905**, **920**, *920*
    NIC, **146**
    OEM for, **106**
    for printers, 910, **927**, **956–958**, *957–958*, 1076
    properties for, **1489**, *1489–1490*
    signing, **1492–1493**, *1492*
    updating, **1300–1303**, *1301–1303*
    viewing, 164
Drivers.cab file, 113
Drivers folder, 1365
Drivers tab, 957–958, *957*
DriverSigningPolicy setting, 146
drives. *See* disks and disk drives
Drop directory, 1171
DS connection objects, 1224
.ds domain, 518
/ds switch in NTBACKUP, 1346
DSA.MSC tool. *See* Active Directory Users and Computers tool
/dsdel option in DNSCMD.EXE, 429–430
DSL, 261, 274

DSMT (Directory Services Migration Tool), 1234, **1244–1245**
    for file resource migration, **1255–1257**, *1256–1257*
    installing and configuring
        Active Directory Configure tab, **1246**, **1249–1450**, *1249*
        General tab, **1246–1247**, *1247*
        Generate Password tab, **1250**, *1250*
        Novell Environment Discover tab, **1247–1248**, *1247*
        Verify tab, **1248–1249**, *1248*
    NDS data in, **1252–1254**, *1252–1253*
    writing objects to Active Directory in, **1254–1255**, *1254–1255*
DTC (Distributed Transaction Coordinator), 1500
dual-boot systems, 782
dumb terminal connections for intranets, **227–228**
DUN (Dial-Up Networking)
    for clients, **1436–1437**, *1436–1437*
    in RAS, 1404
    for VPNs, **1456–1459**, *1456–1459*
duplexing, disk, 748–749, *749*
dwords, 51
Dynamic Bandwidth Control option, 1435
dynamic disks, **760**
    vs. basic disks, **743–744**
    converting basic to, **756–760**, *758–759*, **774**
    converting to basic, **762**
    creating, **760–762**, *760–762*
    deleting, **762**, *762*
    for mirror sets, 765
    moving, **774–776**
    for system recovery, **778–780**, *778*
    in Windows 2000, **773–774**
dynamic DNS. *See* DDNS (dynamic DNS)
Dynamic/Foreign disks indicator, 775
Dynamic Host Configuration Protocol. *See* DHCP (Dynamic Host Configuration Protocol)
dynamic link libraries (DLLs)
    CSE, 673
    direction with, **901–902**
    for spooler, 905
dynamic volume attachments, 66

E

e-commerce online stores, **27**
e-mail, **26–27**
    ASP for, **1172–1174**
    certificates for, **594–595**
    free servers for. *See* IMS (Internet Mail Service) program
    names for, **225–227**
    PKI for, **611–612**

protocols for, **1158–1159**
    SMTP servers for. *See* SMTP servers
$E separator page function, 952
/e switch
    in cipher, 796
    in winnt, 91
ECC (error correcting code) memory, 63–64
Edit Alias dialog box, 852–853, *853*
Edit Phonebook Entry dialog box
    for security, 1438, *1438*
    for VPNs, 1456, *1456*
Edit printer settings, 947
Edit Record dialog box, 399, *399*
Edit Reservation dialog box, 282, *283*
Edit separator pages option, 947
Edit Taskpad View option, 182
Edit user or group permissions to the printer option, 947
editing
    device port settings, 948
    group policies, 689
    mandatory profiles, 1021
    MMC tools, **192**
    NTUSER.DAT file, **722**
    print server port time-outs, **956**
    RDP client connections, **1008**, *1009*
    Registry
        danger in, **53–55**
        REGEDIT vs. REGEDT32, **59**
        remote, **57–58**
    scheduled jobs settings, 1334
    taskpad views, 182
    Terminal Services permissions, 1027
EDU domain, 225
EFS certificates, **614**
EFS Recovery Agent, 588, 595, **798–800**
EFSINFO utility, 797
EIDE adapter IRQ, 1480
ejecting tapes, **1342–1344**
elections for master browsers, **1308–1311**, *1311*
Ellis, James, 589
emergency repair disks (ERDs)
    creating, **1379–1381**
    using, **1391–1393**
EMF (Enhanced Metafile) printer data, 906–907
empty root AD design, **485–486**
emulation, 1067
Enable Authoring setting, 1122
Enable Automatic Partner Configuration option, 346
Enable Automatic Scavenging of Stale Resource Records option, 409
Enable Bandwidth Throttling option, 1110

Enable Burst Handling option, 344
Enable Certificate Trust List option, 613
Enable Client Certificate Mapping option, 1188
Enable Client Certificate Mapping to Windows User
   Accounts option, 1151
enable command, 85, 1385, 1388
Enable computer and user accounts to be trusted for
   delegation right, 662
Enable Content Expiration option, 1116
Enable Context Menus on Taskpads in This Console
   option, 191
Enable DNS for Windows Name Resolution option, 354, 357
Enable Document Footer option, 1113
Enable Forwarders option, 428–429
Enable Gateway option, 1240
Enable Internet Connection Sharing for This Connection
   option, 274
Enable IP Routing option, 254
Enable Library option, 1337
Enable LMHOSTS option, 356
Enable LMHOSTS Lookup option, 354
Enable Logging option
   for FTP sites, 1131
   for NNTP servers, 1147, 1152
   for SMTP servers, 1161
   for Web sites, 1108
Enable NetBIOS over TCP/IP option, 243
Enable Offline Files option, 855–856, 858
Enable On-Demand Dialing option, 274
Enable Process Throttling option, 1110
Enable reminders option, 857
Enable SSL Client Authentication option, 1151
Enable Updates for DNS Clients That Do Not Support
   Dynamic Update option, 319
Enable Web Content on My Desktop option, 962
Enabled option for printer policies, 943
EnableRouter key, 1088
enabling
   Offline Files, **855–857**, *856–857*
   RIS
      for clients, **120**, *121*
      user use of, **128–129**
      services, **1387–1389**
Encapsulating Security Payload (ESP), 284–285
Encrypt Contents to Secure Data option, 800
Encrypted Authentication (CHAP) option, 1432
encryption, **794**
   decrypting files, **800**
   enforcing, **796–797**, *796*
   in IPSec, **284–285**

with Kerberos, 31
key protection in, **797–798**
for Macintosh computers, 1083, 1087–1088
operation of, **794–795**, *794*
of passwords, 29–30, 631
process of, **795–796**
recovering encrypted files, **798–800**
in SSL, **591–593**, 1184, 1186
for Terminal Services client connections, 1026
encryption keys, protecting, **797–798**
End Process option, 1056
end user license agreement (EULA), 93
Enforce Limits option, 1110
Enforce Password History option, 698
enforcing encryption, **796–797**, *796*
Enhanced Metafile (EMF) printer data, 906–907
Enter Commands and Parameters screen, 184, *184*
Enterprise Admins group, 480, 644
Enterprise Admins Properties dialog box, 505, *505*
Enterprise folder, 598
enterprise resources, consolidating, **851**
Entire Network Access for Remote Clients option, 1433
entities in certificates, 593
ENUM IMAGES action, 141
Environment and Operating System screen, 957–958, *958*
Environment tab
   for printer redirection, 929
   for profiles, 738
   for Terminal services, 1023
environment variables
   in scripts, 140
   for Terminal Services clients, 1023, *1023*
Environment Variables dialog box, 1023, *1023*
Environment Variables folder, 1365
ERDs (emergency repair disks)
   creating, **1379–1381**
   using, **1391–1393**
error correcting code (ECC) memory, 63–64
Error events in Event Viewer, 1287, 1290
Error Mapping Properties dialog box, 1118
errors and error handling
   in filesystems, 792
   in IP, **214**
   in TCP, **216**
   in TCP/IP, **197**
   in Web sites, **1118**, *1119*
ESP (Encapsulating Security Payload), 284–285
Ethernet addresses, **200**
Ethernet networks for Macintosh computers, **1066**, 1069–1070
Event ID option, 1290

Event Log category, 694
Event Log Database, 1288
Event Source option, 1290
Event Viewer, **1261**, **1284–1285**
    discarding data in, **1288**, *1289*
    for disk quotas, 801
    filtering data in, **1289–1290**, *1289*
    logs in, **1285–1286**, *1285*
    for printers, 958
    reading data in, **1287–1288**, *1288*
    remote event data in, **1286–1287**, *1286*
    saving and retrieving data in, **1291**, *1291*
Event Viewer folder, 1286
events
    logon, **566–567**
    logs for
        in recovery, **1397**
        in System Tools node, 172
        types of, **1285–1286**, *1285*
    in System Tools node, 172
Everyone group, 649
Exchange, distribution groups with, 640
Exclude Files tab, 1327–1329, *1327*
Exclude Path dialog box, 1328–1329, *1329*
exclusive OR (XOR) arithmetic, 751
Executable Environment for Applications process, 986
executable files in FTP sites, 1139
Execute File permission, 816, 818
Execute mode in Terminal Services, 1039–1040–1214
/execute option in change user, 1041
Execute permission, 1105
Execute Permissions permission, 1112
ExpectedDialupDelay key, 1396
Experience tab, 1013, *1013*
expiration
    DHCP leases, **328–329**
    NNTP servers, **1155–1157**, *1156*
    users, 631
Expires After setting, 387
Explain button in System Monitor, 1264
Explain tab, 943
Export Certificate Wizard, 798
Export option
    for certificates, 798
    for Terminal Services connections, 1008
exporting
    certificates, 798
    private keys, 798
    quotas, 803
    Terminal Services connection settings, 1008

Extend Volume option, 763
Extend Volume Wizard, 763–764, *763*
extended partitions, **746–747**
Extensible Authentication Protocol (EAP) option, 1432
extensions
    for backup file exclusions, 1328–1329
    for Computer Management, 178
    for log files, 1279
    for Macintosh computers, 1090
    in MMC, 170
external DNS, **430–434**, *432*
external RAID boxes, 780
extract command, 1384–1385, 1389

F

$F separator page function, 952
/f switch
    in CHKDSK, 793
    in NTBACKUP, 1346
Failed events in Event Viewer, 1287
Failed indicator, 771
Failed Redundancy indicator, 775
Failure Audit option, 1290
failure recovery in TCP/IP, **197**
fans, 1369
fast memory, 1303
Fast Repair option, **1392–1393**
FAT (file allocation table), 781–782
FAT and FAT32 filesystems, 66, 75–76, **781–785**
    converting to NTFS, **786–787**
    vs. NTFS, **784**
    on system partition, **785**
fault tolerance
    Dfs for, **9**, **840–842**
    in DHCP, **20**
    in DNS, **371–372**, *371*, **375–377**
    in Registry, **56–57**
fault-tolerant systems and areas
    Dfs, **9**, **840–842**
    dynamic disks, **778–780**, *778*
    formatting, 786
    roots and root shares, 843, 1225
    on volumes, 746
Favorites folder, 712
Favorites tab, 170
[FavoritesEX] section, 100, 137
fax services, **20**
FaxServerOperators group, 582
Features tab, 923

FIFO (first-in-first-out) algorithm, 1266
file allocation table (FAT), 781–782
File and Print Services for NetWare (FPNW), 1234, 1244
File and Printer Sharing for Microsoft Networks properties
    dialog box, 1298, *1298*
File and Printer Sharing for Microsoft Networks service, 155,
    1216, 1298, *1298*
File Associations tab, 1090
file-based applications in RAS, **1408–1410**
File Migrate Wizard, 1255–1257, *1256–1257*
File Replication Service (FRS), **9**, 1225
File Replication Service log, 1286
file servers
    benefits of, **26**
    for Macintosh computers, **1070–1071**
file services
    for NetWare, **1243–1244**
    in Web site security, **1210**, **1216**
file shares in GSNW , **1241**, *1241*, *1243*
File Sharing for Microsoft Networks, 80
File System category, 694
File Versions folder, 1366
files and filesystems. *See also* disks and disk drives
    available, **755**
    choosing, **66–67**
    converting, **786–787**
    copying, **105–106**
    FAT and FAT32, **781–785**
    finding, Indexing Service for. *See* Indexing Service
    fixing errors in, 792
    formats for, **781**
    in formatting, **785–786**
    long filenames for, **783**
    migrating. *See* migration
    NTFS, **782–784**
    permissions for. *See* permissions
    replicating. *See* replication
    transferring. *See* FTP sites
Files Open counter, 1272
Filter Properties dialog box, 290–291, *290*, 297, *297*
Filter tab, 1289, *1289*
filtering
    Event Viewer data, **1289–1290**, *1289*
    in Indexing Service, 1189
    in IPSec, **286**, **289–291**, *289–290*, **294–297**, *297*
    for packages, **869**, *870*, **872**, *872–873*
    policies, **564**, **683–685**, *683–684*, 709
Find a Printer in the Directory option, 923
Find and Replace Object Names dialog box, 1253–1254, *1253*
find.asp file, 1198–1200

finding
    Indexing Service for. *See* Indexing Service
    MMC tools, 174–175
    NDS data, **1253–1254**, *1253*
    Registry keys, **53**
    servers, **33–40**, *34–35*, **449–450**
firewalls
    PAT as, **220**
    for Web sites, 1211
first domains for Active Directory, **487–498**, *490–497*
first-in-first-out (FIFO) algorithm, 1266
First Name setting, 624
FirstCountMsgQPeeksSleepBadApp value, 1047
fixboot command, 85, 1385, 1390
fixmbr command, 85, 1385, 1390
Flags value, 1047, 1049
flattemp command, 1023–1024, 1050
Flexible Single Master of Operators. *See* FSMOs (Flexible
    Single Master of Operators)
floplock utility, 1316
floppy disk controller IRQ, 1480
floppy disks and drives
    boot
        creating, **1381–1382**
        with NTFS, 66
    disabling, 1316
    filenames on, 783
    in Macintoshes, 1068
flow control in TCP, **216**
Folder Name screen, 125, *126*
Folder Options dialog box
    for cache settings, 858
    for GUI, 167
    for Offline Files, 855–856, 962
Folder Redirection folder, 681
folders
    encrypting, 796
    home, 632–633
    mounting partitions to, 745
    OUs as, **473**
    redirecting, **691–692**, *693*
    sharing. *See* shares and shared folders
footer files, 1113
For All Users option, 1443, 1445
For Fast Searching option, 1193
Force shutdown from a remote system right, 662
Forced Hardware folder, 1363
foreground processes, 1295
Foreign/Dynamic disks indicator, 775
ForeignSecurityPrincipals container, 621–622

forests, **478–481**, *479*
administrators for, **498–506**, *498–499*, *503–506*
benefits of, 455
enterprise, **1219–1220**, *1220*
global catalogs for, 472
merging, **1220–1221**
roots in, 498, 1219–1220, *1220*
synchronization in, **538–540**
trusts in, **481–485**, *482–483*
Forkize option, 1085
forks in Macintosh computers, 1085
<FORM> command, 142
form settings for print servers, **954–955**, *955*
format command, 1385, 1391
Format dialog box, 772, *772*, 785–786, *785*
Format Partition screen, 753, *754*
Format Volume screen
for formats, 761, *762*
for RAID 5 volumes, 770, *770*
formats, file, 761, *762*, **781–785**
formatting
disks
formats for, **781–785**
tools for, **785–786**, *785*
partitions, 76, **772–773**, *772*
primary, 753, *754*
Recovery Console for, **1390–1391**
Forms tab, 954–955, *955*
forward lookup zones, **369**
Forward Lookup Zones folder, 381, 394, 430
forward name resolution, 369
forward records in DDNS registrations, 407
forward slashes (/)
in FTP sites, 1139
in HTML, 124
forwarders, DNS, **427–430**, *428–429*, 435
Forwarders tab, 428, *429*, 430
forwarding agents, 301
Found New Hardware box, 1484, *1484*
Found New Hardware Wizard, **1492–1495**, *1494–1495*
FPNW (File and Print Services for NetWare), 1234, 1244
FQDNs (Fully Qualified Domain Names), 236
in DNS, 361
for SMTP servers, 1169
FRADs (frame relay access devices), 262
fragmented disks, **787–790**, *788–789*
frame relay
for persistent connections, 262, 264
for RAS, **1415**
frame relay access devices (FRADs), 262

frame-relay Properties dialog box, 561–562, *561*
Free media pool, 1340–1342
free space
fragmentation of, 789
vs. unallocated space, **744**
freeing memory, 1266
Freeze Display button, 1275
Friendly Description and Help Text screen, 118, *119*, 127, *127*
From a Specified Range of Addresses option, 1428
front-side buses, 62
FrontPage Server extensions
configuring, **1122–1123**, *1122*
installing, **1119–1123**
FRS (File Replication Service), 1225
FSMOs (Flexible Single Master of Operators), 470, 526
importance of, **527**
roles of, **528**, 1230
domain naming, **526–527**, **532–533**, *533*
infrastructure and PDC, **534–536**
RID pool, **533–534**, *534*
schema, **528–532**, *529–530*
transferring, **536–538**, *536*
FT (fault-tolerant) root shares, 1225
FTP protocol, port for, 1448
FTP servers, IIS as, **1094**
FTP service performance object, 1500
FTP Site Access Permissions screen, 1129, *1129*
FTP Site Content Directory screen, 1137, *1137*
FTP Site Creation Wizard, **1127–1129**, *1127–1129*
FTP Site Description screen, 1127, *1127*
FTP Site Home Directory screen, 1128, *1128*
FTP sites, **1127**
client types for
command-line, **1140–1142**
graphical, **1142–1143**
creating, **1127–1129**, *1127–1129*
for file transfer, **1138**
organization of, **1139**, *1139*
properties for, **1130–1131**, *1130*
Directory Security tab, **1135**, *1135*
Home Directory tab, **1134–1135**, *1134*
Messages tab, **1133–1134**, *1133*
Security Accounts tab, **1132–1133**, *1132*
virtual directories for, **1136–1138**, *1136–1138*
FTP User Sessions dialog box, 1131, *1131*
Full Control permission, 825
for Macintosh shares, 1075
for shares and shared folders, 812, 819
Full Name setting, 624
FullArmor product, 1223

FullUnattend setting, 97
Fully Automated option, 93
Fully Qualified Domain Names (FQDNs), 236
    in DNS, 361
    for SMTP servers, 1169

G

/g switch in NTBACKUP, 1345, 1347
G3 Power Macs, **1067**
G4 Cube, 1068
G4 Power Macs, **1067–1068**
games, scripts for, 100
garbage collector and tombstone lifetimes, 1357
Gateway Services for NetWare (GSNW), 1234,
    1239–1240, *1240*
    file shares for, **1241**, *1241*
    print shares for, **1242**, *1242*
    security for, **1242–1243**, *1243*
gateways. *See also* routers
    vs. dedicated routers, **260**
    default, **250–252**, *251*, 308
    DHCP for, 308–309
    information needed for, **262**
    ISP connection testing for, **262–263**
    RAS for, **1405**, **1444–1450**, *1445–1447, 1450*
    RRAS for, **263–269**, *263–268*
    WAN connection options for, **260–262**, *260*
    Windows 2000 Server as, **259**
GC (global catalog) servers, **1228–1229**
    domain controllers as, 502–503, **583**
    placement of, **1229–1230**, *1229*
GCs (global catalogs), 458
    purpose of, 642
    and schema, **531–532**
    and universal groups, 470, **472**, 643
    and UPN suffixes, **500–503**, *503*
GDI (Graphics Device Interface), **905**
[General] section, 101
General tab
    alert logs, 1281–1282, *1281–1284*
    backups, **1329–1330**
    counter logs, 1277–1278, *1277*
    DDNS registrations, 410
    devices, **1487–1489**, *1488*
    DHCP, 311, *311*, 317–318, *317*
    DNS, 386, *386*
    DSMT, **1246–1247**, *1247*
    encryption, 795, 800
    folders, 167
    group policies, 676–677, *677–678*

    groups, 636, *637*
    NNTP servers, **1147**, *1147*
    printers, 962
    Remote Desktop clients, 1010, *1011*
    services, 164–165, *165*
    SMTP servers, **1162**, *1162*
    System log, 1288, *1289*
    Terminal Services connections, 1008, *1009*,
        1026–1027, *1026*
    trace logs, 1280
    user profiles, 714, *714*
    users, 627, *627*
Generate Abstracts option, 1191
Generate Password tab, **1250**, *1250*
Generate security audits right, 662
Generate User Password option, 1253
Generation tab, 1191, *1191*
get command, 1142
Get Dfs Referral messages, 851
GetNearestServer packets, 1244
Ghost product, 13, 109, 462
global catalog (GC) servers, **1228–1229**
    domain controllers as, 502–503, **583**
    placement of, **1229–1230**, *1229*
global catalogs (GCs), 458
    purpose of, 642
    and schema, **531–532**
    and universal groups, 470, **472**, 643
    and UPN suffixes, **500–503**, *503*
global groups, 467, 639, **641**
    domain controllers for, **469**
    in Users folder, 469
Global Policy Creator Owners group, 687–688
Global Unique IDs (GUIDs)
    for adapters and connections, 321
    for GPOs, 673, 691
    in GPOTOOL, 707
    for RIS, 125
glue records, **402–404**
goals for Windows 2000, **2–4**
Gopher protocol, 1448
GOV domain, 225
GPCs (Group Policy Containers), 673, 707, 868, **1226**
GPEDIT.MSC console, 619
    adding, 675
    for exporting settings, 695
    focusing, 674–675, *674*, 1223–1224
    folder for, 702, *702*
    opening, 676
    for printers, 940

GPOs. *See* group policies and GPOs
GPOTOOL tool, **707–708**
GPRESULT tool, **707**
GPTs (Group Policy Templates), 707, **1226**
Granted Access option, 916–917
graphical-based setup, **77–81**, *79*
graphical clients for FTP, **1142–1143**
Graphics Device Interface (GDI), **905**
Greenberg, Steve, 982
grounding, 1315
Group Account Migration Wizard, 580, *580–581*
Group Member Options screen, 580, *581*
group memberships for user accounts, **633**, *633–634*
Group option, 636
Group Options screen, 580, *580*
group policies and GPOs, **14–15**, **663–664**
    in Active Directory, 463, 474, **562–566**, **584–585**,
      1222–1224, *1224*
    applying, **673**
    benefits of, **664**
    concepts in, **672–673**
    creating, **676–681**, *677–680*
    delegating administration of, **687–689**, *688*
    filtering, **564**, **683–685**, *683–684*, 709, **872**, *872–873*
    inherited and cumulative, **673–674**, **685**
    logging in for, **565**
    modifying, **1223–1224**
    for network printers, **940–945**, *941*, *944*
    objects for, **674–676**, *674–675*
    order of, **681–683**, *682*
    for packages, 565, 680, **869–871**, *869–871*, **875–877**,
      875–876
    for passwords, **685–687**
    policies for, **702–705**, *703–705*
    vs. profiles, 631
    purpose of, **565–566**
    for RDP client deployment, **1002**
    refresh intervals for, **674**
    Registry for, **708–709**
    removing, **564–565**
    replication of, **1226**
    for rights, 660–661
    over slow links, **705–706**, *706*
    Software Installation in, 867–868
    vs. system policies, 457, **563**, **665–666**
    templates for, **666–672**, *669*
    troubleshooting, **707–709**
    for user accounts, **674–676**, *674–675*
    for user and computer configuration, **689–690**, *689*
      for administrative templates, **696**
      for Control Panel, **697**
      for folder redirection, **691–692**, *693*
      for MMC management, **699–702**, *700–702*
      for passwords and account lockout, **698–699**
      for scripts, **690–691**, *690–691*
      for security, **693–695**, *695*
      for System settings, **697**, *698*
      for windows components, **696–697**
    for ZAP files, **887–888**, *887*
Group Policies tab, 681–682, *682*
Group Policy Containers (GPCs), 673, 707, 868, **1226**
Group Policy Editor, 944
Group Policy folder, 598
Group Policy Objects (GPOs). *See* group policies and GPOs
Group Policy Refresh Intervals for
  Users/Computers/Domain Controllers option, 703
Group Policy Security Settings, 695
Group Policy Slow Link Detection Properties dialog box,
  705, *706*
Group Policy snap-in, 619, 672
    adding, 675
    for exporting settings, 695
    focusing, 674–675, *674*, 1223–1224
    folder for, 702, *702*
    opening, 676
    for printers, 940
Group Policy tab
    access to, 700
    for domains, 676, *677*
    for group policies, 679, *679*, 868, *869*
    for packages, 875, *875*
    for printers, 944
    for users and computers, 689
Group Policy Templates (GPTs), 707, **1226**
group scheduling servers, **27**
group template user profiles, **731–732**
groups, 636
    Active Directory for, **465–466**
      changes to, **582**
      inside groups, **466–472**, *468–471*
      size of, **472–473**
    built-in
      local, **646–651**, *647*
      special, **651**
    creating, **636–638**, *636–639*
    location of, **620**
    login scripts, **652–653**
      assigning, **654**
      example, **654–657**
      languages for, **653–654**

migrating, **580**, *580–581*
nesting, 637, *638*, **643–646**
in NetBIOS, 335–336
for NNTP servers, **1153–1155**, *1154–1155*
vs. OUs, **476**, **652**
policies for. *See* group policies and GPOs
removing users from, 633
scope of, **641–643**
security
    built-in, **646–651**, *647*
    vs. distribution groups, **639–640**
    working with, **643–646**, *644–646*
types of, **639–640**
user rights in, **660–663**, *661*
groupware, 1143
GSNW (Gateway Services for NetWare), 1234,
    1239–1240, *1240*
    file shares for, **1241**, *1241*
    print shares for, **1242**, *1242*
    security for, **1242–1243**, *1243*
GSNW configuration page, 1243
Guest account, 618, **623**
    renaming, 619
    for Web sites, 1211, 1216
Guest authentication mode, 1087
Guests group, 619, **649–650**
GUI. *See also* user interface
    familiarity with, **40**
    modifying, **167–168**
    for trusts, **482–483**, *482–483*
/guiddisplay switch in rsm, 1338–1339
GUIDs (Global Unique IDs)
    for adapters and connections, 321
    for GPOs, 673, 691
    in GPOTOOL, 707
    for RIS, 125
[GUIRunOnce] section, **109**
[GUIUnattended] section, 96–97
GURU tool, 1066
Gutenberg Project, 1141–1142

H

H node in NetBIOS, **333–334**
$H separator page function, 952
HAL.DLL (Hardware Abstraction Layer), 105, 1370
handheld PCs for Terminal Services, **995–996**, **1005**
Handles count, 1292
hard disks. *See* disks and disk drives
hard-linked partitions, 773–774

hardware, **1473–1474**
    adding
        configuration in, **1482–1483**
        drivers for, **1482**
        Plug-and-Play devices, **1483–1485**
        support for, **1481–1482**
    in boot process, **1369**
    conflicts in, 83
    DMA channels for, **1477–1478**
    I/O addresses for, **1474**
    IRQs for, **1478–1481**, *1479*
    managing
        Add/Remove Hardware Wizard for, **1493–1494**,
            1493–1494
        Device Manager for, **1486–1492**, *1486–1487*
        driver signing for, **1492–1493**, *1492*
        Found New Hardware Wizard for, **1493–1495**,
            1494–1495
        profiles for, **1495–1496**, *1496*
        Troubleshooter for, **1496–1497**, *1497*
    preparing, **64**
    for RAS, **1411–1415**
        direct options, **1414–1415**
        frame relay, **1415**
        ISDN, **1413–1414**
        modems, **1411–1414**, **1470–1471**
        X.25, **1415**
    removing, **1485**
    requirements for, **62–64**
    for Terminal Services
        client, **994–996**
        server, **991–994**
    tuning, **1303–1305**
Hardware Abstraction Layer (HAL.DLL), 105, 1370
Hardware Compatibility List (HCL), 64, 77, 1411, 1481–1482
Hardware Profiles screen, 1495–1496, *1496*
hardware RAID vs. software, **780**
Hardware Resources folder, **1362–1363**, *1362*
Hardware tab
    for adding hardware, 1493
    for network adapters, 156, *157*
    for profiles, 1495
Hardware Type screen, 157, *158*
Hardware Wizard, 156–157, 1493
hash command, 1142
hash functions, 590, 1213
HCL (Hardware Compatibility List), 64, 77, 1411,
    1481–1482
headers
    in IMS messages, 1181

in scripts, 97
in TCP/IP, 198
Hellman, Martin, 589
help
 for command prompt, 1374
 in MMC, 169
 for Recovery Console, 86
HELP command, 86
help desk support, Terminal Services for, **984**
hex suffixes in LMHOSTS, **337–338**
hexadecimal number system, **1475–1477**
hfnetchk.exe program, 1206
hidden shares, **834–835**, *834*
Hide File Extensions for Known File Types option, 168
Hide Protected Operating System Files (Recommended)
 option, 168, 859
hiding
 description bars, 190, 621
 resources from network browsers, **1312**
 shared printers, **940**
 taskpad view menus, 190
hierarchies
 in DNS namespace, **360–362**, *362*
 domains, 477–478
 NNTP server groups, **1153–1155**
high-water marks in replication, **548–549**, 551–552
hints file in DNS, 438
HISECDC template, 670
HISECSV template, 670
HISECWS template, 670
hives, 48, **55–57**
HKCU branch, 1039–1040
HKEY_CLASSES_ROOT subtree, 48, 55–56
HKEY_CURRENT_CONFIG subtree, 48
HKEY_CURRENT_USER subtree, 48–49, 55–56
HKEY_LOCAL_MACHINE subtree, 48–49, 52, *52*, 55–56
HKEY_USERS subtree, 48, 55–56, 722–723, *722*
HKLM branch, 1039, 1048
home directories
 for FTP sites, 1128, *1128*, **1134–1135**, *1134*
 for Terminal Services clients, **1020–1021**, *1021*
 for Web sites, **1111–1112**, *1111*
Home Directory tab
 for FTP sites, **1134–1135**, *1134*
 for Web sites, **1111–1112**, *1111*
home folders, 632–633
%home% variable, 1178–1179
host header names, 1102–1104
host names, Internet, **223**
 DNS for, **224–225**

e-mail names in, **225–227**, *226*
 HOSTS file for, **223–224**
host (A) records
 in CACHE.DNS, 440–441
 creating, **389–390**, *389–390*
 in DNS, **370–372**, *371*
hosts
 in DNS, 362
 in intranets, 201
 for multiple virtual Web sites, **1103–1107**
 in remote-control, 1410
 in TCP/IP, **197**
HOSTS file
 in DNS resolution, 352–354, *353*, **418–419**
 limitations of, **223–224**, 362
hot start servers, 1397
hot-swap RAID systems, 780
hotfixes for security, **1205–1207**
hotkey combinations in Terminal Services, 1058
HTTP (HyperText Transfer Protocol)
 ports for, 1102, 1448
 for printing, 914
HTTP Header tab, **1116–1118**, *1117*
HTTP server, IIS as, **1094**
hub-and-spoke design, 348–349, *348*
hubs, 274
hybrid attacks, 1317
HyperText Transfer Protocol (HTTP)
 ports for, 1102, 1448
 for printing, 914

I

I/O addresses, **1474**, 1490
I/O folder, 1363
$I separator page function, 952
/i switch
 in CHKDSK, 793
 in msiexec.exe, 107
I Want to Choose the Installation Partition During Setup
 option, 73
I Want to Set Up My Internet Connection Manually option,
 1418
I386 directory, 72, 105
 extending, **104**
 OEM for, **104–107**
 for RIS files, 118
IANA (Internet Assigned Numbers Authority), 204
IAS (Internet Authentication Service), 1501
IAS Accounting Clients performance object, 1501

IAS Accounting Server performance object, 1501
IAS Authentication Clients performance object, 1501
IAS Authentication Server performance object, 1501
"ICA clients unexpectedly disconnect" error message, 1016
ICANN (Internet Corporation for Assigned Names and Numbers), 204, 224–225, 361, 364
ICMP (Internet Connection Management Protocol), 1501
ICMP performance object, 1501
icons for tasks, 185, *185*
ICS (Internet Connection Sharing), **19–20, 218–220, 269–270**
    activating, **274–275**, *275*
    duplicating, **276–279**, *277–279*
    internal network connections in, **270**
    ISP connections in, **270–274**, *271–273*
    limitations of, **276**
    and NAT, **275–279**, *277–279*, **281–283**, *283*
    and port mapping, **279–280**, *281*
Identification Changes dialog box, 152, *153*, 238, *239*, 380, 971, *971*
[Identification] section, 96–97, 137
Identification settings for FTP sites, **1130**
Identification tab, 965, *966*, 969–970
Identify Additional Servers screen, 894, *894*
Identify local printer name option, 947
Identify network printer name option, 947
Identify the paper source option, 947
Idle Time setting, 1333
Idle Time Before Hanging Up setting, **1423**
Ignore option, 1492
IIS (Internet Information Services), 914, **1094**. *See also* Web sites
    configuration
        default, **1096–1097**, *1097*
        global, **1097–1100**, *1098, 1100*
    functions of, **1094–1095**
    installing, **1096–1097**, *1096–1097*
    managing, 174
    security in, **613–614**, 667
    turning off, **1205, 1207–1208**
IIS Certificate Wizard, **1185–1187**, *1185–1187*
IIS Log File Format, 1161
IIS.MSC tool, 174
iMac computers, **1068–1069**
images
    in FTP transfers, 1142
    in RIS, 131–133, *132–133*
    system
        creating, **125–127**, *126–127*
        delivering, **128**
    limiting, **131**
    Sysprep for, **150**
Images directory, 131
Images tab, 132–133, *132*
IMDB (In-Memory Database), 1501
IMDB Service performance object, 1501
Import Certificate Wizard, 798
Import File option, 1352
Import media pool, 1340–1342
Import MediaPresent dialog box, 1341, *1341*
Import option, 1008
Import Policy option, 695
importing
    bindery and NDS data, **1250–1252**, *1251–1252*
    certificates, 798
    quotas, 803
    security templates, **694–695**, *695*
    Terminal Services connection setting, 1008
IMS (Internet Mail Service) program, **1174**
    batch files for, **1177–1178**
    client setup in, **1180**
    configuring, **1178–1180**, *1178–1179*
    downloading, **1176**
    installing, **1176–1177**
    limitations of, **1175**
    MailSite version, **1180–1181**
    operation of, **1175–1176**
    Registry for, **1177**
    security in, **1181–1182**
    unzipping, **1176**
IN keyword, 402
In-Memory Database (IMDB), 1501
in-place migration, **572–574**
in-place upgrades, 1231
#INCLUDE command, **339**
Increase quotas right, 662
Increase scheduling priority right, 662
Incremental backups, 1326
incremental zone transfers, 1227
Index Files with Unknown Extensions option, 1191
index.html file, 1113
Index News Content option, 1153
Index This Resource option, 1112
Indexing Service, **1189**
    catalogs in
        contents of, **1193**, *1193–1194*
        creating, **1192–1193**, *1192*
        standard, **1192**
    documentation for, **1189**
    managing, **1190–1191**, *1191–1192*

operation of, 1189–1190
permissions in, 1194–1195
querying
    from Manage Computer, 1195–1197, *1195*
    from Web, 1197–1202
inetsrv tool, 174
infinite loops in replication, 549–551
.info domain, 363
Information events in Event Viewer, 1287, 1290
Information Properties dialog box, 1287–1288, *1288*
infrared RAS connections, **1415**
infrastructure
    FSMOs for, **534–536**, 1231
    for RIS, **113**
    services for
        DNS, **1227–1228**
        global catalog servers, **1228–1230**, *1229*
        operations masters, **1230**
inheritance
    in Active Directory planning, **586**
    group policies, **673–674**, **685**
    permissions, **819–820**, *820*
        in DSMT, **1256–1257**, *1257*
        removing, 823
Inheritance Overrides dialog box, 1098, *1098*
Initial Connection dialog box, 1459, *1459*
Initial Settings screen, 117, *118*
Initials setting, 624
Inspect Boot Sector option, **1392**
Inspect Startup Environment option, **1392**
Install Hardware Device Drivers screen, 1302, *1302*, 1489, *1490*
Install Licenses option, 1036
Install Microsoft Windows Network option, 974
Install mode in Terminal Services, **1039–1041**
Install New Modem screen, 1416–1417, *1417*
Install New Modem wizard, 1416, *1416–1417*
/install option in change user, 1041
install.osc file, 144–145
Install the Upgrade Package option, 899
Install This CA Certification Path option, 609
Install This Certificate link, 607
Install User Interface Options settings, 877
installation
    ADMT, **579**
    applications
        for MSIs, **881**
        in multiuser environments, **1039–1041**, *1040*, **1044**
    DHCP, **301–302**, *302*
    disks, **752**

DNS, **380–381**, *381*
DSMT, **1246**, *1246*
FrontPage Server extensions, **1119–1123**
hardware. *See* hardware
IIS, **1096–1097**, *1096–1097*
IMS, **1176–1177**
Macintosh servers, **1071–1073**, *1071–1072*
network adapters, **156–158**, *157–158*
printers, **909–913**, *909–912*, **929–933**
RAS, **1415–1417**, *1416–1417*, **1426–1429**, *1426–1429*
RDP clients, **1000–1001**
Recovery Console, **1378–1379**, *1378*
RIS, **116**, *116*
software. *See* packages
TCP/IP, **230–232**, *231–232*
Windows 2000, **61**
    BIOS preparation in, **65**
    filesystems in, **66–67**
    graphical-based setup, **77–81**, *79*
    hardware preparation, **64**
    network connections and options in, **67–71**
    partitioning in, **65–66**
    planning and preparation, **62**
    post-installation procedures, **82–83**
    preinstallation procedures, **72–74**, *73*
    with RIS. *See* RIS (Remote Installation Services) tool
    server names in, **67**
    Sysprep for, **146–150**
    system hardware requirements for, **62–64**
    text-based setup, **74–77**
    troubleshooting, **83–86**
    unattended. *See* scripts; unattended installation
WINS, **341–342**, *342*
Installation Source Files Location screen, 118, *118*
Installer service, **15–16**
Installers group, RIS for, **129–131**
instances in System Monitor, 1262
integrated zones, **415–418**, *415*
integration with NetWare. *See* NetWare
Intellimirror, 664
inter-site replication, **560–562**, *560–562*
Inter-Site Topology Generator (ISTG), 562
INTERACTIVE group, 651
interface, user. *See* user interface
Interface column in routing table entries, **248–249**
Interface Name screen, 265, *266*, 1464, *1464*
internal DNS, **430–434**, *432*
internal security threats, **1216**
Internet. *See* Web sites

Internet account connection information screen, 272, *272*

Internet account logon information screen, 1420, *1420*

Internet Assigned Numbers Authority (IANA), 204

Internet Authentication Service (IAS), 1501

Internet Connection Management Protocol (ICMP), 1501

Internet Connection Sharing (ICS). *See* ICS (Internet Connection Sharing)

Internet Connection Sharing screen, 1445, *1445*

Internet Connection Sharing Settings dialog box, 1446–1447, *1447*

Internet Connection Wizard, 271–273, *271–272*, **1418–1420**, *1419–1420*

Internet connections, RAS for, **1404–1406**, **1417–1424**, *1418–1425*

Internet Connector Licenses for Terminal Services, **1032–1033**

Internet Connector licensing option, 1025

Internet Corporation for Assigned Names and Numbers (ICANN), 204, 224–225, 361, 364

Internet Explorer, scripts for, **100–101**

Internet Explorer 5 folder, **1365–1366**, *1366*

Internet gateways, **1444–1450**, *1445–1447*, *1450*

Internet host names, **223**
    DNS for, **224–225**
    e-mail names in, **225–227**, *226*
    HOSTS file for, **223–224**

Internet Information Services (IIS), 914, **1094**. *See also* Web sites
    configuration
        default, **1096–1097**, *1097*
        global, **1097–1100**, *1098*, *1100*
    functions of, **1094–1095**
    installing, **1096–1097**, *1096–1097*
    managing, 174
    security in, **613–614**, 667
    turning off, **1205**, **1207–1208**

Internet Information Services folder, 914

Internet Information Services Global performance object, 1502

Internet Mail Service. *See* IMS (Internet Mail Service) program

Internet Packet Exchange/Sequenced Packet Exchange (IPX/SPX) protocol, 28, 1234

Internet printing
    connections for, **924–926**, *925*
    for printer setup, **929**

Internet Printing Protocol (IPP), 914

Internet Protocol (IP), **198–199**, *199*, 1235
    error checking in, **214**
    routers in, **199**, **201–203**
    routing in, **202–203**
    subnets in, **199**

Internet Protocol (TCP/IP) Properties dialog box, 233–234, *233*, 1443–1444, *1444*

Internet service providers (ISPs), 1418–1420
    for gateways and routers, **262–263**
    in ICS, **270–274**, *271–273*

Internet Services Manager, 612

Internetwork Packet Exchange (IPX) protocol, 68, 1234–1235

% Interrupt Time counter, 1270, 1300

interrupts and IRQs, **1478**
    cascading, **1478–1479**, *1479*
    conflicts in, 1483
    for device drivers, 1270, 1300
    listing, 1490
    priority for, **1480–1481**
    and ROM addresses, **1481**

Interrupts/sec counter, 1300

interserver communications, 836

intranets, **227**, 455–456
    connections for
        dumb terminal, **227–228**
        LAN, **228**
        SLIP/PPP, **228**
        terminal, **228–229**, *229*
    IP addresses for, 206, **230**

IP (Internet Protocol), **198–199**, *199*, 1235
    error checking in, **214**
    routers in, **199**, **201–203**
    routing in, **202–203**
    subnets in, **199**

IP Address and Domain Name Restrictions dialog box, 916–917, *917*, 1115–1116, *1116*

IP Address and Port Settings screen, 1101, *1101*, 1127–1128, *1128*

IP Address Assignment screen, 1427, *1427*

IP Address Range screen, 305–306, *305*

IP addresses, **199**, 455, 1419–1420
    CIDR in, **211–214**
    Class A, B, and C, **204–205**, *204*
    DDNS registrations with, **407**
    DHCP for. *See* DHCP (Dynamic Host Configuration Protocol)
    Ethernet, **200**
    for FTP sites, 1127–1128, *1128*, 1130, 1135
    for ICS, 273, *273*
    for IMS, **1175**
    for Internet gateways, 1446, 1450
    for intranets, **230**
    multiple, **244–245**, *244*
    for NNTP servers, 1144–1145, 1147
    for printers, 916–917
    quad format for, **200–201**, *201*
    for RAS, 1427–1428, *1427–1428*, 1438

for RIS, 113
routable and nonroutable, **205–206**
for routing, 1467
for SMTP servers, 1160–1161, 1165–1166, *1165*
special, **207–208**
static, **233–234**, *233*, **407**, **1175**
subnet masks in, **208–210**
subnetting in, **210–211**
for Terminal Services, 1003
for VPNs, 1456, 1458–1459
for Web sites, 1101–1104, 1115–1116, *1116*, 1212
IP domains, 208
IP Filter List dialog box, 289, *290*
IP folder, 561
IP leases in DHCP, **320–321**
duration of, **307**, *307–308*
expiration of, **328–329**
signing, **327–328**, *328*
IP performance object, 1502
IP routing in RRAS, 257
IP Routing option, 1467
IP Settings tab, 244–245, *244*
IPC$ share, **836**
ipconfig /all command, **234–236**, *234*
for DHCP, 328, *328*
for IP addresses, 320
for MAC addresses, 300
for routing, 255, *255*
for WINS, 340
ipconfig /displaydns command, 419
ipconfig /flushdns command, 419–420
ipconfig /registerdns command, 413, 416
ipconfig /release command, **320–321**, 328
ipconfig /renew command, 316, 320, 328
ipconfig /setclassid command, 316–317
IPP (Internet Printing Protocol), 914
IPSec, **284**, 587
actions in, **286**, **291–292**, *291*
authentication in, **286–287**
features in, **298**
filters in, **286**, **289–291**, *289–290*, **294–297**, *297*
for PKI, **610–611**
policies in, **287–289**, *287*
rules in, **286**, 288, **292–297**, *292–294*, *297*
for transmissions
blocking, **284**, **296**
encrypting, **284–285**
permitting, **285**, **296–297**
signing, **285**
in Windows, **287–294**, *287*, *289–294*

IPSec Policy Wizard, 292
IPV6 addresses, 206
IPX (Internetwork Packet Exchange) protocol, 68, 1234–1235
IPX Network Number Assignment settings, 1434
IPX/SPX (Internet Packet Exchange/Sequenced Packet Exchange) protocol, 28, 1234
IRQs (interrupt request levels), **1478**
cascading, **1478–1479**, *1479*
conflicts in, 1483
listing, 1490
priority for, **1480–1481**
and ROM addresses, **1481**
IRQs folder, 1363
ISAPI Filters tab, **1110**, *1110*
ISDN
for persistent connections, 261
for RAS, **1413–1414**
ISPs (Internet service providers), 1418–1420
for gateways and routers, **262–263**
in ICS, **270–274**, *271–273*
ISTG (Inter-Site Topology Generator), 562
Items to Synchronize dialog box, 860, *860*
iterative queries vs. recursive, **424–425**, *425*
IUSR accounts, 1207–1208

J

/j switch in NTBACKUP, 1345
JavaScript language, 654
job numbers in separator pages, 952
Job Object performance object, 1502
Job Object Details performance object, 1502
Jobs folder, 1365
joining
domains, **238–240**, *239*, 970–971
workgroups, **37**
JScript language, 635, 653
junction points, **10–11**, 1355–1356

K

Kahn, Robert, 196
KCC (Knowledge Consistency Checker) program
for DS connection objects, 1224
in replication, **541–542**, *542*
KeepRasConnections registry key, 1470
Kerberos authentication, 8, 286
for networks, **30–32**
for printers, 916
kernel in boot process, **1371**
Kernel Memory section in Task Manager, 1292

.key files, 1044
keyboard shortcuts with RDP clients, **1013–1014**
keyboards
    IRQ for, 1480
    RDP drivers for, 991
keys
    certificate, **589–591**
    Registry, **49–50**, **53**
keywords in shared folders, 517
KiXtart language, 653–654
Knowledge Base articles, 979
Knowledge Consistency Checker (KCC) program
    for DS connection objects, 1224
    in replication, **541–542**, *542*

L

$L separator page function, 952
/l switch in CHKDSK, 793
L0phtCrack utility, 1316–1317
L2F (Layer 2 Forwarding), **1452**
L2TP (Layer 2 Tunneling Protocol), **1452–1459**, *1453–1459*
labeling partitions, **772–773**, *772*
LAN and Demand-Dial Routing option, 1463
LAN connections for intranets, **228**
LAN Manager, 42–43
LAN-to-WAN routing, ICS for. *See* ICS (Internet
    Connection Sharing)
language monitors, 908
Language options, 73
languages, scripting, **653–654**
LANMANNT.BMP, 43
laptop computers
    dynamic disks on, 757
    encryption for, 797–798
LaserPrep files, **1077**
LaserWriter 8 (LW8), 1077
Last Known Good Configuration, 51, **1374–1377**,
    1375–1376
Last Name setting, 624
Layer 2 Forwarding (L2F), **1452**
Layer 2 Tunneling Protocol (L2TP), **1452–1459**, *1453–1459*
lcd command, 1140
LCP (Link Control Protocol) extensions, 1435
LDAP (Lightweight Directory Access Protocol), 449, 553, 620
Lease Duration screen, 307, *307*
leases in DHCP, **320–321**
    duration of, **307**, *307–308*
    expiration of, **328–329**
    signing, **327–328**, *328*

Least Recently Used (LRU) algorithm, 988, 1266
Leave at Remote Computer option, 1011
legacy systems, 332
    logon scripts, 691
    security in, **32–33**
libraries
    DLL
        CSE, 673
        direction with, **901–902**
        for spooler, 905
    in RSM, **1337–1338**
License Agreement, 93, *94*
[LicenseFilePrintData] section, 96–97
licenses, 78, 93
    in installation, **69–70**
    for shared folders, 808
    in Terminal Services, **1029–1030**
        activation in, **1034–1037**, *1035–1036*
        application licensing, **1037**
        client connections, 1025
        session licensing, **1031–1032**
        Terminal Services Licensing tool, **1033–1037**,
            1034–1036
        W2K licensing model, **1030–1031**, *1030*
    for TSAC, 999
Licensing Server Activation screen, 1035, *1035*
Licensing Wizard, **1035–1037**, *1035–1036*
life-cycle management, **851**
Lightweight Directory Access Protocol (LDAP), 449, 553, 620
Limit Connection Size option, 1148
Limit Message Size To setting, 1163
Limit Number of Outbound Messages per Connection To
    setting, 1163
Limit Number of Recipients per Message To setting, 1163
Limit Post Size option, 1148
Limit Session Size To setting, 1163
limited broadcast addresses, 250
Link Control Protocol (LCP) extensions, 1435
link fault tolerance, 840
link tracking method, 727
links
    for Dfs, **845–846**, *845–846*
    for group policies, 672, 678
    for taskpad views, **188–190**, *190*
Links tab, 678
List Folder permission, 816–817
List Folder Contents permissions, 819
listsvc command, 86, 1385, 1388
LMHOSTS file, 243, **337–339**, 342
    in DNS resolution, 352–354, *353*

for domain controllers, 1395
for trusts, 484
Load and unload device drivers right, 662
load balancing
in DNS, **372**
with MetaFrame, **1061–1062**
Load Hive dialog box, 723, *723–724*
Load Hive option, 57, 723, *723*
Load Zone Data on Startup option, 437
Loaded Modules folder, 1365
loading profiles, 738
local Active Directory replication, **540**
crashes in, **544–546**
frequency of, **541**
high-water marks and up-to-date value in, **548–549**,
551–552
infinite loops in, **549–551**
KCC program in, **541–542**, *542*
loops in, **540–542**, *541*
meshes in, **542–543**, *543*
with multiple domain controllers, **552–554**, *552–553*
with one-domain controllers, **546–547**
steps in, **554–556**
topologies in, **543–544**, *544*
update sequence numbers in, **547–549**
Local Area Connection option, 325
Local Area Connection Properties dialog box
for NICs, 231, *232*
for protocols, 154, *154*, 1235, *1235*
for router addresses, 282, *283*
Local Area Network (LAN) Routing Only option, 257,
277, 1463
Local Computer folder, 598
local computers, backing up, **1322–1324**, *1322–1324*
Local Devices setting, 1012
.local domain, 518
local groups, 467–469, 639, **641–643**
built-in, **646–651**, *647*
domain, **468–469**, *469*, 641
machine, **467–468**, *468*
Local or Network Printer screen, 909, *910*, 921, *922*
Local Path field, 1111
Local Policies category, 694
Local Policies folder, 938
"Local policy of this system does not allow you to log in
interactively" error message, 1015
local profiles, **736**
Local Resources tab, 1011–1012, *1012*
Local Security Policy Setting dialog box, 831, *831*

Local Security Policy tool (SECPOL.MSC), 159, **287–288**,
568–569, 619, 660, 666
Local Security Settings dialog box, 287–288, *287*, 569, *569*,
831, *831*
Local Settings folder, 712
local user accounts, 159
Local User option, 725, *725*
Local User Properties dialog box, 725, *725*
Local Users and Groups, 159, 172, 467, *468*
Locate Driver Files screen, 1489, *1490*
Locate Your Printer screen, 922, *922*, 1242, *1242*
Location and Comment screen, 912, *912*, 1079, *1079*, 1081
Lock pages in memory right, 662
locking out Administrator account, 1213
lockout policies
controlling, **159–160**, *159*
group policies for, **698–699**
for Web sites, 1214
Log Access option, 1152
Log Authoring Actions option, 1123
Log Detailed Events option, 344
.LOG extension, 56
log files. *See* logs and logging
Log Files tab, 1278–1280, *1278*
Log on as a batch job right, 663
Log on as a service right, 663
Log On at Startup option, 976
Log on locally right, 663
Log On tab, 165
Log On to Windows NT Domain option, 966
Log On to Windows NT or LAN Manager Domain option,
976
Log Visits option
for FTP sites, 1135
for Web sites, 1112
logging. *See* logs and logging
logging in. *See* logons
logging off
with RDP clients, **1014**
scripts for, 565, 652
Logging tab, 1179
logical drives, **747**, **754–756**, *755–756*, 1323
formatting, **772–773**, *772*
labeling, **772–773**, *772*
logical operators in queries, 1196
logical partitions vs. physical disks, **744–745**
LOGIN action, 141
login.bat script, 654–655
login names in separator pages, 952
login.scr script, 655–657

login scripts, **632–633**, **652–653**
    assigning, **654**
    example, **654–657**
    group policies for, 565
    languages for, **653–654**
Logoff access type, 1029
logoff command in Terminal Services, 1051
logoff function in net, 978
logoffs
    with RDP clients, **1014**
    scripts for, 565, 652
Logon access type, 1029
logon command, 86, 1385
logon function in net, 978
logon hours for users, 629–630, *630*
Logon Information screen, 972
Logon/Logoff tab, 864, *864*
logon names
    in separator pages, 952
    UPNs for, **500**
Logon Properties dialog box, 690, *690*
logon servers, 31, **448–449**, 465
Logon Workstations dialog box, 630, *630*
logons
    under Active Directory, **486–487**
    auditing, **566–567**
    centralized, **448–449**
    for group policies, **565**
    for IMS program, **1177–1178**
    scripts for, **632–633**, **652–653**
        assigning, **654**
        example, **654–657**
        group policies for, 565
        languages for, **653–654**
    and security, **30**
    smart cards for, 588
    with Sysprep, **149**
    troubleshooting, **523–525**, **1393–1396**
    to Windows NT workstations, **970**
%LOGONSERVER% environment variable, 738
logos in Setup, **105**
logs and logging. *See also* Event Viewer; Performance Logs and
  Alerts tool
    in auditing, **569–572**, *570*
    backup
        levels in, 1348
        types of, **1326–1327**, *1327*
        viewing, **1351–1352**, *1351*
    boot, **1377–1378**, *1377*
    for DDNS scavenging, 412

    for DHCP, 317–318
    for disk quotas, 801
    for events
        in recovery, **1397**
        in System Tools node, 172
        types of, **1285–1286**, *1285*
    for FTP sites, 1131
    in IMS, 1179
    for modems, 1471
    for NNTP servers, 1147, 1152
    for print servers, **958**, *959*
    in recovery, **1397**
    restore, **1356**
    for SMTP servers, 1161
    transaction
        in Active Directory, 493
        in NTFS, 790
        size of, 793
    for Web sites, 1108, 1211
    in WINS, 344
long filenames, **783**
lookup zones
    creating, **383–385**, *385*
    in DNS, **369**
loopback adapters, 156
loopback addresses, **207**, 237
loops in local Active Directory replication, **549–551**
loops in replication
    local Active Directory, **540–542**, *541*
    WINS, 349
Low Speed Connection option, 1286
LPT ports, 918
    mapping, 929
    for printers, 948
LPT1 IRQ, 1480
LRU (Least Recently Used) algorithm, 988, 1266
LW8 (LaserWriter 8), 1077

M

M (Mixed) node, **333–334**
    for groups, 645
    migration in, 1231
    and universal groups, **471–472**, *471*
/m switch in winnt32, 89
MAC (Media Access Control) addresses, 200, 300, 455
MACFILE.EXE command, 1073
%MACHINEDOMAIN% environment variable, 140
machines
    accounts for, 129

groups for, **465–473**, *468–469*, *471*
names for, **152**, *153*, **334–336**
Macintosh computers, **1065**
  68K series, **1066**
  advanced options for, **1088–1089**
  cabling for, **1069**
  cross-platform application support for, **1090**
  Ethernet networks for, **1066**, 1069–1070
  iMac, **1068–1069**
  network adapters for, **1069**
  network alternatives for, **1090–1093**
  physical topologies for, **1069–1070**
  Power Macs
    first generation, **1066–1067**
    fourth generation and G3, **1067**
    G4, **1067–1068**
    second and third generation, **1067**
  printers on, **1076–1081**, *1078–1080*, *1082*
  security on, **1086–1088**, 1091
  servers for, **1070–1071**
    accessing, **1082–1086**, *1083–1084*, *1086*
    installing, **1071–1073**, *1071–1072*
  shares on, **1073–1076**, *1074–1076*
MacOS X Server, 1091–1092
Magnifier tool, 74
mail clients, 226
Mail Exchange (MX) records, **373–374**
  creating, **390–391**, *391*
  in zone file formats, **404**
Mail Exchanger (MX) tab, 390, *391*
mail router, 226
Mail Server tab, 1121, *1121*
mailex.asp program, **1172–1174**
MailSite program, **1180–1181**
Main MMC Window, 170, *171*
mainframes, 984
MaintainServerList key, 1311
Make Available Offline option, 857–859
Make Default option, 926
Make New Connection dialog box, 1439, *1439*
Make New Connection icon, 153, 270, 1418
Make New Connection wizard, 1457, *1457*
makeboot command, 72, 1381
/makelocalsource switch in winnt32, 89
.man files, 729, 1021
Manage auditing and security log right, 663
Manage Authorized Servers dialog box, 115, *115*, 303, *303*
Manage Computer, 1190, **1195–1197**, *1195*
Manage Documents permission, 937
Manage Filter Action tab, 291, *291*

Manage Group Policy Links permission, 687–688
Manage IP Lists and Filter Actions dialog box, 289–292, *289*, *291*
Manage Permissions Manually option, 1123
Manage Policy Links permission, 687
Manage Printers permission, 937
Managed By tab, 637
Managing Multiple Remote Access Servers screen, 1428–1429, *1429*
mandatory profiles, 631, **729–731**, 739
  shared, **737**
  summary, **736**
  for Terminal Services clients, 1021
  in Windows 95/98, 740
Manual Caching for Documents setting, 858
manual caching for Offline Files, **858**
Manual Frame Type Detection option, 1236
Manual Repair option, 1391–1392
Manually Configured Server option, 256, 264, 277, 325
map command, 1385, 1391
Map Network Drive dialog box, 836
  for hidden shares, 834, *834*
  for workstations, 972–973, *972*
Map Network Drive option, 967
mapping
  certificates, 614, 1188
  for MIME, 1099
  ports, **279–280**, *281*
  for printers, 927–929
  shared folders, 805, *806*, 834, *834*, 836
  volumes, 746
  in WINS, 342, *342*
  for workstations, 967, 972–973, *972*
market share, Windows 2000 server, **40**
Masquerade Domain setting, 1169
Master Boot Records (MBRs), 774
master browsers, 33, **1308–1311**, *1311*
Master DNS Servers screen, 394, *394*
master file table (MFT), 791
master/resource models, 481
Max Containers in Container setting, 1249
Max Fully Distinguished Name setting, 1248
Max Levels in Tree setting, 1249
Max Object Name Length setting, 1248
Max Objects in Container setting, 1248
Maximize Data Throughput for File Sharing option, 1298
Maximize Data Throughput for Network Applications option, 1298
Maximum Connections message, 1133
Maximum Hop Count setting, 1169

Maximum Password Age setting, 681, 698
MBRs (Master Boot Records), 774
md command, 1385, 1389
Media Access Control (MAC) addresses, 200, 300, 455
Media folder, 1338
media in RSM, **1338–1339**, *1339*, **1342–1345**
media pools in RSM, **1340–1342**, *1341–1342*
member management in Dfs, **848–849**, *849*
Member Of tab
    for groups, 637
    for user accounts, **633**, *633*
member servers, 32
Members tab, 131
    for Enterprise Admins Properties, 505, *505*
    for groups, 637
memory
    for DNS forwarders, 428
    for domain controllers, 487–488
    requirements for, **62–64**, 457
    sharing, **987**
    System Monitor for, **1265–1268**
    for Terminal Services, 991–992
    virtual
        operation of, **1265–1266**
        tuning, **1296–1297**, *1297*
    for Windows terminals, 994
Memory folder, 1363
memory leaks, 1038, 1266
Memory performance object, 1503
Merge Mode option, 705
merging
    domains, **584**
    forests, **1220–1221**
meshes in replication, **542–543**, *543*
Message access type, 1029
messages
    certificates for. *See* certificates
    for print servers, **958**, *959*
    in Terminal Services Manager, **1055–1056**, *1055*
Messages tab
    for FTP sites, **1133–1134**, *1133*
    for SMTP servers, **1162–1164**, *1163*
Messenger service, 336, 1213
<META> commands, 141–145
<META SERVER> command, 143
MetaFrame for Terminal Services, **1061–1062**
Metric column in routing table entries, **249**
metrics, 252
MFT (master file table), 791
Microsoft Authentication option, 1087

Microsoft Certificate Service dialog box, 604–607, *604–608*
Microsoft clearinghouse, 1030
Microsoft Directory Synchronization Services (MSDSS), 1245
Microsoft Disable NetBIOS Option, **314**
Microsoft Encrypted Authentication (MS-CHAP) option, 1432
Microsoft IIS Log Format, 1131
Microsoft Installer (MSI), 15–16, 868, 888
Microsoft LAN Manager, 43
Microsoft License Pak (MLP), 1032
Microsoft Management Console. *See* MMC (Microsoft
    Management Console)
Microsoft Open License program, 1032
Microsoft Point-to-Point Compression (MPPC) protocol,
    1435
Microsoft Release DHCP Lease on Shutdown Option, **314**
Microsoft saved consoles (MSCs), 169–170
Microsoft TCP/IP Properties dialog box
    for DHCP relay agents, 324, *324*
    for Internet gateways, 1450, *1450*
    for workstations, 969, *969*
Microsoft Windows Network dialog box, 975, *975*
Migrate Group SIDs to Target Domain option, 580
migration, **572**
    ADMT for, **578–581**, *580–581*
    clean, **574–577**
    domain, **1231**
        downlevel coexistence in, 1231–1232
        options for, **1231**
    in-place, **572–574**
    NETDOM for, **577**
    with NetWare, **1234**, **1244–1245**
        bindery and NDS data in, **1250–1252**, *1251–1252*
        DSMT for. *See* DSMT (Directory Services
            Migration Tool)
    permissions in, **575–576**
    SID histories in, **575–576**
migration tools for combining elements, **480–481**
MIL domain, 225
MIME (Multipurpose Internet Mail Extensions)
    adding and removing types, 1118
    mappings for, 1099
Minimum (Default) TTL setting, 388
Minimum Password Age option, 698
Minimum Password Length option, 698
mirror sets, **748–749**, *749*
    breaking, **767–768**, 775
    creating, **765–768**, *766*
    deleting, **766–767**, *767*
    guidelines for, **768**
    for system recovery, **778–780**, *778*

Mirrored option, 290–291
Misc tab, 1179, *1179*
Missing indicator, 775
Mixed (M) node, **333–334**
    for groups, 645
    migration in, 1231
    and universal groups, **471–472**, *471*
mkdir command, 1385, 1389
MKS Toolkit, 654
MLP (Microsoft License Pak), 1032
MMC (Microsoft Management Console), **168–169**
    benefits of, **169**
    for certificates, **596–598**, *597–598*
    consoles in
        Computer Management, **171–173**, *171–173*.
          See also Computer Management tool
        creating, **175–178**, *175–179*
        distributing, **192**
        editing, **192**
        packaging, **190–191**, *191*
        taskpad views in. *See* taskpad views
    extensions, 700–701, *701*
    group policies for, **699–702**, *700–702*
    terminology for, **169–170**, *171*
    tools in, **173–175**
Mobile Sync screen, 864
modem drivers for FRADs, 262
ModemLog_modemname.txt file, 1471
modems
    in installation, 79
    log files for, 1471
    for persistent connections, 261
    for RAS, **1411–1414**, **1470–1471**
Modems tab, 1416, 1471
moderated newsgroups, 1148, 1155
modernization, **11–12**
    goals for, **4**
    Plug and Play for, **12**
    user interface, **12**
Modifications tab, 897, *897*
Modify firmware environment values right, 663
Modify permissions, 819
Modify Setup Properties screen, 895, *896*
molecular permissions, **818–819**
monitoring
    DHCP, **319–320**, *320*
    system. *See* Event Viewer; Performance Logs and Alerts
      tool; System Monitor
monitors, print, **908**
more command, 1385

More Info link, 962
Most Fragmented Files window, 790
mounted drives, **10–11**, **745–746**, *746*
MountedDevices key, 776
mounting partitions to folders, 745
mouse port IRQ, 1480
Move dialog box, 638, *639*
Move Server dialog box, 558, *559*
Move Successful Number to Top of List option, 1422
Movetree tool, 1231
moving
    dynamic disks, **774–776**
    encrypted files, **796**
    in FTP, **1140**
    groups, 638, *639*
    paging files, 1296–1927
    servers, 558, *559*
    tapes, **1342**
    user accounts into OUs, **507**
MPPC (Microsoft Point-to-Point Compression) protocol,
    1435
mr900i router, 260
MS-NET tool, 42
.msc extension, 169
MSCLIENT tool, 977
MSCs (Microsoft saved consoles), 169–170
MSDOSInitiated setting, 97
MSDSS (Microsoft Directory Synchronization Services),
    1245
MSDUN13.exe file, 1395
msg command, 1051, **1055–1056**
MsgQBadAppSleepTimeInMillisec value, 1047
MSI (Microsoft Installer), 15–16, 868, 888
.msi files, 15–16, 868
msiexec.exe, 107
MSIs, 868, **879**
    application for
      installing, **881**
      testing, **882**, **885–886**
    clean computers for, **880**
    customizations for, **883–885**, *883–885*
    snapshots for, **880–882**, *880–882*
.mst extension, 888–889
MSTs
    creating, **889–897**, *889–897*
    using, **896–897**, *896–897*
Muglia, Bob, 22
multi-DHCP networks, **329**
multi-WINS networks, **344**
    replication in, **347–349**, *348*

server numbers in, **345**
updating servers in, **346–347**, *346*
multidomain enterprises, **458–459**
building and maintaining, **459–462**, *460–461*
geographically dispersed, **458–459**
size of, **458**
subdomains in, **459**
multidomain structures
forests for, **478–485**, *479*, *482–483*
vs. organizational units, **474–476**
trees for, **477–478**
multihomed computers
for routers, 201, **254–255**, *254*
for WINS servers, **350**
Multilink Connections option, 1434
multimaster model, 458
multimaster replication, 377, 464
vs. single-master, **525–526**
for zones, **415–416**
multiple domain controllers, replication with, **552–554**, *552–553*
Multiple Objects dialog box, 635
multiple permissions for shared folders, **825**
multiple taskpad tools, 180, *180*
multiple virtual Web sites, **1103–1107**
multiprocessor-capable machines, 992
Multipurpose Internet Mail Extensions (MIME)
adding and removing types, 1118
mappings for, 1099
multiuser environments, applications in, **1037**
choosing, **1037–1039**
compatibility scripts for, **1041–1044**
hand-tuning, **1045**
installing, **1039–1041**, *1040*, **1044**
Registry for, **1045–1050**, *1046–1049*
.museum domain, 363
MX (Mail Exchange) records, **373–374**
creating, **390–391**, *391*
in zone file formats, **404**
My Documents folder, 691–692, 712
My Network Places, 38

N

$N separator page function, 952
-n switch in nbtstat, 335, 340
/n switch in NTBACKUP, 1346
NACK (negative acknowledgments) in DHCP, 321
Name and Organization dialog, 78
.name domain, 363

name resolution, **332**, 455
DNS for, 278, **418**, **450**
HOSTS and caches in, **418–421**
preferred DNS servers in, **420–426**, *425*
in NetBIOS, **355–358**, *357*
in TCP/IP, 223
for Terminal Services, 1003–1004
in WINS, **352–355**, *353*
Name Resolution tab, 278
name server (NS) records
in CACHE.DNS, 440–441
in DNS, **372–373**
in zone file format, **402–404**
Name Server (NS) tab, 399, *399*
name servers
for delegation, 399, *399*
for network browsers, **1306–1307**
for zones, 388–389, *388*
Name Servers screen, 399, *399*
Name Servers tab, 388–389, *388*
name services, 1305
Name the Dfs Root screen, 844, *844*
Name Your Printer screen, 910–911, *911*, 1078, *1079*
named pipes, 836
names
administrators, 239, 619, 1214–1215
alerts, 1281
connections, 1446
demand-dialed interfaces, 1463–1464, *1464*
Dfs roots, 844, *844*
disconnecting physical locations from, **8–9**
in DNS, **359–360**. *See also* namespaces
domain controllers, 584
domains, 492–493, **583–585**, 1224, 1227
DHCP for, 308
FSMOs for, **526–527**, **532–533**, *533*, 1230
for TCP/IP, **236–242**, *239–241*
DSMT views, 1251
e-mail, **225–227**, *226*
FTP sites, 1127
Guest account, 619
Indexing Service catalogs, 1192
log files, 1277–1279
machines, **152**, *153*
in NBT, **334–336**
in NetBIOS, **334–336**
newsgroups, 1153–1155
NNTP servers, 1144, 1147
printers, 910–911, 1078, 1081
in Registry, **49–51**, *50*

resolving. *See* name resolution
reverse lookup zones, 369
scopes, 304, *305*
in scripts, 100
server, **67**
shares, 807, 911, 1241
sites, 558
SMTP servers, 1161
tapes, **1342**
taskpad views, 182
tasks, 185, 188
Terminal Services connections, 1004, 1007
trace logs, 1280
trees, **585**
underscores in, 518
users, 499–500, 624. *See also* usernames
zone files, 382–383, 402
zones, 382
namespaces, 477
    DNS, **360**
        hierarchy in, **360–362**, *362*
        second-level domains in, **364–365**
        third-level domains in, **365–366**
        top-level domains in, **362–364**, **518**
    unifying, **455–456**
naming contexts, 543, 1224
Narrator tool, 74
NAT (Network Address Translation), 20
    vs. ICS, **275–276**
    and ICS, **276–279**, *277–279*, **281–283**, *283*
    with IPSec, 298
    vs. PAT, **220–221**
    in routing, 269
National Research and Education Network (NREN), 196
National Science Foundation, 196
Native mode
    for domains, **498**
    for groups, 645–646
    migration in, 1231
    and universal groups, **471–472**, *471*, 642
NBT (NetBIOS over TCP/IP), **332–336**, 1503
NBT Connection performance object, 1503
nbtstat -A command, 335
nbtstat -c command, 356
nbtstat -n command, 335, 340
nbtstat -R command, 356
NCP (Network Control Protocol), 195–196
NCSA Common Log File Format, 1161
NDIS.SYS file, 1378
NDRs (non-delivery reports), 1164

NDS (NetWare Directory Services) data
    in DSMT, **1252–1254**, *1252–1253*
    finding and replacing, **1253–1254**, *1253*
    in NetWare migration, **1250–1252**, *1251–1252*
    passwords for, **1253**
    security for, 33
NEAR operator in queries, 1196
negative acknowledgments (NACK) in DHCP, 321
negative caching, **419–420**
NegativeCacheTime entry, 420
Negotiate Security option, 292
nested groups, 637, *638*, **643–646**
NET.CFG file, 1306
net config server command, 200
net config workstation command, 200
.net domain, 225, 362
net.exe program, 977–978
net logoff command, 978
net logon command, 978
net start command, 539
net stop command, 539
net time command, 538–540
net use command, 330, **837**, 977–978
    for credential conflicts, **837–838**
    for different accounts, **837**
    vs. ping, 329–330
    with WANs, **838**
net use lpt1 command, 918
net user command, 635
net view command, 330
    for browse lists, 35, *35*, 38, 1307–1308, *1308*
    for DOS clients, 978
    for printers, 918
NetBEUI (Network Basic Input/Output System Extended User Interface) protocol, 28, 68
NetBIOS (Network Basic Input-Output System)
    name resolution sequence in, **355–358**, *357*
    names in, 456, 493
    and Winsock, **331–332**
NetBIOS Domain Name screen, 493, *493*, 514, *514*
NetBIOS over TCP/IP (NBT), **332–336**, 1503
NETDOM tool, 484–485, **577**
NetHood folder, 712
NETLOGON directory, 494, 654–655
NETLOGON.DNS file, 520
NETLOGON share, **836**
netsh command, **319**
netstat command, 248
NetWare, **1233**
    clients in

connectivity for, **1238**, *1238*
support for, **1237–1238**, *1237*
file and print services for, 1234, **1243–1244**
GSNW for, 1234, **1239–1240**, *1240*
file shares for, **1241**, *1241*
print shares for, **1242**, *1242*
security for, **1242–1243**, *1243*
integration with, **1233–1234**, **1239**
migration with, **1234**, **1244–1245**
bindery and NDS data in, **1250–1252**, *1251–1252*
DSMT for. *See* DSMT (Directory Services Migration Tool)
protocol support for, **1235–1237**, *1235–1236*
NetWare Directory Services (NDS) data
in DSMT, **1252–1254**, *1252–1253*
finding and replacing, **1253–1254**, *1253*
in NetWare migration, **1250–1252**, *1251–1252*
passwords for, **1253**
security for, 33
NetWare or Compatible Networks window, 1238, *1238*
network adapters
configuring, installing, and removing, **156–158**, *157–158*
for Macintosh computers, **1069**
Network Address Translation (NAT), 20
vs. ICS, **275–276**
and ICS, **276–279**, *277–279*, **281–283**, *283*
with IPSec, 298
vs. PAT, **220–221**
in routing, 269
Network Address Translation (NAT) Properties dialog box, 277–278, *278*
Network and Dial-up Connections information box, 1446, *1446*
Network and Dial-Up Connections window, 222–223
functions of, **166**
for Internet connections, 270, *271*, 273, *273*, 1418, *1418*, 1420, *1421*
for multihomed computers, 254–255, *254*
for protocol installation, 153–154, *154*
for TCP/IP installation, 231, *231*
Network applet
for browser elections, 1311
for DHCP relay agents, 324
for routers, 254
for workstations, 975
network-aware software, 330
Network Basic Input-Output System (NetBIOS)
name resolution sequence in, **355–358**, *357*
names in, 456, 493
and Winsock, **331–332**

Network Basic Input/Output System Extended User Interface (NetBEUI) protocol, 28
network binding, **221–223**
Network Browser, 1082, 1085–1086
network browsers, **1305**
browse services for, **1306–1307**, *1307–1308*
hiding resources from, **1312**
for Macintosh computers, 1082, 1085–1086
master browser elections, **1308–1311**, *1311*
name servers for, **1306–1307**
operation of, **1308**
periodic advertising for, **1306**
refresh interval for, **1312**
static service lists for, **1305–1306**
network cards
drivers for, **146**
MAC addresses for, 455
multiple IP addresses for, **244–245**, *244*
for performance, 1305
for RIS, **111**
in routers, 201
Network Client Administrator utility, 977
Network Connection Type screen
for Internet connections, 270, *271*
for private networks, 1441, *1441*
for VPNs, 1458, *1458*
Network Connection Wizard
for dial-up, 1418
for gateways, 1445–1446, *1445*
for Internet connections, 270, *271*
for private networks, **1441–1443**, *1442*
for VPNs, **1458–1459**, *1458–1459*
Network Connections folder, 1365
Network Control Panel, **152–158**, 964–965, *964–965*
Network Control Protocol (NCP), 195–196
Network Credentials screen, 513, *513*
network default user profiles, **737**
Network dialog box, 964, *965*
Network Directory setting, 1111
Network Drivers dialog box, 974, *975*
NETWORK group, 651
Network Identification tab
for domains, 238, *239*, 240
for names, 152, *153*
for primary DNS servers, 380
for root servers, 442
Network Interface performance object, 1503
network-interface printers, 904
Network Neighborhood, 463
for browse lists, 38

for printers, 920, *921*
for workstations, 967, *967*
Network News servers. *See* NNTP (Network News) servers
network numbers in IP addresses, **207**
Network Path setting, 1241
network resources
for Windows 95/98 workstations, **967**, *967*
for Windows NT workstations, **972–973**, *972*
Network Segment performance object, 1503
Network Settings screen, 95, *95*
Network Setup dialog box, 973, *973*
network shares for RDP clients, **1000**
Network Solutions company, 361
Network Support Program, 42
[Networking] section, 96–97
Networking Services
adjusting, 155, *156*
for DSMT, 1246, *1246*
Networking Services dialog box, 155, *156*
Networking tab, 1443, *1443*
NetworkRangeLowerEnd key, 1089
NetworkRangeUpperEnd key, 1089
networks and networking
backing up, **1325**
client software on, **25**
connections and options for
component selection for, **69**
domain controller upgrades in, **69**
domain membership in, **68–69**
in installation, **67–71**
installation type for, **70–71**
physical, **27**
protocols for, **68**
server licensing in, **69–70**
encryption across, 795
infrastructure improvements in, **5–8**
IP address blocks for, 204–205, *204*
monitoring, **1271–1273**
printers on. *See* printer connections; printers and print
services
protocols for, **28**
purpose of, **23–24**
security for, **29–33**
segmenting, **1299**
server names in, **33–40**, *34–35*
server software on, **25–26**
services for, **155**, *156*
Windows 2000 server benefits for, **40–42**
Networks dialog box, 974, *974*
New Address Range dialog box, 1428

New Alert Settings option, 1281
New Alert Settings From option, 1281
New Alias option, 392
New Answer File or Installation Image screen, 133, *133*
New Authentication Methods Properties dialog box,
293–294, *294*
new capabilities and features, 5
New Class dialog box, 315, *316*
New Connection option, 1007
New Delegation Wizard, 398–399, *398–399*
New Dfs Root Volume option, 842
New Dfs Root Wizard, **842–844**, *842–844*
New Domain Name screen, 492, *493*
New File Share option, 809, 1074
New Filter Action Properties dialog box, 291–292, *291*
New Group Policy Object policy, 676
New Host option, 389
New Interface option, 278
New Log Settings option, 1277, 1280
New Log Settings From option, 1278, 1280
New Mail Exchanger option, 390
New Newsgroup Wizard, 1153–1155, *1154*
New NNTP Expiration Policy Wizard, 1156–1157, *1156*
New NNTP Virtual Directory Wizard, 1157, *1157*
New NNTP Virtual Server Properties dialog box,
1149–1151, *1150*
New NNTP Virtual Server Wizard, **1144–1146**,
1144–1146
New Object-Group dialog box, 507–508, *507*, 636, *637*
New Object-Shared Folder dialog box, 516, *516*
New Object-Site dialog box, 558, *558*
New Object-Site Link dialog box, 561, *561*
New Object-Subnet dialog box, 558, *559*
New Object-User dialog box, 499–500, *499*, 504, *504*,
624–626, *624–626*
New or Existing Answer File screen, 92, *92*
New Phonebook Entry dialog box, 1437, *1437*
New Port option, 955
New Quota Entry option, 802
New Replica option, 847
New Replication Partner option, 347
New Reservation dialog box, 312, *312*
New Resource Record dialog box, 390–393, *391–393*
New Routing Protocol dialog box, 277, *277*
New Rule Properties dialog box, 293, *293*
New Scope Wizard, **304–310**, *305–310*
New Security Method dialog box, 292, *292*
New Share dialog box, 1241, *1241*
New Site option, 558
New SMTP Domain Wizard, 1170–1171, *1170*

New SMTP Virtual Server Wizard, 1159–1161, *1159–1161*
New Static Mapping dialog box, 342, *342*
New Static Route option, 258, 1467
New Task Wizard, **182–186**, *184–186*, 188–189, *188–189*
New Taskpad View Creation Wizard, 181–182, *182*
New Taskpad View option, 187
New User dialog box, 619, *619*
New User option, 148, 619
New Zone Wizard, **381–385**, *381–383*, *385*, 394, *394*
news servers. *See* NNTP (Network News) servers
.nfo extension, 1367
NICs
    drivers for, **146**
    MAC addresses for, 455
    multiple IP addresses for, **244–245**, *244*
    for performance, 1305
    for RIS, **111**
    in routers, 201
NNTP (Network News) servers, **1143–1144**
    creating, **1144–1146**, *1144–1146*
    directories for, 1145
        for groups, 1153
        properties for, **1151–1153**, *1152*
        virtual, **1157**, *1157*
    expiration notices for, **1155–1157**, *1156*
    groups for, **1153–1155**, *1154–1155*
    IIS as, **1095**
    port for, 1144–1145, 1147–1448
    properties for
        Access tab, **1149–1151**, *1150*
        directory, **1151–1153**, *1152*
        General tab, **1147**, *1147*
        NNTP Settings tab, **1148–1149**, *1148*
        Security Account tab, **1149**, *1149*
NNTP Settings tab, **1148–1149**, *1148*
No, I Don't Want to Set Up This Server to Use RADIUS
    Now option, 1429
No, I Need to Add Protocols option, 1427
No Access permission, 1076
"No Domain Controller Found" message, **1393–1396**
No Override option, 676–677, **685**, 708–709
no-refresh intervals for DDNS registrations, **408–410**
NoCopyPrompt option, 1386
node status checks for Dfs, **849–850**, *849*
nodes in NetBIOS, **333–334**
nodes of functionality in GPOs, 1223
noise.enu file, 1196
noise words in queries, **1196–1197**
non-browser servers, 1309
non-delivery reports (NDRs), 1164

non-paged pools, 1266
non-Plug-and-Play devices, 1485
nonroutable addresses, **205–206**, **219–220**
nontransitive trust relationships, 1221
/noreboot switch in winnt32, 89
Normal backups, 1325–1326
normal names in NetBIOS, 335
Not Configured option, 943
NOT operator in queries, 1196
Novell Environment Discover tab, **1247–1248**, *1247*
NREN (National Research and Education Network), 196
NS (name server) records
    in CACHE.DNS, 440–441
    in DNS, **372–373**
    in zone file format, **402–404**
NSLOOKUP in DNS, 384, 396, *396*, **443**, 489
NT, history of, **42–44**
NT 3.51 user profiles, **739–740**, *739–740*
NT 4
    DNS servers in, **521**
    multiple domains with, **460–461**, *460*
    trusts in, **481–482**
NT Advanced Server, 43
NT applications
    permissions for, **900**
    upgrading, **900–902**
NT Diagnostics functions, 167, *167*
NT LAN Manager (NTLM), 8, 1183
NT machines as routers, **253–258**, *254–258*
NT-to-2000 trusts, 484, **579**
NT workstation connections, **968**
    configuring, **968–972**, *968–971*
    network resource access in, **972–973**, *972*
NTBackup program, 58
    automatic backups with, **1345–1347**
    strategies for, **1347–1348**
        differential backups, **1350–1351**
        weekly backups, **1348–1349**
NTBTlog.txt file, 1377, *1377*
NTCONFIG.POL file, 463, 563, 665
NTDetect file
    on boot floppies, 1381
    in boot process, **1370**
    deleting, 84
NTDS.DIT file
    for accounts, 620
    for domain controllers, 468
    for domains, 32, 458, 464–465
    for passwords, 29, 31
    vs. SAM, 448

NTDS Settings folder, 503
  for forcing replication, 552
  for loops, 542, *542*
  for meshes, 543, *543*
NTDS Settings Properties dialog box, 503, *504*, 1229, *1229*
ntdsutil utility, 536
NTFS filesystem, 66, 75–76, **782–784**
  converting FAT to, **786–787**
  encryption in, **794**
    decrypting files, **800**
    enforcing, **796–797**, *796*
    key protection in, **797–798**
    operation of, **794–795**, *794*
    process of, **795–796**
    recovering encrypted files, **798–800**
  vs. FAT and FAT32, **784**
  for fault-tolerant systems, 786
  permissions for, 667, **1207–1208**
  for servers, 488
  transaction logs in, 790
NTFS volumes, extending, 763–764
NTGATEWAY group, 1240
NthCountMsgQPeeksSleepBadApp value, 1047
NTLDR file
  on boot floppies, 1381
  in boot process, **1370**
  deleting, 84
NTLM (NT LAN Manager), 8, 1183
NTOSKRNL file, **1370–1371**
ntpquery.exe tool, 539
NTPRINT.INF file, 927
NTUSER.DAT file
  editing, **722**
  in Registry, 713
NTUSER.DAT.LOG file, 713
NTUSER.MAN file, 729–730
null modems, **1414**
number systems, **1475–1477**
NWConvert tool, 1244
NWLink IPX/SPX/NetBIOS Compatible Transport
  Protocols dialog box, 1236, *1236*
NWLink protocol, 1234, 1236, *1236*

O

Object tab, 512, *512*
objectionable material, 1117–1118, *1117*
objects
  access of, auditing, **567**
  group policy. *See* group policies and GPOs

performance, **1499–1506**
permissions for, **658–659**, *659–660*
in System Monitor, 1262
in zone files, 401
Objects performance object, 1503
Obtain an IP Address Automatically option, 234, 270, 274
Obtain an IP Address from a DHCP Server option, 324, 969
Obtain Client License Key Pack screen, 1036, *1036*
Obtain DNS Server Address Automatically option, 234
ODBC Logging format
  for FTP sites, 1131
  for SMTP servers, 1161
OEM
  for bitmaps and logos, **105**
  for cmdlines.txt, **106–109**
  for directories and copying files, **105–106**
  for drivers, **106**
  for I386, **105–106**
  for RIS, **134**
[OEM_Ads] section, 105
OEMPnPDrivers command, 106, 146
OEMPnPDriversPath command, 106, 146
OEMPreinstall setting, 97, 137
OEMSkipEula setting, 97
OEMSkipWelcome setting, 97
off-line media in RSM, 1337
Office Profile Wizard, 892
Offline Files, **19**, **854**
  accessing, **861**
  as backups, **862–863**, *863*
  caching in, **858–860**, *858*
  cleaning out, **865**
  enabling, **855–857**, *856–857*
  operation of, **854–855**
  preparation for, **859–860**, *859–860*
  problems with, **861**
  synchronizing, **860–865**, *860*, *862*, *864*
Offline Files Settings dialog box, 856–857, *856*, 859
Offline Files Status dialog box, 863, *863*
offline replica members, **848–849**, *849*
OLE Registration folder, 1365
on-demand dialing, 261
On Idle tab, 864, *864*
one-domain controllers, replication with, **546–547**
one-domain enterprises, **457**
110 Alert sensor, 1369
one-way functions, 590
online replica members, **848–849**, *849*
online resources for printer troubleshooting, **962**
Only for Myself option, 1443, 1459

Only Secure Updates option, 386, 415, 417
Only Selected Newsgroups on this Virtual Server option, 1156
Open Database dialog box, 671
Open dialog box in Event Viewer, 1291, *1291*
Open License Authorization, 1032
Open Log File option, 1291
Open Shortest Path First (OSPF) protocol
    for routing, **253**
    TCP/IP support for, 203
Open System Information File option, 1367
Open the MSI File screen, 889, *889*
Open the MST File screen, 889, *890*
Open Transport (OT) technology, 1083
OpenGL format, 1077
opening system information files, **1367**
OpenStep operating system, 1091
[operating systems] section, 779
Operations Manager tool, 571
Operations Master dialog box, 534, *534*
Operations Master option, 530
operations masters, **525**, **1230**
    contacting, 621
    FSMOs as. *See* FSMOs (Flexible Single Master of
      Operators)
Operators tab, **1108–1109**, *1109*
Options dialog box
    for backups, 1325–1326, *1325*
      file exclusions, 1327–1329, *1327*
      General tab, 1329–1330
      logs, 1326–1327, *1327*
    for MMC tools, 191, *191*
Options for domain controller selection dialog box, 1224, *1224*
Options tab
    for Internet connections, 1422–1424, *1423*
    for remote routing, 267, *268*
    for routing, 1468, *1468*
OR operator in queries, 1196
order
    of DNS booting, 437
    of domain searches, 241–242
    of group policies, **681–683**, *682*
.org domain, 225, 362
Organization tab, 628, *629*
organizational units (OUs), 15, **473**
    for accounts, 622
    in Active directory, **473–476**, **584–585**, **1222**
    creating, **507–508**, *507*
    delegating in, 459, **508–513**, *508–510*
    for domains, 452
    as folders, **473**

group policies for, 563
vs. groups, **476**, **652**
moving user accounts into, **507**
vs. multiple domains, **474–476**
for packages, **873–874**
for policies, **474**
for sub-administrators, **474**
for subdomains, **506–510**, *507–510*
%ORGNAME% environment variable, 140
orphaned files, 792
OS/2 operating system, 42–43
osauto.osc file, 144
.osc files, 140–141
oschoice.osc file, 143–145
OSPF (Open Shortest Path First) protocol
    for routing, **253**
    TCP/IP support for, 203
OT (Open Transport) technology, 1083
Other Tools folder, 178
OUs. *See* organizational units (OUs)
Outbound Security for SMTP servers, 1166–1167, *1168*
Outlook, certificates in, 599
overhead in TCP/IP, **197**
overwriting
    logs, 570
    system files, **901**
Owner tab
    for printers, 940, *940*
    of shared folders, 827–828, *827*, *829*
ownership and shared folders permissions, **826–830**,
    827–830

P

P node in NetBIOS, 333–334
-p option in cusrmgr, 636
/p switch in NTBACKUP, 1345, 1347
packages, **867–868**
    assigning, **874–878**, *875–878*
    customizing, **888–897**, *889–897*
    filtering for, **869**, *870*, **872**, *872–873*
    group policies for, 565, 680
    for MMC tools, **190–191**, *191*
    MSIs for, **879**
      application for, **881**, **885–886**
      clean computers for, **880**
      customizations for, **883–885**, *883–885*
      snapshots for, **880–882**, *880–882*
    off-the-shelf applications for, **888**
    OUs for, **873–874**

properties for, **877–878**, *877–878*
publishing, **868–871**, *869–871*
redeploying, **879**, *879*
removing, **878–879**, *878*
for Terminal Services, **1002**
for upgrading applications, **898–902**, *898–900*
ZAP files for, **886–888**, *887*
packet filtering, **294–297**, *297*
packet switching, 227
page faults, 1266
page table entries (PTEs), 1266
paged pools, 1266
pagefile.sys file, 1296
Pages Input/sec counter, 1267
Pages Output/sec counter, 1267
Pages/sec counter, 1267
Paging File performance object, 1504
paging files, 1266
location of, **1296–1297**, *1297*
for performance, 1304
paper jams, 961
parallel cable for RAS, **1415**
parallel ports, 908, 918
mapping, 929
for printers, 948
Parameters key
for IMS program, 1177
for Macintosh computers, 1088–1089
parentheses () in queries, 1196
parity
in memory, 63
stripe sets with, **750–751**, *751*
partitions, 75–76
creating, **65–66**
formatting, **772–773**, *772*
hard-linked, 773–774
labeling, **772–773**, *772*
logical, **744–745**
for Macintosh computers, 1070
for mirror sets, 765–766
primary, **746–747**, **752–753**, *753–754*
Recovery Console for, **1390–1391**
for servers, 488
system
in converting basic disks to dynamic, **757**
disk quotas on, 801
FAT filesystem on, **785**
passfilt.dll file, 685–686
passive opens, 218
Passprop.exe utility, 1213

Password Never Expires option, 626
Password Policy folder, 681, 686
Password Policy options, **698–699**
password-protected screen savers, **1014**
passwords
administrator, 78, 239
in ADMT, 578–581
controlling, **159–160**, *159*
with domain controllers, 459
for DSMT, **1250**, *1250*
encrypting, 29–30, 631
with FSMOs, 535
for FTP sites, 1132–1133, 1141
group policies for, 681, **685–687**, **698–699**
for Guest, 623
in IMS, **1175**, 1180
for Internet gateways, 1446
for local default Administrator account, 94
logon, 448–449
for Macintosh computers, 1084, 1086
migrating, 576
in NDS, **1253**
for NNTP servers, 1150
policies for, **1318–1319**
resetting, **451**, **635–636**
for server protection, **1316–1318**
for services, 165
sniffers for, 30
storing, **29**
for telnet, 1183
for users, *503*, 504, 619, **625–626**
for virtual directories, 1126
vulnerability of, **1316–1318**
for Web sites, 1115, 1211–1214
Passwords Must Meet the Complexity Requirements of Installed Password Filter option, 686, 698
PAT (port address translation), **220**
as firewalls, **220**
vs. NAT, **220–221**
Path Header setting, 1147
paths
for MMC tools, 174–175
for newsgroup postings, 1147
for shortcuts, 727
for Terminal Services, **1020–1024**, *1021*, **1045**
for user profiles, **721**
for virtual directories, 1125
pausing zones, 386
PC-based clients for Terminal Services, **995**, **999**
connections for, **1005–1009**, *1006–1007*, *1009*

deploying, **1001–1002**

installing and configuring, **1000–1001**

network shares for, **1000**

setup disks for, **1000**, *1000*

PCI cards

for performance, 1305

for RIS, **111**

for Terminal Services, 992

PCL.SEP separator page, 951

PDCs (primary domain controllers), 69, 458–459

FSMOs for, 470, **534–536**, **1230**

SAM on, 525

peer-to-peer sharing, **36**

Pending Certificate Request screen, 1187, *1187*

Per-seat licensing, 69–70

Per-server licensing, 70

per-user profiles, 739

Perflogs folder, 1278

Perform Reverse-DNS Lookup on Incoming Messages
option, 1169

performance

with mirror sets, 768

scalability of, **3**

in TCP/IP, 198

in Terminal Services, 991–992, 1026, **1062**

tuning, **1259**

driver updates in, **1300–1303**, *1301–1303*

hardware, **1303–1305**

network browsers. *See* network browsers

processor power, **1295–1296**, *1296*

servers, **1299–1300**

system cache, **1297–1298**, *1298*

Task Manager for, **1291–1295**, *1292–1294*

tools for. *See* Event Viewer; Performance Logs and
Alerts tool; System Monitor

virtual memory, **1296–1297**, *1297*

with VPNs, **1460**

Performance Logs and Alerts tool, 161, **1260–1261**, **1276**

logs in

alert, **1281–1284**, *1281–1284*

counter, **1277–1280**, *1277–1279*, **1284**

creating, **1276**

trace, **1280–1281**, *1280–1281*

types of, **1276**

viewing, **1283–1284**, *1284*

in System Tools node, 172

Performance Monitor, 1211. *See also* System Monitor

performance objects, **1499–1506**

Performance Options dialog box, 1296, *1296*

Performance setting, 1122

Performance tab

in Task Manager, 1292, *1292*

for Web sites, **1109–1110**, *1109*

Performance Tuning settings, 1110

periodic browser advertising, **1306**

periods (.)

in DNS names, 359

in filenames, 783

for root domain, 441

Perl language, 653

Perl2Exe utility, 653

Perlscript engine, 653

Permission Entry dialog box, 130, 512, *512*, 658, *659*

permissions, **32**, 465–466

for delegation, **510–512**, *511–512*

for dial-in RAS, **1429–1430**, *1430*

in DSMT, 1256–1257, *1257*

for FTP sites, 1129, *1129*, 1134–1135, 1137–1138, *1138*

for groups, 647, **660–663**, *661*

in Indexing Service, **1194–1195**

for Macintosh shares, **1074–1076**, *1075–1076*

in migration, **575–576**

for NetWare printers, 1243

for network printers, **933–970**, *934–936*, *938–940*

for NT applications, **900**

for NTFS, 667, **1207–1208**

restoring, 1355

vs. rights, 660

for shares and shared folders, 806–807, 809, **814–815**

assigning, **820–824**, *821–824*

atomic, **817–818**

conflicting, **825**

Deny, **825–826**, *826*

inherited, **819–820**, *820*, 823

molecular, **818–819**

multiple, **825**

ownership in, **826–830**, *827–830*

share, **811–814**, *812–813*

types of, **815–817**, *815*

for Terminal Services client connections, **1027–1029**,
1027–1028

for users, **658–659**, *659–661*

for virtual directories, **1126**, *1126*

for Web sites, **1105–1106**

Permissions screen, 494–495, *496*

Permissions tab

for delegation, 511–512, *511*

for printers, 935–936, *936*

for Terminal Services client connections, **1027–1029**,
1027–1028

Permitted Snap-Ins folder, 700–701
Permitted to Use information option, 719
permitting transmissions, IPSec for, **285**, **296–297**
persistent connections, 261, 1468
persistent mapping for printers, 928
/persistent switch in net use, 918
Personal folder, 712
Phone & Modem Options applet, 1416
Phone Number screen, 267, *267*, 1465, *1465*
Phone Number to Dial screen, 1441, *1442*
phone numbers for Internet connections, 1419, 1421, *1422*
phrases in queries, 1196
Physical Certificate Stores option, 598
Physical Disk performance object, 1504
physical disks vs. logical partitions, **744–745**
physical locations
  disconnecting from names, **8–9**
  in RSM, **1336–1337**, *1336*
Physical Memory section in Task Manager, 1292
physical network connections, 27
physical root for Dfs, **850–851**, *850*
physical security, 1314
physical topologies for Macintosh computers, **1069–1070**
pickname.osc file, 145
Pickup directory, 1171–1172
PICS (Platform for Internet Content Selection), 1117
PIDs (process IDs), 1053–1057, *1054*
ping utility, **236**, *236*
  vs. net use, 329–330
  for speed detection, 705
pinned files and folders, 856, 860–861, 863
Pipeline router, 260
pipes, 836
PKI (Public Key Infrastructure), 3–4
  certificates in, 286, 587
    for e-mail, **611–612**
    EFS, **614**
    IPSec for, **610–611**
    revoking, **614–615**
    for Web browsers, **612–614**
  planning for recovery, **1397–1401**
Platform for Internet Content Selection (PICS), 1117
Platform screen, 92, *93*
platforms, Macintosh computer support across, **1090**
platters, 781
Plug-and-Play devices, **12**, 62, 65
  adding, **1483–1485**
  detecting, 77
  printers, 910
PocketPC operating system, 41

Point-to-Point Protocol (PPP)
  for intranets, **228**
  for RAS, 1425
Point-to-Point Tunneling Protocol (PPTP)
  development of, **1452**
  for VPNs, **1452–1459**, *1453–1459*
pointer (PTR) records
  creating, **393**, *393*
  in DDNS registrations, 407
  in DNS, **374**, *374*
Pointer (PTR) tab, 393, *393*
POLEDIT.EXE program
  for registry, 713, *713*
  for user profiles, **724–726**, *725–726*
policies
  auditing, **567**
  group. *See* group policies and GPOs
  in IPSec, **287–289**, *287*
  OUs for, **474**
  for passwords, **1318–1319**
  system, 14–15, 457, 474, **563**, **665–666**
Policy Processing Options option, 704
politics, 451, **453**, 459
Pool Non-paged Failures counter, 1272
pools
  non-pages, 1266
  printer, **949–950**, *949*
POP3 (Post Office Protocol), 226, 1159
  with IMS, **1175**
  port for, 1448
POP3S.EXE program, 1174
port address translation (PAT), **220**
  as firewalls, **220**
  vs. NAT, **220–221**
port monitors for printing, 908
PortName key, 1089
ports and port numbers
  for FTP sites, 1127–1128, *1128*, 1130, 1142
  for Macintosh printers, 1078, 1080
  mapping, **279–280**, *281*
  for modems, 1417, *1417*
  for NNTP servers, 1144–1145, 1147, 1448
  for printers, 908, 910, 918, **948–950**, *949–950*,
    955–956, *956*
  for RAS, 1414, 1435, *1435*
  for routing, 1463
  for SMTP servers, 1160–1161
  in TCP/IP, **216–218**, 1448
  for VPNs, **1452–1453**, *1453*, 1455
  for Web sites, 1102–1104

Ports Properties dialog box, 1435, *1435*, 1452–1453, *1453*
Ports tab, 948–950, *949*, 955–956
post-installation procedures, **82–83**
Post Office Protocol (POP3), 226, 1159
    with IMS, **1175**
    port for, 1448
PostScript format, 1076–1077
PostScript Printer Description (PPD) files, 1086
potential browsers, 1309
pound signs (#) for separator pages, 952
power conditioners, 1314
Power Macs
    first generation, **1066–1067**
    fourth generation and G3, **1067**
    G4, **1067–1068**
    second and third generation, **1067**
power protection, **1314–1315**
power strips, 1315
power usage, **982**
Power Users group, 619, 650
/POWERDOWN option in tsshutdn, 1060
PPD (PostScript Printer Description) files, 1086
PPP (Point-to-Point Protocol)
    for intranets, **228**
    for RAS, 1425
PPP TCP/IP Settings screen, *1437*, 1438–1439
PPTP (Point-to-Point Tunneling Protocol)
    development of, **1452**
    for VPNs, **1452–1459**, *1453–1459*
PPTP Configuration dialog box, 1455, *1455*
#PRE command, **338**
Pre-Configure Verify Complete dialog box, 1255, *1255*
Pre-Configure Verify Object, 1254, *1254*
Pre-Populate Printer Search Location Text policy, 943
Preboot Execution Environment (PXE) protocol
    for RIS, 121–125, 128
    support for, 64, 87, 111
preconfigured user profiles, **719–722**, *720*, **727**
preferred DNS servers
    authoritative DNS servers found by, **423–426**, *425*
    cache searches by, **420–426**, *425*
    zones in, **421–423**
preferred master browsers, 1309
preinstalling service packs, **104**
preshared keys in PKI, 286, 294
pretty names for newsgroups, 1155
Previous Client Installation Screens Found screen, 133–134, *134*
PRI (Primary Rate Interface), 1413
.pri domain, 518

primary DNS servers
    creating, **379–380**
    in fault tolerance, **375–377**
Primary DNS Suffix for This Computer setting, 380
primary domain controllers (PDCs), 69, 458–459
    FSMOs for, 470, **534–536**, **1230**
    SAM on, 525
primary partitions, **746–747**, **752–753**, *753–754*
Primary Rate Interface (PRI), 1413
primary records in BOOT files, **437–438**
primary WINS servers, 340, 342, 346–347, 349
print devices, 904
Print Directly to the Printer option, 950
Print Manager, 909
Print Operators group, 649
Print permission, 937
print queues in NetWare, 1242
Print Server for Macintosh, **1081**
print services. *See* printer connections; printers and print services
PRINT$ share, 836
Print Sharing for Microsoft Networks, 80
print spoolers, **905–906**, 908
    for Macintosh computers, 1081, *1082*
    print monitor in, **908**
    print processor in, **906–907**
    print provider in, **906**
    print router in, **906**
Print Test Page dialog box, 1079, 1081
PrintAdm tool, 930
Printer Browsing policy, 942
printer connections, **909**
    for clients, **918**
        from DOS, **918**
        from Internet, **924–926**, *925*
        in Terminal Server environment, **926–929**
        from Windows 3.x, **918–920**, *919–920*
        from Windows 95/NT, **920–924**, *921–924*
        from Windows 2000, **921–924**, *922–924*
    printer installation, **909–913**, *909–912*
    for Web, **913–918**, *914–917*
printer graphics driver, 905
printer interface driver, 905
Printer Ports dialog box, 955
Printer Sharing screen, 911, *911*
printers and print services, **903**
    auditing, **937–939**, *938–939*
    connections for. *See* printer connections
    drivers for, **905**
    Graphics Device Interface for, **905**
    hiding, **940**

installing, **909–913**, *909–912*, **929–933**
on Macintosh computers, **1076–1081**, *1078–1080, 1082*, **1085–1086**, *1086*
mapping, 927–929
for NetWare, **1243–1244**
print jobs
    browsers for, **960**
    Printers folder for, **959–960**, *959–960*
print servers for, **26**, **953**, *954*
    drivers for, **956–958**, *957–958*
    forms for, **954–955**, *955*
    for Macintosh computers, **1070–1071**
    messaging and logging for, **958**, *959*
    ports for, **955–956**, *956*
    for Web printing, **914–918**, *914–917*
printer configuration for, **946–947**, *946*
    multiple settings, **948**
    port settings, **948–950**, *949–950*
    priorities, **953**, *954*
    separator pages, **951–953**, *951*
printer troubleshooting
    online resources for, **962**
    problem identification, **961–962**
printing process, **908–909**
redirecting, **926–929**
security for, **933**
    available hours, **933–934**, *934*
    group policy settings, **940–945**, *941*, *944*
    hiding printers, **940**
    permissions, **933–970**, *934–936*, *938–940*
shares for, **1242**, *1242–1243*
spoolers for, **905–908**
for Terminal Services clients, 1023
terminology for, **904**
UPSs for, 1315
in Web site security, **1210**, **1216**
Printers dialog box, 918–920, *919–920*, 924
Printers folder, 906
    for client connections, 920
    for default printers, 926
    for installing printers, 909
    managing printers from, **959–960**, *959–960*
    for online resources, 962
    for redirection, 927
    for Web print servers, 914–917, *914*, *917*
Printers icon, 918
Printers tab, 923
PrintHood folder, 712
priorities
    IRQs, **1480–1481**

printers, **953**, *954*
servers, **1299**
WINS vs. DNS, **355**
Private Bytes counter, 1268
Private Interface Connected to Private Network option, 279
private keys
    for certificates, **589–591**
    exporting, 798
private networks in RAS, **1405**, **1441–1444**, *1442–1444*
private roots in DNS, **441–443**
privilege uses, auditing, **567–568**
privileges. *See* permissions
.pro domain, 363
Process Even If the Group Policy Objects Have Not Changed option, 704
process IDs (PIDs), 1053–1057, *1054*
Process performance object, 1504
processes
    auditing, **568**
    in Terminal Services, 1052
Processes count, 1292
Processes tab, 1056, 1293–1295, *1294*
Processor performance object, 1504
% Processor Time counter, 993, 1269
processors
    for performance, **1304**
    print, **906–907**
    requirements for, **62**
    System Monitor for, **1269–1270**, *1270*
    for Terminal Services, 992
    tuning, **1295–1296**, *1296*
    for Web sites, 1098
    for Windows terminals, 994
Product to Install screen, 92, *92*
ProductID command, **97–98**
ProductOptions key, 1295
Profile Path setting, 717, *717*
profile paths
    for Terminal Services clients, **1020–1022**, *1021*
    for users, 717, *717*
Profile single process right, 663
Profile system performance right, 663
Profile tab
    for Terminal Services clients, 1020
    for user accounts, **631–633**, *632*, 717, *717*
ProfileDlgTimeout Registry entry, 733
profiles
    for hardware, **1495–1496**, *1496*
    user. *See* user profiles
PROFILES directory, 711, *711*

Profiles folder, 1020
ProfilesDir, 100
program groups, 715
Program Groups folder, 1365
Program tab, 1008, *1009*, 1012, *1012*
projects in DSMT, 1245
promoting domain controllers, **162**
Prompt for Name and Password, Certificate, etc. option, 1423
properties for packages, **877–878**, *877–878*
Protocol tab, 290, 297, *297*
protocols, 194, *194*
    adjusting, **153–154**, *154–155*
    in installation, **68**
    for IPSec filters, 290, 297, *297*
    with MetaFrame, **1061**
    for NetWare, **1235–1237**, *1235–1236*
    for networks and networking, **28**
    for RAS clients, 1438–1439
    simplifying, **1299**
    for SMTP servers, **1158–1159**
    for workstations, 964
Protocols and Security screen, 267, *267*, 1465, *1465*
Protocols tab
    for DHCP relay agents, 324
    for routers, 254
    for VPNs, 1454
    for workstations, 969
prototype reconfiguration, **128**
providers
    ISPs, 1418–1420
        for gateways and routers, **262–263**
        in ICS, **270–274**, *271–273*
    print, **906**
    for trace logs, 1280
proxy agents, **351–352**, *351*
Prune Printers That Are Not Automatically Republished
    policy, 943
pruning and grafting, 479
PSCRIPT.SEP separator page, 951
PTEs (page table entries), 1266
PTR (pointer) records
    creating, **393**, *393*
    in DDNS registrations, 407
    in DNS, **374**, *374*
Public Interface Connected to the Internet option, 278
public key encryption, 8, 794
Public Key Infrastructure (PKI), 3–4
    certificates in, 286, 587
        for e-mail, **611–612**
        EFS, **614**

IPSec for, **610–611**
    revoking, **614–615**
    for Web browsers, **612–614**
Public Key Policies category, 694
public keys for certificates, **589–591**
Public Network screen, 1458, *1459*
publishing
    with MetaFrame, **1061**
    packages, **868–871**, *869–871*
    shares, 516, **810–811**
purging WINS records, **350–351**
push/pull partners, 346–349, *348*
PXE (Preboot Execution Environment protocol)
    for RIS, 121–125, 128
    support for, 64, 87, 111
Python language, 653
PythonWin environment, 654

Q

/Q switch in tsprof, 1022
qchain.exe program, 1206
QoS (Quality of Service), 8, 463
quad format for IP addresses, **200–201**, *201*
queries
    Indexing Service
        from Manage Computer, **1195–1197**, *1195*
        from Web, **1197–1202**
    recursive vs. iterative, **424–425**, *425*
Query Information access type, 1029
/query option in change user, 1041
query process command, 1051
query session command, 1051
query termserver command, 1051
Query the Catalog tool, 1195
query user command, 1051
Queue directory, 1171–1172
queues, 904, 1242
quick formats, 753
QuickDraw format, 1076
QuickDraw GX format, 1077
Quit method, 933
Quota Entries folder, 803
Quota Entries management tool, 803
Quota Entries option, 802
Quota tab, 801–803, *801*
quotas, disk, **18**, **800**
    managing, **803–804**
    operation of, **800–801**
    setting up, **801–803**, *801–803*

R

/r switch
    in CHKDSK, 793
    in winnt, 91
/R switch in EFSINFO, 797
-R switch in nbtstat, 356
RADIUS server, 1428–1429, 1431
RAID (Redundant Array of Inexpensive Disks), **743**
    drivers for, 74
    hardware vs. software, **780**
    RAID 5 volumes, **750–751**, *751*
        creating, **768–772**, *769–771*
        stripe sets in, **771–772**, *771*
    SCSI drives for, 1304
RAM
    for DNS forwarders, 428
    for domain controllers, 487–488
    requirements for, **62–64**, 457
    System Monitor for, **1265–1268**
    for Terminal Services, 991–992
    for Windows terminals, 994
random passwords, 636
RAS (Remote Access Service), **1403–1404**
    applications of, **1404–1406**
    bandwidth for, **1406–1410**
    configuration for
        clients, **1436–1440**, *1436–1440*
        servers, **1430–1436**, *1431, 1433–1435*
    connections in
        Internet, **1417–1424**, *1418–1425*
        private network, **1441–1444**, *1442–1444*
        scheduling, 1471–1472
        VPN. *See* VPNs (Virtual Private Networks)
    dial-in permissions for, **1429–1430**, *1430*
    file-based and client-server applications in, **1408–1410**
    hardware requirements for, **1411–1415**
        direct options, 1414–1415
        frame relay, 1415
        ISDN, 1413–1414
        modems, 1411–1414, 1470–1471
        X.25, **1415**
    incoming calls in, **1425–1426**
    installing, **1415–1417**, *1416–1417*, **1426–1429**, *1426–1429*
    for Internet gateways, **1444–1450**, *1445–1447, 1450*
    remote control in, **1410**
    remote node method in, **1406–1407**
    for routing, **1405**, **1460–1461**
        first server setup in, **1461–1469**, *1462–1469*
        sample network, **1461**, *1462*

troubleshooting, **1469–1472**
    user management on, **1440**
    WINS and DNS with, **1472**
RASDIAL command, 1471
Ratings tab, 1117–1118, *1117*
RAW printer data, 906–907
RBFG.exe program, 111, 121–122, 127–128
rd command, 1385, 1389
RDISK utility, 58, 1381
RDP (Remote Desktop Protocol)
    disabling, 1059
    for Terminal Services, **999**
        connections for, **1005–1013**, *1006–1007, 1009–1013*
        deploying, **1001–1002**
        installing and configuring, **1000–1001**
        limitations of, **1013–1014**
        network shares for, **1000**
        setup disks for, **1000**, *1000*
    for thin client sessions, **987–990**
RDP-Tcp dialog box, 1026
Read & Execute permission, 819, 823
Read Attributes permission, 816–817
Read Data permission, 816, 818
Read Extended Attributes permission, 816–817
read-only mode
    CHKDSK in, 792
    for Registry editors, 48
Read Only newsgroups, 1155
read-only user profiles, 729–730
read-only zone copies, **376**
Read permissions
    for FTP sites, 1129, 1134–1135, 1138
    for Macintosh shares, 1076
    for NetWare printers, 1243
    for shares and shared folders, 812, 816, 818–819
    for Web sites, 1105, 1112
Read Permissions permission
    for printers, 937
    for shared folders, 816, 818
/REBOOT option in tsshutdn, 1060
rebooting, 83
    <META> for, 141, 145
    reductions in, **2, 22**
    after Windows NT workstation changes, **971**
Recent folder, 712
reconfiguration, RIS prototype, **128**
record types in DNS, **369–370**, *370*
    A, **370–372**
    CNAME, **373**

MX, **373–374**
NS, **372–373**
PTR, **374**, *374*
SOA, **372**
SRV, **374–375**, 518–520
in zone files, 401
recovering encrypted files, **798–800**
recovery. *See also* backups; Recovery Console; servers
    backups in, **1400–1401**
    boot floppies for, **1381–1382**
    disk failures, **777–780**, *777–778*
    in DNS, **438–444**
    emergency repair disks for, **1379–1381**, **1392–1393**
    guidelines for, **1398–1399**
    planning for, **1397–1401**
    repair options for, **1383**
    services for, **1400**
    in TCP/IP, **197**
    testing plans, **1399–1401**
recovery agents, 588, 595, **798–800**
Recovery Console, **84–86**, 785
    commands in, **1383–1386**
    for fixing boot sectors and boot records, **1390**
    installing, **1378–1379**, *1378*
    for partitions, **1390–1391**
    for replacing files, **1389–1390**
    security settings for, **1386–1387**
    for services, **1387–1389**
Recovery tab, 165, *166*
Recreational Software Advisory Council (RSAC), 1117
recursive queries vs. iterative, **424–425**, *425*
Redeploy Application option, 879
redeploying packages, **879**, *879*
Redial Attempts setting, **1423**
Redial If Line Is Dropped option, **1423–1424**
redirecting
    folders, **691–692**, *693*
    printers, **926–929**
    users to URLs, 1111
Redirector performance object, 1504
redundancy, mirror sets for, 748–749
Redundant Array of Inexpensive Disks (RAID), **743**
    drivers for, 74
    hardware vs. software, **780**
    RAID 5 volumes, **750–751**, *751*
        creating, **768–772**, *769–771*
        stripe sets in, **771–772**, *771*
    SCSI drives for, 1304
refresh intervals
    for DDNS registrations, 408–412, *409*

in DNS, 387
    for group policies, **674**
    for network browsers, **1312**
refreshing
    tapes, **1344–1345**
    in WINS, 340
REG_BINARY data type, 50
REG_DWORD data type, 51
REG.EXE program, 58
REG_EXPAND_SZ data type, 51
.reg files, 1045, 1047
REG_MULTI_SZ data type, 51
REG_SZ data type, 51
REGEDIT editor, 47, 53–54, **59**, 107
REGEDT32 editor, 47, **59**, **722–724**, *722–724*
REGINI.EXE utility, 54, 738
register command, 1051
Register This Connection's Addresses in DNS option, 242
RegisteredOrganization key, 52–53
registers, 1478
registrations, DDNS
    with DHCP, **407**
    scavenging, **408–412**, *408–409*, *411–412*
    with static IP addresses, **407**
    triggering, **406**
    vs. WINS, **412–413**
Registry, **45–47**
    backing up, **58–59**, 1320, 1349
    for browser elections, **1311**
    for DHCP leases, 321
    for DNS forwarders, 430
    for domain logons, 728
    for drive letters, 777
    editing
        danger in, **53–55**
        REGEDIT vs. REGEDT32, **59**
        remote, **57–58**
    on ERDs, 1381
    fault tolerance in, **56–57**
    for group policies, **708–709**
    hives in, **55–57**
    for IMS program, **1177**
    keys in, **49–50**, 53
    for Macintosh computers, **1088–1089**
    for NT applications, **900**
    NTUSER.DAT file in, 713
    permissions for, **667–668**
    for policies, 665
    for processors, 1295
    for profiles, 713–714

for RAS, 1470, 1472
restoring, **58–59**, 1356
subtrees in, **48–49**
for Terminal Services, 1039–1040, **1045–1050**,
    1046–1049
terminology for, **47–48**
for user profiles, **722–724**, *722–724*
value entries, names, values, and data types in, **50–51**, *50*
for WINS and DNS priority, 355
working with, **51–53**, *52*
Registry category, 694
Registry Editor screen, 47–48, *47*
Registry Editors
    for DNS boot order, 437
    REGEDIT, 47, 53, **59**, 107
    REGEDT32, 47, **59**, **722–724**, *722–724*
Registry folder, 598
Relative Identifier (RID) Pool role, **533–534**, *534*, 1231
relative IDs (RIDs), **533–534**, *534*, **536–538**, 621, 1357
relative names in zone files, 402
relay restrictions for SMTP servers, 1166, *1167*
reliability goals, **2**
reliable services, 214
REMINST share, 125
remote access
    installing devices for, **1415–1417**, *1416–1417*
    in RRAS, 257
Remote Access Auto Connection Manager service, **1424**, *1424*
Remote Access Connections (Inbound Only) option, 1435
Remote Access (Inbound Only) option, 1453
Remote Access Server option, 257, 264, 277
Remote Access Service. *See* RAS (Remote Access Service)
Remote Administration mode, **1062–1064**
Remote Boot Disk Generator, 121–122
Remote Client Protocols screen, **1427**, *1427*
remote clients, RAS for, **1405**
remote control, 989
    improvements in, **16**
    in RAS, **1410**
    for Terminal Services clients, **1017–1018**, *1017*
Remote Control access type, 1029
Remote Control dialog box, 1058, *1058*
Remote Control tab, 1017, *1017*
Remote Desktop Connection dialog box, 1010–1013,
    1010–1013
Remote Desktop Protocol (RDP)
    channels in, **988–989**, *989*
    disabling, 1059
    for Terminal Services, **999**
        connections for, **1005–1013**, *1006–1007*, *1009–1013*

deploying, **1001–1002**
installing and configuring, **1000–1001**
limitations of, **1013–1014**
network shares for, **1000**
setup disks for, **1000**, *1000*
for thin client sessions, **987–990**
remote event log data, **1286–1287**, *1286*
Remote Install tab, 120, *121*
Remote Installation Folder Location screen, 117, *117*
Remote Installation Preparation Wizard, **125–127**, *126–127*
Remote Installation Services. *See* RIS (Remote Installation
    Services) tool
Remote Installation Services Setup Wizard, **117–120**,
    117–120, 133–134, *133–134*
remote logins, telnet for, **1182–1184**
remote machines, services on, **162**
remote node method in RAS, **1406–1407**
remote performance monitoring, **1273–1274**, *1274*
remote procedure calls (RPCs), 454, 914
remote Registry editing, **57–58**
Remote Share option, 1146
Remote Storage, **11**
RemoteInstall folder, 118
RemoteRouter dialog box, 267, *268*
removable disk drives as dynamic disks, 756
Removable Storage Manager (RSM), 1330, **1335–1336**
    libraries in, **1337–1338**
    media in, **1338–1339**, *1339*, **1342–1345**
    media pools in, **1340–1342**, *1341–1342*
    physical locations in, **1336–1337**, *1336*
Remove computer from docking station right, 663
Remove Disk option, 775
Remove Mirror dialog box, 766, *767*
Remove Previous Versions screen, 890, *891*
Remove Replica option, 847
Remove Software dialog box, **878–879**, *878*
RemovePrinterConnection method, 932
removing. *See also* deleting
    group policies, **564–565**
    hardware, **1485**
    network adapters, 156
    packages, **878–879**, *878*
    users from groups, 633
rename command, 1385, **1389–1390**
renaming
    Administrator account, 619, **1214–1215**
    domain controllers, 584
    Guest account, 619
    NTUSER.DAT, 729
    tapes, **1342**

renewal intervals in WINS, **340**
repadmin.exe program, 542, 553
repair. *See* recovery
Repair folder, 1393
Repartition command, **98**
REPL$ share, **836**
Replace a process level token right, 663
Replace Mode option, 705
Replace Multi-Valued Properties option, 1250
Replace Owner on Subcontainer and Objects option, 829
Replace Single-Valued Properties option, 1249
replacing files
    damaged, **1389–1390**
    NDS data, **1253–1254**, *1253*
    in restoring, 1354–1355
replicas
    for Distributed File System, **1225–1226**
        configuring, **847**, *847*
        member management, **848–849**, *849*
        process, **848**, *848*
    domain controllers, 162
Replicate This Attribute to the Global Catalog option, 528
replication
    Active Directory, **453–454**, **1224**
        Dfs, **1225–1226**
        GPOs, **1226**
        inter-site, **560–562**, *560–562*
        local. *See* local Active Directory replication
        SYSVOL, **1224–1225**
    in Active Directory-integrated zones, **415–416**
    bandwidth for, **474–475**
    in multi-WINS networks, **347–349**, *348*
    multimaster, 464, **525–526**
    single-master, **525–526**
    for zones, **415–416**
Replication Partners folder, 346–347
Replication Partners Properties dialog box, 346–347, *346*
Replication Policy dialog box, 848, *848*
Replicator group, 619, 649–650
Report option for backups, 1351
Request File Summary screen, 1185, *1186*
requesting certificates, **604–606**, *604–606*
Require Client Certificates option, 613, 1188
Require Secure Channel (SSL) option, 613, 1188
Require SSL Client Authentication option, 1151
Require SSL for Authoring option, 1123
Required Upgrade for Existing Package option, 899
Rescan Disks option, 775
Reseaux IP Europeens (RIPE), 204

Reservation Services Virtual Protocol (RSVP), 1500
Reservations folders, 312
reservations in DHCP, **312**, *312*
Reserve This Public IP Address option, 282
reserved IP addresses, 205
reserving memory, 1266
Reset access type, 1029
Reset Account Lockout Counter After option, 699
reset command, 1051
Reset option for Terminal Services sessions, 1059
Reset Password dialog box, 631, *631*
Reset Password option, 511
Reset Permissions on All Child Objects and Enable
    Propagation of Inheritable Permissions option, 823, 830
reset session command, 1059
resetting
    passwords, **451**, **635–636**
    Terminal Services sessions, 1018, 1059
Resolve File Conflicts dialog box, 862, *862*
resolvers in DNS architecture, **426–427**
Resource Kit, 1214
Resources tab, **1490**, *1491*
Restart option for services, 166
Restart Service Print Spooler dialog box, 1081, *1082*
Restore files and directories right, 663
Restore option, 1048
Restore Progress dialog box, 1356
Restore tab, 1354–1355
Restore Wizard, **1352–1356**, *1353, 1355*
restoring
    backups, **1352**
        authoritative, **1358–1360**
        configuration settings, **1356**
        file selection for, **1353–1356**, *1353, 1355*
        techniques for, **1352–1356**, *1353*
        viewing logs for, **1356**
    Registry, **58–59**, 1048
Restrict access option, 1321
Restrict Newsgroup Visibility option, 1152
Restrict Users to the Explicitly Permitted List of Snap-Ins
    policy, 700–701
Restricted Groups category, 694
Restricted Groups folder, 670
restrictions
    group policies for, 565
    relay, **1166**, *1167*
Resultant Set of Policy (RSOP), 564, 709, 1223
Retrieve The CA Certificate Or Certificate Revocation List
    option, 609, *610*

Retry Interval setting, 387
Reverse Lookup Zone screen, 384, *385*
reverse lookup zones
creating, **383–385**, *385*
in DNS, **369**
Reverse Lookup Zones folder, 381
reverse name resolution, 369
Revert to Basic Disk option, 762
Review Settings screen, 118, *119*, 127, *127*
Revoke Certificate option, 614
Revoked Certificates folder, 614
revoking certificates, **614–615**
RID (Relative Identifier Pool) role, **533–534**, *534*, 1231
RID tab, 534, *534*
RIDs (relative IDs), **533–534**, *534*, **536–538**, 621, 1357
rights. *See* permissions
RIP (Routing Information Protocol), **253**
RIPE (Reseaux IP Europeens), 204
RIPrep images, 111
creating, 125
delivering, **128**
RIPrep program, **125–127**, *126–127*
RIS (Remote Installation Services) tool, **13–14**, 66, **109–111**, 462
Active Directory authorization for, **115–116**, *115–116*
for Client Installation Wizard, **140–145**
for clients, **120**, *121*
enabling user use of, **128–129**
for Installers group, **129–131**
installing, **116**, *116*
limitations of, **111–112**
for NIC drivers, **146**
OEM for, **134**
preparing for, **113–114**
prototype reconfiguration in, **128**
risetup program for, 112, **117–120**, *117–120*
for scripts, **134–139**
for server rollout, **131–134**, *132–134*
starting, **112**
for system images
creating, **125–127**, *126–127*
delivering, **128**
limiting, **131**
in unattended installation, **87**
workstation installation using, **120–125**, *122*
risetup program, 112, **117–120**, *117–120*
ristndrd.sif script, **134–139**, 146
rmdir command, 1385, 1389
roaming profiles. *See* user profiles

rogue DHCP servers, 303, 318
roles of FSMOs, **528**, **1230**
domain naming, **526–527**, **532–533**, *533*
infrastructure and PDC, **534–536**
RID pool, **533–534**, *534*
schema, **528–532**, *529–530*
transferring, **536–538**, *536*
ROM addresses
conflicts in, **1481**
listing, 1490
root directory for FTP sites, 1129
root hints files, 365
Root Hints tab, 429–430
root replica members, 841
root servers, **424**
rooting process, 774
roots
for Dfs, 839–840, **842–844**, *842–845*
connecting and disconnecting from, **850**
links for, **845–846**, *845–846*
physical, **850–851**, *850*
in DNS, 361
empty, **485–486**
forest, 498, 1219–1220, *1220*
private, **441–443**
of trees, 477
virtual, 1124–1125, *1125*
Rossinovich, Mark, 46
round-robin DNS, **371–372**, *371*
routable addresses, **205–206**, **219–220**
route add command, **246–247**, 252–253
Route IP Packets on This Interface option, 267
route print command, **248–250**
Router (Default Gateway) screen, 309, *309*
routers. *See also* gateways
in DHCP operation, **323–326**, *324–326*
in IP, **199**, **201–203**
mail, 226
NT machines as, **253–258**, *254–258*
print, **906**
SAP with, 1306
and subnets, **252–253**
routing, **245–246**, *246*
conflicts in, **251–252**
default gateways in, **250–252**, *251*
default routes in, **247–248**, *248*
in IP, **202–203**
NT machines in, **253–258**, *254–258*
OSPF for, **253**

RAS for, **1405**, **1460–1461**
  first server setup in, **1461–1469**, *1462–1469*
  sample network, **1461**, *1462*
RIP for, **253**
routing tables for. *See* routing tables
static, **258–259**, *258–259*
subnets in, **252–253**
Routing and Remote Access Server Setup Wizard, 256, *256*
  for gateways and routers, 263–264, *263–264*
  for ICS, 277
  for RAS installation, **1426–1429**, *1426–1429*
Routing and Remote Access Service (RRAS), 255–258,
  256–258, 1404
  for DHCP relay agents, 325, *325*
  for gateways and routers, **263–269**, *263–268*
  for ICS, **276–279**, *277–279*
  on-demand dialing in, 261
  for PPP, 228
  for RAS user management, **1440**, *1441*
  for routing, 267, *268*, 1462–1464, *1464*, 1468–1469
Routing Information Protocol (RIP), **253**
Routing Interfaces object, 265, 267
Routing tab, 254
routing tables
  broadcasting, 253
  entries in
    adding, **246–247**
    viewing, **248**, *248*
RPCs (remote procedure calls), 454, 914
RRAS. *See* Routing and Remote Access Service (RRAS)
RSAC (Recreational Software Advisory Council), 1117
RSM (Removable Storage Manager), 1330, **1335–1336**
  libraries in, **1337–1338**
  media in, **1338–1339**, *1339*, **1342–1345**
  media pools in, **1340–1342**, *1341–1342*
  physical locations in, **1336–1337**, *1336*
rsm tool, 1338–1339
RSOP (Resultant Set of Policy), 564, 709, 1223
RSOP modelers, 564
RSVP (Reservation Services Virtual Protocol), 1500
rules in IPSec, **286**, 288, **292–297**, *292–294*, *297*
Run key, 1396
Run Login Script option, 1238
Run Only Allowed Windows Applications Properties dialog
  box, 697, *698*
Run Scripts permission, 1105
runas command, **17–18**
RunLogonScriptSync key, 724
Running Tasks folder, 1365
/rx switch in winnt, 91

S
/s switch
  in GPRESULT, 707
  in winnt32, 89
Safe Mode, **1373–1374**
Safe Mode with Command Prompt, **1374**
Safe Mode with Networking, **1373**
SAM (Security Accounts Manager)
  contents of, 448, 458, 619–620
  limitations of, 29
  on PDCs, 525
  in Registry, 55–56
  uses for, 464–465
  for workstations, 468
Samba utility, 1065
sampling interval for counter logs, 1277–1278
SAP (Service Advertising Protocol), 1306
Save As option in System Monitor, 1275
Save as System Information File option, 1367
Save as Text File option, 1367
Save Key dialog box, 1047, *1047*
Save Log File As option, 1291
Save Selections dialog box, 1331
saving
  backup options, **1331**
  custom consoles, 178
  Event Viewer data, **1291**, *1291*
  Registry keys, **1047–1048**, *1047*
  system configuration, 1367–1368
  System Monitor data, **1274–1275**, *1275*
  user profiles, 733, *735*
  usernames and passwords, 1446
scalability
  Active Directory for, **454–455**
  in DNS, 358
  goals for, **3–4**
Scan for Hardware Changes action, 1492
Scavenge Stale Resource Records option, 408
scavenging
  DDNS registrations, **408–412**, *408–409*, *411–412*
  in WINS, 350–351
Schedule for frame-relay dialog box, 562, *562*
Schedule Job dialog box, 1331–1334, *1333–1334*
Schedule Jobs tab, 1331–1332, *1332*
Schedule tab
  for backups, 1333, *1333*
  for log files, 1279–1280, *1279*
Scheduled Job Options dialog box, 1334–1335, *1335*
Scheduled tab, 865

schedules
 for backups, **1331–1335**, *1331–1335*
 for log files, 1279–1280, *1279*
 for offline file synchronization, 865
 for RAS connections, **1471–1472**
 for replication, 562, *562*, 1225
schema
 changes and conflicts in, **531**
 FSMOs for, **528–532**, *529–530*, 1231
 and GC changes, **531–532**
 modifying, **1220–1221**
 naming contexts, 543, 1224
scope
 in DHCP
  activating, **310–311**, *310–311*
  client options for, **308–309**, *309–310*
  creating, **304**, *305*
  IP address ranges in, **305–306**, *306*
  lease duration in, **307**, *307–308*
  options for, **311–312**, *311*
  superscopes in, **306–307**
 of groups, **641–643**
Scope Name screen, 304, *305*
screen savers
 and performance, 1270, *1270*
 for Terminal Services, **1014**
Script Source Access, 1112
Scripting Host, 654
scripts
 for applications in multiuser environments, **1041–1044**
 for distribution shares, **102–105**
 environment variables in, 140
 group policies for, 565, **690–691**, *690–691*
 improving, **97–101**
 logon, **632–633**, **652–653**
  assigning, **654**
  example, **654–657**
  group policies for, 565
  languages for, **653–654**
 for OEM, **104–107**
 for printer installation, **930–933**
 ProductID in, **97–98**
 for Registry modifications, 54
 RIS for, **134–139**
 Setup Manager for, **91–97**, *92–95*
 trying out, **98–99**
 for unattended installation, **87**
Scripts Policy Processing policy, 706
SCSI applet, 163

SCSI drives, 74
 for Active Directory, 493
 for performance, 488
 for servers, 1304
SDRAM (synchronous dynamic random access memory), 63
Seamless Windows, **1061**
search method for shortcuts, 727
search order for domains, 241–242
search paths for MMC tools, 174–175
searching
 Indexing Service for. *See* Indexing Service
 for MMC tools, 174–175
 for NDS data, **1253–1254**, *1253*
 for Registry keys, **53**
 for servers, **33–40**, *34–35*, **449–450**
secedit.exe (Security Configuration and Analysis tool), **667–672**, *669*, 695
second domains for Active Directory, **498–514**, *498–499*, *503–514*
second-level domains, **364–365**
second name servers, **390**, *391*
second names for Web servers, **391–392**, *392*
secondary records in BOOT files, **438**
secondary servers
 DNS, **375–377**, **393–395**, *394*
 WINS, 340, 342, 346–347, 349
SECPOL.MSC (Local Security Policy tool), 159, **287–288**, 568–569, 619, 660, 666
sections, 97
sectors, 781
 bad, 791–793
 boot, **1390**, 1392
 for dynamic disks, 757
 testing, 791
secure attention sequence, 1372
Secure Communications dialog box, 1188
Secure Server (Require Security) policy, 288
Secure Sockets Layer (SSL)
 certificates in, **1185–1187**, *1185–1187*
 encryption in, **591–593**
 for NNTP servers, 1147, 1151
 port numbers for, **1102–1103**
 for sites and directories, **1188**, *1188*
security
 Active Directory for, **447–449**
 authentication. *See* authentication
 in DDNS, **413–414**, **416–417**
 in DNS, **431**, **434–435**
 domain controllers in, **32**
 domains in, **30–32**

for FTP sites, **1132–1133**, *1132*, **1135**, *1135*
group policies for, **693–695**, *695*
for GSNW configuration, **1242–1243**, *1243*
in IMS program, **1181–1182**
for Indexing Service, **1194–1195**
infrastructure for, **8**
IPSec for. *See* IPSec
in legacy support, **32–33**
and logons, **30**
on Macintosh computers, **1086–1088**, 1091
member servers in, 32
for networks and networking, **29–33**
for NNTP servers, **1149–1151**, *1149–1150*
permissions in. *See* permissions
for printers, 915–916, **933**
    available hours, **933–934**, *934*
    group policy settings, **940–945**, *941*, *944*
    hiding, **940**
    permissions, **933–970**, *934–936*, *938–940*
for RAS clients, **1438**, *1438*
for Recovery Console, **1386–1387**
on Registry keys, 59
for shares, 807
for SMTP servers, **1162**, *1162*, **1164–1168**,
    1164–1165, *1168*
SSL for
    certificates in, **1185–1187**, *1185–1187*
    encryption in, **591–593**
    for NNTP servers, 1147, 1151
    port numbers for, **1102–1103**
    for sites and directories, **1188**, *1188*
in telnet, 1183
for Web sites. *See* Web sites
in zones, 388, **395**, *395*
Security Accounts Manager (SAM)
    contents of, 448, 458, 619–620
    limitations of, 29
    on PDCs, 525
    in Registry, 55–56
    uses for, 464–465
    for workstations, 468
Security Accounts tab, **1132–1133**, *1132*
Security Configuration and Analysis tool (secedit.exe),
    667–672, *669*, 695
security contexts, 165, 998, *998*
Security Credentials screen, 1137, *1137*
security descriptors
    checking, 791
    for Registry keys, 59
Security events, 1285

Security folder, 1366
security groups
    built-in
        local, **646–651**, *647*
        special, **651**
    vs. distribution groups, **639–640**
    working with, **643–646**, *644–646*
security identifiers. *See* SIDs (security identifiers)
SECURITY key, 55–56
Security log, 1285, *1285*
Security Policy Setting dialog box, 661, *661*
security principals, 1231
Security Properties dialog box, 569–570, *570*
Security Settings folder, 695
Security Settings for FTP sites, 1134–1135
Security tab
    for delegation permissions, 511, *511*
    for group policies, 678, *678*, 683–684, *683–684*
    for Installers group, 130
    for NNTP servers, **1149**, *1149*
    for owners, 827–830, *827–830*
    for packages, 869, *870*, 872, *872*, 876, *876*
    for permissions, 659, *659*, 815, *815*, 820–822, *820*,
        822, 825–826, *826*
    for printers, 935, *935*
    for RAS clients, 1438, *1438*
    for shared folders, 820
    for SMTP servers, **1162**, *1162*
security templates, **666–672**, *669*, **694–695**, *695*
Security Translation Wizard, 581
seeding, 1071
SeedingNetwork key, 1089
segmented names in DNS, **359**
segmented networks
    SAP with, 1306
    for server performance, **1299**
Select a device screen, 265, *266*
Select Columns dialog box, 1294, *1294*
Select Computer dialog box
    for Event log data, 1286–1287, *1286*
    for snap-ins, 177, *178*
    for WinChat, 1049, *1049*
Select Counters dialog box, 1277, *1277*, 1282, *1282*
Select Counters from Computer option, 1273
Select Disks page, 763–764, *763*
Select Disks screen, 760–761, *761*, 769, *769*
Select Group Policy Object dialog box, 675, *675*
Select Groups dialog box, 633, *634*
Select key, 1375, *1376*
Select Members by Group option, 635

Select NetWare Logon dialog box, 1237–1238, *1237*

Select Network Adapter dialog box, 968, *968*

Select Network Adapter screen, 158, *159*, 1303, *1303*, 1493, *1494*

Select Network Adapters dialog box, 964, *965*, 1456, *1457*

Select Network Client dialog box, 1237, *1237*

Select Network Component Type dialog box, 155, *156*, 231, *232*, 964, *964*

Select Network Protocol dialog box, 155, *156*, 231, *232*, 1235–1236, *1235*, 1454, *1454*

Select Partition Type screen, 753, *753*, 755, *755*

Select the Dfs Root Type screen, 842, *842*

Select the Host Domain for the Dfs Root screen, 843, *843*

Select the MST File to Save screen, 890, *890*

Select the Printer Port screen, 910, *910*, 1078, *1078*

Select User dialog box, 915, *916*

Select Users, Computers, or Groups dialog box, 821, *821–822*

Select Users, Contacts, Computers, or Groups dialog box, 505, *506*

Select Users or Groups dialog box, 661

Select Volume Type screen, 760, *760*, 764, *764*, 768, *769*

selecting files
> for backup, **1322–1325**, *1322–1324*, **1327–1329**, *1327–1329*
> for restoring backups, **1353–1356**, *1353*, *1355*

Send Copy of Non-delivery Report To setting, 1164

Send Message dialog box, 1055, *1055*

sending messages in Terminal Services Manager, **1055–1056**, *1055*

sendmail program, 225, 1159

SendTo folder, 712, 715

SEP files, **951–953**

Separator Page dialog box, 951, *951*

separator pages for printers, **951**
> choosing, **951**, *951*
> creating, **952–953**

Sequenced Packet Exchange (SPX) protocol, 1234

sequencing in TCP, **215–216**

Serial Line Interface Protocol (SLIP) connections, **228**

serial numbers for zones, 387

serial ports
> mapping, 929
> for printing, 908, 948
> for RAS, 1414

Server Aging/Scavenging Properties dialog box, 408, *408*

Server Certificate screen, 1185, *1185*

server configuration for DHCP, **317–319**, *317–318*

Server Configuration Wizard, 82

Server Extensions Configuration Wizard, 1119–1121, *1119–1121*

Server Extensions tab, 1099–1100, *1100*, **1119–1123**, *1122*

Server IP Address option, 1083

Server Manager, replacement functions for, **160–161**, *161*

Server Name screen, 125, *126*

server numbers in multi-WINS networks, **345**

Server Operators group, 647–650

Server Options dialog box, 311–313, *311*, *313*

Server Options folder, 311

Server performance object, 1504

Server Properties option, 906

Server (Request Security) policy, 288

Server service, 80, 969

Server Sessions counter, 1273

Server Settings folder, **1024–1025**, *1025*

Server tab, 1437, *1437*

Server Tools add-on, 429

Server Types tab, 1439–1440, *1440*

Server Work Queues performance object, 1504

%SERVERNAME% environment variable, 738

servers
> certificates for, 595
> DHCP, 270
>> authorizing, **302–304**, *303–304*
>> for printers, 917
>> for RAS, 1427–1428
>> for Terminal Services, 1003
> DNS. *See* DNS servers
> file
>> benefits of, **26**
>> for Macintosh computers, **1070–1071**
> finding, **33–40**, *34–35*
> GC, **1228–1229**
>> domain controllers as, 502–503, **583**
>> placement of, **1229–1230**, *1229*
> licensing, **69–70**
> for Macintosh computers, **1070–1071**
>> accessing, **1082–1086**, *1083–1084*, *1086*
>> installing, **1071–1073**, *1071–1072*
> names for, **67**
> NNTP. *See* NNTP (Network News) servers
> print, **26**, **953**, *954*
>> drivers for, **956–958**, *957–958*
>> forms for, **954–955**, *955*
>> for Macintosh computers, **1070–1071**
>> messaging and logging for, **958**, *959*
>> ports for, **955–956**, *956*
>> for Web printing, **914–918**, *914–917*
> priority of, **1299**
> protecting
>> environmental hazards, **1315–1316**

limiting access for, **1316**
passwords for, **1316–1318**
power protection for, **1314–1315**
RAS, **1430–1436**, *1431, 1433–1435*
rollouts, RIS for, **131–134**, *132–134*
searching for, **449–450**
in sites, **558–560**, *559*
SMTP. *See* SMTP servers
software for, **25–26**
in Terminal Services, **991–994**
tuning, **1299–1300**
Servers folder, 542, 557
Service Advertising Protocol (SAP), 1306
SERVICE group, 651
service lists, **1305–1306**
service packs
applying, 132
for backups, **1357**
for NTFS, 782
preinstalling, **104**
for Recovery Console, **1379**
for security, **1205–1207**
services
in boot process, **1371**
configuring, 164–165, *165*
enabling and disabling, **1387–1389**
for Internet gateways, 1448–1449
managing, **160–161**, *161*
network, **155**, *156*
on remote machines, **162**
for workstations, 964
Services and Applications node, 171, *172*, **173**
Services Control Panel, replacement functions for, **164–166**, *165–166*
Services folder, 1365
Services for Macintosh (SFM), 1065, 1071, 1090
Services Manager (SMSS.EXE), 1372
Services tab
for Internet gateways, 1448
for workstations, 969, *970*
Services tool, 164–165
session licensing for Terminal Services, **1031–1032**
Session Manager, 986
session shadowing, 989
sessions in Terminal Services, 1052
command-line tools for, **1050–1051**
environment for, **1023**
Terminal Services Manager for. *See* Terminal Services Manager
time-out settings for, **1018–1020**, *1019*

Sessions tab, 1018–1019, *1019*
SessionSpace, 986
Set Aging/Scavenging for All Zones option, 408
Set as Default Protocol option, 974
SET command
in Recovery Console, 1385–1387
for scripts, 656
Set Each Password to the User's Logon Name option, 1250
Set Feature Installation States screen, 891, *892*
Set Information access type, 1029
Set Master option, 848
Set paper orientation option, 947
Set Password option, 619
Set print processor option, 947
Set printer spooling option, 947
Set Schedule option, 1331
Set the hours printer will accept print jobs option, 947
Set the page order option, 947
SetDefaultPrinter method, 930–931
setmail.bat script, 654, 657
Setting up your Internet connection screen, 272, *272*
settings, group policies for, 565
Settings Based On options, 1490
Settings folder, 909
Settings tab
for backups, 1333–1334, *1334*
for redirection, 692, *693*
Setup Boot Disks, 72
setup disks and files, **1000**, *1000*
SETUP key, **1046–1047**
Setup.log file
on ERDs, 1381
for system files, 1392
Setup Manager, **91–97**, *92–95*
setup program
for dynamic disks, **773–774**
for packages, **874–875**, *875*
for Terminal Services, 1002
Setup screen for Macintosh printers, 1086
Setup Wizard
in installation, 81
for Terminal Services, 1003
setupldr.bin file, 1382
SFM (Services for Macintosh), 1065, 1071, 1090
shadow utility, 1051, 1058
Share Name option, 807
Share Names setting, 1241
Share Permissions tab, 812–813, *812–813*
Share This Folder option, 807, 852
Shared Access Application dialog box, 1447–1448, *1447*

Shared Access Service dialog box, 1448–1449, *1449*
Shared Access Settings dialog box, 1448
Shared Folder option, 811
Shared Folders option, 1074, *1074*, 1090
Shared Folders tool, 161
shared mandatory profiles, 631, **737**
Shared System Volume screen, 493, *494*
shares and shared folders, 622, **805–806**, *806*
    Active Directory for, **516–517**, *516*, **810–811**
    auditing, **831–833**, *831–832*
    common, **835–836**, *835*
    connecting, **836–838**
    creating, **806**
        from Computer Management Console, **809–810**, *809–810*
        from Explorer, **807–808**, *807–808*
        publishing shares, **810–811**
    distributed file system for. *See* Distributed File System (Dfs)
    hidden, **834–835**, *834*, **940**
    on Macintosh computers, **1073–1076**, *1074–1076*, **1083–1085**, *1083–1084*
    managing, **160–161**, *161*
    names for, 807, 911, 1241
    Offline Files in. *See* Offline Files
    permissions for. *See* permissions
    publishing, **810–811**
    for roaming profiles, 717
    in System Tools node, 172
    user limits on, **808**
    viewing, 160, *161*
    Web, **852–853**, *852–854*
Shares folder, 809, *809*
sharing. *See also* shares and shared folders
    peer-to-peer, disabling, **36**
    printers, **1076–1081**, *1078–1080*, *1082*, **1085–1086**, *1086*
Sharing option, 807
Sharing tab
    in Explorer, **807–808**, *807*
    for hidden shares, 834, *834*
    for ICS, 274, *275*, *276*
    for Internet gateways, 1446
shell programs, 653
Shiva Encrypted Authentication (SPAP) option, 1432
Shortcut Menu Command screen, 185, *185*, 188–189, *188–189*
shortcuts
    keyboard, **1013–1014**
    in NTFS, 782–783
    for Terminal Services clients, **1013–1014**
    with user profiles, **727**

Show alert message when I start Backup option, 1330
Show alert message when new media is inserted into Removable Storage option, 1330
Show Hidden Files and Folders option, 168
Show/Hide Console Tree option, 190
Show Multiple Schedules option, 1332
Shut down the system right, 663
shutdown scripts, 565, 652
SI (Software Installation), 867, 870, *870*, 886
SIDs (security identifiers), **55–56**
    in backups, 1357
    for contacts, 640
    for deleted accounts, 627
    with drive copiers, 147
    histories, 484, **575–576**
    in migration, **575–576**, 1231
    for printers, 935
    RIDs in, 533
    scrambler programs for, 110
    Sysprep for, 147
    for user accounts, **620–621**
SIDWalker tool, 1231
.sif files, 131
signing
    drivers, **1492–1493**, *1492*
    messages, **590**
    transmissions, **285**
Simple Mail Transfer Protocol (SMTP), 225–226, 1448, 1505
Simple Mail Transfer Protocol (SMTP) servers. *See* SMTP servers
Simple Network Time Protocol (SNTP), 538–539
simple volumes, 747
Single Computer option, 917
Single Instance Store (SIS) service, **113–114**
single large expensive drives (SLEDs), **742**
single-master vs. multimaster replication, **525–526**
SIS (Single Instance Store) service, **113–114**
SIS Common Store folder, 114
Site Link option, 561
Site Manager, 558
sites, **556**
    in Active directory, 477, **556–560**, *557–559*, **584**, **1221**, *1222*
    defining, **558**, *558*
    for domain controllers, 162
    FTP. *See* FTP sites
    group policies for, 563
    operation of, **556**, *557*
    replicating, **560–562**, *560–562*

servers in, **558–560**, *559*
SSL for, **1188**, *1188*
subnets in, **558**, *559*, 1221
virtual, 245
Web. *See* Web sites
Sites and Services snap-in, 1229
Sites folder, 162, 557–558
size
  clusters, 781, 786
  domains, **458**
  groups, **472–473**
  logs, **569–571**, 1279
  mirror sets, 768
  paging files, 1297
  physical disks, 745
  primary partitions, 755
  sectors for dynamic disks, 757
  stripe sets, 764, 769
  system cache, 1298
  transaction logs, 793
  volume sets, **763–764**, *763*
slaves in DNS, **434–435**
SLEDs (single large expensive drives), **742**
SLIP (Serial Line Interface Protocol) connections, **228**
slipstreamed installation, 1379
Slow Link Detection setting, 706
slow links, group policies over, **705–706**, *706*
SlowLinkDetectEnabled Registry entry, 733
SlowLinkTimeout Registry entry, 733
smart cards, 8, 588
Smart Host setting, 1169
Smart UPS series, 1315
smoking, damage from, 1316
SMS (Systems Management Server) tool, 15
SMSS.EXE (Services Manager), 1372
SMTP (Simple Mail Transfer Protocol), 225–226, 1448, 1505
SMTP folder, 561
SMTP Server for Moderated Groups setting, 1148–1149
SMTP Server performance object, 1505
SMTP servers, **1158**
  ASP for, **1172–1174**
  creating, **1159–1161**, *1159–1161*
  directories for, **1171–1172**
  domains for, 1161, *1161*, 1165–1166, *1165*, **1170–1171**, *1170*
  e-mail protocols for, **1158–1159**
  IIS as, **1095**
  properties for
    Access tab, **1164–1166**, *1164*
    Delivery tab, **1166–1169**, *1167*

General tab, **1162**, *1162*
    Messages tab, **1162–1164**, *1163*
    Security tab, **1162**, *1162*
SMTPDS.EXE program, 1174
SMTPRS.EXE program, 1174
snap-ins
  in MMC, 170
  permitted, 700–701, *701*
snapshots for MSIs, **880–882**, *880–882*
sniffers, 30
SNTP (Simple Network Time Protocol), 538–539
SOA (Start of Authority) records
  in DDNS registrations, 407
  in DNS, **372**
  in zone file format, **401–402**
sockets
  in TCP/IP, **216–218**
  in Winsock, **221**, 331
software, certificates for, 595
Software Compression option, 1435
Software Console, 888
Software Environment folder, **1364–1365**, *1364*
SOFTWARE hive, 55–56
software installation. *See* packages
Software Installation (SI), 867, 870, *870*, 886
Software Installation folder, 680, 876, *876*
Software Installation group, 690
software licenses. *See* licenses
software RAID vs. hardware, **780**
Software Settings group, 690
Software Settings node, 689
sorting in Device Manager, 1486, *1487*
sp1network.exe program, **104**, 132
spaces
  in filenames, 783
  in usernames, 624
spammer restrictions, **1166**, *1167*
spamming, 1163
spanned volumes, 747, 775
special built-in groups, **651**
Special Options screen, 73
Specify Default Path and Organization screen, 890, *891*
Specify How Mail Should Be Sent setting, 1123
Specify Partition Size screen, 755, *756*
Specify the Dfs Root Share screen, 843–844, *844*
Specify the Host Server for the Dfs Root screen, 843, *843*
speed
  with mirror sets, 768
  of modems, 1412–1413
.spl extension, 906

Spooler service, 1081
spoolers, **905–906**, **908**
    for Macintosh computers, 1081, *1082*
    print monitor in, **908**
    print processor in, **906–907**
    print provider in, **906**
    print router in, **906**
SPOOLSS.DLL file, 905–906
SPX (Sequenced Packet Exchange) protocol, 1234
square brackets ([]) in scripts, 97
SRV records, **374–375**, 518–520
SSL (Secure Sockets Layer), **1184–1185**
    certificates in, **1185–1187**, *1185–1187*
    encryption in, **591–593**
    for NNTP servers, 1147, 1151
    port numbers for, **1102–1103**
    for sites and directories, **1188**, *1188*
stand-alone Dfs root type, 842
stand-alone Dfs vs. fault-tolerant, **841–842**
stand-alone libraries, 1337
standard primary zones, 1227
Standard Secondary option, 394
standard secondary zones, 1227
Start Menu folder, 691–692, 712, 714–715, *715*
Start Menu Properties dialog box, 692, *693*
Start New Task Wizard option, 183
Start of Authority (SOA) records
    in DDNS registrations, 407
    in DNS, **372**
    in zone file format, **401–402**
Start of Authority (SOA) tab, 386–387, *387*
Start option for DNS servers, 404
Start/Programs menu, 12
start types, 1388–1389
Startup folder, 1396
startup programs, troubleshooting, **1396**
Startup Programs folder, 1365
startup scripts, 565, 652
Startup Settings dialog box, 975–976, *975*
static DNS entries, **238**
static IP addresses, **233–234**, *233*
    DDNS registrations with, **407**
    for IMS, **1175**
static mapping, 342, *342*
Static Route dialog box, 258, *258*, 1467, *1467*
Static Routes option, 258
static routing, **258–259**, *258–259*
static service lists, **1305–1306**
Status Bar check box, clearing, 190
Stop option for DNS servers, 404

storage
    for NNTP servers, 1145–1146, *1145–1146*, 1157
    requirements for, **64**
Storage node, **171–172**, *172*
Store Password Using Reversible Encryption option, 631
Store Passwords Using Reversible Encryption option, 699
StreetTalk service, 21
string data type, 51
stripe sets, **749**, *750*
    creating, **764–765**, *764*
    deleting, 765, **771**
    failed, 771, *771*
    with parity, **750–751**, *751*
styles of taskpad views, 181
SU (Super User) command, 17
sub-administrators
    creating, **450–451**
    OUs for, **474**
subdirectories for FTP sites, 1139
subdomains
    Active Directory for, **459**
    in DNS, 361, **365–366**, **397–400**, *397–399*
    OUs for, **506–510**, *507–510*
subkey services, 49–50
subkeys, 49–50
subnet masks
    in IP addresses, **208–210**
    ordering, **372**
subnets
    in Class C networks, **210–211**
    in IP, **199**, 202
    in routing, **252–253**
    in sites, **558**, *559*, 1221
    in TCP/IP, **197**, 199
subsystems in boot process, **1372**
subtrees in Registry, **48–49**
Success Audit option, 1290
Success events in Event Viewer, 1287
suffixes
    in LMHOSTS, **337–338**
    for user principal names, **500–503**, *503*
Summary folder, 1366
summary information, system, **1361**, *1362*
Summary screen, 496, *496*
super groups, 472
Super User (SU) command, 17
superscopes in DHCP, **306–307**
support.cab file, 577
support information scripts, **101**, *102*
supportability goals, **4**

SuppressWINSNameServers key, 1472
surge protectors, 1315
synchronization
    DNS servers, **376–377**
    forest-wide, **538–540**
    Offline Files, **860–865**, *860, 862, 864*
    in scripts, 656
Synchronization Settings dialog box, 864, *864*
Synchronize all offline files before logging off option, 857
Synchronize directory service data right, 663
synchronous dynamic random access memory (SDRAM), 63
/syspart switch in winnt32, 89
Sysprep program, 13, **88**, **146–147**
    administrative users for, **148–149**
    computer setup for, **148**
    copying images with, **150**
    logging in with, **149**, *149*
    obtaining, **148**
SYSPRINT.SEP separator page, 951
SYSPRTJ.SEP separator page, 951
System applet, 156
system boot files
    backing up, 1320
    restoring, 1356
System Cache Resident Bytes counter, 1298
system caches
    purpose of, 1266
    tuning, **1297–1298**, *1298*
System catalog, 1192
system checks for dynamic disks, 759
system clock, 80
system configuration information, saving, **1367–1368**
system data, transaction logs for, 790
system drive letters, changing, **776–777**
System events, **568**, 1285
system files, overwriting, **901**
SYSTEM group, 651
system hardware requirements, **62–64**
system images
    creating, **125–127**, *126–127*
    delivering, **128**
    limiting, **131**
    Sysprep for, **150**
System Information tool, 167, *167*, **1360–1361**, *1361*
    for components, **1363–1364**, *1364*
    for hardware resources, **1362–1363**, *1362*
    for Internet Explorer 5, **1365–1366**, *1366*
    for saving system configuration, **1367–1368**
    for software environment, **1364–1365**, *1364*
    for summary information, **1361**, *1362*

SYSTEM key, 55–56
System log, 1285, *1285*
    for disk quotas, 801
    properties for, **1288–1290**, *1289*
System Log Properties dialog box, **1288–1290**, *1289*
System Monitor, **1260**, **1262**, *1262*
    charts in, **1263–1264**, *1263*
    counters in, **1264–1273**, *1270*
    for CPU bottlenecks, **1269–1270**, *1270*
    for disk bottlenecks, **1270–1271**
    for memory bottlenecks, **1265–1268**
    for network bottlenecks, **1271–1273**
    for remote performance monitoring, **1273–1274**, *1274*
    saving data in, **1274–1275**, *1275*
    for Terminal Services, **993–994**
system partitions
    in converting basic disks to dynamic, **757**
    disk quotas on, 801
    FAT filesystem on, **785**
System performance object, 1505
system policies, 14–15, 457, 474, **563**, **665–666**
System Policy Editor
    for registry, 713, *713*
    for user profiles, **724–726**, *725–726*
System Properties dialog box
    for device management, 164, *164*
    for domains, 238, *239*
    for names, 152, *153*
    for network adapters, 157, *157*
    for user profiles, 719, *720*
System Services category, 694
System settings, group policies for, **697**, *698*
System State data
    backing up, 1320
    restoring, 1354, 1356
System Tools, 167
    for alerts, 161
    for device management, 164
    for groups, 467
    for Macintosh computers, 1090
System Tools node, 171–172, *172*
system32 directory, 174
systemroot command, 86, 1385
Systems Management Server (SMS) tool, 15
systemstate argument in NTBACKUP, 1345
SYSVOL directory, 494
    backing up, 1320
    for login scripts, 632
    replication of, **1224–1225**
    restoring, 1356

T

$T separator page function, 952
/t switch
    in NTBACKUP, 1346–1347
    in rsm, 1338–1339
tab-delimited (.TSV) files, 1279
tags in HTML, 124
Take ownership of files or other objects right, 663
Take Ownership permission
    for printers, 937
    for shared folders, 816, 818
Take Replica Member Offline/Online option, 849
tape backups
    for remote storage, 11
    with RSM. *See* RSM (Removable Storage Manager)
Tape Device applet, 163
tapes
    ejecting, **1342–1344**
    moving, **1342**
    refreshing, **1344–1345**
    renaming, **1342**
targets, taskpad, 181, *182*
Task Icon screen, 185, *185*
Task Manager, **1291–1295**, *1292–1294*
Taskbar
    configuring, 714
    profile settings for, 713
Taskbar and Start Menu Properties dialog box, 714, *714*
Taskpad Display screen, 181, *182*
Taskpad Navigation Tabs option, 190
Taskpad Target screen, 181, *182*
Taskpad View Creation Wizard, 183
taskpad views, **179–181**, *179–180*
    creating, **181–182**, *182–183*, **187–188**, *188–189*
    links for, **188–190**, *190*
    tasks in, **183–186**, *184–186*
Tasks tab, 183
Tasks to Delegate screen, 509, *509*, 687, *688*
tattooing, 665
TCO (total cost of ownership), 4
TCP (Transmission Control Protocol), **215**
    error detection and correction in, **216**
    flow control in, **216**
    sequencing in, **215–216**
TCP/IP (Transmission Control Protocol/Internet Protocol),
    28, 68, **193**
    design goals in, **197–198**
    DHCP in. *See* DHCP (Dynamic Host Configuration
        Protocol)
    DNS in. *See* DNS (Domain Name Service)

    domains in
        joining, **238–240**, *239*
        names for, **236–242**, *239–241*
    error handling in, **197**
    history of, **194–197**, *194–195*
    ICS for. *See* ICS (Internet Connection Sharing)
    installing, **230–232**, *231–232*
    Internet host names in, **223–227**, *226*
    for intranets, **227–230**, *229*
    IP in. *See* IP (Internet Protocol)
    IPSec for. *See* IPSec
    NetBIOS name resolution sequence in, **355–358**, *357*
    for NetWare, 1236
    network binding in, **221–223**
    PAT in, **220–221**
    ports and sockets in
        for FTP sites, 1127–1128, *1128*, 1130
        for NNTP servers, 1144–1145, 1147
        for SMTP servers, 1160–1161
        for Web sites, 1102–1104
        Winsock, **216–218**, **221**, 1448
    routing in. *See* routing
    testing configuration of, **234–236**, *234, 236*
    Windows 2000 Server as gateway/router in. *See* gateways
    WINS for. *See* WINS (Windows Internet Name Service)
TCP/IP Control Panel, 1083
TCP/IP Filtering option, 295
TCP/IP Properties dialog box
    for DHCP relay agents, 324, *324*
    for Internet gateways, 1450, *1450*
    for workstations, 969, *969*
TCP/IP suite, 198
TCP performance object, 1505
Telephones tab, 627, *628*
Telephony performance object, 1505
telnet protocol
    port for, 1448
    for remote login, **1182–1184**
telnet server, **16**
/tempdrive switch in winnt32, 89
temperature sensors, 1369
templates
    account, 635
    administrative, **696**
    for group policies, **666–672**, *669*
    for print jobs, 954
    security, **694–695**, *695*
Templates folder, 1044
    for RIS images, 131
    in user profiles, 712

Temporarily Available Offline indicator, 860
Temporary Files directory, 1025
temporary folders, **1023–1025**, *1023*
temporary licenses, **1033**
temporary Offline Files, 857, 859
temppf.sys file, 1297
terminal connections for intranets, **228–229**, *229*
terminal emulation, 227
Terminal Server Client, 1005–1008
Terminal Server Edition (TSE), 990, 1295–1296
"Terminal server has exceeded the maximum number of
    allowed connections" error message, 1015
"Terminal server sessions disabled" error message, 1015
terminal servers
    client-side printers in, 926–929
    for thin client sessions, 985–987
    in W2K licensing model, 1030–1031, *1030*
Terminal Services, 14, 979–980
    applications in multiuser environments, **1037**
        choosing, **1037–1039**
        compatibility scripts for, **1041–1044**
        hand-tuning, **1044–1045**
        installing, **1039–1041**, *1040*, **1044**
        Registry for, **1045–1050**, *1046–1049*
    for centralized application deployment, **980–981**
    changing and removing, **998–999**
    client connection settings, **1016**, *1017*
        for all connections, **1024–1029**, *1024–1028*
        path information, **1020–1024**, *1021*, *1023*
        remote control, **1017–1018**, *1017*
        session time-outs, **1018–1020**, *1019*
    client hardware for, **994–996**
    core support for, **996–998**, *996–998*
    handheld PCs for, **1005**
    for help desk support, **984**
    licensing, **1029–1030**
        activation in, **1034–1037**, *1035–1036*
        application licensing, **1037**
        client connections, 1025
        session licensing, **1031–1032**
        Terminal Services Licensing tool, **1033–1037**,
            1034–1036
        W2K licensing model, **1030–1031**, *1030*
    limitations of, **1013–1014**
    MetaFrame for, **1061–1062**
    PC-based RDP clients for, **999**
        connections for, **1005–1009**, *1006–1007*, *1009*
        deploying, **1001–1002**
        installing and configuring, **1000–1001**

network shares for, **1000**
    setup disks for, **1000**, *1000*
for PC-unfriendly environments, **981–982**
power protection for, 1315
processes in, 1295–1296
for processing power, **982–983**
scripts for, 100
server hardware for, **991–994**
session management in, 1052
    command-line tools for, **1050–1051**
    environment for, **1023**
    Terminal Services Manager for. *See* Terminal Services
        Manager
    time-out settings for, **1018–1020**, *1019*
thin client sessions with, **984–985**
    RDP for, **987–990**
    sessions in, **991**
    terminal servers for, **985–987**
troubleshooting, **1015–1016**
TSAC support for, **999**
for user interface, **983**
Windows-based terminals for, **1003–1004**
Terminal Services Advanced Client (TSAC) package, 990
    installing, **999**
    for RDP clients, **999–1002**
    for terminal server connections, 1062
Terminal Services Client, **1006–1008**, *1006–1007*, *1009*
Terminal Services Client Access Licenses (TSCALs), **1032**
Terminal Services Client Creator, 1000
Terminal Services Configuration tool, 929, 1024, *1024*,
    1059, *1060*
Terminal Services dialog box, 997, *997*
Terminal Services Internet Connector Licenses (TSICLs),
    1032–1033
Terminal Services Licensing tool, **1033–1037**, *1034–1036*
Terminal Services Manager, **1051–1052**, *1052*
    gathering information for, **1052–1055**, *1054*
    sending messages in, **1055–1056**, *1055*
    terminating applications in, **1056–1057**
    user sessions in
        controlling, **1057–1058**, *1058*
        ending, **1059–1060**, *1060*
Terminal Services performance object, 1505
Terminal Services Profile tab, 1021, *1021*
Terminal Services Session performance object, 1505
Terminal Services Setup screen, 997–998, *997–998*
[TerminalService] section, 100
terminating Terminal Services sessions, **1014**, **1056–1057**
TermSrvr.mst file, 1044

test mode in ADMT, 578
test WINS servers, **349**
testing
    group policies, 709
    ISP connections, **262–263**
    MSI applications, **882**, **885–886**
    recovery plans, **1399–1401**
    TCP/IP configuration, **234–236**, *234*, *236*
    zones, **396**, *396*
text
    in NDS, finding and replacing, **1253–1254**, *1253*
    saving system information as, **1367–1368**
text-based setup, **74–77**
TEXT printer data, 906–907
Thawte certificate authority, 594
thin client sessions, **984–985**
    RDP for, **987–990**
    sessions in, **991**
    terminal servers for, **985–987**
third-level domains in DNS namespace, **365–366**
Thread count, 1292
Thread performance object, 1506
ThreadPriority key, 1299
tildes (~) in filenames, 783
time
    in separator pages, 952
    synchronizing in scripts, 656
Time between Redial Attempts setting, **1423**
time-outs
    for print server ports, **956**
    for Terminal Services clients, **1018–1020**, *1019*
/TIME parameter in msg, 1055
time to live (TTL) setting
    in Dfs, 851
    in DNS, 387–388
time zones, 80, 95
timer-driver programs, 1270
timer IRQ, 1480–1481
%TIMEZONE% environment variable, 140
.tmp file, 1025
tombstone lifetimes in backups, **1357–1358**
tombstoning WINS records, **350–351**
tools, included, **41–42**
Tools folder, 552, 577
Tools tab, 788–789, *788*
top-level domains in DNS namespace, **362–364**, 518
topologies
    in Active Directory planning, **584**
    in local Active Directory replication, **543–544**, *544*
    for Macintosh computers, **1069–1070**

Total Bytes counter, 993
Total Compressed Bytes counter, 993
total cost of ownership (TCO), 4
Total Protocol Cache Hit Ratio counter, 994
Totals section in Task Manager, 1292
trace logs, **1280–1281**, *1280–1281*
tracert tool, 237
Tracking tab, 1191, *1192*
transaction IDs in DHCP, 322
transaction logs
    in Active Directory, 493
    in NTFS, 790
    size of, 793
transfer protocols, 1095
transferring
    files. *See* FTP sites
    FSMO roles, **536–538**, *536*
    zone data, **377**
transforms, 888
transitive trusts, 461–462, 478
Translate TCP/UDP Headers (Recommended) option, 278
Transmission Control Protocol (TCP), **215**
    error detection and correction in, **216**
    flow control in, **216**
    sequencing in, **215–216**
Transmission Control Protocol/Internet Protocol. *See* TCP/IP
    (Transmission Control Protocol/Internet Protocol)
Traverse Folder permission, 816–817
trees, 455, **477–478**
    with forests, **479–481**
    global catalogs for, 472
    names for, **585**
Troubleshooter Wizard, 1482, 1488, **1496–1497**, *1497*
troubleshooting
    DCPROMO, **523–525**
    DNS, **435–436**
        BOOT files in, **437–440**
        cache.dns file, **440–441**
        DNS boot order, **436–437**
    group policies, **707–709**
    hardware
        System Information tool for. *See* System Information tool
        Troubleshooter for, **1496–1497**, *1497*
    installation, **83–86**
    logons, **523–525**, **1393–1396**
    policies, 709
    printers
        online resources for, **962**
        problem identification, **961–962**

RAS, **1469–1472**
server failures, **1398**
startup programs, **1396**
Terminal Services connections, **1015–1016**
trusts, **483–484**
trust in certificate authorities, **599–602, 608–609**, *609–610*
Trust Relationships dialog box, 482–483, *482*
trusted domains, 481–483
trusting domains, 481–483
trusts and trust relationships, 455, **481**
    ADMT tool for, **579**
    building, **160**
    command line for, **484–485**
    between domains, 452
    for groups, 641
    GUI for, **482–483**, *482–483*
    nontransitive, 1221
    in NT 4, **481–482**
    transitive, 461–462, 478
    troubleshooting, **483–484**
Trusts tab, 483, *483*
TSAC (Terminal Services Advanced Client) package, 990
    installing, **999**
    for RDP clients, **999–1002**
    for terminal server connections, 1062
TSAC page, 999
TSCALs (Terminal Services Client Access Licenses), **1032**
tscon command, 1051
tsdiscon command, 1051, 1059
TSE (Terminal Server Edition), 990, 1295–1296
TSICLs (Terminal Services Internet Connector Licenses),
    1032–1033
tskill command, 1051, 1056–1057
Tsmmcsetup.exe program, 1062
tsprof command, 1022, 1051
tsshutdn command, 1051, 1060
.TSV (tab-delimited files), 1279
TSWEBSETUP.EXE program, 999
TTL (time to live) setting
    in Dfs, 851
    in DNS, 387–388
TTL for This Record setting, 388
tuning
    driver updates in, **1300–1303**, *1301–1303*
    hardware, **1303–1305**
    network browsers. *See* network browsers
    processor power, **1295–1296**, *1296*
    servers, **1299–1300**
    system cache, **1297–1298**, *1298*

tools for. *See* Event Viewer; Performance Logs and Alerts
    tool; System Monitor
    virtual memory, **1296–1297**, *1297*
tunneling in IPSec, 298
two-way trusts, 461–462, 478
txtsetup.sif script, 132
type command, 1385
typical installation, 80
Typical Settings, 94

U

-u option in cusrmgr, 636
$U separator page function, 952
/u switch in EFSINFO, 797
UAM folder, 1087
UAMs (User Authentication Modules), 986, 1070, 1087
/udf switch in winnt32, 90
UDP (User Datagram Protocol)
    in DHCP, 322
    in security, 1214
UDP performance object, 1506
unallocated space vs. free space, **744**
/unattend switch in winnt32, 89–90
unattended.doc file, 100
unattended installation, 86–87
    command-line, **88–91**
    delivery method in, **87**
    scripting for, **87**
    Sysprep for, **88**
[Unattended] section, 96–97, 146
UnattendedInstall setting, 97
Unauthenticated Access option, 1432
UNC (Universal Naming Convention)
    for servers, 35
    in Windows for Workgroups, 976
underscores (_) in names, 235, 518
Unencrypted (clear text) Password (PAP) option, 1432
Uninstall option, 1489
Uninstall the Existing Package option, 899
Uninstall This Application When It Falls Out of the Scope
    of Management option, 872, 877
Uninstall This Application When This GPO No Longer
    Applies to Users or Computers option, 874, 897
universal groups, **469–470**, *470*, 639, **642–643**
    and global catalogs, 470, **472**
    mixed vs. native mode for, **471–472**, *471*
    in Users folder, 469
Universal Naming Convention (UNC)
    for servers, 35
    in Windows for Workgroups, 976

Universal Principal Names. *See* UPNs (user principal names)

Unix, 196

unlimited licenses, **1033**

Unload Hive option, 57, 723

Unrecognized media pool, 1340–1342

unused accounts, deleting and disabling, 1318

up-to-date vectors in replication, **550–552**

Update Associated Pointer (PTR) Record option, 390

Update Data button, 1275

Update Device Driver Wizard, 1302–1303, *1302–1303*

Update Driver option, 1302, 1489

update.exe program, 104

update sequence numbers (USNs)

    in replication, **547–549**

    in restores, 1358

/UPDATE switch in tsprof, 1022

Update User Rights option, 580

updating

    drivers

        for print servers, **958**

        in tuning, **1300–1303**, *1301–1303*

    profile information, **1022**

    servers in multi-WINS networks, **346–347**, *346*

Upgrade Details dialog box, 759, *759*

Upgrade Device Driver Wizard, 1489, *1490*

Upgrade to Dynamic Disk dialog box, 758, *758*

Upgrades tab, 898, *898*

upgrading, 70–71

    applications, **898–902**, *898–900*

    domain controllers, **69**

    vs. wipe-and-replace, 70–71

UPNs (user principal names), 18

    for GCs, 458

    for logon names, **500**

    suffixes for

        and GCs, **500–503**, *503*

        selecting, 624

UPSs, 1314–1315

[URL] section, 100

URLs

    for printers, 922

    for queues, 1242

    in redirection, 1111

% Usage counter, 1268

Usage Peak counter, 1268

Use a Certificate from This Certificate Authority option, 610

Use Add Wizard option, 290–291, 293

Use Automatic Settings option, 1490

Use cached profile on slow connections option, 733

Use Connection Setting from User Settings option, 929

Use DES Encryption Types for This Account option, 631

Use Drive setting, 1241

Use hardware compression option, 1321

Use Local Machine Store option, 605, 610

Use Static Address Pool option, 1433

Use the catalogs on the media to speed up building restore catalogs on disk option, 1330

Use the Following DNS Server Addresses option, 234

Use the Following IP Address option, 234

Use the Same Network Number to All IPX Clients option, 1434

Use This Device option, 1488

Use This Existing File option, 382

Use This Route to Initiate Demand Dial Connections option, 1467

Use Windows Classic Folders option, 167

Usenet. *See* NNTP (Network News) servers

user accounts. *See* users and user accounts

User Authentication Modules (UAMs), 986, 1070, 1087

User Cannot Change Password option, 626

user classes for DHCP, **314–317**, *315–316*

user-configurable profiles, **731–732**

User Configuration node, 689

    vs. Computer Configuration, 696

    group policies for. *See* group policies and GPOs

USER.DA0 file, 740

USER.DAT file, 740

User Datagram Protocol (UDP)

    in DHCP, 322

    in security, 1214

user-defined classes, 315–317, *315–316*

User Group Policy Loopback Processing Mode option, 704–705, *705*

user groups, Active Directory for, **465–473**, *468*, *471*

User Interaction Level, 93, *93*

user interface, **151–152**

    device management, **163–164**, *163–164*

    Disk Administrator functions, **162**, *163*

    domain management functions, **162**

    modernization of, **12**

    Network and Dial-Up Connections tool, **166**

    Network Control Panel functions, **152–158**

    NT Diagnostics functions, **167**, *167*

    Server Manager functions, **160–161**, *161*

    Services Control Panel functions, **164–166**, *165–166*

    Terminal Services for, **983**

    User Manager and User Manager for Domains functions, **159–160**, *159*

User Limit setting, 1241

user limits on shared folders, **808**

user logins for FTP sites, 1131
user logon names, **499–500**, 624
User Manager and User Manager for Domains, 457
    replacement functions for, **158–160**, *159*, 635
    for trusts, 482–483
User Migration Wizard, 578
User mode in MMC, 170
User Must Change Password at Next Logon option,
    625–626, 631
User Must Log On to Change Password option, 699
User Name and Password screen, 1126, *1126*
User Name setting, 619
User option for Event Viewer filtering, 1290
/user option in net use, 837
user principal names (UPNs), 18
    for GCs, 458
    for logon names, **500**
    suffixes for
        and GCs, **500–503**, *503*
        selecting, 624
User Profile Editor tool, 739–740, *740*
user profiles, 49, 631, **709–711**
    cached, **728–729**
    choosing, **732–733**, *733–735*
    comparing, **739–740**, *739–740*
    components of, **711–713**, *711–712*
    configuring, **713–715**, *713–715*, **719–722**, *720*
    creating, **715–719**, *717*
    default, **721–722**, *726*
    distributing, **738**
    group template, **731–732**
    guidelines for, **736–737**
    implementing, **737**
    mandatory, 631, **729–731**, 736–737, 739–740
    paths for, **721**
    preconfigured, **719–722**, *720*, **727**
    Registry for, **722–724**, *722–724*
    saving, 733, *735*
    summary, **736–737**
    System Policy Editor for, **724–726**, *725–726*
    for Terminal Services clients, 1020–1021
    in Windows 95/98, 740
User Profiles tab, 719, *720*, 732
user rights, 565, **660–663**, *661*
user-specific printer settings, **944–945**
[UserData] section, 96–97, 137
USERENV.DLL file, 708, 729
userinit.exe program, 1372
%username% variable, 1178
usernames

for FTP sites, 1131
hacking, 1213
in IMS, 1180
for Internet gateways, 1446
for Macintosh computers, 1084, 1086
for NNTP servers, 1150
rules for, 624
for virtual directories, 1126
for Web sites, 1115, 1213
users and user accounts, **617**
    assigning packages to, **874–878**, *875–878*
    Computer Management for, **617–619**, *618*
    creating, **499–506**, *499*, *503–506*, **623–626**, *624–626*
    domains for, **30–32**
    group policies for. *See* group policies and GPOs
    location of, **620**
    locking out, **698–699**
    managing, **633–635**, *634*
    migrating, **580**, *580–581*
    moving into OUs, **507**
    OUs for, **474**
    permissions for, **658–659**, *659–661*
    prebuilt, **623**
    profiles for. *See* user profiles
    properties for, **626–629**, *627–629*
        Account tab, **629–631**, *629*
        Member Of tab, **633**, *633*
        Profile tab, **631–633**, *632*
    SIDs for, **620–621**
    templates for, 635
    in Terminal Services, 1052
    for Web sites, **1215–1217**
Users folder, 469
    contents of, 473, 504, *504*, 621–622, 647, *647*
    for creating accounts, 619, 624
    on domain controllers, 650
    for Terminal Services client connections, 1016
Users group, 619, 644, 649–650
Users or Groups screen, 508–509, *508–509*, 687, *688*
Users tab, 1057
USNs (update sequence numbers)
    in replication, **547–549**
    in restores, 1358

V

/v switch
    in CHKDSK, 793
    in GPRESULT, 707
    in msg, 1056

values
in Registry, **50–51**, *50*
in scripts, 97
van Velsen, Ruud, 653
variables in scripts, 655–656
.vbs extension, 930
VBScript language, 635, 653
vectors in replication, **550–552**, *553*
vendor classes for DHCP, **312–314**, *313*
verification for backups, 1348
Verify Caller-ID option, 1430
Verify data option, 1321
Verify data after the backup completes option, 1330
Verify tab, **1248–1249**, *1248*
Verify Windows 2000 System Files option, **1392**
verifying messages, **590–591**
VeriSign certificate authority, 594
Version Control setting, 1122
versions of Offline Files, **860**, *860*
VGA mode, Advanced Options menu for, **1377**
video, 94
in iMac computers, 1069
in RDP, 991
in Terminal Services, 992, 1004
View Devices by Connection option, 1486
View Devices by Type option, 1486, *1486*
View From and To option, 1290
view function in net, 978
View Resources by Connection option, 1486
View Resources by Type option, 1486, *1487*
View tab, 168
views
in DSMT, 1245, 1251
taskpad, **179–181**, *179–180*
creating, **181–182**, *182–183*, **187–188**, *188–189*
links for, **188–190**, *190*
tasks in, **183–186**, *184–186*
virtual adapters, 156
Virtual Channels access type, 1029
virtual directories
for FTP sites, **1136–1138**, *1136–1138*
for NNTP servers, **1157**, *1157*
for printers, *914*, 915
for Web sites, **1123–1126**, *1125–1126*
Virtual Directory Alias screen
for FTP sites, 1136–1137, *1136*
for Web sites, 1125, *1125*
Virtual Directory Creation Wizard
for FTP sites, 1136–1138, *1136–1138*
for Web sites, **1125–1126**, *1125–1126*

Virtual Directory tab, *914*, 915
virtual memory
operation of, **1265–1266**
tuning, **1296–1297**, *1297*
Virtual Memory dialog box, 1297, *1297*
Virtual Memory Manager, 986
Virtual Private Networks (VPNs), **1450–1451**
DUN for, **1456–1459**, *1456–1459*
history of, **1452**
performance with, **1460**
PPTP and L2TP for, **1452–1459**, *1453–1459*
RAS for, **1405–1406**
virtual roots, 1124–1125
virtual Web sites, 245, **1103–1107**
Volume Manager, 759–760
volumes and volume sets, **747–748**, *748*
creating, **763–764**, *763*
mapping, 746
size of, **763–764**, *763*
VPNs (Virtual Private Networks), **1450–1451**
DUN for, **1456–1459**, *1456–1459*
history of, **1452**
performance with, **1460**
PPTP and L2TP for, **1452–1459**, *1453–1459*
RAS for, **1405–1406**

W

$W separator page function, 952
/w switch in msg, 1055
W2K licensing model, **1030–1031**, *1030*
W2KRSKT.MSI file, 553
w32tm program, 539
W3C Extended Log Format
for FTP sites, 1131
for SMTP servers, 1161
WANs
in Active Directory planning, **584**
for gateways, **260–262**, *260*
net use command over, **838**
Warn option for driver signing, 1492
Warning events in Event Viewer, 1287, 1290
warning levels for disk quotas, 803
warning.osc file, 144–145
WBTs (Windows-based terminals)
printer redirection with, 928
for Terminal Services, **1003–1004**
Web-Based Printing policy, 943
Web browsers
certificates for, **595**
PKI for, **612–614**

Web catalog, 1192
Web printing
  benefits of, **913–914**
  print servers for, **914–918**, *914–917*
Web servers, second names for, **391–392**, *392*
Web sharing, **852–853**, *852–854*
Web Sharing tab, 852–853, *852–853*
Web Site Access Permissions screen, 1105, *1105*
Web Site Content Directory screen, 1125, *1125*
Web Site Creation Wizard, **1101–1107**, *1101, 1104–1105*
Web Site Home Directory screen, 1104, *1104*
Web Site Identification settings, 1107–1108
Web sites, **1100**
  creating, **1101–1107**, *1101, 1104–1105*
  e-mail servers. *See* IMS (Internet Mail Service) program
  FTP. *See* FTP sites
  NNTP. *See* NNTP (Network News) servers
  properties of, **1107–1108**, *1107–1108*
    Custom Errors tab, **1118**, *1119*
    Directory Security tab, **1113–1116**, *1114*
    Documents tab, **1112–1113**, *1113*
    Home Directory tab, **1111–1112**, *1111*
    HTTP Header tab, **1116–1118**, *1117*
    ISAPI Filters tab, **1110**, *1110*
    Operators tab, **1108–1109**, *1109*
    Performance tab, **1109–1110**, *1109*
    Server Extensions tab, **1119–1123**, *1122*
  querying Indexing Service from, **1197–1202**
  security for, 1113–1116, *1114*, 1203–1205
    attack detection, **1211**
    attack deterrence, **1211–1214**
    file and print services in, **1210, 1216**
    IIS, **1205, 1207–1208**
    internal threats in, **1216**
    nonessential items in, **1208–1210**
    securing accounts, **1215–1217**
    service packs and hotfixes for, **1205–1207**
  SMTP servers. *See* SMTP servers
  SSL for, **1184–1188**, *1185–1188*
  telnet for, **1182–1184**
  virtual, 245, **1103–1107**
  virtual directories for, **1123–1126**, *1125–1126*
Web Sites folder, 176, 178
weekly backups, **1348–1349**
Welcome message for FTP sites, 1133
welcome.osc file, 140–141
Welcome to Setup screen, 75
Welcome to the Windows Components Wizard, 116

well-known ports
  for Internet gateways, 1448
  TCP/IP, 216–217
WFP (Windows File Protection), **901**
What is the name of the backup and the media option, 1321
What to Back Up screen, 1319, *1319*
What to Restore screen, 1352, *1353*
What type of backup should be performed option, 1321
When should the backup run option, 1321
When to Back Up screen, 1332, *1332*
Where to Store the Backup screen, 1320, *1320*
wildcards
  in Indexing Service queries, 1196
  in Recovery Console, 1384, 1386
WIN.ini file, 1396
win_nt.~bt directory, 74, 83
win_nt.~ls directory, 73, 83
Win32 Subsystem process, 986
WinChat, 1049
Windows, IPSec in, **287–294**, *287, 289–294*
Windows 95/98 user profiles, **740**
Windows 95/98 workstation connections, **963**
  Active Directory access in, **968**
  attaching to networks, **965–967**, *966*
  configuring, **964–965**, *964–965*
  network resource access in, **967**, *967*
Windows 2000
  dynamic disks in, **773–774**
  in-place migration in, **573–574**
  multiple domains with, **461–462**, *461*
Windows 2000 Remote Boot Disk Generator dialog box, 121, *122*
Windows 2000 Resource Kit, 53
Windows Authentication option, 1115
Windows-based terminals (WBTs)
  printer redirection with, 928
  for Terminal Services, **1003–1004**
Windows bitmap, 723
windows components, group policies for, **696–697**
Windows Components screen
  in installation, 78–79, *79*
  for Macintosh servers, 1071, *1071*
  for network services, 155, *156*
  for Terminal Services, 996, *996*
Windows Components Wizard, 602–603, *602–603*
  for DHCP, 302
  for DNS service, 380–381
  for DSMT, 1246, *1246*
  for IIS, 1096, *1096*

in installation, 79, *79*
for Macintosh servers, 1071, *1071*
for network services, 155
for RIS, 116, *116*
for Terminal Services, **996–998**, *996–998*
for WINS servers, 341
Windows File Protection (WFP), **901**
Windows for Workgroups workstations connections
attaching to networks, **976**, *976*
configuring, **973–976**, *973–976*
Windows Installation Folder, 73
Windows Installation Image Folder Name screen, 118, *119*,
133, *133*
Windows Installer dialog box, 878, *878*
Windows Internet Name Service. *See* WINS (Windows
Internet Name Service)
Windows Management Instrumentation (WMI), **16**
Windows NT, **42–44**. *See also* NT 4
Windows NT Domain setting, 966
Windows NT Explorer, profile settings for, 713
Windows NT Server, 43
Windows Optional Networking Components Wizard,
155, *156*
Windows Scripting Host (WSH), 635, 653–654, **930**
Windows Security dialog box, 1292
Windows Security Package
for NNTP servers, 1151
for SMTP servers, 1165
Windows Settings folder, 681
Windows Settings group, 689–690
Windows Terminal Services. *See* Terminal Services
Windows Time Service, 80, 538
WinFrame tools, 1050
WinINSTALL Discover dialog box, 880–882, *880–882*
winipcfg command, 320
winlogon.exe program, 1372
winmsd utility, 167, 1361
winnt command, 88, 91, **102–103**
winnt.sif file, 74, 87, 99
winnt32 command, 81, 88, **102–103**
winnt32 options, **88–91**
WINS (Windows Internet Name Service), **242–244**, *242*,
329–332
client failure modes in, **340**
configuring, **342–344**, *343–344*
DHCP for, 308
vs. DNS, **355**
domain controllers with, **350**, 1395
improvements in, **6**

installing, **341–342**, *342*
vs. LMHOSTS, **337–339**
multi-WINS networks, **344**
replication in, **347–349**, *348*
server numbers in, **345**
updating servers in, **346–347**, *346*
name registrations in, **339–340**
name resolution in, **352–355**, *353*
and NBT, **332–336**
nodes in, **333–334**
operating systems for, **339**
problems in, **349–351**
proxy agents in, **351–352**, *351*
with RAS, **1472**
refresh requests in, 340
renewal intervals in, **340**
for Terminal Services, 1003–1004
WINS registrations vs. DDNS, **412–413**
WINS Servers screen, 309, *310*
WINS tab, 242–243, *242*, 388, 1443
Winsock
and NetBIOS, **331–332**
sockets in, **221**
WINSPOOL.DRV driver, 906
WMI (Windows Management Instrumentation), **16**
Word, Offline Files for, **862**
words in Indexing Service queries, 1196
WORKGROUP/DOMAIN selection page, 80
workgroups, **35–38**
joining, **37**
names for, **152**, *153*
Working Set counter, 994, 1268
working sets, 1265
Workstation service, 969
World Wide Web (WWW). *See* Web sites
Write permissions
for FTP sites, 1129, 1134–1135, 1138
for NetWare printers, 1243
for shared folders, 819
for Web sites, 1106, 1112
Write Attributes permission, 816, 818
Write Data permission, 816, 818
Write Extended Attributes permission, 816, 818
write-through caching mechanism, 854
WSH (Windows Scripting Host), 635, 653–654, **930**
wshNetwork object, 930–933
WTS (Windows Terminal Services). *See* Terminal Services
WWW (World Wide Web). *See* Web sites

X

X.25 protocol, **1415**
X.509 standard, 8
/x switch in CHKDSK, 793
XLNT language, 654
XOR (exclusive OR) arithmetic, 751

Y

Yes, All of the Required Protocols Are on This List option,
  1426–1427
Yes, I Want to Use a RADIUS Server option, 1429
"You do not have access to this session" error message, 1015
"Your interactive logon privilege has been disabled" error
  message, 1015

Z

ZAP files, **886–888**, *887*
zero administration information, **462–463**
Zero Administration Windows initiative, 15
Zero Administration Windows tool, 457
Zone Aging/Scavenging Properties dialog box,
  410–411, *411*
Zone File screen, 382–384, *383, 385*
zone files, **400–401**, 437
    A records in, **402**
    CNAME records in, **404**
    in DNS, 369
    manipulating, **404–405**
    MX records in, **404**

names for, 382–383, 402
  NS records in, **402–404**
  SOA records in, **401–402**
Zone Name screen, 382, *382*
zone transfers, 388, 395, *395*, 1227
Zone Transfers tab, 388–389, *389*, 395, *395*
Zone Type screen, 382, *382*, 394, *394*
/ZoneDelete option in DNSCMD.EXE, 429
ZoneList key, 1089
zones in DNS, 369, **377–379**, *378*, 1227–1228. *See also*
  zone files
    Active Directory-integrated, **415**, 1227
        creating, **415**, *415*
        multimaster zone replication in, **415–416**
        problems in, **417–418**
        secure DDNS registration in, **416–417**
    cleaning up, **386–389**, *386–387, 389*
    creating, **381–383**, *381–383*
    in DNS servers, **421–423**
    vs. domains, **367–369**, *368*
    host records for, **389–390**, *389–390*
    installing DNS service for, **380–381**, *381*
    MX records for, **390–391**, *391*
    primary DNS servers for, **379–380**
    PTR records for, **393**, *393*
    reverse lookup, **383–385**, *385*
    second name servers in, 390, *391*, **393–395**, *394*
    security for, **395**, *395*
    testing, **396**, *396*
    transferring data in, **377**
    Web server names in, **391–392**, *392*

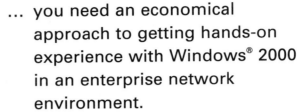

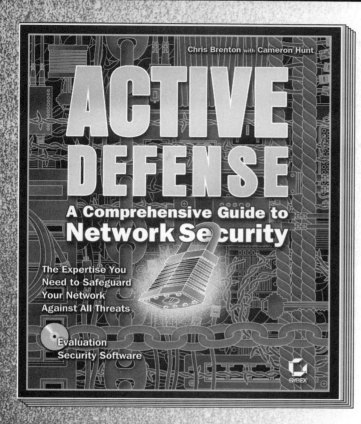

The Mark Minasi
Windows® Administrator Series

First Three Titles of an Expanding Series

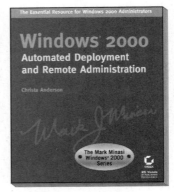

By Jeremy Moskowitz
0-7821-2881-5 • $49.99

By Christa Anderson
0-7821-2885-8 • $49.99

*By J. Peter Bruzzese
and Chris Wolfe*
0-7821-2883-1 • $49.99

- **Mark Minasi** serves as the series editor, chooses topics and authors, and reviews each book

- Concise, focused material based upon real-world implementation of Windows 2000 Server

- Designed to provide Windows 2000 Systems Administrators with specific in-depth technical solutions

Mark Minasi, MCSE, is recognized as one of the world's best teachers of NT/2000. He teaches NT/2000 classes in 15 countries. His best-selling *Mastering Windows 2000 Server* books have more than 500,000 copies in print.

25 YEARS
OF PUBLISHING
EXCELLENCE

SYBEX® WWW.SYBEX.COM

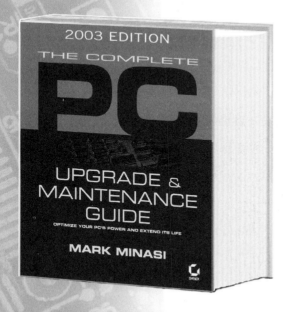